DEDICATION

To the Bench and Bar
whose members preserve and protect
the rule of law in American society

*

PREFACE

Baldwin's™ Ohio Revised Code Annotated has been published and maintained since 1921. Through the years, Banks-Baldwin™ met the changing needs of Code users by continuously improving both editorial content and the level of service provided to subscribers. Now published by West Group in casebound format, *Baldwin's ORC* sets the standard for quality editorial information and user-friendliness. With every content feature known to have value in an annotated Code, and all information presented for maximum user convenience, it is the first state code designed for practice in the 21st century. (Please consult the User's Guide in Volume 1 for additional information.)

Editorial features include:

LEGISLATIVE HISTORY

A complete legislative history, in reverse chronological order, follows each section of law.

UNCODIFIED LAW

Provisions of uncodified law affecting statutory interpretation are printed under related Revised Code sections. See the User's Guide in Volume 1 for a complete explanation of this feature.

HISTORICAL AND STATUTORY NOTES

Editorial notes are inserted where necessary to supplement and clarify legislative history or interpretation; they typically call attention to matters such as Special Endorsements from the Legislative Service Commission, legislative discrepancies, and statutes repealed and reenacted under the same or different section numbers.

"Pre-1953 H 1 Amendments" are noted in reverse chronological order for each section that existed prior to creation of the Revised Code by 1953 House Bill 1.

Amendment notes summarizing the nature and extent of legislative changes to the Revised Code have been editorially prepared and printed under sections of special interest to the Bench and Bar.

UNIFORM LAWS

Uniform Laws and model acts, as promulgated by the National Conference of Commissioners on Uniform State Laws and adopted by the Ohio General Assembly, contain references to identical or similar provisions in West Group's *Uniform Laws Annotated*®. Uniform Laws Tables specify other jurisdictions that have adopted the same Uniform Laws enacted in Ohio.

COMPARATIVE LAWS

Comparative Laws cite selected references to other state statutes on the same or analogous topic.

PREFACE

COMMENTARY

Where appropriate, commentary from the Ohio Legislative Service Commission, the National Conference of Commissioners on Uniform State Laws, committees of the Ohio State Bar Association, and other professional groups is included to assist in statutory interpretation. In addition, selected Rules of Practice carry Staff Notes from the Supreme Court of Ohio.

CROSS REFERENCES

There is an obvious kinship among various laws included in volumes of *Baldwin's Ohio Revised Code Annotated.* Facilitating full use of these interrelationships, time-saving cross references are provided to related or qualifying constitutional, statutory, and court rule provisions.

OHIO ADMINISTRATIVE CODE REFERENCES

Relevant references are provided to the Approved Edition™ of the *Ohio Administrative Code,* the complete compilation of state agency rules published by West Group.

UNITED STATES CODE ANNOTATED

Cross references to federal laws as published in West Group's *United States Code Annotated®* (U.S.C.A.®) are also provided where deemed relevant or useful.

LIBRARY REFERENCES

A special feature that will appeal to users consists of references to West Group's Key Numbers ⚷, WESTLAW® Digest topic numbers, and sections of *Corpus Juris Secundum®* (C.J.S.®). These references open the door to constructions and interpretations of statutory law throughout the country.

In addition, Library References include citations to *Ohio Jurisprudence* (OJur), *American Jurisprudence* (Am Jur), and *American Law Reports* (ALR®). References to OJur, AmJur, and ALR are compiled from the *Ohio Code Research Guide.*

Finally, this feature contains references to West Group's comprehensive line of practice manuals, handbooks, journals, and other secondary sources on specific subjects of law. References in this category cite pertinent parts of these publications where explanatory text, forms, or other practice and study aids can be found.

LAW REVIEW AND JOURNAL COMMENTARIES

Informative articles and discussions in law reviews and bar journals are highlighted for users by references under this heading.

PREFACE

NOTES OF DECISIONS AND OPINIONS

Judicial constructions of the Ohio Revised Code, as contained in the annotations, are prepared and reviewed by the Publisher's editorial staff. Our objectives are to provide thorough and authoritative access to caselaw and agency opinions and to assist users in understanding the application and purpose of the statutes as determined by the courts and the agencies.

Coverage of this material in *Baldwin's ORC Annotated* is the most comprehensive available, including: all reported Ohio court decisions; selected unreported Courts of Appeals decisions since 1981; selected decisions of the Court of Claims; federal cases construing or affecting Ohio law; opinions of the Attorney General; and selected decisions from a number of state agencies, among them the Board of Tax Appeals, Civil Rights Commission, Public Utilities Commission, Ohio Ethics Commission, Unemployment Compensation Review Commission, and Board of Commissioners on Grievances & Discipline.

Closing dates for the annotations in this volume are indicated in the following table:

Reported decisions complete through:
89 Ohio St.3d 139
133 Ohio App.3d 640
104 Ohio Misc.2d 41
31 O.B.R. 610
120 S.Ct. 483
211 F.3d 324
95 F.Supp.2d 744
248 B.R. 784
191 F.R.D. 543
2000 SERB 4-6

Unreported appellate decisions complete through: 4-9-00

Agency opinions and decisions complete through:
SERB 00-003
OAG 00-020
Bd of Commrs on Grievances & Discipline Op 99-001
BTA 99-M-806 (4-7-00)
COC U87-62178 (10-22-87)
CRC 8303 (4-6-00)
EBR [please see now ERAC for decisions of the former Environmental Board of Review]
ERAC 453961-453966 (12-9-99)
Elections Op 98-ELC-04
Ethics Op 99-004
HWFB 94-M-0475 (10-25-98)
Joint Legis Ethics Comm 99-001
PBR 86-MIS-07-1032 (9-25-86)
PUCO 88-716 to 720 GA-AIR (10-17-89)
RBR [please see now RC for decisions of the former Reclamation Board of Review]
RC 98-042
UCBR B98-02318-0000 (4-1-99)

Annotations are grouped by subject matter under descriptive headings, or catchlines, which are numbered and indexed alphabetically. The same arrangement and topic numbers will be used in supplementary pocket parts and in the "Case Notes and Journal References" section of *Baldwin's Ohio Legislative Service Annotated*™ (OLS); thus, Baldwin's Code users will always be able to locate quickly annotations to recent decisions construing a particular point of law. Further research beyond the closing dates indicated above can easily be accomplished by consulting first the annual pocket part, then the cumulative Case Notes and Journal References Table in the current year OLS.

All citations of these constructions give the full name of each case, the standard reporter where the case can be found, and complete case history.

WESTLAW ELECTRONIC RESEARCH GUIDES

WESTLAW electronic research guides have been inserted to facilitate efficient access to West Group's computer assisted legal research system for the latest laws and cases. See page ix.

GENERAL INDEX, RULES INDEX AND VOLUME INDEXES

The General Index is the most comprehensive, precise, reliable, and usable index to Ohio law ever published. It contains multiple, detailed references to the Ohio and U.S. Constitutions, the Ohio Revised Code, and the Ohio rules of practice.

Each title of the Revised Code carries its own index, found in the volume that concludes that title. When two titles are published in the same volume, the Volume Index combines both titles. An index to all rules of practice is found in the last court rule volume.

ANCILLARY RESEARCH AIDS

Other research aids in this set include a User's Guide (in Volume 1); a list of abbreviations; tables of titles and tables of contents; and analyses of chapters and sections.

POCKET PARTS AND LEGISLATIVE SERVICE

Baldwin's Ohio Revised Code Annotated is kept up to date by means of annual cumulative pocket parts and monthly issues of *Baldwin's Ohio Legislative Service Annotated* (OLS). This system assures the fastest possible availability of the laws, rules, and judicial constructions and the fastest access to the full text of decisions and opinions in *Ohio Official Reports* and in WESTLAW electronic research.

ACKNOWLEDGMENT

We express our gratitude and appreciation to members of the Bench and Bar, Ohio's law librarians and law schools, the members and staff of the Ohio Legislative Service Commission, and others whose timely suggestions have contributed materially to the successful planning and development of *Baldwin's Ohio Revised Code Annotated*.

THE PUBLISHER

Cleveland, Ohio
September 2000

WESTLAW ELECTRONIC RESEARCH GUIDE

WESTLAW®, Computer-Assisted Legal Research

WESTLAW is part of the research system provided by West Group. With WESTLAW, you find the same quality and integrity that you have come to expect from West Group books. For the most current and comprehensive legal research, combine the strengths of West Group books and WESTLAW.

WESTLAW Adds to Your Library

Whether you wish to expand or update your research, WESTLAW can help. For instance, WESTLAW is the most current source for case law, including slip opinions and unreported decisions. In addition to case law, the online availability of statutes, statutory indexes, legislation, court rules and orders, administrative materials, looseleaf publications, texts, periodicals, news and business information makes WESTLAW an important asset to any library. Check the online WESTLAW Directory or the print *WESTLAW Database Directory* for a list of available databases and services. Following is a brief description of some of the capabilities that WESTLAW offers.

Natural Language Searching

You can search most WESTLAW databases using WIN®, the revolutionary Natural Language search method. As an alternative to formulating a query using terms and connectors, WIN allows you to simply enter a description of your research issue in plain English:

> What is the government's obligation to warn military personnel of the danger of past exposure to radiation?

WESTLAW then retrieves the set of documents that have the highest statistical likelihood of matching your description.

Retrieving a Specific Document

When you know the citation to a case or statute that is not in your library, use the Find service to retrieve the document on WESTLAW. Access Find and type a citation like the following:

find 620 NE2d 48

find OH ST 1509.37

Updating Your Research

You can use WESTLAW to update your research in many ways:

- Retrieve cases citing a particular statute.
- Update a state or federal statute by accessing the Update service from the displayed statute using the jump marker.

- Retrieve newly enacted legislation by searching in the appropriate legislative service database.
- Retrieve cases not yet reported by searching in case law databases.
- Read the latest U.S. Supreme Court opinions within an hour of their release.
- Update West digests by searching with topic and key numbers.

Determining Case History and Retrieving Citing Cases

KeyCite®: Cases and other legal materials listed in KeyCite Scope can be researched through West Group's KeyCite service on WESTLAW. Use KeyCite to check citations for form, parallel references, prior and later history, and comprehensive citator information, including citations to other decisions and secondary materials.

Additional Information

For more detailed information or assistance, contact your WESTLAW Account Representative or call 1-800-REF-ATTY(1-800-733-2889).

TABLE OF TITLES
BALDWIN'S OHIO REVISED CODE ANNOTATED

*

TABLE OF CONTENTS

*

ABBREVIATIONS

A .... Amended
A B A J .... American Bar Association Journal
Abs .... Ohio Law Abstract
Admin L Rev .... Administrative Law Review, American Bar Association
Akron L Rev .... Akron Law Review
AFSCME .... American Federation of State, County and Municipal Employees
Alb L J Sci & Tech .... Albany Law Journal of Science and Technology
ALR .... American Law Reports Annotated
ALR2d .... American Law Reports Annotated, Second Series
ALR3d .... American Law Reports Annotated, Third Series
ALR4th .... American Law Reports Annotated, Fourth Series
ALR5th .... American Law Reports Annotated, Fifth Series
ALR Fed .... American Law Reports Annotated, Federal
Am .... Amended, Amendment
Am Crim L Rev .... American Criminal Law Review
Am Dec .... American Decisions
Am Jur .... American Jurisprudence
Am Jur 2d .... American Jurisprudence, Second Series
Am L Rec .... American Law Record
Am L Reg .... American Law Register
Am Rep .... American Reports
App .... Appellate Court
App .... Ohio Appellate Reports
App(2d) .... Ohio Appellate Reports, Second Series
App(3d) .... Ohio Appellate Reports, Third Series
App R .... Rules of Appellate Procedure
Ariz L Rev .... Arizona Law Review
Art .... Article
Assn .... Association
A-TF .... Amended and Transferred From
A-TT .... Amended and Transferred To
Auth .... Authority
B .... Weekly Law Bulletin
Babbit's Ohio Mun Serv .... Babbit's Ohio Municipal Service
Baldwin's Ohio Sch L J .... Baldwin's Ohio School Law Journal
Baldwin's Ohio Sch Serv .... Baldwin's Ohio School Service
Bd .... Board
Bldg .... Building
B.R. .... Bankruptcy Reporter
Brook L Rev .... Brooklyn L Rev
BTA .... Ohio Board of Tax Appeals
B U L Rev .... Boston University Law Review
Bull .... Weekly Law Bulletin
Bus Law .... Business Lawyer

ABBREVIATIONS

Cap U L Rev .... Capital University Law Review
Case W Res L Rev .... Case Western Reserve University Law Review
CC.. Ohio Circuit Court Reports
CCA .... United States Circuit Court of Appeals
CC(NS)................................ Ohio Circuit Court Reports, New Series
CCR..................................... Rules of Court of Claims of Ohio
CD .... Ohio Circuit Decisions
CFR...................................... Code of Federal Regulations
CF Stds .... Court Facility Standards
Ch... Chapter
Cin B Ass'n Rep.................. Cincinnati Bar Association Report
Cir .... Circuit Court
Cities & Villages .... Cities and Villages, Ohio Municipal League
CIV DISC............................ Civil Discovery
Civ R .... Rules of Civil Procedure
CJC...................................... Code of Judicial Conduct
C.J.S. .... Corpus Juris Secundum
Clev B J............................... Cleveland Bar Journal
Clev L Rec........................... Cleveland Law Record
Clev L Reg .... Cleveland Law Register
Clev L Rep .... Cleveland Law Reporter
Clev-Marshall L Rev .... Cleveland-Marshall Law Review
Clev St L Rev...................... Cleveland State Law Review
CMR .... Court-Martial Reports
Colum Hum Rts L Rev........ Columbia Human Rights Law Review
Colum J Gender & L .... Columbia Journal of Gender and Law
Colum J L & Soc Probs....... Columbia Journal of Law and Social Problems
Columbus B Briefs .... Columbus Bar Briefs
Co .... Company
COC..................................... Ohio Court of Claims
Comm................................... Commission
Commr .... Commissioner
Com.Pl................................. Common Pleas Court
Conf..................................... Conflicting
Const .... Constitution
Cornell L Rev...................... Cornell Law Review
Corp .... Corporation
CP... Common Pleas Court
CPR .... Code of Professional Responsibility
CRC..................................... Ohio Civil Rights Commission
Crim L J Ohio..................... Criminal Law Journal of Ohio
Crim R .... Rules of Criminal Procedure
CSCR................................... Cincinnati Superior Court Reports
CSS .... Court Security Standards
Ct.. Court
D... Ohio Decisions
Dayton................................. Dayton Reports

ABBREVIATIONS

Dayton B Briefs .... Dayton Bar Briefs
dba .... doing business as
DC .... District Court
Dept..................................... Department
Dick L Rev .... Dickinson Law Review
Dist .... District
Div .... Division
Dom Rel .... Domestic Relations Court
Domestic Rel L J Ohio .... Domestic Relations Journal of Ohio
DPID Reg .... Death Penalty Indigent Defense Regulations
DR .... Disciplinary Rules, Code of Professional Responsibility
D Repr................................. Ohio Decisions, Reprint
Duq L Rev .... Duquesne Law Review
E .... Enacted
EBR..................................... Environmental Board of Review (pre 1997)
EBR..................................... Environmental Review Appeals Commission (1997 and after)
EC.. Ethical Considerations, Code of Professional Responsibility
Ed .... Education
eff. .... Effective
Elections Op .... Ohio Elections Commission Opinions
Envtl L J Ohio .... Environmental Law Journal of Ohio
Envtl Monthly .... Environmental Monthly
ERAC.................................. Environmental Review Appeals Commission
Ethics Op .... Ohio Ethics Commission Opinions
Evid R .... Ohio Rules of Evidence
ex rel .... on the relation of
Fam L Quar .... Family Law Quarterly, American Bar Association
F .... Form
F. .... Federal Reporter
F.2d .... Federal Reporter, Second Series
F.3d .... Federal Reporter, Third Series
F. Cas .... Federal Cases
Fed .... Federal
Fla L Rev .... University of Florida Law Review
Forum .... Forum, American Bar Association
F.R.D. .... Federal Rules Decisions
FR Serv .... Federal Rules Service
FR Serv(2d) .... Federal Rules Service, Second Series
F.Supp.................................. Federal Supplement
GC .... General Code of Ohio
Geo L J................................. Georgetown Law Journal
Gotherman's Ohio Mun Serv .... Gotherman's Ohio Municipal Service
Gov Bar R............................ Supreme Court Rules for the Government of the Bar

ABBREVIATIONS

Gov Jud R	Supreme Court Rules for the Government of the Judiciary
H	House Bill
Harv L Rev	Harvard Law Review
HCR	House Concurrent Resolution
Health L J Ohio	Health Law Journal of Ohio
HJR	House Joint Resolution
HR	House Resolution
HWFB	Hazardous Waste Facility Board
Inc	Incorporated
Ind L J	Indiana Law Journal
Indus Rel Rep	Industrial Relations Report
Iowa L Rev	Iowa Law Review
IRC	Internal Revenue Code
J Fam L	Journal of Family Law (University of Louisville)
J L & Com	Journal of Law and Commerce
J L & Educ	Journal of Law and Education
J L & Health	Journal of Law and Health
J Min L & Pol'y	Journal of Mineral Law and Policy
J Nat Resources & Envtl L	Journal of Natural Resources and Environmental Law
Joint Legis Ethics Comm	Joint Legislative Ethics Commission
Jud Cond	Code of Judicial Conduct
Juv	Juvenile Court
Juv R	Rules of Juvenile Procedure
Ky Bench & B	Kentucky Bench and Bar
Ky L J	Kentucky Law Journal
Lake Legal Views	Lake Legal Views, Lake County Bar Association
Law & Fact	Law & Fact, Cuyahoga County Bar Association
LBA Bull	Louisville Bar Association News Bulletin
L.Ed	Lawyers' Edition, United States Supreme Court Reports
L.Ed.2d	Lawyers' Edition, United States Supreme Court Reports, Second Series
Legal Reference Serv Q	Legal Reference Services Quarterly
Louisville Law	Louisville Lawyer
LRA	Lawyers Reports Annotated
LRA(NS)	Lawyers Reports Annotated, New Series
Ltd	Limited
May Ed R	Mayor's Court Education and Procedure Rules
Md L Rev	Maryland Law Review
Mental Disability L Rep	Mental Disability Law Reporter
Mercer L Rev	Mercer Law Review
Mfg	Manufacturing
Misc	Ohio Miscellaneous Reports
Misc(2d)	Ohio Miscellaneous Reports, Second Series
M J	Military Justice Reporter
Muni	Municipal Court

ABBREVIATIONS

Nat'l L J .... National Law Journal
N D L Rev .... North Dakota Law Review
N.D.Ohio .... Northern District Ohio
N.E. .... Northeastern Reporter
N.E.2d .... Northeastern Reporter, Second Series
NEA .... National Education Association
Neb L Rev .... Nebraska Law Review
N Ky L Rev .... Northern Kentucky Law Review
N Ky St L F .... Northern Kentucky State Law Forum
NP .... Ohio Nisi Prius Reports
NP(NS) .... Ohio Nisi Prius Reports, New Series
Nw U L Rev .... Northwestern University Law Review
O .... Ohio Reports
OAC .... Baldwin's Ohio Administrative Code
OAG .... Opinions of the Ohio Attorney General
OAPSE .... Ohio Association of Public School Employees
OBR .... Ohio Bar Reports
OCA .... Ohio Courts of Appeals Reports
O Const .... Ohio Constitution
OCRC .... Ohio Civil Rights Commission
OEA .... Ohio Education Association
OFD .... Ohio Federal Decisions
OFT .... Ohio Federation of Teachers
Ohio .... Ohio Reports
Ohio App .... Ohio Appellate Reports
Ohio App.2d .... Ohio Appellate Reports, Second Series
Ohio App.3d .... Ohio Appellate Reports, Third Series
Ohio B Ass'n Serv Letter..... Ohio Bar Association Service Letter
Ohio C.C. .... Ohio Circuit Court Reports
Ohio C.C.N.S. .... Ohio Circuit Court Reports, New Series
Ohio C.D. .... Ohio Circuit Decisions
Ohio Civ Prac J .... Ohio Civil Practice Journal
Ohio Ct.Cl. .... Ohio Court of Claims
Ohio Com.Pl. .... Ohio Common Pleas Court
Ohio Dec. .... Ohio Decisions
Ohio Dec. Reprint .... Ohio Decisions, Reprint
Ohio F.Dec. .... Ohio Federal Decisions
Ohio L Rep .... Ohio Law Reporter
Ohio Law .... Ohio Lawyer
Ohio Law Abs. .... Ohio Law Abstract
Ohio Misc. .... Ohio Miscellaneous Reports
Ohio Misc.2d .... Ohio Miscellaneous Reports, Second Series
Ohio N.P. .... Ohio Nisi Prius Reports
Ohio N.P.N.S. .... Ohio Nisi Prius Reports, New Series
Ohio N U L Rev .... Ohio Northern University Law Review
Ohio Sch Boards Ass'n J..... Ohio School Boards Association Journal
Ohio St. .... Ohio State Reports

ABBREVIATIONS

Ohio St.2d .... Ohio State Reports, Second Series
Ohio St.3d .... Ohio State Reports, Third Series
Ohio St B Ass'n Rep .... Ohio State Bar Association Report
Ohio St L J .... Ohio State Law Journal
Ohio Tax Rev .... Ohio Tax Review
Ohio Trial .... Ohio Trial, Ohio Academy of Trial Lawyers Education Foundation
OJur 3d .... Ohio Jurisprudence, Third Series
OLS .... Baldwin's Ohio Legislative Service Annotated
OMR .... Baldwin's Ohio Monthly Record
OO .... Ohio Opinions
OO(2d) .... Ohio Opinions, Second Series
OO(3d) .... Ohio Opinions, Third Series
Or L Rev .... Oregon Law Review
ORC .... Baldwin's Ohio Revised Code
OS .... Ohio State Reports
OS(2d) .... Ohio State Reports, Second Series
OS(3d) .... Ohio State Reports, Third Series
OSLJ .... Ohio State Law Journal
OS Unrep .... Ohio State Unreported
O.Supp. .... Ohio Supplement
Otto .... Otto's Supreme Court Reports
Pa B A Q .... Pennsylvania Bar Association Quarterly
Pa Law .... Pennsylvania Lawyer
Pa St B Ass'n Bull .... Pennsylvania State Bar Association Bulletin
PBR .... Personnel Board of Review
PConf .... Possibly or Partially Conflicting
Pepp L Rev .... Pepperdine Law Review
Prob .... Probate Court
Prob & Trust J .... Probate and Trust Journal
Prob L J Ohio .... Probate Law Journal of Ohio
Civ Discovery Edition .... PRO/GRAM Civil Discovery Edition
Civ Litig Edition .... PRO/GRAM Civil Litigation Edition
PUCO .... Public Utilities Commission of Ohio
R .... Repealed
RBR .... Reclamation Board of Review (pre 1997)
RBR .... Reclamation Commission (1997 and after)
RC .... Ohio Revised Code
R-E .... Repealed and Reenacted
RRD .... RC 119.032 rule review date(s)
Rep R .... Supreme Court Rules for the Reporting of Opinions
RS .... Revised Statutes of Ohio
S .... Senate Bill
St Mary's L J .... St. Mary's Law Journal
SCR .... Senate Concurrent Resolution
S.Ct .... United States Supreme Court Reporter
SCt R .... Rules of Practice of the Supreme Court of Ohio

ABBREVIATIONS

S.D.Ohio .... Southern District Ohio
SERB .... State Employment Relations Board
Shingle .... The Shingle, Philadelphia Bar Association
SJR .... Senate Joint Resolution
SR .... Senate Resolution
Stat .... Statutes
State Employment Rel
Board Q .... State Employment Relations Board Quarterly
Sub .... Substitute
Sup R .... Rules of Superintendence for Courts of Ohio
TC .... Tax Court (United States)
Temp L Q .... Temple Law Quarterly
Temp L Rev .... Temple Law Review
TF .... Transferred From
Title Topics .... Title Topics, Ohio Land Title Association
TJS .... Trial Court Jury Use and Management Standards
Tol B Ass'n News .... Toledo Bar Association Newsletter
Traf R .... Ohio Traffic Rules
Trial .... Trial, Association of Trial Lawyers of America
TT .... Transferred To
Twp .... Township
UCBR .... Unemployment Compensation Board of Review (pre 1997)
UCBR .... Unemployment Compensation Review Commission (1997 and after)
UCC .... Uniform Commercial Code
U Cin L Rev .... University of Cincinnati Law Review
U Colo L Rev .... University of Colorado Law Review
U Dayton L Rev .... University of Dayton Law Review
U Pa L Rev .... University of Pennsylvania Law Review
U Pitt L Rev .... University of Pittsburgh Law Review
U Rich L Rev .... University of Richmond Law Review
U.S. .... United States Supreme Court Reports
USC .... United States Code
USCA .... United States Code Annotated
USLW .... United States Law Week
USP.Q .... United States Patent Quarterly
USP.Q.2d .... United States Patent Quarterly, Second Series
U Tol L Rev .... University of Toledo Law Review
v .... versus
v .... volume, Ohio Laws
VCC R .... Rules of Court of Claims of Ohio, Victims of Crime Compensation Section
Vill L Rev .... Villanova Law Review
W .... Withdrawn
W .... Wright's Ohio Supreme Court Reports
Wall. .... Wallace's Supreme Court Reports

ABBREVIATIONS

Wake Forest L Rev .... Wake Forest Law Review
Washburn L J .... Washburn Law Journal
WL.. Westlaw reference number
W.L.B. .... Weekly Law Bulletin
WLG .... Weekly Law Gazette
WLJ .... Western Law Journal
WLM .... Western Law Monthly
Workers' Compensation J Ohio .... Workers' Compensation Journal of Ohio
W Reserve U L Rev .... Western Reserve University Law Review
Wright .... Wright's Ohio Supreme Court Reports

CITE THIS BOOK

OHIO REV. CODE ANN. § 3101.01 (Baldwin 2000)

*

TITLE XXXI
DOMESTIC RELATIONS—CHILDREN

Complete to September 1, 2000

WESTLAW Computer Assisted Legal Research

WESTLAW supplements your legal research in many ways. WESTLAW allows you to

- update your research with the most current information
- expand your library with additional resources
- retrieve current, comprehensive history and citing references to a case with KeyCite

For more information on using WESTLAW to supplement your research, see the WESTLAW Electronic Research Guide, which follows the Preface.

CHAPTER 3101

Marriage

Cross References

Children, Ch 3109
Common law marriage prohibited, 3105.12
Divorce, legal separation, annulment, dissolution of marriage, Ch 3105
Estates, release from administration, 2113.03
Husband and wife, Ch 3103
Non-spousal artificial insemination, 3111.30 et seq.
Rape, evidence, marriage or cohabitation not defenses to rape charges, 2907.02
State board of uniform state laws, study of marriage and divorce laws, 105.23
Voter registration after name changed by marriage, 3503.19

Library References

Carlin, Baldwin's Ohio Practice, *Merrick-Rippner Probate Law* § 2.3 (1997)
Hausser, Ohio Real Estate Law and Practice (2d Ed.), Text 35.081
Kurtz & Giannelli, Ohio Juvenile Law (1998 Ed.), Text 6.3
Sowald & Morganstern, Baldwin's Ohio Practice, *Domestic Relations Law* § 2.1, 2.6, 7.6 (1997)

WESTLAW Electronic Research

See WESTLAW Electronic Research Guide following the Preface.

Law Review and Journal Commentaries

The Antenuptial Contract in Ohio, Note. 28 Case W Res L Rev 1040 (1978).

Califano v Jobst, Zablocki v Redhail, and the Fundamental Right to Marry, Note. 18 J Fam L 587 (1979-80).

Immigration Marriage Fraud Amendments Of 1988: Locking In By Locking Out?, Note. 27 J Fam L 733 (1988-89).

Irrebuttable Exile Under the Immigration Marriage Fraud Amendments: A Perspective From The Eighth Amendment And International Human Rights Law, Comment. 58 U Cin L Rev 1397 (1990).

Judge's Column, Hon. Francine M. Bruening. (Ed. note: Judge Bruening discusses the pending Ohio Parenting Act.) 20 Lake Legal Views 1 (June 1997).

Nonmarital Relationships and Their Impact on the Institution of Marriage and the Traditional Family Structure, Charles F. Crutchfield. 19 J Fam L 247 (1980-81).

The Ohio Law of Marriage, Hugh A. Ross. 14 W Reserve U L Rev 724 (1963).

Partnership Marriage: The Solution to an Ineffective and Inequitable Law of Support, Joan M. Krauskopf and Rhonda C. Thomas. 35 Ohio St L J 558 (1974).

Property Rights on Termination of Alternative Life Styles: Cohabitation, James T. Flaherty. 10 Cap U L Rev 1 (Fall 1980).

Notes of Decisions and Opinions

1. Common law marriage

The probate court properly vacated the appointment of the applicant as administratrix to the decedent's estate on the grounds that such applicant is not the surviving spouse of the decedent where evidence showed that the decedent had refused to go through with a formal marriage and had signed an oil and gas lease indicating he was single since such is sufficient evidence to refute the claim of common law marriage. Estate of Yerke v Yerke, No. 82 CA 27 (7th Dist Ct App, Mahoning, 4-15-83).

Common law marriages are disfavored in Ohio. Smith-Wilkins on Behalf of Hertzer v. Secretary of Health and Human Services (C.A.6 (Ohio) 1989) 880 F.2d 864.

WHO MAY MARRY

3101.01 Persons who may marry

Male persons of the age of eighteen years, and female persons of the age of sixteen years, not nearer of kin than second cousins, and not having a husband or wife living, may be joined in marriage. A minor must first obtain the consent of the minor's parents, surviving parent, parent who is designated the residential parent and legal custodian of the child by a court of competent jurisdiction, guardian, or any one of the following who has been awarded permanent custody of the minor by a court exercising juvenile jurisdiction:

(A) An adult person;

(B) The department of job and family services or any child welfare organization certified by such department;

(C) A public children services agency.

A minor shall not be required to obtain the consent of a parent who resides in a foreign country, has neglected or abandoned such minor for a period of one year or longer immediately preceding the application for a marriage license, has been adjudged incompetent, is an inmate of a state mental or correctional institution, has been permanently deprived of parental rights and responsibilities for the care of the child and the right to have the child live with the parent and to be the legal custodian of the child by a court exercising juvenile jurisdiction, or has been deprived of parental rights and responsibilities for the care of the child and the right to have the child live with the parent and to be the legal custodian of the child by the appointment of a guardian of the person of the minor by the probate court or by any other court of competent jurisdiction.

(1999 H 471, eff. 7-1-00; 1997 H 408, eff. 10-1-97; 1994 H 571, eff. 10-6-94; 1990 S 3, eff. 4-11-91; 1986 H 428; 1969 S 49; 1953 H 1; GC 8001-1; Source—GC 11181)

Historical and Statutory Notes

Pre-1953 H 1 Amendments: 124 v S 65

Amendment Note: 1999 H 471 substituted "job and family" for "human" in division (B).

Amendment Note: 1997 H 408 substituted "public children services agency" for "county department of human services or a county children services board" in division (C); and made changes to reflect gender neutral language.

Amendment Note: 1994 H 571 substituted "correctional" for "penal" in the final paragraph.

Comparative Laws

Ark.—A.C.A. § 9-11-101.
Ariz.—A.R.S. § 25-102.
Ga.—O.C.G.A. § 19-3-2.
Idaho—I.C. § 32-202.
Iowa—I.C.A. § 595.2.
La.—LSA-R.S. 9:211; LSA-C.C. art. 90.
Mass.—M.G.L.A. c. 207, § 7.
Minn.—M.S.A. § 517.02.
Mo.—V.A.M.S. § 451.090.
Neb.—R.R.S.1943, § 42-102.
N.J.—N.J.S.A. 37:1-6.
N.M.—NMSA 1978, § 40-1-5.
N.Y.—McKinney's Domestic Relations Law § 15-a.
Okl.—43 Okl.St.Ann. § 3.
Tex.—V.T.C.A. Family Code § 2.401.
Wash.—West's RCWA 26.04.010.
Wis.—W.S.A. 765.02.
W.Va.—Code, 48-1-1.

Cross References

Abolition of civil action for breach of promise to marry, 2305.29
Age of majority, 3109.01
Allowance for support of surviving spouse or minor children, 2106.13
Appointment of guardian, 2111.02
Attempt by child to marry without consent, "unruly child", 2151.022
Bigamy, 2919.01
Consent to marry, Juv R 42
Descent and distribution, rights of surviving spouse, 2105.06 et seq.
Divorce, legal separation, annulment, dissolution of marriage, Ch 3105
Dower, Ch 2103
Effect of marriage on existing will, 2107.37
Evidence of marriage; common-law marriage prohibited, 3105.12
Husband and wife, mutual obligations, 3103.01
Interest of husband or wife in property of the other, 3103.04
Jurisdiction of probate court in matters of marriage and guardianship, 2101.24
Juvenile court, jurisdiction regarding applications for consent to marry, 2151.23
Marriage of ward, effect on guardianship, 2111.45
Name change of voter due to marriage, report to board of elections, 3503.19
"Neglected child" defined, 2151.03
Probate court, records of marriage and guardianship, 2101.12
Property ownership rights, effect of marital status, 3103.07
Remarriage, revival of property rights under revoked will, 2107.33
Retirement benefits of spouse, effect of marriage or remarriage, 145.46
Statute of frauds, action on agreement made upon consideration of marriage, 1335.05

Library References

Marriage ⚷4 to 11, 19.
WESTLAW Topic No. 253.
C.J.S. Marriage §§ 4, 7, 9, 13 to 18, 26.

OJur 3d: 45, Family Law § 15 to 17, 19, 26
Am Jur 2d: 52, Marriage § 14 to 26
Common law marriage between parties previously divorced. 82 ALR2d 688
Marriage between persons of the same sex. 63 ALR3d 1199
Validity of marriage as affected by lack of legal authority of person solemnizing it. 13 ALR4th 1323

Baldwin's Ohio School Law, Text 20.9
Carlin, Baldwin's Ohio Practice, *Merrick-Rippner Probate Law* § 106.20, 106.26 (1997)
Sowald & Morganstern, Baldwin's Ohio Practice, *Domestic Relations Law* § 2.16, 2.23, 2.25, 2.26, 2.63, 7.6, 7.7, 7.13, 7.32 (1997)

Law Review and Journal Commentaries

Common Law Marriage, Robert Black. 2 U Cin L Rev 113 (1928).

Common Law Marriage in Ohio, Rosalie M. Moynahan. 5 Ohio St L J 26 (1938); 5 Ohio St L J 175 (1939).

Conflict of laws rules and the interstate recognition of same-sex marriages, Note. 1995 U Ill L Rev 911.

Constitutional Law—The Immigration Marriage Fraud Amendments: Substantive or Procedural Provisions?—Azizi v. Thornburgh, Note. 64 Temp L Rev 1081 (Winter 1991).

A Defense of First-Cousin Marriage, Marvin M. Moore. 10 Clev-Marshall L Rev 136 (1960).

Desperately Seeking Status: Same-Sex Couples Battle for Employment-Linked Benefits. 27 Akron L Rev 253 (Fall 1993).

Domestic relations jurisprudence and the great, slumbering *Baehr*: On definitional preclusion, equal protection, and fundamental interests, Mark Strasser. 64 Fordham L Rev 921 (1995).

For Whom Bell Tolls: On Subsequent Domiciles' Refusing to Recognize Same-Sex Marriages, Mark Strasser. 66 U Cin L Rev 339 (Winter 1998).

High Schools, Marriage, and the Fourteenth Amendment, Laurence W. Knowles. 11 J Fam L 711 (1972).

Legal Rights of Unmarried Heterosexual and Homosexual Couples and Evolving Definitions of "Family," Note. 29 J Fam L 497 (1990-91).

The Loving Decision and the Freedom to Marry, Rev. Robert F. Drinan, S. J. 29 Ohio St L J 358 (1968).

Of Covenants and Conflicts—When "I Do" Means More Than It Used To, But Less Than You Thought, Jason Andrew Macke. 59 Ohio St L J 1377 (1998).

Queer Law: Sexual Orientation Law in The Mid-Eighties, Rhonda R. Rivera. 11 U Dayton L Rev 275 (Winter 1986).

Same Gender Couples: Legal Disabilities and Strategies, Hon. Mike Brigner. 10 Domestic Rel J Ohio 1 (January/February 1998).

Same-Sex Marriage: The Linchpin Issue, G. Sidney Buchanan. 10 U Dayton L Rev 541 (Spring 1985).

Schools—Rules and Regulations Affecting Married Students—Reasonableness and Validity, Note. 16 W Reserve U L Rev 792 (1965).

Teenage Marriage, Misconduct and the Law, William G. Callow. 53 A B A J 541 (1967).

Notes of Decisions and Opinions

---

1. In general

Public policy looks unfavorably on restraints to marriage. Jordan v. Jordan (Ohio App. 4 Dist. 1996) 117 Ohio App.3d 47, 689 N.E.2d 1005, dismissed, appeal not allowed 78 Ohio St.3d 1489, 678 N.E.2d 1227.

Marriage of minor child is an act of emancipation that terminates obligations of domestic relations order as a matter of law. Swanson v. Swanson (Greene 1996) 109 Ohio App.3d 231, 671 N.E.2d 1333.

Marriage valid where made is valid in Ohio, unless expressly prohibited by law. Peefer v. State (Greene 1931) 42 Ohio App. 276, 182 N.E. 117, 12 Ohio Law Abs. 583.

A board of education may adopt a rule prohibiting married students from participating in extracurricular activities. State ex rel. Baker v. Stevenson (Ohio Com.Pl. 1962) 189 N.E.2d 181, 94 Ohio Law Abs. 545, 27 O.O.2d 223.

Where an annulment is justified, the divorce statutes should not be construed as being involved. Nyhuis v. Pierce (Cuyahoga 1952) 114 N.E.2d 75, 65 Ohio Law Abs. 73.

A federal statute concerning immigration fraud, 8 USC 1154(h), meant to prevent marriage for the sole purpose of circumventing immigration laws, does not violate the First, Fifth, or Ninth Amendment by denying the status of an "immediate relative" to an alien who marries during deportation proceedings. Minatsis v. Brown (S.D.Ohio 1989) 713 F.Supp. 1056.

In deciding whether a bankruptcy debtor is married to the recipient of allegedly preferential transfers from him, which would make the recipient an "insider" as a spouse under 11 USC 101(30)(A)(i), the bankruptcy court must answer the question in accordance with state domestic relations law. In re Blankenship (Bkrtcy.N.D.Ohio 1991) 133 B.R. 398.

Ohio does not authorize the performance of marriages by proxy because the statute requires the parties' personal presence; Ohio will, however, recognize proxy marriages performed in another state where such marriages are valid. In re Blankenship (Bkrtcy.N.D.Ohio 1991) 133 B.R. 398.

Cohabitation, which is one nonstatutory factor that may be considered when the validity of a marriage is questioned, means the act of living together and may be based entirely on living together without sexual relations. In re Blankenship (Bkrtcy.N.D.Ohio 1991) 133 B.R. 398.

A probate court may not refuse to issue a marriage license for the reason that there is money due for child support of a previous marriage. OAG 69-051.

A probate court may not refuse to issue a marriage license on the ground of a present inability to support a family. OAG 69-051.

A probate court may not require the evidence of an IQ test or other similar test to prove mental capacity as a prerequisite to the issuance of a marriage license. OAG 69-051.

2. Age of parties and ratification of marriage

Where the parents of a female person under sixteen years of age actively participate in enabling such person to enter into a marriage relationship, such participation constitutes acts tending to cause the child to become a "delinquent child" and the parents "act in a way tending to cause delinquency in such child." State v. Gans (Ohio 1958) 168 Ohio St. 174, 151 N.E.2d 709, 5 O.O.2d 472, certiorari denied 79 S.Ct. 722, 359 U.S. 945, 3 L.Ed.2d 678.

Marriage of Ohio residents in Kentucky, and return to Ohio, followed by cohabitation, held voidable only by infant female, though she was hardly fifteen and had not parent's consent. Peefer v. State (Greene 1931) 42 Ohio App. 276, 182 N.E. 117, 12 Ohio Law Abs. 583.

RC 2101.24 does not indicate that the probate court has authority to determine issues regarding immigration and naturalization and a determination that a marriage is for hire, and intended to circumvent the immigration and naturalization laws, is improper; however, the court has jurisdiction to determine the validity of a marriage where there is no consent by a minor's parent or guardian and no consummation of the marriage. In re Ababseh, No. 95-CA-179, 1996 WL 116148 (7th Dist Ct App, Mahoning, 3-12-96).

Under the statute, the marriage of a girl between twelve and sixteen years of age without the consent of her parents is not void, but only voidable; and it cannot be set aside at suit of the parents without consent of the infant; nor are the parents entitled to an injunction against the consortium of the husband and wife. Klinebell v Hilton, 2 Abs 637 (App, Franklin 1924).

Marriage by a female seventeen years of age and cohabitation by her with her husband renders the marriage valid without the consent of her parents. Allen v. Allen (Ohio Com.Pl. 1923) 21 Ohio Law Rep. 313.

Marriage between persons under the legal age of twenty-one years, but over the common law age of consent, is not void, but only voidable; and where it appears that a minor over common law age of consent enters into a marriage contract and such marriage is consummated by cohabitation, such will be held valid notwithstanding the failure of the minor's parents to consent to such marriage. Pearlman v Pearlman, 27 NP(NS) 46 (1928).

A marriage contracted in Ohio by a female under the age of sixteen years is void, and remains void, unless confirmed by her by cohabitation or by some other ratification, at the time she becomes sixteen years of age or afterwards. State v. Wilcox (Ohio Juv. 1926) 26 Ohio N.P.N.S. 343.

A minor youth who has been committed to the youth services department pursuant to RC 2151.355 and 5139.05 and who wishes to get married must first obtain consent, as required by RC 3101.01 and Juv R 42, from one or both parents, from one of the alternative authorities named in RC 3101.01, or from the juvenile court as provided in Juv R 42(A). The youth services department has no authority to either consent or withhold consent to the marriage of a minor committed to its custody. OAG 89-046.

Amended GC 8023 (RC 3109.01) and GC 11181 (RC 3101.01) apply to all females under twenty-one years of age, and those who were eighteen years of age before the taking effect of these respective amended sections were of full legal age during the period between the date when they became eighteen years of age and the taking effect of said amended sections, and resumed the status of minors upon the taking effect of said amended sections and so remain until they reach the age of twenty-one years. 1923 OAG p 554.

3. —In general, common law marriage

A ceremonial marriage which is void because husband is already married becomes a valid common law marriage upon the death of the first wife and continued cohabitation thereafter, though the death of the first wife may not have been known. Johnson v. Wolford (Ohio 1927) 117 Ohio St. 136, 157 N.E. 385, 5 Ohio Law Abs. 402, 25 Ohio Law Rep. 377.

Where one receiving alimony under a separation agreement, which provides that payments are to cease if such party remarries, enters into a relationship in another state that would constitute a valid marriage in Ohio, such act is a remarriage within the meaning of the agreement. Fahrer v. Fahrer (Hamilton 1973) 36 Ohio App.2d 208, 304 N.E.2d 411, 65 O.O.2d 330.

Where married man and married woman, before either had secured divorce, cohabited together as husband and wife, and continued to do so for period of more than thirty years, and after impediments to their marriage had been removed by divorce or death, pursuant to agreement in the present tense to become husband and wife, a common law marriage existed between them, entitling widow to dower in husband's property. Jenkins v. Jenkins (Sandusky 1928) 30 Ohio App. 336, 164 N.E. 790, 6 Ohio Law Abs. 596.

Existence of common law marriage is to be determined by law of state where it was consummated. Howard v. Central Nat. Bank of Marietta (Washington 1926) 21 Ohio App. 74, 152 N.E. 784, 4 Ohio Law Abs. 700.

Delay of woman, after death of man who had deserted her, to assert common law marriage to him is not conclusive against her, but only a circumstance to be considered. Howard v. Central Nat. Bank of Marietta (Washington 1926) 21 Ohio App. 74, 152 N.E. 784, 4 Ohio Law Abs. 700.

It is not necessarily inconsistent with informal marriage in fact, but only tends to show parties were ashamed of unconventional method adopted, that they said they had been married by an official. Howard v. Central Nat. Bank of Marietta (Washington 1926) 21 Ohio App. 74, 152 N.E. 784, 4 Ohio Law Abs. 700.

Evidence of cohabitation and reputation is admissible in favor of child of parties to prove common law marriage, although surviving party testifies to terms of contract. Howard v. Central Nat. Bank of Marietta (Washington 1926) 21 Ohio App. 74, 152 N.E. 784, 4 Ohio Law Abs. 700.

A child was born as a result of illicit relations which were continued after the subsequent church marriage of the man to another woman and the birth of children as a result of that union. After an interval of seven years the first woman, in order to insure a continuance of support of herself and child and claiming a common law marriage, sued for a divorce and alimony and was granted a decree in the court below. Duhigg v Duhigg, 31 LR 600 (1929).

Common law marriages are disfavored in Ohio. Smith-Wilkins on Behalf of Hertzer v. Secretary of Health and Human Services (C.A.6 (Ohio) 1989) 880 F.2d 864.

Probate court would not recognize validity of an alleged common law marriage where no rights of innocent persons were to be protected and the only reason advanced to sustain such marriage was to establish the right of inheritance. In re Goettge's Estate (Ohio Prob. 1940) 6 Ohio Supp. 89, 32 Ohio Law Abs. 620, 19 O.O. 138.

4. —Requirements; proof, common law marriage

Person seeking to establish common-law marriage must prove four elements: (1) a mutual agreement to marry in praesenti, made by parties competent to marry; (2) cohabitation as husband and wife; (3) holding of themselves out as husband and wife in community in which they live; and (4) being regarded as husband and wife in community in which they live. Kowalik v. Kowalik (Ohio App. 7 Dist. 1997) 118 Ohio App.3d 141, 691 N.E.2d 1152.

Party seeking to establish fact of common-law marriage must do so by proving each and every element thereof by clear and convincing evidence. Kowalik v. Kowalik (Ohio App. 7 Dist. 1997) 118 Ohio App.3d 141, 691 N.E.2d 1152.

Signed marriage license application which stated that applicant had "no wife living" did not fundamentally contradict asserted common-law marriage with woman he was marrying; language in application could be read or understood to ask whether applicant had any other wife and that document was only meant to comply with marriage license statute and statute providing that a person having husband or wife living may not marry another person. Ruscilli v. Ruscilli (Franklin 1993) 90 Ohio App.3d 753, 630 N.E.2d 745, motion to certify overruled 68 Ohio St.3d 1473, 628 N.E.2d 1391.

A common-law marriage may be inferred by cohabitation and community reputation despite a lack of evidence concerning an in presenti agreement to be married. Warren Gen. Hosp. v. Brink (Trumbull 1992) 80 Ohio App.3d 793, 610 N.E.2d 1128.

A common law marriage may be established in Ohio only when each of the following five essential elements is proved by clear and convincing evidence, namely: (1) an agreement of marriage per verba de praesenti; (2) made by parties competent to marry; (3) followed by cohabitation; (4) a holding out as husband and wife; and (5) a reputation as being husband and wife. In re Soeder's Estate (Cuyahoga 1966) 7 Ohio App.2d 271, 220 N.E.2d 547, 36 O.O.2d 404.

Agreement of marriage in praesenti entered into and followed by cohabitation as husband and wife, where contracting parties are treated as such in circle in which they move, constitutes a valid marriage at common law. Holmes v. Pere Marquette R. Co. (Lucas 1927) 28 Ohio App. 297, 162 N.E. 675, 6 Ohio Law Abs. 628.

Agreement to live together as man and wife must be made per verba de praesenti or by words of present tense, and if such agreement is made by words of future tense there can be no common law marriage. Holmes v. Pere Marquette R. Co. (Lucas 1927) 28 Ohio App. 297, 162 N.E. 675, 6 Ohio Law Abs. 628.

Evidence of cohabitation and reputation and conduct of parties, without the testimony of the surviving party, may constitute satisfactory proof of common law marriage. Howard v. Central Nat. Bank of Marietta (Washington 1926) 21 Ohio App. 74, 152 N.E. 784, 4 Ohio Law Abs. 700.

To consummate marriage by verba de praesenti, such words need not be used by both, but the expression thereof by the man, and acquiescence by the woman, is enough. Howard v. Central Nat. Bank of Marietta (Washington 1926) 21 Ohio App. 74, 152 N.E. 784, 4 Ohio Law Abs. 700.

Effect of proof of common law marriage is not destroyed by the man's later adulterous career with another woman. Howard v. Central Nat. Bank of Marietta (Washington 1926) 21 Ohio App. 74, 152 N.E. 784, 4 Ohio Law Abs. 700.

Although surviving party to alleged common law marriage testifies to terms of contract, evidence of cohabitation and reputation and practical construction by parties is admissible in woman's favor; she not testifying that arrangement was not a marriage and ensuing cohabitation meretricious, but to an agreement of doubtful import. Howard v. Central Nat. Bank of Marietta (Washington 1926) 21 Ohio App. 74, 152 N.E. 784, 4 Ohio Law Abs. 700.

Under the circumstances of the case, the man's ambiguous declaration to the woman, "Now we are man and wife," should be treated as a declaration of his marriage in verba de praesenti, and not as an expression of his opinion as to the legal effect of his proposal. Howard v. Central Nat. Bank of Marietta (Washington 1926) 21 Ohio App. 74, 152 N.E. 784, 4 Ohio Law Abs. 700.

The elements to be established by the proponent of the common law marriage are: (a) an agreement to marry in praesenti, (b) made by parties competent to contract, (c) which is accepted by the parties and followed by cohabitation as husband and wife, (d) in the community where they reside as husband and wife, and each element must be proved by "clear and convincing" evidence. Jolley v. Jolley (Ohio Com.Pl. 1975) 46 Ohio Misc. 40, 347 N.E.2d 557, 75 O.O.2d 350.

In order to establish a common law marriage a clear understanding and agreement must be shown between the parties to henceforth live together and treat each other as husband and wife. The agreement must be in praesenti, and not to become effective at some time in the future, and must be followed immediately by cohabitation and probably the holding out of each other to all the world as husband and wife, the woman being thenceforth known under the name of her husband. Schwartz v Schwartz, 11 Abs 483, 35 LR 66 (App, Cuyahoga 1931).

In order to base legal rights on a common law marriage, it must be shown that there was a meeting of minds resulting in a mutual contract and a living together as husband and wife to an extent, as in other marriages, that causes the relation of husband and wife to be recognized and a matter of repute in the community where the parties reside. Gillmore v Dorning, 31 LR 588 (1930).

There is no common law marriage, for purposes of widows' and stepchildrens' eligibility for social security survivor's benefits, between a woman and a man who file separate income tax returns stating they are unmarried and who are not believed to be married by relatives; the fact the woman did not mention the "marriage" on her later license application to marry another man is also significant. Smith-Wilkins on Behalf of Hertzer v. Secretary of Health and Human Services (C.A.6 (Ohio) 1989) 880 F.2d 864.

Ohio recognizes a relationship as a common law marriage only where the parties (1) agree to marriage in praesenti, (2) thereafter live together as husband and wife, and (3) are reputed to be and are treated as husband and wife in the community. Young v. Secretary of Health and Human Services (C.A.6 (Ohio) 1986) 787 F.2d 1064, certiorari denied 107 S.Ct. 585, 479 U.S. 990, 93 L.Ed.2d 587.

In order to sustain a common law marriage, there must be proof of an explicit contract, either in writing or in parol; it must be a contract of marriage at the time of the contract and not a promise in the future; and such contract of marriage must be followed by cohabitation as husband and wife, and, in addition thereto, there must be a holding out to the public by both parties that they are husband and wife. Eagleson v. McKee (Ohio Prob. 1939) 1 Ohio Supp. 321, 33 Ohio Law Abs. 33, 19 O.O. 362, affirmed 33 N.E.2d 417, 33 Ohio Law Abs. 38.

Clear and convincing evidence was required to sustain contention of a valid common law marriage. Eagleson v. McKee (Ohio Prob. 1939) 1 Ohio Supp. 321, 33 Ohio Law Abs. 33, 19 O.O. 362, affirmed 33 N.E.2d 417, 33 Ohio Law Abs. 38.

5. Relatives, marriage of

A common law marriage entered into in Ohio between an uncle and his niece is incestuous and void ab initio. In re Stiles Estate (Ohio 1979) 59 Ohio St.2d 73, 391 N.E.2d 1026, 13 O.O.3d 62.

Although a marriage in Ohio between first cousins is not approved by law, it is not expressly prohibited and made void by any statutory enactment, and, where first cousins by blood, one a resident of Massachusetts and the other a resident of Ohio, are lawfully married in Massachusetts and remove to Ohio to live, such marriage is not void in Ohio, and an action by the Ohio resident instituted in Ohio to annul the marriage on the ground that it is void ab initio cannot be maintained. Mazzolini v. Mazzolini (Ohio 1958) 168 Ohio St. 357, 155 N.E.2d 206, 7 O.O.2d 123.

Marriage between blood first cousins was voidable, rather than void ab initio. Soley v. Soley (Lucas 1995) 101 Ohio App.3d 540, 655 N.E.2d 1381, dismissed, appeal not allowed 73 Ohio St.3d 1410, 651 N.E.2d 1308, certiorari denied 116 S.Ct. 945, 133 L.Ed.2d 870.

Where one has entered into a marriage within the degree of consanguinity prohibited by the law of Ohio, either party to such marriage may obtain a divorce on the statutory ground of fraudulent contract. Such marriage is void ab initio. The relief provided by the statute includes a fraud perpetrated on the law. Basickas v. Basickas (Summit 1953) 93 Ohio App. 531, 114 N.E.2d 270, 51 O.O. 229.

A relator's allegation that he and his wife are first cousins does not entitle the relator to a declaration that his marriage is void ab initio, as a sexual relationship between cousins has never been criminalized as incestuous; thus, a writ of mandamus to dismiss the divorce action and to declare the marriage void will be denied. State ex rel Soley, v Lucas County Court of Common Pleas, No. L-93-232, 1993 WL 334254 (6th Dist Ct App, Lucas, 9-2-93), affirmed by 69 Ohio St.3d 514 (1994).

Marriage between an uncle and niece in Ohio is void ab initio and hence can be collaterally attacked, though both parties to the marriage are dead. Heyse v Michalske, 31 Abs 484 (Prob, Cuyahoga 1940).

6. Homosexual/transsexual marriage

Statute which directly and substantially interferes with the decision to marry will be upheld as complying with due process clause only if it is supported by sufficiently important state interests and closely tailored to effectuate those interests; however, regulations which do not significantly interfere with decision to marry may be legitimately imposed. Pena v. Northeast Ohio Emergency Affiliates, Inc. (Lorain 1995) 108 Ohio App.3d 96, 670 N.E.2d 268, dismissed, appeal not allowed 75 Ohio St.3d 1494, 664 N.E.2d 1291.

Ohio law permits marriage only between two members of the opposite sex, and a homosexual relationship between two women does not constitute a marriage which would permit one woman's former husband to terminate alimony, even where one party has altered her gender through transsexual surgery. Gajovski v. Gajovski (Summit 1991) 81 Ohio App.3d 11, 610 N.E.2d 431, dismissed, jurisdictional motion overruled 62 Ohio St.3d 1415, 577 N.E.2d 660.

Ability to marry is a necessary element of concubinage; therefore, spousal support may not be terminated due to the cohabitation of an obligee wife in a homosexual relationship where the judgment requires that the obligee be in a state of concubinage to justify termination of spousal support. Gajovski v. Gajovski (Summit 1991) 81 Ohio App.3d 11, 610 N.E.2d 431, dismissed, jurisdictional motion overruled 62 Ohio St.3d 1415, 577 N.E.2d 660.

Because RC 3101.01 fails to define "marriage," courts must presume that the legislature used the term in its ordinary sense to mean a heterosexual relationship, and hence a complaint for divorce by one woman against another woman must be dismissed. Irwin v Lupardus, No. 41379 (8th Dist Ct App, Cuyahoga, 6-26-80).

A person's sex is determined at birth by an anatomical examination by the birth attendant and remains the "true sex" of a person despite later gender transformation surgery; thus, a post-operative male to female transsexual is not permitted under Ohio law to marry a male person and a marriage license will not be issued to a post-operative male to female transsexual and another male person. In re Ladrach (Ohio Prob. 1987) 32 Ohio Misc.2d 6, 513 N.E.2d 828.

7. Constitutional issues

Freedom to marry is recognized as one of the vital personal rights essential to the orderly pursuit of happiness by free persons. Pena v. Northeast Ohio Emergency Affiliates, Inc. (Lorain 1995) 108 Ohio App.3d 96, 670 N.E.2d 268, dismissed, appeal not allowed 75 Ohio St.3d 1494, 664 N.E.2d 1291.

Right to marry is both fundamental substantive due process and associational right. Montgomery v. Carr (C.A.6 (Ohio) 1996) 101 F.3d 1117.

Whether governmental action involved is legislative or executive, general or isolated, rational basis scrutiny applies to rationales offered by governmental defendants on claim that plaintiff's associational right to marry has been infringed, unless burden on right to marry is direct and substantial. Montgomery v. Carr (C.A.6 (Ohio) 1996) 101 F.3d 1117.

State action impinging on right to marry is to be reviewed in same fashion whether advanced on theory that it violates substantive due process or advanced on theory that it violates First Amendment's right to intimate association. Montgomery v. Carr (C.A.6 (Ohio) 1996) 101 F.3d 1117.

Public school's antinepotism policy, under which teacher was required to transfer to another school in district when it became known she had married another teacher in building where they both worked, was not substantial burden on their right to marry and thus claim that policy violated teachers' First Amendment associational rights was subject to rational basis scrutiny. Montgomery v. Carr (C.A.6 (Ohio) 1996) 101 F.3d 1117.

Despite contention that it violated public school teachers' First Amendment associational rights, school's antinepotism rule was rationally related to legitimate goals, including avoiding friction if marriage broke down, cutting down on social fraternization, promoting collegiality among teachers, and easing task of managing teachers. Montgomery v. Carr (C.A.6 (Ohio) 1996) 101 F.3d 1117.

8. Bigamist

Alleged common-law wife had standing to bring action to annul her husband's subsequent marriage to another woman. Thomas-Schafer v. Schafer (Hamilton 1996) 111 Ohio App.3d 779, 677 N.E.2d 374.

CONSENT

3101.02 Method of consent

Any consent required under section 3101.01 of the Revised Code shall be personally given before the probate judge or a deputy clerk of the probate court, or certified under the hand of the person consenting, by two witnesses, one of whom must appear before the judge and make oath that he saw the person whose name is annexed to the certificate subscribe it, or heard him acknowledge it.

(129 v 582, eff. 1-10-61; 1953 H 1; GC 8001-2; Source—GC 11190)

Historical and Statutory Notes

Pre-1953 H 1 Amendments: 124 v S 65

Cross References

Consent to marry, Juv R 42
Form and content of acknowledgment, 147.53, 147.54
Juvenile court, jurisdiction regarding applications for consent to marry, 2151.23

Library References

Marriage ⟹19.
WESTLAW Topic No. 253.
C.J.S. Marriage § 26.

OJur 3d: 32, Decedents' Estates § 622; 45, Family Law § 18
Am Jur 2d: 52, Marriage § 15, 16, 27 et seq.

Recognition by foreign state of marriage which, though invalid where contracted, would have been valid if contracted within foreign state. 82 ALR3d 1240

Carlin, Baldwin's Ohio Practice, *Merrick-Rippner Probate Law* § 106.27 (1997)

3101.03 Consent of absent parent or guardian

If the parent or guardian of a minor is a nonresident of, or is absent from, the county in which the marriage license is applied for, he personally may appear before the official upon whose authority marriage licenses are issued, in the county in which he is at the time domiciled, and give his consent in writing to such marriage. The consent must be attested to by two witnesses, certified to by such official, and forwarded to the probate judge of the county in which the license is applied for. The probate judge may administer any oath required, issue and sign such license, and affix the seal of the probate court.

(1972 H 551, eff. 6-22-72; 1953 H 1; GC 8001-3; Source—GC 11191)

Historical and Statutory Notes

Pre-1953 H 1 Amendments: 124 v S 65

Cross References

Consent to marry, Juv R 42
Juvenile court, jurisdiction regarding applications for consent to marry, 2151.23

Library References

Marriage ⟹19.
WESTLAW Topic No. 253.
C.J.S. Marriage § 26.

OJur 3d: 33 Decedents' Estates § 1344; 45, Family Law § 18

Am Jur 2d: 52, Marriage § 15, 16, 27 et seq.

Carlin, Baldwin's Ohio Practice, *Merrick-Rippner Probate Law* § 106.28, 106.29 (1997)

3101.04 Consent of juvenile court

When the juvenile court files a consent to marriage pursuant to the juvenile rules, the probate court may thereupon issue a license, notwithstanding either or both the contracting parties for the marital relation are under the minimum age prescribed in section 3101.01 of the Revised Code. The license shall not issue until section 3101.05 of the Revised Code has been complied with, and until such child has been born, or it is found beyond doubt by the juvenile court that the minor female is pregnant and intends to have the child.

(1996 H 274, eff. 8-8-96; 1974 H 233, eff. 9-23-74; 1972 H 551; 1953 H 1; GC 8001-4; Source—GC 11181-1)

Historical and Statutory Notes

Pre-1953 H 1 Amendments: 124 v S 65

Amendment Note: 1996 H 274 deleted "illegitimate" before "child has been born".

Cross References

Age of majority, 3109.01
Consent to marry, Juv R 42
Jurisdiction of juvenile court regarding applications for consent to marry, 2151.23
Marriage of ward, effect on guardianship, 2111.45

Library References

Marriage ⚷19.
WESTLAW Topic No. 253.
C.J.S. Marriage § 26.

OJur 3d: 45, Family Law § 26
Am Jur 2d: 52, Marriage § 15, 16, 27 et seq.

Carlin, Baldwin's Ohio Practice, *Merrick-Rippner Probate Law* § 105.1, 106.20, 106.26 (1997)
Sowald & Morganstern, Baldwin's Ohio Practice, *Domestic Relations Law* § 2.16 (1997)

Notes of Decisions and Opinions

Consent lacking 1

1. Consent lacking

The marriage of a male person seventeen years of age is void, except under the conditions provided for in this section. Carlton v. Carlton (Wood 1945) 76 Ohio App. 338, 64 N.E.2d 428, 32 O.O. 82.

LICENSE

3101.05 License application; procedures; misrepresentations

(A) The parties to a marriage shall make an application for a marriage license not less than five nor more than thirty days before a license is issued. Each of the persons seeking a marriage license shall personally appear in the probate court within the county where either resides, or, if neither is a resident of this state, where the marriage is expected to be solemnized. If neither party is a resident of this state, the marriage may be solemnized only in the county where the license is obtained. Each party shall make application and shall state upon oath, the party's name, age, residence, place of birth, occupation, social security number, father's name, and mother's maiden name, if known, and the name of the person who is expected to solemnize the marriage. If either party has been previously married, the application shall include the names of the parties to any previous marriage and of any minor children, and if divorced the jurisdiction, date, and case number of the decree. If either applicant is under the age of eighteen years, the judge shall require the applicants to state that they received marriage counseling satisfactory to the court.

Immediately upon receipt of an application for a marriage license, the court shall place the parties' record in a book kept for that purpose. After the expiration of five and not more than thirty days from the date of the application, if the probate judge is satisfied that there is no legal impediment and if one or both of the parties are present, the probate judge shall grant the marriage license.

If the judge is satisfied from the affidavit of a reputable physician in active practice and residing in the county where the probate court is located, that one of the parties is unable to appear in court, by reason of illness or other physical disability, a marriage license may be granted upon application and oath of the other party to the contemplated marriage; but in that case the person who is unable to appear in court, at the time of making application for a marriage license, shall make and file in that court, an affidavit setting forth the information required of applicants for a marriage license. For good cause shown, the probate judge may waive this section with respect to the period between the application and the issuance of a marriage license and may grant the marriage license at any time after the application.

Each marriage license issued shall include the social security number of each party to the marriage, as stated on the marriage license application.

(B) An applicant for a marriage license who knowingly makes a false statement in an application or affidavit prescribed by this section is guilty of falsification under section 2921.13 of the Revised Code.

(C) No licensing officer shall issue a marriage license if the officer has not received the application, affidavit, or other statements prescribed by this section or if the officer has reason to believe that any of the statements in a marriage license application or in an affidavit prescribed by this section is false.

(D) Any fine collected for violation of this section shall be paid to the use of the county together with the costs of prosecution.

(1996 S 269, eff. 7-1-96; 1990 S 3, eff. 4-11-91; 1981 H 694; 1974 H 233; 1972 H 551; 1969 S 135; 129 v 254; 1953 H 1; GC 8001-5; Source—GC 8001-16, 11188)

Historical and Statutory Notes

Pre-1953 H 1 Amendments: 124 v S 65

Amendment Note: 1996 S 269 rewrote divisions (B) and (C); made changes to reflect gender neutral language; and made other nonsubstantive changes. Prior thereto divisions (B) and (C) read:

"(B) No applicant for a marriage license shall misrepresent any of the facts prescribed by this section.

"(C) No licensing officer shall issue a marriage license if he has not received the statements prescribed by this section or if he has reason to believe that any of the facts in those statements or in a marriage license application have been misrepresented."

Comparative Laws

Conn.—C.G.S.A. § 46b-26.
Ga.—O.C.G.A. § 19-3-40 et seq.
Neb.—R.R.S.1943, § 42-104 et seq.
N.J.—N.J.S.A. 37:1-2 et seq.
N.M.—NMSA 1978, § 40-1-11.
Okl.—43 Okl.St.Ann. § 31 et seq.
Wis.—W.S.A. 765.08.
W.Va.—Code, 48-1-6a et seq.

Cross References

Penalty: 3101.99(A)
Prohibition: 2921.13

Falsification, 2921.13
Jurisdiction of probate court to grant marriage licenses, 2101.24

Juvenile court, jurisdiction regarding applications for consent to marry, 2151.23

Marriage license, fees, 2101.16

Minor, consent to marry, Juv R 42

Oaths, 3.20, 3.21

Library References

Marriage ⟹25, 30.
WESTLAW Topic No. 253.
C.J.S. Marriage §§ 27, 28, 32.

OJur 3d: 45, Family Law § 25 to 28
Am Jur 2d: 52, Marriage § 37, 38

Carlin, Baldwin's Ohio Practice, *Merrick-Rippner Probate Law* § 106.20, 106.25 (1997)
Sowald & Morganstern, Baldwin's Ohio Practice, *Domestic Relations Law* § 2.7, 2.8, 2.16, 2.30 (1997)

Law Review and Journal Commentaries

Irrebuttable Exile Under the Immigration Marriage Fraud Amendments: A Perspective From The Eighth Amendment And International Human Rights Law, Comment. 58 U Cin L Rev 1397 (1990).

Marriage License Fees: Are They Constitutional?, Walter E. Harding and Martin R. Levy. 17 J Fam L 703 (1978-79).

Of Covenants and Conflicts—When "I Do" Means More Than It Used To, But Less Than You Thought, Jason Andrew Macke. 59 Ohio St L J 1377 (1998).

Notes of Decisions and Opinions

Common law marriage, effect on application 3
Laboratories 2
Mental capacity 1

---

1. Mental capacity

A probate court may not require the evidence of an IQ test or other similar test to prove mental capacity as a prerequisite to the issuance of a marriage license. OAG 69-051.

2. Laboratories

State department of health in establishing standards by which to determine qualifications of a laboratory to give standard serological test for syphilis, has authority to make and enforce reasonable rules relative to equipment, supervision and personnel of such laboratory. 1947 OAG 1934.

Laboratory approved by state department of health to make serological tests for syphilis may not refuse to accept specimens of blood submitted for tests by licensed physician, except for reasons applicable alike to all physicians; in event laboratory does so refuse, state department of health acting through its director has power and duty to revoke approval of laboratory. 1946 OAG 1199.

3. Common law marriage, effect on application

Signed marriage license application which stated that applicant had "no wife living" did not fundamentally contradict asserted common-law marriage with woman he was marrying; language in application could be read or understood to ask whether applicant had any other wife and that document was only meant to comply with marriage license statute and statute providing that a person having husband or wife living may not marry another person. Ruscilli v. Ruscilli (Franklin 1993) 90 Ohio App.3d 753, 630 N.E.2d 745, motion to certify overruled 68 Ohio St.3d 1473, 628 N.E.2d 1391.

3101.06 Denial of license

No marriage license shall be granted when either of the applicants is under the influence of an intoxicating liquor or controlled substance or is infected with syphilis in a form that is communicable or likely to become communicable.

(1980 H 965, eff. 4-9-81; 1975 H 300; 128 v 573; 1953 H 1; GC 8001-6; Source—GC 11187)

Historical and Statutory Notes

Pre-1953 H 1 Amendments: 124 v S 65

Cross References

Marriage license fees to be used for shelters for victims of domestic violence, 3113.34

Schedules of controlled substances, 3719.41

Ohio Administrative Code References

Controlled substances, OAC Ch 4729-11

Library References

Marriage ⟜4.1, 6, 7, 25(2).
WESTLAW Topic No. 253.
C.J.S. Marriage §§ 4, 7, 13, 15, 16, 27, 28.

OJur 3d: 45, Family Law § 28
Am Jur 2d: 52, Marriage § 37

Validity of marriage as affected by absence of license. 61 ALR2d 847

Eagle, Ohio Mental Health Law (2d Ed.), Text 11.13
Sowald & Morganstern, Baldwin's Ohio Practice, *Domestic Relations Law* § 2.7, 2.8, 2.22, 2.24, 7.14 (1997)

Law Review and Journal Commentaries

The Loving Decision and the Freedom to Marry, Rev. Robert F. Drinan, S.J. 29 Ohio St L J 358 (1968).

Notes of Decisions and Opinions

Ed. Note: *See notes of decisions and opinions at RC 4511.19 regarding construction of the terms "under the influence" and "intoxicating liquor."*

Child support arrearage 3
Financial difficulty 2
Mental capacity 1

---

1. Mental capacity

A probate court may not require the evidence of an IQ test or other similar test to prove mental capacity as a prerequisite to the issuance of a marriage license. OAG 69-051.

2. Financial difficulty

A probate court may not refuse to issue a marriage license on the ground of a present inability to support a family. OAG 69-051.

3. Child support arrearage

A probate court may not refuse to issue a marriage license for the reason that there is money due for child support of a previous marriage. OAG 69-051.

3101.07 Expiration date of license

No marriage license shall be effective nor shall it authorize the performance of a marriage ceremony after the expiration of sixty days from the date of issuance. This provision shall be printed on each license in prominent type.

(1953 H 1, eff. 10-1-53; GC 8001-7; Source—GC 11188-1)

Historical and Statutory Notes

Pre-1953 H 1 Amendments: 124 v S 65

Library References

Marriage ⚷25(.5), 25(2).
WESTLAW Topic No. 253.
C.J.S. Marriage §§ 27, 28.

OJur 3d: 45, Family Law § 27
Am Jur 2d: 52, Marriage § 37 et seq.

Validity of marriage as affected by absence of license. 61 ALR2d 847

Sowald & Morganstern, Baldwin's Ohio Practice, *Domestic Relations Law* § 2.7, 2.9 (1997)

SOLEMNIZATION OF MARRIAGE

3101.08 Who may solemnize

An ordained or licensed minister of any religious society or congregation within this state who is licensed to solemnize marriages, a judge of a county court in accordance with section 1907.18 of the Revised Code, a judge of a municipal court in accordance with section 1901.14 of the Revised Code, a probate judge in accordance with section 2101.27 of the Revised Code, the mayor of a municipal corporation in any county in which such municipal corporation wholly or partly lies, the superintendent of the state school for the deaf, or any religious society in conformity with the rules of its church, may join together as husband and wife any persons who are not prohibited by law from being joined in marriage.

(1990 H 211, eff. 4-11-91; 1990 S 103; 127 v 1039; 1953 H 1; GC 8001-8; Source—GC 11182)

Historical and Statutory Notes

Pre-1953 H 1 Amendments: 124 v S 65

Comparative Laws

Ariz.—A.R.S. § 25-124.
Ark.—A.C.A. § 9-11-213.
Conn.—C.G.S.A. § 46b-22.
Fla.—West's F.S.A. § 741.07.
Idaho—I.C. § 32-303.
Ill.—ILCS 750 5/209.
Iowa—I.C.A. § 595.10.
Ky.—Baldwin's KRS 402.050.
La.—LSA-R.S. 9:202.
Mass.—M.G.L.A. c. 207, § 38.
Mich.—M.C.L.A. § 551.7.
Minn.—M.S.A. § 517.09.
Mo.—V.A.M.S. § 451.100.
N.C.—G.S. § 51-1.
Neb.—R.R.S.1943, § 42-104.
N.J.—N.J.S.A. 37:1-13 et seq.
N.M.—NMSA 1978, § 40-1-2.
N.Y.—McKinney's Domestic Relations Law § 11.
Okl.—43 Okl.St.Ann. § 7.
Tex.—V.T.C.A. Family Code § 2.202.
Wash.—West's RCWA 26.04.050.
W.Va.—Code, 48-1-12.

Cross References

Prohibition: 3101.09

Common law marriage prohibited, 3105.12

County court judges, retention of marriage fees, 1907.26

Jurisdiction of county court judges to perform marriage ceremonies, 1907.18

Jurisdiction of probate court to grant marriage licenses, 2101.24

Powers of municipal court judges, marriage fees, 1901.14

Library References

Marriage ⚷27.
WESTLAW Topic No. 253.
C.J.S. Marriage § 31.

OJur 3d: 45, Family Law § 30
Am Jur 2d: 52, Marriage § 38 to 40

Validity of solemnized marriage as affected by absence of license required by statute. 61 ALR2d 847

Validity of marriage as affected by lack of legal authority of person solemnizing it. 13 ALR4th 1323

Hausser, Ohio Real Estate Law and Practice (2d Ed.), Text 35.081

Sowald & Morganstern, Baldwin's Ohio Practice, *Domestic Relations Law* § 2.9, 2.10 (1997)

Law Review and Journal Commentaries

The Marriage Ceremony, Carl M. Broberg. (Ed. Note: Mayoral authority to perform marriages is discussed.) 44 Cities & Villages 27 (January/February 1996).

Notes of Decisions and Opinions

Justice of the peace 2
Ministers 3
Proxy marriages 1

1. Proxy marriages

Ohio does not authorize the performance of marriages by proxy because the statute requires the parties' personal presence; Ohio will, however, recognize proxy marriages performed in another state where such marriages are valid. In re Blankenship (Bkrtcy.N.D.Ohio 1991) 133 B.R. 398.

2. Justice of the peace

By statute, a justice of the peace has jurisdiction to solemnize marriages within the county in which he was elected. 1928 OAG 1852.

3. Ministers

A minister must be both licensed and currently affiliated with a religious society or congregation in order to perform marriages in Ohio. Wright v Courthouse Facilities Committee, No. L-99-1090, 1999 WL 1022873 (6th Dist Ct App, Lucas, 11-12-99).

3101.09 Prohibition

No person, except those legally authorized, shall attempt to solemnize a marriage, and no marriage shall be solemnized without the issuance of a license.

(1953 H 1, eff. 10-1-53; GC 8001-9; Source—GC 12922)

Historical and Statutory Notes

Pre-1953 H 1 Amendments: 124 v S 65

Cross References

Penalty: 3101.99(B)

Library References

Marriage ⟹26.1, 27.
WESTLAW Topic No. 253.
C.J.S. Marriage §§ 30, 31, 33.

OJur 3d: 45, Family Law § 30
Am Jur 2d: 52, Marriage § 38 to 40

Validity of solemnized marriage as affected by absence of license required by statute. 61 ALR2d 847
Validity of marriage as affected by lack of legal authority of person solemnizing it. 13 ALR4th 1323

3101.10 License to solemnize marriages

A minister upon producing to the secretary of state, credentials of his being a regularly ordained or licensed minister of any religious society or congregation, shall be entitled to receive from the secretary of state a license authorizing him to solemnize marriages in this state so long as he continues as a regular minister in such society or congregation. A minister shall produce for inspection his license to solemnize marriages upon demand of any party to a marriage at which he officiates or proposes to officiate or upon demand of any probate judge.

(1976 H 740, eff. 6-4-76; 1953 H 1; GC 8001-10; Source—GC 11183)

Historical and Statutory Notes

Pre-1953 H 1 Amendments: 124 v S 65

Cross References

Prohibition: 3101.09

Fees to be collected by secretary of state, 111.16

Library References

Marriage ⟹27.
WESTLAW Topic No. 253.
C.J.S. Marriage § 31.

OJur 3d: 45, Family Law § 31

Am Jur 2d: 52, Marriage § 37 et seq.
Validity of marriage as affected by lack of legal authority of person solemnizing it. 13 ALR4th 1323

Carlin, Baldwin's Ohio Practice, *Merrick-Rippner Probate Law* § 106.30 (1997)

Sowald & Morganstern, Baldwin's Ohio Practice, *Domestic Relations Law* § 2.9 (1997)

Notes of Decisions and Opinions

Filing with county 2
Ministers eligible 1
Residency 3

1. Ministers eligible

Member of Jehovah's Witnesses entitled to license authorizing him to solemnize marriages. State ex rel. Hayes v. O'Brien (Ohio 1953) 160 Ohio St. 170, 114 N.E.2d 729, 51 O.O. 384.

A minister must be both licensed and currently affiliated with a religious society or congregation in order to perform marriages in Ohio. Wright v Courthouse Facilities Committee, No. L-99-1090, 1999 WL 1022873 (6th Dist Ct App, Lucas, 11-12-99).

A "reader" in the Christian Science Church is not entitled to the granting of a license to solemnize marriages. 1928 OAG 2797.

2. Filing with county

A probate judge issuing a marriage license may not demand the filing of the minister's license in that county, the minister having been licensed in another county, in addition to the marriage certificate by law returnable for filing in the county issuing the license. 1937 OAG 595.

3. Residency

The statutes of Ohio do not require that the applicant for a license to solemnize marriages within this state be a resident of Ohio, and a nonresident minister of the gospel is entitled to receive such license, provided he produce to the probate judge of any county within this state in which he officiates, credentials of his being a regularly ordained or licensed minister. 1921 OAG p 710.

3101.11 Recording with secretary of state

The secretary of state shall enter the name of a minister licensed to solemnize marriages upon a record kept in the office of the secretary of state.

(1976 H 740, eff. 6-4-76; 1953 H 1; GC 8001-11; Source—GC 11184)

Historical and Statutory Notes

Pre-1953 H 1 Amendments: 124 v S 65

Cross References

Fees to be collected by secretary of state, 111.16

Library References

Marriage ⚷27.
Records ⚷3.
WESTLAW Topic Nos. 253, 326.
C.J.S. Marriage § 31.
C.J.S. Records § 4.

OJur 3d: 45, Family Law § 31

Am Jur 2d: 52, Marriage § 40, 41

Validity of marriage as affected by lack of legal authority of person solemnizing it. 13 ALR4th 1323

Notes of Decisions and Opinions

Validity of license 1

1. Validity of license

When a minister is duly licensed in another county of the state and moves from state, abandoning his charge, he may return, if he is still a regular minister in a religious society or congregation, although said minister has no congregation in this state, and present his Ohio license to the probate judge of any county in this state, who must make a record of it; he may then legally solemnize a marriage. 1949 OAG 715.

3101.12 Record and license as evidence of authority

When the name of a minister licensed to solemnized [*sic*] marriages is entered upon the record by the secretary of state, such record and the license issued under section 3101.10 of the Revised Code shall be evidence that such minister is authorized to solemnize marriages in this state.

(1976 H 740, eff. 6-4-76; 1953 H 1; GC 8001-12; Source—GC 11185)

Historical and Statutory Notes

Pre-1953 H 1 Amendments: 124 v S 65

Library References

Marriage ⚷27, 50(1).
Records ⚷19, 20.

WESTLAW Topic Nos. 253, 326.
C.J.S. Marriage §§ 31, 56 to 60.

C.J.S. Records §§ 30, 31.

OJur 3d: 45, Family Law § 31
Am Jur 2d: 52, Marriage § 40, 41

Validity of marriage as affected by lack of legal authority of person solemnizing it. 13 ALR4th 1323

3101.13 Record of marriage

Except as otherwise provided in this section, a certificate of every marriage solemnized shall be transmitted by the authorized person solemnizing the marriage, within thirty days after the solemnization, to the probate judge of the county in which the marriage license was issued. If, in accordance with section 2101.27 of the Revised Code, a probate judge solemnizes a marriage and if the probate judge issued the marriage license to the husband and wife, he shall file a certificate of that solemnized marriage in his office within thirty days after the solemnization. All such transmitted and filed certificates shall be consecutively numbered and recorded in the order in which they are received.

(1990 H 211, eff. 4-11-91; 1953 H 1; GC 8001-14; Source—GC 8001-13, 11195)

Historical and Statutory Notes

Pre-1953 H 1 Amendments: 124 v S 65

Cross References

Penalty: 3101.99(C)

Certified copies of public records, 3705.23, 3705.24
Probate court to keep record of marriages, 2101.12

Probate judge shall register marriages with office of vital statistics, state department of health, 3705.21

Library References

Records ⟹3.
WESTLAW Topic No. 326.
C.J.S. Records § 4.

OJur 3d: 43, Evidence and Witnesses § 452; 45, Family Law § 32

Am Jur 2d: 52, Marriage § 41

Sowald & Morganstern, Baldwin's Ohio Practice, *Domestic Relations Law* § 2.13, 2.56 (1997)

MISCELLANEOUS PROVISIONS

3101.14 Notice on license of penalty for failure to return certificate

Every marriage license shall have printed upon it in prominent type the notice that, unless the person solemnizing the marriage returns a certificate of the solemnized marriage to the probate court that issued the marriage license within thirty days after performing the ceremony, or, if the person solemnizing the marriage is a probate judge who is acting in accordance with section 2101.27 of the Revised Code and who issued the marriage license to the husband and wife, unless such a probate judge files a certificate of the solemnized marriage in his office within thirty days after the solemnization, he is guilty of a misdemeanor and, upon conviction, may be punished by a fine of fifty dollars. An envelope suitable for returning the certificate of marriage, and addressed to the proper probate court, shall be given with each license, except that this requirement does not apply if a marriage is to be solemnized by a probate judge who is acting in accordance with section 2101.27 of the Revised Code and who issued the marriage license to the husband and wife.

(1990 H 211, eff. 4-11-91; 1953 H 1; GC 8001-15; Source—GC 11189)

Historical and Statutory Notes

Pre-1953 H 1 Amendments: 124 v S 65

Library References

Marriage ⟹31.
WESTLAW Topic No. 253.
C.J.S. Marriage § 35.

OJur 3d: 43, Evidence and Witnesses § 452; 45, Family Law § 32

Am Jur 2d: 52, Marriage § 41

Sowald & Morganstern, Baldwin's Ohio Practice, *Domestic Relations Law* § 2.13 (1997)

3101.15 Correction of certificate of marriage

A person who is not a party to a marriage, when both parties to the marriage are deceased or otherwise unable to correct the certificate of marriage of the parties, and who claims that the facts stated in a certificate of marriage filed in this state are not true may file an application for correction of the certificate in the probate court of the county in which the certificate was filed.

In the application, the applicant shall set forth all of the available facts required on a certificate of marriage and the reasons for making the application, including the reason for the unavailability of the parties to the marriage. The applicant shall verify the application. On the filing of an application under this section, the court may fix a date for a hearing on the application. The date shall not be less than seven days after the filing date. The application shall be supported by the affidavit of at least one person having knowledge of the facts stated in the application, by documentary evidence, or by other evidence as the court considers sufficient. The probate judge may refuse to accept an affidavit or evidence that appears to be submitted for the purpose of falsifying the certificate of marriage. If the probate judge is satisfied that the facts are as stated, the judge shall make an order correcting the certificate of marriage and shall file it in the judge's office.

This section shall not apply to and shall not limit the ability of the parties to a marriage to correct a certificate of marriage in accordance with procedures followed by the probate court.

(1996 H 266, eff. 5-15-96)

3101.99 Penalties

(A) Whoever violates division (B) of section 3101.05 of the Revised Code is guilty of a violation of section 2921.13 of the Revised Code. Whoever violates any other provision of section 3101.05 of the Revised Code is guilty of a minor misdemeanor.

(B) Whoever violates section 3101.09 of the Revised Code shall be fined five hundred dollars and imprisoned not more than six months.

(C) Whoever violates section 3101.13 of the Revised Code shall be fined not more than fifty dollars.

(1990 S 3, eff. 4-11-91; 1953 H 1; GC 8001-16)

Historical and Statutory Notes

Pre-1953 H 1 Amendments: 124 v S 65

Library References

Marriage ⟹30, 53.
WESTLAW Topic No. 253.
C.J.S. Marriage §§ 32, 45.

OJur 3d: 45, Family Law § 25, 28, 30, 32
Am Jur 2d: 52, Marriage § 37, 38
Validity of marriage entered into in jest. 14 ALR2d 624
Validity of marriage as affected by absence of license. 61 ALR2d 847

Conflict of laws as to validity of marriage attacked because of nonage. 71 ALR2d 687
Common law marriage between parties previously divorced. 82 ALR2d 688

Sowald & Morganstern, Baldwin's Ohio Practice, *Domestic Relations Law* § 2.7 (1997)

CHAPTER 3103

Husband and Wife

Cross References

Children, Ch 3109

Non-spousal artificial insemination, 3111.30 et seq.

Ohio Administrative Code References

Joint personal property tax return by husband and wife, OAC 5703-3-05

WESTLAW Electronic Research

See WESTLAW Electronic Research Guide following the Preface.

Law Review and Journal Commentaries

The Case of the Lonely Nurse: The Wife's Action for Loss of Consortium, Note. 18 W Reserve U L Rev 621 (1967).

Interspousal Tort Liability for Infliction of Sexually Transmitted Disease, Note. 29 J Fam L 519 (1990-91).

Judge's Column, Hon. Francine M. Bruening. (Ed. note: Judge Bruening discusses the pending Ohio Parenting Act.) 20 Lake Legal Views 1 (June 1997).

The Ohio Law of Marriage, Hugh A. Ross. 14 W Reserve U L Rev 724 (1963).

The Use of Will Substitutes to Disinherit the Surviving Spouse, William A. Polster. 13 W Reserve U L Rev 674 (1962).

3103.01 Mutual obligations

Husband and wife contract towards each other obligations of mutual respect, fidelity, and support.

(1953 H 1, eff. 10-1-53; GC 8002-1; Source—GC 7995)

Historical and Statutory Notes

Pre-1953 H 1 Amendments: 124 v S 65

Cross References

Adultery a bar to dower, 2103.05

Agreement made upon consideration of marriage to be in writing, 1335.05

Competency of spouses to testify in behalf of or against each other, 2945.42

Dissolution of marriage, release from obligations, 3105.10

Husband and wife, privileged communications and acts, 2317.02, 2921.22

Nonsupport of dependents, 2919.21

Small loans; assignment of personal earnings by married person, 1321.31

Wife may defend for her own or her husband's right, 2307.10

Library References

Husband and Wife ⚿1, 3(.5).
WESTLAW Topic No. 205.
C.J.S. Husband and Wife §§ 2 to 5, 7.

OJur 3d: 45, Family Law § 51; 47, Family Law § 1018

Am Jur 2d: 41, Husband and Wife § 5 to 15

Sowald & Morganstern, Baldwin's Ohio Practice, *Domestic Relations Law* § 4.1, 4.5, 9.1, 11.14, 25.9 (1997)

Law Review and Journal Commentaries

Cohabitation Agreements and Related Documents, Hon. Mike Brigner. 9 Domestic Rel J Ohio 97 (November/December 1997).

Notes of Decisions and Opinions

---

1. In general

Even though loss of consortium claim is derivative in that it depends upon defendant having committed legally cognizable tort upon spouse who suffers bodily injury, it is nonetheless legally separate and independent from claim of spouse who suffered the bodily injury. Schaefer v. Allstate Ins. Co. (Ohio 1996) 76 Ohio St.3d 553, 668 N.E.2d 913.

Policy provision stating that limit of liability for each person was total limit for all damages arising out of bodily injury to one person was unenforceable as applied to claim for uninsured motorist (UM) benefits for insurer's loss of consortium as result of injury to fellow insured; thus, claim for loss of consortium constituted separate compensable injury subject to its own per person limit; overruling *Dues v Hodge*, 36 Ohio St.3d 46, 521 N.E.2d 789; *Tomlinson v. Skolnik*, 44 Ohio St.3d 11, 540 N.E.2d 716. Schaefer v. Allstate Ins. Co. (Ohio 1996) 76 Ohio St.3d 553, 668 N.E.2d 913.

Each person covered by uninsured motorist (UM) policy who is asserting claim for loss of consortium has separate claim subject to separate per person policy limit, and, thus policy provision reaching contrary result is unenforceable; overruling *Dues v Hodge*, 36 Ohio St.3d 46, 521 N.E.2d 789; *Tomlinson v. Skolnik*, 44 Ohio St.3d 11, 540 N.E.2d 716. Schaefer v. Allstate Ins. Co. (Ohio 1996) 76 Ohio St.3d 553, 668 N.E.2d 913.

A spouse may not maintain an action against the other spouse for personal injuries resulting from the negligence of the other spouse where the married parties are living together as husband and wife at the time of the alleged injury. Lyons v. Lyons (Ohio 1965) 2 Ohio St.2d 243, 208 N.E.2d 533, 31 O.O.2d 504.

A married person in applying to the state for aid for the aged thereby obligates his or her estate, upon death, to repay the state, not only the amount of such aid received by him or her but also the amount of aid, if any, received by his or her spouse, and the statutory obligation (GC 7995 Repealed) to repay the aid furnished to the spouse is in the nature of a suretyship obligation without consideration moving directly to such married person, but, where the estate of the spouse is sufficient to repay the aid so furnished to such spouse, the married person or his or her estate is entitled to exoneration as to such aid. Hausser v. Ebinger (Ohio 1954) 161 Ohio St. 192, 118 N.E.2d 522, 53 O.O. 86.

Under this section et seq.: (1) a husband and wife contract toward each other obligations of mutual respect, fidelity and support; (2) the husband is head of family and may choose any reasonable place or mode of living and wife must conform; (3) it is husband's duty to support himself and wife, so long as he is able, and (4) neither spouse has any interest in the other's property, except present right of support, and rights given by statute to a surviving spouse in the property of deceased spouse. Mark v. Mark (Ohio 1945) 145 Ohio St. 301, 61 N.E.2d 595, 30 O.O. 534.

Husband not required to provide other than present support for wife. Mark v. Mark (Ohio 1945) 145 Ohio St. 301, 61 N.E.2d 595, 30 O.O. 534.

Where deceased was chronic invalid and the nature of affliction required that he be constantly watched and assisted and his wife had performed such services frequently from inception of the disease to time of final separation, this was a duty devolving upon her as a wife and in fulfillment of the obligations imposed by this section. Porter v. Lerch (Ohio 1934) 129 Ohio St. 47, 193 N.E. 766, 1 O.O. 356.

A husband or wife may maintain an action for damages against any one who wrongfully and maliciously interferes with the marital relationship. Flandermeyer v. Cooper (Ohio 1912) 85 Ohio St. 327, 98 N.E. 102, 9 Ohio Law Rep. 586, Am.Ann.Cas. 1913A, 983.

A husband and wife have mutual obligations of respect, fidelity, and support; therefore, in order to obtain an award of alimony only on the grounds of gross neglect of duty, the complainant must show that the spouse has breached a duty of mutual respect, fidelity, or support. Vogt v. Vogt (Lucas 1990) 67 Ohio App.3d 197, 586 N.E.2d 242.

Since a discharge in bankruptcy is personal to the bankrupt, a wife is liable for all mutually incurred debt, regardless of the husband's discharge in bankruptcy. Squires Const. Co. v. Smith (Cuyahoga 1982) 8 Ohio App.3d 183, 456 N.E.2d 838, 8 O.B.R. 244.

Decree of divorce which grants to plaintiff-husband custody of four minor children of divorced parties and orders defendant-wife to pay to husband certain specified amounts for support of such children, which amounts had been previously agreed upon in separation agreement approved by court, will be upheld, even though decree does not include finding that husband is unable to support such children. Clover v. Clover (Fairfield 1970) 24 Ohio App.2d 161, 265 N.E.2d 559, 53 O.O.2d 389.

A husband may not contractually compel his wife to deed him certain real property in exchange for services rendered which are of a type obligated by law. Long v Long, No. CA-664 (5th Dist Ct App, Morrow, 8-26-87).

A wife is liable for the funeral expenses and those incurred during her husband's last illness even where she has not directly contracted for them and where the husband has no estate. Smith v. Snapp (Ohio Com.Pl. 1961) 175 N.E.2d 333, 87 Ohio Law Abs. 318, 16 O.O.2d 304.

A husband unable to support himself may compel his wife to contribute to his support, regardless of the existence of right to sue for alimony only. Albert v. Albert (Ohio App. 1916) 29 Ohio C.D. 271, 7 Ohio App. 156, 28 Ohio C.A. 225.

By virtue of this section and upon the grounds of necessity and public policy, it is the duty of the widow to take charge of the body of her deceased husband and see that it is given a decent burial; and where husband leaves no estate, and widow, because of mental disability, is incapable of contracting, the widow's estate is liable for necessary and reasonable expenses incurred in such burial. In re Milholland's Guardianship (Ohio Prob. 1933) 30 Ohio N.P.N.S. 563, 3 Ohio Supp. 121.

It is presumed under Ohio law that a wife's advancements to her husband that result in mutual benefit give her no claim against him, absent an express promise to pay. In re Palermini (Bkrtcy.S.D.Ohio 1990) 113 B.R. 380.

2. Loss of consortium

Loss-of-consortium claim asserted against health insurer by insured's spouse was not subject to contractual arbitration clause where spouse never expressly or impliedly agreed to the contract and neither he nor insured signed anything binding him to contract or clause. Branham v. CIGNA Healthcare of Ohio, Inc. (Ohio 1998) 81 Ohio St.3d 388, 692 N.E.2d 137.

Each person covered by uninsured motorist (UM) policy who is asserting claim for loss of consortium has separate claim subject to separate per person policy limit, and provision in insurance policy which reaches contrary result is unenforceable. Molek v. State Farm Mut. Auto. Ins. Co. (Ohio 1997) 77 Ohio St.3d 392, 674 N.E.2d 689.

When one spouse is injured, other spouse is also damaged and may assert his or her own cause of action against tort-feasor for those damages, i.e., claim for loss of consortium. Schaefer v. Allstate Ins. Co. (Ohio 1996) 76 Ohio St.3d 553, 668 N.E.2d 913.

Action of spouse for loss of consortium and medical expenses arising from bodily injuries suffered by other spouse as result of tort of third party is action for injury to rights of former spouse not arising upon contract, commencement of which is governed by the four-year statute of limitation. Dean v. Angelas (Ohio 1970) 24 Ohio St.2d 99, 264 N.E.2d 911, 53 O.O.2d 282.

A wife has a cause of action for damages for the loss of the consortium of her husband against a person who negligently injures her husband, which injuries deprive her of the consortium of her husband. Clouston v. Remlinger Oldsmobile Cadillac, Inc. (Ohio 1970) 22 Ohio St.2d 65, 258 N.E.2d 230, 51 O.O.2d 96.

Compensation for diminution of earning capacity and subsequent inability to support his family may be recovered by injured husband, and wife may not recover for loss of his society, affection, and assistance. Smith v. Nicholas Bldg. Co. (Ohio 1915) 93 Ohio St. 101, 112 N.E. 204, 13 Ohio Law Rep. 466, Am.Ann.Cas. 1918D, 206.

Wife's claim for loss of consortium is a claim for her own direct injury. Marcum v. Marcum (Ohio App. 2 Dist. 1996) 116 Ohio App.3d 606, 688 N.E.2d 1085.

Determination that wife suffered a loss of consortium was supported by evidence that husband was in a coma for six weeks after the accident and was hospitalized for approximately six months and that wife spent considerable time in caring for her husband after the accident and in assisting him in his recovery from his injuries. Marcum v. Marcum (Ohio App. 2 Dist. 1996) 116 Ohio App.3d 606, 688 N.E.2d 1085.

While spouse's claim for loss of consortium is separate and distinct, the uninjured spouse cannot recover for loss of consortium if there is no cognizable claim under Ohio law that would be available to the injured spouse. Gillum v. Fairgreens Country Club (Jackson 1996) 110 Ohio App.3d 60, 673 N.E.2d 637.

Administrator of driver's estate had no claim, under statute prohibiting sale of intoxicating liquor to intoxicated person, for loss of consortium against country club which allegedly served driver alcohol while he was visibly intoxicated and that alleged negligence of club proximately caused his fatal automobile accident since driver's death was proximately caused by his own intoxication. Gillum v. Fairgreens Country Club (Jackson 1996) 110 Ohio App.3d 60, 673 N.E.2d 637.

Husband's consortium claim, although a separate cause of action, was still dependent upon defendant having committed a legally cognizable tort upon wife. Gaffney v. Powell (Hamilton 1995) 107 Ohio App.3d 315, 668 N.E.2d 951, appeal not allowed 75 Ohio St.3d 1451, 663 N.E.2d 332.

Right to consortium is right that grows out of marriage, is incident to marriage, and cannot exist without marriage. Hite v. Brown (Cuyahoga 1995) 100 Ohio App.3d 606, 654 N.E.2d 452, appeal denied 73 Ohio St.3d 1414, 651 N.E.2d 1311.

Husband had no claim against wife's father for loss of consortium arising from father's alleged molestation of wife, as at least 17 years had passed from last alleged acts of abuse to time husband and wife married. Hite v. Brown (Cuyahoga 1995) 100 Ohio App.3d 606, 654 N.E.2d 452, appeal denied 73 Ohio St.3d 1414, 651 N.E.2d 1311.

A husband's right to recover for loss of his wife's consortium may exist so as to include elements of consortium independent and apart from services of the wife, which the husband replaced by paying a third person to perform. Williams v. Ward (Erie 1969) 18 Ohio App.2d 37, 246 N.E.2d 780, 47 O.O.2d 108.

A wife's loss of consortium claim is not precluded by a waiver of liability for injuries the husband suffers when he falls from a roof while working as a volunteer where the waiver is signed by the husband but is not signed by the wife. Mendelsohn v Habitat For Humanity International, Inc, No. 74342, 1999 WL 401398 (8th Dist Ct App, Cuyahoga, 6-17-99).

Spouse of motorist whose preexisting disk spurs and osteoarthritis due to 33 years of hard labor were aggravated by an automobile accident caused by another's negligence was entitled to an award of $20,000 for loss of consortium. Smelser v. Univ. of Cincinnati (Ohio Ct.Cl. 1999) 99 Ohio Misc.2d 28, 715 N.E.2d 627.

In a state which grants to a husband a right of action for the loss of the consortium of his wife through personal injuries inflicted as a result of the negligence of a third person, it constitutes a denial of the equal protection of the law guaranteed by the fourteenth amendment to deny a wife a similar action for loss of the consortium of her husband under similar circumstances. Steinmetz v. Dworkin Truck Lines, Inc. (Ohio Com.Pl. 1968) 16 Ohio Misc. 273, 242 N.E.2d 686, 45 O.O.2d 155, 45 O.O.2d 345.

Under Ohio law, a wife owes to her husband a duty of consortium, which means the wife's services, aid, comfort, society, and companionship, and the common law recognizes a right in the husband to maintain an action against anyone who tortiously impairs the ability of his wife to fulfill her duty; thus, while a wife may recover personally any earnings lost if she works outside the home, she cannot recover the value of her lost ability to perform household services because it is the husband who is entitled to the value of his wife's lost domestic services that a third person must be hired to perform; similarly, where the husband is injured, the loss resulting from his inability to perform household chores is an item recovered by him and not by his wife. Neyer v. U.S. (C.A.6 (Ohio) 1988) 845 F.2d 641.

Although RC 3103.05 has been construed to grant a husband the right to damages for the loss of his wife's services, a husband does not have an independent right of action for the loss of his wife's consortium, and therefor equal protection of the laws does not require that the wife have such an independent action. Copeland v. Smith Dairy Products Co. (N.D.Ohio 1968) 15 Ohio Misc. 43, 288 F.Supp. 904, 44 O.O.2d 242.

Under Ohio law, claim for loss of "consortium," which consists of society, services, sexual relations and conjugal affection which includes companionship, comfort, love and solace, is derivative action, deriving from spouse's claim for bodily injury. In re Turner (Bkrtcy.S.D.Ohio 1996) 190 B.R. 836.

3. —Cohabiting unmarried persons, mutual obligations

No fiduciary relationship existed between cohabiting individuals. Tarry v. Stewart (Lorain 1994) 98 Ohio App.3d 533, 649 N.E.2d 1, appeal not allowed 71 Ohio St.3d 1502, 646 N.E.2d 1126.

Trial court's refusal to impose constructive trust on property retained by man after termination of cohabitation arrangement with woman did not violate public policy. Tarry v. Stewart (Lorain 1994) 98 Ohio App.3d 533, 649 N.E.2d 1, appeal not allowed 71 Ohio St.3d 1502, 646 N.E.2d 1126.

4. Loss of consortium, parent and child

A parent may state a claim for loss of consortium of his or her child if the loss occurs when the child is a minor. Bock v. Hamilton Cty. Bd. of Park Commrs. (Ohio App. 1 Dist. 1999) 132 Ohio App.3d 726, 726 N.E.2d 509.

Under Ohio law, a plaintiff cannot contractually waive an otherwise valid right of action for loss of consortium held by his relative. Mohney v. USA Hockey, Inc. (N.D.Ohio 1999) 77 F.Supp.2d 859.

3103.02 The head of the family—Repealed

(1974 H 233, eff. 9-23-74; 1953 H 1; GC 8002-2; Source—GC 7996)

Historical and Statutory Notes

Pre-1953 H 1 Amendments: 124 v S 65

3103.03 Duty of married person to support self, spouse, and children; duration of duty to support; third person's recovery of support; funeral expenses of spouse

(A) Each married person must support the person's self and spouse out of the person's property or by the person's labor. If a married person is unable to do so, the spouse of the married person must assist in the support so far as the spouse is able. The biological or adoptive parent of a minor child must support the parent's minor children out of the parent's property or by the parent's labor.

(B) Notwithstanding section 3109.01 of the Revised Code, the parental duty of support to children, including the duty of a parent to pay support pursuant to a child support order, shall continue beyond the age of majority as long as the child continuously attends on a full-time basis any recognized and accredited high school or a court-issued child support order provides that the duty of support continues beyond the age of majority. Except in cases in which a child support order requires the duty of support to continue for any period after the child reaches age nineteen, the order shall not remain in effect after the child reaches age nineteen. That duty of support shall continue during seasonal vacation periods.

(C) If a married person neglects to support the person's spouse in accordance with this section, any other person, in good faith, may supply the spouse with necessaries for the support of the spouse and recover the reasonable value of the necessaries supplied from the married person who neglected to support the spouse unless the spouse abandons that person without cause.

(D) If a parent neglects to support the parent's minor child in accordance with this section and if the minor child in question is unemancipated, any other person, in good faith, may supply the minor child with necessaries for the support of the minor child and recover the reasonable value of the necessaries supplied from the parent who neglected to support the minor child.

(E) If a decedent during the decedent's lifetime has purchased an irrevocable preneed funeral contract pursuant to section 1109.75 of the Revised Code, then the duty of support owed to a spouse pursuant to this section does not include an obligation to pay for the funeral expenses of the deceased spouse. This division does not preclude a surviving spouse from assuming by contract the obligation to pay for the funeral expenses of the deceased spouse.

(1997 H 352, eff. 1-1-98; 1996 H 538, eff. 1-1-97; 1992 S 10, eff. 7-15-92; 1990 S 3, H 346; 1973 S 1; 1953 H 1; GC 8002-3; Source—GC 7997)

Uncodified Law

1990 H 346, § 3, eff. 5-31-90, reads, in part:

(A) Sections 1 and 2 of this act shall apply only to the estates of decedents who die on or after the effective date of this act.

Historical and Statutory Notes

Pre-1953 H 1 Amendments: 124 v S 65

Amendment Note: 1997 H 352 inserted or a court-issued child support order provides that the duty of support continues beyond the age of majority" and added the second sentence in division (B); and made changes to reflect gender neutral language.

Amendment Note: 1996 H 538 substituted "1109.75" for "1107.33" in division (E).

Comparative Laws

Fla.—West's F.S.A. § 61.13.
Ill.—ILCS 750 16/1 et seq.
La.—LSA-R.S. 14:74; LSA-C.C. art. 123.
N.Y.—McKinney's Family Court Act § 411 et seq.

Cross References

Age of majority, 3109.01
Assignment for benefit of creditors by husband not to include property of wife, 1313.17
Child support in divorce, dissolution of marriage, legal separation, or child support proceeding, 3109.05
Dissolution of marriage, release from obligations, 3105.10
Failure to support minor, consent to adoption not required, 3107.07
Grounds for legal separation, 3105.17
Minor can consent to diagnosis and treatment of drug-related condition, parents not liable for payment unless consent, 3719.012
"Neglected child," defined, 2151.03
Nonsupport of dependents, 2919.21
One spouse contracting for improvement to other's land deemed other's agent, when, 1311.10
Parents to support child committed by juvenile court, 2151.36
Payment of support, enforcement procedures, 3113.21
Reciprocal enforcement of support, Ch 3115
Small loans; assignment of personal earnings by married person, 1321.31
Small loans; assignment or order of wages for support, 1321.32, 1321.33

Ohio Administrative Code References

Department of job and family services, child support program, OAC Ch 5101:1-29
Department of job and family services, collection of past due support by federal tax refund offset, OAC Ch 5101:1-30

Library References

Adoption ⚷20.
Children Out-Of-Wedlock ⚷21, 67.
Husband and Wife ⚷4, 19(16), 282 to 284.
Parent and Child ⚷3.1(12), 3.1(13).
WESTLAW Topic Nos. 17, 76H, 205, 285.
C.J.S. Adoption of Persons §§ 134 to 139.
C.J.S. Children Out-of-Wedlock §§ 40 to 43, 122 to 126.
C.J.S. Husband and Wife §§ 48, 54, 238 to 240.
C.J.S. Parent and Child §§ 14, 49, 70, 71.

OJur 3d: 45, Family Law § 61; 47, Family Law § 999, 1018, 1023, 1024, 1027, 1034, 1035
Am Jur 2d: 41, Husband and Wife § 8, 329 et seq.; 59, Parent and Child § 50 et seq.
Parent's obligation to support adult child. 1 ALR2d 910
Construction and application of state statutes providing for reciprocal enforcement of duty to support dependents. 42 ALR2d 768
Parent's obligation to support unmarried minor child who refuses to live with parent. 98 ALR3d 334
Responsibility of noncustodial divorced parent to pay for, or contribute to, cost of child's college education. 99 ALR3d 322
Wife's liability for necessaries furnished husband. 11 ALR4th 1160
Necessity, in action against husband for necessaries furnished wife, of proving husband's failure to provide necessities. 19 ALR4th 432
Modern status of rule that husband is primarily or solely liable for necessaries furnished wife. 20 ALR4th 196
Postsecondary education as within nondivorced parent's child-support obligation. 42 ALR4th 819
Parent's child support liability as affected by other parent's fraudulent misrepresentation regarding sterility or use of birth control, or refusal to abort pregnancy. 2 ALR5th 337

Baldwin's Ohio Legislative Service, 1990 Laws of Ohio, H 346—LSC Analysis, p 5-87
Carlin, Baldwin's Ohio Practice, *Merrick-Rippner Probate Law* § 19.4, 21.79, 89.9, 89.18, 98.31, 108.3, 108.34 (1997)
Klein & Darling, Baldwin's Ohio Practice, *Civil Practice* § 5 (1997)
Sowald & Morganstern, Baldwin's Ohio Practice, *Domestic Relations Law* § 1.7, 3.26, 3.55, 4.1, 4.3, 4.4, 4.5, 4.6,

4.7, 4.10, 4.22, 4.24, 4.26, 9.1, 9.9, 9.12, 11.14, 13.5, 13.6, 14.33, 19.1, 19.3, 19.20, 19.32, 20.10 (1997)

Law Review and Journal Commentaries

Bankruptcy Reform Act of 1994—What the Bankruptcy Code Giveth, Domestic Relations Courts (and Congress) Taketh Away, C.R. "Chip" Bowles. 8 Domestic Rel J Ohio 17 (March/April 1996).

Cohabitation Agreements and Related Documents, Hon. Mike Brigner. 9 Domestic Rel J Ohio 97 (November/December 1997).

Divorce—Liability of Husband to Support Child Awarded to Wife, Note. 7 Ohio St L J 446 (1941).

The Federal Income Tax Consequences of the Legal Obligation of Parents to Support Children, Note. 47 Ohio St L J 753 (1986).

Liability of Husband and of Wife's Estate for Funeral Expenses of Wife, Note. 4 U Cin L Rev 486 (1930).

The Need for Statutes Regulating Artificial Insemination by Donors, Note. 46 Ohio St L J 1055 (198( ).

Parents' Support Obligations to Their Adult Children, Marvin M. Moore. 19 Akron L Rev 183 (Fall 1985).

Paying for Children's Medical Care: Interaction Between Family Law and Cost Containment, Walter J. Wadlington. 36 Case W Res L Rev 1190 (1985-86).

Notes of Decisions and Opinions

---

1. Constitutional issues

Reviewing court's application of amended versions of child support statutes to post-dissolution proceeding did not violate constitutional prohibition on retroactive legislation since amendments did not impose new duty upon ex-husband, but instead merely altered how already existing general duty of support codified by former statute could be enforced. Smith v. Smith (Ohio App. 12 Dist. 1997) 119 Ohio App.3d 15, 694 N.E.2d 476.

The failure of the legislature to include in the Parentage Act a provision for the payment of attorney fees as "costs" in a paternity action seeking to secure child support, denies the unwed mother equal protection of the law when such fees are allowable in a divorce proceeding. McQueen v. Hawkins (Lucas 1989) 63 Ohio App.3d 243, 578 N.E.2d 539.

RC 3103.03 is a gender-based statute that discriminates against men by placing the primary burden of family support on them, denigrating the efforts of women who contribute to the finances of their families and denying equal protection to their husbands; it is not substantially related to important governmental interests, and is therefore unconstitutional. In re Rauscher (Cuyahoga 1987) 40 Ohio App.3d 106, 531 N.E.2d 745.

A father is not relieved of the financial obligation to his child because he does not want him and the father's equal protection challenge fails where he argues, "If it is the woman's constitutional right to have an abortion or give the baby up for adoption, then it should be the constitutional right of the man to have the same decision making powers ... that a man who does not want to be engaged in the parenting role should not be penalized financially because the mother chooses to have and to keep the baby;" relevant consent provisions of the adoption statutes do not treat the mother and father differently, and the spouse or nonmarital partner of a pregnant woman cannot forbid her to terminate her pregnancy since the state cannot delegate to a spouse or nonmarital partner a veto power which the state itself is prohibited from exercising. Bryant v Hacker, No. C-950758, 1996 WL 733143 (1st Dist Ct App, Hamilton, 12-24-96).

Although RC 3103.03 improperly discriminates against males and must, to save its constitutionality, be applied in a gender-neutral manner, neither husband nor wife is unconditionally liable for necessaries furnished to his or her spouse; thus, where medical services rendered to a defendant's husband are not furnished in reliance on the defendant's credit, the defendant is not liable for payment of the debt. St. Elizabeth Medical Center v Kirkland, No. 11257 (2d Dist Ct App, Montgomery, 10-6-89), reversed by 49 OS(3d) 17, 550 NE(2d) 159 (1990).

2. In general

Where a husband is unable to provide for his own support, pursuant to RC 3103.03 a wife must aid in the support of her husband to the extent that she is able. Ohio State University Hosp. v. Kinkaid (Ohio 1990) 48 Ohio St.3d 78, 549 N.E.2d 517, rehearing denied 49 Ohio St.3d 713, 552 N.E.2d 951.

The determination of a wife's ability to aid in the support of her husband is a matter to be decided within the sound discretion of the trial court. Ohio State University Hosp. v. Kinkaid (Ohio 1990) 48 Ohio St.3d 78, 549 N.E.2d 517, rehearing denied 49 Ohio St.3d 713, 552 N.E.2d 951.

Action of spouse for loss of consortium and medical expenses arising from bodily injuries suffered by other spouse as result of tort of third party is action for injury to rights of former spouse not arising upon contract, commencement of which is governed by the four-year statute of limitation. Dean v. Angelas (Ohio 1970) 24 Ohio St.2d 99, 264 N.E.2d 911, 53 O.O.2d 282.

A husband may be held liable for the support of a wife while an inmate of any state benevolent institution, a wife for a husband, a father or mother for a son or daughter, and a son or daughter, or both, for a father or mother. The term "son and daughter" is not limited to minors. State v. Stevens (Ohio 1954) 161 Ohio St. 432, 119 N.E.2d 616, 53 O.O. 343.

A married person in applying to the state for aid for the aged thereby obligates his or her estate, upon death, to repay the state, not only the amount of such aid received by him or her but also the amount of aid, if any, received by his or her spouse, and the statutory obligation (GC 7995 Repealed) to repay the aid furnished to the spouse is in the nature of a suretyship obligation without consideration moving directly to such married person, but, where the estate of the spouse is sufficient to repay the aid so furnished to such spouse, the married person or his or her estate is entitled to exoneration as to such aid. Hausser v. Ebinger (Ohio 1954) 161 Ohio St. 192, 118 N.E.2d 522, 53 O.O. 86.

Marriage does not grant a wife an interest in her husband's real or personal property, except as statutorily granted for support and dower. State v. Garber (Ohio App. 9 Dist. 1998) 125 Ohio App.3d 615, 709 N.E.2d 218.

Parent is not justified in electing lifestyle that would assure his or her inability to pay child support as ordered. In re Adoption of Wagner (Ohio App. 11 Dist. 1997) 117 Ohio App.3d 448, 690 N.E.2d 959, appeal not allowed 78 Ohio St.3d 1516, 679 N.E.2d 311.

Any error by trial court in finding that implied contract for medical services could not exist between patient and her former husband was harmless, where evidence showed that patient could pay monies owed to health center. Fulton Cty. Health Ctr. v. Underwood (Williams 1995) 100 Ohio App.3d 451, 654 N.E.2d 354.

Father's duty of support extends only to his children and his spouse, and there is no provision for support of a person who is the mother of his child but who is not his spouse. Gilpen v. Justice (Fayette 1993) 85 Ohio App.3d 86, 619 N.E.2d 94, motion overruled 67 Ohio St.3d 1410, 615 N.E.2d 1044.

A petition in an action to enforce a duty of support filed in this state by a court of a sister state, which state has adopted the Uniform Support Act, and which petition complies with the requirements of that act in requesting that a common pleas court of this state make an order for support of a wife alleged to have been abandoned in Pennsylvania by her husband, who is not a resident of Ohio, states a good cause of action; and such petition may be tried under the terms of the Ohio Support of Dependents Act. Pennsylvania ex rel. Stobie v. Stobie (Summit 1964) 3 Ohio App.2d 18, 209 N.E.2d 457, 32 O.O.2d 79.

For the purposes of determining cohabitation a showing of mere living together is insufficient, there must be a showing of mutual financial support before spousal support can be terminated. Aldridge v Aldridge, No. CA97-09-025, 1998 WL 640903 (12th Dist Ct App, Preble, 9-21-98).

Prior to the December 31, 1967 amendment to RC 4141.30, an applicant for unemployment compensation could be entitled to benefits for a dependent spouse regardless of the amount of the spouse's earnings. Lewis v. Bureau of Unemployment Compensation (Ohio Com.Pl. 1972) 31 Ohio Misc. 122, 283 N.E.2d 203, 60 O.O.2d 254.

A husband unable to support himself may compel his wife to contribute to his support, regardless of the existence of any right to sue for alimony only. Albert v. Albert (Ohio App. 1916) 29 Ohio C.D. 271, 7 Ohio App. 156, 28 Ohio C.A. 225.

Mother of hockey player, who supported her son's participation in ice hockey and was at the ice rink at the time of his injury, was barred under Ohio law under the doctrine of estoppel by acquiescence from disaffirming the release signed by both hockey player and his father. Mohney v. USA Hockey, Inc. (N.D.Ohio 1999) 77 F.Supp.2d 859.

3. Husband's duty to support wife

It is husband's duty to support himself and his wife so long as he is able to do so, but he is not required to provide other than present support. Mark v. Mark (Ohio 1945) 145 Ohio St. 301, 61 N.E.2d 595, 30 O.O. 534.

The legal obligation of a husband to support his wife out of whatever property he has or may receive is not discharged by his continuing physical disability. State ex rel. Person v. Industrial Commission of Ohio (Ohio 1932) 126 Ohio St. 85, 183 N.E. 920, 37 Ohio Law Rep. 304.

In the amendment of former GC 11990 and 11991 to GC 8003-17 (RC 3105.16) and GC 8003-19 (RC 3105.18), the language omitted and added appears to evince an intention on the part of the legislature to clarify the statutes and not to soften the mandatory duty which is imposed on the husband by GC 8002-3 (RC 3103.03) to provide support for his wife and minor children. Klump v. Klump (Lucas 1954) 96 Ohio App. 93, 121 N.E.2d 273, 54 O.O. 202.

Foreign divorce, granted husband temporarily entering sister state for purpose of obtaining divorce from insane nonresident wife served only constructively, held ineffective so far as regards liability for support of wife. Larrick v. Walters (Noble 1930) 39 Ohio App. 363, 177 N.E. 642, 10 Ohio Law Abs. 508.

When a wife uses her own credit to obtain medical services, her husband is not liable for them. Surgical and Medical Neurology Associates, Inc. v. Levan (Ohio Mun. 1982) 7 Ohio Misc.2d 11, 454 N.E.2d 604, 7 O.B.R. 110.

The word "support" as used in RC 3103.03 includes medical and hospital services arising: (a) where there is a contract between the husband and the medical provider; (b) where the wife is the authorized agent of the husband and pledges his credit; or (c) where the husband fails to perform his legal duty to furnish necessary medical services to his wife. Surgical and Medical Neurology Associates, Inc. v. Levan (Ohio Mun. 1982) 7 Ohio Misc.2d 11, 454 N.E.2d 604, 7 O.B.R. 110.

The fact that a wife was made a free dealer by a Florida court does not relieve the husband of liability for her support and necessities. Tort v. Tort (Ohio Com.Pl. 1966) 9 Ohio Misc. 9, 222 N.E.2d 669, 38 O.O.2d 32.

A husband's liability to support his wife and minor children and his liability for necessaries furnished his wife is not affected by the fact that he may be insane, and wife is entitled to claim such support out of such insane husband's estate for the period from his commitment in state hospital to his discharge even though she was not appointed guardian of husband's estate for some time after his commitment. Martin v. Martin (Cuyahoga 1949) 88 N.E.2d 59, 55 Ohio Law Abs. 31.

4. Spousal support, separate maintenance

A wife is not required to file a divorce or alimony action against her husband in order to compel him to provide her with those legal services that he is obligated to supply under his statutory duty to provide her with "necessaries for her support." (Annotation from former RC 3105.14.) Wolf v. Friedman (Ohio 1969) 20 Ohio St.2d 49, 253 N.E.2d 761, 49 O.O.2d 306.

A surviving spouse, whether male or female, should be required to pay for the deceased spouse's expenses for the last illness and necessities provided by third parties, even though no written contractual obligation exists. Cleveland Metropolitan General Hosp. v. Oleksik (Cuyahoga 1987) 38 Ohio App.3d 21, 525 N.E.2d 831.

The granting of a "legal separation" by the trial court in an action by a wife seeking such relief is a misnomer, and, where such judgment might be construed as absolving the defendant husband from his statutory duty to support the wife, it will be modified accordingly. Cummings v. Cummings (Erie 1959) 111 Ohio App. 447, 173 N.E.2d 159, 15 O.O.2d 64.

A judgment for separate maintenance and support is one in personam and orders a husband to make good his obligation of support based on the duty of a husband to support his wife. Delaney v. Delaney (Cuyahoga 1956) 102 Ohio App. 249, 133 N.E.2d 915, 73 Ohio Law Abs. 545, 2 O.O.2d 271.

An action for separate maintenance and support instituted during a husband's lifetime cannot be maintained after his death where such death occurs before a judgment or order is entered adjudging the rights of the parties. Delaney v. Delaney (Cuyahoga 1956) 102 Ohio App. 249, 133 N.E.2d 915, 73 Ohio Law Abs. 545, 2 O.O.2d 271.

Where in an action for alimony plaintiff obtained a temporary injunction restraining her husband and a daughter by a former marriage from disposing of property allegedly transferred to such daughter, and the defendant husband thereafter died, the action was abated and the order against the daughter properly dismissed. Delaney v. Delaney (Cuyahoga 1956) 102 Ohio App. 249, 133 N.E.2d 915, 73 Ohio Law Abs. 545, 2 O.O.2d 271.

To make an award based entirely on the husband's wealth and ability to pay without giving due consideration to the wife's needs, judged by the standard of living which the parties by common consent had maintained during their married life, constitutes an abuse of discretion and requires a reviewing court to reverse and set aside such an award. Stone v. Stone (Cuyahoga 1954) 98 Ohio App. 240, 122 N.E.2d 404, 57 O.O. 267.

In determining the amount of temporary alimony to be awarded to a wife, including support for a minor child, pending final hearing of the issues presented by the pleadings in a divorce action, the court must give due consideration to the wife's necessities and the husband's means, and where a wife is clearly financially able to prosecute her defense as well as her cross-petition for separate maintenance and support, an order directing the husband to pay wife $5,000 interim attorney fees is unwarranted and the making of such order constitutes an abuse of discretion. Stone v. Stone (Cuyahoga 1954) 98 Ohio App. 240, 122 N.E.2d 404, 57 O.O. 267.

Where an appellant wife has ample funds during an appeal of a divorce action, the appellate court will refrain from awarding her temporary alimony. (See also Phillips v Phillips, 74 Abs 111, 136 NE(2d) 98 (App, Franklin 1956).) Phillips v. Phillips (Franklin 1954) 129 N.E.2d 77, 70 Ohio Law Abs. 552.

5. Funeral expenses, last illness

While assertion that payments decedent's parents made for burial expenses were loan or gift to decedent's wife may have been defense available to wife in any claim made or action for reimbursement brought against her personally, such defense would have no application to claim or action brought against her as personal representative of estate, absent evidence that those defenses were available to estate, as well. Osborne v. Osborne (Greene 1996) 114 Ohio App.3d 412, 683 N.E.2d 365.

Person other than surviving spouse who pays deceased's funeral expenses, not as officious volunteer or meddler but out of necessity of occasion, is entitled to reimbursement from estate of deceased, provided bill is reasonable. Osborne v. Osborne (Greene 1996) 114 Ohio App.3d 412, 683 N.E.2d 365.

Conduct of decedent's parents in paying for burial expenses after decedent's wife told them she had no money to pay those costs did not establish that payments were loan or gift to decedent's estate, so as to excuse estate from its duty of reimbursement. Osborne v. Osborne (Greene 1996) 114 Ohio App.3d 412, 683 N.E.2d 365.

The common-law surviving spouse is liable for the medical expenses incurred by the deceased spouse during the decedent's final illness. Warren Gen. Hosp. v. Brink (Trumbull 1992) 80 Ohio App.3d 793, 610 N.E.2d 1128.

A surviving spouse is not obligated under RC 3103.03, absent a contractual duty, to pay for hospital services rendered to a deceased spouse. Riverside Methodist Hosp. v. Payne (Franklin 1988) 48 Ohio App.3d 123, 548 N.E.2d 987.

Plaintiff's action against the biological father seeking reimbursement for necessaries furnished to plaintiff's wife's children born during his marriage is properly dismissed when it is clear from the record that such action was not brought for the benefit of, nor out of concern for, the children involved. Weinman v Larsh, No. C-810383 (1st Dist Ct App, Hamilton, 3-31-82), affirmed by 5 OS(3d) 85, 5 OBR 138, 448 NE(2d) 1384 (1983).

Surviving spouse was not liable for decedent's funeral expenses beyond amount she already paid, under statute allowing surviving spouse to assume such obligation; surviving spouse did not assume to pay for expenses ex post facto, funeral home did not specifically contract to provide funeral expenses, and surviving spouse emphatically maintained that she could afford only certain amount for funeral and that she assumed her in-laws were liable for any amount beyond that figure. J.C. Battle & Sons Funeral Home, Inc. v. Chambers (Ohio Mun. 1993) 63 Ohio Misc.2d 441, 631 N.E.2d 203.

Funeral expenses for decedent, beyond $1,000 paid by surviving spouse and $410 paid by another party, were unreasonable, and surviving spouse thus was not responsible for them under statute which stated that surviving spouse must assist in support of spouse according to his or her ability to do so; surviving spouse agreed to pay maximum of $1,000 for funeral, decent burial could have been provided for much less than $5,270.03 charged, and funeral home insisted upon, and surviving spouse's brother-in-law agreed to, expensive casket. J.C. Battle & Sons Funeral Home, Inc. v. Chambers (Ohio Mun. 1993) 63 Ohio Misc.2d 441, 631 N.E.2d 203.

Surviving spouse has implied contractual obligation to pay for necessary funeral expenses only to extent they are reasonable; what is reasonable is to be determined on case-by-case basis, is within sound discretion of trial court, and is based on test set forth in statute which states that surviving spouse must assist in support of spouse according to his or her ability to do so. J.C. Battle & Sons Funeral Home, Inc. v. Chambers (Ohio Mun. 1993) 63 Ohio Misc.2d 441, 631 N.E.2d 203.

A surviving spouse is responsible for burial expenses of a deceased spouse, as funeral expenses are "necessaries" as contemplated by RC 3103.03. Davis-Turner Funeral Home, Inc. v. Chaney (Ohio Mun. 1991) 61 Ohio Misc.2d 82, 573 N.E.2d 1242.

The statute making it the duty of a wife, in case of the inability of her husband to support his family, to assist him so far as she is able, imposes liability on her separate estate to pay the expenses of her own last sickness and funeral where her husband is without means to do so. Thornton v. Houck (Gallia 1926) 5 Ohio Law Abs. 533, 32 Ohio Law Rep. 57.

A wife is liable for the funeral expenses and those incurred during her husband's last illness even where she has not directly contracted for them where the husband has no estate. Smith v. Snapp (Ohio Com.Pl. 1961) 175 N.E.2d 333, 87 Ohio Law Abs. 318, 16 O.O.2d 304.

The surviving husband, rather than the deceased wife's estate, is liable for the expenses of her last illness. In re Shields' Estate (Ohio Prob. 1953) 116 N.E.2d 828, 67 Ohio Law Abs. 457.

A contract between husband and wife to live separately for the rest of their lives and releasing him from all claims she had arising out of marriage relation does not relieve him from liability for her funeral expenses. This section recognizes his liability independent of any separate estate. George H. Humphrey & Son v. Huff (Delaware 1914) 25 Ohio C.D. 117, 20 Ohio C.C.(N.S.) 178, 3 Ohio App. 111.

In the absence of a contract with a wife or circumstances which raise a presumption that she intended to charge her separate estate therefor, no liability arises against her even for necessaries required by the family; and tuition fees for services rendered to her child under a contract entered into by her husband cannot be made a charge against her individually. Kruger v Baumgarten, 9 NP(NS) 332, 20 D 434 (1910).

6. —In general, support of children

A nonresident custodial parent has a right to pursue an action for child support against the noncustodial parent in a court of competent jurisdiction in this state when the noncustodial parent is a resident of Ohio and the parties' foreign divorce decree and child custody order do not address the issue of support. Haskins v. Bronzetti (Ohio 1992) 64 Ohio St.3d 202, 594 N.E.2d 582.

The parties to a separation agreement may not abrogate the right of a minor child of the marriage to be supported by either parent; prior to the effective date of RC 3113.215 to 3113.218, the parties could, however, agree to allocate the support obligation between themselves in a manner analogous to an indemnity agreement. In re Dissolution of Marriage of Lazor (Ohio 1991) 59 Ohio St.3d 201, 572 N.E.2d 66.

RC 2151.42, which makes it a criminal offense for the father of an illegitimate child to fail to support such child, does not give rise to a civil action for support on behalf of such child. Baston v. Sears (Ohio 1968) 15 Ohio St.2d 166, 239 N.E.2d 62, 44 O.O.2d 144.

A petition by a minor child, alleging that a defendant wrongfully induced the plaintiff's father to abandon his family, thereby (1) depriving the plaintiff of his father's affection, companionship and guidance and (2) bringing unwanted attention and unwarranted publicity causing embarrassment, humiliation and loss of social standing to the plaintiff, is subject to demurrer on the ground that it fails to state a cause of action. Kane v. Quigley (Ohio 1964) 1 Ohio St.2d 1, 203 N.E.2d 338, 30 O.O.2d 1.

By both statutory and common law of Ohio, parents are charged with obligation of supporting their minor children. State ex rel. Wright v. Industrial Commission (Ohio 1943) 141 Ohio St. 187, 47 N.E.2d 209, 25 O.O. 277.

Court lacked authority to order biological father to provide present and future child support to child who had reached age of majority and was emancipated, even though paternity action had been timely filed within five years after child reached age 18. Snider v. Lillie (Ohio App. 1 Dist. 1997) 131 Ohio App.3d 444, 722 N.E.2d 1036.

Statutory and common law duty on part of parents to support their minor children extends to illegitimate children. Snider v. Lillie (Ohio App. 1 Dist. 1997) 131 Ohio App.3d 444, 722 N.E.2d 1036.

With respect to present and future child support, once child reaches age of majority and becomes emancipated, court is without power to provide child with support, child has no legal right to be supported, and the court no longer has the power to order a parent to pay child support. Snider v. Lillie (Ohio App. 1 Dist. 1997) 131 Ohio App.3d 444, 722 N.E.2d 1036.

One obvious goal of various parentage statutes is to accommodate genetic evidence to ensure that correct parentage determination is made from the outset; duty to support children applies to "biological or adoptive parent," and statutes give precedence to genetic testing over any presumption of legitimacy. Leguillon v. Leguillon (Ohio App. 12 Dist. 1998) 124 Ohio App.3d 757, 707 N.E.2d 571.

Court order providing child support necessarily involves finding by court that obligor is able to pay, and burden is on obligor by allegations and proof to establish his or her inability to pay. Carroll v. Detty (Ross 1996) 113 Ohio App.3d 708, 681 N.E.2d 1383.

Child support is a duty and obligation imposed by statute and common law. Hamilton v. Hamilton (Lucas 1995) 107 Ohio App.3d 132, 667 N.E.2d 1256, appeal not allowed 75 Ohio St.3d 1425, 662 N.E.2d 27.

Ordinarily, child support and visitation are independent matters. Hamilton v. Hamilton (Lucas 1995) 107 Ohio App.3d 132, 667 N.E.2d 1256, appeal not allowed 75 Ohio St.3d 1425, 662 N.E.2d 27.

Trial court had jurisdiction to modify child support provisions of separation agreement which had been incorporated into decree of dissolution, so as to conform support obligation to amended statute governing parental duty to support children, even though separation agreement went into effect more than 13 years before court's action; court had both statutory continuing jurisdiction to modify child support and separate jurisdiction to give effect to statutory command of support statute. Mazzuckelli v. Mazzuckelli (Hamilton 1995) 106 Ohio App.3d 554, 666 N.E.2d 620.

Amended statute governing parental duty to support children should be read to incorporate broad definition of "child support order" contained in statute governing calculation of child support obligation. Mazzuckelli v. Mazzuckelli (Hamilton 1995) 106 Ohio App.3d 554, 666 N.E.2d 620.

Right to receive child support payments was assigned to mother by maternal grandparents, although father was ordered to pay only grandparents and not mother; when custody of child went to mother, duty of support followed child. Wise v. Wise (Butler 1993) 86 Ohio App.3d 702, 621 N.E.2d 1213.

Order allowing attachment of father's employer-sponsored savings plan met requirements of "qualified domestic relations order" (QDRO), and, therefore, general antialienation provision of ERISA was inapplicable; order related to child support, juvenile court made order pursuant to domestic relations law requiring parent to support minor children, and juvenile court had jurisdiction to order child support. Albertson v. Ryder (Lake 1993) 85 Ohio App.3d 765, 621 N.E.2d 480.

A juvenile court does not have jurisdiction to entertain a complaint filed by a county human services department against a child's natural father to establish child support and for reimbursement of ADC payments made to the child's grandmother who had been appointed guardian by a probate court. Lake Cty. Dept. of Human Serv. v. Adams (Lake 1992) 82 Ohio App.3d 494, 612 N.E.2d 766.

A mental health provider which, while in possession of a medical insurance policy covering the policyholder's child, allegedly represents to the parent that the policy will provide coverage for the child's care, but the insurer limits coverage to a specified number of days, may be estopped from seeking payment for services in excess of the policy's limits. Doe v. Blue Cross/Blue Shield of Ohio (Franklin 1992) 79 Ohio App.3d 369, 607 N.E.2d 492.

The estate of a deceased minor child may not claim as damages the child's medical expenses in a medical malpractice action as the child's parents, not the child, are responsible for payment of a child's medical expenses and are therefore the proper party in interest. Blakeman v. Condorodis (Hamilton 1991) 75 Ohio App.3d 393, 599 N.E.2d 776, motion overruled 62 Ohio St.3d 1478, 581 N.E.2d 1099.

The failure of a mother residing in California to support her children residing in Ohio constitutes tortious injury sufficient to confer jurisdiction upon an Ohio court pursuant to Civ R 4.3(A)(3). Wayne Cty. Bur. of Support v. Wolfe (Wayne 1991) 71 Ohio App.3d 765, 595 N.E.2d 421.

The parent of a child adjudicated dependent due to his refusal to seek medical treatment of a venereal disease may be ordered to pay the costs of court-ordered treatment of the venereal disease. In re J.J. (Butler 1990) 64 Ohio App.3d 806, 582 N.E.2d 1138.

A minor who sustains injuries and incurs substantial medical bills is liable for and cannot avoid the debt since emergency medical services constitute necessaries; the custodial parents are likewise liable for the debt under an implied contract because of the duty to support established by RC 3103.03. State of Ohio, University of Cincinnati Hosp. v. Cohen (Hamilton 1989) 57 Ohio App.3d 30, 566 N.E.2d 187.

There is a presumption that a provider of emergency medical services relies on the parents' credit for payment when the injured minor child lives with her parents, and in such an instance, the parents are primarily liable and the minor is secondarily liable; an agreement between the provider and the parents with respect to the terms of the parents' payment does not constitute an accord and satisfaction of the minor's debt when the amount of the debt is liquidated, the parents do not actually agree to pay a lesser amount, and there is no evidence of the parents' performance of the agreement. State of Ohio, University of Cincinnati Hosp. v. Cohen (Hamilton 1989) 57 Ohio App.3d 30, 566 N.E.2d 187.

The term "necessaries" as it appears in RC 3103.03 includes a reasonable allowance for expense money to employ the services of an attorney to prosecute or defend an action in a court concerning the enforcement of the duty of the divorced father to support his minor children. Evans v. Brown (Franklin 1986) 34 Ohio App.3d 56, 516 N.E.2d 1289, 31 O.B.R. 607.

The interest of a beneficiary in the income of a trust that is neither a purely discretionary trust, nor a strict support trust, and that does not expressly exclude the beneficiary's children may be attached for the purpose of paying a judgment against the beneficiary for child support. Matthews v. Matthews (Franklin 1981) 5 Ohio App.3d 140, 450 N.E.2d 278, 5 O.B.R. 320, on reconsideration, reconsideration overruled.

The father of an unemancipated minor child is legally entitled to recover on his uninsured motorist coverage for the wrongful death of that minor child even if such child at the time of the injury and death was not a member of the father's household. Motorists Mut. Ins. Co. v. Speck (Summit 1977) 59 Ohio App.2d 224, 393 N.E.2d 500, 13 O.O.3d 239.

A parent having custody of minor children who is able to fully support such children, and has done so, may not utilize criminal prosecution under RC 2919.21 as a means of enforcing the obligation of the other parent to contribute to the support of their minor children. State v. Oppenheimer (Franklin 1975) 46 Ohio App.2d 241, 348 N.E.2d 731, 75 O.O.2d 404.

Where the circumstances existing at the time of a divorce decree ordering monthly child support payments cease to exist, the legal obligation to make such payments terminates at the same time and not when it is cancelled of record. Hoffmann v. Hoffmann (Hamilton 1972) 32 Ohio App.2d 186, 289 N.E.2d 397, 61 O.O.2d 205.

Aunt who, without court order to do so, assumes custody of minor niece and voluntarily pays for food, clothing, shelter and other necessaries for such minor, but refuses to grant father's request for care and custody of child, cannot recover from father for expenses so incurred. Anderson v. Conn (Lucas 1941) 68 Ohio App. 1, 38 N.E.2d 325, 22 O.O. 45.

Where a wife is divorced from her husband for his aggression, and is given custody of their six-year-old child, the decree making no provision for support of the child or for alimony, and the child does not thereafter live with the father, but with the mother, and the wife voluntarily supports the child and at no time makes demand upon the father to furnish support or to reimburse her therefor, and father makes no promise in reference thereto, the estate of the father, after his decease, is not liable to the mother for the support furnished by the mother after child became adult, though said child was at all times mentally and physically incompetent to support itself. Brunswick v. First-Central Trust Co. (Summit 1940) 66 Ohio App. 242, 32 N.E.2d 855, 33 Ohio Law Abs. 318, 19 O.O. 570.

Where wife was divorced by husband, but given custody of minor daughter, and awarded $1,000 alimony payable in installments, mother was responsible for funeral expenses of minor daughter dying while in mother's control, and suit could not be maintained against father for such expenses. Dodge v. Keller (Cuyahoga 1927) 29 Ohio App. 114, 162 N.E. 750, 6 Ohio Law Abs. 6.

A court appropriately orders a father to pay the guideline child support payment until his son obtains his high school diploma where the father is ordered to pay his son's private high school tuition and the son who was to have graduated from high school in June does not graduate and attends summer school. Guess v Guess, No. 97APF08-1112, 1998 WL 85901 (10th Dist Ct App, Franklin, 2-26-98).

Common law rules that the father is the head of the family and that death terminates his obligation of child support are based on outdated social and sexual stereotypes; the modern trend is for a divorce court to mandate that the obligor designate the child as the beneficiary on the parent's life insurance policy to ensure that the child receive support during minority in the event the obligor parent dies before the child reaches majority. Webb v Webb, No. 16371, 1997 WL 797719 (2d Dist Ct App, Montgomery, 12-31-97).

The father as obligor cannot be credited with social security payments occasioned by the death of the mother and received by the custodial grandparents on behalf of the minor child; such payments should be added to the obligor's annual salary to arrive at an annual child support figure. In re Mudrak, No. 94-B-32, 1997 WL 28557 (7th Dist Ct App, Belmont, 1-22-97).

Pursuant to RC 3103.03, a party who seeks to hold the parent of an unemancipated minor child liable for services rendered to that child has to prove by a preponderance of the evidence that the services were necessary and the charges for same reasonable. Child & Adolescent Service Center v Hambuechen, No. CA-9043 (5th Dist Ct App, Stark, 3-8-93).

Child support benefits received upon a parent's retirement may be credited against the parent's child support obligation because a credit for social security child support payments on retirement merely reflects the fact that the amounts due have been paid, and in no respect alters the obligation of dependant or the award to the children. Curnutte v Delarino, No. 2974 (9th Dist Ct App, Lorain, 9-3-80).

Where the non-custodial parent is ordered to pay child support, to have an abuse of discretion in such a case, there must be a showing of a combination of circumstances where there is an inability to contribute even a nominal amount by the person out of custody, coupled with a showing that the person in custody has an ability to support without help. McCauley v McCauley, No. 79AP-727 (10th Dist Ct App, Franklin, 1-29-80).

While a domestic relations court which grants a divorce has continuing jurisdiction over all matters pertaining to child custody and support, it has no authority to retroactively modify the total amount due and payable under its prior order for support of minor children in this action involving a change of custody. Kuntz v Kuntz, No. 78AP-831 (10th Dist Ct App, Franklin, 7-5-79).

RC 3103.03 does not create a cause of action in favor of a third person against a husband for the supply of necessaries to his minor children. Fifth Third Bank/Visa v. Gilbert (Ohio Mun. 1984) 17 Ohio Misc.2d 14, 478 N.E.2d 1324, 17 O.B.R. 406.

A trial court has jurisdiction to modify a support order as to future installments, whether or not the right is reserved in the decree; but it has no such jurisdiction to modify unpaid installment support payments which have accrued if the child for whose benefit support was awarded was living and not emancipated at the time of the accrual, unless the right to retrospective modification was specifically reserved in the decree. Wedebrook v. Wedebrook (Ohio Com.Pl. 1977) 51 Ohio Misc. 81, 367 N.E.2d 937, 5 O.O.3d 342.

A court granting decree of divorce may change custody of a minor child of parties or increase or decrease provisions for support, maintenance, care and education of such minor child during its minority as changed circumstances require, notwithstanding the unqualified provisions of a separation agreement concerning support, maintenance, care, and education for such child incorporated in decree of divorce. Rutter v. Rutter (Ohio Com.Pl. 1970) 24 Ohio Misc. 7, 261 N.E.2d 202, 53 O.O.2d 32.

A minor defendant is liable for temporary alimony and child support, and a court may award the same upon hearing immediately after the filing of plaintiff's petition and valid and proper service of summons thereon, whether or not a guardian ad litem has as yet been appointed for him. Martens v. Martens (Ohio Com.Pl. 1966) 8 Ohio Misc. 178, 221 N.E.2d 617, 37 O.O.2d 256.

A court does not have jurisdiction to order a parent in a divorce action to pay for a college education for his children. Mitchell v. Mitchell (Cuyahoga 1959) 158 N.E.2d 546, 81 Ohio Law Abs. 88, affirmed in part, reversed in part 170 Ohio St. 507, 166 N.E.2d 396, 11 O.O.2d 281.

Where a father agreed with his children that upon his death or permanent retirement from the family corporation his stock should pass to his two sons, who should thereupon pay half the value thereof to his two daughters, and such retirement and transfer did occur prior to his death, the transfer cannot be attacked as fraudulent by his second wife after his death. MacLean v. J. S. MacLean Co. (Ohio Prob. 1955) 123 N.E.2d 761, 70 Ohio Law Abs. 102, 57 O.O. 454, appeal dismissed 133 N.E.2d 198, 71 Ohio Law Abs. 589, 71 Ohio Law Abs. 590.

It was not error for a court to dismiss a petition for adoption to which the mother had not consented where the evidence showed that the father had supported the child part of the time and that the mother had not known he was not supporting the child at other times. Adoption of Stephen (Darke 1952) 111 N.E.2d 762, 64 Ohio Law Abs. 289.

Ohio statutes make it duty of husband to support his wife and minor children out of his property or by his labor; if he is unable wife must assist him so far as she is able; and no part of ward's estate shall be used for support, maintenance, or education of ward unless ordered or approved by court; there is distinction between parent acting as natural guardian of his minor child with custody of minor's person and position of legal guardian appointed by court for purpose of care and management of estate of such minor. Chertoff v. C.I.R. (C.C.A. 6 1947) 160 F.2d 691, 35 O.O. 399.

Responsibility of mother to support children may be transferred to a trust if justified by language of will creating the trust and the circumstances under which it was made. Cleveland Clinic Foundation v. Humphrys (C.C.A.6 (Ohio) 1938) 97 F.2d 849, certiorari denied 59 S.Ct. 93, 305 U.S. 628, 83 L.Ed. 403.

Calhoun test for determining whether debt is nondischargeable child support obligation did not apply to order entered for sole purpose of designating rights and obligations of unmarried parents with respect to their minor child. In re Kidd (Bkrtcy.S.D.Ohio 1995) 177 B.R. 876.

For purposes of RC 3313.64, the term "guardian" must be given a liberal construction, and can include a person who stands in loco parentis to an adult student. OAG 74-076.

A common-law husband is legally the stepfather of the natural children of his common-law wife where he is not the natural father of those children; consequently he may claim them as dependents for purposes of unemployment compensation under RC 4141.30. In re Gannon, UCBR B89-00802-0000 (3-7-95).

7. —Husband, support of children

It is not an abuse of discretion as a matter of law for the trial court, having jurisdiction of the parties, to order payments by the father for the college education of minor children electing to matriculate in an accredited college. Mitchell v. Mitchell (Ohio 1960) 170 Ohio St. 507, 166 N.E.2d 396, 11 O.O.2d 281.

Father's argument that he did not want child and would have elected either abortion or adoption did not release him from his obligation to pay child support. Bryant v. Hacker (Ohio App. 1 Dist. 1996) 116 Ohio App.3d 860, 689 N.E.2d 609.

Portion of father's child support arrearage payments to child support enforcement agency were properly directed to mother's current husband, though mother had legal custody, where children lived with husband after his separation from mother during period of arrearages; statute allowed court to take appropriate action, and father was not prejudiced since amount of support did not increase. Palmer v. Harrold (Greene 1995) 101 Ohio App.3d 732, 656 N.E.2d 708.

Fact that current husband of children's mother "voluntarily" undertook to contribute to support of children, who were in custody of mother pursuant to divorce decree, did not preclude payment of portion of father's child support arrearages to husband, for period of time in which children lived with husband upon husband's separation from mother. Palmer v. Harrold (Greene 1995) 101 Ohio App.3d 732, 656 N.E.2d 708.

Fathers have duty to support children born to them in wedlock. In re Adoption of Lassiter (Clark 1995) 101 Ohio App.3d 367, 655 N.E.2d 781, dismissed, appeal not allowed 73 Ohio St.3d 1410, 651 N.E.2d 1308.

Drug addiction did not relieve addict from obligation to support his minor child. In re Adoption of Lassiter (Clark 1995) 101 Ohio App.3d 367, 655 N.E.2d 781, dismissed, appeal not allowed 73 Ohio St.3d 1410, 651 N.E.2d 1308.

Father was liable for child support arrearage, although he claimed child's maternal grandparents and mother informed him that he need not make any more payments; father had duty to state as well as to minor child to fulfill his support obligation and, as such, it was not within power of grandparents to relieve him of his duty to support child, and there was no evidence of consideration to support agreement to terminate child support. Wise v. Wise (Butler 1993) 86 Ohio App.3d 702, 621 N.E.2d 1213.

Common law allows cause of action by third persons against father for necessaries provided to minor children in addition to any rights stated in applicable version of support statute. Aharoni v. Michael (Franklin 1991) 74 Ohio App.3d 260, 598 N.E.2d 1215.

A parent has a duty dictated by public policy to take care of his children and a parent will not be totally excused from paying child support without any showing of good faith in making some payment; absent such a showing, failure to pay may be punished by imprisonment. Allen v. Allen (Columbiana 1988) 59 Ohio App.3d 54, 571 N.E.2d 139.

Social security benefits, payable to a mother for the support of her minor children due to the disability of the father, may not be credited toward arrearages of child support payments accrued by the father's violation of his then existing obligation of support. Fuller v. Fuller (Summit 1976) 49 Ohio App.2d 223, 360 N.E.2d 357, 3 O.O.3d 273.

A father's duty to support a minor child includes an obligation to pay reasonable funeral expenses in the event of the child's death prior to reaching the age of majority, and the juvenile court is justified in ordering the continuation of support payments being made by the father until such funeral expenses have been paid. In re Terrell (Cuyahoga 1976) 48 Ohio App.2d 352, 357 N.E.2d 1113, 2 O.O.3d 353.

There is no duty on the father of minor children to make support payments to the mother as decreed by another court pursuant to the Uniform Reciprocal Enforcement of Support Act, where the father has obtained a prior order of custody and the mother has removed the children from the jurisdiction of the court contrary to such order. State of N. J. v. Morales (Franklin 1973) 35 Ohio App.2d 56, 299 N.E.2d 920, 64 O.O.2d 175.

A father may not be relieved of his obligation to support his minor children as a result of their so-called de facto, as distinguished from a de jure, adoption by their mother and stepfather. Logan v. Logan (Lucas 1960) 111 Ohio App. 534, 170 N.E.2d 922, 13 O.O.2d 364.

The obligation of a father to provide reasonably for the support of his minor children until the latter are in condition to provide for themselves is not impaired by a judgment of divorce awarding the mother the custody of the children even though it be silent as to the children's support. Logan v. Logan (Lucas 1960) 111 Ohio App. 534, 170 N.E.2d 922, 13 O.O.2d 364.

Statute which places father and mother on basis of equality with respect to care, custody and control of their offspring, cannot be construed to relieve father of his primary obligation to support his minor children as provided in this section. Kintner v. Kintner (Franklin 1946) 78 Ohio App. 324, 65 N.E.2d 156, 46 Ohio Law Abs. 594, 34 O.O. 41.

Law imposing upon father duty of caring for and supporting his minor children insofar as he is able to do so does not require him to compensate third person who, without father's consent, has assumed obligation of supporting his children. Anderson v. Conn (Lucas 1941) 68 Ohio App. 1, 38 N.E.2d 325, 22 O.O. 45.

Where divorce decree gave children's custody to mother, and required fixed payment for their maintenance, father, in absence of agreement to do so, could not be required to pay for medical services rendered minor child. Harker v. Wolff (Montgomery 1931) 42 Ohio App. 540, 182 N.E. 592, 10 Ohio Law Abs. 470.

A husband may be relieved of the duty imposed by this section to support his minor children by a decree of court pronounced in a divorce proceeding providing for the care and maintenance of the minor children. Rowland v. State (Ohio App. 3 Dist. 1921) 14 Ohio App. 238, 32 Ohio C.A. 75.

A father is liable for medical treatment given without his consent to his son for whom he provides support (1) even though the father and mother are living apart, (2) the mother's consent is given, and (3) the treatment is necessary to stabilize the blood sugar of their son who is diabetic. Children's Hospital Medical Center v Bradley, No. 17723, 1996 WL 525854 (9th Dist Ct App, Summit, 9-18-96).

The juvenile court's authority to order payment of back child support is not defeated by subsequent adoption of the child; however, the court errs by ordering the father to pay support for five months after the child is adopted by the mother's husband. Black v Hart, No. 17524, 1996 WL 304284 (9th Dist Ct App, Summit, 6-5-96).

Where a father was ordered to pay ten dollars a week for support of his two children by a domestic relations court in California and remained current in the payments for ten years, the father remains responsible for the public assistance funds paid by the state to support his children under RC 3103.03 and 5107.05. Human Services Dept v Bond, No. 16256, 1993 WL 526615 (9th Dist Ct App, Summit, 12-15-93).

In an action appealing an order to increase child support, the court may consider the income of the father's present wife in determining his present ability to pay increased child support. Pearson v Pearson, No. 44880 (8th Dist Ct App, Cuyahoga, 12-23-82).

Plaintiff's action against the biological father seeking reimbursement for necessaries furnished to plaintiff's wife's children born during his marriage is properly dismissed when it is clear from the record that such action was not brought for the benefit of, nor out of concern for, the children involved. Weinman v Larsh, No. C-810383 (1st Dist Ct App, Hamilton, 3-31-82), affirmed by 5 OS(3d) 85, 5 OBR 138, 448 NE(2d) 1384 (1983).

A noncustodial father is not liable for an elective abortion performed on his minor daughter, which procedure was neither requested nor authorized by him, and where there was no showing that such parent had refused or neglected to provide for the minor child's support or medical care. Akron City Hospital v. Anderson (Ohio Mun. 1981) 68 Ohio Misc. 14, 428 N.E.2d 472, 22 O.O.3d 238.

Court has jurisdiction and duty to require father to pay adequate support for his minor children whether or not there was an express reservation of continuing jurisdiction in original divorce decree; and where original divorce decree made no order of support, though it approved provisions of separation agreement, modification of support payments may be made without showing changed circumstances. Gilmore v. Gilmore (Ohio Com.Pl. 1971) 28 Ohio Misc. 161, 275 N.E.2d 646, 57 O.O.2d 272.

Separation agreement incorporated into divorce decree in which wife agrees to provide for support of child of parties after it arrives at age of eighteen years, does not relieve husband from duty of providing for such child. Rutter v. Rutter (Ohio Com.Pl. 1970) 24 Ohio Misc. 7, 261 N.E.2d 202, 53 O.O.2d 32.

Where a wife abandons her husband without any aggression on his part and takes her children to another state, the husband cannot be compelled to support such children under the uniform enforcement of support laws where he retains a domicile in Ohio, earns his living in Ohio, and apparently is ready, willing, and able to support his children in Ohio. Buliox v. Buliox (Ohio Com.Pl. 1962) 185 N.E.2d 802, 90 Ohio Law Abs. 251, 21 O.O.2d 30.

A husband's liability to support his wife and minor children and his liability for necessaries furnished his wife is not affected by the fact that he may be insane, and wife is entitled to claim such support out of such insane husband's estate for the period from his commitment in state hospital to his discharge even though she was not appointed guardian of husband's estate for some time after his commitment. Martin v. Martin (Cuyahoga 1949) 88 N.E.2d 59, 55 Ohio Law Abs. 31.

A debt owed by a man to an Ohio agency for assistance payments it made to support his children is a debt for child support and thus cannot be discharged in his bankruptcy proceedings. In re Jones (Bkrtcy.N.D.Ohio 1988) 94 B.R. 99.

8. —Wife, support of children

A wife, who has breached duty imposed upon her by RC 3103.02 to conform to her husband's place of living, may not claim benefit of RC 3103.03, which imposes upon husband absolute duty to support his wife and family. Porter v. Porter (Ohio 1971) 25 Ohio St.2d 123, 267 N.E.2d 299, 54 O.O.2d 260.

Where a husband and wife are divorced, the duty to support minor children is governed by RC 3109.05, so that a wife may be required to contribute to the support of her minor children who are in the custody of their father. Hacker v. Hacker (Fairfield 1981) 5 Ohio App.3d 46, 448 N.E.2d 831, 5 O.B.R. 50.

In an action by a hospital against the parents of a minor child for medical treatment provided to the minor child by the hospital, the mother of the child may not absolve herself of liability to the hospital, a third party, by reason of a provision in the divorce decree requiring the father of the child to pay for all medical expenses incurred by the child. Children's Hospital of Akron v. Johnson (Summit 1980) 68 Ohio App.2d 17, 426 N.E.2d 515, 22 O.O.3d 11.

Where a husband and wife are divorced, the duty to support a minor child is governed by RC 3109.05 and not 3103.03, so that a wife may be required to assume the support of her child which is in the custody of another. Hill v. Hill (Hamilton 1973) 40 Ohio App.2d 1, 317 N.E.2d 250, 69 O.O.2d 1.

Decree of divorce which grants to plaintiff-husband custody of four minor children of divorced parties and orders defendant-wife to pay to husband certain specified amounts for support of such children, which amounts had been previously agreed upon in separation agreement approved by court, will be upheld, even though decree does not include finding that husband is unable to support such children. Clover v. Clover (Fairfield 1970) 24 Ohio App.2d 161, 265 N.E.2d 559, 53 O.O.2d 389.

Liability of husband to support his minor children is primary and that of wife is secondary; wife is not required to support her minor children unless husband is unable to do so. Kintner v. Kintner (Franklin 1946) 78 Ohio App. 324, 65 N.E.2d 156, 46 Ohio Law Abs. 594, 34 O.O. 41.

Where husband and wife are divorced and court made order placing their minor child in custody of third person and fixing support charge at $10 per week, and evidence shows that father is able to support child, it is reversible error for court to order wife to pay to clerk of courts $10 per month to reimburse husband for furnishing full support to child. Kintner v. Kintner (Franklin 1946) 78 Ohio App. 324, 65 N.E.2d 156, 46 Ohio Law Abs. 594, 34 O.O. 41.

Where wife was divorced by husband, but given custody of minor daughter, and awarded $1,000 alimony payable in installments, mother was responsible for funeral expenses of minor daughter dying while in mother's control, and suit could not be maintained against father for such expenses. Dodge v. Keller (Cuyahoga 1927) 29 Ohio App. 114, 162 N.E. 750, 6 Ohio Law Abs. 6.

Where, by decree, custody, care, and support of son was awarded the father, and after the mother's remarriage the son visited her by agreement and was not returned, since she retained him with knowledge that custody had been awarded the father, presumption is that her support was furnished without expectation of recovery and was as gratuity, and no recovery could be had as against the father. Thompson v. Mueller (Hamilton 1927) 28 Ohio App. 51, 161 N.E. 291, 6 Ohio Law Abs. 184.

Trial court properly ordered divorced wife to contribute to support of children where husband was unable to maintain children without assistance, despite fact that settlement agreement imposed no such obligation. Armstrong v. Armstrong (Franklin 1956) 139 N.E.2d 471, 74 Ohio Law Abs. 177.

Where a wife was ordered to contribute to the support of her children, custody of whom was awarded to the father, and the husband moved for judgment against the mother for the arrearages, the court could, in view of the circumstances, deny such motion. Shalosky v. Shalosky (Franklin 1952) 128 N.E.2d 464, 70 Ohio Law Abs. 394.

The duty of a husband to support his wife extends to payment of the expenses of his wife's funeral. Phillips v. Tolerton (Ohio Com.Pl. 1908) 20 Ohio Dec. 249, 9 Ohio N.P.(N.S.) 565, affirmed 82 Ohio St. 403, 92 N.E. 1121, 7 Ohio Law Rep. 645.

As head of the family, the father is primarily responsible for the support of his children, but after his death the mother is bound to support them if she is able, and cannot claim reimbursement for necessaries from the estate left the children by their father; the guardian of the children's estate should not pay such a demand of the mother. Wing v. Hibbert (Ohio Com.Pl. 1897) 8 Ohio Dec. 65, 7 Ohio N.P. 124, affirmed in part, reversed in part 11 Ohio C.D. 190.

Responsibility of mother to support children may be transferred to a trust if justified by language of will creating the trust and the circumstances under which it was made. Cleveland Clinic Foundation v. Humphrys (C.C.A.6 (Ohio) 1938) 97 F.2d 849, certiorari denied 59 S.Ct. 93, 305 U.S. 628, 83 L.Ed. 403.

9. —Child's majority or emancipation, support of children

Eighteen year old student whose grades were withheld due to his father's failure to pay student fees was real party in interest to writ of mandamus seeking to compel school to release his grades and give him credits for classes taken; fact that student had reached age of 18 was not dispositive as he was still attending high school full time and his father still possessed duty to support him. State ex rel. Massie v. Gahanna-Jefferson Pub. Schools Bd. of Edn. (Ohio 1996) 76 Ohio St.3d 584, 669 N.E.2d 839.

The statutory change in the age of majority has no application to pre-1974 support decrees incorporating parental separation agreements. Rosenfeld v. Rosenfeld (Ohio 1976) 47 Ohio St.2d 12, 351 N.E.2d 181, 1 O.O.3d 8.

The statutory change in the age of majority has no application to pre-1974 support decrees. Nokes v. Nokes (Ohio 1976) 47 Ohio St.2d 1, 351 N.E.2d 174, 1 O.O.3d 1.

The legal obligation of the parent to support his children extends to, but not beyond, each child's majority. Thiessen v. Moore (Ohio 1922) 105 Ohio St. 401, 137 N.E. 906, 1 Ohio Law Abs. 245, 20 Ohio Law Rep. 166, 20 Ohio Law Rep. 176.

Parents' common-law duty to support their child continued after child's majority, where child had been blind and mentally impaired, and therefore fully disabled, continuously since birth. Abbas v. Abbas (Ohio App. 7 Dist. 1998) 128 Ohio App.3d 513, 715 N.E.2d 613.

Child support order issued in conjunction with decree of dissolution continued until child reached 18 years of age and ceased to attend a recognized and accredited high school, regardless of whether parties' separation agreement and dissolution decree indicated that support was to terminate when child reached age of majority. Smith v. Smith (Ohio App. 12 Dist. 1997) 119 Ohio App.3d 15, 694 N.E.2d 476.

Emancipation discharges parent from obligation to support minor child, but only so long as minor child is competent to support himself or herself. Swanson v. Swanson (Greene 1996) 109 Ohio App.3d 231, 671 N.E.2d 1333.

Father's obligation to pay child support, under dissolution decree, continued until daughter completed her high school education, even though she already had attained age of majority. Swanson v. Swanson (Greene 1996) 109 Ohio App.3d 231, 671 N.E.2d 1333.

Statute providing for postmajority enforcement of child support orders did not operate retroactively as to father, where, when dissolution decree was entered, statute governing duty to support children required parents to continue paying child support for children attending high school. Swanson v. Swanson (Greene 1996) 109 Ohio App.3d 231, 671 N.E.2d 1333.

Duty to pay court-ordered child support is mandated beyond the age of majority under specified circumstances, and child support enforcement agency has right to see that such duty is appropriately enforced. Mazzuckelli v. Mazzuckelli (Hamilton 1995) 106 Ohio App.3d 554, 666 N.E.2d 620.

Application of amended statute establishing parental duty to support child beyond age of majority so long as child attends accredited high school to case in which support obligation arose some 13 years before statute was amended did not constitute inappropriate retrospective application of statute; when trial court was asked to extend obligation from child's 18th birthday until child graduated from high school, that obligation had yet to be fully carried out under existing law and its dimensions had yet to be fully determined, and, at time of requested extension, trial court had yet to relinquish its statutory continuing jurisdiction to modify child support provisions. Mazzuckelli v. Mazzuckelli (Hamilton 1995) 106 Ohio App.3d 554, 666 N.E.2d 620.

Court is generally without jurisdiction to order a parent to support a child once that child reaches age of majority. Troha v. Troha (Greene 1995) 105 Ohio App.3d 327, 663 N.E.2d 1319.

Parents generally have no duty under Ohio law to provide support, including payment for college expenses, to emancipated children. Troha v. Troha (Greene 1995) 105 Ohio App.3d 327, 663 N.E.2d 1319.

Provision of agreement between former husband and wife which modified provisions of dissolution agreement regarding child support and provided that each would provide for one half of cost of posthigh school education of child at college, graduate, technical, or vocational school, or any institution of higher learning was not vague or ambiguous and was enforceable, even though provision did not specify duration or amount of each party's obligation or location of school. In re Dunn (Clinton 1995) 101 Ohio App.3d 1, 654 N.E.2d 1303.

Referee's failure to find causal connection between child's inability to support himself and child's physical or mental disabilities precluded trial court from determining that parent's support duty continued beyond age of majority. Ulery v. Ulery (Summit 1993) 86 Ohio App.3d 290, 620 N.E.2d 933.

To support finding that parent's duty to support minor children continues beyond age of majority because children are unable to support themselves because of mental or physical disability, trial court must find that child is unable to support himself or herself and that the inability to be self-sufficient results from mental or physical disability. Ulery v. Ulery (Summit 1993) 86 Ohio App.3d 290, 620 N.E.2d 933.

In absence of statutory provision to the contrary, duty of parent to support child ends when child reaches the age of majority. In re Hinko (Cuyahoga 1992) 84 Ohio App.3d 89, 616 N.E.2d 515.

Parents are obligated to support a minor child until the child reaches the age of majority and is legally emancipated, and where a trial court directs that a father pay child support for his minor daughter until she turns eighteen even though a separation agreement provision requires support until she becomes emancipated or graduates from high school, whichever comes first, and the daughter graduates one month before her eighteenth birthday, the trial court's order does not modify the child support absent a showing of a change of circumstances but rather interprets the separation agreement language to mean that "or graduates from high school" has the same definition as "age of majority," which requires support until the minor child's eighteenth birthday. Dudziak v. Dudziak (Cuyahoga 1992) 81 Ohio App.3d 361, 611 N.E.2d 337.

A trial court may not use its contempt powers to seek to enforce a prior child support order by ordering monthly installments to retire arrearages after the children have become emancipated. Crigger v. Crigger (Franklin 1991) 71 Ohio App.3d 410, 594 N.E.2d 67.

A credit against the amount of a prior child support arrearage will not be granted where upon the emancipation of the child in the custody of the arrearage obligee the arrearage obligor does not petition the court to reinstate support obligations due from the arrearage obligee for the support of an unemancipated child in the custody of the support obligor but suspended during the minority of the children because of the near equality of the parties' incomes. Wilmer v. Wilmer (Montgomery 1990) 66 Ohio App.3d 713, 586 N.E.2d 153.

A divorced father's support obligations self-terminate when his child turns eighteen, even though the child has not yet graduated from high school, where the divorce decree incorporating the parties' separation agreement provides for support to continue during the child's minority and no lawful motion to continue support until graduation from high school has been made; therefore, a trial court properly denies the father's motion to terminate his child support obligations, since such motion in reality constitutes a request for an advisory opinion. Behrisch v. Behrisch (Summit 1989) 62 Ohio App.3d 164, 574 N.E.2d 1152.

No cause of action exists for the parents of an emancipated child for the recovery of medical expenses incurred in the care of the emancipated child from an alleged tortfeasor. Kotlar v. House (Portage 1989) 57 Ohio App.3d 26, 566 N.E.2d 701.

Where a divorce decree incorporating a separation agreement is rendered, obligating an obligor to support a child until his age of emancipation, the age of emancipation in effect when the decree is rendered controls. Bauer v. Bauer (Franklin 1989) 57 Ohio App.3d 24, 566 N.E.2d 185.

A parent owes no duty of support to an emancipated epileptic child who is capable of being self-supporting. Cooksey v. Cooksey (Erie 1988) 55 Ohio App.3d 135, 562 N.E.2d 934.

After a man is adjudged a putative father and ordered to pay support until the child is eighteen, pursuant to former RC 3111.17, if the man acknowledges paternity under RC 2105.18, he assumes the obligation imposed by RC 3103.03 to support the child throughout its minority, as minority is defined by RC 3109.01, subject to subsequent amendments to RC 3109.01 and 3103.03. Zweifel v. Price (Franklin 1985) 24 Ohio App.3d 101, 493 N.E.2d 300, 24 O.B.R. 171.

An order in a divorce action that a father pay a child's room, board, and college tuition beyond the child's eighteenth birthday is reversible error. Verplatse v. Verplatse (Hancock 1984) 17 Ohio App.3d 99, 477 N.E.2d 648, 17 O.B.R. 161.

A court in Ohio has no authority to compel a divorced husband to continue paying support for his disabled child who has reached the age of majority. Maphet v. Heiselman (Clermont 1984) 13 Ohio App.3d 278, 469 N.E.2d 92, 13 O.B.R. 343.

Where, as part of a valid agreement, a husband agrees to provide college education for his children and further agrees to keep in effect insurance policies on his life in which such children are beneficiaries, and where such agreement is incorporated in a decree divorcing the husband from his wife, such decree becomes binding upon the husband even though the performance required by the decree may extend beyond the minority of the children. Grant v. Grant (Erie 1977) 60 Ohio App.2d 277, 396 N.E.2d 1037, 14 O.O.3d 249.

RC 3105.10 clothes courts with jurisdiction to incorporate into a court order an agreement to support a child of the parties beyond the age of that child's majority, and such an order may be enforced by contempt proceedings. Bugay v. Bugay (Summit 1977) 53 Ohio App.2d 285, 373 N.E.2d 1263, 7 O.O.3d 336.

Emancipation of child competent to support itself discharges a parent from the obligation for its support. Hoffmann v. Hoffmann (Hamilton 1972) 32 Ohio App.2d 186, 289 N.E.2d 397, 61 O.O.2d 205.

A father's duty to furnish support to a minor child does not cease upon the child's arrival at the age of eighteen. Slawski v. Slawski (Lucas 1934) 49 Ohio App. 100, 195 N.E. 258, 18 Ohio Law Abs. 515, 1 O.O. 201.

Father's duty to support minor child does not stop when child has reached eighteen years. Mieszkalski v. Mieszkalski (Lucas 1932) 44 Ohio App. 152, 184 N.E. 709, 13 Ohio Law Abs. 429, 37 Ohio Law Rep. 435.

A high school student who learns he is not eligible for graduation and (1) has already attained the age of majority, (2) has no intentions of returning to high school after summer recess, and (3) begins working full-time is no longer continuously attending high school and is an emancipated child for whom a parent owes no duty to pay support pursuant to a child support order. Hiltbrand v Hiltbrand, No. 1999AP0115, 1999 WL 547962 (5th Dist Ct App, Tuscarawas, 7-2-99).

Under the Uniform Interstate Family Support Act (UIFSA) an Ohio court is without authority to modify a parent's child support obligation under a New York decree to cease that obligation when the parties' children reach eighteen by applying Ohio law. Vancott-Young v Cummings, No. CA98-09-122, 1999 WL 326149 (12th Dist Ct App, Warren, 5-24-99).

A court errs in overruling a father's motion for return of overpayment of child support where the magistrate uses an incorrect termination date for the support obligation as the twenty-first birthday of the youngest child when the order should have terminated when each child reached age eighteen. Cox v Cox, No. C-970772, 1998 WL 833593 (1st Dist Ct App, Hamilton, 12-4-98).

A child who temporarily leaves the home of a parent will not be considered emancipated for child support purposes if the child remains dependant on a parent for care and attends high school on a full-time basis. Siefker v Siefker, No. 12-97-09, 1997 WL 658995 (3d Dist Ct App, Putnam, 10-23-97).

In order to present a cognizable claim for past child support the appropriate action to establish that claim must have been commenced during the child's minority when the legal duty to support exists. Snider v Lillie, No. C-961014, 1997 WL 663521 (1st Dist Ct App, Hamilton, 10-17-97).

A child support obligation is in effect as long as a child who is eighteen is attending high-school and completes his graduation requirements six weeks after full-time high-school has let out for the summer. O'Brien v O'Brien, No. CA96-11-101, 1997 WL 208133 (12th Dist Ct App, Clermont, 4-28-97).

Even though provisions of the parties' separation agreement incorporated into a divorce decree limit the duration of a noncustodial parent's obligation to pay child support "until the child dies, marries, is emancipated, or reaches the age of majority, whichever occurs first," the noncustodial parent has a statutory obligation to provide support for the child beyond her eighteenth birthday so long as the child continuously attends on a full-time basis any recognized and accredited high school. Farra v Farra, No. 15890, 1996 WL 596536 (2d Dist Ct App, Montgomery, 10-18-96).

Emancipation of a minor discharges a father from his duty of child support; a child is emancipated where she (1) enters an agreement to lease real estate, (2) has utility services for the real estate listed in her name, (3) establishes a checking account in her name from which she pays her rent and utility bills, (4) negotiates with her mother and agrees to complete her high school education, (5) has employment outside the home, and (6) manages money given her by her fiance whom she plans to marry in the near future. Ball v Ball, No. 95-CA-15, 1996 WL 46483 (4th Dist Ct App, Washington, 1-26-96).

Tuition includes only the primary cost of attending college and does not include room, board, and books less any financial aid or scholarships received by the student, in a child support dispute where the parties have a California dissolution judgment and an Ohio court accepts jurisdiction and extends full faith and credit to the California judgment. Weber v Weber, No. 16278, 1994 WL 11039 (9th Dist Ct App, Summit, 1-5-94).

A child who has reached age eighteen but still attends high school fulltime has standing to file a petition on his own behalf to enforce his right to continuing support. Bantz v Bantz, No. 92-CA-0073 (2d Dist Ct App, Greene, 2-10-93).

The parents of an adjudicated delinquent may be ordered to continue to support their child in custodial care until he attains the age of twenty-one. In re Hinko, No. 61394 (8th Dist Ct App, Cuyahoga, 11-19-92).

In accordance with public policy and the statutory grant of broad equitable powers, a domestic relations court may order a noncustodial parent to continue child support payments and medical insurance coverage for a child who has reached majority, where the child is severely handicapped and has been under the jurisdiction of the domestic relations division since the age of six or seven. Mullanney v Mullanney, No. C-820944 (1st Dist Ct App, Hamilton, 1-4-84).

Although RC 3103.03 states that parents have an obligation to support their children until they have completed their high school education, where a support order unambiguously states the father must support each minor child until each child reaches eighteen years of age or is emancipated, the father may discontinue support payments for his son only after the latter turns eighteen years of age, even if the son has not yet finished high school. Morawetz v Morawetz, No. 41857 (8th Dist Ct App, Cuyahoga, 12-20-80).

Where the language of a court order in a divorce action fixes support "until majority," after January 1, 1974, such support order, no matter when made, will terminate as to any child who has attained age eighteen; where the court order fixes support until age twenty-one, such order will be ineffective after January 1, 1974, as to any child who has reached eighteen; where a property settlement agreement provides for payment until majority, a motion to terminate support as to an eighteen-year-old should be sustained after January 1, 1974; where a property settlement agreement provides for payment until age twenty-one, the court may continue to enforce such order. Istnick v. Istnick (Ohio Com.Pl. 1973) 37 Ohio Misc. 91, 307 N.E.2d 922, 66 O.O.2d 244.

Father's duty to support his minor child does not stop when such child has arrived at the age of eighteen years and majority is twenty-one. Rutter v. Rutter (Ohio Com.Pl. 1970) 24 Ohio Misc. 7, 261 N.E.2d 202, 53 O.O.2d 32.

A student who has reached the age of eighteen is entitled to attend school free in the district of his parents' or guardian's actual residence, or, if he works to support himself by his own labor, in the district in which he is employed. OAG 74-076.

Whether or not the parent's duty to support his minor child terminates upon the child's coming of age, where the child is unmarried and living in his father's home and is unable, by reason of physical or mental infirmity, to provide for himself has never been passed on by the courts of this state; although both reason and the weight of authority supports the view that, under such circumstances, the parental rights and duties remain practically unchanged. 1928 OAG p 2282.

10. —Visitation rights, support of children

Where father and his children have been deprived of their rights of visitation with each other by mother's removal of children from this state without father's consent, trial court may condition father's duty to support children upon mother's compliance with reasonable visitation privileges, unless mother is unable fully to support the children. Porter v. Porter (Ohio 1971) 25 Ohio St.2d 123, 267 N.E.2d 299, 54 O.O.2d 260.

The authority vested in a court by RC 3109.05, in extreme circumstances, includes the authority to give relief through a just modification of an order of support, to a parent continuously or repeatedly prevented from exercising a right to visit a child by the child's refusal to visit with him, but such jurisdiction should not be exercised until the court first considers whether to make the child a party pursuant to Civ R 75(B)(2). Foster v. Foster (Franklin 1974) 40 Ohio App.2d 257, 319 N.E.2d 395, 69 O.O.2d 250.

RC 3109.05 does not permit an automatic termination of support if visitation privileges are denied without cause, but requires a determination based upon evidence as to what, if any, modification of support is just, which necessarily includes an evaluation of the needs of a child for support against the right of a parent to visit with such child and a balancing of the equities involved. Foster v. Foster (Franklin 1974) 40 Ohio App.2d 257, 319 N.E.2d 395, 69 O.O.2d 250.

The juvenile court has jurisdiction to require the father of a child whose custody had been given to the mother in a divorce decree to support said child after he has reached his eighteenth birthday, but before he attains the age of twenty-one years, where such continued support beyond the age of eighteen is intended for the purpose of a college education for said child. Calogeras v. Calogeras (Ohio Juv. 1959) 163 N.E.2d 713, 82 Ohio Law Abs. 438, 10 O.O.2d 441.

11. Support of wife by third person ("necessaries")

Legal services rendered to a wife, even in a matter adverse to her husband's interests, may represent "necessaries for her support" within the meaning of RC 3103.03. Wolf v. Friedman (Ohio 1969) 20 Ohio St.2d 49, 253 N.E.2d 761, 49 O.O.2d 306.

Where a petition filed by an attorney alleges (1) that the attorney was employed by defendant's wife to and did render legal services for her in (a) the defense of a criminal charge instituted against her upon the affidavit of the defendant, (b) her complaint that the defendant was performing illegal acts upon her body and that she required protection against his wrongful conduct, (c) her complaint that the defendant refused to support her adequately unless she would return to his home and again submit to illegal acts upon her body, and (d) the opposing of an affidavit executed by the defendant alleging that she was insane; (2) that those services had a reasonable value of a certain amount; and (3) that those services were necessary for her protection and were required for the protection of her rights, and where that petition does not contain any allegations from which it might be inferred that a divorce or alimony action involving the defendant or his wife was then or had been pending, such petition states a cause of action. Wolf v. Friedman (Ohio 1969) 20 Ohio St.2d 49, 253 N.E.2d 761, 49 O.O.2d 306.

A wife is not required to file a divorce or alimony action against her husband in order to compel him to provide her with those legal services that he is obligated to supply under his statutory duty to provide her with "necessaries for her support." Wolf v. Friedman (Ohio 1969) 20 Ohio St.2d 49, 253 N.E.2d 761, 49 O.O.2d 306.

A trial court has authority, after the entry of a divorce decree, to enter an order requiring the divorced husband to pay reasonable expense money to his former wife to enable her to pay attorney fees incurred in post-decree proceedings relative to the support of the minor children of the marriage. Such services are "necessaries." Blum v. Blum (Ohio 1967) 9 Ohio St.2d 92, 223 N.E.2d 819, 38 O.O.2d 224.

A husband is not unconditionally liable for necessaries furnished his wife. To render a husband liable for necessaries furnished his wife, they must have been furnished on his credit. Tille v. Finley (Ohio 1933) 126 Ohio St. 578, 186 N.E. 448, 38 Ohio Law Rep. 479.

There is no statutory requirement that father repay to county department of human services caretaker's support paid to the mother of his child pursuant to Aid to Families with Dependent Children (AFDC), where he has never been married to the mother. Gilpen v. Justice (Fayette 1993) 85 Ohio App.3d 86, 619 N.E.2d 94, motion overruled 67 Ohio St.3d 1410, 615 N.E.2d 1044.

Spouse of indigent patient was jointly and severally liable for debt where hospital was creditor of patient by operation of implied contract; financial resources of both spouses should be available to pay creditor who provides necessary goods and services to either spouse. Cuyahoga Cty. Hospitals v. Price (Cuyahoga 1989) 64 Ohio App.3d 410, 581 N.E.2d 1125.

In a reimbursement suit brought by a county department of human services against a father, a trial court's judgment as to the father's liability for AFDC payments and AFDC-related medicaid arrearages is vacated where it is based on a referee's report but the referee fails to make a specific finding as to the AFDC-related medicaid arrearages and improperly applies the general statute of RC 3103.03 where the specific statute of RC 5107.04(C) applies to the matter. State, ex rel. Morgan Cty. Dept. of Human Services v. Roddy (Morgan 1991) 63 Ohio App.3d 575, 579 N.E.2d 538.

A father's financial responsibility to provide "necessaries" to his family pursuant to RC 3103.03 includes a reasonable allowance for expense money to employ the services of an attorney to prosecute or defend an action in a court concerning the enforcement of a legal duty and obligation of such divorced father to support his minor children; the same rationale for awarding attorney fees for trial proceedings is equally applicable to an award of attorney fees and expenses for appellate proceedings. Evans v. Brown (Franklin 1986) 34 Ohio App.3d 56, 516 N.E.2d 1289, 31 O.B.R. 607.

In an action by third party to recover from husband for necessaries furnished his wife, the questions of whether the husband neglected to make adequate provision for his wife and whether the plaintiff supplied necessaries for her support in good faith are ordinarily for the jury, but where the evidence discloses that the basis of the claim was transportation of the wife upon pleasure trips and that means of transportation were made available by the husband, the court should determine, as a matter of law, that such services were not necessaries. Smith v. Sutter (Huron 1951) 90 Ohio App. 320, 106 N.E.2d 658, 47 O.O. 427.

As regards right of wife to recover for medical services against one causing injuries, husband is bound to pay for medical services rendered to wife as necessities, he not being excused from liability thereof because of this section et seq., establishing husband as the head of the family, permitting spouses to contract with each other, and providing that parties cannot alter legal relations. (Annotation from former RC 3103.02.) Cleveland Ry. Co. v. Kuncic (Cuyahoga 1927) 26 Ohio App. 275, 159 N.E. 96, 5 Ohio Law Abs. 580.

A husband is not liable for necessaries furnished his wife if the merchant furnishing them charged them to the wife and was unaware that she had a husband. Attorneys' Service Co. v. Monk (Ohio App. 4 Dist. 1925) 19 Ohio App. 16.

In an action to recover for medical services furnished by plaintiff to defendant's wife, who at the time such services were rendered was living separate from her husband, the burden is upon the plaintiff to prove that the defendant failed to provide for his wife's support but also that the wife was justified in abandoning defendant because of his misconduct. Morse v. Lewis (Ohio App. 9 Dist. 1921) 15 Ohio App. 108.

A husband is not liable to his wife's father for her support where she abandoned the home provided by her husband because of the presence in it of the husband's aunt and sister, who it was agreed between husband and wife before marriage should be a part of the home. Hardy v. Smith (Ohio App. 8 Dist. 1920) 13 Ohio App. 399, 31 Ohio C.A. 558.

Although RC 3103.03 improperly discriminates against males and must, to save its constitutionality, be applied in a gender-neutral manner, neither husband nor wife is unconditionally liable for necessaries furnished to his or her spouse; thus, where medical services rendered to a defendant's husband are not furnished in reliance on the defendant's credit, the defendant is not liable for payment of the debt. St. Elizabeth Medical Center v Kirkland, No. 11257 (2d Dist Ct App, Montgomery, 10-6-89), reversed by 49 OS(3d) 17, 550 NE(2d) 159 (1990).

A husband is not liable for medical services rendered to his wife where there is no proof that (1) the services were necessary, (2) the services were furnished to the wife upon the husband's credit, (3) there is an express or implied contract between the husband and the physician, or (4) the wife acted as the agent of the husband. Vaneck v Carpenter, No. L-85-347 (6th Dist Ct App, Lucas, 4-25-86).

Where a wife has abandoned her husband, a plaintiff seeking to recover for necessaries furnished her must prove that the abandonment was justified, but where the husband has abandoned his wife, the burden is upon him to justify such abandonment. Creamer v. Payer (Cuyahoga 1952) 113 N.E.2d 883, 65 Ohio Law Abs. 119.

In an action for the furnishing of necessaries to defendant's wife, the defense of the wife's aggression against the sanctity of the marital relationship is an affirmative defense which the defendant must sustain by the preponderance of the evidence. Creamer v. Payer (Cuyahoga 1952) 113 N.E.2d 883, 65 Ohio Law Abs. 119.

A husband's liability to support his wife and minor children and his liability for necessaries furnished his wife is not affected by the fact that he may be insane, and wife is entitled to claim such support out of such insane husband's estate for the period from his commitment in state hospital to his discharge even though she was not appointed guardian of husband's estate for some time after his commitment. Martin v. Martin (Cuyahoga 1949) 88 N.E.2d 59, 55 Ohio Law Abs. 31.

The defendant was liable for necessaries for his wife. The services rendered by a physician were necessary. The calling of a consultant in the interest of a patient is within the implied power of a physician. Downing v. Goldberg (Ohio Com.Pl. 1932) 29 Ohio N.P.N.S. 162.

A rug purchased for $120 to replace one that had been in use eleven years and was rather badly worn and faded, for a home valued at $8,500 in which the husband was earning from $70 to $80 a week, held to have been a necessary which the wife could purchase as agent for the husband. P. H. Harman Co. v. Thornton (Ohio Mun. 1931) 28 Ohio N.P.N.S. 586.

12. Cohabiting couples

Woman who cohabited with man could not recover contributions to that relationship under constructive trust theory. Tarry v. Stewart (Lorain 1994) 98 Ohio App.3d 533, 649 N.E.2d 1, appeal not allowed 71 Ohio St.3d 1502, 646 N.E.2d 1126.

3103.031 Parental duty of support

A biological parent of a child, a man determined to be the natural father of a child under sections 3111.01 to 3111.19 or 3111.20 to 3111.29 of the Revised Code, a parent who adopts a minor child pursuant to Chapter 3107. of the Revised Code, or a parent whose signed acknowledgment of paternity has become final pursuant to section 2151.232, 3111.211, or 5101.314 of the Revised Code assumes the parental duty of support for that child. Notwithstanding section 3109.01 of the Revised Code, the parental duty of support to the child shall continue beyond the age of majority as long as the child continuously attends on a full-time basis any recognized and accredited high school or a court-issued child support order provides that the duty of support continues beyond the age of majority. Except in cases in which a child support order requires the duty of support to continue for any period after the child reaches age nineteen, the order shall not remain in effect after the child reaches age nineteen. That duty of support shall continue during seasonal vacation periods.

(1997 H 352, eff. 1-1-98; 1992 S 10, eff. 7-15-92)

Uncodified Law

1992 S 10, § 5, eff. 7-15-92, reads, in part: Section 3103.031 of the Revised Code, as enacted by this act, shall apply only to a father who signs a child's birth certificate on or after the effective date of this act.

Historical and Statutory Notes

Amendment Note: 1997 H 352 rewrote this section, which prior thereto read:

"A biological parent of a child, a man determined to be the natural father of a child under sections 3111.01 to 3111.19 or 3111.20 to 3111.29 of the Revised Code, a parent who adopts a minor child pursuant to Chapter 3107. of the Revised Code, a parent who acknowledges parentage on the child's birth certificate as provided in section 3705.09 of the Revised Code, or a parent whose signed acknowledgment of paternity is entered upon the probate court's journal under section 2105.18 of the Revised Code assumes the parental duty of support for that child. Notwithstanding section 3109.01 of the Revised Code, the parental duty of support to the child shall continue beyond the age of majority as long as the child continuously attends on a full-time basis any recognized and accredited high school. That duty of support shall continue during seasonal vacation periods."

Library References

Adoption ⚷20.
Children Out-Of-Wedlock ⚷21, 67.
Parent and Child ⚷3.1(12).
WESTLAW Topic Nos. 17, 76H, 285.
C.J.S. Adoption of Persons §§ 134 to 139.
C.J.S. Children Out-of-Wedlock §§ 40 to 43, 122 to 126.
C.J.S. Parent and Child §§ 14, 70, 71.

Carlin, Baldwin's Ohio Practice, *Merrick-Rippner Probate Law* § 19.2, 19.4, 98.31, 108.3, 108.20, 108.33, 108.34 (1997)
Sowald & Morganstern, Baldwin's Ohio Practice, *Domestic Relations Law* § 3.26, 3.35, 3.46, 3.55, 4.6, 4.26, 19.1, 19.2, 19.20, 22.19 (1997)

Law Review and Journal Commentaries

Judge's Column, Hon. Francine M. Bruening. (Ed. note: Judge Bruening discusses the pending Ohio Parenting Act.) 20 Lake Legal Views 1 (June 1997).

Notes of Decisions and Opinions

Constitutional issues 1
Father's duty 2

1. Constitutional issues

A father is not relieved of the financial obligation to his child because he does not want him and the father's equal protection challenge fails where he argues, "If it is the woman's constitutional right to have an abortion or give the baby up for adoption, then it should be the constitutional right of the man to have the same decision making powers ... that a man who does not want to be engaged in the parenting role should not be penalized financially because the mother chooses to have and to keep the baby;" relevant consent provisions of the adoption statutes do not treat the mother and father differently, and the spouse or nonmarital partner of a pregnant woman cannot forbid her to terminate her pregnancy since the state cannot delegate to a spouse or nonmarital partner a veto power which the state itself is prohibited from exercising. Bryant v Hacker, No. C-950758, 1996 WL 733143 (1st Dist Ct App, Hamilton, 12-24-96).

2. Father's duty

Father's argument that he did not want child and would have elected either abortion or adoption did not release him from his obligation to pay child support. Bryant v. Hacker (Ohio App. 1 Dist. 1996) 116 Ohio App.3d 860, 689 N.E.2d 609.

3103.04 Interest in the property of the other

Neither husband nor wife has any interest in the property of the other, except as mentioned in section 3103.03 of the Revised Code, the right to dower, and the right to remain in the mansion house after the death of either. Neither can be excluded from the other's dwelling, except upon a decree or order of injunction made by a court of competent jurisdiction.

(1953 H 1, eff. 10-1-53; GC 8002-4; Source—GC 7998)

Historical and Statutory Notes

Pre-1953 H 1 Amendments: 124 v S 65

Cross References

Assignment for benefit of creditors by husband not to include property of wife, 1313.17
Dispositional hearing, restraining orders, Juv R 34
Divorce, annulment, and legal separation actions, restraining orders, Civ R 75
Divorce, annulment, dissolution of marriage, enforcement of separation agreement, effect on dower, 3105.10, 3105.65
Estate in dower, Ch 2103
Husband and wife must join in chattel mortgage on household property, 1319.06
Injunctions, restraining orders, Civ R 65
Mansion house, rights of surviving spouse, 2106.15
One spouse contracting for improvement to other's land deemed other's agent, when, 1311.10
Real property, dower, Ch 5305
Validity of instruments, release of dower, 5301.071

Library References

Husband and Wife ⚷6(1), 8.
WESTLAW Topic No. 205.
C.J.S. Husband and Wife §§ 10 to 12.

Am Jur 2d: 41, Husband and Wife § 29 et seq.
Pension or retirement benefits as subject to award or division by court in settlement of property rights between spouses. 94 ALR3d 176
Property rights arising from relationship of couple cohabiting without marriage. 3 ALR4th 13
Estate created by deed to persons described as husband and wife but not legally married. 9 ALR4th 1189

Hausser, Ohio Real Estate Law and Practice (2d Ed.), Text 31.10(A)
Sowald & Morganstern, Baldwin's Ohio Practice, *Domestic Relations Law* § 4.1, 4.5, 4.11, 11.14, 25.59 (1997)

Law Review and Journal Commentaries

Bankruptcy Reform Act of 1994—What the Bankruptcy Code Giveth, Domestic Relations Courts (and Congress) Taketh Away, C.R. "Chip" Bowles. 8 Domestic Rel J Ohio 17 (March/April 1996).

Professional Degrees and Spousal Rights, Charles F. Crutchfield. 88 Case & Com 14 (November/December 1983).

Who Needs the Uniform Marital Property Act?, Patrick N. Parkinson. 55 U Cin L Rev 677 (1987).

Notes of Decisions and Opinions

---

1. Trusts

The reservation of income during the life of the settlor coupled with an absolute power to revoke the trust in whole or in part, as well as the right to modify the terms of the settlement and to control investments, bars the wife, upon the settlor's death, from a claimed right to a distributive share of the property in the trust upon her election to take under the statutes of descent and distribution. Smyth v. Cleveland Trust Co. (Ohio 1961) 172 Ohio St. 489, 179 N.E.2d 60, 18 O.O.2d 42.

The reservation of the income during the life of the settlor plus the reservation of the right to amend or revoke causes the settlor not to part with dominion or control over the trust property and this failure to part with dominion and control permits the wife to assert her right under the statutes of descent and distribution to a distributive share of the trust res. Smyth v. Cleveland Trust Co. (Ohio Com.Pl. 1959) 163 N.E.2d 702, 81 Ohio Law Abs. 581, 10 O.O.2d 448, affirmed in part, reversed in part 172 Ohio St. 489, 179 N.E.2d 60, 18 O.O.2d 42.

A trust agreement between a married woman and her father by which she transfers stock in certain corporations to her father may not be set aside by her husband as a fraud on his marital rights. Lamkin v. Robinson (Ohio App. 1922) 35 Ohio C.D. 767, 16 Ohio App. 440, 32 Ohio C.A. 401.

A husband acquires by marriage no interest in the separate personal property of his wife, and if by written instrument she provides that income from stocks acquired by her father but standing in her name shall go to him for life and full ownership pass to him in case of her prior death without issue which subsequently occurred, her husband, who added nothing to the property either by way of investment or management is without ground for complaint of invasion of his marital rights, and as between the husband and the father equity is with the latter. Robinson v. Lamkin (Ohio Super. 1920) 23 Ohio N.P.N.S. 425, affirmed 35 Ohio C.D. 767, 16 Ohio App. 440, 32 Ohio C.A. 401.

2. Rights remaining

Under this section, neither spouse has any interest in property of the other, except present right of support provided for in the preceding section and rights given by statute to a surviving spouse in property of the deceased spouse. Mark v. Mark (Ohio 1945) 145 Ohio St. 301, 61 N.E.2d 595, 30 O.O. 534.

3. Separate property

Marriage does not grant a wife an interest in her husband's real or personal property, except as statutorily granted for support and dower. State v. Garber (Ohio App. 9 Dist. 1998) 125 Ohio App.3d 615, 709 N.E.2d 218.

Ownership of property by one spouse is as distinct from ownership by the other as if the spouses were strangers. State v. Garber (Ohio App. 9 Dist. 1998) 125 Ohio App.3d 615, 709 N.E.2d 218.

As RC 3103.04 prohibits a spouse from gaining an interest in the property of the other spouse by way of the marriage, an insured under a motor vehicle insurance policy is not the "owner" of a vehicle brought into the marriage by his spouse; thus, coverage under the policy is precluded. Hornacek v. Travelers Ins. Co. (Summit 1991) 72 Ohio App.3d 31, 593 N.E.2d 424.

Where stock purchased with nonmarital funds appreciates in value without the efforts of the other spouse and where neither marital funds nor labor was expended to increase the value, the appreciation in the value of such stock is nonmarital property. Walkup v. Walkup (Brown 1986) 31 Ohio App.3d 248, 511 N.E.2d 119, 31 O.B.R. 532.

When a joint and survivorship account is terminated by the mental incompetency of a codepositor, each codepositor, including the incompetent, is entitled to the portion of the funds representing his contribution thereto, and a depositor who has knowledge of a codepositor's mental incompetency prior to such adjudication has no right as against such codepositor to withdraw for his own use more than the portion attributable to his own contribution. In re Webb's Estate (Cuyahoga 1969) 18 Ohio App.2d 287, 249 N.E.2d 83, 47 O.O.2d 452.

Where a codepositor in a joint account has a vested right of survivorship, but does not have true ownership in the account during the lifetime of the other codepositor, his conversion of the funds into an account solely in his own name during the other codepositor's lifetime destroys his right of survivorship and makes him liable to the true owner for the amount converted. In re Webb's Estate (Cuyahoga 1969) 18 Ohio App.2d 287, 249 N.E.2d 83, 47 O.O.2d 452.

Where a father agreed with his children that upon his death or permanent retirement from the family corporation his stock should pass to his two sons, who should thereupon pay half the value thereof to his two daughters, and such retirement and transfer did occur prior to his death, the transfer cannot be attacked as fraudulent by his second wife after his death. MacLean v. J. S. MacLean Co. (Ohio Prob. 1955) 123 N.E.2d 761, 70 Ohio Law Abs. 102, 57 O.O. 454, appeal dismissed 133 N.E.2d 198, 71 Ohio Law Abs. 589, 71 Ohio Law Abs. 590.

Under Ohio law, marriage alone does not confer upon spouse an interest in other spouse's separately titled property. In re Greer (Bkrtcy.N.D.Ohio 1999) 242 B.R. 389.

In allowing husbands and wives to file a single return jointly of income taxes, Congress most definitely did not intend to affect their respective rights to a joint tax refund, which are determined under state law; thus, where the refund arose primarily from withholding of tax from the husband's income in excess of liability the refund is owed by him to that extent under Ohio law, and it is not half the husband's property and half the property of the wife. In re Feitlinger (Bkrtcy.S.D.Ohio 1987) 82 B.R. 860.

A board of education member is prohibited by RC 3313.33 from having any pecuniary interest in a contract of the board of education, including where the member's spouse is a partner in a law firm that is paid to serve as counsel to the board if any of the share of earnings from the contract is used for the support of the board member or the spouse or another dependent of the board member. OAG 89-030.

4. Appreciation in value

Where significant marital funds and labor are expended to improve and maintain nonmarital property, a trial court does not abuse its discretion by apportioning the appreciated value of the property as a marital asset. Walkup v. Walkup (Brown 1986) 31 Ohio App.3d 248, 511 N.E.2d 119, 31 O.B.R. 532.

Increases in the value of nonmarital property do not constitute marital property; however, additions or improvements made by the spending of marital funds or resulting from work furnished by either or both parties during the marriage do constitute marital property; the value of such property is the ratio of the value added and the value of the property immediately before the additions or improvements were made. Palmer v. Palmer (Warren 1982) 7 Ohio App.3d 346, 455 N.E.2d 1049, 7 O.B.R. 444.

5. Contempt

The proper means to enforce a court order of the court of common pleas, division of domestic relations, to vacate the premises is by contempt proceedings in that court and not by a criminal trespass proceeding. State v. Herder (Franklin 1979) 65 Ohio App.2d 70, 415 N.E.2d 1000, 19 O.O.3d 47.

6. Criminal acts

Statute providing that "neither 'husband nor wife' can be excluded from the other's dwelling, except upon a decree or order of injunction made by a court of competent jurisdiction" was intended to address property ownership rights of married persons, which are matters of a civil nature, and was not meant to be enforced criminally and does not affect criminal liabilities. State v. O'Neal (Ohio 2000) 87 Ohio St.3d 402, 721 N.E.2d 73.

A spouse may be criminally liable for trespass and/or burglary in the dwelling of the other spouse who is exercising custody or control over that dwelling. State v. Lilly (Ohio 1999) 87 Ohio St.3d 97, 717 N.E.2d 322.

Statute addressing the privileges of a husband and wife with respect to the property of the other is civil in nature and was not meant to be enforced criminally and does not affect criminal liabilities. State v. Lilly (Ohio 1999) 87 Ohio St.3d 97, 717 N.E.2d 322.

Defendant who used tire iron to knock out windows of pickup truck that had been leased by her husband could be charged with criminal damaging, though defendant could possibly be awarded marital interest in the truck in future if parties divorced; defendant did not have property interest in truck at time of offense, and property interests in truck instead belonged to husband, as the exclusive lessee, and the leasing agency. State v. Garber (Ohio App. 9 Dist. 1998) 125 Ohio App.3d 615, 709 N.E.2d 218.

Statutory ban against exclusion of one spouse from dwelling of another spouse precluded husband's burglary conviction based on his alleged trespass in wife's residence, as, at time of alleged trespass, wife had not obtained court order restricting husband from entering her dwelling. State v. Middleton (Vinton 1993) 85 Ohio App.3d 403, 619 N.E.2d 1113.

An individual may be convicted of arson for burning the property of his spouse although the couple was living together at the time of the incident. State v. Regan (Wayne 1988) 51 Ohio App.3d 214, 555 N.E.2d 987.

In light of the clear policy expression set forth in RC 3103.04, one spouse cannot be criminally liable for trespass in the dwelling of the other, but this does not mean that a spouse may not be liable for criminal acts other than trespass in connection with the gaining of entry to his spouse's dwelling. State v. Herder (Franklin 1979) 65 Ohio App.2d 70, 415 N.E.2d 1000, 19 O.O.3d 47.

7. Exclusion from dwelling

One spouse cannot be held criminally liable for trespassing in dwelling of other spouse unless there exists court order restricting one of the spouses from entering the dwelling of the other. State v. Brooks (Montgomery 1995) 101 Ohio App.3d 260, 655 N.E.2d 418.

The phrase "court of competent jurisdiction" in RC 3103.04 refers to the courts having jurisdiction in domestic relations cases, and not to any court having authority to decide questions touching on property rights, per se. Slansky v. Slansky (Cuyahoga 1973) 33 Ohio App.2d 127, 293 N.E.2d 302, 62 O.O.2d 235.

The municipal courts have power to determine cases in forcible entry and detainer, but they are without jurisdiction to determine domestic relations cases, and may not determine that one or the other may be excluded from the marital home pursuant to RC 3103.04. Slansky v. Slansky (Cuyahoga 1973) 33 Ohio App.2d 127, 293 N.E.2d 302, 62 O.O.2d 235.

The term "dwelling" as used in RC 3103.04 refers to any place of abode that has been used as the matrimonial home, so that a three-year absence from that home by a wife in whose name title is vested does not destroy its character as her "dwelling." Slansky v. Slansky (Cuyahoga 1973) 33 Ohio App.2d 127, 293 N.E.2d 302, 62 O.O.2d 235.

The trial court is not "a court of competent jurisdiction" as defined in RC 3103.04 and is without jurisdiction to exclude a spouse from the marital residence prior to the divorce decree where possession of the marital residence from the date of the spouse's eviction to the date of the divorce decree is not addressed in the decree. Yergan v Yergan, No. 2901-M, 1999 WL 493942 (9th Dist Ct App, Medina, 7-14-99).

8. Other types of claims and actions

There is no "community property" in Ohio. State v. Garber (Ohio App. 9 Dist. 1998) 125 Ohio App.3d 615, 709 N.E.2d 218.

A husband may maintain an action against his wife based on his title in and to property which his wife withholds from him or which she has converted to her own use. Madget v. Madget (Hamilton 1949) 85 Ohio App. 18, 87 N.E.2d 918, 55 Ohio Law Abs. 450, 40 O.O. 37.

A wife cannot maintain an action against husband to recover damages for personal injury caused by his negligence. Leonardi v. Leonardi (Lake 1925) 21 Ohio App. 110, 153 N.E. 93, 4 Ohio Law Abs. 732.

Where husband and wife are living together, wife cannot maintain an action in tort against husband to recover damages for personal injuries sustained through his negligence. Finn v. Finn (Lucas 1924) 19 Ohio App. 302, 3 Ohio Law Abs. 55.

Under this section et seq., evidencing a complete emancipation of the wife in so far as separate property was concerned, except as to dower rights, the wife may bring an action in partition against the husband as to real estate owned jointly. Shively v. Shively (Montgomery 1948) 88 N.E.2d 280, 54 Ohio Law Abs. 527, rehearing denied 88 N.E.2d 615, 54 Ohio Law Abs. 527.

Where wife performs services under contract with another, but in furtherance of her husband's business, she may waive her right to compensation as separate property and allow him to receive the fruits of her labor and bring suit therefor in his own name, and this section does not forbid this. Hess v. Clutz (Ohio App. 1917) 29 Ohio C.D. 497, 8 Ohio App. 57, 28 Ohio C.A. 81.

Mother of hockey player, who supported her son's participation in ice hockey and was at the ice rink at the time of his injury, was barred under Ohio law under the doctrine of estoppel by acquiescence from disaffirming the release signed by both hockey player and his father. Mohney v. USA Hockey, Inc. (N.D.Ohio 1999) 77 F.Supp.2d 859.

Under Ohio law, neither husband nor wife has any interests in property of the other. In re Hoppes (Bkrtcy.N.D.Ohio 1996) 202 B.R. 595.

It is presumed under Ohio law that a wife's advancements to her husband that result in mutual benefit give her no claim against him, absent an express promise to pay. In re Palermini (Bkrtcy.S.D.Ohio 1990) 113 B.R. 380.

An employee on medical leave of absence who is seen doing labor for a company owned by his wife is held to be "employed" in violation of a work rule prohibiting "gainful employment" during a medical leave of absence even though he received no pay for his labor; it is held that he and his wife benefitted from his labor because that work made it unnecessary to pay another individual. In re Moore, UCBR B94-03940-0000 (3-21-95).

3103.05 Contracts

A husband or wife may enter into any engagement or transaction with the other, or with any other person, which either might if unmarried; subject, in transactions between themselves, to the general rules which control the actions of persons occupying confidential relations with each other.

(1953 H 1, eff. 10-1-53; GC 8002-5; Source—GC 7999)

Historical and Statutory Notes

Pre-1953 H 1 Amendments: 124 v S 65

Comparative Laws

Ga.—O.C.G.A. § 19-3-10.
Ill.—ILCS 750 65/6.
Iowa—I.C.A. § 597.18.
Ky.—Baldwin's KRS 404.020.
Mass.—M.G.L.A. c. 209, § 2.
Minn.—M.S.A. § 519.03.
N.C.—G.S. § 52-2.
Neb.—R.R.S.1943, § 42-202.
N.J.—N.J.S.A. 37:2-16 et seq.
N.M.—NMSA 1978, § 40-2-2.
W.Va.—Code, 48-3-8.

Cross References

Agreement made upon consideration of marriage to be in writing, 1335.05
Antenuptial or separation agreement to which decedent a party valid unless set aside; time limits, 2106.22
Assignment of personal earnings; written consent of spouse required, 1321.31
Capacity of married woman to sue and be sued, 2307.09
Fiduciary law, Ch 1339, Ch 2109
Husband and wife must join in chattel mortgage on household property, 1319.06
Judgment against married woman, 2323.09
Liens, work authorized by owner's spouse, 1311.10
Person may insure life of spouse, 3911.11
Policy assigned to a married person, 3911.12
Separation agreements, 3105.63 to 3105.65
Uniform Commercial Code, Ch 1301 to Ch 1309
Wife's right to defend, 2307.10

Library References

Husband and Wife ⚷17, 36.
WESTLAW Topic No. 205.
C.J.S. Husband and Wife §§ 44 to 46, 87.

OJur 3d: 62, Investment Securities and Securities Regulation § 53
Am Jur 2d: 41, Husband and Wife § 124 et seq., 136 et seq., 255 et seq.
Effect of annulment of marriage on rights arising out of acts of or transactions between parties during marriage. 2 ALR2d 637
Recovery of damages for breach of contract to convey homestead where only one spouse signed contract. 5 ALR4th 1310
Failure to disclose extent or value of property owned as ground for avoiding premarital contract. 3 ALR5th 394

Carlin, Baldwin's Ohio Practice, *Merrick-Rippner Probate Law* § 89.18 (1997)
Hausser, Ohio Real Estate Law and Practice (2d Ed.), Text 31.10(A)

Sowald & Morganstern, Baldwin's Ohio Practice, *Domestic Relations Law* § 1.1, 1.4, 1.5, 4.2, 4.5, 4.16, 4.22, 9.1, 9.2, 9.3, 9.22, 9.39, 9.41 (1997)

Law Review and Journal Commentaries

Antenuptial Agreements—New Planning Opportunities, Leon A. Weiss. 56 Clev B J 24 (November 1984).

Bankruptcy Reform Act of 1994—What the Bankruptcy Code Giveth, Domestic Relations Courts (and Congress) Taketh Away, C.R. "Chip" Bowles. 8 Domestic Rel J Ohio 17 (March/April 1996).

Caveat: Antenuptial Agreements Cannot Affect Pension Plan Survivor Benefits, Michael D. Rose. 4 Domestic Rel J Ohio 101 (November/December 1992).

Caveat: Antenuptial Agreements Cannot Affect Pension Plan Survivor Benefits, Michael D. Rose. 2 Prob L J Ohio 121 (July/August 1992).

The Drafting and Enforcement in Ohio of Antenuptial Agreements in Anticipation of Divorce, Will Kuhlmann and Larry D. Rhodebeck. 53 Ohio St B Ass'n Rep 463 (March 24, 1980).

Notes of Decisions and Opinions

---

1. In general

The common law doctrine of the legal identity of husband and wife has been abolished in Ohio, and the wife of a member of a voluntary unincorporated association may maintain an action against the association to recover damages for a tort resulting in her injury. Damm v. Elyria Lodge No. 465, Benev. Protective Order of Elks (Ohio 1952) 158 Ohio St. 107, 107 N.E.2d 337, 48 O.O. 54.

Under GC 7999, compensation for a wife's services performed outside her husband's home, and not in the discharge of her domestic duties or in interference therewith, is recoverable in an action brought therefor in her own name for her own use. Bechtol v. Ewing (Ohio 1913) 89 Ohio St. 53, 105 N.E. 72, 11 Ohio Law Rep. 316, Am.Ann.Cas. 1915C, 1183.

A surviving spouse, whether male or female, should be required to pay for the deceased spouse's expenses for the last illness and necessities provided by third parties, even though no written contractual obligation exists. Cleveland Metropolitan General Hosp. v. Oleksik (Cuyahoga 1987) 38 Ohio App.3d 21, 525 N.E.2d 831.

Where, at the request of a husband who is separated and living at a different address from his wife pending a divorce action, a telephone company attaches an extension on such wife's private telephone line, which private telephone is in her name and paid for by her, and places such extension in the residence of the husband without the wife's knowledge, and where the facts that the parties are living apart pending a divorce and that the wife is paying her own bills are known to the telephone company, such telephone company is severally liable in an action brought by the wife against it for having rendered material aid to another person (the husband) in the commission of a tort (invasion of privacy). LeCrone v. Ohio Bell Tel. Co. (Franklin 1963) 120 Ohio App. 129, 201 N.E.2d 533, 28 O.O.2d 374.

Where a husband persuaded his wife to convey her half interest in property to him upon the belief that she was about to become involved in a law suit, promised to reconvey it and to protect her by his will, and then threatened to kill her if she did not leave the premises, and procured a divorce in which she did not enter an appearance because of threats against her life by him, a cause of action for a constructive trust is set forth. Hasselschwert v. Hasselschwert (Defiance 1951) 90 Ohio App. 331, 106 N.E.2d 786, 47 O.O. 494.

Marriage is the highest consideration for a contract known in law. Rudrick v. Thull (Richland 1931) 39 Ohio App. 69, 177 N.E. 513, 10 Ohio Law Abs. 542, 35 Ohio Law Rep. 36.

When a contract between a man and woman is ambiguous, the construction that is most favorable to the woman should be adopted. Rudrick v. Thull (Richland 1931) 39 Ohio App. 69, 177 N.E. 513, 10 Ohio Law Abs. 542, 35 Ohio Law Rep. 36.

The probate court was within its sound discretion in determining no loan contract existed where a wife-executrix wrote various checks to her husband and there was no written loan agreement, no evidence of interest payments, or a repayment schedule. In re Estate of Sheban, No. 82 CA 33 (7th Dist Ct App, Mahoning, 1-26-83).

The equitable principle requiring a husband to procure independent advice for his wife in transactions between them does not require a showing of a design founded in evil purpose on the part of the husband. In re Marriage of Kesler (Ohio Com.Pl. 1978) 59 Ohio Misc. 33, 392 N.E.2d 905, 13 O.O.3d 105.

Where wife purchases goods and has them charged to her account and delivered to herself and husband for use of family, and payments credited on account are made by wife, wife is liable under this section for payment. Christie v. Dine (Hamilton 1928) 6 Ohio Law Abs. 524.

Under statute providing that husband or wife may enter into any engagement or transaction with the other, which either might, if unmarried, one has right to maintain action at law against other on contract such as a note. In re Lange's Estate (Preble 1949) 91 N.E.2d 546, 56 Ohio Law Abs. 190.

A wife may bring an action in partition against the husband as to real estate owned jointly. Shively v. Shively (Montgomery 1948) 88 N.E.2d 280, 54 Ohio Law Abs. 527, rehearing denied 88 N.E.2d 615, 54 Ohio Law Abs. 527.

An agreement on the part of a wife to refrain from bringing an action against her husband for divorce and alimony constitutes a sufficient consideration for a conveyance of property by him to her, and such conveyance will not be set aside for want of consideration where the wife was not aware at the time the conveyance was made of any fraudulent intent on the part of the husband with respect to creditors. Whitacre v Redmond, 8 LR 165, 24 D 207 (1910).

A husband acquires by marriage no interest in the personal property of his wife, and if by instrument she provides that income from stocks, acquired by her father but standing in her name, shall go to him for life and full title pass to him in case of her prior death without issue, which later occurred, her husband, who added nothing to the property, is without ground of complaint. Robinson v. Lamkin (Ohio Super. 1920) 23 Ohio N.P.N.S. 425, affirmed 35 Ohio C.D. 767, 16 Ohio App. 440, 32 Ohio C.A. 401.

Although, RC 3103.05 has been construed to grant a husband the right to damages for the loss of his wife's services, a husband does not have an independent right of action for the loss of his wife's consortium, and therefore equal protection of the laws does not require that the wife have such an independent action. Copeland v. Smith Dairy Products Co. (N.D.Ohio 1968) 15 Ohio Misc. 43, 288 F.Supp. 904, 44 O.O.2d 242.

2. Antenuptial, postnuptial agreement

The doctrine of constructive fraud is applicable to antenuptial agreements and requires in that connection no proof of fraudulent intent; such agreements must be reviewed for fairness by virtue of the fact that the parties, being engaged to marry, stand in fiduciary relation to one another. Cohen v. Estate of Cohen (Ohio 1986) 23 Ohio St.3d 90, 491 N.E.2d 698, 23 O.B.R. 218.

In a judicial review of an antenuptial agreement, upon motion for modification, at any subsequent separation or divorce proceeding of the parties, provisions setting forth maintenance or sustenance alimony must meet the additional test of conscionability at the time of the divorce or separation. Gross v. Gross (Ohio 1984) 11 Ohio St.3d 99, 464 N.E.2d 500, 11 O.B.R. 400.

Antenuptial agreements containing provisions for disposition of property and setting forth amounts to be paid as sustenance alimony upon a subsequent divorce of the parties are not contrary to public policy; such agreements are valid and enforceable if: (1) they have been entered into freely without fraud, duress, coercion, or overreaching; (2) there was full disclosure, or full knowledge and understanding of the nature, value, and extent of the prospective spouse's property; and (3) if the terms do not promote or encourage divorce or profiteering by divorce. Gross v. Gross (Ohio 1984) 11 Ohio St.3d 99, 464 N.E.2d 500, 11 O.B.R. 400.

If otherwise found to be valid, antenuptial agreements containing provisions for disposition of property and setting forth amounts to be paid as sustenance alimony upon a subsequent divorce of the parties are not abrogated as to either party for marital misconduct after marriage, in the absence of an express provision in the agreement to the contrary. Gross v. Gross (Ohio 1984) 11 Ohio St.3d 99, 464 N.E.2d 500, 11 O.B.R. 400.

Full authority for husband and wife to enter into any agreement or transaction is conferred by this section and that right is limited only by the next section. Mendelson v. Mendelson (Ohio 1930) 123 Ohio St. 11, 173 N.E. 615, 8 Ohio Law Abs. 754, 33 Ohio Law Rep. 321.

This section, the next, and the dower statute, when construed together, do not authorize a post-nuptial contract between husband and wife, by which they release all rights, such as dower, right of distribution, etc., in the property of the other. Du Bois v. Coen (Ohio 1919) 100 Ohio St. 17, 125 N.E. 121, 17 Ohio Law Rep. 63, 17 Ohio Law Rep. 66.

Purported antenuptial agreement was testamentary and was not applicable to divorce proceeding and, thus, upon divorce, husband was not entitled to marital home under agreement; although clause of agreement stated that husband and wife waived any claims "which he or she may acquire by reason of the marriage in the other party's property or estate," clause referred only to testamentary rights and made no reference to division of assets upon divorce. Stokes v. Stokes (Cuyahoga 1994) 98 Ohio App.3d 238, 648 N.E.2d 83.

Where an antenuptial agreement addresses only the disposition of property on the death of one of the spouses, and is silent concerning disposition in the event of divorce, it is error to apply the agreement to determine issues of division of property and spousal support in a divorce proceeding. Devault v. Devault (Franklin 1992) 80 Ohio App.3d 341, 609 N.E.2d 214, motion overruled 65 Ohio St.3d 1444, 600 N.E.2d 686, motion overruled 65 Ohio St.3d 1499, 605 N.E.2d 952.

Strong public policy of encouraging arbitration, rather than resort to litigation, applies to antenuptial agreements, even if party who seeks to enforce arbitration provision commences divorce action. Kelm v. Kelm (Franklin 1992) 73 Ohio App.3d 395, 597 N.E.2d 535.

Where a prenuptial agreement contains no recital of, or an apparent provision for, consideration to support the promisor's obligation; where the absence of such consideration is expressly asserted by the promisor in his responsive pleading; and where nothing further appears to illuminate the issue, the document is properly held to be unenforceable. Conley v. Conley (Hamilton 1975) 45 Ohio App.2d 1, 340 N.E.2d 430, 74 O.O.2d 6.

The existence of a written antenuptial agreement governing property interests between a husband and wife does not preclude a subsequent oral joint venture agreement. Clark v Clark, No. C-820057 (1st Dist Ct App, Hamilton, 11-24-82).

Where a domestic relations court has determined a prenuptial agreement to be unenforceable, a bankruptcy court must abstain from hearing the debtor's complaint seeking a decision on the agreement's validity. In re Baumgartner (Bkrtcy.N.D.Ohio 1986) 57 B.R. 517.

3. Separation agreement

To avoid a contract on the basis of duress, a party must prove coercion by the other party to the contract; it is not enough to show that one assented merely because of difficult circumstances that are not the fault of the other party. Blodgett v. Blodgett (Ohio 1990) 49 Ohio St.3d 243, 551 N.E.2d 1249.

On separation, a husband and wife may enter into an agreement mutually releasing each other from claims for future care, support, and maintenance. Lowman v. Lowman (Ohio 1956) 166 Ohio St. 1, 139 N.E.2d 1, 1 O.O.2d 152.

This section and the next, when construed together, permit a husband and wife contemplating separation to enter into an engagement releasing each other's right to dower and distributive share in the other's property; and they are also authorized to contract for the future support of either of them and their children during such separation. Hoagland v. Hoagland (Ohio 1925) 113 Ohio St. 228, 148 N.E. 585, 3 Ohio Law Abs. 388, 23 Ohio Law Rep. 322.

Contract does not have to be fair or equitable to be enforceable; contracts, including property settlement agreements, can be unfair or favor one side over the other and are still binding and enforceable, so long as they are not procured by fraud, duress, overreaching or undue influence. Walther v. Walther (Hamilton 1995) 102 Ohio App.3d 378, 657 N.E.2d 332.

Elements of undue influence in connection with action to set aside separation agreement are susceptible party, another's opportunity to influence susceptible party, actual or attempted imposition of improper influence, and results showing effect of improper influence. DiPietro v. DiPietro (Franklin 1983) 10 Ohio App.3d 44, 460 N.E.2d 657, 10 O.B.R. 52.

A contract between a husband and wife which divides their property in contemplation of separation, where they agree that its provisions will be incorporated into a divorce decree if granted in the future, is unenforceable where it was a product of duress or undue influence; the husband's threats of bodily harm made to his wife to induce a particular course of action constitute duress, as well as a threat to give false testimony which would bring humiliation, embarrassment, and disgrace upon the wife or her friend, if the wife's will is so overcome as to cause her to perform an act that she was not legally bound to do. Young v. Young (Franklin 1982) 8 Ohio App.3d 52, 455 N.E.2d 1360, 8 O.B.R. 56.

A separation agreement entered into for the sole purpose of a dissolution of marriage is not a valid and binding contract when the dissolution petition is dismissed, but would be a valid and binding contract following dismissal of such petition if it contains language that the agreement shall be binding whether used in a divorce, alimony only, or a dissolution of marriage action, or such similar language evidencing the intent of the parties that it will survive dismissal of a dissolution of marriage petition, and in addition, if it does not contain express language that it was entered into solely for a dissolution of marriage action or express language that the parties intended the separation agreement to survive dismissal of a dissolution of marriage petition, but the actions and conduct of the parties evidence an intention that it will survive dismissal of a dissolution of marriage petition, the separation agreement will continue to be a valid and binding agreement after the dissolution of marriage petition is dismissed. Greiner v. Greiner (Cuyahoga 1979) 61 Ohio App.2d 88, 399 N.E.2d 571, 15 O.O.3d 95.

A court granting a divorce to the wife in an action for divorce and alimony is without authority to modify or alter a contract between the husband and wife whereby the parties in contemplation of separation have released all claims respecting their property rights, support, dower and a distributive share, unless upon allegations and proof of fraud or mistake or evidence showing a violation of the "general rules which control the actions of persons occupying confidential relations with each other." Nellis v. Nellis (Lucas 1955) 98 Ohio App. 247, 129 N.E.2d 217, 57 O.O. 281.

The validity of a separation agreement is controlled by this section, which contains the limitation that such agreement shall be subject "to the general rules which control the actions of persons occupying confidential relations with each other," and the trial court is under no compulsion to approve the agreement. Brewer v. Brewer (Montgomery 1948) 84 Ohio App. 35, 78 N.E.2d 919, 52 Ohio Law Abs. 116, 39 O.O. 89.

RC 3103.05 applies to separation agreements made in connection with the filing of a petition for dissolution of marriage, and where the family's economic circumstances are so substantial and complex that a spouse needs competent professional assistance for a good understanding of such a separation agreement, it may be set aside where such advice has not been had. In re Marriage of Kesler (Ohio Com.Pl. 1978) 59 Ohio Misc. 33, 392 N.E.2d 905, 13 O.O.3d 105.

Where a separation agreement is found voidable, for lack of necessary advice on the part of one spouse, even after it has been approved on the hearing of a petition for dissolution of marriage and one of the former spouses has later married another, the court may propose relief modifying the terms of the separation agreement, which the aggrieved former spouse may elect to receive rather than have the agreement invalidated in its entirety. In re Marriage of Kesler (Ohio Com.Pl. 1978) 59 Ohio Misc. 33, 392 N.E.2d 905, 13 O.O.3d 105.

By virtue of this section and the next, husband and wife are authorized to contract with each other and agree for immediate separation and make provision for support of either and their children during separation. (See also Borst v Borst, 14 Abs 525 (App, Franklin 1933).) Borst v Borst, 20 Abs 184 (App, Franklin 1935).

Under this section and the next, custody of child and separation agreement, if reasonable, proper, and represents fair determination of rights of parties, should be given mature consideration by courts. Mollencamp v Mollencamp, 18 Abs 90 (App, Franklin 1934).

A separation agreement entered into by a husband and wife, followed by separation and providing, in part, for the release by the wife of the right to a year's support and other statutory allowances out of the husband's estate, is valid. In re Carnathan's Estate (Ohio Prob. 1928) 27 Ohio N.P.N.S. 65.

The claim of a debtor in bankruptcy proceedings that over the course of two years he was "unable" to pay more than $75 toward the property settlement of a divorce decree despite his annual salary of $85,000 and ownership of valuable assets is simply unbelievable, although it does not demonstrate that his bankruptcy petition was filed in bad faith; the court will not confirm any plan of this debtor unless it provides for payment of the entire property settlement. In re Markunes (Bkrtcy.S.D.Ohio 1987) 78 B.R. 875.

3103.06 Contracts affecting marriage

A husband and wife cannot, by any contract with each other, alter their legal relations, except that they may agree to an immediate separation and make provisions for the support of either of them and their children during the separation.

(1953 H 1, eff. 10-1-53; GC 8002-6; Source—GC 8000)

Historical and Statutory Notes

Pre-1953 H 1 Amendments: 124 v S 65

Cross References

Agreement made upon consideration of marriage to be in writing, 1335.05

Antenuptial agreement to which decedent a party valid unless set aside; time limits, 2106.22

Dissolution of marriage, provisions of separation agreement, 3105.63 to 3105.65
Dower, Ch 2103
Effect of separation upon voting residence of spouse, 3503.02

Library References

Contracts ⚷111.
Husband and Wife ⚷29, 30, 278(1), 278(2).
Parent and Child ⚷3.1(8).
WESTLAW Topic Nos. 95, 205, 285.
C.J.S. Contracts §§ 235, 245 to 248.
C.J.S. Husband and Wife §§ 61, 68 to 72, 86, 221 to 225, 235, 237.
C.J.S. Parent and Child §§ 60, 61.

Am Jur 2d: 41, Husband and Wife § 126 to 128, 255 et seq.
Annulment of marriage as affecting rights arising out of acts of or transactions between parties during marriage. 2 ALR2d 637
Marriage as extinguishing contractual indebtedness between parties. 45 ALR2d 722
Waiver of right to widow's allowance by antenuptial agreement. 30 ALR3d 858
Spouse's secret intention not to abide by written antenuptial agreement relating to financial matters as ground for annulment. 66 ALR3d 1282
What constitutes contract between husband and wife and third person promotive of divorce or separation. 93 ALR3d 523
Validity and effect, as between former spouses, of agreement releasing parent from payment of child support provided for in an earlier divorce decree. 100 ALR3d 1129
Failure to disclose extent or value of property owned as ground for avoiding premarital contract. 3 ALR5th 394

Carlin, Baldwin's Ohio Practice, *Merrick-Rippner Probate Law* § 98.4, 100.3 (1997)
3 Katz & Giannelli, Baldwin's Ohio Practice, *Criminal Law* § 99.3, 105.10 (1996)
Sowald & Morganstern, Baldwin's Ohio Practice, *Domestic Relations Law* § 1.4, 4.2, 4.22, 9.1, 9.2, 9.3, 9.6, 9.7, 9.8, 9.9, 9.33, 9.39, 12.17 (1997)

Law Review and Journal Commentaries

Antenuptial Agreements [Ohio] in Contemplation of Divorce. 52 Title Topics 3 (May 1985).

The Antenuptial Contract in Ohio, Randolph Carl Oppenheimer. 28 Case W Res L Rev 1040 (1978).

Bankruptcy Reform Act of 1994—What the Bankruptcy Code Giveth, Domestic Relations Courts (and Congress) Taketh Away, C.R. "Chip" Bowles. 8 Domestic Rel J Ohio 17 (March/April 1996).

Developments in Contract Law during the 1980's: The Top Ten, E. Allan Farnsworth. 41 Case W Res L Rev 203 (1990).

The Dischargeability Of Divorce Obligations Under The Bankruptcy Code: Five Faulty Premises In The Application Of Section 523(a)(5), James H. Gold. 39 Case W Res L Rev 455 (1988-89).

The Drafting and Enforcement in Ohio of Antenuptial Agreements in Anticipation of Divorce, Will Kuhlmann and Larry D. Rhodebeck. 53 Ohio St B Ass'n Rep 463 (March 24, 1980).

Judge's Column, Hon. Francine M. Bruening. (Ed. note: Judge Bruening discusses the pending Ohio Parenting Act.) 20 Lake Legal Views 1 (June 1997).

Marriage is a Damnably Serious Business—Especially the Second Time Around, Ellis V. Rippner. 40 Ohio St B Ass'n Rep 291 (1967).

Nonmarital Relationships and Their Impact on the Institution of Marriage and the Traditional Family Structure, Charles F. Crutchfield. 19 J Fam L 247 (1980-81).

Premarital and Remarital Mediation: Complementary Roles for Lawyers and Therapists, Mary-Lynne Fisher and Linda L. McFadden. 24 J Fam L 451 (1985-86).

Notes of Decisions and Opinions

In general 1
Child support 4
Divorce, spousal support 3
Future claims; will 9
Individual identity 10
Prenuptial agreement 2
Separation agreement
  In general 5
  Decree 6
  Legal advice 8
  Modification of decree 7

---

1. In general

Antenuptial agreements containing provisions for disposition of property and setting forth amounts to be paid as sustenance alimony upon a subsequent divorce of the parties are not contrary to public policy; such agreements are valid and enforceable if: (1) they have been entered into freely without fraud, duress, coercion, or overreaching; (2) there was full disclosure, or full knowledge and understanding of the nature, value, and extent of the prospective spouse's property; and (3) if the terms do not promote or encourage divorce or profiteering by divorce. Gross v. Gross (Ohio 1984) 11 Ohio St.3d 99, 464 N.E.2d 500, 11 O.B.R. 400.

A written agreement, executed after marriage by a husband and wife, which recites that it was made for the purpose of setting forth in writing an oral antenuptial agreement between the parties and also recites the terms thereof and affirmatively shows that it is a memorandum of such oral antenuptial agreement, constitutes a sufficient "memorandum or note" of such agreement to comply with the statute of frauds, and is not a contract prohibited by RC 3103.06. In re Weber's Estate (Ohio 1960) 170 Ohio St. 567, 167 N.E.2d 98, 11 O.O.2d 415.

Marriage is terminable only by death or presumption of death, or by judicial decree of divorce, dissolution, or annulment. Langer v. Langer (Ohio App. 2 Dist. 1997)

123 Ohio App.3d 348, 704 N.E.2d 275, cause dismissed 80 Ohio St.3d 1473, 687 N.E.2d 470.

Possibility of sharing in income from a spouse's business, which would be marital income, cannot be consideration for contract between spouses, because one is already entitled to share in marital income. Carlisle v. T & R Excavating, Inc. (Ohio App. 9 Dist. 1997) 123 Ohio App.3d 277, 704 N.E.2d 39.

Where a prenuptial agreement contains no recital of, or an apparent provision for, consideration to support the promisor's obligation; where the absence of such consideration is expressly asserted by the promisor in his responsive pleading; and where nothing further appears to illuminate the issue, the document is properly held to be unenforceable. Conley v. Conley (Hamilton 1975) 45 Ohio App.2d 1, 340 N.E.2d 430, 74 O.O.2d 6.

A husband may not contractually compel his wife to deed him certain real property in exchange for services rendered which are of a type obligated by law. Long v Long, No. CA-664 (5th Dist Ct App, Morrow, 8-26-87).

A spouse who breaches the marital relationship and therefore the antenuptial agreement will not be permitted to enforce the provisions of an antenuptial agreement which are favorable to him. Gross v Gross, No. 82AP-741 (10th Dist Ct App, Franklin, 2-10-83), reversed by 11 OS(3d) 99, 11 OBR 400, 464 NE(2d) 500 (1984).

A postnuptial agreement between spouses domiciled in Ohio is void if not within the exception specified in RC 3103.06, even though it is executed in a state in which agreements of its kind are valid. Brewsaugh v. Brewsaugh (Ohio Com.Pl. 1985) 23 Ohio Misc.2d 19, 491 N.E.2d 748, 23 O.B.R. 184.

An agreement between a father and mother concerning the religious education of children whether made before or after marriage and whether incorporated into a divorce decree or not is judicially unenforceable. Hackett v. Hackett (Ohio Com.Pl. 1957) 146 N.E.2d 477, 77 Ohio Law Abs. 98, 4 O.O.2d 245, affirmed 150 N.E.2d 431, 78 Ohio Law Abs. 485.

2. Prenuptial agreement

No public policy, statute, or case law prevents parties to antenuptial agreements from cutting one another off entirely from any participation in estate of the other upon the death of either. Kinkle v. Kinkle (Ohio 1998) 83 Ohio St.3d 150, 699 N.E.2d 41.

Antenuptial agreement waiving spouse's interest in individual retirement account (IRA) controls over beneficiary designation clause of IRA contract entered into prior to antenuptial agreement. Kinkle v. Kinkle (Ohio 1998) 83 Ohio St.3d 150, 699 N.E.2d 41.

Antenuptial agreement in which husband and wife released all rights to the other's property, and husband listed his individual retirement account (IRA) as an individual asset, superseded existing beneficiary designation clause in IRA contract, which, due to husband's failure to designate beneficiary, called for beneficiary to be surviving spouse or, if there was no surviving spouse, husband's estate. Kinkle v. Kinkle (Ohio 1998) 83 Ohio St.3d 150, 699 N.E.2d 41.

An antenuptial contract voluntarily entered into during the period of engagement is valid when the provision for the wife is fair and reasonable under all the surrounding facts and circumstances. Juhasz v. Juhasz (Ohio 1938) 134 Ohio St. 257, 16 N.E.2d 328, 12 O.O. 57.

When the amount provided for the wife in an antenuptial contract is wholly disproportionate to the property of the prospective husband in the light of all the circumstances and to the amount she would take under the law, the burden is on those claiming the validity of the contract to show that before it was entered into he made full disclosure to her of the nature, extent, and value of his property or that she then had full knowledge thereof without such disclosure. Juhasz v. Juhasz (Ohio 1938) 134 Ohio St. 257, 16 N.E.2d 328, 12 O.O. 57.

Existence of antenuptial agreement rendered "de facto marital termination" exception inapplicable to determination of date of division of marital property, where agreement included waiver of each party's right to claims in property of the other; court was required only to construe antenuptial agreement and enforce rights and duties created thereby. Langer v. Langer (Ohio App. 2 Dist. 1997) 123 Ohio App.3d 348, 704 N.E.2d 275, cause dismissed 80 Ohio St.3d 1473, 687 N.E.2d 470.

Husband was not entitled to equitable relief from his obligation to wife pursuant to antenuptial agreement, despite de facto termination of marriage prior to date set therein for accrual of such obligation, where de facto termination was occasioned by husband's assault on wife and subsequent removal from marital residence and plea of guilty to criminal charge of domestic violence. Langer v. Langer (Ohio App. 2 Dist. 1997) 123 Ohio App.3d 348, 704 N.E.2d 275, cause dismissed 80 Ohio St.3d 1473, 687 N.E.2d 470.

Purported antenuptial agreement was testamentary and was not applicable to divorce proceeding and, thus, upon divorce, husband was not entitled to marital home under agreement; although clause of agreement stated that husband and wife waived any claims "which he or she may acquire by reason of the marriage in the other party's property or estate," clause referred only to testamentary rights and made no reference to division of assets upon divorce. Stokes v. Stokes (Cuyahoga 1994) 98 Ohio App.3d 238, 648 N.E.2d 83.

The consideration of an antenuptial agreement is the marriage contract, and, where parties enter into an antenuptial agreement whereby each relinquishes all rights in the property of the other, and thereafter marry, alimony may properly be awarded to one of the spouses who obtains divorce for the aggression of the other. Dearbaugh v. Dearbaugh (Shelby 1959) 110 Ohio App. 540, 170 N.E.2d 262, 13 O.O.2d 351.

An antenuptial agreement which attempts to save to the wife the right to continue to prosecute such action after marriage is void as against public policy. Tanno v. Eby (Cuyahoga 1946) 78 Ohio App. 21, 68 N.E.2d 813, 46 Ohio Law Abs. 600, 33 O.O. 384.

A court of equity will not cancel for unfairness an antenuptial contract, made during engagement and ratified six years after marriage, whereby the husband and wife each agreed to take nothing from the other's estate, where no evidence is presented as to the respective values of the estates so as to show disparity in the rights surrendered, and the major portion, if not all, of the deceased spouse's estate consisted of real property situated in the county where they resided. Herman v. Soal (Hamilton 1942) 71 Ohio App. 310, 49 N.E.2d 109, 37 Ohio Law Abs. 527, 26 O.O. 188.

A prenuptial contract to pay a $2,000 note to the wife upon the death of the husband, stating that the note is to be a valid lien against his estate, creates an equitable lien against his estate. Whistler v. Allward (Hancock 1936) 57 Ohio App. 147, 12 N.E.2d 299, 23 Ohio Law Abs. 536, 10 O.O. 197.

In an action for arrearages, the trial court rightly denied the right to recover past obligations where the parties had mutually agreed to discharge the continuing obligation to pay support in exchange for a waiver of a continuing visitation right; in an action to reinstate both child support payments and visitation rights, the party seeking reinstatement will not be denied such based on the previous mutual agreement, as the child has an interest in future payments; therefore, such an agreement is binding on both parties as to past obligations, but is not binding on the court as to future payments. In re Dissolution of Marriage of Saltis v Frisby, No. 10345 (9th Dist Ct App, Summit, 1-27-82).

Antenuptial agreements are upheld by the courts in Ohio unless it can be established that one party is guilty of fraud, gross misrepresentation or coercion. Gottfried v Gottfried, No. L-80-256 (6th Dist Ct App, Lucas, 5-22-81).

In the case of a widow who owned property in her own name, conducted her own business affairs, customarily consulted with attorneys, and discussed with both her future husband and an attorney a prenuptial agreement whereby each party released his rights to the property of the other, an antenuptial agreement is binding and valid since a full disclosure of property was made. Hawkins v. Hawkins (Ohio Prob. 1962) 185 N.E.2d 89, 89 Ohio Law Abs. 161, affirmed 176 Ohio St. 469, 200 N.E.2d 300, 27 O.O.2d 435.

An antenuptial agreement cannot be set aside on the grounds that a husband with demonstrated business ability and experience did not understand the agreement which had been read to him. Pniewski v. Przybysz (Cuyahoga 1962) 183 N.E.2d 437, 89 Ohio Law Abs. 385.

Without full disclosure of property holdings by the husband and an adequate provision for the wife in the antenuptial agreement, such agreement is voidable due to fraud in the inducement, and when the wife raises no objections to the agreement by six months after the appointment of the administrator, it must be considered valid. Cantor v. Cantor (Ohio Prob. 1959) 174 N.E.2d 304, 86 Ohio Law Abs. 452, 15 O.O.2d 148.

Where a domestic relations court has determined a prenuptial agreement to be unenforceable, a bankruptcy court must abstain from hearing the debtor's complaint seeking a decision on the agreement's validity. In re Baumgartner (Bkrtcy.N.D.Ohio 1986) 57 B.R. 517.

3. Divorce, spousal support

A decree of divorce, which provides for the minor's custody and support, continues the jurisdiction of the court with respect to the support of the child during its minority, notwithstanding the absence of any express reservation in the decree with respect to and notwithstanding the amount specified for support of the child in a separation agreement; in such instance, the court may increase or decrease the provisions for support of the minor child as circumstances require. Peters v. Peters (Ohio 1968) 14 Ohio St.2d 268, 237 N.E.2d 902, 43 O.O.2d 441.

Where, in a divorce action, permanent alimony is ordered paid by the husband to the wife in a fixed amount per month, payable monthly "hereafter," based upon an agreement between the parties which does not constitute a property settlement and is not related to support of children, and where the alimony order contains no provision for termination of such payments or reservation of jurisdiction by the court, the subsequent marriage of such wife to another man capable of supporting her constitutes an election on her part to be supported by her new husband and an abandonment of the provision for permanent alimony from her divorced husband. Hunt v. Hunt (Ohio 1959) 169 Ohio St. 276, 159 N.E.2d 430, 8 O.O.2d 286.

Where it does not appear that a separation agreement between a husband and a wife is void or that such husband and wife have become reconciled and have returned to cohabitation or that the wife is entitled to any equitable relief from any of the provisions of that agreement, the provisions of such agreement, releasing the husband from any claim by the wife for care, support or maintenance, must be given full effect by the trial court in any proceeding between the parties with respect to alimony. Lowman v. Lowman (Ohio 1956) 166 Ohio St. 1, 139 N.E.2d 1, 1 O.O.2d 152.

On separation, a husband and wife may enter into an agreement releasing their respective rights to dower and distributive shares and releasing each other from claims for care, support or maintenance; where a party to such agreement elects to avoid it, on ground of fraud (other than "fraud in the factum") or for a violation of "the general rules which control the actions of persons occupying confidential relations with each other," such party necessarily seeks equitable relief from the agreement; unless such agreement is void for "fraud in the factum," such relief must be granted before the allowance of alimony. Meyer v. Meyer (Ohio 1950) 153 Ohio St. 408, 91 N.E.2d 892, 41 O.O. 415.

The consideration of an antenuptial agreement is the marriage contract, and, where parties enter into an antenuptial agreement whereby each relinquishes all rights in the property of the other, and thereafter marry, alimony may properly be awarded to one of the spouses who obtains divorce for the aggression of the other. Dearbaugh v. Dearbaugh (Shelby 1959) 110 Ohio App. 540, 170 N.E.2d 262, 13 O.O.2d 351.

Where a decree for permanent alimony incorporates a separation agreement which provides for the release of the husband by the wife from the claim for alimony; that the wife shall not apply for any allowance for counsel fees or alimony in any action for divorce; and releases the husband from all obligations of future support of their minor children, the wife relinquishes her right to support "during the separation"; and, in a subsequent action for divorce in a court other than that which granted such decree for permanent alimony, such other court is without jurisdiction to grant temporary alimony for support of the wife, or to allow temporary support for the minor children. Sinclair v. Sinclair (Preble 1954) 98 Ohio App. 308, 129 N.E.2d 311, 57 O.O. 347.

Where a separation agreement indicates a fixed-sum alimony for ten years and one month, this agreement is in the nature of a property settlement rather than support alimony, and it cannot be terminated on the basis of the wife's remarriage. Ginsburg v Ginsburg, No. 81AP-500 (10th Dist Ct App, Franklin, 10-29-81).

Under this section, a separation agreement which attempts to make settlement of all alimony claims is beyond the statute and effective only as concerns support during the separation, and defendant wife may seek order of court for temporary alimony and legal expenses in divorce action. Davis v. Davis (Montgomery 1943) 51 N.E.2d 288, 39 Ohio Law Abs. 29.

An award of $7000 in attorney fees to the wife in a short-lived, childless marriage after a divorce that simply divided property will be considered by a federal bankruptcy court to be "in the nature of alimony, maintenance or support" and, therefore, not dischargeable in the husband's bankruptcy proceedings. In re Stanjevich (Bkrtcy.S.D.Ohio 1989) 96 B.R. 138.

4. Child support

An agreement between a father and a mother (formerly husband and wife) of minor children, whereby the father, in consideration of his executing and delivering to the wife a written consent to the adoption of the children by their stepfather, is released from his obligation under the decree of divorce to support such children, is valid as between the parties, even though the adoption never takes place and the mother is subsequently divorced from the stepfather; and the mother cannot recover from the father for herself a lump sum judgment for the installments of such child support award which otherwise would have been payable. Tressler v. Tressler (Defiance 1972) 32 Ohio App.2d 79, 288 N.E.2d 339, 61 O.O.2d 85.

Decree of divorce which grants to plaintiff-husband custody of four minor children of divorced parties and orders defendant-wife to pay to husband certain specified amounts for support of such children, which amounts had been previously agreed upon in separation agreement approved by court, will be upheld, even though decree does not include finding that husband is unable to support such children. Clover v. Clover (Fairfield 1970) 24 Ohio App.2d 161, 265 N.E.2d 559, 53 O.O.2d 389.

The continuing jurisdiction that a court of common pleas retains over support orders of minor children in a divorce case, even when the parties have moved from the county over which it has jurisdiction, does not extend to a determination of the rights of such parties under a separation agreement incorporated into the divorce decree when the terms of the separation agreement as to the support of a minor child are different from a subsequent order of the court of common pleas. Harvith v. Harvith (Columbiana 1969) 17 Ohio App.2d 216, 245 N.E.2d 736, 46 O.O.2d 308.

A court of common pleas having jurisdiction over the persons of divorced parents has jurisdiction to determine the rights of such divorced parents under a separation agreement incorporated into the divorce decree made by another court of common pleas in a different county when the other court of common pleas has made a subsequent order increasing the support payments of the minor child of the divorced parents, which was contrary to the terms of such separation agreement. Harvith v. Harvith (Columbiana 1969) 17 Ohio App.2d 216, 245 N.E.2d 736, 46 O.O.2d 308.

A common pleas court having jurisdiction over the determination or approval of support payments for minor children of the parties to a divorce action exercises a continuing jurisdiction to modify the effect of its decree with respect to child support payments by increasing the burden on either of the parties to the divorce action to make such payments, notwithstanding that in its original decree the court approved a separation agreement providing that such burden be borne differently; but its decree modifying provisions for support of such minor children does not operate to relieve either party to the divorce from his or her obligations to the other under the separation agreement. Smith v. Smith (Seneca 1964) 7 Ohio App.2d 4, 218 N.E.2d 473, 36 O.O.2d 27.

Where a decree for permanent alimony incorporates a separation agreement which provides for the release of the husband by the wife from the claim for alimony; that the wife shall not apply for any allowance for counsel fees or alimony in any action for divorce; and releases the husband from all obligations of future support of their minor children, the wife relinquishes her right to support "during the separation"; and, in a subsequent action for divorce in a court other than that which granted such decree for permanent alimony, such other court is without jurisdiction to grant temporary alimony for support of the wife, or to allow temporary support for the minor children. Sinclair v. Sinclair (Preble 1954) 98 Ohio App. 308, 129 N.E.2d 311, 57 O.O. 347.

Judgments entered in different proceedings involving right of wife separated from husband to permanent alimony held not res judicata as to right of action for maintenance and support of minor children. Straub v. Straub (Butler 1928) 29 Ohio App. 373, 163 N.E. 590.

Failure of court to make order for maintenance of minor children on account of husband's inability to pay does not preclude the right to sue and recover on such claim if and when he became able to pay. Straub v. Straub (Butler 1928) 29 Ohio App. 373, 163 N.E. 590.

Where the separation agreement clearly shows the father's obligation for his son's college education, the agreement is enforceable whether the son is emancipated or not if the son desires the education. Kronenberg v Kronenberg, No. 43232 (8th Dist Ct App, Cuyahoga, 6-18-81).

Since funeral expenses are not items of support and where no provision is made for them in the separation agreement, a custodial parent cannot be reimbursed for one-half of the funeral expenses of a child who died in that parent's custody. Partington v Partington, No. 17-80-19 (3d Dist Ct App, Shelby, 4-24-81).

Separation agreement incorporated into divorce decree in which wife agrees to provide for support of child of parties after it arrives at age of eighteen years, does not relieve husband from duty of providing for such child. Rutter v. Rutter (Ohio Com.Pl. 1970) 24 Ohio Misc. 7, 261 N.E.2d 202, 53 O.O.2d 32.

5. —In general, separation agreement

The negligent or willful infliction by a husband of injuries upon his wife's person after execution of a separation agreement between them is no reason for avoiding such agreement. Lowman v. Lowman (Ohio 1956) 166 Ohio St. 1, 139 N.E.2d 1, 1 O.O.2d 152.

A separation agreement does not violate the general rules governing and controlling the actions of persons occupying confidential relations with each other, merely because it provides that the wife is to have custody of the child of the parties and that the husband is to be released from all obligations of future support and for the wife regardless of future consequences and events. Lowman v. Lowman (Ohio 1956) 166 Ohio St. 1, 139 N.E.2d 1, 1 O.O.2d 152.

On separation, a husband and wife may enter into an agreement mutually releasing their respective rights to dower and distributive shares and releasing each other from claims for care, support and maintenance, and such an agreement is enforceable and binding upon the parties thereto until a court has determined that it should be voided for fraud or for violation of the "general rules which control the actions of persons occupying confidential relations with each other." Lowman v. Lowman (Ohio 1956) 166 Ohio St. 1, 139 N.E.2d 1, 1 O.O.2d 152.

The six-month limitation of GC 10512-3 (RC 2131.03), within which the validity of a separation agreement must be attacked by a surviving spouse after the appointment of the executor or administrator of the estate of his deceased spouse, applies to a surviving spouse notwithstanding he was an infant at the time of his marriage, at the time the separation agreement was executed, and during the entire period of limitation. Burlovic v. Farmer (Ohio 1954) 162 Ohio St. 46, 120 N.E.2d 705, 54 O.O. 5.

On separation, a husband and wife may enter into an agreement releasing their respective rights to dower and distributive shares and releasing each other from claims for care, support or maintenance; where a party to such agreement elects to avoid it, on ground of fraud (other than "fraud in the factum") or for a violation of "the general rules which control the actions of persons occupying confidential relations with each other," such party necessarily seeks equitable relief from the agreement; unless such agreement is void for "fraud in the factum," such relief must be granted before the allowance of alimony. Meyer v. Meyer (Ohio 1950) 153 Ohio St. 408, 91 N.E.2d 892, 41 O.O. 415.

Where husband and wife, in contemplation of separation, enter into mutual covenants for release of dower and distributive share, and as part consideration therefor husband pays wife the sum of $5,000, which she accepts, and separation occurs pursuant thereto, such contract, if made in accordance with the rules controlling actions of persons occupying confidential relations is valid. Hoagland v. Hoagland (Ohio 1925) 113 Ohio St. 228, 148 N.E. 585, 3 Ohio Law Abs. 388, 23 Ohio Law Rep. 322.

Written agreement entered by husband and wife in anticipation of possible divorce, under which husband, who operated excavation firm, was obligated to perform excavating services for wife's preschool business as "repayment" for past secretarial services provided by wife, was not enforceable as valid separation agreement, where husband and wife did not separate immediately after executing agreement, but waited several months to do so. Carlisle v. T & R Excavating, Inc. (Ohio App. 9 Dist. 1997) 123 Ohio App.3d 277, 704 N.E.2d 39.

A separation agreement is a contract and its interpretation is a matter of law. Forstner v. Forstner (Lake 1990) 68 Ohio App.3d 367, 588 N.E.2d 285.

A separation agreement is subject to the same rules of construction as other contracts. Forstner v. Forstner (Lake 1990) 68 Ohio App.3d 367, 588 N.E.2d 285.

If there is disagreement over interpreting a certain clause in a separation agreement, the trial court enforcing the agreement may hear the matter, clarify the confusion, and resolve the dispute; a trial court may consider both the intent of the parties and the equities involved. Uram v. Uram (Summit 1989) 65 Ohio App.3d 96, 582 N.E.2d 1060.

A trial court did not abuse its discretion in limiting college costs paid by a former husband to those specific items mentioned in the separation agreement; room and board is not included in an obligation to pay "costs of such items as tuition, fees, and books." Uram v. Uram (Summit 1989) 65 Ohio App.3d 96, 582 N.E.2d 1060.

Separation agreement executed by parties prior to husband's death was enforceable against wife, though husband's death had resulted in dismissal of wife's dissolution action, where agreement provided that it was not executed in consideration of divorce and was intended to be binding on parties independently of any dissolution proceeding. In re Estate of Hogrefe (Henry 1986) 30 Ohio App.3d 238, 507 N.E.2d 414, 30 O.B.R. 397.

Where husband and wife are shareholders of a closely held corporation and where a separation agreement provides that all claims brought by the wife as shareholder against the husband as shareholder are resolved, such agreement effectively bars the corporation, of which the wife is subsequently the sole shareholder, from pursuing the same claims. Knowlton Co. v. Knowlton (Franklin 1983) 10 Ohio App.3d 82, 460 N.E.2d 632, 10 O.B.R. 104.

A separation agreement entered into for the sole purpose of a dissolution of marriage is not a valid and binding contract when the dissolution petition is dismissed, but would be a valid and binding contract following dismissal of such petition if it contains language that the agreement shall be binding whether used in a divorce, alimony only, or a dissolution of marriage action, or such similar language evidencing the intent of the parties that it will survive dismissal of a dissolution of marriage petition, and in addition, if it does not contain express language that it was entered into solely for a dissolution of marriage action or express language that the parties intended the separation agreement to survive dismissal of a dissolution of marriage petition, but the actions and conduct of the parties evidence an intention that it will survive dismissal of a dissolution of marriage petition, the separation agreement will continue to be a valid and binding agreement after the dissolution of marriage petition is dismissed. Greiner v. Greiner (Cuyahoga 1979) 61 Ohio App.2d 88, 399 N.E.2d 571, 15 O.O.3d 95.

It is beyond the power of a wife to release in a separation agreement her right to expense money in a subsequent divorce case. Sinclair v. Sinclair (Preble 1954) 98 Ohio App. 308, 129 N.E.2d 311, 57 O.O. 347.

A separation agreement between husband and wife is binding upon the parties if otherwise legally executed even though the parties thereto are minors. Burlovic v. Farmer (Cuyahoga 1953) 96 Ohio App. 403, 115 N.E.2d 411, 54 O.O. 399, affirmed 162 Ohio St. 46, 120 N.E.2d 705, 54 O.O. 5.

Where parties to a separation agreement include therein an obligation relating to a religious practice, said obligation is unenforceable in a court of law either as a contractual provision or pursuant to the enforcement of a divorce decree which incorporated the terms of such agreement. Steinberg v Steinberg, No. 44125 (8th Dist Ct App, Cuyahoga, 6-24-82).

Where a separation agreement indicates a fixed-sum alimony for ten years and one month, this agreement is in the nature of a property settlement rather than support alimony, and it cannot be terminated on the basis of the wife's remarriage. Ginsburg v Ginsburg, No. 81AP-500 (10th Dist Ct App, Franklin, 10-29-81).

Where a divorce decree incorporates a separation agreement providing that the wife would continue operating her dog-grooming business in the husband's building, the parties' agreement should be interpreted to include an implied covenant that the husband may not compete in the same business in the same building. Hovanek v Hovanek, No. 8-212 (11th Dist Ct App, Lake, 9-30-81).

Where the separation agreement pursuant to divorce states that the father will pay for college education with no further description of its meaning, the term can be construed reasonably to include room and board along with tuition and books. Malkin v Malkin, No. 2919 (11th Dist Ct App, Trumbull, 5-26-81).

Since funeral expenses are not items of support and where no provision is made for them in the separation agreement, a custodial parent cannot be reimbursed for one-half of the funeral expenses of a child who died in that parent's custody. Partington v Partington, No. 17-80-19 (3d Dist Ct App, Shelby, 4-24-81).

A court has jurisdiction, both under common law and by statute, to enforce a separation agreement. Hawgood v. Hawgood (Ohio Com.Pl. 1973) 33 Ohio Misc. 227, 294 N.E.2d 681, 62 O.O.2d 427.

Separation agreement between husband and wife under RC 3103.06 as it applies to custody, support and maintenance of minor child of parties, is executory only and may be revoked by agreement, or by resuming marital relations or by operation of law. Rutter v. Rutter (Ohio Com.Pl. 1970) 24 Ohio Misc. 7, 261 N.E.2d 202, 53 O.O.2d 32.

A written separation agreement between husband and wife, respecting property rights and the surrender of dower interests by both, can be abrogated only by as complete an understanding and meeting of minds as occurred when the original agreement was made. Resumption of marital relations at different times, subsequent to the conclusion of such an agreement, is of little significance so far as establishing an abrogation of the agreement is concerned. Leedy v. Malcolm (Cuyahoga 1930) 8 Ohio Law Abs. 640, 32 Ohio Law Rep. 363.

On the evidence, separation agreement did not bar wife's right to share in insurance proceeds on husband's life. Carpenter v. Carpenter (Ohio Com.Pl. 1962) 185 N.E.2d 502, 89 Ohio Law Abs. 600, 21 O.O.2d 274.

Under this section, a separation agreement which attempts to make settlement of all alimony claims is beyond the statute and effective only as concerns support during the separation, and defendant wife may seek order of court for temporary alimony and legal expenses in divorce action. Davis v. Davis (Montgomery 1943) 51 N.E.2d 288, 39 Ohio Law Abs. 29.

The claim of a debtor in bankruptcy proceedings that over the course of two years he was "unable" to pay more than $75 toward the property settlement of a divorce decree despite his annual salary of $85,000 and ownership of valuable assets is simply unbelievable, although it does not demonstrate that his bankruptcy petition was filed in bad faith; the court will not confirm any plan of this debtor unless it provides for payment of the entire property settlement. In re Markunes (Bkrtcy.S.D.Ohio 1987) 78 B.R. 875.

6. —Decree, separation agreement

Where it does not appear that a separation agreement between a husband and a wife is void or that such husband and wife have become reconciled and have returned to cohabitation or that the wife is entitled to any equitable relief from any of the provisions of that agreement, the provisions of such agreement, releasing the husband from any claim by the wife for care, support or maintenance, must be given full effect by the trial court in any proceeding between the parties with respect to alimony. Lowman v. Lowman (Ohio 1956) 166 Ohio St. 1, 139 N.E.2d 1, 1 O.O.2d 152.

A decree of divorce, which is silent on the subject, does not of its own force terminate a separation agreement previously entered into by the parties. Mendelson v. Mendelson (Ohio 1930) 123 Ohio St. 11, 173 N.E. 615, 8 Ohio Law Abs. 754, 33 Ohio Law Rep. 321.

If the terms of a separation agreement are incorporated into a decree of divorce or alimony, the separation agreement merges into the decree and no longer exists as an independent contract and its terms will be enforced as part of the decree. If a separation agreement is not incorporated by reference into a divorce or alimony decree, nor declared invalid, but only identified and attached as an exhibit to the divorce or alimony decree, the separation agreement will continue to be a valid and binding contract and its terms will not be enforced as part of the decree, but will be enforced as any other contract. Greiner v. Greiner (Cuyahoga 1979) 61 Ohio App.2d 88, 399 N.E.2d 571, 15 O.O.3d 95.

Decree of divorce which grants to plaintiff-husband custody of four minor children of divorced parties and orders defendant-wife to pay to husband certain specified amounts for support of such children, which amounts had been previously agreed upon in separation agreement approved by court, will be upheld, even though decree does not include finding that husband is unable to support such children. Clover v. Clover (Fairfield 1970) 24 Ohio App.2d 161, 265 N.E.2d 559, 53 O.O.2d 389.

Where a decree for permanent alimony incorporates a separation agreement which provides for the release of the husband by the wife from the claim for alimony; that the wife shall not apply for any allowance for counsel fees or alimony in any action for divorce; and releases the husband from all obligations of future support of their minor children, the wife relinquishes her right to support "during the separation"; and, in a subsequent action for divorce in a court other than that which granted such decree for permanent alimony, such other court is without jurisdiction to grant temporary alimony for support of the wife, or to allow temporary support for the minor children. Sinclair v. Sinclair (Preble 1954) 98 Ohio App. 308, 129 N.E.2d 311, 57 O.O. 347.

A trial court in divorce action is under no compulsion to approve a settlement agreement by the parties relative to division of property. Brewer v. Brewer (Montgomery 1948) 84 Ohio App. 35, 78 N.E.2d 919, 52 Ohio Law Abs. 116, 39 O.O. 89.

Separation agreement incorporated into divorce decree in which wife agrees to provide for support of child of parties after it arrives at age of eighteen years, does not relieve husband from duty of providing for such child. Rutter v. Rutter (Ohio Com.Pl. 1970) 24 Ohio Misc. 7, 261 N.E.2d 202, 53 O.O.2d 32.

A husband's liability to a mortgagee bank and to his wife as cosigner of a promissory note is dischargeable in bankruptcy; but where a divorce decree entered after the filing of the bankruptcy petition provides for the husband to pay any deficiency resulting from forced sale of the mortgaged property, the decree creates an independent, postpetition obligation to the wife which is not discharged. In re Neier (Bkrtcy.N.D.Ohio 1985) 45 B.R. 740.

7. —Modification of decree, separation agreement

Decree in a divorce action, unconditionally fixing amount and method of payment by husband for support of a minor child in accordance with a previous contract of separation between the husband and wife providing for complete property settlement and support to their minor child, which contract is specifically approved by the court and made part of the decree, may not, in absence of fraud or mistake, be subsequently modified by the court so as to lessen the amount of support for such minor child. Tullis v. Tullis (Ohio 1941) 138 Ohio St. 187, 34 N.E.2d 212, 20 O.O. 237.

The continuing jurisdiction that a court of common pleas retains over support orders of minor children in a divorce case, even when the parties have moved from the county over which it has jurisdiction, does not extend to a determination of the rights of such parties under a separation agreement incorporated into the divorce decree when the terms of the separation agreement as to the support of a minor child are different from a subsequent order of the court of common pleas. Harvith v. Harvith (Columbiana 1969) 17 Ohio App.2d 216, 245 N.E.2d 736, 46 O.O.2d 308.

A court of common pleas having jurisdiction over the persons of divorced parents has jurisdiction to determine the rights of such divorced parents under a separation agreement incorporated into the divorce decree made by another court of common pleas in a different county when the other court of common pleas has made a subsequent order increasing the support payments of the minor child of the divorced parents, which was contrary to the terms of such separation agreement. Harvith v. Harvith (Columbiana 1969) 17 Ohio App.2d 216, 245 N.E.2d 736, 46 O.O.2d 308.

A common pleas court having jurisdiction over the determination or approval of support payments for minor children of the parties to a divorce action exercises a continuing jurisdiction to modify the effect of its decree with respect to child support payments by increasing the burden on either of the parties to the divorce action to make such payments, notwithstanding that in its original decree the court approved a separation agreement providing that such burden be borne differently; but its decree modifying provisions for support of such minor children does not operate to relieve either party to the divorce from his or her obligations to the other under the separation agreement. Smith v. Smith (Seneca 1964) 7 Ohio App.2d 4, 218 N.E.2d 473, 36 O.O.2d 27.

A court granting a divorce to the wife in an action for divorce and alimony is without authority to modify or alter a contract between the husband and wife whereby the parties in contemplation of separation have released all claims respecting their property rights, support, dower and a distributive share, unless upon allegations and proof of fraud or mistake or evidence showing a violation of the "general rules which control the actions of persons occupying confidential relations with each other." Nellis v. Nellis (Lucas 1955) 98 Ohio App. 247, 129 N.E.2d 217, 57 O.O. 281.

Trial court is not precluded from exercising jurisdiction to modify an alimony award where an alleged separation agreement does not meet the requirements of a valid separation agreement pursuant to RC 3103.06 nor was the agreement written into the divorce decree or incorporated by reference. Strohschein v Strohschein, No. 81AP-784 (10th Dist Ct App, Franklin, 3-9-82).

Where the provision for support is for a definite sum of money to be paid in installments over a specified period of time without any contingencies, this provision constitutes a division of marital assets and is not subject to modification under the continuing jurisdiction of the court. Tasin v Tasin, No. 37707 (8th Dist Ct App, Cuyahoga, 9-28-78).

Where a divorce decree calls for sale of the marital residence when minor children reach a certain age or the premises are abandoned, and where the husband refuses consent to a sale before the minors attain the specified age, a court cannot modify the agreement to provide for execution of a listing agreement and a sale by the husband, but it may entertain an action for partition. Custer v. Custer (Ohio Com.Pl. 1985) 23 Ohio Misc.2d 27, 491 N.E.2d 1145, 23 O.B.R. 250.

A court granting decree of divorce may change custody of a minor child of parties or increase or decrease provisions for support, maintenance, care and education of such minor child during its minority as changed circumstances require, notwithstanding the unqualified provisions of a separation agreement concerning support, maintenance, care and education for such child incorporated in decree of divorce. Rutter v. Rutter (Ohio Com.Pl. 1970) 24 Ohio Misc. 7, 261 N.E.2d 202, 53 O.O.2d 32.

A trial court that approved a separation agreement, thereafter adopted as a part of the judgment in a divorce, alimony and custody action, which agreement contained a provision regarding the custody of a minor child, is not bound by the terms of that agreement in a subsequent hearing on a motion to modify the provisions of the judgment entry. Bastian v. Bastian (Cuyahoga 1959) 160 N.E.2d 133, 81 Ohio Law Abs. 408, 13 O.O.2d 267.

8. —Legal advice, separation agreement

Misconduct on part of the wife does not relieve the husband of fair dealing with respect to any property settlement; because of the dominating influence which a husband exercises over the wife, transactions between them to be valid, particularly as to wife, must be fair and reasonable and voluntarily and understandingly made, and whenever advice of counsel would be of real assistance to the wife relative to the settlement agreement, it is husband's duty to advise wife to seek such counsel. Brewer v. Brewer (Montgomery 1948) 84 Ohio App. 35, 78 N.E.2d 919, 52 Ohio Law Abs. 116, 39 O.O. 89.

3103.05 applies to separation agreements made in connection with the filing of a petition for dissolution of marriage, and where the family's economic circumstances are so substantial and complex that a spouse needs competent professional assistance for a good understanding of such a separation agreement, it may be set aside where such advice has not been had. In re Marriage of Kesler (Ohio Com.Pl. 1978) 59 Ohio Misc. 33, 392 N.E.2d 905, 13 O.O.3d 105.

Where a separation agreement is found voidable, for lack of necessary advice on the part of one spouse, even after it has been approved on the hearing of a petition for dissolution of marriage and one of the former spouses has later married another, the court may propose relief modifying the terms of the separation agreement, which the aggrieved former spouse may elect to receive rather than have the agreement invalidated in its entirety. In re Marriage of Kesler (Ohio Com.Pl. 1978) 59 Ohio Misc. 33, 392 N.E.2d 905, 13 O.O.3d 105.

The equitable principle requiring a husband to procure independent advice for his wife in transactions between them does not require a showing of a design founded in evil purpose on the part of the husband. In re Marriage of Kesler (Ohio Com.Pl. 1978) 59 Ohio Misc. 33, 392 N.E.2d 905, 13 O.O.3d 105.

9. Future claims; will

On separation, a husband and wife may enter into an agreement mutually releasing each other from claims for future care, support and maintenance. Lowman v. Lowman (Ohio 1956) 166 Ohio St. 1, 139 N.E.2d 1, 1 O.O.2d 152.

Where a husband and wife, living together, agreed in writing that for $25,000, evidenced by five notes given to the wife, she would release all her interest in his estate, including her right of distributive share and inchoate dower therein, her executor could not recover against surviving husband on the note last due. Du Bois v. Coen (Ohio 1919) 100 Ohio St. 17, 125 N.E. 121, 17 Ohio Law Rep. 63, 17 Ohio Law Rep. 66.

Post-nuptial contract was ineffective by virtue of this section to bar widow of her dower rights and distributive share and other rights accruing by law to surviving spouse. Hughes v. Reasneor (Darke 1934) 18 Ohio Law Abs. 449.

A husband's liability to a mortgagee bank and to his wife as cosigner of a promissory note is dischargeable in bankruptcy; but where a divorce decree entered after the filing of the bankruptcy petition provides for the husband to pay any deficiency resulting from forced sale of the mortgaged property, the decree creates an independent, postpetition obligation to the wife which is not discharged. In re Neier (Bkrtcy.N.D.Ohio 1985) 45 B.R. 740.

Under this section, a surviving spouse who executes a joint will with her consort during coverture can elect not to take under such will, even if such will is made in pursuance of contract. Passoni v. Breehl (Ohio Prob. 1944) 14 Ohio Supp. 100, 41 Ohio Law Abs. 315, 29 O.O. 220.

10. Individual identity

The common law doctrine of the legal identity of husband and wife has been abolished in Ohio, and the wife of a member of a voluntary unincorporated association may maintain an action against the association to recover damages for a tort resulting in her injury. Damm v. Elyria Lodge No. 465, Benev. Protective Order of Elks (Ohio 1952) 158 Ohio St. 107, 107 N.E.2d 337, 48 O.O. 54.

A partition action cannot be sustained on the basis of a property settlement prior to the trial of the divorce action of the parties. Smith v. Smith (Ohio Com.Pl. 1953) 112 N.E.2d 346, 67 Ohio Law Abs. 489, 50 O.O. 175.

3103.07 Property

A married person may take, hold, and dispose of property, real or personal, the same as if unmarried.

(1953 H 1, eff. 10-1-53; GC 8002-7; Source—GC 8001)

Historical and Statutory Notes

Pre-1953 H 1 Amendments: 124 v S 65

Comparative Laws

Ariz.—A.R.S. § 25-213.
Ark.—A.C.A. § 9-11-505.
Conn.—C.G.S.A. § 46b-36.
Ga.—O.C.G.A. § 19-3-9.
Idaho—I.C. § 32-903.
Iowa—I.C.A. § 597.1.
Ky.—Baldwin's KRS 404.010.
Mass.—M.G.L.A. c. 209, § 1.
Minn.—M.S.A. § 519.02.
Mo.—V.A.M.S. § 451.250.
N.C.—G.S. § 52-1.
Neb.—R.R.S.1943, § 42-201.
N.J.—N.J.S.A. 37:2-12 et seq.
N.Y.—McKinney's Domestic Relations Law § 50.
Wash.—West's RCWA 26.16.020.
Wis.—W.S.A. 766.01.
W.Va.—Code, 48-3-1 et seq.

Cross References

Husband and wife must join in chattel mortgage on household property, 1319.06
Liens, work authorized by owner's spouse, 1311.10
Real property, partition, Ch 5307
Surviving spouse may purchase property, 2106.16

Library References

Husband and Wife ⟹6 to 13, 55.
WESTLAW Topic No. 205.
C.J.S. Husband and Wife §§ 10 to 12, 107.

OJur 3d: 45, Family Law § 47, 61; 46, Family Law § 225; 62, Investment Securities and Securities Regulation § 53
Am Jur 2d: 41, Husband and Wife § 29 et seq., 419 et seq., 531
Joining in subsequent instrument as ratification of or estoppel as to prior instrument affecting real property, ineffective for nonjoinder of spouse. 7 ALR2d 299
Insurable interest of husband or wife in other's property. 27 ALR2d 1059
Conclusiveness of judgment as to property accumulated by man and woman living together in illicit relationship or under void marriage. 31 ALR2d 1314
Rights and incidence where real property purchased with wife's funds is placed in spouses' joint names. 43 ALR2d 917
Notice by lessee's husband of exercise of option to renew lease. 53 ALR2d 1423
Spouse of living co-owner of interest in property as necessary or proper party to partition action. 57 ALR2d 1166
Judgment involving real property against one spouse as binding against other spouse not a party to the proceeding. 58 ALR2d 701
Obligation under property settlement agreement between spouses as dischargeable in bankruptcy. 74 ALR2d 758
Character and incidence of estate created by a deed to persons as husband and wife who are not legally married. 9 ALR4th 1185
Validity and effect of one spouse's conveyance to other spouse of interest in property held as estate by the entireties. 18 ALR5th 230

Hausser, Ohio Real Estate Law and Practice (2d Ed.), Text 31.10(A)
Sowald & Morganstern, Baldwin's Ohio Practice, *Domestic Relations Law* § 4.1, 4.5, 4.16 (1997)

Notes of Decisions and Opinions

Actions against a spouse 2
Actions against third parties 1

1. Actions against third parties

The common law doctrine of the legal identity of husband and wife has been abolished in Ohio, and the wife of a member of a voluntary unincorporated association may maintain an action against the association to recover damages for a tort resulting in her injury. Damm v. Elyria Lodge No. 465, Benev. Protective Order of Elks (Ohio 1952) 158 Ohio St. 107, 107 N.E.2d 337, 48 O.O. 54.

Where, at the request of a husband who is separated and living at a different address from his wife pending a divorce action, a telephone company attaches an extension on such wife's private telephone line, which private telephone is in her name and paid for by her, and places such extension in the residence of the husband without the wife's knowledge, and where the facts that the parties are living apart pending a divorce and that the wife is paying her own bills are known to the telephone company, such telephone company is severally liable in an action brought by the wife against it for having rendered material aid to another person (the husband) in the commission of a tort (invasion of privacy). LeCrone v. Ohio Bell Tel. Co. (Franklin 1963) 120 Ohio App. 129, 201 N.E.2d 533, 28 O.O.2d 374.

2. Actions against a spouse

Marriage does not grant a wife an interest in her husband's real or personal property, except as statutorily granted for support and dower. State v. Garber (Ohio App. 9 Dist. 1998) 125 Ohio App.3d 615, 709 N.E.2d 218.

Ownership of property by one spouse is as distinct from ownership by the other as if the spouses were strangers. State v. Garber (Ohio App. 9 Dist. 1998) 125 Ohio App.3d 615, 709 N.E.2d 218.

An individual may be convicted of arson for burning the property of his spouse although the couple was living together at the time of the incident. State v. Regan (Wayne 1988) 51 Ohio App.3d 214, 555 N.E.2d 987.

A wife may bring an action in partition against the husband as to real estate jointly owned. Shively v. Shively (Montgomery 1948) 88 N.E.2d 280, 54 Ohio Law Abs. 527, rehearing denied 88 N.E.2d 615, 54 Ohio Law Abs. 527.

Under Ohio law, marriage alone does not confer upon spouse an interest in other spouse's separately titled property. In re Greer (Bkrtcy.N.D.Ohio 1999) 242 B.R. 389.

3103.08 Responsibility of spouses for acts of other

Neither husband nor wife, as such, is answerable for the acts of the other.

(1953 H 1, eff. 10-1-53; GC 8002-8; Source—GC 8002)

Historical and Statutory Notes

Pre-1953 H 1 Amendments: 124 v S 65

Comparative Laws

Ga.—O.C.G.A. § 51-1-10.
Iowa—I.C.A. § 597.19.
N.C.—G.S. § 52-12.
N.J.—N.J.S.A. 37:2-8.
N.Y.—McKinney's General Obligations Law § 3-313.
Wash.—West's RCWA 26.16.190.
W.Va.—Code, 48-3-20.

Cross References

Assignment for benefit of creditors by husband not to include property of wife, 1313.17
Civil actions, wife may defend for her own or her husband's right, 2307.10
Judgment against married woman, 2323.09
Liens, work authorized by owner's spouse, 1311.10
Small loans; assignment of personal earnings by married person, 1321.31

Library References

Husband and Wife ⟹53, 54.
WESTLAW Topic No. 205.
C.J.S. Husband and Wife §§ 96, 113.

OJur 3d: 29, Criminal Law § 2891; 45, Family Law § 55; 46, Family Law § 291

Am Jur 2d: 41, Husband and Wife § 144, 323 to 328, 427 to 439

Modern status of interspousal tort immunity in personal injury and wrongful death actions. 92 ALR3d 901

Spouse's liability, after divorce, for community debt contracted by other spouse during marriage. 20 ALR4th 211

Sowald & Morganstern, Baldwin's Ohio Practice, *Domestic Relations Law* § 4.4, 4.38, 9.22 (1997)

Williams, Ohio Consumer Law (2000 Ed.), Text 15.10

Law Review and Journal Commentaries

Bankruptcy Reform Act of 1994—What the Bankruptcy Code Giveth, Domestic Relations Courts (and Congress) Taketh Away, C.R. "Chip" Bowles. 8 Domestic Rel J Ohio 17 (March/April 1996).

Is It Morally Wrong To Depend On the Honesty Of Your Partner Or Spouse? Bankruptcy Dischargeability Of Vicarious Debt, Steven H. Resnicoff. 42 Case W Res L Rev 147 (1992).

Notes of Decisions and Opinions

---

1. Torts

The common law doctrine of the legal identity of husband and wife has been abolished in Ohio, and the wife of a member of a voluntary unincorporated association may maintain an action against the association to recover damages for a tort resulting in her injury. Damm v. Elyria Lodge No. 465, Benev. Protective Order of Elks (Ohio 1952) 158 Ohio St. 107, 107 N.E.2d 337, 48 O.O. 54.

This section abrogated the common law rule which made the husband liable for the negligent acts of his wife as such, so that he is now liable for negligent injuries inflicted by her only when it is shown that she was acting as his servant in the course of her employment. Bretzfelder v. Demaree (Ohio 1921) 102 Ohio St. 105, 130 N.E. 505, 18 Ohio Law Rep. 535, 18 Ohio Law Rep. 536.

Where wife has general permission from husband to use his automobile for her own purposes, proof that the car was his, that she was his wife, and that she took her child with her to religious services, does not, ipso facto, make the husband liable as her master, for negligent injuries inflicted by her in driving the automobile. Bretzfelder v. Demaree (Ohio 1921) 102 Ohio St. 105, 130 N.E. 505, 18 Ohio Law Rep. 535, 18 Ohio Law Rep. 536.

A wife is not liable for her husband's negligence in making repairs to a house owned by them as tenants in common in the absence of proof that he was acting as her agent. Sowers v. Birkhead (Franklin 1958) 108 Ohio App. 507, 157 N.E.2d 459, 80 Ohio Law Abs. 84, 9 O.O.2d 491.

In an action by a minor child against a husband and wife to recover damages for injuries negligently inflicted by the husband while engaged in repairing a house in which each owned an undivided one-half interest, in the absence of any allegation or evidence of the husband's authority to act as agent for his wife in making such repairs it is error for the court to charge the jury that the husband and wife were engaged in a joint enterprise. Sowers v. Birkhead (Franklin 1958) 108 Ohio App. 507, 157 N.E.2d 459, 80 Ohio Law Abs. 84, 9 O.O.2d 491.

2. Contracts

A husband's complicity in arson does not bar his wife's claim as a matter of public policy without regard to the policy's terms; an insured individual's marital relationship with an arsonist does not make her accountable for his misconduct. Attallah v. Midwestern Indem. Co. (Cuyahoga 1988) 49 Ohio App.3d 146, 551 N.E.2d 619.

3. Criminal actions

Where motor vehicle is in a wife's name but is used jointly by both spouses, the wife may permit a warrantless search of it by police officers without the husband's permission. State v. McCarthy (Cuyahoga 1969) 20 Ohio App.2d 275, 253 N.E.2d 789, 49 O.O.2d 364, affirmed 26 Ohio St.2d 87, 269 N.E.2d 424, 55 O.O.2d 161.

A wife, by virtue of her status as a joint occupant and joint controller of the family dwelling, may, in the absence of the husband, allow a warrantless search of the family abode by the police; however, such search should be restricted to the common areas of the home so that the sanctity of the personal effects of the husband will be preserved; a bullet embedded in the wall of a basement is not a personal effect. State v. McCarthy (Cuyahoga 1969) 20 Ohio App.2d 275, 253 N.E.2d 789, 49 O.O.2d 364, affirmed 26 Ohio St.2d 87, 269 N.E.2d 424, 55 O.O.2d 161.

Parents of minor children are not guilty of contempt for failure to comply with an order to produce a child to the court where the whereabouts of the children are unknown to the parents. State v. Hershberger (Wayne 1959) 168 N.E.2d 12, 83 Ohio Law Abs. 63.

Where parents passively resisted an order of the juvenile court, both could be held for contempt, not just the husband. State v. Hershberger (Ohio Juv. 1958) 150 N.E.2d 671, 77 Ohio Law Abs. 487, reversed 168 N.E.2d 12, 83 Ohio Law Abs. 63.

License applicants whose spouses have not been convicted of crimes specified in a municipal licensing ordinance lack standing to challenge the constitutionality of the ordinance's provision denying licences to any person convicted of a named crime or whose spouse has been convicted of a named crime. FW/PBS, Inc. v. City of Dallas (U.S.Tex. 1990) 110 S.Ct. 596, 493 U.S. 215, 107 L.Ed.2d 603, on remand 896 F.2d 864.

4. Debts

Innocent husband could not be held liable for entire amount of wife's fraudulent loan, under unjust enrichment theory based on money had and received due to wife's deposit of loan proceeds in joint account, absent evidence that entire amount was expended exclusively to diminish husband's personal debt; husband had no part in fraud and was unaware of loan, and evidence showed that great share of loan proceeds were used by wife to diminish her own debts for which husband was not personally liable. Natl. City Bank, Norwalk v. Stang (Huron 1992) 84 Ohio App.3d 764, 618 N.E.2d 241.

Husband is not answerable for acts of his wife unless wife acts as his agent or he subsequently ratifies her acts. Society Natl. Bank v. Kienzle (Cuyahoga 1983) 11 Ohio App.3d 178, 463 N.E.2d 1261, 11 O.B.R. 271.

Where merchandise account was in name of deceased wife only and defendant husband's uncontradicted evidence disclosed that he never authorized opening of account with plaintiff, that he furnished wife all cash needed, and that he could find no record of bills showing plaintiff's claim, defendant held entitled to judgment. William Taylor Sons & Co. v. Burton (Cuyahoga 1933) 46 Ohio App. 398, 188 N.E. 874, 15 Ohio Law Abs. 439, 39 Ohio Law Rep. 257.

The common law liability of the husband for the antenuptial debts of his wife has been annulled by the legislation of this state, and a debtor of the husband cannot apply debts due the husband to the payment of the antenuptial debts of the wife. Y. & O. Coal Co. v. Paszka (Ohio App. 1925) 20 Ohio App. 248, 152 N.E. 31, 4 Ohio Law Abs. 82.

Pursuant to a divorce action, a wife who is a co-applicant on a credit card and jointly liable for credit card charges with her husband during the time they are husband and wife is liable for the debts created by her husband during the marriage; RC 3103.18 is not applicable because wife applied for the credit card as a joint applicant and thereby creates her liability for the credit card charges based on the terms of the contract, not on her status as a wife. State Savings Bank v Watts, No. 96APG06-809, 1997 WL 101658 (10th Dist Ct App, Franklin, 3-4-97).

5. Employment matters

An employee on medical leave of absence who is seen doing labor for a company owned by his wife is held to be "employed" in violation of a work rule prohibiting "gainful employment" during a medical leave of absence even though he received no pay for his labor; it is held that he and his wife benefitted from his labor because that work made it unnecessary to pay another individual. In re Moore, UCBR B94-03940-0000 (3-21-95).

An employee fired for possessing marijuana on company property because marijuana was found in the ashtray of his wife's automobile, in which he rode with her to work each day, is fired without just cause under RC 4141.29 where the wife worked for the same employer but had no action taken against her and where the employee denied knowing the drug was present in the car. In re Fox, UCBR B92-00893-0000 (8-26-92).

An employee is fired for just cause after he authorizes his wife to sign his name to health insurance forms that he did not review and that she falsified regardless of whether he had knowledge of the falsification; as an employee required to sign claim forms under an employer-sponsored health plan he cannot escape responsibility by delegating the duty to his wife, and her dishonest acts are imputed to him. In re Mann, UCBR B90-01423-0000 (2-13-91).

After an employee has a minor difference of opinion with his employer, where the worker's wife then appears on the scene and strongly questions the employer's character, ethics, and honesty while her husband stands quietly by, her statements will be attributed to the husband and his dismissal is justified for purposes of RC 4141.29. In re Eichar, UCBR 644839-BR (7-30-86).

6. Agency relationship

Agency relationship is not presumed between husband and wife simply based upon their marital relationship. McSweeney v. Jackson (Ohio App. 4 Dist. 1996) 117 Ohio App.3d 623, 691 N.E.2d 303.

Wife knowingly permitted her husband to conduct sale of their property as though he had full authority, creating agency by estoppel between husband and wife; wife consented to price for selling real estate, identity of buyer was unimportant to wife, as long as they received their money, and wife consented to her husband showing property on their behalf and conducting negotiations. McSweeney v. Jackson (Ohio App. 4 Dist. 1996) 117 Ohio App.3d 623, 691 N.E.2d 303.

CHAPTER 3105

Divorce, Legal Separation, Annulment, Dissolution of Marriage

Section

DIVORCE; GENERAL PROVISIONS

LEGAL SEPARATION; DIVISION OF PROPERTY; SPOUSAL SUPPORT

Cross References

Children, Ch 3109

Common pleas court, division of domestic relations, 2301.03

Divorce, annulment, and legal separation actions, Civ R 75

Divorce, legal separation, or annulment actions stayed by petition for conciliation, 3117.07, 3117.08

Effect of end of marriage on trust powers reserved by grantor, 1339.62

Effect of separation upon voting residence of spouse, 3503.02

General assembly to grant no divorce or exercise judicial power, O Const Art II §32

State board of uniform state laws, study of marriage and divorce laws, 105.23

Uniform Interstate Family Support Act, duties and powers of responding tribunal, 3115.16

Ohio Administrative Code References

Department of job and family services services, child support program, OAC Ch 5101:1-29

Department of job and family services, collection of past due support by federal tax refund offset, OAC Ch 5101:1-30

Library References

Am Jur 2d: 24, Divorce and Separation § 1 to 1010

Sowald & Morganstern, Baldwin's Ohio Practice, *Domestic Relations Law* § 2.62, 7.4, 7.27, 7.36, 13.8, 23.36, 25.13, 27.4 (1997)

WESTLAW Electronic Research

See WESTLAW Electronic Research Guide following the Preface.

Law Review and Journal Commentaries

Amended Substitute Senate Bill 3: Ohio's New Domestic Relations Law, William K. Weisenberg. 5 Ohio Law 28 (March/April 1991).

Annual Survey of Family Law, 1990 Volume 12, compiled by the International Society On Family Law. (Ed. note: articles from Australia, Belgium, Canada, China, Czechoslovakia, England, France, Germany, Greece, Israel, Italy, Jamaica, Japan, Netherlands, Pakistan, Poland, Scotland, South Africa, Spain, Sweden, USSR, United States.) 28 J Fam L 397 (1989-90).

Annual Survey of Family Law, compiled by The International Society On Family Law. (Ed. note: Articles on family law from 23 countries.) 29 J Fam L 277 (1990-91).

The Antenuptial Contract in Ohio, Note. 28 Case W Res L Rev 1040 (1978).

A Case Study in Divorce Law Reform and Its Aftermath, Robert E. McGraw, Gloria J. Sterin and Joseph M. Davis. 20 J Fam L 443 (1981-82).

Children—The Innocent Victims of Family Breakups: How the Family Law Attorney, the Courts, and Society Can Protect Our Children, Michael J. Albano. 26 U Tol L Rev 787 (Summer 1995).

A Constitutional Right to Counsel for Divorce Litigants, William S. McAninch. 14 J Fam L 509 (1975-76).

Court-Connected Marriage Counseling and Divorce—the New York Experience, Jon M.A. McLaughlin. 11 J Fam L 517 (1971).

Divisible Divorce and Rights to Support, Property and Custody, Joan M. Krauskopf. 24 Ohio St L J 346 (1963).

Divorce Investigation Reports in Ohio Child Custody Determinations, Note. 25 Case W Res L Rev 347 (1975).

Divorce Reform, Ohio Style, Alan E. Norris. 47 Ohio St B Ass'n Rep 1031 (1974).

Ferment in Divorce Legislation, H. L. Zuckerman and W. F. Fox. 12 J Fam L 515 (1972-73).

Foreign Migratory Divorces: A Reappraisal, Peter Nash Swisher. 21 J Fam L 9 (1982-83).

From Commandments to Consent: Ohio in the Divorce Reform Era, Henry E. Sheldon, II. 2 Nor Ky St L F 119 (Winter 1974-75).

Interspousal Electronic Surveillance Immunity, Comment. 7 U Tol L Rev 185 (1975).

Interspousal Torts and Divorce: Problems, Policies, Procedures, Note. 27 J Fam L 489 (1989).

Judge's Column, Hon. Francine M. Bruening. (Ed. note: Judge Bruening discusses the pending Ohio Parenting Act.) 20 Lake Legal Views 1 (June 1997).

The Lawyer Turns Peacemaker—with mediation emerging as the most popular form of alternate dispute resolution, the quest for common ground could force attorneys to reinterpret everything they do in the future, Richard C. Reuben. 82 A B A J 54 (August 1996).

A Lawyer's Guide to Marriage Counseling, Charlton S. Smith. 50 A B A J 719 (1964).

Litigation Results—Count on a CPA, Keith J. Libman. 67 Clev B J 12 (October 1996).

Matrimonial Mediation, Alan J. Cornblatt. 23 J Fam L 99 (1984-85).

The New Bankruptcy Reform Act: Its Implications for Family Law Practitioners, Paula L. Schiffer. 19 J Fam L 1 (1980-81).

Non-Fault Divorce in Ohio, Clayton W. Rose, Jr. 31 Ohio St L J 52 (1970).

The Ohio Divorce Reform Act: Half-Stepping to the Modern Drummer, Ronald L. Haldy. 2 Ohio N U L Rev 508 (1975).

The Ohio Divorce Reforms of 1974, Note. 25 Case W Res L Rev 844 (1975).

The Ohio Law of Marriage, Hugh A. Ross. 14 W Reserve U L Rev 724 (1963).

Ohio's Divorce Reform Act—Expectation And Realization, Alan E. Norris. 13 Ohio N U L Rev 173 (1986).

Partition Of Real Property Subject To Divorce Decree?, Robert W. Hausser. 56 Title Topics 5 (September 1989).

Power (Im)Balance and the Failure of Impartiality in Attorney-Mediated Divorce, Nancy Illman Meyers. 27 U Tol L Rev 853 (Summer 1996).

Practical Aspects of Ohio Divorce Proceedings, Anthony R. Fiorette. 10 Clev-Marshall L Rev 482 (1961).

Principles and Guidelines for the Division of Property in Actions for Divorce in Ohio, Domestic Relations Division, Court of Common Pleas, Cuyahoga County, Ohio. 54 Ohio St B Ass'n Rep 491 (March 16, 1981).

Property Rights on Termination of Alternative Life Styles: Cohabitation, James T. Flaherty. 10 Cap U L Rev 1 (Fall 1980).

Refusal to Have Children as a Ground for Divorce or Annulment, Marvin M. Moore. 14 Clev-Marshall L Rev 588 (1965).

Rules of Civil Procedure in Domestic Relations Practice, John R. Milligan. 39 U Cin L Rev 524 (1970).

The Therapeutic Potential of the Divorce Process, J. L. Steinberg. 62 A B A J 617 (1976).

The Violence Against Women Act After United States v. Lopez: Will Domestic Violence Jurisdiction Be Returned to the States?, Note. (Ed. note: Attempted Federal usurpation of this field of state law is discussed.) 44 Clev St L Rev 345 (1996).

Whether Rule 10b-5 Applies to a Property Settlement in a Divorce?, Note. 27 J Fam L 843 (1988-89).

Notes of Decisions and Opinions

1. In general

The principle of Barber v Barber, 21 How 582 (1859) that federal courts have no jurisdiction over suits for divorce, the allowance of alimony, or custody of children remains true and will not be cast aside after nearly a century and a half; however, a district court cannot refuse to exercise diversity jurisdiction over a tort action for damages such as one brought against a former husband and his girlfriend by the former wife based on alleged abuse of the former couple's children. Ankenbrandt v. Richards (U.S.La. 1992) 112 S.Ct. 2206, 504 U.S. 689, 119 L.Ed.2d 468, on remand 973 F.2d 923.

Disputes about domestic matters remain the province of the states. Thompson v. Thompson (U.S.Cal. 1988) 108 S.Ct. 513, 484 U.S. 174, 98 L.Ed.2d 512.

2. Procedural issues

Trial court's denial of wife's motion for continuance of final hearing in husband's action for divorce amounted to abuse of discretion, where court was on notice that wife would likely be without counsel at final hearing if continuance were not granted, matter was set for final hearing mere 65 days after complaint was filed, which time period included both the Thanksgiving and Christmas holidays, and neither party had previously requested continuance or issued subpoenas for witnesses who might have been inconvenienced by any delay in proceedings. Burton v. Burton (Ohio App. 3 Dist. 1999) 132 Ohio App.3d 473, 725 N.E.2d 359.

An Ohio court of common pleas does not have jurisdiction to enforce a divorce decree granted in Oklahoma on issues other than child support, such as payment of marital debts, even if the parties appeared voluntarily. Thorley v. Thorley (Huron 1991) 77 Ohio App.3d 275, 602 N.E.2d 268.

The denial of a motion to dismiss a divorce action for lack of jurisdiction does not constitute a final judgment;

therefore, an appeal of this denial of the motion will not be entertained by an appellate court. Lonigro v. Lonigro (Montgomery 1989) 55 Ohio App.3d 30, 561 N.E.2d 573.

The field of domestic relations is a state matter peculiarly unsuited to control by federal courts and under the principles set forth in Barber v Barber, 62 US 582, 16 LEd 226 (1858), federal courts will refuse to exercise jurisdiction over domestic matters regardless of diversity of state citizenship or the presence of the requisite amount in controversy; federal diversity jurisdiction does exist for suits that are actually tort or contract claims and have only overtones of domestic matters, however, and a constitutional claim that is not frivolous may also invoke federal jurisdiction. Taylor v. Wettstein (S.D.Ohio 1989) 746 F.Supp. 713.

3. Attorney fees

Trial court may order the wife to pay attorney's fees in a divorce action, if the wife has sufficient assets from which to pay said fees. Williams v Williams, Nos. 81 CA 51 and 81 CA 68 (2d Dist Ct App, Greene, 2-26-82).

4. Federal involvement

Rooker Feldman doctrine did not bar former husband's federal action against his former wife, seeking declaration that state divorce decree was void as a violation of due process; action was not inextricably intertwined with state judgment, because former husband's due process allegation did not implicate the merits of the divorce decree, only the procedures leading up to it. Catz v. Chalker (C.A.6 (Ohio) 1998) 142 F.3d 279.

The domestic relations exception to federal jurisdiction applies only where a plaintiff positively sues in federal court for divorce, alimony, or child custody. Catz v. Chalker (C.A.6 (Ohio) 1998) 142 F.3d 279.

Former husband's federal action against his former wife, seeking declaration that state divorce decree was void as a violation of due process, was not a core domestic relations case to which domestic relations exception to federal jurisdiction applied; action did not seek declaration of marital or parental status, but instead presented a constitutional claim in which it was incidental that the underlying action involved a divorce. Catz v. Chalker (C.A.6 (Ohio) 1998) 142 F.3d 279.

DIVORCE; GENERAL PROVISIONS

3105.01 Grounds for divorce

The court of common pleas may grant divorces for the following causes:

(A) Either party had a husband or wife living at the time of the marriage from which the divorce is sought;

(B) Willful absence of the adverse party for one year;

(C) Adultery;

(D) Extreme cruelty;

(E) Fraudulent contract;

(F) Any gross neglect of duty;

(G) Habitual drunkenness;

(H) Imprisonment of the adverse party in a state or federal correctional institution at the time of filing the complaint;

(I) Procurement of a divorce outside this state, by a husband or wife, by virtue of which the party who procured it is released from the obligations of the marriage, while those obligations remain binding upon the other party;

(J) On the application of either party, when husband and wife have, without interruption for one year, lived separate and apart without cohabitation;

(K) Incompatibility, unless denied by either party.

A plea of res judicata or of recrimination with respect to any provision of this section does not bar either party from obtaining a divorce on this ground.

(1994 H 571, eff. 10-6-94; 1990 H 514, eff. 1-1-91; 1989 H 129; 1982 H 477; 1974 H 233, S 348; 1953 H 1; GC 8003-1; Source—GC 11979)

Historical and Statutory Notes

Pre-1953 H 1 Amendments: 124 v S 65

Amendment Note: 1994 H 571 substituted "correctional" for "penal" in division (H).

Comparative Laws

Ariz.—A.R.S. § 25-312.
Ark.—A.C.A. § 9-12-301.
Conn.—C.G.S.A. § 46b-40.
Fla.—West's F.S.A. § 61.052.

Ga.—O.C.G.A. § 19-5-3 et seq.
Idaho—I.C. § 32-603 et seq.
Ind.—West's A.I.C. 31-15-2-3.
La.—LSA-C.C. art. 103.
Mass.—M.G.L.A. c. 208, § 1 et seq.
Me.—19-A M.R.S.A. § 902.
Mich.—M.C.L.A. § 552.6.
Minn.—M.S.A. § 518.06.
Mo.—V.A.M.S. § 452.305.
Neb.—R.R.S.1943, § 42-349, 42-361.
N.J.—N.J.S.A. 2A:34-2.
N.M.—NMSA 1978, § 40-4-1 et seq.
N.Y.—McKinney's Domestic Relations Law § 170.
Okl.—43 Okl.St.Ann. § 101.
Tex.—V.T.C.A. Family Code § 6.001 et seq.
W.Va.—Code, 48-2-2.

Cross References

Bigamy, 2919.01
Divorce action involving custody or care of children, jurisdiction of juvenile court, 2151.23
Duty of married person to support self, spouse, and children duration of duty to assist, 3103.03
General assembly, power to grant divorces only as expressly conferred, O Const Art II §32
Health and hospital insurance coverage after divorce, 1738.23
Husband and wife, mutual obligations, 3103.01
Nonsupport of dependents, 2919.21
Persons who may marry, 3101.01
Registration of divorce with office of vital statistics, department of health, fee, 3705.21
Trust agreement, effect of divorce, 1339.62
Wills, effect of divorce, 2107.33

Library References

Divorce ⚷12 to 38.
WESTLAW Topic No. 134.
C.J.S. Divorce §§ 13 to 70, 77, 78, 139.

OJur 3d: 46, Family Law § 325, 405, 407, 411, 421, 429 to 431, 433 to 436, 438, 549, 811
Am Jur 2d: 24, Divorce and Separation § 20 et seq., 32 et seq., 217, 299, 300
Testimony of children as to grounds of divorce of their parents. 2 ALR2d 1329
Denial of divorce in sister state or foreign country as res judicata in another suit for divorce between the same parties. 4 ALR2d 107
Avoidance of procreation of children as ground for divorce or annulment of marriage. 4 ALR2d 227
Admissibility in divorce action for adultery of wife's statement that husband was not father of her child. 4 ALR2d 567
Delay in bringing suit as affecting right to divorce. 4 ALR2d 1321
Divorce: necessity and sufficiency of corroboration of plaintiff's testimony concerning ground for divorce. 15 ALR2d 170
Antenuptial knowledge relating to alleged grounds as barring right to divorce. 15 ALR2d 670
Requisites of proof of insanity as a ground for divorce. 15 ALR2d 1135
Revival of condoned adultery. 16 ALR2d 585
What constitutes duress sufficient to warrant divorce or annulment of marriage. 16 ALR2d 1430
What amounts to connivance by one spouse at other's adultery. 17 ALR2d 342
Insanity as affecting right to divorce or separation on other grounds. 19 ALR2d 144
Conviction in another jurisdiction as within statute making conviction of crime a ground of divorce. 19 ALR2d 1047
Divorce: acts or omissions of spouse causing other spouse to leave home as desertion by former. 19 ALR2d 1428
Divorce decree as res judicata or estoppel as to previous marital status, against or in favor of third person. 20 ALR2d 1163
Recrimination as defense to divorce sought on ground of incompatibility. 21 ALR2d 1267
Insanity as substantive ground of divorce or separation. 24 ALR2d 873
Racial, religious, or political differences as ground for divorce, separation or annulment. 25 ALR2d 928
Refusal of sexual intercourse as grounds for divorce. 28 ALR2d 499
Wife's failure to follow husband to new domicil as constituting desertion or abandonment as ground for divorce. 29 ALR2d 474
What amounts to habitual intemperance, drunkenness, etc., within statute relating to substantive grounds for divorce. 29 ALR2d 925
Permissibility of counterclaim or cross action for divorce where plaintiff's action is one other than for divorce, separation, or annulment. 30 ALR2d 795
Pendency of prior action for absolute or unlimited divorce between same spouses in same jurisdiction as precluding subsequent action of like nature. 31 ALR2d 442
Condonation of cruel treatment as defense to action for divorce or separation. 32 ALR2d 107
Charge of insanity or attempt to have spouse committed to mental institution as ground for divorce or judicial separation. 33 ALR2d 1230
Written separation agreement as bar to divorce on ground of desertion. 34 ALR2d 954
Sufficiency of allegations of desertion, abandonment, or living apart as ground for divorce, separation or alimony. 57 ALR2d 468
Incompatibility or inability to live together within statutes relating to substantive grounds for divorce. 58 ALR2d 1218
Cohabitation under marriage contracted after divorce decree, later reversed or set aside, as adultery. 63 ALR2d 816
Concealed premarital unchastity or parenthood as ground of divorce or annulment. 64 ALR2d 742
What constitutes impotency as ground for divorce. 65 ALR2d 776
Charging spouse with criminal misconduct as cruelty constituting ground for divorce. 72 ALR2d 1197
Drunkenness, habitual intemperance, or use of drugs as cruelty. 76 ALR2d 419
Homosexuality as ground for divorce. 78 ALR2d 807

Time of pendency of former suit for divorce, annulment, alimony, or maintenance as included in period of desertion. 80 ALR2d 855

Mistreatment of children as ground for divorce. 82 ALR2d 1361

Threats of, or attempts to commit suicide as cruelty or indignity constituting a ground for divorce. 86 ALR2d 422

Insistence of sex relations as cruelty or indignity constituting ground for divorce. 88 ALR2d 553

Acts occurring after commencement of suit for divorce as ground for decree under original complaint. 98 ALR2d 1264

Construction of statute making bigamy or prior lawful subsisting marriage to third person as a ground for divorce. 3 ALR3d 1108

Single act as basis of divorce or separation on ground of cruelty. 7 ALR3d 761

Jurisdiction on constructive or substituted service, in divorce or alimony action, to reach property within state. 10 ALR3d 212

Power of court to grant absolute divorce to both spouses upon showing of mutual fault. 13 ALR3d 1364

Fault of spouse as affecting right to divorce under statute making separation a substantive ground of divorce. 14 ALR3d 502

Retrospective effect of statute prescribing grounds of divorce. 23 ALR3d 626

Separation within statute making separation a substantive ground for divorce. 35 ALR3d 1238

Validity, construction, and effect of "no-fault" divorce statute providing for dissolution of marriage upon finding that relationship is no longer viable. 55 ALR3d 581

Transvestism or transsexualism of spouse as justifying divorce. 82 ALR3d 725

Carlin, Baldwin's Ohio Practice, *Merrick-Rippner Probate Law* § 65.11 (1997)

Sowald & Morganstern, Baldwin's Ohio Practice, *Domestic Relations Law* § 2.25, 2.29, 2.59, 2.63, 4.28, 7.4, 7.7, 7.11, 8.2, 8.7, 11.2, 11.8, 11.9, 11.10, 11.11, 11.12, 11.13, 11.14, 11.15, 11.16, 11.17, 11.18, 11.19, 11.22, 11.24, 11.25, 12.1, 24.8, 25.1, 25.2, 25.9, 25.10, 27.3, 27.4, 27.55 (1997)

Law Review and Journal Commentaries

Children—The Innocent Victims of Family Breakups: How the Family Law Attorney, the Courts, and Society Can Protect Our Children, Michael J. Albano. 26 U Tol L Rev 787 (Summer 1995).

Divorce Reform, Ohio Style, Alan E. Norris. 47 Ohio St B Ass'n Rep 1031 (1974).

Equality and Difference: A Perspective on No-Fault Divorce and Its Aftermath, Herma Hill Kay. 56 U Cin L Rev 1 (1987).

Lov(h)ers: Lesbians as Intimate Partners and Lesbian Legal Theory, Ruthann Robson and S.E. Valentine. 63 Temp L Rev 511 (Fall 1990).

Non-Fault Divorce in Ohio, Clayton W. Rose, Jr. 31 Ohio St L J 52 (1970).

Nothing to Lose But Their Chains: A Survey of the Aguna Problem in American Law, Debbie Eis Sreter. 28 J Fam L 703 (1989-90).

Of Covenants and Conflicts—When "I Do" Means More Than It Used To, But Less Than You Thought, Jason Andrew Macke. 59 Ohio St L J 1377 (1998).

The Violence Against Women Act After United States v. Lopez: Will Domestic Violence Jurisdiction Be Returned to the States?, Note. (Ed. note: Attempted Federal usurpation of this field of state law is discussed.) 44 Clev St L Rev 345 (1996).

Notes of Decisions and Opinions

---

1. In general

Client's divorce settlement did not waive her legal malpractice claim against attorney who had represented her in divorce case; client claimed that she did not recover amounts to which she was entitled as result of attorney's alleged defective representation. Monastra v. D'Amore (Cuyahoga 1996) 111 Ohio App.3d 296, 676 N.E.2d 132, appeal not allowed 77 Ohio St.3d 1479, 673 N.E.2d 142.

In a divorce action, the trial court may either divide the interest in a retirement plan or award it entirely to one party depending on what would be equitable in the circumstances. Welly v. Welly (Williams 1988) 55 Ohio App.3d 111, 562 N.E.2d 914.

In a divorce action, the trial court can reject some of the terms of the separation agreement, make an independent ruling on those issues, and incorporate the independent ruling and partial separation agreement into the divorce decree. Welly v. Welly (Williams 1988) 55 Ohio App.3d 111, 562 N.E.2d 914.

A trial court is granted broad discretion in determining the grounds upon which a divorce shall be granted pursuant to RC 3105.01. Buckles v. Buckles (Franklin 1988) 46 Ohio App.3d 102, 546 N.E.2d 950.

A person found to be incompetent by a Texas court may not bring a divorce action in Ohio in his own name because a guardianship and adjudication of incompetency judgment of another state's court is entitled to full faith and credit under the US Constitution, and an Ohio court cannot readjudicate the ward's competency for the purpose of determining whether the ward may file an action for divorce in his own name. Pace v. Pace (Franklin 1986) 32 Ohio App.3d 47, 513 N.E.2d 1357.

Judgment, in wife's former action for divorce based on gross neglect of duty, awarding wife separate support and maintenance, held res judicata in husband's subsequent divorce action involving same issues. Hanover v. Hanover (Lucas 1929) 34 Ohio App. 483, 171 N.E. 350.

Where plaintiff has unsuccessfully prosecuted divorce action on one statutory ground, he cannot thereafter secure divorce on another ground by proof of happenings which antedated the first action. Siebert v. Siebert (Lucas 1929) 32 Ohio App. 487, 168 N.E. 223, 7 Ohio Law Abs. 435.

Elihu Root's observation is worth recalling, that "About half the practice of a decent lawyer consists of telling ... clients they are d——— fools and should stop ... [that]the law lets you do it but don't. It's a rotten thing to do." Stivison v Goodyear Tire & Rubber Co, No. 95-CA-13, 1996 WL 230037 (4th Dist Ct App, Hocking, 5-6-96), affirmed by 80 Ohio St.3d 498 (1997).

Where the parties prospered financially during a marriage which was of long duration, and the party seeking to enforce the antenuptial agreement was the clear aggressor in causing the breakup of the marriage, because the husband's conduct amounted to a breach of the marital relationship and antenuptial agreement, he will not be permitted to enforce its provisions which limit the wife's entitlement to alimony, property settlement, and expense money. Gross v Gross, No. 82 AP-741 (10th Dist Ct App, Franklin, 2-10-83), reversed by 11 OS(3d) 99, 11 OBR 400, 464 NE(2d) 500 (1984).

Although court may not grant divorce where acts of parties charged were due to lack of mental capacity, divorce may be granted against incompetent spouse for aggressions committed while sane. Butler v. Butler (Ohio Com.Pl. 1984) 19 Ohio Misc.2d 1, 482 N.E.2d 998, 19 O.B.R. 52.

Divorce granted although both parties were guilty of gross misconduct. (See also Phillips v Phillips, 70 Abs 552, 129 NE(2d) 77 (App, Franklin 1954).) Phillips v. Phillips (Franklin 1956) 136 N.E.2d 98, 74 Ohio Law Abs. 111.

Where an annulment is justified, the divorce statutes should not be construed as being involved. Nyhuis v. Pierce (Cuyahoga 1952) 114 N.E.2d 75, 65 Ohio Law Abs. 73.

Insanity in the state of Washington being evidently a statutory ground of divorce, it follows that a divorce granted there upon such ground must be recognized in Ohio, except as to property rights affected, although Ohio does not allow divorces upon that ground. Walters v. Larrick (Ohio Com.Pl. 1930) 28 Ohio N.P.N.S. 281, affirmed 39 Ohio App. 363, 177 N.E. 642, 10 Ohio Law Abs. 508.

Under Ohio law, divorce proceeding, unknown to common law, is created and governed by statute, and party has no right to jury trial nor can party recover damages. Shelar v. Shelar (N.D.Ohio 1995) 910 F.Supp. 1307.

2. —Bigamy, grounds for divorce

Where a decree of divorce is granted on the petition of a woman on the ground that the defendant had a wife living at the time of his marriage with the plaintiff, the court has jurisdiction to grant to the plaintiff alimony and other relief authorized by the statutes on divorce and alimony. Eggleston v. Eggleston (Ohio 1952) 156 Ohio St. 422, 103 N.E.2d 395, 46 O.O. 351.

GC 11979 (RC 3105.01), authorizing the granting of a divorce where "either party had a husband or wife living at the time of the marriage from which the divorce is sought," provides an exclusive remedy in cases involving that situation. Eggleston v. Eggleston (Ohio 1952) 156 Ohio St. 422, 103 N.E.2d 395, 46 O.O. 351.

A wife cannot maintain an action for alimony alone where, because the husband had a wife living at the time of his ceremonial marriage with plaintiff, they were not legally married; but she can maintain an action for divorce on the ground of her husband's undissolved marriage to another at the time of his ceremonial marriage with plaintiff, and in the action for alimony only, the defendant husband may not as a defense to such action obtain a declaratory judgment as to the marital status of the parties, notwithstanding the fact of defendant's prior undissolved marriage was not set out as a ground for alimony by plaintiff wife. Jones v. Jones (Cuyahoga 1962) 115 Ohio App. 358, 180 N.E.2d 847, 20 O.O.2d 441.

Where a decree of divorce is obtained in another state by fraud, a subsequent marriage entered into by one of the parties may be dissolved by an Ohio court, either by a decree of divorce or by an annulment. Schwartz v. Schwartz (Hamilton 1960) 113 Ohio App. 275, 173 N.E.2d 393, 17 O.O.2d 267.

Defendant was entitled to a divorce on a cross-petition against plaintiff where evidence showed that plaintiff had not secured a divorce from previous husband because of discovery that previous husband had a wife living at time of marriage to plaintiff. Kontner v. Kontner (Franklin 1956) 103 Ohio App. 360, 139 N.E.2d 366, 74 Ohio Law Abs. 97, 3 O.O.2d 384, rehearing denied 103 Ohio App. 360, 145 N.E.2d 495, 3 O.O.2d 384.

RC 3105.01, which authorizes the granting of a divorce where "either party had a husband or wife living at the time of the marriage from which the divorce is sought," provides an exclusive remedy where such situation exists. Kontner v. Kontner (Franklin 1956) 103 Ohio App. 360, 139 N.E.2d 366, 74 Ohio Law Abs. 97, 3 O.O.2d 384, rehearing denied 103 Ohio App. 360, 145 N.E.2d 495, 3 O.O.2d 384.

Where plaintiff seeks declaration that his marriage was void by reason of defendant's prior marriage being undissolved, and it appearing the defendant, then a resident of another state, had obtained, with her former husband, a "mail order divorce" from Mexico, neither of the parties ever having been there, court will not recognize Mexico divorce and will declare second marriage void, and plaintiff's knowledge before marriage to defendant of how Mexico divorce was obtained will not defeat his right to such decree. Smith v. Smith (Hamilton 1943) 72 Ohio App. 203, 50 N.E.2d 889, 38 Ohio Law Abs. 531, 27 O.O. 79.

The existence of a prior marriage is a ground for divorce under RC 3105.01(A) and an action for divorce based on such ground will not be dismissed notwithstanding the fact that the subsequent common law marriage is void for lack of competency to marry. Bolin v Bolin, No. 542 (4th Dist Ct App, Jackson, 9-22-87).

The granting of a divorce is proper relief from a marriage entered into when either party had a husband or wife living at the time the marriage was performed.

(See also Abelt v Zeman, 87 Abs 600, 179 NE(2d) 176 (CP, Cuyahoga 1962).) Abelt v. Zeman (Ohio Com.Pl. 1961) 173 N.E.2d 907, 86 Ohio Law Abs. 109, 16 O.O.2d 87.

Where wife, at time of marriage to second husband, mistakenly thought she had been divorced from first husband, but divorce action had been dismissed for want of prosecution, second marriage was void, and wife was entitled as a matter of right to a divorce from second husband, and no fraud or misconduct could be predicated on failure of wife to disclose to court that second marriage was void and that she was in fact a bigamist. Christopher v. Christopher (Ohio Com.Pl. 1950) 94 N.E.2d 50, 56 Ohio Law Abs. 449.

3. —Willful absence, grounds for divorce

Willful absence for a period of less than three years, unattended by aggravating circumstances, is not a cause for divorce and cannot be classed as gross neglect of duty; but desertion for a shorter period, accompanied by aggravating circumstances, may constitute gross neglect duty. Porter v. Lerch (Ohio 1934) 129 Ohio St. 47, 193 N.E. 766, 1 O.O. 356.

In an uncontested divorce proceeding in which there is proof of desertion by defendant husband, trial court has discretionary authority to grant divorce decree to plaintiff wife after considering all appropriate factors including best interests of community and welfare of children without raising defenses not pleaded concerning misconduct of the plaintiff wife subsequent to desertion, and consequently mothers of illegitimate children are not automatically ineligible to divorce husbands who previously deserted them. Newell v. Newell (Stark 1970) 23 Ohio App.2d 149, 261 N.E.2d 278, 52 O.O.2d 178.

In the absence of evidence showing plaintiff in a divorce action guilty of gross neglect of marital duties toward defendant, plaintiff is entitled to a divorce decree on evidence of defendant's willful absence for more than one year. Nelson v. Nelson (Hamilton 1964) 3 Ohio App.2d 293, 210 N.E.2d 137, 32 O.O.2d 391.

The mere refusal of a wife to live with her husband, unaccompanied by aggravating circumstances, constitutes willful absence; but willful absence for a period less than three years, unaccompanied by aggravating circumstances, is not a cause for divorce on the ground of gross neglect of duty. Sullivan v. Sullivan (Greene 1957) 105 Ohio App. 457, 152 N.E.2d 761, 6 O.O.2d 200.

Wife living apart from husband under judgment awarding separate support and maintenance held not willfully absent, precluding divorce on that ground. Hanover v. Hanover (Lucas 1929) 34 Ohio App. 483, 171 N.E. 350.

A husband is not entitled to a decree of divorce from his wife on the ground of willful absence where her absence has been under a decree of court granting her separate support and maintenance. Condon v Condon, 8 App 189, 30 CC(NS) 295 (1917).

Refusal of a wife to move into a new house with the husband constitutes willful absence only, and not gross neglect of duty. Casbarro v. Casbarro (Franklin 1953) 118 N.E.2d 209, 66 Ohio Law Abs. 505.

Conduct of the wife in leaving the husband's domicile and living elsewhere is willful absence rather than gross neglect of duty. Apple v Apple, 28 NP(NS) 620 (1931).

4. —Impotency, grounds for divorce

A decree of divorce granted a husband upon the ground of impotency of his wife, after they had lived together in cordial and affectionate relation for sixteen years and after she had become insane, cannot be said to be based upon the wife's aggression or fault, and does not absolve him from liability to support her; hence, reasonable alimony should be allowed based upon the husband's financial condition and ability to support her and her pecuniary needs, such as will save her from becoming a charge on the charity of her friends, relatives or the state. Knestrick v Knestrick, 1 App 285 (1913).

The trial court's granting of a divorce to the wife-appellee on the grounds of extreme cruelty is not contrary to law or against the manifest weight of the evidence, as plaintiff testified that the defendant was a "sex maniac," and had forced her to have sex against her will. Gallo v Gallo, No. 80-C-62 (7th Dist Ct App, Columbiana, 9-15-81).

Statute does not fix any age with reference to impotency as ground for divorce. Morrison v Morrison, 14 Abs 247 (App, Mahoning 1932).

5. —Extreme cruelty, grounds for divorce

Finding by trial court that the transfer of his personal property by a husband to his children by a former marriage "undermined" the wife's "economic security" is not sufficient to constitute either any gross neglect of duty or extreme cruelty under this section, or any gross neglect of duty under the section on alimony only, where the trial court found no invasion of the wife's right to present support and that the husband was still possessed of unincumbered, improved real estate. Mark v. Mark (Ohio 1945) 145 Ohio St. 301, 61 N.E.2d 595, 30 O.O. 534.

The trial court in a divorce action did not abuse its discretion in finding, based upon the evidence, that a husband had failed to prove gross neglect of duty attended by circumstances of indignity or aggravation, or of extreme cruelty rendering the marital relationship intolerable where, although the husband testified to numerous grievances, they appeared to be either trivial or disputed. Hunt v. Hunt (Montgomery 1989) 63 Ohio App.3d 178, 578 N.E.2d 498.

Although homosexuality is not specifically enumerated as one of the grounds for divorce under RC 3105.01, homosexuality may constitute extreme cruelty or adultery to the other spouse, thereby furnishing grounds for divorce; thus, a defamation action based on allegations of homosexuality within divorce pleadings must fail, since such allegations, bearing a reasonable relationship to the divorce action, are absolutely privileged. Bales v. Hack (Clark 1986) 31 Ohio App.3d 111, 509 N.E.2d 95, 31 O.B.R. 197.

In a divorce action, the propriety of a trial court's consideration of evidence of acts of extreme cruelty which occurred between the filing of the original complaint and the filing of an amended complaint will not be addressed when first challenged on appeal. Verplatse v. Verplatse (Hancock 1984) 17 Ohio App.3d 99, 477 N.E.2d 648, 17 O.B.R. 161.

Evidence that one spouse used abusive, degrading language, and urinated on the other spouse is sufficient, if believed, to prove conduct calculated to permanently destroy the happiness and peace of mind of the offended spouse. Verplatse v. Verplatse (Hancock 1984) 17 Ohio App.3d 99, 477 N.E.2d 648, 17 O.B.R. 161.

A wife's feigning or attempting suicide may constitute extreme cruelty. Glimcher v. Glimcher (Franklin 1971) 29 Ohio App.2d 55, 278 N.E.2d 37, 58 O.O.2d 37.

Unsuccessful and bad faith attempt by wife to commit husband to mental hospital constituted extreme cruelty. Ginn v. Ginn (Lawrence 1960) 112 Ohio App. 259, 175 N.E.2d 848, 16 O.O.2d 164.

The term "extreme cruelty" includes acts and conduct the effect of which is calculated to permanently destroy the peace of mind and happiness of one of the parties to the marriage and thereby render the marital relation intolerable. Buess v. Buess (Hardin 1950) 89 Ohio App. 37, 100 N.E.2d 646, 45 O.O. 331.

"Extreme cruelty," which is ground for divorce, means voluntary or intentional extreme cruelty, and cannot be committed by a lunatic who does not understand the nature of her acts. Heim v. Heim (Lucas 1930) 35 Ohio App. 408, 172 N.E. 451, 8 Ohio Law Abs. 166.

Consistently being late for supper and refusing to divulge one's whereabouts is insufficient as a matter of law to grant a divorce on grounds of gross neglect of duty or extreme cruelty. Wise v Wise, No. L-85-002 (6th Dist Ct App, Lucas, 5-17-85).

Where defendant's increasing obsession with his "new profession as a prophetical evangelist" resulted in expending large sums of money for publishing his religious tracts, neglecting a contracting business with a resultant loss of income, and causing his family worry over his beliefs, there is sufficient evidence to grant a divorce to plaintiff on the grounds of extreme cruelty. Batch v Batch, No. 81-C-52 (7th Dist Ct App, Columbiana, 7-21-82).

A divorce may be granted upon grounds of extreme cruelty even though the defendant's actions were motivated by religious convictions. Hoppes v. Hoppes (Ohio Com.Pl. 1964) 5 Ohio Misc. 159, 214 N.E.2d 860, 34 O.O.2d 329.

Where husband failed to provide for family, struck wife many times, several times in presence of others, and falsely accused wife of infidelity causing family discord, wife is entitled to divorce as matter of law. Sciacca v Sciacca, 69 Abs 514 (App, Franklin 1953).

Excessive drinking is not in and of itself extreme cruelty, but nagging and fighting with a wife while drinking is. Hardt v. Hardt (Mahoning 1961) 182 N.E.2d 9, 88 Ohio Law Abs. 191.

Extreme cruelty defined. Sharkey v. Sharkey (Montgomery 1955) 137 N.E.2d 575, 73 Ohio Law Abs. 321.

Insistence by a wife that her illegitimate child live with her and her husband does not constitute extreme cruelty, where the husband was aware of the existence of the child prior to the marriage. Slyh v. Slyh (Madison 1955) 135 N.E.2d 675, 72 Ohio Law Abs. 537.

The action of a wife in bringing her mother to live with her in cramped quarters with her husband's consent, and in berating him at his place of employment after he had moved to a hotel did not constitute extreme cruelty. Denning v. Denning (Montgomery 1955) 132 N.E.2d 774, 72 Ohio Law Abs. 14.

Evidence that plaintiff, a farmer's wife, performed menial labor around the farm and that her husband displayed a bad temper toward her on occasions did not justify the granting of a divorce on grounds of extreme cruelty. Dean v. Dean (Greene 1954) 126 N.E.2d 819, 70 Ohio Law Abs. 33.

A bona fide attempt at suicide accompanied by prior and subsequent statements of a desire to commit suicide or to be dead, which acts and statements are made known to the other party to the marriage, constitutes extreme cruelty. Liedorff v. Liedorff (Ohio Com.Pl. 1953) 113 N.E.2d 127, 67 Ohio Law Abs. 36.

Excessive indulgence in sexual intercourse is sufficient to constitute extreme cruelty, where indulgence impaired plaintiff's health and her mother corroborated evidence as to plaintiff's health, even though plaintiff did not expressly state that acts upon which she bases her claim were committed against her will. Merta v. Merta (Montgomery 1945) 63 N.E.2d 847, 45 Ohio Law Abs. 186.

"Mental cruelty," consisting of a continued course of aggravating conduct by one party toward the other, a continued course of nagging and opposition and interference with the other's business, may be "extreme cruelty" as well as acts of physical violence; in fact, by their very nature, such acts may have a more serious effect than secondary acts of physical violence. When proven, and especially when accompanied by instances of physical violence of a minor nature, it establishes a legal ground for divorce. Purmort v. Purmort (Ohio Com.Pl. 1933) 32 Ohio N.P.N.S. 313, 17 Ohio Law Abs. 63.

6. —Fraudulent contract, grounds for divorce

Where one has entered into a marriage within the degree of consanguinity prohibited by the law of Ohio, either party to such marriage may obtain a divorce on the statutory ground of fraudulent contract. Such marriage is void ab initio. The relief provided by the statute includes a fraud perpetrated on the law. Basickas v. Basickas (Summit 1953) 93 Ohio App. 531, 114 N.E.2d 270, 51 O.O. 229.

When a man who has had illicit sexual relations with a woman marries her, knowing she was then enceinte, the contract of such a marriage is not fraudulent on part of the woman within meaning of the statute. Kawecki v. Kawecki (Lucas 1941) 67 Ohio App. 34, 35 N.E.2d 865, 21 O.O. 76.

7. —Gross neglect of duty, grounds for divorce

Failure to support, to constitute gross neglect of duty, must exist prior to or at the time the decree for divorce and/or alimony is rendered and may not be predicated upon a possible or probable failure of future support, nor does such possible or probable failure of future support constitute extreme cruelty within the purview of the statutes relating to divorce and alimony. Mark v. Mark (Ohio 1945) 145 Ohio St. 301, 61 N.E.2d 595, 30 O.O. 534.

"Any gross neglect of duty," as used by the statutes, refers to an omission of legal duty. Mark v. Mark (Ohio 1945) 145 Ohio St. 301, 61 N.E.2d 595, 30 O.O. 534.

Finding by trial court that the transfer of his personal property by a husband to his children by a former marriage "undermined" the wife's "economic security" is not sufficient to constitute either any gross neglect of duty or extreme cruelty under this section, or any gross neglect of duty under the section on alimony only, where the trial court found no invasion of the wife's right to present support and that the husband was still possessed of unincumbered, improved real estate. Mark v. Mark (Ohio 1945) 145 Ohio St. 301, 61 N.E.2d 595, 30 O.O. 534.

The term "any gross neglect of duty" is elusive of concrete definition and its application as a cause for divorce must depend upon the circumstances of the particular case. Porter v. Lerch (Ohio 1934) 129 Ohio St. 47, 193 N.E. 766, 1 O.O. 356.

A finding of gross neglect of duty by a husband toward his wife and the trial court's grant of a divorce is proper where the evidence shows that the husband (1) struck and thus physically abused his wife on numerous occasions; (2) was sullen, moody, and constantly argued with his wife; (3) had his wedding ring melted down by a jeweler; (4) verbally abused his wife; and (5) refused to speak to his wife for periods of days and weeks at a time, which resulted in mental anguish and injury to his wife. Moro v. Moro (Cuyahoga 1990) 68 Ohio App.3d 630, 589 N.E.2d 416.

The trial court in a divorce action did not abuse its discretion in finding, based upon the evidence, that a husband had failed to prove gross neglect of duty attended by circumstances of indignity or aggravation, or of extreme cruelty rendering the marital relationship intolerable where, although the husband testified to numerous grievances, they appeared to be either trivial or disputed. Hunt v. Hunt (Montgomery 1989) 63 Ohio App.3d 178, 578 N.E.2d 498.

Poor housekeeping does not constitute gross neglect of duty, unless such neglect is flagrant, heinous, odious, atrocious, shameful, or despicable. Willis v. Willis (Geauga 1984) 19 Ohio App.3d 45, 482 N.E.2d 1274, 19 O.B.R. 112.

The following do not constitute gross neglect of duty: (i) a wife's jealousy because of her husband's attention to other women; (ii) incompatibility, and simple neglect of duty; (iii) neglect by a wife of her housekeeping and child care duties unless such neglect is flagrant, heinous, odious, atrocious, shameful, or despicable; (iv) a wife's complaints to family and friends that her husband is not providing as high a standard of living as she would like; (v) a wife's feigning or attempting suicide; (vi) in the absence of unusual circumstances, nonobservance by one spouse of the other spouse's religious beliefs; (vii) a wife's making of numerous telephone calls and trips to her husband's office, despite the husband's uncontradicted but unsupported testimony that such calls and trips adversely affected his income. Glimcher v. Glimcher (Franklin 1971) 29 Ohio App.2d 55, 278 N.E.2d 37, 58 O.O.2d 37.

Gross neglect of duty depends upon the circumstances of the particular case. Glimcher v. Glimcher (Franklin 1971) 29 Ohio App.2d 55, 278 N.E.2d 37, 58 O.O.2d 37.

An adjudication of incompetence is not a prerequisite to presenting the question of whether the conduct of a defendant charged with gross neglect of duty in a divorce case was the result of a sick mind. (Annotation from former RC 3105.20.) Nelson v. Nelson (Cuyahoga 1958) 108 Ohio App. 365, 154 N.E.2d 653, 79 Ohio Law Abs. 602, 9 O.O.2d 318.

The mere refusal of a wife to live with her husband, unaccompanied by aggravating circumstances, constitutes willful absence; but willful absence for a period less than three years, unaccompanied by aggravating circumstances, is not a cause for divorce on the ground of gross neglect of duty. Sullivan v. Sullivan (Greene 1957) 105 Ohio App. 457, 152 N.E.2d 761, 6 O.O.2d 200.

The term "gross neglect of duty" is to be interpreted in the broad discretion of the trial court. Buess v. Buess (Hardin 1950) 89 Ohio App. 37, 100 N.E.2d 646, 45 O.O. 331.

Time is not of the essence in the gross neglect of duty ground, and it is error for the trial court to refuse to grant a divorce because the defendant's gross neglect of duty had not continued for three years. Coleman v. Coleman (Guernsey 1941) 68 Ohio App. 410, 41 N.E.2d 734, 23 O.O. 126.

Utter neglect of a wife by an indifferent, able-bodied husband for a period of 19 to 28 months amounts to "gross neglect of duty," as a matter of law. Coleman v. Coleman (Guernsey 1941) 68 Ohio App. 410, 41 N.E.2d 734, 23 O.O. 126.

An action for divorce by husband upon the ground that the wife was employed in a gainful occupation aside from her household duties and thereby failed in her duty to make a home for the husband, in which the evidence shows that, by such employment, the wife helped maintain the financial stability of the parties, that the husband's job required him to travel and he was inconvenienced by his wife's working only over small periods of time, that the wife did not remain employed against his express wish, and that she, as a result of working, had become irritable and petulant, presents a question of incompatibility, which is not a ground of divorce in Ohio. Winnard v. Winnard (Franklin 1939) 62 Ohio App. 351, 23 N.E.2d 977, 16 O.O. 51.

Gross neglect of duty as ground for divorce cannot be established by proving willful absence. Hanover v. Hanover (Lucas 1929) 34 Ohio App. 483, 171 N.E. 350.

Consistently being late for supper and refusing to divulge one's whereabouts is insufficient as a matter of law to grant a divorce on grounds of gross neglect of duty or extreme cruelty. Wise v Wise, No. L-85-002 (6th Dist Ct App, Lucas, 5-17-85).

In a suit for divorce brought by the husband where the only evidence of misconduct by the wife was that she kicked in a metal door on property owned by the husband, the trial court erred in granting the divorce on the grounds of the wife's gross neglect of duty. Browning v Browning, No. CA 2838 (5th Dist Ct App, Licking, 6-7-82).

Where the husband shows a lack of attention to his wife, children, to his wife's illness and he belittles her both in private and in public, a granting of a divorce on the grounds of gross neglect of duty is sustained. Pfalzgraf v Pfalzgraf, No. 14-CA-79 (5th Dist Ct App, Fairfield, 10-25-79).

Evidence that a wife worked from time to time because her husband's earnings were insufficient does not constitute evidence of gross neglect. Hamilton v. Hamilton (Montgomery 1952) 114 N.E.2d 487, 65 Ohio Law Abs. 261.

Where the record showed that the defendant refused to live separate and apart from his own family during most of sixteen years of married life; that he refused to take plaintiff out socially; that he spent his time with his mother and male friends; that when he did come home he ignored her presence, spending his time reading the paper; that he was quarrelsome and on one occasion he struck her and that he was selfish, satisfying only his own desires and disregarding her own, gross neglect was established. Harris v. Harris (Franklin 1950) 107 N.E.2d 226, 62 Ohio Law Abs. 249.

"In-law trouble" does not constitute gross neglect of duty so as to warrant granting divorce to complainant unless it so affects the conduct of one of the parties to the marriage as to cause said party to commit a breach of duty toward the other. Miller v. Miller (Franklin 1949) 91 N.E.2d 804, 56 Ohio Law Abs. 280.

Gross neglect of duty is any neglect which is gross, be it one instance or frequent instances. Whether the neglect complained of in a particular case was gross can only be determined from the surrounding circumstances. Faust v Faust, 30 LR 67 (1929).

Breach of pre-nuptial agreement to renounce one's religious faith in consideration of marriage cannot be considered gross neglect of duty, in view of the constitutional provision which guarantees every person the right to worship God as he sees fit. Apple v Apple, 28 NP(NS) 620 (1931).

8. —Imprisonment, grounds for divorce

Imprisonment in the Ohio reformatory at Mansfield or in any other state prison constitutes imprisonment "in a penitentiary" within this section, provided a petition therefor is filed during such imprisonment. Bowers v. Bowers (Ohio 1926) 114 Ohio St. 568, 151 N.E. 750, 4 Ohio Law Abs. 275, 24 Ohio Law Rep. 373.

A wife who has been granted a divorce on the ground of husband's imprisonment in the penitentiary, and thereafter marries him during the term of his sentence, is not entitled to another divorce on the ground of his imprisonment under the same sentence, even though her second marriage to him occurred during the time he was out of the penitentiary on parole, which was subsequently revoked. Miller v Miller, 19 App 518, 4 Abs 108 (1926).

Imprisonment is grounds for divorce under RC 3105.01(I), and as such a trial court does not err in considering the imprisonment of a party to divorce in dividing marital property; thus, an award of all the marital assets, and all the marital debt which exceed the value of the marital assets to the nonincarcerated party to the divorce does not constitute an abuse of discretion. Becker v Becker, No. CA93-04-024, 1993 WL 358147 (12th Dist Ct App, Clermont, 9-13-93).

The fact that both parties to a marriage are incarcerated does not bar the granting of a divorce, and the plaintiff-wife is entitled to a divorce on the ground that her husband is incarcerated even though she is also incarcerated, both being on death row for aggravated murder. Wernert v. Wernert (Ohio Com.Pl. 1991) 61 Ohio Misc.2d 436, 579 N.E.2d 800.

9. —Foreign divorce, grounds for divorce

Where a ground for divorce has been established under RC 3105.01(J) by the plaintiff's testimony and the corroborating evidence of an in rem divorce decree obtained by the plaintiff's spouse in a foreign nation, the court of common pleas has power to award plaintiff alimony in an action for divorce. Rousculp v. Rousculp (Franklin 1968) 17 Ohio App.2d 101, 244 N.E.2d 512, 46 O.O.2d 125.

Where a husband obtains a divorce from a court of a foreign nation which did not have personal jurisdiction of the wife, the court of common pleas has jurisdiction to grant a divorce and alimony to the wife in an action for divorce under RC 3105.01(J). Rousculp v. Rousculp (Franklin 1968) 17 Ohio App.2d 101, 244 N.E.2d 512, 46 O.O.2d 125.

Validity of foreign divorce is to be determined by laws of country in which divorce was obtained, and which at that time had jurisdiction over the parties, unless the law of said foreign domicile offends some positive law of this state. Machransky v. Machransky (Cuyahoga 1927) 31 Ohio App. 482, 166 N.E. 423, 6 Ohio Law Abs. 315.

The trial court erred in dismissing the plaintiff-appellant's complaint for divorce on the grounds that a valid divorce had been granted to the defendant-appellee in a foreign state, because RC 3105.01(J) grants Ohio sufficient minimum contacts to establish in personam jurisdiction over the parties in this case to determine custody; although an Ohio divorce decree cannot be inconsistent with a divorce decree of a foreign state, Ohio can hear questions on the issue of custody, as the foreign court had insufficient minimum contact with the plaintiff-appellant to adjudicate her custody rights over the child. Peterson v Peterson, No. 80AP-667 (10th Dist Ct App, Franklin, 2-3-81).

The court will entertain a complaint for alimony where the defendant obtained a foreign divorce and where the court granting the divorce had no personal jurisdiction of the plaintiff of this alimony action. Linck v. Linck (Ohio Com.Pl. 1972) 31 Ohio Misc. 224, 288 N.E.2d 347, 60 O.O.2d 388.

10. —Living separate and apart, grounds for divorce

As grounds for divorce, living apart for a year is a "no-fault" divorce remedy, against which traditional fault-oriented defenses are unavailing. Mahle v. Mahle (Franklin 1985) 27 Ohio App.3d 326, 500 N.E.2d 907, 27 O.B.R. 383.

That the grant of a divorce will adversely affect one spouse's claim to the other's retirement benefits is not equitable grounds for denying a divorce sought on the basis that the parties have lived separately for a year. Mahle v. Mahle (Franklin 1985) 27 Ohio App.3d 326, 500 N.E.2d 907, 27 O.B.R. 383.

A spouse's conduct is not voluntary, and therefore does not constitute "living separate and apart without cohabitation" within the meaning of RC 3105.01(K), where the spouse: (1) suffers a stroke; (2) enters a hospital for treatment; (3) transfers to a nursing home or health center; and (4) consequently fails to return to the marital home for more than two years. Dailey v. Dailey (Montgomery 1983) 11 Ohio App.3d 121, 463 N.E.2d 427, 11 O.B.R. 176.

Where defendant had been confined to a nursing home for two years, such confinement is not grounds for divorce on the basis of separation since such separation must be voluntary. Dailey v. Dailey (Montgomery 1983) 11 Ohio App.3d 121, 463 N.E.2d 427, 11 O.B.R. 176.

The term "cohabitation," as used in RC 3105.01(K), requires that the parties function as husband and wife sexually, or otherwise, with some regularity, which requirement is not met where the parties engaged in sexual intercourse once during the one-year period. Prather v. Prather (Brown 1983) 9 Ohio App.3d 199, 459 N.E.2d 234, 9 O.B.R. 311.

Since living separately for an extended period of time is a separate ground for divorce, one spouse's refusal to resume cohabitation with the other spouse who had shortly before voluntarily left the family residence does not require a finding either of gross neglect of duty or extreme cruelty. Walters v. Walters (Franklin 1982) 4 Ohio App.3d 162, 446 N.E.2d 1173, 4 O.B.R. 256.

The granting of a divorce under RC 3105.01(K) is within the discretion of the trial judge; thus, where suit is brought by the guardian of a ward previously adjudged incompetent and the suit is opposed by the ward's spouse on the ground that her husband can communicate and does not want the divorce, a divorce will not be granted automatically upon proof of two or more years of physical separation between the parties without cohabitation; the court must first determine whether the ward is competent to testify and what his intentions are regarding the divorce. Boyd v. Edwards (Cuyahoga 1982) 4 Ohio App.3d 142, 446 N.E.2d 1151, 4 O.B.R. 234.

Where a husband and wife reside in separate structures on the same premises with regular visits by one for the sole purpose of helping the other in carrying out household chores, the conduct of the parties does not constitute "living separate and apart without cohabitation" within the meaning of RC 3105.01(K). Bennington v. Bennington (Franklin 1978) 56 Ohio App.2d 201, 381 N.E.2d 1355, 10 O.O.3d 201.

The phrase "continuously confined in a mental institution" as used in RC 3105.01(K) is to be construed to mean that where a person is committed to a mental institution, pursuant to RC Ch 5122, such confinement continues until a person is granted a discharge under RC 5122.21. O'Dell v. O'Dell (Scioto 1977) 55 Ohio App.2d 149, 380 N.E.2d 723, 9 O.O.3d 296.

RC 3105.01(K), effective May 7, 1974, allowing for divorce upon a finding that the husband and wife have, without interruption for two years, lived separate and apart without cohabitation is to be applied retroactively, allowing a party to obtain a divorce for a period of separation occurring prior to the effective date of the statute. Cassaro v. Cassaro (Cuyahoga 1976) 50 Ohio App.2d 368, 363 N.E.2d 753, 4 O.O.3d 320.

The parties' "on again, off again" relationship which consists of (1) intermittent sex, (2) meetings in public bars, and (3) phone calls does not constitute "interruption" in the parties having lived separate and apart without cohabitation for the one year preceding the filing for divorce. Smith v Smith, No. L-96-331, 1997 WL 586707 (6th Dist Ct App, Lucas, 9-19-97).

The guardian of an incompetent ward may amend a divorce complaint to include as grounds living separate and apart for one year, RC 3105.01(K), where the divorce action was pending prior to the ward's incompetence and the ward had vacated the marital home prior to his incompetence; under such circumstances, a divorce may properly be granted on the ground of living separate and apart for one year. Heskett v Heskett, No. 91-CA-05, (2d Dist Ct App, Champaign, 11-25-91).

The one-year period prescribed by RC 3105.01(K) does not begin to run until at least one party voluntarily desires the separation. Coreano v Coreano, No. 47422 (8th Dist Ct App, Cuyahoga, 4-19-84).

An intent to abandon the marital relationship must be established to achieve the separation contemplated by RC 3105.01(K); an incompetent placed in a nursing home by her spouse is incapable of manifesting the requisite intent. Laube v Laube, No. 5-80-3 (3d Dist Ct App, Hancock, 6-17-80).

11. —Adultery, grounds for divorce

Although homosexuality is not specifically enumerated as one of the grounds for divorce under RC 3105.01, homosexuality may constitute extreme cruelty or adultery to the other spouse, thereby furnishing grounds for divorce; thus, a defamation action based on allegations of homosexuality within divorce pleadings must fail, since such allegations, bearing a reasonable relationship to the divorce action, are absolutely privileged. Bales v. Hack (Clark 1986) 31 Ohio App.3d 111, 509 N.E.2d 95, 31 O.B.R. 197.

When a complaint for divorce was filed alleging gross neglect of duty and extreme cruelty, with evidence relative to adultery being admitted without objection, court did not err in granting divorce on ground of adultery. Moser v. Moser (Lorain 1982) 5 Ohio App.3d 193, 450 N.E.2d 741, 5 O.B.R. 427.

12. Procedure

Former husband's filing of numerous original actions challenging the same rulings by judge in his divorce case resulted in abuse of in forma pauperis status, and justified order by Court of Appeals denying husband in forma pauperis status for all future original actions in that Court relating to divorce. State ex rel. Forsyth v. Brigner (Ohio 0000) 86 Ohio St.3d 585, 715 N.E.2d 1164.

Neither the existence of adequate legal remedy for trial court's allegedly erroneous exercise of jurisdiction to vacate dismissal of divorce complaint and enter judgment therein, nor absence of any indication that successor judge was about to exercise jurisdiction to enforce judgment so entered, automatically precluded issuance of writ of prohibition against successor judge's enforcement of judgment. McAuley v. Smith (Ohio 1998) 82 Ohio St.3d 393, 696 N.E.2d 572, on remand.

Complaint seeking writ of prohibition against trial court's enforcement of judgment of divorce alleged set of facts consistent with requested relief; complaint alleged that trial court unconditionally dismissed action for failure of proof, that appeal from dismissal was pending at time trial court reinstated action, that vacation of earlier dismissal was based upon motion for reconsideration, and that trial court therefore patently and unambiguously lacked jurisdiction to reinstate and decide action. McAuley v. Smith (Ohio 1998) 82 Ohio St.3d 393, 696 N.E.2d 572, on remand.

Prohibition would not lie to bar husband from proceeding with divorce action on ground of two year separation where court had entered decree for alimony, support and custody in an earlier action by him in which appeal was pending. State ex rel. Heimann v. George (Ohio 1976) 45 Ohio St.2d 231, 344 N.E.2d 130, 74 O.O.2d 376.

A petition in a divorce action, which alleges bare statutory grounds for divorce without stating in clear and concise language the facts which if proved will sustain such allegations, is subject to a motion to make definite and certain but not to a demurrer. Dansby v. Dansby (Ohio 1956) 165 Ohio St. 112, 133 N.E.2d 358, 59 O.O. 129.

An action for divorce, though more than one statutory cause be relied upon, constitutes a single cause of action; operative facts alleged may support more than one of the causes relied upon and the allegations need not be classified under the respective causes. Arnold v. Arnold (Ohio 1924) 110 Ohio St. 416, 144 N.E. 261, 2 Ohio Law Abs. 374, 22 Ohio Law Rep. 159.

Summary judgment in divorce action fixing de facto date of dissolution of marriage was final order for purposes of determining appellate jurisdiction of Court of Appeals, as judgment affected wife's right under antenuptial agreement to receive payment of $20,000 from husband, which right qualified as substantial right. Langer v. Langer (Ohio App. 2 Dist. 1997) 123 Ohio App.3d 348, 704 N.E.2d 275, cause dismissed 80 Ohio St.3d 1473, 687 N.E.2d 470.

Divorce action was properly dismissed upon death of wife, where no evidence had been heard and no facts had been adjudicated prior to her death. Driggers v. Driggers (Ohio App. 11 Dist. 1996) 115 Ohio App.3d 229, 685 N.E.2d 252.

Any error by trial court in issuing, and then vacating, amended judgment entry after wife appealed original judgment of divorce was outside appellate court's jurisdiction. Mayer v. Mayer (Allen 1996) 110 Ohio App.3d

233, 673 N.E.2d 981, dismissed, appeal not allowed 77 Ohio St.3d 1413, 670 N.E.2d 1002.

Wife was sufficiently competent to participate in divorce proceedings, though she claimed to be on prescribed medications which impaired her full participation and limited her testimonial capacity, where transcript of proceedings indicated that wife's answers were lucid and responsive. Mayer v. Mayer (Allen 1996) 110 Ohio App.3d 233, 673 N.E.2d 981, dismissed, appeal not allowed 77 Ohio St.3d 1413, 670 N.E.2d 1002.

No authority permitted Child Support Enforcement Agency (CSEA) to be a party to divorce decree and consequently, divorce decree was not void and could not be vacated on ground that CSEA had not been named a party at time the action was filed or notified of the proceedings, despite fact that decree was structured in such a way that it permitted mother to receive financial support from both father and the state, by virtue of Aid to Dependent Children (ADC) benefits, in excess of that allowable under the statutory guidelines. Starr v. Starr (Cuyahoga 1996) 109 Ohio App.3d 116, 671 N.E.2d 1097.

Action for divorce abates and cannot be revived if one of the parties thereto dies. Diemer v. Diemer (Cuyahoga 1994) 99 Ohio App.3d 54, 649 N.E.2d 1285.

A separation agreement entered into for the sole purpose of a dissolution of marriage is not a valid and binding contract when the dissolution petition is dismissed, but would be a valid and binding contract following dismissal of such petition if it contains language that the agreement shall be binding whether used in a divorce, alimony only, or a dissolution of marriage action, or such similar language evidencing the intent of the parties that it will survive dismissal of a dissolution of marriage petition, and in addition, if it does not contain express language that it was entered into solely for a dissolution of marriage action or express language that the parties intended the separation agreement to survive dismissal of a dissolution of marriage petition, but the actions and conduct of the parties evidence an intention that it will survive dismissal of a dissolution of marriage petition, the separation agreement will continue to be a valid and binding agreement after the dissolution of marriage petition is dismissed. Greiner v. Greiner (Cuyahoga 1979) 61 Ohio App.2d 88, 399 N.E.2d 571, 15 O.O.3d 95.

In an uncontested divorce proceeding in which there is proof of desertion by defendant husband, trial court has discretionary authority to grant divorce decree to plaintiff wife after considering all appropriate factors including best interests of community and welfare of children without raising defenses not pleaded concerning misconduct of the plaintiff wife subsequent to desertion, and consequently mothers of illegitimate children are not automatically ineligible to divorce husbands who previously deserted them. Newell v. Newell (Stark 1970) 23 Ohio App.2d 149, 261 N.E.2d 278, 52 O.O.2d 178.

Where, in a divorce action in which the grounds alleged for divorce are gross neglect, extreme cruelty and habitual drunkenness, the trial court finds for plaintiff on the ground of gross neglect of duty and makes no separate findings on the other grounds alleged and grants a divorce to plaintiff, and where the court of appeals, on appeal from such judgment, finds that such finding and judgment "is manifestly against the weight of the evidence" and reverses such decree and remands the cause "for retrial, or further proceedings according to law," such trial court may not, solely on the evidence adduced at the original trial and without rehearing any of the evidence, find for plaintiff on the additional grounds of extreme cruelty and habitual drunkenness and enter judgment granting a divorce thereon. Miller v. Miller (Lucas 1960) 114 Ohio App. 234, 181 N.E.2d 282, 19 O.O.2d 108.

Where, upon trial of an action for divorce on the alleged grounds of gross neglect of duty and extreme cruelty, it is brought to the attention of the court that the plaintiff had been previously married, it is error for the court to require plaintiff to prove the legal dissolution of his former marriage before being permitted to offer proof of the allegations in his petition. Treadway v. Treadway (Hamilton 1954) 97 Ohio App. 248, 125 N.E.2d 552, 56 O.O. 35.

A plaintiff in a divorce action is not prejudiced by a court basing the decree for divorce upon one ground only where further grounds are alleged in the petition, the decree being as effectual when based upon one ground as when additional grounds are assigned. (See also Rahn v Rahn, 18 Abs 228 (App, Darke 1934).) Rahn v. Rahn (Darke 1933) 48 Ohio App. 179, 192 N.E. 798, 16 Ohio Law Abs. 169, 1 O.O. 173, motion denied 18 Ohio Law Abs. 228.

The dismissal of a petition for divorce, following a hearing on the merits, in a case where the court had jurisdiction of the persons and subject matter, is a bar to future proceedings in an action in any court, where based on grounds alleged in the petition in the former case or which were known to exist by the plaintiff at the time of filing the first petition. Lewshitz v. Lewshitz (Cuyahoga 1929) 35 Ohio App. 189, 172 N.E. 413, 8 Ohio Law Abs. 232, 31 Ohio Law Rep. 360.

Decree cannot be forced upon defendant not praying for divorce or alimony. Wickham v. Wickham (Lucas 1930) 35 Ohio App. 142, 171 N.E. 864, 8 Ohio Law Abs. 284.

Divorce cannot be granted without evidence showing existence of one of statutory causes, nor upon unsupported testimony or admissions of one party. Hanover v. Hanover (Lucas 1929) 34 Ohio App. 483, 171 N.E. 350.

Petition for divorce alleging statutory grounds of extreme cruelty and gross neglect of duty towards plaintiff stated cause of action, without necessity of pleading facts constituting grounds. Seibel v. Seibel (Hamilton 1927) 30 Ohio App. 198, 164 N.E. 648, 25 Ohio Law Rep. 231.

In a divorce proceeding, failure to object to transfer of the case to another judge constitutes waiver and therefore may not be asserted as error upon appeal. Overman v Overman, No. 44067 (8th Dist Ct App, Cuyahoga, 5-6-82).

In a trial for divorce on extreme cruelty, the trial court may admit evidence of an order to vacate the marital dwelling or evidence concerning the arrest for failure to vacate. Baishnab v Baishnab, No. 43308 (8th Dist Ct App, Cuyahoga, 11-5-81).

Where the parties to a divorce action are incarcerated, the trial may proceed by means of depositions in lieu of personal appearances at trial. Wernert v. Wernert (Ohio Com.Pl. 1991) 61 Ohio Misc.2d 436, 579 N.E.2d 800.

By adoption of the Ohio Rules of Civil Procedure, Ohio Supreme Court has reversed its holding in case of Dansby v Dansby, 165 OS 112 (1956). Carter v. Carter (Ohio Com.Pl. 1970) 24 Ohio Misc. 138, 263 N.E.2d 695, 53 O.O.2d 149.

Civ R 12(E) does not apply to divorce action when complaint sets forth statutory grounds. Carter v. Carter (Ohio Com.Pl. 1970) 24 Ohio Misc. 138, 263 N.E.2d 695, 53 O.O.2d 149.

A plaintiff may unite a cause of action for annulment and a cause of action for divorce in the same petition. Tyminski v. Tyminski (Ohio Com.Pl. 1966) 8 Ohio Misc. 202, 221 N.E.2d 486, 37 O.O.2d 263.

Trial court erred in granting divorce where there was no testimony warranting such relief. Sheldon v. Sheldon (Mahoning 1961) 192 N.E.2d 510, 91 Ohio Law Abs. 517, 27 O.O.2d 191.

If both a petition and a cross-petition filed respectively by a wife and husband plead sufficient facts to state a cause of action for divorce under the statutes, and such facts are established upon trial, the trial court may apply the rule of recrimination and dismiss both the petition and the cross-petition. Sandrene v. Sandrene (Summit 1952) 121 N.E.2d 324, 67 Ohio Law Abs. 481.

13. Insanity of defendant

The granting of a divorce under RC 3105.01(K) is within the discretion of the trial judge; thus, where suit is brought by the guardian of a ward previously adjudged incompetent and the suit is opposed by the ward's spouse on the ground that her husband can communicate and does not want the divorce, a divorce will not be granted automatically upon proof of two or more years of physical separation between the parties without cohabitation; the court must first determine whether the ward is competent to testify and what his intentions are regarding the divorce. Boyd v. Edwards (Cuyahoga 1982) 4 Ohio App.3d 142, 446 N.E.2d 1151, 4 O.B.R. 234.

The phrase "continuously confined in a mental institution" as used in RC 3105.01(K) is to be construed to mean that where a person is committed to a mental institution, pursuant to RC Ch 5122, such confinement continues until a person is granted a discharge under RC 5122.21. O'Dell v. O'Dell (Scioto 1977) 55 Ohio App.2d 149, 380 N.E.2d 723, 9 O.O.3d 296.

The court will not grant a divorce where the acts of the party charged were due to lack of mental capacity, even if such acts, if committed by a person of sound mind, would justify a divorce; the existence of such lack of mental capacity is for the determination of the court or the trier of the facts; and an adjudication of mental incompetence is not a prerequisite to the presenting of the question whether such lack of mental capacity existed. Nelson v. Nelson (Cuyahoga 1958) 108 Ohio App. 365, 154 N.E.2d 653, 79 Ohio Law Abs. 602, 9 O.O.2d 318.

Divorce may be granted against insane person, but only for acts committed while sane. Heim v. Heim (Lucas 1930) 35 Ohio App. 408, 172 N.E. 451, 8 Ohio Law Abs. 166.

Alleged acts of cruelty committed by wife while she was insane and did not understand what she was doing are not cause for divorce. Heim v. Heim (Lucas 1930) 35 Ohio App. 408, 172 N.E. 451, 8 Ohio Law Abs. 166.

"Extreme cruelty," which is ground for divorce, means voluntary or intentional extreme cruelty, and cannot be committed by a lunatic who does not understand the nature of her acts. Heim v. Heim (Lucas 1930) 35 Ohio App. 408, 172 N.E. 451, 8 Ohio Law Abs. 166.

Granting a divorce from an insane woman and divesting her of all interest in her husband's property based on testimony as to trivial matters antedating her insanity is grounds for reversal. McMichael v McMichael, 27 LR 142 (1928).

A decree of divorce may be entered against an insane defendant for aggressions prior to the insanity. Benton v. Benton (Ohio Cir. 1909) 26 Ohio C.D. 613, 16 Ohio C.C.(N.S.) 121.

A divorce granted for fraud in the marriage contract in concealing defendant's congenital insanity from the plaintiff is not void because the act was committed while insane, for if the defendant was insane when he committed the fraud, the marriage is void. Benton v. Benton (Ohio Cir. 1909) 26 Ohio C.D. 613, 16 Ohio C.C.(N.S.) 121.

A petition states sufficient grounds for a decree against an insane defendant, where habitual drunkenness and extreme cruelty are charged as continuing for more than three years prior to the adjudication of the defendant as insane and his commitment to an asylum. Wolcott v. Wolcott (Ohio Cir. 1911) 22 Ohio C.D. 587, 14 Ohio C.C.(N.S.) 437.

Appeal, but not error, lies to an order vacating the appointment of a trustee for an insane defendant in a divorce proceeding and dismissing, without hearing on the merits, a petition which charges statutory grounds for divorce which accrued prior to the adjudging of the defendant as insane. Wolcott v. Wolcott (Ohio Cir. 1911) 22 Ohio C.D. 587, 14 Ohio C.C.(N.S.) 437.

The marriage of an insane husband or wife who has given no cause for divorce and who has become mentally incapacitated since the marriage, cannot be dissolved. Prather v. Prather (Ohio Com.Pl. 1934) 4 Ohio Supp. 243, 33 Ohio Law Abs. 336, 1 O.O. 188.

14. —Incompatibility, not grounds for divorce

Incompatibility under RC 3105.01(K) is not a "ground" that has to be proven so much as a status that must be agreed on by both parties; it is a consensual ground that is not intended to be litigated and thus a wife is not entitled to a divorce on the grounds of incompatibility where her husband testifies at trial that he does not want the parties' marriage to be terminated and still loves her; the wife's testimony that the parties are incompatible amounts to nothing more than a unilateral declaration of a consensual divorce ground that was not intended to be litigated. Lehman v. Lehman (Hocking 1991) 72 Ohio App.3d 68, 593 N.E.2d 447.

A judgment granting a divorce on the ground of gross neglect of duty will be reversed on appeal where the record presents only evidence of incompatibility. Kennedy v. Kennedy (Clermont 1959) 111 Ohio App. 432, 165 N.E.2d 454, 12 O.O.2d 201.

An action for divorce by husband upon the ground that the wife was employed in a gainful occupation aside from her household duties and thereby failed in her duty to make a home for the husband, in which the evidence shows that, by such employment, the wife helped maintain the financial stability of the parties, that the husband's job required him to travel and he was inconvenienced by his wife's working only over small periods of time, that the wife did not remain employed against his express wish, and that she, as a result of working, had become irritable and petulant, presents a question of incompatibility, which is not a ground of divorce in Ohio. Winnard v. Winnard (Franklin 1939) 62 Ohio App. 351, 23 N.E.2d 977, 16 O.O. 51.

The grounds for divorce in Ohio are purely statutory, and a decree should never be granted for incompatibility, disappointment in social and financial aspirations, to satisfy a mere desire to obtain freedom, or for other reasons not statutory. Burke v. Burke (Lucas 1930) 36 Ohio App. 551, 173 N.E. 637, 8 Ohio Law Abs. 682, 33 Ohio Law Rep. 115.

15. Defenses

As grounds for divorce, living apart for a year is a "no-fault" divorce remedy, against which traditional fault-oriented defenses are unavailing. Mahle v. Mahle (Franklin 1985) 27 Ohio App.3d 326, 500 N.E.2d 907, 27 O.B.R. 383.

That the grant of a divorce will adversely affect one spouse's claim to the other's retirement benefits is not equitable grounds for denying a divorce sought on the basis that the parties have lived separately for a year. Mahle v. Mahle (Franklin 1985) 27 Ohio App.3d 326, 500 N.E.2d 907, 27 O.B.R. 383.

In Ohio, a cause of divorce is not barred by lapse of time; and the court will not invade the province of the legislature, and decree a limitation to such a cause, nor will it apply an equitable principle of estoppel, in limitation, where there is no evidence of collusion or condonation. Stark v. Stark (Ohio Com.Pl. 1929) 28 Ohio N.P.N.S. 36, 8 Ohio Law Abs. 287.

Under Ohio doctrine of res judicata or claim preclusion, stipulation of parties to divorce proceeding as to date when marriage ended did not manifest express authority by husband for wife to later raise other claims arising from same subject matter. Shelar v. Shelar (N.D.Ohio 1995) 910 F.Supp. 1307.

16. Federal involvement

The domestic relations exception to federal jurisdiction applies only where a plaintiff positively sues in federal court for divorce, alimony, or child custody. Catz v. Chalker (C.A.6 (Ohio) 1998) 142 F.3d 279.

Former husband's federal action against his former wife, seeking declaration that state divorce decree was void as a violation of due process, was not a core domestic relations case to which domestic relations exception to federal jurisdiction applied; action did not seek declaration of marital or parental status, but instead presented a constitutional claim in which it was incidental that the underlying action involved a divorce. Catz v. Chalker (C.A.6 (Ohio) 1998) 142 F.3d 279.

17. —Living separate and apart involuntarily or under one year, not grounds for divorce

Where defendant had been confined to a nursing home for two years, such confinement is not grounds for divorce on the basis of separation since such separation must be voluntary. Dailey v. Dailey (Montgomery 1983) 11 Ohio App.3d 121, 463 N.E.2d 427, 11 O.B.R. 176.

Where the wife has never intended to sever the marital relationship but has been the helpless victim of disease and temporarily placed out of her residence by the husband for treatment in a nursing home in furtherance of his duty of support, the legislature did not intend that the husband could, by that act, create his own grounds to terminate the marriage. Laube v Laube, No. 5-80-3 (3d Dist Ct App, Hancock, 6-17-80).

The mere fact that husband and wife have separated and intend never to live together again is not a ground for divorce. Apple v Apple, 28 NP(NS) 620 (1931).

18. —Psychological problems, not grounds for divorce

"Chronic dementia" of other spouse is not ground for divorce. Larrick v. Walters (Noble 1930) 39 Ohio App. 363, 177 N.E. 642, 10 Ohio Law Abs. 508.

19. —Irreconcilable estrangement, not grounds for divorce

A divorce cannot be granted in Ohio solely on ground that parties are irreconcilably estranged. Benedict v Benedict, 45 Abs 243 (CP, Delaware 1946).

20. —Refusal of relations, not grounds for divorce

A wife's denial of sexual relations is not per se grounds for divorce where the denial is not absolute and is justified by her suspicions of infidelity on the part of her husband. Moser v. Moser (Allen 1991) 72 Ohio App.3d 575, 595 N.E.2d 518.

21. —Unnatural relations, not grounds for divorce

Abnormal or unnatural sexual acts at the request of the spouse not against the complaining party's will and not shown to be detrimental to her mental or physical health do not constitute a ground for divorce. Johnston v. Johnston (Ohio Com.Pl. 1957) 143 N.E.2d 498, 76 Ohio Law Abs. 29.

3105.011 Equitable powers in domestic relations matters

The court of common pleas including divisions of courts of domestic relations, has full equitable powers and jurisdiction appropriate to the determination of all domestic relations matters. This section is not a determination by the general assembly that such equitable powers and jurisdiction do not exist with respect to any such matter.

(1975 H 370, eff. 8-1-75)

Cross References

Common pleas court, division of domestic relations, 2301.03

Courts of common pleas, powers under constitution, O Const Art IV §1, §4

Divorce action involving custody or care of children, jurisdiction of juvenile court, 2151.23

Library References

Divorce ⟜6, 200, 249.1, 289.

WESTLAW Topic No. 134.

C.J.S. Divorce §§ 5, 10, 15, 97, 98, 312, 314, 508 to 511, 611, 612.

OJur 3d: 46, Family Law § 549, 561

Am Jur 2d: 24, Divorce and Separation § 877

Sowald & Morganstern, Baldwin's Ohio Practice, *Domestic Relations Law* § 2.68, 7.17, 7.18, 7.23, 7.26, 9.35, 12.1, 13.2, 20.32, 27.5, 31.3 (1997)

Law Review and Journal Commentaries

Alimony: Adjudicated Pursuant to Statute or by Judicial Legislation?, Howard S. Lutz. 53 Ohio St B Ass'n Rep 321 (March 3, 1980).

Attorney Fee Awards in Domestic Relations, Hon. V. Michael Brigner. 46 Dayton B Briefs 13 (January 1997).

Attorney Fee Awards in Domestic Relations Court, Hon. Mike Brigner. 9 Domestic Rel J Ohio 1 (January/ February 1997).

Bankruptcy Reform Act of 1994—What the Bankruptcy Code Giveth, Domestic Relations Courts (and Congress) Taketh Away, C.R. "Chip" Bowles. 8 Domestic Rel J Ohio 17 (March/April 1996).

Emergency Custody in Domestic Relations Court: A Proposed Procedural and Substantive Litmus Test, Hon. V. Michael Brigner. 49 Dayton B Briefs 19 (December 1999).

Nothing to Lose But Their Chains: A Survey of the Aguna Problem in American Law, Debbie Eis Sreter. 28 J Fam L 703 (1989-90).

Parents, partners and personal jurisdiction, Rhonda Wasserman. 1995 U Ill L Rev 813.

Notes of Decisions and Opinions

---

1. Jurisdiction

Common pleas court lacked jurisdiction to proceed in divorce action in which it did not decide any issues prior to death of husband, and husband's death occurred prior to scheduled commencement of trial. State ex rel. Litty v. Leskovyansky (Ohio 1996) 77 Ohio St.3d 97, 671 N.E.2d 236.

The subject matter jurisdiction of a trial court to award permanent alimony and to formulate an equitable division of the marital assets commences when either party files a complaint for divorce and a division of the marital property. Bolinger v. Bolinger (Ohio 1990) 49 Ohio St.3d 120, 551 N.E.2d 157.

When case is not primarily of domestic relations nature, it should originally be brought in general division of court of common pleas or assigned by judge thereof. In re Dunn (Clinton 1995) 101 Ohio App.3d 1, 654 N.E.2d 1303.

Domestic relations division of court of common pleas had jurisdiction to determine whether agreement between former husband and wife which purported to modify provisions of marital dissolution agreement regarding child support but which had never been submitted to or approved by court was enforceable contract during action in which wife sought to enforce agreement, even though action sounded in contract, as action was primarily domestic relations matter. In re Dunn (Clinton 1995) 101 Ohio App.3d 1, 654 N.E.2d 1303.

Following wife's death after she filed divorce petition, enforcement of antenuptial agreement fell within jurisdiction of probate division, not domestic relations division, as interpretation and enforcement of the agreement was not a "matter." Diemer v. Diemer (Cuyahoga 1994) 99 Ohio App.3d 54, 649 N.E.2d 1285.

Domestic relations division has plenary jurisdiction to determine equitable division of property between the spouses but that jurisdiction is present only during proceedings for divorce or legal separation and, in the absence of such proceedings, court lacks jurisdiction to distribute property between spouses thus to enforce antenuptial agreement. Diemer v. Diemer (Cuyahoga 1994) 99 Ohio App.3d 54, 649 N.E.2d 1285.

Upon party's filing complaint for legal separation in proper venue, trial court has jurisdiction over parties' assets to determine what constitutes marital property and separate property and how property should be divided between parties. Leathem v. Leathem (Hancock 1994) 94 Ohio App.3d 470, 640 N.E.2d 1210, stay denied 70 Ohio St.3d 1433, 638 N.E.2d 583, dismissed, appeal not allowed 70 Ohio St.3d 1454, 639 N.E.2d 793.

By both statute and common law, Ohio domestic relations courts have and may exercise authority according to established rules of equity. Miller v. Miller (Erie 1993) 92 Ohio App.3d 340, 635 N.E.2d 384, motion overruled 69 Ohio St.3d 1424, 631 N.E.2d 164.

Subject matter jurisdiction of trial court to formulate equitable division of marital assets commences when either party files complaint for divorce and division of marital property. Gibson v. Gibson (Scioto 1993) 87 Ohio App.3d 426, 622 N.E.2d 425.

Although Illinois courts had jurisdiction to entertain husband's divorce action based on his domicile, court nevertheless had to serve wife, who lived out of state, properly with notice of proceeding in order to exercise jurisdiction over her. Johnson v. Johnson (Greene 1993) 86 Ohio App.3d 433, 621 N.E.2d 530.

A domestic relations court has jurisdiction to consider the request of a man who was granted an out-of-state divorce for a temporary restraining order preventing his Ohio employer from withholding part of his pay in response to the other state's support order. Kass v. Cleveland Metro. Gen. Hosp. (Cuyahoga 1989) 65 Ohio App.3d 264, 583 N.E.2d 1012.

Ohio domestic relations court had jurisdiction to consider propriety of representative payee's expenditure of Social Security Administration funds received on behalf of child whose father was disabled; Social Security Administration had no interest in funds once they were paid, and state court jurisdiction was not precluded by statute or nature of particular case. Catlett v. Catlett (Clermont 1988) 55 Ohio App.3d 1, 561 N.E.2d 948, motion overruled 39 Ohio St.3d 730, 534 N.E.2d 357.

A domestic relations court lacks jurisdiction over joint financial ventures of a divorced couple cohabitating as unmarried individuals. Fields v. Fields (Montgomery 1987) 39 Ohio App.3d 187, 530 N.E.2d 933.

In a divorce proceeding involving a spouse for whom a guardian has been appointed by a probate court, the domestic relations court should not order one party to pay the expenses of the guardian as part of its divorce decree, since the guardianship is an issue before the probate court. Caudill v. Caudill (Franklin 1986) 29 Ohio App.3d 51, 502 N.E.2d 703, 29 O.B.R. 53.

After a divorce action has reached final judgment in a domestic relations court, exclusive jurisdiction of the court ends, and a common pleas court, general division, shares concurrent jurisdiction to vacate that judgment. Price v. Price (Cuyahoga 1984) 16 Ohio App.3d 93, 474 N.E.2d 662, 16 O.B.R. 98.

Pursuant to RC 3105.011 and 3105.03, there is no minimum period of domicile as a prerequisite to an action for alimony brought pursuant to RC 3105.17. Gieg v. Gieg (Trumbull 1984) 16 Ohio App.3d 51, 474 N.E.2d 626, 16 O.B.R. 55.

Actions for divorce, alimony, custody, etc., were not known at common law and are purely statutory in nature; the court has no greater jurisdiction or power than is given by statute; the repeal of RC 3105.20 by the legislature divests the domestic relations courts of equity jurisdiction to make divisions of property; accordingly, the trial court is without authority to make a division of property unless it is pursuant to an alimony award under RC 3105.18. (Annotation from former RC 3105.20.) Soyk v. Soyk (Summit 1975) 45 Ohio App.2d 319, 345 N.E.2d 461, 74 O.O.2d 532.

Where the husband in a divorce action dies before the assets have been distributed or the final decree entered, (1) the action abates and the trial court lacks jurisdiction to enter any orders subsequent to his death, (2) restraining orders against the husband are extinguished, and (3) decedent's transfer of his life insurance benefits to his sister is not in violation of the trial court's restraining order prohibiting the husband from transferring or disposing of assets. Ondak v Ondak, No. 74022, 1999 WL 179477 (8th Dist Ct App, Cuyahoga, 4-1-99).

A party in a divorce action is barred by res judicata and collateral estoppel from contesting in an Ohio court whether he was served with process during the divorce proceedings where this same issue has been litigated by a Michigan court when it denied the husband's motion to dismiss the divorce action. Winkler v Stowe, No. 95-CA-763, 1997 WL 30947 (4th Dist Ct App, Jackson, 1-21-97).

The domestic relations court has subject matter jurisdiction to determine a third party's interest in the deferred compensation fund of a person whose spouse seeks to attach the fund for an award of support. Zashin, Rich, Sutula & Monastra v Offenberg, No. 68951, 1995 WL 723345 (8th Dist Ct App, Cuyahoga, 12-7-95).

With respect to the division of domestic relations, "domestic relations matters" within the purview of RC 3105.011 does not encompass parties who are not married and cohabiting. Levy v Levy, No. 77AP-918 (10th Dist Ct App, Franklin, 5-2-78).

The principle of Barber v Barber, 21 How 582 (1859) that federal courts have no jurisdiction over suits for divorce, the allowance of alimony, or custody of children remains true and will not be cast aside after nearly a century and a half; however, a district court cannot refuse to exercise diversity jurisdiction over a tort action for damages such as one brought against a former husband and his girlfriend by the former wife based on alleged abuse of the former couple's children. Ankenbrandt v. Richards (U.S.La. 1992) 112 S.Ct. 2206, 504 U.S. 689, 119 L.Ed.2d 468, on remand 973 F.2d 923.

Under Ohio law, generally, domestic relations forum is not proper forum in which to litigate tort claim. Shelar v. Shelar (N.D.Ohio 1995) 910 F.Supp. 1307.

Divorced wife's removed suit for intentional infliction of emotional distress against her former husband, based upon his alleged conduct during pendency of their divorce proceeding, did not fall within domestic relation exception to diversity jurisdiction. Shelar v. Shelar (N.D.Ohio 1995) 910 F.Supp. 1307.

Federal diversity jurisdiction statute incorporates domestic relations exception, which divests federal courts of power to issue divorce, alimony, and child custody decrees. Shelar v. Shelar (N.D.Ohio 1995) 910 F.Supp. 1307.

Under Ohio law, commencement of divorce proceeding vests divorce court with jurisdiction over all property in which either spouse has interest, regardless of whether such property is separately titled. In re Greer (Bkrtcy.N.D.Ohio 1999) 242 B.R. 389.

2. Immunity

Where a capias is issued for a former husband on his former wife's affidavit and the former husband later brings an action under 42 USC 1983, the former wife is immune as not being a state actor and her attorneys are immune as not acting under color of state law. Kelly v. Whiting (Ohio 1985) 17 Ohio St.3d 91, 477 N.E.2d 1123, 17 O.B.R. 213, 17 O.B.R. 488, concurring opinion 17 Ohio St.3d 254, 479 N.E.2d 254, certiorari denied 106 S.Ct. 532, 474 U.S. 1008, 88 L.Ed.2d 463.

A domestic relations judge is authorized to issue a capias by RC 2705.02, 2705.03, and 3105.011 and is therefore immune to suit in a 42 USC 1983 action and a common law tort action. Kelly v. Whiting (Ohio 1985) 17 Ohio St.3d 91, 477 N.E.2d 1123, 17 O.B.R. 213, 17 O.B.R. 488, concurring opinion 17 Ohio St.3d 254, 479 N.E.2d 254, certiorari denied 106 S.Ct. 532, 474 U.S. 1008, 88 L.Ed.2d 463.

3. Antenuptial agreements

Antenuptial agreements which provide for division of property and contain provisions for sustenance alimony, if otherwise found to be valid, are not abrogated as to either party for marital misconduct arising out of the marriage. Gross v. Gross (Ohio 1984) 11 Ohio St.3d 99, 464 N.E.2d 500, 11 O.B.R. 400.

Where the provisions for maintenance within an antenuptial agreement are unconscionable and voidable by a wife, such provisions should be reviewed by a trial court and it should order alternate provisions. Gross v. Gross (Ohio 1984) 11 Ohio St.3d 99, 464 N.E.2d 500, 11 O.B.R. 400.

Statements by domestic relations court on dismissing wife's divorce petition due to her death which referred to content and interpretation of antenuptial agreement and stated that the court found no language that would give executor or estate any rights upon her death was not an adjudication on the merits and did not determine rights and liabilities of the parties. Diemer v. Diemer (Cuyahoga 1994) 99 Ohio App.3d 54, 649 N.E.2d 1285.

4. Authority

Order entered by domestic relations division which required former husband, who had filed numerous actions that had been found to be deemed meritless following entry of divorce decree, to obtain judge's approval before filing further pleadings with clerk of court, was not an abuse of discretion. State ex rel. Forsyth v. Brigner (Ohio 1999) 86 Ohio St.3d 71, 711 N.E.2d 684, reconsideration denied 86 Ohio St.3d 1468, 715 N.E.2d 569.

Former husband could not take advantage of any error in Court of Appeals' denial of his request for writ of prohibition based on his claim that original provisions of divorce decree were res judicata absent any allegation of change in circumstances, as former husband invited any such error by failing to raise res judicata claim before Court of Appeals and by affirmatively asserting that res judicata was inapplicable. State ex rel. Soukup v. Celebrezze (Ohio 1998) 83 Ohio St.3d 549, 700 N.E.2d 1278.

Common pleas court judge's dismissal of divorce action was not rendered a nullity, for purposes of determining whether court had authority to revive action, by affidavit of disqualification that was pending against him at time of dismissal; affidavit of disqualification did not divest judge of authority to act in administrative or ministerial capacity, and dismissal was ministerial decision which was required following death of husband which occurred prior to adjudication of issues. State ex rel. Litty v. Leskovyansky (Ohio 1996) 77 Ohio St.3d 97, 671 N.E.2d 236.

Common pleas court lacked authority, under its inherent authority to issue nunc pro tunc entry, to reinstate previously dismissed divorce action on ground that it had dismissed action without considering then-pending affidavit of disqualification; reinstatement decision did not reflect what court had actually decided in previous dismissal entry. State ex rel. Litty v. Leskovyansky (Ohio 1996) 77 Ohio St.3d 97, 671 N.E.2d 236.

Although filing of bankruptcy petition stays equitable distribution in divorce case of debtor's interest in marital assets, certain aspects of divorce case, such as dissolution of marriage and child custody issues, are not stayed. State ex rel. Miley v. Parrott (Ohio 1996) 77 Ohio St.3d 64, 671 N.E.2d 24.

Trial court was obligated to reactivate divorce case after bankruptcy court lifted automatic stay affecting Chapter 12 debtor-husband; order inactivating divorce case stated that case would stay inactive until judge "is advised in writing of the stay having been lifted," trial court was advised in writing that bankruptcy court had lifted stay for divorce case, trial court would not be subject to contempt for violating stay after bankruptcy court expressly modified and lifted stay, and divorce case would not be better resolved after conclusion of bankruptcy proceedings. State ex rel. Miley v. Parrott (Ohio 1996) 77 Ohio St.3d 64, 671 N.E.2d 24.

Automatic stay may be lifted or modified for cause. State ex rel. Miley v. Parrott (Ohio 1996) 77 Ohio St.3d 64, 671 N.E.2d 24.

Equity powers of trial court in division of divorcing parties' property do not confer upon that court authority to enter judgment for damages to vehicle titled in one spouse's name where it is neither authorized by domestic relations statute nor demanded by either party. Gibson v. Gibson (Scioto 1993) 87 Ohio App.3d 426, 622 N.E.2d 425.

A court may order a father to pay the professional fees of a mother's experts at a child support hearing to determine if the father should be responsible for medical bills of an emancipated epileptic child under RC 3105.011, so long as the award is not unreasonable, arbitrary, or unconscionable. Cooksey v. Cooksey (Erie 1988) 55 Ohio App.3d 135, 562 N.E.2d 934.

As a court of equity, a domestic relations court may exercise sound discretion and award expenses for lodging, meals, and transportation to a wife who came from Georgia to defend against a motion to reduce child support and to move the court to find the husband in contempt for falling behind in his payments. Harpole v. Harpole (Medina 1986) 27 Ohio App.3d 289, 500 N.E.2d 915, 27 O.B.R. 334.

Court of domestic relations may not issue postdecree temporary restraining order restraining person who has not been made party to action. Van Ho v. Van Ho (Seneca 1984) 17 Ohio App.3d 108, 477 N.E.2d 659, 17 O.B.R. 170.

Although a trial court has equity powers in determining division of property, such powers do not include the power to order a sale of realty which is neither authorized by statute nor demanded by a party. Morgan v. Morgan (Fayette 1984) 16 Ohio App.3d 136, 474 N.E.2d 1216, 16 O.B.R. 143.

A domestic relations court cannot issue an "equitable" order to change the terms of a separation agreement where no change in circumstances has been shown. Roth v Roth, No. F-94-024, 1995 WL 557350 (6th Dist Ct App, Fulton, 9-22-95).

A trial court may issue a restraining order against a husband's interest in his insurance policy, 401(k) plan and IRA to secure his spousal support obligation where the evidence indicates that upon being ordered to pay the support, husband would quit his job or move to Florida; the additional order that the husband maintain a life insurance policy with wife as beneficiary to secure husband's spousal support obligation is improper since the support obligation terminates upon death and the requirement would not secure payment of the support obligation, as husband would be required to be current on the premiums and in the event of an arrearage wife would have to survive husband in order to collect. Addy v Addy, No. 94APF03-421, 1994 WL 521225 (10th Dist Ct App, Franklin, 9-20-94).

The repeal of RC 3105.20, which allowed the court to act equitably in matters concerning "domestic relations," did not affect the court's power to make equitable orders in proceedings for divorce and alimony pursuant to RC 3105.18. (Annotation from former RC 3105.20.) Finnerty v Finnerty, No. 1081 (11th Dist Ct App, Geauga, 3-9-84).

A trial court may amend its divorce decree so as to meet the requirements of Internal Revenue Code §152(e)(2)(A)(i). Soinger v Soinger, No. CA976 (9th Dist Ct App, Medina, 10-29-80).

5. Spousal support

The exercise of the full equity powers and jurisdiction in an alimony or divorce action includes the authority to determine the rights of the parties to alimony and a division of property. (Annotation from former RC 3105.20.) Griste v. Griste (Ohio 1960) 171 Ohio St. 160, 167 N.E.2d 924, 12 O.O.2d 176.

In the exercise of its full equity powers and jurisdiction in a divorce action, the trial court is authorized to adjudicate a complete dissolution of the marriage relationship, including a determination of the rights of the parties to alimony and to a division of property. (Annotation from former RC 3105.20.) Clark v. Clark (Ohio 1956) 165 Ohio St. 457, 136 N.E.2d 52, 60 O.O. 115.

Trial court has wide discretion in making awards of spousal support. Graham v. Graham (Greene 1994) 98 Ohio App.3d 396, 648 N.E.2d 850.

RC 3105.011 and 3105.18 provide ample authority for the attachment of pension benefits to secure the payment of court-ordered alimony. Dayton v. Dayton (Union 1987) 40 Ohio App.3d 17, 531 N.E.2d 324.

A domestic relations court may in the exercise of its discretion utilize the "clean hands" doctrine to deny the payor's motion for modification of future sustenance alimony where the payor is found to be in willful contempt of the court's order to pay that sustenance alimony. Hayden v Hayden, No. 10316 (9th Dist Ct App, Summit, 12-9-81).

6. Division of property

If party in divorce action dies following decree determining property rights and granting divorce but prior to journalization of decree, action does not abate upon the party's death, and decree may be journalized by nunc pro tunc entry. State ex rel. Litty v. Leskovyansky (Ohio 1996) 77 Ohio St.3d 97, 671 N.E.2d 236.

Corporation owned and controlled by divorced husband was in privity with husband and shared such an identity of interest with him that trial court could have concluded that husband adequately represented corporation's legal rights during divorce proceedings and, thus, corporation was collaterally estopped by divorce decree from suing wife, as former employee and part-owner, for conversion and fraud where husband knew that wife had appropriated funds in corporation before entering into settlement with her, had access to all records necessary to discover full extent of any alleged missing funds during divorce proceedings, and had opportunity to structure settlement accordingly. Grant Fritzsche Ent., Inc. v. Fritzsche (Butler 1995) 107 Ohio App.3d 23, 667 N.E.2d 1004.

Trial court did not abuse its discretion in determining that any separate property that husband previously held in marital residence was transmuted into marital property after 50 years of marriage in which both spouses made significant long-term contributions to marriage and marital residence. Leathem v. Leathem (Hancock 1994) 94 Ohio App.3d 470, 640 N.E.2d 1210, stay denied 70 Ohio St.3d 1433, 638 N.E.2d 583, dismissed, appeal not allowed 70 Ohio St.3d 1454, 639 N.E.2d 793.

Trial court in divorce action should have considered damage done by wife to husband's vehicle in court's property division, rather than entering "judgment for damages," which was beyond its statutory authority. Gibson v. Gibson (Scioto 1993) 87 Ohio App.3d 426, 622 N.E.2d 425.

The trial court erred in ordering a husband to pay interest on one-half of an equity payment contained in a dissolution decree to his wife when the referee refused to hear evidence from the husband that the parties had agreed that no interest accrue; equity requires that this evidence be heard. Lehman v Lehman, No. 67483, 1995 WL 264556 (8th Dist Ct App, Cuyahoga, 5-4-95).

An ambiguous property settlement agreement wherein there was no meeting of the minds between counsel or the parties was rightly set aside by the trial court; however, the parties were prejudiced in that they tried their case without knowing whether the separation agreement would or would not be upheld, and the trial court erred in making a division of property and award of alimony with incomplete and inadequate evidence of the value of the marital estate, per RC 3105.18(B). Ovark v Ovark, No. 871 (11th Dist Ct App, Geauga, 12-22-80).

A separation agreement which was made a part of the court's decree will not be subsequently disturbed when the property settlement provided that the value of jointly held land was to be determined by a court appointed appraiser so that each party could claim one half the appraised value; after accepting the appraisal of the court appointed appraiser, the division of property will not be changed even though an offer higher than the appraised value was placed. Cirullo v Cirullo, No. 9741 (9th Dist Ct App, Summit, 10-8-80).

Ex-wife's motion to terminate debtor-husband's purchase option in marital property, on ground that debtor had not made payments required by terms of property settlement agreement, was not "related proceeding" over which bankruptcy court could exercise its "related to" jurisdiction. In re Rose (Bkrtcy.N.D.Ohio 1993) 151 B.R. 128.

7. Child support

Guardianship established for purpose of facilitating child support payments was valid pursuant to implicit authority granted to domestic relations court under statutes granting court equitable powers in domestic relations matters and authority to adjudicate matters in accordance with best interests of child. In re Guardianship of Derakhshan (Lake 1996) 110 Ohio App.3d 190, 673 N.E.2d 954.

Domestic relations court retained subject matter jurisdiction over portion of guardianship estate classified as prepaid child support, and judgment reducing child support arrearages to lump sum was within that court's statutory authority; judgment was issued within scope of court's continuing subject matter jurisdiction regarding child support, supplemental order establishing guardianship estate contained unambiguous language regarding continuing jurisdiction retained by court over funds denominated as prepaid child support and child support order was established before guardianship was established and while court had control over parties. In re Guardianship of Derakhshan (Lake 1996) 110 Ohio App.3d 190, 673 N.E.2d 954.

Absent support order payable through Child Support Enforcement Agency (CSEA), parties to divorce action can deliberately tailor their support obligations in such a way that obligee spouse can still collect public assistance. Starr v. Starr (Cuyahoga 1996) 109 Ohio App.3d 116, 671 N.E.2d 1097.

In accordance with public policy and the statutory grant of broad equitable powers, a domestic relations court may order a noncustodial parent to continue child support payments and medical insurance coverage for a child who has reached majority, where the child is severely handicapped and has been under the jurisdiction of the domestic relations division since the age of six or seven. Mullanney v Mullanney, No. C-820944 (1st Dist Ct App, Hamilton, 1-4-84).

The trial court did not abuse its discretion by its subsequent modification of a support order in favor of the plaintiff-wife, since the defendant-husband failed to show how the fact of his former wife's remarriage justified alteration in the reapportionment of child support obligations. Jeffries v Jeffries, No. 45634 (8th Dist Ct App, Cuyahoga, 5-19-83).

8. Dependency exemption

A domestic relations court may award the state income tax dependency exemption as part of a divorce decree. Hodges v. Hodges (Clark 1988) 43 Ohio App.3d 113, 539 N.E.2d 709.

9. Grounds

That the grant of a divorce will adversely affect one spouse's claim to the other's retirement benefits is not equitable grounds for denying a divorce sought on the basis that the parties have lived separately for a year.

Mahle v. Mahle (Franklin 1985) 27 Ohio App.3d 326, 500 N.E.2d 907, 27 O.B.R. 383.

In the exercise of its full equity powers and jurisdiction, a common pleas court may invoke the "clean hands" doctrine and refuse to grant a divorce in an uncontested action where the plaintiff is guilty of misconduct which would constitute grounds for divorce. (Annotation from former RC 3105.20.) Lewis v. Lewis (Fayette 1956) 103 Ohio App. 129, 144 N.E.2d 887, 3 O.O.2d 199.

10. Defenses

Construing RC 3105.011 in conjunction with RC 3105.10(C), the trial court in domestic relations actions is vested with full equitable powers and may apply the doctrine of clean hands, but where recrimination is pleaded and proved as a defense by a party it does not work a bar upon the trial court for that reason alone to granting a divorce. Helms v Helms, No. 5-81-36 (3d Dist Ct App, Hancock, 10-1-82).

The fact that a character witness of the opposite sex of the party seeking divorce lives at the same address as that party is insufficient to warrant the application of the "clean hands" doctrine absent evidence of conduct in violation of the marriage obligation; on such facts, a dismissal of a complaint for divorce for the stated reason that plaintiff lacked "clean hands" constitutes grounds for reversible error. Helms v Helms, No. 5-81-36 (3d Dist Ct App, Hancock, 10-1-82).

Under Ohio law, divorced wife's property-based claim for intentional infliction of emotional distress against her former husband, for conduct during pendency of their divorce proceeding, arose out of same transaction addressed by divorce proceeding, namely division of couple's property, and therefore equitable-division decree in divorce proceeding and complaint in wife's tort action were offshoots of same basic controversy, for purposes of res judicata. Shelar v. Shelar (N.D.Ohio 1995) 910 F.Supp. 1307.

Under Ohio doctrine of res judicata or claim preclusion, divorced wife's complaint for intentional infliction of emotional distress, for former husband's alleged concealing or misapplying their property during pendency of their divorce proceeding, was barred by equitable decree of divorce, as divorced wife's claims required determination of what property couple owned and who was entitled to what, and divorce court was previously obligated to make such determination. Shelar v. Shelar (N.D.Ohio 1995) 910 F.Supp. 1307.

3105.02 Prohibition against advertising aid in procuring divorce or dissolution of marriage

No person shall advertise, print, publish, distribute, or circulate a circular, pamphlet, card, handbill, advertisement, printed paper, book, newspaper, or notice, or cause such to be done, with the intent to procure or aid in procuring divorces or dissolutions of marriage, either in this state or elsewhere. This section does not apply to the printing or publishing of a notice or advertisement authorized by law.

(1975 H 370, eff. 8-1-75; 1953 H 1; GC 8003-2; Source—GC 13412)

Historical and Statutory Notes

Pre-1953 H 1 Amendments: 124 v S 65

Cross References

Penalty: 3105.99

Courts of record, publication of court calendar, 2701.09

Lawyer may publish information about services; requirements, DR 2-101

Lawyer not to recommend employment of himself or associate, DR 2-103

Library References

Constitutional Law ⟹90.2, 90.3.

WESTLAW Topic No. 92.

C.J.S. Constitutional Law §§ 544, 545, 561, 568, 570, 571, 573, 574, 576, 577, 579, 581.

OJur 3d: 2, Advertising § 8; 46, Family Law § 325

3105.03 Residency requirement and venue; jurisdiction of common pleas court

The plaintiff in actions for divorce and annulment shall have been a resident of the state at least six months immediately before filing the complaint. Actions for divorce and annulment shall be brought in the proper county for commencement of action pursuant to the Rules of Civil Procedure. The court of common pleas shall hear and determine the case, whether the marriage took place, or the cause of divorce or annulment occurred, within or without the state.

Actions for legal separation shall be brought in the proper county for commencement of actions pursuant to the Rules of Civil Procedure.

(1990 H 514, eff. 1-1-91; 1974 H 233; 130 v H 467; 1953 H 1; GC 8003-3; Source—GC 11980)

Historical and Statutory Notes

Pre-1953 H 1 Amendments: 124 v S 65

Comparative Laws

Conn.—C.G.S.A. § 46b-44.
Fla.—West's F.S.A. § 61.021.
Ga.—O.C.G.A. § 19-5-2.
Idaho—I.C. § 32-701.
Ind.—West's A.I.C. 31-15-2-6.
Iowa—I.C.A. § 598.2.
Mass.—M.G.L.A. c. 208, § 4.
Mich.—M.C.L.A. § 552.9 et seq.
Minn.—M.S.A. § 518.07.
Mo.—V.A.M.S. § 452.300.
N.J.—N.J.S.A. 2A:34-9 et seq.
N.M.—NMSA 1978, § 40-4-4.
N.Y.—McKinney's Domestic Relations Law § 231.
Tex.—V.T.C.A. Family Code § 6.301, 6.302 et seq.
W.Va.—Code, 48-2-8.

Cross References

Common pleas court, division of domestic relations, 2301.03
Complaint for divorce, legal separation, and custody of children, Civ R Appendix, Form 20
Divorce action involving custody or care of children, jurisdiction of juvenile court, 2151.23
Divorce, annulment, and legal separation actions, Civ R 75
Plaintiff to furnish security for costs, 2323.30 et seq.
Service of process, out-of-state, Civ R 4.3
Venue in divorce, annulment, or legal separation actions, Civ R 3

Library References

OJur 3d: 46, Family Law § 549, 557, 559
Am Jur 2d: 24, Divorce and Separation § 238 to 243, 267 et seq.
Length or duration of domicil, as distinguished from fact of domicil, as a jurisdictional matter in divorce action. 2 ALR2d 291
Effect on jurisdiction of court to grant divorce, of plaintiff's change of residence pendente lite. 7 ALR2d 1414
Nature and location of one's business or calling as element in determining domicil in divorce cases. 36 ALR2d 756
Right of nonresident wife to maintain action for separate maintenance or alimony alone against resident husband. 36 ALR2d 1369
Power to grant annulment of marriage against nonresident on constructive service. 43 ALR2d 1086
Venue of divorce action in particular county as dependent on residence or domicil for specified time. 54 ALR2d 898
What constitutes residence or domicil within state by citizen of another country for purpose of jurisdiction in divorce. 51 ALR3d 223
Validity of statute imposing durational residency requirements for divorce applicants. 57 ALR3d 221
Validity and construction of statutory provision relating to jurisdiction of court for purpose of divorce for servicemen. 73 ALR3d 431

Klein & Darling, Baldwin's Ohio Practice, *Civil Practice* § 3, 82 (1997)
Sowald & Morganstern, Baldwin's Ohio Practice, *Domestic Relations Law* § 7.26, 7.28, 8.2, 10.2, 11.2, 11.3, 27.4, 27.12, 27.13, 27.18, 27.20, 27.21, 27.29 (1997)

Law Review and Journal Commentaries

Constitutional Law—Equal Protection—Constitutionality of Divorce Durational Residency Statute, Donald Cybulski. 26 Case W Res L Rev 527 (1976).

Jurisdiction: Misunderstood and Abused, Beatrice K. Sowald. 2 Domestic Rel J Ohio 5 (July/August 1990).

Notes of Decisions and Opinions

In general 2
Constitutional issues 1
Jurisdiction 3
Procedure 5
Residence/domicile 4

---

1. Constitutional issues

The one-year residency requirement in RC 3105.03 is not violative of either the Ohio or the United States Constitution. Coleman v. Coleman (Ohio 1972) 32 Ohio St.2d 155, 291 N.E.2d 530, 61 O.O.2d 406.

Six-month residency requirement for filing action for divorce or annulment is constitutional. McMaken v. McMaken (Montgomery 1994) 96 Ohio App.3d 402, 645 N.E.2d 113.

The year's residence requirement of RC 3105.03 is unconstitutional. Monroe v. Monroe (Ohio Com.Pl. 1972) 32 Ohio Misc. 129, 289 N.E.2d 915, 61 O.O.2d 227.

2. In general

A trial court properly declines to exercise jurisdiction on a complaint for divorce and custody where the plaintiff dismissed her complaint in a Texas court immediately prior to filing a complaint in Ohio. Syrios v. Syrios (Summit 1990) 69 Ohio App.3d 246, 590 N.E.2d 759.

Where a husband obtains an ex parte divorce decree before a Florida court which does not grant alimony to the wife, the full faith and credit clause does not bar an Ohio court from subsequently granting alimony to such wife. Armstrong v. Armstrong (Hamilton 1954) 99 Ohio App. 7, 130 N.E.2d 710, 58 O.O. 79, appeal dismissed 161 Ohio St. 390, 119 N.E.2d 72, 53 O.O. 285, affirmed 162 Ohio St. 406, 123 N.E.2d 267, 55 O.O. 234, certiorari granted 75 S.Ct. 604, 349 U.S. 915, 99 L.Ed. 1248, affirmed 76 S.Ct. 629, 350 U.S. 568, 100 L.Ed. 705, 73 Ohio Law Abs. 514, 60 O.O. 268, rehearing denied 76 S.Ct. 832, 351 U.S. 943, 100 L.Ed. 1469.

An action seeking to have declared invalid the one year's residence requirement of RC 3105.03 for filing a divorce complaint is an appropriate one for use of a class action pursuant to Civ R 23. Monroe v. Monroe (Ohio Com.Pl. 1972) 32 Ohio Misc. 129, 289 N.E.2d 915, 61 O.O.2d 227.

The statutory requirement the plaintiff must have been a resident of the state at least one year before filing divorce petition is jurisdictional, and must be averred in petition. Jones v Jones, 22 Abs 193 (App, Pickaway 1936).

An allegation in a petition for divorce and alimony that "the plaintiff has been for more than one year last past a bona fide resident of Hamilton county, state of Ohio," is a sufficient compliance with this section to give jurisdiction, even though the petition is not filed until twenty-three days after being signed and sworn to by plaintiff. Cozart v. Cozart (Ohio Com.Pl. 1920) 22 Ohio N.P.N.S. 483.

3. Jurisdiction

Although filing of bankruptcy petition stays equitable distribution in divorce case of debtor's interest in marital assets, certain aspects of divorce case, such as dissolution of marriage and child custody issues, are not stayed. State ex rel. Miley v. Parrott (Ohio 1996) 77 Ohio St.3d 64, 671 N.E.2d 24.

Trial court was obligated to reactivate divorce case after bankruptcy court lifted automatic stay affecting Chapter 12 debtor-husband; order inactivating divorce case stated that case would stay inactive until judge "is advised in writing of the stay having been lifted," trial court was advised in writing that bankruptcy court had lifted stay for divorce case, trial court would not be subject to contempt for violating stay after bankruptcy court expressly modified and lifted stay, and divorce case would not be better resolved after conclusion of bankruptcy proceedings. State ex rel. Miley v. Parrott (Ohio 1996) 77 Ohio St.3d 64, 671 N.E.2d 24.

Automatic stay may be lifted or modified for cause. State ex rel. Miley v. Parrott (Ohio 1996) 77 Ohio St.3d 64, 671 N.E.2d 24.

Inasmuch as the federal courts have disclaimed any jurisdiction upon the subject of divorce or alimony either as an original proceeding in chancery or as an incident to a divorce, prohibition will not lie to prevent the courts of this state which have jurisdiction of the subject-matter of divorce and alimony, from hearing and determining a suit for divorce or alimony or both against a consular representative accredited by a foreign government to the government of the United States and recognized and accepted by the government of the United States, who is stationed in Ohio. State ex rel. Popovici v. Agler (Ohio 1928) 119 Ohio St. 484, 164 N.E. 524, 7 Ohio Law Abs. 29, 28 Ohio Law Rep. 183, certiorari granted 49 S.Ct. 265, 279 U.S. 828, 73 L.Ed. 979, affirmed 50 S.Ct. 154, 280 U.S. 379, 74 L.Ed. 489.

If plaintiff in divorce action fails to satisfy six-month residency requirement, court has no jurisdiction to grant decree of divorce, and any decree issued is absolutely void. McMaken v. McMaken (Montgomery 1994) 96 Ohio App.3d 402, 645 N.E.2d 113.

Denial of change of venue of a divorce action to the residence county of the parties is improper where the parties do not reside in the county in which the action is filed and it is not shown that the actions forming the basis of the complaint occurred in the county in which the action is pending. Glover v. Glover (Brown 1990) 66 Ohio App.3d 724, 586 N.E.2d 159, motion overruled 55 Ohio St.3d 715, 563 N.E.2d 725.

Where a party to a divorce action admits the other party's assertion of satisfaction of the residency requirement and asserts the same for himself, he is precluded from subsequently seeking vacation of the decree by an assertion that the court lacked jurisdiction. Sturgill v. Sturgill (Montgomery 1989) 61 Ohio App.3d 94, 572 N.E.2d 178.

The Ohio court which granted the divorce decree to parties no longer residents of this state is the proper forum for enforcement of that divorce decree. Weinberger v. Weinberger (Summit 1974) 43 Ohio App.2d 129, 334 N.E.2d 514, 72 O.O.2d 325.

The venue provisions of RC 3105.03 have been superseded by Civ R 3(B), which expands the venue of divorce actions so that, where jurisdictional requirements are met, a divorce action may be brought in the county in which the defendant resides, as well as the county in which the claim for relief arose, or in the county in which the plaintiff has resided for ninety days. Fuller v. Fuller (Franklin 1972) 32 Ohio App.2d 303, 290 N.E.2d 852, 61 O.O.2d 400.

The dismissal of the prayer of a petition for a divorce does not divest the court of jurisdiction to enter a decree for alimony and support. Hobbs v. Hobbs (Greene 1961) 115 Ohio App. 536, 186 N.E.2d 134, 21 O.O.2d 200.

Where a husband who has been a bona fide resident of the county for ninety days but not a resident of the state for the necessary one year files a petition for divorce against his wife, a resident of another state who files an answer and a cross-petition for alimony only, the court, dismissing the petition for want of jurisdiction, has jurisdiction of the wife's cross-petition. Childers v. Childers (Hamilton 1959) 112 Ohio App. 229, 165 N.E.2d 477, 12 O.O.2d 491.

In a petition for divorce, an allegation that plaintiff "has been a resident of the state of Ohio for more than one year, and of the county of Hamilton for more than ninety (90) days," is, because of the omission of an allegation that plaintiff is a bona fide resident of the county, merely an inadequate allegation of a jurisdictional fact which may be cured by amendment of the petition. Jackman v. Jackman (Hamilton 1959) 110 Ohio App. 199, 160 N.E.2d 387, 12 O.O.2d 464.

Husband who moved to county solely to invoke jurisdiction of court therein, and avoid jurisdiction of court in his home county, did not acquire "bona fide" residence within statute requiring divorce actions to be brought in county of which plaintiff has been bona fide resident for thirty days prior thereto. Wolfe v. Wolfe (Lucas 1933) 45 Ohio App. 309, 187 N.E. 86, 14 Ohio Law Abs. 577, 39 Ohio Law Rep. 90, error dismissed 127 Ohio St. 160, 187 N.E. 201, 38 Ohio Law Rep. 481.

A trial court is without jurisdiction to hear an action for divorce where the plaintiff is not a resident of the county or of the state. Malgras v. Malgras (Ohio App. 1 Dist. 1921) 15 Ohio App. 335, 32 Ohio C.A. 374.

Trial court has subject matter jurisdiction to grant wife a divorce due to her being in Ohio for six months but lacks personal jurisdiction over husband to enter spousal support orders or orders affecting his interest in Florida. Cornelius v Cornelius, No. 99CA1494, 1999 WL 999798 (2d Dist Ct App, Darke, 11-5-99).

A plaintiff must satisfy the durational residency requirements under RC 3105.03 for a trial court to acquire subject matter jurisdiction over a divorce action. Wiley v Wiley, No. 17-87-15 (3d Dist Ct App, Shelby, 11-15-88).

Where a plaintiff who has not been a resident of the state of Ohio for one year before the filing of his complaint dismisses the complaint and the amended complaint at the commencement of the trial, after the filing and service of a counterclaim for divorce by the nonresident defendant-spouse, the court retains jurisdiction to rule upon the nonresident defendant's prayer for divorce and custody. Lincoln v. Lincoln (Ohio Com.Pl. 1973) 33 Ohio Misc. 213, 294 N.E.2d 254, 62 O.O.2d 384.

4. Residence/domicile

Prisoner was not entitled to mandamus to compel Court of Common Pleas to hear his complaint for divorce, where prisoner had plain and adequate remedy in ordinary course of law by way of appeal to Court of Appeals and it appeared that prisoner could establish no clear right to relief sought. State ex rel. Saunders v. Court of Common Pleas of Allen County (Ohio 1987) 34 Ohio St.3d 15, 516 N.E.2d 232.

Plaintiff's domicile in divorce action is question of intent and plaintiff's representation will be accepted unless facts and circumstances establish that plaintiff's claimed intent cannot be accepted as true. Polakova v. Polak (Hamilton 1995) 107 Ohio App.3d 745, 669 N.E.2d 498.

Person effectively changes her domicile in divorce action when she actually abandons first domicile, coupled with intention not to return to it, and acquires new domicile. Polakova v. Polak (Hamilton 1995) 107 Ohio App.3d 745, 669 N.E.2d 498.

Foreign citizen with "J" status temporary visa did not have requisite intent to remain in Ohio indefinitely for purposes of conferring jurisdiction in divorce proceeding against noncitizen spouse, though she obtained Ohio driver's license, rented apartment, and paid taxes in Ohio, where she was not legally capable of changing her visa status from temporary "J" status to permanent status, and she would have to return to her native country at some point. Polakova v. Polak (Hamilton 1995) 107 Ohio App.3d 745, 669 N.E.2d 498.

Wife was "resident" of Texas within meaning of statute requiring plaintiff to be resident of state at least six months immediately before filing complaint for divorce or annulment, even though wife stated that she was Ohio resident for six months prior to filing complaint and that she did not intend to move legal residence from Ohio; wife also testified that address was in Texas and that she had moved there three years prior to filing complaint. McMaken v. McMaken (Montgomery 1994) 96 Ohio App.3d 402, 645 N.E.2d 113.

Plaintiff seeking legal separation could avoid 90-day residency requirement for venue in action for divorce, annulment, or legal separation in county in which defendant was resident, and could instead take advantage of a more generous venue provision permitting action to be brought in county in which plaintiff resided, had her principal place of business or regularly and systematically conducted business activities, where there was no other available Ohio forum for action. Taylor v. Taylor (Montgomery 1992) 84 Ohio App.3d 445, 616 N.E.2d 1199.

A husband's act in maintaining Florida automobile tags and title, as well as indicating that state as his "legal residence/domicile" for tax purposes on an air force form is irrelevant in determining his domiciliary residence for jurisdiction over his divorce action. Hager v. Hager (Greene 1992) 79 Ohio App.3d 239, 607 N.E.2d 63.

Where a party to a divorce action admits the other party's assertion of satisfaction of the residency requirement and asserts the same for himself, he is precluded from subsequently seeking vacation of the decree by an assertion that the court lacked jurisdiction. Sturgill v. Sturgill (Montgomery 1989) 61 Ohio App.3d 94, 572 N.E.2d 178.

Where a plaintiff amends a complaint for alimony only to include a complaint for divorce after he has met the minimum residency requirement for jurisdiction over a divorce claim, the amended claim will relate back to the date of the original complaint pursuant to Civ R 15(C) only where the plaintiff has not sought to circumvent the residency requirement of RC 3105.03 by forum shopping. Gieg v. Gieg (Trumbull 1984) 16 Ohio App.3d 51, 474 N.E.2d 626, 16 O.B.R. 55.

Pursuant to RC 3105.011 and 3105.03, there is no minimum period of domicile as a prerequisite to an action for alimony brought pursuant to RC 3105.17. Gieg v. Gieg (Trumbull 1984) 16 Ohio App.3d 51, 474 N.E.2d 626, 16 O.B.R. 55.

The questions of whether the plaintiff in a divorce action became an actual resident of the state of Ohio and whether the plaintiff did so to obtain an Ohio divorce can be considered as to whether the plaintiff is an actual resident of Ohio but, by themselves, are not determinative of whether the plaintiff is a resident of this state. Franklin v. Franklin (Mahoning 1981) 5 Ohio App.3d 74, 449 N.E.2d 457, 5 O.B.R. 186.

Residence within the state for the purposes of RC 3105.03 must be actual and the word "resident" is used in the popular sense and means one who has his place of abode within the state. Franklin v. Franklin (Mahoning 1981) 5 Ohio App.3d 74, 449 N.E.2d 457, 5 O.B.R. 186.

The domicile of a person entering the armed forces is not changed by the mere fact that he changes his place of abode, but such domicile is changed to the new place of abode where there exists on the part of such member of the armed forces an intent to make such change. Draper v. Draper (Franklin 1958) 107 Ohio App. 32, 151 N.E.2d 379, 78 Ohio Law Abs. 5, 7 O.O.2d 354.

If a person has actually removed from one place to another, with an intention of remaining in the latter for an indefinite time and as a place of fixed present domicile, such latter place is to be deemed his place of domicile notwithstanding he may entertain a floating intention to return to his previous domicile at some future period. Redrow v. Redrow (Clermont 1952) 94 Ohio App. 38, 114 N.E.2d 293, 51 O.O. 266.

The word "resident," as used in this section, means one who possesses a domiciliary residence, a residence accompanied by an intention to make the state of Ohio a permanent home. Saalfeld v. Saalfeld (Clermont 1949) 86 Ohio App. 225, 89 N.E.2d 165, 55 Ohio Law Abs. 156, 41 O.O. 94.

A temporary residence, no matter how long it may be extended, does not meet the requirements of the statute. Saalfeld v. Saalfeld (Clermont 1949) 86 Ohio App. 225, 89 N.E.2d 165, 55 Ohio Law Abs. 156, 41 O.O. 94.

Where a permanent bona fide domicile is once established, there is a presumption of fact that such status continues until the contrary is shown by proper proof. Saalfeld v. Saalfeld (Clermont 1949) 86 Ohio App. 225, 89 N.E.2d 165, 55 Ohio Law Abs. 156, 41 O.O. 94.

Where plaintiff in a divorce action alleges she has been a resident of Ohio for more than one year prior to the filing of such action, it is necessary for her to prove not only that she lived in Ohio for more than one year prior to the filing of such action, but that she so lived, entertaining throughout such residence a bona fide intention to make Ohio her domicile; the burden of proof rests upon plaintiff to establish both residence and such concurrent intention by a preponderance of the evidence. Saalfeld v. Saalfeld (Clermont 1949) 86 Ohio App. 225, 89 N.E.2d 165, 55 Ohio Law Abs. 156, 41 O.O. 94.

The word "residence," where used in statutes conferring jurisdiction in divorce actions, means domiciliary residence. Glassman v. Glassman (Hamilton 1944) 75 Ohio App. 47, 60 N.E.2d 716, 42 Ohio Law Abs. 385, 30 O.O. 352.

Domicile of a person entering armed forces of United States remains the same throughout service unless a new domicile is voluntarily selected. Glassman v. Glassman (Hamilton 1944) 75 Ohio App. 47, 60 N.E.2d 716, 42 Ohio Law Abs. 385, 30 O.O. 352.

Husband who moved to county solely to invoke jurisdiction of court therein, and avoid jurisdiction of court in his home county, did not acquire "bona fide" residence within statute requiring divorce actions to be brought in county of which plaintiff has been bona fide resident for thirty days prior thereto. Wolfe v. Wolfe (Lucas 1933) 45 Ohio App. 309, 187 N.E. 86, 14 Ohio Law Abs. 577, 39 Ohio Law Rep. 90, error dismissed 127 Ohio St. 160, 187 N.E. 201, 38 Ohio Law Rep. 481.

Whether petitioner for divorce had recovered her sanity and established bona fide residence in county of forum more than thirty days prior to bringing action held questions of fact. Bishop v. Bishop (Lucas 1931) 40 Ohio App. 493, 179 N.E. 142, 10 Ohio Law Abs. 399.

Where plaintiff was not a resident of this state at the time of the filing of his petition or granting of the divorce decree, as required by statute, the decree was a nullity. Ready v. Ready (Cuyahoga 1927) 25 Ohio App. 432, 158 N.E. 493, 5 Ohio Law Abs. 629.

A wife whose marriage occurred in another state and who has been living with her husband there, may, if justified by his conduct in leaving him, acquire a residence in this state, and after the lapse of one year, obtain a divorce here, which is valid in this state, and the validity of which other states may recognize, although not compelled to do so. Cache v. Cache (Ohio App. 7 Dist. 1919) 12 Ohio App. 140, 30 Ohio C.A. 481.

Jurisdiction and venue of divorce proceedings lie in Ohio despite temporary absence from the state allegedly to flee domestic violence. Reese v Reese, No. 71336, 1997 WL 272368 (8th Dist Ct App, Cuyahoga, 5-22-97).

The spouse of a person in the military does not change residency when living on base because of military service for purposes of meeting the jurisdictional requirements of RC 3105.03. Dobson v Dobson, No. 97CA0217, 1998 WL 519255 (5th Dist Ct App, Stark, 5-18-98).

To satisfy RC 3105.03 as to the statutory meaning of "resident," one must display physical presence and intention to be a resident of this state; once these two elements co-exist, a departure from this state is insignificant, unless the departure is with the intent to change domicil. Drazen v Drazen, No. 9-80-44 (3d Dist Ct App, Marion, 5-8-81).

Where the parties to a divorce action are incarcerated in counties different than that of their residence prior to their incarceration, the county of residence prior to their incarceration is the proper venue for the filing of a divorce action. Wernert v. Wernert (Ohio Com.Pl. 1991) 61 Ohio Misc.2d 436, 579 N.E.2d 800.

It will be presumed that the residence or domicile of a person in military service for purposes of bringing a divorce action is the residence or domicile he had when he entered military service. Spires v. Spires (Ohio Com.Pl. 1966) 7 Ohio Misc. 197, 214 N.E.2d 691, 35 O.O.2d 289.

Terms "resident" and "bona fide resident," as used in statute, have uniformly been construed by courts in this country as meaning domicile. Terms "resident" and "residence," as used in Ohio divorce statutes, mean a domiciliary resident or residence. Baraket v Baraket, 25 Abs 641 (CP, Jefferson 1937).

Where plaintiff's amended petition in a divorce action averred that he had been a resident of Ohio for a year, it was not necessary for his wife in an action on her cross-petition to offer proof of his residence. Payer v. Payer (Cuyahoga 1956) 133 N.E.2d 620, 74 Ohio Law Abs. 124.

The locality of the res, the status of a matrimonial union, with which an action for divorce deals, is the domicile of the parties to the marriage. To give validity to a decree of divorce, it is essential that at least one of the parties must be domiciled in the state of the forum. 1928 OAG 2912.

5. Procedure

Where an annulment action is properly brought, a nonresident defendant may cross-petition for divorce without establishing residence in the state. Lampe v. Lampe (Ohio Com.Pl. 1954) 136 N.E.2d 470, 74 Ohio Law Abs. 122.

Verification of a petition for divorce and alimony twenty-three days before filing it was not a bar to evidence that plaintiff had been a resident of the county for statutory period. Cozart v. Cozart (Ohio Com.Pl. 1920) 22 Ohio N.P.N.S. 483.

Year's residence in state not essential to decree for divorce on cross-petition. Ferguson v. Ferguson (Ohio Insolv. 1910) 11 Ohio N.P.N.S. 679, 55 W.L.B. 158.

3105.04 Residence of spouse

When a person files a petition for divorce or legal separation, the residence of the spouse does not preclude the use of sections 3105.01 to 3105.21 of the Revised Code.

(1990 H 514, eff. 1-1-91; 1978 H 349; 1953 H 1; GC 8003-4; Source—GC 11982)

Historical and Statutory Notes

Pre-1953 H 1 Amendments: 124 v S 65

Cross References

Service of process, out-of-state, Civ R 4.3

Venue in divorce, annulment, or legal separation actions, Civ R 3

Library References

OJur 3d: 46, Family Law § 558, 567
Am Jur 2d: 24, Divorce and Separation § 257 to 262
Length of duration of domicil, as distinguished from fact of domicil, as a jurisdictional matter in divorce action. 2 ALR2d 291
Effect on jurisdiction of court to grant divorce, of plaintiff's change of residence pendente lite. 7 ALR2d 1414
Foreign divorce as subject to attack by spouse in state of which neither spouse is resident. 12 ALR2d 382
Residence or domicil, for purpose of divorce action, of one in armed forces. 21 ALR2d 1163
Recognition as to marital status of foreign divorce decree attacked on ground of lack of domicil, since Williams decision. 28 ALR2d 1303
Foreign divorce as affecting local order previously entered for separate maintenance. 28 ALR2d 1346
Valid foreign divorce decree upon constructive service as precluding action by spouse for alimony, support, or maintenance. 28 ALR2d 1378
Applicability in annulment actions, of residence requirements of divorce actions. 32 ALR2d 734
Right of nonresident wife to maintain action for separate maintenance or alimony alone against resident husband. 36 ALR2d 1369
Lack of insufficiency of allegations of plaintiff's residence or domicil as ground for vacation of, or collateral attack on, divorce decree. 55 ALR2d 1263
What constitutes residence or domicile within state by citizen of another country for purpose of jurisdiction in divorce. 51 ALR3d 223

Sowald & Morganstern, Baldwin's Ohio Practice, *Domestic Relations Law* § 27.15 (1997)

Notes of Decisions and Opinions

Domicile 1
Foreign decrees 2
Nonresident spouse 3

---

1. Domicile

Domicile is a legal relationship between a person and a particular place where the person resides in a particular place at least for some period of time and has the intent to reside in that place permanently or at least indefinitely; residence is encompassed within the definition of domicile; however, a person may have more than one residence but only one domicile. Snelling v. Gardner (Franklin 1990) 69 Ohio App.3d 196, 590 N.E.2d 330.

The legal fiction of common law requiring domicile of wife to follow that of husband cannot be employed to destroy domiciliary rights of a wife who has never been in any domicile of her husband, who never by any voluntary act lost a domicile possessed for many years beyond the statutory requirement in the jurisdiction in which she sues for divorce, whose only absences from her domicile have been attendance upon her husband at the various posts to which under army orders he has been assigned temporarily, who has never been advised by her husband that he has chosen a "place or mode of living" amounting to the establishment of a domicile, who has suffered aggression by the husband entitling her to a divorce, and who has separated from him prior to her institution of an action for divorce, and, where the husband's claim to domicile is predicated upon mere residence prior to his entering the service. Glassman v. Glassman (Hamilton 1944) 75 Ohio App. 47, 60 N.E.2d 716, 42 Ohio Law Abs. 385, 30 O.O. 352.

A wife, upon the aggression of her husband, may select a new domicile, independent and separate from that of her husband. Glassman v. Glassman (Hamilton 1944) 75 Ohio App. 47, 60 N.E.2d 716, 42 Ohio Law Abs. 385, 30 O.O. 352.

In circumstances in which a plaintiff father has the children of the parties with him at the time of the filing for divorce and custody, has had them for several months under the terms of an agreement between the parties, has them at all times during the process of service by publication until the defendant mother surreptitiously persuaded him to permit overnight visitation apart from his home and immediately then absconded with the children to another state, the process of service by publication is completed and when the case comes on for trial, the children's domicile was and remains the domicile of the parent, the father, who had them under these circumstances and the court has jurisdiction to determine the right of custody; but such jurisdiction is not established by the agreement of the parties. Reed v. Reed (Ohio Com.Pl. 1967) 11 Ohio Misc. 93, 229 N.E.2d 113, 40 O.O.2d 327.

A minor wife may acquire a domicile other than her husband's where he is guilty of misconduct. Johnson v. Johnson (Ohio Com.Pl. 1959) 159 N.E.2d 820, 81 Ohio Law Abs. 599, 9 O.O.2d 58.

2. Foreign decrees

A divorce decree entered pro confesso by a foreign court against a nonresident defendant on her failure to appear or answer on constructive service alone is a final decree for divorce to which full faith and credit must be given so long as it remains unreversed, unmodified, and not vacated by the courts of the state in which it was awarded; and such foreign divorce decree is a bar to an action for divorce by such defendant elsewhere, but a decree made by a foreign court in such divorce action enforcing mandatory and prohibitory injunctions barring a wife from all rights based on the marital relations, so far as it attempts to exercise such jurisdiction, is null and void, and the denial of alimony in such divorce decree based solely on constructive service upon the wife by a court of the matrimonial domicile is not entitled to full faith and credit in another state in which the wife resides. Armstrong v. Armstrong (Hamilton 1954) 99 Ohio App. 7, 130 N.E.2d 710, 58 O.O. 79, appeal dismissed 161 Ohio St. 390, 119 N.E.2d 72, 53 O.O. 285, affirmed 162 Ohio St. 406, 123 N.E.2d 267, 55 O.O. 234, certiorari granted 75 S.Ct. 604, 349 U.S. 915, 99 L.Ed. 1248, affirmed 76 S.Ct. 629, 350 U.S. 568, 100 L.Ed. 705, 73 Ohio Law Abs. 514, 60 O.O. 268, rehearing denied 76 S.Ct. 832, 351 U.S. 943, 100 L.Ed. 1469.

3. Nonresident spouse

In a divorce action brought by a wife against a nonresident husband with service by publication, the court may award custody of children within its jurisdiction, but cannot make any award for the support of the children. Noble v. Noble (Ohio Com.Pl. 1959) 160 N.E.2d 426, 80 Ohio Law Abs. 581.

3105.05 Service on residents—Repealed

(1970 H 1201, eff. 7-1-71; 130 v H 467; 1953 H 1; GC 8003-6; Source—GC 11983)

Historical and Statutory Notes

Ed. Note: See now Civ R 4 for provisions analogous to former 3105.05.

Pre-1953 H 1 Amendments: 124 v S 65

3105.06 Notice by publication authorized in certain cases

If the residence of a defendant in an action for divorce, annulment, or legal separation is unknown, or if the defendant is not a resident of this state or is a resident of this state but absent from the state, notice of the pendency of the action shall be given by publication as provided by the Rules of Civil Procedure.

(1990 H 514, eff. 1-1-91; 1979 H 248; 1971 H 602; 1970 H 1201; 130 v H 467; 1953 H 1; GC 8003-7; Source—GC 11984)

Historical and Statutory Notes

Pre-1953 H 1 Amendments: 124 v S 65

Cross References

Actions "authorized by law" for service of summons by publication, 2703.14

Process: service by publication, Civ R 4.4

Library References

OJur 3d: 46, Family Law § 592

Am Jur 2d: 24, Divorce and Separation § 285, 313

Carlin, Baldwin's Ohio Practice, *Merrick-Rippner Probate Law* § 4.23 (1997)

Sowald & Morganstern, Baldwin's Ohio Practice, *Domestic Relations Law* § 7.26, 7.30, 25.76 (1997)

Law Review and Journal Commentaries

Explanation of Amendment to Sec. 3105.06, R.C. (Divorce—Service by Publication), Don C. Bolsinger. 53 Ohio St B Ass'n Rep 176 (February 4, 1980).

Notes of Decisions and Opinions

1. Attorney malpractice

An attorney may not be held liable for malpractice in doing what the law requires in obtaining service of process; however, an attorney is liable for causing the publication of a client's pending divorce in disregard of the client's specific instructions and the written assurance given by the attorney to the client. McInnis v. Hyatt Legal Clinics (Ohio 1984) 10 Ohio St.3d 112, 461 N.E.2d 1295, 10 O.B.R. 437.

2. Jurisdiction

An incompleted service of summons in a divorce action does not vest the court with jurisdiction over the defendant, and such jurisdiction is vested by the completion of personal service of summons and takes precedence over that of another court in a similar action between the same parties where service of summons by publication is incomplete. Gehelo v. Gehelo (Ohio 1953) 160 Ohio St. 243, 116 N.E.2d 7, 52 O.O. 114.

Service by publication is authorized by statute, in an action for divorce, alimony and equitable relief, and the trial court has power to make an alimony decree where the only relief sought is the appropriation of real property of the husband, situated within the county. Reed v. Reed (Ohio 1929) 121 Ohio St. 188, 167 N.E. 684, 7 Ohio Law Abs. 381, 29 Ohio Law Rep. 399.

Ohio code section permitting service by publication on domestic relations defendants who were not residents of Ohio did not mean that out-of-state divorce decree would be allowed full faith and credit even if Ohio residents were served with notice of out-of-state divorce action only by publication, as code section was circumscribed by limitation that notice comply with rules of civil procedure which required that service on out-of-state resident of known residence be made by certified mail. Johnson v. Johnson (Greene 1993) 86 Ohio App.3d 433, 621 N.E.2d 530.

In divorce action brought by Ohio plaintiff against defendant whose last known residence was in foreign country, service by publication in Cleveland paper which did not contain defendant's last known address was defective and did not confer jurisdiction on Ohio trial court to grant default divorce judgment. Demianczuk v. Demianczuk (Cuyahoga 1984) 20 Ohio App.3d 244, 485 N.E.2d 785, 20 O.B.R. 305.

Where defendant in divorce action in Ohio, who was not served with process in accordance with the preceding section, but was served in another state with summons and a certified copy of petition, without filing of an affidavit of nonresidence and without service by publication under this section, personally confers with trial judge before day set for trial, physically appears in courtroom at time of trial and hears plaintiff's evidence and pronouncement of decree, but does not file any answer or enter any appearance by writing in such action, court does not acquire jurisdiction over defendant and its decree is void. O'Dell v. O'Dell (Darke 1945) 78 Ohio App. 60, 64 N.E.2d 126, 33 O.O. 416.

Divorce decree granted to wife against husband who is not resident of state, service being by publication and husband not appearing, is not bar to subsequent action by wife for alimony. Wick v. Wick (Montgomery 1938) 58 Ohio App. 72, 15 N.E.2d 780, 11 O.O. 463.

Statute providing method of service against nonresident defendant in divorce action is mandatory and must be strictly complied with. Beck v. Beck (Coshocton 1933) 45 Ohio App. 507, 187 N.E. 366, 15 Ohio Law Abs. 326, 39 Ohio Law Rep. 203.

In a divorce action brought by a wife against a nonresident husband with service by publication, the court may award custody of children within its jurisdiction, but cannot make any award for the support of the children. Noble v. Noble (Ohio Com.Pl. 1959) 160 N.E.2d 426, 80 Ohio Law Abs. 581.

When it appears that either the defendant is not a resident of this state or his residence is unknown, service by publication is a recognized method of bringing a defendant into the jurisdiction of the courts. McIntosh v. McIntosh (Montgomery 1951) 116 N.E.2d 747, 66 Ohio Law Abs. 211.

Where record is silent on question of whether or not a summons and copy of the petition were mailed to defendant in compliance with the statute, but the judgment entry provides that the defendant was "legally summoned by publication" and failed to appear, and the court was acting as one of general jurisdiction, the judgment entry is controlling on the jurisdictional question, and the judgment cannot be collaterally attacked. In re Lombard's Estate (Madison 1950) 97 N.E.2d 87, 58 Ohio Law Abs. 459, 44 O.O. 357, appeal dismissed 154 Ohio St. 432, 96 N.E.2d 297, 43 O.O. 352.

3. Affidavit

Where certified mail was returned, indicating failure of delivery of process in divorce action, plaintiff's attorney had option of having clerk send complaint by ordinary mail to same address, and it was not necessary to file affidavit with clerk showing reasonable diligence utilized to ascertain defendant's whereabouts. Ferrie v. Ferrie (Medina 1981) 2 Ohio App.3d 122, 440 N.E.2d 1229, 2 O.B.R. 136.

An affidavit for service by publication, under Civ R 4.4, is sufficient if it alleges that service cannot be made because the residence of the defendant is unknown to the affiant and cannot with reasonable diligence be ascertained, and there is no requirement that the affidavit contain a statement that the action in which service by publication is attempted is one where such service is authorized by law. Wilson v. Sinsabaugh (Franklin 1978) 61 Ohio App.2d 224, 401 N.E.2d 454, 15 O.O.3d 365.

By stating that "this affidavit is made in pursuance to law in said cases," an affidavit for service by publication has sufficiently complied with GC 11293 (RC 2703.15). Dexter v. Taylor (Ohio Com.Pl. 1950) 95 N.E.2d 790, 58 Ohio Law Abs. 532, 43 O.O. 236, affirmed 107 N.E.2d 402, 63 Ohio Law Abs. 266, 47 O.O. 398, appeal dismissed 156 Ohio St. 182, 101 N.E.2d 502, 46 O.O. 35.

4. Sufficiency

As officer of court, counsel for wife in divorce proceeding had obligation to investigate why counsel for husband had not appeared for trial and had obligation not to present to trial court judgment entry decree of divorce indicating that husband had notice of trial date when court file clearly indicated that husband had not been provided appropriate notice. Kerns v. Kerns (Franklin 1993) 87 Ohio App.3d 698, 622 N.E.2d 1149, motion overruled 67 Ohio St.3d 1472, 619 N.E.2d 1028.

Trial court should not have granted divorce without notifying husband or his counsel of date set for trial. Kerns v. Kerns (Franklin 1993) 87 Ohio App.3d 698, 622 N.E.2d 1149, motion overruled 67 Ohio St.3d 1472, 619 N.E.2d 1028.

Failure to use reasonable diligence to discover a mother's address invalidates service by publication and is grounds for vacating an adoption decree four years after the decree is entered. In re Adoption of Knipper (Hamilton 1986) 30 Ohio App.3d 214, 507 N.E.2d 436, 30 O.B.R. 371.

Service of summons by publication in a divorce action, not accompanied by any appearance of the defendant for the purpose of contesting the issues raised by the petition, is not sufficient to clothe the court with jurisdiction to decree the payment of money, either by way of support of minor children or by way of alimony. Sutovich v. Sutovich (Hamilton 1964) 120 Ohio App. 473, 200 N.E.2d 716, 29 O.O.2d 371.

In a divorce case, where the affidavit in a service by publication sets forth an address of the defendant where at one time she had resided but the legal advertisement published contains a different address, and a summons and copy of the petition mailed to the first address are returned by the postal department unopened, and where a second affidavit setting forth the second address is filed and a summons and copy of the petition are remailed to such address and actually reach the defendant who does not answer until more than seven months after receiving notice of the action, a ruling by the trial court that defendant was duly served with summons and a copy of the petition is correct, even though there was no second publication of notice after the filing of the second petition. Draper v. Draper (Franklin 1958) 107 Ohio App. 32, 151 N.E.2d 379, 78 Ohio Law Abs. 5, 7 O.O.2d 354.

Where in divorce action with service by publication, the petition and first affidavit recited defendant's last known address, and plaintiff's counsel thereafter determined that she had moved and used the new address in subsequent publications, and defendant had actual notice of the proceeding, the service was sufficient. Draper v. Draper (Franklin 1958) 107 Ohio App. 32, 151 N.E.2d 379, 78 Ohio Law Abs. 5, 7 O.O.2d 354.

Where the plaintiff in a divorce action filed a petition and a copy thereof was mailed to the nonresident defendant and the notice thereof duly published, and an amended petition was then filed, a copy of which was mailed to the defendant, but notice thereof not published, such lack of publication was not a ground for vacating the divorce decree. Hanna v. Hanna (Hamilton 1952) 93 Ohio App. 270, 114 N.E.2d 133, 51 O.O. 18.

In divorce action statute controlling service of summons on nonresident defendants in divorce actions controls over statute that governs service of summons generally. Hendrix v. Hendrix (Ohio Com.Pl. 1951) 103 N.E.2d 317, 60 Ohio Law Abs. 566.

It is not such a defect that it would void a decree on collateral attack when the publication notice, where service is made by publication in an action for divorce and alimony fails to include a reference description of the property attached. Dexter v. Taylor (Ohio Com.Pl. 1950) 95 N.E.2d 790, 58 Ohio Law Abs. 532, 43 O.O. 236, affirmed 107 N.E.2d 402, 63 Ohio Law Abs. 266, 47 O.O. 398, appeal dismissed 156 Ohio St. 182, 101 N.E.2d 502, 46 O.O. 35.

5. Final orders

Although law of Illinois, which was domicile of husband, allowed out-of-state wife to receive notice of divorce action by means of publication, service had to be made by means other than publication where wife's address was known at time of publication, and, thus, Illinois decree was not entitled to full faith and credit. Johnson v. Johnson (Greene 1993) 86 Ohio App.3d 433, 621 N.E.2d 530.

Foreign decree will be afforded full faith and credit only if "the best possible notice" has been served on out-of-state party. Johnson v. Johnson (Greene 1993) 86 Ohio App.3d 433, 621 N.E.2d 530.

An order to deny or overrule a motion to vacate a decree of divorce is a final order. McIntosh v. McIntosh (Montgomery 1951) 116 N.E.2d 747, 66 Ohio Law Abs. 211.

6. Indigent parties

Indigent plaintiff in divorce action may require appropriate public officials to effect service of process by publication in that action without prepayment by indigent plaintiff of costs of publication. State ex rel. Blevins v. Mowrey (Ohio 1989) 45 Ohio St.3d 20, 543 N.E.2d 99.

3105.061 Continuing jurisdiction; notice—Repealed

(1970 H 1201, eff. 7-1-71; 129 v 582; 127 v 422)

Historical and Statutory Notes

Ed. Note: See now Civ R 75(I) for provisions analogous to former 3105.061.

3105.07 Foreign defendants—Repealed

(1970 H 1201, eff. 7-1-71; 130 v H 467; 1953 H 1; GC 8003-8; Source—GC 11979-2)

Historical and Statutory Notes

Ed. Note: See now Civ R 4.5 for provisions analogous to former 3105.07.

Pre-1953 H 1 Amendments: 124 v S 65

3105.08 Conversion of divorce action into dissolution action

At any time before a final judgment is entered in a divorce action, the spouses may convert the action for divorce into an action for dissolution of marriage by filing a motion with the court in which the divorce action is pending for conversion of the divorce action. The motion shall contain a petition for dissolution of marriage that satisfies the requirements of section 3105.63 of the Revised Code. The action for dissolution of marriage then shall proceed in accordance with sections 3105.61 to 3105.65 of the Revised Code with both spouses designated as petitioners. No court fees or costs normally charged upon the filing of an action shall be charged upon the conversion of the action for divorce into an action for dissolution of marriage under this section.

(1990 S 25, eff. 6-13-90)

Historical and Statutory Notes

Ed. Note: Former 3105.08 repealed by 1970 H 1201, eff. 7-1-71; 1969 H 1; 132 v H 316; 130 v H 467; 1953 H 1; GC 8003-9; Source—GC 11979-4; see now Civ R 75(D) for provisions analogous to former 3105.08.

Pre-1953 H 1 Amendments: 124 v S 65

Library References

OJur 3d: 46, Family Law § 612; 47, Family Law § 1198, 1201

Klein & Darling, Baldwin's Ohio Practice, *Civil Practice* § 75 (1997)

Sowald & Morganstern, Baldwin's Ohio Practice, *Domestic Relations Law* § 9.5, 10.2, 10.6, 11.28 (1997)

Notes of Decisions and Opinions

Investigator's reports 1

1. Investigator's reports

Custody investigation reports on both parties' backgrounds are to be admitted into evidence subject to cross-examination of the investigator about the contents of the report so due process rights are protected. Roach v. Roach (Montgomery 1992) 79 Ohio App.3d 194, 607 N.E.2d 35.

3105.09 Hearing—Repealed

(1970 H 1201, eff. 7-1-71; 130 v H 467; 1953 H 1; GC 8003-10; Source—GC 11985)

Historical and Statutory Notes

Ed. Note: See now Civ R 75(J) for provisions analogous to former 3105.09.

Pre-1953 H 1 Amendments: 124 v S 65

3105.091 Conciliation or family counseling order; procedure

(A) At any time after thirty days from the service of summons or first publication of notice in an action for divorce, annulment, or legal separation, or at any time after the filing of a petition for dissolution of marriage, the court of common pleas, upon its own motion or the motion of one of the parties, may order the parties to undergo conciliation for the period of time not exceeding ninety days as the court specifies, and, if children are involved in the proceeding, the court may order the parties to take part in family counseling during the course of the proceeding or for any reasonable period of time as directed by the court. An order requiring conciliation shall set forth the conciliation procedure and name the conciliator. The conciliation procedures may include without limitation referrals to the conciliation judge as provided in Chapter 3117. of the Revised Code, public or private marriage counselors, family service agencies, community health services, physicians, licensed psychologists, or clergymen. The court, in its order requiring the parties to undergo family counseling, may name the counselor and shall set forth the required type of counseling, the length of time for the counseling, and any other specific conditions required by it. The court shall direct and order the manner in which the costs of any conciliation procedures and of any family counseling are to be paid.

(B) No action for divorce, annulment, or legal separation, in which conciliation or family counseling has been ordered, shall be heard or decided until the conciliation or family counseling has concluded and been reported to the court.

(1990 S 3, eff. 4-11-91; 1990 H 514; 1974 H 233)

Cross References

Conciliation of marital controversies, Ch 3117

Plaintiff to furnish security for costs, 2323.30 et seq.

Library References

OJur 3d: 5A, Alternative Dispute Resolution § 175; 46, Family Law § 328, 401, 617, 633

Am Jur 2d: 24, Divorce and Separation § 333, 337 to 339

Validity, construction, and effect of statute providing a "cooling off period" or lapse of time prior to filing of complaint, hearing, or entry of decree in divorce suit. 62 ALR2d 1262

Sowald & Morganstern, Baldwin's Ohio Practice, *Domestic Relations Law* § 6.1, 6.3, 6.9, 7.33, 15.66, 21.16, 25.34 (1997)

Law Review and Journal Commentaries

Children—The Innocent Victims of Family Breakups: How the Family Law Attorney, the Courts, and Society Can Protect Our Children, Michael J. Albano. 26 U Tol L Rev 787 (Summer 1995).

Coercive Conciliation: Judge Paul W. Alexander And The Movement For Therapeutic Divorce, J. Herbie DiFonzo. 25 U Tol L Rev 535 (1994).

Family Conciliation: Draft Rules for the Settlement of Family Disputes, Morris Wolff. 21 J Fam L 213 (1982-83).

3105.10 Power to dissolve marriage; enforcement of separation agreement providing for child support; condonation and recrimination defenses eliminated; effect on dower

(A) The court of common pleas shall hear any of the causes for divorce or annulment charged in the complaint and may, upon proof to the satisfaction of the court, pronounce the marriage contract dissolved and both of the parties released from their obligations.

(B)(1) A separation agreement providing for the support of children eighteen years of age or older is enforceable by the court of common pleas.

(2) A separation agreement that was voluntarily entered into by the parties may be enforceable by the court of common pleas upon the motion of either party to the agreement, if the court determines that it would be in the interests of justice and equity to require enforcement of the separation agreement.

(3) If a court of common pleas has a division of domestic relations, all cases brought for enforcement of a separation agreement under division (B)(1) or (2) of this section shall be assigned to the judges of that division.

(C) A plea of condonation or recrimination is not a bar to a divorce.

(D) Upon the granting of a divorce, on a complaint or counterclaim, by force of the judgment, each party shall be barred of all right of dower in real estate situated within this state of which the other was seized at any time during coverture.

(E) Upon the granting of a judgment for legal separation, when by the force of the judgment real estate is granted to one party, the other party is barred of all right of dower in the real estate and the court may provide that each party shall be barred of all rights of dower in the real estate acquired by either party at any time subsequent to the judgment.

"Dower" as used in this section has the meaning set forth in section 2103.02 of the Revised Code.

(1990 H 514, eff. 1-1-91; 1975 H 370; 1974 H 233; 130 v H 467; 1953 H 1; GC 8003-11; Source—GC 11986)

Historical and Statutory Notes

Pre-1953 H 1 Amendments: 124 v S 65

Cross References

Children's trust fund, additional fee for divorce decree filing, 3109.14

Common pleas court, division of domestic relations, 2301.03

Complaint for divorce, legal separation, and custody of children, Civ R Appendix, Form 20

Conciliation of marital controversies, Ch 3117

Court awarding parental rights and responsibilities, shared parenting, modifications, best interests of child, 3109.04, 3109.041

Divorce action involving custody or care of children, jurisdiction of juvenile court, 2151.23

Divorce, annulment, and legal separation actions, Civ R 75

Duty of married person to support self, spouse, and children, duration of duty to support, 3103.03

General assembly, power to grant divorces only as expressly conferred, O Const Art II §32

Husband and wife, mutual obligations, 3103.01

Reciprocal enforcement of support, Ch 3115

Reciprocal enforcement of support, support pendente lite, 3115.27

Registration of marriages, divorces, annulments, and dissolutions of marriage, 3705.21

Small loans; assignment on order of wages for support, 1321.32, 1321.33

Support of children, authority of court, 3109.05

Uniform child custody jurisdiction law, 3109.21 to 3109.37

Ohio Administrative Code References

Department of job and family services, child support program, OAC Ch 5101:1-29

Department of job and family services, collection of past due support by federal tax refund offset, OAC Ch 5101:1-30

Library References

OJur 3d: 45, Family Law § 170; 46, Family Law § 386, 443, 446, 550, 606, 630, 652, 659, 701, 706; 48, Family Law § 1769

Am Jur 2d: 24, Divorce and Separation § 233, 415 et seq.; 25, Dower and Curtesy § 141 to 148

Validity and effect, as between former spouses, of agreement releasing parent from payment of child support provided for in an earlier divorce decree. 100 ALR3d 1129

Separation agreements: enforceability of provision affecting property rights upon death of one party prior to final judgment of divorce. 67 ALR4th 237

Carlin, Baldwin's Ohio Practice, *Merrick-Rippner Probate Law* § 108.34 (1997)

Klein & Darling, Baldwin's Ohio Practice, *Civil Practice* § 55, 75 (1997)

Sowald & Morganstern, Baldwin's Ohio Practice, *Domestic Relations Law* § 4.28, 7.26, 7.35, 8.2, 8.4, 9.36, 11.8, 11.21, 12.17, 19.20, 20.6, 25.14, 25.64, 27.3 (1997)

Law Review and Journal Commentaries

Divorce and life insurance: Post mortem remedies for breach of a duty to maintain a policy for a designated beneficiary, Kelvin H. Dickinson. 61 Mo L Rev 533 (1996).

The Effect of the Tax Reform Act of 1984 on Divorce Financial Planning, Note. 24 J Fam L 283 (1985-86).

Legal Limbo: The Divorcing Family Between Physical Separation and Legal Separation: A Proposal to Reduce the Mischief, Expense, Waste and Acrimony of the Divorce Process, Jill Coleman. 28 J Fam L 659 (1989-90).

Notes of Decisions and Opinions

1. In general

Separation agreement is not ultimately binding until it is finalized. Schneider v. Schneider (Geauga 1996) 110 Ohio App.3d 487, 674 N.E.2d 769, appeal not allowed 77 Ohio St.3d 1416, 670 N.E.2d 1004.

Finding of fraud, duress, or misrepresentation is not required before separation agreement may be invalidated under statute authorizing court to enforce separation agreement if in interests of justice and equity. Schneider v. Schneider (Geauga 1996) 110 Ohio App.3d 487, 674 N.E.2d 769, appeal not allowed 77 Ohio St.3d 1416, 670 N.E.2d 1004.

Decision to enforce separation agreement is discretionary one and will not be reversed on appeal absent abuse of discretion. Schneider v. Schneider (Geauga 1996) 110 Ohio App.3d 487, 674 N.E.2d 769, appeal not allowed 77 Ohio St.3d 1416, 670 N.E.2d 1004.

A trial court does not err in vacating a divorce decree which does not contain a finding of paternity—which is later disputed by the putative father—and the purported settlement agreement accepted by the court varies from the in-court recitation of its terms and is not signed by the putative father's attorney. LaBonte v. LaBonte (Meigs 1988) 61 Ohio App.3d 209, 572 N.E.2d 704, motion overruled 42 Ohio St.3d 709, 538 N.E.2d 122.

A separation agreement is not signed under duress by a husband who has been in prison for contempt of court for failure to pay child support as well as other expenses and fees and (1) while in prison he initiates a plan suggesting to his spouse that she draw up a separation agreement that he would sign in exchange for her help in getting him out of jail, (2) he inadvertently signs only the acknowledgment and not the separation agreement, and (3) he ratifies the agreement by signing it several days after his release from jail and by making the support payments called for under the agreement. MacNealy v MacNealy, No. 96 CA 125, 1997 WL 674622 (2d Dist Ct App, Clark, 10-31-97).

Sufficiency of evidence to justify a decree of divorce lies largely in the discretion of the trial court. Dursa v. Dursa (Cuyahoga 1958) 150 N.E.2d 306, 78 Ohio Law Abs. 498.

2. Power to dissolve marriage

Although filing of bankruptcy petition stays equitable distribution in divorce case of debtor's interest in marital assets, certain aspects of divorce case, such as dissolution of marriage and child custody issues, are not stayed. State ex rel. Miley v. Parrott (Ohio 1996) 77 Ohio St.3d 64, 671 N.E.2d 24.

Trial court was obligated to reactivate divorce case after bankruptcy court lifted automatic stay affecting Chapter 12 debtor-husband; order inactivating divorce case stated that case would stay inactive until judge "is advised in writing of the stay having been lifted," trial court was advised in writing that bankruptcy court had lifted stay for divorce case, trial court would not be subject to contempt for violating stay after bankruptcy court expressly modified and lifted stay, and divorce case would not be better resolved after conclusion of bankruptcy proceedings. State ex rel. Miley v. Parrott (Ohio 1996) 77 Ohio St.3d 64, 671 N.E.2d 24.

Automatic stay may be lifted or modified for cause. State ex rel. Miley v. Parrott (Ohio 1996) 77 Ohio St.3d 64, 671 N.E.2d 24.

In the hearing of a divorce case, the court must hear and determine the cause, and cannot refer the issues of fact and law to a referee for findings and decision. State ex rel Kleinman v Cleveland, 118 OS 536, 161 NE 918 (1928).

Under former O Const Art 4 § 6, a court of appeals had jurisdiction in error proceedings to reverse a judgment entered in a divorce action upon the grounds that such judgment is contrary to the weight of the evidence. Weeden v. Weeden (Ohio 1927) 116 Ohio St. 524, 156 N.E. 908, 5 Ohio Law Abs. 332, 25 Ohio Law Rep. 336.

Court of appeals has jurisdiction of error proceeding brought to set aside the action of the court of common pleas in overruling a motion to set aside a dismissal of divorce proceeding. Cox v. Cox (Ohio 1922) 104 Ohio St. 611, 136 N.E. 823, 19 Ohio Law Rep. 712, 19 Ohio Law Rep. 740.

No default or consent decree can be made in a divorce case, and if a decree is made after a hearing and entered of record, both parties are released from the marriage contract. There is an affirmative release for each. Of course if new evidence were presented, or the court should on reconsideration arrive at a different conclusion, the decree would be made accordingly. Smith v. Smith (Ohio 1921) 103 Ohio St. 391, 133 N.E. 792, 19 Ohio Law Rep. 395.

In the absence of any express or implied limitation in a divorce decree and separation agreement concerning the "college education" of children, the term "college education" is unambiguous and should be read and interpreted in its broadest sense, subject only to the ability to pay. Forstner v. Forstner (Lake 1990) 68 Ohio App.3d 367, 588 N.E.2d 285.

In an action for divorce, wherein the defendant filed an answer and a counterclaim for alimony, the procedure whereby, by agreement of counsel and the court, the case was tried only on the issue of divorce, with questions of alimony and division of the property deferred, is not conducive to the effective administration of a divorce court, and such method of trial is strongly disapproved. Linz v. Linz (Hamilton 1972) 33 Ohio App.2d 174, 293 N.E.2d 100, 62 O.O.2d 260.

The requirement that the common pleas court shall hear any of the causes for divorce charged in the petition seeking divorce has no application to a hearing on a motion of a divorced husband to amend an order denying him the right to visit his children. Hebden v. Hebden (Franklin 1957) 105 Ohio App. 461, 153 N.E.2d 150, 6 O.O.2d 210.

The common pleas court cannot refer the issues of fact and law in a divorce case therein to a referee, but it may refer motions to terminate or modify former orders for the monthly payments of alimony and support of children, and the referee may hear and make recommendations and reports to the court for approval or disapproval in accordance with the statutes applicable thereto. McGhee v. McGhee (Franklin 1957) 105 Ohio App. 433, 152 N.E.2d 810, 6 O.O.2d 187.

In the hearing of a divorce case, the judge must personally hear and determine the cause, and no reference to another judge or referee can be allowed, even by consent of both parties. Perry v. Perry (Pickaway 1955) 100 Ohio App. 15, 135 N.E.2d 427, 59 O.O. 450.

Where, upon trial of an action for divorce on the alleged grounds of gross neglect of duty and extreme cruelty, it is brought to the attention of the court that the plaintiff had been previously married, it is error for the court to require plaintiff to prove the legal dissolution of his former marriage before being permitted to offer proof of the allegations in his petition. Treadway v. Treadway (Hamilton 1954) 97 Ohio App. 248, 125 N.E.2d 552, 56 O.O. 35.

Only form of divorce that may be decreed by court under this section is absolute divorce. Mathias v. Mathias (Tuscarawas 1946) 78 Ohio App. 330, 70 N.E.2d 276, 34 O.O. 44.

Divorce decree, on amended petition changing action from one for alimony to one for divorce without hearing on amended petition, held erroneously rendered. Thompson v. Thompson (Hamilton 1931) 42 Ohio App. 164, 181 N.E. 272, 12 Ohio Law Abs. 447, 35 Ohio Law Rep. 524.

Trial court's refusal of divorce may be reviewed on weight of evidence, and the judgment reversed. Cassada v. Cassada (Hamilton 1930) 38 Ohio App. 385, 176 N.E. 465, 9 Ohio Law Abs. 135.

The presence in an action for divorce of a cross-petition praying for divorce on the ground of fraudulent contract did not formerly render the action appealable. Raybuck v. Raybuck (Wayne 1927) 25 Ohio App. 365, 157 N.E. 831, 5 Ohio Law Abs. 306.

When a divorce is refused by the trial court and error is prosecuted to the court of appeals, and there is no conflict in the evidence and the judges of the court of appeals are unanimously of the opinion that a divorce should have been granted, the judgment of the trial court should be reversed; and, there being presented only a question of law, the court of appeals may enter the judgment which the trial court should have entered. Widican v. Widican (Summit 1925) 23 Ohio App. 271, 155 N.E. 145, 5 Ohio Law Abs. 762.

The court of appeals has jurisdiction of a proceeding in error to review a judgment dismissing, without hearing, a petition for divorce on the ground of nonresidence of the plaintiff. Schmid v. Schmid (Ohio App. 1 Dist. 1917) 10 Ohio App. 24, 31 Ohio C.A. 429.

Where a husband filed a complaint for divorce and a wife filed a complaint for alimony on the same day and the cases were consolidated, the court erred in granting the wife a divorce on grounds of gross neglect of duty, as she never requested a divorce. Bernasek v Bernasek, No. 82-J-37 (7th Dist Ct App, Jefferson, 3-20-84).

In a divorce action, the fact that four months time elapsed between the final hearing and the issuance of the final decree does not constitute reversible error. Daniels v Daniels, Nos. 3239 and 3236 (9th Dist Ct App, Lorain, 5-12-82).

A nunc pro tunc entry indicating a divorce was granted prior to the death of one of the parties was void, as the pending divorce had not been granted prior to the death of a party; such pending divorce action abated on the date of the death of one of the parties, thus relieving the trial court of jurisdiction to issue the nunc pro tunc order. Parmelee v Laprocina, No. 10135 (9th Dist Ct App, Summit, 7-22-81).

A reviewing court in passing on an assignment of error that a decree of divorce is against the manifest weight of the evidence is warranted in setting aside the decree only when the record does not disclose any evidence of a substantial nature which reasonably supports the judgment. Weinstein v. Weinstein (Cuyahoga 1962) 185 N.E.2d 56, 90 Ohio Law Abs. 199, 27 O.O.2d 115, appeal dismissed 174 Ohio St. 408, 189 N.E.2d 635, 23 O.O.2d 49.

The question of custody of a minor child may not be referred to a referee, and any order made as the result of such a reference is invalid. Rider v. Rider (Mahoning 1957) 152 N.E.2d 361, 78 Ohio Law Abs. 214.

3. Separation agreement regarding child support

A constructive trust is the appropriate remedy to ensure that insurance proceeds are paid to those who were to be named beneficiaries of an insurance policy by the terms of a separation agreement embodied in a divorce decree. Kelly v. Medical Life Ins. Co. (Ohio 1987) 31 Ohio St.3d 130, 509 N.E.2d 411, 31 O.B.R. 289.

The statutory change in the age of majority has no application to pre-1974 support decrees incorporating parental separation agreements. Rosenfeld v. Rosenfeld

(Ohio 1976) 47 Ohio St.2d 12, 351 N.E.2d 181, 1 O.O.3d 8.

The statutory change in the age of majority has no application to pre-1974 support decrees. Nokes v. Nokes (Ohio 1976) 47 Ohio St.2d 1, 351 N.E.2d 174, 1 O.O.3d 1.

Parties to a separation agreement may not abrogate by contract right of minor child of marriage to be supported by either parent. McDonnold v. McDonnold (Lake 1994) 98 Ohio App.3d 822, 649 N.E.2d 1236.

Provision of separation agreement that neither party would be responsible for the support of child in the custody of other party was invalid and of no effect; provision was not within contemplation of statute authorizing husband and wife to agree to immediate separation and to make provisions for support of children during the separation, as agreement did not provide for support of child in custody of other spouse. McDonnold v. McDonnold (Lake 1994) 98 Ohio App.3d 822, 649 N.E.2d 1236.

Former husband's obligation under separation agreement to pay all uninsured medical, dental, optical, and orthodontic expenses for his minor children was nondischargeable in former husband's bankruptcy proceeding as being in nature of support, even though medical expenses did not arise in regular, periodic fashion, and even though medical provider would benefit from payments. Dozer v. Dozer (Ross 1993) 88 Ohio App.3d 296, 623 N.E.2d 1272.

Former husband's child support obligation could be modified even absent showing that former wife was no longer able to provide support over and above former husband's obligation, although child support order provided that former wife shall assume any support of children in excess of former husband's contribution toward support, where separation agreement incorporated into divorce order also provided for modification of child support in event of extraordinary circumstances dramatically affecting children. Parzynski v. Parzynski (Erie 1992) 85 Ohio App.3d 423, 620 N.E.2d 93, dismissed, jurisdictional motion overruled 67 Ohio St.3d 1450, 619 N.E.2d 419, rehearing denied 67 Ohio St.3d 1513, 622 N.E.2d 660.

Where a mother seeks to extend child support payments for the month between a child's high school graduation and her eighteenth birthday, at which time the child becomes emancipated, a motion for relief is unnecessary where the court has continuing jurisdiction and the separation agreement with its child support provision is incorporated into the dissolution agreement and provides for support until the child graduates high school or becomes emancipated, whichever occurs first; the trial court does not have to modify the child support portion of the separation agreement but need only interpret it in light of case law providing for parental obligation of support until the age of majority. Dudziak v. Dudziak (Cuyahoga 1992) 81 Ohio App.3d 361, 611 N.E.2d 337.

A separation agreement adopted by a court in a divorce action which was entered into prior to obtaining a decree of divorce is a binding and enforceable contract which remains enforceable even if the trial court later vacates the accompanying decree of divorce. Bourque v. Bourque (Clermont 1986) 34 Ohio App.3d 284, 518 N.E.2d 49.

A trial court may modify a separation agreement of the parties to an action for divorce in its discretion, unlike separation agreements entered into pursuant to a dissolution of marriage. Bourque v. Bourque (Clermont 1986) 34 Ohio App.3d 284, 518 N.E.2d 49.

A separation agreement clause that a portion of the support payments due from a husband who is a carpenter will be deferred during his seasonal unemployment, strikes, or disability is held to preclude any reduction in support even where the decline in construction over six years halves the husband's income. Oriold v. Oriold (Cuyahoga 1985) 26 Ohio App.3d 122, 498 N.E.2d 1082, 26 O.B.R. 333.

While separation agreement is generally required to be fair and equitable to wife, where parties have dealt at arm's length with each other rather than in confidential relationship, test is whether agreement is product of fraud, duress or undue influence upon party in weaker bargaining position. DiPietro v. DiPietro (Franklin 1983) 10 Ohio App.3d 44, 460 N.E.2d 657, 10 O.B.R. 52.

Separation agreement which is fair and equitable and free from fraud is valid and enforceable; conversely, if separation agreement was procured by fraud or it appears that unfair advantage has been taken of either party thereto in its execution, agreement will not be enforced. Carey v. Carey (Shelby 1983) 9 Ohio App.3d 243, 459 N.E.2d 626, 9 O.B.R. 416.

Where a consent order is entered which changes the custody of minor children but such change never takes place, the trial court, in subsequently considering child support, has jurisdiction to award a lesser amount to the de facto custodial parent than that set forth in a prior order. Ollangg v. Ollangg (Franklin 1979) 64 Ohio App.2d 17, 410 N.E.2d 789, 18 O.O.3d 11.

Where, as part of a valid agreement, a husband agrees to provide college education for his children and further agrees to keep in effect insurance policies on his life in which such children are beneficiaries, and where such agreement is incorporated in a decree divorcing the husband from his wife, such decree becomes binding upon the husband even though the performance required by the decree may extend beyond the minority of the children. Grant v. Grant (Erie 1977) 60 Ohio App.2d 277, 396 N.E.2d 1037, 14 O.O.3d 249.

RC 3105.10 clothes courts with jurisdiction to incorporate into a court order an agreement to support a child of the parties beyond the age of that child's majority, and such an order may be enforced by contempt proceedings. (Annotation from former RC 3105.20.) Bugay v. Bugay (Summit 1977) 53 Ohio App.2d 285, 373 N.E.2d 1263, 7 O.O.3d 336.

A separation agreement loses its contractual nature at the time it is accepted and incorporated by the court into the final divorce decree, and obligations imposed under the agreement are thereafter imposed by the decree and may be enforced by contempt proceedings. Bugay v. Bugay (Summit 1977) 53 Ohio App.2d 285, 373 N.E.2d 1263, 7 O.O.3d 336.

In a dispute between parties pursuant to a separation agreement over reimbursement of college costs, a journal entry is not a final appealable order where it does not (1) determine the action as to college costs, (2) reduce any amount of reimbursement wife may be due for college expenses to judgment such that a garnishment or execution could issue therefrom, or (3) resolve whether wife is entitled to reimbursement. Jack v Jack, No. 96-JE-10, 1997 WL 16173 (7th Dist Ct App, Jefferson, 1-17-97).

The right of a spouse to collect a child support arrearage that accrues prior to her final decree of dissolution is extinguished when the separation agreement imposing the support obligation is incorporated into and becomes the final order of the court. Dula v Canter, No.

17527, 1996 WL 325291 (9th Dist Ct App, Summit, 6-12-96).

Judgment for payment of a child's college expenses provided for in a separation agreement should not be considered child support and collection thereof should not be made through the Child Support Enforcement Agency. Chester v Baker, No. 95-CA-7, 1995 WL 497602 (5th Dist Ct App, Licking, 8-10-95).

Where child support arrearages exist prior to a remarriage of the parties and the parties subsequently divorce for a second time, a general release set forth in a separation agreement incorporated into the second divorce decree discharges a child support arrearage existing at the time of remarriage. Fout v Fout, No. 93AP-865, 1993 WL 485119 (10th Dist Ct App, Franklin, 11-23-93).

A domestic relations court has jurisdiction to determine the validity of a contract between a father and daughter over the age of eighteen, when the contract nullifies the court's decree enforcing a separation agreement that requires the father to pay the daughter's college expenses, if any. Keenan v Keenan, No. L-85-242 (6th Dist Ct App, Lucas, 4-25-86).

Where a separation agreement provides that the father may veto his participation in orthodontic expenses if he does not approve them in advance, the court will find the agreement binding if the agreement is clear and unambiguous. Hamilton v Hamilton, No. 7083 (2d Dist Ct App, Montgomery, 10-19-81).

Wife would not be bound by child support and alimony portions of ostensible oral settlement agreement in divorce action, despite her prior oral agreement to accept terms of settlement agreement; wife had developed severe migraine headache one hour into settlement negotiations, wife revoked her oral acceptance later during same day, and oral agreement was not placed on record, acknowledged by parties under oath, or presented to judge for his consideration. May v. May (Ohio Com.Pl. 1993) 63 Ohio Misc.2d 207, 620 N.E.2d 317.

Chapter 7 debtor's postpetition child support obligation, imposed by prepetition separation agreement was nondischargeable; obligation had effect of insuring that daily needs of children were satisfied even past their minority, given disparity in parties' financial circumstances. In re Friedrich (Bkrtcy.N.D.Ohio 1993) 158 B.R. 675.

Mortgage payments to be made by a husband under a divorce decree that are listed under the heading "alimony" in the decree and that have the effect of providing a home for the couple's children are obligations in the nature of "support" that cannot be discharged in the husband's bankruptcy. In re Costell (Bkrtcy.N.D.Ohio 1987) 75 B.R. 348.

4. Condonation and recrimination in defense

RC 3105.10(C) abolishes the common-law defenses of recrimination or condonation; it does not merely authorize a court to ignore these defenses when the equities of the case so require. Mahle v. Mahle (Franklin 1985) 27 Ohio App.3d 326, 500 N.E.2d 907, 27 O.B.R. 383.

In an uncontested divorce proceeding in which there is proof of desertion by defendant husband, trial court has discretionary authority to grant divorce decree to plaintiff wife after considering all appropriate factors including best interests of community and welfare of children without raising defenses not pleaded concerning misconduct of the plaintiff wife subsequent to desertion, and consequently mothers of illegitimate children are not automatically ineligible to divorce husbands who previously deserted them. (Annotation from former RC 3105.20.) Newell v. Newell (Stark 1970) 23 Ohio App.2d 149, 261 N.E.2d 278, 52 O.O.2d 178.

Where an appellant in an action to vacate a divorce decree is unable to advance any convincing reasons for failing to appear at the divorce hearing, and where appellee's position has been irrevocably changed, it does not constitute an abuse of discretion for a trial court to refuse to vacate the decree despite the fact that appellant is able to produce some evidence that appellee condoned his wife's (the appellant's) conduct and that he stood "in loco parentis" to her child. Wilson v. Wilson (Cuyahoga 1968) 14 Ohio App.2d 148, 237 N.E.2d 421, 43 O.O.2d 340.

Cohabitation will be inferred from the living together of husband and wife; and condonation of aggression will be inferred from cohabitation where the contrary does not appear, but where the evidence discloses that the parties, living in the same house, had no sexual relations during the pendency of an action for divorce, such action should not be dismissed upon the ground that such parties were living in the same house and that the aggression was thereby condoned. Cousino v. Cousino (Lucas 1952) 90 Ohio App. 449, 107 N.E.2d 213, 48 O.O. 121.

Granting of divorce is error where applicant is himself guilty of act which constitutes statutory ground for divorce and recrimination is pleaded. Karpanty v. Karpanty (Lucas 1926) 39 Ohio App. 194, 177 N.E. 521, 5 Ohio Law Abs. 264.

Adulterous acts of husband, continued after wife's condonation of his earlier offenses, held to preclude granting husband divorce for gross neglect of duty, where wife pleaded recrimination. Karpanty v. Karpanty (Lucas 1926) 39 Ohio App. 194, 177 N.E. 521, 5 Ohio Law Abs. 264.

Construing RC 3105.011 in conjunction with RC 3105.10(C), the trial court in domestic relations actions is vested with full equitable powers and may apply the doctrine of clean hands, but where recrimination is pleaded and proved as a defense by a party it does not work a bar upon the trial court for that reason alone to granting a divorce. Helms v Helms, No. 5-81-36 (3d Dist Ct App, Hancock, 10-1-82).

The fact that a character witness of the opposite sex of the party seeking divorce lives at the same address as that party is insufficient to warrant the application of the "clean hands" doctrine absent evidence of conduct in violation of the marriage obligation; on such facts, a dismissal of a complaint for divorce for the stated reason that plaintiff lacked "clean hands" constitutes grounds for reversible error. Helms v Helms, No. 5-81-36 (3d Dist Ct App, Hancock, 10-1-82).

In an action for divorce, trial court erred in dismissing plaintiff's complaint under the "clean hands" doctrine where evidence established only that the plaintiff was living with another man and not that there was conduct in violation of the marriage obligation. Helms v Helms, No. 5-81-36 (3d Dist Ct App, Hancock, 10-1-82).

The so-called doctrine of comparative rectitude does not prevail in Ohio, and where both spouses have been guilty of misconduct which is cause for divorce, neither is entitled to divorce. Sandrene v. Sandrene (Summit 1952) 121 N.E.2d 324, 67 Ohio Law Abs. 481.

5. Dower

A divorced wife who had an inchoate right of dower prior to amendment of the pertinent statutes in 1932 lost such right as a result thereof, and such legislation was valid. Any injustice done her thereby could be remedied by a modification of the alimony award. GC 26 (RC 1.20) has no application to a pending divorce or alimony action where the statute involved relates to inchoate right of dower. Goodman v. Gerstle (Ohio 1952) 158 Ohio St. 353, 109 N.E.2d 489, 49 O.O. 235.

In view of amendment to this section, eff. January 1, 1932, providing that upon granting of a divorce each party shall be barred of all right of dower in real estate of other by force of such judgment, it is unnecessary to incorporate in order of court such bar which arises by operation of law. Huff v. Huff (Wood 1946) 79 Ohio App. 514, 74 N.E.2d 390, 35 O.O. 334.

Where a divorce decree awards the former husband the former wife's interest in the family home and real estate while ordering him to pay her a sum of money secured by a lien on the property, the husband cannot avoid the lien under 11 USC 522(f)(1), which provides that a debtor may avoid judicial liens on an interest in property. Farrey v. Sanderfoot (U.S.Wis. 1991) 111 S.Ct. 1825, 500 U.S. 291, 114 L.Ed.2d 337, on remand 943 F.2d 679.

6. Property division and spousal support

Installment payments made to a custodial parent following a divorce decree do not constitute a division of marital property where: (1) an unidentified portion of the payments are expressly designated as child support; (2) no other provision for spousal support is made in the decree; and (3) the total amount of marital assets are determined to be $7,090, while the total amount of the installment payments exceeds $160,000. Colizoli v. Colizoli (Ohio 1984) 15 Ohio St.3d 333, 474 N.E.2d 280, 15 O.B.R. 458.

In alimony proceedings, the court in awarding alimony is controlled by statute, and is not authorized to exercise general equity powers. Durham v. Durham (Ohio 1922) 104 Ohio St. 7, 135 N.E. 280, 19 Ohio Law Rep. 548.

Trial court's determination that enforcement of separation agreement was contrary to interests of justice and equity was not abuse of discretion, where agreement awarded much larger percentage of marital property to husband and wife claimed that she signed agreement because husband threatened to seek custody of minor child if she fought him in divorce proceeding. Schneider v. Schneider (Geauga 1996) 110 Ohio App.3d 487, 674 N.E.2d 769, appeal not allowed 77 Ohio St.3d 1416, 670 N.E.2d 1004.

Where an antenuptial agreement addresses only the disposition of property on the death of one of the spouses, and is silent concerning disposition in the event of divorce, it is error to apply the agreement to determine issues of division of property and spousal support in a divorce proceeding. Devault v. Devault (Franklin 1992) 80 Ohio App.3d 341, 609 N.E.2d 214, motion overruled 65 Ohio St.3d 1444, 600 N.E.2d 686, motion overruled 65 Ohio St.3d 1499, 605 N.E.2d 952.

A divorce decree will not serve automatically to cut off the rights of a beneficiary to an insurance policy; rather, the decree must plainly indicate the elimination of the named beneficiary from all rights to the life insurance proceeds, or the insured must change the beneficiary of the policy through the procedures set forth in the policy. Reno v. Clark (Van Wert 1986) 33 Ohio App.3d 41, 514 N.E.2d 456.

An action for both divorce and division of property does not require abatement upon death of a party prior to entry of decree; rather, trial court is vested with discretion to either dismiss the action or to enter a judgment nunc pro tunc. Miller v. Trapp (Miami 1984) 20 Ohio App.3d 191, 485 N.E.2d 738, 20 O.B.R. 235.

Where property is not divided by an original divorce decree, no appeal was taken from the decree, and time for appeal has expired, a court of common pleas has no jurisdiction to modify its previous decree. Bean v. Bean (Madison 1983) 14 Ohio App.3d 358, 471 N.E.2d 785, 14 O.B.R. 462.

A divorce decree in effect restoring to the parties their separate property rights, but not coupled with a voluntary separation agreement contemplating a full settlement of their property rights, does not warrant a court finding an implied revocation of a will executed during marriage. Lang v. Leiter (Wood 1956) 103 Ohio App. 119, 144 N.E.2d 332, 3 O.O.2d 184.

A common pleas court, having granted a divorce, may apply equitable principles in making an award of alimony and, with respect to property owned by the parties jointly or in common, may make an equitable division thereof between them. Boehm v. Boehm (Lucas 1956) 101 Ohio App. 145, 138 N.E.2d 418, 1 O.O.2d 83.

Jurisdiction of common pleas courts to award alimony prior to 1953 discussed. Boehm v. Boehm (Lucas 1956) 101 Ohio App. 145, 138 N.E.2d 418, 1 O.O.2d 83.

Decree cannot be forced upon defendant not praying for divorce or alimony. Wickham v. Wickham (Lucas 1930) 35 Ohio App. 142, 171 N.E. 864, 8 Ohio Law Abs. 284.

A decision not to award spousal support to a wife or set aside the separation agreement is supported by evidence (1) that an award of spousal support was bargained away in exchange for a quick uncontested divorce, (2) the wife squandered a substantial share of the marital assets in pursuit of romance in the Bahamas and (3) at the end of the romantic relationship the wife falsely claims that a "confused" state of mind is a basis here to set aside the separation agreement. Overholser v Overholser, No. 97-CA-24, 1998 WL 22040 (2d Dist Ct App, Montgomery, 1-23-98).

A final decree granting a wife free occupancy of the marital home until she remarries is a property division and thus cannot be modified unless justice or equity requires; that the husband has paid all expenses during the twelve years since a decree is not, alone, a circumstance rendering modification necessary. Barcalow v Barcalow, No. 84-B-55 (7th Dist Ct App, Belmont, 6-19-85).

A court's reduction of a husband's equity interest in the former marital property by $2500 to satisfy a child support arrearage of $960 does not constitute modification of a prior property division. Hendershot v Hendershot, No. 84-CA-08 (2d Dist Ct App, Champaign, 10-18-84).

A journal entry reflecting a property settlement agreed to at a pre-trial conference is void, as the court has jurisdiction to divide a couple's property only when it grants a divorce, such jurisdiction not encompassing pre-trial conferences. Daniels v Daniels, No. 2989 (9th Dist Ct App, Lorain, 10-15-80).

Where a divorce case against an insane defendant was dismissed without final hearing, an appeal lay to determine issue made as to property right under earlier statute without deciding whether insanity was bar to divorce. Keerlick v Keerlick, 24 CC(NS) 492, 34 CD 719 (1906).

Postconfirmation change in Chapter 13 debtor's circumstances, when state divorce court ordered debtor's spouse to pay portion of debts thereby increasing money available for distribution to unsecured creditors, was not "unanticipated" change and did not permit modification of debtor's plan to increase payment to unsecured creditors, where debtor was involved in divorce proceeding at time of creditors' meeting and plan confirmation hearing; parties should have anticipated divorce court's order and provided for this contingency in plan. In re Wilson (Bkrtcy.S.D.Ohio 1993) 157 B.R. 389.

Postconfirmation change in Chapter 13 debtor's circumstances, when state divorce court ordered debtor's spouse to pay portion of debts thereby increasing money available for payment to unsecured creditors, was not "substantial" change, and did not permit modification of plan (even assuming that trustee could not have foreseen this development at time plan was confirmed), where debtor's net disposable income increased, as result of divorce court's order, by only $267 per month for 20 months; at time of confirmation hearing, debtor had take-home income of $1,557 per month. In re Wilson (Bkrtcy.S.D.Ohio 1993) 157 B.R. 389.

Where a husband obligated by a divorce decree to pay a joint debt to a lender is able to discharge his own liability on that debt through bankruptcy proceedings, and where he listed the lender as a creditor in those proceedings but did not so list his wife, prompting the wife to return to domestic relations court where she secured a ruling that the husband's obligation to hold her harmless on the debt survived his bankruptcy, the bankruptcy court will not reopen the case to consider the issue decided by the state court, regardless of whether that decision was correct. In re Brice (Bkrtcy.S.D.Ohio 1987) 79 B.R. 310.

Following Williams v Sprigg, 6 OS 585 (1856), a federal court must hold that a women's possession of a home that the latest recorded deed shows is held by her as a tenant by the entireties with her husband is consistent with the record title and therefore imposes no duty on a bona fide purchaser from the husband to inquire and discover that the couple's unrecorded divorce decree states it has the effect of a conveyance of the property from the husband to the wife. In re Costell (Bkrtcy.N.D.Ohio 1987) 75 B.R. 348.

A divorce decree that directs the husband to convey real property to his wife and states the decree itself shall have the effect of a conveyance if the husband neglects to obey must be recorded in the same manner as a deed, or it is fraudulent under RC 5301.25 as against a subsequent bona fide purchaser without knowledge of the decree. In re Costell (Bkrtcy.N.D.Ohio 1987) 75 B.R. 348.

3105.11 Testimony—Repealed

(1970 H 1201, eff. 7-1-71; 130 v H 467; 1953 H 1; GC 8003-12; Source—GC 11988)

Historical and Statutory Notes

Ed. Note: See now Civ R 75(L) for provisions analogous to former 3105.11.

Pre-1953 H 1 Amendments: 124 v S 65

3105.12 Evidence of marriage; common law marriage prohibited

(A) Except as provided in division (B) of this section, proof of cohabitation and reputation of the marriage of a man and woman is competent evidence to prove their marriage, and, in the discretion of the court, that proof may be sufficient to establish their marriage for a particular purpose.

(B)(1) On and after the effective date of this amendment, except as provided in divisions (B)(2) and (3) of this section, common law marriages are prohibited in this state, and the marriage of a man and woman may occur in this state only if the marriage is solemnized by a person described in section 3101.08 of the Revised Code and only if the marriage otherwise is in compliance with Chapter 3101. of the Revised Code.

(2) Common law marriages that occurred in this state prior to the effective date of this amendment and that have not been terminated by death, divorce, dissolution of marriage, or annulment remain valid on and after the effective date of this amendment.

(3) Common law marriages that satisfy all of the following remain valid on and after the effective date of this amendment:

(a) They came into existence prior to the effective date of this amendment, or come into existence on or after that date, in another state or nation that recognizes the validity of common law marriages in accordance with all relevant aspects of the law of that state or nation.

(b) They have not been terminated by death, divorce, dissolution of marriage, annulment, or other judicial determination in this or another state or in another nation.

(4) On and after the effective date of this amendment, all references in the Revised Code to common law marriages or common law marital relationships, including the references in

sections 2919.25, 3113.31, and 3113.33 of the Revised Code, shall be construed to mean only common law marriages as described in divisions (B)(2) and (3) of this section.

(1991 H 32, eff. 10-10-91; 1953 H 1; GC 8003-13; Source—GC 11989)

Historical and Statutory Notes

Pre-1953 H 1 Amendments: 124 v S 65

Comparative Laws

Fla.—West's F.S.A. § 741.211.
Idaho—I.C. § 32-201.
Ill.—ILCS 750 5/214.
Ky.—Baldwin's KRS 402.020.
N.J.—N.J.S.A. 37:1-10.

Cross References

Bigamy, 2919.01
Hearsay exceptions, availability of declarant immaterial, Evid R 803
Persons who may marry, 3101.01

Library References

Marriage ⚷13, 41 to 50.
WESTLAW Topic No. 253.
C.J.S. Marriage §§ 10, 19, 20, 55 to 60.

OJur 3d: 31, Decedents' Estates § 115; 32, Decedents' Estates § 926; 42, Evidence and Witnesses § 233; 43, Evidence and Witnesses § 276; 45, Family Law § 34, 36, 42; 46, Family Law § 656
Am Jur 2d: 24, Divorce and Separation § 356; 52, Marriage § 158 to 161
Common law marriage between parties previously divorced. 82 ALR2d 688
Carlin, Baldwin's Ohio Practice, *Merrick-Rippner Probate Law* § 68.1, 89.18 (1997)
Giannelli & Snyder, Baldwin's Ohio Practice, Evidence § 501.22, 601.8 (1996)
Hausser, Ohio Real Estate Law and Practice (2d Ed.), Text 35.081
Sowald & Morganstern, Baldwin's Ohio Practice, *Domestic Relations Law* § 2.6, 2.35, 2.37, 2.42, 2.50, 2.54, 2.57, 7.6, 7.7, 11.9, 14.24, 35.4 (1997)

Law Review and Journal Commentaries

Nonmarital Relationships and Their Impact on the Institution of Marriage and the Traditional Family Structure, Charles F. Crutchfield. 19 J Fam L 247 (1980-81).

Unmarried Cohabitants: Abandon All Hope, Ye Who Enter Ohio, Hon. Mike Brigner. 9 Domestic Rel J Ohio 75 (September/October 1997).

Notes of Decisions and Opinions

Burden of proof 2
Cohabiting unmarried persons' obligations 4
Elements of common law marriage 1
Evidence 3

---

1. Elements of common law marriage

The fundamental requirement to establish the existence of a common law marriage is a meeting of the minds between the parties who enter into a mutual contract to presently take each other as man and wife; the absence of this agreement precludes the establishment of such a relationship even though the parties live together and openly engage in cohabitation. Nestor v. Nestor (Ohio 1984) 15 Ohio St.3d 143, 472 N.E.2d 1091, 15 O.B.R. 291.

An agreement of marriage followed by living together as husband and wife, establishes a valid marriage at common law. Umbenhower v. Labus (Ohio 1912) 85 Ohio St. 238, 97 N.E. 832, 9 Ohio Law Rep. 554.

Common-law marriages that occurred prior to October 10, 1991, are valid unless terminated by death, divorce, dissolution of marriage, or annulment. State v. Phelps (Cuyahoga 1995) 100 Ohio App.3d 187, 652 N.E.2d 1032.

Although Ohio law now prohibits common-law marriages, the state will recognize as valid all common-law marriages that occurred prior to October 10, 1991. Lyon v. Lyon (Scioto 1993) 86 Ohio App.3d 580, 621 N.E.2d 718.

The essential element of a common-law marriage is a present mutual contract by the parties to be married to each other as husband and wife. Mullins v. Mullins (Paulding 1990) 69 Ohio App.3d 167, 590 N.E.2d 311.

A common law marriage may be established in Ohio only when each of the following five essential elements is proved by clear and convincing evidence: (1) an agreement of marriage per verba de praesenti; (2) made by parties competent to marry; (3) followed by cohabitation; (4) a holding out as husband and wife; and (5) a reputation as being husband and wife. In re Soeder's Estate (Cuyahoga 1966) 7 Ohio App.2d 271, 220 N.E.2d 547, 36 O.O.2d 404.

Proof that a ceremonial marriage has been performed and that the parties have held themselves out as husband and wife for a long time is competent evidence to prove a marriage without proof of the issuance of a marriage license or certificate of such marriage. (See also Kontner v Kontner, 103 App 372, 145 NE(2d) 495 (1956).) Kontner v. Kontner (Franklin 1956) 103 Ohio App. 360, 139 N.E.2d 366, 74 Ohio Law Abs. 97, 3 O.O.2d 384, rehearing denied 103 Ohio App. 360, 145 N.E.2d 495, 3 O.O.2d 384.

Evidence of cohabitation and reputation and conduct of parties, without the testimony of surviving party, held satisfactory proof of common-law marriage. Howard v.

Central Nat. Bank of Marietta (Washington 1926) 21 Ohio App. 74, 152 N.E. 784, 4 Ohio Law Abs. 700.

The elements to be established by the proponent of the common law marriage are: (a) an agreement to marry in praesenti, (b) made by parties competent to contract, (c) which is accepted by the parties and followed by cohabitation as husband and wife, (d) in the community where they reside as husband and wife, and each element must be proved by "clear and convincing" evidence. Jolley v. Jolley (Ohio Com.Pl. 1975) 46 Ohio Misc. 40, 347 N.E.2d 557, 75 O.O.2d 350.

2. Burden of proof

All of the essential elements to a common law marriage must be established by clear and convincing evidence. Nestor v. Nestor (Ohio 1984) 15 Ohio St.3d 143, 472 N.E.2d 1091, 15 O.B.R. 291.

Where evidence before the trial court does not clearly and convincingly establish the parties' intent to establish a common-law marriage, it is proper for the trial court to hold that no such agreement between the parties exists. Mullins v. Mullins (Paulding 1990) 69 Ohio App.3d 167, 590 N.E.2d 311.

Evidence that might not be sufficient to establish a common law marriage for purpose of convicting an accused of bigamy might nevertheless be sufficient to establish such marriage for the purpose of proving the legitimacy of offspring of the persons alleged to have been married. Dirion v. Brewer (Cuyahoga 1925) 20 Ohio App. 298, 151 N.E. 818, 4 Ohio Law Abs. 534.

Although cohabitation, the holding themselves out as husband and wife in the community in which they move, and a reputation as husband and wife in the community in which they live, is not shown, clear and convincing evidence of a mutual agreement to marry in praesenti made by parties competent to marry is sufficient to establish a common law marriage. In re Soeder's Estate (Ohio Prob. 1965) 4 Ohio Misc. 96, 209 N.E.2d 175, 33 O.O.2d 75, reversed 7 Ohio App.2d 271, 220 N.E.2d 547, 36 O.O.2d 404.

3. Evidence

Where term "cohabitation" is used in divorce decree in sense of event which will alter obligations created in decree, court must look to whether parties have assumed obligations, including support, equivalent to those arising from ceremonial marriage. Wallenhurst v. Wallenhurst (Ohio App. 7 Dist. 1996) 116 Ohio App.3d 823, 689 N.E.2d 586.

Proof that ceremonial wedding has been performed allied with holding out as husband and wife for period of time is sufficient to prove marriage under statute governing evidence of marriage. State v. Phelps (Cuyahoga 1995) 100 Ohio App.3d 187, 652 N.E.2d 1032.

Evidence supported finding that man did not reach cohabitation agreement with woman to share expenses and combine incomes and that he did not retain any of the woman's assets after he left. Tarry v. Stewart (Lorain 1994) 98 Ohio App.3d 533, 649 N.E.2d 1, appeal not allowed 71 Ohio St.3d 1502, 646 N.E.2d 1126.

Trial court finding that no present agreement to remarry existed between decedent and his divorced spouse, disqualifying spouse from serving as administrator of decedent's intestate estate as "surviving spouse," was supported by evidence that decedent and former spouse declared themselves single on federal and state income tax forms and bankruptcy petitions, former spouse shipped decedent's possessions to him when he lived in another state, decedent dated other women, and that parties intended to remarry in the future, despite cohabitation immediately before decedent's death. In re Estate of Shepherd (Marion 1994) 97 Ohio App.3d 280, 646 N.E.2d 561.

No valid marriage results from mutual promise to marry in the future followed by cohabitation as husband and wife, even though parties are competent to contract. In re Estate of Shepherd (Marion 1994) 97 Ohio App.3d 280, 646 N.E.2d 561.

Common-law marriages have never been favored in Ohio and, since October 10, 1991, are prohibited altogether. State v. Burkitt (Clark 1993) 89 Ohio App.3d 214, 624 N.E.2d 210, dismissed, jurisdictional motion overruled 67 Ohio St.3d 1501, 622 N.E.2d 650.

There is probative and substantial evidence to support a trial court's judgment that a woman claiming to be a decedent's common-law wife has not established common-law marriage where the two failed to sign purchase documents and income tax returns as reflecting a marital status, no change was made by the decedent to name the woman as the beneficiary of his life insurance or pension benefits, and there is evidence that the deceased had stated that he would not marry the woman and hoped to reconcile with his former wife. In re Estate of Hall (Washington 1990) 67 Ohio App.3d 715, 588 N.E.2d 203.

Where there is no direct proof in reference to formation of contract of marriage in praesenti, testimony regarding cohabitation and community reputation tends to raise inference of marriage; inference is given more or less strength according to circumstances of particular case and is generally strengthened with lapse of time during which parties are living together and cohabitating as man and wife. Fitzgerald v. Mayfield (Adams 1990) 66 Ohio App.3d 298, 584 N.E.2d 13, motion overruled 53 Ohio St.3d 705, 558 N.E.2d 60.

There need not be general reputation to base common law marriage if parties so held out to those with whom they normally come in contact. Gatterdam v. Gatterdam (Franklin 1949) 86 Ohio App. 29, 85 N.E.2d 526, 54 Ohio Law Abs. 271, 40 O.O. 459, appeal dismissed 151 Ohio St. 551, 86 N.E.2d 614, 39 O.O. 347.

Common law marriage in Ohio discussed; fact that relation was originally illicit does not prevent valid marriage to arise by cohabitation and reputation. Ryan v. Ryan (Stark 1948) 84 Ohio App. 139, 86 N.E.2d 44, 39 O.O. 166.

This section, authorizing proof of marriage by evidence of cohabitation and reputation of the marriage of the parties, applies to proof of marriage for the purpose of establishing the legitimacy of the offspring of the parties. Dirion v. Brewer (Cuyahoga 1925) 20 Ohio App. 298, 151 N.E. 818, 4 Ohio Law Abs. 534.

The in praesenti requirement of a common law marriage cannot be defeated by a belief, mistaken or otherwise, that one is already married to the same spouse; thus a common law marriage was established between the parties after an Illinois divorce obtained by the wife in 1968 where the parties continued to live together until 1986 and the wife then filed a second divorce action in Ohio relying on her 1958 marriage. Hatfield v Hatfield, No. 94 CA 07, 1995 WL 23984 (4th Dist Ct App, Gallia, 1-11-95).

Cohabitation and reputation are evidential facts from which the existence of a contract of marriage may be inferred, but an agreement to marry in praesenti is an essential element of a common law marriage: When all the elements essential to a common law marriage are present, the fact that an innocent person will not be benefited or protected thereby will not preclude its establishment. Leibrock v. Leibrock (Ohio Com.Pl. 1952) 107 N.E.2d 418, 63 Ohio Law Abs. 565.

That party discovered existence of common law marriage doctrine did not cause evidence of cohabitation, asserted to constitute common law marriage, to be newly discovered for purposes of motion to reconsider summary judgment order. Huff v. Metropolitan Life Ins. Co. (C.A.6 (Ohio) 1982) 675 F.2d 119.

Where parties cohabited for some time but there was no agreement of marriage in praesenti between them, and few people, if any, with whom they associated knew them as husband and wife, court properly refused to exclude testimony of alleged wife in car theft trial and properly found there was no common law marriage. U. S. v. Goble (C.A.6 (Ky.) 1975) 512 F.2d 458, certiorari denied 96 S.Ct. 220, 423 U.S. 914, 46 L.Ed.2d 143, certiorari denied 96 S.Ct. 221, 423 U.S. 914, 46 L.Ed.2d 143.

4. Cohabiting unmarried persons' obligations

Existence of sexual relationship between unmarried parties living together is not conclusive on issue of cohabitation giving rise to event which will alter obligations created in divorce decree. Wallenhurst v. Wallenhurst (Ohio App. 7 Dist. 1996) 116 Ohio App.3d 823, 689 N.E.2d 586.

Unjust enrichment occurs when party retains money or benefits which in justice and equity belong to another. Tarry v. Stewart (Lorain 1994) 98 Ohio App.3d 533, 649 N.E.2d 1, appeal not allowed 71 Ohio St.3d 1502, 646 N.E.2d 1126.

Trial court's refusal to impose constructive trust on property retained by man after termination of cohabitation arrangement with woman did not violate public policy. Tarry v. Stewart (Lorain 1994) 98 Ohio App.3d 533, 649 N.E.2d 1, appeal not allowed 71 Ohio St.3d 1502, 646 N.E.2d 1126.

3105.13 Legitimacy of children—Repealed

(1982 H 245, eff. 6-29-82; 1953 H 1; GC 8003-14; Source—GC 11987)

Historical and Statutory Notes

Ed. Note: See now 3111.03 for provisions analogous to former 3105.13.

Pre-1953 H 1 Amendments: 124 v S 65

3105.14 and 3105.15 Allowance and custody pendente lite; delay of divorce decree—Repealed

(1970 H 1201, eff. 7-1-71; 132 v H 1; 130 v H 467; 126 v 601; 1953 H 1; GC 8003-15, 8003-16; Source—GC 11979-1, 11994)

Historical and Statutory Notes

Ed. Note: See now Civ R 75(M) and 75(N) for provisions analogous to former 3105.14 and 3105.15, respectively.

Pre-1953 H 1 Amendments: 124 v S 65

3105.16 Restoration of name

When a divorce is granted the court of common pleas shall, if the person so desires, restore any name that the person had before the marriage.

(1978 H 349, eff. 10-25-78; 1953 H 1; GC 8003-17; Source—GC 11190)

Historical and Statutory Notes

Pre-1953 H 1 Amendments: 124 v S 65

Cross References

Change of name, 2717.01
Name change of registered voter, notice to board of elections, 3503.11, 3503.19

Library References

Divorce ⚷313.1, 317.
WESTLAW Topic No. 134.
C.J.S. Divorce §§ 761 to 763, 765, 766, 768.

OJur 3d: 46, Family Law § 702

Am Jur 2d: 24, Divorce and Separation § 882; 29, Divorce and Separation § 419

Sowald & Morganstern, Baldwin's Ohio Practice, *Domestic Relations Law* § 9.23 (1997)

Notes of Decisions and Opinions

Wife's surname 1

1. Wife's surname

After marriage, a woman's legal surname is that of her husband. 1931 OAG 3452.

LEGAL SEPARATION; DIVISION OF PROPERTY; SPOUSAL SUPPORT

3105.17 Grounds for legal separation

(A) Either party to the marriage may file a complaint for divorce or for legal separation, and when filed the other may file a counterclaim for divorce or for legal separation. The court of common pleas may grant divorces for the causes set forth in section 3105.01 of the Revised Code. The court of common pleas may grant legal separation on a complaint or counterclaim, regardless of whether the parties are living separately at the time the complaint or counterclaim is filed, for the following causes:

(1) Either party had a husband or wife living at the time of the marriage from which legal separation is sought;

(2) Willful absence of the adverse party for one year;

(3) Adultery;

(4) Extreme cruelty;

(5) Fraudulent contract;

(6) Any gross neglect of duty;

(7) Habitual drunkenness;

(8) Imprisonment of the adverse party in a state or federal correctional institution at the time of filing the complaint;

(9) On the application of either party, when husband and wife have, without interruption for one year, lived separate and apart without cohabitation;

(10) Incompatibility, unless denied by either party.

(B) The filing of a complaint or counterclaim for legal separation or the granting of a decree of legal separation under this section does not bar either party from filing a complaint or counterclaim for a divorce or annulment or obtaining a divorce or annulment.

(1994 H 571, eff. 10-6-94; 1990 H 514, eff. 1-1-91; 1974 H 233; 1953 H 1; GC 8003-18; Source—GC 11997)

Historical and Statutory Notes

Pre-1953 H 1 Amendments: 124 v S 65

Amendment Note: 1994 H 571 substituted "correctional" for "penal" in division (A)(8).

Cross References

Complaint for divorce, legal separation, and custody of children, Civ R Appendix, Form 20

Divorce, annulment, and legal separation actions, Civ R 75

Divorce, legal separation or annulment actions stayed by petition for conciliation, 3117.07, 3117.08

Divorce or legal separation action involving custody or care of children, jurisdiction of juvenile court, 2151.23

Duty of married person to support self, spouse, and children; duration of duty to support, 3103.03

Husband and wife, mutual obligations, 3103.01

Lottery winner must state under oath whether or not he is in default of support order, 3770.071

Nonsupport of dependents, 2919.21

Library References

Divorce ⟾12 to 38.
WESTLAW Topic No. 134.
C.J.S. Divorce §§ 13 to 70, 77, 78, 139.

OJur 3d: 46, Family Law § 405, 449, 450, 452, 453, 549, 579, 597, 607, 707, 721, 748, 759

Am Jur 2d: 24, Divorce and Separation § 514 et seq.

Misconduct of wife to whom divorce is decreed as affecting allowance of alimony, or amount allowed. 9 ALR2d 1026

Allowance of permanent alimony to wife against whom divorce is granted. 34 ALR2d 313

Right to allowance of permanent alimony in connection with decree of annulment. 81 ALR3d 281

Adulterous wife's right to permanent alimony. 86 ALR3d 97

Fault as consideration in alimony, spousal support, or property division awards pursuant to no-fault divorce. 86 ALR3d 1116

Divorced woman's subsequent sexual relations or misconduct as warranting, alone or with other circumstances, modification of alimony decree. 98 ALR3d 453

Divorced or separated spouse's living with member of opposite sex as affecting other spouse's obligations of alimony or support under separation agreement. 47 ALR4th 38

Insanity as defense to divorce or separation suit—post-1950 cases. 67 ALR4th 277

Carlin, Baldwin's Ohio Practice, *Merrick-Rippner Probate Law* § 98.4 (1997)

Sowald & Morganstern, Baldwin's Ohio Practice, *Domestic Relations Law* § 4.28, 7.36, 8.1, 8.2, 8.4, 8.8, 11.28, 12.1, 13.8, 14.34, 27.3, 27.4, 27.21, 27.55, 29.14 (1997)

Law Review and Journal Commentaries

Children—The Innocent Victims of Family Breakups: How the Family Law Attorney, the Courts, and Society Can Protect Our Children, Michael J. Albano. 26 U Tol L Rev 787 (Summer 1995).

Of Covenants and Conflicts—When "I Do" Means More Than It Used To, But Less Than You Thought, Jason Andrew Macke. 59 Ohio St L J 1377 (1998).

Policyholder May Not Cancel Health Insurance Coverage During Pendency of Action, Pamela J. MacAdams. 3 Domestic Rel J Ohio 151 (November/December 1991).

Notes of Decisions and Opinions

Gross neglect; cruelty 3
Grounds generally 2
Legal separation action 5
Powers and jurisdiction of court 1
Spousal support 4

---

1. Powers and jurisdiction of court

Effect on husband's finances of domestic relations court's interlocutory orders in wife's legal separation action did not establish inadequacy of postjudgment appeal to rectify any alleged errors by that court, as required for husband to obtain writ of prohibition. Fraiberg v. Cuyahoga Cty. Court of Common Pleas, Domestic Relations Div. (Ohio 1996) 76 Ohio St.3d 374, 667 N.E.2d 1189, reconsideration denied 76 Ohio St.3d 1497, 670 N.E.2d 243.

The subject matter jurisdiction of a trial court to award permanent alimony and to formulate an equitable division of the marital assets commences when either party files a complaint for divorce and a division of the marital property. Bolinger v. Bolinger (Ohio 1990) 49 Ohio St.3d 120, 551 N.E.2d 157.

A court is not precluded in the exercise of its equity powers from considering the element of aggression in making an award of alimony. Esteb v. Esteb (Ohio 1962) 173 Ohio St. 259, 181 N.E.2d 462, 19 O.O.2d 80.

A court has the same power in awarding alimony only that it does in awarding alimony where a divorce is granted. Goetzel v. Goetzel (Ohio 1959) 169 Ohio St. 350, 159 N.E.2d 751, 8 O.O.2d 355.

Granting of the prayer of defendant's cross-petition for divorce on same day cross-petition is filed, without service of process on plaintiff or opportunity for her to be fully heard or make defense thereto, is a denial of her day in court, amounts to an abuse of discretion, and is reversible error. Calvert v. Calvert (Ohio 1936) 130 Ohio St. 369, 199 N.E. 473, 4 O.O. 464.

A trial court has no power under RC 3115.23 to order the garnishment of wages to pay alimony. Whitmore v. Whitmore (Wayne 1976) 49 Ohio App.2d 159, 359 N.E.2d 714, 3 O.O.3d 204.

A trial court is without authority to make a division of property unless it is pursuant to an alimony award under RC 3105.18. Soyk v. Soyk (Summit 1975) 45 Ohio App.2d 319, 345 N.E.2d 461, 74 O.O.2d 532.

The dismissal of the prayer of a petition for a divorce does not divest the court of jurisdiction to enter a decree for alimony and support. Hobbs v. Hobbs (Greene 1961) 115 Ohio App. 536, 186 N.E.2d 134, 21 O.O.2d 200.

A defendant may dismiss a cross-petition for divorce before the cause is submitted for decision and it is error for the trial court to disallow such dismissal when the defendant has moved to dismiss before a final submission of the cause. Roberts v. Roberts (Lucas 1961) 113 Ohio App. 33, 177 N.E.2d 281, 17 O.O.2d 38.

The granting of a "legal separation" by the trial court in an action by a wife seeking such relief is a misnomer, and, where such judgment might be construed as absolving the defendant husband from his statutory duty to support the wife, it will be modified accordingly. Cummings v. Cummings (Erie 1959) 111 Ohio App. 447, 173 N.E.2d 159, 15 O.O.2d 64.

Jurisdiction of common pleas courts to award alimony prior to 1953 discussed. Boehm v. Boehm (Lucas 1956) 101 Ohio App. 145, 138 N.E.2d 418, 1 O.O.2d 83.

Whether there is or is not an answer filed to a petition for divorce and alimony or for alimony alone, the cause is adversary and must be submitted and determined on its merits. Gasior v. Gasior (Lucas 1940) 67 Ohio App. 84, 35 N.E.2d 1021, 21 O.O. 105.

Where the parties cannot agree regarding the division of household furnishings, and the referee suggests a division by lottery, and the parties still do not agree, it is not an abuse of discretion for the trial court to adopt the recommendation of the referee. Bokovitz v Bokovitz, No. 1062 (9th Dist Ct App, Medina, 9-23-81).

A court may not make a division of property in an alimony only proceeding because domestic relations courts are without authority, in an alimony only action, to permanently divide the parties' property interests but may only render awards for maintenance and support. Turek v Turek, No. 42307 (8th Dist Ct App, Cuyahoga, 11-13-80).

A wife to whom alimony only has been granted may by her misconduct during the period of judicial separation forfeit her right to the continuing award of alimony. Bishop v. Bishop (Ohio Com.Pl. 1969) 18 Ohio Misc. 177, 248 N.E.2d 641, 47 O.O.2d 417.

Where a wife is granted alimony only, the marriage is not dissolved and the parties have the relationship of husband and wife although they are judicially separated due to the misconduct of the husband. Bishop v. Bishop (Ohio Com.Pl. 1969) 18 Ohio Misc. 177, 248 N.E.2d 641, 47 O.O.2d 417.

Judgment for permanent alimony does not prevent another court from entertaining jurisdiction for an action of divorce and alimony and awarding latter unless prior decree was for a lump sum. Neal v. Neal (Ohio Com.Pl. 1949) 85 N.E.2d 147, 53 Ohio Law Abs. 329.

A petition for alimony alone, by a wife who has not been a resident of the state for a year, gives the court jurisdiction of a cross-petition for divorce by the husband, who is a nonresident, under this section, permitting a cross-petition for divorce to a wife's suit for divorce or alimony. (See also Ferguson v Ferguson, 11 NP(NS) 679, 55 B 1508 (1910).) Arno v Arno, 9 LR 226, 56 B 308 (1911).

Divorce granted in Ohio to husband, without jurisdiction over wife or property in his name, does not determine the right of wife to either alimony or dower in said property. Barberton Savings Bank Co. v. Belford (Ohio Cir. 1911) 22 Ohio C.D. 574, 14 Ohio C.C.(N.S.) 24.

2. Grounds generally

An award of alimony in an action under RC 3105.17 for alimony only requires proof of one of the statutory grounds stated in that statute; the fact of a valid divorce obtained without personal jurisdiction is not a ground under that statute and, where the only evidence to support the statutory grounds is not corroborated as required by RC 3105.11, an award of alimony cannot be granted on the basis of RC 3105.17. Rousculp v. Rousculp (Franklin 1968) 17 Ohio App.2d 101, 244 N.E.2d 512, 46 O.O.2d 125.

Where a husband secures a divorce on the ground that his wife had a husband living at the time of her marriage to him, such cause for divorce is not a ground for alimony under RC 3105.17. (See also Kontner v Kontner, 103 App 372, 145 NE(2d) 495 (1956).) Kontner v. Kontner (Franklin 1956) 103 Ohio App. 360, 139 N.E.2d 366, 74 Ohio Law Abs. 97, 3 O.O.2d 384, rehearing denied 103 Ohio App. 360, 145 N.E.2d 495, 3 O.O.2d 384.

Where wife, in action for divorce brought in the jurisdiction wherein she is domiciled, obtains service upon the husband by publication only, the right to alimony continues until adjudicated, and the decree of divorce in such proceeding is not a bar to subsequent action for alimony. Stephenson v. Stephenson (Cuyahoga 1936) 54 Ohio App. 239, 6 N.E.2d 1005, 22 Ohio Law Abs. 580, 6 O.O. 559.

As respects bar of alimony by foreign divorce, divorce and alimony are separable causes of action. Metzger v. Metzger (Pickaway 1929) 32 Ohio App. 202, 167 N.E. 690, 7 Ohio Law Abs. 298.

Where a husband induces his wife to marry him, leave her home and country, and give up her previous means of support, and then refuses her admittance when she arrives at his home, the court should consider her action for alimony only on the grounds of gross neglect of duty, abandonment without good cause, and ill-treatment by the adverse party, despite the fact that they lived together for only three days following the marriage. Coreano v Coreano, No. 47422 (8th Dist Ct App, Cuyahoga, 4-19-84).

Where the evidence does not show any gross neglect of marital duties and fails to demonstrate such calculated destructive acts as to constitute extreme emotional cruelty, courts may grant a motion to dismiss. Smith v Smith, No. 43527 (8th Dist Ct App, Cuyahoga, 1-14-82).

Subsequent cohabitation of the wife with another man is not grounds for terminating support alimony where the personal relationship does not affect the continued need for alimony. Lester v Lester, No. 81AP-84 (10th Dist Ct App, Franklin, 5-14-81).

In a suit for alimony on the ground of "a separation in consequence of ill-treatment by the adverse party," the ill-treatment complained of must be such as to not only cause the complainant to separate from the other spouse but also such as to justify the complainant in so doing. Maughan v. Maughan (Ohio Com.Pl. 1961) 184 N.E.2d 628, 89 Ohio Law Abs. 282, 21 O.O.2d 121.

A divorce granted in another state against an insane wife in Ohio, dissolves the marriage relation but does not affect property and alimony rights of the wife in Ohio. Walters v. Larrick (Ohio Com.Pl. 1930) 28 Ohio N.P.N.S. 281, affirmed 39 Ohio App. 363, 177 N.E. 642, 10 Ohio Law Abs. 508.

An action for divorce and alimony, brought in the name of an insane husband, by his guardian, cannot be maintained. Prather v. Prather (Ohio Com.Pl. 1934) 4 Ohio Supp. 243, 33 Ohio Law Abs. 336, 1 O.O. 188.

3. Gross neglect; cruelty

Finding by trial court that the transfer of his personal property by a husband to his children by a former marriage "undermined" the wife's "economic security" is not sufficient to constitute either any gross neglect of duty or extreme cruelty under the divorce statute, or any gross neglect of duty under this section, where the trial court found no invasion of the wife's right to present support and that the husband was still possessed of unincumbered, improved real estate. Mark v. Mark (Ohio 1945) 145 Ohio St. 301, 61 N.E.2d 595, 30 O.O. 534.

Failure to support, to constitute gross neglect of duty, must exist prior to or at the time the decree for divorce and/or alimony is rendered and may not be predicated upon a possible or probable failure of future support, nor does such possible or probable failure of future support constitute extreme cruelty within the purview of the statutes relating to divorce and alimony. Mark v. Mark (Ohio 1945) 145 Ohio St. 301, 61 N.E.2d 595, 30 O.O. 534.

"Any gross neglect of duty" as used by the statutes refers to an omission of legal duty. Mark v. Mark (Ohio 1945) 145 Ohio St. 301, 61 N.E.2d 595, 30 O.O. 534.

Where there is evidence of a husband's psychological problems and addiction to alcohol and prescription drugs as well as evidence of the adverse effect of these problems on the marriage, the trial court may properly find the husband grossly neglected his duties and find that therefore the wife is entitled to alimony only she had sought. Vogt v. Vogt (Lucas 1990) 67 Ohio App.3d 197, 586 N.E.2d 242.

Extreme cruelty is not within the grounds for alimony enumerated in this section. McGhee v. McGhee (Montgomery 1945) 64 N.E.2d 254, 45 Ohio Law Abs. 465.

4. Spousal support

Where a separation agreement divides debts between the husband and wife with each party to pay some and hold the other party harmless, a trial court may find that the husband's assumption of debts is in the nature of support and alimony rather than a property division. Thompson v. Thompson (Richland 1986) 27 Ohio App.3d 296, 501 N.E.2d 108, 27 O.B.R. 341.

Where an alimony award contains contingencies which end the obligation to pay, the award is periodic alimony rather than a property division, notwithstanding its statement of definite amounts payable over a definite period, and a reservation of jurisdiction to modify the award is implied. Bean v. Bean (Madison 1983) 14 Ohio App.3d 358, 471 N.E.2d 785, 14 O.B.R. 462.

All orders for temporary alimony are merged in the final decree of divorce and are thereby terminated, unless extended during the pendency of the appeal. Yonally v. Yonally (Summit 1974) 45 Ohio App.2d 122, 341 N.E.2d 602, 74 O.O.2d 134.

The merger of a temporary alimony order in the final decree of divorce does not extinguish the right of the former spouse to collect the arrearage that accrued under the temporary alimony order before the merger occurred. Yonally v. Yonally (Summit 1974) 45 Ohio App.2d 122, 341 N.E.2d 602, 74 O.O.2d 134.

Garnishment provisions of RC 3115.23 do not apply to an award of alimony under RC 3105.17 and 3105.18. McClain v. McClain (Cuyahoga 1971) 26 Ohio App.2d 10, 268 N.E.2d 294, 55 O.O.2d 28.

Where wife, in action for divorce obtains personal service upon defendant, the question of alimony must be litigated therein, and the decree rendered is res judicata on all questions existing between the parties arising out of their marital relationship, including alimony. Stephenson v. Stephenson (Cuyahoga 1936) 54 Ohio App. 239, 6 N.E.2d 1005, 22 Ohio Law Abs. 580, 6 O.O. 559.

The court of common pleas is vested with full equity powers and has broad discretion in the matter of allowing alimony, and an order concerning alimony may be reversed only where the evidence clearly shows an abuse of discretion or a misapprehension of the facts. Lykins v. Lykins (Pike 1964) 198 N.E.2d 779, 93 Ohio Law Abs. 385, 29 O.O.2d 222.

Award of alimony to fifty-one year old physician for aggression of twenty-nine year old wife and property settlement decreed were proper. Sharkey v. Sharkey (Montgomery 1955) 137 N.E.2d 575, 73 Ohio Law Abs. 321.

Where a federal bankruptcy court asks the parties to address the effect of a nunc pro tunc order of an Ohio domestic relations court changing a divorce decree passage from "plaintiff shall retain the 1982 Bonneville" to "plaintiff shall be awarded as alimony, the 1982 Bonneville automobile," the court will conclude from its own review of Ohio law that the nunc pro tunc judgment entry does have retroactive effect. In re Swiczkowski (Bkrtcy.N.D.Ohio 1988) 84 B.R. 487.

The award under a divorce decree of an automobile to the wife and the imposition on the husband of the duty to pay for it as installments of the debt fall due, is in the nature of support and the husband's obligation to the wife is not dischargeable in bankruptcy where the woman also has custody of the children, because "reliable transportation" is "an essential commodity for a family with minor children." In re Swiczkowski (Bkrtcy.N.D.Ohio 1988) 84 B.R. 487.

The circumstances of the parties as they were on the date of a state court decree of divorce control the dischargeability of a husband's obligations under the Bankruptcy Code, 11 USC 523(a)(5); thus, obligations which are plainly alimony, maintenance, and support when viewed in the light of the decree and separation agreement cannot be discharged. Matter of Brown (Bkrtcy.S.D.Ohio 1985) 46 B.R. 612.

5. Legal separation action

A husband and wife have mutual obligations of respect, fidelity, and support; therefore, in order to obtain an award of alimony only on the grounds of gross neglect of duty, the complainant must show that the spouse has breached a duty of mutual respect, fidelity, or support. Vogt v. Vogt (Lucas 1990) 67 Ohio App.3d 197, 586 N.E.2d 242.

In an action for alimony only, if the evidence supports a finding that one of the statutory grounds for alimony only has been proven, the trial court must grant the petition; it has no discretion with regard to this issue. Vogt v. Vogt (Lucas 1990) 67 Ohio App.3d 197, 586 N.E.2d 242.

Pursuant to RC 3105.011 and 3105.03, there is no minimum period of domicile as a prerequisite to an action for alimony brought pursuant to RC 3105.17. Gieg v. Gieg (Trumbull 1984) 16 Ohio App.3d 51, 474 N.E.2d 626, 16 O.B.R. 55.

A complaint for alimony only may be made by the primary wage earner, who would be the party to pay alimony. Gieg v. Gieg (Trumbull 1984) 16 Ohio App.3d 51, 474 N.E.2d 626, 16 O.B.R. 55.

A separation agreement entered into for the sole purpose of a dissolution of marriage is not a valid and binding contract when the dissolution petition is dismissed, but would be a valid and binding contract following dismissal of such petition if it contains language that the agreement shall be binding whether used in a divorce, alimony only, or a dissolution of marriage action, or such similar language evidencing the intent of the parties that it will survive dismissal of a dissolution of marriage petition, and in addition, if it does not contain express language that it was entered into solely for a dissolution of marriage action or express language that the parties intended the separation agreement to survive dismissal of a dissolution of marriage petition, but the actions and conduct of the parties evidence an intention that it will survive dismissal of a dissolution of marriage petition, the separation agreement will continue to be a valid and binding agreement after the dissolution of marriage petition is dismissed. Greiner v. Greiner (Cuyahoga 1979) 61 Ohio App.2d 88, 399 N.E.2d 571, 15 O.O.3d 95.

A wife cannot maintain an action for alimony alone, where, because the husband had a wife living at the time of his ceremonial marriage with plaintiff, they were not legally married, but she can maintain an action for divorce on the ground of her husband's undissolved marriage to another at the time of his ceremonial marriage with plaintiff, and in the action for alimony only, the defendant husband may not as a defense to such action obtain a declaratory judgment as to the marital status of the parties, notwithstanding the fact of defendant's prior undissolved marriage was not set out as a ground for alimony by plaintiff wife. Jones v. Jones (Cuyahoga 1962) 115 Ohio App. 358, 180 N.E.2d 847, 20 O.O.2d 441.

In an alimony action a court may order a division of property. Morrison v. Morrison (Franklin 1956) 102 Ohio App. 376, 143 N.E.2d 591, 2 O.O.2d 392.

Trial court, in action for alimony, may not decree permanent alimony to the wife under this section when the husband and wife continued to live together in the same home under circumstances constituting cohabitation. Smith v. Smith (Montgomery 1949) 86 Ohio App. 479, 92 N.E.2d 418, 56 Ohio Law Abs. 321, 42 O.O. 113.

In action for alimony alone in which alimony is awarded, and divorce decree entered on defendant's cross-petition is then reversed on error proceedings because evidence fails to establish grounds for divorce, the judgment awarding alimony must also be reversed since it was awarded on the theory of permanent alimony based on fact that a divorce had been granted. Welte v.

Welte (Lucas 1935) 50 Ohio App. 484, 198 N.E. 603, 20 Ohio Law Abs. 160, 4 O.O. 193.

Judgment for wife in alimony action bars husband's subsequent action for divorce based on extreme cruelty and neglect of duty committed before decision of alimony case. Picker v. Picker (Sandusky 1933) 46 Ohio App. 82, 187 N.E. 749, 16 Ohio Law Abs. 64, 39 Ohio Law Rep. 269.

In wife's action for alimony based on husband's misconduct which caused separation, general denial raises direct issue of misconduct, ill treatment, neglect of duty, and extreme cruelty, as if they had been specifically pleaded. Picker v. Picker (Sandusky 1933) 46 Ohio App. 82, 187 N.E. 749, 16 Ohio Law Abs. 64, 39 Ohio Law Rep. 269.

An alimony award in a judgment decree of alimony alone, which constitutes a division of the marital assets and liabilities, is not subject to modifications in a subsequent divorce action. Shapiro v Shapiro, No. 80AP-520 (10th Dist Ct App, Franklin, 11-25-80).

A wife to whom alimony only has been granted may by her misconduct during the period of judicial separation forfeit her right to the continuing award of alimony. Bishop v. Bishop (Ohio Com.Pl. 1969) 18 Ohio Misc. 177, 248 N.E.2d 641, 47 O.O.2d 417.

Where a wife is granted alimony only, the marriage is not dissolved and the parties have the relationship of husband and wife although they are judicially separated due to the misconduct of the husband. Bishop v. Bishop (Ohio Com.Pl. 1969) 18 Ohio Misc. 177, 248 N.E.2d 641, 47 O.O.2d 417.

The fact that a husband is making his wife a suitable and regular allowance is a defense to her suit for separate maintenance. Maughan v. Maughan (Ohio Com.Pl. 1961) 184 N.E.2d 628, 89 Ohio Law Abs. 282, 21 O.O.2d 121.

A court will not on a petition for alimony alone anticipate a decree for divorce and the consequent division of the property, unless the facts require it and the judgment expressly shows that the allowance is made as a division of the property and not for support of the wife. Madden v Madden, 11 CC(NS) 238, 21 CD 30 (1908), affirmed by 83 OS 506, 94 NE 1110 (1911).

Where petition was for alimony alone the decree will be modified or terminated by reason of changed conditions, when that right was reserved in the decree to the parties. Madden v Madden, 11 CC(NS) 238, 21 CD 30 (1908), affirmed by 83 OS 506, 94 NE 1110 (1911).

3105.171 Division of marital property; separate property

(A) As used in this section:

(1) "Distributive award" means any payment or payments, in real or personal property, that are payable in a lump sum or over time, in fixed amounts, that are made from separate property or income, and that are not made from marital property and do not constitute payments of spousal support, as defined in section 3105.18 of the Revised Code.

(2) "During the marriage" means whichever of the following is applicable:

(a) Except as provided in division (A)(2)(b) of this section, the period of time from the date of the marriage through the date of the final hearing in an action for divorce or in an action for legal separation;

(b) If the court determines that the use of either or both of the dates specified in division (A)(2)(a) of this section would be inequitable, the court may select dates that it considers equitable in determining marital property. If the court selects dates that it considers equitable in determining marital property, "during the marriage" means the period of time between those dates selected and specified by the court.

(3)(a) "Marital property" means, subject to division (A)(3)(b) of this section, all of the following:

(i) All real and personal property that currently is owned by either or both of the spouses, including, but not limited to, the retirement benefits of the spouses, and that was acquired by either or both of the spouses during the marriage;

(ii) All interest that either or both of the spouses currently has in any real or personal property, including, but not limited to, the retirement benefits of the spouses, and that was acquired by either or both of the spouses during the marriage;

(iii) Except as otherwise provided in this section, all income and appreciation on separate property, due to the labor, monetary, or in-kind contribution of either or both of the spouses that occurred during the marriage;

(iv) A participant account, as defined in section 148.01 of the Revised Code, of either of the spouses, to the extent of the following: the moneys that have been deferred by a continuing member or participating employee, as defined in that section, and that have been transmitted to the Ohio public employees deferred compensation board during the marriage and any income that is derived from the investment of those moneys during the marriage; the moneys that have been deferred by an officer or employee of a municipal corporation and that have been transmitted to the governing board, administrator, depository, or trustee of the deferred compensation program of the municipal corporation during the marriage and any income that is derived from the investment of those moneys during the marriage; or the moneys that have been deferred by an officer or employee of a government unit, as defined in section 148.06 of the Revised Code, and that have been transmitted to the governing board, as defined in that section, during the marriage and any income that is derived from the investment of those moneys during the marriage.

(b) "Marital property" does not include any separate property.

(4) "Passive income" means income acquired other than as a result of the labor, monetary, or in-kind contribution of either spouse.

(5) "Personal property" includes both tangible and intangible personal property.

(6)(a) "Separate property" means all real and personal property and any interest in real or personal property that is found by the court to be any of the following:

(i) An inheritance by one spouse by bequest, devise, or descent during the course of the marriage;

(ii) Any real or personal property or interest in real or personal property that was acquired by one spouse prior to the date of the marriage;

(iii) Passive income and appreciation acquired from separate property by one spouse during the marriage;

(iv) Any real or personal property or interest in real or personal property acquired by one spouse after a decree of legal separation issued under section 3105.17 of the Revised Code;

(v) Any real or personal property or interest in real or personal property that is excluded by a valid antenuptial agreement;

(vi) Compensation to a spouse for the spouse's personal injury, except for loss of marital earnings and compensation for expenses paid from marital assets;

(vii) Any gift of any real or personal property or of an interest in real or personal property that is made after the date of the marriage and that is proven by clear and convincing evidence to have been given to only one spouse.

(b) The commingling of separate property with other property of any type does not destroy the identity of the separate property as separate property, except when the separate property is not traceable.

(B) In divorce proceedings, the court shall, and in legal separation proceedings upon the request of either spouse, the court may, determine what constitutes marital property and what constitutes separate property. In either case, upon making such a determination, the court shall divide the marital and separate property equitably between the spouses, in accordance with this section. For purposes of this section, the court has jurisdiction over all property in which one or both spouses have an interest.

(C)(1) Except as provided in this division or division (E) of this section, the division of marital property shall be equal. If an equal division of marital property would be inequitable, the court shall not divide the marital property equally but instead shall divide it between the spouses in the manner the court determines equitable. In making a division of marital property, the court shall consider all relevant factors, including those set forth in division (F) of this section.

(2) Each spouse shall be considered to have contributed equally to the production and acquisition of marital property.

(3) The court shall provide for an equitable division of marital property under this section prior to making any award of spousal support to either spouse under section 3105.18 of the Revised Code and without regard to any spousal support so awarded.

(4) If the marital property includes a participant account, as defined in section 148.01 of the Revised Code, the court shall not order the division or disbursement of the moneys and income described in division (A)(3)(a)(iv) of this section to occur in a manner that is inconsistent with the law, rules, or plan governing the deferred compensation program involved or prior to the time that the spouse in whose name the participant account is maintained commences receipt of the moneys and income credited to the account in accordance with that law, rules, and plan.

(D) Except as otherwise provided in division (E) of this section or by another provision of this section, the court shall disburse a spouse's separate property to that spouse. If a court does not disburse a spouse's separate property to that spouse, the court shall make written findings of fact that explain the factors that it considered in making its determination that the spouse's separate property should not be disbursed to that spouse.

(E)(1) The court may make a distributive award to facilitate, effectuate, or supplement a division of marital property. The court may require any distributive award to be secured by a lien on the payor's specific marital property or separate property.

(2) The court may make a distributive award in lieu of a division of marital property in order to achieve equity between the spouses, if the court determines that a division of the marital property in kind or in money would be impractical or burdensome.

(3) If a spouse has engaged in financial misconduct, including, but not limited to, the dissipation, destruction, concealment, or fraudulent disposition of assets, the court may compensate the offended spouse with a distributive award or with a greater award of marital property.

(F) In making a division of marital property and in determining whether to make and the amount of any distributive award under this section, the court shall consider all of the following factors:

(1) The duration of the marriage;

(2) The assets and liabilities of the spouses;

(3) The desirability of awarding the family home, or the right to reside in the family home for reasonable periods of time, to the spouse with custody of the children of the marriage;

(4) The liquidity of the property to be distributed;

(5) The economic desirability of retaining intact an asset or an interest in an asset;

(6) The tax consequences of the property division upon the respective awards to be made to each spouse;

(7) The costs of sale, if it is necessary that an asset be sold to effectuate an equitable distribution of property;

(8) Any division or disbursement of property made in a separation agreement that was voluntarily entered into by the spouses;

(9) Any other factor that the court expressly finds to be relevant and equitable.

(G) In any order for the division or disbursement of property or a distributive award made pursuant to this section, the court shall make written findings of fact that support the determination that the marital property has been equitably divided and shall specify the dates it used in determining the meaning of "during the marriage."

(H) Except as otherwise provided in this section, the holding of title to property by one spouse individually or by both spouses in a form of co-ownership does not determine whether the property is marital property or separate property.

(I) A division or disbursement of property or a distributive award made under this section is not subject to future modification by the court.

(J) The court may issue any orders under this section that it determines equitable, including, but not limited to, either of the following types of orders:

(1) An order granting a spouse the right to use the marital dwelling or any other marital property or separate property for any reasonable period of time;

(2) An order requiring the sale or encumbrancing of any real or personal property, with the proceeds from the sale and the funds from any loan secured by the encumbrance to be applied as determined by the court.

(2000 H 628, eff. 9-21-00; 1992 S 300, eff. 11-5-92; 1990 H 514)

Historical and Statutory Notes

Amendment Note: 2000 H 628 substituted "148.01" for "145.71" and "148.06" for "145.74" in division (A)(3)(a)(iv); and substituted "148.01" for "145.71" in division (C)(4).

Cross References

Property held exempt from legal process by person domiciled in state, 2329.66

Public employees deferred compensation program, exemption of benefits from legal process, 148.09

Library References

Divorce ⚷252.2 to 252.5.
WESTLAW Topic No. 134.
C.J.S. Divorce §§ 514 to 527, 529 to 543, 547 to 549, 553 to 561, 563 to 565, 567, 568, 570, 571.

OJur 3d: 45, Exemptions § 48; 46, Family Law § 451, 457, 458, 462 to 464, 468, 470 to 472, 474, 475, 477, 478, 483, 484, 488, 497, 516, 561, 562, 672, 673, 709
Am Jur 2d: 24, Divorce and Separation § 864 et seq.
Rights and incidents where title to real property purchased with wife's funds is taken in spouses' joint names. 43 ALR2d 917
Divorce or separation: consideration of tax liability or consequences in determining alimony or property settlement provisions. 51 ALR3d 461
Evaluation of interest in law firm or medical partnership for purposes of division of property in divorce proceedings. 74 ALR3d 621
Pension or retirement benefits as subject to award or division by court in settlement of property rights between spouses. 94 ALR3d 176
Spouse's professional degree or license as marital property for purposes of alimony, support, or property settlement. 4 ALR4th 1294
Divorce and separation: effect of trial court giving consideration to needs of children in making property division—modern status. 19 ALR4th 239
Spouse's dissipation of marital assets prior to divorce as factor in divorce court's determination of property division. 41 ALR4th 416
Enforceability of premarital agreements governing support or property rights upon divorce or separation as affected by fairness or adequacy of those terms—modern status. 53 ALR4th 161
Divorce: excessiveness or adequacy of combined property division and spousal support awards—modern cases. 55 ALR4th 14
Divorce: propriety of property distribution leaving both parties with substantial ownership interest in same business. 56 ALR4th 862
Divorce property distribution: treatment and method of valuation of future interest in real estate or trust property not realized during marriage. 62 ALR4th 107
Divorce and separation: goodwill in medical or dental practice as property subject to distribution on dissolution of marriage. 76 ALR4th 1025
Valuation of goodwill in accounting practice for purposes of divorce court's property distribution. 77 ALR4th 609
Divorce and separation: goodwill in accounting practice as property subject to distribution on dissolution of marriage. 77 ALR4th 645
Valuation of goodwill in law practice for purposes of divorce court's property distribution. 77 ALR4th 683
Valuation of goodwill in medical or dental practice for purposes of divorce court's property distribution. 78 ALR4th 853
Accrued vacation, holiday time, and sick leave as marital or separate property. 78 ALR4th 1107
Divorce and separation: goodwill in law practice as property subject to distribution on dissolution of marriage. 79 ALR4th 171
Divorce and separation: consideration of tax consequences in distribution of marital property. 9 ALR5th 568

Carlin, Baldwin's Ohio Practice, *Merrick-Rippner Probate Law* § 13.5 (1997)
Klein & Darling, Baldwin's Ohio Practice, *Civil Practice* § 60 (1997)
Sowald & Morganstern, Baldwin's Ohio Practice, *Domestic Relations Law* § 1.7, 2.5, 2.47, 4.16, 4.24, 4.25, 4.28, 4.29, 4.30, 4.31, 4.32, 4.33, 4.34, 4.35, 4.36, 4.37, 5.14, 7.18, 8.4, 8.5, 9.6, 9.15, 9.20, 9.84, 10.3, 11.5, 12.1, 12.2, 12.3, 12.4, 12.5, 12.6, 12.7, 12.8, 12.9, 12.10, 12.11, 12.12, 12.13, 12.14, 12.15, 12.16, 12.18, 12.19, 12.23, 12.25, 12.26, 12.27, 12.29, 12.30, 13.2, 13.3, 13.8, 13.9, 13.16, 13.20, 14.14, 14.16, 14.34, 24.3, 24.7, 25.36, 25.41, 28.1, 29.1, 29.9, 29.40, 30.1, 30.3 (1997)
Wasil, Waite, & Mastrangelo, Ohio Workers' Compensation Law § 11:22

Law Review and Journal Commentaries

Appreciation of Premarital Real Estate—Marital or Separate Property?, Stanley Morganstern and Lynn B. Schwartz. 8 Domestic Rel J Ohio 92 (November/December 1996).

Ascertaining Self-Employment Income, Elaine M. Stoermer. 48 Dayton B Briefs 17 (October 1998).

Bankruptcy Basics—DISCHARGE ... A Simple Word, Not Easily Found, And is the Meaning Plain?, Thomas R. Noland. (Ed. note: The author explains the effect of discharging a debt in bankruptcy court.) 47 Dayton B Briefs 18 (June 1998).

Bankruptcy Reform Act of 1994—What the Bankruptcy Code Giveth, Domestic Relations Courts (and Congress) Taketh Away, C.R. "Chip" Bowles. 8 Domestic Rel J Ohio 17 (March/April 1996).

Buy-Sell Agreements—Valuing Closely Held Business Interests, Patrice R.T. Yarham. 11 Domestic Rel J Ohio 53 (July/August 1999).

Cohabitation Agreements and Related Documents, Hon. Mike Brigner. 9 Domestic Rel J Ohio 97 (November/December 1997).

Court Must Consider Social Security Benefits When Allocating Marital Retirement Benefits. 6 Domestic Rel J Ohio 17 (March/April 1994).

Criminal Law—Forfeiture—Third Circuit Holds Government is Entitled to Forfeiture of Property Interest Held in Tenancy by the Entireties Despite One Spouse's Innocent Owner Defense, United States v 1500 Lincoln Avenue, Comment. 37 Vill L Rev 996 (1992).

Current Pension Issues, Stanley Morganstern. 8 Domestic Rel J Ohio 73 (September/October 1996).

Defining the Business Valuation Expert's Assignment—Establish the Game Plan Before Starting to Play, Rand M. Curtiss. 9 Domestic Rel J Ohio 73 (September/October 1997).

Deposing and Examining Business Valuation Experts: How to Beat Us Up on the Stand, Rand M. Curtiss. 9 Domestic Rel J Ohio 21 (March/April 1997).

Dividing Retirement Benefits: Suggested Clauses, Hon. Judith A. Nicely and Stanley Morganstern. 8 Domestic Rel J Ohio 90 (November/December 1996).

Domestic Relations Corner—Military Benefits in Divorce: A Practitioner's Guide Part 2, Stephen L. De Vita. 45 Dayton B Briefs 19 (March 1996).

Domestic Relations Corner—Military Benefits in Divorce: A Practitioner's Guide Part 1, Stephen L. De Vita. 45 Dayton B Briefs 10 (February 1996).

The Economics of Divorce: Valuing Professional Practices and Licenses, Paul J. Buser. 18 Lake Legal Views 8 (June 1995).

Entrepreneurial Divorce: Warning For Closely Held Companies, Alan Starkoff. 5 Ohio Law 11 (May/June 1991).

Forfeiture of Marital Property Under 21 U.S.C. Sec. 881(a)(7): Irreconcilable Differences?, Anne-Marie Feeley. 37 Vill L Rev 1487 (1992).

How to Value Goodwill as Marital Asset, Sanford K. Ain, et al. 20 Nat'l L J B7 (March 23, 1998).

In Addition to Safeguarding Inheritances, Prenuptial Contracts can Help Attorneys Protect their Firm Ownership Interests, Burton Young, et al. 20 Nat'l L J B7 (December 15, 1997).

The Lawyer Turns Peacemaker—with mediation emerging as the most popular form of alternate dispute resolution, the quest for common ground could force attorneys to reinterpret everything they do in the future, Richard C. Reuben. 82 A B A J 54 (August 1996).

Litigation Results—Count on a CPA, Keith J. Libman. 67 Clev B J 12 (October 1996).

Middendorf—Appreciation of Separate Property Becomes Marital Property by Expenditure of Funds or Labor by Either Spouse, James R. Kirkland. 10 Domestic Rel J Ohio 105 (November/December 1998).

Marital vs. Non-Marital Interests—Valuing Closely Held Corporations, Bernard I. Agin. 8 Domestic Rel J Ohio 37 (May/June 1996).

N.Y. Lawyer Facing Divorce? Beware—State is the only one to value practice and license of professionals as marital property, Ann Davis. 19 Nat'l L J A1 (October 21, 1996).

Of Sausages, Paving Stones, and the Domestic Relations Amendments to the Bankruptcy Codes, John P. Gustafson. 44 Tol B Ass'n News 15 (May 1997).

Ohio Revised Code Section 3105.171: An Equitable Distribution Statute Maintaining Judicial Discretion And Transmutation, Note. 17 U Dayton L Rev 697 (Winter 1992).

Pathfinder: Economic Effects of Divorce on Women, Barbara Laughlin. 14 Legal Reference Serv Q 57 (1995).

The Plain Meaning of the Automatic Stay in Bankruptcy: The Void/Voidable Distinction Revisited, Timothy Arnold Barnes. 57 Ohio St L J 291 (1996).

Practice Pointer—Eighth District Defines Social Security Offset Formula, Pamela J. MacAdams. 8 Domestic Rel J Ohio 57 (July/August 1996).

Suggestions for Better Evaluation of Pensions in Divorce Hearings, Robert Piron. 7 Domestic Rel J Ohio 69 (September/October 1995).

Tax Tips—Disposition of the Marital Home, Stanley Morganstern. 3 Domestic Rel J Ohio 113 (September/October 1991).

Tax Tips—Sale of the Marital Residence, Stanley Morganstern. 3 Domestic Rel J Ohio 146 (November/December 1991).

Tax Tips, Stanley Morganstern. 11 Domestic Rel J Ohio 86 (November/December 1999).

Tax Tips, Stanley Morganstern. (Ed. Note: The federal tax consequences of the transfer of the marital home are discussed.) 11 Domestic Rel J Ohio 56 (July/August 1999).

Tax Tips—Valuation Adjustments for Built-In Gains, Robert G. Turner. 11 Domestic Rel J Ohio 3 (January/February 1999).

Valuation of goodwill in Ohio professional practices, David A. Redle and Ronald J. Kudla. 10 Ohio Law 11 (March/April 1996).

Women and Divorce: The Perils of Pension Division, David L. Baumer and J. C. Poindexter. 57 Ohio St L J 203 (1996).

Notes of Decisions and Opinions

---

1. Equitable division

An unequal division of property may be equitable in view of a separate alimony award. Martin v. Martin (Ohio 1985) 18 Ohio St.3d 292, 480 N.E.2d 1112, 18 O.B.R. 342.

Private agreement between the parties to a divorce proceeding regarding the distribution of marital property does not relieve the trial court of its statutory duty to divide marital property equitably. Szerlip v. Szerlip (Ohio App. 5 Dist. 1998) 129 Ohio App.3d 506, 718 N.E.2d 473.

Wife's mother was necessary party to divorce action, where shares of stock included by trial court in marital assets bore names of wife and wife's mother, and equitable division of such stock between spouses and without determination of extent of wife's mother's interest therein had potential to divest wife's mother of property interest without affording her opportunity to be heard. Koval v. Koval (Ohio App. 11 Dist. 1998) 129 Ohio App.3d 68, 716 N.E.2d 1217.

Wife's allegation that trial judge related anecdote, during settlement negotiations at which only parties and judge were present, concerning other cases in which court had attempted to negotiate settlement but was unable to get parties to agree, and in which court's subsequent decision had resulted in substantially smaller award to party who had objected to settlement terms, without more, was insufficient to support claim that settlement agreement was required to be set aside by reason of duress. Dutton v. Dutton (Ohio App. 7 Dist. 1998) 127 Ohio App.3d 348, 713 N.E.2d 14.

Award to wife of two cars, as part of equitable division of marital property in divorce action, value of which cars were not counted against wife's half of marital estate, adequately compensated wife for lack of interest on amount of property settlement made payable in monthly installments over six-year period. Zeefe v. Zeefe (Ohio App. 8 Dist. 1998) 125 Ohio App.3d 600, 709 N.E.2d 208.

Court is not prohibited from adjusting enforcement of right to suit equities involved when enforcing right conferred by law, also known as "public right," particularly right to share equally in marital property upon divorce, which is expressly made subject of equitable determination. Langer v. Langer (Ohio App. 2 Dist. 1997) 123 Ohio App.3d 348, 704 N.E.2d 275, cause dismissed 80 Ohio St.3d 1473, 687 N.E.2d 470.

Property division must be equitable, and court must address statutory factors in arriving at its division. Neel v. Neel (Cuyahoga 1996) 113 Ohio App.3d 24, 680 N.E.2d 207, dismissed, appeal not allowed 77 Ohio St.3d 1514, 674 N.E.2d 369.

Separate property exists and must be considered in equitably dividing marital estate. Neel v. Neel (Cuyahoga 1996) 113 Ohio App.3d 24, 680 N.E.2d 207, dismissed, appeal not allowed 77 Ohio St.3d 1514, 674 N.E.2d 369.

In order to make equitable division of marital property, trial court should first determine value of marital assets. Donovan v. Donovan (Clermont 1996) 110 Ohio App.3d 615, 674 N.E.2d 1252.

Wife did not have to return benefits received under separation agreement before seeking to rescind such agreement before final divorce was granted, in light of presumption that spouses contributed equally to accumulation of marital assets and had equal right to possess them. Schneider v. Schneider (Geauga 1996) 110 Ohio App.3d 487, 674 N.E.2d 769, appeal not allowed 77 Ohio St.3d 1416, 670 N.E.2d 1004.

Trial courts in domestic relations cases have broad discretion when determining equitable settlement of marital property. Mayer v. Mayer (Allen 1996) 110 Ohio App.3d 233, 673 N.E.2d 981, dismissed, appeal not allowed 77 Ohio St.3d 1413, 670 N.E.2d 1002.

Trial court has broad discretion in establishing equitable division of marital property. Allen v. Allen (Butler 1996) 109 Ohio App.3d 640, 672 N.E.2d 1056.

When determining property distributions upon divorce, trial courts are guided by principles of equitable distribution. Shaffer v. Shaffer (Crawford 1996) 109 Ohio App.3d 205, 671 N.E.2d 1317.

In trial to divide property upon divorce, court is obligated to make division based on principles of equitable distribution, but this does not necessarily mean equal distribution, but only fair and equitable distribution. Walther v. Walther (Hamilton 1995) 102 Ohio App.3d 378, 657 N.E.2d 332.

When presented with task of dividing marital property, trial court is bound by requirements of statute and must divide marital and separate property equitably between parties. James v. James (Greene 1995) 101 Ohio App.3d 668, 656 N.E.2d 399.

Division of marital property incident to divorce, so that incarcerated husband received $46,000, and wife received $20,000, after court assessed $120,000 in lost wages and legal costs against husband, was supported by conclusion that husband's criminal conviction and resulting incarceration rendered equal division of property inequitable. Dragojevic-Wiczen v. Wiczen (Trumbull 1995) 101 Ohio App.3d 152, 655 N.E.2d 222, dismissed, appeal not allowed 72 Ohio St.3d 1539, 650 N.E.2d 479.

Statute governing equitable division of marital assets prohibited trial court from considering spousal support when dividing marital assets. Terry v. Terry (Cuyahoga 1994) 99 Ohio App.3d 228, 650 N.E.2d 184.

Marital property division was equitable, even though wife received all household property and furnishings; parties' stipulation provided that wife would receive household goods and furnishings. Addy v. Addy (Franklin 1994) 97 Ohio App.3d 204, 646 N.E.2d 513.

Equitable division of pension benefits could be accomplished by offsetting wife's potential social security monthly benefit against husband's potential Public Employees Retirement System (PERS) monthly benefit and equitably apportioning balance of PERS monthly benefit between parties. Smith v. Smith (Franklin 1993) 91 Ohio App.3d 248, 632 N.E.2d 555, reconsideration denied, motion to certify overruled 68 Ohio St.3d 1449, 626 N.E.2d 690.

Prior to court of common pleas' dividing marital asset, each party's equitable share of asset must be determined. Smith v. Smith (Franklin 1993) 91 Ohio App.3d 248, 632 N.E.2d 555, reconsideration denied, motion to certify overruled 68 Ohio St.3d 1449, 626 N.E.2d 690.

Marital property must be divided equally, unless equal division would be inequitable, in which case, property must be divided in equitable manner. Getter v. Getter (Montgomery 1993) 90 Ohio App.3d 1, 627 N.E.2d 1043.

Division of marital property was equitable even though husband received assets of greater value, where the assets he received were at greater risk to decline in value and were not as liquid as those received by the wife. Focke v. Focke (Montgomery 1992) 83 Ohio App.3d 552, 615 N.E.2d 327, motion overruled 66 Ohio St.3d 1446, 609 N.E.2d 172.

In a divorce action, a trial court pursuant to RC 3105.171 and 3105.18 must fashion an "equitable" distribution of all marital and separate property belonging to both parties before it determines whether a need for "reasonable spousal support" exists. Krisher v. Krisher (Logan 1992) 82 Ohio App.3d 159, 611 N.E.2d 499.

Only when a divorce is granted to one of the parties can there be an equitable division of their property. Gasior v. Gasior (Lucas 1940) 67 Ohio App. 84, 35 N.E.2d 1021, 21 O.O. 105.

Trial court abused its discretion with its division of marital assets when it deducted child support arrearages before the division of the joint marital funds, resulting in the mother improperly paying back child support from her own share of the marital assets. Pickeral v Pickeral, No. S-98-012, 1999 WL 173678 (6th Dist Ct App, Sandusky, 3-31-99).

To effect an equitable distribution of property a court may award husband's life insurance policies to wife where she is awarded only the cash value of the policies and can decide whether to cash in the policies or maintain them at her own cost. Scalero v Scalero, No. 71738, 1998 WL 23845 (8th Dist Ct App, Cuyahoga, 1-22-98).

A property settlement of 1.2 million dollars of which a significant percentage is liquid assets which are available to the spouse and upon which investment income is available and expected should be considered by the trial court in determining spousal support. Thomas v Thomas, No. 96APE07-949, 1997 WL 254115 (10th Dist Ct App, Franklin, 5-13-97).

Distribution of household goods and personal property is not based upon equity where a wife takes twenty-two per cent of the total household goods when she leaves the marital residence while the husband retains seventy-eight per cent of the items and this unequal distribution is not shown to be equitable. Sellman v Sellman, No. 95CA888, 1996 WL 557553 (4th Dist Ct App, Highland, 9-26-96).

In determining equal division of marital property, a court must consider former employment benefits including (1) severance packages, (2) accrued vacation pay, and (3) stock proceeds from a stock ownership plan. Childs v Childs, No. CA95-03-050, 1996 WL 103781 (12th Dist Ct App, Butler, 3-11-96).

Division of marital property is equitable, even though a wife receives a greater award where (1) the husband committed numerous acts of economic misconduct, including spending from $20 to $100 per week for alcohol during their twenty-two year marriage; (2) the husband was incarcerated for aggravated vehicular homicide, and the wife earned and borrowed money necessary to care for the household and the children in the husband's absence; and (3) the husband currently earns more than twice the salary of the wife, while the wife assumed half of the marital debts. Shinkle v Shinkle, No. CA95-06-034, 1996 WL 12840 (12th Dist Ct App, Clermont, 1-16-96).

An award of all the parties' debts to the husband without explanation is an abuse of discretion. Gray v Gray, No. OT-94-040, 1995 WL 386493 (6th Dist Ct App, Ottawa, 6-30-95).

Division of marital assets is equitable where the husband is awarded less than fifty per cent of the marital property and is burdened with a car payment and the spouse's medical bills in a case where (1) the parties have been married nearly thirty years, (2) the husband is employed but the wife has no immediate prospects for increased employment, (3) the wife is in need of a place to live and does not have sufficient resources to enable her to obtain suitable housing, and (4) more than fifty per cent of the liquidable assets are distributed to the husband. Adams v Adams, No. 93-J-10, 1995 WL 152991 (7th Dist Ct App, Jefferson, 4-4-95).

There is no abuse of discretion where a trial court follows the RC 3105.171 factors in determining property division and values husband's portion of business higher than what parties stipulated to. Blatt v Blatt, No. 61869 (8th Dist Ct App, Cuyahoga, 4-8-93).

Using present value of social security in some cases, where warranted, as full or partial setoff against present value of other party's public pension, is not violation of federal law insofar as it is just one factor, among many, which may or may not be considered, in order to achieve equitable distribution of property when valuing and/or distributing present value of public pension in divorce proceedings. Coats v. Coats (Ohio Com.Pl. 1993) 63 Ohio Misc.2d 299, 626 N.E.2d 707.

Under Ohio law, state divorce court was obligated to determine marital and separate property owned by parties to divorce proceeding; it was then obligated to divide that property equitably while considering any voluntary separation agreement and every relevant and equitable factor. Shelar v. Shelar (N.D.Ohio 1995) 910 F.Supp. 1307.

Ohio courts have broad discretion when equitably dividing property in divorce proceedings, but must address factors listed in Ohio's divorce statutes. Shelar v. Shelar (N.D.Ohio 1995) 910 F.Supp. 1307.

2. Equal division

There is no presumption, rebuttable or irrebuttable, that marital property be divided equally upon divorce; rather, a potentially equal division should be the starting point of the trial court's analysis before it considers the factors listed in RC 3105.18 and all other relevant factors, and consequently a court of common pleas has broad discretion to determine what property division is equitable in a divorce proceeding. The mere fact that a property division is unequal, does not, standing alone, amount to an abuse of discretion. Cherry v. Cherry (Ohio 1981) 66 Ohio St.2d 348, 421 N.E.2d 1293, 20 O.O.3d 318, on remand.

Action for divorce and alimony, seeking relief only against defendant's realty, is action in rem; petition for divorce and alimony, describing husband's realty, with service by publication, confers jurisdiction to appropriate realty for alimony and support. Reed v. Reed (Ohio 1929) 121 Ohio St. 188, 167 N.E. 684, 7 Ohio Law Abs. 381, 29 Ohio Law Rep. 399.

Date on which marriage terminates de jure ordinarily is controlling of court's decision when it determines and divides marital property, as marital property is statutorily defined to include any property, real or personal, acquired by either spouse "during the marriage." Langer v. Langer (Ohio App. 2 Dist. 1997) 123 Ohio App.3d 348, 704 N.E.2d 275, cause dismissed 80 Ohio St.3d 1473, 687 N.E.2d 470.

Trial court's award to husband of dollar-for-dollar credit against division of marital property for improvements to wife's residence paid for by him during marriage was not arbitrary, unreasonable, or unconscionable, absent any evidence permitting determination of difference between fair market value of residence before and after improvements. Barkley v. Barkley (Ohio App. 4 Dist. 1997) 119 Ohio App.3d 155, 694 N.E.2d 989.

Although equal division is starting point for determining division of marital assets and liabilities in divorce proceeding, division need not be equal to be equitable. McQuinn v. McQuinn (Butler 1996) 110 Ohio App.3d 296, 673 N.E.2d 1384.

Division of property upon divorce does not necessarily need to be equal to be equitable. Shaffer v. Shaffer (Crawford 1996) 109 Ohio App.3d 205, 671 N.E.2d 1317.

Once equitable division of pension benefits is made, court of common pleas may divide monthly benefit using qualified domestic relations order (QDRO), and if this is feasible, portion of monthly benefit spouse is entitled to may be reduced to present value utilizing spouse's age and appropriate interest rate. Smith v. Smith (Franklin 1993) 91 Ohio App.3d 248, 632 N.E.2d 555, reconsideration denied, motion to certify overruled 68 Ohio St.3d 1449, 626 N.E.2d 690.

Each parcel of real estate purchased by parties during marriage was marital property, and order dividing net proceeds from sale of that property equally between parties was not inequitable. Getter v. Getter (Montgomery 1993) 90 Ohio App.3d 1, 627 N.E.2d 1043.

A court need not divide a pension equally in a spousal support and property division determination; it may start on an equal basis, and upon a consideration of the duration of the marriage and the assets of parties arrive at a different result. Guziak v. Guziak (Summit 1992) 80 Ohio App.3d 805, 610 N.E.2d 1135, motion overruled 65 Ohio St.3d 1478, 604 N.E.2d 169.

Unequal distribution of marital property is not warranted when based upon a trial court's determination that a husband engages in financial misconduct by wasting the parties' assets by allowing duplexes he purchases to deteriorate to the point of code violation where (1) the properties are in need of improvements to comply with the city code at the time the husband purchases them, (2) such noncompliance is not the result of any misconduct by the husband, and (3) there is no finding by the magistrate that the husband wasted the parties' assets by allowing the duplexes to deteriorate to the point where they are now in code violation. Cuenot v Cuenot, No. 1998CA00205, 1999 WL 254484 (4th Dist Ct App, Stark, 4-12-99).

An equal division of marital property takes place even when it is based upon disparate earning abilities of the parties as when a husband with greater earning ability is also awarded the greater financial obligation of raising three children and maintaining a household; where his documented income is insufficient to meet his financial obligations toward his children, a denial of spousal support to the wife is not an abuse of discretion. Hue v Hue, No. C-940429, 1995 WL 481494 (1st Dist Ct App, Hamilton, 8-16-95).

3. Findings of fact

Any unequal distribution of property in a divorce proceeding requires the trial court to enter written findings of facts supporting its decision; overruling *Day v Day* (Nov. 3, 1997), Licking App. No. 97 CA 27, unreported. Szerlip v. Szerlip (Ohio App. 5 Dist. 1998) 129 Ohio App.3d 506, 718 N.E.2d 473.

Trial court, in making property division in divorce action, erred in failing to make written findings of fact setting forth its characterization of all property, respective values of properties, and rationale and basis for making $50,000 award to wife, so as to enable appellate court to review, as whole, how assets, liabilities, and award resulted in equitable division. Huener v. Huener (Henry 1996) 110 Ohio App.3d 322, 674 N.E.2d 389.

Trial court was required to make written findings of fact to support its division of property in divorce proceeding. Allen v. Allen (Butler 1996) 109 Ohio App.3d 640, 672 N.E.2d 1056.

Remand was required by trial court's failure to make written findings of fact to support its division of property in divorce proceedings. Allen v. Allen (Butler 1996) 109 Ohio App.3d 640, 672 N.E.2d 1056.

Statute requiring trial court to make written findings of fact explaining factors it considered in making determination not to disburse a spouse's separate property to that spouse did not require trial court to make separate written findings of fact and conclusions of law explaining its decision not to award husband, as his separate property, proceeds from sale of house he owned prior to marriage where trial court, within its discretion and judgment, characterized the property in question as marital, and not separate, due to insufficient proof of traceability. Peck v. Peck (Butler 1994) 96 Ohio App.3d 731, 645 N.E.2d 1300.

Husband and wife impliedly waived compliance with statute requiring trial court to make written findings to support determination that marital property had been equitably divided where oral settlement agreement entered into by parties completely settled all marital issues, and parties were aware of their right to have all items of personal property appraised, but chose not to do so prior to reaching complete settlement, in part because of expense involved in acquiring independent appraisals. Pawlowski v. Pawlowski (Franklin 1992) 83 Ohio App.3d 794, 615 N.E.2d 1071.

A trial court fails to follow the statutory mandates of RC 3105.171 when it does not make written findings of fact as to distribution of a wife's $10,000 investment in jointly owned real property. Dewalt v Dewalt, No. 92AP070048+ (1st Dist Ct App, Tuscarawas, 3-17-93).

A court need not make findings of fact supporting an equitable distribution of marital property when a case is filed in December, 1990, and statutory provisions under RC 3105.171 and 3105.18, requiring the findings of faCt App, are effective January 1, 1991. Burke v Burke, No. 490, 1993 WL 63384 (4th Dist Ct App, Meigs, 3-9-93).

4. Separate property

Evidence supported determination that husband's separate interest in stockyard business increased in value by $108,541 during parties' marriage. Middendorf v. Middendorf (Ohio 1998) 82 Ohio St.3d 397, 696 N.E.2d 575.

Party to divorce action seeking to establish that asset or portion of asset is separate property rather than marital property has burden of proof by preponderance of evidence. Zeefe v. Zeefe (Ohio App. 8 Dist. 1998) 125 Ohio App.3d 600, 709 N.E.2d 208.

Evidence that husband drew checks from various accounts prior to marriage and prior to purchase of marital residence was insufficient to establish that husband's alleged premarital contribution of $91,300 down payment on marital residence was traceable and therefore his separate property upon divorce, in absence of any canceled checks or other evidence indicating that withdrawn funds were used for down payment. Zeefe v. Zeefe (Ohio App. 8 Dist. 1998) 125 Ohio App.3d 600, 709 N.E.2d 208.

Husband's testimony during divorce proceeding that he had not intended to transfer half interest in real property to his wife at time he had her name included on deeds was sufficient to support trial court's finding that husband lacked donative intent to transfer present possessory interest required to constitute property bought with his separate assets marital property. Barkley v. Barkley (Ohio App. 4 Dist. 1997) 119 Ohio App.3d 155, 694 N.E.2d 989.

Trial court's characterization of increase in value due to investment earnings on savings and investment plan maintained by husband's employer and constituting husband's separate property as being likewise husband's separate property was not against manifest weight of evidence, absent any indication that increase in plan's value was related to reinvestment of dividends or any labor, monetary, or in-kind contribution by wife. Barkley v. Barkley (Ohio App. 4 Dist. 1997) 119 Ohio App.3d 155, 694 N.E.2d 989.

Increased value that results from passive appreciation of nonmarital property is separate property. Fergus v. Fergus (Ohio App. 7 Dist. 1997) 117 Ohio App.3d 432, 690 N.E.2d 949.

Personal injury settlement was wife's separate property to the extent it compensated wife for loss of consortium. Marcum v. Marcum (Ohio App. 2 Dist. 1996) 116 Ohio App.3d 606, 688 N.E.2d 1085.

Wife was required to trace proceeds of car she owned before marriage in order to be entitled to award of such proceeds. Williams v. Williams (Ohio App. 6 Dist. 1996) 116 Ohio App.3d 320, 688 N.E.2d 30.

Separate real property can be transformed by grantor spouse into marital property by gratuitous transfer to grantee spouse of present interest in property. Helton v. Helton (Ohio App. 2 Dist. 1996) 114 Ohio App.3d 683, 683 N.E.2d 1157.

Characterization, in divorce proceedings, of property as separate or marital is mixed question of law and fact which must be supported by sufficient, credible evidence. Kelly v. Kelly (Hamilton 1996) 111 Ohio App.3d 641, 676 N.E.2d 1210.

Evidence supported finding that parcel of property was advance inheritance that qualified as husband's separate, nonmarital property, though husband testified that property was deeded to both him and his wife three years before divorce action, where no deed to property was submitted by wife's counsel and wife's testimony concerning property was limited to work she performed on property and fact that she shared income from farming property with her husband. Mayer v. Mayer (Allen 1996) 110 Ohio App.3d 233, 673 N.E.2d 981, dismissed, appeal not allowed 77 Ohio St.3d 1413, 670 N.E.2d 1002.

Separate property in Ohio does not automatically become marital property because one spouse contributed to appreciation of property; however, where marital assets are invested in separate property over the years, and parties expended time and effort in improving business, it would not be abuse of discretion for court to declare property a marital asset. Simoni v. Simoni (Cuyahoga 1995) 102 Ohio App.3d 628, 657 N.E.2d 800, appeal not allowed 73 Ohio St.3d 1453, 654 N.E.2d 989.

Where no actions were taken during marriage to change separate property into marital property, spouse is entitled to share in appreciation of other spouse's separate property only where he or she contributed substantial work to improving and maintaining property. Simoni v. Simoni (Cuyahoga 1995) 102 Ohio App.3d 628, 657 N.E.2d 800, appeal not allowed 73 Ohio St.3d 1453, 654 N.E.2d 989.

Automobile which husband inherited from grandparent during parties' marriage was improperly awarded to wife, upon divorce, absent evidence that parties treated automobile as marital asset; fact that wife used automobile during parties' separation pursuant to parties' agreement was insufficient to render asset marital. James v. James (Greene 1995) 101 Ohio App.3d 668, 656 N.E.2d 399.

Trial court did not abuse its discretion in determining that stock options received by husband from his employer were "separate property" of husband and were not subject to division following divorce where option was based on husband's job performance prior to marriage and was not exercised during marriage, even though option was awarded during marriage. Demo v. Demo (Butler 1995) 101 Ohio App.3d 383, 655 N.E.2d 791.

Voluntary Separation Incentive (VSI) payments offered by the armed forces to encourage a reduction in force were more closely analogous to severance benefits than retirement benefits in that VSI benefits, like severance benefits, attempted to compensate separated service member for future lost wages and, accordingly, husband's VSI payments were his separate income and not marital property for purposes of divorce; husband was given ultimatum from his superior to either accept VSI and voluntarily separate or face immediate involuntary separation, husband began receiving VSI payments before trial court made determination and division of marital property, by choosing to accept VSI payments, husband insured higher, more consistent income from which court was able to award child and spousal support, and husband's choice to voluntarily separate did not divest wife of any expectation interest previously awarded to her. McClure v. McClure (Greene 1994) 98 Ohio App.3d 27, 647 N.E.2d 832, appeal not allowed 71 Ohio St.3d 1481, 645 N.E.2d 1260.

Since trial court considered wages of the parties during the pendency of the divorce to be their separate property, husband was entitled to use his separate property to pay for his attorneys during pendency of the divorce proceedings and thus, wife was not entitled to compensation for any alleged dissipation of marital assets. McClure v. McClure (Greene 1994) 98 Ohio App.3d 27, 647 N.E.2d 832, appeal not allowed 71 Ohio St.3d 1481, 645 N.E.2d 1260.

Where spouse suffers compensable injury during marriage, those workers' compensation benefits which compensate for loss of earnings during marriage and for expenses paid from marital assets are marital property subject to division upon divorce, while those benefits which compensate for loss of body part or loss of spouse's future earning capacity are not marital property and are not divisible upon divorce. Hartzell v. Hartzell (Darke 1993) 90 Ohio App.3d 385, 629 N.E.2d 491.

Husband failed to trace down payment for, and cost of improvements to, marital residence to his own nonmarital assets; instead, evidence established that funds came from parties' joint checking account, which also contained unidentified amount of wife's income from her job, and, in any event, fact that husband may have brought an asset into the marriage was merely one factor to be considered in property division. deLevie v. deLevie (Franklin 1993) 86 Ohio App.3d 531, 621 N.E.2d 594, dismissed, jurisdictional motion overruled 67 Ohio St.3d 1409, 615 N.E.2d 1043.

Even if divorce court failed to consider $3,000 which husband had inherited from his mother's estate to be separate property, amount in proportion to size of marital estate, which was valued at over $1 million, was not significant enough to warrant new trial. Frost v. Frost (Franklin 1992) 84 Ohio App.3d 699, 618 N.E.2d 198, motion overruled 66 Ohio St.3d 1489, 612 N.E.2d 1245.

Divorce court did not abuse its discretion in treating husband's law practice as nonmarital property, since it had been established ten years prior to marriage, while finding income generated from practice during course of marriage to be marital asset. Frost v. Frost (Franklin 1992) 84 Ohio App.3d 699, 618 N.E.2d 198, motion overruled 66 Ohio St.3d 1489, 612 N.E.2d 1245.

Determination that 16% of husband's business was marital property, based upon fact that wife worked in business for five of 31 years that husband owned business, was abuse of discretion where business was separate property of husband for many years prior to parties' marriage. Shapiro v. Shapiro (Summit 1992) 83 Ohio App.3d 744, 615 N.E.2d 727.

The transfer of property from a husband to a wife, by gift or other means, makes that property the separate property of the wife unless there is evidence to show otherwise. Pettry v. Pettry (Franklin 1991) 81 Ohio App.3d 30, 610 N.E.2d 443.

In a divorce action, a trial court's determination that the parties' residence is a non-marital asset which should properly be awarded to the husband is not an abuse of discretion, despite the wife's contention that the court only considered the fact that the residence is titled solely in the husband's name, which according to the wife was done on the advice of their attorney so as to prevent termination of her social security benefits, where the court finds that the cash used to purchase the home is directly traceable to the husband's premarital assets, that the home had been maintained as a separate asset of the husband and that the value of the home had depreciated since its purchase. Green v. Green (Erie 1989) 64 Ohio App.3d 37, 580 N.E.2d 513.

Bonds that a husband purchases from an inheritance upon his mother's death are his separate property and his purchase of the bonds does not change the property from separate to marital absent evidence to prove donative intent. Guffey v Guffey, No. 1-99-03, 1999 WL 378358 (3d Dist Ct App, Allen, 6-3-99).

Increase in the value of husband's business during marriage is marital property and wife is entitled to a greater award of such marital property because of the husband's financial misconduct involving the business. Haslem v Haslem, No. 73942, 1999 WL 135277 (8th Dist Ct App, Cuyahoga, 3-11-99).

In the absence of evidence that the parties' joint labor or improvements are responsible for increase in the value of certain real property the increase must be considered passive appreciation and is the separate property of the spouse to whom the purchase price is traceable. Holman v Holman, No. OT-96-029, 1997 WL 458046 (6th Dist Ct App, Ottawa, 8-8-97).

Wife's personal injury settlement is separate property and is not to be considered in dividing the parties' marital property and failure to award a portion of husband's pension would result in an inequitable division of marital assets. Rose v Rose, No. 840, 1997 WL 219136 (5th Dist Ct App, Morrow, 4-11-97).

A trial court incorrectly divides the parties' separate and marital interests in two parcels of real estate by not taking into account a second mortgage and refinancing of one parcel and by imputing rental income which would have otherwise been earned from the other property in which the daughter and grandchild of one of the parties are permitted to live rent free. Charles v Charles, No. 96CA006396, 1997 WL 28247 (9th Dist Ct App, Lorain, 1-22-97).

Custodial accounts that have been held by a child of the previous marriage with the mother as guardian and derive from social security benfits due to the death of the father from the previous marriage are not marital property and the trial court is not required to account for them in making its division of assets in the mother's present marriage and divorce action. Wilson v Wilson, No. 95CA0089, 1996 WL 411631 (9th Dist Ct App, Wayne, 7-24-96).

For purposes of distribution of agricultural assets, a court does not abuse discretion by considering lineage of cattle in order to trace the husband's premarital interest and place a value on the herd where the court concludes that twenty-four of the thirty head of cattle awarded to the husband were descended from cattle he owned before the marriage and were traceable as his premarital property; likewise, there is no distributive value to a bean crop which was sold for more than $30,000 where the proceeds were spent on obligations incurred during the marriage. Bickel v Bickel, Nos. CA95-09-024+, 1996 WL 328715 (12th Dist Ct App, Clinton, 6-17-96).

A trial court errs in (1) finding that the wife's interest in the husband's separate property is the appreciation of the property during the marriage and (2) ordering that pursuant to RC 3105.171(F)(3) the wife, as residential parent, has exclusive use of the residence for six years even though the residence is determined to be the separate property of the husband; however, the court could make the same award either as a division of property pursuant to RC 3105.171(E) or as spousal or child support. Gilt v Gilt, No. 94-CA-513, 1995 WL 498829 (5th Dist Ct App, Holmes, 7-11-95).

The fact that a husband's grandfather put only the husband's name on a certificate of deposit that he gave to the husband is strong evidence that the gift was intended to be to the husband alone; the wife's contention that a joint gift was likely intended since she had helped care for the grandfather is unsupported. Wolfangel v Wolfangel, No. 16868, 1995 WL 312697 (9th Dist Ct App, Summit, 5-24-95).

In a division of marital property where an award of a mobile home in Florida is made to the wife and the husband's nonmarital property, real estate in Pennsylvania, was the source of such property and therefore traceable, such award is error where the court does not address the husband's equity in the Pennsylvania property as being the source of monies used for the purchase of the mobile home. Fritz v Fritz, No. 93-C-66, 1995 WL 75405 (7th Dist Ct App, Columbiana, 2-17-95).

If property is purchased during the marriage with funds from a mortgage on the marital residence, marital property, and cash from the husband's inheritance, the wife's contribution during the marriage by bookkeeping is insufficient to convert his separate property to marital property. Dionne v Dionne, No. CA 9314, 1994 WL 115927 (5th Dist Ct App, Stark, 3-28-94).

Where a husband's father purchases life insurance policies for his son with his own funds and there is no evidence as to who the beneficiaries of the policies are, a trial court errs in awarding a wife one-half interest in the life insurance policies since the policies are not marital property purchased with marital funds and there is no evidence the wife is the designated beneficiary on any of the policies. Mechwart v Mechwart, No. 93AP-92, 1993 WL 379106 (10th Dist Ct App, Franklin, 9-23-93).

A gift of $25,000 equity in a wife's parents' farm, from the parents to the daughter, is separate property; the increase in the value of the farm due to the husband's labors during the marriage is marital property reflected in the division of property. Baker v Baker, No. 477 (4th Dist Ct App, Meigs, 2-10-93).

5. Marital home

Ex-husband and ex-wife entered into a "bailment" under arrangement whereby ex-husband left refrigerator and other items of personal property in former marital residence in order to enhance house's appearance to potential buyers and was permitted to store his car in garage, and ex-wife, in return, was permitted to use the personal items left in house. Vandeventer v. Vandeventer (Ohio App. 12 Dist. 1999) 132 Ohio App.3d 762, 726 N.E.2d 534.

Ex-wife was liable, as bailee of ex-husband's refrigerator in former marital residence, for any damages sustained by ex-husband as result of dent in refrigerator; evidence established that only ex-wife had access to refrigerator, and damage in question showed a failure to exercise ordinary and reasonable care. Vandeventer v. Vandeventer (Ohio App. 12 Dist. 1999) 132 Ohio App.3d 762, 726 N.E.2d 534.

Ex-wife was liable, as bailee of car that ex-husband stored in garage of former marital residence, for damage to car occurring during that bailment; photographs showing all four tires slashed and dents and scratches on body of vehicle, together with evidence that only ex-wife had access to car, established gross negligence on ex-wife's part. Vandeventer v. Vandeventer (Ohio App. 12 Dist. 1999) 132 Ohio App.3d 762, 726 N.E.2d 534.

Fact that ex-husband in one month sent ex-wife two checks, each equal to one-half of mortgage payment due on former marital residence, did not support a finding, on contempt motion by ex-husband, that ex-wife had failed in that month to pay her one-half share of mortgage as required under divorce decree; while ex-wife typically sent mortgage company the full amount due after receiving husband's one-half payment, ex-wife testified that one check from husband during the month in question was to reimburse her for a previous check that had bounced. Vandeventer v. Vandeventer (Ohio App. 12 Dist. 1999) 132 Ohio App.3d 762, 726 N.E.2d 534.

Trial court did not abuse its discretion in permitting wife and two children to remain in marital home following divorce until children were emancipated, even though portion of interest in home represented husband's premarital downpayment made with his separate property, and appreciation of that investment; while husband was entitled to receive appreciated value of his separate property, this did not entitle him to entire residence, substantial portion of which was marital property. Munroe v. Munroe (Ohio App. 8 Dist. 1997) 119 Ohio App.3d 530, 695 N.E.2d 1155.

Husband who had used separate property to make premarital downpayment on home, which was placed in joint names of husband and wife after marriage, was entitled at time of divorce to retain as his separate interest in property that portion of appreciation during marriage which reflected percentage of his separate investment in property. Munroe v. Munroe (Ohio App. 8 Dist. 1997) 119 Ohio App.3d 530, 695 N.E.2d 1155.

Portion of order in divorce action which required former husband to pay one-half of real estate taxes on marital home, possession of which had been awarded to wife, was inconsistent with portion requiring wife to make mortgage payments, which would result in taxes being paid through mortgage escrow, and thus, order applicable to husband would be vacated. Munroe v. Munroe (Ohio App. 8 Dist. 1997) 119 Ohio App.3d 530, 695 N.E.2d 1155.

Court may allow spouse to continue to live in marital residence only upon showing of particularized need, and only for period that is short-term and temporary. Bauser v. Bauser (Ohio App. 2 Dist. 1997) 118 Ohio App.3d 831, 694 N.E.2d 136.

Trial court abused its discretion in preserving marital residence, allowing wife to live in residence for remainder of her life, and ordering husband to pay one-half of maintenance expenses, where wife did not present any need that justified her request that she be allowed to live in marital residence, and both parties had limited monthly income. Bauser v. Bauser (Ohio App. 2 Dist. 1997) 118 Ohio App.3d 831, 694 N.E.2d 136.

Trial court was required to state its reasons for its determination of amount of marital equity in marital residence that husband had brought to the marriage. Fergus v. Fergus (Ohio App. 7 Dist. 1997) 117 Ohio App.3d 432, 690 N.E.2d 949.

Holding of title to property, even by both spouses in form of co-ownership, does not, by itself, determine whether property is marital property. Helton v. Helton (Ohio App. 2 Dist. 1996) 114 Ohio App.3d 683, 683 N.E.2d 1157.

Home that had been husband's separate property when couple married became marital property subject to division upon divorce when husband executed joint survivorship deed to himself and wife with intention that she have present possessory interest, even though primary purpose of conveyance was to avoid estate taxes and probate expense. Helton v. Helton (Ohio App. 2 Dist. 1996) 114 Ohio App.3d 683, 683 N.E.2d 1157.

Husband's mother lacked donative intent with regard to $16,000 transferred to spouses in connection with their purchase of marital home, where wife repaid husband's mother and husband's mother accepted payment. Neel v. Neel (Cuyahoga 1996) 113 Ohio App.3d 24, 680 N.E.2d 207, dismissed, appeal not allowed 77 Ohio St.3d 1514, 674 N.E.2d 369.

Relocation payment, made to husband by husband's employer, which became payable when contract to purchase marital residence was executed, was "marital property" subject to division in divorce proceedings. Kelly v. Kelly (Hamilton 1996) 111 Ohio App.3d 641, 676 N.E.2d 1210.

Husband was entitled, in divorce proceeding, to return of separate property contributed to purchase prior marital residence when dividing proceeds from sale of final marital residence and, thus, error resulted when calculating husband's separate contribution to prior residence as percentage of entire purchase price and calculating separate contribution on final marital residence as percentage of sale price without mortgage. Kelly v. Kelly (Hamilton 1996) 111 Ohio App.3d 641, 676 N.E.2d 1210.

Wife waived her right to review in postdecree proceedings her claim that trial court erred in refusing to require husband to reimburse wife for expenses she incurred in maintaining marital residence during divorce proceedings, where wife failed to object to report of referee pertaining to reimbursement for marital expenses, which was later adopted by trial court. Donovan v. Donovan (Clermont 1996) 110 Ohio App.3d 615, 674 N.E.2d 1252.

Trial court abused its discretion by attempting to divest husband's parents, who were legal owners of marital residence, of their legal title to residence without joining them as parties in divorce action, notwithstanding husband's stipulation admitting that he was "equitable owner" of property; husband had transferred property to parents prior to his marriage to wife, and his parents' holding legal title to property established their interest in it. Huener v. Huener (Henry 1996) 110 Ohio App.3d 322, 674 N.E.2d 389.

Trial court was not bound to order sale of parties' marital residence and rental property upon divorce but could award marital residence to wife and rental property to husband, despite alleged preference of parties for sale, as parties could not agree on distribution of properties and submitted issue to court, which had broad discretion to fashion award so long as award was not unreasonable, arbitrary, or unconscionable. James v. James (Greene 1995) 101 Ohio App.3d 668, 656 N.E.2d 399.

Action of trial court in dividing proceeds from sale of marital home in proportion to initial contributions of husband and wife from their separate funds of two-thirds and one-third respectively was equitable and was not abuse of court's discretion where wife filed for divorce less than 15 months after marriage and wife had bachelor's degree in education and was in process of being recertified to teach. Demo v. Demo (Butler 1995) 101 Ohio App.3d 383, 655 N.E.2d 791.

Loan acceptance fee, change order paid to contractor, and payment to electrical contractor which were paid by husband were directly related to construction of home and were considered part of total purchase price of home in arriving at equitable distribution of property following divorce. Demo v. Demo (Butler 1995) 101 Ohio App.3d 383, 655 N.E.2d 791.

Parties stipulated before trial that former wife should receive family home and, thus, she could not subsequently complain that trial court abused its discretion by accepting stipulation. Terry v. Terry (Cuyahoga 1994) 99 Ohio App.3d 228, 650 N.E.2d 184.

Evidence was insufficient to establish that woman's work on two residences she shared with man resulted in unjust enrichment of man. Tarry v. Stewart (Lorain 1994) 98 Ohio App.3d 533, 649 N.E.2d 1, appeal not allowed 71 Ohio St.3d 1502, 646 N.E.2d 1126.

Purported antenuptial agreement was testamentary and was not applicable to divorce proceeding and, thus, upon divorce, husband was not entitled to marital home under agreement; although clause of agreement stated that husband and wife waived any claims "which he or she may acquire by reason of the marriage in the other party's property or estate," clause referred only to testamentary rights and made no reference to division of assets upon divorce. Stokes v. Stokes (Cuyahoga 1994) 98 Ohio App.3d 238, 648 N.E.2d 83.

Trial court was within its discretion in divorce proceeding in concluding that husband's claim for separate property was not sufficiently traced and was therefore commingled into marital estate during parties' 21—year marriage; although wife conceded that marital residence was purchased with funds husband received from sale of real property he owned prior to marriage, she could not recall amount of funds and presented no specific evidence tracing financial history of asset and husband presented no documentation or other evidence to sufficiently trace that property. Peck v. Peck (Butler 1994) 96 Ohio App.3d 731, 645 N.E.2d 1300.

Trial court did not require personal jurisdiction over trustee of marital residence in order to effectuate its judgment ordering property sold in legal separation proceeding where husband's conveyance of property, which was titled in his name alone, to trustee, with husband and wife designated as income beneficiaries, was void ab initio as attempt to defeat whatever rights wife had in residence as marital property. Leathem v. Leathem (Hancock 1994) 94 Ohio App.3d 470, 640 N.E.2d 1210, stay denied 70 Ohio St.3d 1433, 638 N.E.2d 583, dismissed, appeal not allowed 70 Ohio St.3d 1454, 639 N.E.2d 793.

Trial court did not require either parties' consent or request to order marital residence sold and proceeds divided in legal separation proceeding. Leathem v. Leathem (Hancock 1994) 94 Ohio App.3d 470, 640 N.E.2d 1210, stay denied 70 Ohio St.3d 1433, 638 N.E.2d 583, dismissed, appeal not allowed 70 Ohio St.3d 1454, 639 N.E.2d 793.

Conveyance of marital residence into trust by husband alone was void ab initio where, although property was titled in husband's name alone and wife was named income co-beneficiary, marital residence was marital property before its conveyance; conveyance was attempt to defeat any rights wife may have had in marital residence as marital property. Leathem v. Leathem (Hancock 1994) 94 Ohio App.3d 470, 640 N.E.2d 1210, stay denied 70 Ohio St.3d 1433, 638 N.E.2d 583, dismissed, appeal not allowed 70 Ohio St.3d 1454, 639 N.E.2d 793.

Trial court abused its discretion in ordering equal distribution of proceeds from sale of marital residence between husband and wife, where husband's parents had conveyed property to him four years before marriage. Getter v. Getter (Montgomery 1993) 90 Ohio App.3d 1, 627 N.E.2d 1043.

In divorce proceeding, trial court did not abuse its discretion in ordering that landscaper, who did certain work at marital home, be paid with proceeds from sale of marital home. DiLacqua v. DiLacqua (Summit 1993) 88 Ohio App.3d 48, 623 N.E.2d 118.

In divorce proceeding, trial court abused its discretion in ordering that wife received first $13,150 in net proceeds from sale of marital home due to husband's financial misconduct in failing to pay marital home mortgage payments as ordered by court, which necessitated liquidation of marital assets worth $26,300; although trial court apparently sought to penalize husband for one-half value of marital assets that were lost through his misconduct, order entered actually penalized him only $6,575, since wife would have received half of the proceeds of sale of house regardless as part of division of marital property. DiLacqua v. DiLacqua (Summit 1993) 88 Ohio App.3d 48, 623 N.E.2d 118.

Determination that 43% of parties' home was marital property, based upon fact that wife had lived in home for nine of the twenty-one years that husband owned it, was abuse of discretion where house was separate property of husband years before parties' marriage. Shapiro v. Shapiro (Summit 1992) 83 Ohio App.3d 744, 615 N.E.2d 727.

Trial court properly considered joint mortgage on parties' home when it determined marital equity in home, where court used mortgage to reduce amount of increase in equity which could be attributed to marriage. Baker v. Baker (Summit 1992) 83 Ohio App.3d 700, 615 N.E.2d 699.

Trial court did not abuse its discretion in awarding husband first option to purchase marital real estate; trial court divided equity in marital real estate equally and may have decided to give husband first option based on wife's difficulty in raising funds. Layne v. Layne (Champaign 1992) 83 Ohio App.3d 559, 615 N.E.2d 332.

Division of proceeds from sale of marital home was not abuse of discretion where trial court credited each spouse with separate property in amount of each spouse's contribution to purchase price, and then divided remaining equity in home equally. Babka v. Babka (Summit 1992) 83 Ohio App.3d 428, 615 N.E.2d 247.

Reduction of husband's separate property interest in marital home by $9,000, which represented value from husband's previous home used as portion of down payment on marital home, was not abuse of discretion, where husband and wife lived in previous home for six years before buying marital residence, wife had helped improve and maintain first home, and marital assets were spent on first home. Babka v. Babka (Summit 1992) 83 Ohio App.3d 428, 615 N.E.2d 247.

A trial court abuses its discretion in a divorce action by not making a final disposition of the marital residence where, even though it awards each of the parties a legal half-interest in the property and awards the wife a fifteen-year beneficial interest, the court does not determine how at the end of that fifteen-year period, or at some earlier point, the husband would receive his equity in the home. Rowe v. Rowe (Lucas 1990) 69 Ohio App.3d 607, 591 N.E.2d 716.

A trial court's conclusion that it could not determine what part of a personal settlement check used to purchase the marital residence is for loss of consortium, lost wages, or pain and suffering is not against the weight of the evidence where a settlement check received by the husband is payable to both husband and wife and the proceeds are commingled and used to purchase the marital residence; although the commingling does not destroy the identity of separate property the burden of identifying this distinct property is placed on the husband who claims that the property is separate and where the burden is not met the residence purchased with the funds and titled in the names of both parties is marital property. Cox v Cox, No. CA98-05-007, 1999 WL 74573 (12th Dist Ct App, Fayette, 2-16-99).

Fifty per cent of equity in a marital home is improperly classified as husband's separate property where (1) it is received as part of a divorce from his first wife, (2) he and his second wife own fifty per cent of the home as marital property because marital funds are used to repay the loan in purchasing the one half interest from the first wife, and (3) significant improvements which increase the fair market value of the marital residence are made with marital funds by the husband and his second wife. Friend v Friend, No. 18944, 1998 WL 831471 (9th Dist Ct App, Summit, 11-25-98).

Pursuant to property division in a divorce decree, there is a marital property interest in the parties' home even though it is being purchased under a land installment contract. Hopewell v Hopewell, No. 96CA006436, 1997 WL 79994 (9th Dist Ct App, Lorain, 2-19-97).

Providing a spouse with a distributive award in lieu of her interest in the marital residence is not an abuse of discretion where the spouse presents evidence which traces funds spent on the marital residence and on other purchases back to her inheritance. Obermyer v Obermyer, No. WD-95-048, 1996 WL 28001 (6th Dist Ct App, Wood, 1-26-96).

Where both parties produce evidence that each provided separate property to finance construction of the marital residence, the trial court's award of the marital residence as if it were wholly marital property, without making a finding regarding the traceability of separate property that is claimed by one of the parties, is an abuse of discretion. Rinehart v Rinehart, Nos. 94-CA-26+, 1995 WL 762925 (4th Dist Ct App, Gallia, 12-13-95).

In a case where the trial court finds the marital residence to be the husband's separate property, the wife is entitled to a portion of the marital residence's appreciation during the marriage, if any, where (1) both parties, unmarried, purchase a house and reside together in the house which is placed under both parties' names; (2) following a break-up in the relationship, one party is paid $8500 for her interest in the real estate in exchange for a deed executed to the other party; and (3) the parties marry and divorce. Wright v Wright, No. CA95-03-020, 1995 WL 695028 (12th Dist Ct App, Clermont, 11-27-95).

The trial court's determination that the husband's desire to maintain the couple's large residence does not outweigh the advantages of disentangling their financial affairs is not unreasonable, arbitrary or unconscionable; the resulting sale and unequal division of property ($161,568 to the wife and $133,475 to the husband) is not so inequitable as to be considered an abuse of discretion as the court could have properly considered in its division of marital property whether the husband had been voluntarily underemployed in the years leading up to the parties' divorce. Selders v Selders, No. 2428-M, 1995 WL 655935 (9th Dist Ct App, Medina, 11-8-95).

In a dispute involving interests of the parties in the marital residence, where a husband contributes $7500 plus labor to renovations of the home and contributes to a reduction in the mortgage balance, the home is marital property and the husband is entitled an equitable share. Bockelman v Bockelman, No. L-94-208, 1995 WL 358605 (6th Dist Ct App, Lucas, 6-16-95).

Where husband and wife have made improvements during marriage to their marital residence owned by wife's mother, the trial court errs in awarding husband and wife a $25,000 equitable interest in the home based upon a theory of unjust enrichment in the absence of evidence adduced at trial that these improvements, rather than inflation or general market trends, caused the $25,000 increase in the home's valuation from 1983 to 1993. Urbank v Urbank, No. 16752, 1995 WL 89459 (9th Dist Ct App, Summit, 3-1-95).

An order of division of marital property inequitably charges a wife with a husband's mortgage payments on the marital residence after the date of the parties' separation where the order does not credit the wife with a corresponding interest in the property's increased equity. Rudolph v Rudolph, No. 2880, 1994 WL 721868 (9th Dist Ct App, Wayne, 12-30-94).

Although a wife inherited a home from her first husband and resided in the home with her second husband for ten years, where (1) many improvements were made to the residence with commingled and marital assets as well as the second husband's physical labor; (2) the home was sold and the proceeds commingled and expended during a three and one-half year separation; and (3) another home was purchased with commingled funds, the second home was improperly classified as the wife's separate nonmarital property by a trial court. Shaffer v Shaffer, No. 92-J-18, 1993 WL 390161 (7th Dist Ct App, Jefferson, 9-30-93).

6. Discretion

Trial court was required to take into consideration marital debt arising out of home equity line of credit on wife's residence before dividing marital assets, and its failure to do so was arbitrary, unreasonable, and constituted abuse of discretion. Barkley v. Barkley (Ohio App. 4 Dist. 1997) 119 Ohio App.3d 155, 694 N.E.2d 989.

Trial court did not abuse its discretion in ordering division of property pursuant to divorce awarding husband and wife one-half of marital portion of pension plans of the other spouse and giving each spouse lien on pension fund of the other, requiring that real estate previously awarded to wife be sold and that proceeds from sale would be divided equally after certain deductions were made, and retaining jurisdiction over issue of spousal support. Schafer v. Schafer (Noble 1996) 115 Ohio App.3d 639, 685 N.E.2d 1302.

Trial court is vested with broad discretion in fashioning its division of marital property. Neel v. Neel (Cuyahoga 1996) 113 Ohio App.3d 24, 680 N.E.2d 207, dismissed, appeal not allowed 77 Ohio St.3d 1514, 674 N.E.2d 369.

Generally, there is distinction between court's duty to consider property and court's power to divide that property. Neel v. Neel (Cuyahoga 1996) 113 Ohio App.3d 24, 680 N.E.2d 207, dismissed, appeal not allowed 77 Ohio St.3d 1514, 674 N.E.2d 369.

Trial court has discretion to determine amount spouse must pay in order to reduce arrearage owed by spouse to other spouse. Ricketts v. Ricketts (Butler 1996) 109 Ohio App.3d 746, 673 N.E.2d 156, dismissed, appeal not allowed 76 Ohio St.3d 1473, 669 N.E.2d 856.

Referee's selection of particular date as date to valuate marital home was abuse of discretion; referee's report did not reflect equitable reason for selecting that date as date to valuate marital home, and that date bore no logical relationship to dates typically used in valuating and dividing marital property, such as date of permanent separation, de facto termination date, or date of final hearing. Landry v. Landry (Auglaize 1995) 105 Ohio App.3d 289, 663 N.E.2d 1026.

Although $6,000 amount was high, husband was entitled to attorney fees incurred in enforcing in-court property settlement agreement, where husband's counsel gave repeated notices to both of wife's lawyers that, in event wife tried to repudiate agreement, he intended to seek attorney fees and all time entries submitted as evidence of fees sought were limited to issue of enforcement of agreement. Walther v. Walther (Hamilton 1995) 102 Ohio App.3d 378, 657 N.E.2d 332.

When parties to divorce enter into in-court property settlement agreement, so long as court is satisfied that it was not procured by fraud, duress, overreaching or undue influence, and there is no factual dispute over existence of terms in agreement, court has discretion to accept it without finding it to be fair and equitable. Walther v. Walther (Hamilton 1995) 102 Ohio App.3d 378, 657 N.E.2d 332.

When dividing marital property, trial court has broad discretion to do what is equitable under facts of each case; there are no set rules for determining division of marital property. Terry v. Terry (Cuyahoga 1994) 99 Ohio App.3d 228, 650 N.E.2d 184.

Trial court did not abuse its discretion by awarding mortgaged properties to former wife in division of marital property, in light of award to former wife of potential for nearly $600,000 in cash payments over five-year period that should have been more than adequate to cover approximately $200,000 in mortgage liabilities. Terry v. Terry (Cuyahoga 1994) 99 Ohio App.3d 228, 650 N.E.2d 184.

Trial court abused its discretion in awarding wife, as part of its final entry in divorce proceeding, spousal support of $1500 per month for four years, where award was not based upon conclusion that it was inappropriate for wife to seek employment outside home due to her role as custodian of couple's children and there was insufficient evidence from which trial court could conclude that spousal support in an amount and for a period sufficient to enable wife to complete proposed pharmacy degree program was proper to enable her to obtain appropriate employment. DiLacqua v. DiLacqua (Summit 1993) 88 Ohio App.3d 48, 623 N.E.2d 118.

Domestic relations court is vested with broad discretion to determine what constitutes equitable division of property in divorce proceeding, and its exercise of discretion will not be disturbed on appeal in absence of some demonstration that court abused its discretion. Jelen v. Jelen (Hamilton 1993) 86 Ohio App.3d 199, 620 N.E.2d 224.

Divorce court's failure to order contribution from wife toward expenses husband incurred in maintaining parties' farm was not abuse of discretion, in light of court's failure to require husband to contribute to expenses wife incurred for upkeep of marital residence until its sale. Jelen v. Jelen (Hamilton 1993) 86 Ohio App.3d 199, 620 N.E.2d 224.

Award to wife of marital assets with value corresponding to value of husband's Federal Employees Group Life Insurance policy was not abuse of discretion, given evidence that husband's entitlement to coverage under policy arose by virtue of his employment with federal government during parties' marriage. Jelen v. Jelen (Hamilton 1993) 86 Ohio App.3d 199, 620 N.E.2d 224.

Divorce court, complying with parties' desire for in-kind physical division of household goods and furnishings, did not abuse its discretion in ordering that two-thirds go to wife and one-third to husband on rotation selection basis, and that children's furnishings be excluded from division. Frost v. Frost (Franklin 1992) 84 Ohio App.3d 699, 618 N.E.2d 198, motion overruled 66 Ohio St.3d 1489, 612 N.E.2d 1245.

Trial court enjoys broad, but not unlimited, discretion in fashioning equitable division of marital property; for abuse of discretion to exist, court's attitude must be unreasonable, arbitrary, or unconscionable, and not merely error of law of judgment. Shapiro v. Shapiro (Summit 1992) 83 Ohio App.3d 744, 615 N.E.2d 727.

Trial court has broad discretion in fashioning equitable distribution of marital property. Baker v. Baker (Summit 1992) 83 Ohio App.3d 700, 615 N.E.2d 699.

Trial court did not abuse its discretion in divorce proceeding in not considering potential tax implication and other costs of sales in valuing husband's rental properties, where husband indicated that he would not sell properties in foreseeable future, but rather would manage properties on full-time basis. Baker v. Baker (Summit 1992) 83 Ohio App.3d 700, 615 N.E.2d 699.

"Abuse of discretion," in context of reviewing trial court's division of marital property, connotes more than error of law or judgment, and implies that trial court's attitude is unreasonable, arbitrary, or unconscionable. Baker v. Baker (Summit 1992) 83 Ohio App.3d 700, 615 N.E.2d 699.

Trial court did not abuse its discretion in failing to require husband to pay and save wife harmless from indebtedness on automobile, even though he allegedly promised to do so in pretrial negotiations. Layne v. Layne (Champaign 1992) 83 Ohio App.3d 559, 615 N.E.2d 332.

There are no flat rules for determining property division, and trial court must have discretion to do what is equitable upon the facts and circumstances of each case. Focke v. Focke (Montgomery 1992) 83 Ohio App.3d 552, 615 N.E.2d 327, motion overruled 66 Ohio St.3d 1446, 609 N.E.2d 172.

Reviewing court is limited to determining whether considering totality of circumstances, trial court abused its discretion in making property division; term "abuse of discretion" connotes more than error of law or judgment and implies that court's attitude is unreasonable, arbitrary, or unconscionable. Focke v. Focke (Montgomery 1992) 83 Ohio App.3d 552, 615 N.E.2d 327, motion overruled 66 Ohio St.3d 1446, 609 N.E.2d 172.

Trial court did not abuse discretion by awarding wife one half of parties' marital estate, and denying wife entitlement to share of property previously acquired by husband; marriage had been of short duration, husband's skills and dental practice had been acquired prior to marriage, wife was employable, neither enjoyed high standard of living, and both had significant assets. Verbanic v. Verbanic (Trumbull 1992) 83 Ohio App.3d 327, 614 N.E.2d 1103, cause dismissed 66 Ohio St.3d 1479, 612 N.E.2d 329, rehearing granted 67 Ohio St.3d 1407, 615 N.E.2d 630, reversed 70 Ohio St.3d 41, 635 N.E.2d 1260, reconsideration denied 70 Ohio St.3d 1439, 638 N.E.2d 1042.

"Abuse of discretion" sufficient to support reversal of trial court's distribution of marital assets in divorce case, means more than error of law; decision must be unreasonable, arbitrary or unconscionable. Verbanic v. Verbanic (Trumbull 1992) 83 Ohio App.3d 327, 614 N.E.2d 1103, cause dismissed 66 Ohio St.3d 1479, 612 N.E.2d 329, rehearing granted 67 Ohio St.3d 1407, 615 N.E.2d 630, reversed 70 Ohio St.3d 41, 635 N.E.2d 1260, reconsideration denied 70 Ohio St.3d 1439, 638 N.E.2d 1042.

In a divorce action, the fact that the trial court's decision is rendered six months after trial and no full transcript of proceedings of the trial is available does not alone constitute an abuse of discretion and therefore, where the trial court's judgment entry sets forth detailed findings of fact which are supported by the record and the complaining party has not affirmatively shown that the trial court's conduct or its decision is arbitrary or unreasonable or that any prejudicial error was committed that would require reversal of the trial court's decision, the court's decision is affirmed. Green v. Green (Erie 1989) 64 Ohio App.3d 37, 580 N.E.2d 513.

Trial court has broad discretion in determining division of marital property so long as division is equitable and is arrived at upon consideration of factors enumerated in statute. Schwenk v. Schwenk (Cuyahoga 1982) 2 Ohio App.3d 250, 441 N.E.2d 631, 2 O.B.R. 272.

Award to husband of real estate previously conveyed to wife by husband as part of an alimony decree was an abuse of discretion. (See also Kontner v Kontner, 103 App 372, 145 NE(2d) 495 (1956).) Kontner v. Kontner (Franklin 1956) 103 Ohio App. 360, 139 N.E.2d 366, 74 Ohio Law Abs. 97, 3 O.O.2d 384, rehearing denied 103 Ohio App. 360, 145 N.E.2d 495, 3 O.O.2d 384.

An order permanently restraining husband from competing with the parties' moving and storage business which is awarded to wife is an abuse of discretion where (1) the husband is prohibited from operating, working for, or consulting with any moving and storage business within a fifty-mile radius, (2) the husband has only a high-school education, and (3) his most marketable experience, skills, and expertise lie in the moving and storage industry. Merrick v Merrick, No. 15777, 1997 WL 216583 (2d Dist Ct App, Dayton, 5-2-97).

A trial court abuses its discretion when it fails to rule on a continuance motion and proceeds with the trial where the defendant includes with her motion for continuance a physician's affidavit stating that she is unable to appear for a deposition or for trial without endangering her health or the health of others. Cook v Cook, No. 13849, 1994 WL 237489 (2d Dist Ct App, Montgomery, 6-3-94).

Where a wife began to repeatedly leave the marital home in 1980 and continued to do so for thirteen years, "married" another man and lived with him for a year before getting the marriage annulled, and did not live with her family for the three years prior to the commencement of the divorce action, the trial court does not abuse its discretion in determining, for the purpose of the division of marital property, that the marriage ended in 1980 when the wife's absences first began; under RC 3105.171, the court may select dates that it considers equitable for the period of the marriage, for purposes of determining marital property. Hookway v Hookway, No. 2829, 1994 WL 162343 (9th Dist Ct App, Wayne, 5-4-94).

Where the parties cannot agree regarding the division of household furnishings, and the referee suggests a division by lottery, and the parties still do not agree, it is not an abuse of discretion for the trial court to adopt the recommendation of the referee. Bokovitz v Bokovitz, No. 1062 (9th Dist Ct App, Medina, 9-23-81).

Award of alimony to fifty-one year old physician for aggression of twenty-nine year old wife and property settlement decreed were proper. Sharkey v. Sharkey (Montgomery 1955) 137 N.E.2d 575, 73 Ohio Law Abs. 321.

In an action for separate maintenance and alimony, a court cannot make an equitable division of property, but can allow alimony payable in real and personal property. An interest in a family dwelling can so be awarded and does not constitute a division of property. Glassman v. Glassman (Cuyahoga 1951) 103 N.E.2d 781, 61 Ohio Law Abs. 242.

In action for alimony only where the pleadings fail to present the issue of prior divorce by one of the parties in another jurisdiction, the court has no right to make determination of any question concerning such divorce, and has no authority, after validity of such divorce is questioned in trial of such action for alimony only, to make a division of property. Davis v. Davis (Franklin 1944) 57 N.E.2d 703, 42 Ohio Law Abs. 105.

7. Marital assets

When either spouse makes a labor, money or an in-kind contribution that causes an increase in the value of separate property, that increase in value is marital property. Middendorf v. Middendorf (Ohio 1998) 82 Ohio St.3d 397, 696 N.E.2d 575.

Substantial evidence supported determination that husband's substantial efforts as livestock buyer and co-owner contributed to stockyard's increase in value during his marriage, such that increase in value of husband's separate interest during marriage was marital property to be divided between husband and wife. Middendorf v. Middendorf (Ohio 1998) 82 Ohio St.3d 397, 696 N.E.2d 575.

Increase in value of husband's business during marriage was marital property subject to division upon divorce, rather than husband's separate property, regardless of whether wife significantly contributed to its appreciation. Haslem v. Haslem (Ohio App. 8 Dist. 1999) 133 Ohio App.3d 257, 727 N.E.2d 928.

Stock investment account held jointly by husband and wife was marital property subject to equitable distribution following divorce, even though husband claimed that account was established by parties jointly for sole purpose of providing for the education of their children, where account had not borne children's names since its inception, husband and wife both held a right of survivorship in account and paid income tax on account appreciation, husband testified that account funds were intentionally not placed in a trust for the children, and wife testified that half the money in the account belonged to her. Bowen v. Bowen (Ohio App. 9 Dist. 1999) 132 Ohio App.3d 616, 725 N.E.2d 1165.

Court's failure, in action for divorce, to clearly designate its award of specific marital assets to respective parties on equitable division of marital property required remand for specific delineation of awards, resolution of conflicts in court's journal entries, and determination of amount, if any, owed by husband to wife to equalize property division; majority of marital property was not specifically mentioned in decree, and enumeration of parties' various bank and other financial accounts contained errors in designation of accounts and specification of amounts therein. Zeefe v. Zeefe (Ohio App. 8 Dist. 1998) 125 Ohio App.3d 600, 709 N.E.2d 208.

Personal injury settlement is marital property only to extent that lost earnings and medical expenses have adversely affected marital estate. Munroe v. Munroe (Ohio App. 8 Dist. 1997) 119 Ohio App.3d 530, 695 N.E.2d 1155.

Trial court did not abuse its discretion in determining that $4,000 obtained by husband in settlement of defamation action against his former employer was marital property; while husband initially testified that he did not think lawsuit concerned lost wages, he also testified that underlying incident affected him psychologically and prevented him from working, and because settlement was confidential, there was no evidence as to how damages were allocated. Munroe v. Munroe (Ohio App. 8 Dist. 1997) 119 Ohio App.3d 530, 695 N.E.2d 1155.

Wife's testimony that certain items of personal property given to her by husband during marriage were intended as gifts was insufficient to establish by clear and convincing evidence that husband intended to give up any interest he may have had in such property, as required for finding that property was wife's separate property rather than marital property, where there was also competent, credible evidence to support characterization of property as marital. Barkley v. Barkley (Ohio App. 4 Dist. 1997) 119 Ohio App.3d 155, 694 N.E.2d 989.

Spouse seeking equitable distribution of personal injury compensation paid to other spouse has burden of proving statutory exception for "loss of marital earnings." Bauser v. Bauser (Ohio App. 2 Dist. 1997) 118 Ohio App.3d 831, 694 N.E.2d 136.

Personal injury settlement was marital property to the extent that it included compensation for husband's lost wages, even though he might have received more money if more had been available from tortfeasor or insurer. Marcum v. Marcum (Ohio App. 2 Dist. 1996) 116 Ohio App.3d 606, 688 N.E.2d 1085.

Remand was required so that trial court could make specific findings with regard to life insurance policy that trial court determined was marital asset but awarded to husband without explanation. Neel v. Neel (Cuyahoga 1996) 113 Ohio App.3d 24, 680 N.E.2d 207, dismissed, appeal not allowed 77 Ohio St.3d 1514, 674 N.E.2d 369.

Trial court did not abuse discretion in determining that funds contained in bank savings account were marital property; although account funds were originally derived from husband's premarital holdings in stock portfolio account, evidence indicated parties treated account as joint account, as monies earned by wife were deposited into account during course of marriage to preserve account while husband was unemployed, parties deposited joint tax refunds into account, and there was evidence of other commingling, based on testimony that it was parties' practice to deposit money into that bank savings account and then transfer those funds to their joint checking account. Landry v. Landry (Auglaize 1995) 105 Ohio App.3d 289, 663 N.E.2d 1026.

Retirement benefits or right to receive retirement benefits accumulated during marriage are marital property which must be equitably distributed in divorce. James v. James (Greene 1995) 101 Ohio App.3d 668, 656 N.E.2d 399.

Trial court did not abuse its discretion by dividing marital property so as to award former wife sum certain in cash and real estate and awarding former husband shopping plaza, office building and family business which had potential for significant growth; any growth of assets awarded to husband would depend on his entrepreneurial skills and was not assured, and former husband demonstrated greater investment experience with assets. Terry v. Terry (Cuyahoga 1994) 99 Ohio App.3d 228, 650 N.E.2d 184.

In divorce proceeding, trial court did not abuse its discretion in ordering that psychologist, who, pursuant to agreement of parties, did psychological evaluations of family members, be paid out of marital assets. DiLacqua v. DiLacqua (Summit 1993) 88 Ohio App.3d 48, 623 N.E.2d 118.

Finding that husband's interest in his father's company was marital property was not abuse of discretion; although portion of interest represented premarital labor, divorce court was entitled to determine that nonmarital portion he had, over 27-year duration of marriage, transmuted to marital property. Jelen v. Jelen (Hamilton 1993) 86 Ohio App.3d 199, 620 N.E.2d 224.

Finding that husband's separate cash property, used as down payment for marital residence, became transmuted into marital property during 17-year duration of marriage was not abuse of discretion. Frost v. Frost

(Franklin 1992) 84 Ohio App.3d 699, 618 N.E.2d 198, motion overruled 66 Ohio St.3d 1489, 612 N.E.2d 1245.

Finding that various assets brought into marriage by husband had been substantially transmuted into marital property was not abuse of discretion, given lack of any evidence that assets were treated as husband's separate property throughout duration of 17-year marriage. Frost v. Frost (Franklin 1992) 84 Ohio App.3d 699, 618 N.E.2d 198, motion overruled 66 Ohio St.3d 1489, 612 N.E.2d 1245.

Cash value of life insurance policy separately owned by husband at time of marriage became transmuted into marital property in that, over duration of 17-year marriage, asset acquired purpose of benefitting family unit. Frost v. Frost (Franklin 1992) 84 Ohio App.3d 699, 618 N.E.2d 198, motion overruled 66 Ohio St.3d 1489, 612 N.E.2d 1245.

Evidence that defendant bought property, placed it in his son's name, and permitted son to live in property rent free was sufficient to establish that property was marital property. Baker v. Baker (Summit 1992) 83 Ohio App.3d 700, 615 N.E.2d 699.

Evidence sustained trial court's finding that furs, jewelry, and coin collection presented by husband to wife for her personal use during the marriage were items of marital property rather than the wife's separate property. Focke v. Focke (Montgomery 1992) 83 Ohio App.3d 552, 615 N.E.2d 327, motion overruled 66 Ohio St.3d 1446, 609 N.E.2d 172.

Finding that portions of life insurance policies paid for with marital funds were marital assets was not abuse of discretion, even though husband purchased policies prior to marriage. Babka v. Babka (Summit 1992) 83 Ohio App.3d 428, 615 N.E.2d 247.

Two properties which were divided between divorcing spouses who later remarry each other and create joint tenancies with the right to survivorship in the realty are transformed from separate property into marital property. Moore v. Moore (Summit 1992) 83 Ohio App.3d 75, 613 N.E.2d 1097.

A $5000 gift from a wife's parents meant as a down payment on a house will be considered marital property absent evidence it was a gift solely to the wife. Pettry v. Pettry (Franklin 1991) 81 Ohio App.3d 30, 610 N.E.2d 443.

An inherited motel is a marital asset where both spouses made substantial contributions to the motel as a family asset. Guziak v. Guziak (Summit 1992) 80 Ohio App.3d 805, 610 N.E.2d 1135, motion overruled 65 Ohio St.3d 1478, 604 N.E.2d 169.

Without evidence that a car was bought with separate funds, the court was free to find that the car was purchased with marital assets. Guziak v. Guziak (Summit 1992) 80 Ohio App.3d 805, 610 N.E.2d 1135, motion overruled 65 Ohio St.3d 1478, 604 N.E.2d 169.

Personal injury settlement is "marital property" divisible upon divorce, only to the extent that it reimburses injured spouse for lost earnings and medical expenses that have adverse impact on marital estate; in characterizing settlement proceeds, divorce court was entitled to consider whether injured spouse's medical expenses had, in fact, depleted marital estate, or whether employer or insurer had picked up such expenses. Everhardt v. Everhardt (Lucas 1991) 77 Ohio App.3d 396, 602 N.E.2d 701.

Money received from sale of dental practice is considered marital property, while money received for covenant not to compete is considered a nonmarital asset. Hoeft v. Hoeft (Lucas 1991) 74 Ohio App.3d 809, 600 N.E.2d 746.

Inclusion in the marital estate of the value of $35,000 in cash gifts made by a party to his children out of a joint bank account prior to a decree of divorce or issuance of a restraining order is not an abuse of discretion. Guidubaldi v. Guidubaldi (Portage 1990) 64 Ohio App.3d 361, 581 N.E.2d 621.

Generally, properties acquired by gift, bequest, devise, or descent are considered nonmarital assets, but such nonmarital property may be converted to marital property by transmutation; therefore, where one spouse receives a gift of nine shares of the stock of the family business from his mother, never segregates or otherwise treats the shares any differently than the other fifty shares owned by the parties, conducts all corporate business based on a unified interest of all fifty-nine shares, and freely utilizes corporate assets for personal, family, and household matters, these circumstances suggest transmutation of the nine gift shares of stock. Kuehn v. Kuehn (Clinton 1988) 55 Ohio App.3d 245, 564 N.E.2d 97, motion overruled 41 Ohio St.3d 709, 534 N.E.2d 1212.

A referral fee owed to an attorney-spouse constitutes "deferred compensation" subject to division as a marital asset. Rabbitt v. Rabbitt (Lucas 1988) 43 Ohio App.3d 38, 539 N.E.2d 684, motion overruled 37 Ohio St.3d 708, 532 N.E.2d 141.

Where undisclosed assets are discovered after a divorce is granted and the trial court vacates the entire property settlement, the trial court is then obligated to reconsider its entire decision relating to property issues and not just the division of the previously undisclosed assets. Clymer v Clymer, No. 95APF02-239, 1995 WL 571445 (10th Dist Ct App, Franklin, 9-26-95).

A husband's employment bonus and IRA are marital assets to the parties subject to equitable division and where a husband pays personal living expenses, a $10,000 attorney retainer, and marital debts from the assets, a court errs in dividing the entire amount even though they had already been spent in large part on marital debts, resulting in a substantial disparity in the parties' awards. Jarvis v Jarvis, No. 94APF11-1685, 1995 WL 450254 (10th Dist Ct App, Franklin, 7-25-95).

The trial court does not abuse its discretion in awarding a wife over fifty per cent of the marital assets when the parties had been married for almost thirty years, the wife was a housewife for the majority of the marriage, and she was in need of a place to live and required sustenance alimony. Adams v Adams, No. 93-J-10, 1995 WL 152991 (7th Dist Ct App, Jefferson, 4-4-95).

There is insufficient detail for a trial court to affix a dollar value to a marital asset without explaining how it arrived at the valuation when the trial court then uses the unsubstantiated value to divide the marital asset in a case where the asset involves the value of the parties' ownership interest in a restaurant business represented by forty-nine per cent of its outstanding shares. Rammel v Rammel, No. 14362, 1995 WL 21250 (2d Dist Ct App, Montgomery, 1-20-95).

When the terms of an antenuptial agreement provide that the separately owned real estate of the defendant would only become marital property if the real estate was sold and the proceeds were used for the purchase of other real estate or for the construction of a dwelling house, the mere fact that the real estate was sold during the marriage did not automatically convert the proceeds to marital property. Cook v Cook, No. 13849, 1994 WL 237489 (2d Dist Ct App, Montgomery, 6-3-94).

Notwithstanding Ohio statute restricting assignment or attachment of lottery winnings, proceeds of lottery that was won by Chapter 7 debtor's wife during their marriage constituted "marital property" under Ohio domestic relations statutes, and, thus, debtor had property interest in lottery proceeds at the time they were transferred to wife, prepetition, as part of their marital separation agreement, and this transfer was properly subject to challenge by bankruptcy trustee through the assertion of his avoidance claims. In re Fordu (C.A.6 (Ohio) 1999) 201 F.3d 693.

Under Ohio law, the interest that each spouse acquires upon commencement of divorce action in any separately titled property of the other that is or would qualify as "marital property" is strictly contingent until such time as formal distribution of marital property is made, and is subject to divestment if state court with jurisdiction over parties' property does not enter an order awarding property to the non-title holding spouse. In re Greer (Bkrtcy.N.D.Ohio 1999) 242 B.R. 389.

Chapter 7 debtor's individual retirement account (IRA), as marital asset, was subject to division by state court in divorce proceeding, even though debtor was sole owner of the IRA. In re Donnelly (Bkrtcy.S.D.Ohio 1992) 151 B.R. 787.

8. Retirement funds

Pension or retirement benefits accumulated during course of marriage are marital assets subject to property division in divorce action. Erb v. Erb (Ohio 1996) 75 Ohio St.3d 18, 661 N.E.2d 175, reconsideration denied 75 Ohio St.3d 1452, 663 N.E.2d 333.

When distributing pension or retirement benefits in divorce action, trial court must apply its discretion based upon circumstances of the case, status of parties, nature, terms and conditions of pension or retirement plan, and reasonableness of result. Erb v. Erb (Ohio 1996) 75 Ohio St.3d 18, 661 N.E.2d 175, reconsideration denied 75 Ohio St.3d 1452, 663 N.E.2d 333.

Method of distributing vested pension benefits in divorce proceeding depends upon whether benefits are matured or not. Erb v. Erb (Ohio 1996) 75 Ohio St.3d 18, 661 N.E.2d 175, reconsideration denied 75 Ohio St.3d 1452, 663 N.E.2d 333.

Whether or not vested pension benefits have matured, trial court must not violate terms of pension plan in fashioning division of benefits in divorce proceeding. Erb v. Erb (Ohio 1996) 75 Ohio St.3d 18, 661 N.E.2d 175, reconsideration denied 75 Ohio St.3d 1452, 663 N.E.2d 333.

Qualified domestic relations order (QDRO) entered by court in divorce action which recognized former wife's right to one-half of benefits of police and firefighters retirement plan which had accrued to husband during marriage, and established wife as an alternative payee and assigned her certain retirement benefits otherwise payable to husband, violated statute under which sums of money due to any person under plan are not liable to attachment, garnishment, levy, or seizure, and thus was invalid. Davis v. Davis (Ohio App. 2 Dist. 1998) 131 Ohio App.3d 686, 723 N.E.2d 599.

While court cannot, prior to the participant's retirement, order an immediate, outright division of Police and Fireman's Disability Pension Fund (PFDPF) or deferred compensation benefits, court may equitably divide individual's pension and deferred compensation funds during divorce proceeding and issue orders incidental to accomplishing division. Vaughan v. Vaughan (Ohio App. 4 Dist. 1998) 131 Ohio App.3d 364, 722 N.E.2d 578.

Former wife's one-half interest in former husband's pension and one-half interest in former husband's deferred compensation had actual effect of providing necessary support, where structure of award to former wife indicated that trial court granted such interest to provide for former wife's needs in retirement. Vaughan v. Vaughan (Ohio App. 4 Dist. 1998) 131 Ohio App.3d 364, 722 N.E.2d 578.

Amount of former husband's obligation to former wife created by trial court's order granting former wife one-half interest in his pension and one-half interest in his deferred compensation was not so excessive as to be unreasonable under traditional concepts of support, where approximately nine months prior to divorce, pension was valued at approximately $28,000 and deferred compensation fund amounted to $6,000. Vaughan v. Vaughan (Ohio App. 4 Dist. 1998) 131 Ohio App.3d 364, 722 N.E.2d 578.

Pension and retirement benefits acquired by either spouse during the marriage are marital assets that must be considered in arriving at an equitable division of marital property. Schiavone v. Schiavone (Ohio App. 12 Dist. 1998) 126 Ohio App.3d 780, 711 N.E.2d 694.

Trial court erred in attempting to retain jurisdiction to modify order dividing husband's public employee retirement system (PERS) account, in the event that husband should attempt to discharge in bankruptcy the property settlement order as to PERS account. Schiavone v. Schiavone (Ohio App. 12 Dist. 1998) 126 Ohio App.3d 780, 711 N.E.2d 694.

Vested pension plan accumulated during marriage is marital asset that must be considered in arriving at equitable division of property. Malone v. Malone (Ohio App. 4 Dist. 1998) 126 Ohio App.3d 685, 711 N.E.2d 262.

Trial court's error, in divorce action, in failing to consider wife's pension in arriving at equitable distribution of marital property, required remand for review of parties' retirement benefits and their impact on ultimate division of property, despite failure of both parties to bring pension to trial court's attention. Malone v. Malone (Ohio App. 4 Dist. 1998) 126 Ohio App.3d 685, 711 N.E.2d 262.

Because a division of pension or retirement benefits is a division of marital property, domestic relations court lacks continuing jurisdiction to modify division of pension or retirement benefits. Doolin v. Doolin (Ohio App. 6 Dist. 1997) 123 Ohio App.3d 296, 704 N.E.2d 51, reconsideration denied.

No reservation of continuing jurisdiction existed which would allow domestic relations court to adopt qualified domestic relations orders (QDROs) which modified division of former husband's pension benefits, as agreed to by parties and set forth in divorce decree, and thus, QDROs were void ab initio and could be vacated by trial court pursuant to its inherent authority. Doolin v. Doolin (Ohio App. 6 Dist. 1997) 123 Ohio App.3d 296, 704 N.E.2d 51, reconsideration denied.

Trial court's determination regarding overpayment of portion of former husband's pension benefits to wife, which had occurred as result of domestic relations court's improper entry of qualified domestic relations orders (QDROs) modifying division of husband's pension benefits, was not against manifest weight of the evidence; testimony and documentary evidence was offered to show that wife was still receiving pension benefits specified in improper QDROs. Doolin v. Doolin (Ohio App. 6 Dist. 1997) 123 Ohio App.3d 296, 704 N.E.2d 51, reconsideration denied.

Vested pension plans accumulated during a marriage are marital assets that a trial court must consider to arrive at an equitable property division. Leadingham v. Leadingham (Ohio App. 12 Dist. 1997) 120 Ohio App.3d 496, 698 N.E.2d 465.

Trial court did not abuse its discretion, in dividing parties' pension benefits, by imputing to husband several years of future employment with his former employer that terminated him based on a drug conviction, even though husband claimed his future employment was in question at time of firing due to disabling eye condition, where there was evidence that husband could have continued working for employer if he had not been convicted. Leadingham v. Leadingham (Ohio App. 12 Dist. 1997) 120 Ohio App.3d 496, 698 N.E.2d 465.

Trial court acted within its discretion in considering husband's loss of job and chance to accrue full pension benefits as consequences of his drug conviction in equitably dividing parties' total pension benefits. Leadingham v. Leadingham (Ohio App. 12 Dist. 1997) 120 Ohio App.3d 496, 698 N.E.2d 465.

Trial court properly considered husband's Social Security benefits in dividing parties' total pension benefits, where wife did not participate in the Social Security system. Leadingham v. Leadingham (Ohio App. 12 Dist. 1997) 120 Ohio App.3d 496, 698 N.E.2d 465.

Husband's disability pension income was his separate property and was exempt from equitable division, where there was no evidence that any portion of disability pension was paid in lieu of old-age retirement benefits, or that amount of old-age retirement benefits that husband would otherwise be entitled to receive was diminished by payment of disability pension benefits. Bauser v. Bauser (Ohio App. 2 Dist. 1997) 118 Ohio App.3d 831, 694 N.E.2d 136.

Term "ultimate," as used in separation agreement provision dividing "ultimate value" of husband's retirement fund benefits between husband and wife, covered lump-sum payment received by husband when he elected early retirement, even though he claimed term applied only to what he would receive upon attaining normal retirement age. In Matter of Kincaid (Ohio App. 11 Dist. 1997) 117 Ohio App.3d 148, 690 N.E.2d 47.

Pension plan established during marriage is indeed a marital asset and subject to division like any other marital asset. Mallett v. Mallett (Ohio App. 7 Dist. 1996) 116 Ohio App.3d 139, 687 N.E.2d 17.

Value assigned to pension was supported by figures set forth in written pension evaluation, particularly as no evidence was introduced to contradict exhibit. Mallett v. Mallett (Ohio App. 7 Dist. 1996) 116 Ohio App.3d 139, 687 N.E.2d 17.

Pension and retirement benefits are marital assets subject to division upon divorce or dissolution. Weller v. Weller (Lucas 1996) 115 Ohio App.3d 173, 684 N.E.2d 1284.

Former husband's railroad pension benefits were required to be omitted from division of marital property, and could not be offset against other assets, where such benefits were similar to "Tier I" benefits under Railroad Retirement Act. Loew v. Loew (Trumbull 1996) 114 Ohio App.3d 632, 683 N.E.2d 847.

While Social Security benefits are not true marital assets and are not subject to direct division, they are subject to evaluation and consideration in making equitable distribution of marital assets. Walker v. Walker (Hamilton 1996) 112 Ohio App.3d 90, 677 N.E.2d 1252, appeal not allowed 77 Ohio St.3d 1492, 673 N.E.2d 149.

State courts are prohibited from dividing Social Security benefits, which are allocated according to federal statute, as part of divorce proceeding. Walker v. Walker (Hamilton 1996) 112 Ohio App.3d 90, 677 N.E.2d 1252, appeal not allowed 77 Ohio St.3d 1492, 673 N.E.2d 149.

Court's division of husband's federal postal service retirement benefits, in which court reduced husband's pension plan value by value of benefits that would have accrued under Social Security if he had been participant of Social Security system during marriage, was not abuse of discretion. Walker v. Walker (Hamilton 1996) 112 Ohio App.3d 90, 677 N.E.2d 1252, appeal not allowed 77 Ohio St.3d 1492, 673 N.E.2d 149.

Trial court's order in divorce proceeding awarding husband's pension to husband free and clear of any claim by wife complied with proper guidelines for equitable distribution, though entire pension account was acquired during course of marriage and was marital property, where spouses had few major assets and high outstanding debts, court apportioned all marital debt to husband, and wife, who had few marketable skills and was hampered by multiple physical ailments, received home, van, and household goods free and clear of debt. Mayer v. Mayer (Allen 1996) 110 Ohio App.3d 233, 673 N.E.2d 981, dismissed, appeal not allowed 77 Ohio St.3d 1413, 670 N.E.2d 1002.

Pension and retirement benefits acquired by either spouse during course of marriage are marital assets that must be considered in arriving at equitable division of marital property. Ricketts v. Ricketts (Butler 1996) 109 Ohio App.3d 746, 673 N.E.2d 156, dismissed, appeal not allowed 76 Ohio St.3d 1473, 669 N.E.2d 856.

Trial court has broad discretion in dividing marital property, including pension benefits, but does not have continuing jurisdiction to modify property division incident to divorce decree. Ricketts v. Ricketts (Butler 1996) 109 Ohio App.3d 746, 673 N.E.2d 156, dismissed, appeal not allowed 76 Ohio St.3d 1473, 669 N.E.2d 856.

In determining property division of pension benefits, trial court should attempt to preserve pension or retirement asset in order that each party can procure most benefit, and should attempt to disentangle parties' economic partnership so as to create conclusion and finality to their marriage. Ricketts v. Ricketts (Butler 1996) 109 Ohio App.3d 746, 673 N.E.2d 156, dismissed, appeal not allowed 76 Ohio St.3d 1473, 669 N.E.2d 856.

Qualified domestic relations order (QDRO) is not acceptable method for division of public pension upon divorce, in light of fact that public pension funds are not subject to attachment, garnishment, levy, or seizure under any legal or equitable process including QRDOs relating to property division in divorce action. Ricketts v. Ricketts (Butler 1996) 109 Ohio App.3d 746, 673 N.E.2d 156, dismissed, appeal not allowed 76 Ohio St.3d 1473, 669 N.E.2d 856.

In light of fact that public pension funds do not recognize qualified domestic relations orders (QDROs), trial court may establish formula in divorce decree for future division of public pension when spouse participating in pension plan begins to draw benefits, by calculating amount of future benefits to which nonparticipating spouse is entitled, with payment to be made in installment payments from participating spouse once that spouse begins receiving pension benefits from his or her public pension fund. Ricketts v. Ricketts (Butler 1996) 109 Ohio App.3d 746, 673 N.E.2d 156, dismissed, appeal not allowed 76 Ohio St.3d 1473, 669 N.E.2d 856.

Proper method to determine value of pension benefits for division upon divorce is to compute coverture fraction representing ratio of number of years of employment of employed spouse during marriage to total years of his or her employment. Ricketts v. Ricketts (Butler 1996) 109 Ohio App.3d 746, 673 N.E.2d 156, dismissed, appeal not allowed 76 Ohio St.3d 1473, 669 N.E.2d 856.

Trial court's change in numerator of coverture fraction for computing former wife's share of former husband's monthly pension benefits eight years after entry of divorce decree constituted impermissible modification of pension division in divorce decree, and required recalculation of former wife's share pursuant to terms of decree entitling her to share of monthly benefits based on one half of number of years former husband was employed during marriage divided by total number of years he had in his pension. Ricketts v. Ricketts (Butler 1996) 109 Ohio App.3d 746, 673 N.E.2d 156, dismissed, appeal not allowed 76 Ohio St.3d 1473, 669 N.E.2d 856.

Trial court did not exhibit unreasonable, arbitrary, or unconscionable attitude in permitting gradual repayment of former husband's arrearage owed to former wife for her share of his pension benefits, in light of great reduction in former husband's income as result of his retirement. Ricketts v. Ricketts (Butler 1996) 109 Ohio App.3d 746, 673 N.E.2d 156, dismissed, appeal not allowed 76 Ohio St.3d 1473, 669 N.E.2d 856.

General rule is that pension and retirement benefits are marital assets subject to division as personal property. Schrader v. Schrader (Huron 1995) 108 Ohio App.3d 25, 669 N.E.2d 878.

Domestic relations court, in interest of fashioning fair and equitable award, may deal with pension and retirement benefits flexibly, including reserving authority to modify qualified domestic relations order. Schrader v. Schrader (Huron 1995) 108 Ohio App.3d 25, 669 N.E.2d 878.

Trial court has broad discretion in dividing retirement benefits upon divorce. James v. James (Greene 1995) 101 Ohio App.3d 668, 656 N.E.2d 399.

Treatment of parties' retirement benefits upon divorce was not improper, notwithstanding husband's claim that judgment allowed wife to keep her retirement account intact while requiring husband to liquidate his individual retirement account (IRA), as fact that husband was required to pay distributive monetary award to wife, to equalize assets awarded to parties, did not require husband to liquidate IRA since husband could pay award from other assets. James v. James (Greene 1995) 101 Ohio App.3d 668, 656 N.E.2d 399.

In dividing parties' pension and retirement funds, trial court should have considered wife's social security benefits to avoid penalizing husband who did not participate in social security system and whose pension was considered marital property. Eickelberger v. Eickelberger (Butler 1994) 93 Ohio App.3d 221, 638 N.E.2d 130.

Retirement benefits, including pension rights, vested during course of marriage are "marital assets" to be considered in dividing marital property. Eickelberger v. Eickelberger (Butler 1994) 93 Ohio App.3d 221, 638 N.E.2d 130.

Proper manner in which to consider impact of social security benefits when allocating marital retirement benefits is to determine monthly benefits social security recipient will receive upon retirement. Smith v. Smith (Franklin 1993) 91 Ohio App.3d 248, 632 N.E.2d 555, reconsideration denied, motion to certify overruled 68 Ohio St.3d 1449, 626 N.E.2d 690.

Social security, while not divisible marital asset, must be considered when equitably allocating pension benefits. Smith v. Smith (Franklin 1993) 91 Ohio App.3d 248, 632 N.E.2d 555, reconsideration denied, motion to certify overruled 68 Ohio St.3d 1449, 626 N.E.2d 690.

Use of "distributive award" to divide equitably parties' retirement assets was abuse of discretion, in absence of express determination that division of marital property in-kind or in-money was impracticable or burdensome or that it would be impracticable or burdensome to award wife appropriate share of Public Employees Retirement System (PERS) pension at time of husband's retirement or withdrawal of his account. Smith v. Smith (Franklin 1993) 91 Ohio App.3d 248, 632 N.E.2d 555, reconsideration denied, motion to certify overruled 68 Ohio St.3d 1449, 626 N.E.2d 690.

Use of "distributive award" to divide parties' Public Employees Retirement System (PERS) benefit was abuse of discretion where PERS account could not be withdrawn in whole or in part as long as husband remained employed by state, where husband's interest could not be withdrawn to effectuate division, and where parties did not have substantial other assets with which to set off value of wife's share of husband's pension benefits. Smith v. Smith (Franklin 1993) 91 Ohio App.3d 248, 632 N.E.2d 555, reconsideration denied, motion to certify overruled 68 Ohio St.3d 1449, 626 N.E.2d 690.

When court of common pleas divides nonliquid pension benefit, it is inequitable to order distributive award from current income absent existence of substantial assets or agreement of parties. Smith v. Smith (Franklin 1993) 91 Ohio App.3d 248, 632 N.E.2d 555, reconsideration denied, motion to certify overruled 68 Ohio St.3d 1449, 626 N.E.2d 690.

Premarital deposits by spouse into retirement account and subsequent appreciation on those premarital deposits are separate property, which trial court need not divide upon divorce. Getter v. Getter (Montgomery 1993) 90 Ohio App.3d 1, 627 N.E.2d 1043.

Trial court abused its discretion by refusing to equitably divide wife's retirement account that she opened and made contributions to during marriage. Getter v. Getter (Montgomery 1993) 90 Ohio App.3d 1, 627 N.E.2d 1043.

Upon divorce, teacher could be ordered to pay wife her share of his benefits from state teachers retirement system (STRS) in monthly payments to begin after he retired, rather than in periodic payments to begin immediately or in one lump sum, even though form of award would not serve interest in disentangling parties' financial affairs, where immediate periodic payments or lump sum distribution could not be made without compromising children's interest in remaining in marital home, and STRS would not have recognized order directing it to pay part of benefits to wife. Sprankle v. Sprankle (Medina 1993) 87 Ohio App.3d 129, 621 N.E.2d 1310.

Retirement benefits earned during marriage are marital property. Sprankle v. Sprankle (Medina 1993) 87 Ohio App.3d 129, 621 N.E.2d 1310.

Trial court has broad discretion in dividing spouses' retirement benefits upon divorce; such flexibility is necessary for court to make equitable decision based on relevant factors, such as nature and terms of retirement plan at issue and whether enough marital assets exist to offset nonemployed spouse's share if court decides to assign present value to pension benefit. Sprankle v. Sprankle (Medina 1993) 87 Ohio App.3d 129, 621 N.E.2d 1310.

Wife's share of husband's military retirement pay pursuant to divorce decree which provided that wife was to receive share of pension to which she was legally entitled was one half of fifteen twenty-seconds of benefits, where husband was in military for entire 15 years that parties were married and he retired after 22 years of service. Cherry v. Figart (Clermont 1993) 86 Ohio App.3d 123, 620 N.E.2d 174.

Determination that husband's individual retirement account (IRA) was marital property constituted abuse of discretion where only trial testimony regarding IRA was husband's statement that it was funded prior to marriage. Shapiro v. Shapiro (Summit 1992) 83 Ohio App.3d 744, 615 N.E.2d 727.

Court has broad discretion in dividing retirement benefits accumulated during marriage; equal division is presumed under statute to be equitable division and, in order to reach equitable result, court should attempt to preserve pension or retirement asset in order that each party can procure the most benefit, while disentangling parties' economic partnership so as to create conclusion and finality to marriage. Layne v. Layne (Champaign 1992) 83 Ohio App.3d 559, 615 N.E.2d 332.

Failure to consider relative age of parties in dividing pension funds was not abuse of discretion where pension benefits were included in property settlement; although spousal support statute requires court to consider age of parties and divide pension fund in proportion to that age difference, statute dealing with division of marital property does not require court to consider relative age of parties. Babka v. Babka (Summit 1992) 83 Ohio App.3d 428, 615 N.E.2d 247.

Trial court erred in divorce action when it failed to affix present value to husband's retirement benefits. Connolly v. Connolly (Cuyahoga 1990) 70 Ohio App.3d 738, 591 N.E.2d 1362.

Award to wife of 30% of husband's retirement benefits at time they became payable was equitable, even though wife would receive whatever increase in benefit amount was attributable to husband's postdecree employment, where future earnings were allowed for by means of reduced share of total benefit and jurisdiction was retained over other portions of alimony award. Campitelli v. Campitelli (Stark 1989) 65 Ohio App.3d 307, 583 N.E.2d 1322.

State teachers retirement system (STRS) benefits are not subject to division pursuant to a qualified domestic relations order, but they are marital assets which are to be considered by a trial court in determining an equitable division of property. Guidubaldi v. Guidubaldi (Portage 1990) 64 Ohio App.3d 361, 581 N.E.2d 621.

Assignment of a present value to a pension where the court states the evidence may not represent the present value of the pension plan is an abuse of discretion, since the pension plan must be considered in conjunction with other factors listed in RC 3105.18 and where there is insufficient evidence to determine the present value of the fund and the other factors have not been considered there can be no assignment of a present value until further proceedings are had. Guidubaldi v. Guidubaldi (Portage 1990) 64 Ohio App.3d 361, 581 N.E.2d 621.

Trial court in divorce action was authorized to modify pension fund provision of separation agreement, upon finding that wife did not disclose to husband that she had vested interest in her pension fund valued in excess of $20,000; trial court awarded each party proportionate share of other's pension fund, but agreement stated that parties would keep their own pensions free and clear of any claims thereon by other. Bourque v. Bourque (Clermont 1986) 34 Ohio App.3d 284, 518 N.E.2d 49.

A qualified domestic relation order (QDRO) is not permitted in dividing a husband's pension which is maintained in a police and firemen's disability and pension fund. Ciavarella v Ciavarella, No. 98 CO 53, 1999 WL 979238 (7th Dist Ct App, Columbiana, 10-20-99).

Husband's workers' compensation and employer's pension benefits which are husband's separate property distributed under RC 3105.171 are to be considered when calculating the parties' income for purposes of spousal support. Johnson v Johnson, No. CA99-01-001, 1999 WL 760978 (12th Dist Ct App, Warren, 9-27-99).

Where a retirement plan consists of Part A in which the employee makes no contributions and Part B requiring contributions by the employee, the formula used in a Qualified Domestic Relations Order (QDRO) which accounts for the reasonable growth of the non-employee's share realized from the employee's continued participation in the plan after the divorce cannot also be used as a basis to divide the parties' interests in Part B requiring employee contributions. Hamlin v Hamlin, No. 99-CA-1484, 1999 WL 397328 (2d Dist Ct App, Drake, 6-18-99).

Where parties marry and divorce one another twice and the first divorce decree does not mention husband's vested pension plan the trial court is required to consider pension or retirement benefits that are accumulated during both of the marriages and the consequent impact upon the ultimate division of marital property. Varney v Varney, Nos. 97 CA 809+, 1998 WL 548734 (4th Dist Ct App, Jackson, 8-26-98).

Disability retirement benefits are income rather than marital assets subject to division of property where they are paid to the husband as a form of wage continuation designed to compensate him for wages he would have otherwise received but for his disability. Koba v Koba, No. 70570, 1996 WL 732547 (8th Dist Ct App, Cuyahoga, 12-19-96).

Awarding the wife's pension entirely to the wife, and also half the husband's pension to the wife, while not referring to the wife's own social security benefits, is an abuse of discretion. Biggs v Biggs, No. L-95-214, 1996 WL 464163 (6th Dist Ct App, Lucas, 8-16-96).

Retirement benefits including the survivorship interest is a marital asset that is to be divided because it is earned during the marriage. Wylie v Wylie, No. 95CA18, 1996 WL 292044 (4th Dist Ct App, Lawrence, 6-4-96).

Where a wife's SSI is excluded from the property division calculation as a non-marital asset, the husband's SSI benefits that constitute a portion of his retirement benefits should likewise be excluded and should be free from the wife's twenty-eight per cent interest in his retirement benefits. Henning v Henning, No. 95-CA-31, 1996 WL 239824 (2d Dist Ct App, Miami, 5-10-96).

Award of a proportionate share to the wife of any voluntary separation incentive (VSI) that the husband may receive in the future due to his separation from the Air Force is within a court's discretion where (1) at the time of the divorce, he had completed fifteen years of military service, and (2) if he should elect to leave the service before becoming entitled to retirement benefits and to receive VSI benefits instead, those VSI benefits would be in lieu of the retirement benefits to which he would otherwise become entitled. Denny v Denny, No.

95-CA-87, 1996 WL 173397 (2d Dist Ct App, Greene, 4-12-96).

Unvested pensions earned during the course of marriage are marital assets. Haller v Haller, No. CA95-06-063, 1996 WL 116140 (12th Dist Ct App, Warren, 3-18-96).

In a distribution of marital property, valuation of a husband's pension fund based upon a future value that is not presently available and will not be available to him until he is sixty years old and has canceled the agency agreement with his employer, is error. Davidson v Davidson, No. 95-CA-07, 1996 WL 86254 (2d Dist Ct App, Champaign, 3-1-96).

To determine the value of the marital portion of retirement benefits under the Uniformed Services Former Spouses' Protection Act, 10 USCA 1408, which provides that state law controls whether a pension is marital property and how it is divided, the court should divide the number of years the parties were married during accrual of the pension by the number of years the spouse actually collected credit toward his retirement benefits. Baker v Baker, No. 13-95-36, 1996 WL 16888 (3d Dist Ct App, Seneca, 1-19-96).

While the trial court enjoys the discretion to assess the weight it will give to each party's arguments over the value of STRS pension, the court may not simply accept a party's valuation without explanation; it must determine the appropriate method for valuating the pension as well as clearly describe how it reaches its conclusion. Lynch v Lynch, No. 17170, 1995 WL 655932 (9th Dist Ct App, Summit, 11-8-95).

The division of vested pension benefits need not be equal. Marsala v Marsala, No. 67301, 1995 WL 396360 (8th Dist Ct App, Cuyahoga, 8-6-95).

By ignoring social security benefits, a court has not considered all relevant factors; a division of marital assets and liabilities cannot be deemed equitable where one spouse has a right to social security and made contributions toward it, while the other spouse participated in the state teachers retirement system and is not eligible for social security. Schaefers v Schaefers, No. 91-C-44, 1994 WL 631660 (7th Dist Ct App, Columbiana, 11-10-94).

A pension provision in a divorce decree applies to the person who is the defendant's spouse at the time of the divorce, and a trial court is without jurisdiction to modify the pension provision to include a former spouse to whom the defendant was married before his retirement and whom he remarries after the divorce. Moine v Moine, No. L-93-264, 1994 WL 159784 (6th Dist Ct App, Lucas, 4-29-94).

An award to a wife of a substantial part of a husband's retirement benefits while at the same time refusing to recognize the husband's right to an equitable share of a wife's retirement benefits is not equitable and constitutes an abuse of discretion. Paul v Paul, No. 93-CA-47, 1994 WL 43097 (2d Dist Ct App, Greene, 2-9-94).

When the court divides a nonliquid pension benefit it is inequitable to order a distributive award from current income absent the existence of substantial other assets or an agreement of the parties because it forces a spouse, who lacks significant financial resources to pay from current income the value of a delayed benefit while providing the payee spouse with a present benefit (although reduced), especially in view of the fact the pension can be divided in an alternative manner such as a QDRO ordering division upon retirement or separation from employment. Smith v Smith, No. 93AP-341, 1993 WL 435215 (10th Dist Ct App, Franklin, 10-21-93).

In a divorce action, although retirement pay of military personnel is a personal entitlement and may not be divided, the court may consider such retirement pay in arriving at a fair property disposition. Braund v Braund, No. CA 1073 (2d Dist Ct App, Darke, 10-7-83).

Portion of wife's civil service pension was not exempted from marital estate to extent it was in lieu of social security benefits. Coats v. Coats (Ohio Com.Pl. 1993) 63 Ohio Misc.2d 299, 626 N.E.2d 707.

Formula to determine portion of public pension to be considered as marital property is present value of public pension earned by spouse exempt from social security that exceeds present value of social security benefits actually earned by other spouse; formula should only be applied on case-by-case basis, taking into consideration circumstances of parties such as age, life expectancy, sex, health, income and any other relevant factors. Coats v. Coats (Ohio Com.Pl. 1993) 63 Ohio Misc.2d 299, 626 N.E.2d 707.

In determining present value of civil service pension when dividing marital property for any case in which public or government pension is exempt from social security, it is appropriate to take into consideration present value of actual social security benefits of spouse of party who was exempt from social security because he or she has public or governmental pension plan in lieu of social security, rather than present value of hypothetical social security benefits of exempt party. Coats v. Coats (Ohio Com.Pl. 1993) 63 Ohio Misc.2d 299, 626 N.E.2d 707.

ERISA preemption, community property law, right of pension participant's wife to transfer interest in retirement benefits. Boggs v. Boggs (U.S.La. 1997) 117 S.Ct. 1754, 520 U.S. 833, 138 L.Ed.2d 45, rehearing denied 118 S.Ct. 9, 138 L.Ed.2d 1043, on remand 121 F.3d 168.

Chapter 7 debtor's obligation to pay his former wife a portion of his pension benefits was not nondischargeable under support discharge exception, since state court which granted divorce clearly indicated that pension distribution was not intended to be spousal support award. In re McCafferty (C.A.6 (Ohio) 1996) 96 F.3d 192.

State court presiding over divorce proceedings enjoys complete discretion in determining how best to divide party's retirement benefits. In re McCafferty (C.A.6 (Ohio) 1996) 96 F.3d 192.

Under Ohio law, divorce order which specifically awarded ex-wife a portion of ex-husband's retirement plan awarded ex-wife separate property interest in ex-husband's pension benefits. In re McCafferty (C.A.6 (Ohio) 1996) 96 F.3d 192.

Recognizing constructive trust in favor of Chapter 7 debtor's former wife under state law as to portion of debtor's pension awarded to former wife in divorce decree would not impermissibly hinder bankruptcy policy of equality of distribution among creditors, since pension funds would not have been subject to reach of debtor's creditors under Ohio law. In re McCafferty (C.A.6 (Ohio) 1996) 96 F.3d 192.

Under Ohio law, divorce decree that awarded ex-wife separate property interest in ex-husband's pension benefits created constructive trust in favor of ex-wife, even though payments were not to begin until future date; accordingly, ex-husband retained only bare legal title in designated portion of benefits, with ex-wife being equitable owner, and ex-wife's portion of benefits never became part of ex-husband's Chapter 7 bankruptcy estate. In re McCafferty (C.A.6 (Ohio) 1996) 96 F.3d 192.

Portion of Chapter 7 debtor's military pension awarded prepetition to debtor's former wife in divorce decree was not property of debtor's estate and thus could not be subject to discharge; when portion of pension was awarded, former wife became equitable owner of that portion of pension fund, and that portion became her sole and separate property. Matter of McGraw (Bkrtcy.S.D.Ohio 1994) 176 B.R. 149.

9. Appreciation in value

Wife's efforts that led to appreciation of value in husband's corporation, which was husband's separate property before marriage, did not make entire value of corporation marital property; instead, hearing was required to determine appreciation in value resulting from wife's efforts. Simoni v. Simoni (Cuyahoga 1995) 102 Ohio App.3d 628, 657 N.E.2d 800, appeal not allowed 73 Ohio St.3d 1453, 654 N.E.2d 989.

Evidence that wife performed substantial work in improving husband's rental property, including insulating, staining kitchen cabinets, installing ceiling tile, cleaning, and lawn maintenance was sufficient to support finding in divorce proceeding that wife contributed to appreciation of property. Baker v. Baker (Summit 1992) 83 Ohio App.3d 700, 615 N.E.2d 699.

Evidence that wife worked to improve marital residence was sufficient to support trial court's decision to apportion appreciation of residence in divorce proceeding. Baker v. Baker (Summit 1992) 83 Ohio App.3d 700, 615 N.E.2d 699.

Trial court did not abuse its discretion by using averaging method to determine marital appreciation of two properties in divorce proceeding; although no evidence was presented as to value of properties as of date of marriage, value used for one property was purchase price only months prior to marriage. Baker v. Baker (Summit 1992) 83 Ohio App.3d 700, 615 N.E.2d 699.

Appreciation in value of stock purchased by husband with nonmarital property during the marriage was nonmarital asset; increase in the stock's value was in no part due to any efforts by wife, and no marital funds or labor were expended to increase the stock's value. Walkup v. Walkup (Brown 1986) 31 Ohio App.3d 248, 511 N.E.2d 119, 31 O.B.R. 532.

The appreciation value of property acquired by the husband through an inheritance is not marital property and all money received because of this appreciation belongs to the husband; activities preformed by the wife on the property including maintaining a garden and farming the land do not contribute to the appreciation and value of the real estate. Ebright v Ebright, No. 94CA34, 1995 WL 163299 (5th Dist Ct App, Fairfield, 3-1-95).

Although a marital residence is purchased five years prior to marriage and is titled in the appellee's mother's name, it is held in constructive trust for the appellee and any appreciation in value is considered marital property because of the contribution toward expenses by both spouses during the marriage. Redmond v Redmond, No. 3119, 1994 WL 277941 (2d Dist Ct App, Clark, 6-22-94).

Appreciation in value of a wife's parcel of real property that has served as the couple's residence during the marriage is not considered marital property in itself and a trial court errs in granting the husband a share in the appreciation even though he may have contributed to the appreciation in value through his money, labor, or in-kind contribution. Radcliffe v Radcliffe, No. 14130, 1994 WL 151679 (2d Dist Ct App, Montgomery, 4-27-94).

10. Tax considerations

Trial court acted within its discretion by requiring husband and wife to file joint tax return for prior tax year in order entered in connection with divorce action; husband was not precluded from filing joint return under Internal Revenue Code, and court was required to consider federal tax consequences of its property division. Bowen v. Bowen (Ohio App. 9 Dist. 1999) 132 Ohio App.3d 616, 725 N.E.2d 1165.

Trial court did not have to consider tax consequences in determining present value of husband's pension plan, in light of agreed valuation of known marital assets and other factors that rendered the distribution equitable in its entirety. Fergus v. Fergus (Ohio App. 7 Dist. 1997) 117 Ohio App.3d 432, 690 N.E.2d 949.

Trial court did not abuse its discretion in granting wife income tax refund, given total circumstances surrounding property division. deLevie v. deLevie (Franklin 1993) 86 Ohio App.3d 531, 621 N.E.2d 594, dismissed, jurisdictional motion overruled 67 Ohio St.3d 1409, 615 N.E.2d 1043.

The failure of a trial court to award the dependency exemptions for the parties' three minor children for state and federal tax purposes to the noncustodial parent does not constitute an abuse of discretion where the record clearly reflects that the trial court took no action with respect to the exemptions and the noncustodial parent did not argue allocation of tax exemptions to the trial court, nor did he present evidence of the benefit he would derive by being able to use them. Goode v. Goode (Franklin 1991) 70 Ohio App.3d 125, 590 N.E.2d 439.

If the overall distribution of marital property in a divorce judgment is equitable, a trial court does not abuse its discretion in allocating a joint tax liability to just one of the parties. Rowe v. Rowe (Lucas 1990) 69 Ohio App.3d 607, 591 N.E.2d 716.

A trial court may not award in a postdecree proceeding the state and federal income tax exemption for dependent children, which was part of the division of property in a divorce proceeding. Mettler v. Mettler (Ross 1988) 61 Ohio App.3d 14, 572 N.E.2d 127.

Tax refunds created by net operating losses which carry back to years during the marriage are separate property and an ex-spouse is not entitled to half of the tax refunds where the right to the refund accrued after the de facto date of the termination of the marriage and the spouse did not share in suffering the net operating loss which generated the right to the refund. Office v Office, No. 15298, 1997 WL 18043 (2d Dist Ct App, Montgomery, 1-17-97).

A wife's federal tax earned income credit for a child of a previous marriage is marital property acquired during the marriage where (1) the husband assumes complete responsibility for the child and (2) the child has had no relationship or financial support from his natural father. Derr v Derr, No. CA95-06-010, 1996 WL 131156 (12th Dist Ct App, Preble, 3-25-96).

11. Appellate review

Appellate review of trial court's application of test for determining whether debt not specifically designated as alimony, maintenance, or support is actually in nature of alimony, maintenance, or support presents mixed question of law and fact, and Court of Appeals therefore reviews factual findings for clear error and legal conclusions de novo. Vaughan v. Vaughan (Ohio App. 4 Dist. 1998) 131 Ohio App.3d 364, 722 N.E.2d 578.

Appellate court should view a trial court's division of marital property in a divorce proceeding as a whole in determining whether an equitable and fair division has been achieved. Szerlip v. Szerlip (Ohio App. 5 Dist. 1998) 129 Ohio App.3d 506, 718 N.E.2d 473.

In allocating property between parties to divorce, trial court must indicate basis of its award in sufficient detail to enable reviewing court to determine whether award is fair, equitable, and in accordance with the law. Neel v. Neel (Cuyahoga 1996) 113 Ohio App.3d 24, 680 N.E.2d 207, dismissed, appeal not allowed 77 Ohio St.3d 1514, 674 N.E.2d 369.

Mathematical error that occurred in divorce proceeding when calculating value of husband's separate contribution to marital home was corrected on appeal. Kelly v. Kelly (Hamilton 1996) 111 Ohio App.3d 641, 676 N.E.2d 1210.

Appellate court reviews overall appropriateness of trial court's property division in divorce proceedings under abuse of discretion standard. Kelly v. Kelly (Hamilton 1996) 111 Ohio App.3d 641, 676 N.E.2d 1210.

After reviewing totality of circumstances in divorce proceedings, trial court's decision regarding distribution of property will not be overturned absent abuse of discretion. Mayer v. Mayer (Allen 1996) 110 Ohio App.3d 233, 673 N.E.2d 981, dismissed, appeal not allowed 77 Ohio St.3d 1413, 670 N.E.2d 1002.

Appellate court must not disturb trial court's decision to make distributive award of party's separate property in divorce proceeding absent abuse of discretion. Swartz v. Swartz (Warren 1996) 110 Ohio App.3d 218, 673 N.E.2d 972.

Decision of trial court in dividing marital property will not be disturbed on appeal absent an abuse of discretion. Landry v. Landry (Auglaize 1995) 105 Ohio App.3d 289, 663 N.E.2d 1026.

When reviewing trial court's marital property division, reviewing court is limited to determining whether, considering totality of circumstances, trial court abused its discretion in fashioning award; term "abuse of discretion" implies that court's attitude is unreasonable, arbitrary, or unconscionable. James v. James (Greene 1995) 101 Ohio App.3d 668, 656 N.E.2d 399.

Reviewing court should not review discrete aspects of property division upon divorce out of context of entire award, but should consider distribution within context of entire award. James v. James (Greene 1995) 101 Ohio App.3d 668, 656 N.E.2d 399.

Appellate review of trial court's classification of property as marital or separate is based on whether determination is supported by manifest weight of evidence. James v. James (Greene 1995) 101 Ohio App.3d 668, 656 N.E.2d 399.

Scope of review of division of marital property is limited to determination of whether trial court abused its discretion. Terry v. Terry (Cuyahoga 1994) 99 Ohio App.3d 228, 650 N.E.2d 184.

When husband initially appealed divorce judgment to Court of Appeals and argued that property division was incorrect based on one theory, but failed to argue it was incorrect based on other theories, and case was remanded for limited purpose of considering effect of husband's medical condition on child support obligation, trial court's original property division was the law of the case; fact that issue of child support was reversed and remanded did serendipitously reopen all previously closed issues for presentation of new theory. Singleton v. Singleton (Summit 1994) 95 Ohio App.3d 467, 642 N.E.2d 708.

Trial court in divorce action had to indicate basis for its award in sufficient detail to enable reviewing court to determine that award was fair, equitable and in accordance with law, notwithstanding any question as to applicability of statute requiring written findings of fact supporting determination that marital property has been equitably divided. Gibson v. Gibson (Scioto 1993) 87 Ohio App.3d 426, 622 N.E.2d 425.

In determining whether trial court abused its discretion when dividing parties' marital assets, reviewing court cannot examine valuation and division of particular asset or liability in isolation; rather, reviewing court must view property division in its entirety, consider totality of circumstances, and determine whether property division reflects unreasonable, arbitrary or unconscionable attitude on part of domestic relations court. Jelen v. Jelen (Hamilton 1993) 86 Ohio App.3d 199, 620 N.E.2d 224.

Appellate court should not review discrete aspects of marital property division out of context of entire award. Baker v. Baker (Summit 1992) 83 Ohio App.3d 700, 615 N.E.2d 699.

Reviewing court may modify or review marital property division only if it finds that trial court abused its discretion in dividing property. Baker v. Baker (Summit 1992) 83 Ohio App.3d 700, 615 N.E.2d 699.

When applying abuse of discretion standard in reviewing property division, court is not free to merely substitute its judgment for that of trial court but must be guided by presumption that findings of trial court are correct. Focke v. Focke (Montgomery 1992) 83 Ohio App.3d 552, 615 N.E.2d 327, motion overruled 66 Ohio St.3d 1446, 609 N.E.2d 172.

Civ R 60(A) authorizes the correction of clerical mistakes only in a judgment entry, and substantive changes in judgments, orders, and decrees are not within its purview, since such a substantial change may not be made without affording notice to the parties and an opportunity to be heard; therefore, where a trial court makes a sua sponte amendment to a judgment entry dividing marital property, and the amendment represents a substantial change in the division of marital property which prejudices one spouse by leaving her a minority shareholder, the court's action is reversible error. Kuehn v. Kuehn (Clinton 1988) 55 Ohio App.3d 245, 564 N.E.2d 97, motion overruled 41 Ohio St.3d 709, 534 N.E.2d 1212.

12. Valuation

Ex-husband did not suffer economically from dent sustained by his refrigerator during bailment with ex-wife, where refrigerator was purchased for $1,100 and ex-husband was able to resell it for $800. Vandeventer v. Vandeventer (Ohio App. 12 Dist. 1999) 132 Ohio App.3d 762, 726 N.E.2d 534.

Determination by trial court in making division of property in divorce action that parties owed debt to wife's father in amount of $12,000 was supported by testimony of wife that loans had been made in approximately that amount, and by testimony of wife's father that, while there was no documentation of accumulated debt, he expected repayment. Bowen v. Bowen (Ohio App. 9 Dist. 1999) 132 Ohio App.3d 616, 725 N.E.2d 1165.

Husband, by privately agreeing with his wife to a particular division of household goods in their divorce proceeding, did not waive any right to demand that the trial court assess the value of the goods, at least where the private agreement contained no mention of such a waiver. Szerlip v. Szerlip (Ohio App. 5 Dist. 1998) 129 Ohio App.3d 506, 718 N.E.2d 473.

Wife's noncompliance with an agreement she had entered with her husband to divide their household goods in a particular way in their divorce proceeding precluded her from arguing in equity that the husband's assent to the agreement should estop him from appealing the trial court's error in not assessing the value of the goods. Szerlip v. Szerlip (Ohio App. 5 Dist. 1998) 129 Ohio App.3d 506, 718 N.E.2d 473.

Trial court abused its discretion by awarding jewelry to wife as part of division of marital property following divorce without first setting a value on that jewelry. Badovick v. Badovick (Ohio App. 8 Dist. 1998) 128 Ohio App.3d 18, 713 N.E.2d 1066.

Fact that final settlement agreement valuation of certain marital assets was identical to valuation appearing in husband's pretrial statement, and that property division was favorable to husband, without more, was not evidence of coercion and undue influence of wife sufficient to require that agreement be set aside on wife's motion. Dutton v. Dutton (Ohio App. 7 Dist. 1998) 127 Ohio App.3d 348, 713 N.E.2d 14.

When determining value of marital asset, domestic relations court is not required to use particular valuation method. Zeefe v. Zeefe (Ohio App. 8 Dist. 1998) 125 Ohio App.3d 600, 709 N.E.2d 208.

Testimony of husband's expert as to valuation of husband's auto parts business formed adequate basis for valuation adopted by court in its equitable division of marital property in divorce action, and could reasonably have been found more accurate and more reasonable than testimony of wife's expert; husband's expert had substantial experience in evaluating over 800 businesses in his career and, unlike wife's expert, personally viewed all three store locations. Zeefe v. Zeefe (Ohio App. 8 Dist. 1998) 125 Ohio App.3d 600, 709 N.E.2d 208.

Trial court was not required to consider value of missing marital property in making equitable distribution, where court left open for future distribution missing property that might later be found and postjudgment pleadings reflected that husband had filed a police report on the missing property. Fergus v. Fergus (Ohio App. 7 Dist. 1997) 117 Ohio App.3d 432, 690 N.E.2d 949.

Trial court has discretion to value property as of date other than actual date of divorce. Neel v. Neel (Cuyahoga 1996) 113 Ohio App.3d 24, 680 N.E.2d 207, dismissed, appeal not allowed 77 Ohio St.3d 1514, 674 N.E.2d 369.

Trial court has broad discretion to determine value of marital property. Donovan v. Donovan (Clermont 1996) 110 Ohio App.3d 615, 674 N.E.2d 1252.

Trial court acted within its discretion in accepting husband's valuation of lot given to parties by wife's parents, rather than accepting wife's valuation; wife and her father testified that they intentionally understated value of lot to avoid taxes and that they understated value so that husband and wife would have more equity with which to obtain loan. Donovan v. Donovan (Clermont 1996) 110 Ohio App.3d 615, 674 N.E.2d 1252.

Use of final divorce hearing date for valuation of marital assets, rather than de facto date of end of marriage, was not unreasonable, arbitrary, or unconscionable, where no special situation was present. Schneider v. Schneider (Geauga 1996) 110 Ohio App.3d 487, 674 N.E.2d 769, appeal not allowed 77 Ohio St.3d 1416, 670 N.E.2d 1004.

Decision to use final divorce hearing date for valuation of marital assets, rather than alternative date, is discretionary and will not be reversed on appeal absent abuse of discretion. Schneider v. Schneider (Geauga 1996) 110 Ohio App.3d 487, 674 N.E.2d 769, appeal not allowed 77 Ohio St.3d 1416, 670 N.E.2d 1004.

Trial court enjoys broad discretion in determining value of marital asset, but this discretion is not limitless; task of appellate court in reviewing valuation of asset is not to require adoption of any particular method of valuation, but to determine whether, based on all relevant facts and circumstances, court abused its discretion in arriving at value. James v. James (Greene 1995) 101 Ohio App.3d 668, 656 N.E.2d 399.

Valuation of husband's business upon divorce was improper, where court failed to take into account buy-sell provision which, rather than permitting sale on open market, required either co-owner to first offer shares to other co-owner, and court did not consider low level of compensation which business provided to co-owners. James v. James (Greene 1995) 101 Ohio App.3d 668, 656 N.E.2d 399.

Divorce referee's valuation of bank account maintained in connection with installment contract sale, in which money was deposited by purchasers and withdrawn by husband to make mortgage payments on subject property, was proper where value was based on amount in account as of hearing date and as presented by husband in testimony and pretrial statement, notwithstanding husband's claim that account should be valued at minimum amount necessary to keep account open. James v. James (Greene 1995) 101 Ohio App.3d 668, 656 N.E.2d 399.

Trial court's valuation of parties' automobiles was supported by evidence, though automobiles were valued higher than value asserted by husband at trial, where first automobile was valued at amount set forth in husband's pretrial statement and second automobile was valued at amount between that set forth in pretrial statement and amount which husband testified to at trial. James v. James (Greene 1995) 101 Ohio App.3d 668, 656 N.E.2d 399.

Trial court was not required to consider estimated taxes which husband would incur by selling property, in valuing rental property awarded to husband upon divorce, as tax liability was speculative where property was subject to option contract and husband failed to show that option was likely to be exercised. James v. James (Greene 1995) 101 Ohio App.3d 668, 656 N.E.2d 399.

In dividing vested retirement benefits upon divorce, court must determine present value of benefits if they are to be divided immediately through liquidation of fund, offset against other marital property, or periodic payments from employed spouse, but court need not determine present value of benefits which will not be distributed until benefits are paid to employed spouse; under such circumstances, projected value, rather than present value, is critical. Sprankle v. Sprankle (Medina 1993) 87 Ohio App.3d 129, 621 N.E.2d 1310.

Trial court could reject testimony of wife's expert witness as to projected annual amount of husband's benefit from state teachers retirement system (STRS), where expert said that calculations were complicated and that he had done them correctly but did not explain exactly how he arrived at his figure. Sprankle v. Sprankle (Medina 1993) 87 Ohio App.3d 129, 621 N.E.2d 1310.

In divorce of parties to common-law marriage, trial court did not abuse discretion in refusing to admit testimony on value of motor vehicle at time of final hearing where record revealed that parties filed joint pretrial statements setting value of motor vehicle at $10,000. Lyon v. Lyon (Scioto 1993) 86 Ohio App.3d 580, 621 N.E.2d 718.

Disinterested and qualified appraiser appointed to report to the court on the matter of value is a form of "special master" and his or her fees may be taxed to the parties as costs. Focke v. Focke (Montgomery 1992) 83 Ohio App.3d 552, 615 N.E.2d 327, motion overruled 66 Ohio St.3d 1446, 609 N.E.2d 172.

Trial court did not abuse its discretion in adopting corporation's retained earnings value as the value of corporation for purposes of division of marital property, where it was the only basis of valuation offered by the parties, and court was free to choose between the values offered based on different years according to the weight of the evidence. Focke v. Focke (Montgomery 1992) 83 Ohio App.3d 552, 615 N.E.2d 327, motion overruled 66 Ohio St.3d 1446, 609 N.E.2d 172.

Where evidence demonstrates that marital asset has significant value, question of its value should be submitted for valuation to knowledgeable person who is a stranger to the proceedings. Focke v. Focke (Montgomery 1992) 83 Ohio App.3d 552, 615 N.E.2d 327, motion overruled 66 Ohio St.3d 1446, 609 N.E.2d 172.

If parties to a divorce action agree at a preliminary property division hearing to use that day's newspaper as the authority on stock values, a subsequent division of the stock will not be disturbed even if the value drops between the first and final hearings. Wolding v. Wolding (Logan 1992) 82 Ohio App.3d 235, 611 N.E.2d 860.

Selection of the trial date as the date of valuation of marital assets is inequitable where the parties have been separated for an extended period and one of the parties has dissipated marital assets for personal use. Spychalski v. Spychalski (Lucas 1992) 80 Ohio App.3d 10, 608 N.E.2d 802.

A specific valuation of property is necessary to facilitate appellate review in cases where the division of property is contested, but where the vast majority of the property is distributed pursuant to the parties' prior agreement, specific valuation is not as essential; moreover, a court's distribution of property not covered by a stipulation will not be overturned where a party fails to offer any evidence of the property's value at trial so as to prove that the court's distribution was inequitable. Goode v. Goode (Franklin 1991) 70 Ohio App.3d 125, 590 N.E.2d 439.

Where the evidence reveals assets that represent a significant portion of the marital assets, their value should be submitted for valuation to a knowledgeable person who is a stranger to the proceedings; a trial court errs in failing to order expert testimony as to the value of a significant marital asset. Mochko v. Mochko (Cuyahoga 1990) 63 Ohio App.3d 671, 579 N.E.2d 773.

Civ R 70 cannot be used as a substitute for Civ R 60(B) to modify or vacate the terms of a divorce decree which orders that stocks currently held by the parties in their joint or individual names be divided equally using the values as of a certain date and that the parties cooperate in the creation and execution of the QDRO for the equal division and distribution of the stock; a Civ R 70 motion is not a proper vehicle to use where (1) there is no evidence of failure to comply with the order, (2) there is a decrease in the valuation of the stock between the date of the agreement and the date of implementation of the agreement, and (3) one party requests the other to bear the risk of the decrease. Freeman v Freeman, No. 97APF05-706, 1997 WL 781999 (10th Dist Ct App, Franklin, 12-16-97).

An award of attorney fees with an order that the husband pay an $8000 debt to the wife's parents is unreasonable and unfairly duplicative; furthermore, in determining the parties' marital assets in separate credit union and retirement accounts, a trial court errs when it double-counts the funds by adding fluctuating balances from different dates from the same account and uncashed checks withdrawn and later redeposited into that account. Thomas v Thomas, No. 94-CA-18, 1995 WL 137015 (2d Dist Ct App, Greene, 3-31-95).

Trial court must make findings of valuation concerning crops and cattle located on the parties' farm and specifically determine what portions of the different pieces of real property, including the farm and assets, constitute separate property and what portions constitute marital property. Bickel v Bickel, No. CA93-11-031, 1994 WL 562011 (12th Dist Ct App, Clinton, 10-17-94).

A court order for parties to accept a non-consensual sale of real property at a price unreasonably below fair market value is an abuse of discretion which prevents the parties from obtaining a fair price for their property where the court uses a figure of $8000 below the lowest valuation and there is evidence the low valuation was arrived at by inappropriate methods. Mullen v Mullen, No. 65254, 1994 WL 163955 (8th Dist Ct App, Cuyahoga, 4-28-94).

Under Ohio law, former wife was entitled to damages for her ex-husband's conversion of property which was subject of equitable distribution award, consisting of award of $500 which represented value of property which husband had sold and could no longer deliver, together with interest at state judgment rate of ten percent on determined value of property of which wife was deprived for more than two years by husband's unauthorized retention thereof. In re Neumann (Bkrtcy.N.D.Ohio 1995) 182 B.R. 502.

13. Financial misconduct

Distributive award of husband's separate assets or greater award of marital property to wife upon divorce was warranted by reason of husband's dissipation and concealment of marital property; husband systematically siphoned cash from his business, converted money to gold, and allegedly gave it to a friend to be used to purchase real estate in Serbia, and also personally cashed at least $15,992.60 in checks from vendors that were not recorded in corporate business records or tax returns. Haslem v. Haslem (Ohio App. 8 Dist. 1999) 133 Ohio App.3d 257, 727 N.E.2d 928.

In dividing property divorce court could require spouse to pay full amount of post-separation debts of approximately $26,090.17 that he incurred without informing other spouse in order to pay off parties' marital home, his personal automobile, and his credit-card debt and to purchase time-share condominium in Europe. Stafinsky v. Stafinsky (Ohio App. 11 Dist. 1996) 116 Ohio App.3d 781, 689 N.E.2d 112.

Trial court's determination that husband engaged in dissipation of marital assets was not against manifest weight of the evidence, where husband acknowledged at trial that he had not only been taking $800 per month from marital business account to reimburse himself for managing marital rental properties, as he had been authorized to do, but also had been taking an additional $714 per month from that account to reimburse himself for spousal support that was being withheld from social security and pension benefits. Modon v. Modon (Ohio App. 9 Dist. 1996) 115 Ohio App.3d 810, 686 N.E.2d 355, appeal not allowed 78 Ohio St.3d 1442, 676 N.E.2d 1187.

Divorce court correctly ordered husband to pay wife one-half of proceeds from land contract payoff that he received while case was pending, based on finding that husband failed to reliably account for his use of proceeds from contract payoff; husband was unable to produce written or oral evidence of exactly how he had spent the funds, and he admitted at trial that he had placed proceeds into marital business account which he was found to have dissipated in part. Modon v. Modon (Ohio App. 9 Dist. 1996) 115 Ohio App.3d 810, 686 N.E.2d 355, appeal not allowed 78 Ohio St.3d 1442, 676 N.E.2d 1187.

While trial court has discretion in finding that spouse has engaged in financial misconduct and, in turn, in granting offended spouse distributive award or greater share of marital property, in doing so, trial court needs to indicate basis for its award in sufficient detail to enable reviewing court to determine that award is fair, equitable and in accordance with law. Huener v. Huener (Henry 1996) 110 Ohio App.3d 322, 674 N.E.2d 389.

Finding that husband dissipated entire amount of proceeds from sale of marital stock was not abuse of discretion, notwithstanding husband's claim that some of proceeds were spent on marital debts, where husband failed to provide accounting as to how proceeds were spent. James v. James (Greene 1995) 101 Ohio App.3d 668, 656 N.E.2d 399.

Trial court may compensate spouse with distributive award or greater award of marital property if court finds that the other spouse has engaged in financial misconduct, including dissipation, destruction, concealment, or fraudulent disposition of assets. Babka v. Babka (Summit 1992) 83 Ohio App.3d 428, 615 N.E.2d 247.

Financial misconduct does not occur when one spouse leaves the marital residence and the other spouse as the sole occupant stops making the mortgage payments where both parties are owners of the marital residence and are equally responsible for the payments and taxes; and so a court does not err in assessing each of the parties one half of the tax assessment and deficiency judgments in a foreclosure action. Phillips v Phillips, No. 99 CA 1495, 2000 WL 282306 (2d Dist Ct App, Darke, 3-17-00).

A husband engages in financial misconduct and is required to compensate wife for the loss of her property including furniture and appliances valued in excess of $37,000 which is lost in a fire where the insurance company compensates the parties for the loss of this property but instead of replacing the lost possessions husband spends the insurance proceeds on repairs and improvements to the house and does not share with his wife his belief that the marriage was over until the renovations were made and the proceeds spent; meanwhile wife and her children are forced to (1) leave the temporary housing provided them after the fire, (2) move into a house with no furniture or appliances, and (3) sleep on the floor for six months while husband is able to leave the marriage with a completely furbished house. Kita v Kita, No. 19256, 1999 WL 1068450 (9th Dist Ct App, Summit, 11-24-99).

Under Ohio law, divorce court was empowered to redress husband's alleged misconduct in concealment and misapplication of property during pendency of divorce proceeding, despite husband and wife's agreement not to litigate claims arising after stipulated end of marriage. Shelar v. Shelar (N.D.Ohio 1995) 910 F.Supp. 1307.

Under Ohio law, amount to which one spouse is entitled in equitable division of property can only be ascertained by court upon full hearing of all facts and surroundings concerning parties; court cannot ignore damage that one spouse has done to other's property nor dissipation or concealment of assets. Shelar v. Shelar (N.D.Ohio 1995) 910 F.Supp. 1307.

Under Ohio law, divorce judgment equitably dividing spouses' property may preclude later claims alleging wrongful withholding of property during divorce. Shelar v. Shelar (N.D.Ohio 1995) 910 F.Supp. 1307.

Under Ohio law, divorced wife's intentional infliction of emotional distress claims based on former husband's conduct during pendency of their divorce proceeding were not barred, pursuant to doctrine of issue preclusion, by divorce court's adjudication of issues relating to equitable division of their marital property, including divorced wife's allegations of concealment and dissipation of assets during pendency of marriage, though such allegations were essential to judgment of divorce court, where it could not be determined whether all issues concerning alleged concealment or misapplication of property were litigated and necessarily determined. Shelar v. Shelar (N.D.Ohio 1995) 910 F.Supp. 1307.

14. Distributive award

Distributive award may be made to facilitate, effectuate, or supplement a division of marital property, or in lieu of a division of marital property to achieve equity between the spouses, or to compensate one spouse for the financial misconduct of the other spouse. Marcum v. Marcum (Ohio App. 2 Dist. 1996) 116 Ohio App.3d 606, 688 N.E.2d 1085.

In any order for a distributive award, or for the division or disbursement of property, the court must make written findings of fact that support its determination that the marital property has been equitably divided. Marcum v. Marcum (Ohio App. 2 Dist. 1996) 116 Ohio App.3d 606, 688 N.E.2d 1085.

Based upon available assets of marriage, trial court's distributive award of former husband's separate property, a farm, to former wife, awarding only life estate to former husband and entire remainder interest to former wife, was grossly disproportionate as supplement to property division and was abuse of discretion; trial court awarded former husband assets valued at about $24,735, plus life estate in farm, and former wife received assets valued at about $24,600, plus vested remainder in farm, thereby bringing total accumulated value of all assets awarded to former wife in property distribution to $180,930, and trial court failed to make written findings of fact to support distributive award. Swartz v. Swartz (Warren 1996) 110 Ohio App.3d 218, 673 N.E.2d 972.

Court may order distributive award to one spouse from other spouse's separate property if it is equitable to do so. Swartz v. Swartz (Warren 1996) 110 Ohio App.3d 218, 673 N.E.2d 972.

In divorce proceeding, trial court has broad discretion to determine whether distributive award of party's separate property is equitable and appropriate. Swartz v. Swartz (Warren 1996) 110 Ohio App.3d 218, 673 N.E.2d 972.

Distributive award of former husband's separate property, valued at about $156,330, to former wife, in order to provide wife with some form of spousal support, was not authorized by statute. Swartz v. Swartz (Warren 1996) 110 Ohio App.3d 218, 673 N.E.2d 972.

Failure to credit motor vehicle debt to husband's account after wife traded in motor vehicle toward purchase of new vehicle did not make distribution of debt in divorce proceedings so inequitable as to constitute abuse of discretion. Shaffer v. Shaffer (Crawford 1996) 109 Ohio App.3d 205, 671 N.E.2d 1317.

Division of marital property which awarded wife 55% of assets and husband 45% of assets was not abuse of discretion, in light of husband's pursuit of foreign divorce and obstruction of proceedings. Soley v. Soley (Lucas 1995) 101 Ohio App.3d 540, 655 N.E.2d 1381, dismissed, appeal not allowed 73 Ohio St.3d 1410, 651 N.E.2d 1308, certiorari denied 116 S.Ct. 945, 133 L.Ed.2d 870.

Divorce court did not abuse its discretion in awarding wife portion of husband's law firm's cash account as part of its division of marital property. Frost v. Frost (Franklin 1992) 84 Ohio App.3d 699, 618 N.E.2d 198, motion overruled 66 Ohio St.3d 1489, 612 N.E.2d 1245.

Distribution to wife of husband's share of proceeds from sale of marital home was not abuse of discretion where majority of other marital assets consisted of life insurance policies and retirement accounts, and court ordered distribution of husband's share of marital home's equity to avoid disturbing those assets; court may make distributive award to facilitate equal division of property. Babka v. Babka (Summit 1992) 83 Ohio App.3d 428, 615 N.E.2d 247.

Provision for the award of attorney fees is present only in RC 3105.18 and not RC 3105.171, therefore, trial court improperly categorized award of attorney fees as part of the property award instead of as spousal support. Perorazio v Perorazio, No. 96 CO 60, 1999 WL 159218 (7th Dist Ct App, Columbiana, 3-17-99).

Finding that husband dissipated marital assets is not an abuse of discretion where his accounting of expenditures is not complete, accurate, or sufficiently credible to justify his contention that assets from a 401(k) savings plan were spent on marital debts. King v King, No. 95CA44, 1997 WL 106898 (4th Dist Ct App, Washington, 3-4-97).

Distribution of a marital business to the wife in the parties' property division is unreasonable where the wife claims (1) the valuation of the small business is nonexistent without the husband's participation because any goodwill of the business was dependent on him, (2) she lacks the expertise to operate the business, (3) the referee assigns a value that is no longer valid because the husband allowed the value of the business to diminish during the divorce proceeding. Webb v Webb, No. 9-96-6, 1996 WL 355059 (3d Dist Ct App, Marion, 6-28-96).

In a divorce proceeding where the parties were married for forty-three years, the fact that the wife had a terminal illness did not render the court's decision to award her any of the assets that the parties had obtained during their long marriage an abuse of discretion. Blynn v Blynn, No. 2422-M, 1995 WL 688810 (9th Dist Ct App, Medina, 11-22-95).

Divorce court's equitable distribution order, which required husband to divide certain assets with his ex-wife, imposed bailment relationship on husband, who had to hold property in question in trust for his former wife. In re Neumann (Bkrtcy.N.D.Ohio 1995) 182 B.R. 502.

15. Antenuptial agreement effect

Trial court could determine that antenuptial agreement executed day before small informal wedding was enforceable against wife, even though the contract never specifically mentioned divorce, and even though attorney who drafted agreement was from same firm as attorney that represented wife in her prior divorce, where agreement referred to "support" and "division of property," wife was given opportunity to consult with independent counsel but refused, and there was evidence that wife read and understood agreement before signing it. Fletcher v. Fletcher (Ohio 1994) 68 Ohio St.3d 464, 628 N.E.2d 1343.

"Circumstances" that must be disclosed in connection with antenuptial agreement refers not to legal rights, but to assets. Fletcher v. Fletcher (Ohio 1994) 68 Ohio St.3d 464, 628 N.E.2d 1343.

Supreme Court must affirm trial court's determination that prenuptial agreement is valid if there is some evidence in record to establish that agreement was entered into freely without fraud, duress, coercion, or overreaching; there was full disclosure, or full knowledge and understanding of nature, value and extent of prospective spouse's property; and terms do not promote or encourage divorce or profiteering by divorce. Fletcher v. Fletcher (Ohio 1994) 68 Ohio St.3d 464, 628 N.E.2d 1343.

When antenuptial agreement provides disproportionately less than party challenging it would have received under equitable distribution, burden is on party claiming validity of contract to show that other party entered into it with benefit of full knowledge or disclosure of proponent's assets; however, burden of proving fraud, duress, coercion or overreaching remains with party challenging agreement. Fletcher v. Fletcher (Ohio 1994) 68 Ohio St.3d 464, 628 N.E.2d 1343.

Evidence in divorce proceeding was sufficient to establish that parties' antenuptial agreement had been rescinded; parties failed to produce agreement at trial, wife testified that husband had instructed his attorney to destroy agreement so that wife would sign loans to pay off debts of husband's corporation, and parties' estate planner testified that they did not mention existence of antenuptial agreement when he did estate planning for them. Simoni v. Simoni (Cuyahoga 1995) 102 Ohio App.3d 628, 657 N.E.2d 800, appeal not allowed 73 Ohio St.3d 1453, 654 N.E.2d 989.

Following wife's death after she filed divorce petition, enforcement of antenuptial agreement fell within jurisdiction of probate division, not domestic relations division, as interpretation and enforcement of the agreement was not a "matter." Diemer v. Diemer (Cuyahoga 1994) 99 Ohio App.3d 54, 649 N.E.2d 1285.

Domestic relations division has plenary jurisdiction to determine equitable division of property between the spouses but that jurisdiction is present only during proceedings for divorce or legal separation and, in the absence of such proceedings, court lacks jurisdiction to distribute property between spouses thus to enforce antenuptial agreement. Diemer v. Diemer (Cuyahoga 1994) 99 Ohio App.3d 54, 649 N.E.2d 1285.

Where an antenuptial agreement addresses only the parties' separate property, a $3,000 distributive award covering a spouse's contribution to the other spouse's home improvement and a $1,000 distributive award reimbursing one spouse's payment of the other spouse's premarital tax debt are proper. Adams v. Chambers (Butler 1992) 82 Ohio App.3d 462, 612 N.E.2d 746.

Investment in cattle and accrual of retirement benefits during marriage give rise to marital property, which is subject to distribution when the antenuptial agreement does not forbid distribution of marital property. Adams v. Chambers (Butler 1992) 82 Ohio App.3d 462, 612 N.E.2d 746.

A trial court's judgment crediting one-half the marital debt against the wife's prenuptial award despite the provision in the prenuptial agreement granting her $100,000 upon divorce did not contradict the terms of the prenuptial agreement and was not precluded by it where the prenuptial agreement, although addressing the parties' separate premarital liabilities, does not discuss responsibility for marital debts, the court was unable to determine what portion of the couple's tax liability should be attributed to each party, it was equitable that the parties share the tax liability equally. Mulvey v Mulvey, No. 17707, 1996 WL 724759 (9th Dist Ct App, Summit, 12-4-96).

16. Duration of marriage

Statutory presumption exists that the proper date for termination of marriage, for purposes of division of marital property, is the date of the final divorce hearing. Bowen v. Bowen (Ohio App. 9 Dist. 1999) 132 Ohio App.3d 616, 725 N.E.2d 1165.

While statute permits trial court to select date of separation as a de facto date of termination of marriage, for purposes of equitable division of marital property, in place of statutory presumption that date of final divorce hearing is termination date, such action is clearly not mandated. Bowen v. Bowen (Ohio App. 9 Dist. 1999) 132 Ohio App.3d 616, 725 N.E.2d 1165.

Trial court acted within its discretion by selecting first day of trial in divorce action as date of termination of marriage, for purposes of making equitable division of marital property, even though testimony was presented that parties felt that functioning of marital unit had ceased upon their separation over a year earlier. Bowen v. Bowen (Ohio App. 9 Dist. 1999) 132 Ohio App.3d 616, 725 N.E.2d 1165.

In divorce cases, court will presume that the date of the final hearing is the appropriate termination date of the marriage, for purposes of division of marital property, unless the court in its discretion uses a de facto termination date. Badovick v. Badovick (Ohio App. 8 Dist. 1998) 128 Ohio App.3d 18, 713 N.E.2d 1066.

Divorce court may use de facto date for termination of marriage when such date would be equitable; otherwise, it is presumed that termination date is date of final hearing. Stafinsky v. Stafinsky (Ohio App. 11 Dist. 1996) 116 Ohio App.3d 781, 689 N.E.2d 112.

Date of final divorce hearing could be chosen over separation date as date of termination of marriage. Stafinsky v. Stafinsky (Ohio App. 11 Dist. 1996) 116 Ohio App.3d 781, 689 N.E.2d 112.

Trial court did not abuse its discretion in determining that any separate property that husband previously held in marital residence was transmuted into marital property after 50 years of marriage in which both spouses made significant long-term contributions to marriage and marital residence. Leathem v. Leathem (Hancock 1994) 94 Ohio App.3d 470, 640 N.E.2d 1210, stay denied 70 Ohio St.3d 1433, 638 N.E.2d 583, dismissed, appeal not allowed 70 Ohio St.3d 1454, 639 N.E.2d 793.

Husband did not waive his right to produce evidence on existence of and duration of alleged common-law marriage by failing to make specific objection to referee's finding on motion for order of temporary spousal support that common-law marriage occurred in or about December 1960; such finding was beyond scope of temporary spousal support hearing and requirement of report and recommendation was not applicable to that hearing. Lyon v. Lyon (Scioto 1993) 86 Ohio App.3d 580, 621 N.E.2d 718.

Trial court had discretion to determine that end of marriage was at time of filing of court's decision, six months after date of hearing. deLevie v. deLevie (Franklin 1993) 86 Ohio App.3d 531, 621 N.E.2d 594, dismissed, jurisdictional motion overruled 67 Ohio St.3d 1409, 615 N.E.2d 1043.

In devising equitable division of property in divorce proceeding, fact that property was brought to marriage by one party is not determinative of disposition of property, but must be considered in relation to other relevant factors, including duration of marriage. Jelen v. Jelen (Hamilton 1993) 86 Ohio App.3d 199, 620 N.E.2d 224.

A court does not err in "tacking" parties' two marriages for purposes of property division where a husband and wife are separated for only six months out of thirty-four years of married life. Krisher v. Krisher (Logan 1992) 82 Ohio App.3d 159, 611 N.E.2d 499.

17. Trusts, constructive

Where a divorce judgment entry provides that certain "property shall be placed in ... trust," and a former spouse fails to transfer the property deeds into a trust, such failure does not undermine validity of the trust, so a constructive trust is established, and the former spouse is estopped from claiming interest in the property and a purchaser may reasonably rely upon the agreement, a public record, in the belief that the trustee has authority to sell the property and a trial court order for specific performance of the real estate purchase agreement is proper. Shaheen v. Vassilakis (Cuyahoga 1992) 82 Ohio App.3d 311, 612 N.E.2d 435.

A husband who executes a quit claim deed to his wife has the burden of proving that the deed is not meant to be an outright complete transfer of his interest in the property to his wife, but instead is intended to establish a type of trust. Pettry v. Pettry (Franklin 1991) 81 Ohio App.3d 30, 610 N.E.2d 443.

Transfer of marital property by only one spouse during the pendency of the divorce action into a trust constitutes an attempt to defeat property rights of the other spouse in the marital property, and constitutes economic misconduct. Oatey v Oatey, Nos. 67809+, 1996 WL 200273 (8th Dist Ct App, Cuyahoga, 4-25-96).

Chapter 7 debtor was constructive trustee of portion of his military pension awarded to debtor's former wife pursuant to domestic relations court order; prepetition order could be considered as a judicial determination by a court in a separate proceeding that debtor's property be held in constructive trust for the benefit of another. Matter of McGraw (Bkrtcy.S.D.Ohio 1994) 176 B.R. 149.

18. In general

Form of title to real property is relevant to, but not conclusive of, classification of property as either marital or separate, and property held jointly may therefore ultimately be determined to be separate; effect of statute governing characterization of property on divorce is to negate presumption of gift resulting from joint title, but not to preclude such finding upon appropriate factual context. Barkley v. Barkley (Ohio App. 4 Dist. 1997) 119 Ohio App.3d 155, 694 N.E.2d 989.

Stock acquired after parties separated was not a marital asset. Neel v. Neel (Cuyahoga 1996) 113 Ohio App.3d

24, 680 N.E.2d 207, dismissed, appeal not allowed 77 Ohio St.3d 1514, 674 N.E.2d 369.

Trial court's division of assets and liabilities of parties was not erroneous in divorce proceeding; trial court properly and carefully divided parties' marital assets and, in doing so, considered all factors set forth in governing statute, and trial court's property division was not so arbitrary, unreasonable, or unconscionable as to connote abuse of discretion. McQuinn v. McQuinn (Butler 1996) 110 Ohio App.3d 296, 673 N.E.2d 1384.

Contract does not have to be fair or equitable to be enforceable; contracts, including property settlement agreements, can be unfair or favor one side over the other and are still binding and enforceable, so long as they are not procured by fraud, duress, overreaching or undue influence. Walther v. Walther (Hamilton 1995) 102 Ohio App.3d 378, 657 N.E.2d 332.

Neither change of heart nor poor legal advice is ground to set aside property settlement agreement; party may not unilaterally repudiate binding agreement. Walther v. Walther (Hamilton 1995) 102 Ohio App.3d 378, 657 N.E.2d 332.

Settlement agreements are favored in the law, and where parties enter into such agreement in presence of court, agreement constitutes binding contract. Walther v. Walther (Hamilton 1995) 102 Ohio App.3d 378, 657 N.E.2d 332.

Based on actions during marriage, spouses can transform nature of property from separate to marital. James v. James (Greene 1995) 101 Ohio App.3d 668, 656 N.E.2d 399.

Divorce decree is insufficient and incomplete if it does not dispose of all property of marriage. James v. James (Greene 1995) 101 Ohio App.3d 668, 656 N.E.2d 399.

Following termination of lesbian relationship with defendant, plaintiff was not entitled to legal or equitable division of property accumulated by parties' joint efforts during time they lived together, where there were no written contracts or agreements governing parties' relationship, and defendant never conveyed any intention to reimburse plaintiff for money spent on renovating defendant's property; absent marriage contract or similar agreement, trial court had no authority to divide property. Seward v. Mentrup (Clermont 1993) 87 Ohio App.3d 601, 622 N.E.2d 756.

New statute, which modified prior alimony statute and provided that division of marital property would be equal unless it would be inequitable, would not be applied retroactively to cases which were filed prior to its effective date. Lyon v. Lyon (Scioto 1993) 86 Ohio App.3d 580, 621 N.E.2d 718.

After commencement of action and absent any clear legislative intent otherwise, parties must proceed under substantive law applicable upon date of filing action. Lyon v. Lyon (Scioto 1993) 86 Ohio App.3d 580, 621 N.E.2d 718.

Elihu Root's observation is worth recalling, that "About half the practice of a decent lawyer consists of telling ... clients they are d——— fools and should stop ... [that]the law lets you do it but don't. It's a rotten thing to do." Stivison v Goodyear Tire & Rubber Co, No. 95-CA-13, 1996 WL 230037 (4th Dist Ct App, Hocking, 5-6-96), affirmed by 80 Ohio St.3d 498 (1997).

Under Ohio law, once division of property is fixed by court, both spouses are legally entitled to the share respectively allotted to them. In re McCafferty (C.A.6 (Ohio) 1996) 96 F.3d 192.

District court was not required to abstain from exercising jurisdiction in interpleader action filed to resolve claims to funds subject to order of state domestic relations court, where Internal Revenue Service (IRS) was named as defendant, and domestic relations court did not specifically assert jurisdiction over funds until almost a year after action was removed to federal court. Eastside MRI v. Jaenson (N.D.Ohio 1993) 824 F.Supp. 118.

Bankruptcy law's purpose is to provide honest debtor with fresh start and to insure that debtor's creditors receive equitable dividend from bankruptcy estate. In re Moghrabi (Bkrtcy.N.D.Ohio 1996) 197 B.R. 258.

Chapter 7 debtor's obligation to make annual payments to his former wife under separation agreement was nondischargeable as support where agreement characterized debtor's obligation as alimony, at time of dissolution there was disparity in parties's financial situations, payments were to terminate on death or remarriage of wife, and debtor deducted annual payments for income tax purposes even though payments were secured by life insurance policy and were to continue as charge against debtor's estate. In re Hobbs (Bkrtcy.N.D.Ohio 1996) 197 B.R. 254.

Bankruptcy court's determination of parties' intent at time of dissolution, for purposes of resolving whether debt was nondischargeable as support, does not turn on one party's post hoc explanation as to his state of mind at time of agreement, even if uncontradicted, but rather, critical inquiry is shared intent of parties at time obligation arose. In re Hobbs (Bkrtcy.N.D.Ohio 1996) 197 B.R. 254.

Creditor seeking nondischargeability of debtor's obligation to make payments bears burden of establishing that obligation should be excepted from discharge by preponderance of evidence. In re Hobbs (Bkrtcy.N.D.Ohio 1996) 197 B.R. 254.

19. Bankruptcy

Nondebtor-wife did not possess adequate remedy at law by litigating her property rights in husband's pending Chapter 12 case, so that writ of procedendo should be granted to reactivate divorce case after bankruptcy court lifted automatic stay; issues in pending divorce and Chapter 12 cases were interrelated but distinct, bankruptcy court could not grant divorce or award child custody, child and spousal support, or visitation, bankruptcy court lifted stay so that trial court would resolve divorce matter, including determination of division of marital property, and absent writ of procedendo, divorce action would be subject of potential judicial gridlock. State ex rel. Miley v. Parrott (Ohio 1996) 77 Ohio St.3d 64, 671 N.E.2d 24.

Although filing of bankruptcy petition stays equitable distribution in divorce case of debtor's interest in marital assets, certain aspects of divorce case, such as dissolution of marriage and child custody issues, are not stayed. State ex rel. Miley v. Parrott (Ohio 1996) 77 Ohio St.3d 64, 671 N.E.2d 24.

Trial court was obligated to reactivate divorce case after bankruptcy court lifted automatic stay affecting Chapter 12 debtor-husband; order inactivating divorce case stated that case would stay inactive until judge "is advised in writing of the stay having been lifted," trial court was advised in writing that bankruptcy court had lifted stay for divorce case, trial court would not be subject to contempt for violating stay after bankruptcy court expressly modified and lifted stay, and divorce case would not be better resolved after conclusion of bankruptcy proceedings. State ex rel. Miley v. Parrott (Ohio 1996) 77 Ohio St.3d 64, 671 N.E.2d 24.

Automatic stay may be lifted or modified for cause. State ex rel. Miley v. Parrott (Ohio 1996) 77 Ohio St.3d 64, 671 N.E.2d 24.

Although husband's obligation to pay wife her share of his pension plan directly as part of property settlement in divorce might not qualify as exception to discharge under Bankruptcy Code, wife's separate property interest in pension would neither be part of husband's bankruptcy estate nor be subject to jurisdiction of bankruptcy courts, and, thus, discharge of husband's obligation to pay wife directly would not affect wife's ownership interest in pension itself. Erb v. Erb (Ohio 1996) 75 Ohio St.3d 18, 661 N.E.2d 175, reconsideration denied 75 Ohio St.3d 1452, 663 N.E.2d 333.

Former husband's obligation to former wife, created by award to former wife of one-half interest in his pension and one-half interest in his deferred compensation, did not constitute "debt" for purposes of determining its dischargeability in bankruptcy, where award was made prior to former husband's filing for bankruptcy. Vaughan v. Vaughan (Ohio App. 4 Dist. 1998) 131 Ohio App.3d 364, 722 N.E.2d 578.

Chapter 7 debtor's obligation under divorce decree to hold his former wife harmless from certain debts was not support or maintenance, for purposes of dischargeability determination, where it was not designated as such in the divorce decree, even though former wife's financial situation would be materially adversely affected if she were forced to pay the debt. In re Findley (Bkrtcy.N.D.Ohio 2000) 245 B.R. 526.

Chapter 7 debtor's obligation under divorce decree to hold his former wife harmless from certain debts was nondischargeable where debtor's pension could have been used to pay the debt, debtor had possible equity in his home, liquidation of debtor's interests in pension and home would not significantly impair his standard of living, and debtor filed bankruptcy petition only three months after agreeing to hold former wife harmless from the debts. In re Findley (Bkrtcy.N.D.Ohio 2000) 245 B.R. 526.

Chapter 7 debtor was not entitled to discharge his obligation to former spouse to pay her $500 per month as part of property settlement in divorce action, on theory that benefit of discharge to debtor outweighed any detriment to former spouse, where debtor was presently earning roughly $30,000 per year and had ability to pay at least $100 per month pending projected increase in his income, while former spouse was earning only $13,000 per year and, not having worked during parties' marriage, did not appear to be able to significantly increase her income; however, based on his present inability to make full payments of $500 per month, debtor would be required to pay only $100 per month pending projected increase in his income. In re Miley (Bkrtcy.N.D.Ohio 1998) 228 B.R. 651.

In assessing, for debt dischargeability purposes, debtor's ability to pay divorce-related debt not in nature of support, bankruptcy court would consider only debtor's income, expenses and share of joint expenses, and would not consider income or expenses of debtor's new spouse, where new spouse was providing post-majority support to children of prior marriage; while it would be inequitable not to allow debtor's new spouse to provide such support to her own children, it would likewise be inequitable to allow new spouse's nonlegal obligations to her children to interfere with debtor's legal obligations to his former wife and his children's household. In re Melton (Bkrtcy.N.D.Ohio 1998) 228 B.R. 641, reconsideration denied 238 B.R. 686.

Debtor may be granted partial discharge of divorce-related debt not in nature of support, where debtor has ability to pay debt only in part. In re Melton (Bkrtcy.N.D.Ohio 1998) 228 B.R. 641, reconsideration denied 238 B.R. 686.

Debtor had ability to make payments of $200.00 per month for period of five years on his and his ex-wife's credit card debt, and his obligation, pursuant to property settlement provision of divorce decree, to be responsible for this joint debt would be declared nondischargeable to this extent, where debtor had excess monthly income over expenses in amount of approximately $200.00, and his income and expenses appeared to be stable. In re Melton (Bkrtcy.N.D.Ohio 1998) 228 B.R. 641, reconsideration denied 238 B.R. 686.

Chapter 7 debtor's former husband lacked standing to file nondischargeability complaint as to debt owed to him for attorney fees he incurred in divorce proceeding, where husband had failed to schedule, in his Chapter 7 case, debt he owed to attorney and debt owed to him by former wife; unscheduled, unadministered asset became property of husband's bankruptcy estate, and could be pursued only by trustee of husband's estate. In re Cundiff (6th Cir.BAP (Ohio) 1998) 227 B.R. 476.

Chapter 7 debtor's obligation to pay one-half of promissory note executed in favor of his former wife's mother for down payment on parties' marital residence was not excepted from discharge; debtor did not incur any additional obligation to former wife to pay her portion of joint obligation under the note to her mother, nor did former wife acquire any right to payment or enforcement of obligation under divorce decree, and so obligation at issue was to a third party, not to debtor's former wife. In re Bartholomew (Bkrtcy.S.D.Ohio 1998) 226 B.R. 849.

Debtor's financial condition at time of trial should be the starting point in assessing, for dischargeability purposes, debtor's ability to pay divorce-related obligation not in nature of support. In re Cooke (Bkrtcy.N.D.Ohio 1997) 213 B.R. 830.

Upon determining that debtor does not have ability to pay divorce-related obligation not in nature of support, bankruptcy court need proceed no further and should allow this debt to be discharged in bankruptcy; it is only when debtor has ability to pay obligation that court must consider whether benefit to debtor of discharging debt outweighs detriment to creditor. In re Cooke (Bkrtcy.N.D.Ohio 1997) 213 B.R. 830.

Absent "hold harmless" clause in Chapter 7 debtor's divorce decree or separation agreement, joint debt to third party, which was neither owed to debtor's former spouse nor listed as support obligation, was not excepted from discharge as support obligation. In re Gibson (Bkrtcy.N.D.Ohio 1997) 210 B.R. 113, affirmed in part, reversed in part 219 B.R. 195.

Under Ohio law, proceeds of lottery that was won by Chapter 7 debtor's wife during their marriage, and prior to their separation or to commencement of dissolution action, constituted "marital property," in which debtor had interest sufficient to support fraudulent conveyance claim by bankruptcy trustee, in exercise of his strong-arm powers, when debtor waived any claim to future lottery proceeds as part of marital separation agreement. In re Fordu (6th Cir.BAP (Ohio) 1997) 209 B.R. 854.

Adversary proceeding brought by Chapter 7 trustee to set aside certain transfers made by debtor in connection with dissolution of his marriage would be remanded to bankruptcy court for further findings on trustee's third and fourth causes of action, where record on appeal did not afford Bankruptcy Appellate Panel a clear understanding of basis for bankruptcy court's decision dismissing those causes of action. In re Fordu (6th Cir.BAP (Ohio) 1997) 209 B.R. 854.

In his capacity as representative of creditors seeking to set aside alleged fraudulent conveyance resulting when debtor waived certain claims as part of marital separation agreement, Chapter 7 trustee did not stand in privity with debtor and was not collaterally estopped from arguing that debtor did not receive reasonably equivalent value for waiving these claims simply because state court had found, in dissolution proceeding, that distribution of property effected by parties' agreement was fair, just and equitable. In re Fordu (6th Cir.BAP (Ohio) 1997) 209 B.R. 854.

Chapter 7 trustee was not collaterally estopped from arguing, for purposes of his fraudulent conveyance claim, that debtor did not receive reasonably equivalent value for waiving his claims in marital separation agreement to future lottery proceeds payable to his wife, simply because dissolution court had found that distribution of property effected by parties' agreement was fair, just and equitable; in dissolution as opposed to divorce proceeding, state court lacked any authority under Ohio law to unilaterally change provisions of parties' agreement. In re Fordu (6th Cir.BAP (Ohio) 1997) 209 B.R. 854.

Discharging divorce judgment debt for valuable reptiles taken by Chapter 7 debtor would benefit debtor more than it would harm debtor's former husband, where debtor was unemployed and had two minor children, debtor's current husband did not have significant income or assets that would aid debtor in repaying judgment, and former husband had no dependents and earned steady income from his employment as charter captain and from his operation of produce stand. In re Wynn (Bkrtcy.N.D.Ohio 1997) 205 B.R. 97.

State divorce court judgment compensating Chapter 7 debtor's husband for debtor's removal of valuable reptiles from marital home was not in the nature of alimony or support; language of judgment did not indicate that state court intended to impose support obligation, debtor had less income that husband and had duty to support two minor children, judgment was not designed to furnish husband with necessities of life, and judgment was in lump sum. In re Wynn (Bkrtcy.N.D.Ohio 1997) 205 B.R. 97.

Basic principle that, even when brought under guise of federal question action, suit whose substance is domestic relations generally will not be entertained in federal court cannot be applied with bright line certainty when bankruptcy law is involved; however, bankruptcy court authority should not be exercised when it its clear that bankruptcy action is merely continuation of previously litigated dispute between divorced spouses. In re Griffith (Bkrtcy.N.D.Ohio 1996) 203 B.R. 422.

Bankruptcy court should not put itself in position where its purpose is to second guess previous decision of domestic relations court. In re Griffith (Bkrtcy.N.D.Ohio 1996) 203 B.R. 422.

Debtor who seeks reexamination of issue previously considered by state domestic relations court is acting with improper motivation, and such action violates spirit of Bankruptcy Code. In re Griffith (Bkrtcy.N.D.Ohio 1996) 203 B.R. 422.

Chapter 13 debtor filed petition in bad faith, warranting its dismissal, where debtor proposed plan that provided very low monthly payments with vague pledge that all claims would eventually be paid and required creditors to wait up to 54 months to receive payment, debtor did not accurately state debts in plan, and debtor filed petition to avoid sale of farm pursuant to state domestic relations decision. In re Griffith (Bkrtcy.N.D.Ohio 1996) 203 B.R. 422.

Although individual retirement account (IRA) was marital asset subject to division in any divorce action involving debtor, Ohio statutes governing equitable distribution of property in divorce did not apply to determination of whether IRA was property of debtor's bankruptcy estate. In re Hoppes (Bkrtcy.N.D.Ohio 1996) 202 B.R. 595.

Chapter 7 debtor who sought to discharge nonsupport divorce debts to former wife, who objected to discharge, had burden of establishing either inability to pay or that discharge would result in benefit to debtor that would outweigh detriment to former wife. In re Henderson (Bkrtcy.N.D.Ohio 1996) 200 B.R. 322.

Bankruptcy court should review debtor's financial condition at time of trial in making determination under discharge exception for nonsupport divorce debts. In re Henderson (Bkrtcy.N.D.Ohio 1996) 200 B.R. 322.

Chapter 7 debtor's obligation to provide for postdivorce decree repairs, maintenance, upkeep, mortgage payments, taxes, and insurance on former marital residence represented nondischargeable property settlement under discharge exception for nonsupport divorce debts, even though debtor's former wife had paid portion of debtor's obligation to repay mortgages; debtor had ability to pay obligation with future income that was not necessary to be expended for maintenance or support of debtor and his dependent, and discharging debtor's obligation to make mortgage payments would not result in benefit to debtor that outweighed detrimental consequences to debtor's former wife. In re Henderson (Bkrtcy.N.D.Ohio 1996) 200 B.R. 322.

Chapter 7 debtor's debt to her former husband's parents for loan they had provided as down payment on marital home was not dischargeable under discharge exception for divorce debts that are property settlements; discharge exception applied only to debts owed to spouse or former spouse, not third parties. In re Finaly (Bkrtcy.S.D.Ohio 1995) 190 B.R. 312.

Home mortgage debt, for which both Chapter 7 debtor and her former husband were jointly indebted, was not dischargeable under exception to discharge for divorce debts that are property settlements, at least to the extent that debtor owed the debt to the mortgagee rather than to her former spouse, even though the mortgage obligation was addressed in marital termination agreement. In re Finaly (Bkrtcy.S.D.Ohio 1995) 190 B.R. 312.

Parents of Chapter 7 debtor's former husband did not have standing to assert claim that debt owed to them for providing down payment on debtor's marital home was nondischargeable; discharge exception for divorce debts stemming from property settlements applied only to debts owed to debtor's spouse or former spouse, not former spouse's parents. In re Finaly (Bkrtcy.S.D.Ohio 1995) 190 B.R. 312.

Joint marital debts that Chapter 7 debtor assumed under divorce judgment entry came within discharge exception for support, where former wife's retention of house was necessary as support for minor children, nonpayment of debts could result in attachment of house by creditors, former wife lacked sufficient income to enable her to pay marital debts, and hold harmless provision of entry stated that bankruptcy filing should not be undertaken if it would affect former wife's right of ownership in house. In re Chapman (Bkrtcy.N.D.Ohio 1995) 187 B.R. 573.

Merely because divorce judgment entry stated that Chapter 7 debtor's assumption of certain debt shall be as and for spousal support, and provision wherein debtor assumed other marital debts contained no such language, did not show that it was indisputable that parties intended to create property settlement with regard to other marital debts, and that discharge exception for support was inapplicable to those other debts. In re Chapman (Bkrtcy.N.D.Ohio 1995) 187 B.R. 573.

For purposes of exception to discharge for debts incurred in course of divorce, debtor's former spouse, as creditor, must merely establish that relevant debt is incurred by debtor in course of divorce or separation or in connection with separation agreement, divorce decree or other court order; upon such showing, burden of proof will necessarily shift to debtor who must either prove inability to pay debt or that discharge would result in benefit to debtor that outweighs detrimental consequences to debtor's spouse or children. In re Carroll (Bkrtcy.S.D.Ohio 1995) 187 B.R. 197.

Exception to discharge for obligations incurred by debtor in course of divorce concerns relative positions of parties as of date of filing of bankruptcy petition, not as of date of divorce. In re Carroll (Bkrtcy.S.D.Ohio 1995) 187 B.R. 197.

Balancing test used for discharge exemption for debts incurred in course of divorce, but not in nature of support, favored discharge of joint debts and debts otherwise assumed by Chapter 7 debtor under divorce decree, when neither debtor or his ex-wife could pay debts and debtor would have to expend funds reasonably necessary for his maintenance and support in order to pay them; debtor was unemployed or underemployed since divorce, debt could not be collected from either party, and, although debtor omitted certain assets from schedules and made prepetition expenditures on things other than debt payment, any recovery on those amounts would inure to estate, not debtor, and evidence of fraud or bad faith was lacking. In re Woodworth (Bkrtcy.N.D.Ohio 1995) 187 B.R. 174.

Chapter 7 debtor's ex-wife, as creditor, bore burden of proof on her adversary complaint seeking to determine dischargeability of debts incurred in course of divorce, but not in nature of spousal or child support. In re Woodworth (Bkrtcy.N.D.Ohio 1995) 187 B.R. 174.

When debtor fails to turn over property divided under domestic relations court order, that property may be subject to constructive trust or equitable lien in favor of spouse. Matter of McGraw (Bkrtcy.S.D.Ohio 1994) 176 B.R. 149.

Bankruptcy court has discretion to lift or modify automatic stay to permit debtor's divorce proceeding to continue in state court; such relief would permit state court to exercise its domestic relations authority to determine equitable ownership of marital assets. In re Donnelly (Bkrtcy.S.D.Ohio 1992) 151 B.R. 787.

Bankruptcy court modified automatic stay for purpose of permitting state domestic relations court to apportion marital property between Chapter 7 debtor and his wife in divorce proceeding so that bankruptcy court could then determine whether debtor's individual retirement account (IRA) was subject to claim of exemption brought by wife who may or may not need the IRA for support, depending on what the state domestic relations court would award to the wife. In re Donnelly (Bkrtcy.S.D.Ohio 1992) 151 B.R. 787.

Ex-wife's motion to terminate debtor-husband's purchase option in marital property, on ground that debtor had not made payments required by terms of property settlement agreement, was not "core proceeding" that bankruptcy court could finally determine, since ex-wife's claim did not invoke substantive rights provided under Bankruptcy Code and was not claim which could arise only in context of bankruptcy proceedings. In re Rose (Bkrtcy.N.D.Ohio 1993) 151 B.R. 128.

Ex-wife's motion to terminate debtor-husband's purchase option in marital property, on ground that debtor had not made payments required by terms of property settlement agreement, was not "related proceeding" over which bankruptcy court could exercise its "related to" jurisdiction. In re Rose (Bkrtcy.N.D.Ohio 1993) 151 B.R. 128.

A husband who transfers his interest in a marital residence to his wife on the advice of his attorney, as part of a separation agreement, and files a bankruptcy petition two months later without mentioning the transfer on his bankruptcy statement of financial affairs, thereby fraudulently and knowingly makes a false oath, and one that is material because the creditors and trustee are entitled to know what property has passed through the debtor's hands during the period preceding bankruptcy; for swearing falsely, the debtor is denied discharge of his debts in bankruptcy. In re Bluestone (Bkrtcy.N.D.Ohio 1989) 102 B.R. 103.

Where a husband obligated by a divorce decree to pay a joint debt to a lender is able to discharge his own liability on that debt through bankruptcy proceedings, and where he listed the lender as a creditor in those proceedings but did not so list his wife, prompting the wife to return to domestic relations court where she secured a ruling that the husband's obligation to hold her harmless on the debt survived his bankruptcy, the bankruptcy court will not reopen the case to consider the issue decided by the state court, regardless of whether that decision was correct. In re Brice (Bkrtcy.S.D.Ohio 1987) 79 B.R. 310.

20. Legal malpractice

Client failed to indicate evidence that her attorney could have presented in divorce proceeding to show that she had performed services which increased value of marital residence, as required to maintain malpractice action against attorney for failing to obtain award based on her interest in residence; statement of client's expert, that he understood that evidence could have been presented to establish that client had improved residence, did not demonstrate that expert had personal knowledge of such evidence. Petersen, Ibold & Wantz v. Whiting (Geauga 1996) 109 Ohio App.3d 738, 673 N.E.2d 151, appeal not allowed 76 Ohio St.3d 1491, 670 N.E.2d 240.

Even if client could have established that attorney could have presented evidence in divorce proceeding to show that client performed services which increased value of marital residence, client failed to establish value of such services to establish that she had suffered damages as result of omission of such evidence, as required to maintain malpractice action against attorney. Petersen, Ibold & Wantz v. Whiting (Geauga 1996) 109 Ohio App.3d 738, 673 N.E.2d 151, appeal not allowed 76 Ohio St.3d 1491, 670 N.E.2d 240.

Client failed to establish that attorney's method for computing client's interest in her husband's pension plan, which involved computing ratio of number of years of employment of employed spouse during marriage to total years of his or her employment, was below commonly accepted method of practice at time, as required to maintain malpractice action against attorney for failing to obtain records of husband's payments to plan. Petersen, Ibold & Wantz v. Whiting (Geauga 1996) 109 Ohio App.3d 738, 673 N.E.2d 151, appeal not allowed 76 Ohio St.3d 1491, 670 N.E.2d 240.

Former spouse of Air Force master sergeant failed to prove that any acts or omissions by military counsel representing her in preparing separation and property settlement agreement amounted to legal malpractice, though qualified domestic relations practitioners in Ohio, where both parties resided and agreement was enforced, testified that counsel did not provide competent representation to spouse in negotiating agreement, where no evidence was submitted regarding how counsel was unqualified, incompetent, or less than zealous in his representation. Knisley v. U.S. (S.D.Ohio 1993) 817 F.Supp. 680.

21. Federal issues

Order issued in divorce proceeding that directed government pension fund, exempted from ERISA, to pay wife portion of husband's pension benefits at her election, regardless of whether husband had retired, violated terms of retirement plan, inasmuch as actual retirement was condition precedent to payment of benefits, and thus pension fund lacked authority to pay retirement benefits until husband retired, even though husband had met all conditions necessary to receive immediate payment upon his retirement. Erb v. Erb (Ohio 1996) 75 Ohio St.3d 18, 661 N.E.2d 175, reconsideration denied 75 Ohio St.3d 1452, 663 N.E.2d 333.

Order issued in divorce proceeding that directed government pension fund to pay wife her share of husband's pension benefits at her election, regardless of whether husband had retired, provided for option not available under pension fund's terms, in that husband's retirement was condition precedent for payment of benefits, and thus order could not qualify as qualified domestic relations order (QDRO). Erb v. Erb (Ohio 1996) 75 Ohio St.3d 18, 661 N.E.2d 175, reconsideration denied 75 Ohio St.3d 1452, 663 N.E.2d 333.

Wife was entitled to offset for hypothetical social security benefits she would have accrued if she had participated in social security as against marital portion of her public pension account. Neel v. Neel (Cuyahoga 1996) 113 Ohio App.3d 24, 680 N.E.2d 207, dismissed, appeal not allowed 77 Ohio St.3d 1514, 674 N.E.2d 369.

Spouse's interest in future social security benefits cannot be divided directly as a marital asset but must be evaluated and considered by court in equitably distributing marital assets. Neel v. Neel (Cuyahoga 1996) 113 Ohio App.3d 24, 680 N.E.2d 207, dismissed, appeal not allowed 77 Ohio St.3d 1514, 674 N.E.2d 369.

Under *Cornbleth* formula for dividing spouses' pensions, present value of public pension plan participant's hypothetical social security benefit is computed and deducted from present value of public pension, the present marital portion of which is then derived and included in marital estate for distribution. Neel v. Neel (Cuyahoga 1996) 113 Ohio App.3d 24, 680 N.E.2d 207, dismissed, appeal not allowed 77 Ohio St.3d 1514, 674 N.E.2d 369.

Congress by enacting provision of Uniformed Services Spouses Protection Act, which authorizes court which has entered dissolution decree for marriage involving member of military to divide military retirement pay for pay periods beginning after June 25, 1981, in accordance with law of jurisdiction, did not intend to override state law, but instead intended to overrule decision of United States Supreme Court in *McCarty* by making it clear that state law could provide for division of military retirement pay after June 25, 1981, without offending federal law. Hester v. Hester (Miami 1996) 110 Ohio App.3d 727, 675 N.E.2d 63, appeal not allowed 77 Ohio St.3d 1445, 671 N.E.2d 1284.

Federal law ban on treating "Tier I" benefits under Railroad Retirement Act, which approximated Social Security benefits, as marital property subject to division at divorce also precluded offsetting value of Tier I benefits against other marital assets in making division of property. Tarbet v. Tarbet (Summit 1994) 97 Ohio App.3d 674, 647 N.E.2d 254.

The Former Spouses Protection Act does not grant state courts the power to treat as property divisible upon divorce military retirement pay that has been waived to receive veterans' disability benefits. Kutzke v Kutzke, No. 95-CA-66, 1996 WL 173399 (2d Dist Ct App, Greene, 4-12-96).

An award of the dependency tax exemption to a wife who does not have custody is error where the parents have comparable incomes in the same tax bracket. Wolfangel v Wolfangel, No. 16868, 1995 WL 312697 (9th Dist Ct App, Summit, 5-24-95).

Ohio law governed res judicata effect of Ohio equitable-division decree in divorced wife's removed suit against former husband for intentional infliction of emotional distress. Shelar v. Shelar (N.D.Ohio 1995) 910 F.Supp. 1307.

Action by former spouse of Air Force master sergeant against the United States under Federal Tort Claims Act for failing to provide adequate training, supervision, or equipment to military counsel representing her in negotiating property settlement and separation agreement was precluded by the discretionary function exception to the Act. Knisley v. U.S. (S.D.Ohio 1993) 817 F.Supp. 680.

Action under Federal Tort Claims Act arising from alleged legal malpractice by military counsel in preparing marital separation agreement on behalf of former spouse of Air Force master sergeant was barred by foreign country exception to federal jurisdiction, where all legal services at issue were performed in Belgium. Knisley v. U.S. (S.D.Ohio 1993) 817 F.Supp. 680.

22. Procedural issues

Statute regarding equitable division of marital and separate property applies prospectively only to those divorce cases filed after its effective date, January 1, 1991. Schulte v. Schulte (Ohio 1994) 71 Ohio St.3d 41, 641 N.E.2d 719.

Trial court did not abuse its discretion in applying standard formula and equally dividing value of marital contributions toward marital residence upon divorce, despite wife's contention that either entire value of marital residence should have been considered marital property or her share should have been equitably increased because of husband's financial misconduct, where parties stipulated to values of home and of separate and marital contributions to value thereof. Haslem v. Haslem (Ohio App. 8 Dist. 1999) 133 Ohio App.3d 257, 727 N.E.2d 928.

Wife waived any claimed error concerning magistrate's alleged failure to account for husband's spousal-support arrearage and magistrate's award of two large assets to husband in the property division in divorce case, where wife failed to object to any findings and dispositions of property recommended in magistrate's decision. Hansen v. Hansen (Ohio App. 1 Dist. 1999) 132 Ohio App.3d 795, 726 N.E.2d 557.

Failure of a trial court to determine the value of the marital properties it divides in a divorce proceeding is reversible error. Szerlip v. Szerlip (Ohio App. 5 Dist. 1998) 129 Ohio App.3d 506, 718 N.E.2d 473.

While the trial court retains its ability to enforce its division of marital property, the trial court may not reserve the right to modify the order. Schiavone v. Schiavone (Ohio App. 12 Dist. 1998) 126 Ohio App.3d 780, 711 N.E.2d 694.

Former husband's motion to vacate judgment incorporating qualified domestic relations orders (QDROs) which were void ab initio, due to domestic relations court's lack of continuing jurisdiction to modify division of husband's pension benefits, did not have to comply with requisites which generally govern motions for relief from judgment. Doolin v. Doolin (Ohio App. 6 Dist. 1997) 123 Ohio App.3d 296, 704 N.E.2d 51, reconsideration denied.

Trial court's division of marital property and debt and its award of spousal support constituted arbitrary abuse of discretion where trial court failed to indicate factual basis for its award in its judgment entry, and there was lack of evidence in the record supporting conclusion that trial court considered mandatory statutory factors. Vanderpool v. Vanderpool (Ohio App. 9 Dist. 1997) 118 Ohio App.3d 876, 694 N.E.2d 164.

Trial court did not abuse its discretion in overruling former wife's motion to vacate divorce decree which failed to credit her with portion of former husband's railroad pension, where motion was filed more than eight years after decree was filed, wife offered no explanation for her unreasonable delay, there was no evidence of willful concealment by husband, wife admitted that court was precluded from valuing and dividing the benefits, and wife provided few evidential materials. Loew v. Loew (Trumbull 1996) 114 Ohio App.3d 632, 683 N.E.2d 847.

Wife's motion for relief from judgment on ground that her trial counsel inadvertently erred in calculating value of marital estate, thus preventing parties from achieving their mutually agreed goal of equal division of marital property, demonstrated ground for relief of excusable neglect and inadvertence; there was no evidence that mathematical miscalculation was anything more than inadvertent error. Krysa v. Sieber (Cuyahoga 1996) 113 Ohio App.3d 572, 681 N.E.2d 949, dismissed, appeal not allowed 77 Ohio St.3d 1490, 673 N.E.2d 147.

Testimony that husband's attorney was aware of intention to divide marital assets equally, if believed, was sufficient to show that wife had right to relief from agreed judgment based on her attorney's material mistake in property division calculations. Krysa v. Sieber (Cuyahoga 1996) 113 Ohio App.3d 572, 681 N.E.2d 949, dismissed, appeal not allowed 77 Ohio St.3d 1490, 673 N.E.2d 147.

Divorce decree providing that parties had settled all issues between them and that husband was to retain military pension as his own was res judicata with regard to husband's claim that, while he and wife were still married, wife had forged his name on pension checks and wrongly converted them. Blymiller v. Blymiller (Carroll 1996) 111 Ohio App.3d 644, 676 N.E.2d 1212.

For purposes of rule permitting third party who possesses or claims interest in property from which party in divorce action seeks award of support to join as party, "interest" includes legal ownership. Huener v. Huener (Henry 1996) 110 Ohio App.3d 322, 674 N.E.2d 389.

For purposes of rule permitting third party who possesses or claims interest in property from which party to divorce action seeks award of support to join as party, joinder is within discretion of trial court, and its purpose is to allow individuals to join whose interests need to be protected. Huener v. Huener (Henry 1996) 110 Ohio App.3d 322, 674 N.E.2d 389.

Trial court's finding in divorce proceedings that parcel of property was separate, nonmarital property of husband was not "surprise" sufficient for grant of new trial, though husband did not raise issue of property's status before trial, where there was no stipulation or agreement between parties in record concerning marital status of parcel. Mayer v. Mayer (Allen 1996) 110 Ohio App.3d 233, 673 N.E.2d 981, dismissed, appeal not allowed 77 Ohio St.3d 1413, 670 N.E.2d 1002.

Deed allegedly demonstrating joint ownership of property did not warrant new trial regarding division of property at divorce, where deed was available at time of divorce hearing and could have been submitted then. Mayer v. Mayer (Allen 1996) 110 Ohio App.3d 233, 673 N.E.2d 981, dismissed, appeal not allowed 77 Ohio St.3d 1413, 670 N.E.2d 1002.

Preferred treatment of qualified domestic relations order is that in interest of finality of judgments and disentanglement of parties, jurisdiction to modify order should not ordinarily be reserved. Schrader v. Schrader (Huron 1995) 108 Ohio App.3d 25, 669 N.E.2d 878.

Qualified domestic relations order which provided that court could create, conform, and maintain order was reservation of power so that court might maintain effectiveness of order, but was not express reservation of jurisdiction to modify terms of order, and therefore trial court lacked jurisdiction to modify order. Schrader v. Schrader (Huron 1995) 108 Ohio App.3d 25, 669 N.E.2d 878.

Domestic relations court lacks jurisdiction to revisit division of property in divorce or dissolution unless its final judgment or decree contains express reservation of continuing jurisdiction. Schrader v. Schrader (Huron 1995) 108 Ohio App.3d 25, 669 N.E.2d 878.

On remand, reconsideration of division of marital property was required where it was apparent that, based on figures contained in loan statement, that marital residence down payment amount was $67,800, and that referee mistook $65,200 loan figure contained in statement for amount of down payment; thus referee's final property division overstated husband's equity in marital residence, skewing final division of marital property. Landry v. Landry (Auglaize 1995) 105 Ohio App.3d 289, 663 N.E.2d 1026.

Guideline for establishing what is marital property and what is not marital property is statutory and must be followed by court in its determination. Simoni v. Simoni (Cuyahoga 1995) 102 Ohio App.3d 628, 657 N.E.2d 800, appeal not allowed 73 Ohio St.3d 1453, 654 N.E.2d 989.

Although trial court made no finding that in-court property settlement agreement was fair and equitable, court properly made agreement part of its divorce judgment, where referee found no evidence of fraud, overreaching, undue influence or coercion. Walther v. Walther (Hamilton 1995) 102 Ohio App.3d 378, 657 N.E.2d 332.

Upon party's filing complaint for legal separation in proper venue, trial court has jurisdiction over parties' assets to determine what constitutes marital property and separate property and how property should be divided between parties. Leathem v. Leathem (Hancock 1994) 94 Ohio App.3d 470, 640 N.E.2d 1210, stay denied 70 Ohio St.3d 1433, 638 N.E.2d 583, dismissed, appeal not allowed 70 Ohio St.3d 1454, 639 N.E.2d 793.

A trial court may journalize an in-court settlement agreement in a divorce action without holding an evidentiary hearing on one of the party's subsequent objections. Kelley v. Kelley (Cuyahoga 1991) 76 Ohio App.3d 505, 602 N.E.2d 400.

An order by a trial court pursuant to a divorce decree requiring liquidation and sale of a restaurant owned by a husband, wife and the wife's mother to be completed within sixty days or be auctioned in a sheriff's sale is an abuse of discretion and fails to give the wife a reasonable chance for a fair, timely and voluntary sale. Davis v Davis, No. 14-95-11, 1995 WL 417065 (3d Dist Ct App, Union, 7-14-95).

A former spouse lacks standing to pursue a fraud action in regard to the transfer of marital property until she has a legally protected interest in that property, which does not occur until entry of judgment regarding the transfer; the statute of limitations does not begin to run until she attempts to execute on that judgment and discovers the damage done to her. Schnorf v Society Bank, No. L-94-120, 1995 WL 217533 (6th Dist Ct App, Lucas, 4-14-95).

In a division of marital property, an option agreement for reconveyance of three acres of land which does not include a legal description of the three acres is not void for vagueness where a fence surrounds the land and the parties know exactly which three acres are involved, so that every detail relating to the description of the land is not required and the option agreement is valid. McCarty v McCarty, No. 94 CA 575, 1994 WL 718404 (4th Dist Ct App, Adams, 12-21-94).

Where parties have a divorce action pending in the domestic relations division and in the interim, the wife files an action in the general division asking to be named a partner and to be awarded an ownership interest in her husband's partnership, the domestic relations court, under the doctrine of concurrent jurisdiction, does not have the authority to determine the wife's claims since the claims the wife presented in the general division action are not the same as those raised in the divorce action. Robinson v Robinson, No. L-94-095, 1994 WL 573803 (6th Dist Ct App, Lucas, 10-14-94).

Trial court abuses its discretion when it declares defendant's inheritance to be his separate property without attempting to trace the amount that is identifiably separate where defendant received a $75,000 inheritance in 1967 and put the money in a joint account, used $20,000 as a down payment on a home, and used more money from the inheritance for household expenses. Freytag v Freytag, No. CA93-11-223, 1994 WL 424135 (12th Dist Ct App, Butler, 8-15-94).

Where a dissolution decree provides for a property settlement, a contempt order is void where the court fails to provide the obligor with a proper opportunity to purge that contempt but instead offers the opportunity to make monthly payments; such order is constitutionally and statutorily prohibited in that any future violations of the court's order must each be attacked through a separate charge of contempt and opportunity given the accused to be heard. Miller v Miller, No. 93WD061, 1994 WL 159537 (6th Dist Ct App, Wood, 4-29-94).

23. Commingled assets

Divorce court correctly determined that full amount of personal injury settlement received by parties was marital property, where husband and wife chose to receive settlement proceeds in one check, thereby commingling their separate and marital property, and husband failed to adequately trace what part of settlement proceeds was compensation to him for his permanent injuries, pain and suffering, and medical expenses. Modon v. Modon (Ohio App. 9 Dist. 1996) 115 Ohio App.3d 810, 686 N.E.2d 355, appeal not allowed 78 Ohio St.3d 1442, 676 N.E.2d 1187.

With respect to statute providing that commingling of separate property and marital property does not destroy the identity of separate property so long as the separate property can be traced, burden of tracing separate property is on party claiming its existence. Modon v. Modon (Ohio App. 9 Dist. 1996) 115 Ohio App.3d 810, 686 N.E.2d 355, appeal not allowed 78 Ohio St.3d 1442, 676 N.E.2d 1187.

Awarding $20,000 to the husband as his separate property is error where the husband fails to meet his burden of proving that separate property exists, which includes submitting sufficient evidence on the issue of tracing, when he testifies that there was a $20,000 bank account in existence at that time of the marriage that his parents set up for him and that the balance had gone down during the marriage, leaving only $3,866.13 which he did not say had stayed in the account from the time of the marriage. Guenther v Guenther, No. 2827, 1994 WL 577751 (9th Dist Ct App, Wayne, 10-19-94).

24. Constitutional issues

A trial court commits reversible error when a husband is not provided with opportunity to be heard as to the issues of property division and child custody at his divorce trial under circumstances that (1) he is present in the courtroom without counsel while seated in the back of the room, (2) he waves his arms in objection and the trial judge requests that the defendant either stop waving his arms or leave the courtroom, and (3) the defendant verbally objects to a particular statement, to which the judge responds, "Just be quiet. I'm taking testimony up here at this time," after which trial continues without defendant's participation and proceeds to grant judgment in favor of the plaintiff following her presentation of evidence. Skaggs v Skaggs, No. 9-94-60, 1995 WL 368838 (3d Dist Ct App, Marion, 6-22-95).

25. Jurisdictional issues

An Ohio court may accord full faith and credit solely to the portion of a Florida decree which dissolves a marital relationship and not to the portion which divides the parties' marital assets where the requirements of Florida's long-arm statute for division of property in connection with an action to dissolve a marriage are not satisfied, leaving the Florida court without personal jurisdiction over the Ohio resident spouse. Atkinson v Atkinson, No. 95-CA-8, 1995 WL 723037 (2d Dist Ct App, Miami, 12-6-95).

26. Unmarried couple as partnership business

An unmarried, cohabiting couple is not a "partnership" under RC 1705.06 and thus neither person is entitled to an accounting after the couple breaks up where (1) they had sold a jointly-owned home and used the proceeds including profit to buy a farming business, (2) they had shared business profits as their living expenses and paid bills from a joint account where profits were placed, but (3) they filed separate tax returns and the businesses were listed only on the man's returns. Froelich v Feeney, No. 11-96-4, 1996 WL 368227 (3d Dist Ct App, Paulding, 6-24-96).

27. Annulment property division distinguished

Property rights of litigants in annulment proceeding are only those that attach to persons in individual capacity, and are not same rights usually affiliated with husband and wife in divorce proceeding. Liming v. Liming (Ohio App. 4 Dist. 1996) 117 Ohio App.3d 617, 691 N.E.2d 299.

Magistrate's division of marital property upon grant of annulment, which division was based upon statutory principles applicable only to divorce and legal separation proceedings, was reversible error. Liming v. Liming (Ohio App. 4 Dist. 1996) 117 Ohio App.3d 617, 691 N.E.2d 299.

28. —Student loans, debts outside of bankruptcy

Student loans incurred by one spouse during the marriage should be considered marital debt to be equitably divided pursuant to RC 3105.171 rather than separate property because equity requires the debtor spouse to bear the full responsibility for repaying her student loans where (1) the benefits of the degree are solely the spouse's because the income generated by the degree will be realized only after the divorce, (2) the spouse did not work while attending school so the family was deprived of the $12,000 annual income she previously generated, and (3) no evidence is provided that any loan monies remaining after school expenses were paid were used to support the family. Webb v Webb, No. CA97-09-167, 1998 WL 820838 (12th Dist Ct App, Butler, 11-30-98).

29. —Debt incurred after de facto termination of marriage, debts outside of bankruptcy

Trial court abused its discretion by listing $8,000 loan taken by wife against value of her automobile, which occurred after de facto termination of marriage, as a marital debt, for purposes of division of marital property following divorce, where wife paid $6,000 of loan amount to her attorney and bought furniture with the remaining amount. Badovick v. Badovick (Ohio App. 8 Dist. 1998) 128 Ohio App.3d 18, 713 N.E.2d 1066.

30. Modification of property division

While the general rule is that property division may not be subsequently modified, trial court had jurisdiction and authority to modify property division where such modification was an exercise of the court's ability to punish for contempt. Dombroski v Dombroski, No. 506, 1999 WL 783975 (7th Dist Ct App, Harrison, 9-28-99).

3105.18 Spousal support

(A) As used in this section, "spousal support" means any payment or payments to be made to a spouse or former spouse, or to a third party for the benefit of a spouse or a former spouse, that is both for sustenance and for support of the spouse or former spouse. "Spousal support" does not include any payment made to a spouse or former spouse, or to a third party for the benefit of a spouse or former spouse, that is made as part of a division or distribution of property or a distributive award under section 3105.171 of the Revised Code.

(B) In divorce and legal separation proceedings, upon the request of either party and after the court determines the division or disbursement of property under section 3105.171 of the Revised Code, the court of common pleas may award reasonable spousal support to either party. During the pendency of any divorce, or legal separation proceeding, the court may award reasonable temporary spousal support to either party.

An award of spousal support may be allowed in real or personal property, or both, or by decreeing a sum of money, payable either in gross or by installments, from future income or otherwise, as the court considers equitable.

Any award of spousal support made under this section shall terminate upon the death of either party, unless the order containing the award expressly provides otherwise.

(C)(1) In determining whether spousal support is appropriate and reasonable, and in determining the nature, amount, and terms of payment, and duration of spousal support, which is payable either in gross or in installments, the court shall consider all of the following factors:

(a) The income of the parties, from all sources, including, but not limited to, income derived from property divided, disbursed, or distributed under section 3105.171 of the Revised Code;

(b) The relative earning abilities of the parties;

(c) The ages and the physical, mental, and emotional conditions of the parties;

(d) The retirement benefits of the parties;

(e) The duration of the marriage;

(f) The extent to which it would be inappropriate for a party, because that party will be custodian of a minor child of the marriage, to seek employment outside the home;

(g) The standard of living of the parties established during the marriage;

(h) The relative extent of education of the parties;

(i) The relative assets and liabilities of the parties, including but not limited to any court-ordered payments by the parties;

(j) The contribution of each party to the education, training, or earning ability of the other party, including, but not limited to, any party's contribution to the acquisition of a professional degree of the other party;

(k) The time and expense necessary for the spouse who is seeking spousal support to acquire education, training, or job experience so that the spouse will be qualified to obtain appropriate employment, provided the education, training, or job experience, and employment is, in fact, sought;

(l) The tax consequences, for each party, of an award of spousal support;

(m) The lost income production capacity of either party that resulted from that party's marital responsibilities;

(n) Any other factor that the court expressly finds to be relevant and equitable.

(2) In determining whether spousal support is reasonable and in determining the amount and terms of payment of spousal support, each party shall be considered to have contributed equally to the production of marital income.

(D) In an action brought solely for an order for legal separation under section 3105.17 of the Revised Code, any continuing order for periodic payments of money entered pursuant to this section is subject to further order of the court upon changed circumstances of either party.

(E) If a continuing order for periodic payments of money as alimony is entered in a divorce or dissolution of marriage action that is determined on or after May 2, 1986, and before January 1, 1991, or if a continuing order for periodic payments of money as spousal support is entered in a divorce or dissolution of marriage action that is determined on or after January 1, 1991, the court that enters the decree of divorce or dissolution of marriage does not have jurisdiction to modify the amount or terms of the alimony or spousal support unless the court determines that the circumstances of either party have changed and unless one of the following applies:

(1) In the case of a divorce, the decree or a separation agreement of the parties to the divorce that is incorporated into the decree contains a provision specifically authorizing the court to modify the amount or terms of alimony or spousal support.

(2) In the case of a dissolution of marriage, the separation agreement that is approved by the court and incorporated into the decree contains a provision specifically authorizing the court to modify the amount or terms of alimony or spousal support.

(F) For purposes of divisions (D) and (E) of this section, a change in the circumstances of a party includes, but is not limited to, any increase or involuntary decrease in the party's wages, salary, bonuses, living expenses, or medical expenses.

(G) Each order for alimony made or modified by a court shall include as part of the order a general provision, as described in division (A)(1) of section 3113.21 of the Revised Code, requiring the withholding or deduction of income or assets of the obligor under the order as described in division (D) of section 3113.21 of the Revised Code or another type of appropriate requirement as described in division (D)(3), (D)(4), or (H) of that section, to ensure that withholding or deduction from the income or assets of the obligor is available from the commencement of the support order for collection of the support and of any arrearages that occur; a statement requiring all parties to the order to notify the child support enforcement agency in writing of their current mailing address, current residence address, current residence telephone number, current driver's license number, and of any changes to that information; and a notice that the requirement to notify the agency of all changes to that information continues until further notice from the court.

If any person required to pay alimony under an order made or modified by a court on or after December 1, 1986, and before January 1, 1991, or any person required to pay spousal support under an order made or modified by a court on or after January 1, 1991, is found in contempt of court for failure to make alimony or spousal support payments under the order, the court that makes the finding, in addition to any other penalty or remedy imposed, shall assess all court costs arising out of the contempt proceeding against the person and shall require the person to pay any reasonable attorney's fees of any adverse party, as determined by the court, that arose in relation to the act of contempt.

(H) In divorce or legal separation proceedings, the court may award reasonable attorney's fees to either party at any stage of the proceedings, including, but not limited to, any appeal, any proceeding arising from a motion to modify a prior order or decree, and any proceeding to enforce a prior order or decree, if it determines that the other party has the ability to pay the attorney's fees that the court awards. When the court determines whether to award reasonable attorney's fees to any party pursuant to this division, it shall determine whether either party will be prevented from fully litigating that party's rights and adequately protecting that party's interests if it does not award reasonable attorney's fees.

(1997 H 352, eff. 1-1-98; 1993 H 173, eff. 12-31-93; 1990 S 3, H 514; 1988 H 708; 1987 H 231; 1986 H 509, H 358; 1974 H 233; 1953 H 1; GC 8003-19; Source—GC 8003-17, 11991)

Uncodified Law

1986 H 358, § 3, eff. 5-2-86, reads: The amendments to sections 3105.18, 3105.63, and 3105.65 of the Revised Code made by Section 1 of this act do not affect divorces or dissolutions of marriage that were determined prior to the effective date of this act, and do not affect awards of alimony or, when authorized by statutory or common law of this state, modifications of awards of alimony in such divorces or dissolutions of marriage.

Historical and Statutory Notes

Pre-1953 H 1 Amendments: 124 v S 65

Amendment Note: 1997 H 352 deleted "on or after December 31, 1993," before "shall include", substituted "income" for "wages" twice and "(D)(3), (D)(4)" for "(D)(6), (D)(7)", and inserted "current residence telephone number, current driver's license number,", in the first paragraph in division (G); and made changes to reflect gender neutral language and other nonsubstantive changes.

Amendment Note: 1993 H 173 rewrote the first paragraph of division (G) before the first semi-colon, which previously read:

"(G) Each order for alimony made or modified by a court on or after December 1, 1986, and before January 1, 1991, and each order for spousal support made or modified by a court on or after January 1, 1991, shall be accompanied by one or more orders described in division (D) or (H) of section 3113.21 of the Revised Code, whichever is appropriate under the requirements of that section".

Cross References

Administration of child support orders by child support enforcement agencies, 3113.218

Bureau of child support, programs, 5101.31

Calculation of amount of child support obligation, 3113.215

Child support enforcement agencies, compliance, 2301.35

Contempt action for failure to pay support, 2705.031, 2705.05

Divorce, annulment, and legal separation actions, Civ R 75

Divorce, dissolution of marriage, legal separation, or child support proceeding; order for child support, factors to be considered, 3109.05

Divorce or legal separation action involving custody or care of children, jurisdiction of juvenile court, 2151.23

Effect of end of marriage on trust powers reserved by grantor, 1339.62

Interfering with action to issue or modify support order, 2919.231

Issuance of new child support orders, interest and costs, 3113.219

Lottery winner, oath regarding default of support order, hearing, deduction order, 3770.071

Public employees retirement system, benefits of spouse, effect of divorce, annulment, or marriage dissolution, 145.46

Right to spousal support exempt from execution of judgment, 2329.66
Separation agreements and dissolutions of marriage, continuing jurisdiction of court, modification of spousal support, 3105.65
Small loans; assignment or order of wages for support, 1321.32, 1321.33
Stay pending completion of conciliation proceedings, 3117.08
Support orders, enforcement, 2301.34 et seq.

Ohio Administrative Code References

Department of job and family services, child support program, OAC Ch 5101:1-29
Department of job and family services, collection of past due support by federal tax refund offset, OAC Ch 5101:1-30

Library References

Divorce ⟹231 to 247.
WESTLAW Topic No. 134.
C.J.S. Divorce §§ 369 to 419, 421 to 426, 429, 430, 432 to 434, 437 to 439, 442, 474, 475, 481 to 487.

OJur 3d: 46, Family Law § 321, 366, 375, 378 to 380, 399, 400, 451, 457, 475, 498 to 500, 504, 512, 513, 515 to 517, 519 to 529, 532, 534, 537 to 539, 543, 561, 562, 579, 672, 673, 675, 678 to 681, 686, 710, 737, 738, 740 to 742, 744, 746, 748, 766, 768, 781, 1222, 1300, 1301, 1306, 1308; 48, Family Law § 1754, 1756
Am Jur 2d: 24, Divorce and Separation § 514 et seq., 624 et seq., 746 et seq.
Validity of provision of separation agreement for cessation or diminution of payments for wife's support upon specified event. 4 ALR2d 732
Misconduct of wife to whom divorce is decreed as affecting allowance of alimony, or amount allowed. 9 ALR2d 1026
Change in financial condition or needs of husband or wife as ground for modification of decree for alimony or maintenance. 18 ALR2d 10
What law governs validity, effect, and construction of separation or property settlement agreements. 18 ALR2d 760
Pension of husband as resource which court may consider in determining amount of alimony. 22 ALR2d 1421
Valid foreign divorce granted upon constructive service as precluding action by spouse for alimony, support, or maintenance. 28 ALR2d 1378
Allowance of permanent alimony to wife against whom divorce is granted. 34 ALR2d 313
Death of husband as affecting alimony. 39 ALR2d 1406
Remarriage of wife as affecting husband's obligation under separation agreement to support her or to make other money payments to her. 48 ALR2d 318
Review of discretion as to declaration of lien for security of periodical payments for support or alimony. 59 ALR2d 666, 681
Allowance of alimony in lump sum in action for separate maintenance without divorce. 61 ALR2d 946
Husband's right to alimony, maintenance, suit money, or attorney's fees. 66 ALR2d 880
Review of discretion of court with respect to grant to husband of alimony, maintenance, suit money, or attorneys' fees. 66 ALR2d 888, 895
Construction and effect of clause in divorce decree providing for payment of former wife's future medical expenses. 71 ALR2d 1236
Allocation or apportionment of previous combined award of alimony and child support. 78 ALR2d 1110
Construction and effect of provision in separation agreement that wife is to have portion of "income," "total income," "net income," and the like. 79 ALR2d 609
Adequacy or excessiveness of amount of money awarded as separate maintenance, alimony, or support for wife where no absolute divorce is or has been granted. 1 ALR3d 208
Adequacy or excessiveness of amount of money granted as combined award of alimony and child support. 2 ALR3d 537
Assumption or denial of jurisdiction of action involving matrimonial disputes. 9 ALR3d 545
Right of one spouse, over objection, to voluntarily dismiss claim for divorce, annulment, or similar marital relief. 16 ALR3d 283
Validity and construction of provision for arbitration of disputes as to alimony or support payments, or child visitation or custody matters. 18 ALR3d 1264
Annulment of later marriage as reviving prior husband's obligation under alimony decree or separation agreement. 45 ALR3d 1033
Effect of remarriage of spouses to each other on permanent alimony provisions in final divorce decree. 52 ALR3d 1334
Accountability for good will of professional practice in actions arising from divorce or separation. 52 ALR3d 1344
Provision in divorce decree that one party obtain or maintain life insurance for benefit of other party or child. 59 ALR3d 9
Wife's possession of independent means as affecting her right to alimony pendente lite. 60 ALR3d 728
Power of court to modify decree for alimony or support to spouse which was based on agreement of parties. 61 ALR3d 520
Provision in divorce decree requiring husband to pay certain percentage of future salary increases as additional alimony or child support. 74 ALR3d 493
Evaluation of interest in law firm or medical partnership for purposes of division of property in divorce proceedings. 74 ALR3d 621
Right to allowance of permanent alimony in connection with decree of annulment. 81 ALR3d 281
Statute expressly allowing alimony to wife, but not expressly allowing alimony to husband, as unconstitutional sex discrimination. 85 ALR3d 940
Adulterous wife's right to permanent alimony. 86 ALR3d 97
Fault as consideration in alimony, spousal support, or property division awards pursuant to no-fault divorce. 86 ALR3d 1116
Pension or retirement benefits as subject to award or division by court in settlement of property rights between spouses. 94 ALR3d 176
Propriety in divorce proceedings of awarding rehabilitative alimony. 97 ALR3d 740

Spouse's professional degree or license as marital property for purposes of alimony, support, or property settlement. 4 ALR4th 1294

Laches or acquiescence as defense, so as to bar recovery of arrearages of permanent alimony or child support. 5 ALR4th 1015

Husband's death as affecting periodic payment provision of separation agreement. 5 ALR4th 1153

Validity and enforceability of escalation clause in divorce decree relating to alimony and child support. 19 ALR4th 830

Excessiveness or adequacy of amount of money awarded as permanent alimony following divorce. 28 ALR4th 786

Divorce: excessiveness or adequacy of combined property division and spousal support awards—modern cases. 55 ALR4th 14

Divorce and separation: excessiveness or adequacy of trial court's property award—modern cases. 56 ALR4th 12

Divorce and separation: goodwill in medical or dental practice as property subject to distribution on dissolution of marriage. 76 ALR4th 1025

Valuation of goodwill in accounting practice for purposes of divorce court's property distribution. 77 ALR4th 609

Divorce and separation: goodwill in accounting practice as property subject to distribution on dissolution of marriage. 77 ALR4th 645

Valuation of goodwill in law practice for purposes of divorce court's property distribution. 77 ALR4th 683

Valuation of goodwill in medical or dental practice for purposes of divorce court's property distribution. 78 ALR4th 853

Accrued vacation, holiday time, and sick leave as marital or separate property. 78 ALR4th 1107

Death of obligor spouse as affecting alimony. 79 ALR4th 10

Divorce and separation: goodwill in law practice as property subject to distribution on dissolution of marriage. 79 ALR4th 171

Bankruptcy: wife's claim to alimony or other allowances in divorce or separation suit as passing, or exempt from passing, to trustee in wife's bankruptcy, under § 70(a) of Bankruptcy Act (11 USC § 110(a)). 10 ALR Fed 881

3 Katz & Giannelli, Baldwin's Ohio Practice, *Criminal Law* § 109.12 (1996)

Klein & Darling, Baldwin's Ohio Practice, *Civil Practice* § 60 (1997)

Sowald & Morganstern, Baldwin's Ohio Practice, *Domestic Relations Law* § 1.7, 2.47, 4.24, 4.25, 4.28, 4.35, 4.36, 4.37, 7.17, 8.2, 8.4, 8.5, 8.7, 8.8, 9.5, 9.6, 9.15, 9.20, 9.27, 9.35, 9.37, 9.100, 10.3, 10.15, 10.15.1, 12.1, 12.2, 12.10, 12.11, 12.12, 12.13, 12.16, 12.18, 12.20, 13.1, 13.2, 13.3, 13.5, 13.6, 13.8, 13.9, 13.15, 13.17, 13.18, 13.20, 13.21, 13.23, 13.24, 13.25, 13.26, 13.27, 13.31, 13.35, 13.38, 14.1, 14.2, 14.5, 14.6, 14.10, 14.14, 14.16, 14.17, 14.18, 14.20, 14.21, 14.22, 14.26, 14.27, 14.28, 14.30, 14.34, 15.58, 20.6, 23.15, 24.2, 24.7, 24.16, 25.13, 25.28, 25.36, 25.57, 27.5, 27.21, 27.22, 27.55, 28.1, 28.4, 28.8, 29.1, 29.9, 29.32, 30.1, 30.3, 32.29 (1997)

Law Review and Journal Commentaries

Alimony: Adjudicated Pursuant to Statute or by Judicial Legislation?, Howard S. Lutz. 53 Ohio St B Ass'n Rep 321 (March 3, 1980).

Alimony Payments Under the Internal Revenue Code, David S. Bloomfield. 14 Cap U L Rev 491 (Summer 1985).

Alimony, Till Death Do Us Part, Note. 27 J Fam L 859 (1988-89).

Antenuptial Agreements—New Planning Opportunities, Leon A. Weiss. 56 Clev B J 24 (November 1984).

Ascertaining Self-Employment Income, Elaine M. Stoermer. 48 Dayton B Briefs 17 (October 1998).

Asset Valuation/The Valuation of Stock Options in Divorce and Dissolution Cases, Deborah R. Akers. 2 Domestic Rel J Ohio 69 (September/October 1990).

Attorney Fee Awards in Domestic Relations, Hon. V. Michael Brigner. 46 Dayton B Briefs 13 (January 1997).

Attorney Fee Awards in Domestic Relations Court, Hon. V. Michael Brigner. 46 Dayton B Briefs 13 (February 1997).

Attorney Fee Awards in Domestic Relations Court, Hon. Mike Brigner. 9 Domestic Rel J Ohio 1 (January/February 1997).

Balance Need and Ability to Pay in Spousal Support Orders, Pamela J. MacAdams. 9 Domestic Rel J Ohio 44 (May/June 1997).

Bankruptcy Basics—DISCHARGE ... A Simple Word, Not Easily Found, And is the Meaning Plain?, Thomas R. Noland. (Ed. note: The author explains the effect of discharging a debt in bankruptcy court.) 47 Dayton B Briefs 18 (June 1998).

Bankruptcy Reform Act of 1994—What the Bankruptcy Code Giveth, Domestic Relations Courts (and Congress) Taketh Away, C.R. "Chip" Bowles. 8 Domestic Rel J Ohio 17 (March/April 1996).

Business Owner's Compensation and Valuation, Robert G. Turner, Jr. 11 Domestic Rel J Ohio 24 (March/April 1999).

BWC and Self-Insured Employer Liability for Spousal and Child Support, C. Jeffrey Waite. 11 Domestic Rel J Ohio 17 (March/April 1999).

A Case Study in Divorce Law Reform and Its Aftermath, Robert E. McGraw, Gloria J. Sterin and Joseph M. Davis. 20 J Fam L 443 (1981-82).

Classification Of Personal Injury Awards In Divorce Actions, Note. 27 J Fam L 453 (1989).

Cohabitation Agreements and Related Documents, Hon. Mike Brigner. 9 Domestic Rel J Ohio 97 (November/December 1997).

Cohabitation by an Alimony Recipient Revisited, J. Thomas Oldham. 20 J Fam L 615 (1981-82).

Contingencies on Division of Property are Improper, Pamela J. MacAdams. 3 Domestic Rel J Ohio 63 (May/June 1991).

The Court's Authority to Assign Assets, Ann B. Oldfather. 20 Trial (American Trial Lawyers' Assn) 66 (March 1984).

Current State of Alimony in Ohio, Judith A. Nicely. 1 Domestic Rel J Ohio 3 (July/August 1989).

Deferred Property Division Payments, Stanley Morganstern. 4 Domestic Rel J Ohio 86 (September/October 1992).

Defining the Business Valuation Expert's Assignment—Establish the Game Plan Before Starting to Play, Rand M. Curtiss. 9 Domestic Rel J Ohio 73 (September/October 1997).

Deposing and Examining Business Valuation Experts: How to Beat Us Up on the Stand, Rand M. Curtiss. 9 Domestic Rel J Ohio 21 (March/April 1997).

The Dischargeability Of Divorce Obligations Under The Bankruptcy Code: Five Faulty Premises In The Application Of Section 523(a)(5), James H. Gold. 39 Case W Res L Rev 455 (1988-89).

Domestic Relations Corner—Military Benefits in Divorce: A Practitioner's Guide Part 2, Stephen L. De Vita. 45 Dayton B Briefs 19 (March 1996).

Domestic Relations Corner—Military Benefits in Divorce: A Practitioner's Guide Part 1, Stephen L. De Vita. 45 Dayton B Briefs 10 (February 1996).

Do Professional Degrees and Licenses Earned During Marriage Constitute Marital Property?: An Irrelevant Issue, Note. 48 Ohio St L J 1171 (1987).

Economics of Divorce: Alimony and Property Awards, Note. 43 U Cin L Rev 133 (1974).

The Economics of Divorce: Valuing Professional Practices and Licenses, Paul J. Buser. 18 Lake Legal Views 8 (June 1995).

The Economics of Divorce: Valuing Professional Practices and Licenses, Part I, Paul J. Buser. 18 Lake Legal Views 11 (May 1995).

Economists in Marital Contests, Allan G. King. 20 Trial (American Trial Lawyers' Assn) 46 (March 1984).

The Effect of the Tax Reform Act of 1984 on Divorce Financial Planning, Note. 24 J Fam L 283 (1985-86).

The Effect of Unmarried Cohabitation by a Former Spouse Upon His or Her Right to Continue to Receive Alimony, J. Thomas Oldham. 17 J Fam L 249 (1978-79).

Extinguishing the Right to Collect Temporary Alimony and Support—Merger of Interlocutory Orders with Final Decrees. 52 Law & Fact 9 (November, 1978).

Gross v Gross: Ohio's First Step Toward Allowing Private Ordering of the Marital Relationship, Comment. 47 Ohio St L J 235 (1986).

Guidelines in Alimony and Support for Ohio, Judge John R. Milligan. 52 Ohio St B Ass'n Rep 2009 (12-3-79).

How to Value Goodwill as Marital Asset, Sanford K. Ain, et al. 20 Nat'l L J B7 (March 23, 1998).

In Addition to Safeguarding Inheritances, Prenuptial Contracts can Help Attorneys Protect their Firm Ownership Interests, Burton Young, et al. 20 Nat'l L J B7 (December 15, 1997).

Is Alimony Mandatory When Divorce is at Aggression of the Husband?, Comment. 7 Ohio St L J 83 (December 1940).

Is It Morally Wrong To Depend On the Honesty Of Your Partner Or Spouse? Bankruptcy Dischargeability Of Vicarious Debt, Steven H. Resnicoff. 42 Case W Res L Rev 147 (1992).

Judicial Activism in Domestic Relations Cases, Hon. V. Michael Brigner. (Ed. note: Judge Brigner lists the powers of a judge hearing custody, support, and visitation matters.) 45 Dayton B Briefs 22 (January 1996).

The Lawyer Turns Peacemaker—with mediation emerging as the most popular form of alternate dispute resolution, the quest for common ground could force attorneys to reinterpret everything they do in the future, Richard C. Reuben. 82 A B A J 54 (August 1996).

Litigation Results—Count on a CPA, Keith J. Libman. 67 Clev B J 12 (October 1996).

Marital Partnership And The Case For Permanent Alimony, Sally F. Goldfarb. 27 J Fam L 351 (1989).

Modification of Spousal Support: A Survey of a Confusing Area of the Law, Note. 17 J Fam L 711 (1978-79).

Nobody Gets Married for the First Time Anymore—A Primer on the Tax Implications of Support Payments in Divorce, C. Garrison Lepow. 25 Duq L Rev 43 (Fall 1986).

Once More Into The Breach, Dear Friends: The 1986 Reforms Of The Reformed Bankruptcy Reform Act, Michael J. Herbert. 16 Cap U L Rev 325 (Spring 1987).

Orr v Orr: A Husband's Constitutional Right Not to Pay Alimony, Comment. 41 Ohio St L J 1061 (1980).

Partition Of Real Property Subject To Divorce Decree?, Robert W. Hausser. 56 Title Topics 5 (September 1989).

Pathfinder: Economic Effects of Divorce on Women, Barbara Laughlin. 14 Legal Reference Serv Q 57 (1995).

The Plain Meaning of the Automatic Stay in Bankruptcy: The Void/Voidable Distinction Revisited, Timothy Arnold Barnes. 57 Ohio St L J 291 (1996).

Policyholder May Not Cancel Health Insurance Coverage During Pendency of Action, Pamela J. MacAdams. 3 Domestic Rel J Ohio 151 (November/December 1991).

Professional Degrees and Spousal Rights, Charles F. Crutchfield. 88 Case & Com 14 (November/December 1983).

Proof of Former Wife's Unchastity as a Factor in a Proceeding to Modify an Alimony Award Based Upon Agreement of the Parties, Wolfe v Wolfe, Note. 8 U Tol L Rev 783 (Spring 1977).

Proving The Value Of Goodwill Of A Spouse's Closely-Held Commercial Corporation In A Divorce Proceeding, Note. 25 J Fam L 549 (1986-87).

Qualified Domestic Relations Order: "Family Law" & "Benefit Plan" Lawyers Must Know This Creature of the 1984 Retirement Equity Act, Mac Lee Henney. 59 Ohio St B Ass'n Rep 878 (June 2, 1986).

Qualified Domestic Relations Orders, Philip Zukowski and Mary Eaves. 35 Dayton B Briefs 12 (June/July 1986).

A Radical Theory of Jurisprudence: The "Decisionmaker" as the Source of Law—The Ohio Supreme Court's Adoption of the Spendthrift Trust Doctrine as a Model, Gerald P. Moran. 30 Akron L Rev 393 (Spring 1997).

The Reasonableness of Attorney's Fees to be Awarded in Domestic Proceedings, William K. McCarter and Sean A. McCarter. 19 Lake Legal Views 10 (September 1996).

Rehabilitative Alimony in Ohio, Comment. 16 Ohio N U L Rev 173 (1989).

Retirement Benefits—Not Just Another Asset to be Assigned a Value and Traded, Mary G. Sotera. 1 Domestic Rel J Ohio 1 (July/August 1989).

Security for Spousal Support, Richard L. Innis. 4 Domestic Rel J Ohio 61 (July/August 1992).

Separation Agreements and the Modification of Alimony Awards in Ohio: Wolfe v Wolfe, Comment. 38 Ohio St L J 735 (1977).

Should a Professional Degree be Considered a Marital Asset Upon Divorce?, Dr. Marvin M. Moore. 15 Akron L Rev 543 (Winter 1982).

Spousal And Child Support Payment Provisions In Chapter 13 Plans, Michaela M. White. 16 Cap U L Rev 369 (Spring 1987).

Spousal Support—Guidelines or Methodology?, Bernard I. Agin. 5 Domestic Rel J Ohio 17 (March/April 1993).

Spousal Support: The Other Ohio Lottery, Leslie Herndon Spillane. 24 Ohio N U L Rev 281 (1998).

Tax Consequences of Attorney Fees, Awards, and Payments, Stanley Morganstern. 4 Domestic Rel J Ohio 29 (March/April 1992).

Tax Tips—Alimony Recomputation, Stanley Morganstern. 4 Domestic Rel J Ohio 71 (July/August 1992).

Tax Tips—Disposition of the Marital Home, Stanley Morganstern. 3 Domestic Rel J Ohio 113 (September/October 1991).

Tax Tips—"Spousal Support"—Lesterized Payments, Stanley Morganstern. 4 Domestic Rel J Ohio 43 (May/June 1992).

'Til Graduation Do We Part—The Professional Degree Acquired During Marriage as Marital Property Upon Dissolution: An Evaluation and Recommendation for Ohio, Comment. 56 U Cin L Rev 227 (1987).

Valuation of goodwill in Ohio professional practices, David A. Redle and Ronald J. Kudla. 10 Ohio Law 11 (March/April 1996).

The Valuation of Limited Partnerships in Divorce and Dissolution Matters, Deborah R. Akers. 3 Domestic Rel J Ohio 141 (November/December 1991).

The Way We Were: Reinstatement Of Alimony After Annulment Of Spouse's "Remarriage," Note. 28 J Fam L 289 (1990).

What Divorce Court Giveth, Bankruptcy Court Taketh Away: A Review of the Dischargeability of Marital Support Obligations, Sandra D. Freeburger and Claude Bowles. 24 J Fam L 587 (1985-86).

When Experts Disagree, Bernard I. Agin. 4 Domestic Rel J Ohio 67 (July/August 1992).

Women and Divorce: The Perils of Pension Division, David L. Baumer and J. C. Poindexter. 57 Ohio St L J 203 (1996).

Notes of Decisions and Opinions

---

1. In general

Permanent sustenance alimony is in the nature of support, and the attachment of conditions to its continuance is reasonable considering that the need for support may change, thus altering the payor's obligation; however, such conditions are not acceptable as limitations on the division of marital property. Zimmie v. Zimmie (Ohio 1984) 11 Ohio St.3d 94, 464 N.E.2d 142, 11 O.B.R. 396.

A decree in a divorce action disposing of real property is not subject to collateral attack in an action for partition. Arbogast v. Arbogast (Ohio 1956) 165 Ohio St. 459, 136 N.E.2d 54, 60 O.O. 116.

When imposing spousal support order in first instance, domestic relations court's order must show that it considered all statutory factors. Kucmanic v. Kucmanic (Ohio App. 8 Dist. 1997) 119 Ohio App.3d 609, 695 N.E.2d 1205.

Award of spousal support could only be made retroactive to date on which complaint was filed in divorce action. Munroe v. Munroe (Ohio App. 8 Dist. 1997) 119 Ohio App.3d 530, 695 N.E.2d 1155.

Right to interest on unpaid installments of alimony accrues on date each installment matures or becomes due, and runs until paid. Munroe v. Munroe (Ohio App. 8 Dist. 1997) 119 Ohio App.3d 530, 695 N.E.2d 1155.

Trial court has broad discretion concerning award of spousal support. Tremaine v. Tremaine (Montgomery 1996) 111 Ohio App.3d 703, 676 N.E.2d 1249, appeal not allowed 77 Ohio St.3d 1480, 673 N.E.2d 142.

Determination that former husband's income had increased, rather than decreased, and that his testimony to the contrary was not credible was supported by evidence that former husband had concealed income and diverted income to his son. Tremaine v. Tremaine (Montgomery 1996) 111 Ohio App.3d 703, 676 N.E.2d 1249, appeal not allowed 77 Ohio St.3d 1480, 673 N.E.2d 142.

Former husband's inability to pay full amount of spousal support and property division awards did not excuse his complete failure to pay anything at all, and, therefore incarceration for contempt was warranted by his failure to pay what he could, by his failure to maintain bank account and life insurance as ordered, and by his efforts to conceal his assets. Tremaine v. Tremaine (Montgomery 1996) 111 Ohio App.3d 703, 676 N.E.2d 1249, appeal not allowed 77 Ohio St.3d 1480, 673 N.E.2d 142.

Trial court has broad discretion in determining whether award of spousal support is appropriate. Swartz v. Swartz (Warren 1996) 110 Ohio App.3d 218, 673 N.E.2d 972.

Distributive award of former husband's separate property, valued at about $156,330, to former wife, in order to provide wife with some form of spousal support, was not authorized by statute. Swartz v. Swartz (Warren 1996) 110 Ohio App.3d 218, 673 N.E.2d 972.

Client failed to indicate evidence that her attorney could have presented in divorce proceeding to show her entitlement to spousal support, as required to maintain malpractice action against attorney for failing to obtain spousal support for her. Petersen, Ibold & Wantz v. Whiting (Geauga 1996) 109 Ohio App.3d 738, 673 N.E.2d 151, appeal not allowed 76 Ohio St.3d 1491, 670 N.E.2d 240.

Nonpayment of spousal support is classed as a "civil contempt." Marden v. Marden (Butler 1996) 108 Ohio App.3d 568, 671 N.E.2d 331.

Portion of contempt order that conditioned suspension of former husband's jail sentence upon timely future payments toward his monthly spousal support obligation did not allow husband opportunity to purge himself of contempt and was thus void. Marden v. Marden (Butler 1996) 108 Ohio App.3d 568, 671 N.E.2d 331.

Recipient of former husband's divorce settlement payment was an escrow agent, and thus could be held liable for breach of fiduciary duty, where agreement specified that recipient was receiving money as "escrow agent," check made out by husband listed recipient as "escrow agent," and recipient deposited check into an account bearing names of recipient and former wife. Spalding v. Coulson (Cuyahoga 1995) 104 Ohio App.3d 62, 661 N.E.2d 197.

Former husband's payment directly to wife, as part of divorce settlement, was irrelevant to issue of whether escrow agent, who held another part of husband's settlement payment pending resolution of certain issues, breached his fiduciary duties by disbursing funds prior to resolution of disputed issues, contrary to terms of escrow agreement. Spalding v. Coulson (Cuyahoga 1995) 104 Ohio App.3d 62, 661 N.E.2d 197.

Husband's statements to domestic relations court that divorce judgment had been discharged and satisfied did not estop husband to claim that escrow agent had breached fiduciary duty by improperly disbursing escrow funds, which husband had paid in partial satisfaction of divorce settlement; at time of statements, husband was unaware of improper disbursement. Spalding v. Coulson (Cuyahoga 1995) 104 Ohio App.3d 62, 661 N.E.2d 197.

Contribution is appropriate remedy where two parties are liable for debt and its payment by one party discharges their joint liability and relieves other party from burden. Mallin v. Mallin (Cuyahoga 1995) 102 Ohio App.3d 717, 657 N.E.2d 856.

Alimony comprises two components including division of marital assets and liabilities, and periodic payments for sustenance and support, and thus, trial court has equitable authority to divide and distribute marital estate, and then consider whether award of sustenance alimony would be appropriate. Terry v. Terry (Cuyahoga 1994) 99 Ohio App.3d 228, 650 N.E.2d 184.

Purpose of spousal support is to provide for financial needs of ex-spouse; if ex-spouse is living with another person, and that person provides financial support or is supported, then underlying need for spousal support is reduced or does not exist. Moell v. Moell (Ottawa 1994) 98 Ohio App.3d 748, 649 N.E.2d 880, appeal not allowed 72 Ohio St.3d 1407, 647 N.E.2d 496.

New statute, which modified prior alimony statute and provided that division of marital property would be equal unless it would be inequitable, would not be applied retroactively to cases which were filed prior to its effective date. Lyon v. Lyon (Scioto 1993) 86 Ohio App.3d 580, 621 N.E.2d 718.

In making award of spousal support, trial court is required to indicate basis for its award in sufficient detail to enable reviewing court to determine that award is fair, equitable, and in accordance with the law. Layne v. Layne (Champaign 1992) 83 Ohio App.3d 559, 615 N.E.2d 332.

An Ohio court of common pleas does not have jurisdiction to enforce a divorce decree granted in Oklahoma on issues other than child support, such as payment of marital debts, even if the parties appeared voluntarily. Thorley v. Thorley (Huron 1991) 77 Ohio App.3d 275, 602 N.E.2d 268.

A trial court is not required to order the purchase of life insurance to secure an award of alimony. Nori v. Nori (Butler 1989) 58 Ohio App.3d 69, 568 N.E.2d 730.

A court may order an award of sustenance alimony where no specific demand for alimony has been made if such an award is warranted. Carr v. Carr (Wayne 1989) 46 Ohio App.3d 132, 546 N.E.2d 226.

It is within the discretion of a trial court to order that the payor of sustenance alimony keep his former spouse as a beneficiary of his life insurance policy as long as he is required to pay alimony. Gore v. Gore (Summit 1985) 27 Ohio App.3d 141, 499 N.E.2d 1281, 27 O.B.R. 173.

Where a trial court does not specify the reasons behind an award which differs from a referee's recommendation, it will be presumed that the factors listed in RC 3105.18(B) were considered. Russell v. Russell (Warren 1984) 14 Ohio App.3d 408, 471 N.E.2d 810, 14 O.B.R. 526.

Support alimony can be distinguished from property alimony by the following means: (1) an award of support alimony is made pursuant to the husband's duty to provide sustenance in contrast with the right of the wife to a share of the marital property; (2) an award of support alimony is not made in any definite amount, in contrast to the definite nature of a property settlement; and (3) an award of support alimony is made independently of any other award, including a property division. St. Clair v. St. Clair (Lorain 1983) 9 Ohio App.3d 195, 459 N.E.2d 243, 9 O.B.R. 306.

Under the statutes dealing with alimony, including the division of property, there is no general burden of proof and each side has the burden of going forward with evidence as to any factor which it wants considered. Stetler v. Stetler (Mercer 1982) 6 Ohio App.3d 29, 452 N.E.2d 344, 6 O.B.R. 138.

Although the court has the responsibility to weigh the evidence presented on the relevant factors, when applying its broad discretion with relation to all relevant factors, it is not required, as to any one factor, to make its order of award and/or distribution conform to a preponderance of evidence on such factor, and a party cannot complain if a listed factor has not been considered on which neither party offered any evidence. Stetler v. Stetler (Mercer 1982) 6 Ohio App.3d 29, 452 N.E.2d 344, 6 O.B.R. 138.

RC 3105.18 directs the procedures to be followed by trial courts in contested proceedings and is not applicable to uncontested proceedings where the parties have stipulated an "in-court" settlement. Thomas v. Thomas (Licking 1982) 5 Ohio App.3d 94, 449 N.E.2d 478, 5 O.B.R. 208.

An alimony judgment should separately state the amount imposed for alimony and for child support. Zaciewski v. Zaciewski (Lucas 1960) 113 Ohio App. 318, 178 N.E.2d 258, 86 Ohio Law Abs. 601, 17 O.O.2d 331.

Alimony may be awarded only upon satisfactory proof of the charges set forth in the petition therefor. Witkorowski v. Witkorowski (Lucas 1951) 89 Ohio App. 424, 102 N.E.2d 896, 46 O.O. 259.

Court's power to award alimony or divide property is statutory. Budai v. Budai (Hamilton 1930) 38 Ohio App. 79, 175 N.E. 624, 9 Ohio Law Abs. 371, 34 Ohio Law Rep. 83.

Elihu Root's observation is worth recalling, that "About half the practice of a decent lawyer consists of telling ... clients they are d——— fools and should stop ... [that]the law lets you do it but don't. It's a rotten thing to do." Stivison v Goodyear Tire & Rubber Co, No. 95-CA-13, 1996 WL 230037 (4th Dist Ct App, Hocking, 5-6-96), affirmed by 80 Ohio St.3d 498 (1997).

Where a term of the divorce decree provided that the husband shall keep his wife as insured on the husband's medical insurance with his employer and subsequently the husband's company and insurer refused to provide such coverage, the trial court properly refused to hold such husband in contempt. However, the trial court erred in failing to order such husband to provide his wife with equivalent medical insurance at his own expense. Jewett v Jewett, No. CA-82-06 (5th Dist Ct App, Muskingum, 7-23-82).

In a divorce and property division proceeding, defendant's failure to move for separate findings of fact and conclusions of law is a bar to asserting the claim that the property division orders of the trial court were based on an "inadequately developed and preserved record." Hall v Hall, No. C-810869 (1st Dist Ct App, Hamilton, 7-21-82).

Where trial court awards physical possession of the marital premises to one spouse for the purpose of providing a home for minor children, upon such spouse's remarriage the new husband may not be required to pay rent to the non-resident spouse where the non-resident spouse's rights or interests in the marital premises are not jeopardized. Wise v Paul, No. CA-1569 (5th Dist Ct App, Tuscarawas, 4-9-82).

An order for the payment of alimony under RC 3105.18, including an order for the payment of temporary alimony, is a "support order" as defined in RC 2301.34(B) and, pursuant to RC 2301.36, payments made pursuant to such an order are to be made payable to the child support enforcement agency as trustee for the person entitled to receive such payments. OAG 88-094.

2. Jurisdiction/discretion of court

The subject matter jurisdiction of a trial court to award permanent alimony and to formulate an equitable division of the marital assets commences when either party files a complaint for divorce and a division of the marital property. Bolinger v. Bolinger (Ohio 1990) 49 Ohio St.3d 120, 551 N.E.2d 157.

In allocating property between the parties to a divorce and in making an award of sustenance alimony, the trial court must indicate the basis for its award in sufficient detail to enable a reviewing court to determine that the award is fair, equitable and in accordance with the law. Kaechele v. Kaechele (Ohio 1988) 35 Ohio St.3d 93, 518 N.E.2d 1197.

Whether to award interest upon obligations arising out of the division of marital property is within the discretion of the trial court. Koegel v. Koegel (Ohio 1982) 69 Ohio St.2d 355, 432 N.E.2d 206, 23 O.O.3d 320.

A trial court, in determining divorce litigants' inter se property rights in a joint savings account accumulated during marriage, does not abuse its discretion when it bases its award upon the account balance in existence at the time of the parties' permanent separation. Berish v. Berish (Ohio 1982) 69 Ohio St.2d 318, 432 N.E.2d 183, 23 O.O.3d 296.

There is no presumption, rebuttable or irrebuttable, that marital property be divided equally upon divorce; rather, a potentially equal division should be the starting point of the trial court's analysis before it considers the factors listed in RC 3105.18 and all other relevant factors, and consequently a court of common pleas has broad discretion to determine what property division is equitable in a divorce proceeding. The mere fact that a property division is unequal, does not, standing alone, amount to an abuse of discretion. Cherry v. Cherry (Ohio 1981) 66 Ohio St.2d 348, 421 N.E.2d 1293, 20 O.O.3d 318, on remand.

In the exercise of its full equity powers and jurisdiction in a divorce action, the trial court is authorized to adjudicate a complete dissolution of the marriage relationship, including a determination of the rights of the parties to alimony and to a division of property. Clark v. Clark (Ohio 1956) 165 Ohio St. 457, 136 N.E.2d 52, 60 O.O. 115.

The allowance of permanent alimony is left to the sound discretion of the trial court, subject to review by the court of appeals upon the questions of the weight of the evidence and abuse of discretion. Dennison v. Dennison (Ohio 1956) 165 Ohio St. 146, 134 N.E.2d 574, 59 O.O. 210.

Where a decree of divorce is granted on the petition of a woman on the ground that the defendant had a wife living at the time of his marriage with the plaintiff, the court has jurisdiction to grant to the plaintiff alimony and other relief authorized by the statutes on divorce and alimony. Eggleston v. Eggleston (Ohio 1952) 156 Ohio St. 422, 103 N.E.2d 395, 46 O.O. 351.

An action by a wife for alimony and support of her child against the husband, who deserted the family and became a nonresident, is substantially one in rem; and the court has jurisdiction at its commencement to grant a preliminary injunction preventing the disposition of the property by the defendant pending the suit, and, on completion of the service by publication, to decree the relief sought. Benner v. Benner (Ohio 1900) 63 Ohio St. 220, 44 W.L.B. 291, 58 N.E. 569.

Trial court did not abuse its discretion in finding husband in contempt of spousal support provisions of divorce decree, where husband deliberately and intentionally kept his net income as low as possible by keeping his federal income tax withholding high and starting individual retirement account (IRA) through wage withholding, thereby limiting amount his employer was permitted to attach and submit to child support enforcement agency, and where wife was unable to pay mortgages on marital residence because husband did not pay his full support obligation. Arthur v. Arthur (Ohio App. 5 Dist. 1998) 130 Ohio App.3d 398, 720 N.E.2d 176.

Trial court may not require spouse required to pay spousal support to secure obligation with insurance policy on his life where award of support is terminable upon obligor's death. Moore v. Moore (Ohio App. 9 Dist. 1997) 120 Ohio App.3d 488, 698 N.E.2d 459.

Court is not required to reserve jurisdiction to terminate spousal support in event of cohabitation. Jordan v. Jordan (Ohio App. 4 Dist. 1996) 117 Ohio App.3d 47, 689 N.E.2d 1005, dismissed, appeal not allowed 78 Ohio St.3d 1489, 678 N.E.2d 1227.

Trial court has broad discretion to determine whether award of spousal support is appropriate and its decision will not be disturbed absent an abuse of discretion. Carman v. Carman (Butler 1996) 109 Ohio App.3d 698, 672 N.E.2d 1093.

While applying statutory factors in determining amount and extent of sustenance alimony, trial court enjoys tremendous power of discretion; however, this power of discretion is not unlimited, and is subject to appellate court reversal whenever abuse of discretion is found. Simoni v. Simoni (Cuyahoga 1995) 102 Ohio App.3d 628, 657 N.E.2d 800, appeal not allowed 73 Ohio St.3d 1453, 654 N.E.2d 989.

When trial court is faced with challenge of awarding sum-certain sustenance alimony or dividing marital property in divorce proceeding, it is guided by law, but controlled by equity. Simoni v. Simoni (Cuyahoga 1995) 102 Ohio App.3d 628, 657 N.E.2d 800, appeal not allowed 73 Ohio St.3d 1453, 654 N.E.2d 989.

Trial courts have broad discretion in formulating spousal support awards, and reviewing court should not alter award absent finding that trial court abused its discretion. Poe v. Poe (Logan 1995) 102 Ohio App.3d 581, 657 N.E.2d 589.

There was no abuse of discretion in providing that spousal support of $450 per month for 42-year-old wife should continue until attainment of retirement age, absent earlier remarriage or death of either party, where parties had been married for 20 years, wife took care of parties' children and until recent years did not develop employment outside the home, she would have children at home for at least six more years, and court had reserved jurisdiction over spousal support. Poe v. Poe (Logan 1995) 102 Ohio App.3d 581, 657 N.E.2d 589.

Trial court did not abuse its discretion in determining that expenses incurred by wife prior to marriage for cleaning and repairing antique clock given to couple, costs of purchase by wife of her own wedding band and remounting of her grandmother's diamond ring, payment by wife of expenses for husband's move into marital home, and rebate checks for appliances and overpayment to title company which were deposited into husband's account were amounts expended for marital purposes and that wife was not entitled to reimbursement. Demo v. Demo (Butler 1995) 101 Ohio App.3d 383, 655 N.E.2d 791.

Trial court abuses its discretion in making award of spousal support when its decision is unreasonable, arbitrary, or unconscionable. Graham v. Graham (Greene 1994) 98 Ohio App.3d 396, 648 N.E.2d 850.

Trial court did not err in failing to follow law of case on remand by ordering spousal support for period of 12 years, though Court of Appeals stated that wife probably should receive indefinite spousal support, but it did not state that trial court abused its discretion in awarding spousal support for period of nine years; trial court was obligated to set forth sufficient reasoning for its original award of spousal support to permit review on appeal, but it was not obligated to award indefinite support. Graham v. Graham (Greene 1994) 98 Ohio App.3d 396, 648 N.E.2d 850.

Temporary restraining order (TRO) against husband's interest in certain companies in order to secure his spousal support obligation was proper; there was uncontroverted evidence that husband did not want to pay wife spousal support in excess of $500 per month and that, should court order support above that amount, husband would quit his job and/or move to Florida. Addy v. Addy (Franklin 1994) 97 Ohio App.3d 204, 646 N.E.2d 513.

In dividing marital property, trial court has authority and discretion to do what is equitable upon facts and circumstances of each case, and "equitable" need not mean "equal." Addy v. Addy (Franklin 1994) 97 Ohio App.3d 204, 646 N.E.2d 513.

Domestic relations court did not have jurisdiction to issue permanent injunction restraining former husband from selling or disposing of property after underlying divorce action has been terminated through journalization of final judgment. Gullia v. Gullia (Cuyahoga 1994) 93 Ohio App.3d 653, 639 N.E.2d 822, cause dismissed 70 Ohio St.3d 1409, 637 N.E.2d 6, dismissed, jurisdictional motion overruled 70 Ohio St.3d 1409, 637 N.E.2d 7.

Trial court abused its discretion in finding former husband in arrears on temporary alimony and support obligations absent evidence showing that former husband violated order requiring those payments. Gullia v. Gullia (Cuyahoga 1994) 93 Ohio App.3d 653, 639 N.E.2d 822, cause dismissed 70 Ohio St.3d 1409, 637 N.E.2d 6, dismissed, jurisdictional motion overruled 70 Ohio St.3d 1409, 637 N.E.2d 7.

Trial court lacked jurisdiction to proceed with show cause hearing where former husband had not been served with former wife's motion to show cause. Gullia v. Gullia (Cuyahoga 1994) 93 Ohio App.3d 653, 639 N.E.2d 822, cause dismissed 70 Ohio St.3d 1409, 637 N.E.2d 6, dismissed, jurisdictional motion overruled 70 Ohio St.3d 1409, 637 N.E.2d 7.

Trial court's award of spousal support of $75,000 per year to former wife, for period of eight years, payable in monthly installments, though generous, was not an abuse of discretion; marriage had lasted 27 years, former wife basically worked as business manager and bookkeeper for former husband's physical therapy business, for which she never received more than $5,400 per year, and in one year former husband earned $420,000 from physical therapy business. McCoy v. McCoy (Cuyahoga 1993) 91 Ohio App.3d 570, 632 N.E.2d 1358, appeal dismissed 68 Ohio St.3d 1457, 627 N.E.2d 562.

Trial courts have broad discretion to make property, alimony, and sustenance alimony awards. Turner v. Turner (Franklin 1993) 90 Ohio App.3d 161, 628 N.E.2d 110, motion overruled 68 Ohio St.3d 1430, 624 N.E.2d 1067.

Reasonable amount of spousal support should be awarded when appropriate; in making such determination, court should consider all statutory factors. Turner v. Turner (Franklin 1993) 90 Ohio App.3d 161, 628 N.E.2d

110, motion overruled 68 Ohio St.3d 1430, 624 N.E.2d 1067.

Permanent spousal support award of $5,000 a month was not abuse of discretion because it only left husband with $1,770 a month to put toward his other expenses. Turner v. Turner (Franklin 1993) 90 Ohio App.3d 161, 628 N.E.2d 110, motion overruled 68 Ohio St.3d 1430, 624 N.E.2d 1067.

Appellate court should not alter property, alimony, and sustenance alimony awards absent finding that trial court abused its discretion, i.e., finding that trial court's determination was unreasonable, arbitrary, or unconscionable; nor may appellate court substitute its judgment on factual or discretionary issues for that of trial court. Turner v. Turner (Franklin 1993) 90 Ohio App.3d 161, 628 N.E.2d 110, motion overruled 68 Ohio St.3d 1430, 624 N.E.2d 1067.

Trial court did not abuse its discretion in its distribution of marital debts, where marriage was of short duration, with both parties being highly educated professionals, and parties possessed equal earning capacity. deLevie v. deLevie (Franklin 1993) 86 Ohio App.3d 531, 621 N.E.2d 594, dismissed, jurisdictional motion overruled 67 Ohio St.3d 1409, 615 N.E.2d 1043.

Trial court enjoys wide latitude in awarding spousal support and its decisions are reversible only for abuse of discretion; abuse of discretion connotes more than error of law or judgment and implies that court's attitude is unreasonable, arbitrary or unconscionable. Layne v. Layne (Champaign 1992) 83 Ohio App.3d 559, 615 N.E.2d 332.

Trial court abused its descretion in ordering definite termination after less than four years of spousal support awarded to wife who was in poor health after 26 year marriage and who had not been employed outside home. Layne v. Layne (Champaign 1992) 83 Ohio App.3d 559, 615 N.E.2d 332.

Although trial court must consider statutory factors in determining whether award of spousal support is appropriate, amount of support is discretionary with court. Babka v. Babka (Summit 1992) 83 Ohio App.3d 428, 615 N.E.2d 247.

Where there is good faith confusion over the requirements of the dissolution decree, a court has the power to enforce its decree of dissolution of marriage, hear the matter, clarify the confusion, and resolve the dispute. Bond v. Bond (Summit 1990) 69 Ohio App.3d 225, 590 N.E.2d 348.

Whenever a clause in a separation agreement is deemed to be ambiguous, it is the responsibility of the trial court to interpret it; the trial court has broad discretion in clarifying ambiguous language by considering not only the intent of the parties but the equities involved. Bond v. Bond (Summit 1990) 69 Ohio App.3d 225, 590 N.E.2d 348.

A trial court errs in failing to award sustenance alimony where the wife's income is slightly more than minimum wage, she is awarded an equity interest in the marital home payable upon the husband's sale at an unknown date, and the husband's counsel admits in closing argument that the wife needs rehabilitative alimony. Mochko v. Mochko (Cuyahoga 1990) 63 Ohio App.3d 671, 579 N.E.2d 773.

A court may order an award of sustenance alimony where no specific demand for alimony has been made if such an award is warranted. Carr v. Carr (Wayne 1989) 46 Ohio App.3d 132, 546 N.E.2d 226.

A court has the authority to award alimony in the form of a division of property under RC 3105.18, even where no specific demand for alimony has been made, so long as the recipient is "entitled" to the award granted. McLaughlin v. McLaughlin (Seneca 1986) 30 Ohio App.3d 242, 507 N.E.2d 423, 30 O.B.R. 401.

The allowance of alimony is within the sound discretion of the trial court. Lathrop v. Lathrop (Preble 1982) 5 Ohio App.3d 240, 451 N.E.2d 546, 5 O.B.R. 526.

Actions for divorce, alimony, custody, etc., were not known at common law and are purely statutory in nature; the court has no greater jurisdiction or power than is given by statute; the repeal of RC 3105.20 by the legislature divests the domestic relations courts of equity jurisdiction to make divisions of property; accordingly, the trial court is without authority to make a division of property unless it is pursuant to an alimony award under RC 3105.18. (Equitable powers returned by enactment of RC 3105.011 (1975 H 370, eff. 8-1-75)). Soyk v. Soyk (Summit 1975) 45 Ohio App.2d 319, 345 N.E.2d 461, 74 O.O.2d 532.

A trial court is without authority to make a division of property unless it is pursuant to an alimony award under RC 3105.18. Soyk v. Soyk (Summit 1975) 45 Ohio App.2d 319, 345 N.E.2d 461, 74 O.O.2d 532.

Where a ground for divorce has been established under RC 3105.01(J) by the plaintiff's testimony and the corroborating evidence of an in rem divorce decree obtained by the plaintiff's spouse in a foreign nation, the court of common pleas has power to award plaintiff alimony in an action for divorce. Rousculp v. Rousculp (Franklin 1968) 17 Ohio App.2d 101, 244 N.E.2d 512, 46 O.O.2d 125.

An award of alimony in an amount which greatly exceeds what defendant is able to pay and without any evidence to support it but evidence that defendant has sizeable debts, no assets and no job, is an abuse of discretion and will be reversed. Campbell v. Campbell (Hamilton 1968) 17 Ohio App.2d 87, 244 N.E.2d 525, 46 O.O.2d 101.

The court of common pleas has broad discretion in the matter of allowing alimony in an action for divorce or alimony, and an order concerning alimony in such action may be reversed only where the evidence clearly shows an abuse of discretion or a misapprehension of the facts. Ginn v. Ginn (Lawrence 1960) 112 Ohio App. 259, 175 N.E.2d 848, 16 O.O.2d 164.

Where the defendant in a divorce action is a nonresident of Ohio and is not amenable to personal service and there is no property owned by such defendant in Ohio, the trial court does not have jurisdiction to pass upon the question of alimony; and where such defendant, in an action filed subsequent to the termination of the divorce action, is reinvested with title to property in Ohio, the situation existing at the time of the divorce action is not changed and the jurisdiction of the court in the divorce action is not changed thereby, so that an action to partition such property is not res judicata as to a subsequent action for alimony. Hasselschwert v. Hasselschwert (Defiance 1956) 103 Ohio App. 202, 145 N.E.2d 224, 3 O.O.2d 269.

A common pleas court, having granted a divorce, may apply equitable principles in making an award of alimony and, with respect to property owned by the parties jointly or in common, may make an equitable division thereof between them. Boehm v. Boehm (Lucas 1956) 101 Ohio App. 145, 138 N.E.2d 418, 1 O.O.2d 83.

A court's cavalier approach in ordering the parties to "flip a coin" to determine the order of selection from four remaining items of marital property is not an abuse of discretion where there is no prejudice to either party and the items are of disparate value. Neal v Neal, No. 96APE02-150, 1996 WL 550379 (10th Dist Ct App, Franklin, 9-30-96).

A husband who is ordered to pay nonmodifiable permanent spousal support is entitled to a new trial based upon newly discovered evidence after he loses his job of twenty-two years, the judgment entry is not filed until two years after the trial before a referee, where the referee does not recommend that the trial court retain jurisdiction to modify the spousal support award. Bender v Bender, No. 2224-M, 1994 WL 149247 (9th Dist Ct App, Medina, 4-27-94).

A court has the authority to order a lump sum payment for the purchase of health insurance as part of an alimony award even absent a request for such in the demand for alimony or the pleadings. Stone v Stone, No. 1872 (4th Dist Ct App, Lawrence, 11-23-88).

A trial court abuses its discretion where it awards nine per cent of the marital property to the husband and ninety-one per cent of the marital property to the wife, thereby depriving the husband of his means of earning a livelihood. Farmer v Farmer, No. 9-103 (11th Dist Ct App, Lake, 4-6-84).

In a divorce proceeding, trial court's decision to delay sale of ninety-year-old marital home until youngest son had completed high school was not an abuse of discretion. Overman v Overman, No. 44067 (8th Dist Ct App, Cuyahoga, 5-6-82).

In a divorce action, trial court has jurisdiction over all property brought into the marriage by either party including a nonmarital asset which one party owned exclusively prior to the marriage. Crawford v Crawford, No. 7508 (2d Dist Ct App, Montgomery, 4-23-82).

Where most of the assets to be divided are the product of the wife's inheritance and industry, the wife faces future medical bills as a result of her husband shooting her, and the husband's immediate needs are being satisfied by the state in prison, it is not an abuse of discretion by the court to award seventy-five per cent of the net proceeds of the sale of the parties' home to the wife and only twenty-five per cent to the husband. Mowery v Mowery, No. 81AP-343 (10th Dist Ct App, Franklin, 10-29-81).

In a divorce proceeding, the court has jurisdiction to make a division of property and an award of alimony, but where the children have reached majority, and there has been no prior provision for support of children, the court has no authority to make a retroactive award for support over and above that which was paid without any award having been requested. Winegardner v Winegardner, No. 26-CA-80 (5th Dist Ct App, Fairfield, 7-29-81).

A journal entry reflecting a property settlement agreed to at a pre-trial conference is void, as the court has jurisdiction to divide a couple's property only when it grants a divorce, such jurisdiction not encompassing pre-trial conferences. Daniels v Daniels, No. 2989 (9th Dist Ct App, Lorain, 10-15-80).

The allowance of permanent alimony is left to the sound discretion of the trial court, subject to review by the court of appeals upon the questions of the weight of the evidence and abuse of discretion. Weinstein v. Weinstein (Cuyahoga 1962) 185 N.E.2d 56, 90 Ohio Law Abs. 199, 27 O.O.2d 115, appeal dismissed 174 Ohio St. 408, 189 N.E.2d 635, 23 O.O.2d 49.

Partition of property may not be ordered in a divorce action. Flatter v. Flatter (Darke 1954) 130 N.E.2d 145, 71 Ohio Law Abs. 89.

A partition action cannot be sustained on the basis of a property settlement prior to the trial of the divorce action of the parties. Smith v. Smith (Ohio Com.Pl. 1953) 112 N.E.2d 346, 67 Ohio Law Abs. 489, 50 O.O. 175.

3. Temporary spousal support

In a domestic relations action, interlocutory orders are merged within the final decree, and the right to enforce such interlocutory orders does not extend beyond the decree, unless they have been reduced to a separate judgment or they have been considered by the trial court and specifically referred to within the decree. Colom v. Colom (Ohio 1979) 58 Ohio St.2d 245, 389 N.E.2d 856, 12 O.O.3d 242.

Where a court of appeals has made an order granting temporary alimony to a wife for her sustenance during the pendency of an appeal before it from a final order and decree which granted a divorce and awarded permanent alimony to the wife, and where such final order and decree is affirmed on that appeal, payments of amounts for such temporary alimony must be credited against amounts due from such permanent alimony. Bentz v. Bentz (Ohio 1961) 171 Ohio St. 535, 173 N.E.2d 129, 15 O.O.2d 1.

Absence from appellate record of transcript of divorce court's hearing on motion to increase temporary spousal support precluded appellate review of referee's finding that such increase was appropriate, even assuming obligor spouse timely filed objections to the finding. Stafinsky v. Stafinsky (Ohio App. 11 Dist. 1996) 116 Ohio App.3d 781, 689 N.E.2d 112.

Obligor spouse's failure to object to divorce referee's finding that increase in temporary spousal-support obligation was appropriate precluded appellate review of that finding. Stafinsky v. Stafinsky (Ohio App. 11 Dist. 1996) 116 Ohio App.3d 781, 689 N.E.2d 112.

Trial court did not abuse its discretion in divorce action in imposing award to former wife of monthly spousal support payments without specific termination date. Hutchinson v. Hutchinson (Clermont 1996) 113 Ohio App.3d 863, 682 N.E.2d 698.

Wife was not entitled to temporary rehabilitative alimony, where wife had ability to earn over $50,000 per year, had advanced educational degrees, and had earning capability that exceeded that of husband. Walker v. Walker (Hamilton 1996) 112 Ohio App.3d 90, 677 N.E.2d 1252, appeal not allowed 77 Ohio St.3d 1492, 673 N.E.2d 149.

Time limit did not have to be placed on award of spousal maintenance made in divorce proceedings, despite wife's training as registered nurse, where marriage lasted approximately 25 years, wife's maximum earning capacity was limited due to her need to take care of and tutor dyslexic child, and wife would be in her fifties by time her minor children became emancipated. Shaffer v. Shaffer (Crawford 1996) 109 Ohio App.3d 205, 671 N.E.2d 1317.

Trial court could increase amount of spousal support between temporary and final support order; purpose of temporary order is to provide economically disadvantaged spouse means of maintenance during pendency of action, while final order is rendered only after hearing is held and court considers evidence presented in light of statutory factors. Soley v. Soley (Lucas 1995) 101 Ohio App.3d 540, 655 N.E.2d 1381, dismissed, appeal not allowed 73 Ohio St.3d 1410, 651 N.E.2d 1308, certiorari denied 116 S.Ct. 945, 133 L.Ed.2d 870.

Trial court order which converted payments previously ordered to be made by husband to wife for household expenses to sum certain, and ordered payment by wage withholding, was not impermissible modification of temporary support order. Soley v. Soley (Lucas 1995) 101 Ohio App.3d 540, 655 N.E.2d 1381, dismissed, appeal not allowed 73 Ohio St.3d 1410, 651 N.E.2d 1308, certiorari denied 116 S.Ct. 945, 133 L.Ed.2d 870.

Finding that husband received service of notice of contempt hearing in connection with alleged failure to abide by temporary spousal support order was supported by evidence, notwithstanding husband's claim that he was out of country when service of notice was made at husband's office and called court to explain situation. Soley v. Soley (Lucas 1995) 101 Ohio App.3d 540, 655 N.E.2d 1381, dismissed, appeal not allowed 73 Ohio St.3d 1410, 651 N.E.2d 1308, certiorari denied 116 S.Ct. 945, 133 L.Ed.2d 870.

Trial court did not abuse its discretion in directing husband to pay as temporary support during divorce proceeding child support, spousal support, amount to bring mortgage on marital home current, and mortgage payments thereafter as they became due. DiLacqua v. DiLacqua (Summit 1993) 88 Ohio App.3d 48, 623 N.E.2d 118.

Husband did not waive his right to produce evidence on existence of and duration of alleged common-law marriage by failing to make specific objection to referee's finding on motion for order of temporary spousal support that common-law marriage occurred in or about December 1960; such finding was beyond scope of temporary spousal support hearing and requirement of report and recommendation was not applicable to that hearing. Lyon v. Lyon (Scioto 1993) 86 Ohio App.3d 580, 621 N.E.2d 718.

All orders for temporary alimony are merged in the final decree of divorce and are thereby terminated, unless extended during the pendency of the appeal. Yonally v. Yonally (Summit 1974) 45 Ohio App.2d 122, 341 N.E.2d 602, 74 O.O.2d 134.

Temporary alimony pending appeal may be granted to either party for sustenance and/or expense money during the pendency of the appeal, and it may be granted in a divorce action or alimony action, whether or not the final judgment contains an order for permanent alimony, but if the final judgment of the trial court provides for permanent alimony, and on appeal temporary alimony pending appeal is awarded, any amounts paid as temporary alimony pending appeal are deducted and set off from the award of permanent alimony if there is an affirmance of the trial court's judgment. Rahm v. Rahm (Cuyahoga 1974) 39 Ohio App.2d 74, 315 N.E.2d 495, 68 O.O.2d 225.

A trial court's three year limitation of spousal support corresponding to the period before the youngest child can go to school is not an abuse of discretion after the trial court carefully considers (1) monthly expenses the parties would be responsible to pay following the divorce, (2) that the combined income could be insufficient to meet all of the needs of the parties, and (3) that a "shortfall" could result in any distribution. Calevro v Calevro, No. L-98-1303, 1999 WL 128379 (6th Dist Ct App, Lucas, 3-12-99).

A trial court may award temporary spousal support during the pendency of a divorce action under RC 3105.18 despite the existence of a prenuptial agreement to the contrary. Mulvey v Mulvey, No. 17707, 1996 WL 724759 (9th Dist Ct App, Summit, 12-4-96).

A wife's misrepresentation that her annual income was $14,000 when it was actually $39,000, although a significant misrepresentation, had no effect on the amount of temporary spousal support the husband should pay where his annual income was $404,330 and the disparity in the parties' incomes warranted the temporary support order made. Mulvey v Mulvey, No. 17707, 1996 WL 724759 (9th Dist Ct App, Summit, 12-4-96).

Husband's poverty is no defense to wife's application for temporary alimony, where divorce action is brought by husband. Davis v. Davis (Montgomery 1943) 51 N.E.2d 288, 39 Ohio Law Abs. 29.

4. Sources of spousal support

Absent an agreement between payor and payee spouses, it is improper to include in an award of sustenance alimony a clause requiring the payor to pay alimony based on a fixed percentage of the payor's income, gross or otherwise, when the award is in the form of a penalty or is not based on the payee's need. Kunkle v. Kunkle (Ohio 1990) 51 Ohio St.3d 64, 554 N.E.2d 83.

Alimony may be based on the future personal earnings of the husband and is not limited to a consideration of property in his possession. The phrase, "out of her husband's property," in this section is essentially directory in its nature. Lape v. Lape (Ohio 1918) 99 Ohio St. 143, 124 N.E. 51, 16 Ohio Law Rep. 465.

Where insured was obligated under divorce decree to maintain his ex-wife as beneficiary of life insurance, and insured died after naming another individual as beneficiary, imposition of constructive trust on the life insurance proceeds was appropriate remedy to ensure that proceeds were paid to ex-wife in accordance with divorce decree, even if named beneficiary had been innocent party to insured's actions; ex-wife had equitable right to insurance proceeds which was superior to the legal right of named beneficiary. Bailey v. Prudential Ins. Co. of America (Ohio App. 10 Dist. 1997) 124 Ohio App.3d 31, 705 N.E.2d 389.

Where insured was obligated under divorce decree to maintain his ex-wife as beneficiary of life insurance, and insured died after naming another individual as beneficiary, ex-wife was not required to exhaust any potential remedy against insured's estate before seeking to impose constructive trust on the life insurance proceeds. Bailey v. Prudential Ins. Co. of America (Ohio App. 10 Dist. 1997) 124 Ohio App.3d 31, 705 N.E.2d 389.

Trial court erred in ordering husband to maintain $50,000 life insurance policy to secure his spousal support obligations; order for spousal support terminated upon wife's death or remarriage and, thus, requiring husband to maintain life insurance policy would not necessarily secure payment of husband's spousal support obligation, as it would require husband to keep current on premiums and, in event of arrearage, require wife to survive husband in order to collect. Addy v. Addy (Franklin 1994) 97 Ohio App.3d 204, 646 N.E.2d 513.

State teachers retirement system (STRS) benefits are not subject to division pursuant to a qualified domestic relations order, but they are marital assets which are to be considered by a trial court in determining an equitable division of property. Guidubaldi v. Guidubaldi (Portage 1990) 64 Ohio App.3d 361, 581 N.E.2d 621.

A court in making a division of property may properly award nonmarital property including gifts, devises, or bequests, along with property brought to the marriage if in considering all of the factors of RC 3105.18 such an award is necessary to make an equitable division. Buckles v. Buckles (Franklin 1988) 46 Ohio App.3d 102, 546 N.E.2d 950.

Alimony may be awarded out of the future personal earnings of the husband. Gage v. Gage (Cuyahoga 1955) 101 Ohio App. 483, 129 N.E.2d 486, 73 Ohio Law Abs. 277, 1 O.O.2d 413, affirmed 165 Ohio St. 462, 136 N.E.2d 56, 60 O.O. 117.

Alimony may be awarded out of the future personal earnings of the husband and made payable in installments, and such award may be made in addition to an allowance out of the husband's personal or real property, or both. Klump v. Klump (Lucas 1954) 96 Ohio App. 93, 121 N.E.2d 273, 54 O.O. 202.

The cash surrender value or the right to receive the endowment proceeds of an insurance policy, wherein insured reserves such immediate rights as to make a "change of beneficiary," procure "cash loans," and take advantage of "surrender options," is property of the insured which a court may require insured to convert into proceeds to be paid to his wife as alimony. Foulks v. Foulks (Stark 1934) 49 Ohio App. 291, 197 N.E. 201, 19 Ohio Law Abs. 323, 3 O.O. 207.

In action for divorce and alimony, testimony regarding the amount or value of property owned by defendant previous to time of the divorce is admissible for purpose of obtaining a complete picture of the married life of the parties, although its exclusion may not constitute prejudicial error, as alimony can be based only on the value of the real and personal estate of the defendant at the time of divorce. (See also Rahn v Rahn, 18 Abs 228 (App, Darke 1934).) Rahn v. Rahn (Darke 1933) 48 Ohio App. 179, 192 N.E. 798, 16 Ohio Law Abs. 169, 1 O.O. 173, motion denied 18 Ohio Law Abs. 228.

RC 3105.18 precludes (1) any effort by the trial court to make spousal support a charge against an obligor's estate or (2) to require him to obtain or maintain insurance upon his life for the benefit of his former spouse or (3) require any security for the payment of spousal support. Hartman v Hartman, No. CA96-04-008, 1996 WL 622560 (12th Dist Ct App, Preble, 10-28-96).

The domestic relations court has subject matter jurisdiction to determine a third party's interest in the deferred compensation fund of a person whose spouse seeks to attach the fund for an award of support. Zashin, Rich, Sutula & Monastra v Offenberg, No. 68951, 1995 WL 723345 (8th Dist Ct App, Cuyahoga, 12-7-95).

A trial court's order that a husband maintain a life insurance policy with the wife as beneficiary to secure husband's spousal support obligation is an abuse of discretion since spousal support terminates upon the death of either party; requiring a husband to maintain such a policy would not secure payment of the support obligation, as the husband would be required to be current on the premiums, and in the event of an arrearage the wife would have to survive the husband to collect. Addy v Addy, No. 94APF03-421, 1994 WL 521225 (10th Dist Ct App, Franklin, 9-20-94).

Where a divorce decree calls for alimony payments based on fifty percent of a spouse's adjusted income, the term "adjusted income," although ambiguous by itself, will be construed to mean income after adjustments for state, federal, and local taxes, where both spouses testify to such an interpretation and the divorce decree requires the submission of state, federal, and local income tax returns each year to the spouse receiving the alimony. Kellogg v Kellogg, No. 7681 (2d Dist Ct App, Montgomery, 7-8-82).

In a divorce proceeding, take-home pay is not the equivalent of "relative earning abilities of the parties" for purposes of awarding a property settlement nor is take-home pay the determinative factor in arriving at an order for child support. Hanney v Hanney, No. OT-81-25 (6th Dist Ct App, Ottawa, 5-7-82).

Although workers compensation awards and social security payments are exempt from attachment, a court may order lifetime alimony of $150 a month to the wife when a court does not designate the payment's source. Horne v Horne, No. 347 (4th Dist Ct App, Pike, 12-14-81).

It is an abuse of discretion for the trial court to consider inherited property of the wife as if it were marital property subject to division because courts regularly do make such a separation in the process of determining an equitable division of marital property under RC 3105.18. McDade v McDade, No. 376 (12th Dist Ct App, Warren, 9-16-81).

Where a decree for divorce is granted to a wife on account of the aggression of her husband, an allowance of alimony may be based on future personal earnings or wages of the husband. In such a case the court is not necessarily limited to a consideration of property in possession of the husband at time of decree. Thompson v. Thompson (Montgomery 1951) 110 N.E.2d 17, 63 Ohio Law Abs. 444.

Insured's designation of current wife as beneficiary of his Federal Employees Group Life Insurance (FEGLI) policy took precedence over prior state divorce decree mandating designation of former wife as irrevocable beneficiary, where designation of current wife was proper under FEGLI statute. Matthews v. Matthews (N.D.Ohio 1996) 926 F.Supp. 650.

5. —In general, factors to consider in award

At minimum, trial court fashioning division of marital property must address statutorily enumerated factors in arriving at its decision; to do otherwise is abuse of discretion. Bisker v. Bisker (Ohio 1994) 69 Ohio St.3d 608, 635 N.E.2d 308.

A trial court should attempt to preserve a pension or retirement asset in order that each party can procure the most benefit, and the court should attempt to disentangle the parties' economic partnership so as to create a conclusion and finality to the marriage. Hoyt v. Hoyt (Ohio 1990) 53 Ohio St.3d 177, 559 N.E.2d 1292.

Except in cases involving a marriage of long duration, parties of advanced age, or a homemaker-spouse who has had little opportunity to develop meaningful employment outside the home, where a payee spouse has the resources, ability, and potential to be self-supporting, an award of sustenance alimony should provide for the termination of the award, within a reasonable time and upon a date certain, in order to place a definitive limit upon the parties' rights and responsibilities. Kunkle v. Kunkle (Ohio 1990) 51 Ohio St.3d 64, 554 N.E.2d 83.

In making a sustenance alimony award, the trial court must consider all the factors listed in RC 3105.18(B) and not base its determination upon any one of those factors taken in isolation. Kaechele v. Kaechele (Ohio 1988) 35 Ohio St.3d 93, 518 N.E.2d 1197.

Under amended version of spousal support statute, "need" is no longer basis for a spousal support award, nor is it significant whether spouse "deserves" the support; only relevant question is what is "appropriate and reasonable" under the circumstances. Bowen v. Bowen (Ohio App. 9 Dist. 1999) 132 Ohio App.3d 616, 725 N.E.2d 1165.

Trial court's division of marital property and debt and its award of spousal support constituted arbitrary abuse of discretion where trial court failed to indicate factual basis for its award in its judgment entry, and there was lack of evidence in the record supporting conclusion that trial court considered mandatory statutory factors. Vanderpool v. Vanderpool (Ohio App. 9 Dist. 1997) 118 Ohio App.3d 876, 694 N.E.2d 164.

Trial court properly considered aid wife received from her male friend in declining to reduce or terminate husband's alimony obligation; wife did not claim expenses for items that friend provided. Mottice v. Mottice (Ohio App. 9 Dist. 1997) 118 Ohio App.3d 731, 693 N.E.2d 1179.

Discussion of statutory factors in divorce court's spousal-support order was inadequate, necessitating remand, where order merely recited that court had considered statutory factors and did not even reference parties' income levels. Stafinsky v. Stafinsky (Ohio App. 11 Dist. 1996) 116 Ohio App.3d 781, 689 N.E.2d 112.

Competent, credible evidence in the record established wife's need for spousal support, particularly in view of her unemployed status, limited income, limited educational background, limited employment experience, and custodial responsibilities for her four young children; in addition, given trial court's allocation of separate property to husband, a source of funds existed for payment of lump sum spousal support award. Marcum v. Marcum (Ohio App. 2 Dist. 1996) 116 Ohio App.3d 606, 688 N.E.2d 1085.

Trial court must not base spousal support decision on any one of the statutory factors taken in isolation. Williams v. Williams (Ohio App. 6 Dist. 1996) 116 Ohio App.3d 320, 688 N.E.2d 30.

Trial court must consider all statutory factors in making a sustenance alimony award. Mallett v. Mallett (Ohio App. 7 Dist. 1996) 116 Ohio App.3d 139, 687 N.E.2d 17.

Court must consider all relevant statutory factors in determining whether to modify spousal support and should not consider any one factor in isolation. Tremaine v. Tremaine (Montgomery 1996) 111 Ohio App.3d 703, 676 N.E.2d 1249, appeal not allowed 77 Ohio St.3d 1480, 673 N.E.2d 142.

When considering award of spousal support, court should consider all 14 statutory factors and award only an amount which is appropriate and reasonable, not an amount based upon need. Schultz v. Schultz (Franklin 1996) 110 Ohio App.3d 715, 675 N.E.2d 55.

Trial courts are required to apply statutory factors when determining whether award of spousal support is appropriate, and to indicate in final decree of divorce underlying basis for award in sufficient detail to enable appellate court to determine whether award was appropriate. Schneider v. Schneider (Geauga 1996) 110 Ohio App.3d 487, 674 N.E.2d 769, appeal not allowed 77 Ohio St.3d 1416, 670 N.E.2d 1004.

Decision to award spousal support to wife in divorce proceedings was supported by evidence that following marriage of long duration, husband had much higher level of education, income, and income potential, wife had been homemaker throughout marriage and was going to continue her education for approximately four additional years, and wife's annual needs far exceeded her present income. Schneider v. Schneider (Geauga 1996) 110 Ohio App.3d 487, 674 N.E.2d 769, appeal not allowed 77 Ohio St.3d 1416, 670 N.E.2d 1004.

Either the record or trial court's decision with respect to spousal support must indicate basis for award in detail sufficient to permit appellate review; thus, as long as record contains adequate support for award, trial court need not state its rationale in divorce decree itself; overruling *Davis v Davis*, Fayette App. No. CA90—04—003, 1990 WL 183497 and *Duncil v. Duncil*, Warren App. Nos. CA92—09—084 and CA92—09—088, 1993 WL 137025. Carman v. Carman (Butler 1996) 109 Ohio App.3d 698, 672 N.E.2d 1093.

Among factors court may consider when determining whether amount of spousal support at divorce is appropriate and reasonable are income of parties, relative earning abilities of parties, and extent to which it would be inappropriate for party, because of being custodian of minor child of marriage, to seek employment outside home. Shaffer v. Shaffer (Crawford 1996) 109 Ohio App.3d 205, 671 N.E.2d 1317.

Trial court did not abuse its discretion in ordering husband to pay wife $375 per month in spousal support, considering parties' incomes, their relative earning abilities, their age and physical condition, their retirement benefits, duration of marriage, their standard of living during marriage and wife's lost income production capacity. Alder v. Alder (Butler 1995) 105 Ohio App.3d 524, 664 N.E.2d 609.

Trial court must evaluate evidence in accordance with each factor that trial court must consider when making award of spousal support and then weigh need for support against ability to pay. Graham v. Graham (Greene 1994) 98 Ohio App.3d 396, 648 N.E.2d 850.

Upon divorce, assets of economic partnership must be divided and distributed in equitable manner. Clark v. Joseph (Summit 1994) 95 Ohio App.3d 207, 642 N.E.2d 36.

Ordering that former husband pay $7,000 for attorney fees directly to attorney of former husband's girlfriend, who was cross-appellant in divorce proceedings, was abuse of discretion; award had to be paid to former girlfriend. Gullia v. Gullia (Cuyahoga 1994) 93 Ohio App.3d 653, 639 N.E.2d 822, cause dismissed 70 Ohio St.3d 1409, 637 N.E.2d 6, dismissed, jurisdictional motion overruled 70 Ohio St.3d 1409, 637 N.E.2d 7.

Trial court did not abuse its discretion in awarding spousal support to wife based on disparity in income, after excluding husband's evidence, where husband's willful failure to provide court-ordered discovery impeded wife in proving amount of husband's income. Getter v. Getter (Montgomery 1993) 90 Ohio App.3d 1, 627 N.E.2d 1043.

Substantial disparity in parties' incomes is important factor to consider in determining appropriateness and amount of spousal support. Getter v. Getter (Montgomery 1993) 90 Ohio App.3d 1, 627 N.E.2d 1043.

Trial court's property division was reasonable, in light of duration of marriage, earning capacity of parties, and debts incurred by parties in pursuing divorce litigation. deLevie v. deLevie (Franklin 1993) 86 Ohio App.3d 531, 621 N.E.2d 594, dismissed, jurisdictional motion overruled 67 Ohio St.3d 1409, 615 N.E.2d 1043.

Trial court abused its descretion in ordering definite termination after less than four years of spousal support awarded to wife who was in poor health after 26 year marriage and who had not been employed outside home. Layne v. Layne (Champaign 1992) 83 Ohio App.3d 559, 615 N.E.2d 332.

In considering all relevant factors in statute governing court's award of spousal support, court must evaluate evidence germane to each applicable factor, then weigh need for support against ability to pay. Layne v. Layne (Champaign 1992) 83 Ohio App.3d 559, 615 N.E.2d 332.

Trial court did not indicate basis of its award of spousal support to wife in sufficient detail to allow Court of Appeals to determine if it was fair and equitable, and remand was thus appropriate; trial court did not articulate rationale other than to state award was based upon wife's present inability to work, and made no findings as to other relevant statutory factors pertaining to wife's needs. Layne v. Layne (Champaign 1992) 83 Ohio App.3d 559, 615 N.E.2d 332.

A trial court does not abuse its discretion in failing to grant a wife sustenance alimony where the wife does not present evidence relating to the relevant statutory factors in RC 3105.18. Ellars v. Ellars (Franklin 1990) 69 Ohio App.3d 712, 591 N.E.2d 783.

A trial court's failure to set forth the basis for its award of sustenance alimony warrants vacation of the award and a remand of the matter to the trial court for a redetermination of the award and the inclusion of a basis for the award. Moro v. Moro (Cuyahoga 1990) 68 Ohio App.3d 630, 589 N.E.2d 416.

In the awarding of alimony, tax-shelter consequences may be considered as a factor. Birath v. Birath (Franklin 1988) 53 Ohio App.3d 31, 558 N.E.2d 63, motion overruled 39 Ohio St.3d 730, 534 N.E.2d 357.

A law degree is not marital property, although it may be taken into account in the determination of an equitable alimony award under RC 3105.18; the degree is not tangible property that can be conveyed and any attempt at precise evaluation would require an unacceptable amount of speculation and an assumption that the degreed spouse would prosper and remain in the field; if the assumption were wrong the property award still could not be modified. Josselson v. Josselson (Cuyahoga 1988) 52 Ohio App.3d 60, 557 N.E.2d 835, appeal dismissed 41 Ohio St.3d 721, 535 N.E.2d 305, appeal dismissed 41 Ohio St.3d 726, 536 N.E.2d 381.

Sustenance alimony and property-division alimony are two different types of alimony, and in deciding whether to award either or both types of alimony, a trial court must consider every factor listed in RC 3105.18(B). Pacht v. Jadd (Franklin 1983) 13 Ohio App.3d 363, 469 N.E.2d 918, 13 O.B.R. 444.

The provision of RC 3105.18(B)(3) which requires a trial court to consider retirement and pension benefits in connection with an alimony award does not require the court to divide the retirement funds or potential benefits between the parties at the time of the divorce decree where to do so would destroy the value of the property right and the division of assets is equitable in other respects. Blair v. Blair (Franklin 1983) 11 Ohio App.3d 117, 463 N.E.2d 423, 11 O.B.R. 171.

In an action for divorce and alimony the court may allow alimony as it deems reasonable, having due regard to property which came to either the husband or the wife by their marriage, the earning capacity of either and the value of the real and personal estate of either at the time of the decree in such action. Hill v. Hill (Mahoning 1955) 100 Ohio App. 281, 136 N.E.2d 131, 60 O.O. 230.

Trial court does not abuse its discretion in awarding minimal spousal support in the amount of $150 a month for five years or until the death of either party or the remarriage or cohabitation of the spouse where the reasons for the court's decision include (1) the length of the marriage, (2) the increase in the standard of living that results from the spouse's inheritance, and (3) the fact that the difference in the incomes of the parties is unlikely to change. Myers v Myers, No. L-99-1168, 2000 WL 331573 (6th Dist Ct App, Lucas, 3-31-00).

Financial misconduct does not occur when one spouse leaves the marital residence and the other spouse as the sole occupant stops making the mortgage payments where both parties are owners of the marital residence and are equally responsible for the payments and taxes; and so a court does not err in assessing each of the parties one half of the tax assessment and deficiency judgments in a foreclosure action. Phillips v Phillips, No. 99 CA 1495, 2000 WL 282306 (2d Dist Ct App, Darke, 3-17-00).

Trial court abused its discretion in arriving at the award for spousal support, where the award for spousal support was arbitrary and not supported by the trial record. McEaneney v McEaneney, No. 19555, 2000 WL 141060 (9th Dist Ct App, Summit, 2-2-00).

A property settlement of 1.2 million dollars of which a significant percentage is liquid assets which are available to the spouse and upon which investment income is available and expected should be considered by the trial court in determining spousal support. Thomas v Thomas, No. 96APE07-949, 1997 WL 254115 (10th Dist Ct App, Franklin, 5-13-97).

Absent evidence of one spouse's need for support and the other spouse's ability to pay, the trial court abuses its discretion in awarding spousal support. Murphy v Murphy, No. 15693, 1996 WL 629522 (2d Dist Ct App, Montgomery, 11-1-96).

Spousal support is warranted where it is based upon the wife's (1) employment related arthritis, (2) limited education and earning potential, (3) overcrowded living conditions, and (4) responsibilities as custodial and residential parent for three of the four children for at least three years; in addition, the husband was awarded a residence with no mortgage and the award is less than $50 per week and scheduled to terminate in three years. Slivka v Slivka, No. 69146, 1996 WL 100854 (8th Dist Ct App, Cuyahoga, 3-7-96).

Where a court grants a wife spousal support and requires the husband to make the monthly marital debt payments in its Civ R 75(M) temporary order then, upon hearing, enters a modification order that reduces the husband's spousal support payments but does not specifically state who is to pay the monthly marital debt, a court's failure to continue spousal support in the final divorce decree because the wife fails to make the monthly marital debt payments between the time of the temporary order and the final hearing is error where the wife clearly demonstrates need for support under the factors enumerated in RC 3105.18. Rockford v Rockford, No. H-93-026, 1994 WL 455673 (6th Dist Ct App, Huron, 8-19-94).

Court's comment at trial prior to hearing evidence indicating a predetermination to divide parties' income equally was not error where judgment entry confirms court based its decision on consideration of factors in RC 3105.18. Sollberger v Sollberger, No. 15796, 1993 WL 84546 and 1993 WL 86762 (9th Dist Ct App, Summit, 3-17-93).

Where a domestic relations judge awards alimony in a remanded cause on the basis of evidence of expenses that is five years old, because the payee spouse did not appear, the judgment is unsupported by probative, material evidence and the cause may be remanded a second time. Adler v Adler, No. 10-211 (11th Dist Ct App, Lake, 9-13-85).

The burden of presenting relevant evidence as to the factors to be considered in awarding alimony is upon the parties to the suit and not upon the trial court. Briganti v Briganti, No. 82 CA 31 (7th Dist Ct App, Mahoning, 12-20-82), affirmed by 9 OS(3d) 220, 9 OBR 529, 459 NE(2d) 896 (1984).

A court's award of alimony is determined by other factors besides a possible need for sustenance, such as the duration of the marriage, the standard of living of the parties established during the marriage, the property brought to the marriage by either party, the contribution of a spouse as homemaker, and the relative situation of the parties. Hosford v Hosford, No. 40380 (8th Dist Ct App, Cuyahoga, 3-6-80).

Where the trial court fails to consider the relative earning abilities of the parties, the physical condition of the parties, the relative assets and liabilities of the parties, and several other factors, the trial court errs in awarding the wife the entire house while not holding her liable on the mortgage and in awarding the wife $3,500 as well as $750 for attorneys' fees. Smith v Smith, No. 40347 (8th Dist Ct App, Cuyahoga, 2-7-80).

On petition of wife for separate maintenance and support, station of life of parties and their accustomed manner of living were pertinent in determining amount husband should pay, but financial ability of husband to provide means of maintaining wife and children in way to which they were accustomed or which would be more desirable would control award. Hill v. Hill (Franklin 1953) 115 N.E.2d 399, 65 Ohio Law Abs. 572.

Amount of the estates of the respective parties when married, respective abilities to work and earn money in the future, and past earnings may be considered on question of alimony. Bryant v. Bryant (Mahoning 1949) 91 N.E.2d 275, 56 Ohio Law Abs. 107.

6. —Relative earning ability, factors to consider in award

A professional degree or license is not marital property and the present value of the projected future earnings of the degreed spouse is not a marital asset subject to division upon divorce. Although not an asset, the future value of a professional degree or license acquired by one of the parties during the marriage is an element to be considered in reaching an equitable award of alimony in accordance with RC 3105.18. Stevens v. Stevens (Ohio 1986) 23 Ohio St.3d 115, 492 N.E.2d 131, 23 O.B.R. 273.

Increase in former wife's annual income from $11,444 to $16,120, and decrease in her monthly expenses from $1,969 to $1,402, was within contemplation of parties at time of divorce and did not constitute substantial change in circumstances justifying termination or modification of former husband's spousal support obligation; trial court's findings contemplated increase in wife's earning potential, husband's earning capacity still greatly exceeded wife's, and elimination of mortgage payments for which wife shared responsibility was contemplated at time of divorce. Moore v. Moore (Ohio App. 9 Dist. 1997) 120 Ohio App.3d 488, 698 N.E.2d 459.

Award of $600 per month in spousal support to wife for period of six years following divorce was not an abuse of discretion; husband had gross annual income of over $50,000, while wife's gross income was $16,200, and although wife was also receiving $716.65 in monthly child support, she was obligated to meet monthly mortgage payments on marital home. Munroe v. Munroe (Ohio App. 8 Dist. 1997) 119 Ohio App.3d 530, 695 N.E.2d 1155.

Trial court's award in divorce action of $1,000 per month in spousal support payments to former wife was not abuse of discretion, in light of great disparity in income and work-related benefits between former wife and husband, 30-year length of marriage, and former wife's focus on rearing children instead of developing lucrative career. Hutchinson v. Hutchinson (Clermont 1996) 113 Ohio App.3d 863, 682 N.E.2d 698.

Wife was entitled to permanent spousal support upon divorce, where marriage spanned 20 years, wife was in midfifties, and wife was qualified for only unskilled or semiskilled work due to lack of fluency in English. Soley v. Soley (Lucas 1995) 101 Ohio App.3d 540, 655 N.E.2d 1381, dismissed, appeal not allowed 73 Ohio St.3d 1410, 651 N.E.2d 1308, certiorari denied 116 S.Ct. 945, 133 L.Ed.2d 870.

Trial court did not abuse its discretion in determining that seven-year period of continuing spousal support would provide sufficient transitional period in which former wife could resolve alleged personal physical and mental problems and reenter job market; former wife had recently earned graduate degree in counseling and human services, and was licensed to work as social worker under direction of licensed psychologist or medical doctor. Terry v. Terry (Cuyahoga 1994) 99 Ohio App.3d 228, 650 N.E.2d 184.

Award of spousal support, totaling $6,000 before taxes over a period of two years, was reasonable and not an abuse of discretion considering that husband's annual income was approximately $46,000, wife's annual income was approximately $29,000, husband received an interest in various employer-sponsored pension plans which were not available to wife through her employer, and wife had only a high school education while husband had completed at least two years of college. Peck v. Peck (Butler 1994) 96 Ohio App.3d 731, 645 N.E.2d 1300.

Wife had sufficient "need" for spousal support to justify award of $600 per month, though trial court found that she was self-supporting and was capable of living well within her current income of approximately $32,000 per year, where wife was planning on spending great deal of money and time to give herself education which would fulfill requirements of her present job. Adams v. Adams (Marion 1994) 95 Ohio App.3d 419, 642 N.E.2d 677.

To extent one spouse has ability to pay necessary fees incurred by other spouse in divorce action, while spouse incurring those fees lacks that ability, it is appropriate for court to shift fees to spouse who can afford to pay them because of previous contributions made to marital partnership by spouse lacking ability to pay. Clark v. Joseph (Summit 1994) 95 Ohio App.3d 207, 642 N.E.2d 36.

Awarding former wife approximately two thirds of marital property while ordering former husband to pay real estate tax delinquency on marital residence, alleged temporary support arrearage, and part of former wife's attorney fees and part of husband's girlfriend's attorney fees was abuse of discretion where trial court failed to consider former husband's ability to pay the obligations, which had decreased due to drop in income following his bankruptcy. Gullia v. Gullia (Cuyahoga 1994) 93 Ohio App.3d 653, 639 N.E.2d 822, cause dismissed 70 Ohio St.3d 1409, 637 N.E.2d 6, dismissed, jurisdictional motion overruled 70 Ohio St.3d 1409, 637 N.E.2d 7.

Trial court committed abuse of discretion in awarding to former wife $25,000 for attorney fees and $30,000 per year for life or until remarriage where husband's net income had not exceeded $27,500 since his bankruptcy some years earlier. Gullia v. Gullia (Cuyahoga 1994) 93 Ohio App.3d 653, 639 N.E.2d 822, cause dismissed 70 Ohio St.3d 1409, 637 N.E.2d 6, dismissed, jurisdictional motion overruled 70 Ohio St.3d 1409, 637 N.E.2d 7.

Trial court's failure to consider wife's calculated earning ability as teacher of $1,250 a month when awarding wife permanent spousal support of $5,000 a month was not abuse of discretion, in light of current job market for teachers in area. Turner v. Turner (Franklin 1993) 90 Ohio App.3d 161, 628 N.E.2d 110, motion overruled 68 Ohio St.3d 1430, 624 N.E.2d 1067.

Trial court's decision not to award wife sustenance alimony was supported by evidence, which indicated that she was earning salary of $47,000 as teacher prior to separation, that husband was earning $62,909.64, and that prior to separation wife withdrew $14,400 from parties' credit union account and transferred it to account belonging to her parents. Ingalls v. Ingalls (Cuyahoga 1993) 88 Ohio App.3d 570, 624 N.E.2d 368.

Award of spousal support to wife, which was taxable income to her and tax deductible by husband, was not abuse of discretion, despite fact court had already awarded wife substantial investment and passive income assets; there was evidence that wife was not capable of gainful employment, either part-time or full-time. Frost v. Frost (Franklin 1992) 84 Ohio App.3d 699, 618 N.E.2d 198, motion overruled 66 Ohio St.3d 1489, 612 N.E.2d 1245.

Divorce court is within its discretion to arrive at amounts of spousal support and child support based on different calculations, since calculation for child support is based upon actual wages earned, whereas calculation of spousal support is determined by earning capacity. Frost v. Frost (Franklin 1992) 84 Ohio App.3d 699, 618 N.E.2d 198, motion overruled 66 Ohio St.3d 1489, 612 N.E.2d 1245.

Trial court abused its discretion in ordering definite termination after less than four years of spousal support awarded to wife who was in poor health after 26 year marriage and who had not been employed outside home. Layne v. Layne (Champaign 1992) 83 Ohio App.3d 559, 615 N.E.2d 332.

Award to wife of spousal support in amount of $1,500 monthly for 24 months, and $1,000 per month for additional 24 months, was not abuse of discretion where trial court stated that it had considered statutory factors in determining wife's entitlement to spousal support award, wife earned substantially less than husband, and evidence indicated that wife would be unable to meet her expenses on her current salary. Babka v. Babka (Summit 1992) 83 Ohio App.3d 428, 615 N.E.2d 247.

A trial court properly rules as to a wife's earning potential where the evidence supports the factual conclusion that the wife's potential income is that which she currently earns, and that full-time employment would be inappropriate for her at the present time due to her responsibilities as a custodial parent for the parties' three minor children, in particular, the parties' son who is subject to epileptic seizures which are expected to worsen during puberty. Goode v. Goode (Franklin 1991) 70 Ohio App.3d 125, 590 N.E.2d 439.

In a divorce action, the failure of a trial court to award a wife the parties' residence as alimony in gross does not constitute an abuse of discretion where it is clear that the court considered the statutory factors, as well as all other factors in reaching its determination as to both the division of property and support; the wife, who was forty-six years old, had a ninth grade education, no marketable skills and was totally and permanently disabled with no other source of income besides welfare, and the husband who was forty-four years old, had a high school degree and was employed as a taxicab driver with an annual income of less than $7,000 a year with no health insurance or retirement program through his work. Green v. Green (Erie 1989) 64 Ohio App.3d 37, 580 N.E.2d 513.

A trial court errs in failing to award sustenance alimony where the wife's income is slightly more than minimum wage, she is awarded an equity interest in the marital home payable upon the husband's sale at an unknown date, and the husband's counsel admits in closing argument that the wife needs rehabilitative alimony. Mochko v. Mochko (Cuyahoga 1990) 63 Ohio App.3d 671, 579 N.E.2d 773.

A sole practitioner's law practice is not a marital asset and is to be considered in determining alimony only insofar as it affects the attorney's earning capacity. Josselson v. Josselson (Cuyahoga 1988) 52 Ohio App.3d 60, 557 N.E.2d 835, appeal dismissed 41 Ohio St.3d 721, 535 N.E.2d 305, appeal dismissed 41 Ohio St.3d 726, 536 N.E.2d 381.

The fact that one spouse obtained a medical degree during a marriage should be considered when applying RC 3105.18 to insure an equitable alimony award; however, the "value" of a medical degree is not divisible between two parties upon any exact basis. Gebhart v. Gebhart (Montgomery 1984) 14 Ohio App.3d 107, 470 N.E.2d 205, 14 O.B.R. 121.

A license to practice medicine and a teaching certificate do not constitute divisible marital assets and are not to be considered by the trial court under RC 3105.18(B)(9); however, the trial court may consider such license and certificate as they affect other factors listed in RC 3105.18(B), such as the parties' relative earning capacities, educations, and expectations. Pacht v. Jadd (Franklin 1983) 13 Ohio App.3d 363, 469 N.E.2d 918, 13 O.B.R. 444.

To determine the reasonable amount of alimony under RC 3105.18(B), "[t]he relative earning abilities of the parties" should be considered, rather than the failure to seek or obtain employment; where a party is unemployed, in the absence of evidence that employment cannot be obtained, his or her earning ability is deemed to be that which such party could earn if employment were sought. Haninger v. Haninger (Franklin 1982) 8 Ohio App.3d 286, 456 N.E.2d 1228, 8 O.B.R. 380.

An award of spousal support is not appropriate where the husband is imprisoned for abusing the parties' oldest daughter and it can safely be presumed that (1) he would be released from prison at age sixty-three, (2) he would be unable to support himself by working due to his age and disability, and (3) he will need his pension and his share of the equity from the marital residence for living expenses. Kelly v Kelly, No. CA97-11-099, 1998 WL 281344 (12th Dist Ct App, Clermont, 6-1-98).

Spousal support in the amount of $1000 per month is not an abuse of discretion based upon (1) wife's support of husband while he obtains his undergraduate education, (2) wife's lost income production capacity as a result of her substantial marital and parental responsibilities, and (3) a close margin between wife's income and expenses. Rheude v Rheude, No. CA96-10-084, 1997 WL 226207 (12th Dist Ct App, Clermont, 5-5-97).

An award and finding of need for permanent spousal support of $600 per month is supported by evidence of (1) husband's earnings in excess of twice the amount of his spouse, (2) his retirement benefits being considerably more than the spouse's, and (3) the spouse at age 50 without a college degree has little likelihood of earning a self-supporting income. Shepherd v Shepherd, No. 70134, 1996 WL 631051 (8th Dist Ct App, Cuyahoga, 10-31-96).

A trial judge is in no position to balance the payee's need with the payor's ability to pay in making an independent assessment of the appropriate amount of spousal support where the referee fails to set forth the necessary factual findings regarding (1) the husband's income as sole proprietor of a business, (2) his income from sources other than the business, or (3) his earning ability. Miller v Miller, No. 14540, 1994 WL 730560 (2d Dist Ct App, Montgomery, 12-28-94).

Where a trial court fails to consider the relative earning abilities of the parties and the duration of their marriage, the award of spousal support will be reversed. Edgell v Edgell, No. 2945 (2d Dist Ct App, Clark, 3-3-93).

A trial court errs in awarding as alimony a fixed percentage of an obligee's social security benefits. Edwards v Edwards, No. 651 (4th Dist Ct App, Jackson, 8-26-91).

A spouse's solo law practice is not a marital asset since it cannot be freely bought or sold as property due to ethical constraints; however, the value of a solo law practice is primarily in its earning capacity, and a party's earning ability is one of the factors under RC 3105.18(B)(1) which a court must consider. Josselson v Josselson, No. 54542 (8th Dist Ct App, Cuyahoga, 10-27-88).

There is no requirement for a separate valuation as an asset of a license to practice law which was acquired during marriage, so long as the effect of the license is properly considered in determining the relative earning capacities of the parties. Adkins v Adkins, No. 82-CA-32 (4th Dist Ct App, Pickaway, 8-30-84).

In a divorce proceeding trial court abused its discretion in awarding child support and alimony payments without requiring evidence of both parties' wages. Geiner v Geiner, No. WD-82-11 (6th Dist Ct App, Wood, 8-13-82).

Where a divorce decree calls for alimony payments based on fifty percent of a spouse's adjusted income, the term "adjusted income," although ambiguous by itself, will be construed to mean income after adjustments for state, federal, and local taxes, where both spouses testify to such an interpretation and the divorce decree requires the submission of state, federal, and local income tax returns each year to the spouse receiving the alimony. Kellogg v Kellogg, No. 7681 (2d Dist Ct App, Montgomery, 7-8-82).

In a divorce proceeding, take-home pay is not the equivalent of "relative earning abilities of the parties" for purposes of awarding a property settlement nor is take-home pay the determinative factor in arriving at an order for child support. Hanney v Hanney, No. OT-81-25 (6th Dist Ct App, Ottawa, 5-7-82).

Even though a judgment decree did not specifically make a finding of need, the fact that the wife has only recently gotten into the job market after twenty-two years as a homemaker, wife and mother is an inference sufficient to sustain the necessity for an award. Pasterczyk v Pasterczyk, No. 43595 (8th Dist Ct App, Cuyahoga, 12-24-81).

Where the wife earns only half of what her husband earns at the time of the trial, has custodial responsibility for the parties' child in addition to a fifteen-year-old daughter from a previous marriage, and the parties had modest accumulations during their marriage, it is not an abuse of discretion for the court to award the wife substantially all of the assets and to hold the husband liable for marital debts attributable to the assets. Loucka v Loucka, No. 43302 (8th Dist Ct App, Cuyahoga, 10-15-81).

An award of alimony coupled with the provision of a debt-free home to the wife does not indicate an abuse of discretion by the trial court where the wife has no earning capacity, no employment, and emotional problems due to the death of her son, especially since the decree specifically states that after five years the alimony shall be reconsidered by the court. Crowell v Crowell, No. F-81-2 (6th Dist Ct App, Fulton, 9-25-81).

The condition subsequent to an alimony award that such alimony will cease upon the attainment of age eighteen by the parties' son is an unreasonable condition, as child support is separately provided and the alimony award is in the nature of support to the plaintiff-appellant; also, the condition subsequent to an alimony award that such will cease upon the gainful employment of the recipient at an annual salary in excess of $10,000 is unreasonable, considering the plaintiff-appellant's accustomed standard of living and the current rate of inflation, therefore benefits shall terminate if the appellant receives an annual income in excess of $20,000. Woods v Woods, No. 79-CA-2 (2d Dist Ct App, Fayette, 8-15-80).

Where a physician has completed the necessary educational requirements to qualify to practice medicine, the amount he actually earns while in residency is not fairly indicative of his "earning capacity" as that term is used in RC 3105.18. Daniels v. Daniels (Montgomery 1961) 185 N.E.2d 773, 90 Ohio Law Abs. 161, 20 O.O.2d 458.

Trial court, in determining what constituted a reasonable alimony award to husband in his divorce suit, properly considered its special findings that wife was a trained and skilled registered nurse, in a good state of health, and of the age of 29 years, while husband was of the age of 51 years, in ill health, and might not be able to resume his medical practice for quite some period of time, if ever. Sharkey v. Sharkey (Montgomery 1955) 137 N.E.2d 575, 73 Ohio Law Abs. 321.

Where a decree for divorce is granted to a wife on account of aggression of her husband, allowance of alimony may be based on future personal earnings or wages of husband, and court is not limited to consideration of property in possession of husband at time of decree. Washington v. Washington (Montgomery 1950) 103 N.E.2d 300, 61 Ohio Law Abs. 52.

A former husband having $1800 left as monthly net income after paying child support cannot discharge in bankruptcy his obligation under the separation agreement to pay $7050 of joint credit card debts where his former wife's earnings are less than her expenses; in such a case, the court will determine that the obligation is in the nature of support and hence not dischargeable. In re Eikenberg (Bkrtcy.N.D.Ohio 1989) 107 B.R. 139.

7. —Ages, physical and emotional condition, factors to consider in award

Trial court did not abuse its discretion in determining that payment of sustenance alimony in amount of $2,000 per month to wife was "necessary," where wife was over 60 years old and had physical health problems, she could no longer work, her expenses exceeded alimony payments, and husband earned approximately $120,000 per year from medical practice and earned about $50,000 from retirement account in one year. Mottice v. Mottice (Ohio App. 9 Dist. 1997) 118 Ohio App.3d 731, 693 N.E.2d 1179.

Trial court's decision to award spousal support to former wife, in form of distributive award of remainder interest in former husband's separate property, was abuse of discretion; former husband was 71 years old and was suffering from advanced lung cancer, but former wife was 54 years old, in good health, and able to work. Swartz v. Swartz (Warren 1996) 110 Ohio App.3d 218, 673 N.E.2d 972.

Former wife was properly allowed to testify, as part of determining alimony and property division awards, regarding knee injury she sustained after parties' separation, despite absence of expert testimony, where former wife's testimony was about her own medical condition and former wife was subject to cross-examination. Gullia v. Gullia (Cuyahoga 1994) 93 Ohio App.3d 653, 639 N.E.2d 822, cause dismissed 70 Ohio St.3d 1409, 637 N.E.2d 6, dismissed, jurisdictional motion overruled 70 Ohio St.3d 1409, 637 N.E.2d 7.

Ordering husband to pay permanent spousal support of $5,000 a month was not abuse of discretion, despite wife's teaching degree, where wife had health problems which seriously impeded her employment chances. Turner v. Turner (Franklin 1993) 90 Ohio App.3d 161, 628 N.E.2d 110, motion overruled 68 Ohio St.3d 1430, 624 N.E.2d 1067.

Failure to consider relative age of parties in dividing pension funds was not abuse of discretion where pension benefits were included in property settlement; although spousal support statute requires court to consider age of parties and divide pension fund in proportion to that age difference, statute dealing with division of marital property does not require court to consider relative age of parties. Babka v. Babka (Summit 1992) 83 Ohio App.3d 428, 615 N.E.2d 247.

A property settlement awarding a seventy-one-year-old party a pension plan with a present value approximately equal to the value of the marital home awarded to the other spouse is inequitable where the pension cannot be converted into a lump-sum payment, since a seventy-one-year-old pensioner receiving a monthly benefit of $751 is unlikely to receive the present value of the asset during his lifetime. Ralston v. Ralston (Hamilton 1989) 61 Ohio App.3d 346, 572 N.E.2d 791.

A trial court is given broad discretion in determining the appropriate scope of an alimony award based upon the particular facts and circumstances of each case, and where the parties have been married twenty-nine years, both are of an advanced age, and the homemaker spouse has had little opportunity to develop a career as her husband objected to her working during the marriage, the trial court may award alimony terminable only upon certain contingencies such as the death or remarriage of the recipient of the award or further order of the court. Noll v. Noll (Sandusky 1989) 55 Ohio App.3d 160, 563 N.E.2d 44.

Where an award of sustenance alimony is "non-modifiable" under the terms of a final decree of divorce, it is error for a court to deny a motion for a new trial based on the newly discovered evidence that the moving party sustained physical injuries rendering him incapable of working. Marksbury v. Marksbury (Erie 1988) 46 Ohio App.3d 17, 545 N.E.2d 651.

A court may vacate a judgment concerning alimony when it transpires that the court in rendering the judgment had failed to consider a deposition on a party's health which was relevant under RC 3105.18(B)(2) and was acknowledged to be part of the record. Reichert v. Reichert (Summit 1985) 23 Ohio App.3d 67, 491 N.E.2d 376, 23 O.B.R. 112.

Spousal support of $2000 per month is appropriate to wife who is under a medical disability which currently prevents her from working to support herself and severely limits any potential income; in addition, the court rules appropriately concerning husband's objections to wife's physical condition when a question called for an opinion concerning medical causation and husband's objection was sustained and when the question called for wife to testify concerning her own first-hand experience of her physical condition the objection was overruled because her own experience of her physical condition was not in the nature of opinion testimony requiring expertise pursuant to Evid R 702. Mills v Mills, No. 17637, 1999 WL 1082646 (2d Dist Ct App, Montgomery, 12-3-99).

An indefinite term of spousal support in the amount of $1,750 per month to a wife of twenty-five years who is unemployed and suffers from multiple sclerosis is not an abuse of discretion. Carruth v Carruth, No. 2761-M, 1999 WL 33430 (9th Dist Ct App, Medina, 1-27-99).

Award of eight years of spousal support to a seventy-two-year-old wife who was in a marriage of long duration and is a homemaker-spouse with little opportunity to develop a meaningful employment outside the home is an abuse of discretion where during the marriage she is subjected to (1) threats by her husband and his family to kill her by letting the brake fluid out of her car, (2) her husband's attempts to poison and electrocute her, and (3) her husband's son lurking around the house by hiding in bushes and feeding the dogs treats so they would not chase him. Taylor v Taylor, No. 97 CA 2537, 1998 WL 603142 (4th Dist Ct App, Scioto, 8-4-98).

Reduction of spousal support is warranted where the husband is a sixty-nine-year-old self-employed electrical designer who has to reduce his working hours from a previous workload of seventy hours per week to forty hours due to a heart attack and subsequent open heart surgery. Frederick v Frederick, No. 72156, 1998 WL 83222 (8th Dist Ct App, Cuyahoga, 2-26-98).

Spousal support of over $2000 per month for an indefinite period is not unreasonable considering that the payee (1) suffers from depression caused by unresolved issues from her childhood, (2) cannot function without antidepressant medication, (3) will need medical support for the next several years, and (4) may have trouble maintaining employment due to memory and concentration problems, moodiness and absenteeism caused by her illness. Smith v Smith, No. 97 CA 12, 1998 WL 46682 (2d Dist Ct App, Champaign, 2-6-98).

A trial court's errors in judgment in its division of marital assets or the award of sustenance alimony to appellee for three years is not an abuse of discretion considering appellee's health, earning power of the parties, and the nature of the marital assets. Barr v Barr, No. CA5469 (5th Dist Ct App, Stark, 6-24-81).

Where a totally disabled wife receives $876 a month gross income, but where the court did not consider the wife's monthly gasoline and maintenance expenses for her automobile, or her monthly clothing allotment, it is an abuse of discretion for the trial court not to have awarded sustenance alimony in this particular case. Reincheld v Reincheld, No. 80AP-286 (10th Dist Ct App, Franklin, 10-23-80).

The trial court erred in failing to award permanent sustenance alimony to a permanently totally disabled party, even though a favorable property settlement was granted to such party, as the facts show that the disabled party earned significantly less income than the healthy party who was able to work, and the trial court failed to consider certain monthly maintenance expenses. Reincheld v Reincheld, No. 80AP-286 (10th Dist Ct App, Franklin, 10-23-80).

8. —Retirement benefits, factors to consider in award

Vested pension plan accumulated during marriage is marital asset that must be considered in arriving at equitable division of property. Bisker v. Bisker (Ohio 1994) 69 Ohio St.3d 608, 635 N.E.2d 308.

Where record did not indicate that trial court ever reviewed retirement benefits of parties in fashioning division of marital property, at either first or second divorce proceeding, orders were incorrect as matter of law; court's failure to conduct independent review of marital assets during first divorce proceeding was error which could not be corrected by parties' subsequent remarriage. Bisker v. Bisker (Ohio 1994) 69 Ohio St.3d 608, 635 N.E.2d 308.

When considering a fair and equitable distribution of pension or retirement benefits in a divorce, the trial court must apply its discretion based on (1) the circumstances of the case; (2) the status of the parties; (3) the nature, terms, and conditions of the pension or retirement plan; and (4) the reasonableness of the result. Hoyt v. Hoyt (Ohio 1990) 53 Ohio St.3d 177, 559 N.E.2d 1292.

A trial court should attempt to preserve a pension or retirement asset in order that each party can procure the most benefit, and the court should attempt to disentangle the parties' economic partnership so as to create a conclusion and finality to the marriage. Hoyt v. Hoyt (Ohio 1990) 53 Ohio St.3d 177, 559 N.E.2d 1292.

A vested pension plan accumulated during marriage is a marital asset and must be considered in conjunction with other factors listed under RC 3105.18 and other relevant factors in dividing marital assets and liabilities to ensure that the result reached is equitable. Holcomb v. Holcomb (Ohio 1989) 44 Ohio St.3d 128, 541 N.E.2d 597.

An equal division of military retirement benefits among the parties to a divorce action is not an abuse of discretion. Teeter v. Teeter (Ohio 1985) 18 Ohio St.3d 76, 479 N.E.2d 890, 18 O.B.R. 106.

Provision of divorce decree stating that wife would receive spousal support in amount representing the difference between 43.24% of husband's gross military retirement pay and 43.24% of his disposable military retirement pay did not violate Uniformed Services Former Spouses' Protection Act. Blissit v. Blissit (Ohio App. 2 Dist. 1997) 122 Ohio App.3d 727, 702 N.E.2d 945.

The Uniformed Services Former Spouses' Protection Act does not preclude parties to a divorce from using gross military retired pay to calculate an agreed-upon sum for spousal support. Blissit v. Blissit (Ohio App. 2 Dist. 1997) 122 Ohio App.3d 727, 702 N.E.2d 945.

Former wife's contributions to pension account, to savings account, and to charity were not expenses to be deducted from her income in determining her need for spousal support; furthermore, income from pension had to be included. Carnahan v. Carnahan (Ohio App. 12 Dist. 1997) 118 Ohio App.3d 393, 692 N.E.2d 1086.

Trial court was required to give former husband credit, in determining his ability to pay spousal support, for pension funds that were awarded to him in the divorce and that he used to reduce his monthly housing expenses; failure to do so penalized former husband for using his own money to lower his monthly housing expense. Carnahan v. Carnahan (Ohio App. 12 Dist. 1997) 118 Ohio App.3d 393, 692 N.E.2d 1086.

Trial court could properly consider ex-husband's previously divided pension benefits as a source of income for spousal support purposes. Lindsay v. Curtis (Ohio App. 12 Dist. 1996) 115 Ohio App.3d 742, 686 N.E.2d 313.

There was no abuse of discretion in the trial court's refusal to terminate ex-husband's spousal support obligation and requiring him to pay $156 per week, given that the parties were married for 37 years and were now in their sixties, that wife was a homemaker during the entire marriage and had extensive medical problems, and that husband received net severance benefit of $37,000 and was receiving total of $2,127 per month from Social Security and pension. Lindsay v. Curtis (Ohio App. 12 Dist. 1996) 115 Ohio App.3d 742, 686 N.E.2d 313.

There was no abuse of discretion by the trial court in finding ex-husband in contempt for admitted failure to pay spousal support following retirement. Lindsay v. Curtis (Ohio App. 12 Dist. 1996) 115 Ohio App.3d 742, 686 N.E.2d 313.

Marriage did not end on date of separation of husband and wife, but rather continued until date of final hearing in divorce action, and thus trial court's valuation of retirement funds as of date of hearing for purpose of property division was proper; after they separated, husband and wife divided family responsibilities, saw each other regularly, spent holidays together with family, and maintained conjugal relationship, husband continued to pay significant portion of family's expenses while wife remained primarily responsible for children, and when wife filed prior complaint for divorce, husband convinced her to dismiss it. Hutchinson v. Hutchinson (Clermont 1996) 113 Ohio App.3d 863, 682 N.E.2d 698.

Order permitting agency that distributed husband's civil service pension checks to deduct fee to cover its costs of complying with order withholding portion of those checks to pay husband's alimony obligation did not amount to modification of alimony award. Holloman v. Holloman (Montgomery 1993) 91 Ohio App.3d 279, 632 N.E.2d 575.

Trial court's failure to value former husband's nonvested pension and failure to award former wife his military survivor benefits, in awarding former wife one half of military retirement pay from date of marriage through end of 1990, was not unreasonable; evidence indicated that pension would not become vested until early 1992, transcript showed that former wife's counsel stipulated on record that parties were in agreement concerning provision of military pension, and division of pension plan appeared to conform to agreement. Ingalls v. Ingalls (Cuyahoga 1993) 88 Ohio App.3d 570, 624 N.E.2d 368.

Failure to consider relative age of parties in dividing pension funds was not abuse of discretion where pension benefits were included in property settlement; although spousal support statute requires court to consider age of parties and divide pension fund in proportion to that age difference, statute dealing with division of marital property does not require court to consider relative age of parties. Babka v. Babka (Summit 1992) 83 Ohio App.3d 428, 615 N.E.2d 247.

Equal division of husband's pension funds, without taking into account monies which would be lost by forced early withdrawal from funds, was not abuse of discretion where trial court did not order husband to withdraw assets from his pension funds, but rather ordered that husband's proceeds from sale of marital residence be distributed to wife in order to avoid early withdrawal penalties and protect pension funds. Babka v. Babka (Summit 1992) 83 Ohio App.3d 428, 615 N.E.2d 247.

A court need not divide a pension equally in a spousal support and property division determination; it may start on an equal basis, and upon a consideration of the duration of the marriage and the assets of parties arrive at a different result. Guziak v. Guziak (Summit 1992) 80 Ohio App.3d 805, 610 N.E.2d 1135, motion overruled 65 Ohio St.3d 1478, 604 N.E.2d 169.

An award of half of a PERS pension income to the payee spouse is alimony to be deducted from the payor spouse's gross income and included in the payee spouse's gross income; thus, the court need not further apportion tax liability from PERS payments. Guziak v. Guziak (Summit 1992) 80 Ohio App.3d 805, 610 N.E.2d 1135, motion overruled 65 Ohio St.3d 1478, 604 N.E.2d 169.

A trial court errs in awarding a spouse forty per cent of a spouse's retirement benefits which has the effect of awarding the nonowner spouse all of the benefits determined to be marital assets where it appears that the court was attempting to effect an equal division of the benefits. Connolly v. Connolly (Cuyahoga 1990) 70 Ohio App.3d 738, 591 N.E.2d 1362.

Where alimony awarded to a former wife was based partially on the rationale that the alimony award compensated the wife for retirement savings accrued by her and her former husband during their thirty-year marriage, and where there was no express reservation of jurisdiction to modify alimony, a refusal by the trial court to modify the alimony order is proper. Mullins v. Mullins (Paulding 1990) 69 Ohio App.3d 167, 590 N.E.2d 311.

A trial court does not abuse its discretion in awarding a wife, as part of an alimony settlement, thirty per cent of the husband's retirement benefits when they become payable where the court allows for any inequity that might result from an increase in the husband's benefits through his post-divorce employment by awarding the wife only the reduced thirty per cent share of the total benefits and by retaining continuing jurisdiction over the other portions of the alimony award. Campitelli v. Campitelli (Stark 1989) 65 Ohio App.3d 307, 583 N.E.2d 1322.

A spouse's pension or retirement plan, to the extent it was accumulated during the marriage, is a marital asset subject to division and must be considered in determining an award of alimony. Diefenthaler v. Diefenthaler (Ottawa 1989) 63 Ohio App.3d 845, 580 N.E.2d 477.

When pension and retirement plans are not terminated at the time of the divorce, the future tax consequences can only be estimated since it is not known at the time of divorce what the tax rates will be, or what the employee spouse's taxable income will be at the time of distribution, and whether the value of a party's pension and retirement plans which are not immediately terminated should be reduced by estimated future tax consequences on distribution and by how much is a factor best left to the discretion of the trial court after hearing all the evidence and any expert testimony as to those tax consequences. Noll v. Noll (Sandusky 1989) 55 Ohio App.3d 160, 563 N.E.2d 44.

In a divorce action, the trial court may either divide the interest in a retirement plan or award it entirely to one party depending on what would be equitable in the circumstances. Welly v. Welly (Williams 1988) 55 Ohio App.3d 111, 562 N.E.2d 914.

In awarding alimony the court has discretion to consider the future distribution to one spouse of a proportionate share of the other spouse's pension fund under a qualified domestic relations order, as an alternative to equitably dividing and distributing pension benefits given the parties' needs and means. Powell v. Powell (Lucas 1989) 49 Ohio App.3d 56, 550 N.E.2d 538.

An unvested pension may be a marital asset under RC 3105.18 and in determining whether the unvested pension is a marital asset the court should consider the time left before the pension becomes vested, the length of the marriage between the parties, and the contributions of the parties both primarily and secondarily to the pension plan. Lemon v. Lemon (Hocking 1988) 42 Ohio App.3d 142, 537 N.E.2d 246.

A trial court's failure to consider whether or not a spouse's pension plan may properly be subject to a "qualified domestic relations order" pursuant to 29 USC 1056 constitutes an abuse of discretion. Day v. Day (Franklin 1988) 40 Ohio App.3d 155, 532 N.E.2d 201.

Husband's workers' compensation and employer's pension benefits which are husband's separate property distributed under RC 3105.171 are to be considered when calculating the parties' income for purposes of spousal support. Johnson v Johnson, No. CA99-01-001, 1999 WL 760978 (12th Dist Ct App, Warren, 9-27-99).

In a distribution of marital property, valuation of a husband's pension fund based upon a future value that is not presently available and will not be available to him until he is sixty years old and has canceled the agency agreement with his employer, is error. Davidson v Davidson, No. 95-CA-07, 1996 WL 86254 (2d Dist Ct App, Champaign, 3-1-96).

A court order regarding distribution of the husband's share of the wife's pension in which the court determines that the sums due will be paid as spousal support so that the husband will be protected if the wife files for bankruptcy must be vacated when the court fails to consider the factors for awarding spousal support enumerated in RC 3105.18. Reitano v Reitano, No. 50-CA-1993, 1994 WL 369412 (5th Dist Ct App, Fairfield, 6-27-94).

Forfeiture of pension rights does not necessarily demonstrate a need for spousal support in any given amount. Alder v Alder, No. CA93-10-209, 1994 WL 178373 (12th Dist Ct App, Butler 5-9-94).

There is no abuse of discretion in ordering the liquidation of a husband's pension plan to pay lump sum alimony and placing the rest of the assets in receivership when that remedy was warranted by the husband closing his solo law practice and his reluctance to pay temporary support; however, the payment must comply with the terms of the pension plan and with ERISA. Josselson v Josselson, No. 54542 (8th Dist Ct App, Cuyahoga, 10-27-88).

Where the court has ordered a husband to pay his wife $75 per week alimony until the husband's death, the wife's death, the wife's remarriage, or further order of the court, based on factors listed in RC 3105.18, it may take into consideration the husband's prospective retirement benefits and modify the award to make it reviewable upon the husband's retirement. Wise v Wise, No. L-86-085 (6th Dist Ct App, Lucas, 3-20-87).

Trial court abused its discretion in finding that a spouse's contribution to a public employees' retirement fund was not to be considered a factor in the division of marital property or alimony award. Briganti v Briganti, No. 82 CA 31 (7th Dist Ct App, Mahoning, 12-20-82), affirmed by 9 OS(3d) 220, 9 OBR 529, 459 NE(2d) 896 (1984).

In determining a husband's retirement benefits, the husband must be allowed to introduce evidence of the loss of a lung before judicial notice of the husband's life expectancy from the United States Life Table may be taken. Halter v Halter, No. 438 (7th Dist Ct App, Carroll, 8-5-81).

Under RC 3105.18, a trial court in a divorce action must consider the pension funds of the parties, but it need not dispose of such funds in any predetermined manner because to hold otherwise would place unwarranted restrictions on the court's exercise of discretion. Brooksieker v Brooksieker, No. D-68611 (8th Dist Ct App, Cuyahoga, 4-26-79).

In an action for divorce, the vested interest of a spouse in a profit-sharing and pension plan which was earned during the marriage is a marital asset subject to division by the court. Bohnlein v. Bohnlein (Ohio Com.Pl. 1983) 11 Ohio Misc.2d 16, 463 N.E.2d 666, 11 O.B.R. 179.

Military retirement pay waived by a veteran of the service to qualify for an equivalent amount of veterans' disability benefits cannot be treated by a state court as property divisible upon divorce under the Uniformed Services Former Spouses Protection Act, 10 USC 1408; under 10 USC 1408(C)(1), state courts may treat disposable retirement pay as community property but not total retirement pay. Mansell v. Mansell (U.S.Cal. 1989) 109 S.Ct. 2023, 490 U.S. 581, 104 L.Ed.2d 675, on remand 217 Cal.App.3d 219, 265 Cal.Rptr. 227, review denied.

9. —Expectancies and inheritances, factors to consider in award

Courts should not give too much weight to the possibility of inheritance unless the expectation is fairly certain; where it is of a highly speculative nature, it should not be considered until actually received. Cherry v. Cherry (Ohio 1981) 66 Ohio St.2d 348, 421 N.E.2d 1293, 20 O.O.3d 318, on remand.

In determining the value of the real and personal estate of a party, the court should give due regard to evidence that the party is a legatee and devisee of an estate which is in the process of administration at the time of the decree. Ziegler v. Ziegler (Ohio 1957) 166 Ohio St. 406, 143 N.E.2d 589, 2 O.O.2d 348.

An inheritance is a proper factor to consider in awarding sustenance alimony but it is not a current asset subject to division. Buckles v. Buckles (Franklin 1988) 46 Ohio App.3d 102, 546 N.E.2d 950.

It is an abuse of discretion for the trial court to consider inherited property of the wife as if it were marital property subject to division because courts regularly do make such a separation in the process of determining an equitable division of marital property under RC 3105.18. McDade v McDade, No. 376 (12th Dist Ct App, Warren, 9-16-81).

Although RC 3105.18 permits the trial court in a divorce proceeding to consider as a relevant factor in determining alimony for either party the expectancies and inheritances of the parties, the wife's mother is not in contempt of court if she refuses to answer questions pertaining to her net worth. In re Shapiro, No. L-76-076 (6th Dist Ct App, Lucas, 4-16-76).

10. —Duration of marriage, factors to consider in award

A marriage of long duration, in and of itself, will permit a trial court to award spousal support of indefinite duration following divorce without abusing its discretion. Bowen v. Bowen (Ohio App. 9 Dist. 1999) 132 Ohio App.3d 616, 725 N.E.2d 1165.

Seven-year spousal support award was not abuse of discretion, in light of 23-year duration of marriage and wide disparity in incomes between parties. Schneider v. Schneider (Geauga 1996) 110 Ohio App.3d 487, 674 N.E.2d 769, appeal not allowed 77 Ohio St.3d 1416, 670 N.E.2d 1004.

Spousal support award of $350 per month for four years was supported by evidence that husband's gross income was more than four times that of wife, that parties had been married for 12 years, and that wife's schedule did not permit her to work more hours. Carman v. Carman (Butler 1996) 109 Ohio App.3d 698, 672 N.E.2d 1093.

Trial court did not abuse discretion by awarding wife one half of parties' marital estate, and denying wife entitlement to share of property previously acquired by husband; marriage had been of short duration, husband's skills and dental practice had been acquired prior to marriage, wife was employable, neither enjoyed high standard of living, and both had significant assets. Verbanic v. Verbanic (Trumbull 1992) 83 Ohio App.3d 327, 614 N.E.2d 1103, cause dismissed 66 Ohio St.3d 1479, 612 N.E.2d 329, rehearing granted 67 Ohio St.3d 1407, 615 N.E.2d 630, reversed 70 Ohio St.3d 41, 635 N.E.2d 1260, reconsideration denied 70 Ohio St.3d 1439, 638 N.E.2d 1042.

A court may consider for spousal support purposes that a relationship lasted for seventeen years, during which time the spouses had divorced once before for a period of five months, in awarding spousal support of indefinite duration in their second divorce action; the fact that the first divorce after twelve years provided for no spousal support does not prevent the court from considering the earlier years of marriage as a "factor" in determining spousal support based on the second marriage. Moore v. Moore (Summit 1992) 83 Ohio App.3d 75, 613 N.E.2d 1097.

A court need not divide a pension equally in a spousal support and property division determination; it may start on an equal basis, and upon a consideration of the duration of the marriage and the assets of parties arrive at a different result. Guziak v. Guziak (Summit 1992) 80 Ohio App.3d 805, 610 N.E.2d 1135, motion overruled 65 Ohio St.3d 1478, 604 N.E.2d 169.

A trial court is given broad discretion in determining the appropriate scope of an alimony award based upon the particular facts and circumstances of each case, and where the parties have been married twenty-nine years, both are of an advanced age, and the homemaker spouse has had little opportunity to develop a career as her husband objected to her working during the marriage, the trial court may award alimony terminable only upon certain contingencies such as the death or remarriage of the recipient of the award or further order of the court. Noll v. Noll (Sandusky 1989) 55 Ohio App.3d 160, 563 N.E.2d 44.

In view of the parties' thirty-three year marriage the court errs in ordering automatic termination of spousal support upon wife's sixty-fifth birthday where the rational is based upon the assumption that she would then begin receiving social security at the rate of $637 per month; instead, the trial court should retain jurisdiction and allow the parties to seek modification of spousal support in the event of unforeseeable circumstances. Parsons v Parsons, No. 99AP-485, 1999 WL 1262056 (10th Dist Ct App, Franklin, 12-28-99).

The trial court properly ordered a sixty-six year old retiree ex-husband to pay spousal support to his fifty-seven year old ex-wife even though she left the husband ten years previously and now lives with another man where 1) the parties' marriage lasted twenty-six years, 2) the husband enjoys a $3200 monthly tax free income while the wife makes $7.00 per hour with no retirement benefits, 3) the wife helped the husband recover from his stroke, and 4) the man the wife lives with has an income of only $425 a month, as cohabitation of the dependent spouse does not automatically require termination of the support award but is one factor in deciding whether the dependent spouse would have a further need for support. Schulte v Schulte, No. CA95-12-222, 1996 WL 723530 (12th Dist Ct App, Butler, 12-16-96).

An order to pay spousal support for the same number of years that the parties had been married is not an abuse of discretion even though no children were born of the marriage and the wife did not contribute to the husband's education given the disparity in the parties' income and the impact the wife's ailing health has had and will continue to have on her earning capability. Ellman v Ellman, No. 95-CA-0115, 1996 WL 562815 (2d Dist Ct App, Greene, 9-27-96).

Where record of trial court's award of spousal support revealed that parties' marriage lasted twenty years—only one of statutory factors listed in RC 3105.18(C)(1)—and lacked any information relevant to other statutory factors, trial court erred in awarding spousal support without determining the current income and expenses of each party. Campbell v Campbell, No. 92-CA-39, 1993 WL 307535 (4th Dist Ct App, Gallia, 8-13-93).

An alimony award of $300 per month is an abuse of discretion where payor is earning $36,000 per year and the parties were married for forty-three years, notwithstanding that the children of the marriage reside with payor. Lloyd v Lloyd, No. 3320 (9th Dist Ct App, Lorain, 9-1-82).

A court's award of alimony is determined by other factors besides a possible need for sustenance, such as the duration of the marriage, the standard of living of the parties established during the marriage, the property brought to the marriage by either party, the contribution of a spouse as homemaker, and the relative situation of the parties. Hosford v Hosford, No. 40380 (8th Dist Ct App, Cuyahoga, 3-6-80).

11. —Party as custodian of minor child, factors to consider in award

Trial court acted within its discretion in divorce proceedings when it declined to impute full-time earnings to wife in determining proper award of spousal support, though wife was registered nurse, in light of wife's status as custodian of two minor children of marriage, one of whom suffered from dyslexia and required considerable parental tutoring. Shaffer v. Shaffer (Crawford 1996) 109 Ohio App.3d 205, 671 N.E.2d 1317.

Trial court improperly considered child support guidelines in modifying spousal support, where child from marriage was emancipated before original complaint was filed. Graham v. Graham (Greene 1994) 98 Ohio App.3d 396, 648 N.E.2d 850.

In making property division, court was entitled to consider that wife would have custody of child. deLevie v. deLevie (Franklin 1993) 86 Ohio App.3d 531, 621 N.E.2d 594, dismissed, jurisdictional motion overruled 67 Ohio St.3d 1409, 615 N.E.2d 1043.

To treat former husband's business debts as marital debts to reduce the value of marital assets before awarding the bulk of the assets to the former husband is not improper where the former husband (1) has sole financial responsibility for the four minor children, (2) is responsible for substantial debt encumbering those assets and for $11,200 outstanding on a loan for the former wife's vehicle, and (3) is engaged in a medical practice which is financially troubled, and where there is evidence that the former wife's failure to repair or maintain the house contributed only to a dimunition in its value and that the assets of the former husband's business were used to pay off substantial credit card debts incurred by the former wife for purchases of gasoline and of other items that she returned for cash. Thornton v. Thornton (Wyandot 1990) 70 Ohio App.3d 317, 590 N.E.2d 1375.

The tax exemption for dependent children awarded to the custodial parent as part of the division of property may not be subsequently modified by a court. Mettler v. Mettler (Ross 1988) 61 Ohio App.3d 14, 572 N.E.2d 127.

An equal division of marital property takes place even when it is based upon disparate earning abilities of the parties as when a husband with greater earning ability is also awarded the greater financial obligation of raising three children and maintaining a household; where his documented income is insufficient to meet his financial obligations toward his children, a denial of spousal support to the wife is not an abuse of discretion. Hue v Hue, No. C-940429, 1995 WL 481494 (1st Dist Ct App, Hamilton, 8-16-95).

The trial court erred to the prejudice of the wife-appellant when it limited the alimony award to a period of three years, where the facts showed the wife had custody of two minor children and no particular work skills, and the husband-appellee was a licensed physician presently in residence at a small salary; under RC 3105.18(B)(6), it would still be inappropriate for the wife to work outside the home due to the ages of the children; RC 3105.18(B)(1) requires the court to consider the husband's probable future earning ability; therefore, the trial court's alimony award for a limited three year period was neither reasonable nor equitable as required by RC 3105.18(A). West v West, No. 5830 (2d Dist Ct App, Mongtomery, 6-23-78).

12. —Standard of living, factors to consider in award

Award of spousal support in divorce action, which merely stated that wife was to receive support in amount of $2,550 per month, failed to explain basis of award with required specificity and required remand, where trial court demonstrably failed to consider possible sources of husband's income aside from his reasonable salary and support award taken together with wife's salary did not meet what trial court found to be her needs. Zeefe v. Zeefe (Ohio App. 8 Dist. 1998) 125 Ohio App.3d 600, 709 N.E.2d 208.

Amount and duration of spousal support were inadequate in light of great disparity between parties' earning abilities and great disparity between the standard of living the parties enjoyed during the marriage compared to the standard of living wife could expect to maintain following the marriage on such a small amount of spousal support. Williams v. Williams (Ohio App. 6 Dist. 1996) 116 Ohio App.3d 320, 688 N.E.2d 30.

Spousal support award need not equalize parties' standard of living. Tremaine v. Tremaine (Montgomery 1996) 111 Ohio App.3d 703, 676 N.E.2d 1249, appeal not allowed 77 Ohio St.3d 1480, 673 N.E.2d 142.

Spouse is not entitled as matter of law to continuous luxurious lifestyle as lived by parties during marriage. Simoni v. Simoni (Cuyahoga 1995) 102 Ohio App.3d 628, 657 N.E.2d 800, appeal not allowed 73 Ohio St.3d 1453, 654 N.E.2d 989.

Awarding wife sustenance alimony without evidence of hardship demonstrated by wife was abuse of discretion in divorce proceeding; sustenance alimony was awarded so wife could maintain luxurious lifestyle that parties lived during marriage, even though both parties had substantial income-creating assets and wife would receive $49,000 in first year following divorce. Simoni v. Simoni (Cuyahoga 1995) 102 Ohio App.3d 628, 657 N.E.2d 800, appeal not allowed 73 Ohio St.3d 1453, 654 N.E.2d 989.

Evidence supported $1,000 per month permanent sustenance alimony award to wife; marriage lasted 30 years, wife earned annual salary of $19,100 per year while husband earned $52,000 per year, and wife was not required to resign from union or charge her son, daughter, and grandson rent in order to bring her standard of living to similar level to that existing when parties were married. Addy v. Addy (Franklin 1994) 97 Ohio App.3d 204, 646 N.E.2d 513.

Statute allowing mother who seeks child support from her husband as part of divorce proceeding to recover attorney fees without similar opportunity for the mother seeking child support from father in paternity action did not violate equal protection; statute had substantial relationship to important government interest of insuring that divorcing spouses are treated fairly and allowed to become self-supporting, or provided sufficient income to maintain lifestyles as close as possible to those which were attained during their marriages. Clark v. Joseph (Summit 1994) 95 Ohio App.3d 207, 642 N.E.2d 36.

The fact that an ex-spouse voluntarily incurs additional debt by purchasing a home in support of his lifestyle is not a sufficient change in circumstance to terminate alimony to his first wife whose income is at poverty level and who has little hope of advancement at work. Thacker v. Thacker (Cuyahoga 1991) 74 Ohio App.3d 348, 598 N.E.2d 1183.

Substantial increase of an obligor's income alone is insufficient to merit an increase in spousal support, as the obligee must show a change of circumstances, such as increased need; where it has previously been determined that the court-ordered support is just and proper despite the obligor's ability to afford a larger award, a substantial increase in the obligor's income from $250,000 per year to $3.2 million per year is insufficient to merit a modification of spousal support to sustain a predivorce standard of living for the obligee. Gross v. Gross (Franklin 1990) 64 Ohio App.3d 815, 582 N.E.2d 1144, motion overruled 55 Ohio St.3d 706, 563 N.E.2d 300, rehearing denied 55 Ohio St.3d 723, 564 N.E.2d 502.

Parity as a goal of alimony expressed in RC 3105.18 is not a mathematical equality but an equitable term. Buckles v. Buckles (Franklin 1988) 46 Ohio App.3d 102, 546 N.E.2d 950.

Post-divorce spousal support during the time that the parties continue to live together along with five unemancipated children until sale of the marital residence is not an abuse of discretion where there is no indication that after the divorce the husband would continue to make certain household expenditures he typically made during the marriage. Powers v Powers, No. CA95-11-197, 1996 WL 263633 (12th Dist Ct App, Butler, 5-20-96).

It is reversible error for a trial court to award an amount of sustenance alimony that would not allow a wife to meet her monthly expenses, let alone permit her to become self-sufficient, without specific findings of fact justifying the decision and reflecting the court's consideration of all factors listed in RC 3105.18(C). Henninger v Henninger, No. 1303, 1993 WL 143765 (2d Dist Ct App, Darke, 5-4-93).

A party's share of the marital assets and periodic alimony must be sufficient to maintain a lifestyle comparable to the one achieved during the marriage. Metro v Metro, No. 42849 (8th Dist Ct App, Cuyahoga, 5-21-81).

The condition subsequent to an alimony award that such alimony will cease upon the attainment of age eighteen by the parties' son is an unreasonable condition, as child support is separately provided and the alimony award is in the nature of support to the plaintiff-appellant; also, the condition subsequent to an alimony award that such will cease upon the gainful employment of the recipient at an annual salary in excess of $10,000 is unreasonable, considering the plaintiff-appellant's accustomed standard of living and the current rate of inflation, therefore benefits shall terminate if the appellant receives an annual income in excess of $20,000. Woods v Woods, No. 79-CA-2 (2d Dist Ct App, Fayette, 8-15-80).

13. —Relative extent of education, factors to consider in award

A professional degree or license is not marital property and the present value of the projected future earnings of the degreed spouse is not a marital asset subject to division upon divorce. Although not an asset, the future value of a professional degree or license acquired by one of the parties during the marriage is an element to be considered in reaching an equitable award of alimony in accordance with RC 3105.18. Stevens v. Stevens (Ohio 1986) 23 Ohio St.3d 115, 492 N.E.2d 131, 23 O.B.R. 273.

Despite wife's present ability to obtain employment, trial court did not abuse its discretion in ordering husband to pay rehabilitative spousal support to wife in the amount of $400 per month for two years for educational purposes. McClure v. McClure (Greene 1994) 98 Ohio App.3d 27, 647 N.E.2d 832, appeal not allowed 71 Ohio St.3d 1481, 645 N.E.2d 1260.

The fact that one spouse obtained a medical degree during a marriage should be considered when applying RC 3105.18 to insure an equitable alimony award; however, the "value" of a medical degree is not divisible between two parties upon any exact basis. Gebhart v. Gebhart (Montgomery 1984) 14 Ohio App.3d 107, 470 N.E.2d 205, 14 O.B.R. 121.

A license to practice medicine and a teaching certificate do not constitute divisible marital assets and are not to be considered by the trial court under RC

3105.18(B)(9); however, the trial court may consider such license and certificate as they affect other factors listed in RC 3105.18(B), such as the parties' relative earning capacities, educations, and expectations. Pacht v. Jadd (Franklin 1983) 13 Ohio App.3d 363, 469 N.E.2d 918, 13 O.B.R. 444.

For purposes of an award of alimony, a spouse's license to practice medicine is an asset. The license itself, however, is not subject to precise division; rather, it is one factor to be considered in the award of alimony. Lira v. Lira (Cuyahoga 1980) 68 Ohio App.2d 164, 428 N.E.2d 445, 22 O.O.3d 231.

RC 3105.18(C)(1)(j) requires the trial court to consider the contribution of one spouse toward the education or earning ability of the other spouse, including the acquisition of a professional degree; a trial court properly considers this factor in awarding spousal support. Evans v Evans, No. 95CA006038, 1995 WL 752688 (9th Dist Ct App, Lorain, 12-20-95).

In divorce action brought by wife of physician in residency training, court properly considered fact that wife's family had advanced funds for medical education. Daniels v. Daniels (Montgomery 1961) 185 N.E.2d 773, 90 Ohio Law Abs. 161, 20 O.O.2d 458.

14. —Relative assets and liabilities, factors to consider in award

Increase in former wife's cash assets, resulting from her receipt of her share of proceeds from sale of residence, constituted substantial change of circumstances justifying modification of former husband's spousal support obligation under divorce decree, where investment of former wife's additional cash assets at rate of six percent would yield annual income which was slightly more than 40% of former husband's current spousal support obligation. Joseph v. Joseph (Ohio App. 2 Dist. 1997) 122 Ohio App.3d 734, 702 N.E.2d 949.

Increase in former wife's income decreased her need for support and warranted some modification of spousal support; however, trial court also could consider whether wife's annual living expenses had increased and, if they had, whether increase was such that support should have continued at or near amount ordered by the court. Tremaine v. Tremaine (Montgomery 1996) 111 Ohio App.3d 703, 676 N.E.2d 1249, appeal not allowed 77 Ohio St.3d 1480, 673 N.E.2d 142.

Trial court did not abuse its discretion in awarding less spousal support to former wife upon divorce than she requested, in light of speculative nature of some of wife's future expenses, and in light of $250,000 of anticipated proceeds wife would receive from ordered sale of company owned by parties. Terry v. Terry (Cuyahoga 1994) 99 Ohio App.3d 228, 650 N.E.2d 184.

There was insufficient financial data with respect to husband's alleged debt to his professional corporation to support finding that award of permanent spousal support to wife of $5,000 a month was abuse of discretion, despite husband's contention that debt reduced actual money per month that he had to work with, absent any evidence of total amount of "office advance" that husband's corporation had lent to him or evidence as to whether debt was one that had to be repaid and, if so, over what time period and under what terms. Turner v. Turner (Franklin 1993) 90 Ohio App.3d 161, 628 N.E.2d 110, motion overruled 68 Ohio St.3d 1430, 624 N.E.2d 1067.

Fact that husband had paid less temporary support than permanent support award did not necessarily establish that permanent award amounted to abuse of discretion, particularly where court's order affected parties' financial situations in more ways than amount of monthly support by requiring wife to be responsible for her own health insurance and mortgage. Turner v. Turner (Franklin 1993) 90 Ohio App.3d 161, 628 N.E.2d 110, motion overruled 68 Ohio St.3d 1430, 624 N.E.2d 1067.

Court's error as to husband's state income tax obligation did not require recalculation of spousal support where the error would in no way affect the wife's own need for support and would have only a marginal impact on the ability of the husband to pay support in a greater amount. Focke v. Focke (Montgomery 1992) 83 Ohio App.3d 552, 615 N.E.2d 327, motion overruled 66 Ohio St.3d 1446, 609 N.E.2d 172.

Failure of the court of common pleas to order a husband to continue to pay his former wife's medical insurance is proper despite her fragile health where the following conditions exist: (1) the husband earns $45,000 per year and pays sustenance alimony of $400 per month; (2) the wife earns $15,000 per year; (3) the husband has custody of the couple's younger child for which the wife does not pay child support; and (4) the wife receives $316.20 in child support per month for the couple's older child, whom the husband says has been emancipated. Pettry v. Pettry (Franklin 1991) 81 Ohio App.3d 30, 610 N.E.2d 443.

A husband's personal injury settlement of a lump sum of $68,000 plus $1,200 per month for thirty years to compensate injuries received on the job while the parties were married is considered marital property only to the extent that it reimburses medical expenses and lost wages; where insurance covered the expenses, and the family lost no funds because of disability pay, most of the lump sum is not a marital asset. Everhardt v. Everhardt (Lucas 1991) 77 Ohio App.3d 396, 602 N.E.2d 701.

A court's determination declining to award a former wife sustenance alimony and postponing the former husband's obligation to pay $300 alimony monthly to assist her in furthering her education is not improper where the husband (1) has sole financial responsibility for the four minor children, (2) is responsible for the bulk of the marital assets but also substantial debt encumbering those assets and for $11,200 outstanding on a loan for the former wife's vehicle, and (3) is engaged in a medical practice which is financially troubled which must sustain for the family and the three-year alimony obligation to the former wife, and where there is evidence that the former wife's profligate purchases and failure to maintain the family assets contributed to the family's financial difficulties. Thornton v. Thornton (Wyandot 1990) 70 Ohio App.3d 317, 590 N.E.2d 1375.

An award of sustenance alimony is unreasonable where the court (1) adopts a referee's report accepting the obligee's expenses and needs as reasonable and views the obligor's similar expenses and needs as excessive, (2) fails to consider that some of the obligee's expenses and needs are temporary, and (3) fails to reserve jurisdiction to modify the award. Chikar v. Chikar (Clermont 1989) 61 Ohio App.3d 772, 573 N.E.2d 1160.

A court does not commit abuse of discretion when it denies a motion to reduce an award of alimony where the payor's alleged inability to pay results from the payor's act of voluntarily incurring additional debt. Shanley v. Shanley (Cuyahoga 1989) 46 Ohio App.3d 100, 546 N.E.2d 477.

For purposes of an award of alimony, a spouse's license to practice medicine is an asset. The license itself, however, is not subject to precise division; rather, it is one factor to be considered in the award of alimony. Lira v. Lira (Cuyahoga 1980) 68 Ohio App.2d 164, 428 N.E.2d 445, 22 O.O.3d 231.

In determining an alimony award the court should take into consideration the monthly payments which a husband receives although those payments were generated from a sale of property awarded to the husband in the property settlement. Beyer v. Beyer (Cuyahoga 1979) 64 Ohio App.2d 280, 413 N.E.2d 844, 18 O.O.3d 267.

Social security received by a party is an "asset" and must be taken into account in determining an alimony award. Beyer v. Beyer (Cuyahoga 1979) 64 Ohio App.2d 280, 413 N.E.2d 844, 18 O.O.3d 267.

Reviewing court may modify judgment for alimony where it appears that trial court did not have due regard for defendant's real and personal estate. Chastang v. Mutual Life Ins. Co. of N.Y. (Franklin 1946) 77 Ohio App. 433, 65 N.E.2d 873, 49 Ohio Law Abs. 513, 33 O.O. 298, rehearing denied 68 N.E.2d 240, affirmed 147 Ohio St. 341, 71 N.E.2d 270, 34 O.O. 257.

A spousal support award of $2200 per month with gradual reduction over eight years is fair, equitable and in accordance with the law where (1) the parties have been married twenty-five years, (2) husband's annual income is $107,000 and the spouse's income is $10,500, (3) during the eight years the husband worked on his medical degree his wife helped him get through several crises caused by his addiction to alcohol and other drugs, and (4) wife's monthly debt obligations including two mortgage payments exceed the amount of spousal support. Platt v Platt, No. 96CA1735, 1996 WL 655790 (4th Dist Ct App, Athens, 11-6-96).

Where a husband and wife move to a farm owned by the husband's father and where the husband, wife, and father jointly operate the farm, pay the expenses, and pay a mortgage, a gift of the farm from the father to the husband/son does not preclude inclusion of the farm in a division of property award pursuant to a divorce. Harrod v Harrod, No. 83-CA-22 (5th Dist Ct App, Knox, 7-3-84).

It is an abuse of discretion to deny a motion to enlarge the record to include tax liabilities, where they were being litigated at the time the referee filed his report but were settled shortly thereafter, and where the court has a duty to consider all of the liabilities of the parties in dividing the marital assets. Smith v Smith, No. 9-279 (11th Dist Ct App, Lake, 6-29-84).

Where a wife's contribution as a homemaker allows her husband to devote unusually long hours to his business and where the wife accompanies her husband on frequent business trips which contribute to the goodwill of the business, any increase in the value of the business not attributable to inflation is considered to be a result of the joint efforts of the marriage partners and, therefore, a marital asset. Wischmeier v Wischmeier, Nos. 47493 and 47494 (8th Dist Ct App, Cuyahoga, 6-7-84).

A trial court need not award sustenance alimony to a wife when she chooses to let her income-producing investment properties lie fallow. Block v Block, No. 1048 (9th Dist Ct App, Medina, 8-27-81).

An employee's refusal to accept overtime work because of a concern that doing so will increase his income and result in higher alimony and child support payments is just cause for an employer to fire the employee under RC 4141.29. In re Cobb, UCBR B95-01393-0000 (8-10-95).

15. —Property brought to marriage, factors to consider in award

Husband failed to trace down payment for, and cost of improvements to, marital residence to his own nonmarital assets; instead, evidence established that funds came from parties' joint checking account, which also contained unidentified amount of wife's income from her job, and, in any event, fact that husband may have brought an asset into the marriage was merely one factor to be considered in property division. deLevie v. deLevie (Franklin 1993) 86 Ohio App.3d 531, 621 N.E.2d 594, dismissed, jurisdictional motion overruled 67 Ohio St.3d 1409, 615 N.E.2d 1043.

In a divorce action, a trial court's determination that the parties' residence is a non-marital asset which should properly be awarded to the husband is not an abuse of discretion, despite the wife's contention that the court only considered the fact that the residence is titled solely in the husband's name, which according to the wife was done on the advice of their attorney so as to prevent termination of her social security benefits, where the court finds that the cash used to purchase the home is directly traceable to the husband's premarital assets, that the home had been maintained as a separate asset of the husband and that the value of the home had depreciated since its purchase. Green v. Green (Erie 1989) 64 Ohio App.3d 37, 580 N.E.2d 513.

There is no mandate that property brought to the marriage by either party be excluded from the division of marital assets upon divorce. Carpenter v. Carpenter (Lorain 1988) 61 Ohio App.3d 584, 573 N.E.2d 698, motion overruled 42 Ohio St.3d 704, 536 N.E.2d 1174.

A court in making a division of property may properly award nonmarital property including gifts, devises, or bequests, along with property brought to the marriage if in considering all of the factors of RC 3105.18 such an award is necessary to make an equitable division. Buckles v. Buckles (Franklin 1988) 46 Ohio App.3d 102, 546 N.E.2d 950.

In determining the division of property in divorce proceedings, the fact that certain property was brought into the marriage by one party is not necessarily determinative of the disposition of said property, but should be considered in relation to all other relevant factors, including those specifically set forth in RC 3105.18. Sanzenbacher v. Sanzenbacher (Lucas 1981) 3 Ohio App.3d 180, 444 N.E.2d 454, 3 O.B.R. 206.

Both amount of property husband brought to marriage and extent to which joint efforts of parties increased his estate are elements in fixing alimony allowance. Garber v. Garber (Montgomery 1938) 28 Ohio Law Abs. 589.

16. —Contribution as homemaker, factors to consider in award

Economic success of partnership created by marriage depends not only upon respective financial contributions of partners, but also on wide range of nonremunerated services to joint enterprise, such as homemaking, raising children, and providing emotional and moral support necessary to sustain other spouse in coping with vicissitudes of life outside home. Clark v. Joseph (Summit 1994) 95 Ohio App.3d 207, 642 N.E.2d 36.

Failure to consider a spouse's contribution as a homemaker is prejudicial error. Smith v Smith, No. 9-279 (11th Dist Ct App, Lake, 6-29-84).

Where a wife's contribution as a homemaker allows her husband to devote unusually long hours to his business and where the wife accompanies her husband on frequent business trips which contribute to the goodwill of the business, any increase in the value of the business not attributable to inflation is considered to be a result of the joint efforts of the marriage partners and, therefore, a marital asset. Wischmeier v Wischmeier, Nos. 47493 and 47494 (8th Dist Ct App, Cuyahoga, 6-7-84).

Where the court concludes that the husband should receive the bulk of the value of the residential property because he paid for it, and the court ignores the fact that it was acquired during the marriage, and the husband was enabled to pay for it because of the wife's efficiency as a homemaker and her financial contributions, the court has abused its discretion by failing to apply the factors required by law in RC 3105.18. Warren v Warren, No. 5-80-47 (3d Dist Ct App, Hancock, 7-31-81).

17. —In general, assets: value or valuation

Determination as to when to apply valuation date of marital assets other than date of actual divorce is within trial court's discretion and cannot be disturbed on appeal absent demonstration of abuse of discretion. Gullia v. Gullia (Cuyahoga 1994) 93 Ohio App.3d 653, 639 N.E.2d 822, cause dismissed 70 Ohio St.3d 1409, 637 N.E.2d 6, dismissed, jurisdictional motion overruled 70 Ohio St.3d 1409, 637 N.E.2d 7.

De facto termination date of marriage should have been used, for purposes of determining value of marital property, where after parties separated, they had separate residences, separate business activities and used separate bank accounts, and neither party attempted reconciliation. Gullia v. Gullia (Cuyahoga 1994) 93 Ohio App.3d 653, 639 N.E.2d 822, cause dismissed 70 Ohio St.3d 1409, 637 N.E.2d 6, dismissed, jurisdictional motion overruled 70 Ohio St.3d 1409, 637 N.E.2d 7.

An alimony award based on a percentage of the husband's business profits, which had been determined in 1986, is not affected by a subsequent law holding such awards contrary to law because to apply the law retrospectively would create havoc in the judicial system. Proctor v. Proctor (Allen 1991) 77 Ohio App.3d 99, 601 N.E.2d 113.

Inclusion in the marital estate of the value of $35,000 in cash gifts made by a party to his children out of a joint bank account prior to a decree of divorce or issuance of a restraining order is not an abuse of discretion. Guidubaldi v. Guidubaldi (Portage 1990) 64 Ohio App.3d 361, 581 N.E.2d 621.

A divorce decree awarding specified marital property to one spouse and "the balance of the property" to the other spouse may be modified to fairly and completely dispose of newly disclosed property after it is found that the parties did not disclose the full extent of marital property. Schroeder v. Schroeder (Putnam 1988) 52 Ohio App.3d 117, 557 N.E.2d 145.

A referral fee owed to an attorney-spouse constitutes "deferred compensation" subject to division as a marital asset. Rabbitt v. Rabbitt (Lucas 1988) 43 Ohio App.3d 38, 539 N.E.2d 684, motion overruled 37 Ohio St.3d 708, 532 N.E.2d 141.

Reviewing court may modify judgment for alimony where it appears trial court did not have due regard for defendant's real and personal estate. Chastang v. Mutual Life Ins. Co. of N.Y. (Franklin 1946) 77 Ohio App. 433, 65 N.E.2d 873, 49 Ohio Law Abs. 513, 33 O.O. 298, rehearing denied 68 N.E.2d 240, affirmed 147 Ohio St. 341, 71 N.E.2d 270, 34 O.O. 257.

18. —Specific categories, assets: value or valuation

As part of the division of marital property in a divorce proceeding, a domestic relations court may award the dependency exemption permitted in 26 USC 151, to the noncustodial parent. Such an order does not conflict with 26 USC 152, nor with the Sixteenth Amendment to the US Constitution. Hughes v. Hughes (Ohio 1988) 35 Ohio St.3d 165, 518 N.E.2d 1213, certiorari denied 109 S.Ct. 124, 488 U.S. 846, 102 L.Ed.2d 97.

A professional degree or license is not marital property and the present value of the projected future earnings of the degreed spouse is not a marital asset subject to division upon divorce. Although not an asset, the future value of a professional degree or license acquired by one of the parties during the marriage is an element to be considered in reaching an equitable award of alimony in accordance with RC 3105.18. Stevens v. Stevens (Ohio 1986) 23 Ohio St.3d 115, 492 N.E.2d 131, 23 O.B.R. 273.

A trial court, in determining the division of property pursuant to the factors contained in RC 3105.18 and all other relevant factors, does not abuse its discretion by apportioning the appreciation in value of nonmarital property as a marital asset, where significant marital funds and labor are expended to improve and maintain such property. Worthington v. Worthington (Ohio 1986) 21 Ohio St.3d 73, 488 N.E.2d 150, 21 O.B.R. 371.

Permanent sustenance alimony is in the nature of support, and the attachment of conditions to its continuance is reasonable considering that the need for support may change, thus altering the payor's obligation; however, such conditions are not acceptable as limitations on the division of marital property. Zimmie v. Zimmie (Ohio 1984) 11 Ohio St.3d 94, 464 N.E.2d 142, 11 O.B.R. 396.

To treat former husband's business debts as marital debts to reduce the value of marital assets before awarding the bulk of the assets to the former husband is not improper where the former husband (1) has sole financial responsibility for the four minor children, (2) is responsible for substantial debt encumbering those assets and for $11,200 outstanding on a loan for the former wife's vehicle, and (3) is engaged in a medical practice which is financially troubled, and where there is evidence that the former wife's failure to repair or maintain the house contributed only to a dimunition in its value and that the assets of the former husband's business were used to pay off substantial credit card debts incurred by the former wife for purchases of gasoline and of other items that she returned for cash. Thornton v. Thornton (Wyandot 1990) 70 Ohio App.3d 317, 590 N.E.2d 1375.

A court's determination declining to award a former wife sustenance alimony and postponing the former husband's obligation to pay $300 alimony monthly to assist her in furthering her education is not improper where the husband (1) has sole financial responsibility for the four minor children, (2) is responsible for the bulk of the marital assets but also substantial debt encumbering those assets and for $11,200 outstanding on a loan for the former wife's vehicle, and (3) is engaged in a medical practice which is financially troubled which must sustain for the family and the three-year alimony obligation to the former wife, and where there is evidence that the former wife's profligate purchases and failure to maintain the family assets contributed to the family's financial difficulties. Thornton v. Thornton (Wyandot 1990) 70 Ohio App.3d 317, 590 N.E.2d 1375.

A money market fund is properly determined to be a marital asset subject to division by a trial court on the granting of a divorce where testimony adduced at trial demonstrates that (1) the money market account was established and funded during the marriage; (2) on previous occasions, the husband had withdrawn funds from the money market account to establish an IRA for his wife; and (3) the husband indicated to his wife that the money market account was to be used for purposes of retirement on behalf of both parties. Moro v. Moro (Cuyahoga 1990) 68 Ohio App.3d 630, 589 N.E.2d 416.

A spouse's pension or retirement plan, to the extent it was accumulated during the marriage, is a marital asset subject to division and must be considered in determining an award of alimony. Diefenthaler v. Diefenthaler (Ottawa 1989) 63 Ohio App.3d 845, 580 N.E.2d 477.

A divorce decree awarding specified marital property to one spouse and "the balance of the property" to the other spouse may be modified to fairly and completely dispose of newly disclosed property after it is found that the parties did not disclose the full extent of marital property. Schroeder v. Schroeder (Putnam 1988) 52 Ohio App.3d 117, 557 N.E.2d 145.

A sole practitioner's law practice is not a marital asset and is to be considered in determining alimony only insofar as it affects the attorney's earning capacity. Josselson v. Josselson (Cuyahoga 1988) 52 Ohio App.3d 60, 557 N.E.2d 835, appeal dismissed 41 Ohio St.3d 721, 535 N.E.2d 305, appeal dismissed 41 Ohio St.3d 726, 536 N.E.2d 381.

A marital residence bought by a husband before a marriage may be awarded to a wife with custody of the children in view of a low monthly mortgage payment and the fact that the husband is reimbursed for his purchase money and half the appreciation of the home's value during the marriage. Ranz v. Ranz (Hamilton 1988) 51 Ohio App.3d 66, 554 N.E.2d 142.

An unvested pension may be a marital asset under RC 3105.18 and in determining whether the unvested pension is a marital asset the court should consider the time left before the pension becomes vested, the length of the marriage between the parties, and the contributions of the parties both primarily and secondarily to the pension plan. Lemon v. Lemon (Hocking 1988) 42 Ohio App.3d 142, 537 N.E.2d 246.

The unilateral decision of one spouse to leave the marital residence does not constitute a de facto termination of the marriage for purposes of determining whether assets acquired after the separation of the parties are marital property subject to equitable division or nonmarital property to be excluded from the division of property. Day v. Day (Franklin 1988) 40 Ohio App.3d 155, 532 N.E.2d 201.

Although military retirement benefits were not subject to property division before the amendment to 10 USC 1408(c)(1), eff. 2-1-83, such benefits were subject to consideration by the court in rendering an equitable property division; property division decrees before the amendment are therefore not necessarily inequitable. Alexander v. Alexander (Franklin 1985) 20 Ohio App.3d 94, 484 N.E.2d 1068, 20 O.B.R. 115.

Where marital assets approach $1,400,000 and the husband offers speculative evidence that he may have to pay $400,000 in a bankruptcy action in which he is involved as a creditor, an order that the wife receive $300,000 as a property settlement is not an abuse of discretion. Verplatse v. Verplatse (Hancock 1984) 17 Ohio App.3d 99, 477 N.E.2d 648, 17 O.B.R. 161.

A license to practice medicine and a teaching certificate do not constitute divisible marital assets and are not to be considered by the trial court under RC 3105.18(B)(9); however, the trial court may consider such license and certificate as they affect other factors listed in RC 3105.18(B), such as the parties' relative earning capacities, educations, and expectations. Pacht v. Jadd (Franklin 1983) 13 Ohio App.3d 363, 469 N.E.2d 918, 13 O.B.R. 444.

In a divorce proceeding where a wife contributed small amounts of money towards repairs and minor improvements of a home owned by her husband before the marriage, the referee properly concludes that any substantial increase in value was due to inflation and therefore such appreciation is not a marital asset. Palmer v. Palmer (Warren 1982) 7 Ohio App.3d 346, 455 N.E.2d 1049, 7 O.B.R. 444.

The trial court is not required to label its order in a domestic relations case as either sustenance alimony or a division of marital assets. Slorgie v. Slorgie (Wayne 1982) 5 Ohio App.3d 202, 450 N.E.2d 721, 5 O.B.R. 465.

For purposes of an award of alimony, a spouse's license to practice medicine is an asset. The license itself, however, is not subject to precise division; rather, it is one factor to be considered in the award of alimony. Lira v. Lira (Cuyahoga 1980) 68 Ohio App.2d 164, 428 N.E.2d 445, 22 O.O.3d 231.

A medical license may also be subject to consideration as property brought to the marriage by a spouse; however, its greatest significance may be its effect on the relative earning abilities of the parties. Lira v. Lira (Cuyahoga 1980) 68 Ohio App.2d 164, 428 N.E.2d 445, 22 O.O.3d 231.

Social security received by a party is an "asset" and must be taken into account in determining an alimony award. Beyer v. Beyer (Cuyahoga 1979) 64 Ohio App.2d 280, 413 N.E.2d 844, 18 O.O.3d 267.

Post-divorce lottery winnings constitute a change of circumstances sufficient to justify modification of spousal support in an appropriate case; thus an increase is justified where progression of the obligee's multiple sclerosis requires significant supplemental services and improvements to her home to allow her to remain in an independent living situation where jurisdiction to modify support is present and where, at the time of the divorce, the obligee's support needs exceeded the obligor's ability to pay. Foster v Foster, No. 96CA1767, 1997 WL 583567 (4th Dist Ct App, Washington, 9-23-97).

A spousal support obligation that terminates upon the death of either party renders an order requiring the husband to maintain a life insurance policy inappropriate ab initio. Shaw v Shaw, No. CA96-05-013, 1996 WL 551423 (12th Dist Ct App, Fayette, 9-30-96).

A stock certificate representing interest on corporate stock that is issued only in the husband's name and acquired as a gift is the husband's separate nonmarital property; however, appreciation on the shares which results from the joint efforts of both marriage partners must be considered marital property. Estate of Dunlap v Dunlap, Nos. C-940033 and C-940050, 1996 WL 134543 (1st Dist Ct App, Hamilton, 3-27-96).

Life insurance is inappropriate for spousal support payments by requiring the husband to maintain his wife as a beneficiary and providing her with a spousal support award after his death; in addition, it is error to designate a portion of spousal support which provides an additional thirty per cent of any income the husband receives above $100,000 without regard to what the status of the wife's needs and other statutory factors may be in the future.

Robiner v Robiner, No. 67195, 1995 WL 723269 (8th Dist Ct App, Cuyahoga, 12-7-95).

Including a doctor's employment agreement in the marital estate is error where it is assigned goodwill value due to increase in referrals after the doctor joins the corporation since an increase in the profitability of a business due to the efforts and accomplishments of an employee is goodwill as to the business itself and not to that employee. Burma v Burma, No. 65052, 1994 WL 530876 (8th Dist Ct App, Cuyahoga, 9-29-94).

The net amount remaining after tax is the proper base for division of vacation pay. Alder v Alder, No. CA93-10-209, 1994 WL 178373 (12th Dist Ct App, Butler 5-9-94).

Where the marital residence was purchased with separate funds of the husband, a trial court may award the wife half of the appreciation on the property for her services as homemaker, particularly when the evidence does not establish the wife was compensated for her fourteen years of homemaking services. Edgell v Edgell, No. 2945 (2d Dist Ct App, Clark, 3-3-93).

RC 1701.91 provides the exclusive means for judicial dissolution of a corporation; hence, a corporation cannot be dissolved judicially as part of a division of marital property. Harrow v Harrow, No. 3674 (11th Dist Ct App, Trumbull, 1-15-88).

A court does not violate the provisions of RC Ch 1775 by equally dividing the interest of a partner in a Michigan partnership, between him and his spouse pursuant to a divorce, in lieu of awarding the spouse the cash value, where all the partners are amenable to such division. Randall v Randall, No. 9-85-28 (3d Dist Ct App, Marion, 3-31-87).

Where a husband and wife move to a farm owned by the husband's father and where the husband, wife, and father jointly operate the farm, pay the expenses, and pay a mortgage, a gift of the farm from the father to the husband/son does not preclude inclusion of the farm in a division of property award pursuant to a divorce. Harrod v Harrod, No. 83-CA-22 (5th Dist Ct App, Knox, 7-3-84).

For purposes of division of property, corporate shares which have been transferred by a spouse to his children can not be included as the spouse's property, as they could be for federal tax purposes pursuant to Internal Revenue Code § 318(a)(1), 26 USCA 312. Smith v Smith, No. 9-279 (11th Dist Ct App, Lake, 6-29-84).

Where a wife's contribution as a homemaker allows her husband to devote unusually long hours to his business and where the wife accompanies her husband on frequent business trips which contribute to the goodwill of the business, any increase in the value of the business not attributable to inflation is considered to be a result of the joint efforts of the marriage partners and, therefore, a marital asset. Wischmeier v Wischmeier, Nos. 47493 and 47494 (8th Dist Ct App, Cuyahoga, 6-7-84).

Furs, jewelry, personal effects, and a car, which are shown to be gifts from a husband to his wife, are not marital property. Wischmeier v Wischmeier, Nos. 47493 and 47494 (8th Dist Ct App, Cuyahoga, 6-7-84).

In a divorce proceeding where there is evidence that defendant did not transfer his entire ownership interest of stock to his son, the trial court may treat such stock as being owned by the defendant for the purposes of dividing the marital property. Albaugh v Albaugh, No. 81AP-637 (10th Dist Ct App, Franklin, 7-22-82).

In a divorce action, trial court has jurisdiction over all property brought into the marriage by either party including a nonmarital asset which one party owned exclusively prior to the marriage. Crawford v Crawford, No. 7508 (2d Dist Ct App, Montgomery, 4-23-82).

In a divorce action, where husband has not made any financial or other contribution of service or otherwise to the nonmarital asset of his wife's business, trial court abused its discretion in awarding such husband a portion of the appreciation in value of the wife's business. Crawford v Crawford, No. 7508 (2d Dist Ct App, Montgomery, 4-23-82).

Where the commingling of plaintiff's marital property and defendant's separate property renders their residence a marital asset, it does not necessarily follow that plaintiff is entitled to one-half its value because the division need not be equal to be equitable. Black v Black, No. 43005 (8th Dist Ct App, Cuyahoga, 6-4-81).

In an action for divorce, the vested interest of a spouse in a profit-sharing and pension plan which was earned during the marriage is a marital asset subject to division by the court. Bohnlein v. Bohnlein (Ohio Com.Pl. 1983) 11 Ohio Misc.2d 16, 463 N.E.2d 666, 11 O.B.R. 179.

Where a divorce was granted upon constructive service, possession by the plaintiff therein of insurance policies belonging to the defendant did not justify the court in awarding her all right and title in the policies. Whitelaw v. Whitelaw (Cuyahoga 1952) 113 N.E.2d 105, 65 Ohio Law Abs. 11.

In an action for separate maintenance and alimony, a court cannot make an equitable division of property, but can allow alimony payable in real and personal property. An interest in a family dwelling can so be awarded and does not constitute a division of property. (Annotation from former RC 3105.21.) Glassman v. Glassman (Cuyahoga 1951) 103 N.E.2d 781, 61 Ohio Law Abs. 242.

19. —Valuation, assets: value or valuation

Trial court did not abuse its discretion in divorce action by awarding to former husband the insurance policy on his life and his auto club pension, even in absence of evidence as to valuation of those assets, at least where the assets were only minor part of total award and trial court gave consideration to appropriate statutory factors with limited record available. Briganti v. Briganti (Ohio 1984) 9 Ohio St.3d 220, 459 N.E.2d 896, 9 O.B.R. 529.

A trial court, in determining divorce litigants' inter se property rights in a joint savings account accumulated during marriage, does not abuse its discretion when it bases its award upon the account balance in existence at the time of the parties' permanent separation. Berish v. Berish (Ohio 1982) 69 Ohio St.2d 318, 432 N.E.2d 183, 23 O.O.3d 296.

In determining the value of the real and personal estate of a party, the court should give due regard to evidence that the party is a legatee and devisee of an estate which is in the process of administration at the time of the decree. Ziegler v. Ziegler (Ohio 1957) 166 Ohio St. 406, 143 N.E.2d 589, 2 O.O.2d 348.

Trial court's excessive award of marital property to former wife, based on overvaluation of former husband's interest in physical therapy partnership, would be affirmed upon condition that former wife accept remittitur from $725,041.44 to $435,480 with respect to her share in former husband's interest in therapy business. McCoy v. McCoy (Cuyahoga 1993) 91 Ohio App.3d 570, 632 N.E.2d 1358, appeal dismissed 68 Ohio St.3d 1457, 627 N.E.2d 562.

If parties to a divorce action agree at a preliminary property division hearing to use that day's newspaper as the authority on stock values, a subsequent division of the stock will not be disturbed even if the value drops between the first and final hearings. Wolding v. Wolding (Logan 1992) 82 Ohio App.3d 235, 611 N.E.2d 860.

A trial court errs in failing to assign a present value to a pension plan which it divides by means of proportionate shares. Connolly v. Connolly (Cuyahoga 1990) 70 Ohio App.3d 738, 591 N.E.2d 1362.

Assignment of a present value to a pension where the court states the evidence may not represent the present value of the pension plan is an abuse of discretion, since the pension plan must be considered in conjunction with other factors listed in RC 3105.18 and where there is insufficient evidence to determine the present value of the fund and the other factors have not been considered there can be no assignment of a present value until further proceedings are had. Guidubaldi v. Guidubaldi (Portage 1990) 64 Ohio App.3d 361, 581 N.E.2d 621.

The value of a spouse's fully vested pension or retirement plan is the present value of future benefits to be received, not the amount of accumulated contributions. Diefenthaler v. Diefenthaler (Ottawa 1989) 63 Ohio App.3d 845, 580 N.E.2d 477.

Where the evidence reveals assets that represent a significant portion of the marital assets, their value should be submitted for valuation to a knowledgeable person who is a stranger to the proceedings; a trial court errs in failing to order expert testimony as to the value of a significant marital asset. Mochko v. Mochko (Cuyahoga 1990) 63 Ohio App.3d 671, 579 N.E.2d 773.

A county auditor's tax duplicate constitutes sufficient evidence of the value of realty. Carpenter v. Carpenter (Lorain 1988) 61 Ohio App.3d 584, 573 N.E.2d 698, motion overruled 42 Ohio St.3d 704, 536 N.E.2d 1174.

A tax shelter is valued not as physical property but primarily by tax savings that will be realized in the future. Birath v. Birath (Franklin 1988) 53 Ohio App.3d 31, 558 N.E.2d 63, motion overruled 39 Ohio St.3d 730, 534 N.E.2d 357.

An economist's testimony about the future value of a husband's pharmacy and law degrees is admissible as a basis for an award of sustenance alimony to the wife where she paid the majority of the expenses of his education, which continued for six of the seven years they lived together, and where the testimony is necessary to provide an indication of his true earning ability in light of his voluntary underemployment in the form of working just part-time and apparent lack of effort to locate full-time work. Ranz v. Ranz (Hamilton 1988) 51 Ohio App.3d 66, 554 N.E.2d 142.

A trial court's failure to individually determine the value of each piece of property considered in an alimony determination constitutes error. Buckles v. Buckles (Franklin 1988) 46 Ohio App.3d 102, 546 N.E.2d 950.

The inclusion of the value of goodwill of a medical practice in marital assets is proper and does not make the medical degree a marital asset; further, a court may consider both future earnings capacity and professional goodwill without being accused of considering exactly the same assets twice. Kahn v. Kahn (Montgomery 1987) 42 Ohio App.3d 61, 536 N.E.2d 678.

In rendering judgment on a division of marital property, a trial court must make findings of value so that an appellate court can review the propriety of the judgment. Eisler v. Eisler (Geauga 1985) 24 Ohio App.3d 151, 493 N.E.2d 975, 24 O.B.R. 240.

Where parties fail to present evidence of the value of a particular asset, the court should instruct the parties to do so; it is reversible error to decree a division of property where there is no evidence whatsoever of an asset's value. Willis v. Willis (Geauga 1984) 19 Ohio App.3d 45, 482 N.E.2d 1274, 19 O.B.R. 112.

A trial court in determining the nature and amount of alimony, whether as a division of the marital assets or for sustenance and support, must consider all relevant factors, including the retirement benefits of the parties, and if, in the judgment of a reviewing court the value placed on this asset is against the manifest weight of the evidence, that court may either modify or reverse the property division. Moser v. Moser (Lorain 1982) 5 Ohio App.3d 193, 450 N.E.2d 741, 5 O.B.R. 427.

A finding of fact in a divorce action as to the equity of the parties in jointly owned real property, although possibly erroneous because based upon acceptance of the valuation report of the court-appointed appraiser as conclusive and because of failure of the court to insert into the record evidentiary detail as to the amount due on the mortgate, is not prejudicial where the settlement arrived at is eminently just and reasonable under all the demonstrated circumstances. Creelman v. Creelman (Hamilton 1966) 8 Ohio App.2d 55, 220 N.E.2d 684, 37 O.O.2d 56.

In an action for alimony where the property of the parties consists of many parcels of real estate and substantial personal property, amounting in the aggregate to a probable value of $325,000 or more, the decree is erroneous requiring a reversal, when the trial court decrees a division of the property of the parties, and orders an allowance of alimony, without a prior determination as to the reasonable or fair market value of such property. Roberts v. Roberts (Lucas 1961) 113 Ohio App. 33, 177 N.E.2d 281, 17 O.O.2d 38.

In action for divorce and alimony, testimony regarding the amount or value of property owned by defendant previous to time of the divorce is admissible for purpose of obtaining a complete picture of the married life of the parties, although its exclusion may not constitute prejudicial error, as alimony can be based only on the value of the real and personal estate of the defendant at the time of divorce. (See also Rahn v Rahn, 18 Abs 228 (App, Darke 1934).) Rahn v. Rahn (Darke 1933) 48 Ohio App. 179, 192 N.E. 798, 16 Ohio Law Abs. 169, 1 O.O. 173, motion denied 18 Ohio Law Abs. 228.

In a domestic relations action dividing property, apportioning debts, and awarding spousal support, a trial court errs when it fails to assign a value to unimproved acreage given the parties dispute over the value of the property. Berry v Berry, No. CA14776, 1995 WL 570561 (2d Dist Ct App, Montgomery, 9-29-95).

When a court fails to specify in its judgment entry which debts are marital debts and the valuation of these debts, and also fails to address the issue of the dates of the marriage, the court fails to make findings of fact sufficient for a reviewing court to determine that the spousal support award is fair, equitable, and in accordance with law. Gillespie v Gillespie, No. 65518, 1994 WL 317785 (8th Dist Ct App, Cuyahoga, 6-30-94).

There is no requirement for a separate valuation as an asset of a license to practice law which was acquired during marriage, so long as the effect of the license is properly considered in determining the relative earning capacities of the parties. Adkins v Adkins, No. 82-CA-32 (4th Dist Ct App, Pickaway, 8-30-84).

Where a couple separated in 1962, and the original divorce action was dismissed and they had no contact thereafter except at weddings and funerals, the de facto termination of the marriage took place at the time of the separation, despite the fact that the final divorce action was not filed until twenty years later; valuation of marital property should be made as of the separation rather than the final divorce action. Herman v Herman, No. 46186 (8th Dist Ct App, Cuyahoga, 2-16-84).

The trial court erred in strictly using an averaging approach to arrive at a value for shares in a closely held corporation in determining alimony payments and property distribution between the spouses. Moeller v Moeller, No. 1-81-66 (3d Dist Ct App, Allen, 2-17-83).

In a property settlement pursuant to a marriage dissolution, the trial court erred by failing to consider the appreciated value of marital property rather than the initial purchase price. Van Vleet v Van Vleet, No. L-82-021 (6th Dist Ct App, Lucas, 7-30-82).

In determining the fair market value of property subject to division in a divorce action, trial court need not admit testimony concerning the criteria used by the Internal Revenue Service. Hadley v Hadley, No. 81AP-149 (10th Dist Ct App, Franklin, 2-25-82).

In a division of marital property in a divorce action, determination of the fair market value of a partnership does not require that such property be evaluated in terms of a "forced sale" or "distress sale" where other evidence does not support such a finding. Hadley v Hadley, No. 81AP-149 (10th Dist Ct App, Franklin, 2-25-82).

In a property settlement following a divorce decree, trial court abused its discretion in failing to consider the value of a jointly owned chiropractic practice and the extent of the parties' contribution to the practice. Hahne v Hahne, No. 993 (12th Dist Ct App, Clermont, 1-29-82).

Where the trial court awards the wife both houses owned by the parties and awards the husband the parties' business, this is an abuse of the court's discretion where there is inadequate evidence in the record to establish the value of the property owned by the parties upon which to base a meaningful review. Trendafilov v Trendafilov, No. L-80-402 (6th Dist Ct App, Lucas, 8-7-81).

Where the court awards the marital residence to the wife absent evidence in the record as to the current fair market value, the court's division of the marital property is unreasonable. Yesberger v Yesberger, No. 42560 (8th Dist Ct App, Cuyahoga, 2-12-81).

20. Reasonable/unreasonable award

Except in cases involving a marriage of long duration, parties of advanced age, or a homemaker-spouse who has had little opportunity to develop meaningful employment outside the home, where a payee spouse has the resources, ability, and potential to be self-supporting, an award of sustenance alimony should provide for the termination of the award, within a reasonable time and upon a date certain, in order to place a definitive limit upon the parties' rights and responsibilities. Kunkle v. Kunkle (Ohio 1990) 51 Ohio St.3d 64, 554 N.E.2d 83.

An award of sustenance alimony must not exceed an amount which is reasonable. Kunkle v. Kunkle (Ohio 1990) 51 Ohio St.3d 64, 554 N.E.2d 83.

An unequal division of property may be equitable in view of a separate alimony award. Martin v. Martin (Ohio 1985) 18 Ohio St.3d 292, 480 N.E.2d 1112, 18 O.B.R. 342.

An equal division of military retirement benefits among the parties to a divorce action is not an abuse of discretion. Teeter v. Teeter (Ohio 1985) 18 Ohio St.3d 76, 479 N.E.2d 890, 18 O.B.R. 106.

There is no presumption, rebuttable or irrebuttable, that marital property be divided equally upon divorce; rather, a potentially equal division should be the starting point of the trial court's analysis before it considers the factors listed in RC 3105.18 and all other relevant factors, and consequently a court of common pleas has broad discretion to determine what property division is equitable in a divorce proceeding. The mere fact that a property division is unequal, does not, standing alone, amount to an abuse of discretion. Cherry v. Cherry (Ohio 1981) 66 Ohio St.2d 348, 421 N.E.2d 1293, 20 O.O.3d 318, on remand.

It was inequitable and an abuse of discretion to require former husband making $19,000 annually to pay $7,200 each year to support former wife who was earning almost $40,000 annually. Carnahan v. Carnahan (Ohio App. 12 Dist. 1997) 118 Ohio App.3d 393, 692 N.E.2d 1086.

Award of spousal support to former wife for period of six years was unreasonable, despite former wife's demanding task of raising infant twins; mother had been self-supporting before brief marriage and would suffer no unusual hardship in seeking employment after children stopped breast-feeding. Bowen v. Thomas (Marion 1995) 102 Ohio App.3d 196, 656 N.E.2d 1328.

Trial court's award of sustenance alimony in amount of $30,000 per year until former wife remarried or died had to be remanded for more specific findings of fact and conclusions of law where trial court did not adequately set forth basis for its award. Gullia v. Gullia (Cuyahoga 1994) 93 Ohio App.3d 653, 639 N.E.2d 822, cause dismissed 70 Ohio St.3d 1409, 637 N.E.2d 6, dismissed, jurisdictional motion overruled 70 Ohio St.3d 1409, 637 N.E.2d 7.

Trial court did not abuse its discretion in failing to rule on whether husband was entitled to share in wife's income tax refunds, where hearing concluded before any refund would have been determined and husband did not attempt to obtain court's consideration of this issue during period between conclusion of hearing and release of court's decision and judgment entry. deLevie v. deLevie (Franklin 1993) 86 Ohio App.3d 531, 621 N.E.2d 594, dismissed, jurisdictional motion overruled 67 Ohio St.3d 1409, 615 N.E.2d 1043.

It was not unreasonable for trial court to grant wife five years to pay husband his share of home equity, given costs to wife of litigating the divorce, fact that she was assuming the mortgage and other costs associated with ownership of home, and that she was assuming debts incurred in connection with husband's medical school education. deLevie v. deLevie (Franklin 1993) 86 Ohio App.3d 531, 621 N.E.2d 594, dismissed, jurisdictional motion overruled 67 Ohio St.3d 1409, 615 N.E.2d 1043.

In a divorce action, a trial court pursuant to RC 3105.171 and 3105.18 must fashion an "equitable" distribution of all marital and separate property belonging to both parties before it determines whether a need for "reasonable spousal support" exists. Krisher v. Krisher (Logan 1992) 82 Ohio App.3d 159, 611 N.E.2d 499.

A trial court errs in awarding the same amount of sustenance alimony on remand as it did in the original divorce decree since the court in the prior case specifically held that the amount of the award constituted an abuse of discretion and reversed the trial court on that issue; the law-of-the-case doctrine applies as the court was faced with identical facts and issues on remand.

Kaechele v. Kaechele (Franklin 1991) 72 Ohio App.3d 267, 594 N.E.2d 641.

A trial court's monthly alimony award of $2200 to a wife is not supported by its findings of fact where in several germane areas, i.e., (1) the determination of the husband's base salary, (2) the wife's employment potential and her health, (3) the spouses' finances, and (4) the amount of money necessary for the wife to maintain her standard of living to which she had become accustomed, the court's findings of fact are so slanted and misleading as to be against the weight of the evidence, which is the direct result of the court adopting the findings of fact prepared by the husband rather than considering the issues and writing its own findings using those suggested by the parties as a guide. Kaechele v. Kaechele (Franklin 1991) 72 Ohio App.3d 267, 594 N.E.2d 641.

An eight-year award of spousal support to a wife who is currently employed part-time as a licensed practical nurse is reasonable and supported by the evidence where (1) the wife testifies that she has completed one and one-quarter years toward a degree as a registered nurse and that in order to obtain a degree she would need to attend nursing school for approximately eight years on a part-time basis; (2) the evidence indicates that the parties' three minor children should be out of school within eight years, thus alleviating some of the wife's responsibilities as a custodial parent and allowing her additional time to devote to employment; and (3) the trial court reserves jurisdiction to modify its order of support on proof of a substantial change of circumstances. Goode v. Goode (Franklin 1991) 70 Ohio App.3d 125, 590 N.E.2d 439.

A husband may be ordered by a trial court to provide, through his employment, health insurance coverage for his wife for a period of three years after their divorce; RC 3105.18(B) allows a trial court to consider all relevant facts in determining the nature, amount, and terms of payment of spousal support and the fact that the wife had difficulty obtaining insurance through her current employer due, in part, to the high cost of individual coverage further supports the trial court's award. Goode v. Goode (Franklin 1991) 70 Ohio App.3d 125, 590 N.E.2d 439.

A sustenance alimony award in the amount of $200 a week plus two per cent of the husband's salary is unreasonable where (1) the wife is self-supporting, is awarded the major portion of the marital property, and has her own pension; (2) her health problems do not interfere with her employment; and (3) the husband is ordered to pay the entire obligation for an invalid tax shelter; even though the parties are almost the same age, the marriage was of long duration, the husband's income is approximately twice as much as the wife's, and the wife may be entitled to an equivalent standard of living as established by the marriage, she is not entitled to an alimony award that leaves the husband without sufficient funds to cover his living expenses. Rowe v. Rowe (Lucas 1990) 69 Ohio App.3d 607, 591 N.E.2d 716.

Awarding divorced wife sustenance alimony without setting forth definite date upon which that award would terminate was not an abuse of discretion; parties had been married for 35 years at time of divorce, husband, age 56, held full and part-time position with approximately $1,548 of disposable income per month while wife, age 57, was employed full time with approximately $758 of disposable income per month and was unable to further supplement her income due to health problems. Pendleton v. Pendleton (Sandusky 1989) 65 Ohio App.3d 763, 585 N.E.2d 479.

A trial court does not abuse its discretion in awarding partial sustenance alimony to a wife in excess of the amount she has requested and the amount the evidence shows she had been spending per month where (1) this evidence is based on very marginal living by the wife and does not include certain expenses that had previously been the husband's responsibility; (2) the wife would be liable for income taxes on the alimony; (3) the amount awarded is about one-half of the husband's employment income, and the husband has additional income from rental property; (4) the husband had insisted that the wife not work during the marriage, and she thus feels that he cannot insist on her working after the divorce; and (5) the court retains continuing jurisdiction over the award and can thus cure any future inequity. Campitelli v. Campitelli (Stark 1989) 65 Ohio App.3d 307, 583 N.E.2d 1322.

Where the present value of a spouse's pension plan is approximately $235,000 and constitutes approximately seventy per cent of all marital assets, a trial court commits an abuse of discretion in awarding all of the pension plan benefits to the husband and failing to award sustenance alimony to the wife; such a division is unreasonable. Diefenthaler v. Diefenthaler (Ottawa 1989) 63 Ohio App.3d 845, 580 N.E.2d 477.

An award of sustenance alimony is unreasonable where the court (1) adopts a referee's report accepting the obligee's expenses and needs as reasonable and views the obligor's similar expenses and needs as excessive, (2) fails to consider that some of the obligee's expenses and needs are temporary, and (3) fails to reserve jurisdiction to modify the award. Chikar v. Chikar (Clermont 1989) 61 Ohio App.3d 772, 573 N.E.2d 1160.

A court abuses its discretion in the award of alimony where (1) an award of alimony is insufficient to assist a spouse in the transition from homemaker to head of household and working parent, (2) the amount of the award denies the spouse the chance to remain home with her two-year-old son during his formative years, (3) the standard of living enjoyed during the marriage far exceeds the standard of living available to the spouse under the award, (4) the award fails to provide competitive interest on periodic payments spread over an eleven-year period, and (5) the award unreasonably undervalues the husband's interest in his professional corporation. Collier v. Collier (Crawford 1987) 36 Ohio App.3d 130, 521 N.E.2d 849.

It is within the discretion of a trial court to order that the payor of sustenance alimony keep his former spouse as a beneficiary of his life insurance policy as long as he is required to pay alimony. Gore v. Gore (Summit 1985) 27 Ohio App.3d 141, 499 N.E.2d 1281, 27 O.B.R. 173.

An award of sustenance alimony of $2500 per month to be paid by a party whose net worth is about $8,000,000 and whose income in recent years has been over $250,000 annually is not so low as to constitute an abuse of discretion where the court reasonably considered the factors listed in RC 3105.18, where the award is consistent with evidence on the recipient's expenses, and where the recipient has some moderate earning capacity. (See also 11 OS(3d) 99, 11 OBR 400, 464 NE(2d) 500 (1984).) Gross v. Gross (Franklin 1985) 23 Ohio App.3d 172, 492 N.E.2d 476, 23 O.B.R. 415.

An award of alimony in an amount which greatly exceeds what defendant is able to pay and without any evidence to support it but evidence that defendant has sizeable debts, no assets and no job, is an abuse of discretion and will be reversed. Campbell v. Campbell (Hamilton 1968) 17 Ohio App.2d 87, 244 N.E.2d 525, 46 O.O.2d 101.

A finding of fact in a divorce action as to the equity of the parties in jointly owned real property, although possibly erroneous because based upon acceptance of the valuation report of the court-appointed appraiser as conclusive and because of failure of the court to insert into the record evidentiary detail as to the amount due on the mortgate, is not prejudicial where the settlement arrived at is eminently just and reasonable under all the demonstrated circumstances. Creelman v. Creelman (Hamilton 1966) 8 Ohio App.2d 55, 220 N.E.2d 684, 37 O.O.2d 56.

It is an abuse of discretion, in an action for divorce awarded the wife because of the husband's aggression, for the trial court to order the wife's place of residence (the principal asset of the parties) sold and the assets of the parties divided equally, where the wife's earnings contributed to the purchase of such property and the effect of such order would be to relieve the husband of all future obligations of support. Johnson v. Johnson (Cuyahoga 1962) 115 Ohio App. 387, 181 N.E.2d 494, 20 O.O.2d 457.

In an action for alimony where the property of the parties consists of many parcels of real estate and substantial personal property, amounting in the aggregate to a probable value of $325,000 or more, the decree is erroneous requiring a reversal, when the trial court decrees a division of the property of the parties, and orders an allowance of alimony, without a prior determination as to the reasonable or fair market value of such property. Roberts v. Roberts (Lucas 1961) 113 Ohio App. 33, 177 N.E.2d 281, 17 O.O.2d 38.

In a judgment relative to the division of property in a divorce and alimony action, which provided that a certain business remain in the name of the wife, that certain realty held in joint and survivorship title be conveyed to the wife within thirty days, and that if the husband fails to make the proper conveyances, he shall pay in lieu thereof $500 per month as alimony, and awarded the wife the household goods, that part of the judgment ordering plaintiff to pay defendant alimony in the amount of $500 per month constituted an abuse of discretion and being so closely related to the remainder of the judgment, the entire judgment failed. Pickering v. Pickering (Logan 1959) 111 Ohio App. 458, 173 N.E.2d 156, 15 O.O.2d 103.

Alimony award held not excessive where husband's testimony as to his assets was evasive. Hill v. Hill (Mahoning 1955) 100 Ohio App. 281, 136 N.E.2d 131, 60 O.O. 230.

Where husband and wife had a common understanding whereby both contributed all their earnings to a common fund and, after expenses were paid, investments were made in both names, and wife contributed a substantial amount to the common fund and investments, and divorce is granted to the husband because of aggression of the wife, an order of division of property whereby the wife receives approximately one-half of the property jointly accumulated is fair to both parties. Brewer v. Brewer (Montgomery 1948) 84 Ohio App. 35, 78 N.E.2d 919, 52 Ohio Law Abs. 116, 39 O.O. 89.

In calculating an obligor's annual income for the computation of child and spousal support, the trial court is not required to rely exclusively on the obligor's gross income as reported on his previous tax return. Showalter v Showalter, No. CA95-11-082, 1996 WL 679681 (12th Dist Ct App, Clermont, 11-25-96).

A spousal support award of $150 per month requires a trial court's explanation where circumstances include (1) the court's property award permitting the husband to retain nearly all of the parties' real property, (2) the spouse having no advanced education or work experience other than homemaking skills acquired throughout the marriage, and (3) the husband is seventy-two years old and the wife is in her mid-fifties. Nance v Nance, No. 95CA553, 1996 WL 104741 (4th Dist Ct App, Pike, 3-6-96).

A court does not abuse its discretion in awarding $600 per month to the wife where the husband receives gross retirement benefits of $1724 per month and where the court has considered and applied the statutory requirements found in RC 3108.15 in making its award. Stone v Stone, No. 1872 (4th Dist Ct App, Lawrence, 11-23-88).

A trial court abuses its discretion where it awards nine per cent of the marital property to the husband and ninety-one per cent of the marital property to the wife, thereby depriving the husband of his means of earning a livelihood. Farmer v Farmer, No. 9-103 (11th Dist Ct App, Lake, 4-6-84).

In a divorce action, where the trial court's order provides that the plaintiff will have the use and occupancy of the jointly owned residence while the defendant pays the mortgage and taxes and further orders such residence to be sold and the equity equally divided between the parties upon the termination of the custody of the minor children living in the house, such provision is an order for sustenance alimony and as such must meet the requirements of necessity and reasonableness. Lyons v Lyons, No. 82AP-949 (10th Dist Ct App, Franklin, 6-28-83).

An alimony award of $300 per month is an abuse of discretion where payor is earning $36,000 per year and the parties were married for forty-three years, notwithstanding that the children of the marriage reside with payor. Lloyd v Lloyd, No. 3320 (9th Dist Ct App, Lorain, 9-1-82).

Where the wife is awarded the parties' home but is responsible for all of the ensuing payments of the mortgage, taxes, interest, and insurance on the home, the trial court's award is thus quite equitable, and there is no abuse of discretion. Overman v Overman, No. 44067 (8th Dist Ct App, Cuyahoga, 5-6-82).

Where most of the assets to be divided are the product of the wife's inheritance and industry, that the wife faces future medical bills as a result of her husband shooting her, and that the husband's immediate needs are being satisfied by the state in prison, it is not an abuse of discretion by the court to award seventy-five per cent of the net proceeds of the sale of the parties' home to the wife and only twenty-five per cent to the husband. Mowery v Mowery, No. 81AP-343 (10th Dist Ct App, Franklin, 10-29-81).

Where the wife earns only half of what her husband earns at the time of the trial, has custodial responsibility for the parties' child in addition to a fifteen-year-old daughter from a previous marriage, and the parties had only modest accumulations during their marriage, it is not an abuse of discretion for the court to award the wife substantially all of the assets and to hold the husband liable for marital debts attributable to the assets. Loucka v Loucka, No. 43302 (8th Dist Ct App, Cuyahoga, 10-15-81).

Where the trial court's order would leave the wife without sufficient support or means to care for herself, the court's order constitutes an abuse of discretion under RC 3105.18. Adams v Adams, No. 383 (12th Dist Ct App, Warren, 8-31-81).

Where the commingling of plaintiff's marital property and defendant's separate property renders their residence a marital asset, it does not necessarily follow that plaintiff is entitled to one-half its value because the division need not be equal to be equitable. Black v Black, No. 43005 (8th Dist Ct App, Cuyahoga, 6-4-81).

A party's share of the marital assets and periodic alimony must be sufficient to maintain a lifestyle comparable to the one achieved during the marriage. Metro v Metro, No. 42849 (8th Dist Ct App, Cuyahoga, 5-21-81).

Where the court awards the marital residence to the wife absent evidence in the record as to the current fair market value, the court's division of the marital property is unreasonable. Yesberger v Yesberger, No. 42560 (8th Dist Ct App, Cuyahoga, 2-12-81).

An alimony award of $750 in money to wife of defendant earning $4,800 per year was not an abuse of discretion. Cullers v. Cullers (Miami 1953) 134 N.E.2d 869, 72 Ohio Law Abs. 348.

Lump-sum alimony of $3,500 against a fifty-two-year-old defendant earning four to five thousand dollars a year held reasonable. Duff v. Duff (Montgomery 1954) 126 N.E.2d 466, 69 Ohio Law Abs. 496.

An award of alimony, in a divorce decree on account of the aggression of the husband, of one year's earnings is inadequate. Thompson v. Thompson (Montgomery 1951) 110 N.E.2d 17, 63 Ohio Law Abs. 444.

Reviewing court may modify the judgment of the trial court by increasing award of alimony upon concluding from record that trial judge did not have due regard to defendant's real and personal estate at time of divorce and award of alimony, and that such award is inadequate and insufficient. Henry v. Henry (Huron 1951) 100 N.E.2d 283, 59 Ohio Law Abs. 494, 46 O.O. 365, reversed 157 Ohio St. 319, 105 N.E.2d 406, 47 O.O. 189.

A former husband's agreement in divorce proceedings to pay $8929.16 in credit card debts run up by his former wife on accounts held in her name alone is in the nature of support and cannot be discharged in bankruptcy where the husband's annual take-home earnings of $15,785 leave him about $190 each month after paying his expenses, while the former wife is presently not working, earned $8000 in 1988, and is supported by her family and friends; the man is allowed to discharge the interest debt on these credit accounts, however, in light of the fact the former wife is just twenty-six years old, has a college degree, and is employable: it would be manifestly unreasonable under traditional concepts of what constitutes "support" to hold him responsible for the accruing interest. In re Sermersheim (Bkrtcy.N.D.Ohio 1989) 97 B.R. 885.

21. Agreement of parties

"Incident to a termination of their marriage," as used in arbitration clause of parties' antenuptial agreement, covered both temporary and permanent spousal and/or child support. Kelm v. Kelm (Ohio 1993) 68 Ohio St.3d 26, 623 N.E.2d 39.

If otherwise found to be valid, antenuptial agreements containing provisions for disposition of property and setting forth amounts to be paid as sustenance alimony upon a subsequent divorce of the parties are not abrogated as to either party for marital misconduct after marriage, in the absence of an express provision in the agreement to the contrary. Gross v. Gross (Ohio 1984) 11 Ohio St.3d 99, 464 N.E.2d 500, 11 O.B.R. 400.

Antenuptial agreements containing provisions for disposition of property and setting forth amounts to be paid as sustenance alimony upon a subsequent divorce of the parties are not contrary to public policy; such agreements are valid and enforceable if: (1) they have been entered into freely without fraud, duress, coercion, or overreaching; (2) there was full disclosure, or full knowledge and understanding of the nature, value, and extent of the prospective spouse's property; and (3) if the terms do not promote or encourage divorce or profiteering by divorce. Gross v. Gross (Ohio 1984) 11 Ohio St.3d 99, 464 N.E.2d 500, 11 O.B.R. 400.

In a judicial review of an antenuptial agreement at any subsequent separation or divorce proceeding of the parties, provisions setting forth maintenance or sustenance alimony must meet the additional test of conscionability at the time of the divorce or separation. Gross v. Gross (Ohio 1984) 11 Ohio St.3d 99, 464 N.E.2d 500, 11 O.B.R. 400.

The holding in Wolfe as to alimony awards pursuant to an agreement of the parties is to be applied prospectively only to decrees entered after June 23, 1976. Supanick v. Supanick (Ohio 1981) 66 Ohio St.2d 360, 421 N.E.2d 1301, 20 O.O.3d 325, certiorari denied 102 S.Ct. 642, 454 U.S. 1084, 70 L.Ed.2d 620.

A separation agreement of the parties loses its nature as a contract the moment it is adopted by the court and incorporated into a decree of divorce. Wolfe v. Wolfe (Ohio 1976) 46 Ohio St.2d 399, 350 N.E.2d 413, 75 O.O.2d 474.

Where a wife, in a divorce action instituted by her husband, seeks alimony only and also pleads an agreement by the husband to convey certain real property to her and asks the court to compel her husband to specifically perform that agreement, a decree, allowing her alimony in a certain amount each month but not mentioning said agreement or said real estate, constitutes an adjudication that such wife has no right to compel her husband to specifically perform that agreement to convey that real estate. Goetzel v. Goetzel (Ohio 1959) 169 Ohio St. 350, 159 N.E.2d 751, 8 O.O.2d 355.

A court may enter a decree approving an agreement made between husband and wife adjusting alimony. Sponseller v. Sponseller (Ohio 1924) 110 Ohio St. 395, 144 N.E. 48, 2 Ohio Law Abs. 374, 22 Ohio Law Rep. 159.

Wife was not in contempt of divorce decree by reason of her failure to make mortgage payments on marital residence as required under such decree, where decree also required husband to provide her with funds to make such payments as part of his support obligation, and where husband willfully and intentionally failed to meet his support obligations. Arthur v. Arthur (Ohio App. 5 Dist. 1998) 130 Ohio App.3d 398, 720 N.E.2d 176.

Divorce decree was to be modified to reflect spouses' agreement at hearing that the survivor benefit plan payable to wife would not be assignable or transferable by wife during her life or upon her death. Blissit v. Blissit (Ohio App. 2 Dist. 1997) 122 Ohio App.3d 727, 702 N.E.2d 945.

Trial court properly adopted divorce decree stating that children's transportation costs would be shared by spouses only for children's spring break, summer and Christmas visits with husband, despite husband's contention that spouses had agreed at hearing to split transportation costs for all visits. Blissit v. Blissit (Ohio App. 2 Dist. 1997) 122 Ohio App.3d 727, 702 N.E.2d 945.

Trial court's determination that enforcement of separation agreement was contrary to interests of justice and equity was not abuse of discretion, where agreement awarded much larger percentage of marital property to husband and wife claimed that she signed agreement because husband threatened to seek custody of minor child if she fought him in divorce proceeding. Schneider v. Schneider (Geauga 1996) 110 Ohio App.3d 487, 674 N.E.2d 769, appeal not allowed 77 Ohio St.3d 1416, 670 N.E.2d 1004.

Former husband's alimony obligation did not terminate upon former wife's remarriage, where parties' agreement specified definite amount to be paid for definite period of time and award was parties' agreement regarding division of property. McClusky v. Nelson (Summit 1994) 94 Ohio App.3d 746, 641 N.E.2d 807.

Where alimony award is for payment of sum certain in installments over definite period of time and is payable without contingencies, that amount is part of property division, no matter what the parties or the court actually called the award. McClusky v. Nelson (Summit 1994) 94 Ohio App.3d 746, 641 N.E.2d 807.

Where an antenuptial agreement addresses only the disposition of property on the death of one of the spouses, and is silent concerning disposition in the event of divorce, it is error to apply the agreement to determine issues of division of property and spousal support in a divorce proceeding. Devault v. Devault (Franklin 1992) 80 Ohio App.3d 341, 609 N.E.2d 214, motion overruled 65 Ohio St.3d 1444, 600 N.E.2d 686, motion overruled 65 Ohio St.3d 1499, 605 N.E.2d 952.

A settlement agreement providing for a husband to pay one half of his annual "net income" to his wife that does not provide a clear definition of "net income" must be remanded to the trial court to determine the parties' intent. Patterson v. Patterson (Franklin 1991) 72 Ohio App.3d 818, 596 N.E.2d 534.

A property settlement provision contained in a separation agreement which is subsequently incorporated into a divorce decree is enforceable by contempt proceedings. Weaver v. Weaver (Ross 1987) 36 Ohio App.3d 210, 522 N.E.2d 574.

A property settlement agreement provision may be waived by actions occurring after the agreement is entered into by the parties but before such agreement is incorporated into the final divorce decree. Weaver v. Weaver (Ross 1987) 36 Ohio App.3d 210, 522 N.E.2d 574.

Where a separation agreement incorporated into a decree of dissolution grants the wife a right of first refusal upon the husband's sale of his 1970 Corvette, the husband is in breach of such provision if he transfers the title to a third party in order to secure a debt pursuant to an alleged "constructive trust." Linehan v. Linehan (Cuyahoga 1986) 34 Ohio App.3d 124, 517 N.E.2d 967.

Where a separation agreement incorporated into a decree of dissolution provides for the termination of alimony upon the death or remarriage of the recipient but certain provisions for life insurance contain no such limitation, it is not error for the court to find that the purpose of the insurance provisions is to fund the alimony payments and thus such provisions terminate along with the obligation to pay alimony upon the remarriage of the recipient spouse. Linehan v. Linehan (Cuyahoga 1986) 34 Ohio App.3d 124, 517 N.E.2d 967.

In a dissolution brought under RC 3105.61 et seq., the trial court may grant alimony, but only upon the agreement of both spouses to the terms of alimony which the court has approved; RC 3105.18 does not grant authority to the trial court to decide the terms of alimony independent of such agreement. Ashley v. Ashley (Cuyahoga 1981) 1 Ohio App.3d 80, 439 N.E.2d 911, 1 O.B.R. 359.

An in-court agreement of the parties concerning property division and alimony adopted by the court as its judgment thereon is enforceable by the court and may be incorporated into the judgment entry even in the absence of a written agreement or an approval of the judgment entry signed by a party of his attorney. Holland v. Holland (Franklin 1970) 25 Ohio App.2d 98, 266 N.E.2d 580, 54 O.O.2d 175.

Where a wife institutes an action for alimony only and, at the time of such hearing, enters into an agreement with her husband for support, and such agreement is then approved by the trial court and made a part of the judgment entry in the alimony only action, a trial court, in a new action later instituted by the wife for divorce and alimony (the parties never having lived together after the institution of the first action for alimony only), may not modify such agreement and grant an additional award to such wife, in the absence of a finding of fraud, undue influence, duress or other similar feature in the execution of the original separation agreement. Garn v. Garn (Wayne 1960) 111 Ohio App. 498, 173 N.E.2d 904, 15 O.O.2d 218.

Agreement between parties for alimony at time of divorce, if carried into decree, is not subject to modification. Oral evidence is permissible to prove the agreement, and that it was carried into decree. Folz v. Folz (Hamilton 1932) 42 Ohio App. 135, 181 N.E. 658, 12 Ohio Law Abs. 67, 36 Ohio Law Rep. 433.

Judgment, in divorce action, unconditionally fixing amount of alimony and method of payment pursuant to contract of parties executed during pendency of action, is not subject to modification after term in absence of fraud or mistake. Kettenring v. Kettenring (Lucas 1928) 29 Ohio App. 62, 163 N.E. 43, 6 Ohio Law Abs. 722.

Where a husband makes a voluntary, deliberate choice to enter into a settlement agreement and requests that the court incorporate the agreement into a dissolution; when the agreement states that spousal support is to be secured with the husband's life insurance policy; when, per the agreement, spousal support is modified due to the husband's retirement, it would be inequitable to set aside the life insurance clause of the agreement merely because hindsight now indicates that the husband made an unwise decision and the husband must continue with his contractual obligations without additional modification, per the agreement. Ryan v Ryan, No. 19347, 1999 WL 980572 (9th Dist Ct App, Summit, 10-27-99).

A decision not to award spousal support to a wife or set aside the separation agreement is supported by evidence (1) that an award of spousal support was bargained away in exchange for a quick uncontested divorce, (2) the wife squandered a substantial share of the marital assets in pursuit of romance in the Bahamas and (3) at the end of the romantic relationship the wife falsely claims that a "confused" state of mind is a basis here to set aside the separation agreement. Overholser v Overholser, No. 97-CA-24, 1998 WL 22040 (2d Dist Ct App, Montgomery, 1-23-98).

Income that results from withdrawal of retirement investments is not considered wage income from which spousal support can be paid pursuant to a separation agreement whereby a spouse expects her support to end if the husband retires and has no more wage income; on the other hand, unemployment compensation is money received in lieu of wages and may be considered as such by the trial court. Sanders v Sanders, No. WD-96-005, 1996 WL 549232 (6th Dist Ct App, Wood, 9-30-96).

An antenuptial agreement providing for the disposition or devolution of property and payments for sustenance upon the death of one or other of the spouses, and not specifically calling for its application to a divorce proceeding, will not be found to apply to a divorce proceeding between the parties. Devault v Devault, No. 91AP-1089 (10th Dist Ct App, Franklin, 5-28-92).

Where a separation agreement required the husband to keep the ex-wife as a beneficiary of his life insurance policy, and he secretly changed the beneficiary and then subsequently died, the trial court correctly ordered distribution of the insurance proceeds to the ex-wife. Dahunsi v Aetna Life Insurance Co, No. 80-C-32 (7th Dist Ct App, Columbiana, 4-24-81).

Where a party was expressly given an opportunity to object to an in-court settlement agreement and did not, the party may not later challenge the settlement as being unjust, unfair or inequitable where those allegations were not raised previously. Bauer v Bauer, No. 42805 (8th Dist Ct App, Cuyahoga, 4-2-81).

A wife's challenge to a pretrial separation agreement made on the basis that she signed the agreement under coercion and duress from her husband and former attorney is unwarranted based on her subsequent failures to object to the referee's report and failure to contest the divorce. Buza v Buza, No. 9866 (9th Dist Ct App, Summit, 2-25-81).

An ambiguous property settlement agreement wherein there was no meeting of the minds between counsel or the parties was rightly set aside by the trial court; however, the parties were prejudiced in that they tried their case without knowing whether the separation agreement would or would not be upheld, and the trial court erred in making a division of property and award of alimony with incomplete and inadequate evidence of the value of the marital estate, per RC 3105.18(B). Ovark v Ovark, No. 871 (11th Dist Ct App, Geauga, 12-22-80).

Separation agreement which has been incorporated into a decree for alimony may be attacked only by proving the voidability of such decree. Davis v. Davis (Ohio Com.Pl. 1970) 24 Ohio Misc. 17, 258 N.E.2d 277, 51 O.O.2d 388, 53 O.O.2d 48.

In divorce case, where parties are properly before the court, the court of common pleas is vested with ample authority, under the code, to make a full and complete settlement of the property rights between the parties. In such case, the court has power in dealing with the question of alimony and property rights, to make and enter a decree, unimpeded by the provisions of a prior voluntary agreement between the parties as to support of the wife, unless confirmed by a decree of the court, and such agreement may be affirmed, modified, cancelled and annulled. Such agreement does not preclude all further inquiry or abrogate the power of the court. Stark v. Stark (Ohio Com.Pl. 1929) 28 Ohio N.P.N.S. 36, 8 Ohio Law Abs. 287.

22. Attorney fees

For purposes of arbitration provision of antenuptial agreement, attorney fees were part of "support" to which wife was entitled. Kelm v. Kelm (Ohio 1993) 68 Ohio St.3d 26, 623 N.E.2d 39.

Two parties in a non-commercial transaction may lawfully contract to require, in a suit between them, the payment by the unsuccessful party of the prevailing party's attorney fees. Nottingdale Homeowners' Ass'n, Inc. v. Darby (Ohio 1987) 33 Ohio St.3d 32, 514 N.E.2d 702.

A trial court may under proper circumstances award alimony to a wife although a divorce is granted to the husband by reason of the wife's aggression, which alimony may include an allowance from future earnings and an allowance for expenses including reasonable attorney fees. Gage v. Gage (Ohio 1956) 165 Ohio St. 462, 136 N.E.2d 56, 60 O.O. 117.

Evidence of wife's income and other financial resources adduced at property division hearing during divorce proceedings supported court's finding that wife was able to pay husband's attorney fees. Hansen v. Hansen (Ohio App. 1 Dist. 1999) 132 Ohio App.3d 795, 726 N.E.2d 557.

Ex-husband's award of attorney fees was properly limited under local rule to $200 after ex-wife was found in contempt of divorce decree, though ex-husband testified he incurred additional expenses in attorney fees, where ex-husband did not demonstrate the actual services performed or their reasonable value and failed to introduce evidence through independent testimony or documentation. Vandeventer v. Vandeventer (Ohio App. 12 Dist. 1999) 132 Ohio App.3d 762, 726 N.E.2d 534.

Payment of attorney fees is primarily the function of the party who retains the attorney, and is not an equal obligation of both parties. Bowen v. Bowen (Ohio App. 9 Dist. 1999) 132 Ohio App.3d 616, 725 N.E.2d 1165.

Former wife was not entitled to award of attorney fees in connection with divorce action, even though husband earned substantially more than wife, where both parties had to borrow money to finance litigation, and no showing was made that wife was unable to pursue justice adequately without an award, and that her litigation costs were reasonable. Bowen v. Bowen (Ohio App. 9 Dist. 1999) 132 Ohio App.3d 616, 725 N.E.2d 1165.

Trial court did not abuse its discretion in ordering husband to pay $7,500 of wife's attorney fees incurred in course of divorce action, where such sum represented only a portion of $23,000 total fees supported by wife's evidence. Arthur v. Arthur (Ohio App. 5 Dist. 1998) 130 Ohio App.3d 398, 720 N.E.2d 176.

Statute permitting trial court to award reasonable attorney fees from one party in divorce action to another does not permit court to determine amount of fees between client and her own attorney. Zeefe v. Zeefe (Ohio App. 8 Dist. 1998) 125 Ohio App.3d 600, 709 N.E.2d 208.

Domestic relations court exceeded its jurisdiction in determining amount of fee wife's attorney was entitled to collect from wife in divorce action. Zeefe v. Zeefe (Ohio App. 8 Dist. 1998) 125 Ohio App.3d 600, 709 N.E.2d 208.

Statute under which court may award reasonable attorney fees to either party at any stage of divorce or legal separation proceedings contemplates a prospective award, in that it requires that trial court determine that party will be prevented from fully litigating his or her rights if an award of fees is not made. Seagraves v. Seagraves (Ohio App. 2 Dist. 1997) 125 Ohio App.3d 98, 707 N.E.2d 1165.

Order awarding former wife attorney fees and expenses incurred in divorce action was improper to extent that it encompassed fees and costs incurred prior to date her motion for fees was filed, as husband had not received notice of intent to seek such relief. Seagraves v. Seagraves (Ohio App. 2 Dist. 1997) 125 Ohio App.3d 98, 707 N.E.2d 1165.

Wife was not entitled to award of attorney fees when trial court overruled husband's objections to magistrate's proposed divorce decree and adopted decree, though some of husband's objections challenged language in proposed decree to which he had not objected at hearing, where spouses had expressly agreed at hearing that they would each pay their own attorney fees, and some of husband's objections raised issues upon which proposed decree differed from that to which spouses had agreed or about which there was some ambiguity at hearing. Blissit v. Blissit (Ohio App. 2 Dist. 1997) 122 Ohio App.3d 727, 702 N.E.2d 945.

Award of alimony may be made in form of allowance for reasonable attorney fees; where such an award is made, consideration must be given to reasonableness of fee award and to criteria used in granting of alimony award. Munroe v. Munroe (Ohio App. 8 Dist. 1997) 119 Ohio App.3d 530, 695 N.E.2d 1155.

Trial court did not abuse its discretion in requiring former husband to pay attorney fees of $5,000 to wife in connection with divorce action, even though court failed to recognize that husband also owed additional $7,500 in fees to his prior counsel. Munroe v. Munroe (Ohio App. 8 Dist. 1997) 119 Ohio App.3d 530, 695 N.E.2d 1155.

Award of interest of five percent on attorney fees, which were awarded to wife as form of spousal support in connection with divorce action, was an abuse of discretion, as there had been no willful noncompliance by husband, and husband was entitled to be given option of paying off attorney fees without incurring interest obligation he would incur by awaiting sale of marital home. Munroe v. Munroe (Ohio App. 8 Dist. 1997) 119 Ohio App.3d 530, 695 N.E.2d 1155.

Statute does not authorize award of interest on attorney fees issued as part of support order in divorce action, but merely states that fees must be reasonable. Munroe v. Munroe (Ohio App. 8 Dist. 1997) 119 Ohio App.3d 530, 695 N.E.2d 1155.

Where award of alimony is made in form of attorney fee award, only questions for inquiry on appeal are whether factual conclusions upon which trial court based exercise of its discretion were against manifest weight of evidence, or whether there was an abuse of discretion. Munroe v. Munroe (Ohio App. 8 Dist. 1997) 119 Ohio App.3d 530, 695 N.E.2d 1155.

Attorney fees are awarded in divorce proceedings as part of alimony. Williams v. Williams (Ohio App. 6 Dist. 1996) 116 Ohio App.3d 320, 688 N.E.2d 30.

Wife was entitled to award of attorney fees in light of husband's far greater ability to pay them. Williams v. Williams (Ohio App. 6 Dist. 1996) 116 Ohio App.3d 320, 688 N.E.2d 30.

Trial court did not abuse its discretion in denying wife's request for attorney fees, where court was fully apprised of all facts influencing award and there was no indication that wife was prevented from fully litigating her rights and protecting her interests absent an award of attorney fees. Neel v. Neel (Cuyahoga 1996) 113 Ohio App.3d 24, 680 N.E.2d 207, dismissed, appeal not allowed 77 Ohio St.3d 1514, 674 N.E.2d 369.

Appellate review of attorney fee awards is limited to determining whether factual considerations upon which award was based are supported by manifest weight of the evidence or domestic relations court abused its discretion; "abuse of discretion" implies more than error of law or judgment and implies that court's attitude is unreasonable, arbitrary, or unconscionable. Neel v. Neel (Cuyahoga 1996) 113 Ohio App.3d 24, 680 N.E.2d 207, dismissed, appeal not allowed 77 Ohio St.3d 1514, 674 N.E.2d 369.

Court did not abuse its discretion in denying wife's request for payment of legal fees in divorce action, where record reflected that court and referee considered reasonableness of demand, need of each party and their ability to pay. Walker v. Walker (Hamilton 1996) 112 Ohio App.3d 90, 677 N.E.2d 1252, appeal not allowed 77 Ohio St.3d 1492, 673 N.E.2d 149.

Award of attorney fees is within sound discretion of trial court. Schultz v. Schultz (Franklin 1996) 110 Ohio App.3d 715, 675 N.E.2d 55.

Award of attorney fees will not be disturbed absent abuse of trial court's discretion. Schultz v. Schultz (Franklin 1996) 110 Ohio App.3d 715, 675 N.E.2d 55.

It was not unreasonable, given mother's income, to award mother less than half of the attorney fees incurred in postdivorce child support modification proceeding, despite disparity between her income and that of father. Schultz v. Schultz (Franklin 1996) 110 Ohio App.3d 715, 675 N.E.2d 55.

Award of $9,000 attorney fees to wife in divorce proceedings was not abuse of discretion, in light of total legal expenses of $17,822 and husband's greater ability to pay. Schneider v. Schneider (Geauga 1996) 110 Ohio App.3d 487, 674 N.E.2d 769, appeal not allowed 77 Ohio St.3d 1416, 670 N.E.2d 1004.

Husband's claim that amount of attorney fees awarded to wife in divorce proceedings was excessive did not have to be addressed on appeal, where husband did not argue such claim in his brief. Schneider v. Schneider (Geauga 1996) 110 Ohio App.3d 487, 674 N.E.2d 769, appeal not allowed 77 Ohio St.3d 1416, 670 N.E.2d 1004.

Decision whether to award attorney fees is within sound discretion of trial court. Carman v. Carman (Butler 1996) 109 Ohio App.3d 698, 672 N.E.2d 1093.

Trial court was not required to make specific findings of fact and conclusions of law with regard to award of attorney fees to wife, where husband did not request such findings and conclusions and where record was adequate to permit appellate review. Carman v. Carman (Butler 1996) 109 Ohio App.3d 698, 672 N.E.2d 1093.

Partial award of attorney fees to wife was supported by evidence that husband earned more than five times as much as wife earned, that after payment of bills and expenses wife did not have any remaining funds, and that hourly rate charged by attorney and amount of time spent by attorney were reasonable. Carman v. Carman (Butler 1996) 109 Ohio App.3d 698, 672 N.E.2d 1093.

Decision with respect to attorney fees will be affirmed unless trial court's attitude is unreasonable, arbitrary, or unconscionable. Carman v. Carman (Butler 1996) 109 Ohio App.3d 698, 672 N.E.2d 1093.

Trial court may award reasonable attorney fees in divorce or legal separation proceeding, if court determines that other party has ability to pay fees awarded.

Shaffer v. Shaffer (Crawford 1996) 109 Ohio App.3d 205, 671 N.E.2d 1317.

Burden rests on party seeking attorney fees in divorce or separation proceeding to demonstrate reasonableness of those fees. Shaffer v. Shaffer (Crawford 1996) 109 Ohio App.3d 205, 671 N.E.2d 1317.

Awarding wife $1,000 in attorney fees in divorce proceedings was supported by the evidence that wife's attorney fees exceeded $4,000 and that husband had ability to pay amount awarded. Shaffer v. Shaffer (Crawford 1996) 109 Ohio App.3d 205, 671 N.E.2d 1317.

Trial court's award of attorney fees in divorce proceeding was void, since it lacked subject matter jurisdiction. Polakova v. Polak (Hamilton 1995) 107 Ohio App.3d 745, 669 N.E.2d 498.

Validity of assignment of divorce settlement payment from former wife to her former attorney was supported by attorney's affidavit, in which he set forth that wife had signed assignment in his presence, and by evidence that attorney had provided legal services to wife for which attorney had not been paid. Spalding v. Coulson (Cuyahoga 1995) 104 Ohio App.3d 62, 661 N.E.2d 197.

Former husband's allegation that escrow agent disbursed money, which had been paid to escrow agent as part of divorce settlement, to unintended parties, stated cause of action for breach of fiduciary duty and for punitive damages, including attorney fees. Spalding v. Coulson (Cuyahoga 1995) 104 Ohio App.3d 62, 661 N.E.2d 197.

Indemnification of former husband by escrow agent was not permitted, where husband had paid divorce settlement funds to escrow agent, rather than to wife's former attorney, despite wife's assignment of settlement amount to attorney; escrow agent's breach of fiduciary duty by improperly disbursing escrow funds was a separate wrongful act from husband's failure to comply with obligations set forth in assignment and agreement. Spalding v. Coulson (Cuyahoga 1995) 104 Ohio App.3d 62, 661 N.E.2d 197.

Husband's obligation to pay his former wife, as type of additional alimony ordered by divorce court, a portion of attorney fees that wife incurred in connection with their divorce was separate and apart from wife's own contractual obligations to divorce counsel, and was not affected, under common-law principles of contribution, by discharge of wife's attorney fee obligation in bankruptcy. Mallin v. Mallin (Cuyahoga 1995) 102 Ohio App.3d 717, 657 N.E.2d 856.

Former husband who had been ordered, pursuant to terms of divorce decree, to reimburse his ex-wife for portion of her legal expenses would not be relieved of that obligation, under equitable principles of unjust enrichment, though wife's underlying obligation to attorneys had been discharged in bankruptcy; husband's failure to contribute to his ex-wife's attorney fees was, in part, responsible for forcing wife into bankruptcy, and equity would not be served by allowing husband to utilize wife's discharge to escape his own obligation to contribute to his ex-wife's attorney fees as additional form of alimony. Mallin v. Mallin (Cuyahoga 1995) 102 Ohio App.3d 717, 657 N.E.2d 856.

Although $6,000 amount was high, husband was entitled to attorney fees incurred in enforcing in-court property settlement agreement, where husband's counsel gave repeated notices to both of wife's lawyers that, in event wife tried to repudiate agreement, he intended to seek attorney fees and all time entries submitted as evidence of fees sought were limited to issue of enforcement of agreement. Walther v. Walther (Hamilton 1995) 102 Ohio App.3d 378, 657 N.E.2d 332.

Trial court did not abuse its discretion in declining to order former husband to pay portion of wife's attorney fees following divorce where wife was college graduate who was certified to teach in state, lived with her parents, had minimal living expenses and no child care expenses, and had assets from retirement plans, individual retirement account (IRA), savings, and her share from sale of marital home and was able to litigate her rights and protect her interests. Demo v. Demo (Butler 1995) 101 Ohio App.3d 383, 655 N.E.2d 791.

Incarcerated husband was not entitled to be physically present at divorce proceeding, despite disposition of marital property at proceeding, where husband did not move court for attorney fees so that he could have been represented by counsel at trial, did not present his factual case by way of deposition, and did not cross-examine wife, or other relevant parties, by deposition or interrogatories. Dragojevic-Wiczen v. Wiczen (Trumbull 1995) 101 Ohio App.3d 152, 655 N.E.2d 222, dismissed, appeal not allowed 72 Ohio St.3d 1539, 650 N.E.2d 479.

Evidence of nominal amount of attorney fees and reasonableness of charge is unnecessary in divorce or legal separation proceeding. Woloch v. Foster (Miami 1994) 98 Ohio App.3d 806, 649 N.E.2d 918.

Trial court on remand could not require former husband to pay former wife's costs of filing and transcript fees as part of award of appellate attorney fees in divorce action, after Court of Appeals previously had required that wife pay husband's costs of appeal. Farley v. Farley (Cuyahoga 1994) 97 Ohio App.3d 351, 646 N.E.2d 875, dismissed, jurisdictional motion overruled 71 Ohio St.3d 1500, 646 N.E.2d 1124.

Evidence of former wife's marital assets and current expenses did not establish her relative inability to pay her attorney fees for purposes of supporting award of attorney fees in divorce action, absent any evidence concerning wife's present income. Farley v. Farley (Cuyahoga 1994) 97 Ohio App.3d 351, 646 N.E.2d 875, dismissed, jurisdictional motion overruled 71 Ohio St.3d 1500, 646 N.E.2d 1124.

Mechanical computation of award of attorney fees by multiplying number of hours spent by hourly rate of counsel failed to establish reasonableness of fees as required to support award in divorce action, especially in light of counsel's tactics of filing motions for reconsideration and new trial without requisite support for such motions. Farley v. Farley (Cuyahoga 1994) 97 Ohio App.3d 351, 646 N.E.2d 875, dismissed, jurisdictional motion overruled 71 Ohio St.3d 1500, 646 N.E.2d 1124.

Payment of attorney fees is often necessary part of terminating marital partnership. Clark v. Joseph (Summit 1994) 95 Ohio App.3d 207, 642 N.E.2d 36.

Where court awards attorney fees in divorce proceeding, such award must be entered in favor of party litigant and not directly in favor of party's attorney. Gullia v. Gullia (Cuyahoga 1994) 93 Ohio App.3d 653, 639 N.E.2d 822, cause dismissed 70 Ohio St.3d 1409, 637 N.E.2d 6, dismissed, jurisdictional motion overruled 70 Ohio St.3d 1409, 637 N.E.2d 7.

Trial court is precluded from making required factual determination of reasonableness of attorney fees charged by party's counsel in divorce proceeding when party, through his or her attorney, provides no evidence to court showing nature of services rendered, difficulty of services performed, or any other required information. McCoy v. McCoy (Cuyahoga 1993) 91 Ohio App.3d 570, 632

N.E.2d 1358, appeal dismissed 68 Ohio St.3d 1457, 627 N.E.2d 562.

Trial court's award of $96,000 attorney fees to former wife, who requested $100,000, was not an abuse of discretion; former wife's counsel offered itemized evidence of services rendered, difficulties encountered, and reasonableness of work and hourly rates charged, and such evidence was supported by expert testimony of experienced domestic relations practitioner. McCoy v. McCoy (Cuyahoga 1993) 91 Ohio App.3d 570, 632 N.E.2d 1358, appeal dismissed 68 Ohio St.3d 1457, 627 N.E.2d 562.

Trial court did not abuse its discretion in awarding former wife $500 in attorney fees incurred during pendency of her motion for contempt and husband's motion, which included request for relief from final judgment and request to modify visitation and allocation of federal income tax dependency exemption, even though husband was entitled to relief from prior judgment as to amount of spousal support; trial court did not abuse its discretion in finding husband was in contempt, referee's report stated that wife testified to reasonableness of attorney fees and that she incurred at least $500 in necessary fees, and trial court adopted report. Goode v. Goode (Franklin 1993) 89 Ohio App.3d 405, 624 N.E.2d 788.

Trial court did not abuse its discretion in finding former husband to be in contempt of divorce decree for failing to pay $1,000 of wife's attorney fees as ordered in decree, even though husband claimed he made no attempt to pay fees because matter was under appeal and he did not receive statement from wife's attorney; husband signed decree and received copy of it, giving him knowledge of order to pay fees. Goode v. Goode (Franklin 1993) 89 Ohio App.3d 405, 624 N.E.2d 788.

Award of $4,000 attorney fees to former wife in divorce proceeding was not unreasonable, even though wife's attorney presented documents indicating that he was entitled to fee of $16,581.25; trial court considered fact that former wife had withdrawn $14,400 from marital account and transferred it to her parents. Ingalls v. Ingalls (Cuyahoga 1993) 88 Ohio App.3d 570, 624 N.E.2d 368.

Failure of divorce decree to specify time for former husband to pay former wife's attorney fees justified decision not to hold former husband in contempt for failure to pay the fees. Patton v. Patton (Licking 1993) 87 Ohio App.3d 844, 623 N.E.2d 235.

Whether to award attorney fees in postdivorce action lies in discretion of trial court. Parzynski v. Parzynski (Erie 1992) 85 Ohio App.3d 423, 620 N.E.2d 93, dismissed, jurisdictional motion overruled 67 Ohio St.3d 1450, 619 N.E.2d 419, rehearing denied 67 Ohio St.3d 1513, 622 N.E.2d 660.

Award to wife of $35,000 in attorney fees was not abuse of discretion. Frost v. Frost (Franklin 1992) 84 Ohio App.3d 699, 618 N.E.2d 198, motion overruled 66 Ohio St.3d 1489, 612 N.E.2d 1245.

Award of attorney fees is matter within sound discretion of trial court; decision to not award fees may not be reversed absent clear abuse of discretion. Layne v. Layne (Champaign 1992) 83 Ohio App.3d 559, 615 N.E.2d 332.

One party's inability to pay his or her attorney fees is not sufficient justification for ordering adverse party to pay. Layne v. Layne (Champaign 1992) 83 Ohio App.3d 559, 615 N.E.2d 332.

Trial court's award to mother of costs and attorney fees incurred in contempt action for father's failure to pay court-ordered child support was not warranted; trial court made none of required findings on record to support award and it appeared that court made award as one of remedies permitted in relation to act of contempt and contempt was improper because father received no summons or order. In re Yeauger (Union 1992) 83 Ohio App.3d 493, 615 N.E.2d 289.

It is within trial court's discretion to award attorney fees in divorce action. Babka v. Babka (Summit 1992) 83 Ohio App.3d 428, 615 N.E.2d 247.

Fact that affidavit of wife's counsel, requesting specific amount of attorney fees, was improperly admitted in divorce action did not preclude award of attorney fees; trial court may properly award attorney fees in divorce action, absent affidavit or other evidence, if amount of work and time spent on case is apparent. Babka v. Babka (Summit 1992) 83 Ohio App.3d 428, 615 N.E.2d 247.

Statute providing that in divorce or legal separation proceedings, court may award reasonable attorney fees to either party at any stage of the proceeding if either party would be prevented from fully litigating his rights and adequately protecting his interests if it does not award attorney fees does not categorically establish "special proceeding," for purposes of statute defining appealable "final order" to include order that affects substantial right made in special proceeding. Oatey v. Oatey (Cuyahoga 1992) 83 Ohio App.3d 251, 614 N.E.2d 1054.

Under prior law, prejudgment orders in domestic relations actions, including attorney fee awards, generally constituted ordinary proceedings in domestic relations actions from which appeal could not be taken until final disposition of case. Oatey v. Oatey (Cuyahoga 1992) 83 Ohio App.3d 251, 614 N.E.2d 1054.

Under prior law, attorney fee awards authorized during course of domestic relations proceedings prior to final judgment, during appeals, or in proceedings to modify or enforce domestic relations orders were generally characterized as component of alimony or as necessaries supplied to party's spouse or children, although some awards were not in fact made as part of alimony or child support obligations. Oatey v. Oatey (Cuyahoga 1992) 83 Ohio App.3d 251, 614 N.E.2d 1054.

Statute authorizing domestic relations courts to order payment of reasonable interim attorney fees for completed services upon proper application from time to time during course of proceedings did not authorize payment of prospective attorney fees at inception of case. Oatey v. Oatey (Cuyahoga 1992) 83 Ohio App.3d 251, 614 N.E.2d 1054.

Parties' ability to pay reasonable court-ordered attorney fees encompassed more than parties' current income flow or credit limitations and could include court-ordered asset sale under appropriate circumstances after considering other alternatives to adequately protect parties' respective interests. Oatey v. Oatey (Cuyahoga 1992) 83 Ohio App.3d 251, 614 N.E.2d 1054.

Domestic relations court is not prohibited from ordering commercially reasonable sale of marital property to satisfy reasonable court-ordered interim attorney fee awards for completed services. Oatey v. Oatey (Cuyahoga 1992) 83 Ohio App.3d 251, 614 N.E.2d 1054.

Husband's ability to post $100,000 supersedeas bond within two weeks of journalization of order to stay execution of order of domestic relations court requiring husband to sell property to pay wife's attorney fees in advance did not demonstrate that husband's claimed inability to pay attorney fees was sham. Oatey v. Oatey (Cuyahoga 1992) 83 Ohio App.3d 251, 614 N.E.2d 1054.

Domestic relations court relied upon and decided its order for attorney fees in case pursuant to guidelines specified in statute which was enacted and became effective after motion for attorney fees was filed, where order expressly stated that matter was heard and decided after effective date and pursuant to amended statute. Oatey v. Oatey (Cuyahoga 1992) 83 Ohio App.3d 251, 614 N.E.2d 1054.

Prior law sanctioned motions for attorney fees during course of domestic relations proceedings prior to final judgment, during appeals, or in proceedings to modify or enforce domestic relations order. Oatey v. Oatey (Cuyahoga 1992) 83 Ohio App.3d 251, 614 N.E.2d 1054.

Under prior law, discretion of domestic relations court in awarding attorney fees in course of domestic relations proceedings prior to final judgment, during appeals, or in proceedings to modify or enforce domestic relations orders was guided by parties' respective needs and ability to pay. Oatey v. Oatey (Cuyahoga 1992) 83 Ohio App.3d 251, 614 N.E.2d 1054.

Award of reasonable attorney fees in domestic relations action must be predicated upon evidence submitted by movant demonstrating reasonable value of actual services performed and itemized to party. Oatey v. Oatey (Cuyahoga 1992) 83 Ohio App.3d 251, 614 N.E.2d 1054.

Domestic relations court's order mandating payment by husband of $50,000 within seven days to wife's attorney and place $50,000 in escrow for future attorney fees was abuse of discretion, given that prior to filing of motion for interim attorney fees and costs counsel for wife had received $1,500 retainer and billed wife total of $3,177.68 for services rendered and had presented bill at hearing for additional services in amount of $24,970, absent any testimony of reasonableness of any other fees in the original or supplemental invoices. Oatey v. Oatey (Cuyahoga 1992) 83 Ohio App.3d 251, 614 N.E.2d 1054.

Domestic relations court's order of immediate wholesale sacrifice sale of real property without regard to market conditions in order for party to divorce action to pay attorney fees of opposing party constitutes abuse of discretion. Oatey v. Oatey (Cuyahoga 1992) 83 Ohio App.3d 251, 614 N.E.2d 1054.

Trial court could award attorney fees in postdivorce decree proceeding; finding of changed circumstances, of specific requests for additional alimony or of contempt was not necessary for award of fees. Cattren v. Cattren (Cuyahoga 1992) 83 Ohio App.3d 111, 614 N.E.2d 770.

The court found that an award of $7,000 in attorney fees as part of an award of spousal support was not excessive given the complexity and duration of the divorce case. Guziak v. Guziak (Summit 1992) 80 Ohio App.3d 805, 610 N.E.2d 1135, motion overruled 65 Ohio St.3d 1478, 604 N.E.2d 169.

A trial court errs in neither awarding attorney fees as part of a wife's alimony nor increasing the amount of alimony so as to make it more possible for her to pay her own attorney fees where it is determined that the court's alimony award is so low as to constitute an abuse of discretion. Kaechele v. Kaechele (Franklin 1991) 72 Ohio App.3d 267, 594 N.E.2d 641.

A trial court's order requiring a husband to contribute $1,000 to the payment of his wife's attorney fees is not unreasonable or unconscionable given the nominal amount of the award; the wife stated that as of one month prior to trial she had incurred attorney fees in the amount of $2500. Goode v. Goode (Franklin 1991) 70 Ohio App.3d 125, 590 N.E.2d 439.

An award of attorney fees to an obligee in a spousal support modification proceeding will be vacated where the appellate court determines that there was no basis for modification of support; attorney fees are not to be awarded to a completely unsuccessful litigant. Gross v. Gross (Franklin 1990) 64 Ohio App.3d 815, 582 N.E.2d 1144, motion overruled 55 Ohio St.3d 706, 563 N.E.2d 300, rehearing denied 55 Ohio St.3d 723, 564 N.E.2d 502.

Failure to award attorney fees to a party constitutes an abuse of discretion where the party demonstrates that the opposing party has the ability to pay the attorney fees, has superior income, and was awarded the greater amount of the marital assets. Mochko v. Mochko (Cuyahoga 1990) 63 Ohio App.3d 671, 579 N.E.2d 773.

The award of attorney fees is a matter left to the sound discretion of the court, notwithstanding the fact that the parties have stipulated as to the reasonableness of the fees. Nori v. Nori (Butler 1989) 58 Ohio App.3d 69, 568 N.E.2d 730.

An alimony award may include an allowance for reasonable attorney fees. Birath v. Birath (Franklin 1988) 53 Ohio App.3d 31, 558 N.E.2d 63, motion overruled 39 Ohio St.3d 730, 534 N.E.2d 357.

An award of less than the full amount of attorney fees in a post-dissolution proceeding is not an abuse of discretion where the court takes into consideration the relative ability of the parties to pay attorney fees. Linehan v. Linehan (Cuyahoga 1986) 34 Ohio App.3d 124, 517 N.E.2d 967.

A clause in a separation agreement requiring the party in default to pay the other party's attorney fees in an enforcement action is not enforceable. (See now Nottingdale Homeowners' Assn, Inc v Darby, 33 OS(3d) 32, 514 NE(2d) 702 (1987).) Snyder v. Snyder (Cuyahoga 1985) 27 Ohio App.3d 1, 499 N.E.2d 320, 27 O.B.R. 1.

Under certain circumstances, attorney fees may be awarded for an appeal from an alimony modification or child support proceeding; however, the more appropriate forum to evaluate such claims is the courts of common pleas, although Civ R 75 grants discretionary power to the courts of appeals to award these fees. Lee v. Lee (Cuyahoga 1983) 10 Ohio App.3d 113, 460 N.E.2d 710, 10 O.B.R. 137.

A trial court may award appellate attorney fees as alimony if five conditions exist: (1) the dependent spouse is in need of such assistance; (2) the supporting spouse is able to pay; (3) the bringing or resisting of the appeal by the dependent spouse is done in good faith; (4) the dependent spouse's position on appeal is based on reasonable grounds; and (5) the fees allowed are reasonable. Lee v. Lee (Cuyahoga 1983) 10 Ohio App.3d 113, 460 N.E.2d 710, 10 O.B.R. 137.

Where a court awards attorney fees in a divorce proceeding, the award must be entered in favor of a party litigant and not directly in favor of the party's attorney. Stout v. Stout (Hamilton 1982) 3 Ohio App.3d 279, 445 N.E.2d 253, 3 O.B.R. 325.

In determining an award of attorney fees as alimony, the time and labor of the attorney for the prevailing party is only one of the many factors to be given consideration; where the record discloses that alimony awarded as attorney fees by the trial court was determined solely by multiplying the number of hours worked by the minimum hourly fee established by the bar association, such an award constitutes prejudicial error which requires reversal. Swanson v. Swanson (Cuyahoga 1976) 48 Ohio App.2d 85, 355 N.E.2d 894, 2 O.O.3d 65.

An order in a divorce action for payment by the husband of his wife's attorney fees directly to her attorney is invalid and a violation thereof does not constitute contempt. (Annotation from former RC 3105.14.) Beach v. Beach (Montgomery 1955) 99 Ohio App. 428, 130 N.E.2d 164, 59 O.O. 187.

Provision for the award of attorney fees is present only in RC 3105.18 and not RC 3105.171, therefore, trial court improperly categorized award of attorney fees as part of the property award instead of as spousal support. Perorazio v Perorazio, No. 96 CO 60, 1999 WL 159218 (7th Dist Ct App, Columbiana, 3-17-99).

Although testimony should be taken to justify an award of attorney fees no one could contest that attorney fees in the amount of $1750 is reasonable and necessary in prosecution of a divorce proceeding in which (1) the court is required to determine the parties' rights after a twenty-five year marriage, (2) property must be decided equitably, (3) temporary and permanent alimony is considered, (4) the custody of the parties' child is determined, and (5) the proceeding is extensively litigated over a two-year period. Petrusch v Petrusch, No. 15960, 1997 WL 102014 (2d Dist Ct App, Montgomery, 3-7-97).

Refusal to award attorney fees to the wife in a spousal support modification proceeding is not an abuse of discretion where there may be little question as to the husband's ability to pay; on the other hand, the wife fails to present any evidence of her inability to adequately protect her interests without this financial assistance given her full-time salary of $24,000 and spousal support of $15,000. Towne v Towne, No. 17772, 1996 WL 688155 (9th Dist Ct App, Summit, 11-27-96).

Award of attorney fees to a spouse in the amount of $2000 is justified where she is subjected "to a legal barrage absolutely unjustified by the issues" whereby the husband maintains a deliberate strategy of burying the wife under a mountain of paper in the hope that she would not be able to maintain her position in the litigation because of an inability to pay counsel to represent her. Jackson v Jackson, No. 15795, 1996 WL 647636 (2d Dist Ct App, Montgomery, 11-8-96).

An award of $2000 in attorney fees for handling a matter of noncompliance with a divorce decree is error in absence of the attorney's customary billing rate, its reasonableness, and evidence that the time expended by the attorney in his representation of the client was reasonably necessary. LeBlanc v LeBlanc, No. 95-CA-43, 1996 WL 283939 (2d Dist Ct App, Greene, 5-31-96).

In a divorce proceeding where the plaintiff submits documentation that her legal fees are over $74,000.00 and the parties stipulate that the fees are reasonable, a trial court does not abuse its discretion in awarding attorney fees of only $7,500.00 where the record indicates that the court bases its decision upon the totality of the circumstances and finds that based upon the division of assets plaintiff is able to protect her interests and an award of more than $7,500.00 would be inappropriate. Arena v Arena, No. 94APF09-1338, 1995 WL 571429 (10th Dist Ct App, Franklin, 9-29-95).

An award for attorney fees is not to include a $750 retainer fee in addition to billing for time expended where the $750 sum is consumed by the time spent on pending motions and where a journal entry provides that the indebtedness of each party to his or her present or former legal counsel would be paid by the party who benefits from the legal services. Sateren v Sateren, No. 94APF10-1561, 1995 WL 238426 (10th Dist Ct App, Franklin, 4-20-95).

An award of attorney fees with an order that the husband pay an $8000 debt to the wife's parents is unreasonable and unfairly duplicative; furthermore, in determining the parties' marital assets in separate credit union and retirement accounts, a trial court errs when it double-counts the funds by adding fluctuating balances from different dates from the same account and uncashed checks withdrawn and later redeposited into that account. Thomas v Thomas, No. 94-CA-18, 1995 WL 137015 (2d Dist Ct App, Greene, 3-31-95).

A challenge to a post-divorce decree for attorney fees has merit where the award of fees is based on a mechanical formula of multiplying the number of hours expended by the hourly rate of counsel, a method deficient as a matter of law since it is based on only one factor of consideration. Farley v Farley, No. 66455, 1994 WL 695916 (8th Dist Ct App, Cuyahoga, 9-29-94).

An award of attorney fees that is based on a mechanical formula of multiplying the number of hours expended by the hourly rate of counsel is deficient as a matter of law; a trial court must pay close attention to all proceedings and their origin to ensure that attorneys are not engaging in prolonged litigation tactics on behalf of their client on the belief that the other party will automatically bear the costs. Farley v Farley, No. 66455, 1994 WL 695916 (8th Dist Ct App, Cuyahoga, 9-29-94).

An award of $9000 in fees and $1000 in expert fees is an abuse of discretion where (1) wife's counsel fails to offer testimony on the issues of his hourly rate and the complexity of the case, and (2) a spouse incurs fees for one year prior to the filing of her complaint for negotiations and sessions not relevant to the proceeding. Dodenhoff v Dodenhoff, No. 66100, 1994 WL 463839 (8th Dist Ct App, Cuyahoga, 8-25-94).

An award of $1000 attorney fees is not an abuse of discretion even in the absence of specific evidence to support the amount where it is apparent from the record that counsel spent a considerable amount of time and effort preparing and presenting a client's case. Kreger v Kreger, No. 91CA005073 (9th Dist Ct App, Lorain, 12-11-91).

Attorney's fees may be awarded notwithstanding a party's refusal of an offer to settle. Lloyd v Lloyd, No. 3320 (9th Dist Ct App, Lorain, 9-1-82).

Court reversed an award of $12,000 of attorney's fees because there was no evidence in the record demonstrating the number of hours or nature of the services rendered, nor evidence justifying the need under RC 3105.18. Cerovski v Cerovski, No. 43213 (8th Dist Ct App, Cuyahoga, 8-27-81).

Divorce attorney who represented indigent wife in contesting divorce petition filed by her husband was not entitled to recover his legal fees from husband, on theory that they constituted "necessaries" provided for wife's support; no determination had been made as to necessity or reasonableness of legal expenses in question, and even assuming that such a determination had been made, right to recover legal expenses from husband was right personal to wife, which could not be exercised by wife's attorney. Rust v. Takacs (Ohio Mun. 1994) 70 Ohio Misc.2d 1, 650 N.E.2d 193.

Any determination as to necessity and reasonableness of legal expenses incurred by spouse in divorce action, for purposes of holding other spouse liable therefor on "necessaries" theory, is matter best left to divorce court.

Rust v. Takacs (Ohio Mun. 1994) 70 Ohio Misc.2d 1, 650 N.E.2d 193.

Right to recover legal expenses as "necessaries" provided for spouse's support is right personal to supported spouse, which may not be asserted by spouse's attorney. Rust v. Takacs (Ohio Mun. 1994) 70 Ohio Misc.2d 1, 650 N.E.2d 193.

Law firm that represented Chapter 7 debtor in state court divorce action did not have standing to bring adversary proceeding to except debtor's attorney fee obligation to firm from discharge, as divorce-related obligation not in nature of support. In re Wenneman (Bkrtcy.N.D.Ohio 1997) 210 B.R. 115.

An attorney who represented a wife in her divorce suit that was concluded three days after the wife files in bankruptcy violates the wife's bankruptcy discharge order by continuing to demand payment and threatening to take action; no damages will be awarded, however, since the wife in this case lacked clean hands because she discovered that the attorney was not listed as a creditor on her bankruptcy schedule but did not act to amend it. In re Heuring (Bkrtcy.N.D.Ohio 1992) 139 B.R. 856.

23. Death of payor, payee

Sustenance alimony awarded in a specific amount for a definite period of time, whether encompassed in an agreement between the payor and payee or decreed by court order, is chargeable against the payor's estate to the extent such award is not fully paid at the death of the payor. Kunkle v. Kunkle (Ohio 1990) 51 Ohio St.3d 64, 554 N.E.2d 83.

An award of sustenance alimony for a fixed period of time and for a definite amount is not rendered indefinite even though the award is made subject to the payee's death, remarriage, or cohabitation. Kunkle v. Kunkle (Ohio 1990) 51 Ohio St.3d 64, 554 N.E.2d 83.

By virtue of two amendments in 1951, a court granting a divorce may, in the expressly sanctioned exercise of general equity power and jurisdiction and regardless of the "aggression" of either party, embody in the judgment an order for the payment of alimony in future installments, which order will be operative according to its terms against the estate of the party charged with such payments after his death. De Milo v. Watson (Ohio 1957) 166 Ohio St. 433, 143 N.E.2d 707, 2 O.O.2d 433.

Where, upon granting a divorce to the wife for aggressions of the husband, there is an equitable division of the husband's real and personal estate made, and portion retained by husband is ordered to be "held and owned by him, free and clear from the inchoate dower estate" of the wife, and wife is further awarded, as alimony, $100 per month, payments to continue so long as she remains unmarried, in absence of contract or statutory provision to the contrary, such decree with respect to the installment alimony payments will be held not to embrace periods beyond the death of the husband. Snouffer v. Snouffer (Ohio 1937) 132 Ohio St. 617, 9 N.E.2d 621, 9 O.O. 14.

Trial court abused its discretion in ordering that permanent spousal award be a charge against husband's estate in event that he died before wife. Alder v. Alder (Butler 1995) 105 Ohio App.3d 524, 664 N.E.2d 609.

Trial court's ordering of "security" in form of life insurance for spousal support to former wife was unwarranted, as decree did not indicate that support would continue beyond death of either party. McCoy v. McCoy (Cuyahoga 1993) 91 Ohio App.3d 570, 632 N.E.2d 1358, appeal dismissed 68 Ohio St.3d 1457, 627 N.E.2d 562.

Where a divorce proceeding is pending and a court issues an ex parte temporary restraining order prohibiting the husband from changing the beneficiary of a life insurance policy naming his wife as beneficiary and where the husband changes the beneficiary on such life insurance policy in violation of the court's restraining order prior to his death and a final adjudication of the rights of the parties, the husband's death abates the divorce action and the ex parte restraining order, making the life insurance proceeds properly payable to the newly designated beneficiary. Hook v. Hook (Cuyahoga 1987) 35 Ohio App.3d 51, 519 N.E.2d 687.

An award of alimony, which is to terminate only on the recipient's death and which is subject to modification by the court, is justifiable based on factors such as the recipient's age, lack of work experience, and contribution to the marriage, as well as the duration of the marriage. Koepke v. Koepke (Lucas 1983) 12 Ohio App.3d 80, 466 N.E.2d 570, 12 O.B.R. 278.

Where a separation agreement incorporated into a decree provides for support of the other party during that party's lifetime, the agreement will constitute a charge against the obligor's estate. White v. White (Erie 1975) 48 Ohio App.2d 72, 355 N.E.2d 816, 2 O.O.3d 48.

Where separation agreement, binding on both parties and their executors, provides that one party pay to other specific monthly amount, and requires such party to purchase insurance which in hands of party or his estate should constitute security for future payments, payor's estate is liable for continued payments. McKenzie v. Moore (Hamilton 1971) 28 Ohio App.2d 134, 275 N.E.2d 880, 57 O.O.2d 198.

Alimony payments are a personal obligation and not binding on estate of deceased husband; distinguished decree for share in estate. Platt v. Davies (Franklin 1947) 82 Ohio App. 182, 77 N.E.2d 486, 50 Ohio Law Abs. 225, 37 O.O. 533.

A domestic relations court is empowered to order that alimony payable for the life of the recipient be a charge upon the estate of the deceased payor. Heer v Heer, No. 84AP-1144 (10th Dist Ct App, Franklin, 7-11-85).

24. Appeal

Following reversal of spousal support award on appeal in divorce action, former wife was not entitled to writs of mandamus or prohibition to require trial judge to comply with and not proceed contrary to Court of Appeals' remand order, where there was no evidence that judge had proceeded contrary to mandate of Court of Appeals, judge had discretion in discovery matters and in determining appropriate spousal support award, any errors committed by judge would be remediable on appeal, and judge did not unnecessarily delay in ruling on former wife's pending motions. Berthelot v. Dezso (Ohio 1999) 86 Ohio St.3d 257, 714 N.E.2d 888.

In allocating property between the parties to a divorce and in making an award of sustenance alimony, the trial court must indicate the basis for its award in sufficient detail to enable a reviewing court to determine that the award is fair, equitable and in accordance with the law. Kaechele v. Kaechele (Ohio 1988) 35 Ohio St.3d 93, 518 N.E.2d 1197.

An order in an action for alimony overruling defendant's motion to be dismissed as a party defendant and dismissing a temporary restraining order issued against such defendant to maintain the status quo, is not a final appealable order. (Annotation from former RC 3105.20.)

Petrus v. Petrus (Ohio 1964) 176 Ohio St. 305, 199 N.E.2d 579, 27 O.O.2d 233.

Where a court of appeals has made an order granting temporary alimony to a wife for her sustenance during the pendency of an appeal before it from a final order and decree which granted a divorce and awarded permanent alimony to the wife, and where such final order and decree is affirmed on that appeal, payments of amounts for such temporary alimony must be credited against amounts due from such permanent alimony. Bentz v. Bentz (Ohio 1961) 171 Ohio St. 535, 173 N.E.2d 129, 15 O.O.2d 1.

A court of appeals cannot reverse and remand a decision of a trial court in a divorce action awarding alimony and providing for a division of property solely upon the ground that the trial court abused its discretion in the apportionment of property between the parties. Conner v. Conner (Ohio 1959) 170 Ohio St. 85, 162 N.E.2d 852, 9 O.O.2d 480.

In an appeal on questions of law from a judgment awarding alimony to a wife where a divorce is granted because of the husband's aggression, the court of appeals may not ordinarily substitute its judgment as to what it deems reasonable as an allowance of alimony for the trial court's judgment. A unanimous judgment of the court of appeals substantially increasing such alimony will be construed as a reversal on the weight of the evidence. Henry v. Henry (Ohio 1952) 157 Ohio St. 319, 105 N.E.2d 406, 47 O.O. 189.

Appellate review of reasonableness of trial court's award of temporary support in divorce action was precluded by form of award, where trial court addressed temporary child support and spousal support together without indicating which portion of $3,200 monthly award was allocated to each. Zeefe v. Zeefe (Ohio App. 8 Dist. 1998) 125 Ohio App.3d 600, 709 N.E.2d 208.

Initial overriding consideration with respect to review of alimony award is financial ability of individual in question to meet demands of any award; not only must award be within individual's ability to pay, but it must also leave that individual means to maintain his own health and well-being by obtaining proper food, shelter and clothing, and it must not burden him to extent his incentive to pay is destroyed. Munroe v. Munroe (Ohio App. 8 Dist. 1997) 119 Ohio App.3d 530, 695 N.E.2d 1155.

Trial court making spousal-support award must review statutory factors that support such order and then indicate basis for awarding support in sufficient detail to facilitate adequate appellate review. Stafinsky v. Stafinsky (Ohio App. 11 Dist. 1996) 116 Ohio App.3d 781, 689 N.E.2d 112.

Spousal support order will not be disturbed on appeal absent an abuse of trial court's discretion. Tremaine v. Tremaine (Montgomery 1996) 111 Ohio App.3d 703, 676 N.E.2d 1249, appeal not allowed 77 Ohio St.3d 1480, 673 N.E.2d 142.

Decision regarding spousal support will not be disturbed on appeal absent abuse of discretion. Swartz v. Swartz (Warren 1996) 110 Ohio App.3d 218, 673 N.E.2d 972.

Trial court has broad discretion in determining spousal support and is subject to reversal on appeal only if abuse of discretion is demonstrated. Alder v. Alder (Butler 1995) 105 Ohio App.3d 524, 664 N.E.2d 609.

Reviewing court will presume that trial court considered all statutory factors in determining whether to award spousal support, and all other relevant factors. Alder v. Alder (Butler 1995) 105 Ohio App.3d 524, 664 N.E.2d 609.

In determining whether trial court abused its discretion in awarding sustenance alimony, reviewing court considers totality of the circumstances before arriving at decision to reverse trial court judgment. Simoni v. Simoni (Cuyahoga 1995) 102 Ohio App.3d 628, 657 N.E.2d 800, appeal not allowed 73 Ohio St.3d 1453, 654 N.E.2d 989.

Order of domestic relations court directing husband to liquidate numerous condominiums within 60 days, distribute $50,000 of proceeds to wife's attorney and place additional $50,000 in escrow to ensure payment of wife's possible future attorney fees and expenses so impacted with finality rights of respective parties as to constitute order made in "special proceeding" warranting immediate appeal prior to final disposition of entire case. Oatey v. Oatey (Cuyahoga 1992) 83 Ohio App.3d 251, 614 N.E.2d 1054.

Order to liquidate business assets and real estate to facilitate subsequent division of property and to pay attorney fees prior to final disposition of divorce proceeding constitutes final appealable order. Oatey v. Oatey (Cuyahoga 1992) 83 Ohio App.3d 251, 614 N.E.2d 1054.

Appellate review of attorney fee awards in domestic relations actions is not intended to deny awards of reasonable attorney fees and is limited to determining whether factual considerations upon which award was based are supported by manifest weight of evidence, or domestic relations court abused its discretion. Oatey v. Oatey (Cuyahoga 1992) 83 Ohio App.3d 251, 614 N.E.2d 1054.

The time in which to file an appeal of postdivorce decree rulings is suspended by the filing of the motion for a new trial. Haase v. Haase (Cuyahoga 1990) 64 Ohio App.3d 758, 582 N.E.2d 1107.

When a trial court makes an alimony award, it must set forth in the judgment, with sufficient detail, the basis for the award so that a reviewing court can properly review the judgment. Schneider v. Schneider (Lucas 1989) 61 Ohio App.3d 164, 572 N.E.2d 221.

Failure of the supported spouse to appeal the original order fixing duration of sustenance alimony constitutes a waiver of any right of the supported spouse to alimony beyond the period stated in the original judgment of divorce, which fixed alimony. Norris v. Norris (Stark 1982) 13 Ohio App.3d 248, 469 N.E.2d 76, 13 O.B.R. 310.

Under certain circumstances, attorney fees may be awarded for an appeal from an alimony modification or child support proceeding; however, the more appropriate forum to evaluate such claims is the courts of common pleas, although Civ R 75 grants discretionary power to the courts of appeals to award these fees. Lee v. Lee (Cuyahoga 1983) 10 Ohio App.3d 113, 460 N.E.2d 710, 10 O.B.R. 137.

A trial court may award appellate attorney fees as alimony if five conditions exist: (1) the dependent spouse is in need of such assistance; (2) the supporting spouse is able to pay; (3) the bringing or resisting of the appeal by the dependent spouse is done in good faith; (4) the dependent spouse's position on appeal is based on reasonable grounds; and (5) the fees allowed are reasonable. Lee v. Lee (Cuyahoga 1983) 10 Ohio App.3d 113, 460 N.E.2d 710, 10 O.B.R. 137.

Temporary alimony pending appeal may be granted to either party for sustenance and/or expense money during the pendency of the appeal, and it may be granted in a divorce action or alimony action, whether or not the final judgment contains an order for permanent alimony, but if the final judgment of the trial court provides for permanent alimony, and on appeal temporary alimony pending appeal is awarded, any amounts paid as temporary alimony pending appeal are deducted and set off from the award of permanent alimony if there is an affirmance of the trial court's judgment. Rahm v. Rahm (Cuyahoga 1974) 39 Ohio App.2d 74, 315 N.E.2d 495, 68 O.O.2d 225.

An appeal in an alimony proceeding is on questions of law only. Williams v. Williams (Miami 1959) 109 Ohio App. 399, 166 N.E.2d 422, 11 O.O.2d 286.

In an action for divorce and alimony it is prejudicial error for the trial court to admit in evidence and consider a letter from a physician as to the physical condition of the wife where there is no opportunity to cross-examine the physician. Johnson v. Johnson (Warren 1957) 104 Ohio App. 211, 143 N.E.2d 625, 4 O.O.2d 373.

A trial court that disregards an appeals court order to limit a total spousal support award to fifty-five per cent of the husband's disposable earnings and to modify a journal entry to specify the age limit of the children as beneficiaries to a life insurance policy will be instructed on remand to make the required modifications. Gillespie v Gillespie, No. 68197, 1996 WL 125582 (8th Dist Ct App, Cuyahoga, 3-21-96).

Where a decree resolves issues of divorce and custody and sets the matter of marital assets, alimony and child support for a later date, this does not constitute a final appealable order, so no appeal can be taken from the award of a divorce decree and custody of the children to appellee. Eligado v Eligado, No. 43635 (8th Dist Ct App, Cuyahoga, 11-25-81).

Where the decision appealed by the appellant is not a final and appealable order for purposes of Civ R 54(B), the court of appeals need not reach the merit of the case, but it can make observations where there was abuse of discretion in an alimony award and recommend that the trial court consider those observations in reconsideration of that case. Metro v Metro, No. 42849 (8th Dist Ct App, Cuyahoga, 5-21-81).

An appellate court, reversing an order denying a divorce decree, cannot award alimony, but must remand the controversy to the trial court. Sciacca v Sciacca, 69 Abs 514 (App, Franklin 1953).

The allowance of permanent alimony is left to the sound discretion of the trial court, subject to review by the court of appeals upon the questions of the weight of the evidence and abuse of discretion. Weinstein v. Weinstein (Cuyahoga 1962) 185 N.E.2d 56, 90 Ohio Law Abs. 199, 27 O.O.2d 115, appeal dismissed 174 Ohio St. 408, 189 N.E.2d 635, 23 O.O.2d 49.

25. —In general, modification

Civ R 60(B)(4) and 60(B)(5) may not be used to vacate an alimony award thought to be insufficient by a party as a device for modifying the award after an earlier appeal from the alimony award has failed. Crouser v. Crouser (Ohio 1988) 39 Ohio St.3d 177, 529 N.E.2d 1251.

Where a divorce was granted to a wife and alimony granted to her as agreed by the parties, the amount of alimony may not be modified upon the motion of the husband, absent fraud or mistake. Law v. Law (Ohio 1901) 64 Ohio St. 369, 45 W.L.B. 364, 60 N.E. 560.

Trial court erred in declining to retain jurisdiction to modify amount of spousal support to be paid to wife until termination date of support award, where any failure on part of husband to pay amounts ordered would frustrate wife's attempt to complete her schooling within time frame anticipated by trial court in calculating reductions in, and eventual termination of, support award. Arthur v. Arthur (Ohio App. 5 Dist. 1998) 130 Ohio App.3d 398, 720 N.E.2d 176.

Order awarding former wife alimony arrearage was required to be modified to reflect the 21 months the former wife cohabited with her former husband after the parties' divorce, where trial court, without explanation, used 16 month cohabitation period when awarding arrearage, despite finding that parties had cohabited for 21 months. In Matter of Shanyfelt (Ohio App. 3 Dist. 1997) 118 Ohio App.3d 243, 692 N.E.2d 642.

Divorce judgment stating that "alimony shall continue until further order of this court" specifically authorized court to modify amount or terms of alimony. Merkle v. Merkle (Mahoning 1996) 115 Ohio App.3d 748, 686 N.E.2d 316.

Trial court had authority to make spousal support modification relate back to date contempt action was filed, but arrearages accruing before that date had to remain in effect. Merkle v. Merkle (Mahoning 1996) 115 Ohio App.3d 748, 686 N.E.2d 316.

Burden of showing that modification of spousal support is warranted is on party who seeks it. Tremaine v. Tremaine (Montgomery 1996) 111 Ohio App.3d 703, 676 N.E.2d 1249, appeal not allowed 77 Ohio St.3d 1480, 673 N.E.2d 142.

Periodic alimony payment provided for by separation agreement incorporated into decree of dissolution cannot be modified by court after agreement is merged into decree. Rohrbacher v. Rohrbacher (Lucas 1992) 83 Ohio App.3d 569, 615 N.E.2d 338.

Trial court's allegedly inadvertent exclusion, from final order in divorce action, of its earlier order that husband and wife would be required to share cost of repairs to marital home would not be considered by Court of Appeals; if exclusion of repairs from final order was due to oversight, proper method of correcting error would be in trial court, not through appellate process. Babka v. Babka (Summit 1992) 83 Ohio App.3d 428, 615 N.E.2d 247.

A trial court is without authority to modify a property division in a separation agreement which has been incorporated into a dissolution of marriage decree. Bond v. Bond (Summit 1990) 69 Ohio App.3d 225, 590 N.E.2d 348.

A local rule of court concerning modification of foreign decrees may not be used as a vehicle for modifying an out-of-state divorce decree in response to the husband's claim of accord and satisfaction regarding the decree's support order where the other state's court has not relinquished jurisdiction, as shown by the court's letter stating that its state's statutes prevented the court from relinquishing jurisdiction. Kass v. Cleveland Metro. Gen. Hosp. (Cuyahoga 1989) 65 Ohio App.3d 264, 583 N.E.2d 1012.

A party is barred from subsequent attempts to modify an alimony award when a prior determination was made that the award was not modifiable and the party failed to appeal the prior determination. Panzarello v. Panzarello (Medina 1989) 61 Ohio App.3d 364, 572 N.E.2d 803.

A substantial change in circumstances is required for the modification of a sustenance alimony award, and upon finding a substantial change of circumstance, the trial court must determine whether sustenance alimony is still necessary and, if so, what amount is reasonable considering all relevant factors, including those listed in RC 3105.18(B). Leighner v. Leighner (Franklin 1986) 33 Ohio App.3d 214, 515 N.E.2d 625.

In assessing the relevant factors in a sustenance alimony modification proceeding, the court must take into account the reality that a marriage relationship no longer exists and refer to the standard of living established during the marriage. Thus, ordinarily, the alimony recipient will not be entitled to share in the increased earnings of the alimony obligor, except to the extent that these increased earnings now enable the obligor to pay a share which will support a reasonable predivorce standard of living for the alimony recipient. Leighner v. Leighner (Franklin 1986) 33 Ohio App.3d 214, 515 N.E.2d 625.

An award of alimony, which is to terminate only on the recipient's death and which is subject to modification by the court, is justifiable based on factors such as the recipient's age, lack of work experience, and contribution to the marriage, as well as the duration of the marriage. Koepke v. Koepke (Lucas 1983) 12 Ohio App.3d 80, 466 N.E.2d 570, 12 O.B.R. 278.

While a spouse may have no right to share in the other spouse's improved circumstances attained after the divorce, the financially dependent spouse may well be entitled to financial support sufficient to maintain his or her standard of living enjoyed before the divorce, where the financially supportive spouse is economically capable of providing such support. Lee v. Lee (Cuyahoga 1983) 10 Ohio App.3d 113, 460 N.E.2d 710, 10 O.B.R. 137.

Where alimony awards for a definite amount of money without contingencies have been granted pursuant to an agreement of the parties, Ohio courts will not modify them. Vaught v. Vaught (Clermont 1981) 2 Ohio App.3d 264, 441 N.E.2d 811, 2 O.B.R. 293.

The granting of a "legal separation" by the trial court in an action by a wife seeking such relief is a misnomer, and, where such judgment might be construed as absolving the defendant husband from his statutory duty to support the wife, it will be modified accordingly. Cummings v. Cummings (Erie 1959) 111 Ohio App. 447, 173 N.E.2d 159, 15 O.O.2d 64.

In alimony suit, decree allowing alimony in installments may thereafter be modified as to future installments and so as to have retroactive effect. Pace v. Pace (Morrow 1931) 41 Ohio App. 130, 180 N.E. 81, 11 Ohio Law Abs. 563.

Information about a significant increase in income following a significant decrease should be considered by the trial court when deciding on modification of spousal support and a spouse is entitled to a hearing on a Civ R 60(B) motion seeking relief from a ruling accelerating the reduction in spousal support where she seeks to recover the support lost as a result of the accelerated reduction. Costakos v Costakos, No. 97APF04-553, 1997 WL 607477 (10th Dist Ct App, Franklin, 9-30-97).

A separation agreement incorporated into a decree of dissolution of marriage may not be modified under Civ R 60(B) without vacating the entire decree of dissolution; where one or both parties have remarried such relief is impossible, since the remarried party has acted in reliance on the dissolution. Henry v Edwards, No. 15205, 1996 WL 220885 (2d Dist Ct App, Montgomery, 5-3-96).

A domestic relations court cannot issue an "equitable" order to change the terms of a separation agreement where no change in circumstances has been shown. Roth v Roth, No. F-94-024, 1995 WL 557350 (6th Dist Ct App, Fulton, 9-22-95).

A final decree granting a wife free occupancy of the marital home until she remarries is a property division and thus cannot be modified unless justice or equity requires; that the husband has paid all expenses during the twelve years since a decree is not, alone, a circumstance rendering modification necessary. Barcalow v Barcalow, No. 84-B-55 (7th Dist Ct App, Belmont, 6-19-85).

A domestic relations court may in the exercise of its discretion utilize the "clean hands" doctrine to deny the payor's motion for modification of future sustenance alimony where the payor is found to be in willful contempt of the court's order to pay that sustenance alimony. Hayden v Hayden, No. 10316 (9th Dist Ct App, Summit, 12-9-81).

A payment of $400 a month for sixty months is in fact a division of marital assets and not alimony, hence the payment is not subject to modification. Kick v Kick, No. 1739 (9th Dist Ct App, Wayne, 9-30-81).

A wife may seek an interpretation of the provisions of a separation agreement, but she may not ask the trial court to alter, modify or reconsider the provisions of a separation agreement concerning the division of property. Channell v Channell, No. CA-2771 (5th Dist Ct App, Licking, 9-25-81).

Where a wife receives $100 in alimony per week so that she can resume her interrupted college education and become economically independent, a court cannot modify the decree because it is more in the nature of a property division and not sustenance support. Walke v Walke, No. 408 (4th Dist Ct App, Jackson, 6-12-81).

Once it is established to the court's satisfaction that the award of alimony is for sustenance, then the court has power to modify the award, and wife's motion that the court is without jurisdiction to modify will be denied. Burley v Burley, No. 42712 (8th Dist Ct App, Cuyahoga, 4-9-81).

Where there is a separate and independent division of property and a statement that alimony would be paid at the rate of $100 per month for thirty-six months, the latter division, even though reducible to a lump sum, was held to be periodic alimony, subject to modification due to the changed circumstance of the wife's remarriage. Estes v Estes, No. C-800226 (1st Dist Ct App, Hamilton, 4-8-81).

Where the court authorizes the sale of a parcel of land, but it cannot be determined whether the award is a division of property or a division of property pursuant to an alimony order under RC 3105.18, the award will be reversed and remanded to the trial court for modifications. Scherer v Scherer, No. 41934 (8th Dist Ct App, Cuyahoga, 11-6-80).

Where a motion is made to modify a separation agreement alimony clause calling for $200 per month until death or remarriage, a court cannot grant the motion since the imposition of a time period would, in effect, be a judicial modification of a separation agreement which the court cannot do without consent of the parties or without an express reservation of continuing jurisdiction to do so. Kelly v Kelly, No. 37476 (8th Dist Ct App, Cuyahoga, 6-22-78).

Decree for alimony can be opened, vacated or modified only by a proceeding for that purpose in court in which it was rendered. Davis v. Davis (Ohio Com.Pl. 1970) 24 Ohio Misc. 17, 258 N.E.2d 277, 51 O.O.2d 388, 53 O.O.2d 48.

A final judgment for alimony in gross is not subject to modification. Aultman v. Aultman (Cuyahoga 1960) 167 N.E.2d 377, 83 Ohio Law Abs. 543.

Failure to separate an award of alimony into alimony for the wife and support money for the children is not prejudicial error, since such an order could be modified upon a proper showing. Hutson v. Hutson (Fayette 1954) 128 N.E.2d 673, 70 Ohio Law Abs. 511.

26. —Termination of support, modification

Absent a showing that a trial court abused its discretion, a termination of sustenance alimony payments in a modification proceeding should not be disturbed. Blakemore v. Blakemore (Ohio 1983) 5 Ohio St.3d 217, 450 N.E.2d 1140, 5 O.B.R. 481.

Where in a divorce action payment of alimony is ordered which in effect is part of an overall property settlement, extending for a period of eleven years and then terminating, the subsequent remarriage of the divorced wife does not constitute an abandonment of her right to alimony. Dailey v. Dailey (Ohio 1960) 171 Ohio St. 133, 167 N.E.2d 906, 12 O.O.2d 161.

General rule is that spousal support awards should terminate upon a date certain, in order to place a definitive limit on the parties' rights and responsibilities; however, potential exceptions to rule include cases involving a marriage of long duration, or where a homemaker-spouse has little opportunity to develop meaningful employment outside the home. Bowen v. Bowen (Ohio App. 9 Dist. 1999) 132 Ohio App.3d 616, 725 N.E.2d 1165.

Trial court's failure to establish a termination date for spousal support does not result in an award for life, where the court retains jurisdiction to reduce or terminate the support award at any time based on a change in either party's circumstances. Bowen v. Bowen (Ohio App. 9 Dist. 1999) 132 Ohio App.3d 616, 725 N.E.2d 1165.

Trial court's failure to establish specific termination date for award of spousal support in connection with divorce judgment did not render award improper, where parties' marriage of 20 years was one of long duration that came within exception to requirement that support awards have a definite termination date, and court retained jurisdiction to reduce or terminate award at any time based on a change of circumstances. Bowen v. Bowen (Ohio App. 9 Dist. 1999) 132 Ohio App.3d 616, 725 N.E.2d 1165.

Where payee spouse has resources, ability and potential to be self-supporting, award of sustenance alimony in divorce action should provide for termination of award, within reasonable time and upon date certain, in order to place definitive limit upon parties' rights and responsibilities, except in cases involving marriage of long duration, parties of advanced age or homemaker-spouse with little opportunity to develop meaningful employment outside home. Arthur v. Arthur (Ohio App. 5 Dist. 1998) 130 Ohio App.3d 398, 720 N.E.2d 176.

Without showing of financial support by new partner or for new partner, merely living with unrelated member of opposite sex is insufficient, in and of itself, to require termination of spousal support for cohabitation, where divorce decree provides for such termination. In re Dissolution of Marriage of Briggs (Ohio App. 9 Dist. 1998) 129 Ohio App.3d 346, 717 N.E.2d 1110.

Former wife was not "cohabiting" with male companion, as such term was used in divorce decree as condition for termination of spousal support; wife and companion owned separate homes in two different states, each being solely responsible for all expenses related to his or her respective home, were registered to vote in different states, never held themselves out as being married, maintained separate finances and bank accounts, and did not otherwise obtain financial benefits of remarriage by reason of their relationship. In re Dissolution of Marriage of Briggs (Ohio App. 9 Dist. 1998) 129 Ohio App.3d 346, 717 N.E.2d 1110.

Husband's anticipated retirement did not provide basis for reduction or termination of spousal support obligation, where husband did not present evidence as to when he would retire or as to his expected income and expenses on retirement. Mottice v. Mottice (Ohio App. 9 Dist. 1997) 118 Ohio App.3d 731, 693 N.E.2d 1179.

Spousal support should terminate within reasonable time, where payee spouse has resources, ability, and potential to be self-supporting, except in cases involving marriage of long duration, parties of advanced age, or homemaker spouse with little opportunity to develop meaningful employment outside the home. Schultz v. Schultz (Franklin 1996) 110 Ohio App.3d 715, 675 N.E.2d 55.

Termination of spousal support was warranted in light of former wife's current resources and income. Schultz v. Schultz (Franklin 1996) 110 Ohio App.3d 715, 675 N.E.2d 55.

Court with authority to modify spousal support award has discretion to terminate award. Ricketts v. Ricketts (Butler 1996) 109 Ohio App.3d 746, 673 N.E.2d 156, dismissed, appeal not allowed 76 Ohio St.3d 1473, 669 N.E.2d 856.

Trial court did not abuse its discretion in not retaining jurisdiction over spousal support issue when terminating former husband's spousal support obligation; trial court initially imposed spousal support of $75 per week while retaining jurisdiction over issue, then reduced support to $50 per week, and then terminated support. Ricketts v. Ricketts (Butler 1996) 109 Ohio App.3d 746, 673 N.E.2d 156, dismissed, appeal not allowed 76 Ohio St.3d 1473, 669 N.E.2d 856.

Termination of spousal support payments in modification proceeding should not be disturbed, absent showing that trial court abused its discretion. Ricketts v. Ricketts (Butler 1996) 109 Ohio App.3d 746, 673 N.E.2d 156, dismissed, appeal not allowed 76 Ohio St.3d 1473, 669 N.E.2d 856.

Husband's motions to terminate spousal support and to vacate finding of contempt for failure to pay support, based on fact that husband and wife were first cousins, were properly deemed moot after trial court entered final decree finding that marriage between cousins was voidable, not void, since motion for relief from judgment must be supported, at least, by demonstration of meritorious defense if relief is granted. Soley v. Soley (Lucas 1995) 101 Ohio App.3d 540, 655 N.E.2d 1381, dismissed, appeal not allowed 73 Ohio St.3d 1410, 651 N.E.2d 1308, certiorari denied 116 S.Ct. 945, 133 L.Ed.2d 870.

Trial court did not abuse its discretion in determining that establishing termination date for former husband's spousal support obligation would be inappropriate; parties had been married for 22 years, wife's financial situation limited her to taking one evening course at college per semester, there was evidence that her annual salary would be no more than $20,000 once she obtained degree, and she did not have resources and immediate potential to be self-supporting, despite claim that evidence established that she had in fact become self-supporting. Vanke v. Vanke (Franklin 1994) 93 Ohio App.3d 373, 638 N.E.2d 630.

At a later modification proceeding, if there is no set termination date in a divorce decree, the court should consider whether spousal support should be set to terminate based on the payee-spouse's resources, ability, and potential to be self-supporting. Vanke v. Vanke (Franklin 1992) 80 Ohio App.3d 576, 609 N.E.2d 1328.

A trial court errs in failing to reserve jurisdiction to modify an alimony award terminable on a date certain. Nori v. Nori (Butler 1989) 58 Ohio App.3d 69, 568 N.E.2d 730.

Where an alimony award contains contingencies which end the obligation to pay, the award is periodic alimony rather than a property division, notwithstanding its statement of definite amounts payable over a definite period, and a reservation of jurisdiction to modify the award is implied. Bean v. Bean (Madison 1983) 14 Ohio App.3d 358, 471 N.E.2d 785, 14 O.B.R. 462.

Remarriage of a party who receives spousal support does not automatically terminate an ex-spouse's obligation to pay the support as ordered where (1) the spousal support ordered by the trial court at the time of divorce is associated with an unequal distribution of marital property in favor of the obligor, (2) the obligee has a medical condition which affects earning ability, and (3) the spousal support payments are related to the obligor's child support obligation. Taylor v Taylor, No. 97-BA-10, 1998 WL 473340 (7th Dist Ct App, Belmont, 8-4-98).

A court abuses discretion when it concludes that a former husband is voluntarily unemployed and in denying his motion for termination of spousal support where he is injured in an explosion and has difficulty performing his duties as CEO of a corporation because of his diminished capacity due to the explosion. Pogoloff v Pogoloff, No. L-96-258, 1997 WL 416288 (6th Dist Ct App, Lucas, 7-18-97).

Exception to the general rule that alimony should have a definite termination date is warranted where (1) the parties are married for eighteen years, (2) the wife does not have a college degree and can expect to make only $13,000 to $20,000 a year whereas the husband is able to earn over $800,000 a year, and (3) the wife is forty-six years old and receives counseling for mental health problems. Burma v Burma, No. 68838, 1996 WL 157332 (8th Dist Ct App, Cuyahoga, 4-4-96).

Termination of spousal support is supported by (1) an interest-free loan of $5000 from the support recipient's cohabitant, (2) a joint checking account, (3) a shared household fund in which the parties deposit spare change, (4) each party paying one-half of the utilities, groceries, and household expenses, (5) sharing in household chores, (6) traveling together on day trips and overnight vacations to visit mutual friends, and (7) including one another in family gatherings. Slack v Slack, No. 94 CA 2050, 1995 WL 670041 (4th Dist Ct App, Ross, 11-4-95).

A retroactive order to terminate spousal support eighteen months prior to the filing of the motion to terminate is appropriate where the parties agree in a separation agreement that spousal support would terminate upon cohabitation and evidence substantiates the cohabitation; furthermore, the request for overpayments in the motion to terminate support places the party on notice of potential liability and there is no violation of due process rights. Jennings v Jennings, No. 68782, 1995 WL 628336 (8th Dist Ct App, Cuyahoga, 10-26-95).

In accordance with a divorce decree, cohabitation by a wife with a nonrelative male for more than thirty days triggers termination of alimony because the paramour has voluntarily undertaken a duty of total support, or has otherwise assumed obligations equivalent to those arising from a ceremonial marriage. Peace v Peace, No. L-94-342, 1995 WL 490985 (6th Dist Ct App, Lucas, 9-18-95).

The trial court did not err in denying the defendant-husband's motion to terminate or modify alimony, in that the alimony award was for a definite amount, to terminate at a certain date; inclusion in an alimony award of terminating conditions will not render such award indefinite where the outer limit of the parties rights and liabilities may be ascertained. Burgess v Burgess, No. L-82-200 (6th Dist Ct App, Lucas, 10-1-82).

A husband may not get a decrease in alimony payments even when the wife has a new job and higher income if such income and employment were within the expectation of the parties at the time, and the agreement does not specify that the earnings would be a basis for termination. Fox v Fox, No. 43636 (8th Dist Ct App, Cuyahoga, 1-28-82).

Where the judgment ordering alimony decreed that the alimony would end when the wife earned an excess of $500 gross income for two months, it is not error to grant plaintiff's motion to terminate rather than to grant defendant's motion to modify on a sliding scale. Conner v Conner, No. CA5491 (5th Dist Ct App, Stark, 6-10-81).

It is an abuse of discretion for the trial judge to omit to provide for a decrease in alimony at a date certain and to provide some terminal point for the alimony award other than the death or remarriage of the appellee or further order of the court. Mattoni v Mattoni, No. L-79-129 (6th Dist Ct App, Lucas, 2-22-80).

The trial court erred in terminating the plaintiff-appellant's weekly alimony payments and monthly mortgage payments, as the court did not find that the plaintiff-appellant's need for support had changed, yet the defendant-appellee's income had increased; the trial court abused its discretion in terminating the alimony payments, as the court's assumption that some portion of those payments might be used by the plaintiff-appellant to support her illegitimate child was unfounded. Moore v Moore, No. 78AP-755 (10th Dist Ct App, Franklin, 6-19-79).

27. —Change in circumstances, modification

Trial court abused its discretion by modifying husband's spousal support obligation in divorce action three months after entry of order that initially established obligation, where court failed to provide any reasons for decision that would constitute a change of circumstances warranting modification. Bowen v. Bowen (Ohio App. 9 Dist. 1999) 132 Ohio App.3d 616, 725 N.E.2d 1165.

Periodic reductions in spousal maintenance payable to wife corresponded with reasonably anticipated changes in her expenses and income, and did not amount to abuse of trial court's discretion to set duration and amount of maintenance. Arthur v. Arthur (Ohio App. 5 Dist. 1998) 130 Ohio App.3d 398, 720 N.E.2d 176.

Even after the party moving for reduction of spousal support under divorce decree demonstrates a substantial change of circumstances, the burden does not shift to the obligee spouse to demonstrate a continuing need for support or that the existing award is unnecessary or unreasonable; the burden of persuasion with respect to the modification sought remains with the movant. Joseph v.

Joseph (Ohio App. 2 Dist. 1997) 122 Ohio App.3d 734, 702 N.E.2d 949.

Trial court erred in failing to remove from former husband's spousal support obligation requirement that he secure obligation with policy of life insurance, where husband's increased difficulty and expense in obtaining life insurance due to medical condition constituted substantial change in circumstances justifying review of original obligation and obligation to pay support was terminable upon his death. Moore v. Moore (Ohio App. 9 Dist. 1997) 120 Ohio App.3d 488, 698 N.E.2d 459.

Domestic relations court's spousal support modification order, which found that husband's current medical condition prevented him from working enough overtime to keep his income at same level it had been at time of divorce, adequately set forth basis for conclusion that changed circumstances justified modification, even though other statutory factors were not mentioned. Kucmanic v. Kucmanic (Ohio App. 8 Dist. 1997) 119 Ohio App.3d 609, 695 N.E.2d 1205.

Trial court did not abuse its discretion by failing to make individual findings of fact as to husband's allegedly failing health in denying his request to reduce or terminate his spousal support obligation; court implicitly considered his health in ruling that husband's anticipated retirement did not constitute substantial change as required to support modification of alimony. Mottice v. Mottice (Ohio App. 9 Dist. 1997) 118 Ohio App.3d 731, 693 N.E.2d 1179.

"Change of circumstances" includes, but is not limited to any increase or involuntary decrease in former spouse's wages, salary, bonuses, living expenses, or medical expenses. Carnahan v. Carnahan (Ohio App. 12 Dist. 1997) 118 Ohio App.3d 393, 692 N.E.2d 1086.

Reduction of more than $50,000 per year in former husband's income was such change in circumstance as might warrant modification of spousal support. Carnahan v. Carnahan (Ohio App. 12 Dist. 1997) 118 Ohio App.3d 393, 692 N.E.2d 1086.

New spouse's income can be considered in determining whether circumstances have changed but cannot be used to determine the spousal support obligor's ability to pay. Carnahan v. Carnahan (Ohio App. 12 Dist. 1997) 118 Ohio App.3d 393, 692 N.E.2d 1086.

Determination of the amount of spousal support is different from a determination that there was a substantial change in circumstances to warrant a modification. Carnahan v. Carnahan (Ohio App. 12 Dist. 1997) 118 Ohio App.3d 393, 692 N.E.2d 1086.

Evidence supported finding that husband's reduction in income was voluntary, and thus did not justify reduction in spousal support payments arising out of divorce decree, where husband reduced his income so that he could enhance his professional practice. Wallenhurst v. Wallenhurst (Ohio App. 7 Dist. 1996) 116 Ohio App.3d 823, 689 N.E.2d 586.

Former husband was entitled to alimony modification based on decrease in his income due to his inability to work the number of hours required for his job coupled with former wife's postdivorce employment. Merkle v. Merkle (Mahoning 1996) 115 Ohio App.3d 748, 686 N.E.2d 316.

Change in circumstances necessary to modify spousal support must be one that is substantial and not contemplated at time of earlier order. Tremaine v. Tremaine (Montgomery 1996) 111 Ohio App.3d 703, 676 N.E.2d 1249, appeal not allowed 77 Ohio St.3d 1480, 673 N.E.2d 142.

A domestic relations court enjoys continuing jurisdiction to modify or terminate a sustenance alimony award where the agreement at issue expressly requires a former wife to notify the husband when she gains employment and expressly provides for modification in the future. Kearns v. Kearns (Summit 1990) 69 Ohio App.3d 305, 590 N.E.2d 797.

Early retirement of a spousal support obligor and a resulting significant reduction of income necessitated by a severe medical condition constitutes sufficient cause for modification of spousal support such that denial of modification is an abuse of discretion. Haase v. Haase (Cuyahoga 1990) 64 Ohio App.3d 758, 582 N.E.2d 1107.

A court does not commit abuse of discretion when it denies a motion to reduce an award of alimony where the payor's alleged inability to pay results from the payor's act of voluntarily incurring additional debt. Shanley v. Shanley (Cuyahoga 1989) 46 Ohio App.3d 100, 546 N.E.2d 477.

There is no change in circumstances sufficient to require a reduction in alimony where the payor discontinues his high-paying job in order to establish his own business, which business initially produces a significantly lower income. Haynie v. Haynie (Cuyahoga 1984) 19 Ohio App.3d 288, 484 N.E.2d 750, 19 O.B.R. 459.

In an action seeking modification of alimony where the trial court finds only that there has been a substantial change in the circumstances of the obligor/spouse as relates to his ability to pay without finding that there has been a change in the need of the obligee/spouse, the court commits reversible error in ordering the modification. Norris v. Norris (Stark 1982) 13 Ohio App.3d 248, 469 N.E.2d 76, 13 O.B.R. 310.

Where a modified order of sustenance support not only increases the amount of spousal support but also extends the original period during which sustenance alimony is to be paid, the extension is improper absent a showing of a dramatic change in circumstances. Norris v. Norris (Stark 1982) 13 Ohio App.3d 248, 469 N.E.2d 76, 13 O.B.R. 310.

It is not an abuse of discretion to modify an alimony award to provide a four-fold increase, where the income of the supporting party has increased six-fold, and the original decree provided for review in anticipation of such increased income. Lira v. Lira (Cuyahoga 1983) 12 Ohio App.3d 69, 465 N.E.2d 1353, 12 O.B.R. 211.

Inquiry regarding the existence of changed circumstances pursuant to RC 3105.18 must begin from the time that the existing order was entered; the trial court abuses its discretion when it inquires solely into events which have happened since an intervening hearing on a party's unsuccessful attempt to modify sustenance alimony. Bingham v. Bingham (Franklin 1983) 9 Ohio App.3d 191, 459 N.E.2d 231, 9 O.B.R. 302.

An award of a certain sum each month as alimony subject to modification if the financial status of the recipient is changed is final except for the specific reservation, although, where a change in such condition is found to exist, changes in other conditions may be considered in determining the feasibility of such modification. Ward v. Ward (Montgomery 1956) 104 Ohio App. 105, 140 N.E.2d 906, 74 Ohio Law Abs. 408, 4 O.O.2d 177.

Court may amend its decree for alimony only when there has been a material change in the circumstances of the parties. Nash v. Nash (Medina 1945) 77 Ohio App. 155, 65 N.E.2d 728, 32 O.O. 409.

A decree of divorce between wife who is eighty-six years old and husband who is eighty-nine that stipulates each party is to receive his or her separate property free and clear of any claims of the other party any time in the future is basis for denial of wife's motion for modification of support due to infirmity from old age despite husband's cost of living increases in his Social Security and STRS pensions. Schwab v Schwab, No. 1998CA00315, 1999 WL 668847 (5th Dist Ct App, Stark, 8-23-99).

A CPA with a history of successful employment in the health care area, upon being informed that in four months the income with his current employer will cease, cannot know what his income will be in four months and the trial court abuses discretion in dismissing defendant's motion for reduction of spousal support by not permitting the magistrate to complete the scheduled hearing and consider all the statutory criteria. Talley v Talley, No. 98AP-1368, 1999 WL 536638 (10th Dist Ct App, Franklin, 7-27-99).

A decision to modify spousal support to $600 per month despite the husband's involuntary decrease in income is warranted where his financial circumstances are much better than those of the wife who remains unemployed and on medication for a bi-polar disorder. Smith v Smith, No. 98CA2615, 1999 WL 482398 (4th Dist Ct App, Scioto, 6-29-99).

A trial court abuses its discretion by failing to consider a motion for new trial in a divorce and spousal support action based on newly discovered evidence which indicate a change in circumstances when evidence shows the referee relied on a finding that it would be unlikely for the wife to gain full-time employment in fashioning his spousal support recommendation, and subsequent to the support determination the wife did acquire full-time employment. Rogers v Rogers, No. 95-CA-7, 1995 WL 461262 (2d Dist Ct App, Miami, 8-2-95).

Modification of a spousal support obligation is supported by a change of circumstances evidenced by (1) employment which undergoes change within a six-month period from an executive sales position grossing $60,000 a year to a state of unemployment, (2) unsuccessful efforts to find new employment, (3) attempts to start a new business, and (4) the business operating at a loss as of the date of hearing. Conrad v Conrad, No. 66780, 1994 WL 723738 (8th Dist Ct App, Cuyahoga, 12-29-94).

The trial court's modification order adjusting the husband's spousal support obligation from $1,000 per month to $500 per month for one year, with the remaining $500 per month going into arrearage, is illusory, arbitrary, and unreasonable, given that (1) the husband has lost his $60,000 per year job, efforts at reemployment are unsuccessful, and a business which he starts is operating at a loss; (2) there is no evidence that the husband is voluntarily unemployed or underemployed; (3) there is no explanation or rational analysis in the referee's report to support a finding that imputes income of $30,000 per year to the husband or a finding that the husband would have available $12,000 per year to pay in spousal support; and (4) the order deprives the husband of sufficient funds to cover his monthly living expenses. Conrad v Conrad, No. 66780, 1994 WL 723738 (8th Dist Ct App, Cuyahoga, 12-29-94).

Retirement constitutes a change of circumstances which justifies reduction or termination of a sustenance alimony obligation where a vocational school employee's retirement is not voluntary due to termination of the teacher's instructional program. Stewart v Stewart, No. 94 CA 15, 1994 WL 718355 (4th Dist Ct App, Gallia, 12-27-94).

The reduction of a husband's sustenance alimony obligation after his voluntary retirement does not constitute an abuse of discretion. Melhorn v Melhorn, No. 11139 (2d Dist Ct App, Montgomery, 1-30-89).

Where a husband's income is reduced one-half by his retirement, and he seeks a reduction of alimony, a court may refuse the modification on the grounds that the husband, age fifty-six, is not required to retire, and therefore the change in financial circumstances is not beyond the husband's control. Bauer v Bauer, No. CA 7596 (2d Dist Ct App, Montgomery, 4-15-82).

A court may not order an increase in alimony when the husband acquires ownership of a corporation because the time and circumstances of that future event are too uncertain to serve as the basis for an automatic change in periodic alimony payments, particularly since the court cannot reasonably anticipate other circumstances which might affect the level of alimony payments at that unknown future date. Hakeman v Hakeman, No. 43475 (8th Dist Ct App, Cuyahoga, 12-17-81).

Where a separation agreement provides for the court to review the question of alimony in the event husband's salary is reduced to two-thirds of what he once earned, and where husband quits his job rather than having lost his job, the court may refuse to modify the alimony. Pappas v Pappas, No. 3234 (9th Dist Ct App, Lorain, 12-2-81).

Where the husband has suffered a heart attack, bankruptcy and loss of his job, a court may not allow a motion to modify alimony because the decree was dated prior to the Wolfe decision which is only applied prospectively. Parsons v Parsons, No. 9937 (9th Dist Ct App, Summit, 4-1-81).

Where the wife's income has dramatically increased but her expenses have similarly increased, the court will deny husband's motion for a reduction of alimony payments because he has not demonstrated a change of circumstances. Learmonth v Learmonth, No. 80AP-537 (10th Dist Ct App, Franklin, 3-3-81).

Wife's motion for increase in alimony based on the sole change in circumstance of husband's increased income is not grounds for an increase in alimony. Steinbrenner v Steinbrenner, No. 1609 (9th Dist Ct App, Wayne, 12-19-79).

In an action for modification of alimony and child support, where the income of a spouse who was in a professional school during the marriage increased greatly following the divorce, alimony will be limited to the predivorce living standard, unless (1) the original alimony award was decreased because of the provider's inability to completely maintain two households; (2) the original alimony payments no longer can maintain the same standard of living due to inflation; or (3) the dependent spouse has been rendered less independent because of infirmity or some other reason. Colizoli v Colizoli, 9 OBR 242 (App, Cuyahoga 1983), modified by 15 Ohio St.3d 333, 15 O.B.R. 458, 474 N.E.2d 280 (1984).

A court of common pleas may modify an alimony decree upon a showing of changed conditions of the parties even though such decree does not provide that it is subject to further order of the court. Braund v. Braund (Cuyahoga 1962) 183 N.E.2d 641, 89 Ohio Law Abs. 365.

28. Jurisdiction for modification

A decreeing court does not have continuing jurisdiction to modify a sustenance alimony award that was made for a fixed period of years even though the award is subject to termination in the event of death, remarriage, or cohabitation unless the decreeing court expressly reserves jurisdiction to modify. Ressler v. Ressler (Ohio 1985) 17 Ohio St.3d 17, 476 N.E.2d 1032, 17 O.B.R. 14.

Where sustenance already is for ascertainable amount over an ascertainable number of years, the court has no jurisdiction to modify the alimony portion of an award. Colizoli v. Colizoli (Ohio 1984) 15 Ohio St.3d 333, 474 N.E.2d 280, 15 O.B.R. 458.

Just as a trial court lacks authority to set the amount of alimony in a dissolution, the court lacks jurisdiction to modify alimony in a dissolution. McClain v. McClain (Ohio 1984) 15 Ohio St.3d 289, 473 N.E.2d 811, 15 O.B.R. 421.

An alimony award which constitutes a division of the marital assets and liabilities is not subject to modification under the continuing jurisdiction of the court. Wolfe v. Wolfe (Ohio 1976) 46 Ohio St.2d 399, 350 N.E.2d 413, 75 O.O.2d 474.

Where, upon granting a divorce, a court awards alimony to a wife, pursuant to an agreement of the parties, to be paid until the condition subsequent of remarriage or death of the wife, and such award is for her sustenance and support and independent of any award arising by adjustment of the property rights of the parties, reservation of jurisdiction to modify the award will be implied in the decree. Wolfe v. Wolfe (Ohio 1976) 46 Ohio St.2d 399, 350 N.E.2d 413, 75 O.O.2d 474.

Evidence did not establish that husband was coerced into signing divorce judgment entry that did not contain reservation of jurisdiction to modify spousal support, where record gave every indication that husband signed the entry freely and voluntarily without any improper pressure or tactics from opposing counsel. Cermak v. Cermak (Ohio App. 7 Dist. 1998) 126 Ohio App.3d 589, 710 N.E.2d 1191, dismissed, appeal not allowed 82 Ohio St.3d 1450, 695 N.E.2d 1148.

Trial court lacked jurisdiction to modify or terminate husband's spousal support obligation set forth in judgment of divorce, where judgment did not contain specific provision reserving jurisdiction to modify spousal support. Cermak v. Cermak (Ohio App. 7 Dist. 1998) 126 Ohio App.3d 589, 710 N.E.2d 1191, dismissed, appeal not allowed 82 Ohio St.3d 1450, 695 N.E.2d 1148.

Decreeing court does not have continuing jurisdiction to modify a spousal support award of fixed duration unless the decreeing court expressly reserves such jurisdiction. Kopich v. Kopich (Ohio App. 1 Dist. 1998) 126 Ohio App.3d 332, 710 N.E.2d 350, motion to certify allowed 82 Ohio St.3d 1442, 695 N.E.2d 265, appeal allowed 82 Ohio St.3d 1443, 695 N.E.2d 266, cause dismissed 85 Ohio St.3d 1450, 708 N.E.2d 723.

Trial court had jurisdiction to modify amount of spousal support obligation which was established in separation agreement, and which was incorporated into divorce decree, where last paragraph of divorce decree contained language stating "ALL UNTIL FURTHER ORDER OF THIS COURT." Kopich v. Kopich (Ohio App. 1 Dist. 1998) 126 Ohio App.3d 332, 710 N.E.2d 350, motion to certify allowed 82 Ohio St.3d 1442, 695 N.E.2d 265, appeal allowed 82 Ohio St.3d 1443, 695 N.E.2d 266, cause dismissed 85 Ohio St.3d 1450, 708 N.E.2d 723.

Trial court did not retain jurisdiction to modify spousal support where divorce decree provided that court retained jurisdiction to terminate spousal support in event of wife's death, remarriage, or return to full-time employment. Jordan v. Jordan (Ohio App. 4 Dist. 1996) 117 Ohio App.3d 47, 689 N.E.2d 1005, dismissed, appeal not allowed 78 Ohio St.3d 1489, 678 N.E.2d 1227.

Trial court can retain jurisdiction to terminate spousal support on occurrence of certain events without retaining power to modify spousal support for change in circumstances. Jordan v. Jordan (Ohio App. 4 Dist. 1996) 117 Ohio App.3d 47, 689 N.E.2d 1005, dismissed, appeal not allowed 78 Ohio St.3d 1489, 678 N.E.2d 1227.

Notwithstanding public policy in favor of marriage, former wife's cohabitation with man did not equate to "marriage" for purposes of trial court's retention of jurisdiction to terminate spousal support if wife remarried. Jordan v. Jordan (Ohio App. 4 Dist. 1996) 117 Ohio App.3d 47, 689 N.E.2d 1005, dismissed, appeal not allowed 78 Ohio St.3d 1489, 678 N.E.2d 1227.

Decision whether to retain jurisdiction to modify spousal support award is within trial court's discretion. Ricketts v. Ricketts (Butler 1996) 109 Ohio App.3d 746, 673 N.E.2d 156, dismissed, appeal not allowed 76 Ohio St.3d 1473, 669 N.E.2d 856.

Trial court does not have continuing jurisdiction to modify spousal support award, even though award is subject to termination in event of death, remarriage, or cohabitation, unless court expressly reserves jurisdiction to modify. Ricketts v. Ricketts (Butler 1996) 109 Ohio App.3d 746, 673 N.E.2d 156, dismissed, appeal not allowed 76 Ohio St.3d 1473, 669 N.E.2d 856.

Failure to alter award of spousal support after changing distribution of property to provide for sale of marital residence, which wife would no longer have to maintain, was not abuse of discretion in divorce proceedings, where trial court retained jurisdiction to modify spousal support based on changed circumstances. Shaffer v. Shaffer (Crawford 1996) 109 Ohio App.3d 205, 671 N.E.2d 1317.

Decreeing court does not have continuing jurisdiction to modify spousal support unless court expressly reserves jurisdiction to modify. Marden v. Marden (Butler 1996) 108 Ohio App.3d 568, 671 N.E.2d 331.

Trial court could make spousal support order upon divorce nonmodifiable by refusing to retain jurisdiction. Soley v. Soley (Lucas 1995) 101 Ohio App.3d 540, 655 N.E.2d 1381, dismissed, appeal not allowed 73 Ohio St.3d 1410, 651 N.E.2d 1308, certiorari denied 116 S.Ct. 945, 133 L.Ed.2d 870.

Trial court abused its discretion by failing to reserve jurisdiction to modify indefinite award of sustenance alimony; statute requires domestic relations court to specifically reserve jurisdiction to subsequently modify sustenance alimony award. Gullia v. Gullia (Cuyahoga 1994) 93 Ohio App.3d 653, 639 N.E.2d 822, cause dismissed 70 Ohio St.3d 1409, 637 N.E.2d 6, dismissed, jurisdictional motion overruled 70 Ohio St.3d 1409, 637 N.E.2d 7.

Where trial court at time of divorce decree did not reserve jurisdiction to modify amount or terms of alimony or spousal support and husband did not make any direct appeal of that order, trial court lacked jurisdiction to modify order on husband's motion to modify spousal support in light of changed circumstances. Johnson v. Johnson (Knox 1993) 88 Ohio App.3d 329, 623 N.E.2d 1294.

Divorce court was required to determine whether spousal support award was permanent, or if not, then to provide date certain for its termination; court erred in reserving jurisdiction for review of spousal support for specified period of time. Frost v. Frost (Franklin 1992) 84 Ohio App.3d 699, 618 N.E.2d 198, motion overruled 66 Ohio St.3d 1489, 612 N.E.2d 1245.

A court may not determine that an award of alimony is unwarranted, yet retain continuing jurisdiction over alimony. Wolding v. Wolding (Logan 1992) 82 Ohio App.3d 235, 611 N.E.2d 860.

It is an abuse of discretion for a trial court to reserve jurisdiction over a party's unvested interest in a military pension. King v. King (Warren 1992) 78 Ohio App.3d 599, 605 N.E.2d 970.

In an action for modification of an alimony award in a decree finalized before 1986, the trial court retains jurisdiction over the issue when the total amount, $900 per month until remarriage, death or cohabitation, is unascertainable. Dickson v. Dickson (Ashtabula 1991) 74 Ohio App.3d 70, 598 N.E.2d 58.

When a court awards sustenance alimony for a number of years or "until further order of the Court," that court has expressly retained jurisdiction to modify both the amount of alimony and the length of time during which the alimony is to be paid. Meinke v. Meinke (Lucas 1989) 56 Ohio App.3d 171, 565 N.E.2d 875.

Provision of separation agreement incorporated into dissolution decree stating that in event of dissolution or in event either party procured divorce, court granting divorce had jurisdiction for modification purposes did not confer jurisdiction upon court of common pleas to modify alimony provision of separation agreement; specific language granted continuing jurisdiction only to court granting the divorce, and no divorce was granted inasmuch as parties terminated their marriage through dissolution procedures. Neidenthal v. Neidenthal (Franklin 1987) 41 Ohio App.3d 379, 535 N.E.2d 714.

A court's lack of authority to modify an alimony order due to its failure to expressly reserve jurisdiction over the issues renders a modification of the order voidable by a timely appeal, but not void. Purpura v. Purpura (Cuyahoga 1986) 33 Ohio App.3d 237, 515 N.E.2d 27.

Jurisdiction to modify an award of alimony includes the jurisdiction to terminate sustenance alimony when the dependent spouse no longer needs that assistance. Purpura v. Purpura (Cuyahoga 1986) 33 Ohio App.3d 237, 515 N.E.2d 27.

An award of sustenance alimony need not have a definite termination date but may continue until further order of the court, if guesswork involved in setting a definite date could result in hardship to either party. Gore v. Gore (Summit 1985) 27 Ohio App.3d 141, 499 N.E.2d 1281, 27 O.B.R. 173.

A court has continuing jurisdiction to modify a decree of alimony if the parties agree to continuing jurisdiction in a separation agreement incorporated into a decree of dissolution of marriage. Merrill v. Merrill (Summit 1985) 26 Ohio App.3d 201, 499 N.E.2d 13, 26 O.B.R. 422.

Where a change in circumstances that would affect alimony occurs during a fourteen-month delay between submission of an alimony case to a court and the entry of judgment, it is an abuse of discretion to deny a motion for a new trial on grounds of newly discovered evidence, where the court is otherwise without jurisdiction to modify an alimony award for a definite amount. Knox v. Knox (Stark 1986) 26 Ohio App.3d 17, 498 N.E.2d 236, 26 O.B.R. 186.

A trial court has continuing jurisdiction over sustenance alimony judgments which are not the product of agreement between the parties, and the court may, pursuant to such jurisdiction, increase the amount of spousal support where it is found that there is a substantial increase in the obligee's need for sustenance and in the obligor's ability to pay. Norris v. Norris (Stark 1982) 13 Ohio App.3d 248, 469 N.E.2d 76, 13 O.B.R. 310.

Trial court had no jurisdiction to make modification in alimony, where separation agreement incorporated into dissolution decree did not include provision permitting court to modify alimony. DiPietro v. DiPietro (Franklin 1983) 10 Ohio App.3d 44, 460 N.E.2d 657, 10 O.B.R. 52.

Party seeking to vacate or modify alimony award may properly proceed by filing a motion for release of judgment or by filing a motion to invoke continuing jurisdiction of domestic relations court. McKinnon v. McKinnon (Franklin 1983) 9 Ohio App.3d 220, 459 N.E.2d 590, 9 O.B.R. 370.

Where no agreement has been made as to a permanent alimony award between the parties, and trial court makes an alimony award after hearing all the evidence, court has implied continuing jurisdiction to modify award for permanent alimony due to changed circumstances, even though it did not expressly reserve jurisdiction to do so. McDonagh v. McDonagh (Lucas 1982) 4 Ohio App.3d 207, 447 N.E.2d 758, 4 O.B.R. 311.

If the parties to a divorce proceeding agree to an indefinite amount of permanent alimony and the trial court finds that the agreement as to permanent alimony is fair, just and equitable and therefore incorporates it into the journal entry, but does not reserve continuing jurisdiction to modify said award, the trial court does not have authority to modify the decree for permanent alimony because of changed circumstances, but if there is no agreement between the parties as to permanent alimony of an indefinite amount, and the trial court makes an alimony award after hearing all the evidence, but the court does not expressly reserve jurisdiction to modify, it is implied that the trial court does have continuing jurisdiction to modify the award for permanent alimony because of change of circumstances. Popovic v. Popovic (Cuyahoga 1975) 45 Ohio App.2d 57, 341 N.E.2d 341, 74 O.O.2d 94.

An order for temporary alimony pending litigation is merged into the final judgment in a divorce or alimony action, and any temporary order and arrearages incident thereto is terminated when final judgment is entered; the final judgment replaces all that transpired before it, so that once the trial court enters final judgment it cannot reinstate any order it may have made for temporary alimony pending the litigation because it has lost jurisdiction and, therefore, has no authority to make such an order. Rahm v. Rahm (Cuyahoga 1974) 39 Ohio App.2d 74, 315 N.E.2d 495, 68 O.O.2d 225.

A court of common pleas retains jurisdiction to modify or vacate a decree of alimony upon a proper showing of changed conditions and circumstances of the parties, where such decree was not for a definite amount payable in installments or payable only for a limited number of installments, or was not based upon an agreement of the parties as to a division of property, which was affirmed by the court and incorporated into the decree. Bulloch v. Bulloch (Franklin 1969) 21 Ohio App.2d 76, 255 N.E.2d 299, 50 O.O.2d 142.

Where a court of common pleas, division of domestic relations, decrees separate maintenance for a husband and wife and orders the husband to make regular installment payments, in the nature of alimony, to the wife and to also make weekly child-support payments to her, and where such alimony and child-support orders are not, pursuant to agreement of the parties, a division of property or a fixed sum in settlement of the ultimate property rights of the parties at that time, the court has continuing jurisdiction to entertain a motion, filed after term, to modify the alimony and child-support payments orders due to a change in circumstances. Caudill v. Caudill (Butler 1969) 20 Ohio App.2d 100, 252 N.E.2d 186, 49 O.O.2d 118.

Where the provisions of a separation agreement as to alimony and for the future adjustment of alimony payments by the court are incorporated by reference in a divorce decree, the court has continuing jurisdiction to decide any questions relating thereto. Williams v. Williams (Miami 1959) 112 Ohio App. 412, 176 N.E.2d 288, 16 O.O.2d 322.

Court of common pleas retains jurisdiction to modify or vacate a decree of alimony upon a proper showing of changed condition and circumstances of the parties, where such decree was not for a definite amount payable in installments or payable only for a limited number of installments, or was not based upon an agreement of the parties as to a division of property which was affirmed by the court and incorporated into the decree. Clelland v. Clelland (Franklin 1959) 110 Ohio App. 546, 166 N.E.2d 428, 82 Ohio Law Abs. 515, 13 O.O.2d 354.

Where alimony in a lump sum has been awarded to wife in her action for alimony only, and journal entry expressly states that so far as support of child is concerned it is held open until further order of court, but there is no such statement in decree with reference to support of wife and no statement retaining jurisdiction over allowance for further alimony, court has no jurisdiction over allowance of further alimony to wife in an application for additional alimony filed by way of cross-petition in her husband's subsequent action for divorce. Robertson v. Robertson (Scioto 1938) 61 Ohio App. 458, 22 N.E.2d 744, 15 O.O. 286.

Common pleas court cannot vacate alimony decree entered in another county. Fessenden v. Fessenden (Wayne 1928) 32 Ohio App. 16, 165 N.E. 746, 6 Ohio Law Abs. 716, 28 Ohio Law Rep. 166.

In a child custody case the court does not improperly consider the mother's religious affiliation in determining that she should not be designated the residential parent for all the children where the court centers its concerns around the quality of education the children receive at a church-affiliated school rather than the religious philosophy of the church itself including (1) the below average class sizes, (2) the problems with teacher staffing, (3) the lack of teacher experience, (4) the lack of curriculum, and (5) the sheltered lifestyle. Arthur v Arthur, Nos. 97CA0071 and 98CA0023, 1998 WL 751701 (5th Dist Ct App, Fairfield, 10-22-98).

A trial court is without jurisdiction to terminate a spousal support obligation where the court has made no reservation of jurisdiction to reinstate the award based upon a change of circumstances after the termination date. Grevey v Grevey, No. CA96-04-074, 1997 WL 30573 (12th Dist Ct App, Butler, 1-27-97).

The language "all until further order of the court" appearing at the very end of the decree of divorce is sufficient to retain trial court jurisdiction over the award of spousal support. Kirkwood v Kirkwood, No. C-950940, 1996 WL 496947 (1st Dist Ct App, Hamilton, 9-4-96).

Failure of a trial court to retain jurisdiction over the issue of sustenance alimony awarded to a spouse in a marriage of long duration who is completely and indefinitely disabled constitutes an abuse of discretion. Easton v Tabet, Nos. 1995CA00313 and 1995CA00296, 1996 WL 488794 (5th Dist Ct App, Stark, 8-12-96).

Jurisdiction to determine whether a husband's spousal support obligation should be modified is retained where (1) the jurisdictional limitation of RC 3105.18 does not apply because the divorce decree was issued prior to the statutory revision that added the limiting language, (2) the $680 monthly payments are separate from the division of property and are intended to support the spouse, (3) the total support obligation is indefinite because the decree does not provide that payments will terminate on a particular date. Kirschner v Kirschner, No. C.A. 94CA005966, 1995 WL 500096 (9th Dist Ct App, Lorain, 8-23-95).

Language located at the end of a separation agreement under the section "Further Provisions" which states "This Agreement is, however, subject to review and modification and to further order of this Court," is sufficient language to invoke continuing jurisdiction of the trial court to modify spousal support. Stadelman-Wells v Wells, No. 94APF09-1361, 1995 WL 238419 (10th Dist Ct App, Franklin, 4-20-95).

Where a trial court expressly reserves the right to modify a spousal support award that is for a fixed period in the original divorce proceeding, later terminates that award due to the wife's cohabitation and does not reserve jurisdiction over the spousal support issue, that court has no jurisdiction to reinstate a spousal support award upon the husband's initiation of bankruptcy proceedings. Charlton v Charlton, No. 218, 1994 WL 583092 (7th Dist Ct App, Noble, 10-11-94).

A motion for alimony modification is properly denied if the trial court does not explicitly reserve jurisdiction to modify in the separation agreement incorporated into the dissolution of marriage decree. Edwards v Edwards, No. 14022, 1994 WL 95253 (2d Dist Ct App, Montgomery, 3-23-94).

Paragraph in divorce decree conditioning payment of alimony on payment of mortgage and insurance premiums is not a reservation of jurisdiction to modify the terms of amount of alimony; therefore, court's modification of alimony violated RC 3105.18. Benincasa v Benincasa, No. CA-93-20, 1993 WL 535259 (5th Dist Ct App, Muskingum, 12-6-93).

Where a court issuing a divorce decree fails to reserve jurisdiction to modify the amount of spousal support in case of changed circumstances and no direct appeal is made of that order, under RC 3105.18(E) the court has no jurisdiction to later modify the support amount. Johnson v Johnson, No. 92-CA-32, 1993 WL 274283 (5th Dist Ct App, Knox, 6-21-93).

A trial court's failure to expressly reserve continuing jurisdiction to modify a sustenance alimony award, not terminable after a definite period of time, upon a finding of changed circumstances, constitutes an abuse of discretion. Colwell v Colwell, No. CA88-03-043 (12th Dist Ct App, Butler, 10-11-88).

Where sustenance alimony is awarded pursuant to a decree or a separation agreement and the award is for a definite amount for a definite period of time, the award is not rendered indefinite because contingencies are attached which could reduce the total amount of sustenance alimony payable and a trial court has no jurisdiction to modify such award. Didomenico v Didomenico, No. CA84-10-009 (12th Dist Ct App, Fayette, 7-8-85).

A divorce decree which ordered the "transfer of hospitalization coverage" to the wife was a property alimony award, and therefore not subject to the continuing jurisdiction of the court or amenable to modification. Mayle v Mayle, No. CA 6268 (5th Dist Ct App, Stark, 2-13-84).

Trial court has continuing jurisdiction to settle a dispute between divorced parties as to which party is entitled to certain personal property, where the entitlements to the personal property were not provided for in the decree for divorce. Meeks v Meeks, No. L-82-085 (6th Dist Ct App, Lucas, 7-23-82).

Trial court is not precluded from exercising jurisdiction to modify an alimony award where an alleged separation agreement does not meet the requirements of a valid separation agreement pursuant to RC 3103.06 nor was the agreement written into the divorce decree or incorporated by reference. Strohschein v Strohschein, No. 81AP-784 (10th Dist Ct App, Franklin, 3-9-82).

An award of alimony for a definite amount for 121 months or until death with no reservation of jurisdiction is a property division rather than support alimony, and thus the trial court does not have continuing jurisdiction to modify. Maher v Maher, No. 43456 (8th Dist Ct App, Cuyahoga, 11-12-81).

Where alimony was sustenance for the wife and in definite amount and independent of property settlement, and where the husband's employment had been terminated and created a marked change in his financial condition, the court has continuing jurisdiction to modify the alimony provision. Davis v Davis, No. 1568 (2d Dist Ct App, Clark, 10-21-81).

In a case where the award for support is for a definite amount, and the support obligation terminates on a certain date, the trial court may properly deny appellant's motion to modify the alimony award because the award is not subject to modification. Szymkowiak v Calabrese, No. L-81-008 (6th Dist Ct App, Lucas, 10-16-81).

A motion for an order of public sale of real property which is not pursuant to an original order is actually a motion for modification of the divorce decree and under the continuing jurisdiction of the court. Martino v Martino, No. 14-80-15 (3d Dist Ct App, Union, 4-24-81).

An alimony award in a judgment decree of alimony alone, which constitutes a division of the marital assets and liabilities, is not subject to modifications in a subsequent divorce action. Shapiro v Shapiro, No. 80AP-520 (10th Dist Ct App, Franklin, 11-25-80).

The trial court erred in denying defendant-appellant's motion to modify a separation agreement on the grounds that said agreement lacked a reservation to modify alimony, because the separation agreement enumerated four financial obligations to support the award, three of which had been satisfied at the time the motion to modify was filed; therefore, the separation agreement clearly implied that a right to modification was contemplated when the enumerated conditions met fruition. Park v Park, No. CA 9538 (9th Dist Ct App, Summit, 7-2-80).

Where the provision for support is for a definite sum of money to be paid in installments over a specified period of time without any contingencies, this provision constitutes a division of marital assets and is not subject to modification under the continuing jurisdiction of the court. Tasin v Tasin, No. 37707 (8th Dist Ct App, Cuyahoga, 9-28-78).

Tax exemptions for children are "marital property," notwithstanding the fact that the separation agreement incorporated within the dissolution decree treats the exemptions as a component of child support; therefore, a court lacks subject matter jurisdiction to subsequently modify the award of the exemptions. In re Lee (Ohio Com.Pl. 1989) 58 Ohio Misc.2d 4, 567 N.E.2d 1350.

29. Post-divorce unchastity or remarriage

When a dependent divorced spouse remarries, the obligation of the first spouse to pay sustenance alimony terminates as a matter of law unless: (1) the sustenance alimony constitutes a property settlement, (2) the payment is related to child support, or (3) the parties have executed a separation agreement in contemplation of divorce that expressly provides for the continuation of sustenance alimony after the dependent party remarries. Dunaway v. Dunaway (Ohio 1990) 53 Ohio St.3d 227, 560 N.E.2d 171.

Post-divorce unchastity upon the part of the former wife is not grounds for automatically terminating the alimony award but may be considered in a subsequent modification proceeding insofar as it is relevant to the issues of continued need for such alimony and the amount. Wolfe v. Wolfe (Ohio 1976) 46 Ohio St.2d 399, 350 N.E.2d 413, 75 O.O.2d 474.

Where, in a divorce action, permanent alimony is ordered paid by the husband to the wife in a fixed amount per month, payable monthly "hereafter," based upon an agreement between the parties which does not constitute a property settlement and is not related to support of children, and where the alimony order contains no provision for termination of such payments or reservation of jurisdiction by the court, the subsequent marriage of such wife to another man capable of supporting her constitutes an election on her part to be supported by her new husband and an abandonment of the provision for permanent alimony from her divorced husband. Hunt v. Hunt (Ohio 1959) 169 Ohio St. 276, 159 N.E.2d 430, 8 O.O.2d 286.

Remarriage of one who owes spousal support does not warrant a modification of the spousal support payments, but the second spouse's income can be considered when there is an allegation of a change in circumstances. Carnahan v. Carnahan (Ohio App. 12 Dist. 1997) 118 Ohio App.3d 393, 692 N.E.2d 1086.

Award of spousal support to wife was not barred by fact that wife had been cohabiting with another man during the marriage, where court found that wife had a need for spousal support, and there was no evidence that wife and other man shared living expenses. Nemeth v. Nemeth (Ohio App. 7 Dist. 1997) 117 Ohio App.3d 554, 690 N.E.2d 1338.

When considering evidence with regards to cohabitation, trial court in divorce case should look to three principal factors: (1) an actual living together (2) of sustained duration (3) with shared expenses with respect to financing and day-to-day incidental expenses; in addition, trial court may also consider other relevant criteria including both behavior and intent of the parties. Nemeth v. Nemeth (Ohio App. 7 Dist. 1997) 117 Ohio App.3d 554, 690 N.E.2d 1338.

Trial court properly applied all factors set forth in statute and did not err or abuse its discretion in awarding wife spousal support of $675 per month for 18 months, notwithstanding wife's complaint that since marriage was one of long duration and she was a homemaker spouse, duration of support should not have been limited to 18 months, and that limitation was based solely upon court's finding that she was cohabiting with another male during the marriage. Nemeth v. Nemeth (Ohio App. 7 Dist. 1997) 117 Ohio App.3d 554, 690 N.E.2d 1338.

Competent evidence supported finding that wife did not cohabit prior to her remarriage, so as to justify termination of husband's spousal support obligation under divorce decree, even though wife and boyfriend took vacations together and spent many times together, where there was no evidence that wife was supported in whole or in part by boyfriend. Wallenhurst v. Wallenhurst (Ohio App. 7 Dist. 1996) 116 Ohio App.3d 823, 689 N.E.2d 586.

Without a showing of financial support, fact that former spouse is living with another is insufficient to permit termination of alimony on ground of cohabitation. Moell v. Moell (Ottawa 1994) 98 Ohio App.3d 748, 649 N.E.2d 880, appeal not allowed 72 Ohio St.3d 1407, 647 N.E.2d 496.

Whether particular living arrangement arises to level of "cohabitation," for purposes of cohabitation clause in divorce decree, is factual question to be initially determined by trial court which should look to three key principal factors: actual living together; of sustained duration; with shared expenses with respect to financing and day-to-day incidental expenses. Moell v. Moell (Ottawa 1994) 98 Ohio App.3d 748, 649 N.E.2d 880, appeal not allowed 72 Ohio St.3d 1407, 647 N.E.2d 496.

Neither presence nor absence of sexual relationship is dispositive of issue of cohabitation for purposes of cohabitation clause in divorce decree. Moell v. Moell (Ottawa 1994) 98 Ohio App.3d 748, 649 N.E.2d 880, appeal not allowed 72 Ohio St.3d 1407, 647 N.E.2d 496.

Trial court did not abuse its discretion in denying former husband's motion to terminate spousal support on ground of cohabitation; evidence supported conclusion that former wife and companion had not assumed mutual obligations of financial support required to establish cohabitation; with exception of food, no expenses were shared, each keeping his or her own separate accounts and finances, and neither received any substantial direct monetary support from the other; moreover, overwhelming reason why companion moved into former wife's home was to provide care after former wife suffered debilitating stroke. Moell v. Moell (Ottawa 1994) 98 Ohio App.3d 748, 649 N.E.2d 880, appeal not allowed 72 Ohio St.3d 1407, 647 N.E.2d 496.

Evidence supported finding that ex-wife and man with whom she lived following divorce were not "living in a state of concubinage" within meaning of provision of divorce decree terminating alimony upon occurrence of such event; although there was evidence that ex-wife and man had sexual relationship and went out socially and that man made some rent, utility and car payments for ex-wife, their relationship did not rise to level of one approximating marriage inasmuch as man did not receive mail at ex-wife's residence, and ex-wife and man usually ate meals separately, slept separately, and did not hold themselves out as husband and wife. Dial v. Dial (Summit 1993) 92 Ohio App.3d 513, 636 N.E.2d 361.

In cases involving divorce decree providing that spousal support will terminate upon recipient's cohabitation, question of recipient's cohabitation is to be determined by trier of fact of the case. Piscione v. Piscione (Lorain 1992) 85 Ohio App.3d 273, 619 N.E.2d 1030, motion overruled 65 Ohio St.3d 1493, 605 N.E.2d 393.

For purposes of divorce decrees providing that spousal support would terminate upon recipient's cohabitation, "cohabitation" requires some regularity of functioning as would husband and wife, either sexually or otherwise, and typically involves man and woman living together in same household and behaving as would husband and wife. Piscione v. Piscione (Lorain 1992) 85 Ohio App.3d 273, 619 N.E.2d 1030, motion overruled 65 Ohio St.3d 1493, 605 N.E.2d 393.

Trial court's finding that wife entered into "living arrangement similar to marriage," for purposes of divorce decree providing that spousal support would terminate upon wife's entering into such arrangement, was against manifest weight of evidence, even though wife and another man unquestionably were involved in serious relationship and spent great deal of time together; evidence that man had free access to wife's house, that he at one time kept several changes of clothing at wife's house, that he had ongoing sexual relationship with wife, that he attended church and went on vacations with wife and her children, and that he acted as supervisor and protector of children did not indicate that relationship rose to level similar to marriage. Piscione v. Piscione (Lorain 1992) 85 Ohio App.3d 273, 619 N.E.2d 1030, motion overruled 65 Ohio St.3d 1493, 605 N.E.2d 393.

Former husband's obligation to make alimony payments to wife terminated as matter of law on date wife remarried where divorce decree explicitly provided for trial court to retain jurisdiction to modify the order in the event of a significant change in circumstances, such as the wife's remarriage, decree contained separate provisions regarding property division and child support, and parties did not explicitly agree that alimony payments would continue after wife remarried, even though trial court originally awarded wife permanent alimony in recognition of physical and mental abuse she had suffered at hands of husband. VonAhlefeld v. VonAhlefeld (Butler 1993) 85 Ohio App.3d 220, 619 N.E.2d 495.

Ability to marry is a necessary element of concubinage; therefore, spousal support may not be terminated due to the cohabitation of an obligee wife in a homosexual relationship where the judgment requires that the obligee be in a state of concubinage to justify termination of spousal support. Gajovski v. Gajovski (Summit 1991) 81 Ohio App.3d 11, 610 N.E.2d 431, dismissed, jurisdictional motion overruled 62 Ohio St.3d 1415, 577 N.E.2d 660.

Termination of alimony is held too harsh a remedy although the woman recipient lives in a state of concubinage but the evidence fails to establish that the male paramour has undertaken any obligation of supporting her although he is a beneficiary of the alimony; the focus should be whether an appreciable amount of the sustenance alimony directly benefits the paramour and, if this is the case, this may be considered a change of circumstances warranting modification of the award. Perri v. Perri (Montgomery 1992) 79 Ohio App.3d 845, 608 N.E.2d 790, stay denied 64 Ohio St.3d 1426, 594 N.E.2d 968, dismissed, jurisdictional motion overruled 65 Ohio St.3d 1430, 600 N.E.2d 675.

The term cohabitation necessarily implies support; thus, alimony is properly terminated where it is shown that the recipient is also receiving financial assistance from a paramour. Thomas v. Thomas (Franklin 1991) 76 Ohio App.3d 482, 602 N.E.2d 385.

A former wife's post-divorce cohabitation in a family relationship with another is not a ground for automatic termination of alimony except to the extent that it bears upon the former wife's continued need for support. Thornton v. Thornton (Wyandot 1990) 70 Ohio App.3d 317, 590 N.E.2d 1375.

Termination of alimony is proper when the decree awarding alimony provides for modification upon the recipient's cohabitation "with an unrelated male who does provide support for the obligee" and the obligee does in fact cohabit with an unrelated male who provides some support, although the amount is less than the alimony award; a trial court is correct in construing an order providing for termination of alimony upon cohabitation and receipt of support from the cohabitant so as not to require any particular level of support, but simply that the cohabitant be providing some support to the obligee, in order to trigger the termination of alimony. Miller v. Miller (Montgomery 1989) 61 Ohio App.3d 269, 572 N.E.2d 742.

Evidence adduced at trial is sufficient to establish cohabitation where it is shown that (1) a vehicle belonging to the former wife's male friend was seen in front of the former wife's residence, in the driveway, or in the garage on numerous occasions and at various hours of the day and night; (2) the former wife and her male friend went on week-end trips together; (3) the former wife and her male friend admitted engaging in sexual intercourse together; and (4) the male friend received mail at the former wife's residence on at least one occasion. Bussey v. Bussey (Warren 1988) 55 Ohio App.3d 117, 563 N.E.2d 37.

Where a divorce decree uses the term "cohabitation" in the sense of an event which will change obligations created by the decree, the court must inquire whether the parties have assumed obligations, including support, similar to those which arise from a ceremonial marriage; the existence of a sexual relationship between unmarried parties who live together is not conclusive on the issue of cohabitation. (See also Bussey v Bussey, 55 App(3d) 117 (Warren 1988).) Taylor v. Taylor (Hamilton 1983) 11 Ohio App.3d 279, 465 N.E.2d 476, 11 O.B.R. 459.

With respect to dissolution decrees which permit termination of alimony upon "cohabitation" of alimony recipient with person of opposite sex, "cohabitation" requires some regularity of functioning as would husband and wife, either sexually or otherwise, and usually will be manifested by man and woman living together in same household and behaving as would husband and wife, although there need not be actual assertion of marriage. Fuller v. Fuller (Franklin 1983) 10 Ohio App.3d 253, 461 N.E.2d 1348, 10 O.B.R. 366.

Where, at the time a permanent alimony decree is entered, in conjunction with the granting of a divorce, the parties contemplate the wife's remarriage and intend the decree to be a permanent division of property, with monthly payments thereunder applied to an outstanding mortgage and to terminate at a fixed date, it is not subject to modification after a remarriage of the wife. Drossman v. Drossman (Erie 1975) 48 Ohio App.2d 81, 355 N.E.2d 891, 2 O.O.3d 63.

Where the right to receive alimony from a former spouse has terminated because the alimony recipient has remarried, such right to alimony is not revived by an annulment of the second marriage where the second marriage was merely voidable and not void, ab initio. Darling v. Darling (Cuyahoga 1975) 44 Ohio App.2d 5, 335 N.E.2d 708, 73 O.O.2d 5.

Where one receiving alimony under a separation agreement, which provides that payments are to cease if such party remarries, enters into a relationship in another state that would constitute a valid marriage in Ohio, such act is a remarriage within the meaning of the agreement. Fahrer v. Fahrer (Hamilton 1973) 36 Ohio App.2d 208, 304 N.E.2d 411, 65 O.O.2d 330.

For the purposes of determining cohabitation a showing of mere living together is insufficient, there must be a showing of mutual financial support before spousal support can be terminated. Aldridge v Aldridge, No. CA97-09-025, 1998 WL 640903 (12th Dist Ct App, Preble, 9-21-98).

Testimony establishing that an ex-wife is now living with another man and "doing things like husband and wife" and is being supported by and living on a full-time basis with this man along with the stipulation by the ex-wife that she is cohabiting with this man establishes cohabitation and justifies the termination of spousal support. Yacovone v Yacovone, No. 97-CA-66, 1998 WL 598127 (2d Dist Ct App, Miami, 9-11-98).

Failure to award spousal support is not an abuse of discretion based upon a former wife's cohabitation with a person of the opposite sex who is eighty-three years of age who takes care of her food and housing needs in addition to $14,000 given to her in the divorce which could be used to generate some income, and at a modest interest rate of six per cent, would generate sufficient income to meet her prescription drug expenses. Moore v Moore, No. CA-97-02-002, 1997 WL 727490 (12th Dist Ct App, Fayette, 11-24-97).

Cohabitation is manifested when a former wife moves into the residence of an unrelated male; a trial court abuses discretion in terminating spousal support prior to that time even though (1) she stays at the friend's house a couple of times a week, (2) sometimes "stayed the night," and (3) keeps clothing and toiletries at the friend's house prior to her moving in. Dingey v Dingey, No. 96-CA-14, 1997 WL 64036 (2d Dist Ct App, Champaign, 2-14-97).

Denial of spousal support because of cohabitation with an eighty-one-year-old brother-in-law is not supported by evidence of (1) a Christmas card with the message "all I want for Christmas is you ..." and signed with the brother-in-law's initials, (2) a photograph of his house with the former wife's inscription reading "this is our new home where we live now," (3) general surveillance by private detectives of the couple's comings and goings, and (4) neighbors' testimony that the former wife was seen driving by the marital home several times a week accompanied by an older gentleman. Moore v Moore, No. CA95-05-013, 1996 WL 42329 (12th Dist Ct App, Fayette, 2-5-96).

Evidence of cohabitation is insufficient to terminate an obligation to pay spousal support where obligations including support equivalent to those obligations that arise from a ceremonial marriage have not been assumed by the parties, as in a case where a former spouse, the plaintiff, cohabitates with a man not her husband who (1) spends weekends at the plaintiff's residence for a period over three years (2) lives with his mother during the week (3) eats meals with the plaintiff (4) drives her car (5) keeps some clothes in the plaintiff's closet in her home (6) makes no contribution to plaintiff's support and it is further established that (7) there is a sexual relationship between the parties. Knowlton v Knowlton, No. 712, 1994 WL 10631 (7th Dist Ct App, Monroe, 1-11-94).

Where a decree provides for an end to alimony payments if an ex-wife cohabits, and where the ex-wife is unchaste and her paramour lives at her house and her apartment whenever he is "in town on business" but he contributes toward nothing but the food he eats, it is not an abuse of discretion to find the alimony necessary to maintain the ex-wife's "quality of life" and to order the ex-husband jailed for failure to pay it. Savino v Savino, No. CA-9164 (2d Dist Ct App, Montgomery, 4-26-85).

Cohabitation on the part of a former wife is not grounds for automatic termination of an alimony award and the court errs in ordering, in a decree, that alimony will terminate upon cohabitation, but cohabitation may be considered as one factor in a modification proceeding. Ruedele v Ruedele, Nos. 83AP-872 and 83AP-895 (10th Dist Ct App, Franklin, 6-19-84).

Automatic terminations of alimony are improper when they are not based on factors which show that the divorced wife's need for alimony has terminated; thus, a trial court abused its discretion when it approved a provision terminating monthly alimony payments if the wife entered into "a relationship substantially similar to marriage." Finnerty v Finnerty, No. 1081 (11th Dist Ct App, Geauga, 3-9-84).

Where a dissolution decree provided that a wife's installment payments to her husband would become fully due upon the wife's cohabitation with a member of the opposite sex, a finding of cohabitation must be supported by evidence that the couple is living together, that such living together is of a sustained duration and that the expenses of maintaining the residence and incidental day-to-day expenses are shared. Birthelmer v Birthelmer, No. L-83-046 (6th Dist Ct App, Lucas, 7-15-83).

Where trial court awards physical possession of the marital premises to one spouse for the purpose of providing a home for minor children, upon such spouse's remarriage the new husband may not be required to pay rent to the non-resident spouse where the non-resident spouse's rights or interests in the marital premises are not jeopardized. Wise v Paul, No. CA-1569 (5th Dist Ct App, Tuscarawas, 4-9-82).

In a divorce proceeding, where trial court awards a spouse a lump sum alimony award to be paid in monthly amounts and does not identify such award as "sustenance alimony" or provide that the award would cease upon spouse's remarriage or death, such award is deemed to be a permanent division of property and a subsequent remarriage has no effect upon spouse's duty to pay such alimony. Wise v Paul, No. CA-1569 (5th Dist Ct App, Tuscarawas, 4-9-82).

Post-divorce unchastity or similar conduct is merely a circumstance to be considered along with specified factors and does not automatically require a termination of an alimony award where there is no direct proof that the relationship affected the wife's need for support. Lash v Lash, No. 81AP-507 (10th Dist Ct App, Franklin, 10-6-81).

Where a wife remarries and lives with her new husband in a house whose mortgage and utility bills are being paid by the former husband, a court will relieve the former husband of those obligations. Lutes v Lutes, No. 10071 (9th Dist Ct App, Summit, 7-29-81).

The trial court rightfully denied the defendant-payor's motion to modify the alimony decree on the grounds that the plaintiff-payee was cohabitating with a third party, because the separation agreement incorporated into the divorce decree did not include cohabitation as a contingency; if the proper judgment is granted for the wrong reason it is not prejudicial. Skidmore v Skidmore, No. 876 (11th Dist Ct App, Geauga, 8-4-80).

30. Aggression

Although RC 3105.18 does not list marital misconduct as a factor to be considered in alimony awards, it may be a relevant factor. Zimmie v. Zimmie (Ohio 1984) 11 Ohio St.3d 94, 464 N.E.2d 142, 11 O.B.R. 396.

A court is not precluded in the exercise of its equity powers from considering the element of aggression in making an award of alimony. Esteb v. Esteb (Ohio 1962) 173 Ohio St. 259, 181 N.E.2d 462, 19 O.O.2d 80.

The legislature, by completely eliminating reference to "aggression" on the part of either the husband or the wife from the statute on alimony as it presently reads, intended that such factor not be considered in determining the amount of alimony or division of property to be allowed a spouse in a divorce case; property that came to either by their marriage, the earning capacity of either, and the value of the real or personal estate of either are the elements now to be considered in determining the alimony or division of property. Esteb v. Esteb (Ohio 1962) 173 Ohio St. 259, 181 N.E.2d 462, 19 O.O.2d 80.

Where a divorce is granted by reason of the aggression of the wife, the court can adjudge to her such share of the husband's real or personal property, or both, as it deems just; or the husband should be allowed such alimony out of the real and personal property of the wife as the court deems reasonable. Arbogast v. Arbogast (Ohio 1956) 165 Ohio St. 459, 136 N.E.2d 54, 60 O.O. 116.

A trial court, in the exercise of its full equity powers and jurisdiction, may award alimony to a wife who is divorced by her husband on the ground of adultery, and the amount of such an alimony award is not excessive if the trial court, having due regard to the items set forth in RC 3105.18, does not abuse its discretion. Rabin v. Rabin (Montgomery 1962) 118 Ohio App. 446, 195 N.E.2d 377, 25 O.O.2d 355.

Under GC 11993 (Repealed), the court is permitted to give wife a share of the husband's property, even though divorce is granted to husband because of the wife's aggression. Brewer v. Brewer (Montgomery 1948) 84 Ohio App. 35, 78 N.E.2d 919, 52 Ohio Law Abs. 116, 39 O.O. 89.

Where husband and wife had a common understanding whereby both contributed all their earnings to a common fund and, after expenses were paid, investments were made in both names, and wife contributed a substantial amount to the common fund and investments, and divorce is granted to the husband because of aggression of the wife, an order of division of property whereby the wife receives approximately one-half of the property jointly accumulated is fair to both parties. Brewer v. Brewer (Montgomery 1948) 84 Ohio App. 35, 78 N.E.2d 919, 52 Ohio Law Abs. 116, 39 O.O. 89.

Court which granted husband divorce because of wife's aggression could enforce order that wife convey home to husband by decree which would act as conveyance. Ball v. Ball (Stark 1933) 47 Ohio App. 547, 192 N.E. 364, 17 Ohio Law Abs. 592, 40 Ohio Law Rep. 407.

Upon the vacating of a judgment of divorce granted to the husband for the wife's aggression, on petition brought for such purpose, it is error to grant the wife alimony without a rehearing upon the merits of the action for divorce. Kristo v. Kristo (Cuyahoga 1926) 23 Ohio App. 29, 154 N.E. 59, 5 Ohio Law Abs. 279.

Marital fault is to be given minimal consideration, and a court abuses its discretion in making a grossly disproportionate property division of this basis. Zaller v Zaller, No. 10-035 (11th Dist Ct App, Lake, 6-29-84).

Fault of a party may be considered as one factor in making an equitable award, but it is error for a court to make a distribution of marital property based solely or predominantly on fault. Wischmeier v Wischmeier, Nos. 47493 and 47494 (8th Dist Ct App, Cuyahoga, 6-7-84).

Although a court may consider marital misconduct or aggression in making an award of alimony, even though it is not one of the factors specifically set forth under RC 3105.18(B), if the court determines that marital misconduct should be given little or no weight in comparison with other factors, that determination shall not be overturned absent a showing of abuse of discretion. Zimmie v Zimmie, Nos. 43299, 44803, and 44804 (8th Dist Ct App, Cuyahoga, 2-3-83), reversed by 11 OS(3d) 94, 11 OBR 396, 464 NE(2d) 142 (1984).

Where the trial court found that a husband had engaged in adultery for five years preceding the filing of a complaint for divorce by the wife, the trial court erred in considering the adulterous conduct in making an award of alimony to the wife. Wilson v Wilson, No. 751 (12th Dist Ct App, Madison, 10-6-82).

It is error for the trial court to adopt a referee's final report which deletes all reference of wife's aggression. Brulin v Brulin, No. 6-232 (11th Dist Ct App, Lake, 10-30-78).

Where there is a valid, binding antenuptial agreement, it will be the controlling document regarding an alimony award, and unless aggression is a basis for setting aside the agreement, the wife is not entitled to an award of alimony. Benza v Benza, No. 171 (1st Dist Ct App, Warren, 3-29-78).

Where the husband's drinking habits give rise to the wife's grounds for divorce, this aggression may also be considered by the trial judge as he equitably determines alimony. Tennent v Tennent, No. 1430 (9th Dist Ct App, Wayne, 7-28-76).

A denial of alimony and support money to a wife for whose aggression the divorce was granted is not contrary to law. Bradbury v. Bradbury (Franklin 1950) 118 N.E.2d 681, 66 Ohio Law Abs. 321.

An award of alimony, in a divorce decree on account of the aggression of the husband, of one year's earnings is inadequate. Thompson v. Thompson (Montgomery 1951) 110 N.E.2d 17, 63 Ohio Law Abs. 444.

Where a decree for divorce is granted to a wife on account of the aggression of her husband, an allowance of alimony may be based on future personal earnings or wages of the husband. In such a case the court is not necessarily limited to a consideration of property in possession of the husband at time of decree. Thompson v. Thompson (Montgomery 1951) 110 N.E.2d 17, 63 Ohio Law Abs. 444.

31. Husband's spousal support

Where a divorce is granted by reason of the aggression of the wife, the court can adjudge to her such share of the husband's real or personal property, or both, as it deems just; or the husband should be allowed such alimony out of the real and personal property of the wife as the court deems reasonable. Arbogast v. Arbogast (Ohio 1956) 165 Ohio St. 459, 136 N.E.2d 54, 60 O.O. 116.

Where divorce is granted on husband's cross-petition, the court may grant alimony to the husband even though not specifically prayed for. Rainsburg v. Rainsburg (Marion 1946) 80 Ohio App. 303, 75 N.E.2d 481, 36 O.O. 13.

GC 11992 (Repealed) is not applicable where parties are joint owners of substantially all the property involved. Huff v. Huff (Wood 1946) 79 Ohio App. 514, 74 N.E.2d 390, 35 O.O. 334.

Divorce granted husband on his cross-petition in wife's suit for divorce, alimony and custody of their children, awarding to wife custody of the children and small monthly allowance, and awarding to husband, who was earning a large salary, a lump sum, almost sufficient to pay the alimony awarded to the wife for support of the children, and made a lien on the wife's residence property, where the husband did not ask for alimony, works an injustice on the wife, and such decree will be modified by eliminating the alimony awarded to the husband. Henke v. Henke (Hamilton 1938) 61 Ohio App. 416, 22 N.E.2d 655, 28 Ohio Law Abs. 357, 15 O.O. 268.

Court decreeing divorce to wife for aggression of husband could make award to husband in wife's real estate, where husband had but little property or means. Budai v. Budai (Hamilton 1930) 38 Ohio App. 79, 175 N.E. 624, 9 Ohio Law Abs. 371, 34 Ohio Law Rep. 83.

The finding by a court that the placing of property in wife's name, where the business activities of the husband render such course prudent for protection of the family, established the legal title in her, did not create a status which would prevent, under doctrine of res adjudicata, an award in subsequent divorce proceedings of one of the properties to the husband as alimony. Gaffney v. Gaffney (Ohio App. 1929) 32 Ohio App. 274, 167 N.E. 897, 28 Ohio Law Rep. 493.

Husband age forty-five who is permanently and totally disabled as a result of his heart attack is not entitled to spousal support from wife age fifty-two who is working and earning a salary and is able to earn additional income from dog grooming services where (1) the husband is able to sustain himself on social security disability payments of $896 per month, (2) he has no expenses associated with property ownership or employment, and (3) his social security benefits will increase on a regular basis to cover the increased cost of living as calculated by the social security administration. Young v Young, No. 96-CO-26, 1998 WL 30074 (7th Dist Ct App, Columbiana, 1-22-98).

In a divorce action, where husband has not made any financial or other contribution of service or otherwise to the nonmarital asset of his wife's business, trial court abused its discretion in awarding such husband a portion of the appreciation in value of the wife's business. Crawford v Crawford, No. 7508 (2d Dist Ct App, Montgomery, 4-23-82).

This section does not require husband to set forth in pleadings nature and extent of property he owns, but it is contemplated that the court will find whether he is possessed of little or no property and the circumstances of the husband and wife, from the evidence presented in the case. Kelly v Kelly, 19 Abs 338 (App, Mahoning 1935).

GC 11992 and 11993 (Repealed) are the only sections wherein any allowance can be made to husband when divorce is granted him. This allowance is by way of alimony and none other. (See also Nelson v Nelson, 14 Abs 34 (App, Franklin 1933).) Nelson v Nelson, 14 Abs 510 (App, Franklin 1933).

Award to husband may be made on good cause without any specific prayer for alimony. Potter v. Potter (Franklin 1946) 65 N.E.2d 666, 46 Ohio Law Abs. 357.

Alimony may be awarded to the husband under GC 11992 (Repealed), although a divorce is refused him, he being destitute and helpless and the family property being in the wife's name. Albert v. Albert (Ohio App. 1916) 29 Ohio C.D. 271, 7 Ohio App. 156, 28 Ohio C.A. 225.

32. Dower

A divorced wife who had an inchoate right of dower prior to amendment of the pertinent statutes in 1932, lost such right as a result thereof, and such legislation was valid. Any injustice done her thereby could be remedied by a modification of the alimony award. GC 26 (RC 1.20) has no application to a pending divorce or alimony action where the statute involved relates to inchoate right of dower. Goodman v. Gerstle (Ohio 1952) 158 Ohio St. 353, 109 N.E.2d 489, 49 O.O. 235.

Where wife is granted divorce and alimony for aggression of husband, and husband prosecutes error, and judgment is reversed as to alimony, it is error for trial court, upon retrial, to deprive wife of dower in the husband's property. Kundert v. Kundert (Summit 1927) 24 Ohio App. 342, 156 N.E. 237, 5 Ohio Law Abs. 99.

Real estate acquired after divorce from wife is not subject to dower right of such divorced wife. Spaulding v. Spaulding (Ohio App. 1 Dist. 1919) 11 Ohio App. 143, 30 Ohio C.A. 475.

33. Lien of decree

By principles of subrogation, one who advances money for payment of taxes on real estate acquires a lien against the real estate superior to one for alimony, decreed to be a specific lien and charge against the estate. McNealy v. Cochran (Licking 1937) 59 Ohio App. 254, 17 N.E.2d 670, 12 O.O. 525.

Lien for alimony installments, decreed to be a specific lien and charge against real estate prior in point of time to a judgment, execution and levy against such real estate, is a superior lien to that of the intervening judgment, although all the alimony installments became due after the intervening judgment, and the judgment for the installments due and execution thereon were subsequent to the intervening judgment. McNealy v. Cochran (Licking 1937) 59 Ohio App. 254, 17 N.E.2d 670, 12 O.O. 525.

34. Lis pendens

If petition for divorce and alimony describes property or property is in some way taken into possession of court, court may make application of property to a finding for alimony, and pending the decision the proceeding is lis pendens and prevents the assertion of judgment liens obtained after the beginning of the divorce proceeding. Parker v. Parker (Franklin 1938) 56 N.E.2d 527, 28 Ohio Law Abs. 49.

35. Constructive service

Service of summons by publication in a divorce action, not accompanied by any appearance of the defendant for the purpose of contesting the issues raised by the petition, is not sufficient to clothe the court with jurisdiction to decree the payment of money, either by way of support of minor children or by way of alimony. Sutovich v. Sutovich (Hamilton 1964) 120 Ohio App. 473, 200 N.E.2d 716, 29 O.O.2d 371.

Where wife, having previously obtained an alimony decree only, payable in installments, brings suit in the same court to obtain a lump-sum judgment, service by publication upon her non-resident husband will not give the court jurisdiction to grant a personal judgment against such defendant. Whitaker v. Whitaker (Cuyahoga 1936) 52 Ohio App. 223, 3 N.E.2d 667, 21 Ohio Law Abs. 599, 6 O.O. 316.

Service by publication provides a basis for jurisdiction over the defendant in an action for alimony sufficient to permit a decree charging real estate of the defendant which is mentioned in the petition, located in this state, with the payment of a sum for alimony. Shonk v. Shonk (Ohio Com.Pl. 1968) 16 Ohio Misc. 123, 241 N.E.2d 178, 45 O.O.2d 86.

Where a divorce was granted upon constructive service, possession by the plaintiff therein of insurance policies belonging to the defendant did not justify the court in awarding her all right and title in the policies. Whitelaw v. Whitelaw (Cuyahoga 1952) 113 N.E.2d 105, 65 Ohio Law Abs. 11.

Court is without authority to award property which was not described in pleadings or taken into custody of the court, as and for permanent alimony where jurisdiction is based on service by publication. Parker v. Parker (Franklin 1938) 56 N.E.2d 527, 28 Ohio Law Abs. 49.

The fact that in Ohio a court, after constructive service, may award alimony out of real estate in another county in Ohio where jurisdiction is invoked by specifically describing the real estate in the petition, does not indicate any trend in this state to enlarge jurisdiction in alimony cases to point of making it possible to award money as alimony where defendant is not served personally and has no property in this state. Gross v Wickfeldt, 28 NP(NS) 333 (1931).

A decree awarding a sum of money as alimony in a case in which defendant was a nonresident of the state, had no property in this state, and was served by publication, is invalid. In a proceeding to enforce such decree it is immaterial whether the proceeding is brought in same state in which decree was awarded or in a different state, the constitutional question involved being the due process clause rather than the full faith and credit clause. Such proceeding cannot be maintained even if brought in the same court in which the decree was rendered. Gross v Wickfeldt, 28 NP(NS) 333 (1931).

36. Enforcement

The doctrine of laches does not apply in an action for past-due child support and alimony payments, despite the fact that no action has been taken by the wife in over thirty-five years, where: (1) the wife actively pursued the delinquent husband in court twelve years after entrance of the support order, thereby indicating her non-acquiescence in the husband's failure to make payments; and (2) the husband was not materially prejudiced by the delay in bringing the claim. Connin v. Bailey (Ohio 1984) 15 Ohio St.3d 34, 472 N.E.2d 328, 15 O.B.R. 134.

A property settlement provision in a decree of divorce or dissolution is enforceable by contempt proceedings; such proceeding does not involve "debt" as used in the constitutional prohibition against imprisonment for debt. Harris v. Harris (Ohio 1979) 58 Ohio St.2d 303, 390 N.E.2d 789, 12 O.O.3d 291.

Trial court's order that former husband be imprisoned for contempt for failure to pay spousal support, but that jail sentence would be stayed on condition that husband make some payment on current support each month, was an enforcement of terms of original dissolution decree, not a modification thereof. Marden v. Marden (Butler 1996) 108 Ohio App.3d 568, 671 N.E.2d 331.

An appellant complaining of a discrepancy between the trial court's calculation of spousal support arrearages, as adapted from the referee's report, and actual testimony at trial, must transmit a transcript of the proceedings to the appellate court; if the record is without such a transcript and fails to demonstrate reversible error, the appellate court is bound by a presumption of regularity in the proceedings and cannot find that a discrepancy in fact exists. Vanke v. Vanke (Franklin 1992) 80 Ohio App.3d 576, 609 N.E.2d 1328.

A referee's report that an obligor's failure to make alimony and child support payments may not be contemptuous and stating that the obligor suffered financial setbacks constitutes insufficient evidence to sustain a contempt finding. Kelley v. Kelley (Cuyahoga 1991) 76 Ohio App.3d 505, 602 N.E.2d 400.

A trial court abuses its discretion in ordering a husband to pay temporary alimony arrearages where there is no indication in the record that any claim was made by the wife that the husband was in arrears, but rather, the trial court independently procures an unauthenticated statement from a county child support enforcement agency, and based on that statement, the court issues the order for a lump-sum temporary alimony arrearage payment. Rowe v. Rowe (Lucas 1990) 69 Ohio App.3d 607, 591 N.E.2d 716.

Imprisonment for failure to pay spousal support arrearages where the appellate court has determined that the support obligation is excessive constitutes imprisonment for debt and must be vacated. Haase v. Haase (Cuyahoga 1990) 64 Ohio App.3d 758, 582 N.E.2d 1107.

Payment of mortgage arrearages owed by a spousal support obligee by an obligor whose name appears on the mortgage obligation does not constitute a gift to the ex-spouse where it is demonstrated that the payments were made only to protect the spousal support obligor's credit rating; under these circumstances, it is an abuse of discretion to fail to credit the mortgage payments against the spousal support obligation. Haase v. Haase (Cuyahoga 1990) 64 Ohio App.3d 758, 582 N.E.2d 1107.

The administrator of an alimony obligor's pension plan may properly be joined as a party to an action to secure payment of alimony, although the obligee has waived all rights to the obligor's pension plan. Roach v. Roach (Cuyahoga 1989) 61 Ohio App.3d 315, 572 N.E.2d 772.

Although a Florida dissolution decree obtained by parties who lived in Ohio both before and after its issuance says it "shall be construed and governed" in accordance with Florida law, in later proceedings in Ohio court Ohio law presumably controls any change of custody for a child who resides in Ohio, while Florida law controls the meaning of the decree and the agreement it incorporates. Zigmont v. Toto (Cuyahoga 1988) 47 Ohio App.3d 181, 547 N.E.2d 1208, cause dismissed 38 Ohio St.3d 715, 533 N.E.2d 783.

Where a Florida dissolution decree incorporating a settlement states it shall be construed and governed in accordance with Florida law and the parties, who resided in Ohio both before and after the decree, are endeavoring to settle later litigation in an Ohio court, that court does not err by not announcing before accepting a settlement whether Florida or Ohio law would control the case; a party has no right to know the court's disposition toward an issue before the party negotiates a settlement. Zigmont v. Toto (Cuyahoga 1988) 47 Ohio App.3d 181, 547 N.E.2d 1208, cause dismissed 38 Ohio St.3d 715, 533 N.E.2d 783.

An auction of marital property to complete a property settlement, while sometimes necessary, should not ordinarily be ordered where there is a reasonable chance of a fair, timely, and voluntary sale; divorce is usually a losing proposition for the parties involved as it is, and an order for a sale of property made before the parties are even given an opportunity to see the property on the open market will be reversed. Van Fossen v. Van Fossen (Summit 1988) 47 Ohio App.3d 175, 547 N.E.2d 1237.

RC 3105.011 and 3105.18 provide ample authority for the attachment of pension benefits to secure the payment of court-ordered alimony. Dayton v. Dayton (Union 1987) 40 Ohio App.3d 17, 531 N.E.2d 324.

A pension plan is a proper party-defendant in an action for the attachment of pension benefits to secure the payment of a court-ordered alimony obligation and, as such, service upon the agent of the plan is sufficient to secure service on the plan; there is no need to serve the plan administrator or trustee pursuant to 29 USC 1132(d). Dayton v. Dayton (Union 1987) 40 Ohio App.3d 17, 531 N.E.2d 324.

Although 29 USC 1056(d)(1) prohibits the assignment or alienation of pension plan benefits, it does not prevent enforcement of a state court order attaching pension benefits to satisfy an outstanding alimony obligation. Dayton v. Dayton (Union 1987) 40 Ohio App.3d 17, 531 N.E.2d 324.

A property settlement provision contained in a separation agreement which is subsequently incorporated into a divorce decree is enforceable by contempt proceedings. Weaver v. Weaver (Ross 1987) 36 Ohio App.3d 210, 522 N.E.2d 574.

Attorney fees may be awarded where delinquent payments are enforced by being reduced to a lump sum for execution, as well as where enforcement is by a contempt proceeding. Saeks v. Saeks (Montgomery 1985) 24 Ohio App.3d 67, 493 N.E.2d 280, 24 O.B.R. 122.

Under its power to enforce a decree of dissolution incorporating a separation agreement, a court may order business income distributed according to the agreement and disregard the corporate structure created by one party with the knowledge that it would reduce his alimony liability. Saeks v. Saeks (Montgomery 1985) 24 Ohio App.3d 67, 493 N.E.2d 280, 24 O.B.R. 122.

Civ R 65(A) does not extend the equitable powers of domestic relations courts to encompass persons not parties to an action; thus an order restraining a husband's former employer from disbursing back salary until a motion concerning unpaid alimony is heard is reversible error where the former employer is not a party to the action. Van Ho v. Van Ho (Seneca 1984) 17 Ohio App.3d 108, 477 N.E.2d 659, 17 O.B.R. 170.

It is within power of court to reduce arrearages on alimony and child support to a lump-sum judgment which is enforceable against a party the same as any other judgment. Davis v. Davis (Cuyahoga 1983) 12 Ohio App.3d 38, 465 N.E.2d 917, 12 O.B.R. 125.

The court in a domestic relations case does not abuse its discretion under RC 3105.18 when it appoints a receiver, pursuant to RC 2735.01, to sell stock that had been awarded to one of the parties in the property settlement, in order to satisfy judgments against that party. Golick v. Golick (Cuyahoga 1983) 9 Ohio App.3d 106, 458 N.E.2d 459, 9 O.B.R. 159.

An alimony award for the payment of a sum certain in installments over a definite period of time without contingencies, when based on agreement by the parties, is part of the division of property, regardless of how denominated; thus, it vests when it is merged into the final divorce decree and is, therefore, a valid claim against the deceased spouse's estate. Vaught v. Vaught (Clermont 1981) 2 Ohio App.3d 264, 441 N.E.2d 811, 2 O.B.R. 293.

A husband, by a written separation agreement incorporated in a divorce decree, may contract to support his wife as long as she lives, and where the intent of the parties is clear and the wife survives her husband, such obligation extends beyond the death of the husband and obligates his estate and any fund intended to be so impressed for the duration of her life. White v. White (Erie 1975) 48 Ohio App.2d 72, 355 N.E.2d 816, 2 O.O.3d 48.

Where separation agreement, binding on both parties and their executors, provides that one party pay to other specific monthly amount, and requires such party to purchase insurance which in hands of party or his estate should constitute security for future payments, payor's estate is liable for continued payments. McKenzie v. Moore (Hamilton 1971) 28 Ohio App.2d 134, 275 N.E.2d 880, 57 O.O.2d 198.

An award of alimony in a divorce decree, although partaking of the nature of an ordinary judgment which does not order a party to pay anything but simply adjudicates the amount owing, goes further and is a direct command to the party to pay the sum or sums therein mentioned, and the court has the power to punish such party for contempt and send him to jail, where he fails to comply with such order. Peters v. Peters (Butler 1962) 115 Ohio App. 443, 183 N.E.2d 431, 21 O.O.2d 68, 26 O.O.2d 66.

Where a wife obtains an order for alimony payable in installments in an action for alimony only in this state and therafter takes up residence in another state and subsequently petitions a court of general jurisdiction for and obtains a decree of absolute divorce in that state, if she fails to ask for permanent alimony in such proceeding or fails to bring to attention of that court the orders theretofore procured in this state, she will be deemed to have waived her claims thereto and will be forever barred from asserting any claim for alimony thereafter in this state and forever barred from maintaining any action in this state to recover past due and unpaid installments that accrued on the original installment order prior to the divorce decree. Whitaker v. Whitaker (Cuyahoga 1936) 52 Ohio App. 223, 3 N.E.2d 667, 21 Ohio Law Abs. 599, 6 O.O. 316.

Jurisdiction of court entering decree for alimony in installments may be invoked by motion or by independent proceeding to reduce decree to decree in gross having force of judgment upon which execution may issue. Pace v. Pace (Morrow 1931) 41 Ohio App. 130, 180 N.E. 81, 11 Ohio Law Abs. 563.

Where amount of alimony was absolutely fixed by agreement of parties and judgment of court and was not subject to change, court of common pleas of another county had jurisdiction of action to recover accrued and unpaid amounts of judgment therefor. Kettenring v. Kettenring (Lucas 1928) 29 Ohio App. 62, 163 N.E. 43, 6 Ohio Law Abs. 722.

A laches defense based upon a fifteen-month delay in filing a contempt motion to assert spousal support precludes full recovery of delinquent support where the delay results in material prejudice to the husband who incurs unwarranted support arrearage each month the former spouse fails to assert her rights. Coder v Coder, No. 15566, 1996 WL 257215 (2d Dist Ct App, Montgomery, 5-17-96).

Where a trust contained a spendthrift clause which allowed the trustee to pay interest or principal for the support of the beneficiary's spouse or children, disbursements could be made from a trust to an ex-spouse, on behalf of the beneficiary, to satisfy a judgment that was characterized as "for the benefit of the children"; disbursements could not be made to satisfy a portion of a judgment that could be characterized as alimony. Board v Board, No. C-810395 (1st Dist Ct App, Hamilton, 4-7-82).

Although the husband has a history of failing to comply with court orders on alimony payments, this does not mean that the court can use this as justification for not terminating alimony, and further, it is an abuse of discretion for the court to refuse to put a termination date on alimony payments. Forkapa v Forkapa, No. L-80-305 (6th Dist Ct App, Lucas, 6-26-81).

The trial court correctly found the appellant-obligor guilty of contempt for failure to pay alimony, as the appellant-obligor's defense to inability to pay holds no weight, due to the fact that the alleged contemptor voluntarily placed himself in his present financial condition, making him unable to pay; advice of counsel is no justification for contempt. Mileti v Mileti, Nos. CA6617 and 6729 (2d Dist Ct App, Montgomery, 11-20-80).

Court which has rendered a decree of alimony concerning delivery of specific property retains continuing jurisdiction to award lump-sum money judgment necessary to enforce obligations established in original decree. Collins v. Smith (Ohio Com.Pl. 1971) 26 Ohio Misc. 231, 270 N.E.2d 377, 55 O.O.2d 370.

Where the defendant husband in a divorce action is in arrears in his support payments and the wife seeks to reach his interest in an estate in the process of administration, she may obtain a lump-sum judgment and execute thereon or institute proceedings in aid of execution or a creditor's bill, but cannot obtain an order directing the executors of the estate to pay the money directly to her. (Annotation from former RC 3105.20.) Stemple v. Stemple (Ohio Com.Pl. 1967) 12 Ohio Misc. 147, 230 N.E.2d 677, 41 O.O.2d 203.

The fact a man is without money or property at time decree for alimony is entered against him, does not absolve him from payment of the judgment out of future earnings, and failure so to do renders him subject to proceedings in contempt. Jaffa v Jaffa, 7 Abs 590 (App, Cuyahoga 1929).

It is no defense to a prosecution for failure to pay temporary alimony that the unpaid portion was owed to a relative of defendant's by the plaintiff. Hutson v. Hutson (Ohio Com.Pl. 1954) 120 N.E.2d 618, 68 Ohio Law Abs. 131.

It is no defense to a prosecution for contempt for violation of a temporary alimony award order that the defendant was unemployed and had no income from which to pay the amount due. Hutson v. Hutson (Ohio Com.Pl. 1954) 120 N.E.2d 618, 68 Ohio Law Abs. 131.

Alimony liability of nonresident husband served by publication, though inchoate at commencement of divorce suit, may be enforced by injunction order against his bank deposit in local bank, consistently with due process of law guaranteed by U.S.C.A.Const. Amend. 14. Pennington v. Fourth Nat. Bank of Cincinnati, Ohio (U.S.Ohio 1917) 37 S.Ct. 282, 243 U.S. 269, 61 L.Ed. 713.

A domestic relations judge who finds a former husband in contempt and jails him is engaging in a "judicial act" for purposes of the former husband's civil rights suit against the judge under 42 USC 1983 and the judge's defense of absolute judicial immunity, even though the judge knew from the beginning there was no affidavit for the capias. Filip v. Flanagan (N.D.Ohio 1989) 729 F.Supp. 1149.

37. Action for spousal support only

A court has the same power in awarding alimony only that it does in awarding alimony where a divorce is granted. Goetzel v. Goetzel (Ohio 1959) 169 Ohio St. 350, 159 N.E.2d 751, 8 O.O.2d 355.

In a proceeding involving claim for alimony only, court is without power to make award to wife which is to be determinative of all her rights to her husband's property. Materazzo v. Materazzo (Ohio 1941) 139 Ohio St. 36, 37 N.E.2d 967, 21 O.O. 548.

Upon petition of the wife for alimony alone, the court is confined to making an award as alimony for her maintenance and support during separation, and is not authorized to make an equitable division of the husband's property. Durham v. Durham (Ohio 1922) 104 Ohio St. 7, 135 N.E. 280, 19 Ohio Law Rep. 548.

Where a court of common pleas, division of domestic relations, decrees separate maintenance for a husband and wife and orders the husband to make regular installment payments, in the nature of alimony, to the wife and to also make weekly child-support payments to her, and where such alimony and child-support orders are not, pursuant to agreement of the parties, a division of property or a fixed sum in settlement of the ultimate property rights of the parties at that time, the court has continuing jurisdiction to entertain a motion, filed after term, to modify the alimony and child-support payments orders due to a change in circumstances. (Annotation from former RC 3105.20.) Caudill v. Caudill (Butler 1969) 20 Ohio App.2d 100, 252 N.E.2d 186, 49 O.O.2d 118.

The court of common pleas has the authority to make a division of property in an action for alimony only. Brewer v. Brewer (Warren 1962) 117 Ohio App. 263, 183 N.E.2d 250, 24 O.O.2d 60.

A wife cannot maintain an action for alimony alone, where, because the husband had a wife living at the time of his ceremonial marriage with plaintiff, they were not legally married; but she can maintain an action for divorce on the ground of her husband's undissolved marriage to another at the time of his ceremonial marriage with plaintiff. In an action by the wife for alimony only, the defendant husband may not as a defense to such action obtain a declaratory judgment as to the marital status of the parties, notwithstanding the fact of defendant's prior undissolved marriage was not set out as a ground for alimony by plaintiff wife. Jones v. Jones (Cuyahoga 1962) 115 Ohio App. 358, 180 N.E.2d 847, 20 O.O.2d 441.

Where a wife institutes an action for alimony only and, at the time of such hearing, enters into an agreement with her husband for support, and such agreement is then approved by the trial court and made a part of the judgment entry in the alimony only action, a trial court, in a new action later instituted by the wife for divorce and alimony (the parties never having lived together after the institution of the first action for alimony only), may not modify such agreement and grant an additional award to such wife, in the absence of a finding of fraud, undue influence, duress or other similar feature in the execution of the original separation agreement. Garn v. Garn (Wayne 1960) 111 Ohio App. 498, 173 N.E.2d 904, 15 O.O.2d 218.

In an alimony action a court may order a division of property. (Annotation from former RC 3105.20.) Morrison v. Morrison (Franklin 1956) 102 Ohio App. 376, 143 N.E.2d 591, 2 O.O.2d 392.

The distinction made between proceedings for divorce and alimony and alimony alone and the power of the court to award alimony in an action for alimony alone were not modified or overruled by the enactment of GC 8003-19 (RC 3105.18) in 1951. Hetrick v. Hetrick (Ottawa 1954) 101 Ohio App. 334, 139 N.E.2d 674, 1 O.O.2d 282.

Upon a petition of the wife for alimony alone, the trial court is not authorized to make an equitable division of property of the respective spouses, but is confined to making an award of alimony for her maintenance and support. Zatko v. Zatko (Lucas 1953) 100 Ohio App. 223, 136 N.E.2d 358, 60 O.O. 200.

Upon an appeal from a judgment rendered upon a petition by the wife for alimony alone, which judgment in effect makes a division of property, the court of appeals will modify the judgment by eliminating that portion thereof relating to the division of property and, upon a finding that the lower court has not abused its discretion in making the award to the wife as alimony, will affirm the judgment as modified. Zatko v. Zatko (Lucas 1953) 100 Ohio App. 223, 136 N.E.2d 358, 60 O.O. 200.

It is error for a trial court to grant a divorce to a wife in a suit by her for alimony and custody of minor children, where her only request for divorce is in the prayer of her reply to an answer and cross-petition of the husband for divorce. Gasior v. Gasior (Lucas 1940) 67 Ohio App. 84, 35 N.E.2d 1021, 21 O.O. 105.

Where alimony in a lump sum has been awarded to wife in her action for alimony only, and journal entry expressly states that so far as support of child is concerned it is held open until further order of court, but there is no such statement in decree with reference to support of wife and no statement retaining jurisdiction over allowance for further alimony, court has no jurisdiction over allowance of further alimony to wife in an application for additional alimony filed by way of cross-petition in her husband's subsequent action for divorce. Robertson v. Robertson (Scioto 1938) 61 Ohio App. 458, 22 N.E.2d 744, 15 O.O. 286.

Where a wife obtains an order for alimony payable in installments in an action for alimony only in this state and therafter takes up residence in another state and subsequently petitions a court of general jurisdiction for and obtains a decree of absolute divorce in that state, if she fails to ask for permanent alimony in such proceeding or fails to bring to attention of that court the orders theretofore procured in this state, she will be deemed to have waived her claims thereto and will be forever barred from asserting any claim for alimony thereafter in this state and forever barred from maintaining any action in this state to recover past due and unpaid installments that accrued on the original installment order prior to the divorce decree. Whitaker v. Whitaker (Cuyahoga 1936) 52 Ohio App. 223, 3 N.E.2d 667, 21 Ohio Law Abs. 599, 6 O.O. 316.

Husband is not relieved of primary duty of supporting wife out of his property and labor by wrongful abandonment of wife. Wife is not deprived of right to alimony because earning money, where husband's income and property are ample therefor. Coleman v. Coleman (Ottawa 1930) 37 Ohio App. 474, 175 N.E. 38, 8 Ohio Law Abs. 481.

In action for alimony alone, wife's separate income should be considered in determining fair allowance to wife from husband's property. Coleman v. Coleman

(Ottawa 1930) 37 Ohio App. 474, 175 N.E. 38, 8 Ohio Law Abs. 481.

The right to alimony arises from marriage relation and is not founded on contract, express or implied, but on duty of husband to support wife. Coleman v. Coleman (Ottawa 1930) 37 Ohio App. 474, 175 N.E. 38, 8 Ohio Law Abs. 481.

The primary duty rests upon the husband to support his wife while they are living together as husband and wife, even though she may have property of her own, and he may not be relieved of that duty by his own wrongful act in abandoning the wife without cause. The law is clearly settled in Ohio that the authority of the court in allowing alimony in an action for alimony alone is much more limited than when dealing with alimony where divorce has been granted. Coleman v. Coleman (Ottawa 1930) 37 Ohio App. 474, 175 N.E. 38, 8 Ohio Law Abs. 481.

The court in an alimony alone action may, statutorily, make a division of property; there is no statutory mandate which requires a division of property. Poulias v Poulias, No. CA84-10-118 (12th Dist Ct App, Butler, 1-13-86).

A court may not make a division of property in an alimony only proceeding because domestic relations courts are without authority, in an alimony only action, to permanently divide the parties' property interests but may only render awards for maintenance and support. Turek v Turek, No. 42307 (8th Dist Ct App, Cuyahoga, 11-13-80).

In an action for alimony only, a court is not authorized to make a permanent division of property of the spouses, but has power to render an award for maintenance and support only, and consequently, a trial court's award as alimony of the husband's one-half interest in the marital home to the wife is meant to last until further order of the court, and jurisdiction of the cause is retained for modification of the judgment upon application supported by evidence of changed circumstances. Martin v Martin, No. 39881 (8th Dist Ct App, Cuyahoga, 12-13-79).

A wife to whom alimony only has been granted may by her misconduct during the period of judicial separation forfeit her right to the continuing award of alimony. Bishop v. Bishop (Ohio Com.Pl. 1969) 18 Ohio Misc. 177, 248 N.E.2d 641, 47 O.O.2d 417.

Where a wife is granted alimony only, the marriage is not dissolved and the parties have the relationship of husband and wife although they are judicially separated due to the misconduct of the husband. Bishop v. Bishop (Ohio Com.Pl. 1969) 18 Ohio Misc. 177, 248 N.E.2d 641, 47 O.O.2d 417.

Courts in Ohio are restricted by statutes in fixing alimony in an action brought to recover alimony alone. Segal v Segal, 16 Abs 452 (App, Hamilton 1934).

Where petition is filed for alimony only, court has no authority to make a division of property, by reason of limitations on GC 11997 (RC 3105.17) provided in GC 11998 (RC 3105.21). Davis v. Davis (Franklin 1944) 57 N.E.2d 703, 42 Ohio Law Abs. 105.

In action for alimony only where the pleadings fail to present the issue of prior divorce by one of the parties in another jurisdiction, the court has no right to make determination of any question concerning such divorce, and has no authority, after validity of such divorce is questioned in trial of such action for alimony only, to make a division of property. Davis v. Davis (Franklin 1944) 57 N.E.2d 703, 42 Ohio Law Abs. 105.

38. —In general, effect of bankruptcy

The automatic stay provision as provided for in 11 USC 362 does not violate US Const Am 10 insofar as it stays a state court contempt action to enforce a divorce decree deciding marital property. Barnett v. Barnett (Ohio 1984) 9 Ohio St.3d 47, 458 N.E.2d 834, 9 O.B.R. 165.

A decree awarding alimony to a wife on granting her a divorce is not a debt from which the bankrupt is released by his discharge. Lemert v. Lemert (Ohio 1905) 72 Ohio St. 364, 74 N.E. 194, 106 Am.St.Rep. 621, 2 Ohio Law Rep. 535, 3 Ohio Law Rep. 20, 2 Am.Ann.Cas. 914.

Under discharge exception for alimony, maintenance, or support, label given to particular obligation in separation agreement or divorce decree is not dispositive of nature of obligation. Ballinger v. Ballinger (Madison 1995) 107 Ohio App.3d 358, 668 N.E.2d 979.

Court order in divorce action requiring husband to pay weekly sums of $50 and in addition to pay in one lump sum more than $8,000 for such interest as wife possessed in certain corporation was, with respect to weekly and lump sum payments, an order in nature of alimony within meaning of Ohio statute and Bankruptcy Act, and husband's subsequent discharge in bankruptcy did not relieve him of his obligation to pay lump sum. Kadel v. Kadel (Ohio Com.Pl. 1969) 21 Ohio Misc. 232, 250 N.E.2d 420, 49 O.O.2d 179, 50 O.O.2d 460.

Bankruptcy does not discharge husband from payments he agreed to make in a separation agreement with his wife after their divorce, though payments were to be made to third parties because such payments are alimony under GC 11991 (RC 3105.18). Reed v. Reed (Franklin 1935) 20 Ohio Law Abs. 491.

There may be times when a bankruptcy court should not lift the automatic stay that was imposed on a state divorce proceeding when one spouse filed a bankruptcy petition, e.g., where the court suspects the spouses of collusion to stage a divorce to avoid the just claims of creditors. In re White (C.A.6 (Ohio) 1988) 851 F.2d 170.

In determining whether discharging a marital debt would result in a benefit to debtor that outweighs the detrimental consequences to debtor's former spouse or children, court engages in so-called "who will suffer more" analysis, reviewing the financial status of debtor and former spouse, and then comparing their relative standards of living to determine the true benefit of debtor's possible discharge against any hardship the spouse, former spouse, and/or children would suffer as a result of debtor's discharge. In re Miller (Bkrtcy.N.D.Ohio 2000) 247 B.R. 412.

Debt consisting of half of the funds in a Chapter 7 debtor's 401(K) plan was excepted from discharge as nonsupport divorce debt where debtor, as a part of his bankruptcy petition, listed the full value of the 401(K) plan as his personal property, thus ostensibly demonstrating that he had the ability to pay his debt to his former wife, former wife submitted affidavit affirming that the soundness of her financial situation was, at least in part, dependent upon her receiving possession of the 401(K) funds awarded to her in the parties' divorce, and debtor, who had a surplus in his income versus expenses of about $400 per month, presented no evidence tending to show that former wife enjoyed a higher standard of living than he, or that he needed immediate access to all funds in the 401(k) plan in order to meet basic living expenses. In re Adams (Bkrtcy.N.D.Ohio 1999) 241 B.R. 880.

Debt owed by Chapter 7 debtor to creditor, his former spouse, was excepted from discharge as nonsupport divorce debt where, although both debtor and creditor were experiencing difficult financial times, creditor was not employed, was on full disability, and was living a spartan-like lifestyle, borrowing money from relatives in order to eat and living in various parts of the country to avoid becoming a burden on her family, while debtor, who was college-educated with an advanced degree, was employed, any restrictions on debtor's employment field were self-imposed, and debtor, who had remarried, had the benefit of his current spouse's income. In re Hallagan (Bkrtcy.N.D.Ohio 1999) 241 B.R. 544.

Chapter 7 debtor failed to prove that discharging $36,000 nonsupport divorce debt would result in benefit to him that would outweigh detrimental consequences to his former wife and, thus, debt was nondischargeable, where annual adjusted gross income of former wife, who had high school education and earned $9 per hour at retail store, had dropped to $4,193, former wife was involved in serious accident that affected her ability to work and resulted in $25,000 in medical expenses, she had not received settlement offer in her pending personal injury action, former wife had to borrow funds from relatives to meet day-to-day expenses, and, after deducting other expenses, debtor had approximately $1,750 per month to make $750 payment to former wife and to pay any out-of-pocket expenses for his twins' medical treatment. In re Barnes (Bkrtcy.S.D.Ohio 1998) 218 B.R. 409.

Chapter 11 debtor's treatment of his obligation to make periodic payments to his former wife, prior to her remarriage, as "alimony" obligation on his federal tax returns was not inconsistent with his position, in dischargeability proceeding, that he never intended that alimony should continue after wife remarried, and did not estop debtor from maintaining that whatever continuing obligation he had to make payments to his wife after she remarried should not be regarded as "alimony," for debt dischargeability purposes. In re Edwards (Bkrtcy.S.D.Ohio 1997) 216 B.R. 796.

Obligation arising under "alimony" provision of separation agreement was not in nature of "alimony, maintenance, or support," and could be discharged in former husband's Chapter 11 case, at least to the extent of alimony payable after the ex-wife remarried; evidence was presented that debtor-husband, who was not represented by attorney, had never intended that his obligation to pay alimony would continue after his ex-wife's remarriage. In re Edwards (Bkrtcy.S.D.Ohio 1997) 216 B.R. 796.

While it may look to state substantive law for guidance, what constitutes alimony, maintenance, or support, for debt dischargeability purposes, is determined under bankruptcy law and not under law of state. In re Edwards (Bkrtcy.S.D.Ohio 1997) 216 B.R. 796.

Statutory exception to discharge for divorce-related obligations not in nature of support confers standing to object to discharge only upon spouse, former spouse or dependent of debtor. In re Wenneman (Bkrtcy.N.D.Ohio 1997) 210 B.R. 115.

Basic principle that, even when brought under guise of federal question action, suit whose substance is domestic relations generally will not be entertained in federal court cannot be applied with bright line certainty when bankruptcy law is involved; however, bankruptcy court authority should not be exercised when it its clear that bankruptcy action is merely continuation of previously litigated dispute between divorced spouses. In re Griffith (Bkrtcy.N.D.Ohio 1996) 203 B.R. 422.

Bankruptcy court should not put itself in position where its purpose is to second guess previous decision of domestic relations court. In re Griffith (Bkrtcy.N.D.Ohio 1996) 203 B.R. 422.

Debtor who seeks reexamination of issue previously considered by state domestic relations court is acting with improper motivation, and such action violates spirit of Bankruptcy Code. In re Griffith (Bkrtcy.N.D.Ohio 1996) 203 B.R. 422.

Chapter 13 debtor filed petition in bad faith, warranting its dismissal, where debtor proposed plan that provided very low monthly payments with vague pledge that all claims would eventually be paid and required creditors to wait up to 54 months to receive payment, debtor did not accurately state debts in plan, and debtor filed petition to avoid sale of farm pursuant to state domestic relations decision. In re Griffith (Bkrtcy.N.D.Ohio 1996) 203 B.R. 422.

Federal and state courts have concurrent jurisdiction to hear questions of dischargeability arising out of alimony and child support exception. In re Baker (Bkrtcy.S.D.Ohio 1996) 195 B.R. 883.

Where state court has not yet determined property interests involved, it is appropriate for bankruptcy court to defer to that state court for determination of dischargeability under alimony and child support exception. In re Baker (Bkrtcy.S.D.Ohio 1996) 195 B.R. 883.

In general, federal courts defer to state courts in domestic relations matters, but this deference is limited to matters where the matter is more suitably handled by state courts. In re Baker (Bkrtcy.S.D.Ohio 1996) 195 B.R. 883.

Factors that court may consider in determining whether debtor's right to payment in pension plan is reasonably necessary for support of debtor, for exemption purposes, include, debtor's present and anticipated living expenses; debtor's present and anticipated income from all sources; debtor's age; debtor's health; debtor's ability to work and earn living; debtor's job skills, training, and education; debtor's other assets, including exempt assets; liquidity of other assets; debtor's ability to save for retirement; special needs of debtor; and debtor's financial obligations, e.g., alimony or support. In re Webb (Bkrtcy.S.D.Ohio 1995) 189 B.R. 144.

When obligation is specifically denominated as alimony and obligation was intended to serve as alimony, obligation is nondischargeable. In re Leslie (Bkrtcy.N.D.Ohio 1995) 181 B.R. 317.

If divorce decree created debt rather than property interest in spouse's favor, any award to spouse not in nature of alimony, maintenance or support would be dischargeable to debtor's spouse. In re Piasecki (Bkrtcy.N.D.Ohio 1994) 171 B.R. 49.

If circumstances of debtor have changed from time that divorce decree obligation ensued to present, making payment untenable, bankruptcy court may consider debtor's current general ability to pay as it relates to continuing obligation to assume joint debts, when determining whether debt is nondischargeable spousal support or alimony. In re Friedrich (Bkrtcy.N.D.Ohio 1993) 158 B.R. 675.

To be excepted from discharge on ground debt is in nature of alimony, support or maintenance, debt must be: (1) directly payable to spouse, former spouse or child of debtor, (2) designated as alimony to, maintenance for, or support of such spouse or child, (3) result of separation agreement, divorce decree, or property settlement agreement, and (4) actually in nature of alimony, maintenance or support. In re Friedrich (Bkrtcy.N.D.Ohio 1993) 158 B.R. 675.

Bankruptcy court has authority to adjust and alter amount of payments owed for spousal and child support if it finds the payments to be unreasonably burdensome to Chapter 13 debtor; however, it is only appropriate to make such a modification if original state court award was unreasonable or if there has been detrimental change in financial circumstances from time divorce decree was entered to time of petition filing. Matter of Bush (Bkrtcy.S.D.Ohio 1993) 154 B.R. 69.

A separation agreement stating it fully satisfies both parties' rights to alimony and a judgment entry indicating the parties waive all rights and claims to alimony, when taken together, are ambiguous and do not express an intent of the parties for or against alimony; in any event, federal bankruptcy courts do not consider themselves bound by the characterization of payments as alimony or a property settlement by the parties or by a state court. In re Eikenberg (Bkrtcy.N.D.Ohio 1989) 107 B.R. 139.

In determining whether an award of support in a divorce decree is necessary or excessive and subject to discharge in a former husband's bankruptcy proceedings, the bankruptcy court will consider the circumstances considered by Ohio domestic relations courts in deciding what amounts to award as alimony and child support, such as those listed in RC 3105.18 and 3109.05. In re Angel (Bkrtcy.S.D.Ohio 1989) 105 B.R. 825.

A man whose earnings from an apparently failing business in which he is a partner have dropped from $35,000 per year to $18,000 and who has taken cash advances against future salary in order to meet support obligations under a divorce decree will not be granted relief in his bankruptcy proceedings, on the ground changed circumstances have lessened his ability to pay support or the ground that ordered support is excessive, with respect to obligations to pay $150 weekly child support, $200 weekly alimony, medical insurance, the former wife's auto costs for two years, half the children's tuition at a private school, and an additional $2000 per year for five years; the court considers that "there is no indication" the former husband, "an apparently able-bodied, middle-aged man is incapable of earning a respectable income." In re Angel (Bkrtcy.S.D.Ohio 1989) 105 B.R. 825.

A husband who transfers his interest in a marital residence to his wife on the advice of his attorney, as part of a separation agreement, and files a bankruptcy petition two months later without mentioning the transfer on his bankruptcy statement of financial affairs, thereby fraudulently and knowingly makes a false oath, and one that is material because the creditors and trustee are entitled to know what property has passed through the debtor's hands during the period preceding bankruptcy; for swearing falsely, the debtor is denied discharge of his debts in bankruptcy. In re Bluestone (Bkrtcy.N.D.Ohio 1989) 102 B.R. 103.

Where a former husband who earns $30,000 annually pays $295 monthly on a first mortgage, $320 monthly in child support, half of household utilities, and $100 monthly for college expenses of a son now living with him, it is "manifestly unreasonable" to make him also pay $275 monthly on a second mortgage, particularly in light of the fact he is unable to continue working a second job that enabled him to make the payment for several years. In re Schreiber (Bkrtcy.S.D.Ohio 1989) 99 B.R. 380.

A former husband's agreement in divorce proceedings to pay $8929.16 in credit card debts run up by his former wife on accounts held in her name alone is in the nature of support and cannot be discharged in bankruptcy where the husband's annual take-home earnings of $15,785 leave him about $190 each month after paying his expenses, while the former wife is presently not working, earned $8000 in 1988, and is supported by her family and friends; the man is allowed to discharge the interest debt on these credit accounts, however, in light of the fact the former wife is just twenty-six years old, has a college degree, and is employable: it would be manifestly unreasonable under traditional concepts of what constitutes "support" to hold him responsible for the accruing interest. In re Sermersheim (Bkrtcy.N.D.Ohio 1989) 97 B.R. 885.

Any part of a support award that is not "manifestly unreasonable under traditional concepts of support" and that is owing but unpaid from the entry of the state court divorce decree until commencement of the former husband's federal bankruptcy case will not be affected by the former husband's discharge in bankruptcy; he remains responsible for the arrearage and must make arrangements with his former wife for payment. In re Caughenbaugh (Bkrtcy.S.D.Ohio 1988) 92 B.R. 255.

Where a former husband's income has declined dramatically since a divorce decree and now amounts to $1321 monthly, from which he claims to spend $1285 monthly on necessities exclusive of the $600 monthly support he was ordered to pay his former wife, and where the former wife has income of $400 monthly and monthly expenses of $625, the bankruptcy court will find it "manifestly unreasonable under traditional concepts of support" to make the former husband pay the support decreed; instead, the former husband is found able to pay $80 weekly henceforth by effecting economies, and the remainder of the obligation is held subject to his discharge in bankruptcy. In re Caughenbaugh (Bkrtcy.S.D.Ohio 1988) 92 B.R. 255.

A party claiming that an award in a divorce decree constitutes "support" has the burden of proving it is support money even though the parties termed it such in the separation agreement; thus, absent evidence of the parties' intentions and of a former wife's assets, education, and needs, a bankruptcy court will not find an award of $4000 monthly for 126 months to be "support" payments that cannot be discharged in the former husband's bankruptcy proceedings. In re Skaggs (Bkrtcy.S.D.Ohio 1988) 91 B.R. 1018.

A monthly support award of $2000 is considered "manifestly excessive" by the federal bankruptcy court when the former husband charged with paying it is now disabled and has a monthly income of just $778; the court will review the former husband's budget and decide to what extent the support payment should be adjusted. In re Skaggs (Bkrtcy.S.D.Ohio 1988) 91 B.R. 1018.

A father who signed private school tuition contracts with his wife, was thereafter divorced by her, was sued by her and lost a judgment for the tuition amount, and who soon afterward filed for bankruptcy, is relieved of liability for the wife's judgment where the divorce decree provided for support and did not mention the contracts, and there is no proof the state court awarding the judgment considered the sum to be support. In re Motley (Bkrtcy.N.D.Ohio 1987) 69 B.R. 406.

A plaintiff's divorce attorney who imposes his fee upon the defendant husband in the divorce decree cannot shield this debt from discharge in the husband's bankruptcy by terming his fee a payment "as and for alimony and property division," because this subterfuge does not render the fee a genuine, nondischargeable debt in the nature of alimony or support. In re Shaw (Bkrtcy.N.D.Ohio 1986) 66 B.R. 399.

A husband's obligation under a divorce decree to pay the wife's attorney is alimony and cannot be discharged by the husband's bankruptcy where the total sum of the husband's obligations under the decree is not large enough to justify a finding the obligation is really part of a property settlement. In re Sigworth (Bkrtcy.N.D.Ohio 1986) 60 B.R. 137.

The obligation of a husband under a divorce decree to pay a sum certain to the wife as a "settlement of all assets subject to equitable distribution" is not dischargeable in the husband's bankruptcy to the extent that his payments are designated to (1) pay the wife's attorney fees, and (2) replenish a trust for the parties' child that the husband had raided, as these payments are in the nature of support. Matter of Heck (Bkrtcy.S.D.Ohio 1985) 53 B.R. 402.

A husband's liability to a mortgagee bank and to his wife as cosigner of a promissory note is dischargeable in bankruptcy; but where a divorce decree entered after the filing of the bankruptcy petition provides for the husband to pay any deficiency resulting from forced sale of the mortgaged property, the decree creates an independent, postpetition obligation to the wife which is not discharged. In re Neier (Bkrtcy.N.D.Ohio 1985) 45 B.R. 740.

A husband's obligation under a divorce decree to not incur further debts on joint credit accounts is imposed to maintain and support the former wife's individual credit standing; hence, where the husband breaches the obligation by incurring further debts, for which his former wife stands solely liable because of the husband's bankruptcy, the former wife acquires a cause of action against her spouse for the breach which is nondischargeable to the extent of credit charges since the date of the decree. In re Hiller (Bkrtcy.N.D.Ohio 1984) 44 B.R. 764.

Debts on a joint credit card which a husband is obliged to pay under a divorce decree are not maintenance or support and are dischargeable in the husband's bankruptcy proceeding where there is no evidence of the nature of the credit purchases and where the import of the decree is that the parties divide property and go their own ways; the wife's cause of action against her spouse for breach of the decree leaving her solely liable to creditors is also discharged, as she was aware of the petition and had opportunity to submit a claim. In re Hiller (Bkrtcy.N.D.Ohio 1984) 44 B.R. 764.

39. —Daily support needs—nondischargeable, effect of bankruptcy

In determining whether debtor's obligation is in nature of alimony, maintenance, or support, and consequently nondischargeable, bankruptcy court must determine that there was intent to create support obligation, obligation has effect of providing support necessary to satisfy daily needs of former spouse and any children of marriage, and amount of support represented by obligation at issue is not so excessive that it is manifestly unreasonable under traditional concepts of support. Ballinger v. Ballinger (Madison 1995) 107 Ohio App.3d 358, 668 N.E.2d 979.

In determining that Chapter 7 debtor's obligation, pursuant to divorce decree, to pay minor child's medical and school expenses was nondischargeable support, trial court was not obligated to independently examine bills that resulted in judgment to enforce divorce decree to determine if each of bills was in nature of support; though judgment ordering debtor to pay child's medical and school expenses and determining amount of expenses was by default, debtor was properly served with notice of proceedings, debtor failed to file answer or raise affirmative defense of dischargeability in bankruptcy, and debtor never moved to vacate judgment or contest it in any way. Rizzen v. Spaman (Lucas 1995) 106 Ohio App.3d 95, 665 N.E.2d 283, dismissed, appeal not allowed 74 Ohio St.3d 1509, 659 N.E.2d 1286.

Chapter 7 debtor's obligation to pay ex-wife's medical insurance, as ordered in divorce decree, as well as uncovered medical expenses incurred before entry of judgment to enforce divorce decree, was nondischargeable support; debtor's failure to meet divorce decree obligation to provide ex-wife with health insurance policy resulted in ex-wife's incurring medical bills not covered by insurance. Rizzen v. Spaman (Lucas 1995) 106 Ohio App.3d 95, 665 N.E.2d 283, dismissed, appeal not allowed 74 Ohio St.3d 1509, 659 N.E.2d 1286.

Chapter 7 debtor's ex-wife was not entitled to have debtor pay amount of ex-wife's uncovered medical expenses from time of judgment enforcing divorce decree to date of ex-wife's remarriage, even though uncovered medical expenses incurred before judgment were nondischargeable; under terms of original divorce decree, debtor was obligated to pay only ex-wife's medical insurance premiums, not any uncovered medical expenses, and award of medical expenses pursuant to judgment enforcing divorce decree was, therefore, not an order to pay all of ex-wife's uncovered medical expenses, but only a judgment for damages incurred by ex-wife due to debtor's failure to maintain ex-wife's medical insurance. Rizzen v. Spaman (Lucas 1995) 106 Ohio App.3d 95, 665 N.E.2d 283, dismissed, appeal not allowed 74 Ohio St.3d 1509, 659 N.E.2d 1286.

Trial court properly ordered Chapter 7 debtor to pay cost of debtor's ex-wife's medical insurance premiums, which was nondischargeable support, even though ex-wife had since remarried; ex-wife's remarriage did not remove debtor's obligation to repay ex-wife for support that he was obligated to maintain before ex-wife's remarriage. Rizzen v. Spaman (Lucas 1995) 106 Ohio App.3d 95, 665 N.E.2d 283, dismissed, appeal not allowed 74 Ohio St.3d 1509, 659 N.E.2d 1286.

In determining if debt is in the nature of support and, thus, is not dischargeable, court must ascertain whether state court or parties to divorce intended to create obligation to provide support through the assumption of joint debts, if assumption was intended as support, whether such assumption has the effect of providing support necessary to ensure that the daily needs of the former spouse and any children of the marriage are satisfied, and, if so, whether the amount of support represented by the assumption is not so excessive that it is manifestly unreasonable under traditional concepts of support. Snyder v. Snyder (Ashtabula 1995) 105 Ohio App.3d 69, 663 N.E.2d 695.

Chapter 7 debtor's $4,501.81 debt to former wife for one half of child's college expenses was in nature of support, and thus, came within the discharge exception for alimony, maintenance, or support. In re Dissolution of Marriage of Coplin (Van Wert 1995) 102 Ohio App.3d 212, 656 N.E.2d 1338.

Debt arising from Chapter 7 debtor's obligation under divorce decree to make loan payments on wife's vehicle came within the exception to discharge for maintenance or support where wife needed car to maintain her employment, and debtor's assumption of debt made it possible for wife to earn additional support for herself and her children. Smith v. Smith (Ashtabula 1992) 81 Ohio App.3d 641, 611 N.E.2d 987.

Where an obligation imposed by a divorce decree is imposed with the intent of the court or the parties to create an obligation to provide support through the assumption of the joint debts, the debt assumption is necessary to the daily support of the former spouse, and the obligation is not unreasonably excessive, the debt constitutes alimony and as such is nondischargeable in bankruptcy. Clark v. Clark (Franklin 1987) 40 Ohio App.3d 177, 532 N.E.2d 158.

A trial court finding that an order for one spouse to pay certain joint debts of the parties constitutes an obligation in the nature of alimony due to the disparate earnings of the parties and the amount of debt is not erroneous and is not discharged by a general discharge in bankruptcy. Clemons v Clemons, No. 92AP-1196, 1993 WL 271000 (10th Dist Ct App, Franklin, 7-13-93).

Where the court finds that one party's assumption of a joint debt is necessary for the other party's daily support, and such support is not unreasonably excessive under traditional notions of alimony, such obligation was intended to be in the nature of alimony. Clark v Clark, No. 86AP-869 (10th Dist Ct App, Franklin, 6-23-87).

When state court or parties to divorce do not intend to create obligation in nature of support, that obligation cannot be deemed nondischargeable under support discharge exception. In re McCafferty (C.A.6 (Ohio) 1996) 96 F.3d 192.

Chapter 7 debtor's portion of a marital debt owed to former wife's father was not a nondischargeable support obligation; there was no indication of a great deal disparity in parties' earning power or that former wife had a significant need for spousal support, given her relatively young age and apparent good health at the time parties' marriage ended, debtor's obligation did not end upon former wife's death or remarriage, length of parties' marriage was relatively short, parties' divorce decree specifically stated that neither party was obligated to pay the other party spousal support, and so bankruptcy court could not find that it was state court's intent to create a support obligation. In re McClelland (Bkrtcy.N.D.Ohio 2000) 247 B.R. 423.

For purposes of comparing parties' prospective standards of living to determine whether divorce obligations are dischargeable, each party's projected income should be measured by his or her realistic earning potential, not by lifestyle or other choices which restrict income. In re Findley (Bkrtcy.N.D.Ohio 2000) 245 B.R. 526.

Chapter 7 debtor's payments to his adult daughter, although laudatory, were voluntary and had to be deducted in considering debtor's ability to pay, for purposes of the discharge exception for nonsupport divorce debt. In re Slygh (Bkrtcy.N.D.Ohio 2000) 244 B.R. 410.

State court intended for Chapter 7 debtor's assumption of parties' credit card debt to provide support to his former wife, for purposes of determining whether obligation was nondischargeable support; court permitted debtor to retain his exempt retirement accounts and all monies contained therein in exchange for his obligation to relieve former wife from a large portion of the unsecured debt incurred by parties during their marriage, allowing debtor to discharge his credit card debt would effectively reform state court divorce decree to provide that he receive a greater portion of the marital assets, state court was keenly aware that debtor was a prime candidate for a bankruptcy filing, and state court presumably was aware that support obligations arising from a divorce are nondischargeable in bankruptcy. In re Luman (Bkrtcy.N.D.Ohio 1999) 238 B.R. 697.

Pursuant to the "present needs analysis" of the *Calhoun* test, in determining whether debtor's assumption of debt pursuant to parties' divorce decree has the actual effect of providing necessary support to former spouse, court must look to the practical effect of discharge upon the nondebtor spouse's ability to sustain daily needs; in other words, if, without the loan assumption, the nondebtor spouse could not maintain the daily necessities of life, such as food, housing, and transportation, effect of the loan assumption may be found in the nature of support, for nondischargeability purposes. In re Luman (Bkrtcy.N.D.Ohio 1999) 238 B.R. 697.

Although, in undertaking the "present needs" analysis for determining whether a debtor's assumption of debt pursuant to parties' divorce decree has the actual effect of providing necessary support to former spouse, evidence tending to show that an imminent collection action is about to be commenced against former spouse would be helpful to his or her case, there is no per se rule that such evidence is absolutely needed; rather, better approach is to have nondebtor spouse demonstrate that there exists a real possibility that creditors of joint debt assumed by debtor will initiate collection activities against nondebtor spouse. In re Luman (Bkrtcy.N.D.Ohio 1999) 238 B.R. 697.

Chapter 7 debtor's assumption of joint credit card debt pursuant to parties' divorce decree had the actual effect of providing necessary support to former wife, for purposes of determining whether obligation was in the nature of nondischargeable support; former wife was barely getting by financially, with more than a $400 shortfall between her occupation income versus her monthly expenses, and any increase in former wife's monthly expenses could have had dire consequences on her ability to provide for the basic necessities for herself and her child. In re Luman (Bkrtcy.N.D.Ohio 1999) 238 B.R. 697.

Under third step of *Calhoun* test for determining whether payments made by a debtor pursuant to a divorce decree are in the nature of nondischargeable support, Chapter 7 debtor's assumption of credit card debt in the amount of $20,451.73 was not manifestly unreasonable under traditional concepts of support; debtor's annual income was approximately $32,000, it was feasible that debtor could actually experience a positive monthly cash flow if extra income were imputed to debtor and debtor would reduce some of his questionable expenses, such as an expenditure for cable television, and nondebtor spouse was the residential parent of parties' child. In re Luman (Bkrtcy.N.D.Ohio 1999) 238 B.R. 697.

Unlike the other exceptions to discharge, which are construed narrowly, the exception for alimony, maintenance, or support is given a broad construction so as to promote the congressional policy that favors enforcement of obligations for spousal and child support. In re Luman (Bkrtcy.N.D.Ohio 1999) 238 B.R. 697.

In determining whether debts jointly incurred by a couple during their marriage are thereafter dischargeable by only one of the parties after the marriage has ended, court must balance two important, but very diametric, public policy concerns, namely, the strong public policy concern of giving deserving debtors a fresh start, versus the equally as strong public policy against permitting debtors to discharge their support obligations to their former dependents. In re Luman (Bkrtcy.N.D.Ohio 1999) 238 B.R. 697.

Nondebtor spouse who seeks to hold a debt nondischargeable under the discharge exception for alimony, maintenance, or support must, at a minimum, establish that the following three elements are met: (1) debt(s) must have arisen "in connection" with a separation agreement, divorce decree, or other order of a court of record; (2) underlying debt(s) must actually be owed to the former spouse or child; and (3) debt(s) owed to the former spouse must actually be in the "nature of alimony or support." In re Luman (Bkrtcy.N.D.Ohio 1999) 238 B.R. 697.

Debts arising from a property settlement are not encompassed within the discharge exception for those debts contained in a divorce decree or separation agreement which are for the maintenance and support of debtor's child or former spouse. In re Luman (Bkrtcy.N.D.Ohio 1999) 238 B.R. 697.

Purpose of third step of the *Calhoun* test for determining whether payments by debtor pursuant to divorce decree are in the nature of nondischargeable support, which requires court to examine whether amount of support provision is so excessive so as to be manifestly unreasonable under the traditional concepts of support, is to prevent a debtor from effectively contracting away his or her right and opportunity for a fresh start under the Bankruptcy Code. In re Luman (Bkrtcy.N.D.Ohio 1999) 238 B.R. 697.

In determining whether a debtor's assumption of debt pursuant to a divorce decree is in the nature of nondischargeable alimony, maintenance, or support, bankruptcy courts consider such relevant factors as the following: (1) disparity of earning power between the parties; (2) need for economic support and stability; (3) presence of minor children; (4) marital fault; (5) nature of the obligations assumed; (6) structure and language of parties' agreement or court's decree; (7) whether other lump sum or periodic payments were also provided; (8) length of the marriage; (9) age, health, and work skills of the parties; (10) whether obligation terminates upon the death or remarriage of the parties; (11) adequacy of support absent the debt assumption; and (12) evidence of negotiations or other understandings as to intended purposes of the assumption. In re Luman (Bkrtcy.N.D.Ohio 1999) 238 B.R. 697.

Although a "hold harmless" provision in a separation agreement or divorce decree is strong evidence of an intent to create a support obligation, the lack thereof does not necessarily indicate that the underlying obligation is not in the nature of support, for nondischargeability purposes. In re Luman (Bkrtcy.N.D.Ohio 1999) 238 B.R. 697.

Discharge exception for nonsupport divorce debt is limited in two very important respects: first, it does not apply when debtor does not have "the ability to pay" the debt from income not reasonably to be expended in support of debtor or dependents of debtor, and second, it does not apply when discharging such debt would result in a benefit to debtor that outweighs the detrimental consequences to debtor's spouse, former spouse, or child. In re Melton (Bkrtcy.N.D.Ohio 1999) 238 B.R. 686.

Debtor may be found to have the ability to pay a nonsupport divorce debt, but would still be entitled to a discharge if the benefit of discharge to debtor outweighs the detrimental consequences to his or her former spouse. In re Melton (Bkrtcy.N.D.Ohio 1999) 238 B.R. 686.

Under so-called balancing test, court must undertake a two-step analysis when determining the dischargeability of a nonsupport debt incurred vis-a-vis a divorce: first, court determines the benefit to debtor of receiving a bankruptcy discharge, and detriment to creditor-spouse if discharge is granted and, next, court must weigh the benefit and the detriment against each other, so that if court determines that debtor's benefit outweighs creditor's detriment, debt must be discharged, but if court concludes that creditor's detriment outweighs debtor's benefit, debt remains nondischargeable. In re Melton (Bkrtcy.N.D.Ohio 1999) 238 B.R. 686.

In weighing benefit to debtor of receiving a bankruptcy discharge versus detriment to creditor-spouse if discharge is granted, for purposes of the discharge exception for nonsupport divorce debt, court uses "standard of living test": first, court determines parties' relative standards of living on the basis of their financial status, second, court compares parties' respective standards of living to determine the true benefit of debtor's possible discharge against any hardship that former spouse would suffer, and third, court asks whether debtor's standard of living would be greater than or approximately equal to that of former spouse if debt is not discharged, and if so, then debt is nondischargeable. In re Melton (Bkrtcy.N.D.Ohio 1999) 238 B.R. 686.

In determining parties' relative standards of living, for purposes of weighing the benefit to debtor of receiving a discharge versus the detriment to a creditor-spouse if discharge is granted, under the discharge exception for nonsupport divorce debt, court should consider, at a minimum, the following: (1) amount of debt involved, including all payment terms; (2) current income of debtor, objecting creditor, and their respective spouses; (3) current expenses of debtor, objecting creditor, and their respective spouses; (4) current assets, including exempt assets, of debtor, objecting creditor, and their respective spouses; (5) current liabilities, excluding those discharged by debtor's bankruptcy, of debtor, objecting creditor, and their respective spouses; (6) health, job skills, training, age, and education of debtor, objecting creditor, and their respective spouses; (7) dependents of debtor, objecting creditor, and their respective spouses, their ages, and any special needs which they may have; (8) any changes in financial conditions of debtor and objecting creditor which may have occurred since entry of the divorce decree; (9) amount of debt which has been or will be discharged in debtor's bankruptcy; (10) whether objecting creditor is eligible for relief under the Bankruptcy Code; and (11) whether parties have acted in good faith in the filing of the bankruptcy and the litigation of the nondischargeability issues. In re Melton (Bkrtcy.N.D.Ohio 1999) 238 B.R. 686.

Although incorrect factual conclusions regarding creditor-former wife's income were contained in court's original memorandum opinion and decision, resulting upward adjustment in her income did not change court's determination that, pursuant to the "standard of living" test, benefit of discharge to Chapter 7 debtor did not outweigh the detrimental consequences of discharge to creditor; even with adjustment in creditor's income, each party had about $200 per month in disposable income, creditor resided with parties' children whereas debtor, who had remarried, had a party with whom he could share his household expenses and whose income had been otherwise disregarded by the court in reaching its decision, and debtor's financial difficulties were alleviated by discharge of unsecured debts totaling more than $60,000.00. In re Melton (Bkrtcy.N.D.Ohio 1999) 238 B.R. 686.

Debtor failed to establish that he did not have ability to pay non-support marital debt arising out of property settlement incorporated into dissolution decree, as required for exception to nondischargeability, where debtor artificially diminished his ability to repay debt by quitting job with annual income of $48,000 and assisting his new wife in her business, in return for her supporting him as dependant. In re Molino (6th Cir.BAP (Ohio) 1998) 225 B.R. 904.

Debtor failed to establish, for purposes of exception to nondischargeability of non-support marital debt, that discharge of debt would confer benefit upon him that outweighed detrimental consequences to his ex-wife, even though his income was $40 to $90 per week while his ex-wife's income was $30,000 per year; debtor voluntarily reduced his income and he failed to provide evidence regarding assets of debtor's new spouse, expenses of ex-wife and her new spouse, income of new spouses, liabilities of ex-wife and new spouses, and ex-wife's health, training, and education. In re Molino (6th Cir.BAP (Ohio) 1998) 225 B.R. 904.

Though there is nothing wrong with debtor voluntarily repaying prepetition debts which have or could have been discharged, such payments do not rise to level of expenses which are reasonably necessary to be expended for maintenance and support, for purposes of statute setting forth discharge exception for nonsupport divorce debt. In re Perkins (Bkrtcy.N.D.Ohio 1998) 221 B.R. 186.

In determining whether debtor has ability to pay nonsupport divorce debt, so as to except debt from nondischargeability, bankruptcy courts apply "disposable income" test, which considers: (1) debtor's "disposable income" as measured at time of trial, (2) presence of more lucrative employment opportunities which might enable debtor to fully satisfy divorce-related obligation, (3) extent to which debtor's burden of debt will be lessened in near term, (4) extent to which debtor previously has made good faith effort towards satisfying debt in question, (5) amount of debts which creditor is seeking to have held nondischargeable, and repayment terms and conditions of those debts, (6) value and nature of any property debtor retained after bankruptcy filing, (7) amount of reasonable and necessary expenses which debtor must incur for support of debtor, debtor's dependents, and continuation, preservation, and operation of debtor's business, if any, (8) income of debtor's new spouse, if any, as such income should be included in calculation of debtor's disposable income, and (9) any evidence of probable changes in debtor's expenses. In re Barnes (Bkrtcy.S.D.Ohio 1998) 218 B.R. 409.

Chapter 7 debtor failed to prove that he was unable to pay $36,000 nonsupport divorce debt in monthly installments of $750 as required by divorce decree and, thus, debt was nondischargeable, where debtor's take-home pay was in neighborhood of $4,400 per month, debtor paid $750 per month to rent home, debtor's other monthly expenses totaled $1,892, and only evidence that debtor was unable to pay obligation was testimony of debtor's domestic attorney who opined that forcing debtor to pay debt would be devastating to him and his two children and would force him to take second job. In re Barnes (Bkrtcy.S.D.Ohio 1998) 218 B.R. 409.

Exceptions to nondischargeability for nonsupport divorce debts are best treated as affirmative defenses which debtors must plead and establish; thus, creditor-plaintiff need only establish that debt was incurred by debtor in course of marital action and is not in nature of support, and burden then shifts to debtor to prove either that he or she does not have ability to pay debt or that its discharge would result in benefit to him or her greater than harm to plaintiff. In re Barnes (Bkrtcy.S.D.Ohio 1998) 218 B.R. 409.

Absent "hold harmless" clause in Chapter 7 debtor's divorce decree or separation agreement, joint debt to third party, which was neither owed to debtor's former spouse nor listed as support obligation, was not excepted from discharge as support obligation. In re Gibson (Bkrtcy.N.D.Ohio 1997) 210 B.R. 113, affirmed in part, reversed in part 219 B.R. 195.

Chapter 7 debtor's obligation, pursuant to so-called "stock buyout" agreement executed by parties in connection with their separation and wife's surrender of her stock in family-owned business, to pay wife $450 per week for the next 12 years, was nondischargeable as being in nature of "alimony, maintenance or, support," given 31-year length of parties' marriage and limited other sources of income available to wife as person with no formal training, no savings and no work experience other than with family business, given wife's present need for support at time of her nondischargeability complaint, and given evidence of husband's past and present ability, as party who controlled trucking companies with multimillion dollar cash flows, to pay alimony despite his gratuitous transfers of assets and attempts to voluntarily reduce his salary. In re Custer (Bkrtcy.N.D.Ohio 1997) 208 B.R. 675.

Even assuming that Chapter 7 debtor's weekly payment obligation of $450 to his former wife, pursuant to so-called "stock buyout" agreement incorporated into final marital dissolution decree, was not excepted from discharge as being in nature of "alimony, maintenance or, support," obligation could be excepted from discharge as divorce-related obligation not in nature of support, given evidence that, despite modest salary drawn by debtor from his new wife's businesses so as to allegedly minimize his problems with the Internal Revenue Service (IRS), debtor exercised control over businesses and their cash flow which provided him with ability to make these weekly payments, and given evidence that, in light of debtor's and his current wife's financial circumstances relative to those of his former spouse, benefit to debtor of discharging obligation would not outweigh detriment to former spouse. In re Custer (Bkrtcy.N.D.Ohio 1997) 208 B.R. 675.

In deciding whether benefit to debtor of discharging divorce-related debt not in nature of support outweighs detrimental consequences to former spouse, such that obligation may be discharged, bankruptcy court may consider financial circumstances of debtor's new spouse if debtor has remarried. In re Custer (Bkrtcy.N.D.Ohio 1997) 208 B.R. 675.

Under nonsupport exception to discharge, debtor's former spouse, as party seeking to except debt from discharge, must merely establish that debt was incurred by debtor in course of divorce or separation; burden then shifts to debtor to show either that he or she is unable to pay debt, or that discharge would result in benefit to debtor that outweighs detrimental consequences to former spouse. In re Custer (Bkrtcy.N.D.Ohio 1997) 208 B.R. 675.

Chapter 7 debtor's divorce decree obligation to make weekly payments to former wife was nondischargeable support, even though payments were nonmodifiable and not tax-deductible to debtor; parties intended to create support obligation at time of divorce, separation agreement, which was incorporated into divorce decree, characterized obligation as support, debtor intended payments to provide former wife with funds for health insurance, and debtor earned about $37,000 per year on date of decree while former wife was unemployed. In re Henderson (Bkrtcy.N.D.Ohio 1996) 200 B.R. 322.

Bankruptcy law's purpose is to provide honest debtor with fresh start and to insure that debtor's creditors receive equitable dividend from bankruptcy estate. In re Moghrabi (Bkrtcy.N.D.Ohio 1996) 197 B.R. 258.

Chapter 7 debtor's obligation to make annual payments to his former wife under separation agreement was nondischargeable as support where agreement characterized debtor's obligation as alimony, at time of dissolution there was disparity in parties's financial situations, payments were to terminate on death or remarriage of wife, and debtor deducted annual payments for income tax purposes even though payments were secured by life insurance policy and were to continue as charge against debtor's estate. In re Hobbs (Bkrtcy.N.D.Ohio 1996) 197 B.R. 254.

Bankruptcy court's determination of parties' intent at time of dissolution, for purposes of resolving whether debt was nondischargeable as support, does not turn on one party's post hoc explanation as to his state of mind at time of agreement, even if uncontradicted, but rather, critical inquiry is shared intent of parties at time obligation arose. In re Hobbs (Bkrtcy.N.D.Ohio 1996) 197 B.R. 254.

Creditor seeking nondischargeability of debtor's obligation to make payments bears burden of establishing that obligation should be excepted from discharge by preponderance of evidence. In re Hobbs (Bkrtcy.N.D.Ohio 1996) 197 B.R. 254.

Chapter 7 debtor's obligation under divorce decree to repay credit card debts incurred during marriage represented nondischargeable support obligation, where parties intended to create support obligation in view of their relative financial circumstances, former wife's custody of their minor child, and 14-year duration of marriage, and where obligation to repay debts would have actual effect of providing former wife and child with necessary support, since former wife's monthly expenses exceeded her total monthly income. In re Williams (Bkrtcy.N.D.Ohio 1995) 189 B.R. 678.

Fact that Chapter 7 debtor's former wife had refinanced credit card debts, which debtor was obliged under divorce decree to repay, did not affect nondischargeability of those obligations under discharge exception for alimony, maintenance, and support. In re Williams (Bkrtcy.N.D.Ohio 1995) 189 B.R. 678.

State and federal courts have concurrent jurisdiction to determine whether debt is excepted from discharge under spousal and child support exception. Matter of Tremaine (Bkrtcy.S.D.Ohio 1995) 188 B.R. 380.

In proceedings to determine dischargeability under child and spousal support exception where bankruptcy court and state court have concurrent jurisdiction to determine issue, general rule is that court in which issue is first presented, or capable of presentation, through proper filings and proceedings will continue proceedings to conclusion. Matter of Tremaine (Bkrtcy.S.D.Ohio 1995) 188 B.R. 380.

Bankruptcy court would abstain, in favor of state domestic relations court, from determining whether debts owed to Chapter 7 debtor's former wife were nondischargeable under spousal support exception, in light of related proceeding pending in state court system, appearance of forum shopping by debtor, and lack of finality caused by debtor's pursuit of state court appellate proceedings that diminished, if not eliminated, any meaningful determination of dischargeability by bankruptcy court; appellate proceeding had reached advanced stages in state court system, but had not finally established amount of divorce decree debts, and absence of finality in amount of obligations precluded determination of nature of debt. Matter of Tremaine (Bkrtcy.S.D.Ohio 1995) 188 B.R. 380.

Debt owed by debtor-husband to former wife for arrearage on house expense payments ordered by divorce judgment was clearly in nature of "support" and nondischargeable. In re Sanders (Bkrtcy.N.D.Ohio 1995) 187 B.R. 588.

When determining whether parties or state court intended to create support obligation in divorce judgment, bankruptcy court may consider any relevant evidence including those factors used by state courts to make factual determination of intent to create "support." In re Sanders (Bkrtcy.N.D.Ohio 1995) 187 B.R. 588.

Usually, inquiry as to whether parties or state divorce court intended to create nondischargeable "support" obligation in divorce judgment is made by considering each debt which was to be assumed in divorce entry individually, especially when contested obligations are secured by specific items of property or incurred for specifically delineated services or items of property; however, sometimes it is necessary to determine whether in scheme of obligations imposed by decree, payment of those debts effectively operates as nondischargeable maintenance and support. In re Sanders (Bkrtcy.N.D.Ohio 1995) 187 B.R. 588.

If support obligation is found to be excessive, fourth prong of *Calhoun* inquiry tests extent to which support is excessive and directs bankruptcy court to reduce nondischargeable support obligation by amount of excess. In re Sanders (Bkrtcy.N.D.Ohio 1995) 187 B.R. 588.

Merely because spousal and child support were otherwise provided for in divorce judgment entry did not establish that Chapter 7 debtor's assumption of marital debts under decree was not intended to provide support, and that discharge exception for support was inapplicable. In re Chapman (Bkrtcy.N.D.Ohio 1995) 187 B.R. 573.

Although discharging joint debts and thereby causing creditors to seek payment from Chapter 7 debtor's ex-wife would cause ex-wife to expend funds reasonably necessary for her maintenance, such factors could not be considered in determining whether debts should be discharged under discharge exemption for debts incurred in course of divorce, but not in nature of spousal or child support. In re Woodworth (Bkrtcy.N.D.Ohio 1995) 187 B.R. 174.

For purposes of applying discharge exception for support, maintenance or alimony in divorce cases other than those involving hold-harmless provisions, assumptions of loans or other hybrid provisions, if court makes determination that there was intent to create obligation for alimony, maintenance or support, obligation is nondischargeable. In re Pinkstaff (Bkrtcy.N.D.Ohio 1994) 163 B.R. 504.

If obligation is specifically denominated as alimony and obligation was intended to serve as alimony, obligation is nondischargeable. In re Pinkstaff (Bkrtcy.N.D.Ohio 1994) 163 B.R. 504.

Debtor's obligation to pay former wife's water bill fell within exception to discharge for maintenance, alimony and support where divorce decree demonstrated state divorce court's intent to impose support obligation on debtor for water bill based on its finding of financial necessity, relative financial condition of parties, and fact that former wife was charged with providing for child. In re Pinkstaff (Bkrtcy.N.D.Ohio 1994) 163 B.R. 504.

Fact that water bill, which state court determined that debtor had to pay for former wife, represented obligation for necessities of life imposed by divorce court prior to divorce decree compelled conclusion that debtor's obligation to pay water bill represented nondischargeable support. In re Pinkstaff (Bkrtcy.N.D.Ohio 1994) 163 B.R. 504.

Attorney fees can represent nondischargeable alimony, maintenance or support because award of attorney fees may be essential to spouse's ability to sue or defend matrimonial action and therefore a necessity. In re Pinkstaff (Bkrtcy.N.D.Ohio 1994) 163 B.R. 504.

Debtor's obligation under divorce decree to pay former wife's attorney fees incurred in divorce proceedings fell within exception to discharge for support where decree specifically characterized the obligation as alimony and decree included finding of financial necessity, disparity in income between parties, and fact that former wife was charged with caring for child. In re Pinkstaff (Bkrtcy.N.D.Ohio 1994) 163 B.R. 504.

Periodic payments from Chapter 7 debtor to his former wife of $1,800 per month for 21 months and $1,000 per month for three more months, which were provided for in judgment entry of divorce pursuant to negotiated settlement, were intended for spousal support and were reasonable, and so were nondischargeable; payments were referred to as "spousal support," judgment included distinct apportionment of parties' personal and real property, payments were terminable upon wife's death, wife did not collect regular paycheck during marriage and needed ongoing source of support for her sustenance, and amount of payments was not excessive based upon evidence regarding parties' income and lifestyle. In re Sandoval (Bkrtcy.N.D.Ohio 1992) 161 B.R. 796.

Chapter 7 debtor's separation agreement obligation to pay one half of former wife's college expenses while she obtained postdissolution college degree was in nature of support, and thus nondischargeable; obligation was intended to provide support, and debtor's assumption of obligation was not so excessive that it was manifestly unreasonable under traditional concepts of support. In re Friedrich (Bkrtcy.N.D.Ohio 1993) 158 B.R. 675.

In order for divorce decree obligation to assume debts to be found to be nondischargeable spousal support or alimony, parties must have intended that obligation have effect and purpose of providing support for spouse, support must be necessary to insure that daily needs of former spouse and any children of marriage are satisfied, and amount of obligation assumed must not be so excessive that it is manifestly unreasonable under traditional concepts of support. In re Friedrich (Bkrtcy.N.D.Ohio 1993) 158 B.R. 675.

In determining whether debt is nondischargeable as being in nature of alimony, maintenance, or support, bankruptcy court, with exception of cases involving hold-harmless agreements and assumption of marital debt, will decline to make extensive intrusions into the law of domestic relations, absent clear congressional mandate to do so. In re Gibson (Bkrtcy.S.D.Ohio 1993) 157 B.R. 366.

Change in debtor's circumstances does not affect whether his obligation for arrearages owed to former spouse is nondischargeable. In re Gibson (Bkrtcy.S.D.Ohio 1993) 157 B.R. 366.

Cases which involve past-due obligations that are clearly in nature of support are not subject to *Calhoun's* four-prong test, which includes analysis of "present needs," in determining whether obligation is nondischargeable as being in nature of alimony, maintenance or support. In re Gibson (Bkrtcy.S.D.Ohio 1993) 157 B.R. 366.

Calhoun's four-prong test for determining whether debt is nondischargeable as being in nature of alimony, maintenance of support, which includes analysis of "present needs" and "change of circumstances," is not applicable to case involving spousal support arrearages. In re Gibson (Bkrtcy.S.D.Ohio 1993) 157 B.R. 366.

In determining whether obligation is nondischargeable as being in nature of alimony, maintenance, or support, initial inquiry must be to ascertain whether state court or parties to divorce intended to create obligation to provide support; in making such determination, bankruptcy court may consider any relevant evidence, including those factors utilized by state courts to make factual determination of intent to create support. In re Gibson (Bkrtcy.S.D.Ohio 1993) 157 B.R. 366.

Among factors that may be examined by court in determining whether state court or parties to divorce intended to create obligation to provide support, and thus, whether obligation is nondischargeable, include: nature of obligations; structure and language of parties' agreement or court's decree; whether other lump-sum or periodic payments were also provided; length of marriage; existence of children from marriage; relative earning powers of parties; age, health and work skills of parties; adequacy of support absent debt assumption; and evidence of negotiation or other understandings as to intended purpose of payments. In re Gibson (Bkrtcy.S.D.Ohio 1993) 157 B.R. 366.

Debtor's obligation of $15,600 represented arrearages for spousal support or maintenance, and, therefore, obligation was nondischargeable, even though debtor contended that former wife did not require full amount for support in light of her postdissolution earnings, and that debtor's financial condition prevented him from paying support; internal structure of separation agreement indicated parties' intent that debtor would pay $300 as monthly support or maintenance, and testimony indicated that purpose of support was to provide former wife with sufficient security to remain in financially uncertain real estate business and to become financially self-supporting. In re Gibson (Bkrtcy.S.D.Ohio 1993) 157 B.R. 366.

Bankruptcy court has authority to adjust and alter amount of payments owed for spousal and child support if it finds the payments to be unreasonably burdensome to Chapter 13 debtor; however, it is only appropriate to make such a modification if original state court award was unreasonable or if there has been detrimental change in financial circumstances from time divorce decree was entered to time of petition filing. Matter of Bush (Bkrtcy.S.D.Ohio 1993) 154 B.R. 69.

Any relevant evidence may be considered in determining, for nondischargeability purposes, whether state court or parties intended to create obligation for support through assumption of joint debts. In re Semler (Bkrtcy.N.D.Ohio 1992) 147 B.R. 137.

Intent of state court or parties is relevant in determining whether obligation is in nature of alimony, maintenance or support, and thus nondischargeable; if intent behind assumption of joint debts was not to provide support, obligation is dischargeable. In re Semler (Bkrtcy.N.D.Ohio 1992) 147 B.R. 137.

A former husband's obligation to pay the former wife's divorce attorney fees is a debt for support not dischargeable in his bankruptcy proceeding where the state court awarded the fees because of the former wife's mental and physical condition, her inability to support herself, and sale of the marital residence. In re Hodges (Bkrtcy.N.D.Ohio 1991) 139 B.R. 846.

The separation agreement obligation of a husband with a $15,000 annual income to pay the balance due on the automobile loan of his wife with a $3389 yearly income is in the form of support to enable her to work and have transportation; as such, the debt is held not dischargeable in the husband's bankruptcy proceedings. In re Spangler (Bkrtcy.N.D.Ohio 1992) 139 B.R. 684.

A husband's agreement to pay his wife's attorney fees in a divorce is deemed a support payment that cannot be discharged in the husband's bankruptcy proceedings where (1) the wife is unemployed at the time of divorce and apparently needs all support payments to meet the necessities of the children and herself, (2) the wife is never told that any portion of the support payment is a property settlement, and (3) the award is necessary to provide support and is not so manifestly unreasonable as to offend traditional concepts of support. In re Rudicil (Bkrtcy.N.D.Ohio 1991) 125 B.R. 747.

A "sustenance alimony" payment of $1950 per month to a wife will be deemed "support," so that arrearages cannot be discharged in the husband's bankruptcy proceedings as a "property settlement," where the woman testifies without refutation that she needs all the money to live, that her electricity has been shut off, and that family members periodically give her money. In re Rudicil (Bkrtcy.N.D.Ohio 1991) 125 B.R. 747.

In a Chapter 7 bankruptcy case, an obligation in a divorce decree to assume a second mortgage on the marital residence is nondischargeable as being in the nature of alimony or support where the assumption has the effect of providing necessary support to ensure that daily needs of the former spouse are satisfied, and the amount of the assumption is not so excessive as to render it unreasonable under traditional concepts of support, especially since the loan proceeds apparently went to finance the debtor's business, and the payment the debtor was to make to the bank on the loan was a periodic payment which is no different than if he would have made payments directly to his former spouse and she made the loan payments. In re Szuch (Bkrtcy.N.D.Ohio 1990) 117 B.R. 296.

A divorce decree obligation and arrearages intended to secure daily needs of a former wife are not dischargeable in the former husband's bankruptcy proceedings. In re Solomito (Bkrtcy.S.D.Ohio 1990) 112 B.R. 25.

A former husband's obligation under a divorce decree to assume a home improvement loan and credit card debt, and to pay a fixed sum, is nondischargeable in his bankruptcy proceedings where the evidence as a whole suggests that the state judge meant to create a support obligation for the former spouse who was in school and had no separate job or resources at the time. In re Lariccia (Bkrtcy.N.D.Ohio 1989) 110 B.R. 822.

A debtor's obligations after a divorce decree provide necessary support and are not dischargeable in his bankruptcy proceedings where they are to (1) pay half of a mortgage, property taxes, and house insurance; (2) repay educational loans; (3) pay for attorney fees caused by his untimely actions during litigation; (4) pay children's college expenses as ordered by a state court; and (5) pay half the present value of his pension. In re Portaro (Bkrtcy.N.D.Ohio 1989) 108 B.R. 142.

A former husband having $1800 left as monthly net income after paying child support cannot discharge in bankruptcy his obligation under the separation agreement to pay $7050 of joint credit card debts where his former wife's earnings are less than her expenses; in such a case, the court will determine that the obligation is in the nature of support and hence not dischargeable. In re Eikenberg (Bkrtcy.N.D.Ohio 1989) 107 B.R. 139.

A marital obligation will not be discharged in bankruptcy proceedings where (1) the state court or the parties intended to create an obligation to provide alimony, maintenance, or support; (2) this obligation truly has the effect of support by supplying the daily needs of the spouse and children; and (3) the amount of the obligation is not "manifestly unreasonable" in light of either state law or the bankruptcy concept of a "fresh start." In re Schreiber (Bkrtcy.S.D.Ohio 1989) 99 B.R. 380.

An award of $7000 in attorney fees to the wife in a short-lived, childless marriage after a divorce that simply divided property will be considered by a federal bankruptcy court to be "in the nature of alimony, maintenance or support" and, therefore, not dischargeable in the husband's bankruptcy proceedings. In re Stanjevich (Bkrtcy.S.D.Ohio 1989) 96 B.R. 138.

An obligation imposed on a husband by a divorce decree to pay debts representing outstanding balances for such everyday necessities as rent, electricity, heat, telephone, and trash collection is an obligation of support that cannot be discharged in the husband's bankruptcy proceedings, in light of the fact he earns $32,500 annually while the wife is not employed and has minor children at home. In re Alford (Bkrtcy.N.D.Ohio 1988) 95 B.R. 493.

The award under a divorce decree of an automobile to the wife and the imposition on the husband of the duty to pay for it as installments of the debt fall due, is in the nature of support and the husband's obligation to the wife is not dischargeable in bankruptcy where the woman also has custody of the children, because "reliable transportation" is "an essential commodity for a family with minor children." In re Swiczkowski (Bkrtcy.N.D.Ohio 1988) 84 B.R. 487.

Where a husband assumed a joint debt in a separation agreement and the circumstances indicate the wife was in need of support, it may be presumed in the husband's bankruptcy proceedings that the separation agreement provision was intended as support, thereby rendering the husband's obligation nondischargeable. In re Pitzen (Bkrtcy.N.D.Ohio 1986) 73 B.R. 10.

Where a separation agreement provides that a laborer earning more than $28,000 yearly pay a $4,700 second mortgage on the home of the wife and children while she pays the first mortgage, taxes, and other expenses, and where the wife's new husband maintains his own separate residence, the first husband's obligation is "support" for shelter, at least for the minor children, is not unreasonable in relation to his income, and as a result is not discharged by his bankruptcy. In re Mizen (Bkrtcy.N.D.Ohio 1987) 72 B.R. 251.

Where a separation agreement obligated a husband to pay the rent, utilities, and college expenses of the wife, who also was given custody of the couple's child, but the husband fell into arrears on the obligation, his later bankruptcy will not discharge the arrearage even though (1) he regained custody of the child within six months of the divorce, (2) the wife began sharing expenses with a "roommate," and (3) the wife completed school and now supports herself; the debt represented payments in the nature of support, which are not dischargeable. Matter of Rowles (Bkrtcy.N.D.Ohio 1986) 66 B.R. 628.

Where a joint marital debt assumed by a husband under a dissolution decree is secured by a mortgage on the house in which the wife and the child in her custody live, the husband's obligation is in the nature of support and cannot be discharged in bankruptcy. In re Wright (Bkrtcy.S.D.Ohio 1985) 51 B.R. 630.

Where a single sum is awarded to a wife who indicates an aversion to periodic payments from fear they will not be paid and who is receiving public assistance, and where little property was acquired during the course of the marriage, there is sufficient evidence to determine that the sum is alimony and, therefore, not dischargeable in bankruptcy. In re Kline (Bkrtcy.N.D.Ohio 1984) 42 B.R. 141, 15 O.B.R. 130.

40. —"Hold harmless" agreements, effect of bankruptcy

Where a separation agreement divides debts between the husband and wife with each party to pay some and hold the other party harmless, a trial court may find that the husband's assumption of debts is in the nature of support and alimony rather than a property division and not dischargeable in bankruptcy. Thompson v. Thompson (Richland 1986) 27 Ohio App.3d 296, 501 N.E.2d 108, 27 O.B.R. 341.

Order of court in divorce action, decreeing that defendant husband deliver certain personal property to plaintiff wife, and save her harmless from any obligations against such property, constitutes decree of alimony, so that obligation to reimburse her for claims she was required to pay is not discharged by his being adjudged bankrupt. Collins v. Smith (Ohio Com.Pl. 1971) 26 Ohio Misc. 231, 270 N.E.2d 377, 55 O.O.2d 370.

The typical "hold harmless" clause involving the assumption of joint obligations found in most separation agreements and divorce decrees can, under certain circumstances, create nondischargeable debt to third parties; the issue of whether a debt is in the nature of alimony, maintenance, or support as opposed to a property settlement is to be determined by federal bankruptcy law. In re Calhoun (C.A.6 (Ohio) 1983) 715 F.2d 1103.

Debtor's obligation to hold his former wife harmless on a loan securing the family home might be considered nondischargeable as support or alimony despite the existence of separate and distinct support provisions in the property settlement agreement. Stout v. Prussel (C.A.9 (Cal.) 1982) 691 F.2d 859.

Ex-husband's obligation to his ex-wife, incorporated in divorce decree, to pay and indemnify and hold ex-wife absolutely harmless from all existing obligations constituted alimony, maintenance and support for ex-wife or child, and hence was a debt not dischargeable in bankruptcy, even though award to wife was not specifically designated as alimony. In re Waller (C.A.6 (Ohio) 1974) 494 F.2d 447.

Chapter 7 debtor's $20,000 debt assumption and hold harmless obligation, arising from separation agreement incorporated in his divorce decree, was nondischargeable; divorce decree expressly stated that allocation of assets and liabilities was, in part, to provide for former wife's maintenance and support, and that if she were required for any reason to pay debts assigned to debtor, effect would be to cause former wife to be in need of additional support, hold harmless obligation was thus viewed by both parties and domestic court as intended for former wife's support, hold harmless obligation had the actual effect of providing support, and there was no suggestion that amount of support provided was unreasonable. In re Slygh (Bkrtcy.N.D.Ohio 2000) 244 B.R. 410.

Chapter 7 debtor failed to show that, if his $20,000 hold harmless obligation were discharged as nonsupport divorce debt, benefit to him would exceed the detriment to his former wife; debtor had long and effective work history with his employer with periodic pay increases, debtor had a demonstrated ability to increase his income through overtime work, $90,000 gross income projection for debtor was realistic, debtor's income greatly exceeded former wife's gross monthly income of $2,833 from her job and $1,284.84 from debtor for child support, and there was no evidence that former wife had any potential to increase her income from her job or to otherwise supplement her income. In re Slygh (Bkrtcy.N.D.Ohio 2000) 244 B.R. 410.

Although a "hold harmless" provision in a separation agreement or divorce decree is strong evidence of an intent to create a support obligation, the lack thereof does not necessarily indicate that the underlying obligation is not in the nature of support, for nondischargeability purposes. In re Luman (Bkrtcy.N.D.Ohio 1999) 238 B.R. 697.

Chapter 7 debtor was not entitled to discharge a divorce-related obligation which was not in nature of support, consisting of her obligation to make payments on vehicle which she had been awarded by divorce court and to hold former husband harmless on debt, on theory that benefits of granting debtor a discharge outweighed any detriment to former spouse; debtor's extravagant expenditures after discharging more than $11,000 in unsecured debt, as compared with former husband's modest lifestyle, and fact that discharge would only serve to provide debtor with additional discretionary income, belied any claim of balance of benefits tipping in debtor's favor. In re Dunn (Bkrtcy.S.D.Ohio 1998) 225 B.R. 393.

Debtor failed to show that he was entitled to discharge of his obligation to hold his former spouse harmless on mutual debts of their marriage; former spouse's income, even considering child support payment income, was substantially less than debtor's, with former spouse's gross income totalling approximately $22,240 per year, while debtor's gross income potential was $31,000 per year. In re Perkins (Bkrtcy.N.D.Ohio 1998) 221 B.R. 186.

Debtor's obligation to hold former spouse harmless on mutual debts of their marriage was incurred in connection with separation agreement and was not excepted from discharge as alimony, maintenance, or support, and, thus, former spouse met her initial burden under discharge exception for nonsupport divorce debt. In re Perkins (Bkrtcy.N.D.Ohio 1998) 221 B.R. 186.

Property settlement obligation imposed on Chapter 7 debtor under separation agreement incorporated into judgment of divorce, which required debtor to assume joint marital indebtedness and to hold his former wife harmless thereon, was dischargeable in bankruptcy as nonsupport obligation which debtor did not have ability to pay, where expenses of debtor and his new spouse, at time of hearing on dischargeability complaint, exceeded their monthly income, and where debtor's situation would not improve, even after anticipated payoff of his debt to the Internal Revenue Service (IRS), to extent sufficient to permit debtor to make any payment on property settlement obligation. In re Cooke (Bkrtcy.N.D.Ohio 1997) 213 B.R. 830.

Where separation agreement or divorce decree fails to provide "hold harmless" provision regarding one or more debts, former spouse is not entitled to indemnification or reimbursement where debtor fails to pay joint obligation to third party. In re Gibson (Bkrtcy.N.D.Ohio 1997) 210 B.R. 113, affirmed in part, reversed in part 219 B.R. 195.

Chapter 7 debtor's divorce decree obligation to pay and hold former wife harmless as to credit card debts was nondischargeable property settlement under discharge exception for nonsupport divorce debts; debtor had ability to pay obligation with future income that was not necessary to be expended for maintenance or support of debtor and his dependent, and discharging debtor's obligation to make credit card payments would not result in benefit to debtor that outweighed detrimental consequences to debtor's former wife. In re Henderson (Bkrtcy.N.D.Ohio 1996) 200 B.R. 322.

Evidentiary hearing would be required to determine whether Chapter 7 debtor's obligation to her former husband under their marital termination agreement, which provided that debtor would "hold harmless" her former spouse for $425 per month for monthly mortgage payment, was a nondischargeable property settlement. In re Finaly (Bkrtcy.S.D.Ohio 1995) 190 B.R. 312.

Fact that nondebtor-wife was able to keep her baby grand piano under divorce decree did not render obligation of debtor-husband to hold wife harmless from business debts so excessive as to lose benefit of nondischargeability as support. In re Sanders (Bkrtcy.N.D.Ohio 1995) 187 B.R. 588.

Provision in divorce judgment requiring husband to hold wife harmless from husband's business debts was intended as nondischargeable "support" for parties' children. In re Sanders (Bkrtcy.N.D.Ohio 1995) 187 B.R. 588.

Spouse of debtor does not have to sell off all possessions of value in order to be eligible under bankruptcy law to retain nondischargeability benefit of hold harmless obligation intended to provide support. In re Sanders (Bkrtcy.N.D.Ohio 1995) 187 B.R. 588.

To extent that debtor's former wife was able to afford to maintain her equity in Florida condominium following divorce, nondischargeable support provided to wife and parties' children by debtor-husband's obligation in divorce decree to hold wife harmless from business debts was so excessive as to be unreasonable under traditional concepts of support, requiring reduction, especially considering husband's relative income both now and at time of divorce. In re Sanders (Bkrtcy.N.D.Ohio 1995) 187 B.R. 588.

To determine amount by which nondischargeable support obligation arising out of debtor-husband's obligation under divorce judgment to hold wife harmless from business debts had to be reduced on ground that it was excessive due to wife's ability to make payments to maintain condominium, bankruptcy court would reduce to lump sum $214 per month wife had been paying on condominium; to do this, court would consider present value of five-year monthly annuity of $214 and judgment rate of 10% for lack of more appropriate method of accomplishing this goal. In re Sanders (Bkrtcy.N.D.Ohio 1995) 187 B.R. 588.

Hold harmless obligation found in divorce decree regarding joint marital debts can be found to be nondischargeable spousal support. In re Chapman (Bkrtcy.N.D.Ohio 1995) 187 B.R. 573.

In determining whether obligation is nondischargeable as being in nature of alimony, maintenance, or support, bankruptcy court's inquiry should be limited to nature of obligation at time it was undertaken, except in those cases involving hold-harmless provisions, assumptions of loan, or other hybrid provisions. In re Gibson (Bkrtcy.S.D.Ohio 1993) 157 B.R. 366.

Only in cases involving hold-harmless agreements or assumption of marital debts does *Calhoun's* four-prong test, including analysis of "present needs" and "change of circumstances," apply in determining whether obligation is nondischargeable as being in nature of alimony, maintenance, or support. In re Gibson (Bkrtcy.S.D.Ohio 1993) 157 B.R. 366.

In order to be excepted from discharge, hold harmless provisions requiring debtor to assume marital debt and hold spouse harmless, imposed by separation agreement or divorce decree, must actually be in nature of alimony, maintenance or support. In re Semler (Bkrtcy.N.D.Ohio 1992) 147 B.R. 137.

Husband's obligation to assume debts and hold wife harmless was not intended to provide alimony, maintenance or support, and thus debt was dischargeable, where marriage was of short duration, no children were produced, debt assumption was not styled as support, parties were represented by counsel, and no marital or family circumstances or disparity in earning power indicated necessity for support payments. In re Semler (Bkrtcy.N.D.Ohio 1992) 147 B.R. 137.

A wife's obligation in a divorce decree to hold her husband harmless on a second mortgage is held not in the nature of alimony, maintenance, or support in light of his greater earning capacity and the wife's custody of the children; as a result, her obligation may be discharged in her bankruptcy proceedings. In re Mallin (Bkrtcy.N.D.Ohio 1992) 137 B.R. 673.

After a former wife is held in contempt for violating a separation agreement by not paying her share of an escrow deficit when the marital residence was sold, a state court judgment requiring her to pay her former husband will be considered a property division obligation that she can discharge in her bankruptcy proceeding rather than a nondischargeable support obligation. In re Lever (Bkrtcy.N.D.Ohio 1992) 137 B.R. 243.

A provision in a divorce decree requiring a debtor to hold harmless the former spouse on certain debts of the marriage may constitute alimony if it has the effect of providing alimony, for purposes of determining whether the debts may be discharged in the debtor's bankruptcy proceedings. In re Keeran (Bkrtcy.N.D.Ohio 1990) 112 B.R. 881.

The obligation of a debtor under a divorce decree to hold his former wife harmless on mortgages she cosigned on rental property the state court awarded to the debtor can be discharged in the debtor's bankruptcy proceedings where not intended as support. In re Portaro (Bkrtcy.N.D.Ohio 1989) 108 B.R. 142.

The Bankruptcy Code at 11 USC 523(a)(5) is apparently devised to prevent a debtor from discharging in bankruptcy obligations to support his former wife and children imposed on him under the divorce decree even if the "support" is in the form of paying a debt jointly owed by the man and woman to a third party; thus, a debtor's agreement to hold his former wife harmless on joint debts cannot be discharged in bankruptcy to the extent his agreement is found to be "in payment of alimony, maintenance or support." In re Shelton (Bkrtcy.S.D.Ohio 1988) 92 B.R. 268.

Obligations imposed on a former husband under a divorce decree, to hold his wife harmless on a mortgage and to pay her a sum certain as her share of equity in their former residence, do not have the effect of providing necessary support to the former wife where her new husband enjoys a large income and her former husband's income is less than his expenses; the obligations are, therefore, dischargeable in bankruptcy. Matter of Seta (Bkrtcy.S.D.Ohio 1984) 45 B.R. 8.

41. —Property division, effect of bankruptcy

For purposes of discharge exception for alimony, maintenance, or support, when settlement agreement fails to provide for spousal support, court may presume that so-called property settlement is intended for support, when circumstances indicate that recipient spouse needs support. Ballinger v. Ballinger (Madison 1995) 107 Ohio App.3d 358, 668 N.E.2d 979.

Chapter 7 debtor's obligation, pursuant to divorce decree, to pay any tax liability resulting from tax returns of debtor and his former wife was in nature of property settlement and, therefore, did not come within discharge exception for alimony, maintenance, or support. Rizzen v. Spaman (Lucas 1995) 106 Ohio App.3d 95, 665 N.E.2d 283, dismissed, appeal not allowed 74 Ohio St.3d 1509, 659 N.E.2d 1286.

Finding that Chapter 7 debtor's obligation, pursuant to divorce decree, to make mortgage payments was in nature of property settlement and, therefore, dischargeable was abuse of discretion, as payments were to assist ex-wife in meeting her financial obligations in support of herself and minor child and, therefore, were nondischargeable support. Rizzen v. Spaman (Lucas 1995) 106 Ohio App.3d 95, 665 N.E.2d 283, dismissed, appeal not allowed 74 Ohio St.3d 1509, 659 N.E.2d 1286.

Chapter 7 debtor-husband's assumption of joint credit card debt under divorce decree was not in the nature of spousal support but, rather, was in the nature of property allocation, so that the debt was dischargeable, where decree explicitly stated that neither party was to pay spousal support to the other, wife obtained titles to marital residence and van and assumed approximately $37,000 in debt, husband obtained title to automobile along with approximately $9,800 in debt, at time of divorce wife's gross income was $16,500 and husband's was $36,000, parties' conflicting testimony regarding their respective beliefs as to the nature of husband's assumption of the joint credit card debt was insufficient to clearly indicate intention to create spousal support obligation, and, in light of wife's disposable monthly income of $364 at time of divorce, there was no evidence that support was necessary to meet daily needs of wife or parties' two minor children. Snyder v. Snyder (Ashtabula 1995) 105 Ohio App.3d 69, 663 N.E.2d 695.

Just as valuation and division of particular marital asset or liability must be viewed in context of entire property division, disparity in allocation of parties' debts must also be viewed with the entire division of property, for purposes of determining whether assumption of joint debt was in the nature of spousal support and thus is nondischargeable. Snyder v. Snyder (Ashtabula 1995) 105 Ohio App.3d 69, 663 N.E.2d 695.

Although, in broad sense, support results from assumption of joint marital debt even if the assumption was actually a division of property because funds are made available for other purposes including necessary support, it is clear from the Bankruptcy Code and its legislative history that Congress could not have intended that all assumptions of joint debt would be nondischargeable. Snyder v. Snyder (Ashtabula 1995) 105 Ohio App.3d 69, 663 N.E.2d 695.

Where a divorce decree awards the former husband the former wife's interest in the family home and real estate while ordering him to pay her a sum of money secured by a lien on the property, the husband cannot avoid the lien under 11 USC 522(f)(1), which provides that a debtor may avoid judicial liens on an interest in property. Farrey v. Sanderfoot (U.S.Wis. 1991) 111 S.Ct. 1825, 500 U.S. 291, 114 L.Ed.2d 337, on remand 943 F.2d 679.

A separation agreement provision that the husband pay his wife a fixed sum for ten years is a "property settlement in connection with alimony" not dischargeable in the husband's bankruptcy proceeding where the agreement does not otherwise provide for support, the wife is sixty years old, and she was never employed while married. In re Singer (C.A.6 (Ohio) 1986) 787 F.2d 1033.

After ascertaining debtor's disposable income, for purposes of determining his or her "ability to pay," under the first exception to nondischargeability provided in the discharge exception for nonsupport divorce debt, court must determine, after considering the total amount of indebtedness involved, whether debtor has a sufficient amount of disposable income available to pay the marital debt(s) within a reasonable amount of time. In re Miller (Bkrtcy.N.D.Ohio 2000) 247 B.R. 412.

If debtor has a sufficient amount of disposable income available to pay marital debt(s) within a reasonable amount of time, then debt is nondischargeable under the discharge exception for nonsupport divorce debt. In re Miller (Bkrtcy.N.D.Ohio 2000) 247 B.R. 412.

In determining whether debtor has a sufficient amount of disposable income available to pay marital debt(s) within a reasonable amount of time, court should be cautious of dedicating all debtor's disposable income to repayment of marital debt, as unexpected expenses, such as car repairs, may arise. In re Miller (Bkrtcy.N.D.Ohio 2000) 247 B.R. 412.

If debtor has some disposable income available, but marital debt is simply too large to expect debtor to realistically pay the entire debt in a reasonable period of time, court may consider discharging a portion of the marital debt, if circumstances of the particular case would make it equitable to do so. In re Miller (Bkrtcy.N.D.Ohio 2000) 247 B.R. 412.

Debtor had the "ability to pay" a $7,844.60 marital debt arising from the post-dissolution operation of his excavating business, within meaning of the discharge exception for nonsupport divorce debt; debtor had disposable income of $755.00 per month, debt would be paid off in less than two years if debtor devoted just half of his disposable income to its repayment, and, given amount of debtor's disposable income, partial discharge of the debt was not appropriate. In re Miller (Bkrtcy.N.D.Ohio 2000) 247 B.R. 412.

In determining the dischargeability of debtor's obligation to assume and hold his former wife harmless on a marital debt arising from the post-dissolution operation of debtor's excavating business, court's analysis was not changed by debtor's lack of malicious intent in making former wife jointly liable on the debt, nor by former wife's own failure to exercise due care in neglecting to give creditor proper and timely notice that she would no longer be liable for such debts. In re Miller (Bkrtcy.N.D.Ohio 2000) 247 B.R. 412.

State divorce court judgment compensating Chapter 7 debtor's husband for debtor's removal of valuable reptiles from marital home was not in the nature of alimony or support; language of judgment did not indicate that state court intended to impose support obligation, debtor had less income that husband and had duty to support two minor children, judgment was not designed to furnish husband with necessities of life, and judgment was in lump sum. In re Wynn (Bkrtcy.N.D.Ohio 1997) 205 B.R. 97.

Merely because divorce judgment entry stated that Chapter 7 debtor's assumption of certain debt shall be as and for spousal support, and provision wherein debtor assumed other marital debts contained no such language, did not show that it was indisputable that parties intended to create property settlement with regard to other marital debts, and that discharge exception for support was inapplicable to those other debts. In re Chapman (Bkrtcy.N.D.Ohio 1995) 187 B.R. 573.

Balancing test used for discharge exemption for debts incurred in course of divorce, but not in nature of support, favored discharge of joint debts and debts otherwise assumed by Chapter 7 debtor under divorce decree, when neither debtor or his ex-wife could pay debts and debtor would have to expend funds reasonably necessary for his maintenance and support in order to pay them; debtor was unemployed or underemployed since divorce, debt could not be collected from either party, and, although debtor omitted certain assets from schedules and made prepetition expenditures on things other than debt payment, any recovery on those amounts would inure to estate, not debtor, and evidence of fraud or bad faith was lacking. In re Woodworth (Bkrtcy.N.D.Ohio 1995) 187 B.R. 174.

Upon filing of divorce decree, former spouse's interest in pension becomes sole and separate property of that spouse, not debt. In re Piasecki (Bkrtcy.N.D.Ohio 1994) 171 B.R. 49.

Irrespective of how it is labeled, court may presume that so-called property settlement is intended for support, and so is nondischargeable in bankruptcy, when circumstances of case indicate that recipient spouse needs support. In re Sandoval (Bkrtcy.N.D.Ohio 1992) 161 B.R. 796.

Chapter 7 debtor's divorce decree obligation to pay joint debts was nondischargeable spousal support or maintenance rather than dischargeable property settlement; although debt was characterized in separation agreement as property settlement, disparity in parties' income and wife's residential needs indicated that debtor's assumption of obligation was intended as support. In re Friedrich (Bkrtcy.N.D.Ohio 1993) 158 B.R. 675.

Where the terms of a divorce decree indicate that the parties did not intend the husband's assumption of the mortgage on rental property to be support for his former wife, the obligation arises from a property settlement and will not be denied discharge in the husband's bankruptcy proceedings as "support." In re Cornett (Bkrtcy.N.D.Ohio 1990) 123 B.R. 776.

A divorce decree that appears to contemplate sale of the marital residence and an equal sharing of the net proceeds is dividing property in this respect rather than imposing a support obligation on any party; as a result, a provision calling for the husband to make mortgage payments does not create a support obligation and the obligation may be discharged in the husband's bankruptcy along with any arrearage. In re Shelton (Bkrtcy.S.D.Ohio 1988) 92 B.R. 268.

Where a state court in a divorce case gave judgment against the husband for $12,800 without stating whether the sum was a property division or for support, a federal bankruptcy court will find the state judge meant the award to be a property division dischargeable in bankruptcy upon the facts of the case that the husband was aged fifty-three years, educated through ninth grade, and receiving workers' compensation because unable to work, while the wife was thirty-three years old, had attended college for two years, and was incapacitated by an automobile accident. In re Harrison (Bkrtcy.S.D.Ohio 1988) 82 B.R. 900.

A divorce decree that a husband turn thirty per cent of his military pension over to his wife gives her an ownership interest in the funds that is not affected by the husband's bankruptcy petition or discharge, since that thirty per cent interest is not property of the husband. In re Mace (Bkrtcy.S.D.Ohio 1987) 82 B.R. 864.

Whether a debt owed by one former spouse to the other is dischargeable in bankruptcy proceedings because it represents a property division, or not dischargeable because it represents alimony, maintenance, or support depends upon (1) the intentions of the state court or the parties as to the purpose of the payment, (2) the use of the money, and (3) the reasonableness of the obligation in light of traditional notions of support and of the party's resources at the time of the award and thereafter; if the parties or state court intended the payment to be a division of property, the inquiry ends there and the debt is dischargeable. In re Mace (Bkrtcy.S.D.Ohio 1987) 82 B.R. 864.

The claim of a debtor in bankruptcy proceedings that over the course of two years he was "unable" to pay more than $75 toward the property settlement of a divorce decree despite his annual salary of $85,000 and ownership of valuable assets is simply unbelievable, although it does not demonstrate that his bankruptcy petition was filed in bad faith; the court will not confirm any plan of this debtor unless it provides for payment of the entire property settlement. In re Markunes (Bkrtcy.S.D.Ohio 1987) 78 B.R. 875.

Where an Ohio divorce decree awards the wife "all right, title and interest in the household furnishings, goods and effects" except articles specified as the husband's property, a bankruptcy court will find firearms bought by the husband or inherited from his father but not listed as his in the decree to be the property of the wife, and therefore available to be sold to pay her debts. In re Welch (Bkrtcy.S.D.Ohio 1986) 70 B.R. 5.

Where a wife releases her interest in realty under a separation agreement in return for the husband's promise to pay a fixed sum for ten and one-half years unconditionally, the payments are in the nature of a property settlement and therefore dischargeable in the husband's bankruptcy even though the agreement termed the payments alimony and allowed the husband the income tax deduction associated with such payments. In re Mallisk (Bkrtcy.N.D.Ohio 1986) 64 B.R. 39.

Where a husband and wife jointly borrow money to buy personalty then divorce with the husband receiving the property and required to hold the wife harmless on the obligation, the debt is a property settlement and may be discharged in the husband's bankruptcy; a debt for money borrowed during marriage to effect repairs to a residence retained by the wife after the divorce is support, however, and cannot be discharged. In re Shimp (Bkrtcy.N.D.Ohio 1986) 59 B.R. 553.

A husband's obligation under a divorce decree to pay the wife a sum that represents a division of the husband's pension fund is not in the nature of support and may therefore be discharged in bankruptcy. Matter of Heck (Bkrtcy.S.D.Ohio 1985) 53 B.R. 402.

The debt of one spouse to another on a promissory note given under a divorce decree to compensate for the difference in value between properties allocated thereunder is dischargeable in bankruptcy in the absence of proof that the obligation was intended as alimony or support and truly represents necessary support payments. In re Brandstadt (Bkrtcy.N.D.Ohio 1984) 45 B.R. 538.

A promissory note given by a husband to his wife pursuant to a divorce decree, which appears to secure repayment of property brought by the wife into the marriage, is a compromise between the parties concerning a property dispute and, as such, is a debt dischargeable in bankruptcy. In re Hiller (Bkrtcy.N.D.Ohio 1984) 44 B.R. 764.

A divorce decree provision requiring a husband to transfer one-half of a farm owned by him as tenant-in-common with his father, or a sum equal in value, to his former wife is a property settlement and, therefore, is dischargeable in bankruptcy where the decree otherwise provides sufficient support to the former spouse. In re Hansen (Bkrtcy.N.D.Ohio 1984) 44 B.R. 654.

42. —Procedural issues, effect of bankruptcy

State and federal courts have concurrent jurisdiction to determine whether debt to child or former spouse should be excepted from discharge as one for alimony, maintenance or support. Bratton v. Frederick (Defiance 1996) 109 Ohio App.3d 13, 671 N.E.2d 1030.

In deciding whether obligation should be excepted from discharge, as one for alimony, maintenance or support, court should inquire whether parties intended to create obligation of support, whether obligation has effect of providing necessary support, and whether amount awarded is so excessive as to be manifestly unreasonable under traditional concepts of support. Bratton v. Frederick (Defiance 1996) 109 Ohio App.3d 13, 671 N.E.2d 1030.

State courts and bankruptcy courts have concurrent jurisdiction to determine whether debt comes within discharge exception for alimony, maintenance, or support. Ballinger v. Ballinger (Madison 1995) 107 Ohio App.3d 358, 668 N.E.2d 979.

Under discharge exception for alimony, maintenance, or support, if court determines that amount of debtor's obligation is unreasonable, then court must determine how much of obligation is reasonable and therefore nondischargeable. Ballinger v. Ballinger (Madison 1995) 107 Ohio App.3d 358, 668 N.E.2d 979.

Chapter 7 debtor's obligation to reimburse ex-spouse after she paid boat debt, which debtor had been ordered to pay pursuant to divorce decree, came within discharge exception for alimony, maintenance, or support; at time of dissolution proceedings, debtor's spouse was in need of support, and amount of debt assumed by debtor was not unreasonable or excessive. Ballinger v. Ballinger (Madison 1995) 107 Ohio App.3d 358, 668 N.E.2d 979.

Appellate court reviews factual determination of whether obligation constitutes nondischargeable support obligation for clear error and reviews legal conclusions de novo. Ballinger v. Ballinger (Madison 1995) 107 Ohio App.3d 358, 668 N.E.2d 979.

In determining whether specific obligation is actually in nature of alimony, maintenance, or support, for nondischargeability purposes, state courts have concurrent jurisdiction with bankruptcy courts. Rizzen v. Spaman (Lucas 1995) 106 Ohio App.3d 95, 665 N.E.2d 283, dismissed, appeal not allowed 74 Ohio St.3d 1509, 659 N.E.2d 1286.

In determining whether debt meets standards of discharge exception for alimony, maintenance, or support, federal law controls, guided in part by state law. Rizzen v. Spaman (Lucas 1995) 106 Ohio App.3d 95, 665 N.E.2d 283, dismissed, appeal not allowed 74 Ohio St.3d 1509, 659 N.E.2d 1286.

Under law of Sixth Circuit, in determining whether obligation imposed by divorce decree is in nature of alimony, maintenance, or support, for nondischargeability purposes, court must first determine whether state court or parties to divorce intended to create obligation to provide support through assumption of joint debts; if initial question is answered in affirmative, court must determine whether such assumption has effect of providing support necessary to ensure that daily needs of former spouse and any children of marriage are satisfied, and if this second question is answered in affirmative, court must then determine that amount of support represented by assumption is not so excessive that it is manifestly unreasonable under traditional concepts of support. Rizzen v. Spaman (Lucas 1995) 106 Ohio App.3d 95, 665 N.E.2d 283, dismissed, appeal not allowed 74 Ohio St.3d 1509, 659 N.E.2d 1286.

Award of partial attorney fees to Chapter 7 debtor's ex-wife was not abuse of discretion in ex-wife's action to enforce divorce decree. Rizzen v. Spaman (Lucas 1995) 106 Ohio App.3d 95, 665 N.E.2d 283, dismissed, appeal not allowed 74 Ohio St.3d 1509, 659 N.E.2d 1286.

Remand for redetermination judgment was appropriate remedy, where trial court, in determining nondischargeability of divorce debts, failed to give Chapter 7 debtor credit for sum that debtor's ex-wife had previously collected from debtor. Rizzen v. Spaman (Lucas 1995) 106 Ohio App.3d 95, 665 N.E.2d 283, dismissed, appeal not allowed 74 Ohio St.3d 1509, 659 N.E.2d 1286.

Although state law cannot be completely ignored, issue of when assumption of joint debts is "in the nature of alimony, maintenance, or support," as opposed to division of communal property, is to be determined by federal bankruptcy law. Snyder v. Snyder (Ashtabula 1995) 105 Ohio App.3d 69, 663 N.E.2d 695.

Party objecting to discharge of debt has the burden of proving his or her objection. Snyder v. Snyder (Ashtabula 1995) 105 Ohio App.3d 69, 663 N.E.2d 695.

State courts have concurrent jurisdiction with federal courts to determine dischargeability of debts under discharge exception for alimony, maintenance, or support. In re Dissolution of Marriage of Coplin (Van Wert 1995) 102 Ohio App.3d 212, 656 N.E.2d 1338.

In determining dischargeability under discharge exception for alimony, maintenance, or support, initial inquiry is whether parties intended to create obligation for support, next inquiry is whether obligation has effect of providing necessary support, and finally, court must determine that amount of support is not so excessive that it is manifestly unreasonable under traditional concepts of support. In re Dissolution of Marriage of Coplin (Van Wert 1995) 102 Ohio App.3d 212, 656 N.E.2d 1338.

Trial court abused its discretion in entering final decree in divorce proceeding that provided for spousal support for wife in amount of $2,000 per month during period between entry of decree and date upon which marital home was sold, since indefinite nature of order invited abuse. DiLacqua v. DiLacqua (Summit 1993) 88 Ohio App.3d 48, 623 N.E.2d 118.

One legitimate way of preserving status quo, which is a purpose of award of reasonable spousal support during pendency of divorce proceeding, is to ensure that mortgage payments continue to be made on marital home. DiLacqua v. DiLacqua (Summit 1993) 88 Ohio App.3d 48, 623 N.E.2d 118.

Where a former husband opposes a motion for contempt based on failure to pay debts under a separation agreement by asserting that his obligation was discharged in bankruptcy, the domestic relations court may nonetheless find him in contempt where the bankruptcy order neither specifically relieves him of the obligation nor states whether the obligation is part of the property settlement or in the nature of alimony. Jacobs v Jacobs, No. CA-2031 (2d Dist Ct App, Clark, 11-15-85).

A state statute exempting homestead property from forced sale that has been construed to be inapplicable to liens that existed before property acquired its homestead status under an amendment concerning condominiums does not preclude the debtor whose condominium is subject to the pre-existing lien from invoking 11 USC 522 to avoid the lien, which is based in this case upon a judgment owed to his former wife; the question under 11 USC 522(f) is not whether the lien impairs an exemption to which the debtor is in fact entitled but whether it impairs an exemption to which he would have been entitled but for the lien itself. Owen v. Owen (U.S.Fla. 1991) 111 S.Ct. 1833, 500 U.S. 305, 114 L.Ed.2d 350, on remand 961 F.2d 170.

Although matters concerning divorce and alimony have been excepted from federal court jurisdiction based on diversity of the parties' state citizenship since Barber v Barber, 62 US 582, 16 LEd(2d) 226(1859), this rule does not bar a husband's claim in federal court that the former wife intentionally inflicted emotional distress on him by taking their child to another state and denying him visitation rights, or that she interfered with his employment by writing letters to his employer; the court may also hear his counterclaim for enforcement of a state judgment concerning arrearages in alimony and child support. Drewes v. Ilnicki (C.A.6 (Ohio) 1988) 863 F.2d 469.

Because the individual's rights to property are matters of state law it is proper for the bankruptcy court to lift the automatic stay imposed when one spouse filed a federal bankruptcy petition after the other spouse had filed a divorce action in state court; the stay is lifted so the state court may proceed to exercise its exclusive authority in domestic matters, including power to divide marital property, and once the state court decides what property belongs to the bankruptcy petitioner the bankruptcy court may then exercise its exclusive jurisdiction over the petitioner's property. In re White (C.A.6 (Ohio) 1988) 851 F.2d 170.

Question of what constitutes alimony, maintenance, or support within meaning of the Bankruptcy Code's discharge exception is a matter of federal, not state, law. In re Slygh (Bkrtcy.N.D.Ohio 2000) 244 B.R. 410.

"Balance of benefits" exception to nondischargeability of divorce-related obligations not in nature of support should not be applied in manner which would permit debtor to receive discharge of debt owed former spouse based solely upon an assertion that repayment of obligation would cause a reduction in debtor's standard of living which is below one that is suitable for debtor's own tastes, but which is equal to or above that of nondebtor former spouse, who lives modestly within his or her means. In re Dunn (Bkrtcy.S.D.Ohio 1998) 225 B.R. 393.

Best way to apply balancing test required by discharge exception for nonsupport divorce debt is to review financial status of debtor and creditor and compare their relative standards of living to determine true benefit of debtor's possible discharge against any hardship that spouse, former spouse, and/or children would suffer as result of debtor's discharge. In re Perkins (Bkrtcy.N.D.Ohio 1998) 221 B.R. 186.

Determination by state divorce court, upon finding that parties had complied with appropriate procedural requirements for a dissolution of their marriage, in entering decree that incorporated the permanent alimony provision of parties' separation agreement, was not a "final judgment or decree rendered upon the merits," and would not be given preclusive effect on question of whether obligation was in nature of "alimony," for debt dischargeability purposes. In re Edwards (Bkrtcy.S.D.Ohio 1997) 216 B.R. 796.

Chapter 7 debtor's former wife, who objected to debtor's complaint seeking to discharge marital obligations, had burden of establishing that debtor's debt to former wife should be excepted from discharge under discharge exception for support, alimony, or maintenance by preponderance of the evidence. In re Henderson (Bkrtcy.N.D.Ohio 1996) 200 B.R. 322.

In adversary proceeding brought by Chapter 7 debtor, seeking to discharge his obligation under divorce decree to repay credit card debts incurred during marriage, debtor's former wife bore burden of proof by preponderance of evidence of showing applicability of discharge exception for alimony, maintenance, or support. In re Williams (Bkrtcy.N.D.Ohio 1995) 189 B.R. 678.

For purposes of determining whether divorce created obligation that falls within exception to discharge for maintenance, alimony or support, court must analyze relative financial condition of parties at time of divorce. In re Pinkstaff (Bkrtcy.N.D.Ohio 1994) 163 B.R. 504.

In determining whether obligation is in nature of spousal support or property settlement for purposes of determining dischargeability of obligation in bankruptcy, court must look beyond language of divorce decree to intent of parties and substance of obligation. In re Sandoval (Bkrtcy.N.D.Ohio 1992) 161 B.R. 796.

Standard of what constitutes nondischargeable spousal support or maintenance is matter of federal bankruptcy law, not state law concerning domestic relations. In re Friedrich (Bkrtcy.N.D.Ohio 1993) 158 B.R. 675.

For purpose of determining whether spousal obligation is in nature of maintenance, and thus nondischargeable, federal bankruptcy law controls determination characterizing the obligation; however, reference to state law can provide guidance. In re Semler (Bkrtcy.N.D.Ohio 1992) 147 B.R. 137.

To establish that a debt under a divorce decree is support and therefore not dischargeable in the debtor's bankruptcy, the obligee spouse must show a support obligation was intended and that the amount is not manifestly unreasonable under traditional notions of support. In re Cacolici (Bkrtcy.N.D.Ohio 1989) 108 B.R. 578.

A separation agreement provision that "[i]n the event he should file a bankruptcy petition under Chapter 7 or Chapter 13, she will not contest his discharge on previously joint debts" is ineffective; attempts before a bankruptcy petition is filed to secure a waiver of the right to contest the discharge of a debt after the petition is filed are unenforceable. In re Eikenberg (Bkrtcy.N.D.Ohio 1989) 107 B.R. 139.

A former husband seeking a "hardship discharge" from his obligation to pay $600 each month to creditors under his "Chapter 13" bankruptcy plan will be found by a "somewhat reluctant" court to have shown that his inability to complete payment is caused by circumstances for which he cannot justly be held accountable where: (1) he pays $1020 each month for child support, (2) he now earns "significantly less" as a commissioned stockbroker than the $48,000 salary he was paid by another brokerage firm that went out of business in 1988, and (3) he has married another woman who receives about $280 monthly as child support from her former husband; the discharge is nonetheless denied under 11 USC 328(b), however, in light of the fact the former husband has not shown that his general unsecured creditors, who have thus far received only .008% payment have gotten as much as they would have if he filed under "Chapter 7," and in light of the fact he has not attempted to modify the plan by reducing the 100% payment promised to creditors rather than ceasing further payment altogether. In re Schleppi (Bkrtcy.S.D.Ohio 1989) 103 B.R. 901.

A former wife who moves the domestic relations court to find her former husband in contempt for not paying certain liabilities imposed by their divorce agreement, after she has been notified by telephone that the man has filed a bankruptcy petition, willfully violates the automatic stay of 11 USC 362 and is liable for damages including costs and attorney fees, and possibly for punitive damages as well. In re Sermersheim (Bkrtcy.N.D.Ohio 1989) 97 B.R. 885.

A determination in state court that a party's responsibilities under a separation agreement are alimony and thus not dischargeable in bankruptcy estops any collateral attack in bankruptcy court on the nature of the obligation where the state judge used the same standard as bankruptcy judges for deciding when a payment constitutes alimony. In re Polley (Bkrtcy.S.D.Ohio 1987) 74 B.R. 68.

The debts of an individual who files for bankruptcy under Chapter 13 may all be discharged unless shown specifically excepted under 11 USC 523; the burden of showing a debt not dischargeable is on the creditor. Accordingly, an obligation of a bankrupt former husband imposed by a separation agreement and decree will be discharged unless the former wife proves the debt within a statutory exception such as 11 USC 523 (a)(5), concerning debts in the nature of alimony or support. In re Shaw (Bkrtcy.N.D.Ohio 1986) 66 B.R. 399.

Modification of a state court decree as to alimony and support will no longer be ordered by a federal bankruptcy court; thus, a judgment against a debtor for unpaid alimony will not be discharged despite "changed circumstances," as the effect of such a change is for state court determination. Matter of Brown (Bkrtcy.S.D.Ohio 1985) 46 B.R. 612.

43. Findings of fact

Determination of traceability of premarital contribution to purchase of asset is finding of fact. Zeefe v. Zeefe (Ohio App. 8 Dist. 1998) 125 Ohio App.3d 600, 709 N.E.2d 208.

Trial court does not need to list each factor and comment on factors considered in determining whether and how much to modify spousal support unless there is a request for findings of fact and conclusions of law. Carnahan v. Carnahan (Ohio App. 12 Dist. 1997) 118 Ohio App.3d 393, 692 N.E.2d 1086.

Lump sum spousal support award was not a "distributive award" from separate property and, therefore, did not have to be supported by findings of fact that must be entered to support such awards. Marcum v. Marcum (Ohio App. 2 Dist. 1996) 116 Ohio App.3d 606, 688 N.E.2d 1085.

Finding that there was present need for spousal support in specified amount was insufficient to meet requirement that trial court set forth the basis for its decision to award support. Mallett v. Mallett (Ohio App. 7 Dist. 1996) 116 Ohio App.3d 139, 687 N.E.2d 17.

Trial court was not required to make specific findings of fact regarding its award of spousal support to wife, particularly as husband did not request such findings. Carman v. Carman (Butler 1996) 109 Ohio App.3d 698, 672 N.E.2d 1093.

When spouse does not request findings of fact and conclusions of law concerning award of spousal support, reviewing court presumes that trial court considered all statutory factors and all other relevant facts. Carman v. Carman (Butler 1996) 109 Ohio App.3d 698, 672 N.E.2d 1093.

Absent request for findings of fact and conclusions of law, it is not necessary that trial court list and comment on each factor it must consider in determining whether spousal support is appropriate and reasonable. Alder v. Alder (Butler 1995) 105 Ohio App.3d 524, 664 N.E.2d 609.

To enable reviewing court to determine if award of spousal support is fair, equitable, and in accordance with law, trial court must indicate basis for its award in sufficient detail to permit proper appellate review. Graham v. Graham (Greene 1994) 98 Ohio App.3d 396, 648 N.E.2d 850.

Trial court abused its discretion in modifying spousal support award on remand to $810 per month for 12 years without setting forth sufficient reasoning for its decision, where remand order directed trial court to set forth its reasoning for its original award to allow proper review. Graham v. Graham (Greene 1994) 98 Ohio App.3d 396, 648 N.E.2d 850.

A court need not make findings of fact supporting an equitable distribution of marital property when a case is filed in December, 1990, and statutory provisions under RC 3105.171 and 3105.18, requiring the findings of fact are effective January 1, 1991. Burke v Burke, No. 490, 1993 WL 63384 (4th Dist Ct App, Meigs, 3-9-93).

44. —Contempt order, effect of bankruptcy

Chapter 7 petition filed by debtor on eve of his imprisonment for contempt for failing to pay divorce-related obligation to his former spouse would not be dismissed as "bad faith" filing, where debtor had significant debt in addition to that owed to former spouse, and it did not appear that petition was filed only to prevent debtor from being jailed for contempt. In re Custer (Bkrtcy.N.D.Ohio 1997) 208 B.R. 675.

45. Annulment distinguished from divorce

Statute governing award of attorney fees in divorce or legal separation proceedings was inapplicable to annulment proceeding. Liming v. Liming (Ohio App. 4 Dist. 1996) 117 Ohio App.3d 617, 691 N.E.2d 299.

46. Federal non-bankruptcy involvement

The domestic relations exception to federal jurisdiction applies only where a plaintiff positively sues in federal court for divorce, alimony, or child custody. Catz v. Chalker (C.A.6 (Ohio) 1998) 142 F.3d 279.

3105.19 and 3105.20 Alimony proceedings, joinder; injunction and equity powers of court—Repealed

(1970 H 1201, eff. 7-1-71; 132 v S 54; 1953 H 1; GC 8003-20, 8003-21; Source—GC 11995, 11996)

Historical and Statutory Notes

Ed. Note: See now Civ R 75(B) and 75(H) for provisions analogous to former 3105.19 and 3105.20.

Pre-1953 H 1 Amendments: 124 v S 65

CHILD CUSTODY AND SUPPORT

3105.21 Custody and support of children; support orders

(A) Upon satisfactory proof of the causes in the complaint for divorce, annulment, or legal separation, the court of common pleas shall make an order for the disposition, care, and maintenance of the children of the marriage, as is in their best interests, and in accordance with section 3109.04 of the Revised Code.

(B) Upon the failure of proof of the causes in the complaint, the court may make the order for the disposition, care, and maintenance of any dependent child of the marriage as is in the child's best interest, and in accordance with section 3109.04 of the Revised Code.

(C) Each order for child support made or modified under this section shall include as part of the order a general provision, as described in division (A)(1) of section 3113.21 of the Revised Code, requiring the withholding or deduction of income or assets of the obligor under the order as described in division (D) of section 3113.21 of the Revised Code, or another type of appropriate requirement as described in division (D)(3), (D)(4), or (H) of that section, to ensure that withholding or deduction from the income or assets of the obligor is available from the commencement of the support order for collection of the support and of any arrearages that occur; a statement requiring all parties to the order to notify the child support enforcement agency in writing of their current mailing address, current residence address, current residence telephone number, current driver's license number, and any changes to that information; and a notice that the requirement to notify the agency of all changes to that information continues until further notice from the court. Any court of common pleas that makes or modifies an order for child support under this section shall comply with sections 3113.21 to 3113.219 of the Revised Code. If any person required to pay child support under an order made under this section on or after April 15, 1985, or modified on or after December 1, 1986, is found in contempt of court for failure to make support payments under the order, the court that makes the finding, in addition to any other penalty or remedy imposed, shall assess all court costs arising out of the contempt proceeding against the person and require the person to pay any reasonable attorney's fees of any adverse party, as determined by the court, that arose in relation to the act of contempt.

(D) Notwithstanding section 3109.01 of the Revised Code, if a court issues a child support order under this section, the order shall remain in effect beyond the child's eighteenth birthday as long as the child continuously attends on a full-time basis any recognized and accredited high school or the order provides that the duty of support of the child continues beyond the child's eighteenth birthday. Except in cases in which the order provides that the duty of support continues for any period after the child reaches age nineteen, the order shall not remain in effect after the child reaches age nineteen. Any parent ordered to pay support under a child support order issued under this section shall continue to pay support under the order, including during seasonal vacation periods, until the order terminates.

(1997 H 352, eff. 1-1-98; 1993 H 173, eff. 12-31-93; 1992 S 10; 1990 H 514, H 591; 1988 H 708; 1987 H 231; 1986 H 509; 1984 H 614; 1974 H 233)

Historical and Statutory Notes

Ed. Note: Former 3105.21 repealed by 1970 H 1201, eff. 7-1-71; 130 v H 467; 1953 H 1; GC 8003-22; Source—GC 11998.

Pre-1953 H 1 Amendments: 124 v S 65

Amendment Note: 1997 H 352 deleted "on or after December 31, 1993," before "shall include", substituted "income" for "wages" twice and "(D)(3), (D)(4)" for "(D)(6), (D)(7)", inserted "current residence telephone number, current driver's license number,", and deleted "on or after April 12, 1990," before "shall comply", in division (C); inserted "or the order provides that the duty of support of the child continues beyond the child's eighteenth birthday" and added the second sentence in division (D); and made other nonsubstantive changes.

Amendment Note: 1993 H 173 rewrote division (C) before the first semi-colon, which previously read:

"(C) Each order for child support made or modified under this section on or after December 1, 1986, shall be accompanied by one or more orders described in division (D) or (H) of section 3113.21 of the Revised Code, whichever is appropriate under the requirements of that section".

Cross References

Administration of child support orders by child support enforcement agencies, 3113.218

Calculation of amount of child support obligation, 3113.215

Contempt action for failure to pay support, 2705.031, 2705.05

Court awarding parental rights and responsibilities, shared parenting, modifications, best interests of child, 3109.04, 3109.041

Division of child support, 5101.31 et seq.

Divorce, annulment, and legal separation actions; investigation in parental rights and responsibilities proceedings, Civ R 75

Divorce or alimony action involving custody or care of children, jurisdiction of juvenile court, 2151.23

Domestic violence, support order, 3113.31

Equal rights of parents to parental rights and responsibilities toward children, 3109.03

Health insurance coverage for children, 3113.217

Husband and wife natural guardians of minor children, 2111.08

Interfering with action to issue or modify support order, 2919.231

Lottery winner must state under oath whether or not he is in default of support order, 3770.071

Neglect and abandonment of dependents, failure to pay maintenance cost of child, 3113.06

Nonsupport of dependents, 2919.21

Notice of default on child support order sent to professional licensing boards, 2301.373

Parentage action, support order, 3111.13, 3111.15

Reciprocal enforcement of support, Ch 3115

Reciprocal enforcement of support, support pendente lite, 3115.27

Small loans; assignment or order of wages for support, 1321.32, 1321.33

Support orders, enforcement, 2301.34 et seq.

Uniform child custody jurisdiction law, 3109.21 to 3109.37

Ohio Administrative Code References

Department of job and family services, child support program, OAC Ch 5101:1-29

Department of job and family services, collection of past due support by federal tax refund offset, OAC Ch 5101:1-30

Library References

Divorce ⚷289 to 310.
Marriage ⚷64.
WESTLAW Topic Nos. 134, 253.
C.J.S. Divorce §§ 611 to 630, 632 to 705, 708, 719 to 736.
C.J.S. Marriage § 79.

OJur 3d: 46, Family Law § 564, 567, 711; 47, Family Law § 1144, 1198, 1201, 1222, 1300, 1301, 1306, 1308; 62, Investment Securities and Securities Regulation § 53

Am Jur 2d: 24, Divorce and Separation § 772 to 878, 963 to 1097; 59, Parent and Child § 50 to 84

Nonresidence as affecting one's right to custody of child. 15 ALR2d 432

Court's power as to custody and visitation of children in marriage annulment proceedings. 63 ALR2d 1008

Right of wife to allowance for expense money and attorney's fees in action by or against husband, without divorce, for child custody. 82 ALR2d 1008

Right of mother to custody of illegitimate child. 98 ALR2d 417

Power of court which denied divorce, legal separation, or annulment, to award custody or make provisions for support of child. 7 ALR3d 1096

Right of putative father to custody of illegitimate child. 45 ALR3d 216

Wife's possession of independent means as affecting her right to child support pendente lite. 60 ALR3d 832
Child's right of action for loss of support, training, parental attention, or the like, against a third person negligently injuring parent. 69 ALR3d 528
Modern status of maternal preference rule or presumption in child custody cases. 70 ALR3d 262
Statutory change of age of majority as affecting preexisting status or rights. 75 ALR3d 228
Provision in divorce decree requiring husband to pay certain percentage of future salary increases as additional alimony or child support. 75 ALR3d 493
Who has custody or control of child within terms of penal statute punishing cruelty or neglect by one having custody or control. 75 ALR3d 933
Validity, construction, and application of statute imposing upon stepparent obligation to support child. 75 ALR3d 1129
Obtaining jurisdiction over nonresident parent in filiation or support proceeding. 76 ALR3d 708
Effect, in subsequent proceedings, of paternity findings or implications in divorce or annulment decree or in support or custody order made incident thereto. 78 ALR3d 846
Right of indigent parent to appointed counsel in proceeding for involuntary termination of parental rights. 80 ALR3d 1141
Determination of paternity of child as within scope of proceeding under Uniform Reciprocal Enforcement of Support Act. 81 ALR3d 1175
Father's liability for support of child furnished after divorce decree which awarded custody to mother but made no provision for support. 91 ALR3d 530
Validity, construction, and application of Uniform Child Custody Jurisdiction Act. 96 ALR3d 968
Parent's obligation to support unmarried minor child who refuses to live with parent. 98 ALR3d 334
Propriety of decree in proceeding between divorced parents to determine mother's duty to pay support for children in custody of father. 98 ALR3d 1146
Right to require psychiatric or mental examination for party seeking to obtain or retain custody of child. 99 ALR3d 268
Responsibility of noncustodial divorced parent to pay for, or contribute to, costs of child's college education. 99 ALR3d 322
Validity and effect, as between former spouses, of agreement releasing parent from payment of child support provided for in an earlier divorce decree. 100 ALR3d 1129
Admissibility of social worker's expert testimony on custody issue. 1 ALR4th 837
Parent's physical disability or handicap as factor in custody award or proceedings. 3 ALR4th 1044
Spouse's professional degree or license as marital property for purposes of alimony, support, or property settlement. 4 ALR4th 1294
Laches or acquiescence as defense, so as to bar recovery of arrearages of permanent alimony or child support. 5 ALR4th 1015
Initial award or denial of child custody to homosexual or lesbian parent. 6 ALR4th 1297
Removal by custodial parents of child from jurisdiction in violation of court order as justifying termination, suspension, or reduction of child support payments. 8 ALR4th 1231
Award of custody of child where contest is between natural parent and stepparent. 10 ALR4th 767
Race as factor in custody award or proceedings. 10 ALR4th 796
Desire of child as to geographical location of residence or domicile as factor in awarding custody or terminating parental rights. 10 ALR4th 827
Right of incarcerated mother to retain custody of infant in penal institution. 14 ALR4th 748
Necessity of requiring presence in court of both parties in proceedings relating to custody or visitation of children. 15 ALR4th 864
Propriety of awarding joint custody of children. 17 ALR4th 1013
Effect of trial court giving consideration to needs of children in making property division. 19 ALR4th 239
Validity and enforceability of escalation clause in divorce decree relating to alimony and child support. 19 ALR4th 830
Propriety of awarding custody of child to parent residing or intending to reside in foreign country. 20 ALR4th 677
Smoking as factor in child custody and visitation cases. 36 ALR5th 377

Baldwin's Ohio Legislative Service, 1990 Laws of Ohio, H 591—LSC Analysis, p 5-576
Carlin, Baldwin's Ohio Practice, *Merrick-Rippner Probate Law* § 19.2, 105.11, 108.1, 108.3, 108.13, 108.20, 108.33, 108.34 (1997)
3 Katz & Giannelli, Baldwin's Ohio Practice, *Criminal Law* § 109.9, 109.12 (1996)
Kurtz & Giannelli, Ohio Juvenile Law (1998 Ed.), Text 3.2
Sowald & Morganstern, Baldwin's Ohio Practice, *Domestic Relations Law* § 3.31, 4.26, 7.19, 7.35, 8.6, 10.3, 15.3, 19.1, 19.23, 20.1, 21.3, 21.8, 23.15, 24.2, 25.36 (1997)

Law Review and Journal Commentaries

Bankruptcy Reform Act of 1994—What the Bankruptcy Code Giveth, Domestic Relations Courts (and Congress) Taketh Away, C.R. "Chip" Bowles. 8 Domestic Rel J Ohio 17 (March/April 1996).

A Case For Joint Custody After The Parent's Divorce, Note. 17 J Fam L 741 (1978-79).

Custody and the Cohabitating Parent, Note. 20 J Fam L 697 (1981-82).

Divorce Reform, Ohio Style, Alan E. Norris. 47 Ohio St B Ass'n Rep 1031 (9-16-74).

Joint Custody and the Right to Travel: Legal and Psychological Implications, Paula M. Raines. 24 J Fam L 625 (1985-86).

Keeping Kids Out of Court. (Ed. note: Arbitration of custody disputes, but courts reserve the right to review awards.) 19 Nat'l L J B8 (May 5, 1997).

Nobody Gets Married for the First Time Anymore—A Primer on the Tax Implications of Support Payments in Divorce, C. Garrison Lepow. 25 Duq L Rev 43 (Fall 1986).

Parental Support of Post-Majority Children in College: Changes and Challenges, Enid L. Veron. 17 J Fam L 645 (1978-79).

Remedies for Parental Kidnapping in Federal Court: A Comment Applying the Parental Kidnapping Prevention Act in Support of Judge Edwards, Joan M. Krauskopf. 45 Ohio St L J 429 (1984).

State Intervention in the Family: Making a Federal Case Out of It, Martin Guggenheim. 45 Ohio St L J 399 (1984).

Notes of Decisions and Opinions

---

1. In general

The phrase "failure of proof" in RC 3105.21(B) is broad enough to encompass a dismissal for lack of prosecution. State ex rel. Easterday v. Zieba (Ohio 1991) 58 Ohio St.3d 251, 569 N.E.2d 1028.

Judgment setting amount and repayment terms of former husband's child support arrearage was supported by testimony of agent of the Child Support Enforcement Agency, despite former husband's contention that, at the conclusion of trial, both parties agreed that the order was erroneous; no stipulation to that effect appeared in the record. Mallett v. Mallett (Ohio App. 7 Dist. 1996) 116 Ohio App.3d 139, 687 N.E.2d 17.

Divorce decree provided no basis for conclusion that parties had contemplated that their child would continue to attend particular private religious school such that ex-husband's support obligation was limited to portion of tuition for attending that school; rather than restricting expense or religious affiliation of school child would attend, decree merely stated that ex-husband was to pay one half of child's educational costs, "including private elementary school." Wesselman v. Wesselman (Butler 1993) 88 Ohio App.3d 338, 623 N.E.2d 1300.

A judgment entry in a divorce action finding that a child was born during the marriage and ordering the husband to pay child support is not conclusive as to the paternity of the child where the husband had denied such paternity in the divorce action and the decree did not explicitly find that a parent and child relationship existed; res judicata is inapplicable in a subsequent paternity action filed by the putative father absent a specific finding that a parent and child relationship existed; therefore, a juvenile court errs in dismissing the subsequent paternity action. LaBonte v. LaBonte (Meigs 1988) 61 Ohio App.3d 209, 572 N.E.2d 704, motion overruled 42 Ohio St.3d 709, 538 N.E.2d 122.

A court has no jurisdiction to issue an order of custody and support under RC 3105.21(B) after a complaint for divorce has been voluntarily dismissed with no proof having been offered. Lilly v. Lilly (Montgomery 1985) 26 Ohio App.3d 192, 499 N.E.2d 21, 26 O.B.R. 412.

Divorce Reform Act R.C. §§3105.21, 3109.04 mandates best interest of child test as sole test for selecting custodial parent. Charles v. Charles (Franklin 1985) 23 Ohio App.3d 109, 491 N.E.2d 378, 23 O.B.R. 175.

Pursuant to a divorce decree by which a husband is ordered to maintain his wife as the beneficiary of $10,000 of life insurance and the former husband, before his death, names a new beneficiary, the former wife is entitled to have a constructive trust imposed on the $10,000 in life insurance proceeds for which she has an equitable interest and she is not required to first exhaust any potential remedy against the estate. Bailey v Prudential Insurance Co of America, No. 97APE04-593, 1997 WL 661928 (10th Dist Ct App, Franklin, 10-23-97).

Where trial court awards physical possession of the marital premises to one spouse for the purpose of providing a home for minor children, upon such spouse's remarriage the new husband may not be required to pay rent to the non-resident spouse where the non-resident spouse's rights or interests in the marital premises are not jeopardized. Wise v Paul, No. CA-1569 (5th Dist Ct App, Tuscarawas, 4-9-82).

The test as to relief from the duty of support is the "inability" of a parent to provide support; hence, a voluntary termination of employment arising from a personal affair does not constitute an inability. Bellamy v Bellamy, No. 583 (5th Dist Ct App, Morrow, 11-10-81).

2. Support and maintenance

A decree of divorce, which provides for the custody and support of minor children of the divorced parties, continues the jurisdiction of the court with respect to the support of such children during their minority, notwithstanding the absence of any express reservation in the decree with respect thereto and notwithstanding the amount specified for support of such children in such decree had been adjudged pursuant to a separation agreement approved by the court in that decree, and in such an instance, the court may increase or decrease the provisions for support of such minor children as changed circumstances may require. (Annotation from former RC 3105.21.) Peters v. Peters (Ohio 1968) 14 Ohio St.2d 268, 237 N.E.2d 902, 43 O.O.2d 441.

The provision of RC 3105.08 that the trial court in a divorce proceeding "shall cause an investigation to be made as to the character, family relations, past conduct, earning ability, and financial worth of the parties to the action" where "there are children under 14 years of age involved," is not a jurisdictional prerequisite to the making of an order for the "maintenance of the children of the marriage" under RC 3105.21, and such order is not void when made without such prior investigation. (Annotation from former RC 3105.21.) Rolls v. Rolls (Ohio 1967) 9 Ohio St.2d 59, 223 N.E.2d 604, 38 O.O.2d 159.

In a divorce action, it is not abuse of discretion as a matter of law for the trial court, having jurisdiction of the parties, to order payments by the father for the college education of minor children electing to matriculate in an accredited college. (Annotation from former RC 3105.21.) Mitchell v. Mitchell (Ohio 1960) 170 Ohio St. 507, 166 N.E.2d 396, 11 O.O.2d 281.

In a divorce, alimony, custody, support and maintenance proceeding, the court is without power to make a decree with reference to the maintenance of minor children beyond the date when such children shall arrive at their majority, and a decree which attempts to direct the course of succession to the title of real estate after the death of the parents is in that respect ultra vires and void and may be attacked in a collateral proceeding. (Annotation from former RC 3105.21.) Thiessen v. Moore (Ohio

1922) 105 Ohio St. 401, 137 N.E. 906, 1 Ohio Law Abs. 245, 20 Ohio Law Rep. 166, 20 Ohio Law Rep. 176.

Individual signators to a separation agreement may not modify the rights of third-party beneficiaries without their consent and those beneficiaries may enforce the beneficial provisions of the agreement; thus, a former wife cannot waive the right to college expenses for her younger child under a separation agreement which merged into a divorce decree by not enforcing the college expense provision on behalf of an older child since both children are third-party beneficiaries of the agreement whose rights cannot be waived by anyone other then themselves and the failure of the older child to pursue his rights does not preclude the younger child from doing so. Wolfinger v. Ocke (Shelby 1991) 72 Ohio App.3d 193, 594 N.E.2d 139.

Where a divorce decree is silent as to parochial schooling of children and public schools are available at little or no cost, a father's tuition payments do not constitute funds necessary for actual support of the children. Mihna v. Mihna (Cuyahoga 1989) 48 Ohio App.3d 303, 549 N.E.2d 558.

Where a divorce decree requires that a father name the child of the parties as "primary, irrevocable beneficiary" of several life insurance policies in effect at the time of the divorce, the fact that the father changes jobs and thereafter changes life insurance policies maintained through his employer does not defeat the child's irrevocable rights, and where the father named his parents as beneficiaries in the life insurance policy maintained through his new employer, an action for the proceeds of such policy on behalf of the child will prevail. Studley v. Studley (Cuyahoga 1986) 32 Ohio App.3d 1, 513 N.E.2d 811.

A court in Ohio has no authority to compel a divorced husband to continue paying support for his disabled child who has reached the age of majority. Maphet v. Heiselman (Clermont 1984) 13 Ohio App.3d 278, 469 N.E.2d 92, 13 O.B.R. 343.

Compliance with common pleas court order fixing amount of support payments for minor child of divorced parents is a bar to prosecution for nonsupport in juvenile court. (Annotation from former RC 3105.21.) State v. Holl (Auglaize 1971) 25 Ohio App.2d 75, 266 N.E.2d 587, 54 O.O.2d 114.

A father cannot by contract escape his responsibility for adequate support of a minor child, and a mother cannot barter away the child's right to such support. (Annotation from former RC 3105.21.) Byrd v. Byrd (Montgomery 1969) 20 Ohio App.2d 183, 252 N.E.2d 644, 49 O.O.2d 248.

In a divorce proceeding, where an issue is raised as to the paternity of a minor child born during wedlock, the child is presumed to be the child of the husband; and this presumption can only be overcome by clear and convincing evidence that there was no sexual connection between the husband and wife during the time in which the child must have been conceived. (Annotation from former RC 3105.21.) Rose v. Rose (Marion 1968) 16 Ohio App.2d 123, 242 N.E.2d 677, 45 O.O.2d 372.

A court may not order accrued child-support payments from a divorced father remitted because the mother refused to permit him to visit the child. (Annotation from former RC 3105.21.) Lenzer v. Lenzer (Hamilton 1962) 115 Ohio App. 442, 183 N.E.2d 144, 21 O.O.2d 67.

A court, after dismissing a petition for divorce, has no jurisdiction to make an order relating to the future support of a minor child of the parties, but may make an order providing for payment of any delinquent installments of support which accrued prior to the dismissal of such petition. (Annotation from former RC 3105.21.) Szaras v. Szaras (Cuyahoga 1959) 110 Ohio App. 103, 161 N.E.2d 903, 83 Ohio Law Abs. 481, 12 O.O.2d 266.

In a husband's action for divorce, in which the wife's cross-petition raises the issue of the paternity of her child, a finding by the trial court that the evidence is insufficient to prove that the husband is not the father of the child is a determination that the child was conceived by the parties as husband and wife, and it is the duty of such court to make an order for the disposition, care and maintenance of the child. (Annotation from former RC 3105.21.) Whitecotton v. Whitecotton (Lucas 1955) 103 Ohio App. 149, 144 N.E.2d 678, 3 O.O.2d 210.

Where the court refuses to grant a divorce decree, it is without jurisdiction to make an order relating to the support and custody of minor children of the parties. (Annotation from former RC 3105.21.) Lewis v. Lewis (Fayette 1956) 103 Ohio App. 129, 144 N.E.2d 887, 3 O.O.2d 199.

A husband may be relieved of the duty imposed by this section to support his minor children by a decree of court pronounced in a divorce proceeding providing for the care and maintenance of the minor children. (Annotation from former RC 3105.21.) Rowland v. State (Ohio App. 3 Dist. 1921) 14 Ohio App. 238, 32 Ohio C.A. 75.

Judgment for payment of a child's college expenses provided for in a separation agreement should not be considered child support and collection thereof should not be made through the Child Support Enforcement Agency. Chester v Baker, No. 95-CA-7, 1995 WL 497602 (5th Dist Ct App, Licking, 8-10-95).

Absent specific agreement to pay child support beyond majority in the separation agreement, the term "cost of higher education" means those special costs a student incurs beyond living expenses and cannot include room and board. Frazier v Frazier, No. 2919 (5th Dist Ct App, Licking, 2-14-83).

A trial court may not order child support payments beyond the date the child committed suicide because child support is not part of a property settlement but is solely for the benefit of the child. Herman v Herman, Nos. 343 and 384 (12th Dist Ct App, Warren, 6-24-81).

A court granting decree of divorce may change custody of a minor child of parties or increase or decrease provisions for support, maintenance, care and education of such minor child during its minority as changed circumstances require, notwithstanding the unqualified provisions of a separation agreement concerning support, maintenance, care and education for such child incorporated in decree of divorce. (Annotation from former RC 3105.21.) Rutter v. Rutter (Ohio Com.Pl. 1970) 24 Ohio Misc. 7, 261 N.E.2d 202, 53 O.O.2d 32.

Separation agreement between husband and wife under RC 3103.06 as it applies to custody, support and maintenance of minor child of parties, is executory only and may be revoked by agreement, or by resuming marital relations or by operation of law. (Annotation from former RC 3105.21.) Rutter v. Rutter (Ohio Com.Pl. 1970) 24 Ohio Misc. 7, 261 N.E.2d 202, 53 O.O.2d 32.

Separation agreement incorporated into divorce decree in which wife agrees to provide for support of child of parties after it arrives at age of eighteen years, does not relieve husband from duty of providing for such child. (Annotation from former RC 3105.21.) Rutter v. Rutter (Ohio Com.Pl. 1970) 24 Ohio Misc. 7, 261 N.E.2d 202, 53 O.O.2d 32.

Where the defendant husband in a divorce action is in arrears in his support payments and the wife seeks to reach his interest in an estate in the process of administration, she may obtain a lump-sum judgment and execute thereon or institute proceedings in aid of execution or a creditor's bill, but cannot obtain an order directing the executors of the estate to pay the money directly to her. (Annotation from former RC 3105.21.) Stemple v. Stemple (Ohio Com.Pl. 1967) 12 Ohio Misc. 147, 230 N.E.2d 677, 41 O.O.2d 203.

Where a wife was ordered to contribute to the support of her children, custody of whom was awarded to the father, and the husband moved for judgment against the mother for the arrearages, the court could, in view of the circumstances, deny such motion. (See Annotation from former RC 3105.21.) Shalosky v. Shalosky (Franklin 1952) 128 N.E.2d 464, 70 Ohio Law Abs. 394.

A former husband's contention that his former wife, her attorney, and the domestic relations judge conspired to violate his constitutional rights by using Ohio law to get his money and have him imprisoned after he voluntarily signed a payment agreement and then breached it is "so far from being based on a plausible legal theory" that the man will be ordered to pay the former wife's attorney fees on appeal in federal court. Agg v. Flanagan (C.A.6 (Ohio) 1988) 855 F.2d 336.

A former husband ordered to make support payments to his former wife cannot simply stop payment without seeking modification of the order and then, after his wages are assigned to cover the payments, challenge the constitutionality of the wage assignment in federal court by arguing he had a good reason to cease making payments; if he believed the amount was too high he should have challenged it when the order was issued. Agg v. Flanagan (C.A.6 (Ohio) 1988) 855 F.2d 336.

An obligation imposed on a husband by a divorce decree to pay debts representing outstanding balances for such everyday necessities as rent, electricity, heat, telephone, and trash collection is an obligation of support that cannot be discharged in the husband's bankruptcy proceedings, in light of the fact he earns $32,500 annually while the wife is not employed and has minor children at home. In re Alford (Bkrtcy.N.D.Ohio 1988) 95 B.R. 493.

3. Parental rights and responsibilities

A domestic relations court has jurisdiction under RC 3105.21(B) to determine custody despite dismissal of a divorce action for lack of prosecution. State ex rel. Easterday v. Zieba (Ohio 1991) 58 Ohio St.3d 251, 569 N.E.2d 1028.

RC 3105.21(B) affords a domestic relations court authority to determine custody of a child, as between his parents and another relative, even though that court has dismissed the parent's divorce action; if after dismissing the divorce action, the domestic relations court elects to certify the matter of custody to juvenile court, under RC 3105.21(B) and 3109.04 the domestic relations court must specifically find custody in neither parent to be in the child's best interest, or all jurisdiction over the matter is lost. State ex rel. Easterday v. Zieba (Ohio 1991) 58 Ohio St.3d 251, 569 N.E.2d 1028.

A probate court has jurisdiction to hear and determine an adoption proceeding relating to a minor child notwithstanding the fact that the custody of such child is at the time within the continuing jurisdiction of a divorce court. (Annotation from former RC 3105.21.) (See also In re Biddle, 81 Abs 529, 163 NE(2d) 188 (Ohio App 1958).) In re Adoption of Biddle (Ohio 1958) 168 Ohio St. 209, 152 N.E.2d 105, 6 O.O.2d 4, on remand 163 N.E.2d 188, 81 Ohio Law Abs. 529.

The prohibition of RC 3109.04(B)(1) against modification of a prior custody decree unless there has been a change in circumstances applies when the prior decree was rendered under the provisions of RC 3105.21(B) upon the failure of proof of the causes in a complaint for divorce. Dickrede v. Dickrede (Allen 1984) 14 Ohio App.3d 292, 470 N.E.2d 925, 14 O.B.R. 349.

Because the best interests of a child are of overriding importance, a trial court does not err in granting a motion for relief from judgment pursuant to Civ R 60(B)(5) which is filed, almost four years after the dissolution of marriage was granted, in order to decide custody of the child whose existence in utero was concealed from the father and the court at the time of the dissolution. In re Marriage of Watson (Lorain 1983) 13 Ohio App.3d 344, 469 N.E.2d 876, 13 O.B.R. 424.

In a custody action involving a child conceived and born while the parties were married, a stipulation and affidavit to the effect that the husband is not the father of the child are insufficient as a matter of law to overcome the presumption of legitimacy of such child. Nelson v. Nelson (Franklin 1983) 10 Ohio App.3d 36, 460 N.E.2d 653, 10 O.B.R. 44.

Mother who has been awarded custody of her children in previous court proceeding is entitled to be informed of reasons behind an order divesting her of such custody rendered by court or its appointed referee. (Annotation from former RC 3105.21.) Currens v. Currens (Hamilton 1970) 26 Ohio App.2d 215, 270 N.E.2d 362, 55 O.O.2d 360.

Evidence that a woman, while separated from but still married to her husband, openly consorted with another man, permitting him to frequent her apartment in the small hours of the morning and sleep there on occasion, will support a finding that she is, thereby, unfit to retain custody of a minor child of the parties and that custody of such child should be in the husband. (Annotation from former RC 3105.21.) Bingham v. Bingham (Hamilton 1968) 14 Ohio App.2d 202, 237 N.E.2d 620, 43 O.O.2d 403.

Except when the question of custody is incidental to the separation of parents, their right to custody cannot be taken away unless the grounds as recognized by statute, in general that the child is dependent, neglected or delinquent or that the parent is unfit, are present to support a proper exercise of the police power. (Annotation from former RC 3105.21.) Holderle v. Holderle (Franklin 1967) 11 Ohio App.2d 148, 229 N.E.2d 79, 40 O.O.2d 305.

In an action for divorce, a court may not deny the relief sought in the petition, or cross-petition, for a divorce, and retain jurisdiction under RC 3105.21, respecting the custody of a minor child. (Annotation from former RC 3105.21.) Holderle v. Holderle (Franklin 1967) 11 Ohio App.2d 148, 229 N.E.2d 79, 40 O.O.2d 305.

The overruling of a motion to set aside a default judgment, awarding a decree of divorce and custody of the minor children, and disapproving the separation agreement wherein the parties agreed that the movant was to be awarded the custody of the children, is not an abuse of discretion, where it appears that the movant was present at the divorce proceeding, but stood mute, and there is no evidence of fraud, collusion or an abuse of discretion in the granting of the decree. (Annotation from former RC 3105.21.) Dreitzler v. Dreitzler (Ross 1961) 115 Ohio App. 231, 184 N.E.2d 679, 20 O.O.2d 311.

An award of custody of a child in a divorce action is conclusive only as to the parties to such action, and the remedy of habeas corpus is available to obtain such child where a party other than the parties to the divorce action is involved; and it is not necessary to apply to the court which originally awarded custody of such child. (Annotation from former RC 3105.21.) In re Howland (Highland 1961) 115 Ohio App. 186, 184 N.E.2d 228, 20 O.O.2d 277.

Jurisdiction over custody of minor obtained by court of common pleas in divorce action is continuing and exclusive but only between parties to action and does not bar subsequent jurisdiction in the juvenile court. (Annotation from former RC 3105.21.) McFadden v. Kendall (Auglaize 1946) 81 Ohio App. 107, 77 N.E.2d 625, 36 O.O. 414.

Court may not award custody of children to other than parents on any basis other than the unfitness of both parents. (Annotation from former RC 3105.21.) Luebkeman v. Luebkeman (Montgomery 1945) 75 Ohio App. 566, 61 N.E.2d 638, 43 Ohio Law Abs. 17, 31 O.O. 319.

In a divorce proceeding in which an issue is raised as to the paternity of a minor child born during wedlock, where there is clear and convincing evidence of sexual relations between husband and wife during the time in which the child must have been conceived, the presumption of RC 3111.03 becomes essentially conclusive and cannot be rebutted by genetic tests which are, by statute, to be used only with respect to an alleged father, not a presumed father. Hulett v Hulett, No. 87AP-330 (10th Dist Ct App, Franklin, 11-17-87).

In an action for divorce, the court may not deny the principal relief sought, that is, the granting a divorce, and retain jurisdiction to determine an incidental matter respecting the custody of a minor child. (Annotation from former RC 3105.21.) Cowgill v. Cowgill (Highland 1960) 172 N.E.2d 721, 85 Ohio Law Abs. 185, 17 O.O.2d 138.

In a divorce action a court has jurisdiction to award custody of minor children even though no divorce is granted. (Annotation from former RC 3105.21.) Cowgill v. Cowgill (Ohio Com.Pl. 1960) 171 N.E.2d 769, 84 Ohio Law Abs. 406, reversed 172 N.E.2d 721, 85 Ohio Law Abs. 185, 17 O.O.2d 138.

In a divorce action brought by a wife against a nonresident husband with service by publication, the court may award custody of children within its jurisdiction, but cannot make any award for the support of the children. (Annotation from former RC 3105.21.) Noble v. Noble (Ohio Com.Pl. 1959) 160 N.E.2d 426, 80 Ohio Law Abs. 581.

A court does not have the power under the statutes respecting custody of minor children of divorced parents to place restrictions concerning the right of such divorced parent to remarry, the necessity to have a relative reside in the home of such parent to whom custody is awarded, and restrict such parent in the choice of school to which the children shall be sent. (Annotation from former RC 3105.21.) Selby v. Selby (Summit 1952) 124 N.E.2d 772, 69 Ohio Law Abs. 257.

Failure of court to provide for custody of a child in a divorce action constitutes prejudicial error. (Annotation from former RC 3105.21.) Mierowitz v. Mierowitz (Mahoning 1946) 71 N.E.2d 526, 47 Ohio Law Abs. 104.

Where divorce has been refused and petition dismissed, jurisdiction is terminated and no order can be made as to custody of children, since that is a matter incidental to the divorce proceeding; effort to obtain custody by habeas corpus unsuccessful. (Annotation from former RC 3105.21.) In re Bettis, 28 NP(NS) 304 (1930).

In a habeas corpus proceeding attacking the right of a mother to retain possession of her minor children, an Ohio court need not give full faith and credit to a Wisconsin decree awarding custody of the children to their father when that decree is obtained by the father in an ex parte divorce action in a Wisconsin court which had no personal jurisdiction over the mother. (Annotation from former RC 3105.21.) May v. Anderson (U.S.Ohio 1953) 73 S.Ct. 840, 345 U.S. 528, 97 L.Ed. 1221, 67 Ohio Law Abs. 468, 52 O.O. 45.

4. Appeal

Where the court of common pleas in a divorce action dismisses the action for insufficient evidence and without making a determination on the merits, it lacks the power and authority to certify the question of the custody of the minor child of the parties to the juvenile court, and the juvenile court is without power to accept such question. (Annotation from former RC 3105.21.) Haynie v. Haynie (Ohio 1959) 169 Ohio St. 467, 159 N.E.2d 765, 8 O.O.2d 476.

In proceeding on motion for change of custody, judgment that defers issue of child support for future determination is not "final appealable order." Kouns v. Pemberton (Lawrence 1992) 84 Ohio App.3d 499, 617 N.E.2d 701, motion overruled 66 Ohio St.3d 1489, 612 N.E.2d 1245.

A husband who voluntarily agrees pursuant to a pretrial agreement to pay one half of his children's uninsured medical and dental bills may not assign as error on appeal the trial court's order to that effect. Goode v. Goode (Franklin 1991) 70 Ohio App.3d 125, 590 N.E.2d 439.

The dismissal of the prayer of a petition for a divorce does not divest the court of jurisdiction to enter a decree for alimony and support. (Annotation from former RC 3105.21.) Hobbs v. Hobbs (Greene 1961) 115 Ohio App. 536, 186 N.E.2d 134, 21 O.O.2d 200.

A judgment for plaintiff wife in an action for alimony will not be disturbed by a reviewing court on the ground of insufficiency of corroborative testimony, where such corroborative testimony supports a limited portion of the overall testimony of plaintiff concerning the aggressions of the defendant husband during their married life and tends in the slightest degree to substantiate the direct testimony of the plaintiff. (Annotation from former RC 3105.21.) Hobbs v. Hobbs (Greene 1961) 115 Ohio App. 536, 186 N.E.2d 134, 21 O.O.2d 200.

Where husband and wife have been divorced and custody of their minor child under ten years of age awarded the mother, upon the mother's death, such custody does not devolve upon the father, nor upon probate court of the father's residence, but is still exclusively under control of the court granting the divorce. (Annotation from former RC 3105.21.) In re Hampshire (Ohio App. 5 Dist. 1922) 17 Ohio App. 139.

In circumstances in which a plaintiff father has the children of the parties with him at the time of the filing for divorce and custody, has had them for several months under the terms of an agreement between the parties, has them at all times during the process of service by publication until the defendant mother surreptitiously persuaded him to permit overnight visitation apart from his home and immediately then absconded with the children to another state, the process of service by publication is completed and when the case comes on for trial, the children's domicile was and remains the domicile of the parent, the father, who had them under these circumstances and the court has jurisdiction to determine the right of custody; but such jurisdiction is not established by the agreement of the parties. (Annotation from former RC 3105.21.) Reed v. Reed (Ohio Com.Pl. 1967) 11 Ohio Misc. 93, 229 N.E.2d 113, 40 O.O.2d 327.

A court does not have jurisdiction to order a parent in a divorce action to pay for a college education for his children. (Annotation from former RC 3105.21.) Mitchell v. Mitchell (Cuyahoga 1959) 158 N.E.2d 546, 81 Ohio Law Abs. 88, affirmed in part, reversed in part 170 Ohio St. 507, 166 N.E.2d 396, 11 O.O.2d 281.

In an appeal from an order of a trial court granting a change of custody of the children of divorced parents an appellate court will not substitute its judgment for that of the trial court. (Annotation from former RC 3105.21.) Shalosky v. Shalosky (Franklin 1952) 128 N.E.2d 464, 70 Ohio Law Abs. 394.

5. Powers and jurisdiction of court

Domestic relations court lacks jurisdiction to exercise further jurisdiction in marital dissolution proceeding if parties voluntarily dismissed their claims, and writ of prohibition will issue to prevent exercise of jurisdiction. State ex rel. Fogle v. Steiner (Ohio 1995) 74 Ohio St.3d 158, 656 N.E.2d 1288.

Parties' voluntary dismissal of marital dissolution proceedings was effective, even though it did not contain signature of paternal grandmother who was awarded temporary custody of children during dissolution proceedings, and therefore, mother's complaint seeking writ of prohibition preventing domestic relations court from exercising further jurisdiction over custody issues in divorce proceedings was not frivolous, and sua sponte dismissal of writs without notice was abuse of discretion, in view of evidence that paternal grandmother was not joined as party to proceedings prior to dismissal notice. State ex rel. Fogle v. Steiner (Ohio 1995) 74 Ohio St.3d 158, 656 N.E.2d 1288.

A domestic relations court has jurisdiction under RC 3105.21(B) to determine custody despite dismissal of a divorce action for lack of prosecution. State ex rel. Easterday v. Zieba (Ohio 1991) 58 Ohio St.3d 251, 569 N.E.2d 1028.

RC 3105.21(B) affords a domestic relations court authority to determine custody of a child, as between his parents and another relative, even though that court has dismissed the parent's divorce action; if after dismissing the divorce action, the domestic relations court elects to certify the matter of custody to juvenile court, under RC 3105.21(B) and 3109.04 the domestic relations court must specifically find custody in neither parent to be in the child's best interest, or all jurisdiction over the matter is lost. State ex rel. Easterday v. Zieba (Ohio 1991) 58 Ohio St.3d 251, 569 N.E.2d 1028.

Divorce court should have credited the husband, as child-support obligor, with a $2,200 child-support payment made on his behalf by a court-appointed receiver. Szerlip v. Szerlip (Ohio App. 5 Dist. 1998) 129 Ohio App.3d 506, 718 N.E.2d 473.

Guardianship established for purpose of facilitating child support payments was valid pursuant to implicit authority granted to domestic relations court under statutes granting court equitable powers in domestic relations matters and authority to adjudicate matters in accordance with best interests of child. In re Guardianship of Derakhshan (Lake 1996) 110 Ohio App.3d 190, 673 N.E.2d 954.

Domestic relations court retained subject matter jurisdiction over portion of guardianship estate classified as prepaid child support, and judgment reducing child support arrearages to lump sum was within that court's statutory authority; judgment was issued within scope of court's continuing subject matter jurisdiction regarding child support, supplemental order establishing guardianship estate contained unambiguous language regarding continuing jurisdiction retained by court over funds denominated as prepaid child support and child support order was established before guardianship was established and while court had control over parties. In re Guardianship of Derakhshan (Lake 1996) 110 Ohio App.3d 190, 673 N.E.2d 954.

Trial court acted within its discretion in divorce proceedings when it retained jurisdiction to make future support orders for adult child of marriage who suffered from dyslexia, although child worked and lived outside family home, where dyslexia severely limited child's reading ability and was first diagnosed when child was a minor. Shaffer v. Shaffer (Crawford 1996) 109 Ohio App.3d 205, 671 N.E.2d 1317.

Trial court may not place limitations on parent's obligation to pay for educational expenses where divorce decree does not contain such limitations. Wesselman v. Wesselman (Butler 1993) 88 Ohio App.3d 338, 623 N.E.2d 1300.

In view of fact that divorce decree unambiguously called for ex-husband to pay one half of parties' child's educational costs, trial court could not subsequently limit ex-husband's obligation based upon his allegedly limited financial means. Wesselman v. Wesselman (Butler 1993) 88 Ohio App.3d 338, 623 N.E.2d 1300.

An order of an Ohio domestic relations court granting a divorce and custody of two children to their father after the mother moves to England and fails to appear at the hearing is at the most voidable for jurisdictional error over the custody issue and a writ of habeas corpus is not applicable. Harvey v. Bentley (Montgomery 1991) 74 Ohio App.3d 375, 599 N.E.2d 284.

Because the best interests of a child are of overriding importance, a trial court does not err in granting a motion for relief from judgment pursuant to Civ R 60(B)(5) which is filed, almost four years after the dissolution of marriage was granted, in order to decide custody of the child whose existence in utero was concealed from the father and the court at the time of the dissolution. In re Marriage of Watson (Lorain 1983) 13 Ohio App.3d 344, 469 N.E.2d 876, 13 O.B.R. 424.

A court in Ohio has no authority to compel a divorced husband to continue paying support for his disabled child who has reached the age of majority. Maphet v. Heiselman (Clermont 1984) 13 Ohio App.3d 278, 469 N.E.2d 92, 13 O.B.R. 343.

The common pleas court is without power to order, in a divorce decree, a father to support a child of the divorced parties after such child reaches the age of twenty-one years. (Annotation from former RC 3105.21.)

Sylvester v. Sylvester (Hamilton 1969) 21 Ohio App.2d 58, 254 N.E.2d 699, 50 O.O.2d 104.

An Ohio juvenile court, in a dependency proceeding pursuant to RC 2151.27 et seq., has no jurisdiction to interfere with a mother's legal custody of her children, in the absence of proof and a finding of unfitness of such parent, merely for the purpose of releasing such children to the officers of the court of a foreign state, and the court need not give full faith and credit to a Michigan decree where that decree was obtained by the husband in an ex parte custody determination, subsequent to a divorce decree, in which the Michigan court had no personal jurisdiction over the nonresident wife. (Annotation from former RC 3105.21.) In re Messner (Huron 1969) 19 Ohio App.2d 33, 249 N.E.2d 532, 48 O.O.2d 31.

RC 3105.20 does not deny the court of common pleas in any matter concerning domestic relations the exercise of "its full equity powers and jurisdiction," but there must be a statutory basis upon which to exercise those powers before they may be put into execution. (Annotation from former RC 3105.21.) Haynie v. Haynie (Summit 1958) 108 Ohio App. 342, 161 N.E.2d 549, 9 O.O.2d 301, affirmed 169 Ohio St. 467, 159 N.E.2d 765, 8 O.O.2d 476.

Jurisdiction of common pleas court in divorce action is continuing jurisdiction. (Annotation from former RC 3105.21.) Dodge v. Keller (Cuyahoga 1927) 29 Ohio App. 114, 162 N.E. 750, 6 Ohio Law Abs. 6.

Common law rules that the father is the head of the family and that death terminates his obligation of child support are based on outdated social and sexual stereotypes; the modern trend is for a divorce court to mandate that the obligor designate the child as the beneficiary on the parent's life insurance policy to ensure that the child receive support during minority in the event the obligor parent dies before the child reaches majority. Webb v Webb, No. 16371, 1997 WL 797719 (2d Dist Ct App, Montgomery, 12-31-97).

Trial court lacks jurisdiction to make any order respecting an original or modified decree of child support unless it is in connection with a divorce or alimony action pending in that court since child support must remain incidental to the alimony or divorce action. Anderson v Anderson, No. 5-81-16 (3d Dist Ct App, Hancock, 1-19-82).

A court may make minor children of a pending divorce parties to the action and appoint a guardian ad litem to represent them where the interests of the minor children are or may may be substantially different from either or both of the parents. (Annotation from former RC 3105.21.) Barth v. Barth (Ohio Com.Pl. 1967) 12 Ohio Misc. 141, 225 N.E.2d 866, 39 O.O.2d 83, 41 O.O.2d 166.

RC 3105.21 gives the court no authority over the children of one party, but not of the marriage. (Annotation from former RC 3105.21.) Hartshorne v. Hartshorne (Columbiana 1959) 185 N.E.2d 329, 89 Ohio Law Abs. 243.

A court has no jurisdiction to make any order respecting visitation with children unless the plaintiff seeks a divorce or alimony in such petition. (Annotation from former RC 3105.21.) Cable v. Cable (Ohio Com.Pl. 1955) 127 N.E.2d 433, 70 Ohio Law Abs. 187, 57 O.O. 495.

This section, giving common pleas courts jurisdiction over children in divorce suits, was not superseded by the juvenile court statutes. The common pleas jurisdiction continued and precludes the juvenile court. (Annotation from former RC 3105.21.) Cleveland Protestant Orphan Asylum v. Soule (Sandusky 1915) 26 Ohio C.D. 135, 24 Ohio C.C.(N.S.) 151, 5 Ohio App. 67.

Although matters concerning divorce and alimony have been excepted from federal court jurisdiction based on diversity of the parties' state citizenship since Barber v Barber, 62 US 582, 16 LEd(2d) 226(1859), this rule does not bar a husband's claim in federal court that the former wife intentionally inflicted emotional distress on him by taking their child to another state and denying him visitation rights, or that she interfered with his employment by writing letters to his employer; the court may also hear his counterclaim for enforcement of a state judgment concerning arrearages in alimony and child support. Drewes v. Ilnicki (C.A.6 (Ohio) 1988) 863 F.2d 469.

6. Modification

Trial court properly applied child support statute in determining whether to modify child support, even though motion was filed and reinstated prior to statute's effective date, where hearings on motion and filing of trial court's decision and judgment entry took place after its effective date. Parzynski v. Parzynski (Erie 1992) 85 Ohio App.3d 423, 620 N.E.2d 93, dismissed, jurisdictional motion overruled 67 Ohio St.3d 1450, 619 N.E.2d 419, rehearing denied 67 Ohio St.3d 1513, 622 N.E.2d 660.

Trial court did not abuse its discretion in ordering that increase in former husband's child support obligation apply retroactively to date that former wife's modification motion was first filed, even though motion had been dismissed due to failure of former wife to comply with local rules, motion was not reinstated until later date, and former husband did not obtain proper service of motion until later date. Parzynski v. Parzynski (Erie 1992) 85 Ohio App.3d 423, 620 N.E.2d 93, dismissed, jurisdictional motion overruled 67 Ohio St.3d 1450, 619 N.E.2d 419, rehearing denied 67 Ohio St.3d 1513, 622 N.E.2d 660.

To modify a child support agreement, the court must go through a two-step analysis: (1) determining if there has been a change in circumstances, and (2) if so, reanalyzing the amount of support necessary. Dudziak v. Dudziak (Cuyahoga 1992) 81 Ohio App.3d 361, 611 N.E.2d 337.

A former husband's obligation under a divorce decree to make payments to each of his children while they attended college is not terminated by language in a child custody and support modification order which provides for support payments to end when each child reaches age eighteen or ceases to continually attend a recognized high school on a full-time basis, whichever occurs last. Wolfinger v. Ocke (Shelby 1991) 72 Ohio App.3d 193, 594 N.E.2d 139.

Court-ordered child support is for the benefit of the children and future obligations cannot be waived by the parents; however, the custodial parent is empowered in certain circumstances to forgive past arrearages. Nelson v. Nelson (Lake 1990) 65 Ohio App.3d 800, 585 N.E.2d 502.

A local rule of court concerning modification of foreign decrees may not be used as a vehicle for modifying an out-of-state divorce decree in response to the husband's claim of accord and satisfaction regarding the decree's support order where the other state's court has not relinquished jurisdiction, as shown by the court's letter stating that its state's statutes prevented the court from relinquishing jurisdiction. Kass v. Cleveland Metro.

Gen. Hosp. (Cuyahoga 1989) 65 Ohio App.3d 264, 583 N.E.2d 1012.

A modification of an existing support order is justified where the moving party demonstrates a substantial change of circumstances which renders unreasonable an order which was once reasonable; evidence constituting a substantial change of circumstances justifing modification of an original support order includes the wife's fraudulent misrepresentation that the child she was carrying at the time of marriage was that of her husband and the results of blood test excluding the moving party as the father. Carson v. Carson (Brown 1989) 62 Ohio App.3d 670, 577 N.E.2d 391, motion overruled 46 Ohio St.3d 716, 546 N.E.2d 1334.

The prohibition of RC 3109.04(B)(1) against modification of a prior custody decree unless there has been a change in circumstances applies when the prior decree was rendered under the provisions of RC 3105.21(B) upon the failure of proof of the causes in a complaint for divorce. Dickrede v. Dickrede (Allen 1984) 14 Ohio App.3d 292, 470 N.E.2d 925, 14 O.B.R. 349.

Social security benefits which a handicapped child receives under the supplemental security income program provided in 42 USC 1381 et seq., neither alter the father's obligation for his support nor constitute a change of circumstances warranting a modification of the support order for such child entered in a divorce action. Oatley v. Oatley (Lucas 1977) 57 Ohio App.2d 226, 387 N.E.2d 245, 11 O.O.3d 260.

Social security benefits, payable to a mother for the support of her minor children due to the disability of the father, may not be credited toward arrearages of child support payments accrued by the father's violation of his then existing obligation of support. Fuller v. Fuller (Summit 1976) 49 Ohio App.2d 223, 360 N.E.2d 357, 3 O.O.3d 273.

Where a father's yearly salary has measurably lessened due to a change in job, it is error for the court to base a child-support award on the higher salary rather than what the salary was at the time of the hearing. Brady v Brady, No. CA 1974 (5th Dist Ct App, Richland, 4-15-81).

7. Visitation

Testimony from the guardian ad litem, the court-appointed psychologist, and the noncustodial parent supported a divorce court's decision to adopt the standard visitation schedule set forth in its local rules in place of one privately agreed to by the parties that provided the husband with a more liberal visitation schedule, despite the husband's claim that he consented to the wife's custody over their children only after she agreed to the private schedule. Szerlip v. Szerlip (Ohio App. 5 Dist. 1998) 129 Ohio App.3d 506, 718 N.E.2d 473.

A parent who is not the residential parent has a right to have continuing contact with the children, and in a final judgment entry decree of divorce, a trial court errs in failing to make an order for visitation between a father and his minor son, by instead ordering visitation according to a schedule recommended by the child's counsellor. Mayo v Mayo, No. 1351, 1995 WL 139747 (2d Dist Ct App, Darke, 3-29-95).

Where the original divorce decree did not prohibit an out-of-state move by the custodial parent, both parents should bear equally the cost and time of transportation for visitation purposes; the custodial parent should not be penalized for having made the move by being made to bear a disproportionate share of the transportation burden. Pitcher v Pitcher, No. 83AP-530 (10th Dist Ct App, Franklin, 2-28-84).

A father whose visitation rights are denied because of his former wife's false accusations of child abuse has no liberty interest in continued companionship and association with his child under the federal constitution that is cognizable in a civil rights suit under 42 USC 1983 or 1985. Norton v. Cobb (N.D.Ohio 1990) 744 F.Supp. 798.

ANNULMENT

3105.31 Grounds for annulment

A marriage may be annulled for any of the following causes existing at the time of the marriage:

(A) That the party in whose behalf it is sought to have the marriage annulled was under the age at which persons may be joined in marriage as established by section 3101.01 of the Revised Code, unless after attaining such age such party cohabited with the other as husband or wife;

(B) That the former husband or wife of either party was living and the marriage with such former husband or wife was then and still is in force;

(C) That either party has been adjudicated to be mentally incompetent, unless such party after being restored to competency cohabited with the other as husband or wife;

(D) That the consent of either party was obtained by fraud, unless such party afterwards, with full knowledge of the facts constituting the fraud, cohabited with the other as husband or wife;

(E) That the consent to the marriage of either party was obtained by force, unless such party afterwards cohabited with the other as husband or wife;

(F) That the marriage between the parties was never consummated although otherwise valid.

(130 v H 467, eff. 9-24-63)

Comparative Laws

Ark.—A.C.A. § 9-12-201.
Conn.—C.G.S.A. § 46b-40.
Ga.—O.C.G.A. § 19-4-1 et seq.
Idaho—I.C. § 32-501 et seq.
Ill.—ILCS 750 5/301 et seq.
Ky.—Baldwin's KRS 403.120.
Mass.—M.G.L.A. c. 207, § 15.
Mich.—M.C.L.A. § 552.1.
Neb.—R.R.S.1943, § 42-119.
N.M.—NMSA 1978, § 40-1-9.
Wis.—W.S.A. 767.03.

Cross References

Bigamy, 2919.01
Consent to marry, Juv R 42
Divorce, annulment, and legal separation actions, Civ R 75
Health and hospital insurance after annulment, 1738.23
Reciprocal enforcment of support, support pendente lite, 3115.27
Registration of marriages, divorces, annulments, and dissolutions of marriage, 3705.21
Stay of annulment action pending completion of conciliation proceedings, 3117.07, 3117.08
Trust agreement, effect of annulment, 1339.62
Wills, effect of annulment, 2107.33

Library References

Marriage ⚿58(1) to 58(8).
WESTLAW Topic No. 253.
C.J.S. Marriage §§ 15, 16, 18, 36 to 42, 65.

Am Jur 2d: 4, Annulment of Marriage § 1 et seq.
Avoidance of procreation of children as ground for divorce or annulment of marriage. 4 ALR2d 227
Validity of marriage as affected by intention of the parties that it should only be a matter of form or jest. 14 ALR2d 624
What constitutes duress sufficient to warrant annulment of marriage. 16 ALR2d 1430
Racial, religious, or political differences as ground for divorce, separation, or annulment. 25 ALR2d 928
Refusal of sexual intercourse as ground for annulment. 28 ALR2d 499
What constitutes intoxication sufficient to warrant annulment of marriage. 57 ALR2d 1250
Concealed premarital unchastity or parenthood as ground of divorce or annulment. 64 ALR2d 742
Mental incompetency of defendant at time of action as precluding annulment of marriage. 97 ALR2d 483
Concealment of or misrepresentation as to prior marital status as ground for annulment of marriage. 15 ALR3d 759
Concealment or misrepresentation relating to religion as ground for annulment. 44 ALR3d 972
What constitutes mistake in the identity of one of the parties to warrant annulment of marriage. 50 ALR3d 1295
Incapacity for sexual intercourse as ground for annulment. 52 ALR3d 589
Spouse's secret intention not to abide by written antenuptial agreement relating to financial matters as ground for annulment. 66 ALR3d 1282
Divorce or annulment as affecting will previously executed by husband or wife. 71 ALR3d 1297
Effect, in subsequent proceedings, of paternity findings or implications in divorce or annulment decree or in support or custody order made incident thereto. 78 ALR3d 846
Right to allowance of permanent alimony in connection with decree of annulment. 81 ALR3d 281
Recognition by forum state of marriage which, although invalid where contracted, would have been valid if contracted within forum state. 82 ALR3d 1240
Estate created by deed to persons described as husband and wife but not legally married. 9 ALR4th 1189
Validity of marriage as affected by lack of legal authority of person solemnizing it. 13 ALR4th 1323
Homosexuality, transvestism, and similar sexual practices as grounds for annulment of marriage. 68 ALR4th 1069

Carlin, Baldwin's Ohio Practice, *Merrick-Rippner Probate Law* § 100.4 (1997)
Sowald & Morganstern, Baldwin's Ohio Practice, *Domestic Relations Law* § 2.14, 2.24, 2.25, 2.26, 2.29, 2.59, 2.60, 2.62, 2.63, 7.2, 7.4, 7.5, 7.6, 7.7, 7.8, 7.9, 7.10, 7.11, 7.23, 7.26, 7.35, 11.9, 11.13, 27.4 (1997)

Law Review and Journal Commentaries

Refusal to Have Children as a Ground for Divorce or Annulment, Marvin M. Moore. 14 Clev-Marshall L Rev 588 (September 1965).

Notes of Decisions and Opinions

---

1. Consummation

RC 3105.31(F) does not require that a condition exist prior to marriage which would prevent consummation of the marriage and which continues throughout the marriage to the point of annulment; the fact that the marriage was not consummated is sufficient to support a decree of annulment. Lang v. Reetz-Lang (Franklin 1985) 22 Ohio App.3d 77, 488 N.E.2d 929, 22 O.B.R. 176.

2. Effect of annulment

Property rights of litigants in annulment proceeding are only those that attach to persons in individual capacity, and are not same rights usually affiliated with husband and wife in divorce proceeding. Liming v. Liming (Ohio App. 4 Dist. 1996) 117 Ohio App.3d 617, 691 N.E.2d 299.

Property division in annulment is not based on legal status such as marriage, but is more like adjustment of property interests between parties, similar in nature to dissolution of business partnership. Liming v. Liming (Ohio App. 4 Dist. 1996) 117 Ohio App.3d 617, 691 N.E.2d 299.

Judgment annulling marriage should place parties in same position that they would have been in had annulled marriage not taken place, returning property interests to each party to whatever extent is possible. Liming v. Liming (Ohio App. 4 Dist. 1996) 117 Ohio App.3d 617, 691 N.E.2d 299.

Where a plaintiff transferred by antenuptial agreement his real estate to husband and wife as tenants by the entireties in consideration of marriage, and where the marriage was later annulled under RC 3105.31(F) because of the wife's knowing avoidance if not outright refusal of consummation, the agreement is unenforceable for want of consideration and the plaintiff is properly restored to full ownership of the real property. Lang v. Reetz-Lang (Franklin 1985) 22 Ohio App.3d 77, 488 N.E.2d 929, 22 O.B.R. 176.

Where the right to receive alimony from a former spouse has terminated because the alimony recipient has remarried, such right to alimony is not revived by an annulment of the second marriage where the second marriage was merely voidable and not void, ab initio. Darling v. Darling (Cuyahoga 1975) 44 Ohio App.2d 5, 335 N.E.2d 708, 73 O.O.2d 5.

3. Fraud

A marriage is fraudulently induced and may be annulled where a pregnant woman intentionally misrepresents the paternity of her child and the man induced to marry her reasonably relies on the woman's representations; such action is not barred on the grounds that the parties engaged in pre-marital sexual relations. Slavin v Slavin, No. 49087 (8th Dist Ct App, Cuyahoga, 6-27-85).

A plaintiff husband may not obtain an annulment from a defendant wife upon the ground that she fraudulently or wrongfully represented that she was pregnant in order to induce the marriage if plaintiff had engaged in sexual intercourse with defendant prior to such marriage. Tyminski v. Tyminski (Ohio Com.Pl. 1966) 8 Ohio Misc. 202, 221 N.E.2d 486, 37 O.O.2d 263.

Where a woman is pregnant at the time of a marriage with another man, and conceals her condition, and the fraud is not discovered until after the marriage, the marriage may be voided, if separation takes place immediately after the discovery; but where a man knows of the prenuptial pregnancy of his wife, it is no ground for divorce or annulment; and where a man marries without knowledge of his wife's pregnancy, annulment will be denied if prior to the marriage he had sexual relations with her. Anderson v. Anderson (Ohio Com.Pl. 1966) 8 Ohio Misc. 97, 219 N.E.2d 317, 37 O.O.2d 108.

4. Procedure

The trial court erred in deciding on a motion for summary judgment before the date set for the inspection and copying of documents pursuant to the plaintiff's request for inspection of certain documents held in the custody of the defendant's attorney. Levine v Levine, No. 82AP-200 (10th Dist Ct App, Franklin, 7-13-82).

A plaintiff may unite a cause of action for annulment and a cause of action for divorce in the same petition. Tyminski v. Tyminski (Ohio Com.Pl. 1966) 8 Ohio Misc. 202, 221 N.E.2d 486, 37 O.O.2d 263.

5. Age

Where a marriage contract between parties is not consummated by cohabitation and has not been ratified by the parties after they reach the age of majority, or in fact at any time, an annulment is proper. Abelt v. Zeman (Ohio Com.Pl. 1962) 179 N.E.2d 176, 87 Ohio Law Abs. 600, 18 O.O.2d 379.

6. Cohabitation

While in a suit to annul a marriage, a court may take into consideration whether there has been cohabitation or not, the fact that there has been none subsequent to the marriage is not of controlling importance, particularly where there has been prior sexual intercourse, or if the defendant is ready and willing to live with the plaintiff and he refuses. Anderson v. Anderson (Ohio Com.Pl. 1966) 8 Ohio Misc. 97, 219 N.E.2d 317, 37 O.O.2d 108.

7. Earlier marriage still in force

Alleged common-law wife had standing to bring action to annul her husband's subsequent marriage to another woman. Thomas-Schafer v. Schafer (Hamilton 1996) 111 Ohio App.3d 779, 677 N.E.2d 374.

8. Attorney fees

Attorney fees may be awarded in cases involving fraud, if award of punitive or exemplary damages would be appropriate; this requires case of gross or malicious fraud or something showing very corrupt state of affairs. Liming v. Liming (Ohio App. 4 Dist. 1996) 117 Ohio App.3d 617, 691 N.E.2d 299.

Magistrate's finding in action for annulment of marriage that husband had made "a fraudulent representation" to wife that he was a widower was insufficient, without more, to permit wife to recover her attorney fees. Liming v. Liming (Ohio App. 4 Dist. 1996) 117 Ohio App.3d 617, 691 N.E.2d 299.

Considering relative assets of parties in proceeding for annulment of marriage, trial court did not abuse its discretion in not awarding wife her attorney fees, despite husband's arguably fraudulent claim prior to marriage that he was widower. Liming v. Liming (Ohio App. 4 Dist. 1996) 117 Ohio App.3d 617, 691 N.E.2d 299.

3105.32 Time limitations for bringing annulment actions

An action to obtain a decree of nullity of a marriage must be commenced within the periods and by the parties as follows:

(A) For the cause mentioned in division (A) of section 3105.31 of the Revised Code, by the party to the marriage who was married under the age at which persons may be joined in marriage as established by section 3101.01 of the Revised Code, within two years after arriving at such age; or by a parent, guardian, or other person having charge of such party at any time before such party has arrived at such age;

(B) For the cause mentioned in division (B) of section 3105.31 of the Revised Code, by either party during the life of the other or by such former husband or wife;

(C) For the cause mentioned in division (C) of section 3105.31 of the Revised Code, by the party aggrieved or a relative or guardian of the party adjudicated mentally incompetent at any time before the death of either party;

(D) For the cause mentioned in division (D) of section 3105.31 of the Revised Code, by the party aggrieved within two years after the discovery of the facts constituting fraud;

(E) For the cause mentioned in division (E) of section 3105.31 of the Revised Code, by the party aggrieved within two years from the date of the said marriage;

(F) For the cause mentioned in division (F) of section 3105.31 of the Revised Code, by the party aggrieved within two years from the date of the marriage.

(130 v H 467, eff. 9-24-63)

Cross References

Time of hearing in annulment action, Civ R 75

Library References

Marriage ⟹60(2).
WESTLAW Topic No. 253.
C.J.S. Marriage § 68.

OJur 3d: 62, Investment Securities and Securities Regulation § 53
Am Jur 2d: 4, Annulment of Marriage § 67 et seq.
Limitation of actions for annulment of marriage. 52 ALR2d 1163

Time of pendency of former suit for divorce, annulment, alimony, or maintenance as included in period of desertion. 80 ALR2d 855

Sowald & Morganstern, Baldwin's Ohio Practice, *Domestic Relations Law* § 2.24, 7.2, 7.4, 7.5, 7.6, 7.7, 7.8, 7.9, 7.10, 7.11, 7.29, 7.32, 7.35, 7.36 (1997)

Notes of Decisions and Opinions

Mental competency 1

1. Mental competency

RC 3105.32 provides that only a party aggrieved may sue to have a marriage annulled on the grounds of mental incapacity, and although a relative of a mental incompetent may sue for an annulment while the putative incompetent is alive, such right terminates with the death of the incompetent spouse. Hall v. Nelson (Summit 1987) 41 Ohio App.3d 138, 534 N.E.2d 929.

3105.33 Legitimacy of children when marriage annulled; custody and support—Repealed

(1982 H 245, eff. 6-29-82; 130 v H 467)

Historical and Statutory Notes

Ed. Note: See now 3111.03 for provisions analogous to former 3105.33.

3105.34 Restoration of name

If the court determines that a marriage is void or that a judgment of nullity ought to be granted, the court may in its discretion, and regardless of whether or not a request therefor was included in the prayer of the complaint as a part of such judgment, restore any name that the person had before the marriage.

(1978 H 349, eff. 10-25-78; 130 v H 467)

Cross References

Name change of registered voter, notice to board of elections, 3503.11, 3503.19

Proceedings to change name of person, 2717.01

Library References

Marriage ⟹65, 67.

WESTLAW Topic No. 253.

C.J.S. Marriage §§ 81, 83.

OJur 3d: 70, Names § 14
Am Jur 2d: 4, Annulment of Marriage § 93; 24, Divorce and Separation § 419

Sowald & Morganstern, Baldwin's Ohio Practice, *Domestic Relations Law* § 7.2, 7.4, 7.5, 7.21, 7.35 (1997)

DISSOLUTION OF MARRIAGE

3105.61 Dissolution of marriage

The court of common pleas may grant a dissolution of marriage.

(1974 H 233, eff. 9-23-74)

Cross References

Decree of presumption of death, dissolution of marriage, 2121.04
Fee for issuance of certificate, 2303.20
Health and hospital insurance coverage after dissolution, 1738.23
Registration of dissolutions of marriage with office of vital statistics, department of health, fee, 3705.21
Trust agreement, effect of dissolution of marriage, 1339.62
Wills, effect of dissolution of marriage, 2107.33

Library References

Divorce ⟹6.
WESTLAW Topic No. 134.
C.J.S. Divorce §§ 5, 10, 15, 97, 98.

OJur 3d: 46, Family Law § 549, 708
Am Jur 2d: 24, Divorce and Separation § 29 to 31, 171.5, 238 to 243, 274, 280, 340, 347, 354
Length or duration of domicil, as distinguished from fact of domicil, as a jurisdictional matter in divorce action. 2 ALR2d 291
Effect on jurisdiction of court to grant divorce, of plaintiff's change of residence pendente lite. 7 ALR2d 1414
Nature and location of one's business or calling as element in determining domicil in divorce cases. 36 ALR2d 756
Right of nonresident wife to maintain action for separate maintenance or alimony alone against resident husband. 36 ALR2d 1369
What constitutes residence or domicil within state by citizen of another country for purpose of jurisdiction in divorce. 51 ALR3d 223
Validity, construction and effect of "no-fault" divorce statutes providing for dissolution of marriage upon finding that relationship is no longer viable. 55 ALR3d 581
Validity of statute imposing durational residency requirements for divorce applicants. 57 ALR3d 221
Validity and construction of statutory provision relating to jurisdiction of court for purpose of divorce for servicemen. 73 ALR3d 431
Validity, construction and effect of "no-fault" divorce statutes providing for dissolution of marriage upon finding that relationship is no longer viable. 86 ALR3d 1116

Sowald & Morganstern, Baldwin's Ohio Practice, *Domestic Relations Law* § 10.1, 10.6, 27.3 (1997)

Law Review and Journal Commentaries

Children—The Innocent Victims of Family Breakups: How the Family Law Attorney, the Courts, and Society Can Protect Our Children, Michael J. Albano. 26 U Tol L Rev 787 (Summer 1995).

Divorce Reform, Ohio Style, Alan E. Norris. 47 Ohio St B Ass'n Rep 1031 (9-16-74).

Property Rights on Termination of Alternative Life Styles: Cohabitation, James T. Flaherty. 10 Cap U L Rev 1 (Fall 1980).

Notes of Decisions and Opinions

In general 2
Separation agreement 1

---

1. Separation agreement

A separation agreement entered into for the sole purpose of a dissolution of marriage is not a valid and binding contract when the dissolution petition is dismissed, but would be a valid and binding contract following dismissal of such petition if it contains language that the agreement shall be binding whether used in a divorce, alimony only, or a dissolution of marriage action, or such similar language evidencing the intent of the parties that it will survive dismissal of a dissolution of marriage petition, and in addition, if it does not contain express language that it was entered into solely for a dissolution of marriage action or express language that the parties intended the separation agreement to survive dismissal of a dissolution of marriage petition, but the actions and conduct of the parties evidence an intention that it will survive dismissal of a dissolution of marriage petition, the separation agreement will continue to be a valid and binding agreement after the dissolution of marriage petition is dismissed. Greiner v. Greiner (Cuyahoga 1979) 61 Ohio App.2d 88, 399 N.E.2d 571, 15 O.O.3d 95.

2. In general

Dissolution is creature of statute that is based upon parties' consent; it is mutuality component of dissolution that distinguishes it from termination of marriage by divorce. In re Whitman (Ohio 1998) 81 Ohio St.3d 239, 690 N.E.2d 535.

In order for court to be empowered to grant dissolution, parties must agree to dissolution of their marriage and to terms of their separation agreement which provide for division of property, alimony, custody, child support and visitation; if parties do not agree to both prerequisites, they do not qualify for dissolution and may seek divorce pursuant to ground listed in statute, thereby invoking adversary process. Ashley v. Ashley (Cuyahoga 1981) 1 Ohio App.3d 80, 439 N.E.2d 911, 1 O.B.R. 359.

Absent a judgment following actual litigation, a dissolution decree cannot be accorded issue-preclusive effect under Ohio law. In re Fordu (C.A.6 (Ohio) 1999) 201 F.3d 693.

Under Ohio law, claim-preclusive effect may be granted to a dissolution decree. In re Fordu (C.A.6 (Ohio) 1999) 201 F.3d 693.

3105.62 Residency requirement; venue

One of the spouses in an action for dissolution of marriage shall have been a resident of the state for at least six months immediately before filing the petition. Actions for dissolution of marriage shall be brought in the proper county for commencement of actions pursuant to the Rules of Civil Procedure. An action for dissolution of marriage may be brought pursuant to a motion for conversion of a divorce action into an action for dissolution of marriage pursuant to section 3105.08 of the Revised Code. For purposes of service of process, both parties in an action for dissolution of marriage shall be considered as defendants and subject to service of process as defendants pursuant to the Rules of Civil Procedure.

(1990 S 25, eff. 6-13-90; 1975 H 1; 1974 H 233)

Cross References

Commencement of action, venue, Civ R 3

Service of process, Civ R 4 et seq.

Library References

Divorce ⚷58 to 66.
WESTLAW Topic No. 134.
C.J.S. Divorce §§ 96 to 113.

OJur 3d: 46, Family Law § 392, 396, 557, 558, 576, 588
Am Jur 2d: 24, Divorce and Separation § 29 to 31, 238 to 243, 267 to 270, 274, 280, 340, 347, 354
Length or duration of domicil, as distinguished from fact of domicil, as a jurisdictional matter in divorce action. 2 ALR2d 291
Effect on jurisdiction of court to grant divorce, of plaintiff's change of residence pendente lite. 7 ALR2d 1414
Nature and location of one's business or calling as element in determining domicil in divorce cases. 36 ALR2d 756
Right of nonresident wife to maintain action for separate maintenance or alimony alone against resident husband. 36 ALR2d 1369
What constitutes residence or domicil within state by citizen of another country for purpose of jurisdiction in divorce. 51 ALR3d 223
Validity of statute imposing durational residency requirements for divorce applicants. 57 ALR3d 221
Validity and construction of statutory provision relating to jurisdiction of court for purpose of divorce for servicemen. 73 ALR3d 431

Sowald & Morganstern, Baldwin's Ohio Practice, *Domestic Relations Law* § 10.2, 10.6, 11.28, 25.12, 27.18, 27.21, 27.29, 27.31 (1997)

Notes of Decisions and Opinions

Military spouse 1

1. Military spouse

Under Soldiers' and Sailors' Civil Relief Act, former husband's motion to stay dissolution proceedings in Ohio while he was stationed in Persian Gulf, and unable to obtain leave to attend any proceedings, should not have been denied without explanation in the record; Act had to be enforced to provide service personnel with its safeguards. Olsen v. Olsen (Cuyahoga 1993) 87 Ohio App.3d 12, 621 N.E.2d 830.

3105.63 Petition for dissolution; separation agreement

(A)(1) A petition for dissolution of marriage shall be signed by both spouses and shall have attached and incorporated a separation agreement agreed to by both spouses. The separation agreement shall provide for a division of all property; spousal support; if there are minor children of the marriage, the allocation of parental rights and responsibilities for the care of the minor children, the designation of a residential parent and legal custodian of the minor children, child support, and visitation rights; and, if the spouses so desire, an authorization for the court to modify the amount or terms of spousal support provided in the separation agreement. If there are minor children of the marriage, the spouses may address the allocation of the parental rights and responsibilities for the care of the minor children by including in the separation agreement a plan under which both parents will have shared rights and responsibilities for the care of the minor children. The spouses shall file the plan with the petition for dissolution of marriage and shall include in the plan the provisions described in division (G) of section 3109.04 of the Revised Code.

(2) The division of property in the separation agreement shall include any participant account, as defined in section 148.01 of the Revised Code, of either of the spouses, to the extent of the following:

(a) The moneys that have been deferred by a continuing member or participating employee, as defined in that section, and that have been transmitted to the Ohio public employees deferred compensation board during the marriage and any income that is derived from the investment of those moneys during the marriage;

(b) The moneys that have been deferred by an officer or employee of a municipal corporation and that have been transmitted to the governing board, administrator, depository, or trustee of the deferred compensation program of the municipal corporation during the marriage and any income that is derived from the investment of those moneys during the marriage;

(c) The moneys that have been deferred by an officer or employee of a government unit, as defined in section 148.06 of the Revised Code, and that have been transmitted to the governing board, as defined in that section, during the marriage and any income that is derived from the investment of those moneys during the marriage.

(3) The separation agreement shall not require or permit the division or disbursement of the moneys and income described in division (A)(2) of this section to occur in a manner that is inconsistent with the law, rules, or plan governing the deferred compensation program involved or prior to the time that the spouse in whose name the participant account is maintained commences receipt of the moneys and income credited to the account in accordance with that law, rules, and plan.

(B) An amended separation agreement may be filed at any time prior to or during the hearing on the petition for dissolution of marriage. Upon receipt of a petition for dissolution of marriage, the court may cause an investigation to be made pursuant to the Rules of Civil Procedure.

(C) If a petition for dissolution of marriage contains an authorization for the court to modify the amount or terms of spousal support provided in the separation agreement, the modification shall be in accordance with section 3105.18 of the Revised Code.

(2000 H 628, eff. 9-21-00; 1992 S 300, eff. 11-5-92; 1990 S 3, H 514; 1986 H 358; 1975 H 370; 1974 H 233)

Uncodified Law

1986 H 358, § 3: See Uncodified Law under 3105.18.

Historical and Statutory Notes

Amendment Note: 2000 H 628 substituted "148.01" for "145.71" in the introductory paragraph in division (A)(2); and substituted "148.06" for "145.74" in division (A)(2)(c).

Comparative Laws

Ariz.—A.R.S. § 25-317.
Ind.—West's A.I.C. 31-15-2-17.
Neb.—R.R.S.1943, § 42-366.

Cross References

Child support guidelines, 3113.215
Conciliation of marriage, Ch 3117
Contracts affecting marriage, 3103.06
Divorce, annulment, legal separation and related proceedings, Civ R 75
Factors determining amount of child support, support orders, visitation rights, 3109.05
Presumptions as to father and child relationship, 3111.03
Property held exempt from legal process by person domiciled in state, 2329.66
Public employees deferred compensation program, exemption of benefits from legal process, 148.09
Reciprocal enforcement of support, support pendente lite, 3115.27
Right of either parent to parental rights and responsibilities toward children, 3109.03
Separation agreement to which decedent a party valid unless set aside; time limits, 2106.22
Shared parenting, request for, modification, 3109.04, 3109.041

Spousal support, modification, grounds for, 3105.18
Uniform child custody jurisdiction law, 3109.21 to 3109.37
Wills, effect of separation agreement, 2107.33

Library References

Divorce ⟹88 to 108.
Husband and Wife ⟹278.
WESTLAW Topic Nos. 134, 205.
C.J.S. Divorce §§ 143 to 161.
C.J.S. Husband and Wife §§ 221 to 225, 235, 237.

OJur 3d: 45, Exemptions § 48; 46, Family Law § 364, 391, 393, 400, 401, 603, 604, 610, 746
Am Jur 2d: 24, Divorce and Separation § 29 to 31, 238 to 243, 274, 280, 294 to 315, 340, 347, 354
Length or duration of domicil, as distinguished from fact of domicil, as a jurisdictional matter in divorce action. 2 ALR2d 291
Effect on jurisdiction of court to grant divorce, of plaintiff's change of residence pendente lite. 7 ALR2d 1414
Nature and location of one's business or calling as element in determining domicil in divorce cases. 36 ALR2d 756
Right of nonresident wife to maintain action for separate maintenance or alimony alone against resident husband. 36 ALR2d 1369
What constitutes residence or domicil within state by citizen of another country for purpose of jurisdiction in divorce. 51 ALR3d 223
Validity of statute imposing durational residency requirements for divorce applicants. 57 ALR3d 221
Validity and construction of statutory provision relating to jurisdiction of court for purpose of divorce for servicemen. 73 ALR3d 431
Husband's death as affecting periodic payment provision of separation agreement. 5 ALR4th 1153

Klein & Darling, Baldwin's Ohio Practice, *Civil Practice* § 60 (1997)
Sowald & Morganstern, Baldwin's Ohio Practice, *Domestic Relations Law* § 4.28, 9.2, 9.3, 9.6, 9.9, 9.27, 10.6, 10.14, 10.15, 10.15.1, 12.1, 14.5, 14.6, 14.10, 14.14, 15.3, 15.19, 25.12, 29.40 (1997)

Law Review and Journal Commentaries

Divorce Mediation: A Nonadversary Procedure for the No-Fault Divorce, Patricia L. Winks. 19 J Fam L 615 (1981-82).

Gross v Gross: Ohio's First Step Toward Allowing Private Ordering of the Marital Relationship, Comment. 47 Ohio St L J 235 (1986).

Notes of Decisions and Opinions

---

1. Insurance

Where a separation agreement embodied in a divorce decree mandates insurance coverage and unambiguously designates a purpose for which insurance proceeds are to be used by certain beneficiaries, a constructive trust for that designated purpose is the appropriate remedy to ensure that the proceeds are used for the purpose intended under the agreement. Aetna Life Ins. Co. v. Hussey (Ohio 1992) 63 Ohio St.3d 640, 590 N.E.2d 724, decision clarified on rehearing 64 Ohio St.3d 1207, 595 N.E.2d 942.

A constructive trust is the appropriate remedy to ensure that insurance proceeds are paid to those who were to be named beneficiaries of an insurance policy by the terms of a separation agreement embodied in a divorce decree. Kelly v. Medical Life Ins. Co. (Ohio 1987) 31 Ohio St.3d 130, 509 N.E.2d 411, 31 O.B.R. 289.

Where the parties to a separation agreement that is incorporated into a decree of dissolution specifically address the issue of life insurance and express their intent to release all rights which each may have as beneficiary under the policies of the other, such language is sufficient to eliminate each party as beneficiary of the other, although no specific change of beneficiary is actually made to the policies. Phillips v. Pelton (Ohio 1984) 10 Ohio St.3d 52, 461 N.E.2d 305, 10 O.B.R. 314.

Separation agreement which specifically addresses life insurance need not include words "life insurance beneficiary" to effectuate elimination of former spouse as beneficiary. Lelux v. Chernick (Ohio App. 10 Dist. 1997) 119 Ohio App.3d 6, 119 Ohio St.3d 6, 694 N.E.2d 471.

Language of separation agreement was sufficient to eliminate husband and wife as beneficiary of the other, notwithstanding fact that no subsequent specific change of beneficiary was filed, where they specifically directed their attention to issues of retirement accounts and life insurance policies and expressed their intention to release any and all claims to assets of the other. Lelux v. Chernick (Ohio App. 10 Dist. 1997) 119 Ohio App.3d 6, 119 Ohio St.3d 6, 694 N.E.2d 471.

2. Child support

The parties to a separation agreement may not abrogate the right of a minor child of the marriage to be supported by either parent; prior to the effective date of RC 3113.215 to 3113.218, the parties could, however, agree to allocate the support obligation between themselves in a manner analogous to an indemnity agreement. In re Dissolution of Marriage of Lazor (Ohio 1991) 59 Ohio St.3d 201, 572 N.E.2d 66.

Where the parties to a separation agreement agree that the obligation to make child support payments will terminate when the child reaches the "age of majority," the obligation to make support payments terminates when the child reaches his or her eighteenth birthday unless the parties specify some other definition of the phrase "age of majority." In re Dissolution of Marriage of Lazor (Ohio 1991) 59 Ohio St.3d 201, 572 N.E.2d 66.

Separation agreements providing for support of children beyond age of majority, including provisions to pay for the college education of the children, are valid and enforceable if they have been incorporated into a divorce decree. Troha v. Troha (Greene 1995) 105 Ohio App.3d 327, 663 N.E.2d 1319.

Armed forces retirement pay may not be divided to satisfy a property settlement upon dissolution of a marriage. However, such retirement pay "may be subject to legal process to enforce child support or alimony obligations." Williams v Williams, Nos. 81 CA 51 and 81 CA 68 (2d Dist Ct App, Greene, 2-26-82).

3. Legal representation

An attorney who represents a spouse in the negotiation of a separation agreement relative to a marriage dissolution action does not simultaneously and automatically represent the interests of a minor child of the marriage. Scholler v. Scholler (Ohio 1984) 10 Ohio St.3d 98, 462 N.E.2d 158, 10 O.B.R. 426.

Evidence in proceeding to set aside dissolution decree was sufficient to establish that counsel for husband represented both parties and that document in which wife purportedly waived counsel was meaningless; husband's counsel was social friend of both parties and had represented them both in prior legal matters, and husband had initially retained attorney to represent both parties, and did not inform wife that attorney represented only husband until day they signed separation agreement. McSweeney v. McSweeney (Franklin 1996) 112 Ohio App.3d 355, 678 N.E.2d 969.

Fact issues as to whether divorce counsel was negligent in failing to provide for promissory note in separation agreement, and as to whether such negligence damaged client, were for jury in legal malpractice action. Mobberly v. Hendricks (Medina 1994) 98 Ohio App.3d 839, 649 N.E.2d 1247.

Where legal counsel would be preferable, if not necessary, to protect each party's rights pursuant to complex issues involving a separation agreement, a trial court errs in denying a continuance to obtain new counsel and granting the motion of present counsel to withdraw. Hughes v Hughes, No. 73843, 1998 WL 855608 (8th Dist Ct App, Cuyahoga, 12-10-98).

4. Spousal support

Ex-husband was entitled to a setoff of his spousal support obligation after ex-wife withdrew $105,000 from joint account two years after marriage had terminated; since parties had specified in separation agreement that all joint accounts had already been divided between them but had apparently overlooked account in question, proper amount of setoff was difference between $105,00 and one-half of the account balance on date that separation agreement was executed. Morgan v. Morgan (Ohio App. 7 Dist. 1998) 127 Ohio App.3d 142, 711 N.E.2d 1059.

Periodic alimony payment provided for by separation agreement incorporated into decree of dissolution cannot be modified by court after agreement is merged into decree. Rohrbacher v. Rohrbacher (Lucas 1992) 83 Ohio App.3d 569, 615 N.E.2d 338.

In a dissolution brought under RC 3105.61 et seq., the trial court may grant alimony, but only upon the agreement of both spouses to the terms of alimony which the court has approved; RC 3105.18 does not grant authority to the trial court to decide the terms of alimony independent of such agreement. Ashley v. Ashley (Cuyahoga 1981) 1 Ohio App.3d 80, 439 N.E.2d 911, 1 O.B.R. 359.

A separation agreement incorporated into a decree of dissolution of marriage may not be modified under Civ R 60(B) without vacating the entire decree of dissolution; where one or both parties have remarried such relief is impossible, since the remarried party has acted in reliance on the dissolution. Henry v Edwards, No. 15205, 1996 WL 220885 (2d Dist Ct App, Montgomery, 5-3-96).

The common pleas court has no jurisdiction under Ohio law to render a modified alimony decree where the original amount was determined in a separation agreement included in a decree of dissolution; consequently, an alimony increase in an amended decree is not a ground for the husband's estate to claim an increased estate tax deduction. Trent v. U.S. (C.A.6 (Ohio) 1990) 893 F.2d 846, rehearing denied, certiorari denied 111 S.Ct. 54, 498 U.S. 814, 112 L.Ed.2d 29.

Lump-sum judgment arising out of Chapter 7 debtor's separation agreement obligation to assume loans was in nature of alimony, support or maintenance and thus was nondischargeable, despite drop in debtor's income between time of separation agreement and bankruptcy filing; lump-sum judgment reflected past obligations of debtor, rather than any future, current or continuing obligations, and thus debtor's current situation was irrelevant. In re Northcutt (Bkrtcy.N.D.Ohio 1993) 158 B.R. 658.

Lump-sum judgment, reflecting debtor's separation agreement obligations for house payments and health insurance premiums, was nondischargeable as being for alimony, support or maintenance; health insurance payments were in nature of support, and, although proviso on mortgage payments fell within real property division section of agreement, payment was necessary in order to provide housing for former wife and children. In re Northcutt (Bkrtcy.N.D.Ohio 1993) 158 B.R. 658.

5. Separation agreement

Separation agreement is binding contract between the parties. In re Whitman (Ohio 1998) 81 Ohio St.3d 239, 690 N.E.2d 535.

In dissolution proceeding, if parties have incorporated into separation agreement a clause that allows court to modify agreement by court order, and court has approved this agreement and incorporated it into decree of dissolution, court has continuing jurisdiction to enforce this clause. In re Whitman (Ohio 1998) 81 Ohio St.3d 239, 690 N.E.2d 535.

If consent or mutuality did not exist when parties entered into separation agreement because of fraud or material mistake or misrepresentation, then there was no agreement upon which dissolution decree could have been based, and this lack of mutuality undermines integrity of dissolution proceeding and may constitute sufficient grounds to set aside decree under rule governing relief by motion from judgment. In re Whitman (Ohio 1998) 81 Ohio St.3d 239, 690 N.E.2d 535.

Separation agreement incorporated into divorce decree, awarding wife the marital residence, automobile, and couple's stock accounts, and requiring husband to pay wife one-half of his income until either spouse died or wife remarried, to pay for an addition to marital residence, and to pay the mortgage, was not unconscionable; husband had opportunity to review agreement with legal counsel of his choice and acknowledged in writing his choice not to do so, he did not allege he was coerced into signing agreement, and his annual gross income at time of agreement was $536,000 while wife's was $10,000. Biscardi v. Biscardi (Ohio App. 7 Dist. 1999) 133 Ohio App.3d 288, 727 N.E.2d 949.

Trial court had jurisdiction to revisit issue of pension benefits and to clarify meaning of qualified domestic relations order (QDRO) and separation agreement, where separation agreement specified that QDRO was to convey to each party one-half of total sums of husband's pension plan at time of distribution but QDRO stated that husband was to receive 50% of the basic vested monthly pension benefit, and where neither separation agreement nor QDRO addressed issue of temporary benefits. Weller v. Weller (Lucas 1996) 115 Ohio App.3d 173, 684 N.E.2d 1284.

Trial court may clarify disputed terms of separation agreement as they relate to division of property. Weller v. Weller (Lucas 1996) 115 Ohio App.3d 173, 684 N.E.2d 1284.

Evidence was sufficient to support finding that wife signed separation agreement due to intimidation on part of husband; wife testified that husband had history of verbal and physical abuse during marriage and that she feared losing her job because he was her ultimate supervisor at work. McSweeney v. McSweeney (Franklin 1996) 112 Ohio App.3d 355, 678 N.E.2d 969.

Decision to enforce separation agreement is discretionary one and will not be reversed on appeal absent abuse of discretion. Schneider v. Schneider (Geauga 1996) 110 Ohio App.3d 487, 674 N.E.2d 769, appeal not allowed 77 Ohio St.3d 1416, 670 N.E.2d 1004.

Separation agreement is a contract and, as such, is subject to same rules of construction that apply to other contracts. Troha v. Troha (Greene 1995) 105 Ohio App.3d 327, 663 N.E.2d 1319.

Separation agreement is a contract and is therefore subject to same rules of construction that apply to other contracts. Tapp v. Tapp (Montgomery 1995) 105 Ohio App.3d 159, 663 N.E.2d 944, dismissed, appeal not allowed 74 Ohio St.3d 1418, 655 N.E.2d 738.

Finding that wife signed separation agreement under duress was supported by evidence that agreement was drafted by husband and his attorney, that husband had threatened to take all three of the children from wife unless she assented to the agreement, and that there had been repeated acts of actual and threatened abuse by husband during the marriage. Quebodeaux v. Quebodeaux (Lorain 1995) 102 Ohio App.3d 502, 657 N.E.2d 539.

Separation agreement between husband and wife was supported by adequate consideration, even if distribution of marital assets were disproportionate in husband's favor, because agreement embodied mutual release of rights and obligations of marriage and wife failed to present any evidence of fraud in inducement of agreement. Brown v. Brown (Geauga 1993) 90 Ohio App.3d 781, 630 N.E.2d 763, cause dismissed 68 Ohio St.3d 1441, 626 N.E.2d 124.

Trial court could construe ambiguous term "cohabitation" in separation agreement incorporated into divorce decree by trial court's own prior judgment to determine that former wife's living in same home with her daughter and daughter's boyfriend was not "cohabitation" that would terminate former husband's spousal support obligation. Dickerson v. Dickerson (Lucas 1993) 87 Ohio App.3d 848, 623 N.E.2d 237.

Separation agreement referring to general principles of particular appellate decision to determine meaning of "cohabitation" that would terminate spousal support obligation was ambiguous, and trial court permissibly considered equities of case as well as parties' intent in determining whether cohabitation had occurred. Dickerson v. Dickerson (Lucas 1993) 87 Ohio App.3d 848, 623 N.E.2d 237.

In dissolution proceeding, separation agreement formulated by parties and incorporated into decree of dissolution must provide for division of marital property, spousal support, child custody and visitation, and child support. Rohrbacher v. Rohrbacher (Lucas 1992) 83 Ohio App.3d 569, 615 N.E.2d 338.

In a divorce action, the trial court can reject some of the terms of the separation agreement, make an independent ruling on those issues, and incorporate the independent ruling and partial separation agreement into the divorce decree. Welly v. Welly (Williams 1988) 55 Ohio App.3d 111, 562 N.E.2d 914.

When separation agreement purports to divide all assets and debts equally between parties and grants to husband any property not specifically referenced therein, wife may not obtain relief from judgment to make reference to husband's military pension where any mistakes in drafting separation agreement were result of her inexcusable neglect or carelessness. In re Marriage of Wise (Franklin 1988) 46 Ohio App.3d 82, 545 N.E.2d 1314.

A separation agreement, which includes a specific provision requiring disclosure of the agreement to a court in the event either party initiates an action for divorce, dissolution of marriage, or for alimony only, will be held to survive the death of one of the parties to the agreement and the resulting dismissal of a pending dissolution proceeding; consequently, a covenant within the separation agreement providing that the agreement is a full settlement of the rights of each party in the estate of the other is binding and extinguishes all statutory rights of the surviving spouse where decedent dies intestate. In re Estate of Hogrefe (Henry 1986) 30 Ohio App.3d 238, 507 N.E.2d 414, 30 O.B.R. 397.

A separation agreement which is incorporated into a dissolution decree must include a division of all property owned by the parties, not just jointly owned property. In re Murphy (Hamilton 1983) 10 Ohio App.3d 134, 461 N.E.2d 910, 10 O.B.R. 184.

While separation agreement is generally required to be fair and equitable to wife, where parties have dealt at arm's length with each other rather than in confidential relationship, test is whether agreement is product of fraud, duress or undue influence upon party in weaker bargaining position. DiPietro v. DiPietro (Franklin 1983) 10 Ohio App.3d 44, 460 N.E.2d 657, 10 O.B.R. 52.

Where a petition for dissolution is withdrawn simultaneously with the filing of a complaint for divorce, a separation agreement is not rendered ineffective where the agreement contains language showing the parties' intention that the separation agreement should survive a dismissal of the dissolution petition. Carey v. Carey (Shelby 1983) 9 Ohio App.3d 243, 459 N.E.2d 626, 9 O.B.R. 416.

A separation agreement entered into for the sole purpose of a dissolution of marriage is not a valid and binding contract when the dissolution petition is dismissed, but would be a valid and binding contract following dismissal of such petition if it contains language that the agreement shall be binding whether used in a divorce, alimony only, or a dissolution of marriage action, or such similar language evidencing the intent of the parties that it will survive dismissal of a dissolution of marriage petition, and in addition, if it does not contain express language that it was entered into solely for a dissolution of marriage action or express language that the parties intended the separation agreement to survive dismissal of a dissolution of marriage petition, but the actions and conduct of the parties evidence an intention that it will survive dismissal of a dissolution of marriage petition, the separation agreement will continue to be a valid and binding agreement after the dissolution of marriage petition is dismissed. Greiner v. Greiner (Cuyahoga 1979) 61 Ohio App.2d 88, 399 N.E.2d 571, 15 O.O.3d 95.

RC 3105.63 requires that a Separation Agreement provide for a division of all property, and where a Separation Agreement filed with and adopted by the court fails to state when or if the former marital residence is to be quit claimed to one of the parties, the final divorce decree of the parties is voidable and may be attacked solely by a motion to vacate. Morgan v Morgan, No. 93-C-36 (7th Dist Ct App, Columbiana, 6-14-94).

Ex-wife, who, pursuant to separation agreement which was incorporated into divorce decree, owed ex-husband $5,000 at time of his death, was not precluded from asserting setoff for amount ex-husband was required to pay ex-wife under agreement, even though she did not file claim against ex-husband's estate, where amount ex-wife owed ex-husband was greater than amount ex-husband owed ex-wife such that any claim filed by ex-wife would only indicate that she owed ex-husband's estate money. Estate of Ruehl v. Ruehl (Ohio Mun. 1993) 63 Ohio Misc.2d 260, 623 N.E.2d 741.

Under Ohio law, where judgment entry incorporates separation agreement, separation agreement merges into, and is superseded by, domestic relations court's order. In re Gibson (6th Cir.BAP (Ohio) 1998) 219 B.R. 195.

Under Ohio law, upon merger of separation agreement into domestic relations court's final decree, all causes of action under separation agreement are extinguished and replaced by postjudgment remedies to enforce decree. In re Gibson (6th Cir.BAP (Ohio) 1998) 219 B.R. 195.

6. Enforcement

Trial court's discretion to grant motion for relief from property settlement incorporated into dissolution decrees is limited to motions based on mistake, newly discovered evidence, and fraud; limitation provides permanency to any dissolution that has remained unchallenged for one year, and preserves rights of moving party to relief without sacrificing general finality of dissolution decree and without creating any undue hardship for opposing party. In re Whitman (Ohio 1998) 81 Ohio St.3d 239, 690 N.E.2d 535.

Trial court did not have jurisdiction to order that certificate of deposit (CD) accounts in the name of divorced parties' younger child be turned over to father pursuant to separation agreement under which CDs in the name of each child were to be used to pay for children's college educations, even though court adopted and approved the separation agreement; accounts in question were the separate property of the child. Troha v. Troha (Greene 1995) 105 Ohio App.3d 327, 663 N.E.2d 1319.

In enforcing separation agreement that has been incorporated into a divorce decree, trial court has authority to hear the matter, clarify any confusion over interpretation to be given a particular clause, and resolve the dispute. Troha v. Troha (Greene 1995) 105 Ohio App.3d 327, 663 N.E.2d 1319.

Separation agreement that is the product of duress will be held to be unenforceable. Quebodeaux v. Quebodeaux (Lorain 1995) 102 Ohio App.3d 502, 657 N.E.2d 539.

Trial court properly declined to hold former husband in contempt of previously issued court order requiring former husband to pay expenses as required by separation agreement; parties disputed whether expenses were dischargeable in former husband's bankruptcy proceeding. Dozer v. Dozer (Ross 1993) 88 Ohio App.3d 296, 623 N.E.2d 1272.

When a separation agreement is incorporated into a dissolution decree by the court, provisions in the separation agreement are enforceable just as any court decree or order. Dudziak v. Dudziak (Cuyahoga 1992) 81 Ohio App.3d 361, 611 N.E.2d 337.

Where a separation agreement incorporated into a decree of dissolution grants the wife a right of first refusal upon the husband's sale of his 1970 Corvette, the husband is in breach of such provision if he transfers the title to a third party in order to secure a debt pursuant to an alleged "constructive trust." Linehan v. Linehan (Cuyahoga 1986) 34 Ohio App.3d 124, 517 N.E.2d 967.

A clause in a separation agreement requiring the party in default to pay the other party's attorney fees in an enforcement action is not enforceable. Snyder v. Snyder (Cuyahoga 1985) 27 Ohio App.3d 1, 499 N.E.2d 320, 27 O.B.R. 1.

Separation agreement incorporated into dissolution decree, providing that husband would transfer to wife and his two daughters any inheritance he received from his parents, was not entered into through fraud or imposition and was supported by adequate consideration, and thus, was valid and enforceable, where husband offered and wife accepted an uncertain inheritance and where husband's obvious intent was to sweeten wife's acceptance of the dissolution in order to expedite its conclusion; fact that husband believed his parents had disinherited him was irrelevant. Bednar v. Bednar (Summit 1984) 20 Ohio App.3d 176, 485 N.E.2d 834, 20 O.B.R. 219.

If the terms of a separation agreement are incorporated into a decree of divorce or alimony, the separation agreement merges into the decree and no longer exists as an independent contract and its terms will be enforced as part of the decree. If a separation agreement is not incorporated by reference into a divorce or alimony decree, nor declared invalid, but only identified and attached as an exhibit to the divorce or alimony decree, the separation agreement will continue to be a valid and binding contract and its terms will not be enforced as part of the decree, but will be enforced as any other contract. Greiner v. Greiner (Cuyahoga 1979) 61 Ohio App.2d 88, 399 N.E.2d 571, 15 O.O.3d 95.

A wife does not waive her rights as surviving spouse of the decedent although she signs a separation agreement which was to be appended to a petition for dissolution where the decedent does not sign the separation agreement before his death and the parties never file a petition for dissolution. Estate of Evans v Evans, No. F-96-040, 1997 WL 438254 (6th Dist Ct App, Fulton, 8-1-97).

Children named as beneficiaries pursuant to a separation agreement that becomes part of the final dissolution decree have an equitable right to insurance proceeds which is superior to the legal rights of designated beneficiaries named in the policy. Yuda v Saumer, No. 65829, 1994 WL 385945 (8th Dist Ct App, Cuyahoga, 7-21-94).

Where a separation agreement provides that the husband will pay for his son's tuition at an approved college and the referee concludes that the husband's obligation is to pay for room and board at a college the husband did not approve, the trial court erred in adopting the referee's report where there are no findings in the referee's report to support his conclusions. In re Hadaway, No. C-820991 (1st Dist Ct App, Hamilton, 11-16-83).

Where parties to a separation agreement include therein an obligation relating to a religious practice, said obligation is unenforceable in a court of law either as a contractual provision or pursuant to the enforcement of a divorce decree which incorporated the terms of such agreement. Steinberg v Steinberg, No. 44125 (8th Dist Ct App, Cuyahoga, 6-24-82).

Marital debts assumed by a spouse under the terms of a separation agreement incorporated in a decree of dissolution cannot be discharged in bankruptcy. In re Troup (C.A.6 (Ohio) 1984) 730 F.2d 464.

7. Interpretation

Trial court has the authority to clarify the terms and conditions of a marital separation agreement, consider the intentions of the parties, and establish the equities between them. Robinson v. Rodi (Ohio App. 7 Dist. 1998) 129 Ohio App.3d 550, 718 N.E.2d 504.

As a contract, a separation agreement must be interpreted in accordance with the parties' intention. Troha v. Troha (Greene 1995) 105 Ohio App.3d 327, 663 N.E.2d 1319.

Trial court erred in striking from separation agreement a provision by which funds from certificate of deposit (CD) accounts in the names of parties' children were to be used to pay for children's college education, even though court lacked authority to order that the CDs be used for such expenses; both the language of agreement and testimony in record revealed parties' intent that husband would not be responsible for paying balance of college costs until children had depleted CD funds and other funds specified in agreement, and court should have construed provision as condition precedent to husband's obligation to pay balance of costs. Troha v. Troha (Greene 1995) 105 Ohio App.3d 327, 663 N.E.2d 1319.

Language in separation agreement, under which husband agreed that he would be responsible for balance of payment on children's college educations after expenditure of $3,850 in savings bond owned by him, after payment of those expenses from certificate of deposit (CD) accounts in the names of the children, and after payment of proceedings from sale of vacation properties clearly reflected parties' intention that husband's obligation to pay balance of the college costs was contingent upon depletion of the specified funds. Troha v. Troha (Greene 1995) 105 Ohio App.3d 327, 663 N.E.2d 1319.

Clause in separation agreement was ambiguous, and thus subject to interpretation by considering parties' intent as well as equities involved, where it provided that certificates of deposit (CDs) in the names of each of parties' two children were to be used for the children's college education before husband's duty to pay the balance arose; provision could be interpreted to mean that the CDs of both children must first be used for older child's education before husband's duty to pay balance arose, or to mean that each child's CD must be used for his or her own college expenses. Troha v. Troha (Greene 1995) 105 Ohio App.3d 327, 663 N.E.2d 1319.

Clause in separation agreement, providing that certificates of deposit (CDs) in the names of each of parties' two children were to be used for the children's college education before husband's duty to pay the balance arose, was interpreted to mean that each child's CD must be used for his or her own education; any other interpretation would risk compromising funds for younger child's education if some unforeseen event occurred to prevent father from contributing toward child's college expenses, and further, it would be inequitable to make younger child use her funds to pay for older sibling's expenses, as younger child's account consisted mostly of funds received as settlement for dog-bite injury. Troha v. Troha (Greene 1995) 105 Ohio App.3d 327, 663 N.E.2d 1319.

When a clause in a separation agreement is ambiguous, court can resolve the dispute by considering not only the intent of the parties, but also the equities involved. Troha v. Troha (Greene 1995) 105 Ohio App.3d 327, 663 N.E.2d 1319.

Even if husband's failure to make payment to wife in exchange for interest in real property by time specified in separation agreement constituted breach of agreement, such breach was not material, where wife did not indicate that agreement hinged on husband's timely payment; purpose of agreement would not have been defeated by husband's action. Brown v. Brown (Geauga 1993) 90 Ohio App.3d 781, 630 N.E.2d 763, cause dismissed 68 Ohio St.3d 1441, 626 N.E.2d 124.

Where terms of separation agreement incorporated into decree of divorce are confusing or ambiguous, court is accorded broad discretion to clarify those terms and can resolve dispute by considering not only intent of parties but also equities involved. Rohrbacher v. Rohrbacher (Lucas 1992) 83 Ohio App.3d 569, 615 N.E.2d 338.

Ambiguities of language in a separation contract are construed against the party who prepared the contract. Uram v. Uram (Summit 1989) 65 Ohio App.3d 96, 582 N.E.2d 1060.

A separation agreement incorporated into a dissolution of marriage decree which provides that the "husband agrees to pay the real estate taxes on the real estate" requires payment of any and all special assessments billed on the tax duplicate as well as the amount of property taxes. Burkey v. Burkey (Summit 1986) 31 Ohio App.3d 108, 508 N.E.2d 1012, 31 O.B.R. 179.

With respect to dissolution decrees which permit termination of alimony upon "cohabitation" of alimony recipient with person of opposite sex, "cohabitation" requires some regularity of functioning as would husband and wife, either sexually or otherwise, and usually will be manifested by man and woman living together in same household and behaving as would husband and wife, although there need not be actual assertion of marriage. Fuller v. Fuller (Franklin 1983) 10 Ohio App.3d 253, 461 N.E.2d 1348, 10 O.B.R. 366.

When a spouse receiving spousal support remarries, her spousal support will terminate unless (1) the support constitutes a property settlement, (2) the support is related to child support, or (3) the parties expressly agree in their separation agreement that the support payments will survive the payee spouse's remarriage; where the parties' separation agreement does not expressly provide that support is to continue after the spouse remarries, it is error for the court to consider letters and notations of communications evidencing negotiations between the parties prior to the separation agreement at issue being adopted which contradict the unambiguous terms of that separation agreement. Whalen v Whalen, No.

1994-CA-0001, 1994 WL 477825 (5th Dist Ct App, Stark, 8-22-94).

8. Vacation of decree

Trial court may grant relief from judgment as to property division in separation agreement without vacating decree of dissolution where parties to dissolution have expressly agreed in separation agreement that agreement may be modified by court order and agreement has been incorporated into decree. In re Whitman (Ohio 1998) 81 Ohio St.3d 239, 690 N.E.2d 535.

On ex-wife's motion for relief from judgment on ground of mistake of fact as to property owned by couple at time of dissolution, trial court could elect to modify property division rather than vacate entire dissolution decree, where parties had specifically reserved to court the power to modify separation agreement with language that agreement should not be altered "unless it is done so in writing, signed by both parties, or by Court Order." In re Whitman (Ohio 1998) 81 Ohio St.3d 239, 690 N.E.2d 535.

Where a separation agreement omitted assets both substantial in amount and material to an informed agreement regarding the equitable division of property, the dissolution decree is thereby rendered voidable, and the decree may be vacated by motion for relief filed pursuant to Civ R 60(B)(5). In re Murphy (Hamilton 1983) 10 Ohio App.3d 134, 461 N.E.2d 910, 10 O.B.R. 184.

A dissolution of a marriage under RC 3105.61 et seq. which is contingent upon the parties mutually agreeing on (1) a dissolution and (2) a separation agreement that is approved by the court cannot be countenanced where a court subsequently orders the agreement to be vacated based on incomplete disclosure by one of the parties; to set aside the agreement requires the vacating of the dissolution. Ashley v. Ashley (Cuyahoga 1981) 1 Ohio App.3d 80, 439 N.E.2d 911, 1 O.B.R. 359.

When one or both of the parties have remarried Civ R 60(B) is not the proper recourse where a party requests that the dissolution decree be vacated because the incorporated separation agreement omitted substantial and material pieces of property; instead, the aggrieved party may seek relief in an action for accounting, declaratory judgment, conversion, damages, or unjust enrichment. Whitman v Whitman, No. 5-95-47, 1996 WL 276379 (3d Dist Ct App, Hancock, 5-14-96).

Failure of a party to a separation agreement to disclose all assets, as required by RC 3105.63, may constitute fraud on the court, under Civ R 60(B)(5), and it is error to deny relief without an evidentiary hearing. In re Dissolution of the Marriage of Frecker, No. 83AP-382 (10th Dist Ct App, Franklin, 3-6-84).

Where a party fails to file timely objections to a referee's report, the party waives his or her right to appeal on that issue. Morris v Morris, No. 43528 (8th Dist Ct App, Cuyahoga, 12-3-81).

Where the record shows that the husband obtained the consent of the wife to a separation agreement by use of threats, and where the record shows that the agreement does not dispose of all assets of the marriage in violation of RC 3105.63, which calls for a division of all property, the court may grant a motion to vacate judgment of a dissolution pursuant to Civ R 60(B)(3) on the grounds of inequity and unconscionability. Norton v Norton, No. 979 (11th Dist Ct App, Ashtabula, 11-5-79).

3105.64 Appearance; acknowledgment of satisfaction with agreement

(A) Except as provided in division (B) of this section, not less than thirty nor more than ninety days after the filing of a petition for dissolution of marriage, both spouses shall appear before the court and each spouse shall acknowledge under oath that he has voluntarily entered into the separation agreement appended to the petition, that he is satisfied with its terms, and that he seeks dissolution of the marriage.

(B) If an action for divorce is converted to an action for dissolution of marriage pursuant to section 3105.08 of the Revised Code and if the conversion occurs more than thirty days after the filing of the original petition in the divorce action, the appearance and acknowledgement requirements of division (A) of this section may be satisfied at the time of the conversion or at a time that is not more than ninety days after the conversion.

(1990 S 25, eff. 6-13-90; 1974 H 233)

Cross References

Stay pending completion of conciliation proceedings, 3117.07, 3117.08

Library References

Divorce ⚷36, 81.
WESTLAW Topic No. 134.
C.J.S. Divorce §§ 20, 21, 126.

OJur 3d: 46, Family Law § 397, 633, 638
Am Jur 2d: 24, Divorce and Separation § 29 to 31, 238 to 243, 274, 280, 340, 347, 354
Length or duration of domicil, as distinguished from fact of domicil, as a jurisdictional matter in divorce action. 2 ALR2d 291
Effect on jurisdiction of court to grant divorce, of plaintiff's change of residence pendente lite. 7 ALR2d 1414
Nature and location of one's business or calling as element in determining domicil in divorce cases. 36 ALR2d 756
Right of nonresident wife to maintain action for separate maintenance or alimony alone against resident husband. 36 ALR2d 1369

What constitutes residence or domicil within state by citizen of another country for purpose of jurisdiction in divorce. 51 ALR3d 223

Validity of statute imposing durational residency requirements for divorce applicants. 57 ALR3d 221

Validity and construction of statutory provision relating to jurisdiction of court for purpose of divorce for servicemen. 73 ALR3d 431

Sowald & Morganstern, Baldwin's Ohio Practice, *Domestic Relations Law* § 10.3, 10.6, 11.28, 27.11 (1997)

Notes of Decisions and Opinions

1. Waiting period

Trial court had jurisdiction to entertain motion to convert dissolution action into divorce action beyond 30—to—90—day period within which parties must appear, acknowledge satisfaction with separation agreement and consent to dissolution. Smith v. Smith (Highland 1995) 101 Ohio App.3d 62, 654 N.E.2d 1342.

The thirty-day waiting period in RC 3105.64 is mandatory, but where it is not used, the dissolution decree is not void but merely voidable. Starr v. Starr (Madison 1985) 26 Ohio App.3d 134, 498 N.E.2d 1092, 26 O.B.R. 346.

The ninety-day time limit under RC 3105.64 does not require dismissal of a dissolution action still pending at that time and, pursuant to RC 3105.65, the parties are not required to file motions to convert a dissolution action into a divorce action within the first ninety days after they file the petition for dissolution. Smith v Smith, No. 94 CA 847, 1995 WL 57380 (4th Dist Ct App, 2-8-95).

The RC 3105.64 thirty- to-ninety-day time period relates only to the appearance and acknowledgment of the parties, not to the jurisdiction of the trial court so that a court, beyond the ninety-day point, has jurisdiction to enter a dissolution decree and has jurisdiction to entertain a motion to convert the dissolution action into an action for divorce. Smith v Smith, No. 94 CA 847, 1995 WL 57380 (4th Dist Ct App, Highland, 2-8-95).

2. Relief from judgment

Evidence did not establish that reversionary clause in separation agreement incorporated into divorce decree, pursuant to which ex-wife retained reversionary interest in former marital residence should particular individual occupy residence overnight, was result of duress and undue influence, despite ex-husband's contention that restraining order that had been obtained to prevent him from selling or transferring assets and ex-wife's attorney's threatened pursuit of contempt motion left him no alternative but to agree to reversionary clause. Beechler v. Beechler (Fayette 1994) 95 Ohio App.3d 121, 641 N.E.2d 1189.

Where a separation agreement is voluntarily entered into and signed, a Civ R 60(B) motion for relief from a divorce decree that incorporates the agreement will be denied. Kilbreath v Kilbreath, No. CA-9074 (5th Dist Ct App, Stark, 3-29-93).

3105.65 Dismissal of petition or approval of agreement and grant of dissolution; effect of decree; continuing jurisdiction; modification of spousal support; conversion of dissolution action into divorce action

(A) If, at the time of the hearing, either spouse is not satisfied with the separation agreement or does not wish a dissolution of the marriage and if neither spouse files a motion pursuant to division (C) of this section to convert the action to an action for divorce, the court shall dismiss the petition and refuse to validate the proposed separation agreement.

(B) If, upon review of the testimony of both spouses and of the report of the investigator pursuant to the Rules of Civil Procedure, the court approves the separation agreement and any amendments to it agreed upon by the parties, it shall grant a decree of dissolution of marriage that incorporates the separation agreement. If the separation agreement contains a plan for the exercise of shared parenting by the spouses, the court shall review the plan in accordance with the provisions of division (D)(1) of section 3109.04 of the Revised Code that govern the review of a pleading or motion requesting shared parenting jointly submitted by both spouses to a marriage. A decree of dissolution of marriage has the same effect upon the property rights of the parties, including rights of dower and inheritance, as a decree of divorce. The court has full power to enforce its decree and retains jurisdiction to modify all matters pertaining to the allocation of parental rights and responsibilities for the care of the children, to the designation of a residential parent and legal custodian of the children, to child support, and to visitation. The court, only in accordance with division (E)(2) of section 3105.18 of the Revised Code, may modify the amount or terms of spousal support.

(C) At any time before a decree of dissolution of marriage has been granted under division (B) of this section, either spouse may convert the action for dissolution of marriage into a divorce action by filing a motion with the court in which the action for dissolution of marriage is pending for conversion of the action for dissolution of marriage. The motion shall contain a complaint for divorce that contains grounds for a divorce and that otherwise complies with the Rules of Civil Procedure and this chapter. The divorce action then shall proceed in accordance with the Rules of Civil Procedure in the same manner as if the motion had been the original complaint in the action, including, but not limited to, the issuance and service of summons pursuant to Civil Rules 4 to 4.6, except that no court fees shall be charged upon conversion of the action for dissolution of marriage into a divorce action under this division.

(1990 S 3, eff. 4-11-91; 1990 H 514, S 25; 1986 H 358; 1975 H 370; 1974 H 233)

Uncodified Law

1986 H 358, § 3: See Uncodified Law under 3105.18.

Cross References

Additional fees for filing decree of dissolution, children's trust fund, 3109.14
Child support guidelines, 3113.215
Divorce, annulment, legal separation, and related proceedings, Civ R 75
Dower, Ch 2103
Parental rights and responsibilities, shared parenting, child support, 3109.04, 3109.041, 3109.05
Reciprocal enforcement of support, support pendente lite, 3115.27
Retirement benefits of spouse, effect of dissolution of marriage, 145.46
Separation agreement to which decedent a party valid unless set aside; time limits, 2106.22
Stay pending completion of conciliation proceedings, 3117.07, 3117.08
Uniform child custody jurisdiction law, 3109.21 to 3109.37

Ohio Administrative Code References

Department of job and family services, child support program, OAC Ch 5101:1-29
Department of job and family services, collection of past due support by federal tax refund offset, OAC Ch 5101:1-30

Library References

Divorce ⟜36, 138 to 139 1/2, 154.
WESTLAW Topic No. 134.
C.J.S. Divorce §§ 20, 21, 201 to 204, 222, 223.

OJur 3d: 46, Family Law § 321, 398, 400, 402, 603, 613, 696, 708, 714, 749; 47, Family Law § 1180; 62, Investment Securities and Securities Regulation § 53
Am Jur 2d: 24, Divorce and Separation § 29 to 31, 238 to 243, 274, 280, 340, 342 to 351, 354, 415 to 513
Length or duration of domicil, as distinguished from fact of domicil, as a jurisdictional matter in divorce action. 2 ALR2d 291
Effect on jurisdiction of court to grant divorce, of plaintiff's change of residence pendente lite. 7 ALR2d 1414
Nature and location of one's business or calling as element in determining domicil in divorce cases. 36 ALR2d 756
Right of nonresident wife to maintain action for separate maintenance or alimony alone against resident husband. 36 ALR2d 1369
What constitutes residence or domicil within state by citizen of another country for purpose of jurisdiction in divorce. 51 ALR3d 223
Validity of statute imposing durational residency requirements for divorce applicants. 57 ALR3d 221
Validity and construction of statutory provision relating to jurisdiction of court for purpose of divorce for servicemen. 73 ALR3d 431

Klein & Darling, Baldwin's Ohio Practice, *Civil Practice* § 60 (1997)
Sowald & Morganstern, Baldwin's Ohio Practice, *Domestic Relations Law* § 9.8, 9.9, 9.27, 9.35, 9.36, 10.3, 10.7, 10.14, 10.15, 10.15.1, 11.28, 14.5, 14.6, 14.10, 14.12, 14.13, 15.3, 15.6, 15.8, 15.19, 20.6, 20.10, 24.2, 24.6, 25.13 (1997)

Law Review and Journal Commentaries

Modification of Alimony—Dissolution, Judith A. Nicely. 1 Domestic Rel J Ohio 9 (September/October 1989).

Notes of Decisions and Opinions

1. In general

A modification of an existing support order is justified where the moving party demonstrates a substantial change of circumstances which renders unreasonable an order which was once reasonable; evidence constituting a substantial change of circumstances justifing modification of an original support order includes the wife's fraudulent misrepresentation that the child she was carrying at the time of marriage was that of her husband and the results of blood test excluding the moving party as the father. Carson v. Carson (Brown 1989) 62 Ohio App.3d 670, 577 N.E.2d 391, motion overruled 46 Ohio St.3d 716, 546 N.E.2d 1334.

Where a divorce decree incorporating a separation agreement is rendered, obligating an obligor to support a child until his age of emancipation, the age of emancipation in effect when the decree is rendered controls. Bauer v. Bauer (Franklin 1989) 57 Ohio App.3d 24, 566 N.E.2d 185.

As part of its enforcement powers, a trial court has the power to hear a matter, clarify confusion, and resolve a dispute concerning the interpretation of a confusing provision within a separation agreement. In re Marriage of Seders (Summit 1987) 42 Ohio App.3d 155, 536 N.E.2d 1190.

A trial court may modify a separation agreement of the parties to an action for divorce in its discretion, unlike separation agreements entered into pursuant to a dissolution of marriage. Bourque v. Bourque (Clermont 1986) 34 Ohio App.3d 284, 518 N.E.2d 49.

Where a separation agreement incorporated into a decree of dissolution provides for the termination of alimony upon the death or remarriage of the recipient but certain provisions for life insurance contain no such limitation, it is not error for the court to find that the purpose of the insurance provisions is to fund the alimony payments and thus such provisions terminate along with the obligation to pay alimony upon the remarriage of the recipient spouse. Linehan v. Linehan (Cuyahoga 1986) 34 Ohio App.3d 124, 517 N.E.2d 967.

Under its power to enforce a decree of dissolution incorporating a separation agreement, a court may order business income distributed according to the agreement and disregard the corporate structure created by one party with the knowledge that it would reduce his alimony liability. Saeks v. Saeks (Montgomery 1985) 24 Ohio App.3d 67, 493 N.E.2d 280, 24 O.B.R. 122.

Separation agreement was not rendered ineffective by withdrawal of petition for dissolution and simultaneously filing of complaint in divorce where agreement contained language evidencing intent of parties that separation agreement should survive dismissal of dissolution petition. Carey v. Carey (Shelby 1983) 9 Ohio App.3d 243, 459 N.E.2d 626, 9 O.B.R. 416.

A court does not retain jurisdiction to modify periodic alimony payments provided for in a separation agreement incorporated in a decree of dissolution of marriage. Leonti v. Leonti (Summit 1983) 8 Ohio App.3d 129, 456 N.E.2d 584, 8 O.B.R. 185.

2. Jurisdiction

Pursuant to RC 3105.65(B), a court is without jurisdiction to modify or terminate an award of alimony set forth in a separation agreement incorporated into a decree of dissolution of marriage, absent a reservation of jurisdiction in the agreement. In re Adams (Ohio 1989) 45 Ohio St.3d 219, 543 N.E.2d 797.

A court of common pleas does not have jurisdiction to modify a provision for periodic sustenance alimony payments contained within a dissolution of marriage decree. (See also Werk v Werk, 17 OS(3d) 143, 17 OBR 286, 477 NE(2d) 1150 (1985).) McClain v. McClain (Ohio 1984) 15 Ohio St.3d 289, 473 N.E.2d 811, 15 O.B.R. 421.

Withdrawal from high school by child who was in custody of former husband on day child turned 18 years of age terminated wife's duty to pay child support, and divested trial court of jurisdiction to order wife to pay child support or to modify child support agreement; child's subsequent enrollment in vocational school did not resurrect order, as obligation continues after age 18 only if child continuously attends high school. Gleason v. Gleason (Ohio App. 4 Dist. 1998) 129 Ohio App.3d 563, 718 N.E.2d 512.

If child does not continuously attend high school on a full-time basis after turning 18, parent's duty to provide child support ends, and trial court loses subject matter jurisdiction. Gleason v. Gleason (Ohio App. 4 Dist. 1998) 129 Ohio App.3d 563, 718 N.E.2d 512.

Trial court lacked jurisdiction in postdissolution proceeding to modify terms of property division based on alleged oral premarital agreement under which husband was to pay wife $800 per month for performing household services, where separation agreement that was incorporated into dissolution judgment made no mention of alleged premarital agreement and did not expressly reserve jurisdiction of trial court relative to any future division of property. Morgan v. Morgan (Ohio App. 7 Dist. 1998) 127 Ohio App.3d 142, 711 N.E.2d 1059.

Following entry of divorce decree, domestic relations court did not have original or continuing jurisdiction to consider issue of paternity raised by former wife's child, who was born after the divorce. Fitzpatrick v. Fitzpatrick (Ohio App. 12 Dist. 1998) 126 Ohio App.3d 476, 710 N.E.2d 778, dismissed, appeal not allowed 82 Ohio St.3d 1441, 695 N.E.2d 264.

Trial court lacked jurisdiction to modify terms of property settlement originally set forth in separation agreement and thereafter adopted and incorporated into divorce decree, to order sale of marital residence at lower price than that contemplated in property settlement, absent any ambiguity or confusion in original agreement; original agreement was mutual and included contingency plan in event marital residence could not be sold for price contemplated. Proctor v. Proctor (Ohio App. 3 Dist. 1997) 122 Ohio App.3d 56, 701 N.E.2d 36.

Trial court lacked jurisdiction to modify provisions of decree of dissolution of marriage with respect to division of marital property where decree included release of any interests that any party might then have or might thereafter have in assets of the other, and did not reserve jurisdiction to modify its provisions with respect to division of marital property. Hester v. Hester (Miami 1996) 110 Ohio App.3d 727, 675 N.E.2d 63, appeal not allowed 77 Ohio St.3d 1445, 671 N.E.2d 1284.

Trial court had jurisdiction to modify child support provisions of separation agreement which had been incorporated into decree of dissolution, so as to conform support obligation to amended statute governing parental duty to support children, even though separation agreement went into effect more than 13 years before court's action; court had both statutory continuing jurisdiction to modify child support and separate jurisdiction to give effect to statutory command of support statute. Mazzuckelli v. Mazzuckelli (Hamilton 1995) 106 Ohio App.3d 554, 666 N.E.2d 620.

Application of amended statute establishing parental duty to support child beyond age of majority so long as child attends accredited high school to case in which support obligation arose some 13 years before statute was amended did not constitute inappropriate retrospective application of statute; when trial court was asked to extend obligation from child's 18th birthday until child graduated from high school, that obligation had yet to be fully carried out under existing law and its dimensions had yet to be fully determined, and, at time of requested extension, trial court had yet to relinquish its statutory continuing jurisdiction to modify child support provisions. Mazzuckelli v. Mazzuckelli (Hamilton 1995) 106 Ohio App.3d 554, 666 N.E.2d 620.

Trial court had jurisdiction to enforce provision of decree of dissolution distributing share of husband's military retirement pay to wife, even though husband's rights in pension had not vested at time of decree; provision was part of separation agreement which was incorporated into decree and parties did not appeal decree, provision in separation agreement was prospective and acknowledged that pension had not yet vested, at time decree was entered, husband had already completed three fourths of years of service required for his rights to become vested, and parties did not consider value of benefits to be speculative. Cherry v. Figart (Clermont 1993) 86 Ohio App.3d 123, 620 N.E.2d 174.

Trial court has full power to enforce provisions of separation agreement which has been incorporated into decree of dissolution. Cherry v. Figart (Clermont 1993) 86 Ohio App.3d 123, 620 N.E.2d 174.

Court has jurisdiction to enforce and/or modify terms of separation agreement which relate to matters of child custody, child support and visitation. Rohrbacher v. Rohrbacher (Lucas 1992) 83 Ohio App.3d 569, 615 N.E.2d 338.

Statute granting court full power and jurisdiction to modify terms of separation agreement relating to matters of child support applies only during a child's minority; court is without jurisdiction to order parent to support child when that child reaches age of majority and is not attending an accredited high school on fulltime basis. Rohrbacher v. Rohrbacher (Lucas 1992) 83 Ohio App.3d 569, 615 N.E.2d 338.

During child's minority, domestic relations court has jurisdiction to alter provisions of its decree which relate to college education of child upon proper motion of or consent of parties but once child reaches age of majority, court is without jurisdiction to modify those provisions without consent of child of the parties. Rohrbacher v. Rohrbacher (Lucas 1992) 83 Ohio App.3d 569, 615 N.E.2d 338.

Trial court has broad discretion in clarifying ambiguous language in separation agreement by considering not only intent of parties but equities involved. Bond v. Bond (Summit 1990) 69 Ohio App.3d 225, 590 N.E.2d 348.

Trial court did not abuse its discretion in refusing to transfer jurisdiction over dissolution of marriage proceeding to court in divorced husband's new county of residence, even though that court had consented to accept jurisdiction; trial court had jurisdiction of matter for approximately ten years prior to transfer motion, and concluded that it was better able to deal with various issues in case. Bieniek v. Bieniek (Medina 1985) 27 Ohio App.3d 28, 499 N.E.2d 356, 27 O.B.R. 29.

A domestic relations court does not have jurisdiction pursuant to RC 3105.65 to modify either the alimony or property division provisions of a separation agreement. Anderson v. Anderson (Greene 1984) 13 Ohio App.3d 194, 468 N.E.2d 784, 13 O.B.R. 242.

In a case where a court neglects to divide two remaining burial lots pursuant to dissolving a marriage, where a foreign state court having in personam jurisdiction over the parties orders the conveyance of both lots located in Ohio to the former wife, that decree is entitled to res judicata effect in an Ohio action brought by the former husband against his former wife for illegal internment in burying her second husband in one of the lots. Short v Hinman, No. 97 CA 1443, 1998 WL 57345 (2d Dist Ct App, Montgomery, 2-13-98).

Where the terms of a separation agreement provide that the husband will commence alimony payments of $1000 per month and continue until the amount paid to wife equals fifty per cent of the net worth of the husband's car dealership, the court has no jurisdiction to modify the $1000 per month payment to a $1,000,000 lump-sum. Womelsdorf v Reichert, No. C-950224, 1996 WL 61072 (1st Dist Ct App, Hamilton, 2-14-96).

Ohio retains jurisdiction over disputes involving visitation under the terms of a dissolution decree where Ohio is the decree-issuing state and the party seeking visitation (1) leaves the jurisdiction for one year following the dissolution decree, (2) returns and maintains residence in Ohio, and (3) is an Ohio resident when he files his visitation contempt motion; in addition, a case involving child visitation matters between parties residing in different states constitutes a special proceeding affecting substantial rights of all the parties involved and the trial court's order denying a party's motion to dismiss the motion for contempt is a final appealable order. Shiver v Shiver, No. C-950239, 1995 WL 757838 (1st Dist Ct App, Hamilton, 12-20-95).

The ninety-day time limit under RC 3105.64 does not require dismissal of a dissolution action still pending at that time and, pursuant to RC 3105.65, the parties are not required to file motions to convert a dissolution action into a divorce action within the first ninety days after they file the petition for dissolution. Smith v Smith, No. 94 CA 847, 1995 WL 57380 (4th Dist Ct App, 2-8-95).

A motion for alimony modification is properly denied if the trial court does not explicitly reserve jurisdiction to modify in the separation agreement incorporated into the dissolution of marriage decree. Edwards v Edwards, No. 14022, 1994 WL 95253 (2d Dist Ct App, Montgomery, 3-23-94).

RC 3105.65(B) does not give a trial court jurisdiction to modify a property division provided for in a separation agreement which was incorporated in a decree of dissolution. Hubbell v Hubbell, No. CA-656 (5th Dist Ct App, Morrow, 1-26-87).

RC 3105.65 does not confer jurisdiction on a trial court to modify the disposition of the marital home when disposed of in a settlement agreement incorporated in a final decree. Brown v Brown, No. E-84-31 (6th Dist Ct App, Erie, 3-15-85).

RC 3105.65(B) does not confer upon the common pleas court the jurisdiction to modify periodic alimony payments provided for in a separation agreement, even if the separation agreement provided such a provision. In re Fugazzi, No. 82AP-174 and 82AP-184 (10th Dist Ct App, Franklin, 6-2-83).

Trial court does not retain jurisdiction to modify periodic alimony payments provided for in a separation agreement incorporated in a decree of dissolution of marriage even where the separation agreement provides for court review of alimony payments. In re Fugazzi, Nos. 82AP-174 and 82AP-184 (10th Dist Ct App, Franklin, 6-2-83).

Tax exemptions for children are "marital property," notwithstanding the fact that the separation agreement incorporated within the dissolution decree treats the exemptions as a component of child support; therefore, a court lacks subject matter jurisdiction to subsequently modify the award of the exemptions. In re Lee (Ohio Com.Pl. 1989) 58 Ohio Misc.2d 4, 567 N.E.2d 1350.

A trial court has jurisdiction to modify a support order as to future installments, whether or not the right is reserved in the decree; but it has no such jurisdiction to modify unpaid installment support payments which have accrued if the child for whose benefit support was awarded was living and not emancipated at the time of the accrual, unless the right to retrospective modification was specifically reserved in the decree. Wedebrook v. Wedebrook (Ohio Com.Pl. 1977) 51 Ohio Misc. 81, 367 N.E.2d 937, 5 O.O.3d 342.

3. Agreement of parties

Under RC 3105.65(B), as amended by 1975 H 370, eff. 8-1-75, a court may retain jurisdiction to modify alimony payments provided for in a separation agreement by parties to a dissolution where the parties have agreed to such continuing jurisdiction and the agreement has been incorporated in a decree of dissolution of marriage. Colley v. Colley (Ohio 1989) 43 Ohio St.3d 87, 538 N.E.2d 410.

Wife's right to receive lump sum payment upon dissolution of marriage, as provided in antenuptial agreement, accrued on date of termination of marriage de jure, rather than on date marriage was allegedly de facto terminated by removal of husband from marital home following his assault on wife. Langer v. Langer (Ohio App. 2 Dist. 1997) 123 Ohio App.3d 348, 704 N.E.2d 275, cause dismissed 80 Ohio St.3d 1473, 687 N.E.2d 470.

Husband's death following filing of petition for marital dissolution did not affect binding nature of separation agreement between husband and wife, where agreement provided that it would continue to be binding even if final decree were not issued in proceeding to dissolve marriage. Brown v. Brown (Geauga 1993) 90 Ohio App.3d 781, 630 N.E.2d 763, cause dismissed 68 Ohio St.3d 1441, 626 N.E.2d 124.

Provisions in dissolution decree requiring party to pay other party's attorney fees if legal proceedings are instituted to enforce terms of decree are valid and enforceable. Wesselman v. Wesselman (Butler 1993) 88 Ohio App.3d 338, 623 N.E.2d 1300.

Trial court could apply statutory child support guidelines to separation agreement, following agreement to extent it could while complying with guidelines, and did not thereby abrogate agreement in dissolution of marriage action; agreement provided it was reviewable by court according to terms set forth by law and trial court accommodated agreement and guidelines by permitting deviation from guidelines to extent husband had agreed to make payments which guidelines contemplated as being responsibility of wife. In re Marriage of Stearns (Franklin 1993) 88 Ohio App.3d 264, 623 N.E.2d 711.

If terms of separation agreement are incorporated into decree of dissolution, agreement merges into decree and no longer exists as independent contract; its terms will therefore be enforced as part of decree. Cherry v. Figart (Clermont 1993) 86 Ohio App.3d 123, 620 N.E.2d 174.

Separation agreement incorporated into dissolution decree was binding and was res judicata on issue of property division, where parties did not appeal decree. Cherry v. Figart (Clermont 1993) 86 Ohio App.3d 123, 620 N.E.2d 174.

RC 3105.65(B) does not confer upon a court of common pleas jurisdiction to modify periodic alimony payments provided for in the separation agreement incorporated in the dissolution decree, at least in the absence of a provision in the separation agreement for such modification. Neidenthal v. Neidenthal (Franklin 1987) 41 Ohio App.3d 379, 535 N.E.2d 714.

A court has continuing jurisdiction to modify a decree of alimony if the parties agree to continuing jurisdiction in a separation agreement incorporated into a decree of dissolution of marriage. Merrill v. Merrill (Summit 1985) 26 Ohio App.3d 201, 499 N.E.2d 13, 26 O.B.R. 422.

RC 3105.65(B) does not confer jurisdiction upon a court of common pleas to modify periodic alimony payments provided for in a separation agreement incorporated in a decree of dissolution of marriage, at least in the absence of a provision in the separation agreement for such modification. Alban v. Alban (Franklin 1981) 1 Ohio App.3d 146, 439 N.E.2d 963, 1 O.B.R. 454.

In a dissolution brought under RC 3105.61 et seq., the trial court may grant alimony, but only upon the agreement of both spouses to the terms of alimony which the court has approved; RC 3105.18 does not grant authority to the trial court to decide the terms of alimony independent of such agreement. Ashley v. Ashley (Cuyahoga 1981) 1 Ohio App.3d 80, 439 N.E.2d 911, 1 O.B.R. 359.

The element of consideration necessary for an accord and satisfaction is not satisfied by the promisee husband in regard to his obligation to reimburse his wife for income taxes she incurs pursuant to a separation agreement where there is no loss to the promisee husband and there is no benefit to the promisor wife who accepts $15,000 in full settlement if she does not attempt to recover the $62,000 against her husband to which she is legally entitled. White v White, No. 5-94-31, 1995 WL 114147 (3d Dist Ct App, Hancock, 3-17-95).

The trial court retains jurisdiction to modify alimony payments provided for in a separation agreement which was incorporated in a decree of dissolution, even though the agreement does not specifically provide for such jurisdiction. Werk v Werk, No. CA83-07-049 (12th Dist Ct App, Warren, 4-30-84).

Where a separation agreement incorporated in a decree of dissolution states that the husband will pay all educational expenses including room and board of his adult children, such agreement does not apply to expenses for room and board while such children are living with their mother. In re Fugazzi, Nos. 82AP-174 and 82AP-184 (10th Dist Ct App, Franklin, 6-2-83).

A trial court does not have the right to alter, modify or in any way change a separation agreement of persons who are parties to a dissolution unless the changes are agreed upon by the parties. In re Dissolution of Marriage of Black, No. F-80-7 (6th Dist Ct App, Fulton, 2-13-81).

4. Procedural issues

When party has petitioned for relief from decree of dissolution, remarriage of opposing party is not complete bar to relief, but should be considered by trial court in determining whether such relief is equitable, and motivation of party filing motion can also be considered. In re Whitman (Ohio 1998) 81 Ohio St.3d 239, 690 N.E.2d 535.

The doctrine of res judicata can be invoked to give conclusive effect to a determination of parentage contained in a dissolution decree or a legitimation order, thereby barring a subsequent paternity action brought pursuant to RC Ch 3111. In re Gilbraith (Ohio 1987) 32 Ohio St.3d 127, 512 N.E.2d 956.

The "it is no longer equitable" clause of Civ R 60(B)(4) will not relieve a litigant from the consequences of his voluntary, deliberate choice to enter into a separation agreement in a dissolution of marriage proceeding. Knapp v. Knapp (Ohio 1986) 24 Ohio St.3d 141, 493 N.E.2d 1353, 24 O.B.R. 362.

Any determination of support by trial court in former wife's prior action under Uniform Reciprocal Enforcement of Support Act (URESA) was unaffected by subsequent court proceedings which modified support order, unless subsequent order specifically provided for alteration in the URESA payment. In Matter of Shanyfelt (Ohio App. 3 Dist. 1997) 118 Ohio App.3d 243, 692 N.E.2d 642.

In former wife's action to recover child support and alimony arrearages from former husband, trial court had jurisdiction to grant judgment on terms of parties' original separation agreement, although trial court in another county had previously entered judgment on same issues in former wife's action under Uniform Reciprocal Enforcement of Support Act (URESA). In Matter of Shanyfelt (Ohio App. 3 Dist. 1997) 118 Ohio App.3d 243, 692 N.E.2d 642.

Where disputed clause in separation agreement is subject to more than one interpretation, that is, is ambiguous, court has broad discretion in clarifying ambiguous language by considering not only intent of parties but also equities involved. Weller v. Weller (Lucas 1996) 115 Ohio App.3d 173, 684 N.E.2d 1284.

Evidence supported trial court's finding that former husband failed to prove that his son, who was born with spina bifida and was over 18 years of age, was emancipated for child support purposes; examining physician felt that son would require lifelong assistance and close observation as well as ongoing individualized care from team of specialists; former wife, who was custodial parent, testified she believed son's physical and mental condition made him unemployable; and trial court stated that husband offered no proof that son could perform jobs suggested by husband or that employer would hire son for them. Powell v. Powell (Athens 1996) 111 Ohio App.3d 418, 676 N.E.2d 556.

Motion to convert action for dissolution to divorce action filed three months after hearing on petition for dissolution and almost five months after petition for dissolution was filed was timely under section of dissolution statute providing that motions to convert may be filed at any time before decree of dissolution has been granted. Smith v. Smith (Highland 1995) 101 Ohio App.3d 62, 654 N.E.2d 1342.

Trial court did not retroactively apply statutory child support guidelines in contravention of State and Federal Constitutions when it modified child support set forth in separation agreement which had been incorporated into decree of dissolution of marriage; agreement expressly provided for review by appropriate domestic relations court and effect of trial court's order modifying previous child support provisions was only to make changes from date of original filing of motion for modification of child support. In re Marriage of Stearns (Franklin 1993) 88 Ohio App.3d 264, 623 N.E.2d 711.

Trial court was within its discretion in failing to find husband in contempt, in dissolution of marriage proceeding in which wife sought modification of husband's child support obligation, on ground that husband deposited funds for children's educational expenses into accounts under his control instead of under wife's control as provided in separation agreement incorporated into dissolution decree; neither party had clean hands, as wife had improperly used money from account for children's educational expenses to pay taxes. In re Marriage of Stearns (Franklin 1993) 88 Ohio App.3d 264, 623 N.E.2d 711.

Despite fact that former wife labeled her motion as motion to amend decree of dissolution which incorporated property division provisions of separation agreement, trial court had jurisdiction over motion, even if decree contained no express reservation of jurisdiction to modify; former wife did not seek to amend provisions of decree regarding property division, but merely to enforce agreement of parties. Cherry v. Figart (Clermont 1993) 86 Ohio App.3d 123, 620 N.E.2d 174.

Court does not have jurisdiction to modify terms of property division set forth in separation agreement by parties to dissolution absent express reservation of jurisdiction. Cherry v. Figart (Clermont 1993) 86 Ohio App.3d 123, 620 N.E.2d 174.

A complete in-court separation agreement read into the record and agreed to by both parties may be reduced to judgment by filing of a judgment entry prepared by one of the parties where the other party fails to produce a judgment entry for filing. Gulling v. Gulling (Lorain 1990) 70 Ohio App.3d 410, 591 N.E.2d 349, cause dismissed 60 Ohio St.3d 706, 573 N.E.2d 674.

In a divorce action, the trial court can reject some of the terms of the separation agreement, make an independent ruling on those issues, and incorporate the independent ruling and partial separation agreement into the divorce decree. Welly v. Welly (Williams 1988) 55 Ohio App.3d 111, 562 N.E.2d 914.

A person who has benefited from a decree of dissolution of marriage by relying on it for purposes of remarriage may not attack the judgment of dissolution. Anderson v. Anderson (Greene 1984) 13 Ohio App.3d 194, 468 N.E.2d 784, 13 O.B.R. 242.

If the terms of a separation agreement are incorporated into a decree of divorce or alimony, the separation agreement merges into the decree and no longer exists as an independent contract and its terms will be enforced as part of the decree. If a separation agreement is not incorporated by reference into a divorce or alimony decree, nor declared invalid, but only identified and attached as an exhibit to the divorce or alimony decree, the separation agreement will continue to be a valid and binding contract and its terms will not be enforced as part of the decree, but will be enforced as any other contract. Greiner v. Greiner (Cuyahoga 1979) 61 Ohio App.2d 88, 399 N.E.2d 571, 15 O.O.3d 95.

In a motion for relief from judgment for payment of child support a party must demonstrate that it is no longer equitable that the child support order should have prospective application (1) after a finding of nonpaternity where the child is born during the marriage and the party has no reason to contest paternity, (2) it was not foreseeable to contest paternity at the time of the dissolution of marriage, and (3) it would be inequitable to continue the enforcement of the parentage order when it is clear that the party is not the child's father. Gross v Guenther, No. CA98-08-165, 1999 WL 450210 (12th Dist Ct App, Butler, 6-1-99).

The RC 3105.64 thirty- to-ninety-day time period relates only to the appearance and acknowledgment of the parties, not to the jurisdiction of the trial court so that a court, beyond the ninety-day point, has jurisdiction to enter a dissolution decree and has jurisdiction to entertain a motion to convert the dissolution action into an action for divorce. Smith v Smith, No. 94 CA 847, 1995 WL 57380 (4th Dist Ct App, Highland, 2-8-95).

A party may seek relief under Civ R 60(B)(4) where it would be inequitable for nonmodifiable periodic alimony payments incorporated into a decree of dissolution to have prospective enforcement. Knapp v Knapp, No. 84-CA-7 (4th Dist Ct App, Pickaway, 8-20-85), reversed by 24 OS(3d) 141, 24 OBR 362, 493 NE(2d) 1353 (1986).

Where a court-approved separation agreement provided for the payment of a sum of money, secured by a second mortgage on real estate, and the mortgage was later released in exchange for a cognovit note for the same amount at higher interest, the note was not a payment, modification, or settlement of the order of the court, nor was it an election to rely exclusively on the note; rather the note was a change in the form of evidence of the original judicial obligation, and the court was not deprived of its continuing jurisdiction by such a change. O'Quinn v O'Quinn, No. 8325 (2d Dist Ct App, Montgomery, 1-11-84).

In a dissolution action, until there has been a custody determination by a court based on the best interests of the child, the trial court may modify the prior custody award which was decreed simply as a part of the separation agreement, without compliance with the terms of RC 3109.04. Hoehn v Hoehn, No. 899 (11th Dist Ct App, Geauga, 12-30-80).

Under Ohio law, decree of dissolution of marriage is not "final judgment or decree rendered upon the merits," and cannot be given preclusive effect. In re Edwards (Bkrtcy.S.D.Ohio 1997) 216 B.R. 796.

Under Ohio law, court can accord preclusive effect to dissolution decree. In re Fordu (6th Cir.BAP (Ohio) 1997) 209 B.R. 854.

5. Dismissal

Evidence that, when separation agreement was entered, parties' marital assets had not been fully accounted for or properly valued and that wife had not been adequately representing her interests, but had only signed separation agreement because husband intimidated her established that wife had meritorious defense or claim to present if relief were granted, as required for relief from judgment. McSweeney v. McSweeney (Franklin 1996) 112 Ohio App.3d 355, 678 N.E.2d 969.

Evidence was sufficient to establish that wife could not have discovered, with exercise of due diligence, essential financial facts at time separation agreement was entered into and dissolution decree awarded, as required for relief from judgment; wife had history of being intimidated by husband, who was her ultimate superior at work, testified that she felt coerced and under duress when she signed separation agreement, and only started to look out for her own interests after she had received counseling for approximately six months after dissolution. McSweeney v. McSweeney (Franklin 1996) 112 Ohio App.3d 355, 678 N.E.2d 969.

Although dissolution statute requires trial court to dismiss action if party appears at hearing and indicates dissatisfaction with terms of separation agreement, statute does not require immediate dismissal of action, and if a party has filed motion to convert action into divorce action, court must grant motion to convert. Smith v. Smith (Highland 1995) 101 Ohio App.3d 62, 654 N.E.2d 1342.

Dual representation of the parties to a separation agreement, material nondisclosure of the value of the marital home, and the fact that the movant was undergoing psychotherapy prior to and during the dissolution warrant vacation of a dissolution of marriage incorporating the separation agreement. Longstreet v. Longstreet (Cuyahoga 1989) 57 Ohio App.3d 55, 566 N.E.2d 708.

A dissolution of a marriage under RC 3105.61 et seq. which is contingent upon the parties mutually agreeing on (1) a dissolution and (2) a separation agreement that is approved by the court cannot be countenanced where a court subsequently orders the agreement to be vacated based on incomplete disclosure by one of the parties; to set aside the agreement requires the vacating of the dissolution. Ashley v. Ashley (Cuyahoga 1981) 1 Ohio App.3d 80, 439 N.E.2d 911, 1 O.B.R. 359.

A separation agreement entered into for the sole purpose of a dissolution of marriage is not a valid and binding contract when the dissolution petition is dismissed, but would be a valid and binding contract following dismissal of such petition if it contains language that the agreement shall be binding whether used in a divorce, alimony only, or a dissolution of marriage action, or such similar language evidencing the intent of the parties that it will survive dismissal of a dissolution of marriage petition, and in addition, if it does not contain express language that it was entered into solely for a dissolution of marriage action or express language that the parties intended the separation agreement to survive dismissal of a dissolution of marriage petition, but the actions and conduct of the parties evidence an intention that it will survive dismissal of a dissolution of marriage petition, the separation agreement will continue to be a valid and binding agreement after the dissolution of marriage petition is dismissed. Greiner v. Greiner (Cuyahoga 1979) 61 Ohio App.2d 88, 399 N.E.2d 571, 15 O.O.3d 95.

6. Federal issues

Trial court did not abuse its discretion by failing to give former husband credit for son's Supplemental Security Income (SSI) benefits when calculating husband's child support arrearage and obligation as to son, who was born with spina bifida; trial court's judgment was not unreasonable, arbitrary, or unconscionable, Court of Appeals would not substitute its judgment for that of trial court, and facts did not support conclusion that child support award was inequitable or resulted in windfall. Powell v. Powell (Athens 1996) 111 Ohio App.3d 418, 676 N.E.2d 556.

Congress by enacting provision of Uniformed Services Spouses Protection Act, which authorizes court which has entered dissolution decree for marriage involving member of military to divide military retirement pay for pay periods beginning after June 25, 1981, in accordance with law of jurisdiction, did not intend to override state law, but instead intended to overrule decision of United States Supreme Court in *McCarty* by making it clear that state law could provide for division of military retirement pay after June 25, 1981, without offending federal law. Hester v. Hester (Miami 1996) 110 Ohio App.3d 727, 675 N.E.2d 63, appeal not allowed 77 Ohio St.3d 1445, 671 N.E.2d 1284.

Under Ohio law, agreed dissolution decree entered by Ohio domestic relations court, which dissolved debtor's marriage and recited that parties' separation agreement was fair, just and equitable, did not have claims preclusive effect as to Chapter 7 trustee's fraudulent transfer and preference claims seeking to recover lottery proceeds won by debtor's wife during their marriage and to which debtor waived any claim under separation agreement, since trustee was not in privity with debtor in the dissolution proceeding. In re Fordu (C.A.6 (Ohio) 1999) 201 F.3d 693.

Chapter 7 trustee's actual fraudulent transfer claims could not have been litigated in Ohio marriage dissolution proceeding, as would be required for dissolution decree to have claims preclusive effect in subsequent fraudulent transfer proceedings, since trustee's complaint alleged that debtor transferred his interest in wife's lottery proceeds, as part of parties' separation agreement, with intent to hinder, delay and/or defraud his creditors, and, as an alleged willing participant in this scheme, debtor would not have acted to protect the interest of those same creditors in the dissolution proceeding. In re Fordu (C.A.6 (Ohio) 1999) 201 F.3d 693.

Determination by state appellate courts, that they did not have jurisdiction to relieve Chapter 11 debtor-husband of effects of permanent alimony provision incorporated into final dissolution decree, was not a "final judgment or decree rendered upon the merits," and would not be given preclusive effect in dischargeability proceeding. In re Edwards (Bkrtcy.S.D.Ohio 1997) 216 B.R. 796.

HEALTH AND HOSPITALIZATION INSURANCE COVERAGE

3105.71 Health insurance coverage for spouse and dependents to continue beyond termination of marriage

(A) If a party to an action for divorce, annulment, dissolution of marriage, or legal separation was the named insured or subscriber under, or the policyholder, certificate holder, or contract holder of, a policy, contract, or plan of health insurance that provided health insurance coverage for that party's spouse and dependents immediately prior to the filing of the action, that party shall not cancel or otherwise terminate or cause the termination of such coverage for which the spouse and dependents would otherwise be eligible until the court determines that the party is no longer responsible for providing such health insurance coverage for that party's spouse and dependents.

(B) If the party responsible for providing health insurance coverage for that party's spouse and dependents under division (A) of this section fails to provide that coverage in accordance with that division, the court shall issue an order that includes all of the following:

(1) A requirement that the party make payment to that party's spouse in the amount of any premium that party failed to pay or contribution that party failed to make that resulted in that party's failure to provide health insurance coverage in compliance with division (A) of this section;

(2) A requirement that the party make payment to that party's spouse for reimbursement of any hospital, surgical, and medical expenses incurred as a result of that party's failure to comply with division (A) of this section;

(3) A requirement that, if the party fails to comply with divisions (B)(1) and (2) of this section, the employer of the party deduct from the party's earnings an amount necessary to make any payments required under divisions (B)(1) and (2) of this section.

(C) If the party responsible for providing health insurance coverage for that party's spouse and dependents under division (A) of this section cancels or otherwise terminates or causes the termination of such coverage for which the spouse and dependents would otherwise be eligible, the spouse may apply to the insurer, health insuring corporation, or other third-party payer that provided the coverage for a policy or contract of health insurance. The spouse and dependents shall have the same rights and be subject to the same limitations as a person applying for or covered under a converted or separate policy under section 3923.32 of the Revised Code upon the divorce, annulment, dissolution of marriage, or the legal separation of the spouse from the named insured.

(1997 S 67, eff. 6-4-97; 1990 H 737, eff. 4-11-91)

Historical and Statutory Notes

Amendment Note: 1997 S 67 replaced a reference to health maintenance organizations with language pertaining to health insuring corporations in division (C); and made changes to reflect gender neutral language.

Library References

Divorce ⟹237, 240, 247.
WESTLAW Topic No. 134.
C.J.S. Divorce §§ 373 to 378, 380 to 390, 399, 400, 405 to 413.

Am Jur 2d: 24, Divorce and Separation § 630

Notes of Decisions and Opinions

Termination of coverage 1

1. Termination of coverage

Trial court's denial of former husband's motion to terminate requirement in divorce decree that he pay for wife's health insurance coverage was not unreasonable, notwithstanding fact that it was determined that stipulation erroneously understated wife's income; appropriateness of providing wife with insurance was not affected by misstatement as to wife's income, wife was not eligible for health insurance from her employer since she worked part-time, and working full-time was inappropriate for wife. Goode v. Goode (Franklin 1993) 89 Ohio App.3d 405, 624 N.E.2d 788.

3105.72 Record of action to include social security numbers of parties

The record of any action instituted under this chapter shall include the social security numbers of both parties to the action.

(1997 H 352, eff. 1-1-98)

Library References

OJur 3d: 46, Family Law § 337, 356, 391, 403, 449

PENALTY

3105.99 Penalty

(A)[1] Whoever violates section 3105.02 of the Revised Code shall be fined not less than twenty-five nor more than five hundred dollars or imprisoned not more than six months, or both.

(1953 H 1, eff. 10-1-53; GC 8003-23; Source—GC 13412)

Historical and Statutory Notes

Pre-1953 H 1 Amendments: 124 v S 65

Library References

Constitutional Law ⟜90.2, 90.3.
WESTLAW Topic No. 92.
C.J.S. Constitutional Law §§ 544, 545, 561, 568, 570, 571, 573, 574, 576, 577, 579, 581.

OJur 3d: 46, Family Law § 325

CHAPTER 3107

Adoption

Section

GENERAL PROVISIONS

[1]So in original; there is no paragraph (B).

Uniform Adoption Act

Table of Jurisdictions Wherein Act Has Been Adopted

For text of Uniform Act, and variation notes and annotation materials for adopting jurisdictions, see Uniform Laws Annotated, Master Edition, Volume 9, Pt. I.

Jurisdiction	Statutory Citation
Arkansas	A.C.A. § 9-9-201 to 9-9-224.
North Dakota	NDCC 14-15-01 to 14-15-23.

Comparative Laws

Ariz.—A.R.S. § 8-101 et seq.
Ark.—A.C.A. § 9-9-201.
Fla.—West's F.S.A. § 63.012 et seq.
Ga.—O.C.G.A. § 19-8-1 et seq.
Idaho—I.C. § 16-1501 et seq.
Ill.—ILCS 750 50/1 et seq.
Ind.—West's A.I.C. 31-19-2-1 et seq.
Iowa—I.C.A. § 600.1 et seq.
Ky.—Baldwin's KRS 199.470 et seq.
Mass.—M.G.L.A. c. 210, § 1 et seq.
Me.—18-A M.R.S.A. § 9-101 et seq.
Mich.—M.C.L.A. § 710.21 et seq.
Minn.—M.S.A. § 259.21 et seq.
Mo.—V.A.M.S. § 453.010 et seq.
N.C.—G.S. § 48-1-100 et seq.
Neb.—R.R.S.1943, § 43-101 et seq.
N.J.—N.J.S.A. 9:3-37 et seq.
N.Y.—McKinney's Domestic Relations Law § 109 et seq.
Tenn.—T.C.A. § 36-1-101 et seq.
Tex.—V.T.C.A. Family Code § 162.001 et seq.
Wis.—W.S.A. 48.81 et seq.
W.Va.—Code, 48-4-1 et seq.

Cross References

Children, Ch 3109
Confidentiality of adoption files, courts, Sup R 55
Custody of children, notice of dispositional hearing to prospective adoptive parent, 2151.424

Department of job and family services, division of social administration; care and placement of children; interstate compact on placement of children, 5103.09 to 5103.17, 5103.20 to 5103.28
Designation of heir-at-law, 2105.15
Hearsay exceptions, statements regarding declarant's own adoption, Evid R 804
Parentage, Ch 3111
Parental duty of support, 3103.031
Placement for adoption of children from other states, 2151.39
Powers and duties of county children services board, 5153.16
Registering adoptions; access of adopted individual to birth certificate, 3705.12
Wills, status of pretermitted heirs, 2107.34

Ohio Administrative Code References

ADC-related medicaid, eligibility of adopted children, OAC 5101:1-39-741, 5101:1-39-742, 5101:1-39-772

Adoption assistance for children in permanent and temporary custody, OAC Ch 5101:2-47

AdoptOhio agency, services and responsibilities, OAC Ch 5101:2-48

Department of job and family services, child care agencies, boarding homes, and child care institutions, OAC Ch 5101:2-5 to Ch 5101:2-9
Subsidized adoptions, OAC Ch 5101:2-44
Temporary or permanent custody and placement of children, interstate placements by individuals and courts, OAC Ch 5101:2-42

Library References

Carlin, Baldwin's Ohio Practice, *Merrick-Rippner Probate Law* § 98.2, 98.3, 98.8, 98.31, 108.3 (1997)

Sowald & Morganstern, Baldwin's Ohio Practice, *Domestic Relations Law* § 19.2 (1997)

WESTLAW Electronic Research

See WESTLAW Electronic Research Guide following the Preface.

Law Review and Journal Commentaries

Adoption and Religious Control, Rita E. Hauser. 54 A B A J 771 (August 1968).

Adoption Laws of Ohio: a Critical and Comparative Study, William Yost. 21 Clev St L Rev 1 (September 1972).

Adoption Reform in Ohio, Note. 24 Clev St L Rev 146 (Winter 1975).

Adoption Rights of Natural Parents and Those of Non-parents in Adoption Proceedings, Note. 14 J Fam L 318 (1975).

Adoptions and Their Legal Consequences, John H. Woehrmann. 34 Clev B J 161 (July 1963).

Cohabitants And Constructive Trusts—Comparative Approaches, Robert L. Stenger. 27 J Fam L 373 (1989).

The Emergence Of Wrongful Adoption As A Cause Of Action, Note. 27 J Fam L 475 (1989).

Family Law—Ohio's Statutory Requirement of Legal Guardian Consent to Adoption and Its Effect on the Jurisdiction of the Probate Court, Note. 36 Ohio St L J 451 (1975).

The Historical Background of the American Law of Adoption, Stephen B. Presser. 11 J Fam L 443 (1972).

The Interracial Adoption Implications of Drummond v Fulton County Department of Family and Children Services, Comment. 17 J Fam L 117 (1978-79).

The Law of Adoption in Ohio, Beverly E. Sylvester. 2 Cap U L Rev 23 (1973).

Race And Child Placement: The Best Interests Test And The Cost Of Discretion, Twila L. Perry. 29 J Fam L 51 (1990-91).

Racial Matching and the Adoption Dilemma: Alternatives for the Hard to Place, Note. 17 J Fam L 333 (1978-79).

The Revised Law of Adoption in Ohio, Beverly E. Sylvester. 7 Cap U L Rev 219 (1977).

Transracial Adoption: A Critical View Of The Courts' Present Standards, Note. 28 J Fam L 303 (1990).

Notes of Decisions and Opinions

---

1. Cause of action

No breach of contract suit by adoptive parents against an adoption agency is recognized in Ohio and nowhere in the statutes dealing with adoptions has the general assembly expressly created any cause of action for damages in such a situation; the only cause of action by adoptive parents against adoption agencies sounds in fraud. Allen v. Childrens Services (Cuyahoga 1990) 58 Ohio App.3d 41, 567 N.E.2d 1346, motion overruled 54 Ohio St.3d 709, 561 N.E.2d 944.

2. Parentage

Proceedings under RC Ch 3111 and adoption are not the exclusive legal mechanisms by which paternity may be determined to provide a basis for child support and custody orders; an acknowledgement of paternity under RC 2105.18 provides a sufficient legal basis for such orders. In re Custody of Davis (Guernsey 1987) 41 Ohio App.3d 81, 534 N.E.2d 945.

3. Equitable adoption

In a suit to determine heirs for the purpose of distributing a decedent's estate under the laws of intestate succession, the doctrine of equitable adoption does not apply if there is no evidence of a purported contract or agreement to adopt, and the trial court's order of escheat to the state was proper. Boulger v Unknown Heirs of Robertson, No. 951 (4th Dist Ct App, Ross, 7-1-83).

GENERAL PROVISIONS

3107.01 Definitions

Note: See also following version of this section, eff. 10-5-00.

As used in sections 3107.01 to 3107.19 of the Revised Code:

(A) "Agency" means any public or private organization certified, licensed, or otherwise specially empowered by law or rule to place minors for adoption.

(B) "Attorney" means a person who has been admitted to the bar by order of the Ohio supreme court.

(C) "Child" means a son or daughter, whether by birth or by adoption.

(D) "Court" means the probate courts of this state, and when the context requires, means the court of any other state empowered to grant petitions for adoption.

(E) "Identifying information" means any of the following with regard to a person: first name, last name, maiden name, alias, social security number, address, telephone number, place of employment, number used to identify the person for the purpose of the statewide education management information system established pursuant to section 3301.0714 of the Revised Code, and any other number federal or state law requires or permits to be used to identify the person.

(F) "Minor" means a person under the age of eighteen years.

(G) "Putative father" means a man, including one under age eighteen, who may be a child's father and to whom all of the following apply:

(1) He is not married to the child's mother at the time of the child's conception or birth;

(2) He has not adopted the child;

(3) He has not been determined, prior to the date a petition to adopt the child is filed, to have a parent and child relationship with the child by a court proceeding pursuant to sections 3111.01 to 3111.19 of the Revised Code, a court proceeding in another state, an administrative agency proceeding pursuant to sections 3111.20 to 3111.29 of the Revised Code, or an administrative agency proceeding in another state;

(4) He has not acknowledged paternity of the child pursuant to section 5101.314 of the Revised Code.

(1997 H 352, eff. 1-1-98; 1997 H 408, eff. 10-1-97; 1996 H 274, eff. 9-18-96; 1996 H 419, eff. 9-18-96; 1976 H 156, eff. 1-1-77)

Note: See also following version of this section, eff. 10-5-00.

3107.01 Definitions

Note: See also preceding version of this section, in effect until 10-5-00.

As used in sections 3107.01 to 3107.19 of the Revised Code:

(A) "Agency" means any public or private organization certified, licensed, or otherwise specially empowered by law or rule to place minors for adoption.

(B) "Attorney" means a person who has been admitted to the bar by order of the Ohio supreme court.

(C) "Child" means a son or daughter, whether by birth or by adoption.

(D) "Court" means the probate courts of this state, and when the context requires, means the court of any other state empowered to grant petitions for adoption.

(E) "Foster caregiver" has the same meaning as in section 5103.02 of the Revised Code.

(F) "Identifying information" means any of the following with regard to a person: first name, last name, maiden name, alias, social security number, address, telephone number, place of employment, number used to identify the person for the purpose of the statewide education management information system established pursuant to section 3301.0714 of the Revised Code, and any other number federal or state law requires or permits to be used to identify the person.

(G) "Minor" means a person under the age of eighteen years.

(H) "Putative father" means a man, including one under age eighteen, who may be a child's father and to whom all of the following apply:

(1) He is not married to the child's mother at the time of the child's conception or birth;

(2) He has not adopted the child;

(3) He has not been determined, prior to the date a petition to adopt the child is filed, to have a parent and child relationship with the child by a court proceeding pursuant to sections 3111.01 to 3111.19 of the Revised Code, a court proceeding in another state, an administrative agency proceeding pursuant to sections 3111.20 to 3111.29 of the Revised Code, or an administrative agency proceeding in another state;

(4) He has not acknowledged paternity of the child pursuant to section 5101.314 of the Revised Code.

(2000 H 448, eff. 10-5-00; 1997 H 352, eff. 1-1-98; 1997 H 408, eff. 10-1-97; 1996 H 274, eff. 9-18-96; 1996 H 419, eff. 9-18-96; 1976 H 156, eff. 1-1-77)

Note: See also preceding version of this section, in effect until 10-5-00.

Uncodified Law

1996 H 419, § 5: See Uncodified Law under 3107.06.

Historical and Statutory Notes

Ed. Note: Former 3107.01 repealed by 1976 H 156, eff. 1-1-77; 1973 S 1; 1953 H 1; GC 8004-1; Source—GC 10512-9.

Pre-1953 H 1 Amendments: 124 v S 65

Amendment Note: 2000 H 448 added new division (E) and redesignated former divisions (E) through (G) as new divisions (F) through (H).

Amendment Note: 1997 H 352 substituted "5101.314" for "2105.18" in division (G)(4).

Amendment Note: 1997 H 408 deleted former division (G); and redesignated former division (H) as new division (G). Prior to deletion, former division (G) read:

"(G)'Private child placing agency,' 'private noncustodial agency,' and 'public children services agency' have the same meanings as in section 2151.011 of the Revised Code."

Amendment Note: 1996 H 274 added division (H)(4).

Amendment Note: 1996 H 419 rewrote this section, which previously read:

"As used in sections 3107.01 to 3107.19 of the Revised Code, unless the context otherwise requires:

"(A) 'Child' means a son or daughter, whether by birth or by adoption;

"(B) 'Court' means the probate courts of this state, and when the context requires, means the court of any other state empowered to grant petitions for adoption;

"(C) 'Minor' means a person under the age of eighteen years;

"(D) 'Agency' means any public or private organization certified, licensed, or otherwise specially empowered by law or rule to place minors for adoption."

Cross References

Age of majority, 3109.01
Conditions for juvenile court approving parent's agreement for childs' adoption, identifying information defined, 5103.151
Department of human resources, division of social administration, placing of children, 5103.16
Duty of parents to support children of unemancipated minor children, 3109.19
Jurisdiction of juvenile court, 2151.23
Jurisdiction of probate court, 2101.24

Ohio Administrative Code References

AdoptOhio, adoption, OAC Ch 5101:2-48

Library References

Adoption ⟹1.
WESTLAW Topic No. 17.
C.J.S. Adoption of Persons §§ 2 to 4.
OJur 3d: 32, Decedents' Estates § 622; 47, Family Law § 898, 901, 906, 910
Am Jur 2d: 2, Adoption § 1, 11

What constitutes "duress" in obtaining parent's consent to adoption of child or surrender of child to adoption agency. 74 ALR3d 527

Baldwin's Ohio Legislative Service, 1996 H 419—LSC Analysis, 3/L-336

Carlin, Baldwin's Ohio Practice, *Merrick-Rippner Probate Law* § 3.2, 98.2, 98.5, 98.27, 98.29, 98.39, 98.53 (1997)
Sowald & Morganstern, Baldwin's Ohio Practice, *Domestic Relations Law* § 3.9, 22.19 (1997)

Law Review and Journal Commentaries

Advertising for Adoption Placement: Gray Market Activities in a Gray Area of Constitutional Protection, Comment. 25 Duq L Rev 129 (Fall 1986).

Ohio House Bill 419: Increased Openness in Adoption Records Law, Wendy L. Weiss. 45 Clev St L Rev 101 (1997).

Notes of Decisions and Opinions

---

1. In general

Goal of adoption statutes is to protect best interests of children, which is best accomplished in cases where adoption is necessary by providing child with permanent and stable home and ensuring that adoption process is completed in expeditious manner. In re Adoption of Zschach (Ohio 1996) 75 Ohio St.3d 648, 665 N.E.2d 1070, reconsideration denied 76 Ohio St.3d 1410, 666 N.E.2d 569, certiorari denied 117 S.Ct. 582, 136 L.Ed.2d 513.

Adoption is a function which requires the exercise of the judicial power which is vested in the courts of Ohio pursuant to O Const Art IV §4. (Annotation from former RC 3107.06.) State ex rel. Portage County Welfare Dept. v. Summers (Ohio 1974) 38 Ohio St.2d 144, 311 N.E.2d 6, 67 O.O.2d 151.

The main purpose of adoption is to find homes for children, not children for families. (Annotation from former RC 3107.01.) (See also In re Harshey, 40 App(2d) 157, 318 NE(2d) 544 (1974).) In re Harshey (Cuyahoga 1975) 45 Ohio App.2d 97, 341 N.E.2d 616, 74 O.O.2d 120.

The adoption of children exists in this country only by virtue of statute. There is no common law adoption. (Annotation from former RC 3107.01.) Belden v. Armstrong (Summit 1951) 93 Ohio App. 307, 113 N.E.2d 693, 51 O.O. 62.

Adoption is purely statutory, and statutory provisions should be strictly complied with. (Annotation from former RC 3107.01.) In re Privette (Franklin 1932) 45 Ohio App. 51, 185 N.E. 435, 12 Ohio Law Abs. 652, 38 Ohio Law Rep. 90.

The statutes of Ohio do not require, as a condition of the adoption of a minor child, either that child be a citizen of the United States, or that its natural parents, or either of them, be citizens. (Annotation from former RC 3107.01.) 1920 OAG p 1038.

2. Jurisdiction

Original and exclusive jurisdiction over adoption proceedings is vested specifically in the probate court pursuant to RC Ch 3107. (Annotation from former RC 3107.01.) State ex rel. Portage County Welfare Dept. v. Summers (Ohio 1974) 38 Ohio St.2d 144, 311 N.E.2d 6, 67 O.O.2d 151.

The refusal of consent to an adoption by a "certified organization," as defined in RC 3107.01(C), does not impair the jurisdiction of the probate court, but the recommendations and the reports, filed pursuant to RC 3107.05 and 3107.10, are to be considered, in conjunction with all other evidence adduced in the proceeding, by the court in deciding the issues presented by RC 3107.09. (Annotation from former RC 3107.01.) State ex rel. Portage County Welfare Dept. v. Summers (Ohio 1974) 38 Ohio St.2d 144, 311 N.E.2d 6, 67 O.O.2d 151.

Probate court has duty of making adoption ruling based on all evidence presented to it, and such evidence can include testimony of natural parent. In re Adoption of Lassiter (Clark 1995) 101 Ohio App.3d 367, 655 N.E.2d 781, dismissed, appeal not allowed 73 Ohio St.3d 1410, 651 N.E.2d 1308.

While natural parents entrusted with the permanent custody of their children may deprive a probate court of jurisdiction to enter a decree of adoption by withholding their consent to the adoption, the refusal of consent to an adoption by a "certified agency" as defined in RC 3107.01(C) does not impair the jurisdiction of the probate court to fully hear and determine an adoption proceeding. (Annotation from former RC 3107.01.) (See also In re Harshey, 45 App(2d) 97, 341 NE(2d) 616 (1975).) In re Harshey (Cuyahoga 1974) 40 Ohio App.2d 157, 318 N.E.2d 544, 69 O.O.2d 165.

By this section, exclusive jurisdiction is conferred upon probate court in proceedings for adoption. (Annotation from former RC 3107.01.) Eastman v Brewer, 20 Abs 597 (App, Cuyahoga 1935).

3. Consent

Where parents, by contract, surrender the permanent custody and control of their child to an approved child care agency with authority to give consent to the adoption of such child under GC 1352-12 (RC 5103.15), such approved child care agency is the only one authorized to give consent to adoption, as long as the contract of permanent surrender remains in force, and is a necessary party to a proceeding to adopt such child. (Annotation from former RC 3107.01.) In re Bolling's Adoption (Cuyahoga 1948) 83 Ohio App. 1, 82 N.E.2d 135, 52 Ohio Law Abs. 572, 38 O.O. 122.

An order stating that the consent of a natural parent to the adoption of her child is not necessary is a "final appealable order" within the meaning of RC 2505.02 since such an order affects a substantial right, and a court therefore cannot vacate a consent order sua sponte. In re Adoption of Daniel B, No. L-93-306, 1994 WL 374196 (6th Dist Ct App, Lucas, 6-15-94).

Refusal of consent to an adoption by an individual or agency having permanent custody of a child, does not deprive the court of jurisdiction, but raises the issues of the best interest and welfare of the child. (Annotation from former RC 3107.01.) In re Haun (Ohio Prob. 1971) 31 Ohio Misc. 9, 277 N.E.2d 258, 58 O.O.2d 336, 60

O.O.2d 154, affirmed 31 Ohio App.2d 63, 286 N.E.2d 478, 60 O.O.2d 163.

Mother of illegitimate child has right to withdraw her consent to adoption of her child at any time before court acts upon such consent and in so doing dismisses the petition for the adoption of the child and deprives the court of proceeding further with the case. (Annotation from former RC 3107.01.) In re Adoption of Rubin, 33 Abs 108 (Prob, Belmont 1941).

Probate court cannot decree an adoption, unless mother of child files written consent with court, and mother may withdraw such consent any time before decree. (Annotation from former RC 3107.01.) State ex rel Scholder v Scholder, 2 Abs 471, 22 OLR 608 (App, Summit 1924).

4. Inheritance

Contract to receive child by adoption and as apprentice, to be maintained, clothed, educated, and treated like natural child of persons receiving child, does not show intention to adopt child as heir. (Annotation from former RC 3107.01.) Sisson v. Irish (Cuyahoga 1926) 23 Ohio App. 462, 155 N.E. 168, 4 Ohio Law Abs. 768, 6 Ohio Law Abs. 470.

Contract to receive child by adoption and as apprentice, containing no tangible rights with respect to heirship in existence at time of contract and no reference to property which might come into possession or ownership at later date, cannot be specifically enforced. (Annotation from former RC 3107.01.) Sisson v. Irish (Cuyahoga 1926) 23 Ohio App. 462, 155 N.E. 168, 4 Ohio Law Abs. 768, 6 Ohio Law Abs. 470.

5. Right to counsel

No action to recover damages for breach of a contract of marriage will lie where the parties are related as first cousins. Reed v. Reed (Ohio 1892) 49 Ohio St. 654, 29 W.L.B. 48, 32 N.E. 750.

Approval by the court of the permanent surrender of a child is purely an administrative matter, and not in the nature of an adversary proceeding; the court has no duty to advise the mother of her right to counsel or to appoint a lawyer for her in the event of indigency. (Annotation from former RC 3107.01.) In re K. (Ohio Juv. 1969) 31 Ohio Misc. 218, 282 N.E.2d 370, 60 O.O.2d 134, 60 O.O.2d 388.

3107.011 Representation by agency or attorney

A person seeking to adopt a minor shall utilize an agency or attorney to arrange the adoption. Only an agency or attorney may arrange an adoption. An attorney may not represent with regard to the adoption both the person seeking to adopt and the parent placing a child for adoption.

Any person may informally aid or promote an adoption by making a person seeking to adopt a minor aware of a minor who will be or is available for adoption.

(1996 H 419, eff. 9-18-96)

Library References

Am Jur 2d: 2, Adoption § 9 to 13, 47

Adoption of child in absence of statutorily required consent of public or private agency or institution. 83 ALR3d 373

Criminal liability of one arranging for adoption of child through other than licensed child placement agency ("baby broker acts"). 3 ALR4th 468

Required parties in adoption proceedings. 48 ALR4th 860

Baldwin's Ohio Legislative Service, 1996 H 419—LSC Analysis, 3/L-336

Carlin, Baldwin's Ohio Practice, *Merrick-Rippner Probate Law* § 98.2 (1997)

Sowald & Morganstern, Baldwin's Ohio Practice, *Domestic Relations Law* § 3.9 (1997)

Notes of Decisions and Opinions

1. —Relative, person "arranging" adoption

A grandmother who arranges the adoption of her grandchild with a prospective adoptive parent violates RC 3107.011 and in such a case it is beyond the trial court's discretion to impose a penalty and to exclude the interested person as a prospective adoptive parent based on the grandmother's violation. In re Adoption of Baby Doe, No. 19279, 1999 WL 241379 (9th Dist Ct App, Summit, 4-14-99).

3107.012 Home study assessor; requirements

Note: See also following version of this section, eff. 10-5-00.

(A) Except as provided in division (B) of this section, only an individual who meets all of the following requirements may perform the duties of an assessor under sections 3107.031, 3107.082, 3107.09, 3107.12, and 5103.152 of the Revised Code:

(1) The individual must be in the employ of, appointed by, or under contract with a court, public children services agency, private child placing agency, or private noncustodial agency;

(2) The individual must be one of the following:

(a) A professional counselor or social worker licensed under Chapter 4757. of the Revised Code;

(b) A psychologist licensed under Chapter 4732. of the Revised Code;

(c) A student working to earn a post-secondary degree who conducts assessor's duties under the supervision of a professional counselor or social worker licensed under Chapter 4757. of the Revised Code or a psychologist licensed under Chapter 4732. of the Revised Code;

(d) A civil service employee engaging in social work without a license under Chapter 4757. of the Revised Code, as permitted by division (A)(5) of section 4757.41 of the Revised Code.

(3) The individual must complete education programs in accordance with rules adopted under section 3107.013 of the Revised Code.

(B) An individual in the employ of, appointed by, or under contract with a court prior to September 18, 1996, to conduct adoption investigations of prospective adoptive parents may perform the duties of an assessor under sections 3107.031, 3107.082, 3107.09, 3107.12, and 5103.152 of the Revised Code if the individual complies with division (A)(3) of this section regardless of whether the individual meets the requirement of division (A)(2) of this section.

(C) A court, public children services agency, private child placing agency, or private noncustodial agency may employ, appoint, or contract with an assessor in the county in which a petition for adoption is filed and in any other county or location outside this state where information needed to complete or supplement the assessor's duties may be obtained. More than one assessor may be utilized for an adoption.

(1998 H 446, eff. 8-5-98; 1996 H 419, eff. 9-18-96)

Note: See also following version of this section, eff. 10-5-00.

3107.012 Application for adoption by foster caregiver seeking to adopt foster child

Note: See also preceding version of this section, in effect until 10-5-00.

(A) A foster caregiver may use the application prescribed under division (B) of this section to obtain the services of an agency to arrange an adoption for the foster caregiver if the foster caregiver seeks to adopt the foster caregiver's foster child who has resided in the foster caregiver's home for at least twelve months prior to the date the foster caregiver submits the application to the agency.

(B) The department of job and family services shall prescribe an application for a foster caregiver to use under division (A) of this section. The application shall not require that the foster caregiver provide any information the foster caregiver already provided the department, or undergo an inspection the foster caregiver already underwent, to obtain a foster home certificate under section 5103.03 of the Revised Code.

(C) An agency that receives an application prescribed under division (B) of this section from a foster caregiver authorized to use the application shall not require, as a condition of the agency accepting or approving the application, that the foster caregiver undergo a criminal records check under section 2151.86 of the Revised Code as a prospective adoptive parent. The agency shall inform the foster caregiver, in accordance with division (G) of section 2151.86 of the Revised Code, that the foster caregiver must undergo the criminal records check before a court may issue a final decree of adoption or interlocutory order of adoption under section 3107.14 of the Revised Code.

(2000 H 448, eff. 10-5-00)

Note: See also preceding version of this section, in effect until 10-5-00.

Historical and Statutory Notes

Ed. Note: Former 3107.012 amended and recodified as 3107.014 by 2000 H 448, eff. 10-5-00; 1998 H 446, eff. 8-5-98; 1996 H 419, eff. 9-18-96.

3107.013 Education programs for assessors

Note: See also following version of this section, eff. 10-5-00.

Not later than ninety days after the effective date of this section, the director of job and family services shall adopt rules in accordance with Chapter 119. of the Revised Code governing the education programs an individual must complete for the purpose of division (A)(3) of section 3107.012 of the Revised Code. The education programs shall include courses on adoption placement practice, federal and state adoption assistance programs, and post adoption support services.

(1999 H 471, eff. 7-1-00; 1996 H 419, eff. 6-20-96)

Note: See also following version of this section, eff. 10-5-00.

3107.013 Information about adoption

Note: See also preceding version of this section, in effect until 10-5-00.

An agency arranging an adoption pursuant to an application submitted to the agency under section 3107.012 of the Revised Code for a foster caregiver seeking to adopt the foster caregiver's foster child shall offer to provide the foster caregiver information about adoption, including information about state adoption law, adoption assistance available pursuant to section 5153.163 of the Revised Code and Title IV-E of the "Social Security Act," 94 Stat. 501, 42 U.S.C.A. 670 (1980), as amended, and other adoption issues the department of job and family services identifies. If the foster caregiver informs the agency that the foster caregiver wants the information, the agency shall provide the information to the foster caregiver in accordance with rules the department of job and family services shall adopt in accordance with Chapter 119. of the Revised Code.

(2000 H 448, eff. 10-5-00)

Note: See also preceding version of this section, in effect until 10-5-00.

Historical and Statutory Notes

Ed. Note: Former 3107.013 amended and recodified as 3107.015 by 2000 H 448, eff. 10-5-00; 1999 H 471, eff. 7-1-00; 1996 H 419, eff. 6-20-96.

3107.014 Home study assessor; requirements

(A) Except as provided in division (B) of this section, only an individual who meets all of the following requirements may perform the duties of an assessor under sections 3107.031, 3107.082, 3107.09, 3107.12, 5103.0324, and 5103.152 of the Revised Code:

(1) The individual must be in the employ of, appointed by, or under contract with a court, public children services agency, private child placing agency, or private noncustodial agency;

(2) The individual must be one of the following:

(a) A professional counselor or social worker licensed under Chapter 4757. of the Revised Code;

(b) A psychologist licensed under Chapter 4732. of the Revised Code;

(c) A student working to earn a post-secondary degree who conducts assessor's duties under the supervision of a professional counselor or social worker licensed under Chapter 4757. of the Revised Code or a psychologist licensed under Chapter 4732. of the Revised Code;

(d) A civil service employee engaging in social work without a license under Chapter 4757. of the Revised Code, as permitted by division (A)(5) of section 4757.41 of the Revised Code;

(e) A former employee of a public children services agency who, while so employed, conducted the duties of an assessor.

(3) The individual must complete education programs in accordance with rules adopted under section 3107.015 of the Revised Code.

(B) An individual in the employ of, appointed by, or under contract with a court prior to September 18, 1996, to conduct adoption investigations of prospective adoptive parents may perform the duties of an assessor under sections 3107.031, 3107.082, 3107.09, 3107.12, 5103.0324, and 5103.152 of the Revised Code if the individual complies with division (A)(3) of this section regardless of whether the individual meets the requirement of division (A)(2) of this section.

(C) A court, public children services agency, private child placing agency, or private noncustodial agency may employ, appoint, or contract with an assessor in the county in which a petition for adoption is filed and in any other county or location outside this state where information needed to complete or supplement the assessor's duties may be obtained. More than one assessor may be utilized for an adoption.

(2000 H 448, eff. 10-5-00)

Historical and Statutory Notes

Ed. Note: 3107.014 is former 3107.012, amended and recodified by 2000 H 448, eff. 10-5-00; 1998 H 446, eff. 8-5-98; 1996 H 419, eff. 9-18-96.

Amendment Note: 2000 H 448 inserted "5103.0324" in divisions (A) and (B); added new division (A)(2)(e); and substituted "3107.015" for "3107.013" in division (A)(3).

Amendment Note: 1998 H 446 substituted "in the employ of, appointed by," for "employed by" and inserted "court," in division (A)(1); substituted "division (A)(5) of section 4757.41" for "division (E) of section 4757.16" in division (A)(2)(d); rewrote division (B); and added division (C). Prior to amendment, division (B) read:

"(B) An individual employed by a court prior to the effective date of this section to conduct home studies of prospective adoptive parents may conduct home studies under section 3107.031 of the Revised Code if the individual complies with division (A)(3) of this section."

Cross References

Probate courts, appointment of assessors, 2101.11

Library References

Am Jur 2d: 2, Adoption § 147

Baldwin's Ohio Legislative Service, 1996 H 419—LSC Analysis, 3/L-336

Carlin, Baldwin's Ohio Practice, *Merrick-Rippner Probate Law* § 98.2, 98.21, 98.26 (1997)

Sowald & Morganstern, Baldwin's Ohio Practice, *Domestic Relations Law* § 3.9 (1997)

3107.015 Education programs for assessors

Not later than ninety days after June 20, 1996, the director of job and family services shall adopt rules in accordance with Chapter 119. of the Revised Code governing the education programs an individual must complete for the purpose of division (A)(3) of section 3107.014 of the Revised Code. The education programs shall include courses on adoption placement practice, federal and state adoption assistance programs, and post adoption support services.

(2000 H 448, eff. 10-5-00)

Historical and Statutory Notes

Ed. Note: 3107.015 is former 3107.013, amended and recodified by 2000 H 448, eff. 10-5-00; 1999 H 471, eff. 7-1-00; 1996 H 419, eff. 6-20-96.

Amendment Note: 2000 H 448 substituted "June 20, 1996" for "the effective date of this section" and "3107.014" for "3107.012".

Amendment Note: 1999 H 471 substituted "director of job and family services" for "department of human services".

Ohio Administrative Code References

Adoption agency staffing, OAC 5101:2-48-06

AdoptOhio, agency agreements, OAC 5101:2-48-04

Postfinalization services, OAC 5101:2-48-18

Library References

Baldwin's Ohio Legislative Service, 1996 H 419—LSC Analysis, 3/L-336

Carlin, Baldwin's Ohio Practice, *Merrick-Rippner Probate Law* § 98.2 (1997)

3107.016 Schedule of education programs

The department of job and family services shall develop a schedule of education programs that meet the requirements established in rules adopted pursuant to section 3107.015 of the Revised Code. The schedule shall include enough programs to provide all agencies equal access to the programs. The department shall distribute the schedule to all agencies.

(2000 H 448, eff. 10-5-00)

3107.02 Persons who may be adopted

Note: See also following version of this section, eff. 10-5-00.

(A) Any minor may be adopted.

(B) An adult may be adopted under any of the following conditions:

(1) If he is totally and permanently disabled;

(2) If he is determined to be a mentally retarded person as defined in section 5123.01 of the Revised Code;

(3) If he had established a child-foster parent or child-stepparent relationship with the petitioners as a minor, and he consents to the adoption.

(C) When proceedings to adopt a minor are initiated by the filing of a petition, and the eighteenth birthday of the minor occurs prior to the decision of the court, the court shall require the person who is to be adopted to submit a written statement of consent or objection to the adoption. If an objection is submitted, the petition shall be dismissed, and if a consent is submitted, the court shall proceed with the case, and may issue an interlocutory order or final decree of adoption.

(1984 H 71, eff. 9-20-84; 1981 H 1; 1976 H 156)
Note: See also following version of this section, eff. 10-5-00.

3107.02 Persons who may be adopted

Note: See also preceding version of this section, in effect until 10-5-00.

(A) Any minor may be adopted.

(B) An adult may be adopted under any of the following conditions:

(1) If the adult is totally and permanently disabled;

(2) If the adult is determined to be a mentally retarded person as defined in section 5123.01 of the Revised Code;

(3) If the adult had established a child-foster caregiver or child-stepparent relationship with the petitioners as a minor, and the adult consents to the adoption.

(C) When proceedings to adopt a minor are initiated by the filing of a petition, and the eighteenth birthday of the minor occurs prior to the decision of the court, the court shall require the person who is to be adopted to submit a written statement of consent or objection to the adoption. If an objection is submitted, the petition shall be dismissed, and if a consent is submitted, the court shall proceed with the case, and may issue an interlocutory order or final decree of adoption.

(2000 H 448, eff. 10-5-00; 1984 H 71, eff. 9-20-84; 1981 H 1; 1976 H 156)
Note: See also preceding version of this section, in effect until 10-5-00.

Historical and Statutory Notes

Ed. Note: Former 3107.02 repealed by 1976 H 156, eff. 1-1-77; 1953 H 1; GC 8004-2; Source—GC 10512-10; see now 3107.03 for provisions analogous to former 3107.02.

Pre-1953 H 1 Amendments: 124 v S 65

Amendment Note: 2000 H 448 substituted "caregiver" for "parent" in division (B)(3); and made changes to reflect gender neutral language.

Cross References

Department of job and family services, division of social administration; care and placement of children; interstate compact on placement of children, 5103.09 to 5103.17, 5103.20 to 5103.28

Department of job and family services, lists of prospective adoptive children and parents, 5103.154

Designation of heir-at-law, 2105.15

Placement for adoption of children from other states, 2151.39

Powers and duties of county children services board, 5153.16

Ohio Administrative Code References

AdoptOhio, adoption, OAC Ch 5101:2-48

Eligibility of child for subsidized adoption, OAC 5101:2-44-05

Library References

Adoption ⟜5.

WESTLAW Topic No. 17.

C.J.S. Adoption of Persons §§ 18 to 24.

OJur 3d: 47, Family Law § 903, 906

Am Jur 2d: 2, Adoption § 10, 11, 54

Mental illness and the like of parents as ground for adoption of their children. 45 ALR2d 1379

Adoption of child in absence of statutorily required consent of public or private agency or institution. 83 ALR3d 373

Carlin, Baldwin's Ohio Practice, *Merrick-Rippner Probate Law* § 15.28, 17.3, 98.2, 98.4, 98.5, 98.53 (1997)

Notes of Decisions and Opinions

Adoption of adult 3
Eligibility to adopt 2
Rights of adoptee 1

---

1. Rights of adoptee

An adult who is adopted pursuant to RC 3107.02(B)(3), and thus is a "child" by definition under RC 3107.01(A), has the same status and the same rights as a person who is a minor at the time of adoption. Solomon v. Central Trust Co. of Northeastern Ohio, N.A. (Ohio 1992) 63 Ohio St.3d 35, 584 N.E.2d 1185.

2. Eligibility to adopt

Under RC 3107.03(B), an unmarried adult in Ohio is an eligible person to adopt those persons specified in RC 3107.02. In re Adoption of Charles B. (Ohio 1990) 50 Ohio St.3d 88, 552 N.E.2d 884.

While an unmarried adult in Ohio is eligible to adopt, the right is permissive and not absolute as both RC 3107.02 and 3107.03 use the verb "may." In re Adoption of Charles B. (Ohio 1990) 50 Ohio St.3d 88, 552 N.E.2d 884.

3. Adoption of adult

Evidence that petitioners and an eighteen-year-old orphan had developed strong emotional ties, mutual affection for each other, and a showing that petitioners' children and the adult orphan had developed a sibling relationship is insufficient to support a petition for the adoption of an adult based upon a child-foster parent or child-stepparent relationship established during the minority of such adult where there is no evidence that petitioners contributed financial support, provided schooling, medical care, or a residence to the adult orphan. In re Adoption of Huitzil (Butler 1985) 29 Ohio App.3d 222, 504 N.E.2d 1173, 29 O.B.R. 267.

Relationship involving emotional support, guidance, love, and affection existed between birth father and adult child, during child's minority and into his majority, such that father would be permitted to adopt child, who had previously been adopted by step-father pursuant to birth father's consent. Matter of Huskins (Ohio Com.Pl. 1997) 89 Ohio Misc.2d 13, 692 N.E.2d 1105.

3107.03 Persons who may adopt

The following persons may adopt:

(A) A husband and wife together, at least one of whom is an adult;

(B) An unmarried adult;

(C) The unmarried minor parent of the person to be adopted;

(D) A married adult without the other spouse joining as a petitioner if any of the following apply:

(1) The other spouse is a parent of the person to be adopted and supports the adoption;

(2) The petitioner and the other spouse are separated under section 3103.06 or 3105.17 of the Revised Code;

(3) The failure of the other spouse to join in the petition or to support the adoption is found by the court to be by reason of prolonged unexplained absence, unavailability, incapacity, or circumstances that make it impossible or unreasonably difficult to obtain either the support or refusal of the other spouse.

(1996 H 419, eff. 9-18-96; 1976 H 156, eff. 1-1-77)

Historical and Statutory Notes

Ed. Note: 3107.03 is analogous to former 3107.02, repealed by 1976 H 156, eff. 1-1-77.

Ed. Note: Former 3107.03 repealed by 1976 H 156, eff. 1-1-77; 1969 S 49; 1953 H 1; GC 8004-3; Source—GC 10512-11; see now 3107.05 for provisions analogous to former 3107.03.

Pre-1953 H 1 Amendments: 124 v S 65

Amendment Note: 1996 H 419 substituted "supports," "support," and "support" for "consents to," "consent to," and "consent," respectively, in divisions (D)(1) and (3).

Cross References

Department of job and family services, lists of prospective adoptive children and parents, 5103.154
Department of job and family services, placing of children, assumption of responsibility for expenses, 5103.16
Designation of heir-at-law, 2105.15
Parent and child relationship, definition and establishment, 3111.01, 3111.02
Powers and duties of county children services board, 5153.16

Ohio Administrative Code References

AdoptOhio, adoption, OAC Ch 5101:2-48
Eligibility of adoptive parents for subsidized adoption, OAC 5101:2-44-06

Library References

Adoption ⚷4.
WESTLAW Topic No. 17.
C.J.S. Adoption of Persons §§ 13 to 17, 23, 24.

OJur 3d: 47, Family Law § 903
Am Jur 2d: 2, Adoption § 10, 11, 54
Race as factor in adoption proceedings. 54 ALR2d 909
Requirements as to residence or domicil of adoptee or adoptive parent for purposes of adoption. 33 ALR3d 176
Religion as factor in adoption proceedings. 48 ALR3d 383
Adoption of child in absence of statutorily required consent of public or private agency or institution. 83 ALR3d 373
Age of prospective parents as factor in adoption proceedings. 84 ALR3d 665

Marital status of prospective adopting parents as factor in adoption proceeding. 2 ALR4th 555

Adoption of child by same-sex partners. 27 ALR5th 54

Baldwin's Ohio Legislative Service, 1996 H 419—LSC Analysis, 3/L-336

Carlin, Baldwin's Ohio Practice, *Merrick-Rippner Probate Law* § 98.2, 98.3, 98.4, 98.8 (1997)

Sowald & Morganstern, Baldwin's Ohio Practice, *Domestic Relations Law* § 2.73 (1997)

Law Review and Journal Commentaries

An Alternative Placement for Children in Adoption Law: Allowing Homosexuals the Right to Adopt, Comment. 18 Ohio N U L Rev 631 (1992).

In Re Adoption Of Charles B.—A Tough Act To Follow, Note. 24 Akron L Rev 447 (Fall 1990).

Open Adoption in Kentucky: Public Attitudes, the Present Law, and Proposed Changes, Elizabeth Lewis Rompf and John H. Rompf, Jr. III Ky Children's Rts J 11 (Spring 1993).

The Opportunities, Or Lack Thereof, For Homosexual Adults To Adopt Children—*In re Adoption of Charles B*, 50 Ohio St. 3d 88, 553 N.E.2d 884 (1990), Note. 16 U Dayton L Rev 471 (Winter 1991).

Race And Child Placement: The Best Interests Test And The Cost Of Discretion, Twila L. Perry. 29 J Fam L 51 (1990-91).

The Right of the Thwarted Father to Veto the Adoption of His Child, Comment. 62 U Cin L Rev 1695 (Spring 1994).

Notes of Decisions and Opinions

Ethnic heritage 4
Jurisdiction 2
Natural parent adoption 3
Stepparent 5
Unmarried adult 1

1. Unmarried adult

Under RC 3107.03(B), an unmarried adult in Ohio is an eligible person to adopt those persons specified in RC 3107.02. In re Adoption of Charles B. (Ohio 1990) 50 Ohio St.3d 88, 552 N.E.2d 884.

While an unmarried adult in Ohio is eligible to adopt, the right is permissive and not absolute as both RC 3107.02 and 3107.03 use the verb "may." In re Adoption of Charles B. (Ohio 1990) 50 Ohio St.3d 88, 552 N.E.2d 884.

The concepts of homosexuality and adoption are so inherently mutually exclusive and inconsistent, if not hostile, that the legislature never considered it necessary to enact an express ineligibility provision; however, homosexuals are ineligible to adopt as a matter of law. In re Adoption of Charles B., No. CA-3382 (5th Dist Ct App, Licking, 10-28-88), reversed by 50 OS(3d) 88, 552 NE(2d) 884 (1990).

2. Jurisdiction

A probate court has jurisdiction to hear and determine an adoption proceeding relating to a minor child notwithstanding the fact that the custody of such child is at the time within the continuing jurisdiction of a divorce court. (Annotation from former RC 3107.02.) In re Adoption of Biddle (Ohio 1958) 168 Ohio St. 209, 152 N.E.2d 105, 6 O.O.2d 4, on remand 163 N.E.2d 188, 81 Ohio Law Abs. 529.

Jurisdiction in adoption cases and in cases of placement of minors is vested in the probate court by RC 3107.02 as to the former, and RC 5103.16 as to the latter. (Annotation from former RC 3107.02.) In re McTaggart (Cuyahoga 1965) 2 Ohio App.2d 214, 207 N.E.2d 562, 31 O.O.2d 336, on rehearing 4 Ohio App.2d 359, 212 N.E.2d 663, 33 O.O.2d 447.

3. Natural parent adoption

The natural parent of a legitimate child may not seek to adopt his natural child to terminate the other natural parent's parental rights. In re Adoption of Kohorst (Paulding 1992) 75 Ohio App.3d 813, 600 N.E.2d 843, motion overruled 65 Ohio St.3d 1466, 602 N.E.2d 1174.

4. Ethnic heritage

Ethnic heritage of a child and prospective adoptive parents may be considered as a factor in adoption placements, but may not be used as the sole or determinative criterion; the opportunity to adopt a child may not be denied merely because the prospective adoptive parents are Caucasian and the child is African-American. In re Moorehead (Montgomery 1991) 75 Ohio App.3d 711, 600 N.E.2d 778.

5. Stepparent

Adoption of children by stepfather was in their best interest; there was evidence that children were being raised in loving and stable environment, and visitations with natural father had been confusing and disconcerting to them, and at hearing both children expressed desire to terminate their relationship with natural father and to be raised by stepfather. In re Adoption of Deems (Crawford 1993) 91 Ohio App.3d 552, 632 N.E.2d 1347, cause dismissed 70 Ohio St.3d 1451, 639 N.E.2d 460.

Trial court's finding that stepfather's adoption of child was in child's best interest was not against manifest weight of the evidence; county children's services board recommended that adoption proceed, child's maternal grandmother and her mother testified that child considered stepfather to be her father, that he spent time playing with her and taking her various places, and provided healthy, stable home for child. In re Adoption of Cline (Trumbull 1993) 89 Ohio App.3d 450, 624 N.E.2d 1083.

3107.031 Home study

Note: See also following version of this section, eff. 10-5-00.

An assessor shall conduct a home study for the purpose of ascertaining whether a person seeking to adopt a minor is suitable to adopt. A written report of the home study shall be filed with the court at least ten days before the petition for adoption is heard.

The report shall contain the opinion of the assessor as to whether the person who is the subject of the report is suitable to adopt a minor and other information and documents specified in rules adopted by the director of job and family services under section 3107.032 of the Revised Code. The assessor shall not consider the person's age when determining whether the person is suitable to adopt if the person is old enough to adopt as provided by section 3107.03 of the Revised Code.

An assessor may request departments or agencies within or outside this state to assist in the home study as may be appropriate and to make a written report to be included with and attached to the report to the court. The assessor shall make similar home studies and reports on behalf of other assessors designated by the courts of this state or another place.

Upon order of the court, the costs of the home study and other proceedings shall be paid by the person seeking to adopt, and, if the home study is conducted by a public agency or public employee, the part of the cost representing any services and expenses shall be taxed as costs and paid into the state treasury or county treasury, as the court may direct.

On request, the assessor shall provide the person seeking to adopt a copy of the report of the home study. The assessor shall delete from that copy any provisions concerning the opinion of other persons, excluding the assessor, of the person's suitability to adopt a minor.

(1999 H 471, eff. 7-1-00; 1996 H 274, eff. 9-18-96; 1996 H 419, eff. 9-18-96)

Note: See also following version of this section, eff. 10-5-00.

3107.031 Home study

Note: See also preceding version of this section, in effect until 10-5-00.

Except as otherwise provided in this section, an assessor shall conduct a home study for the purpose of ascertaining whether a person seeking to adopt a minor is suitable to adopt. A written report of the home study shall be filed with the court at least ten days before the petition for adoption is heard.

The report shall contain the opinion of the assessor as to whether the person who is the subject of the report is suitable to adopt a minor and other information and documents specified in rules adopted by the director of job and family services under section 3107.032 of the Revised Code. The assessor shall not consider the person's age when determining whether the person is suitable to adopt if the person is old enough to adopt as provided by section 3107.03 of the Revised Code.

An assessor may request departments or agencies within or outside this state to assist in the home study as may be appropriate and to make a written report to be included with and attached to the report to the court. The assessor shall make similar home studies and reports on behalf of other assessors designated by the courts of this state or another place.

Upon order of the court, the costs of the home study and other proceedings shall be paid by the person seeking to adopt, and, if the home study is conducted by a public agency or public employee, the part of the cost representing any services and expenses shall be taxed as costs and paid into the state treasury or county treasury, as the court may direct.

On request, the assessor shall provide the person seeking to adopt a copy of the report of the home study. The assessor shall delete from that copy any provisions concerning the opinion of other persons, excluding the assessor, of the person's suitability to adopt a minor.

This section does not apply to a foster caregiver seeking to adopt the foster caregiver's foster child if the foster child has resided in the foster caregiver's home for at least twelve months prior to the date the foster caregiver submits an application prescribed under division (B) of section 3107.012 of the Revised Code to the agency arranging the adoption.

(2000 H 448, eff. 10-5-00; 1999 H 471, eff. 7-1-00; 1996 H 274, eff. 9-18-96; 1996 H 419, eff. 9-18-96)

Note: See also preceding version of this section, in effect until 10-5-00.

Historical and Statutory Notes

Ed. Note: 3107.031 is former 3107.12, amended and recodified by 1996 H 419, eff. 9-18-96; 1984 H 84, eff. 3-19-85; 1978 S 340; 1976 H 156.

Amendment Note: 2000 H 448 substituted "Except as otherwise provided in this section, an" for "an"; and added the last paragraph.

Amendment Note: 1999 H 471 substituted "director of job and family services" for "department of human services" in the second paragraph.

Amendment Note: 1996 H 274 deleted "Except when a stepparent adopts a stepchild," from the beginning of the first paragraph.

Amendment Note: 1996 H 419 rewrote this section, which formerly read:

"(A) An investigation shall be made by the department of human services, an agency, or other person appointed by the court into the conditions and antecedents of a minor sought to be adopted and of the petitioner, for the purpose of ascertaining whether the adoptive home is a suitable home for the minor and whether the proposed adoption is in the best interest of the minor. If the minor is in the custody of the department or an agency, the department or agency shall perform the investigation.

"(B) A written report of the investigation as described in division (C) of this section shall be filed with the court at least ten days before the petition for adoption is heard.

"(C) The report of the investigation shall contain, in addition to any other information that the court requires regarding the petitioner or the minor sought to be adopted, the following information:

"(1) The physical and mental health, emotional stability, and personal integrity of the petitioner and the ability of the petitioner to provide for the needs of the minor;

"(2) The physical, mental, and developmental condition of the minor;

"(3) The minor's family background, including names and identifying data regarding the biological or other legal parents, and, except when the adoption is by a stepparent or grandparent, the social and medical histories described in division (D) of this section, to the extent that they can be prepared;

"(4) The reasons for the minor's placement with persons other than his biological or other legal parents, their attitude toward the proposed adoption, and the circumstances under which the minor came to be placed in the home of the petitioner;

"(5) The attitude of the minor toward the proposed adoption in any case in which the minor's age makes this feasible;

"(6) The recommendation of the investigator as to the granting or denial of the petition for adoption.

"(D)(1) The department of human services shall prescribe, and shall supply for purposes of an investigation pursuant to division (A) of this section, forms for the taking of the social and medical histories of the biological parents of minors sought to be adopted.

"(2) Except when an adoption is by a stepparent or grandparent, the department, an agency, and any other person appointed by a court to make an investigation pursuant to division (A) of this section, to the extent possible, shall record the social and medical histories of the biological parents of the minor sought to be adopted, using the forms prescribed pursuant to division (D)(1) of this section. The investigator shall not include on the forms the names of the biological parents or other ancestors of the minor, or any identifying data that would allow a person, except the court or the investigator, to determine the identity of the biological parents or other ancestors.

"(3) The social history of the biological parents of a minor sought to be adopted shall describe and identify the ethnic, racial, religious, marital, physical characteristics, educational, cultural, talent and hobby, and work experience background of the biological parents of the minor. The medical history of the biological parents of a minor sought to be adopted shall identify major diseases, malformations, allergies, ear or eye defects, major conditions, and major health problems of the biological parents that are or may be congenital or familial. These histories may include other social and medical information relative to the biological parents, and shall include social and medical information relative to the minor's other ancestors.

"The social and medical histories may be obtained through interviews with the biological parents or other persons, and from any available records if a parent or any legal guardian of a parent consents to the release of information contained in a record. If the investigator considers it necessary, it may request that a parent undergo a medical examination. In obtaining social and medical histories of a biological parent, an investigator shall inform the biological parent, or a person other than a biological parent who provides information pursuant to this section, of the purpose and use of the histories and of his right to correct or expand the histories at any time.

"(4) A biological parent, or a person other than a biological parent who provided information in the preparation of the social and medical histories of the biological parents of a minor, may cause, in accordance with this division, the histories to be corrected or expanded to include different or additional types of information. A biological parent or such a person may cause the histories to be corrected or expanded at any time prior or subsequent to the adoption of the minor, including, but not limited to, at any time after the minor becomes an adult. A biological parent may cause the histories to be corrected or expanded even if he did not provide any information to the investigator at the time the histories were prepared.

"To cause the histories to be corrected or expanded, a biological parent or such a person shall provide the information that he wishes to have included, or shall specify the information that he wishes to have corrected, to one of the following, whichever is appropriate under the circumstances:

"(a) subject to division (D)(4)(b) of this section, if the biological parent or person knows the investigator that prepared the histories, to the investigator;

"(b) if the biological parent or person does not know the investigator that prepared the histories, if he ascertains that the investigator has ceased to exist, or if an investigator other than the department of human services refuses to assist him, to the clerk of the court involved in the adoption or, if that court is not known, to the department of health.

"If an investigator receives information from a biological parent or such a person pursuant to division (D)(4)(a) of this section and is willing to assist the biological parent or person, it shall determine whether the information is of a type that divisions (D)(2) and (3) of this section permit to be included in the histories and, to the best of its ability, whether the information is accurate. If it determines the information is of a permissible type and accurate, the investigator shall cause the histories to be corrected or expanded to reflect the information. If, at the time the information is received, the histories have been filed with the court as required by division (D)(6) of this section, the clerk of the court shall cooperate with the investigator in the correcting or expanding of the histories.

"If the department of health or a clerk receives information from a biological parent or such a person pursuant to division (D)(4)(b) of this section, it shall determine whether the information is of a type that divisions (D)(2) and (3) of this section permit to be included in the histories and, to the best of its ability, whether the information is accurate. If a clerk determines the information is of a permissible type and accurate, he shall cause the histories to be corrected or expanded to reflect the information. If the department of health so determines, the clerk of the court involved shall cooperate with the department in the correcting or expanding of the histories.

"(5) An investigator shall comply, to the extent possible, with division (D)(3) of this section, but neither the failure of the investigator to obtain all or any part of the information mentioned in that division nor the refusal of a biological parent to supply information shall invalidate, delay, or otherwise affect the adoption.

"(6) An investigator shall file, as part of the report required by division (B) of this section, the social and medical histories of the biological parents prepared, to the extent possible, pursuant to divisions (D)(2) and (3) of this section. The court promptly shall provide a copy of the social and medical histories filed with it to the petitioner. No interlocutory order or final decree of adoption shall be entered by a court, in a case involving the adoption of a minor, if either the histories of his biological parents have not been so filed or the copy of the histories has not been so provided.

"(E) The department of human services, an agency, or a person, when required to make an investigation pursuant to division (A) of this section, may request departments or agencies within or outside this state to make or assist in the investigation as may be appropriate and to make a written report which shall be included with and attached to the report to the court. The department, an agency, or a person appointed to make an investigation pursuant to division (A) of this section shall make similar investigations and reports on behalf of departments, agencies, or persons designated by the courts of this state or another place.

"(F) Upon order of the court, the costs of the investigation and other proceedings shall be paid by the petitioner, and, if the investigation is conducted by a public agency or public employee, the part of the cost representing any services and expenses shall be taxed as costs and paid into the state treasury or county treasury, as the court may direct."

Cross References

Availability of adoption records, 149.43
Certificate of adoption for person born in foreign country, inspection, 3705.12
Courts, confidentiality of adoption files, Sup R 55
Placement of child for adoption, criteria, 5103.16
Placing of child in public or private institution, agreements to be in writing, social and medical histories required, 5103.15
Probate courts, appointment of assessors, 2101.11

Ohio Administrative Code References

Approval of a family foster home for adoptive placement, OAC 5101:2-48-11
Completion of the homestudy report, OAC 5101:2-48-12

Library References

Adoption ⟹9.1, 13.
Infants ⟹208, 226.
WESTLAW Topic Nos. 17, 211.
C.J.S. Adoption of Persons §§ 10 to 12, 49, 50, 73, 88 to 97.
C.J.S. Infants §§ 51, 52, 57 to 85.

OJur 3d: 47, Family Law § 928 to 930

Am Jur 2d: 2, Adoption § 59

Baldwin's Ohio Legislative Service, 1996 H 419—LSC Analysis, 3/L-336
Carlin, Baldwin's Ohio Practice, *Merrick-Rippner Probate Law* § 98.2 (1997)

Law Review and Journal Commentaries

Deboer v Schmidt: Disregarding the Child's Best Interests in Adoption Proceedings, Note. 23 Cap U L Rev 1099 (1994).

The Interracial Adoption Implications of Drummond v Fulton County Department of Family and Children Services, Comment. 17 J Fam L 117 (1978-79).

Racial Matching and the Adoption Dilemma: Alternatives for the Hard to Place, Note. 17 J Fam L 333 (1978-79).

S.B. 340: Disclosure of Social and Medical History of the Biological Parents of an Adopted Child, Note. 4 U Dayton L Rev 533 (Summer 1979).

Will *Palmore v. Sidoti* Preclude the Use of Race as a Factor in Denying an Adoption?, Note. 24 J Fam L 497 (1985-86).

Wrongful Adoption: Adoption Agency Held Liable for Fraudulent Representations: *Burr v. Stark County Board of Commissioners*, Note. 56 U Cin L Rev 343 (1987).

Notes of Decisions and Opinions

---

1. Agency

The refusal of consent to an adoption by a "certified organization," as defined in RC 3107.01(C), does not impair the jurisdiction of the probate court, but the recommendations and the reports, filed pursuant to RC 3107.05 and 3107.10, are to be considered, in conjunction with all other evidence adduced in the proceeding, by the court in deciding the issues presented by RC 3107.09. (Annotation from former RC 3107.05.) State ex rel. Portage County Welfare Dept. v. Summers (Ohio 1974) 38 Ohio St.2d 144, 311 N.E.2d 6, 67 O.O.2d 151.

2. Investigator

Where natural father refuses to consent to adoption of his child by a third party, bifurcated procedure is followed; first, hearing on issue of necessity of consent is held, and in second stage, court determines whether adoption is in best interest of child after home study investigation. (Annotation from former RC 3107.12.) In re Adoption of Cline (Trumbull 1993) 89 Ohio App.3d 450, 624 N.E.2d 1083.

The failure of the human services department to include the name of the investigator on its report prior to an adoption hearing is merely a clerical oversight and not error. (Annotation from former RC 3107.12.) In re Adoption of Howell (Lawrence 1991) 77 Ohio App.3d 80, 601 N.E.2d 92, motion overruled 62 Ohio St.3d 1508, 583 N.E.2d 1320.

When authorized by the probate court under RC 5103.16 to make an investigation of a proposed placement, or when appointed by a probate court under RC 3107.04 and 3107.05 to act as the next friend of a child being adopted, a child welfare board has the duty to carry out the court's request. (Annotation from former RC 3107.05.) 1962 OAG 2747.

3. Ethnic heritage

Ethnic heritage of a child and prospective adoptive parents may be considered as a factor in adoption placements, but may not be used as the sole or determinative criterion; the opportunity to adopt a child may not be denied merely because the prospective adoptive parents are Caucasian and the child is African-American. (Annotation from former RC 3107.12.) In re Moorehead (Montgomery 1991) 75 Ohio App.3d 711, 600 N.E.2d 778.

Order denying adoption reversed where such order was based on the fact that the adopting father was Caucasian, his wife Japanese, the natural mother of English descent, and the natural father Puerto Rican. (Annotation from former RC 3107.05.) In re Adoption of Baker (Cuyahoga 1962) 117 Ohio App. 26, 185 N.E.2d 51, 90 Ohio Law Abs. 125, 22 O.O.2d 459.

4. Report

The probate judge has primary responsibility for deciding whether to allow an adoption but great weight should be given the report and investigation made under RC 3107.12. (Annotation from former RC 3107.12.) In re Adoption of Labo (Shelby 1988) 47 Ohio App.3d 57, 546 N.E.2d 1384.

In granting or denying an application for adoption, great weight should be accorded to the report and recommendation of the next friend appointed pursuant to RC 3107.04. (Annotation from former RC 3107.04.) In re Adoption of Baker (Cuyahoga 1962) 117 Ohio App. 26, 185 N.E.2d 51, 90 Ohio Law Abs. 125, 22 O.O.2d 459.

A reviewing court is without authority to require filing, as a part of the transcript, a so-called "next friend's report" to the probate court. (Annotation from former RC 3107.05.) In re Adoption of Kane (Stark 1952) 91 Ohio App. 327, 108 N.E.2d 176, 48 O.O. 407.

5. Costs

The adopting parents of an illegitimate child are liable only for the cost of the adoption proceeding, and not for expenses incurred by the child welfare board for prenatal care or delivery or for the care of the mother and child after birth. (Annotation from former RC 3107.05.) 1955 OAG 5956.

6. Guardian ad litem

Appointment of guardian ad litem for minor who was subject of adoption proceedings was not required, since interest of child in adoption is protected by appointment of agency or persons who inquire into conditions and antecedents of person sought to be adopted and of petitioner for adoption. (Annotation from former RC 3107.12.) In re Adoption of Carnes (Portage 1983) 8 Ohio App.3d 435, 457 N.E.2d 903, 8 O.B.R. 560.

3107.032 Rules for conducting home study

Not later than ninety days after June 20, 1996, the director of job and family services shall adopt rules in accordance with Chapter 119. of the Revised Code specifying the manner in which a home study is to be conducted and the information and documents to be included in a home study report.

(1999 H 471, eff. 7-1-00; 1996 H 419, eff. 6-20-96)

Historical and Statutory Notes

Amendment Note: 1999 H 471 substituted "June 20, 1996" for "the effective date of this section" and "director of job and family services" for "department of human services".

Ohio Administrative Code References

Approval of a family foster home for adoptive placement, OAC 5101:2-48-11

Completion of the homestudy report, OAC 5101:2-48-12

Release of identifying and nonidentifying information, OAC 5101:2-48-20

Library References

Baldwin's Ohio Legislative Service, 1996 H 419—LSC Analysis, 3/L-336

Carlin, Baldwin's Ohio Practice, *Merrick-Rippner Probate Law* § 98.2 (1997)

3107.04 Venue; caption of petition for adoption

(A) A petition for adoption shall be filed in the court in the county in which the person to be adopted was born, or in which, at the time of filing the petition, the petitioner or the person to be adopted or parent of the person to be adopted resides, or in which the petitioner is stationed in military service, or in which the agency having the permanent custody of the person to be adopted is located.

(B) If the court finds in the interest of justice that the case should be heard in another forum, the court may stay the proceedings or dismiss the petition in whole or in part on any conditions that are just, or certify the case to another court.

(C) The caption of a petition for adoption shall be styled, "In the matter of adoption of ___________". The person to be adopted shall be designated in the caption under the name by which he is to be known if the petition is granted.

(1976 H 156, eff. 1-1-77)

Historical and Statutory Notes

Ed. Note: Former 3107.04 repealed by 1976 H 156, eff. 1-1-77; 1975 S 145; 1953 H 1; GC 8004-4; Source—GC 10512-12; see now 3107.11 for provisions analogous to former 3107.04.

Pre-1953 H 1 Amendments: 124 v S 65

Cross References

Department of job and family services, division of social administration; care and placement of children; interstate compact on placement of children, 5103.09 to 5103.17, 5103.20 to 5103.28

Powers and duties of county children services board, 5153.16

Library References

Adoption ⟹10, 11.
WESTLAW Topic No. 17.
C.J.S. Adoption of Persons §§ 74 to 77, 87.

OJur 3d: 47, Family Law § 924

Am Jur 2d: 2, Adoption § 10, 11, 48 to 57

Carlin, Baldwin's Ohio Practice, *Merrick-Rippner Probate Law* § 3.23, 98.2, 98.24 (1997)

Notes of Decisions and Opinions

Jurisdiction 1

---

1. Jurisdiction

Where the mother of a baby and two adoptive parents are Lucas county residents and the baby is born in Lucas county, the Wood county probate court has no jurisdiction over the adoption of the baby. In re Adoption of Murphy (Wood 1988) 53 Ohio App.3d 14, 557 N.E.2d 827.

3107.05 Petition; documents to be filed with clerk

(A) A petition for adoption shall be prepared and filed according to the procedure for commencing an action under the Rules of Civil Procedure. It shall include the following information:

(1) The date and place of birth of the person to be adopted, if known;

(2) The name of the person to be adopted, if known;

(3) The name to be used for the person to be adopted;

(4) The date of placement of a minor and the name of the person placing the minor;

(5) The full name, age, place, and duration of residence of the petitioner;

(6) The marital status of the petitioner, including the date and place of marriage, if married;

(7) The relationship to the petitioner of the person to be adopted;

(8) That the petitioner has facilities and resources suitable to provide for the nurture and care of the person to be adopted, and that it is the desire of the petitioner to establish the relationship of parent and child with the person to be adopted;

(9) A description and estimate of value of all property of the person to be adopted;

(10) The name and address, if known, of any person whose consent to the adoption is required, but who has not consented, and facts that explain the lack of the consent normally required to the adoption.

(B) A certified copy of the birth certificate of the person to be adopted, if available, and ordinary copies of the required consents, and relinquishments of consents, if any, shall be filed with the clerk.

(1976 H 156, eff. 1-1-77)

Historical and Statutory Notes

Ed. Note: 3107.05 is analogous to former 3107.03, repealed by 1976 H 156, eff. 1-1-77.

Ed. Note: Former 3107.05 repealed by 1976 H 156, eff. 1-1-77; 1969 S 49; 1953 H 1; GC 8004-5; Source—GC 10512-13; see now 3107.12 for provisions analogous to former 3107.05.

Pre-1953 H 1 Amendments: 124 v S 65

Cross References

Birth certificates, 3705.10 to 3705.15
Commencement of action, service of process, Civ R 3 to 4.6
Fee for filing petition for adoption, 2101.16

Ohio Administrative Code References

Application for subsidized adoption, OAC 5101:2-44-04

Library References

Adoption ⇨9.1, 11.
WESTLAW Topic No. 17.
C.J.S. Adoption of Persons §§ 49, 73, 76, 77, 87.

OJur 3d: 47, Family Law § 923, 924
Am Jur 2d: 2, Adoption § 10, 11, 54
Change of child's name in adoption proceeding. 53 ALR2d 927
Restricting access to judicial records of concluded adoption proceedings. 83 ALR3d 800
Restricting access to judicial records of pending adoption proceedings. 83 ALR3d 824

Carlin, Baldwin's Ohio Practice, *Merrick-Rippner Probate Law* § 98.2, 98.3, 98.21, 98.24, 98.56, 98.57 (1997)
Klein & Darling, Baldwin's Ohio Practice, *Civil Practice* § 1, 4 (1997)

Law Review and Journal Commentaries

The Right of the Thwarted Father to Veto the Adoption of His Child, Comment. 62 U Cin L Rev 1695 (Spring 1994).

Notes of Decisions and Opinions

Consent 5
Custody affidavit 1
Denial of petition 3
Duties of petitioners 4
"Person" defined 6
Placement date 2

---

1. Custody affidavit

Grandparents seeking to adopt their grandchild are not required to file an affidavit of custody since adoption proceedings do not determine custody. In re Adoption of Howell (Lawrence 1991) 77 Ohio App.3d 80, 601 N.E.2d 92, motion overruled 62 Ohio St.3d 1508, 583 N.E.2d 1320.

RC 3107.05 does not require that a custodial affidavit be filed in conjunction with a petition for adoption. In re Adoption of Reams (Franklin 1989) 52 Ohio App.3d 52, 557 N.E.2d 159, dismissed 50 Ohio St.3d 707, 553 N.E.2d 684.

2. Placement date

In an adoption proceeding initiated by the child's grandparents, the placement date is determined to be the date that she was left in the care of the grandparents, which was considered to be a temporary placement since no adoption was intended at the time. In re Adoption of Howell (Lawrence 1991) 77 Ohio App.3d 80, 601 N.E.2d 92, motion overruled 62 Ohio St.3d 1508, 583 N.E.2d 1320.

3. Denial of petition

After conducting a hearing pursuant to RC 3107.09, the probate court improperly denies a petition for adoption of a four-year-old boy in the custody of the county welfare department, when the court finds that the petitioners meet all the requirements of suitability as adoptive parents, but denies the petition for adoption on the grounds that the granting of the adoption would violate the integrity of a waiting list allegedly maintained by the welfare department, where at the adoption hearing there was no evidence establishing the existence or administration of such a waiting list and no evidence that the waiting list contained suitable applicants ready, willing, and able to adopt the child in question. (Annotation from former RC 3107.03.) In re Harshey (Cuyahoga 1975) 45 Ohio App.2d 97, 341 N.E.2d 616, 74 O.O.2d 120.

A petition for adoption, duly filed in accordance with RC 3107.03, is not properly dismissed without a hearing on the merits merely upon a finding by the probate court that a certified agency has not consented to the adoption as required in RC 3107.06. (Annotation from former RC 3107.03.) (See also In re Harshey, 45 App(2d) 97, 341 NE(2d) 616 (1975).) In re Harshey (Cuyahoga 1974) 40 Ohio App.2d 157, 318 N.E.2d 544, 69 O.O.2d 165.

4. Duties of petitioners

The requirements of RC 5103.16 relating to the duty of parents applying to probate court for approval of a proposed placement for adoption do not apply to a situation where prospective adoptive parents in accordance with RC 3107.03 have duly petitioned for the adoption of a child whose permanent custody has been entrusted to the county welfare department. (Annotation from former RC 3107.06.) (See also In re Harshey, 45 App(2d) 97, 341 NE(2d) 616 (1975).) In re Harshey (Cuyahoga 1974) 40 Ohio App.2d 157, 318 N.E.2d 544, 69 O.O.2d 165.

The adopting parents of an illegitimate child are liable only for the cost of the adoption proceeding and not for expenses incurred by the child welfare board for prenatal care or delivery or for the care of the mother and child after birth. (Annotation from former RC 3107.03.) 1955 OAG 5956.

5. Consent

Dismissal of particular petition for child's adoption does not invalidate biological mother's consent to adoption executed in connection therewith; prior statutory references to applicability of consent to one adoption petition only were deleted during legislative revisions, applicable statutes do not place time limit on effectiveness of consent, consent is viable until the court grants a motion to withdraw it, and consent to adoption and petition for adoption must be two separate legal documents. In re Adoption of Koszycki (Ohio App. 1 Dist. 1999) 133 Ohio App.3d 434, 728 N.E.2d 437.

Consent to adoption and petition for adoption must be two separate legal documents. In re Adoption of Koszycki (Ohio App. 1 Dist. 1999) 133 Ohio App.3d 434, 728 N.E.2d 437.

Biological mother's consent to child's adoption survived dismissal of prospective adoptive parents' first petition for adoption and could be used in support of their second petition. In re Adoption of Koszycki (Ohio App. 1 Dist. 1999) 133 Ohio App.3d 434, 728 N.E.2d 437.

Where a mother, as sole parent, files an "application for placement" and a written waiver and consent to adoption in the probate court to place her newborn baby with a married couple whose identity she did not know but who were procured by an intermediary at her request with adoption in mind, appears in person before such court for approval of such placement, and the probate court, after an independent investigation of the proposed placement by a qualified person, determines that it is in the best interest of the child and approves of record the proposed placement, and the child is delivered to the married couple pursuant to the order of the court, the mother, as petitioner in a habeas corpus action filed in the court of common pleas to regain custody of her child, is estopped from claiming that the probate court was without jurisdiction by reason of an insufficient application in not identifying by names the placement parents; and a finding by the court of common pleas of lack of such jurisdiction is reversible error. (Annotation from former RC 3107.02.) In re McTaggart (Cuyahoga 1965) 4 Ohio App.2d 359, 212 N.E.2d 663, 33 O.O.2d 447.

In an adoption proceeding, written consent of child to the adoption was not required to be filed of record by former statutes, and where record disclosed that such consent was given, it was presumed that consent was legally executed. (Annotation from former RC 3107.03.) In re Dickman's Estate (Mercer 1946) 81 Ohio App. 281, 79 N.E.2d 172, 37 O.O. 125.

The petition to adopt and the consent to adoption are two separate documents and so a natural parent's consent to adoption survives dismissal of a contemporaneously filed petition for adoption and may be used to support a subsequent petition filed by the same petitioners concerning adoption of the same child. In re Adoption of Koszycki, No. C-980741, 1999 WL 299904 (1st Dist Ct App, Hamilton, 5-14-99).

6. "Person" defined

Word "person" as used in statute is to be construed as having meaning ordinarily given that word, to wit, a "human being." (Annotation from former RC 3107.03.) 1944 OAG 6716.

3107.051 Submission of petition for adoption

(A) Except as provided in division (B) of this section, a person seeking to adopt a minor, or the agency or attorney arranging the adoption, shall submit a petition for the minor's adoption no later than ninety days after the date the minor is placed in the person's home. Failure to file a petition within the time provided by this division does not affect a court's jurisdiction to hear the petition and is not grounds for denying the petition.

(B) This section does not apply if any of the following apply:

(1) The person seeking to adopt the minor is the minor's stepparent;

(2) The minor was not originally placed in the person's home with the purpose of the person adopting the minor;

(3) The minor is a "child with special needs," as defined by the director of job and family services in accordance with section 5153.163 of the Revised Code.

(1999 H 471, eff. 7-1-00; 1996 H 419, eff. 9-18-96)

Historical and Statutory Notes

Amendment Note: 1999 H 471 substituted "director of job and family services" for "department of human services" in division (B)(3).

Library References

Am Jur 2d: 2, Adoption § 130

Baldwin's Ohio Legislative Service, 1996 H 419—LSC Analysis, 3/L-336

Carlin, Baldwin's Ohio Practice, *Merrick-Rippner Probate Law* § 98.2, 98.24, 98.56 (1997)

CONSENTS AND PUTATIVE FATHER REGISTRY

3107.06 Consents required

Unless consent is not required under section 3107.07 of the Revised Code, a petition to adopt a minor may be granted only if written consent to the adoption has been executed by all of the following:

(A) The mother of the minor;

(B) The father of the minor, if any of the following apply:

(1) The minor was conceived or born while the father was married to the mother;

(2) The minor is his child by adoption;

(3) Prior to the date the petition was filed, it was determined by a court proceeding pursuant to sections 3111.01 to 3111.19 of the Revised Code, a court proceeding in another state, an administrative proceeding pursuant to sections 3111.20 to 3111.29 of the Revised Code, or an administrative proceeding in another state that he has a parent and child relationship with the minor;

(4) He acknowledged paternity of the child and that acknowledgment has become final pursuant to section 2151.232, 3111.211, or 5101.314 of the Revised Code.

(C) The putative father of the minor;

(D) Any person or agency having permanent custody of the minor or authorized by court order to consent;

(E) The juvenile court that has jurisdiction to determine custody of the minor, if the legal guardian or custodian of the minor is not authorized by law or court order to consent to the adoption;

(F) The minor, if more than twelve years of age, unless the court, finding that it is in the best interest of the minor, determines that the minor's consent is not required.

(1997 H 352, eff. 1-1-98; 1996 H 274, eff. 9-18-96; 1996 H 419, eff. 9-18-96; 1988 H 790, eff. 3-16-89; 1986 H 476; 1982 H 245; 1976 H 156)

Uncodified Law

1996 H 419, § 5, eff. 6-20-96, reads: The amendment made by this act to sections 3107.06 and 3107.07 of the Revised Code concerning a putative father, as defined in section 3107.01 of the Revised Code, consenting to his child's adoption apply only if the child is born on or after January 1, 1997. Whether a putative father's consent to the adoption of his child born prior to January 1, 1997, is required shall be determined in accordance with sections 3107.06 and 3107.07 of the Revised Code as those sections exist immediately prior to their amendment by this act.

Historical and Statutory Notes

Ed. Note: Former 3107.06 repealed by 1976 H 156, eff. 1-1-77; 1975 S 145; 1969 S 49; 130 v S 155; 129 v 498; 126 v 392; 1953 H 1; GC 8004-6; Source—GC 10512-14; see now 3107.07 and 3107.09 for provisions analogous to former 3107.06.

Pre-1953 H 1 Amendments: 124 v S 65

Amendment Note: 1997 H 352 rewrote division (B)(4), which prior thereto read:

"(4) He acknowledged paternity of the child pursuant to section 2105.18 of the Revised Code."

Amendment Note: 1996 H 274 added division (B)(4).

Amendment Note: 1996 H 419 rewrote division (B); added new divison (C); redesignated former divisions (C) through (E) as divisions (D) through (F), respectively; and deleted former section (F). Prior to amendment and deletion, divisions (B) and (F) read:

"(B) The father of the minor, if the minor was conceived or born while the father was married to the mother, if the minor is his child by adoption, or if the minor has been established to be his child by a court proceeding;

* * *

"(F) Subject to division (B) of section 3107.07 of the Revised Code, the putative father, if he:

"(1) Is alleged to be the father of the minor in proceedings brought under sections 3111.01 to 3111.19 of the Revised Code at any time before the placement of the minor in the home of the petitioner;

"(2) Has acknowledged the child in a writing sworn to before a notary public at any time before the placement of the minor in the home of the petitioner;

"(3) Has signed the birth certificate of the child as an informant as provided in section 3705.09 of the Revised Code;

"(4) Has filed an objection to the adoption with the agency having custody of the minor or the department of human services at any time before the placement of the minor in the home of the petitioner, or with the probate court or the department of human services within thirty days of the filing of a petition to adopt the minor or its placement in the home of the petitioner, whichever occurs first."

Comparative Laws

Ariz.—A.R.S. § 8-106 et seq.
Ark.—A.C.A. § 9-9-206 et seq.
Fla.—West's F.S.A. § 63.062 et seq.
Idaho—I.C. § 16-1503 et seq.
Ill.—ILCS 750 50/8 et seq.
Ind.—West's A.I.C. 31-19-4-10 et seq.
Iowa—I.C.A. § 600.7.
Ky.—Baldwin's KRS 199.500.
Mass.—M.G.L.A. c. 210, § 2 et seq.
Me.—18-A M.R.S.A. § 9-302.
Mich.—M.C.L.A. § 710.43.
Minn.—M.S.A. § 259.24.
Mo.—V.A.M.S. § 453.040.
N.C.—G.S. § 48-3-601 et seq.
N.Y.—McKinney's Domestic Relations Law § 111.
Okl.—10 Okl.St.Ann. § 7503-2.1.
Tenn.—T.C.A. § 36-1-108 et seq.
Tex.—V.T.C.A. Family Code § 162.010, 162.011.

Cross References

Custody of child by public agency, 2151.38
Department of job and family services, division of social administration, placing of children; interstate compact on placement of children, 5103.09 to 5103.17, 5103.20 to 5103.28
Jurisdiction of juvenile court, 2151.23
Placement of children from other states, 2151.39
Powers and duties of county children services board, 5153.16

Ohio Administrative Code References

Child care agencies, placement of children in foster homes, adoption, and permanent custody, OAC 5101:2-5-99

Library References

Adoption ⟹7 to 7.8.
WESTLAW Topic No. 17.
C.J.S. Adoption of Persons §§ 51 to 72.

OJur 3d: 47, Family Law § 908, 915; 48, Family Law § 1491
Am Jur 2d: 2, Adoption § 23 et seq., 30 to 39
Annulment or vacation of adoption decree by adopting parent or natural parent consenting to adoption. 2 ALR2d 887
Sufficiency of parent's consent to adoption of child. 24 ALR2d 1127
Consent of natural parents as essential to adoption where parents are divorced. 47 ALR2d 824
Necessity of securing consent of parents of illegitimate child to its adoption. 51 ALR2d 497
Adoption of adult. 21 ALR3d 1012
What constitutes undue influence in obtaining a parent's consent to adoption of child. 50 ALR3d 918
Right of natural parent to withdraw valid consent to adoption of child. 74 ALR3d 421
Mistake or want of understanding as ground for revocation of consent to adoption or of agreement releasing infant to adoption placement agency. 74 ALR3d 489
What constitutes "duress" in obtaining parent's consent to adoption of child or surrender of child to adoption agency. 74 ALR3d 527
Parent's involuntary confinement, or failure to care for child as result thereof, as permitting adoption without parental consent. 78 ALR3d 712
Adoption of child in absence of statutorily required consent of public or private agency or institution. 83 ALR3d 373
Natural parent's parental rights as affected by consent to child's adoption by other natural parent. 37 ALR4th 724
Necessity and sufficiency of consent to adoption by spouse of adopting parent. 38 ALR4th 768
Required parties in adoption proceedings. 48 ALR4th 860

Baldwin's Ohio Legislative Service, 1996 H 419—LSC Analysis, 3/L-336
Carlin, Baldwin's Ohio Practice, *Merrick-Rippner Probate Law* § 98.2, 98.13, 98.29, 98.30, 98.31, 98.33, 98.34, 98.37, 98.38, 98.40, 98.56, 105.13, 107.79 (1997)
Klein & Darling, Baldwin's Ohio Practice, *Civil Practice* § 5 (1997)
Kurtz & Giannelli, Ohio Juvenile Law (1998 Ed.), Text 27.10
Sowald & Morganstern, Baldwin's Ohio Practice, *Domestic Relations Law* § 3.46, 22.19 (1997)

Law Review and Journal Commentaries

Adoption—Consent—A Court May Enter a Final Decree of Adoption without the Consent of a Certified Child Welfare Agency When the Adoption Is in the Child's Best Interest, Note. 41 U Cin L Rev 704 (1972).

Awarding Child Support Against the Impoverished Parent: Straying from Statutory Guidelines and Using SSI in Setting the Amount, Note. 83 Ky L J 653 (1994-95).

Family Law—Ohio's Statutory Requirement of Legal Guardian Consent to Adoption and Its Effect on the Jurisdiction of the Probate Court, Note. 36 Ohio St L J 451 (1975).

Judicial Review of Adoption Agency Decisions, Note. 25 Case W Res L Rev 650 (Spring 1975).

The Law of Adoption in Ohio, Beverly E. Sylvester. 2 Cap U L Rev 23 (1973).

Lehr v Robertson: Putting the Genie Back in the Bottle: the Supreme Court Limits the Scope of the Putative Father's Right to Notice, Hearing, and Consent in the Adoption of His Illegitimate Child, Note. 15 U Tol L Rev 1501 (Summer 1984).

Seeking the wisdom of Solomon: Defining the rights of unwed fathers in newborn adoptions, Scott A. Resnik. 20 Seton Hall Legis J 363 (1996).

Termination of Parental Rights in Adoption Cases: Focusing on the Child, Comment. 14 J Fam L 547 (1975-76).

Notes of Decisions and Opinions

---

1. In general

Valid consent to adoption is one which has been freely, knowingly, and voluntarily given with full understanding of adoption process and consequences of one's actions. In re Adoption of Zschach (Ohio 1996) 75 Ohio St.3d 648, 665 N.E.2d 1070, reconsideration denied 76 Ohio St.3d 1410, 666 N.E.2d 569, certiorari denied 117 S.Ct. 582, 136 L.Ed.2d 513.

To preserve right to withheld consent to child's adoption and avoid finding that requirement of father's consent shall be excused, putative father who has signed birth certificate must file objection to adoption with court, department or agency having custody of child, but his objection need not be filed within 30 days of earlier of date of filing of adoption petition or placement of child. In re Adoption of Greer (Ohio 1994) 70 Ohio St.3d 293, 638 N.E.2d 999.

The one-year period of nonsupport prescribed by RC 3107.07(A) which obviates the requirement to obtain parental consent to an adoption pursuant to RC 3107.06 commences on the date that parentage has been judicially established. In re Adoption of Sunderhaus (Ohio 1992) 63 Ohio St.3d 127, 585 N.E.2d 418, rehearing denied 63 Ohio St.3d 1442, 589 N.E.2d 46.

Consent to adoption is voluntary where both consenting parents have attained the age of majority, attend college, and are fully aware of their rights to retain the child and the consequences of signing the consent form. Morrow v. Family & Community Services of Catholic Charities, Inc. (Ohio 1986) 28 Ohio St.3d 247, 504 N.E.2d 2, 28 O.B.R. 327.

Judgment entry on issue of whether child's biological father had been in communication with child during year prior to filing of petition for child's adoption by husband of child's mother was partial final judgment; while final and appealable when entered, it was appealable alternatively 30 days after court rendered final order on all issues in case. In re Adoption of Eblin (Ohio App. 3 Dist. 1998) 126 Ohio App.3d 774, 711 N.E.2d 319, appeal allowed 82 Ohio St.3d 1482, 696 N.E.2d 1088, cause dismissed 83 Ohio St.3d 1454, 700 N.E.2d 617.

Father of child has same adoption rights with respect to adoption of child as mother, with few narrowly defined exceptions. Bryant v. Hacker (Ohio App. 1 Dist. 1996) 116 Ohio App.3d 860, 689 N.E.2d 609.

Prescriptive one-year period after which natural father may be deemed to have abandoned child so that natural father's consent is not necessary to child's adoption commences running not upon birth of child, but upon determination of paternity, so that father's actions regarding communication and support were to be analyzed from date of declaration of paternity, where father's parentage action was filed and determined prior to filing of adoption petition. In re Adoption of Sherry (Medina 1995) 107 Ohio App.3d 830, 669 N.E.2d 551.

Putative father's failure to strictly comply with time limits of statute due to misleading notice sent out by court did not preclude his filing of objection to adoption within time frame set out in notice and delay was excusable due to putative father's incarceration. In re Adoption of Bowes (Lake 1995) 105 Ohio App.3d 574, 664 N.E.2d 963.

Mother's notification to putative father concerning proposed adoption satisfied due process, justifying dismissal of putative father's untimely objection to adoption; putative father was not entitled to additional notice from probate court of child's placement with adoptive parents, absent evidence that putative father had participated in rearing of child or had otherwise provided any care or support, and there was no evidence that putative father was prevented from filing objection because of either fraud or legal disability. In re Adoption of Baby Boy Dearing (Medina 1994) 98 Ohio App.3d 197, 648 N.E.2d 57, dismissed, appeal not allowed 71 Ohio St.3d 1492, 646 N.E.2d 467.

Parental consent to adoption is generally a jurisdictional prerequisite. Celestino v. Schneider (Lucas 1992) 84 Ohio App.3d 192, 616 N.E.2d 581.

A father who has supported his illegitimate child must receive notice of an application for adoption; where the father has not been notified until after the thirty-day objection period of RC 3107.06(F)(4), his objection is timely if filed within thirty days of his notice of the proceedings. In re Adoption of Holt (Hamilton 1991) 75 Ohio App.3d 450, 599 N.E.2d 812.

The natural father of a child, the subject of an adoption proceeding, who, as an active member of the armed forces is stationed in another state, is not entitled to notice of the proposed placement or adoption of his child where the father is not married to the mother of the child, has made no attempt to acknowledge his paternity prior to an untimely filed objection to the adoption, and where there is no evidence that the father was prevented from timely filing an adoption due to fraud or legal disability. In re Adoption of Baby Girl Hudnall (Franklin 1991) 71 Ohio App.3d 376, 594 N.E.2d 45.

The consent of the natural father is not required in an adoption proceeding under RC 3107.06 and 3107.07 where (1) the father abandoned the mother and child when the child was three; (2) the mother was granted a divorce eight months later and retained full custody of the child; (3) the natural father did not contact the mother until three years after the divorce, after the petitioner had filed the adoption petition, although the mother and the petitioner did not marry until five months later; and (4) the father refused to consent to the adoption; the court's consideration of only one of two dates for calculation of the requisite one-year period during which the parent fails without justifiable cause to communicate with the minor or to provide for the maintenance and support is error, as the entire one-year period should be examined, not just a portion. In re Adoption of Jones (Medina 1990) 70 Ohio App.3d 576, 591 N.E.2d 823.

A probate court could conclude that a petitioner has not carried his burden on the issue of "justifiable cause" for his failure to communicate with his child in RC 3107.07(A) where the natural father establishes prior to the filing of the petition that he was an alcoholic with suicidal tendencies, that once in recovery the father secured employment and tried to contact his ex-wife to arrange for visits with and support payments to the child, that he made contact through an attorney rather than to have a face-to-face confrontation with his ex-wife, and that his ex-wife largely rebuffed his advances, failed to encourage visitation, and employed the adoption process largely as a means of severing his parental rights; the term "justifiable cause" in RC 3107.07 is not a readily defined term and must be determined from the surrounding circumstances of each case. In re Adoption of Jones (Medina 1990) 70 Ohio App.3d 576, 591 N.E.2d 823.

Even where a probate court finds that the natural father's consent to an adoption is not necessary, a determination of what is in the child's best interests is still required prior to termination of parental rights. In re Adoption of Jones (Medina 1990) 70 Ohio App.3d 576, 591 N.E.2d 823.

The consent of a natural parent to an adoption must be of the parent's own volition, free from duress or other extraordinary circumstances, and with full understanding of the adoption process. In re Adoption of Infant Girl Banda (Franklin 1988) 53 Ohio App.3d 104, 559 N.E.2d 1373.

The acceptance of attorney fees from adoptive parents by the attorney of the natural mother does not invalidate the consent of the natural mother where she was fully informed of such fees and where the consent was not induced by coercion or undue influence. In re Adoption of Infant Girl Banda (Franklin 1988) 53 Ohio App.3d 104, 559 N.E.2d 1373.

RC 2151.353, permitting the state to receive permanent custody of a "dependent child" whose parent is jailed, does not conflict with RC 3107.07; where the child is a "dependent child" under RC 2151.04 the state has authority to obtain permanent custody under RC 2151.353, and once parental rights have been terminated under RC Ch 2151, it is provided by RC 3107.06(D) that this parent's consent to adoption is no longer necessary. In re Dillard (Montgomery 1988) 48 Ohio App.3d 263, 549 N.E.2d 213.

A probate court is without jurisdiction to hear a case, and properly dismisses a petition for adoption of a child in the custody of a natural parent, where the natural parent has not consented to the adoption as required in RC 3107.06(B). (Annotation from former RC 3107.06.) (See also In re Harshey, 45 App(2d) 97, 341 NE(2d) 616 (1975).) In re Harshey (Cuyahoga 1974) 40 Ohio App.2d 157, 318 N.E.2d 544, 69 O.O.2d 165.

A consent to adoption required by section may be obtained prior to the time the petition to adopt is filed; sno exclusive method of executing such consent is defined by statute, and, where the consent is in writing, verified or acknowledged and filed in the court, compliance with the terms of the statute is accomplished. (Annotation from former RC 3107.06.) In re Burdette (Summit 1948) 83 Ohio App. 368, 83 N.E.2d 813, 38 O.O. 429.

Statute is mandatory, and must be followed strictly in order to effect a legal adoption. (Annotation from former RC 3107.06.) Martin v. Fisher (Mercer 1927) 25 Ohio App. 372, 158 N.E. 287, 5 Ohio Law Abs. 596.

A natural father's consent is required for adoption by a stepparent where the father has justifiable cause to fail to provide maintenance and support to his children due to a spinal cord injury which severely limits his earning ability. In re Adoption of Richison, No. 17488, 1999 WL 375587 (2d Dist Ct App, Montgomery, 6-11-99).

Pursuant to the explicit language of RC 3107.07, failure by a parent to communicate with his or her child is sufficient to authorize adoption without that parent's consent only if there is a complete absence of communication for the statutorily defined one-year period. Bryant v Van Auken, No. 97CA635, 1997 WL 766460 (4th Dist Ct App, Washington, 12-9-97).

A natural unmarried father who was in the physical presence of his child twice within the one-year period immediately preceding the filing of a petition for adoption by the mother's husband constitutes communication with the child and the consent of the natural father in order to effect the adoption is required. In re Adoption of Doe, No. H-93-11, 1993 WL 434681 (6th Dist Ct App, Huron, 10-29-93).

Where notice of an adoption petition sent to a putative father states that any objections must be filed on or before the hearing date, rather than within thirty days of the filing of the adoption petition, and the putative father files objections to the adoption eleven days prior to the hearing, it is a violation of due process for the trial court to find the putative father's consent unnecessary for failure to timely object. In re Adoption of Greer, No. 5-92-34 (3d Dist Ct App, Hancock, 3-16-93).

Natural parent may relinquish or consent to give up rights and duties of parentage. Belsito v. Clark (Ohio Com.Pl. 1994) 67 Ohio Misc.2d 54, 644 N.E.2d 760.

In proceeding for adoption of child of divorced parents, on ground that father had consented to adoption, and on ground that mother had willfully failed to properly support and maintain child for more than two years prior to filing of petition for adoption, burden of proof was on petitioners. Adoption of Stephen (Darke 1952) 111 N.E.2d 762, 64 Ohio Law Abs. 289.

Under statute providing that no final decree of adoption shall be made unless by consent of parents or unless both parents have willfully failed to support the child for over two years, mere failure, in and of itself, to pay support of minor children does not constitute willfulness. Poet v. Rosinski (Cuyahoga 1951) 102 N.E.2d 19, 60 Ohio Law Abs. 513, appeal dismissed 155 Ohio St. 510, 99 N.E.2d 320, 44 O.O. 460.

Adoption, failure to terminate parental rights of natural parents. DeBoer by Darrow v. DeBoer (U.S.Mich. 1993) 114 S.Ct. 1, 509 U.S. 1301, 125 L.Ed.2d 755.

When the natural parents of children sought to be adopted are living and under no legal disability to assume parental custody over the same, their written consent to the adoption proceedings is a necessary statutory requirement of GC 8025 (Repealed). (Annotation from former RC 3107.06.) 1921 OAG p 955.

2. Powers and jurisdiction of court

Parental consent to adoption order is jurisdictional prerequisite which, if absent, allows order to be attacked as void. In re Adoption of Zschach (Ohio 1996) 75 Ohio

St.3d 648, 665 N.E.2d 1070, reconsideration denied 76 Ohio St.3d 1410, 666 N.E.2d 569, certiorari denied 117 S.Ct. 582, 136 L.Ed.2d 513.

Valid consent to adoption is jurisdictional prerequisite to issuance of adoption order. In re Adoption of Zschach (Ohio 1996) 75 Ohio St.3d 648, 665 N.E.2d 1070, reconsideration denied 76 Ohio St.3d 1410, 666 N.E.2d 569, certiorari denied 117 S.Ct. 582, 136 L.Ed.2d 513.

Parental consent to an adoption is a jurisdictional prerequisite which, if absent, allows adoption to be attacked as void in a habeas corpus proceeding. Barnebey v. Zschach (Ohio 1995) 71 Ohio St.3d 588, 646 N.E.2d 162.

Probate court order allowing adoption to proceed without putative father's consent was a final, appealable order as an order that affected a substantial right made in a special proceeding. In re Adoption of Greer (Ohio 1994) 70 Ohio St.3d 293, 638 N.E.2d 999.

RC 3107.06(D) may not operate to divest the probate court of its necessary judicial power to fully hear and determine an adoption proceeding. (Annotation from former RC 3107.06.) State ex rel. Portage County Welfare Dept. v. Summers (Ohio 1974) 38 Ohio St.2d 144, 311 N.E.2d 6, 67 O.O.2d 151.

Where there is substantial evidence in the record to support the conclusion of the probate court on a factual question involved in a case, a finding by the court of appeals that there is no such substantial evidence in the record may, where reasonable minds could find either way on such factual question, be regarded as a conclusion by the court of appeals that the finding of the probate court is against the weight of the evidence. (Annotation from former RC 3107.06.) In re Adoption of Lewis (Ohio 1966) 8 Ohio St.2d 25, 222 N.E.2d 628, 37 O.O.2d 376.

A probate court has jurisdiction to hear and determine an adoption proceeding relating to a minor child notwithstanding the fact that the custody of such child is at the time within the continuing jurisdiction of a divorce court. (Annotation from former RC 3107.06.) In re Adoption of Biddle (Ohio 1958) 168 Ohio St. 209, 152 N.E.2d 105, 6 O.O.2d 4, on remand 163 N.E.2d 188, 81 Ohio Law Abs. 529.

Except in those instances specified in GC 8004-6 (RC 3107.06), a probate court had no power to make a final decree or interlocutory order of adoption of a child where it affirmatively appears that there was not filed with the court a written consent to the adoption by the living mother of such child; and the requirement of such a consent was not dispensed with in an instance where a juvenile court had previously made a valid determination that such child was "neglected." (Annotation from former RC 3107.06.) In re Ramsey (Ohio 1956) 164 Ohio St. 567, 132 N.E.2d 469, 58 O.O. 431.

A probate court's failure to consider a putative father's objection to adoption which is filed before entry of the final decree of adoption is not erroneous where the putative father's objection is not filed within thirty days of placement of the minor as set forth in RC 3107.06(F); thus, the putative father's consent was not necessary in order for the court to proceed with the adoption. In re Adoption of Hall (Franklin 1991) 72 Ohio App.3d 503, 595 N.E.2d 473.

The continuing jurisdiction in a divorce action of the court of common pleas, domestic relations division, to determine the custody of a minor child does not deprive the court of common pleas, probate division, of jurisdiction in adoption proceedings relating to that child. Syversten v. Carrelli (Cuyahoga 1979) 67 Ohio App.2d 105, 425 N.E.2d 930, 21 O.O.3d 418.

RC 3107.06 does not mandate that the ongoing jurisdiction of a Kentucky juvenile court bars the issuance of an adoption order by the probate division of an Ohio court of common pleas. In re Johnson (Hamilton 1978) 56 Ohio App.2d 265, 382 N.E.2d 1176, 10 O.O.3d 278.

Strict statutory compliance with RC 3107.06(B) is required. (Annotation from former RC 3107.06.) (See also In re Harshey, 45 App(2d) 97, 341 NE(2d) 616 (1975).) In re Harshey (Cuyahoga 1974) 40 Ohio App.2d 157, 318 N.E.2d 544, 69 O.O.2d 165.

Order denying adoption reversed where such order was based on the fact that the adopting father was Caucasian, his wife Japanese, the natural mother of English descent, and the natural father Puerto Rican. (Annotation from former RC 3107.06.) In re Adoption of Baker (Cuyahoga 1962) 117 Ohio App. 26, 185 N.E.2d 51, 90 Ohio Law Abs. 125, 22 O.O.2d 459.

While courts in one state will enforce a valid custody decree of foreign court rendered in divorce action, in so far as it determines the status of the child at the time it was issued, yet such courts may, if they have jurisdiction, change such award upon facts which have arisen subsequent to the first decree, without consent of such foreign court. (Annotation from former RC 3107.06.) In re Adoption of Wyant (Henry 1942) 72 Ohio App. 249, 51 N.E.2d 221, 40 Ohio Law Abs. 164, 27 O.O. 105.

While the consent required by RC 3107.06 is not a prerequisite for granting jurisdiction to the probate court in an adoption proceeding, compliance with the statute is. (Annotation from former RC 3107.02.) In re Dickhaus (Ohio Com.Pl. 1974) 41 Ohio Misc. 1, 321 N.E.2d 800, 70 O.O.2d 24.

The legality of a placement of a child with persons other than his parents is governed by the statute in effect at the time such placement is made. (Annotation from former RC 3107.06.) In re Adoption of Wright (Ohio Prob. 1968) 15 Ohio Misc. 354, 240 N.E.2d 923, 44 O.O.2d 509.

Where, in divorce proceedings, one parent is awarded custody of child, consent of that parent, under GC 10512-11 (RC 3107.03), together with consent of court granting divorce, is sufficient consent to adoption of such child, and once such court has granted consent, it loses jurisdiction of child, and subsequent vacation of such consent is ineffective to revest jurisdiction or to prevent adoption. (Annotation from former RC 3107.06.) In re Stromberg's Adoption (Montgomery 1944) 58 N.E.2d 88, 41 Ohio Law Abs. 133.

Where a minor child has been awarded to his mother in divorce proceedings, and the mother remarries, her husband adopting the child, the court which granted the divorce loses jurisdiction over the child to make an order affecting its future custody by virtue of GC 10512-11 (RC 3107.03), but still retains jurisdiction of the parties interested in the modification of the support order. (Annotation from former RC 3107.06.) Kosen v. Kosen (Cuyahoga 1942) 42 N.E.2d 778, 36 Ohio Law Abs. 156, 23 O.O. 449, appeal dismissed 140 Ohio St. 131, 42 N.E.2d 647, 23 O.O. 459.

A decree of adoption which only shows consent of one of the natural parents, where the statute requires both unless the other is accounted for, is not subject to collateral attack to defeat the right to be the heir of the foster parent; compliance with the requirement is not jurisdictional and is presumed. (Annotation from former RC 3107.06.) Taylor v Bushnell, 29 CC(NS) 497, 35 CD 642 (1919).

An Ohio probate court is without jurisdiction to act in adoption proceedings where parties in interest are nonresidents of the state of Ohio, and a former decree unrevoked of a court of another state has awarded the custody of said minor to a foster parent. Such court originally determining such matters has a continuing jurisdiction in the same. (Annotation from former RC 3107.06.) 1921 OAG p 955.

3. Consent of institution, etc.

When public agency subjects natural parent, who is minor, single, and unrepresented by counsel, to undue influence, and as result of that undue influence, parent signs agreement permanently surrendering her child, parent's consent to agreement is invalid and custody of child remains with parent. In re Adoption of Zschach (Ohio 1996) 75 Ohio St.3d 648, 665 N.E.2d 1070, reconsideration denied 76 Ohio St.3d 1410, 666 N.E.2d 569, certiorari denied 117 S.Ct. 582, 136 L.Ed.2d 513.

Unless statutory requirement to consent of adoption is excused by virtue of failure of putative father to file objection, a putative father who has signed birth certificate as informant has statutory right to withhold consent to adoption of that child, thereby barring child's adoption by another. In re Adoption of Greer (Ohio 1994) 70 Ohio St.3d 293, 638 N.E.2d 999.

A child, surrendered by its parents into the permanent custody of an institution established for the purpose of aiding, caring for and placing children in homes, under a written agreement pursuant to RC 5103.15, which agreement provides that the institution may appear in any legal proceeding for the adoption of such child and consent to the child's adoption, continues as an heir of its parents, either natural or adoptive, until such time as the child has been legally adopted pursuant to RC Ch 3107. (Annotation from former RC 3107.06.) Maurer v. Becker (Ohio 1971) 26 Ohio St.2d 254, 271 N.E.2d 255, 55 O.O.2d 486.

Where the parents of a child make an agreement surrendering such child into the permanent custody of an association or institution of this state, established for the purposes of aiding, caring for, and placing children in homes, and approved and certified by the division of social administration of the department of public welfare, in writing on a form prescribed and furnished by such division, and authorizes the association or institution to appear in any proceeding for the legal adoption of such child and consent to its adoption without fraud or misrepresentation, and the association or institution accepts, the agreement is irrevocable except with the consent of the association or institution even though one of the parents was a minor. (Annotation from former RC 3107.06.) Kozak v. Lutheran Children's Aid Soc. (Ohio 1955) 164 Ohio St. 335, 130 N.E.2d 796, 58 O.O. 125.

Paternity was established, within meaning of adoption statute requiring father's consent, when administrative determination of parentage was made, even though order did not become final for 30 days. In re Adoption of Hudnell (Ross 1996) 113 Ohio App.3d 296, 680 N.E.2d 1055.

Accidental meeting between father and child was "communication" for purposes of adoption statutes requiring parent's consent unless parent has failed without justifiable cause to communicate with child during the year preceding the adoption petition. In re Adoption of Hudnell (Ross 1996) 113 Ohio App.3d 296, 680 N.E.2d 1055.

Father's duty to support child did not begin until date administrative parentage determination became final, nearly a month after mother and stepfather petitioned to adopt child, and, therefore, father's earlier failure to support child did not obviate need to obtain father's consent to adoption. In re Adoption of Hudnell (Ross 1996) 113 Ohio App.3d 296, 680 N.E.2d 1055.

Finding that parent's consent to adoption is unnecessary is final, appealable order. In re Adoption of Hudnell (Ross 1996) 113 Ohio App.3d 296, 680 N.E.2d 1055.

Statutory requirement that juvenile court give its consent to adoption where court has jurisdiction over child and child's guardian is not authorized to give consent does not give court greater power and involvement in adoption proceeding than guardian or agency would have. State ex rel. Hitchcock v. Cuyahoga Cty. Court of Common Pleas, Probate Div. (Cuyahoga 1994) 97 Ohio App.3d 600, 647 N.E.2d 208.

The required consent for an adoption may be executed any time from seventy-two hours after the birth of a child to be adopted until the time the adoption petition is granted, and there is no jurisdictional defect if the required consent is not executed prior to the hearing on the adoption petition or prior to the close of the petitioner's case; thus, where the guardian of children sought to be adopted gives her written consent well before the adoption petition is granted, the trial court has jurisdiction to grant the adoption petition even though the consent was not given prior to the close of the petitioner's case. In re Adoption of Jordan (Preble 1991) 72 Ohio App.3d 638, 595 N.E.2d 963.

A probate court errs in stating it will uphold the denial of consent to adoption by a human services department absent an abuse of discretion by such department, since this constitutes an impermisible delegation of judicial power to the department; the court must independently determine whether an adoption should be granted. In re Adoption of Yoder (Tuscarawas 1989) 62 Ohio App.3d 820, 577 N.E.2d 692, motion overruled 45 Ohio St.3d 710, 545 N.E.2d 905.

The main purpose of adoption is to find homes for children, not children for families. (Annotation from former RC 3107.06.) (See also In re Harshey, 40 App(2d) 157, 318 NE(2d) 544 (1974).) In re Harshey (Cuyahoga 1975) 45 Ohio App.2d 97, 341 N.E.2d 616, 74 O.O.2d 120.

RC 5103.16 is intended to provide a measure of judicial control over so-called "independent" placements for adoption, not conducted under the aegis of an authorized agency such as the county welfare department, and such measure of control can be accomplished by requiring, inter alia, that parents of a child seeking to make such an independent placement for adoption personally apply to and appear before the proper probate court for approval of the placement. (Annotation from former RC 3107.06.) (See also In re Harshey, 45 App(2d) 97, 341 NE(2d) 616 (1975).) In re Harshey (Cuyahoga 1974) 40 Ohio App.2d 157, 318 N.E.2d 544, 69 O.O.2d 165.

While natural parents entrusted with the permanent custody of their children may deprive a probate court of jurisdiction to enter a decree of adoption by withholding their consent to the adoption, the refusal of consent to an adoption by a "certified agency" as defined in RC 3107.01(C) does not impair the jurisdiction of the probate court to fully hear and determine an adoption proceeding. (Annotation from former RC 3107.06.) (See also In re Harshey, 45 App(2d) 97, 341 NE(2d) 616 (1975).) In re Harshey (Cuyahoga 1974) 40 Ohio App.2d 157, 318 N.E.2d 544, 69 O.O.2d 165.

A petition for adoption, duly filed in accordance with RC 3107.03 is not properly dismissed without a hearing on the merits merely upon a finding by the probate court that a certified agency has not consented to the adoption as required in RC 3107.06. (Annotation from former RC 3107.06.) (See also In re Harshey, 45 App(2d) 97, 341 NE(2d) 616 (1975).) In re Harshey (Cuyahoga 1974) 40 Ohio App.2d 157, 318 N.E.2d 544, 69 O.O.2d 165.

Where adoptive parents clearly meet all of the agency's standards concerning maturity, stability, financial ability to carry responsibility, and love of the child, and where the agency placed the child with the adoptive parents from birth to the present time as foster parents, the denial of agency consent based solely upon the age of the adoptive parents is unreasonable, arbitrary, and capricious, and violates the spirit of the whole adoption system while holding to the letter of part of it. (Annotation from former RC 3107.06.) In re Haun (Cuyahoga 1972) 31 Ohio App.2d 63, 286 N.E.2d 478, 60 O.O.2d 163.

The refusal of an agency to consent to an adoption does not deprive the probate court of jurisdiction even when such refusal is not arbitrary, unreasonable, or capricious, and is but an element for consideration in the probate court's determination of the qualifications of the adoptive parents and the best interests of the child. (Annotation from former RC 3107.06.) In re Haun (Cuyahoga 1972) 31 Ohio App.2d 63, 286 N.E.2d 478, 60 O.O.2d 163.

A department of human services does not act in a "wanton or reckless manner" by its decision to place a foster child for adoption in a home other than that of the foster parents. Jay T v Williams County Human Services Dept, No. 94WM000007, 1995 WL 19112 (6th Dist Ct App, Williams, 1-20-95).

Where evidence shows that the social services agency has no substantial reasons for withholding the answer and consent required by RC 3107.06, the court will order the answer and consent filed when the court determines it is in the best interest of the child, but if substantial reasons exist for withholding such answer and consent, and the court is satisfied that it is not in the best interest of the child to require it, the petition for adoption will be denied. (Annotation from former RC 3107.06.) In re Dickhaus (Ohio Com.Pl. 1974) 41 Ohio Misc. 1, 321 N.E.2d 800, 70 O.O.2d 24.

While the consent required by RC 3107.06 is not a prerequisite for granting jurisdiction to the probate court in an adoption proceeding, compliance with the statute is. (Annotation from former RC 3107.06.) In re Dickhaus (Ohio Com.Pl. 1974) 41 Ohio Misc. 1, 321 N.E.2d 800, 70 O.O.2d 24.

An answer and consent signed and verified by the executive secretary of the child welfare board is sufficient compliance with RC 3107.06 to authorize the court to enter a decree of adoption. (Annotation from former RC 3107.06.) In re Adoption of Wyatt (Ohio Prob. 1965) 4 Ohio Misc. 47, 210 N.E.2d 925, 33 O.O.2d 27.

The consent to adoption of a county child welfare board required under RC 3107.06 can be given by a majority of a quorum of the board, but not by the executive secretary to the board. (Annotation from former RC 3107.06.) OAG 65-24.

Under the provisions of GC 8025 (Repealed), a New York society can give the legal consent to the adoption in Ohio of a child, if and when said society has received the certificate mentioned in GC 1352-1 (RC 5103.03) and has fully complied with the provisions of GC 1677 (Repealed). (Annotation from former RC 3107.06.) 1922 OAG p 518.

4. Withdrawal of consent

A petition in habeas corpus seeking to revoke a natural parent's consent to an adoption will be denied where the issues raised have already been determined in an action to revoke consent and an appeal from such action. McGinty v. Jewish Children's Bureau (Ohio 1989) 46 Ohio St.3d 159, 545 N.E.2d 1272.

Revocation of a natural parent's consent to adoption is not shown where, after repeated questioning, the custodial parent testifies that it may be in the child's best interest to become reacquainted with the noncustodial parent before the child decides whether he wants to be adopted by a stepparent. In re Adoption of Carletti (Muskingum 1992) 78 Ohio App.3d 244, 604 N.E.2d 243, motion overruled 65 Ohio St.3d 1457, 602 N.E.2d 253.

Where a mother, as sole parent, files an "application for placement" and a written waiver and consent to adoption in the probate court to place her newborn baby with a married couple whose identity she did not know but who were procured by an intermediary at her request with adoption in mind, appears in person before such court for approval of such placement, and the probate court, after an independent investigation of the proposed placement by a qualified person determines that it is in the best interest of the child and approves of record the proposed placement, and the child is delivered to the married couple pursuant to the order of the court, the mother, as petitioner in a habeas corpus action filed in the court of common pleas to regain custody of her child, is estopped from claiming that the probate court was without jurisdiction by reason of an insufficient application in not identifying by names the placement parents; and a finding by the court of common pleas of lack of such jurisdiction is reversible error. (Annotation from former RC 3107.06.) In re McTaggart (Cuyahoga 1965) 4 Ohio App.2d 359, 212 N.E.2d 663, 33 O.O.2d 447.

Where one of the parents had been awarded divorce and custody of child, and other parent had failed or refused to support such child for two consecutive years prior to proceeding to adopt child, the consent, under the statute, of former to such adoption is sufficient, notwithstanding failure of court which awarded such divorce and custody to approve such consent; and as the consents prescribed by subdivisions (a) and (d) of the second provision of the statute are cumulative, consent complying with former subdivision need not comply with latter. (Annotation from former RC 3107.06.) In re Adoption of Wyant (Henry 1942) 72 Ohio App. 249, 51 N.E.2d 221, 40 Ohio Law Abs. 164, 27 O.O. 105.

An interlocutory order of adoption is erroneously entered after the putative father of the minor child who signed the birth certificate objects to the adoption, and consequently, a mother's motion to withdraw her consent to the adoption is not time barred pursuant to RC 3107.09. In re Adoption of Zschach, Nos. 1994CA-14+, 1994 WL 728626 (5th Dist Ct App, Fairfield, 12-19-94), reversed by 75 Ohio St.3d 648 (1996).

Approval by the court of the permanent surrender of a child is purely an administrative matter, and not in the nature of an adversary proceeding; the court has no duty to advise the mother of her right to counsel or to appoint a lawyer for her in the event of indigency. (Annotation from former RC 3107.06.) In re K. (Ohio Juv. 1969) 31 Ohio Misc. 218, 282 N.E.2d 370, 60 O.O.2d 134, 60 O.O.2d 388.

Mother of illegitimate child has right to withdraw her consent to an adoption of her child at any time before the court acts upon such consent and in so doing dismisses the petition for the adoption of the child and deprives the court of proceeding further with the case. (Annotation from former RC 3107.06.) In re Adoption of Rubin, 33 Abs 108 (Prob, Belmont 1941).

Consent to the adoption of an illegitimate child may be withdrawn by the mother. (Annotation from former RC 3107.06.) In re O--- (Ohio Juv. 1964) 199 N.E.2d 765, 95 Ohio Law Abs. 101, 28 O.O.2d 165.

Placement of an illegitimate child for adoption and subsequent withdrawal of consent thereto by the mother does not of itself warrant a finding that the child is neglected. (Annotation from former RC 3107.06.) In re O--- (Ohio Juv. 1964) 199 N.E.2d 765, 95 Ohio Law Abs. 101, 28 O.O.2d 165.

Consent to adoption by the mother of a child is necessary in order to confer jurisdiction to enter the adoption order, and the lack of such consent may be asserted in a habeas corpus proceeding. (Annotation from former RC 3107.06.) In re Martin (Cuyahoga 1957) 140 N.E.2d 623, 76 Ohio Law Abs. 219.

Consent of the mother in writing at the time of the decree, if she is accessible, is necessary to a decree for adoption by petition; and her previous consent may be revoked at any time before decree. (Annotation from former RC 3107.06.) State ex rel Scholder v Scholder, 22 LR 608 (1924).

A mother who is a minor under twenty-one years of age may lawfully give her consent to the adoption of her child, under this section, and may also surrender such child under GC 1352-12 and 1352-13 (RC 5103.15 and 5103.16). (Annotation from former RC 3107.06.) 1930 OAG 1584.

5. Objections to adoptions, construed

Putative father's attempt to condition his consent to adoption upon his retention of permanent visitation rights was not written objection to adoption, required to preserve his right to contest adoption. In re Adoption of Zschach (Ohio 1996) 75 Ohio St.3d 648, 665 N.E.2d 1070, reconsideration denied 76 Ohio St.3d 1410, 666 N.E.2d 569, certiorari denied 117 S.Ct. 582, 136 L.Ed.2d 513.

The filing of the acknowledgement of paternity pursuant to RC 2105.18 accompanied by the filing of an objection to adoption pursuant to RC 3107.06(F)(4) is sufficient to place the father within the purview of RC 3107.07(A) as a parent and not within RC 3107(B). In re Adoption of Dickson, No. 94-CA-57, 1995 WL 495450 (5th Dist Ct App, Fairfield, 5-19-95).

Verbal objections made over the telephone by a putative father to the department of human services do not constitute the "filing" of an objection satisfying RC 3107.06. In re Adoption of Eckleberry, No. 94APF10-1523, 1995 WL 311409 (10th Dist Ct App, Franklin, 5-11-95).

6. Constitutional issues

A putative father who fails to preserve his rights to contest an adoption by filing an objection within the time limits prescribed by RC 3107.06 has no parental rights and, as such, is due no process. In re Adoption of Eckleberry, No. 94APF10-1523, 1995 WL 311409 (10th Dist Ct App, Franklin, 5-11-95).

3107.061 Adoption of child without putative father's consent

A man who has sexual intercourse with a woman is on notice that if a child is born as a result and the man is the putative father, the child may be adopted without his consent pursuant to division (B) of section 3107.07 of the Revised Code.

(1996 H 419, eff. 6-20-96)

Library References

Am Jur 2d: 2, Adoption § 113

Natural parent's parental rights as affected by consent to child's adoption by other natural parent. 37 ALR4th 724

Required parties in adoption proceedings. 48 ALR4th 860

Baldwin's Ohio Legislative Service, 1996 H 419—LSC Analysis, 3/L-336

Carlin, Baldwin's Ohio Practice, *Merrick-Rippner Probate Law* § 98.2, 98.29 (1997)

Law Review and Journal Commentaries

Ohio House Bill 419: Increased Openness in Adoption Records Law, Wendy L. Weiss. 45 Clev St L Rev 101 (1997).

3107.062 Putative father registry

The department of job and family services shall establish a putative father registry. To register, a putative father must complete a registration form prescribed under section 3107.065 of the Revised Code and submit it to the department. The registration form shall include the putative father's name; the address or telephone number at which he wishes to receive, pursuant to section 3107.11 of the Revised Code, notice of a petition to adopt the minor he claims as his child; and the name of the mother of the minor.

A putative father may register before or not later than thirty days after the birth of the child. No fee shall be charged for registration.

On receipt of a completed registration form, the department shall indicate on the form the date of receipt and file it in the putative father registry. The department shall maintain registration forms in a manner that enables it to access a registration form using either the name of the putative father or of the mother.

(1999 H 471, eff. 7-1-00; 1996 H 274, eff. 9-18-96; 1996 H 419, eff. 9-18-96)

Historical and Statutory Notes

Amendment Note: 1999 H 471 substituted "job and family" for "human" in the first paragraph.

Amendment Note: 1996 H 274 substituted "not later than thirty days" for ", to the extent provided by division (B)(1) of section 3107.07 of the Revised Code," in the second paragraph.

Cross References

Availability of state government public records, public records defined, 149.43
Examination of putative father registry, 5101.313
Personal information systems, right to inspection of putative father registry, 1347.08
Uniform Interstate Family Support Act, bases for jurisdiction over nonresident, 3115.03

Ohio Administrative Code References

Putative father registry, OAC 5101:2-48-02

Library References

Am Jur 2d: 2, Adoption § 113
Natural parent's parental rights as affected by consent to child's adoption by other natural parent. 37 ALR4th 724
Required parties in adoption proceedings. 48 ALR4th 860
Baldwin's Ohio Legislative Service, 1996 H 419—LSC Analysis, 3/L-336
Carlin, Baldwin's Ohio Practice, *Merrick-Rippner Probate Law* § 98.2, 98.31, 98.37 (1997)
Sowald & Morganstern, Baldwin's Ohio Practice, *Domestic Relations Law* § 23.32 (1997)

Law Review and Journal Commentaries

Ohio House Bill 419: Increased Openness in Adoption Records Law, Wendy L. Weiss. 45 Clev St L Rev 101 (1997).

3107.063 Request to search registry

A mother or an agency or attorney arranging a minor's adoption may request at any time that the department of job and family services search the putative father registry to determine whether a man is registered as the minor's putative father. The request shall include the mother's name. On receipt of the request, the department shall search the registry. If the department determines that a man is registered as the minor's putative father, it shall provide the mother, agency, or attorney a certified copy of the man's registration form. If the department determines that no man is registered as the minor's putative father, it shall provide the mother, agency, or attorney a certified written statement to that effect. The department shall specify in the statement the date the search request was submitted. No fee shall be charged for searching the registry.

Division (B) of section 3107.17 of the Revised Code does not apply to this section.

(1999 H 471, eff. 7-1-00; 1996 H 274, eff. 9-18-96; 1996 H 419, eff. 9-18-96)

Historical and Statutory Notes

Amendment Note: 1999 H 471 substituted "job and family" for "human" in the first paragraph.

Amendment Note: 1996 H 274 deleted "Not sooner than thirty one days after the birth of a minor," from the beginning of, and inserted "at any time" in, the first sentence in the first paragraph; and made other nonsubstantive changes.

Library References

Am Jur 2d: 2, Adoption § 113

Natural parent's parental rights as affected by consent to child's adoption by other natural parent. 37 ALR4th 724
Required parties in adoption proceedings. 48 ALR4th 860
Baldwin's Ohio Legislative Service, 1996 H 419—LSC Analysis, 3/L-336
Carlin, Baldwin's Ohio Practice, *Merrick-Rippner Probate Law* § 98.2 (1997)

3107.064 Required search of registry prior to adoption; exceptions

(A) Except as provided in division (B) of this section, a court shall not issue a final decree of adoption or finalize an interlocutory order of adoption unless the mother placing the minor for adoption or the agency or attorney arranging the adoption files with the court a certified document provided by the department of job and family services under section 3107.063 of the Revised Code. The court shall not accept the document unless the date the department places on the document pursuant to that section is thirty-one or more days after the date of the minor's birth.

(B) The document described in division (A) of this section is not required if any of the following apply:

(1) The mother was married at the time the minor was conceived or born;

(2) The parent placing the minor for adoption previously adopted the minor;

(3) Prior to the date a petition to adopt the minor is filed, a man has been determined to have a parent and child relationship with the minor by a court proceeding pursuant to sections 3111.01 to 3111.19 of the Revised Code, a court proceeding in another state, an administrative agency proceeding pursuant to sections 3111.20 to 3111.29 of the Revised Code, or an administrative agency proceeding in another state;

(4) The minor's father acknowledged paternity of the minor and that acknowledgment has become final pursuant to section 2151.232, 3111.211, or 5101.314 of the Revised Code;

(5) A public children services agency has permanent custody of the minor pursuant to Chapter 2151. or division (B) of section 5103.15 of the Revised Code after both parents lost or surrendered parental rights, privileges, and responsibilities over the minor.

(1999 H 471, eff. 7-1-00; 1997 H 352, eff. 1-1-98; 1996 H 274, eff. 9-18-96; 1996 H 419, eff. 9-18-96)

Historical and Statutory Notes

Amendment Note: 1999 H 471 substituted "job and family" for "human" in division (A).

Amendment Note: 1997 H 352 rewrote division (B)(4), which prior thereto read:

"(4) The minor's father acknowledged paternity of the minor pursuant to section 2105.18 of the Revised Code."

Amendment Note: 1996 H 274 added the second sentence in division (A); added division (B)(4); and redesignated former division (B)(4) as division (B)(5).

Library References

Am Jur 2d: 2, Adoption § 69 to 73, 113, 125
Natural parent's parental rights as affected by consent to child's adoption by other natural parent. 37 ALR4th 724
Required parties in adoption proceedings. 48 ALR4th 860
Baldwin's Ohio Legislative Service, 1996 H 419—LSC Analysis, 3/L-336
Carlin, Baldwin's Ohio Practice, *Merrick-Rippner Probate Law* § 19.4, 98.2, 98.30, 98.31, 98.33, 98.37 (1997)
Sowald & Morganstern, Baldwin's Ohio Practice, *Domestic Relations Law* § 22.19 (1997)

3107.065 Rules, registration form, and informational campaign for registry

Not later than ninety days after the effective date of this section, the director of job and family services shall do both of the following:

(A) Adopt rules in accordance with Chapter 119. of the Revised Code governing the putative father registry. The rules shall establish the registration form to be used by a putative father under section 3107.062 of the Revised Code.

(B) Establish a campaign to promote awareness of the putative father registry. The campaign shall include informational materials about the registry.

(1999 H 471, eff. 7-1-00; 1996 H 419, eff. 6-20-96)

Historical and Statutory Notes

Amendment Note: 1999 H 471 substituted "director of job and family services" for "department of human services" in the introductory paragraph.

Library References

Baldwin's Ohio Legislative Service, 1996 H 419—LSC Analysis, 3/L-336

Carlin, Baldwin's Ohio Practice, *Merrick-Rippner Probate Law* § 98.2 (1997)

3107.07 Consents not required

Consent to adoption is not required of any of the following:

(A) A parent of a minor, when it is alleged in the adoption petition and the court finds after proper service of notice and hearing, that the parent has failed without justifiable cause to communicate with the minor or to provide for the maintenance and support of the minor as required by law or judicial decree for a period of at least one year immediately preceding either the filing of the adoption petition or the placement of the minor in the home of the petitioner.

(B) The putative father of a minor if either of the following applies:

(1) The putative father fails to register as the minor's putative father with the putative father registry established under section 3107.062 of the Revised Code not later than thirty days after the minor's birth;

(2) The court finds, after proper service of notice and hearing, that any of the following are the case:

(a) The putative father is not the father of the minor;

(b) The putative father has willfully abandoned or failed to care for and support the minor;

(c) The putative father has willfully abandoned the mother of the minor during her pregnancy and up to the time of her surrender of the minor, or the minor's placement in the home of the petitioner, whichever occurs first.

(C) Except as provided in section 3107.071 of the Revised Code, a parent who has entered into a voluntary permanent custody surrender agreement under division (B) of section 5103.15 of the Revised Code;

(D) A parent whose parental rights have been terminated by order of a juvenile court under Chapter 2151. of the Revised Code;

(E) A parent who is married to the petitioner and supports the adoption;

(F) The father, or putative father, of a minor if the minor is conceived as the result of the commission of rape by the father or putative father and the father or putative father is convicted of or pleads guilty to the commission of that offense. As used in this division, "rape" means a violation of section 2907.02 of the Revised Code or a similar law of another state.

(G) A legal guardian or guardian ad litem of a parent judicially declared incompetent in a separate court proceeding who has failed to respond in writing to a request for consent, for a period of thirty days, or who, after examination of the written reasons for withholding consent, is found by the court to be withholding consent unreasonably;

(H) Any legal guardian or lawful custodian of the person to be adopted, other than a parent, who has failed to respond in writing to a request for consent, for a period of thirty days, or who, after examination of the written reasons for withholding consent, is found by the court to be withholding consent unreasonably;

(I) The spouse of the person to be adopted, if the failure of the spouse to consent to the adoption is found by the court to be by reason of prolonged unexplained absence, unavailability, incapacity, or circumstances that make it impossible or unreasonably difficult to obtain the consent or refusal of the spouse;

(J) Any parent, legal guardian, or other lawful custodian in a foreign country, if the person to be adopted has been released for adoption pursuant to the laws of the country in which the person resides and the release of such person is in a form that satisfies the requirements of the immigration and naturalization service of the United States department of justice for purposes of immigration to the United States pursuant to section 101(b)(1)(F) of the "Immigration and Nationality Act," 75 Stat. 650 (1961), 8 U.S.C. 1101(b)(1)(F), as amended or reenacted.

(K) Except as provided in divisions (G) and (H) of this section, a juvenile court, agency, or person given notice of the petition pursuant to division (A)(1) of section 3107.11 of the Revised Code that fails to file an objection to the petition within fourteen days after proof is filed pursuant to division (B) of that section that the notice was given;

(L) Any guardian, custodian, or other party who has temporary custody of the child.

(1999 H 176, eff. 10-29-99; 1998 H 484, eff. 3-18-99; 1996 H 274, eff. 9-18-96; 1996 H 419, eff. 9-18-96; 1986 H 428, eff. 12-23-86; 1980 S 205; 1977 H 1; 1976 H 156)

Uncodified Law

1996 H 419, § 5: See Uncodified Law under 3107.06.

Historical and Statutory Notes

Ed. Note: 3107.07 contains provisions analogous to former 3107.06, repealed by 1976 H 156, eff. 1-1-77.

Ed. Note: Former 3107.07 repealed by 1976 H 156, eff. 1-1-77; 1953 H 1; GC 8004-7; Source—GC 10512-17.

Pre-1953 H 1 Amendments: 124 v S 65

Amendment Note: 1999 H 176 substituted "(A)(1)" for "(A)(2)" in division (K).

Amendment Note: 1998 H 484 added division (L).

Amendment Note: 1996 H 274 deleted ", or for reasons beyond his control, other than lack of knowledge of the minor's birth, is not able to register within that time period and fails to register not later than ten days after it becomes possible to register" from the end of division (B)(1).

Amendment Note: 1996 H 419 rewrote divisions (B) and (C); added divisions (E), (F), and (K); redesignated former divisions (E) through (H) as (G) through (J), respectively; and made changes to reflect gender neutral language throughout. Prior to amendment, divisions (B) and (C) read:

"(B) The putative father of a minor if the putative father fails to file an objection with the court, the department of human services, or the agency having custody of the minor as provided in division (F)(4) of section 3107.06 of the Revised Code, or files an objection with the court, department, or agency and the court finds, after proper service of notice and hearing, that he is not the father of the minor, or that he has willfully abandoned or failed to care for and support the minor, or abandoned the mother of the minor during her pregnancy and up to the time of her surrender of the minor, or its placement in the home of the petitioner, whichever occurs first;

"(C) A parent who has relinquished his right to consent under section 5103.15 of the Revised Code;"

Cross References

Department of job and family services, division of social administration, placing of children; interstate compact on placement of children, 5103.09 to 5103.17, 5103.20 to 5103.28

Married persons to support self, spouse and children, duration of duty to support, 3103.03

Support of children, 3109.05

Library References

Adoption ⚷7 to 7.8.
WESTLAW Topic No. 17.
C.J.S. Adoption of Persons §§ 51 to 72.

OJur 3d: 62, Investment Securities and Securities Regulation § 53

Am Jur 2d: 2, Adoption § 23 et seq.

Right of natural parent to withdraw valid consent to adoption of child. 74 ALR3d 421

Mistake or want of understanding as ground for revocation of consent to adoption or of agreement releasing infant to adoption placement agency. 74 ALR3d 489

What constitutes "duress" in obtaining parent's consent to adoption of child or surrender of child to adoption agency. 74 ALR3d 527

Parent's involuntary confinement, or failure to care for child as result thereof, as permitting adoption without parental consent. 78 ALR3d 712

Adoption of child in absence of statutorily required consent of public or private agency or institution. 83 ALR3d 373

Baldwin's Ohio Legislative Service, 1996 H 419—LSC Analysis, 3/L-336

Carlin, Baldwin's Ohio Practice, *Merrick-Rippner Probate Law* § 19.10, 98.2, 98.6, 98.8, 98.29, 98.30, 98.31, 98.33, 98.37, 98.38, 98.39, 98.41, 98.43 (1997)
Klein & Darling, Baldwin's Ohio Practice, *Civil Practice* § 4 (1997)
Sowald & Morganstern, Baldwin's Ohio Practice, *Domestic Relations Law* § 3.46, 18.20 (1997)

Law Review and Journal Commentaries

Adoption—Abandonment and Failure to Support as Grounds for Dispensing With the Natural Parent's Consent, Note. 14 J Fam L 139 (1975).

Awarding Child Support Against the Impoverished Parent: Straying from Statutory Guidelines and Using SSI in Setting the Amount, Note. 83 Ky L J 653 (1994-95).

Children Born Out Of Wedlock And Nonsupport—Valid Statutory Grounds For Termination Of Parental Rights?, Note. 25 J Fam L 755 (1986-87).

Contested Adoptions, Glenn E. Forbes. 12 Lake Legal Views 9 (February 1989).

Defining the "Best Interests": Constitutional Protections in Involuntary Adoptions, Erwin Chemerinsky. 18 J Fam L 79 (1979-80).

Lehr v Robertson: Putative Fathers Revisited, Note. 11 Ohio N U L Rev 385 (1984).

Lehr v Robinson: Putting the Genie Back in the Bottle: the Supreme Court Limits the Scope of the Putative Father's Right to Notice, Hearing, and Consent in the Adoption of His Illegitimate Child, Comment. 15 U Tol L Rev 1501 (Summer 1984).

Protecting the Putative Father's Rights After Stanley v Illinois: Problems In Implementation, Note. 13 J Fam L 115 (1973-74).

Seeking the wisdom of Solomon: Defining the rights of unwed fathers in newborn adoptions, Scott A. Resnik. 20 Seton Hall Legis J 363 (1996).

Termination of Parental Rights in Adoption Cases: Focusing on the Child, Comment. 14 J Fam L 547 (1975-76).

Notes of Decisions and Opinions

---

1. In general

Probate court order allowing adoption to proceed without putative father's consent was a final, appealable order as an order that affected a substantial right made in a special proceeding. In re Adoption of Greer (Ohio 1994) 70 Ohio St.3d 293, 638 N.E.2d 999.

The question of whether justifiable cause for failure to pay child support has been proven by clear and convincing evidence in a particular case is a determination for the probate court and will not be disturbed on appeal unless such determination is against the manifest weight of the evidence. In re Adoption of Masa (Ohio 1986) 23 Ohio St.3d 163, 492 N.E.2d 140, 23 O.B.R. 330.

The marriage of a natural parent and the subsequent bringing of a minor into the home with the stepparent will not initiate ab initio the placement of a minor for the purposes of RC 3107.07(A). In determining whether a placement pursuant to RC 3107.07(A) has occurred, a court should consider the facts of each particular case while remaining mindful that the paramount concern is the best interest of the child. In re Adoption of Kreyche (Ohio 1984) 15 Ohio St.3d 159, 472 N.E.2d 1106, 15 O.B.R. 304.

RC 3107.07(A) does not impose any new duty nor does it remove any vested right. In re Adoption of McDermitt (Ohio 1980) 63 Ohio St.2d 301, 408 N.E.2d 680, 17 O.O.3d 195.

Judgment entry on issue of whether child's biological father had been in communication with child during year prior to filing of petition for child's adoption by husband of child's mother was partial final judgment; while final and appealable when entered, it was appealable alternatively 30 days after court rendered final order on all issues in case. In re Adoption of Eblin (Ohio App. 3 Dist. 1998) 126 Ohio App.3d 774, 711 N.E.2d 319, appeal allowed 82 Ohio St.3d 1482, 696 N.E.2d 1088, cause dismissed 83 Ohio St.3d 1454, 700 N.E.2d 617.

Judgment that the consent of a natural parent is not required for the adoption of a minor by another is a final order subject to appellate review. In re Doe (Ohio App. 9 Dist. 1997) 123 Ohio App.3d 505, 704 N.E.2d 608, stay denied 80 Ohio St.3d 1470, 687 N.E.2d 298, dismissed, jurisdictional motion overruled 81 Ohio St.3d 1443, 690 N.E.2d 15.

Natural parent's consent to minor child's adoption would be required if he or she provided maintenance and support for, and communicated with, child within one year prior to filing of adoption petition. In re Adoption of Wagner (Ohio App. 11 Dist. 1997) 117 Ohio App.3d 448, 690 N.E.2d 959, appeal not allowed 78 Ohio St.3d 1516, 679 N.E.2d 311.

Finding that party's consent to adoption is not required is final appealable order. In re Adoption of Wagner (Ohio App. 11 Dist. 1997) 117 Ohio App.3d 448, 690 N.E.2d 959, appeal not allowed 78 Ohio St.3d 1516, 679 N.E.2d 311.

Finding that parent's consent to adoption is unnecessary is final, appealable order. In re Adoption of Hudnell (Ross 1996) 113 Ohio App.3d 296, 680 N.E.2d 1055.

Prescriptive one-year period after which natural father may be deemed to have abandoned child so that natural father's consent is not necessary to child's adoption commences running not upon birth of child, but upon determination of paternity, so that father's actions regarding communication and support were to be analyzed from date of declaration of paternity, where father's parentage action was filed and determined prior to filing of adoption petition. In re Adoption of Sherry (Medina 1995) 107 Ohio App.3d 830, 669 N.E.2d 551.

Termination of natural parent's right to object to adoption of child is very serious matter, requiring strict adherence to controlling statute. In re Adoption of

Kuhlmann (Hamilton 1994) 99 Ohio App.3d 44, 649 N.E.2d 1279.

Probate court's judgment to dispense with parent's consent to adoption will not be reversed as being against "manifest weight of the evidence" if it is supported by some competent, credible evidence. In re Adoption of Kuhlmann (Hamilton 1994) 99 Ohio App.3d 44, 649 N.E.2d 1279.

Natural father who did not consent to adoption of his child was given reasonable opportunity to present evidence concerning child's best interest at final hearing; notice of hearing was sent and received by counsel for father on at least two, if not three, separate occasions, and father did not proffer testimony of witnesses he claimed he would have called if he had had notice of hearing. In re Adoption of Cline (Trumbull 1993) 89 Ohio App.3d 450, 624 N.E.2d 1083.

Statute citing circumstances in which natural parent's consent to adoption is not required imposes dual responsibility upon "non-petitioning" natural parent to both communicate with minor child and provide maintenance and support. In re Adoption of Cline (Trumbull 1993) 89 Ohio App.3d 450, 624 N.E.2d 1083.

A probate court errs in considering only one of two dates specified by RC 3107.07(A) regardless of policy implications where the statute contemplates the calculation of the requisite year from either the filing of the adoption petition or the placement of the child in the petitioner's home; RC 1.02(F) does not apply to alter the meaning of a provision where the statutory language is plain and unambiguous or if application of the rule would render a passage senseless. In re Adoption of Jones (Medina 1990) 70 Ohio App.3d 576, 591 N.E.2d 823.

The one-year time requirement of RC 3107.07(A) is not to be applied to RC 3107.07(B). In re Adoption of Hart (Lucas 1989) 62 Ohio App.3d 544, 577 N.E.2d 77, motion overruled 45 Ohio St.3d 704, 543 N.E.2d 810.

In calculating the one-year lack of support and communication by a natural father that is a condition of adoption without a natural parent's consent, the time before the adjudication of an illegitimate child's paternity may be considered. In re Adoption of Taylor (Medina 1989) 61 Ohio App.3d 500, 573 N.E.2d 156, motion overruled 43 Ohio St.3d 712, 541 N.E.2d 78.

RC 2151.353, permitting the state to receive permanent custody of a "dependent child" whose parent is jailed, does not conflict with RC 3107.07; where the child is a "dependent child" under RC 2151.04 the state has authority to obtain permanent custody under RC 2151.353, and once parental rights have been terminated under RC Ch 2151, it is provided by RC 3107.06(D) that this parent's consent to adoption is no longer necessary. In re Dillard (Montgomery 1988) 48 Ohio App.3d 263, 549 N.E.2d 213.

A ruling by the court that the consent of a natural parent is not required in an adoption proceeding filed pursuant to RC Ch 3107 is a final appealable order, since it constitutes "an order affecting a substantial right made in a special proceeding" within the meaning of RC 2505.02. In re Adoption of Jorgensen (Hancock 1986) 33 Ohio App.3d 207, 515 N.E.2d 622.

A finding that the consent of a natural parent is not required for an adoption under RC 3107.07(A) does not constitute consent to the adoption but merely "provides for cutting off the statutory right of a parent to withhold his consent to the adoption of the child," leaving all other parental rights and obligations intact. Therefore, the exclusion of a natural parent from the final hearing on whether or not adoption is in the best interest of the child renders meaningless the requirement of RC 3107.11 that a natural parent who has lost the right to withhold consent to the adoption be given notice of the time and place of the best interest hearing, and an adoption under such circumstances must be reversed. In re Adoption of Jorgensen (Hancock 1986) 33 Ohio App.3d 207, 515 N.E.2d 622.

A bifurcated procedure is required where the natural parent of a minor child refuses to consent to adoption of that child by a third party whereby (1) initially, the probate court determines the issue of necessity of consent, (2) a judgment on the issue of consent only is filed, and (3) in the second stage, the best interest of the child standard is utilized; failure to conduct a hearing on the issue of whether the proposed adoption is in the best interest of the child is error. In re Adoption of Zachary H, No. WM 96-013, 1997 WL 103808 (6th Dist Ct App, Williams, 3-7-97).

Diapers, toys, clothing and medical insurance constitute maintenance and support within the meaning of RC 3107.07 and there was evidence to show natural mother provided support, however meager, to child within one year of adoption petition filing. In re Adoption of Mills, No. CA93-04-036, 1993 WL 430473 (12th Dist Ct App, Warren, 10-25-93).

Statute making nonconsenting parent's consent to adoption unnecessary if he has failed to pay child support or communicate with child for one year prior to petition must be strictly construed to protect interests of natural parent. In re Serre (Ohio Com.Pl. 1996) 77 Ohio Misc.2d 29, 665 N.E.2d 1185.

Under RC 3107.07(A) the consent to an adoption is not required of a parent who has been found by the court to have failed without justifiable cause to communicate with or support the minor for a period of at least one year either immediately preceding the filing of the adoption petition or immediately preceding the placement of the minor in the home of the petitioner, and the words "whichever occurs first" are deemed to refer or pertain to such parent's failure during either period rather than to the relative dates of filing and placement. In re Adoption of Taylor (Ohio Com.Pl. 1977) 55 Ohio Misc. 15, 380 N.E.2d 370, 7 O.O.3d 167, 9 O.O.3d 350.

2. Failure to support

An unmarried parent is subject to the support obligation to which RC 3107.07(A) refers only where a paternity determination has been rendered pursuant to RC 3111.08(B) or 3111.12. In re Adoption of Sunderhaus (Ohio 1992) 63 Ohio St.3d 127, 585 N.E.2d 418, rehearing denied 63 Ohio St.3d 1442, 589 N.E.2d 46.

The one-year period of nonsupport prescribed by RC 3107.07(A) which obviates the requirement to obtain parental consent to an adoption pursuant to RC 3107.06 commences on the date that parentage has been judicially established. In re Adoption of Sunderhaus (Ohio 1992) 63 Ohio St.3d 127, 585 N.E.2d 418, rehearing denied 63 Ohio St.3d 1442, 589 N.E.2d 46.

The question of whether a natural parent's failure to support his or her child has been proven by the petitioner by clear and convincing evidence to have been without justifiable cause is a determination for the probate court, and will not be disturbed on appeal unless such determination is against the manifest weight of the evidence. In re Adoption of Bovett (Ohio 1987) 33 Ohio St.3d 102, 515 N.E.2d 919.

In order to properly support and maintain her child within the meaning of RC 3107.06, a mother has a duty to give personal care and attention to that child and, if able to do so, to provide financial support for the child, even though the child is being properly supported and maintained by someone else, and whether such mother has legal custody and actual possession of the child, either such custody or such possession, or neither such custody nor such possession. (Annotation from former RC 3107.06.) In re Adoption of Lewis (Ohio 1966) 8 Ohio St.2d 25, 222 N.E.2d 628, 37 O.O.2d 376.

To preserve the right to consent to the adoption of his or her children, a natural parent must justify his or her failure to support for substantially the entire one-year period preceding the petition for adoption; it is not enough to show that some time during the year a failure to support was justified, but it must instead be demonstrated that no modicum of support reasonably could have been provided at any time during the year. In re Adoption of Kilbane (Ohio App. 8 Dist. 1998) 130 Ohio App.3d 203, 719 N.E.2d 1012.

Stepfather established by clear and convincing evidence that his stepchildren's biological father had failed to support the children without justifiable cause for one-year statutory period preceding stepfather's petition for adoption, and thus biological father's consent was not required for proposed adoption; biological father did not make any support payments until just prior to filing of adoption petition, and his claim that he was unemployed through most of year was contradicted by other evidence in record. In re Adoption of Kilbane (Ohio App. 8 Dist. 1998) 130 Ohio App.3d 203, 719 N.E.2d 1012.

Natural mother's two payments of $10 each in October and November 1994 constituted support and maintenance of child, for purposes of October 1995 hearing on whether her consent to stepmother's adoption petition was required, even though payments were made to child support agency in wrong county and receipt of payments was delayed by nearly a year. In re Fetzer (Ohio App. 3 Dist. 1997) 118 Ohio App.3d 156, 692 N.E.2d 219, dismissed, appeal not allowed 78 Ohio St.3d 1513, 679 N.E.2d 309.

So long as natural parent complies with duty to support child for any period during the one year immediately preceding adoption petition, then she has not failed to support for purposes of statute listing circumstances in which natural parent's consent to adoption is not required. In re Fetzer (Ohio App. 3 Dist. 1997) 118 Ohio App.3d 156, 692 N.E.2d 219, dismissed, appeal not allowed 78 Ohio St.3d 1513, 679 N.E.2d 309.

Alleged payments made by natural father for provision of health coverage for minor child did not constitute "maintenance and support," for purposes of statute permitting adoption of child without natural parent's consent if parent has failed to support child without justifiable cause for year prior to adoption petition, where father failed to reveal existence of health coverage to child's mother, child derived no benefit from payments as result of father's concealment, and earlier health insurance card that mother did receive from father was rejected when she attempted to use it. In re Adoption of Wagner (Ohio App. 11 Dist. 1997) 117 Ohio App.3d 448, 690 N.E.2d 959, appeal not allowed 78 Ohio St.3d 1516, 679 N.E.2d 311.

Finding that natural father failed, without justifiable cause, to provide maintenance and support for his minor child, so that his consent to child's adoption by stepfather was not necessary, was supported by evidence that father was obligated to pay $150 per week, or $7,800 per year, in child support, that father's total income for year in question was $13,443.81, that father paid total of $329.40, or less than three percent of his income, in support for his two children, and that father failed to obtain employment commensurate with his level of education. In re Adoption of Wagner (Ohio App. 11 Dist. 1997) 117 Ohio App.3d 448, 690 N.E.2d 959, appeal not allowed 78 Ohio St.3d 1516, 679 N.E.2d 311.

Trial court was not bound or required to find that natural father's incarceration was justifiable cause for nonsupport, so as to require his consent to adoption. Dallas v. Dotson (Lorain 1996) 113 Ohio App.3d 484, 681 N.E.2d 464, dismissed, appeal not allowed 77 Ohio St.3d 1515, 674 N.E.2d 370.

Under statute providing that natural parent's consent to adoption is not required where that parent has failed, without justifiable cause, to support child for period of "at least one year," trial court was not required to limit its review to period of one year. Dallas v. Dotson (Lorain 1996) 113 Ohio App.3d 484, 681 N.E.2d 464, dismissed, appeal not allowed 77 Ohio St.3d 1515, 674 N.E.2d 370.

Father's duty to support child did not begin until date administrative parentage determination became final, nearly a month after mother and stepfather petitioned to adopt child, and, therefore, father's earlier failure to support child did not obviate need to obtain father's consent to adoption. In re Adoption of Hudnell (Ross 1996) 113 Ohio App.3d 296, 680 N.E.2d 1055.

Party alleging that need for parent's consent to adoption has been obviated by nonsupport has burden to prove by clear and convincing evidence that parent has failed to support child for requisite one-year period. In re Adoption of Hudnell (Ross 1996) 113 Ohio App.3d 296, 680 N.E.2d 1055.

Child who was subject of adoption petition had been legitimized by natural father, as required to commence period of nonsupport permitting court to approve adoption without consent of natural parent. In re Adoption of Lassiter (Clark 1995) 101 Ohio App.3d 367, 655 N.E.2d 781, dismissed, appeal not allowed 73 Ohio St.3d 1410, 651 N.E.2d 1308.

Legitimation of child granted pursuant to code section in effect at time of legitimation was sufficient to trigger one-year period of nonsupport found in subsequently adopted code section which obviated need to obtain parental consent to adoption, as language in new code section did not change or modify law, but merely clarified it. In re Adoption of Lassiter (Clark 1995) 101 Ohio App.3d 367, 655 N.E.2d 781, dismissed, appeal not allowed 73 Ohio St.3d 1410, 651 N.E.2d 1308.

Father assumed duty of supporting son, and one-year period of nonsupport obviating need to obtain parental consent to adoption began to run, when father acknowledged paternity and trial court granted legitimacy. In re Adoption of Lassiter (Clark 1995) 101 Ohio App.3d 367, 655 N.E.2d 781, dismissed, appeal not allowed 73 Ohio St.3d 1410, 651 N.E.2d 1308.

Probate court order finding that natural father's consent was not required for son's adoption, due to natural father's failure to support son for one year prior to adoption petition, was final appealable order. In re Adoption of Lassiter (Clark 1995) 101 Ohio App.3d 367, 655 N.E.2d 781, dismissed, appeal not allowed 73 Ohio St.3d 1410, 651 N.E.2d 1308.

Natural mother's alleged ignorance of law requiring her to support child was not justifiable cause for nonsupport of child, for purposes of mother's right to object to adoption of child. In re Adoption of Kuhlmann (Hamilton 1994) 99 Ohio App.3d 44, 649 N.E.2d 1279.

Once failure of natural parent to provide support has been proven by petitioner seeking adoption, court must then decide whether failure was justified, and such determination will not be disturbed on appeal unless against manifest weight of evidence. In re Adoption of Kuhlmann (Hamilton 1994) 99 Ohio App.3d 44, 649 N.E.2d 1279.

In determining whether failure to support child is justified, so as to permit parent to object to adoption, parent who is willing to support but unable to do so may have "justification," but parent who is unwilling but able to support does not. In re Adoption of Kuhlmann (Hamilton 1994) 99 Ohio App.3d 44, 649 N.E.2d 1279.

Evidence, which indicated that at one time mother was homeless and unable to pay any support, but that she was not indigent during one-year period prior to adoption petition, failed to establish "justification" for mother's nonpayment of support, and thus, mother was precluded from objecting to adoption; evidence indicated that mother worked briefly for temporary employment service, and then worked at another job where she received at least two raises, one of which was merit raise. In re Adoption of Kuhlmann (Hamilton 1994) 99 Ohio App.3d 44, 649 N.E.2d 1279.

Natural father's single payment of $20 for child support in year preceding filing of adoption petition by putative father did not constitute maintenance and support required to make natural father's consent to adoption necessary; payment was less than half of natural father's child support obligation for a single week. In re Adoption of Knight (Franklin 1994) 97 Ohio App.3d 670, 647 N.E.2d 251.

Natural father's payment, in year preceding filing of adoption petition by putative father, of $300 to child's psychologist for counseling to work on problem of child's fear of visiting natural father, did not constitute maintenance and support required to make natural father's consent to adoption necessary. In re Adoption of Knight (Franklin 1994) 97 Ohio App.3d 670, 647 N.E.2d 251.

Natural father's purchase of health insurance for child, in year preceding filing of adoption petition by putative father, did not constitute maintenance and support required to make natural father's consent to adoption necessary, where natural father did not reveal existence of insurance to child or child's mother, and insurance thus did not benefit child. In re Adoption of Knight (Franklin 1994) 97 Ohio App.3d 670, 647 N.E.2d 251.

Natural father had not shown facially justifiable cause for terminating employment, and his consent to adoption was consequently not required by virtue of his having failed to make court-ordered support payments, even though he claimed that he had left work to help his parents in operation of their farm, and former wife and children would have continued to be supported if they had remained in farm residence where they were being provided for during marriage. In re Adoption of Deems (Crawford 1993) 91 Ohio App.3d 552, 632 N.E.2d 1347, cause dismissed 70 Ohio St.3d 1451, 639 N.E.2d 460.

Evidence that putative father neither paid nor offered to pay natural mother's medical bills associated with pregnancy was insufficient to establish that father had abandoned mother, and, thus, that mother could place child for adoption without father's consent, where no evidence showed that father was made aware of medical bills or that mother would have accepted his assistance, and all indications were that mother and her parents would have refused any assistance. In re Adoption of Klonowski (Stark 1993) 87 Ohio App.3d 352, 622 N.E.2d 376.

Monies involuntarily intercepted from father's federal income tax refund, and then used to support child, constituted "support" for purposes of statute obviating necessity for parental consent to adoption in cases of parent's unjustifiable failure to provide "maintenance" and "support" for child for period of one year prior to filing of adoption petition; fact that money was derived from interception of income tax refund, rather than from voluntary payment or withholding from wages, did not render payment something other than payment for support of maintenance, regardless of degree of voluntariness involved. In re Adoption of Kessler (Huron 1993) 87 Ohio App.3d 317, 622 N.E.2d 354.

In deciding whether natural parent has failed to provide support and maintenance for at least one year prior to the filing of adoption petition, such that parent's consent is not prerequisite to adoption, court's inquiry is not whether parent can be held in contempt for failing to provide support, but whether parent's failure to support as ordered is of such magnitude as to be the equivalent of abandonment. Celestino v. Schneider (Lucas 1992) 84 Ohio App.3d 192, 616 N.E.2d 581.

Any contribution toward child support, no matter how meager, satisfies maintenance and support requirements of adoption provision and preserves natural parent's consent as jurisdictional prerequisite to child's adoption. Celestino v. Schneider (Lucas 1992) 84 Ohio App.3d 192, 616 N.E.2d 581.

The one partial payment that father made on his court-ordered child support obligation, in amount of $36, qualified as "support and maintenance" for purposes of adoption petition filed by natural mother's new husband; trial court could not dispense with natural father's consent as prerequisite to adoption, on theory that father had failed to provide support and maintenance. Celestino v. Schneider (Lucas 1992) 84 Ohio App.3d 192, 616 N.E.2d 581.

A probate court does not err when it concludes that a payment of one-week support after notice of intention to file an adoption petition and immediately before the petition is filed is not support within the meaning of RC 3107.07(A). In re Adoption of Carletti (Muskingum 1992) 78 Ohio App.3d 244, 604 N.E.2d 243, motion overruled 65 Ohio St.3d 1457, 602 N.E.2d 253.

In an adoption wherein the natural grandparents seek to adopt their granddaughter whose father is deceased and whose mother has not seen or supported her in three years, it is in the best interest of the child to have a guardian ad litem, and the trial court's failure to appoint one is error. In re Adoption of Howell (Lawrence 1991) 77 Ohio App.3d 80, 601 N.E.2d 92, motion overruled 62 Ohio St.3d 1508, 583 N.E.2d 1320.

A stepmother petitioning to adopt her stepchild has the burden of proving that the natural mother's failure to provide support is unjustifiable after the natural mother comes forward with some evidence justifying her failure to provide support. In re Adoption of Dues (Montgomery 1990) 69 Ohio App.3d 498, 591 N.E.2d 257.

A trial court's finding that a child's natural father's consent to the child's adoption is not required on the ground that the father failed to provide for the maintenance and support of the child as required by law or judicial decree for a period of at least one year immediately preceding the filing of the adoption petition is erroneous where it is shown that the father made payments through the bureau of support totaling $130 during the one year preceding the filing of the adoption petition. Vecchi v. Thomas (Montgomery 1990) 67 Ohio App.3d 688, 588 N.E.2d 186.

Willful failure by a putative father of a child born out of wedlock to support the child for a substantial period of time prior to the filing of an adoption petition can result in the conclusion that the consent of this putative father is not required for the adoption. In re Adoption of Youngpeter (Hancock 1989) 65 Ohio App.3d 172, 583 N.E.2d 360.

A father's duty of support includes "necessaries," such as expenses for pregnancy and confinement of the mother attendant to the birth of a child. In re Adoption of Youngpeter (Hancock 1989) 65 Ohio App.3d 172, 583 N.E.2d 360.

A putative father's payment of medical bills attendant to a child's birth within one year of the filing of a petition for adoption qualifies as "support" for purposes of the duty of support of a minor child; since the putative father's duty of support is met, his consent is required for adoption. In re Adoption of Youngpeter (Hancock 1989) 65 Ohio App.3d 172, 583 N.E.2d 360.

Willful abandonment and failure to support a child will be found where (1) the father provides no support to the mother of the child either before or after the birth; (2) the father does not pay for the expenses of the birth; and (3) although the mother, child, and father temporarily reside in the father's parents' home, the father fails to support the child and continues to date another woman. In re Adoption of Hart (Lucas 1989) 62 Ohio App.3d 544, 577 N.E.2d 77, motion overruled 45 Ohio St.3d 704, 543 N.E.2d 810.

A natural father's duty to support a child arises at birth, particularly where he acknowledges paternity, and where the natural father unjustifiably fails to communicate with or support a child for one year prior to the filing of an adoption petition, his consent to the adoption of his illegitimate child is unnecessary. In re Adoption of Taylor (Medina 1989) 61 Ohio App.3d 500, 573 N.E.2d 156, motion overruled 43 Ohio St.3d 712, 541 N.E.2d 78.

A child can be adopted under RC 3107.07(A) without the consent of a natural parent if the parent failed without just cause to pay child support even though the parent communicated with the child and sent gifts; interference by the child's stepfather with the father's telephone calls and written correspondence with his child are held insufficient cause for the father's failure to pay support in light of the court's conclusion that "ultimately it was [the child's] own choice to discontinue contact" because of the father's lack of "real interest." In re Adoption of Labo (Shelby 1988) 47 Ohio App.3d 57, 546 N.E.2d 1384.

The purchase of toys and clothes valued at approximately $133 is insufficient to fulfill a natural parent's duty of support where the gifts are not requested and they provide no real value of support because the child has sufficient toys and clothes; consequently, the consent of the natural parent is not required in an action for adoption. In re Adoption of Strawser (Franklin 1987) 36 Ohio App.3d 232, 522 N.E.2d 1105.

The fact that a natural father places his child on a medical insurance policy through his employer at a cost of $6 per month is insufficient to constitute care and support of the child pursuant to RC 3107.07(B) where the nominal contribution is neither used nor within the knowledge of the child's natural mother for two or three years prior to the filing of an adoption petition. In re Adoption of Strawser (Franklin 1987) 36 Ohio App.3d 232, 522 N.E.2d 1105.

Where a man establishes himself as a child's father in a paternity action brought pursuant to RC Ch 3111, the father's duty to support the child is retroactive to birth of the child for determining the father's failure to support the child for purposes of RC 3107.07(A). In re Adoption of Foster (Van Wert 1985) 22 Ohio App.3d 129, 489 N.E.2d 1070, 22 O.B.R. 331.

Where the record indicates that a nonconsenting parent made some contribution, although meager, to the support of her children within the one year immediately preceding the filing of the adoption proceedings, the parent will not be held to have abandoned her parental responsibilities and it is not error for the trial court to find that the parent's consent can not be dispensed with. In re Adoption of Salisbury (Franklin 1982) 5 Ohio App.3d 65, 449 N.E.2d 519, 5 O.B.R. 161.

RC 3107.07 must be strictly construed to protect the rights of the natural parents; thus, so long as the nonconsenting parent complies with his duty to support the child for any period during the one year immediately preceding the filing of the petition, the parent has not failed to provide support for one year and has not abandoned his parental responsibilities to the extent that he will be deemed to have forfeited his parental rights. In re Adoption of Anthony (Franklin 1982) 5 Ohio App.3d 60, 449 N.E.2d 511, 5 O.B.R. 156.

Absent an allegation that the natural parent failed to communicate with his child, in order for the natural parent to maintain his right to avoid an adoption of his child by withholding consent, the natural parent must pay the full amount of support required by judicial decree for at least one of the twelve months immediately preceding the filing of the adoption petition or else show "justifiable cause" for failure to pay for at least one of those months. In re Adoption of Burton (Warren 1981) 3 Ohio App.3d 251, 444 N.E.2d 1061, 3 O.B.R. 283.

Evidence that the mother of a child born out of wedlock paid nothing for the support of the child does not establish "willful failure" to support, nor can any inference be drawn therefrom to that effect where there is positive evidence that the mother was not financially able to contribute to the support of the child, and the petitioner for adoption, with whom the child was placed, never requested or expected any assistance, payment or contribution by the mother. (Annotation from former RC 3107.06.) In re Adoption of Peters (Lucas 1961) 113 Ohio App. 173, 177 N.E.2d 541, 17 O.O.2d 141.

A father has not "willfully failed to properly support" his minor child for a period of more than two years, where for almost fourteen months of such time he fulfills his obligations of support, and does furnish some, but not enough, "support" for nine months more and there is no evidence of a willful failure to furnish enough "support," and the consent of the father to the adoption of such child is necessary. (Annotation from former RC 3107.06.) In re Adoption of De Vore (Franklin 1959) 111 Ohio App. 1, 167 N.E.2d 381, 83 Ohio Law Abs. 14, 13 O.O.2d 376.

A parent, who for more than seven years prior to the filing of a petition for the adoption of her child has refused to contribute to the support of such child except for occasional Christmas presents, has "willfully failed to properly support and maintain" such child; and the consent of such parent to the adoption is not required. (Annotation from former RC 3107.06.) In re Adoption of Krisher (Fairfield 1958) 107 Ohio App. 109, 157 N.E.2d 123, 7 O.O.2d 465.

In a proceeding for adoption, instituted by the filing of such petition, where the evidence discloses that a nonconsenting parent willfully neglected to properly support and maintain such child for a period of time far in excess of two years, and where there is no evidence to show that the petitioners for adoption are not suitably qualified to support and maintain the child, or that the adoption is not for the best interests of the child, or that the child is not suitable for adoption, the consent of such nonconsenting parent is not required and the adoption will be granted. (Annotation from former RC 3107.06.) In re Adoption of Shaw (Brown 1950) 91 Ohio App. 347, 108 N.E.2d 236, 48 O.O. 427.

Where petition for adoption alleged that the mother "has not supported" child "for two consecutive years," but does not allege that mother "has failed or refused to support the child" for such length of time, as prescribed by statute, and there is no proof of a failure or refusal to support, it is reversible error for court to render decree of adoption without mother's consent thereto, and court's finding that mother is not a proper person to have custody of the child is unjustifiable where court ruled that testimony relative to mother's reputation was incompetent and evidence as to her moral qualifications was very limited. (Annotation from former RC 3107.06.) In re Goodfleisch (Franklin 1943) 73 Ohio App. 17, 53 N.E.2d 913, 40 Ohio Law Abs. 432, 27 O.O. 542.

Trial court erroneously construed "maintenance" and "support" to include only monetary payments in the form of child support, so where natural father provided his daughter with necessities in the course of exercising his visitation privileges with her, such non-monetary contributions fulfilled his duty to support. In re Adoption of McNutt, No. 99 CA 2633, 1999 WL 787921 (4th Dist Ct App, Scioto, 9-27-99).

In a step-parent adoption petition, consent of the natural father is necessary where he provides $200.00 in support in the year preceding the adoption petition; whether some funds deposited by the father's mother were a gift to her son or wages earned by her son is of no consequence where the funds were deposited in his name with the Bureau of Support. In re Adoption of Alexander, No. 1366, 1995 WL 570555 (2d Dist Ct App, Darke, 9-29-95).

Where a natural father pays three premiums of $173 toward health insurance coverage for himself and his child for a few months, but fails to reveal the existence of the health insurance to the child or the child's mother and as a result the health insurance never benefits the child, the insurance payments do not constitute sufficient support and maintenance of the child to make the natural father's consent necessary for the child's proposed adoption. In re Adoption of Knight, No. 94APF06-875, 1994 WL 672999 (10th Dist Ct App, Franklin, 11-29-94).

A putative father has no legal duty to support his child until the duty is established in a paternity action; therefore, where paternity proceedings have not been instituted, failure to support, pursuant to RC 3107.07(A), does not provide a basis for determining that the father's consent to adoption is not required. In re Adoption of Sunderhaus, No. CA89-12-176 (12th Dist Ct App, Butler, 10-15-90), affirmed by 63 OS(3d) 127, 585 NE(2d) 418 (1992).

The failure of the natural father to pay weekly child support payments to his son does not constitute failure to provide for his maintenance and support under RC 3107.07(A) where the father provides the son with clothes, toys and meals during visitation periods. In re Adoption of Pinkava, No. L-88-034 (6th Dist Ct App, Lucas, 1-13-89).

The involuntary withholding of one support payment from the wages of the natural father in the previous year is not sufficient support to require the consent of the natural father to the adoption of his child under RC 3107.07(A). In re Adoption of Thomas, No. CA-3311 (5th Dist Ct App, Licking, 12-22-87).

Where a child's natural father is disabled and cannot work, supporting the child on social security disability payments alone does not constitute a failure to support under RC 3107.07, and the consent of the natural father is required for adoption. In re Adoption of Davis, No. 402 (4th Dist Ct App, Pike, 10-21-87).

In adoption proceedings where a natural father, unemployed for three years, is willing yet unable to provide support for his children, the failure to support is justified and his consent to the adoption is necessary. In re Rickus, No. CA-7089 (5th Dist Ct App, Stark, 8-24-87).

Where there has been no judicial determination of parentage, the acknowledged natural father of a child born out of wedlock, who has signed the birth certificate, has no legal obligation to support his child and cannot be found to have violated a legal duty, thereby dispensing with his consent in an adoption proceeding. Amstutz v Braden, No. L-85-191 (6th Dist Ct App, Lucas, 12-27-85).

The payment of three partial weekly support payments and one full payment three days prior to the filing of an adoption petition is sufficient to maintain the requirement of consent of the natural parent to the adoption petition. In re Adoption of Mackall, No. 1365 (9th Dist Ct App, Medina, 4-24-85).

Where a putative father sends two checks totalling thirty dollars for the support of a child just prior to the filing of a petition for adoption and where this constitutes the only support ever offered or given, a finding that the putative father has failed to care for and support the minor child is justified and renders his consent to the adoption unnecessary. In re Adoption of Rouleau, No. 1058 (4th Dist Ct App, Ross, 8-31-84).

Where a non-custodial parent chooses a particular life style that prevents her from being able to provide for the maintenance and support of her minor child for at least one year, such parent's consent to the adoption of the child is not required. In re Adoption of Adolphson, No. 82-C-19 (7th Dist Ct App, Columbiana, 3-4-83).

Where the natural father made a lump sum payment of child support, accruing over a fourteen month period, three days before the stepfather filed a petition for adoption, such payment is sufficient to require the consent of the natural father to the adoption petition where the natural father has been in communication with his child. In re Adoption of Wallace, No. 82-CA-24 (5th Dist Ct App, Muskingum, 7-20-82).

Where the natural father has made four weeks of child support payments and has visited with his children once during the year immediately preceding the filing of an adoption petition by the child's stepfather, the natural father's consent to the adoption may not be dispensed with under RC 3107.07. Anthony v Arick, No. 81AP-907 (10th Dist Ct App, Franklin, 5-13-82).

Nonconsenting parent should not be allowed to thwart operation of statute making his consent to adoption unnecessary if he has failed to pay child support or communicate with child for one year prior to petition by making one or two token support payments just prior to adoption petition. In re Serre (Ohio Com.Pl. 1996) 77 Ohio Misc.2d 29, 665 N.E.2d 1185.

Although natural father's income was not enough to allow him to make full support payments, two partial support payments totalling $70 within week of stepfather's filing of adoption petition were insufficient to require natural father's consent to petition; payments equalled about one percent of natural father's income, and natural father made no attempt to seek reduction of support order. In re Serre (Ohio Com.Pl. 1996) 77 Ohio Misc.2d 29, 665 N.E.2d 1185.

Where a divorce court decreed that the mother assume financial responsibility for the children and imposed no legal obligation upon the father for their support, the failure of the father to pay support was not the willful failure to perform a legal duty, so long as the mother was willing and able to provide the required support; and the adoption of the children cannot be granted without the consent of the father. (Annotation from former RC 3107.06.) In re Adoption of McCoy (Ohio Com.Pl. 1972) 31 Ohio Misc. 195, 287 N.E.2d 833, 60 O.O.2d 356.

Where a couple petition for adoption of their grandson, who has lived in their home during his mother's separation and divorce from his father, and in their custody since her death, claiming that the consent of the father is not required because of willful failure to support the child for more than two years immediately preceding filing the petition, as specified in RC 3107.06, the burden of proving such willful failure is not sustained by evidence that the petitioners, financially able to support the child without hardship, had never requested any payment from the father, although he had told them on numerous occasions to call on him if they needed any money for the boy's care, and he did maintain an interest otherwise in his son's welfare, even seeking to have the boy live in his own home. (Annotation from former RC 3107.06.) In re Adoption of Wright (Ohio Prob. 1968) 15 Ohio Misc. 354, 240 N.E.2d 923, 44 O.O.2d 509.

Small sporadic payments for support of children does not constitute such support as to make the consent of the payor thereof a prerequisite to adoption. (Annotation from former RC 3107.06.) In re Adoptions of Zinsmeister (Ohio Prob. 1961) 178 N.E.2d 849, 87 Ohio Law Abs. 129.

Payment by a divorced father under a $25 per week support order of only $1,500 over a two and one-half year period constituted willful failure to support such children within the meaning of RC 3107.06. (Annotation from former RC 3107.06.) In re Adoptions of Zinsmeister (Ohio Prob. 1961) 178 N.E.2d 849, 87 Ohio Law Abs. 129.

3. Failure to communicate

Pursuant to the explicit language of RC 3107.07(A), failure by a parent to communicate with his or her child is sufficient to authorize adoption without that parent's consent only if there is a complete absence of communication for the statutorily defined one-year period. In re Adoption of Holcomb (Ohio 1985) 18 Ohio St.3d 361, 481 N.E.2d 613, 18 O.B.R. 419.

In the phrase "communicate with the minor child or to provide maintenance and support of the minor" the word "or" cannot be construed to mean "and." In re Adoption of McDermitt (Ohio 1980) 63 Ohio St.2d 301, 408 N.E.2d 680, 17 O.O.3d 195.

A mother who does not have custody of her child has a duty to give some personal care and attention to that child even though the child is being properly supported and maintained by his father, so that where she knows of her duty to give some personal care and attention to her child, is able to do so, and completely fails to give any care or attention to such child, such failure may justify a finding that she willfully failed to properly "maintain the child" within the meaning of those words as used in RC 3107.06(B)(4). (Annotation from former RC 3107.06.) Johnson v. Varney (Ohio 1965) 2 Ohio St.2d 161, 207 N.E.2d 558, 31 O.O.2d 316.

The phrase in RC 3107.06, "properly support and maintain," implies personal care and attention by the parent having custody as well as mere financial support. (Annotation from former RC 3107.06.) (See also In re Biddle, 81 Abs 529, 163 NE(2d) 190 (App, Franklin 1959).) In re Adoption of Biddle (Ohio 1958) 168 Ohio St. 209, 152 N.E.2d 105, 6 O.O.2d 4, on remand 163 N.E.2d 188, 81 Ohio Law Abs. 529.

"Failure to communicate" portion of the statute providing that consent to adoption is not required where parent has failed without justifiable cause to communicate with child is an objective standard, and courts should not read into the phrase such qualifiers as "meaningfully," "substantially," "significantly," or "regularly." In re Doe (Ohio App. 9 Dist. 1997) 123 Ohio App.3d 505, 704 N.E.2d 608, stay denied 80 Ohio St.3d 1470, 687 N.E.2d 298, dismissed, jurisdictional motion overruled 81 Ohio St.3d 1443, 690 N.E.2d 15.

Uncontested facts established that father failed to communicate with child for one-year statutory period, for purposes of dispensing with father's consent to adoption of child by stepfather. In re Doe (Ohio App. 9 Dist. 1997) 123 Ohio App.3d 505, 704 N.E.2d 608, stay denied 80 Ohio St.3d 1470, 687 N.E.2d 298, dismissed, jurisdictional motion overruled 81 Ohio St.3d 1443, 690 N.E.2d 15.

Natural mother did not have justifiable cause for failure to communicate with son in year prior to stepmother's filing of adoption petition, and therefore her consent to adoption was not necessary; although father and stepmother did not make any effort to voluntarily allow natural mother to visit son, nothing was done to conceal child's whereabouts, natural mother never attempted to contact son either in person or through any written communication, and she never attempted to establish any visitation rights to her son until after adoption petition was filed. In re Fetzer (Ohio App. 3 Dist. 1997) 118 Ohio App.3d 156, 692 N.E.2d 219, dismissed, appeal not allowed 78 Ohio St.3d 1513, 679 N.E.2d 309.

Natural mother waived any objection to probate court's jurisdiction to hear issue, in stepmother's adoption proceeding, of whether natural mother had failed without justifiable cause to communicate with child, where mother orally stipulated that communication issue was to be determined by probate court and produced evidence on that issue at hearing. In re Fetzer (Ohio App. 3 Dist. 1997) 118 Ohio App.3d 156, 692 N.E.2d 219, dismissed, appeal not allowed 78 Ohio St.3d 1513, 679 N.E.2d 309.

Accidental meeting between father and child was "communication" for purposes of adoption statutes requiring parent's consent unless parent has failed without justifiable cause to communicate with child during the year preceding the adoption petition. In re Adoption of Hudnell (Ross 1996) 113 Ohio App.3d 296, 680 N.E.2d 1055.

For purposes of statute allowing adoption without consent of noncustodial parent if parent failed without justifiable cause to communicate with child for over one year preceding adoption petition, term "communicate" must be given its ordinary and accepted meaning. In re Adoption of Hedrick (Cuyahoga 1996) 110 Ohio App.3d 622, 674 N.E.2d 1256.

Essence of "communication," for purposes of statute allowing adoption without consent of noncustodial parent if parent failed without justifiable cause to communicate with child for over one year preceding adoption petition, is the passing of thought from mind of one person to mind of another; message not received or successfully passed to mind of another is not communicated, nor does unsuccessful attempt to communicate constitute communication. In re Adoption of Hedrick (Cuyahoga 1996) 110 Ohio App.3d 622, 674 N.E.2d 1256.

Natural father did not communicate with child during requisite one-year period preceding adoption petition filed by mother's husband where letters and cards sent to child by father through father's mother were never received by child and never read. In re Adoption of Hedrick (Cuyahoga 1996) 110 Ohio App.3d 622, 674 N.E.2d 1256.

In examining whether noncustodial parent's failure to communicate with child within requisite one-year period preceding adoption petition was justified, court is not restricted to focusing only on events occurring during period; court must also examine preceding events bearing on parent's failure to communicate with child. In re Adoption of Hedrick (Cuyahoga 1996) 110 Ohio App.3d 622, 674 N.E.2d 1256.

Natural father did not have justifiable cause for failing to communicate with child during requisite one-year period preceding adoption petition filed by mother's husband even though father's mother, through whom father sent letters and cards to child at undisclosed address, did not forward letters and cards for fear that her contact with child would be cut off. In re Adoption of Hedrick (Cuyahoga 1996) 110 Ohio App.3d 622, 674 N.E.2d 1256.

Two-part responsibility upon parent is imposed by statute, in order to avoid termination of right to object to adoption: to provide support and to communicate with child. In re Adoption of Kuhlmann (Hamilton 1994) 99 Ohio App.3d 44, 649 N.E.2d 1279.

In an adoption wherein the natural grandparents seek to adopt their granddaughter whose father is deceased and whose mother has not seen or supported her in three years, it is in the best interest of the child to have a guardian ad litem, and the trial court's failure to appoint one is error. In re Adoption of Howell (Lawrence 1991) 77 Ohio App.3d 80, 601 N.E.2d 92, motion overruled 62 Ohio St.3d 1508, 583 N.E.2d 1320.

Clear and convincing evidence exists to support a trial court's conclusion that a natural mother failed to communicate with her two sons for the requisite one-year period prior to the children's guardian's filing an adoption petition; the mother saw her children only once at a school Christmas program and the only interaction between the mother and the children consisted of a wave, a smile, or a nod, which does not constitute communication within the meaning of RC 3107.07(A) since a wave, smile, or nod does not convey information. In re Adoption of Jordan (Preble 1991) 72 Ohio App.3d 638, 595 N.E.2d 963.

No justifiable cause existed for a natural mother's failure to communicate with her two children for over a one-year period despite the mother's claim that interference from the children's guardian kept her from visiting the children, as the mother cited only one occasion where she called about a month before the adoption petition was filed to arrange a time to see her children, but according to the mother, the guardian hung up on her, since this one incident does not constitute significant interference with communication between the mother and her children and the guardian reaction was justified because the natural mother became abusive on the phone; moreover, no other instances existed where the mother attempted to visit her children even though she knew their address and phone number and worked only 200 yards from where the children were living, and she never tried to speak to her children on the phone. In re Adoption of Jordan (Preble 1991) 72 Ohio App.3d 638, 595 N.E.2d 963.

The consent of the natural father is not required in an adoption proceeding under RC 3107.06 and 3107.07 where (1) the father abandoned the mother and child when the child was three; (2) the mother was granted a divorce eight months later and retained full custody of the child; (3) the natural father did not contact the mother until three years after the divorce, after the petitioner had filed the adoption petition, although the mother and the petitioner did not marry until five months later; and (4) the father refused to consent to the adoption; the court's consideration of only one of two dates for calculation of the requisite one-year period during which the parent fails without justifiable cause to communicate with the minor or to provide for the maintenance and support is error, as the entire one-year period should be examined, not just a portion. In re Adoption of Jones (Medina 1990) 70 Ohio App.3d 576, 591 N.E.2d 823.

A natural father's duty to support a child arises at birth, particularly where he acknowledges paternity, and where the natural father unjustifiably fails to communicate with or support a child for one year prior to the filing of an adoption petition, his consent to the adoption of his illegitimate child is unnecessary. In re Adoption of Taylor (Medina 1989) 61 Ohio App.3d 500, 573 N.E.2d 156, motion overruled 43 Ohio St.3d 712, 541 N.E.2d 78.

Adoption without a parent's consent is authorized by the failure of the parent to communicate with his child only if the failure to communicate is complete, tantamount to a complete abandonment of current interest in the child. Matter of Adoption of Hupp (Cuyahoga 1982) 9 Ohio App.3d 128, 458 N.E.2d 878, 9 O.B.R. 192.

RC 3107.07 requires that, in order for there to be a failure of communication, there must have been a complete absence of communication for a period of at least one year immediately prior to the filing of the petition. In re Adoption of Anthony (Franklin 1982) 5 Ohio App.3d 60, 449 N.E.2d 511, 5 O.B.R. 156.

Pursuant to the explicit language of RC 3107.07, failure by a parent to communicate with his or her child is sufficient to authorize adoption without that parent's consent only if there is a complete absence of communication for the statutorily defined one-year period. Bryant v Van Auken, No. 97CA635, 1997 WL 766460 (4th Dist Ct App, Washington, 12-9-97).

Sending of a birthday card along with photographs and a letter during the year preceding adoption adequately supports a finding of communication for purposes of RC 3107.07 and preserves the natural father's right not to consent to adoption of his daughter by her stepfather. In re Petition to Adopt Christie, No. 96CA0049, 1997 WL 119556 (9th Dist Ct App, Wayne, 3-12-97).

A natural father's incarceration which prevents him from seeking his child's whereabouts is justiciable cause for failure to communicate for a period of one year immediately preceding the filing of an adoption petition by the child's stepfather. In re Adoption of Cockerham, No. 1996 CA 0247, 1997 WL 118267 (5th Dist Ct App, Stark, 1-27-97).

Where a natural father's testimony stating he sent cards and packages to his children in the one-year period immediately preceding the filing of a petition for adoption conflicts with the children's testimony they did not recall receiving the alleged card and packages, the natural father failed to communicate with his children for a one-year period and the consent of the natural father is unnecessary for the adoption. In re Adoption of Doe, No. H-93-12, 1993 WL 551530 (6th Dist Ct App, Huron, 12-30-93).

The trial court correctly holds that a parent's written consent to adoption is required where the parent made repeated attempts to exercise his visitation rights and was thwarted in each instance by some objection raised or limitation placed thereon by the custodial parent. In re Adoption of Meagley, No. 1-83-45 (3d Dist Ct App, Allen, 5-14-84).

Telephone conversations between a mother and minor child constitute communication of a parent with a child within the purview of RC 3107.07(A) and therefore the consent of such mother is required for the adoption of such child. In re Adoption of Kreyche, No. 1258 (11th Dist Ct App, Portage, 3-18-83), affirmed by 15 OS(3d) 159, 15 OBR 304, 472 NE(2d) 1106 (1984).

Natural father's motion to show cause to enforce his visitation rights was not "communication with the child," for purposes of statute making nonconsenting parent's consent to adoption unnecessary if he has failed to pay child support or communicate with child for one year prior to petition. In re Serre (Ohio Com.Pl. 1996) 77 Ohio Misc.2d 29, 665 N.E.2d 1185.

Natural father failed to show justifiable cause for his failure to communicate with his child, and thus his consent to child's adoption was not necessary; mother testified that she concealed her residence from father because he had threatened her and physically abused her in the past but that she agreed to father's supervised visitations with child in another place, and child's registration in school under petitioner's surname in order to conceal her whereabouts did not preclude father from contacting child through child's grandmother. In re Serre (Ohio Com.Pl. 1996) 77 Ohio Misc.2d 29, 665 N.E.2d 1185.

Significant interference by custodial parent with communication between child and noncustodial parent or significant discouragement of such communication is required to establish justifiable cause to excuse noncustodial parent's failure to communicate with child for one year, and make noncustodial parent's consent a prerequisite to adoption. In re Serre (Ohio Com.Pl. 1996) 77 Ohio Misc.2d 29, 665 N.E.2d 1185.

The two-year requirement of RC 3107.06(B)(4) is not tolled by fact that child was living away from parents by agreement with them, or merely because parents made telephone calls discussing return of child or because parents were in financial difficulty for a portion of the period and unable to contribute to child's support. (Annotation from former RC 3107.06.) In re Adoption of Sargent (Ohio Com.Pl. 1970) 28 Ohio Misc. 261, 272 N.E.2d 206, 57 O.O.2d 135, 57 O.O.2d 494.

4. Justifiable cause

Under RC 3107.07(A), the probate court shall determine the issue of justifiable cause by weighing the evidence of the natural parent's circumstances for the statutory period for which he or she failed to provide support. The court shall determine whether the parent's failure to support the child for that period as a whole (and not just a portion thereof) was without justifiable cause. In re Adoption of Bovett (Ohio 1987) 33 Ohio St.3d 102, 515 N.E.2d 919.

A natural mother collecting public assistance and cohabiting with an employed man is not unable to pay $5 weekly support for her child in the custody of paternal grandparents; the lack of payment is thus unjustifiable. In re Adoption of Lay (Ohio 1986) 25 Ohio St.3d 41, 495 N.E.2d 9, 25 O.B.R. 66.

Where the record discloses that neither the custodial parent nor the party seeking to adopt has provided current address or telephone information concerning the children to a non-consenting parent residing thousands of miles distant, justifiable cause for lack of communication is established, and an adoption order based upon a contrary finding will reversed. In re Adoption of Holcomb (Ohio 1985) 18 Ohio St.3d 361, 481 N.E.2d 613, 18 O.B.R. 419.

Evidence that child's biological father had not had contact with child for one year prior to filing of petition to dispense with his consent to child's adoption by mother's husband was less than clear and convincing and could not form basis for granting petition, where biological father contended that he had attempted to contact child from prison but that his efforts were continually frustrated by child's mother, and where trial court improperly placed burden of proving justifiable cause for failure to communicate on biological father. In re Adoption of Eblin (Ohio App. 3 Dist. 1998) 126 Ohio App.3d 774, 711 N.E.2d 319, appeal allowed 82 Ohio St.3d 1482, 696 N.E.2d 1088, cause dismissed 83 Ohio St.3d 1454, 700 N.E.2d 617.

Natural parent's failure to either support or communicate with his or her minor child within year prior to filing of adoption petition would abrogate need for parent's consent to adoption if trial court also decided that such failure was without justifiable cause. In re Adoption of Wagner (Ohio App. 11 Dist. 1997) 117 Ohio App.3d 448, 690 N.E.2d 959, appeal not allowed 78 Ohio St.3d 1516, 679 N.E.2d 311.

Evidence supported finding that natural father was without "justifiable cause" for failure to support child during one-year period prior to adoption petition and, thus, his consent was not required for adoption; natural father was experiencing financial hardship but it was clear from fairly significant support paid for his other two children and fact that he was able to pay attorney fees for both divorce and bankruptcy proceedings that he had some discretionary income which he could have divided among his three children and contributed toward support of child who was to be adopted. In re Adoption of Cline (Trumbull 1993) 89 Ohio App.3d 450, 624 N.E.2d 1083.

Determination of whether justifiable cause for natural parent's failure to pay child support has been proven by clear and convincing evidence, for purposes of determining whether natural parent's consent to adoption is required, can be disturbed on appeal only if determination is against manifest weight of the evidence; hence, judgment will not be overturned if supported by some competent and credible evidence. In re Adoption of Cline (Trumbull 1993) 89 Ohio App.3d 450, 624 N.E.2d 1083.

If petitioner for adoption presents evidence that natural parent has failed to support child for one-year period, parent must justify his or her failure to support for substantially entire one-year period to avoid nonconsensual adoption; it is not enough to show that sometime during year failure to support was justified; it must be demonstrated that no modicum of support reasonably could have been provided at any time during year. In re Adoption of Kessler (Huron 1993) 87 Ohio App.3d 317, 622 N.E.2d 354.

Assuming that father failed to provide support for his child for one-year period necessary to obviate necessity of father's consent to child's adoption by another, failure could not be deemed unjustifiable where father was unemployed and was unable to find new employment, outside of temporary job that lasted six weeks; there was no evidence as to amount father earned during time period from temporary job or from other jobs or of his ability to pay support. In re Adoption of Kessler (Huron 1993) 87 Ohio App.3d 317, 622 N.E.2d 354.

Where a stepfather and the custodial parent make a concerted effort to thwart an incarcerated father's efforts to communicate with his children by refusing to accept his calls and returning his letters to his children unopened, the father's failure to communicate with his children is justified and even though the stepfather and the custodial parent believe their actions are in the children's best interest, they cannot prohibit communication and then claim the benefits of their efforts under RC 3107.07(A). In re Adoption of Lauck (Summit 1992) 82 Ohio App.3d 348, 612 N.E.2d 459, motion overruled 65 Ohio St.3d 1499, 605 N.E.2d 952.

A probate court could conclude that a petitioner has not carried his burden on the issue of "justifiable cause" for his failure to communicate with his child in RC 3107.07(A) where the natural father establishes prior to the filing of the petition that he was an alcoholic with suicidal tendencies, that once in recovery the father secured employment and tried to contact his ex-wife to arrange for visits with and support payments to the child, that he made contact through an attorney rather than to have a face-to-face confrontation with his ex-wife, and that his ex-wife largely rebuffed his advances, failed to encourage visitation, and employed the adoption process largely as a means of severing his parental rights; the term "justifiable cause" in RC 3107.07 is not a readily defined term and must be determined from the surrounding circumstances of each case. In re Adoption of Jones (Medina 1990) 70 Ohio App.3d 576, 591 N.E.2d 823.

Where a mother refuses to permit visitation by a father on one occasion, and fails to provide the father with the child's name and address, the father did not completely fail to communicate with the child for purposes of ascertaining whether his consent is required for adoption of the child by the mother's new husband. In re Adoption of Youngpeter (Hancock 1989) 65 Ohio App.3d 172, 583 N.E.2d 360.

Where a woman with custody of children moves them to California and refuses to give their address or telephone number to the father despite the urgings of the domestic relations judge, and where the repeated efforts of the father, the post office, and the telephone company to locate the woman and the children are unsuccessful, a petition by the woman's new husband to adopt the children and eliminate the father's parental rights without his consent, based on an assertion that the father failed without justifiable cause to communicate and failed to pay child support, must be granted without regard to the father's opposition where he had not gone back to court and succeeded at having the support obligation halted, even though (1) mail he sent to the children was returned on at least two occasions, (2) he had paid support in a timely manner until the woman disappeared, and (3) the woman made no attempt to collect any money after taking the children away from their father: "interference" with visitation rights is not an "excuse" for unilateral refusal to pay support. In re Adoptions of Bruce (Montgomery 1989) 56 Ohio App.3d 126, 564 N.E.2d 1110.

A child can be adopted under RC 3107.07(A) without the consent of a natural parent if the parent failed without just cause to pay child support even though the parent communicated with the child and sent gifts; interference by the child's stepfather with the father's telephone calls and written correspondence with his child are held insufficient cause for the father's failure to pay support in light of the court's conclusion that "ultimately it was [the child's] own choice to discontinue contact" because of the father's lack of "real interest." In re Adoption of Labo (Shelby 1988) 47 Ohio App.3d 57, 546 N.E.2d 1384.

A natural father has justifiable cause for failure to support his child, within the meaning of RC 3107.07(A), if the mother has denied visitation and refused some of his tendered contributions toward support of the child. In re Adoption of Foster (Van Wert 1985) 22 Ohio App.3d 129, 489 N.E.2d 1070, 22 O.B.R. 331.

While sincere voluntary effort to cure illness or improve lifestyle may be viewed as justifiable cause for failure to pay child support, natural father's four-month stay in a drug rehabilitation facility does not excuse nonsupport where he has failed to pay support before his commitment or after his release. In re Adoption of Stidham, No. 16930, 1998 WL 656567 (2d Dist Ct App, Montgomery, 9-25-98).

A mother's refusal to accept payment for the child's tuition is justifiable cause for the natural father's failure to support his child and his consent to adoption by the mother's current husband is necessary where in addition the court fails to schedule a hearing to determine the amount of support which results in the father being unable to make any payments to the child support enforcement agency which would not accept payment without a court order. In re Adoption of Williams, No. CT97-0038, 1998 WL 346853 (5th Dist Ct App, Muskingum, 6-4-98).

Probate court's denial of Civ R 60(B) motion to vacate adoption order is not error when record shows clear and convincing evidence that father lacked a justifiable cause for failing to communicate with child during year immediately preceding adoption. In re Adoption of Linn, No. 64243 (8th Dist Ct App, Cuyahoga, 4-29-93).

The consent of a natural parent who fails to communicate with or provide support to her children for a full year prior to the filing of an adoption petition is required where such failure to communicate or support is due to the incarceration of the natural parent. In re Adoption of Thompson, No. 27-CA-87 (5th Dist Ct App, Fairfield, 1-7-88).

That natural father received annual earnings between $3,000 and $4,000 from public assistance and sporadic employment does not constitute justifiable cause for failure to pay any child support or communicate with his child pursuant to RC 3107.07. In re Adoption of Bitner, No. 81-CA-77 (7th Dist Ct App, Mahoning, 2-24-82).

Where natural father deposited child support payments into an escrow account pursuant to approval of the court of another state, such a failure to pay child support directly to the mother constitutes "justifiable cause" under RC 3107.07(A). In re Adoption of Howard, No. 81-02-0013 (12th Dist Ct App, Butler, 1-13-82).

In RC 3107.07(A), providing that consent to an adoption is not required of a parent of a minor when the court finds that the parent has failed without justifiable cause to communicate with the minor "or" to provide for the maintenance and support of the minor, the word "or" should be read "and." In re Adoption of Taylor (Ohio Com.Pl. 1977) 55 Ohio Misc. 15, 380 N.E.2d 370, 7 O.O.3d 167, 9 O.O.3d 350.

5. Burden of proof

Pursuant to RC 3107.07(A), the petitioner for adoption has the burden of proving, by clear and convincing evidence, both (1) that the natural parent has failed to support the child for the requisite one-year period, and (2) that this failure was without justifiable cause. Once the petitioner has established, by clear and convincing evidence, that the natural parent has failed to support the child for at least the requisite one-year period, the burden of going forward with the evidence shifts to the natural parent to show some facially justifiable cause for such failure. The burden of proof, however, remains with the petitioner. In re Adoption of Bovett (Ohio 1987) 33 Ohio St.3d 102, 515 N.E.2d 919.

A petitioner for adoption has the burden of proving, by clear and convincing evidence, that the natural parent has failed to communicate with the child for one year, and that there was no justifiable cause for this failure. In re Adoption of Gibson (Ohio 1986) 23 Ohio St.3d 170, 492 N.E.2d 146, 23 O.B.R. 336.

Pursuant to RC 3107.07(A), the petitioner for adoption has the burden of proving, by clear and convincing evidence, that the natural parent has failed to support the child for the requisite one-year period and that this failure was without justifiable cause. In re Adoption of Masa (Ohio 1986) 23 Ohio St.3d 163, 492 N.E.2d 140, 23 O.B.R. 330.

The party petitioning for adoption has the burden of proving, by clear and convincing evidence, that the parent failed to communicate with the child during the requisite one-year period and that there was no justifiable cause for the failure of communication. In re Adoption of Holcomb (Ohio 1985) 18 Ohio St.3d 361, 481 N.E.2d 613, 18 O.B.R. 419.

Marriage of a natural parent does not automatically initiate a placement for adoption purposes, pursuant to RC 3107.07, where the natural parent did not have permanent custody of the child at the time of his marriage and the placement of the child in the home of her father was not originally for the purpose of adoption. In re Adoption of Kreyche (Ohio 1984) 15 Ohio St.3d 159, 472 N.E.2d 1106, 15 O.B.R. 304.

Trial court erroneously placed burden of proof, on issue of whether child's biological father communicated with child during statutory one-year period prior to filing of adoption petition by child's mother's husband, on biological father; trial court required biological father, who had been incarcerated during statutory period on conviction related to domestic violence against child's mother, to prove that there was justifiable cause for his failure, if any, to communicate with child from prison. In re Adoption of Eblin (Ohio App. 3 Dist. 1998) 126 Ohio App.3d 774, 711 N.E.2d 319, appeal allowed 82 Ohio St.3d 1482, 696 N.E.2d 1088, cause dismissed 83 Ohio St.3d 1454, 700 N.E.2d 617.

Although the nonconsenting parent is responsible for articulating a justifiable cause for failure to communicate with child, in action to dispense with parent's consent to adoption, no burden is placed upon nonconsenting parent to establish that the failure to communicate was justifiable. In re Doe (Ohio App. 9 Dist. 1997) 123 Ohio App.3d 505, 704 N.E.2d 608, stay denied 80 Ohio St.3d 1470, 687 N.E.2d 298, dismissed, jurisdictional motion overruled 81 Ohio St.3d 1443, 690 N.E.2d 15.

Clear and convincing evidence did not establish that father's failure to communicate with his child for one-year period was unjustified, as required for stepfather to adopt child without father's consent, where mother and stepfather failed to appear at meeting to discuss father's visitation rights, and father thereafter sought relief in courts to enforce and augment his visitation rights. In re Doe (Ohio App. 9 Dist. 1997) 123 Ohio App.3d 505, 704 N.E.2d 608, stay denied 80 Ohio St.3d 1470, 687 N.E.2d 298, dismissed, jurisdictional motion overruled 81 Ohio St.3d 1443, 690 N.E.2d 15.

Before probate court can reach issue of whether natural parent had justifiable cause for not supporting or communicating with child, for purposes of determining whether natural parent's consent to adoption petition is necessary, it is incumbent upon petitioner to show, by clear and convincing evidence, that natural parent failed to support or communicate with child for requisite one-year period. In re Fetzer (Ohio App. 3 Dist. 1997) 118 Ohio App.3d 156, 692 N.E.2d 219, dismissed, appeal not allowed 78 Ohio St.3d 1513, 679 N.E.2d 309.

Once adoption petitioner has established, by clear and convincing evidence, that natural parent has failed to support or communicate with child for at least one year, burden of going forward with evidence shifts to natural parent to show some facially justifiable cause for failure; however, burden of proof remains with petitioner. In re Fetzer (Ohio App. 3 Dist. 1997) 118 Ohio App.3d 156, 692 N.E.2d 219, dismissed, appeal not allowed 78 Ohio St.3d 1513, 679 N.E.2d 309.

Once party who has filed adoption petition has established failure of minor child's natural parent to either provide support for, or communicate with, child, burden of going forward with evidence shifts to natural parent to show some facially justifiable cause for such failure. In re Adoption of Wagner (Ohio App. 11 Dist. 1997) 117 Ohio App.3d 448, 690 N.E.2d 959, appeal not allowed 78 Ohio St.3d 1516, 679 N.E.2d 311.

When adoption petition has been filed so that natural parent faces termination of his or her parental rights, burden of proof is on petitioner to establish by clear and convincing evidence that natural parent failed to communicate with or support, without justifiable cause, his or her minor child during one-year period prior to adoption petition. In re Adoption of Wagner (Ohio App. 11 Dist. 1997) 117 Ohio App.3d 448, 690 N.E.2d 959, appeal not allowed 78 Ohio St.3d 1516, 679 N.E.2d 311.

Once petitioner for adoption has established by clear and convincing evidence that natural parent has failed to support child for requisite one-year period, burden of going forward with evidence shifts to natural parent to show some facially justifiable cause for that failure, though burden of proof remains with petitioner. Dallas v. Dotson (Lorain 1996) 113 Ohio App.3d 484, 681 N.E.2d

464, dismissed, appeal not allowed 77 Ohio St.3d 1515, 674 N.E.2d 370.

Trial judge's comment, in contested adoption proceeding, that burden of proof switched to noncustodial parent after petitioner proved by clear and convincing evidence a lack of communication without justifiable cause was harmless error where noncustodial parent was provided full and fair hearing and judge as trier of fact had sufficient evidence to satisfy petitioner's burden of proof. In re Adoption of Hedrick (Cuyahoga 1996) 110 Ohio App.3d 622, 674 N.E.2d 1256.

Petitioner seeking adoption without natural parent's consent must prove by clear and convincing evidence that natural parent has not only failed to support child for statutory period but that failure was without justifiable cause; furthermore, petitioner had burden of proving that natural parent's failure to provide support is not justified after natural parent provides some evidence to justify failure to provide support. In re Adoption of Lassiter (Clark 1995) 101 Ohio App.3d 367, 655 N.E.2d 781, dismissed, appeal not allowed 73 Ohio St.3d 1410, 651 N.E.2d 1308.

Probate court's finding, in support of conclusion that one year of nonsupport obviated need for father's approval of son's adoption, that father had at least some income but still did not pay any support was not against manifest weight of evidence. In re Adoption of Lassiter (Clark 1995) 101 Ohio App.3d 367, 655 N.E.2d 781, dismissed, appeal not allowed 73 Ohio St.3d 1410, 651 N.E.2d 1308.

Probate court's determination regarding justifiable cause for failing to support minor child as would toll one-year period of nonsupport obviating need to obtain parental consent to adoption will not be disturbed on appeal unless it is against manifest weight of evidence. In re Adoption of Lassiter (Clark 1995) 101 Ohio App.3d 367, 655 N.E.2d 781, dismissed, appeal not allowed 73 Ohio St.3d 1410, 651 N.E.2d 1308.

Once petitioner seeking adoption has proven by clear and convincing evidence the failure to support child within required one-year period, natural parent has burden of going forward with some evidence to show that failure was justified; burden of proof remains with petitioner. In re Adoption of Kuhlmann (Hamilton 1994) 99 Ohio App.3d 44, 649 N.E.2d 1279.

Petitioner seeking adoption has burden of establishing, by clear and convincing evidence, natural parents' noncompliance with either support requirement or communication with child requirement. In re Adoption of Kuhlmann (Hamilton 1994) 99 Ohio App.3d 44, 649 N.E.2d 1279.

Adoption petitioner, seeking to establish that consent of natural parent is not required because natural parent has neglected support obligation, is required to prove at adoption hearing that natural parent's failure to support was without justifiable cause. In re Adoption of Deems (Crawford 1993) 91 Ohio App.3d 552, 632 N.E.2d 1347, cause dismissed 70 Ohio St.3d 1451, 639 N.E.2d 460.

Once adoption petitioner, seeking to establish that consent of natural parent is not required because natural parent has failed to support child, has shown by clear and convincing evidence that natural parent has failed to support child for at least one-year period, burden of going forward with evidence shifts to natural parent to show some facially justifiable cause for failure, with ultimate burden of proof remaining with petitioner. In re Adoption of Deems (Crawford 1993) 91 Ohio App.3d 552, 632 N.E.2d 1347, cause dismissed 70 Ohio St.3d 1451, 639 N.E.2d 460.

Because cases in which consent to adoption may not be required may involve termination of fundamental parental rights, burden of proof is on petitioner seeking adoption to establish by clear and convincing evidence that natural parent failed to support, without justifiable cause, minor child during one-year period prior to adoption petition; then, once petitioner has established a failure, burden of going forward with evidence is on natural parent to show some facially justifiable cause for the failure. In re Adoption of Cline (Trumbull 1993) 89 Ohio App.3d 450, 624 N.E.2d 1083.

Burden of proving abandonment is upon natural mother who seeks to place child for adoption without putative father's consent. In re Adoption of Klonowski (Stark 1993) 87 Ohio App.3d 352, 622 N.E.2d 376.

Petitioner for adoption who seeks to utilize statute in lieu of parent's consent to adoption has burden of proving by clear and convincing evidence that natural parent has not only failed to support child for statutory period but that such failure was without justifiable cause. In re Adoption of Kessler (Huron 1993) 87 Ohio App.3d 317, 622 N.E.2d 354.

Burden is on parties petitioning to adopt child to demonstrate that natural parent's consent is not prerequisite to adoption, on ground that natural parent has failed to provide support and maintenance for at least one year before petition was filed. Celestino v. Schneider (Lucas 1992) 84 Ohio App.3d 192, 616 N.E.2d 581.

Even after court determines that consent of natural parent is not necessary for child's adoption, court must still determine whether adoption is in best interest of child. Celestino v. Schneider (Lucas 1992) 84 Ohio App.3d 192, 616 N.E.2d 581.

Even where a probate court finds that the natural father's consent to an adoption is not necessary, a determination of what is in the child's best interests is still required prior to termination of parental rights. In re Adoption of Jones (Medina 1990) 70 Ohio App.3d 576, 591 N.E.2d 823.

In addressing the RC 3107.07(A) requirement that the failure to communicate or support must be without justifiable cause, the trial court may place no burden upon the nonconsenting parent to establish that his failure was justifiable. In re Adoption of Anthony (Franklin 1982) 5 Ohio App.3d 60, 449 N.E.2d 511, 5 O.B.R. 156.

The showing of a mere failure to make payment for the support and maintenance of a child will not support a finding that such failure was willful, and the burden of proof of such willfulness is on the petitioner charging such failure. (Annotation from former RC 3107.06.) In re Adoption of Baker (Hardin 1955) 100 Ohio App. 146, 136 N.E.2d 147, 60 O.O. 137.

When evidence of failure to pay child support is shown, the burden of proof shifts to the parent not paying child support to go forward with evidence to show that such lack of support was not willful. In re Adoption of Bitner, No. 81-CA-77 (7th Dist Ct App, Mahoning, 2-24-82).

Once adoption petitioner has established, by clear and convincing evidence, that natural parent has failed to support or communicate with child for at least one year, burden of going forward with evidence shifts to natural parent to show some facially justifiable cause for such failure; however, burden of proof remains with petitioner. In re Serre (Ohio Com.Pl. 1996) 77 Ohio Misc.2d 29, 665 N.E.2d 1185.

Adoption petitioner offered competent, credible testimony showing natural father's failure to communicate with child without justifiable cause and thus burden of going forward shifted to father to show some facially justifiable cause for such failure. In re Serre (Ohio Com.Pl. 1996) 77 Ohio Misc.2d 29, 665 N.E.2d 1185.

6. Putative father

Putative father's attempt to condition his consent to adoption upon his retention of permanent visitation rights was not written objection to adoption, required to preserve his right to contest adoption. In re Adoption of Zschach (Ohio 1996) 75 Ohio St.3d 648, 665 N.E.2d 1070, reconsideration denied 76 Ohio St.3d 1410, 666 N.E.2d 569, certiorari denied 117 S.Ct. 582, 136 L.Ed.2d 513.

Nothing short of written objection to adoption proceeding suffices to preserve putative father's right to contest adoption. In re Adoption of Zschach (Ohio 1996) 75 Ohio St.3d 648, 665 N.E.2d 1070, reconsideration denied 76 Ohio St.3d 1410, 666 N.E.2d 569, certiorari denied 117 S.Ct. 582, 136 L.Ed.2d 513.

Where putative father fails to demonstrate full commitment to responsibilities of parenthood, state should not be compelled to listen to his opinion of where child's best interests lie. In re Adoption of Zschach (Ohio 1996) 75 Ohio St.3d 648, 665 N.E.2d 1070, reconsideration denied 76 Ohio St.3d 1410, 666 N.E.2d 569, certiorari denied 117 S.Ct. 582, 136 L.Ed.2d 513.

Putative father was not entitled to notice and hearing before probate court's finalization of adoption that deprived him of right to visitation; father's constitutionally protected interests were adequately safeguarded in being given opportunity to object to adoption of his putative child, but failing to object and thereby demonstrate his full commitment to responsibilities of parenthood. In re Adoption of Zschach (Ohio 1996) 75 Ohio St.3d 648, 665 N.E.2d 1070, reconsideration denied 76 Ohio St.3d 1410, 666 N.E.2d 569, certiorari denied 117 S.Ct. 582, 136 L.Ed.2d 513.

To preserve right to withheld consent to child's adoption and avoid finding that requirement of father's consent shall be excused, putative father who has signed birth certificate must file objection to adoption with court, department or agency having custody of child, but his objection need not be filed within 30 days of earlier of date of filing of adoption petition or placement of child. In re Adoption of Greer (Ohio 1994) 70 Ohio St.3d 293, 638 N.E.2d 999.

Unless statutory requirement to consent of adoption is excused by virtue of failure of putative father to file objection, a putative father who has signed birth certificate as informant has statutory right to withhold consent to adoption of that child, thereby barring child's adoption by another. In re Adoption of Greer (Ohio 1994) 70 Ohio St.3d 293, 638 N.E.2d 999.

Significant interference by a custodial parent with communication between the noncustodial parent and the child, or significant discouragement of such communication, is required to establish justifiable cause for the noncustodial parent's failure to communicate with the child. The question of whether justifiable cause exists in a particular case is a factual determination for the probate court and will not be disturbed upon appeal unless such determination is unsupported by clear and convincing evidence. In re Adoption of Holcomb (Ohio 1985) 18 Ohio St.3d 361, 481 N.E.2d 613, 18 O.B.R. 419.

Paternity was established, within meaning of adoption statute requiring father's consent, when administrative determination of parentage was made, even though order did not become final for 30 days. In re Adoption of Hudnell (Ross 1996) 113 Ohio App.3d 296, 680 N.E.2d 1055.

Administrative determination of parentage was "court proceeding," within meaning of adoption statute requiring consent of father whose parentage is established in court proceeding. In re Adoption of Hudnell (Ross 1996) 113 Ohio App.3d 296, 680 N.E.2d 1055.

Statute section governing consent of putative fathers, rather than section applicable to consent of one whose status as parent had been legally adjudicated, was appropriate to apply to issue of whether putative father's consent was required for adoption of minor child. In re Adoption of Bowes (Lake 1995) 105 Ohio App.3d 574, 664 N.E.2d 963.

Putative father had common-law duty to support his child for purposes of father's right to object to adoption of child by another, even if there had been no specific court-ordered support of child. In re Adoption of Bowes (Lake 1995) 105 Ohio App.3d 574, 664 N.E.2d 963.

It is quality of relationship between putative parent and child, and not amount of money spent on child by putative parent, which determines whether putative father has acquired parental interest in child for purposes of statute section requiring consent of person with parental interest in child to adoption of child. In re Adoption of Bowes (Lake 1995) 105 Ohio App.3d 574, 664 N.E.2d 963.

Willful failure to fulfill common-law duty of support for substantial period of time prior to filing of adoption petition can result in determination that putative father's consent to adoption is not required. In re Adoption of Bowes (Lake 1995) 105 Ohio App.3d 574, 664 N.E.2d 963.

There was some competent credible evidence to support trial court's finding that putative father had cared for and had not willfully failed to support child under statutory provision allowing putative father to object to adoption where testimony showed that putative father's income was between $0 and $6,000 per year since child's birth, and that father had provided repair and other in kind services to child's mother and had been incarcerated part of time since child's birth. In re Adoption of Bowes (Lake 1995) 105 Ohio App.3d 574, 664 N.E.2d 963.

Burden is on party seeking adoption to prove by clear and convincing evidence that putative parent willfully failed to monetarily support child. In re Adoption of Bowes (Lake 1995) 105 Ohio App.3d 574, 664 N.E.2d 963.

Trial court's conclusion that putative father abandoned natural mother during term of her pregnancy, and, thus, that mother could place child for adoption without putative father's consent, was against manifest weight of evidence and was unsupported by clear and convincing evidence; evidence overwhelmingly demonstrated that it was mother that forsook all contact with father, and that father's attempts to reconcile his relationship with mother were met with resistance, threats, and deceit. In re Adoption of Klonowski (Stark 1993) 87 Ohio App.3d 352, 622 N.E.2d 376.

A probate court's failure to consider a putative father's objection to adoption which is filed before entry of the final decree of adoption is not erroneous where the putative father's objection is not filed within thirty days of placement of the minor as set forth in RC 3107.06(F); thus, the putative father's consent was not necessary in order for the court to proceed with the adoption. In re Adoption of Hall (Franklin 1991) 72 Ohio App.3d 503, 595 N.E.2d 473.

RC 3107.07(A), which sets forth the circumstances under which the consent of a parent is not required in an adoption proceeding, does not apply to an acknowledged natural father of a child who was not married to the mother of the child at the time of the child's birth and who has not been established to be the child's father in a paternity proceeding under RC Ch 3111; rather, the provisions of RC 3107.07(B) apply. In re Adoption of Toth (Summit 1986) 33 Ohio App.3d 265, 515 N.E.2d 950.

Where a man establishes himself as a child's father in a paternity action brought pursuant to RC Ch 3111, the father's duty to support the child is retroactive to birth of the child for determining the father's failure to support the child for purposes of RC 3107.07(A). In re Adoption of Foster (Van Wert 1985) 22 Ohio App.3d 129, 489 N.E.2d 1070, 22 O.B.R. 331.

Justifiable cause for a noncustodial parent's failure to communicate with his child exists where the custodial parent interfered to a significant degree with communication between the noncustodial parent and the child, and a showing is made that the failure was neither voluntary nor intentional. Matter of Adoption of Hupp (Cuyahoga 1982) 9 Ohio App.3d 128, 458 N.E.2d 878, 9 O.B.R. 192.

Purchasing Christmas presents and including the child on a medical insurance policy at work are not sufficient to require consent of the putative father for adoption by the child's stepfather. In re Adoption of Hilary Marie B, No. WM-97-013, 1997 WL 586741 (6th Dist Ct App, Williams, 9-19-97).

Where a father has signed the birth certificate as an informant, making him the child's putative father, a decision of the juvenile court finding that consent to adoption is not needed is unlawful in that it violates RC 3107.07 by failing to find that the party is not the natural father or that he willfully abandoned or failed to care for and support the minor. In re Adoption of Hilary Marie B, No. WM-96-014, 1996 WL 715453 (6th Dist Ct App, Williams, 12-13-96).

The filing of the acknowledgement of paternity pursuant to RC 2105.18 accompanied by the filing of an objection to adoption pursuant to RC 3107.06(F)(4) is sufficient to place the father within the purview of RC 3107.07(A) as a parent and not within RC 3107(B). In re Adoption of Dickson, No. 94-CA-57, 1995 WL 495450 (5th Dist Ct App, Fairfield, 5-19-95).

A putative father as that term is used in RC 3107.07 is not a "father" or "parent" as those words are used in RC 3107.06, 3111.01, and 5103.15. In re Adoption of Eckleberry, No. 94APF10-1523, 1995 WL 311409 (10th Dist Ct App, Franklin, 5-11-95).

Where there has been no judicial determination of parentage, the acknowledged natural father of a child born out of wedlock, who has signed the birth certificate, has no legal obligation to support his child and cannot be found to have violated a legal duty, thereby dispensing with his consent in an adoption proceeding. Amstutz v Braden, No. L-85-191 (6th Dist Ct App, Lucas, 12-27-85).

Where a putative father sends two checks totalling thirty dollars for the support of a child just prior to the filing of a petition for adoption and where this constitutes the only support ever offered or given, a finding that the putative father has failed to care for and support the minor child is justified and renders his consent to the adoption unnecessary. In re Adoption of Rouleau, No. 1058 (4th Dist Ct App, Ross, 8-31-84).

State's failure to give putative father, who never developed any significant custodial, personal, or financial relationship with out-of-wedlock child and who did not seek to establish legal ties with child until after she was two years old, notice and opportunity to be heard prior to entering adoption order did not violate putative father's due process or equal protection rights; the equal protection clause does not prevent state from treating natural parent who has established custodial relationship with child differently from natural parent who has never established any custodial, personal, or financial relationship with child. (Ed. note: New York law construed in light of federal constitution.) Lehr v. Robertson (U.S.N.Y. 1983) 103 S.Ct. 2985, 463 U.S. 248, 77 L.Ed.2d 614.

7. Willful failure

The fact of incarceration in a penal institution does not constitute a willful failure to properly support and maintain a child, within the meaning of RC 3107.06(B)(4), so as to vitiate the requirement of consent by both natural parents prior to the entry of a decree of adoption. (Annotation from former RC 3107.06.) In re Schoeppner's Adoption (Ohio 1976) 46 Ohio St.2d 21, 345 N.E.2d 608, 75 O.O.2d 12.

A parent may be found to have "willfully failed" to support, within the meaning of RC 3107.06, where such parent, knowing of the duty and being able to provide such support, voluntarily and intentionally fails to do so. (Annotation from former RC 3107.06.) In re Adoption of Lewis (Ohio 1966) 8 Ohio St.2d 25, 222 N.E.2d 628, 37 O.O.2d 376.

The words, "willfully failed to properly support and maintain," as used in RC 3107.06 in regard to circumstances in which consent of a parent to adoption of a child is not necessary, imply more than a mere failure to provide financial support; such failure must be intentional. (Annotation from former RC 3107.06.) In re Adoption of Earhart (Miami 1961) 117 Ohio App. 73, 190 N.E.2d 468, 23 O.O.2d 156.

A petition, in the proceeding for the adoption of a child, which does not allege that the parents "willfully" failed to properly support and maintain their child, is not in compliance with the requirements of RC 3107.06, and fails to state a good cause of action. (Annotation from former RC 3107.06.) In re Gates' Adoption (Shelby 1948) 84 Ohio App. 269, 85 N.E.2d 597, 53 Ohio Law Abs. 315, 39 O.O. 379.

Natural parents who placed a child with the sister of the mother several hours after its birth and permitted such sister and her husband to care for such child and did not contribute to its support did not "willfully fail" to support such child within the meaning of GC 8004-6 (RC 3107.06). (Annotation from former RC 3107.06.) Adoption of Wedl (Ohio Prob. 1952) 114 N.E.2d 311, 65 Ohio Law Abs. 231.

3107.071 Parental consent required despite voluntary permanent custody surrender agreement; exceptions

If a parent enters into a voluntary permanent custody surrender agreement under division (B)(2) of section 5103.15 of the Revised Code on or after the effective date of this section, the parent's consent to the adoption of the child who is the subject of the agreement is required unless all of the following requirements are met:

(A) In the case of a parent whose child, if adopted, will be an adopted person as defined in section 3107.45 of the Revised Code:

(1) The parent does all of the following:

(a) Signs the component of the form prescribed under division (A)(1)(a) of section 3107.083 of the Revised Code;

(b) Checks either the "yes" or "no" space provided on the component of the form prescribed under division (A)(1)(b) of section 3107.083 of the Revised Code and signs that component;

(c) If the parent is the mother, completes and signs the component of the form prescribed under division (A)(1)(c) of section 3107.083 of the Revised Code.

(2) The agency provides the parent the opportunity to sign, if the parent chooses to do so, the components of the form prescribed under divisions (A)(1)(d), (e), and (f) of section 3107.083 of the Revised Code;

(3) The agency files with the juvenile and probate courts the form prescribed under division (A)(1) of section 3107.083 of the Revised Code signed by the parent, provides a copy of the form signed by the parent to the parent, and keeps a copy of the form signed by the parent in the agency's records.

The court shall keep a copy of the form signed by the parent in the court records.

(B) In the case of a parent whose child, if adopted, will be an adopted person as defined in section 3107.39 of the Revised Code:

(1) The parent does both of the following:

(a) Signs the component of the form prescribed under division (B)(1)(a) of section 3107.083 of the Revised Code;

(b) If the parent is the mother, completes and signs the component of the form prescribed under division (B)(1)(b) of section 3107.083 of the Revised Code.

(2) The agency provides the parent the opportunity to sign, if the parent chooses to do so, the components of the form prescribed under divisions (B)(1)(c), (d), and (e) of section 3107.083 of the Revised Code at the time the parent enters into the agreement with the agency;

(3) The agency files the form signed by the parent with the juvenile and probate courts, provides a copy of the form signed by the parent to the parent, and keeps a copy of the form signed by the parent in the agency's records.

The court shall keep a copy of the form signed by the parent in the court records.

(1999 H 471, eff. 7-1-00; 1996 H 419, eff. 9-18-96)

Historical and Statutory Notes

Amendment Note: 1999 H 471 deleted "by the department of human services" after "prescribed" in divisions (A)(1)(a) and (B)(1)(a); and made other nonsubstantive changes.

Ohio Administrative Code References

Acceptance of permanent custody by permanent surrender, OAC 5101:2-42-09

Library References

Baldwin's Ohio Legislative Service, 1996 H 419—LSC Analysis, 3/L-336

Carlin, Baldwin's Ohio Practice, *Merrick-Rippner Probate Law* § 98.2, 98.35, 98.37 (1997)

3107.08 Execution of consent

(A) The required consent to adoption may be executed at any time after seventy-two hours after the birth of a minor, and shall be executed in the following manner:

(1) If by the person to be adopted, in the presence of the court;

(2) If by a parent of the person to be adopted, in accordance with section 3107.081 of the Revised Code;

(3) If by an agency, by the executive head or other authorized representative, in the presence of a person authorized to take acknowledgments;

(4) If by any other person, in the presence of the court or in the presence of a person authorized to take acknowledgments;

(5) If by a juvenile court, by appropriate order.

(B) A consent which does not name or otherwise identify the prospective adoptive parent is valid if it contains a statement by the person giving consent that it was voluntarily executed irrespective of disclosure of the name or other identification of the prospective adoptive parent.

(1996 H 419, eff. 9-18-96; 1976 H 156, eff. 1-1-77)

Historical and Statutory Notes

Ed. Note: Former 3107.08 repealed by 1976 H 156, eff. 1-1-77; 1975 S 145; 1953 H 1; GC 8004-8; Source—GC 10512-16.

Pre-1953 H 1 Amendments: 124 v S 65

Amendment Note: 1996 H 419 added division (A)(2); redesignated former divisions (A)(2) through (4) as (A)(3) through (5), respectively; substituted "acknowledgments" for "acknowledgements" in divisions (A)(3) and (4); deleted "except a minor" following "If by any other person" in division (A)(4); added "juvenile" in division (A)(5); deleted former division (A)(5), which read: "(5) If by a minor parent, pursuant to section 5103.16 of the Revised Code"; substituted "adoptive" for "adopting" twice in division (B); and made a nonsubstantive change.

Cross References

County children services board, powers and duties, 5153.16

Department of job and family services, division of social administration; care and placement of children; interstate compact on placement of children, 5103.09 to 5103.17, 5103.20 to 5103.28

Notaries public and commissioners, acknowledgments, Ch 147

Library References

Adoption ⚷7.5.

WESTLAW Topic No. 17.

C.J.S. Adoption of Persons §§ 51 et seq., 68 et seq.

OJur 3d: 47, Family Law § 912; 48, Family Law § 1544

Am Jur 2d: 2, Adoption § 43 to 47

What constitutes undue influence in obtaining a parent's consent to adoption of child. 50 ALR3d 918

What constitutes "duress" in obtaining parent's consent to adoption of child or surrender of child to adoption agency. 74 ALR3d 527

Validity of birth parent's "blanket" consent to adoption which fails to identify adoptive parents. 15 ALR5th 1

Baldwin's Ohio Legislative Service, 1996 H 419—LSC Analysis, 3/L-336

Carlin, Baldwin's Ohio Practice, *Merrick-Rippner Probate Law* § 98.2, 98.21, 98.35, 98.36 (1997)

Notes of Decisions and Opinions

1. Time of consent

The required consent for an adoption may be executed any time from seventy-two hours after the birth of a child to be adopted until the time the adoption petition is granted, and there is no jurisdictional defect if the required consent is not executed prior to the hearing on the adoption petition or prior to the close of the petitioner's case; thus, where the guardian of children sought to be adopted gives her written consent well before the adoption petition is granted, the trial court has jurisdiction to grant the adoption petition even though the consent was not given prior to the close of the petitioner's case. In re Adoption of Jordan (Preble 1991) 72 Ohio App.3d 638, 595 N.E.2d 963.

2. Nature of consent

Consent to adoption of minor child was freely given by natural parents, for purpose of probate court's subject-matter jurisdiction to enter final order of adoption; natural parents had attained age of majority and had completed all but one semester of college, adoption of child had been considered even prior to its birth, both parents were before court of law and were fully aware of their rights to retain child and were fully aware that by signing consent form they were permanently surrendering their rights to child, and there was no evidence that they did not understand consequences of their actions. Morrow v. Family & Community Services of Catholic Charities, Inc. (Ohio 1986) 28 Ohio St.3d 247, 504 N.E.2d 2, 28 O.B.R. 327.

Statute regarding execution of biological mother's consent to child's adoption does not require that a petition be filed prior to the execution and does not require that the consent to adopt provide a name or identify the adoptive parent, as long as it contains a statement that it is voluntarily executed irrespective of such disclosure. In re Adoption of Koszycki (Ohio App. 1 Dist. 1999) 133 Ohio App.3d 434, 728 N.E.2d 437.

The petition to adopt and the consent to adoption are two separate documents and so a natural parent's consent to adoption survives dismissal of a contemporaneously filed petition for adoption and may be used to support a subsequent petition filed by the same petitioners concerning adoption of the same child. In re Adoption of Koszycki, No. C-980741, 1999 WL 299904 (1st Dist Ct App, Hamilton, 5-14-99).

3107.081 Conditions for court acceptance of parental consent

(A) Except as provided in divisions (B), (E), and (F) of this section, a parent of a minor, who will be, if adopted, an adopted person as defined in section 3107.45 of the Revised Code, shall do all of the following as a condition of a court accepting the parent's consent to the minor's adoption:

(1) Appear personally before the court;

(2) Sign the component of the form prescribed under division (A)(1)(a) of section 3107.083 of the Revised Code;

(3) Check either the "yes" or "no" space provided on the component of the form prescribed under division (A)(1)(b) of section 3107.083 of the Revised Code and sign that component;

(4) If the parent is the mother, complete and sign the component of the form prescribed under division (A)(1)(c) of section 3107.083 of the Revised Code.

At the time the parent signs the components of the form prescribed under divisions (A)(1)(a), (b), and (c) of section 3107.083 of the Revised Code, the parent may sign, if the parent chooses to do so, the components of the form prescribed under divisions (A)(1)(d), (e), and (f) of that section. After the parent signs the components required to be signed and any discretionary components the parent chooses to sign, the parent, or the attorney arranging the adoption, shall file the form and parent's consent with the court. The court or attorney shall give the parent a copy of the form and consent. The court and attorney shall keep a copy of the form and consent in the court and attorney's records of the adoption.

The court shall question the parent to determine that the parent understands the adoption process, the ramifications of consenting to the adoption, each component of the form prescribed under division (A)(1) of section 3107.083 of the Revised Code, and that the minor and adoptive parent may receive identifying information about the parent in accordance with section 3107.47 of the Revised Code unless the parent checks the "no" space provided on the component of the form prescribed under division (A)(1)(b) of section 3107.083 of the Revised Code or has a denial of release form filed with the department of health under section 3107.46 of the Revised Code. The court also shall question the parent to determine that the parent's consent to the adoption and any decisions the parent makes in filling out the form prescribed under division (A)(1) of section 3107.083 of the Revised Code are made voluntarily.

(B) The parents of a minor, who is less than six months of age and will be, if adopted, an adopted person as defined in section 3107.45 of the Revised Code, may consent to the minor's adoption without personally appearing before a court if both parents do all of the following:

(1) Execute a notarized statement of consent to the minor's adoption before the attorney arranging the adoption;

(2) Sign the component of the form prescribed under division (A)(1)(a) of section 3107.083 of the Revised Code;

(3) Check either the "yes" or "no" space provided on the component of the form prescribed under division (A)(1)(b) of section 3107.083 of the Revised Code and sign that component.

At the time the parents sign the components of the form prescribed under divisions (A)(1)(a) and (b) of section 3107.083 of the Revised Code, the mother shall complete and sign the component of the form prescribed under division (A)(1)(c) of that section and the attorney arranging the adoption shall provide the parents the opportunity to sign, if they choose to do so, the components of the form prescribed under divisions (A)(1)(d), (e), and (f) of that section. At the time the petition to adopt the minor is submitted to the court, the attorney shall file the parents' consents and forms with the court. The attorney shall give the parents a copy of the consents and forms. At the time the attorney files the consents and forms with the court, the attorney also shall file with the court all other documents the director of job and family services requires by rules adopted under division (D) of section 3107.083 of the Revised Code to be filed with the court. The court and attorney shall keep a copy of the consents, forms, and documents in the court and attorney's records of the adoption.

(C) Except as provided in divisions (D), (E), and (F) of this section, a parent of a minor, who will be, if adopted, an adopted person as defined in section 3107.39 of the Revised Code, shall do all of the following as a condition of a court accepting the parent's consent to the minor's adoption:

(1) Appear personally before the court;

(2) Sign the component of the form prescribed under division (B)(1)(a) of section 3107.083 of the Revised Code;

(3) If the parent is the mother, complete and sign the component of the form prescribed under division (B)(1)(b) of section 3107.083 of the Revised Code.

At the time the parent signs the components prescribed under divisions (B)(1)(a) and (b) of section 3107.083 of the Revised Code, the parent may sign, if the parent chooses to do so, the components of the form prescribed under divisions (B)(1)(c), (d), and (e) of that section. After the parent signs the components required to be signed and any discretionary components the parent chooses to sign, the parent, or the attorney arranging the adoption, shall file the form and parent's consent with the court. The court or attorney shall give the parent a copy of the form and consent. The court and attorney shall keep a copy of the form and consent in the court and attorney's records of the adoption.

The court shall question the parent to determine that the parent understands the adoption process, the ramifications of consenting to the adoption, and each component of the form prescribed under division (B)(1) of section 3107.083 of the Revised Code. The court also shall question the parent to determine that the parent's consent to the adoption and any decisions the parent makes in filling out the form are made voluntarily.

(D) The parent of a minor who is less than six months of age and will be, if adopted, an adopted person as defined in section 3107.39 of the Revised Code may consent to the minor's adoption without personally appearing before a court if the parent does all of the following:

(1) Executes a notarized statement of consent to the minor's adoption before the attorney arranging the adoption;

(2) Signs the component of the form prescribed under division (B)(1)(a) of section 3107.083 of the Revised Code;

(3) If the parent is the mother, completes and signs the component of the form prescribed under division (B)(1)(b) of section 3107.083 of the Revised Code.

At the time the parent signs the components of the form prescribed under divisions (B)(1)(a) and (b) of section 3107.083 of the Revised Code, the attorney arranging the adoption shall provide the parent the opportunity to sign, if the parent chooses to do so, the components of the form prescribed under divisions (B)(1)(c), (d), and (e) of that section. At the time the petition to adopt the minor is submitted to the court, the attorney shall file the parent's consent and form with the court. The attorney shall give the parent a copy of the consent and form. At the time the attorney files the consent and form with the court, the attorney also shall file with the court all other documents the director of job and family services requires by rules adopted under division (D) of section 3107.083 of the Revised Code to be filed with the court. The court and attorney shall keep a copy of the consent, form, and documents in the court and attorney's records of the adoption.

(E) If a minor is to be adopted by a stepparent, the parent who is not married to the stepparent may consent to the minor's adoption without appearing personally before a court if the parent executes consent in the presence of a person authorized to take acknowledgments. The attorney arranging the adoption shall file the consent with the court and give the parent a copy of the consent. The court and attorney shall keep a copy of the consent in the court and attorney's records of the adoption.

(F) If a parent of a minor to be adopted resides in another state, the parent may consent to the minor's adoption without appearing personally before a court if the parent executes consent in the presence of a person authorized to take acknowledgments. The attorney arranging the adoption shall file the consent with the court and give the parent a copy of the consent. The court and attorney shall keep a copy of the consent in the court and attorney's records of the adoption.

(1999 H 471, eff. 7-1-00; 1996 H 274, eff. 9-18-96; 1996 H 419, eff. 9-18-96)

Historical and Statutory Notes

Amendment Note: 1999 H 471 deleted "by the department of human services" after "prescribed" in divisions (A)(2), (B)(2), (C)(2), and (D)(2); substituted "director of job and family services" for "department of human services" in the final paragraphs in divisions (B) and (D); and made other nonsubstantive changes.

Amendment Note: 1996 H 274 substituted "At the time the petition to adopt the minor is submitted to the court" for "Not later than two business days after the parents execute consent and sign the components of the form required to be signed and any discretionary components the parents choose to sign" in the final paragraph in division (B); and for "Not later than two business days after the parents execute consent and signs the components of the form required to be signed and any discretionary components the parent chooses to sign" in the final paragraph in division (D).

Library References

Am Jur 2d: 2, Adoption § 60 et seq., 207 to 212

What constitutes undue influence in obtaining a parent's consent to adoption of child. 50 ALR3d 918

Comment Note.—Right of natural parent to withdraw valid consent to adoption of child. 74 ALR3d 421

Mistake or want of understanding as ground for revocation of consent to adoption or of agreement releasing infant to adoption placement agency. 74 ALR3d 489

What constitutes "duress" in obtaining parent's consent to adoption of child or surrender of child to adoption agency. 74 ALR3d 527

Restricting access to judicial records of concluded adoption proceedings. 83 ALR3d 800

Restricting access to judicial records of pending adoption proceedings. 83 ALR3d 824

Validity of birth parent's "blanket" consent to adoption which fails to identify adoptive parents. 15 ALR5th 1

Baldwin's Ohio Legislative Service, 1996 H 419—LSC Analysis, 3/L-336

Carlin, Baldwin's Ohio Practice, *Merrick-Rippner Probate Law* § 98.2 (1997)

Law Review and Journal Commentaries

Ohio House Bill 419: Increased Openness in Adoption Records Law, Wendy L. Weiss. 45 Clev St L Rev 101 (1997).

3107.082 Assessor's meeting with parent prior to parent's consent to adoption

Not less than seventy-two hours prior to the date a parent executes consent to the adoption of the parent's child under section 3107.081 of the Revised Code, an assessor shall meet in person with the parent and do both of the following unless the child is to be adopted by a stepparent or the parent resides in another state:

(A) Provide the parent with a copy of the written materials about adoption prepared under division (C) of section 3107.083 of the Revised Code, discuss with the parent the adoption process and ramifications of a parent consenting to a child's adoption, and provide the parent the opportunity to review the materials and to ask questions about the materials, discussion, and related matters;

(B) Unless the child, if adopted, will be an adopted person as defined in section 3107.39 of the Revised Code, inform the parent that the child and the adoptive parent may receive, in accordance with section 3107.47 of the Revised Code, identifying information about the parent that is contained in the child's adoption file maintained by the department of health unless the parent checks the "no" space provided on the component of the form prescribed under division (A)(1)(b) of section 3107.083 of the Revised Code or signs and has filed with the department a denial of release form prescribed under section 3107.50 of the Revised Code.

(1999 H 471, eff. 7-1-00; 1996 H 419, eff. 9-18-96)

Historical and Statutory Notes

Amendment Note: 1999 H 471 deleted "by the department of human services" after "prepared" in division (A).

Cross References

Probate courts, appointment of assessors, 2101.11

Library References

Baldwin's Ohio Legislative Service, 1996 H 419—LSC Analysis, 3/L-336

Carlin, Baldwin's Ohio Practice, *Merrick-Rippner Probate Law* § 98.2, 98.13 (1997)

3107.083 Form authorizing release of information

Not later than ninety days after June 20, 1996, the director of job and family services shall do all of the following:

(A)(1) For a parent of a child who, if adopted, will be an adopted person as defined in section 3107.45 of the Revised Code, prescribe a form that has the following six components:

(a) A component the parent signs under section 3107.071, 3107.081, or 5103.151 of the Revised Code to indicate the requirements of section 3107.082 or 5103.152 of the Revised Code have been met. The component shall be as follows:

"Statement Concerning Ohio Law and Adoption Materials

By signing this component of this form, I acknowledge that it has been explained to me, and I understand, that, if I check the space on the next component of this form that indicates that I authorize the release, the adoption file maintained by the Ohio Department of Health, which contains identifying information about me at the time of my child's birth, will be released, on request, to the adoptive parent when the adoptee is at least age eighteen but younger than age twenty-one and to the adoptee when he or she is age twenty-one or older. It has also been explained to me, and I understand, that I may prohibit the release of identifying information about me contained in the adoption file by checking the space on the next component of this form that indicates that I do not authorize the release of the identifying information. It has additionally been explained to me, and I understand, that I may change my mind regarding the decision I make on the next component of this form at any time and as many times as I desire by signing, dating, and having filed with the Ohio Department of Health a denial of release form or authorization of release form prescribed and provided by the Department of Health and providing the Department two items of identification.

By signing this component of this form, I also acknowledge that I have been provided a copy of written materials about adoption prepared by the Ohio Department of Job and Family Services, the adoption process and ramifications of consenting to adoption or entering into a voluntary permanent custody surrender agreement have been discussed with me, and I have been provided the opportunity to review the materials and ask questions about the materials and discussion.

Signature of biological parent:____

Signature of witness:______________________________________

Date:______________________________________"

(b) A component the parent signs under section 3107.071, 3107.081, or 5103.151 of the Revised Code regarding the parent's decision whether to allow identifying information about the parent contained in an adoption file maintained by the department of health to be released to the parent's child and adoptive parent pursuant to section 3107.47 of the Revised Code. The component shall be as follows:

"Statement Regarding Release of Identifying Information

The purpose of this component of this form is to allow a biological parent to decide whether to allow the Ohio Department of Health to provide an adoptee and adoptive parent identifying information about the adoptee's biological parent contained in an adoption file maintained by the Department. Please check one of the following spaces:

___YES, I authorize the Ohio Department of Health to release identifying information about me, on request, to the adoptive parent when the adoptee is at least age eighteen but younger than age twenty-one and to the adoptee when he or she is age twenty-one or older.

___NO, I do not authorize the release of identifying information about me to the adoptive parent or adoptee.

Signature of biological parent:______________________________________

Signature of witness:______________________________________

Date:______________________________________"

(c) A component the parent, if the mother of the child, completes and signs under section 3107.071, 3107.081, or 5103.151 of the Revised Code to indicate, to the extent of the mother's knowledge, all of the following:

(i) Whether the mother, during her pregnancy, was a recipient of the medical assistance program established under Chapter 5111. of the Revised Code or other public health insurance program and, if so, the dates her eligibility began and ended;

(ii) Whether the mother, during her pregnancy, was covered by private health insurance and, if so, the dates the coverage began and ended, the name of the insurance provider, the type of coverage, and the identification number of the coverage;

(iii) The name and location of the hospital, freestanding birth center, or other place where the mother gave birth and, if different, received medical care immediately after giving birth;

(iv) The expenses of the obstetrical and neonatal care;

(v) Whether the mother has been informed that the adoptive parent or the agency or attorney arranging the adoption are to pay expenses involved in the adoption, including expenses the mother has paid and expects to receive or has received reimbursement, and, if so, what expenses are to be or have been paid and an estimate of the expenses;

(vi) Any other information related to expenses the department determines appropriate to be included in this component.

(d) A component the parent may sign to authorize the agency or attorney arranging the adoption to provide to the child or adoptive parent materials, other than photographs of the parent, that the parent requests be given to the child or adoptive parent pursuant to section 3107.68 of the Revised Code.

(e) A component the parent may sign to authorize the agency or attorney arranging the adoption to provide to the child or adoptive parent photographs of the parent pursuant to section 3107.68 of the Revised Code.

(f) A component the parent may sign to authorize the agency or attorney arranging the adoption to provide to the child or adoptive parent the first name of the parent pursuant to section 3107.68 of the Revised Code.

(2) State at the bottom of the form that the parent is to receive a copy of the form the parent signed.

(3) Provide copies of the form prescribed under this division to probate and juvenile courts, public children services agencies, private child placing agencies, private noncustodial agencies, attorneys, and persons authorized to take acknowledgments.

(B)(1) For a parent of a child who, if adopted, will become an adopted person as defined in section 3107.39 of the Revised Code, prescribe a form that has the following five components:

(a) A component the parent signs under section 3107.071, 3107.081, or 5103.151 of the Revised Code to attest that the requirement of division (A) of section 3107.082 or division (A) of section 5103.152 of the Revised Code has been met;

(b) A component the parent, if the mother of the child, completes and signs under section 3107.071, 3107.081, or 5103.151 of the Revised Code to indicate, to the extent of the mother's knowledge, all of the following:

(i) Whether the mother, during her pregnancy, was a recipient of the medical assistance program established under Chapter 5111. of the Revised Code or other public health insurance program and, if so, the dates her eligibility began and ended;

(ii) Whether the mother, during her pregnancy, was covered by private health insurance and, if so, the dates the coverage began and ended, the name of the insurance provider, the type of coverage, and the identification number of the coverage;

(iii) The name and location of the hospital, freestanding birth center, or other place where the mother gave birth and, if different, received medical care immediately after giving birth;

(iv) The expenses of the obstetrical and neonatal care;

(v) Whether the mother has been informed that the adoptive parent or the agency or attorney arranging the adoption are to pay expenses involved in the adoption, including expenses the mother has paid and expects to receive or has received reimbursement for, and, if so, what expenses are to be or have been paid and an estimate of the expenses;

(vi) Any other information related to expenses the department determines appropriate to be included in the component.

(c) A component the parent may sign to authorize the agency or attorney arranging the adoption to provide to the child or adoptive parent materials, other than photographs of the parent, that the parent requests be given to the child or adoptive parent pursuant to section 3107.68 of the Revised Code.

(d) A component the parent may sign to authorize the agency or attorney arranging the adoption to provide to the child or adoptive parent photographs of the parent pursuant to section 3107.68 of the Revised Code.

(e) A component the parent may sign to authorize the agency or attorney arranging the adoption to provide to the child or adoptive parent the first name of the parent pursuant to section 3107.68 of the Revised Code.

(2) State at the bottom of the form that the parent is to receive a copy of the form the parent signed.

(3) Provide copies of the form prescribed under this division to probate and juvenile courts, public children services agencies, private child placing agencies, private noncustodial agencies, and attorneys.

(C) Prepare the written materials about adoption that are required to be given to parents under division (A) of section 3107.082 and division (A) of section 5103.152 of the Revised Code. The materials shall provide information about the adoption process, including ramifications of a parent consenting to a child's adoption or entering into a voluntary permanent custody surrender agreement. The materials also shall include referral information for professional counseling and adoption support organizations. The director shall provide the materials to assessors.

(D) Adopt rules in accordance with Chapter 119. of the Revised Code specifying the documents that must be filed with a probate court under divisions (B) and (D) of section 3107.081 of the Revised Code and a juvenile court under divisions (C) and (E) of section 5103.151 of the Revised Code.

(1999 H 471, eff. 7-1-00; 1996 H 419, eff. 6-20-96)

Historical and Statutory Notes

Amendment Note: 1999 H 471 substituted "June 20, 1996" for "the effective date of this section" and "director of job and family services" for "department of human services" in the introductory paragraph; substituted "Job and Family" for "Human" in the form in division (A)(1); and substituted "director" for "department" in division (C).

Cross References

Assessor's meeting with birth parent prior to parent's consenting to adoption, written materials, 5103.152

Conditions for juvenile court approving parent's agreement for child's adoption, form, 5103.151

Ohio Administrative Code References

Acceptance of permanent custody by permanent surrender, OAC 5101:2-42-09

AdoptOhio photo listing web page, listing and withdrawing children and families with the "Ohio Adoption Photo Listing" (OAPL), OAC 5101:2-48-07

Release of identifying and nonidentifying information, OAC 5101:2-48-20

Library References

Baldwin's Ohio Legislative Service, 1996 H 419—LSC Analysis, 3/L-336

Carlin, Baldwin's Ohio Practice, *Merrick-Rippner Probate Law* § 98.2 (1997)

Law Review and Journal Commentaries

Ohio House Bill 419: Increased Openness in Adoption Records Law, Wendy L. Weiss. 45 Clev St L Rev 101 (1997).

3107.084 Withdrawal of consent

(A) A consent to adoption is irrevocable and cannot be withdrawn after the entry of an interlocutory order or after the entry of a final decree of adoption when no interlocutory order has been entered. The consent of a minor is not voidable by reason of the minor's age.

(B) A consent to adoption may be withdrawn prior to the entry of an interlocutory order or prior to the entry of a final decree of adoption when no interlocutory order has been entered if the court finds after hearing that the withdrawal is in the best interest of the person to be adopted and the court by order authorizes the withdrawal of consent. Notice of the hearing shall be given to the petitioner, the person seeking the withdrawal of consent, and the agency placing the minor for adoption.

(1996 H 419, eff. 9-18-96)

Historical and Statutory Notes

Ed. Note: 3107.084 is former 3107.09, amended and recodified by 1996 H 419, eff. 9-18-96; 1976 H 156, eff. 1-1-77.

Amendment Note: 1996 H 419 amended this section by substituting "the minor's age" for "his minority" at the end of division (A).

Library References

Adoption ⟹7.6(1) to 7.6(3).
WESTLAW Topic No. 17.
C.J.S. Adoption of Persons §§ 51 et seq., 70 et seq.

OJur 3d: 47, Family Law § 914
Am Jur 2d: 2, Adoption § 46, 47
Comment Note—Right of natural parent to withdraw valid consent to adoption of child. 74 ALR3d 421

Baldwin's Ohio Legislative Service, 1996 H 419—LSC Analysis, 3/L-336

Carlin, Baldwin's Ohio Practice, *Merrick-Rippner Probate Law* § 98.2 (1997)

Notes of Decisions and Opinions

1. Agency consent

The refusal of consent to an adoption by a "certified organization," as defined in RC 3107.01(C), does not impair the jurisdiction of the probate court, but the recommendations and the reports, filed pursuant to RC 3107.05 and 3107.10, are to be considered, in conjunction with all other evidence adduced in the proceeding, by the court in deciding the issues presented by RC 3107.09. (Annotation from former RC 3107.01.) State ex rel. Portage County Welfare Dept. v. Summers (Ohio 1974) 38 Ohio St.2d 144, 311 N.E.2d 6, 67 O.O.2d 151.

2. Burden of proof

Biological mother who signed adoption consent form had burden to establish duress or undue influence by clear and convincing evidence. (Annotation from former RC 3107.09.) In re Rabatin (Geauga 1992) 83 Ohio App.3d 836, 615 N.E.2d 1099.

Once a natural mother has entered her consent to an adoption in open court, any claim of duress or undue influence must be established by clear and convincing evidence. (Annotation from former RC 3107.09.) In re Adoption of Infant Boy (Allen 1989) 60 Ohio App.3d 80, 573 N.E.2d 753.

3. Grounds for revocation

A change of heart on the part of a natural mother who consented to an adoption is insufficient ground to revoke her consent. (Annotation from former RC 3107.09.) In re Adoption of Infant Boy (Allen 1989) 60 Ohio App.3d 80, 573 N.E.2d 753.

A court considering a motion to withdraw consent to an adoption cannot properly consider the best interests of the various family members. (Annotation from former RC 3107.09.) In re Adoption of Infant Boy (Allen 1989) 60 Ohio App.3d 80, 573 N.E.2d 753.

4. Minor parent

A minor parent may consent to the adoption of her child, and such consent may not be withdrawn after the entry of an interlocutory order, or after the final decree, of adoption. (Annotation from former RC 3107.06.) In re Burdette (Summit 1948) 83 Ohio App. 368, 83 N.E.2d 813, 38 O.O. 429.

5. Denial of petition

After conducting a hearing pursuant to RC 3107.09, the probate court improperly denies a petition for adoption of a four-year-old boy in the custody of the county welfare department, when the court finds that petitioners meet all the requirements of suitability as adoptive parents, but denies the petition for adoption on the grounds that the granting of the adoption would violate the integrity of a waiting list allegedly maintained by the welfare department, where at the adoption hearing there was no evidence adduced establishing the existence or administration of such a waiting list and no evidence that the waiting list contained suitable applicants ready, willing, and able to adopt the child in question. (Annotation from former RC 3107.06.) (See also In re Harshey, 40 App(2d) 157, 318 NE(2d) 544 (1974).) In re Harshey (Cuyahoga 1975) 45 Ohio App.2d 97, 341 N.E.2d 616, 74 O.O.2d 120.

6. Timing of withdrawal

Biological mother's consent to adoption was not product of fraud or undue influence; thus, she was not allowed to withdraw her consent after final order of adoption. (Annotation from former RC 3107.09.) In re Adoption of Zschach (Ohio 1996) 75 Ohio St.3d 648, 665 N.E.2d 1070, reconsideration denied 76 Ohio St.3d 1410, 666 N.E.2d 569, certiorari denied 117 S.Ct. 582, 136 L.Ed.2d 513.

Consent to adoption is viable until the court grants a motion to withdraw it, which must be filed before the entry of an interlocutory order or the entry of a final order of adoption. In re Adoption of Koszycki (Ohio App. 1 Dist. 1999) 133 Ohio App.3d 434, 728 N.E.2d 437.

An interlocutory order of adoption is erroneously entered after the putative father of the minor child who signed the birth certificate objects to the adoption, and consequently, a mother's motion to withdraw her consent to the adoption is not time barred pursuant to RC 3107.09. (Annotation from former RC 3107.09.) In re Adoption of Zschach, Nos. 1994CA-14+, 1994 WL 728626 (5th Dist Ct App, Fairfield, 12-19-94), reversed by 75 Ohio St.3d 648 (1996).

The condition of RC 3107.09(B) that consent to adoption may be withdrawn upon a finding that the withdrawal is in the best interests of the child applies after an application for placement has been filed pursuant to RC 5103.16 and the consent has been executed in compliance with RC 3107.08, even though no adoption petition has yet been filed. (Annotation from former RC 3107.09.) In re Adoption of Frank, No. 85CA54 (2d Dist Ct App, Greene, 3-11-86).

3107.085 Temporary custody—Repealed

(1996 H 274, eff. 8-8-96; 1996 H 419, eff. 9-18-96)

HISTORY OF BIOLOGICAL PARENTS

3107.09 Social and medical histories of biological parents

(A) The department of job and family services shall prescribe and supply forms for the taking of social and medical histories of the biological parents of a minor available for adoption.

(B) An assessor shall record the social and medical histories of the biological parents of a minor available for adoption, unless the minor is to be adopted by the minor's stepparent or grandparent. The assessor shall use the forms prescribed pursuant to division (A) of this section. The assessor shall not include on the forms identifying information about the biological parents or other ancestors of the minor.

(C) A social history shall describe and identify the age; ethnic, racial, religious, marital, and physical characteristics; and educational, cultural, talent and hobby, and work experience background of the biological parents of the minor. A medical history shall identify major diseases, malformations, allergies, ear or eye defects, major conditions, and major health problems of the biological parents that are or may be congenital or familial. These histories may include other social and medical information relative to the biological parents and shall include social and medical information relative to the minor's other ancestors.

The social and medical histories may be obtained through interviews with the biological parents or other persons and from any available records if a biological parent or any legal guardian of a biological parent consents to the release of information contained in a record. An assessor who considers it necessary may request that a biological parent undergo a medical examination. In obtaining social and medical histories of a biological parent, an assessor shall inform the biological parent, or a person other than a biological parent who provides information pursuant to this section, of the purpose and use of the histories and of the biological parent's or other person's right to correct or expand the histories at any time.

(D) A biological parent, or another person who provided information in the preparation of the social and medical histories of the biological parents of a minor, may cause the histories to be corrected or expanded to include different or additional types of information. The biological parent or other person may cause the histories to be corrected or expanded at any time prior or subsequent to the adoption of the minor, including any time after the minor becomes an adult. A biological parent may cause the histories to be corrected or expanded even if the biological parent did not provide any information to the assessor at the time the histories were prepared.

To cause the histories to be corrected or expanded, a biological parent or other person who provided information shall provide the information to be included or specify the information to be corrected to whichever of the following is appropriate under the circumstances:

(1) Subject to division (D)(2) of this section, if the biological parent or other person knows the assessor who prepared the histories, to the assessor;

(2) If the biological parent or person does not know the assessor or finds that the assessor has ceased to perform assessments, to the court involved in the adoption or, if that court is not known, to the department of health.

An assessor who receives information from a biological parent or other person pursuant to division (D)(1) of this section shall determine whether the information is of a type that divisions (B) and (C) of this section permit to be included in the histories. If the assessor determines the information is of a permissible type, the assessor shall cause the histories to be corrected or expanded to reflect the information. If, at the time the information is received, the histories have been filed with the court as required by division (E) of this section, the court shall cooperate with the assessor in correcting or expanding the histories.

If the department of health or a court receives information from a biological parent or other person pursuant to division (D)(2) of this section, it shall determine whether the information is of a type that divisions (B) and (C) of this section permit to be included in the histories. If a court determines the information is of a permissible type, the court shall cause the histories to be corrected or expanded to reflect the information. If the department of health so determines, the court involved shall cooperate with the department in the correcting or expanding of the histories.

An assessor or the department of health shall notify a biological parent or other person in writing if the assessor or department determines that information the biological parent or other person provided or specified for inclusion in a history is not of a type that may be included in a history. On receipt of the notice, the biological parent or other person may petition the court involved in the adoption to make a finding as to whether the information is of a type that may be included in a history. On receipt of the petition, the court shall issue its finding without holding a hearing. If the court finds that the information is of a type that may be included in a history, it shall cause the history to be corrected or expanded to reflect the information.

(E) An assessor shall file the social and medical histories of the biological parents prepared pursuant to divisions (B) and (C) of this section with the court with which a petition to adopt the biological parents' child is filed. The court promptly shall provide a copy of the social and medical histories filed with it to the petitioner. In a case involving the adoption of a minor by any person other than the minor's stepparent or grandparent, a court may refuse to issue an interlocutory order or final decree of adoption if the histories of the biological parents have not been so filed, unless the assessor certifies to the court that information needed to prepare the histories is unavailable for reasons beyond the assessor's control.

(1999 H 471, eff. 7-1-00; 1996 H 419, eff. 9-18-96)

Historical and Statutory Notes

Ed. Note: Former 3107.09 amended and recodified as 3107.084 by 1996 H 419, eff. 9-18-96; 1976 H 156, eff. 1-1-77.

Ed. Note: Prior 3107.09 repealed by 1976 H 156, eff. 1-1-77; 1969 S 49; 1953 H 1; GC 8004-9; Source—GC 10512-18; see now 3107.14 for provisions analogous to former 3107.09.

Pre-1953 H 1 Amendments: 124 v S 65

Amendment Note: 1999 H 471 substituted "job and family" for "human" in division (A).

Cross References

Adoption registration, contents of file, 3705.12
Placement of child in institution, custody agreement, 5103.15
Probate courts, appointment of assessors, 2101.11

Ohio Administrative Code References

Requirement of ODHS 1616 "social and medical history", OAC 5101:2-48-03

Library References

OJur 3d: 47, Family Law § 914
Am Jur 2d: 2, Adoption § 147

Baldwin's Ohio Legislative Service, 1996 H 419—LSC Analysis, 3/L-336

Carlin, Baldwin's Ohio Practice, *Merrick-Rippner Probate Law* § 98.2, 98.3, 98.32, 98.35, 98.36 (1997)

3107.091 Biological parent may add medical and social history to records concerning adopted person

(A) As used in this section, "biological parent" means a biological parent whose offspring, as a minor, was adopted and with respect to whom a medical and social history was not prepared prior or subsequent to the adoption.

(B) A biological parent may request the department of job and family services to provide the biological parent with a copy of the social and medical history forms prescribed by the department pursuant to section 3107.09 of the Revised Code. The department, upon receipt of such a request, shall provide the forms to the biological parent, if the biological parent indicates that the forms are being requested so that the adoption records of the biological parent's offspring will include a social and medical history of the biological parent.

In completing the forms, the biological parent may include information described in division (C) of section 3107.09 of the Revised Code, but shall not include identifying information. When the biological parent has completed the forms to the extent the biological parent wishes to provide information, the biological parent shall return them to the department. The department shall review the completed forms, and shall determine whether the information included by the biological parent is of a type permissible under divisions (B) and (C) of section 3107.09 of the Revised Code and, to the best of its ability, whether the information is accurate. If it determines that the forms contain accurate, permissible information, the department, after excluding from the forms any information the department deems impermissible, shall file them with the court that entered the interlocutory order or final decree of adoption in the adoption case. If the department needs assistance in determining that court, the department of health, upon request, shall assist it.

The department of job and family services shall notify the biological parent in writing if it excludes from the biological parent's social and medical history forms information deemed impermissible. On receipt of the notice, the biological parent may petition the court with which the forms were filed to make a finding as to whether the information is permissible. On receipt of the petition, the court shall issue its finding without holding a hearing. If the court finds the information is permissible, it shall cause the information to be included on the forms.

Upon receiving social and medical history forms pursuant to this section, a court shall cause them to be filed in the records pertaining to the adoption case.

Social and medical history forms completed by a biological parent pursuant to this section may be corrected or expanded by the biological parent in accordance with division (D) of section 3107.09 of the Revised Code.

Access to the histories shall be granted in accordance with division (D) of section 3107.17 of the Revised Code.

(1999 H 471, eff. 7-1-00; 1996 H 419, eff. 9-18-96)

Historical and Statutory Notes

Ed. Note: 3107.091 is former 3107.121, amended and recodified by 1996 H 419, eff. 9-18-96; 1984 H 84, eff. 3-19-85.

Amendment Note: 1999 H 471 substituted "job and family" for "human" in the first and third paragraphs in division (B).

Amendment Note: 1996 H 419 amended this section (former 3107.121) by substituting "the biological parent" and "the biological parent's" for "he," "him," and "his" throughout the section; substituting "3107.09" for "3107.12" throughout the section; substituting "information" for "data as described in division (D)(2) of that section" in the first sentence of the second paragraph of division (B); substituting "information the department deems impermissible" for "impermissible information" and "divisions (B) and (C) of section 3107.09" for "divisions (D)(2) and (3) of section 3107.12" in the second paragraph of division (B); adding the third paragraph of division (B); deleting "the clerk of" preceding "a court shall cause them to be filed" in the fourth paragraph of division (B); and substituting "division (D) of section 3107.09" for "division (D)(4) of section 3107.12" in the fifth paragraph of divison (B).

Cross References

Adoption registration, contents of file, 3705.12
Availability of adoption records, 149.43
Courts, confidentiality of adoption files, Sup R 55

Ohio Administrative Code References

Requirement of ODHS 1616 "Social and Medical History", OAC 5101:2-48-03

Library References

Records ⚷32.
WESTLAW Topic No. 326.
C.J.S. Records §§ 65, 67 to 75.

OJur 3d: 47, Family Law § 930
Am Jur 2d: 2, Adoption § 59

Baldwin's Ohio Legislative Service, 1996 H 419—LSC Analysis, 3/L-336
Carlin, Baldwin's Ohio Practice, *Merrick-Rippner Probate Law* § 98.2 (1997)

ACCOUNTING TO COURT

3107.10 Accounting; disbursements; summary to be sent to department

(A) Notwithstanding section 3107.01 of the Revised Code, as used in this section, "agency" does not include a public children services agency.

(B) An agency or attorney, whichever arranges a minor's adoption, shall file with the court a preliminary estimate accounting not later than the time the adoption petition for the minor is filed with the court. The agency or attorney, whichever arranges the adoption, also shall file a final accounting with the court before a final decree of adoption is issued or an interlocutory order of adoption is finalized for the minor. The agency or attorney shall complete and file accountings in a manner acceptable to the court.

An accounting shall specify all disbursements of anything of value the petitioner, a person on the petitioner's behalf, and the agency or attorney made and has agreed to make in connection with the minor's permanent surrender under division (B) of section 5103.15 of the Revised Code, placement under section 5103.16 of the Revised Code, and adoption under this chapter. The agency or attorney shall include in an accounting an itemization of each expense listed in division (C) of this section. The itemization of the expenses specified in divisions (C)(3) and (4) of this section shall show the amount the agency or attorney charged or is going to charge for the services and the actual cost to the agency or attorney of providing the services. An accounting shall indicate whether any expenses listed in division (C) of this section do not apply to the adoption proceeding for which the accounting is filed.

The agency or attorney shall include with a preliminary estimate accounting and a final accounting a written statement signed by the petitioner that the petitioner has reviewed the accounting and attests to its accuracy.

(C) No petitioner, person acting on a petitioner's behalf, or agency or attorney shall make or agree to make any disbursements in connection with the minor's permanent surrender, placement, or adoption other than for the following:

(1) Physician expenses incurred on behalf of the birth mother or minor in connection with prenatal care, delivery, and confinement prior to or following the minor's birth;

(2) Hospital or other medical facility expenses incurred on behalf of the birth mother or minor in connection with the minor's birth;

(3) Expenses charged by the attorney arranging the adoption for providing legal services in connection with the placement and adoption, including expenses incurred by the attorney pursuant to sections 3107.031, 3107.081, 3107.082, 3107.09, and 3107.12 of the Revised Code;

(4) Expenses charged by the agency arranging the adoption for providing services in connection with the permanent surrender and adoption, including the agency's application fee and the expenses incurred by the agency pursuant to sections 3107.031, 3107.09, 3107.12, 5103.151, and 5103.152 of the Revised Code;

(5) Temporary costs of routine maintenance and medical care for a minor required under section 5103.16 of the Revised Code if the person seeking to adopt the minor refuses to accept placement of the minor;

(6) Guardian ad litem fees incurred on behalf of the minor in any court proceedings;

(7) Foster care expenses incurred in connection with any temporary care and maintenance of the minor;

(8) Court expenses incurred in connection with the minor's permanent surrender, placement, and adoption.

(D) If a court determines from an accounting that an amount that is going to be disbursed for an expense listed in division (C) of this section is unreasonable, the court may order a reduction in the amount to be disbursed. If a court determines from an accounting that an unreasonable amount was disbursed for an expense listed in division (C) of this section, the court may order the person who received the disbursement to refund to the person who made the disbursement an amount the court orders.

If a court determines from an accounting that a disbursement for an expense not permitted by division (C) of this section is going to be made, the court may issue an injunction prohibiting the disbursement. If a court determines from an accounting that a disbursement for an expense not permitted by division (C) of this section was made, the court may order the person who received the disbursement to return it to the person who made the disbursement.

If a court determines that a final accounting does not completely report all the disbursements that are going to be made or have been made in connection with the minor's permanent surrender, placement, and adoption, the court shall order the agency or attorney to file with the court an accounting that completely reports all such disbursements.

The agency or attorney shall file the final accounting with the court not later than ten days prior to the date scheduled for the final hearing on the adoption. The court may not issue a final decree of adoption or finalize an interlocutory order of adoption of a minor until at least ten days after the agency or attorney files the final accounting.

(E) At the conclusion of each adoption proceeding, the court shall prepare a summary of the proceeding, and on or before the tenth day of each month, send copies of the summaries for all proceedings concluded during the preceding calendar month to the department of job and family services. The summary shall contain:

(1) A notation of the nature and approximate value or amount of anything paid in connection with the proceeding, compiled from the final accounting required by division (B) of this section and indicating the category of division (C) of this section to which any payment relates;

(2) If the court has not issued a decree because of the requirements of division (D) of this section, a notation of that fact and a statement of the reason for refusing to issue the decree, related to the financial data summarized under division (E)(1) of this section;

(3) If the adoption was arranged by an attorney, a notation of that fact.

The summary shall contain no information identifying by name any party to the proceeding or any other person, but may contain additional narrative material that the court considers useful to an analysis of the summary.

(F) This section does not apply to an adoption by a stepparent whose spouse is a biological or adoptive parent of the minor.

(1999 H 471, eff. 7-1-00; 1996 H 274, eff. 9-18-96; 1996 H 419, eff. 9-18-96; 1986 H 428, eff. 12-23-86; 1978 H 832; 1976 H 156)

Historical and Statutory Notes

Ed. Note: Former 3107.10 repealed by 1976 H 156, eff. 1-1-77; 1953 H 1; GC 8004-10; Source—GC 10512-19; see now 3107.14 for provisions analogous to former 3107.10.

Pre-1953 H 1 Amendments: 124 v S 65

Amendment Note: 1999 H 471 substituted "job and family" for "human" in the introductory paragraph in division (E).

Amendment Note: 1996 H 274 substituted "may" for "shall" in the fourth paragraph in division (D).

Amendment Note: 1996 H 419 rewrote this section, which prior thereto read:

"(A) The petitioner in any proceeding for the adoption of a minor shall file, before the petition is heard, a full accounting in a manner acceptable to the court of all disbursements of anything of value made or agreed to be made by or on behalf of the petitioner in connection with the placement or adoption of the minor. The accounting shall show any payments made or to be made by or on behalf of the petitioner in connection with the placement or adoption.

"(B) A petitioner shall not make or agree to make any disbursements in connection with the placement or adoption of a minor other than for the following:

"(1) Physician expenses incurred in connection with prenatal care and confinement or in connection with the birth of the minor to be adopted;

"(2) Hospital expenses incurred in connection with the birth of the minor to be adopted;

"(3) Attorneys' fees incurred in providing legal services in connection with the placement of the minor to be adopted or in connection with legal services provided to initiate and pursue the adoption proceedings;

"(4) Agency expenses incurred for providing services in connection with the adoption or in connection with placement services provided by an agency under section 5103.16 of the Revised Code;

"(5) Temporary costs of routine maintenance and medical care for a minor required under section 5103.16

of the Revised Code if the person seeking to adopt the minor refuses to accept placement of the minor.

"(C) The court shall review and approve, prior to the entry of any decree of adoption, all expenses made or agreed to be made by a petitioner in connection with the adoption of a minor. The court shall not issue a decree of adoption if after a hearing it determines that any of the expenses incurred by the petitioner were unreasonable or were for services other than those permitted under division (B) of this section or if after a hearing it determines that the petitioner has failed to report all of the expenses incurred in connection with the placement or adoption of the minor.

"(D) At the conclusion of each adoption proceeding, the court shall prepare a summary of the proceeding, and on or before the tenth day of each month, send copies of the summaries for all proceedings concluded during the preceding calendar month to the department of human services. The summary shall contain:

"(1) A notation of the nature and approximate value or amount of anything paid in connection with the proceeding, compiled from the accounting required by division (A) of this section and indicating the category of division (B) of this section to which any payment relates;

"(2) If the court has not issued a decree because of the requirements of division (C) of this section, a notation of that fact and a statement of the reason for refusing to issue the decree, related to the financial data summarized under division (D)(1) of this section;

"(3) If placement in the petitioners' home was privately arranged under section 5103.16 of the Revised Code, a notation of that fact.

"The summary shall contain no information identifying by name any party to the proceeding or any other person, but may contain additional narrative material that the court considers useful to an analysis of the summary.

"(E) This section does not apply to an adoption by a stepparent whose spouse is a biological or adoptive parent of the minor."

Cross References

Job and family services department, report on summaries submitted, 2151.416

Library References

Adoption ⟜7.5, 9.1, 13.
WESTLAW Topic No. 17.
C.J.S. Adoption of Persons §§ 49, 50, 51 et seq., 68 et seq., 73, 88 to 97.

OJur 3d: 47, Family Law § 925

Baldwin's Ohio Legislative Service, 1996 H 419—LSC Analysis, 3/L-336
Carlin, Baldwin's Ohio Practice, *Merrick-Rippner Probate Law* § 98.2, 98.3, 98.27, 98.30, 98.48 (1997)
Greenbaum, Lawyer's Guide to the Ohio Code of Professional Responsibility, Text 5.139

Notes of Decisions and Opinions

1. Accounting

Although an accounting is mandatory before the adoption petition is heard, its late filing is not reversible error when the child had been placed with her natural grandparents and the mother had shown no prejudicial effect. In re Adoption of Howell (Lawrence 1991) 77 Ohio App.3d 80, 601 N.E.2d 92, motion overruled 62 Ohio St.3d 1508, 583 N.E.2d 1320.

2. Attorneys' fees

RC 3107.10 does not prohibit adoptive parents from paying the legal expenses of the birth mother, but the attorney must, in accordance with DR 5-107(A), disclose their intention to his client, the birth mother, before he accepts such payment. In re Adoption of Infant Girl Banda (Franklin 1988) 53 Ohio App.3d 104, 559 N.E.2d 1373.

COURT PROCEEDINGS

3107.11 Hearing and notice

(A) After the filing of a petition to adopt an adult or a minor, the court shall fix a time and place for hearing the petition. The hearing may take place at any time more than thirty days after the date on which the minor is placed in the home of the petitioner. At least twenty days before the date of hearing, notice of the filing of the petition and of the time and place of hearing shall be given by the court to all of the following:

(1) Any juvenile court, agency, or person whose consent to the adoption is required by this chapter but who has not consented;

(2) A person whose consent is not required as provided by division (A), (G), (H), or (I) of section 3107.07 of the Revised Code and has not consented;

(3) Any guardian, custodian, or other party who has temporary custody or permanent custody of the child.

Notice shall not be given to a person whose consent is not required as provided by division (B), (C), (D), (E), (F), or (J) of section 3107.07, or section 3107.071, of the Revised Code. Second notice shall not be given to a juvenile court, agency, or person whose consent is not required as provided by division (K) of section 3107.07 of the Revised Code because the court, agency, or person failed to file an objection to the petition within fourteen days after proof was filed pursuant to division (B) of this section that a first notice was given to the court, agency, or person pursuant to division (A)(1) of this section.

(B) All notices required under this section shall be given as specified in the Rules of Civil Procedure. Proof of the giving of notice shall be filed with the court before the petition is heard.

(1999 H 176, eff. 10-29-99; 1998 H 484, eff. 3-18-99; 1996 H 419, eff. 9-18-96; 1986 H 428, eff. 12-23-86; 1978 H 832; 1976 H 156)

Historical and Statutory Notes

Ed. Note: 3107.11 is analogous to former 3107.04, repealed by 1976 H 156, eff. 1-1-77.

Ed. Note: Former 3107.11 repealed by 1976 H 156, eff. 1-1-77; 130 v H 202; 1953 H 1; GC 8004-11; Source—GC 10512-20; see now 3107.14 and 3107.19 for provisions analogous to former 3107.11.

Pre-1953 H 1 Amendments: 124 v S 65

Amendment Note: 1999 H 176 deleted former division (A)(1); redesignated former divisions (A)(2) through (A)(4) as new divisions (A)(1) through (A)(3); deleted "The notice to the department of human services shall be accompanied by a copy of the petition." from the beginning of the final paragraph in division (A); and substituted "(A)(1)" for "(A)(2)" in the final paragraph in division (A). Prior to deletion, former division (A)(1) read:

"(1) The department of human services."

Amendment Note: 1998 H 484 added division (A)(4).

Amendment Note: 1996 H 419 added "juvenile" to division (A)(2); substituted "consent is not required as provided by division (A), (G), (H), or (I) of section 3107.07 of the Revised Code and has not consented." for "consent is dispensed with upon any ground mentioned in divisions (A), (E), (F), and (G) of section 3107.07 of the Revised Code, but who has not consented." in division (A)(3); and added the second and third sentences of the second paragraph of division (A)(3).

Cross References

Department of job and family services, division of social administration; care and placement of children; interstate compact on placement of children, 5103.09 to 5103.17, 5103.20 to 5103.28

Service and filing of pleadings and other papers subsequent to original complaint, Civ R 5

Library References

Adoption ⟹12, 13.
WESTLAW Topic No. 17.
C.J.S. Adoption of Persons §§ 49, 50, 78 to 86, 88 to 97.

OJur 3d: 47, Family Law § 927
Am Jur 2d: 2, Adoption § 55 to 67
Admissibility of social worker's expert testimony on custody issue. 1 ALR4th 837

Baldwin's Ohio Legislative Service, 1996 H 419—LSC Analysis, 3/L-336
Carlin, Baldwin's Ohio Practice, *Merrick-Rippner Probate Law* § 98.2, 98.37, 98.42, 98.43 (1997)
Klein & Darling, Baldwin's Ohio Practice, *Civil Practice* § 4 (1997)

Notes of Decisions and Opinions

1. Notice

Among protections accorded natural parent where adoption of child is proposed are right to adequate notice and opportunity to be heard before any parental rights which may exist are terminated. State ex rel. Smith v. Smith (Ohio 1996) 75 Ohio St.3d 418, 662 N.E.2d 366.

Even if probate court makes determination that parent's consent to adoption is not required, court must still go on to make determination that adoption is in best interest of child, and parent whose consent to adoption has been found unnecessary still must be given notice of the best-interest hearing. In re Adoption of Kuhlmann (Hamilton 1994) 99 Ohio App.3d 44, 649 N.E.2d 1279.

Biological mother was presumed to have actual notice of adoption and to have effectively waived notice requirement where mother signed adoption consent form which contained waiver of notice of hearing on petition for adoption and mother presented no evidence showing that she was unable to read or otherwise could not understand consent form. In re Rabatin (Geauga 1992) 83 Ohio App.3d 836, 615 N.E.2d 1099.

Trial court's failure to notify Department of Human Services prior to hearing on petition filed by grandparents seeking to adopt grandchild was not prejudicial error where natural mother placed child with grandparents, and Department of Human Services was not involved in adoption. In re Adoption of Howell (Lawrence 1991) 77 Ohio App.3d 80, 601 N.E.2d 92, motion overruled 62 Ohio St.3d 1508, 583 N.E.2d 1320.

Section which provides for notice of the adoption hearing to be given to the parent of the child does not require the issuance of a summons to such parent; GC 10501-21 (RC 2101.26, 2101.27, 2101.28), as amended, eff. 9-29-45, provides for the manner in which notice is to be given. (Annotation from former RC 3107.04.) In re Burdette (Summit 1948) 83 Ohio App. 368, 83 N.E.2d 813, 38 O.O. 429.

2. "Best-interest" test

An adoption proceeding is a two-step process involving a "consent" phase and a "best-interest" phase; thus, a trial court errs when it fails to hold a best-interest hearing even though parental consent was not required for the adoption since the natural parents have an overriding interest in being heard on the issue of whether the proposed adoption would be in the child's best interest. In re Adoption of Jordan (Preble 1991) 72 Ohio App.3d 638, 595 N.E.2d 963.

A finding that the consent of a natural parent is not required for an adoption under RC 3107.07(A) does not constitute consent to the adoption but merely "provides for cutting off the statutory right of a parent to withhold his consent to the adoption of the child," leaving all other parental rights and obligations intact. Therefore, the exclusion of a natural parent from the final hearing on whether or not adoption is in the best interest of the child renders meaningless the requirement of RC 3107.11 that a natural parent who has lost the right to withhold consent to the adoption be given notice of the time and place of the best interest hearing, and an adoption under such circumstances must be reversed. In re Adoption of Jorgensen (Hancock 1986) 33 Ohio App.3d 207, 515 N.E.2d 622.

3. Temporary custody

There was no competent, credible evidence showing that due process rights of foster parents were violated by county department of human services' decision to place foster child with different couple for purposes of permanent adoption; there was testimony that adoptive parents had taken child with understanding that custody was temporary, until child was returned to birth mother or placed with another couple, and county had policies prohibiting adoption by couple that was fertile or had more than one adopted or natural child. Tingley v. Williams Cty. Dept. of Human Serv. (Williams 1995) 100 Ohio App.3d 385, 654 N.E.2d 148, dismissed, appeal not allowed 72 Ohio St.3d 1528, 649 N.E.2d 838, certiorari denied 116 S.Ct. 773, 133 L.Ed.2d 725.

Where a final decree of adoption is vacated due to a defect in service, a prior order granting temporary custody to the adoptive parents remains in full force and effect precluding the need for a new temporary custody order; thus, a trial court errs in failing to dismiss a subsequent duplicative temporary custody petition. In re Knipper (Hamilton 1987) 39 Ohio App.3d 35, 528 N.E.2d 1319.

4. Hearing

Former foster parents' dilatory filing of complaint which sought writ of prohibition preventing probate court from holding finalization hearing in adoption of former foster child by third parties warranted dismissal of prohibition; juvenile court order endeavoring to stop adoption proceedings was filed approximately one month before adoption proceedings but complaint in prohibition was not filed until two and a half hours before adoption hearing was to commence. State ex rel. Hitchcock v. Cuyahoga Cty. Court of Common Pleas, Probate Div. (Cuyahoga 1994) 97 Ohio App.3d 600, 647 N.E.2d 208.

It is not abuse of discretion for a trial court in an adoption proceeding to grant a motion to reopen such case, after the hearing but before judgment, for the submission of a so-called "stipulation of facts," the contents of which are admitted to be substantially true and which evidence goes to the heart of the only issue before the court. (Annotation from former RC 3107.04.) In re Adoption of Earhart (Miami 1961) 117 Ohio App. 73, 190 N.E.2d 468, 23 O.O.2d 156.

Appointment of a next friend under statute throws out a protecting arm of the court in the best interests of the minor and does not deny to one contesting an adoption the right of cross-examination. (Annotation from former RC 3107.04.) In re Todhunter's Adoption (Franklin 1941) 35 N.E.2d 992, 33 Ohio Law Abs. 567.

3107.12 Prefinalization assessment and report

Note: See also following version of this section, eff. 10-5-00.

(A) Except as provided in division (B) of this section, an assessor shall conduct a prefinalization assessment of a minor and petitioner before a court issues a final decree of adoption or finalizes an interlocutory order of adoption for the minor. On completion of the assessment, the assessor shall prepare a written report of the assessment and provide a copy of the report to the court before which the adoption petition is pending.

The report of a prefinalization assessment shall include all of the following:

(1) The adjustment of the minor and the petitioner to the adoptive placement;

(2) The present and anticipated needs of the minor and the petitioner, as determined by a review of the minor's medical and social history, for adoption-related services, including assistance under Title IV-E of the "Social Security Act," 94 Stat. 501 (1980), 42 U.S.C.A. 670, as amended, or section 5153.163 of the Revised Code and counseling, case management services, crisis services, diagnostic services, and therapeutic counseling.

(3) The physical, mental, and developmental condition of the minor;

(4) If known, the minor's biological family background, including identifying information about the biological or other legal parents;

(5) The reasons for the minor's placement with the petitioner, the petitioner's attitude toward the proposed adoption, and the circumstances under which the minor was placed in the home of the petitioner;

(6) The attitude of the minor toward the proposed adoption, if the minor's age makes this feasible;

(7) If the minor is an Indian child, as defined in 25 U.S.C.A. 1903(4), how the placement complies with the "Indian Child Welfare Act of 1978," 92 Stat. 3069, 25 U.S.C.A. 1901, as amended.

The assessor shall file the prefinalization report with the court not later than twenty days prior to the date scheduled for the final hearing on the adoption unless the court determines there is good cause for filing the report at a later date.

(B) This section does not apply if the petitioner is the minor's stepparent, unless a court, after determining a prefinalization assessment is in the best interest of the minor, orders that an assessor conduct a prefinalization assessment.

(C) The director of job and family services shall adopt rules in accordance with Chapter 119. of the Revised Code defining "counseling," "case management services," "crisis services," "diagnostic services," and "therapeutic counseling" for the purpose of this section.

(1999 H 471, eff. 7-1-00; 1998 H 446, eff. 8-5-98; 1996 H 274, eff. 9-18-96; 1996 H 419, eff. 9-18-96)

Note: See also following version of this section, eff. 10-5-00.

3107.12 Prefinalization assessment and report

Note: See also preceding version of this section, in effect until 10-5-00.

(A) Except as provided in division (B) of this section, an assessor shall conduct a prefinalization assessment of a minor and petitioner before a court issues a final decree of adoption or finalizes an interlocutory order of adoption for the minor. On completion of the assessment, the assessor shall prepare a written report of the assessment and provide a copy of the report to the court before which the adoption petition is pending.

The report of a prefinalization assessment shall include all of the following:

(1) The adjustment of the minor and the petitioner to the adoptive placement;

(2) The present and anticipated needs of the minor and the petitioner, as determined by a review of the minor's medical and social history, for adoption-related services, including assistance under Title IV-E of the "Social Security Act," 94 Stat. 501 (1980), 42 U.S.C.A. 670, as amended, or section 5153.163 of the Revised Code and counseling, case management services, crisis services, diagnostic services, and therapeutic counseling.

(3) The physical, mental, and developmental condition of the minor;

(4) If known, the minor's biological family background, including identifying information about the biological or other legal parents;

(5) The reasons for the minor's placement with the petitioner, the petitioner's attitude toward the proposed adoption, and the circumstances under which the minor was placed in the home of the petitioner;

(6) The attitude of the minor toward the proposed adoption, if the minor's age makes this feasible;

(7) If the minor is an Indian child, as defined in 25 U.S.C.A. 1903(4), how the placement complies with the "Indian Child Welfare Act of 1978," 92 Stat. 3069, 25 U.S.C.A. 1901, as amended.

The assessor shall file the prefinalization report with the court not later than twenty days prior to the date scheduled for the final hearing on the adoption unless the court determines there is good cause for filing the report at a later date.

(B) This section does not apply if the petitioner is the minor's stepparent, unless a court, after determining a prefinalization assessment is in the best interest of the minor, orders that an assessor conduct a prefinalization assessment. This section also does not apply if the petitioner is the minor's foster caregiver and the minor has resided in the petitioner's home as the foster caregiver's foster child for at least twelve months prior to the date the petitioner submits an application prescribed under division (B) of section 3107.012 of the Revised Code to the agency arranging the adoption.

(C) The director of job and family services shall adopt rules in accordance with Chapter 119. of the Revised Code defining "counseling," "case management services," "crisis services," "diagnostic services," and "therapeutic counseling" for the purpose of this section.

(2000 H 448, eff. 10-5-00; 1999 H 471, eff. 7-1-00; 1998 H 446, eff. 8-5-98; 1996 H 274, eff. 9-18-96; 1996 H 419, eff. 9-18-96)

Note: See also preceding version of this section, in effect until 10-5-00.

Historical and Statutory Notes

Ed. Note: Former 3107.12 amended and recodified as 3107.031 by 1996 H 419, eff. 9-18-96; 1984 H 84, eff. 3-19-85; 1978 S 340; 1976 H 156.

Ed. Note: Prior 3107.12 repealed by 1976 H 156, eff. 1-1-77; 1953 H 1; GC 8004-12; Source—GC 10512-21; see now 3107.14 for provisions analogous to former 3107.12.

Pre-1953 H 1 Amendments: 124 v S 65

Amendment Note: 2000 H 448 added the last sentence in division (B)

Amendment Note: 1999 H 471 substituted "director of job and family services" for "department of human services" in division (C).

Amendment Note: 1998 H 446 designated new division (A) and inserted "Except as provided in division (B) of this section," in the first paragraph therein; redesignated former divisions (A) through (G) as new divisions (A)(1) through (A)(7); added new division (B); designated new division (C); and made other nonsubstantive changes.

Amendment Note: 1996 H 274 deleted "Except in the case of a stepparent adopting a stepchild," from the beginning of the first paragraph.

Cross References

Probate courts, appointment of assessors, 2101.11

Ohio Administrative Code References

Prefinalization services, OAC 5101:2-48-17

Library References

Am Jur 2d: 2, Adoption § 119, 147; 41, Indians § 150 to 153

Baldwin's Ohio Legislative Service, 1996 H 419—LSC Analysis, 3/L-336

Carlin, Baldwin's Ohio Practice, *Merrick-Rippner Probate Law* § 98.2, 98.4, 98.8, 98.21, 98.26, 98.27, 98.28, 98.30, 98.43, 98.46, 98.48 (1997)

3107.121 Biological parent may add medical and social history to records concerning adopted person—Repealed

(1996 H 419, eff. 9-18-96; 1984 H 84, eff. 3-19-85)

Historical and Statutory Notes

Ed. Note: Former 3107.121 amended and recodified as 3107.091 by 1996 H 419, eff. 9-18-96.

3107.13 Residence in adoptive home

Note: See also following version of this section, eff. 10-5-00.

(A) A final decree of adoption shall not be issued and an interlocutory order of adoption does not become final, until the person to be adopted has lived in the adoptive home for at least six months after placement by an agency, or for at least six months after the department of job and family services or the court has been informed of the placement of the person with the petitioner, and the department or court has had an opportunity to observe or investigate the adoptive home, or in the case of adoption by a stepparent, until at least six months after the filing of the petition, or until the child has lived in the home for at least six months.

(B) In the case of a foster parent adopting a foster child or person adopting a child to whom the person is related, the court shall apply the amount of time the child lived in the foster parent's or relative's home prior to the date the foster parent or relative files the petition to adopt the child toward the six-month waiting period established by division (A) of this section.

(1999 H 471, eff. 7-1-00; 1996 H 419, eff. 9-18-96; 1986 H 428, eff. 12-23-86; 1980 S 205; 1976 H 156)

Note: See also following version of this section, eff. 10-5-00.

3107.13 Residence in adoptive home

Note: See also preceding version of this section, in effect until 10-5-00.

(A) A final decree of adoption shall not be issued and an interlocutory order of adoption does not become final, until the person to be adopted has lived in the adoptive home for at least six months after placement by an agency, or for at least six months after the department of job and family services or the court has been informed of the placement of the person with the petitioner, and the department or court has had an opportunity to observe or investigate the adoptive home, or in the case of adoption by a stepparent, until at least six months after the filing of the petition, or until the child has lived in the home for at least six months.

(B) In the case of a foster caregiver adopting a foster child or person adopting a child to whom the person is related, the court shall apply the amount of time the child lived in the foster caregiver's or relative's home prior to the date the foster caregiver or relative files the petition to adopt the child toward the six-month waiting period established by division (A) of this section.

(2000 H 448, eff. 10-5-00; 1999 H 471, eff. 7-1-00; 1996 H 419, eff. 9-18-96; 1986 H 428, eff. 12-23-86; 1980 S 205; 1976 H 156)

Note: See also preceding version of this section, in effect until 10-5-00.

Historical and Statutory Notes

Ed. Note: Former 3107.13 repealed by 1976 H 156, eff. 1-1-77; 1971 S 267; 132 v S 326; 129 v 1566; 1953 H 1; GC 8004-13; Source—GC 10512-23; see now 3107.15 for provisions analogous to former 3107.13.

Pre-1953 H 1 Amendments: 124 v S 65

Amendment Note: 2000 H 448 substituted "caregiver" for "parent" throughout the section.

Amendment Note: 1999 H 471 substituted "job and family" for "human" in division (A).

Amendment Note: 1996 H 419 designated division (A) and added division (B).

Cross References

Residency requirements for public school attendance, 3313.64

Ohio Administrative Code References

AdoptOhio, agency responsibilities, OAC 5101:2-48-01

Library References

Adoption ⚿14.

Infants ⚿226.

WESTLAW Topic Nos. 17, 211.

C.J.S. Adoption of Persons §§ 10 to 12, 98 to 102, 124 to 128.

C.J.S. Infants §§ 57, 70 to 82, 84.

OJur 3d: 31, Decedents' Estates § 534; 47, Family Law § 933

Baldwin's Ohio Legislative Service, 1996 H 419—LSC Analysis, 3/L-336

Carlin, Baldwin's Ohio Practice, *Merrick-Rippner Probate Law* § 43.16, 43.23, 98.2, 98.48, 98.52, 98.53 (1997)

Hausser, Ohio Real Estate Law and Practice (2d Ed.), Text 1.05, 1.08

Law Review and Journal Commentaries

Inheritance Rights of Adopted Children: A Review of Recent Cases, Angela G. Carlin. 3 Prob L J Ohio 52 (March/April 1993).

Notes of Decisions and Opinions

1. Decree vacated

An order vacating a final decree of adoption pursuant to Civ R 60(B) is a final appealable order. In re Adoption of Davis, No. 851 (4th Dist Ct App, Ross, 1-4-82).

2. Death of adoptive parent

Where a child is placed in a prospective adoptive home but the father dies before the child has resided therein for six months and hence the adoption has not been completed, the child is not entitled to social security benefits. (Annotation from former RC 3107.09.) Spiegel v. Flemming (N.D.Ohio 1960) 181 F.Supp. 185, 89 Ohio Law Abs. 562, 13 O.O.2d 225.

3107.14 Court's discretion; final decree or interlocutory order

Note: See also following version of this section, eff. 10-5-00.

(A) The petitioner and the person sought to be adopted shall appear at the hearing on the petition, unless the presence of either is excused by the court for good cause shown.

(B) The court may continue the hearing from time to time to permit further observation, investigation, or consideration of any facts or circumstances affecting the granting of the petition, and may examine the petitioners separate and apart from each other.

(C) If, at the conclusion of the hearing, the court finds that the required consents have been obtained or excused and that the adoption is in the best interest of the person sought to be adopted as supported by the evidence, it may issue, subject to division (B)(1) of section 2151.86, section 3107.064, and division (E) of section 3107.09 of the Revised Code, and any other limitations specified in this chapter, a final decree of adoption or an interlocutory order of adoption, which by its own terms automatically becomes a final decree of adoption on a date specified in the order, which, except as provided in division (B) of section 3107.13 of the Revised Code, shall not be less than six months or more than one year from the date of issuance of the order, unless sooner vacated by the court for good cause shown. In determining whether the adoption is in the best interest of the person sought to be adopted, the court shall not consider the age of the petitioner if the petitioner is old enough to adopt as provided by section 3107.03 of the Revised Code.

In an interlocutory order of adoption, the court shall provide for observation, investigation, and a further report on the adoptive home during the interlocutory period.

(D) If the requirements for a decree under division (C) of this section have not been satisfied or the court vacates an interlocutory order of adoption, or if the court finds that a person sought to be adopted was placed in the home of the petitioner in violation of law, the court shall dismiss the petition and may determine the agency or person to have temporary or permanent custody of the person, which may include the agency or person that had custody prior to the filing of the petition or the petitioner, if the court finds it is in the best interest of the person as supported by the evidence, or if the person is a minor, the court may certify the case to the juvenile court of the county where the minor is then residing for appropriate action and disposition.

(1998 H 446, eff. 8-5-98; 1996 H 419, eff. 9-18-96; 1984 H 84, eff. 3-19-85; 1976 H 156)

Note: See also following version of this section, eff. 10-5-00.

3107.14 Court's discretion; final decree or interlocutory order

Note: See also preceding version of this section, in effect until 10-5-00.

(A) The petitioner and the person sought to be adopted shall appear at the hearing on the petition, unless the presence of either is excused by the court for good cause shown.

(B) The court may continue the hearing from time to time to permit further observation, investigation, or consideration of any facts or circumstances affecting the granting of the petition, and may examine the petitioners separate and apart from each other.

(C) If, at the conclusion of the hearing, the court finds that the required consents have been obtained or excused and that the adoption is in the best interest of the person sought to be adopted as supported by the evidence, it may issue, subject to division (C)(1) of section 2151.86, section 3107.064, and division (E) of section 3107.09 of the Revised Code, and any other limitations specified in this chapter, a final decree of adoption or an interlocutory order of adoption, which by its own terms automatically becomes a final decree of adoption on a date specified in the order, which, except as provided in division (B) of section 3107.13 of the Revised Code, shall not be less than six months or more than one year from the date of issuance of the order, unless sooner vacated by the court for good cause shown. In determining whether the adoption is in the best interest of the person sought to be adopted, the court shall not consider the age of the petitioner if the petitioner is old enough to adopt as provided by section 3107.03 of the Revised Code.

In an interlocutory order of adoption, the court shall provide for observation, investigation, and a further report on the adoptive home during the interlocutory period.

(D) If the requirements for a decree under division (C) of this section have not been satisfied or the court vacates an interlocutory order of adoption, or if the court finds that a person sought to be adopted was placed in the home of the petitioner in violation of law, the court shall dismiss the petition and may determine the agency or person to have temporary or permanent custody of the person, which may include the agency or person that had custody prior to the filing of the petition or the petitioner, if the court finds it is in the best interest of the person as supported by the evidence, or if the person is a minor, the court may certify the case to the juvenile court of the county where the minor is then residing for appropriate action and disposition.

(2000 H 448, eff. 10-5-00; 1998 H 446, eff. 8-5-98; 1996 H 419, eff. 9-18-96; 1984 H 84, eff. 3-19-85; 1976 H 156)

Note: See also preceding version of this section, in effect until 10-5-00.

Historical and Statutory Notes

Ed. Note: 3107.14 contains provisions analogous to former 3107.08 to 3107.12, repealed by 1976 H 156, eff. 1-1-77.

Ed. Note: Former 3107.14 repealed by 1976 H 156, eff. 1-1-77; 130 v H 202; 1953 H 1; GC 8004-14; Source—GC 10512-22; see now 3107.17 for provisions analogous to former 3107.14.

Pre-1953 H 1 Amendments: 124 v S 65

Amendment Note: 2000 H 448 substituted "(C)" for "(B)" after "subject to division" in division (C).

Amendment Note: 1998 H 446 inserted "division (B)(1) of section 2151.86," in the first paragraph in division (C); and made other nonsubstantive changes.

Amendment Note: 1996 H 419 substituted "as supported by the evidence, it may issue, subject to section 3107.064, division (E) of section 3107.09 of the Revised Code," for "it may issue, subject to division (D)(6) of section 3107.12 of the Revised Code" in division (C); added "except as provided in division (B) of section 3107.13 of the Revised Code," preceding "shall not be less than six months or more than one year" in division (C); added the second sentence in the first paragraph of division (C); added "as supported by the evidence," preceding "or if the person is a minor" in division (D); and made other nonsubstantive changes.

Cross References

Prohibition: 3107.65(B)

Adoption, recognition of decrees from other countries, 3107.18

Department of job and family services, division of social administration, placing of children, 5103.16

Powers and duties of county children services board, 5153.16

Residency requirements for public school attendance, 3313.64

Ohio Administrative Code References

Temporary or permanent custody and placement of children, interstate placements by individuals and courts, OAC Ch 5101:2-42

Library References

Adoption ⚿13, 14.
WESTLAW Topic No. 17.
C.J.S. Adoption of Persons §§ 49, 50, 88 to 102, 124 to 128.

OJur 3d: 47, Family Law § 931, 934, 935
Am Jur 2d: 2, Adoption § 65 et seq.

Baldwin's Ohio Legislative Service, 1996 H 419—LSC Analysis, 3/L-336
Carlin, Baldwin's Ohio Practice, *Merrick-Rippner Probate Law* § 98.2, 98.8, 98.22, 98.44, 98.46, 98.47, 98.48, 98.49, 105.12 (1997)
Kurtz & Giannelli, Ohio Juvenile Law (1998 Ed.), Text 13.11

Law Review and Journal Commentaries

Belsito v Clark: Ohio's Battle with "Motherhood," Dawn Wenk. 28 U Tol L Rev 247 (Fall 1996).

Child's Relationship with Biological Father's Family Not Precluding Adoption by Stepfather, Pamela J. MacAdams. 4 Domestic Rel J Ohio 41 (May/June 1992).

Notes of Decisions and Opinions

---

1. Constitutional issues

If biological father fails to accept responsibilities of parenthood, no continuing constitutionally protected interest will be recognized from mere existence of biological link. In re Adoption of Zschach (Ohio 1996) 75 Ohio St.3d 648, 665 N.E.2d 1070, reconsideration denied 76 Ohio St.3d 1410, 666 N.E.2d 569, certiorari denied 117 S.Ct. 582, 136 L.Ed.2d 513.

Failure to notify natural mother that investigation report had been filed in stepmother's adoption action did not violate natural mother's due process rights; no statutory authority required service of report on parties involved, and report was primarily for use of court in assessing quality of adoptive home. In re Fetzer (Ohio App. 3 Dist. 1997) 118 Ohio App.3d 156, 692 N.E.2d 219, dismissed, appeal not allowed 78 Ohio St.3d 1513, 679 N.E.2d 309.

Even if probate court makes determination that parent's consent to adoption is not required, court must still go on to make determination that adoption is in best interest of child, and parent whose consent to adoption has been found unnecessary still must be given notice of the best-interest hearing. In re Adoption of Kuhlmann (Hamilton 1994) 99 Ohio App.3d 44, 649 N.E.2d 1279.

Ethnic heritage of a child and prospective adoptive parents may be considered as a factor in adoption placements, but may not be used as the sole or determinative criterion; the opportunity to adopt a child may not be denied merely because the prospective adoptive parents are Caucasian and the child is African-American. In re Moorehead (Montgomery 1991) 75 Ohio App.3d 711, 600 N.E.2d 778.

RC 3107.14(D), to the extent that it allows a probate court to award permanent custody of a child to a nonparent without a determination that the parent has relinquished custody or that the parent is unsuitable, is an unconstitutional infringement of the parent's fundamental interest in the custody of the child. In re Adoption of Mays (Hamilton 1986) 30 Ohio App.3d 195, 507 N.E.2d 453, 30 O.B.R. 338.

2. In general

Natural mother had an adequate legal remedy to contest adoption by filing a motion in probate court during pendency of adoption proceedings alleging that consent to adoption was invalid; therefore, natural mother was not entitled to a writ of habeas corpus. Barnebey v. Zschach (Ohio 1995) 71 Ohio St.3d 588, 646 N.E.2d 162.

Under RC 3107.14, adoption matters must be decided on a case-by-case basis through the able exercise of discretion by the trial court giving due consideration to all known factors in determining what is the best interest of the person to be adopted. In re Adoption of Charles B. (Ohio 1990) 50 Ohio St.3d 88, 552 N.E.2d 884.

The natural parent of a legitimate child may not seek to adopt his natural child to terminate the other natural parent's parental rights. In re Adoption of Kohorst (Paulding 1992) 75 Ohio App.3d 813, 600 N.E.2d 843, motion overruled 65 Ohio St.3d 1466, 602 N.E.2d 1174.

An adoption proceeding is a two-step process involving a "consent" phase and a "best-interest" phase; thus, a trial court errs when it fails to hold a best-interest hearing even though parental consent was not required for the adoption since the natural parents have an overriding interest in being heard on the issue of whether the proposed adoption would be in the child's best interest. In re Adoption of Jordan (Preble 1991) 72 Ohio App.3d 638, 595 N.E.2d 963.

The function of RC 5103.16 is to prevent black-market adoptions which is not the case where a mother moves her child into the prospective adoptive home to parties who have agreed to adopt the child and would also care for the child until the adoption process is completed. In re Adoption of a Child by Michael S. and Shirley S, No. H-98-009, 1998 WL 769788 (6th Dist Ct App, Huron, 11-6-98).

A bifurcated procedure is required where the natural parent of a minor child refuses to consent to adoption of that child by a third party whereby (1) initially, the probate court determines the issue of necessity of consent, (2) a judgment on the issue of consent only is filed, and (3) in the second stage, the best interest of the child standard is utilized; failure to conduct a hearing on the issue of whether the proposed adoption is in the best interest of the child is error. In re Adoption of Zachary

H, No. WM 96-013, 1997 WL 103808 (6th Dist Ct App, Williams, 3-7-97).

A natural parent cannot be the sole adoptive parent of a natural child even with the consent of other natural parent as a matter of law. In re Adoption of Graham (Ohio Com.Pl. 1980) 63 Ohio Misc. 22, 409 N.E.2d 1067, 16 O.O.3d 347, 17 O.O.3d 341.

3. Approval of placement: jurisdiction

Within the meaning of RC 3107.09, a child is "legally placed in the home of the petitioner" when such child was brought there voluntarily by the parent immediately after birth and so maintained there after such parent was subsequently awarded legal custody in a divorce action, and under such circumstances the probate court is the "proper court" to determine whether the placement was "beneficial to the child." (Annotation from former RC 3107.09.) In re Adoption of Biddle (Ohio 1958) 168 Ohio St. 209, 152 N.E.2d 105, 6 O.O.2d 4, on remand 163 N.E.2d 188, 81 Ohio Law Abs. 529.

Court's decision to allow adoption was presumptively proper, where investigator's report favorably indicated that adoptive parents could provide loving, stable environment in which child would thrive in every realm of life and court entered final order of adoption following interlocutory decree and investigator's report. In re Rabatin (Geauga 1992) 83 Ohio App.3d 836, 615 N.E.2d 1099.

For purposes of statute which provides that final decree of adoption may not be issued until child has lived in adoptive home for at least six months, date on which adoption petition was filed could be used as start of six-month period where child's natural mother had placed child with paternal grandparents, there was no indication that mother intended to place child in grandparents' home for adoption, and grandparents later sought to adopt child after mother failed to support or contact child for several years. In re Adoption of Howell (Lawrence 1991) 77 Ohio App.3d 80, 601 N.E.2d 92, motion overruled 62 Ohio St.3d 1508, 583 N.E.2d 1320.

A trial court's conclusion that the placement of a child with foster parents for purposes of adoption is not in the child's best interest because of the issue of confidentiality is against the manifest weight of the evidence where all the evidence of record is positive to the adoption and the investigator's report recommends the placement; "confidentiality" was never demonstrated to be a necessary factor in evaluating the suitability of either any adoption or specifically this adoption and there was no evidence presented to the court to indicate that the lack of confidentiality would cause problems at the present or a future date. In re Reichenbach (Portage 1991) 71 Ohio App.3d 730, 595 N.E.2d 399.

The trial court's denial of a child's placement with foster parents for purposes of adoption based on the fact that the foster parents established a relationship with the child and that the placement would diminish the integrity of the foster care system is against the manifest weight of the evidence where (1) no specific policy prohibiting such a placement was put into evidence via judicial notice or otherwise, (2) no testimony indicated that the best interests of the child were offended, and (3) the facts of the case do not support the contention that the foster parents were using the foster care system to adopt a child, since during the five years they had fostered fourteen children they had never sought to adopt any of them as they had three children of their own and did not seek to adopt the present child until they became aware that the child's grandmother was searching for adoptive parents for her. In re Reichenbach (Portage 1991) 71 Ohio App.3d 730, 595 N.E.2d 399.

Where adoptive parents clearly meet all of the agency's standards concerning maturity, stability, financial ability to carry responsibility, and love of the child, and where the agency placed the child with the adoptive parents from birth to the present time as foster parents, the denial of agency consent based solely upon the age of the adoptive parents is unreasonable, arbitrary, and capricious, and violates the spirit of the whole adoption system while holding to the letter of part of it. (Annotation from former RC 3107.09.) In re Haun (Cuyahoga 1972) 31 Ohio App.2d 63, 286 N.E.2d 478, 60 O.O.2d 163.

The legality of a placement of a child with persons other than his parents is governed by the statute in effect at the time such placement is made. (Annotation from former RC 3107.08.) In re Adoption of Wright (Ohio Prob. 1968) 15 Ohio Misc. 354, 240 N.E.2d 923, 44 O.O.2d 509.

The probate court no longer has authority to approve an illegal placement of a child in the best interest of said child. (Annotation from former RC 3107.08.) In re Boyd's Adoption (Ohio Prob. 1962) 185 N.E.2d 331, 89 Ohio Law Abs. 202.

RC 5103.16 and 2151.04 effect by implication a partial repeal of RC 3107.08, and by such sections it is required that the parents of a child apply to the probate court for placement of the child for adoption prior to the placement. (Annotation from former RC 3107.08.) In re Boyd's Adoption (Ohio Prob. 1962) 185 N.E.2d 331, 89 Ohio Law Abs. 202.

Though the division of social administration of the department of public welfare is not a necessary party to adoption proceedings, its responsibility for enforcing certain laws concerning placement or adoption causes it to be a person in interest entitled to notice of an illegal placement and thus a proper party to such proceedings. (Annotation from former RC 3107.08.) 1962 OAG 2747.

Under RC 5103.16 probate courts may approve the proposed placement of children under the procedures set forth in that statute; probate courts may also, under RC 3107.08, during an adoption proceeding, and upon a finding that the child being adopted was placed in the home of the petitioner in violation of the laws relating to the placement of children, determine whether the placement is for the best interest of the child and either approve or disapprove it. (Annotation from former RC 3107.08.) 1962 OAG 2747.

4. Decree; jurisdiction

A trial judge fails to base his adoption decisions on a consideration of the best interests of the children involved when he denies foster parents' petition for adoption based on a consideration of the children's biological grandparents' visitation rights. In re Adoption of Ridenour (Ohio 1991) 61 Ohio St.3d 319, 574 N.E.2d 1055.

The refusal of consent to an adoption by a "certified organization," as defined in RC 3107.01(C), does not impair the jurisdiction of the probate court, but the recommendations and the reports, filed pursuant to RC 3107.05 and 3107.10, are to be considered, in conjunction with all other evidence adduced in the proceeding, by the court in deciding the issues presented by RC 3107.09. (Annotation from former RC 3107.09.) State ex rel. Portage County Welfare Dept. v. Summers (Ohio 1974) 38 Ohio St.2d 144, 311 N.E.2d 6, 67 O.O.2d 151.

A probate court has jurisdiction to hear and determine an adoption proceeding relating to a minor child notwithstanding the fact that the custody of such child is at the time within the continuing jurisdiction of a divorce court. (Annotation from former RC 3107.09.) In re Adoption of Biddle (Ohio 1958) 168 Ohio St. 209, 152 N.E.2d 105, 6 O.O.2d 4, on remand 163 N.E.2d 188, 81 Ohio Law Abs. 529.

After conducting a hearing pursuant to RC 3107.09, the probate court improperly denies a petition for adoption of a four-year-old boy in the custody of the county welfare department, when the court finds that petitioners meet all the requirements of suitability as adoptive parents, but denies the petition for adoption on the grounds that the granting of the adoption would violate the integrity of a waiting list allegedly maintained by the welfare department, where at the adoption hearing there was no evidence adduced establishing the existence or administration of such a waiting list and no evidence that the waiting list contained suitable applicants ready, willing, and able to adopt the child in question. (Annotation from former RC 3107.09.) (See also In re Harshey, 40 App(2d) 157, 318 NE(2d) 544 (1974).) In re Harshey (Cuyahoga 1975) 45 Ohio App.2d 97, 341 N.E.2d 616, 74 O.O.2d 120.

The refusal of an agency to consent to an adoption does not deprive the probate court of jurisdiction even when such refusal is not arbitrary, unreasonable, or capricious, and is but an element for consideration in the probate court's determination of the qualifications of the adoptive parents and the best interests of the child. (Annotation from former RC 3107.09.) In re Haun (Cuyahoga 1972) 31 Ohio App.2d 63, 286 N.E.2d 478, 60 O.O.2d 163.

It is not an abuse of discretion for a trial court in an adoption proceeding to grant a motion to reopen such case, after the hearing but before judgment, for the submission of a so-called "stipulation of facts," the contents of which are admitted to be substantially true and which evidence goes to the heart of the only issue before the court. (Annotation from former RC 3107.11.) In re Adoption of Earhart (Miami 1961) 117 Ohio App. 73, 190 N.E.2d 468, 23 O.O.2d 156.

In proceeding involving validity of decree of adoption, court of appeals must rely wholly on record before it. (Annotation from former RC 3107.09.) McClain v. Lyon (Morrow 1926) 24 Ohio App. 279, 156 N.E. 529, 6 Ohio Law Abs. 60.

Adoption proceedings are wholly statutory, and statutes must be clearly followed to give probate court jurisdiction to decree adoption. (Annotation from former RC 3107.09.) McClain v. Lyon (Morrow 1926) 24 Ohio App. 279, 156 N.E. 529, 6 Ohio Law Abs. 60.

Under GC 8030 and 8030-1 (Repealed), where probate court was without jurisdiction in first instance in adoption proceedings, such proceedings were not merely voidable, but were void. (Annotation from former RC 3107.09.) McClain v. Lyon (Morrow 1926) 24 Ohio App. 279, 156 N.E. 529, 6 Ohio Law Abs. 60.

Where evidence shows that the social services agency has no substantial reasons for withholding the answer and consent required by RC 3107.06, the court will order the answer and consent filed when the court determines it is in the best interest of the child, but if substantial reasons exist for withholding such answer and consent, and the court is satisfied that it is not in the best interest of the child to require it, the petition for adoption will be denied. (Annotation from former RC 3107.09.) In re Dickhaus (Ohio Com.Pl. 1974) 41 Ohio Misc. 1, 321 N.E.2d 800, 70 O.O.2d 24.

Where a child is placed in a prospective adoptive home but the father dies before the child has resided therein for six months and hence the adoption has not been completed, the child is not entitled to social security benefits. Spiegel v. Flemming (N.D.Ohio 1960) 181 F.Supp. 185, 89 Ohio Law Abs. 562, 13 O.O.2d 225.

5. Disposition of child if petition dismissed

Lack of agency involvement or court approval of initial placement of child with adoptive parent did not require dismissal of adoption petition, where biological parents were active participants in placement, contacting adoptive parent as "a friend" after they engaged in unsuccessful negotiations to place child with three sets of prospective adoptive parents. In re Adoption of Zschach (Ohio 1996) 75 Ohio St.3d 648, 665 N.E.2d 1070, reconsideration denied 76 Ohio St.3d 1410, 666 N.E.2d 569, certiorari denied 117 S.Ct. 582, 136 L.Ed.2d 513.

The certification of a cause from the probate court to the juvenile court under the provisions of section does not constitute a complaint against the parents that the child which was the subject of the adoption proceedings is a dependent, delinquent or neglected child, and a judgment by the juvenile court finding that such child is a dependent child, made without the filing of a complaint against the parents, is void ab initio for lack of jurisdiction. (Annotation from former RC 3107.12.) State ex rel. Clark v. Allaman (Ohio 1950) 154 Ohio St. 296, 95 N.E.2d 753, 43 O.O. 190.

The provision of former section (part of the Adoption Code), that "if for any reason whatsoever the petition shall be dismissed or the court shall deny or revoke its interlocutory order of adoption or deny a final decree of adoption ... the cause shall be certified to the juvenile court of the county where the child is then residing for appropriate action and disposition by such court," authorizes and requires the juvenile court, upon receiving such certification, to make proper investigation within its statutory jurisdiction to determine who has the responsibility for the care of such child. (Annotation from former RC 3107.12.) State ex rel. Clark v. Allaman (Ohio 1950) 154 Ohio St. 296, 95 N.E.2d 753, 43 O.O. 190.

Upon rendering a judgment denying a petition for adoption, the court must certify the cause to the juvenile court in the county in which the child is residing, for appropriate action and disposition. (Annotation from former RC 3107.12.) In re Adoption of Peters (Lucas 1961) 113 Ohio App. 173, 177 N.E.2d 541, 17 O.O.2d 141.

Where, in an action to vacate an adoption decree upon the ground that the next friend of the child fraudulently concealed the fact that the child was mentally defective, the court sustained a motion to quash service upon the next friend, the action to vacate was not terminated in its entirety, and hence the order was not final. (Annotation from former RC 3107.12.) In re Adoption of Sladky (Franklin 1958) 109 Ohio App. 120, 161 N.E.2d 554, 81 Ohio Law Abs. 264, 10 O.O.2d 304.

Where a petition for the adoption of an illegitimate child was filed in the probate court and the child's mother gave her consent in writing to such adoption, but the petitioners withdrew their petition before any action thereon was taken, the court, upon issuing an order that the petition be withdrawn and the cause dismissed, is without authority to certify the cause to the juvenile court for disposition under section in such case; there was no proper basis for certification from the probate court to the juvenile court; and, no complaint having been filed charging the child to be a dependent child or any other form of complaint originating in the juvenile court, that court was without jurisdiction to determine that the child was a dependent child or to make an order depriving the mother of custody and committing the child to the custody of a detention home. (Annotation from former RC 3107.12.) State ex rel. Clark v. Allaman (Montgomery 1950) 87 Ohio App. 101, 90 N.E.2d 394, 57 Ohio Law Abs. 17, 42 O.O. 330, affirmed 154 Ohio St. 296, 95 N.E.2d 753, 43 O.O. 190.

Under the provisions of section upon a proper certification of the case to the juvenile court, jurisdiction is conferred upon such court to determine the custody of the child. (Annotation from former RC 3107.12.) State ex rel. Sparto v. Williams (Darke 1949) 86 Ohio App. 377, 86 N.E.2d 501, 55 Ohio Law Abs. 341, 41 O.O. 474.

A declaration or finding in a proceeding begun by an adopting father under provisions of GC 10512-21 (RC 3107.12), that an adoption is null and void on grounds therein set forth, operates prospectively only and does not cut off rights acquired by the adopted child prior to such declaration. In such case, in an action under GC 10509-95 (RC 2123.01) to determine who is entitled to next estate of inheritance of adopting mother, who died prior to such declaration without issue or surviving spouse, the adopted child is entitled to the next estate of inheritance of the deceased adopting mother. (Annotation from former RC 3107.12.) Steiner v. Rainer (Mahoning 1941) 69 Ohio App. 6, 42 N.E.2d 684, 23 O.O. 306.

Where a child is placed for adoption and the mother's consent is subsequently withdrawn, a certification of the case to the juvenile court upon dismissal of the petition does not of itself give the juvenile court jurisdiction to determine the child's custody. (Annotation from former RC 3107.12.) In re O--- (Ohio Juv. 1964) 199 N.E.2d 765, 95 Ohio Law Abs. 101, 28 O.O.2d 165.

Where probate court denies decree for adoption, section requires that the cause be certified to juvenile court for appropriate action, but probate judge, even though in the county he was also juvenile judge, may not proceed from the adoption hearing directly to his capacity as juvenile judge and dispose of question of custody in absence of evidence submitted to him as juvenile judge relating to custody or in absence of stipulation that the evidence offered in the adoption proceeding was to be submitted to juvenile court. (Annotation from former RC 3107.12.) In re Sparto's Adoption (Darke 1948) 82 N.E.2d 328, 52 Ohio Law Abs. 189.

3107.141 Order to redo or supplement report or history; appointment of different assessor

After an assessor files a home study report under section 3107.031, a social and medical history under section 3107.09, or a prefinalization assessment report under section 3107.12 of the Revised Code, or the department of job and family services files a social and medical history under section 3107.091 of the Revised Code, a court may do either or both of the following if the court determines the report or history does not comply with the requirements governing the report or history or, in the case of a home study or prefinalization assessment report, does not enable the court to determine whether an adoption is in the best interest of the minor to be adopted:

(A) Order the assessor or department to redo or supplement the report or history in a manner the court directs;

(B) Appoint a different assessor to redo or supplement the report or history in a manner the court directs.

(1999 H 471, eff. 7-1-00; 1998 H 446, eff. 8-5-98)

Historical and Statutory Notes

Amendment Note: 1999 H 471 substituted "job and family" for "human" in the introductory paragraph.

Library References

Carlin, Baldwin's Ohio Practice, *Merrick-Rippner Probate Law* § 98.26 (1997)

3107.15 Effects of final decree

(A) A final decree of adoption and an interlocutory order of adoption that has become final as issued by a court of this state, or a decree issued by a jurisdiction outside this state as recognized pursuant to section 3107.18 of the Revised Code, shall have the following effects as to all matters within the jurisdiction or before a court of this state, whether issued before or after the effective date of this amendment:

(1) Except with respect to a spouse of the petitioner and relatives of the spouse, to relieve the biological or other legal parents of the adopted person of all parental rights and responsi-

bilities, and to terminate all legal relationships between the adopted person and the adopted person's relatives, including the adopted person's biological or other legal parents, so that the adopted person thereafter is a stranger to the adopted person's former relatives for all purposes including inheritance and the interpretation or construction of documents, statutes, and instruments, whether executed before or after the adoption is decreed, which do not expressly include the person by name or by some designation not based on a parent and child or blood relationship;

(2) To create the relationship of parent and child between petitioner and the adopted person, as if the adopted person were a legitimate blood descendant of the petitioner, for all purposes including inheritance and applicability of statutes, documents, and instruments, whether executed before or after the adoption is decreed, and whether executed or created before or after the effective date of this amendment, which do not expressly exclude an adopted person from their operation or effect.

(B) Notwithstanding division (A) of this section, if a parent of a child dies without the relationship of parent and child having been previously terminated and a spouse of the living parent thereafter adopts the child, the child's rights from or through the deceased parent for all purposes, including inheritance and applicability or construction of documents, statutes, and instruments, are not restricted or curtailed by the adoption.

(C) An interlocutory order of adoption, while it is in force, has the same legal effect as a final decree of adoption. If an interlocutory order of adoption is vacated, it shall be as though void from its issuance, and the rights, liabilities, and status of all affected persons that have not become vested are governed accordingly.

(1996 S 129, eff. 5-30-96; 1976 H 156, eff. 1-1-77)

Historical and Statutory Notes

Ed. Note: 3107.15 contains provisions analogous to former 3107.13, repealed by 1976 H 156, eff. 1-1-77.

Amendment Note: 1996 S 129 inserted "or a decree issued by a jurisdiction outside this state as recognized pursuant to section 3107.18 of the Revised Code" and "whether issued before or after the effective date of this amendment" in division (A); inserted "and whether executed or created before or after the effective date of this amendment" in division (A)(2); and made changes to reflect gender neutral language and other nonsubstantive changes throughout.

Cross References

Descent and distribution, 2105.06
Dower, Ch 2103
Estate tax, Ch 5731

Ohio Administrative Code References

Acceptance of permanent custody by permanent surrender, OAC 5101:2-42-09

Library References

Adoption ⟹14, 20 to 24.
WESTLAW Topic No. 17.
C.J.S. Adoption of Persons §§ 98 to 102, 124 to 128, 134 to 139, 146 to 153.

OJur 3d: 31, Decedents' Estates § 38, 100; 32, Decedents' Estates § 528, 535, 540, 547, 622, 789, 793; 34, Decedents' Estates § 1688; 41, Estates, Powers, and Restraints on Alienation § 37; 47, Family Law § 934, 940, 946; 53, Guardian and Ward § 43; 91, Trusts § 126

Am Jur 2d: 2, Adoption § 83 et seq.

What law, in point of time, governs as to inheritance from or through adoptive parent. 18 ALR2d 960

Adoption as affecting right of inheritance through or from natural parent or other natural kin. 37 ALR2d 333

Right of adopted child to inherit from kindred of adoptive parent. 43 ALR2d 1183

Children of adopted child, or adopted children of natural child, as "lineal descendants" within provisions of inheritance, succession, or estate tax statutes respecting exemption and tax rates. 51 ALR2d 854

What law, in point of time, governs inheritance from or through adopted person. 52 ALR2d 1228

Child adopted by another as beneficiary of action or settlement for wrongful death of natural parent. 67 ALR2d 745

Law governing effect, with respect to inheritance, of foreign contract to adopt. 80 ALR2d 1128

Adopted child as within class in testamentary gift. 86 ALR2d 12

Adopted child as within class named in deed or inter vivos trust instrument. 86 ALR2d 115

Conflict of laws as to adoption as affecting descent and distribution of decedent's estate. 87 ALR2d 1240

Right of children of adopted child to inherit from adopting parent. 94 ALR2d 1200

Action for death of adoptive parent, by or for benefit of adopted or equitably adopted child. 94 ALR2d 1237; 97 ALR3d 347

Adoption by third person as excluding one who otherwise answers to the description of a testamentary beneficiary. 96 ALR2d 639

Right of adopted child to inherit from intestate natural grandparent. 60 ALR3d 631

Adopted child as subject to protection of statute regarding rights of children pretermitted by will, or statute preventing disinheritance of child. 43 ALR4th 947

Adoption as precluding testamentary gift under natural relative's will. 71 ALR4th 374

Adopted child as within class named in testamentary gift. 36 ALR5th 395

Adopted child as within class named deed or inter vivos trust instrument. 37 ALR5th 237

Carlin, Baldwin's Ohio Practice, *Merrick-Rippner Probate Law* § 15.28, 17.2, 30.25, 30.231, 43.16, 43.23, 43.25, 98.2, 98.3, 98.8, 98.31, 98.38, 98.48, 98.52, 98.53, 98.54, 108.15 (1997)

Hausser, Ohio Real Estate Law and Practice (2d Ed.), Text 1.05

Sowald & Morganstern, Baldwin's Ohio Practice, *Domestic Relations Law* § 18.4.1, 21.6 (1997)

Law Review and Journal Commentaries

Belsito v Clark: Ohio's Battle with "Motherhood," Dawn Wenk. 28 U Tol L Rev 247 (Fall 1996).

Browsing Among the Later Probate Authorities, Harry L. Deibel. 22 Ohio St B Ass'n Rep 243 (1949).

Grandparent Visitation Rights in Ohio After Grandchild Adoption: Is It Time to Move in a New Direction?, Note. 46 Clev St L Rev 385 (1998).

In re Adoption of Ridenour, Note. 18 Ohio N U L Rev 719 (1992).

Inheritance from an Adopted Child, Robert R. Augsburger. 1 W Reserve U L Rev 133 (1949).

Inheritance Rights of Adopted Children: A Review of Recent Cases, Angela G. Carlin. 3 Prob L J Ohio 52 (March/April 1993).

An Interpretation of Ohio Law on Maternal Status in Gestational Surrogacy Disputes: Belsito v. Clark, Note. 21 U Dayton L Rev 229 (Fall 1995).

Little Red Riding Hood is Missing—Grandparent Visitation Not Authorized After Stepparent Adoption, Richard L. Innis. 7 Domestic Rel J Ohio 17 (March/April 1995).

Right of Adopted Child to Inherit Through its Adoptive Parents, John P. McMahon. 7 Ohio St L J 441 (September 1941).

There's More than the Wolf Keeping Little Red Riding Hood from Her Grandparents, Hon. Russell A. Steiner. 5 Domestic Rel J Ohio 93 (November/December 1993).

Wills Can Be Made "Unbreakable," Ellis V. Rippner. 6 Clev-Marshall L Rev 336 (May 1957).

Notes of Decisions and Opinions

Child's right to inherit
- **In general 2**
- **As issue or lineal descendant 3**
- **From and through natural parent 4**
- **Trusts 5**

Death of adopted child 7
Effect of decree: in general 1
Rights of adopting parents 6
Visitation 8

---

1. Effect of decree: in general

Mother was not entitled to writ of prohibition to prevent juvenile court judge from proceeding with father's parentage action, based on foreign adoption decree, since foreign adoption law did not require notice to father before adoption of child out-of-wedlock and therefore may not have been enforced under comity as being repugnant to state law, jurisdiction was not divested even if action was barred on res judicata grounds, and inadequacy of postjudgment appeal was not established. State ex rel. Smith v. Smith (Ohio 1996) 75 Ohio St.3d 418, 662 N.E.2d 366.

Putative paternal grandparents were not qualified to seek court-ordered right to visit their putative biological grandchild, until alleged paternity of grandchild was established by putative father filing legitimation petition or by paternity action to determine if putative father was father of child. In re Martin (Ohio 1994) 68 Ohio St.3d 250, 626 N.E.2d 82.

Even if putative father was father of child, putative paternal grandparents were not entitled to court-ordered right to visit child who had been adopted by maternal grandparents, as statute which provides that adoption of child terminates all legal relationships between adopted child and his relatives does not distinguish between adoption by strangers and nonstrangers. In re Martin (Ohio 1994) 68 Ohio St.3d 250, 626 N.E.2d 82.

The common law rule known as "stranger to the adoption" was abrogated as to wills, including trusts established by wills, as of the effective date of GC 8004-13, even though the doctrine remained viable as to trust instruments until the amendments to former RC 3107.13 effective in 1972. Central Trust Co. of Northern Ohio, N.A. v. Smith (Ohio 1990) 50 Ohio St.3d 133, 553 N.E.2d 265.

Following an adoption, RC 3107.15(A)(1) does not operate in a retroactive manner to relieve the payor spouse of all past due child support arrearages not reduced to judgment prior to adoption. Bercaw v. Bercaw (Ohio 1989) 45 Ohio St.3d 160, 543 N.E.2d 1197.

Given the absence of an expression by the general assembly to the contrary, RC 3107.15 shall be applied prospectively only, and subsequent to its effective date, January 1, 1977, to those documents, statutes, and instruments, whether executed before or after an adoption is decreed, which do not expressly exclude the adopted person from the laws' or instruments' operation and effect. Ohio Citizens Bank v. Mills (Ohio 1989) 45 Ohio St.3d 153, 543 N.E.2d 1206.

3107.13 is constitutional. In re Millward's Estate (Ohio 1957) 166 Ohio St. 243, 141 N.E.2d 462, 2 O.O.2d 61.

GC 5334 (RC 5731.09), prescribing exemptions from succession taxes, and GC 5335 (RC 5731.12), prescribing rates of such taxes as applicable to certain categories of persons named therein, are not in pari materia with section, relating to the adoption of children and the inheritable rights of such children. (Annotation from former RC 3107.13.) In re Friedman's Estate (Ohio 1950) 154 Ohio St. 1, 93 N.E.2d 273, 42 O.O. 97.

Adoption of child by adult who was not child's stepparent would terminate parental rights of biological parent by operation of law, in accordance with unambiguous language and meaning of adoption statutes, notwithstanding that unmarried adult seeking to adopt child was lesbian partner of child's biological mother and was otherwise eligible to adopt child. In re Adoption of Doe (Ohio App. 9 Dist. 1998) 130 Ohio App.3d 288, 719 N.E.2d 1071.

Best interest of the child test pertains to adoption process, not to legal effects of adoption on parental rights. In re Adoption of Doe (Ohio App. 9 Dist. 1998) 130 Ohio App.3d 288, 719 N.E.2d 1071.

Adoption of child born out of wedlock by mother's spouse did not relieve child's biological father of support obligations incurred and unpaid prior to child's adoption, even though no support obligation was reduced to judgment prior to child's adoption and child was emancipated at time she brought action for support; biological father's obligation commenced at child's birth and continued until her adoption, and child's right to pursue support for such time period was not extinguished by her adoption. Hudgins v. Mitchell (Ohio App. 9 Dist. 1998) 128 Ohio App.3d 403, 715 N.E.2d 213.

Adoption terminates all legal relationships between adopted person and natural family, making adopted person stranger to former relatives. Sawyer v. Lebanon Citizens Natl. Bank (Warren 1995) 105 Ohio App.3d 464, 664 N.E.2d 571, dismissed, appeal not allowed 74 Ohio St.3d 1476, 657 N.E.2d 783.

Where a final decree of adoption is vacated due to a defect in service, a prior order granting temporary custody to the adoptive parents remains in full force and effect precluding the need for a new temporary custody order; thus, a trial court errs in failing to dismiss a subsequent duplicative temporary custody petition. In re Knipper (Hamilton 1987) 39 Ohio App.3d 35, 528 N.E.2d 1319.

The juvenile court's authority to order payment of back child support is not defeated by subsequent adoption of the child; however, the court errs by ordering the father to pay support for five months after the child is adopted by the mother's husband. Black v Hart, No. 17524, 1996 WL 304284 (9th Dist Ct App, Summit, 6-5-96).

The "stranger to the adoption" doctrine is not a rule of construction which should be given effect. (Annotation from former RC 3107.13.) Cleveland Trust Co. v. Schumacher (Ohio Com.Pl. 1973) 35 Ohio Misc. 118, 298 N.E.2d 913, 64 O.O.2d 394.

A child adopted in a foreign state or country may take under local statutes of descent and distribution, if such foreign state or country had jurisdiction to fix his status with respect to his adoptive parents, but this rule of international comity is subject to the condition that the law, with regard to adoption, of the state in which the real and personal property is situated, does not differ essentially from the law of the state in which the adoption was had, so that local public policy is not violated by recognizing and giving effect to the adoption proceedings of the foreign state or country. (Annotation from former RC 3107.13.) National City Bank of Cleveland v. Judkins (Ohio Com.Pl. 1964) 8 Ohio Misc. 119, 219 N.E.2d 456, 37 O.O.2d 200.

2. —In general, child's right to inherit

Former RC 3107.13 provided that a legally adopted child, for all purposes under laws of this state, including laws and wills governing inheritance and succession, shall have the same status and rights as a natural born child of the adoptive parents. Central Trust Co. of Northern Ohio, N.A. v. Smith (Ohio 1990) 50 Ohio St.3d 133, 553 N.E.2d 265.

Where a testator uses the term "heirs of the body" as a term of limitation in a class gift to exclude adopted beneficiaries, such term in the absence of contrary intent constitutes an express exclusion of adopted persons under RC 3107.15. Tootle v. Tootle (Ohio 1986) 22 Ohio St.3d 244, 490 N.E.2d 878, 22 O.B.R. 420.

A child, surrendered by its parents into the permanent custody of an institution established for the purpose of aiding, caring for and placing children in homes, under a written agreement pursuant to RC 5103.15, which agreement provides that the institution may appear in any legal proceeding for the adoption of such child and consent to the child's adoption, continues as an heir of its parents, either natural or adoptive, until such time as the child has been legally adopted pursuant to RC Ch 3107. (Annotation from former RC 3107.07.) Maurer v. Becker (Ohio 1971) 26 Ohio St.2d 254, 271 N.E.2d 255, 55 O.O.2d 486.

A legally adopted child's right of inheritance is governed by the law in effect at the time of the parent's death and not by the law in effect at the time of the adoption. (Annotation from former RC 3107.13.) In re Millward's Estate (Ohio 1957) 166 Ohio St. 243, 141 N.E.2d 462, 2 O.O.2d 61.

Where, in providing for his "heirs at law" after a life interest, a testator indicates his intention that such heirs should be determined at the date of the expiration of such life interest, then the statutory law in effect at the expiration of such life interest should be applied in determining such heirs of the testator unless by the provisions of the will or surrounding circumstances a contrary intention is indicated, even though such statutory law will permit an adopted child of the testator's daughter to take and the statutory law in effect at the testator's death would not have permitted such adopted child to take and even though such adopted child was not either born or adopted until long after the testator's death. (Annotation from former RC 3107.13.) Tiedtke v. Tiedtke (Ohio 1952) 157 Ohio St. 554, 106 N.E.2d 637, 47 O.O. 411.

Where a testator bequeathed property to "each of my then living grandchildren, whether born prior or subsequent to my decease," there is a presumption, in the absence of any language in the will to the contrary, that the testator intended only the blood children of his children to partake of his bounty. (Annotation from former RC 3107.13.) Third Nat. Bank & Trust Co. v. Davidson (Ohio 1952) 157 Ohio St. 355, 105 N.E.2d 573, 47 O.O. 257.

An adopted child is entitled to the same rights as a child begotten in lawful wedlock, including the right to have a will revoked. (Annotation from former RC 3107.13.) Surman v. Surman (Ohio 1926) 114 Ohio St. 579, 151 N.E. 708, 4 Ohio Law Abs. 276, 24 Ohio Law Rep. 374.

With respect to instruments executed after the effective date, in 1951, of the provisions of GC 8004-13 (RC 3107.13), children adopted by children of the testator are to be included in a class gift to his "grandchildren," in the absence of other language within the same instrument evidencing a contrary intent. (Annotation from former RC 3107.13.) Conkle v. Conkle (Coshocton 1972) 31 Ohio App.2d 44, 285 N.E.2d 883, 60 O.O.2d 144.

In a proceeding to determine heirship in an administration of decedent's estate, where issue is validity of a judgment of adoption, an attack on such judgment on ground that court rendering it had no jurisdiction is a collateral attack, and in such case, where a complete record of adoption proceeding was made according to statute, original papers in the proceeding were not admissible in determination of heirship proceeding as a part of record of former proceeding, and such original papers could not be used to impeach record of adoption proceeding. (Annotation from former RC 3107.09.) In re Dickman's Estate (Mercer 1946) 81 Ohio App. 281, 79 N.E.2d 172, 37 O.O. 125.

A bequest to grandchildren of the testatrix should be construed to include the adopted children of a child of the testatrix, where the adoptions occurred between the time of the execution of the will and the death of the testatrix, she knew and approved of the adoptions, and, having the ability to change the will, the testatrix failed to do so. (Annotation from former RC 3107.13.) Weitzel v. Weitzel (Ohio Prob. 1968) 16 Ohio Misc. 105, 239 N.E.2d 263, 45 O.O.2d 55, 45 O.O.2d 83.

A child adopted in a foreign state or country may take under local statutes of descent and distribution, if such foreign state or country had jurisdiction to fix his status with respect to his adoptive parents, but this rule of international comity is subject to the condition that the law with regard to adoption of the state in which the real and personal property is situated, does not differ essentially from the law of the state in which the adoption was had, so that local public policy is not violated by recognizing and giving effect to the adoption proceedings of the foreign state or country. (Annotation from former RC 3107.09.) National City Bank of Cleveland v. Judkins (Ohio Com.Pl. 1964) 8 Ohio Misc. 119, 219 N.E.2d 456, 37 O.O.2d 200.

Where an adoptive parent has obtained a decree of adoption and taken the adopted child into his own home, his presumptive heirs, personal representatives, as well as himself, are estopped thereafter from asserting the adoption was invalid due to an irregularity in the adoption proceedings, which is not jurisdictional. (Annotation from former RC 3107.09.) National City Bank of Cleveland v. Judkins (Ohio Com.Pl. 1964) 8 Ohio Misc. 119, 219 N.E.2d 456, 37 O.O.2d 200.

Adopted daughter held entitled to the share her deceased adopting parent would have inherited, the same as if she were a natural child of such parent. (Annotation from former RC 3107.13.) Shearer v Gasstman, 15 Abs 103 (Prob, Franklin 1933).

Validity of an adoption proceeding cannot be collaterally attacked in a proceeding to determine heirship. Wachuta v. Wachuta (Ohio Com.Pl. 1954) 122 N.E.2d 677, 69 Ohio Law Abs. 324, 55 O.O. 293.

An adopted child's right to inherit is governed by the statutes in force at the time of decedent's death and not those in force at the time he was adopted. (Annotation from former RC 3107.13.) Staley v. Honeyman (Miami 1950) 98 N.E.2d 429, 59 Ohio Law Abs. 203, affirmed 157 Ohio St. 61, 104 N.E.2d 172, 47 O.O. 67.

An adopted child inherits no interest in the estate of a relative of the adopting parent in which as a child of the blood he would be entitled to share. (Annotation from former RC 3107.13.) Hollencamp v Greulich, 27 NP(NS) 344 (1928).

Where granddaughter of testator was adopted by daughter of testator in New York, effect of such adoption obviously being governed by law of that state, right of inheritance is determinable by law in force at time of foster parents' death, and child had right of inheritance from foster parent, as she would under Ohio law, and she takes one-third of estate as granddaughter of testator and one-third as granddaughter through adoption of testator, to wit, adopted daughter of daughter of testator. (Annotation from former RC 3107.13.) Hollister v. Witherbee (Ohio Com.Pl. 1937) 2 Ohio Supp. 345, 24 Ohio Law Abs. 312, 9 O.O. 37.

Since GC 10503-18 (RC 2105.21) provides for disposition of estates of a husband and wife who died within three days of each other as though they had survived each other, their adopted child of the age of ten years would be entitled to a year's allowance and an allowance of property not deemed assets from the estate of each. (Annotation from former RC 3107.13.) Harrison v. Hillegas (Ohio Prob. 1939) 1 Ohio Supp. 160, 28 Ohio Law Abs. 404, 13 O.O. 523.

3. —As issue or lineal descendant, child's right to inherit

The succession of an adopted child of a child of a decedent in the estate of the latter is not taxable under the provisions of RC 5731.09 and 5731.12 as passing to a person as a lineal descendant of such decedent. (Annotation from former RC 3107.13.) In re Friedman's Estate (Ohio 1950) 154 Ohio St. 1, 93 N.E.2d 273, 42 O.O. 97.

When a settlor established a trust in 1924 which, by subsequent modification in 1933, left property to the "lawful issue" of his son or their "surviving heirs of the body," the settlor's intent was to limit devolution of his property to blood relatives, even though two children adopted by the settlor's son after the settlor's death were thereby excluded, and under such facts, the 1932 adoption statute does not create a presumption of inclusion for adopted children even though no affirmative statement of exclusion is embodied in the trust instrument; and an adopted child is deemed to be excluded from a class of beneficiaries under a trust where the settlor was a stranger to the adoption and had not otherwise manifested an intent to include adopted children. (Annotation from former RC 3107.13.) National City Bank of Cleveland v. Mitchell (Cuyahoga 1968) 13 Ohio App.2d 141, 234 N.E.2d 916, 42 O.O.2d 262.

A testamentary provision for "lineal descendants of my blood" furnishes "other clear identification," as required by RC 3107.13(B), of the children of testator's predeceased son, without naming them, so as to enable them to succeed to a designated portion of testator's estate, although such children were previously adopted by nonrelatives. (Annotation from former RC 3107.13.) Saintignon v. Saintignon (Darke 1966) 5 Ohio App.2d 133, 214 N.E.2d 124, 34 O.O.2d 243.

Where a testator who died in 1925 provided for a life estate for his children with a remainder to their "living issue," and said testator's son died in 1952, a child of said son adopted in 1912 was included within the meaning of "living issue." (Annotation from former RC 3107.13.)

Cook v. Crabill (Greene 1959) 110 Ohio App. 45, 164 N.E.2d 425, 82 Ohio Law Abs. 164, 12 O.O.2d 220.

Order of adoption creates parent-child relationship for all purposes, including inheritances, regardless of date of instrument under which gifts are given; effects of adoption apply retroactively to any instrument which does not expressly exclude adopted person. Fifth Third Bank v. Crosley (Ohio Com.Pl. 1996) 79 Ohio Misc.2d 10, 669 N.E.2d 904, affirmed.

Terms such as child, children, grandchild, heirs of body, issue, or heirs appearing in will or trust exclude adopted child, absent contrary intention within instrument itself. Fifth Third Bank v. Crosley (Ohio Com.Pl. 1996) 79 Ohio Misc.2d 10, 669 N.E.2d 904, affirmed.

Class gifts to "only lawful issue of blood of Trustor" unambiguously excluded adopted children from class of beneficiaries. Fifth Third Bank v. Crosley (Ohio Com.Pl. 1996) 79 Ohio Misc.2d 10, 669 N.E.2d 904, affirmed.

Class gift to settlor's "lawful issue ... includ(ing) children, grandchildren and more remote descendants" included settlor's adopted grandchildren; there was no express prohibition against adoptees being included in class of beneficiaries. Fifth Third Bank v. Crosley (Ohio Com.Pl. 1996) 79 Ohio Misc.2d 10, 669 N.E.2d 904, affirmed.

Adopted children of testator's son were "issue" of testator, entitled to share in class gift to "each of my (testator's) issue per stirpes" upon termination of testamentary trust. Fifth Third Bank v. Crosley (Ohio Com.Pl. 1996) 79 Ohio Misc.2d 10, 669 N.E.2d 904, affirmed.

RC 3107.13 enables adopted children to inherit through an adopting parent, and one who can inherit through another is a lineal descendant of the testator, even though adopted. (Annotation from former RC 3107.13.) Schneider v. Dorr (Ohio Prob. 1965) 3 Ohio Misc. 103, 210 N.E.2d 311, 32 O.O.2d 391.

Adopted daughter cannot participate in distribution of an estate where testator limited estate to brother's "issue." (Annotation from former RC 3107.13.) Reinhard v. Reinhard (Franklin 1936) 23 Ohio Law Abs. 306.

Where a devise is made to a devisee with a provision that in the event of his death leaving issue, his issue shall take his share, an adopted child may take as such "issue." (Annotation from former RC 3107.13.) Graves v. Graves (Ohio Prob. 1956) 155 N.E.2d 540, 79 Ohio Law Abs. 262.

Where testator's only lineal descendant was his granddaughter, who had been adopted by her stepfather who had married the testator's daughter-in-law after the death of the testator's son, the testator died without issue or the lineal descendant of issue, and charitable bequests executed within a year of testator's death are valid. (Annotation from former RC 3107.13.) Campbell v. Musart Soc. of Cleveland Museum of Art (Ohio Prob. 1956) 131 N.E.2d 279, 72 Ohio Law Abs. 46, 2 O.O.2d 517.

4. —From and through natural parent, child's right to inherit

A child, surrendered by its parents into the permanent custody of an institution established for the purpose of aiding, caring for and placing children in homes, under a written agreement pursuant to RC 5103.15, which agreement provides that the institution may appear in any legal proceeding for the adoption of such child and consent to the child's adoption, continues as an heir of its parents, either natural or adoptive, until such time as the child has been legally adopted pursuant to RC Ch 3107. (Annotation from former RC 3107.13.) Maurer v. Becker (Ohio 1971) 26 Ohio St.2d 254, 271 N.E.2d 255, 55 O.O.2d 486.

Under the provisions of former RC 3107.13, for the purpose of inheritance to, through, and from a legally adopted child, such child shall be treated the same as if he were the natural child of his adopting parents, and shall cease to be treated as the child of his natural parents for the purposes of intestate succession; such child's right of inheritance is governed by the law in effect at the time of the parent's death and not by the law in effect at the time of the adoption. In re Millward's Estate (Ohio 1957) 166 Ohio St. 243, 141 N.E.2d 462, 2 O.O.2d 61.

A legally adopted child may not inherit from an intestate natural parent. (Annotation from former RC 3107.13.) In re Millward's Estate (Ohio 1957) 166 Ohio St. 243, 141 N.E.2d 462, 2 O.O.2d 61.

By terms of statute reciting that adopted child shall be capable of inheriting property expressly limited by will or by operation of law to child, heir or next of kin of adopting parent, adopted child was enabled to inherit property through as well as from his adopting parent whether property passed by will or by operation of law. (Annotation from former RC 3107.13.) Flynn v. Bredbeck (Ohio 1946) 147 Ohio St. 49, 68 N.E.2d 75, 33 O.O. 243.

Introduction of evidence that patient's minor daughter was adopted by her stepfather after patient's death was prejudicial error in patient's estate's medical malpractice action, as status of daughter was fixed at time of patient's death, before his daughter's adoption, and child's statutory rights derived from and through patient were not restricted by child's subsequent adoption. Ulmer v. Ackerman (Allen 1993) 87 Ohio App.3d 137, 621 N.E.2d 1315, dismissed, jurisdictional motion overruled 67 Ohio St.3d 1434, 617 N.E.2d 685.

The provisions of RC 3107.13 preclude an adopted child, who has again been adopted subsequent to the deaths of the first adopting parents and prior to the death of an ancestor of a first adopting parent, from inheriting under the statute of descent and distribution through the first adopting parent from the first adopting parent's ancestor who died subsequent to the second adoption. (Annotation from former RC 3107.13.) Evans v. Freter (Tuscarawas 1969) 20 Ohio App.2d 8, 251 N.E.2d 513, 49 O.O.2d 4.

An adopted child is entitled to inherit not only from adopting parent, but also through such parent from a deceased sister of the adopting parent. (Annotation from former RC 3107.13.) White v. Meyer (Cuyahoga 1940) 66 Ohio App. 549, 37 N.E.2d 546, 33 Ohio Law Abs. 151, 21 O.O. 38.

Foster children can inherit from their foster parents, but they cannot inherit through them; and, where a man dies intestate, leaving no wife or children, the foster children of his deceased sister are not entitled to share in his estate. (Annotation from former RC 3107.13.) Pickering v. Koesling (Cuyahoga 1928) 30 Ohio App. 201, 164 N.E. 537, 6 Ohio Law Abs. 507, 27 Ohio Law Rep. 18.

A child who becomes vested in interest, but not in possession, of an expectant estate in land limited to the "heirs of the body" as a natural descendant and survivor of the grantee of an estate in fee tail prior to his adoption by others does not have his right as the vested owner of such expectant estate cut off by reason of the adoption statute. (Annotation from former RC 3107.13.) Eisenmann v. Eisenmann (Ohio Com.Pl. 1976) 52 Ohio Misc. 119, 370 N.E.2d 788, 6 O.O.3d 449.

Under RC 3107.13 a child adopted by his stepfather before his natural father's death may inherit through his natural father from estate of the latter's mother. (Annotation from former RC 3107.13.) First Nat. Bank of East Liverpool v. Collar (Ohio Com.Pl. 1971) 27 Ohio Misc. 88, 272 N.E.2d 916, 56 O.O.2d 302.

RC 3107.13, although generally denying adopted child legal status of child of his natural parents, expressly prevents debarring of such child from taking under will of natural parent, when he is identified by name or otherwise clearly identified as intended beneficiary. (Annotation from former RC 3107.13.) Seeley v. Bedillion (Ohio Com.Pl. 1969) 23 Ohio Misc. 4, 260 N.E.2d 639, 51 O.O.2d 128, 52 O.O.2d 14.

An adopted child cannot take under the statute of descent and distribution from a parent of his natural parent. (Annotation from former RC 3107.13.) Frantz v. Florence (Ohio Com.Pl. 1954) 131 N.E.2d 630, 72 Ohio Law Abs. 222.

Where testator's only lineal descendant was his granddaughter, who had been adopted by her stepfather who had married the testator's daughter-in-law after the death of the testator's son, the testator died without issue or the lineal descendant of issue, and charitable bequests executed within a year of testator's death are valid. (Annotation from former RC 3107.13.) Campbell v. Musart Soc. of Cleveland Museum of Art (Ohio Prob. 1956) 131 N.E.2d 279, 72 Ohio Law Abs. 46, 2 O.O.2d 517.

An adopted child may inherit collaterally through his adoptive parent as well as from such parent. (Annotation from former RC 3107.13.) Staley v. Honeyman (Miami 1950) 98 N.E.2d 429, 59 Ohio Law Abs. 203, affirmed 157 Ohio St. 61, 104 N.E.2d 172, 47 O.O. 67.

Where children of a deceased mother have been adopted by their natural grandparents and one of the grandparents dies, such children cannot inherit from their grandmother and adopted mother in a two-fold capacity but take only as children of the adopting grandmother, because in such a situation the smaller interest receivable by them will be merged in the larger, so that the most they can receive is the larger of the two interests. (Annotation from former RC 3107.13.) Paul v. Paul (Ohio Prob. 1940) 2 Ohio Supp. 349, 31 Ohio Law Abs. 453, 17 O.O. 392.

By the terms of RC 3107.15, if a parent of a child dies without the relationship of parent and child having been previously terminated, and a spouse of the living parent thereafter adopts the child, the child's rights through the deceased parent to survivor's benefits under RC Ch 145 are not restricted or curtailed by the adoption, notwithstanding RC 145.45(B)(4). OAG 79-079.

5. —Trusts, child's right to inherit

A testator who creates a trust that provides for termination at the death of a life beneficiary and distribution of trust assets to the "then living children" of the beneficiary is presumed to know that the legislative definition of children will be determined at the time the class closes and that the definition may include adult adoptees even though adult adoptions were not authorized at the time the trust was created. Solomon v. Central Trust Co. of Northeastern Ohio, N.A. (Ohio 1992) 63 Ohio St.3d 35, 584 N.E.2d 1185.

Where there is no specific language in a trust provision of a will prohibiting an adopted child from taking under the trust, a child adopted by a trust beneficiary, after the testator's death, may take under the term of the instrument as a member of the class of "then living children" of the beneficiary, even though the adoptee was an adult at the time of his adoption. Solomon v. Central Trust Co. of Northeastern Ohio, N.A. (Ohio 1992) 63 Ohio St.3d 35, 584 N.E.2d 1185.

Provisions of RC 3107.13, as in effect since 1951, which establish rights of adopted children to inherit, do not create presumption that settlor of inter vivos trust created in 1930 intended to include adopted child as beneficiary where settlor is stranger to adoption proceedings and did not otherwise express intention to include adopted children. (Annotation from former RC 3107.13.) Central Trust Co. v. Bovey (Ohio 1971) 25 Ohio St.2d 187, 267 N.E.2d 427, 54 O.O.2d 297.

The intention of settlor of an inter vivos trust created in 1930, in providing gift of portion of corpus of trust to "child or children ... surviving the daughter then dying," should be determined in light of law existing at time of creation of the trust; an adopted child will not be deemed to be "child ... surviving the daughter ..." of settlor where, under law of intestacy at time of creation of trust applicable by analogy, term "child" included only blood relatives. (Annotation from former RC 3107.13.) Central Trust Co. v. Bovey (Ohio 1971) 25 Ohio St.2d 187, 267 N.E.2d 427, 54 O.O.2d 297.

Irrevocable trust for benefit of minor children created with proceeds from wrongful death of their natural mother did not terminate on subsequent adoption of children; interests of children in trust vested when shares of all beneficiaries were adjusted in wrongful death proceeding and children were proper beneficiaries. Sawyer v. Lebanon Citizens Natl. Bank (Warren 1995) 105 Ohio App.3d 464, 664 N.E.2d 571, dismissed, appeal not allowed 74 Ohio St.3d 1476, 657 N.E.2d 783.

An adopted grandchild is entitled to share in a trust as a beneficiary where the grandchild is adopted after the death of the settlor but before the eldest biological grandchild reaches the age of thirty, the time at which the trustee is directed to begin payments from the trust corpus and the time at which the class of beneficiaries closes. Bank One, Youngstown, N.A. v. Heltzel (Trumbull 1991) 76 Ohio App.3d 524, 602 N.E.2d 412, motion overruled 63 Ohio St.3d 1458, 590 N.E.2d 753.

When a settlor established a trust in 1924 which, by subsequent modification in 1933, left property to the "lawful issue" of his son or their "surviving heirs of the body," the settlor's intent was to limit devolution of his property to blood relatives, even though two children adopted by the settlor's son after the settlor's death were thereby excluded, and under such facts, the 1932 adoption statute does not create a presumption of inclusion for adopted children even though no affirmative statement of exclusion is embodied in the trust instrument; and an adopted child is deemed to be excluded from a class of beneficiaries under a trust where the settlor was a stranger to the adoption and had not otherwise manifested an intent to include adopted children. (Annotation from former RC 3107.13.) National City Bank of Cleveland v. Mitchell (Cuyahoga 1968) 13 Ohio App.2d 141, 234 N.E.2d 916, 42 O.O.2d 262.

Where it was determined in action to construe will that upon the death of a life tenant leaving no surviving children, the principal and income should be divided among the testator's heirs, and the life tenant died leaving an adopted child surviving, such adopted child takes the corpus of the trust. (Annotation from former RC 3107.13.) Tiedtke v. Tiedtke (Lucas 1951) 91 Ohio App.

442, 108 N.E.2d 578, 49 O.O. 36, appeal denied 156 Ohio St. 187, 101 N.E.2d 500, 46 O.O. 58, affirmed 157 Ohio St. 554, 106 N.E.2d 637, 47 O.O. 411.

Rights of adopted children to take under trust deed antedating adoption were fixed by statute in effect when they were adopted, not statute as subsequently amended. (Annotation from former RC 3107.13.) Rodgers v. Miller (Franklin 1932) 43 Ohio App. 198, 182 N.E. 654, 12 Ohio Law Abs. 23, 36 Ohio Law Rep. 310.

Under trust deed, adopted children of settlor's deceased son held not entitled to take as "children" or "issue" of settlor's deceased child. (Annotation from former RC 3107.13.) Rodgers v. Miller (Franklin 1932) 43 Ohio App. 198, 182 N.E. 654, 12 Ohio Law Abs. 23, 36 Ohio Law Rep. 310.

Repeal of "stranger to the adoption" doctrine in RC 3107.13 applied to trust modified after its effective date. (Annotation from former RC 3107.13.) Cleveland Trust Co. v. Schumacher (Ohio Com.Pl. 1973) 35 Ohio Misc. 118, 298 N.E.2d 913, 64 O.O.2d 394.

6. Rights of adopting parents

Adopting parents allowed to recover for the wrongful death of adopted child. (Annotation from former RC 3107.13.) Ransom v. New York, C. & St. L.R. Co. (Ohio 1915) 93 Ohio St. 223, 112 N.E. 586, 13 Ohio Law Rep. 514, 13 Ohio Law Rep. 566.

Since a presumption of law arises from a decree of adoption that all provisions of law relating thereto have been complied with and such exists until overcome by proof to the contrary adopting parents are entitled to custody of their adopted child, to the exclusion of all other persons, until some lawful reason for a change in the child's custody is made to appear by competent evidence. (Annotation from former RC 3107.07.) Martin v. Fisher (Mercer 1927) 25 Ohio App. 372, 158 N.E. 287, 5 Ohio Law Abs. 596.

Where an adoptive parent has obtained a decree of adoption and taken the adopted child into his own home, his presumptive heirs, personal representatives, as well as himself, are estopped thereafter from asserting the adoption was invalid due to an irregularity in the adoption proceedings, which is not jurisdictional. (Annotation from former RC 3107.13.) National City Bank of Cleveland v. Judkins (Ohio Com.Pl. 1964) 8 Ohio Misc. 119, 219 N.E.2d 456, 37 O.O.2d 200.

The natural mother and adoptive father of a decedent are entitled to share equally in his estate. (Annotation from former RC 3107.13.) Mancino v. Smith (Ohio Prob. 1964) 201 N.E.2d 93, 95 Ohio Law Abs. 51, 30 O.O.2d 282.

That an adopting parent perpetrated a fraud by adopting a child, and then using such child's estate for its support, even if true, would not invalidate the adoption or change the application of the laws of descent and distribution. (Annotation from former RC 3107.13.) Vodrey v. Quigley (Ohio Prob. 1956) 139 N.E.2d 108, 74 Ohio Law Abs. 29, affirmed 143 N.E.2d 162, 75 Ohio Law Abs. 65.

7. Death of adopted child

Although the adopted child of a childless couple dies before the adopting parents, if it leaves issue the issue or its devisee inherits to the exclusion of collaterals. The primary purpose of GC 8029 and 8030 (Repealed) being to make the child the same as a natural child, unless it dies first without issue. (Annotation from former RC 3107.07.) Kroff v. Amrhein (Ohio 1916) 94 Ohio St. 282, 114 N.E. 267, 14 Ohio Law Rep. 204.

Where adopted child dies before his adopting parent, the issue of the adopted child inherits from the adopting parent. (Annotation from former RC 3107.13.) Kroff v. Amrhein (Ohio 1916) 94 Ohio St. 282, 114 N.E. 267, 14 Ohio Law Rep. 204.

Where adopted child dies intestate, leaving no spouse or issue, his property passes to his blood kin and not to his kin by adoption, even though such property was inherited by the adopted child from his adopting mother and brother by adoption and is identifiable as identical. (Annotation from former RC 3107.13.) National Bank of Lima v. Hancock (Allen 1948) 85 Ohio App. 1, 88 N.E.2d 67, 40 O.O. 30.

An adoption terminates any right of the relatives of the natural mother to inherit from the adopted child, and where the adopting parent is deceased, the heirs of such adopting parent will take. (Annotation from former RC 3107.13.) (See also Vodrey v Quigley, 74 Abs 29, 139 NE(2d) 108 (Prob, Columbiana 1956).) Vodrey v. Quigley (Columbiana 1956) 143 N.E.2d 162, 75 Ohio Law Abs. 65.

Where a child has been validly adopted, a blood relative is deprived of all rights of intestate succession, regardless of whether the natural parents were alive at the time of such adoption. (Annotation from former RC 3107.13.) Vodrey v. Quigley (Ohio Prob. 1956) 139 N.E.2d 108, 74 Ohio Law Abs. 29, affirmed 143 N.E.2d 162, 75 Ohio Law Abs. 65.

8. Visitation

Biological father's allegations, that appeal was not complete, beneficial, and speedy, and thus was not adequate remedy to prevent Court of Common Pleas from granting visitation to biological mother following issuance of adoption decree that terminated her parental rights, and that irreparable harm to child and to relationship between biological father would result should visitation proceedings not be stopped, stated cause of action in complaint seeking writ of prohibition. State ex rel. Kaylor v. Bruening (Ohio 1997) 80 Ohio St.3d 142, 684 N.E.2d 1228.

Although Court of Common Pleas had basic statutory jurisdiction to grant visitation to biological parent, it was patently and unambiguously divested by adoption statute of jurisdiction to proceed on biological mother's motions relating to visitation following adoption decree terminating her parental rights, and writ of prohibition preventing Court from doing so thus was appropriate. State ex rel. Kaylor v. Bruening (Ohio 1997) 80 Ohio St.3d 142, 684 N.E.2d 1228.

Even if juvenile court had authority to set postadoption terms and conditions in granting permanent custody of children to county children services board, it could not require that visitation by biological grandparents continue following adoption of children by stranger. In re Adoption of Ridenour (Ohio 1991) 61 Ohio St.3d 319, 574 N.E.2d 1055.

Trial court lacked authority to grant paternal grandparents visitation with children of divorced parents after the children were adopted by their stepfather subsequent to their father's death; while a statute preserved the right of grandparent visitation when a surviving spouse remarried, it did not provide for the preservation of visitation rights after an adoption by a stepparent. Foor v. Foor (Ohio App. 12 Dist. 1999) 133 Ohio App.3d 250, 727 N.E.2d 618.

Relatives of parents whose parental rights are terminated have no standing to assert visitation rights. Farley v. Farley (Licking 1992) 85 Ohio App.3d 113, 619 N.E.2d 427.

Juvenile court does not have authority to grant paternal grandparents visitation rights with grandchild after grandchild has been adopted by stepfather. Krnac v. Starman (Medina 1992) 83 Ohio App.3d 578, 615 N.E.2d 344, dismissed, jurisdictional motion overruled 66 Ohio St.3d 1485, 612 N.E.2d 1241.

A domestic relations court which granted a divorce retains jurisdiction for the purposes of granting visitation rights as required by the best interest of any children born as issue of the marriage regardless of the existence or venue of a subsequent stepparent adoption proceeding. Bente v. Hill (Clermont 1991) 73 Ohio App.3d 151, 596 N.E.2d 1042, dismissed, jurisdictional motion overruled 62 Ohio St.3d 1422, 577 N.E.2d 1105.

Maternal grandparents could be granted visitation with their grandchildren where grandchildren were adopted by paternal grandmother and her husband; court was permitted to grant visitation on case by case basis, considering all relevant facts and taking best interests of children as guiding principle. In re Pennington (Scioto 1988) 55 Ohio App.3d 99, 562 N.E.2d 905.

Where a child's parent dies, the surviving parent remarries, and the surviving parent's new spouse adopts the child, a court may grant visitation rights to relatives of the deceased parent pursuant to RC 3109.11 over the objections of the child's parents, notwithstanding RC 3107.15. In re Thornton (Franklin 1985) 24 Ohio App.3d 152, 493 N.E.2d 977, 24 O.B.R. 241.

RC 3107.15 does not prohibit an order pursuant to RC 3109.05, granting visitation rights to a biological paternal grandparent after adoption of a child by a stepfather, when the biological father's whereabouts are unknown. Welsh v. Laffey (Butler 1984) 16 Ohio App.3d 110, 474 N.E.2d 681, 16 O.B.R. 117.

The power of the court to order visitation and companionship rights to relatives under RC 3109.11 is not divested or terminated by the adoption of the child of a deceased parent by a stepparent, pursuant to RC 3107.13, and such adoption is merely a factor which the court must consider in determining the best interest of the child under RC 3109.11. (Annotation from former RC 3107.13.) Graziano v. Davis (Mahoning 1976) 50 Ohio App.2d 83, 361 N.E.2d 525, 4 O.O.3d 55.

A trial court has no authority to grant grandparents' visitation rights following a stepparent adoption. Foor v Foor, No. CA98-06-007, 1999 WL 247144 (12th Dist Ct App, Preble, 4-26-99).

The legislature has not provided the juvenile court with the authority to grant visitation rights to biological grandparents following an adoption of a grandchild by a stepparent even where the parental rights of the grandparents' child have been terminated through death. In re Apple, No. 93-VA-59, 1994 WL 515116 (2d Dist Ct App, Miami, 9-21-94).

3107.16 Appeals; finality of decree

(A) Appeals from the probate court are subject to the Rules of Appellate Procedure and, to the extent not in conflict with those rules, Chapter 2505. of the Revised Code. Unless there is good cause for delay, appeals shall be heard on an expedited basis.

(B) Subject to the disposition of an appeal, upon the expiration of one year after an adoption decree is issued, the decree cannot be questioned by any person, including the petitioner, in any manner or upon any ground, including fraud, misrepresentation, failure to give any required notice, or lack of jurisdiction of the parties or of the subject matter, unless, in the case of the adoption of a minor, the petitioner has not taken custody of the minor, or, in the case of the adoption of a minor by a stepparent, the adoption would not have been granted but for fraud perpetrated by the petitioner or the petitioner's spouse, or, in the case of the adoption of an adult, the adult had no knowledge of the decree within the one-year period.

(1996 H 419, eff. 9-18-96; 1986 H 412, eff. 3-17-87; 1976 H 156)

Historical and Statutory Notes

Amendment Note: 1996 H 419 added the second sentence to division (A).

Library References

Adoption ⚷14 to 16.

WESTLAW Topic No. 17.

C.J.S. Adoption of Persons §§ 98 to 128.

OJur 3d: 47, Family Law § 955

Am Jur 2d: 2, Adoption § 68 to 82

Validity and construction of statutes imposing time limitations upon actions to vacate or set aside an adoption decree or judgment. 83 ALR2d 945

Baldwin's Ohio Legislative Service, 1996 H 419—LSC Analysis, 3/L-336

Carlin, Baldwin's Ohio Practice, *Merrick-Rippner Probate Law* § 98.2, 98.30, 98.35, 98.43, 98.50 (1997)

Notes of Decisions and Opinions

1. Constitutional issues

Statute providing that decrees of adoption are uncontestable after one year was not unconstitutional as applied to biological mother, where mother freely and knowingly signed adoption consent form which contained waiver of notice of hearing on petition for adoption, mother had actual notice of adoption proceedings, and mother had adequate posttermination opportunity to contest adoption placement, since she learned of adoption decree at least one month before expiration of one-year period. In re Rabatin (Geauga 1992) 83 Ohio App.3d 836, 615 N.E.2d 1099.

RC 3107.16(B) is unconstitutional insofar as it bars a biological parent from attacking a decree of adoption more than one year after it is issued, where the adopting parents failed to use reasonable diligence in their efforts to locate the biological parent's address. In re Adoption of Knipper (Hamilton 1986) 30 Ohio App.3d 214, 507 N.E.2d 436, 30 O.B.R. 371.

Adoption, jurisdiction of Supreme Court, review of state court's interpretation of state law. O'Connell v. Kirchner (U.S.Ill. 1995) 115 S.Ct. 891, 513 U.S. 1303, 130 L.Ed.2d 873.

Adoption, federal due process rights of adoptive parents and child, habeas corpus ordering surrender of custody. O'Connell v. Kirchner (U.S.Ill. 1995) 115 S.Ct. 891, 513 U.S. 1303, 130 L.Ed.2d 873.

2. Habeas corpus

Where a natural mother alleges that she has been unlawfully deprived of her child upon signing a permanent surrender agreement, pursuant to RC 5103.15, in response to undue pressure, a writ of habeas corpus seeking the return of the child is proper where an informal request for the vacation of a court entry consenting to the permanent surrender agreement has been denied rendering a formal motion for vacation futile, and the appeal process from a formal denial is an inadequate remedy at law where an expeditious resolution is required to challenge a possible adoption and a speedy permanent placement of the child is sought. Marich v. Knox County Dept. of Human Services/Children Services Unit (Ohio 1989) 45 Ohio St.3d 163, 543 N.E.2d 776, rehearing denied 45 Ohio St.3d 715, 545 N.E.2d 909.

Where the natural parent of minor children was not represented by counsel during neglect, dependency and temporary custody proceedings but was represented by counsel at the parental rights termination and permanent custody proceedings, such parent is barred from bringing a habeas corpus action more than one year after the final decrees of adoption were issued for the minor children. Beard v Williams County Dept of Social Services, No. WMS-83-3 (6th Dist Ct App, Williams, 7-15-83).

3. Challenge of decree

Natural father's contention, on appeal of adoption order, that record contained no clear and convincing evidence of marriage between child's mother and stepfather, was assigned and briefed but was not addressed at trial, and thus Court of Appeals was not required to address it, but would do so, since matter of adoption was so important. In re Adoption of Lassiter (Clark 1995) 101 Ohio App.3d 367, 655 N.E.2d 781, dismissed, appeal not allowed 73 Ohio St.3d 1410, 651 N.E.2d 1308.

Judgment that consent of natural father was not required for adoption of child by third party was not a final appealable order and, thus, natural father's dismissal of his former appeal on consent ruling was not res judicata regarding consent. In re Adoption of Cline (Trumbull 1993) 89 Ohio App.3d 450, 624 N.E.2d 1083.

Statute providing that decree of adoption is uncontestable after one year applied to biological mother's motion for relief from judgment, not rule of civil procedure governing relief from judgment or order on ground of fraud or misrepresentation, where mother had signed adoption consent form which gave her actual notice of adoption proceedings. In re Rabatin (Geauga 1992) 83 Ohio App.3d 836, 615 N.E.2d 1099.

Where a putative father receives notice of adoption proceedings after they have been instituted, but before the final decree is rendered, and is given an opportunity to contest the adoption, neither RC 3107.16(B) nor In re Adoption of Knipper, 30 App(3d) 214, 30 OBR 371, 507 NE(2d) 436 (Hamilton 1986), apply. In re Adoption of Hart (Lucas 1989) 62 Ohio App.3d 544, 577 N.E.2d 77, motion overruled 45 Ohio St.3d 704, 543 N.E.2d 810.

An adoption decree, defective because it violated a biological parent's due process rights, may be vacated more than four years after the decree was journalized under Civ R 60(B)(5). In re Adoption of Knipper (Hamilton 1986) 30 Ohio App.3d 214, 507 N.E.2d 436, 30 O.B.R. 371.

4. Fraud

Biological mother's consent to adoption was not product of fraud or undue influence; thus, she was not allowed to withdraw her consent after final order of adoption. In re Adoption of Zschach (Ohio 1996) 75 Ohio St.3d 648, 665 N.E.2d 1070, reconsideration denied 76 Ohio St.3d 1410, 666 N.E.2d 569, certiorari denied 117 S.Ct. 582, 136 L.Ed.2d 513.

Biological father's cause of action for fraudulent adoption accrued, for limitations purposes, when he discovered that biological mother of child had placed child for adoption, rather than when court decided that his consent to adoption was not required; elements of cause of action for fraud were established when father was on notice that child might be his and that he could lose his parental rights. Copeland v. Delvaux (Lucas 1993) 89 Ohio App.3d 1, 623 N.E.2d 569, dismissed, jurisdictional motion overruled 67 Ohio St.3d 1510, 622 N.E.2d 657.

Injury, in action for fraudulent adoption, is loss of parenthood. Copeland v. Delvaux (Lucas 1993) 89 Ohio App.3d 1, 623 N.E.2d 569, dismissed, jurisdictional motion overruled 67 Ohio St.3d 1510, 622 N.E.2d 657.

Biological mother's claim of fraud in securing her consent to adoption was not sufficient to exempt her from one-year limitation applicable to challenges to adoption decrees, even if adoptive parents' financial and personal situation may have changed after expiration of one-year period; there was no evidence that mother was unable to understand adoption consent form when she signed it, there was no evidence of fraud or misrepresentation at time of adoption, and there was no evidence of adverse conditions which mother alleged were found by court's investigator. In re Rabatin (Geauga 1992) 83 Ohio App.3d 836, 615 N.E.2d 1099.

5. Paternity

Knowledge of a mother regarding the paternity of her child whom she has put up for adoption cannot be imputed to the prospective adoptive parents. In re Adoption of Hart (Lucas 1989) 62 Ohio App.3d 544, 577 N.E.2d 77, motion overruled 45 Ohio St.3d 704, 543 N.E.2d 810.

3107.161 Contested adoption; factors considered; best interest of child

(A) As used in this section, "the least detrimental available alternative" means the alternative that would have the least long-term negative impact on the child.

(B) When a court makes a determination in a contested adoption concerning the best interest of a child, the court shall consider all relevant factors including, but not limited to, all of the following:

(1) The least detrimental available alternative for safeguarding the child's growth and development;

(2) The age and health of the child at the time the best interest determination is made and, if applicable, at the time the child was removed from the home;

(3) The wishes of the child in any case in which the child's age and maturity makes this feasible;

(4) The duration of the separation of the child from a parent;

(5) Whether the child will be able to enter into a more stable and permanent family relationship, taking into account the conditions of the child's current placement, the likelihood of future placements, and the results of prior placements;

(6) The likelihood of safe reunification with a parent within a reasonable period of time;

(7) The importance of providing permanency, stability, and continuity of relationships for the child;

(8) The child's interaction and interrelationship with the child's parents, siblings, and any other person who may significantly affect the child's best interest;

(9) The child's adjustment to the child's current home, school, and community;

(10) The mental and physical health of all persons involved in the situation;

(11) Whether any person involved in the situation has been convicted of, pleaded guilty to, or accused of any criminal offense involving any act that resulted in a child being abused or neglected; whether the person, in a case in which a child has been adjudicated to be an abused or neglected child, has been determined to be the perpetrator of the abusive or neglectful act that is the basis of the adjudication; whether the person has been convicted of, pleaded guilty to, or accused of a violation of section 2919.25 of the Revised Code involving a victim who at the time of the commission of the offense was a member of the person's family or household; and whether the person has been convicted of, pleaded guilty to, or accused of any offense involving a victim who at the time of the commission of the offense was a member of the person's family or household and caused physical harm to the victim in the commission of the offense.

(C) A person who contests an adoption has the burden of providing the court material evidence needed to determine what is in the best interest of the child and must establish that the child's current placement is not the least detrimental available alternative.

(1996 S 292, eff. 11-6-96; 1996 H 419, eff. 9-18-96)

Uncodified Law

1996 S 292, § 4, eff. 11-6-96, reads: The repeal by this act of division (C) of section 3107.161 of the Revised Code shall not be construed to change the public policy of this state regarding the status of a child in a contested adoption and whether the child may be represented by independent counsel as the public policy existed immediately prior to the enactment of Am. Sub. H.B. 419 of the 121st General Assembly.

Historical and Statutory Notes

Amendment Note: 1996 S 292 added division (A); redesignated former division (A) as division (B); added division (B)(1); redesignated former divisions (A)(1) through (A)(10) as divisions (B)(2) through (B)(11); redesignated former division (B) as division (C); and deleted former division (C), which previously read:

"(C) A child in a contested adoption has full party status and may be represented by independent counsel."

Library References

Am Jur 2d: 2, Adoption § 134 to 147
Required parties in adoption proceedings. 48 ALR4th 860

Baldwin's Ohio Legislative Service, 1996 H 419—LSC Analysis, 3/L-336
Carlin, Baldwin's Ohio Practice, *Merrick-Rippner Probate Law* § 98.2 (1997)

RECORDS

3107.17 Confidentiality; records; access to histories of biological parents; rights of parties concerning proposed correction or expansion; procedures

(A) All hearings held under sections 3107.01 to 3107.19 of the Revised Code shall be held in closed court without the admittance of any person other than essential officers of the court, the parties, the witnesses of the parties, counsel, persons who have not previously consented to an adoption but who are required to consent, and representatives of the agencies present to perform their official duties.

(B)(1) Except as provided in divisions (B)(2) and (D) of this section and sections 3107.39 to 3107.44 and 3107.60 to 3107.68 of the Revised Code, no person or governmental entity shall knowingly reveal any information contained in a paper, book, or record pertaining to a placement under section 5103.16 of the Revised Code or to an adoption that is part of the permanent record of a court or maintained by the department of job and family services, an agency, or attorney without the consent of a court.

(2) An agency or attorney may examine the agency's or attorney's own papers, books, and records pertaining to a placement or adoption without a court's consent for official administrative purposes. The department of job and family services may examine its own papers, books, and records pertaining to a placement or adoption, or such papers, books, and records of an agency, without a court's consent for official administrative, certification, and eligibility determination purposes.

(C) The petition, the interlocutory order, the final decree of adoption, and other adoption proceedings shall be recorded in a book kept for such purposes and shall be separately indexed. The book shall be a part of the records of the court, and all consents, affidavits, and other papers shall be properly filed.

(D) All forms that pertain to the social or medical histories of the biological parents of an adopted person and that were completed pursuant to section 3107.09 or 3107.091 of the Revised Code shall be filed only in the permanent record kept by the court. During the minority of the adopted person, only the adoptive parents of the person may inspect the forms. When an adopted person reaches majority, only the adopted person may inspect the forms. Under the circumstances described in this division, an adopted person or the adoptive parents are entitled to inspect the forms upon requesting the clerk of the court to produce them.

(E)(1) The department of job and family services shall prescribe a form that permits any person who is authorized by division (D) of this section to inspect forms that pertain to the social or medical histories of the biological parents and that were completed pursuant to section 3107.09 or 3107.091 of the Revised Code to request notice if any correction or expansion of either such history, made pursuant to division (D) of section 3107.09 of the Revised Code, is made a part of the permanent record kept by the court. The form shall be designed to facilitate the provision of the information and statements described in division (E)(3) of this section. The department shall provide copies of the form to each court. A court shall provide a copy of the request form to each adoptive parent when a final decree of adoption is entered and shall explain to each adoptive parent at that time that an adoptive parent who completes and files the form will be notified of any correction or expansion of either the social or medical history of the biological parents of the adopted person made during the minority of the adopted person that is made a part of the permanent record kept by the court, and that, during the adopted person's minority, the adopted person may inspect the forms that pertain to those histories. Upon request, the court also shall provide a copy of the request form to any adoptive parent during the minority of the adopted person and to an adopted person who has reached the age of majority.

(2) Any person who is authorized to inspect forms pursuant to division (D) of this section who wishes to be notified of corrections or expansions pursuant to division (D) of section 3107.09 of the Revised Code that are made a part of the permanent record kept by the court shall file with the court, on a copy of the form prescribed by the department of job and family services pursuant to division (E)(1) of this section, a request for such notification that contains the information and statements required by division (E)(3) of this section. A request may be filed at any time if the person who files the request is authorized at that time to inspect forms that pertain to the social or medical histories.

(3) A request for notification as described in division (E)(2) of this section shall contain all of the following information:

(a) The adopted person's name and mailing address at that time;

(b) The name of each adoptive parent, and if the adoptive person is a minor at the time of the filing of the request, the mailing address of each adoptive parent at that time;

(c) The adopted person's date of birth;

(d) The date of entry of the final decree of adoption;

(e) A statement requesting the court to notify the person who files the request, at the address provided in the request, if any correction or expansion of either the social or medical history of the biological parents is made a part of the permanent record kept by the court;

(f) A statement that the person who files the request is authorized, at the time of the filing, to inspect the forms that pertain to the social and medical histories of the biological parents;

(g) The signature of the person who files the request.

(4) Upon the filing of a request for notification in accordance with division (E)(2) of this section, the clerk of the court in which it is filed immediately shall insert the request in the permanent record of the case. A person who has filed the request and who wishes to update it with respect to a new mailing address may inform the court in writing of the new address. Upon its receipt, the court promptly shall insert the new address into the permanent record by attaching it to the request. Thereafter, any notification described in this division shall be sent to the new address.

(5) Whenever a social or medical history of a biological parent is corrected or expanded and the correction or expansion is made a part of the permanent record kept by the court, the court shall ascertain whether a request for notification has been filed in accordance with division (E)(2) of this section. If such a request has been filed, the court shall determine whether, at that time, the person who filed the request is authorized, under division (D) of this section, to inspect the forms that pertain to the social or medical history of the biological parents. If the court determines that the person who filed the request is so authorized, it immediately shall notify the person that the social or medical history has been corrected or expanded, that it has been made a part of the permanent record kept by the court, and that the forms that pertain to the records may be inspected in accordance with division (D) of this section.

(1999 H 471, eff. 7-1-00; 1996 H 419, eff. 9-18-96; 1984 H 84, eff. 3-19-85; 1978 H 832, S 340; 1976 H 156)

Historical and Statutory Notes

Ed. Note: 3107.17 contains provisions analogous to former 3107.14, repealed by 1976 H 156, eff. 1-1-77.

Amendment Note: 1999 H 471 substituted "job and family" for "human" in divisions (B)(1), (B)(2), (E)(1), and (E)(2).

Amendment Note: 1996 H 419 rewrote division (B); deleted "probate" preceding "court" in divisions (C) and (E)(1); substituted "section 3107.09 or 3107.091 of the Revised Code" for "division (D) of section 3107.12 or section 3107.121 of the Revised Code" in division (D); substituted "section 3107.09 or 3107.091 of the Revised Code to request notice if any correction or expansion of either such history, made pursuant to division (D) of section 3107.09 of the Revised Code" for "division (D) of section 3107.12 or section 3107.121 of the Revised Code to request that he be notified if any correction or expansion of either such history, made pursuant to division (D)(4) of section 3107.12 of the Revised Code" in division (E)(1); substituted "division (D) of section 3107.09 of the Revised Code" for "division (D)(4) of section 3107.12 of the Revised Code" in division (E)(2); and made changes to reflect gender neutral language throughout the section. Prior to amendment, former division (B) read:

"(B) All papers, books, and records pertaining to a placement under section 5103.16 of the Revised Code or an adoption, whether part of the permanent record of the court or of a file in the department of human services or in an agency, are, except as provided in division (D) of this section, subject to inspection only upon consent of the court."

Comparative Laws

Idaho—I.C. § 16-1511.
Ill.—ILCS 750 50/18.
Ind.—West's A.I.C. 31-19-19-1 et seq.
Iowa—I.C.A. § 600.24.
Ky.—Baldwin's KRS 199.570.
Mass.—M.G.L.A. c. 210, § 5c.
Me.—18-A M.R.S.A. § 9-310.
Mo.—V.A.M.S. § 453.120.
N.C.—G.S. § 48-25.
N.J.—N.J.S.A. 9:3-51.
Wis.—W.S.A. 48.93.

Cross References

Penalty: 3107.99
Prohibition: 3107.65(A)

Availability of adoption records, 149.43
Courts, confidentiality of adoption files, Sup R 55
Jurisdiction of juvenile court, 2151.23
Maternity hospital record of children given out or adopted, 3711.08
Personal information systems; rights of subjects, or possible subjects, to inspection, 1347.08
Probate court, record and index of adoptions, 2101.12

Ohio Administrative Code References

Adoptive family case record, OAC 5101:2-48-22
Preservation of adoptive child case record, OAC 5101:2-48-23
Requirement of ODHS 1616 "Social and Medical History", OAC 5101:2-48-03

Library References

Infants ⟹133.
Records ⟹17.
WESTLAW Topic Nos. 211, 326.
C.J.S. Criminal Law § 2008.
C.J.S. Infants §§ 57, 69 to 85.
C.J.S. Records § 34.

OJur 3d: 47, Family Law § 931, 936, 937
Am Jur 2d: 2, Adoption § 58
Restricting access to judicial records of concluded adoption proceedings. 83 ALR3d 800
Restricting access to judicial records of pending adoption proceedings. 83 ALR3d 824

Baldwin's Ohio Legislative Service, 1996 H 419—LSC Analysis, 3/L-336
Baldwin's Ohio School Law, Text 44.5
Carlin, Baldwin's Ohio Practice, *Merrick-Rippner Probate Law* § 30.25, 98.2, 98.28, 98.44 (1997)

Law Review and Journal Commentaries

Ohio House Bill 419: Increased Openness in Adoption Records Law, Wendy L. Weiss. 45 Clev St L Rev 101 (1997).

The Open Adoption Records Movement: Constitutional Cases And Legislative Compromise, Note. 26 J Fam L 395 (1987-88).

A Reasonable Approach to the Adoptee's Sealed Record Dilemma, Michael L. Hanley. 2 Ohio N U L Rev 542 (1975).

Secrecy and genetics in adoption law and practice, Demosthenes A. Lorandos. 27 Loy U Chi L J 277 (1996).

Notes of Decisions and Opinions

Confidentiality 2
Contempt 1
Record keeping 3

---

1. Contempt

Contempt proceedings ex parte are a proper means for a court to protect the secrecy of adoption records. State ex rel. Wolff v. Donnelly (Ohio 1986) 24 Ohio St.3d 1, 492 N.E.2d 810, 24 O.B.R. 1.

2. Confidentiality

Trial court's order permitting counsel to inspect and discover contents of adoption records would be affirmed, where actual documents at issue were not before Court of Appeals, and thus it could not be determined whether trial court abused its discretion in permitting counsel to inspect their contents; in absence of adequate record, validity of trial court's action had to be presumed. Cochran v. Northeast Ohio Adoption Serv. (Portage 1993) 85 Ohio App.3d 750, 621 N.E.2d 470.

More specific statute concerning county department of human services records pertaining particularly to adoptions and placements was applicable to issue whether adoption records were confidential and not discoverable, rather than more general statute providing that records required to be kept by such agency be confidential, and open to inspection to other persons only upon written permission of executive secretary. Cochran v. Northeast Ohio Adoption Serv. (Portage 1993) 85 Ohio App.3d 750, 621 N.E.2d 470.

The department of health is under no particular statutory duty to ensure the confidentiality of any adoption records in the possession of local registrars; rather, under RC 3107.17, the department is only obligated to maintain the confidentiality of its own records, and it is not responsible for any adoption records kept by local registrars. Grothouse v. Ohio Dept. of Health (Franklin 1992) 80 Ohio App.3d 258, 608 N.E.2d 1183.

3. Record keeping

Proposed placements by a probate court under RC 5103.16 are "other adoption proceedings" as that phrase is used in RC 3107.14 and, therefore, all papers that are a part of the record in such placement proceedings should be separately recorded and indexed, and kept in the manner provided for under RC 3107.14. (Annotation from former RC 3107.14.) 1962 OAG 2747.

Proceedings in adoption cases should be separately recorded in a book kept for that purpose and separately indexed and should not be journalized or generally recorded. (Annotation from former RC 3107.14.) 1959 OAG 652.

A probate court may make up the record required by RC 2101.12, 3107.14, 5123.37, 5123.38, and 5731.48 by microfilming or other duplication process authorized by RC 9.01, provided the originals are maintained on file and until they are eventually destroyed in accordance with RC 149.38. (Annotation from former RC 3107.14.) 1955 OAG 5667.

3107.18 Recognition of decrees of other jurisdictions and countries

Note: See also following version of this section, eff. 10-10-00.

(A) Except when giving effect to such a decree would violate the public policy of this state, a court decree terminating the relationship of parent and child, or establishing the relationship by adoption, issued pursuant to due process of law by a court of any jurisdiction outside this state, whether within or outside the United States, shall be recognized in this state, and the rights and obligations of the parties as to all matters within the jurisdiction of this state, including without limitation, those matters specified in section 3107.15 of the Revised Code, shall be determined as though the decree were issued by a court of this state. A decree or certificate of adoption that is issued under the laws of a foreign country and that is verified and approved by the immigration and naturalization service of the United States shall be recognized in this state. Nothing in this section prohibits a court from issuing a final decree of adoption or interlocutory order of adoption pursuant to section 3107.14 of the Revised Code for a person the petitioner has adopted pursuant to a decree or certificate of adoption recognized in this state that was issued outside the United States.

(B) If a child born in a foreign country is placed with adoptive parents or an adoptive parent in this state for the purpose of adoption and if the adoption previously has been finalized in the country of the child's birth, the adoptive parent or parents may bring a petition in the probate court in their county of residence, requesting that the court issue a final decree of adoption or an interlocutory order of adoption pursuant to section 3701.14 [*sic*] of the Revised Code. In a proceeding on the petition, proof of finalization of the adoption outside the United States is prima facie evidence of the consent of the parties who are required to give consent even if the foreign decree or certificate of adoption was issued with respect to only one of two adoptive parents who seek to adopt the child in this state.

(C) At the request of a person who has adopted a person pursuant to a decree or certificate of adoption recognized in this state that was issued outside the United States, the court of the county in which the person making the request resides shall order the department of health to issue a foreign birth record for the adopted person under division (A)(4) of section 3705.12 of the Revised Code. The court may specify a change of name for the child and, if a physician has recommended a revision of the birth date, a revised birth date. The court shall send to the department with its order a copy of the foreign adoption decree or certificate of adoption and, if the foreign decree or certificate of adoption is not in English, a translation certified as to its accuracy by the translator and provided by the person who requested the order.

(1996 H 274, eff. 9-18-96; 1996 H 419, eff. 9-18-96; 1996 H 266, eff. 5-15-96; 1976 H 156, eff. 1-1-77)

Note: See also following version of this section, eff. 10-10-00.

3107.18 Recognition of decrees of other jurisdictions and countries

Note: See also preceding version of this section, in effect until 10-10-00.

(A) Except when giving effect to such a decree would violate the public policy of this state, a court decree terminating the relationship of parent and child, or establishing the relationship by adoption, issued pursuant to due process of law by a court of any jurisdiction outside this state, whether within or outside the United States, shall be recognized in this state, and the rights and obligations of the parties as to all matters within the jurisdiction of this state, including, without limitation, those matters specified in section 3107.15 of the Revised Code, shall be determined as though the decree were issued by a court of this state. A decree or certificate of adoption that is issued under the laws of a foreign country and that is verified and approved by the immigration and naturalization service of the United States shall be recognized in this state. Nothing in this section prohibits a court from issuing a final decree of adoption or interlocutory order of adoption pursuant to section 3107.14 of the Revised Code for a person the petitioner has adopted pursuant to a decree or certificate of adoption recognized in this state that was issued outside the United States.

(B) If a child born in a foreign country is placed with adoptive parents or an adoptive parent in this state for the purpose of adoption and if the adoption previously has been finalized in the country of the child's birth, the adoptive parent or parents may bring a petition in the probate court in their county of residence requesting that the court issue a final decree of adoption or an interlocutory order of adoption pursuant to section 3107.14 of the Revised Code. In a proceeding on the petition, proof of finalization of the adoption outside the United States is prima-facie evidence of the consent of the parties who are required to give consent even if the foreign decree or certificate of adoption was issued with respect to only one of two adoptive parents who seek to adopt the child in this state.

(C) At the request of a person who has adopted a person pursuant to a decree or certificate of adoption recognized in this state that was issued outside the United States, the court of the county in which the person making the request resides shall order the department of health to issue a foreign birth record for the adopted person under division (A)(4) of section 3705.12 of the Revised Code. The court may specify a change of name for the child and, if a physician has recommended a revision of the birth date, a revised birth date. The court shall send to the department with its order a copy of the foreign adoption decree or certificate of adoption and, if the foreign decree or certificate of adoption is not in English, a translation certified as to its accuracy by the translator and provided by the person who requested the order.

(2000 S 173, eff. 10-10-00; 1996 H 274, eff. 9-18-96; 1996 H 419, eff. 9-18-96; 1996 H 266, eff. 5-15-96; 1976 H 156, eff. 1-1-77)

Note: See also preceding version of this section, in effect until 10-10-00.

Historical and Statutory Notes

Amendment Note: 2000 S 173 substituted "3107.14" for "3701.14"; and made other nonsubstantive changes.

Amendment Note: 1996 H 274 deleted "of common pleas" before "of the county" in division (C).

Amendment Note: 1996 H 419 designated division (A); added the second and third sentences to division (A); and added divisions (B) and (C).

Amendment Note: 1996 H 266 designated division (A) and added the second and third sentences therein; and added divisions (B) and (C).

Cross References

Adoption registration, issuance of foreign birth record on receipt of order, 3705.12

Interstate compact on placement of children, 5103.22 to 5103.28

Placement of children from other states, 2151.39

Ohio Administrative Code References

Interstate placements of children into or from Ohio, OAC 5101:2-42-20 to 5101:2-42-26

Placement for adoption in Ohio of foreign-born children, OAC 5101:2-42-27

Library References

Adoption ⚷25.
WESTLAW Topic No. 17.
C.J.S. Adoption of Persons §§ 144, 154.

OJur 3d: 47, Family Law § 939
Change of child's name in adoption proceeding. 53 ALR2d 927
Validity and application of statute authorizing change in record of birthplace of adopted child. 14 ALR4th 739

Baldwin's Ohio Legislative Service, 1996 H 419—LSC Analysis, 3/L-336
Carlin, Baldwin's Ohio Practice, *Merrick-Rippner Probate Law* § 98.2, 98.6, 98.51 (1997)
Sowald & Morganstern, Baldwin's Ohio Practice, *Domestic Relations Law* § 3.46 (1997)

Notes of Decisions and Opinions

Exceptions to recognition of foreign decree 1

1. Exceptions to recognition of foreign decree

Mother was not entitled to writ of prohibition to prevent juvenile court judge from proceeding with father's parentage action, based on foreign adoption decree, since foreign adoption law did not require notice to father before adoption of child out-of-wedlock and therefore may not have been enforced under comity as being repugnant to state law, jurisdiction was not divested even if action was barred on res judicata grounds, and inadequacy of postjudgment appeal was not established. State ex rel. Smith v. Smith (Ohio 1996) 75 Ohio St.3d 418, 662 N.E.2d 366.

Recognition and effectiveness of foreign adoption decree are subject to condition that decree not be repugnant to laws of state. State ex rel. Smith v. Smith (Ohio 1996) 75 Ohio St.3d 418, 662 N.E.2d 366.

3107.19 Information forwarded to human services department

If the adopted person was born in this state or outside the United States, the court shall forward all of the following to the department of health within thirty days after an adoption decree becomes final:

(A) A copy of the adopted person's certificate of adoption;

(B) The form prescribed under division (A)(1) of section 3107.083 of the Revised Code, if a parent filled out and signed the form pursuant to section 3107.071, 3107.081, or 5103.151 of the Revised Code;

(C) A statement of whether the adopted person is an adopted person as defined in section 3107.39 or 3107.45 of the Revised Code.

If the adopted person was born in another state of the United States, the court shall forward a copy of the adopted person's certificate of adoption to that state's vital statistics office within thirty days after an adoption decree becomes final.

(1999 H 176, eff. 10-29-99; 1996 H 419, eff. 9-18-96; 1986 H 428, eff. 12-23-86; 1976 H 156)

Historical and Statutory Notes

Ed. Note: 3107.19 is analogous to provisions of former 3107.11, repealed by 1976 H 156, eff. 1-1-77.

Amendment Note: 1999 H 176 deleted "Within thirty days after an adoption decree becomes final, the court shall forward a copy of the decree to the department of human services of this state for statistical purposes." from the beginning of the introductory paragraph; and substituted "within thirty days after an adoption decree becomes final" for "at the time of forwarding the adoption decree to the department of human services" in the introductory and final paragraphs.

Amendment Note: 1996 H 419 rewrote this section, which prior thereto read:

"Within thirty days after an adoption decree becomes final, the clerk of the court shall prepare an application for a birth record of the adopted person and forward the application to the appropriate vital statistics office of the place, if known, where the adopted person was born, and forward a copy of the decree to the department of human services of this state for statistical purposes."

Comparative Laws

Ark.—A.C.A. § 9-9-219.
Mich.—M.C.L.A. § 710.67.

Cross References

Adoption registration, items sent by probate court, 3705.12
Registration of adoptions, status of records as to access, 3705.12

Library References

Health and Environment ⚷34.
WESTLAW Topic No. 199.

C.J.S. Health and Environment § 41.

OJur 3d: 47, Family Law § 938

Change of child's name in adoption proceeding. 53 ALR2d 927

Validity and application of statute authorizing change in record of birthplace of adopted child. 14 ALR4th 739

Baldwin's Ohio Legislative Service, 1996 H 419—LSC Analysis, 3/L-336

Carlin, Baldwin's Ohio Practice, *Merrick-Rippner Probate Law* § 98.2, 98.48 (1997)

ACCESS TO ADOPTION RECORDS BY ADOPTEES

3107.38 Adoptee's written request or petition to see adoption file

(A) As used in this section:

(1) "Adoption file" means the file maintained by the department of health under section 3705.12 of the Revised Code.

(2) "Items of identification" include a motor vehicle driver's or commercial driver's license, an identification card issued under sections 4507.50 to 4507.52 of the Revised Code, a marriage application, a social security card, a credit card, a military identification card, or an employee identification card.

(B) An adopted person whose birth occurred in this state and whose adoption was decreed prior to January 1, 1964, may do either or both of the following:

(1) Submit a written request to the department of health for the department to provide the adopted person with a copy of the contents of the adopted person's adoption file. The request shall provide the adopted person's address, notarized signature, and be accompanied by two items of identification of the adopted person. If the adopted person submits such a request, the fee required by section 3705.241 of the Revised Code is paid, and the department has an adoption file for the adopted person, the department shall mail to the adopted person, at the address provided in the request, a copy of the contents of the adopted person's adoption file.

(2) File a petition pursuant to section 3107.41 of the Revised Code for the release of information regarding the adopted person's name by birth and the identity of the adopted person's biological parent and biological sibling.

(1996 H 419, eff. 9-18-96)

Cross References

Adoption registration, release of file contents, 3705.12

Fees for copying adoption file, contents, 3705.241

Library References

Am Jur 2d: 2, Adoption § 207 to 211

Restricting access to judicial records of concluded adoption proceedings. 83 ALR3d 800

Baldwin's Ohio Legislative Service, 1996 H 419—LSC Analysis, 3/L-336

3107.39 Definitions

As used in sections 3107.39 to 3107.44 of the Revised Code:

(A) "Adopted person" means a person who, as a minor, was adopted and who, prior to September 18, 1996, became available or potentially available for adoption. For the purpose of this division, a person was available or potentially available for adoption prior to September 18, 1996, if, prior to that date, either of the following occurred:

(1) At least one of the person's biological parents executed consent to person's adoption;

(2) A probate court entered a finding that the consent of at least one of the person's biological parents to the person's adoption was not needed as determined pursuant to section 3107.07 of the Revised Code.

(B) "Adopted sibling" means an adopted person who has a biological sibling.

(C) "Agency" means any public or private organization that is certified by the department of job and family services to place minors for adoption.

(D) "Biological parent" means a parent, by birth, of an adopted person.

(E) "Biological sibling" means a sibling, by birth, of an adopted person.

(F) "Effective release" means a release that is filed by a biological parent or biological sibling of an adopted person, and with respect to which a withdrawal of release has not been filed by that biological parent or biological sibling.

(G) "File of releases" means the file that is established by the department of health pursuant to division (C) of section 3107.40 of the Revised Code.

(H) "Final decree of adoption" includes an interlocutory order of adoption that has become final.

(I) "Identifying information" has the same meaning as in section 3107.01 of the Revised Code.

(J) "Offspring" means a child, by birth, of a person.

(K) "Petition for release of information" means the petition filed in a probate court in accordance with section 3107.41 of the Revised Code.

(L) "Release" means the form that is filed, pursuant to division (B) of section 3107.40 of the Revised Code, by a biological parent or biological sibling with the department of health and that contains the information, statement, and matter required by division (B)(3) of that section.

(M) "Withdrawal of release" means the form that is filed, pursuant to division (D) of section 3107.40 of the Revised Code, by a biological parent or biological sibling with the department of health and that contains the information, statement, and matter required by division (D)(3) of that section.

(1999 H 471, eff. 7-1-00; 1996 H 419, eff. 9-18-96; 1988 H 790, eff. 3-16-89; 1984 H 84)

Historical and Statutory Notes

Amendment Note: 1999 H 471 substituted "September 18, 1996" for "the effective date of this amendment" twice in the introductory paragraph in division (A); and substituted "job and family" for "human" in division (C).

Amendment Note: 1996 H 419 rewrote this section, which prior thereto read:

"As used in sections 3107.39 to 3107.44 of the Revised Code:

"(A) 'Adopted person' means a person who, as a minor, was adopted pursuant to a final decree of adoption entered by a court.

"(B) 'Agency' means any public or private organization that is certified by the department of human services to place minors for adoption.

"(C) 'Biological parent' means a parent, by birth, of an adopted person and, for purposes of section 3107.40 of the Revised Code, includes a parent, by birth, of a minor who has been placed for adoption.

"(D) 'Biological sibling' means a sibling, by birth, of an adopted person and, for purposes of section 3107.40 of the Revised Code, includes a sibling, by birth, of a minor who has been placed for adoption.

"(E) 'Effective release' means a release that is filed by a biological parent or biological sibling of an adopted person, and with respect to which a withdrawal of release has not been filed by that biological parent or biological sibling.

"(F) 'File of releases' means the file that is established by the department of health pursuant to division (C) of section 3107.40 of the Revised Code.

"(G) 'Final decree of adoption' includes an interlocutory order of adoption that has become final.

"(H) 'Identifying information' means information that is described in either of the following categories:

"(1) Information that is likely to assist an adopted person in identifying his name by birth or one or both of his biological parents and that is described in any of the following categories:

"(a) The information is contained in the copy of the adopted person's original birth record that is obtained by an agency pursuant to an order of a probate judge to the department of health to provide the agency with a copy of the person's original birth record.

"(b) If the probate court in which the petition for release of identifying information is filed is the court that entered the final decree of adoption in the adoption proceedings pertaining to the adopted person, the information is contained in the adoption records of that court. Such information includes, but is not limited to, the addresses of the adopted person's biological parents at the time of the entry of the decree.

"(c) The information is contained in a release filed by a biological parent of the adopted person and is obtained by an agency pursuant to division (B)(2) of section 3107.41 of the Revised Code.

"(d) The information is contained in a probate court's or agency's records and relates to any deceased biological parent of the adopted person.

"(2) If the adopted person's original birth record contains the name of only one of his biological parents, a statement that informs the adopted person of this fact.

"'Identifying information' does not include information that pertains to a biological sibling of the adopted person.

"(I) 'Offspring' means a child, by birth, of a person.

"(J) 'Adopted sibling' means a sibling, by birth, of a person who has been adopted or in relation to whom an adoption petition has been filed.

"(K) 'Petition for release of information' means the petition filed in a probate court in accordance with section 3107.41 of the Revised Code.

"(L) 'Release' means the form that is filed, pursuant to division (B) of section 3107.40 of the Revised Code, by a biological parent or biological sibling with the department of health and that contains the information, statement, and matter required by division (B)(3) of that section.

"(M) 'Withdrawal of release' means the form that is filed, pursuant to division (D) of section 3107.40 of the Revised Code, by a biological parent or biological sibling with the department of health and that contains the information, statement, and matter required by division (D)(3) of that section."

Cross References

Assessor's meeting with birth parent prior to parent's consenting to adoption, adopted person defined, 5103.152

Conditions for juvenile court approving parent's agreement for child's adoption, adopted person defined, 5103.151

Probate court, procedure; adoption information, fees, 2101.16

Library References

Records ⚷32 to 34, 50 to 68.
WESTLAW Topic No. 326.
C.J.S. Records §§ 63 to 65, 67 to 75, 86, 93 to 131.

OJur 3d: 47, Family Law § 937

Baldwin's Ohio Legislative Service, 1996 H 419—LSC Analysis, 3/L-336

Carlin, Baldwin's Ohio Practice, *Merrick-Rippner Probate Law* § 98.1, 98.28 (1997)

Law Review and Journal Commentaries

Ohio House Bill 419: Increased Openness in Adoption Records Law, Wendy L. Weiss. 45 Clev St L Rev 101 (1997).

3107.40 Release of identifying information; consent of biological parents or siblings; procedures; withdrawal of release

(A) The department of health shall prescribe a form that permits any biological parent to authorize the release of identifying information, in accordance with section 3107.41 of the Revised Code, to the biological parent's offspring and a form that permits any biological sibling to authorize the release of specified information, in accordance with section 3107.41 of the Revised Code, to the biological sibling's adopted sibling. The forms shall be designed in a manner that permits the biological parent or biological sibling, whichever is applicable, to supply the information, statement, and matter required by division (B)(3) of this section. The department shall prepare written instructions that explain to biological parents and biological siblings the manner in which the applicable form is to be completed; the information, statement, and matter required by division (B)(3) of this section; and the manner in which the completed form is to be filed by a biological parent or biological sibling with the department.

The department shall provide copies of the forms and the instructions to agencies located in, and to the probate courts of, this state. Upon request of any biological parent or biological sibling, the department shall provide the parent or sibling with a copy of the applicable form and the instructions. If an agency or a probate court has copies of the applicable form and the instructions available, the agency or probate court shall provide, upon request, a copy of the applicable form and the instructions to any biological parent or biological sibling.

(B)(1) Any biological parent or biological sibling who wishes to obtain a copy of the applicable form prescribed and the instructions prepared by the department pursuant to division (A) of this section, may obtain them from the department or from an agency located in, or a probate court of, this state, if the agency or probate court has copies of the form and instructions available.

(2) Any biological parent who wishes to authorize the release of identifying information, in accordance with section 3107.41 of the Revised Code, to the biological parent's offspring, and any biological sibling who wishes to authorize the release of specified information, in accordance with section 3107.41 of the Revised Code, to the biological sibling's adopted sibling shall file with the department, on a copy of the applicable form prescribed by it pursuant to division

(A) of this section, a release that contains the information, statement, and matter required by division (B)(3) of this section. A release may be filed with the department at any time.

(3) A release shall contain at least the following:

(a) For a biological parent:

(i) The complete name of the biological parent who is filing the release, at the time of its filing with the department and at the time the adoption petition for the biological parent's offspring was filed, if the biological parent knows when the petition was filed;

(ii) The complete name and date of birth, as set forth in the original birth record, of the offspring of the biological parent to whom the biological parent authorizes the release of identifying information in accordance with section 3107.41 of the Revised Code;

(iii) A statement authorizing the release of identifying information, in accordance with section 3107.41 of the Revised Code, to that offspring;

(iv) The written signature of the biological parent, the biological parent's residential mailing address, and the date upon which the release is filed with the department.

(b) For a biological sibling:

(i) The complete name of the biological sibling who is filing the release, at the time of its filing with the department and at the time the adoption petition for the biological sibling's adopted sibling was filed, if the biological sibling knows when the petition was filed;

(ii) The complete name and date of birth, as set forth in the original birth record, of the adopted sibling to whom the biological sibling authorizes the release of the specified information in accordance with section 3107.41 of the Revised Code;

(iii) A statement authorizing the release of the information specified in the release, in accordance with section 3107.41 of the Revised Code, to that adopted sibling;

(iv) The signature of the biological sibling, the biological sibling's residential mailing address, and the date upon which the release is filed with the department.

(4)(a) A release of a biological parent also may contain information that is not required by division (B)(3)(a) of this section and that the biological parent wishes to reveal, in accordance with section 3107.41 of the Revised Code, to the biological parent's offspring. This information shall not include information pertaining to the other biological parent of the offspring or information pertaining to a biological sibling of the offspring.

(b) A release of a biological sibling also may contain information that is not required by division (B)(3)(b) of this section and that the biological sibling wishes to reveal, in accordance with section 3107.41 of the Revised Code, to the biological sibling's adopted sibling. This information shall not include information pertaining to either biological parent of the adopted person or information pertaining to any biological sibling of the adopted person other than the sibling filing the release.

(C) The department shall establish and maintain a file of releases that shall be organized in the manner described in this section and be used in accordance with section 3107.41 of the Revised Code. If any biological parent or biological sibling files with the department a release that has been completed in accordance with the applicable provisions of division (B) of this section, the department shall accept it and place it in the file of releases in accordance with this division.

The department shall place each release accepted pursuant to this division in the file of releases in alphabetical order, according to the surname of the offspring or adopted sibling to whom it pertains, as set forth in the release. The department shall maintain an index to the file of releases that shall list each offspring and each adopted sibling in alphabetical order, according to the surname set forth in the release. The department also shall maintain a separate, alphabetical index to the file of releases that shall list each biological parent and each biological sibling who files a release according to the biological parent's or biological sibling's name at the time of the filing of the release or, if the release indicates that the biological parent or biological sibling had a different name at the time of the filing of an adoption petition, according to the biological parent's or biological sibling's name at that time; and that shall cross-reference each biological parent and each biological sibling listing to the listing of the biological parent's offspring or biological sibling's adopted sibling, whichever is applicable, that is contained in the other index to the file of releases.

(D)(1) The department of health shall prescribe a form that permits any biological parent or biological sibling who has filed a release with the department pursuant to division (B) of this section to withdraw the release. The form shall be designed in a manner that permits the biological parent or biological sibling to supply the information, statement, and matter required by division (D)(3) of this section. Upon request of any biological parent or biological sibling who has filed a release with the department pursuant to division (B) of this section, the department shall provide a copy of the form to the biological parent or biological sibling.

(2) At any time after filing a release with the department, a biological parent or biological sibling may withdraw the release by filing with the department, on a form prescribed by it pursuant to division (D)(1) of this section, a withdrawal of release that contains the information, statement, and matter required by division (D)(3) of this section.

(3) A withdrawal of release shall contain all the following:

(a) The information that the biological parent set forth in the release in accordance with divisions (B)(3)(a)(i) and (ii) of this section, or that the biological sibling set forth in the release in accordance with divisions (B)(3)(b)(i) and (ii) of this section, whichever is applicable;

(b) A statement withdrawing the authorization of the biological parent to release identifying information, in accordance with section 3107.41 of the Revised Code, to the biological parent's offspring, or withdrawing the authorization of the biological sibling to release specified information, in accordance with section 3107.41 of the Revised Code, to the biological sibling's adopted sibling, whichever is applicable;

(c) The written signature of the biological parent or biological sibling, the biological parent's or biological sibling's residential mailing address, and the date upon which the withdrawal of release is filed with the department.

(4) If any biological parent or biological sibling who previously filed a release with the department, files with the department a withdrawal of release that has been completed in accordance with division (D)(3) of this section, the department shall accept the withdrawal of release and place it in the file of releases together with and attached to the release previously filed by the biological parent or biological sibling. Upon request of the biological parent or biological sibling, the department shall provide the biological parent or biological sibling with a copy of the withdrawal of release.

Upon the withdrawal of a release, the department shall note in the index to the file of releases that lists each biological parent and biological sibling who files a release, the fact that the biological parent or biological sibling has filed the withdrawal of release. This notation shall be placed in the index next to the biological parent's or biological sibling's name and the cross-reference to the listing of the biological parent's offspring or the biological sibling's adopted sibling in the other index to the file of releases.

(1996 H 419, eff. 9-18-96; 1988 H 790, eff. 3-16-89; 1984 H 84)

Historical and Statutory Notes

Amendment Note: 1996 H 419 deleted divisions (A)(1) and (2) and redesignated division (A)(3) as division (A); rewrote divisions (B)(3)(a)(i) and (B)(3)(b)(i); and made changes to reflect gender neutral language. Prior to amendment, divisions (A)(1) and (2), (B)(3)(a)(i) and (B)(3)(b)(i), respectively, read:

"(A)(1) The department of human services shall prescribe the procedure to be used by agencies for informing the biological parents of their right to file a form that permits them to authorize the release of identifying information to their offspring, in accordance with section 3107.41 of the Revised Code. The procedure shall include instructions for advising the biological parents of their right to authorize the release of identifying information at the time of the transfer of permanent custody, in accordance with section 5103.15 or Chapter 2151. of the Revised Code, or when a consent to adoption is filed, whichever occurs first.

"(2) A probate court that is acting upon an application filed pursuant to section 5103.16 of the Revised Code shall prescribe the procedure for notification of the biological parents of their right to file a form that permits them to authorize the release of identifying information to their offspring, in accordance with section 3107.41 of the Revised Code.

* * *

"(i) The complete name of the biological parent who is filing the release, at the time of its filing with the department; and, if prior to the filing of the release, an adoption petition has been filed or a final decree of adoption entered relative to the offspring described in division (B)(3)(a)(ii) of this section, and the biological parent is aware of the adoption proceedings, the complete name of that biological parent at the time of the filing of the adoption petition;

* * *

"(i) The complete name of the biological sibling who is filing the release, at the time of its filing with the department and, if prior to the filing of the release, an adoption petition has been filed or a final decree of adoption entered regarding the adopted sibling described in division (B)(3)(b)(ii) of this section and the biological sibling is aware of the adoption proceedings, the complete name of that biological sibling at the time of the filing of the adoption petition[.]"

Cross References

Availability of public records, 149.43
Courts, confidentiality of adoption files, Sup R 55
Probate court, procedure; adoption information, fees, 2101.16
Registration of adoption, original birth record no longer a public record, 3705.12

Ohio Administrative Code References

Release of identifying and nonidentifying information, OAC 5101:2-48-17

Library References

Records ⟹32.
WESTLAW Topic No. 326.
C.J.S. Records §§ 65, 67 to 75.

OJur 3d: 47, Family Law § 937

Baldwin's Ohio Legislative Service, 1996 H 419—LSC Analysis, 3/L-336
Carlin, Baldwin's Ohio Practice, *Merrick-Rippner Probate Law* § 98.1, 98.28 (1997)

Law Review and Journal Commentaries

Ohio House Bill 419: Increased Openness in Adoption Records Law, Wendy L. Weiss. 45 Clev St L Rev 101 (1997).

3107.41 Rights of an adult who believes he is an adopted person; birth record; procedures

(A)(1) Any person who is twenty-one years of age or older and who believes he is an adopted person may file a petition for the release of information regarding his name by birth, and the identity of his biological parents and biological siblings, as follows:

(a) If the person is a resident of this state, the petition shall be filed in the probate court of the county in which he resides or in the probate court that entered the final decree of adoption in the adoption proceedings pertaining to him;

(b) If the person is not a resident of this state, the petition shall be filed in the probate court that entered the final decree of adoption in the adoption proceedings pertaining to him, or, if the person does not know which probate court entered that decree, in the probate court of any county.

(2) The petition shall be accompanied by the fee that the probate court has fixed pursuant to division (E) of section 2101.16 of the Revised Code.

(B)(1) Upon the filing of a petition for the release of such information and the payment of the fee fixed by the probate court, the probate judge to whom the petition is assigned shall do each of the following:

(a) Appoint the agency that was involved in the adoption proceeding to perform the tasks described in divisions (B)(2), (C), and (D) of this section, or if no agency was involved in the proceeding, it is not possible to determine the agency involved, or the court determines that it is not feasible for the agency involved in the proceeding to perform those tasks, appoint any agency to perform those tasks;

(b) Issue an order to the department of health that requires it to provide the agency appointed pursuant to division (B)(1)(a) of this section with a copy of the original birth record of the petitioner or with the identity of the court involved in the petitioner's adoption if the department does not possess the original birth record of the petitioner;

(c) Give a certified copy of the order issued pursuant to division (B)(1)(b) of this section to the appointed agency;

(d) Require the appointed agency to perform the tasks described in division (B)(2) of this section within the time that the judge shall prescribe, which time shall be no later than ninety days from the date of appointment or as extended by the judge for good cause shown.

(2)(a) An agency appointed pursuant to division (B)(1) of this section shall present, by mail or in another reasonable manner, the certified copy of the order issued pursuant to division (B)(1) of this section to the department of health. Upon receipt of the order, the department shall provide the agency with a copy of the original birth record of the petitioner, if any. If the department possesses no original birth record of the petitioner, it shall inform the agency, in writing, of this fact and shall provide the agency with the identity of the court that was involved in the petitioner's adoption, and the agency, upon receipt of this information, shall present, by mail or in another reasonable manner, a copy of the order issued pursuant to division (B)(1) of this section and a copy of the information provided by the department to that court and shall request the court to provide the agency with a copy of the original birth record of the petitioner. Upon receipt of the copy of the order and the copy of the information provided by the department, the court shall provide the agency with a copy of the original birth record of the petitioner, if any. If the court possesses no copy of the original birth record of the petitioner, it shall inform the agency of this fact, and, if the court determines that the petitioner was born outside of this state, the department also shall inform the agency of the petitioner's state of birth and shall provide the agency with any pertinent information contained in its file that normally is noted on a birth record in this state.

(b) If the agency receives a copy of the petitioner's original birth record, it shall inspect the record. If the agency determines, upon the inspection, that the petitioner is not an adopted person, it shall report this determination to the probate court in writing. If it determines, upon the inspection, that the petitioner is an adopted person, it shall contact the department of health and request the department to determine whether the file of releases contains a release or releases filed by one or both of the petitioner's biological parents and authorizing the release of identifying information to him, to determine whether the file of releases contains a release or releases filed by any biological sibling of the petitioner and authorizing the release of specified information to him, to determine whether a withdrawal of release also has been filed with respect to any such release, and to provide the agency with a copy of each release with respect to which a withdrawal of release has not been filed. If the agency determines, upon the inspection, that the petitioner is an adopted person, the agency also shall review its records to determine whether they indicate that one or both of the petitioner's biological parents as indicated on the petitioner's original birth record are deceased.

Upon receipt of an agency's request as described in this division, the department of health shall search the file of releases to determine whether it contains a release or releases filed by one or both of the petitioner's biological parents and authorizing the release of identifying information to him, to determine whether it contains a release or releases filed by any biological sibling of the petitioner and authorizing the release of specified information to him, and to determine whether a withdrawal of release also has been filed with respect to any such release. The department promptly shall inform the agency, in writing, of its findings and provide the agency with a copy of each such release with respect to which a withdrawal of release has not been filed.

(c) If the department of health informs an agency either that the file of releases does not contain a release or releases filed by one or both of the petitioner's biological parents that authorize the release of identifying information to him and does not contain a release or releases filed by any biological sibling of the petitioner that authorize the release of specified information to him or that it contains at least one such release but a withdrawal of release has been filed that negates each such release, the agency shall report its determination that the petitioner is an adopted person and the findings of the department to the probate court, in writing, and shall attach to the report the copy of the petitioner's original birth record. If the department informs the agency that the file of releases contains a release or releases filed by one or both of the petitioner's biological parents that authorize the release of identifying information to him for which no withdrawal has been filed or contains a release or releases filed by any biological sibling of the petitioner for which no withdrawal has been filed, and provides the agency with a copy of each such release, the agency shall report its determination that the petitioner is an adopted person and the findings of the department to the probate court, in writing, and shall attach to the report the copy of the petitioner's original birth record and the copy of each release provided by the department. In either case, if the agency after its review of records, has determined that one or both of the petitioner's biological parents as indicated on the petitioner's original birth record are deceased, the agency also shall report that fact to the probate court, in writing, and shall identify the deceased parent or parents.

If the department informs the agency that it possesses no original birth record of the petitioner, the agency shall report that fact and the identity of the court that was involved in the petitioner's adoption, as provided by the department, to the probate court, in writing; if the court that was involved in the adoption informs the agency that it possesses no copy of the original birth record of the petitioner, the agency also shall report that fact to the probate court, in writing; and if the court that was involved in the adoption informs the agency that the petitioner was born outside of this state, the agency also shall report that fact and the identity of the other state to the probate court, in writing.

(d) An agency shall perform all tasks required of it by division (B)(2) of this section within the time prescribed by the probate judge pursuant to division (B)(1)(d) of this section.

(C) Upon receipt of an agency's report submitted pursuant to division (B)(2) of this section, the probate judge shall review the records of the court to determine whether they indicate that one or both of the petitioner's biological parents as indicated on the petitioner's original birth record are deceased, and shall do whichever of the following is appropriate:

(1) If the agency determined that the petitioner is not an adopted person, or if no original birth record was possessed by the department of health and no copy of such record was possessed by the court that was involved in the petitioner's adoption, the judge shall enter an order dismissing the petition, which order shall state the reason for the dismissal.

(2) If the agency determined that the petitioner is an adopted person, if the department of health informed the agency either that the file of releases does not contain a release or releases filed by one or both of the petitioner's biological parents that authorize the release of identifying information to him and does not contain a release or releases filed by any biological sibling that authorizes the release of specified information to him or that the file of releases contains at least one such release but a withdrawal of release has been filed that negates each such release, if the agency did not inform the court that it had determined that one or both of the petitioner's biological parents as indicated on the petitioner's original birth record were deceased, and if the court did not determine that one or both of the petitioner's biological parents as indicated on that record were deceased, the judge shall order that the petition remain pending until withdrawn by the petitioner and order the department of health to note its pendency in the file of releases according to the surname of the petitioner as set forth in his original birth record; shall inform the petitioner that he is an adopted person and, if known, of the county in which the adoption proceedings occurred; shall inform the petitioner that information regarding his name by birth and the identity of his biological parents and biological siblings may not be released at that time because the file of releases at that time does not contain an effective release that authorizes the release of any such information to him; and shall inform the petitioner that, upon the subsequent filing of a release by or the death of either of his biological parents, or the subsequent filing of a release by any of his biological

siblings, the petition will be acted upon within thirty days of the filing in accordance with division (E) of this section.

(3) If the agency determined that the petitioner is an adopted person and either the agency informed the court that it had determined that one or both of the petitioner's biological parents as indicated on the petitioner's original birth record were deceased or the court determined that one or both of the petitioner's biological parents as indicated on that record were deceased, the judge shall proceed as follows:

(a) The judge shall inform the petitioner that he is an adopted person and, if known, of the county in which the adoption proceedings occurred;

(b) The judge shall inform the petitioner that one or both of his biological parents, whichever is applicable, is deceased, provided that the information provided under this requirement shall not identify either biological parent of the petitioner;

(c) If two biological parents were indicated on the petitioner's original birth record, if only one of those biological parents is deceased, and if an effective release of the surviving biological parent that authorizes the release of identifying information to the petitioner was provided the agency by the department of health, the judge shall comply with division (C)(4) of this section in relation to the surviving biological parent, and the judge may enter an order granting the petition in relation to the deceased biological parent and requiring the agency and the department of health to release identifying information in relation to the deceased biological parent, subject to the limitations of division (D)(2) of this section and within the time prescribed by the judge;

(d) If two biological parents were indicated on the petitioner's original birth record, if only one of those biological parents is deceased, and if either no effective release of the surviving biological parent that authorizes the release of identifying information to the petitioner is contained in the file of releases or such an effective release is contained in the file but the judge does not enter an order of a type described in division (C)(3)(c) of this section, the judge shall inform the petitioner that one of his biological parents is deceased, shall order that the petition remain pending until withdrawn by the petitioner and order the department of health to note its pendency in the file of releases according to the surname of the petitioner as set forth in his original birth record, and shall inform the petitioner that upon the subsequent filing of a release by or the death of the surviving biological parent, the petition will be acted on in accordance with division (E) of this section;

(e) If two biological parents were indicated on the petitioner's original birth record and both of them are deceased or if only one biological parent was indicated on that record and is deceased, the judge may enter an order granting the petition in relation to each such deceased biological parent and requiring the agency and the department of health to release identifying information in relation to each such deceased biological parent to the petitioner, subject to the limitations of division (D)(2) of this section and within the time prescribed by the judge; if the judge does not enter such an order the petition shall be dismissed;

(f) The judge shall comply with division (C)(4)(d) of this section in relation to any biological sibling of the petitioner who has filed a release that authorizes the release of information to the petitioner and that has not been withdrawn.

(4) If the agency determined that the petitioner is an adopted person and the department of health provided the agency with a copy of each release that authorizes the release of identifying information or specified information to him, the judge shall do each of the following that applies:

(a) Enter an order granting the petition in relation to each biological parent who has filed a release that has not been withdrawn;

(b) Inform the petitioner that he is an adopted person and, if known, of the county in which the adoption proceedings occurred;

(c) In relation to a biological parent:

(i) Require the agency to release identifying information to the petitioner, subject to the limitations of division (D)(2) of this section and within the time prescribed by the judge;

(ii) If an effective release of only one of the petitioner's biological parents that authorizes the release of information to him is contained in the file of releases and either the agency has informed the court that it has determined that the other biological parent is deceased or the court has determined that the other biological parent is deceased, comply with division (C)(3) of this section in relation to the deceased biological parent;

(iii) If an effective release of only one of the petitioner's biological parents that authorizes the release of identifying information to him is contained in the file of releases, if the agency has not informed the court that it has determined that the other biological parent is deceased, and if the court has not determined that the other biological parent is deceased, order that the petition remain pending as to the other biological parent until withdrawn by the petitioner and order the department of health to note its pendency in the file of releases according to the surname of the petitioner as set forth in his original birth record, and inform the petitioner that, upon the subsequent filing of a release by or the death of that biological parent or the filing of a release by any biological sibling, the petition will be acted upon within thirty days of the filing in accordance with division (E) of this section.

(d) In relation to a biological sibling:

(i) If the agency or the court has determined that each biological parent indicated on the petitioner's original birth record is deceased or has filed a release authorizing the release of identifying information to the petitioner that has not been withdrawn, enter an order granting the petition in relation to the biological sibling, require the agency to release the information specified in the biological sibling's release to the petitioner, subject to the limitations of division (D)(2) of this section and within the time prescribed by the judge;

(ii) Order that the petition remain pending until withdrawn by the petitioner and order the department of health to note its pendency in the file of releases according to the surname of the petitioner as set forth in his original birth record, and inform the petitioner that, upon the subsequent filing of a release by any biological sibling or biological parent whose effective release is not contained in the file, the petition will be acted upon within thirty days in accordance with division (E) of this section.

(D)(1) Each agency that is required by an order of a probate judge entered under division (C)(3) or (4) of this section to release information to a petitioner shall do both of the following:

(a) Gather all the information that is subject to the order that it is permitted to release;

(b) Subject to the limitations of division (D)(2) of this section and within the time prescribed by the judge, release to the petitioner the information that is subject to the order that it is permitted to release.

(2)(a) Except as otherwise provided in this division, if a biological parent of a petitioner is deceased or an effective release of a biological parent of a petitioner is contained in the file of releases, and an agency is required by an order of a probate judge entered under division (C)(3) or (4) of this section to release identifying information pertaining to that biological parent to the petitioner, the agency shall not release to the petitioner any identifying information pertaining to a surviving biological parent who filed a withdrawal of release, a surviving biological parent who did not file a release, or a deceased biological parent other than in the circumstances described in division (C)(3) of this section, or any information pertaining to a biological sibling of the petitioner. The agency shall release identifying information pertaining to any biological parent of the petitioner who the probate court's or agency's records indicates is deceased in accordance with an order to do so issued under division (C)(3) of this section, and if a biological sibling has filed an effective release, shall release the information specified in the release, in accordance with any order issued under division (C)(4) of this section requiring the release.

(b) Except as otherwise provided in this division, if an effective release of a biological sibling of a petitioner is in the file of releases and an agency is required by an order of a probate judge entered under division (C)(4) of this section to release information specified in the release of that biological sibling to the petitioner, the agency shall not release to the petitioner any information pertaining to a biological sibling of the petitioner who filed a withdrawal of release or who did not file a release, or any identifying information pertaining to a biological parent of the petitioner. The agency shall release identifying information pertaining to any biological parent of the petitioner who the probate court's or agency's records indicate is deceased in accordance with an order to do so issued under division (C)(3) of this section, and shall release identifying information pertaining to any biological parent who has filed an effective release, in accordance with any order issued by a probate judge under division (C)(4) of this section requiring the release of identifying information.

(E) The petition of a petitioner to whom no information is released in relation to a biological parent in accordance with an order entered pursuant to division (C)(2) of this section, or in accordance with division (C)(3) or (4) of this section, shall remain pending until withdrawn by the petitioner. The petition of a petitioner to whom identifying information is released concerning only one biological parent in accordance with an order entered pursuant to division (C)(3) or (4) of this section shall remain pending as to the other biological parent and as to biological siblings until withdrawn by the petitioner. At the same time as it enters the order under division (C)(2), (3), or (4) of this section, the probate court in which the petition is pending shall order the department of health promptly to provide both the agency appointed pursuant to division (B)(1) of this section and the court with a copy of each release that subsequently is filed by one or both of the petitioner's biological parents, or by the petitioner's other biological parent, whichever is applicable, or by a biological sibling of the petitioner, and that authorizes the release of identifying information to the petitioner, and promptly to notify the agency and the court of the death of a surviving biological parent as indicated on the petitioner's original birth record for whom no identifying information had been released relative to the petition for release, of which the department gains knowledge. Upon receipt of a copy of any such release or of notice of the death of any such biological parent, the probate judge, within thirty days of the date on which the release was filed with the department or the date on which the department gained knowledge of the death, shall do each thing listed in divisions (C)(3)(a) to (f) or (4)(a) to (d) of this section that applies.

Any petitioner who has filed a petition with the probate court that is to remain pending under this division and who wishes to update it with respect to a new mailing address may inform the department in writing, through the court, of the new address. The court shall promptly file the writing with the department and provide the department with the petitioner's name as set forth in his original birth record. The department shall attach the writing to the notation of pendency of the petition contained in the file of releases. Any petitioner who has filed a petition with the probate court that is to remain pending under this division may file a written withdrawal of the petition with the court at any time. Upon the filing of such a withdrawal, the court shall enter an order dismissing the petition, and shall notify both the agency appointed pursuant to division (B)(1) of this section and the department of health of the withdrawal, and upon receipt of such a notice, the department does not have to provide copies of any subsequently filed releases to the agency or the court, as otherwise would be required by this division.

(F) An agency that performs any task described in this division relative to or in connection with a petition for the release of identifying information filed under this section may be reimbursed a reasonable portion of the fee charged for the filing of that petition, in accordance with division (D) of section 2101.16 of the Revised Code, for any services it renders in performing any such task.

(1989 S 46, eff. 1-1-90; 1988 H 790; 1984 H 84)

Cross References

Adoption information, jurisdiction of probate court, 2101.24
Availability of public records, 149.43
Certificate of adoption for person born in foreign country, inspection; registration of adoption, new birth record issued, 3705.12
Courts, confidentiality of adoption files, Sup R 55
Department of job and family services, division of social administration; care and placement of children; interstate compact on placement of children, 5103.09 to 5103.17, 5103.20 to 5103.28
Placement of children from other states, 2151.39
Powers and duties of county children services board, 5153.16
Probate court, procedure, adoption information, fees, 2101.16
Registration of births, 3705.09

Library References

Records ⚷32 to 34, 50 to 68.
WESTLAW Topic No. 326.
C.J.S. Records §§ 63 to 65, 67 to 75, 86, 93 to 131.
Carlin, Baldwin's Ohio Practice, *Merrick-Rippner Probate Law* § 98.1, 98.28 (1997)

OJur 3d: 47, Family Law § 937

3107.42 Records declared not public

(A) The following records are not public records subject to inspection or copying under section 149.43 of the Revised Code:

(1) The file of releases;

(2) The indices to the file of releases;

(3) Releases and withdrawals of releases in the file of releases, and information contained in them;

(4) Probate court and agency records pertaining to proceedings under sections 3107.39 to 3107.44 of the Revised Code.

(B) No adopted person who is the subject of personal information contained in a record listed in division (A) of this section may inspect or copy all or part of any such record.

(1984 H 84, eff. 3-19-85)

Cross References

Availability of public records, 149.43
Courts, confidentiality of adoption files, Sup R 55
Personal information systems, rights of subjects or possible subjects to inspection, 1347.08

Library References

Records ⚷32 to 34.
WESTLAW Topic No. 326.
C.J.S. Records §§ 63 to 65, 67 to 75, 86.

OJur 3d: 80, Records and Recording § 22

Baldwin's Ohio School Law, Text 44.2, 44.5

Carlin, Baldwin's Ohio Practice, *Merrick-Rippner Probate Law* § 98.1, 98.28 (1997)
Gotherman & Babbit, Ohio Municipal Law, Text 6.12(A)
Ohio Administrative Law Handbook and Agency Directory, OAC Vol 17, Text 7.8

3107.43 Revealing information without statutory authority; penalty

(A) No employee or officer of the department of health shall knowingly reveal whether any release or withdrawal of release is included in the file of releases, knowingly provide a copy of any release or withdrawal of release in the files of releases, or knowingly reveal any information contained in any release or withdrawal of release in the file of releases, to any person unless authorized to do so by sections 3107.39 to 3107.44 of the Revised Code.

(B)(1) No agency, officer of an agency, or employee of an agency shall knowingly reveal any information regarding the name by birth of an adopted person or the identity of an adopted person's biological parents or biological siblings to a person who filed a petition for the release of such information unless a probate judge has entered an order under division (C)(3) or (4) of section 3107.41 of the Revised Code requiring the agency, officer, or employee to release such information to the petitioner.

(2) No agency required to release information regarding the name by birth of an adopted person or the identity of an adopted person's biological parents or biological siblings to a

petitioner by an order entered by a probate judge under division (C)(3) or (4) of section 3107.41 of the Revised Code, officer of such an agency, or employee of such an agency shall knowingly reveal any information in violation of division (D)(2) of section 3107.41 of the Revised Code.

(C) Whoever violates this section is guilty of a minor misdemeanor.

(1984 H 84, eff. 3-19-85)

Cross References

Personal information systems, civil cause of action for harm done, criminal penalties, 1347.10, 1347.99

Ohio Administrative Code References

Social services, release of identifying information from adoption record, OAC 5101:2-48-27

Library References

Records ⚷50.
WESTLAW Topic No. 326.
C.J.S. Records §§ 93 to 96.

Carlin, Baldwin's Ohio Practice, *Merrick-Rippner Probate Law* § 98.1, 98.28 (1997)

3107.44 Rights of adult who believes he is adopted; release of information to petitioner; immunity from liability

No agency, officer of an agency, or employee of an agency that releases any information to a petitioner pursuant to an order entered by a probate judge under division (C)(3) or (4) of section 3107.41 of the Revised Code is liable in damages in a civil action to any person for injury, death, or loss allegedly arising from the release of the information to the petitioner, or is criminally liable for the release of the information to the petitioner, if the agency, officer, or employee makes a good faith effort to comply with division (D) of section 3107.41 of the Revised Code in its release of that information.

(1984 H 84, eff. 3-19-85)

Cross References

Civil liabilities of officers and employees, 9.86

Library References

Records ⚷50.
WESTLAW Topic No. 326.
C.J.S. Records §§ 93 to 96.

Carlin, Baldwin's Ohio Practice, *Merrick-Rippner Probate Law* § 98.1, 98.28 (1997)

ACCESS TO ADOPTION RECORDS BY BIRTH PARENTS AND SIBLINGS

3107.45 Definitions

As used in sections 3107.45 to 3107.53 of the Revised Code:

(A) "Adopted person" means a person who, as a minor, was adopted but is not an "adopted person" as defined in section 3107.39 of the Revised Code.

(B) "Adoption file" means the file maintained by the department of health under section 3705.12 of the Revised Code.

(C) "Adoptive parent" means a person who adopted an adopted person.

(D) "Authorization of release form" means the form prescribed under division (A)(2) of section 3107.50 of the Revised Code.

(E) "Birth parent" means the biological parent of an adopted person.

(F) "Birth sibling" means a biological sibling of an adopted person.

(G) "Denial of release form" means either of the following:

(1) The component of the form prescribed under division (A)(1)(b) of section 3107.083 if the birth parent checked the "no" space provided on that component.

(2) The form prescribed under division (A)(1) of section 3107.50 of the Revised Code.

(H) "Effective denial of release form" means a denial of release form that has not been rescinded by an authorization of release form pursuant to division (B) of section 3107.46 of the Revised Code.

(I) "Final decree of adoption" includes an interlocutory order of adoption that has become final.

(J) "Identifying information" has the same meaning as in section 3107.01 of the Revised Code.

(K) "Items of identification" include a motor vehicle driver's or commercial driver's license, an identification card issued under sections 4507.50 to 4507.52 of the Revised Code, a marriage application, a social security card, a credit card, a military identification card, or an employee identification card.

(1996 H 419, eff. 9-18-96)

Cross References

Conditions for juvenile court approving parent's agreement for child's adoption, adopted person defined, 5103.151

Fees for copying adoption file, adoption records fund, 3705.241

Ohio Administrative Code References

Forms used in the system of vital statistics, OAC 3701-5-02

Library References

Baldwin's Ohio Legislative Service, 1996 H 419—LSC Analysis, 3/L-336

Law Review and Journal Commentaries

Ohio House Bill 419: Increased Openness in Adoption Records Law, Wendy L. Weiss. 45 Clev St L Rev 101 (1997).

3107.46 Denial or authorization of release form; rescinding of form

(A) A birth parent who did not check, pursuant to section 3107.071, 3107.081, or 5103.151 of the Revised Code, the "no" space provided on the component of the form prescribed pursuant to division (A)(1)(b) of section 3107.083 of the Revised Code may sign, date, and have filed with the department of health a denial of release form prescribed under section 3107.50 of the Revised Code. A birth parent who signs an authorization of release form under division (B) of this section may rescind that form by signing, dating, and having filed with the department of health a denial of release form prescribed under section 3107.50 of the Revised Code. If, at the time of submitting the denial of release form, the birth parent provides the department two items of identification, the department shall file the form in the adoption file of the adopted person indicated on the form.

(B) If an adoption file contains a birth parent's denial of release form, the birth parent may rescind that form by signing, dating, and having filed with the department of health an authorization of release form. If, at the time of submitting the authorization of release form, the birth parent provides the department two items of identification, the department shall file the form in the adoption file of the adopted person indicated on the form.

(C) After a birth parent submits a denial of release form or an authorization of release form under this section, the department of health shall provide the birth parent a copy of the form.

(D) A birth parent may rescind an authorization of release form pursuant to division (A) of this section and rescind a denial of release form pursuant to division (B) of this section as many times as the birth parent wishes.

(1996 H 419, eff. 9-18-96)

Cross References

Adoption registration, release of file contents, 3705.12

Library References

Am Jur 2d: 2, Adoption § 208
Restricting access to judicial records of concluded adoption proceedings. 83 ALR3d 800
Restricting access to judicial records of pending adoption proceedings. 83 ALR3d 824
Baldwin's Ohio Legislative Service, 1996 H 419—LSC Analysis, 3/L-336

3107.47 Adoptee or adoptee's parents requesting copy of adoption file

(A) An adopted person age twenty-one or older, or an adoptive parent of an adopted person at least age eighteen but under age twenty-one, may submit a request to the department of health for a copy of the contents of the adopted person's adoption file. If the adopted person includes with the request the adopted person's notarized signature and copies of two items of identification, or the adoptive parent includes with the request the adoptive parent's notarized signature and copies of two items of identification, the department shall do the following:

(1) If there is not an effective denial of release form for either birth parent in the adopted person's adoption file and the fee required by section 3705.241 of the Revised Code is paid, provide the adopted person or adoptive parent a copy of the contents of the adopted person's adoption file;

(2) If there is an effective denial of release form for each birth parent in the adopted person's adoption file, refuse to provide the adopted person or adoptive parent a copy of the contents of the adopted person's adoption file;

(3) If there is an effective denial of release form for only one of the birth parents in the adopted person's adoption file and the fee required by section 3705.241 of the Revised Code is paid, provide the adopted person or adoptive parent a copy of the contents of the adopted person's adoption file with all identifying information about the birth parent for whom there is an effective denial of release form deleted.

(B) If an adopted person or adoptive parent is denied a copy of the contents of the adopted person's adoption file or receives a copy of the contents with identifying information about one of the birth parents deleted, the department of health shall inform the adopted person or adoptive parent that it will notify the adopted person or adoptive parent if the department subsequently receives an authorization of release form from one or both birth parents and the adopted person or adoptive parent submits to the department a request to be notified. An adopted person or adoptive parent who submits a request to be notified shall provide the department the adopted person's or adoptive parent's address and notify the department of any change of address. An adopted person or adoptive parent who subsequently decides not to be notified may submit a statement with the department for the department not to notify the adopted person or adoptive parent.

The department shall notify the adopted person or adoptive parent if the department receives an authorization of release form from one or both birth parents and the adopted person or adoptive parent submitted a request to be notified and has not subsequently submitted a statement not to be notified. If the adopted person or adoptive parent contacts the department after being notified and indicates a desire to receive the information the department may provide, the department shall provide the adopted person or adoptive parent information in accordance with division (A) of this section.

(1996 H 419, eff. 9-18-96)

Cross References

Prohibition: 3107.65(A)

Adoption registration, release of file contents, 3705.12

Assessor's meeting with birth parent prior to parent's consenting to adoption, identifying information about parent, 5103.152

Fees for copying adoption file, contents, 3705.241

Ohio Administrative Code References

Forms used in the system of vital statistics, OAC 3701-5-02

Library References

Am Jur 2d: 2, Adoption § 208

Restricting access to judicial records of concluded adoption proceedings. 83 ALR3d 800

Restricting access to judicial records of pending adoption proceedings. 83 ALR3d 824

Baldwin's Ohio Legislative Service, 1996 H 419—LSC Analysis, 3/L-336

3107.48 Adoptee's request that health department assist birth parents or siblings in finding adoptee's name by adoption

(A) An adopted person age twenty-one or older may submit a request with the department of health for the department to assist the adopted person's birth parent or birth sibling in finding the adopted person's name by adoption pursuant to section 3107.49 of the Revised Code. The adopted person shall submit the request on a form prescribed by the department under section 3107.51 of the Revised Code. If the adopted person provides all the information required by section 3107.51 of the Revised Code on the form, the department shall file it in the adopted person's adoption file and assist the birth parent or birth sibling in finding the adopted person's name by adoption unless the adopted person rescinds the request pursuant to division (B) of this section.

(B) An adopted person who has requested under division (A) of this section that the department of health assist the adopted person's birth parent or birth sibling in finding the adopted person's name by adoption pursuant to section 3107.49 of the Revised Code may rescind the request and prohibit the department from assisting the birth parent or birth sibling in finding the adopted person's name by adoption pursuant to section 3107.49 of the Revised Code. The department shall remove the request from the adopted person's adoption file and destroy the request to rescind the request if the adopted person does both of the following:

(1) Makes a written request to the department;

(2) Provides to the department the adopted person's residence address, notarized signature, and two items of identification of the adopted person.

(C) An adopted person may submit requests under division (A) of this section and rescind requests under division (B) of this section as many times as the adopted person wishes.

(1996 H 419, eff. 9-18-96)

Cross References

Adoption registration, contents of file, 3705.12

Ohio Administrative Code References

Forms used in the system of vital statistics, OAC 3701-5-02

Library References

Am Jur 2d: 2, Adoption § 208

Restricting access to judicial records of concluded adoption proceedings. 83 ALR3d 800

Restricting access to judicial records of pending adoption proceedings. 83 ALR3d 824

Baldwin's Ohio Legislative Service, 1996 H 419—LSC Analysis, 3/L-336

3107.49 Birth parent or sibling's request for assistance in finding adoptee's name by adoption

(A) A birth parent, or birth sibling age twenty-one or older, may submit a request to the department of health for assistance in finding an adopted person's name by adoption. The department shall examine the adopted person's adoption file to determine the adopted person's name by adoption and provide the birth parent or birth sibling with the adopted person's name by adoption if all of the following are the case:

(1) The adopted person's adoption file contains a request submitted by the adopted person under division (A) of section 3107.48 of the Revised Code that the department assist the birth parent or birth sibling in finding the adopted person's name by adoption;

(2) The adopted person was the child of the birth parent or sibling of the birth sibling before the adoption;

(3) In the case of a request by a birth parent, the court that issued the adopted person's final decree of adoption sends the department, in accordance with division (B) of this section, a notice stating that the birth parent's parental rights concerning the adopted person were not involuntarily terminated pursuant to Chapter 2151. of the Revised Code;

(4) The request is in writing and includes the birth parent's or birth sibling's residence address and notarized signature, one or more items of identification of the birth parent or birth sibling, and the adopted person's name and date of birth as it appears on the original birth record;

(5) The department has an adoption file for the adopted person and is able to determine the adopted person's name by adoption from the file's contents.

(B) If a birth parent requests assistance from the department of health in finding an adopted person's name by adoption, the department shall request the court that issued the adopted person's final decree of adoption to determine whether the birth parent's parental rights concerning the adopted person were involuntarily terminated pursuant to Chapter 2151. of the Revised Code. The department shall provide to the court any information the department has and the court needs to make the determination. On request from the department, the court shall make the determination. After making the determination, the court shall send a notice to the department stating whether the birth parent's parental rights were so involuntarily terminated.

(C) If a birth parent or birth sibling does not know all the information about the adopted person that the department needs to be able to find the adopted person's adoption file, the department shall, if it is known which court issued the adopted person's final decree of adoption, ask the court to find the information about the adopted person from its records. The department shall provide to the court any information the department receives from the birth parent or birth sibling that the court needs to find the information. On the department's request, the court shall provide to the department any information the court has that will aid the department in finding the adopted person's adoption file.

(D) If a birth parent or birth sibling is denied assistance in finding an adopted person's name by adoption because the adopted person's adoption file does not contain a request submitted by the adopted person under division (A) of section 3107.48 of the Revised Code, the department shall inform the birth parent or birth sibling that it will notify the birth parent or birth sibling if the adopted person subsequently submits a request under division (A) of section 3107.48 of the Revised Code and the birth parent or birth sibling submits to the department a request to be notified. A birth parent or birth sibling who submits a request to be notified shall provide the department the birth parent's or birth sibling's address and shall notify the department of any change of address. A birth parent or birth sibling who subsequently decides not to be notified may submit a statement with the department for the department not to notify the birth parent or birth sibling. The department shall notify the birth parent or birth sibling if the adopted person submits a request under division (A) of section

3107.48 of the Revised Code and the birth parent or birth sibling has submitted a request to be notified and not subsequently submitted a statement not to be notified.

(1996 H 419, eff. 9-18-96)

Cross References

Adoption registration, release of file contents, 3705.12

Library References

Am Jur 2d: 2, Adoption § 208
Restricting access to judicial records of concluded adoption proceedings. 83 ALR3d 800
Restricting access to judicial records of pending adoption proceedings. 83 ALR3d 824
Baldwin's Ohio Legislative Service, 1996 H 419—LSC Analysis, 3/L-336

3107.50 Denial of release form; authorization of release form

(A) Not later than ninety days after the effective date of this section, the department of health shall prescribe the following forms:

(1) A denial of release form to be used by a birth parent under division (A) of section 3107.46 of the Revised Code. The form shall explain that the birth parent may rescind the denial of release at any time by signing, dating, and having filed with the department of health an authorization of release form pursuant to division (B) of section 3107.46 of the Revised Code.

(2) An authorization of release form to be used by a birth parent under division (B) of section 3107.46 of the Revised Code. The form shall state that the birth parent may rescind the authorization of release at any time by signing, dating, and having filed with the department of health a denial of release form pursuant to division (A) of that section.

(B) On request of a birth parent, the department shall provide a copy of a denial of release form or authorization of release form to the birth parent.

(1996 H 419, eff. 6-20-96)

Cross References

Assessor's meeting with birth parent prior to parent's consenting to adoption, denial of release form, 5103.152

Library References

Am Jur 2d: 2, Adoption § 208
Restricting access to judicial records of concluded adoption proceedings. 83 ALR3d 800
Restricitng access to judicial records of pending adoption proceedings. 83 ALR3d 824
Baldwin's Ohio Legislative Service, 1996 H 419—LSC Analysis, 3/L-336

3107.51 Form for adoptee's requesting assistance for birth parents or siblings finding adoptee's name by adoption

(A) Not later than ninety days after the effective date of this section, the department of health shall prescribe a form with which an adopted person may make a request under division (A) of section 3107.48 of the Revised Code. The form shall require all of the following information:

(1) The residence address of the adopted person;

(2) The adopted person's name and date of birth as it appears on the adopted person's new birth record;

(3) The notarized signature of the adopted person;

(4) Any other information considered necessary by the department.

(B) The form shall include instructions that explain how it is to be completed and filed with the department. The department shall include on the form information that advises the adopted person that the adopted person may, in accordance with division (B) of section 3107.48 of the Revised Code, rescind the request at any time, and shall include instructions on how to do so.

(C) On request of an adopted person, the department shall provide the adopted person with a copy of the form.

(1996 H 419, eff. 6-20-96)

Library References

Am Jur 2d: 2, Adoption § 208
Restricting access to judicial records of concluded adoption proceedings. 83 ALR3d 800
Restricting access to judicial records of pending adoption proceedings. 83 ALR3d 824
Baldwin's Ohio Legislative Service, 1996 H 419—LSC Analysis, 3/L-336

3107.52 Records not public

(A) The department of health's records pertaining to proceedings under sections 3107.45 to 3107.53 of the Revised Code are not public records subject to inspection or copying under section 149.43 of the Revised Code.

(B) No person who is the subject of personal information contained in a record listed in division (A) of this section may inspect or copy all or part of any such record except pursuant to section 3107.47 of the Revised Code.

(1996 H 419, eff. 9-18-96)

Cross References

Availability of state government public records, public records defined, 149.43

Library References

Am Jur 2d: 2, Adoption § 208
Restricting access to judicial records of concluded adoption proceedings. 83 ALR3d 800
Restricting access to judicial records of pending adoption proceedings. 83 ALR3d 824
Baldwin's Ohio Legislative Service, 1996 H 419—LSC Analysis, 3/L-336
Baldwin's Ohio School Law, Text 44.2, 44.5

3107.53 No liability for release of information

No officer or employee of the department of health who releases any information contained in an adopted person's adoption file or provides a copy of the contents of an adopted person's adoption file to a person who requests the copy pursuant to section 3107.47 or 3107.49 of the Revised Code is liable in damages in a civil action to any person for injury, death, or loss allegedly arising from the release to the person or is criminally liable for the release if the officer or employee releases the information or copy in accordance with section 3107.47 or 3107.49 of the Revised Code.

(1996 H 419, eff. 9-18-96)

Library References

Am Jur 2d: 2, Adoption § 208
Restricting access to judicial records of concluded adoption proceedings. 83 ALR3d 800
Restricitng access to judicial records of pending adoption proceedings. 83 ALR3d 824
Baldwin's Ohio Legislative Service, 1996 H 419—LSC Analysis, 3/L-336

OPEN ADOPTIONS

3107.60 Definitions

As used in sections 3107.60 to 3107.68 of the Revised Code:

(A) "Agency," "attorney," and "identifying information" have the same meanings as in section 3107.01 of the Revised Code.

(B) "Nonidentifying information" means any information that is not identifying information, including all of the following:

(1) A birth parent's age at the time the birth parent's child is adopted;

(2) The medical and genetic history of the birth parents;

(3) The age, sex, and medical and genetic history of an adopted person's birth sibling and extended family members;

(4) A person's heritage and ethnic background, educational level, general physical appearance, religion, occupation, and cause of death;

(5) Any information that may be included in a social and medical history as specified in divisions (B) and (C) of section 3107.09 of the Revised Code.

(1996 H 419, eff. 9-18-96)

Library References

Baldwin's Ohio Legislative Service, 1996 H 419—LSC Analysis, 3/L-336

Carlin, Baldwin's Ohio Practice, *Merrick-Rippner Probate Law* § 98.27 (1997)

Law Review and Journal Commentaries

Ohio House Bill 419: Increased Openness in Adoption Records Law, Wendy L. Weiss. 45 Clev St L Rev 101 (1997).

3107.61 Profiles of prospective adoptive parents shown to birth parent

At the request of a birth parent who voluntarily chooses to have a child placed for adoption, the agency or attorney arranging the child's placement and adoption may provide the birth parent profiles of prospective adoptive parents who an assessor has recommended pursuant to a home study under section 3107.031 of the Revised Code be approved to adopt a child. At the request of the birth parent, the agency or attorney may include identifying information about a prospective adoptive parent in the profile if the prospective adoptive parent agrees to the inclusion of the identifying information. If a birth parent chooses a prospective adoptive parent from a profile, the agency or attorney shall give that prospective adoptive parent priority when determining with whom the agency or attorney will place the child.

(1996 H 419, eff. 9-18-96)

Ohio Administrative Code References

Child study inventory, OAC 5101:2-48-21

Provision of information to adoptive family, OAC 5101:2-48-15

Library References

Am Jur 2d: 2, Adoption § 43, 44, 47

Criminal liability of one arranging for adoption of child through other than licensed child placement agency ("baby broker acts"). 3 ALR4th 468

Baldwin's Ohio Legislative Service, 1996 H 419—LSC Analysis, 3/L-336

Law Review and Journal Commentaries

Ohio House Bill 419: Increased Openness in Adoption Records Law, Wendy L. Weiss. 45 Clev St L Rev 101 (1997).

3107.62 Nonbinding open adoption option

An agency or attorney arranging a child's adoptive placement shall inform the child's birth parent and prospective adoptive parent that the birth parent and prospective adoptive parent may enter into a nonbinding open adoption in accordance with section 3107.63 of the Revised Code.

(1996 H 274, eff. 9-18-96; 1996 H 419, eff. 9-18-96)

Historical and Statutory Notes

Amendment Note: 1996 H 274 deleted "or 3107.64" after "3107.63".

Ohio Administrative Code References

Provision of information to adoptive family, OAC 5101:2-48-15

Library References

Am Jur 2d: 2, Adoption § 43, 44, 47
Criminal liability of one arranging for adoption of child through other than licensed child placement agency ("baby broker acts"). 3 ALR4th 468
Baldwin's Ohio Legislative Service, 1996 H 419—LSC Analysis, 3/L-336
Carlin, Baldwin's Ohio Practice, *Merrick-Rippner Probate Law* § 98.27 (1997)

Law Review and Journal Commentaries

Ohio House Bill 419: Increased Openness in Adoption Records Law, Wendy L. Weiss. 45 Clev St L Rev 101 (1997).

3107.63 Birth parent requesting open adoption of child voluntarily placed for adoption

(A) A birth parent who voluntarily chooses to have the birth parent's child placed for adoption may request that the agency or attorney arranging the child's adoptive placement provide for the birth parent and prospective adoptive parent to enter into an open adoption with terms acceptable to the birth parent and prospective adoptive parent. Except as provided in division (B) of this section, the agency or attorney shall provide for the open adoption if the birth parent and prospective adoptive parent agree to the terms of the open adoption.

(B) An agency or attorney arranging a child's adoptive placement may refuse to provide for the birth parent and prospective adoptive parent to enter into an open adoption. If the agency or attorney refuses, the agency or attorney shall offer to refer the birth parent to another agency or attorney the agency or attorney knows will provide for the open adoption.

(1996 H 419, eff. 9-18-96)

Library References

Am Jur 2d: 2, Adoption § 43, 44, 47
Criminal liability of one arranging for adoption of child through other than licensed child placement agency ("baby broker acts"). 3 ALR4th 468
Baldwin's Ohio Legislative Service, 1996 H 419—LSC Analysis, 3/L-336
Carlin, Baldwin's Ohio Practice, *Merrick-Rippner Probate Law* § 98.27 (1997)

Law Review and Journal Commentaries

Ohio House Bill 419: Increased Openness in Adoption Records Law, Wendy L. Weiss. 45 Clev St L Rev 101 (1997).

3107.64 Birth parent requesting open adoption of child involuntarily placed for adoption—Repealed

(1996 H 274, eff. 8-8-96; 1996 H 419, eff. 9-18-96)

3107.65 Prohibitions in open adoptions

(A) No open adoption shall do any of the following:

(1) Provide for the birth parent to share with the prospective adoptive parent parental control and authority over the child placed for adoption or in any manner limit the adoptive parent's full parental control and authority over the adopted child;

(2) Deny the adoptive parent or child access to forms pertaining to the social or medical histories of the birth parent if the adoptive parent or child is entitled to them under section 3107.17 of the Revised Code;

(3) Deny the adoptive parent or child access to a copy of the contents of the child's adoption file if the adoptive parent or child is entitled to them under section 3107.47 of the Revised Code;

(4) Deny the adoptive parent, child, birth parent, birth sibling, or other relative access to nonidentifying information that is accessible pursuant to section 3107.66 of the Revised Code or to materials, photographs, or information that is accessible pursuant to section 3107.68 of the Revised Code;

(5) Provide for the open adoption to be binding or enforceable.

(B) A probate court may not refuse to approve a proposed placement pursuant to division (D)(1) of section 5103.16 of the Revised Code or to issue a final decree of adoption or interlocutory order of adoption under section 3107.14 of the Revised Code on the grounds that the birth parent and prospective adoptive parent have entered into an open adoption unless the court issues a finding that the terms of the open adoption violate division (A) of this section or are not in the best interest of the child. A probate court may not issue a final decree of adoption or interlocutory order of adoption that nullifies or alters the terms of an open adoption unless the court issues a finding that the terms violate division (A) of this section or are not in the best interest of the child.

(C) Subject to divisions (A) and (B) of this section, an open adoption may provide for the exchange of any information, including identifying information, and have any other terms. All terms of an open adoption are voluntary and any person who has entered into an open adoption may withdraw from the open adoption at any time. An open adoption is not enforceable. At the request of a person who has withdrawn from an open adoption, the court with jurisdiction over the adoption shall issue an order barring any other person who was a party to the open adoption from taking any action pursuant to the open adoption.

(1996 H 274, eff. 9-18-96; 1996 H 419, eff. 9-18-96)

Historical and Statutory Notes

Amendment Note: 1996 H 274 deleted "or relative" after "birth parent" in division (A)(1); and deleted ", or relative of the child to be adopted and prospective adoptive parent," after "adoptive parent" in division (B).

Library References

Am Jur 2d: 2, Adoption § 43, 44, 47

Criminal liability of one arranging for adoption of child through other than licensed child placement agency ("baby broker acts"). 3 ALR4th 468

Baldwin's Ohio Legislative Service, 1996 H 419—LSC Analysis, 3/L-336

Carlin, Baldwin's Ohio Practice, *Merrick-Rippner Probate Law* § 98.27 (1997)

Law Review and Journal Commentaries

Ohio House Bill 419: Increased Openness in Adoption Records Law, Wendy L. Weiss. 45 Clev St L Rev 101 (1997).

3107.66 Written request for information on adoption

(A) As used in this section, "adopted person," "adoptive parent," "birth parent," and "birth sibling" have the same meanings as in section 3107.45 of the Revised Code.

(B) An adopted person age eighteen or older, an adoptive parent of an adopted person under age eighteen, or an adoptive family member of a deceased adopted person may submit a written request to the agency or attorney who arranged the adopted person's adoption, or the probate court that finalized the adopted person's adoption, for the agency, attorney, or court to provide the adopted person, adoptive parent, or adoptive family member information about the adopted person's birth parent or birth sibling contained in the agency's, attorney's, or court's adoption records that is nonidentifying information. Except as provided in division (C) of this section, the agency, attorney, or court shall provide the adopted person, adoptive parent, or adoptive family member the information sought within a reasonable amount of time. The agency, attorney, or court may charge a reasonable fee for providing the information.

A birth parent of an adopted person, a birth sibling age eighteen or older, or a birth family member of a deceased birth parent may submit a written request to the agency or attorney who arranged the adopted person's adoption, or the probate court that finalized the adoption, for the agency, attorney, or court to provide the birth parent, birth sibling, or birth family member information about the adopted person or adoptive parent contained in the agency's, attorney's, or court's adoption records that is nonidentifying information. Except as provided in division (C) of this section, the agency, attorney, or court shall provide the birth parent, birth sibling, or birth family member the information sought within a reasonable amount of time. The agency, attorney, or court may charge a reasonable fee for providing the information.

(C) An agency or attorney that has permanently ceased to arrange adoptions is not subject to division (B) of this section. If the adoption records of such an agency or attorney are held by a probate court, person, or other governmental entity pursuant to section 3107.67 of the Revised Code, the adopted person, adoptive parent, adoptive family member, birth parent, birth sibling, or birth family member may submit the written request that otherwise would be submitted to the agency or attorney under division (B) of this section to the court, person, or other governmental entity that holds the records. On receipt of the request, the court, person, or other governmental entity shall provide the information that the agency or attorney would have been required to provide within a reasonable amount of time. The court, person, or other governmental entity may charge a reasonable fee for providing the information.

(D) Prior to providing nonidentifying information pursuant to division (B) or (C) of this section, the person or governmental entity providing the information shall review the record to ensure that all identifying information about any person contained in the record is deleted.

(1996 H 419, eff. 9-18-96)

Cross References

Prohibition: 3107.65(A)

Library References

Am Jur 2d: 2, Adoption § 207 to 210

Restricting access to judicial records of concluded adoption proceedings. 83 ALR3d 800

Restricting access to judicial records of pending adoption proceedings. 83 ALR3d 824

Baldwin's Ohio Legislative Service, 1996 H 419—LSC Analysis, 3/L-336

Law Review and Journal Commentaries

Ohio House Bill 419: Increased Openness in Adoption Records Law, Wendy L. Weiss. 45 Clev St L Rev 101 (1997).

3107.67 Agency or attorney providing probate court with adoption records upon permanently ceasing to arrange adoptions

(A) For the purpose of division (C) of section 3107.66 of the Revised Code, an agency or attorney that arranged an adoption shall provide the probate court that finalized the adoption with the agency's or attorney's records of the adoption when the agency or attorney permanently ceases to arrange adoptions.

If an agency permanently ceases to arrange adoptions because the person operating the agency has died or become incapacitated or the attorney ceases to arrange adoptions because the attorney has died or become incapacitated, the person responsible for disposing of the agency's or attorney's records shall provide the court with the adoption records. If no one is responsible for disposing of the records, the person responsible for administering the estate or managing the resources of the attorney or the person who operated the agency shall provide the court with the adoption records.

If the attorney who permanently ceases to arrange adoptions is in practice with another attorney, the attorney may provide the adoption records to the other attorney rather than the court if the other attorney agrees to act in the place of the first attorney for the purpose of section 3107.66 of the Revised Code. The person responsible for the practice of the first attorney shall provide the adoption records to the probate court that finalized the adoption when the practice no longer includes an attorney who agrees to act in the first attorney's place for the purpose of section 3107.66 of the Revised Code.

(B) A probate court that receives adoption records under division (A) of this section may transfer the records to a person or governmental entity that voluntarily accepts the records. If the court finds a person or governmental entity that accepts the adoption records, the court shall maintain a directory for the purpose of informing a person seeking the records where the records are held.

(1996 H 419, eff. 9-18-96)

Library References

Am Jur 2d: 2, Adoption § 207; 66, Records and Recording Laws § 2 to 5, 23, 27, 29

Baldwin's Ohio Legislative Service, 1996 H 419—LSC Analysis, 3/L-336

3107.68 Birth parent providing information and photographs

A birth parent who signs the component of the form prescribed pursuant to division (A)(1)(d), or (B)(1)(c), of section 3107.083 of the Revised Code shall provide the materials the birth parent requests be given to the birth parent's child or adoptive parent to the agency or attorney arranging the adoption. At the request of the birth parent's child or adoptive parent, the agency or attorney shall provide the materials to the child or adoptive parent.

A birth parent who signs the component of the form prescribed pursuant to division (A)(1)(e), or (B)(1)(d), of section 3107.083 of the Revised Code shall provide the photographs of the birth parent that the birth parent requests be given to the birth parent's child or adoptive parent to the agency or attorney arranging the adoption. At the request of the birth parent's child or adoptive parent, the agency or attorney shall provide the photographs to the child or adoptive parent.

If a birth parent has signed the component of the form prescribed pursuant to division (A)(1)(f), or (B)(1)(e), of section 3107.083 of the Revised Code authorizing the agency or attorney that arranged the adoption of the birth parent's child to provide the child or adoptive parent the first name of the birth parent, the agency or attorney may provide the birth parent's first name to the child or adoptive parent at the request of the child or adoptive parent.

An agency or attorney arranging a child's adoption shall provide the adoptive parent the child's social security number.

(1996 H 419, eff. 9-18-96)

Cross References

Prohibition: 3107.65(A)

Ohio Administrative Code References

Provision of information to adoptive family, OAC 5101:2-48-15

Library References

Baldwin's Ohio Legislative Service, 1996 H 419—LSC Analysis, 3/L-336

PENALTIES

3107.99 Penalties

Whoever violates division (B)(1) of section 3107.17 of the Revised Code is guilty of a misdemeanor of the third degree.

(1996 H 419, eff. 9-18-96)

Library References

Baldwin's Ohio Legislative Service, 1996 H 419—LSC Analysis, 3/L-336

CHAPTER 3109

Children

Section

Cross References

Adoption, Ch 3107
Child support guidelines, 3113.215
Domestic violence, criminal sanctions, 2919.25 to 2919.271
Juvenile court, Ch 2151
Neglect, abandonment, or domestic violence, Ch 3113
Non-spousal artificial insemination, 3111.30 et seq.
School child, treatment by city or general health district board of health only on request of parent or guardian, 3709.22
Uniform Interstate Family Support Act, duties and powers of responding tribunal, 3115.16

Ohio Administrative Code References

Abused and neglected children, supportive services for, OAC Ch 5101:2-39
Child support program, OAC Ch 5101:1-29
Children's protective services, OAC Ch 5101:2-34
Collection of past due support by federal tax refund offset, OAC Ch 5101:1-30

Library References

Carlin, Baldwin's Ohio Practice, *Merrick-Rippner Probate Law* § 98.2, 108.13 (1997)
Sowald & Morganstern, Baldwin's Ohio Practice, *Domestic Relations Law* § 16.1, 23.36 (1997)

WESTLAW Electronic Research

See WESTLAW Electronic Research Guide following the Preface.

Law Review and Journal Commentaries

Annual Survey of Family Law, 1990 Volume 12, compiled by the International Society On Family Law. (Ed. note: articles from Australia, Belgium, Canada, China, Czechoslovakia, England, France, Germany, Greece, Israel, Italy, Jamaica, Japan, Netherlands, Pakistan, Poland, Scotland, South Africa, Spain, Sweden, USSR, United States.) 28 J Fam L 397 (1989-90).

Annual Survey of Family Law, compiled by The International Society On Family Law. (Ed. note: Articles on family law from 23 countries.) 29 J Fam L 277 (1990-91).

Child Custody Jurisdiction in Ohio—Implementing the Uniform Child Custody Jurisdiction Act, Comment. 12 Akron L Rev 121 (Summer 1978).

Children—The Innocent Victims of Family Break-ups: How the Family Law Attorney, the Courts, and Society Can Protect Our Children, Michael J. Albano. 26 U Tol L Rev 787 (Summer 1995).

Fragmenting and Reassembling the World: Of Flying Squirrels, Augmented Persons, and Other Monsters, Michael H. Shapiro. (Ed. note: The moral dimensions of abortion, genetic engineering, and other products of modern technology are explored.) 51 Ohio St L J 331 (1990).

Judge's Column, Hon. Francine M. Bruening. (Ed. note: Judge Bruening discusses the pending Ohio Parenting Act.) 20 Lake Legal Views 1 (June 1997).

The Lawyer Turns Peacemaker—with mediation emerging as the most popular form of alternate dispute resolution, the quest for common ground could force attorneys to reinterpret everything they do in the future, Richard C. Reuben. 82 A B A J 54 (August 1996).

Ligation Litigation, Brian Murphy, Leo C. Downing. 25 J Fam L 729 (1986-87).

Litigation Results—Count on a CPA, Keith J. Libman. 67 Clev B J 12 (October 1996).

Notes of Decisions and Opinions

Federal jurisdiction 1

---

1. Federal jurisdiction

Although filing of bankruptcy petition stays equitable distribution in divorce case of debtor's interest in marital assets, certain aspects of divorce case, such as dissolution of marriage and child custody issues, are not stayed. State ex rel. Miley v. Parrott (Ohio 1996) 77 Ohio St.3d 64, 671 N.E.2d 24.

Trial court was obligated to reactivate divorce case after bankruptcy court lifted automatic stay affecting Chapter 12 debtor-husband; order inactivating divorce case stated that case would stay inactive until judge "is advised in writing of the stay having been lifted," trial court was advised in writing that bankruptcy court had lifted stay for divorce case, trial court would not be subject to contempt for violating stay after bankruptcy court expressly modified and lifted stay, and divorce case would not be better resolved after conclusion of bankruptcy proceedings. State ex rel. Miley v. Parrott (Ohio 1996) 77 Ohio St.3d 64, 671 N.E.2d 24.

Automatic stay may be lifted or modified for cause. State ex rel. Miley v. Parrott (Ohio 1996) 77 Ohio St.3d 64, 671 N.E.2d 24.

The principle of Barber v Barber, 21 How 582 (1859) that federal courts have no jurisdiction over suits for divorce, the allowance of alimony, or custody of children remains true and will not be cast aside after nearly a century and a half; however, a district court cannot refuse to exercise diversity jurisdiction over a tort action for damages such as one brought against a former husband and his girlfriend by the former wife based on alleged abuse of the former couple's children. Ankenbrandt v. Richards (U.S.La. 1992) 112 S.Ct. 2206, 504 U.S. 689, 119 L.Ed.2d 468, on remand 973 F.2d 923.

Disputes about domestic matters remain the province of the states. Thompson v. Thompson (U.S.Cal. 1988) 108 S.Ct. 513, 484 U.S. 174, 98 L.Ed.2d 512.

The field of domestic relations is a state matter peculiarly unsuited to control by federal courts and under the principles set forth in Barber v Barber, 62 US 582, 16 LEd 226 (1858), federal courts will refuse to exercise jurisdiction over domestic matters regardless of diversity of state citizenship or the presence of the requisite amount in controversy; federal diversity jurisdiction does exist for suits that are actually tort or contract claims and have only overtones of domestic matters, however, and a constitutional claim that is not frivolous may also invoke federal jurisdiction. Taylor v. Wettstein (S.D.Ohio 1989) 746 F.Supp. 713.

GENERAL PROVISIONS

3109.01 Age of majority

All persons of the age of eighteen years or more, who are under no legal disability, are capable of contracting and are of full age for all purposes.

(1973 S 1, eff. 1-1-74; 1953 H 1; GC 8005-1; Source—GC 8023)

Historical and Statutory Notes

Pre-1953 H 1 Amendments: 124 v S 65

Cross References

Age and schooling certificates, over-age certificates, release of certificates, 3331.15

Age does not bar student loan, 3351.09

Anatomical gifts, age requirement, 2108.02

Disability assistance program, eligibility requirements, 5115.05

Duty of married person to support self, spouse, and children, wife to assist, 3103.03

Fiduciary law, power of appointment, age limit, 1339.151

"Legal disability" defined, 2131.02

Minor can consent to diagnosis and treatment of drug-related condition, parents not liable for payment unless consent, 3719.012

Minor's contract for life insurance, 3911.08

Parental duty of support continuing beyond age of majority where child attending high school, 2151.23, 3105.21, 3111.13, 3111.20, 3113.04, 3113.31

Persons who may marry, 3101.01

Prohibitions regarding purchase of liquor, 4301.63 et seq.

Seventeen-year-olds may donate blood, 2108.21

Small loans, assignment of wages by minor invalid without consent of parent or guardian, 1321.31

Voters, age requirements, O Const Art V §1; 3503.011

Who may make a will, 2107.02

Library References

Infants ⚷1.

WESTLAW Topic No. 211.

C.J.S. Infants §§ 2 to 4.

OJur 3d: 47, Family Law § 818, 999; 62, Investment Securities and Securities Regulation § 53

Am Jur 2d: 42, Infants § 3, 4, 6

Statutory change of age of majority as affecting pre-existing status or rights. 75 ALR3d 228

Carlin, Baldwin's Ohio Practice, *Merrick-Rippner Probate Law* § 19.4, 19.6, 19.7, 61.2, 105.1, 105.11, 106.20, 108.3, 108.13, 108.20, 108.34, 108.35 (1997)

Dill Calloway, Ohio Nursing Law, Text 11.02(E)

Hausser, Ohio Real Estate Law and Practice (2d Ed.), Text 31.09(I)

Sowald & Morganstern, Baldwin's Ohio Practice, *Domestic Relations Law* § 2.16, 7.1, 7.6, 16.1, 27.11 (1997)

White, Ohio Landlord Tenant Law (1999 Ed.), Text 2.22

Williams, Ohio Consumer Law (2000 Ed.), Text 1.1

Law Review and Journal Commentaries

What Lawyers Should Know About the New Age of Majority, Stanley J. Aronoff. 46 Ohio St B Ass'n Rep 1551 (10-7-73).

Notes of Decisions and Opinions

In general 2
Age of majority for females from eighteen to twenty-one 6
Alcohol purchasing under age 21 7
Constitutional issues 1
Disaffirming contracts 5
Parental discipline 8
Personal injury action 4
Support decree 3

---

1. Constitutional issues

The amendment to RC 3109.01 changing the age of majority from twenty-one years to eighteen years is constitutional and applies to an injured person who reached eighteen years of age after the effective date of the amendment. Scheer v. Air-Shields, Inc. (Hamilton 1979) 61 Ohio App.2d 205, 401 N.E.2d 478, 15 O.O.3d 321.

The amendment to RC 3109.01 changing the age of majority from twenty-one years to eighteen years is constitutional and applies to an injured person who is eighteen years of age on the effective date of the amendment. Durham v. Anka Research Ltd. (Hamilton 1978) 60 Ohio App.2d 239, 396 N.E.2d 799, 14 O.O.3d 222.

The effect of a statutory amendment reducing the age of majority from twenty-one to eighteen in shortening the period of limitations governing the actions of minors is remedial in nature and does not violate O Const Art II §28, prohibiting retroactive laws, provided a reasonable time is still permitted to bring the action. Ledwell v. May Co. (Ohio Com.Pl. 1977) 54 Ohio Misc. 43, 377 N.E.2d 798, 7 O.O.3d 138, 8 O.O.3d 347.

Statute, as amended (110 v 125) effective 7-18-23, raising the age of majority of females from eighteen to twenty-one years, is unconstitutional to the extent that it attempted to divest females who had attained the age of eighteen before such date of the right to convey real estate. Gigger v. Kelly (Ohio Com.Pl. 1923) 24 Ohio N.P.N.S. 499.

2. In general

Court lacked authority to order biological father to provide present and future child support to child who had reached age of majority and was emancipated, even though paternity action had been timely filed within five years after child reached age 18. Snider v. Lillie (Ohio App. 1 Dist. 1997) 131 Ohio App.3d 444, 722 N.E.2d 1036.

With respect to present and future child support, once child reaches age of majority and becomes emancipated, court is without power to provide child with support, child has no legal right to be supported, and the court no longer has the power to order a parent to pay child support. Snider v. Lillie (Ohio App. 1 Dist. 1997) 131 Ohio App.3d 444, 722 N.E.2d 1036.

Time in which to bring a claim to establish paternity is five years longer than period of father's duty to support, which expires when child reaches age 18. Snider v. Lillie (Ohio App. 1 Dist. 1997) 131 Ohio App.3d 444, 722 N.E.2d 1036.

Withdrawal from high school by child who was in custody of former husband on day child turned 18 years of age terminated wife's duty to pay child support, and divested trial court of jurisdiction to order wife to pay child support or to modify child support agreement; child's subsequent enrollment in vocational school did not resurrect order, as obligation continues after age 18 only if child continuously attends high school. Gleason v. Gleason (Ohio App. 4 Dist. 1998) 129 Ohio App.3d 563, 718 N.E.2d 512.

If child does not continuously attend high school on a full-time basis after turning 18, parent's duty to provide child support ends, and trial court loses subject matter jurisdiction. Gleason v. Gleason (Ohio App. 4 Dist. 1998) 129 Ohio App.3d 563, 718 N.E.2d 512.

"Emancipation" is the entire surrender by parent of right to care, custody, and earnings of minor child as well as renunciation of parental duties. Swanson v. Swanson (Greene 1996) 109 Ohio App.3d 231, 671 N.E.2d 1333.

Emancipation applies only to minor children. Swanson v. Swanson (Greene 1996) 109 Ohio App.3d 231, 671 N.E.2d 1333.

A parent owes no duty of support to an emancipated epileptic child who is capable of being self-supporting. Cooksey v. Cooksey (Erie 1988) 55 Ohio App.3d 135, 562 N.E.2d 934.

A statutory amendment lowering the age of majority from twenty-one to eighteen operates prospectively from its effective date to remove the disability of minority of all persons who are eighteen to twenty-one years of age on such effective date. Ledwell v. May Co. (Ohio Com.Pl. 1977) 54 Ohio Misc. 43, 377 N.E.2d 798, 7 O.O.3d 138, 8 O.O.3d 347.

Persons under the age of legal capacity to contract may become a "guest," within the meaning of RC 4515.02, so that a child who rides in an automobile, without any consideration for such ride having been received by its owner, is a "guest" although neither parent nor guardian consented to such ride. Kemp v. Parmley (Ohio Com.Pl. 1967) 17 Ohio Misc. 23, 243 N.E.2d 779, 46 O.O.2d 18, affirmed 16 Ohio St.2d 3, 241 N.E.2d 169, 45 O.O.2d 67.

RC 737.15 and 737.16 permit the appointment of otherwise qualified persons of the age of eighteen to the offices of village marshal, deputy marshal, policeman, night watchman and special policeman. OAG 78-058.

RC 509.01 and 505.49 permit the appointment of otherwise qualified persons of the age of eighteen to township police positions, unless, in the operation of a police district, pursuant to RC 505.48 et seq., the board of trustees under RC 505.49 has acted by a two-thirds vote to establish a higher age requirement. OAG 78-058.

RC 311.04 permits the appointment of an otherwise qualified person of the age of eighteen to the office of deputy sheriff. OAG 78-058.

RC 124.41 requires that all persons originally appointed as policemen or policewomen in a city or civil service township police department be at least twenty-one years of age. OAG 78-058.

3. Support decree

Where the parties to a separation agreement agree that the obligation to make child support payments will terminate when the child reaches the "age of majority," the obligation to make support payments terminates when the child reaches his or her eighteenth birthday unless the parties specify some other definition of the phrase "age of majority." In re Dissolution of Marriage of Lazor (Ohio 1991) 59 Ohio St.3d 201, 572 N.E.2d 66.

Common-law duty imposed on parents to support their minor children may be found by a court of domestic relations having jurisdiction of the matter to continue beyond age of majority if the children are unable to support themselves because of mental or physical disabilities which existed before attaining the age of majority. Castle v. Castle (Ohio 1984) 15 Ohio St.3d 279, 473 N.E.2d 803, 15 O.B.R. 413.

The statutory change in the age of majority has no application to pre-1974 support decrees incorporating parental separation agreements. Rosenfeld v. Rosenfeld (Ohio 1976) 47 Ohio St.2d 12, 351 N.E.2d 181, 1 O.O.3d 8.

The statutory change in the age of majority has no application to pre-1974 support decrees. Nokes v. Nokes (Ohio 1976) 47 Ohio St.2d 1, 351 N.E.2d 174, 1 O.O.3d 1.

Determination of whether a child support obligation in a pre-1974 divorce decree was altered by statutory amendments lowering of the age of majority depends on whether the decree, explicitly or implicitly, enumerated the duration of the obligation; if it did, the lowering of the age of majority did not change that obligation, but if it did not, the lowering of the age of majority meant that the support obligation ended when the child or children at issue reached the age of eighteen. Cox v. Cox (Ohio App. 1 Dist. 1998) 130 Ohio App.3d 609, 720 N.E.2d 946.

Ex-father's child support obligation, pursuant to divorce decree entered prior to statutory amendments that lowered age of majority from twenty-one to eighteen, terminated when youngest child reached age eighteen, where decree did not state a duration for support order but referred to parties' "minor children." Cox v. Cox (Ohio App. 1 Dist. 1998) 130 Ohio App.3d 609, 720 N.E.2d 946.

Parents' common-law duty to support their child continued after child's majority, where child had been blind and mentally impaired, and therefore fully disabled, continuously since birth. Abbas v. Abbas (Ohio App. 7 Dist. 1998) 128 Ohio App.3d 513, 715 N.E.2d 613.

Marriage of minor child is an act of emancipation that terminates obligations of domestic relations order as a matter of law. Swanson v. Swanson (Greene 1996) 109 Ohio App.3d 231, 671 N.E.2d 1333.

To extent that emancipation relieves parent of duty of support, it does so only with respect to parent's duty to support minor child; emancipation is irrelevant to any duty of support that may exist after child reaches age of majority. Swanson v. Swanson (Greene 1996) 109 Ohio App.3d 231, 671 N.E.2d 1333.

Emancipation discharges parent from obligation to support minor child, but only so long as minor child is competent to support himself or herself. Swanson v. Swanson (Greene 1996) 109 Ohio App.3d 231, 671 N.E.2d 1333.

Minor's employment does not terminate child support obligation as a matter of law, and mere capability of minor child to earn money on his or her own behalf is no ground for termination or reduction of child support order. Swanson v. Swanson (Greene 1996) 109 Ohio App.3d 231, 671 N.E.2d 1333.

Determination of whether obligation to provide child support pursuant to divorce decree entered prior to statutory amendment lowering age of majority from 21 to 18 is affected by amendment depends upon whether decree, explicitly or implicitly, enumerates duration of obligation of support; if it does, obligation is not changed by lowering of age; if it does not, lowering means that support obligation ends when child reaches age 18. Motley v. Motley (Summit 1995) 102 Ohio App.3d 67, 656 N.E.2d 995.

Where divorce decree did not include enumeration of duration of husband's child support obligation, but only provided that it would continue until further order of court, obligation ended when each child reached age 18, even though original divorce decree was entered prior to statutory amendment lowering age of majority from 21 to 18. Motley v. Motley (Summit 1995) 102 Ohio App.3d 67, 656 N.E.2d 995.

During child's minority, domestic relations court has jurisdiction to alter provisions of its decree which relate to college education of child upon proper motion of or consent of parties but once child reaches age of majority, court is without jurisdiction to modify those provisions without consent of child of the parties. Rohrbacher v. Rohrbacher (Lucas 1992) 83 Ohio App.3d 569, 615 N.E.2d 338.

A father is obligated to support a child until she reaches majority at age eighteen, at which time she becomes legally emancipated despite a separation agreement stating that the father's support would end when the child graduated high school or became emancipated, whichever came first, where the child graduates one month before her eighteenth birthday. Dudziak v. Dudziak (Cuyahoga 1992) 81 Ohio App.3d 361, 611 N.E.2d 337.

Age of majority in effect at time of entry of dissolution decree that contained child support obligation controlled determination of child's emancipation based on attainment of age of majority. Bauer v. Bauer (Franklin 1989) 57 Ohio App.3d 24, 566 N.E.2d 185.

After a man is adjudged a putative father and ordered to pay support until the child is eighteen, pursuant to former RC 3111.17, if the man acknowledges paternity under RC 2105.18, he assumes the obligation imposed by RC 3103.03 to support the child throughout its minority, as minority is defined by RC 3109.01, subject to subsequent amendments to RC 3109.01 and 3103.03. Zweifel v. Price (Franklin 1985) 24 Ohio App.3d 101, 493 N.E.2d 300, 24 O.B.R. 171.

An order in a divorce action that a father pay a child's room, board, and college tuition beyond the child's eighteenth birthday is reversible error. Verplatse v. Verplatse (Hancock 1984) 17 Ohio App.3d 99, 477 N.E.2d 648, 17 O.B.R. 161.

A court in Ohio has no authority to compel a divorced husband to continue paying support for his disabled child who has reached the age of majority. Maphet v. Heiselman (Clermont 1984) 13 Ohio App.3d 278, 469 N.E.2d 92, 13 O.B.R. 343.

The statutory change in the age of majority operates prospectively only and does not affect the provisions of pre-1974 support decrees. Price v. Price (Darke 1983) 12 Ohio App.3d 42, 465 N.E.2d 922, 12 O.B.R. 129.

Where, as part of a valid agreement, a husband agrees to provide college education for his children and further agrees to keep in effect insurance policies on his life in which such children are beneficiaries, and where such agreement is incorporated in a decree divorcing the husband from his wife, such decree becomes binding upon the husband even though the performance required by the decree may extend beyond the minority of the children. Grant v. Grant (Erie 1977) 60 Ohio App.2d 277, 396 N.E.2d 1037, 14 O.O.3d 249.

RC 3105.10 clothes courts with jurisdiction to incorporate into a court order an agreement to support a child of the parties beyond the age of that child's majority, and such an order may be enforced by contempt proceedings. Bugay v. Bugay (Summit 1977) 53 Ohio App.2d 285, 373 N.E.2d 1263, 7 O.O.3d 336.

Where the age of legal majority is reduced by the legislature, a party to a divorce settlement, under which he is bound to support minor children until they become emancipated, is relieved of any obligation beyond that age designated by the new act. Allison v. Allison (Warren 1975) 44 Ohio App.2d 230, 337 N.E.2d 666, 73 O.O.2d 243.

A high school student who learns he is not eligible for graduation and (1) has already attained the age of majority, (2) has no intentions of returning to high school after summer recess, and (3) begins working full-time is no longer continuously attending high school and is an emancipated child for whom a parent owes no duty to pay support pursuant to a child support order. Hiltbrand v Hiltbrand, No. 1999AP0115, 1999 WL 547962 (5th Dist Ct App, Tuscarawas, 7-2-99).

A court errs in overruling a father's motion for return of overpayment of child support where the magistrate uses an incorrect termination date for the support obligation as the twenty-first birthday of the youngest child when the order should have terminated when each child reached age eighteen. Cox v Cox, No. C-970772, 1998 WL 833593 (1st Dist Ct App, Hamilton, 12-4-98).

By stating that a parent must provide child support for "the parties' two minor children," the parties' pre-1974 divorce decree implicitly provides a duration for the support obligation which is the age of twenty-one, the statutorily defined age of majority at the time the decree was entered. Quillen v Deaton, No. CA97-07-147, 1998 WL 42234 (12th Dist Ct App, Butler, 2-2-98).

Parents can agree to provide post-divorce support for emancipated children by way of an annuity to provide for the children's college education. Strong v Strong, No. L-96-044, 1997 WL 89105 (6th Dist Ct App, Lucas, 2-28-97).

A trial court's extension of support beyond a child's eighteenth birthday violates the terms of the couple's 1978 divorce agreement and reliance on present day RC 3109.05(E) is misplaced as that section's language, requiring support issued pursuant to this section to continue past the age of majority so long as the child is in high school, was enacted years after the divorce decree was issued and is not controlling. Wendling v Wendling, No. 68837, 1996 WL 50825 (8th Dist Ct App, Cuyahoga, 2-8-96).

The 1974 amendment to RC 3109.01 lowering the age of majority to eighteen years will be applied so that a pre-1974 support order will terminate upon the child reaching the age of eighteen years, absent a separation agreement provision concerning termination of support at a different time. Colvin v Colvin, No. 10120 (2d Dist Ct App, Montgomery, 3-5-87).

RC 3109.01 which effectuates a change of the age of majority to eighteen effective January 1, 1974 has no effect upon pre-1974 child support decrees. Coleman v Coleman, No. L-82-005 (6th Dist Ct App, Lucas, 5-7-82).

In an action to extend child support provisions to cover the children from age eighteen to twenty-one, the trial court does have authority to entertain the motion to modify the original divorce decree and extend the time of the husband's support obligation. Kufrin v Kufrin, No. 42926 (8th Dist Ct App, Cuyahoga, 4-23-81).

Where the language of a court order in a divorce action fixes support "until majority," after January 1, 1974, such support order—no matter when made—will terminate as to any child who has attained age eighteen; where the court order fixes support until age twenty-one, such order will be ineffective after January 1, 1974, as to any child who has reached eighteen; where a property settlement agreement provides for payment until majority, a motion to terminate support as to an eighteen-year-old should be sustained after January 1, 1974; where a property settlement agreement provides for payment until age twenty-one, the court may continue to enforce such order. Istnick v. Istnick (Ohio Com.Pl. 1973) 37 Ohio Misc. 91, 307 N.E.2d 922, 66 O.O.2d 244.

Father's duty to support his minor child does not stop when such child has arrived at the age of eighteen years. Rutter v. Rutter (Ohio Com.Pl. 1970) 24 Ohio Misc. 7, 261 N.E.2d 202, 53 O.O.2d 32.

Separation agreement incorporated into divorce decree in which wife agrees to provide for support of child of parties after it arrives at age of eighteen years, does not relieve husband from duty of providing for such child. Rutter v. Rutter (Ohio Com.Pl. 1970) 24 Ohio Misc. 7, 261 N.E.2d 202, 53 O.O.2d 32.

A father is primarily responsible for the support of his minor children, and that support continues under the law of Ohio until the child is twenty-one years of age or is otherwise emancipated. Burney v. Vance (Ohio Com.Pl. 1969) 17 Ohio Misc. 307, 246 N.E.2d 371, 46 O.O.2d 427.

Determination of the age at which a person becomes an adult for the purpose of enforcing the provisions of the reciprocal support act, depends upon the state in which the child is living and the state in which the father is living, and not in the state in which the original divorce was granted. Burney v. Vance (Ohio Com.Pl. 1969) 17 Ohio Misc. 307, 246 N.E.2d 371, 46 O.O.2d 427.

The uniform support act covers children who are minors, and under RC 3115.22 is in addition to and not in substitution of any other remedies authorized by law. Burney v. Vance (Ohio Com.Pl. 1969) 17 Ohio Misc. 307, 246 N.E.2d 371, 46 O.O.2d 427.

The juvenile court has jurisdiction to require the father of a child whose custody had been given to the mother in a divorce decree to support said child after he has reached his eighteenth birthday, but before he attains the age of twenty-one years, where such continued support beyond the age of eighteen is intended for the purpose of a college education for said child. Calogeras v. Calogeras (Ohio Juv. 1959) 163 N.E.2d 713, 82 Ohio Law Abs. 438, 10 O.O.2d 441.

4. Personal injury action

A plaintiff in a personal injury action who was injured in an accident occurring prior to January 1, 1974, while he was under the age of 21, must litigate his claim within two years after the January 1, 1974 amendment to RC 3109.01, lowering the age of majority to 18 years, or within two years after his eighteenth birthday, whichever is later. Cook v. Matvejs (Ohio 1978) 56 Ohio St.2d 234, 383 N.E.2d 601, 10 O.O.3d 384.

A plaintiff in a personal injury action who was injured in an accident occurring prior to January 1, 1974, while he was under the age of twenty-one, must litigate his claim within two years after the January 1, 1974, amendment to RC 3109.01, lowering the age of majority to eighteen years. Dickerson v. Ferrell (Richland 1976) 53 Ohio App.2d 160, 372 N.E.2d 619, 7 O.O.3d 161.

Mother of hockey player, who supported her son's participation in ice hockey and was at the ice rink at the time of his injury, was barred under Ohio law under the doctrine of estoppel by acquiescence from disaffirming the release signed by both hockey player and his father. Mohney v. USA Hockey, Inc. (N.D.Ohio 1999) 77 F.Supp.2d 859.

5. Disaffirming contracts

A minor can void a contract whether or not she is married. Bramley's Water Conditioning v. Hagen (Portage 1985) 27 Ohio App.3d 300, 501 N.E.2d 38, 27 O.B.R. 356.

Infant before or within reasonable time after coming of age may disaffirm contract not for necessaries. Infant who, on attaining majority, elected to disaffirm contract for purchase of automobile, made disaffirmance effective by returning car to seller without notifying seller's assignee. Hoffman v. Edson Co. (Cuyahoga 1929) 37 Ohio App. 262, 173 N.E. 307, 7 Ohio Law Abs. 388.

A minor can withdraw from contract without placing other party in statu quo, where it is impossible to do so. Eagle Dairy Co. v. Dylag (Cuyahoga 1929) 33 Ohio App. 113, 168 N.E. 754, 7 Ohio Law Abs. 358, 30 Ohio Law Rep. 361.

Infant misrepresenting his age upon purchasing automobile may plead minority to avoid contract and may recover payments made without any diminution. Summit Auto Co. v. Jenkins (Summit 1925) 20 Ohio App. 229, 153 N.E. 153, 4 Ohio Law Abs. 50, 24 Ohio Law Rep. 392.

To maintain action on contract for necessaries made with minor, transaction must be fair and reasonable, made in good faith by plaintiff, and without knowledge of defendant's lack of capacity to contract; "necessaries" are defined as food, medicine, clothing, shelter or personal services usually considered reasonably essential for preservation and enjoyment of life. Parkwood OB/GYN Inc. v. Hess (Ohio Mun. 1995) 70 Ohio Misc.2d 32, 650 N.E.2d 533.

Although medical services provided to minor constituted "necessary" services, medical clinic was precluded from recovering on contract for services, since clinic knew minor's date of birth when services were rendered and therefore had knowledge of minor's incapacity to contract. Parkwood OB/GYN Inc. v. Hess (Ohio Mun. 1995) 70 Ohio Misc.2d 32, 650 N.E.2d 533.

Contracts of minor are voidable at minor's election upon reaching majority or reasonable time thereafter; only exceptions are those authorized by law, those entered in performance of legal duty, and those for purchase of necessities. Parkwood OB/GYN Inc. v. Hess (Ohio Mun. 1995) 70 Ohio Misc.2d 32, 650 N.E.2d 533.

Under this section, no minor can make a valid contract unless it be for necessaries, or for some other purpose which law permits. No provision permits a minor parent to contract away a child. GC 10512-11 (RC 3107.03) permits parent to give consent to adoption, and GC 1352-12 (RC 5103.15) permits parents to place children with state department of public welfare, and while no age is mentioned in these sections, consent of minor parents is sufficient because these sections place no limitation as to age of parents. As contracting away a child is not an adoption case, or a placement with department of public welfare, this section would thereby restrict minor parent from making contract in question. In re Swentosky, 25 Abs 601 (Prob, Tuscarawas 1937).

Where minor purchases an automobile, giving notes in part payment therefor, and continues to use it and make payments thereon for more than six months after attaining majority, it is too late to disaffirm his contract of purchase, and he is bound thereby. Herschede Motor Car Co. v. Bangham (Ohio Com.Pl. 1926) 26 Ohio N.P.N.S. 232.

6. Age of majority for females from eighteen to twenty-one

A deed by female persons over the age of eighteen but under twenty-one years of age, executed at a time when the amendment of this section, changing the majority of females from eighteen to twenty-one was effective, is voidable and may be set aside. Coleman v. Coleman

(Hamilton 1935) 51 Ohio App. 221, 200 N.E. 197, 19 Ohio Law Abs. 661, 4 O.O. 172.

Legislature acted within its power in passing statute increasing age of majority of females from eighteen to twenty-one years and the statute is not retroactive. Pickering v. Peskind (Cuyahoga 1930) 43 Ohio App. 401, 183 N.E. 301, 13 Ohio Law Abs. 312, 31 Ohio Law Rep. 439.

Right of action for tort, by female who became eighteen on January 7, 1923, then accrued and being a property right, could not be taken away by statute becoming effective July 18, 1923, increasing age of majority of females to twenty-one years. Pickering v. Peskind (Cuyahoga 1930) 43 Ohio App. 401, 183 N.E. 301, 13 Ohio Law Abs. 312, 31 Ohio Law Rep. 439.

The amendment to the statute, fixing age of majority of females at twenty-one, is not retroactive and does not affect existing rights of property of women who became eighteen years of age prior to the date the amendment became effective. Pickering v. Peskind (Cuyahoga 1930) 43 Ohio App. 401, 183 N.E. 301, 13 Ohio Law Abs. 312, 31 Ohio Law Rep. 439.

It is error for trial court to dismiss action for divorce on ground that plaintiff is a minor, being a female under twenty-one years of age at time of trial, where she was of legal age at time of filing the action, and subsequent thereto but before trial, the legislature amended the statute, changing the age of majority of females from eighteen to twenty-one years. Tigner v. Tigner (Hamilton 1923) 19 Ohio App. 297, 2 Ohio Law Abs. 571.

In an action to extend child support provisions to cover the children from age eighteen to twenty-one, the trial court does have authority to entertain the motion to modify the original divorce decree and extend the time of the husband's support obligation. Kufrin v Kufrin, No. 42926 (8th Dist Ct App, Cuyahoga, 4-23-81).

7. Alcohol purchasing under age 21

No cause of action exists against liquor permit holder on part of a voluntarily intoxicated patron who is "underage" pursuant to statute but who has attained the age of majority, or on part of patron's representative, for patron's self-inflicted injury or death which is due to intoxication. Klever v. Canton Sachsenheim, Inc. (Ohio 1999) 86 Ohio St.3d 419, 715 N.E.2d 536.

Nineteen-year-old motorist who sustained fatal injuries in single-vehicle accident which occurred while motorist was driving after becoming intoxicated at wedding reception was not protected by Dramshop Act, and thus, motorist's representative could not maintain wrongful death action under Dramshop Act against club which had hosted reception and served alcohol to motorist. Klever v. Canton Sachsenheim, Inc. (Ohio 1999) 86 Ohio St.3d 419, 715 N.E.2d 536.

A state's decision to limit the consumption of alcoholic beverages to persons twenty-one years and older is a lawful exercise of a state's police power and is rationally related to a legitimate state interest in keeping inexperienced and young drivers from driving on the streets of Ohio while under the influence of alcohol. State v Powers, Nos. 9-98-08 to 9-98-10, 1998 WL 720694 (3d Dist Ct App, Marion, 10-16-98).

8. Parental discipline

Parental-discipline defense is not applicable where the victim has reached age eighteen and is not mentally or physically handicapped. State v Miller, No. C-980846, 1999 WL 631033 (1st Dist Ct App, Hamilton, 8-20-99).

3109.02 Veteran's exception

Any person who is eligible for a loan under the Servicemen's Readjustment Act of 1944, any amendments thereto or re-enactment thereof, the Veterans Readjustment Assistance Act of 1952, any amendments thereto or re-enactment thereof, the Act of September 2, 1958, Public Law 85-857, 72 Stat. 1105, any amendments thereto or re-enactment thereof, or the Veterans' Readjustment Benefits Act of 1966, any amendments thereto or re-enactments thereof, whether or not he or his spouse is a minor, may, in his name and without any order of court or the intervention of a guardian or trustee, execute any instruments, take title to real property, borrow money thereon, and do all other acts necessary to secure to him all rights and benefits under said acts, or any regulations thereunder, in as full and ample manner as if he and his spouse had attained the age of eighteen years. No person eligible for such loan, or his spouse, is, by reason only of such minority, incompetent to acquire title to property by contract or to borrow thereon; and no instrument made in connection with acquiring title to real estate or making such loan shall be voidable on the grounds of minority of such person or his spouse.

Any person who has qualified under said acts or any regulations thereunder and has secured a loan and taken title to real property thereunder is capable of disposing of such property by deed or other conveyance, notwithstanding the fact that he or his spouse is a minor, and no such deed or other conveyance shall be voidable on the grounds of minority of such person or his spouse.

(1973 S 1, eff. 1-1-74; 132 v H 909; 125 v 99; 1953 H 1; GC 8005-2; Source—GC 8023-1)

Historical and Statutory Notes

Pre-1953 H 1 Amendments: 124 v S 65

Library References

Armed Services ⚷108 to 112, 123(1), 123(2).
Infants ⚷46 to 58.
WESTLAW Topic Nos. 34, 211.
C.J.S. Armed Services §§ 260, 261, 264, 267.
C.J.S. Infants §§ 113, 114, 122, 166 to 188, 191.

OJur 3d: 47, Family Law § 829
Am Jur 2d: 42, Infants § 63

White, Ohio Landlord Tenant Law (1999 Ed.), Text 2.22

Notes of Decisions and Opinions

Unimproved lots 1

1. Unimproved lots

The spouse of a serviceman, who is a minor and who joins with her husband in executing a promissory note in payment of the purchase price of three unimproved lots, as a separate consideration for same and apart from the consideration paid for an adjacent dwelling house purchased concurrently although constituting one transaction, upon arriving at her majority, may disaffirm her legal obligation of liability on such note. Lambright v. Heck (Wood 1949) 86 Ohio App. 456, 93 N.E.2d 45, 42 O.O. 64.

Where one "who is eligible for a loan under the Servicemen's Readjustment Act of 1944" purchases a dwelling house and three unimproved lots adjacent, and who obtains a loan under the act on the lot improved with a dwelling house, and who in the same transaction executes a promissory note in payment of the purchase price of three unimproved lots, the provisions of the act have no application in determining the validity of the promissory note. Lambright v. Heck (Wood 1949) 86 Ohio App. 456, 93 N.E.2d 45, 42 O.O. 64.

PARENTAL RIGHTS AND RESPONSIBILITIES

3109.03 Equal rights of parents to parental rights and responsibilities toward children

When husband and wife are living separate and apart from each other, or are divorced, and the question as to the parental rights and responsibilities for the care of their children and the place of residence and legal custodian of their children is brought before a court of competent jurisdiction, they shall stand upon an equality as to the parental rights and responsibilities for the care of their children and the place of residence and legal custodian of their children, so far as parenthood is involved.

(1990 S 3, eff. 4-11-91; 1953 H 1; GC 8005-3; Source—GC 8032)

Historical and Statutory Notes

Pre-1953 H 1 Amendments: 124 v S 65

Cross References

Action for divorce, annulment, or legal separation, custody and support of children, 3105.21
Husband and wife are natural guardians of minor children, 2111.08
Provision for allocation of parental rights and responsibilities in separation agreement attached to petition for dissolution of marriage, 3105.63

Library References

Parent and Child ⚷1, 2(1) to 2(3.7), 3.1(1) to 3.1(3).
WESTLAW Topic No. 285.
C.J.S. Parent and Child §§ 2 to 4, 10 to 30, 49, 50, 53 to 56, 59.

Am Jur 2d: 59, Parent and Child § 25 et seq., 44, 45
Right to punish for contempt for failure to obey custody order either beyond power or jurisdiction of court or merely erroneous. 12 ALR2d 1095
Nonresidence as affecting one's right to custody of child. 15 ALR2d 432
Alienation of child's affections as affecting custody award. 32 ALR2d 1005
Annulment: court's power as to support and maintenance of children in marriage annulment proceedings. 63 ALR2d 1029
Mental health of contesting parent as factor in award of child custody. 74 ALR2d 1073
Right of mother to custody of illegitimate child. 98 ALR2d 417
Comment Note—Propriety of separating children by awarding custody to different parents. 98 ALR2d 926
Propriety of court conducting private interview with child in determining custody. 99 ALR2d 954
Child's wishes as factor in awarding custody. 4 ALR3d 1396
Award of custody of child to parent against whom divorce is decreed. 23 ALR3d 6
Award of custody of child where contest is between child's father and grandparent. 25 ALR3d 7
Award of custody of child where contest is between child's mother and grandparent. 29 ALR3d 366
Award of custody of child where contest is between child's grandparent and one other than the child's parent. 30 ALR3d 290
Award of custody of child where contest is between child's parents and grandparents. 31 ALR3d 1187
Right of putative father to custody of illegitimate child. 45 ALR3d 216

Right, in child custody proceedings, to cross-examine investigating officer whose report is used by court in its decision. 59 ALR3d 1337

Modern status of maternal preference rule or presumption in child custody cases. 70 ALR3d 262

Who has custody or control of child within terms of penal statute punishing cruelty or neglect by one having custody or control. 75 ALR3d 933

Effect, in subsequent proceedings, of paternity findings or implications in divorce or annulment decree or in support or custody order made incident thereto. 78 ALR3d 846

Parent's involuntary confinement, or failure to care for child as result thereof, as evincing neglect, unfitness, or the like in dependency or divestiture proceeding. 79 ALR3d 417

Validity, construction, and application of Uniform Child Custody Jurisdiction Act. 96 ALR3d 968

Right to require psychiatric or mental examination for party seeking to obtain or retain custody of child. 99 ALR3d 268

Custodial parent's sexual relations with third person as justifying modification of child custody order. 100 ALR3d 625

Admissibility of social worker's expert testimony on child custody issues. 1 ALR4th 837

Parent's physical disability or handicap as factor in custody award or proceedings. 3 ALR4th 1044

Award of custody of child where contest is between natural parent and stepparent. 10 ALR4th 767

Race as factor in custody award or proceedings. 10 ALR4th 796

Desire of child as to geographical location of residence or domicile as factor in awarding custody or terminating parental rights. 10 ALR4th 827

Right of incarcerated mother to retain custody of infant in penal institution. 14 ALR4th 748

Necessity of requiring presence in court of both parties in proceedings relating to custody or visitation of children. 15 ALR4th 864

Propriety of awarding joint custody of children. 17 ALR4th 1013

Propriety of awarding custody of child to parent residing or intending to reside in foreign country. 20 ALR4th 677

Religion as factor in child custody and visitation cases. 22 ALR4th 971

Parent's transsexuality as factor in award of custody of children, visitation rights, or termination of parental rights. 59 ALR4th 1170

Child custody: separating children by custody awards to different parents—post-1975 cases. 67 ALR4th 354

Parental rights of man who is not biological or adoptive father of child but was husband or cohabitant of mother when child was conceived or born. 84 ALR4th 655

Child custody and visitation rights of person infected with AIDS. 86 ALR4th 211

Authority of court, upon entering default judgment, to make orders for child custody or support which were not specifically requested in pleadings of prevailing party. 5 ALR5th 863

Continuity of residence as factor in contest between parent and nonparent for custody of child who has been residing with nonparent—modern status. 15 ALR5th 692

Smoking as factor in child custody and visitation cases. 36 ALR5th 377

Sowald & Morganstern, Baldwin's Ohio Practice, *Domestic Relations Law* § 7.19, 15.10, 21.24, 21.26, 25.30 (1997)

Law Review and Journal Commentaries

Bankruptcy Reform Act of 1994—What the Bankruptcy Code Giveth, Domestic Relations Courts (and Congress) Taketh Away, C.R. "Chip" Bowles. 8 Domestic Rel J Ohio 17 (March/April 1996).

Child custody disputes between lesbians: Legal strategies and their limitations, Nicole Berner. 10 Berkeley Women's L J 31 (1995).

The Child Dependency Exemption And Divorced Parents: What Is "Custody"?, David J. Benson. 18 Cap U L Rev 57 (Spring 1989).

Children—The Innocent Victims of Family Breakups: How the Family Law Attorney, the Courts, and Society Can Protect Our Children, Michael J. Albano. 26 U Tol L Rev 787 (Summer 1995).

Custody Disputes Following the Dissolution of Interracial Marriages: Best Interests of the Child or Judicial Racism?, Colleen McKinley. 19 J Fam L 97 (1980-81).

Enforcement Of Surrogate Mother Contracts: Case Law, The Uniform Acts, and State and Federal Legislation, James T. Flaherty. 36 Clev St L Rev 223 (1988).

Judges' Column, Hon. Francine Bruening. (Ed. note: Judge Bruening discusses the Child Support Reorganization Act of House Bill 352, effective 1-1-98.) 21 Lake Legal Views 1 (June 1998).

Report of the Family Law Committee (Uniform Child Custody Jurisdiction Act). 49 Ohio St B Ass'n Rep 611 (5-17-76).

Standard of Proof in Proceedings to Terminate Parental Rights, Note. 31 Clev St L Rev 679 (1982).

Notes of Decisions and Opinions

---

1. Constitutional issues

Father was not denied fair trial in custody determination proceedings by being denied right to proceed pro se; father claimed right to proceed pro se as cocounsel, father was represented by counsel throughout proceedings, father ignored instructions to file papers only through his attorney, trial court recognized obligation to rule on all motions filed by counsel, and father did not indicate how he was prejudiced by failure of court to rule on several pro se motions. Rife v. Morgan (Clark 1995) 106 Ohio App.3d 843, 667 N.E.2d 450.

Father was not prejudiced by minimal participation of mother's counsel in evidentiary hearing in custody determination, despite mother's apparent agreement that custody should be with maternal grandparents, and thus, he was not denied a fair trial or due process of law. Rife v. Morgan (Clark 1995) 106 Ohio App.3d 843, 667 N.E.2d 450.

Father was not denied due process in custody determination by trial court's appointment of counsel for guardian ad litem without affording father an opportunity to be heard, where guardian ad litem was to be subjected to cross-examination. Rife v. Morgan (Clark 1995) 106 Ohio App.3d 843, 667 N.E.2d 450.

Father was not denied a fair trial in custody determination by trial court's refusal to permit his child to be cross-examined during evidentiary hearing, where remand from previous appeal of trial court's award of custody to maternal grandparents was limited to requiring trial court to allow cross-examination of guardian ad litem. Rife v. Morgan (Clark 1995) 106 Ohio App.3d 843, 667 N.E.2d 450.

Father in custody proceeding was not prejudiced by trial court's failure to rule on motions to allow newly discovered evidence and for finding of contempt against child's maternal grandmother, and thus was not denied a fair trial, where trial court recognized that it had not yet ruled upon motions and matter had been remanded to trial court from earlier appeal only for purpose of allowing father to cross-examine guardian ad litem. Rife v. Morgan (Clark 1995) 106 Ohio App.3d 843, 667 N.E.2d 450.

Father in custody proceeding was not prejudiced by trial court's implicit overruling of father's motion to remove guardian ad litem for child, and thus was not denied a fair trial, where father did not explain how he was prejudiced and matter had been remanded to trial court from earlier appeal only for purpose of allowing father to cross-examine guardian ad litem. Rife v. Morgan (Clark 1995) 106 Ohio App.3d 843, 667 N.E.2d 450.

Father in custody proceeding was not prejudiced by trial court's failure to rule on pro se motions for findings of contempt against school, social worker, and children's home after remand from earlier appeal to allow father opportunity to cross-examine guardian ad litem, and thus was not denied a fair trial, where father did not explain how he was prejudiced, motions did not implicate limited purpose of remand, and there was no reason to conclude that trial court would not eventually rule on motions. Rife v. Morgan (Clark 1995) 106 Ohio App.3d 843, 667 N.E.2d 450.

Father who lost custody of his child was not denied a fair trial or equal protection by trial court's failure to obtain complete record of prior proceedings to resolve authenticity objection to report used by father's counsel on cross-examination of guardian ad litem, where father's counsel convinced trial court that document was authentic and counsel was allowed to use report. Rife v. Morgan (Clark 1995) 106 Ohio App.3d 843, 667 N.E.2d 450.

Appellate court, on appeal after remand to allow father in custody proceeding to cross-examine guardian ad litem, would not address argument by father that trial court had denied him a fair trial by withholding the record of its discussions with child; discussion appeared to be germane to prior appeal from court's original judgment, and any problem with securing record should have been addressed during pendency of prior appeal. Rife v. Morgan (Clark 1995) 106 Ohio App.3d 843, 667 N.E.2d 450.

A trial court commits reversible error when a husband is not provided with opportunity to be heard as to the issues of property division and child custody at his divorce trial under circumstances that (1) he is present in the courtroom without counsel while seated in the back of the room, (2) he waves his arms in objection and the trial judge requests that the defendant either stop waving his arms or leave the courtroom, and (3) the defendant verbally objects to a particular statement, to which the judge responds, "Just be quiet. I'm taking testimony up here at this time," after which trial continues without defendant's participation and proceeds to grant judgment in favor of the plaintiff following her presentation of evidence. Skaggs v Skaggs, No. 9-94-60, 1995 WL 368838 (3d Dist Ct App, Marion, 6-22-95).

There is no substantive federal constitutional right to physical possession of a child; a parent's right to custody or visitation with a child, however, is a constitutionally protected liberty interest that cannot be interfered with absent due process of law. Scarso v. Cuyahoga County Dept. of Human Services (N.D.Ohio 1989) 747 F.Supp. 381, affirmed in part and remanded 917 F.2d 1305.

2. Child support

A custodial parent is not entitled to reimbursement for child support from the noncustodial parent where no support order is made or requested at the time custody is awarded. Meyer v. Meyer (Ohio 1985) 17 Ohio St.3d 222, 478 N.E.2d 806, 17 O.B.R. 455.

Trial court did not abuse its discretion by ordering that commencement of former wife's child support obligation begin at time when all three children of couple began residing with former husband, even though husband had been designated as residential parent for two of children eight months earlier. Bowen v. Bowen (Ohio App. 9 Dist. 1999) 132 Ohio App.3d 616, 725 N.E.2d 1165.

A custodial parent is not entitled to reimbursement for child support from the non-custodial parent where no support order is made or requested at the time custody is awarded. Bowen v. Bowen (Ohio App. 9 Dist. 1999) 132 Ohio App.3d 616, 725 N.E.2d 1165.

Evidence supported trial court's determination that father should pay entire amount of child support owed under dissolution decree, even though child had moved in with her boyfriend; mother testified that she used money received to pay child's expenses, and child testified that she remained dependent upon mother for support after she left her mother's home. Swanson v. Swanson (Greene 1996) 109 Ohio App.3d 231, 671 N.E.2d 1333.

Where a wife abandons her husband without any aggression on his part and takes her children to another state, the husband cannot be compelled to support such children under the uniform enforcement of support laws where he retains a domicile in Ohio, earns his living in Ohio, and apparently is ready, willing and able to support his children in Ohio. Buliox v. Buliox (Ohio Com.Pl. 1962) 185 N.E.2d 802, 90 Ohio Law Abs. 251, 21 O.O.2d 30.

3. Unmarried parents

Statute specifying that husband and wife who are divorced or living separate and apart shall stand upon equality as to parental rights and responsibilities and shall have equal rights to custody in absence of agreement or binding court order does not deal with rights of putative father who has neither acknowledged paternity nor supported the child. State v. Hill (Ohio 1996) 75 Ohio St.3d 195, 661 N.E.2d 1068, reconsideration denied 75 Ohio St.3d 1453, 663 N.E.2d 333, certiorari denied 117 S.Ct. 241, 136 L.Ed.2d 170, denial of post-conviction relief affirmed, dismissed, appeal not allowed 81 Ohio St.3d 1468, 690 N.E.2d 1288.

When the alleged natural father of an illegitimate child, who has participated in the nurturing process of the child, files a complaint seeking custody of the child under RC 2151.23(A)(2), and the mother admits that he is the natural father of the child, the natural father has equality of standing with the mother with respect to the custody of the child, and the court shall determine which parent shall have the legal custody of the child, taking into account what would be in the best interests of the child. In re Byrd (Ohio 1981) 66 Ohio St.2d 334, 421 N.E.2d 1284, 20 O.O.3d 309.

Although parents who are suitable persons generally have paramount right to custody of their minor children, rights and interests of natural parents are not absolute. In re Hiatt (Adams 1993) 86 Ohio App.3d 716, 621 N.E.2d 1222.

A trial court abuses its discretion when it awards the father custody of the two minor children of the unmarried couple where (1) the mother supported the couple and children through part-time employment during the eight years they were together but the father was not regularly employed and rarely spent quality time with the children; (2) the father took the children on vacation to Florida and, after the mother informed him over the telephone that she wished to terminate their relationship, he refused to let the mother see them or often even to speak to them on the telephone; and (3) once in Florida, the father changed his residence, found employment, enrolled the children in school, affiliated with a church, and began to spend time with the children. In re Markham (Meigs 1990) 70 Ohio App.3d 841, 592 N.E.2d 896, dismissed, jurisdictional motion overruled 60 Ohio St.3d 702, 573 N.E.2d 118.

The father of a child born out of wedlock is not entitled to visitation with such child over the objections of the mother, who has legal custody, unless he clearly establishes that such would be in the best interests of the child. In re Connolly (Franklin 1974) 43 Ohio App.2d 38, 332 N.E.2d 376, 72 O.O.2d 194.

4. Full faith and credit

Where a court of another state has awarded custody of a minor child pursuant to a valid in personam order, and there is no evidence of a subsequent change in circumstances affecting the best interests of the child, the courts of this state will give full faith and credit to that order. Williams v. Williams (Ohio 1975) 44 Ohio St.2d 28, 336 N.E.2d 426, 73 O.O.2d 121.

5. Moral conduct of parents

A court's inquiry into the moral conduct or standards of a custodial parent is limited to a determination of the effect of such conduct on the child. In re Rex (Seneca 1981) 3 Ohio App.3d 198, 444 N.E.2d 482, 3 O.B.R. 226.

A mother's having surreptitiously relocated a child is one of several factors for a court to consider in making a custody determination and it does not err in vacating a child custody portion of a divorce decree which awards sole custody to the father where evidence is insufficient to support a granting of permanent custody to either parent and the court has heard very little evidence concerning the best interests of the child. Eichenberger v Eichenberger, No. 95APF04-456, 1995 WL 632059 (10th Dist Ct App, Franklin, 10-24-95).

6. Jurisdiction

An Ohio juvenile court, in a dependency proceeding pursuant to RC 2151.27 et seq., has no jurisdiction to interfere with a mother's legal custody of her children, in the absence of proof and a finding of unfitness of such parent, merely for the purpose of releasing such children to the officers of the court of a foreign state, and the court need not give full faith and credit to a Michigan decree where that decree was obtained by the husband in an ex parte custody determination, subsequent to a divorce decree, in which the Michigan court had no personal jurisdiction over the nonresident wife. In re Messner (Huron 1969) 19 Ohio App.2d 33, 249 N.E.2d 532, 48 O.O.2d 31.

The Lucas County court of common pleas, division of domestic relations, is a court of competent jurisdiction to determine care, custody, and control of minor children. Witkorowski v. Witkorowski (Lucas 1951) 89 Ohio App. 424, 102 N.E.2d 896, 46 O.O. 259.

7. Married parents

When a divorce is denied, the parties are still married and they have equal rights as to custody of minor children, and both are responsible for care and support, and, until such time as a separate complaint or application is made to a court of competent jurisdiction, the provisions of RC 3109.03 and 3109.04 may not be invoked. Holderle v. Holderle (Franklin 1967) 11 Ohio App.2d 148, 229 N.E.2d 79, 40 O.O.2d 305.

8. Divorced parents

Where in a divorce action in which neither party is found to be unsuited for custody, custody is awarded to the mother, and the court pursuant to agreement of the parties orders that the child continue to reside with the paternal grandparents, and each party thereafter seeks modification of the order, the agreement is waived and the court must award physical custody to the mother in the absence of a showing that she is not suitable. La Ferier v. Garey (Lucas 1954) 98 Ohio App. 37, 128 N.E.2d 168, 57 O.O. 157.

Under the provisions of GC 8032 (RC 3109.03), when the parents are divorced and the question as to the custody of their child is before the court, the parents "stand upon an equality as to the care, custody and control" of their child. Ludy v. Ludy (Franklin 1948) 84 Ohio App. 195, 82 N.E.2d 775, 53 Ohio Law Abs. 47, 39 O.O. 241, rehearing denied 84 N.E.2d 120, 53 Ohio Law Abs. 47.

Visitation rights as to children of divorced parents must be considered without regard to the child's religious training, for all Christian denominations stand on the same footing in the eye of the law. Angel v. Angel (Ohio Com.Pl. 1956) 140 N.E.2d 86, 74 Ohio Law Abs. 531, 2 O.O.2d 136.

Trial court was justified in awarding custody of children eleven, ten, and six to the father because of the mother's emotional instability. Herzog v. Herzog (Montgomery 1955) 132 N.E.2d 754, 72 Ohio Law Abs. 22.

Custody of minor children in a divorce proceeding may be given to the father's sister, even though the divorce was granted for his aggression, where the mother's health is such that she should not have the children. Peterson v. Peterson (Ohio Com.Pl. 1954) 123 N.E.2d 546, 69 Ohio Law Abs. 459, 55 O.O. 134.

The remarriage of divorced parents terminates the jurisdiction of the divorce court over the custody of their minor children. Lockard v. Lockard (Ohio Com.Pl. 1951) 102 N.E.2d 747, 63 Ohio Law Abs. 549, 49 O.O. 163.

Where the natural parents of a minor child are divorced, custody of the child being given to the mother, and the mother remarries and her husband adopts the child, and then the mother and adoptive father are divorced, and custody is awarded to the adoptive father, and the natural father seeks custody, and prior to hearing the mother and adoptive father are remarried, the court loses jurisdiction over the custody of the child. Lockard v. Lockard (Ohio Com.Pl. 1951) 102 N.E.2d 747, 63 Ohio Law Abs. 549, 49 O.O. 163.

The judgment of a state court divesting a natural mother of the custody of her young child because of her remarriage to a man of a different race violates the Equal Protection Clause of US Const Am 14. (Ed. note: Florida law construed in light of federal constitution.) Palmore v. Sidoti (U.S.Fla. 1984) 104 S.Ct. 1879, 466 U.S. 429, 80 L.Ed.2d 421.

9. Tender years doctrine

While RC 3109.03 eliminates the presumption that the mother is the proper custodian of a child of tender years, the age of the child and the child's relationship with the mother are factors to be considered under RC 3109.04(C); and a trial court's failure to consider the child's tender years constitutes an abuse of discretion. Berry v Berry, No. CA88-11-081 (12th Dist Ct App, Clermont, 3-12-90).

10. Habeas corpus

On the evidence in a habeas corpus action the court will permit two boys to remain with their father rather than being given to their mother or separated. Trout v. Trout (Ohio Com.Pl. 1956) 136 N.E.2d 474, 73 Ohio Law Abs. 91, appeal dismissed 167 Ohio St. 476, 149 N.E.2d 728, 5 O.O.2d 156.

11. Interests of child

The welfare of the child is considered when the question of custody of such child arises between the parents who stand on an equality, or when the parents are found to be unfit and the court is required to grant custody to a third person. Ludy v. Ludy (Franklin 1948) 84 Ohio App. 195, 82 N.E.2d 775, 53 Ohio Law Abs. 47, 39 O.O. 241, rehearing denied 84 N.E.2d 120, 53 Ohio Law Abs. 47.

12. Voluntary relinquishment

Natural parent has paramount right to custody of his or her child as against nonparent, but exception exists providing that abandonment, contractual relinquishment, or total inability to provide support may be a forfeiture of natural parent's paramount right to custody. Miller v. Miller (Hocking 1993) 86 Ohio App.3d 623, 621 N.E.2d 745.

Whether relinquishing custody should be forfeiture of right of custody of parent is question of fact, and any contractual custody arrangement is not necessarily as matter of law a relinquishment of right of custody; there are situations where parent might make contractual arrangement for care and custody of child that cannot be construed to be forfeiture of custodial rights. Miller v. Miller (Hocking 1993) 86 Ohio App.3d 623, 621 N.E.2d 745.

3109.04 Court awarding parental rights and responsibilities; shared parenting; modifications; best interests of child; child's wishes

(A) In any divorce, legal separation, or annulment proceeding and in any proceeding pertaining to the allocation of parental rights and responsibilities for the care of a child, upon hearing the testimony of either or both parents and considering any mediation report filed pursuant to section 3109.052 of the Revised Code and in accordance with sections 3109.21 to 3109.36 of the Revised Code, the court shall allocate the parental rights and responsibilities for the care of the minor children of the marriage. Subject to division (D)(2) of this section, the court may allocate the parental rights and responsibilities for the care of the children in either of the following ways:

(1) If neither parent files a pleading or motion in accordance with division (G) of this section, if at least one parent files a pleading or motion under that division but no parent who filed a pleading or motion under that division also files a plan for shared parenting, or if at least one parent files both a pleading or motion and a shared parenting plan under that division but no plan for shared parenting is in the best interest of the children, the court, in a manner consistent with the best interest of the children, shall allocate the parental rights and responsibilities for the care of the children primarily to one of the parents, designate that parent as the residential parent and the legal custodian of the child, and divide between the parents the other rights and responsibilities for the care of the children, including, but not limited to, the responsibility to provide support for the children and the right of the parent who is not the residential parent to have continuing contact with the children.

(2) If at least one parent files a pleading or motion in accordance with division (G) of this section and a plan for shared parenting pursuant to that division and if a plan for shared parenting is in the best interest of the children and is approved by the court in accordance with division (D)(1) of this section, the court may allocate the parental rights and responsibilities for the care of the children to both parents and issue a shared parenting order requiring the

parents to share all or some of the aspects of the physical and legal care of the children in accordance with the approved plan for shared parenting. If the court issues a shared parenting order under this division and it is necessary for the purpose of receiving public assistance, the court shall designate which one of the parents' residences is to serve as the child's home. The child support obligations of the parents under a shared parenting order issued under this division shall be determined in accordance with section 3113.215 of the Revised Code.

(B)(1) When making the allocation of the parental rights and responsibilities for the care of the children under this section in an original proceeding or in any proceeding for modification of a prior order of the court making the allocation, the court shall take into account that which would be in the best interest of the children. In determining the child's best interest for purposes of making its allocation of the parental rights and responsibilities for the care of the child and for purposes of resolving any issues related to the making of that allocation, the court, in its discretion, may and, upon the request of either party, shall interview in chambers any or all of the involved children regarding their wishes and concerns with respect to the allocation.

(2) If the court interviews any child pursuant to division (B)(1) of this section, all of the following apply:

(a) The court, in its discretion, may and, upon the motion of either parent, shall appoint a guardian ad litem for the child.

(b) The court first shall determine the reasoning ability of the child. If the court determines that the child does not have sufficient reasoning ability to express his wishes and concern with respect to the allocation of parental rights and responsibilities for the care of the child, it shall not determine the child's wishes and concerns with respect to the allocation. If the court determines that the child has sufficient reasoning ability to express his wishes or concerns with respect to the allocation, it then shall determine whether, because of special circumstances, it would not be in the best interest of the child to determine the child's wishes and concerns with respect to the allocation. If the court determines that, because of special circumstances, it would not be in the best interest of the child to determine the child's wishes and concerns with respect to the allocation, it shall not determine the child's wishes and concerns with respect to the allocation and shall enter its written findings of fact and opinion in the journal. If the court determines that it would be in the best interests of the child to determine the child's wishes and concerns with respect to the allocation, it shall proceed to make that determination.

(c) The interview shall be conducted in chambers, and no person other than the child, the child's attorney, the judge, any necessary court personnel, and, in the judge's discretion, the attorney of each parent shall be permitted to be present in the chambers during the interview.

(3) No person shall obtain or attempt to obtain from a child a written or recorded statement or affidavit setting forth the child's wishes and concerns regarding the allocation of parental rights and responsibilities concerning the child. No court, in determining the child's best interest for purposes of making its allocation of the parental rights and responsibilities for the care of the child or for purposes of resolving any issues related to the making of that allocation, shall accept or consider a written or recorded statement or affidavit that purports to set forth the child's wishes and concerns regarding those matters.

(C) Prior to trial, the court may cause an investigation to be made as to the character, family relations, past conduct, earning ability, and financial worth of each parent and may order the parents and their minor children to submit to medical, psychological, and psychiatric examinations. The report of the investigation and examinations shall be made available to either parent or his counsel of record not less than five days before trial, upon written request. The report shall be signed by the investigator, and the investigator shall be subject to cross-examination by either parent concerning the contents of the report. The court may tax as costs all or any part of the expenses for each investigation.

If the court determines that either parent previously has been convicted of or pleaded guilty to any criminal offense involving any act that resulted in a child being a neglected child, that either parent previously has been determined to be the perpetrator of the neglectful act that is the basis of an adjudication that a child is a neglected child, or that there is reason to believe that either parent has acted in a manner resulting in a child being a neglected child, the court shall consider that fact against naming that parent the residential parent and against granting a shared parenting decree. When the court allocates parental rights and responsibilities for the care of children or determines whether to grant shared parenting in any proceeding, it shall consider whether either parent has been convicted of or pleaded guilty to a violation of section 2919.25 of the Revised Code involving a victim who at the time of the commission of the offense was a member of the family or household that is the subject of the proceeding, has been convicted of or pleaded guilty to any other offense involving a victim who at the time of the commission of the offense was a member of the family or household that is the subject of the proceeding and caused physical harm to the victim in the commission of the offense, or has been determined to be the perpetrator of the abusive act that is the basis of an adjudication that a child is an abused child. If the court determines that either parent has been convicted of or pleaded guilty to a violation of section 2919.25 of the Revised Code involving a victim who at the time of the commission of the offense was a member of the family or household that is the subject of the proceeding, has been convicted of or pleaded guilty to any other offense involving a victim who at the time of the commission of the offense was a member of the family or household that is the subject of the proceeding and caused physical harm to the victim in the commission of the offense, or has been determined to be the perpetrator of the abusive act that is the basis of an adjudication that a child is an abused child, it may designate that parent as the residential parent and may issue a shared parenting decree or order only if it determines that it is in the best interest of the child to name that parent the residential parent or to issue a shared parenting decree or order and it makes specific written findings of fact to support its determination.

(D)(1)(a) Upon the filing of a pleading or motion by either parent or both parents, in accordance with division (G) of this section, requesting shared parenting and the filing of a shared parenting plan in accordance with that division, the court shall comply with division (D)(1)(a)(i), (ii), or (iii) of this section, whichever is applicable:

(i) If both parents jointly make the request in their pleadings or jointly file the motion and also jointly file the plan, the court shall review the parents' plan to determine if it is in the best interest of the children. If the court determines that the plan is in the best interest of the children, the court shall approve it. If the court determines that the plan or any part of the plan is not in the best interest of the children, the court shall require the parents to make appropriate changes to the plan to meet the court's objections to it. If changes to the plan are made to meet the court's objections, and if the new plan is in the best interest of the children, the court shall approve the plan. If changes to the plan are not made to meet the court's objections, or if the parents attempt to make changes to the plan to meet the court's objections, but the court determines that the new plan or any part of the new plan still is not in the best interest of the children, the court may reject the portion of the parents' pleadings or deny their motion requesting shared parenting of the children and proceed as if the request in the pleadings or the motion had not been made. The court shall not approve a plan under this division unless it determines that the plan is in the best interest of the children.

(ii) If each parent makes a request in his pleadings or files a motion and each also files his own separate plan, the court shall review each plan filed to determine if either is in the best interest of the children. If the court determines that one of the filed plans is in the best interest of the children, the court may approve the plan. If the court determines that neither filed plan is in the best interest of the children, the court may order each parent to submit appropriate changes to his own plan or both of the filed plans to meet the court's objections, or may select one of the filed plans and order each parent to submit appropriate changes to the selected plan to meet the court's objections. If changes to the plan or plans are submitted to meet the court's objections, and if any of the filed plans with the changes is in the best interest of the children, the court may approve the plan with the changes. If changes to the plan or plans are not submitted to meet the court's objections, or if the parents submit changes to the plan or plans to meet the court's objections but the court determines that none of the filed plans with the submitted changes is in the best interest of the children, the court may reject the portion of the parents' pleadings or deny their motions requesting shared parenting of the children and proceed as if the requests in the pleadings or the motions had not been made. If the court approves a plan under this division, either as originally filed or with submitted changes, or if the court rejects the portion of the parents' pleadings or denies their motions requesting shared parenting under this division and proceeds as if the requests in the pleadings or the motions had not been made, the court shall enter in the record of the case findings of fact and conclusions of law as to the reasons for the approval or the rejection or denial. Division (D)(1)(b) of this section applies in relation to the approval or disapproval of a plan under this division.

(iii) If each parent makes a request in his pleadings or files a motion but only one parent files his own plan, or if only one parent makes a request in his pleadings or files a motion and also files a plan, the court in the best interest of the children may order the other parent to file a plan for shared parenting in accordance with division (G) of this section. The court shall review each plan filed to determine if any plan is in the best interest of the children. If the court determines that one of the filed plans is in the best interest of the children, the court may approve the plan. If the court determines that no filed plan is in the best interest of the children, the court may order each parent to submit appropriate changes to his own plan or both of the filed plans to meet the court's objections or may select one filed plan and order each parent to submit appropriate changes to the selected plan to meet the court's objections. If changes to the plan or plans are submitted to meet the court's objections, and if any of the filed plans with the changes is in the best interest of the children, the court may approve the plan with the changes. If changes to the plan or plans are not submitted to meet the court's objections, or if the parents submit changes to the plan or plans to meet the court's objections but the court determines that none of the filed plans with the submitted changes is in the best interest of the children, the court may reject the portion of the parents' pleadings or deny the parents' motion or reject the portion of the parents' pleadings or deny their motions requesting shared parenting of the children and proceed as if the request or requests or the motion or motions had not been made. If the court approves a plan under this division, either as originally filed or with submitted changes, or if the court rejects the portion of the pleadings or denies the motion or motions requesting shared parenting under this division and proceeds as if the request or requests or the motion or motions had not been made, the court shall enter in the record of the case findings of fact and conclusions of law as to the reasons for the approval or the rejection or denial. Division (D)(1)(b) of this section applies in relation to the approval or disapproval of a plan under this division.

(b) The approval of a plan under division (D)(1)(a)(ii) or (iii) of this section is discretionary with the court. The court shall not approve more than one plan under either division and shall not approve a plan under either division unless it determines that the plan is in the best interest of the children. If the court, under either division, does not determine that any filed plan or any filed plan with submitted changes is in the best interest of the children, the court shall not approve any plan.

(c) Whenever possible, the court shall require that a shared parenting plan approved under division (D)(1)(a)(i), (ii), or (iii) of this section ensure the opportunity for both parents to have frequent and continuing contact with the child, unless frequent and continuing contact with any parent would not be in the best interest of the child.

(d) If a court approves a shared parenting plan under division (D)(1)(a)(i), (ii), or (iii) of this section, the approved plan shall be incorporated into a final shared parenting decree granting the parents the shared parenting of the children. Any final shared parenting decree shall be issued at the same time as and shall be appended to the final decree of dissolution, divorce, annulment, or legal separation arising out of the action out of which the question of the allocation of parental rights and responsibilities for the care of the children arose.

No provisional shared parenting decree shall be issued in relation to any shared parenting plan approved under division (D)(1)(a)(i), (ii), or (iii) of this section. A final shared parenting decree issued under this division has immediate effect as a final decree on the date of its issuance, subject to modification or termination as authorized by this section.

(2) If the court finds, with respect to any child under eighteen years of age, that it is in the best interest of the child for neither parent to be designated the residential parent and legal custodian of the child, it may commit the child to a relative of the child or certify a copy of its findings, together with as much of the record and the further information, in narrative form or otherwise, that it considers necessary or as the juvenile court requests, to the juvenile court for further proceedings, and, upon the certification, the juvenile court has exclusive jurisdiction.

(E)(1)(a) The court shall not modify a prior decree allocating parental rights and responsibilities for the care of children unless it finds, based on facts that have arisen since the prior decree or that were unknown to the court at the time of the prior decree, that a change has occurred in the circumstances of the child, his residential parent, or either of the parents subject to a shared parenting decree, and that the modification is necessary to serve the best interest of the child. In applying these standards, the court shall retain the residential parent designated by the prior decree or the prior shared parenting decree, unless a modification is in the best interest of the child and one of the following applies:

(i) The residential parent agrees to a change in the residential parent or both parents under a shared parenting decree agree to a change in the designation of residential parent.

(ii) The child, with the consent of the residential parent or of both parents under a shared parenting decree, has been integrated into the family of the person seeking to become the residential parent.

(iii) The harm likely to be caused by a change of environment is outweighed by the advantages of the change of environment to the child.

(b) One or both of the parents under a prior decree allocating parental rights and responsibilities for the care of children that is not a shared parenting decree may file a motion requesting that the prior decree be modified to give both parents shared rights and responsibilities for the care of the children. The motion shall include both a request for modification of the prior decree and a request for a shared parenting order that complies with division (G) of this section. Upon the filing of the motion, if the court determines that a modification of the prior decree is authorized under division (E)(1)(a) of this section, the court may modify the prior decree to grant a shared parenting order, provided that the court shall not modify the prior decree to grant a shared parenting order unless the court complies with divisions (A) and (D)(1) of this section and, in accordance with those divisions, approves the submitted shared parenting plan and determines that shared parenting would be in the best interest of the children.

(2) In addition to a modification authorized under division (E)(1) of this section:

(a) Both parents under a shared parenting decree jointly may modify the terms of the plan for shared parenting approved by the court and incorporated by it into the shared parenting decree. Modifications under this division may be made at any time. The modifications to the plan shall be filed jointly by both parents with the court, and the court shall include them in the plan, unless they are not in the best interest of the children. If the modifications are not in the best interests of the children, the court, in its discretion, may reject the modifications or make modifications to the proposed modifications or the plan that are in the best interest of the children. Modifications jointly submitted by both parents under a shared parenting decree shall be effective, either as originally filed or as modified by the court, upon their inclusion by the court in the plan. Modifications to the plan made by the court shall be effective upon their inclusion by the court in the plan.

(b) The court may modify the terms of the plan for shared parenting approved by the court and incorporated by it into the shared parenting decree upon its own motion at any time if the court determines that the modifications are in the best interest of the children or upon the request of one or both of the parents under the decree. Modifications under this division may be made at any time. The court shall not make any modification to the plan under this division, unless the modification is in the best interest of the children.

(c) The court may terminate a prior final shared parenting decree that includes a shared parenting plan approved under division (D)(1)(a)(i) of this section upon the request of one or both of the parents or whenever it determines that shared parenting is not in the best interest of the children. The court may terminate a prior final shared parenting decree that includes a shared parenting plan approved under division (D)(1)(a)(ii) or (iii) of this section if it determines, upon its own motion or upon the request of one or both parents, that shared parenting is not in the best interest of the children. If modification of the terms of the plan for shared parenting approved by the court and incorporated by it into the final shared parenting decree is attempted under division (E)(2)(a) of this section and the court rejects the modifications, it may terminate the final shared parenting decree if it determines that shared parenting is not in the best interest of the children.

(d) Upon the termination of a prior final shared parenting decree under division (E)(2)(c) of this section, the court shall proceed and issue a modified decree for the allocation of parental rights and responsibilities for the care of the children under the standards applicable under divisions (A), (B), and (C) of this section as if no decree for shared parenting had been granted and as if no request for shared parenting ever had been made.

(F)(1) In determining the best interest of a child pursuant to this section, whether on an original decree allocating parental rights and responsibilities for the care of children or a modification of a decree allocating those rights and responsibilities, the court shall consider all relevant factors, including, but not limited to:

(a) The wishes of the child's parents regarding his care;

(b) If the court has interviewed the child in chambers pursuant to division (B) of this section regarding the child's wishes and concerns as to the allocation of parental rights and responsibilities concerning the child, the wishes and concerns of the child, as expressed to the court;

(c) The child's interaction and interrelationship with his parents, siblings, and any other person who may significantly affect the child's best interest;

(d) The child's adjustment to his home, school, and community;

(e) The mental and physical health of all persons involved in the situation;

(f) The parent more likely to honor and facilitate visitation and companionship rights approved by the court;

(g) Whether either parent has failed to make all child support payments, including all arrearages, that are required of that parent pursuant to a child support order under which that parent is an obligor;

(h) Whether either parent previously has been convicted of or pleaded guilty to any criminal offense involving any act that resulted in a child being an abused child or a neglected child; whether either parent, in a case in which a child has been adjudicated an abused child or a neglected child, previously has been determined to be the perpetrator of the abusive or neglectful act that is the basis of an adjudication; whether either parent previously has been convicted of or pleaded guilty to a violation of section 2919.25 of the Revised Code involving a victim who at the time of the commission of the offense was a member of the family or household that is the subject of the current proceeding; whether either parent previously has been convicted of or pleaded guilty to any offense involving a victim who at the time of the commission of the offense was a member of the family or household that is the subject of the current proceeding and caused physical harm to the victim in the commission of the offense; and whether there is reason to believe that either parent has acted in a manner resulting in a child being an abused child or a neglected child;

(i) Whether the residential parent or one of the parents subject to a shared parenting decree has continuously and willfully denied the other parent his or her right to visitation in accordance with an order of the court;

(j) Whether either parent has established a residence, or is planning to establish a residence, outside this state.

(2) In determining whether shared parenting is in the best interest of the children, the court shall consider all relevant factors, including, but not limited to, the factors enumerated in division (F)(1) of this section, the factors enumerated in division (B)(3) of section 3113.215 of the Revised Code, and all of the following factors:

(a) The ability of the parents to cooperate and make decisions jointly, with respect to the children;

(b) The ability of each parent to encourage the sharing of love, affection, and contact between the child and the other parent;

(c) Any history of, or potential for, child abuse, spouse abuse, other domestic violence, or parental kidnapping by either parent;

(d) The geographic proximity of the parents to each other, as the proximity relates to the practical considerations of shared parenting;

(e) The recommendation of the guardian ad litem of the child, if the child has a guardian ad litem.

(3) When allocating parental rights and responsibilities for the care of children, the court shall not give preference to a parent because of that parent's financial status or condition.

(G) Either parent or both parents of any children may file a pleading or motion with the court requesting the court to grant both parents shared parental rights and responsibilities for the care of the children in a proceeding held pursuant to division (A) of this section. If a pleading or motion requesting shared parenting is filed, the parent or parents filing the pleading or motion also shall file with the court a plan for the exercise of shared parenting by both parents. If each parent files a pleading or motion requesting shared parenting but only one parent files his own plan or if only one parent files a pleading or motion requesting shared parenting and also files a plan, the other parent as ordered by the court shall file with the court a plan for the exercise of shared parenting by both parents. The plan for shared parenting shall be filed with the petition for dissolution of marriage, if the question of parental rights and responsibilities for the care of the children arises out of an action for dissolution of marriage, or, in other cases, at a time at least thirty days prior to the hearing on the issue of the parental rights and responsibilities for the care of the children. A plan for shared parenting shall include provisions covering all factors that are relevant to the care of the children, including, but not limited to, provisions covering factors such as physical living arrangements, child support obligations, provision for the children's medical and dental care, school placement, and the parent with which the children will be physically located during legal holidays, school holidays, and other days of special importance.

(H) If an appeal is taken from a decision of a court that grants or modifies a decree allocating parental rights and responsibilities for the care of children, the court of appeals shall give the case calendar priority and handle it expeditiously.

(I) As used in this section, "abused child" has the same meaning as in section 2151.031 of the Revised Code, and "neglected child" has the same meaning as in section 2151.03 of the Revised Code.

(J) As used in the Revised Code, "shared parenting" means that the parents share, in the manner set forth in the plan for shared parenting that is approved by the court under division (D)(1) and described in division (K)(6) of this section, all or some of the aspects of physical and legal care of their children.

(K) For purposes of the Revised Code:

(1) A parent who is granted the care, custody, and control of a child under an order that was issued pursuant to this section prior to April 11, 1991, and that does not provide for shared parenting has "custody of the child" and "care, custody, and control of the child" under the order, and is the "residential parent," the "residential parent and legal custodian," or the "custodial parent" of the child under the order.

(2) A parent who primarily is allocated the parental rights and responsibilities for the care of a child and who is designated as the residential parent and legal custodian of the child under an order that is issued pursuant to this section on or after April 11, 1991, and that does not provide for shared parenting has "custody of the child" and "care, custody, and control of the child" under the order, and is the "residential parent," the "residential parent and legal custodian," or the "custodial parent" of the child under the order.

(3) A parent who is not granted custody of a child under an order that was issued pursuant to this section prior to April 11, 1991, and that does not provide for shared parenting is the "parent who is not the residential parent," the "parent who is not the residential parent and legal custodian," or the "noncustodial parent" of the child under the order.

(4) A parent who is not primarily allocated the parental rights and responsibilities for the care of a child and who is not designated as the residential parent and legal custodian of the child under an order that is issued pursuant to this section on or after April 11, 1991, and that does not provide for shared parenting is the "parent who is not the residential parent," the "parent who is not the residential parent and legal custodian," or the "noncustodial parent" of the child under the order.

(5) Unless the context clearly requires otherwise, if an order is issued by a court pursuant to this section and the order provides for shared parenting of a child, both parents have "custody of the child" or "care, custody, and control of the child" under the order, to the extent and in the manner specified in the order.

(6) Unless the context clearly requires otherwise and except as otherwise provided in the order, if an order is issued by a court pursuant to this section and the order provides for shared parenting of a child, each parent, regardless of where the child is physically located or with whom the child is residing at a particular point in time, as specified in the order, is the "residential parent," the "residential parent and legal custodian," or the "custodial parent" of the child.

(7) Unless the context clearly requires otherwise and except as otherwise provided in the order, a designation in the order of a parent as the residential parent for the purpose of determining the school the child attends, as the custodial parent for purposes of claiming the child as a dependent pursuant to section 152(e) of the "Internal Revenue Code of 1986," 100 Stat. 2085, 26 U.S.C.A. 1, as amended, or as the residential parent for purposes of receiving public assistance pursuant to division (A)(2) of this section, does not affect the designation pursuant to division (K)(6) of this section of each parent as the "residential parent," the "residential parent and legal custodian," or the "custodial parent" of the child.

(1994 H 415, eff. 11-9-94; 1993 S 115, eff. 10-12-93; 1990 S 3, H 514, H 591; 1983 H 93; 1981 S 39, H 71; 1977 S 135; 1975 H 370, H 1; 1974 H 740, H 233; 131 v H 745; 1953 H 1; GC 8005-4; Source—GC 8033)

Historical and Statutory Notes

Pre-1953 H 1 Amendments: 124 v S 65

Amendment Note: 1994 H 415 rewrote division (E)(2); substituted "the parent with which the children will be physically located during legal holidays, school holidays, and other days of special importance" for "visitation" in division (G); inserted "and described in division (K)(6)" in division (J); substituted "each" for "the" and inserted ", regardless of where the child is phsyically located or" in division (K)(6); and rewrote division (K)(7). Prior to amendment, divisions (E)(2) and (K)(7) read:

"(2) In addition to a modification authorized under division (E)(1) of this section:

"(a) Both parents under a shared parenting decree jointly may modify the terms of the plan for shared parenting approved by the court and incorporated by it into the shared parenting decree. Modifications under this division may be made in relation to a final decree at any time and may be made in relation to a provisional decree issued prior to April 11, 1991, at any time prior to sixty days after the date of issuance of the provisional decree. The modifications to the plan shall be filed jointly by both parents with the court, and the court shall include them in the plan, unless they are not in the best interest of the children, in which case the court may reject the modifications. Modifications jointly submitted by both parents under a shared parenting decree shall be effective upon their inclusion by the court in the plan. A modification to a provisional plan issued prior to April 11, 1991, that is made under this division does not affect or extend the ninety-day period during which the provisional plan may be terminated upon motion of either parent or the court itself.

"(b) The court may modify the terms of the plan for shared parenting approved by the court and incorporated by it into the shared parenting decree upon the request of one or both of the parents under the decree. Modifications under this division may be made in relation to a final decree at any time and may be made in relation to a provisional decree issued prior to April 11, 1991, at any time prior to sixty days after the date of issuance of the provisional decree. The court shall not make any modification to the plan under this division, unless the modification is in the best interest of the children and, if the plan was approved under division (D)(1)(a)(i) of this section, unless both parents agree to the modification. A modification to a provisional plan issued prior to April 11, 1991, that is made under this division does not affect or extend the ninety-day period during which the provisional plan may be terminated upon motion of either parent or the court itself, as described in divisions (E)(2)(c), (d), and (e) of this section.

"(c) The court shall terminate a provisional shared parenting decree issued prior to April 11, 1991, if either parent or the court itself makes a motion to terminate the provisional decree at any time prior to the expiration of ninety days after the date of its issuance. The court itself may make a motion to terminate a provisional decree only if it has reason to believe that the plan incorporated into the provisional decree is not in the best interest of the children and that it cannot be modified so as to be in the best interest of the children or if it has reason to believe that shared parenting itself is not in the best interest of the children. If the court has reason to believe that the plan incorporated into the provisional decree is not in the best interest of the children but that it can be modified so as to be in the best interest of the children, the plan may be modified in accordance with division (E)(2)(a) or (b) of this section regardless of whether the sixty-day period that normally applies in relation to modification of provisional decrees under those divisions has expired. If a provisional decree is terminated under this division, the court shall proceed in accordance with division (E)(2)(e) of this section. If neither parent nor the court itself makes a motion to terminate a provisional decree prior to the expiration of the ninety-day period, the provisional decree immediately and without need for further action shall become final on the ninetieth day after the date of its issuance, subject to modification or termination authorized by this section. Division (E)(2)(c) of this section does not apply in relation to a final shared parenting decree.

"(d) The court may terminate a prior final shared parenting decree that includes a shared parenting plan approved under division (D)(1)(a)(i) of this section upon the request of one or both of the parents or whenever it determines that shared parenting is not in the best interest of the children. The court may terminate a prior final shared parenting decree that includes a shared parenting plan approved under division (D)(1)(a)(ii) or (iii) of this section if it determines, upon its own motion or upon the request of one or both parents, that shared parenting is not in the best interest of the children. If modification of the terms of the plan for shared parenting approved by the court and incorporated by it into the final shared parenting decree is attempted under division (E)(2)(a) of this section and the court rejects the modifications, it may terminate the final shared parenting decree if it determines that shared parenting is not in the best interest of the children.

"(e) Upon the termination of a provisional shared parenting decree issued prior to April 11, 1991, or a prior final shared parenting decree under division (E)(2)(c) or (d) of this section, the court shall proceed and issue a modified decree for the allocation of parental rights and responsibilities for the care of the children under the standards applicable under divisions (A), (B), and (C) of this section as if no decree for shared parenting had been granted and as if no request for shared parenting ever had been made.

* * *

"(7) Unless the context clearly requires otherwise and except as otherwise provided in the order, if an order is issued by a court pursuant to this section and the order provides for shared parenting of a child, the parent with whom the child is not to reside at a particular point in time, as specified in the order, is the 'parent who is not the residential parent,' the 'parent who is not the residential parent and legal custodian,' or the 'noncustodial parent' of the child at that point in time."

Amendment Note: 1993 S 115 substituted "April 11, 1991" for "the effective date of this amendment" in division (E); changed a reference to section 3109.05(A) to a reference to section 3113.215(B)(3) in the first paragraph of division (F)(2); and substituted "April 11, 1991" for "the effective date of this amendment" in division (K).

Cross References

Boards of education, residency for attendance purposes, acceptance of certain tuition requirements, enforcement, 3313.64

Child support guidelines, 3113.215

Criminal interference with custody, 2919.23

Dismissal of petition or approval of agreement, 3105.65

Divorce, annulment, and legal separation actions, custody and support of children, 3105.21; Civ R 75

Juvenile courts, exercise of jurisdiction in custody matters, 2151.23

Report of investigations conducted by court made available to all parties, 2317.39

Separation agreements, petition for dissolution, shared parenting plan, 3105.63

Taking of child into custody by juvenile court, Juv R 6

Tuition exemption, qualified former spouse of fire fighter or law enforcement officer killed in line of duty, 3333.26

Library References

Divorce ⟹298(1) to 298(6), 299, 301, 303(1) to 303(8).
Husband and Wife ⟹278, 279.
Infants ⟹78(1), 78(7).
Marriage ⟹64.
Parent and Child ⟹2(3) to 2(18).
WESTLAW Topic Nos. 134, 205, 211, 253, 285.
C.J.S. Divorce §§ 618 to 630, 632 to 634, 637 to 640, 648 to 664.
C.J.S. Husband and Wife §§ 221 to 225, 227, 235, 237.
C.J.S. Infants §§ 223 to 229.
C.J.S. Marriage § 79.
C.J.S. Parent and Child §§ 19 to 42, 44 to 46, 48.

OJur 3d: 5A, Alternative Dispute Resolution § 174
Am Jur 2d: 59, Parent and Child § 28 to 33, 44, 45
Nonresidence as affecting one's right to custody of child. 15 ALR2d 432
Alienation of child's affections as affecting custody award. 32 ALR2d 1005
Religion as factor in awarding custody of child. 66 ALR2d 1410
"Split," "divided," or "alternate" custody of children. 92 ALR2d 695
Right of mother to custody of illegitimate child. 98 ALR2d 417
Comment Note—Propriety of separating children by awarding custody to different parents. 98 ALR2d 926
Propriety of court conducting private interview with child in determining custody. 99 ALR2d 954
Child's wishes as factor in awarding custody. 4 ALR3d 1396
Award of custody of child to parent against whom divorce is decreed. 23 ALR3d 6
Right of putative father to custody of illegitimate child. 45 ALR3d 216
Right, in child custody proceedings, to cross-examine investigating officer whose report is used by court in its decision. 59 ALR3d 1337
Modern status of maternal preference rule or presumption in child custody cases. 70 ALR3d 262
Validity, construction, and application of Uniform Child Custody Jurisdiction Act. 96 ALR3d 968
Right to require psychiatric or mental examination for party seeking to obtain or retain custody of child. 99 ALR3d 268
Custodial parent's sexual relations with third person as justifying modification of child custody order. 100 ALR3d 625
Admissibility of social worker's expert testimony on child custody issues. 1 ALR4th 837
Parent's physical disability or handicap as factor in custody award or proceedings. 3 ALR4th 1044
Award of custody of child where contest is between natural parent and stepparent. 10 ALR4th 767
Race as factor in custody award or proceedings. 10 ALR4th 796
Desire of child as to geographical location of residence or domicile as factor in awarding custody or terminating parental rights. 10 ALR4th 827
Right of incarcerated mother to retain custody of infant in penal institution. 14 ALR4th 748
Necessity of requiring presence in court of both parties in proceedings relating to custody or visitation of children. 15 ALR4th 864
Propriety of awarding joint custody of children. 17 ALR4th 1013
Effect of trial court giving consideration to needs of children in making property division. 19 ALR4th 239
Propriety of awarding custody of child to parent residing or intending to reside in foreign country. 20 ALR4th 677
Religion as factor in child custody and visitation cases. 22 ALR4th 971
Parent's transsexuality as factor in award of custody of children, visitation rights, or termination of parental rights. 59 ALR4th 1170
Mother's status as "working mother" as factor in awarding child custody. 62 ALR4th 259
Divorce: voluntary contributions to child's education expenses as factor justifying modification of spousal support award. 63 ALR4th 436
Child custody: separating children by custody awards to different parents—post-1975 cases. 67 ALR4th 354
Child custody and visitation rights of person infected with AIDS. 86 ALR4th 211
Authority of court, upon entering default judgment, to make orders for child custody or support which were not specifically requested in pleadings of prevailing party. 5 ALR5th 863
Parent's use of drugs as factor in award of custody of children, visitation rights, or termination of parental rights. 20 ALR5th 534
Age of parent as factor in awarding custody. 34 ALR5th 57

Baldwin's Ohio Legislative Service, 1990 Laws of Ohio, H 591—LSC Analysis, p 5-576
Carlin, Baldwin's Ohio Practice, *Merrick-Rippner Probate Law* § 105.3, 105.4, 105.11, 105.13, 107.101, 107.106, 107.122, 108.13, 108.14, 108.15, 108.29 (1997)
Giannelli & Snyder, Baldwin's Ohio Practice, Evidence § 702.8 (1996)
Klein & Darling, Baldwin's Ohio Practice, *Civil Practice* § 60 (1997)
Kurtz & Giannelli, Ohio Juvenile Law (1998 Ed.), Text 3.2, 3.3, 12.4, 13.11, 15.2, 22.5, 27.2, 27.7, 31.4, 31.6
Sowald & Morganstern, Baldwin's Ohio Practice, *Domestic Relations Law* § 3.33, 3.57, 7.19, 8.6, 9.35, 10.3, 11.6, 15.1, 15.3, 15.7, 15.9, 15.11, 15.12, 15.15, 15.16, 15.17, 15.19, 15.20, 15.21, 15.33, 15.34, 15.35, 15.36, 15.37, 15.38, 15.39, 15.41, 15.43, 15.44, 15.46, 15.47, 15.49, 15.51, 15.52, 15.55, 15.58, 15.60, 15.67, 16.1, 16.3, 16.4, 16.5, 16.6, 16.7, 16.8, 16.10, 16.16, 16.17, 16.18, 16.19, 17.2, 17.8, 18.21, 18.23, 18.24, 18.25, 19.11, 20.6, 21.3, 21.6, 21.9, 21.15, 21.20, 21.26, 24.2, 25.21, 25.30, 25.32, 25.33, 25.41, 26.21, 37.19, 37.20, 37.21, 37.29 (1997)

Law Review and Journal Commentaries

Allocation of Dependency Tax Exemptions to Noncustodial Parents: When and Why, Pamela J. MacAdams. 4 Domestic Rel J Ohio 65 (July/August 1992).

Artificial insemination: In the child's best interest? 5 Alb L J Sci & Tech 321 (1996).

A Case Study in Divorce Law Reform and Its Aftermath, Robert E. McGraw, Gloria J. Sterin and Joseph M. Davis. 20 J Fam L 443 (1981-82).

Child Custody Determination—A Better Way!, Sheldon G. Kirshner. 17 J Fam L 275 (1978-79).

Child custody disputes between lesbians: Legal strategies and their limitations, Nicole Berner. 10 Berkeley Women's L J 31 (1995).

The Child Dependency Exemption And Divorced Parents: What Is "Custody"?, David J. Benson. 18 Cap U L Rev 57 (Spring 1989).

Children And Cults: A Practical Guide, Susan Linda. 29 J Fam L 591 (May 1991).

Children At Risk In The Politics Of Child Custody Suits: Acknowledging Their Needs For Nurture, Arlene Browand Huber. 32 J Fam L 33 (Winter 1994).

Children—The Innocent Victims of Family Breakups: How the Family Law Attorney, the Courts, and Society Can Protect Our Children, Michael J. Albano. 26 U Tol L Rev 787 (Summer 1995).

The Child's Advocate—Changing Roles in Changing Times, Ilana Horowitz Ratner. 7 Domestic Rel J Ohio 1 (January/February 1995).

Confessions of a Judicial Activist, Hon. Ronald L. Solove. [Ed. note: Judge Solove discusses and advocates custody mediation.] 54 Ohio St L J 797 (1993).

Custody Case Basics, Hon. Michael V. Brigner. 47 Dayton B Briefs 15 (December 1997).

Custody and the Cohabitating Parent, Note. 20 J Fam L 697 (1981-82).

Custody Disputes Following the Dissolution of Interracial Marriages: Best Interests of the Child or Judicial Racism?, Colleen McKinley. 19 J Fam L 97 (1980-81).

Custody in Ohio—A New Concept for an Age-Old Problem, V. Sinclair Lewis. 3 Domestic Rel J Ohio 57 (May/June 1991).

Custody of Children—Child's Right of Choice under Ohio G.C. Section 8033, Comment. 7 Ohio St L J 246 (March 1941).

Custody Rights Of Gay And Lesbian Parents, Comment. 36 Vill L Rev 1665 (1991).

Divorce And Amended Section 152(e) Of The Internal Revenue Code: Do State Courts Have The Power To Allocate Dependency Exemptions?, Note. 29 J Fam L 901 (August 1991).

Divorce Reform, Ohio Style, Alan E. Norris. 47 Ohio St B Ass'n Rep 1031 (9-16-74).

Family, Church And State: An Essay On Constitutionalism And Religious Authority, Carol Weisbrod. 26 J Fam L 741 (1987-88).

Gay Parents: A Legal Oxymoron In Ohio?, Comment. 18 Cap U L Rev 277 (Summer 1989).

Grandparent Visitation: Can the Parent Refuse?, Kathleen S. Bean. 24 J Fam L 393 (1985-86).

Illinois Court Overturns Mandatory Parent Education Class, Paul J. Buser. 18 Lake Legal Views 8 (August 1995).

In all its Variations, the Father's Rights Movement is Saying One Thing ... Make Room for Daddy, Stephanie B. Goldberg. 83 A B A J 48 (February 1997).

In Whose Best Interests? Legal Standards on Relocation of the Custodial Parent, Karen Tapp. III Ky Children's Rts J 19 (Spring 1993).

Interference with Visitation as an Independent Tort, Note. 24 J Fam L 481 (1985-86).

Interminable Child Neglect/Custody Cases: Are There Better Alternatives?, Sheila Reynolds and Roy B. Lacoursiere. 21 J Fam L 239 (1982-83).

Irreconcilable Differences: When Children Sue Their Parents For "Divorce", Note. 32 J Fam L 67 (1993-94).

The Issue of Stability in the Modification of Custody Decisions: Factor or Determinant?, Constance W. Cole. 29 Vill L Rev 1095 (1983-84).

Joint Custody: A Jaundiced View, Gary N. Skoloff. 20 Trial 52 (March 1984).

Joint Custody: A View From the Bench, Hon. Jerry Hayes. 2 Domestic Rel J Ohio 71 (September/October 1990).

Joint Custody and the Right to Travel: Legal and Psychological Implications, Paula M. Raines. 24 J Fam L 625 (1985-86).

Joint Custody: Constitutional Imperatives, Holly L. Robinson. 54 U Cin L Rev 27 (1985).

Joint Custody: Recent Research and Overloaded Courtrooms Inspire New Solutions to Custody Disputes, Diane Trombetta. 19 J Fam L 213 (1980-81).

Judge's Column, Hon. Francine M. Bruening. (Ed. note: Judge Bruening goes through RC 3109.04 step-by-step in this guide for practitioners.) 17 Lake Legal Views 1 (June 1994).

Judicial Activism in Domestic Relations Cases, Hon. V. Michael Brigner. (Ed. note: Judge Brigner lists the powers of a judge hearing custody, support, and visitation matters.) 45 Dayton B Briefs 22 (January 1996).

Keeping Kids Out of Court. (Ed. note: Arbitration of custody disputes, but courts reserve the right to review awards.) 19 Nat'l L J B8 (May 5, 1997).

Out of State Move as Change in Circumstances—Eaches Court Requires More, James R. Kirkland. 9 Domestic Rel J Ohio 79 (September/October 1997).

Parenting Order Must not be Based on Future Possibilities, Pamela J. MacAdams. 4 Domestic Rel J Ohio 28 (March/April 1992).

The Plight of the Interstate Child in American Courts, Leona Mary Hudak. 9 Akron L Rev 257 (Fall 1975).

The Power Of State Courts To Award The Federal Dependency Exemption Upon Divorce, David J. Benson. 16 U Dayton L Rev 29 (Fall 1990).

Practice Pointer—In Camera Interviews—Parents Have No Right to Access Transcript; Courts Not Required to Make Findings of Fact, Lynn B. Schwartz. 7 Domestic Rel J Ohio 84 (November/December 1995).

Primary Caretaker Doctrine, Stanley Morganstern. 1 Domestic Rel J Ohio 2 (September/October 1989).

The Proper Role of Psychology in Child Custody Disputes, Thomas R. Litwack, Gwendolyn L. Gerber and C. Abraham Fenster. 18 J Fam L 269 (1979-80).

Pro-Rating Child Support for Shared Parenting, James R. Kirkland. 6 Domestic Rel J Ohio 82 (November/December 1994).

Protecting The Interests Of Children In Divorce Mediation, Gary Paquin. 26 J Fam L 279 (1987-88).

Psychological Parents vs. Biological Parents: The Courts' Response to New Directions in Child Custody Dispute Resolution, Note. 17 J Fam L 545 (1978-79).

Reframing Child Custody Decisionmaking, Naomi R. Cahn. 58 Ohio St L J 1 (1997).

Relocation Issues—Part II—The Law in Selected States, Hon. Cheryl S. Karner. 5 Domestic Rel J Ohio 57 (July/August 1993).

Relocation of the Children After the Divorce, Hon. Cheryl S. Karner. 64 Law & Fact 6 (January-February 1990).

Remedies for Parental Kidnapping in Federal Court: A Comment Applying the Parental Kidnapping Prevention Act in Support of Judge Edwards, Joan M. Krauskopf. 45 Ohio St L J 429 (1984).

Representation for Children in Custody Decisions: All That Glitters Is Not Gault, Donald N. Bersoff. 15 J Fam L 27 (1976-77).

Rethinking Joint Custody, Elizabeth Scott and Andre Derdeyn. 45 Ohio St L J 455 (1984).

Shared Parenting—Modification Easier After 11-9-94, Richard L. Innis. 6 Domestic Rel J Ohio 81 (November/December 1994).

Should the Ill Effects of Environmental Tobacco Smoke Exposure Affect Child-Custody Decisions?, Note. 32 J Fam L 115 (1993-94).

Smoking And Parenting: Can They Be Adjudged Mutually Exclusive Activities?, Note. 42 Case W Res L Rev 1025 (Summer 1992).

State Intervention in the Family: Making a Federal Case Out of It, Martin Guggenheim. 45 Ohio St L J 399 (1984).

Tax Tips—Award of Dependency Exemptions, Stanley Morganstern. 3 Domestic Rel J Ohio 89 (July/August 1991).

Termination of Parental Rights in Adoption Cases: Focusing on the Child, Comment. 14 J Fam L 547 (1975-76).

Trial Court May Not Adopt Its Own Shared Parenting Plan, Pamela J. MacAdams. 5 Domestic Rel J Ohio 76 (September/October 1993).

Unhappy Families: Special Considerations In Custody Cases Involving Handicapped Children, Note. 24 J Fam L 59 (1985-86).

Visitation Interference: Legal Solutions for Fathers, Hon. V. Michael Brigner. 49 Dayton B Briefs 19 (November 1999).

The Voice of a Child: Independent Legal Representation of Children in Private Custody Disputes When Sexual Abuse Is Alleged, Kerin S. Bischoff. 138 U Pa L Rev 1383 (May 1990).

Within The Best Interests Of The Child: The Factor Of Parental Status In Custody Disputes Arising From Surrogacy Contracts, Irma S. Russell. 27 J Fam L 585 (1988-89).

Would Abolishing the Natural Parent Preference in Custody Disputes Be in Everyone's Best Interest?, Note. 29 J Fam L 539 (1990-91).

"You Get the House. I Get the Car. You Get the Kids. I Get Their Souls." The Impact of Spiritual Custody Awards on the Free Exercise Rights of Custodial Parents, Comment. 138 U Pa L Rev 583 (December 1989).

Notes of Decisions and Opinions

---

1. In general

There is no provision in RC 3109.04 for a "physical custodian" and a trial court errs as a matter of law by awarding "physical custody" of a child to a parent without statutory authority. In re Ghadr, Nos. 95CA22 and 96CA6, 1997 WL 133299 (4th Dist Ct App, Hocking, 3-19-97).

2. —Juvenile court and custody of abused, neglected or dependent children, custody or visitation issues in proceedings other than divorce

When a juvenile court makes a custody determination under RC 2151.23 and 2151.353, it must do so in accordance with RC 3109.04. In re Poling (Ohio 1992) 64 Ohio St.3d 211, 594 N.E.2d 589.

In a RC 2151.23(A)(2) child custody proceeding between a parent and a nonparent, the hearing officer may not award custody to the nonparent without first making a finding of parental unsuitability—that is, without first determining that a preponderance of the evidence shows that the parent abandoned the child, that the parent contractually relinquished custody of the child, that the parent has become totally incapable of supporting or caring for the child, or that an award of custody to the parent would be detrimental to the child. In re Perales (Ohio 1977) 52 Ohio St.2d 89, 369 N.E.2d 1047, 6 O.O.3d 293.

To the extent that RC 3109.04 proceedings may grant custody in the "best interest" of the child without a finding of parental unsuitablity, it is error to apply the "best interest" test of custody provided for in RC 3109.04 proceedings to a case involving proceedings under RC 2151.23. In re Perales (Ohio 1977) 52 Ohio St.2d 89, 369 N.E.2d 1047, 6 O.O.3d 293.

Juvenile court may not award legal custody to nonparent unless it first determines that both of the child's parents are unsuitable. Davis v. Wilson (Ohio App. 12 Dist. 1997) 123 Ohio App.3d 19, 702 N.E.2d 1227.

Juvenile court's exercise of jurisdiction over child custody and abuse complaint filed by mother and grandmother was subject to terms of Uniform Child Custody Jurisdiction Act (UCCJA), given that there was pending divorce and custody proceeding in Kentucky. In re Simons (Ohio App. 2 Dist. 1997) 118 Ohio App.3d 622, 693 N.E.2d 1111.

Father had standing to assert on appeal that trial court erred in not granting legal custody of children to one of his relatives rather than granting permanent custody to county children services agency, even though none of relatives had appealed, where by granting permanent custody to agency, father lost residual parental rights, privileges and obligations. In re Hiatt (Adams 1993) 86 Ohio App.3d 716, 621 N.E.2d 1222.

While there is no statutory mandate that factors for determining best interest of child in custody disputes arising from divorce actions be considered in custody proceedings incident to dependency action, juvenile courts should consider totality of circumstances, including those factors, to extent they are applicable. In re Pryor (Athens 1993) 86 Ohio App.3d 327, 620 N.E.2d 973.

Failure of common pleas court to make finding that natural parents were unfit custodians of child did not preclude certification of child custody case to juvenile court, where case was certified pursuant to statute giving juvenile court discretion whether to accept certification, rather than statute pursuant to which juvenile court must accept certification based on finding that it is in best interest of child for neither parent to have custody. In re Whaley (Athens 1993) 86 Ohio App.3d 304, 620 N.E.2d 954.

Because RC 2151.23 is a jurisdictional statute without any substantive law test, the common-law parental-suitability test is to be applied when a non-parent seeks custody of a child; the "best-interest" test of RC 3109.04 applies only to divorce-custody proceedings. Reynolds v. Goll (Lorain 1992) 80 Ohio App.3d 494, 609 N.E.2d 1276.

An order placing children in custody of children's services is in error absent a finding of unsuitability of the mother and consideration of the best interest of the children. Truitt v. Truitt (Preble 1989) 65 Ohio App.3d 126, 583 N.E.2d 331.

When a case concerning a child is transferred or certified from another court, such certification does not constitute a complaint in the juvenile court that such a child is neglected, dependent, or abused, and those dispositions provided for under RC 2151.353 pertaining to neglected, dependent, or abused children, including an award of permanent custody to a county welfare department which has assumed the administration of child welfare, are not applicable to such a child, disposition thereof being subject to and controlled by RC 3109.04. In re Snider (Defiance 1984) 14 Ohio App.3d 353, 471 N.E.2d 516, 14 O.B.R. 420.

Where a juvenile court grants the temporary custody of a minor child, with the consent of his parents, to a nonrelative, after the father had unrestricted custody pursuant to a divorce decree, RC 3109.04(B) and 3109.04(C), as effective September 23, 1974, are not applicable to prevent the court's consideration of a motion filed by the father, in the same court, for the restoration of custody. Leininger v. Leininger (Fulton 1975) 48 Ohio App.2d 21, 355 N.E.2d 508, 2 O.O.3d 15.

Except when the question of custody is incidental to the separation of parents, their right to custody cannot be taken away unless the grounds as recognized by statute, in general that the child is dependent, neglected or delinquent or that the parent is unfit, are present to support a proper exercise of the police power. Holderle v. Holderle (Franklin 1967) 11 Ohio App.2d 148, 229 N.E.2d 79, 40 O.O.2d 305.

A juvenile court which acquires jurisdiction of a minor child of persons who are subsequently divorced has exclusive jurisdiction of such minor, and the common pleas court wherein such divorce is granted has no jurisdiction to make any order respecting the custody of such child. Patton v. Patton (Muskingum 1963) 1 Ohio App.2d 1, 203 N.E.2d 662, 30 O.O.2d 49.

Where a neglected child proceeding is instituted in the juvenile court by a parent of such child, and a divorce action is later instituted by such parent, the juvenile court has exclusive original jurisdiction to determine whether the child is neglected, the power to determine his custody and the authority to place the child with a relative. In re Small (Darke 1960) 114 Ohio App. 248, 181 N.E.2d 503, 19 O.O.2d 128.

RC 3109.04 is not applicable to a neglected child proceeding under RC 2151.27. In re Small (Darke 1960) 114 Ohio App. 248, 181 N.E.2d 503, 19 O.O.2d 128.

In exercising its jurisdiction under RC 2151.23(A)(2) to determine custody of children, a juvenile court must rely on the standards in RC 3109.04. In re Brazell (Ohio Com.Pl. 1986) 27 Ohio Misc.2d 7, 499 N.E.2d 925, 27 O.B.R. 68.

RC 3109.04 is applicable to a proceeding for change of custody under the Juvenile Court Act. In re Custody of Smelser (Ohio Com.Pl. 1969) 22 Ohio Misc. 41, 257 N.E.2d 769, 51 O.O.2d 31, 51 O.O.2d 75.

As used in 4507.07, "custody" refers to any relationship in which a person stands in loco parentis to a minor, whether or not that person has legal custody of the minor. OAG 72-087.

3. —"Primary caregiver" preference and "Tender years" doctrine, allocation of rights and responsibilities: Initial Allocation—"Best interest" and Specific Factors

When forming a custody order, a trial court should give due consideration to which parent performed the role of primary caregiver. Bechtol v. Bechtol (Ohio 1990) 49 Ohio St.3d 21, 550 N.E.2d 178, rehearing denied 49 Ohio St.3d 718, 552 N.E.2d 952, opinion corrected 51 Ohio St.3d 701, 554 N.E.2d 899.

Substantial amount of credible and competent evidence supported trial court's decision to name former wife primary caregiver of parties' child in connection with divorce proceeding; wife had been child's primary caregiver before divorce, and social worker, psychologist, and psychology trainee all gave opinion testimony that wife should continue to be primary caregiver. Badovick v. Badovick (Ohio App. 8 Dist. 1998) 128 Ohio App.3d 18, 713 N.E.2d 1066.

Ohio courts must give due consideration to which parent was primary caregiver in fashioning custody award. Marshall v. Marshall (Ohio App. 3 Dist. 1997) 117 Ohio App.3d 182, 690 N.E.2d 68.

A trial court abuses its discretion when it awards the father custody of the two minor children of the unmarried couple where (1) the mother supported the couple and children through part-time employment during the eight years they were together but the father was not regularly employed and rarely spent quality time with the children; (2) the father took the children on vacation to Florida and, after the mother informed him over the telephone that she wished to terminate their relationship, he refused to let the mother see them or often even to speak to them on the telephone; and (3) once in Florida, the father changed his residence, found employment, enrolled the children in school, affiliated with a church, and began to spend time with the children. In re Markham (Meigs 1990) 70 Ohio App.3d 841, 592 N.E.2d 896, dismissed, jurisdictional motion overruled 60 Ohio St.3d 702, 573 N.E.2d 118.

The primary caretaker doctrine, although not a dispositive rule in Ohio, is a factor that can properly be considered when reviewing other statutory factors relating to custody. Roth v. Roth (Lucas 1989) 65 Ohio App.3d 768, 585 N.E.2d 482.

The primary caregiver doctrine is part of the best interest of the child and is included in the language of RC 3109.04(C)(3), "the child's interaction and interrelationship with his parents." Thompson v. Thompson (Washington 1987) 31 Ohio App.3d 254, 511 N.E.2d 412, 31 O.B.R. 538.

A trial court commits reversible error by presuming that a mother is entitled to custody of a child of tender years. Charles v. Charles (Franklin 1985) 23 Ohio App.3d 109, 491 N.E.2d 378, 23 O.B.R. 175.

To determine the best interests of a child of tender years in an original award of custody, it is within the sound discretion of the trial court to strongly consider which parent was the primary caretaker of the child, in addition to considering the factors set forth in RC 3109.04(C). In re Maxwell (Darke 1982) 8 Ohio App.3d 302, 456 N.E.2d 1218, 8 O.B.R. 409.

Custody of the parties' daughter granted to the natural father is within the court's discretion after considering (1) the mother's limited contact with the child over the previous two years, (2) the mother's decision to abscond with the child to North Carolina where the mother is residing, (3) most of the child's extended family, including the maternal grandparents, live in Ohio, and (4) the active role played by the father's present wife in helping him raise his daughter. Michael v Chesnut, No. 96-CA-72, 1997 WL 254142 (2d Dist Ct App, Greene, 5-16-97).

While RC 3109.03 eliminates the presumption that the mother is the proper custodian of a child of tender years, the age of the child and the child's relationship with the mother are factors to be considered under RC 3109.04(C); and a trial court's failure to consider the child's tender years constitutes an abuse of discretion. Berry v Berry, No. CA88-11-081 (12th Dist Ct App, Clermont, 3-12-90).

Where custody of a minor child was originally awarded to the child's mother, subsequently the child's father obtained custody with the mother's consent, and later the mother filed a motion to return custody of the child to her, the trial court erred in granting such motion based solely on the tender years doctrine. Kiskis v Kiskis, No. 330 (4th Dist Ct App, Meigs, 12-1-83).

Being the primary caretaker of the children does not lead to a presumption that the particular parent should be the residential parent but should be considered with other statutory factors; in addition, where there is documentation that an obligor is under a duty to support two other children, the trial court must consider such obligation when calculating the current child support obligation. Kunkle v Lupardus, No. 96-P-0014, 1997 WL 158104 (11th Dist Ct App, Portage, 3-28-97).

Under statute, one parent is not preferred over other, and court is authorized to award custody to either parent, taking into account that which would be for best interests, and while courts, in awarding custody of children of tender years, most times prefer mother over father, where circumstances warrant, it is always in furtherance of what court conceives to be for children's best interests. Riggs v. Riggs (Franklin 1954) 124 N.E.2d 835, 69 Ohio Law Abs. 263.

4. —Filing request with court as prerequisite, shared parenting: joint custody

A satisfactory shared parenting plan must be filed with the court for adoption, and otherwise, the court will not adopt any plan. Bowen v. Bowen (Ohio App. 9 Dist. 1999) 132 Ohio App.3d 616, 725 N.E.2d 1165.

Trial court in divorce action could not adopt shared parenting plan that was not submitted by either party, and that, while derived from a plan submitted by former wife, was nonetheless a product of court's own creation. Bowen v. Bowen (Ohio App. 9 Dist. 1999) 132 Ohio App.3d 616, 725 N.E.2d 1165.

Statutory requirement that shared parenting plan must be filed at least 30 days prior to hearing on parental rights and responsibilities is directory, not mandatory, although statutory deadline does implicate party's right to due process; although trial court may relieve party of statutory deadline and grant party's request to file shared parenting plan within 30 days prior to hearing, other party must have adequate opportunity to respond to plan. Harris v. Harris (Miami 1995) 105 Ohio App.3d 671, 664 N.E.2d 1304.

Where neither party files a written motion or a shared parenting plan pursuant to RC 3109.04, a request for shared parenting is denied. Bache v Bache, No. 92-AP-090071 (5th Dist Ct App, Tuscarawas, 5-6-93).

A court may not award joint custody of a child to his parents where the parents have not requested or consented to joint custody, and an award of joint custody without the consent of the parties will be reversed. Mani v Mani, No. CA-7861 (5th Dist Ct App, Stark, 12-11-89).

Where a joint custody plan is not submitted by either parent and there is no mutual consent by the parents to a joint custody agreement ordered by the court, the provisions of the joint custody statute are not applicable and the trial court errs in awarding joint custody. Monroe v Presgraves, No. CA-2847 (5th Dist Ct App, Licking, 10-29-82).

5. —Child's wishes and interview with judge, allocation of rights and responsibilities: Modification after original allocation—"Change in circumstances" and Specific Factors

Statute prohibiting use in custody and visitation proceedings of statements and affidavits purporting to set forth child's preference concerning allocation of parental responsibilities also applied in mandamus proceeding which arose out of custody proceeding; harm to child from demand that he choose between his parents was valid concern in any proceeding. State ex rel. Papp v. James (Ohio 1994) 69 Ohio St.3d 373, 632 N.E.2d 889.

When elder of two children whose custody has previously been awarded to divorced parent becomes ten years of age and thereafter chooses as custodian the other parent who is not disqualified by unfitness, there is a change of conditions as to the younger child and it is for the court to determine whether it is for the best interest of the children to be separated and to fix custody of the younger child accordingly. Dailey v. Dailey (Ohio 1945) 146 Ohio St. 93, 64 N.E.2d 246, 32 O.O. 29.

When a child in custody of divorced parent by virtue of a previous order of court arrives at age of ten years and, in court proceeding involving modification of previous order, chooses as custodian the other parent who is not unfitted for charge by reason of moral depravity, etc., there is a change of conditions requiring modification of previous order. Dailey v. Dailey (Ohio 1945) 146 Ohio St. 93, 64 N.E.2d 246, 32 O.O. 29.

Trial court which performed in camera interview of child in connection with motion seeking modification of parental rights and responsibilities established by order in divorce action did not abuse its discretion by failing to ask child ultimate question regarding whether he would prefer to live with his mother or his father; method of questioning did not violate letter or spirit of statute, and judge asked questions sufficient to ascertain child's wishes and concerns with respect to allocation of rights and responsibilities. Inscoe v. Inscoe (Ohio App. 4 Dist. 1997) 121 Ohio App.3d 396, 700 N.E.2d 70.

Trial court which had conducted in camera interview of minor child, in connection with motion for modification of parental rights and responsibilities established by prior order in divorce action, erred by sealing interview from parties; no statutory basis exists for denying parents access to transcript of their child's in camera interview. Inscoe v. Inscoe (Ohio App. 4 Dist. 1997) 121 Ohio App.3d 396, 700 N.E.2d 70.

Trial court considering parents' post-divorce cross-motions to determine child's school district was statutorily obligated to appoint guardian ad litem for child, where mother requested interview of child and filed motion for appointment of guardian. Badgett v. Badgett (Ohio App. 7 Dist. 1997) 120 Ohio App.3d 448, 698 N.E.2d 84.

Trial court considering parents' post-divorce cross-motions to determine child's school district was statutorily obligated to interview child, even though neither party filed written motion requesting interview, where mother's counsel orally requested an interview, and counsel objected several times to lack of interview. Badgett v. Badgett (Ohio App. 7 Dist. 1997) 120 Ohio App.3d 448, 698 N.E.2d 84.

Record should have been made of trial court's in-chambers interview of children on issue of change of custody following divorce; statute listing persons allowed to be present at interview requires that court stenographer and/or other recording device be present upon timely request; overruling *Crabbs v Crabbs*, 1992 WL

195417. Patton v. Patton (Licking 1993) 87 Ohio App.3d 844, 623 N.E.2d 235.

Issues involving child custody and visitation are peculiarly within the very broad discretion of the trial court since the knowledge obtained through contact with and observation of the parties cannot be conveyed to a reviewing court through the printed word and therefore, a court is required to find a change of circumstances subsequent to the prior custody award to allow a change of custody and although a child's arrival at the statutory age accompanied by his election of the parent who does not presently have custody and would not be deemed unfit is a change of circumstances, a trial court is permitted to deny the wishes of the child when conditions surrounding the custody change indicate it is not in the best interests of the child and the benefit of the custody change would not outweigh the harm caused by such change. Bawidamann v. Bawidamann (Montgomery 1989) 63 Ohio App.3d 691, 580 N.E.2d 15.

To determine the best interests of a child in an action where one parent is seeking to modify custody, where both parents are deemed fit, and where the child has expressed a preference or election pursuant to RC 3109.04 the trial court must look to the totality of the circumstances surrounding the change and therefore, where a trial court finds that a father's allegation of an unhealthy environment provided by his children's mother is untrue and that the father has exerted a subtle manipulative power over his children and that his actions are based more on his desire for revenge than for the well being of the children, the court does not abuse its discretion in finding that custody of the children should remain with the mother, even though both parents are fit to have custody and the children elect to live with their father. Bawidamann v. Bawidamann (Montgomery 1989) 63 Ohio App.3d 691, 580 N.E.2d 15.

In a proceeding to vacate a prior custody decree pursuant to Civ R 60(B), a trial court may use its sound discretion in deciding whether to allow a child under eleven years of age to testify, pursuant to RC 3109.04(C)(2), regarding the child's preferred custodian. Wade v. Wade (Wayne 1983) 10 Ohio App.3d 167, 461 N.E.2d 30, 10 O.B.R. 220.

A trial court may consider the factors set out in RC 3109.04 when ruling on a motion for relief from judgment of a custody decree pursuant to Civ R 60(B); specifically, the expressed desire of a nine-year-old child to live with her mother is insufficient to meet the requirement of a change in circumstances as set forth in RC 3109.04. Wade v. Wade (Wayne 1983) 10 Ohio App.3d 167, 461 N.E.2d 30, 10 O.B.R. 220.

In an action seeking a change of child custody, a presumption is created by RC 3109.04 favoring retention of the current custodian; such presumption is especially strong if the children are twelve or older, and want to stay with the current custodial parent. Kraus v. Kraus (Cuyahoga 1983) 10 Ohio App.3d 63, 460 N.E.2d 680, 10 O.B.R. 73.

Circumstances short of a parent being found unfit may necessitate the denial of a change of custody where the child expresses a preference or makes an election pursuant to RC 3109.04 because the change may not be in the best interests of the child. Venable v. Venable (Cuyahoga 1981) 3 Ohio App.3d 421, 445 N.E.2d 1125, 3 O.B.R. 498.

Where both parents are fit and suitable and a child has expressed a preference, the court may still deny a change of custody upon a determination that the change is not in the best interest of the child. Venable v. Venable (Cuyahoga 1981) 3 Ohio App.3d 421, 445 N.E.2d 1125, 3 O.B.R. 498.

A change of circumstance sufficient to justify a change of custody exists where a child over the age of eleven expresses a strengthening desire to live with her noncustodial parent. In re Reynolds (Hamilton 1982) 2 Ohio App.3d 309, 441 N.E.2d 1141, 2 O.B.R. 341.

Burden of proof is upon the parent seeking modification of decree awarding custody of child, at the child's election, to the other parent, to show unfitness of such other parent. Schwalenberg v. Schwalenberg (Columbiana 1940) 65 Ohio App. 217, 29 N.E.2d 617, 18 O.O. 397.

A court properly conducts an in camera interview of a child now fifteen years old who has lived with her father for ten years and presently chooses to live with her mother and stepfather where the court determines that (1) the child is capable of expressing her wishes in an intelligent and rational manner, (2) she chooses to live with her mother and stepfather so that she might foster a better relationship with them and her half siblings, (3) she finds it difficult to participate in after school activities because of the location of her private school, (4) due to her father's and stepmother's jobs and lifestyles her interaction with them is very limited, and (5) her father is planning to move to Arizona. Zygela v Euler, No. L-97-1123, 1997 WL 770972 (6th Dist Ct App, Lucas, 12-5-97).

A father's continued payment of child support while he has extended summer visitation with his son is not inappropriate; in addition, a court is within its discretion in finding that an eight-year-old child lacks sufficient reasoning ability to make an informed choice with respect to who would be his residential parent. Dicke v Dicke, No. 1-95-23, 1995 WL 657112 (3d Dist Ct App, Allen, 11-7-95).

A twelve-year-old child's election to live with the noncustodial parent must be granted unless there is a finding that it is detrimental to the child's best interests, and a court does not abuse its discretion in modifying custody of minor children when the evidence supports a finding that modification is necessary to serve the minors' best interests. Collins v Collins, No. 42688 (8th Dist Ct App, Cuyahoga, 3-19-81).

Court has no jurisdiction to modify or vacate a prior order "sua sponte" where no motion to change custody is pending and where no notice is given to the parties; in addition, a change of custody cannot be based solely upon the expressed wishes of a nine-and-one-half-year-old child. In re Remmer, No. 52712 (8th Dist Ct App, Cuyahoga, 7-2-87).

Courts have traditionally defined the phrase "change in circumstances" in RC 3109.04 to denote an event, occurrence, or situation which has a material and adverse effect upon the child, and that requirement of a change in circumstances of either the residential parent or the child is to prevent the continued relitigation of issues previously raised and considered by the trial court; and although the former RC 3109.04 permitted a court to allow any child who was twelve years of age or older to choose the parent with whom he wants to live, under the amended version of RC 3109.04 a change in the child's wishes and concerns regarding a residential parent standing alone is not a change of circumstances, though it is one factor in determining whether there has been such a change. Moyer v Moyer, No. 96APF05-659, 1996 WL 729859 (10th Dist Ct App, Franklin, 12-17-96).

While a court is not bound by the preference of a ten-year-old child when ruling on a motion for change of custody, RC 3109.04 does not preclude the court from considering it. Gordon v Gordon, No. 1334 (4th Dist Ct App, Athens, 10-19-87).

It is improper to grant a change of custody solely on the expressed wishes of a nine-year-old child, although the child's preference may be a consideration; the requisite statutory factors should be investigated and weighed. In re Remmer, No. 52712 (8th Dist Ct App, Cuyahoga, 7-2-87).

The expressed desire of a child who is nearly ten years old to reside with his mother is insufficient to warrant separation from his father who has had custody since the child was two years old where (1) the child suffers from attention deficit disorder and hyperactivity and is prescribed Ritalin, (2) when not taking Ritalin he is disruptive at school and unable to learn, (3) the mother refuses to give the medication while the child is staying with her for a short period so the father takes the medication to his son's school for it to be administered, and (4) the child's relationship with his father is normal and healthy. Basinger v Basinger, No. 98-T-0080, 1999 WL 266606 (11th Dist Ct App, Trumbull, 4-30-99).

In a mother's motion for change in custody with respect to her daughter who is nearly nine at the time of hearing on the motion, a trial court commits reversible error by excluding the testimony of the child without first conducting a voir dire examination to determine the child's competency to testify; in addition, the mother's failure to proffer what her daughter's testimony would have been had she been allowed to testify does not preclude the mother from raising the issue on appeal without having to resort to the plain error rule. Baird v Gillispie, No. 99-CA-12, 2000 WL 43493 (2d Dist Ct App, Miami, 1-21-00).

Upon hearing of a motion for change of custody of a child now fifteen years old previously granted to the father, the expression of the child of the preference to live with his mother is a sufficient change in conditions to require consideration of the motion, and the child's preference between parents should be a major factor in the determination of what will be in his best interest. In re Custody of Smelser (Ohio Com.Pl. 1969) 22 Ohio Misc. 41, 257 N.E.2d 769, 51 O.O.2d 31, 51 O.O.2d 75.

Court did not err in refusing to change custody of fourteen-year-old daughter from father to mother, even though daughter requested such change, where mother had carried on adulterous relationship with individual whom she subsequently married. Watson v. Watson (Columbiana 1956) 146 N.E.2d 443, 76 Ohio Law Abs. 348.

In proceeding for change of custody of eight year old child awarded to father by divorce decree, wherein evidence established abuse and misuse of child by father's present wife, denial of change of custody on ground that child in conference with trial judge stated she desired to stay with father had effect of making 8 year old child choose between her parents though she was not capable of being sworn as a witness, and was prejudicially erroneous. Newman v. Newman (Cuyahoga 1951) 104 N.E.2d 707, 61 Ohio Law Abs. 438.

In a wrongful death action brought by the administrator of the estate of a divorced woman who did not have custody of her children, a federal trial court does not err by refusing to instruct the jury that when the children reached the age of twelve an Ohio court could let them choose under RC 3109.04 which parent to live with; the administrator's argument that it is "reasonable and probable that ... each ... would have selected the mother" is unfounded, and the proposed change would require the jury to speculate. Bowman v. Koch Transfer Co. (C.A.6 (Ohio) 1988) 862 F.2d 1257.

6. —Child's "best interest" in general, allocation of rights and responsibilities: Modification after original allocation—"Change in circumstances" and Specific Factors

Term "shall," as used in statute enumerating factors to be considered in determining children's best interest, is mandatory and requires trial court to consider such factors in entering or modifying an order allocating parental rights and responsibilities. Dilworth v. Dilworth (Ohio App. 2 Dist. 1996) 115 Ohio App.3d 537, 685 N.E.2d 847.

In considering a change of custody RC 3109.04 requires only a finding of a "change of circumstances" before a trial court can determine the best interest of the child and a court that bases its finding upon a substantial change of circumstances errs. Willis v Willis, No. 70937, 1997 WL 272377 (8th Dist Ct App, Cuyahoga, 5-22-97).

7. —Arbitration agreements for disputes, shared parenting: joint custody

Dispute over mother's relocation involved matter of child custody that was not arbitrable, even though parties' shared parenting agreement provided for arbitration of parties' disputes. Pulfer v. Pulfer (Allen 1996) 110 Ohio App.3d 90, 673 N.E.2d 656, dismissed, appeal not allowed 77 Ohio St.3d 1412, 670 N.E.2d 1001.

8. Arbitration, generally

Matters of child custody may only be decided by trial court and are not subject to arbitration despite any agreement entered into by parties. Pulfer v. Pulfer (Allen 1996) 110 Ohio App.3d 90, 673 N.E.2d 656, dismissed, appeal not allowed 77 Ohio St.3d 1412, 670 N.E.2d 1001.

9. —Visitation, allocation of rights and responsibilities: Initial Allocation—"Best interest" and Specific Factors

Trial court has considerable discretion to decide domestic relations issues, including visitation; discretion requires only that decisions not be unreasonable, arbitrary or unconscionable. Jacobs v. Jacobs (Wayne 1995) 102 Ohio App.3d 568, 657 N.E.2d 580.

Possibility that parties could seek further modification of child visitation order did not justify imposition of midweek visitation which trial court expressly found to be "unfair." Jacobs v. Jacobs (Wayne 1995) 102 Ohio App.3d 568, 657 N.E.2d 580.

The father of a child born out of wedlock is not entitled to visitation with such child over the objections of the mother, who has legal custody, unless he clearly establishes that such would be in the best interests of the child. In re Connolly (Franklin 1974) 43 Ohio App.2d 38, 332 N.E.2d 376, 72 O.O.2d 194.

A court errs in denying a noncustodial parent's right of visitation where there is no independent proof through a psychological evaluation and through a report of a guardian ad litem that visitation with the father would jeopardize the child's safety, welfare, and well-being. Kreuzer v Kreuzer, No. 96-CA-131, 1997 WL 432224 (2d Dist Ct App, Greene, 8-1-97).

10. —Paternity issues, allocation of rights and responsibilities: Initial Allocation—"Best interest" and Specific Factors

When the alleged natural father of an illegitimate child, who has participated in the nurturing process of the child, files a complaint seeking custody of the child under RC 2151.23(A)(2), and the mother admits that he is the natural father of the child, the natural father has equality of standing with the mother with respect to the custody of the child, and the court shall determine which parent shall have the legal custody of the child, taking into account what would be in the best interests of the child. In re Byrd (Ohio 1981) 66 Ohio St.2d 334, 421 N.E.2d 1284, 20 O.O.3d 309.

Legal custodians of child, who obtained custody from child's mother, were in privity with mother, and so were barred by res judicata from litigating issue of paternity of child that had been decided in divorce decree. Broxterman v. Broxterman (Hamilton 1995) 101 Ohio App.3d 661, 656 N.E.2d 394.

Legal parentage, not to be confused with biological parentage, must be established before the issue of custody can properly be decided where the child is the product of artificial insemination of a married woman by a man not her husband. In re Adoption of Reams (Franklin 1989) 52 Ohio App.3d 52, 557 N.E.2d 159, dismissed 50 Ohio St.3d 707, 553 N.E.2d 684.

A judgment in a paternity action has the effect of a prior determination of custody; therefore, a subsequent change of custody pursuant to a petition by the natural father must be based on a finding of changed circumstances. In re Yates (Franklin 1984) 18 Ohio App.3d 95, 481 N.E.2d 646, 18 O.B.R. 458.

In a husband's action for divorce, in which the wife's cross-petition raises the issue of the paternity of her child, a finding by the trial court that the evidence is insufficient to prove that the husband is not the father of the child is a determination that the child was conceived by the parties as husband and wife, and it is the duty of such court to make an order for the disposition, care and maintenance of the child. Whitecotton v. Whitecotton (Lucas 1955) 103 Ohio App. 149, 144 N.E.2d 678, 3 O.O.2d 210.

Exclusion as the father through genetic testing constitutes clear and convincing evidence that overcomes the presumption of paternity created under RC 3111.03 and where the defendant is excluded as the father there is no minor issue of the marriage and RC 3109.04 no longer provides the court of common pleas with subject matter jurisdiction to make a ruling on custody; instead the issue of custody becomes subject matter exclusive to the juvenile court pursuant to RC 2151.23, and consequently, the "best interest of the child" standard in determining custody does not apply. Thompson v Thompson, No. 94CA859, 1995 WL 481480 (4th Dist Ct App, Highland, 8-16-95).

Where an unmarried mother leaves a child less than two years old with the child's maternal grandmother in an inappropriate environment and the mother does not disclose her location for six months and does not return until eight or nine months passed, and upon returning the mother institutes a paternity action but does not address the custody of the child, a trial court properly determines the custody of the child under the best interest of the child standard used in initial custody determinations when presented with the respective custody motions of the adjudged father and natural mother of the child. In re Webster, No. 92CA1559, 1993 WL 373784 (4th Dist Ct App, Athens, 9-14-93).

Pursuant to a parentage action where the issue of who would have custody of the child is never before the court or addressed in an agreement between the parties, it is error for the trial court to address issues of child support and visitation without first making a determination as to which parent will have custody. State ex rel Ellen v Deal, No. 94APF04-549, 1994 WL 723377 (10th Dist Ct App, Franklin, 12-27-94).

A judgment establishing paternity and imposing a duty to support on the father may also imply a determination of custody to the mother, so that a motion to determine custody filed years later by the father should be determined according to the standards for change in custody set forth in RC 3109.04(B)(1). In re Brazell (Ohio Com.Pl. 1986) 27 Ohio Misc.2d 7, 499 N.E.2d 925, 27 O.B.R. 68.

The mother of an illegitimate child has a right of custody that is superior to that of the putative father. In re H. (Ohio Com.Pl. 1973) 37 Ohio Misc. 123, 305 N.E.2d 815, 66 O.O.2d 178, 66 O.O.2d 368.

11. —Investigations and psychological evaluations, generally, allocation of rights and responsibilities: Modification after ori ginal allocation—"Change in circumstances" and Specific Factors

Any error in admitting posthearing psychological report into evidence, under seal, without allowing cross-examination of its author, in connection with motion for modification of parental rights and responsibilities established by order in divorce action, was harmless, where copies of report were ultimately released to parties, and report did not change result of case. Inscoe v. Inscoe (Ohio App. 4 Dist. 1997) 121 Ohio App.3d 396, 700 N.E.2d 70.

Trial court did not err in considering home study report as evidence in the absence of sworn testimony in proceeding regarding modification of child custody decree, given that statutes and rule authorized trial court to consider court-ordered investigation reports as evidence. Sayre v. Hoelzle-Sayre (Seneca 1994) 100 Ohio App.3d 203, 653 N.E.2d 712, appeal allowed 70 Ohio St.3d 1426, 638 N.E.2d 88, appeal dismissed as improvidently allowed 72 Ohio St.3d 1218, 651 N.E.2d 430.

Custody investigation reports as to the character, earning ability, financial worth, past conduct and family relations of both parties to the action are to be made available to each party's counsel at least seven days before trial under Civ R 75 and five days under RC 3109.04. Roach v. Roach (Montgomery 1992) 79 Ohio App.3d 194, 607 N.E.2d 35.

Custody investigation reports on both parties' backgrounds are to be admitted into evidence subject to cross-examination of the investigator about the contents of the report so due process rights are protected. Roach v. Roach (Montgomery 1992) 79 Ohio App.3d 194, 607 N.E.2d 35.

It is within the sound discretion of the court to decline to order a home investigation of both parties before ordering a change of custody. Stone v. Stone (Warren 1983) 9 Ohio App.3d 6, 457 N.E.2d 919, 9 O.B.R. 6.

In a custody dispute where the noncustodial parent undergoes a court-ordered psychological evaluation, the trial court does not abuse its discretion by declining to order the noncustodial parent's second wife to undergo an evaluation as well. In re Reynolds (Hamilton 1982) 2 Ohio App.3d 309, 441 N.E.2d 1141, 2 O.B.R. 341.

Upon a motion to modify custody provisions of a divorce decree, a court is not limited to any particular line of inquiry, nor is it bound by strict legal rules governing the introduction of evidence, and while hearsay evidence alone is insufficient to support a modification of a custody order, the court may properly consider reports of court-appointed social workers. Woodruff v. Woodruff (Ohio Com.Pl. 1965) 7 Ohio Misc. 87, 217 N.E.2d 264, 36 O.O.2d 165.

12. —In general, shared parenting: joint custody

During divorce proceeding, trial court is required to allocate parental rights and responsibilities for care of minor children pursuant to statute, and has two options when doing so: court may designate one parent as residential parent and legal custodian who bears primary rights and responsibilities for care of the children; or court may issue shared parenting order requiring parents to share all or some aspects of physical and legal care of the children. Arthur v. Arthur (Ohio App. 5 Dist. 1998) 130 Ohio App.3d 398, 720 N.E.2d 176.

Competent, credible evidence supported trial court's determination that shared parenting agreement was fair and reasonable and in best interest of children; record indicated that in addition to parties' own joint plan and trial court's observation of parties, trial court had before it detailed psychological evaluations of both parties and children. Evans v. Evans (Butler 1995) 106 Ohio App.3d 673, 666 N.E.2d 1176, dismissed, appeal not allowed 75 Ohio St.3d 1448, 663 N.E.2d 330.

Award of shared parenting was not an abuse of discretion; trial court could reasonably have concluded from evidence presented at hearing, including husband's testimony regarding his sobriety and his alcoholism rehabilitation program, that husband's alcoholism was not an appropriate reason to deny shared custody, and husband's demanding work schedule did not require that he be denied shared custody, given testimony that husband would seek other employment, if necessary, to preserve relationship with children and feasibility of tailoring parenting arrangement to accommodate husband's work schedule. Harris v. Harris (Miami 1995) 105 Ohio App.3d 671, 664 N.E.2d 1304.

Trial court did not have to reject husband's shared parenting plan based on his omission of statutorily required elements, as those issues had already been addressed by trial court in final decree of divorce issued before court adopted shared parenting plan. Harris v. Harris (Miami 1995) 105 Ohio App.3d 671, 664 N.E.2d 1304.

Trial court erred in granting shared parenting on terms not set forth in shared-parenting plan submitted to court by one party or other. McClain v. McClain (Summit 1993) 87 Ohio App.3d 856, 623 N.E.2d 242.

"Shared parenting" of children by divorced couples means that parents literally share some, or all, of aspects of physical and legal care of their children. Snouffer v. Snouffer (Meigs 1993) 87 Ohio App.3d 89, 621 N.E.2d 879.

Pursuant to Civ R 75(P) and RC 3109.04, it is mandatory for the trial court to award custody of minor children to one of the parents where a divorce is granted, unless neither parent is a suitable person to have custody. McVay v. McVay (Columbiana 1974) 44 Ohio App.2d 370, 338 N.E.2d 772, 73 O.O.2d 415.

13. —Findings of fact and conclusions of law, allocation of rights and responsibilities: Modification after original allocation—"Change in circumstances" and Specific Factors

Mother who has been awarded custody of her children in previous court proceeding is entitled to be informed of reasons behind an order divesting her of such custody rendered by court or its appointed referee. Currens v. Currens (Hamilton 1970) 26 Ohio App.2d 215, 270 N.E.2d 362, 55 O.O.2d 360.

14. —"Residential parent" rights and duties, allocation of rights and responsibilities: Initial Allocation—"Best interest" and Specific Factors

Although a party exercising visitation rights might gain temporary physical control over the child for that purpose, such control does not constitute "child custody" because the legal authority to make fundamental decisions about the child's welfare remains with the custodial party and because the child eventually must be returned to the more permanent setting provided by that party. Braatz v. Braatz (Ohio 1999) 85 Ohio St.3d 40, 706 N.E.2d 1218.

Where evidence conclusively shows that mother of minor child is not suitable person to have custody of such child, and where an award of custody to mother would constitute abuse of discretion, it is erroneous, as a matter of law, for common pleas court to award "physical" custody of child to grandmother and "legal" custody to mother; under such circumstances court of appeals is not required to remand cause for new trial but may order custody awarded to father. Baxter v. Baxter (Ohio 1971) 27 Ohio St.2d 168, 271 N.E.2d 873, 56 O.O.2d 104.

Former husband's proposed move out of state with children amounted to change of circumstances requiring trial court to inquire, upon former wife's motion for modification of parental rights and responsibilities originally established in judgment of divorce, into whether change of custody would be in children's best interests, where children had close relationships with members of extended family resident in state on both sides of the family and no connection with state to which former husband proposed to move, and where proposed move would undoubtedly impact children's ability to continue their family relationships. Zinnecker v. Zinnecker (Ohio App. 12 Dist. 1999) 133 Ohio App.3d 378, 728 N.E.2d 38.

Change of residence on part of residential parent that has no direct impact on child amounts to slight or inconsequential change in circumstances, while move that directly impacts child in some demonstrable way constitutes substantive change sufficient to meet threshold showing, on nonresidential parent's motion for modification of parental rights and responsibilities, that change of circumstances has occurred warranting further inquiry to determine whether change of custody is in best interest of child. Zinnecker v. Zinnecker (Ohio App. 12 Dist. 1999) 133 Ohio App.3d 378, 728 N.E.2d 38.

Where a divorce decree, voluntarily agreed to by both parties, gives legal custody of minor children to their father but leaves the immediate care and control with their mother, it is not error for the domestic relations court to approve a change of schools requested by the mother, since the immediate welfare of the children is in her hands. Majnaric v. Majnaric (Summit 1975) 46 Ohio App.2d 157, 347 N.E.2d 552, 75 O.O.2d 250.

Court could not allocate responsibilities for the care of the children primarily to one parent without designating that parent as the residential parent since RC 3109.04 is directory rather than discretionary. In the matter of Clark, No. 74663, 1999 WL 166018 (8th Dist Ct App, Cuyahoga, 3-25-99).

15. Ethics of divorce attorneys

Elihu Root's observation is worth recalling, that "About half the practice of a decent lawyer consists of telling ... clients they are d——— fools and should stop ... [that]the law lets you do it but don't. It's a rotten thing to do." Stivison v Goodyear Tire & Rubber Co, No. 95-CA-13, 1996 WL 230037 (4th Dist Ct App, Hocking, 5-6-96), affirmed by 80 Ohio St.3d 498 (1997).

16. —Death of undivorced parents, custody or visitation issues in proceedings other than divorce

Where husband and wife have been divorced and custody of their minor child under ten years of age awarded the mother, upon the mother's death, such custody does not devolve upon the father, nor upon probate court of the father's residence, but is still exclusively under control of the court granting the divorce. (Annotation from former RC 3105.21.) In re Hampshire (Ohio App. 5 Dist. 1922) 17 Ohio App. 139.

RC 3109.04(A) deals exclusively with divorce and is not applicable in a custody action brought by children's grandmother after the children's parents were killed in an airplane accident. In re Caneen, No. 654 (7th Dist Ct App, Monroe, 3-23-89).

17. —Investigations and psychological evaluations in general, allocation of rights and responsibilities: Initial Allocation—"B est interest" and Specific Factors

Wife was not entitled to introduce testimony of licensed social worker as an expert witness in proceedings to determine which party should be son's custodial parent; social worker only briefly met with son for five minutes, social worker met with husband on only two occasions in context of counseling with parties' daughter, and trial court heard testimony from all parties involved and also conducted in camera interview with son and daughter. Donovan v. Donovan (Clermont 1996) 110 Ohio App.3d 615, 674 N.E.2d 1252.

Statute and rule which provide for admission of court-ordered investigation reports involving child custody and divorce matters and permit cross-examination of the parties concerning contents of reports import the use of such reports as testimony. Sayre v. Hoelzle-Sayre (Seneca 1994) 100 Ohio App.3d 203, 653 N.E.2d 712, appeal allowed 70 Ohio St.3d 1426, 638 N.E.2d 88, appeal dismissed as improvidently allowed 72 Ohio St.3d 1218, 651 N.E.2d 430.

Where a court in a child custody hearing authorizes a custodial investigation and bases its decision entirely on the findings therefrom while excluding other available evidence, such decision is invalid. Hillard v. Hillard (Butler 1971) 29 Ohio App.2d 20, 277 N.E.2d 557, 58 O.O.2d 14.

The power of the court to order psychological evaluations of parties to a custody dispute under RC 3109.04 is advisory and not mandatory. Heyob v Newman, No. 638 (4th Dist Ct App, Highland, 12-8-87).

In a custody hearing, it is within the discretion of the trial court to refuse to consider an investigative report prepared by the county welfare department. Garza v Garza, No. S-81-28 (6th Dist Ct App, Sandusky, 5-14-82).

Pursuant to RC 3109.04, a trial court is required to review the mental and physical health of all parties concerned in addressing issues of parental rights and responsibilities and it does not abuse discretion in ordering a mental health counseling facility to disclose medical records where a case presents an ongoing issue regarding a parent's visitation and companionship rights with the parties' minor children and whether the visitation would be in the children's best interests. Smith v Smith, No. 94-B-55, 1997 WL 467554 (7th Dist Ct App, Belmont, 8-8-97).

Trial court was justified in awarding custody of children eleven, ten, and six to the father because of the mother's emotional instability. Herzog v. Herzog (Montgomery 1955) 132 N.E.2d 754, 72 Ohio Law Abs. 22.

18. —"Unfitness" of parent as factor, allocation of rights and responsibilities: Modification after original allocation—"Change in circumstances" and Specific Factors

Trial court abuses its discretion when it uses document filed in compliance with local rule as only evidence to remove child from mother's custody. Masters v. Masters (Ohio 1994) 69 Ohio St.3d 83, 630 N.E.2d 665.

In a change-of-custody proceeding initiated by a motion in a divorce action, as between the parents of the children, it is not necessary for the court to determine a parent is unfit to be a custodian prior to ordering change of custody, but only that the change of circumstances occurring since the prior order of the court justifies such change of custody for the best interests of the children. (Annotation from former RC 3105.21.) Beamer v. Beamer (Seneca 1969) 17 Ohio App.2d 89, 244 N.E.2d 775, 46 O.O.2d 118.

Where a child's mother has been determined to be an unsuitable parent, the father gives physical custody of the child to the maternal grandmother, the child undergoes brain surgery and is left with a soft skull, and the mother's boyfriend has a propensity for violence, an award of custody of the child to the maternal grandmother is proper despite the lack of a finding that the child's father is an unsuitable parent where such award of custody to a nonparent is in the best interest of the child. Mannering v Mannering, No. 559 (4th Dist Ct App, Jackson, 5-3-89).

Where a minor child was entrusted to friends because the mother was unfit, and the father subsequently remarried and reclaimed the child, a court may not award custody to any person other than the father except upon a finding of the father's unfitness. Garabrandt v. Garabrandt (Ohio Com.Pl. 1953) 114 N.E.2d 919, 65 Ohio Law Abs. 380, 51 O.O. 319.

19. —In general, states' sovereign rights in domestic relations

Disputes about domestic matters remain the province of the states. Thompson v. Thompson (U.S.Cal. 1988) 108 S.Ct. 513, 484 U.S. 174, 98 L.Ed.2d 512.

States retain power to require disabled veterans to use their federal benefits to support their children, as the benefits are not restricted to use for veterans' support; it follows that a veteran's refusal to pay can be punished in state court by contempt. (Ed. note: Tennessee law construed in light of federal constitution.) Rose v. Rose (U.S.Tenn. 1987) 107 S.Ct. 2029, 481 U.S. 619, 95 L.Ed.2d 599.

20. —Habeas corpus, custody or visitation issues in proceedings other than divorce

Although filing of bankruptcy petition stays equitable distribution in divorce case of debtor's interest in marital assets, certain aspects of divorce case, such as dissolution of marriage and child custody issues, are not stayed. State ex rel. Miley v. Parrott (Ohio 1996) 77 Ohio St.3d 64, 671 N.E.2d 24.

Trial court was obligated to reactivate divorce case after bankruptcy court lifted automatic stay affecting Chapter 12 debtor-husband; order inactivating divorce case stated that case would stay inactive until judge "is advised in writing of the stay having been lifted," trial court was advised in writing that bankruptcy court had lifted stay for divorce case, trial court would not be subject to contempt for violating stay after bankruptcy court expressly modified and lifted stay, and divorce case would not be better resolved after conclusion of bankruptcy proceedings. State ex rel. Miley v. Parrott (Ohio 1996) 77 Ohio St.3d 64, 671 N.E.2d 24.

Automatic stay may be lifted or modified for cause. State ex rel. Miley v. Parrott (Ohio 1996) 77 Ohio St.3d 64, 671 N.E.2d 24.

Pursuant to RC 2151.23(A), the juvenile court has jurisdiction to determine the custody of a child alleged to be abused, neglected, or dependent, when that child is not the ward of any court in this state; this jurisdiction includes children subject to a divorce decree granting custody pursuant to RC 3109.04. In re Poling (Ohio 1992) 64 Ohio St.3d 211, 594 N.E.2d 589.

A domestic relations court has jurisdiction under RC 3105.21(B) to determine custody despite dismissal of a divorce action for lack of prosecution. State ex rel. Easterday v. Zieba (Ohio 1991) 58 Ohio St.3d 251, 569 N.E.2d 1028.

RC 3105.21(B) affords a domestic relations court authority to determine custody of a child, as between his parents and another relative, even though that court has dismissed the parent's divorce action; if after dismissing the divorce action, the domestic relations court elects to certify the matter of custody to juvenile court, under RC 3105.21(B) and 3109.04 the domestic relations court must specifically find custody in neither parent to be in the child's best interest, or all jurisdiction over the matter is lost. State ex rel. Easterday v. Zieba (Ohio 1991) 58 Ohio St.3d 251, 569 N.E.2d 1028.

Where a court of another state has awarded custody of a minor child pursuant to a valid in personam order, and there is no evidence of a subsequent change in circumstances affecting the best interests of the child, the courts of this state will give full faith and credit to that order. Williams v. Williams (Ohio 1975) 44 Ohio St.2d 28, 336 N.E.2d 426, 73 O.O.2d 121.

RC 3105.20 does not deny the court of common pleas in any matter concerning domestic relations the exercise of "its full equity powers and jurisdiction," but there must be a statutory basis upon which to exercise those powers before they may be put into execution. Haynie v. Haynie (Ohio 1959) 169 Ohio St. 467, 159 N.E.2d 765, 8 O.O.2d 476.

A probate court has jurisdiction to hear and determine an adoption proceeding relating to a minor child notwithstanding the fact that the custody of such child is at the time within the continuing jurisdiction of a divorce court. (See also In re Biddle, 81 Abs 529, 163 NE(2d) 190 (App, Franklin 1959).) In re Adoption of Biddle (Ohio 1958) 168 Ohio St. 209, 152 N.E.2d 105, 6 O.O.2d 4, on remand 163 N.E.2d 188, 81 Ohio Law Abs. 529.

Although divorce action was completed, jurisdiction over paternity action that was brought as postdecree motion was proper in Court of Domestic Relations, not solely in Juvenile Court, since other postdecree matters were still pending. Broxterman v. Broxterman (Hamilton 1995) 101 Ohio App.3d 661, 656 N.E.2d 394.

Common pleas courts which have already issued orders concerning parental rights and responsibilities do not lose jurisdiction after the death of the custodial parent and must resolve the case in the best interests of the children under RC 3109.04. In re Dunn (Auglaize 1992) 79 Ohio App.3d 268, 607 N.E.2d 81, dismissed, jurisdictional motion overruled 65 Ohio St.3d 1416, 598 N.E.2d 1168.

Although a Florida dissolution decree obtained by parties who lived in Ohio both before and after its issuance says it "shall be construed and governed" in accordance with Florida law, in later proceedings in Ohio court Ohio law presumably controls any change of custody for a child who resides in Ohio, while Florida law controls the meaning of the decree and the agreement it incorporates. Zigmont v. Toto (Cuyahoga 1988) 47 Ohio App.3d 181, 547 N.E.2d 1208, cause dismissed 38 Ohio St.3d 715, 533 N.E.2d 783.

A court, in ordering dismissal of a complaint for divorce at a party's request, may not issue an order of child custody and support as "terms and conditions" of dismissal under Civ R 41(A)(2), since the purpose of that provision is to permit an order that leaves the parties as if the action had not been brought. Lilly v. Lilly (Montgomery 1985) 26 Ohio App.3d 192, 499 N.E.2d 21, 26 O.B.R. 412.

Where the domestic relations division of a common pleas court concludes a divorce action with judgment entries including one finding that custody of a child to neither parent is in the child's best interest and certifies its findings to the juvenile court for further proceedings pursuant to RC 3109.04(A), the certification order is a final appealable order. Robinson v. Robinson (Franklin 1984) 19 Ohio App.3d 323, 484 N.E.2d 710, 19 O.B.R. 496.

When a parent having legal custody of minor children takes up residence with such children outside the state, an Ohio court has continuing jurisdiction to modify the original custody order. Murck v. Murck (Cuyahoga 1976) 47 Ohio App.2d 292, 353 N.E.2d 917, 1 O.O.3d 355.

Where a child, whose original custody was determined by an out-of-state court, presently resides in Ohio, a court of this state has jurisdiction to determine whether it is in the best interests of the child to give full faith and credit to the out-of-state order. Purcell v. Purcell (Hamilton 1975) 47 Ohio App.2d 258, 353 N.E.2d 882, 1 O.O.3d 316.

Where a court, having acquired jurisdiction over a child by virtue of a divorce action between the child's parents, certifies the matter of the child's custody to a juvenile court, the consent of the juvenile court having been first obtained, the juvenile court has exclusive jurisdiction over the child's custody by virtue of RC 3109.06 and 2151.23(D) and a finding of unfitness of the parents or that there is no suitable relative to have custody is not a necessary prerequisite to such certification, and while such certification shall be deemed to be the complaint in the juvenile court, it does not constitute a complaint in the juvenile court that such child is dependent or neglected and those dispositions provided for under RC 2151.353, 2151.354, and 2151.355 are not applicable to the disposition of such a child, disposition thereof being subject to and controlled by RC 3109.04. In re Height (Van Wert 1975) 47 Ohio App.2d 203, 353 N.E.2d 887, 1 O.O.3d 279.

When a mother having legal custody of a minor child is domiciled in another state with such child, an Ohio court does not have continuing jurisdiction to modify the original custody order, but if such child resides in Ohio, even though he may be domiciled in another state with the parent having legal custody, the courts of Ohio will have continuing jurisdiction to hear a motion for modification of custody. Heiney v. Heiney (Columbiana 1973) 40 Ohio App.2d 571, 321 N.E.2d 611, 69 O.O.2d 519.

When a divorce is denied, the parties are still married and they have equal rights as to custody of minor children, and both are responsible for care and support, and, until such time as a separate complaint or application is made to a court of competent jurisdiction, the provisions of RC 3109.03 and 3109.04 may not be invoked. Holderle v. Holderle (Franklin 1967) 11 Ohio App.2d 148, 229 N.E.2d 79, 40 O.O.2d 305.

An award of custody of a child in a divorce action is conclusive only as to the parties to such action, and the remedy of habeas corpus is available to obtain such child where a party other than the parties to the divorce action is involved; and it is not necessary to apply to the court which originally awarded custody of such child. In re Howland (Highland 1961) 115 Ohio App. 186, 184 N.E.2d 228, 20 O.O.2d 277.

In a case where a foreign decree of dissolution stipulates that the father gives up custody and visitation rights in exchange for the mother's agreement to forego child support payments, the father's motion to adopt the foreign decree is granted and Ohio is the proper forum to litigate the issue of custody where it is the child's home state. Kirby v Nakanishi, No. 68671, 1995 WL 753944 (8th Dist Ct App, Cuyahoga, 12-20-95).

Where a trial court feels an award of custody to either parent at the time of granting a divorce is not in the best interests of the child, an order indicating that one of the parties has temporary possession of a minor child for one year is not a final appealable order under Civ R 55(b). Shun v Shun, No. 43075 (8th Dist Ct App, Cuyahoga, 8-6-81).

Since an award of custody pendente lite to the father on a motion for temporary custody is not a custody decree, the award can be modified without a showing of changed circumstance. Garnet v Garnet, No. 80CA31 (7th Dist Ct App, Mahoning, 3-2-81).

A domestic relations court has continuing jurisdiction over the issue of child custody although the divorce decree did not address the issue of custody. Huxley v Huxley, No. 1903 (9th Dist Ct App, Wayne, 5-23-84).

Though husband had insufficient contacts with Ohio to provide Ohio court with in personam jurisdiction for purposes of division of property and support, Ohio had jurisdiction under Ohio statutes to make custody determination, where mother and child were present in Ohio; very presence of child in Ohio, meeting requirements of the Uniform Child Custody Jurisdiction Act (UCCJA) made clear the necessity of custody order. Schroeder v. Vigil-Escalera Perez (Ohio Com.Pl. 1995) 76 Ohio Misc.2d 25, 664 N.E.2d 627.

A common pleas court has no jurisdiction to make any order respecting the care and custody or visitation with minor children unless in the prayer of the petition the plaintiff asks for a divorce or alimony. Crum v. Howard (Ohio Com.Pl. 1956) 137 N.E.2d 654, 73 Ohio Law Abs. 111, 1 O.O.2d 399.

Where the natural parents of a minor child are divorced, custody of the child being given to the mother, and the mother remarries and her husband adopts the child, and then the mother and adoptive father are divorced, and custody is awarded to the adoptive father, and the natural father seeks custody, and prior to hearing the mother and adoptive father are remarried, the court loses jurisdiction over the custody of the child. Lockard v. Lockard (Ohio Com.Pl. 1951) 102 N.E.2d 747, 63 Ohio Law Abs. 549, 49 O.O. 163.

The remarriage of divorced parents terminates the jurisdiction of the divorce court over the custody of their minor children. Lockard v. Lockard (Ohio Com.Pl. 1951) 102 N.E.2d 747, 63 Ohio Law Abs. 549, 49 O.O. 163.

21. —Appeal, emergency and temporary orders

Emergency order temporarily designating father as residential parent was interlocutory in nature and, therefore, not immediately appealable. Brooks v. Brooks (Ohio App. 10 Dist. 1996) 117 Ohio App.3d 19, 689 N.E.2d 987.

22. —Agreement of parties, effect, allocation of rights and responsibilities: Initial Allocation—"Best interest" and Specific Factors

Agreed entry awarding temporary and permanent custody of children was interlocutory prior to its integration as part of final divorce decree and thus court, in determining custody provision of final decree, was required to apply "best interest of child" standard, and it had discretion to accept, reject or modify parties' agreement; statute authorizing change of custody only upon showing of changed circumstances was applicable only where parties sought to modify prior, final custody decree. Frost v. Frost (Franklin 1992) 84 Ohio App.3d 699, 618 N.E.2d 198, motion overruled 66 Ohio St.3d 1489, 612 N.E.2d 1245.

A court must consider the factors listed in RC 3109.04(C) and make an independent original determination of custody, not merely adopt the provisions of a separation agreement in a divorce action, and a court's failure to do so is an abuse of discretion. Clark v Clark, No. 11021 (2d Dist Ct App, Montgomery, 1-18-89).

In the event of a dissolution of marriage, as contrasted with divorce, child custody is determined by whatever separation agreement is approved by the court and incorporated into its dissolution decree, the parties having the right to amend the agreement prior to or during the hearing on the petition for dissolution. Davidson v Davidson, No. 4-79-7 (3d Dist Ct App, Defiance, 2-20-80).

A trial court that approved a separation agreement, thereafter adopted as a part of the judgment in a divorce, alimony and custody action, which agreement contained a provision regarding the custody of a minor child, is not bound by the terms of that agreement in a subsequent hearing on a motion to modify the provisions of the judgment entry. Bastian v. Bastian (Cuyahoga 1959) 160 N.E.2d 133, 81 Ohio Law Abs. 408, 13 O.O.2d 267.

An agreement between husband and wife, parties to a divorce action, that the custody of their child should be given to a third person, is enforceable, subject only to judicial determination that the custodian was in every way a proper person to have the care of the child. Rowe v. Rowe (Franklin 1950) 97 N.E.2d 223, 58 Ohio Law Abs. 497, 44 O.O. 224.

23. —Appeal, allocation of rights and responsibilities: Modification after original allocation—"Change in circumstances" and Specific Factors

Determination of trial judge as to whether "change of circumstances" warranting change in custody has occurred should not be disturbed on appeal absent abuse of discretion. Davis v. Flickinger (Ohio 1997) 77 Ohio St.3d 415, 674 N.E.2d 1159.

Trial court's order that parties to proceeding for modification of custody provisions of divorce decree undergo physical and psychological testing did not affect substantial right and was not immediately appealable; trial court had broad discretion to order testing, tests ordered were not intrusive, and blanket assertion that order was final and appealable did not demonstrate that appeal from final custody determination would not adequately afford meaningful or effective remedy. Montecalvo v. Montecalvo (Ohio App. 11 Dist. 1999) 126 Ohio App.3d 377, 710 N.E.2d 379, motion dismissed 85 Ohio St.3d 1455, 708 N.E.2d 1010.

Father's claims that home study report and doctor's report did not indicate that he was unfit for custody of his child was not an issue for appeal of trial court's decision on remand from prior appeal to maintain custody with maternal grandparents; reports were before trial court in connection with original decision awarding custody and any contentions as to those reports should have been raised in earlier appeal. Rife v. Morgan (Clark 1995) 106 Ohio App.3d 843, 667 N.E.2d 450.

Trial court did not abuse its discretion in overruling mother's motion for change of custody of parties' three daughters; there was evidence to support trial court's determination that change in circumstances had not occurred, and no evidence to show that modification of custody would be in best interest of children. Clyborn v. Clyborn (Hardin 1994) 93 Ohio App.3d 192, 638 N.E.2d 112.

Decisions concerning change of custody of minor children will not be reversed absent showing that trial court abused its discretion. Perz v. Perz (Lucas 1993) 85 Ohio App.3d 374, 619 N.E.2d 1094, motion overruled 67 Ohio St.3d 1423, 616 N.E.2d 506.

In proceeding on motion for change of custody, judgment that defers issue of child support for future determination is not "final appealable order." Kouns v. Pemberton (Lawrence 1992) 84 Ohio App.3d 499, 617 N.E.2d 701, motion overruled 66 Ohio St.3d 1489, 612 N.E.2d 1245.

The denial of a motion for modification of a custody order will not be reversed on the ground that the conditions described in RC 3109.04 exist unless the evidence compels that conclusion. Pryer v. Pryer (Hardin 1984) 20 Ohio App.3d 170, 485 N.E.2d 268, 20 O.B.R. 205.

24. —In general, emergency and temporary orders

RC 3109.04(B)(1) does not apply to a parent's motion to extinguish an award of custody to a non-parent that is temporary both in its denomination and in terms of the length of time elapsing between the award and the parent's motion to terminate the award. In re Custody of Carpenter (Greene 1987) 41 Ohio App.3d 182, 534 N.E.2d 1216.

In a proceeding to award temporary custody of a child, the governing principle is the best interest of the child under RC 3109.04; limitation of examination concerning events in the child's life before the proceeding began is therefore prejudicial error. Mercer v Channell, No. 509 (4th Dist Ct App, Jackson, 5-14-86).

25. —In general, allocation of rights and responsibilities: Modification after original allocation—"Change in circumstances" and Specific Factors

In determining whether change of circumstances has occurred so as to warrant change in custody initially established by decree allocating parental rights and responsibilities, trial judge, as trier of fact, must have wide latitude in considering all issues and evidence before him or her which support such change. Davis v. Flickinger (Ohio 1997) 77 Ohio St.3d 415, 674 N.E.2d 1159.

Statute governing modification of decrees allocating parental rights and responsibilities, while requiring that change in circumstances justifying change of custody be change of substance and not slight or inconsequential, does not require "substantial" change in circumstances; word "substantial" does not appear in statute, and intent of statute is to spare children from constant tug of war between their parents and provide stability to custodial status of children. Davis v. Flickinger (Ohio 1997) 77 Ohio St.3d 415, 674 N.E.2d 1159.

The family reunification law set forth in RC 2151.414 has no relevance and does not apply to motions for a change of custody under RC 3109.04; RC 2151.414 is limited to matters pertaining to a motion for permanent custody of a child by a county department, board, or certified organization that has temporary custody of the child. Miller v. Miller (Ohio 1988) 37 Ohio St.3d 71, 523 N.E.2d 846, clarification denied 43 Ohio St.3d 710, 540 N.E.2d 728.

Court is not warranted in modifying a previous order fixing custody of children where there is neither a change of conditions nor a discovery of material facts existent at the time of entering previous order and then unknown to court; but upon proof of such change or discovery of material facts, court is empowered to make an order of modification when warranted by evidence. Dailey v. Dailey (Ohio 1945) 146 Ohio St. 93, 64 N.E.2d 246, 32 O.O. 29.

Pursuant to statute, trial court cannot order modification of custody decree without evidence that change in circumstances has occurred and that child's best interest is served by modification; change in circumstances requirement fosters continuity and stability in child's life, and also serves court's interest by discouraging relitigation of same issues. Waggoner v. Waggoner (Wayne 1996) 111 Ohio App.3d 1, 675 N.E.2d 541, dismissed, appeal not allowed 77 Ohio St.3d 1445, 671 N.E.2d 1284.

Mere possibility of change in circumstances in the future will not ordinarily suffice to support modification of child custody decree. Waggoner v. Waggoner (Wayne 1996) 111 Ohio App.3d 1, 675 N.E.2d 541, dismissed, appeal not allowed 77 Ohio St.3d 1445, 671 N.E.2d 1284.

In deciding whether change in circumstances sufficient to warrant modification of child custody decree exists, court is required by statute to weigh harm against advantages that would likely result from change; implicit in balancing test is recognition that disruption in child's regular residence and care is harmful, and to balance that harm, court must be able to justify risk in part through change in circumstances requirement. Waggoner v. Waggoner (Wayne 1996) 111 Ohio App.3d 1, 675 N.E.2d 541, dismissed, appeal not allowed 77 Ohio St.3d 1445, 671 N.E.2d 1284.

Court cannot modify prior decree that allocates parental rights and responsibilities for care of child, including parental rights to continuing contact with that child, unless it finds that change in circumstances has occurred and that modification is necessary to serve best interest of child. Jacobs v. Jacobs (Wayne 1995) 102 Ohio App.3d 568, 657 N.E.2d 580.

Modification of visitation order to impose court's standard visitation schedule is not per se just and reasonable, as court must consider whether there has been change of circumstances and whether modification is in best interest of child. Jacobs v. Jacobs (Wayne 1995) 102 Ohio App.3d 568, 657 N.E.2d 580.

Trial court's use of term "substantial" in its findings in support of denial of mother's motion for change of custody did not indicate that trial court improperly required mother to demonstrate "substantial" change of circumstances rather than simply a change of circumstances. Clyborn v. Clyborn (Hardin 1994) 93 Ohio App.3d 192, 638 N.E.2d 112.

Under "best interest of the child" test, custody will not be modified unless party can prove that change of custody will be in best interest of child, and mere assertion that it will not be detrimental is insufficient. Miller v. Miller (Hocking 1993) 86 Ohio App.3d 623, 621 N.E.2d 745.

There must be some substantial change of circumstance that is significant to question of child custody before reexamination of best interest of child is appropriate. Perz v. Perz (Lucas 1993) 85 Ohio App.3d 374, 619 N.E.2d 1094, motion overruled 67 Ohio St.3d 1423, 616 N.E.2d 506.

Modification of parental rights is not warranted unless there is some competent credible evidence to effect that there has been change in circumstances, modification is in best interest of child, and any harm likely to be caused by change in environment is outweighed by advantages. Holm v. Smilowitz (Athens 1992) 83 Ohio App.3d 757, 615 N.E.2d 1047.

By adopting one party's judgment entry modifying children's custody in the absence of an agreement of the parents or a finding that the statutory factors justify a change, a domestic relations court exceeds its authority. Zigmont v. Toto (Cuyahoga 1988) 47 Ohio App.3d 181, 547 N.E.2d 1208, cause dismissed 38 Ohio St.3d 715, 533 N.E.2d 783.

The grant of final custody after a temporary custody order is issued pending a final divorce decree does not constitute a modification of an existing order; therefore, the provisions of RC 3109.04(B) are inapplicable. Thompson v. Thompson (Washington 1987) 31 Ohio App.3d 254, 511 N.E.2d 412, 31 O.B.R. 538.

A judgment in a paternity action has the effect of a prior determination of custody; therefore, a subsequent change of custody pursuant to a petition by the natural father must be based on a finding of changed circumstances. In re Yates (Franklin 1984) 18 Ohio App.3d 95, 481 N.E.2d 646, 18 O.B.R. 458.

The prohibition of RC 3109.04(B)(1) against modification of a prior custody decree unless there has been a change in circumstances applies when the prior decree was rendered under the provisions of RC 3105.21(B) upon the failure of proof of the causes in a complaint for divorce. Dickrede v. Dickrede (Allen 1984) 14 Ohio App.3d 292, 470 N.E.2d 925, 14 O.B.R. 349.

A parent seeking a transfer of custody must establish that: (1) the circumstances of the child or the custodial parent have changed since the original custody order was entered; (2) the child's best interests will be served by the modification; and (3) the present environment of the child poses a significant danger to "his physical health or his mental, moral, or emotional development and the harm likely to be caused by a change in environment is outweighed by the advantages of the change." Stone v. Stone (Warren 1983) 9 Ohio App.3d 6, 457 N.E.2d 919, 9 O.B.R. 6.

Under former RC 3109.04(B) (now RC 3109.04(B)(1)), facts "unknown to the court at the time of the prior decree" may include facts known to the adverse party, but not the court, at the time of the prior decree. Wyss v. Wyss (Franklin 1982) 3 Ohio App.3d 412, 445 N.E.2d 1153, 3 O.B.R. 479.

In a custody action subsequent to the original custody order, the trial court does not abuse its discretion by limiting the evidence to events which occurred after the original custody order was made. In re Reynolds (Hamilton 1982) 2 Ohio App.3d 309, 441 N.E.2d 1141, 2 O.B.R. 341.

Where a court in a change-of-custody action determines it is no longer equitable that a judgment continue to have prospective application, it may change such, notwithstanding RC 3109.04(B) and even though none of the exceptions in that statute exist. Sexton v. Sexton (Morrow 1978) 60 Ohio App.2d 339, 397 N.E.2d 425, 14 O.O.3d 297.

A court of common pleas does not have absolute discretion to change a previous award of custody of a minor child; such a change must be based on a finding of a "change of conditions." McVay v. McVay (Columbiana 1974) 44 Ohio App.2d 370, 338 N.E.2d 772, 73 O.O.2d 415.

In a change-of-custody proceeding initiated by motion in a divorce action as between the parents of the children, it is not necessary for the court to determine a parent is unfit to be a custodian prior to ordering change of custody, but only that a change of circumstances occurring since the prior order of the court justifies such change of custody for the best interests of the children. Beamer v. Beamer (Seneca 1969) 17 Ohio App.2d 89, 244 N.E.2d 775, 46 O.O.2d 118.

A finding that a change in circumstances had occurred was required to modify an award of custody and if the statutory factors required for such modification are not found, the court may not look only to the best interests of the child or children in making that modification. In re Phillip Kilkenny, Stewart Kilkenny, Dependent Children, No. 99CA77, 2000 WL 145924 (2d Dist Ct App, Greene, 2-11-00).

In an action for custody modification, a showing that the child would be better off with the non-custodial parent is not sufficient; there must be a change in circumstances before the change of custody can be considered. Cummins v Voorheis, No. 1325 (4th Dist Ct App, Scioto, 6-10-81).

Where the only prior custody decree is the one at the time of the divorce, the noncustodial parent may attempt to show a change of circumstances occurring since the original decree under RC 3109.04(B). Hlutke v Hlutke, No. 3000 (9th Dist Ct App, Lorain, 11-5-80).

In order to effect a change of custody it is incumbent upon the trial court to find pursuant to RC 3109.04 that it is in the child's interest to change custody and that the advantages of a change in environment outweigh the harm likely to be caused thereby. Smith v Smith, No.

CA98-04-005, 1998 WL 857523 (12th Dist Ct App, Fayette, 12-14-98).

26. —In general, allocation of rights and responsibilities: Initial Allocation—"Best interest" and Specific Factors

Permanent custody order was "judgment," for purposes of rule requiring court to issue written findings of fact and conclusions of law supporting judgment, regardless of when order was entered. State ex rel. Papp v. James (Ohio 1994) 69 Ohio St.3d 373, 632 N.E.2d 889.

Trial court has broad discretion in cases relating to custody of children for it is in the best position to gain knowledge of the parties and it is delegated with the authority to decide disputes of fact and weigh testimony and credibility of witnesses. Sayre v. Hoelzle-Sayre (Seneca 1994) 100 Ohio App.3d 203, 653 N.E.2d 712, appeal allowed 70 Ohio St.3d 1426, 638 N.E.2d 88, appeal dismissed as improvidently allowed 72 Ohio St.3d 1218, 651 N.E.2d 430.

RC 3109.04(B) requires findings of a change in circumstance upon modification of a final custody decree only, and not upon modification of an interlocutory custody order. Schoffner v. Schoffner (Auglaize 1984) 19 Ohio App.3d 208, 483 N.E.2d 1190, 19 O.B.R. 352.

27. —Modification, emergency and temporary orders

RC 3109.04(B)(1) does not apply to a parent's motion to extinguish an award of custody to a non-parent that is temporary both in its denomination and in terms of the length of time elapsing between the award and the parent's motion to terminate the award. In re Custody of Carpenter (Greene 1987) 41 Ohio App.3d 182, 534 N.E.2d 1216.

An interlocutory order regarding child custody entered pursuant to Civ R 75(M) is by its very nature temporary and may be modified upon the entering of the final divorce decree; RC 3109.04(A), rather than RC 3109.04(B), applies to the final determination of custody as well as such inherently temporary orders. Spence v. Spence (Franklin 1981) 2 Ohio App.3d 280, 441 N.E.2d 822, 2 O.B.R. 310.

Where a mother grants voluntary temporary custody to an infant's paternal grandparents, the proper standard to be used by the court in determining an award of custody upon the filing of a petition by the mother is the fitness of the mother, not the best interests of the child standard in RC 3109.04(B). In re Curry, No. 89AP-550 (10th Dist Ct App, Franklin, 11-21-89).

RC 3109.04(B) does not apply where a parent files to obtain custody after an award of temporary custody to a non-parent. An agreement to allow temporary custody is not a knowing surrender of parents' natural right to preferential treatment in a custody proceeding. In re Carpenter, No. 87-CA-3 (2d Dist Ct App, Greene, 7-27-87).

A two-year interval between a grant of temporary child custody to a relative and the parent's attempt to regain custody is insufficient to find that the parent has relinquished her parental rights and so the court does not err in concluding that the natural parent is a suitable parent who has not relinquished legal custody of her daughter. In re Wilson, No. 98-CA-19, 1999 WL 252799 (2d Dist Ct App, Miami, 4-30-99).

28. —Visitation interference, allocation of rights and responsibilities: Modification after original allocation—"Change in circumstances" and Specific Factors

Trial court's modification of original custody decree to designate father of child born out of wedlock as child's residential parent was supported by substantial evidence; mother requested complete termination of father's visitation rights, mother and her new husband were hostile to child's father, child entered kindergarten subsequent to issuance of original decree, and mother and new husband refused to modify visitation agreement to permit father to spend time with child under child's new school schedule. Davis v. Flickinger (Ohio 1997) 77 Ohio St.3d 415, 674 N.E.2d 1159.

Request by mother of minor child born out of wedlock for complete termination of father's visitation rights could be considered by trial court in evaluating best interest of child as required by custody statute, as such request added to hostility between child's parents and demonstrated mother's disregard for best interest of child. Davis v. Flickinger (Ohio 1997) 77 Ohio St.3d 415, 674 N.E.2d 1159.

Trial court could consider, in determining whether to modify custodial status of child born out of wedlock, change in circumstances created by maturing of child; child entered kindergarten subsequent to original decree, and residential parent was unwilling to provide any substitute arrangements that would enable nonresidential parent to spend as much time with child as before child was in kindergarten. Davis v. Flickinger (Ohio 1997) 77 Ohio St.3d 415, 674 N.E.2d 1159.

Trial court could consider, in determining whether to modify custodial status of child born out of wedlock, issue of which parent was more likely to honor and facilitate visitation, and factor that issue into best interest of child. Davis v. Flickinger (Ohio 1997) 77 Ohio St.3d 415, 674 N.E.2d 1159.

Evidence supported determination that mother's interference with visitation constituted a "change in circumstances" warranting custody modification, despite father's child support arrearages, and even though guardian ad litem had found that the children were thriving while living with mother; father was currently paying child support and diligently working on reducing his arrearages, he had been forced to seek court intervention to enjoy visitation on at least three separate occasions while mother had custody, and the children were of relatively tender years, and had shown great flexibility in adjusting to new environments. Clark v. Smith (Ohio App. 3 Dist. 1998) 130 Ohio App.3d 648, 720 N.E.2d 973.

Evidence in child custody modification proceeding supported determination that father did not interfere with visitation between mother and children, despite incident in which father's cohabitant took the children to Kentucky to see her brother's graduation, during which time mother could not reach them; father testified that he attempted to call mother and let her know the children would be out of town. Clark v. Smith (Ohio App. 3 Dist. 1998) 130 Ohio App.3d 648, 720 N.E.2d 973.

Custodial parent's interference with visitation by a noncustodial parent may be considered as part of a "change in circumstances" which would allow for modification of custody. Clark v. Smith (Ohio App. 3 Dist. 1998) 130 Ohio App.3d 648, 720 N.E.2d 973.

Custodial parent's interference with visitation by noncustodial parent may be considered "change of circumstances" which would allow for modification of custody. Mitchell v. Mitchell (Ohio App. 2 Dist. 1998) 126 Ohio App.3d 500, 710 N.E.2d 793.

For purposes of custodial parent's request that noncustodial parent be sanctioned for filing motion for modification of custody lacking basis in law or fact, custodial parent's alleged denial of visitation to noncustodial parent, supported by evidence in record, constituted "change of circumstances" sufficient, standing alone, to provide legal basis for noncustodial parent's motion. Mitchell v. Mitchell (Ohio App. 2 Dist. 1998) 126 Ohio App.3d 500, 710 N.E.2d 793.

A trial court is without authority to modify a mother's custody because of her failure to encourage or implement regular visitation with grandparents pursuant to a court's visitation order. Truitt v. Truitt (Preble 1989) 65 Ohio App.3d 126, 583 N.E.2d 331.

Child custody may not be altered as a sanction for contempt of court. Truitt v. Truitt (Preble 1989) 65 Ohio App.3d 126, 583 N.E.2d 331.

Termination of a mother's custody for her bitterness and uncooperativeness regarding a grandparent's visitation order is unwarranted. Truitt v. Truitt (Preble 1989) 65 Ohio App.3d 126, 583 N.E.2d 331.

Modification of a custody order is not among the available sanctions under RC 2705.05(A) as punishment for contempt; a trial court may not as a sanction for contempt of court arising from a custodial parent's interference with a noncustodial parent's visitation rights transfer the authority to the noncustodial parent to grant permission to a minor child to apply for a driver's license or to participate in extracurricular school activities as these changes actually modify custody, which is not a sanction authorized by RC 2705.05(A). Fry v. Fry (Paulding 1989) 64 Ohio App.3d 519, 582 N.E.2d 11.

Custody of children may not be changed merely as a sanction for contempt of a court order. Sontag v Sontag, No. C-800223 (1st Dist Ct App, Hamilton, 4-15-81).

It is in the best interest of a fourteen-year-old child with Down's Syndrome to be removed from the custody of his mother who has been his primary caretaker since birth and to designate the father as legal custodian and residential parent where it is found that (1) the mother has willfully denied the father's visitation rights and (2) the father is the parent more likely to facilitate visitation. Deimling v Messer, No. CA97-07-070, 1998 WL 117208 (12th Dist Ct App, Clermont, 3-16-98).

The court may award custody to a mother who previously interfered with visitation rights and who is accused of immoral conduct where the court considers all relevant factors concerning the best interests of the child, there is no evidence that the mother's alleged immoral conduct had any impact on the one and one-half year old child, and an intention is stated to tolerate no further interference with visitation. McDonald v Johnston, No. 1-95-37, 1995 WL 695086 (3d Dist Ct App, Allen, 11-22-95).

The denial of visitation by the custodial parent to the noncustodial parent is not sufficient grounds to justify a change in custody under RC 3109.04(B). In re Lehman, No. 87AP020012 (5th Dist Ct App, Tuscarawas, 7-20-87).

Pursuant to a motion for change of custody hearing, a custodial parent's prior citation for contempt in violating the visitation rights of the other parent is not sufficient to establish a change of circumstances under RC 3109.04(B). Mundschenk v Mundschenk, No. 81AP-406 (10th Dist Ct App, Franklin, 3-25-82).

29. —Immorality of parent: fornication, cohabitation and the like, allocation of rights and responsibilities: Modification after original allocation—"Change in circumstances" and Specific Factors

Evidence in child custody modification proceedings supported finding that, since the parties' divorce, circumstances in the living arrangements and familial relationship of the children had gone through "substan[illegible] changes"; since the divorce, mother had st[illegible] cohabitating with a man she subsequently marrie[illegible] father was cohabitating with a woman in Conn[illegible] and had changed residences. Clark v. Smith (Ohi[illegible] Dist. 1998) 130 Ohio App.3d 648, 720 N.E.2d [illegible]

Trial court could order former spouses n[illegible] overnight romantic guests when children we[illegible] despite former wife's contention that the [illegible] impermissibly based on notions of morality, w[illegible] night visits had adverse impact on the childre[illegible] v. Dilworth (Ohio App. 2 Dist. 1996) 115 O[illegible] 537, 685 N.E.2d 847.

Where an action seeking a change of custo[illegible]d, based on the fact that the custodial parent (the mother) has allowed her boyfriend to live in the marital home, an order of change of custody is erroneous where the evidence does not clearly show that the boyfriend's presence has an adverse impact on the children's physical, mental, emotional, or moral development. Kraus v. Kraus (Cuyahoga 1983) 10 Ohio App.3d 63, 460 N.E.2d 680, 10 O.B.R. 73.

Where a custodial parent is married to the person with whom she previously lived and there is no evidence that the child was materially adversely affected by the paramour relationship, change of custody may not be properly ordered as a penalty for the past misconduct of the custodial parent. Wyss v. Wyss (Franklin 1982) 3 Ohio App.3d 412, 445 N.E.2d 1153, 3 O.B.R. 479.

In light of the needs of a child for a stable environment, the modification of a prior custody order under RC 3109.04(B) can only be made where the harm caused by the change is outweighed by the advantage of such change. In re Rex (Seneca 1981) 3 Ohio App.3d 198, 444 N.E.2d 482, 3 O.B.R. 226.

A court's inquiry into the moral conduct or standards of a custodial parent is limited to a determination of the effect of such conduct on the child. Whaley v. Whaley (Lawrence 1978) 61 Ohio App.2d 111, 399 N.E.2d 1270, 15 O.O.3d 136.

In light of the needs of a child for a stable environment, the modification of a prior custody order under RC 3109.04(B) can only be made where the harm caused by the change is outweighed by the advantages of such change. Whaley v. Whaley (Lawrence 1978) 61 Ohio App.2d 111, 399 N.E.2d 1270, 15 O.O.3d 136.

A former wife's new baby and intimate relationship with the opposite sex do not amount to a change of substance and do not constitute a sufficient change of circumstance in the former wife's life to warrant reexamination of the custody issue or award of custody to the former husband. Marshall v Marshall, No. 97 10 0067, 1998 WL 725941 (3d Dist Ct App, Allen, 9-8-98).

It is an abuse of discretion requiring reversal for a court to order a modification of child custody based on a finding that the former husband has entered into an openly gay lifestyle since the last custody hearing and it has adversely affected the parties' minor child where no evidence in the record supports such a conclusion, and a psychologist's report noting that the prejudices and biases that are generally aimed at persons with alternative sexual orientations may put the child at greater risk for emotional distress cannot be given any effect since a parent's sexual preference, standing alone, is not a sufficient basis to modify the allocation of parental rights and responsibilities. Inscoe v Inscoe, No. 95 CA 12, 1997 WL 346199 (4th Dist Ct App, Meigs, 6-18-97).

Where there is reliable, probative, and credible evidence that the parties' minor child's emotional problems were the result of the parties' rancorous marriage relationship, and was not the result of the wife's living with a male companion, a new trial court hearing to change custody will not be granted. Mann v Mann, No. 45157 (8th Dist Ct App, Cuyahoga, 7-21-83).

The trial court did not err in granting custody to the mother, even though there was evidence that she was cohabitating with a man subsequent to her divorce; alleged immoral conduct must be shown to have a direct or probable adverse impact on the welfare of the child in order to justify a change of custody. Mann v Mann, No. 45157 (8th Dist Ct App, Cuyahoga, 7-21-83).

Where the custodial parent engaged in nonmarital sexual conduct, the trial court erred in ordering a change of custody absent any evidence that such conduct had a direct adverse impact on the child, especially where there is no indication that the child lacked proper care. In re Demangone, No. 81-CA-38 (2d Dist Ct App, Greene, 7-30-82).

A court cannot change the custody of a child to punish a parent whom the court believes has behaved immorally. DeMangone v DeMangone, No. 81-CA-38 (2d Dist Ct App, Greene, 2-22-82).

In a custody action, evidence showing that a mother was living with men to whom she was not married, drank excessively and used marijuana, is only relevant if it can be demonstrated that such conduct has an adverse impact on the best interests of the child. Horsley v Horsley, No. 803 (4th Dist Ct App, Ross, 7-14-81).

The trial court did not err in granting a change of custody from the custodial parent who had two sequential common law marriages, to the non-custodial parent who was established in a sound second marriage; a court's inquiry into the moral conduct of the custodial parent is limited to the determination of the affect of such conduct on the child. Zubay v Zubay, No. 79-C-48 (7th Dist Ct App, Columbiana, 11-26-80).

Where a custodial mother openly engages in homosexual activities in the presence of her minor daughter, a change of custody is in order because such activities endanger the child's physical health and mental, moral, and emotional development. Haton v Haton, No. WD-80-30 (6th Dist Ct App, Wood, 11-21-80).

Where a mother neglects to give her child corrective shoes for the prevention of scolosis, and where the child is afraid of the mother's new live-in boyfriend, a change of custody is in the best interest of the child. In re Lambeth, No. 78CA168 (7th Dist Ct App, Mahoning, 8-27-79).

Where the custodial mother establishes a lesbian household, there has been a substantial change in the circumstances of the children warranting a modification of a prior custody decree. Starnes v Starnes, No. 5029 (5th Dist Ct App, Stark, 6-19-79).

A court need not classify certain conduct as a "wicked sin" or "mere indiscretion;" the best test to determine a change of custody for reasons of morality is whether the residential parent's conduct has had a direct or probable adverse impact on the welfare of the child. Jasper v Jasper, No. C-940481, 1995 WL 540110 (1st Dist Ct App, Hamilton, 9-13-95).

A mother's lesbian relationship bears upon her fitness and ability to provide proper parenting where she allows her children to be exposed to her sexual orientation and activities and the relationship alienates the children and unnecessarily competes with the children's time with their mother so that custody is awarded to the father. Phillips v Phillips, No. CA94-03-005, 1995 WL 115426 (12th Dist Ct App, Preble, 3-20-95).

Where a custodial mother violates a court order granting custody so long as no male person shall be in the mother's house between midnight and 7:00 a.m., and in fact she admits sleeping in bed with four different men during the time, the court will award a change of custody due to the effect on the child. Wallace v Wallace, No. 81-C-32 (7th Dist Ct App, Columbiana, 2-26-82).

The custody of an illegitimate child will not be taken from the mother and awarded to the father merely upon the basis that the wife has contracted an interracial marriage. In re H. (Ohio Com.Pl. 1973) 37 Ohio Misc. 123, 305 N.E.2d 815, 66 O.O.2d 178, 66 O.O.2d 368.

Court did not err in refusing to change custody of fourteen-year-old daughter from father to mother, even though daughter requested such change, where mother had carried on adulterous relationship with individual whom she subsequently married. Watson v. Watson (Columbiana 1956) 146 N.E.2d 443, 76 Ohio Law Abs. 348.

30. —Child's wishes and interview with judge, allocation of rights and responsibilities: Initial Allocation—"Best interest" and Specific Factors

Upon mother's motion in custody proceeding, trial court was required to appoint guardian ad litem for child before it could interview child. State ex rel. Papp v. James (Ohio 1994) 69 Ohio St.3d 373, 632 N.E.2d 889.

Mother was not entitled to writ of mandamus to compel trial court in custody proceeding to appoint guardian ad litem for child; although mother had clear right to have trial court appoint guardian ad litem for child it sought to privately interview in custody proceedings, appeal was adequate remedy for violation of that right. State ex rel. Papp v. James (Ohio 1994) 69 Ohio St.3d 373, 632 N.E.2d 889.

The statute is mandatory insofar as it allows children ten years of age or more to choose parent with whom they prefer to live, except that court shall determine their custodian when parent so selected is unfitted by reason of moral depravity, habitual drunkenness or incapacity. Dailey v. Dailey (Ohio 1945) 146 Ohio St. 93, 64 N.E.2d 246, 32 O.O. 29.

Trial court allocating parental rights and responsibilities must, pursuant to statute, interview child if either party requests interview; interview is discretionary only if no party requests it. Badgett v. Badgett (Ohio App. 7 Dist. 1997) 120 Ohio App.3d 448, 698 N.E.2d 84.

Trial court must make record of any in camera interview with children involved in custody proceedings, to be kept under seal for review on appeal; audio recording, video recording, or stenographic record must be made, and no other person other than child and court personnel authorized by judge may be present with judge in chambers. Donovan v. Donovan (Clermont 1996) 110 Ohio App.3d 615, 674 N.E.2d 1252.

In determining the best interests of the child one factor to be considered is her wish to live with her father; where both parents live in the same school district, have homes and jobs to provide ample support for their children, and neither has any emotional problems, the trial court's naming the father as the residential parent is not arbitrary, capricious, or unreasonable. Williams v. Williams (Hardin 1992) 80 Ohio App.3d 477, 609 N.E.2d 617.

In a case in which both unmarried parents of two minor children seek custody after their relationship ends, a trial court errs in interviewing the children in chambers out of the presence of the parties and off the record where the children are eight and six years of age. In re Markham (Meigs 1990) 70 Ohio App.3d 841, 592 N.E.2d 896, dismissed, jurisdictional motion overruled 60 Ohio St.3d 702, 573 N.E.2d 118.

An award of custody of the eldest minor child of the marriage to the former husband is proper despite the child's election of the former wife as custodian where substantial evidence negated the child's election, including evidence that the home where the former wife was the caretaker was unsanitary and that she periodically left the children unattended, including the youngest who was handicapped; the paramount consideration is always the best interest of the child, and the child's election is only one factor to be considered in the trial court's custody determination, which is to be given the utmost deference. Thornton v. Thornton (Wyandot 1990) 70 Ohio App.3d 317, 590 N.E.2d 1375.

RC 3109.04(C) requires the court to determine whether it is in the child's best interests to allow him to elect to choose his custodial parent, not whether the choice made by the child is in his best interests under RC 3109.04(C). Buckles v. Buckles (Franklin 1988) 46 Ohio App.3d 102, 546 N.E.2d 950.

Where one child is of an age to make a choice, such election does not mean that siblings must also be placed with same parent. Glimcher v. Glimcher (Franklin 1971) 29 Ohio App.2d 55, 278 N.E.2d 37, 58 O.O.2d 37.

Privilege of child to choose parent with which he wishes to live exists only where court finds that both parents have capacity to properly care for child. Godbey v. Godbey (Hamilton 1942) 70 Ohio App. 450, 44 N.E.2d 810, 36 Ohio Law Abs. 511, 25 O.O. 184.

A letter which states a child's preference for custodial parent, which is addressed to the attorney of a party, rather than to the court, does not constitute a valid election under RC 3109.04(A). McFiggen v McFiggen, No. 46996 (8th Dist Ct App, Cuyahoga, 2-2-84).

In designating the residential parent, a court abuses discretion in adopting the findings and recommendations of the referee over the preference of the minor children to live with their mother in light of a repetitive theme throughout the proceedings of her activities with other men and her failure to be a "dutiful" wife and mother with respect to (1) her employment outside the home, (2) fewer "home cooked meals," (3) the husband being forced to take a more active role in the care of their children and home, and (4) failure to attend and meet the standards of the husband's church; the law imposes no religious standards for wives and mothers, and such evidence has no relevance other than to paint the wife and mother in a bad light. Sellman v Sellman, No. 95CA888, 1996 WL 557553 (4th Dist Ct App, Highland, 9-26-96).

The wishes of a child twelve years of age or older is a factor the court must consider, but not controlling upon it. Fisk v Fisk, No. CA85-03-009 (12th Dist Ct App, Preble, 8-12-85).

The trial court is obligated to conduct an in camera interview with the children with respect to their wishes regarding custody upon the request of one of the parties prior to entry of the final decree. Bauer v Bauer, No. CA97-01-003, 1997 WL 368371 (12th Dist Ct App, Warren, 6-30-97).

In allocating parental rights and responsibilities it is discretionary with the judge in the absence of a motion from any of the parties to interview minor children in chambers; however, when either party moves the court to interview the children in chambers, it is mandatory that the judge conduct the interview. Troll v Troll, No. 94-B-17, 1996 WL 19079 (7th Dist Ct App, Belmont, 1-17-96).

A court does not commit error by assuming that a four-year-old child lacks the reasoning capacity to express her own wishes without questioning her, or by failing to make a record of its interviews with two older children, as RC 3109.04 indicates that the interviews are to be confidential and are not to be disclosed to the parents. Linger v Linger, No. 92-CA-120, 1993 WL 274318 (5th Dist Ct App, Licking, 6-30-93).

A child's choice of custodian, made pursuant to RC 3109.04(A), is not binding on the court, but is merely one factor for the court to consider in determining the best interests of the child. In re Brazell (Ohio Com.Pl. 1986) 27 Ohio Misc.2d 7, 499 N.E.2d 925, 27 O.B.R. 68.

Court is bound by this section to consider preference expressed by child over ten years of age as to which of divorced parents child desires to live with, and failure so to do is reversible error. Mollencamp v Mollencamp, 18 Abs 90 (App, Franklin 1934).

Failure of trial court to consider preference of child over ten years of age in determining question of custody, is reversible error. Holland v. Holland (Cuyahoga 1947) 75 N.E.2d 489, 49 Ohio Law Abs. 237.

31. —Child's "best interest" in general, allocation of rights and responsibilities: Initial Allocation—"Best interest" and Specific Factors

Where child custody determination in habeas corpus proceeding is simply between child's natural parents, and neither party has judicial order awarding custody, court will determine what custody award will be in child's best interests. Pegan v. Crawmer (Ohio 1996) 76 Ohio St.3d 97, 666 N.E.2d 1091.

Divorce courts have discretion in matters of child custody, in accordance with statutory elements, standards and factors focusing on best interests of child. Marshall v. Marshall (Ohio App. 3 Dist. 1997) 117 Ohio App.3d 182, 690 N.E.2d 68.

Irrespective of terminology involved, ultimate goal of court in considering request to modify child custody decree is the same: to determine what is best for the child. Waggoner v. Waggoner (Wayne 1996) 111 Ohio App.3d 1, 675 N.E.2d 541, dismissed, appeal not allowed 77 Ohio St.3d 1445, 671 N.E.2d 1284.

Since there was no prior formal award of custody, trial court's judgment entry awarding legal custody of child to father was an initial award of custody, as opposed to modification of prior custodial arrangement, and as such, no showing of change of circumstances was required and trial court properly applied the best interest standard. In re Wells (Butler 1995) 108 Ohio App.3d 41, 669 N.E.2d 887.

Trial court is bound to consider best interests of child when determining which parent should have custody of minor child in divorce proceeding. Rowe v. Franklin

(Hamilton 1995) 105 Ohio App.3d 176, 663 N.E.2d 955, appeal not allowed 74 Ohio St.3d 1464, 656 N.E.2d 1299.

Under RC 3109.04 as presently constituted, the custodian of a child is selected with reference to the best interest of the child. Thrasher v. Thrasher (Summit 1981) 3 Ohio App.3d 210, 444 N.E.2d 431, 3 O.B.R. 240.

Under the provisions of GC 8033 (RC 3109.04), when the question of custody arises between the parents, "the court shall decide which one of them shall have the care, custody and control of such offspring, taking into account that which would be for their best interests." Ludy v. Ludy (Franklin 1948) 84 Ohio App. 195, 82 N.E.2d 775, 53 Ohio Law Abs. 47, 39 O.O. 241, rehearing denied 84 N.E.2d 120, 53 Ohio Law Abs. 47.

An initial grant of custody requires application of the best interest of the child standard and in a case where there is no order for support after paternity is established, and therefore no "prior decree" which grants custody of the parties' child to either party, the trial court properly applies the best interest standard. David W. v Amy S, No. H-95-029, 1996 WL 76054 (6th Dist Ct App, Huron, 2-23-96).

A child custody case that involves no prior paternity adjudication or support order does not require a showing of a change in circumstances and custody is awarded to the father in the best interest of the child. Barker v Helton, No. CA94-11-207, 1995 WL 540423 (12th Dist Ct App, Butler, 9-11-95).

32. —Appeal, allocation of rights and responsibilities: Initial Allocation—"Best interest" and Specific Factors

Award of custody supported by substantial amount of credible and competent evidence will not be reversed on appeal as being against weight of evidence; finding of error in law is legitimate ground for reversal, but difference of opinion on credibility of witnesses and evidence is not. Davis v. Flickinger (Ohio 1997) 77 Ohio St.3d 415, 674 N.E.2d 1159.

A permanent custody award supported by substantial evidence will not be reversed on appeal as being against the weight of the evidence. Bechtol v. Bechtol (Ohio 1990) 49 Ohio St.3d 21, 550 N.E.2d 178, rehearing denied 49 Ohio St.3d 718, 552 N.E.2d 952, opinion corrected 51 Ohio St.3d 701, 554 N.E.2d 899.

Where a court of appeals finds that a trial court's adoption of a referee's report in a custody proceeding constitutes an abuse of discretion, it is error for the appellate court to independently weigh the evidence and rule on the custody motion; instead, the appellate court must remand the case for a new trial. Miller v. Miller (Ohio 1988) 37 Ohio St.3d 71, 523 N.E.2d 846, clarification denied 43 Ohio St.3d 710, 540 N.E.2d 728.

"Abuse of discretion," such as will permit appellate court to disturb custody decision of divorce court, connotes more than error of law or judgment; it implies that divorce court's attitude is unreasonable, arbitrary or unconscionable. Marshall v. Marshall (Ohio App. 3 Dist. 1997) 117 Ohio App.3d 182, 690 N.E.2d 68.

Appellate court must uphold custody decision absent an abuse of discretion and, therefore, may not independently review the weight of the evidence in the majority of cases. Miller v. Miller (Seneca 1996) 115 Ohio App.3d 336, 685 N.E.2d 319.

Trial court's judgment in custody matters enjoys presumption of correctness. Butler v. Butler (Auglaize 1995) 107 Ohio App.3d 633, 669 N.E.2d 291.

When award of custody is supported by some competent, credible evidence, that award will not be reversed by reviewing court as being against the weight of the evidence. Evans v. Evans (Butler 1995) 106 Ohio App.3d 673, 666 N.E.2d 1176, dismissed, appeal not allowed 75 Ohio St.3d 1448, 663 N.E.2d 330.

When there is no evidence to the contrary, appellate court will presume that trial court considered all relevant factors in determining custody. Evans v. Evans (Butler 1995) 106 Ohio App.3d 673, 666 N.E.2d 1176, dismissed, appeal not allowed 75 Ohio St.3d 1448, 663 N.E.2d 330.

Trial court's decision in custody matters will be reversed only upon a showing of abuse of discretion. Evans v. Evans (Butler 1995) 106 Ohio App.3d 673, 666 N.E.2d 1176, dismissed, appeal not allowed 75 Ohio St.3d 1448, 663 N.E.2d 330.

Trial court's decision concerning custody in divorce cannot be reversed by reviewing court absent abuse of discretion. Rowe v. Franklin (Hamilton 1995) 105 Ohio App.3d 176, 663 N.E.2d 955, appeal not allowed 74 Ohio St.3d 1464, 656 N.E.2d 1299.

Abuse of discretion standard for reviewing trial court's decision in child custody matters means that discretion which trial court enjoys in custody matters should be accorded the utmost respect, and, consequently, it is improper for appellate court to independently review weight of the evidence in the majority of cases. Sayre v. Hoelzle-Sayre (Seneca 1994) 100 Ohio App.3d 203, 653 N.E.2d 712, appeal allowed 70 Ohio St.3d 1426, 638 N.E.2d 88, appeal dismissed as improvidently allowed 72 Ohio St.3d 1218, 651 N.E.2d 430.

An appeal from an order regarding the custody of a child is conditional upon giving bond. Call v. Call (Franklin 1958) 107 Ohio App. 516, 160 N.E.2d 307, 81 Ohio Law Abs. 243, 9 O.O.2d 54.

On an appeal where the appellant had supplied only a few pages of the transcript, the appellate court could not determine whether there had been an abuse of discretion by the trial court. The partial transcript did not demonstrate that there was not sufficient evidence to support the basis for the trial court's decision. A reviewing court will not disturb an exercise of discretion unless the above is plain and manifestly shown, and the complaining party's rights have been prejudiced. Guard v Guard, No. 1123 (11th Dist Ct App, Ashtabula, 6-10-83).

A Civ R 35(A) order for further psychological examination is a final appealable order and affects a substantial right when made in a custody and divorce proceeding. Shoff v Shoff, No. 95APF01-8, 1995 WL 450249 (10th Dist Ct App, Franklin, 7-27-95).

The issue of credit for child support that is raised for the first time in an objection to a referee's report should not be reviewed by an appellate court. Myers v Mantia, No. 93-CA-44, 1994 WL 277859 (2d Dist Ct App, Miami, 6-22-94).

Where custody of minor children is originally granted to the maternal grandparents and a subsequent court order grants custody to the father, both awards of custody constitute final, appealable orders and, therefore, preclude the mother from asserting assignments of error in a proceeding which is not a timely appeal of those orders. Torbeck v Torbeck, No. C-810827 (1st Dist Ct App, Hamilton, 7-21-82).

On the evidence in a habeas corpus action the court will permit two boys to remain with their father rather than being given to their mother or separated. (Annotation from former RC 3105.21.) Trout v. Trout (Ohio Com.Pl. 1956) 136 N.E.2d 474, 73 Ohio Law Abs. 91, appeal dismissed 167 Ohio St. 476, 149 N.E.2d 728, 5 O.O.2d 156.

33. Conflicting plans, shared parenting: joint custody

Where both parties submit shared parenting plans, court may determine that one of the submitted plans is in the best interest of the children and adopt that plan verbatim; however, barring adoption of one of the submitted plans, court may only make suggestions for modification of the plans to the parties, and if the parties do not make appropriate changes, or if the court is not satisfied with the changes that are resubmitted following the suggestions for modification, then the court may deny the request for shared parenting of the children. Bowen v. Bowen (Ohio App. 9 Dist. 1999) 132 Ohio App.3d 616, 725 N.E.2d 1165.

Trial court acted within its discretion in adopting shared parenting plan in which child would reside with former husband during school year and with former wife during summer months, rather than wife's plan, under which child would have resided with wife and husband would have been permitted alternating weekend visitation and extended visitation during summer months. Donovan v. Donovan (Clermont 1996) 110 Ohio App.3d 615, 674 N.E.2d 1252.

Trial court did not abuse its discretion in refusing to grant shared parenting, in view of parties' unwillingness to agree on basic decisions regarding child's upbringing, most notably in area of religious education. deLevie v. deLevie (Franklin 1993) 86 Ohio App.3d 531, 621 N.E.2d 594, dismissed, jurisdictional motion overruled 67 Ohio St.3d 1409, 615 N.E.2d 1043.

A trial court abuses its discretion at a hearing on a shared parenting plan in denying a motion for a new trial where after settlement negotiations lasted until midnight the night before the hearing, and the ex-wife was not informed until the trial had begun that the ex-husband had not accepted the agreement, and arrived at the courthouse after the hearing had already concluded, since the law clearly establishes both parents should be given the opportunity to present evidence at a hearing for an order of shared parenting and the ex-wife was denied the right to a fair trial because she was refused the chance to present evidence at the hearing. Nash v Nash, No. 96CA006433, 1996 WL 724760 (9th Dist Ct App, Hamilton, 12-4-96).

34. —Discretion of court, shared parenting: joint custody

Trial court has broad authority to order shared parenting, and its decision in that regard is discretionary. Donovan v. Donovan (Clermont 1996) 110 Ohio App.3d 615, 674 N.E.2d 1252.

The choice of proposing shared parenting is on the parties, not the court, and a trail judge has no authority to force shared parenting where it has not been requested; a previous temporary custody plan, although evidence of the factors in RC 3109.04(L) is not a "formal request." Torch v Torch, No. 93 TC 030134, 1996 WL 363429 (5th Dist Ct App, Tuscarawas, 6-19-96).

35. —Education and school performance, allocation of rights and responsibilities: Modification after original allocation—"Change in circumstances" and Specific Factors

Trial court's decision to grant father's motion for modification of custody by designating father as the residential parent and legal custodian of children was clearly substantiated based on school psychologist's evaluation of children who were home-schooled by mother and who had deficient proficiency results on exams, and testimony by father. Sayre v. Hoelzle-Sayre (Seneca 1994) 100 Ohio App.3d 203, 653 N.E.2d 712, appeal allowed 70 Ohio St.3d 1426, 638 N.E.2d 88, appeal dismissed as improvidently allowed 72 Ohio St.3d 1218, 651 N.E.2d 430.

A trial court does not abuse its discretion in modifying a prior custody order when there is some evidence to support the trial court's finding of a change in circumstances in that the children's schooling is very poor while in the mother's custody and the father can offer a better educational environment, which is in the children's best interests. Paparodis v Paparodis, No. 88-CA-119 (7th Dist Ct App, Mahoning, 3-23-89).

36. —Both parents fit: relative advantages of each one, allocation of rights and responsibilities: Initial Allocation—"Best interest" and Specific Factors

Wife's residence with her parents, and her parents' strong commitment to child, were relevant to determination of best interests of child and to award of custody in action for divorce. Davis v. Wilson (Ohio App. 12 Dist. 1997) 123 Ohio App.3d 19, 702 N.E.2d 1227.

Trial court is not required to make finding that one of child's parents is unsuitable before it may consider child's relationship with his or her grandparents as one factor in its best interest analysis in rendering award of custody incident to divorce proceeding. Davis v. Wilson (Ohio App. 12 Dist. 1997) 123 Ohio App.3d 19, 702 N.E.2d 1227.

Trial court did not abuse its discretion in refusing to grant husband sole custody of child, where either parent would have been fit person for custody. deLevie v. deLevie (Franklin 1993) 86 Ohio App.3d 531, 621 N.E.2d 594, dismissed, jurisdictional motion overruled 67 Ohio St.3d 1409, 615 N.E.2d 1043.

An award of custody to a father will be upheld as in the best interest of the child where the mother is irresponsible with money, lacks control over her impulses, and has poor judgment. Apgar v. Apgar (Cuyahoga 1984) 21 Ohio App.3d 193, 486 N.E.2d 1181, 21 O.B.R. 206.

The welfare of the child is considered when the question of custody of such child arises between the parents who stand on an equality, or when the parents are found to be unfit and the court is required to grant custody to a third person. Ludy v. Ludy (Franklin 1948) 84 Ohio App. 195, 82 N.E.2d 775, 53 Ohio Law Abs. 47, 39 O.O. 241, rehearing denied 84 N.E.2d 120, 53 Ohio Law Abs. 47.

37. —Psychological evidence: in general, allocation of rights and responsibilities: Initial Allocation—"Best interest" and Specific Factors

Divorce court was within its discretion to disregard psychologist's recommendation and base its child custody decision on other evidence. Frost v. Frost (Franklin 1992) 84 Ohio App.3d 699, 618 N.E.2d 198, motion overruled 66 Ohio St.3d 1489, 612 N.E.2d 1245.

38. —Immorality of parent: adultery, cohabitation, and the like, allocation of rights and responsibilities: Initial Allocation—"Best interest" and Specific Factors

A court's inquiry into moral conduct of custodial parent in a dependent/neglect action is limited to a determination of the effect such conduct has on the child. In re

Burrell (Ohio 1979) 58 Ohio St.2d 37, 388 N.E.2d 738, 12 O.O.3d 43.

Evidence was insufficient to support determination that sexual orientation of former husband, who had custody of child of marriage and who was living in openly homosexual relationship, had directly and adversely affected child since prior custody decision, as would warrant modification of parental rights and responsibilities on that basis; investigator recommended that child continue to live with husband, psychologist did not make any recommendation regarding custody and did not find that child had been adversely affected, and no witnesses testified that husband's sexual orientation had adversely affected child. Inscoe v. Inscoe (Ohio App. 4 Dist. 1997) 121 Ohio App.3d 396, 700 N.E.2d 70.

Parent's sexual orientation, standing alone, has no relevance to decision concerning allocation of parental rights and responsibilities. Inscoe v. Inscoe (Ohio App. 4 Dist. 1997) 121 Ohio App.3d 396, 700 N.E.2d 70.

In determining whether parental nonmarital sexual conduct is having direct harmful effect on child, as will give that conduct relevance in connection with allocation of parental rights and responsibilities, primary focus should be on child's present physical and psychological welfare and developmental potential; unless accompanied by clearly adverse collateral consequences, moral impact should be ignored. Inscoe v. Inscoe (Ohio App. 4 Dist. 1997) 121 Ohio App.3d 396, 700 N.E.2d 70.

Former judge, who had entered visitation order in connection with divorce proceeding, was properly precluded from testifying, at hearing on subsequent motion for modification of parental rights and responsibilities, with regard to whether he was aware of former husband's sexual orientation at time of prior hearing; matter in question was one judge had learned solely in his official capacity as judge, and husband, who stated that his sexual orientation was discussed at prior hearing, failed to show that no other witness could testify about judge's awareness. Inscoe v. Inscoe (Ohio App. 4 Dist. 1997) 121 Ohio App.3d 396, 700 N.E.2d 70.

Order limiting the overnight stays of former spouses' romantic friends was straightforward and comprehensible and provided adequate notice to the parties as to the scope and nature of the mandate. Dilworth v. Dilworth (Ohio App. 2 Dist. 1996) 115 Ohio App.3d 537, 685 N.E.2d 847.

Order preventing former spouses from having romantic guests stay overnight when the children were present modified custody provisions of divorce decree, despite trial court's statement that order served merely to remind former spouses of trial court's policy concerning parental conduct. Dilworth v. Dilworth (Ohio App. 2 Dist. 1996) 115 Ohio App.3d 537, 685 N.E.2d 847.

Trial court was required to consider, and to enter findings concerning, statutory factors for determining best interests of children before it could adopt magistrate's order preventing former spouses from having romantic guests stay overnight when the children were present. Dilworth v. Dilworth (Ohio App. 2 Dist. 1996) 115 Ohio App.3d 537, 685 N.E.2d 847.

Awarding custody of child to father based on mother's move to pursue career, attending law school, and engaging in sexual conduct with recently separated man, resulting in pregnancy, was an abuse of discretion absent showing that mother's conduct had direct adverse impact on best interests of child. Rowe v. Franklin (Hamilton 1995) 105 Ohio App.3d 176, 663 N.E.2d 955, appeal not allowed 74 Ohio St.3d 1464, 656 N.E.2d 1299.

Although court is not obligated to wear blinders as to parent's morals, including sexual conduct, when determining best interests of child in custody dispute, consideration of parent's life-styles and moral values is limited to determination of direct or probable effect of parental conduct on physical, mental, emotional, and social development of child. Rowe v. Franklin (Hamilton 1995) 105 Ohio App.3d 176, 663 N.E.2d 955, appeal not allowed 74 Ohio St.3d 1464, 656 N.E.2d 1299.

The award of custody of male children to a father who admits to a past homosexual liaison is improper where the mother is fit to be granted custody despite her recent drug use. Glover v. Glover (Brown 1990) 66 Ohio App.3d 724, 586 N.E.2d 159, motion overruled 55 Ohio St.3d 715, 563 N.E.2d 725.

In making an initial award of custody, the trial court is bound to consider the best interests of the child. A court is not required to find that the mother's lesbian relationship will have an adverse impact on the child in order to award custody to the father; rather, the court need only consider the effects of the mother's relationship upon the child. Mohrman v. Mohrman (Sandusky 1989) 57 Ohio App.3d 33, 565 N.E.2d 1283.

A court's inquiry into the moral conduct or standards of a custodial parent is limited to a determination of the effect of such conduct on the child. In re Rex (Seneca 1981) 3 Ohio App.3d 198, 444 N.E.2d 482, 3 O.B.R. 226.

A court's inquiry into the moral conduct or standards of a custodial parent is limited to a determination of the effect of such conduct on the child. Whaley v. Whaley (Lawrence 1978) 61 Ohio App.2d 111, 399 N.E.2d 1270, 15 O.O.3d 136.

Evidence that a woman, while separated from but still married to her husband, openly consorted with another man, permitting him to frequent her apartment in the small hours of the morning and sleep there on occasion, will support a finding that she is, thereby, unfit to retain custody of a minor child of the parties and that custody of such child should be in the husband. Bingham v. Bingham (Hamilton 1968) 14 Ohio App.2d 202, 237 N.E.2d 620, 43 O.O.2d 403.

Cohabitation cannot be the sole determining factor in denying custody to a parent. Williams v Williams, No. 85AP-293 (10th Dist Ct App, Franklin, 8-27-85).

There are three possible rules to apply in an initial custody determination when the party seeking custody is cohabiting with a person not his or her spouse: (1) it is an automatic disqualification; (2) it is but one factor to consider in "best interests"; (3) it is not to be considered at all, absent specific proof of harm to the child. Wilder v Wilder, No. 84AP-604 (10th Dist Ct App, Franklin, 2-5-85).

Where the issue is the appropriate residential parent for the youngest child whose father is not the husband in the divorce action it is reasonable to restrict the evidence to events and circumstances that affect the child within his lifetime; evidence of the mother's past sexual misconduct to show that she is not an appropriate residential parent is irrelevant. Eitel v Eitel, No. 95CA11, 1996 WL 482703 (4th Dist Ct App, Pickaway, 8-23-96).

39. —Moving or relocation, allocation of rights and responsibilities: Initial Allocation—"Best interest" and Specific Factors

A trial court's award of custody of the parties' minor child to the father constitutes an abuse of discretion where the mother is the primary caretaker of the child and the court fails to consider the child's tender years, which is a relevant factor meriting consideration in determining the child's best interest, and additionally, the court improperly relies on possible future circumstances which are placed before the court through the testimony of a clinical psychologist who recommends that the father be awarded custody because he is concerned with the mother's financial and emotional instability caused by her having to relocate and find a job with limited employment qualifications. Seibert v. Seibert (Clermont 1990) 66 Ohio App.3d 342, 584 N.E.2d 41, motion overruled 53 Ohio St.3d 705, 558 N.E.2d 60.

If the best interests of the child will be served, custody will be awarded to nonresidents, either in an original custody award or in a modification of a standing custody award; a nonresident or one intending to become a nonresident will not be deprived of custody of a child merely because of her nonresidence. In re Marriage of Barber (Cuyahoga 1983) 8 Ohio App.3d 372, 457 N.E.2d 360, 8 O.B.R. 485.

40. —Guardian ad litem, allocation of rights and responsibilities: Modification after original allocation—"Change in circumstances" and Specific Factors

Civ R 75(B)(2) leaves the appointment of a guardian ad litem for the child in a change of custody proceeding to the sound discretion of the trial court. Stone v. Stone (Warren 1983) 9 Ohio App.3d 6, 457 N.E.2d 919, 9 O.B.R. 6.

41. —Racial matters, allocation of rights and responsibilities: Initial Allocation—"Best interest" and Specific Factors

Where mother appealed the award of custody of minor child to the father claiming the court used race as a determinative factor, the court of appeals found that the determinative factors were other than race. Hayes v Hayes, No. CA-5551 (5th Dist Ct App, Stark, 7-29-81).

42. —Remarriage effect, allocation of rights and responsibilities: Modification after original allocation—"Change in circumstances" and Specific Factors

A court does not have the power under the statutes respecting custody of minor children of divorced parents to place restrictions concerning the right of such divorced parent to remarry, the necessity to have a relative reside in the home of such parent to whom custody is awarded, and restrict such parent in the choice of school to which the children shall be sent. Selby v. Selby (Summit 1952) 124 N.E.2d 772, 69 Ohio Law Abs. 257.

43. —Child support, shared parenting: joint custody

Former RC 3113.215(B)(4), which required a trial court to modify a joint custody support order that was ten per cent less than the amount set by the child support guidelines, is an exception to former RC 3109.04(B)(2)(b), which prohibited a court from modifying a joint custody support order without the consent of both custodians. Martin v. Martin (Ohio 1993) 66 Ohio St.3d 110, 609 N.E.2d 537.

Court of common pleas had jurisdiction to modify child support award contained within agreed joint custody plan pursuant to wife's motion based upon husband's increased income and Uniform Child Support Guidelines which were adopted after original plan, despite husband's lack of consent. Santantonio v. Santantonio (Lorain 1993) 88 Ohio App.3d 201, 623 N.E.2d 670, motion overruled 67 Ohio St.3d 1506, 622 N.E.2d 653.

The parent in a shared parenting plan with the greater child support obligation, after being given credit for the time that the child lives with him or her, is the obligor parent, and the obligor parent is required to pay as child support only the difference between his or her greater obligation and the other parent's lesser obligation. Leis v Leis, No. 96-CA-20, 1997 WL 335145 (2d Dist Ct App, Miami, 6-20-97).

A residential parent is entitled to a reduction of the child support obligation in proportion to the time the children reside with the parent. Beard v Beard, No. 96-P-0011, 1997 WL 184766 (11th Dist Ct App, Portage, 4-4-97).

44. —Split custody: each parent with a child, allocation of rights and responsibilities: Initial Allocation—"Best interest" and Specific Factors

Trial court did not abuse its discretion in ordering split custody of parties' four minor children in divorce action, with wife having residential custody of parties' daughters and husband having residential custody of parties' sons; although split custody arrangements are not generally encouraged, in case sub judice sons had interests outside school which were best furthered by their residence with husband, and visitation schedule gave all children substantial time with their nonresidential parents. Arthur v. Arthur (Ohio App. 5 Dist. 1998) 130 Ohio App.3d 398, 720 N.E.2d 176.

In the absence of compelling evidence to the contrary, it is in the best interests of siblings to grow up in an environment in which they may interact and share experiences with one another. Kasten v Kasten, No. CA87-02-011 (12th Dist Ct App, Warren, 11-23-87).

The election of one child, aged twelve years, to live with his mother should not determine the custody of another, younger child but it is a factor the trial judge may consider in deciding what arrangement will best serve the interest of the younger child. Brown v Long, No. 8469 (2d Dist Ct App, Montgomery, 7-27-84).

45. —Education and school performance, allocation of rights and responsibilities: Initial Allocation—"Best interest" and Specific Factors

Quality of education parties' children would receive at school operated by wife's church was legitimate consideration in determining residential custody, and consideration thereof did not amount to improper consideration of wife's religious affiliation, where public school children would attend while in husband's custody offered programs for gifted students and wide curriculum, and where court expressed concerns with church-operated school's below-average class sizes, problems with teacher staffing, lack of teacher experience, lack of curriculum, and sheltered lifestyle. Arthur v. Arthur (Ohio App. 5 Dist. 1998) 130 Ohio App.3d 398, 720 N.E.2d 176.

Post-divorce motions filed by mother and father to determine child's school district dealt with allocation of parental rights and responsibilities for care of child, and thus fell within scope of statute governing court's allocation of such rights and responsibilities. Badgett v. Badgett (Ohio App. 7 Dist. 1997) 120 Ohio App.3d 448, 698 N.E.2d 84.

46. —Creation after initial decree issued, shared parenting: joint custody

To modify divorce decree in order to implement shared parenting plan, trial court must determine that such modification is in best interest of child and that there has been a change in circumstances. Neel v. Neel (Cuyahoga 1996) 113 Ohio App.3d 24, 680 N.E.2d 207, dismissed, appeal not allowed 77 Ohio St.3d 1514, 674 N.E.2d 369.

Trial court could not modify custody provisions of divorce decree to provide for shared parenting plan, absent change of circumstances and showing that such modification was in best interest of child, particularly as parties' relationship had deteriorated to such an extent that cooperation between them was highly unlikely. Neel v. Neel (Cuyahoga 1996) 113 Ohio App.3d 24, 680 N.E.2d 207, dismissed, appeal not allowed 77 Ohio St.3d 1514, 674 N.E.2d 369.

47. —Procedural issues, shared parenting: joint custody

In choosing shared parenting plan in divorce proceeding, trial court was not required to issue findings of fact pertaining to in camera interview it conducted with parties' children, where there were no special circumstances. Donovan v. Donovan (Clermont 1996) 110 Ohio App.3d 615, 674 N.E.2d 1252.

Wife's due process rights were not violated by divorce court's consideration of husband's motion for shared parenting, filed on day of custody hearing, or by manner in which custody hearing was conducted, as wife was not thereby prejudiced; husband's alternative request for shared parenting was filed more than 30 days before hearing and indicated that specific terms would be discussed at hearing, both parties had requested sole custody and wife was thus undoubtedly prepared to address relative strengths and weaknesses of parties' parenting skills, wife had more than two months between first and second days of hearing to further prepare case against shared parenting, and trial court did not adopt plan initially submitted by husband but gave wife ample opportunity to present her own plan once it decided that shared parenting was in best interests of children. Harris v. Harris (Miami 1995) 105 Ohio App.3d 671, 664 N.E.2d 1304.

Trial court should not have rejected wife's shared parenting plan based on plan's incorporation of referee's recommendation as to child support and inclusion of items provided elsewhere or not customary in jurisdiction, as wife's plan addressed issues relevant to care of children which were not outside scope of shared parenting plan contemplated by statute, and trial court's own failure to follow statutory procedure in issuing final decree of divorce, which resolved some issues related to child custody and support, before adopting shared parenting plan made it uncertain which provisions parties needed to include in proposals requested by court. Harris v. Harris (Miami 1995) 105 Ohio App.3d 671, 664 N.E.2d 1304.

Statute providing that courts shall allocate parental rights and responsibilities for care of minor children of marriage terminating in divorce "upon hearing the testimony of either or both parents" precluded court from adopting shared parenting plan submitted by former wife without holding hearing and entertaining objections to plan by former husband. Snouffer v. Snouffer (Meigs 1993) 87 Ohio App.3d 89, 621 N.E.2d 879.

A referee's interim report is by nature incomplete and indicates that there is to be a final report at some future time and a domestic relations court abuses discretion when it denies a father's motion for shared parenting on the basis of this report where the order is stamped as a final appealable order but the referee states within the report that it is interim. Thieken v Spoerl, No. CA94-11-201, 1995 WL 470535 (12th Dist Ct App, Butler, 8-7-95).

48. —Parent's refusal to consider, as factor in custody, shared parenting: joint custody

A trial court abuses its discretion by trying to require a mother to accept joint custody and by considering her failure to agree to joint custody as a material factor in the court's decision to award sole custody to the father. Ellars v. Ellars (Franklin 1990) 69 Ohio App.3d 712, 591 N.E.2d 783.

49. —Termination, shared parenting: joint custody

A joint custody plan can only work so long as both parents continue to hold to the proposition that joint custody is in the best interest of all parties; thus, if either parent concludes that joint custody is no longer viable, the court may terminate joint custody upon request. Blair v. Blair (Tuscarawas 1986) 34 Ohio App.3d 345, 518 N.E.2d 950.

Where joint custody is terminated pursuant to the request of the parties, the court is empowered to issue a modified custody decree based on the best interest of the child just as if no decree for joint custody had ever been requested or granted. Blair v. Blair (Tuscarawas 1986) 34 Ohio App.3d 345, 518 N.E.2d 950.

Proper issue on termination of joint custody, where both agree it should be terminated is best interest of the child under RC 3109.04(C). Shrider v Shrider, No. 87AP-229 (10th Dist Ct App, Franklin, 7-14-87).

50. —Modification, shared parenting: joint custody

Evidence of changed circumstances since adoption of shared parenting plan incident to divorce, while sufficient to support modification of plan, was insufficient to justify trial court's sua sponte modification of plan in manner not contemplated by either former spouse and not supported by any evidence in hearing record concerning statutory factors applicable to determination of children's best interests; both former spouses wanted sole custody, court modified plan to provide for custody changing each school year, and court's modification did not address dispute as to which school children should attend, which originally brought matter before court. Bunten v. Bunten (Ohio App. 3 Dist. 1998) 126 Ohio App.3d 443, 710 N.E.2d 757.

Evidence that both parties to shared parenting plan had remarried since original divorce decree was effected, with attendant changes in obligations to children and step-children, that former wife had left full-time employment outside home to stay with children and work as daycare provider, and that children were reaching school age, making original arrangement in which former spouses alternated as "residential" parent on month-to-month basis detrimental to stability of children's educations, was sufficient to establish change in circumstances warranting modification of shared parenting plan. Bunten v. Bunten (Ohio App. 3 Dist. 1998) 126 Ohio App.3d 443, 710 N.E.2d 757.

Unless modification of child custody decree is sought from shared parenting order, statutory change in circumstances requirement relates to circumstances of child or residential parent. Waggoner v. Waggoner (Wayne 1996)

111 Ohio App.3d 1, 675 N.E.2d 541, dismissed, appeal not allowed 77 Ohio St.3d 1445, 671 N.E.2d 1284.

Fact that trial court, in addition to finding shared parenting agreement fair, reasonable and in best interest of children, also found that there had been no change in circumstance that would support a motion to modify did not invalidate trial court's finding that plan served children's best interests. Evans v. Evans (Butler 1995) 106 Ohio App.3d 673, 666 N.E.2d 1176, dismissed, appeal not allowed 75 Ohio St.3d 1448, 663 N.E.2d 330.

A request by a party to a shared parenting agreement that it be modified from the children living six months with each parent to them living with the mother the entire year except for six weeks in the summer when they would live with their father is governed by RC 3109.04(E)(1)(a) rather than RC 3109.04(E)(2)(b) since the proposed modification of the agreement substantially changes the allocation of the parties' parental rights and responsibilities, and therefore "change of circumstances" is the appropriate standard, and age of the children alone is not a sufficient factor to find a change of circumstances, since if age was sufficient there would be no reason to impose this requirement as children always grow older. Fisher v Campbell, No. CA96-11-248, 1997 WL 349013 (12th Dist Ct App, Butler, 6-23-97).

A mother's modified version of a shared parenting plan is in the children's best interest where it establishes continuity and a routine to follow by having the children reside with the mother every weeknight during the school year and reside overnight with the father during the summer months. Yunker v Yunker, No. CA95-07-041, 1996 WL 71497 (12th Dist Ct App, Clermont, 2-20-96).

A trial court may modify a shared parenting decree without the approval of both or either parent when it concludes that it is in the best interests of the child and a change of circumstance has occurred. Davis v Davis, No. 14184, 1994 WL 277903 (2d Dist Ct App, Montgomery, 6-24-94).

A trial court errs in granting a husband's motion to modify a transportation provision of the parties' shared parenting agreement regarding visitation where (1) he appears with counsel and the wife appears without counsel and is deprived of adequate opportunity to present her case, (2) there is no evidence that the modification was necessary to serve the best interest of the child, and (3) the court's decision is wrongly based on its finding that the husband was fully employed which itself was based on his unsworn, unsubstantiated assertion. Schoettle v Bering, No. CA95-07-011, 1996 WL 189027 (12th Dist Ct App, Brown, 4-22-96).

51. —Moral and religious issues, shared parenting: joint custody

A father's proclivity to cross-dressing is not evidence that he would not be a fit, loving, and capable parent and a shared parenting plan in such case is proper where it establishes (1) the mother as residential parent for nine months, (2) the father as residential parent for three months, and (3) a provision for modification once the child becomes school age. Mayfield v Mayfield, No. 96AP030032, 1996 WL 489043 (5th Dist Ct App, Tuscarawas, 8-14-96).

An original shared parenting plan made part of a divorce decree can continue when the mother has moved to New York and intends to teach and instruct the minor child in Orthodox Judaism over the father's objections; however, the court's decision to have the child spend all of the holiday periods with the mother is an abuse of discretion because it impedes the father's ability to share religious holidays and traditions with his son in equal measure. Davidovics v Shore, No. 75589, 1999 WL 561569 (8th Dist Ct App, Cuyahoga, 7-29-99).

In a custody dispute involving parties raised as Jehovah Witnesses, a plan of shared parenting in accordance with the recommendations of a court-appointed psychologist is adopted by the trial court in light of the court's continuing jurisdiction and in view of evidence presented by the father who has left the religious sect that (1) the church "shuns" those who have left, (2) family members are restricted in the kinds of interaction they can have with a former church member, and (3) such disfellowship will interfere with his relationship with the children unless he is made the residential parent. Reier v Reier, No. 1372, 1996 WL 339943 (2d Dist Ct App, Darke, 6-21-96).

52. —Nonparent as custodian, allocation of rights and responsibilities: Initial Allocation—"Best interest" and Specific Factors

Evidence supported trial court's decision that it was in best interests of 11-year-old child to remain with nonparents who had cared for her since she was a week old; guardian ad litem, court investigator and psychologist all testified that nonparents should be granted custody with liberal visitation by biological father. Reynolds v. Goll (Ohio 1996) 75 Ohio St.3d 121, 661 N.E.2d 1008.

Trial court's finding of abandonment by and unsuitability of biological father was supported by competent evidence; court heard extensive testimony over two days which supported that father had abandoned his daughter by leaving her under care of another family with very limited visitation and no financial support other than medical insurance. Reynolds v. Goll (Ohio 1996) 75 Ohio St.3d 121, 661 N.E.2d 1008.

RC 3105.21(B) affords a domestic relations court authority to determine custody of a child, as between his parents and another relative, even though that court has dismissed the parent's divorce action; if after dismissing the divorce action, the domestic relations court elects to certify the matter of custody to juvenile court, under RC 3105.21(B) and 3109.04 the domestic relations court must specifically find custody in neither parent to be in the child's best interest, or all jurisdiction over the matter is lost. State ex rel. Easterday v. Zieba (Ohio 1991) 58 Ohio St.3d 251, 569 N.E.2d 1028.

A parent's consent to guardianship over his child by the child's grandparents constitutes a forfeiture of the parent's rights to custody to the extent that a later change-of-custody motion may be decided according to the best interests of the child, and without a finding of the parent's unsuitability. Masitto v. Masitto (Ohio 1986) 22 Ohio St.3d 63, 488 N.E.2d 857, 22 O.B.R. 81.

Where court found natural parent of child had renounced custody she had forfeited her right to paramount custody, and court could award custody to a third party if a preponderance of the evidence indicated abandonment, contractual release of custody, inability to support or other unsuitability. In re Young (Ohio 1979) 58 Ohio St.2d 90, 388 N.E.2d 1235, 12 O.O.3d 93.

Natural paternity alone is insufficient to support a claim in habeas corpus where the child is well cared for by grandparents and the natural parent abandoned the child and for nine years did nothing for her. Hughes v. Scaffide (Ohio 1979) 58 Ohio St.2d 88, 388 N.E.2d 1233, 12 O.O.3d 92.

Insofar as Civ R 75(P), which requires the court to find, prior to committing a child to a relative, that both parents are unsuitable to have custody, abridges the child's statutory right under RC 3109.04 to be committed to a relative where commitment to a parent would be contrary to the child's best interest, such rule is invalid under the provisions of O Const Art IV §5. Boyer v. Boyer (Ohio 1976) 46 Ohio St.2d 83, 346 N.E.2d 286, 75 O.O.2d 156, certiorari denied 97 S.Ct. 245, 429 U.S. 889, 50 L.Ed.2d 172.

In determining who shall have the care, custody, and control of a child under eighteen years of age, even though the child's parents are not found to be unfit or unsuitable, the court may commit the child to a relative of the child where the court finds that custody to neither parent is in the best interest of the child. Boyer v. Boyer (Ohio 1976) 46 Ohio St.2d 83, 346 N.E.2d 286, 75 O.O.2d 156, certiorari denied 97 S.Ct. 245, 429 U.S. 889, 50 L.Ed.2d 172.

Under RC 3109.04, common pleas court has no authority to award custody of minor child to its grandmother unless it has found that "neither parent is a suitable person to have custody," and such lack of authority may not be obviated by describing commitment as "physical" rather than "legal" custody. Baxter v. Baxter (Ohio 1971) 27 Ohio St.2d 168, 271 N.E.2d 873, 56 O.O.2d 104.

Following death of mother to whom trial court had awarded custody in divorce proceeding, dispute over custody of children between father and children's maternal uncle fell within coverage of statute allowing custody to be awarded to relative other than parent "when it is in the best interest of the child," rather than under statute establishing jurisdiction of juvenile courts to determine custody of child not ward of another court of state. Schneeberger v. Baker (Summit 1996) 113 Ohio App.3d 805, 682 N.E.2d 661, appeal not allowed 77 Ohio St.3d 1525, 674 N.E.2d 376.

Evidence supported award of custody of child to stepmother, rather than to cousin of mother and her husband; stepmother had attended many parenting skills training classes, and was a licensed foster home provider; by contrast, cousin and her husband ignored recommendations that child be taken to particular school and to day-care, and did not comply with court order requiring them to attend parenting skills training classes. In re Whaley (Athens 1993) 86 Ohio App.3d 304, 620 N.E.2d 954.

Where both parents had voluntarily relinquished custody of child, and child custody proceeding involved only competing claims of nonparents to custody, court did not have to make a finding of parental unsuitability prior to awarding custody to stepmother. In re Whaley (Athens 1993) 86 Ohio App.3d 304, 620 N.E.2d 954.

Custody may not be awarded to a nonparent without a judicial finding that the custodial parent is unsuitable. Truitt v. Truitt (Preble 1989) 65 Ohio App.3d 126, 583 N.E.2d 331.

As between a parent and non-parent, a parent may be denied custody only if a preponderance of the evidence indicates abandonment, contractual relinquishment of custody, total inability to provide care or support, or that the parent is otherwise unsuitable so that an award of custody to the parent would be detrimental to the child, and although RC 3109.04(C) does not apply to temporary custody orders, the factors enumerated therein are factors which the court may consider in determining the suitability or unsuitability of the parent. In re Custody of Carpenter (Greene 1987) 41 Ohio App.3d 182, 534 N.E.2d 1216.

In a child custody dispute brought under RC 3109.04 between the child's parent and a nonparent, a suitable parent has a paramount right to custody so long as such custody causes no detriment to the child. Thrasher v. Thrasher (Summit 1981) 3 Ohio App.3d 210, 444 N.E.2d 431, 3 O.B.R. 240.

An award of custody of a child in a divorce action is conclusive only as to the parties to such action, and the remedy of habeas corpus is available to obtain such child where a party other than the parties to the divorce action is involved; and it is not necessary to apply to the court which originally awarded custody of such child. In re Howland (Highland 1961) 115 Ohio App. 186, 184 N.E.2d 228, 20 O.O.2d 277.

The welfare of the child is considered when the question of custody of such child arises between the parents who stand on an equality, or when the parents are found to be unfit and the court is required to grant custody to a third person. Ludy v. Ludy (Franklin 1948) 84 Ohio App. 195, 82 N.E.2d 775, 53 Ohio Law Abs. 47, 39 O.O. 241, rehearing denied 84 N.E.2d 120, 53 Ohio Law Abs. 47.

A court may not award custody of children to any other person than their parents unless a finding is made of the unfitness of the parents to have their children's custody as provided by this section. Luebkeman v. Luebkeman (Montgomery 1945) 75 Ohio App. 566, 61 N.E.2d 638, 43 Ohio Law Abs. 17, 31 O.O. 319.

A court is not obligated to find parents unfit before awarding custody to the child's grandmother where the child (1) has adjusted to life at his grandmother's house, (2) is participating in school and community activities and (3) the grandmother is making an effort to preserve the child's relationships with the father and his extended family. Wright v Wright, No. 67884, 1995 WL 614500 (8th Dist Ct App, Cuyahoga, 10-19-95).

Where a mother grants voluntary temporary custody to an infant's paternal grandparents, the proper standard to be used by the court in determining an award of custody upon the filing of a petition by the mother is the fitness of the mother, not the best interests of the child standard in RC 3109.04(B). In re Curry, No. 89AP-550 (10th Dist Ct App, Franklin, 11-21-89).

Where a child's mother has been determined to be an unsuitable parent, the father gives physical custody of the child to the maternal grandmother, the child undergoes brain surgery and is left with a soft skull, and the mother's boyfriend has a propensity for violence, an award of custody of the child to the maternal grandmother is proper despite the lack of a finding that the child's father is an unsuitable parent where such award of custody to a nonparent is in the best interest of the child. Mannering v Mannering, No. 559 (4th Dist Ct App, Jackson, 5-3-89).

A court must make a finding of parental unsuitability prior to assuming jurisdiction under RC 3109.04 to award permanent custody of a child to a nonparent relative. Fronk v Arison, No. 1167 (11th Dist Ct App, Ashtabula, 10-26-84).

A complainant who is not a parent of the minor child does not have standing to bring an action under RC 3109.04. Young v Young, No. 29-CA-92 (5th Dist Ct App, Fairfield, 4-26-93).

53. —Nonparent as custodian, allocation of rights and responsibilities: Modification after origi-

nal allocation—"Change in circumstances" and Specific Factors

A parent's consent to guardianship over his child by the child's grandparents constitutes a forfeiture of the parent's rights to custody to the extent that a later change-of-custody motion may be decided according to the best interests of the child, and without a finding of the parent's unsuitability. Masitto v. Masitto (Ohio 1986) 22 Ohio St.3d 63, 488 N.E.2d 857, 22 O.B.R. 81.

A common pleas court has no authority in a divorce proceeding, after having first awarded custody of a child to its mother, to later change the legal custody of that child when under eighteen from its mother to its grandmother, where the child has not been abandoned by the mother and it does not find that the mother is not "a suitable person to have custody" of such child, notwithstanding that it determines that the mother is not as suitable as the grandmother and that changing such custody to the grandmother will be for the child's best interest. Grandon v. Grandon (Ohio 1955) 164 Ohio St. 234, 129 N.E.2d 819, 57 O.O. 462.

Father had no justiciable concern in whether trial court discharged guardian ad litem after determination was made to maintain custody with maternal grandparents. Rife v. Morgan (Clark 1995) 106 Ohio App.3d 843, 667 N.E.2d 450.

Trial court's determination that best interest of children warranted continuation of custody with paternal grandparents, rather than change of custody to mother, was supported by evidence; evidence indicated that mother originally consented to grandparents having custody, that she had not paid much, if anything, in support, that children had lived with grandparents for about ten years, and that children had received lower grades when they lived with their parents during three-month trial period, although both children said they wanted to live with mother. Miller v. Miller (Hocking 1993) 86 Ohio App.3d 623, 621 N.E.2d 745.

Trial court's finding that mother contractually relinquished custody of child to paternal grandparents, thus requiring application of best interest standard to determine whether mother was entitled to change of custody, was supported by evidence; evidence indicated that both children had lived with paternal grandparents since infancy and that mother and her ex-husband had filed a motion to award custody to paternal grandparents. Miller v. Miller (Hocking 1993) 86 Ohio App.3d 623, 621 N.E.2d 745.

Where the natural father placed his infant daughter in the care of nonrelatives during and after the natural mother's protracted final illness, that father's paramount right to custody may be terminated only upon a finding of unsuitability. Reynolds v. Goll (Lorain 1992) 80 Ohio App.3d 494, 609 N.E.2d 1276.

Where a parent or parents have consented to a change of custody to a nonparent and this change of custody was effected by way of a judicially approved contractual agreement, the parent or parents have relinquished the paramount right to custody and the proper test on a motion to change custody by a parent or parents is the best interest of the child pursuant to RC 3109.04(B). In re Whiting (Ottawa 1990) 70 Ohio App.3d 183, 590 N.E.2d 859.

Where the parents of a child voluntarily grant custody of a child to other family members, a change of the child's circumstances is required to be shown where the mother seeks to regain custody of the child; a change in the mother's circumstances is insufficient. In re Whiting (Ottawa 1990) 70 Ohio App.3d 183, 590 N.E.2d 859.

Even where the circumstances have changed, and a previously unfit mother is now better suited to take care of her children, the court does not have to remove custody from the grandmother because the mere fact that a natural parent is fit, though it is certainly one factor that may enter into judicial consideration, does not automatically entitle the natural parent to custody of her child since the best interests and welfare of that child are of paramount importance. Hanson v Hanson, No. 519 (7th Dist Ct App, Monroe, 9-28-79).

Where possession of a child over 14 years has been voluntarily relinquished by a father to a blood relative under an agreement where possession is not to be taken away and where the child has been properly reared and is content and the child is well adjusted, the wishes of the child raise a presumption that the child's best interest will be served by not being changed, in the absence of showing that such change would be beneficial to the child's welfare. Ex parte Justice (Ohio Com.Pl. 1956) 135 N.E.2d 285, 72 Ohio Law Abs. 323.

Where a minor child was entrusted to friends because the mother was unfit, and the father subsequently remarried and reclaimed the child, a court may not award custody to any person other than the father except upon a finding of the father's unfitness. Garabrandt v. Garabrandt (Ohio Com.Pl. 1953) 114 N.E.2d 919, 65 Ohio Law Abs. 380, 51 O.O. 319.

54. —Disabled adult child, allocation of rights and responsibilities: Modification after original allocation—"Change in circumstances" and Specific Factors

Trial court that awarded custody of parties' fully disabled adult child pursuant to divorce retained jurisdiction to modify its custody order and child support awarded therein, where award of custody amounted to recognition by court of fact that child was under permanent legal disability due to extent of his physical and mental disabilities. Abbas v. Abbas (Ohio App. 7 Dist. 1998) 128 Ohio App.3d 513, 715 N.E.2d 613.

55. —Constitutional issues, allocation of rights and responsibilities: Modification after original allocation—"Change in circumstances" and Specific Factors

An order changing child custody for no reason other than the vacation of the original decree, by virtue of Civ R 60(B), would violate the express prohibition by O Const Art IV §5(B) of modification of substantive rights by operation of procedural rules, inasmuch as a change of custody must be based upon a finding either that a condition described at RC 3109.04(B) exists or that a de facto change has already taken place; consequently, a motion to vacate a custody decree will be treated as a motion for modification of custody when appropriate. Tatom v. Tatom (Montgomery 1984) 19 Ohio App.3d 198, 482 N.E.2d 1339, 19 O.B.R. 306.

56. —Dangerous environment: false allegations of abuse, effect, allocation of rights and responsibilities: Modification after o riginal allocation—"Change in circumstances" and Specific Factors

Ex-wife's unsubstantiated allegations that ex-husband abused children was a change of circumstances warranting change of custody from ex-wife to ex-husband. Beekman v. Beekman (Pike 1994) 96 Ohio App.3d 783, 645 N.E.2d 1332.

Unsubstantiated allegations of sexual abuse by noncustodial parent are a change of circumstances that may be grounds on which to modify a prior custody award. Beekman v. Beekman (Pike 1994) 96 Ohio App.3d 783, 645 N.E.2d 1332.

57. —Probation, custody or visitation issues in proceedings other than divorce

The factors set forth in RC 3109.04(C) with respect to determining the child's best interest in custody cases apply equally to visitation cases. The trial court must weigh these and other relevant factors in determining the child's best interest in visitation cases. In re Whitaker (Ohio 1988) 36 Ohio St.3d 213, 522 N.E.2d 563.

Specific rules for determining when a court may modify custody decree are not equally applicable to modification of visitation rights. Appleby v. Appleby (Ohio 1986) 24 Ohio St.3d 39, 492 N.E.2d 831, 24 O.B.R. 81.

Child's change in age from two and one-half years to nine years, father's desire to spend more time with child, and parties' de facto modification of holiday visitation schedule did not constitute changed circumstances warranting modification of father's visitation schedule as set forth in agreement upon marital dissolution. Jacobs v. Jacobs (Wayne 1995) 102 Ohio App.3d 568, 657 N.E.2d 580.

Change in nonresidential parent's circumstances is relevant in proceeding to modify visitation schedule only if prior decree was shared parenting decree. Jacobs v. Jacobs (Wayne 1995) 102 Ohio App.3d 568, 657 N.E.2d 580.

Trial court erred in failing to consider uncontroverted testimony of child's treating psychologist, on father's motion to modify visitation schedule, as statute required consideration of physical and mental health of all persons involved and testimony was only evidence submitted on child's mental health. Jacobs v. Jacobs (Wayne 1995) 102 Ohio App.3d 568, 657 N.E.2d 580.

Trial court's failure to determine that modification of visitation schedule was in child's best interests was erroneous on father's motion for modification of divorce decree. Jacobs v. Jacobs (Wayne 1995) 102 Ohio App.3d 568, 657 N.E.2d 580.

Parties' agreement to modify prior visitation schedule may be sufficient change of circumstances to justify court's modification of schedule to conform with that agreement, provided it is in best interest of child; agreement, however, should not be used as change in circumstances that justifies discontinuation of entire visitation schedule without reference to parties' mutually demonstrated desires. Jacobs v. Jacobs (Wayne 1995) 102 Ohio App.3d 568, 657 N.E.2d 580.

Trial court enjoys a broader measure of discretion in setting visitation than in awarding or modifying custody; although domestic relations practitioners and judges routinely consider visitation modification in the context of the presence or absence of changed circumstances, there is no requirement that they do so. Roudebush v. Roudebush (Franklin 1984) 20 Ohio App.3d 380, 486 N.E.2d 849, 20 O.B.R. 485.

Municipal court order modifying visitation as part of defendant's probation was void as matters of visitation are within the sole jurisdiction of courts of common pleas, and even assuming the defendant agreed to supervised visitation as part of a plea agreement, a party can not agree to submit a court's subject matter jurisdiction and, as a result, the municipal court could not enforce the new conditions because it lacked the subject matter jurisdiction to do so. Rocky River v Taylor, No. 75621, 75661, 2000 WL 193234 (8th Dist Ct App, Cuyahoga, 2-17-00).

Without a shared parenting plan, a change in circumstances of the non-custodial parent may not be considered changed circumstances pursuant to RC 3109.04 and thus a change in the visitation schedule does not affect custody and consequently does not warrant a change therein. Yasher v Yasher, No. 65545, 1994 WL 97694 (8th Dist Ct App, Cuyahoga, 3-24-94).

A residential parent's motion to terminate visitation and the motion of the nonresidential parent to set specific visitation times do not concern custodial issues, and a court errs by granting a motion to modify custody in a case where testimony and evidence do not rise to the level of a substantial change of circumstance but rather indicate the nonresidential parent's increasing demand for additional visitation. Davis v Flickinger, No. 94AP110077, 1995 WL 557132 (5th Dist Ct App, Tuscarawas, 9-19-95), reversed by 77 OS(3d) 415 (1997).

58. —Age; maturing of child, allocation of rights and responsibilities: Modification after original allocation—"Change in circumstances" and Specific Factors

Change in age of child subject to custody decree, without more, is not sufficient factor to permit modification of decree for change in circumstances. Davis v. Flickinger (Ohio 1997) 77 Ohio St.3d 415, 674 N.E.2d 1159.

Change in child's age is alone not dispositive of right to modify prior child custody decree. Waggoner v. Waggoner (Wayne 1996) 111 Ohio App.3d 1, 675 N.E.2d 541, dismissed, appeal not allowed 77 Ohio St.3d 1445, 671 N.E.2d 1284.

Passage of time during significant portion of child's life, i.e., from age of 11 months to age of five and one-half years, combined with other pertinent factors, particularly child's relationship with her parents, relative stability of each parent's life, and fact that mother had had two incidents of unruly behavior requiring involvement by police from time of original custody order, supported finding of changed circumstances requiring further inquiry by trial court into redetermination of parental rights and responsibilities. Butler v. Butler (Auglaize 1995) 107 Ohio App.3d 633, 669 N.E.2d 291.

Passage of time, alone, is not sufficient to find change of circumstances and relitigate issue of custody. Butler v. Butler (Auglaize 1995) 107 Ohio App.3d 633, 669 N.E.2d 291.

Change in circumstances supporting modification of visitation order generally should not be predicated upon change in child's age, but child's age is properly considered as relevant factor in determination of child's best interests. Jacobs v. Jacobs (Wayne 1995) 102 Ohio App.3d 568, 657 N.E.2d 580.

Passage of children from infancy to early adolescence was sufficient "change of circumstance" to warrant inquiry into question of whether interests of children would best be served by their remaining with custodial parent, or by changing custody. Perz v. Perz (Lucas 1993) 85 Ohio App.3d 374, 619 N.E.2d 1094, motion overruled 67 Ohio St.3d 1423, 616 N.E.2d 506.

A combination of facts including (1) the child's age of twelve years, (2) the child's preference to reside primarily with his father, and (3) the long history of difficulty between the parties is sufficient for a finding of a change of circumstances in order for the court to address its decision to change residential parents. Khulenberg v Davis, No. CA96-07-143, 1997 WL 527647 (12th Dist Ct App, Butler, 8-25-97).

The passage of children from infancy to early adolescence is a sufficient change of circumstances to warrant an inquiry into the question of whether the interests of the children would best be served by remaining with the current custodial parent, or by a change in custody; thus, a trial court's refusal to make a determination as to the best interests of the children on a motion for a change of custody constitutes an abuse of discretion. Perz v Perz, No. L-92-183 (6th Dist Ct App, Lucas, 3-19-93).

59. —Procedural issues, hearings, evidence: in general, allocation of rights and responsibilities: Modification after original allocation—"Change in circumstances" and Specific Factors

Mistaken finding of fact regarding child custody modification, erroneously stating the date of the parties' divorce, was not relevant to the custody determination. Clark v. Smith (Ohio App. 3 Dist. 1998) 130 Ohio App.3d 648, 720 N.E.2d 973.

Mistaken finding of fact regarding child custody modification, erroneously stating that a shared-parenting plan was adopted in the divorce decree, was not prejudicial error; trial court was aware that mother was the residential parent and that father was granted visitation by the original divorce decree. Clark v. Smith (Ohio App. 3 Dist. 1998) 130 Ohio App.3d 648, 720 N.E.2d 973.

Requirement by referee that former wife, who sought modification of decree which awarded custody of children to former husband, show "change of circumstances substantial enough to warrant this modification" did not impose impermissibly heavy burden of proof on wife. Waggoner v. Waggoner (Wayne 1996) 111 Ohio App.3d 1, 675 N.E.2d 541, dismissed, appeal not allowed 77 Ohio St.3d 1445, 671 N.E.2d 1284.

Evidence supported trial court's determination that former wife had not shown change of circumstances sufficient to warrant modification of decree which awarded custody of all six children to former wife; much the same evidence had been before court when it last decided custody two years previously, and evidence of bitterness between parties did not demonstrate change in circumstances, as situation had been ongoing since dissolution of marriage. Waggoner v. Waggoner (Wayne 1996) 111 Ohio App.3d 1, 675 N.E.2d 541, dismissed, appeal not allowed 77 Ohio St.3d 1445, 671 N.E.2d 1284.

Generally, prior notice of change of custody ought to be given to both parties so that they have enough time to make arrangements and expedite transfers; however, where it appears that demonstrated recalcitrance of one party may interfere with orderly transfer, court might permit a more summary transfer. Beekman v. Beekman (Pike 1994) 96 Ohio App.3d 783, 645 N.E.2d 1332.

Trial court's order granting father's motion for change in parental rights and responsibilities met requirements of statute governing such motions, despite fact trial court viewed motion as motion to modify disposition and failed to include specific statutory language in order and, thus, order was valid where referees report, adopted by trial court, contained sufficient facts to find that change in circumstances had occurred, that modification would be in best interests of child, and that harm of changing child's environment was outweighed by benefits of changing environment. In re Kennedy (Marion 1994) 94 Ohio App.3d 414, 640 N.E.2d 1176.

Best interest of the child test for modification of custody is a weight of the evidence question and, if judgment of trial court is supported by competent probative evidence, Court of Appeals must affirm trial court's decision. Miller v. Miller (Hocking 1993) 86 Ohio App.3d 623, 621 N.E.2d 745.

Court referee did not abuse her discretion in limiting time for hearing on father's motion to modify custody to one and one-half hours per party, where a number of depositions were submitted into evidence, both mother and another witness testified at length as to merits of father's motion, and there was no indication in record of what any additional evidence presented by mother might have shown. Holm v. Smilowitz (Athens 1992) 83 Ohio App.3d 757, 615 N.E.2d 1047.

In considering a motion for change of custody, it is error for a court to exclude evidence of circumstances occurring after a specified date, where relevant evidence is thereby excluded. Van Hook v. Van Hook (Summit 1985) 26 Ohio App.3d 188, 499 N.E.2d 365, 26 O.B.R. 408.

A motion for relief from judgment pursuant to Civ R 60(B) has no application to an action for a change of custody under RC 3109.04. Mundschenk v Mundschenk, No. 81AP-406 (10th Dist Ct App, Franklin, 3-25-82).

60. —Split custody: each parent with a child, allocation of rights and responsibilities: Modification after original allocation—"Change in circumstances" and Specific Factors

Custody modification was unwarranted, despite mother's contention that younger child's relationship with elder sibling deteriorated after each parent was designated residential parent of one child, where younger child was acclimated to father's home, school, and community, child was performing well at school, children were close despite seven-year age difference, children were together every weekend and one night every week under custody provisions of divorce decree, and father was not shown to be unsuitable to have custody. Miller v. Miller (Seneca 1996) 115 Ohio App.3d 336, 685 N.E.2d 319.

61. —Custody while case is pending, effect, allocation of rights and responsibilities: Initial Allocation—"Best interest" and Specific Factors

Direct adverse impact of custodial mother's conduct on child was standard that applied when making initial custody determination some 18 months after parties separated and mother assumed custody; interests in refraining from moving child between parents are same as in postdecree modification decisions. Rowe v. Franklin (Hamilton 1995) 105 Ohio App.3d 176, 663 N.E.2d 955, appeal not allowed 74 Ohio St.3d 1464, 656 N.E.2d 1299.

62. —Poisoning of child's relationship with other parent, allocation of rights and responsibilities: Modification after origina l allocation—"Change in circumstances" and Specific Factors

Where evidence shows that after initial decree residential parent is not living up to court's presumption and is attempting to poison relationship between ex-spouse and child, this is a change of circumstances that warrants modification of prior custody decree. Beekman v. Beekman (Pike 1994) 96 Ohio App.3d 783, 645 N.E.2d 1332.

63. Retroactive or prospective effect of amendments

Although courts must give due consideration to which parent was primary caregiver in fashioning custody award in divorce proceeding, no presumptive quality is to be given to primary caregiver doctrine, assuming that it applies, in custody modification proceeding. Holm v. Smilowitz (Athens 1992) 83 Ohio App.3d 757, 615 N.E.2d 1047.

Although the current version of RC 3109.04 was not in effect at the time the complaint was filed, and the court mistakenly applied it and its criteria for a best interest of the child determination anyway, this error does not require reversal where there was no prejudice and the decision was proper under the prior statute. Williams v. Williams (Hardin 1992) 80 Ohio App.3d 477, 609 N.E.2d 617.

RC 3109.04(B) and 3109.04(C), effective September 23, 1974, affect substantial vested rights of parents and their children and will not be applied retroactively. Leininger v. Leininger (Fulton 1975) 48 Ohio App.2d 21, 355 N.E.2d 508, 2 O.O.3d 15.

64. —Standard of living improvement, effect, allocation of rights and responsibilities: Modification after original allocation—"Change in circumstances" and Specific Factors

In proceeding by mother for modification of an order granting custody of three minor sons to father, fact that shortly prior to the hearing maternal grandparents purchased a residence, that maternal grandmother testified that if custody were given to mother, she would furnish home for mother and children and would furnish financial support if needed of $60 per week, that there was no binding obligation on part of grandparents, and that the claimed changed conditions were prospective in character were to be considered by trial judge in determining whether evidence showed sufficient change to warrant modification. Harper v. Harper (Greene 1954) 98 Ohio App. 359, 129 N.E.2d 471, 57 O.O. 389.

65. —Support order, allocation of rights and responsibilities: Modification after original allocation—"Change in circumstances" and Specific Factors

While a domestic relations court which grants a divorce has continuing jurisdiction over all matters pertaining to child custody and support, it has no authority to retroactively modify the total amount due and payable under its prior order for support of minor children in an action involving a change of custody. Kuntz v Kuntz, No. 78AP-831 (10th Dist Ct App, Franklin, 7-5-79).

66. —Racial matters, allocation of rights and responsibilities: Modification after original allocation—"Change in circumstances" and Specific Factors

The custody of an illegitimate child will not be taken from the mother and awarded to the father merely upon the basis that the wife has contracted an interracial marriage. In re H. (Ohio Com.Pl. 1973) 37 Ohio Misc. 123, 305 N.E.2d 815, 66 O.O.2d 178, 66 O.O.2d 368.

67. —Dangerous environment: actual acts, allocation of rights and responsibilities: Modification after original allocation—"Change in circumstances" and Specific Factors

Child's best interests would be served by natural father retaining custody, where child was found wandering in street while in custody of mother, mother had been convicted of theft, and mother had been convicted of child endangering with respect to one of her other children. Pegan v. Crawmer (Ohio 1996) 76 Ohio St.3d 97, 666 N.E.2d 1091.

Pursuant to former RC 3109.04(B)(1)(c), a party seeking a modification of custody must show that some action by the custodial parent presently endangers the child or, with a reasonable degree of certainty, will manifest itself and endanger the child in the future if the child is not removed from his or her present environment immediately. Gardini v. Moyer (Ohio 1991) 61 Ohio St.3d 479, 575 N.E.2d 423, rehearing denied 62 Ohio St.3d 1419, 577 N.E.2d 663.

Unsubstantiated allegation that former wife's current husband committed sexual abuse against former wife's children did not alone warrant change of custody to former husband; rather, unsubstantiated allegations of sexual abuse by their stepfather was only one factor that court could consider when determining whether change in circumstances had occurred. Stover v. Plumley (Gallia 1996) 113 Ohio App.3d 839, 682 N.E.2d 683.

Trial court did not abuse its discretion in modifying custody order so as to designate father residential parent to child; evidence showed that child was underdeveloped in several respects for her age, that mother's temperament was volatile and had caused her to be involved in two physical altercations, and that father would provide stable environment for child, and trial court specifically stated that it considered statutory factors in reaching its determination that it was in child's best interest to designate father as residential parent. Butler v. Butler (Auglaize 1995) 107 Ohio App.3d 633, 669 N.E.2d 291.

Trial court which modified child custody decree by designating father as the residential parent and legal custodian of children complied with statute governing modification of custody by concluding that harm to the children, if they stayed with mother, was outweighed by the advantages of giving custody to father. Sayre v. Hoelzle-Sayre (Seneca 1994) 100 Ohio App.3d 203, 653 N.E.2d 712, appeal allowed 70 Ohio St.3d 1426, 638 N.E.2d 88, appeal dismissed as improvidently allowed 72 Ohio St.3d 1218, 651 N.E.2d 430.

When modifying child custody decree, trial court must make some finding that the harm is outweighed by the advantages of changing the environment. Sayre v. Hoelzle-Sayre (Seneca 1994) 100 Ohio App.3d 203, 653 N.E.2d 712, appeal allowed 70 Ohio St.3d 1426, 638 N.E.2d 88, appeal dismissed as improvidently allowed 72 Ohio St.3d 1218, 651 N.E.2d 430.

Deficient proficiency results on exams taken by children who were home-schooled by parent, alone, may constitute grounds for change of custody as custody may be modified in situations where child's development will be affected by condition in his present environment. Sayre v. Hoelzle-Sayre (Seneca 1994) 100 Ohio App.3d 203, 653 N.E.2d 712, appeal allowed 70 Ohio St.3d 1426, 638 N.E.2d 88, appeal dismissed as improvidently allowed 72 Ohio St.3d 1218, 651 N.E.2d 430.

Improvement in mother's emotional state since she was allegedly "coerced" to relinquish custody of her children to father did not warrant modification in custody; change in circumstances of the child or residential parent was required. Clyborn v. Clyborn (Hardin 1994) 93 Ohio App.3d 192, 638 N.E.2d 112.

A trial court errs in granting an ex-husband's motion to modify custody by awarding him custody of the minor children of the marriage where (1) there is conflicting evidence concerning the amount of time and care that the mother gave to the children; (2) after the divorce the mother and children lived first with her parents, while she worked in Chillicothe, and later with her sister and brother-in-law in Bainbridge, while she worked in Columbus; and (3) because her job required her to work later hours, she often stayed overnight in Columbus; the ex-husband's showing that the children would be "better off" with him is insufficient to support modification of a prior custody decree absent a showing that the children's present environment endangers significantly their physical health or mental, moral, or emotional development and that the harm likely to result from the change in environment is outweighed by the advantages of the proposed change. Well v. Well (Ross 1990) 70 Ohio App.3d 606, 591 N.E.2d 843, motion overruled 59 Ohio St.3d 720, 572 N.E.2d 696.

Evidence supports awarding custody of minor children of a marriage to the former husband despite the former wife's assertion that she was the primary caretaker where the trial court finds that she had not fulfilled her duties as caretaker because (1) the home was filthy and unsanitary based on results of investigations of a state agency finding (a) a dead mouse and dog feces on the floor where the youngest child, who was handicapped, played; (b) dirty bedroom and linens of the former wife; and (c) children's clothing scattered around the house; (2) the general impression that the children were left unattended, even the youngest child, and their conduct was unrestrained; (3) the former wife's failure to obtain CPR certification to properly care for the youngest child; and (4) the former wife's failure to participate in family outings and activities; the trial court further found that the former wife failed to recognize that there were problems and was thus unmotivated to remedy them. Thornton v. Thornton (Wyandot 1990) 70 Ohio App.3d 317, 590 N.E.2d 1375.

Modification of a shared parenting plan and change of custody to the child's father is warranted where (1) the mother leaves her three-year-old child in the care of her present husband who falls asleep while taking care of the child, (2) dog feces are found in the child's bedroom and on her sheets and toys at the mother's home, (3) police become involved in the mother's fighting with her present husband, and (4) the mother changes her residence at least six times over a period of two years. Dedic v Dedic, No. 98CA0008, 1999 WL 33445 (9th Dist Ct App, Wayne, 1-27-99).

Change of custody is awarded to the father based upon testimony concerning (1) the child not being fed or cared for by the mother, (2) the presence of cockroaches in the home and dirty dishes stacked high in the kitchen, and (3) bruises on the child's body. Rhoads v Rhoads, No. 97 CA 944, 1998 WL 548759 (4th Dist Ct App, Highland, 8-24-98).

In a motion to modify custody, the trial court does not err in concluding that the teenaged child's best interest is served by continuing to have the child remain in the father's custody, and apparently disbelieved testimony by the teenager that the father used drugs, made threats about using plastic explosives to blow up people, and that the child slept on a mattress on the floor in a house with no heat, when the court also considered the father's contrary testimony and evidence that since the child had voluntarily moved in with his mother, his grades and school attendance were very poor. Clutter v Reidy, No. 95-JE-20, 1996 WL 342194 (7th Dist Ct App, Jefferson, 6-20-96).

Where a child frequently exhibits inappropriate behavior and such behavior is attributable to the environment provided by the custodial parent, a court is justified in granting a motion for change of custody. Circelli v Petrunak, No. 47847 (8th Dist Ct App, Cuyahoga, 6-7-84).

A change of custody is awarded to the father even though he had little contact with the child for seven years after the divorce, where it is shown that during the time the mother had custody, she tried to commit suicide, and she had failed to work with the son concerning problems in school; here, the advantage of a change outweighs the harm caused by a change. Krueck v Walters, No. L-81-064 (6th Dist Ct App, Lucas, 10-2-81).

A court may change custody from the mother to the father when the mother shows an inability to provide a stable environment for the child; this outweighs the benefits the child could receive by remaining with her mother and continuing in a fluctuating lifestyle. Cholewa v Cholewa, No. 42942 (8th Dist Ct App, Cuyahoga, 3-19-81).

In a custody action, evidence showing that a mother was living with men to whom she was not married, drank excessively and used marijuana, is only relevant if it can be demonstrated that such conduct has an adverse impact on the best interests of the child. Horsley v Horsley, No. 803 (4th Dist Ct App, Ross, 7-14-81).

The judgment of a state court divesting a natural mother of the custody of her young child because of her remarriage to a man of a different race violates the Equal Protection Clause of US Const Am 14. (Ed. note: Florida law construed in light of federal constitution.) Palmore v. Sidoti (U.S.Fla. 1984) 104 S.Ct. 1879, 466 U.S. 429, 80 L.Ed.2d 421.

68. —Moving or relocation, allocation of rights and responsibilities: Modification after original allocation—"Change in circumstances" and Specific Factors

Trial court abused its discretion by modifying custody of child by changing custodial parent from wife to husband after dissolution of marriage, where only evidence supporting its conclusion was filing of motion to remove child from state, which reflected desire to leave state and had to be filed according to local rule. Masters v. Masters (Ohio 1994) 69 Ohio St.3d 83, 630 N.E.2d 665.

Filing of motion to remove child from state that merely reflects mother's desire to leave state does not on its own constitute "substantial change" in circumstances under statute governing child custody. Masters v. Masters (Ohio 1994) 69 Ohio St.3d 83, 630 N.E.2d 665.

Fact that mother took children out of state and moved twice thereafter while not disclosing place of residence to husband justified trial court's awarding custody to husband. Ross v. Ross (Ohio 1980) 64 Ohio St.2d 203, 414 N.E.2d 426, 18 O.O.3d 414.

Divorce court may consider nonresidence of one of the spouses in determining what custody award will be in best interests of child, but nonresidence alone should not deprive parent of custody. Marshall v. Marshall (Ohio App. 3 Dist. 1997) 117 Ohio App.3d 182, 690 N.E.2d 68.

Divorce court's custody order, which focused on wife's failure to return with children to Ohio, contrary to court's order, as basis for awarding custody to husband, was abuse of discretion, where wife was primary caretaker, where she had moved with children, only in response to husband's admitted physical abuse, in order to be near her relatives, and where wife had not attempted to secret children from husband or otherwise to frustrate his visitation rights. Marshall v. Marshall (Ohio App. 3 Dist. 1997) 117 Ohio App.3d 182, 690 N.E.2d 68.

Mother seeking to relocate minor children pursuant to terms of divorce decree as modified failed to meet her burden of establishing that relocation was in children's best interests, where mother failed to rebut conclusion of expert approved by both parties that children's present residence offered accessibility of day-to-day contact with persons significant to children and that relocation would disrupt children's relationships with their father and other family members. Rozborski v. Rozborski (Ohio App. 8 Dist. 1996) 116 Ohio App.3d 29, 686 N.E.2d 546.

Moving party bears burden of establishing, according to statutory guidelines, whether requested relocation is in best interest of child. Rozborski v. Rozborski (Ohio App. 8 Dist. 1996) 116 Ohio App.3d 29, 686 N.E.2d 546.

Finding that modification of custody to make father residential parent was in child's best interest was supported by evidence that child did not establish strong interpersonal relationships with her maternal relatives in Utah, child's ties to North Carolina, where father lived, predated her move with mother to Utah, child had frequent social interaction with children in North Carolina, mother continuously and willfully interfered with father's visitation rights and was not likely to honor his visitation rights in future, and father indicated that he desired that mother have access to child. Holm v. Smilowitz (Athens 1992) 83 Ohio App.3d 757, 615 N.E.2d 1047.

Where movement out of state by the custodial parent in order to obtain employment will result in no more than an increase in travel costs and time to the noncustodial parent, the trial court erred in refusing to grant the custodial parent permission to leave the state. Schwartz v. Schwartz (Lake 1982) 8 Ohio App.3d 311, 456 N.E.2d 1272, 8 O.B.R. 419.

The removal of a child from the state by his custodial parent is a factor that may be considered if it adversely affects the best interests of the child to the extent set forth by RC 3109.04(B)(3), but it does not per se require a change in custody or shift the burden of proof. Schmidt v. Schmidt (Franklin 1982) 7 Ohio App.3d 175, 454 N.E.2d 970, 7 O.B.R. 221.

In a change of custody action, the removal of the child from the state by his custodial parent is a factor that may be considered if it adversely affects the best interests of the child to the extent set forth by RC 3109.04(B)(3), but it does not per se require a change in custody or shift the burden of proof. Schmidt v. Schmidt (Franklin 1982) 7 Ohio App.3d 175, 454 N.E.2d 970, 7 O.B.R. 221.

Where the custodial parent disrupts the residence of her children for a period of two weeks, such a disruption is not sufficient evidence to grant a change of custody under RC 3109.04. Wyss v. Wyss (Franklin 1982) 3 Ohio App.3d 412, 445 N.E.2d 1153, 3 O.B.R. 479.

Where the custodial parent moves out of state and the children resettle with a new stepparent and enroll in a new school, sufficient change of circumstance does not exist to allow a court to change custody of the children to an in-state parent. Vincenzo v. Vincenzo (Lake 1982) 2 Ohio App.3d 307, 441 N.E.2d 1139, 2 O.B.R. 339.

When a remarried mother removes children in her custody from the country of their father's residence to a foreign country, there is a sufficient change of conditions to warrant a court's modifying its original order to change the custody of the children from the mother to the father. Wallace v. Wallace (Lorain 1974) 49 Ohio App.2d 31, 358 N.E.2d 1369, 3 O.O.3d 105.

Finding that changing custody of child from father to mother would not be for best interest of child and that child would be immediately removed from this state is equivalent to finding that mother lacked capacity to care properly for child within territorial jurisdiction of court. Godbey v. Godbey (Hamilton 1942) 70 Ohio App. 450, 44 N.E.2d 810, 36 Ohio Law Abs. 511, 25 O.O. 184.

A trial court is required to develop a shared parenting order pursuant to the father's motion where the child (1) has become acquainted and accustomed to the father's home, (2) has developed friendships with neighbors in the father's community and school district, (3) has a large extended family in the area, (4) has no friends or extended family within the state where the mother plans to move, and (5) would be required to adjust to a new school, neighbors, friends, and community. Thieken v Spoerl, No. CA95-11-186, 1996 WL 263583 (12th Dist Ct App, Butler, 5-20-96).

Relocation of the residential parent due to the current husband's job transfer and increased employment opportunities for wife is not legal basis for finding a change of circumstances where the move is not for the improper purpose of interfering with visitation even though the child will not be able to see the father, grandparents, or cousins as often as before absent proof that harm from the move will exceed the normal expected problems of moving; having held there is thus no change of circumstances whatever from the move, the court refuses to proceed to consider what action is in the best interest of the child. Thatcher v Thatcher, No. 10-97-08, 1997 WL 619808 (3d Dist Ct App, Mercer, 10-6-97).

In making its decision to grant custody to the father, the trial court errs by placing undue emphasis on the fact that the mother left Ohio and established residence out of state under circumstances where (1) the mother is the primary caregiver, (2) she leaves the marital home because of spousal abuse, (3) she provides the father with an address and telephone number and does not thwart any efforts at visitation, and (4) the father elects not to visit even though he had vacation time. Marshall v Marshall, No. CA96-05-0033, 1997 WL 22859 (3d Dist Ct App, Allen, 1-15-97).

Where a mother has left the state taking a child and the court enters a shared parenting order that the child be returned to Cuyahoga County and reside with the mother if she returns also, but reside with the father if the mother elects to not return, this order does not violate the mother's "constitutional right to travel;" the order concerns the child's best interests and residence, interferes with no one's travel, and it is essential here to remove this child from the negative atmosphere of the mother's efforts to alienate the child from her father. Marsala v Marsala, No. 67301, 1995 WL 396360 (8th Dist Ct App, Cuyahoga, 8-6-95).

A court may consider a parent's move from Ohio in determining the best interests of the child but this should not be the only factor depriving a parent of custody. Rowe v Franklin, No. C-930522+, 1995 WL 392503 (1st Dist Ct App, Hamilton, 6-28-95).

A trial court order restricting any move of the minor children to within 50 miles from the parties current home infringes upon the custodial parent's constitutionally protected freedom to live where she chooses. Smeltzer v Smeltzer, No. 92-C-50, 1993 WL 488235 (7th Dist Ct App, Columbiana, 11-24-93).

The pending remarriage and relocation of a custodial parent coupled with the loss to the child of contact with the child's local support network including grandparents can be factors justifying a change in custody. Franklin v Franklin, No. CA-8696 (2d Dist Ct App, Montgomery, 9-12-84).

Where there is no substantive evidence presented as to living conditions or schooling, removal of a child to another state is justification for a change of custody; however, mere contemplation of removal is not justification for modification. Evick v Evick, No. 81CA39 (7th Dist Ct App, Mahoning, 1-25-82).

The removal of a child to another state which affects the best interest of the child constitutes sufficient reason to justify a change of custody pursuant to RC 3109.04(B). Evick v Evick, No. 81 CA 39 (7th Dist Ct App, Mahoning, 1-25-82).

In an action for permission to remove a child from the jurisdiction and the noncustodial father, the court determined that the mutual benefit of the father/child visitation right is more in the child's best interests than the mother's change of residence. Jamison v Jamison, No. C-800829 (1st Dist Ct App, Hamilton, 11-10-81).

The fact that the father is planning to move out of state and that the mother is now a fit parent for the child is not sufficient in itself to warrant a change in custody under RC 3109.04(B). Gooch v Mathews, No. 1479 (5th Dist Ct App, Tuscarawas, 6-9-81).

Where there is evidence that the mother is moving to another state to be near a male friend, and that the child reacts unfavorably to the friend, such facts represent a change in circumstances, so it is not necessary that the court find the custodial parent unfit, but only that the court find the best interest of the child requires a change of custody. Hahner v Hahner, No. 7-166 (11th Dist Ct App, Lake, 3-31-80).

A party seeking modification of a custody and visitation order to delete the restriction against the removal of the child from the county and to change the noncustodial parent's visitation rights from frequent weekday and weekend contact to a long-distance visitation schedule bears the burden of affirmatively demonstrating by a preponderance of the evidence that the changes sought are in the best interests of the child pursuant to consideration of the factors set forth in RC 3109.04(C)(1) through RC 3109.04(C)(5). Powe v. Powe (Ohio Com.Pl. 1987) 38 Ohio Misc.2d 5, 525 N.E.2d 845.

69. —"Integration" into one parent's family, allocation of rights and responsibilities: Modification after original allocation—"Change in circumstances" and Specific Factors

While mother of illegitimate child had sole physical custody of child for a year and a half following child's birth, albeit with at least one interruption, mother did not have de facto residential custody of child for purposes of custody determination. In re Wells (Butler 1995) 108 Ohio App.3d 41, 669 N.E.2d 887.

In a child custody action between a mother and stepmother, custody may not be awarded to the nonparent without a showing of parental unsuitability by a preponderance of the evidence, not merely determining if the best interests of the children would be served; therefore, an award of custody to the stepmother instead of the mother, who remarried after leaving her husband and their two children, is based upon the detrimental effect living with the mother would have on the children, not on society's judgment of her, since the children do not view their natural mother as a parental figure and are integrated into the stepmother's community. In re Dunn (Auglaize 1992) 79 Ohio App.3d 268, 607 N.E.2d 81, dismissed, jurisdictional motion overruled 65 Ohio St.3d 1416, 598 N.E.2d 1168.

A motion for change of custody from a father is granted the mother where the court analyzes evidence including testimony from both parents and a teacher sufficient to find that the circumstances of the children had changed in the four-month long time period that the father leaves the children with their mother to go on a camping trip and to find a new babysitter, and that the children had become integrated into their mother's homelife and family. Wirt v Wirt, No. 95CA0041, 1996 WL 170362 (9th Dist Ct App, Wayne, 4-10-96).

It is not in the best interest of a child to change her residential parent when the evidence presented at trial indicates that the child is living a happy, well-adjusted life with her father, step -brother and -sister, that the child is bonded closely with her step-brother, that the step-sister's alcohol abuse has not affected the child's mental state and that the father, rather than the mother, would be the most likely to facilitate visitation with the child. Kreimes v Schmidt, No. E-93-80, 1994 WL 518133 (6th Dist Ct App, Erie, 9-23-94).

Where a custodial parent deliberately delays psychological testing ordered by the court pursuant to a motion for change of custody, it is not error for the referee to consider the integration of the child into the custodial parent's family during this period and a denial of change of custody based on a referee's recommendation citing this integration as a favorable factor is proper. Bartholomew v Bartholomew, No. CA-7133 (5th Dist Ct App, Stark, 8-24-87).

Where a custodial parent moves out of state upon remarriage and integration into the noncustodial parent's family takes place as a result of the children residing with the noncustodial parent until the custodial parent obtains mandatory court approval to move the children out of state, the children's integration into the noncustodial parent's family is voluntary and with the consent of the custodial parent. Brown v Schrull, No. 4139 (9th Dist Ct App, Lorain, 4-22-87).

Integration with consent does not require consent to change custody, only consent to the placement and retention that constitutes integration. Tighe v Tighe, No. 11844 (9th Dist Ct App, Summit, 3-27-85).

Where custodial parent permits the child to visit with non-custodial parent in excess of court ordered visitation rights to such an extent that the child becomes integrated with the family of the non-custodial parent, trial court does not abuse its discretion in changing custody pursuant to RC 3109.04. Morris v Morris, No. 970 (11th Dist Ct App, Geauga, 3-31-82).

70. —Federal involvement, states' sovereign rights in domestic relations

The domestic relations exception to federal jurisdiction applies only where a plaintiff positively sues in federal court for divorce, alimony, or child custody. Catz v. Chalker (C.A.6 (Ohio) 1998) 142 F.3d 279.

71. —Expert testimony required or not, allocation of rights and responsibilities: Modification after original allocation—"Change in circumstances" and Specific Factors

Professional testimony need not be presented on the issue of the probable relative harm and advantages to be caused by a change in custody. Stone v. Stone (Warren 1983) 9 Ohio App.3d 6, 457 N.E.2d 919, 9 O.B.R. 6.

72. —Time period considered, allocation of rights and responsibilities: Modification after original allocation—"Change in circumstances" and Specific Factors

Evidence admissible under RC 3109.04(B) may be excluded by limiting admissible evidence to activities which occurred within a reasonable time immediately preceding a change of custody hearing, especially when its probative value is outweighed by considerations of undue delay. Schmidt v. Schmidt (Franklin 1982) 7 Ohio App.3d 175, 454 N.E.2d 970, 7 O.B.R. 221.

In a custody action subsequent to the original custody order, the trial court does not abuse its discretion by limiting the evidence to events which occurred after the original custody order was made. In re Reynolds (Hamilton 1982) 2 Ohio App.3d 309, 441 N.E.2d 1141, 2 O.B.R. 341.

In proceeding seeking modification of decree awarding custody of a child, at child's election, it is not error for court to refuse evidence of parent's habits earlier than one year immediately preceding the hearing, as this matter rests in the sound discretion of the trial court. Schwalenberg v. Schwalenberg (Columbiana 1940) 65 Ohio App. 217, 29 N.E.2d 617, 18 O.O. 397.

In a change of custody hearing, trial court does not commit prejudicial error in hearing upon remand by admitting evidence concerning matters which preceded the previous hearing. Gooch v Mathews, No. CA-1571 (5th Dist Ct App, Tuscarawas, 4-9-82).

73. —Privileged communications, allocation of rights and responsibilities: Modification after original allocation—"Change in circumstances" and Specific Factors

The doctor-patient privilege established by RC 2317.02(B) is effective in an action for modification of child custody, and a private physician or psychologist retained by the movant for modification cannot be deposed with respect to treatment administered before the filing of the motion unless the privilege is waived. Brown v Long, No. 8469 (2d Dist Ct App, Montgomery, 7-27-84).

74. Attorney fees

Expert testimony of attorney was inadmissible, in hearing on attorney fee requests made pursuant to cross-motions for custody of children, to determine whether former wife's motion for change of custody was warranted under existing law or could be supported by good-faith argument for extension, modification, or reversal of existing law. Mitchell v. Mitchell (Ohio App. 2 Dist. 1998) 126 Ohio App.3d 500, 710 N.E.2d 793.

It is not an abuse of discretion to award an ex-wife her reasonable attorney fees incurred in resisting a motion to modify custody. Cohen v. Cohen (Lake 1983) 8 Ohio App.3d 109, 456 N.E.2d 581, 8 O.B.R. 143.

There is no statute and no provision for attorney fees to be awarded to custodial parent who resists a motion to visit brought by grandparents. Midkiff v Midkiff, No. CA86-10-025 (12th Dist Ct App, Madison, 7-20-87).

A court has the power to order a husband to pay his ex-wife's attorney's fees in post divorce decree proceedings involving the custody of the parties' child. Roberts v Roberts, No. 47635 (8th Dist Ct App, Cuyahoga, 5-24-84).

75. —Expert testimony required or not, allocation of rights and responsibilities: Initial Allocation—"Best interest" and Specific Factors

In custody cases where the best interests of the child are at issue, RC 3109.04 does not require that expert testimony be presented. Mohrman v. Mohrman (Sandusky 1989) 57 Ohio App.3d 33, 565 N.E.2d 1283.

76. —Guardian ad litem, allocation of rights and responsibilities: Initial Allocation—"Best interest" and Specific Factors

"Adoption" is not a custody proceeding and may only become one at such time that a guardian, as opposed to a guardian ad litem, is appointed to protect the child's best interest. In re Adoption of Reams (Franklin 1989) 52 Ohio App.3d 52, 557 N.E.2d 159, dismissed 50 Ohio St.3d 707, 553 N.E.2d 684.

A court may make minor children of a pending divorce parties to the action and appoint a guardian ad litem to represent them where the interests of the minor children are or may be substantially different from either or both of the parents. Barth v. Barth (Ohio Com.Pl. 1967) 12 Ohio Misc. 141, 225 N.E.2d 866, 39 O.O.2d 83, 41 O.O.2d 166.

77. —Guardianship effect, allocation of rights and responsibilities: Initial Allocation—"Best interest" and Specific Factors

Termination of a guardianship of seven months' duration, where the mother has not contracted away her rights, should be determined pursuant to a good cause test not a best interest standard. In re Spriggs, No. 89-CA-1803 (4th Dist Ct App, Scioto, 4-24-90).

78. —Religion, allocation of rights and responsibilities: Initial Allocation—"Best interest" and Specific Factors

A parent may not be denied custody of a child on the basis of the parent's religious practices unless there is probative evidence that those practices will adversely affect the mental or physical health of the child; evidence that the child will not be permitted to participate in certain social or patriotic activities is not sufficient to prove possible harm. Pater v. Pater (Ohio 1992) 63 Ohio St.3d 393, 588 N.E.2d 794.

A court may not restrict a noncustodial parent's right to expose his or her child to religious beliefs, unless the conflict between the parents' religious beliefs is affecting the child's general welfare. Pater v. Pater (Ohio 1992) 63 Ohio St.3d 393, 588 N.E.2d 794.

In deciding the custody of minor children, the court may consider the religious practices of a parent in making the custody determination without violating the parent's constitutional right to the free exercise of religion; the parent may be found unsuitable after such consideration without a finding of actual harm to the children. Birch v. Birch (Ohio 1984) 11 Ohio St.3d 85, 463 N.E.2d 1254, 11 O.B.R. 327.

Parent may not be denied custody on basis of his or her religious practices unless such practices adversely affect mental or physical well-being of child. Arthur v. Arthur (Ohio App. 5 Dist. 1998) 130 Ohio App.3d 398, 720 N.E.2d 176.

A court may consider the parents' religious convictions in awarding custody as those convictions relate to the determination of what is in the best interests of the child; the court does not thereby violate the parties' constitutional rights. Klamo v. Klamo (Butler 1988) 56 Ohio App.3d 15, 564 N.E.2d 1078.

In a child custody case the court does not improperly consider the mother's religious affiliation in determining that she should not be designated the residential parent for all the children where the court centers its concerns around the quality of education the children receive at a church-affiliated school rather than the religious philosophy of the church itself including (1) the below average class sizes, (2) the problems with teacher staffing, (3) the lack of teacher experience, (4) the lack of curriculum, and (5) the sheltered lifestyle. Arthur v Arthur, Nos. 97CA0071 and 98CA0023, 1998 WL 751701 (5th Dist Ct App, Fairfield, 10-22-98).

The provisions of a separation agreement, dealing with the promise of the mother to see to it that the daughter placed in her custody be reared in the Catholic faith and attend a school affiliated with the Catholic church, cannot be enforced by judicial decree. (Annotation from former RC 3105.21.) Hackett v. Hackett (Lucas 1958) 150 N.E.2d 431, 78 Ohio Law Abs. 485.

79. —Procedural issues, hearings, evidence: in general, allocation of rights and responsibilities: Initial Allocation—"Best interest" and Specific Factors

Failure of husband to verify habeas corpus petition that he filed in Court of Appeals to contest trial court's award of custody of parties' minor daughter to wife in divorce action precluded any entitlement to relief. Evans v. Klaeger (Ohio 1999) 87 Ohio St.3d 260, 719 N.E.2d 546.

Unexcused absence of mother who voluntarily left courtroom after being summoned to the stand as father's witness did not afford her grounds to object to the proceeding of the hearing on father's motion for modification of child custody decree, and, consequently, trial court did not abuse its discretion by holding the hearing despite mother's absence. Sayre v. Hoelzle-Sayre (Seneca 1994) 100 Ohio App.3d 203, 653 N.E.2d 712, appeal allowed 70 Ohio St.3d 1426, 638 N.E.2d 88, appeal dismissed as improvidently allowed 72 Ohio St.3d 1218, 651 N.E.2d 430.

Cross-examination testimony by stepmother about alleged domestic violence committed by father was properly excluded in child custody case as irrelevant to question whether stepmother or cousin of mother should have custody of child, as father no longer resided with stepmother; moreover, although evidence might have been relevant to issue whether father's motion for visitation should have been granted, it was beyond scope of cross-examination, as direct examination did not address question of father's visitation. In re Whaley (Athens 1993) 86 Ohio App.3d 304, 620 N.E.2d 954.

A statement by the court in its judgment entry that it carefully considered all the evidence presented to the referee and made an independent review of the facts shows that the referee's decision was not merely "rubber-stamped." Roach v. Roach (Montgomery 1992) 79 Ohio App.3d 194, 607 N.E.2d 35.

In a custody dispute, a trial court fails to comply with Civ R 53 where it chooses to adopt the referee's report without any modification even though the report contains no findings of fact on the issue of allocation of parental rights and responsibilities upon which the court can independently determine the best interest of the children and analyze the custody issue. Jordan v Jordan, No. 95CA2333, 1996 WL 310039 (4th Dist Ct App, Scioto, 6-6-96).

80. —Findings of fact and conclusions of law, emergency and temporary orders

Magistrates are not required to issue findings of fact and conclusions of law when, during pendency of divorce action, they make temporary award of child custody to parent who has been convicted of offense involving family member that resulted in physical harm to that victim; rather, statute that requires findings and conclusions when custody is awarded to such parent applies only to final decrees. State ex rel. Thompson v. Spon (Ohio 1998) 83 Ohio St.3d 551, 700 N.E.2d 1281.

81. —Habeas corpus, allocation of rights and responsibilities: Initial Allocation—"Best interest" and Specific Factors

Husband was not entitled to seek habeas corpus relief from judgment entered in divorce action granting permanent custody of minor child to wife, as he had an adequate remedy by way of appeal. Evans v. Klaeger (Ohio 1999) 87 Ohio St.3d 260, 719 N.E.2d 546.

Habeas corpus relief is exception rather than general rule in child custody actions. Pegan v. Crawmer (Ohio 1996) 76 Ohio St.3d 97, 666 N.E.2d 1091.

To prevail on petition for writ of habeas corpus in child custody case, petitioner must establish that child is being unlawfully detained, and petitioner has superior legal right to custody of child. Pegan v. Crawmer (Ohio 1996) 76 Ohio St.3d 97, 666 N.E.2d 1091.

82. —"Unsuitability" of parent, allocation of rights and responsibilities: Initial Allocation—"Best interest" and Specific Factors

"Unsuitability" of parent to have custody of child does not necessarily connote any moral or character weakness, but rather, is designed to indicate that contractual relinquishment of custody, abandonment, complete inability to provide care or support, or that parental custody would be detrimental to child, has been proved by preponderance of evidence. Schneeberger v. Baker (Summit 1996) 113 Ohio App.3d 805, 682 N.E.2d 661, appeal not allowed 77 Ohio St.3d 1525, 674 N.E.2d 376.

83. —Court-appointed experts, shared parenting: joint custody

Trial court does not err by submitting its chosen shared parenting plan to psychologist for review. Donovan v. Donovan (Clermont 1996) 110 Ohio App.3d 615, 674 N.E.2d 1252.

84. —Violations, shared parenting: joint custody

Wife could not be found in contempt of shared parenting agreement before shared parenting decree was entered. Evans v. Evans (Butler 1995) 106 Ohio App.3d 673, 666 N.E.2d 1176, dismissed, appeal not allowed 75 Ohio St.3d 1448, 663 N.E.2d 330.

85. —Appeal, shared parenting: joint custody

Wife waived for appellate review claim that trial court erred in denying her motion to set aside shared parenting agreement, where wife failed to raise objection before trial court. Evans v. Evans (Butler 1995) 106 Ohio App.3d 673, 666 N.E.2d 1176, dismissed, appeal not allowed 75 Ohio St.3d 1448, 663 N.E.2d 330.

Plain-error doctrine did not apply to wife's claim that trial court erred in denying her motion to set aside shared parenting agreement absent any indication in record that there had been a miscarriage of justice or that wife was prejudiced by trial court's decision to adopt shared parenting agreement. Evans v. Evans (Butler 1995) 106 Ohio App.3d 673, 666 N.E.2d 1176, dismissed, appeal not allowed 75 Ohio St.3d 1448, 663 N.E.2d 330.

86. —Constitutional issues, shared parenting: joint custody

Shared parenting order requiring custodial parent to request court order prior to relocating children concerned residence and visitation of children, and did not unconstitutionally prohibit custodial parent from travelling; custodial parent was never ordered to stay in county, and in fact agreed to stay there as part of shared parenting plan. Rozborski v. Rozborski (Ohio App. 8 Dist. 1996) 116 Ohio App.3d 29, 686 N.E.2d 546.

87. —Constitutional issues, allocation of rights and responsibilities: Initial Allocation—"Best interest" and Specific Factors

Findings in support of determination that it was in best interests of children for custody to be awarded to their maternal uncle, rather than their father, following their mother's death necessarily also tended to prove that father was unsuitable to have custody, and implicit finding of unsuitability precluded father from establishing violation of his fundamental right under State and Federal Constitutions to custody of his children as against third parties. Schneeberger v. Baker (Summit 1996) 113 Ohio App.3d 805, 682 N.E.2d 661, appeal not allowed 77 Ohio St.3d 1525, 674 N.E.2d 376.

Father in custody dispute with children's maternal uncle, which fell within statute allowing award of custody to relative other than parent when in best interest of child, was not similarly situated to parent involved in custody dispute under statute establishing jurisdiction of juvenile courts over various matters, which required explicit finding of unsuitability before awarding custody to any nonparent, as opposed to only relatives, and father's right to equal protection of law was therefore not violated by lack of explicit finding of unsuitability in connection with award of custody to maternal uncle. Schneeberger v. Baker (Summit 1996) 113 Ohio App.3d 805, 682 N.E.2d 661, appeal not allowed 77 Ohio St.3d 1525, 674 N.E.2d 376.

A court's decision to require the residential parent to live close enough to the non-residential parent to facilitate visitation deals with the custody of the parties' children and does not prohibit either party from travelling state to state or relocating; the residential parent is merely prohibited from taking the children with her if she decides to relocate and the prohibition does not violate the residential parent's right to travel. Alvari v Alvari, No. 99CA05, 2000 WL 133849 (4th Dist Ct App, Lawrence, 2-2-00).

A residential parent is in contempt of court for changing the religious practice of the parties' minor child in violation of a previously issued standard order of visitation which conditions any change in the child's religious practices on agreement of the parents and approval of the court; the visitation order does not unconstitutionally prohibit either parent the freedom to choose a religion or to enjoy the right to expose their child to such religion. Cappelli v Cappelli, No. 97 CA 15, 1998 WL 811346 (7th Dist Ct App, Mahoning, 11-16-98).

Former husband's federal action against his former wife, seeking declaration that state divorce decree was void as a violation of due process, was not a core domestic relations case to which domestic relations exception to federal jurisdiction applied; action did not seek declaration of marital or parental status, but instead presented a constitutional claim in which it was incidental that the underlying action involved a divorce. Catz v. Chalker (C.A.6 (Ohio) 1998) 142 F.3d 279.

88. —Visitation generally, allocation of rights and responsibilities: Modification after original allocation—"Change in circumstances" and Specific Factors

Modification of child visitation is governed by statute that specifically addresses visitation rights, rather than by statute that governs child custody, i.e., "parental rights and responsibilities." Braatz v. Braatz (Ohio 1999) 85 Ohio St.3d 40, 706 N.E.2d 1218.

An extended visitation order at issue was not the equivalent of a formal modification of a prior custody decree. State ex rel. Scordato v. George (Ohio 1981) 65 Ohio St.2d 128, 419 N.E.2d 4, 19 O.O.3d 318.

Trial court acted within its discretion in refusing to find former husband in contempt for his technical violation of custody order from divorce proceeding in picking up parties' children at former wife's home on evening which was not one of his scheduled visitation nights, where former wife was in hospital that evening, children were left at home without adult present, and children telephoned former husband. Brooks v. Brooks (Ohio App. 10 Dist. 1996) 117 Ohio App.3d 19, 689 N.E.2d 987.

The mere statement of a twelve-year-old child of divorced parents that she did not want to see her father again was insufficient evidence to justify a complete refusal to permit such father to visit her, and a statement by the mother's counsel that defendant had been guilty of misconduct toward his step-daughter was of no probative value. Marsh v. Marsh (Franklin 1954) 126 N.E.2d 468, 69 Ohio Law Abs. 539.

3109.041 Shared parenting modification to decree entered before specific authority in law

(A) Parties to any custody decree issued pursuant to section 3109.04 of the Revised Code prior to the effective date of this amendment may file a motion with the court that issued the decree requesting the issuance of a shared parenting decree in accordance with division (G) of section 3109.04 of the Revised Code. Upon the filing of the motion, the court shall determine whether to grant the parents shared rights and responsibilities for the care of the children in accordance with divisions (A), (D)(1), and (E)(1) of section 3109.04 of the Revised Code.

(B) A custody decree issued pursuant to section 3109.04 of the Revised Code prior to the effective date of this amendment that granted joint care, custody, and control of the children to the parents shall not be affected or invalidated by, and shall not be construed as being affected or invalidated by, the provisions of section 3109.04 of the Revised Code relative to the granting of a shared parenting decree or a decree allocating parental rights and responsibilities for the care of children on and after the effective date of this amendment. The decree issued prior to the effective date of this amendment shall remain in full force and effect, subject to modification or termination pursuant to section 3109.04 of the Revised Code as that section exists on and after the effective date of this amendment.

(C) As used in this section, "joint custody" and "joint care, custody, and control" have the same meaning as "shared parenting."

(1990 S 3, eff. 4-11-91; 1981 S 39, H 71)

Library References

Divorce ⟹303(1), 303(2).
Parent and Child ⟹2(18).
WESTLAW Topic Nos. 134, 285.
C.J.S. Divorce §§ 648, 650 to 653.
C.J.S. Parent and Child §§ 44 to 46, 48.

Age of parent as factor in awarding custody. 34 ALR5th 57

Carlin, Baldwin's Ohio Practice, *Merrick-Rippner Probate Law* § 105.11, 107.122 (1997)
Sowald & Morganstern, Baldwin's Ohio Practice, *Domestic Relations Law* § 7.19, 15.1, 16.17 (1997)

Notes of Decisions and Opinions

1. Effective date

Statute authorizing "shared parenting" custody decrees was applicable to divorce case pending on its effective date. Frost v. Frost (Franklin 1992) 84 Ohio App.3d 699, 618 N.E.2d 198, motion overruled 66 Ohio St.3d 1489, 612 N.E.2d 1245.

A mediation provision in a joint custody decree of September 30, 1986 is enforceable pursuant to RC 3109.041; however, the parties waive their right to have nonpayment of medical expenses submitted to mediation where one of the parties files a motion for contempt with the court and the other party fails to request mediation and actively participates in the proceedings. Dugach v Dugach, No. 93-L-073, 1995 WL 237040 (11th Dist Ct App, Lake, 3-31-95).

2. Discretion of court

Custody award was abuse of discretion where there was no evidence that court had considered and rejected party's motion and proposed plan for shared parenting. Frost v. Frost (Franklin 1992) 84 Ohio App.3d 699, 618 N.E.2d 198, motion overruled 66 Ohio St.3d 1489, 612 N.E.2d 1245.

3. Out-of-state child

Where a mother has left the state taking a child and the court enters a shared parenting order that the child be returned to Cuyahoga County and reside with the mother if she returns also, but reside with the father if the mother elects to not return, this order does not violate the mother's "constitutional right to travel;" the order concerns the child's best interests and residence, interferes with no one's travel, and it is essential here to remove this child from the negative atmosphere of the mother's efforts to alienate the child from her father. Marsala v Marsala, No. 67301, 1995 WL 396360 (8th Dist Ct App, Cuyahoga, 8-6-95).

4. In general

To modify divorce decree in order to implement shared parenting plan, trial court must determine that such modification is in best interest of child and that there has been a change in circumstances. Neel v. Neel (Cuyahoga 1996) 113 Ohio App.3d 24, 680 N.E.2d 207, dismissed, appeal not allowed 77 Ohio St.3d 1514, 674 N.E.2d 369.

Trial court could not modify custody provisions of divorce decree to provide for shared parenting plan, absent change of circumstances and showing that such modification was in best interest of child, particularly as parties' relationship had deteriorated to such an extent that cooperation between them was highly unlikely. Neel v. Neel (Cuyahoga 1996) 113 Ohio App.3d 24, 680 N.E.2d 207, dismissed, appeal not allowed 77 Ohio St.3d 1514, 674 N.E.2d 369.

In a child custody case the court does not improperly consider the mother's religious affiliation in determining that she should not be designated the residential parent for all the children where the court centers its concerns around the quality of education the children receive at a church-affiliated school rather than the religious philosophy of the church itself including (1) the below average class sizes, (2) the problems with teacher staffing, (3) the lack of teacher experience, (4) the lack of curriculum, and (5) the sheltered lifestyle. Arthur v Arthur, Nos. 97CA0071 and 98CA0023, 1998 WL 751701 (5th Dist Ct App, Fairfield, 10-22-98).

3109.042 Designation of residential parent and legal custodian

An unmarried female who gives birth to a child is the sole residential parent and legal custodian of the child until a court of competent jurisdiction issues an order designating another person as the residential parent and legal custodian. A court designating the residential parent and legal custodian of a child described in this section shall treat the mother and father as standing upon an equality when making the designation.

(1997 H 352, eff. 1-1-98)

Ohio Administrative Code References

CSEA paternity process, OAC 5101:1-32-02

Library References

OJur 3d: 47, Family Law § 1073

Baldwin's Ohio School Law, Text 23.2

Carlin, Baldwin's Ohio Practice, *Merrick-Rippner Probate Law* § 108.13 (1997)

Sowald & Morganstern, Baldwin's Ohio Practice, *Domestic Relations Law* § 3.10, 3.33, 7.19, 15.55 (1997)

3109.05 Support orders; medical needs

(A)(1) In a divorce, dissolution of marriage, legal separation, or child support proceeding, the court may order either or both parents to support or help support their children, without regard to marital misconduct. In determining the amount reasonable or necessary for child support, including the medical needs of the child, the court shall comply with sections 3113.21 to 3113.219 of the Revised Code.

(2) The court, in accordance with sections 3113.21 and 3113.217 of the Revised Code, shall include in each support order made under this section the requirement that one or both of the parents provide for the health care needs of the child to the satisfaction of the court, and the court shall include in the support order a requirement that all support payments be made through the division of child support in the department of job and family services.

(3) Each order for child support made or modified under this section shall include as part of the order a general provision, as described in division (A)(1) of section 3113.21 of the Revised Code, requiring the withholding or deduction of income or assets of the obligor under the order as described in division (D) or (H) of section 3113.21 of the Revised Code, or another type of appropriate requirement as described in division (D)(3), (D)(4), or (H) of that section, to ensure that withholding or deduction from the income or assets of the obligor is available from the commencement of the support order for collection of the support and of any arrearages that occur; a statement requiring both parents to notify the child support enforcement agency in writing of their current mailing address; current residence address, current residence telephone number, current driver's license number, and any changes to that information, and a notice that the requirement to notify the agency of all changes to that information continues until further notice from the court. The court shall comply with sections 3113.21 to 3113.219 of the Revised Code when it makes or modifies an order for child support under this section.

(B) The juvenile court has exclusive jurisdiction to enter the orders in any case certified to it from another court.

(C) If any person required to pay child support under an order made under division (A) of this section on or after April 15, 1985, or modified on or after December 1, 1986, is found in contempt of court for failure to make support payments under the order, the court that makes the finding, in addition to any other penalty or remedy imposed, shall assess all court costs arising out of the contempt proceeding against the person and require the person to pay any reasonable attorney's fees of any adverse party, as determined by the court, that arose in relation to the act of contempt and, on or after July 1, 1992, shall assess interest on any unpaid amount of child support pursuant to section 3113.219 of the Revised Code.

(D) The court shall not authorize or permit the escrowing, impoundment, or withholding of any child support payment ordered under this section or any other section of the Revised Code because of a denial of or interference with a right of companionship or visitation granted in an order issued under this section, section 3109.051, 3109.11, 3109.12, or any other section of the Revised Code, or as a method of enforcing the specific provisions of any such order dealing with visitation.

(E) Notwithstanding section 3109.01 of the Revised Code, if a court issues a child support order under this section, the order shall remain in effect beyond the child's eighteenth birthday as long as the child continuously attends on a full-time basis any recognized and accredited high school or the order provides that the duty of support of the child continues beyond the child's eighteenth birthday. Except in cases in which the order provides that the duty of support continues for any period after the child reaches age nineteen, the order shall not remain in effect after the child reaches age nineteen. Any parent ordered to pay support under a child support order issued under this section shall continue to pay support under the order, including during seasonal vacation periods, until the order terminates.

(1999 H 471, eff. 7-1-00; 1997 H 352, eff. 1-1-98; 1993 H 173, eff. 12-31-93; 1993 S 115; 1992 S 10; 1990 S 3, H 514, H 591, H 15; 1988 H 708; 1987 H 231; 1986 H 509; 1984 H 614; 1981 H 694, H 71; 1974 H 233; 1971 H 163, H 544; 1953 H 1; GC 8005-5; Source—GC 8034)

Historical and Statutory Notes

Pre-1953 H 1 Amendments: 124 v S 65

Amendment Note: 1999 H 471 substituted "job and family" for "human" in division (A)(2).

Amendment Note: 1997 H 352 substituted "division of child support in the department of human services" for "child support enforcement agency" in division (A)(2); deleted "on or after December 31, 1993," before "shall include", substituted "income" for "wages" twice and "(D)(3), (D)(4)" for "(D)(6), (D)(7)", and inserted "current residence telephone number, current driver's license number,", in division (A)(3); inserted "or the order provides that the duty of support of the child continues beyond the child's eighteenth birthday" and added the second sentence in division (E); and made other nonsubstantive changes.

Amendment Note: 1993 H 173 rewrote division (A)(3) before the first semi-colon, which previously read:

"(3) Each order for child support made or modified under this section on or after December 1, 1986, shall be accompanied by one or more orders described in division (D) or (H) of section 3113.21 of the Revised Code, whichever is appropriate under the requirements of that section".

Amendment Note: 1993 S 115 rewrote division (A)(1), which previously read:

"(A)(1) In a divorce, dissolution of marriage, legal separation, or child support proceeding, the court may order either or both parents to support or help support their children, without regard to marital misconduct. In determining the amount reasonable or necessary for child support, including the medical needs of the child, the court shall comply with sections 3113.21 to 3113.219 of the Revised Code and shall consider all relevant factors, including, but not limited to, all of the following:

"(a) The financial resources and the earning ability of the child;

"(b) The relative financial resources, other assets and resources, and needs of the residential parent and of the parent who is not the residential parent, when a decree for shared parenting is not issued;

"(c) The standard of living and circumstances of each parent and the standard of living the child would have enjoyed had the marriage continued;

"(d) The physical and emotional condition and needs of the child;

"(e) The financial resources, other assets and resources, and needs of both parents, when a decree for shared parenting is issued;

"(f) The need and capacity of the child for an education, and the educational opportunities that would have been available to him had the circumstances requiring a court order for his support not arisen;

"(g) The earning ability of each parent;

"(h) The age of the child;

"(i) The responsibility of each parent for the support of others;

"(j) The value of services contributed by the residential parent."

Comparative Laws

Ariz.—A.R.S. § 25-320.
Ark.—A.C.A. § 9-12-312.
Conn.—C.G.S.A. § 46b-84.
Ga.—O.C.G.A. § 19-6-17.
Ill.—ILCS 750 5/505.
Ind.—West's A.I.C. 31-16-6-1 et seq.
Ky.—Baldwin's KRS 403.210.
La.—LSA-C.C. art. 227.
Mass.—M.G.L.A. c. 208, § 28.
Mich.—M.C.L.A. § 552.151 et seq.
Mo.—V.A.M.S. § 452.340.
Neb.—R.R.S.1943, § 42-364 et seq.
N.J.—N.J.S.A. 2A:34-23.
N.M.—NMSA 1978, § 40-4-7.
Wash.—West's RCWA 26.09.100.
Wis.—W.S.A. 767.25.
W.Va.—Code, 48-2-15.

Cross References

Administration of child support orders by child support enforcement agencies, 3113.218
Bureau of child support, 5101.31 et seq.
Calculation of amount of child support obligation, 3113.215
Child support enforcement, 2301.34 et seq.
Child support enforcement agencies, compliance, 2301.35
Collection of past-due child support from tax refunds, 5101.32, 5101.321
Contempt action for failure to pay support, 2705.031, 2705.05
Criminal interference with custody, 2919.23

Criminal nonsupport of dependents, 2919.21
Department of job and family services, division of social administration; care and placement of children, 5103.09 to 5103.17
Failure to support minor, consent to adoption not required, 3107.07
Health insurance coverage for children, 3113.217
Interfering with action to issue or modify support order, 2919.231
Juvenile courts, exercise of jurisdiction in child support matters, 2151.23
Lottery winner must state under oath whether or not he is in default of support order, 3770.071
Notice of default on child support order sent to professional licensing boards, 2301.373
Parents to support child committed by juvenile court, 2151.36
Payment of child support through withholding of earnings, workers' compensation benefits, unemployment compensation benefits, retirement benefits, or bank account, fees, 3113.211
Powers and duties of county children services board, 5153.16
Procedures for collection of past-due child support from state income tax refunds, 5747.121
Reciprocal enforcement of support, Ch 3115
Reciprocal enforcement of support, suspension of visitation rights, 3115.21
Relief pending appeal of child support order, Civ R 75
Wage assignments for support of spouse or children, 1321.33

Ohio Administrative Code References

Child support enforcement agency's responsibility in custody situations, OAC 5101:1-29-01
Medical support; health insurance, OAC 5101:1-29-35 to 5101:1-29-361

Library References

Divorce ⚷306, 308, 309.1, 309.2(1) to 309.2(4), 309.6.
Marriage ⚷64.
Parent and Child ⚷3.1(1) to 3.1(12), 3.3(7), 3.3(8).
WESTLAW Topic Nos. 134, 253, 285.
C.J.S. Divorce §§ 665 to 671, 673 to 683, 700 to 705, 708, 719 to 730, 736.
C.J.S. Marriage § 79.
C.J.S. Parent and Child §§ 14, 49 to 62, 65 to 71, 80 to 84, 89.

Am Jur 2d: 23, Desertion and Nonsupport § 51 et seq.; 24, Divorce and Separation § 827 to 875, 1018 et seq.; 59, Parent and Child § 45, 50 et seq.
Parent's obligation to support adult child. 1 ALR2d 910
Support provisions of judicial decree or order as limit of father's liability for expenses of child. 7 ALR2d 491
Maintenance of suit by child, independently of statute, against parent for support. 13 ALR2d 1142
Death of parent as affecting decree for support of child. 18 ALR2d 1126
Father's duty under divorce or separation decree to support child as affected by latter's induction into military service. 20 ALR2d 1414
Conflict of laws as to right of child or third person against parent for support of child. 34 ALR2d 1460
When statute of limitations begins to run on contractual obligation to pay for minor's support. 52 ALR2d 1125
Pleading and burden of proof, in contempt proceedings, as to ability to comply with order for payment of alimony or child support. 53 ALR2d 591
Validity and effect, as between former spouses, of agreement releasing father from payment of child support provided for in an earlier divorce decree. 57 ALR2d 1139; 100 ALR3d 1129
Marriage of minor child as terminating support provisions in divorce or similar decree. 58 ALR2d 355
Father's liability for support of child furnished after entry of decree of divorce not providing for support. 69 ALR2d 203; 91 ALR3d 530
Statute of limitations, laches, or acquiescence as defense to action or proceeding for alimony or support of child allowed by court order or decree. 70 ALR2d 1250; 5 ALR4th 1015
What law governs validity and enforceability of contract made for support of illegitimate child. 87 ALR2d 1306
Adequacy of amount of money awarded as child support. 1 ALR3d 324
Excessiveness of amount of money awarded as child support. 1 ALR3d 382
Power of divorce court, after child attained majority, to enforce by contempt proceedings payment of arrears of child support. 32 ALR3d 888
What voluntary acts of child, other than marriage or entry into military service, terminate parent's obligation to support. 32 ALR3d 1055
Death of putative father as precluding action for determination of paternity or for child support. 58 ALR3d 188
Wife's possession of independent means as affecting her right to child support pendente lite. 60 ALR3d 832
Divorce power of court to modify decree for support of child which was based on agreement of parties. 61 ALR3d 657
Provision in divorce decree requiring husband to pay certain percentage of future salary increases as additional alimony or child support. 75 ALR3d 493
Validity, construction, and application of statute imposing upon stepparent obligation to support child. 75 ALR3d 1129
Long-arm statutes: obtaining jurisdiction over nonresident parent in filiation or support proceeding. 76 ALR3d 708
Effect, in subsequent proceedings, of paternity findings or implications in divorce or annulment decree or in support or custody order made incidental thereto. 78 ALR3d 846
Father's liability for support of child furnished after divorce decree which awarded custody to mother but made no provision for support. 91 ALR3d 530
Parent's obligation to support unmarried minor child who refuses to live with parent. 98 ALR3d 334
Propriety of decree in proceeding between divorced parents to determine mother's duty to pay support for children in custody of father. 98 ALR3d 1146

Responsibility of noncustodial divorced parent to pay for, or contribute to, costs of child's college education. 99 ALR3d 322

Visitation rights of persons other than natural parents or grandparents. 1 ALR4th 1270

Spouse's professional degree or license as marital property for purposes of alimony, support, or property settlement. 4 ALR4th 1294

Laches or acquiescence as defense, so as to bar recovery of arrearages of permanent alimony or child support. 5 ALR4th 1015

Removal by custodial parents of child from jurisdiction in violation of court order as justifying termination, suspension, or reduction of child support payments. 8 ALR4th 1231

Child's right of action for loss of support, training, parental attention, or the like, against a third person negligently injuring parent. 11 ALR4th 549

Constitutionality of gender-based classifications in criminal laws proscribing nonsupport of spouse or child. 14 ALR4th 717

Validity and enforceability of escalation clause in divorce decree relating to alimony and child support. 19 ALR4th 830

Excessiveness or adequacy of money awarded as child support. 27 ALR4th 864

Child support: court's authority to reinstitute parent's support obligation after terms of prior decree have been fulfilled. 48 ALR4th 952

Authority of court, upon entering default judgment, to make orders for child custody or support which were not specifically requested in pleadings of prevailing party. 5 ALR5th 863

Baldwin's Ohio Legislative Service, 1990 Laws of Ohio, H 591—LSC Analysis, p 5-576

Carlin, Baldwin's Ohio Practice, *Merrick-Rippner Probate Law* § 105.11, 107.122, 108.1, 108.15, 108.34, 108.35, 108.36 (1997)

3 Katz & Giannelli, Baldwin's Ohio Practice, *Criminal Law* § 109.9, 109.12 (1996)

Sowald & Morganstern, Baldwin's Ohio Practice, *Domestic Relations Law* § 3.31, 3.34, 4.24, 4.26, 7.19, 9.9, 9.11, 13.23, 14.29, 15.14, 16.17, 18.21, 19.1, 19.7, 19.10, 19.11, 19.14, 19.23, 20.1, 20.6, 20.18, 20.26, 20.27, 20.37, 21.2, 21.25, 22.5, 23.15, 24.2, 24.6, 25.29, 25.56, 25.57, 31.14 (1997)

Law Review and Journal Commentaries

Abusing the Power to Regulate: The Child Support Recovery Act of 1992, Comment. (Ed. note: Federal encroachment into traditional fields of State criminal law is discussed.) 46 Case W Res L Rev 935 (Spring 1996).

Agreement to Provide College Education—Clear, Unambiguous Language Required, Lynn B. Schwartz. 8 Domestic Rel J Ohio 40 (May/June 1996).

Ascertaining Self-Employment Income, Elaine M. Stoermer. 48 Dayton B Briefs 17 (October 1998).

Awarding Child Support Against the Impoverished Parent: Straying from Statutory Guidelines and Using SSI in Setting the Amount, Note. 83 Ky L J 653 (1994-95).

Bankruptcy Basics—DISCHARGE ... A Simple Word, Not Easily Found, And is the Meaning Plain?, Thomas R. Noland. (Ed. note: The author explains the effect of discharging a debt in bankruptcy court.) 47 Dayton B Briefs 18 (June 1998).

Bankruptcy Reform Act of 1994—What the Bankruptcy Code Giveth, Domestic Relations Courts (and Congress) Taketh Away, C.R. "Chip" Bowles. 8 Domestic Rel J Ohio 17 (March/April 1996).

Business Owner's Compensation and Valuation, Robert G. Turner, Jr. 11 Domestic Rel J Ohio 24 (March/April 1999).

BWC and Self-Insured Employer Liability for Spousal and Child Support, C. Jeffrey Waite. 11 Domestic Rel J Ohio 17 (March/April 1999).

A Case Study in Divorce Law Reform and Its Aftermath, Robert E. McGraw, Gloria J. Sterin and Joseph M. Davis. 20 J Fam L 443 (1981-82).

The Child Dependency Exemption And Divorced Parents: What Is "Custody"?, David J. Benson. 18 Cap U L Rev 57 (Spring 1989).

Child Support Deviation Calculation, David K. Ross. 17 Lake Legal Views 9 (December 1994).

Children—The Innocent Victims of Family Breakups: How the Family Law Attorney, the Courts, and Society Can Protect Our Children, Michael J. Albano. 26 U Tol L Rev 787 (Summer 1995).

Completed Child Support Worksheet Must be Made Part of Court Record, Pamela J. MacAdams. 5 Domestic Rel J Ohio 1 (January/February 1993).

Divorce Reform, Ohio Style, Alan E. Norris. 47 Ohio St B Ass'n Rep 1031 (9-16-74).

Family Law: Construing Ohio Revised Code § 3109.05, Note. 4 Cap U L Rev 283 (1975).

Family Law: Ohio's New Child Support Guidelines: Amended Substitute House Bill Number 591, 1990 Ohio Legis. Serv. 5-546 (Baldwin), Note. 16 U Dayton L Rev 521 (Winter 1991).

The Federal Income Tax Consequences of the Legal Obligation of Parents to Support Children, Note. 47 Ohio St L J 753 (1986).

Grandparent Visitation: The Best Interests of the Grandparent, Child, and Society, Erica L. Strawman. 30 U Tol L Rev 31 (Fall 1998).

Guidelines in Alimony and Support for Ohio, Hon. John R. Milligan. 52 Ohio St B Ass'n Rep 2009 (12-3-79).

Illinois Court Overturns Mandatory Parent Education Class, Paul J. Buser. 18 Lake Legal Views 8 (August 1995).

Judges' Column, Hon. Francine Bruening. (Ed. note: Judge Bruening discusses the Child Support Reorganization Act of House Bill 352, effective 1-1-98.) 21 Lake Legal Views 1 (June 1998).

Judicial Activism in Domestic Relations Cases, Hon. V. Michael Brigner. (Ed. note: Judge Brigner lists the powers of a judge hearing custody, support, and visitation matters.) 45 Dayton B Briefs 22 (January 1996).

The Lawyer Turns Peacemaker—with mediation emerging as the most popular form of alternate dispute resolution, the quest for common ground could force attorneys to reinterpret everything they do in the future, Richard C. Reuben. 82 A B A J 54 (August 1996).

Learning From Social Sciences: A Model For Reformation of the Laws Affecting Stepfamilies, David R. Fine and Mark A. Fine. 97 Dick L Rev 49 (Fall 1992).

Litigation Results—Count on a CPA, Keith J. Libman. 67 Clev B J 12 (October 1996).

Little Red Riding Hood is Missing—Grandparent Visitation Not Authorized After Stepparent Adoption, Richard L. Innis. 7 Domestic Rel J Ohio 17 (March/April 1995).

The New Child Support Act—1993 S.B. 115, Richard L. Innis. 5 Domestic Rel J Ohio 73 (September/October 1993).

Nobody Gets Married for the First Time Anymore—A Primer on the Tax Implications of Support Payments in Divorce, C. Garrison Lepow. 25 Duq L Rev 43 (Fall 1986).

Ohio's Child Support Guidelines Revisited, Hon. Lillian M. Kern. 3 Ohio Law 12 (January/February 1989).

Ohio's Mandatory Child Support Guidelines: Child Support or Spousal Maintenance?, Note. 42 Case W Res L Rev 297 (1992).

Origins and Development of the Law of Parental Child Support, Donna Schuele. 27 J Fam L 807 (1988-89).

Parents Who Abandon or Fail to Support their Children and Apportionment of Wrongful Death Damages, Note. 27 J Fam L 871 (1988-89).

Pathfinder: Economic Effects of Divorce on Women, Barbara Laughlin. 14 Legal Reference Serv Q 57 (1995).

Paying for Children's Medical Care: Interaction Between Family Law and Cost Containment, Walter J. Wadlington. 36 Case W Res L Rev 1190 (1985-86).

The Plain Meaning of the Automatic Stay in Bankruptcy: The Void/Voidable Distinction Revisited, Timothy Arnold Barnes. 57 Ohio St L J 291 (1996).

The Power Of State Courts To Award The Federal Dependency Exemption Upon Divorce, David J. Benson. 16 U Dayton L Rev 29 (Fall 1990).

The Reasonableness of Attorney's Fees to be Awarded in Domestic Proceedings, William K. McCarter and Sean A. McCarter. 19 Lake Legal Views 10 (September 1996).

The Significance Of A Divorced Father's Remarriage In Adjudicating A Motion To Modify His Child Support Obligations, Marvin M. Moore. 18 Cap U L Rev 483 (Winter 1989).

Standard of Proof in Proceedings to Terminate Parental Rights, Note. 31 Clev St L Rev 679 (1982).

Support Obligations Beyond Majority, Stanley Morganstern. 6 Domestic Rel J Ohio 33 (May/June 1994).

Tax Consequences of Attorney Fees, Awards, and Payments, Stanley Morganstern. 4 Domestic Rel J Ohio 29 (March/April 1992).

Total of Spousal Support Deducted from Payor's Gross in Child Support Computation, Pamela J. MacAdams. 5 Domestic Rel J Ohio 42 (May/June 1993).

Validity of Agreements Between Parties to Suspend Support Payments, Pamela J. MacAdams. 3 Domestic Rel J Ohio 12 (January/February 1991).

Notes of Decisions and Opinions

---

1. Constitutional issues

Judicial enforcement of a separation agreement incorporated into a divorce decree calling for the parent without custody to pay tuition for his child's religious education does not offend O Const Art I §7, which concerns freedom of religion. Rand v. Rand (Ohio 1985) 18 Ohio St.3d 356, 481 N.E.2d 609, 18 O.B.R. 415.

Reviewing court's application of amended versions of child support statutes to post-dissolution proceeding did not violate constitutional prohibition on retroactive legislation since amendments did not impose new duty upon ex-husband, but instead merely altered how already existing general duty of support codified by former statute could be enforced. Smith v. Smith (Ohio App. 12 Dist. 1997) 119 Ohio App.3d 15, 694 N.E.2d 476.

Statute providing for enforcement of child support orders past child's age of majority is remedial, not substantive, and thus does not violate constitutional prohibition against retroactive laws. Swanson v. Swanson (Greene 1996) 109 Ohio App.3d 231, 671 N.E.2d 1333.

Trial court's decision to impute to father his "potential" income for purposes of child support was not per se abuse of discretion. In re Yeauger (Union 1992) 83 Ohio App.3d 493, 615 N.E.2d 289.

Ohio domestic relations court had jurisdiction to consider propriety of representative payee's expenditure of Social Security Administration funds received on behalf of child whose father was disabled; Social Security Administration had no interest in funds once they were paid, and state court jurisdiction was not precluded by statute or nature of particular case. Catlett v. Catlett (Clermont 1988) 55 Ohio App.3d 1, 561 N.E.2d 948, motion overruled 39 Ohio St.3d 730, 534 N.E.2d 357.

After a child has reached the age of majority and support money yet unpaid and owing is reduced to a lump-sum judgment during a civil proceeding, the judgment becomes a debt for which imprisonment is prohibited pursuant to O Const Art I §15. Bauer v. Bauer (Franklin 1987) 39 Ohio App.3d 39, 528 N.E.2d 964.

A decree in a divorce action, ordering the payment of money for the support of a minor child, is not a judgment for the payment of money nor is it a debt within the constitutional inhibition against imprisonment for debt, but is in the nature of an order for the payment of alimony, and contempt will lie for willful failure to comply with its terms. Slawski v. Slawski (Lucas 1934) 49 Ohio App. 100, 195 N.E. 258, 18 Ohio Law Abs. 515, 1 O.O. 201.

A defendant is not exposed to double jeopardy when criminally convicted for child non-support following his civil contempt citation in the divorce proceedings. State v Yacovella, No. 69487, 1996 WL 38898 (8th Dist Ct App, Cuyahoga, 2-1-96).

RC 3109.05, in allowing visitation rights to grandparents, does not violate the Equal Protection Clause by treating divorced parents differently than married parents because divorced parents are not a suspect classification and because it promotes a legitimate state interest in protecting the best interests of children. Andrews v Andrews, No. CA88-03-035 (12th Dist Ct App, Butler, 11-28-88).

Judicial enforcement of a separation agreement that requires the noncustodial parent to pay tuition for his children's education at a religiously oriented school does not constitute unconstitutional state support of such religiously oriented school under either the Establishment or Free Exercise Clauses of the US Constitution, or the religious freedom provision of the Ohio Constitution. Rand v Rand, No. 47712 (8th Dist Ct App, Cuyahoga, 6-28-84), affirmed by 18 OS(3d) 356, 18 OBR 415, 481 NE(2d) 609 (1985).

Where defendant is unemployed and his sole income is from aid to dependent children, an order to pay child support for an illegitimate child does not violate 42 USC 601 or the Supremacy Clause of the US Constitution. Goode v Wilburn, No. 1542 (4th Dist Ct App, Lawrence, 3-25-82).

Where it is presumed under state law that a noncustodial parent is able to make support payments and a state court has held this ability an element of the offense of contempt for not obeying a court order to make the payments, the Due Process Clause of the Fourteenth Amendment to the federal constitution does not necessarily prevent use of the presumption if the parent could discharge the contempt judgment by paying his support arrearage, since this possibility would render the proceeding civil in nature. (Ed. note: California law construed in light of federal constitution.) Hicks on Behalf of Feiock v. Feiock (U.S.Cal. 1988) 108 S.Ct. 1423, 485 U.S. 624, 99 L.Ed.2d 721, on remand 215 Cal.App.3d 141, 263 Cal.Rptr. 437, review denied.

There is no substantive federal constitutional right to physical possession of a child; a parent's right to custody or visitation with a child, however, is a constitutionally protected liberty interest that cannot be interfered with absent due process of law. Scarso v. Cuyahoga County Dept. of Human Services (N.D.Ohio 1989) 747 F.Supp. 381, affirmed in part and remanded 917 F.2d 1305.

A suit against state officials for injunctive and declaratory relief for violations of Social Security Act requirements at 42 USC 651 to 669 that states adopt plans for child support enforcement to remain eligible for aid to families with dependent children funds is not barred by US Const Am 11. Carelli v. Howser (S.D.Ohio 1990) 733 F.Supp. 271, reversed 923 F.2d 1208, rehearing denied.

2. In general

Trial court acted within its discretion in refusing to find former husband in contempt for his alleged violation of divorce decree in not making any payment toward certain medical bill of parties' child; decree required former wife to provide former husband with "such information as could be submitted to former husband's insurance carrier," and former husband testified that he had needed "explanation of benefits" form from former wife's insurer showing what portion of bill was paid and what claims were denied in order to submit bill for payment to his insurance carrier. Brooks v. Brooks (Ohio App. 10 Dist. 1996) 117 Ohio App.3d 19, 689 N.E.2d 987.

Father's argument that he did not want child and would have elected either abortion or adoption did not release him from his obligation to pay child support. Bryant v. Hacker (Ohio App. 1 Dist. 1996) 116 Ohio App.3d 860, 689 N.E.2d 609.

Child support is a duty and obligation imposed by statute and common law. Hamilton v. Hamilton (Lucas 1995) 107 Ohio App.3d 132, 667 N.E.2d 1256, appeal not allowed 75 Ohio St.3d 1425, 662 N.E.2d 27.

Reference to 3109.05 was presumed to be intended to refer to 3109.051, in statute providing that whenever court issues child support order, it shall include in order specific provisions for regular, holiday, vacation, and special visitation in accordance with 3109.05, 3109.11, or 3109.12 of the Revised Code or in accordance with any other applicable section of the Revised Code, since 3109.05 deals exclusively with child support, whereas 3109.051 deals exclusively with visitation or companionship rights. Tobens v. Brill (Auglaize 1993) 89 Ohio App.3d 298, 624 N.E.2d 265.

Medical expenses are child support. Rohrbacher v. Rohrbacher (Lucas 1992) 83 Ohio App.3d 569, 615 N.E.2d 338.

A defendant who fails to avail himself of the opportunity to defend against his former wife's motion for child support modification and custody determination, to challenge an alleged error in the admission of bureau of support records, and to bring the objection to the trial court's attention waives that objection. Hostetler v. Kennedy (Wayne 1990) 69 Ohio App.3d 299, 590 N.E.2d 793.

Trial court abused its discretion by setting up savings account for child born out-of-wedlock to be funded by father and be disbursed as court ordered, where account was not based on child's current needs or support. Bailey v. Mitchell (Cuyahoga 1990) 67 Ohio App.3d 441, 587 N.E.2d 358.

Obligation of father to support his minor children after his divorce is granted is obligation cast upon him by law and not by decree of divorce. Verplatse v. Verplatse (Hancock 1984) 17 Ohio App.3d 99, 477 N.E.2d 648, 17 O.B.R. 161.

Elihu Root's observation is worth recalling, that "About half the practice of a decent lawyer consists of telling ... clients they are d——— fools and should stop ... [that]the law lets you do it but don't. It's a rotten thing to do." Stivison v Goodyear Tire & Rubber Co, No. 95-CA-13, 1996 WL 230037 (4th Dist Ct App, Hocking, 5-6-96), affirmed by 80 Ohio St.3d 498 (1997).

Where trial court merely recites that the statutory factors set forth in RC 3109.05 have been considered without a specific showing of the basis upon which a modification of a child support order is made, the judgment of the trial court will be reversed and remanded for a showing of such a basis. Coleman v Coleman, No. L-82-005 (6th Dist Ct App, Lucas, 5-7-82).

The principle of Barber v Barber, 21 How 582 (1859) that federal courts have no jurisdiction over suits for divorce, the allowance of alimony, or custody of children remains true and will not be cast aside after nearly a century and a half; however, a district court cannot refuse to exercise diversity jurisdiction over a tort action for damages such as one brought against a former husband and his girlfriend by the former wife based on alleged abuse of the former couple's children. Ankenbrandt v.

Richards (U.S.La. 1992) 112 S.Ct. 2206, 504 U.S. 689, 119 L.Ed.2d 468, on remand 973 F.2d 923.

3. Jurisdiction

Four years after dissolution of parties' marriage, Court of Common Pleas did not have jurisdiction to decide parentage and ultimately award child support for child conceived after dissolution through artificial insemination. Bailey v. Bailey (Lawrence 1996) 109 Ohio App.3d 569, 672 N.E.2d 747.

In order for trial court to maintain continuing jurisdiction over issue of child support, there must have been minor child either born or conceived prior to entry of final judgment in dissolution. Bailey v. Bailey (Lawrence 1996) 109 Ohio App.3d 569, 672 N.E.2d 747.

Court of Appeals could not say that domestic relations court abused its discretion in suspending father's child support obligation, notwithstanding statute prohibiting court from authorizing or permitting withholding of child support payment based on denial of or interference with visitation rights; mother took children to her native England, out of reach of American courts, with specific intent of denying father and children their mutual rights of companionship, children were being adequately supported, and it was in best interest of children that father had financial resources to pursue his rights of companionship in English courts. Miller v. Miller (Erie 1993) 92 Ohio App.3d 340, 635 N.E.2d 384, motion overruled 69 Ohio St.3d 1424, 631 N.E.2d 164.

Judgment in form of child support and alimony can be awarded as part of valid divorce decree where court obtains jurisdiction over real or personal property of defendant and, in essence, transforms nature of award to in rem or quasi in rem. Meadows v. Meadows (Hancock 1992) 73 Ohio App.3d 316, 596 N.E.2d 1146.

A domestic relations court which granted a divorce retains jurisdiction for the purposes of granting visitation rights as required by the best interest of any children born as issue of the marriage regardless of the existence or venue of a subsequent stepparent adoption proceeding. Bente v. Hill (Clermont 1991) 73 Ohio App.3d 151, 596 N.E.2d 1042, dismissed, jurisdictional motion overruled 62 Ohio St.3d 1422, 577 N.E.2d 1105.

The failure to support one's minor children constitutes a tortious act or omission in Ohio conferring in personam jurisdiction; thus, in personam jurisdiction exists over a nonresident mother whose children are in the care of guardians who are receiving aid to dependent children for purposes of a support action brought against the mother by a county bureau of support. Wayne Cty. Bur. of Support v. Wolfe (Wayne 1991) 71 Ohio App.3d 765, 595 N.E.2d 421.

Transfer of jurisdiction of a case concerning enforcement of an order for child support is within the discretion of the court to refuse, even though the desired transferee court consents to the transfer. Bieniek v. Bieniek (Medina 1985) 27 Ohio App.3d 28, 499 N.E.2d 356, 27 O.B.R. 29.

In any case where a court of common pleas has made an award of custody or an order for support, or both, of minor children, that court may certify the case to the juvenile court of any county in the state for further proceedings. Pylant v. Pylant (Huron 1978) 61 Ohio App.2d 247, 401 N.E.2d 940, 15 O.O.3d 407.

The authority vested in a court by 3109.05, in extreme circumstances, includes the authority to give relief, through a just modification of an order of support, to a parent continuously or repeatedly prevented from exercising a right to visit a child by the child's refusal to visit with him; but such jurisdiction should not be exercised until the court first considers whether to make the child a party pursuant to Civ R 75(B)(2). Foster v. Foster (Franklin 1974) 40 Ohio App.2d 257, 319 N.E.2d 395, 69 O.O.2d 250.

When the question of custody only comes before a court, under the authority granted in 2151.23(A)(2), that court has jurisdiction to include in the award of custody an order for the support of such child. Kolody v. Kolody (Summit 1960) 110 Ohio App. 260, 169 N.E.2d 34, 13 O.O.2d 25.

This section confers jurisdiction to hear a motion for modification of a foreign decree of child support when the child is an Ohio resident. Bowden v Bowden, No. L-84-212 (6th Dist Ct App, Lucas, 12-14-84).

A court has no jurisdiction to modify a visitation decree where the party was not served pursuant to Civ R 75(I). Jenkins v Jenkins, No. 1504 (4th Dist Ct App, Lawrence, 12-9-81).

RC 3109.05 does not impliedly permit the retroactive application of a support order to a time prior to the institution of the divorce proceedings, because the trial court lacks jurisdiction to retroactively apply an award of child support to a time prior to the court's subject matter jurisdiction; to maintain an action for support prior to a court order for child support, one must file an action based on the common law seeking compensation for necessaries furnished to the minor child. Liggins v Liggins, No. 796 (4th Dist Ct App, Ross, 11-9-81).

Where the father received no notice pursuant to the rules of procedure that the continuing jurisdiction of the court had been invoked to modify his visitation rights, the court of appeals will reverse because the father is entitled to attend such a hearing with a clear understanding of its purpose. Harris v Harris, No. 1593 (2d Dist Ct App, Clark, 10-22-81).

While a domestic relations court which grants a divorce has continuing jurisdiction over all matters pertaining to child custody and support, it has no authority to retroactively modify the total amount due and payable under its prior order for support of minor children in this action involving a change of custody. Kuntz v Kuntz, No. 78AP-831 (10th Dist Ct App, Franklin, 7-5-79).

Court has jurisdiction and duty to require father to pay adequate support for his minor children whether or not there was an express reservation of continuing jurisdiction in original divorce decree; and where original divorce decree made no order of support, though it approved provisions of separation agreement, modification of support payments may be made without showing changed circumstances. (Annotation from former RC 3105.21.) Gilmore v. Gilmore (Ohio Com.Pl. 1971) 28 Ohio Misc. 161, 275 N.E.2d 646, 57 O.O.2d 272.

4. Support award

Trial court did not abuse its discretion in formulating award for reimbursement of medical expenses in light of former wife's evidence consisting primarily of her own testimony, dental bills, and her handwritten list of medical expenses as submitted on her federal income tax return. Dunbar v. Dunbar (Ohio 1994) 68 Ohio St.3d 369, 627 N.E.2d 532.

Nonresident custodial parent had right to pursue action against resident noncustodial parent for child support in court of competent jurisdiction in state, where foreign divorce decree and child custody order did not address issue of support. Haskins v. Bronzetti (Ohio 1992) 64 Ohio St.3d 202, 594 N.E.2d 582.

Deviation from the child support guidelines, set forth in C P Sup R 75, by using a father's net income where the father's living expenses are substantially higher than the mother's due to geographic differences does not constitute an abuse of discretion. Booth v. Booth (Ohio 1989) 44 Ohio St.3d 142, 541 N.E.2d 1028.

A custodial parent is not entitled to reimbursement for child support from the noncustodial parent where no support order is made or requested at the time custody is awarded. Meyer v. Meyer (Ohio 1985) 17 Ohio St.3d 222, 478 N.E.2d 806, 17 O.B.R. 455.

Finding of domestics relations court, on ex-husband's motion for return of overpayment of child support, that support order was in-gross order that ex-husband was required to pay in fall until youngest child reached age of emancipation, was not abuse of discretion, where divorce decree failed to specify support obligation as to each child. Cox v. Cox (Ohio App. 1 Dist. 1998) 130 Ohio App.3d 609, 720 N.E.2d 946.

Juvenile court was required by statute to consider father's finances as they related to determination of future support payments for child who was born out-of-wedlock and was receiving Aid to Families with Dependent Children (AFDC). Gilpen v. Justice (Fayette 1993) 85 Ohio App.3d 86, 619 N.E.2d 94, motion overruled 67 Ohio St.3d 1410, 615 N.E.2d 1044.

Divorce court is required to consider financial resources and earning ability of child, including interest income earned on child's accumulated assets, when setting amount of child support. Frost v. Frost (Franklin 1992) 84 Ohio App.3d 699, 618 N.E.2d 198, motion overruled 66 Ohio St.3d 1489, 612 N.E.2d 1245.

Although trial court is required by statute in fixing child support under guidelines to consider financial resources and earning ability of minor child, including social security benefits paid either to child or child's representative payee, it is unreasonable to permit one parent to receive windfall and be totally relieved of child support obligation which would otherwise be allocated to that parent under child support guidelines solely because of social security benefits to or for benefit of minor child. McNeal v. Cofield (Franklin 1992) 78 Ohio App.3d 35, 603 N.E.2d 436.

In a case in which the unmarried parents of two minor children both seek custody after the relationship between the parties has terminated, a trial court does not err in making a child support determination without an evidentiary hearing where the judge met with counsel for the parties and requested information about the party's incomes; this information coupled with the testimony presented at the hearing was a sufficient basis on which the court could make its determination and a further hearing was not necessary. In re Markham (Meigs 1990) 70 Ohio App.3d 841, 592 N.E.2d 896, dismissed, jurisdictional motion overruled 60 Ohio St.3d 702, 573 N.E.2d 118.

It is an abuse of discretion for a trial court to order a father to put money into a savings account which is set up by the court and which is for his son to be disbursed as the court may order where this order does not serve as support for the current needs of the child. Bailey v. Mitchell (Cuyahoga 1990) 67 Ohio App.3d 441, 587 N.E.2d 358.

Court-ordered support is for benefit of children, rather than custodial parent, and cannot be waived by parents. Nelson v. Nelson (Lake 1990) 65 Ohio App.3d 800, 585 N.E.2d 502.

In the absence of factors making it inequitable, the right to interest under RC 1343.03(A) on unpaid child support accrues on the date each installment becomes due, and runs until paid; such interest may be included in a lump-sum judgment for child support arrearages. Allen v. Allen (Summit 1990) 62 Ohio App.3d 621, 577 N.E.2d 126.

Proper amount of child support is that amount necessary to maintain for children standard of living they would have enjoyed had marriage continued, and amount includes consideration of financial resources and needs of both custodial and noncustodial parent. Birath v. Birath (Franklin 1988) 53 Ohio App.3d 31, 558 N.E.2d 63, motion overruled 39 Ohio St.3d 730, 534 N.E.2d 357.

The amount of child support necessary is the amount needed to maintain for the children the standard of living they would have had if the marriage had continued, with consideration given to other factors like the financial resources and needs of the custodial and the noncustodial parents. Birath v. Birath (Franklin 1988) 53 Ohio App.3d 31, 558 N.E.2d 63, motion overruled 39 Ohio St.3d 730, 534 N.E.2d 357.

A family maintenance provision, where no portion of the amount is specifically fixed as child support, incorporated within a divorce decree in order to take advantage of tax benefits, may not be reduced by the amount intended by the parties as child support upon the death or the emancipation of the child, where the provision provides for a reduction or termination of the support only if the receiving spouse reaches a certain income level. Rittgers v. Rittgers (Fairfield 1986) 38 Ohio App.3d 115, 528 N.E.2d 571.

Known and reasonably anticipated medical needs of a child must be provided for in every support order, and it is not sufficient for a trial court to assume, as a basis for its order, that payments for medical expenses made voluntarily by one parent will continue. Gorman v. Gorman (Franklin 1986) 28 Ohio App.3d 85, 501 N.E.2d 1234, 28 O.B.R. 128.

A loss of income to a supporting parent does not require a proportional reduction in his support obligation. Snyder v. Snyder (Cuyahoga 1985) 27 Ohio App.3d 1, 499 N.E.2d 320, 27 O.B.R. 1.

No direct evidence of value is required to support an award of only $8 per week per child in satisfaction of a father's common-law duty to provide his children with the necessities of life. Kulcsar v. Petrovic (Wayne 1984) 20 Ohio App.3d 104, 484 N.E.2d 1365, 20 O.B.R. 126.

Where a husband and wife are divorced, the duty to support minor children is governed by RC 3109.05, so that a wife may be required to contribute to the support of her minor children who are in the custody of their father. Hacker v. Hacker (Fairfield 1981) 5 Ohio App.3d 46, 448 N.E.2d 831, 5 O.B.R. 50.

In determining the amount of child support which is reasonable and necessary under RC 3109.05(A), the trial court first must determine the child's needs, after considering all relevant factors, including those listed in RC 3109.05(A); the determination of need must then be tempered by ascertaining the amount which is reasonable in view of the overall financial condition of the parents and the child. Bright v. Collins (Franklin 1982) 2 Ohio App.3d 421, 442 N.E.2d 822, 2 O.B.R. 514.

Minor children are third party beneficiaries of provisions in a divorce decree granting support payments for their benefit, and such benefits may not be modified by the parties to the detriment of the minors. Rhoades v. Rhoades (Hamilton 1974) 40 Ohio App.2d 559, 321 N.E.2d 242, 69 O.O.2d 488.

Where a husband and wife are divorced, the duty to support a minor child is governed by 3109.05 and not 3103.03, so that a wife may be required to assume the support of her child who is in the custody of another. Hill v. Hill (Hamilton 1973) 40 Ohio App.2d 1, 317 N.E.2d 250, 69 O.O.2d 1.

Common law rules that the father is the head of the family and that death terminates his obligation of child support are based on outdated social and sexual stereotypes; the modern trend is for a divorce court to mandate that the obligor designate the child as the beneficiary on the parent's life insurance policy to ensure that the child receive support during minority in the event the obligor parent dies before the child reaches majority. Webb v Webb, No. 16371, 1997 WL 797719 (2d Dist Ct App, Montgomery, 12-31-97).

Where a noncustodial mother inherits sixty thousand dollars, the trial court does not abuse its discretion in denying the father's motion for child support, notwithstanding that the father was ordered to pay support before he gained custody, where the father does not show that he is unable to provide for his children's needs and where the court finds that the mother desires use of the money for her own purposes. Griffith v Griffith, No. CA-84-07-078 (12th Dist Ct App, Butler, 12-17-84).

A cost-of-living clause in a separation agreement providing for automatic increases in child support is valid, as the ability of a domestic relations court to modify for a change of circumstances exists despite the clause. Gui v Brown, No. CA-6392 (5th Dist Ct App, Stark, 11-26-84).

It is an abuse of discretion to order that a noncustodial parent, without disabilities, who has been out of the employment market for twelve years, must pay child support whether or not employed. Zaller v Zaller, No. 10-035 (11th Dist Ct App, Lake, 6-29-84).

Inflation alone will not justify a modification in a support award, but where the custodial parent has experienced increased food, fuel, and educational expenses, and the noncustodial parent has received a pay raise sufficient to cover the increase in support, a modification is justified under RC 3109.05. Frierott v Frierott, No. 2-82-18 (3d Dist Ct App, Auglaize, 1-10-84).

Where a minor child uses the surname of her stepfather but no legal steps have been taken to change such child's surname, the use of the surname does not relieve the noncustodial parent's obligation to pay child support. Houser v Houser, No. CA-2887 (5th Dist Ct App, Licking, 9-24-82).

In a divorce proceeding trial court abused its discretion in awarding child support and alimony payments without requiring evidence of both parties' wages. Geiner v Geiner, No. WD-82-11 (6th Dist Ct App, Wood, 8-13-82).

In a divorce proceeding, take-home pay is not the equivalent of "relative earning abilities of the parties" for purposes of awarding a property settlement nor is take-home pay the determinative factor in arriving at an order for child support. Hanney v Hanney, No. OT-81-25 (6th Dist Ct App, Ottawa, 5-7-82).

An order to pay child support is proper only if the trial court determines the appropriateness of the amount of child support by considering the required factors under RC 3109.05. Botticello v Botticello, No. 7372 (2d Dist Ct App, Montgomery, 1-7-82).

The court defines dental, optical and pharmaceutical services as medical expenses, but optical expenses include only those services provided by an opthalmologist and not glasses furnished by an optometrist. Minick v Minick, No. OT-81-3 (6th Dist Ct App, Ottawa, 8-14-81).

Although RC 3109.05 requires that the financial resources and needs of both the custodial and noncustodial parent be considered in determining a reasonable child-support amount, it is an abuse of discretion to require the mother to pay twenty-three per cent of her meager $110 per week income for child support. Logsdon v Logsdon, No. 80AP-919 (10th Dist Ct App, Franklin, 7-21-81).

Where a court of appeals does not have testimony concerning the amount required to support the children, the need of the father for additional support for the children, and the needs of the mother, an award of forty-five dollars per month child support is deemed as adequate and not an abuse of discretion. Adams v Adams, No. 81AP-233 (10th Dist Ct App, Franklin, 5-28-81).

Where the non-custodial parent is ordered to pay child support, to have an abuse of discretion in such a case, there must be a showing of a combination of circumstances where there is an inability to contribute even a nominal amount by the person out of custody, coupled with a showing that the person in custody has an ability to support without help. McCauley v McCauley, No. 79AP-727 (10th Dist Ct App, Franklin, 1-29-80).

An automatic escalator clause in a child support decree is improper if not based on future earning capability or future needs of the child. Royse v. Royse (Ohio Com.Pl. 1984) 23 Ohio Misc.2d 5, 491 N.E.2d 397, 23 O.B.R. 113.

In determining if there has been a material change in circumstances justifying an increase in child support, a trial court may consider changes in the: (1) take-home pay of the parties, (2) cost-of-living index, and (3) other support obligations of the parties. Neukam v. Neukam (Ohio Com.Pl. 1983) 13 Ohio Misc.2d 4, 468 N.E.2d 391, 13 O.B.R. 76.

5. —In general, modification of support

Public policy underlying statutory provision for modification of child support is that parental relationships and obligations continue after parents divorce each other and that children have right to expect same support and care they could have reasonably expected if their parents had remained married. Colizoli v. Colizoli (Ohio 1984) 15 Ohio St.3d 333, 474 N.E.2d 280, 15 O.B.R. 458.

Former wife's voluntary decision to quit her guidance counseling job and take another one that paid $15,000 less but was in a community closer to her home and children did not warrant imputing potential income to her in determining whether to modify her $550 monthly child support obligation, where she was still working as a counselor and was earning the most she could in the closer community. Shank v. Shank (Ohio App. 3 Dist. 1997) 122 Ohio App.3d 189, 701 N.E.2d 439, appeal not allowed 80 Ohio St.3d 1471, 687 N.E.2d 299.

Requiring wife to pay first $100 of extraordinary medical expenses per year per child rather than first $150, with balance to be paid 20% by wife and 80% by husband, did not violate local rule stating that custodial parent would pay ordinary health care expenses not exceeding $150 per year per child, and in fact any deviation from local rule benefitted husband by excusing him from paying any portion of first $100 of uninsured extraordinary expenses. Shaffer v. Shaffer (Crawford 1996) 109 Ohio App.3d 205, 671 N.E.2d 1317.

Former husband's failure to pay past due and owing college expenses and medical expenses, as required under separation agreement and modification order, justified contempt finding; former husband's motion to modify filed after contempt proceeding was instituted was not viable defense and husband offered no evidence of alleged inability to pay. Rohrbacher v. Rohrbacher (Lucas 1992) 83 Ohio App.3d 569, 615 N.E.2d 338.

Generally, changed circumstances relied upon to obtain modification of child support order must not have been within knowledge or contemplation of court when decree was entered, and must be substantial. Osborne v. Osborne (Meigs 1992) 81 Ohio App.3d 666, 611 N.E.2d 1003.

Modification of award of child support normally requires two-step determination: determination whether there has been change of circumstance and, if so, redetermination of amount of child support. Osborne v. Osborne (Meigs 1992) 81 Ohio App.3d 666, 611 N.E.2d 1003.

To modify a child support agreement, the court must go through a two-step analysis: (1) determining if there has been a change in circumstances, and (2) if so, reanalyzing the amount of support necessary. Dudziak v. Dudziak (Cuyahoga 1992) 81 Ohio App.3d 361, 611 N.E.2d 337.

Incarceration of a child support obligor, standing alone, does not warrant a finding of change of circumstances; arrearages accrued during the incarceration of the obligor can be paid after release by way of a supplement to the original order. Cole v. Cole (Erie 1990) 70 Ohio App.3d 188, 590 N.E.2d 862.

Denial of modification of child support despite the incarceration of the obligor does not constitute cruel and unusual punishment as continuation of the support order does not constitute a fine, nor is the denial a violation of equal protection as a support order may remain in force on one who is voluntarily unemployed; incarceration is the result of a voluntary willful act. Cole v. Cole (Erie 1990) 70 Ohio App.3d 188, 590 N.E.2d 862.

The intentional act of a parent which results in incarceration is not voluntary, and a motion for termination or modification of support because of this change in circumstances is justifiable; a father's incarceration bears a close resemblance to a situation where an employer terminates an individual's employment. Peters v. Peters (Warren 1990) 69 Ohio App.3d 275, 590 N.E.2d 777, motion overruled 57 Ohio St.3d 711, 568 N.E.2d 697.

To modify child support, court must apply two-step analysis that determines whether change of circumstances exists and, if so, redetermines appropriate amount of child support under statutes and under child support guidelines. Miller v. Barker (Cuyahoga 1989) 64 Ohio App.3d 649, 582 N.E.2d 647.

A modification of an existing support order is justified where the moving party demonstrates a substantial change of circumstances which renders unreasonable an order which was once reasonable; evidence constituting a substantial change of circumstances justifing modification of an original support order includes the wife's fraudulent misrepresentation that the child she was carrying at the time of marriage was that of her husband and the results of blood test excluding the moving party as the father. Carson v. Carson (Brown 1989) 62 Ohio App.3d 670, 577 N.E.2d 391, motion overruled 46 Ohio St.3d 716, 546 N.E.2d 1334.

Evidence of the inflation rate and its effect on the financial resources of the parents and the needs of the child may be considered within the entire context of proving the existence of changes in circumstances necessary to justify modification of an existing support order. Bright v. Collins (Franklin 1982) 2 Ohio App.3d 421, 442 N.E.2d 822, 2 O.B.R. 514.

In order to justify an increase in an existing support order, there must be a finding supported by evidence that either (1) the amount necessary for child support is greater than it was at the time of the original order, or (2) a greater amount is reasonable in view of the parents' increased resources. Bright v. Collins (Franklin 1982) 2 Ohio App.3d 421, 442 N.E.2d 822, 2 O.B.R. 514.

The determination of child support must be achieved in two steps: first, the monetary amount necessary for the child's support in the standard of living he would have enjoyed had the marriage continued, including the child's educational needs and opportunities, must be established; then, the support obligation must be divided equitably between the parents in proportions reasonable under all circumstances, including the financial resources and needs of both parents. In many instances it would be unreasonable to require the parents to pay the full amount necessary to support the child in the standard of living he would have enjoyed had the marriage continued. Cheek v. Cheek (Franklin 1982) 2 Ohio App.3d 86, 440 N.E.2d 831, 2 O.B.R. 95.

To determine child support, the monetary amount necessary for the support of the children in a standard of living commensurate with the incomes of their parents should first be established; then the proportionate share of the child support so established that each parent equitably should bear should be set. In re Machmer (Franklin 1981) 2 Ohio App.3d 84, 440 N.E.2d 829, 2 O.B.R. 93.

Where the evidence shows the father's income has increased by 50 per cent in the past five years and the mother's income has increased by 250 per cent, the trial court erred by not finding a substantial change in circumstances. In re Machmer (Franklin 1981) 2 Ohio App.3d 84, 440 N.E.2d 829, 2 O.B.R. 93.

An order of a divorce court increasing the support payments required of a father for the declared purpose of "the support of the children" is a valid order, notwithstanding one of the children is a high school graduate, intends to acquire a college education, has had part-time employment and saves some of his earnings toward a college education. (Annotation from former RC 3105.21.) Ford v. Ford (Miami 1959) 109 Ohio App. 495, 167 N.E.2d 787, 12 O.O.2d 67.

A trial court did not abuse its discretion in an action to modify a child support order by finding a substantial change in circumstances justifying a ninety-two per cent increase in the father's obligation where his gross income has increased twenty-five per cent and his teenage daughter's financial needs have increased since the divorce due to her involvement in extra-curricular high-school activities, and her driving expenses and increased clothing costs over the previous three years. Holt v Troha, No. 96-CA-19, 1996 WL 430866 (2d Dist Ct App, Greene, 8-2-96).

A trial court abuses its discretion when it orders the suspension of a child support obligation for a period of eighteen months due to the residential parent's noncompliance with the visitation schedule. Roberts v Roberts, No. 95 APF01-33, 1995 WL 432612 (10th Dist Ct App, Franklin, 7-20-95).

Where the circumstances of a non-custodial parent have improved subsequent to the divorce, and child support costs have increased, fault should not be attributed to the custodial parent because she chose to take a lower paying job in order to be able to live with her parents. Pitcher v Pitcher, No. 83AP-530 (10th Dist Ct App, Franklin, 2-28-84).

A motion to terminate a child support decree will be denied where a man marries a pregnant woman with full knowledge of her condition, because the law conclusively presumes that he is father of the child, and even a failure to permit or admit blood tests to disprove paternity is not in error. Humphrey v Humphrey, No. C-800312 (1st Dist Ct App, Hamilton, 5-6-81).

Upon a motion to modify custody provisions of a divorce decree, a court is not limited to any particular line of inquiry, nor is it bound by strict legal rules governing the introduction of evidence, and, while hearsay evidence alone is insufficient to support a modification of a custody order, the court may properly consider reports of court-appointed social workers. (Annotation from former RC 3105.21.) Woodruff v. Woodruff (Ohio Com.Pl. 1965) 7 Ohio Misc. 87, 217 N.E.2d 264, 36 O.O.2d 165.

6. —Remarriage, modification of support

A trial court's consideration of the income of a divorced father's new wife for the purpose of determining the amount of income the divorced father could pay in child support did not deny the new wife due process by taking her income without affording her notice or an opportunity to be heard since as she is not required to make child support payments for her husband, either directly or indirectly, she has not suffered any loss of property; court's decision was based on the rational conclusion that the divorced father's marriage to a wage-earning spouse will provide him with additional money for child support that might otherwise be required for his personal household expenses. Esber v. Esber (Medina 1989) 63 Ohio App.3d 394, 579 N.E.2d 222.

In a modification of child support action, a trial court's determination of the amount of child support a divorced father should pay is reasonable and will not be disturbed based on a divorced father's argument that the court should not have considered all of his new wife's income, but only the amount of her income he actually received where the new wife's income was not the trial court's sole consideration but in addition, the court noted that the divorced father was trying to hide his true financial status. Esber v. Esber (Medina 1989) 63 Ohio App.3d 394, 579 N.E.2d 222.

Remarriage of the custodial parent may be considered in determining whether to reduce the supporting parent's obligation. Snyder v. Snyder (Cuyahoga 1985) 27 Ohio App.3d 1, 499 N.E.2d 320, 27 O.B.R. 1.

RC 3109.05(E) requires that a court, in determining the "financial resources and needs of the noncustodial parent," consider the father's remarriage and its resulting new obligations, together with the other factors delineated in RC 3109.05, before either granting or denying a change in a previous child support order. Martin v. Martin (Summit 1980) 69 Ohio App.2d 78, 430 N.E.2d 962, 23 O.O.3d 102.

The trial court did not abuse its discretion by its subsequent modification of a support order in favor of the plaintiff-wife, since the defendant-husband failed to show how the fact of his former wife's remarriage justified alteration in the reapportionment of child support obligations. Jeffries v Jeffries, No. 45634 (8th Dist Ct App, Cuyahoga, 5-19-83).

In an action appealing an order to increase child support, the court may consider the income of the father's present wife in determining his present ability to pay increased child support. Pearson v Pearson, No. 44880 (8th Dist Ct App, Cuyahoga, 12-23-82).

7. —Unemployment, modification of support

Income decrease resulting from obligor's voluntary unemployment or underemployment may be rejected by court as substantial change of circumstances for modification of child support. Woloch v. Foster (Miami 1994) 98 Ohio App.3d 806, 649 N.E.2d 918.

Reduction of child support obligor's income as result of voluntary choice does not necessarily demonstrate voluntary underemployment; test is not only whether change is voluntary, but also whether it was made with due regard to obligor's income-producing abilities and duty to provide for continuing needs of children. Woloch v. Foster (Miami 1994) 98 Ohio App.3d 806, 649 N.E.2d 918.

A parent has a duty dictated by public policy to take care of his children and a parent will not be totally excused from paying child support without any showing of good faith in making some payment; absent such a showing, failure to pay may be punished by imprisonment. Allen v. Allen (Columbiana 1988) 59 Ohio App.3d 54, 571 N.E.2d 139.

A court may reduce the amount of life insurance to be maintained for the benefit of a minor child where it is shown that the insured party has since been unemployed, as the unemployment of the payor/spouse constitutes a change of circumstances sufficient to allow the modification of child support provisions originally set forth in a separation agreement. Linehan v. Linehan (Cuyahoga 1986) 34 Ohio App.3d 124, 517 N.E.2d 967.

Voluntary termination of employment at the request of a parent's new spouse does not constitute an inability to support and therefore does not constitute a change of circumstances justifying the modification or termination of an earlier support order. Boltz v. Boltz (Summit 1986) 31 Ohio App.3d 214, 509 N.E.2d 1274, 31 O.B.R. 484.

Imputation of a $36,000 annual salary to a husband who is capable of working as an attorney is an abuse of discretion absent evidence that he is voluntarily underemployed and failed to look for work within his profession; whether defendant should be required to obtain work outside his area of expertise is a factual determination depending on whether it appears he will be unable to find work as an attorney, or whether temporary work outside his profession will interfere with looking for a job. English v Rubino, No. 68901, 1996 WL 157342 (8th Dist Ct App, Cuyahoga, 4-4-96).

It is an abuse of discretion to order that a noncustodial parent, without disabilities, who has been out of the employment market for twelve years, must pay child support whether or not employed. Zaller v Zaller, No. 10-035 (11th Dist Ct App, Lake, 6-29-84).

In a paternity action, an order to pay child support is properly made when trial court considers all factors listed under RC 3109.05 even though defendant is unemployed and supported totally by the federal aid to dependent children program. Goode v Wilburn, No. 1542 (4th Dist Ct App, Lawrence, 3-25-82).

Where the father has been laid off from his job, it is not an abuse of discretion to deny a motion for modification of child support because the fact that he would not be held in contempt to pay while he remains unemployed prevents unnecessary hardship on the appellant. Szymkowiak v Calabrese, No. L-81-008 (6th Dist Ct App, Lucas, 10-16-81).

A court may suspend support payment obligations when the father loses his job; the change in the financial condition of a parent may warrant a modification of the support decree. In re Dissolution of Marriage of Sandor, No. 10043 (9th Dist Ct App, Summit, 7-1-81).

When seeking a decrease in or termination of child support, a party fails to show that the loss of his job constituted a material change in circumstances where the period of unemployment was not more than a year and the party failed to show: (1) that he quit for good cause, (2) that he was laid off because of lack of work; or (3) that chances for new employment were highly unlikely. Smith v. Smith (Ohio Com.Pl. 1983) 12 Ohio Misc.2d 22, 467 N.E.2d 913, 12 O.B.R. 495.

8. —Benefits paid by third party, modification of support

Social security payments for a child's benefit must be considered in connection with child support payments ordered to be made by the parent whose retirement triggers the payments, but this does not justify crediting the entire monthly benefit amount to child support, nor is the determination of necessary child support unaffected by the receipt of the benefits; the proper method is to deduct all or part of the benefit amount from the guideline-determined necessary support based on the child's best interest and equity to both parents. McNeal v. Cofield (Franklin 1992) 78 Ohio App.3d 35, 603 N.E.2d 436.

A domestic relations court does not abuse its discretion in ordering a representative payee to place in trust for the benefit of a child the excess social security funds not needed for her current needs. Catlett v. Catlett (Clermont 1988) 55 Ohio App.3d 1, 561 N.E.2d 948, motion overruled 39 Ohio St.3d 730, 534 N.E.2d 357.

An Ohio domestic relations court may consider the propriety of a representative payee's expenditure of social security disability benefits received on behalf of a child. Catlett v. Catlett (Clermont 1988) 55 Ohio App.3d 1, 561 N.E.2d 948, motion overruled 39 Ohio St.3d 730, 534 N.E.2d 357.

Social security payments received on behalf of a minor child as a result of a parent's disability may be credited toward that parent's support obligation commencing at such time as the benefit is received and not exceeding the monthly support obligation set forth in the decree of divorce, and such credit is not a retroactive modification of a child support order, but is merely a credit against the arrearage. Pride v. Nolan (Hamilton 1987) 31 Ohio App.3d 261, 511 N.E.2d 408, 31 O.B.R. 546.

When an obligor's estate is bound to pay child support after the obligor's death, social security death benefits paid to the child should be credited against the support obligation. Gilford v. Wurster (Lorain 1983) 24 Ohio App.3d 77, 493 N.E.2d 258, 24 O.B.R. 145.

Social security benefits which a handicapped child receives under the supplemental security income program do not alter the noncustodial parent's obligation for his support nor constitute a change of circumstances warranting a modification of child support order. Oatley v. Oatley (Lucas 1977) 57 Ohio App.2d 226, 387 N.E.2d 245, 11 O.O.3d 260.

Social security payments received by a child for a parent's disability should be considered in calculating child support where the disabled parent is the obligee. Edmonds v Edmonds, No. 93CA1604, 1994 WL 514890 (4th Dist Ct App, Athens, 9-22-94).

The receipt by a child of supplemental security income neither alters the father's obligation nor constitutes a change of circumstances warranting a modification of support. Justice v Justice, No. CA-3250 (5th Dist Ct App, Licking, 6-24-87).

Where a minor child is receiving veterans administration benefits payable to the custodial parent for the support of such child due to the death of the child's stepfather, the noncustodial parent is not entitled to offset the amount of such benefits against the noncustodial parent's obligation to pay child support. Houser v Houser, No. CA-2887 (5th Dist Ct App, Licking, 9-24-82).

The trial court did not err when it declined to hold the appellee in contempt of court for child support arrearages as it chose to credit the social security benefits received on behalf of the minor children to the arrearage that accrued after the social security disability payments began; since the monies received exceeded the amount owed under the child support order, the trial court did not err in refusing to reduce the alleged arrearage to judgment. Yuhasz v Yuhasz, No. 42193 (8th Dist Ct App, Cuyahoga, 11-28-80).

Child support benefits received upon a parent's retirement may be credited against the parent's child support obligation because a credit for social security child support payments on retirement merely reflects the fact that the amounts due have been paid, and in no respect alters the obligation of the parent or the award to the children. Curnutte v Delarino, No. 2974 (9th Dist Ct App, Lorain, 9-3-80).

Where a father who has been ordered to make child support payments becomes totally and permanently disabled, and unconditioned Social Security payments for the benefit of minor children are paid to the divorced mother, the father is entitled to credit such payments by the government against his liability for child support under the divorce decree, but the father is entitled to credit, however, only up to the extent of his obligation for monthly payments of child support, but not exceeding it; the excess paid each month must be regarded under the divorce decree as a gratuity to the children. Loucks v Loucks, No. 18619 (6th Dist Ct App, Ottawa, 6-13-80).

Seven years of child support arrearages cannot be discharged in bankruptcy even where the husband ceased payment because the wife began receiving $465 each month for the children from her next husband's social security, and she then gave the children to her mother to raise yet only gave her mother $150 each month for doing so. In re Troxell (Bkrtcy.S.D.Ohio 1986) 67 B.R. 328.

9. —Guidelines, modification of support

Motion for modification of child support requires trial court to decide whether movant has demonstrated substantial change of circumstances; if substantial change of circumstances is demonstrated, court should make modification appropriate to statutory factors. Woloch v. Foster (Miami 1994) 98 Ohio App.3d 806, 649 N.E.2d 918.

Trial court which adopted shared-parenting plan granting residential status to father during school year and to mother during summer months could properly determine that strict application of child support guidelines would be inappropriate and accordingly deny child support to father under circumstances that parties stipulated that cost of children's parochial education would be shared in proportion to their relative incomes, both parties were required to carry medical insurance for children, and parties were required to share cost of clothing, school supplies and other ordinary expenses. Eickelberger v. Eickelberger (Butler 1994) 93 Ohio App.3d 221, 638 N.E.2d 130.

A trial court errs when it orders a divorced mother to pay child support in accordance with the child support guidelines based on her income from a prior year without the benefit of evidence of the individualized criteria set forth in RC 3109.05. Carter v. Carter (Clermont 1989) 62 Ohio App.3d 167, 574 N.E.2d 1154.

Although the child support guidelines set forth in CP Sup R 75 are intended to be used by a court to indicate the appropriate level of child support to be ordered, the court still retains broad discretion to deviate from the guidelines if it substantiates its decision by stating its findings of fact; consequently, a child support order which deviates more than forty per cent from the guidelines may not be an abuse of discretion where the child support obligor incurs increased necessary living expenses due to relocation and remarriage. Hurdelbrink v. Hurdelbrink (Lucas 1989) 45 Ohio App.3d 5, 544 N.E.2d 700, motion overruled 44 Ohio St.3d 715, 542 N.E.2d 1112.

Although fact that level of child support called for by application of new guidelines would exceed by ten-percent level of child support provided for in preguidelines dissolution decree would be sufficient to justify increase in child support, father was entitled to evidentiary hearing on issue because guidelines were merely guidelines and did not supplant statutory requirement that court consider all relevant factors in determining amount reasonable or necessary for child support. Wogoman v. Wogoman (Miami 1989) 44 Ohio App.3d 34, 541 N.E.2d 128.

The guidelines set forth in CP Sup R 75 are just that—guidelines; they are not intended to supplant the requirement in RC 3109.05 that courts must consider all relevant factors in determining the amount reasonable or necessary for child support, including the factors expressly stated in the statute. Wogoman v. Wogoman (Miami 1989) 44 Ohio App.3d 34, 541 N.E.2d 128.

In considering amount which is reasonable and necessary to support a child when a change of circumstances has occurred, needs of child must first be determined, guided by statutory factors, and determination of amount found to be necessary must be tempered by ascertaining the amount of child support which is reasonable in view of the overall financial picture of the parents and of the child. Zacek v. Zacek (Franklin 1983) 11 Ohio App.3d 91, 463 N.E.2d 391, 11 O.B.R. 143.

The child support guidelines are not a mathematical straitjacket, and the refusal of a domestic relations court to consider evidence supporting deviation from the guidelines constitutes an abuse of discretion. Oyer v Oyer, No. CA88-03-007 (12th Dist Ct App, Madison, 9-19-88).

On a motion to reduce a child support obligation, where the trial court finds a change of circumstances but orders only a minimal reduction in support not in conformity with the support guidelines, the modification order will be remanded for computation in accordance with the guidelines, absent findings of fact warranting the deviation. Kozloski v Kozloski, No. CA87-10-141 (12th Dist Ct App, Butler, 6-30-88).

The use of child support guidelines to obtain calculation of child support level, without prorating custodial parent's proportion and without considering other factors, is an abuse of discretion. Johnson-Wagner v Wagner, No. CA2304 (2d Dist Ct App, Clark, 6-29-87).

When using child support guidelines, court must compute formula correctly. Further, a prior agreement regarding child support adjustments cannot bind the court or the parties for future child support which continues to be subject to the court's jurisdiction. Gross v Gross, No. 49018 (8th Dist Ct App, Cuyahoga, 5-30-85).

The trial court erred in ordering child support modification based solely upon the cost of living index without actual evidence of increased costs of child care expenses. Nichols v Nichols, No. 992 (11th Dist Ct App, Geauga, 5-28-82).

Where a judgment for child support is tied to the consumer price index, and the father seeks credit for overpayment of his obligation, the trial court erred by allowing the credit because the child is the true party in interest and the child's needs have increased, and further, the father has the ability to pay the increased support. Firebaugh v Firebaugh, No. L-81-016 (6th Dist Ct App, Lucas, 8-28-81).

10. —Sole responsibility/waiver, modification of support

In an action seeking modification of a child support order, the initial determination is whether the order can (rather than should) be modified, requiring a finding of a substantial change in circumstances; in the unusual circumstance where one parent has expressly agreed to assume sole responsibility for the future support of the parties' children, if that parent later seeks to modify the order, the question is whether his circumstances have changed so much that he can no longer provide the entire support of the children; factors to be considered in such a determination include his assets which may be used to satisfy the support obligation, his income, his ability to earn extra income, and whether he can free up financial resources for the support of the children by limiting his own standard of living. Bahgat v. Bahgat (Franklin 1982) 8 Ohio App.3d 291, 456 N.E.2d 1239, 8 O.B.R. 386.

Where a noncustodial mother inherits sixty thousand dollars, the trial court does not abuse its discretion in denying the father's motion for child support, notwithstanding that the father was ordered to pay support before he gained custody, where the father does not show that he is unable to provide for his children's needs and where the court finds that the mother desires use of the money for her own purposes. Griffith v Griffith, No. CA-84-07-078 (12th Dist Ct App, Butler, 12-17-84).

In an action for arrearages, the trial court rightly denied the right to recover past obligations where the parties had mutually agreed to discharge the continuing obligation to pay support in exchange for a waiver of a continuing visitation right; in an action to reinstate both child support payments and visitation rights, the party seeking reinstatement will not be denied such based on the previous mutual agreement, as the child has an interest in future payments; therefore, such an agreement is binding on both parties as to past obligations, but is not binding on the court as to future payments. In re Dissolution of Marriage of Saltis v Frisby, No. 10345 (9th Dist Ct App, Summit, 1-27-82).

Trial court may order defendant-father to pay child support when plaintiff-mother's waiver of child support is conditioned upon defendant-father's refraining from exercising visitation and evidence that visitation was requested and exercised by defendant is shown. Botticello v Botticello, No. 7372 (2d Dist Ct App, Montgomery, 1-7-82).

Where the trial court enters a divorce order incorporating a separation agreement in which the plaintiff-mother waived all rights to child support in exchange for which the father waived his visitation rights, said order may be modified to establish a child support obligation without finding of a change of circumstances. Botticello v Botticello, No. 7372 (2d Dist Ct App, Montgomery, 1-7-82).

Where a mother waives her right to child support payments in exchange for father's foregoing of his visitation rights, the mother may not subsequently demand a lump sum judgment for the unpaid child support. Church v Church, No. 80X23 (4th Dist Ct App, Washington, 8-12-81).

An action for child support arrearages accumulated over sixteen years was rightly denied, in that the trial court found that the plaintiff-mother was estopped from asserting such claim in that she had waived the right to child support payments to avoid contact with the defendant-father, who had waived his visitation rights to avoid the child support payments. Long v Long, No. 9590 (9th Dist Ct App, Summit, 10-22-80).

A court may reinstate an order for support and visitation rights, though the parties to the divorce signed an affidavit stating their intent to terminate the support and relinquish certain visitation rights. Green v. Green (Ohio Com.Pl. 1972) 31 Ohio Misc. 69, 286 N.E.2d 328, 60 O.O.2d 216.

States retain power to require disabled veterans to use their federal benefits to support their children, as the benefits are not restricted to use for veterans' support; it follows that a veteran's refusal to pay can be punished in state court by contempt. (Ed. note: Tennessee law construed in light of federal constitution.) Rose v. Rose (U.S.Tenn. 1987) 107 S.Ct. 2029, 481 U.S. 619, 95 L.Ed.2d 599.

11. —Retroactivity, modification of support

Custodial parent was not entitled to retroactive child support, where no support order was issued at time he was awarded custody subsequent to divorce and no motion seeking support was pending. Hannas v. Hannas (Ohio App. 11 Dist. 1997) 123 Ohio App.3d 378, 704 N.E.2d 294.

Evidence that husband committed fraud in misrepresenting amount of his annual income justified making order for increased child support effective from date of dissolution decree, rather than date from filing of motion of increase; if support figure could be retroactively ordered only to date of wife's motion, husband would still retain benefits of fraud he perpetrated upon wife and the court between dates of dissolution decree and wife's motion, which anomalous result would not be sanctioned. Osborne v. Osborne (Meigs 1992) 81 Ohio App.3d 666, 611 N.E.2d 1003.

Absent some special circumstance, an order of a trial court modifying child support should be retroactive to the date such modification was first requested; the effective date of modification must coincide with some significant event in the litigation, and an arbitrary date may not be employed. State, ex rel. Draiss, v. Draiss (Medina 1990) 70 Ohio App.3d 418, 591 N.E.2d 354.

A trial court does not abuse its discretion by ordering an increase in child support to be retroactive to the date the motion for modification was filed, since disposition of such motions often takes a substantial length of time. Murphy v. Murphy (Franklin 1984) 13 Ohio App.3d 388, 469 N.E.2d 564, 13 O.B.R. 471.

When a father who has custody of a child and a court-ordered obligation of support transfers the child to the custody of its mother, the obligation of support remains, so that the mother's motion for support, made after a lapse of time since the transfer, is not to be denied as a motion for a retroactive order or modification. Royse v. Royse (Ohio Com.Pl. 1984) 23 Ohio Misc.2d 5, 491 N.E.2d 397, 23 O.B.R. 113.

A trial court has jurisdiction to modify a support order as to future installments, whether or not the right is reserved in the decree; but it has no such jurisdiction to modify unpaid installment support payments which have accrued if the child for whose benefit support was awarded was living and not emancipated at the time of the accrual, unless the right to retrospective modification was specifically reserved in the decree. Wedebrook v. Wedebrook (Ohio Com.Pl. 1977) 51 Ohio Misc. 81, 367 N.E.2d 937, 5 O.O.3d 342.

12. —Change in parental rights and responsibilities, modification of support

Former husband's court-ordered child support obligation for daughter who was initially placed in custody of his former wife did not terminate merely because custody of daughter was transferred to husband. Lytle v. Lytle (Ohio App. 10 Dist. 1998) 130 Ohio App.3d 697, 720 N.E.2d 1007.

When support is paid in accordance with child support order, courts are reluctant to order a refund to obligor because of facts and circumstances learned after support has been paid; to avoid that prospect, support orders should require obligee to notify obligor of any change in circumstances underlying the support order. Swanson v. Swanson (Greene 1996) 109 Ohio App.3d 231, 671 N.E.2d 1333.

Trial court could not order ex-husband to visit his multihandicapped child as a form of child support; determination of child support obligation was governed by comprehensive statutory scheme that did not provide for visitation as a form of support. Hamilton v. Hamilton (Lucas 1995) 107 Ohio App.3d 132, 667 N.E.2d 1256, appeal not allowed 75 Ohio St.3d 1425, 662 N.E.2d 27.

Reduction in former husband's income as result of voluntary resignation to start his own company was not shown to be substantial change of circumstances and, therefore, did not entitle former husband to modification of child support; trial court could conclude that former husband failed to give adequate weight to duty to support children. Woloch v. Foster (Miami 1994) 98 Ohio App.3d 806, 649 N.E.2d 918.

Child who was ordered out of his mother's home and then enrolled in Federal Job Corps program was not yet emancipated, for purposes of determining whether former husband's child support obligation continued; mother continued to provide child with money and assistance, child went to live with his father and then his uncle upon leaving his mother's home, and mother provided child with money for long-distance phone calls when child was in program, and paid for his bus ticket when he left program. In re Owens (Clark 1994) 96 Ohio App.3d 429, 645 N.E.2d 130.

Trial court's adding on remand only $500 to $2,200 sustenance alimony award already determined by Court of Appeals to be inadequate was abuse of discretion, where trial court, on remand, adopted Court of Appeals' findings and determined wife's monthly expenses to be approximately $4,000; consideration of award to wife of portion of bonus to which husband was entitled through his employment, which was more in nature of division of property, did not render alimony award reasonable. Kaechele v. Kaechele (Franklin 1992) 83 Ohio App.3d 468, 615 N.E.2d 273.

Where a consent order is entered which changes the custody of minor children but such change never takes place, the trial court, in subsequently considering child support, has jurisdiction to award a lesser amount to the de facto custodial parent other than that set forth in a prior order. Ollangg v. Ollangg (Franklin 1979) 64 Ohio App.2d 17, 410 N.E.2d 789, 18 O.O.3d 11.

Where the custodial parent does not provide child support and the child resides with the noncustodial parent who provides full support in kind while the child attends high school, the custodial parent is not entitled to support arrearage for such time as full support is provided by the noncustodial parent; since the noncustodial parent is providing child support, the amount he was ordered to pay should be credited to the arrearage for that time. Peterson v Hunt, No. 1-98-25, 1998 WL 720690 (3d Dist Ct App, Allen, 10-15-98).

A child who temporarily leaves the home of a parent will not be considered emancipated for child support purposes if the child remains dependant on a parent for care and attends high school on a full-time basis. Siefker v Siefker, No. 12-97-09, 1997 WL 658995 (3d Dist Ct App, Putnam, 10-23-97).

False testimony of an adverse party in a divorce proceeding, that the husband was the father of a child fourteen years before, does not warrant a finding of fraud upon the court; this is intrinsic fraud, time-barred by the one-year statute of limitations of Civ 60(B)(3). Still v Still, No. 95CA15, 1996 WL 362259 (4th Cist Ct App, Gallia, 6-25-96).

Denial of an obligor's motion to terminate his child support obligation for his nineteen-year-old severely handicapped child is error where the court fails to recognize the child's ability to support himself from a trust fund in excess of $200,000 received as settlement of a medical malpractice action that occurred after the child's parents divorced. Mitchell v Mitchell, No. E-93-77, 1994 WL 518183 (6th Dist Ct App, Erie, 9-23-94).

A child support order will not be amended retroactively on the ground that minor children who lived with their mother at the time of a joint custody order took up residence with their father less than a month thereafter, where it is found that the order for payment of child support to the mother was made in contemplation of the children living with the father. Palladino v Palladino, No. 48378 (8th Dist Ct App, Cuyahoga, 12-27-84).

13. —Dependency tax exemptions, modification of support

Dependency exemption provided by Internal Revenue Code may be awarded to noncustodial parent when that allocation would produce net tax savings for parents, thereby furthering best interest of child. Singer v. Dickinson (Ohio 1992) 63 Ohio St.3d 408, 588 N.E.2d 806.

As part of the division of marital property in a divorce proceeding, a domestic relations court may award the dependency exemption permitted in 26 USC 151, to the noncustodial parent. Such an order does not conflict with 26 USC 152, nor with the Sixteenth Amendment to the US Constitution. Hughes v. Hughes (Ohio 1988) 35 Ohio St.3d 165, 518 N.E.2d 1213, certiorari denied 109 S.Ct. 124, 488 U.S. 846, 102 L.Ed.2d 97.

When determining whether awarding dependency tax exemption to nonresidential parent would produce a net tax savings for the parents, a trial court should review all pertinent factors, including the parents' gross incomes, the exemptions and deductions to which the parents are otherwise entitled, and the relevant federal, state and local income tax rates. Corple v. Corple (Ohio App. 7 Dist. 1997) 123 Ohio App.3d 31, 702 N.E.2d 1234.

Trial court abused its discretion in divorce proceeding by awarding husband, who was nonresidential parent, the dependency tax exemption for parties' minor child, where record did not indicate that trial court found net tax savings to parties or that best interest of child was furthered in awarding exemption to husband. Corple v. Corple (Ohio App. 7 Dist. 1997) 123 Ohio App.3d 31, 702 N.E.2d 1234.

Husband's challenge to trial court's failure to award him income tax exemptions for minor children of marriage in judgment of divorce was waived by husband's failure to object to referee's report on this issue. Shaffer v. Shaffer (Crawford 1996) 109 Ohio App.3d 205, 671 N.E.2d 1317.

Trial court did not err in splitting children's tax exemptions between father and mother even though father, pursuant to shared-parenting plan, was residential parent of children for nine months of year. Eickelberger v. Eickelberger (Butler 1994) 93 Ohio App.3d 221, 638 N.E.2d 130.

As alternative to contempt to enforce award of dependency tax exemption, court may consider that exemption when considering parents' financial resources; where noncustodial parent would experience greater tax benefit from exemption he should generally receive it, and when custodial parent refuses to surrender exemption at order of court, noncustodial parent's support obligation may be reduced accordingly. Esber v. Esber (Medina 1989) 63 Ohio App.3d 394, 579 N.E.2d 222.

Since a trial court may properly award the dependency exemption to either parent in the best interest of the child, even where the parents were never married, the dependency exemption is a matter concerning the duty of support pursuant to RC 3109.05, and not the division of property, and accordingly, the trial court retains jurisdiction over the award of this exemption during the minority of the child. Esber v. Esber (Medina 1989) 63 Ohio App.3d 394, 579 N.E.2d 222.

In an action for the modification of child support, a trial court errs in ruling that it lacks jurisdiction to allocate the child dependency tax exemption and therefore, on remand, the court must consider the tax exemption issue and determine whether the exemption benefits the children best in the hands of their custodial mother or their noncustodial father and then whether any increase or decrease in support is necessary. Esber v. Esber (Medina 1989) 63 Ohio App.3d 394, 579 N.E.2d 222.

Although a contempt of court action in a state court could be used to force an unwilling parent to part with his tax exemption when the court considers that an award of the tax exemption to the other parent would be in the best interest of the child, as an alternative solution the court may consider the tax exemption when considering the financial resources of the parents pursuant to RC 3109.05 and where the noncustodial parent would experience the greater tax benefit from the exemption, he should generally receive the exemption since the additional disposable income generated can be considered for additional child support, and when the custodial parent refuses to surrender the exemption at the order of the court, the court may reduce the noncustodial parent's support obligation accordingly. Esber v. Esber (Medina 1989) 63 Ohio App.3d 394, 579 N.E.2d 222.

Where there was no provision in divorce decree concerning which parent was entitled to claim dependency exemptions for minor children, trial court could consider whether noncustodial parent's inability to claim dependency exemption would result in a substantial reduction in income so as to warrant reduction of child support obligation. Mettler v. Mettler (Ross 1988) 61 Ohio App.3d 14, 572 N.E.2d 127.

The tax exemption for dependent children awarded to the custodial parent as part of the division of property may not be subsequently modified by a court. Mettler v. Mettler (Ross 1988) 61 Ohio App.3d 14, 572 N.E.2d 127.

Trial court abused its discretion by ordering that tax dependency exemption alternate between the custodial parent and non-residential parent as the record and transcript did not reveal any evidence regarding any tax savings that would result from awarding the tax dependency exemption to one parent or the other. Pentzer v Pentzer, No. CA99-09-026, 2000 WL 190019 (12th Dist Ct App, Fayette, 2-14-00).

An award of the dependency tax exemption to the noncustodial parent which appears in the property division section of the divorce decree is not properly linked to the amount of the child support obligation, nor is it to be modified upon modification of child support. Kozloski v Kozloski, No. CA87-10-141 (12th Dist Ct App, Butler, 6-30-88).

An award of the dependency tax exemption to a wife who does not have custody is error where the parents have comparable incomes in the same tax bracket. Wolfangel v Wolfangel, No. 16868, 1995 WL 312697 (9th Dist Ct App, Summit, 5-24-95).

Tax exemptions for children are "marital property," notwithstanding the fact that the separation agreement incorporated within the dissolution decree treats the exemptions as a component of child support; therefore, a court lacks subject matter jurisdiction to subsequently modify the award of the exemptions. In re Lee (Ohio Com.Pl. 1989) 58 Ohio Misc.2d 4, 567 N.E.2d 1350.

The child support guidelines, C P Sup R 75, do not address the issue of tax exemptions; accordingly, there is no provision for taking into account the tax exemptions and the tax ramifications of child support in considering at what level to place child support. (Annotation from former C P Sup R 75.) In re Lee (Ohio Com.Pl. 1989) 58 Ohio Misc.2d 4, 567 N.E.2d 1350.

Where a taxpayer's former wife is the lessee of real estate and pays her ex-husband a fixed rental, she is entitled to be credited with the lodging support for the minor children in determining whether the wife or husband has provided more than one-half support of the children for purposes of federal income tax dependency exemptions, since she has the right to use and possession of the property. Klofta v. U. S. (N.D.Ohio 1970) 333 F.Supp. 781, 64 O.O.2d 291.

14. Support beyond majority; college expenses

A domestic relations court retains jurisdiction over parties in a divorce, dissolution, or separation proceeding to continue or to modify support payments for a mentally or physically disabled child, who was so disabled before he or she attained the statutory age of majority, as if the child were still an infant. Castle v. Castle (Ohio 1984) 15 Ohio St.3d 279, 473 N.E.2d 803, 15 O.B.R. 413.

The statutory change in the age of majority can have no application to the subject decretal support obligations because such change, in and of itself, has no effect on pre-1974 support decrees. Nokes v. Nokes (Ohio 1976) 47 Ohio St.2d 1, 351 N.E.2d 174, 1 O.O.3d 1.

In a divorce action, it is not abuse of discretion as a matter of law for the trial court, having jurisdiction of the parties, to order payments by the father for the college education of minor children electing to matriculate in an accredited college. Mitchell v. Mitchell (Ohio 1960) 170 Ohio St. 507, 166 N.E.2d 396, 11 O.O.2d 281.

Where as part of a valid agreement, a husband agrees to provide a college education for his children and further agrees to keep in effect insurance policies on his life in which such children are beneficiaries, and where such agreement is incorporated in a decree divorcing the husband from his wife, such decree becomes binding on the husband even though the performance required by the decree may extend beyond the minority of the children. (Annotation from former RC 3105.20.) Robrock v. Robrock (Ohio 1958) 167 Ohio St. 479, 150 N.E.2d 421, 5 O.O.2d 165.

Court may order support for child until it attains majority. Josh v. Josh (Ohio 1929) 120 Ohio St. 151, 165 N.E. 717.

Withdrawal from high school by child who was in custody of former husband on day child turned 18 years of age terminated wife's duty to pay child support, and divested trial court of jurisdiction to order wife to pay child support or to modify child support agreement; child's subsequent enrollment in vocational school did not resurrect order, as obligation continues after age 18 only if child continuously attends high school. Gleason v. Gleason (Ohio App. 4 Dist. 1998) 129 Ohio App.3d 563, 718 N.E.2d 512.

Voluntary contributions by child support obligor to education of adult children are not an appropriate consideration in calculation of child support obligations, and do not entitle obligor to reduction in child support obligations. State ex rel. Scioto County Child Support Enforcement Agency v.Gardner (Scioto 1996) 113 Ohio App.3d 46, 680 N.E.2d 221.

Party seeking relief from child support order bears burden of proving that child is emancipated. Powell v. Powell (Athens 1996) 111 Ohio App.3d 418, 676 N.E.2d 556.

Whether child is emancipated, so as to relieve parent from obligation of support, depends upon particular facts and circumstances of each individual case. Powell v. Powell (Athens 1996) 111 Ohio App.3d 418, 676 N.E.2d 556.

In determining whether child is emancipated for child support purposes, unique facts and circumstances of each case must be evaluated. Powell v. Powell (Athens 1996) 111 Ohio App.3d 418, 676 N.E.2d 556.

Father's obligation to pay child support, under dissolution decree, continued until daughter completed her high school education, even though she already had attained age of majority. Swanson v. Swanson (Greene 1996) 109 Ohio App.3d 231, 671 N.E.2d 1333.

Trial court did not abuse its discretion in requiring father to pay child support under dissolution decree until adult child graduated from high school, even though child could have graduated from high school a year earlier than she did, where additional year of high school prepared child for job. Swanson v. Swanson (Greene 1996) 109 Ohio App.3d 231, 671 N.E.2d 1333.

Court is generally without jurisdiction to order a parent to support a child once that child reaches age of majority. Troha v. Troha (Greene 1995) 105 Ohio App.3d 327, 663 N.E.2d 1319.

Parents generally have no duty under Ohio law to provide support, including payment for college expenses, to emancipated children. Troha v. Troha (Greene 1995) 105 Ohio App.3d 327, 663 N.E.2d 1319.

Courts are generally without jurisdiction to order parents to support children who have attained age of majority except where parties have entered into separation agreement that provides their child with support beyond age of majority and agreement is incorporated into divorce or dissolution decree. Tapp v. Tapp (Montgomery 1995) 105 Ohio App.3d 159, 663 N.E.2d 944, dismissed, appeal not allowed 74 Ohio St.3d 1418, 655 N.E.2d 738.

Court of Common Pleas had proper jurisdiction to enforce a separation agreement pursuant to which husband agreed to pay for daughter's college education. Tapp v. Tapp (Montgomery 1995) 105 Ohio App.3d 159, 663 N.E.2d 944, dismissed, appeal not allowed 74 Ohio St.3d 1418, 655 N.E.2d 738.

Ex-husband unreasonably withheld approval of his daughter's choice of college under separation agreement, incorporated into dissolution decree, rendering ex-husband responsible for payment of all expenses incurred by or for daughter's college education in four-year undergraduate program, where only college program he approved was that of a community college which only provided a two-year program. Tapp v. Tapp (Montgomery 1995) 105 Ohio App.3d 159, 663 N.E.2d 944, dismissed, appeal not allowed 74 Ohio St.3d 1418, 655 N.E.2d 738.

Trial court lacked jurisdiction to order former husband to maintain trust fund for child's college education after former husband won lottery, even though former husband had voluntarily established trust fund; there was no separation agreement or any other enforceable agreement by which former husband had agreed to fund trust for child's college education. Pratt v. McCullough (Warren 1995) 100 Ohio App.3d 479, 654 N.E.2d 372, appeal not allowed 72 Ohio St.3d 1540, 650 N.E.2d 481.

Parent's obligations to pay medical expenses of child ceases at time child obtains age of majority and is not enrolled fulltime in accredited high school unless separation agreement incorporated into decree of divorce or dissolution provides otherwise. Rohrbacher v. Rohrbacher (Lucas 1992) 83 Ohio App.3d 569, 615 N.E.2d 338.

Parents are obligated to support a minor child until the child reaches the age of majority and is legally emancipated, and where a trial court directs that a father pay child support for his minor daughter until she turns eighteen even though a separation agreement provision requires support until she becomes emancipated or graduates from high school, whichever comes first, and the daughter graduates one month before her eighteenth birthday, the trial court's order does not modify the child support absent a showing of a change of circumstances but rather interprets the separation agreement language to mean that "or graduates from high school" has the same definition as "age of majority," which requires support until the minor child's eighteenth birthday. Dudziak v. Dudziak (Cuyahoga 1992) 81 Ohio App.3d 361, 611 N.E.2d 337.

Where a mother seeks to extend child support payments for the month between a child's high school graduation and her eighteenth birthday, at which time the child becomes emancipated, a motion for relief is unnecessary where the court has continuing jurisdiction and the separation agreement with its child support provision is incorporated into the dissolution agreement and provides for support until the child graduates high school or becomes emancipated, whichever occurs first; the trial court does not have to modify the child support portion of the separation agreement but need only interpret it in light of case law providing for parental obligation of support until the age of majority. Dudziak v. Dudziak (Cuyahoga 1992) 81 Ohio App.3d 361, 611 N.E.2d 337.

A father is obligated to support a child until she reaches majority at age eighteen, at which time she becomes legally emancipated despite a separation agreement stating that the father's support would end when the child graduated high school or became emancipated, whichever came first, where the child graduates one month before her eighteenth birthday. Dudziak v. Dudziak (Cuyahoga 1992) 81 Ohio App.3d 361, 611 N.E.2d 337.

A child who enters the United States coast guard academy on a full scholarship with stipend for the pursuit of a baccalaureate is a full-time college student for the purposes of a support order provision which requires child support payments to continue during college study. Howard v. Howard (Clermont 1992) 80 Ohio App.3d 832, 610 N.E.2d 1152.

Domestic relations court had authority to give effect to former husband's agreement which was incorporated in divorce decree and required him to support incompetent adult child, although domestic relations court never had jurisdiction over child. O'Connor v. O'Connor (Franklin 1991) 71 Ohio App.3d 541, 594 N.E.2d 1081, motion overruled 62 Ohio St.3d 1409, 577 N.E.2d 362.

A domestic relations court may enforce the provisions of an agreement incorporated to a divorce decree that a parent provide financial support for an incompetent adult child, notwithstanding the fact that the child is an adult at the time the decree is issued and may utilize the child support guidelines to determine the appropriate amount of support. O'Connor v. O'Connor (Franklin 1991) 71 Ohio App.3d 541, 594 N.E.2d 1081, motion overruled 62 Ohio St.3d 1409, 577 N.E.2d 362.

While domestic relations court in divorce, dissolution, legal separation or child support proceeding has authority to order either or both parents to aid or support their children, the court does not have power to make decree regarding support of minor children beyond date when child reaches age of majority. Crigger v. Crigger (Franklin 1991) 71 Ohio App.3d 410, 594 N.E.2d 67.

A trial court's broad interpretation of the word "tuition" as used in a parties' separation agreement to include the undergraduate fee and the general fee listed on a university fee statement for purposes of the amount of tuition an ex-husband is required to pay as part of his child support is not unreasonable, arbitrary, or unconscionable; the general fee is a fee assessed against all students for admission into college and is not an optional fee. Baker v. Baker (Wood 1990) 68 Ohio App.3d 402, 588 N.E.2d 944.

A trial court did not abuse its discretion in limiting college costs paid by a former husband to those specific items mentioned in the separation agreement; room and board is not included in an obligation to pay "costs of such items as tuition, fees, and books." Uram v. Uram (Summit 1989) 65 Ohio App.3d 96, 582 N.E.2d 1060.

A divorced father's support obligations self-terminate when his child turns eighteen, even though the child has not yet graduated from high school, where the divorce decree incorporating the parties' separation agreement provides for support to continue during the child's minority and no lawful motion to continue support until graduation from high school has been made; therefore, a trial court properly denies the father's motion to terminate his child support obligations, since such motion in reality constitutes a request for an advisory opinion. Behrisch v. Behrisch (Summit 1989) 62 Ohio App.3d 164, 574 N.E.2d 1152.

Age of majority in effect at time of entry of dissolution decree that contained child support obligation controlled determination of child's emancipation based on attainment of age of majority. Bauer v. Bauer (Franklin 1989) 57 Ohio App.3d 24, 566 N.E.2d 185.

Father had no duty to provide continued support for his epileptic son, after son graduated from high school; there was evidence that extent of disability did not prevent son from being employable, and he in fact held a part-time job. Cooksey v. Cooksey (Erie 1988) 55 Ohio App.3d 135, 562 N.E.2d 934.

A divorce decree requiring one parent to pay a child's tuition expenses at a designated university may reasonably be interpreted to require payment of an equivalent amount toward tuition costs of another university which the child and custodial parent choose. Evans v. Brown (Franklin 1985) 23 Ohio App.3d 97, 491 N.E.2d 384, 23 O.B.R. 163.

The court that granted a divorce has no subject matter jurisdiction to provide for the support of a child of the divorced parties once the child reaches the age of majority. Maphet v. Heiselman (Clermont 1984) 13 Ohio App.3d 278, 469 N.E.2d 92, 13 O.B.R. 343.

Question of when a child is emancipated so as to relieve a parent from the obligation of support depends upon particular facts and circumstances of each case. Price v. Price (Darke 1983) 12 Ohio App.3d 42, 465 N.E.2d 922, 12 O.B.R. 129.

Where the children of a marriage have reached the age of majority, the trial court cannot enforce an existing child support order by exercising its contempt power; however, the child support obligee may collect any support arrearage by garnishment, attachment, or execution on the lump sum judgments previously granted. Thompson v. Albers (Clermont 1981) 1 Ohio App.3d 139, 439 N.E.2d 955, 1 O.B.R. 446.

RC 3105.10 clothes courts with jurisdiction to incorporate into a court order an agreement to support a child of the parties beyond the age of that child's majority, and such an order may be enforced by contempt proceedings. Bugay v. Bugay (Summit 1977) 53 Ohio App.2d 285, 373 N.E.2d 1263, 7 O.O.3d 336.

Where the age of legal majority is reduced by the legislature, a party to a divorce settlement, under which he is bound to support minor children until they become emancipated, is relieved of any obligation beyond that age designated by the new act. Allison v. Allison (Warren 1975) 44 Ohio App.2d 230, 337 N.E.2d 666, 73 O.O.2d 243.

An order of a divorce court increasing the support payments required of a father for the declared purpose of "the support of the children" is a valid order, notwithstanding one of the children is a high school graduate, intends to acquire a college education, has had part-time employment and saves some of his earnings toward a college education. (Annotation from former RC 3105.21.) Ford v. Ford (Miami 1959) 109 Ohio App. 495, 167 N.E.2d 787, 12 O.O.2d 67.

An eighteen-year-old student who withdraws from high school and enrolls in the Job Corps where he intends to complete his final year of high school is not emancipated because his mother's continued financial support for clothes, tools and personal items demonstrates that she had not relinquished parental control consistent with her son's emancipation. Johnson v Johnson, No. 17858, 1999 WL 1206690 (2d Dist Ct App, Montgomery, 12-17-99).

A child who quits school when he turns eighteen in March and leaves home in June is emancipated notwithstanding emotional problems and financial assistance from his mother in paying his bills and a court's decision to terminate support for the period after the child quits school and before he leaves home is not an abuse of discretion. Palmer v Palmer, No. 16986, 1999 WL 22747 (2d Dist Ct App, Montgomery, 1-22-99).

A child support obligation is in effect as long as a child who is eighteen is attending high-school and completes his graduation requirements six weeks after full-time high-school has let out for the summer. O'Brien v O'Brien, No. CA96-11-101, 1997 WL 208133 (12th Dist Ct App, Clermont, 4-28-97).

A child support obligation that remains in effect beyond a child's eighteenth birthday until graduation from high school does not apply to the child's attendance at a community college for attainment of college credits towards a high school diploma. Roy v Fitzgerald, No. 96 CA 43, 1997 WL 219172 (5th Dist Ct App, Guernsey, 3-27-97).

Parents can agree to provide post-divorce support for emancipated children by way of an annuity to provide for the children's college education. Strong v Strong, No. L-96-044, 1997 WL 89105 (6th Dist Ct App, Lucas, 2-28-97).

A trial court's extension of support beyond a child's eighteenth birthday violates the terms of the couple's 1978 divorce agreement and reliance on present day RC 3109.05(E) is misplaced as that section's language, requiring support issued pursuant to this section to continue past the age of majority so long as the child is in high school, was enacted years after the divorce decree was issued and is not controlling. Wendling v Wendling, No. 68837, 1996 WL 50825 (8th Dist Ct App, Cuyahoga, 2-8-96).

Judgment for payment of a child's college expenses provided for in a separation agreement should not be considered child support and collection thereof should not be made through the Child Support Enforcement Agency. Chester v Baker, No. 95-CA-7, 1995 WL 497602 (5th Dist Ct App, Licking, 8-10-95).

An obligor is not entitled to a credit towards child support where a child receives a full college tuition scholarship and the separation agreement that provides child support of $225 per month per child and continues as to that child until graduation from college is a binding contract, and the parties did not contemplate and provide in the agreement for one of the children receiving a scholarship. Urban v Spriestersbach, No. 13-94-26, 1995 WL 81975 (3d Dist Ct App, 2-28-95).

A divorce decree that contains a provision that the husband has the college education obligation for the parties' child providing he is financially able to pay it fails to specify an objective standard to be used to determine when the husband is "financially able" and is vague and unenforceable. Hartlieb v Hartlieb, No. 64635, 1994 WL 30427 (8th Dist Ct App, Cuyahoga, 2-3-94).

The trial court may reinstate support obligations including medical expenses for a handicapped child after prior termination of the order. Bragg v Gorby, No. 86-C-37 (7th Dist Ct App, Columbiana, 6-30-87).

Where a child was injured in an auto accident after he was eighteen, but before graduation, after completing all the requirements for graduation, the duty to support does not continue. Blandon v Blandon, No. CA86-12-173 (12th Dist Ct App, Butler, 6-29-87).

Where a separation agreement provides that the father shall pay the cost of a child's college education, and the agreement is silent as to whether that education must be at a public or private institution, the father is required to pay the full cost of the child's college education at the private institution attended. Rand v Rand, No. 47712 (8th Dist Ct App, Cuyahoga, 6-28-84), affirmed by 18 OS(3d) 356, 18 OBR 415, 481 NE(2d) 609 (1985).

In accordance with public policy and the statutory grant of broad equitable powers, a domestic relations court may order a noncustodial parent to continue child support payments and medical insurance coverage for a child who has reached majority, where the child is severely handicapped and has been under the jurisdiction of the domestic relations division since the age of six or seven. Mullanney v Mullanney, No. C-820944 (1st Dist Ct App, Hamilton, 1-4-84).

Where an unrepresented husband/father signed an ambiguous separation agreement which contractually obligated him to pay room and board for his emancipated children, such agreement's ambiguity shall be resolved in favor of the father as being limited to the obligation to pay for educationally related expenses, such as dormitory room and board rather than room and board at the wife's home, as such intention was demonstrated by the limiting word "educational" in the separation agreement. In re Fugazzi, No. 82AP-174 and 82AP-184 (10th Dist Ct App, Franklin, 6-2-83).

Absent specific agreement to pay child support beyond majority in the separation agreement, the term "cost of higher education" means those special costs a student incurs beyond living expenses and cannot include room and board. Frazier v Frazier, No. 2919 (5th Dist Ct App, Licking, 2-14-83).

As part of a separation agreement, the parties may contract for their children to receive education at a parochial school with tuition payment to be made by a designated party. Braun v Braun, No. L-80-156 (6th Dist Ct App, Lucas, 2-20-81).

Determination of the age at which a person becomes an adult for the purpose of enforcing the provisions of the reciprocal support act, depends upon the state in which the child is living and the state in which the father is living, and not in the state in which the original divorce was granted. Burney v. Vance (Ohio Com.Pl. 1969) 17 Ohio Misc. 307, 246 N.E.2d 371, 46 O.O.2d 427.

A father is primarily responsible for the support of his minor children, and that support continues under the law of Ohio until the child is twenty-one years of age or is otherwise emancipated. Burney v. Vance (Ohio Com.Pl. 1969) 17 Ohio Misc. 307, 246 N.E.2d 371, 46 O.O.2d 427.

15. Agreement of the parties

Parties to separation agreement may not abrogate right of minor child of marriage to be supported by either parent. In re Dissolution of Marriage of Lazor (Ohio 1991) 59 Ohio St.3d 201, 572 N.E.2d 66.

The parties to a separation agreement may not abrogate the right of a minor child of the marriage to be supported by either parent; prior to the effective date of RC 3113.215 to 3113.218, the parties could, however, agree to allocate the support obligation between themselves in a manner analogous to an indemnity agreement. In re Dissolution of Marriage of Lazor (Ohio 1991) 59 Ohio St.3d 201, 572 N.E.2d 66.

The court must be satisfied that the child support provision in a separation agreement represents compliance with the husband's duty of support. Scholler v. Scholler (Ohio 1984) 10 Ohio St.3d 98, 462 N.E.2d 158, 10 O.B.R. 426.

The full equity powers and jurisdiction lodged in the court of common pleas by RC 3105.21 extend to orders made for the disposition, care, maintenance and support of minor children, so that in a divorce action, the court in making an order for the disposition, care, maintenance and support of minor children of the parties, may incorporate in its decree the terms of an agreement entered into between such parties that the husband support a child past the age of majority even though the court, in the absence of an agreement of the parties, would not have the power to make the resultant decree. Robrock v. Robrock (Ohio 1958) 167 Ohio St. 479, 150 N.E.2d 421, 5 O.O.2d 165.

Lesbian mother's agreement, to accept full financial responsibility for children in exchange for father impregnating mother, was circumstance "which ought reasonably to relieve father" of child support obligation between date of birth and date amicable and cooperative parenting arrangement broke down and, thus, trial court's refusal to order child support to commence at birth was not an abuse of discretion. Myers v. Moschella (Hamilton 1996) 112 Ohio App.3d 75, 677 N.E.2d 1243.

Children remained "third-party beneficiaries" of separation agreement which created benefits for them, even after agreement was merged into divorce decree; merger did not alter agreement, but rather, only affected enforcement and ability to alter agreement. Wolfinger v. Ocke (Shelby 1991) 72 Ohio App.3d 193, 594 N.E.2d 139.

A domestic relations court may enforce the provisions of an agreement incorporated to a divorce decree that a parent provide financial support for an incompetent adult child, notwithstanding the fact that the child is an adult at the time the decree is issued and may utilize the child support guidelines to determine the appropriate amount of support. O'Connor v. O'Connor (Franklin 1991) 71 Ohio App.3d 541, 594 N.E.2d 1081, motion overruled 62 Ohio St.3d 1409, 577 N.E.2d 362.

A child's right to insurance policy proceeds is vested by a separation agreement providing that a husband "shall keep or cause to be kept" a life insurance policy with his child as "primary, irrevocable beneficiary"; this right is enforceable in equity and cannot be defeated by the husband's failure to maintain the policy as required. Thomas v. Studley (Cuyahoga 1989) 59 Ohio App.3d 76, 571 N.E.2d 454.

Where parents of a child continue their disputes and animosity toward each other after the dissolution of their marriage and such conflict causes their child psychological problems, the parents' agreement to share medical expenses of the child includes the costs of the child's psychological treatment. Sterbling v. Sterbling (Clermont 1987) 35 Ohio App.3d 68, 519 N.E.2d 673.

A parent may agree to extend his obligation to support a child beyond the parent's death, in which case the support obligation becomes a charge, against the estate; language in the agreement that it is binding on the parties' estates, heirs, executors, and administrators is sufficient to bind the estate. Gilford v. Wurster (Lorain 1983) 24 Ohio App.3d 77, 493 N.E.2d 258, 24 O.B.R. 145.

Where a separation agreement provides that a parent will pay for education costs at a school to be agreed on by both parties, upon the death of a party, that party's discretion to agree on a choice of schools is to be exercised by the court. Gilford v. Wurster (Lorain 1983) 24 Ohio App.3d 77, 493 N.E.2d 258, 24 O.B.R. 145.

Where a court accepts as fair and reasonable an agreement of the parties that a husband support his children beyond the age of majority the court may enforce it within the provisions of RC 3105.10. Bugay v. Bugay (Summit 1977) 53 Ohio App.2d 285, 373 N.E.2d 1263, 7 O.O.3d 336.

An agreement between a father and a mother (formerly husband and wife) of minor children, whereby the father, in consideration of his executing and delivering to the wife a written consent to the adoption of the children by their stepfather, is released from his obligation under the decree of divorce to support such children, is valid as between the parties, even though the adoption never takes place and the mother is subsequently divorced from the stepfather; and the mother cannot recover from the father for herself a lump-sum judgment for the installments of such child support award which otherwise would have been payable. (Annotation from former RC 3107.06.) Tressler v. Tressler (Defiance 1972) 32 Ohio App.2d 79, 288 N.E.2d 339, 61 O.O.2d 85.

A cost-of-living clause in a separation agreement providing for automatic increases in child support is valid, as the ability of a domestic relations court to modify for a change of circumstances exists despite the clause. Gui v Brown, No. CA-6392 (5th Dist Ct App, Stark, 11-26-84).

In an action for arrearages, the trial court rightly denied the right to recover past obligations where the parties had mutually agreed to discharge the continuing obligation to pay support in exchange for a waiver of a continuing visitation right; in an action to reinstate both child support payments and visitation rights, the party seeking reinstatement will not be denied such based on the previous mutual agreement, as the child has an interest in future payments; therefore, such an agreement is binding on both parties as to past obligations, but is not binding on the court as to future payments. In re Dissolution of Marriage of Saltis v Frisby, No. 10345 (9th Dist Ct App, Summit, 1-27-82).

Where the trial court enters a divorce order incorporating a separation agreement in which the plaintiff-mother waived all rights to child support in exchange for which the father waived his visitation rights, said order may be modified to establish a child support obligation without a finding of a change of circumstances. Botticello v Botticello, No. 7372 (2d Dist Ct App, Montgomery, 1-7-82).

A once unemployed mother now earning $520 per month is not grounds for a reduction of child support since the possibility of the mother's employment could have been reasonably expected such that it is not a change of circumstances, and further, because such contingency was not in the agreement. Swartz v Swartz, No. 948 (11th Dist Ct App, Geauga, 9-30-81).

Where a separation agreement states that child-support payments shall terminate as each child becomes emancipated, and further provides that the modification will either be agreed upon or submitted to the court, the matter must be submitted to the court as a changing circumstance. McFadden v McFadden, No. 80AP-626 (10th Dist Ct App, Franklin, 7-28-81).

16. Support payment to third party

For purposes of ex-husband's motion for return of overpayment of child support, payments that he made pursuant to a voluntary agreement with county welfare department after a child was born subsequent to parties' divorce would not be deemed a gift, despite lack of court order mandating those payments; unrefuted evidence showed payments were made to discharge child support obligation, and equitable considerations further supported crediting ex-husband for voluntary expenditures made on behalf of child. Cox v. Cox (Ohio App. 1 Dist. 1998) 130 Ohio App.3d 609, 720 N.E.2d 946.

Voluntary payments made by a noncustodial parent directly to a child are not to be considered payments in lieu of support where the divorce decree orders that support payments be made through the court. Evans v. Brown (Franklin 1985) 23 Ohio App.3d 97, 491 N.E.2d 384, 23 O.B.R. 163.

A supporting parent is not necessarily entitled to credit against arrearages for insurance premium payments made on account of the children but not required by the terms of the support decree. Ferrere v. Ferrere (Cuyahoga 1984) 20 Ohio App.3d 82, 484 N.E.2d 753, 20 O.B.R. 102.

The obligee (the state) can collect only in accordance with Ch 5121; when both parents are obligated under Ch 5121, the question of what share each of two divorced parents will pay is a matter to be determined from the divorce decree. State, Dept. of Mental Health & Mental Retardation, Bureau of Support v. Wiedemann (Ohio App. 12 Dist. 1980) 1 Ohio App.3d 27, 437 N.E.2d 1212, 1 O.B.R. 17.

The domestic relations court has clear authority to place the burden of child support as it shall deem best, within the scope of discretion allowed in 3109.05; but this authority does not eliminate or in any way affect the liability of both parents for the support of a minor patient under 5121.06 and the related sections of the Revised Code. State, Dept. of Mental Health & Mental Retardation, Bureau of Support v. Wiedemann (Ohio App. 12 Dist. 1980) 1 Ohio App.3d 27, 437 N.E.2d 1212, 1 O.B.R. 17.

In an action by a hospital against the parents of a minor child for medical treatment provided to the minor child by the hospital, the mother of the child may not absolve herself of liability to the hospital, a third party, by reason of a provision in the divorce decree requiring the father of the child to pay for all medical expenses incurred by the child. Children's Hospital of Akron v. Johnson (Summit 1980) 68 Ohio App.2d 17, 426 N.E.2d 515, 22 O.O.3d 11.

Where a husband and wife are divorced, the duty to support a minor child is governed by RC 3109.05 and not 3103.03, so that a wife may be required to assume the support of her child which is in the custody of another. Hill v. Hill (Hamilton 1973) 40 Ohio App.2d 1, 317 N.E.2d 250, 69 O.O.2d 1.

It is not error to grant a judgment for arrearages for nonpayment of child support for the six year period between emancipation of the child and a final judgment because there was no agreement between the parties that the appellant would not pay child support; also, it was not error to grant interest on the arrearages for that period of time involved. Colister v Colister, No. 43048 (8th Dist Ct App, Cuyahoga, 6-4-81).

Mothers who bring a civil rights action under 42 USC 1983 seeking no monetary relief but requesting that the court permanently enjoin the defendants, various county and state officials responsible for administering child support enforcement services, from failing to provide these services under state law and the Social Security Act, have failed to state a claim upon which relief can be granted; the plaintiffs sought only a "hurry-up" order, and unearthed no acts of noncompliance beyond those already found in an audit by the secretary of health and human services. Carelli v. Howser (C.A.6 (Ohio) 1991) 923 F.2d 1208, rehearing denied.

A divorce decree that appears to contemplate sale of the marital residence and an equal sharing of the net proceeds is dividing property in this respect rather than imposing a support obligation on any party; as a result, a provision calling for the husband to make mortgage payments does not create a support obligation and the obligation may be discharged in the husband's bankruptcy along with any arrearage. In re Shelton (Bkrtcy.S.D.Ohio 1988) 92 B.R. 268.

17. Remedy for noncompliance with support

A nonresident custodial parent has a right to pursue an action for child support against the noncustodial parent in a court of competent jurisdiction in this state when the noncustodial parent is a resident of Ohio and the parties' foreign divorce decree and child custody order do not address the issue of support. Haskins v. Bronzetti (Ohio 1992) 64 Ohio St.3d 202, 594 N.E.2d 582.

The appellate court erred in reversing the trial court's rejection of a defense of laches in a suit to recover child support arrearages where there was substantial disagreement in the evidence regarding both opportunity to bring suit and the question of prejudice. Kinney v. Mathias (Ohio 1984) 10 Ohio St.3d 72, 461 N.E.2d 901, 10 O.B.R. 361.

The payee of an installment child-support order or judgment, issued in conjunction with a divorce decree, is not precluded by a statutory limitation of time, by laches, or by loss of jurisdiction by the court making the order, from having unpaid and delinquent installments thereon reduced to a "lump-sum judgment," upon which execution may be lawfully levied, because fourteen years elapsed since the last payment on the order was due or because the court lost custodial jurisdiction of the child when he reached the age of twenty-one. (Annotation from former RC 3105.20.) Smith v. Smith (Ohio 1959) 168 Ohio St. 447, 156 N.E.2d 113, 7 O.O.2d 276.

Former husband could be found in contempt for failure to remain current on medical payments and failure to maintain dental insurance for children in violation of separation agreement incorporated in judgment. Woloch v. Foster (Miami 1994) 98 Ohio App.3d 806, 649 N.E.2d 918.

Divorced mother was entitled to recover aggregate total of medical bills incurred by children, not merely out-of-pocket expenses, from father, regardless of whether expenses were covered by insurance procured by mother's new spouse; father failed to pay for any of children's medical expenses, prompting mother to acquire insurance for children and to incur uninsured out-of-pocket medical costs, and father was responsible under separation agreement for all medical, dental, hospital and surgical expenses that exceeded $15 per occurrence. Stracker v. Stracker (Lorain 1994) 94 Ohio App.3d 261, 640 N.E.2d 611.

Former husband's failure to pay past due and owing college expenses and medical expenses, as required under separation agreement and modification order, justified contempt finding; former husband's motion to modify filed after contempt proceeding was instituted was not viable defense and husband offered no evidence of alleged inability to pay. Rohrbacher v. Rohrbacher (Lucas 1992) 83 Ohio App.3d 569, 615 N.E.2d 338.

While award of attorney fees to wife in divorce proceeding may have been reasonable, trial court's failure to do so did not constitute abuse of discretion, given that Court of Appeals increased wife's sustenance alimony award from $2,700 to $3,500 and trial court awarded to wife portion of bonus to which husband was entitled through his employment. Kaechele v. Kaechele (Franklin 1992) 83 Ohio App.3d 468, 615 N.E.2d 273.

Reviewing court's affirmance of trial court order requiring ex-wife to pay ex-husband's portion of mortgage payments she received upon sale of marital home directly to county child support enforcement agency to pay for ex-husband's arrearage in child support was law of the case and precluded finding that ex-husband was still obligated on entire amount of arrearage without setoff for mortgage payment amounts; however, order did not mention future child support payments and did not preclude holding ex-husband liable for arrearages occurring after date of order. Schneider v. Schneider (Clermont 1992) 83 Ohio App.3d 423, 615 N.E.2d 244.

The doctrine of laches prevents an award of child support arrearage to a mother who deliberately kept the child from the father for eighteen years where she and her new family moved several times out of state and never requested payment during those years; these actions materially prejudiced the father's rights. Ferree v. Sparks (Warren 1991) 77 Ohio App.3d 185, 601 N.E.2d 568.

Insufficient minimum contacts exist with Ohio to warrant assumption of personal jurisdiction over a father in a child support action where the parties are married and reside in California, the mother removes herself and the children to Ohio and obtains a divorce in an Ohio court, the father has only briefly visited Ohio twice to visit his children, and he owns no property in Ohio. Meadows v. Meadows (Hancock 1992) 73 Ohio App.3d 316, 596 N.E.2d 1146.

In a contempt action brought by a wife against her ex-husband for failure to pay child support, the ex-husband's defense of laches does not prevent a trial court's willful contempt finding against him, even though the wife's action is brought eleven years after the children became emancipated and twenty years after the divorce, custody, and support decree was entered, where the husband never successfully disputes that his ex-wife did not know or had never learned of his address in another state or any other particulars about his existence there and never indicates how the delay in enforcing the support order has materially or legally prejudiced him. Johnson v. Johnson (Portage 1991) 71 Ohio App.3d 713, 595 N.E.2d 388.

A wife's action against her ex-husband for contempt for failure to pay child support is a civil contempt proceeding in which proof of willfulness is not a prerequisite. Johnson v. Johnson (Portage 1991) 71 Ohio App.3d 713, 595 N.E.2d 388.

Child support arrearages may not be ordered to be paid where the obligor's only source of income is from public assistance received for the benefit of his other children as aid for dependent children benefits are not subject to attachment. Crigger v. Crigger (Franklin 1991) 71 Ohio App.3d 410, 594 N.E.2d 67.

A trial court may not use its contempt powers to seek to enforce a prior child support order by ordering monthly installments to retire arrearages after the children have become emancipated. Crigger v. Crigger (Franklin 1991) 71 Ohio App.3d 410, 594 N.E.2d 67.

A defendant who fails to avail himself of the opportunity to defend against his former wife's motion for child support modification and custody determination, to challenge an alleged error in the admission of bureau of support records, and to bring the objection to the trial court's attention waives that objection. Hostetler v. Kennedy (Wayne 1990) 69 Ohio App.3d 299, 590 N.E.2d 793.

Before a person can be incarcerated for failure to pay child support and arrearages pursuant to a trial court's order, it is first necessary that a judge review and approve the referee's written report with his factual determination that the person has not purged himself of his contempt sentence by making a substantial effort to seek work by a certain date. State ex rel. Burns v. Haines (Montgomery 1989) 55 Ohio App.3d 168, 563 N.E.2d 52.

Where a noncustodial parent owes child support arrearages from the date of original decree until the change of custody, a trial court may set off the child support obligation of the new noncustodial parent against the arrearage due the current obligor; however, it is error to only allow one-half of the current obligor's weekly obligation to be set off against the arrearage due. Krause v. Krause (Butler 1987) 35 Ohio App.3d 18, 518 N.E.2d 1221.

Uniform Reciprocal Enforcement of Support Act does not authorize suspension of support order by reason of denial or interference with visitation rights. Brown v. Brown (Warren 1984) 16 Ohio App.3d 26, 474 N.E.2d 613, 16 O.B.R. 28.

Father could not excuse his failure to pay child support required by separation agreement merely because of mother's denial of visitation rights. Flynn v. Flynn (Madison 1984) 15 Ohio App.3d 34, 472 N.E.2d 388, 15 O.B.R. 57.

RC 3105.10 clothes courts with jurisdiction to incorporate into a court order an agreement to support a child of the parties beyond the age of that child's majority, and such an order may be enforced by contempt proceedings. (Annotation from former RC 3105.20.) Bugay v. Bugay (Summit 1977) 53 Ohio App.2d 285, 373 N.E.2d 1263, 7 O.O.3d 336.

Where circumstances indicate an inability on the part of the noncustodial parent to pay child support, such parent cannot be deprived of his right of visitation solely by reason of his inability to pay. Johnson v. Johnson (Summit 1977) 52 Ohio App.2d 180, 368 N.E.2d 1273, 6 O.O.3d 170.

A parent having custody of minor children who is able to fully support such children, and has done so, may not utilize criminal prosecution under 2919.21 as a means of enforcing the obligation of the other parent to contribute to the support of their minor children. State v. Oppenheimer (Franklin 1975) 46 Ohio App.2d 241, 348 N.E.2d 731, 75 O.O.2d 404.

RC 3109.05 does not permit an automatic termination of support if visitation privileges are denied without cause, but requires a determination based upon evidence as to what, if any, modification of support is just, which necessarily includes an evaluation of the needs of a child for support against the right of a parent to visit with such child and a balancing of the equities involved. Foster v. Foster (Franklin 1974) 40 Ohio App.2d 257, 319 N.E.2d 395, 69 O.O.2d 250.

There is no duty on the father of minor children to make support payments to the mother as decreed by another court pursuant to the uniform reciprocal enforcement of support act, where the father has obtained a prior order of custody and the mother has removed the children from the jurisdiction of the court contrary to such order. (Annotation from former RC 3103.02.) State of N. J. v. Morales (Franklin 1973) 35 Ohio App.2d 56, 299 N.E.2d 920, 64 O.O.2d 175.

Compliance with common pleas court order fixing amount of support payments for minor child of divorced parents is a bar to prosecution for nonsupport in juvenile court. State v. Holl (Auglaize 1971) 25 Ohio App.2d 75, 266 N.E.2d 587, 54 O.O.2d 114.

Where for many years the plaintiff in a divorce proceeding failed to enforce installment payments of support money for a minor child, ordered in a decree granting a divorce to plaintiff, the unpaid installments become vested when due, and the court has no power to reduce the amount found to be due where the evidence does not indicate any intention on the part of the plaintiff to waive, relinquish, or abandon her rights under the support order. (Annotation from former RC 3105.20.) Brunner v. Williams (Franklin 1955) 100 Ohio App. 144, 135 N.E.2d 908, 60 O.O. 136.

The duty to pay child support is unaffected by any interference with rights of visitation, and no estoppel to claim child support arrears from a father may be inferred from the mother's withholding of visitation with the child. French v French, No. 9-95-7, 1995 WL 328110 (3d Dist Ct App, Marion, 5-30-95).

A court may recognize the defense of laches in an action for past due child support; however, the obligor must prove he was materially prejudiced. The court will not infer prejudice from the mere lapse of time or inconvenience in having to meet an obligor. Garrison v Garrison, No. 10256 (2d Dist Ct App, Montgomery, 6-5-87).

A court may not use its contempt power to force a public employees retirement system member to withdraw money from PERS in order to pay child support arrearages since PERS moneys are exempt from execution, attachment, garnishment, or other process of law. Baecker v Baecker, No. CA-9810 (2d Dist Ct App, Montgomery, 11-6-86).

A court cannot order withholding of funds from a member of the public employees retirement system until he has requested a refund or is entitled to receive retirement benefits, and a court cannot compel a party to a child support action to make such a request to pay arrearages. Baecker v Baecker, No. CA-9810 (2d Dist Ct App, Montgomery, 11-6-86).

Trial court may order defendant-father to pay child support when plaintiff-mother's waiver of child support is conditioned upon defendant-father's refraining from exercising visitation and evidence that visitation was requested and exercised by defendant is shown. Botticello v Botticello, No. 7372 (2d Dist Ct App, Montgomery, 1-7-82).

The uniform support act covers children who are minors, and under 3115.22 is in addition to and not in substitution of any other remedies authorized by law. Burney v. Vance (Ohio Com.Pl. 1969) 17 Ohio Misc. 307, 246 N.E.2d 371, 46 O.O.2d 427.

Where a wife abandons her husband without any aggression on his part and takes her children to another state, the husband cannot be compelled to support such children under the uniform enforcement of support laws where he retains a domicile in Ohio, earns his living in Ohio, and apparently is ready, willing and able to support his children in Ohio. (Annotation from former RC 3103.02.) Buliox v. Buliox (Ohio Com.Pl. 1962) 185 N.E.2d 802, 90 Ohio Law Abs. 251, 21 O.O.2d 30.

Although matters concerning divorce and alimony have been excepted from federal court jurisdiction based on diversity of the parties' state citizenship since Barber v Barber, 62 US 582, 16 LEd(2d) 226(1859), this rule does not bar a husband's claim in federal court that the former wife intentionally inflicted emotional distress on him by taking their child to another state and denying him visitation rights, or that she interfered with his employment by writing letters to his employer; the court may also hear his counterclaim for enforcement of a state judgment concerning arrearages in alimony and child support. Drewes v. Ilnicki (C.A.6 (Ohio) 1988) 863 F.2d 469.

In a federal suit based on diversity of citizenship the principle that federal courts will not hear domestic relations disputes does not apply where the claim is that an employer who withheld wages to satisfy an Ohio court's support order converted the funds instead of turning them over to the Cuyahoga support enforcement agency; the federal court will not be delving into the plaintiff's domestic affairs here, the level or appropriateness of the support payments is not at issue, the state court's orders are not questioned, and it is merely alleged that the employer converted withheld wages. Ungrady v. Burns Intern. Sec. Services, Inc. (N.D.Ohio 1991) 767 F.Supp. 849.

Where an indigent individual is ordered to appear and show cause why he should not be held in contempt for failure to pay support, and where the penalty that may be inflicted includes incarceration, due process requires that the indigent be informed he has a right to appointed counsel, and that such counsel be appointed on request before an appearance to show cause is required. Johnson v. Zurz (N.D.Ohio 1984) 596 F.Supp. 39.

The fact that children to whom a support order relates have reached the age of majority does not prevent a finding that a debt based on arrearages cannot be discharged in the obligor's bankruptcy proceedings. In re Ridgway (Bkrtcy.N.D.Ohio 1989) 108 B.R. 154.

18. Procedural issues

Appeal was adequate remedy at law after trial court refused to dismiss mother's motion to modify child support, in alleged violation of parties' agreement to mediate postdivorce disputes before resorting to court action, making mandamus and prohibition unavailable to husband to challenge court's interlocutory decision; although husband claimed that appeal would not be complete, beneficial and speedy, reviewing court could determine that trial judge erred in proceeding on postdivorce motion without parties first resorting to mediation and could vacate any support modification order. State ex rel. Hunter v. Patterson (Ohio 1996) 75 Ohio St.3d 512, 664 N.E.2d 524.

Statutory right to interest on delinquent child-support payments upon judicial finding that support order had not been paid did not apply to support order that was neither issued nor modified on or after effective date specified in statute. Dunbar v. Dunbar (Ohio 1994) 68 Ohio St.3d 369, 627 N.E.2d 532.

Where there is evidence that a woman has borne, during wedlock, illegitimate children by a man other than her husband, the husband lacks standing either under RC Ch 3111 or the common law to bring an action against the alleged natural father for past necessaries furnished to the children. Weinman v. Larsh (Ohio 1983) 5 Ohio St.3d 85, 448 N.E.2d 1384, 5 O.B.R. 138.

A petition by a minor child, alleging that a defendant wrongfully induced the plaintiff's father to abandon his family thereby (1) depriving the plaintiff of his father's affection, companionship and guidance and (2) bringing unwanted attention and unwarranted publicity causing embarrassment, humiliation and loss of social standing to the plaintiff, is subject to demurrer on the ground that it fails to state a cause of action. Kane v. Quigley (Ohio 1964) 1 Ohio St.2d 1, 203 N.E.2d 338, 30 O.O.2d 1.

Unappealed entry of juvenile court, finding that ex-husband owed no arrearage on support payments for child born to the parties after their divorce decree was entered, was res judicata, and therefore domestic relations court lacked authority, in ruling on husband's motion for return of overpayment of support paid under divorce decree, to find that he still owed $2,500 in support for the child born after the marriage. Cox v. Cox (Ohio App. 1 Dist. 1998) 130 Ohio App.3d 609, 720 N.E.2d 946.

Child support arrearages not incorporated into final decree of divorce are waived and temporary orders are merged into final decree. Brooks v. Brooks (Ohio App. 10 Dist. 1996) 117 Ohio App.3d 19, 689 N.E.2d 987.

Former husband could not be found in contempt of court's order directing him to pay one half of children's uninsured medical expenses, where husband never received actual notice or notice by service of court's order. Sancho v. Sancho (Union 1996) 114 Ohio App.3d 636, 683 N.E.2d 849.

Trial court did not abuse its discretion in ordering father to provide health insurance for child if it was available to him at reasonable cost, even absent investigation to determine whether father had satisfactory health insurance coverage; based upon history of case, trial court already knew that father had health care coverage. Yost v. Unanue (Stark 1996) 109 Ohio App.3d 294, 671 N.E.2d 1374.

Statute providing for postmajority enforcement of child support orders did not operate retroactively as to father, where, when dissolution decree was entered, statute governing duty to support children required parents to continue paying child support for children attending high school. Swanson v. Swanson (Greene 1996) 109 Ohio App.3d 231, 671 N.E.2d 1333.

Appellate courts should exercise great restraint when asked to reverse or modify child support orders for reasons that are fact sensitive. Swanson v. Swanson (Greene 1996) 109 Ohio App.3d 231, 671 N.E.2d 1333.

In paternity action filed by Child Support Enforcement Agency (CSEA), trial court could not order mother, who was not represented by attorney, to seek employment, where matter was not addressed in pleadings, no evidence was presented at hearing on issue, and trial court did not determine whether such order was in best interests of children. Dorsett v. Wheeler (Paulding 1995) 101 Ohio App.3d 716, 656 N.E.2d 698.

Trial court did not abuse its discretion in temporarily suspending child support while it was waiting for continuation of hearing on former husband's motion to terminate child support; court suspended payments because child's needs were being met by government during child's tenure with Federal Job Corps. In re Owens (Clark 1994) 96 Ohio App.3d 429, 645 N.E.2d 130.

In determining whether parent has duty to support mentally or physically disabled child beyond age of 18, court must make factual determination as to whether child is so physically or mentally disabled as to be incapable of maintaining himself or herself. In re Owens (Clark 1994) 96 Ohio App.3d 429, 645 N.E.2d 130.

Shared-parenting order in divorce action was not improper on theory it encouraged excessive entanglement between parties in requiring parties to cooperate and communicate by sharing expenses. Eickelberger v. Eickelberger (Butler 1994) 93 Ohio App.3d 221, 638 N.E.2d 130.

Failure to include child support worksheet in record on appeal required reversal and remand for completion of worksheet. McClain v. McClain (Summit 1993) 87 Ohio App.3d 856, 623 N.E.2d 242.

An action by the state to collect money paid by ADC to a mother for the past support of her children differs from the mother's own action to enforce present and future support; thus, an action for present and future action is not barred by res judicata. Crittendon v. Crittendon (Summit 1992) 82 Ohio App.3d 484, 612 N.E.2d 759.

A referee's report need not recite all the evidence, or absence of evidence, regarding each and every factor mentioned in RC 3109.05 and 3113.215. Smith v. Smith (Scioto 1991) 75 Ohio App.3d 679, 600 N.E.2d 396.

A trial court modifying child support sufficiently complies with a request for findings of fact and conclusions of law where it appends a prior decision of the court which determined the facts of the case and set out the law applicable to the case and the circumstances contemplated by the prior decision have not changed. Riepenhoff v. Riepenhoff (Jackson 1990) 64 Ohio App.3d 135, 580 N.E.2d 846.

The rules of superintendence are merely internal housekeeping rules, to be used as guidelines to facilitate the administration of justice and although they do not give any rights to individual defendants, to the extent that they are applied in an action for the determination of child support, they should be applied correctly and not used as a substitute for the judicial discretion mandated by RC 3109.05. Esber v. Esber (Medina 1989) 63 Ohio App.3d 394, 579 N.E.2d 222.

A motion for child support necessarily raises the issue of the medical needs of the child; a motion expressly pertaining to medical needs is not a prerequisite to consideration of the issue. Gorman v. Gorman (Franklin 1986) 28 Ohio App.3d 85, 501 N.E.2d 1234, 28 O.B.R. 128.

A court, in ordering dismissal of a complaint for divorce at a party's request, may not issue an order of child custody and support as "terms and conditions" of dismissal under Civ R 41(A)(2), since the purpose of that provision is to permit an order that leaves the parties as if the action had not been brought. Lilly v. Lilly (Montgomery 1985) 26 Ohio App.3d 192, 499 N.E.2d 21, 26 O.B.R. 412.

Trial court order holding father responsible for his daughter's medical bills incurred in giving birth to illegitimate child was not erroneous on ground that natural father of illegitimate child was obligated, pursuant to public policy of state, to pay such expenses, where in accordance with decretal support order as modified, father was responsible for all medical, dental, optical and hospital expenses of child in excess of $50 during any one year. Nuckols v. Nuckols (Wood 1983) 12 Ohio App.3d 94, 467 N.E.2d 259, 12 O.B.R. 400.

In an action for modification of child support, the "relevant factors" set out in RC 3109.05 must be considered, and an order of modification based solely upon evidence of the supporting parent's resources and needs is improperly granted. Cooper v. Cooper (Van Wert 1983) 10 Ohio App.3d 143, 460 N.E.2d 1137, 10 O.B.R. 194.

In an action to determine support under RC 3109.05, the burden of going forward with necessary evidence may vary depending on the circumstances of the case, but generally each party is responsible for bringing forth evidence as to his or her needs. Factors about which neither party adduces evidence may be deemed by the trial court to have no significance. Cheek v. Cheek (Franklin 1982) 2 Ohio App.3d 86, 440 N.E.2d 831, 2 O.B.R. 95.

3109.05 applies to modification proceedings as well as original proceedings. Martin v. Martin (Summit 1980) 69 Ohio App.2d 78, 430 N.E.2d 962, 23 O.O.3d 102.

RC 3109.05 does not permit an automatic termination of support if visitation privileges are denied without cause, but requires a determination based upon evidence as to what, if any, modification of support is just, which necessarily includes an evaluation of the needs of a child for support against the right of a parent to visit with such child and a balancing of the equities involved. Foster v. Foster (Franklin 1974) 40 Ohio App.2d 257, 319 N.E.2d 395, 69 O.O.2d 250.

A trial court's assertion that it is not required to record child support proceedings unless requested by a party is erroneous and contrary to the requirements of Civ R 53(D)(2). Moyers v Moyers, No. 98-A-0080, 1999 WL 418007 (11th Dist Ct App, Ashtabula, 6-18-99).

A child support order does not survive the death of the payor parent unless the payor parent consents to continuation of child support after his death and so a trial court abuses discretion by ordering the obligor to maintain life insurance as security for his child support obligation. Whitt v Whitt, No. 98CA12, 1999 WL 3938 (5th Dist Ct App, Fairfield, 12-24-98).

The adoption of the child support guidelines found in CP Sup R 75 has extinguished the burden of demonstrating a change of circumstances in order to obtain modification of a child support order. Andreas v Andreas, No. CA-7559 (5th Dist Ct App, Stark, 11-7-88).

When using child support guidelines, court must compute formula correctly. Further, a prior agreement regarding child support adjustments cannot bind the court or the parties for future child support which continues to be subject to the court's jurisdiction. Gross v Gross, No. 49018 (8th Dist Ct App, Cuyahoga, 5-30-85).

It is error for a court to modify a child support order to exclude a child because of the non-paternity of the payor, when the issue of paternity is first raised by oral motion at a hearing to determine whether there has been a change in circumstances sufficient to warrant modification of the original decree. Hines v Hines, No. C-830772 (1st Dist Ct App, Hamilton, 7-25-84).

For purposes of comparing parties' prospective standards of living to determine whether divorce obligations are dischargeable, each party's projected income should be measured by his or her realistic earning potential, not by lifestyle or other choices which restrict income. In re Findley (Bkrtcy.N.D.Ohio 2000) 245 B.R. 526.

19. Bankruptcy effect

While federal law is controlling in determining dischargeability of debt as alleged support obligation, state law may be used as source of guidance in developing federal standards for determining nature of debt. Bratton v. Frederick (Defiance 1996) 109 Ohio App.3d 13, 671 N.E.2d 1030.

Former Chapter 7 debtor's obligation to pay legal and travel expenses incurred by his ex-wife in enforcing support obligations of parties' divorce decree was likewise in nature of "support," so as not to be dischargeable in bankruptcy. Bratton v. Frederick (Defiance 1996) 109 Ohio App.3d 13, 671 N.E.2d 1030.

Former Chapter 7 debtor's obligation, pursuant to terms of divorce decree, to procure medical insurance for his children and to pay for certain medical expenses was in nature of "child support," so as not to be dischargeable in bankruptcy. Bratton v. Frederick (Defiance 1996) 109 Ohio App.3d 13, 671 N.E.2d 1030.

Forgiveness of indebtedness by medical practitioners who had provided services to former Chapter 7 debtor's children did not affect debtor's obligation, pursuant to terms of divorce decree, to pay childrens' medical expenses, so that evidence of medical providers' forgiveness of indebtedness was properly excluded as irrelevant in proceeding brought to determine dischargeability of debtor's debt. Bratton v. Frederick (Defiance 1996) 109 Ohio App.3d 13, 671 N.E.2d 1030.

Court of Appeals would set sustenance alimony award pursuant to 1986 divorce at $3,500 per month, where trial court had determined wife's monthly expenses to be approximately $4,000, wife suggested award in amount of $3,500, and husband offered no suggestion other than trial court's award of $2,700, which was found by Court of Appeals to constitute abuse of discretion. Kaechele v. Kaechele (Franklin 1992) 83 Ohio App.3d 468, 615 N.E.2d 273.

Nondebtor spouse who seeks to hold a debt nondischargeable under the discharge exception for alimony, maintenance, or support must, at a minimum, establish that the following three elements are met: (1) debt(s) must have arisen "in connection" with a separation agreement, divorce decree, or other order of a court of record; (2) underlying debt(s) must actually be owed to the former spouse or child; and (3) debt(s) owed to the former spouse must actually be in the "nature of alimony or support." In re Luman (Bkrtcy.N.D.Ohio 1999) 238 B.R. 697.

Debts arising from a property settlement are not encompassed within the discharge exception for those debts contained in a divorce decree or separation agreement which are for the maintenance and support of debtor's child or former spouse. In re Luman (Bkrtcy.N.D.Ohio 1999) 238 B.R. 697.

Purpose of third step of the *Calhoun* test for determining whether payments by debtor pursuant to divorce decree are in the nature of nondischargeable support, which requires court to examine whether amount of support provision is so excessive so as to be manifestly unreasonable under the traditional concepts of support, is to prevent a debtor from effectively contracting away his or her right and opportunity for a fresh start under the Bankruptcy Code. In re Luman (Bkrtcy.N.D.Ohio 1999) 238 B.R. 697.

In determining whether a debtor's assumption of debt pursuant to a divorce decree is in the nature of nondischargeable alimony, maintenance, or support, bankruptcy courts consider such relevant factors as the following: (1) disparity of earning power between the parties; (2) need for economic support and stability; (3) presence of minor children; (4) marital fault; (5) nature of the obligations assumed; (6) structure and language of parties' agreement or court's decree; (7) whether other lump sum or periodic payments were also provided; (8) length of the marriage; (9) age, health, and work skills of the parties; (10) whether obligation terminates upon the death or remarriage of the parties; (11) adequacy of support absent the debt assumption; and (12) evidence of negotiations or other understandings as to intended purposes of the assumption. In re Luman (Bkrtcy.N.D.Ohio 1999) 238 B.R. 697.

Under third step of *Calhoun* test for determining whether payments made by a debtor pursuant to a divorce decree are in the nature of nondischargeable support, Chapter 7 debtor's assumption of credit card debt in the amount of $20,451.73 was not manifestly unreasonable under traditional concepts of support; debtor's annual income was approximately $32,000, it was feasible that debtor could actually experience a positive monthly cash flow if extra income were imputed to debtor and debtor would reduce some of his questionable expenses, such as an expenditure for cable television, and nondebtor spouse was the residential parent of parties' child. In re Luman (Bkrtcy.N.D.Ohio 1999) 238 B.R. 697.

Although a "hold harmless" provision in a separation agreement or divorce decree is strong evidence of an intent to create a support obligation, the lack thereof does not necessarily indicate that the underlying obligation is not in the nature of support, for nondischargeability purposes. In re Luman (Bkrtcy.N.D.Ohio 1999) 238 B.R. 697.

Federal and state courts have concurrent jurisdiction to hear questions of dischargeability arising out of alimony and child support exception. In re Baker (Bkrtcy.S.D.Ohio 1996) 195 B.R. 883.

Where state court has not yet determined property interests involved, it is appropriate for bankruptcy court to defer to that state court for determination of dischargeability under alimony and child support exception. In re Baker (Bkrtcy.S.D.Ohio 1996) 195 B.R. 883.

In general, federal courts defer to state courts in domestic relations matters, but this deference is limited to matters where the matter is more suitably handled by state courts. In re Baker (Bkrtcy.S.D.Ohio 1996) 195 B.R. 883.

State and federal courts have concurrent jurisdiction to determine whether debt is excepted from discharge under spousal and child support exception. Matter of Tremaine (Bkrtcy.S.D.Ohio 1995) 188 B.R. 380.

In proceedings to determine dischargeability under child and spousal support exception where bankruptcy court and state court have concurrent jurisdiction to determine issue, general rule is that court in which issue is first presented, or capable of presentation, through proper filings and proceedings will continue proceedings to conclusion. Matter of Tremaine (Bkrtcy.S.D.Ohio 1995) 188 B.R. 380.

Bankruptcy court would abstain, in favor of state domestic relations court, from determining whether debts owed to Chapter 7 debtor's former wife were nondischargeable under spousal support exception, in light of related proceeding pending in state court system, appearance of forum shopping by debtor, and lack of finality caused by debtor's pursuit of state court appellate proceedings that diminished, if not eliminated, any meaningful determination of dischargeability by bankruptcy court; appellate proceeding had reached advanced stages in state court system, but had not finally established amount of divorce decree debts, and absence of finality in amount of obligations precluded determination of nature of debt. Matter of Tremaine (Bkrtcy.S.D.Ohio 1995) 188 B.R. 380.

Provision in divorce judgment requiring husband to hold wife harmless from husband's business debts was intended as nondischargeable "support" for parties' children. In re Sanders (Bkrtcy.N.D.Ohio 1995) 187 B.R. 588.

Joint marital debts that Chapter 7 debtor assumed under divorce judgment entry came within discharge exception for support, where former wife's retention of house was necessary as support for minor children, nonpayment of debts could result in attachment of house by creditors, former wife lacked sufficient income to enable her to pay marital debts, and hold harmless provision of entry stated that bankruptcy filing should not be undertaken if it would affect former wife's right of ownership in house. In re Chapman (Bkrtcy.N.D.Ohio 1995) 187 B.R. 573.

Merely because spousal and child support were otherwise provided for in divorce judgment entry did not establish that Chapter 7 debtor's assumption of marital debts under decree was not intended to provide support, and that discharge exception for support was inapplicable. In re Chapman (Bkrtcy.N.D.Ohio 1995) 187 B.R. 573.

Calhoun test for determining whether debt is nondischargeable child support obligation did not apply to order entered for sole purpose of designating rights and obligations of unmarried parents with respect to their minor child. In re Kidd (Bkrtcy.S.D.Ohio 1995) 177 B.R. 876.

"Right to receive," as expressed in Ohio statute exempting from claims of creditors right to receive spousal support, child support, allowance or other maintenance to extent necessary to support person or his dependents, includes payments previously ordered, but not yet due, as well as payments due, but not paid as of date of bankruptcy filing; because parent to whom arrearage is owed has first responsibility to use arrearages for benefit of child, arrearages may be held exempt from claims of creditors to extent such usage is reasonably necessary support, determination which is factual issue requiring an evidentiary hearing. In re Davis (Bkrtcy.S.D.Ohio 1994) 167 B.R. 104.

Chapter 13 debtor's right to payment of past-due child support was part of her bankruptcy estate. In re Davis (Bkrtcy.S.D.Ohio 1994) 167 B.R. 104.

Adjustment of Chapter 13 debtor's obligation under marital separation agreement to make college assistance payments for children's education pursuant to marital separation agreement was not appropriate where debtor's financial position had improved from time of separation agreement when he was unemployed until time of petition filing when debtor was earning $3,000 per month and was remarried to wife who also worked. Matter of Bush (Bkrtcy.S.D.Ohio 1993) 154 B.R. 69.

To determine if college assistance payments for children's education are dischargeable, courts must examine whether intent of state court or the parties was to create a support obligation, whether the support provision has actual effect of providing necessary support, whether amount of support is so excessive as to be unreasonable under traditional concepts of support, and if amount of support is unreasonable what part should be characterized as nondischargeable in bankruptcy. Matter of Bush (Bkrtcy.S.D.Ohio 1993) 154 B.R. 69.

Chapter 13 debtor's obligation under marital separation agreement to make college assistance payments for his children's educations fell within the exception to discharge for support; payments were intended to be support, and they were not overly burdensome on debtor. Matter of Bush (Bkrtcy.S.D.Ohio 1993) 154 B.R. 69.

Bankruptcy court has authority to adjust and alter amount of payments owed for spousal and child support if it finds the payments to be unreasonably burdensome to Chapter 13 debtor; however, it is only appropriate to make such a modification if original state court award was unreasonable or if there has been detrimental change in financial circumstances from time divorce decree was entered to time of petition filing. Matter of Bush (Bkrtcy.S.D.Ohio 1993) 154 B.R. 69.

Support payments do not have to be in form of monthly payments to be considered nondischargeable "support." In re Oberley (Bkrtcy.N.D.Ohio 1993) 153 B.R. 179.

Medical expenses incurred due to birth of debtor's child were nondischargeable as "support." In re Oberley (Bkrtcy.N.D.Ohio 1993) 153 B.R. 179.

In determining whether debt is nondischargeable as "support," courts are required to determine if debt is so high that it is considered unreasonable under "traditional concepts of support." In re Oberley (Bkrtcy.N.D.Ohio 1993) 153 B.R. 179.

Debtor's obligation to pay $5 per week to county department of human services for child's past medical expenses was not unreasonable burden on debtor, and, accordingly, obligation could be found nondischargeable as "support," even though it would take debtor over 200 years to pay off entire debt based on weekly payments of $5. In re Oberley (Bkrtcy.N.D.Ohio 1993) 153 B.R. 179.

Absent showing that current needs of child support payee are unmet, Chapter 13 plan providing for 100 percent payment of arrearages over life of plan is acceptable. In re Walter (Bkrtcy.N.D.Ohio 1993) 153 B.R. 38.

Because child support obligations are typically nondischargeable, in instances where Chapter 13 plan calls for less than full payment of arrearages, relief from automatic stay may be available to allow payee or appropriate governmental agency to pursue only those amounts not provided for in plan. In re Walter (Bkrtcy.N.D.Ohio 1993) 153 B.R. 38.

A retroactive $15 per week child support obligation imposed on the father in a paternity suit begun when the child was aged sixteen years cannot be discharged in the father's bankruptcy action. In re Smith (Bkrtcy.N.D.Ohio 1992) 139 B.R. 864.

The fact that a man and woman remarry ten years after they divorced has no effect on the arrearage for child support that he owes her and that she had assigned to the county while she collected aid to dependent children during the time that the couple was divorced. In re Lhamon (Bkrtcy.N.D.Ohio 1991) 139 B.R. 849.

An $11,000 obligation resulting from the compromise of a paternity action is a support payment to the child that cannot be discharged in the father's bankruptcy action where the amount was based on analysis of what would have been required for support had a declaration of paternity applied from the date of birth to the time of the agreement and from certain medical expenses relating to the birth. In re Wilson (Bkrtcy.S.D.Ohio 1989) 109 B.R. 283.

In determining whether an award of support in a divorce decree is necessary or excessive and subject to discharge in a former husband's bankruptcy proceedings, the bankruptcy court will consider the circumstances considered by Ohio domestic relations courts in deciding what amounts to award as alimony and child support, such as those listed in RC 3105.18 and 3109.05. In re Angel (Bkrtcy.S.D.Ohio 1989) 105 B.R. 825.

A man whose earnings from an apparently failing business in which he is a partner have dropped from $35,000 per year to $18,000 and who has taken cash advances against future salary in order to meet support obligations under a divorce decree will not be granted relief in his bankruptcy proceedings, on the ground changed circumstances have lessened his ability to pay support or the ground that ordered support is excessive, with respect to obligations to pay $150 weekly child support, $200 weekly alimony, medical insurance, the former wife's auto costs for two years, half the children's tuition at a private school, and an additional $2000 per year for five years; the court considers that "there is no indication" the former husband, "an apparently able-bodied, middle-aged man is incapable of earning a respectable income." In re Angel (Bkrtcy.S.D.Ohio 1989) 105 B.R. 825.

Unpaid child support that accrued before the support obligation ended and that would have supported the children if paid when due is a debt that cannot be discharged in the father's bankruptcy. In re Matyac (Bkrtcy.S.D.Ohio 1989) 102 B.R. 125.

The Bankruptcy Code at 11 USC 523(a)(5) is apparently devised to prevent a debtor from discharging in bankruptcy obligations to support his former wife and children imposed on him under the divorce decree even if the "support" is in the form of paying a debt jointly owed by the man and woman to a third party; thus, a debtor's agreement to hold his former wife harmless on joint debts cannot be discharged in bankruptcy to the extent his agreement is found to be "in payment of alimony, maintenance or support." In re Shelton (Bkrtcy.S.D.Ohio 1988) 92 B.R. 268.

An obligation imposed on a father under a divorce decree to maintain medical insurance covering children is considered an obligation of support and thus cannot be discharged in his bankruptcy proceedings. In re Shelton (Bkrtcy.S.D.Ohio 1988) 92 B.R. 268.

Any part of a support award that is not "manifestly unreasonable under traditional concepts of support" and that is owing but unpaid from the entry of the state court divorce decree until commencement of the former husband's federal bankruptcy case will not be affected by the former husband's discharge in bankruptcy; he remains responsible for the arrearage and must make arrangements with his former wife for payment. In re Caughenbaugh (Bkrtcy.S.D.Ohio 1988) 92 B.R. 255.

Where a former husband's income has declined dramatically since a divorce decree and now amounts to $1321 monthly, from which he claims to spend $1285 monthly on necessities exclusive of the $600 monthly support he was ordered to pay his former wife, and where the former wife has income of $400 monthly and monthly expenses of $625, the bankruptcy court will find it "manifestly unreasonable under traditional concepts of support" to make the former husband pay the support decreed; instead, the former husband is found able to pay $80 weekly henceforth by effecting economies, and the remainder of the obligation is held subject to his discharge in bankruptcy. In re Caughenbaugh (Bkrtcy.S.D.Ohio 1988) 92 B.R. 255.

A party claiming that an award in a divorce decree constitutes "support" has the burden of proving it is support money even though the parties termed it such in the separation agreement; thus, absent evidence of the parties' intentions and of a former wife's assets, education, and needs, a bankruptcy court will not find an award of $4000 monthly for 126 months to be "support" payments that cannot be discharged in the former husband's bankruptcy proceedings. In re Skaggs (Bkrtcy.S.D.Ohio 1988) 91 B.R. 1018.

A monthly support award of $2000 is considered "manifestly excessive" by the federal bankruptcy court when the former husband charged with paying it is now disabled and has a monthly income of just $778; the court will review the former husband's budget and decide to what extent the support payment should be adjusted. In re Skaggs (Bkrtcy.S.D.Ohio 1988) 91 B.R. 1018.

Where a separation agreement provides that a laborer earning more than $28,000 yearly pay a $4,700 second mortgage on the home of the wife and children while she pays the first mortgage, taxes, and other expenses, and where the wife's new husband maintains his own separate residence, the first husband's obligation is "support" for shelter, at least for the minor children, is not unreasonable in relation to his income, and as a result is not discharged by his bankruptcy. In re Mizen (Bkrtcy.N.D.Ohio 1987) 72 B.R. 251.

A father who signed private school tuition contracts with his wife, was thereafter divorced by her, was sued by her and lost a judgment for the tuition amount, and who soon afterward filed for bankruptcy, is relieved of liability for the wife's judgment where the divorce decree provided for support and did not mention the contracts, and there is no proof the state court awarding the judgment considered the sum to be support. In re Motley (Bkrtcy.N.D.Ohio 1987) 69 B.R. 406.

Seven years of child support arrearages cannot be discharged in bankruptcy even where the husband ceased payment because the wife began receiving $465 each month for the children from her next husband's social security, and she then gave the children to her mother to raise yet only gave her mother $150 each month for doing so. In re Troxell (Bkrtcy.S.D.Ohio 1986) 67 B.R. 328.

An obligation for child support arrearages will be discharged in bankruptcy, as between the debtor and the mother, where the obligation arose by agreement in settlement of a paternity proceeding in which the debtor denied paternity, and where no evidence of paternity is before the bankruptcy court. Matter of Gray (Bkrtcy.S.D.Ohio 1984) 41 B.R. 759.

20. Attorney fees

Two parties, in a noncommercial transaction, may lawfully contract to require the payment by the unsuccessful party in a subsequent suit between them, of the prevailing party's attorney fees. Nottingdale Homeowners' Ass'n, Inc. v. Darby (Ohio 1987) 33 Ohio St.3d 32, 514 N.E.2d 702.

The awarding of attorney fees in proceedings on a motion after a decree of divorce is within the sound discretion of the trial court, and a showing of necessity is not a prerequisite to an award. Rand v. Rand (Ohio 1985) 18 Ohio St.3d 356, 481 N.E.2d 609, 18 O.B.R. 415.

A trial court has authority, after the entry of a divorce decree, to enter an order requiring the divorced husband to pay reasonable expense money to his former wife to enable her to pay attorney fees incurred in post-decree proceedings relative to the support of the minor children of the marriage. Blum v. Blum (Ohio 1967) 9 Ohio St.2d 92, 223 N.E.2d 819, 38 O.O.2d 224.

Under terms of divorce decree, ex-wife could recover attorney fees incurred in instituting contempt proceedings to enforce ex-husband's obligation to pay one half of costs of parties' child's education, notwithstanding ex-husband's contention that amount he owed was in dispute; even if amount was in dispute, there was no dispute that ex-husband had failed to pay any portion of child's educational expenses during relevant period. Wesselman v. Wesselman (Butler 1993) 88 Ohio App.3d 338, 623 N.E.2d 1300.

An award of attorney fees is improper where the court fails to determine (1) the time and labor involved, (2) the fee customarily charged in the locality, and (3) the nature and length of the professional relationship with the client. Hockenberry v. Hockenberry (Henry 1992) 75 Ohio App.3d 806, 600 N.E.2d 839.

Where a husband moving for a reduction in child support does not come to the hearing on his motion, an award of attorney fees to the wife without a showing of necessity but based instead on the husband's failure to prosecute is not an abuse of discretion. Harpole v. Harpole (Medina 1986) 27 Ohio App.3d 289, 500 N.E.2d 915, 27 O.B.R. 334.

A clause in a separation agreement requiring the party in default to pay the other party's attorney fees in an enforcement action is not enforceable. Snyder v. Snyder (Cuyahoga 1985) 27 Ohio App.3d 1, 499 N.E.2d 320, 27 O.B.R. 1.

A noncustodial parent may not recover attorney fees upon successfully defending, on procedural grounds only, a post-decree enforcement action for child support, where procedural errors by the party seeking enforcement were not the result of bad faith. Montgomery County Welfare Dept. v. Bobo (Montgomery 1984) 21 Ohio App.3d 69, 486 N.E.2d 222, 21 O.B.R. 74.

Where a divorced wife obtains an order modifying a support order and the defendant husband appeals and loses such appeal, the court is authorized to grant her an allowance for reasonable expenses in connection with such appeal. (Annotation from former RC 3105.14.) Ward v. Ward (Montgomery 1956) 104 Ohio App. 105, 140 N.E.2d 906, 74 Ohio Law Abs. 408, 4 O.O.2d 177.

The provisions of RC 3109.05(C) awarding costs and attorney fees are mandatory where there is a finding of contempt for failure to pay child support. Holyak v Holyak, No. 411 (7th Dist Ct App, Harrison, 5-22-89).

Where a request for an increase in support is met with resistance and litigation is required, the expense of such litigation is in the nature of additional child support necessary for the child to have the standard of living commensurate with the parent's income. Hummer v Hummer, No. 86AP-293 (10th Dist Ct App, Franklin, 8-28-86).

Where post-divorce proceedings to enforce the support obligation of the noncomplying noncustodial parent are necessary, it is not an abuse of discretion for the court to award attorney fees to the complainant spouse regardless of her ability to pay such fees. Rand v Rand, No. 47712 (8th Dist Ct App, Cuyahoga, 6-28-84), affirmed by 18 OS(3d) 356, 18 OBR 415, 481 NE(2d) 609 (1985).

21. Imprisonment effect

Imprisonment because of criminal conduct is "voluntary" and, as such, will no longer be considered a "change in circumstances" justifying modification of a child support obligation; contempt proceedings should not go forward while the man is already jailed, however. Richardson v Ballard, 113 App(3d) 552, 681 NE(2d) 507 (Bulter 1996).

22. Income of obligor generally

An obligor who deliberately redirects part of his income to his new wife to avoid child support obligations perpetrates a fraud upon the court which consequently awards retroactive support payments to remedy the results of the scheme to defraud the court. Leffel v Leffel, No. 97-CA-20, 1997 WL 666102 (2d Dist Ct App, Clark, 10-24-97).

23. Federal non-bankruptcy involvement

The domestic relations exception to federal jurisdiction applies only where a plaintiff positively sues in federal court for divorce, alimony, or child custody. Catz v. Chalker (C.A.6 (Ohio) 1998) 142 F.3d 279.

3109.051 Visitation rights

(A) If a divorce, dissolution, legal separation, or annulment proceeding involves a child and if the court has not issued a shared parenting decree, the court shall consider any mediation report filed pursuant to section 3109.052 of the Revised Code and, in accordance with division (C) of this section, shall make a just and reasonable order or decree permitting each parent who is not the residential parent to visit the child at the time and under the conditions that the court directs, unless the court determines that it would not be in the best interest of the child to permit that parent to visit the child and includes in the journal its findings of fact and conclusions of law. Whenever possible, the order or decree permitting the visitation shall ensure the opportunity for both parents to have frequent and continuing contact with the child, unless frequent and continuing contact by either parent with the child would not be in the best interest of the child. The court shall include in its final decree a specific schedule of visitation for that parent. Except as provided in division (E)(6) of section 3113.31 of the Revised Code, if the court, pursuant to this section, grants any person companionship or visitation rights with respect to any child, it shall not require the public children services agency to provide supervision of or other services related to that person's exercise of companionship or visitation rights with respect to the child. This section does not limit the power of a juvenile court pursuant to Chapter 2151. of the Revised Code to issue orders with respect to children who are alleged to be abused, neglected, or dependent children or to make dispositions of children who are adjudicated abused, neglected, or dependent children or of a common pleas court to issue orders pursuant to section 3113.31 of the Revised Code.

(B)(1) In a divorce, dissolution of marriage, legal separation, annulment, or child support proceeding that involves a child, the court may grant reasonable companionship or visitation rights to any grandparent, any person related to the child by consanguinity or affinity, or any other person other than a parent, if all of the following apply:

(a) The grandparent, relative, or other person files a motion with the court seeking companionship or visitation rights.

(b) The court determines that the grandparent, relative, or other person has an interest in the welfare of the child.

(c) The court determines that the granting of the companionship or visitation rights is in the best interest of the child.

(2) A motion may be filed under division (B)(1) of this section during the pendency of the divorce, dissolution of marriage, legal separation, annulment, or child support proceeding or, if a motion was not filed at that time or was filed at that time and the circumstances in the case have changed, at any time after a decree or final order is issued in the case.

(C) When determining whether to grant companionship or visitation rights to a parent, grandparent, relative, or other person pursuant to this section or section 3109.11 or 3109.12 of the Revised Code, when establishing a specific visitation schedule, and when determining other visitation matters under this section or section 3109.11 or 3109.12 of the Revised Code, the court shall consider any mediation report that is filed pursuant to section 3109.052 of the Revised Code and shall consider all other relevant factors, including, but not limited to, all of the factors listed in division (D) of this section. In considering the factors listed in division (D) of this section for purposes of determining whether to grant visitation rights, establishing a specific visitation schedule, determining other visitation matters under this section or under section 3109.11 or 3109.12 of the Revised Code, and resolving any issues related to the making of any determination with respect to visitation rights or the establishment of any specific visitation schedule, the court, in its discretion, may interview in chambers any or all involved children regarding their wishes and concerns. If the court interviews any child concerning the child's wishes and concerns regarding those visitation matters, the interview shall be conducted in chambers, and no person other than the child, the child's attorney, the judge, any necessary court personnel, and, in the judge's discretion, the attorney of each parent shall be permitted to be present in the chambers during the interview. No person shall obtain or attempt to obtain from a child a written or recorded statement or affidavit setting forth the wishes and concerns of the child regarding those visitation matters. A court, in considering the factors listed in division (D) of this section for purposes of determining whether to grant any visitation rights, establishing a visitation schedule, determining other visitation matters under this section or under section 3109.11 or 3109.12 of the Revised Code, or resolving any issues related to the making of any determination with respect to visitation rights or the establishment of any specific visitation schedule, shall not accept or consider a written or recorded statement or affidavit that purports to set forth the child's wishes or concerns regarding those visitation matters.

(D) In determining whether to grant companionship or visitation rights to a parent, grandparent, relative, or other person pursuant to this section or section 3109.11 or 3109.12 of the Revised Code, in establishing a specific visitation schedule, and in determining other visitation matters under this section or section 3109.11 or 3109.12 of the Revised Code, the court shall consider all of the following factors:

(1) The prior interaction and interrelationships of the child with the child's parents, siblings, and other persons related by consanguinity or affinity, and with the person who requested companionship or visitation if that person is not a parent, sibling, or relative of the child;

(2) The geographical location of the residence of each parent and the distance between those residences, and if the person who requested companionship or visitation is not a parent, the geographical location of that person's residence and the distance between that person's residence and the child's residence;

(3) The child's and parents' available time, including, but not limited to, each parent's employment schedule, the child's school schedule, and the child's and the parents' holiday and vacation schedule;

(4) The age of the child;

(5) The child's adjustment to home, school, and community;

(6) If the court has interviewed the child in chambers, pursuant to division (C) of this section, regarding the wishes and concerns of the child as to visitation by the parent who is not the residential parent or companionship or visitation by the grandparent, relative, or other person who requested the companionship or visitation, as to a specific visitation schedule, or as to other visitation matters, the wishes and concerns of the child, as expressed to the court;

(7) The health and safety of the child;

(8) The amount of time that will be available for the child to spend with siblings;

(9) The mental and physical health of all parties;

(10) Each parent's willingness to reschedule missed visitation and to facilitate the other parent's visitation rights, and if the person who requested companionship or visitation is not a parent, the willingness of that person to reschedule missed visitation;

(11) In relation to visitation by a parent, whether either parent previously has been convicted of or pleaded guilty to any criminal offense involving any act that resulted in a child being an abused child or a neglected child; whether either parent, in a case in which a child has been adjudicated an abused child or a neglected child, previously has been determined to be the perpetrator of the abusive or neglectful act that is the basis of the adjudication; and whether there is reason to believe that either parent has acted in a manner resulting in a child being an abused child or a neglected child;

(12) In relation to requested companionship or visitation by a person other than a parent, whether the person previously has been convicted of or pleaded guilty to any criminal offense involving any act that resulted in a child being an abused child or a neglected child; whether the person, in a case in which a child has been adjudicated an abused child or a neglected child, previously has been determined to be the perpetrator of the abusive or neglectful act that is the basis of the adjudication; whether either parent previously has been convicted of or pleaded guilty to a violation of section 2919.25 of the Revised Code involving a victim who at the time of the commission of the offense was a member of the family or household that is the subject of the current proceeding; whether either parent previously has been convicted of an offense involving a victim who at the time of the commission of the offense was a member of the family or household that is the subject of the current proceeding and caused physical harm to the victim in the commission of the offense; and whether there is reason to believe that the person has acted in a manner resulting in a child being an abused child or a neglected child;

(13) Whether the residential parent or one of the parents subject to a shared parenting decree has continuously and willfully denied the other parent's right to visitation in accordance with an order of the court;

(14) Whether either parent has established a residence or is planning to establish a residence outside this state;

(15) Any other factor in the best interest of the child.

(E) The remarriage of a residential parent of a child does not affect the authority of a court under this section to grant visitation rights with respect to the child to the parent who is not the residential parent or to grant reasonable companionship or visitation rights with respect to the child to any grandparent, any person related by consanguinity or affinity, or any other person.

(F)(1) If the court, pursuant to division (A) of this section, denies visitation to a parent who is not the residential parent or denies a motion for reasonable companionship or visitation rights filed under division (B) of this section and the parent or movant files a written request for findings of fact and conclusions of law, the court shall state in writing its findings of fact and conclusions of law in accordance with Civil Rule 52.

(2) On or before July 1, 1991, each court of common pleas, by rule, shall adopt standard visitation guidelines. A court shall have discretion to deviate from its standard visitation guidelines based upon factors set forth in division (D) of this section.

(G)(1) If the residential parent intends to move to a residence other than the residence specified in the visitation order or decree of the court, the parent shall file a notice of intent to relocate with the court that issued the order or decree. Except as provided in divisions (G)(2), (3), and (4) of this section, the court shall send a copy of the notice to the parent who is not the residential parent. Upon receipt of the notice, the court, on its own motion or the motion of the parent who is not the residential parent, may schedule a hearing with notice to both parents to determine whether it is in the best interest of the child to revise the visitation schedule for the child.

(2) When a court grants visitation or companionship rights to a parent who is not the residential parent, the court shall determine whether that parent has been convicted of or pleaded guilty to a violation of section 2919.25 of the Revised Code involving a victim who at the time of the commission of the offense was a member of the family or household that is the subject of the proceeding, has been convicted of or pleaded guilty to any other offense involving a victim who at the time of the commission of the offense was a member of the family or household that is the subject of the proceeding and caused physical harm to the victim in the commission of the offense, or has been determined to be the perpetrator of the abusive act that is the basis of an adjudication that a child is an abused child. If the court determines that that parent has not been so convicted and has not been determined to be the perpetrator of an abusive act that is the basis of a child abuse adjudication, the court shall issue an order stating that a copy of any notice of relocation that is filed with the court pursuant to division (G)(1) of this section will be sent to the parent who is given the visitation or companionship rights in accordance with division (G)(1) of this section.

If the court determines that the parent who is granted the visitation or companionship rights has been convicted of or pleaded guilty to a violation of section 2919.25 of the Revised Code involving a victim who at the time of the commission of the offense was a member of the family or household that is the subject of the proceeding, has been convicted of or pleaded guilty to any other offense involving a victim who at the time of the commission of the offense was a member of the family or household that is the subject of the proceeding and caused physical harm to the victim in the commission of the offense, or has been determined to be the perpetrator of the abusive act that is the basis of an adjudication that a child is an abused child, it shall issue an order stating that that parent will not be given a copy of any notice of relocation that is filed with the court pursuant to division (G)(1) of this section unless the court determines that it is in the best interest of the children to give that parent a copy of the notice of relocation, issues an order stating that that parent will be given a copy of any notice of relocation filed pursuant to division (G)(1) of this section, and issues specific written findings of fact in support of its determination.

(3) If a court, prior to April 11, 1991, issued an order granting visitation or companionship rights to a parent who is not the residential parent and did not require the residential parent in that order to give the parent who is granted the visitation or companionship rights notice of any change of address and if the residential parent files a notice of relocation pursuant to division (G)(1) of this section, the court shall determine if the parent who is granted the

visitation or companionship rights has been convicted of or pleaded guilty to a violation of section 2919.25 of the Revised Code involving a victim who at the time of the commission of the offense was a member of the family or household that is the subject of the proceeding, has been convicted of or pleaded guilty to any other offense involving a victim who at the time of the commission of the offense was a member of the family or household that is the subject of the proceeding and caused physical harm to the victim in the commission of the offense, or has been determined to be the perpetrator of the abusive act that is the basis of an adjudication that a child is an abused child. If the court determines that the parent who is granted the visitation or companionship rights has not been so convicted and has not been determined to be the perpetrator of an abusive act that is the basis of a child abuse adjudication, the court shall issue an order stating that a copy of any notice of relocation that is filed with the court pursuant to division (G)(1) of this section will be sent to the parent who is granted visitation or companionship rights in accordance with division (G)(1) of this section.

If the court determines that the parent who is granted the visitation or companionship rights has been convicted of or pleaded guilty to a violation of section 2919.25 of the Revised Code involving a victim who at the time of the commission of the offense was a member of the family or household that is the subject of the proceeding, has been convicted of or pleaded guilty to any other offense involving a victim who at the time of the commission of the offense was a member of the family or household that is the subject of the proceeding and caused physical harm to the victim in the commission of the offense, or has been determined to be the perpetrator of the abusive act that is the basis of an adjudication that a child is an abused child, it shall issue an order stating that that parent will not be given a copy of any notice of relocation that is filed with the court pursuant to division (G)(1) of this section unless the court determines that it is in the best interest of the children to give that parent a copy of the notice of relocation, issues an order stating that that parent will be given a copy of any notice of relocation filed pursuant to division (G)(1) of this section, and issues specific written findings of fact in support of its determination.

(4) If a parent who is granted visitation or companionship rights pursuant to this section or any other section of the Revised Code is authorized by an order issued pursuant to this section or any other court order to receive a copy of any notice of relocation that is filed pursuant to division (G)(1) of this section or pursuant to court order, if the residential parent intends to move to a residence other than the residence address specified in the visitation or companionship order, and if the residential parent does not want the parent who is granted the visitation or companionship rights to receive a copy of the relocation notice because the parent with visitation or companionship rights has been convicted of or pleaded guilty to a violation of section 2919.25 of the Revised Code involving a victim who at the time of the commission of the offense was a member of the family or household that is the subject of the proceeding, has been convicted of or pleaded guilty to any other offense involving a victim who at the time of the commission of the offense was a member of the family or household that is the subject of the proceeding and caused physical harm to the victim in the commission of the offense, or has been determined to be the perpetrator of the abusive act that is the basis of an adjudication that a child is an abused child, the residential parent may file a motion with the court requesting that the parent who is granted the visitation or companionship rights not receive a copy of any notice of relocation. Upon the filing of the motion, the court shall schedule a hearing on the motion and give both parents notice of the date, time, and location of the hearing. If the court determines that the parent who is granted the visitation or companionship rights has been so convicted or has been determined to be the perpetrator of an abusive act that is the basis of a child abuse adjudication, the court shall issue an order stating that the parent who is granted the visitation or companionship rights will not be given a copy of any notice of relocation that is filed with the court pursuant to division (G)(1) of this section or that the residential parent is no longer required to give that parent a copy of any notice of relocation unless the court determines that it is in the best interest of the children to give that parent a copy of the notice of relocation, issues an order stating that that parent will be given a copy of any notice of relocation filed pursuant to division (G)(1) of this section, and issues

specific written findings of fact in support of its determination. If it does not so find, it shall dismiss the motion.

(H)(1) Subject to division (F)(2) of section 2301.35 and division (F) of section 3319.321 of the Revised Code, a parent of a child who is not the residential parent of the child is entitled to access, under the same terms and conditions under which access is provided to the residential parent, to any record that is related to the child and to which the residential parent of the child legally is provided access, unless the court determines that it would not be in the best interest of the child for the parent who is not the residential parent to have access to the records under those same terms and conditions. If the court determines that the parent of a child who is not the residential parent should not have access to records related to the child under the same terms and conditions as provided for the residential parent, the court shall specify the terms and conditions under which the parent who is not the residential parent is to have access to those records, shall enter its written findings of facts and opinion in the journal, and shall issue an order containing the terms and conditions to both the residential parent and the parent of the child who is not the residential parent. The court shall include in every order issued pursuant to this division notice that any keeper of a record who knowingly fails to comply with the order or division (H) of this section is in contempt of court.

(2) Subject to division (F)(2) of section 2301.35 and division (F) of section 3319.321 of the Revised Code, subsequent to the issuance of an order under division (H)(1) of this section, the keeper of any record that is related to a particular child and to which the residential parent legally is provided access shall permit the parent of the child who is not the residential parent to have access to the record under the same terms and conditions under which access is provided to the residential parent, unless the residential parent has presented the keeper of the record with a copy of an order issued under division (H)(1) of this section that limits the terms and conditions under which the parent who is not the residential parent is to have access to records pertaining to the child and the order pertains to the record in question. If the residential parent presents the keeper of the record with a copy of that type of order, the keeper of the record shall permit the parent who is not the residential parent to have access to the record only in accordance with the most recent order that has been issued pursuant to division (H)(1) of this section and presented to the keeper by the residential parent or the parent who is not the residential parent. Any keeper of any record who knowingly fails to comply with division (H) of this section or with any order issued pursuant to division (H)(1) of this section is in contempt of court.

(3) The prosecuting attorney of any county may file a complaint with the court of common pleas of that county requesting the court to issue a protective order preventing the disclosure pursuant to division (H)(1) or (2) of this section of any confidential law enforcement investigatory record. The court shall schedule a hearing on the motion and give notice of the date, time, and location of the hearing to all parties.

(I) A court that issues a visitation order or decree pursuant to this section, section 3109.11 or 3109.12 of the Revised Code, or any other provision of the Revised Code shall determine whether the parent granted the right of visitation is to be permitted access, in accordance with section 5104.011 of the Revised Code, to any child day-care center that is, or that in the future may be, attended by the children with whom the right of visitation is granted. Unless the court determines that the parent who is not the residential parent should not have access to the center to the same extent that the residential parent is granted access to the center, the parent who is not the residential parent and who is granted visitation or companionship rights is entitled to access to the center to the same extent that the residential parent is granted access to the center. If the court determines that the parent who is not the residential parent should not have access to the center to the same extent that the residential parent is granted such access under division (C) of section 5104.011 of the Revised Code, the court shall specify the terms and conditions under which the parent who is not the residential parent is to have access to the center, provided that the access shall not be greater than the access that is provided to the residential parent under division (C) of section 5104.011 of the Revised Code, the court shall enter its written findings of fact and opinions in the journal, and the court shall include the terms and conditions of access in the visitation order or decree.

(J)(1) Subject to division (F) of section 3319.321 of the Revised Code, when a court issues an order or decree allocating parental rights and responsibilities for the care of a child, the parent of the child who is not the residential parent of the child is entitled to access, under the same terms and conditions under which access is provided to the residential parent, to any student activity that is related to the child and to which the residential parent of the child legally is provided access, unless the court determines that it would not be in the best interest of the child to grant the parent who is not the residential parent access to the student activities under those same terms and conditions. If the court determines that the parent of the child who is not the residential parent should not have access to any student activity that is related to the child under the same terms and conditions as provided for the residential parent, the court shall specify the terms and conditions under which the parent who is not the residential parent is to have access to those student activities, shall enter its written findings of facts and opinion in the journal, and shall issue an order containing the terms and conditions to both the residential parent and the parent of the child who is not the residential parent. The court shall include in every order issued pursuant to this division notice that any school official or employee who knowingly fails to comply with the order or division (J) of this section is in contempt of court.

(2) Subject to division (F) of section 3319.321 of the Revised Code, subsequent to the issuance of an order under division (J)(1) of this section, all school officials and employees shall permit the parent of the child who is not the residential parent to have access to any student activity under the same terms and conditions under which access is provided to the residential parent of the child, unless the residential parent has presented the school official or employee, the board of education of the school, or the governing body of the chartered nonpublic school with a copy of an order issued under division (J)(1) of this section that limits the terms and conditions under which the parent who is not the residential parent is to have access to student activities related to the child and the order pertains to the student activity in question. If the residential parent presents the school official or employee, the board of education of the school, or the governing body of the chartered nonpublic school with a copy of that type of order, the school official or employee shall permit the parent who is not the residential parent to have access to the student activity only in accordance with the most recent order that has been issued pursuant to division (J)(1) of this section and presented to the school official or employee, the board of education of the school, or the governing body of the chartered nonpublic school by the residential parent or the parent who is not the residential parent. Any school official or employee who knowingly fails to comply with division (J) of this section or with any order issued pursuant to division (J)(1) of this section is in contempt of court.

(K) If any person is found in contempt of court for failing to comply with or interfering with any order or decree granting companionship or visitation rights that is issued pursuant to this section, section 3109.11 or 3109.12 of the Revised Code, or any other provision of the Revised Code, the court that makes the finding, in addition to any other penalty or remedy imposed, shall assess all court costs arising out of the contempt proceeding against the person and require the person to pay any reasonable attorney's fees of any adverse party, as determined by the court, that arose in relation to the act of contempt, and may award reasonable compensatory visitation to the person whose right of visitation was affected by the failure or interference if such compensatory visitation is in the best interest of the child. Any compensatory visitation awarded under this division shall be included in an order issued by the court and, to the extent possible, shall be governed by the same terms and conditions as was the visitation that was affected by the failure or interference.

(L) Any person who requests reasonable companionship or visitation rights with respect to a child under this section, section 3109.11 or 3109.12 of the Revised Code, or any other provision of the Revised Code may file a motion with the court requesting that it waive all or any part of the costs that may accrue in the proceedings under this section, section 3109.11, or section 3109.12 of the Revised Code. If the court determines that the movant is indigent and that the waiver is in the best interest of the child, the court, in its discretion, may waive payment of all or any part of the costs of those proceedings.

(M) The juvenile court has exclusive jurisdiction to enter the orders in any case certified to it from another court.

(N) As used in this section:

(1) "Abused child" has the same meaning as in section 2151.031 of the Revised Code, and "neglected child" has the same meaning as in section 2151.03 of the Revised Code.

(2) "Record" means any record, document, file, or other material that contains information directly related to a child, including, but not limited to, any of the following:

(a) Records maintained by public and nonpublic schools;

(b) Records maintained by facilities that provide child day-care, as defined in section 5104.01 of the Revised Code, publicly funded child day-care, as defined in section 5104.01 of the Revised Code, or pre-school services operated by or under the supervision of a school district board of education or a nonpublic school;

(c) Records maintained by hospitals, other facilities, or persons providing medical or surgical care or treatment for the child;

(d) Records maintained by agencies, departments, instrumentalities, or other entities of the state or any political subdivision of the state, other than a child support enforcement agency. Access to records maintained by a child support enforcement agency is governed by division (F)(2) of section 2301.35 of the Revised Code.

(3) "Confidential law enforcement investigatory record" has the same meaning as in section 149.43 of the Revised Code.

(1997 H 408, eff. 10-1-97; 1996 H 274, eff. 8-8-96; 1991 H 155, eff. 7-22-91; 1990 S 3, H 15)

Historical and Statutory Notes

Amendment Note: 1997 H 408 substituted "division (F)(2) of section 2301.35" for "division (G)(2) of section 2301.35" in divisions (H)(1), (H)(2), and (N)(2)(d); and made changes to reflect gender neutral language.

Amendment Note: 1996 H 274 added the fourth and fifth sentences in division (A); substituted "legal separation" for "alimony" in division (B)(2); and made changes to reflect gender neutral language.

Cross References

Contempt for failure to comply or interference with visitation order, 2705.031

County children services boards, powers and duties, 5153.16

Library References

Divorce ⟹299.
Marriage ⟹64.
Parent and Child ⟹2(17).
WESTLAW Topic Nos. 134, 253, 285.
C.J.S. Divorce §§ 618, 619, 632 to 634.
C.J.S. Marriage § 79.
C.J.S. Parent and Child §§ 41, 42.

OJur 3d: 5A, Alternative Dispute Resolution § 174
Denial or restriction of visitation rights to parent charged with sexually abusing child. 1 ALR5th 776

Baldwin's Ohio School Law, Text 31.3

Carlin, Baldwin's Ohio Practice, *Merrick-Rippner Probate Law* § 98.3, 105.11, 107.122, 107.9, 108.15 (1997)
Klein & Darling, Baldwin's Ohio Practice, *Civil Practice* § 52 (1997)
Sowald & Morganstern, Baldwin's Ohio Practice, *Domestic Relations Law* § 3.34, 9.9, 9.10, 9.35, 11.43, 16.11, 18.2, 18.3, 18.4, 18.6, 18.8, 18.10, 18.11, 18.12, 18.13, 18.15, 18.16, 18.17, 18.18, 18.19, 18.24, 18.26, 18.27, 21.2, 21.3, 21.6, 21.7, 21.11, 21.23, 24.2, 25.41, 25.57, 37.21, 37.29, 37.31 (1997)

Law Review and Journal Commentaries

Children Born Out Of Wedlock And Nonsupport—Valid Statutory Grounds For Termination Of Parental Rights?, Note. 25 J Fam L 755 (1986-87).

Constitutional questions regarding grandparent visitation and due process standards. 60 Mo L Rev 195 (1995).

A Father's Right to Visit His Illegitimate Child, Note. 27 Ohio St L J 738 (Fall 1966).

Grandparent Visitation Rights in Ohio After Grandchild Adoption: Is It Time to Move in a New Direction?, Note. 46 Clev St L Rev 385 (1998).

Grandparents' Rights in Ohio After H.B. 15, Richard J. Innis. 2 Domestic Rel J Ohio 33 (May/June 1990).

Grandparent Visitation: The Best Interests of the Grandparent, Child, and Society, Erica L. Strawman. 30 U Tol L Rev 31 (Fall 1998).

Grandparents' Visitation Rights in Ohio: A Procedural Quagmire, Comment. 56 U Cin L Rev 295 (1987).

In re Adoption of Ridenour, Note. 18 Ohio N U L Rev 719 (1992).

Judges' Column, Hon. Francine Bruening. (Ed. note: Judge Bruening discusses the Child Support Reorganization Act of House Bill 352, effective 1-1-98.) 21 Lake Legal Views 1 (June 1998).

Judicial Activism in Domestic Relations Cases, Hon. V. Michael Brigner. (Ed. note: Judge Brigner lists the powers of a judge hearing custody, support, and visitation matters.) 45 Dayton B Briefs 22 (January 1996).

Keeping Kids Out of Court. (Ed. note: Arbitration of custody disputes, but courts reserve the right to review awards.) 19 Nat'l L J B8 (May 5, 1997).

Relocation Issues: Part I—Development of Ohio Law, Hon. Cheryl S. Karner. 5 Domestic Rel J Ohio 37 (May/June 1993).

Sibling Rights to Visitation: A Relationship Too Valuable to Be Denied, Comment. 27 U Tol L Rev 259 (Fall 1995).

There's More than the Wolf Keeping Little Red Riding Hood from Her Grandparents, Hon. Russell A. Steiner. 5 Domestic Rel J Ohio 93 (November/December 1993).

Visitation Interference: Legal Solutions for Fathers, Hon. V. Michael Brigner. 49 Dayton B Briefs 19 (November 1999).

Visitation Rights of a Grandparent Over the Objection of a Parent: The Best Interests of the Child, Note. 15 J Fam L 51 (1976-77).

Visitation Rights Of An AIDS Infected Parent, Note. 27 J Fam L 715 (1988-89).

Wide-Open Grandparent Visitation Statutes: Is the Door Closing?, Comment. 62 U Cin L Rev 1659 (Spring 1994).

Notes of Decisions and Opinions

---

1. Constitutional issues

At common law, grandparents had no right of access to, or constitutional right of association with, their grandchildren. Gaffney v. Menrath (Ohio App. 1 Dist. 1999) 132 Ohio App.3d 113, 724 N.E.2d 507.

There is a federal constitutional basis upon which parental autonomy can be asserted, with respect to grandparent visitation. Gaffney v. Menrath (Ohio App. 1 Dist. 1999) 132 Ohio App.3d 113, 724 N.E.2d 507.

Broadly drawn order forbidding "visitation in the presence of nonrelative adults of the opposite sex" was necessary to further state's compelling interest in protecting children from myriad possibilities of multiple adulterous relationships and the evidentiary problems associated with establishing the existence or nonexistence of said relationships, and, therefore, order infringed on, but did not violate, husband's constitutional right to freedom of association. Boggs v. Boggs (Ohio App. 5 Dist. 1997) 118 Ohio App.3d 293, 692 N.E.2d 674.

Trial court has considerable discretion to decide domestic relations issues, including visitation; discretion requires only that decisions not be unreasonable, arbitrary or unconscionable. Jacobs v. Jacobs (Wayne 1995) 102 Ohio App.3d 568, 657 N.E.2d 580.

Possibility that parties could seek further modification of child visitation order did not justify imposition of midweek visitation which trial court expressly found to be "unfair." Jacobs v. Jacobs (Wayne 1995) 102 Ohio App.3d 568, 657 N.E.2d 580.

Modification of visitation order to impose court's standard visitation schedule is not per se just and reasonable, as court must consider whether there has been change of circumstances and whether modification is in best interest of child. Jacobs v. Jacobs (Wayne 1995) 102 Ohio App.3d 568, 657 N.E.2d 580.

Parties' agreement to modify prior visitation schedule may be sufficient change of circumstances to justify court's modification of schedule to conform with that agreement, provided it is in best interest of child; agreement, however, should not be used as change in circumstances that justifies discontinuation of entire visitation schedule without reference to parties' mutually demonstrated desires. Jacobs v. Jacobs (Wayne 1995) 102 Ohio App.3d 568, 657 N.E.2d 580.

RC 3109.05(B) does not violate the Equal Protection Clause by differentiating between divorced and nondivorced parents in that a court may grant visitation rights to third persons interested in the welfare of a child of divorced parents nor does RC 3109.05(B) violate the Due Process Clause since such visitation rights do not unduly interfere with the home life of the parent or child. Hollingsworth v. Hollingsworth (Franklin 1986) 34 Ohio App.3d 13, 516 N.E.2d 1250.

A court's decision to require the residential parent to live close enough to the non-residential parent to facilitate visitation deals with the custody of the parties' children and does not prohibit either party from travelling state to state or relocating; the residential parent is merely prohibited from taking the children with her if she decides to relocate and the prohibition does not violate the residential parent's right to travel. Alvari v Alvari, No. 99CA05, 2000 WL 133849 (4th Dist Ct App, Lawrence, 2-2-00).

Grandparent visitation that is granted where the parents are divorced does not impermissibly impinge upon constitutional rights of the residential parent who remarries and whose relationship with his parents deteriorates because they do not accept their son's decision to remarry or to include his stepchildren in family outings; when parties obtain a divorce the state is involved and RC 3109.051(B) is properly invoked. Gaffney v Menrath, No. C-971041, 1999 WL 34600 (1st Dist Ct App, Hamilton, 1-29-99).

Absent a finding that a noncustodial parent is unfit or that visitation may be harmful to the children, a visitation order which provides for one hour per week visitation in the custodial parent's home and four hours per week visitation in a grandparent's home is punitive on its face and constitutes an abuse of discretion. Harter v Harter, No. CA-8785 (5th Dist Ct App, Stark, 10-26-92).

Constitutional religious rights are not violated by a child visitation decree giving the noncustodial parent visitation rights on holidays and one Sunday per month, where the custodial parent observes no religious holidays but Sundays. Johnson v Johnson, No. C-830653 (1st Dist Ct App, Hamilton, 7-11-84).

2. In general

Although a party exercising visitation rights might gain temporary physical control over the child for that purpose, such control does not constitute "child custody" because the legal authority to make fundamental decisions about the child's welfare remains with the custodial party and because the child eventually must be returned to the more permanent setting provided by that party. Braatz v. Braatz (Ohio 1999) 85 Ohio St.3d 40, 706 N.E.2d 1218.

Modification of child visitation is governed by statute that specifically addresses visitation rights, rather than by statute that governs child custody, i.e., "parental rights and responsibilities." Braatz v. Braatz (Ohio 1999) 85 Ohio St.3d 40, 706 N.E.2d 1218.

Trial court did not abuse its discretion by deviating from local rule providing for noncustodial parent to receive six weeks of visitation with child during summer months, and instead allowing former husband only two weeks of visitation, where opinion testimony of psychologist and psychology trainee, to which husband did not object, indicated that child's development could regress if she was transferred to husband for the summer months. Badovick v. Badovick (Ohio App. 8 Dist. 1998) 128 Ohio App.3d 18, 713 N.E.2d 1066.

Nonresidential parent's statutory right to access to records relating to care of child is self-executing, and court needs to take action only if it intends to deny access to records. Badovick v. Badovick (Ohio App. 8 Dist. 1998) 128 Ohio App.3d 18, 713 N.E.2d 1066.

Statute governing nonresidential parent's right of access to child's day care facility is not self-executing and places mandatory duty on the court to determine the nonresidential parent's right to access. Badovick v. Badovick (Ohio App. 8 Dist. 1998) 128 Ohio App.3d 18, 713 N.E.2d 1066.

Ordinarily, child support and visitation are independent matters. Hamilton v. Hamilton (Lucas 1995) 107 Ohio App.3d 132, 667 N.E.2d 1256, appeal not allowed 75 Ohio St.3d 1425, 662 N.E.2d 27.

Visitation is a right or privilege that is normally, but not always, granted to nonresidential parent. Hamilton v. Hamilton (Lucas 1995) 107 Ohio App.3d 132, 667 N.E.2d 1256, appeal not allowed 75 Ohio St.3d 1425, 662 N.E.2d 27.

Because visitation is a right, not a duty, trial court cannot force nonresidential parent to visit his or her child. Hamilton v. Hamilton (Lucas 1995) 107 Ohio App.3d 132, 667 N.E.2d 1256, appeal not allowed 75 Ohio St.3d 1425, 662 N.E.2d 27.

For purposes of statute providing that court "shall" consider any mediation report filed if divorce proceeding involves child and if court has not issued shared parenting decree, the word "shall" indicates that the statute is mandatory, but statute becomes mandatory only if mediation report is filed. McClure v. McClure (Greene 1994) 98 Ohio App.3d 27, 647 N.E.2d 832, appeal not allowed 71 Ohio St.3d 1481, 645 N.E.2d 1260.

In divorce action, trial court did not abuse its discretion in entering judgment, in accordance with the apparent agreement of the parties, stating that visitation with child might be granted to father at some future date upon finding by father's treating physician that visitation would be appropriate; father was present in courtroom when attorneys entered into agreement regarding child visitation, father did not object to this agreement, and there was nothing in the record to support father's contention that he did not consent to agreement entered by his attorney. McClure v. McClure (Greene 1994) 98 Ohio App.3d 27, 647 N.E.2d 832, appeal not allowed 71 Ohio St.3d 1481, 645 N.E.2d 1260.

Reference to 3109.05 was presumed to be intended to refer to 3109.051, in statute providing that whenever court issues child support order, it shall include in order specific provisions for regular, holiday, vacation, and special visitation in accordance with 3109.05, 3109.11, or 3109.12 of the Revised Code or in accordance with any other applicable section of the Revised Code, since 3109.05 deals exclusively with child support, whereas 3109.051 deals exclusively with visitation or companionship rights. Tobens v. Brill (Auglaize 1993) 89 Ohio App.3d 298, 624 N.E.2d 265.

Visitation to an incarcerated parent is not prohibited by statute. Tobens v. Brill (Auglaize 1993) 89 Ohio App.3d 298, 624 N.E.2d 265.

Trial court did not abuse its discretion in granting unsupervised visitation privileges to father after it awarded permanent custody to stepmother, despite contention of relative of child that record contained evidence that father committed domestic violence against stepmother before they were married, and committed domestic violence against woman he lived with after he left stepmother; record contained no evidence that incidents of domestic violence ever had an effect on child who was not present at either incident; moreover, although some witnesses testified that they suspected father abused child, no witness testified that any such abuse had in fact occurred. In re Whaley (Athens 1993) 86 Ohio App.3d 304, 620 N.E.2d 954.

Parental rights of visitation are within sound discretion of trial court, and its discretion must be exercised in manner which best protects interest of child. In re Whaley (Athens 1993) 86 Ohio App.3d 304, 620 N.E.2d 954.

Standard court must use in making its decision whether to order visitation is whether visitation is in child's best interest. Holley v. Higgins (Franklin 1993) 86 Ohio App.3d 240, 620 N.E.2d 251.

Divorce court erred in failing to set forth visitation schedule between father and daughter; although son's custody was contested, daughter's custody was not and there was no evidence upon which court could deny reasonable visitation of father with either child. Frost v. Frost (Franklin 1992) 84 Ohio App.3d 699, 618 N.E.2d 198, motion overruled 66 Ohio St.3d 1489, 612 N.E.2d 1245.

A visitation order that affords the nonresidential father of two young children two three-week periods of summer visitation does not constitute an abuse of discretion by virtue of the fact that it requires that the children be returned to the residential parent between the visitation periods for one week where the father is a career military officer currently stationed in the United States who may be assigned to an extended tour of service in Europe, even though this will require the children to endure four, rather than two, transatlantic flights. King v. King (Warren 1992) 78 Ohio App.3d 599, 605 N.E.2d 970.

Where there is clear and convincing evidence that a proposed visitation arrangement will be harmful to the welfare of the children, a trial court abuses its discretion in failing to impose sufficient restrictions to ensure the children's well-being. Bodine v. Bodine (Franklin 1988) 38 Ohio App.3d 173, 528 N.E.2d 973.

A noncustodial parent may not be denied overnight visitation privileges solely on the grounds of the parent's homosexuality. Conkel v. Conkel (Pickaway 1987) 31 Ohio App.3d 169, 509 N.E.2d 983, 31 O.B.R. 335.

Proof of changed circumstances is not required to support modification of a visitation order. Roudebush v. Roudebush (Franklin 1984) 20 Ohio App.3d 380, 486 N.E.2d 849, 20 O.B.R. 485.

The trial court did not abuse its discretion by limiting a visitation schedule to one week at Christmas and two weeks in the summer, where the child was only three years old and lived approximately two hundred miles distant from the noncustodial parent. In re Marriage of Barber (Cuyahoga 1983) 8 Ohio App.3d 372, 457 N.E.2d 360, 8 O.B.R. 485.

Age must be a central consideration in determining when a minor's reluctance in visiting with the noncustodial parent is enough to prevent visitation. Smith v. Smith (Franklin 1980) 70 Ohio App.2d 87, 434 N.E.2d 749, 24 O.O.3d 100.

The father of a child born out of wedlock is not entitled to visitation with such child over the objections of the mother, who has legal custody, unless he clearly establishes that such would be in the best interests of the child. In re Connolly (Franklin 1974) 43 Ohio App.2d 38, 332 N.E.2d 376, 72 O.O.2d 194.

In allocating visitation rights a court does not abuse discretion in not requiring a former spouse to share responsibility for transportation of a minor child between Dayton and Indianapolis when her current husband receives a job promotion and transfer which involves a two and one-half hour drive and eliminates weekday visitation; on the contrary, a magistrate achieves an equitable result by ordering the non-custodial parent to transport the child to and from Indianapolis and also orders a reduction of that parent's support obligation by $40 per month to compensate for transportation costs. Brown v Brown, No. 16039, 1997 WL 531223 (2d Dist Ct App, Montgomery, 8-29-97).

The residential parent's filing of the statutorily required notice of intent to relocate does not grant to the court the authority to prevent the party's relocation to another state; the court may only modify the visitation schedule to comport with the increased distance between the parties. Spain v Spain, No. 8-94-30, 1995 WL 380067 (3d Dist Ct App, Logan, 6-21-95).

Where a child age two years four months hardly knows his father, a visitation order which promotes gradual bonding by way of a six-month period during which father and child have one 48-hour, unsupervised visit per month near the child's home and then allows for seven weeks extended visitation periods in four intervals at the father's home in Texas does not constitute an abuse of discretion. Haudenschield v Brakora, No. 13749, 1993 WL 277846 (2d Dist Ct App, Montgomery, 7-20-93).

Trial court may order a noncustodial parent to visit his child, picking her up from her mother for alternate weekends, where such visitation is ordered for the purpose of providing care and maintenance in a nonmonetary form. Bragg v Gorby, No. 86-C-31 (7th Dist Ct App, Columbiana, 6-30-87).

Where the original decree did not prohibit an out-of-state move by the custodial parent, both parents should bear equally the cost and time of transportation for visitation purposes; the custodial parent should not be penalized for having made the move by being made to bear a disproportionate share of the transportation burden. Pitcher v Pitcher, No. 83AP-530 (10th Dist Ct App, Franklin, 2-28-84).

"Liberal" visitation rights are modified by the pattern of visitation developed by agreement of the parties since the divorce. Hauck v Hauck, No. D-108, 619 (8th Dist Ct App, Cuyahoga, 3-31-83).

Where there is a combination of a father's occasional intoxication and his children's multiple school activities, the court may order the father to make arrangements with the children for visitation without abusing its discretion. Kliner v Kliner, No. 81-J-19 (7th Dist Ct App, Jefferson, 2-2-82).

In an action for permission to remove a child from the jurisdiction and the noncustodial father, the court determined that the mutual benefit of the father/child visitation right is more in the child's best interests than the mother's change of residence. Jamison v Jamison, No. C-800829 (1st Dist Ct App, Hamilton, 11-10-81).

The trial court did not err in requiring the defendant-appellant determined to be the father in a paternity proceeding to prove that visitation with his child would be in the child's best interest; there is no presumption that a reputed father's visitation would be in the best interests of an illegitimate child. Kuhmer v Gibson, No. 924 (11th Dist Ct App, Geauga, 9-30-81).

Visitation by two-year-old with her father while father was incarcerated awaiting trial for aggravated murder of child's mother was not in best interests of child, given very limited nature of visitation that could take place between father and child in highly restricted setting, child's young age, and extreme trauma to which she had already been subjected. In re Erica (Ohio Com.Pl. 1994) 65 Ohio Misc.2d 17, 640 N.E.2d 623.

On the evidence the court will not require a child to be sent to her father in another state in the exercise of his rights of visitation. Anonymous v. Anonymous (Ohio Com.Pl. 1962) 180 N.E.2d 205, 88 Ohio Law Abs. 398, 18 O.O.2d 282.

Visitation rights as to children of divorced parents must be considered without regard to the child's religious training, for all Christian denominations stand on the same footing in the eye of the law. Angel v. Angel (Ohio Com.Pl. 1956) 140 N.E.2d 86, 74 Ohio Law Abs. 531, 2 O.O.2d 136.

When a county children services board is ordered by a court to provide supervision of visitation in a domestic relations case, the county children services board is obligated to provide that supervision unless and until the order is changed, and the county children services board may not charge the court for costs incurred in carrying out the order, except as provided in the order; refusal to comply with the court's order may be the basis for a contempt proceeding. OAG 92-072.

3. Interference with visitation

Trial court acted within its discretion, when granting parties' divorce, in ordering wife to transport parties' minor child 600 miles to visit husband every time child had three-day weekend from school, where wife had moved outside state during pendency of divorce action without court's permission, and trial court found that wife was attempting to influence child away from husband and that wife may have been able to find comparable job without moving. Corple v. Corple (Ohio App. 7 Dist. 1997) 123 Ohio App.3d 31, 702 N.E.2d 1234.

Court's determination that father was not in violation of child visitation order was not against manifest weight of evidence, despite mother's testimony that she had been repeatedly denied telephone access with children and father's admission that he violated visitation order by not being available to answer telephone on several evenings. Davis v. Davis (Jefferson 1996) 115 Ohio App.3d 623, 685 N.E.2d 1292.

Contempt citation was supported by evidence that mother willfully impeded or obstructed court-ordered visitation, even though trial court later conceded that monthly visitation had been rendered impracticable by mother's move with child to another state; fact that judgment may have appeared impracticable in retrospect did not sanction mother's defiance of visitation order. Holm v. Smilowitz (Athens 1992) 83 Ohio App.3d 757, 615 N.E.2d 1047.

Custodial parent's interference with visitation by noncustodial parent may be considered as part of "change of circumstances" which would warrant modification of custody. Holm v. Smilowitz (Athens 1992) 83 Ohio App.3d 757, 615 N.E.2d 1047.

Question for jury was presented as to whether maternal grandparents had interfered with father's court-ordered visitation with his children, in father's action under interference with possessory interest in minor statute; there was evidence that the grandparents knew that the divorce court had ordered that father have visitation with his children when the grandparents took the grandchildren and their daughter with them to their home in Tennessee. Brown v. Denny (Montgomery 1991) 72 Ohio App.3d 417, 594 N.E.2d 1008.

Trial court did not have authority to modify or change mother's custody of children based upon her failure to encourage or implement regular visitation with grandparents as to whom court had provided visitation rights. Truitt v. Truitt (Preble 1989) 65 Ohio App.3d 126, 583 N.E.2d 331.

Modification of a custody order is not among the available sanctions under RC 2705.05(A) as punishment for contempt; a trial court may not as a sanction for contempt of court arising from a custodial parent's interference with a noncustodial parent's visitation rights transfer the authority to the noncustodial parent to grant permission to a minor child to apply for a driver's license or to participate in extracurricular school activities as these changes actually modify custody, which is not a sanction authorized by RC 2705.05(A). Fry v. Fry (Paulding 1989) 64 Ohio App.3d 519, 582 N.E.2d 11.

Suspension of a child support obligation pending three undisturbed visitation periods is not a permissible sanction for interference with a visitation order. Fry v. Fry (Paulding 1989) 64 Ohio App.3d 519, 582 N.E.2d 11.

A court should rigorously use its many powers to discourage a custodial parent from interfering with court-ordered visitation. The custodial parent should be aware that those powers include civil or criminal contempt with fines or imprisonment. Davis v. Davis (Cuyahoga 1988) 55 Ohio App.3d 196, 563 N.E.2d 320.

Modification of a visitation order is not an available sanction for a party's contempt of the order by interfering with visitation; modification of a custody order may be accomplished only after a motion invoking the court's continuing jurisdiction, notice, and a hearing on the motion. Andrulis v. Andrulis (Summit 1985) 26 Ohio App.3d 164, 498 N.E.2d 1380, 26 O.B.R. 383.

Neither RC 3115.21(B) nor 3109.05(B) authorizes the suspension of a support order or the forgiveness of past due unpaid support because of denial or interference with the obligor's visitation rights. Brown v. Brown (Warren 1984) 16 Ohio App.3d 26, 474 N.E.2d 613, 16 O.B.R. 28.

A custodial parent's denial of visitation rights does not excuse refusal by the supporting parent to obey an order requiring support payments; such denial of visitation rights could be the basis for a motion to reduce support payments. Flynn v. Flynn (Madison 1984) 15 Ohio App.3d 34, 472 N.E.2d 388, 15 O.B.R. 57.

Where a noncustodial parent's delay in re-establishing visitation with his child is due to his inability to locate the child, even though he made diligent efforts to do so, the equitable concept of laches should not be applied to curtail his visitation rights. McGill v. McGill (Montgomery 1982) 3 Ohio App.3d 455, 445 N.E.2d 1163, 3 O.B.R. 535.

If a court establishes a visitation schedule concerning the minor children of the parties, in the absence of proof showing that visitation with the noncustodial parent would cause physical or mental harm to the children or a showing of some justification for preventing visitation, the custodial parent must do more than merely encourage the minor children to visit the noncustodial parent, and until the children can affirmatively and independently decide not to have any visitation with the noncustodial parent, the custodial parent must follow a court order requiring the custodial parent to deliver the children to the noncustodial parent for visitation. Smith v. Smith (Franklin 1980) 70 Ohio App.2d 87, 434 N.E.2d 749, 24 O.O.3d 100.

A non-custodial parent is not required as a condition of exercising visitation to present himself at the prescribed time after the custodial parent has made it clear that she will not permit visitation nor is he obliged to seek a reaffirmation of the order when it becomes possible and convenient for him to begin exercising visitation in accordance with its terms. Tangeman v Tangeman, No. 99-CA-53, 2000 WL 217284 (2d Dist Ct App, Greene, 2-25-00).

A trial court abuses its discretion when it orders the suspension of a child support obligation for a period of eighteen months due to the residential parent's noncompliance with the visitation schedule. Roberts v Roberts, No. 95 APF01-33, 1995 WL 432612 (10th Dist Ct App, Franklin, 7-20-95).

The duty to pay child support is unaffected by any interference with rights of visitation, and no estoppel to claim child support arrears from a father may be inferred from the mother's withholding of visitation with the child. French v French, No. 9-95-7, 1995 WL 328110 (3d Dist Ct App, Marion, 5-30-95).

It is the absolute duty of the custodial parent to have the children participate in visitation, and parents must immediately attempt to resolve any conflicts that arise through the court or another appropriate party; consequently, a mother who fails to comply with a visitation order and actively interferes with visitation will be found in contempt. Dickard v Ringenbach, No. 66136, 1994 WL 449424 (8th Dist Ct App, Cuyahoga, 8-18-94).

Where the noncustodial mother of children moves to another state and refuses to return the children to the custodial father after an extended visitation period in defiance of court orders, the court is within its authority to modify visitation to ensure that the custodial father's rights are not jeopardized. Stehura v Stehura, No. 1333 (11th Dist Ct App, Ashtabula, 2-26-88).

Where a welfare department does not complete an investigation of alleged abuse by a noncustodial father, within thirty days as required by RC 2151.421 but instead waits nearly one year to close the case because of the complaining mother's refusal to cooperate and the department's failure to take any of the steps available to it to secure cooperation, the father who was deprived of visitation for the entire period should have sought a writ of mandamus ordering the investigation to proceed and cannot sue the department in US district court under 42 USC 1983. Haag v. Cuyahoga County (N.D.Ohio 1985) 619 F.Supp. 262, affirmed 798 F.2d 1414.

4. Visitation with grandparents and others

Statute permitting court in divorce, dissolution of marriage, legal separation, annulment, or child support proceeding that involves child to grant visitation rights to "any other person other than a parent," does not apply following adoption. State ex rel. Kaylor v. Bruening (Ohio 1997) 80 Ohio St.3d 142, 684 N.E.2d 1228.

A juvenile court abuses its discretion by ordering that visitation with adopted children's biological grandparents shall continue post-adoption. In re Adoption of Ridenour (Ohio 1991) 61 Ohio St.3d 319, 574 N.E.2d 1055.

In general, grandparental visitation rights do not vest until occurrence of disruptive precipitating event, such as parental death or divorce; absent disruptive event, common-law view of deferring to parental autonomy in raising child is observed despite moral or social obligations that encourage contact between grandparents and grandchildren. In re Gibson (Ohio 1991) 61 Ohio St.3d 168, 573 N.E.2d 1074.

Grandparents may be granted visitation rights under RC 3109.11 and 3109.05(B) if the trial court finds that such visitation is in the child's best interest. In re Whitaker (Ohio 1988) 36 Ohio St.3d 213, 522 N.E.2d 563.

Trial court lacked authority to grant paternal grandparents visitation with children of divorced parents after the children were adopted by their stepfather subsequent to their father's death; while a statute preserved the right of grandparent visitation when a surviving spouse remarried, it did not provide for the preservation of visitation rights after an adoption by a stepparent. Foor v. Foor (Ohio App. 12 Dist. 1999) 133 Ohio App.3d 250, 727 N.E.2d 618.

Assuming that adjudicated father's petition for modification of his child support obligation was properly before Juvenile Court, fact that such petition was pending did not vest Juvenile Court with jurisdiction to entertain paternal grandmother's petition for grandparental visitation pursuant to domestic relations statute, where statute setting forth Juvenile Court's jurisdiction in parentage actions did not reference domestic relations statute, and where child's mother was unmarried. Borkosky v. Mihailoff (Ohio App. 3 Dist. 1999) 132 Ohio App.3d 508, 725 N.E.2d 694.

Parental authority of husband who divorced and then remarried was not impermissibly infringed by the granting of grandparent visitation rights with respect to husband's children from his first marriage. Gaffney v. Menrath (Ohio App. 1 Dist. 1999) 132 Ohio App.3d 113, 724 N.E.2d 507.

Statutory grandparent visitation rights are not limited to situations in which the visitation interests of the parents of the nonresidential parent have been adversely threatened; rather, each set of grandparents has the right to invoke the statute. Gaffney v. Menrath (Ohio App. 1 Dist. 1999) 132 Ohio App.3d 113, 724 N.E.2d 507.

In addition to the statutory factors for finding that grandparent visitation is in the best interests of the child, the trial court must consider the extent to which the autonomy of either parent may be undermined and the impact on the then-existing family situation. Gaffney v. Menrath (Ohio App. 1 Dist. 1999) 132 Ohio App.3d 113, 724 N.E.2d 507.

Trial court did not abuse its discretion in granting stepfather visitation rights with ex-wife's child from previous marriage, where guardian ad litem recommended that stepfather be granted visitation rights, and stepfather was only real father child had for six of her 11 years. Shannon v. Shannon (Ohio App. 9 Dist. 1997) 122 Ohio App.3d 346, 701 N.E.2d 771.

Paternal grandparents were divested of visitation and companionship rights with grandchild where their son, child's father, was deceased and mother's new spouse had adopted the child; stepparent adoption terminated child's relationship with paternal grandparents for all purposes and fact that adoption occurred after death of child's father did not change this conclusion. Beard v. Pannell (Sandusky 1996) 110 Ohio App.3d 572, 674 N.E.2d 1225, appeal not allowed 77 Ohio St.3d 1447, 671 N.E.2d 1285.

Statute providing that marriage of the surviving parent of child does not affect authority of court to grant reasonable companionship or visitation rights to grandparents preserves the right of grandparent visitation when the surviving spouse remarries, but it does not provide for the preservation of grandparent visitation rights after adoption of child by stepparent. Beard v. Pannell (Sandusky 1996) 110 Ohio App.3d 572, 674 N.E.2d 1225, appeal not allowed 77 Ohio St.3d 1447, 671 N.E.2d 1285.

Grandparent visitation rights are statutorily provided and, thus, any changes in this area must be initiated by General Assembly. Beard v. Pannell (Sandusky 1996) 110 Ohio App.3d 572, 674 N.E.2d 1225, appeal not allowed 77 Ohio St.3d 1447, 671 N.E.2d 1285.

In general, grandparent visitation is in child's best interest. Holley v. Higgins (Franklin 1993) 86 Ohio App.3d 240, 620 N.E.2d 251.

Trial court's decision to allow maternal grandmother visitation with granddaughter who was in custody of father was not an abuse of discretion, despite fact that grandmother had previously been convicted of grand theft; grandmother had paid her debt to society more than 16 years ago and record indicated she had been a model citizen and mother since then; moreover, offense for which grandmother was convicted did not result in child abuse or neglect, and thus was not an issue for consideration by trial court under applicable statute. Holley v. Higgins (Franklin 1993) 86 Ohio App.3d 240, 620 N.E.2d 251.

Relatives of parents whose parental rights are terminated have no standing to assert visitation rights. Farley v. Farley (Licking 1992) 85 Ohio App.3d 113, 619 N.E.2d 427.

Juvenile court does not have authority to grant paternal grandparents visitation rights with grandchild after grandchild has been adopted by stepfather. Krnac v. Starman (Medina 1992) 83 Ohio App.3d 578, 615 N.E.2d

344, dismissed, jurisdictional motion overruled 66 Ohio St.3d 1485, 612 N.E.2d 1241.

After suspending a father's visitation rights, a trial court may also suspend the paternal grandparents' visitation rights until further court order where the grandparents live only 500 feet from the child's father, the father is at their house every day, and the grandparents do not acknowledge the ill effects of the father's treatment of the child and reinforce the father's conduct. Johntonny v. Malliski (Geauga 1990) 67 Ohio App.3d 709, 588 N.E.2d 200, motion to certify overruled 55 Ohio St.3d 715, 563 N.E.2d 725.

A court must decide whether visitation by grandparents is in a child's best interest, and refusal to grant visitation to a grandparent will not be disturbed on appeal where the grandparent has allowed the father to be alone with the child despite an agreement with the father not to do so and where the grandparent is likely to have close contact with the father, who has threatened violence to the child and subjected the child to scenes of extreme violence against the mother. Drennen v. Drennen (Erie 1988) 52 Ohio App.3d 121, 557 N.E.2d 149.

A trial court's jurisdiction to modify a visitation order and grant visitation rights to any other person includes the authority to add persons not originally parties to the action. Hollingsworth v. Hollingsworth (Franklin 1986) 34 Ohio App.3d 13, 516 N.E.2d 1250.

RC 3109.05(B) specifically states that a court in its discretion may grant reasonable companionship or visitation rights "to any other person having an interest in the welfare of the child." This broad category includes any person regardless of the relationship to the custodial or noncustodial parent since the determinative factor in the award is the welfare of the child, not the relationship the person has to or with either parent. Hollingsworth v. Hollingsworth (Franklin 1986) 34 Ohio App.3d 13, 516 N.E.2d 1250.

RC 3107.15 does not prohibit an order pursuant to RC 3109.05, granting visitation rights to a biological paternal grandparent after adoption of a child by a stepfather, when the biological father's whereabouts are unknown. Welsh v. Laffey (Butler 1984) 16 Ohio App.3d 110, 474 N.E.2d 681, 16 O.B.R. 117.

Where a divorced mother of a minor child, having been given custody thereof, has not abandoned the child, has not agreed that the paternal grandparents shall have visitation rights with such child, and where such child has not been living with such grandparents, a court exceeds its authority in granting visitation rights to such grandparents upon a motion for modification of visitation rights filed by the divorced father. Shriver v. Shriver (Union 1966) 7 Ohio App.2d 169, 219 N.E.2d 300, 36 O.O.2d 308.

A trial court has no authority to grant grandparents' visitation rights following a stepparent adoption. Foor v Foor, No. CA98-06-007, 1999 WL 247144 (12th Dist Ct App, Preble, 4-26-99).

A partner in a lesbian relationship does not have an obligation to pay child support insofar as she is not the biological, natural or adoptive mother of her partner's child and her attempt to file a child support proceeding in order to claim visitation rights pursuant to RC 3109.051 must fail. Liston v Pyles, No. 97APF01-137, 1997 WL 467327 (10th Dist Ct App, Franklin, 8-12-97).

Paternal grandparents who are granted leave to intervene as parties in their son's divorce action solely for the purpose of obtaining visitation with their grandchildren do not have any rights in the determination of custody and placement of the children and no right to notice of dismissal of a motion for reallocation of parental rights and responsibilities. Hughes v Hughes, No. 95APF12-1570, 1996 WL 325486 (10th Dist Ct App, Franklin, 6-11-96).

Restriction upon a father's visitation rights is justified by testimony of the childrens' treating therapists and a record of physical and sexual abuse of the children by the father and his girlfriend. In re Lamb, No. CA95-01-006, 1996 WL 56077 (12th Dist Ct App, Butler, 2-12-96).

Since RC 3109.051 allows an individual related to a child by marriage or any other person other than a parent to file a motion requesting companionship rights, a trial court errs in dismissing a stepfather as a party by ruling that a stepparent lacks standing to contest any issues regarding companionship rights or the allocation of parental rights and responsibilities. Corn v Corn, No. 15-95-1, 1995 WL 551102 (3d Dist Ct App, Van Wert, 9-15-95).

Although a juvenile court determined that the plaintiff was not the father of a child in a prior proceeding, the domestic relations court errs in determining that it did not have jurisdiction of the plaintiff's claim of visitation and companionship rights since RC 3109.051 expressly permits nonparents to obtain visitation and companionship rights with respect to a minor child in connection with a divorce or legal separation. Cassim v Cassim, No. 94APF12-1771, 1995 WL 546926 (10th Dist Ct App, Franklin, 9-14-95).

After temporary custody of grandchildren has been awarded to the county children services, the trial court may exercise its discretion and determine whether the grandparents should be allowed to intervene in the proceedings by considering the timeliness of the motion filed by the grandparents, as well as the persuasiveness of the argument the grandparents seek to assert regarding visitation. In re Deleon, No. 94APF5-763, 1994 WL 714465 (10th Dist Ct App, Franklin, 12-22-94).

The legislature has not provided the juvenile court with the authority to grant visitation rights to biological grandparents following an adoption of a grandchild by a stepparent even where the parental rights of the grandparents' child have been terminated through death. In re Apple, No. 93-VA-59, 1994 WL 515116 (2d Dist Ct App, Miami, 9-21-94).

Grandparents are not statutorily entitled to visitation of their grandchildren and a court must consider the factors enumerated in RC 3109.11 as well as the best interest and wishes of the children; consequent denial of visitation to a grandmother is neither an automatic ground for reversal nor an abuse of discretion. In re Skinner, No. 93CA547, 1994 WL 93149 (4th Dist Ct App, Adams, 3-23-94).

The power given courts by RC 3109.05(B) to grant visitation rights to individuals other than parents is not limited in exercise to the "divorce, dissolution of marriage, alimony, or child support proceeding" provided under RC 3109.05(A); consequently, paternal grandparents may seek visitation rights under RC 3109.05(B) after their son consents to termination of his parental rights and the grandchild is placed for adoption with a maternal uncle. Brandt v DeGroff, No. WMS-85-21 (6th Dist Ct App, Williams, 10-17-86).

5. Procedural issues

Father who sought modification of his child visitation rights under divorce decree was not required to show that there had been change in circumstances; however, trial court was required to consider 15 statutory factors, and, in its sound discretion, determine visitation that was in child's best interest; abrogating *Jacobs v Jacobs*, 102 Ohio App.3d 568, 657 N.E.2d 580. Braatz v. Braatz (Ohio 1999) 85 Ohio St.3d 40, 706 N.E.2d 1218.

Biological father's allegations, that appeal was not complete, beneficial, and speedy, and thus was not adequate remedy to prevent Court of Common Pleas from granting visitation to biological mother following issuance of adoption decree that terminated her parental rights, and that irreparable harm to child and to relationship between biological father would result should visitation proceedings not be stopped, stated cause of action in complaint seeking writ of prohibition. State ex rel. Kaylor v. Bruening (Ohio 1997) 80 Ohio St.3d 142, 684 N.E.2d 1228.

Although Court of Common Pleas had basic statutory jurisdiction to grant visitation to biological parent, it was patently and unambiguously divested by adoption statute of jurisdiction to proceed on biological mother's motions relating to visitation following adoption decree terminating her parental rights, and writ of prohibition preventing Court from doing so thus was appropriate. State ex rel. Kaylor v. Bruening (Ohio 1997) 80 Ohio St.3d 142, 684 N.E.2d 1228.

An in camera interview of a child may be an appropriate method by which the trial court determines the child's best interest in visitation cases, even if one of the parties objects to such an interview. In re Whitaker (Ohio 1988) 36 Ohio St.3d 213, 522 N.E.2d 563.

Modification of visitation rights is governed by RC 3109.05 and the specific rules for determining when a court may modify a custody decree are not equally applicable to modification of visitation rights. Appleby v. Appleby (Ohio 1986) 24 Ohio St.3d 39, 492 N.E.2d 831, 24 O.B.R. 81.

An extended visitation order at issue was not the equivalent of a formal modification of a prior custody decree. State ex rel. Scordato v. George (Ohio 1981) 65 Ohio St.2d 128, 419 N.E.2d 4, 19 O.O.3d 318.

Trial court's failure to schedule visitation by child with former husband on both child's birthday and former husband's birthday, as required by local rules, was improper, and matter would be remanded to allow order to be amended to incorporate visitation, where nothing indicated that court intentionally decided to omit such visitation, and wife did not suggest that such visitation would be against child's best interests. Badovick v. Badovick (Ohio App. 8 Dist. 1998) 128 Ohio App.3d 18, 713 N.E.2d 1066.

Trial court that granted wife's first divorce had subject matter jurisdiction over stepfather's motion for visitation with wife's child by first marriage; stepfather properly invoked court's continuing jurisdiction over divorce by filing motion for visitation with original court, rather than with court that granted divorce of stepfather and wife. Shannon v. Shannon (Ohio App. 9 Dist. 1997) 122 Ohio App.3d 346, 701 N.E.2d 771.

Denial of husband's motion for temporary visitation rights in separation action was interlocutory order that was not appealable, and that could not be made appealable by findings that appeal should be undertaken forthwith and that there was no just cause for delay, since that denial did not preclude different judgment upon final determination of case, and denial of motion was not such a distinct portion of action as to constitute separate claim. Cassim v. Cassim (Franklin 1994) 98 Ohio App.3d 576, 649 N.E.2d 28, on subsequent appeal, dismissed, appeal not allowed 75 Ohio St.3d 1404, 661 N.E.2d 754.

Since no mediation report was filed and there was no indication that any mediation occurred, trial court could not have erred by failing to consider mediation report pursuant to statute providing that, if divorce proceeding involves child and if court has not issued shared parenting decree, court shall consider any mediation report filed. McClure v. McClure (Greene 1994) 98 Ohio App.3d 27, 647 N.E.2d 832, appeal not allowed 71 Ohio St.3d 1481, 645 N.E.2d 1260.

Trial court's "decision on divorce" and its "final judgment and decree of divorce" were sufficient to constitute statement of the court's findings of facts and conclusions of law in the case for purposes of statute requiring court to journalize its findings of fact and conclusions of law when court determines that it would not be in best interest of child to permit parent to visit child. McClure v. McClure (Greene 1994) 98 Ohio App.3d 27, 647 N.E.2d 832, appeal not allowed 71 Ohio St.3d 1481, 645 N.E.2d 1260.

By agreeing to waive his right to visitation with child, father waived his right to statement of trial court's findings of fact and conclusions of law pursuant to statute requiring court to journalize its findings of fact and conclusions of law when court determines that it would not be in best interest of child to permit parent to visit child. McClure v. McClure (Greene 1994) 98 Ohio App.3d 27, 647 N.E.2d 832, appeal not allowed 71 Ohio St.3d 1481, 645 N.E.2d 1260.

In divorce action, trial court was not bound to adopt opinion of father's treating physician as to appropriateness of father's visitation with child and thus, trial court would not have abused its discretion in denying father visitation with child even if father had not agreed to waive his visitation; physician diagnosed father with major depression, posttraumatic stress disorder, and multiple personality disorders, physician testified that father's prognosis was fair and that father required continuing psychiatric treatment, and physician stated that posttraumatic stress disorder and personality disorders could be lifelong problems for father. McClure v. McClure (Greene 1994) 98 Ohio App.3d 27, 647 N.E.2d 832, appeal not allowed 71 Ohio St.3d 1481, 645 N.E.2d 1260.

Trial court's allocation of transportation expenses for visitation was unreasonable, insofar as court, in determining parties' income, subtracted father's child support obligation and added the same to mother's income. Gatliff v. Gatliff (Hancock 1993) 89 Ohio App.3d 391, 624 N.E.2d 779.

In determining visitation schedule, trial court was not required to continue any temporary arrangements made during pendency of divorce. deLevie v. deLevie (Franklin 1993) 86 Ohio App.3d 531, 621 N.E.2d 594, dismissed, jurisdictional motion overruled 67 Ohio St.3d 1409, 615 N.E.2d 1043.

A domestic relations court which granted a divorce retains jurisdiction for the purposes of granting visitation rights as required by the best interest of any children born as issue of the marriage regardless of the existence or venue of a subsequent stepparent adoption proceeding. Bente v. Hill (Clermont 1991) 73 Ohio App.3d 151, 596 N.E.2d 1042, dismissed, jurisdictional motion overruled 62 Ohio St.3d 1422, 577 N.E.2d 1105.

A trial court may, pursuant to motions to modify and/or enforce visitation and companionship filed following a dissolution, order the parties and their children to undergo mental examinations, as the mental health of the parties and the children is relevant to the children's best interests as to visitation, but the court may order such examinations under Civ R 35(A) only on motion by one of the parties and after evidence has been presented to show good cause for each examination requested; moreover, the court must also specify the time, place, manner, conditions, and scope of any examinations ordered. Brossia v. Brossia (Wood 1989) 65 Ohio App.3d 211, 583 N.E.2d 978.

When a parent seeks to modify a previous visitation arrangement, it is that party who bears the burden of proof as to whether the prior arrangement was not in the best interests of the children; in the same way, the presumption that a parent is fit does not automatically entitle a parent to any visitation schedule desired as the parent must still establish that the schedule is in the children's best interests. Bodine v. Bodine (Franklin 1988) 38 Ohio App.3d 173, 528 N.E.2d 973.

One not a party to an original divorce action may obtain visitation rights through a court's continuing inherent jurisdiction, provided that proper notice is given pursuant to RC 3109.05(B), which provides that "reasonable companionship or visitation rights may be granted to any other person having an interest in the welfare of the child." Hollingsworth v. Hollingsworth (Franklin 1986) 34 Ohio App.3d 13, 516 N.E.2d 1250.

A stepfather may invoke the continuing jurisdiction of the court in a divorce action between the mother and natural father of a child pursuant to Civ R 75(I), in order to obtain an award of visitation rights with a stepchild under RC 3109.05, which permits the court to grant such rights to "any other person having an interest in the welfare of the child." Hutton v. Hutton (Lorain 1984) 21 Ohio App.3d 26, 486 N.E.2d 129, 21 O.B.R. 28.

The authority vested in a court by RC 3109.05, in extreme circumstances, includes the authority to give relief, through a just modification of an order of support, to a parent continuously or repeatedly prevented from exercising a right to visit a child by the child's refusal to visit with him; but such jurisdiction should not be exercised until the court first considers whether to make the child a party pursuant to Civ R 75(B)(2). Foster v. Foster (Franklin 1974) 40 Ohio App.2d 257, 319 N.E.2d 395, 69 O.O.2d 250.

Where a divorce court has by its decree discharged its duty under 3109.05 with respect to the determination of visitation rights of the parent deprived of a minor child's custody, by merely accepting as its order as to visitation that to which the parties have agreed, but without specifically determining what would be for the child's best interest and welfare, and the parents thereafter disagree and a motion for modification is filed by the parent deprived of custody, the court is not bound by the agreement, and, though there are no changed conditions or circumstances which would otherwise justify the court in modifying or changing the previous order, the court must determine that which is for the best interest and welfare of the child and, in the exercise of its discretion, may modify the visitation rights accordingly. Miller v. Miller (Hancock 1966) 7 Ohio App.2d 22, 218 N.E.2d 630, 36 O.O.2d 69.

The burden of proof that visitation would not be in the child's best interest is on the person opposing visitation and there is no requirement to show a change of circumstances in any request to change visitation rights. In re Nichols, No. CA97-11-102, 1998 WL 295937 (12th Dist Ct App, Clermont, 6-8-98).

A definite child visitation schedule should be provided by the court where the parties harbor animosity towards one another and are unable to agree upon a summer schedule of visitation for the nonresidential parent; likewise, a trial court errs in failing to award the nonresidential parent six weeks of extended summer visitation with the minor child of the parties as provided by local rule without showing good cause why such visitation should not be permitted. Leas v Leech, No. 95-J-5, 1996 WL 451374 (7th Dist Ct App, Jefferson, 8-9-96).

Telephone visitation between a father and his children is not limited by scheduling his telephone calls to the children and eliminating daily phone calls, which reduces conflict between the parties' households. Darner v Bach, No. CA95-06-069, 1996 WL 71490 (12th Dist Ct App, Warren, 2-20-96).

A residential parent's motion to terminate visitation and the motion of the nonresidential parent to set specific visitation times do not concern custodial issues, and a court errs by granting a motion to modify custody in a case where testimony and evidence do not rise to the level of a substantial change of circumstance but rather indicate the nonresidential parent's increasing demand for additional visitation. Davis v Flickinger, No. 94AP110077, 1995 WL 557132 (5th Dist Ct App, Tuscarawas, 9-19-95), reversed by 77 OS(3d) 415 (1997).

Trial court erred in denying grandparents post stepparent adoption visitation rights with their grandchildren as the adoption does not prevent them from having standing and they can show an interest in the children's welfare under RC 3109.051. Sweeney v Sweeney, No. CA93-02-004, 1993 WL 414186 (12th Dist Ct App, Fayette, 10-18-93), reversed by 71 Ohio St. 3d 169 (1994).

Trial court did not abuse its discretion in modifying visitation schedule and not adopting standard visitation schedule applicable to parents living within 150 miles of each other, where RC 3109.051(F)(2) gave trial court authority to deviate from its standard visitation guidelines and trial court considered factors set forth in RC 3109.051(D). Snyder v Snyder, No. S-92-30, 1993 WL 356939 (6th Dist Ct App, Sandusky, 9-17-93).

A trial court's failure to provide for any visitation schedule due to a noncustodial parent's current incarceration without exploring options which would allow the incarcerated parent to visit his children prior to his release from incarceration or to establish a schedule effective upon his release constitutes an abuse of discretion and will be reversed and remanded. Tobens v Brill, No. 2-93-3, 1993 WL 312913 (3d Dist Ct App, Auglaize, 8-19-93).

Because a trial court may modify visitation (as distinguished from custody and support) without a change of circumstances, a judgment fixing visitation is not a final appealable order and an appeal therefrom will be dismissed. Tolerton v Tolerton, No. 92-CA-9, 1993 WL 221254 (5th Dist Ct App, Licking, 6-1-93).

A court has no jurisdiction to modify a visitation decree where the party was not served pursuant to Civ R 75(I). Jenkins v Jenkins, No. 1504 (4th Dist Ct App, Lawrence, 12-9-81).

Where the father received no notice pursuant to the rules of procedure that the continuing jurisdiction of the court had been invoked to modify his visitation rights, the court of appeals will reverse because the father is entitled to attend such a hearing with a clear understanding of its purpose. Harris v Harris, No. 1593 (2d Dist Ct App, Clark, 10-22-81).

6. Termination of visitation

Trial court abused its discretion in denying all visitation because former husband was incarcerated and then requiring former husband to request visitation upon his release. Tobens v. Brill (Auglaize 1993) 89 Ohio App.3d 298, 624 N.E.2d 265.

Enforcement of a court-approved settlement of a prior visitation modification proceeding terminating the father's visitation rights if the father again engaged in offenses relating to alcohol or drugs is proper where the court determines that termination of visitation rights is in the child's best interest in light of the father's subsequent DWI offenses. Brown v. Brown (Hancock 1992) 78 Ohio App.3d 416, 604 N.E.2d 1380.

Clear and convincing evidence supports the trial court's decision to suspend a father's visitation where (1) the child's intense dislike and fear of his father is shown, (2) there is evidence that a serious problem exists between the father and child due to the child's perceptions of his father's constant fault-finding and lack of empathy with him, and (3) the father has failed to cooperate in therapy and has not acknowledged the existence of a problem. Johntonny v. Malliski (Geauga 1990) 67 Ohio App.3d 709, 588 N.E.2d 200, motion to certify overruled 55 Ohio St.3d 715, 563 N.E.2d 725.

A parent's incarceration for a term of years constitutes an extraordinary circumstance, as do (1) unfitness of the noncustodial parent, and (2) harm to the child caused by visitation. In re Hall (Franklin 1989) 65 Ohio App.3d 88, 582 N.E.2d 1055.

Imprisonment of a parent for a term of years for a violent crime, while an extraordinary circumstance which supports denial of visitation, does not necessarily preclude visitation; visitation may occur, but only if it is in the best interests of the child, a circumstance which must be proven by the incarcerated parent. In re Hall (Franklin 1989) 65 Ohio App.3d 88, 582 N.E.2d 1055.

Visitation of a noncustodial parent in prison which requires transporting a young child there on a regular frequent basis gives rise to an inference of harm to the child so that this visitation is not in the child's best interest; such an inference should not be drawn only if the incarcerated noncustodial parent proves that visitation at the place of imprisonment is not harmful to the child, but is in the child's best interest. In re Hall (Franklin 1989) 65 Ohio App.3d 88, 582 N.E.2d 1055.

In a proceeding for termination of visitation, where expert testimony establishes that the children would be harmed by knowledge of their father's homosexuality, it is an abuse of discretion not to terminate visitation rights or impose conditions that would guarantee that the children not acquire that knowledge. Roberts v. Roberts (Franklin 1985) 22 Ohio App.3d 127, 489 N.E.2d 1067, 22 O.B.R. 328.

While visitation rights may be entirely denied under extraordinary circumstances, a child's unwillingness and fear to visit the noncustodial parent should be discounted if they result from influence of the custodial parent, or ignorance due to the child's age or lack of familiarity with the noncustodial parent. Pettry v. Pettry (Cuyahoga 1984) 20 Ohio App.3d 350, 486 N.E.2d 213, 20 O.B.R. 454.

Visitation rights may be completely denied only on a showing of such extraordinary circumstances as the unfitness of the noncustodial parent, or that visitation would harm the children, and the burden of proof of such circumstances is on the party contesting visitation privileges. Pettry v. Pettry (Cuyahoga 1984) 20 Ohio App.3d 350, 486 N.E.2d 213, 20 O.B.R. 454.

Where a minor child is less than two years old at the time of the divorce hearing, the mother is still nursing him, the father has difficulty handling the child, and the father has frequently failed to show up for scheduled visitations, the trial court's order granting custody to the mother and limiting the father's visitation rights is not unreasonable, arbitrary, or unconscionable. Lathrop v. Lathrop (Preble 1982) 5 Ohio App.3d 240, 451 N.E.2d 546, 5 O.B.R. 526.

The fact that a nonresidential parent is imprisoned for a term of years is an extraordinary circumstance which will ordinarily support the denial of visitation, and such visitation is usually presumed not in the best interest of a child unless there is some evidence to the contrary; therefore, where a noncustodial parent is incarcerated for aggravated robbery, a serious offense of violence under Ohio law, and has not demonstrated to the satisfaction of the court that there is any reason whatsoever why visitation with him while he is incarcerated would serve the best interests of the parties' minor children, denial of visitation is not an abuse of discretion. Lowe v Lowe, No. CA97-02-003, 1997 WL 349033 (12th Dist Ct App, Butler, 6-23-97).

A mother's visitation rights may be suspended due to her physical and emotional harm to her children evidenced by (1) hitting and pinching, (2) pulling the daughter's hair, (3) depriving them of food as punishment of her husband, and (4) physically attacking the husband in front of the children; a court may reinstate visitation after a period free of the mother's negative behavior. Pisani v Pisani, Nos. 67814+, 1996 WL 28572 (8th Dist Ct App, Cuyahoga, 1-25-96).

Ex-husband's sex change from male to female constituted a substantial change of circumstances that justified temporary termination of a previously ordered right to visitation of minor children until evidence of their growth and maturity could be presented to the trial court. Cisek v Cisek, No. 80-CA-113 (7th Dist Ct App, Mahoning, 7-20-82).

The mere statement of a twelve-year-old child of divorced parents that she did not want to see her father again was insufficient evidence to justify a complete refusal to permit such father to visit her, and a statement by the mother's counsel that defendant had been guilty of misconduct toward his step-daughter was of no probative value. Marsh v. Marsh (Franklin 1954) 126 N.E.2d 468, 69 Ohio Law Abs. 539.

7. Age of child

Child's change in age from two and one-half years to nine years, father's desire to spend more time with child, and parties' de facto modification of holiday visitation schedule did not constitute changed circumstances warranting modification of father's visitation schedule as set forth in agreement upon marital dissolution. Jacobs v. Jacobs (Wayne 1995) 102 Ohio App.3d 568, 657 N.E.2d 580.

Change in circumstances supporting modification of visitation order generally should not be predicated upon change in child's age, but child's age is properly considered as relevant factor in determination of child's best interests. Jacobs v. Jacobs (Wayne 1995) 102 Ohio App.3d 568, 657 N.E.2d 580.

3109.052 Mediation order; report

(A) If a proceeding for divorce, dissolution, legal separation, annulment, or the allocation of parental rights and responsibilities for the care of a child involves one or more children, if the parents of the children do not agree upon an appropriate allocation of parental rights and responsibilities for the care of their children or do not agree upon a specific schedule of visitation for their children, the court may order the parents to mediate their differences on those matters in accordance with mediation procedures adopted by the court by local rule. When the court determines whether mediation is appropriate in any proceeding, it shall consider whether either parent previously has been convicted of or pleaded guilty to a violation of section 2919.25 of the Revised Code involving a victim who at the time of the commission of the offense was a member of the family or household that is the subject of the proceeding, whether either parent previously has been convicted of or pleaded guilty to an offense involving a victim who at the time of the commission of the offense was a member of the family or household that is the subject of the proceeding and caused physical harm to the victim in the commission of the offense, and whether either parent has been determined to be the perpetrator of the abusive act that is the basis of an adjudication that a child is an abused child. If either parent has been convicted of or pleaded guilty to a violation of section 2919.25 of the Revised Code involving a victim who at the time of the commission of the offense was a member of the family or household that is the subject of the proceeding, has been convicted of or pleaded guilty to any other offense involving a victim who at the time of the commission of the offense was a member of the family or household that is the subject of the proceeding and caused physical harm to the victim in the commission of the offense, or has been determined to be the perpetrator of the abusive act that is the basis of an adjudication that a child is an abused child, the court may order mediation only if the court determines that it is in the best interests of the parties to order mediation and makes specific written findings of fact to support its determination.

If a court issues an order pursuant to this division requiring mediation, it also may order the parents to file a mediation report within a specified period of time and order the parents to pay the cost of mediation, unless either or both of the parents file a motion requesting that the court waive that requirement. Upon the filing of a motion requesting the waiver of that requirement, the court, for good cause shown, may waive the requirement that either or both parents pay the cost of mediation or may require one of the parents to pay the entire cost of mediation. Any mediation procedures adopted by local court rule for use under this division shall include, but are not limited to, provisions establishing qualifications for mediators who may be employed or used and provisions establishing standards for the conduct of the mediation.

(B) If a mediation order is issued under division (A) of this section and the order requires the parents to file a mediation report, the mediator and each parent who takes part in mediation in accordance with the order jointly shall file a report of the results of the mediation process with the court that issued the order under that division. A mediation report shall indicate only whether agreement has been reached on any of the issues that were the subject of the mediation, and, if agreement has been reached, the content and details of the agreement. No mediation report shall contain any background information concerning the mediation process or any information discussed or presented in the process. The court shall consider the mediation report when it allocates parental rights and responsibilities for the care of children under section 3109.04 of the Revised Code and when it establishes a specific schedule of visitation under section 3109.051 of the Revised Code. The court is not bound by the mediation report and shall consider the best interest of the children when making that allocation or establishing the visitation schedule.

(C) If a mediation order is issued under division (A) of this section, the mediator shall not be made a party to, and shall not be called as a witness or testify in, any action or proceeding, other than a criminal, delinquency, child abuse, child neglect, or dependent child action or proceeding, that is brought by or against either parent and that pertains to the mediation process, to any information discussed or presented in the mediation process, to the allocation of parental rights and responsibilities for the care of the parents' children, or to the awarding of visitation rights in relation to their children. The mediator shall not be made a party to, or be called as a witness or testify in, such an action or proceeding even if both parents give their prior consent to the mediator being made a party to or being called as a witness or to testify in the action or proceeding.

(D) Division (A) of this section does not apply to either of the following:

(1) Any proceeding, or the use of mediation in any proceeding that is not a proceeding for divorce, dissolution, legal separation, annulment, or the allocation of parental rights and responsibilities for the care of a child;

(2) The use of mediation in any proceeding for divorce, dissolution, legal separation, annulment, or the allocation of parental rights and responsibilities for the care of a child, in relation to issues other than the appropriate allocation of parental rights and responsibilities for the care of the parents' children and other than a specific visitation schedule for the parents' children.

(1990 S 3, eff. 4-11-91)

Cross References

Mediation communications privileged, exceptions, 2317.023

Privileged communications, 2317.02

Library References

Arbitration ⚷1, 2, 3.1, 4.1.
WESTLAW Topic No. 33.
C.J.S. Arbitration §§ 2 to 4, 6, 11.

OJur 3d: 5A, Alternative Dispute Resolution § 174
Validity and construction of provision for arbitration of disputes as to alimony or support payments, or child visitation or custody matters. 18 ALR3d 1264

Carlin, Baldwin's Ohio Practice, *Merrick-Rippner Probate Law* § 105.11, 107.122 (1997)

Klein & Darling, Baldwin's Ohio Practice, *Civil Practice* § 52 (1997)

Kurtz & Giannelli, Ohio Juvenile Law (1998 Ed.), Text 12.4

Sowald & Morganstern, Baldwin's Ohio Practice, *Domestic Relations Law* § 6.1, 6.3, 6.4, 6.7, 15.65, 16.1, 16.9, 18.10, 18.16, 21.2, 21.6, 21.15, 25.41, 37.18 (1997)

Law Review and Journal Commentaries

Can We Talk?, Hon. Francine M. Bruening. (Ed. Note: Mediation is discussed.) 19 Lake Legal Views 1 (June 1996).

Keeping Kids Out of Court. (Ed. note: Arbitration of custody disputes, but courts reserve the right to review awards.) 19 Nat'l L J B8 (May 5, 1997).

Ohio Divorce Mediation, C. Terrence Knapp. 4 Domestic Rel J Ohio 21 (March/April 1992).

3109.053 Mandatory parenting classes and counseling as condition of allocation of parental rights and responsibilities

Note: See also following version of this section, eff. 10-5-00.

In any divorce, legal separation, or annulment proceeding and in any proceeding pertaining to the allocation of parental rights and responsibilities for the care of a child, the court may require, by rule or otherwise, that the parents attend classes on parenting or other related issues or obtain counseling before the court issues an order allocating the parental rights and responsibilities for the care of the minor children of the marriage. If the court orders the parents to attend classes or obtain counseling, the court shall impose the cost of the classes and counseling on, and may allocate the costs between, the parents, except that if the court determines that both parents are indigent, the court shall not impose the cost of the classes or counseling on the parents.

(1996 H 368, eff. 9-10-96)

Note: See also following version of this section, eff. 10-5-00.

3109.053 Mandatory parenting classes and counseling as condition of allocation of parental rights and responsibilities

Note: See also preceding version of this section, in effect until 10-5-00.

In any divorce, legal separation, or annulment proceeding and in any proceeding pertaining to the allocation of parental rights and responsibilities for the care of a child, the court may require, by rule or otherwise, that the parents attend classes on parenting or other related issues or obtain counseling before the court issues an order allocating the parental rights and responsibilities for the care of the minor children of the marriage. If a court in any proceeding requires parents to attend classes on parenting or other related issues or to obtain counseling, the court may require that the parents' children attend the classes or counseling with the parents. If the court orders the parents to attend classes or obtain counseling, the court shall impose the cost of the classes and counseling on, and may allocate the costs between, the parents, except that if the court determines that both parents are indigent, the court shall not impose the cost of the classes or counseling on the parents.

(2000 H 537, eff. 10-5-00; 1996 H 368, eff. 9-10-96)

Note: See also preceding version of this section, in effect until 10-5-00.

Historical and Statutory Notes

Amendment Note: 2000 H 537 inserted the second sentence in the section.

Library References

Carlin, Baldwin's Ohio Practice, *Merrick-Rippner Probate Law* § 105.11, 107.122 (1997)

Sowald & Morganstern, Baldwin's Ohio Practice, *Domestic Relations Law* § 21.6 (1997)

3109.06 Certification to juvenile court

Any court, other than a juvenile court, that has jurisdiction in any case respecting the allocation of parental rights and responsibilities for the care of a child under eighteen years of age and the designation of the child's place of residence and legal custodian or in any case respecting the support of a child under eighteen years of age, may, on its own motion or on motion of any interested party, with the consent of the juvenile court, certify the record in the case or so much of the record and such further information, in narrative form or otherwise, as the court deems necessary or the juvenile court requests, to the juvenile court for further proceedings; upon the certification, the juvenile court shall have exclusive jurisdiction.

In cases in which the court of common pleas finds the parents unsuitable to have the parental rights and responsibilities for the care of the child or children and unsuitable to provide the place of residence and to be the legal custodian of the child or children, consent of the juvenile court shall not be required to such certification. This section applies to actions pending on August 28, 1951.

In any case in which a court of common pleas, or other court having jurisdiction, has issued an order that allocates parental rights and responsibilities for the care of minor children and designates their place of residence and legal custodian of minor children, has made an order for support of minor children, or has done both, the jurisdiction of the court shall not abate upon the death of the person awarded custody but shall continue for all purposes during the minority of the children. The court, upon its own motion or the motion of either parent or of any interested person acting on behalf of the children, may proceed to make further disposition of the case in the best interests of the children and subject to sections 3109.42 to 3109.48 of the Revised Code. If the children are under eighteen years of age, it may certify them, pursuant to this section, to the juvenile court of any county for further proceedings. After certification to a juvenile court, the jurisdiction of the court of common pleas, or other court, shall cease, except as to any payments of spousal support due for the spouse and support payments due and unpaid for the children at the time of the certification.

Any disposition made pursuant to this section, whether by a juvenile court after a case is certified to it, or by any court upon the death of a person awarded custody of a child, shall be made in accordance with sections 3109.04 and 3109.42 to 3109.48 of the Revised Code. If an appeal is taken from a decision made pursuant to this section that allocates parental rights and responsibilities for the care of a minor child and designates the child's place of residence and legal custodian, the court of appeals shall give the case calendar priority and handle it expeditiously.

(1999 H 191, eff. 10-20-99; 1990 S 3, eff. 4-11-91; 1990 H 514; 1983 H 93; 1953 H 1; GC 8005-6; Source—GC 8034-1)

Historical and Statutory Notes

Pre-1953 H 1 Amendments: 124 v S 65

Amendment Note: 1999 H 191 inserted "and subject to sections 3109.42 to 3109.48 of the Revised Code" in the third paragraph; inserted "and 3109.42 to 3109.48" in the fourth paragraph; and made other nonsubstantive changes.

Cross References

Allowance of spousal support modification, 3105.18
Jurisdiction of juvenile court, 2151.23
Taking of child into custody by juvenile court, Juv R 6

Library References

Courts ⚿483 to 488.
WESTLAW Topic No. 106.
C.J.S. Courts §§ 193 to 199.

Liability of parent for support of child institutionalized by juvenile court. 59 ALR3d 636
Validity and effect, as between former spouses, of agreement releasing parent from payment of child support provided for in an earlier divorce decree. 100 ALR3d 1129

Carlin, Baldwin's Ohio Practice, *Merrick-Rippner Probate Law* § 105.3, 105.11, 105.13, 107.106, 107.122, 108.34 (1997)

Klein & Darling, Baldwin's Ohio Practice, *Civil Practice* § 24 (1997)

Kurtz & Giannelli, Ohio Juvenile Law (1998 Ed.), Text 3.2, 13.11, 31.6

Sowald & Morganstern, Baldwin's Ohio Practice, *Domestic Relations Law* § 15.51, 15.56, 18.23, 21.26 (1997)

Law Review and Journal Commentaries

The Custody Contest Between a Parent and a Nonparent, Don C. Bolsinger. 2 Domestic Rel J Ohio 51 (July/August 1990).

The Voice of a Child: Independent Legal Representation of Children in Private Custody Disputes When Sexual Abuse Is Alleged, Kerin S. Bischoff. 138 U Pa L Rev 1383 (May 1990).

Notes of Decisions and Opinions

Appeal 6
Child support 5
Continuing jurisdiction 1
Death of parent 4
Juvenile court jurisdiction 3
Procedure 2

---

1. Continuing jurisdiction

RC 3105.21(B) affords a domestic relations court authority to determine custody of a child, as between his parents and another relative, even though that court has dismissed the parent's divorce action; if after dismissing the divorce action, the domestic relations court elects to certify the matter of custody to juvenile court, under RC 3105.21(B) and 3109.04 the domestic relations court must specifically find custody in neither parent to be in the child's best interest, or all jurisdiction over the matter is lost. State ex rel. Easterday v. Zieba (Ohio 1991) 58 Ohio St.3d 251, 569 N.E.2d 1028.

Where in a divorce action custody of a minor child is awarded by the court, that court retains jurisdiction over custody of the child, and in a subsequent divorce action between the custodial parent and a successor spouse, the court hearing that action has no jurisdiction over custody of such child. Loetz v. Loetz (Ohio 1980) 63 Ohio St.2d 1, 406 N.E.2d 1093, 17 O.O.3d 1.

When a parent having legal custody of minor children takes up residence with such children outside the state, an Ohio court has continuing jurisdiction to modify the original custody order. Murck v. Murck (Cuyahoga 1976) 47 Ohio App.2d 292, 353 N.E.2d 917, 1 O.O.3d 355.

When a mother having legal custody of a minor child is domiciled in another state with such child, an Ohio court does not have continuing jurisdiction to modify the original custody order, but if such child resides in Ohio, even though he may be domiciled in another state with the parent having legal custody, the courts of Ohio will have continuing jurisdiction to hear a motion for modification of custody. Heiney v. Heiney (Columbiana 1973) 40 Ohio App.2d 571, 321 N.E.2d 611, 69 O.O.2d 519.

Where a common pleas court, having made an award of custody and an order for the support of a minor child, certifies the same to juvenile court for further proceedings and the jurisdiction of the juvenile court attaches before the minor is eighteen years of age, the jurisdiction of that court continues until the minor attains the age of twenty-one. Slawski v. Slawski (Lucas 1934) 49 Ohio App. 100, 195 N.E. 258, 18 Ohio Law Abs. 515, 1 O.O. 201.

This section in no wise affects jurisdiction of regular branch of common pleas court to hear, determine and retain jurisdiction in custodial and support orders in divorce cases; however, it authorizes court upon determination of the advisability so to do to relinquish this jurisdiction to the juvenile court, whereupon it is provided that it ceases. Metz v. Metz (Franklin 1934) 17 Ohio Law Abs. 531.

2. Procedure

The Ohio Rules of Civil Procedure do not apply to a custody proceeding in the juvenile division of a court of common pleas; rather, such proceedings are governed by the Ohio Rules of Juvenile Procedure. Squires v. Squires (Preble 1983) 12 Ohio App.3d 138, 468 N.E.2d 73, 12 O.B.R. 460.

In any case where a court of common pleas has made an award of custody or an order for support, or both, of minor children, that court may certify the case to the juvenile court of any county in the state for further proceedings. Pylant v. Pylant (Huron 1978) 61 Ohio App.2d 247, 401 N.E.2d 940, 15 O.O.3d 407.

Where a court, having acquired jurisdiction over a child by virtue of a divorce action between the child's parents, certifies the matter of the child's custody to a juvenile court, the consent of the juvenile court having been first obtained, the juvenile court has exclusive jurisdiction over the child's custody by virtue of RC 3109.06 and 2151.23(D) and a finding of unfitness of the parents or that there is no suitable relative to have custody is not a necessary prerequisite to such certification, and while such certification shall be deemed to be the complaint in the juvenile court, it does not constitute a complaint in the juvenile court that such child is dependent or neglected and those dispositions provided for under RC 2151.353, 2151.354, and 2151.355 are not applicable to the disposition of such a child, disposition thereof being subject to and controlled by RC 3109.04. In re Height (Van Wert 1975) 47 Ohio App.2d 203, 353 N.E.2d 887, 1 O.O.3d 279.

A common pleas court has no jurisdiction to make any order respecting the care and custody or visitation with minor children unless in the prayer of the petition the plaintiff asks for a divorce or alimony. Crum v. Howard (Ohio Com.Pl. 1956) 137 N.E.2d 654, 73 Ohio Law Abs. 111, 1 O.O.2d 399.

3. Juvenile court jurisdiction

Failure of common pleas court to make finding that natural parents were unfit custodians of child did not preclude certification of child custody case to juvenile court, where case was certified pursuant to statute giving juvenile court discretion whether to accept certification, rather than statute pursuant to which juvenile court must accept certification based on finding that it is in best interest of child for neither parent to have custody. In re Whaley (Athens 1993) 86 Ohio App.3d 304, 620 N.E.2d 954.

Where a juvenile court grants the temporary custody of a minor child, with the consent of his parents, to a non-relative, after the father had unrestricted custody pursuant to a divorce decree, RC 3109.04(B) and 3109.04(C), as effective September 23, 1974, are not applicable to prevent the court's consideration of a motion filed by the father, in the same court, for the restoration of custody. Leininger v. Leininger (Fulton 1975) 48 Ohio App.2d 21, 355 N.E.2d 508, 2 O.O.3d 15.

There is no statutory provision for any juvenile court to certify a case back to the common pleas court; when a case is once certified to a juvenile court, it has exclusive jurisdiction, and the jurisdiction of the common pleas court ceases. Handelsman v. Handelsman (Columbiana 1958) 108 Ohio App. 30, 160 N.E.2d 543, 9 O.O.2d 101.

Order of common pleas court in divorce case affecting custody of minor is effective until reversed or modified, although case relating to minor is transferred to juvenile court. Sonnenberg v. State (Franklin 1931) 40 Ohio App. 475, 178 N.E. 855, 10 Ohio Law Abs. 271.

Express consent of the juvenile court is an essential prerequisite to the acquiring of jurisdiction over children upon certification of an award of custody and support by the common pleas court. Cline v. Cline (Fayette 1955) 137 N.E.2d 633, 73 Ohio Law Abs. 289.

Where common pleas court has, in divorce action, made an order as to custody of minor child, and has certified the case to juvenile court for further proceedings, the common pleas court's jurisdiction ceases and sole jurisdiction is vested in juvenile court under section. In such case, objection to jurisdiction of common pleas court after such certification may be made at any time in further proceedings relating to custody. Agler v. Agler (Franklin 1944) 64 N.E.2d 854, 44 Ohio Law Abs. 289.

When orders made in the common pleas court or probate court as to the care and custody of minor children are certified to the juvenile court, the juvenile court may then exercise jurisdiction over said minors in the same manner as in cases originally brought in said juvenile court. No new jurisdiction is conferred except the authority to proceed in said cases, in the same manner, and with the same powers, as if said cases had been adjudicated in the juvenile court. 1925 OAG 2310.

4. Death of parent

Following death of mother to whom trial court had awarded custody in divorce proceeding, dispute over custody of children between father and children's maternal uncle fell within coverage of statute allowing custody to be awarded to relative other than parent "when it is in the best interest of the child," rather than under statute establishing jurisdiction of juvenile courts to determine custody of child not ward of another court of state. Schneeberger v. Baker (Summit 1996) 113 Ohio App.3d 805, 682 N.E.2d 661, appeal not allowed 77 Ohio St.3d 1525, 674 N.E.2d 376.

Where the parent to whom custody of minor children has been awarded by a divorce court subsequently dies during their minority, custody is to be awarded on the death of that parent as the court may have determined in the best interests of the children; in such event it is not necessary for the court to find that the surviving parent is not a suitable person to have custody before awarding custody to another person. Gordon v. Gordon (Hardin 1973) 33 Ohio App.2d 257, 294 N.E.2d 239, 62 O.O.2d 375.

Where the trial court awarded custody of minor children to the father following a divorce action, it had jurisdiction following the death of such father to determine custody upon personal service upon the mother in another state by the local sheriff. Kirkpatrick v. Kirkpatrick (Ohio Com.Pl. 1956) 139 N.E.2d 119, 74 Ohio Law Abs. 14.

5. Child support

Where a parent, against whom an order to pay for the support of a minor child is made, is before the court, the court has the power to order such parent to support such child, even though the child is not physically within the state where the award of support is made. Handelsman v. Handelsman (Columbiana 1958) 108 Ohio App. 30, 160 N.E.2d 543, 9 O.O.2d 101.

A trial court has jurisdiction to modify a support order as to future installments, whether or not the right is reserved in the decree; but it has no such jurisdiction to modify unpaid installment support payments which have accrued if the child for whose benefit support was awarded was living and not emancipated at the time of the accrual, unless the right to retrospective modification was specifically reserved in the decree. Wedebrook v. Wedebrook (Ohio Com.Pl. 1977) 51 Ohio Misc. 81, 367 N.E.2d 937, 5 O.O.3d 342.

6. Appeal

Although it is the general rule that when an appeal is taken from a trial court that court is divested of jurisdiction, except to take action in aid of the appeal, until the case is remanded to it by the appellate court, the best interests of the children sometimes might better be served if the appellate court postpones its resolution of the questions raised by the assignments of error until the juvenile court is re-invested with jurisdiction to review the entire matter of custody in light of the possibility that the passage of some twenty-two months has worked a change in conditions regarding the children's best interest. In the Matter of Wallace, Nos. 360 and 361 (1st Dist Ct App, Clinton, 2-14-79).

No bond is required in the appeal of a child custody case. Reynolds v. Reynolds (Ross 1964) 200 N.E.2d 890, 94 Ohio Law Abs. 289, 30 O.O.2d 380.

3109.07 Appeal to the court of appeals

An appeal to the court of appeals may be had pursuant to the Rules of Appellate Procedure and, to the extent not in conflict with those rules, Chapter 2505. of the Revised Code.

(1986 H 412, eff. 3-17-87; 129 v 291; 1953 H 1; GC 8005-7; Source—GC 8035)

Historical and Statutory Notes

Pre-1953 H 1 Amendments: 124 v S 65

Cross References

Relief pending appeal, Civ R 75

Library References

Divorce ⟹312.1.
Marriage ⟹66.
Parent and Child ⟹2(20), 3.3(10).
WESTLAW Topic Nos. 134, 253, 285.
C.J.S. Divorce §§ 737, 738, 745.
C.J.S. Marriage § 82.
C.J.S. Parent and Child §§ 47, 48, 88, 89.

Am Jur 2d: 4, Appeal and Error § 136

Notes of Decisions and Opinions

Bond 1
Procedure 2

---

1. Bond

The giving of the bond specified in RC 3109.07 is a condition precedent to an appeal of the kind provided for therein. Volz v. Volz (Ohio 1957) 167 Ohio St. 141, 146 N.E.2d 734, 4 O.O.2d 136.

A motion to dismiss an appeal from the overruling of a motion to change the custody of a child will be sustained where no bond is filed within twenty days from the order appealed from. Call v. Call (Franklin 1958) 107 Ohio App. 516, 160 N.E.2d 307, 81 Ohio Law Abs. 243, 9 O.O.2d 54.

An appeal from an order regarding the custody of a child is conditional upon giving bond. Call v. Call (Franklin 1958) 107 Ohio App. 516, 160 N.E.2d 307, 81 Ohio Law Abs. 243, 9 O.O.2d 54.

Where no bond is filed in an appeal on law and fact from a juvenile court order relating to custody of minor children, the appeal will be retained on questions of law only. Bachtel v. Bachtel (Lucas 1954) 97 Ohio App. 521, 127 N.E.2d 761, 56 O.O. 469.

2. Procedure

The word "appeal," as used in GC 8005-7 (RC 3109.07), has the meaning specified in subdivision (A) of 2505.01. Volz v. Volz (Ohio 1957) 167 Ohio St. 141, 146 N.E.2d 734, 4 O.O.2d 136.

In proceeding on motion for change of custody, judgment that defers issue of child support for future determination is not "final appealable order." Kouns v. Pemberton (Lawrence 1992) 84 Ohio App.3d 499, 617 N.E.2d 701, motion overruled 66 Ohio St.3d 1489, 612 N.E.2d 1245.

Where trial court, as part of final determination of divorce action, found it not to be in best interest of child to award custody to either parent and certified issue of custody to juvenile court, certification order was properly appealable as part of divorce judgment and constituted a final appealable order. Robinson v. Robinson (Franklin 1984) 19 Ohio App.3d 323, 484 N.E.2d 710, 19 O.B.R. 496.

Where a special statute prescribes the method of appeal from a particular order, such statute is controlling and the general statutes providing for appeal have no application; and compliance with the general statute, but not with the special statute, is not sufficient to perfect such appeal, and hence RC 3109.07 prescribes the only method by which an appeal may be effected from an order fixing the custody of a child. Gregg v. Mitchell (Scioto 1955) 99 Ohio App. 350, 133 N.E.2d 645, 59 O.O. 133, appeal dismissed 163 Ohio St. 330, 126 N.E.2d 809, 56 O.O. 288.

Where custody of minor children is originally granted to the maternal grandparents and a subsequent court order grants custody to the father, both awards of custody constitute final, appealable orders and, therefore, preclude the mother from asserting assignments of error in a proceeding which is not a timely appeal of those orders. Torbeck v Torbeck, No. C-810827 (1st Dist Ct App, Hamilton, 7-21-82).

3109.08 Release of dower rights—Repealed

(1973 S 1, eff. 1-1-74; 130 v S 193)

LIABILITY OF PARENTS

3109.09 Damages recoverable against parent of minor who willfully damages property or commits theft offense; community service

(A) As used in this section, "parent" means one of the following:

(1) Both parents unless division (A)(2) or (3) of this section applies;

(2) The parent designated the residential parent and legal custodian pursuant to an order issued under section 3109.04 of the Revised Code that is not a shared parenting order;

(3) The custodial parent of a child born out of wedlock with respect to whom no custody order has been issued.

(B) Any owner of property, including any board of education of a city, local, exempted village, or joint vocational school district, may maintain a civil action to recover compensatory damages not exceeding ten thousand dollars and court costs from the parent of a minor if the minor willfully damages property belonging to the owner or commits acts cognizable as a "theft offense," as defined in section 2913.01 of the Revised Code, involving the property of the owner. The action may be joined with an action under Chapter 2737. of the Revised Code against the minor, or the minor and the minor's parent, to recover the property regardless of value, but any additional damages recovered from the parent pursuant to this section shall be limited to compensatory damages not exceeding ten thousand dollars, as authorized by this section. A finding of willful destruction of property or of committing acts cognizable as a theft offense is not dependent upon a prior finding that the child is a delinquent child or upon the child's conviction of any criminal offense.

(C)(1) If a court renders a judgment in favor of a board of education of a city, local, exempted village, or joint vocational school district in an action brought pursuant to division (B) of this section, if the board of education agrees to the parent's performance of community service in lieu of full payment of the judgment, and if the parent who is responsible for the payment of the judgment agrees to voluntarily participate in the performance of community service in lieu of full payment of the judgment, the court may order the parent to perform community service in lieu of providing full payment of the judgment.

(2) If a court, pursuant to division (C)(1) of this section, orders a parent to perform community service in lieu of providing full payment of a judgment, the court shall specify in its order the amount of the judgment, if any, to be paid by the parent, the type and number of hours of community service to be performed by the parent, and any other conditions necessary to carry out the order.

(D) This section shall not apply to a parent of a minor if the minor was married at the time of the commission of the acts or violations that would otherwise give rise to a civil action commenced under this section.

(E) Any action brought pursuant to this section shall be commenced and heard as in other civil actions.

(F) The monetary limitation upon compensatory damages set forth in this section does not apply to a civil action brought pursuant to section 2307.70 of the Revised Code.

(1996 H 601, eff. 10-29-96; 1992 H 154, eff. 7-31-92; 1990 S 3; 1988 H 708; 1986 H 158, S 316; 1978 H 456; 1969 S 10; 132 v H 257; 131 v H 159)

Historical and Statutory Notes

Amendment Note: 1996 H 601 added divisions (A) and (A)(1) to (A)(3); redesignated former divisions (A) to (E) as divisions (B) to (F) respectively; substituted "ten thousand dollars" for "six thousand dollars" throughout and "parent of a minor" for "parents who have the parental rights and responsibilities for the care of a minor, and are the residential parents and legal custodians of a minor" in division (B); substituted "This section shall not apply to a parent" for "For purposes of this section, the parents of a minor do not have parental rights and responsibilities for the care of the minor and are not the residential parents and legal custodians of the minor" and "would otherwise give" for "gave" in division (D); changed references from"parents" to "parent" throughout; made changes to reflect gender neutral language; and made other nonsubstantive changes.

Comparative Laws

Ill.—ILCS 740 115/1 et seq.
Ind.—West's A.I.C. 34-31-4-1, 34-31-4-2.
Ky.—Baldwin's KRS 405.025.
Mich.—M.C.L.A. § 600.2913.

Cross References

Delinquent child, defined, 2151.02
Disposition of delinquent child, 2151.355
Liability of parents for acts of delinquent child, 2151.411
Vandalism, criminal damaging or endangering, 2909.05, 2909.06
Victims' rights pamphlet, publication and distribution, 109.42

Library References

Parent and Child ⚷13(1), 13(2).
WESTLAW Topic No. 285.
C.J.S. Parent and Child §§ 123 to 126.

OJur 3d: 58, Insurance § 965; 62, Investment Securities and Securities Regulation § 53; 70, Negligence § 35
Am Jur 2d: 59, Parent and Child § 130 to 137
Validity and construction of statutes making parents liable for torts committed by their minor children. 8 ALR3d 612
Parents' liability for injury or damage intentionally inflicted by minor child. 54 ALR3d 974
Liability of parent for injury caused by child riding a bicycle. 70 ALR3d 611
Carrier's liability for injury or death of infant passenger as affected by fact that child was in custody of parent or other adult. 74 ALR3d 1171
Criminal responsibility of parent for act of child. 12 ALR4th 673
Jurisdiction or power of juvenile court to order parent of juvenile to make restitution for juvenile's offense. 66 ALR4th 985

Baldwin's Ohio School Law, Text 38.12
Carlin, Baldwin's Ohio Practice, *Merrick-Rippner Probate Law* § 107.61, 107.83, 107.96, 108.41 (1997)
Kurtz & Giannelli, Ohio Juvenile Law (1998 Ed.), Text 24.8, 29.3

Law Review and Journal Commentaries

Fundamentally Speaking: Application of Ohio's Domestic Violence Laws in Parental Discipline Cases—A Parental Perspective, Richard Garner. 30 U Tol L Rev 1 (Fall 1998).

Intra-Family Immunities and the Law of Torts in Ohio, John E. Sullivan. 18 W Reserve U L Rev 447 (January 1967).

Liability of Parents for the Willful Torts of Their Children Under Ohio Revised Code Section 3109.09, Stuart A. Laven. 24 Clev St L Rev 1 (Winter 1975).

Motorist Mutual Insurance Co v Bill, 56 OS(2d) 258, 383 NE(2d) 880 (1978): A Limitation on Parental Liability and Willful Acts, Susan J. Scheutzow. 9 Cap U L Rev 749 (Summer 1980).

New student discipline options enacted, Daniel A. Jaffe. 40 Ohio Sch Boards Ass'n J 2 (October 1996).

Parents' Support Obligations to Their Adult Children, Marvin M. Moore. 19 Akron L Rev 183 (Fall 1985).

Property Owner's Civil Action for Minor's Theft, Ron Mount. 4 U Dayton L Rev 539 (1979).

Statutory Vicarious Parental Liability: Review and Reform, Note. 32 Case W Res L Rev 559 (1982).

Student Misconduct—New Weapons for Schools, Richard J. Dickinson. 8 Baldwin's Ohio Sch L J 29 (July/August 1996).

Tort Law: Parental Liability and the Extension of Social Host Liability to Minors—*Huston v. Konieczny*, 52 Ohio St. 3d 214, 556 N.E.2d 505 (1990), Note. 16 U Dayton L Rev 827 (Spring 1991).

Notes of Decisions and Opinions

---

1. In general

Although no basis existed for imposing liability on parents of teenage children who witnessed but did not report fire started by another teenager, material fact issue existed as to liability of children themselves, precluding summary judgment for them. Am. Economy Ins. Co. v. Knowles (Ohio App. 2 Dist. 1996) 113 Ohio App.3d 71, 680 N.E.2d 237.

No statutory authority exists authorizing the payment of guardian ad litem fees from county funds in a civil action involving negligent or intentional acts of an indigent minor in causing fire damage to a rental unit. Nationwide Mut. Ins. Co. v. Wymer (Franklin 1986) 33 Ohio App.3d 318, 515 N.E.2d 987.

In an action brought against a parent and his child for damages caused by a fire in a rental unit, where the court finds the child alone liable for such damages in that the child was responsible for starting the fire, the fees and expenses of a court-appointed guardian ad litem are properly charged to the indigent minor child and not to his parent, as part of the court costs. Nationwide Mut. Ins. Co. v. Wymer (Franklin 1986) 33 Ohio App.3d 318, 515 N.E.2d 987.

RC 3109.09 is in derogation of the common law and must be strictly construed. Nationwide Ins. Co. v. Love (Lucas 1984) 22 Ohio App.3d 9, 488 N.E.2d 226, 22 O.B.R. 43.

Under RC 3109.09, a noncustodial parent cannot recover from an ex-spouse and custodial parent for a theft of the noncustodial parent's property by the parties' minor child. Hartford Acc. & Indem. Co. v. Borchers (Franklin 1982) 3 Ohio App.3d 452, 445 N.E.2d 1160, 3 O.B.R. 532.

When a person trespasses on the lands of another, while the trespass continues, he owes a duty of care to the owner of the premises; such duty includes the obligation to protect the property from harm as a result of the trespass. Wigton v. Lavender (Delaware 1980) 70 Ohio App.2d 241, 436 N.E.2d 1378, 24 O.O.3d 349.

RC 3109.09 creates an exception to the common law principle that liability will not be imposed upon parents for the intentional torts of their minor children, and must be strictly construed and its application limited to those situations involving intentional acts of destruction. Travelers Indem. Co. v. Brooks (Lucas 1977) 60 Ohio App.2d 37, 395 N.E.2d 494, 14 O.O.3d 19.

Where a minor child is validly married, has established his own residence apart from his parents, and is self-supporting, he is no longer within the custody and control of his parents for purposes of establishing liability pursuant to RC 3109.10. Albert v. Ellis (Cuyahoga 1978) 59 Ohio App.2d 152, 392 N.E.2d 1309, 13 O.O.3d 188.

The two-year statute of limitations set forth in RC 2305.10 applies to civil actions to recover compensatory damages for injury to property brought under RC 3109.09. Rudnay v. Corbett (Cuyahoga 1977) 53 Ohio App.2d 311, 374 N.E.2d 171, 7 O.O.3d 416.

The Ohio legislature primarily intended RC 3109.09 to establish a civil cause of action, providing for compensatory damages to innocent victims of minor delinquents, against the parents having custody and control of a minor who willfully damages the property of another. Rudnay v. Corbett (Cuyahoga 1977) 53 Ohio App.2d 311, 374 N.E.2d 171, 7 O.O.3d 416.

The Ohio youth commission is not a parent, within the meaning of RC 3109.09, to incarcerated children so as to allow an action in the court of claims for the willful destruction of property. Hahn v. Brown (Franklin 1976) 51 Ohio App.2d 177, 367 N.E.2d 884, 5 O.O.3d 323.

Minor's taking of her mother's automobile without permission and her willful driving of automobile without authority or license was not behavior upon which court was to focus in action against mother pursuant to parental liability statute to recover damages arising out of minor's crash of automobile into building but, rather, subsequent act of wrecking automobile was behavior at issue. State Auto. Mut. Ins. Co. v. Newman (Ohio Mun. 1994) 65 Ohio Misc.2d 23, 640 N.E.2d 627.

"Willful conduct" under parental liability statute means intentional doing of act which occasions injury and resulting damage; there must be intent to cause injury. State Auto. Mut. Ins. Co. v. Newman (Ohio Mun. 1994) 65 Ohio Misc.2d 23, 640 N.E.2d 627.

Where two or more children, all covered by RC 3109.09, combine to do damage, the parents are responsible in the amount set forth in the statute for each of said children, and where such acts are committed between October 6, 1965, and October 10, 1965, by four such minor children, the parents are responsible up to the extent of $1,000. Lewis v. Martin (Ohio Com.Pl. 1968) 16 Ohio Misc. 18, 240 N.E.2d 913, 45 O.O.2d 22.

The amendment to RC 3109.09, effective October 24, 1967, which raises the limit of liability of a parent from $250 to $800, is not retroactive, and any damages done prior to that time are limited to the older section, namely, $250. Lewis v. Martin (Ohio Com.Pl. 1968) 16 Ohio Misc. 18, 240 N.E.2d 913, 45 O.O.2d 22.

The parents who are responsible under RC 3109.09 may be joined in the same action with their minor children, and where such children unite in a common willful destruction of property, the minors are jointly and severally liable for the damages, and the parents are jointly and severally liable with said children to the extent of the parents' responsibility under said section. Lewis v. Martin (Ohio Com.Pl. 1968) 16 Ohio Misc. 18, 240 N.E.2d 913, 45 O.O.2d 22.

Neither a county children services board nor a foster parent appointed and certified by a county children services board pursuant to RC 5153.16 and accompanying regulations is a "parent" under RC 3109.09 or 3109.10; accordingly, neither the board nor a foster parent is liable under RC 3109.09 or 3109.10 for the willful damage to or theft of property, or willful or malicious assault of a person, committed by a child in their custody. OAG 87-082.

2. Insurance

A homeowner's insurance policy that provides coverage for "property damage caused by an occurrence," which latter term is defined in the policy as "an accident," does not obligate the insurer to pay the claim of an insured under the policy who incurs liability under RC 3109.09 for intentional damage caused by another separately insured under the same policy, absent other clear indicia of such obligation in the insurance contract. Randolf v. Grange Mut. Cas. Co. (Ohio 1979) 57 Ohio St.2d 25, 385 N.E.2d 1305, 11 O.O.3d 110.

A subrogated insurer may maintain an action against the parents in custody and control of a minor who willfully damages the property of an owner. Motorists Mut. Ins. Co. v. Bill (Ohio 1978) 56 Ohio St.2d 258, 383 N.E.2d 880, 10 O.O.3d 398.

A subrogated insurance company may bring an action pursuant to RC 3109.09 for recovery, within the limits of the statute, of amounts paid out under the insurance policy. Peterson v. Slone (Ohio 1978) 56 Ohio St.2d 255, 383 N.E.2d 886, 10 O.O.3d 396.

The homeowners insurance of the parents of a minor wrongdoer is required to defend and/or pay a claim under RC 3109.09. Liberty Mut. Ins. Co. v. Davis (Ohio Mun. 1977) 52 Ohio Misc. 26, 368 N.E.2d 336, 6 O.O.3d 108.

A subrogated insurance company may maintain an action under RC 3109.09 against the parents of a minor wrongdoer. Liberty Mut. Ins. Co. v. Davis (Ohio Mun. 1977) 52 Ohio Misc. 26, 368 N.E.2d 336, 6 O.O.3d 108.

3. Willful damage

As used in RC 3109.09, "willfully damages property" means the intentional doing of the act which occasions the damage and resulting loss, coupled with the intent or purpose of causing the damage; and in order that parents may be found liable for the tortious acts of their minor children, both the initial act, as well as the subsequent damage, must be found to have been intentional. Motorists Mut. Ins. Co. v. Bill (Ohio 1978) 56 Ohio St.2d 258, 383 N.E.2d 880, 10 O.O.3d 398.

Recovery cannot be had under RC 3109.09 against a minor involved in an automobile accident on the basis that the initial stealing of the automobile was willful. Peterson v. Slone (Ohio 1978) 56 Ohio St.2d 255, 383 N.E.2d 886, 10 O.O.3d 396.

Statute that imposes liability upon parents for destructive acts of child only applies to minor who "willfully damages property," which means intentional doing of act that occasions injury and resulting damage. Am. Economy Ins. Co. v. Knowles (Ohio App. 2 Dist. 1996) 113 Ohio App.3d 71, 680 N.E.2d 237.

When a minor under age steals an automobile, and, in attempting to elude the owner and others seeking to thwart his theft, throws the automobile gears into reverse, floors the gas pedal and precipitously in the darkness on an unfamiliar road backs the automobile over a curb into a tree, damaging the car, such recklessness constitutes "willfully" damaging the property of the "owner" within the meaning of RC 3109.09 and causes the parents having the custody and control of such minor to be liable under such statute for the damage caused by the minor. Central Mut. Ins. Co. v. Rabideau (Lucas 1977) 60 Ohio App.2d 5, 395 N.E.2d 367, 14 O.O.3d 5.

The father of a minor cannot be held legally accountable on an oral contract made by his son and his son's friends to repair plaintiff's car where there is no finding that the son willfully damaged or stole the car and (1) the son's friend refuses to let the plaintiff see her car when she refuses to give him an additional $100, (2) the owner is forced to have her vehicle towed because the defendants remove the ignition, and (3) the plaintiff is not seeking to recover for the additional damage to the vehicle over and above her claim for contractual damages; therefore, removal of the ignition is not the result of willful damage by the son for which his father can be held legally accountable. Allison v Boehringer, No. 14862, 1995 WL 225448 (2d Dist Ct App, Montgomery, 4-12-95).

As used in RC 3109.09, the term "damages" is intended to include loss by reason of a theft. Liberty Mut. Ins. Co. v. Davis (Ohio Mun. 1977) 52 Ohio Misc. 26, 368 N.E.2d 336, 6 O.O.3d 108.

"Willful damaging" of property under Ohio statute imposing liability on parents when minor willfully damages property means intentional doing of act which occasions damages and resulting loss, coupled with intent or purpose of causing damage and, to impose liability upon parent, both initial act and subsequent damage must be found to be intentional. Byrd v. Brandeburg (N.D.Ohio 1996) 922 F.Supp. 60.

4. Theft provision

Unauthorized use of a motor vehicle by a minor may constitute a theft offense subjecting the minor's parents to liability for damage to an automobile operated without the owner's consent. Evans v. Graham (Franklin 1991) 71 Ohio App.3d 417, 594 N.E.2d 71.

The unauthorized use of an automobile is a "theft offense" under RC 2913.01 and therefore grounds under RC 3109.09 for an action by the owner of an automobile against the parents of a child who willfully damages the vehicle while joyriding. Nationwide Ins. Co. v. Love (Lucas 1984) 22 Ohio App.3d 9, 488 N.E.2d 226, 22 O.B.R. 43.

An award of attorney fees in a civil suit under RC 3109.09 against the parents of a minor who damages a stolen automobile while joyriding is without adequate evidentiary support and must be reversed where it is not established that the damage was intentionally inflicted. Nationwide Ins. Co. v. Love (Lucas 1984) 22 Ohio App.3d 9, 488 N.E.2d 226, 22 O.B.R. 43.

Parental liability arises under the "theft provision" of RC 3109.09, as amended by 1978 H 456, eff. 5-23-78, when the child has engaged in conduct which is the equivalent of theft and the property is thereafter damaged, regardless of whether the child acted in a willful or unwillful manner at the time the property was actually damaged. Schirmer v. Losacker (Hamilton 1980) 70 Ohio App.2d 138, 434 N.E.2d 1388, 24 O.O.3d 171.

The parents with custody and control of a minor who commits acts cognizable as a "theft offense" and thereby damages the property involved are liable to the property owner under RC 3109.09 regardless of whether the damage was negligent or intentional. West American Ins. Co. v. Carter (Ohio Mun. 1989) 50 Ohio Misc.2d 20, 553 N.E.2d 1099.

5. Parent's negligence

At common law, a parent is not ordinarily liable for damages caused by a child's wrongful conduct; however, liability can attach when the injury committed by the child is the foreseeable consequence of a parent's negligent act. In those circumstances, liability arises from the parent's conduct. Huston v. Konieczny (Ohio 1990) 52 Ohio St.3d 214, 556 N.E.2d 505.

Statute dealing with parental liability for child's willful damage of property was not basis for imposing liability on parents in connection with fire started by one teenager and witnessed but not reported by parents' teenage children; there was no evidence that parents' children actively participated or agreed with teenager who started fire to set fire that caused damage to store, or any evidence connecting parents with their children's alleged conduct. Am. Economy Ins. Co. v. Knowles (Ohio App. 2 Dist. 1996) 113 Ohio App.3d 71, 680 N.E.2d 237.

Fire that was started by teenager in presence of, but without active participation of, parents' teenage children was not foreseeable consequence of any negligent acts of parents such that they could be held liable; parents did not provide their children with dangerous instrumentality, did not direct or sanction any prior wrongdoing, and any parental negligence or lack of supervision and control did not have as foreseeable consequence fire or similar catastrophe. Am. Economy Ins. Co. v. Knowles (Ohio App. 2 Dist. 1996) 113 Ohio App.3d 71, 680 N.E.2d 237.

There are three situations in which parents might incur liability for conduct of child: (1) when parents negligently entrust child with instrument that becomes source of danger; (2) when parents know of child's wrongdoing and consent to it, direct it, or sanction it; and (3) when parents fail to exercise reasonable control over child when parent knows, or should know, that injury to another is probable consequence. Am. Economy Ins. Co. v. Knowles (Ohio App. 2 Dist. 1996) 113 Ohio App.3d 71, 680 N.E.2d 237.

At common law, parent is not liable for damages caused by child's wrongful conduct, and in order to be excepted from such general proposition, child's alleged misconduct must, at very least, be within reasonable comprehension of alleged negligence of parents. Am. Economy Ins. Co. v. Knowles (Ohio App. 2 Dist. 1996) 113 Ohio App.3d 71, 680 N.E.2d 237.

A parent who negligently fails to supervise his child by permitting the child to violate a municipal curfew may be liable for damages caused during the child's unauthorized use of a motor vehicle if it can be shown that the damage caused by the child is a foreseeable consequence of violation of the curfew. Evans v. Graham (Franklin 1991) 71 Ohio App.3d 417, 594 N.E.2d 71.

A child under seven years of age is incapable, as a matter of law, of committing an intentional tort; therefore, a property owner has no cause of action against the parents of such a child under RC 3109.09 where: (1) the parents had been warned that the child had gone onto the plaintiff's property and thrown objects into a sewer drain; and (2) the child had subsequently committed the same acts, causing serious property damage; however, the property owner may have a cause of action in negligence against the parents. D'Amico v. Burns (Cuyahoga 1984) 13 Ohio App.3d 325, 469 N.E.2d 1016, 13 O.B.R. 402.

Although parents are generally not liable for wrongful conduct of their children, parent can be liable for his own negligent act when injury caused by child is foreseeable to parent. Boyd v. Watson (Ohio Com.Pl. 1996) 83 Ohio Misc.2d 88, 680 N.E.2d 251.

Parent can be liable for negligent entrustment when he entrusts his child with instrumentality which, because of child's immaturity or lack of experience, may become source of danger to others. Boyd v. Watson (Ohio Com.Pl. 1996) 83 Ohio Misc.2d 88, 680 N.E.2d 251.

Parental liability for negligent entrustment may occur when parent entrusts child with instrumentality that is dangerous per se, or when he entrusts child with instrumentality that is not dangerous per se, but becomes dangerous due to child's immaturity or inexperience. Boyd v. Watson (Ohio Com.Pl. 1996) 83 Ohio Misc.2d 88, 680 N.E.2d 251.

Parent may be liable for negligent supervision when parent fails to exercise proper parental control over his child, and parent knows, or should know from his knowledge of child's habits or tendencies, that failure to exercise such control poses unreasonable risk that child will injure others. Boyd v. Watson (Ohio Com.Pl. 1996) 83 Ohio Misc.2d 88, 680 N.E.2d 251.

Parent may be liable for consenting to, directing, or sanctioning his child's wrongdoing. Boyd v. Watson (Ohio Com.Pl. 1996) 83 Ohio Misc.2d 88, 680 N.E.2d 251.

Home residents established liability of parents for actions of their minor child under Ohio statute imposing liability when minor "willfully damages" property; evidence that minor was found delinquent of attempted arson, which crime required proof of intent, and unrebutted statements of affiant demonstrated minor's intention to throw Molotov cocktail at residents' home, and use of Molotov cocktail itself demonstrated intention to cause fire damage to home. Byrd v. Brandeburg (N.D.Ohio 1996) 922 F.Supp. 60.

6. Emotional distress damages

Under Ohio parental liability statute, parents of minor defendant who participated in racially-motivated fire bombing of plaintiff's house were liable for property damage caused by incident, but not for plaintiff's emotional distress. Byrd v. Brandeburg (N.D.Ohio 1996) 932 F.Supp. 198.

7. Attorney fees

Under Ohio parental liability statute, attorney fees could be collected from parents of minor defendant who participated in racially-motivated fire bombing of plaintiff's house, where plaintiffs brought action under Fair Housing Act. Byrd v. Brandeburg (N.D.Ohio 1996) 932 F.Supp. 198.

3109.10 Liability of parents for assaults by their children

As used in this section, "parent" has the same meaning as in section 3109.09 of the Revised Code.

Any person is entitled to maintain an action to recover compensatory damages in a civil action, in an amount not to exceed ten thousand dollars and costs of suit in a court of competent jurisdiction, from the parent of a child under the age of eighteen if the child willfully and maliciously assaults the person by a means or force likely to produce great bodily harm. A finding of willful and malicious assault by a means or force likely to produce great bodily harm is not dependent upon a prior finding that the child is a delinquent child.

Any action brought pursuant to this section shall be commenced and heard as in other civil actions for damages.

The monetary limitation upon compensatory damages set forth in this section does not apply to a civil action brought pursuant to section 2307.70 of the Revised Code.

(1996 H 601, eff. 10-29-96; 1995 H 18, eff. 11-24-95; 1990 S 3, eff. 4-11-91; 1986 S 316; 1969 S 11)

Historical and Statutory Notes

Amendment Note: 1996 H 601 inserted the first paragraph; substituted "ten thousand dollars" for "six thousand dollars", deleted "parents who have the parental rights and responsibilities for the care of a child under the age of eighteen, and from any" following "jurisdiction, from the" and "who is the residential parent and legal custodian" preceding "of a child" in the second paragraph; and made other nonsubstantive changes.

Amendment Note: 1995 H 18 substituted "six" for "two", "parent" for "parents", and "custodian" for "custodians"; added "from any parent", "is", and "under the age of eighteen"; and made nonsubstantive changes.

Cross References

Assault, 2903.11 et seq.
Delinquent child, defined, 2151.02
Disposition of delinquent child, 2151.355
Liability of parents for acts of delinquent child, 2151.411
Victims' rights pamphlet, publication and distribution, 109.42

Library References

Parent and Child ⚷13(1), 13(2).
WESTLAW Topic No. 285.
C.J.S. Parent and Child §§ 123 to 126.

Am Jur 2d: 59, Parent and Child § 130 to 137
Validity and construction of statutes making parents liable for torts committed by their minor children. 8 ALR3d 612
Parents' liability for injury or damage intentionally inflicted by minor child. 54 ALR3d 974
Criminal responsibility of parent for act of child. 12 ALR4th 673

Baldwin's Ohio School Law, Text 38.12
Carlin, Baldwin's Ohio Practice, *Merrick-Rippner Probate Law* § 107.61, 107.83, 107.96, 108.41 (1997)
Kurtz & Giannelli, Ohio Juvenile Law (1998 Ed.), Text 24.8, 29.3

Law Review and Journal Commentaries

Statutory Vicarious Parental Liability: Review and Reform, Note. 32 Case W Res L Rev 559 (1982).

Student Misconduct—New Weapons for Schools, Richard J. Dickinson. 8 Baldwin's Ohio Sch L J 29 (July/August 1996).

Notes of Decisions and Opinions

Act by third person 3
Bankruptcy 8
"Damages" defined 7
Divorced parents 1
Married child 5
Negligence established 4
Negligence not established 10
"Parent" construed 2
Procedural issues 9
Statute of limitations 6

---

1. Divorced parents

A mother who has custody and control of her seventeen-year-old son is liable for his intentional act of assault and battery arising out of his throwing of a snowball which subsequently hits a person resulting in injury. Labadie v. Semler (Lucas 1990) 66 Ohio App.3d 540, 585 N.E.2d 862.

A father is properly found not to have custody and control of his seventeen-year-old son so as to make him not liable for his son's intentional tort where the evidence shows that (1) the father and mother were divorced, (2) the mother was awarded custody of the son in the divorce proceedings, (3) the father has not lived with the mother and his son for approximately four years, (4) the father did not participate in the disciplining of his son, and (5) the father was not involved in any major decisions made with regard to his son's education. Labadie v. Semler (Lucas 1990) 66 Ohio App.3d 540, 585 N.E.2d 862.

RC 3109.10 does not require a father to submit a legal document to a court showing that he does not have custody of his seventeen-year-old son in an action brought against both him and the child's mother in which an attempt is made to hold them statutorily liable for the intentional acts of their son. Labadie v. Semler (Lucas 1990) 66 Ohio App.3d 540, 585 N.E.2d 862.

2. "Parent" construed

A stepparent, without legal right of custody or obligation of control over a minor, does not constitute a "parent" within the meaning of RC 3109.10. Gosnell v. Middlebrook (Marion 1988) 55 Ohio App.3d 93, 563 N.E.2d 32.

Neither a county children services board nor a foster parent appointed and certified by a county children services board pursuant to RC 5153.16 and accompanying regulations is a "parent" under RC 3109.09 or 3109.10; accordingly, neither the board nor a foster parent is liable under RC 3109.09 or 3109.10 for the willful damage to or theft of property, or willful or malicious assault of a person, committed by a child in their custody. OAG 87-082.

3. Act by third person

Owner of firearm should not be held absolutely liable for any injury that occurs when he permits or leaves firearm accessible to children. Nearor v. Davis (Ohio App. 1 Dist. 1997) 118 Ohio App.3d 806, 694 N.E.2d 120, appeal not allowed 79 Ohio St.3d 1460, 681 N.E.2d 442.

A parent is not liable for injuries sustained by a victim of crime where his minor child who is experienced in the handling of firearms lends a firearm to a friend for the stated purpose of lawful hunting but instead the borrower uses the firearm to rob a grocery store and neither the child nor the parent is aware of the borrower's criminal history; in that situation the intervening willful, malicious and criminal act was not intended nor foreseeable by the gun owner. Bilicic v. Brake (Ashtabula 1989) 64 Ohio App.3d 304, 581 N.E.2d 586, motion overruled 49 Ohio St.3d 713, 552 N.E.2d 950.

4. Negligence established

Statutory limitation on a parent's vicarious liability for the torts of his or her children did not apply to claims asserted against father of minor child who was alleged to have sexually assaulted children he was babysitting, where court found that father had acted negligently and wantonly toward plaintiffs, and that father's acts were the direct and proximate cause of injuries for which recovery was sought. Cuervo v. Snell (Ohio App. 10 Dist. 1998) 131 Ohio App.3d 560, 723 N.E.2d 139.

Parent's negligent entrustment of gun to child can include not only presenting gun to child, but also having gun accessible to child. Nearor v. Davis (Ohio App. 1 Dist. 1997) 118 Ohio App.3d 806, 694 N.E.2d 120, appeal not allowed 79 Ohio St.3d 1460, 681 N.E.2d 442.

Where parents permit their inexperienced or irresponsible minor child to keep or have access to an inherently dangerous instrumentality, under circumstances which should put them on notice that the instrumentality might become a source of danger to others, reasonable minds could conclude that the parents were negligent in their acquiescence, and that they should be answerable in legal damages for an injury occasioned by the child's use of such instrumentality. McGinnis v. Kinkaid (Cuyahoga 1981) 1 Ohio App.3d 4, 437 N.E.2d 313, 1 O.B.R. 45.

Parents of minor child may be liable for torts of child if parents fail to exercise proper parental control over child and parents knew, or should have known, from their knowledge of habits or tendencies of child that failure to exercise such control posed unreasonable risk that child would injure others. Doe v. Kahrs (Ohio Com.Pl. 1995) 75 Ohio Misc.2d 7, 662 N.E.2d 101.

Parents can be held liable for torts of their child when they permit their inexperienced or irresponsible minor child to keep or have access to inherently dangerous instrumentality, under circumstances that should put them on notice that instrumentality may become source of danger to others. Doe v. Kahrs (Ohio Com.Pl. 1995) 75 Ohio Misc.2d 7, 662 N.E.2d 101.

5. Married child

Where a minor child is validly married, has established his own residence apart from his parents, and is self-supporting, he is no longer within the custody and control of his parents for purposes of establishing liability pursuant to RC 3109.10. Albert v. Ellis (Cuyahoga 1978) 59 Ohio App.2d 152, 392 N.E.2d 1309, 13 O.O.3d 188.

6. Statute of limitations

The one-year statute of limitation for assault, covered by RC 2305.11, is applicable to RC 3109.10. Liddy v. Smole (Shelby 1978) 56 Ohio App.2d 205, 381 N.E.2d 1335, 10 O.O.3d 203.

7. "Damages" defined

As used in RC 3109.09, the term "damages" is intended to include loss by reason of a theft. Liberty Mut. Ins. Co. v. Davis (Ohio Mun. 1977) 52 Ohio Misc. 26, 368 N.E.2d 336, 6 O.O.3d 108.

8. Bankruptcy

A debt arising from a parent's liability under RC 3109.10 for a willful, malicious assault by his minor child may be discharged in the parent's bankruptcy proceedings, although debts resulting from a willful, malicious injury caused by the debtor cannot be discharged in the debtor's bankruptcy; the minor child's conduct will not be imputed to the parents. In re Whitacre (Bkrtcy.N.D.Ohio 1988) 93 B.R. 584.

9. Procedural issues

Statute which limits a parent's vicarious liability for the torts of his or her children does not protect a parent from liability for his or her own conduct. Cuervo v. Snell (Ohio App. 10 Dist. 1998) 131 Ohio App.3d 560, 723 N.E.2d 139.

Claim that judgment entered against defendant in action arising from alleged acts of sexual assault by his minor child while babysitting exceeded statutory limitation on a parent's vicarious liability for assaults by his or her children was waived by defendant's failure to raise issue when court entered the default judgment assessing liability, or when defendant learned that the court had entered a damages judgment against him. Cuervo v. Snell (Ohio App. 10 Dist. 1998) 131 Ohio App.3d 560, 723 N.E.2d 139.

Minor defendant in tort action is responsible for paying fee of court-appointed guardian ad litem. Thatcher v. Fields (Ohio App. 10 Dist. 1997) 118 Ohio App.3d 63, 691 N.E.2d 1103.

Trial court had no authority to shift, to party that prevailed on his tort claims against minor defendant, the responsibility for paying fee of guardian ad litem appointed to represent minor defendant's interests in tort action. Thatcher v. Fields (Ohio App. 10 Dist. 1997) 118 Ohio App.3d 63, 691 N.E.2d 1103.

Material issue of fact as to whether parents of two minors who allegedly sexually abused another child knew or should have known that at least one of their sons had propensity to engage in aberrant sexual behavior precluded summary judgment for minors' parents in negligent supervision action. Doe v. Kahrs (Ohio Com.Pl. 1995) 75 Ohio Misc.2d 7, 662 N.E.2d 101.

10. Negligence not established

Gun being accessible to teenage child does not necessarily constitute danger to others so as to subject parent to liability for negligent entrustment. Nearor v. Davis (Ohio App. 1 Dist. 1997) 118 Ohio App.3d 806, 694 N.E.2d 120, appeal not allowed 79 Ohio St.3d 1460, 681 N.E.2d 442.

Teenage child's prior instances of misconduct, none of which to parents' knowledge involved firearms, did not make it "foreseeable" that he would fatally shoot his friend with loaded revolver parents had left under their mattress, and thus parents were not liable for negligent entrustment; instances of misconduct included possible involvement in receiving stolen property, possible marijuana use, declining grades at school, disobeying house rule prohibiting visitors when parents were gone, and driving mother's car without her permission and without license or permit. Nearor v. Davis (Ohio App. 1 Dist. 1997) 118 Ohio App.3d 806, 694 N.E.2d 120, appeal not allowed 79 Ohio St.3d 1460, 681 N.E.2d 442.

Pornographic material was not "dangerous instrumentality," and thus parents of minors who allegedly sexually assaulted minor victim could not be held liable under negligent entrustment claim based on minors' alleged access to such material. Doe v. Kahrs (Ohio Com.Pl. 1995) 75 Ohio Misc.2d 7, 662 N.E.2d 101.

Generally, parents cannot be held liable for independent torts of their child unless parents are in some way connected to child's wrongdoing, either actively or passively. Doe v. Kahrs (Ohio Com.Pl. 1995) 75 Ohio Misc.2d 7, 662 N.E.2d 101.

Parents cannot be held liable for negligent supervision of their children when parents do not know of children's propensity to engage in sort of conduct that causes plaintiff's injury. Doe v. Kahrs (Ohio Com.Pl. 1995) 75 Ohio Misc.2d 7, 662 N.E.2d 101.

In absence of any evidence indicating that parents knew or should have known that their son was sexually abusing a minor, parents cannot be held liable for negligent supervision as result of their child's sexually abusing minor plaintiff. Doe v. Kahrs (Ohio Com.Pl. 1995) 75 Ohio Misc.2d 7, 662 N.E.2d 101.

VISITATION RIGHTS OF RELATIVES

3109.11 Visitation rights of grandparents and other relatives when parent deceased

If either the father or mother of an unmarried minor child is deceased, the court of common pleas of the county in which the minor child resides may grant the parents and other relatives of the deceased father or mother reasonable companionship or visitation rights with respect to the minor child during the child's minority if the parent or other relative files a complaint requesting reasonable companionship or visitation rights and if the court determines that the granting of the companionship or visitation rights is in the best interest of the minor child. In determining whether to grant any person reasonable companionship or visitation rights with respect to any child, the court shall consider all relevant factors, including, but not limited to, the factors set forth in division (D) of section 3109.051 of the Revised Code. Divisions (C), (K), and (L) of section 3109.051 of the Revised Code apply to the determination of reasonable companionship or visitation rights under this section and to any order granting any such rights that is issued under this section.

The remarriage of the surviving parent of the child does not affect the authority of the court under this section to grant reasonable companionship or visitation rights with respect to the child to a parent or other relative of the child's deceased father or mother.

If the court denies a request for reasonable companionship or visitation rights made pursuant to this section and the complainant files a written request for findings of fact and conclusions of law, the court shall state in writing its findings of fact and conclusions of law in accordance with Civil Rule 52.

Except as provided in division (E)(6) of section 3113.31 of the Revised Code, if the court, pursuant to this section, grants any person companionship or visitation rights with respect to any child, it shall not require the public children services agency to provide supervision of or other services related to that person's exercise of companionship or visitation rights with respect to the child. This section does not limit the power of a juvenile court pursuant to Chapter 2151. of the Revised Code to issue orders with respect to children who are alleged to be abused, neglected, or dependent children or to make dispositions of children who are adjudicated abused, neglected, or dependent children or of a common pleas court to issue orders pursuant to section 3113.31 of the Revised Code.

(1996 H 274, eff. 8-8-96; 1990 S 3, eff. 4-11-91; 1990 H 15; 1971 H 163)

Historical and Statutory Notes

Amendment Note: 1996 H 274 added the fourth paragraph; and made changes to reflect gender neutral language.

Cross References

Child support order to include provisions for visitation, 3113.215

Contempt for failure to comply or interference with visitation order, 2705.031

County children services boards, powers and duties, 5153.16

Day care centers, access of parents, 5104.011

Library References

Infants ⟹19.3(4).
Parent and Child ⟹2(17).
WESTLAW Topic Nos. 211, 285.
C.J.S. Infants §§ 22 to 25.
C.J.S. Parent and Child §§ 41, 42.

Am Jur 2d: 59, Parent and Child § 45
Grandparents' visitation rights. 90 ALR3d 222
Visitation rights of persons other than natural parents or grandparents. 1 ALR4th 1270

Carlin, Baldwin's Ohio Practice, *Merrick-Rippner Probate Law* § 98.8, 107.9, 108.15 (1997)

Klein & Darling, Baldwin's Ohio Practice, *Civil Practice* § 52 (1997)

Sowald & Morganstern, Baldwin's Ohio Practice, *Domestic Relations Law* § 18.2, 18.6, 18.7, 18.10, 18.18, 19.11, 21.2 (1997)

Law Review and Journal Commentaries

The Child's Right to Visit Grandparents, Henry H. Foster and Doris Jonas Freed. 20 Trial (American Trial Lawyers' Assn) 38 (March 1984).

Grandparents' Rights in Ohio After H.B. 15, Richard J. Innis. 2 Domestic Rel J Ohio 33 (May/June 1990).

Grandparent Visitation: The Best Interests of the Grandparent, Child, and Society, Erica L. Strawman. 30 U Tol L Rev 31 (Fall 1998).

Grandparents' Visitation Rights in Ohio: A Procedural Quagmire, Comment. 56 U Cin L Rev 295 (1987).

Open Adoption: Can Visitation With Natural Family Members Be In The Child's Best Interest?, Note. 30 J Fam L 471 (February 1992).

Visitation Rights of a Grandparent Over the Objection of a Parent: The Best Interests of the Child, Note. 15 J Fam L 51 (1976-77).

Notes of Decisions and Opinions

1. Factors

The factors set forth in RC 3109.04(C) with respect to determining the child's best interest in custody cases apply equally to visitation cases. The trial court must weigh these and other relevant factors in determining the child's best interest in visitation cases. In re Whitaker (Ohio 1988) 36 Ohio St.3d 213, 522 N.E.2d 563.

Grandparents are not statutorily entitled to visitation of their grandchildren and a court must consider the factors enumerated in RC 3109.11 as well as the best interest and wishes of the children; consequent denial of visitation to a grandmother is neither an automatic ground for reversal nor an abuse of discretion. In re Skinner, No. 93CA547, 1994 WL 93149 (4th Dist Ct App, Adams, 3-23-94).

2. Best interest of child

Grandparents may be granted visitation rights under RC 3109.11 and 3109.05(B) if the trial court finds that such visitation is in the child's best interest. In re Whitaker (Ohio 1988) 36 Ohio St.3d 213, 522 N.E.2d 563.

Trial court in proceeding in which maternal grandmother sought visitation privileges with granddaughter did not abuse its discretion in compelling father who had custody of child to tell child about her mother's death from a drug overdose; it was in child's best interest to know what happened to her mother and such information was best learned from concerned parent rather than from some other source, such as siblings. Holley v. Higgins (Franklin 1993) 86 Ohio App.3d 240, 620 N.E.2d 251.

Maternal grandparents may be granted visitation rights, pursuant to RC 3109.11, where the children's father consents to an adoption of the children by their paternal grandparents. The court shall consider the best interest of the children when considering such a request. In re Pennington (Scioto 1988) 55 Ohio App.3d 99, 562 N.E.2d 905.

The companionship and visitation rights vested by RC 3109.11 are neither absolute nor unqualified but are conditioned upon the finding by the proper court that such rights are in the best interest of the child. Graziano v. Davis (Mahoning 1976) 50 Ohio App.2d 83, 361 N.E.2d 525, 4 O.O.3d 55.

The companionship and visitation rights of relatives granted in RC 3109.11 are subservient to the best interests of the minor child. In re Griffiths (Mahoning 1975) 47 Ohio App.2d 238, 353 N.E.2d 884, 1 O.O.3d 307.

In general, the visitation and companionship of a child's grandparents are in a child's best interests, and so where a thirteen year old child, rightly or wrongly, resents or dislikes his grandparents to such a degree that court enforced association cannot be reasonably expected to modify his attitude toward them and can only result in an intensification of his resentment and dislike, the usual benefits of visitation and the necessary elements of companionship do not exist and the best interests of the child require the court to deny visitation rights to such grandparents. In re Griffiths (Mahoning 1975) 47 Ohio App.2d 238, 353 N.E.2d 884, 1 O.O.3d 307.

The companionship and visitation rights vested by RC 3109.11 are neither absolute nor unqualified but are conditioned upon the finding by a court of competent jurisdiction that such rights are in the best interests of the child. In re Griffiths (Mahoning 1975) 47 Ohio App.2d 238, 353 N.E.2d 884, 1 O.O.3d 307.

3. Adoption

Trial court lacked authority to grant paternal grandparents visitation with children of divorced parents after the children were adopted by their stepfather subsequent to their father's death; while a statute preserved the right of grandparent visitation when a surviving spouse remarried, it did not provide for the preservation of visitation rights after an adoption by a stepparent. Foor v. Foor (Ohio App. 12 Dist. 1999) 133 Ohio App.3d 250, 727 N.E.2d 618.

Statute providing that marriage of the surviving parent of child does not affect authority of court to grant reasonable companionship or visitation rights to grandparents preserves the right of grandparent visitation when the surviving spouse remarries, but it does not provide for the preservation of grandparent visitation rights after adoption of child by stepparent. Beard v. Pannell (Sandusky 1996) 110 Ohio App.3d 572, 674 N.E.2d 1225, appeal not allowed 77 Ohio St.3d 1447, 671 N.E.2d 1285.

Where a child's parent dies, the surviving parent remarries, and the surviving parent's new spouse adopts the child, a court may grant visitation rights to relatives of the deceased parent pursuant to RC 3109.11 over the objections of the child's parents, notwithstanding RC 3107.15. In re Thornton (Franklin 1985) 24 Ohio App.3d 152, 493 N.E.2d 977, 24 O.B.R. 241.

The power of the court to order visitation and companionship rights to relatives under RC 3109.11 is not divested or terminated by the adoption of the child of a deceased parent by a stepparent, pursuant to RC 3107.13, and such adoption is merely a factor which the court must consider in determining the best interest of the child under RC 3109.11. Graziano v. Davis (Mahoning 1976) 50 Ohio App.2d 83, 361 N.E.2d 525, 4 O.O.3d 55.

Trial court has no authority to grant visitation rights to paternal grandparents where the relationship between the father and child has been terminated pursuant to RC 3107.07. In re Adoption of Bitner, No. 81-CA-77 (7th Dist Ct App, Mahoning, 2-24-82).

A relative does not have a preferential right over a pre-adoptive parent in determining who should adopt a child. In re Dickhaus (Ohio Com.Pl. 1974) 41 Ohio Misc. 1, 321 N.E.2d 800, 70 O.O.2d 24.

4. Rights of child

If one parent of an unmarried minor child is deceased, RC 3109.11 vests in the relatives of the deceased parent reasonable companionship and visitation rights to the child during its minority, and vests in the child the right to the companionship and visitation of its relatives. Graziano v. Davis (Mahoning 1976) 50 Ohio App.2d 83, 361 N.E.2d 525, 4 O.O.3d 55.

If the father or mother of an unmarried minor child is deceased, RC 3109.11 vests in the relatives of the deceased person reasonable companionship and visitation rights to the minor child during the minority and vests in the minor child the right to the companionship and visitation of its relatives. In re Griffiths (Mahoning 1975) 47 Ohio App.2d 238, 353 N.E.2d 884, 1 O.O.3d 307.

5. Constitutional issues

RC 3109.11, allowing a court to order reasonable companionship and visitation rights with a minor child to relatives of a deceased parent, is not facially unconstitutional. Burton v Jones, Nos. CA86-04-046 and CA86-06-087 (12th Dist Ct App, Butler, 4-27-87).

3109.12 Visitation rights of grandparents and other relatives when child's mother unmarried

(A) If a child is born to an unmarried woman, the parents of the woman and any relative of the woman may file a complaint requesting the court of common pleas of the county in which the child resides to grant them reasonable companionship or visitation rights with the child. If a child is born to an unmarried woman and if the father of the child has acknowledged the child and that acknowledgment has become final pursuant to section 2151.232, 3111.211, or 5101.314 of the Revised Code or has been determined in an action under Chapter 3111. of the Revised Code to be the father of the child, the father, the parents of the father, and any relative of the father may file a complaint requesting the court of common pleas of the county in which the child resides to grant them reasonable companionship or visitation rights with respect to the child.

(B) The court may grant the companionship or visitation rights requested under division (A) of this section, if it determines that the granting of the companionship or visitation rights is in the best interest of the child. In determining whether to grant any person reasonable companionship or visitation rights with respect to any child, the court shall consider all relevant factors, including, but not limited to, the factors set forth in division (D) of section 3109.051 of the Revised Code. Divisions (C), (K), and (L) of section 3109.051 of the Revised Code apply to the determination of reasonable companionship or visitation rights under this section and to any order granting any such rights that is issued under this section.

The marriage or remarriage of the mother or father of a child does not affect the authority of the court under this section to grant the natural father, the parents or relatives of the natural father, or the parents or relatives of the mother of the child reasonable companionship or visitation rights with respect to the child.

If the court denies a request for reasonable companionship or visitation rights made pursuant to division (A) of this section and the complainant files a written request for findings of fact and conclusions of law, the court shall state in writing its findings of fact and conclusions of law in accordance with Civil Rule 52.

Except as provided in division (E)(6) of section 3113.31 of the Revised Code, if the court, pursuant to this section, grants any person companionship or visitation rights with respect to any child, it shall not require the public children services agency to provide supervision of or other services related to that person's exercise of companionship or visitation rights with respect to the child. This section does not limit the power of a juvenile court pursuant to Chapter 2151. of the Revised Code to issue orders with respect to children who are alleged to be abused, neglected, or dependent children or to make dispositions of children who are adjudicated abused, neglected, or dependent children or of a common pleas court to issue orders pursuant to section 3113.31 of the Revised Code.

(1997 H 352, eff. 1-1-98; 1996 H 274, eff. 8-8-96; 1990 S 3, eff. 4-11-91; 1990 H 15)

Historical and Statutory Notes

Amendment Note: 1997 H 352 inserted "and that acknowledgment has become final" and substituted "2151.232, 3111.211, or 5101.314" for "2105.18" in division (A).

Amendment Note: 1996 H 274 added the fourth paragraph in division (B).

Cross References

Acknowledgment of paternity, 2105.18
Child support order to include provisions for visitation, 3113.215
Contempt for failure to comply or interference with visitation order, 2705.031
County children services boards, powers and duties, 5153.16
Day care centers, access of parents, 5104.011
Parent and child relationship, effect of judgment determining, 3111.13

Library References

Children Out-Of-Wedlock ⚷20.
Infants ⚷19.3(4).
Parent and Child ⚷2(17).
WESTLAW Topic Nos. 76H, 211, 285.
C.J.S. Children Out-of-Wedlock §§ 11, 12, 34 to 39.
C.J.S. Infants §§ 22 to 25.
C.J.S. Parent and Child §§ 41, 42.
Carlin, Baldwin's Ohio Practice, *Merrick-Rippner Probate Law* § 19.2, 98.31, 98.48, 98.84, 107.9, 108.13, 108.15, 108.20 (1997)
Klein & Darling, Baldwin's Ohio Practice, *Civil Practice* § 52 (1997)
Sowald & Morganstern, Baldwin's Ohio Practice, *Domestic Relations Law* § 3.8, 3.34, 18.2, 18.8, 18.10, 18.18, 19.11, 21.2, 22.19 (1997)

Law Review and Journal Commentaries

Grandparents' Rights in Ohio After H.B. 15, Richard J. Innis. 2 Domestic Rel J Ohio 33 (May/June 1990).

Notes of Decisions and Opinions

1. Procedural issues

Putative paternal grandparents were not qualified to seek court-ordered right to visit their putative biological grandchild, until alleged paternity of grandchild was established by putative father filing legitimation petition or by paternity action to determine if putative father was father of child. In re Martin (Ohio 1994) 68 Ohio St.3d 250, 626 N.E.2d 82.

Even if putative father was father of child, putative paternal grandparents were not entitled to court-ordered right to visit child who had been adopted by maternal grandparents, as statute which provides that adoption of child terminates all legal relationships between adopted child and his relatives does not distinguish between adoption by strangers and nonstrangers. In re Martin (Ohio 1994) 68 Ohio St.3d 250, 626 N.E.2d 82.

In general, grandparental visitation rights do not vest until occurrence of disruptive precipitating event, such as parental death or divorce; absent disruptive event, common-law view of deferring to parental autonomy in raising child is observed despite moral or social obligations that encourage contact between grandparents and grandchildren. In re Gibson (Ohio 1991) 61 Ohio St.3d 168, 573 N.E.2d 1074.

Assuming that adjudicated father's petition for modification of his child support obligation was properly before Juvenile Court, fact that such petition was pending did not vest Juvenile Court with jurisdiction to entertain paternal grandmother's petition for grandparental visitation pursuant to domestic relations statute, where statute setting forth Juvenile Court's jurisdiction in parentage actions did not reference domestic relations statute, and where child's mother was unmarried. Borkosky v. Mihailoff (Ohio App. 3 Dist. 1999) 132 Ohio App.3d 508, 725 N.E.2d 694.

Juvenile court of county other than that of child's residence lacked jurisdiction to entertain paternal grandmother's motion for grandparental visitation, where child's mother was unmarried and child's paternity had been established through adjudication. Borkosky v. Mihailoff (Ohio App. 3 Dist. 1999) 132 Ohio App.3d 508, 725 N.E.2d 694.

After Human Leukocyte Antigen (HLA) tests conclusively excluded plaintiff as father, there was no basis for permitting juvenile court to grant plaintiff visitation rights, where plaintiff had not acknowledged his paternity with probate court following child's birth. Sherburn v. Reichert (Van Wert 1994) 97 Ohio App.3d 120, 646 N.E.2d 255.

The burden of proof that visitation would not be in the child's best interest is on the person opposing visitation and there is no requirement to show a change of circumstances in any request to change visitation rights. In re Nichols, No. CA97-11-102, 1998 WL 295937 (12th Dist Ct App, Clermont, 6-8-98).

A partner in a lesbian relationship does not have an obligation to pay child support insofar as she is not the biological, natural or adoptive mother of her partner's child and her attempt to file a child support proceeding in order to claim visitation rights pursuant to RC 3109.051 must fail. Liston v Pyles, No. 97APF01-137, 1997 WL 467327 (10th Dist Ct App, Franklin, 8-12-97).

Grandparents' visitation rights are granted where the mother's marriage to the biological father after the child is born coupled with the establishment of paternity after the marriage does not vest the parties with the right of parental autonomy which does not apply to a mother and father who have not been married throughout the child's lifetime. Stout v Kline, No. 96-CA-71, 1997 WL 219099 (5th Dist Ct App, Richland, 3-28-97).

PREVENTION OF CHILD ABUSE AND CHILD NEGLECT

Cross References

"Abused child," defined, 2151.031
Child abuse and domestic violence, criminal sanctions, 2919.22 to 2919.271
Department of human services, division of social administration; care and placement of children, 5103.09 to 5103.17
Estate taxes, deduction for bequest for prevention of cruelty to children, 5731.17
Guardian ad litem for abused and neglected children, 2151.281
Injury or neglect of child, persons required to report, 2151.421
Neglect, abandonment, or domestic violence, Ch 3113
Powers and duties of county children services board, 5153.16
Protective services for children, 5101.46

Library References

Dill Calloway, Ohio Nursing Law, Text 5.02(A)

3109.13 Child abuse or neglect prevention programs

Note: See also following version of this section, eff. 1-1-01.

As used in sections 3109.13 to 3109.18 of the Revised Code, "child abuse and child neglect prevention programs" means programs designed to prevent child abuse and child neglect, including, but not limited to, any of the following:

(A) Community-based public awareness programs that pertain to child abuse or child neglect;

(B) Community-based educational programs that pertain to prenatal care, perinatal bonding, child development, basic child care, care of children with special needs, or coping with family stress;

(C) Community-based programs that relate to care and treatment in child abuse or child neglect crisis situations; aid to parents who potentially may abuse or neglect their children; child abuse or child neglect counseling; support groups for parents who potentially may abuse or neglect their children, and support groups for their children; or early identification of families in which there is a potential for child abuse or child neglect;

(D) Programs that train and place volunteers in programs that pertain to child abuse or child neglect;

(E) Programs that may develop and make available to boards of education curricula and educational materials on basic child care and parenting skills, or programs that would provide both teacher and volunteer training programs.

(1984 H 319, eff. 12-26-84)

Note: See also following version of this section, eff. 1-1-01.

3109.13 Child abuse or neglect prevention programs defined

Note: See also preceding version of this section, in effect until 1-1-01.

As used in sections 3109.13 to 3109.18 of the Revised Code, child abuse and child neglect prevention programs means programs designed to prevent child abuse and child neglect, including, but not limited to, any of the following:

(A) Public awareness programs that pertain to child abuse or child neglect;

(B) Community-based, family-focused support services and activities that do any of the following:

(1) Build parenting skills;

(2) Promote parental behaviors that lead to healthy and positive personal development of parents and children;

(3) Promote individual, family, and community strengths;

(4) Provide information, education, or health activities that promote the well-being of families and children.

(C) Programs that train and place volunteers in programs that pertain to child abuse or child neglect.

(1999 H 283, eff. 1-1-01; 1984 H 319, eff. 12-26-84)
Note: See also preceding version of this section, in effect until 1-1-01.

Historical and Statutory Notes

Amendment Note: 1999 H 283 rewrote the section, which prior thereto read:

"As used in sections 3109.13 to 3109.18 of the Revised Code, 'child abuse and child neglect prevention programs' means programs designed to prevent child abuse and child neglect, including, but not limited to, any of the following:

"(A) Community-based public awareness programs that pertain to child abuse or child neglect;

"(B) Community-based educational programs that pertain to prenatal care, perinatal bonding, child development, basic child care, care of children with special needs, or coping with family stress;

"(C) Community-based programs that relate to care and treatment in child abuse or child neglect crisis situations; aid to parents who potentially may abuse or neglect their children; child abuse or child neglect counseling; support groups for parents who potentially may abuse or neglect their children, and support groups for their children; or early identification of families in which there is a potential for child abuse or child neglect;

"(D) Programs that train and place volunteers in programs that pertain to child abuse or child neglect;

"(E) Programs that may develop and make available to boards of education curricula and educational materials on basic child care and parenting skills, or programs that would provide both teacher and volunteer training programs."

Ohio Administrative Code References

Child abuse and neglect, supportive services, OAC Ch 5101:2-39

Children's trust fund; administration, OAC Ch 5101:5-1

Library References

Infants ⟜13, 17, 131.
WESTLAW Topic No. 211.
C.J.S. Infants §§ 5, 8, 9, 31, 33, 42, 50, 51, 53, 54, 92, 93, 95 to 98.

Am Jur 2d: 42, Infants § 16, 17

Dill Calloway, Ohio Nursing Law, Text 5.02(A)

3109.14 Additional fees for birth and death records; children's trust fund

Note: See also following version of this section, eff. 1-1-01.

As used in this section, "birth record" and "certification of birth" have the meanings given in section 3705.01 of the Revised Code.

The director of health, a person authorized by the director, a local commissioner of health, or a local registrar of vital statistics shall charge and collect for each copy of a birth record and for each certification of birth a fee of two dollars, and for each copy of a death record a fee of two dollars, in addition to the fee imposed by section 3705.24 or any other section of the Revised Code. A local commissioner of health or a local registrar of vital statistics may retain an amount of each additional fee collected, not to exceed three per cent of the amount of the additional fee, to be used for costs directly related to the collection of the fee and the forwarding of the fee to the treasurer of state.

Upon the filing for a divorce decree under section 3105.10 or a decree of dissolution under section 3105.65 of the Revised Code, a court of common pleas shall charge and collect a fee of ten dollars in addition to any other court costs or fees. The county clerk of courts may retain an amount of each additional fee collected, not to exceed three per cent of the amount of the additional fee, to be used for costs directly related to the collection of the fee and the forwarding of the fee to the treasurer of state.

The additional fees collected, but not retained, under this section during each month shall be forwarded not later than the twentieth day of the immediately following month to the treasurer of state, who shall deposit the fees in the state treasury to the credit of the children's trust fund, which is hereby created.

The treasurer of state shall invest the moneys in the fund, and all earnings resulting from investment of the fund shall be credited to the fund, except that actual administrative costs incurred by the treasurer of state in administering the fund may be deducted from the earnings resulting from investments. The amount that may be deducted shall not exceed three per cent of the total amount of fees credited to the fund in each fiscal year, except that the children's trust fund board may approve an amount for actual administrative costs exceeding three per cent but not exceeding four per cent of such amount. The balance of the investment earnings shall be credited to the fund. Moneys credited to the fund shall be used only for the purposes described in sections 3109.17 and 3109.18 of the Revised Code.

(1998 H 426, eff. 7-22-98; 1988 H 790, eff. 3-16-89; 1985 H 201; 1984 H 319)
Note: See also following version of this section, eff. 1-1-01.

3109.14 Additional fees for birth and death records; children's trust fund

Note: See also preceding version of this section, in effect until 1-1-01.

(A) As used in this section, birth record and certification of birth have the meanings given in section 3705.01 of the Revised Code.

(B)(1) The director of health, a person authorized by the director, a local commissioner of health, or a local registrar of vital statistics shall charge and collect for each certified copy of a birth record and for each certification of birth a fee of two dollars, and for each copy of a death record a fee of two dollars, in addition to the fee imposed by section 3705.24 or any other section of the Revised Code. A local commissioner of health or a local registrar of vital statistics may retain an amount of each additional fee collected, not to exceed three per cent of the amount of the additional fee, to be used for costs directly related to the collection of the fee and the forwarding of the fee to the treasurer of state.

(2) Upon the filing for a divorce decree under section 3105.10 or a decree of dissolution under section 3105.65 of the Revised Code, a court of common pleas shall charge and collect a fee of ten dollars in addition to any other court costs or fees. The county clerk of courts may retain an amount of each additional fee collected, not to exceed three per cent of the amount of the additional fee, to be used for costs directly related to the collection of the fee and the forwarding of the fee to the treasurer of state.

(C) The additional fees collected, but not retained, under this section during each month shall be forwarded not later than the tenth day of the immediately following month to the treasurer of state, who shall deposit the fees in the state treasury to the credit of the children's trust fund, which is hereby created. A person or government entity that fails to forward the fees in a timely manner, as determined by the treasurer of state, shall forward to the treasurer of state, in addition to the fees, a penalty equal to ten per cent of the fees.

The treasurer of state shall invest the moneys in the fund, and all earnings resulting from investment of the fund shall be credited to the fund, except that actual administrative costs incurred by the treasurer of state in administering the fund may be deducted from the earnings resulting from investments. The amount that may be deducted shall not exceed three per cent of the total amount of fees credited to the fund in each fiscal year, except that the children's trust fund board may approve an amount for actual administrative costs exceeding three per cent but not exceeding four per cent of such amount. The balance of the investment earnings shall be credited to the fund. Moneys credited to the fund shall be used only for the purposes described in sections 3109.13 to 3109.18 of the Revised Code.

(1999 H 283, eff. 1-1-01; 1998 H 426, eff. 7-22-98; 1988 H 790, eff. 3-16-89; 1985 H 201; 1984 H 319)
Note: See also preceding version of this section, in effect until 1-1-01.

Historical and Statutory Notes

Amendment Note: 1999 H 283 designated divisions (A), (B)(1), (B)(2), and (C); inserted "certified" in division (B)(1); substituted "tenth" for "twentieth" and added the second sentence in the first paragraph in division (C); and substituted "3109.13 to 3109.18" for "3109.17 and 3109.18" in the second paragraph in division (C).

Amendment Note: 1998 H 426 substituted "collected" for "that he collects" in the second and third paragraphs; and substituted "twentieth" for "fifth" in the fourth paragraph.

Cross References

Heirloom certifications of birth, fee, 3705.24

Information supplied from public records, 3705.23

Ohio Administrative Code References

Children's trust fund; administration, OAC Ch 5101:5-1

Library References

Clerks of Courts ⚷11.
Divorce ⚷192.
States ⚷122, 127.
WESTLAW Topic Nos. 79, 134, 360.
C.J.S. Courts §§ 242, 244.
C.J.S. Divorce § 301.
C.J.S. States §§ 224, 228.

Dill Calloway, Ohio Nursing Law, Text 5.02(A)

Notes of Decisions and Opinions

1. Procedure

The fees collected by the appropriate clerks of court pursuant to 1984 H 319, eff. 12-26-84, and 1984 S 219, eff. 1-8-85, are to be collected only in cases filed subsequent to the effective dates of those acts. OAG 85-057.

The fee collected pursuant to RC 3109.14 by the county clerk of courts "[u]pon the filing for a divorce decree ... or a decree of dissolution" is to be collected upon the filing of the complaint for divorce or the petition for dissolution. OAG 85-057.

The fee collected by the county clerk of courts pursuant to RC 3109.14 must be forwarded to the treasurer of state, irrespective of the subsequent dismissal of the action which generated the fee; further, the fee must be forwarded to the treasurer of state not later than the fifth day of the month immediately following the month in which the fee is collected.

3109.15 Children's trust fund board

Note: See also following version of this section, eff. 1-1-01.

There is hereby created within the department of job and family services the children's trust fund board consisting of thirteen members. The director of health and the director of job and family services shall be members of the board. Seven public members shall be appointed by the governor. These members shall be persons with demonstrated knowledge in programs for children, shall be representative of the demographic composition of this state, and, to the extent practicable, shall be representative of the following categories: the educational community; the legal community; the social work community; the medical community; the voluntary sector; and professional providers of child abuse and child neglect services. Five of these members shall be residents of counties where the population exceeds four hundred thousand; no more than one such member shall be a resident of the same county. Two members of the board shall be members of the house of representatives appointed by the speaker of the house of representatives and shall be members of two different political parties. Two members of the board shall be members of the senate appointed by the president of the senate and shall be members of two different political parties. All members of the board appointed by the speaker of the house of representatives or the president of the senate shall serve until the expiration of the sessions of the general assembly during which they were appointed. They may be reappointed to an unlimited number of successive terms of two years at the pleasure of the speaker of the house of representatives or president of the senate. Of the public members first appointed, three shall serve for terms of four years; two shall serve for terms of three years; and two shall serve for terms of two years. Thereafter, public members shall serve terms of three years. Each member shall serve until the member's successor is appointed. No public member may serve more than two consecutive terms, regardless of whether such terms were full or partial terms. All vacancies on the board shall be filled for the balance of the unexpired term in the same manner as the original appointment.

Any public member of the board may be removed by the governor for misconduct, incompetency, or neglect of duty after first being given the opportunity to be heard in the member's own behalf.

Each member of the board shall serve without compensation but shall be reimbursed for all actual and necessary expenses incurred in the performance of official duties.

The speaker of the house of representatives and the president of the senate shall jointly appoint the board chairperson from among the legislative members of the board.

This section is an interim section effective until January 1, 2001.

(1999 H 471, § 1, eff. 7-1-00; 1987 H 171, eff. 7-1-87; 1984 H 319)
Note: See also following version of this section, eff. 1-1-01.

3109.15 Children's trust fund board

Note: See also preceding version of this section, in effect until 1-1-01.

There is hereby created within the department of job and family services the children's trust fund board consisting of fifteen members. The directors of alcohol and drug addiction services, health, and job and family services shall be members of the board. Eight public members shall be appointed by the governor. These members shall be persons with demonstrated knowledge in programs for children, shall be representative of the demographic composition of this state, and, to the extent practicable, shall be representative of the following categories: the educational community; the legal community; the social work community; the medical community; the voluntary sector; and professional providers of child abuse and child neglect services. Five of these members shall be residents of counties where the population exceeds four hundred thousand; no more than one such member shall be a resident of the same county. Two members of the board shall be members of the house of representatives appointed by the speaker of the house of representatives and shall be members of two different political parties. Two members of the board shall be members of the senate appointed by the president of the senate and shall be members of two different political parties. All members of the board appointed by the speaker of the house of representatives or the president of the senate shall serve until the expiration of the sessions of the general assembly during which they were appointed. They may be reappointed to an unlimited number of successive terms of two years at the pleasure of the speaker of the house of representatives or president of the senate. Public members shall serve terms of three years. Each member shall serve until the member's successor is appointed. No public member may serve more than two consecutive terms, regardless of whether such terms were full or partial terms. All vacancies on the board shall be filled for the balance of the unexpired term in the same manner as the original appointment.

Any member of the board may be removed by the member's appointing authority for misconduct, incompetency, or neglect of duty after first being given the opportunity to be heard in the member's own behalf. Pursuant to section 3.17 of the Revised Code, a member, except a member of the general assembly or a judge of any court in the state, who fails to attend at least three-fifths of the regular and special meetings held by the board during any two-year period forfeits the member's position on the board.

Each member of the board shall serve without compensation but shall be reimbursed for all actual and necessary expenses incurred in the performance of official duties.

The speaker of the house of representatives and the president of the senate shall jointly appoint the board chairperson from among the legislative members of the board.

(1999 H 471, § 3, eff. 1-1-01; 1999 H 471, § 1, eff. 7-1-00; 1999 H 283, eff. 1-1-01; 1987 H 171, eff. 7-1-87; 1984 H 319)
Note: See also preceding version of this section, in effect until 1-1-01.

Uncodified Law

1996 H 670, § 27: See Uncodified Law under 101.84 for provisions regarding expiration of agencies.

Historical and Statutory Notes

Amendment Note: 1999 H 471, § 3, eff. 1-1-01, substituted "job and family" for "human" twice in the first paragraph.

Amendment Note: 1999 H 471, § 1, eff. 7-1-00, substituted "job and family" for "human" twice in the first paragraph; added the final paragraph; and made changes to reflect gender neutral language and other nonsubstantive changes.

Amendment Note: 1999 H 283 rewrote the section, which prior thereto read:

"There is hereby created within the department of human services the children's trust fund board consisting of thirteen members. The director of health and the director of human services shall be members of the board. Seven public members shall be appointed by the governor. These members shall be persons with demonstrated knowledge in programs for children, shall be representative of the demographic composition of this state, and, to the extent practicable, shall be representative of the following categories: the educational community; the legal community; the social work community; the medical community; the voluntary sector; and professional providers of child abuse and child neglect services. Five of these members shall be residents of counties where the population exceeds four hundred thousand; no more than one such member shall be a resident of the same county. Two members of the board shall be members of the house of representatives appointed by the speaker of the house of representatives and shall be members of two different political parties. Two members of the board shall be members of the senate appointed by the president of the senate and shall be members of two different political parties. All members of the board appointed by the speaker of the house of representatives or the president of the senate shall serve until the expiration of the sessions of the general assembly during which they were appointed. They may be reappointed to an unlimited number of successive terms of two years at the pleasure of the speaker of the house of representatives or president of the senate. Of the public members first appointed, three shall serve for terms of four years; two shall serve for terms of three years; and two shall serve for terms of two years. Thereafter, public members shall serve terms of three years. Each member shall serve until his successor is appointed. No public member may serve more than two consecutive terms, regardless of whether such terms were full or partial terms. All vacancies on the board shall be filled for the balance of the unexpired term in the same manner as the original appointment.

"Any public member of the board may be removed by the governor for misconduct, incompetency, or neglect of duty after first being given the opportunity to be heard in his own behalf.

"Each member of the board shall serve without compensation but shall be reimbursed for all actual and necessary expenses incurred by him in the performance of his official duties.

"The speaker of the house of representatives and the president of the senate shall jointly appoint the board chairman from among the legislative members of the board."

Cross References

Wellness block grant program, administrative agent of, 121.371

Ohio Administrative Code References

Children's trust fund; administration, OAC Ch 5101:5-1

Library References

Infants ⚷17.
WESTLAW Topic No. 211.
C.J.S. Infants §§ 8, 9.

Dill Calloway, Ohio Nursing Law, Text 5.02(A)

Notes of Decisions and Opinions

Board members' status 1

---

1. Board members' status

The Ohio children's trust fund board is invested with independent power under RC 3109.16 and 3109.17 to allocate public funds and perform other sovereign duties on behalf of the state; its members are accordingly "public officials" for purposes of RC 2921.42.

3109.16 Powers and duties

Note: See also following version of this section, eff. 1-1-01.

The children's trust fund board, upon the recommendation of the director of job and family services, shall approve the employment of the staff that will administer the programs of the board. The department of job and family services shall provide budgetary, procurement, accounting, and other related management functions for the board. An amount not to exceed three per cent of the total amount of fees deposited in the children's trust fund in each fiscal year may be used for costs directly related to these administrative functions of the department. With the approval of the board, an amount exceeding three per cent, but not exceeding four per cent, of the total amount of fees credited to the fund in each fiscal year may be used for costs directly related to these administrative functions.

The board shall meet at the call of the chairperson to conduct its official business. All business transactions of the board shall be conducted in public meetings. The votes of at least seven board members are required to approve the state plan for the allocation of funds from the children's trust fund.

The board may apply for and accept federal funds for the purposes of sections 3109.13 to 3109.18 of the Revised Code. In addition, the board may accept gifts and donations from any source, including individuals, philanthropic foundations or organizations, corporations, or corporation endowments. The acceptance and use of federal funds shall not entail any commitment or pledge of state funds, nor obligate the general assembly to continue the programs or activities for which the federal funds are made available. All funds received in the manner described in this section shall be transmitted to the treasurer of state, who shall credit them to the children's trust fund created in section 3109.14 of the Revised Code.

This section is an interim section effective until January 1, 2001.

(1999 H 471, § 1, eff. 7-1-00; 1994 H 335, eff. 12-9-94; 1987 H 171, eff. 7-1-87; 1985 H 201; 1984 H 319)

Note: See also following version of this section, eff. 1-1-01.

3109.16 Powers and duties

Note: See also preceding version of this section, in effect until 1-1-01.

The children's trust fund board, upon the recommendation of the director of job and family services, shall approve the employment of the staff that will administer the programs of the board. The department of job and family services shall provide budgetary, procurement, accounting, and other related management functions for the board. An amount not to exceed three per cent of the total amount of fees deposited in the children's trust fund in each fiscal year may be used for costs directly related to these administrative functions of the department. Each fiscal year, the board shall approve a budget for administrative expenditures for the next fiscal year.

The board shall meet at the call of the chairperson to conduct its official business. All business transactions of the board shall be conducted in public meetings. Eight members of the board constitute a quorum. A majority of the quorum is required to approve the state plan for the allocation of funds from the children's trust fund.

The board may apply for and accept federal and other funds for the purpose of funding child abuse and child neglect prevention programs. In addition, the board may accept gifts and donations from any source, including individuals, philanthropic foundations or organizations, corporations, or corporation endowments. The acceptance and use of federal funds shall not entail any commitment or pledge of state funds, nor obligate the general assembly to continue the programs or activities for which the federal funds are made available. All funds received in the manner described in this section shall be transmitted to the treasurer of state, who shall credit them to the children's trust fund created in section 3109.14 of the Revised Code.

(2000 H 448, § 6, eff. 1-1-01; 1999 H 471, § 3, eff. 1-1-01; 1999 H 471, § 1, eff. 7-1-00; 1999 H 283, eff. 1-1-01; 1994 H 335, eff. 12-9-94; 1987 H 171, eff. 7-1-87; 1985 H 201; 1984 H 319)

Note: See also preceding version of this section, in effect until 1-1-01.

Historical and Statutory Notes

Amendment Note: 2000 H 448, § 6, substituted "three" for "five" in the first paragraph.

Amendment Note: 1999 H 471, § 3, eff. 1-1-01, substituted "job and family" for "human" twice in the first paragraph.

Amendment Note: 1999 H 471, § 1, eff. 7-1-00, substituted "job and family" for "human" twice in the first paragraph; substituted "chairperson" for "chairman" in the second paragraph; and added the final paragraph.

Amendment Note: 1999 H 283 rewrote the section, which prior thereto read:

"The children's trust fund board, upon the recommendation of the director of human services, shall approve the employment of the staff that will administer the programs of the board. The department of human services shall provide budgetary, procurement, accounting, and other related management functions for the board. An amount not to exceed three per cent of the total amount of fees deposited in the children's trust fund in each fiscal year may be used for costs directly related to these administrative functions of the department. With the approval of the board, an amount exceeding three per cent, but not exceeding four per cent, of the total amount of fees credited to the fund in each fiscal year may be used for costs directly related to these administrative functions.

"The board shall meet at the call of the chairman to conduct its official business. All business transactions of the board shall be conducted in public meetings. The votes of at least seven board members are required to approve the state plan for the allocation of funds from the children's trust fund.

"The board may apply for and accept federal funds for the purposes of sections 3109.13 to 3109.18 of the Revised Code. In addition, the board may accept gifts and donations from any source, including individuals, philanthropic foundations or organizations, corporations, or corporation endowments. The acceptance and use of federal funds shall not entail any commitment or pledge of state funds, nor obligate the general assembly to continue the programs or activities for which the federal funds are made available. All funds received in the manner described in this section shall be transmitted to the treasurer of state, who shall credit them to the children's trust fund created in section 3109.14 of the Revised Code."

Amendment Note: 1994 H 335 inserted "any source, including" and ", corporations, or corporation endowments" in the second sentence in the final paragraph.

Ohio Administrative Code References

Children's trust fund; administration, OAC Ch 5101:5-1

Library References

Infants ⚷17.
WESTLAW Topic No. 211.
C.J.S. Infants §§ 8, 9.

Dill Calloway, Ohio Nursing Law, Text 5.02(A)

3109.17 State plan for allocation of funds; powers and duties of board

Note: See also following version of this section, eff. 1-1-01.

(A) For each fiscal biennium beginning on the first day of July of each odd-numbered year, the children's trust fund board shall establish a biennial state plan for the allocation of funds in the children's trust fund. The plan shall ensure that equal opportunity exists for the establishment of child abuse and child neglect prevention programs and the use of moneys from the fund to provide assistance in all geographic areas of this state and to provide assistance to members of all social and economic groups of this state. The plan shall be transmitted to the governor, the president of the senate, and the speaker of the house of representatives and shall be made available to the general public.

(B) In developing and carrying out a plan, the children's trust fund board shall, in accordance with Chapter 119. of the Revised Code, do all of the following:

(1) Develop and adopt the state plan for the allocation of funds and develop criteria, including standards for cost and program effectiveness, for county or district allocation plans and for individual projects in counties or districts that do not have a child abuse and child neglect advisory board;

(2) Establish criteria, including standards for cost and program effectiveness, for child abuse and child neglect prevention programs;

(3) Make grants to public or private agencies or schools for the purpose of child abuse and child neglect prevention programs. The board may consider factors such as need, geographic location, diversity, coordination with or improvement of existing services, maintenance of local funding efforts, and extensive use of volunteers. Children's trust fund moneys shall be allocated among all counties according to a formula based on the ratio of the number of children under the age of eighteen in the county to the number of children under the age of eighteen in the state, as shown in the most recent federal decennial census of population; provided, that

each county receiving trust fund moneys shall receive a minimum of ten thousand dollars per funding year.

(4) Approve each county or district allocation plan and individual project in whole or in part if it is in compliance with the criteria established under this section and under section 3109.18 of the Revised Code. If an allocation plan or individual project is rejected in whole or in part, the board shall:

(a) Cite specific reasons for rejection;

(b) When appropriate, offer recommendations and technical assistance to bring the plan or project into compliance, holding the funds until the plan or project is finally approved or rejected.

(5) Notify each advisory board or individual applicant in writing whether the allocation plan or individual project has been approved in whole or in part not later than sixty days after submission of the plan or project to the children's trust fund board;

(6) Regularly review and monitor the expenditure of moneys from the children's trust fund;

(7) Consult with appropriate state agencies to help determine the probable effectiveness and fiscal soundness of and need for proposed community-based child abuse and child neglect prevention programs;

(8) Facilitate the exchange of information between groups concerned with programs for children in this state;

(9) Provide for statewide educational and public informational conferences and workshops for the purpose of developing appropriate public awareness regarding the problems of families and children, encouraging professional persons and groups to recognize and deal with problems of families and children, making information regarding the problems of families and children and the prevention of these problems available to the general public in order to encourage citizens to become involved in the prevention of such problems, and encouraging the development of community prevention programs;

(10) Establish a procedure for a written annual internal evaluation of the functions, responsibilities, and performance of the board. The evaluation shall be coordinated with the state plan. The evaluation shall be transmitted to the governor, the president of the senate, and the speaker of the house of representatives and shall be made available to the general public.

(1994 H 715, eff. 7-22-94; 1985 H 201, eff. 7-1-85; 1984 H 319)
Note: See also following version of this section, eff. 1-1-01.

3109.17 State plan for comprehensive child abuse and child neglect prevention; powers and duties of board; reports

Note: See also preceding version of this section, in effect until 1-1-01.

(A) For each fiscal biennium, the children's trust fund board shall establish a biennial state plan for comprehensive child abuse and child neglect prevention. The plan shall be transmitted to the governor, the president and minority leader of the senate, and the speaker and minority leader of the house of representatives and shall be made available to the general public.

(B) In developing and carrying out the state plan, the children's trust fund board shall, in accordance with Chapter 119. of the Revised Code, do all of the following:

(1) Ensure that an opportunity exists for assistance through child abuse and child neglect prevention programs to persons throughout the state of various social and economic backgrounds;

(2) Before the thirtieth day of October of each year, notify each child abuse and child neglect prevention advisory board of the amount estimated to be block granted to that advisory board for the following fiscal year.

(3) Develop criteria for county or district comprehensive allocation plans, including criteria for determining the plans' effectiveness;

(4) Review county or district comprehensive allocation plans;

(5) Make a block grant to each child abuse and child neglect prevention advisory board for the purpose of funding child abuse and child neglect prevention programs. The block grants shall be allocated among advisory boards according to a formula based on the ratio of the number of children under age eighteen in the county or multicounty district to the number of children under age eighteen in the state, as shown in the most recent federal decennial census of population. Subject to the availability of funds, each advisory board shall receive a minimum of ten thousand dollars per fiscal year. In the case of an advisory board that serves a multicounty district, the advisory board shall receive, subject to available funds, a minimum of ten thousand dollars per fiscal year for each county in the district. Block grants shall be disbursed to the advisory boards twice annually. At least fifty per cent of the amount of the block grant allocated to an advisory board for a fiscal year shall be disbursed to the advisory board not later than the thirtieth day of September. The remainder of the block grant allocated to the advisory board for that fiscal year shall be disbursed before the thirty-first day of March.

If the children's trust fund board determines, based on county or district performance or on the annual report submitted by an advisory board, that the advisory board is not operating in accordance with the criteria established in division (B)(3) of this section, it may revise the allocation of funds that the advisory board receives.

(6) Provide for the monitoring of expenditures from the children's trust fund and of programs that receive money from the children's trust fund;

(7) Establish reporting requirements for advisory boards;

(8) Collaborate with appropriate persons and government entities and facilitate the exchange of information among those persons and entities for the purpose of child abuse and child neglect prevention;

(9) Provide for the education of the public and professionals for the purpose of child abuse and child neglect prevention.

(C) The children's trust fund board shall prepare a report for each fiscal biennium that evaluates the expenditure of money from the children's trust fund. On or before January 1, 2002, and on or before the first day of January of a year that follows the end of a fiscal biennium of this state, the board shall file a copy of the report with the governor, the president and minority leader of the senate, and the speaker and minority leader of the house of representatives.

(D) In addition to the duties described in this section and in section 3109.16 of the Revised Code, the children's trust fund board shall perform the duties described in section 121.371 of the Revised Code with regard to the wellness block grant program.

(1999 H 283, eff. 1-1-01; 1994 H 715, eff. 7-22-94; 1985 H 201, eff. 7-1-85; 1984 H 319)

Note: See also preceding version of this section, in effect until 1-1-01.

Historical and Statutory Notes

Amendment Note: 1999 H 283 rewrote the section, which prior thereto read:

"(A) For each fiscal biennium beginning on the first day of July of each odd-numbered year, the children's trust fund board shall establish a biennial state plan for the allocation of funds in the children's trust fund. The plan shall ensure that equal opportunity exists for the establishment of child abuse and child neglect prevention programs and the use of moneys from the fund to provide assistance in all geographic areas of this state and to provide assistance to members of all social and economic groups of this state. The plan shall be transmitted to the governor, the president of the senate, and the speaker of the house of representatives and shall be made available to the general public.

"(B) In developing and carrying out a plan, the children's trust fund board shall, in accordance with Chapter 119. of the Revised Code, do all of the following:

"(1) Develop and adopt the state plan for the allocation of funds and develop criteria, including standards for cost and program effectiveness, for county or district allocation plans and for individual projects in counties or districts that do not have a child abuse and child neglect advisory board;

"(2) Establish criteria, including standards for cost and program effectiveness, for child abuse and child neglect prevention programs;

"(3) Make grants to public or private agencies or schools for the purpose of child abuse and child neglect prevention programs. The board may consider factors such as need, geographic location, diversity, coordination with or improvement of existing services, maintenance of local funding efforts, and extensive use of volunteers. Children's trust fund moneys shall be allocated among all counties according to a formula based on the ratio of the number of children under the age of eighteen in the county to the number of children under the age of eighteen in the state, as shown in the most recent federal decennial census of population; provided, that each county receiving trust fund moneys shall receive a minimum of ten thousand dollars per funding year.

"(4) Approve each county or district allocation plan and individual project in whole or in part if it is in compliance with the criteria established under this section and under section 3109.18 of the Revised Code. If an allocation plan or individual project is rejected in whole or in part, the board shall:

"(a) Cite specific reasons for rejection;

"(b) When appropriate, offer recommendations and technical assistance to bring the plan or project into compliance, holding the funds until the plan or project is finally approved or rejected.

"(5) Notify each advisory board or individual applicant in writing whether the allocation plan or individual project has been approved in whole or in part not later than sixty days after submission of the plan or project to the children's trust fund board;

"(6) Regularly review and monitor the expenditure of moneys from the children's trust fund;

"(7) Consult with appropriate state agencies to help determine the probable effectiveness and fiscal soundness of and need for proposed community-based child abuse and child neglect prevention programs;

"(8) Facilitate the exchange of information between groups concerned with programs for children in this state;

"(9) Provide for statewide educational and public informational conferences and workshops for the purpose of developing appropriate public awareness regarding the problems of families and children, encouraging professional persons and groups to recognize and deal with problems of families and children, making information regarding the problems of families and children and the prevention of these problems available to the general public in order to encourage citizens to become involved in the prevention of such problems, and encouraging the development of community prevention programs;

"(10) Establish a procedure for a written annual internal evaluation of the functions, responsibilities, and performance of the board. The evaluation shall be coordinated with the state plan. The evaluation shall be transmitted to the governor, the president of the senate, and the speaker of the house of representatives and shall be made available to the general public."

Amendment Note: 1994 H 715 rewrote the first sentence of division (A); inserted ", including standards for cost and program effectiveness," in divisions (B)(1) and (B)(2); deleted "substantial" before "compliance" throughout division (B)(4); and deleted "annual" before "state plan" in division (B)(10). Prior to amendment, the first sentence of division (A) read:

"Each year, beginning within one year after the appointment of its first members, the children's trust fund board shall develop a state plan for the allocation of funds in the children's trust fund."

Ohio Administrative Code References

Child abuse and neglect, supportive services, OAC Ch 5101:2-39
Children's trust fund; administration, OAC Ch 5101:5-1
Grant and interagency agreement request procedure, OAC 5101-9-57

Library References

Infants ⚷17.
States ⚷127.
WESTLAW Topic Nos. 211, 360.
C.J.S. Infants §§ 8, 9.
C.J.S. States § 228.

Dill Calloway, Ohio Nursing Law, Text 5.02(A)

Notes of Decisions and Opinions

Board authority 1

1. Board authority

The children's trust fund board does not have the authority to prohibit schools or school districts which allow corporal punishment from receiving funds from the children's trust fund.

3109.18 Child abuse and child neglect prevention advisory boards

Note: See also following version of this section, eff. 1-1-01.

(A) Each board of county commissioners in the following counties shall establish a child abuse and child neglect advisory board: Cuyahoga, Franklin, Hamilton, Lucas, Montgomery, and Summit. The boards of county commissioners of the remaining counties may establish a child abuse and child neglect advisory board or the boards of county commissioners of two or more contiguous counties may form a multicounty district to be served by a multicounty child abuse and child neglect advisory board.

Each child abuse and child neglect advisory board shall consist of an odd number of members who represent both public and private child serving agencies, and persons with demonstrated knowledge in programs for children, such as persons from the educational community, parent groups, juvenile justice, and the medical community. Of the members first appointed, at least one shall serve for a term of three years, at least one for a term of two years, and at least one for a term of one year. Thereafter, each member shall serve a term of three years. Each member shall serve until the member's successor is appointed. All vacancies on the board shall be filled for the balance of the unexpired term in the same manner as the original appointment. Each board shall meet at least quarterly.

Each board of county commissioners may incur reasonable costs not to exceed three per cent of the funding allocated to the county or district under section 3109.17 of the Revised Code, for the purpose of carrying out the functions of the advisory board.

(B) Annually, each child abuse and child neglect advisory board shall:

(1) Give effective public notice to all potential applicants about the availability of funds from the children's trust fund. The notification shall include an estimate of the amount of money available for grants within each county or district, the date of at least one public hearing, the deadline for submitting applications for grants, and information on obtaining a copy of the application form;

(2) Review all applications received using criteria established by the children's trust fund board under section 3109.17 of the Revised Code and any criteria developed by the child abuse and child neglect advisory board, and develop an allocation plan for the county or district;

(3) Submit the allocation plan to the children's trust fund board, with evidence of compliance with this section and with section 3109.17 of the Revised Code;

(4) Upon notification by the children's trust fund board that the allocation plan is in compliance with the criteria established by the boards, monitor the operation of the allocation plan;

(5) Establish procedures for evaluating programs in the county or district, including reporting requirements for grant recipients.

Applicants from counties that are not served by a child abuse and child neglect advisory board shall apply for funding to the children's trust fund board.

(C) A recipient of a grant from the children's trust fund shall use the grant funds only to fund child abuse and child neglect prevention programs. A recipient of a grant may use the grant funds only for the expansion of existing programs or the creation of new programs.

Any grant funds that are not spent by the counties or the recipient of the funds within the time specified by the terms of the grant shall be returned to the treasurer of state. The treasurer of state shall deposit such unspent moneys into the children's trust fund to be spent for purposes consistent with the state plan adopted under section 3109.17 of the Revised Code.

(D) Applications for grants from the children's trust fund shall be on forms prescribed by the department of job and family services and, after any review required by division (B) of this section, shall be submitted to the children's trust fund board by the date required in the schedule established by rules adopted by the board. Each application shall include at least the following:

(1) Information showing that the applicant meets the eligibility requirements of section 3109.17 of the Revised Code;

(2) If the applicant is a corporation, a list of the trustees of the corporation;

(3) A specification of the amount of money requested;

(4) A summary of the program that the applicant intends to provide with funds from the grant;

(5) Any other information required by rules adopted by the children's trust fund board.

Each recipient of a grant from the children's trust fund shall file two copies of an annual report with the county or district advisory board. If no such board serves the recipient's county of residence, the recipient shall file two copies of an annual report with the children's trust fund board. The annual report shall describe the program provided by the recipient, indicate the manner in which the grant funds were expended, include the results of an independent audit of the funds, and include other information that the granting board or the department may require. If a public agency is a recipient of a grant, the results of the most recent audit of the funds conducted under Chapter 117. of the Revised Code shall be considered to be the results of the independent audit of the funds that must be included in the annual report. The granting boards shall annually file one copy of each annual report with the department, which shall compile the reports received pursuant to this section.

This section is an interim section effective until January 1, 2001.

(1999 H 471, § 1, eff. 7-1-00; 1987 H 171, eff. 7-1-87; 1986 H 428; 1985 H 201; 1984 H 319)
Note: See also following version of this section, eff. 1-1-01.

3109.18 Child abuse and child neglect prevention advisory boards

Note: See also preceding version of this section, in effect until 1-1-01.

(A)(1) A board of county commissioners may establish a child abuse and child neglect prevention advisory board or may designate the county family and children first council to serve as the child abuse and child neglect prevention advisory board. The boards of county commissioners of two or more contiguous counties may instead form a multicounty district to be served by a child abuse and child neglect prevention advisory board or may designate a regional family and children first council to serve as the district child abuse and child neglect prevention advisory board. Each advisory board shall meet at least twice a year.

(2) The county auditor is hereby designated as the auditor and fiscal officer of the advisory board. In the case of a multicounty district, the boards of county commissioners that formed the district shall designate the auditor of one of the counties as the auditor and fiscal officer of the advisory board.

(B) Each county that establishes an advisory board or, in a multicounty district, the county the auditor of which has been designated as the auditor and fiscal agent of the advisory board, shall establish a fund in the county treasury known as the county or district children's trust fund. The advisory board shall deposit all funds received from the children's trust fund board into that fund, and the auditor shall distribute money from the fund at the request of the advisory board.

(C) Each January, the board of county commissioners of a county that has established an advisory board or, in a multicounty district, the board of county commissioners of the county the auditor of which has been designated as the auditor and fiscal agent for the advisory board, shall appropriate the amount described in division (B)(2) of section 3109.17 of the Revised Code for distribution by the advisory board to child abuse and child neglect prevention programs.

(D)(1) Except in the case of a county or regional family and children first council that is designated to serve as a child abuse and child neglect prevention advisory board, each advisory board shall consist of an odd number of members from both the public and private sectors, including all of the following:

(a) A representative of an agency responsible for the administration of children's services in the county or district;

(b) A provider of alcohol or drug addiction services or a representative of a board of alcohol, drug addiction, and mental health services that serves the county or district;

(c) A provider of mental health services or a representative of a board of alcohol, drug addiction, and mental health services that serves the county or district;

(d) A representative of a board of mental retardation and developmental disabilities that serves the county or district;

(e) A representative of the educational community appointed by the superintendent of the school district with largest enrollment in the county or multicounty district.

(2) The following groups and entities may be represented on the advisory board:

(a) Parent groups;

(b) Juvenile justice officials;

(c) Pediatricians, health department nurses, and other representatives of the medical community;

(d) School personnel;

(e) Counselors;

(f) Head start agencies;

(g) Child day-care providers;

(h) Other persons with demonstrated knowledge in programs for children.

(3) Of the members first appointed, at least one shall serve for a term of three years, at least one for a term of two years, and at least one for a term of one year. Thereafter, each member shall serve a term of three years. Each member shall serve until the member's successor is appointed. All vacancies on the board shall be filled for the balance of the unexpired term in the same manner as the original appointment.

(E) Each board of county commissioners may incur reasonable costs not to exceed five per cent of the block grant allocated to the county or district under section 3109.17 of the Revised Code, for the purpose of carrying out the functions of the advisory board.

(F) Each child abuse and child neglect prevention advisory board shall do all of the following:

(1) Develop a comprehensive allocation plan for the purpose of preventing child abuse and child neglect and submit the plan to the children's trust fund board;

(2) Notify potential applicants about the availability of funds from the children's trust fund;

(3) Review all applications received using any criteria developed by the child abuse and child neglect prevention advisory board;

(4) Consistent with the plan developed pursuant to division (F)(1) of this section, make grants to child abuse and child neglect prevention programs. In making grants to child abuse and child neglect prevention programs, the advisory board may consider factors such as need, geographic location, diversity, coordination with or improvement of existing services, maintenance of local funding efforts, and extensive use of volunteers.

(5) Establish reporting requirements for grant recipients.

(G) Each advisory board shall assist the children's trust fund board in monitoring programs that receive money from the children's trust fund and shall perform such other duties for the local administration of the children's trust fund as the children's trust fund board requires.

(H) A recipient of a grant from the children's trust fund shall use the grant funds only to fund child abuse and child neglect prevention programs. Any grant funds that are not spent by the recipient of the funds within the time specified by the terms of the grant shall be returned to the county treasurer. Any grant funds returned that are not redistributed by the advisory board within the time specified by the terms of the original grant shall be returned to the treasurer of state. The treasurer of state shall deposit such unspent moneys into the children's trust fund to be spent for purposes consistent with the state plan adopted under section 3109.17 of the Revised Code.

(I) Applications for grants from the children's trust fund shall be made to the advisory board on forms prescribed by the department of job and family services.

(J)(1) Each recipient of a children's trust fund grant from an advisory board shall file with the advisory board a copy of an annual report that includes the information required by the advisory board.

(2) Each advisory board shall file with the children's trust fund board a copy of an annual report regarding the county or district comprehensive allocation plan that contains the information required by the children's trust fund board.

(2000 H 448, § 6, eff. 1-1-01; 1999 H 471, § 3, eff. 1-1-01; 1999 H 471, § 1, eff. 7-1-00; 1999 H 283, eff. 1-1-01; 1987 H 171, eff. 7-1-87; 1986 H 428; 1985 H 201; 1984 H 319)
Note: See also preceding version of this section, in effect until 1-1-01.

Uncodified Law

1999 H 283, § 136, eff. 6-30-99, reads:

The amendments to section 3109.18 of the Revised Code by this act shall not affect the term of any member of a child abuse and child neglect advisory board serving on the effective date of this section. Vacancies on the board shall be filled in accordance with section 3109.18 of the Revised Code.

Historical and Statutory Notes

Amendment Note: 2000 H 448, § 6, substituted "five" for "three" in division (E).

Amendment Note: 1999 H 471, § 3, eff. 1-1-01, substituted "job and family" for "human" in division (I).

Amendment Note: 1999 H 471, § 1, eff. 7-1-00, substituted "the member's" for "his" in the second paragraph in division (A); substituted "job and family" for "human" in the introductory paragraph in division (D); and added the final paragraph.

Amendment Note: 1999 H 283 rewrote the section, which prior thereto read:

"(A) Each board of county commissioners in the following counties shall establish a child abuse and child neglect advisory board: Cuyahoga, Franklin, Hamilton, Lucas, Montgomery, and Summit. The boards of county commissioners of the remaining counties may establish a child abuse and child neglect advisory board or the boards of county commissioners of two or more contiguous counties may form a multicounty district to be served by a multicounty child abuse and child neglect advisory board.

"Each child abuse and child neglect advisory board shall consist of an odd number of members who represent both public and private child serving agencies, and persons with demonstrated knowledge in programs for children, such as persons from the educational community, parent groups, juvenile justice, and the medical community. Of the members first appointed, at least one shall serve for a term of three years, at least one for a term of two years, and at least one for a term of one year. Thereafter, each member shall serve a term of three years. Each member shall serve until his successor is appointed. All vacancies on the board shall be filled for the balance of the unexpired term in the same manner as the original appointment. Each board shall meet at least quarterly.

"Each board of county commissioners may incur reasonable costs not to exceed three per cent of the funding allocated to the county or district under section 3109.17 of the Revised Code, for the purpose of carrying out the functions of the advisory board.

"(B) Annually, each child abuse and child neglect advisory board shall:

"(1) Give effective public notice to all potential applicants about the availability of funds from the children's trust fund. The notification shall include an estimate of the amount of money available for grants within each county or district, the date of at least one public hearing, the deadline for submitting applications for grants, and information on obtaining a copy of the application form;

"(2) Review all applications received using criteria established by the children's trust fund board under section 3109.17 of the Revised Code and any criteria developed by the child abuse and child neglect advisory board, and develop an allocation plan for the county or district;

"(3) Submit the allocation plan to the children's trust fund board, with evidence of compliance with this section and with section 3109.17 of the Revised Code;

"(4) Upon notification by the children's trust fund board that the allocation plan is in compliance with the criteria established by the boards, monitor the operation of the allocation plan;

"(5) Establish procedures for evaluating programs in the county or district, including reporting requirements for grant recipients.

"Applicants from counties that are not served by a child abuse and child neglect advisory board shall apply for funding to the children's trust fund board.

"(C) A recipient of a grant from the children's trust fund shall use the grant funds only to fund child abuse and child neglect prevention programs. A recipient of a grant may use the grant funds only for the expansion of existing programs or the creation of new programs.

"Any grant funds that are not spent by the counties or the recipient of the funds within the time specified by the terms of the grant shall be returned to the treasurer of state. The treasurer of state shall deposit such unspent moneys into the children's trust fund to be spent for purposes consistent with the state plan adopted under section 3109.17 of the Revised Code.

"(D) Applications for grants from the children's trust fund shall be on forms prescribed by the department of human services and, after any review required by division (B) of this section, shall be submitted to the children's trust fund board by the date required in the schedule established by rules adopted by the board. Each application shall include at least the following:

"(1) Information showing that the applicant meets the eligibility requirements of section 3109.17 of the Revised Code;

"(2) If the applicant is a corporation, a list of the trustees of the corporation;

"(3) A specification of the amount of money requested;

"(4) A summary of the program that the applicant intends to provide with funds from the grant;

"(5) Any other information required by rules adopted by the children's trust fund board.

"Each recipient of a grant from the children's trust fund shall file two copies of an annual report with the county or district advisory board. If no such board serves the recipient's county of residence, the recipient shall file two copies of an annual report with the children's trust fund board. The annual report shall describe the program provided by the recipient, indicate the manner in which the grant funds were expended, include the results of an independent audit of the funds, and include other information that the granting board or the department may require. If a public agency is a recipient of a grant, the results of the most recent audit of the funds conducted under Chapter 117. of the Revised Code shall be considered to be the results of the independent audit of the funds that must be included in the annual report. The granting boards shall annually file one copy of each annual report with the department, which shall compile the reports received pursuant to this section."

Ohio Administrative Code References

Children's trust fund; administration, OAC Ch 5101:5-1

Library References

Infants ⚿17.
WESTLAW Topic No. 211.
C.J.S. Infants §§ 8, 9.

Dill Calloway, Ohio Nursing Law, Text 5.02(A)

3109.19 Duty of parents to support children of unemancipated minor children

(A) As used in this section, "minor" has the same meaning as in section 3107.01 of the Revised Code.

(B)(1) If a child is born to parents who are unmarried and unemancipated minors, a parent of one of the minors is providing support for the minors' child, and the minors have not signed an acknowledgment of paternity or a parent and child relationship has not been established between the child and the male minor, the parent who is providing support for the child may request a determination of the existence or nonexistence of a parent and child relationship between the child and the male minor pursuant to Chapter 3111. of the Revised Code.

(2) If a child is born to parents who are unmarried and unemancipated minors, a parent of one of the minors is providing support for the child, and the minors have signed an acknowledgment of paternity that has become final pursuant to section 2151.232, 3111.211, or 5101.314 of the Revised Code or a parent and child relationship has been established between the child and the male minor pursuant to Chapter 3111. of the Revised Code, the parent who is providing support for the child may file a complaint requesting that the court issue an order or may request the child support enforcement agency of the county in which the child resides to issue an administrative order requiring all of the minors' parents to pay support for the child.

(C)(1) On receipt of a complaint filed under division (B)(2) of this section, the court shall schedule a hearing to determine, in accordance with sections 3113.21 to 3113.219 of the Revised Code, the amount of child support the minors' parents are required to pay, the method of paying the support, and the method of providing for the child's health care needs. On receipt of a request under division (B)(2) of this section, the agency shall schedule a hearing to determine, in accordance with sections 3111.23 to 3111.28 and 3113.215 of the Revised Code, the amount of child support the minors' parents are required to pay, the method of paying the support, and the method of providing for the child's health care needs. At the conclusion of the hearing, the court or agency shall issue an order requiring the payment of support of the child and provision for the child's health care needs. The court or agency shall calculate the child support amount using the income of the minors' parents instead of the income of the minors. If any of the minors' parents are divorced, the court or agency shall calculate the child support as if they were married, and issue a child support order requiring the parents to pay a portion of any support imposed as a separate obligation. If a child support order issued pursuant to section 2151.23, 2151.231, 2151.232, 3111.13, 3111.20, 3111.211, or 3111.22 of the Revised Code requires one of the minors to pay support for the child, the amount the minor is required to pay shall be deducted from any amount that minor's parents are required to pay pursuant to an order issued under this section. The hearing shall be held not later than sixty days after the day the complaint is filed or the request is made nor earlier than thirty days after the court or agency gives the minors' parents notice of the action.

(2) An order issued by an agency for the payment of child support shall include a notice stating all of the following: that the parents of the minors may object to the order by filing a complaint pursuant to division (B)(2) of this section with the court requesting that the court issue an order requiring the minors' parents to pay support for the child and provide for the child's health care needs; that the complaint may be filed no later than thirty days after the date of the issuance of the agency's order; and that, if none of the parents of the minors file a complaint pursuant to division (B)(2) of this section, the agency's order is final and enforceable by a court and may be modified and enforced only in accordance with sections 3111.23 to 3111.28 and sections 3113.21 to 3113.219 of the Revised Code.

(D) An order issued by a court or agency under this section shall remain in effect, except as modified pursuant to sections 3113.21 to 3113.219 of the Revised Code with respect to a court-issued child support order or pursuant to sections 3111.23 to 3111.28 and 3113.215 of the Revised Code with respect to an administrative child support order, until the occurrence of any of the following:

(1) The minor who resides with the parents required to pay support under this section reaches the age of eighteen years, dies, marries, enlists in the armed services, is deported, gains legal or physical custody of the child, or is otherwise emancipated.

(2) The child who is the subject of the order dies, is adopted, is deported, or is transferred to the legal or physical custody of the minor who lives with the parents required to pay support under this section.

(3) The minor's parents to whom support is being paid pursuant to this section is no longer providing any support for the child.

(E)(1) The minor's parents to whom support is being paid under a child support order issued by a court pursuant to this section shall notify, and the minor's parents who are paying support may notify the child support enforcement agency of the occurrence of any event described in division (D) of this section. A willful failure to notify the agency as required by this division is contempt of court. Upon receiving notification pursuant to this division, the agency shall comply with division (G)(4) of section 3113.21 of the Revised Code.

(2) The minor's parents to whom support is being paid under a child support order issued by the agency pursuant to this section shall notify, and the minor's parents who are paying support may notify the child support enforcement agency of the occurrence of any event described in division (D) of this section. Upon receiving notification pursuant to this division, the agency shall comply with division (E)(4) of section 3111.23 of the Revised Code.

(1997 H 352, eff. 1-1-98; 1995 H 167, eff. 11-15-95)

Historical and Statutory Notes

Amendment Note: 1997 H 352 inserted "that has become final" and substituted "2151.232, 3111.211, or 5101.314" for "2105.18" in division (A)(2); inserted "and the method of providing for the child's health care needs" twice and "2151.231, 2151.232,", and substituted "3111.211" for "3111.21", in division (C)(1); inserted "and provide for the child's health care needs" in division (C)(2); and made other nonsubstantive changes.

Cross References

Child support enforcement agencies, as social security Title IV-D agency, 2301.35

Interfering with action to issue or modify support order, 2919.231

Support order defined, 2301.34

Library References

Am Jur 2d: 41, Illegitimate Children § 39, 89 to 92; 59, Parent & Child § 123

Carlin, Baldwin's Ohio Practice, *Merrick-Rippner Probate Law* § 18.2, 108.34, 108.44 (1997)

3 Katz & Giannelli, Baldwin's Ohio Practice, *Criminal Law* § 109.12 (1996)

Sowald & Morganstern, Baldwin's Ohio Practice, *Domestic Relations Law* § 3.10, 3.44, 3.51, 22.19 (1997)

Law Review and Journal Commentaries

R.C. 3109.19: Grandparent's Duty to Support Grandchild—Support for Children of Unemancipated Minor Children, Pamela J. MacAdams. 8 Domestic Rel J Ohio 42 (May/June 1996).

UNIFORM CHILD CUSTODY JURISDICTION LAW

Uniform Child Custody Jurisdiction Act

Table of Jurisdictions Wherein Act Has Been Adopted

For text of Uniform Act, and variation notes and annotation materials for adopting jurisdictions, see Uniform Laws Annotated, Master Edition, Volume 9, Pt. I.

Jurisdiction	Statutory Citation
Arizona	A.R.S. § 25-431 to 25-454.
Delaware	13 Del.C. § 1901 to 1925.
District of Columbia	D.C.Code 1981, § 16-4501 to 16-4524.
Florida	West's F.S.A. § 61.1302 to 61.1348.
Georgia	O.C.G.A. § 19-9-40 to 19-9-64.
Hawaii	HRS § 583-1 to 583-26.
Idaho	I.C. § 32-1101 to 32-1126.
Illinois	750 ILCS 35/1 to 35/26.
Indiana	West's A.I.C. 31-17-3-1 to 31-17-3-25.
Kansas	K.S.A. 38-1301 to 38-1326.
Kentucky	KRS 403.400 to 403.630.
Louisiana	LSA-R.S. 13:1700 to 13:1724.
Maryland	Code, Family Law, § 9-201 to 9-224.
Massachusetts	M.G.L.A. c. 209B, § 1 to 14.
Michigan	M.C.L.A. § 600.651 to 600.673.
Mississippi	Code 1972, § 93-23-1 to 93-23-47.
Missouri	V.A.M.S. § 452.440 to 452.550.
Nebraska	R.R.S.1943, § 43-1201 to 43-1225.
Nevada	N.R.S. 125A.010 to 125A.250.
New Hampshire	RSA 458-A:1 to 458-A:25.
New Jersey	N.J.S.A. 2A:34-28 to 2A:34-52.
New Mexico	NMSA 1978, § 40-10-1 to 40-10-24.
New York	McKinney's Domestic Relations Law, § 75-a to 75-z.
Pennsylvania	23 Pa.C.S.A. § 5341 to 5366.
Rhode Island	Gen.Laws 1956, § 15-14-1 to 15-14-26.
South Carolina	Code 1976, § 20-7-782 to 20-7-830.
South Dakota	SDCL 26-5A-1 to 26-5A-26.
Utah	U.C.A.1953, § 78-45c-1 to 78-45c-26.
Vermont	15 V.S.A. § 1031 to 1051.
Virgin Islands	16 V.I.C. § 115 to 139.
Virginia	Code 1950, § 20-125 to 20-146.
Washington	West's RCWA 26.27.010 to 26.27.910.
West Virginia	Code, 48-10-1 to 48-10-26.
Wisconsin	W.S.A. 822.01 to 822.25.
Wyoming	Wyo.Stat.Ann., § 20-5-101 to 20-5-125.

Cross References

Divorce, legal separation, and dissolution of marriage actions, child custody provisions, spousal support, 3105.10, 3105.21, 3105.63, 3105.65

Jurisdiction of juvenile court, 2151.23

Relation of visitation rights to child support, 3113.215

Ohio Administrative Code References

Location efforts regarding parental kidnapping and child custody determination, OAC 5101:1-30-04

Library References

Right to attorneys' fees in proceeding, after absolute divorce, for modification of child custody or support order. 57 ALR4th 710

What types of proceedings or determinations are governed by the Uniform Child Custody Jurisdiction Act (UCCJA) or the Parental Kidnapping Prevention Act (PKPA). 78 ALR4th 1028

Applicability of Uniform Child Custody Jurisdiction Act (UCCJA) to temporary custody orders. 81 ALR4th 1101

Child custody: when does state that issued previous custody determination have continuing jurisdiction under Uniform Child Custody Jurisdiction Act (UCCJA) or Parental Kidnapping Prevention Act (PKPA). 28 USC § 1738A, 83 ALR4th 742

Sowald & Morganstern, Baldwin's Ohio Practice, *Domestic Relations Law* § 7.19, 7.31, 11.6, 15.7, 15.51, 15.67, 17.1, 17.15, 21.3, 27.9 (1997)

Law Review and Journal Commentaries

A Brief Analysis of the Uniform Child Custody Jurisdiction Act, Charles W. Geron. 51 Ohio St B Ass'n Rep 347 (3-27-78).

Uniform Child Custody Jurisdiction Act: Its Provisions and Effects in Ohio, Note. 7 Cap U L Rev 453 (1977).

Notes of Decisions and Opinions

Procedure 2
Purpose 1

---

1. Purpose

Intent of legislature in adopting Uniform Child Custody Jurisdiction Act (UCCJA) was to avoid jurisdictional conflict and to promote cooperation between state courts in custody matters so that decree is rendered in state that can best decide best interest of child. Justis v. Justis (Ohio 1998) 81 Ohio St.3d 312, 691 N.E.2d 264.

The Uniform Child Custody Jurisdiction Act was adopted to resolve jurisdictional disputes between two states, each of which could properly exercise jurisdiction over a child's custody. Daerr v. Daerr (Medina 1987) 41 Ohio App.3d 206, 534 N.E.2d 1229.

2. Procedure

The Uniform Child Custody Jurisdiction Act, RC 3109.21 to RC 3109.37, is a body of substantive law affecting a court's authority to determine matters of custody and support, and therefore it may not be applied retroactively. Overbee v. Overbee (Hamilton 1986) 31 Ohio App.3d 179, 509 N.E.2d 960, 31 O.B.R. 345.

3109.21 Definitions

As used in sections 3109.21 to 3109.37 of the Revised Code:

(A) "Contestant" means a parent of a child who claims a right to be the residential parent and legal custodian of the child or claims visitation rights with respect to the child, or a person, other than a parent of a child, who claims a right to custody or visitation rights with respect to the child.

(B) "Parenting determination" means a court decision and court orders and instructions that, in relation to the parents of a child, allocates parental rights and responsibilities for the care of the child, including any designation of visitation rights, and designates a residential parent and legal custodian of the child or that, in relation to any other person, provides for the custody of a child, including visitation rights. It does not include a decision relating to child support or any other monetary obligation of any person.

(C) "Parenting proceeding" includes proceedings in which a parenting determination is one of several issues, such as an action for divorce or separation, and includes child neglect and dependency proceedings.

(D) "Decree" or "parenting decree" means a parenting determination contained in a judicial decree or order made in a parenting proceeding, and includes an initial decree and a modification decree.

(E) "Home state" means the state in which the child, immediately preceding the time involved, lived with his parents, a parent, or a person acting as parent, for at least six consecutive months, and in the case of a child less than six months old the state in which the child lived from birth with any of the persons mentioned. Periods of temporary absence of any of the named persons are counted as part of the six-month or other period.

(F) "Initial decree" means the first parenting decree concerning a particular child.

(G) "Modification decree" means a parenting decree that modifies or replaces a prior decree, whether made by the court that rendered the prior decree or by another court.

(H) "Physical custody" means actual possession and control of a child.

(I) "Person acting as parent" means a person, other than a parent, who has physical custody of a child and who either has been awarded custody by a court or claims a right to custody.

(1990 S 3, eff. 4-11-91; 1977 S 135)

Cross References

Guardian of the person or the estate, 2111.06

Library References

Divorce ⟾289, 290, 303(1), 402(2), 402(8).
Infants ⟾18, 196.
Parent and Child ⟾2(5).
WESTLAW Topic Nos. 134, 211, 285.
C.J.S. Courts § 249 et seq.
C.J.S. Divorce §§ 611, 612, 648, 650, 826, 845.
C.J.S. Infants §§ 5 to 7, 10, 12, 17, 42, 53, 54.
C.J.S. Parent and Child § 32.

OJur 3d: 53, Guardian and Ward § 32
Am Jur 2d: 42, Infants § 33 to 41
Validity, construction, and application of Uniform Child Custody Jurisdiction Act. 96 ALR3d 968
Necessity of requiring presence in court of both parties in proceedings relating to custody or visitation of children. 15 ALR4th 864
What types of proceedings or determinations are governed by the Uniform Child Custody Jurisdiction Act (UCCJA) or the Parental Kidnapping Prevention Act (PKPA). 78 ALR4th 1028
Applicability of Uniform Child Custody Jurisdiction Act (UCCJA) to temporary custody orders. 81 ALR4th 1101
Child custody: when does state that issued previous custody determination have continuing jurisdiction under Uniform Child Custody Jurisdiction Act (UCCJA) or Parental Kidnapping Prevention Act (PKPA), 28 USC § 1738A. 83 ALR4th 742
Significant connection jurisdiction of court under § 3(a)(2) of the Uniform Child Custody Jurisdiction Act (UCCJA) and the Parental Kidnapping Prevention Act (PKPA), 28 USC § 1738A(c)(2)(B). 5 ALR5th 550
Abandonment and emergency jurisdiction of court under § 3(a)(3) of the Uniform Child Custody Jurisdiction Act (UCCJA) and the Parental Kidnapping Prevention Act (PKPA), 28 USC § 1738A(c)(2)(C). 5 ALR5th 788
Home state jurisdiction of court under § 3(a)(1) of the Uniform Child Custody Jurisdiction Act (UCCJA) or the Parental Kidnapping Prevention Act (PKPA), 28 USC § 1738A(c)(2)(A). 6 ALR5th 1
Default jurisdiction of court under § 3(a)(4) of the Uniform Child Custody Jurisdiction Act (UCCJA) or the Parental Kidnapping Prevention Act (PKPA), 28 USC § 1738A(c)(2)(D). 6 ALR5th 69
Parties' misconduct as ground for declining jurisdiction under § 8 of the Uniform Child Custody Jurisdiction Act (UCCJA). 16 ALR5th 650

Carlin, Baldwin's Ohio Practice, *Merrick-Rippner Probate Law* § 62.33, 62.51, 62.53, 66.10, 105.1, 107.106, 108.13, 108.17, 108.34 (1997)
Kurtz & Giannelli, Ohio Juvenile Law (1998 Ed.), Text 12.4, 13.9, 13.11
Sowald & Morganstern, Baldwin's Ohio Practice, *Domestic Relations Law* § 15.3, 15.67, 16.1, 17.1, 17.2, 17.4, 21.3, 25.82 (1997)

Law Review and Journal Commentaries

Child Welfare—Outside the Interstate Compact on the Placement of Children—Placement of a Child with a Natural Parent, McComb v Wambaugh, Comment. 37 Vill L Rev 896 (1992).

Keeping Kids Out of Court. (Ed. note: Arbitration of custody disputes, but courts reserve the right to review awards.) 19 Nat'l L J B8 (May 5, 1997).

Notes of Decisions and Opinions

Adoption 3
Guardianship 1
Jurisdiction 5
Parenting determination 2
Visitation 4

---

1. Guardianship

The Uniform Child Custody Jurisdiction Act, as adopted in Ohio, is applicable to and must be complied with in a guardianship termination proceeding. In re Wonderly's Guardianship (Ohio 1981) 67 Ohio St.2d 178, 423 N.E.2d 420, 21 O.O.3d 111.

2. Parenting determination

Former spouses' court-approved shared parenting agreement was "initial decree," within meaning of statutes setting forth standards for determining initial custody orders and later modifications; consequently, showing of changed circumstances was necessary to justify later change in custody. Miller v. Miller (Seneca 1996) 115 Ohio App.3d 336, 685 N.E.2d 319.

Trial court acted unreasonably in misclassifying custody order as initial decree, rather than modification, and in basing modification solely on children's best interests. Miller v. Miller (Seneca 1996) 115 Ohio App.3d 336, 685 N.E.2d 319.

Custody must be an issue before the Uniform Child Custody Jurisdiction Act (UCCJA) can apply; an out-of-state support order cannot be certified under UCCJA even when the order concerns visitation rights. Snelling v. Gardner (Franklin 1990) 69 Ohio App.3d 196, 590 N.E.2d 330.

A custody decree or court determination that is entitled to recognition in Ohio under Uniform Child Custody Jurisdiction Act includes a finding of child neglect and dependency by another state's court. Squires v. Squires (Preble 1983) 12 Ohio App.3d 138, 468 N.E.2d 73, 12 O.B.R. 460.

A writ of habeas corpus is a "custody decree" or "custody determination" within the meaning of RC 3109.21(B) and (D), and therefore a Louisiana court may choose to enforce an Ohio writ of habeas corpus, pursuant to the uniform child custody jurisdiction law. Davis v Davis, Nos. 47377 and 47378 (8th Dist Ct App, Cuyahoga, 4-19-84).

Any person has standing to bring an action for child custody under RC 2151.23; such a person need not be a parent, need not have established paternity and need not have legitimized the child. Harris v Hopper, No. L-81-187 (6th Dist Ct App, Lucas, 1-15-82).

3. Adoption

"Adoption" is not a custody proceeding and may only become one at such time that a guardian, as opposed to a guardian ad litem, is appointed to protect the child's best interest. In re Adoption of Reams (Franklin 1989) 52 Ohio App.3d 52, 557 N.E.2d 159, dismissed 50 Ohio St.3d 707, 553 N.E.2d 684.

4. Visitation

Uniform Child Custody Jurisdiction Act provisions requiring that each party in a parentage proceeding must file an affidavit containing certain enumerated information did not apply to stepfather's motion for visitation with ex-wife's child by previous marriage, where stepfather was not seeking custody of child. Shannon v. Shannon (Ohio App. 9 Dist. 1997) 122 Ohio App.3d 346, 701 N.E.2d 771.

An Ohio court has authority to modify a New Jersey court decree as to visitation with children residing in Ohio even where the decree lacks sufficient finality to entitle it to full faith and credit as to child support and alimony. Auberry v Auberry, No. 13966 (9th Dist Ct App, Summit, 2-15-89).

5. Jurisdiction

Custody decree rendered by juvenile court in Ohio was binding on grandmother who had taken children from Ohio to Louisiana, given fact that both Ohio and Louisiana had adopted the Uniform Child Custody Jurisdiction Act, R.C. §3109.01 et seq., and given fact that record indicated that grandmother was properly served; thus, mother could enforce custody decree through Louisiana courts and issuance of an extraordinary writ of habeas corpus was unnecessary and duplicative. In re Davis (Ohio 1985) 18 Ohio St.3d 226, 480 N.E.2d 775, 18 O.B.R. 285.

Former wife's petition to transfer jurisdiction over child custody matters from court of state in which dissolution was originally entered, and for modification of visitation and child support originally established in dissolution decree, did not place parenting determination at issue, and Uniform Child Custody Jurisdiction Act (UCCJA) was therefore inapplicable. In re Monroe (Ohio App. 7 Dist. 1999) 133 Ohio App.3d 294, 727 N.E.2d 953.

West Virginia court from which divorce decree originated maintained continuing jurisdiction with respect to child custody and visitation issues, where hearing was held in West Virginia court on former husband's motion to modify child support and order entered thereon two months before former wife filed petition to transfer jurisdiction to Ohio. In re Monroe (Ohio App. 7 Dist. 1999) 133 Ohio App.3d 294, 727 N.E.2d 953.

In determining jurisdiction under Uniform Child Custody Jurisdiction Act (UCCJA), two-step process is used in which court first determines if Ohio has jurisdiction, and then determines whether Ohio should exercise that jurisdiction. In re Skrha (Cuyahoga 1994) 98 Ohio App.3d 487, 648 N.E.2d 908.

Uniform Child Custody Jurisdiction Act (UCCJA) acts to statutorily ensure same type of recognition of interstate continuing custody jurisdiction as is afforded intrastate continuing custody jurisdiction. Boehn v. Shurtliff (Huron 1993) 90 Ohio App.3d 363, 629 N.E.2d 478.

Where Kentucky court initially awards custody of child to mother, and where mother and child subsequently move to Ohio and reside in Ohio for nearly two years, Ohio becomes "home state" within meaning of Uniform Child Custody Jurisdiction Act. In re Reynolds (Hamilton 1982) 2 Ohio App.3d 309, 441 N.E.2d 1141, 2 O.B.R. 341.

If a child is not the ward of any other court, trial court has jurisdiction over custody proceedings where the trial court's state has been the child's home state within six months before commencement of the proceeding, the child has developed significant connections with the state by virtue of the former residence, and the plaintiff, who acknowledges that he is the child's natural father, resides in the state. Harris v Hopper, No. L-81-187 (6th Dist Ct App, Lucas, 1-15-82).

3109.22 Prerequisites to jurisdiction

(A) No court of this state that has jurisdiction to make a parenting determination relative to a child shall exercise that jurisdiction unless one of the following applies:

(1) This state is the home state of the child at the time of commencement of the proceeding, or this state had been the child's home state within six months before commencement of the proceeding and the child is absent from this state because of his removal or retention by a parent who claims a right to be the residential parent and legal custodian of a child or by any other person claiming his custody or is absent from this state for other reasons, and a parent or person acting as parent continues to live in this state;

(2) It is in the best interest of the child that a court of this state assumes jurisdiction because the child and his parents, or the child and at least one contestant, have a significant connection with this state, and there is available in this state substantial evidence concerning the child's present or future care, protection, training, and personal relationships;

(3) The child is physically present in this state and either has been abandoned or it is necessary in an emergency to protect the child because he has been subjected to or threatened with mistreatment or abuse or is otherwise neglected or dependent;

(4) It appears that no other state would have jurisdiction under prerequisites substantially in accordance with division (A) (1), (2), or (3) of this section, or a court in another state has declined to exercise jurisdiction on the ground that this state is the more appropriate forum to

make a parenting determination relative to the child, and it is in the best interest of the child that this court assume jurisdiction.

(B) Except as provided in divisions (A)(3) and (4) of this section, physical presence in this state of the child, or of the child and one of the contestants, is not alone sufficient to confer jurisdiction on a court of this state to make a parenting determination relative to the child.

(C) Physical presence of the child, while desirable, is not a prerequisite for jurisdiction to make a parenting determination relative to the child.

(1990 S 3, eff. 4-11-91; 1977 S 135)

Cross References

Divorce, legal separation, and dissolution of marriage actions, child custody provisions, spousal support, 3105.10, 3105.21, 3105.63, 3105.65

Jurisdiction of juvenile court, 2151.23

Library References

Divorce ⚷289, 290, 303(1), 402(2), 402(8).
Infants ⚷18, 196.
Parent and Child ⚷2(5).
WESTLAW Topic Nos. 134, 211, 285.
C.J.S. Courts § 249 et seq.
C.J.S. Divorce §§ 611, 612, 648, 650, 826, 845.
C.J.S. Infants §§ 5 to 7, 10, 12, 17, 42, 53, 54.
C.J.S. Parent and Child § 32.

OJur 3d: 53, Guardian and Ward § 32

Am Jur 2d: 24, Divorce and Separation § 772 to 782; 42, Infants § 33 to 41; 59, Parent and Child § 41

Validity, construction, and application of Uniform Child Custody Jurisdiction Act. 96 ALR3d 968

Necessity of requiring presence in court of both parties in proceedings relating to custody or visitation of children. 15 ALR4th 864

What types of proceedings or determinations are governed by the Uniform Child Custody Jurisdiction Act (UCCJA) or the Parental Kidnapping Prevention Act (PKPA). 78 ALR4th 1028

Applicability of Uniform Child Custody Jurisdiction Act (UCCJA) to temporary custody orders. 81 ALR4th 1101

Child custody: when does state that issued previous custody determination have continuing jurisdiction under Uniform Child Custody Jurisdiction Act (UCCJA) or Parental Kidnapping Prevention Act (PKPA), 28 USC § 1738A. 83 ALR4th 742

Significant connection jurisdiction of court under § 3(a)(2) of the Uniform Child Custody Jurisdiction Act (UCCJA) and the Parental Kidnapping Prevention Act (PKPA), 28 USC § 1738A(c)(2)(B). 5 ALR5th 550

Abandonment and emergency jurisdiction of court under § 3(a)(3) of the Uniform Child Custody Jurisdiction Act (UCCJA) and the Parental Kidnapping Prevention Act (PKPA), 28 USC § 1738A(c)(2)(C). 5 ALR5th 788

Home state jurisdiction of court under § 3(a)(1) of the Uniform Child Custody Jurisdiction Act (UCCJA) or the Parental Kidnapping Prevention Act (PKPA), 28 USC § 1738A(c)(2)(A). 6 ALR5th 1

Default jurisdiction of court under § 3(a)(4) of the Uniform Child Custody Jurisdiction Act (UCCJA) or the Parental Kidnapping Prevention Act (PKPA), 28 USC § 1738A(c)(2)(D). 6 ALR5th 69

Parties' misconduct as ground for declining jurisdiction under § 8 of the Uniform Child Custody Jurisdiction Act (UCCJA). 16 ALR5th 650

Carlin, Baldwin's Ohio Practice, *Merrick-Rippner Probate Law* § 62.33, 62.51, 62.53, 66.10, 105.1, 107.106, 108.13, 108.17, 108.34 (1997)

Kurtz & Giannelli, Ohio Juvenile Law (1998 Ed.), Text 12.4

Sowald & Morganstern, Baldwin's Ohio Practice, *Domestic Relations Law* § 15.3, 17.1, 17.2, 17.3, 17.5, 17.6, 21.3, 21.4, 25.82 (1997)

Notes of Decisions and Opinions

---

1. Jurisdiction proper

Jurisdiction of Ohio court over interstate custody dispute was proper under terms of Uniform Child Custody Jurisdiction Act (UCCJA); Ohio was children's home state at time proceeding was commenced, children's father and grandparents resided in Ohio, substantial evidence concerning children's present and future care, protection, and personal relationships was located within Ohio, counselors in Ohio had longstanding relationship with children, and two contestants for custody resided in Ohio. Justis v. Justis (Ohio 1998) 81 Ohio St.3d 312, 691 N.E.2d 264.

Where an Ohio court assumes jurisdiction in a suit to modify an out-of-state custody decree pursuant to RC 3109.22(A)(4), and there is no statute specifically prohibiting the assumption of jurisdiction by the Ohio court, a writ of prohibition preventing the Ohio court from proceeding in the change-of-custody action will not lie. State ex rel. Aycock v. Mowrey (Ohio 1989) 45 Ohio St.3d 347, 544 N.E.2d 657.

Fact that Common Pleas Court had issued temporary restraining order did not compel finding that it had issued "initial decree" and thus could no longer decline to exercise jurisdiction under Uniform Child Custody Jurisdiction Act (UCCJA); Court had inherent authority to issue temporary restraining order that it perceived as necessary to alleviate emergency situation, and then to dissolve restraining order upon determination that it would not be in best interest of children to assume jurisdiction. In re Skrha (Cuyahoga 1994) 98 Ohio App.3d 487, 648 N.E.2d 908.

Determining custody under Uniform Child Custody Jurisdiction Act (UCCJA) is within discretion of trial court. In re Skrha (Cuyahoga 1994) 98 Ohio App.3d 487, 648 N.E.2d 908.

Court issuing injunction has inherent authority to modify or vacate its own injunctive decree. In re Skrha (Cuyahoga 1994) 98 Ohio App.3d 487, 648 N.E.2d 908.

Determination on issue of jurisdiction in child custody case should only be made after hearing on facts relevant to provisions of Uniform Child Custody Jurisdiction Act. Powers v. Powers (Crawford 1994) 95 Ohio App.3d 352, 642 N.E.2d 451.

Evidence sustained finding that North Carolina was state with jurisdiction to determine custody of children under Uniform Child Custody Jurisdiction Act; North Carolina court had already issued temporary order placing custody of children in mother, North Carolina was children's home state, and North Carolina was state where there existed most substantial evidence concerning children's past and present care and future welfare. Powers v. Powers (Crawford 1994) 95 Ohio App.3d 352, 642 N.E.2d 451.

Trial court's decision to exercise emergency jurisdiction in order to transfer custody of children from father to mother was supported by evidence; father had fabricated allegations of sexual abuse of children to justify taking children from their home and to persuade trial court to initially issue ex parte order granting custody to father, and father's statements and demeanor indicated that he was likely to flee with children again if custody was not transferred to mother. Powers v. Powers (Crawford 1994) 95 Ohio App.3d 352, 642 N.E.2d 451.

Exclusive continuing jurisdiction exists under Uniform Child Custody Jurisdiction Act (UCCJA) so long as child or parent resides in state which rendered original decree. Boehn v. Shurtliff (Huron 1993) 90 Ohio App.3d 363, 629 N.E.2d 478.

The Uniform Child Custody Jurisdiction Act (UCCJA), rather than Ohio Civil Procedure Rule invoking continuing jurisdiction, was applicable law when determining whether Ohio or Illinois courts had jurisdiction over dispute concerning modifications of custody and visitation provisions of Ohio divorce decree. Mayor v. Mayor (Cuyahoga 1991) 71 Ohio App.3d 789, 595 N.E.2d 436.

Ohio courts had jurisdiction, pursuant to Uniform Child Custody Jurisdiction Act, to resolve postdissolution judgment motion for relief predicated on wife's concealment of her pregnancy at time of dissolution, as Ohio had real and significant contacts with both parents and child, Colorado, where child was born, had already expressly declined to exercise jurisdiction, and New Mexico, where mother and child resided after separation, lacked any substantial and permanent contacts with them. In re Marriage of Watson (Lorain 1983) 13 Ohio App.3d 344, 469 N.E.2d 876, 13 O.B.R. 424.

A juvenile court has jurisdiction to determine custody of a child under RC 3109.22(A), where the child had lived with her father and stepmother in Ohio for almost eight months immediately before the custody action was filed, and was enrolled in school and active in extracurricular activities. Minton v. McManus (Summit 1983) 9 Ohio App.3d 165, 458 N.E.2d 1292, 9 O.B.R. 231.

Where a child has been residing and attending school in Ohio and both she and the custodial parent have been receiving counseling from Ohio mental health services, it is in the child's best interests that litigation concerning her custody occur in Ohio; thus, Ohio courts have jurisdiction over the custody action, even though the original custody order was made by a Kentucky court. In re Reynolds (Hamilton 1982) 2 Ohio App.3d 309, 441 N.E.2d 1141, 2 O.B.R. 341.

The primary focus in determining the best forum to adjudicate custody is to select the forum which is in the best interest of the child, and although the Cuyahoga County Juvenile Court could exercise jurisdiction over a case involving a child living with her aunt and uncle, now in Idaho, for four years, because her father resides in Ohio and has petitioned the Cuyahoga County Juvenile Court for custody of his daughter, it is not mandatory that it do so where the court determines that (1) Idaho is the child's home state, (2) the child's guardians reside in Idaho and have no ties with Ohio, and (3) substantial evidence of the child's "present and future care, protection, training and personal relationships is more readily available" in Idaho, and where the father has neither proffered evidence nor indicated in his brief any material outside the record which would tend to contradict the existing record or discredit the lower court's decision, despite the father's unsubstantiated allegations that the child has been medically, physically, and educationally neglected and has been beaten, humiliated, intimidated, and exploited in the legal guardian's home in Idaho. In re Nath, No. 70926, 1997 WL 321137 (8th Dist Ct App, Cuyahoga, 6-12-97).

A court that renders a divorce decree maintains jurisdiction to change the designation of residential parent from the mother to the father based upon the mother's interference with visitation as evidenced by the child's living in seven different counties in six different states before he is four years old; in addition, the father continues to reside in the same location as before the parties' marriage. Gloeckner v Gloeckner, No. 94-C-61, 1995 WL 763302 (7th Dist Ct App, Columbiana, 12-22-95).

Where a child's mother was properly served with notice as required by RC 3109.23 and appeared at all proceedings; the child's mother caused her child to come to Ohio to live in 1987 and acquiesced in her child remaining in Ohio for three and one-half years before taking action to avoid losing custody of the child; and the child's mother by virtue of allowing her child to remain in the jurisdiction for nearly four years established the level of minimum contact required for personal jurisdiction. In re Brooks, No. L-92-152, 1993 WL 403542 (6th Dist Ct App, Lucas, 10-8-93).

Despite Florida court's inherent power to modify its previous order and grandparents' continuing residency in Florida, where Florida is not the child's home state and substantial evidence concerning the child's present or future care, protection, training, and personal relationships is not available in Florida, Ohio has jurisdiction under RC 3109.22. Churchill v Wood, No. 91-CA-91, 1993 WL 102634 (2d Dist Ct App, Greene, 4-7-93).

An Ohio court has authority to modify a New Jersey court decree as to visitation with children residing in Ohio even where the decree lacks sufficient finality to entitle it to full faith and credit as to child support and alimony. Auberry v Auberry, No. 13966 (9th Dist Ct App, Summit, 2-15-89).

Where a child's father residing in Ohio has visitation rights and alleges that the child suffers from sexual abuse while residing with his mother in a foreign state, the Uniform Child Custody Jurisdiction Act gives an Ohio court jurisdiction to hold an evidentiary hearing on the allegations. In re Scarso, No. 53315 (8th Dist Ct App, Cuyahoga, 2-4-88).

An Ohio court may, consistent with RC 3109.22, exercise jurisdiction over a motion for change of custody where the child spent his formative years in Ohio, has most of his friends in Ohio, and wishes for both parents and himself to reside in Ohio. Gordon v Gordon, No. 1334 (4th Dist Ct App, Athens, 10-19-87).

If a child is not the ward of any other court, trial court has jurisdiction over custody proceedings where the trial court's state has been the child's home state within six months before commencement of the proceeding, the child has developed significant connections with the state by virtue of the former residence, and the plaintiff, who acknowledges that he is the child's natural father, resides in the state. Harris v Hopper, No. L-81-187 (6th Dist Ct App, Lucas, 1-15-82).

Though husband had insufficient contacts with Ohio to provide Ohio court with in personam jurisdiction for purposes of division of property and support, Ohio had jurisdiction under Ohio statutes to make custody determination, where mother and child were present in Ohio; very presence of child in Ohio, meeting requirements of the Uniform Child Custody Jurisdiction Act (UCCJA) made clear the necessity of custody order. Schroeder v. Vigil-Escalera Perez (Ohio Com.Pl. 1995) 76 Ohio Misc.2d 25, 664 N.E.2d 627.

Even though children resided with their mother in West Virginia, Ohio court had jurisdiction under Uniform Child Custody Jurisdiction Act over contempt, visitation, and change of child custody matter, where parties previously had entered into consent order in Ohio for custody and visitation, Ohio had at least equal family ties as compared to West Virginia, and substantial evidence concerning children's care, protection, training, and relationship was located in Ohio. Willis v. Willis (Ohio Com.Pl. 1985) 25 Ohio Misc.2d 1, 495 N.E.2d 478, 25 O.B.R. 50.

2. Jurisdiction improper

An Ohio court is not a convenient forum for a guardianship termination proceeding where the foreign contestants have been guardians of and have had custody of the children for over nine years and have integrated the children into their own family, notwithstanding the facts that (1) the same Ohio court originally appointed the foreign guardians and (2) the other contestants are Ohio residents. In re Wonderly's Guardianship (Ohio 1981) 67 Ohio St.2d 178, 423 N.E.2d 420, 21 O.O.3d 111.

Juvenile court did not abuse its discretion, under the Uniform Child Custody Jurisdiction Act (UCCJA), in declining to exercise jurisdiction over child custody and abuse complaint filed by mother and grandmother, given that there was pending custody proceeding in Kentucky and Ohio was inconvenient forum, where father resided in Kentucky, most of alleged abuse occurred in Kentucky, nearly all witnesses were in Kentucky, Kentucky was child's home at time mother commenced divorce and custody proceeding in that state, and Kentucky court had been regularly holding hearings in that action. In re Simons (Ohio App. 2 Dist. 1997) 118 Ohio App.3d 622, 693 N.E.2d 1111.

Common Pleas Court did not abuse its discretion in declining to exercise jurisdiction under Uniform Child Custody Jurisdiction Act (UCCJA); although Court could have exercised jurisdiction under section of UCCJA providing for exercise of jurisdiction in best interest of children, children's mere presence in state was not sufficient to exercise jurisdiction under that section, and Court was free to determine that other factors listed in that section were not met. In re Skrha (Cuyahoga 1994) 98 Ohio App.3d 487, 648 N.E.2d 908.

An order of an Ohio domestic relations court granting a divorce and custody of two children to their father after the mother moves to England and fails to appear at the hearing is at the most voidable for jurisdictional error over the custody issue and a writ of habeas corpus is not applicable. Harvey v. Bentley (Montgomery 1991) 74 Ohio App.3d 375, 599 N.E.2d 284.

An Ohio juvenile court properly exercises discretion in declining to exercise jurisdiction over a custody and abuse complaint and instead defers to Kentucky under the Uniform Child Custody Jurisdiction Act (UCCJA) where jurisdiction of the Kentucky court is invoked by filing of the action for divorce and child custody in Kentucky which has substantial evidence concerning the child. Johnson v Montgomery County Children's Services, No. 16020, 1997 WL 102015 (2d Dist Ct App, Montgomery, 3-7-97).

The juvenile court in Ohio does not have jurisdiction to determine custody of a child who lived in Virginia the past two years and is not physically present in Ohio during pendency of the action. Rupert v Landis, No. 93-J-27, 1995 WL 138911 (7th Dist Ct App, Jefferson, 3-22-95).

An Ohio court is prohibited from exercising subject matter jurisdiction by granting a wife's motion to dismiss a husband's complaint for divorce and child custody where the wife's complaint for divorce and child custody, filed in Michigan, is pending in Michigan at the time she files her motion to dismiss the husband's Ohio action, so that pursuant to RC 3109.24 the court is required at the very least to communicate with the Michigan court to avoid jurisdictional conflicts and to establish the more appropriate forum under RC 3109.22 for litigating the child custody issue. Hochmuth v Hochmuth, No. H-94-13, 1995 WL 12070 (6th Dist Ct App, Huron, 1-13-95).

Where a party to a divorce action does not live in Ohio and has no minimum contacts with the state of Ohio, an Ohio common pleas court has no personal jurisdiction over the party and any child custody and child support orders in connection with the divorce are invalid because decisions concerning custody and child support require personal jurisdiction over the parties which will be bound by the order. Smith v Smith, No. 92-CA-13, 1993 WL 370824 (5th Dist Ct App, Guernsey, 9-3-93).

Trial court lacks jurisdiction to make any order respecting an original or modified decree of child support unless it is in connection with a divorce or alimony action pending in that court since child support must remain incidental to the alimony or divorce action. Anderson v Anderson, No. 5-81-16 (3d Dist Ct App, Hancock, 1-19-82).

A child permanently domiciled in a foreign state with a custodial parent does not establish "significant connection" with Ohio under the meaning in RC 3109.22(A)(3) when under a valid visitation agreement, such child visits the non-custodial parent who is permanently domiciled in Ohio. In re Heritage, No. C-800683 (1st Dist Ct App, Hamilton, 8-26-81).

3. Due Process Clause

The presence of a child and one spouse in Illinois is not enough, in and of itself, to give an Illinois court jurisdiction under the Due Process Clause over the other spouse such that an Ohio court is bound by its custody decree. Pasqualone v. Pasqualone (Ohio 1980) 63 Ohio St.2d 96, 406 N.E.2d 1121, 17 O.O.3d 58.

4. Enforcement

Father, who resided in France and had custody of child pursuant to order of French court, was entitled to order returning child to France under ICARA, where child's habitual residence was France and child was wrongfully retained by mother in Ohio. Crall-Shaffer v. Shaffer (Hamilton 1995) 105 Ohio App.3d 369, 663 N.E.2d 1346.

An Ohio juvenile court may not assume original jurisdiction if custody has been finally adjudicated in another state, and no request for decree modification has been made since the authority to enforce is different from the authority to modify, and the juvenile court is required to determine the enforcement issue under the applicable law and not conduct a hearing to expand its decision to include modification. In re McClurg (Butler 1992) 78 Ohio App.3d 465, 605 N.E.2d 418, dismissed, jurisdictional motion overruled 64 Ohio St.3d 1429, 594 N.E.2d 971.

An Ohio court of common pleas does not have jurisdiction to enforce a divorce decree granted in Oklahoma on issues other than child support, such as payment of marital debts, even if the parties appeared voluntarily. Thorley v. Thorley (Huron 1991) 77 Ohio App.3d 275, 602 N.E.2d 268.

5. Foreign decree

Former wife's petition to transfer jurisdiction over child custody matters from court of state in which dissolution was originally entered, and for modification of visitation and child support originally established in dissolution decree, did not place parenting determination at issue, and Uniform Child Custody Jurisdiction Act (UCCJA) was therefore inapplicable. In re Monroe (Ohio App. 7 Dist. 1999) 133 Ohio App.3d 294, 727 N.E.2d 953.

West Virginia court from which divorce decree originated maintained continuing jurisdiction with respect to child custody and visitation issues, where hearing was held in West Virginia court on former husband's motion to modify child support and order entered thereon two months before former wife filed petition to transfer jurisdiction to Ohio. In re Monroe (Ohio App. 7 Dist. 1999) 133 Ohio App.3d 294, 727 N.E.2d 953.

Ohio domestic relations court did not have jurisdiction under Uniform Child Custody Jurisdiction Act (UCCJA) to modify Virginia child custody order, where Ohio was not child's home state, child was not physically present in state, it was not in child's best interests to invoke jurisdiction in Ohio, and Virginia had jurisdiction to enforce divorce degree and custody order and had not declined jurisdiction to modify such judgments. Kachele v. Kachele (Ohio App. 8 Dist. 1996) 115 Ohio App.3d 609, 685 N.E.2d 1283.

Pennsylvania law contains statutory provisions substantially in accord with Uniform Child Custody Jurisdiction Act (UCCJA), and thus, state court should give full faith and credit to Pennsylvania decree. Strothers v. Lambert (Cuyahoga 1996) 113 Ohio App.3d 449, 680 N.E.2d 1326.

Father waived claim that Kansas court's previous granting of father's petition for divorce and child custody precluded Ohio common pleas court from determining custody, where father failed to raise issue in timely appeal from Ohio judgment entry in which mother was appointed legal custodian and residential parent of children, since argument that one court was better suited to determine which parent should have custody did not involve resolution of whether Ohio court had subject matter jurisdiction, but rather raised issue of which state's courts had best forum to determine custody of children. Gurtner v. Gurtner (Van Wert 1994) 94 Ohio App.3d 236, 640 N.E.2d 596.

An Ohio court has no jurisdiction to "define and clarify a vague order" of visitation imposed by a foreign court where the child and mother have never resided in Ohio, but the child's father, with whom the child does not reside, currently resides in Ohio. State, ex rel. Adache, v. Avellone (Lake 1991) 70 Ohio App.3d 521, 591 N.E.2d 420.

Ohio courts of common pleas have no power in an extradition proceeding to review and reverse an order of a foreign juvenile and domestic relations court on either statutory or constitutional grounds. State ex rel. Gilpin v. Stokes (Hamilton 1984) 19 Ohio App.3d 99, 483 N.E.2d 179, 19 O.B.R. 186.

A foreign state properly exercises jurisdiction, and an Ohio court will enforce a judgment thereof, where that foreign state is the residence of the child in question. Fox v Fox, No. 87AP100074 (5th Dist Ct App, Tuscarawas, 3-29-88).

6. Concurrent jurisdiction

RC 2151.23(A) confers concurrent jurisdiction on an Ohio court where a court of another state has previously assumed and exercised jurisdiction pursuant to RC 3109.21 to 3109.36. Squires v. Squires (Preble 1983) 12 Ohio App.3d 138, 468 N.E.2d 73, 12 O.B.R. 460.

7. Parental Kidnapping Protection Act

Pursuant to federal Parental Kidnapping Prevention Act (PKPA), in order for state court to modify existing parenting decree issued by another state court or child custody decree from another state, courts of state seeking to modify decree must have jurisdiction to make child custody determination, and courts of original state must no longer have jurisdiction, or must have declined to exercise such jurisdiction. Justis v. Justis (Ohio 1998) 81 Ohio St.3d 312, 691 N.E.2d 264.

Federal Parental Kidnapping Prevention Act (PKPA) provides for exclusive jurisdiction over interstate custody disputes, and eliminates possibility of concurrent jurisdiction by preventing second state from modifying custody decree where original home state has continuing jurisdiction. Justis v. Justis (Ohio 1998) 81 Ohio St.3d 312, 691 N.E.2d 264.

Ohio court having continuing jurisdiction over interstate custody dispute had authority to issue contempt order against children's mother for her failure to abide by terms of its prior parenting determination modifying custody. Justis v. Justis (Ohio 1998) 81 Ohio St.3d 312, 691 N.E.2d 264.

North Carolina court lacked jurisdiction, under federal Parental Kidnapping Prevention Act (PKPA), to modify parenting determination made by Ohio court, where Ohio courts had jurisdiction over custody dispute under Ohio laws and Ohio remained residence of two contestants for custody. Justis v. Justis (Ohio 1998) 81 Ohio St.3d 312, 691 N.E.2d 264.

States are required, pursuant to federal Parental Kidnapping Prevention Act (PKPA), to afford full faith and credit to valid child custody orders of another state court. Justis v. Justis (Ohio 1998) 81 Ohio St.3d 312, 691 N.E.2d 264.

Terms of federal Parental Kidnapping Prevention Act (PKPA) preventing second state from modifying custody decree where original home state has continuing jurisdiction prevail over jurisdictional provisions of Uniform Child Custody Jurisdiction Act (UCCJA) as adopted by Ohio, as PKPA attempts to limit circumstances under which court may modify custody decree of another state. Justis v. Justis (Ohio 1998) 81 Ohio St.3d 312, 691 N.E.2d 264.

Under Uniform Child Custody Jurisdiction Act (UCCJA) as adopted in Ohio, read together with jurisdictional provisions of federal Parental Kidnapping Prevention Act (PKPA), state court rendering initial custody decree has exclusive jurisdiction over ongoing custody dispute if state has continuing jurisdiction, and so long as state complies with jurisdictional requirements under state law and under PKPA, its orders are entitled to full faith and credit by any other state. Justis v. Justis (Ohio 1998) 81 Ohio St.3d 312, 691 N.E.2d 264.

RC 3109.22(A) is not preempted by the Parental Kidnapping Prevention Act (PKPA), 28 USC 1738A(d) in those instances where an Ohio court assumes jurisdiction over a child custody case pursuant to law, notwithstanding the fact that the parties are no longer residents of Ohio, and in agreement with any sister state having potentially competing jurisdictional claims. Holm v Smilowitz, No. 1520 (4th Dist Ct App, Athens, 11-16-92).

The Uniform Child Custody Jurisdiction Act (UCCJA) and the Parental Kidnapping Prevention Act (PKPA) were inapplicable to international custody dispute. Schroeder v. Vigil-Escalera Perez (Ohio Com.Pl. 1995) 76 Ohio Misc.2d 25, 664 N.E.2d 627.

8. Enforcement of Foreign Judgments Act

In matters of child custody, the Uniform Child Custody Jurisdiction Act, RC 3109.21 to 3109.37, governs procedure involving foreign judgments and supersedes the Enforcement of Foreign Judgments Act, RC 2329.021 to 2329.027. Fox v Fox, No. 87AP100074 (5th Dist Ct App, Tuscarawas, 3-29-88).

9. Hague Convention

State court had original concurrent jurisdiction over father's Hague Convention petition pursuant to ICARA. Crall-Shaffer v. Shaffer (Hamilton 1995) 105 Ohio App.3d 369, 663 N.E.2d 1346.

Mother's decision not to participate in hearing on father's Hague Convention petition pursuant to ICARA did not make hearing and subsequent order in favor of father invalid; mother had notice of hearing and opportunity to be heard, and mother's objection to trial court's assertion of jurisdiction over petition was overruled but preserved for appeal. Crall-Shaffer v. Shaffer (Hamilton 1995) 105 Ohio App.3d 369, 663 N.E.2d 1346.

Mother received proper notice and service of father's petition for return of child under Hague Convention on Civil Aspects of International Child Abduction and had opportunity to present defense, although mother claimed she did not receive mail service of petition until three days prior to magistrate's hearing, as mother had constructive notice; mother was informed more than two months before hearing that petition would be filed, counsel for both parties had correspondence regarding petition, and there was no prejudice by magistrate's failure to grant continuance. Ciotola v. Fiocca (Ohio Com.Pl. 1997) 86 Ohio Misc.2d 24, 684 N.E.2d 763.

In order to determine under Hague Convention whether foreign country is appropriate country for purposes of determining custody and return of child, court must consider whether that country was habitual residence of child and whether removal of child from that country or her retention in the United States was wrongful. Schroeder v. Vigil-Escalera Perez (Ohio Com.Pl. 1995) 76 Ohio Misc.2d 25, 664 N.E.2d 627.

Habitual residence of child can be altered for purposes of Hague Convention only by change of geography and passage of time, not by changes of parental affection and responsibility, and change in geography must occur before questionable removal of child from one country to another; focus should be on child, not parents, and past experience, not future intentions, must be examined, but desires and actions of parents cannot be ignored when child was, at time of removal or retention, an infant. Schroeder v. Vigil-Escalera Perez (Ohio Com.Pl. 1995) 76 Ohio Misc.2d 25, 664 N.E.2d 627.

Ohio was habitual residence of child prior to filing of action involving custody, within meaning of Hague Convention, though child had lived for three months in Spain with her Spanish father and American mother before removal to the United States, where removal was with the knowledge and consent of the father and, though mother and the baby had return tickets, father acquiesced and agreed that mother and child would remain in the United States and child had been in the United States for some six months before the pleading of alleged wrongful retention. Schroeder v. Vigil-Escalera Perez (Ohio Com.Pl. 1995) 76 Ohio Misc.2d 25, 664 N.E.2d 627.

Date when custody of child became issue, upon father's filing of motion to dismiss mother's action seeking custody, was proper date for examining alleged wrongfulness of retention of child in the United States for purposes of Hague Convention. Schroeder v. Vigil-Escalera Perez (Ohio Com.Pl. 1995) 76 Ohio Misc.2d 25, 664 N.E.2d 627.

Even if Spain was habitual residence of child prior to child's removal to the United States by mother, removal was not wrongful under Hague Convention, where father knew at all times where mother and child were, acquiesced in removal and retention of child in the United States, and did not ask for return of child until six months after child was removed, and where father made no effort to see or visit minor child, though encouraged by the mother to do so. Schroeder v. Vigil-Escalera Perez (Ohio Com.Pl. 1995) 76 Ohio Misc.2d 25, 664 N.E.2d 627.

A child's "habitual residence" for purposes of the Hague Convention on the Civil Aspects of International Child Abduction, 42 USC 11603(e)(2), must not be confused with domicile, and to determine the habitual residence a court must focus on the child rather than the parents and examine past experience instead of future intentions; consequently, a child born in Germany to a German father and an American servicewoman who lived exclusively in Germany except for short vacations until the mother removed him to her parents' home in Ohio has habitual residence in Germany despite the child's United States citizenship, the listing of Ironton, Ohio as his permanent address, and the stated intention of the mother to return to the United States. Friedrich v. Friedrich (C.A.6 (Ohio) 1993) 983 F.2d 1396.

10. Appeals

An order entered in a proceeding for change of custody is a final, appealable order if it affects substantial right. Haskins v. Haskins (Montgomery 1995) 104 Ohio App.3d 58, 660 N.E.2d 1260.

Trial court's denial of father's motion to dismiss custody action, brought under Uniform Child Custody Jurisdiction Act, on grounds that courts in another state had jurisdiction, was not an appealable final judgment; jurisdictional determination was ultimately reviewable for error upon conclusion of proceeding. Haskins v. Haskins (Montgomery 1995) 104 Ohio App.3d 58, 660 N.E.2d 1260.

In proceeding on motion for change of custody, judgment that defers issue of child support for future determination is not "final appealable order." Kouns v. Pemberton (Lawrence 1992) 84 Ohio App.3d 499, 617 N.E.2d 701, motion overruled 66 Ohio St.3d 1489, 612 N.E.2d 1245.

3109.23 Notice of parenting proceeding; proof of service

(A) Before making a parenting decree, the court shall give reasonable notice of the parenting proceeding and opportunity to be heard to the contestants, any parent whose parental rights previously have not been terminated, and any person or public agency who has physical custody of the child. If any of these persons or the public agency is outside this state, notice and opportunity to be heard shall be given in accordance with division (B) of this section.

(B) Notice required for the exercise of jurisdiction over a person or public agency outside this state shall be given either in accordance with the Rules of Civil Procedure governing service of process within this state or by one of the following methods:

(1) In the manner prescribed by the law of the place in which the service is made for service of process in that place in an action in any of its courts of general jurisdiction;

(2) As directed by the court, including publication, if other means of notification are ineffective.

(C) Notice under division (B) of this section shall be served, mailed, delivered, or last published at least twenty days before any hearing in this state.

(D) Proof of service outside this state may be made by affidavit of the individual who made the service or in the manner prescribed by the Rules of Civil Procedure governing service of process within this state, the order pursuant to which the service is made, or the law of the place in which the service is made. If service is made by mail, proof may be a receipt signed by the addressee or other evidence of delivery to the addressee.

(E) Notice is not required if a person submits to the jurisdiction of the court.

(1990 S 3, eff. 4-11-91; 1977 S 135)

Cross References

Service of process, Civ R 4 to 4.6

Ohio Administrative Code References

Federal parent locator service, OAC 5101:1-30-01, 5101:1-30-03 to 5101:1-30-05

Library References

Divorce ⚿301, 303(3), 402(8).
Infants ⚿19.3(1), 198.
Parent and Child ⚿2(6).
WESTLAW Topic Nos. 134, 211, 285.
C.J.S. Divorce §§ 637 to 640, 648, 654 to 657, 661 to 663, 845.
C.J.S. Infants §§ 19, 20, 22, 23, 27, 56.
C.J.S. Parent and Child § 33.

OJur 3d: 53, Guardian and Ward § 32
Am Jur 2d: 24, Divorce and Separation § 791; 42, Infants § 33 to 41; 59, Parent and Child § 42

Validity, construction, and application of Uniform Child Custody Jurisdiction Act. 96 ALR3d 968
Necessity of requiring presence in court of both parties in proceedings relating to custody or visitation of children. 15 ALR4th 864
What types of proceedings or determinations are governed by the Uniform Child Custody Jurisdiction Act (UCCJA) or the Parental Kidnapping Prevention Act (PKPA). 78 ALR4th 1028
Applicability of Uniform Child Custody Jurisdiction Act (UCCJA) to temporary custody orders. 81 ALR4th 1101

Child custody: when does state that issued previous custody determination have continuing jurisdiction under Uniform Child Custody Jurisdiction Act (UCCJA) or Parental Kidnapping Prevention Act (PKPA), 28 USC § 1738A. 83 ALR4th 742

Significant connection jurisdiction of court under § 3(a)(2) of the Uniform Child Custody Jurisdiction Act (UCCJA) and the Parental Kidnapping Prevention Act (PKPA), 28 USC § 1738A(c)(2)(B). 5 ALR5th 550

Abandonment and emergency jurisdiction of court under § 3(a)(3) of the Uniform Child Custody Jurisdiction Act (UCCJA) and the Parental Kidnapping Prevention Act (PKPA), 28 USC § 1738A(c)(2)(C). 5 ALR5th 788

Home state jurisdiction of court under § 3(a)(1) of the Uniform Child Custody Jurisdiction Act (UCCJA) or the Parental Kidnapping Prevention Act (PKPA), 28 USC § 1738A(c)(2)(A). 6 ALR5th 1

Default jurisdiction of court under § 3(a)(4) of the Uniform Child Custody Jurisdiction Act (UCCJA) or the Parental Kidnapping Prevention Act (PKPA), 28 USC § 1738A(c)(2)(D). 6 ALR5th 69

Parties' misconduct as ground for declining jurisdiction under § 8 of the Uniform Child Custody Jurisdiction Act (UCCJA). 16 ALR5th 650

Carlin, Baldwin's Ohio Practice, *Merrick-Rippner Probate Law* § 62.33, 62.51, 62.53, 66.10, 105.1, 107.106, 108.13, 108.17, 108.34 (1997)

Kurtz & Giannelli, Ohio Juvenile Law (1998 Ed.), Text 12.4

Sowald & Morganstern, Baldwin's Ohio Practice, *Domestic Relations Law* § 15.3, 17.1, 17.13, 25.82 (1997)

Notes of Decisions and Opinions

---

1. Service by publication

Service by publication is proper in a case in which a county children's services board files a motion for permanent custody of a mother's children where the board adequately establishes that it exercised reasonable diligence in attempting to locate the mother; the mother's history of sporadic contact coupled with her inability to obtain stable housing, ten addresses within one year, or provide the board with an address to send notices made it extremely impractical, if not impossible, to serve the mother in any other manner than by publication. In re Cowling (Summit 1991) 72 Ohio App.3d 499, 595 N.E.2d 470.

2. Notice lacking

Where a final judgment denying a change of custody has been entered and the court has only a visitation motion before it, it is violative of due process for the court to subsequently sua sponte change the custody order since notice of the proposed action was not provided to the parties involved. In re Remmer, No. 52712 (8th Dist Ct App, Cuyahoga, 7-2-87).

3. Standing

Any person has standing to bring an action for child custody under RC 2151.23; such a person need not be a parent, need not have established paternity and need not have legitimized the child. Harris v Hopper, No. L-81-187 (6th Dist Ct App, Lucas, 1-15-82).

4. Timing

RC 3109.23(C) must be interpreted to require "at least twenty days before any hearing in this state" from the time the notice of the hearing is "served, mailed [or] delivered." Sontag v Sontag, No. C-800223 (1st Dist Ct App, Hamilton, 4-15-81).

3109.24 Pendency of proceedings in another state

(A) A court of this state shall not exercise its jurisdiction, if at the time of filing the petition a parenting proceeding concerning the child was pending in a court of another state exercising jurisdiction substantially in conformity with sections 3109.21 to 3109.36 of the Revised Code, unless the proceeding is stayed by the court of the other state because this state is a more appropriate forum or for other reasons.

(B) Before hearing the petition in a parenting proceeding, the court shall examine the pleadings and other information supplied by the parties under section 3109.27 of the Revised Code and shall consult the child parenting and custody registry established under division (A) of section 3109.33 of the Revised Code concerning the pendency of parenting proceedings with respect to the child in other states. If the court has reason to believe that parenting proceedings may be pending in another state, it shall direct an inquiry to the state court administrator or other appropriate official of the other state.

(C) If a court is informed during the course of a parenting proceeding that a parenting proceeding concerning the child was pending in a court of another state before the court assumed jurisdiction, it shall stay the proceeding and communicate with the court in which the other proceeding is pending for the purpose of litigating the issue in the more appropriate forum and to ensure that information is exchanged in accordance with sections 3109.34 to 3109.36 of the Revised Code. If a court of this state has made a parenting decree before being informed of a pending proceeding in a court of another state, it immediately shall inform that court of the fact. If a court of this state is informed that a proceeding was commenced in another state after it assumed jurisdiction, it shall inform the other court for the purpose of litigating the issues in the more appropriate forum.

(1990 S 3, eff. 4-11-91; 1977 S 135)

Cross References

Reciprocal enforcement of support, contents of complaint, venue, 3115.09

Library References

Divorce ⟹289, 290, 303(1), 402(2), 402(8).
Infants ⟹18, 196.
Parent and Child ⟹2(5).
WESTLAW Topic Nos. 134, 211, 285.
C.J.S. Courts § 249 et seq.
C.J.S. Divorce §§ 611, 612, 648, 650, 826, 845.
C.J.S. Infants §§ 5 to 7, 10, 12, 17, 42, 53, 54.
C.J.S. Parent and Child § 32.

OJur 3d: 53, Guardian and Ward § 32
Am Jur 2d: 42, Infants § 33 to 41
Validity, construction, and application of Uniform Child Custody Jurisdiction Act. 96 ALR3d 968
Necessity of requiring presence in court of both parties in proceedings relating to custody or visitation of children. 15 ALR4th 864
What types of proceedings or determinations are governed by the Uniform Child Custody Jurisdiction Act (UCCJA) or the Parental Kidnapping Prevention Act (PKPA). 78 ALR4th 1028
Applicability of Uniform Child Custody Jurisdiction Act (UCCJA) to temporary custody orders. 81 ALR4th 1101
Child custody: when does state that issued previous custody determination have continuing jurisdiction under Uniform Child Custody Jurisdiction Act (UCCJA) or Parental Kidnapping Prevention Act (PKPA), 28 USC § 1738A. 83 ALR4th 742
Significant connection jurisdiction of court under § 3(a)(2) of the Uniform Child Custody Jurisdiction Act (UCCJA) and the Parental Kidnapping Prevention Act (PKPA), 28 USC § 1738A(c)(2)(B). 5 ALR5th 550
Abandonment and emergency jurisdiction of court under § 3(a)(3) of the Uniform Child Custody Jurisdiction Act (UCCJA) and the Parental Kidnapping Prevention Act (PKPA), 28 USC § 1738A(c)(2)(C). 5 ALR5th 788
Home state jurisdiction of court under § 3(a)(1) of the Uniform Child Custody Jurisdiction Act (UCCJA) or the Parental Kidnapping Prevention Act (PKPA), 28 USC § 1738A(c)(2)(A). 6 ALR5th 1
Default jurisdiction of court under § 3(a)(4) of the Uniform Child Custody Jurisdiction Act (UCCJA) or the Parental Kidnapping Prevention Act (PKPA), 28 USC § 1738A(c)(2)(D). 6 ALR5th 69
Parties' misconduct as ground for declining jurisdiction under § 8 of the Uniform Child Custody Jurisdiction Act (UCCJA). 16 ALR5th 650
Pending proceeding in another state as ground for declining jurisdiction under § 6(a) of the Uniform Child Custody Jurisdiction Act (UCCJA) or the Parental Kidnapping Prevention Act (PKPA). 28 USC § 1738A(g), 20 ALR5th 700

Carlin, Baldwin's Ohio Practice, *Merrick-Rippner Probate Law* § 62.33, 62.51, 62.53, 66.10, 105.1, 107.106, 108.13, 108.17, 108.34 (1997)
Kurtz & Giannelli, Ohio Juvenile Law (1998 Ed.), Text 12.4
Sowald & Morganstern, Baldwin's Ohio Practice, *Domestic Relations Law* § 17.1, 17.9, 17.10 (1997)

Notes of Decisions and Opinions

Bankruptcy effect 5
Communication between states 2
Due Process Clause 1
Federal jurisdiction 4
Stay of proceedings 3

---

1. Due Process Clause

An Ohio court is not bound by an Illinois custody decree under the Full Faith and Credit Clause of the United States Constitution unless the Illinois court has sufficient jurisdiction over the person of the non-Illinois party under the Due Process Clause. Pasqualone v. Pasqualone (Ohio 1980) 63 Ohio St.2d 96, 406 N.E.2d 1121, 17 O.O.3d 58.

The presence of a child and one spouse in Illinois is not enough, in and of itself, to give an Illinois court jurisdiction under the Due Process Clause over the other spouse such that an Ohio court is bound by its custody decree. Pasqualone v. Pasqualone (Ohio 1980) 63 Ohio St.2d 96, 406 N.E.2d 1121, 17 O.O.3d 58.

Juvenile court's ex parte communications with Kentucky court concerning status of the two pending child custody proceedings was authorized by law under Ohio's Uniform Child Custody Jurisdiction Act (UCCJA), and did not violate any party's due process rights, where there was no evidence that judges exchanged evidence or discussed substantive issues of pending cases. In re Simons (Ohio App. 2 Dist. 1997) 118 Ohio App.3d 622, 693 N.E.2d 1111.

2. Communication between states

RC 3109.24 provides that when custody proceedings are pending in another state, the proceedings are to be stayed and the courts are to communicate with one another for the purpose of deciding which is the more appropriate forum for litigating the issue of custody. Daerr v. Daerr (Medina 1987) 41 Ohio App.3d 206, 534 N.E.2d 1229.

RC 3109.24(C) contemplates that jurisdiction be exercised only after there has been "some cooperation, exchange of information and communication" between two states. Daerr v. Daerr (Medina 1987) 41 Ohio App.3d 206, 534 N.E.2d 1229.

RC 3109.24 contemplates that an Ohio court will not exercise jurisdiction in a custody proceeding which is already pending in another state until there has been some communication, exchange of information, and cooperation between the two states; where the court of the other state has already exercised jurisdiction, an Ohio court may not also exercise jurisdiction; in any case, an Ohio court may not exercise jurisdiction unless it is in the best interests of the child. Squires v. Squires (Preble 1983) 12 Ohio App.3d 138, 468 N.E.2d 73, 12 O.B.R. 460.

An Ohio court is prohibited from exercising subject matter jurisdiction by granting a wife's motion to dismiss a husband's complaint for divorce and child custody where the wife's complaint for divorce and child custody, filed in Michigan, is pending in Michigan at the time she files her motion to dismiss the husband's Ohio action, so that pursuant to RC 3109.24 the court is required at the very least to communicate with the Michigan court to avoid jurisdictional conflicts and to establish the more appropriate forum under RC 3109.22 for litigating the child custody issue. Hochmuth v Hochmuth, No. H-94-13, 1995 WL 12070 (6th Dist Ct App, Huron, 1-13-95).

If both parties aver that a parenting proceeding is pending in another state under RC 3109.24, an Ohio court may not exercise its jurisdiction unless it first communicates with the other court, and unless the other court stays its parenting proceedings. Andres v Andres, No. E-92-32, 1993 WL 155631 (6th Dist Ct App, Erie, 5-14-93).

3. Stay of proceedings

Temporary custody of a child may not be awarded by the trial court when a custody action is pending in the court of another state unless the other state stays its proceedings or is not exercising its jurisdiction substantially in conformity with RC 3109.21 to 3109.26. Anderson v Anderson, No. 5-81-16 (3d Dist Ct App, Hancock, 1-19-82).

A stay of child custody proceedings in a court of this state where a court in another state has already acquired jurisdiction over the matter does not act to stay the custody proceedings in this state indefinitely or forever; rather, the stay prohibition of RC 3109.24 must be interpreted to mean "stayed for a reasonable time, until the out-of-state court either acts, or has had adequate opportunity to act." Reed v. Reed (Ohio Com.Pl. 1987) 41 Ohio Misc.2d 13, 535 N.E.2d 761.

4. Federal jurisdiction

The Parental Kidnaping Prevention Act of 1980, 28 USC 1738A, establishes no private right of action in federal court to resolve a conflict between custody decrees of two courts in different states. Thompson v. Thompson (U.S.Cal. 1988) 108 S.Ct. 513, 484 U.S. 174, 98 L.Ed.2d 512.

5. Bankruptcy effect

Even assuming that seller may have perfected its security interest in Chapter 7 debtor's equipment by taking possession of equipment, following debtor's default, during 90-day preference period, this perfection, which occurred more than ten days after security agreement was executed, did not relate back to date that agreement was executed, and was itself avoidable by trustee as preferential transfer. In re Fox (Bkrtcy.N.D.Ohio 1998) 229 B.R. 160.

3109.25 Inconvenient forum; more appropriate forum

(A) A court that has jurisdiction to make an initial or modification decree may decline to exercise its jurisdiction any time before making a decree if it finds that it is an inconvenient forum to make a parenting determination under the circumstances of the case and that a court of another state is a more appropriate forum.

(B) A finding of inconvenient forum may be made upon the court's own motion or upon motion of a party or a guardian ad litem or other representative of the child.

(C) In determining if it is an inconvenient forum, the court shall consider if it is in the interest of the child that another state assume jurisdiction. For this purpose it may take into account, but is not limited to, any of the following factors:

(1) If another state is or recently was the child's home state;

(2) If another state has a closer connection with the child and his family or with the child and one or more of the contestants;

(3) If substantial evidence concerning the child's present or future care, protection, training, and personal relationships is more readily available in another state;

(4) If the parties have agreed on another forum that is no less appropriate.

(D) Before determining whether to decline or retain jurisdiction, the court may communicate with a court of another state and exchange information pertinent to the assumption of jurisdiction by either court for the purpose of assuring that jurisdiction is exercised by the more appropriate court and that a forum is available to the parties.

(E) If the court finds that it is an inconvenient forum and that a court of another state is a more appropriate forum, it may dismiss the proceedings, or may stay the proceedings upon condition that a custody proceeding be promptly commenced in another named state or upon any other conditions that may be just and proper, including the condition that a moving party stipulate his consent and submission to the jurisdiction of the other forum.

(F) The court may decline to exercise its jurisdiction, if a parenting determination is incidental to an action for divorce or another proceeding, while retaining jurisdiction over the divorce or other proceeding.

(G) If it appears to the court that it clearly is an inappropriate forum, it may require the party who commenced the proceedings to pay, in addition to the costs of the proceedings in this state, necessary travel and other expenses, including attorney's fees, incurred by other parties or their witnesses. Payment shall be made to the clerk of the court for remittance to the proper party.

(H) Upon dismissal or stay of proceedings under this section, the court shall inform the court found to be the more appropriate forum of this fact, or if the court which would have jurisdiction in the other state is not certainly known, shall transmit the information to the clerk of the court for forwarding to the appropriate court.

(I) Any communication received from another state informing this state of a finding of inconvenient forum because a court of this state is the more appropriate forum shall be filed in the parenting and custody registry of the appropriate court. Upon assuming jurisdiction, the court of this state shall inform the original court of this fact.

(1990 S 3, eff. 4-11-91; 1977 S 135)

Cross References

Reciprocal enforcement of support, contents of complaint, venue, 3115.09

Library References

Divorce ⟹289, 290, 303(1), 402(2), 402(8).
Infants ⟹18, 196.
Parent and Child ⟹2(5).
WESTLAW Topic Nos. 134, 211, 285.
C.J.S. Divorce §§ 611, 612, 648, 650, 826, 845.
C.J.S. Infants §§ 5 to 7, 10, 12, 17, 42, 53, 54.
C.J.S. Parent and Child §§ 32.

OJur 3d: 53, Guardian and Ward § 32
Am Jur 2d: 42, Infants § 33 to 41
Validity, construction, and application of Uniform Child Custody Jurisdiction Act. 96 ALR3d 968
Necessity of requiring presence in court of both parties in proceedings relating to custody or visitation of children. 15 ALR4th 864
What types of proceedings or determinations are governed by the Uniform Child Custody Jurisdiction Act (UCCJA) or the Parental Kidnapping Prevention Act (PKPA). 78 ALR4th 1028
Applicability of Uniform Child Custody Jurisdiction Act (UCCJA) to temporary custody orders. 81 ALR4th 1101
Child custody: when does state that issued previous custody determination have continuing jurisdiction under Uniform Child Custody Jurisdiction Act (UCCJA) or Parental Kidnapping Prevention Act (PKPA), 28 USC § 1738A. 83 ALR4th 742
Significant connection jurisdiction of court under § 3(a)(2) of the Uniform Child Custody Jurisdiction Act (UCCJA) and the Parental Kidnapping Prevention Act (PKPA), 28 USC § 1738A(c)(2)(B). 5 ALR5th 550
Abandonment and emergency jurisdiction of court under § 3(a)(3) of the Uniform Child Custody Jurisdiction Act (UCCJA) and the Parental Kidnapping Prevention Act (PKPA), 28 USC § 1738A(c)(2)(C). 5 ALR5th 788
Home state jurisdiction of court under § 3(a)(1) of the Uniform Child Custody Jurisdiction Act (UCCJA) or the Parental Kidnapping Prevention Act (PKPA), 28 USC § 1738A(c)(2)(A). 6 ALR5th 1
Default jurisdiction of court under § 3(a)(4) of the Uniform Child Custody Jurisdiction Act (UCCJA) or the Parental Kidnapping Prevention Act (PKPA), 28 USC § 1738A(c)(2)(D). 6 ALR5th 69
Parties' misconduct as ground for declining jurisdiction under § 8 of the Uniform Child Custody Jurisdiction Act (UCCJA). 16 ALR5th 650
Inconvenience of forum as ground for declining jurisdiction under § 7 of the Uniform Child Custody Jurisdiction Act (UCCJA). 21 ALR5th 396

Carlin, Baldwin's Ohio Practice, *Merrick-Rippner Probate Law* § 62.33, 62.51, 62.53, 66.10, 105.1, 107.106, 108.13, 108.17, 108.34 (1997)
Kurtz & Giannelli, Ohio Juvenile Law (1998 Ed.), Text 12.4
Sowald & Morganstern, Baldwin's Ohio Practice, *Domestic Relations Law* § 17.1, 17.2, 17.9, 17.10, 17.11, 17.13, 17.16 (1997)

Notes of Decisions and Opinions

Child support 4
Constitutional issues
Due process 6
Guardianship 1
Hearing 3
Ohio as inconvenient forum 2
Ohio as more convenient forum 5

---

1. Guardianship

An Ohio court is not a convenient forum for a guardianship termination proceeding where the foreign contestants have been guardians of and have had custody of the children for over nine years and have integrated the children into their own family, notwithstanding the facts that (1) the same Ohio court originally appointed the foreign guardians and (2) the other contestants are Ohio residents. In re Wonderly's Guardianship (Ohio 1981) 67 Ohio St.2d 178, 423 N.E.2d 420, 21 O.O.3d 111.

2. Ohio as inconvenient forum

Juvenile court did not abuse its discretion, under the Uniform Child Custody Jurisdiction Act (UCCJA), in declining to exercise jurisdiction over child custody and abuse complaint filed by mother and grandmother, given that there was pending custody proceeding in Kentucky and Ohio was inconvenient forum, where father resided in Kentucky, most of alleged abuse occurred in Kentucky, nearly all witnesses were in Kentucky, Kentucky was child's home at time mother commenced divorce and custody proceeding in that state, and Kentucky court had been regularly holding hearings in that action. In re Simons (Ohio App. 2 Dist. 1997) 118 Ohio App.3d 622, 693 N.E.2d 1111.

In an action brought by an ex-husband for modification of visitation, support, and custody and to show cause after his ex-wife moved to Illinois, the ex-wife has not consented to jurisdiction in Ohio where (1) her motion to dismiss filed in the action is based on opposition to jurisdiction, and (2) her counsel files a notice of appearance to apprise the court of where to send any additional information; even if the ex-wife did consent to jurisdiction, this consent does not preclude the Ohio and Illinois courts from determining which forum is most convenient for the best interest of the child. Mayor v. Mayor (Cuyahoga 1991) 71 Ohio App.3d 789, 595 N.E.2d 436.

Illinois, rather than Ohio, is the more convenient forum for determining an ex-husband's motions for modification of visitation, support, and custody and to show cause after his ex-wife moved to Illinois, even though the Ohio Uniform Child Custody Jurisdiction Act did not divest the Ohio court of jurisdiction over the matter since Illinois had become the child's home state and had a closer connection with the child than Ohio and there was substantial evidence in Illinois regarding the child's care, relationships, schooling, and future. Mayor v. Mayor (Cuyahoga 1991) 71 Ohio App.3d 789, 595 N.E.2d 436.

An Ohio juvenile court properly exercises discretion in declining to exercise jurisdiction over a custody and abuse complaint and instead defers to Kentucky under the Uniform Child Custody Jurisdiction Act (UCCJA) where jurisdiction of the Kentucky court is invoked by filing of the action for divorce and child custody in Kentucky which has substantial evidence concerning the child. Johnson v Montgomery County Children's Services, No. 16020, 1997 WL 102015 (2d Dist Ct App, Montgomery, 3-7-97).

An Ohio court may decline to exercise its jurisdiction to determine unresolved custody and visitation issues and find that it is in the best interest of the parties' minor children that a South Carolina court is a more appropriate forum where the children have resided in South Carolina for more than two years, are undergoing psychological treatment, are enrolled in school, and maintain relationships and activities in South Carolina. Conner v Renz, Nos. 94CA1605+, 1994 WL 725151 (4th Dist Ct App, Athens, 12-29-94).

An Ohio court is not a convenient forum for hearing a custody complaint filed by grandparents having temporary custody of a child in Ohio, where the residence of the child, the custodial parent, and the evidence is in another state. Spencer v Spencer, No. CA83-04-010 (12th Dist Ct App, Preble, 4-23-84).

3. Hearing

Common Pleas Court did not abuse its discretion in finding that Alaska was more convenient forum than Ohio to hear custody proceeding under Uniform Child Custody Jurisdiction Act (UCCJA); Court carefully considered factors listed in section of UCCJA related to finding of inconvenient forum, and Court's failure to take sworn testimony on the issue was not error, since Court would likely have reached same conclusion after taking sworn testimony. In re Skrha (Cuyahoga 1994) 98 Ohio App.3d 487, 648 N.E.2d 908.

A trial court's failure to conduct an evidentiary hearing before dismissing an ex-husband's motions for modification of visitation, support, and custody and to show cause for lack of jurisdiction is not erroneous since although it would have been a better practice to have conducted a hearing, the hearing would in all likelihood have lead to the conclusion that the state where the ex-wife was currently residing with the child is the more convenient forum. Mayor v. Mayor (Cuyahoga 1991) 71 Ohio App.3d 789, 595 N.E.2d 436.

4. Child support

RC 3109.25 which provides for transfers of custody matters based on forum inconvenience applies exclusively to custody matters; therefore, it does not provide a basis on which a trial court may transfer a support modification proceeding. Satava v. Gerhard (Lake 1990) 66 Ohio App.3d 598, 585 N.E.2d 899.

5. Ohio as more convenient forum

Ohio may be the proper forum to make a child custody determination where (1) the mother has filed a motion for change of custody in North Carolina and the father then files a petition for custody in Ohio, (2) there is an extended absence from North Carolina of all the parties, and (3) the North Carolina trial court has not been exercising its jurisdiction substantially in compliance with the Uniform Child Custody Jurisdiction Act. In re Prysock, No. 94APF12-1811, 1995 WL 360311 (10th Dist Ct App, Franklin, 6-13-95).

Ohio was proper venue and was not an inconvenient forum to determine custody between mother living in Ohio and father who was citizen and resident of Spain, where mother lived in Ohio with family members and had no plans to leave, while father's employment required him to travel throughout Europe, and where substantial evidence concerning child's future care was not more readily available elsewhere. Schroeder v. Vigil-Escalera Perez (Ohio Com.Pl. 1995) 76 Ohio Misc.2d 25, 664 N.E.2d 627.

In a dispute over visitation rights, an Ohio court may retain jurisdiction, even though the defendant and children reside in another state, where the parties have recently entered into a consent order in the court, thereby indicating that they consider family ties to Ohio to be strong. Willis v. Willis (Ohio Com.Pl. 1985) 25 Ohio Misc.2d 1, 495 N.E.2d 478, 25 O.B.R. 50.

6. —Due process, constitutional issues

Juvenile court's ex parte communications with Kentucky court concerning status of the two pending child custody proceedings was authorized by law under Ohio's Uniform Child Custody Jurisdiction Act (UCCJA), and did not violate any party's due process rights, where there was no evidence that judges exchanged evidence or discussed substantive issues of pending cases. In re Simons (Ohio App. 2 Dist. 1997) 118 Ohio App.3d 622, 693 N.E.2d 1111.

3109.26 Improperly obtained custody

(A) If the petitioner for an initial decree has wrongfully taken the child from another state or has engaged in similar conduct, the court may decline to exercise jurisdiction, if this is just and proper under the circumstances.

(B) Unless required in the interest of the child, the court shall not exercise its jurisdiction to modify a parenting decree of another state if the petitioner, without consent of the parent who is designated the residential parent and legal custodian or another person entitled to custody, has improperly removed the child from the physical custody of the parent who is designated the residential parent and legal custodian or another person entitled to custody or has improperly retained the child after a visit or other temporary relinquishment of physical custody. If the petitioner has violated any other provision of a parenting decree of another state, the court may decline to exercise its jurisdiction, if this is just and proper under the circumstances.

(C) In appropriate cases, a court dismissing a petition under this section may charge the petitioner with necessary travel and other expenses, including attorney's fees, incurred by other parties or their witnesses.

(1990 S 3, eff. 4-11-91; 1977 S 135)

Cross References

Criminal child stealing, 2905.04

Criminal interference with custody, 2919.23

Ohio Administrative Code References

Location efforts regarding parental kidnapping and child custody determination, OAC 5101:1-30-04

Library References

Divorce ⚿289, 290, 303(1), 402(2), 402(8).
Infants ⚿18, 196.
Parent and Child ⚿2(5).
WESTLAW Topic Nos. 134, 211, 285.
C.J.S. Divorce §§ 611, 612, 648, 650, 826, 845.
C.J.S. Infants §§ 5 to 7, 10, 12, 17, 42, 53, 54.
C.J.S. Parent and Child § 32.

OJur 3d: 53, Guardian and Ward § 32
Am Jur 2d: 42, Infants § 33 to 41
Validity, construction, and application of Uniform Child Custody Jurisdiction Act. 96 ALR3d 968
Necessity of requiring presence in court of both parties in proceedings relating to custody or visitation of children. 15 ALR4th 864
Kidnapping or related offense by taking or removing of child by or under authority of parent or one in loco parentis. 20 ALR4th 823
What types of proceedings or determinations are governed by the Uniform Child Custody Jurisdiction Act (UCCJA) or the Parental Kidnapping Prevention Act (PKPA). 78 ALR4th 1028
Applicability of Uniform Child Custody Jurisdiction Act (UCCJA) to temporary custody orders. 81 ALR4th 1101
Child custody: when does state that issued previous custody determination have continuing jurisdiction under Uniform Child Custody Jurisdiction Act (UCCJA) or Parental Kidnapping Prevention Act (PKPA), 28 USC § 1738A. 83 ALR4th 742
Significant connection jurisdiction of court under § 3(a)(2) of the Uniform Child Custody Jurisdiction Act (UCCJA) and the Parental Kidnapping Prevention Act (PKPA), 28 USC § 1738A(c)(2)(B). 5 ALR5th 550
Abandonment and emergency jurisdiction of court under § 3(a)(3) of the Uniform Child Custody Jurisdiction Act (UCCJA) and the Parental Kidnapping Prevention Act (PKPA), 28 USC § 1738A(c)(2)(C). 5 ALR5th 788
Home state jurisdiction of court under § 3(a)(1) of the Uniform Child Custody Jurisdiction Act (UCCJA) or the Parental Kidnapping Prevention Act (PKPA), 28 USC § 1738A(c)(2)(A). 6 ALR5th 1
Default jurisdiction of court under § 3(a)(4) of the Uniform Child Custody Jurisdiction Act (UCCJA) or the Parental Kidnapping Prevention Act (PKPA), 28 USC § 1738A(c)(2)(D). 6 ALR5th 69
Parties' misconduct as ground for declining jurisdiction under § 8 of the Uniform Child Custody Jurisdiction Act (UCCJA). 16 ALR5th 650
Recognition and enforcement of out-of-state custody decree under § 13 of the Uniform Child Custody Jurisdiction Act (UCCJA) or the Parental Kidnapping Prevention Act (PKPA), 28 USCS § 1738A(a). 40 ALR5th 227

Carlin, Baldwin's Ohio Practice, *Merrick-Rippner Probate Law* § 62.33, 62.51, 62.53, 66.10, 105.1, 107.106, 108.13, 108.17, 108.34 (1997)
Kurtz & Giannelli, Ohio Juvenile Law (1998 Ed.), Text 12.4
Sowald & Morganstern, Baldwin's Ohio Practice, *Domestic Relations Law* § 17.1, 17.9, 17.12, 17.13, 17.16 (1997)

Law Review and Journal Commentaries

The Parental Kidnapping Prevention Act: Constitutionality and Effectiveness, Note. 33 Case W Res L Rev 89 (1982).

Notes of Decisions and Opinions

1. Parental Kidnapping Prevention Act

Child custody jurisdictional statutes should not be applied to allow retention or removal of child in violation of valid custody order. State ex rel. Aycock v. Mowrey (Ohio 1989) 45 Ohio St.3d 347, 544 N.E.2d 657.

Violations of Parental Kidnapping Prevention Act (PKPA) do not arise until there are two different states entering conflicting custody decrees. Holm v. Smilowitz (Athens 1992) 83 Ohio App.3d 757, 615 N.E.2d 1047.

Purpose of section of Parental Kidnapping Prevention Act (PKPA) providing that jurisdiction of court of state which made child custody determination continues so long as state remains residence of child or of any contestant is to determine whether state can modify child custody determination made previously by another state; it was not intended to act as a bar to state's assuming jurisdiction outside context of full faith and credit problem. Holm v. Smilowitz (Athens 1992) 83 Ohio App.3d 757, 615 N.E.2d 1047.

Court of common pleas properly declined to exercise jurisdiction over wife's complaint for divorce and custody, where mother had previously dismissed her Texas complaint for divorce and left Texas with the children to seek more sympathetic forum in Ohio. Syrios v. Syrios (Summit 1990) 69 Ohio App.3d 246, 590 N.E.2d 759.

Provision of Uniform Child Custody Jurisdiction Act for recognition and enforcement of decrees of courts of other states did not require trial court, in custody proceeding, to recognize divorce decree of Scotland court which awarded custody of child to former wife. Minton v. McManus (Summit 1983) 9 Ohio App.3d 165, 458 N.E.2d 1292, 9 O.B.R. 231.

The Parental Kidnaping Prevention Act of 1980, 28 USC 1738A, establishes no private right of action in federal court to resolve a conflict between custody decrees of two courts in different states. Thompson v. Thompson (U.S.Cal. 1988) 108 S.Ct. 513, 484 U.S. 174, 98 L.Ed.2d 512.

2. Visitation

Where a non-custodial parent filed a petition for a temporary restraining order together with an application to determine custody of the child, RC 3109.26 is applicable to preclude jurisdiction where the non-custodial parent retained physical custody of the child beyond the terms of a valid visitation agreement, even though such petition was filed during the visitation period when the non-custodial parent had the right to physical custody of the child. In re Heritage, No. C-800683 (1st Dist Ct App, Hamilton, 8-26-81).

When a petitioner has improperly retained custody of a child after a visit or other temporary relinquishment of physical custody by the person entitled thereto, the court may decline to exercise its jurisdiction if this is just and proper under the circumstances in accordance with RC 3109.26(B). Matter of Potter (Ohio Com.Pl. 1978) 56 Ohio Misc. 17, 377 N.E.2d 536, 10 O.O.3d 214.

3. Interest of the child

"Grave risk" exception to requirement that unlawfully abducted child be returned to his or her country of residency is applicable only when risk is posed by general environment of child's home country, not by specific environment in which child will live. In re Petition for Writ of Habeas Corpus for Coffield (Portage 1994) 96 Ohio App.3d 52, 644 N.E.2d 662.

Although evidence concerning possible harm caused by separation of child from parent who had abducted him from his country of residence three years earlier would be relevant in plenary custody proceeding, it was not relevant, in action under the International Child Abduction Remedies Act (ICARA), to question of whether child would be placed at "grave risk" if he was returned to his native Australia. In re Petition for Writ of Habeas Corpus for Coffield (Portage 1994) 96 Ohio App.3d 52, 644 N.E.2d 662.

The mere showing by a petitioner who wrongfully retains custody that he now provides a better environment for a child as opposed to the party granted custody under the original out of state decree does not, per se, meet the "best interest" standard set forth in the Uniform Child Custody Jurisdiction Act. Matter of Potter (Ohio Com.Pl. 1978) 56 Ohio Misc. 17, 377 N.E.2d 536, 10 O.O.3d 214.

In appropriate circumstances, a court, in the "interest of the child," may exercise limited jurisdiction to enforce an original custody decree of a sister state to which it gives full faith and credit. Matter of Potter (Ohio Com.Pl. 1978) 56 Ohio Misc. 17, 377 N.E.2d 536, 10 O.O.3d 214.

3109.27 Facts to be pleaded

(A) Each party in a parenting proceeding, in the party's first pleading or in an affidavit attached to that pleading, shall give information under oath as to the child's present address, the places where the child has lived within the last five years, and the name and present address of each person with whom the child has lived during that period. In this pleading or affidavit, each party also shall include all of the following information:

(1) Whether the party has participated as a party, a witness, or in any other capacity in any other litigation, in this or any other state, that concerned the allocation, between the parents of the same child, of parental rights and responsibilities for the care of the child and the

designation of the residential parent and legal custodian of the child or that otherwise concerned the custody of the same child;

(2) Whether the party has information of any parenting proceeding concerning the child pending in a court of this or any other state;

(3) Whether the party knows of any person who is not a party to the proceeding and has physical custody of the child or claims to be a parent of the child who is designated the residential parent and legal custodian of the child or to have visitation rights with respect to the child or to be a person other than a parent of the child who has custody or visitation rights with respect to the child;

(4) Whether the party previously has been convicted of or pleaded guilty to any criminal offense involving any act that resulted in a child being an abused child or a neglected child or previously has been determined, in a case in which a child has been adjudicated an abused child or a neglected child, to be the perpetrator of the abusive or neglectful act that was the basis of the adjudication.

(B) If the declaration under division (A)(1), (2), (3), or (4) of this section is in the affirmative, the court may require the declarant to give additional information under oath. The court may examine the parties under oath as to details of the information furnished and as to other matters pertinent to the court's jurisdiction and the disposition of the case.

(C) Each party has a continuing duty to inform the court of any parenting proceeding concerning the child in this or any other state of which the party obtained information during this proceeding.

(D) A public children services agency, acting pursuant to a complaint or an action on a complaint filed under section 2151.27 of the Revised Code, is not subject to the requirements of this section.

(E) As used in this section, "abused child" has the same meaning as in section 2151.031 of the Revised Code, and "neglected child" has the same meaning as in section 2151.03 of the Revised Code.

(1996 H 274, eff. 8-8-96; 1990 S 3, eff. 4-11-91; 1977 S 135)

Historical and Statutory Notes

Amendment Note: 1996 H 274 added division (D); and redesignated former division (D) as division (E).

Cross References

Complaint for divorce, alimony, and custody of children, Civ R Appendix, Form 20

Library References

Divorce ⟾301, 303(3), 402(8).
Infants ⟾19.3(1).
Parent and Child ⟾2(7).
WESTLAW Topic Nos. 134, 211, 285.
C.J.S. Divorce §§ 637 to 640, 648, 654 to 657, 661 to 663, 845.
C.J.S. Infants §§ 19, 20, 22, 23, 27.
C.J.S. Parent and Child §§ 34, 35.

OJur 3d: 53, Guardian and Ward § 32
Am Jur 2d: 24, Divorce and Separation § 792; 42, Infants § 33 to 41
Validity, construction, and application of Uniform Child Custody Jurisdiction Act. 96 ALR3d 968
Necessity of requiring presence in court of both parties in proceedings relating to custody or visitation of children. 15 ALR4th 864
What types of proceedings or determinations are governed by the Uniform Child Custody Jurisdiction Act (UCCJA) or the Parental Kidnapping Prevention Act (PKPA). 78 ALR4th 1028
Applicability of Uniform Child Custody Jurisdiction Act (UCCJA) to temporary custody orders. 81 ALR4th 1101
Child custody: when does state that issued previous custody determination have continuing jurisdiction under Uniform Child Custody Jurisdiction Act (UCCJA) or Parental Kidnapping Prevention Act (PKPA), 28 USC § 1738A. 83 ALR4th 742
Significant connection jurisdiction of court under § 3(a)(2) of the Uniform Child Custody Jurisdiction Act (UCCJA) and the Parental Kidnapping Prevention Act (PKPA), 28 USC § 1738A(c)(2)(B). 5 ALR5th 550
Abandonment and emergency jurisdiction of court under § 3(a)(3) of the Uniform Child Custody Jurisdiction Act (UCCJA) and the Parental Kidnapping Preven-

tion Act (PKPA), 28 USC § 1738A(c)(2)(C). 5 ALR5th 788
Home state jurisdiction of court under § 3(a)(1) of the Uniform Child Custody Jurisdiction Act (UCCJA) or the Parental Kidnapping Prevention Act (PKPA), 28 USC § 1738A(c)(2)(A). 6 ALR5th 1
Default jurisdiction of court under § 3(a)(4) of the Uniform Child Custody Jurisdiction Act (UCCJA) or the Parental Kidnapping Prevention Act (PKPA), 28 USC § 1738A(c)(2)(D). 6 ALR5th 69
Parties' misconduct as ground for declining jurisdiction under § 8 of the Uniform Child Custody Jurisdiction Act (UCCJA). 16 ALR5th 650
Carlin, Baldwin's Ohio Practice, *Merrick-Rippner Probate Law* § 62.33, 62.51, 62.53, 66.10, 105.1, 107.4, 107.82, 107.106, 107.118, 108.13, 108.17, 108.34 (1997)
Kurtz & Giannelli, Ohio Juvenile Law (1998 Ed.), Text 12.4, 13.9, 28.2
Sowald & Morganstern, Baldwin's Ohio Practice, *Domestic Relations Law* § 3.33, 3.57, 5.7, 5.9, 7.19, 7.31, 7.33, 7.37, 10.8, 15.3, 15.5, 16.2, 17.1, 17.2, 17.10, 17.13, 21.3 (1997)

Notes of Decisions and Opinions

---

1. Jurisdictional requirement

Mother was not entitled to habeas corpus relief from domestic relations court's custody order, which was premised on continuing jurisdiction of juvenile court that issued initial paternity order, even though neither party to paternity action filed jurisdictionally required child custody affidavit in paternity action, since issue was raised for first time on appeal and record did not include pleadings filed in paternity action. Pegan v. Crawmer (Ohio 1996) 76 Ohio St.3d 97, 666 N.E.2d 1091.

Each party in parentage proceeding which included custody and visitation determinations was required to file child custody affidavit. Pegan v. Crawmer (Ohio 1996) 76 Ohio St.3d 97, 666 N.E.2d 1091.

Domestic relations court could exercise continuing jurisdiction to modify child custody based on father's second postjudgment motion for change of custody, even though father had appealed dismissal of first motion for change of custody due to his failure to attach required child custody affidavit, where domestic relations court granted temporary custody to father pending hearing on second motion before father filed notice of appeal from court's dismissal of first motion, domestic relations court did not proceed on second motion until after reviewing court had resolved appeal concerning dismissal of first motion, and father filed required child custody affidavit with second motion. Pegan v. Crawmer (Ohio 1996) 76 Ohio St.3d 97, 666 N.E.2d 1091.

Requirement that parent bringing action for custody inform court at outset of proceedings of any knowledge he has of custody proceedings pending in other jurisdictions is mandatory jurisdictional requirement of such action. Pegan v. Crawmer (Ohio 1996) 76 Ohio St.3d 97, 666 N.E.2d 1091.

When a county welfare department brings a complaint for permanent custody in the juvenile court, its failure to provide the affidavit required by RC 3109.27(A) is not a jurisdictional defect. In re Palmer (Ohio 1984) 12 Ohio St.3d 194, 465 N.E.2d 1312, 12 O.B.R. 259, certiorari denied 105 S.Ct. 918, 469 U.S. 1162, 83 L.Ed.2d 930.

The requirement in RC 3109.27 that a parent bringing an action for custody inform the court at the outset of the proceedings of any knowledge he has of custody proceedings pending in other jurisdictions is a mandatory jurisdictional requirement of such an action. Pasqualone v. Pasqualone (Ohio 1980) 63 Ohio St.2d 96, 406 N.E.2d 1121, 17 O.O.3d 58.

Facts that neither Ohio nor Kentucky courts had made efforts to prevent removal of child from mother, and that there had been no finding that child was in imminent danger in mother's care were irrelevant to issue of whether Ohio juvenile court abused its discretion under the Uniform Child Custody Jurisdiction Act (UCCJA) in declining to exercise jurisdiction over custody and abuse complaint. In re Simons (Ohio App. 2 Dist. 1997) 118 Ohio App.3d 622, 693 N.E.2d 1111.

Purposes of jurisdictional affidavit are to avoid jurisdictional disputes and conflicts with other courts and to facilitate speedy resolution of custody disputes so that children are not victims of jurisdictional tugs of war. In Matter of Porter (Marion 1996) 113 Ohio App.3d 580, 681 N.E.2d 954.

Trial court had jurisdiction over mother's motion to vacate temporary custody order, even though mother did not file jurisdictional affidavit until after paternal grandmother had moved out of state, where mother's motion was filed after court had been exercising continuing jurisdiction for seven years, parties had acknowledged facts sufficient to invoke court's jurisdiction, paternal grandmother did not object to mother's affidavit, and no custody proceeding was pending in any other state. In Matter of Porter (Marion 1996) 113 Ohio App.3d 580, 681 N.E.2d 954.

In proceeding instituted by grandparents seeking to adopt their grandchild, grandparents' failure to file custody affidavit until after hearing on their adoption petition was harmless error; affidavit was not required under circumstances, and thus there was no question as to its timeliness. In re Adoption of Howell (Lawrence 1991) 77 Ohio App.3d 80, 601 N.E.2d 92, motion overruled 62 Ohio St.3d 1508, 583 N.E.2d 1320.

Uniform Child Custody Jurisdiction Act did not have retroactive application, and wife's failure to file custody affidavit at time of divorce proceedings did not divest trial court of jurisdiction to decide issue of custody, where Act took effect 14 days after wife filed her divorce complaint. Overbee v. Overbee (Hamilton 1986) 31 Ohio App.3d 179, 509 N.E.2d 960, 31 O.B.R. 345.

A court obtains exclusive jurisdiction over a child custody proceeding when it acquires subject matter jurisdiction and personal jurisdiction, by proper personal service, before any other court so acquires jurisdiction, even though the affidavit required by RC 3109.27 is not filed with the complaint, so long as that affidavit is filed within a reasonable time. Cook v. Court of Common Pleas of Marion County (Marion 1986) 28 Ohio App.3d 82, 502 N.E.2d 245, 28 O.B.R. 124.

The requirement as to when the parenting affidavit pursuant to RC 3109.27 is filed is directory not mandatory so that a trial court has jurisdiction to modify custody even though an affidavit is filed the day after the filing of the motion to modify custody. Rose v Spjut, No. 95CA6, 1996 WL 275083 (4th Dist Ct App, Hocking, 5-24-96).

Where record of lower court shows an absence of any allegation of child abuse or neglect, pleading that fact was not material to trial court's jurisdiction; and as there was substantial compliance with requirements of RC 3109.27(A), trial court had jurisdiction in divorce and custody proceedings. Dorski v Dorski, No. 93 OT008, 1993 WL 372235 (6th Dist Ct App, Ottawa, 9-24-93).

A custody order granted pursuant to a motion for change of custody is not invalidated in that all information required by RC 3109.27 was not included in that motion; the trial court's jurisdiction was not erroneously exercised when the motion failed to comply with RC 3109.27, as the party filing the motion did not affirmatively deny that other custody actions were pending; the omission of the child's residence for the last five years was immaterial; the absence of information as to the present address of the child and the parent with physical possession is attributable to the fact that such parent had recently left the state without notice to the parent seeking custody. In re Hites, No. 1701 (9th Dist Ct App, Wayne, 4-22-81).

2. Authority to enforce

Trial court could summarily grant mother's motion to terminate temporary custody order that was based on agreement placing child with paternal grandmother during mother's absence from state, even though mother and grandmother had extended the order by further private agreement for years after mother returned to state. In Matter of Porter (Marion 1996) 113 Ohio App.3d 580, 681 N.E.2d 954.

An Ohio juvenile court may not assume original jurisdiction if custody has been finally adjudicated in another state, and no request for decree modification has been made since the authority to enforce is different from the authority to modify, and the juvenile court is required to determine the enforcement issue under the applicable law and not conduct a hearing to expand its decision to include modification. In re McClurg (Butler 1992) 78 Ohio App.3d 465, 605 N.E.2d 418, dismissed, jurisdictional motion overruled 64 Ohio St.3d 1429, 594 N.E.2d 971.

Where mother and child resided out-of-state for over seven years, and father failed to file his change in custody affidavit required by RC 3109.27, court lacked jurisdiction and erred in dismissing mother's motion to dismiss for want of jurisdiction and lack of convenient forum. Moodispaugh v Moodispaugh, No. CA-787, 1993 WL 500302 (5th Dist Ct App, Morrow, 11-26-93).

3109.28 Persons claiming rights to be made parties

If the court learns from information furnished by the parties pursuant to section 3109.27 of the Revised Code or from other sources that a person not a party to the parenting proceeding has physical custody of the child, claims to be a parent of the child who has parental rights and responsibilities for the care of the child and who has been designated the residential parent and legal custodian of the child, claims to be any other person with custody of the child, or claims to have visitation rights with respect to the child, it shall order that person to be joined as a party and to be duly notified of the pendency of the proceeding and of his joinder as a party. If the person joined as a party is outside this state he shall be served with process or otherwise notified in accordance with division (B) of section 3109.23 of the Revised Code.

(1990 S 3, eff. 4-11-91; 1977 S 135)

Cross References

Joinder of persons needed for just adjudication, compulsory joinder, Civ R 19, 19.1

Library References

Divorce ⟹301, 303(3), 402(8).
Infants ⟹19.3(1).
Parent and Child ⟹2(6), 2(7)
WESTLAW Topic Nos. 134, 211, 285.
C.J.S. Divorce §§ 637 to 640, 648, 654 to 657, 661 to 663, 845.
C.J.S. Infants §§ 19, 20, 22, 23, 27.
C.J.S. Parent and Child §§ 33 to 35.

OJur 3d: 53, Guardian and Ward § 32
Am Jur 2d: 24, Divorce and Separation § 799 to 804; 42, Infants § 33 to 41
Validity, construction, and application of Uniform Child Custody Jurisdiction Act. 96 ALR3d 968
Necessity of requiring presence in court of both parties in proceedings relating to custody or visitation of children. 15 ALR4th 864
Standing of foster parent to seek termination of rights of foster child's natural parents. 21 ALR4th 535
What types of proceedings or determinations are governed by the Uniform Child Custody Jurisdiction Act (UCCJA) or the Parental Kidnapping Prevention Act (PKPA). 78 ALR4th 1028
Applicability of Uniform Child Custody Jurisdiction Act (UCCJA) to temporary custody orders. 81 ALR4th 1101
Child custody: when does state that issued previous custody determination have continuing jurisdiction under Uniform Child Custody Jurisdiction Act (UCCJA) or Parental Kidnapping Prevention Act (PKPA), 28 USC § 1738A. 83 ALR4th 742
Significant connection jurisdiction of court under § 3(a)(2) of the Uniform Child Custody Jurisdiction Act (UCCJA) and the Parental Kidnapping Prevention Act (PKPA), 28 USC § 1738A(c)(2)(B). 5 ALR5th 550
Abandonment and emergency jurisdiction of court under § 3(a)(3) of the Uniform Child Custody Jurisdiction

Act (UCCJA) and the Parental Kidnapping Prevention Act (PKPA), 28 USC § 1738A(c)(2)(C). 5 ALR5th 788

Home state jurisdiction of court under § 3(a)(1) of the Uniform Child Custody Jurisdiction Act (UCCJA) or the Parental Kidnapping Prevention Act (PKPA), 28 USC § 1738A(c)(2)(A). 6 ALR5th 1

Default jurisdiction of court under § 3(a)(4) of the Uniform Child Custody Jurisdiction Act (UCCJA) or the Parental Kidnapping Prevention Act (PKPA), 28 USC § 1738A(c)(2)(D). 6 ALR5th 69

Parties' misconduct as ground for declining jurisdiction under § 8 of the Uniform Child Custody Jurisdiction Act (UCCJA). 16 ALR5th 650

Carlin, Baldwin's Ohio Practice, *Merrick-Rippner Probate Law* § 62.33, 62.51, 62.53, 66.10, 105.1, 107.106, 108.13, 108.17, 108.34 (1997)

Kurtz & Giannelli, Ohio Juvenile Law (1998 Ed.), Text 12.4

Sowald & Morganstern, Baldwin's Ohio Practice, *Domestic Relations Law* § 3.57, 17.1 (1997)

Notes of Decisions and Opinions

Rights of grandparents 1

1. Rights of grandparents

Grandparents without any legal right to custody of or visitation with grandchildren, obtained through statute, court order, or other legal means, have no right under RC 3109.28 to intervene in a proceeding to terminate the parents' rights to the children. In re Schmidt (Ohio 1986) 25 Ohio St.3d 331, 496 N.E.2d 952, 25 O.B.R. 386.

3109.29 Personal appearance of parties may be required

(A) The court may order any party to a parenting proceeding who is in this state to appear personally before the court. If that party has physical custody of the child, the court may order that he appear personally with the child.

(B) If a party to a parenting proceeding whose presence is desired by the court is outside this state with or without the child, the court may order that the notice given under division (B) of section 3109.23 of the Revised Code include a statement directing that party to appear personally with or without the child and declaring that failure to appear may result in a decision adverse to that party.

(C) If a party to a parenting proceeding who is outside this state is directed to appear under division (B) of this section or desires to appear personally before the court with or without the child, the court may require another party to pay to the clerk of the court travel and other necessary expenses for the appearance of the party and the child who are outside this state, if this is just and proper under the circumstances.

(1990 S 3, eff. 4-11-91; 1977 S 135)

Ohio Administrative Code References

Federal parent locator service, OAC 5101:1-30-01, 5101:1-30-03 to 5101:1-30-05

Library References

Divorce ⟹301, 303(3), 402(8).
Infants ⟹19.3(1).
Parent and Child ⟹2(6).
WESTLAW Topic Nos. 134, 211, 285.
C.J.S. Divorce §§ 637 to 640, 648, 654 to 657, 661 to 663, 845.
C.J.S. Infants §§ 19, 20, 22, 23, 27.
C.J.S. Parent and Child § 33.

OJur 3d: 53, Guardian and Ward § 32

Am Jur 2d: 42, Infants § 33 to 41

Validity, construction, and application of Uniform Child Custody Jurisdiction Act. 96 ALR3d 968

Necessity of requiring presence in court of both parties in proceedings relating to custody or visitation of children. 15 ALR4th 864

What types of proceedings or determinations are governed by the Uniform Child Custody Jurisdiction Act (UCCJA) or the Parental Kidnapping Prevention Act (PKPA). 78 ALR4th 1028

Applicability of Uniform Child Custody Jurisdiction Act (UCCJA) to temporary custody orders. 81 ALR4th 1101

Child custody: when does state that issued previous custody determination have continuing jurisdiction under Uniform Child Custody Jurisdiction Act (UCCJA) or Parental Kidnapping Prevention Act (PKPA), 28 USC § 1738A. 83 ALR4th 742

Significant connection jurisdiction of court under § 3(a)(2) of the Uniform Child Custody Jurisdiction Act (UCCJA) and the Parental Kidnapping Prevention Act (PKPA), 28 USC § 1738A(c)(2)(B). 5 ALR5th 550

Abandonment and emergency jurisdiction of court under § 3(a)(3) of the Uniform Child Custody Jurisdiction Act (UCCJA) and the Parental Kidnapping Prevention Act (PKPA), 28 USC § 1738A(c)(2)(C). 5 ALR5th 788

Home state jurisdiction of court under § 3(a)(1) of the Uniform Child Custody Jurisdiction Act (UCCJA) or

the Parental Kidnapping Prevention Act (PKPA), 28 USC § 1738A(c)(2)(A). 6 ALR5th 1
Default jurisdiction of court under § 3(a)(4) of the Uniform Child Custody Jurisdiction Act (UCCJA) or the Parental Kidnapping Prevention Act (PKPA), 28 USC § 1738A(c)(2)(D). 6 ALR5th 69
Parties' misconduct as ground for declining jurisdiction under § 8 of the Uniform Child Custody Jurisdiction Act (UCCJA). 16 ALR5th 650
Carlin, Baldwin's Ohio Practice, *Merrick-Rippner Probate Law* § 62.33, 62.51, 62.53, 66.10, 105.1, 107.106, 108.13, 108.17, 108.34 (1997)
Kurtz & Giannelli, Ohio Juvenile Law (1998 Ed.), Text 12.4
Sowald & Morganstern, Baldwin's Ohio Practice, *Domestic Relations Law* § 3.57, 17.1, 17.13 (1997)

Notes of Decisions and Opinions

Cost of appearance 1

1. Cost of appearance
In child custody proceeding, trial court did not abuse its discretion in denying former wife's motion to require former husband, who commenced the action, to pay necessary expenses of her trip from California to appear in the proceeding. Minton v. McManus (Summit 1983) 9 Ohio App.3d 165, 458 N.E.2d 1292, 9 O.B.R. 231.

3109.30 Parties bound by decrees

(A) A parenting decree rendered by a court of this state that exercises its jurisdiction in conformity with sections 3109.21 to 3109.36 of the Revised Code binds all parties who have been served in this state or notified in accordance with division (B) of section 3109.23 of the Revised Code, or who have submitted to the jurisdiction of the court, and who have been given an opportunity to be heard. As to these parties, the parenting decree is conclusive as to all issues of law and fact decided and as to the parenting determination made, unless and until that determination is modified pursuant to law.

(B) The courts of this state shall recognize and enforce an initial or modification decree of a court of another state if that court assumed jurisdiction under statutory provisions substantially in accordance with sections 3109.21 to 3109.36 of the Revised Code or if the decree was made under factual circumstances meeting the jurisdictional standards of sections 3109.21 to 3109.36 of the Revised Code, so long as the decree has not been modified in accordance with jurisdictional standards substantially similar to those of these sections.

(1990 S 3, eff. 4-11-91; 1977 S 135)

Library References

Divorce ⚷302, 402(1) to 402(8).
Infants ⚷19.3(4).
Parent and Child ⚷2(18).
WESTLAW Topic Nos. 134, 211, 285.
C.J.S. Divorce §§ 641 to 645, 648, 826, 827, 845.
C.J.S. Infants §§ 22 to 25.
C.J.S. Parent and Child §§ 44 to 46, 48.

OJur 3d: 53, Guardian and Ward § 32
Am Jur 2d: 24, Divorce and Separation § 795; 42, Infants § 33 to 41, 56, 57; 59, Parent and Child § 44
Validity, construction, and application of Uniform Child Custody Jurisdiction Act. 96 ALR3d 968
Necessity of requiring presence in court of both parties in proceedings relating to custody or visitation of children. 15 ALR4th 864
What types of proceedings or determinations are governed by the Uniform Child Custody Jurisdiction Act (UCCJA) or the Parental Kidnapping Prevention Act (PKPA). 78 ALR4th 1028
Applicability of Uniform Child Custody Jurisdiction Act (UCCJA) to temporary custody orders. 81 ALR4th 1101
Child custody: when does state that issued previous custody determination have continuing jurisdiction under Uniform Child Custody Jurisdiction Act (UCCJA) or Parental Kidnapping Prevention Act (PKPA), 28 USC § 1738A. 83 ALR4th 742
Significant connection jurisdiction of court under § 3(a)(2) of the Uniform Child Custody Jurisdiction Act (UCCJA) and the Parental Kidnapping Prevention Act (PKPA), 28 USC § 1738A(c)(2)(B). 5 ALR5th 550
Abandonment and emergency jurisdiction of court under § 3(a)(3) of the Uniform Child Custody Jurisdiction Act (UCCJA) and the Parental Kidnapping Prevention Act (PKPA), 28 USC § 1738A(c)(2)(C). 5 ALR5th 788
Home state jurisdiction of court under § 3(a)(1) of the Uniform Child Custody Jurisdiction Act (UCCJA) or the Parental Kidnapping Prevention Act (PKPA), 28 USC § 1738A(c)(2)(A). 6 ALR5th 1
Default jurisdiction of court under § 3(a)(4) of the Uniform Child Custody Jurisdiction Act (UCCJA) or the Parental Kidnapping Prevention Act (PKPA), 28 USC § 1738A(c)(2)(D). 6 ALR5th 69
Parties' misconduct as ground for declining jurisdiction under § 8 of the Uniform Child Custody Jurisdiction Act (UCCJA). 16 ALR5th 650
Carlin, Baldwin's Ohio Practice, *Merrick-Rippner Probate Law* § 62.33, 62.51, 62.53, 66.10, 105.1, 107.106, 108.13, 108.17, 108.34 (1997)

Kurtz & Giannelli, Ohio Juvenile Law (1998 Ed.), Text 12.4

Sowald & Morganstern, Baldwin's Ohio Practice, *Domestic Relations Law* § 17.1, 17.15 (1997)

Notes of Decisions and Opinions

1. Jurisdiction

The presence of a child and one spouse in Illinois is not enough, in and of itself, to give an Illinois court jurisdiction under the Due Process Clause over the other spouse such that an Ohio court is bound by its custody decree. Pasqualone v. Pasqualone (Ohio 1980) 63 Ohio St.2d 96, 406 N.E.2d 1121, 17 O.O.3d 58.

Other than father's self-serving statements that mother had moved to Maryland and only returned to Pennsylvania to file her petition for emergency custody of children, record was devoid of any evidence that Pennsylvania had lost jurisdiction, and thus, trial court properly granted mother's motion to register Pennsylvania order awarding her emergency interim custody, pursuant to Uniform Child Custody Jurisdiction Act (UCCJA). Strothers v. Lambert (Cuyahoga 1996) 113 Ohio App.3d 449, 680 N.E.2d 1326.

2. Enforcement

Under the Uniform Child Custody Jurisdiction Act and the Parental Kidnapping Prevention Act, which both Ohio and Kentucky have adopted, the Ohio juvenile court is required to recognize and enforce a Kentucky custody decree without a hearing as long as Kentucky has proper jurisdiction, which is found if it granted the marriage dissolution and incorporated custody issue, despite a competing custody petition filed in Ohio, especially when the Ohio petitioners have submitted to Kentucky's jurisdiction by becoming parties in that proceeding. In re McClurg (Butler 1992) 78 Ohio App.3d 465, 605 N.E.2d 418, dismissed, jurisdictional motion overruled 64 Ohio St.3d 1429, 594 N.E.2d 971.

The finding by another state court that a child is neglected and dependent is entitled to recognition in Ohio if the requirements of RC 3109.30(B) are met. Squires v. Squires (Preble 1983) 12 Ohio App.3d 138, 468 N.E.2d 73, 12 O.B.R. 460.

In child custody cases, the provisions of RC 3109.30 do not require Ohio courts to recognize the decrees of foreign nations. Minton v. McManus (Summit 1983) 9 Ohio App.3d 165, 458 N.E.2d 1292, 9 O.B.R. 231.

The lower court erred in enforcing a foreign state court's modification order, where neither the child, the custodial parents, nor the natural parents had resided in the foreign state for one year before the modification order. Roth v Hatfield, Nos. 82CA19 to 82CA21 (4th Dist Ct App, Gallia, 12-28-83).

The trial court acted contrary to law when it exercised its jurisdiction to grant a temporary restraining order to a non-custodial parent who was attempting to enjoin the custodial parent from enforcing a valid foreign custody decree, as RC 3109.30(B) required the trial court to recognize and enforce valid decrees of foreign states, and RC 3109.31(A) prevented the trial court from lawfully commencing to exercise its jurisdiction to modify a valid foreign custody decree. In re Heritage, No. C-800683 (1st Dist Ct App, Hamilton, 8-26-81).

3109.31 Modification of decree of another court

(A) If a court of another state has made a parenting decree, a court of this state shall not modify that decree, unless it appears to the court of this state that the court that rendered the decree does not now have jurisdiction under jurisdictional prerequisites substantially in accordance with sections 3109.21 to 3109.36 of the Revised Code, or has declined to assume jurisdiction to modify the decree, and the court of this state has jurisdiction.

(B) If a court of this state is authorized under division (A) of this section and section 3109.26 of the Revised Code to modify a parenting decree of another state, it shall give due consideration to the transcript of the record and other documents of all previous proceedings submitted to it in accordance with division (B) of section 3109.36 of the Revised Code.

(1990 S 3, eff. 4-11-91; 1977 S 135)

Cross References

Divorce, annulment, and legal separation actions; modification of decree allocating parental rights and responsibilities, Civ R 75

Library References

Divorce ⚷402(1) to 402(8).
Infants ⚷19.3(4).
Parent and Child ⚷2(19).
WESTLAW Topic Nos. 134, 211, 285.
C.J.S. Divorce §§ 826, 827, 845.
C.J.S. Infants §§ 22 to 25.
C.J.S. Parent and Child § 43.

OJur 3d: 53, Guardian and Ward § 32

Am Jur 2d: 24, Divorce and Separation § 812 et seq.; 42, Infants § 33 to 41, 57; 59, Parent and Child § 44

Validity, construction, and application of Uniform Child Custody Jurisdiction Act. 96 ALR3d 968

Necessity of requiring presence in court of both parties in proceedings relating to custody or visitation of children. 15 ALR4th 864

What types of proceedings or determinations are governed by the Uniform Child Custody Jurisdiction Act

(UCCJA) or the Parental Kidnapping Prevention Act (PKPA). 78 ALR4th 1028

Applicability of Uniform Child Custody Jurisdiction Act (UCCJA) to temporary custody orders. 81 ALR4th 1101

Child custody: when does state that issued previous custody determination have continuing jurisdiction under Uniform Child Custody Jurisdiction Act (UCCJA) or Parental Kidnapping Prevention Act (PKPA), 28 USC § 1738A. 83 ALR4th 742

Significant connection jurisdiction of court under § 3(a)(2) of the Uniform Child Custody Jurisdiction Act (UCCJA) and the Parental Kidnapping Prevention Act (PKPA), 28 USC § 1738A(c)(2)(B). 5 ALR5th 550

Abandonment and emergency jurisdiction of court under § 3(a)(3) of the Uniform Child Custody Jurisdiction Act (UCCJA) and the Parental Kidnapping Prevention Act (PKPA), 28 USC § 1738A(c)(2)(C). 5 ALR5th 788

Home state jurisdiction of court under § 3(a)(1) of the Uniform Child Custody Jurisdiction Act (UCCJA) or the Parental Kidnapping Prevention Act (PKPA), 28 USC § 1738A(c)(2)(A). 6 ALR5th 1

Default jurisdiction of court under § 3(a)(4) of the Uniform Child Custody Jurisdiction Act (UCCJA) or the Parental Kidnapping Prevention Act (PKPA), 28 USC § 1738A(c)(2)(D). 6 ALR5th 69

Parties' misconduct as ground for declining jurisdiction under § 8 of the Uniform Child Custody Jurisdiction Act (UCCJA). 16 ALR5th 650

Full faith and credit "last-in-time" rules as applicable to sister state divorce or custody judgment which is inconsistent with the forum state's earlier judgment. 36 ALR5th 527

Carlin, Baldwin's Ohio Practice, *Merrick-Rippner Probate Law* § 62.33, 62.51, 62.53, 66.10, 105.1, 107.106, 108.13, 108.17, 108.34 (1997)

Kurtz & Giannelli, Ohio Juvenile Law (1998 Ed.), Text 12.4

Sowald & Morganstern, Baldwin's Ohio Practice, *Domestic Relations Law* § 17.1, 17.8, 17.15 (1997)

Law Review and Journal Commentaries

Child Welfare—Outside the Interstate Compact on the Placement of Children—Placement of a Child with a Natural Parent, McComb v Wambaugh, Comment. 37 Vill L Rev 896 (1992).

Notes of Decisions and Opinions

1. Personal jurisdiction

An Ohio court is not bound by an Illinois custody decree under the Full Faith and Credit Clause of the United States Constitution unless the Illinois court has sufficient jurisdiction over the person of the non-Illinois party under the Due Process Clause. Pasqualone v. Pasqualone (Ohio 1980) 63 Ohio St.2d 96, 406 N.E.2d 1121, 17 O.O.3d 58.

The presence of a child and one spouse in Illinois is not enough, in and of itself, to give an Illinois court jurisdiction under the Due Process Clause over the other spouse such that an Ohio court is bound by its custody decree. Pasqualone v. Pasqualone (Ohio 1980) 63 Ohio St.2d 96, 406 N.E.2d 1121, 17 O.O.3d 58.

2. Subject matter jurisdiction

Ohio domestic relations court did not have jurisdiction under Uniform Child Custody Jurisdiction Act (UCCJA) to modify Virginia child custody order, where Ohio was not child's home state, child was not physically present in state, it was not in child's best interests to invoke jurisdiction in Ohio, and Virginia had jurisdiction to enforce divorce degree and custody order and had not declined jurisdiction to modify such judgments. Kachele v. Kachele (Ohio App. 8 Dist. 1996) 115 Ohio App.3d 609, 685 N.E.2d 1283.

Common pleas court lacked jurisdiction to hear custody complaint filed by children's grandparents, since father was still resident of Utah, and thus Utah court which had awarded custody to children's father had continuing jurisdiction over children's custody under Uniform Child Custody Jurisdiction Act (UCCJA). Boehn v. Shurtliff (Huron 1993) 90 Ohio App.3d 363, 629 N.E.2d 478.

Court's decision regarding subject matter jurisdiction under Uniform Child Custody Jurisdiction Act (UCCJA) should only be made after plenary hearing and full explanation of facts essential to decision. Bowen v. Britton (Pike 1993) 84 Ohio App.3d 473, 616 N.E.2d 1217.

Failure to hold evidentiary hearing on father's complaint requesting modification of foreign state divorce decree, so as to change custody of three of parties' four minor children, on ground that trial court lacked subject matter jurisdiction over custody issue, was abuse of discretion; trial court should afford parties opportunity to have full evidentiary hearing prior to deciding whether to assume jurisdiction under Uniform Child Custody Jurisdiction Act (UCCJA) provisions over motion to modify custody decree entered in another state. Bowen v. Britton (Pike 1993) 84 Ohio App.3d 473, 616 N.E.2d 1217.

It is within trial court's discretion to assume jurisdiction in change of custody proceeding pursuant to Uniform Child Custody Jurisdiction Act (UCCJA), and thus trial court's decision as to whether to exercise jurisdiction pursuant to UCCJA should only be reversed upon showing of abuse of discretion; "abuse of discretion" connotes more than error of law or judgment, and implies that court's attitude is unreasonable, arbitrary, or unconscionable. Bowen v. Britton (Pike 1993) 84 Ohio App.3d 473, 616 N.E.2d 1217.

Ohio courts did not lack subject matter jurisdiction to modify child custody which had been awarded pursuant to divorce decree entered by Ohio court, even though child and both her parents had left Ohio; Parental Kidnapping Prevention Act (PKPA) did not preempt Ohio's version of Uniform Child Custody Jurisdiction Act (UCCJA), since Utah, which was state to which mother and child had moved, declined to exercise jurisdiction in deference to Ohio's exercise of jurisdiction. Holm v. Smilowitz (Athens 1992) 83 Ohio App.3d 757, 615 N.E.2d 1047.

The trial court acted contrary to law when it exercised its jurisdiction to grant a temporary restraining order to a non-custodial parent who was attempting to enjoin the custodial parent from enforcing a valid foreign custody decree, as RC 3109.30(B) required the trial court to recognize and enforce valid decrees of foreign states, and RC 3109.31(A) prevented the trial court from lawfully commencing to exercise its jurisdiction to modify a valid foreign custody decree. In re Heritage, No. C-800683 (1st Dist Ct App, Hamilton, 8-26-81).

3. Jurisdiction proper in Ohio

Mere presence of prior custody decree entered by another state does not per se preclude Ohio court from subsequently exercising jurisdiction over motion to modify foreign custody decree, especially where neither parents nor children have resided in foreign state for several years. Bowen v. Britton (Pike 1993) 84 Ohio App.3d 473, 616 N.E.2d 1217.

Where a child has been residing and attending school in Ohio and both she and the custodial parent have been receiving counseling from Ohio mental health services, it is in the child's best interests that litigation concerning her custody occur in Ohio; thus, Ohio courts have jurisdiction over the custody action, even though the original custody order was made by a Kentucky court. In re Reynolds (Hamilton 1982) 2 Ohio App.3d 309, 441 N.E.2d 1141, 2 O.B.R. 341.

An Ohio court has authority to modify a New Jersey court decree as to visitation with children residing in Ohio even where the decree lacks sufficient finality to entitle it to full faith and credit as to child support and alimony. Auberry v Auberry, No. 13966 (9th Dist Ct App, Summit, 2-15-89).

4. Federal jurisdiction

The Parental Kidnaping Prevention Act of 1980, 28 USC 1738A, establishes no private right of action in federal court to resolve a conflict between custody decrees of two courts in different states. Thompson v. Thompson (U.S.Cal. 1988) 108 S.Ct. 513, 484 U.S. 174, 98 L.Ed.2d 512.

3109.32 Filing decree from another state

(A) A certified copy of a parenting decree of another state may be filed in the office of the clerk of any court of this state that renders parenting decrees. The clerk shall treat the decree in the same manner as a parenting decree of an appropriate court of this state. Until modified, a parenting decree so filed has the same effect and shall be enforced in like manner as a parenting decree rendered by a court of this state.

(B) A person violating a parenting decree of another state which makes it necessary to enforce the decree in this state may be required to pay necessary travel and other expenses, including attorney's fees, incurred by the parent who is designated the residential parent and legal custodian or his witnesses or by any other party entitled to the custody or his witnesses.

(1990 S 3, eff. 4-11-91; 1977 S 135)

Library References

Divorce ⚷402(1) to 402(8).
Infants ⚷19.3(4).
Parent and Child ⚷2(19).
WESTLAW Topic Nos. 134, 211, 285.
C.J.S. Divorce §§ 826, 827, 845.
C.J.S. Infants §§ 22 to 25.
C.J.S. Parent and Child § 43.

OJur 3d: 53, Guardian and Ward § 32
Am Jur 2d: 42, Infants § 33 to 41
Validity, construction, and application of Uniform Child Custody Jurisdiction Act. 96 ALR3d 968
Necessity of requiring presence in court of both parties in proceedings relating to custody or visitation of children. 15 ALR4th 864
What types of proceedings or determinations are governed by the Uniform Child Custody Jurisdiction Act (UCCJA) or the Parental Kidnapping Prevention Act (PKPA). 78 ALR4th 1028
Applicability of Uniform Child Custody Jurisdiction Act (UCCJA) to temporary custody orders. 81 ALR4th 1101
Child custody: when does state that issued previous custody determination have continuing jurisdiction under Uniform Child Custody Jurisdiction Act (UCCJA) or Parental Kidnapping Prevention Act (PKPA), 28 USC § 1738A. 83 ALR4th 742
Significant connection jurisdiction of court under § 3(a)(2) of the Uniform Child Custody Jurisdiction Act (UCCJA) and the Parental Kidnapping Prevention Act (PKPA), 28 USC § 1738A(c)(2)(B). 5 ALR5th 550
Abandonment and emergency jurisdiction of court under § 3(a)(3) of the Uniform Child Custody Jurisdiction Act (UCCJA) and the Parental Kidnapping Prevention Act (PKPA), 28 USC § 1738A(c)(2)(C). 5 ALR5th 788
Home state jurisdiction of court under § 3(a)(1) of the Uniform Child Custody Jurisdiction Act (UCCJA) or the Parental Kidnapping Prevention Act (PKPA), 28 USC § 1738A(c)(2)(A). 6 ALR5th 1
Default jurisdiction of court under § 3(a)(4) of the Uniform Child Custody Jurisdiction Act (UCCJA) or the Parental Kidnapping Prevention Act (PKPA), 28 USC § 1738A(c)(2)(D). 6 ALR5th 69
Parties' misconduct as ground for declining jurisdiction under § 8 of the Uniform Child Custody Jurisdiction Act (UCCJA). 16 ALR5th 650

Carlin, Baldwin's Ohio Practice, *Merrick-Rippner Probate Law* § 62.33, 62.51, 62.53, 66.10, 105.1, 107.106, 108.13, 108.17, 108.34 (1997)
Kurtz & Giannelli, Ohio Juvenile Law (1998 Ed.), Text 12.4
Sowald & Morganstern, Baldwin's Ohio Practice, *Domestic Relations Law* § 17.1, 17.2, 17.8, 17.15, 17.16, 25.82 (1997)

Whiteside, Ohio Appellate Practice (2000 Ed.), Text 10.36

Notes of Decisions and Opinions

Habeas corpus 1

1. Habeas corpus

In an action to enforce an out-of-state custody decree it is error for the court to grant a writ of habeas corpus sought in conjunction with or as a substitute for a statutory remedy and discretionary appeal. Luchene v. Wagner (Ohio 1984) 12 Ohio St.3d 37, 465 N.E.2d 395, 12 O.B.R. 32.

3109.33 Registry of parenting and custody documents

(A) The clerk of each court that renders a parenting decree shall maintain a parenting and custody registry in which he shall enter the following:

(1) Certified copies of parenting decrees of other states received for filing;

(2) Communications as to the pendency of parenting proceedings in other states;

(3) Communications concerning a finding of inconvenient forum by a court of another state;

(4) Other communications or documents concerning parenting proceedings in another state that may affect the jurisdiction of a court of this state or the disposition to be made by it in a parenting proceeding.

(B) A clerk who maintains a registry under division (A) of this section, at the request of the court of another state or at the request of any person who is affected by or has a legitimate interest in a parenting decree, shall certify and forward a copy of the decree to that court or person.

(1990 S 3, eff. 4-11-91; 1977 S 135)

Cross References

Juvenile court, clerk of courts, 2151.12

Library References

Records ⟹32.
WESTLAW Topic No. 326.
C.J.S. Records §§ 65, 67 to 75.

OJur 3d: 53, Guardian and Ward § 32
Am Jur 2d: 42, Infants § 33 to 41
Validity, construction, and application of Uniform Child Custody Jurisdiction Act. 96 ALR3d 968
Necessity of requiring presence in court of both parties in proceedings relating to custody or visitation of children. 15 ALR4th 864
What types of proceedings or determinations are governed by the Uniform Child Custody Jurisdiction Act (UCCJA) or the Parental Kidnapping Prevention Act (PKPA). 78 ALR4th 1028
Applicability of Uniform Child Custody Jurisdiction Act (UCCJA) to temporary custody orders. 81 ALR4th 1101
Child custody: when does state that issued previous custody determination have continuing jurisdiction under Uniform Child Custody Jurisdiction Act (UCCJA) or Parental Kidnapping Prevention Act (PKPA), 28 USC § 1738A. 83 ALR4th 742
Significant connection jurisdiction of court under § 3(a)(2) of the Uniform Child Custody Jurisdiction Act (UCCJA) and the Parental Kidnapping Prevention Act (PKPA), 28 USC § 1738A(c)(2)(B). 5 ALR5th 550
Abandonment and emergency jurisdiction of court under § 3(a)(3) of the Uniform Child Custody Jurisdiction Act (UCCJA) and the Parental Kidnapping Prevention Act (PKPA), 28 USC § 1738A(c)(2)(C). 5 ALR5th 788
Home state jurisdiction of court under § 3(a)(1) of the Uniform Child Custody Jurisdiction Act (UCCJA) or the Parental Kidnapping Prevention Act (PKPA), 28 USC § 1738A(c)(2)(A). 6 ALR5th 1
Default jurisdiction of court under § 3(a)(4) of the Uniform Child Custody Jurisdiction Act (UCCJA) or the Parental Kidnapping Prevention Act (PKPA), 28 USC § 1738A(c)(2)(D). 6 ALR5th 69
Parties' misconduct as ground for declining jurisdiction under § 8 of the Uniform Child Custody Jurisdiction Act (UCCJA). 16 ALR5th 650

Carlin, Baldwin's Ohio Practice, *Merrick-Rippner Probate Law* § 62.33, 62.51, 62.53, 66.10, 105.1, 107.106, 108.13, 108.17, 108.34 (1997)

Kurtz & Giannelli, Ohio Juvenile Law (1998 Ed.), Text 12.4

Sowald & Morganstern, Baldwin's Ohio Practice, *Domestic Relations Law* § 17.1, 17.10, 17.13, 17.14, 17.15 (1997)

3109.34 Ancillary proceedings in other state

(A) A court of this state may request the appropriate court of another state to hold a hearing to adduce evidence, to order a party to produce or give evidence under other procedures of that state, or to have social studies made with respect to the allocation of parental rights and responsibilities for the care of a child involved in parenting proceedings pending in the court of this state, with respect to the designation of a parent as the residential parent and legal custodian of the child, and with respect to the custody of the child in any other person, and to forward to the court of this state certified copies of the transcript of the record of the hearing, the evidence otherwise adduced, or any social studies prepared in compliance with the request. The cost of the services may be assessed against the parties or, if necessary, paid from the county treasury and taxed as costs in the case.

(B) A court of this state may request the appropriate court of another state to order a party to parenting proceedings pending in the court of this state to appear in the proceedings, and if that party has physical custody of the child, to appear with the child. The request may state that travel and other necessary expenses of the party and of the child whose appearance is desired will be assessed against another party or will otherwise be paid.

In addition to other procedural devices available to a party, any party to a parenting proceeding or a guardian ad litem or other representative of the child may adduce testimony of witnesses, including parties and the child, by deposition or otherwise, in another state. The court on its own motion may direct that the testimony of a person be taken in another state and may prescribe the manner in which and the terms upon which the testimony shall be taken.

(1990 S 3, eff. 4-11-91; 1977 S 135)

Library References

Divorce ⚷289, 290.
Infants ⚷18.
Parent and Child ⚷2(5).
WESTLAW Topic Nos. 134, 211, 285.
C.J.S. Divorce §§ 611, 612.
C.J.S. Infants §§ 5 to 7, 10, 12, 17.
C.J.S. Parent and Child § 32.

OJur 3d: 53, Guardian and Ward § 32
Am Jur 2d: 42, Infants § 33 to 41
Validity, construction, and application of Uniform Child Custody Jurisdiction Act. 96 ALR3d 968
Necessity of requiring presence in court of both parties in proceedings relating to custody or visitation of children. 15 ALR4th 864
What types of proceedings or determinations are governed by the Uniform Child Custody Jurisdiction Act (UCCJA) or the Parental Kidnapping Prevention Act (PKPA). 78 ALR4th 1028
Applicability of Uniform Child Custody Jurisdiction Act (UCCJA) to temporary custody orders. 81 ALR4th 1101
Child custody: when does state that issued previous custody determination have continuing jurisdiction under Uniform Child Custody Jurisdiction Act (UCCJA) or Parental Kidnapping Prevention Act (PKPA), 28 USC § 1738A. 83 ALR4th 742
Significant connection jurisdiction of court under § 3(a)(2) of the Uniform Child Custody Jurisdiction Act (UCCJA) and the Parental Kidnapping Prevention Act (PKPA), 28 USC § 1738A(c)(2)(B). 5 ALR5th 550
Abandonment and emergency jurisdiction of court under § 3(a)(3) of the Uniform Child Custody Jurisdiction Act (UCCJA) and the Parental Kidnapping Prevention Act (PKPA), 28 USC § 1738A(c)(2)(C). 5 ALR5th 788
Home state jurisdiction of court under § 3(a)(1) of the Uniform Child Custody Jurisdiction Act (UCCJA) or the Parental Kidnapping Prevention Act (PKPA), 28 USC § 1738A(c)(2)(A). 6 ALR5th 1
Default jurisdiction of court under § 3(a)(4) of the Uniform Child Custody Jurisdiction Act (UCCJA) or the Parental Kidnapping Prevention Act (PKPA), 28 USC § 1738A(c)(2)(D). 6 ALR5th 69
Parties' misconduct as ground for declining jurisdiction under § 8 of the Uniform Child Custody Jurisdiction Act (UCCJA). 16 ALR5th 650

Carlin, Baldwin's Ohio Practice, *Merrick-Rippner Probate Law* § 62.33, 62.51, 62.53, 66.10, 105.1, 107.106, 108.13, 108.17, 108.34 (1997)

Kurtz & Giannelli, Ohio Juvenile Law (1998 Ed.), Text 12.4

Sowald & Morganstern, Baldwin's Ohio Practice, *Domestic Relations Law* § 17.1, 17.14 (1997)

Law Review and Journal Commentaries

Child Welfare—Outside the Interstate Compact on the Placement of Children—Placement of a Child with a Natural Parent, McComb v Wambaugh, Comment. 37 Vill L Rev 896 (1992).

Notes of Decisions and Opinions

Habeas corpus 1

1. Habeas corpus

A writ of habeas corpus will not issue on the request of an Ohio parent granted custody of children who were removed to a foreign state by their grandmother; absent extraordinary circumstances RC 3109.34(B) is the proper remedy. In re Davis (Ohio 1985) 18 Ohio St.3d 226, 480 N.E.2d 775, 18 O.B.R. 285.

3109.35 Ancillary proceedings in this state for courts of other state

(A) Upon request of the court of another state, the courts of this state that render parenting decrees may order a person in this state to appear at a hearing to adduce evidence or to produce or give evidence under other procedures available in this state or may order social studies to be made for use in a parenting proceeding in another state. A certified copy of the transcript of the record of the hearing or the evidence otherwise adduced and any social studies prepared shall be forwarded by the clerk of the court to the requesting court.

(B) A person within this state may voluntarily give his testimony or statement in this state for use in a parenting proceeding outside this state.

(C) Upon request of the court of another state, a court of this state may order a person in this state to appear alone or with the child in a parenting proceeding in another state. The court may condition compliance with the request upon assurance by the other state that travel and other necessary expenses will be advanced or reimbursed.

(1990 S 3, eff. 4-11-91; 1977 S 135)

Library References

Divorce ⟹289, 290.
Infants ⟹18.
Parent and Child ⟹2(5).
WESTLAW Topic Nos. 134, 211, 285.
C.J.S. Divorce §§ 611, 612.
C.J.S. Infants §§ 5 to 7, 10, 12, 17.
C.J.S. Parent and Child § 32.

OJur 3d: 53, Guardian and Ward § 32
Am Jur 2d: 42, Infants § 33 to 41
Validity, construction, and application of Uniform Child Custody Jurisdiction Act. 96 ALR3d 968
Necessity of requiring presence in court of both parties in proceedings relating to custody or visitation of children. 15 ALR4th 864
What types of proceedings or determinations are governed by the Uniform Child Custody Jurisdiction Act (UCCJA) or the Parental Kidnapping Prevention Act (PKPA). 78 ALR4th 1028
Applicability of Uniform Child Custody Jurisdiction Act (UCCJA) to temporary custody orders. 81 ALR4th 1101
Child custody: when does state that issued previous custody determination have continuing jurisdiction under Uniform Child Custody Jurisdiction Act (UCCJA) or Parental Kidnapping Prevention Act (PKPA), 28 USC § 1738A. 83 ALR4th 742
Significant connection jurisdiction of court under § 3(a)(2) of the Uniform Child Custody Jurisdiction Act (UCCJA) and the Parental Kidnapping Prevention Act (PKPA), 28 USC § 1738A(c)(2)(B). 5 ALR5th 550
Abandonment and emergency jurisdiction of court under § 3(a)(3) of the Uniform Child Custody Jurisdiction Act (UCCJA) and the Parental Kidnapping Prevention Act (PKPA), 28 USC § 1738A(c)(2)(C). 5 ALR5th 788
Home state jurisdiction of court under § 3(a)(1) of the Uniform Child Custody Jurisdiction Act (UCCJA) or the Parental Kidnapping Prevention Act (PKPA), 28 USC § 1738A(c)(2)(A). 6 ALR5th 1
Default jurisdiction of court under § 3(a)(4) of the Uniform Child Custody Jurisdiction Act (UCCJA) or the Parental Kidnapping Prevention Act (PKPA), 28 USC § 1738A(c)(2)(D). 6 ALR5th 69
Parties' misconduct as ground for declining jurisdiction under § 8 of the Uniform Child Custody Jurisdiction Act (UCCJA). 16 ALR5th 650

Carlin, Baldwin's Ohio Practice, *Merrick-Rippner Probate Law* § 62.33, 62.51, 62.53, 66.10, 105.1, 107.106, 108.13, 108.17, 108.34 (1997)

Kurtz & Giannelli, Ohio Juvenile Law (1998 Ed.), Text 12.4

Sowald & Morganstern, Baldwin's Ohio Practice, *Domestic Relations Law* § 17.14 (1997)

Law Review and Journal Commentaries

Child Welfare—Outside the Interstate Compact on the Placement of Children—Placement of a Child with a Natural Parent, McComb v Wambaugh, Comment. 37 Vill L Rev 896 (1992).

3109.36 Preservation and certification of records

(A) In any parenting proceeding in this state, the court shall preserve the pleadings, orders and decrees, any record that has been made of its hearings, social studies, and other pertinent documents until the child reaches eighteen years of age. Upon appropriate request of the court of another state, the court shall forward to the other court certified copies of any or all of such documents.

(B) If a parenting decree has been rendered in another state concerning a child involved in a parenting proceeding pending in a court of this state, the court of this state upon taking jurisdiction of the case shall request of the court of the other state a certified copy of the transcript of any court record and other documents mentioned in division (A) of this section.

(1990 S 3, eff. 4-11-91; 1977 S 135)

Library References

Records ⚿32.
WESTLAW Topic No. 326.
C.J.S. Records §§ 65, 67 to 75.

OJur 3d: 53, Guardian and Ward § 32
Am Jur 2d: 42, Infants § 33 to 41
Validity, construction, and application of Uniform Child Custody Jurisdiction Act. 96 ALR3d 968
Necessity of requiring presence in court of both parties in proceedings relating to custody or visitation of children. 15 ALR4th 864
What types of proceedings or determinations are governed by the Uniform Child Custody Jurisdiction Act (UCCJA) or the Parental Kidnapping Prevention Act (PKPA). 78 ALR4th 1028
Applicability of Uniform Child Custody Jurisdiction Act (UCCJA) to temporary custody orders. 81 ALR4th 1101
Child custody: when does state that issued previous custody determination have continuing jurisdiction under Uniform Child Custody Jurisdiction Act (UCCJA) or Parental Kidnapping Prevention Act (PKPA), 28 USC § 1738A. 83 ALR4th 742
Significant connection jurisdiction of court under § 3(a)(2) of the Uniform Child Custody Jurisdiction Act (UCCJA) and the Parental Kidnapping Prevention Act (PKPA), 28 USC § 1738A(c)(2)(B). 5 ALR5th 550
Abandonment and emergency jurisdiction of court under § 3(a)(3) of the Uniform Child Custody Jurisdiction Act (UCCJA) and the Parental Kidnapping Prevention Act (PKPA), 28 USC § 1738A(c)(2)(C). 5 ALR5th 788
Home state jurisdiction of court under § 3(a)(1) of the Uniform Child Custody Jurisdiction Act (UCCJA) or the Parental Kidnapping Prevention Act (PKPA), 28 USC § 1738A(c)(2)(A). 6 ALR5th 1
Default jurisdiction of court under § 3(a)(4) of the Uniform Child Custody Jurisdiction Act (UCCJA) or the Parental Kidnapping Prevention Act (PKPA), 28 USC § 1738A(c)(2)(D). 6 ALR5th 69
Parties' misconduct as ground for declining jurisdiction under § 8 of the Uniform Child Custody Jurisdiction Act (UCCJA). 16 ALR5th 650

Carlin, Baldwin's Ohio Practice, *Merrick-Rippner Probate Law* § 62.33, 62.51, 62.53, 66.10, 105.1, 107.106, 108.13, 108.17, 108.34 (1997)
Kurtz & Giannelli, Ohio Juvenile Law (1998 Ed.), Text 12.4
Sowald & Morganstern, Baldwin's Ohio Practice, *Domestic Relations Law* § 16.1, 17.14 (1997)

3109.37 Priority of handling of jurisdictional challenge

Upon the request of a party to a parenting proceeding which raises a question of existence or exercise of jurisdiction under sections 3109.21 to 3109.36 of the Revised Code, the case shall be given calendar priority and handled expeditiously.

(1990 S 3, eff. 4-11-91; 1977 S 135)

Library References

OJur 3d: 53, Guardian and Ward § 32
Am Jur 2d: 42, Infants § 33 to 41
Validity, construction, and application of Uniform Child Custody Jurisdiction Act. 96 ALR3d 968
Necessity of requiring presence in court of both parties in proceedings relating to custody or visitation of children. 15 ALR4th 864
What types of proceedings or determinations are governed by the Uniform Child Custody Jurisdiction Act (UCCJA) or the Parental Kidnapping Prevention Act (PKPA). 78 ALR4th 1028
Applicability of Uniform Child Custody Jurisdiction Act (UCCJA) to temporary custody orders. 81 ALR4th 1101
Child custody: when does state that issued previous custody determination have continuing jurisdiction under Uniform Child Custody Jurisdiction Act (UCCJA) or Parental Kidnapping Prevention Act (PKPA), 28 USC § 1738A. 83 ALR4th 742
Significant connection jurisdiction of court under § 3(a)(2) of the Uniform Child Custody Jurisdiction Act (UCCJA) and the Parental Kidnapping Prevention Act (PKPA), 28 USC § 1738A(c)(2)(B). 5 ALR5th 550
Abandonment and emergency jurisdiction of court under § 3(a)(3) of the Uniform Child Custody Jurisdiction Act (UCCJA) and the Parental Kidnapping Prevention Act (PKPA), 28 USC § 1738A(c)(2)(C). 5 ALR5th 788
Home state jurisdiction of court under § 3(a)(1) of the Uniform Child Custody Jurisdiction Act (UCCJA) or the Parental Kidnapping Prevention Act (PKPA), 28 USC § 1738A(c)(2)(A). 6 ALR5th 1
Default jurisdiction of court under § 3(a)(4) of the Uniform Child Custody Jurisdiction Act (UCCJA) or the

Parental Kidnapping Prevention Act (PKPA), 28 USC § 1738A(c)(2)(D). 6 ALR5th 69
Parties' misconduct as ground for declining jurisdiction under § 8 of the Uniform Child Custody Jurisdiction Act (UCCJA). 16 ALR5th 650

Carlin, Baldwin's Ohio Practice, *Merrick-Rippner Probate Law* § 62.33, 62.51, 62.53, 66.10, 105.1, 107.106, 108.13, 108.17, 108.34 (1997)

Notes of Decisions and Opinions

Enforcement 2
Guardianship 1
Modification 3

1. Guardianship

The Uniform Child Custody Jurisdiction Act, as adopted in Ohio, is applicable to and must be complied with in a guardianship termination proceeding. In re Wonderly's Guardianship (Ohio 1981) 67 Ohio St.2d 178, 423 N.E.2d 420, 21 O.O.3d 111.

2. Enforcement

An Ohio juvenile court may not assume original jurisdiction if custody has been finally adjudicated in another state, and no request for decree modification has been made since the authority to enforce is different from the authority to modify, and the juvenile court is required to determine the enforcement issue under the applicable law and not conduct a hearing to expand its decision to include modification. In re McClurg (Butler 1992) 78 Ohio App.3d 465, 605 N.E.2d 418, dismissed, jurisdictional motion overruled 64 Ohio St.3d 1429, 594 N.E.2d 971.

3. Modification

Failure to hold evidentiary hearing on father's complaint requesting modification of foreign state divorce decree, so as to change custody of three of parties' four minor children, on ground that trial court lacked subject matter jurisdiction over custody issue, was abuse of discretion; trial court should afford parties opportunity to have full evidentiary hearing prior to deciding whether to assume jurisdiction under Uniform Child Custody Jurisdiction Act (UCCJA) provisions over motion to modify custody decree entered in another state. Bowen v. Britton (Pike 1993) 84 Ohio App.3d 473, 616 N.E.2d 1217.

Court's decision regarding subject matter jurisdiction under Uniform Child Custody Jurisdiction Act (UCCJA) should only be made after plenary hearing and full explanation of facts essential to decision. Bowen v. Britton (Pike 1993) 84 Ohio App.3d 473, 616 N.E.2d 1217.

It is within trial court's discretion to assume jurisdiction in change of custody proceeding pursuant to Uniform Child Custody Jurisdiction Act (UCCJA), and thus trial court's decision as to whether to exercise jurisdiction pursuant to UCCJA should only be reversed upon showing of abuse of discretion; "abuse of discretion" connotes more than error of law or judgment, and implies that court's attitude is unreasonable, arbitrary, or unconscionable. Bowen v. Britton (Pike 1993) 84 Ohio App.3d 473, 616 N.E.2d 1217.

TASK FORCE ON FAMILY LAW AND CHILDREN

3109.401 Task force on family law and children; creation

(A) The general assembly finds the following:

(1) That the parent and child relationship is of fundamental importance to the welfare of a child, and that the relationship between a child and each parent should be fostered unless inconsistent with the child's best interests;

(2) That parents have the responsibility to make decisions and perform other parenting functions necessary for the care and growth of their children;

(3) That the courts, when allocating parenting functions and responsibilities with respect to the child in a divorce, dissolution, legal separation, annulment, or any other proceeding addressing the allocation of parental rights and responsibilities, must determine the child's best interests;

(4) That the courts and parents must take into consideration the following general principles when allocating parental rights and responsibilities and developing appropriate terms for parenting plans:

(a) Children are served by a parenting arrangement that best provides for a child's safety, emotional growth, health, stability, and physical care.

(b) Exposure of the child to harmful parental conflict should be minimized as much as possible.

(c) Whenever appropriate, parents should be encouraged to meet their responsibilities to their children through agreements rather than by relying on judicial intervention.

(d) When a parenting plan provides for mutual decision-making responsibility by the parents but they are unable to make decisions mutually, they should make a good faith effort to utilize the mediation process as required by the parenting plan.

(e) In apportioning between the parents the daily physical living arrangements of the child and the child's location during legal and school holidays, vacations, and days of special importance, a court should not impose any type of standard schedule unless a standard schedule meets the needs of the child better than any proposed alternative parenting plan.

(B) It is, therefore, the purpose of Chapter 3109. of the Revised Code, when it is in the child's best interest, to foster the relationship between the child and each parent when a court allocates parental rights and responsibilities with respect to the child in a divorce, dissolution, legal separation, annulment, or any other proceeding addressing the allocation of parental rights and responsibilities.

(C) There is hereby created the task force on family law and children consisting of twenty-four members. The Ohio state bar association shall appoint three members who shall be attorneys with extensive experience in the practice of family law. The Ohio association of domestic relations judges shall appoint three members who shall be domestic relations judges. The Ohio association of juvenile and family court judges shall appoint three members who shall be juvenile or family court judges. The chief justice of the supreme court shall appoint eight members, three of whom shall be persons who practice in the field of family law mediation, two of whom shall be persons who practice in the field of child psychology, one of whom shall be a person who represents parent and child advocacy organizations, one of whom shall be a person who provides parenting education services, and one of whom shall be a magistrate employed by a domestic relations or juvenile court. The speaker of the house of representatives shall appoint two members who shall be members of the house of representatives and who shall be from different political parties. The president of the senate shall appoint two members who shall be members of the senate and who shall be from different political parties. The governor shall appoint two members who shall represent child caring agencies. One member shall be the director of job and family services or the director's designee. The chief justice shall designate one member of the task force to chair the task force.

The appointing authorities and persons shall make appointments to the task force on family law and children within thirty days after September 1, 1998. Section 101.84 of the Revised Code does not apply to the task force.

(D) The task force on family law and children shall do all of the following:

(1) Appoint and fix the compensation of any technical, professional, and clerical employees and perform any services that are necessary to carry out the powers and duties of the task force on family law and children. All employees of the task force shall serve at the pleasure of the task force.

(2) By July 1, 2001, submit to the speaker and minority leader of the house of representatives and to the president and the minority leader of the senate a report of its findings and recommendations on how to create a more civilized and constructive process for the parenting of children whose parents do not reside together. The recommendations shall propose a system to do all of the following:

(a) Put children first;

(b) Provide families with choices before they make a decision to obtain or finalize a divorce, dissolution, legal separation, or annulment;

(c) Redirect human services to intervention and prevention, rather than supporting the casualties of the current process;

(d) Avoid needless conflict between the participants;

(e) Encourage problem solving among the participants;

(f) Force the participants to act responsibly;

(g) Shield both the participants and their children from lasting emotional damage.

(3) Gather information on and study the current state of family law in this state;

(4) Collaborate and consult with entities engaged in family and children's issues including, but not limited to, the Ohio association of child caring agencies, the Ohio family court feasibility study, and the Ohio courts futures commission;

(5) Utilize findings and outcomes from pilot projects conducted by the Ohio family court feasibility study to explore alternatives in creating a more civilized and constructive process for the parenting of children whose parents do not reside together with an emphasis on the areas of mediation and obtaining visitation compliance.

(E) Courts of common pleas shall cooperate with the task force on family law and children in the performance of the task force's duties described in division (D) of this section.

(1999 H 471, eff. 7-1-00; 2000 S 245, eff. 3-30-00; 1998 H 770, eff. 6-17-98; 1998 S 112, eff. 9-1-98)

Uncodified Law

2000 S 245, § 89, eff. 6-30-00, reads, in part:

Sections 169.02, 329.07, 3109.401, 3314.08, 5101.325, 5107.05, 5107.161, 5107.162, and 5111.23 of the Revised Code are amended by this act and also by H.B. 471 of the 123rd General Assembly effective July 1, 2000. The amendments of H.B. 471 are included in this act to confirm the intention to retain them, but they are not intended to be effective until July 1, 2000.

Historical and Statutory Notes

Amendment Note: 1999 H 471 substituted "job and family" for "human" in the first paragraph in division (C).

Amendment Note: 2000 S 245 substituted "September 1, 1998" for "the effective date of this section" in the second paragraph in division (C) and "July 1, 2001" for "December 31, 1999" in division (D)(2).

Amendment Note: 1998 H 770 rewrote the second paragraph in division (C); and made other nonsubstantive changes. Prior to amendment, the second paragraph in division (C) read:

"The appointing authorities and persons shall make initial appointments to the task force on family law and children within thirty days after the effective date of this section. Initial appointments to the task force shall be for terms ending July 1, 1999. Thereafter, terms of office shall be for two years, with each term ending on the first day of July of the following odd-numbered year. Members who are members of the general assembly shall hold office until the end of the term for which the member was appointed or until the person ceases to be a member of the general assembly, whichever occurs first. The director of human services shall hold office until the director ceases to be director of human services. Each member shall hold office from the date of the person's appointment until the end of the term for which the member was appointed. Members may be reappointed. Vacancies shall be filled in the manner provided for original appointments. Any member appointed to fill a vacancy occurring prior to the expiration date of the term for which the member's predecessor was appointed shall hold office as a member for the remainder of that term. A member shall continue in office subsequent to the expiration date of the member's term until the member's successor takes office or until a period of sixty days has elapsed, whichever occurs first. Section 101.84 of the Revised Code does not apply to the task force."

Library References

OJur 3d: 47, Family Law § 814 et seq., 1018 et seq.

PARENT CONVICTED OF KILLING OTHER PARENT

3109.41 Definitions

As used in sections 3109.41 to 3109.48 of the Revised Code:

(A) A person is "convicted of killing" if the person has been convicted of or pleaded guilty to a violation of section 2903.01, 2903.02, or 2903.03 of the Revised Code.

(B) "Custody order" means an order designating a person as the residential parent and legal custodian of a child under section 3109.04 of the Revised Code or any order determining custody of a child under section 2151.23, 2151.33, 2151.353, 2151.354, 2151.355, 2151.356, 2151.415, 2151.417, or 3113.31 of the Revised Code.

(C) "Visitation order" means an order issued under division (B)(1)(c) of section 2151.33 or under section 2151.412, 3109.051, 3109.12, or 3113.31 of the Revised Code.

(1999 H 191, eff. 10-20-99)

3109.42 Unavailability of custody for parent convicted of killing other parent

Except as provided in section 3109.47 of the Revised Code, if a parent is convicted of killing the other parent of a child, no court shall issue a custody order designating the parent as the residential parent and legal custodian of the child or granting custody of the child to the parent.

(1999 H 191, eff. 10-20-99)

3109.43 Unavailability of visitation rights for parent convicted of killing other parent

Except as provided in section 3109.47 of the Revised Code, if a parent is convicted of killing the other parent of a child, no court shall issue a visitation order granting the parent visitation rights with the child.

(1999 H 191, eff. 10-20-99)

3109.44 Notice of conviction

Upon receipt of notice that a visitation order is pending or has been issued granting a parent visitation rights with a child or a custody order is pending or has been issued designating a parent as the residential parent and legal custodian of a child or granting custody of a child to a parent prior to that parent being convicted of killing the other parent of the child, the court in which the parent is convicted of killing the other parent shall immediately notify the court that issued the visitation or custody order of the conviction.

(1999 H 191, eff. 10-20-99)

3109.45 Termination of visitation order upon receipt of notice of conviction

On receipt of notice under section 3109.44 of the Revised Code, a court that issued a visitation order described in that section shall terminate the order.

(1999 H 191, eff. 10-20-99)

3109.46 Termination of custody order upon receipt of notice of conviction; deemed new complaint for custody

If the court to which notice is sent under section 3109.44 of the Revised Code is a juvenile court that issued a custody order described in that section, the court shall retain jurisdiction over the order. If the court to which notice is sent is not a juvenile court but the court issued a custody order described in that section, the court shall transfer jurisdiction over the custody order to the juvenile court of the county in which the child has a residence or legal settlement.

On receipt of the notice in cases in which the custody order was issued by a juvenile court or after jurisdiction is transferred, the juvenile court with jurisdiction shall terminate the custody order.

The termination order shall be treated as a complaint filed under section 2151.27 of the Revised Code alleging the child subject of the custody order to be a dependent child. If a juvenile court issued the terminated custody order under a prior juvenile proceeding under Chapter 2151. of the Revised Code in which the child was adjudicated an abused, neglected, dependent, unruly, or delinquent child or a juvenile traffic offender, the court shall treat the termination order as a new complaint.

(1999 H 191, eff. 10-20-99)

3109.47 Custody or visitation order when in best interest of child

(A) A court may do one of the following with respect to a parent convicted of killing the other parent of a child if the court determines, by clear and convincing evidence, that it is in the best interest of the child and the child consents:

(1) Issue a custody order designating the parent as the residential parent and legal custodian of the child or granting custody of the child to that parent;

(2) Issue a visitation order granting that parent visitation rights with the child.

(B) When considering the ability of a child to consent and the validity of a child's consent under this section, the court shall consider the wishes of the child, as expressed directly by the child or through the child's guardian ad litem, with due regard for the maturity of the child.

(1999 H 191, eff. 10-20-99)

3109.48 Court order and consent of custodian required for visitation

No person, with the child of the parent present, shall visit the parent who has been convicted of killing the child's other parent unless a court has issued an order granting the parent visitation rights with the child and the child's custodian or legal guardian consents to the visit.

(1999 H 191, eff. 10-20-99)

CHAPTER 3111

Parentage

Section

PRELIMINARY PROVISIONS

PRACTICE AND PROCEDURE

ADMINISTRATIVE SUPPORT ORDERS

Uniform Parentage Act

Table of Jurisdictions Wherein Act Has Been Adopted

For text of Uniform Act, and variation notes and annotation materials for adopting jurisdictions, see Uniform Laws Annotated, Master Edition, Volume 9B.

Jurisdiction	Statutory Citation
Alabama	Code 1975, § 26-17-1 to 26-17-22.
California	West's Ann.Cal.Fam. Code, § 7600 to 7730.
Colorado	West's C.R.S.A. § 19-4-101 to 19-4-130.
Delaware	13 Del.C. § 801 to 819.
Hawaii	HRS § 584-1 to 584-26.
Illinois	750 ILCS 45/1 to 45/26.
Kansas	K.S.A. 38-1110 to 38-1138.
Minnesota	M.S.A. § 257.51 to 257.75.
Missouri	V.A.M.S. § 210.817 to 210.853.
Montana	MCA 40-6-101 to 40-6-135.
Nevada	N.R.S. 126.011 to 126.371.
New Jersey	N.J.S.A. 9:17-38 to 9:17-59.
New Mexico	NMSA 1978 § 40-11-1 to 40-11-23.
North Dakota	NDCC 14-17-01 to 14-17-26.
Rhode Island	Gen. Laws 1956, § 15-8-1 to 15-8-28.
Washington	West's RCWA 26.26.010 to 26.26.905.
Wyoming	Wyo.Stat.Ann., § 14-2-101 to 14-2-120.

Cross References

Acknowledgment of paternity, rescission, 5101.314

Action for child support order, existence of parent-child relationship, 2151.231

Adoption, Ch 3107

Capability of children born out of wedlock to inherit, 2105.17

Child support enforcement agencies, administrative officers, 2301.358

Child support enforcement agencies establishing genetic testing programs, rules, 2301.35

Child support enforcement agencies providing phlebotomists and examiners for genetic tests, 2301.356

Children, Ch 3109

County court of common pleas, domestic relations divisions, 2301.03

Duty of parents to support children of unemancipated minor children, 3109.19

Job and family services department preparing acknowledgment of paternity affidavits, 5101.324
Issuance of new child support orders, interest and costs, 3113.219
Jurisdiction of juvenile court, orders for child support, 2151.23
Juvenile courts, action for child support order before acknowledgment becomes final, 2151.232
Juvenile rules, exceptions, Juv R 1
Parental duty of support, 3103.031
Procedure for father to establish relationship to his child, 2105.18
Reciprocal enforcement of support, adjudication of paternity issue, genetic testing, 3115.24
Relief from final judgment, court order, or administrative determination, 3113.2111
Uniform Interstate Family Support Act, duties and powers of responding tribunal, 3115.16
Uniform Interstate Family Support Act, proceeding to determine parentage, 3115.52
Vital statistics, birth certificate of legitimatized child, 3705.09

Ohio Administrative Code References

CSEA paternity process, OAC 5101:1-32-02
Federal parent locator service, efforts to locate when paternity not established, OAC 5101:1-30-06 et seq.

Library References

Carlin, Baldwin's Ohio Practice, *Merrick-Rippner Probate Law* § 15.30, 17.2, 19.1, 19.2, 19.3, 19.7, 19.9, 19.10, 19.11, 30.26, 38.4, 98.31, 98.38, 98.48, 105.1, 105.2, 106.5, 108.3, 108.15, 108.19, 108.20, 108.24, 108.28, 108.31, 108.33 (1997)
Klein & Darling, Baldwin's Ohio Practice, *Civil Practice* § 1, 5 (1997)
Kurtz & Giannelli, Ohio Juvenile Law (1998 Ed.), Text 20.3
Sowald & Morganstern, Baldwin's Ohio Practice, *Domestic Relations Law* § 3.1, 3.2, 3.5, 3.8, 3.9, 3.13, 3.36, 3.43, 3.46, 3.47, 17.13, 18.8, 21.2, 21.3, 22.4, 23.14, 23.36 (1997)

WESTLAW Electronic Research

See WESTLAW Electronic Research Guide following the Preface.

Law Review and Journal Commentaries

Belsito v Clark: Ohio's Battle with "Motherhood," Dawn Wenk. 28 U Tol L Rev 247 (Fall 1996).

The Contractual Allocation of Procreative Resources and Parental Rights: The Natural Endowment Critique, William J. Wagner. 41 Case W Res L Rev 1 (1990).

The *Davis* Dilemma: How to Prevent Battles over Frozen Preembryos, Note. 41 Case W Res L Rev 543 (1991).

DNA Data Banking: The Dangerous Erosion Of Privacy, E. Donald Shapiro and Michele L. Weinberg. 38 Clev St L Rev 455 (1990).

Fragmenting and Reassembling the World: Of Flying Squirrels, Augmented Persons, and Other Monsters, Michael H. Shapiro. (Ed. note: The moral dimensions of abortion, genetic engineering, and other products of modern technology are explored.) 51 Ohio St L J 331 (1990).

Frozen Embryos: What They Are And How Should The Law Treat Them?, Comment. 38 Clev St L Rev 585 (1990).

Legal Implications of In Vitro Fertilization with Donor Eggs: A Research Guide, Note. 13 Legal Reference Serv Q 5 (1994).

Multiplication and Division—New Math for the Courts: New Reproductive Technologies Create Potential Legal Time Bombs, Comment. 95 Dick L Rev 155 (Fall 1990).

New Wine In Old Skins: Using Paternity-Suit Settlements To Facilitate Surrogate Motherhood, Natalie Loder Clark. 25 J Fam L 483 (1986-87).

Prior Agreements for Disposition of Frozen Embryos. 51 Ohio St L J 407 (1990).

Regulating Genetic Engineering In An Era Of Increased Judicial Deference: A Proper Balance Of The Federal Powers, William H. von Oehsen III. 40 Admin L Rev 303 (Summer 1988).

Should Indigent Putative Fathers be Provided Court Appointed Counsel in Ohio Paternity Proceedings?, Daniel S. Cade. 10 Ohio N U L Rev 473 (1983).

Stiver v Parker: The Siege on Surrogacy, Note. 22 Cap U L Rev 527 (Spring 1993).

Surrogate Parenting: What We Can Learn From Our British Counterparts, Note. 39 Case W Res L Rev 217 (1988-89).

Technology And Motherhood: Legal And Ethical Issues In Human Egg Donation, John A. Robertson. 39 Case W Res L Rev 1 (1988-89).

Would Abolishing the Natural Parent Preference in Custody Disputes Be in Everyone's Best Interest?, Note. 29 J Fam L 539 (1990-91).

Notes of Decisions and Opinions

---

1. Laches

The equitable doctrine of laches may be applicable in parentage cases, even though filed within the statute of limitations, but only if the defendant can show material prejudice. Wright v. Oliver (Ohio 1988) 35 Ohio St.3d 10, 517 N.E.2d 883.

2. Res judicata

The doctrine of res judicata can be invoked to give conclusive effect to a determination of parentage contained in a dissolution decree or a legitimation order, thereby barring a subsequent paternity action brought pursuant to RC Ch 3111. In re Gilbraith (Ohio 1987) 32 Ohio St.3d 127, 512 N.E.2d 956.

RC Ch 3111, as re-enacted by 1982 H 245, eff. 6-29-82, has no application to paternity actions in which judgment was entered prior to that date. Johnson v. Adams (Ohio 1985) 18 Ohio St.3d 48, 479 N.E.2d 866, 18 O.B.R. 83.

Legal custodians of child, who obtained custody from child's mother, were in privity with mother, and so were barred by res judicata from litigating issue of paternity of child that had been decided in divorce decree. Broxterman v. Broxterman (Hamilton 1995) 101 Ohio App.3d 661, 656 N.E.2d 394.

Child was not in privity with his mother in divorce action, and so was not barred by res judicata from bringing paternity action, even though paternity had been decided in divorce decree; although interests of child and mother coincided over support, their interests may have diverged on child's right to know identity of his biological father, and his potential rights of inheritance from his biological father. Broxterman v. Broxterman (Hamilton 1995) 101 Ohio App.3d 661, 656 N.E.2d 394.

After decree of divorce or dissolution has been entered which includes adjudication or agreement as to parentage and parental rights and obligations, postdecree paternity action cannot be brought on child's behalf absent express determination by court that such action is in best interest of child. Broxterman v. Broxterman (Hamilton 1995) 101 Ohio App.3d 661, 656 N.E.2d 394.

A paternity adjudication under RC Ch 3111 has the effect of res judicata on the determination of next of kin under the descent and distribution statute, RC 2105.06. In re Estate of River, No. 1386 (4th Dist Ct App, Ross, 12-23-87).

3. Right of action

An action which alleges that a woman has conceived, during wedlock, an illegitimate child by a man other than her husband may not be maintained by the husband as an action for past necessaries furnished, against the alleged natural father of such child. Weinman v. Larsh (Ohio 1983) 5 Ohio St.3d 85, 448 N.E.2d 1384, 5 O.B.R. 138.

4. Probate court acknowledgment

Proceedings under RC Ch 3111 and adoption are not the exclusive legal mechanisms by which paternity may be determined to provide a basis for child support and custody orders; an acknowledgement of paternity under RC 2105.18 provides a sufficient legal basis for such orders. In re Custody of Davis (Guernsey 1987) 41 Ohio App.3d 81, 534 N.E.2d 945.

5. Artificial insemination

Where a husband and wife agree to conceive a child by means of artificial insemination, and a child so conceived is born to the parties, it is against public policy for a court to enter a judgment establishing the husband's non-paternity in connection with a divorce of the parties and the remarriage of the mother. Brooks v. Fair (Van Wert 1988) 40 Ohio App.3d 202, 532 N.E.2d 208.

6. Indigent defendants

The decisions of State ex rel Cody v Toner, 8 OS(3d) 22, 8 OBR 255, 456 NE(2d) 813 (1983), cert denied 466 US 938, 104 SCt 1912, 80 LEd(2d) 461 (1984), and Anderson v Jacobs, 68 OS(2d) 67, 428 NE(2d) 419 (1981), that the state must provide appointed counsel and blood grouping tests to indigent defendants who face the state as an adversary in paternity proceedings are to be applied retroactively and may therefore be the basis for vacation of judgment pursuant to Civ R 60(B). Keeney v. Lawson (Hamilton 1984) 19 Ohio App.3d 318, 484 N.E.2d 745, 19 O.B.R. 491.

Paternity proceedings brought under RC Ch 3111 are civil in nature and are neither criminal nor quasi-criminal proceedings; consequently, indigent defendants do not have a constitutional right to court-appointed counsel. Sheppard v. Mack (Cuyahoga 1980) 68 Ohio App.2d 95, 427 N.E.2d 522, 22 O.O.3d 104.

In parentage proceedings where the complainant-mothers and their children are recipients of public assistance, the state public defender must, in accordance with RC 120.18, 120.28, and 120.33, partially reimburse the counties for the cost of representing indigent paternity defendants who face the state as an adversary. OAG 85-090.

7. Procedure

In a paternity proceeding brought in juvenile court pursuant to RC Ch 3111, a motion for summary judgment will not lie. De Salvo v. Sukalski (Geauga 1983) 8 Ohio App.3d 337, 457 N.E.2d 349, 8 O.B.R. 448.

Disputes about domestic matters remain the province of the states. Thompson v. Thompson (U.S.Cal. 1988) 108 S.Ct. 513, 484 U.S. 174, 98 L.Ed.2d 512.

PRELIMINARY PROVISIONS

Library References

Sowald & Morganstern, Baldwin's Ohio Practice, *Domestic Relations Law* § 3.2, 3.4, 3.5, 3.7, 3.10, 3.42, 15.6, 19.2, 22.4 (1997)

3111.01 Definition

(A) As used in sections 3111.01 to 3111.29 of the Revised Code, "parent and child relationship" means the legal relationship that exists between a child and the child's natural or adoptive parents and upon which those sections and any other provision of the Revised Code confer or impose rights, privileges, duties, and obligations. The "parent and child relationship" includes the mother and child relationship and the father and child relationship.

(B) The parent and child relationship extends equally to all children and all parents, regardless of the marital status of the parents.

(1992 S 10, eff. 7-15-92; 1986 H 476; 1982 H 245)

Uncodified Law

1992 S 10, § 5, eff. 7-15-92, reads, in part: Sections 3111.01 to 3111.19 of the Revised Code, as enacted or amended by this act, shall apply only to an action brought under sections 3111.01 to 3111.19 of the Revised Code on or after the effective date of this act.

1982 H 245, § 3: See Uncodified Law under 3111.04.

Historical and Statutory Notes

Ed. Note: Former 3111.01 repealed by 1982 H 245, eff. 6-29-82; 1975 S 145; 127 v 1039; 1953 H 1; GC 8006-1; Source—GC 12110.

Pre-1953 H 1 Amendments: 124 v S 65

Cross References

Adoption, putative father defined, 3107.01
Adoption, search of putative father registry prior to adoption, exemptions, 3107.064
Age and schooling certificate, responsibility of parent, 3331.14
"Child without proper parental care," defined, 2151.05
Diagnosis and treatment of minor for drug or alcohol related condition, liability of parent for expenses, 3719.012
DNA database, disclosure of information, 109.573
Driver's license for minor, obligation of parent, 4507.07
Duty of married person to support self, spouse, and children, duration of duty to support, 3103.03
Liability of parent for acts of delinquent child, 2151.411
Liability of parent of minor who willfully damages property or commits theft offense, 3109.09
Liability of parents for assaults by their children, 3109.10

Library References

Children Out-Of-Wedlock ⚷1.
Parent and Child ⚷1.
WESTLAW Topic Nos. 76H, 285.
C.J.S. Children Out-of-Wedlock §§ 2 to 11.
C.J.S. Parent and Child §§ 2 to 4, 10.

OJur 3d: 47, Family Law § 891, 892, 908, 956, 958, 962, 963, 968, 973, 978, 979, 991, 1001

Carlin, Baldwin's Ohio Practice, *Merrick-Rippner Probate Law* § 18.2, 18.3, 19.1, 19.2, 19.3, 19.4, 19.5, 19.6, 19.7, 19.8, 19.9, 19.10, 19.12, 38.4, 98.29, 98.30, 98.31, 105.2, 107.28, 108.19, 108.20, 108.22, 108.23, 108.24, 108.27, 108.28, 108.31, 108.34 (1997)

Klein & Darling, Baldwin's Ohio Practice, *Civil Practice* § 1 (1997)

Sowald & Morganstern, Baldwin's Ohio Practice, *Domestic Relations Law* § 3.1, 3.10, 7.20 (1997)

Law Review and Journal Commentaries

Belsito v Clark: Ohio's Battle with "Motherhood," Dawn Wenk. 28 U Tol L Rev 247 (Fall 1996).

Enforcement Of Surrogate Mother Contracts: Case Law, The Uniform Acts, and State and Federal Legislation, James T. Flaherty. 36 Clev St L Rev 223 (1988).

Establishing Parentage After Senate Bill 10, Pamela J. MacAdams. 4 Domestic Rel J Ohio 81 (September/October 1992).

An Interpretation of Ohio Law on Maternal Status in Gestational Surrogacy Disputes: Belsito v. Clark, Note. 21 U Dayton L Rev 229 (Fall 1995).

Notes of Decisions and Opinions

Consortium loss through injury 3
Mother's marital status 1
Wrongful death action 2

---

1. Mother's marital status

Adulterine bastard is one begotten of the mother's adulterous intercourse, and proceedings ordained by RC 3111.01 et seq. are available to such a child and its mother regardless of the marital status of mother at delivery. (Annotation from former RC 3111.01.) Franklin v. Julian (Ohio 1972) 30 Ohio St.2d 228, 283 N.E.2d 813, 59 O.O.2d 264.

Under this section, complainant must be an "unmarried woman" and have been "delivered of or pregnant with a bastard child," but, after birth of still-born child, she cannot comply with these conditions relative to such child, because she has not been "delivered of a bastard child" as word child is commonly used, nor is she pregnant "with a bastard child," and in order for her to maintain action for support, maintenance and necessary expenses caused by pregnancy, complaint must be filed before dead foetus was expelled from mother's womb. (Annotation from former RC 3111.01.) Seldenright v Jenkins, 22 Abs 576 (Prob, Tuscarawas 1936).

2. Wrongful death action

In a wrongful death action against a truck driver and driver's employer involving a collision between the truck driver and a motorist, dismissal is proper on the basis that the plaintiff could not maintain a wrongful death suit on behalf of an alleged minor child of the motorist where the plaintiff and the motorist were not married, the motorist did not in probate court formally acknowledge the child as his with consent of the mother, and the motorist did not designate the child as his heir-at-law, adopt the child, or make provision for the child in his will, and, although a parentage action was brought by the plaintiff and her son, the action was brought after the death of the motorist; thus, as a matter of law, the child cannot inherit from the decedent's estate, including any recovery from the wrongful death action. Hunter-Martin v. Winchester Transp., Inc. (Shelby 1991) 71 Ohio App.3d 273, 593 N.E.2d 383, motion overruled 62 Ohio St.3d 1408, 577 N.E.2d 361.

3. Consortium loss through injury

A minor child has a cause of action for loss of parental consortium against a third-party tortfeasor who negligently or intentionally causes physical injury to the child's parent, based upon prospective application of Gallimore v. Children's Hosp. (1993), 67 Ohio St.3d 244, so that minor children whose mother is injured in a motor vehicle collision have consortium claims against the driver of the vehicle who has caused the collision. Goodrick v Didovic, No. 65093, 1994 WL 173643 (8th Dist Ct App, Cuyahoga, 5-5-94).

3111.02 Parent and child relationship; how established; reciprocity

(A) The parent and child relationship between a child and the child's natural mother may be established by proof of her having given birth to the child or pursuant to sections 3111.01 to 3111.19 or 3111.20 to 3111.29 of the Revised Code. The parent and child relationship between a child and the natural father of the child may be established by an acknowledgment of paternity as provided in section 5101.314 of the Revised Code, and pursuant to sections 3111.01 to 3111.19 or 3111.20 to 3111.29 of the Revised Code. The parent and child relationship between a child and the adoptive parent of the child may be established by proof of adoption or pursuant to Chapter 3107. of the Revised Code.

(B) A court that is determining a parent and child relationship pursuant to this chapter shall give full faith and credit to a parentage determination made under the laws of this state or another state, regardless of whether the parentage determination was made pursuant to a voluntary acknowledgement of paternity, an administrative procedure, or a court proceeding.

(1997 H 352, eff. 1-1-98; 1994 S 355, eff. 12-9-94; 1992 S 10, eff. 7-15-92; 1986 H 476; 1982 H 245)

Uncodified Law

1994 S 355, § 5: See Uncodified Law under 3111.08.

1992 S 10, § 5: See Uncodified Law under 3111.01.

1982 H 245, § 3: See Uncodified Law under 3111.04.

Historical and Statutory Notes

Ed. Note: Former 3111.02 repealed by 1982 H 245, eff. 6-29-82; 127 v 1039; 1953 H 1; GC 8006-2; Source—GC 12125; see now 3111.04 for provisions analogous to former 3111.02.

Pre-1953 H 1 Amendments: 124 v S 65

Amendment Note: 1997 H 352 substituted "an acknowledgment of paternity" for "a probate court entering an acknowledgment upon its journal" and "5101.314" for "2105.18" in division (A).

Amendment Note: 1994 S 355 designated division (A) and added division (B).

Cross References

Birth certificates, 3705.06 et seq.
Records of births, proof, exception to hearsay rule, Evid R 803

Library References

Adoption ⟹17.
Children Out-Of-Wedlock ⟹6, 12, 13.
Parent and Child ⟹1.
WESTLAW Topic Nos. 17, 76H, 285.
C.J.S. Adoption of Persons §§ 130 to 132.
C.J.S. Children Out-of-Wedlock §§ 20 to 22, 25, 26, 28.
C.J.S. Parent and Child §§ 2 to 4, 10.

OJur 3d: 47, Family Law § 962, 966
Am Jur 2d: 59, Parent and Child § 2 to 5
Parental rights of man who is not biological or adoptive father of child but was husband or cohabitant of mother when child was conceived or born. 84 ALR4th 655

Carlin, Baldwin's Ohio Practice, *Merrick-Rippner Probate Law* § 18.2, 18.3, 19.1, 19.2, 19.3, 19.4, 19.5, 19.6, 19.7, 19.8, 19.10, 19.12, 38.4, 98.2, 98.29, 98.30, 98.31, 105.2, 108.19, 108.20, 108.22, 108.23, 108.24, 108.27, 108.28, 108.31, 108.34 (1997)
Klein & Darling, Baldwin's Ohio Practice, *Civil Practice* § 1 (1997)
Sowald & Morganstern, Baldwin's Ohio Practice, *Domestic Relations Law* § 3.9, 3.10, 3.43, 23.14 (1997)

Law Review and Journal Commentaries

Anna J. v. Mark C.: Proof Of The Imminent Need For Surrogate Motherhood Regulation, Note. 30 J Fam L 493 (February 1992).

Enforcement Of Surrogate Mother Contracts: Case Law, The Uniform Acts, and State and Federal Legislation, James T. Flaherty. 36 Clev St L Rev 223 (1988).

Modern Reproductive Technology and Motherhood: The Search for Common Ground and the Recognition of Difference, Comment. 62 U Cin L Rev 1623 (Spring 1994).

Practice Pointer—Effects of 1994 Am. S.B. 355, Richard L. Innis. 7 Domestic Rel J Ohio 6 (January/February 1995).

Surrogate Parenting: What We Can Learn From Our British Counterparts, Note. 39 Case W Res L Rev 217 (1988-89).

Technology And Motherhood: Legal And Ethical Issues In Human Egg Donation, John A. Robertson. 39 Case W Res L Rev 1 (1988-89).

Notes of Decisions and Opinions

In general 1
Action by child 3
Action by husband 2

1. In general

RC 3111.02 to 3111.04, 3111.09, and 3111.10 are in pari materia and must be construed together. Hulett v. Hulett (Ohio 1989) 45 Ohio St.3d 288, 544 N.E.2d 257.

"In loco parentis" is relationship which person assumes toward child not his own, holding him out to world as member of his family toward whom he owes discharge of parental duties; person standing in loco parentis to child is one who put himself in position of lawful parent assuming obligations incident to parental relation, without going through formalities necessary to legal adoption. Evans v. Ohio State Univ. (Ohio App. 10 Dist. 1996) 112 Ohio App.3d 724, 680 N.E.2d 161, appeal not allowed 77 Ohio St.3d 1494, 673 N.E.2d 149.

When person accepts custody of child, that person stands in loco parentis to child, accepting all rights and responsibilities that go with that status. Evans v. Ohio State Univ. (Ohio App. 10 Dist. 1996) 112 Ohio App.3d 724, 680 N.E.2d 161, appeal not allowed 77 Ohio St.3d 1494, 673 N.E.2d 149.

Key factors of "in loco parentis" relationship are intentional assumption of obligations incidental to parental relationship, especially support and maintenance. Evans v. Ohio State Univ. (Ohio App. 10 Dist. 1996) 112 Ohio App.3d 724, 680 N.E.2d 161, appeal not allowed 77 Ohio St.3d 1494, 673 N.E.2d 149.

R.C. Chapter 3111 paternity proceedings or adoption are not the exclusive methods by which paternity may be determined. In re Custody of Davis (Guernsey 1987) 41 Ohio App.3d 81, 534 N.E.2d 945.

Under statute governing establishment of parent and child relationship, maternity can be established by identifying natural mother through birth process or by other means, including DNA blood tests. Belsito v. Clark (Ohio Com.Pl. 1994) 67 Ohio Misc.2d 54, 644 N.E.2d 760.

When child is delivered by gestational surrogate who has been impregnated through process of in vitro fertilization, natural parents of child shall be identified by determination as to which individuals have provided genetic imprint for that child, and if individuals who have been identified as genetic parents have not relinquished or waived their rights to assume legal status of natural parents, they shall be considered natural and legal parents of that child. Belsito v. Clark (Ohio Com.Pl. 1994) 67 Ohio Misc.2d 54, 644 N.E.2d 760.

2. Action by husband

Where a man expressly acknowledges paternity of a child in a separation agreement incorporated into a judgment for dissolution, both parties to the separation agreement were represented by counsel, and the parties agreed to the man's child support obligation, a subsequent paternity action to establish that the man is not the child's biological father is barred by res judicata. Kashnier v. Donelly (Medina 1991) 81 Ohio App.3d 154, 610 N.E.2d 519.

A judgment entry in a divorce action finding that a child was born during the marriage and ordering the husband to pay child support is not conclusive as to the paternity of the child where the husband had denied such paternity in the divorce action and the decree did not explicitly find that a parent and child relationship existed; res judicata is inapplicable in a subsequent paternity action filed by the putative father absent a specific finding that a parent and child relationship existed; therefore, a juvenile court errs in dismissing the subsequent paternity action. LaBonte v. LaBonte (Meigs 1988) 61 Ohio App.3d 209, 572 N.E.2d 704, motion overruled 42 Ohio St.3d 709, 538 N.E.2d 122.

The two methods for a father to secure companionship rights with an illegitimate child are (1) to acknowledge his paternity or (2) have his paternity determined in an action pursuant to RC Ch 3111; where it is undisputed that a putative father who seeks visitation rights, did not acknowledge his paternity with the probate court following the child's birth and HLA tests conclusively exclude him as the father, there is no statutory basis permitting the juvenile court to order visitation rights. Sherburn v Reichert, No. 15-94-3, 1994 WL 581539 (3d Dist Ct App, Van Wert, 10-13-94).

3. Action by child

Minor child has cause of action for loss of parental consortium against third-party tort-feasor who negligently or intentionally injures child's parent. Coleman v. Sandoz Pharmaceuticals Corp. (Ohio 1996) 74 Ohio St.3d 492, 660 N.E.2d 424.

Derivative claim for loss of parental consortium that is filed by intervening minor child can be brought against additional defendants in event that parent's case in chief has only one defendant. Coleman v. Sandoz Pharmaceuticals Corp. (Ohio 1996) 74 Ohio St.3d 492, 660 N.E.2d 424.

Child has statutory right to bring paternity action and has separate and distinct claim from that of his mother. Rees v. Heimberger (Cuyahoga 1989) 60 Ohio App.3d 45, 573 N.E.2d 189, dismissed 47 Ohio St.3d 702, 547 N.E.2d 986, rehearing denied 48 Ohio St.3d 707, 550 N.E.2d 483, certiorari denied 110 S.Ct. 1827, 494 U.S. 1088, 108 L.Ed.2d 956.

3111.03 Presumptions as to father and child relationship

(A) A man is presumed to be the natural father of a child under any of the following circumstances:

(1) The man and the child's mother are or have been married to each other, and the child is born during the marriage or is born within three hundred days after the marriage is terminated by death, annulment, divorce, or dissolution or after the man and the child's mother separate pursuant to a separation agreement.

(2) The man and the child's mother attempted, before the child's birth, to marry each other by a marriage that was solemnized in apparent compliance with the law of the state in which the marriage took place, the marriage is or could be declared invalid, and either of the following applies:

(a) The marriage can only be declared invalid by a court and the child is born during the marriage or within three hundred days after the termination of the marriage by death, annulment, divorce, or dissolution;

(b) The attempted marriage is invalid without a court order and the child is born within three hundred days after the termination of cohabitation.

(3) The man and the child's mother, after the child's birth, married or attempted to marry each other by a marriage solemnized in apparent compliance with the law of the state in which the marriage took place, and either of the following occurs:

(a) The man has acknowledged his paternity of the child in a writing sworn to before a notary public;

(b) The man is required to support the child by a written voluntary promise or by a court order.

(4) An acknowledgment of paternity filed with the division of child support in the department of job and family services becomes final pursuant to section 2151.232, 3111.211, or 5101.314 of the Revised Code.

(5) A court or administrative body, pursuant to section 3111.09, 3111.22, or 3115.52 of the Revised Code or otherwise, has ordered that genetic tests be conducted or the natural mother and alleged natural father voluntarily agreed to genetic testing pursuant to former section 3111.21 of the Revised Code to determine the father and child relationship and the results of the genetic tests indicate a probability of ninety-nine per cent or greater that the man is the biological father of the child.

(B)(1) A presumption arises under division (A)(3) of this section regardless of the validity or invalidity of the marriage of the parents. A presumption that arises under this section can only be rebutted by clear and convincing evidence that includes the results of genetic testing, except that a presumption that arises under division (A)(1) or (2) of this section is conclusive as provided in division (A) of section 3111.37 of the Revised Code and cannot be rebutted. If two or more conflicting presumptions arise under this section, the court shall determine, based upon logic and policy considerations, which presumption controls. If a determination described in division (B)(3) of this section conflicts with a presumption that arises under this section the determination is controlling.

(2) Notwithstanding division (B)(1) of this section, a presumption that arises under division (A)(4) of this section may only be rebutted as provided in division (B)(2) of section 5101.314 of the Revised Code.

(3) Notwithstanding division (A)(5) of this section, a final and enforceable determination finding the existence of a father and child relationship pursuant to former section 3111.21 or section 3111.22 of the Revised Code that is based on the results of genetic tests ordered pursuant to either of those sections, is not a presumption.

(C) A presumption of paternity that arose pursuant to this section prior to January 1, 1998, shall remain valid on and after that date unless rebutted pursuant to division (B) of this section. This division does not apply to a determination described in division (B)(3) of this section.

(1999 H 471, eff. 7-1-00; 1997 H 352, eff. 1-1-98; 1992 S 10, eff. 7-15-92; 1990 S 3; 1988 H 790; 1986 H 476; 1982 H 245)

Uncodified Law

1992 S 10, § 5: See Uncodified Law under 3111.01.

1982 H 245, § 3: See Uncodified Law under 3111.04.

Historical and Statutory Notes

Ed. Note: 3111.03 contains provisions analogous to former 3105.13 and 3105.33, repealed by 1982 H 245, eff. 6-29-82.

Ed. Note: Former 3111.03 repealed by 1982 H 245, eff. 6-29-82; 1953 H 1; GC 8006-3; Source—GC 12134; see now 3111.04 for provisions analogous to former 3111.03.

Pre-1953 H 1 Amendments: 124 v S 65

Amendment Note: 1999 H 471 substituted "job and family" for "human" in division (A)(4); and substituted "January 1, 1998" for "the effective date of this amendment" in division (C).

Amendment Note: 1997 H 352 deleted former division (A)(3)(b); redesignated former division (A)(3)(c) as new division (A)(3)(b); deleted former division (A)(4); redesignated former divisions (A)(5) and (A)(6) as new divisions (A)(4) and (A)(5) and rewrote those divisions; designated division (B)(1) and added the fourth sentence therein; added divisions (B)(2), (B)(3), and (C); and made other nonsubstantive changes. Prior to amendment, former divisions (A)(3)(b) and (A)(4) through (A)(6) read:

"(b) The man, with his consent, is named as the child's father on the child's birth certificate;"

"(4) The man, with his consent, signs the child's birth certificate as an informant as provided in section 3705.09 of the Revised Code.

"(5) A court enters upon its journal an acknowledgment of paternity pursuant to section 2105.18 of the Revised Code.

"(6) A court or administrative body, pursuant to section 3111.09 or 3115.24 of the Revised Code or otherwise, has ordered that genetic tests be conducted or the natural mother and alleged natural father voluntarily agreed to genetic testing pursuant to section 3111.21 or 3111.22 of the Revised Code to determine the father and child relationship and the results of the genetic tests indicate a probability of ninety-five per cent or greater that the man is the biological father of the child."

Cross References

Hospital staff sending signed and notarized acknowledgment of paternity to child support division, 2301.357, 3727.17

Non-spousal artificial insemination, husband rather than donor regarded as natural father of child, 3111.37

Non-spousal insemination, effect of physician's failure to comply with statutes, 3111.38

Notarizing and filing acknowledgment of paternity regarding man known to be presumed father, 5101.314

Presumptions in general in civil actions and proceedings, Evid R 301

Registrar sending signed and notarized acknowledgment of paternity to child support division, 3705.091

Relief from final judgment, court order, or administrative determination, 3113.2111

Solemnization of marriage, 3101.08 to 3101.13

Ohio Administrative Code References

Collection of past due support by federal tax refund offset, OAC 5101:1-30-775

Library References

Children Out-Of-Wedlock ⟹3, 12, 43.
WESTLAW Topic No. 76H.
C.J.S. Children Out-of-Wedlock §§ 13 to 17, 25, 26, 51, 100.

OJur 3d: 47, Family Law § 965, 966, 991, 1007, 1017
Am Jur 2d: 10, Bastards § 10 et seq.
Blood grouping tests. 46 ALR2d 1000
Proof of husband's impotency or sterility as rebutting presumption of legitimacy. 84 ALR3d 495
Who may dispute presumption of legitimacy of child conceived or born during wedlock. 90 ALR3d 1032

Carlin, Baldwin's Ohio Practice, *Merrick-Rippner Probate Law* § 18.2, 18.3, 19.1, 19.2, 19.3, 19.4, 19.5, 19.6, 19.7, 19.8, 19.9, 19.10, 19.12, 38.4, 98.29, 98.30, 98.31, 98.48, 105.2, 108.13, 108.15, 108.19, 108.20, 108.22, 108.23, 108.24, 108.27, 108.28, 108.31, 108.34 (1997)
Giannelli & Snyder, Baldwin's Ohio Practice, Evidence § 301.15 (1996)
Klein & Darling, Baldwin's Ohio Practice, *Civil Practice* § 1 (1997)
Sowald & Morganstern, Baldwin's Ohio Practice, *Domestic Relations Law* § 2.58, 3.10, 3.12, 3.13, 3.14, 3.16, 3.18, 3.21, 3.43, 3.47, 7.4, 7.20, 11.9, 22.4, 22.5, 22.13, 22.19 (1997)

Law Review and Journal Commentaries

Artificial Insemination: Donor Rights In Situations Involving Unmarried Recipients, Note. 26 J Fam L 793 (1987-88).

The Biological Father's Right to Require a Pregnant Woman to Undergo Medical Treatment Necessary to Sustain Fetal Life, Comment. 94 Dick L Rev 199 (Fall 1989).

The Burden of Proof in a Paternity Proceeding, Note. 25 J Fam L 357 (1986-87).

The DNA Paternity Test: Legislating the Future Paternity Action, E. Donald Shapiro, Stewart Reifler, Claudia L. Psome. 7 J L & Health 1 (1992-93).

Enforcement Of Surrogate Mother Contracts: Case Law, The Uniform Acts, and State and Federal Legislation, James T. Flaherty. 36 Clev St L Rev 223 (1988).

The Need for Statutes Regulating Artificial Insemination by Donors, Note. 46 Ohio St L J 1055 (1986).

Paternity: Rebuttable Presumption, Lawrence G. Sheehe, Jr. 63 Law & Fact 10 (November-December 1989).

Protecting a Husband's Parental Rights When His Wife Disputes the Presumption of Legitimacy, Note. 28 J Fam L 115 (1989-90).

Smith v. Cole: Triumph in Family Court, Comment. 40 Case W Res L Rev 1157 (1989-90).

When Does Divorce Decree Bar Parentage Action?, Pamela J. MacAdams. 8 Domestic Rel J Ohio 95 (November/December 1996).

Notes of Decisions and Opinions

---

1. In general

RC 3111.02 to 3111.04, 3111.09, and 3111.10 are in pari materia and must be construed together. Hulett v. Hulett (Ohio 1989) 45 Ohio St.3d 288, 544 N.E.2d 257.

Genetic tests indicating greater than 95% probability that putative father was not child's biological father gave rise to presumption of nonpaternity. Riddle v. Riddle (Ohio Com.Pl. 1992) 63 Ohio Misc.2d 43, 619 N.E.2d 1201.

2. Rebutting presumption of paternity

Pursuant to RC 3111.03(A)(1), a man is presumed to be the natural father of a child where the man and the child's mother are or have been married to each other and the child is born during the marriage; however, such presumption may be rebutted by clear and convincing evidence to the contrary. Hulett v. Hulett (Ohio 1989) 45 Ohio St.3d 288, 544 N.E.2d 257.

While every child conceived in wedlock is presumed legitimate, such presumption is not conclusive and may be rebutted by clear and convincing evidence that there were no sexual relations between husband and wife during the time in which the child must have been conceived, and a complaint for determination of paternity is sufficient if the plaintiff alleges he is the natural father of the child. Joseph v. Alexander (Ohio 1984) 12 Ohio St.3d 88, 465 N.E.2d 448, 12 O.B.R. 77.

In divorce action involving pregnant wife, parties' agreed entry, pursuant to which wife dropped any claim against husband with regard to unborn child, was insufficient to overcome statutory presumption of legitimacy, where domestic relations court adopted the agreed entry without holding hearing and receiving evidence to rebut presumption of legitimacy, divorce decree made finding of nonpaternity, and husband did not undertake obligation for child support. Fitzpatrick v. Fitzpatrick (Ohio App. 12 Dist. 1998) 126 Ohio App.3d 476, 710 N.E.2d 778, dismissed, appeal not allowed 82 Ohio St.3d 1441, 695 N.E.2d 264.

Laches is equitable defense to paternity action. Seegert v. Zietlow (Cuyahoga 1994) 95 Ohio App.3d 451, 642 N.E.2d 697.

Presumption of paternity resulting from genetic testing may only be rebutted by clear and convincing evidence. Filkins v. Cales (Logan 1993) 86 Ohio App.3d 61, 619 N.E.2d 1156, motion overruled 67 Ohio St.3d 1422, 616 N.E.2d 506.

Doctor's inconsistent testimony that child's estimated gestational age at birth was about 34 weeks, which would have placed probable date of conception one month before mother and putative father had intercourse, did not rise to level of clear and convincing evidence required to rebut presumption of paternity established by genetic test results which disclosed that there was 98.5% probability that putative father was biological father of child. Filkins v. Cales (Logan 1993) 86 Ohio App.3d 61, 619 N.E.2d 1156, motion overruled 67 Ohio St.3d 1422, 616 N.E.2d 506.

Where a child is conceived and born during the marriage of a husband and wife, the husband is presumed to be the father of the child even though the husband had a vasectomy prior to the conception of the child, since the husband failed to return for a sperm test after the vasectomy, and even though the wife admits having had a sexual relationship with another man. Walkup v. Walkup (Brown 1986) 31 Ohio App.3d 248, 511 N.E.2d 119, 31 O.B.R. 532.

In a custody action involving a child conceived and born while the parties were married, a stipulation and affidavit to the effect that the husband is not the father of the child are insufficient as a matter of law to overcome the presumption of legitimacy of such child. Nelson v. Nelson (Franklin 1983) 10 Ohio App.3d 36, 460 N.E.2d 653, 10 O.B.R. 44.

A complainant mother in a bastardy action, who was married at the time of her child's conception, must establish, by clear and convincing evidence, that her husband was not the father of the child, and, by a preponderance of the evidence, that the defendant was the father of the child, and in such case, a verdict for the complainant mother finding the defendant to be the father of such child is against the manifest weight of the evidence where such evidence shows that complainant's husband had actual physical access to complainant at the time of the child's conception, and that, following the husband's subsequent divorce from complainant, he took her into his home and, when the child was born, took her to the hospital, visited her there frequently, did not protest the use of his name as the father of the child, and brought the mother and child to his home after their release from the hospital. (Annotation from former RC 3111.01.) State ex rel. Satterfield v. Sullivan (Franklin 1962) 115 Ohio App. 347, 185 N.E.2d 47, 20 O.O.2d 419.

The presumption that a child conceived during wedlock is legitimate can be overcome by evidence which is strong and convincing. (Annotation from former RC 3111.15.) Quasion v. Friedman (Montgomery 1959) 110 Ohio App. 166, 169 N.E.2d 28, 12 O.O.2d 430.

A presumption that the husband is the natural father of a child is rebutted by genetic testing that indicates a 99.96 per cent probability that the mother's live-in boyfriend is the child's father and by testimony of the mother indicating (1) the child's baby picture is identical to that of the boyfriend, (2) the threesome functions as a family, (3) the friend keeps the child when the mother works evenings and visits the child every weekend, and (4) the husband was involved in three other marriages without bearing children and doctors advise him that he is unable to produce a child. Chenoweth v Chenoweth, No. 16700, 1998 WL 127591 (2d Dist Ct App, Montgomery, 3-20-98).

A husband's paternity is rebuttable by a genetic test and a putative father may bring a parentage action where the mother was, and continues to be, married to another man at the time the child was conceived. Crawford County Child Support Enforcement Agency v Sprague, No. 3-97-13, 1997 WL 746770 (3d Dist Ct App, Crawford, 12-5-97).

False testimony of an adverse party in a divorce proceeding, that the husband was the father of a child fourteen years before, does not warrant a finding of fraud upon the court; this is intrinsic fraud, time-barred by the one-year statute of limitations of Civ 60(B)(3). Still v Still, No. 95CA15, 1996 WL 362259 (4th Cist Ct App, Gallia, 6-25-96).

Exclusion as the father through genetic testing constitutes clear and convincing evidence that overcomes the presumption of paternity created under RC 3111.03 and where the defendant is excluded as the father there is no minor issue of the marriage and RC 3109.04 no longer provides the court of common pleas with subject matter jurisdiction to make a ruling on custody; instead the issue of custody becomes subject matter exclusive to the juvenile court pursuant to RC 2151.23, and consequently, the "best interest of the child" standard in determining custody does not apply. Thompson v Thompson, No. 94CA859, 1995 WL 481480 (4th Dist Ct App, Highland, 8-16-95).

Evidence a defendant had sexual relations with a child's mother approximately nine months prior to the birth of the child, HLA test results producing a 99.93% probability the defendant is the father of the child, and testimony the mother's husband was incarcerated with no access to an intimate relationship with the mother for months prior to and after the approximate time of conception constitutes clear and convincing evidence rebutting the presumption that the mother's husband is the father of the child and a failure to obtain an HLA test of the husband does not preclude a judgment finding the defendant to be the natural father of the child. Feister v Lee, No. 93AP060037, 1993 WL 472868 (5th Dist Ct App, Tuscarawas, 11-1-93).

Appellate court distinguished an "alleged" father from a "presumed" father. Where there is clear and convincing evidence of sexual relations between husband and wife during possible conception period, the presumption of RC 3111.03 becomes essentially conclusive and not rebutted by genetic tests which are to be used only with respect to an alleged father, not a presumed father. Hulett v Hulett, No. 87AP-330 (10th Dist Ct App, Franklin, 11-17-87).

The presumption of paternity set forth in RC 3111.03 is overcome by clear and convincing evidence, such as the birth of a biracial child to a married couple of the same race. Murph v Murph, No. 10262 (2d Dist Ct App, Montgomery, 7-16-87).

The presumption that a child conceived in wedlock is legitimate cannot be rebutted except by evidence that the spouses had no sexual relations during the time in which the child was conceived. Joseph v Alexander, No. CA-6781 (5th Dist Ct App, Stark, 5-5-86).

RC 3111.03 abolishes the conclusive presumption of paternity established by Hall v Rosen, 50 OS(2d) 135 (1977), and provides that the presumption of paternity may be refuted by clear and convincing evidence; this provision should be applied retroactively. Johnson v Adams, No. 81 X 29 (4th Dist Ct App, Washington, 2-3-84), affirmed by 18 OS(3d) 48, 18 OBR 83, 479 NE(2d) 866 (1985).

Trial court properly dismissed for failure to state a claim for relief plaintiff's suit to be declared father of a minor child where the defendant-parents were lawfully married at the time of such child's conception. N.J. v B.A, No. CA-6088 (5th Dist Ct App, Stark, 8-15-83).

Presumption of paternity created by putative father's marriage to mother at time of child's birth and his signature on birth certificate conflicted with presumption of nonpaternity created by genetic test results indicating more than 95% probability of nonpaternity, requiring use of logic and analysis of policy considerations in determining what presumption should control. Riddle v. Riddle (Ohio Com.Pl. 1992) 63 Ohio Misc.2d 43, 619 N.E.2d 1201.

A provision of a state evidence code which presumes that a child born to a married woman living with her husband, who is neither impotent nor sterile, is a child of the marriage does not violate the due process rights of a man who wishes to establish his paternity of a child born to the wife of another man nor infringe upon the constitutional right of the child to maintain a relationship with her natural father. (Ed. note: California law construed in light of federal constitution.) Michael H. v. Gerald D. (U.S.Cal. 1989) 109 S.Ct. 2333, 491 U.S. 110, 105 L.Ed.2d 91, rehearing denied 110 S.Ct. 22, 492 U.S. 937, 106 L.Ed.2d 634, rehearing denied 111 S.Ct. 1645, 499 U.S. 984, 113 L.Ed.2d 739, motion to amend denied 112 S.Ct. 1931, 504 U.S. 905, 118 L.Ed.2d 538.

3. Evidence

Clear and convincing evidence sufficient to overcome the presumption of paternity contained in RC 3111.03(A)(1) may be adduced through any or all of the enumerated methods prescribed by RC 3111.10, including the submission of genetic test results. Hulett v. Hulett (Ohio 1989) 45 Ohio St.3d 288, 544 N.E.2d 257.

Mother established prima facie parent-child relationship between putative father and daughter by preponderance of evidence in view of fact that genetic test disclosed 98.5% probability that he was biological father of child, that mother had sexual intercourse with putative father twice during alleged month of conception, that, although she had sexual intercourse with one other man during that month, genetic blood testing excluded him as biological father of child, and that putative father admitted under cross-examination that it was possible that he had sexual intercourse with child's mother during month of conception and they did not use any form of contraceptive. Filkins v. Cales (Logan 1993) 86 Ohio App.3d 61, 619 N.E.2d 1156, motion overruled 67 Ohio St.3d 1422, 616 N.E.2d 506.

A presumption of paternity does not arise under RC 3111.03(A)(3)(a) when a man states he is the natural father of a child in an affidavit supporting a change of name for the child if the man does not marry the child's mother afterwards. McMullen v. Muir (Cuyahoga 1986) 34 Ohio App.3d 241, 517 N.E.2d 1381.

Genetic test results are admissible without the need for foundation testimony or further proof of authenticity or accuracy where the biological father fails to file a written objection to the report of the court-ordered genetic test results and does not dispute that he received a copy. Joy B. v Glen D, No. OT-99-002, 1999 WL 575945 (6th Dist Ct App, Wood, 8-6-99).

4. Marriage during pregnancy

A man who marries a woman while she is pregnant is presumed to be the natural father of any child born from the pregnancy; however, this presumption can be rebutted by clear and convincing evidence. Johnson v. Adams (Ohio 1985) 18 Ohio St.3d 48, 479 N.E.2d 866, 18 O.B.R. 83.

The biological father of a child cannot be held for her support where the mother, during pregnancy, contracts marriage with another man, who marries her with full knowledge of her condition and thereby consents to stand in loco parentis to such child and to being the father of the child. (Annotation from former RC 3111.17.) Hall v. Rosen (Ohio 1977) 50 Ohio St.2d 135, 363 N.E.2d 725, 4 O.O.3d 336.

Under common law, child was "child of the marriage" of parties, where child was born during marriage and parties continued to live together for slightly less than one year after child was born. Cassim v. Cassim (Franklin 1994) 98 Ohio App.3d 576, 649 N.E.2d 28, on subsequent appeal, dismissed, appeal not allowed 75 Ohio St.3d 1404, 661 N.E.2d 754.

Term "child of the marriage," as used in rules and statute with respect to divorce and separation, includes child who is born to wife during marriage and, thus, who is presumptively the child of the husband. Cassim v. Cassim (Franklin 1994) 98 Ohio App.3d 576, 649 N.E.2d 28, on subsequent appeal, dismissed, appeal not allowed 75 Ohio St.3d 1404, 661 N.E.2d 754.

A man who marries a pregnant woman can rebut the presumption of paternity by presenting clear and convincing evidence of fraud and nonpaternity. Carson v. Carson (Brown 1989) 62 Ohio App.3d 670, 577 N.E.2d 391, motion overruled 46 Ohio St.3d 716, 546 N.E.2d 1334.

Where a man marries a woman who is pregnant by another man, and there is no showing of fraud in the inception of the marriage, the husband is conclusively presumed to be the father of the child. (Annotation from former RC 3111.01.) Burse v. Burse (Hamilton 1976) 48 Ohio App.2d 244, 356 N.E.2d 755, 2 O.O.3d 197.

Where a man marries a woman with full knowledge that she is pregnant by another, and the child is born during their marriage, and subsequently the woman obtains a divorce, the divorced husband may be ordered to support such minor child, inasmuch as by such marriage the husband deprives the wife of the right to institute a bastardy action against the child's natural father. (Annotation from former RC 3111.01.) Gustin v. Gustin (Montgomery 1958) 108 Ohio App. 171, 161 N.E.2d 68, 9 O.O.2d 204.

Civ R 60 relief from agreed judgment entry stipulating that parties in divorce had no issue born of the marriage was proper where, once the stipulation is disregarded, the husband claims the child born to his wife is his daughter. Wingenfeld v Wingenfeld, No. 63942, 1993 WL 497074 (8th Dist Ct App, Cuyahoga, 12-2-93).

A motion to terminate a child support decree will be denied where a man marries a pregnant woman with full knowledge of her condition, because the law conclusively presumes that he is father of the child, and even a failure to permit or admit blood tests to disprove paternity is not in error. Humphrey v Humphrey, No. C-800312 (1st Dist Ct App, Hamilton, 5-6-81).

5. Appeals

A divorce decree that entered judgment on the custody and support of an older child but deferred the question of support for an unborn child pending a determination of paternity is a final appealable order where a speedy determination and review of the custody question for the older child outweighed the danger of piecemeal appeals or harm to the prompt and orderly disposition of litigation, and the court expressly found that there was no just reason for delay. Evicks v. Evicks (Lawrence 1992) 79 Ohio App.3d 657, 607 N.E.2d 1090.

6. Wrongful death

Putative father of minor child who had died in automobile accident was entitled to receive wrongful death proceeds awarded as result of child's death, even though putative father had failed to satisfy technical requirements for establishing parent-child relationship, where following child's death both mother and putative father testified that he was in fact child's natural father. Matter of Estate of Pulford (Ohio App. 11 Dist. 1997) 122 Ohio App.3d 92, 701 N.E.2d 58.

In a wrongful death action against a truck driver and driver's employer involving a collision between the truck driver and a motorist, dismissal is proper on the basis that the plaintiff could not maintain a wrongful death suit on behalf of an alleged minor child of the motorist where the plaintiff and the motorist were not married, the motorist did not in probate court formally acknowledge the child as his with consent of the mother, and the motorist did not designate the child as his heir-at-law, adopt the child, or make provision for the child in his will, and, although a parentage action was brought by the plaintiff and her son, the action was brought after the death of the motorist; thus, as a matter of law, the child cannot inherit from the decedent's estate, including any recovery from the wrongful death action. Hunter-Martin v. Winchester Transp., Inc. (Shelby 1991) 71 Ohio App.3d 273, 593 N.E.2d 383, motion overruled 62 Ohio St.3d 1408, 577 N.E.2d 361.

7. Res judicata/estoppel

Duly notorized declaration of paternity signed by one putative father did not have force of final judgment and did not bar, on res judicata grounds, subsequent legitimation action against second putative father; declaration of paternity had never been filed with probate court. Collett v. Cogar (Ohio 1988) 35 Ohio St.3d 114, 518 N.E.2d 1202.

The doctrine of res judicata can be invoked to give conclusive effect to determination of parentage contained in dissolution decree or legitimation order, thereby barring a subsequent paternity action brought pursuant to parentage statute. In re Gilbraith (Ohio 1987) 32 Ohio St.3d 127, 512 N.E.2d 956.

Under doctrine of res judicata, putative father's second motion for relief from judgment of paternity, based on results of genetic blood test which excluded him from being father of child, was barred by virtue of denial of his first motion for relief from judgment which had been specifically based on ground of newly discovered evidence; grounds for both motions were identical, i.e., newly discovered evidence. Matter of Kay B. v. Timothy C. (Ohio App. 6 Dist. 1997) 117 Ohio App.3d 598, 690 N.E.2d 1366.

Legitimation order filed in probate court with consent of mother did not bar subsequent parentage action wherein mother sought child support arrearages; application of doctrine of res judicata would violate state's strong public policy favoring protection of children and their support, health, maintenance and welfare, and would also violate equal protection. Lewis v. Chapin (Cuyahoga 1994) 93 Ohio App.3d 695, 639 N.E.2d 848.

Child was not barred under doctrine of res judicata from pursuing parentage action on basis that father acknowledged existence of parent-child relationship and that mother consented to filing of legitimacy order, as child was not a party or in privity with a party to the legitimacy order. Lewis v. Chapin (Cuyahoga 1994) 93 Ohio App.3d 695, 639 N.E.2d 848.

An appellant in a divorce action may not raise the issue of paternity fifteen months after the decree, stating that another man fathered his children, by claiming that genetic testing was not available under prior law when he had offered no clear and convincing evidence on the issue. Weber v. Weber (Fulton 1991) 74 Ohio App.3d 396, 599 N.E.2d 288.

A judgment entry in a divorce action finding that a child was born during the marriage and ordering the husband to pay child support is not conclusive as to the paternity of the child where the husband had denied such paternity in the divorce action and the decree did not explicitly find that a parent and child relationship existed; res judicata is inapplicable in a subsequent paternity action filed by the putative father absent a specific finding that a parent and child relationship existed; therefore, a juvenile court errs in dismissing the subsequent paternity action. LaBonte v. LaBonte (Meigs 1988) 61 Ohio App.3d 209, 572 N.E.2d 704, motion overruled 42 Ohio St.3d 709, 538 N.E.2d 122.

Doctrines of laches and equitable estoppel precluded mother from claiming that putative father, who was married to her at time of birth and had signed birth certificate, was not child's biological father based on genetic results; mother had allowed putative father to believe that he was child's father for more than five years, allowed him to financially contribute to care and support of child, participated in development of intimate father/son relationship, and represented to putative father's parents that they were child's grandparents and allowed them to develop relationship with child. Riddle v. Riddle (Ohio Com.Pl. 1992) 63 Ohio Misc.2d 43, 619 N.E.2d 1201.

Common Pleas Court has inherent authority, when considering best interests of minor child, to estop mother from using genetic testing to disestablish child's paternity with his or her presumed father. Riddle v. Riddle (Ohio Com.Pl. 1992) 63 Ohio Misc.2d 43, 619 N.E.2d 1201.

8. Artificial insemination

Where a husband and wife agree to conceive a child by means of artificial insemination, and a child so conceived is born to the parties, it is against public policy for a court to enter a judgment establishing the husband's non-paternity in connection with a divorce of the parties and the remarriage of the mother. Brooks v. Fair (Van Wert 1988) 40 Ohio App.3d 202, 532 N.E.2d 208.

Failure to comply with medical requirements of artificial insemination statutes would prevent mother from invoking nonspousal artificial insemination statute to obtain dismissal of sperm donor's complaint to determine paternity, custody, support, and visitation. C.O. v. W.S. (Ohio Com.Pl. 1994) 64 Ohio Misc.2d 9, 639 N.E.2d 523.

Even if artificial insemination statute establishing legal relationship between donor and mother applied, statute was unconstitutional as applied to donor and child insofar as it could be read to absolutely extinguish donor's efforts to assert rights and responsibilities of being father in case in which mother had solicited participation of donor, who was known to her, and donor and mother agreed that there would be relationship between donor and child. C.O. v. W.S. (Ohio Com.Pl. 1994) 64 Ohio Misc.2d 9, 639 N.E.2d 523.

Artificial insemination statute establishing legal relationship between donor and mother would not apply to prevent paternity adjudication where unmarried woman solicited participation of donor, who was known to her, and where donor and woman agreed that there would be relationship between donor and child. C.O. v. W.S. (Ohio Com.Pl. 1994) 64 Ohio Misc.2d 9, 639 N.E.2d 523.

9. Judgment of paternity

Putative father's motion for relief from judgment of paternity, based on recently obtained results of genetic blood test which excluded him from being father of child, was based on newly discovered evidence and, therefore, was untimely when it was filed more than one year after entry of judgment. Matter of Kay B. v. Timothy C. (Ohio App. 6 Dist. 1997) 117 Ohio App.3d 598, 690 N.E.2d 1366.

A judgment pursuant to former RC 3111.17 which sets visitation rights and support duties of a man who has signed a birth certificate as informant, even though both he and the mother admit he is not the natural father, may be properly vacated to relieve the child and mother from the determination of paternity implicit in the judgment. In re Smith (Miami 1984) 16 Ohio App.3d 75, 474 N.E.2d 632, 16 O.B.R. 79.

A determination of a "reputed father" under RC 3111.17 does not convert that finding into a finding of a "natural father" under RC 2105.18, nor does such a determination give the mother authority either as agent for the father or by operation of law to file an application for legitimation under RC 2105.18 and acknowledge that the alleged father is the natural father of the child. (Annotation from former RC 3111.17.) In re Minor of Martin (Cuyahoga 1977) 51 Ohio App.2d 21, 365 N.E.2d 892, 5 O.O.3d 141.

Statements of counsel indicating that the client concedes he is the father and "there is no dispute that the child in question is the defendant's" and that he is the father of the child conceived by him and the victim of his attack are sufficient for conviction of domestic violence based upon an admitted fact and not upon a presumption of paternity. State v Rowland, No. 96 CA 135, 1997 WL 446861 (2d Dist Ct App, Greene, 8-8-97).

PRACTICE AND PROCEDURE

Library References

Sowald & Morganstern, Baldwin's Ohio Practice, *Domestic Relations Law* § 3.2, 3.4, 3.5, 3.7, 3.10, 3.42, 15.6, 19.2, 22.4 (1997)

3111.04 Action to determine father and child relationship

(A) An action to determine the existence or nonexistence of the father and child relationship may be brought by the child or the child's personal representative, the child's mother or her personal representative, a man alleged or alleging himself to be the child's father, the child support enforcement agency of the county in which the child resides if the child's mother is a recipient of public assistance or of services under Title IV-D of the "Social Security Act," 88 Stat. 2351 (1975), 42 U.S.C.A. 651, as amended, or the alleged father's personal representative.

(B) An agreement does not bar an action under this section.

(C) If an action under this section is brought before the birth of the child and if the action is contested, all proceedings, except service of process and the taking of depositions to perpetuate testimony, may be stayed until after the birth.

(D) A recipient of public assistance or of services under Title IV-D of the "Social Security Act," 88 Stat. 2351 (1975), 42 U.S.C.A. 651, as amended, shall cooperate with the child support enforcement agency of the county in which a child resides to obtain an administrative determination pursuant to section 3111.22 of the Revised Code, or, if necessary, a court determination pursuant to sections 3111.01 to 3111.19 of the Revised Code, of the existence or nonexistence of a parent and child relationship between the father and the child. If the recipient fails to cooperate, the agency may commence an action to determine the existence or nonexistence of a parent and child relationship between the father and the child pursuant to sections 3111.01 to 3111.19 of the Revised Code.

(E) As used in this section, "public assistance" means medical assistance under Chapter 5111. of the Revised Code, assistance under Chapter 5107. of the Revised Code, or disability assistance under Chapter 5115. of the Revised Code.

(1997 H 352, eff. 1-1-98; 1992 S 10, eff. 7-15-92; 1982 H 245)

Uncodified Law

1992 S 10, § 5: See Uncodified Law under 3111.01.

1982 H 245, § 3, eff. 6-29-82, reads: An action may be commenced pursuant to sections 3111.01 to 3111.19 of the Revised Code, as enacted by Section 1 of this act, to establish the father and child relationship, or the mother and child relationship, irrespective of whether a child is born prior to, or on or after, the effective date of this act.

Historical and Statutory Notes

Ed. Note: Former 3111.04 repealed by 1982 H 245, eff. 6-29-82; 127 v 1039; 125 v 184; 1953 H 1; GC 8006-4; Source—GC 12111. 3111.04 contains provisions analogous to former 3111.02 and 3111.03, repealed by 1982 H 245, eff. 6-29-82.

Pre-1953 H 1 Amendments: 124 v S 65

Amendment Note: 1997 H 352 rewrote this section, which prior thereto read:

"(A) An action to determine the existence or nonexistence of the father and child relationship may be brought by the child or the child's personal representative, the child's mother or her personal representative, a man alleged or alleging himself to be the child's father, the child support enforcement agency of the county in which the child resides if the child's mother is a recipient of public assistance as defined in section 2301.351 of the Revised Code or of services under Title IV-D of the "Social Security Act," 88 Stat. 2351 (1975), 42 U.S.C.A. 651, as amended, or the alleged father's personal representative.

"(B) An agreement does not bar an action under this section.

"(C) If an action under this section is brought before the birth of the child and if the action is contested, all proceedings, except service of process and the taking of depositions to perpetuate testimony, may be stayed until after the birth.

"(D) A recipient of public assistance as defined in section 2301.351 of the Revised Code or of services under Title IV-D of the "Social Security Act," 88 Stat. 2351 (1975), 42 U.S.C.A. 651, as amended, shall request the child support enforcement agency of the county in which a child resides to make an administrative determination of the existence or nonexistence of a parent and child relationship between the father and the child pursuant to section 3111.22 of the Revised Code before the recipient commences an action to determine the existence or nonexistence of that parent and child relationship."

Cross References

Guardian of the person or the estate, 2111.06
Procedure for father to establish relationship to his child, 2105.18
Reciprocal enforcement of support, defense of nonpaternity, adjudication of paternity issue, 3115.24

Library References

Action ⟹68.
Children Out-Of-Wedlock ⟹22, 30, 34.
WESTLAW Topic Nos. 13, 76H.
C.J.S. Actions §§ 243 to 247.
C.J.S. Children Out-of-Wedlock §§ 44 to 46, 49, 51, 70, 85 to 93.

OJur 3d: 47, Family Law § 956, 966, 968 to 970
Am Jur 2d: 10, Bastards § 75 to 77, 99
Maintainability of bastardy proceedings by infant prosecutrix in her own name and right. 50 ALR2d 1029
Right of nonresident mother to maintain bastardy proceedings. 57 ALR2d 689
Effect of marriage of woman to one other than defendant upon her right to institute or maintain bastardy proceeding. 98 ALR2d 256
Right of illegitimate child to maintain action to determine paternity. 19 ALR4th 1082

Carlin, Baldwin's Ohio Practice, *Merrick-Rippner Probate Law* § 17.2, 18.2, 18.3, 19.1, 19.2, 19.3, 19.4, 19.5, 19.6, 19.7, 19.8, 19.9, 19.10, 19.12, 38.4, 98.29, 98.30, 98.31, 105.2, 108.19, 108.20, 108.22, 108.23, 108.24, 108.27, 108.28, 108.31, 108.34 (1997)
Klein & Darling, Baldwin's Ohio Practice, *Civil Practice* § 1 (1997)
Sowald & Morganstern, Baldwin's Ohio Practice, *Domestic Relations Law* § 3.8, 3.9, 3.10, 3.13, 3.47, 22.18 (1997)

Law Review and Journal Commentaries

Bankruptcy Reform Act of 1994—What the Bankruptcy Code Giveth, Domestic Relations Courts (and Congress) Taketh Away, C.R. "Chip" Bowles. 8 Domestic Rel J Ohio 17 (March/April 1996).

The Burden of Proof in a Paternity Proceeding, Note. 25 J Fam L 357 (1986-87).

The Constitutional Rights of Unwed Fathers Before and After *Lehr v. Robertson,* Elizabeth Buchanan. 45 Ohio St L J 313 (1984).

Fathers, Biological and Anonymous, and Other Legal Strangers: Determination of Parentage and Artificial Insemination by Donor Under Ohio Law, Susan Garner Eisenman. 45 Ohio St L J 383 (1984).

Finality in Parentage Findings: Perfection or Finality?, Pamela J. MacAdams. 10 Domestic Rel J Ohio 19 (March/April 1998).

Gideon's Trumpet Revisited: Protecting the Rights of Indigent Defendants in Paternity Actions, Mark D. Esterle. 24 J Fam L 1 (1985-86).

Looking to Unwed Dads to Fill the Public Purse: A Disturbing Wave in Welfare Reform, Roger J.R. Levesque. 32 J Fam L 1 (Winter 1994).

Should Indigent Putative Fathers be Provided Court Appointed Counsel in Ohio Paternity Proceedings?, Daniel S. Cade. 10 Ohio N U L Rev 473 (1983).

Usefulness of Polygraph Results in Paternity Investigations when Used In Conjunction With Exclusionary Blood Tests and a Sixty-Day Conception Period, Richard J. Phannenstill. 21 J Fam L 69 (1982-83).

Notes of Decisions and Opinions

---

1. Constitutional issues

Even if Parentage Act precluded illegitimate children from claiming inheritance rights from and through their natural fathers absent inter vivos adjudication of paternity, inheritance scheme would not violate equal protection as to illegitimate children, as illegitimate child had several options through which to effectuate inheritance rights during father's lifetime, including acknowledgment, legitimation and right of action by child to establish paternity. Brookbank v. Gray (Ohio 1996) 74 Ohio St.3d 279, 658 N.E.2d 724.

Denial of court-appointed counsel for indigent paternity defendant who faced state as adversary, when complainant mother and her child were recipients of public assistance, violated due process guarantees of State and Federal Constitutions, as private interests of both putative father and child were substantial, substantial interest and integrity of paternity determination itself could be damaged were defendant to be denied counsel during proceedings, and state's financial stake in providing defendant with court-appointed counsel was insignificant relative to private interests involved. State ex rel. Cody v. Toner (Ohio 1983) 8 Ohio St.3d 22, 456 N.E.2d 813, 8 O.B.R. 255, certiorari denied 104 S.Ct. 1912, 466 U.S. 938, 80 L.Ed.2d 461.

Statute which did not expressly prohibit mother from bringing parentage action after child became adult and father's right to visitation had expired did not violate father's right to equal protection; father's failure to obtain visitation rights resulted from his own inaction rather than from parentage statutes, and, moreover, mother's action was barred under doctrine of laches. Park v. Ambrose (Ross 1993) 85 Ohio App.3d 179, 619 N.E.2d

469, dismissed, jurisdictional motion overruled 67 Ohio St.3d 1409, 615 N.E.2d 1043.

A county department of human services has no standing to (1) initiate a law suit to determine parentage after a mother assigned her right to receive child support to the agency to receive ADC, or (2) declare RC 3111.14 unconstitutional for not protecting the rights of illegitimate children because there is no general public interest in pecuniary reimbursement. State ex rel. Athens Cty. Dept. of Human Serv. v. Wolf (Athens 1991) 77 Ohio App.3d 619, 603 N.E.2d 252.

Rules that state is constitutionally required to provide appointed counsel and blood grouping tests to indigent putative father who faces state as adversary in paternity proceedings are to be applied retroactively. Keeney v. Lawson (Hamilton 1984) 19 Ohio App.3d 318, 484 N.E.2d 745, 19 O.B.R. 491.

It is a violation of the equal protection clauses of the United States and Ohio constitutions to allow the aid and support of the child support enforcement agency in an action for child support brought by parents who have established their parentage through the probate court and residential parents who are on public assistance while denying the aid and support of the child support enforcement agency to parents who have established their parentage through the administrative process. Cuyahoga County Support Enforcement Agency v Lozada, Nos. 67463+, 1995 WL 386965 (8th Dist Ct App, Cuyahoga, 6-29-95).

Paternity statute, which granted putative fathers standing to assert paternity when there was presumption of legitimacy, was unconstitutional infringement on fundamental interests of family of child born during mother's marriage to her husband without sufficient governmental purpose to justify the infringement for due process purposes, where putative father had no relationship with child, and mother and husband intended to nurture and raise child in their unitary family. Merkel v. Doe (Ohio Com.Pl. 1993) 63 Ohio Misc.2d 490, 635 N.E.2d 70.

2. In general

A probate judge in common pleas court has no subject matter jurisdiction to determine paternity as an ancillary claim to heirship against the estate of his alleged father. Martin v. Davidson (Ohio 1990) 53 Ohio St.3d 240, 559 N.E.2d 1348.

While every child conceived in wedlock is presumed legitimate, such presumption is not conclusive and may be rebutted by clear and convincing evidence that there were no sexual relations between husband and wife during the time in which the child must have been conceived, and a complaint for determination of paternity is sufficient if the plaintiff alleges he is the natural father of the child. Joseph v. Alexander (Ohio 1984) 12 Ohio St.3d 88, 465 N.E.2d 448, 12 O.B.R. 77.

An adulterine bastard is one begotten of the mother's adulterous intercourse and the proceedings ordained by RC 3111.01 et seq. (bastardy proceedings) are available to such a child and its mother regardless of the marital status of the mother at delivery. (Annotation from former RC 3111.01.) Franklin v. Julian (Ohio 1972) 30 Ohio St.2d 228, 283 N.E.2d 813, 59 O.O.2d 264.

Bastardy proceedings are governed wholly by statute, and under the provisions of the general code, a woman, to make a valid complaint in bastardy, must have been unmarried at the time of the birth of the alleged bastard child. (Annotation from former RC 3111.01.) State ex rel. Hoerres v. Wilkoff (Ohio 1952) 157 Ohio St. 286, 105 N.E.2d 39, 47 O.O. 174.

Trial court had subject matter jurisdiction to award child support retroactive to child's date of birth in paternity proceeding brought more than 20 years after child was born. Park v. Ambrose (Ross 1993) 85 Ohio App.3d 179, 619 N.E.2d 469, dismissed, jurisdictional motion overruled 67 Ohio St.3d 1409, 615 N.E.2d 1043.

When the state acts on a paternity complaint, a court should at the outset of the case determine whether the defendant is indigent and whether counsel should be appointed in his behalf. Rees v. Heimberger (Cuyahoga 1989) 60 Ohio App.3d 45, 573 N.E.2d 189, dismissed 47 Ohio St.3d 702, 547 N.E.2d 986, rehearing denied 48 Ohio St.3d 707, 550 N.E.2d 483, certiorari denied 110 S.Ct. 1827, 494 U.S. 1088, 108 L.Ed.2d 956.

Where a husband and wife agree to conceive a child by means of artificial insemination, and a child so conceived is born to the parties, it is against public policy for a court to enter a judgment establishing the husband's non-paternity in connection with a divorce of the parties and the remarriage of the mother. Brooks v. Fair (Van Wert 1988) 40 Ohio App.3d 202, 532 N.E.2d 208.

RC 3111.04(A) may not be used to determine the nonexistence of a parent-child relationship retroactively, although it may be applied retroactively to establish the existence of such relationship. Brooks v. Fair (Van Wert 1988) 40 Ohio App.3d 202, 532 N.E.2d 208.

A complainant/mother in an appeal from civil paternity proceedings is not entitled to a court-appointed counsel or a transcript provided at public expense because there is no possibility of the mother or child involved being deprived of their physical liberty should the appeal fail. State ex rel. Armstrong v. Hall (Marion 1986) 33 Ohio App.3d 1, 514 N.E.2d 424.

The presumption of paternity of a man signing a birth certificate as informant pursuant to RC 3705.14 may be overcome by the admissions of the man and the mother that he is not the natural father. In re Smith (Miami 1984) 16 Ohio App.3d 75, 474 N.E.2d 632, 16 O.B.R. 79.

The action provided by the statutes of Ohio whereby the mother may institute proceedings against the father of an illegitimate child is found in this section, which action may be maintained only by an unmarried woman. (Annotation from former RC 3111.01.) Sullivan v. Wilkoff (Mahoning 1939) 63 Ohio App. 269, 26 N.E.2d 460, 17 O.O. 32.

Right of action exists under the statute irrespective of whether the child is stillborn or born alive. (Annotation from former RC 3111.17.) State ex rel. Discus v. Van Dorn (Crawford 1937) 56 Ohio App. 82, 10 N.E.2d 14, 24 Ohio Law Abs. 104, 8 O.O. 393.

A creditor has no civil cause of action against a reputed father for necessaries furnished a bastard child. (Annotation from former RC 3111.17.) Hoffer v. White (Warren 1935) 53 Ohio App. 187, 4 N.E.2d 595, 20 Ohio Law Abs. 288, 5 O.O. 73.

A justice of the peace has no authority to discharge accused in a bastardy proceeding on ground that it appears from an examination of the complainant that prior to the filing of her complaint she and accused had entered into a private agreement by which accused had paid her an amount equal to the amount the common pleas court would charge the reputed father for maintenance of child. (Annotation from former RC 3111.04.) Walker v. Chandler (Ohio App. 7 Dist. 1921) 15 Ohio App. 292.

An individual may file a paternity action against the estate of a deceased putative parent, as the action is not barred by the death of the alleged parent. Martin v Davidson; vacated by 53 OS(3d) 240, 559 NE(2d) 1348 (1990), No. 13840 (9th Dist Ct App, Summit, 4-19-89).

The presumption that a child conceived in wedlock is legitimate cannot be rebutted except by evidence that the spouses had no sexual relations during the time in which the child was conceived. Joseph v Alexander, No. CA-6781 (5th Dist Ct App, Stark, 5-5-86).

A woman whose child was conceived and born during lawful marriage may, after death of her husband and while unmarried, institute and maintain a bastardy proceeding under the statute, charging another than her former husband with being the father of the child. (Annotation from former RC 3111.01.) (See also State ex rel Hoerres v Wilkoff, 157 OS 286, 105 NE(2d) 39 (1952); overruled by Franklin v Julian, 30 OS(2d) 228, 283 NE(2d) 813 (1972).) State ex rel. Sprungle v. Bard (Cuyahoga 1950) 98 N.E.2d 63, 59 Ohio Law Abs. 129.

Bastardy action does not abate because complainant gave birth to still-born child, as complaint was filed long before dead fetus was born, and complainant is entitled to trial to determine whether she is entitled to judgment "for support, maintenance and necessary expenses caused by pregnancy," as provided for under this section. (Annotation from former RC 3111.17.) Seldenright v. Jenkins (Ohio Prob. 1936) 3 Ohio Supp. 36, 22 Ohio Law Abs. 576, 7 O.O. 127.

3. Procedural issues

RC 3111.02 to 3111.04, 3111.09, and 3111.10 are in pari materia and must be construed together. Hulett v. Hulett (Ohio 1989) 45 Ohio St.3d 288, 544 N.E.2d 257.

The doctrine of res judicata can be invoked to give conclusive effect to a determination of parentage contained in a dissolution decree or a legitimation order, thereby barring a subsequent paternity action brought pursuant to RC Ch 3111. In re Gilbraith (Ohio 1987) 32 Ohio St.3d 127, 512 N.E.2d 956.

Husband of mother of natural father's children did not have standing to maintain action to determine existence and nonexistence of father and child relationship between children and natural father. Weinman v. Larsh (Ohio 1983) 5 Ohio St.3d 85, 448 N.E.2d 1384, 5 O.B.R. 138.

Res judicata did not bar former wife's child, who was found in divorce decree to be illegitimate, from bringing parentage action in juvenile court; child was not party to divorce action, and child was not in privity with former wife. Fitzpatrick v. Fitzpatrick (Ohio App. 12 Dist. 1998) 126 Ohio App.3d 476, 710 N.E.2d 778, dismissed, appeal not allowed 82 Ohio St.3d 1441, 695 N.E.2d 264.

Court deciding whether adjudicated father should be estopped from challenging relationship by means of motion for relief from parentage determination may examine factors including: whether adjudicated father had reason to suspect parentage and whether he acted reasonably after first developing his suspicions; whether adjudicated father established relationship with child and nature of parties' relationship; likely future of any relationship; and chance of finding and establishing relationship with child's biological father. Leguillon v. Leguillon (Ohio App. 12 Dist. 1998) 124 Ohio App.3d 757, 707 N.E.2d 571.

After decree of divorce or dissolution has been entered which includes adjudication or agreement as to parentage and parental rights and obligations, postdecree paternity action on child's behalf is subject to overriding consideration of child's best interest. Leguillon v. Leguillon (Ohio App. 12 Dist. 1998) 124 Ohio App.3d 757, 707 N.E.2d 571.

Determination of parentage in agreed dissolution decree or legitimation order will bar subsequent paternity action. Cornell v. Brumfield (Ohio App. 4 Dist. 1996) 115 Ohio App.3d 259, 685 N.E.2d 270.

Agreed settlement entry of previous parentage action between parents of minor child and judgment of support entered as result of action brought by child to establish parent-child relationship were not mutually exclusive and were capable of simultaneous enforcement, as parentage claims of child and his mother were separate and distinct. Cornell v. Brumfield (Ohio App. 4 Dist. 1996) 115 Ohio App.3d 259, 685 N.E.2d 270.

Mother's compromise agreement with alleged father did not bar later paternity action brought on behalf of child to recover prospective support and by Department of Human Services to recover birthing expenses, where child was not party to compromise agreement. Payne v. Cartee (Ross 1996) 111 Ohio App.3d 580, 676 N.E.2d 946, appeal not allowed 77 Ohio St.3d 1482, 673 N.E.2d 143.

Child was not party to his mother's prior divorce action, so as to bar subsequent paternity action on res judicata grounds. State ex rel. Smith v. Smith (Cuyahoga 1996) 110 Ohio App.3d 336, 674 N.E.2d 398, appeal not allowed 76 Ohio St.3d 1496, 670 N.E.2d 243.

County child support enforcement agency was not in privity with mother in prior divorce proceeding, so as to bar agency from bringing subsequent paternity action on grounds of res judicata; agency would not succeed to estate or interest formerly held by mother, but had interest in determining existence of parent-child relationship between child who was not named in divorce decree and mother's former husband. State ex rel. Smith v. Smith (Cuyahoga 1996) 110 Ohio App.3d 336, 674 N.E.2d 398, appeal not allowed 76 Ohio St.3d 1496, 670 N.E.2d 243.

Absent showing that alleged father requested leave, stay of paternity and child support proceedings was not required, under Soldiers' and Sailors' Civil Relief Act, by reason of alleged father's military service. Phelps v. Fowler (Cuyahoga 1995) 107 Ohio App.3d 263, 668 N.E.2d 558, appeal not allowed 75 Ohio St.3d 1452, 663 N.E.2d 332.

Alleged father lacked standing to argue that conflict of interest resulted from joint representation of mother, child, and the Department of Health and Human Services in suit to determine paternity and past-due child support. Phelps v. Fowler (Cuyahoga 1995) 107 Ohio App.3d 263, 668 N.E.2d 558, appeal not allowed 75 Ohio St.3d 1452, 663 N.E.2d 332.

Despite mother's contention that father's failure to participate in administrative determination of parentage precluded court of common pleas from exercising jurisdiction over parentage action, given apparent conflict in jurisdictional statutes, court of common pleas was not so patently and unambiguously devoid of subject matter jurisdiction that Court of Appeals would issue writ of prohibition prohibiting court of common pleas from exercising jurisdiction while final judgment was pending. State ex rel. Dixon v. Clark Cty. Court of Common Pleas, Juv. Div. (Clark 1995) 103 Ohio App.3d 523, 660 N.E.2d 486.

Fact that prosecutor from child support enforcement agency signed paternity complaint did not establish that action was brought by the agency rather than mother so that court was without jurisdiction. Ransome v. Lampman (Miami 1995) 103 Ohio App.3d 8, 658 N.E.2d 313, dismissed, appeal not allowed 73 Ohio St.3d 1449, 654 N.E.2d 985.

In paternity action filed by Child Support Enforcement Agency (CSEA), record supported finding of paternity, where father admitted paternity at hearing and blood tests of parties concluded probability of paternity at approximately 99 percent. Dorsett v. Wheeler (Paulding 1995) 101 Ohio App.3d 716, 656 N.E.2d 698.

In paternity action filed by Child Support Enforcement Agency (CSEA), trial court, if not CSEA's attorney, had affirmative duty to inquire into status of mother's legal representation, though CSEA's complaint named mother and children as plaintiffs, as CSEA's attorney did not represent mother's interests during hearing and trial court expressly found that mother appeared without counsel. Dorsett v. Wheeler (Paulding 1995) 101 Ohio App.3d 716, 656 N.E.2d 698.

In paternity action filed by Child Support Enforcement Agency (CSEA) on behalf of mother and children, father could not be required to reimburse CSEA for governmental financial assistance given to mother and her children, where CSEA was never made party to action and there was no evidence in record to support amount awarded to CSEA. Dorsett v. Wheeler (Paulding 1995) 101 Ohio App.3d 716, 656 N.E.2d 698.

While Ohio Department of Human Resources (ODHR) has authority to seek recoupment for its monetary expenditures for support of its recipients, proper procedure must be employed to recover such expenditures. Dorsett v. Wheeler (Paulding 1995) 101 Ohio App.3d 716, 656 N.E.2d 698.

Legal custodians of child, who obtained custody from child's mother, were in privity with mother, and so were barred by res judicata from litigating issue of paternity of child that had been decided in divorce decree. Broxterman v. Broxterman (Hamilton 1995) 101 Ohio App.3d 661, 656 N.E.2d 394.

Child was not in privity with his mother in divorce action, and so was not barred by res judicata from bringing paternity action, even though paternity had been decided in divorce decree; although interests of child and mother coincided over support, their interests may have diverged on child's right to know identity of his biological father, and his potential rights of inheritance from his biological father. Broxterman v. Broxterman (Hamilton 1995) 101 Ohio App.3d 661, 656 N.E.2d 394.

After decree of divorce or dissolution has been entered which includes adjudication or agreement as to parentage and parental rights and obligations, postdecree paternity action cannot be brought on child's behalf absent express determination by court that such action is in best interest of child. Broxterman v. Broxterman (Hamilton 1995) 101 Ohio App.3d 661, 656 N.E.2d 394.

In action to determine father and child relationship with minor child, after successful final determination in that case establishing existence of father-child relationship, father was not entitled as a matter of right to file motion in that proceeding seeking visitation rights with minor child. Burns v. Darnell (Franklin 1995) 100 Ohio App.3d 419, 654 N.E.2d 169.

Putative father could not challenge paternity order more than 30 days after administrative determination and did not have right to HLA testing. State ex rel. Fulton Cty. Dept. of Human Serv. v. Kenneth J. (Fulton 1994) 99 Ohio App.3d 475, 651 N.E.2d 27.

County Support Enforcement Agency has no independent authority to initiate action to establish putative father's parentage without mother's initial request for administrative determination. State ex rel. Gillion v. Reese (Cuyahoga 1994) 97 Ohio App.3d 315, 646 N.E.2d 852, appeal not allowed 71 Ohio St.3d 1466, 644 N.E.2d 1388.

Mother's "dilatory" conduct did not amount to unexplained or unreasonable delay and, thus, laches did not bar her paternity action against putative father; mother testified that she notified putative father in person when she was pregnant, mother instituted parentage action eight months after giving birth, action was voluntarily dismissed five and one-half years later for failure to serve summons on putative father within one year of filing action and mother refiled action only two months later. Seegert v. Zietlow (Cuyahoga 1994) 95 Ohio App.3d 451, 642 N.E.2d 697.

Putative father was not "materially prejudiced" by mother's alleged dilatory conduct in bringing paternity proceedings and, thus, laches did not bar that action; putative father's generic assertion of hardship arising from allegedly excessive award was insufficient to rise to level of material prejudice, and, despite putative father's claim that he had lost all rights of visitation, custody and participation in direction of child's growth and development during her formative years, child was nine years old and had many formative years remaining. Seegert v. Zietlow (Cuyahoga 1994) 95 Ohio App.3d 451, 642 N.E.2d 697.

Parentage must be determined prior to death of putative father to the extent that parent-child relationship is being established under chapter governing descent and distribution; however, parent-child relationship may be established after death of putative father under chapter governing paternity actions. In re Estate of Hicks (Erie 1993) 90 Ohio App.3d 483, 629 N.E.2d 1086.

A judgment entry in a divorce action finding that a child was born during the marriage and ordering the husband to pay child support is not conclusive as to the paternity of the child where the husband had denied such paternity in the divorce action and the decree did not explicitly find that a parent and child relationship existed; res judicata is inapplicable in a subsequent paternity action filed by the putative father absent a specific finding that a parent and child relationship existed; therefore, a juvenile court errs in dismissing the subsequent paternity action. LaBonte v. LaBonte (Meigs 1988) 61 Ohio App.3d 209, 572 N.E.2d 704, motion overruled 42 Ohio St.3d 709, 538 N.E.2d 122.

Although a proper party may intervene in an existing parentage action brought under RC 3111.04, a proper party may not bring a Civ R 60(B) motion to vacate a judgment in an action to which he was never a party. Hardman v. Chiaramonte (Summit 1987) 39 Ohio App.3d 9, 528 N.E.2d 1270.

Unlike a custody proceeding under RC 3109.27, there is no statutory requirement that a party bringing an RC Ch 3111 parentage action provide notice of related proceedings in other courts. Hardman v. Chiaramonte (Summit 1987) 39 Ohio App.3d 9, 528 N.E.2d 1270.

Under Uniform Parentage Act, child, child's mother, alleged father of child, or their personal representatives may bring action in juvenile court to effect determination of paternity and to provide for custody and support. Manley v. Howard (Marion 1985) 25 Ohio App.3d 1, 495 N.E.2d 436, 25 O.B.R. 30.

A plaintiff claiming to be the natural father of a child born to a woman while she was married to another man may assert that claim in an action brought pursuant to the Uniform Parentage Act, RC Ch 3111, even though the child was determined to be the issue of the marriage during an earlier divorce suit in which the plaintiff was not a party, and the juvenile court has jurisdiction over the plaintiff's claim. Gatt v. Gedeon (Cuyahoga 1984) 20 Ohio App.3d 285, 485 N.E.2d 1059, 20 O.B.R. 376.

A judgment pursuant to former RC 3111.17 which sets visitation rights and support duties of a man who has signed a birth certificate as informant, even though both he and the mother admit he is not the natural father, may be properly vacated to relieve the child and mother from the determination of paternity implicit in the judgment. In re Smith (Miami 1984) 16 Ohio App.3d 75, 474 N.E.2d 632, 16 O.B.R. 79.

Determination of paternity in a bastardy proceeding is not a prerequisite to the prosecution of a parent under RC 2903.08 for nonsupport of an illegitimate child. (Annotation from former RC 3111.08.) State v. Medley (Miami 1960) 111 Ohio App. 352, 172 N.E.2d 143, 14 O.O.2d 328.

A husband's paternity is rebuttable by a genetic test and a putative father may bring a parentage action where the mother was, and continues to be, married to another man at the time the child was conceived. Crawford County Child Support Enforcement Agency v Sprague, No. 3-97-13, 1997 WL 746770 (3d Dist Ct App, Crawford, 12-5-97).

A prior divorce decree does not bar a child support enforcement agency from initiating its own action to establish a parent-child relationship between a minor child and the former husband and to request the court order the former husband to pay current and future child support, including health insurance. State v Smith, No. 69379, 1996 WL 139707 (8th Dist Ct App, Cuyahoga, 3-28-96).

A forty-two year old man who voluntarily files a petition to be declared the father, even though he knows that he may be infertile, is not entitled to Civ R 60(B) relief from the agreed order declaring him to be the father where the sole ground for relief is the infertility which he knew about since he was nineteen years old. Snyder v Fulkrod, No. 17224, 1995 WL 734021 (9th Dist Ct App, Summit, 12-13-95).

Paternity is a special proceeding under RC 2505.02, but a judgment related to paternity, in itself, does not affect a substantial right until the trial court issues a support order based upon the judgment of defendant's paternity, so that a defendant's motion to vacate the judgment, filed thirty-three days after the final order, entitles the defendant to a hearing on the merits of his motion. Adams v Jett, No. 14636, 1995 WL 51060 (2d Dist Ct App, Montgomery, 2-8-95).

Father fails to allege a basis for relief under Civ R 60(B) by his failure to allege fraud after blood tests showed that he could not be the child's biological father. In re Belden, No. 92 CA 21, 1993 WL 179254 (2d Dist Ct App, Miami, 5-25-93).

Although a county department of human services may intervene in a parentage action for purposes of collecting or recovering support, a county department of human services does not have standing to initiate a parentage action. State ex rel Athens County Human Services Dept v Wolf, No. 1462 (4th Dist Ct App, Athens, 10-9-91).

4. Child's action

Where there is no prior judgment of paternity, the doctrine of res judicata does not act as a bar to a legitimation action subsequently brought by or on behalf of a child under RC Ch 3111. Collett v. Cogar (Ohio 1988) 35 Ohio St.3d 114, 518 N.E.2d 1202.

A child born out of wedlock may not bring a paternity proceeding under RC Ch 3111, but such child does have the same common law right to bring a civil action against his father for support and maintenance as does a legitimate child, incident to which the court shall make a determination on the issue of paternity, and so the unmarried mother's dismissal of her action under RC Ch 3111 with prejudice is not a bar to the minor child's separate common law action for support and maintenance from his putative father. (Annotation from former RC 3111.01.) Johnson v. Norman (Ohio 1981) 66 Ohio St.2d 186, 421 N.E.2d 124, 20 O.O.3d 196.

RC 2151.42, which makes it a criminal offense for the father of an illegitimate child to fail to support such a child, does not give rise to a civil action for support on behalf of such child. (Annotation from former RC 3111.03.) Baston v. Sears (Ohio 1968) 15 Ohio St.2d 166, 239 N.E.2d 62, 44 O.O.2d 144.

Where a minor commences an action under RC 3111.01 and no attack is made upon her capacity to sue until after a verdict is rendered finding the defendant guilty, the trial court has the power to permit the minor to amend her complaint to show her minority by adding the affidavit of her mother, as next friend, to the complaint and to conform the complaint and proceedings to the facts proved when the amendment does not substantially change the claim, and failure to do so constitutes error. (Annotation from former RC 3111.03.) Taylor v. Scott (Ohio 1959) 168 Ohio St. 391, 155 N.E.2d 884, 7 O.O.2d 243.

Right of a child to bring an action to establish paternity is separate and distinct from its mother's right to bring such an action, and a mother's agreement not to establish paternity cannot bind the child. Snider v. Lillie (Ohio App. 1 Dist. 1997) 131 Ohio App.3d 444, 722 N.E.2d 1036.

Former wife's child, who was born after former wife and former husband divorced, was not bound by domestic relations court's finding of illegitimacy in divorce decree, and he could bring separate paternity action against former husband. Fitzpatrick v. Fitzpatrick (Ohio App. 12 Dist. 1998) 126 Ohio App.3d 476, 710 N.E.2d 778, dismissed, appeal not allowed 82 Ohio St.3d 1441, 695 N.E.2d 264.

The right of a child to bring an action to establish paternity is separate and distinct from a mother's right to bring such an action. Fitzpatrick v. Fitzpatrick (Ohio App. 12 Dist. 1998) 126 Ohio App.3d 476, 710 N.E.2d 778, dismissed, appeal not allowed 82 Ohio St.3d 1441, 695 N.E.2d 264.

Where a mother enters into agreement not to establish paternity with an alleged father, the child is not bound by the agreement and may subsequently bring a paternity action against the alleged father. Fitzpatrick v. Fitzpatrick (Ohio App. 12 Dist. 1998) 126 Ohio App.3d 476, 710 N.E.2d 778, dismissed, appeal not allowed 82 Ohio St.3d 1441, 695 N.E.2d 264.

Child's claim in parentage action is separate and distinct from that of the mother. State ex rel. Donovan v. Zajac (Ohio App. 11 Dist. 1998) 125 Ohio App.3d 245,

708 N.E.2d 254, dismissed, appeal not allowed 81 Ohio St.3d 1521, 692 N.E.2d 1023.

Child is not barred by paternity adjudication from bringing action to determine existence or nonexistence of father-child relationship; although adjudication may bar father from challenging relationship under doctrine of res judicata, child may still challenge relationship since he or she was arguably not in privity with parties to original action. Leguillon v. Leguillon (Ohio App. 12 Dist. 1998) 124 Ohio App.3d 757, 707 N.E.2d 571.

Court determining whether to permit child to bring his or her own action to seek or challenge adjudication of paternity should consider appointment of guardian ad litem to aid in determining child's best interests. Leguillon v. Leguillon (Ohio App. 12 Dist. 1998) 124 Ohio App.3d 757, 707 N.E.2d 571.

Juvenile court did not abuse its discretion by permitting mother to proceed as child's next friend in his paternity action, where such action was prosecuted solely on son's behalf, there was no showing that she might fail to vigorously pursue child's action, and guardian ad litem was appointed three days after determination that alleged father was, in fact, child's father. Payne v. Cartee (Ross 1996) 111 Ohio App.3d 580, 676 N.E.2d 946, appeal not allowed 77 Ohio St.3d 1482, 673 N.E.2d 143.

Mother's claim is distinct and separate from that of child for purposes of determining whether judgment in mother's paternity action presents res judicata bar to later action by child. Payne v. Cartee (Ross 1996) 111 Ohio App.3d 580, 676 N.E.2d 946, appeal not allowed 77 Ohio St.3d 1482, 673 N.E.2d 143.

Child was not in privity with mother with regard to compromise agreement reached in mother's paternity action, and, therefore, doctrine of equitable estoppel did not apply to a child's paternity action, regardless of whether alleged father relied on any of mother's representations with regard to effect of compromise. Payne v. Cartee (Ross 1996) 111 Ohio App.3d 580, 676 N.E.2d 946, appeal not allowed 77 Ohio St.3d 1482, 673 N.E.2d 143.

Doctrine of laches did not apply to child's paternity action, even though alleged father had dramatically changed his obligations in life by getting married and having a new family, absent showing that alleged father incurred these new family obligations in reliance on terms of compromise agreement with mother. Payne v. Cartee (Ross 1996) 111 Ohio App.3d 580, 676 N.E.2d 946, appeal not allowed 77 Ohio St.3d 1482, 673 N.E.2d 143.

Assuming that probate court's finding that woman was intestate's biological child was supported by competent, credible evidence, woman failed to establish that she was "legitimized" in one of recognized manners and thus had no right to intestate's estate; only method by which woman could affirmatively seek relief would have been under Parentage Act which required that parentage action be brought in juvenile court which woman had failed to do. In re Estate of Hicks (Erie 1993) 90 Ohio App.3d 483, 629 N.E.2d 1086.

Implied agreement between mother and father, if any, did not bar award of child support in child's action to establish paternity. Park v. Ambrose (Ross 1993) 85 Ohio App.3d 179, 619 N.E.2d 469, dismissed, jurisdictional motion overruled 67 Ohio St.3d 1409, 615 N.E.2d 1043.

Pursuant to RC 3111.04, a child has a right to bring a paternity action in his own name; thus, a child's claim is separate and distinct from that of his mother. Rees v. Heimberger (Cuyahoga 1989) 60 Ohio App.3d 45, 573 N.E.2d 189, dismissed 47 Ohio St.3d 702, 547 N.E.2d 986, rehearing denied 48 Ohio St.3d 707, 550 N.E.2d 483, certiorari denied 110 S.Ct. 1827, 494 U.S. 1088, 108 L.Ed.2d 956.

A child born out of wedlock may seek to inherit from his natural father by establishing paternity through RC 3111.04 or by the procedures established under RC Ch 2105. Garrison v. Smith (Lucas 1988) 55 Ohio App.3d 14, 561 N.E.2d 1041.

A testator's illegitimate child can contest the will if a parent-child relationship was established during the testator's life. Birman v. Sproat (Miami 1988) 47 Ohio App.3d 65, 546 N.E.2d 1354.

An illegitimate child may bring a civil action under common-law against his father for support and maintenance, and mother of the illegitimate child may maintain a separate cause of action against father for cost of past support of the child as well as for future support. Kulcsar v. Petrovic (Wayne 1984) 20 Ohio App.3d 104, 484 N.E.2d 1365, 20 O.B.R. 126.

A minor cannot bring a bastardy action. (Annotation from former RC 3111.03.) State ex rel. Love v. Jones (Hamilton 1953) 98 Ohio App. 45, 128 N.E.2d 228, 57 O.O. 161.

A minor child is not barred from instituting a later action to determine paternity when a prior action brought in her name has reached judgment through a stipulated agreement. Ransome v Lampman, Nos. 94-CA-20+, 1995 WL 136983, 2d Dist Ct App, Miami, 3-31-95).

Adult child who had learned of identity of her birth father as an adult was not entitled to award of retroactive support, where at time of child's birth, child's mother and her husband, who could not conceive a child, mutually agreed with birth father, whose affair with mother had resulted in child's conception, that child would be raised by mother and her husband as if child were their natural child, husband remained committed to child throughout her childhood, and child was raised in a middle-class lifestyle with all of her basic needs met. Hugershoff v. Loecy (Ohio Com.Pl. 1999) 103 Ohio Misc.2d 58, 725 N.E.2d 378.

To determine the rights, status, and legal relations of an illegitimate child in regard to the alleged father, such child may, by his next friend, maintain an action for declaratory judgment. (Annotation from former RC 3111.01.) Maiden v. Maiden (Ohio Com.Pl. & Juv. 1955) 153 N.E.2d 460, 78 Ohio Law Abs. 551, 11 O.O.2d 362.

A bastardy proceeding cannot be instituted and maintained by the state of Ohio, nor by a complainant while she is a minor. (Annotation from former RC 3111.03.) State ex rel. Love v. Jones (Ohio Com.Pl. 1953) 111 N.E.2d 607, 65 Ohio Law Abs. 595, 50 O.O. 249, affirmed 98 Ohio App. 45, 128 N.E.2d 228, 57 O.O. 161.

3111.05 Limitation of action

An action to determine the existence or nonexistence of the father and child relationship may not be brought later than five years after the child reaches the age of eighteen. Neither section 3111.04 of the Revised Code nor this section extends the time within which a right of inheritance or a right to a succession may be asserted beyond the time provided by Chapter 2105., 2107., 2113., 2117., or 2123. of the Revised Code.

(1982 H 245, eff. 6-29-82)

Uncodified Law

1992 S 10, § 5: See Uncodified Law under 3111.01.

1982 H 245, § 3: See Uncodified Law under 3111.04.

Historical and Statutory Notes

Ed. Note: Former 3111.05 repealed by 1982 H 245, eff. 6-29-82; 127 v 1039; 125 v 184; 1953 H 1; GC 8006-5; Source—GC 12112.

Pre-1953 H 1 Amendments: 124 v S 65

Library References

Children Out-Of-Wedlock ⚷38.
WESTLAW Topic No. 76H.
C.J.S. Children Out-of-Wedlock §§ 46, 67, 81, 82.

OJur 3d: 47, Family Law § 971; 62, Investment Securities and Securities Regulation § 53
Am Jur 2d: 10, Bastards § 78, 79
Statute of limitations in illegitimacy or bastardy proceedings. 59 ALR3d 685
Statutes limiting time for commencement of action to establish paternity of illegitimate child as violating child's constitutional rights. 16 ALR4th 926

Carlin, Baldwin's Ohio Practice, *Merrick-Rippner Probate Law* § 17.2, 18.2, 18.3, 19.1, 19.2, 19.3, 19.4, 19.5, 19.6, 19.7, 19.8, 19.10, 19.12, 38.4, 98.29, 98.30, 98.31, 105.2, 108.19, 108.20, 108.21, 108.22, 108.23, 108.24, 108.27, 108.28, 108.31 (1997)
Klein & Darling, Baldwin's Ohio Practice, *Civil Practice* § 1 (1997)
Sowald & Morganstern, Baldwin's Ohio Practice, *Domestic Relations Law* § 3.23 (1997)

Law Review and Journal Commentaries

Practice Pointer—Application of the Doctrine of Laches in Parentage Actions, Pamela J. MacAdams. 9 Domestic Rel J Ohio 9 (January/February 1997).

Notes of Decisions and Opinions

Constitutional issues 1
Laches 2
Limit for bringing action 4
Res judicata 3

---

1. Constitutional issues

The provision of RC 3111.05 limiting actions to determine paternity to five years after the child reaches eighteen is not unconstitutional on its face. Pound v Fracker, No. CA-3018 (5th Dist Ct App, Licking, 5-22-84).

A limitations period of six years for bringing paternity suits claiming the defendant is the father of an illegitimate child is held "not substantially related to [the state] interest in avoiding the litigation of stale or fraudulent claims" and held to deny the equal Protection of the laws secured by the Fourteenth Amendment to the federal constitution, in view of the state's law allowing legitimate children to seek support from their parents at any time. (Ed. note: Pennsylvania statute construed in light of federal constitution.) Clark v. Jeter (U.S.Pa. 1988) 108 S.Ct. 1910, 486 U.S. 456, 100 L.Ed.2d 465.

2. Laches

Laches may be applicable in parentage actions filed prior to the expiration of the statute of limitations, but only if the defendant can show material prejudice. Wright v. Oliver (Ohio 1988) 35 Ohio St.3d 10, 517 N.E.2d 883.

Complaint seeking adjudication of paternity and back child support, brought one month prior to child's attaining age of majority, was not barred by doctrine of laches, as putative father was not materially prejudiced by delay; adjudicated father did not claim loss of evidence helpful to his case or change in his position that would not have occurred had child's mother not delayed in asserting her rights, and had been aware of child's existence and likelihood of his paternity since her birth. State ex rel. Donovan v. Zajac (Ohio App. 11 Dist. 1998) 125 Ohio App.3d 245, 708 N.E.2d 254, dismissed, appeal not allowed 81 Ohio St.3d 1521, 692 N.E.2d 1023.

Laches is not a defense in an action for paternity and child support brought fourteen years after the child's birth where the defendant (1) is contacted by the county child support enforcement agency before the child's birth and informed of his putative parentage, (2) is informed by his own mother, shortly after the birth, that the child's mother had advised her that he was the putative father, (3) makes no attempt to verify whether or not he is the father, and (4) is not materially prejudiced by delay in bringing the action. Cooper v Russell, No. CA94-11-095, 1995 WL 520773 (12th Dist Ct App, Warren, 9-5-95).

Adult child born out of wedlock was not barred by doctrine of laches from seeking support and other statutory relief from father, even though such a claim by child's mother was barred due to her initial decision not to seek child support, and delay of over 23 years in asserting such a claim, where child did not unreasonably delay in bringing claim after becoming aware of her birth father's identity. Hugershoff v. Loecy (Ohio Com.Pl. 1999) 103 Ohio Misc.2d 58, 725 N.E.2d 378.

Mother of adult child was barred by doctrine of laches from pursuing claim for child support and other statutory relief arising out of parentage action against estate of deceased father, where mother, her husband, and father were aware early on of father's paternity, but had entered mutual understanding that child would be raised by mother and her husband without any interference from father, and mother, after initially making decision not to pursue child support, had waited for over 23 years before bringing suit. Hugershoff v. Loecy (Ohio Com.Pl. 1999) 103 Ohio Misc.2d 58, 725 N.E.2d 378.

3. Res judicata

The doctrine of res judicata can be invoked to give conclusive effect to a determination of parentage contained in a dissolution decree or a legitimation order, thereby barring a subsequent paternity action brought pursuant to RC Ch 3111. In re Gilbraith (Ohio 1987) 32 Ohio St.3d 127, 512 N.E.2d 956.

Legitimation order filed in probate court with consent of mother did not bar subsequent parentage action wherein mother sought child support arrearages; application of doctrine of res judicata would violate state's strong public policy favoring protection of children and their support, health, maintenance and welfare, and would also violate equal protection. Lewis v. Chapin (Cuyahoga 1994) 93 Ohio App.3d 695, 639 N.E.2d 848.

Child was not barred under doctrine of res judicata from pursuing parentage action on basis that father acknowledged existence of parent-child relationship and that mother consented to filing of legitimacy order, as child was not a party or in privity with a party to the legitimacy order. Lewis v. Chapin (Cuyahoga 1994) 93 Ohio App.3d 695, 639 N.E.2d 848.

4. Limit for bringing action

Court lacked authority to order biological father to provide present and future child support to child who had reached age of majority and was emancipated, even though paternity action had been timely filed within five years after child reached age 18. Snider v. Lillie (Ohio App. 1 Dist. 1997) 131 Ohio App.3d 444, 722 N.E.2d 1036.

Time in which to bring a claim to establish paternity is five years longer than period of father's duty to support, which expires when child reaches age 18. Snider v. Lillie (Ohio App. 1 Dist. 1997) 131 Ohio App.3d 444, 722 N.E.2d 1036.

Child may bring action to establish paternity and pursue past support obligation even after any present support obligation has been eliminated due to child's reaching majority. Hudgins v. Mitchell (Ohio App. 9 Dist. 1998) 128 Ohio App.3d 403, 715 N.E.2d 213.

Statute of limitations for parentage action does not begin to run until child reaches age of majority. Lewis v. Chapin (Cuyahoga 1994) 93 Ohio App.3d 695, 639 N.E.2d 848.

Failure of temporary administrator of intestate's estate to assert that alleged biological daughter of intestate should have been barred by statute of limitations provision applicable to paternity actions from establishing parentage for purposes of descent and distribution resulted in waiver of that defense. In re Estate of Hicks (Erie 1993) 90 Ohio App.3d 483, 629 N.E.2d 1086.

Parentage action brought by adult child within five years after she reached majority was timely regardless of limitations period in effect when child was born. Park v. Ambrose (Ross 1993) 85 Ohio App.3d 179, 619 N.E.2d 469, dismissed, jurisdictional motion overruled 67 Ohio St.3d 1409, 615 N.E.2d 1043.

Limitations period for parentage actions is five years after child reaches 18 years of age regardless of whether prior parentage statutes in effect when child was born would otherwise have barred action. Park v. Ambrose (Ross 1993) 85 Ohio App.3d 179, 619 N.E.2d 469, dismissed, jurisdictional motion overruled 67 Ohio St.3d 1409, 615 N.E.2d 1043.

The four-year statute of limitations of RC 2305.09(D) is inapplicable to a parentage action; rather, RC 3111.05, providing that a parentage action shall not be brought later than five years following a child reaching the age of eighteen, is controlling, even if the child was born before the effective date of RC 3111.05. Marcy v. McCommons (Ashtabula 1988) 55 Ohio App.3d 191, 563 N.E.2d 315.

The statute of limitations of RC 3111.05 is properly applied to an action commenced under RC Ch 2105 to determine heirship, where the action is essentially a paternity action. Garrison v. Smith (Lucas 1988) 55 Ohio App.3d 14, 561 N.E.2d 1041.

The limitation of actions brought under RC Ch 3111 is governed by RC 3111.05, and not by RC 2305.09. Manley v. Howard (Marion 1985) 25 Ohio App.3d 1, 495 N.E.2d 436, 25 O.B.R. 30.

An action for support brought by a mother of an illegitimate child which was time-barred by RC 2305.09 before the enactment of RC Ch 3111 by 1982 H 245, eff. 6-29-82, is not revived by that enactment. Manley v. Howard (Marion 1985) 25 Ohio App.3d 1, 495 N.E.2d 436, 25 O.B.R. 30.

Putative daughter was entitled to establish her paternity for purposes of inheritance, despite death of her alleged father. Meckstroth v. Robinson (Ohio Com.Pl. 1996) 83 Ohio Misc.2d 57, 679 N.E.2d 744.

3111.06 Jurisdiction

(A) The juvenile court has original jurisdiction of any action authorized under sections 3111.01 to 3111.19 of the Revised Code. An action may be brought under those sections in the juvenile court of the county in which the child, the child's mother, or the alleged father resides or is found or, if the alleged father is deceased, of the county in which proceedings for the probate of the alleged father's estate have been or can be commenced, or of the county in which the child is being provided support by the county department of job and family services of that county. An action pursuant to sections 3111.01 to 3111.19 of the Revised Code to object to an administrative order issued pursuant to former section 3111.21 or section 3111.22 of the Revised Code determining the existence or nonexistence of a parent and child relationship that has not become final and enforceable, may be brought only in the juvenile court of the county in which the child support enforcement agency that issued the order is located. If an action for divorce, dissolution, or legal separation has been filed in a court of common pleas, that court of common pleas has original jurisdiction to determine if the parent and child relationship exists between one or both of the parties and any child alleged or presumed to be the child of one or both of the parties.

(B) A person who has sexual intercourse in this state submits to the jurisdiction of the courts of this state as to an action brought under sections 3111.01 to 3111.19 of the Revised Code with respect to a child who may have been conceived by that act of intercourse. In addition to any other method provided by the Rules of Civil Procedure, personal jurisdiction may be acquired by personal service of summons outside this state or by certified mail with proof of actual receipt.

(1999 H 471, eff. 7-1-00; 1997 H 352, eff. 1-1-98; 1990 H 514, eff. 1-1-91; 1986 H 476; 1982 H 245)

Uncodified Law

1992 S 10, § 5: See Uncodified Law under 3111.01.

1982 H 245, § 3: See Uncodified Law under 3111.04.

Historical and Statutory Notes

Ed. Note: Former 3111.06 repealed by 1982 H 245, eff. 6-29-82; 127 v 1039; 125 v 184; 1953 H 1; GC 8006-6; Source—GC 12113. 3111.06 contains provisions analogous to former 3111.08, repealed by 1982 H 245, eff. 6-29-82.

Pre-1953 H 1 Amendments: 124 v S 65

Amendment Note: 1999 H 471 substituted "county department of job and family services" for "department of human services" in division (A).

Amendment Note: 1997 H 352 added the third sentence in division (A); and made changes to reflect gender neutral language.

Cross References

Jurisdiction of juvenile court, 2151.23

Service of process, Civ R 4 to 4.6

Library References

Children Out-Of-Wedlock ⚷36.
WESTLAW Topic No. 76H.
C.J.S. Children Out-of-Wedlock §§ 47, 83.

OJur 3d: 47, Family Law § 973; 48, Family Law § 1554
Am Jur 2d: 10, Bastards § 76

Carlin, Baldwin's Ohio Practice, *Merrick-Rippner Probate Law* § 18.2, 18.3, 19.1, 19.2, 19.3, 19.4, 19.5, 19.6, 19.7, 19.8, 19.10, 19.12, 38.4, 98.29, 98.30, 98.31, 105.2, 108.19, 108.20, 108.21, 108.22, 108.23, 108.24, 108.27, 108.28, 108.31 (1997)

Klein & Darling, Baldwin's Ohio Practice, *Civil Practice* § 1 (1997)

Sowald & Morganstern, Baldwin's Ohio Practice, *Domestic Relations Law* § 3.8, 3.49, 15.6, 21.3, 22.19, 23.3, 23.6 (1997)

Law Review and Journal Commentaries

Service of Process on Out-of-State Obligors, Don C. Bolsinger. 3 Domestic Rel J Ohio 1 (January/February 1991).

Notes of Decisions and Opinions

Personal jurisdiction 2
Subject matter jurisdiction 1

---

1. Subject matter jurisdiction

Juvenile courts have original jurisdiction over parentage actions. State ex rel. Willacy v. Smith (Ohio 1997) 78 Ohio St.3d 47, 676 N.E.2d 109.

Postjudgment appeal was adequate remedy at law in juvenile court parentage action, precluding putative father from challenging juvenile court's exercise of subject matter jurisdiction by seeking writ of prohibition or mandamus, absent patent and unambiguous lack of jurisdiction, despite numerous interlocutory orders and alleged absence of mechanism to guarantee reimbursement of putative father's temporary child support payments. State ex rel. Willacy v. Smith (Ohio 1997) 78 Ohio St.3d 47, 676 N.E.2d 109.

Jurisdiction was not patently and unambiguously lacking in juvenile court parentage action brought by natural mother against child's putative father, barring putative father's mandamus and prohibition action challenging juvenile court's subject matter jurisdiction, although mother was married to another man at time child was born; mother's complaint sufficiently alleged that child was born out of wedlock by stating that his conception and birth resulted from her affair with putative father, giving juvenile court basic statutory jurisdiction to proceed. State ex rel. Willacy v. Smith (Ohio 1997) 78 Ohio St.3d 47, 676 N.E.2d 109.

Court of common pleas has jurisdiction to determine paternity of child born out of wedlock in conjunction with wrongful death claim; juvenile court's jurisdiction over such issues is not exclusive. Brookbank v. Gray (Ohio 1996) 74 Ohio St.3d 279, 658 N.E.2d 724.

A probate judge in common pleas court has no subject matter jurisdiction to determine paternity as an ancillary claim to heirship against the estate of his alleged father. Martin v. Davidson (Ohio 1990) 53 Ohio St.3d 240, 559 N.E.2d 1348.

Following entry of divorce decree, domestic relations court did not have original or continuing jurisdiction to consider issue of paternity raised by former wife's child, who was born after the divorce. Fitzpatrick v. Fitzpatrick (Ohio App. 12 Dist. 1998) 126 Ohio App.3d 476, 710 N.E.2d 778, dismissed, appeal not allowed 82 Ohio St.3d 1441, 695 N.E.2d 264.

Domestic relations courts have original jurisdiction to consider parentage issues during pendency of divorce, dissolution, or legal separation actions. Leguillon v. Leguillon (Ohio App. 12 Dist. 1998) 124 Ohio App.3d 757, 707 N.E.2d 571.

Juvenile division had jurisdiction over child's paternity action filed after mother's paternity action was dismissed with prejudice by general division and before alleged father filed motion to reopen the action in the general division. Payne v. Cartee (Ross 1996) 111 Ohio App.3d 580, 676 N.E.2d 946, appeal not allowed 77 Ohio St.3d 1482, 673 N.E.2d 143.

General division of Common Pleas Court exhausted its exclusive jurisdiction over paternity action by dismissing action with prejudice, and, therefore, juvenile division had concurrent jurisdiction over child's later filed paternity action against same alleged father. Payne v. Cartee (Ross 1996) 111 Ohio App.3d 580, 676 N.E.2d 946, appeal not allowed 77 Ohio St.3d 1482, 673 N.E.2d 143.

Where divorce action is no longer pending, domestic relations court does not have necessary jurisdiction to hear paternity action. State ex rel. Smith v. Smith (Cuyahoga 1996) 110 Ohio App.3d 336, 674 N.E.2d 398, appeal not allowed 76 Ohio St.3d 1496, 670 N.E.2d 243.

Paternity action brought by state after final judgment was entered in mother's divorce action was required to be brought in Juvenile Court, rather than in Domestic Relations Division of the common pleas court. State ex rel. Smith v. Smith (Cuyahoga 1996) 110 Ohio App.3d 336, 674 N.E.2d 398, appeal not allowed 76 Ohio St.3d 1496, 670 N.E.2d 243.

Legal custodians of child, who obtained custody from child's mother, were in privity with mother, and so were barred by res judicata from litigating issue of paternity of child that had been decided in divorce decree. Broxterman v. Broxterman (Hamilton 1995) 101 Ohio App.3d 661, 656 N.E.2d 394.

Although divorce action was completed, jurisdiction over paternity action that was brought as postdecree motion was proper in Court of Domestic Relations, not solely in Juvenile Court, since other postdecree matters were still pending. Broxterman v. Broxterman (Hamilton 1995) 101 Ohio App.3d 661, 656 N.E.2d 394.

When divorce action is pending between the putative parents of child, court considering that action has original jurisdiction to determine whether parent-child relationship exists between a party and the child; however, divorce action is not subject to statutory genetic testing mandates until jurisdiction of the court to determine paternity is invoked by pleadings which put existence or nonexistence of father-child relationship in issue. McClure v. McClure (Greene 1994) 98 Ohio App.3d 27, 647 N.E.2d 832, appeal not allowed 71 Ohio St.3d 1481, 645 N.E.2d 1260.

Juvenile court, in determining paternity, had jurisdiction to decide state's action for aid furnished by state for support and medical expenses of children born out-of-wedlock. Brightwell v. Easter (Summit 1994) 93 Ohio App.3d 425, 638 N.E.2d 1067.

Trial court did not have jurisdiction, after filing of appeal, to modify qualified domestic relations order (QDRO) in paternity action to take into account tax consequences that had not been previously considered; trial court modified judgment on appeal by changing amount of judgment, and, thus, interfered with Court of Appeals' ability to affirm, modify or reverse judgment on appeal. Albertson v. Ryder (Lake 1993) 85 Ohio App.3d 765, 621 N.E.2d 480.

Trial court had subject matter jurisdiction to award child support retroactive to child's date of birth in paternity proceeding brought more than 20 years after child was born. Park v. Ambrose (Ross 1993) 85 Ohio App.3d 179, 619 N.E.2d 469, dismissed, jurisdictional motion overruled 67 Ohio St.3d 1409, 615 N.E.2d 1043.

Both general division of Court of Common Pleas, in dissolution action, and juvenile division, in paternity action, have authority to decide paternity issue. LaBonte v. LaBonte (Meigs 1988) 61 Ohio App.3d 209, 572 N.E.2d 704, motion overruled 42 Ohio St.3d 709, 538 N.E.2d 122.

A plaintiff claiming to be the natural father of a child born to a woman while she was married to another man may assert that claim in an action brought pursuant to the Uniform Parentage Act, RC Ch 3111, even though the child was determined to be the issue of the marriage during an earlier divorce suit in which the plaintiff was not a party, and the juvenile court has jurisdiction over the plaintiff's claim. Gatt v. Gedeon (Cuyahoga 1984) 20 Ohio App.3d 285, 485 N.E.2d 1059, 20 O.B.R. 376.

A juvenile court's original jurisdiction over parentage actions does not exclude the jurisdiction of a court of common pleas. Standifer v. Arwood (Warren 1984) 17 Ohio App.3d 241, 479 N.E.2d 304, 17 O.B.R. 508.

A domestic relations court is the proper forum to determine matters of paternity during the pendency of a divorce action. Roebuck v Roebuck, No. 54986 (8th Dist Ct App, Cuyahoga, 2-2-89).

2. Personal jurisdiction

Court rejected state's argument that failure to support an illegitimate child constitutes a tortious act which would extend personal jurisdiction over a nonresident defendant in a parental action when the defendant had never been in Ohio. State ex rel. Stone v. Court of Common Pleas of Cuyahoga County, Juvenile Div. (Ohio 1984) 14 Ohio St.3d 32, 470 N.E.2d 899, 14 O.B.R. 333.

A bastardy proceeding can be maintained against an Ohio resident notwithstanding that the child was conceived and born in another state and that the mother and child were never residents of Ohio, regardless of the laws of the other state. (Annotation from former RC 3111.08.) Yuin v. Hilton (Ohio 1956) 165 Ohio St. 164, 134 N.E.2d 719, 59 O.O. 219.

Ohio courts did not have long-arm jurisdiction over putative father in paternity case; mother acknowledged that conception had occurred in Texas, and putative father had never entered state or had any contacts with Ohio. Gaisford v. Swanson (Paulding 1992) 83 Ohio App.3d 457, 615 N.E.2d 266.

Insufficient contacts with Ohio are present to confer personal jurisdiction over a defendant in an Ohio court in a paternity action where the child was not conceived in Ohio and the parties did not live in a marital relationship in Ohio, although the defendant transported the mother to Ohio prior to the child's birth, visited the mother and child in Ohio, and sent support payments to Ohio. Massey-Norton v. Trammel (Franklin 1989) 61 Ohio App.3d 394, 572 N.E.2d 821, dismissed 44 Ohio St.3d 714, 542 N.E.2d 1110.

Where paternity proceedings are instituted by a plaintiff who claims to be the biological father of an illegitimate child, the mother's claim that she did not consent to sexual intercourse at the time the child was conceived is irrelevant to obtaining personal jurisdiction over her under RC 3111.06. Van Pham v. Redle (Summit 1985) 29 Ohio App.3d 213, 504 N.E.2d 1147, 29 O.B.R. 258.

Refusing or failing to pay necessary monetary support for dependent, minor children is a tortious "act or omission in this state" sufficient to create a basis for in personam jurisdiction under Civ R 4.3(A)(3). Upole v Caldwell, No. WD-84-23 (6th Dist Ct App, Wood, 9-14-84).

A bastardy action may be brought against an Ohio defendant by a woman who is not a resident of Ohio. (Annotation from former RC 3111.01.) Smith v. Smith (Ohio Com.Pl. 1965) 11 Ohio Misc. 25, 224 N.E.2d 925, 40 O.O.2d 136.

3111.07 Necessary parties; intervenors

(A) The natural mother, each man presumed to be the father under section 3111.03 of the Revised Code, each man alleged to be the natural father, and, if the party who initiates the action is a recipient of public assistance as defined in section 3111.04 of the Revised Code or if the responsibility for the collection of support for the child who is the subject of the action has been assumed by the child support enforcement agency under Title IV-D of the "Social Security Act," 88 Stat. 2351 (1975), 42 U.S.C.A. 651, as amended, the child support enforcement agency of the county in which the child resides shall be made parties to the action brought pursuant to sections 3111.01 to 3111.19 of the Revised Code or, if not subject to the jurisdiction of the court, shall be given notice of the action pursuant to the Rules of Civil Procedure and shall be given an opportunity to be heard. The court may align the parties. The child shall be made a party to the action unless a party shows good cause for not doing so. Separate counsel shall be appointed for the child if the court finds that the child's interests conflict with those of the mother.

If the person bringing the action knows that a particular man is not or, based upon the facts and circumstances present, could not be the natural father of the child, the person bringing the action shall not allege in the action that the man is the natural father of the child and shall not make the man a party to the action.

(B) If an action is brought pursuant to sections 3111.01 to 3111.19 of the Revised Code and the child to whom the action pertains is or was being provided support by the department of job and family services, a county department of job and family services, or another public agency, the department, county department, or agency may intervene for purposes of collecting or recovering the support.

(1999 H 471, eff. 7-1-00; 1997 H 352, eff. 1-1-98; 1992 S 10, eff. 7-15-92; 1990 H 591; 1986 H 428, H 476; 1982 H 245)

Uncodified Law

1992 S 10, § 5: See Uncodified Law under 3111.01.

1982 H 245, § 3: See Uncodified Law under 3111.04.

Historical and Statutory Notes

Ed. Note: Former 3111.07 repealed by 1982 H 245, eff. 6-29-82; 127 v 1039; 125 v 184; 1953 H 1; GC 8006-7; Source—GC 12114; see now 3111.19 for provisions analogous to former 3111.07.

Pre-1953 H 1 Amendments: 124 v S 65

Amendment Note: 1999 H 471 substituted "job and family" for "human" twice in division (B).

Amendment Note: 1997 H 352 substituted "3111.04" for "2301.351" in the first paragraph in division (A).

Cross References

Compulsory joinder, Civ R 19.1
Guardian of the person or the estate, 2111.06
Guardians ad litem, 2151.281
Juvenile court proceedings, right to counsel, guardian ad litem, Juv R 4
Service of process, Civ R 4 to 4.6

Library References

Children Out-Of-Wedlock ⚷30, 34.
WESTLAW Topic No. 76H.
C.J.S. Children Out-of-Wedlock §§ 46, 49, 70, 85 to 93.

OJur 3d: 35, Declaratory Judgments and Related Proceedings § 32; 47, Family Law § 974, 975

Am Jur 2d: 10, Bastards § 80 et seq., 85, 86, 104 et seq., 114, 116, 118, 123 et seq.

Race or color of child as admissible in evidence on issue of legitimacy or paternity, or as basis of rebuttal or exception to presumption of legitimacy. 32 ALR3d 1303

Bastardy proceedings; Propriety of exhibition of child to jury to show family resemblance, or lack of it, on issue of paternity. 55 ALR3d 1087

Admissibility, in disputed paternity proceedings, of evidence to rebut mother's claim of prior chastity. 59 ALR3d 659

Admissibility or compellability of blood test to establish testee's nonpaternity for purpose of challenging testee's parental rights. 87 ALR4th 572

Baldwin's Ohio Legislative Service, 1990 Laws of Ohio, H 591—LSC Analysis, p 5-576

Carlin, Baldwin's Ohio Practice, *Merrick-Rippner Probate Law* § 18.2, 18.3, 19.1, 19.2, 19.3, 19.4, 19.5, 19.6, 19.7, 19.8, 19.10, 19.12, 29.3, 38.4, 98.29, 98.30, 98.31, 105.2, 108.19, 108.20, 108.22, 108.23, 108.24, 108.25, 108.27, 108.28, 108.31 (1997)

Klein & Darling, Baldwin's Ohio Practice, *Civil Practice* § 1 (1997)

Sowald & Morganstern, Baldwin's Ohio Practice, *Domestic Relations Law* § 3.10, 3.30, 3.40, 3.51, 22.4, 22.16, 22.18 (1997)

Notes of Decisions and Opinions

---

1. Child as a party

The purpose of a paternity proceeding under RC Ch 3111 is to provide a remedy for the unmarried mother of a minor child born out of wedlock, and the action may be commenced only by the unmarried mother or her legal representative; the child born out of wedlock is not a party to such action. (Annotation from former RC 3111.17.) Johnson v. Norman (Ohio 1981) 66 Ohio St.2d 186, 421 N.E.2d 124, 20 O.O.3d 196.

A child born out of wedlock may not bring a paternity proceeding under RC Ch 3111, but such child does have the same common-law right to bring a civil action against his father for support and maintenance as does a legitimate child, incident to which the court shall make a determination on the issue of paternity, and so the unmarried mother's dismissal of her action under RC Ch 3111 with prejudice is not a bar to the minor child's separate common-law action for support and maintenance from his putative father. (Annotation from former RC 3111.01.) Johnson v. Norman (Ohio 1981) 66 Ohio St.2d 186, 421 N.E.2d 124, 20 O.O.3d 196.

Bastardy proceedings are governed by the procedure provided for the trial of civil cases, and an action brought by a minor must comply with RC 2307.11. (Annotation from former RC 3111.03.) Taylor v. Scott (Ohio 1959) 168 Ohio St. 391, 155 N.E.2d 884, 7 O.O.2d 243.

2. Alleged father as defendant

Jurisdiction was not patently and unambiguously lacking in juvenile court parentage action brought by natural mother against child's putative father, barring putative father's mandamus and prohibition action challenging juvenile court's subject matter jurisdiction, although mother was married to another man at time child was born; mother's complaint sufficiently alleged that child was born out of wedlock by stating that his conception and birth resulted from her affair with putative father, giving juvenile court basic statutory jurisdiction to proceed. State ex rel. Willacy v. Smith (Ohio 1997) 78 Ohio St.3d 47, 676 N.E.2d 109.

A woman who is unmarried (not having a lawful husband) and pregnant may, under the statute, institute a bastardy proceeding charging another than her former husband with being the father of the child, even though child was conceived during the existence of a lawful marriage. (Annotation from former RC 3111.01.) State ex rel. Walker v. Clark (Ohio 1944) 144 Ohio St. 305, 58 N.E.2d 773, 29 O.O. 450.

In action to establish parent and child relationship, only proper parties are natural mother, presumed father, and alleged natural father. Vance v. Banks (Cuyahoga 1994) 94 Ohio App.3d 475, 640 N.E.2d 1214, appeal not allowed 70 Ohio St.3d 1447, 639 N.E.2d 115, certiorari denied 115 S.Ct. 1144, 513 U.S. 1170, 130 L.Ed.2d 1103.

Where the trial court determined that a minor child was conclusively presumed to be the child of the parties who were married to each other at her birth, but neither the child nor the man alleged by the husband to be the father of the child were joined as parties, the judgment is not binding since all necessary parties were not before the court. Corder v Corder, No. CA-1591 (5th Dist Ct App, Tuscarawas, 9-13-82).

3. Intervenor

Derivative claim for loss of parental consortium that is filed by intervening minor child can be brought against additional defendants in event that parent's case in chief has only one defendant. Coleman v. Sandoz Pharmaceuticals Corp. (Ohio 1996) 74 Ohio St.3d 492, 660 N.E.2d 424.

Attorney violates disciplinary rule prohibiting attorney from giving advice to person who is not represented by lawyer and whose interests may conflict with those of attorney's client by arranging for appointment of guardian ad litem for child allegedly fathered by client and arranging for guardian to sign, on behalf of child, consent judgment entry dismissing parentage action with prejudice. Disciplinary Counsel v. Rich (Ohio 1994) 69 Ohio St.3d 470, 633 N.E.2d 1114.

Public reprimand, rather than one-year suspension, is warranted by attorney's violation of disciplinary rule prohibiting him from giving advice to person who is not represented by lawyer and whose interests may conflict with those of his client, where violation consists of arranging for appointment of guardian ad litem for child allegedly fathered by client and arranging for guardian to sign, on behalf of child, consent judgment entry dismissing parentage action with prejudice. Disciplinary Counsel v. Rich (Ohio 1994) 69 Ohio St.3d 470, 633 N.E.2d 1114.

Trial court was not required to enter judgment in favor of Department of Human Services (DHS) in mother's action for determination of paternity and for back child support, where DHS was not named as party and did not intervene to recover amounts paid in public assistance to mother and child; better practice, however, would have been for DHS to intervene rather than to bring separate action. State ex rel. Donovan v. Zajac (Ohio App. 11 Dist. 1998) 125 Ohio App.3d 245, 708 N.E.2d 254, dismissed, appeal not allowed 81 Ohio St.3d 1521, 692 N.E.2d 1023.

Although a proper party may intervene in an existing parentage action brought under RC 3111.04, a proper party may not bring a Civ R 60(B) motion to vacate a judgment in an action to which he was never a party. Hardman v. Chiaramonte (Summit 1987) 39 Ohio App.3d 9, 528 N.E.2d 1270.

Although a county department of human services may intervene in a parentage action for purposes of collecting or recovering support, a county department of human services does not have standing to initiate a parentage action. State ex rel Athens County Human Services Dept v Wolf, No. 1462 (4th Dist Ct App, Athens, 10-9-91).

4. Agency as a party

County child support enforcement agency was entitled to participate in parentage action following admission of paternity and in absence of evidence of past child support, as agency was necessary party and adjudicated father suffered no prejudice from agency's participation. State ex rel. Donovan v. Zajac (Ohio App. 11 Dist. 1998) 125 Ohio App.3d 245, 708 N.E.2d 254, dismissed, appeal not allowed 81 Ohio St.3d 1521, 692 N.E.2d 1023.

Trial court's dismissal of child support enforcement agency as party in five child support actions where parentage was established through administrative proceedings violated equal protection clauses of State and Federal Constitutions; statutory scheme, which permits agency to be party in support actions where parentage is established through probate court and where parents are on public assistance, but which does not specifically permit agency to be party when parentage is established through administrative proceedings, did not have rational basis, since enforcement agency can only effectuate its duty to protect best interests of child and public fisc by being joined as party in all child support enforcement actions. Cuyahoga Cty. Support Enforcement Agency v. Lozada (Cuyahoga 1995) 102 Ohio App.3d 442, 657 N.E.2d 372.

The child support enforcement agency is to be considered a proper party to all actions for the collection of child support and dismissal of the agency violates the constitutional guarantee of equal protection. State Child Support Enforcement Agency v Seals, No. 69249, 1996 WL 239886 (8th Dist Ct App, Cuyahoga, 5-9-96).

3111.08 Civil nature of action to establish father and child relationship; judgment; default judgment

(A) An action brought pursuant to sections 3111.01 to 3111.19 of the Revised Code to declare the existence or nonexistence of the father and child relationship is a civil action and shall be governed by the Rules of Civil Procedure unless a different procedure is specifically provided by those sections.

(B) If an action is brought against a person to declare the existence or nonexistence of the father and child relationship between that person and a child and the person in his answer admits the existence or nonexistence of the father and child relationship as alleged in the action, the court shall enter judgment in accordance with section 3111.13 of the Revised Code. If the person against whom the action is brought fails to plead or otherwise defend against the action, the opposing party may make an oral or written motion for default judgment pursuant to the Rules of Civil Procedure. The court shall render a judgment by default against the person after hearing satisfactory evidence of the truth of the statements in the complaint.

(1994 S 355, eff. 12-9-94; 1992 S 10, eff. 7-15-92; 1990 H 591; 1986 H 476; 1982 H 245)

Uncodified Law

1994 S 355, § 5, eff. 12-9-94, reads: The provisions of this act that apply to actions brought under Chapter 3111. of the Revised Code to determine paternity apply only to actions initiated on or after the effective date of this act.

1992 S 10, § 5: See Uncodified Law under 3111.01.

1982 H 245, § 3: See Uncodified Law under 3111.04.

Historical and Statutory Notes

Ed. Note: Former 3111.08 repealed by 1982 H 245, eff. 6-29-82; 1976 H 390; 127 v 1039; 1953 H 1; GC 8006-8; Source—GC 12115; see now 3111.06 for provisions analogous to former 3111.08.

Pre-1953 H 1 Amendments: 124 v S 65

Amendment Note: 1994 S 355 rewrote division (B), which previously read:

"(B) If an action is brought against a person to declare the existence or nonexistence of the father and child relationship between that person and a child and the person in his answer admits the existence or nonexistence of the father and child relationship as alleged in the action, the court shall enter judgment in accordance with section 3111.13 of the Revised Code. If the person against whom the action is brought does not admit the existence or nonexistence of the father and child relationship, the court, upon its own motion, may order, and, upon the motion of any party to the action, shall order genetic tests to be taken in accordance with section 3111.09 of the Revised Code. If genetic tests are ordered upon the motion of a party or the court, the court shall order that the child's mother, the child, the alleged father, and any other defendant submit to the genetic tests in accordance with section 3111.09 of the Revised Code. A willful failure to submit to genetic tests as ordered by the court is contempt of court. If the person against whom the action is brought does not appear personally or by counsel at a pretrial hearing scheduled under section 3111.11 of the Revised Code, the opposing party may file a written motion for default judgment against the person. The motion, along with a notice of the date and time when it is to be heard, shall be served upon the person in the same manner as is provided for service of a complaint under the Rules of Civil Procedure. The court may render a judgment by default against the person after hearing satisfactory evidence of the truth of the statements in the complaint."

Cross References

Default judgment, Civ R 55

Service of process, Civ R 4 to 4.6

Library References

Children Out-Of-Wedlock ⚷30, 58.
WESTLAW Topic No. 76H.
C.J.S. Children Out-of-Wedlock §§ 46, 70, 75, 76, 92, 93.

OJur 3d: 35, Declaratory Judgments and Related Proceedings § 32
Am Jur 2d: 10, Bastards § 80 et seq., 85, 86, 104 et seq., 114, 116, 118, 123 et seq.
Race or color of child as admissible in evidence on issue of legitimacy or paternity, or as basis of rebuttal or exception to presumption of legitimacy. 32 ALR3d 1303
Bastardy proceedings; Propriety of exhibition of child to jury to show family resemblance, or lack of it, on issue of paternity. 55 ALR3d 1087
Admissibility, in disputed paternity proceedings, of evidence to rebut mother's claim of prior chastity. 59 ALR3d 659
Proof of husband's impotency or sterility as rebutting presumption of legitimacy. 84 ALR3d 495
Admissibility, weight and sufficiency of Human Leukocyte Antigen (HLA) tissue typing tests in paternity cases. 37 ALR4th 167
Admissibility and weight of blood-grouping tests in disputed paternity cases. 43 ALR4th 579

Baldwin's Ohio Legislative Service, 1990 Laws of Ohio, H 591—LSC Analysis, p 5-576
Carlin, Baldwin's Ohio Practice, *Merrick-Rippner Probate Law* § 18.2, 18.3, 19.1, 19.2, 19.3, 19.4, 19.5, 19.6, 19.7, 19.8, 19.10, 19.12, 38.4, 98.29, 98.30, 98.31, 98.38, 105.2, 108.19, 108.20, 108.22, 108.23, 108.24, 108.26, 108.27, 108.28, 108.31 (1997)
Klein & Darling, Baldwin's Ohio Practice, *Civil Practice* § 1 (1997)
Sowald & Morganstern, Baldwin's Ohio Practice, *Domestic Relations Law* § 3.11, 3.21, 3.28, 23.6 (1997)

Notes of Decisions and Opinions

Appeals 5
Constitutional issues 1
Default judgment 7
Defendants 6
Evidence 3
Procedure 4
Support 2

---

1. Constitutional issues

Indigent paternity defendant has a constitutional right to appointed counsel when the state is a plaintiff in a paternity action. Douglas v. Boykin (Ohio App. 12 Dist. 1997) 121 Ohio App.3d 140, 699 N.E.2d 123.

Putative father validly waived his right to counsel at paternity hearing, despite the absence of a transcript, where magistrate made handwritten notation that putative father was advised of his right to counsel and blood testing and that he waived those rights, and putative father signed report. Douglas v. Boykin (Ohio App. 12 Dist. 1997) 121 Ohio App.3d 140, 699 N.E.2d 123.

The requirement to submit to the withdrawal of blood to determine paternity is not susceptible to a right of privacy challenge, and as such, a court may find one who refuses to comply with such an order in contempt. McCarty v. Kimmel (Montgomery 1989) 62 Ohio App.3d 775, 577 N.E.2d 665.

The state of Ohio having granted by statute to all defendants in bastardy proceedings, which are "quasi criminal" in nature, the right to a blood test to determine paternity, cannot deny this right to those defendants who are unable to pay the required fee in advance, without violating the equal protection clause of the United States Constitution, because such a defendant's ability to pay in advance bears no rational relationship to his guilt or innocence, and to discriminate upon this basis constitutes that type of invidious discrimination which is constitutionally prohibited; it is mandatory that the trial court tax as costs the expense of a blood test requested by appropriate motion by an indigent in a bastardy action. (Annotation from former RC 3111.16.) Walker v. Stokes (Cuyahoga 1975) 45 Ohio App.2d 275, 344 N.E.2d 159, 74 O.O.2d 402.

Former GC 12110 (RC 3111.01) authorizing arresting officer in bastardy proceeding to pursue into any county of the state a person charged in an affidavit with being the father of a bastard child, and to arrest and bring him before the court to answer the complaint, is constitutional. (Annotation from former RC 3111.01.) Barnett v. Boice (Franklin 1930) 37 Ohio App. 549, 175 N.E. 620, 10 Ohio Law Abs. 157.

An agreed judgment entry which finds a defendant to be the "reputed father" of a child and orders support does not constitute a valid legal determination of paternity and does not give rise to a statutory obligation of support; therefore, an order for support without a prior valid determination of paternity must be vacated and remanded. Glass v Campbell, No. 15-92-18 (3d Dist Ct App, Van Wert, 5-27-93).

The ruling that RC 3111.17 and 3111.18 are unconstitutional as a denial of the equal protection clause of the US Const Am 14 insofar as the sections provide for the imprisonment of an indigent defendant adjudged to be the reputed father of plaintiff's illegitimate child solely because of his inability to pay the award ordered by the court removed the last vestige of a criminal or quasi-criminal case from paternity proceedings. (Annotation from former RC 3111.17.) Bigsby v. Bates (Ohio Com.Pl. 1978) 59 Ohio Misc. 51, 391 N.E.2d 1384, 11 O.O.3d 262, 13 O.O.3d 260.

2. Support

An unmarried parent is subject to the support obligation to which RC 3107.07(A) refers only where a paternity determination has been rendered pursuant to RC

3111.08(B) or 3111.12. In re Adoption of Sunderhaus (Ohio 1992) 63 Ohio St.3d 127, 585 N.E.2d 418, rehearing denied 63 Ohio St.3d 1442, 589 N.E.2d 46.

Juvenile court, in determining paternity, had jurisdiction to decide state's action for aid furnished by state for support and medical expenses of children born out-of-wedlock. Brightwell v. Easter (Summit 1994) 93 Ohio App.3d 425, 638 N.E.2d 1067.

Mother established prima facie parent-child relationship between putative father and daughter by preponderance of evidence in view of fact that genetic test disclosed 98.5% probability that he was biological father of child, that mother had sexual intercourse with putative father twice during alleged month of conception, that, although she had sexual intercourse with one other man during that month, genetic blood testing excluded him as biological father of child, and that putative father admitted under cross-examination that it was possible that he had sexual intercourse with child's mother during month of conception and they did not use any form of contraceptive. Filkins v. Cales (Logan 1993) 86 Ohio App.3d 61, 619 N.E.2d 1156, motion overruled 67 Ohio St.3d 1422, 616 N.E.2d 506.

Mother's burden of proof in paternity action was to establish existence of parent-child relationship between putative father and daughter by preponderance of evidence. Filkins v. Cales (Logan 1993) 86 Ohio App.3d 61, 619 N.E.2d 1156, motion overruled 67 Ohio St.3d 1422, 616 N.E.2d 506.

A person is not entitled to relief under Civ R 60(B)(2) or (5) from a judgment of paternity and child support where he signed the child's birth certificate and an administrative order indicating he was the child's biological father even though he knew he was not the biological father because the mother was two months pregnant when he began dating her, and therefore a recent DNA test result showing a 0.00 chance he was the father is not "new evidence" under Civ R 60(B)(2), the specific provision of the rule that prevails over the more general section, (B)(5); although it may appear unfair to require an individual to pay child support for a child not biologically his own, there must be some finality to a judgment and one cannot choose to be a parent and then change his or her mind when the relationship is dissolved. Shaffer v Rusnak, No. 97 CA 26, 1998 WL 429624 (5th Dist Ct App, Guernsey, 7-1-98).

Claim for support and other statutory relief from father by child born out of wedlock is separate and distinct from that of her mother. Hugershoff v. Loecy (Ohio Com.Pl. 1999) 103 Ohio Misc.2d 58, 725 N.E.2d 378.

Bastardy proceeding has for its primary object fixing of sum of money to be paid by accused to complainant "for her support, maintenance, and necessary expenses caused by pregnancy and childbirth." (Annotation from former RC 3111.17.) Seldenright v. Jenkins (Ohio Prob. 1936) 3 Ohio Supp. 36, 22 Ohio Law Abs. 576, 7 O.O. 127.

3. Evidence

To overcome the presumption that a child born during a marriage is a child of the husband, the evidence must be clear and convincing that the spouses had no sexual relations during the possible period of conception. Joseph v. Alexander (Ohio 1984) 12 Ohio St.3d 88, 465 N.E.2d 448, 12 O.B.R. 77.

Juvenile court may enter judgment in paternity action upon satisfactory evidence of paternity. Lewis v. Chapin (Cuyahoga 1994) 93 Ohio App.3d 695, 639 N.E.2d 848.

Paternity of a child is proven by a preponderance of the evidence where (1) evidence is introduced of sexual intercourse within the period of conception; (2) expert testimony is given concerning the probability of defendant's paternity based on genetic testing; and (3) expert testimony is given regarding the probability of defendant's paternity based on the physical characteristics and ethnic ancestry of the parties. Grove v. Mattison (Franklin 1988) 61 Ohio App.3d 252, 572 N.E.2d 731, dismissed 42 Ohio St.3d 706, 537 N.E.2d 226.

The standard of proof of paternity is a preponderance of the evidence. Domigan v. Gillette (Clark 1984) 17 Ohio App.3d 228, 479 N.E.2d 291, 17 O.B.R. 494.

Father fails to allege a basis for relief under Civ R 60(B) by his failure to allege fraud after blood tests showed that he could not be the child's biological father. In re Belden, No. 92 CA 21, 1993 WL 179254 (2d Dist Ct App, Miami, 5-25-93).

4. Procedure

Statute allowing parties in paternity action to enter compromise agreement subject to court approval supersedes rule allowing dismissal by stipulation without court approval. State ex rel. Fowler v. Smith (Ohio 1994) 68 Ohio St.3d 357, 626 N.E.2d 950.

Prosecutions of complaints relating to bastardy are, unless specified otherwise therein, governed by the procedure provided for the trial of civil cases. (Annotation from former RC 3111.01.) State ex rel. Wise v. Chand (Ohio 1970) 21 Ohio St.2d 113, 256 N.E.2d 613, 50 O.O.2d 322.

Bastardy proceedings are governed by the procedure provided for the trial of civil cases, and an action brought by a minor must comply with RC 2307.11. (Annotation from former RC 3111.03.) Taylor v. Scott (Ohio 1959) 168 Ohio St. 391, 155 N.E.2d 884, 7 O.O.2d 243.

When divorce action is pending between the putative parents of child, court considering that action has original jurisdiction to determine whether parent-child relationship exists between a party and the child; however, divorce action is not subject to statutory genetic testing mandates until jurisdiction of the court to determine paternity is invoked by pleadings which put existence or nonexistence of father-child relationship in issue. McClure v. McClure (Greene 1994) 98 Ohio App.3d 27, 647 N.E.2d 832, appeal not allowed 71 Ohio St.3d 1481, 645 N.E.2d 1260.

Common pleas court has inherent power to estop mother from using genetic testing to disestablish child's paternity with his or her presumed father under doctrine of laches, but there must be finding of material prejudice to invoke the doctrine. Sherburn v. Reichert (Van Wert 1994) 97 Ohio App.3d 120, 646 N.E.2d 255.

Eligibility for genetic test in paternity action is not guaranteed, and court can find defendant has fathered child without genetic test results if defendant fails to submit to blood test. Harvey v. Mynatt (Summit 1994) 94 Ohio App.3d 619, 641 N.E.2d 291.

Assuming that putative father's request for blood testing in letter sent to court after receiving complaint in paternity action could be considered motion for genetic test, motion was not made in timely fashion, where letter was sent to court two days after father's answer to paternity complaint was due and court did not receive letter until one week after answer was due. Harvey v. Mynatt (Summit 1994) 94 Ohio App.3d 619, 641 N.E.2d 291.

Although a parentage action brought by a natural mother takes place in a juvenile division of the common pleas court, the civil rules apply rather than the juvenile rules; thus, a motion for judgment on the pleadings under Civ R 12(C) is permissible in a parentage action. Nelson v. Pleasant (Lawrence 1991) 73 Ohio App.3d 479, 597 N.E.2d 1137.

Although a proper party may intervene in an existing parentage action brought under RC 3111.04, a proper party may not bring a Civ R 60(B) motion to vacate a judgment in an action to which he was never a party. Hardman v. Chiaramonte (Summit 1987) 39 Ohio App.3d 9, 528 N.E.2d 1270.

A bastardy action is essentially civil in nature, and the failure of the defendant in such action to testify may be the subject of comment to the jury. (Annotation from former RC 3111.01.) Smith v. Lautenslager (Hamilton 1968) 15 Ohio App.2d 212, 240 N.E.2d 109, 44 O.O.2d 371.

Motion for summary judgment does not lie in a paternity proceeding in juvenile court. De Salvo v. Sukalski (Geauga 1983) 8 Ohio App.3d 337, 457 N.E.2d 349, 8 O.B.R. 448.

The caption or title of an action or proceeding instituted by the filing of a complaint under the bastardy act and dealing with an award to the complainant should contain only the names of the complainant and accused. (Annotation from former RC 3111.01.) State ex rel. Love v. Jones (Hamilton 1953) 98 Ohio App. 45, 128 N.E.2d 228, 57 O.O. 161.

While some of the procedure in a bastardy case is similar to that in a criminal case, the proceeding is a civil one. (Annotation from former RC 3111.01.) Durst v. Griffith (Hocking 1932) 43 Ohio App. 44, 182 N.E. 519, 12 Ohio Law Abs. 522, 37 Ohio Law Rep. 183.

Bastardy proceeding is quasi-criminal proceeding, but is so far civil that, where verdict of three-fourths of jurors is allowed in any civil case, it is also allowed in such proceeding, and it is not necessary to furnish proof beyond reasonable doubt, preponderance of evidence being sufficient. (Annotation from former RC 3111.15.) Schneider v. State (Cuyahoga 1929) 33 Ohio App. 125, 168 N.E. 568.

A motion for summary judgment may lie in paternity proceedings in juvenile court. State ex rel Drews v Ambrosi, No. 73761, 1998 WL 563993 (8th Dist Ct App, Cuyahoga, 9-3-98).

In a parentage action, a trial court commits plain error when it considers a document submitted by the county support enforcement agency entitled "Plaintiff's Written Interrogatories for Oral Deposition," where the document does not comprise (1) an interrogatory because it was served on a nonparty, (2) a deposition because the defendant did not receive notice as required by Civ R 31, and (3) an affidavit because the answers were not given under oath. Stilwell v Van Meter, No. 95-CA-66, 1996 WL 27846 (2d Dist Ct App, Clark, 1-24-96).

The trial court errs in affirming the order of parentage where the notice of the order is not properly served, thereby denying the parties the thirty days from the date of the order to object. Howard v Heineman, No. 94CAF12039, 1995 WL 495483 (5th Dist Ct App, Delaware, 6-30-95).

The Ohio Rules of Civil Procedure apply to parentage actions; thus, an answer must be filed by the person against whom the action is brought, and a failure to properly plead the affirmative defense of laches bars its defense at trial. Eppley v Bratton, No. 94 CA 7, 1994 WL 668111 (5th Dist Ct App, Coshocton, 11-7-94).

Actions under RC 3111.01 to 3111.24 relating to paternity proceedings are, unless specified otherwise therein, governed by the Rules of Civil Procedure. (Annotation from former RC 5111.08.) Bigsby v. Bates (Ohio Com.Pl. 1978) 59 Ohio Misc. 51, 391 N.E.2d 1384, 11 O.O.3d 262, 13 O.O.3d 260.

In bastardy proceedings burden of proof is on defendant to prove that complainant had entered into common law marriage at time of filing of affidavit. (Annotation from former RC 3111.17.) State ex rel. Allen v. Wagoner (Trumbull 1961) 182 N.E.2d 328, 88 Ohio Law Abs. 218.

5. Appeals

An order mandating genetic testing in a parentage action is not a final appealable order as it is not determinative of the parentage action. McCarty v. Kimmel (Montgomery 1989) 62 Ohio App.3d 775, 577 N.E.2d 665.

6. Defendants

When the state acts on a paternity complaint, a court should at the outset of the case determine whether the defendant is indigent and whether counsel should be appointed in his behalf. Rees v. Heimberger (Cuyahoga 1989) 60 Ohio App.3d 45, 573 N.E.2d 189, dismissed 47 Ohio St.3d 702, 547 N.E.2d 986, rehearing denied 48 Ohio St.3d 707, 550 N.E.2d 483, certiorari denied 110 S.Ct. 1827, 494 U.S. 1088, 108 L.Ed.2d 956.

The court of domestic relations of Franklin County has authority, under this section, to issue its warrant for the arrest of a nonresident of the county charged with being the father of a bastard child, conceived and born in another state, and to serve such warrant upon the person named therein in a sister county of the state and bring such person into Franklin County for trial. (Annotation from former RC 3111.01.) Barnett v. Boice (Franklin 1930) 37 Ohio App. 549, 175 N.E. 620, 10 Ohio Law Abs. 157.

An unmarried, pregnant woman may institute a bastardy proceeding charging one other than her former husband with being the father of the child, even though such child was conceived during the existence of a lawful marriage. (Annotation from former RC 3111.01.) State ex rel. Sprungle v. Bard (Cuyahoga 1950) 98 N.E.2d 63, 59 Ohio Law Abs. 129.

7. Default judgment

Failure to inform putative father of court's intent to enter finding of paternity on his refusal to submit to genetic testing precluded finding of paternity by default, where putative father appeared before trial court for purpose of contesting paternity; adjudication was available only as sanction for willful refusal to submit to genetic testing, and not under statutory provision governing default paternity judgments. Marsh v. Clay (Ohio App. 8 Dist. 1998) 125 Ohio App.3d 518, 708 N.E.2d 1073.

Trial court obtained personal jurisdiction over putative father by virtue of county's properly served complaint and by virtue of putative father's answer, and, therefore, court had jurisdiction to enter default judgment against putative father despite his contention that he was never properly served with motion for default judgment. Austin v. Payne (Lorain 1995) 107 Ohio App.3d 818, 669 N.E.2d 543.

Trial court was not required to allow putative father to receive genetic test to determine if he was father of child born out of wedlock prior to entering default judgment in paternity action brought by county child support enforcement agency, despite putative father's request for blood test in letter sent to court after father received copy of paternity complaint, where letter was sent after father's answer to complaint was due, and father failed to appear and contest motion for default judgment after receipt of notice of default hearing. Harvey v. Mynatt (Summit 1994) 94 Ohio App.3d 619, 641 N.E.2d 291.

Defendant who was in default of answer and had failed to appear in parentage action was not entitled to notice of filing of motion for default. Long v. Bartlett (Franklin 1992) 73 Ohio App.3d 764, 598 N.E.2d 197.

In an action to establish a father-child relationship where the mother, prior to her pregnancy, enlists in the United States Navy and is on active duty during the time of default proceedings which result in an order that she pay child support, the trial court fails to comply with the protections of the Soldiers' and Sailors' Civil Relief Act by allowing her attorney to withdraw prior to the default proceeding, leaving her without representation, and despite the fact that she had notice of the action, the Soldiers' and Sailors' Act affords active duty service persons entitlement to legal representation which is separate and apart from the notice issue. State ex rel Burden v Smith, No. 94APF06-877, 1994 WL 714505 (10th Dist Ct App, Franklin, 12-22-94).

Where no answer is filed to a complaint alleging paternity, the trial court errs in entering judgment by default without first conducting the pretrial hearing provided under RC 3111.11. Potts v Wilson, No. 409 (4th Dist Ct App, Adams, 5-30-85).

3111.09 Genetic tests and DNA records

(A)(1) In any action instituted under sections 3111.01 to 3111.19 of the Revised Code, the court, upon its own motion, may order and, upon the motion of any party to the action, shall order the child's mother, the child, the alleged father, and any other person who is a defendant in the action to submit to genetic tests. Instead of or in addition to genetic testing ordered pursuant to this section, the court may use the following information to determine the existence of a parent and child relationship between the child and the child's mother, the alleged father, or another defendant:

(a) A DNA record of the child's mother, the child, the alleged father, or any other defendant that is stored in the DNA database pursuant to section 109.573 of the Revised Code;

(b) Results of genetic tests conducted on the child, the child's mother, the alleged father, or any other defendant pursuant to former section 3111.21 or section 3111.22 of the Revised Code.

If the court intends to use the information described in division (A)(1)(a) of this section, it shall order the superintendent of the bureau of criminal identification and investigation to disclose the information to the court. If the court intends to use the genetic test results described in division (A)(1)(b) of this section, it shall order the agency that ordered the tests to provide the report of the genetic test results to the court.

(2) If the child support enforcement agency is not made a party to the action, the clerk of the court shall schedule the genetic testing no later than thirty days after the court issues its order. If the agency is made a party to the action, the agency shall schedule the genetic testing in accordance with the rules adopted by the director of job and family services pursuant to section 2301.35 of the Revised Code. If the alleged father of a child brings an action under sections 3111.01 to 3111.19 of the Revised Code and if the mother of the child willfully fails to submit to genetic testing or if the mother is the custodian of the child and willfully fails to submit the child to genetic testing, the court, on the motion of the alleged father, shall issue an order determining the existence of a parent and child relationship between the father and the child without genetic testing. If the mother or other guardian or custodian of the child brings an action under sections 3111.01 to 3111.19 of the Revised Code and if the alleged father of the child willfully fails to submit himself to genetic testing or, if the alleged father is the custodian of the child and willfully fails to submit the child to genetic testing, the court shall issue an order determining the existence of a parent and child relationship between the father and the child without genetic testing. If a party shows good cause for failing to submit to genetic testing or for failing to submit the child to genetic testing, the court shall not consider the failure to be willful.

(3) Except as provided in division (A)(4) of this section, any fees charged for the tests shall be paid by the party that requests them, unless the custodian of the child is represented by the child support enforcement agency in its role as the agency providing enforcement of child support orders under Title IV-D of the "Social Security Act," 88 Stat. 2351 (1975), 42 U.S.C.

651, as amended, the custodian is a participant in Ohio works first under Chapter 5107. of the Revised Code for the benefit of the child, or the defendant in the action is found to be indigent, in which case the child support enforcement agency shall pay the costs of genetic testing. The child support enforcement agency, within guidelines contained in that federal law, shall use funds received pursuant to Title IV-D of the "Social Security Act," 88 Stat. 2351 (1975), 42 U.S.C. 651, as amended, to pay the fees charged for the tests.

Except as provided in division (A)(4) of this section, if there is a dispute as to who shall pay the fees charged for genetic testing, the child support enforcement agency shall pay the fees, but neither the court nor the agency shall delay genetic testing due to a dispute as to who shall pay the genetic testing fees. The child support enforcement agency or the person who paid the fees charged for the genetic testing may seek reimbursement for the genetic testing fees from the person against whom the court assesses the costs of the action. Any funds used in accordance with this division by the child support enforcement agency shall be in addition to any other funds that the agency is entitled to receive as a result of any contractual provision for specific funding allocations for the agency between the county, the state, and the federal government.

(4) If, pursuant to former section 3111.21 or section 3111.22 of the Revised Code, the agency has previously conducted genetic tests on the child, child's mother, alleged father, or any other defendant and the current action pursuant to section 3111.01 to 3111.19 of the Revised Code has been brought to object to the result of those previous tests, the agency shall not be required to pay the fees for conducting genetic tests pursuant to this section on the same persons.

(B)(1) The genetic tests shall be made by qualified examiners who are authorized by the court or the department of job and family services. An examiner conducting a genetic test, upon the completion of the test, shall send a complete report of the test results to the clerk of the court that ordered the test or, if the agency is a party to the action, to the child support enforcement agency of the county in which the court that ordered the test is located.

(2) If a court orders the superintendent of the bureau of criminal identification and investigation to disclose information regarding a DNA record stored in the DNA database pursuant to section 109.573 of the Revised Code, the superintendent shall send the information to the clerk of the court that issued the order or, if the agency is a party to the action, to the child support enforcement agency of the county in which the court that issued the order is located.

(3) If a court orders the child support enforcement agency to provide the report of the genetic test results obtained pursuant to former section 3111.21 or section 3111.22 of the Revised Code, the agency shall send the information to the person or government entity designated by the court that issued the order.

(4) The clerk, agency, or person or government entity under division (B)(3) of this section that receives a report or information pursuant to division (B)(1), (2), or (3) of this section shall mail a copy of the report or information to the attorney of record for each party or, if a party is not represented by an attorney, to the party. The clerk, agency, or person or government entity under division (B)(3) of this section that receives a copy of the report or information shall include with the report or information sent to an attorney of record of a party or a party a notice that the party may object to the admission into evidence of the report or information by filing a written objection as described in division (D) of section 3111.12 of the Revised Code with the court that ordered the tests or ordered the disclosure of the information no later than fourteen days after the report or information was mailed to the attorney of record or to the party. The examiners may be called as witnesses to testify as to their findings. Any party may demand that other qualified examiners perform independent genetic tests under order of the court. The number and qualifications of the independent examiners shall be determined by the court.

(C) Nothing in this section prevents any party to the action from producing other expert evidence on the issue covered by this section, but, if other expert witnesses are called by a party to the action, the fees of these expert witnesses shall be paid by the party calling the witnesses and only ordinary witness fees for these expert witnesses shall be taxed as costs in the action.

(D) If the court finds that the conclusions of all the examiners are that the alleged father is not the father of the child, the court shall enter judgment that the alleged father is not the father of the child. If the examiners disagree in their findings or conclusions, the court shall determine the father of the child based upon all the evidence.

(E) As used in sections 3111.01 to 3111.29 of the Revised Code:

(1) "Genetic tests" and "genetic testing" mean either of the following:

(a) Tissue or blood tests, including tests that identify the presence or absence of common blood group antigens, the red blood cell antigens, human lymphocyte antigens, serum enzymes, serum proteins, or genetic markers;

(b) Deoxyribonucleic acid typing of blood or buccal cell samples.

"Genetic test" and "genetic testing" may include the typing and comparison of deoxyribonucleic acid derived from the blood of one individual and buccal cells of another.

(2) "DNA record" and "DNA database" have the same meanings as in section 109.573 of the Revised Code.

(1999 H 471, eff. 7-1-00; 1997 H 352, eff. 1-1-98; 1997 H 408, eff. 10-1-97; 1996 H 357, eff. 9-19-96; 1995 H 5, eff. 8-30-95; 1994 S 355, eff. 12-9-94; 1992 S 10, eff. 7-15-92; 1990 H 591; 1988 H 708; 1987 H 231; 1986 H 476; 1982 H 245)

Uncodified Law

1994 S 355, § 5: See Uncodified Law under 3111.08.

1992 S 10, § 5: See Uncodified Law under 3111.01.

1982 H 245, § 3: See Uncodified Law under 3111.04.

Historical and Statutory Notes

Ed. Note: Former 3111.09 repealed by 1982 H 245, eff. 6-29-82; 1953 H 1; GC 8006-9; Source—GC 12116. 3111.09 contains provisions analogous to former 3111.16, repealed by 1982 H 245, eff. 6-29-82.

Pre-1953 H 1 Amendments: 124 v S 65

Amendment Note: 1999 H 471 substituted "director of job and family services" for "department of human services" in division (A)(2); and substituted "job and family" for "human" in division (B)(1).

Amendment Note: 1997 H 352 split division (A) into paragraphs; designated division (A)(1) and rewrote that division; designated division (A)(2) and inserted "on the motion of the alleged father" therein; designated division (A)(3) and inserted "Except as provided in division (A)(4) of this section," at the beginning thereof; added division (A)(4) and new division (B)(3); redesignated former division (B)(3) as new division (B)(4) and inserted "or person or government entity under division (B) of this section" twice and ", (2), or (3)" therein; deleted "or jury" before "shall determine" in division (D); and made other nonsubstantive changes.

Amendment Note: 1997 H 408 split the paragraphs in division (A); and substituted "participant in Ohio works first" for "recipient of aid to dependent children" in the second paragraph in division (A).

Amendment Note: 1996 H 357 substituted "either of the following:" for "a series of serological" in division (E)(1); designated and rewrote division (E)(1)(a); and added division (E)(1)(b) and the final paragraph in division (E)(1). Prior to amendment, the provisions now contained in division (E)(1)(a) read"tests, that are either immunological or biochemical or both immunological and biochemical in nature, and that are specifically selected because of their known genetic transmittance. 'Genetic tests' and 'genetic testing' include, but are not limited to, tests for the presence or absence of the common blood group antigens, the red blood cell antigens, human lymphocyte antigens, serum enzymes, and serum proteins and for the comparison of the deoxyribonucleic acid."

Amendment Note: 1995 H 5 added the third sentence in division (A); designated division (B)(1); added division (B)(2); designated division (B)(3); added all references to DNA record information and deleted "(1)" after "(D)" in the second sentence in division (B)(3); designated division (E)(1); added division (E)(2); and made other nonsubstantive changes.

Amendment Note: 1994 S 355 added the second through the fourth sentence in division (B).

Cross References

Child support enforcement agencies, 2301.34 to 2301.41

Hearsay exceptions, records of vital statistics, Evid R 803

Testimony by experts, Evid R 702

Ohio Administrative Code References

Genetic testing, OAC 5101:1-30-29

Library References

Children Out-Of-Wedlock ⚿45, 58.
WESTLAW Topic No. 76H.
C.J.S. Children Out-of-Wedlock §§ 51, 75, 76.

OJur 3d: 35, Declaratory Judgments and Related Proceedings § 32
Am Jur 2d: 10, Bastards § 80 et seq., 85, 86, 104 et seq., 114, 116, 118, 123 et seq.
Race or color of child as admissible in evidence on issue of legitimacy or paternity, or as basis of rebuttal or exception to presumption of legitimacy. 32 ALR3d 1303
Bastardy proceedings; Propriety of exhibition of child to jury to show family resemblance, or lack of it, on issue of paternity. 55 ALR3d 1087
Proof of husband's impotency or sterility as rebutting presumption of legitimacy. 84 ALR3d 495
Admissibility, weight and sufficiency of Human Leukocyte Antigen (HLA) tissue typing tests in paternity cases. 37 ALR4th 167
Admissibility and weight of blood-grouping tests in disputed paternity cases. 43 ALR4th 579

Baldwin's Ohio Legislative Service, 1995 H 5—LSC Analysis, p 5/L-336
Baldwin's Ohio Legislative Service, 1990 Laws of Ohio, H 591—LSC Analysis, p 5-576
Carlin, Baldwin's Ohio Practice, *Merrick-Rippner Probate Law* § 18.2, 18.3, 19.1, 19.2, 19.3, 19.4, 19.5, 19.6, 19.7, 19.8, 19.10, 19.12, 38.4, 98.29, 98.30, 98.31, 105.2, 106.5, 108.19, 108.20, 108.22, 108.23, 108.24, 108.26, 108.27, 108.28, 108.31, 108.36 (1997)
Klein & Darling, Baldwin's Ohio Practice, *Civil Practice* § 1 (1997)
Sowald & Morganstern, Baldwin's Ohio Practice, *Domestic Relations Law* § 3.16, 3.17, 3.18, 3.19, 3.21, 3.42, 22.4 (1997)

Law Review and Journal Commentaries

DNA Data Banking: The Dangerous Erosion Of Privacy, E. Donald Shapiro and Michele L. Weinberg. 38 Clev St L Rev 455 (1990).

DNA Identification Testing: Assessing The Threat To Privacy, Dan L. Burke. 24 U Tol L Rev 87 (Fall 1992).

The DNA Paternity Test: Legislating the Future Paternity Action, E. Donald Shapiro, Stewart Reifler, Claudia L. Psome. 7 J L & Health 1 (1992-93).

An Interpretation of Ohio Law on Maternal Status in Gestational Surrogacy Disputes: Belsito v. Clark, Note. 21 U Dayton L Rev 229 (Fall 1995).

A Layman's Guide to the Use of Blood Group Analysis in Paternity Testing, E. G. Reisner and T. A. Bolk. 20 J Fam L 657 (1981-82).

Uniform Parentage Act: Ohio Recognizes Genetic Testing's Validity To Rebut The Presumption That The Natural Mother's Husband Is Not The Father—Hulett v. Hulett, 45 Ohio St. 3d 288, 544 N.E. 2d 257 (1989), Note. 16 U Dayton L Rev 497 (Winter 1991).

Usefulness of Polygraph Results in Paternity Investigations When Used In Conjunction With Exclusionary Blood Tests and a Sixty-Day Conception Period, Richard J. Phannenstill. 21 J Fam L 69 (1982-83).

Notes of Decisions and Opinions

---

1. In general

Putative father whose nonpaternity was conclusively established by genetic testing conducted more than one year after entry of paternity judgment was not entitled to relief from that judgment on ground that it was no longer equitable to enforce it; putative father was aware of parentage proceedings against him and that genetic testing could be performed, but he chose to ignore these initial proceedings and, in doing so, made voluntary, deliberate choice not to seek genetic testing until after finding of parentage and until after he was notified of support arrearage. Cuyahoga Support Enforcement Agency v. Guthrie (Ohio 1999) 84 Ohio St.3d 437, 705 N.E.2d 318.

RC 3111.02 to 3111.04, 3111.09, and 3111.10 are in pari materia and must be construed together. Hulett v. Hulett (Ohio 1989) 45 Ohio St.3d 288, 544 N.E.2d 257.

One obvious goal of various parentage statutes is to accommodate genetic evidence to ensure that correct parentage determination is made from the outset; duty to support children applies to "biological or adoptive parent," and statutes give precedence to genetic testing over any presumption of legitimacy. Leguillon v. Leguillon (Ohio App. 12 Dist. 1998) 124 Ohio App.3d 757, 707 N.E.2d 571.

Common pleas court has inherent power to estop mother from using genetic testing to disestablish child's paternity with his or her presumed father under doctrine of laches, but there must be finding of material prejudice to invoke the doctrine. Sherburn v. Reichert (Van Wert 1994) 97 Ohio App.3d 120, 646 N.E.2d 255.

Assuming that putative father's request for blood testing in letter sent to court after receiving complaint in paternity action could be considered motion for genetic test, motion was not made in timely fashion, where letter was sent to court two days after father's answer to paternity complaint was due and court did not receive letter until one week after answer was due. Harvey v. Mynatt (Summit 1994) 94 Ohio App.3d 619, 641 N.E.2d 291.

RC 3111.09 and 3111.10, as enacted by 1982 H 245, eff. 6-29-82, do not affect substantive rights, and thus may be applied retrospectively to abrogate the usage of the provision under former RC 3111.16 that test results be receivable in evidence only when favorable to the defendant. Standifer v. Arwood (Warren 1984) 17 Ohio App.3d 241, 479 N.E.2d 304, 17 O.B.R. 508.

Putative father would not be allowed, three years after judgment finding him to be child's father, which adjudication he had originally sought, to dismiss complaint or to have genetic testing done to determine whether he was biological father, notwithstanding physician's statement in affidavit that it was highly unlikely that plaintiff could be child's father; there would be no current benefit to child to change her position as plaintiff's daughter, procedural rule did not contemplate dismissal of action, at plaintiff's request, three years after rendering of final appealable order in plaintiff's favor, and plaintiff had failed to request genetic testing when he could have properly done so, at which time request would have been granted. Frederick v. Alltop (Ohio Com.Pl. 1996) 80 Ohio Misc.2d 13, 672 N.E.2d 1123.

"Natural parent" refers to child and parent being of same blood or related by blood or genetics. Belsito v. Clark (Ohio Com.Pl. 1994) 67 Ohio Misc.2d 54, 644 N.E.2d 760.

Common Pleas Court has inherent authority, when considering best interests of minor child, to estop mother from using genetic testing to disestablish child's paternity with his or her presumed father. Riddle v. Riddle (Ohio Com.Pl. 1992) 63 Ohio Misc.2d 43, 619 N.E.2d 1201.

Presumption of paternity created by putative father's marriage to mother at time of child's birth and his signature on birth certificate conflicted with presumption of nonpaternity created by genetic test results indicating more than 95% probability of nonpaternity, requiring use of logic and analysis of policy considerations in determining what presumption should control. Riddle v. Riddle (Ohio Com.Pl. 1992) 63 Ohio Misc.2d 43, 619 N.E.2d 1201.

2. HLA tests

Results of human leukocyte antigen blood test are admissible to determine paternity. Strack v. Pelton (Ohio 1994) 70 Ohio St.3d 172, 637 N.E.2d 914.

Motion for relief from paternity determination in divorce judgment based on genetic test results showing that husband was not father of child was untimely when made nearly nine years after judgment became final and five years after results of test became admissible; fact that motion was filed shortly after receiving results of genetic testing was irrelevant. Strack v. Pelton (Ohio 1994) 70 Ohio St.3d 172, 637 N.E.2d 914.

Human leukocyte antigen (HLA) tests are basically genetic comparison examinations rather than blood grouping tests, and constitute relevant evidence to establish the probability of paternity. Owens v. Bell (Ohio 1983) 6 Ohio St.3d 46, 451 N.E.2d 241, 6 O.B.R. 65.

Failure to inform putative father of court's intent to enter finding of paternity on his refusal to submit to genetic testing precluded finding of paternity by default, where putative father appeared before trial court for purpose of contesting paternity; adjudication was available only as sanction for willful refusal to submit to genetic testing, and not under statutory provision governing default paternity judgments. Marsh v. Clay (Ohio App. 8 Dist. 1998) 125 Ohio App.3d 518, 708 N.E.2d 1073.

Some form of adversarial hearing is required before trial court may make paternity determination based upon putative father's willful refusal to submit to genetic testing; statute provides party opportunity to explain why refusal to submit to genetic testing was not willful. Marsh v. Clay (Ohio App. 8 Dist. 1998) 125 Ohio App.3d 518, 708 N.E.2d 1073.

Once Human Leukocyte Antigen (HLA) test excluded plaintiff as father, juvenile court lacked discretion to consider other evidence of paternity, such as mother's misleading plaintiff into believing he was the natural father, and was required to enter judgment that plaintiff was not the father. Sherburn v. Reichert (Van Wert 1994) 97 Ohio App.3d 120, 646 N.E.2d 255.

Results of Human Leukocyte Antigen (HLA) test excluding plaintiff as father were correctly before juvenile court for its review, where court had sua sponte ordered the test. Sherburn v. Reichert (Van Wert 1994) 97 Ohio App.3d 120, 646 N.E.2d 255.

Eligibility for genetic test in paternity action is not guaranteed, and court can find defendant has fathered child without genetic test results if defendant fails to submit to blood test. Harvey v. Mynatt (Summit 1994) 94 Ohio App.3d 619, 641 N.E.2d 291.

Trial court was not required to allow putative father to receive genetic test to determine if he was father of child born out of wedlock prior to entering default judgment in paternity action brought by county child support enforcement agency, despite putative father's request for blood test in letter sent to court after father received copy of paternity complaint, where letter was sent after father's answer to complaint was due, and father failed to appear and contest motion for default judgment after receipt of notice of default hearing. Harvey v. Mynatt (Summit 1994) 94 Ohio App.3d 619, 641 N.E.2d 291.

Genetic tests indicating greater than 95% probability that putative father was not child's biological father gave rise to presumption of nonpaternity. Riddle v. Riddle (Ohio Com.Pl. 1992) 63 Ohio Misc.2d 43, 619 N.E.2d 1201.

3. Indigent defendant

The denial of blood grouping tests to an indigent paternity defendant, who is unable to prepay for such tests, and who faces the state as an adversary when the complainant-mother and her child are recipients of public assistance, violates the due process guarantee of US Const Am 14. (Annotation from former RC 3111.01.) Anderson v. Jacobs (Ohio 1981) 68 Ohio St.2d 67, 428 N.E.2d 419, 22 O.O.3d 268.

It is an abuse of discretion to assess the costs of human leukocyte antigen testing, incurred in a paternity proceeding, against an indigent putative father whose test results definitively exclude him as the biological father of the child. Little v. Stoops (Clinton 1989) 65 Ohio App.3d 758, 585 N.E.2d 475.

The putative father in a paternity proceeding is denied due process where the referee grants him approximately five weeks in which to have genetic blood tests done at the putative father's expense; this period of time is insufficient to permit the putative father with an income of $300 per week to accumulate funds to defray the $280 cost of the tests. Hamilton County Dept. of Human Services v. Ball (Hamilton 1986) 36 Ohio App.3d 89, 521 N.E.2d 462.

The decisions of State ex rel Cody v Toner, 8 OS(3d) 22, 8 OBR 255, 456 NE(2d) 813 (1983), cert denied 466 US 938, 104 SCt 1912, 80 LEd(2d) 461 (1984), and Anderson v Jacobs, 68 OS(2d) 67, 428 NE(2d) 419 (1981), that the state must provide appointed counsel and blood grouping tests to indigent defendants who face the state as an adversary in paternity proceedings are to be applied retroactively and may therefore be the basis for vacation of judgment pursuant to Civ R 60(B). Keeney v. Lawson (Hamilton 1984) 19 Ohio App.3d 318, 484 N.E.2d 745, 19 O.B.R. 491.

Where the defendant in a paternity action knowingly and voluntarily plead guilty, never requested genetic tests, and did not tell the court that he was indigent, the trial court was not required to inform the defendant of his constitutional right to the state's prepayment of the cost of the genetic tests. Edwards v. Porter (Lorain 1983) 8 Ohio App.3d 277, 456 N.E.2d 1347, 8 O.B.R. 370.

The state of Ohio having granted by statute to all defendants in bastardy proceedings, which are "quasi criminal" in nature, the right to a blood test to determine paternity, cannot deny this right to those defendants who are unable to pay the required fee in advance, without violating the equal protection clause of the United States Constitution, because such a defendant's ability to pay in advance bears no rational relationship to his guilt or innocence, and to discriminate upon this basis constitutes that type of invidious discrimination which is constitutionally prohibited; it is mandatory that the trial court tax as costs the expense of a blood test requested by appropriate motion by an indigent in a bastardy action. (Annotation from former RC 3111.16.) Walker v. Stokes (Cuyahoga 1975) 45 Ohio App.2d 275, 344 N.E.2d 159, 74 O.O.2d 402.

4. Bloodgrouping tests

Where blood-grouping tests may be required to determine whether a party or any person involved can be excluded as being the father of a child and law authorizes admission of such evidence only where results of test establish nonpaternity, the results of such blood-grouping tests, where a mere possibility of parentage is thereby disclosed, are not competent, and their admission is prejudicial. (Annotation from former RC 3111.16.) State ex rel. Freeman v. Morris (Ohio 1951) 156 Ohio St. 333, 102 N.E.2d 450, 46 O.O. 188.

As a paternity proceeding is neither a criminal nor a quasi-criminal action, it is not a denial of due process or equal protection of the law as guaranteed by the US Const Am 14, to require by rule of court that the defendant pay in advance for the costs of blood grouping tests granted pursuant to the defendant's motion. (Annotation from former RC 3111.16.) Bigsby v. Bates (Ohio Com.Pl. 1978) 59 Ohio Misc. 51, 391 N.E.2d 1384, 11 O.O.3d 262, 13 O.O.3d 260.

5. Evidence

For purposes of the rule providing for relief from judgment based on newly discovered evidence, results of a paternity test, not obtained and thus not provided until after an adjudication of the existence of a parent-and-child relationship are not "newly discovered evidence." Cuyahoga Support Enforcement Agency v. Guthrie (Ohio 1999) 84 Ohio St.3d 437, 705 N.E.2d 318.

On trial of a bastardy proceeding instituted by unmarried woman whose child was conceived during existence of a prior marital relation, plaintiff, to establish the nonpaternity of her former husband, may call as a witness a qualified expert who may be permitted to testify that the findings and result of a standard and recognized blood-grouping test made by him from blood of plaintiff, the child, and her former husband, excluded the former husband as the father of the child; findings and result of such test admitted in evidence are not conclusive of nonpaternity, but may be considered for whatever weight they may have in proving that fact. (Annotation from former RC 3111.16.) State ex rel. Walker v. Clark (Ohio 1944) 144 Ohio St. 305, 58 N.E.2d 773, 29 O.O. 450.

Juvenile court must consider genetic evidence regarding paternity of child, even in absence of proffer by the parties. Sherburn v. Reichert (Van Wert 1994) 97 Ohio App.3d 120, 646 N.E.2d 255.

Paternity of a child is proven by a preponderance of the evidence where (1) evidence is introduced of sexual intercourse within the period of conception; (2) expert testimony is given concerning the probability of defendant's paternity based on genetic testing; and (3) expert testimony is given regarding the probability of defendant's paternity based on the physical characteristics and ethnic ancestry of the parties. Grove v. Mattison (Franklin 1988) 61 Ohio App.3d 252, 572 N.E.2d 731, dismissed 42 Ohio St.3d 706, 537 N.E.2d 226.

Results from genetic testing which could have been made available prior to final judgment and are not made available until after final judgment are not newly discovered evidence for purposes of Civ R 60(B)(2). Hardman v. Chiaramonte (Summit 1987) 39 Ohio App.3d 9, 528 N.E.2d 1270.

While the scientific laws of blood-grouping are not "immutable," where the testifying expert was qualified, the testing procedures were technologically correct, the results were consistent and the interpretation sound, this evidence may be considered and may be given sufficient weight to overcome lay testimony to the contrary, including the testimony of the parties. (Annotation from former RC 3111.16.) Garrett v. Garrett (Hamilton 1977) 54 Ohio App.2d 25, 374 N.E.2d 654, 8 O.O.3d 41.

Where alleged father of a bastard child offers in evidence the testimony of an expert witness who made what is known as the Landsteiner-Bernstein blood group testing of the blood of the mother and child and the reputed father, which disclosed that the reputed father could not be the father of the child, it is not error for court to refuse the admission of such testimony as conclusive evidence, but to admit it along with other evidence for whatever weight it may have to prove thc nonpaternity of the alleged father. (Annotation from former RC 3111.16.) State ex rel. Slovak v. Holod (Guernsey 1939) 63 Ohio App. 16, 24 N.E.2d 962, 16 O.O. 257.

Genetic test results are admissible without the need for foundation testimony or further proof of authenticity or accuracy where the biological father fails to file a written objection to the report of the court-ordered genetic test results and does not dispute that he received a copy. Joy B. v Glen D, No. OT-99-002, 1999 WL 575945 (6th Dist Ct App, Wood, 8-6-99).

6. Appeals

An order mandating genetic testing in a parentage action is not a final appealable order as it is not determinative of the parentage action. McCarty v. Kimmel (Montgomery 1989) 62 Ohio App.3d 775, 577 N.E.2d 665.

7. Contempt

Trial court's statement to putative father that his failure to submit to genetic testing might result in contempt citation punishable by either fine or imprisonment did not in any way constitute notice that his failure to submit to genetic testing would result in paternity determination, as prerequisite to entry of paternity determination as sanction for willful refusal to submit to testing. Marsh v. Clay (Ohio App. 8 Dist. 1998) 125 Ohio App.3d 518, 708 N.E.2d 1073.

The requirement to submit to the withdrawal of blood to determine paternity is not susceptible to a right of privacy challenge, and as such, a court may find one who refuses to comply with such an order in contempt. McCarty v. Kimmel (Montgomery 1989) 62 Ohio App.3d 775, 577 N.E.2d 665.

Sanctions other than dismissal of paternity proceeding would have been more appropriate when mother failed to appear at center for genetic testing, especially where there was no showing that delay was intentional, and neither state nor child could control mother's conduct; trial court could have found mother in contempt of court, rescheduled test, and had her pay cost of testing. Dukes v. Cole (Lorain 1985) 23 Ohio App.3d 65, 491 N.E.2d 374, 23 O.B.R. 110.

A putative father is entitled to notice of the court's intent to enter a finding of paternity upon his refusal to submit to genetic testing because a possible long-term obligation of child support is far different from the simple contempt warning for willful refusal to take the test and the party must be given the chance to come before the court and explain his refusal. Marsh v Clay, No. 71665, 1998 WL 23849 (8th Dist Ct App, Cuyahoga, 1-22-98).

3111.10 Admissible evidence

In an action brought under sections 3111.01 to 3111.19 of the Revised Code, evidence relating to paternity may include:

(A) Evidence of sexual intercourse between the mother and alleged father at any possible time of conception;

(B) An expert's opinion concerning the statistical probability of the alleged father's paternity, which opinion is based upon the duration of the mother's pregnancy;

(C) Genetic test results, weighted in accordance with evidence, if available, of the statistical probability of the alleged father's paternity;

(D) Medical evidence relating to the alleged father's paternity of the child based on tests performed by experts. If a man has been identified as a possible father of the child, the court may, and upon the request of a party shall, require the child, the mother, and the man to submit to appropriate tests. Any fees charged for the tests shall be paid by the party that requests them unless the court orders the fees taxed as costs in the action.

(E) All other evidence relevant to the issue of paternity of the child.

(1986 H 476, eff. 9-24-86; 1982 H 245)

Uncodified Law

1992 S 10, § 5: See Uncodified Law under 3111.01.

1982 H 245, § 3: See Uncodified Law under 3111.04.

Historical and Statutory Notes

Ed. Note: Former 3111.10 repealed by 1982 H 245, eff. 6-29-82; 127 v 1039; 1953 H 1; GC 8006-10; Source—GC 12117.

Pre-1953 H 1 Amendments: 124 v S 65

Cross References

Relevancy and its limits, Evid R 401 to 411

Library References

Children Out-Of-Wedlock ⟹42.1 to 50.
WESTLAW Topic No. 76H.
C.J.S. Children Out-of-Wedlock §§ 51, 75, 76, 99 to 106.

OJur 3d: 35, Declaratory Judgments and Related Proceedings § 32
Am Jur 2d: 10, Bastards § 80 et seq., 85, 86, 104 et seq., 114, 116, 118, 123 et seq.
Race or color of child as admissible in evidence on issue of legitimacy or paternity, or as basis of rebuttal or exception to presumption of legitimacy. 32 ALR3d 1303
Bastardy proceedings; Propriety of exhibition of child to jury to show family resemblance, or lack of it, on issue of paternity. 55 ALR3d 1087
Admissibility, in disputed paternity proceedings, of evidence to rebut mother's claim of prior chastity. 59 ALR3d 659
Proof of husband's impotency or sterility as rebutting presumption of legitimacy. 84 ALR3d 495
Admissibility, weight and sufficiency of Human Leukocyte Antigen (HLA) tissue typing tests in paternity cases. 37 ALR4th 167

Admissibility and weight of blood-grouping tests in disputed paternity cases. 43 ALR4th 579

Carlin, Baldwin's Ohio Practice, *Merrick-Rippner Probate Law* § 18.2, 18.3, 19.1, 19.2, 19.3, 19.4, 19.5, 19.6, 19.7, 19.8, 19.10, 19.12, 38.4, 98.29, 98.30, 98.31, 105.2, 108.19, 108.20, 108.22, 108.23, 108.24, 108.27, 108.28, 108.31 (1997)

Giannelli & Snyder, Baldwin's Ohio Practice, Evidence § 702.14 (1996)

Klein & Darling, Baldwin's Ohio Practice, *Civil Practice* § 1 (1997)

Sowald & Morganstern, Baldwin's Ohio Practice, *Domestic Relations Law* § 3.12, 3.14, 3.16, 3.20, 3.42 (1997)

Law Review and Journal Commentaries

Chromosome Testing—New, Improved Paternity Tests?, Note. 28 J Fam L 753 (1989-90).

DNA Data Banking: The Dangerous Erosion Of Privacy, E. Donald Shapiro and Michele L. Weinberg. 38 Clev St L Rev 455 (1990).

'Genetically' Altered Admissibility: Legislative Notice Of DNA Typing, Note. 39 Clev St L Rev 415 (1991).

The Need for Statutes Regulating Artificial Insemination by Donors, Note. 46 Ohio St L J 1055 (1986).

Notes of Decisions and Opinions

---

1. In general

RC 3111.02 to 3111.04, 3111.09, and 3111.10 are in pari materia and must be construed together. Hulett v. Hulett (Ohio 1989) 45 Ohio St.3d 288, 544 N.E.2d 257.

Paternity of a child is proven by a preponderance of the evidence where (1) evidence is introduced of sexual intercourse within the period of conception; (2) expert testimony is given concerning the probability of defendant's paternity based on genetic testing; and (3) expert testimony is given regarding the probability of defendant's paternity based on the physical characteristics and ethnic ancestry of the parties. Grove v. Mattison (Franklin 1988) 61 Ohio App.3d 252, 572 N.E.2d 731, dismissed 42 Ohio St.3d 706, 537 N.E.2d 226.

RC 3111.09 and 3111.10, as enacted by 1982 H 245, eff. 6-29-82, do not affect substantive rights, and thus may be applied retrospectively to abrogate the usage of the provision under former RC 3111.16 that test results be receivable in evidence only when favorable to the defendant. Standifer v. Arwood (Warren 1984) 17 Ohio App.3d 241, 479 N.E.2d 304, 17 O.B.R. 508.

2. Burden of proof

Clear and convincing evidence sufficient to overcome the presumption of paternity contained in RC 3111.03(A)(1) may be adduced through any or all of the enumerated methods prescribed by RC 3111.10, including the submission of genetic test results. Hulett v. Hulett (Ohio 1989) 45 Ohio St.3d 288, 544 N.E.2d 257.

The facts upon which a hypothetical question to an expert witness is premised must be established by the party calling the witness by a preponderance of the evidence; it is up to the jury to determine whether the preponderance test has been met. Camden v. Miller (Clark 1986) 34 Ohio App.3d 86, 517 N.E.2d 253.

A state statute establishing the burden of proof in civil paternity actions as a preponderance of the evidence rather than clear and convincing evidence does not deprive the defendant of due process of law. (Ed. note: Pennsylvania statute construed in light of federal constitution.) Rivera v. Minnich (U.S.Pa. 1987) 107 S.Ct. 3001, 483 U.S. 574, 97 L.Ed.2d 473.

3. HLA tests

Results of human leukocyte antigen blood test are admissible to determine paternity. Strack v. Pelton (Ohio 1994) 70 Ohio St.3d 172, 637 N.E.2d 914.

Human leukocyte antigen (HLA) tests are basically genetic comparison examinations rather than blood grouping tests, and constitute relevant evidence to establish the probability of paternity. Owens v. Bell (Ohio 1983) 6 Ohio St.3d 46, 451 N.E.2d 241, 6 O.B.R. 65.

Results of Human Leukocyte Antigen (HLA) test excluding plaintiff as father were correctly before juvenile court for its review, where court had sua sponte ordered the test. Sherburn v. Reichert (Van Wert 1994) 97 Ohio App.3d 120, 646 N.E.2d 255.

Human leukocyte antigen blood test results are admissible in an action to determine paternity where the following foundational requirements have been established: (1) the blood tested was in fact that of the defendant, the plaintiff, and the child; (2) the test results were based upon reliable blood samples; and (3) there was an unbroken chain of custody from the time the samples were taken to the time they were analyzed. Camden v. Miller (Clark 1986) 34 Ohio App.3d 86, 517 N.E.2d 253.

The plaintiff in a paternity action must present proper foundational evidence to introduce results of court-ordered Human Leukocyte Antigen (HLA) blood testing, such as evidence that the blood tested was actually that of the defendant, the mother and the child, since there is no special statutory provision exempting the admission of HLA tests from the basic foundational requirements set forth in the Ohio Rules of Evidence. McElroy v Gilbert, No. 92 CA 9, 1994 WL 527119 (7th Dist Ct App, Mahoning, 9-27-94).

4. Other relevant evidence

Juvenile court must consider genetic evidence regarding paternity of child, even in absence of proffer by the parties. Sherburn v. Reichert (Van Wert 1994) 97 Ohio App.3d 120, 646 N.E.2d 255.

Under RC 3111.10(E), a jury view of the child whose paternity is disputed, for purposes of comparing its physical characteristics and appearances with the alleged father, is permissible. Domigan v. Gillette (Clark 1984) 17 Ohio App.3d 228, 479 N.E.2d 291, 17 O.B.R. 494.

A proposed witness in a paternity action need not be rejected or grounds of public policy when such witness is the child whose paternity is under inquiry. Philpot v. Williams (Hamilton 1983) 8 Ohio App.3d 241, 456 N.E.2d 1315, 8 O.B.R. 314.

Evidence obtained by accused under the statute must be considered as defensive matter; if accused wishes to introduce such, he must offer it during the presentation of his own case. (Annotation from former RC 3111.04.) State ex rel. Brannon v. Turner (Franklin 1947) 81 Ohio App. 47, 77 N.E.2d 255, 49 Ohio Law Abs. 446, 36 O.O. 359.

Proper interpretation of this section is that accused shall be permitted to ask complainant any question which within rules of evidence is competent, relevant or material to complaint of prosecuting witness or which under such rules may have any tendency to establish defense. (Annotation from former RC 3111.04.) Mabra v. State ex rel. Settles (Clark 1935) 21 Ohio Law Abs. 190.

In a prosecution for nonsupport of an illegitimate child, an adjudication of paternity in a bastardy action is admissible, but does not constitute conclusive proof. (Annotation from former RC 3111.17.) State v. Lockwood (Cuyahoga 1959) 160 N.E.2d 131, 84 Ohio Law Abs. 257.

5. Sexual intercourse with others

Evidence in a bastardy action of complainant's sexual relations with other persons at a time which could not have resulted in the conception complained or of her bad character in general is inadmissible. (Annotation from former RC 3111.04.) Taylor v. Mosley (Ohio Juv. 1961) 178 N.E.2d 55, 87 Ohio Law Abs. 335, 17 O.O.2d 439.

3111.11 Pretrial procedures

If the person against whom an action is brought pursuant to sections 3111.01 to 3111.19 of the Revised Code does not admit in his answer the existence or nonexistence of the father and child relationship, the court shall hold a pretrial hearing, in accordance with the Civil Rules, at a time set by the court. At the pretrial hearing, the court shall notify each party to the action that the party may file a motion requesting the court to order the child's mother, the alleged father, and any other person who is a defendant in the action to submit to genetic tests and, if applicable, to the appropriate tests referred to in section 3111.10 of the Revised Code. When the court determines that all pretrial matters have been completed, the action shall be set for trial.

(1986 H 476, eff. 9-24-86; 1982 H 245)

Uncodified Law

1992 S 10, § 5: See Uncodified Law under 3111.01.

1982 H 245, § 3: See Uncodified Law under 3111.04.

Historical and Statutory Notes

Ed. Note: Former 3111.11 repealed by 1982 H 245, eff. 6-29-82; 1953 H 1; GC 8006-11; Source—GC 12118.

Pre-1953 H 1 Amendments: 124 v S 65

Library References

Children Out-Of-Wedlock ⟾39, 54.
WESTLAW Topic No. 76H.
C.J.S. Children Out-of-Wedlock §§ 50, 72 to 74, 92, 94, 110.

OJur 3d: 35, Declaratory Judgments and Related Proceedings § 32
Am Jur 2d: 10, Bastards § 80 et seq., 85, 86, 104 et seq., 114, 116, 118, 123 et seq.
Race or color of child as admissible in evidence on issue of legitimacy or paternity, or as basis of rebuttal or exception to presumption of legitimacy. 32 ALR3d 1303
Bastardy proceedings; Propriety of exhibition of child to jury to show family resemblance, or lack of it, on issue of paternity. 55 ALR3d 1087
Admissibility, in disputed paternity proceedings, of evidence to rebut mother's claim of prior chastity. 59 ALR3d 659
Proof of husband's impotency or sterility as rebutting presumption of legitimacy. 84 ALR3d 495
Admissibility, weight and sufficiency of Human Leukocyte Antigen (HLA) tissue typing tests in paternity cases. 37 ALR4th 167
Admissibility and weight of blood-grouping tests in disputed paternity cases. 43 ALR4th 579

Carlin, Baldwin's Ohio Practice, *Merrick-Rippner Probate Law* § 18.2, 18.3, 19.1, 19.2, 19.3, 19.4, 19.5, 19.6, 19.7, 19.8, 19.10, 19.12, 38.4, 98.29, 98.30, 98.31, 105.2, 108.19, 108.20, 108.22, 108.23, 108.24, 108.26, 108.27, 108.28, 108.31 (1997)
Klein & Darling, Baldwin's Ohio Practice, *Civil Practice* § 1 (1997)
Sowald & Morganstern, Baldwin's Ohio Practice, *Domestic Relations Law* § 3.11 (1997)

Notes of Decisions and Opinions

1. Default judgment

Defendant who was in default of answer and had failed to appear in parentage action was not entitled to notice of filing of motion for default. Long v. Bartlett (Franklin 1992) 73 Ohio App.3d 764, 598 N.E.2d 197.

Where no answer is filed to a complaint alleging paternity, the trial court errs in entering judgment by default without first conducting the pretrial hearing provided under RC 3111.11. Potts v Wilson, No. 409 (4th Dist Ct App, Adams, 5-30-85).

2. Waiver of defenses

The Ohio Rules of Civil Procedure apply to parentage actions; thus, an answer must be filed by the person against whom the action is brought, and a failure to properly plead the affirmative defense of laches bars its defense at trial. Eppley v Bratton, No. 94 CA 7, 1994 WL 668111 (5th Dist Ct App, Coshocton, 11-7-94).

3111.111 Temporary support order pending action objecting to parentage determination

If an action is brought pursuant to sections 3111.01 to 3111.19 of the Revised Code to object to a determination made pursuant to former section 3111.21 or section 3111.22 of the

Revised Code that the alleged father is the natural father of a child, the court, on its own motion or on the motion of either party, shall issue a temporary order for the support of the child pursuant to section 3113.21 to 3113.219 of the Revised Code requiring the alleged father to pay support to the natural mother or the guardian or legal custodian of the child. The order shall remain in effect until the court issues a judgment in the action pursuant to section 3111.13 of the Revised Code that determines the existence or nonexistence of a father and child relationship. If the court, in its judgment, determines that the alleged father is not the natural father of the child, the court shall order the person to whom the temporary support was paid under the order to repay the alleged father all amounts paid for support under the temporary order.

(1997 H 352, eff. 1-1-98)

Library References

OJur 3d: 47, Family Law § 977

Carlin, Baldwin's Ohio Practice, *Merrick-Rippner Probate Law* § 18.3, 19.2, 19.3, 19.7, 19.10, 19.10.1, 105.2, 108.20, 108.27, 108.29, 108.30, 108.34 (1997)

Sowald & Morganstern, Baldwin's Ohio Practice, *Domestic Relations Law* § 3.39 (1997)

3111.12 Testimony; admissibility of genetic test results or DNA records

(A) In an action under sections 3111.01 to 3111.19 of the Revised Code, the mother of the child and the alleged father are competent to testify and may be compelled to testify by subpoena. If a witness refuses to testify upon the ground that the testimony or evidence of the witness might tend to incriminate the witness and the court compels the witness to testify, the court may grant the witness immunity from having the testimony of the witness used against the witness in subsequent criminal proceedings.

(B) Testimony of a physician concerning the medical circumstances of the mother's pregnancy and the condition and characteristics of the child upon birth is not privileged.

(C) Testimony relating to sexual access to the mother by a man at a time other than the probable time of conception of the child is inadmissible in evidence, unless offered by the mother.

(D) If, pursuant to section 3111.09 of the Revised Code, a court orders genetic tests to be conducted, orders disclosure of information regarding a DNA record stored in the DNA database pursuant to section 109.573 of the Revised Code, or intends to use a report of genetic test results obtained from tests conducted pursuant to former section 3111.21 or section 3111.22 of the Revised Code, a party may object to the admission into evidence of any of the genetic test results or of the DNA record information by filing a written objection with the court that ordered the tests or disclosure or intends to use a report of genetic test results. The party shall file the written objection with the court no later than fourteen days after the report of the test results or the DNA record information is mailed to the attorney of record of a party or to a party. The party making the objection shall send a copy of the objection to all parties.

If a party files a written objection, the report of the test results or the DNA record information shall be admissible into evidence as provided by the Rules of Evidence. If a written objection is not filed, the report of the test results or the DNA record information shall be admissible into evidence without the need for foundation testimony or other proof of authenticity or accuracy.

(E) If a party intends to introduce into evidence invoices or other documents showing amounts expended to cover pregnancy and confinement and genetic testing, the party shall notify all other parties in writing of that intent and include copies of the invoices and documents. A party may object to the admission into evidence of the invoices or documents by filing a written objection with the court that is hearing the action no later than fourteen days after the notice and the copies of the invoices and documents are mailed to the attorney of record of each party or to each party.

If a party files a written objection, the invoices and other documents shall be admissible into evidence as provided by the Rules of Evidence. If a written objection is not filed, the invoices or other documents are admissible into evidence without the need for foundation testimony or other evidence of authenticity or accuracy.

(F) A juvenile court shall give priority to actions under sections 3111.01 to 3111.19 of the Revised Code and shall issue an order determining the existence or nonexistence of a parent and child relationship no later than one hundred twenty days after the date on which the action was brought in the juvenile court.

(1997 H 352, eff. 1-1-98; 1995 H 5, eff. 8-30-95; 1994 S 355, eff. 12-9-94; 1992 S 10, eff. 7-15-92; 1986 H 476; 1982 H 245)

Uncodified Law

1994 S 355, § 5: See Uncodified Law under 3111.08.

1992 S 10, § 5: See Uncodified Law under 3111.01.

1982 H 245, § 3: See Uncodified Law under 3111.04.

Historical and Statutory Notes

Ed. Note: Former 3111.12 repealed by 1982 H 245, eff. 6-29-82; 1953 H 1; GC 8006-12; Source—GC 12119. 3111.12 contains provisions analogous to former 3111.15, repealed by 1982 H 245, eff. 6-29-82.

Pre-1953 H 1 Amendments: 124 v S 65

Amendment Note: 1997 H 352 rewrote divisions (D) and (E), which prior thereto read:

"(D) If, pursuant to section 3111.09 of the Revised Code, a court orders genetic tests to be conducted or orders disclosure of information regarding a DNA record stored in the DNA database pursuant to section 109.573 of the Revised Code, a party may object to the admission into evidence of the report of the test results or of the DNA record information by filing a written objection with the court that ordered the tests or disclosure. The party shall file the written objection with the court no later than fourteen days after the report of the test results or the DNA record information is mailed to the attorney of record of a party or to a party. The party making the objection shall send a copy of the objection to all parties.

"If a party files a written objection, the report of the test results or the DNA record information shall be admissible into evidence as provided by the Rules of Evidence. If a written objection is not filed, the report of the test results or the DNA record information shall be admissible into evidence without the need for foundation testimony or other proof of authenticity or accuracy.

"(E) Any party to an action brought pursuant to sections 3111.01 to 3111.19 of the Revised Code may demand a jury trial by filing the demand within three days after the action is set for trial. If a jury demand is not filed within the three-day period, the trial shall be by the court.

"If the action is tried to a jury, the verdict of the jury is limited only to the parentage of the child, and all other matters involved in the action shall be determined by the court following the rendering of the verdict."

Amendment Note: 1995 H 5 added all references to DNA record information in division (D); and made changes to reflect gender neutral language.

Amendment Note: 1994 S 355 added division (D); and redesignated former divisions (D) and (E) as divisions (E) and (F).

Cross References

Common pleas court to grant transactional immunity, procedure, exceptions, 2945.44

Jury trial of right, Civ R 38

Reciprocal enforcement of support proceedings, self-incrimination, immunity, 3115.19

Right against compulsory self-incrimination, O Const Art I §10

Right of trial by jury, O Const Art I §5

Testimony regarding witness credibility, not waiver of privilege against self-incrimination, Evid R 608

Ohio Administrative Code References

Genetic testing, OAC 5101:1-30-29

Library References

Children Out-Of-Wedlock ⟸57.

WESTLAW Topic No. 76H.

C.J.S. Children Out-of-Wedlock §§ 110, 111, 113, 114.

OJur 3d: 35, Declaratory Judgments and Related Proceedings § 32

Am Jur 2d: 10, Bastards § 80 et seq., 85, 86, 104 et seq., 114, 116, 118, 123 et seq.

Race or color of child as admissible in evidence on issue of legitimacy or paternity, or as basis of rebuttal or exception to presumption of legitimacy. 32 ALR3d 1303

Bastardy proceedings; Propriety of exhibition of child to jury to show family resemblance, or lack of it, on issue of paternity. 55 ALR3d 1087

Admissibility, in disputed paternity proceedings, of evidence to rebut mother's claim of prior chastity. 59 ALR3d 659

Proof of husband's impotency or sterility as rebutting presumption of legitimacy. 84 ALR3d 495

Admissibility, weight and sufficiency of Human Leukocyte Antigen (HLA) tissue typing tests in paternity cases. 37 ALR4th 167

Admissibility and weight of blood-grouping tests in disputed paternity cases. 43 ALR4th 579
Paternity proceedings: right to jury trial. 51 ALR4th 565

Carlin, Baldwin's Ohio Practice, *Merrick-Rippner Probate Law* § 18.2, 18.3, 19.1, 19.2, 19.3, 19.4, 19.5, 19.6, 19.7, 19.8, 19.10, 19.12, 38.4, 98.29, 98.30, 98.31, 98.38, 105.2, 106.5, 108.19, 108.20, 108.22, 108.23, 108.24, 108.26, 108.27, 108.28, 108.31 (1997)

Klein & Darling, Baldwin's Ohio Practice, *Civil Practice* § 1, 38 (1997)
Sowald & Morganstern, Baldwin's Ohio Practice, *Domestic Relations Law* § 3.11, 3.14, 3.15, 3.18, 3.19, 3.37 (1997)

Notes of Decisions and Opinions

---

1. Support obligation

An unmarried parent is subject to the support obligation to which RC 3107.07(A) refers only where a paternity determination has been rendered pursuant to RC 3111.08(B) or 3111.12. In re Adoption of Sunderhaus (Ohio 1992) 63 Ohio St.3d 127, 585 N.E.2d 418, rehearing denied 63 Ohio St.3d 1442, 589 N.E.2d 46.

2. Procedure

Bastardy statutes do not contemplate the punishment of criminal act but only enforcement of moral duty of reimbursing complainant for expense of and maintaining child; verdict of guilty against putative father may be rendered upon the concurrence of three-fourths or more members of jury. (Annotation from former RC 3111.15.) State ex rel. Gill v. Volz (Ohio 1951) 156 Ohio St. 60, 100 N.E.2d 203, 45 O.O. 63.

The trial of an action in bastardy is governed by the code of civil procedure, so far as it is applicable, and the complainant has the right under the Constitution and statutes to have the issues raised therein tried by a jury. (Annotation from former RC 3111.15.) State ex rel. Wonderland v. Shuba (Lucas 1951) 91 Ohio App. 64, 107 N.E.2d 407, 48 O.O. 240.

In bastardy proceeding, it is not error for the trial court to enter judgment on the verdict of a jury at once, and within the three-day period for filing a motion for new trial. (Annotation from former RC 3111.17.) State ex rel. Adkins v. Mefford (Hamilton 1944) 75 Ohio App. 215, 61 N.E.2d 635, 43 Ohio Law Abs. 349, 30 O.O. 554.

Since, under this section, as amended effective April 5, 1923, bastardy complaint by mother is not bar to prosecution of father for failure to support child, charge that proceeding by mother was not wholly in her interest, but was also to protect state from care of child, constituted prejudicial error. (Annotation from former RC 3111.17.) Pummell v. State (Vinton 1926) 22 Ohio App. 340, 154 N.E. 745, 5 Ohio Law Abs. 293.

Genetic test results are admissible without the need for foundation testimony or further proof of authenticity or accuracy where the biological father fails to file a written objection to the report of the court-ordered genetic test results and does not dispute that he received a copy. Joy B. v Glen D, No. OT-99-002, 1999 WL 575945 (6th Dist Ct App, Wood, 8-6-99).

3. Jury trial

The language in RC 3111.12(D) requiring a jury demand in a paternity suit to be made "within three days after the action is set for trial" means "not later than" three days after a trial date is set and does not require that the demand be filed within the three-day period, and a jury demand was timely and proper when it was filed months before a trial date was set. Abbott v. Potter (Jackson 1992) 78 Ohio App.3d 335, 604 N.E.2d 804.

The requirement in RC 3111.12(D) that a jury demand in a paternity suit be made not later than three days after a trial date is set does not clearly conflict with the requirement in Civ R 38(B) that a jury demand be made not later than fourteen days after service of the last pleading directed to the issue, and in such case the statute rather than the rule controls the time within which to make a jury demand. Abbott v. Potter (Jackson 1992) 78 Ohio App.3d 335, 604 N.E.2d 804.

The trial court abuses its discretion by refusing a defendant in a paternity action a jury trial when his request had been granted at pretrial, even though his payment of a jury deposit was not made within the time period prescribed by local rule and the court did not return the deposit but applied it to costs. Wade v. Oglesby (Huron 1991) 74 Ohio App.3d 560, 599 N.E.2d 748.

The granting of a new trial in a bastardy case is not an abuse of discretion as being unreasonable, arbitrary or unconscionable, where, after verdict and judgment, it is discovered that one of the jurors had previously been a defendant in a paternity suit and had remained silent when the jury was asked on voir dire examination whether any one of them had ever "been involved in a paternity case." (Annotation from former RC 3111.15.) Strader v. Mendenhall (Clark 1959) 110 Ohio App. 231, 167 N.E.2d 504, 83 Ohio Law Abs. 23, 13 O.O.2d 13.

Unless otherwise specified, paternity actions are governed by the Ohio rules of civil procedure and, thus, a defendant who fails to demand a jury trial pursuant to Civ R 38, but instead makes a request for the first time on the day of trial, waives his right to a jury trial. (Annotation from former RC 3111.15.) Lent v Stull, No. 81 X 7 (4th Dist Ct App, Washington, 2-25-82).

4. Burden of proof

Finding in divorce action that husband is father of two children born during marriage may not be used to resolve disputed paternity issue involving those two children in subsequent criminal nonsupport trial. State v. Cole (Hamilton 1994) 94 Ohio App.3d 629, 641 N.E.2d 732, appeal not allowed 70 Ohio St.3d 1416, 637 N.E.2d 12.

RC 3111.12(C) does not impermissibly shift the burden of proof to defendants in paternity actions. Grove v. Mattison (Franklin 1988) 61 Ohio App.3d 252, 572 N.E.2d 731, dismissed 42 Ohio St.3d 706, 537 N.E.2d 226.

5. Testimony

In paternity action, child whose paternity is under inquiry is not incompetent to testify. Philpot v. Williams

(Hamilton 1983) 8 Ohio App.3d 241, 456 N.E.2d 1315, 8 O.B.R. 314.

In a bastardy proceeding where there is a direct conflict in the evidence as to whether complainant and defendant had sexual relations about the time the child was conceived, the question is one for the jury, and it is the jury's prerogative to believe the complainant and disbelieve the defendant. (Annotation from former RC 3111.15.) Wells v. Fulton (Montgomery 1953) 96 Ohio App. 178, 121 N.E.2d 437, 54 O.O. 171, 54 O.O. 240.

An accused in a bastardy case may be called by counsel for complainant, and, over defendant's objection, be compelled to testify under cross-examination, either orally or by deposition, but cannot be forced to testify or to give evidence in such proceeding, when to do so would tend to incriminate him. (Annotation from former RC 3111.04.) Taylor v. Mosley (Ohio Juv. 1961) 178 N.E.2d 55, 87 Ohio Law Abs. 335, 17 O.O.2d 439.

Where a defendant in a bastardy action testified on cross-examination but not on direct, plaintiff was not entitled to an instruction that the jury could take into consideration such failure to testify. (Annotation from former RC 3111.15.) State ex rel. Johnson v. Mooney (Cuyahoga 1961) 171 N.E.2d 918, 86 Ohio Law Abs. 105.

A defendant in a bastardy action may be compelled to testify against himself. (Annotation from former RC 3111.01.) State ex rel. Hetzler v. Snyder (Ohio Mun. 1950) 109 N.E.2d 54, 63 Ohio Law Abs. 42.

6. Time limit of 120 days for order

RC 3111.12(F) is directory in nature in that parentage cases are to be decided in one hundred and twenty (120) days and does not provide for an express dismissal of the case if that time frame is not met. State ex rel Lawrence County Child Support Enforcement Agency v Ward, No. 95CA40, 1996 WL 668832 (4th Dist Ct App, Lawrence, 11-18-96).

3111.13 Effects of judgment; supplemental release; support orders; contempt

Note: See also following version of this section, eff. 10-27-00.

(A) The judgment or order of the court determining the existence or nonexistence of the parent and child relationship is determinative for all purposes.

(B) If the judgment or order of the court is at variance with the child's birth record, the court may order that a new birth record be issued under section 3111.18 of the Revised Code.

(C) The judgment or order may contain any other provision directed against the appropriate party to the proceeding, concerning the duty of support, the furnishing of bond or other security for the payment of the judgment, or any other matter in the best interest of the child. The judgment or order shall direct the father to pay all or any part of the reasonable expenses of the mother's pregnancy and confinement. After entry of the judgment or order, the father may petition that he be designated the residential parent and legal custodian of the child or for visitation rights in a proceeding separate from any action to establish paternity. Additionally, if the mother is unmarried, the father, the parents of the father, any relative of the father, the parents of the mother, and any relative of the mother may file a complaint pursuant to section 3109.12 of the Revised Code requesting the granting under that section of reasonable companionship or visitation rights with respect to the child.

The judgment or order shall contain any provision required by section 3111.14 of the Revised Code.

(D) Support judgments or orders ordinarily shall be for periodic payments that may vary in amount. In the best interest of the child, a lump-sum payment or the purchase of an annuity may be ordered in lieu of periodic payments of support.

(E) In determining the amount to be paid by a parent for support of the child and the period during which the duty of support is owed, a court enforcing the obligation of support shall comply with sections 3113.21 to 3113.219 of the Revised Code.

(F)(1) Each order for child support made or modified under this section shall include as part of the order a general provision, as described in division (A)(1) of section 3113.21 of the Revised Code, requiring the withholding or deduction of income or assets of the obligor under the order as described in division (D) or (H) of section 3113.21 of the Revised Code, or another type of appropriate requirement as described in division (D)(3), (D)(4), or (H) of that section, to ensure that withholding or deduction from the income or assets of the obligor is available from the commencement of the support order for collection of the support and of any arrearages that occur; a statement requiring all parties to the order to notify the child support enforcement agency in writing of their current mailing address, current residence address, current residence telephone number, current driver's license number, and any changes to that information; and a notice that the requirement to notify the agency of all changes to that information continues until further notice from the court. Any court that makes or modifies an order for child support under this section shall comply with sections 3113.21 to 3113.219 of the Revised Code. If any person required to pay child support under an order made under this section on or after April 15, 1985, or modified on or after December 1, 1986, is found in contempt of court for failure to make support payments under the order, the court that makes the finding, in addition to any other penalty or remedy imposed, shall assess all court costs arising out of the contempt proceeding against the person and require the person to pay any reasonable attorney's fees of any adverse party, as determined by the court, that arose in relation to the act of contempt.

(2) Notwithstanding section 3109.01 of the Revised Code, if a court issues a child support order under this section, the order shall remain in effect beyond the child's eighteenth birthday as long as the child continuously attends on a full-time basis any recognized and accredited high school or the order provides that the duty of support of the child continues beyond the child's eighteenth birthday. Except in cases in which the order provides that the duty of support continues for any period after the child reaches nineteen years of age, the order shall not remain in effect after the child reaches age nineteen. Any parent ordered to pay support under a child support order issued under this section shall continue to pay support under the order, including during seasonal vacation periods, until the order terminates.

(3) When a court determines whether to require a parent to pay an amount for that parent's failure to support a child prior to the date the court issues an order requiring that parent to pay an amount for the current support of that child, it shall consider all relevant factors, including, but not limited to, any monetary contribution either parent of the child made to the support of the child prior to the court issuing the order requiring the parent to pay an amount for the current support of the child.

(G) As used in this section, "birth record" has the same meaning as in section 3705.01 of the Revised Code.

(H) Unless the court has reason to believe that a person named in the order is a potential victim of domestic violence, any order issued pursuant to this section finding the existence of a parent and child relationship shall contain the full names, addresses, and social security numbers of the mother and father of the child and the full name and address of the child.

(1997 H 352, eff. 1-1-98; 1993 H 173, eff. 12-31-93; 1993 S 115; 1992 S 10; 1990 S 3, H 591, H 15; 1988 H 790, H 708; 1987 H 231; 1986 H 509; 1984 H 614; 1982 H 245)

Note: See also following version of this section, eff. 10-27-00.

3111.13 Effects of judgment; support orders; contempt; prohibitions on certain arrearages

Note: See also preceding version of this section, in effect until 10-27-00.

(A) The judgment or order of the court determining the existence or nonexistence of the parent and child relationship is determinative for all purposes.

(B) If the judgment or order of the court is at variance with the child's birth record, the court may order that a new birth record be issued under section 3111.18 of the Revised Code.

(C) Except as otherwise provided in this section, the judgment or order may contain any other provision directed against the appropriate party to the proceeding, concerning the duty of support, the furnishing of bond or other security for the payment of the judgment, or any other matter in the best interest of the child. The judgment or order shall direct the father to pay all or any part of the reasonable expenses of the mother's pregnancy and confinement. After entry of the judgment or order, the father may petition that he be designated the residential parent and legal custodian of the child or for visitation rights in a proceeding separate from any action to establish paternity. Additionally, if the mother is unmarried, the father, the parents of the father, any relative of the father, the parents of the mother, and any relative of the mother may file a complaint pursuant to section 3109.12 of the Revised Code requesting the granting under that section of reasonable companionship or visitation rights with respect to the child.

The judgment or order shall contain any provision required by section 3111.14 of the Revised Code.

(D) Support judgments or orders ordinarily shall be for periodic payments that may vary in amount. In the best interest of the child, a lump-sum payment or the purchase of an annuity may be ordered in lieu of periodic payments of support.

(E) In determining the amount to be paid by a parent for support of the child and the period during which the duty of support is owed, a court enforcing the obligation of support shall comply with sections 3113.21 to 3113.219 of the Revised Code.

(F)(1) Each order for child support made or modified under this section shall include as part of the order a general provision, as described in division (A)(1) of section 3113.21 of the Revised Code, requiring the withholding or deduction of income or assets of the obligor under the order as described in division (D) or (H) of section 3113.21 of the Revised Code, or another type of appropriate requirement as described in division (D)(3), (D)(4), or (H) of that section, to ensure that withholding or deduction from the income or assets of the obligor is available from the commencement of the support order for collection of the support and of any arrearages that occur; a statement requiring all parties to the order to notify the child support enforcement agency in writing of their current mailing address, current residence address, current residence telephone number, current driver's license number, and any changes to that information; and a notice that the requirement to notify the agency of all changes to that information continues until further notice from the court. Any court that makes or modifies an order for child support under this section shall comply with sections 3113.21 to 3113.219 of the Revised Code. If any person required to pay child support under an order made under this section on or after April 15, 1985, or modified on or after December 1, 1986, is found in contempt of court for failure to make support payments under the order, the court that makes the finding, in addition to any other penalty or remedy imposed, shall assess all court costs arising out of the contempt proceeding against the person and require the person to pay any reasonable attorney's fees of any adverse party, as determined by the court, that arose in relation to the act of contempt.

(2) Notwithstanding section 3109.01 of the Revised Code, if a court issues a child support order under this section, the order shall remain in effect beyond the child's eighteenth birthday as long as the child continuously attends on a full-time basis any recognized and accredited high school or the order provides that the duty of support of the child continues beyond the child's eighteenth birthday. Except in cases in which the order provides that the duty of support continues for any period after the child reaches nineteen years of age, the order shall not remain in effect after the child reaches age nineteen. Any parent ordered to pay support under a child support order issued under this section shall continue to pay support under the order, including during seasonal vacation periods, until the order terminates.

(3) When a court determines whether to require a parent to pay an amount for that parent's failure to support a child prior to the date the court issues an order requiring that parent to pay an amount for the current support of that child, it shall consider all relevant factors, including, but not limited to, any monetary contribution either parent of the child made to the support of the child prior to the court issuing the order requiring the parent to pay an amount for the current support of the child.

(4)(a) A court shall not require a parent to pay an amount for that parent's failure to support a child prior to the date the court issues an order requiring that parent to pay an amount for the current support of that child or to pay all or any part of the reasonable expenses of the mother's pregnancy and confinement, if both of the following apply:

(i) At the time of the initial filing of an action to determine the existence of the parent and child relationship with respect to that parent, the child was over three years of age.

(ii) Prior to the initial filing of an action to determine the existence of the parent and child relationship with respect to that parent, the alleged father had no knowledge and had no reason to have knowledge of his alleged paternity of the child.

(b) For purposes of division (F)(4)(a)(ii) of this section, the mother of the child may establish that the alleged father had or should have had knowledge of the paternity of the child by showing, by a preponderance of the evidence, that she performed a reasonable and documented effort to contact and notify the alleged father of his paternity of the child.

(c) A party is entitled to obtain modification of an existing order for arrearages under this division regardless of whether the judgment, court order, or administrative support order from which relief is sought was issued prior to, on, or after the effective date of this amendment.

(G) As used in this section, "birth record" has the same meaning as in section 3705.01 of the Revised Code.

(H) Unless the court has reason to believe that a person named in the order is a potential victim of domestic violence, any order issued pursuant to this section finding the existence of a parent and child relationship shall contain the full names, addresses, and social security numbers of the mother and father of the child and the full name and address of the child.

(2000 H 242, eff. 10-27-00; 1997 H 352, eff. 1-1-98; 1993 H 173, eff. 12-31-93; 1993 S 115; 1992 S 10; 1990 S 3, H 591, H 15; 1988 H 790, H 708; 1987 H 231; 1986 H 509; 1984 H 614; 1982 H 245)
Note: See also preceding version of this section, in effect until 10-27-00.

Uncodified Law

2000 H 242, § 3, eff. 10-27-00, reads:

The General Assembly hereby declares that it is a person's or male minor's substantive right to obtain relief from a final judgment, court order, or administrative determination or order that determines that the person or male minor is the father of a child or that requires the person or male minor to pay child support for a child. The person or male minor may obtain relief from a final judgment, court order, or administrative determination or order only if relief is granted based on genetic evidence that the person or male minor is not the father of the child who is the subject of the judgment, order, or determination.

1992 S 10, § 5: See Uncodified Law under 3111.01.

1982 H 245, § 3: See Uncodified Law under 3111.04.

Historical and Statutory Notes

Ed. Note: Former 3111.13 repealed by 1982 H 245, eff. 6-29-82; 1953 H 1; GC 8006-13; Source—GC 12120. 3111.13 contains provisions analogous to former 3111.17, repealed by 1982 H 245, eff. 6-29-82.

Pre-1953 H 1 Amendments: 124 v S 65

Amendment Note: 2000 H 242 substituted "Except as otherwise provided in this section, the" for "the"in division (C); and added new division (F)(4).

Amendment Note: 1997 H 352 deleted "division (B) of" before "section 3111.14" in the second paragraph in division (C); deleted "on or after December 31, 1993," before "shall include", substituted "income" for "wages" twice and "(D)(3), (D)(4)" for "(D)(6), (D)(7)", inserted "current residence telephone number, current driver's license number,", and deleted "on or after April 12, 1990," before "shall comply", in division (F)(1); inserted "or the order provides that the duty of support of the child continues beyond the child's eighteenth birthday" and added the second sentence in division (F)(2); added division (H); and made other nonsubstantive changes.

Amendment Note: 1993 H 173 rewrote division (F)(1) before the first semi-colon, which previously read:

"(F)(1) Each order for child support made or modified under this section on or after December 1, 1986, shall be accompanied by one or more orders described in division (D) or (H) of section 3113.21 of the Revised Code, whichever is appropriate under the requirements of that section".

Amendment Note: 1993 S 115 rewrote division (E), which previously read:

"(E) In determining the amount to be paid by a parent for support of the child and the period during which the duty of support is owed, a court enforcing the obligation of support shall comply with sections 3113.21 to 3113.219 of the Revised Code, and shall consider all relevant factors, including, but not limited to, all of the following:

"(1) The physical and emotional condition and needs of the child;

"(2) The standard of living and circumstances of each parent and the standard of living the child would have enjoyed had the parents been married;

"(3) The relative financial resources, other assets and resources, and needs of each parent;

"(4) The earning ability of each parent;

"(5) The need and capacity of the child for education, and the educational opportunities that would have been available to him had the parents been married;

"(6) The age of the child;

"(7) The financial resources and the earning ability of the child;

"(8) The responsibility of each parent for the support of others;

"(9) The value of services contributed by the parent who is the residential parent and legal custodian."

Cross References

Acknowledgment of paternity, support order filed with child support division, 5101.314

Administration of child support orders by child support enforcement agencies, 3113.218

Automated system to support enforcement of child support, 5101.322

Calculation of amount of child support obligation, 3113.215

Child support enforcement agency, adoption of rules, 2301.35

Contempt action for failure to pay support, 2705.031, 2705.05

Criminal nonsupport of dependents, 2919.21

Duty of parents to support children of unemancipated minor children, 3109.19

Health insurance coverage for children, 3113.217

Interfering with action to issue or modify support order, 2919.231

Lottery winner to state under oath whether or not he is in default of support order, hearing, deduction order, 3770.071

Notice of default on child support order sent to professional licensing boards, 2301.373

Payment of child support to bureau of support, procedures on default, 2301.37

Support order defined, 2301.34

Vital statistics, birth record of legitimatized child, 3705.09

Ohio Administrative Code References

Child support program, OAC Ch 5101:1-29

Collection of past due support by federal tax refund offset, OAC Ch 5101:1-30

Library References

Children Out-Of-Wedlock ⚿64 to 68.

WESTLAW Topic No. 76H.

C.J.S. Children Out-of-Wedlock §§ 120 to 127.

OJur 3d: 47, Family Law § 959, 976, 996-999, 1003, 1049, 1050 to 1052, 1198, 1201, 1222, 1295, 1300, 1301, 1306, 1308

Am Jur 2d: 10, Bastards § 99, 127

Baldwin's Ohio Legislative Service, 1990 Laws of Ohio, H 591—LSC Analysis, p 5-576

Carlin, Baldwin's Ohio Practice, *Merrick-Rippner Probate Law* § 18.2, 18.3, 19.1, 19.2, 19.3, 19.4, 19.5, 19.6, 19.7, 19.8, 19.10, 19.11, 19.12, 38.4, 98.29, 98.30, 98.31, 98.38, 105.2, 107.128, 108.1, 108.13, 108.19, 108.20, 108.22, 108.23, 108.24, 108.26, 108.27, 108.28, 108.29, 108.31, 108.32, 108.34, 108.35, 108.37 (1997)

3 Katz & Giannelli, Baldwin's Ohio Practice, *Criminal Law* 109.9, 109.12 (1996)

Klein & Darling, Baldwin's Ohio Practice, *Civil Practice* § 1 (1997)

Kurtz & Giannelli, Ohio Juvenile Law (1998 Ed.), Text 27.14

Sowald & Morganstern, Baldwin's Ohio Practice, *Domestic Relations Law* § 3.1, 3.33, 3.34, 3.35, 3.36, 3.37, 3.42, 3.48, 3.49, 3.58, 19.1, 19.7, 19.23, 21.3, 21.8 (1997)

Law Review and Journal Commentaries

Family Law—Support—The Natural Father of a Child Born Out of Wedlock May Not Assert as a Defense Against His Support Obligation the Mother's Deliberate Misrepresentation That She Was Using Contraception, Note. 29 Vill L Rev 185 (1983-84).

Looking to Unwed Dads to Fill the Public Purse: A Disturbing Wave in Welfare Reform, Roger J.R. Levesque. 32 J Fam L 1 (Winter 1994).

Practice Pointer: Nonmodifiable Child Support Via Annuity, Pamela J. MacAdams. 2 Domestic Rel J Ohio 70 (September/October 1990).

Support Issues in Paternity Cases, Pamela J. MacAdams. 7 Domestic Rel J Ohio 81 (November/December 1995).

Notes of Decisions and Opinions

---

1. Constitutional issues

The obligation created by the statute is not a debt within the meaning of O Const Art I §15. (Annotation from former RC 3111.17.) Belding v. State (Ohio 1929) 121 Ohio St. 393, 169 N.E. 301, 8 Ohio Law Abs. 28, 30 Ohio Law Rep. 546.

Statute which did not expressly prohibit mother from bringing parentage action after child became adult and father's right to visitation had expired did not violate father's right to equal protection; father's failure to obtain visitation rights resulted from his own inaction rather than from parentage statutes, and, moreover, mother's action was barred under doctrine of laches. Park v. Ambrose (Ross 1993) 85 Ohio App.3d 179, 619 N.E.2d 469, dismissed, jurisdictional motion overruled 67 Ohio St.3d 1409, 615 N.E.2d 1043.

To the extent that an expense is incurred due to a custodial parent's decision to raise a minor in a particular religion, a support order which includes such expense does not impinge upon the rights guaranteed by the Establishment Clause of the First Amendment. However, while it is reasonable to assume, absent evidence to the contrary, that one-half of a parent's ordinary expenses for food, shelter, clothing, transportation, and so forth is expended for the support of a minor, there is no such presumption with respect to extraordinary expenses such as religious or charitable donations. These discretionary expenditures must be supported by evidence which tends to establish that the expenses are incurred on behalf of the child. Dunson v. Aldrich (Franklin 1988) 54 Ohio App.3d 137, 561 N.E.2d 972.

A person is not entitled to relief under Civ R 60(B)(2) or (5) from a judgment of paternity and child support where he signed the child's birth certificate and an administrative order indicating he was the child's biological father even though he knew he was not the biological father because the mother was two months pregnant when he began dating her, and therefore a recent DNA test result showing a 0.00 chance he was the father is not "new evidence" under Civ R 60(B)(2), the specific provision of the rule that prevails over the more general section, (B)(5); although it may appear unfair to require an individual to pay child support for a child not biologically his own, there must be some finality to a judgment and one cannot choose to be a parent and then change his or her mind when the relationship is dissolved. Shaffer v Rusnak, No. 97 CA 26, 1998 WL 429624 (5th Dist Ct App, Guernsey, 7-1-98).

Right of indigent putative father to court-appointed counsel in paternity case does not extend to hearings to determine amount of support once paternity has been established. Geauga Cty. Dept. of Human Serv. v. Hall (Ohio Com.Pl. 1995) 68 Ohio Misc.2d 75, 647 N.E.2d 579.

2. In general

Pursuant to RC 3111.13(C), a court of common pleas may determine the surname by which the child shall be known after establishment of the existence of the parent and child relationship, and a showing that the name determination is in the best interest of the child. Bobo v. Jewell (Ohio 1988) 38 Ohio St.3d 330, 528 N.E.2d 180.

In determining the best interest of the child concerning the surname to be used when parents who have never been married contest a surname, the court should consider: (1) the length of time that the child has used a surname; (2) the effect of a name change on the father-child relationship and on the mother-child relationship; (3) the identification of the child as part of a family unit; (4) the embarassment, discomfort, or inconvenience that may result when a child bears a surname different from the custodial parent's; (5) the preference of the child if the child is of an age and maturity to express a meaningful preference; and (6) any other factor relevant to the child's best interest. Courts should consider only those factors present in the particular circumstances of each case. Bobo v. Jewell (Ohio 1988) 38 Ohio St.3d 330, 528 N.E.2d 180.

Purpose of paternity statute is to compel father of illegitimate child to bear expenses of childbirth and child support so that mother will not be solely responsible for that support and so that child will not be financial burden on state. Seegert v. Zietlow (Cuyahoga 1994) 95 Ohio App.3d 451, 642 N.E.2d 697.

A parentage action brought by a natural mother against a putative father is barred by res judicata where the parties have previously entered into an agreement signed and journalized by the court, providing for the father to pay the mother $20 a week until the minor child's eighteenth birthday and for the mother to release the father from all claims against him; the fact that the agreement failed to determine the parent/child relationship did not render it void since RC 3111.19 expressly provides that the agreement need not make such a determination. Nelson v. Pleasant (Lawrence 1991) 73 Ohio App.3d 479, 597 N.E.2d 1137.

A juvenile court errs in not entertaining evidence on the issue of attorney fees and in failing, within its sound discretion, to make a reasonable award of attorney fees under the mandate of RC 3111.13(F) to a mother after it has found a father in contempt for nonpayment of child support. Miller v. Barker (Cuyahoga 1989) 64 Ohio App.3d 649, 582 N.E.2d 647.

A court is not granted authority by RC Ch 3111 to award attorney fees in a paternity proceeding. Dunson v. Aldrich (Franklin 1988) 54 Ohio App.3d 137, 561 N.E.2d 972.

Term "child" as used in descent and distribution statute R.C. §2105.06, providing that "child" could inherit property from parent, includes child born out-of-wedlock as well as legitimate child, if parent-child relationship has been established prior to death of father under procedures for determination of paternity under Parentage Act. Beck v. Jolliff (Knox 1984) 22 Ohio App.3d 84, 489 N.E.2d 825, 22 O.B.R. 237.

A judgment in a paternity action has the effect of a prior determination of custody; therefore, a subsequent change of custody pursuant to a petition by the natural father must be based on a finding of changed circumstances. In re Yates (Franklin 1984) 18 Ohio App.3d 95, 481 N.E.2d 646, 18 O.B.R. 458.

The support and maintenance award under RC 3111.17 is dependent on both the mother's needs and the father's ability to pay. Edwards v. Sadusky (Summit 1982) 4 Ohio App.3d 297, 448 N.E.2d 506, 4 O.B.R. 548.

The word "children," as it appears in the substitute beneficiary clause of a group life insurance policy, is to be construed to mean all offspring, regardless of whether they are born in or out of wedlock. (Annotation from former RC 3111.01.) Butcher v. Pollard (Cuyahoga 1972) 32 Ohio App.2d 1, 288 N.E.2d 204, 61 O.O.2d 1.

The mother of a bastard child is its natural guardian, has the legal right to its custody, and is legally responsible for its care and support. (Annotation from former RC 3111.01.) In re Gary (Cuyahoga 1960) 112 Ohio App. 331, 167 N.E.2d 509, 83 Ohio Law Abs. 486, 14 O.O.2d 431.

The mother of an illegitimate child has a right of custody that is superior to that of the putative father. In re H. (Ohio Com.Pl. 1973) 37 Ohio Misc. 123, 305 N.E.2d 815, 66 O.O.2d 178, 66 O.O.2d 368.

The custody of an illegitimate child will not be taken from the mother and awarded to the father merely upon the basis that the wife has contracted an interracial marriage. (Annotation from former RC 3107.05.) In re H. (Ohio Com.Pl. 1973) 37 Ohio Misc. 123, 305 N.E.2d 815, 66 O.O.2d 178, 66 O.O.2d 368.

Establishment of paternity pursuant to RC Ch 3111 confers upon a child born out of wedlock the same rights of inheritance under RC 2105.06(A) as a child born within wedlock. Beck v Jolliff, 20 OBR 129 (App, Knox 1984).

3. Procedural issues

Juvenile court possessed jurisdiction to make custody and visitation order in paternity judgment, under statute allowing order determining existence of parent and child relationship to contain any other provision directed against appropriate party to proceeding, concerning matter in best interest of child. Pegan v. Crawmer (Ohio 1996) 76 Ohio St.3d 97, 666 N.E.2d 1091.

Amended sections of R.C. §3111.01 et seq., governing paternity proceedings, that became effective on or after June 29, 1982, have no application to paternity actions in which a judgment was entered prior to effective date. Johnson v. Adams (Ohio 1985) 18 Ohio St.3d 48, 479 N.E.2d 866, 18 O.B.R. 83.

While every child conceived in wedlock is presumed legitimate, such presumption is not conclusive and may be rebutted by clear and convincing evidence that there were no sexual relations between husband and wife during the time in which the child must have been conceived, and a complaint for determination of paternity is sufficient if the plaintiff alleges he is the natural father of the child. Joseph v. Alexander (Ohio 1984) 12 Ohio St.3d 88, 465 N.E.2d 448, 12 O.B.R. 77.

When the alleged natural father of an illegitimate child, who has participated in the nurturing process of the child, files a complaint seeking custody of the child under RC 2151.23(A)(2), and the mother admits that he is the natural father of the child, the natural father has equality of standing with the mother with respect to the custody of the child, and the court shall determine which parent shall have the legal custody of the child, taking into account what would be in the best interests of the child. In re Byrd (Ohio 1981) 66 Ohio St.2d 334, 421 N.E.2d 1284, 20 O.O.3d 309.

An adjudication in a bastardy proceeding is not conclusive upon the state unless expressly made so by statute, and the state has power to prosecute criminal proceedings for nonsupport of an illegitimate child at any time before, after and independently of an adjudication in a bastardy proceeding, and wholly independently of any finding therein made, or judgment therein rendered, with respect to the question of paternity. (Annotation from former RC 3111.01.) State v. Schwartz (Ohio 1940) 137 Ohio St. 371, 30 N.E.2d 551, 19 O.O. 90.

Juvenile court's statutory jurisdiction to render final judgment in parentage action includes power to enter order of paternity and order of child support, and also to determine issues of custody and visitation arising from parentage action. Borkosky v. Mihailoff (Ohio App. 3 Dist. 1999) 132 Ohio App.3d 508, 725 N.E.2d 694.

While generally some adjudication or acknowledgement of paternity is necessary for court to invoke its statutory power to order child support, the right to find out who one's father is (or is not) is separate and distinct from the right to support from one's father. Snider v. Lillie (Ohio App. 1 Dist. 1997) 131 Ohio App.3d 444, 722 N.E.2d 1036.

Dismissal of paternity action without prejudice was proper upon mother's failure to prosecute, where dismissal with prejudice would have foreclosed valid claim of county child support enforcement agency for reimbursement of monies expended for child support. State ex rel. Cody v. Bradley (Ohio App. 2 Dist. 1997) 123 Ohio App.3d 397, 704 N.E.2d 307.

Trial court did not abuse its discretion in denying putative father's motion for relief from judgment for child support arrearages, even though court granted relief from judgment of paternity and for future support, where motion was based on newly discovered evidence in form of genetic tests that excluded him as father and that he was impotent, and motion was made more than one year after judgment was entered. Douglas v. Boykin (Ohio App. 12 Dist. 1997) 121 Ohio App.3d 140, 699 N.E.2d 123.

Trial court was required to consider support being paid by father of minor child to child's mother pursuant to agreed settlement entry of previous parentage action in calculating support payable under judgment entered in child's subsequent action to establish parent-child relationship; while prior action was not res judicata with respect to issue of support, both actions served same purpose in that they required payment of money for benefit of child, and child was only entitled to single "support." Cornell v. Brumfield (Ohio App. 4 Dist. 1996) 115 Ohio App.3d 259, 685 N.E.2d 270.

Child support obligor who fails to comply with child support order has burden to prove inability to pay, and it is not prerequisite to finding of contempt that violation be purposeful, willing, or intentional. Watson v. Wolsonovich (Ohio App. 7 Dist. 1996) 112 Ohio App.3d 565, 679 N.E.2d 350.

Child and Department of Human Services were not in privity with mother, and, therefore, judgment rendered in mother's paternity action did not present res judicata bar to later action by child and Department. Payne v. Cartee (Ross 1996) 111 Ohio App.3d 580, 676 N.E.2d 946, appeal not allowed 77 Ohio St.3d 1482, 673 N.E.2d 143.

Mother's claim against alleged father was distinct from Department of Human Services' claim for reimbursement of birthing expenses, for purposes of determining whether judgment rendered in mother's paternity action barred Department's later claim. Payne v. Cartee (Ross 1996) 111 Ohio App.3d 580, 676 N.E.2d 946, appeal not allowed 77 Ohio St.3d 1482, 673 N.E.2d 143.

Juvenile court's judgment establishing paternity and setting visitation but not addressing issue of support was not final, as would support extraordinary writ of prohibition, where issue of support was before juvenile court. State ex rel. Dixon v. Clark Cty. Court of Common Pleas, Juv. Div. (Clark 1995) 103 Ohio App.3d 523, 660 N.E.2d 486.

In paternity action filed by Child Support Enforcement Agency (CSEA), trial court could not change surnames of children without first determining whether name change was in best interests of children. Dorsett v. Wheeler (Paulding 1995) 101 Ohio App.3d 716, 656 N.E.2d 698.

Subsequent to order establishing paternity, father must file separate complaint in separate action if he wishes to seek visitation with the child, and father cannot merely file motion for visitation in paternity proceedings. Burns v. Darnell (Franklin 1995) 100 Ohio App.3d 419, 654 N.E.2d 169.

Trial court in paternity action did not err in overruling motion to transfer father's request for visitation where denial was predicated upon failure of father-plaintiff to file separate action seeking visitation, rather than because motion was filed in wrong county. Burns v. Darnell (Franklin 1995) 100 Ohio App.3d 419, 654 N.E.2d 169.

Juvenile court has jurisdiction in parentage action to award retroactive or back child support for period of time prior to date upon which parent-child relationship is judicially established. Seegert v. Zietlow (Cuyahoga 1994) 95 Ohio App.3d 451, 642 N.E.2d 697.

Juvenile court may enter judgment in paternity action upon satisfactory evidence of paternity. Lewis v. Chapin (Cuyahoga 1994) 93 Ohio App.3d 695, 639 N.E.2d 848.

Juvenile court, in determining paternity, had jurisdiction to decide state's action for aid furnished by state for support and medical expenses of children born out-of-wedlock. Brightwell v. Easter (Summit 1994) 93 Ohio App.3d 425, 638 N.E.2d 1067.

Trial court which adopted shared-parenting plan granting residential status to father during school year and to mother during summer months could properly determine that strict application of child support guidelines would be inappropriate and accordingly deny child support to father under circumstances that parties stipulated that cost of children's parochial education would be shared in proportion to their relative incomes, both parties were required to carry medical insurance for children, and parties were required to share cost of clothing, school supplies and other ordinary expenses. Eickelberger v. Eickelberger (Butler 1994) 93 Ohio App.3d 221, 638 N.E.2d 130.

Trial court did not err in splitting children's tax exemptions between father and mother even though father, pursuant to shared-parenting plan, was residential parent of children for nine months of year. Eickelberger v. Eickelberger (Butler 1994) 93 Ohio App.3d 221, 638 N.E.2d 130.

Shared-parenting order in divorce action was not improper on theory it encouraged excessive entanglement between parties in requiring parties to cooperate and communicate by sharing expenses. Eickelberger v. Eickelberger (Butler 1994) 93 Ohio App.3d 221, 638 N.E.2d 130.

Mother's laches will not be imputed to child so as to bar child's claim for support in parentage action. Park v. Ambrose (Ross 1993) 85 Ohio App.3d 179, 619 N.E.2d 469, dismissed, jurisdictional motion overruled 67 Ohio St.3d 1409, 615 N.E.2d 1043.

Mother's inaction during child's minority did not bar adult child's claim for retroactive support in parentage action brought by child. Park v. Ambrose (Ross 1993) 85 Ohio App.3d 179, 619 N.E.2d 469, dismissed, jurisdictional motion overruled 67 Ohio St.3d 1409, 615 N.E.2d 1043.

Child's claim for support in parentage action is separate and distinct from claim of mother. Park v. Ambrose (Ross 1993) 85 Ohio App.3d 179, 619 N.E.2d 469, dismissed, jurisdictional motion overruled 67 Ohio St.3d 1409, 615 N.E.2d 1043.

It is court, and not county department of human services, that is charged with determining child support and related payments by parent following parentage action with respect to child receiving Aid to Families with Dependent Children (AFDC). Gilpen v. Justice (Fayette 1993) 85 Ohio App.3d 86, 619 N.E.2d 94, motion overruled 67 Ohio St.3d 1410, 615 N.E.2d 1044.

A party who fails to answer a paternity complaint has no right to notice prior to entry of a default judgment. Long v. Bartlett (Franklin 1992) 73 Ohio App.3d 764, 598 N.E.2d 197.

The validity of an RC 2105.18 acknowledgment of paternity may not be attacked in defending an action for custody and support. In re Custody of Davis (Guernsey 1987) 41 Ohio App.3d 81, 534 N.E.2d 945.

The provision in RC 3111.17 for a court order requiring the reputed father to give security for support payments is one of several remedies available to secure payment of the judgment and it is within the sound discretion of the juvenile court. Edwards v. Sadusky (Summit 1982) 4 Ohio App.3d 297, 448 N.E.2d 506, 4 O.B.R. 548.

Determination of paternity in a bastardy proceeding is not a prerequisite to the prosecution of a parent under RC 2903.08 for nonsupport of an illegitimate child. (Annotation from former RC 3111.17.) State v. Medley (Miami 1960) 111 Ohio App. 352, 172 N.E.2d 143, 14 O.O.2d 328.

An order designating paternal grandparents as legal custodians is void ab initio where the action seeking custody is initiated by a motion in a parentage proceeding; furthermore, RC 3111.13 contemplates an entirely new proceeding after the determination of paternity by which the father would be the named plaintiff and the mother would be the named defendant and where the mother is never served with a summons and copies of a complaint seeking custody the trial court does not have personal jurisdiction over her and does not have the authority to render the custody determination. Mary B. v Zollie M, No. L-96-120, 1997 WL 90612 (6th Dist Ct App, Lucas, 2-28-97).

The juvenile court's authority to order payment of back child support is not defeated by subsequent adoption of the child; however, the court errs by ordering the father to pay support for five months after the child is adopted by the mother's husband. Black v Hart, No. 17524, 1996 WL 304284 (9th Dist Ct App, Summit, 6-5-96).

Pursuant to a parentage action where the issue of who would have custody of the child is never before the court or addressed in an agreement between the parties, it is error for the trial court to address issues of child support and visitation without first making a determination as to which parent will have custody. State ex rel Ellen v Deal, No. 94APF04-549, 1994 WL 723377 (10th Dist Ct App, Franklin, 12-27-94).

An agreed judgment entry which finds a defendant to be the "reputed father" of a child and orders support does not constitute a valid legal determination of paternity and does not give rise to a statutory obligation of support; therefore, an order for support without a prior valid determination of paternity must be vacated and remanded. Glass v Campbell, No. 15-92-18 (3d Dist Ct App, Van Wert, 5-27-93).

Court in which paternity proceeding is pending had subject matter jurisdiction to award back child support to an adult child. Hugershoff v. Loecy (Ohio Com.Pl. 1998) 103 Ohio Misc.2d 55, 725 N.E.2d 376.

A judgment establishing paternity and imposing a duty to support on the father may also imply a determination of custody to the mother, so that a motion to determine custody filed years later by the father should be determined according to the standards for change in custody set forth in RC 3109.04(B)(1). In re Brazell (Ohio Com.Pl. 1986) 27 Ohio Misc.2d 7, 499 N.E.2d 925, 27 O.B.R. 68.

There is a distinction between a "putative" father and a father who has been adjudicated as such by his own admission, in that a father adjudicated as such by his own admission has legal standing to seek custody of his illegitimate child against the world, including the mother. (Annotation from former RC 3111.01.) In re Wright (Ohio Com.Pl. 1977) 52 Ohio Misc. 4, 367 N.E.2d 931, 6 O.O.3d 31.

The reputed father who has paid or given security as ordered by court for maintenance of the child, under this section, is not liable to proceedings under GC 13008 (RC 3113.01), for nonsupport. (Annotation from former RC 3111.17.) 1917 (Pt 2) OAG 601.

4. Amount of support payments

Child born out of wedlock was not entitled to half of award of back child support owed by her adjudicated father, and entire award was required to go to mother, in absence of any evidence that mother had not spent funds awarded on necessities for raising child and where mother's action for back child support was not barred by laches. State ex rel. Donovan v. Zajac (Ohio App. 11 Dist. 1998) 125 Ohio App.3d 245, 708 N.E.2d 254, dismissed, appeal not allowed 81 Ohio St.3d 1521, 692 N.E.2d 1023.

Parent obliged to make periodic payments of child support cannot also be required to fund future needs trust for child's benefit; while court may require that parent make lump-sum payment or purchase annuity for child's benefit, such payment or annuity is in lieu of periodic support payments. Frazier v. Daniels (Ohio App. 1 Dist. 1997) 118 Ohio App.3d 425, 693 N.E.2d 289.

Juvenile court did not abuse its discretion in parentage action by calculating back child support owed for each year of child's life by use of worksheets with reference to applicable law for each given year, due to dramatic changes in parties' financial situations since child's birth. Seegert v. Zietlow (Cuyahoga 1994) 95 Ohio App.3d 451, 642 N.E.2d 697.

Father failed to demonstrate abuse of discretion by juvenile court in parentage proceeding in awarding $3,900 in current child support for year of 1993; pursuant to statutory guidelines, "rebuttably presumed" correct amount was $4,542 for 1993 and, despite father's claims to contrary, his disposable income exceeded amount of child support for that year. Seegert v. Zietlow (Cuyahoga 1994) 95 Ohio App.3d 451, 642 N.E.2d 697.

Juvenile court was required to award to state in paternity actions full amount of past aid provided to children born out of wedlock, and award of amount less than all aid furnished to children was improper. Brightwell v. Easter (Summit 1994) 93 Ohio App.3d 425, 638 N.E.2d 1067.

Awards against fathers of children born out-of-wedlock to state for reimbursement of support and medical expenses paid on behalf of children were not modifiable. Brightwell v. Easter (Summit 1994) 93 Ohio App.3d 425, 638 N.E.2d 1067.

Social security payments for a child's benefit must be considered in connection with child support payments ordered to be made by the parent whose retirement triggers the payments, but this does not justify crediting the entire monthly benefit amount to child support, nor is the determination of necessary child support unaffected by the receipt of the benefits; the proper method is to deduct all or part of the benefit amount from the guideline-determined necessary support based on the child's best interest and equity to both parents. McNeal v. Cofield (Franklin 1992) 78 Ohio App.3d 35, 603 N.E.2d 436.

Trial court abused its discretion by setting up savings account for child born out-of-wedlock to be funded by father and be disbursed as court ordered, where account was not based on child's current needs or support. Bailey v. Mitchell (Cuyahoga 1990) 67 Ohio App.3d 441, 587 N.E.2d 358.

A juvenile court does not impermissibly order a father to pay child support without consideration of the applicable statutory provisions and child support guidelines issued by the state supreme court where the statement of proceedings shows that the court inquired of counsel and the parties regarding the subjects required by the statutory provisions and the guidelines and that it, based on its inquiries, found the parties' circumstances had sufficiently changed to order a modification of support. Miller v. Barker (Cuyahoga 1989) 64 Ohio App.3d 649, 582 N.E.2d 647.

Where evidence of a defendant's monthly child support expenses from a prior marriage are before the court, absent evidence to the contrary, a reviewing court will presume that the court properly considered the evidence in fashioning a child support award pursuant to RC 3111.13. Dunson v. Aldrich (Franklin 1988) 54 Ohio App.3d 137, 561 N.E.2d 972.

An award of child support made pursuant to RC 3111.13(E) must countenance both parents' financial status and the father's ability to pay. In making this award, it is appropriate for the trial court to first ascertain the amount necessary to support the child and then to fashion an award which is reasonable in light of the factors listed in RC 3111.13(E). Dunson v. Aldrich (Franklin 1988) 54 Ohio App.3d 137, 561 N.E.2d 972.

In the absence of evidence to the contrary, it is not an abuse of discretion for the court to assume that one-half of the plaintiff-mother's necessary monthly expenses are incurred on behalf of her child. Dunson v. Aldrich (Franklin 1988) 54 Ohio App.3d 137, 561 N.E.2d 972.

The phrase "support and maintenance," as it was used in RC 3111.17(Repealed), did not include within its meaning lost wages as a consequence of a pregnancy. (Annotation from former RC 3111.17.) Jelen v. Price (Cuyahoga 1983) 9 Ohio App.3d 174, 458 N.E.2d 1267, 9 O.B.R. 284.

In paternity proceedings, the juvenile court may consider insurance payments and disability benefits received by the mother of an illegitimate child in determining her need for medical expenses and support during pregnancy, delivery, and post-natal convalescence. Edwards v. Sadusky (Summit 1982) 4 Ohio App.3d 297, 448 N.E.2d 506, 4 O.B.R. 548.

Under section, the obligation of the bond therein prescribed is confined to payment of support, maintenance, and necessary expenses of the complainant caused by the pregnancy and childbirth together with the cost of prosecution, and does not run to any reasonable sum fixed by the court for support and maintenance of the child until it becomes eighteen years of age. (Annotation from former RC 3111.17.) State ex rel. Adkins v. Mefford (Hamilton 1944) 75 Ohio App. 215, 61 N.E.2d 635, 43 Ohio Law Abs. 349, 30 O.O. 554.

A juvenile court must use the child support guidelines when determining the amount of child support to be awarded. In re Stewart, No. 88 CA 15 (2d Dist Ct App, Greene, 11-23-88).

Where a father has been disabled and unemployed for four years preceding a support hearing, and has no income at the time of the hearing, it is consistent with RC 3111.13 for the court to decline to order support payments, with the proviso that if the father were to become employed or obtain a source of income, a hearing would be held at such time to determine support payments. Fedor v DiBacco, No. 83 CA 46 (7th Dist Ct App, Mahoning, 1-11-84).

5. Time of liability for support

Trial court calculating adjudicated father's back child support obligation with respect to child born in October erred in including payments for January through September of year of child's birth in calculation, because there was no duty to support child before her birth. State ex rel. Donovan v. Zajac (Ohio App. 11 Dist. 1998) 125 Ohio App.3d 245, 708 N.E.2d 254, dismissed, appeal not allowed 81 Ohio St.3d 1521, 692 N.E.2d 1023.

Trial court erred in requiring adjudicated father to pay back child support, covering period of 21 years, in lump sum payment; father was entitled to payment schedule over reasonable period of time, not less than three years. State ex rel. Donovan v. Zajac (Ohio App. 11 Dist. 1998) 125 Ohio App.3d 245, 708 N.E.2d 254, dismissed, appeal not allowed 81 Ohio St.3d 1521, 692 N.E.2d 1023.

Remand for recalculation of adjudicated father's back child support obligation was required, where trial court erroneously applied guidelines enacted when child was nine years old to calculate father's obligation as of her date of birth. State ex rel. Donovan v. Zajac (Ohio App. 11 Dist. 1998) 125 Ohio App.3d 245, 708 N.E.2d 254, dismissed, appeal not allowed 81 Ohio St.3d 1521, 692 N.E.2d 1023.

Trial court clearly has discretion to award support from date of child's birth. Frazier v. Daniels (Ohio App. 1 Dist. 1997) 118 Ohio App.3d 425, 693 N.E.2d 289.

Back child support may be ordered in paternity proceeding to date of child's birth. Beach v. Poole (Muskingum 1996) 111 Ohio App.3d 710, 676 N.E.2d 1254, appeal not allowed 77 Ohio St.3d 1482, 673 N.E.2d 143.

While trial court does not have authority to order child support until there is legal determination of parentage, once that determination is made, putative father can be ordered to pay support retroactive to date of child's birth; date of judicial establishment of parentage is not date putative father became child's father, as putative father was child's natural father from date of child's birth. Beach v. Poole (Muskingum 1996) 111 Ohio App.3d 710, 676 N.E.2d 1254, appeal not allowed 77 Ohio St.3d 1482, 673 N.E.2d 143.

In parentage action, absent a defense, court may award child support from date of child's birth to date of paternity adjudication. Lewis v. Chapin (Cuyahoga 1994) 93 Ohio App.3d 695, 639 N.E.2d 848.

Trial court had subject matter jurisdiction to award child support retroactive to child's date of birth in paternity proceeding brought more than 20 years after child was born. Park v. Ambrose (Ross 1993) 85 Ohio App.3d 179, 619 N.E.2d 469, dismissed, jurisdictional motion overruled 67 Ohio St.3d 1409, 615 N.E.2d 1043.

Mother's claim for retroactive child support was barred under doctrine of laches, where mother failed to seek support until child was adult and had not permitted father to have any input in child's upbringing. Park v. Ambrose (Ross 1993) 85 Ohio App.3d 179, 619 N.E.2d 469, dismissed, jurisdictional motion overruled 67 Ohio St.3d 1409, 615 N.E.2d 1043.

A natural father's duty to support a child arises at birth, particularly where he acknowledges paternity, and where the natural father unjustifiably fails to communicate with or support a child for one year prior to the filing of an adoption petition, his consent to the adoption of his illegitimate child is unnecessary. In re Adoption of Taylor (Medina 1989) 61 Ohio App.3d 500, 573 N.E.2d 156, motion overruled 43 Ohio St.3d 712, 541 N.E.2d 78.

In the absence of a specific finding that the equitable amount that a paternity defendant should pay toward child support has not varied since the birth of the child, it is inappropriate for a court to utilize the current finding as to appropriate child support and arbitrarily determine the amount due for support since the birth of the child by multiplying the number of weeks involved by the current child support amount. Dunson v. Aldrich (Franklin 1988) 54 Ohio App.3d 137, 561 N.E.2d 972.

Child support must be awarded from the date of the child's birth to the date of the paternity adjudication. Edwards v. Sadusky (Summit 1982) 4 Ohio App.3d 297, 448 N.E.2d 506, 4 O.B.R. 548.

Where support payments for the period from the date of a child's birth to the date of adjudication are prayed for and proved, the court abuses its discretion by failing to make an award of child support for that period, unless there is an affirmative demonstration of some circumstance which reasonably could relieve the father of this obligation and the child of this entitlement. (Annotation from former RC 3111.17.) Baugh v. Carver (Hamilton 1981) 3 Ohio App.3d 139, 444 N.E.2d 58, 3 O.B.R. 157.

The court in a bastardy action has jurisdiction to order support payments to commence with the birth of the child, even though the complaint was filed subsequent to the birth of the child. (Annotation from former RC 3111.01.) Weaver v. Chandler (Franklin 1972) 31 Ohio App.2d 243, 287 N.E.2d 917, 60 O.O.2d 405.

A person adjudged to be the reputed father of an illegitimate child before such child attains the age of eighteen years is liable for support of the child from the time of its birth until such adjudication. (Annotation from former RC 3111.17.) Willis v. Wilson (Lawrence 1947) 83 Ohio App. 311, 80 N.E.2d 175, 51 Ohio Law Abs. 122, 38 O.O. 1.

RC 3111.13(C) confers jurisdiction on the court to determine whether an order of retroactive support is appropriate when brought after the child is emancipated. Spires v Moore, No. CT98-0040, 2000 WL 1545 (5th Dist Ct App, Muskingum, 11-24-99).

An award of child support retroactive to the child's date of birth is denied where the mother (1) repeatedly prevents the father from having access to the child, (2) refuses to return telephone calls, (3) neglects to provide the father pictures or information of the child's well-being, and (4) states she does not believe the father deserves information about or contact with the child. Tod W. v Erika P, No. WD-99-013, 1999 WL 728087 (6th Dist Ct App, Wood, 9-17-99).

A parent who makes significant financial contributions towards the care of his son for nine years prior to the date the complaint for support is filed is relieved of his support obligation for the nine year period where (1) the child has had severe mental and physical disabilities since birth and is confined to a wheelchair, (2) a good faith relationship exists between the mother and father before the support complaint is filed such that the child's financial needs were apparently met, and (3) there is reason to expect that the father's support obligation may last well beyond the time that the child reaches the age of majority. Shocky v Blackburn, No. CA98-07-085, 1999 WL 326174 (12th Dist Ct App, Warren, 5-17-99).

A minor has a right to an award of retroactive child support independent of his mother's claim. Crawley-Kinley v Price, No. C-940920, 1996 WL 107569 (1st Dist Ct App, Hamilton, 3-13-96).

Where an order of paternity has been vacated after a subsequent HLA test, it is error for the court to order relief from the support obligation retroactive to the date of the original order when the adjudged father failed to obtain appropriate HLA testing for three years after the original order. Haney v Feltner, No. C-830715 (1st Dist Ct App, Hamilton, 7-3-84).

Court is not required to award child support retroactively from the time paternity is determined, and discretion is left with the court. Hugershoff v. Loecy (Ohio Com.Pl. 1999) 103 Ohio Misc.2d 58, 725 N.E.2d 378.

Payment for the support of an illegitimate child starts from the time of the child's birth. (Annotation from former RC 3111.01 and 3111.17.) State ex rel. Raydel v. Raible (Ohio Com.Pl. 1953) 112 N.E.2d 568, 64 Ohio Law Abs. 438, affirmed 117 N.E.2d 480, 69 Ohio Law Abs. 356, appeal dismissed 162 Ohio St. 74, 120 N.E.2d 590, 54 O.O. 18.

6. Federal tax refund offset

Birthing expenses, which are defined in state statute as proper part of child support order, may be recouped from parent's federal tax refund under federal statute requiring past-due child support to be withheld from federal income tax refunds. Gladysz v. King (Clark 1995) 103 Ohio App.3d 1, 658 N.E.2d 309, appeal not allowed 73 Ohio St.3d 1428, 652 N.E.2d 801.

County child support enforcement agency could not collect monies pursuant to federal statute requiring past-due child support to be withheld from obligor's federal income tax refunds as there was no "past due" child support where father was not in default of obligation fixed by court to pay one-half expenses of mother's pregnancy despite fact that father had not yet extinguished that debt. Gladysz v. King (Clark 1995) 103 Ohio App.3d 1, 658 N.E.2d 309, appeal not allowed 73 Ohio St.3d 1428, 652 N.E.2d 801.

3111.14 Fees for experts; court costs

The court may order reasonable fees for experts and other costs of the action and pretrial proceedings, including genetic tests, to be paid by the parties in proportions and at times determined by the court. The court may order the proportion of any party to be paid by the court, and, before or after payment by any party or the county, may order all or part of the fees and costs to be taxed as costs in the action.

(1992 S 10, eff. 7-15-92; 1990 H 591; 1982 H 245)

Uncodified Law

1992 S 10, § 5: See Uncodified Law under 3111.01.

1982 H 245, § 3: See Uncodified Law under 3111.04.

Historical and Statutory Notes

Ed. Note: Former 3111.14 repealed by 1982 H 245, eff. 6-29-82; 1953 H 1; GC 8006-14; Source—GC 12121. 3111.14 contains provisions analogous to former 3111.17, repealed by 1982 H 245, eff. 6-29-82.

Pre-1953 H 1 Amendments: 124 v S 65

Cross References

Board of county commissioners may pay expert witness fee, 307.52

Ohio Administrative Code References

Genetic testing, OAC 5101:1-30-29

Library References

Children Out-Of-Wedlock ⚿75.
WESTLAW Topic No. 76H.
C.J.S. Children Out-of-Wedlock §§ 52, 75, 140, 141.

OJur 3d: 47, Family Law § 1001

Baldwin's Ohio Legislative Service, 1990 Laws of Ohio, H 591—LSC Analysis, p 5-576

Carlin, Baldwin's Ohio Practice, *Merrick-Rippner Probate Law* § 18.2, 18.3, 19.1, 19.2, 19.3, 19.4, 19.5, 19.6, 19.7, 19.8, 19.10, 19.11, 19.12, 38.4, 98.29, 98.30, 98.31, 105.2, 108.19, 108.20, 108.22, 108.23, 108.24, 108.27, 108.28, 108.31 (1997)

Klein & Darling, Baldwin's Ohio Practice, *Civil Practice* § 1 (1997)

Sowald & Morganstern, Baldwin's Ohio Practice, *Domestic Relations Law* § 3.19, 3.31 (1997)

Notes of Decisions and Opinions

---

1. Indigent defendant

The denial of blood grouping tests to an indigent paternity defendant, who is unable to prepay for such tests, and who faces the state as an adversary when the complainant-mother and her child are recipients of public assistance, violates the due process guarantee of US Const Am 14. (Annotation from former RC 3111.01.) Anderson v. Jacobs (Ohio 1981) 68 Ohio St.2d 67, 428 N.E.2d 419, 22 O.O.3d 268.

Where the defendant in a paternity action knowingly and voluntarily plead guilty, never requested genetic tests, and did not tell the court that he was indigent, the trial court was not required to inform the defendant of his constitutional right to the state's prepayment of the cost of the genetic tests. Edwards v. Porter (Lorain 1983) 8 Ohio App.3d 277, 456 N.E.2d 1347, 8 O.B.R. 370.

GC 12123 (RC 3111.17) did not authorize an award of attorney's fees. (Annotation from former RC 3111.17.) State ex rel. Raydel v. Raible (Cuyahoga 1954) 117

N.E.2d 480, 69 Ohio Law Abs. 356, appeal dismissed 162 Ohio St. 74, 120 N.E.2d 590, 54 O.O. 18.

2. Attorney fees

Failure of legislature to include in parentage act a provision for payment of attorney fees as "costs" in paternity actions involving child support orders denied unmarried mother equal protection of the law because payment of attorney fees as "costs" was statutorily available in divorce proceedings. McQueen v. Hawkins (Lucas 1989) 63 Ohio App.3d 243, 578 N.E.2d 539.

RC 3111.14 does not provide for an award of attorney fees. Sutherland v. Sutherland (Franklin 1989) 61 Ohio App.3d 154, 572 N.E.2d 215.

A court is not granted authority by RC Ch 3111 to award attorney fees in a paternity proceeding. Dunson v. Aldrich (Franklin 1988) 54 Ohio App.3d 137, 561 N.E.2d 972.

3. Guardian ad litem fees

While RC 3111.14 does not expressly mention guardian ad litem fees, such fees may be awarded if they are found to constitute "reasonable fees for experts" or "other costs of the action." Sutherland v. Sutherland (Franklin 1989) 61 Ohio App.3d 154, 572 N.E.2d 215.

4. HLA tests

In paternity action in which results of genetic testing clearly excluded indigent putative father as natural father of child, costs of genetic testing were properly taxable against mother and would thus be paid by county child support agency under statute authorizing payment of court costs by local social service agency when custodian was recipient of Aid for Dependent Children and defendant was found to be indigent. Little v. Stoops (Clinton 1989) 65 Ohio App.3d 758, 585 N.E.2d 475.

The cost of an HLA test to determine paternity is a necessary litigating expense and it is reversible error not to tax such cost to a nonindigent plaintiff who does not prevail at trial. Reed v Pace, No. 48612 (8th Dist Ct App, Cuyahoga, 4-18-85).

5. Bankruptcy effect

Although bankruptcy matters are inherently proceedings in equity and must foster equitable results, bankruptcy court would not second-guess judgment rendered by state court in establishing Chapter 7 debtor-biological father's debt for paternity action expenses where debtor was not placed in any worse position than that which existed before bankruptcy and debtor had opportunity to argue merits of debt allocation before the state court. In re Lamb (Bkrtcy.N.D.Ohio 1996) 198 B.R. 511.

3111.15 Enforcement of support order

(A) If the existence of the father and child relationship is declared or if paternity or a duty of support has been adjudicated under sections 3111.01 to 3111.19 of the Revised Code or under prior law, the obligation of the father may be enforced in the same or other proceedings by the mother, the child, or the public authority that has furnished or may furnish the reasonable expenses of pregnancy, confinement, education, support, or funeral, or by any other person, including a private agency, to the extent that any of them may furnish, has furnished, or is furnishing these expenses.

(B) The court may order support payments to be made to the mother, the clerk of the court, or a person or agency designated to administer them for the benefit of the child under the supervision of the court.

(C) Willful failure to obey the judgment or order of the court is a civil contempt of the court.

(1986 H 476, eff. 9-24-86; 1982 H 245)

Uncodified Law

1992 S 10, § 5: See Uncodified Law under 3111.01.

1982 H 245, § 3: See Uncodified Law under 3111.04.

Historical and Statutory Notes

Ed. Note: Former 3111.15 repealed by 1982 H 245, eff. 6-29-82; 125 v 184; 1953 H 1; GC 8006-15; Source—GC 12122; see now 3111.12 for provisions analogous to former 3111.15. 3111.15 contains provisions analogous to former 3111.17, repealed by 1982 S 245, eff. 6-29-82.

Pre-1953 H 1 Amendments: 124 v S 65

Cross References

Automated system to support enforcement of child support, 5101.322

Calculation of amount of child support obligation, 3113.215

Contempt action for failure to pay support, 2705.031, 2705.05

Court of common pleas, bureau of support, 2301.34 et seq.

Criminal nonsupport of dependents, 2919.21

Lottery winner to state under oath whether or not he is in default of support order, hearing, deduction order, 3770.071

Payment of support through withholding of earnings, workers' compensation benefits, unemployment compensation benefits, retirement benefits, or bank account, 3113.21

Small loans; assignment or order of wages for support, 1321.32, 1321.33

Ohio Administrative Code References

Child support program, OAC Ch 5101:1-29
Collection of past due support by federal tax refund offset, OAC Ch 5101:1-30

Library References

Children Out-Of-Wedlock ⟹69.
WESTLAW Topic No. 76H.
C.J.S. Children Out-Of-Wedlock §§ 128, 129.

OJur 3d: 47, Family Law § 1049, 1285
Am Jur 2d: 10, Bastards § 128

Carlin, Baldwin's Ohio Practice, *Merrick-Rippner Probate Law* § 18.2, 18.3, 19.1, 19.2, 19.3, 19.4, 19.5, 19.6, 19.7, 19.8, 19.10, 19.12, 38.4, 98.29, 98.30, 98.31, 105.2, 108.19, 108.20, 108.22, 108.23, 108.24, 108.27, 108.28, 108.30, 108.31 (1997)
Klein & Darling, Baldwin's Ohio Practice, *Civil Practice* § 1 (1997)
Sowald & Morganstern, Baldwin's Ohio Practice, *Domestic Relations Law* § 3.35 (1997)

Law Review and Journal Commentaries

Bankruptcy Reform Act of 1994—What the Bankruptcy Code Giveth, Domestic Relations Courts (and Congress) Taketh Away, C.R. "Chip" Bowles. 8 Domestic Rel J Ohio 17 (March/April 1996).

Notes of Decisions and Opinions

Bankruptcy 4
Duty to support 1
Imprisonment of defendant 2
Indigent defendants 5
Right of action 3

---

1. Duty to support

Trial court clearly has discretion to award support from date of child's birth. Frazier v. Daniels (Ohio App. 1 Dist. 1997) 118 Ohio App.3d 425, 693 N.E.2d 289.

Back child support may be ordered in paternity proceeding to date of child's birth. Beach v. Poole (Muskingum 1996) 111 Ohio App.3d 710, 676 N.E.2d 1254, appeal not allowed 77 Ohio St.3d 1482, 673 N.E.2d 143.

While trial court does not have authority to order child support until there is legal determination of parentage, once that determination is made, putative father can be ordered to pay support retroactive to date of child's birth; date of judicial establishment of parentage is not date putative father became child's father, as putative father was child's natural father from date of child's birth. Beach v. Poole (Muskingum 1996) 111 Ohio App.3d 710, 676 N.E.2d 1254, appeal not allowed 77 Ohio St.3d 1482, 673 N.E.2d 143.

Purpose of paternity statute is to compel father of illegitimate child to bear expenses of childbirth and child support so that mother will not be solely responsible for that support and so that child will not be financial burden on state. Seegert v. Zietlow (Cuyahoga 1994) 95 Ohio App.3d 451, 642 N.E.2d 697.

Juvenile court has jurisdiction in parentage action to award retroactive or back child support for period of time prior to date upon which parent-child relationship is judicially established. Seegert v. Zietlow (Cuyahoga 1994) 95 Ohio App.3d 451, 642 N.E.2d 697.

Any right by mother to receive $50 from father's monthly child support obligation, which was to be paid to county department of human services, did not confer upon mother right to enforce father's child support obligation, which had been assigned to department by operation of law due to mother's receipt of aid to dependent children; mother's right to receive certain amount from amount collected required satisfaction of certain conditions and could be enforced only after amount had been collected. Vance v. Banks (Cuyahoga 1994) 94 Ohio App.3d 475, 640 N.E.2d 1214, appeal not allowed 70 Ohio St.3d 1447, 639 N.E.2d 115, certiorari denied 115 S.Ct. 1144, 513 U.S. 1170, 130 L.Ed.2d 1103.

Motion for order to show cause why parent should not be held in contempt for failure to comply with court order to support child can be enforced only by party who provided or provides support. Vance v. Banks (Cuyahoga 1994) 94 Ohio App.3d 475, 640 N.E.2d 1214, appeal not allowed 70 Ohio St.3d 1447, 639 N.E.2d 115, certiorari denied 115 S.Ct. 1144, 513 U.S. 1170, 130 L.Ed.2d 1103.

Juvenile court, in determining paternity, had jurisdiction to decide state's action for aid furnished by state for support and medical expenses of children born out-of-wedlock. Brightwell v. Easter (Summit 1994) 93 Ohio App.3d 425, 638 N.E.2d 1067.

Awards against fathers of children born out-of-wedlock to state for reimbursement of support and medical expenses paid on behalf of children were not modifiable. Brightwell v. Easter (Summit 1994) 93 Ohio App.3d 425, 638 N.E.2d 1067.

A natural father's duty to support a child arises at birth, particularly where he acknowledges paternity, and where the natural father unjustifiably fails to communicate with or support a child for one year prior to the filing of an adoption petition, his consent to the adoption of his illegitimate child is unnecessary. In re Adoption of Taylor (Medina 1989) 61 Ohio App.3d 500, 573 N.E.2d 156, motion overruled 43 Ohio St.3d 712, 541 N.E.2d 78.

Where the father is ordered to pay as support ten per cent of any and all commissions, overrides and bonuses, such an order is in conformity with RC 3111.17. (Annotation from former RC 3111.17.) Misquitta v Misquitta, No. 1188 (7th Dist Ct App, Columbiana, 8-17-78).

2. Imprisonment of defendant

The provisions of RC 3111.17 and 3111.18 are unconstitutional as a denial of the Equal Protection Clause guaranteed by US Const Am XIV, insofar as these sections provide for the imprisonment of an indigent defendant adjudged to be the reputed father of the plaintiff's illegitimate child solely because of his inability to pay the support award ordered by the court. (Annotation from former RC 3111.17.) Walker v. Stokes (Cuyahoga 1977) 54 Ohio App.2d 119, 375 N.E.2d 1258, 8 O.O.3d 237.

The language of RC 3111.17 providing that the defendant shall be jailed if he "neglects or refuses" to pay the award ordered by the court does not authorize the jailing of an indigent defendant; before the defendant can be jailed because he "neglects or refuses" to pay or secure the award ordered by the court, he must be accorded the opportunity to prove that he is unable to pay or secure the award. (Annotation from former RC 3111.17.) Bigsby v. Bates (Ohio Com.Pl. 1978) 59 Ohio Misc. 51, 391 N.E.2d 1384, 11 O.O.3d 262, 13 O.O.3d 260.

A defendant who fails to pay an award for maternity expenses in a bastardy action may be committed to jail. (Annotation from former RC 3111.17.) Crawford v. Hasberry (Ohio Juv. 1962) 186 N.E.2d 522, 90 Ohio Law Abs. 205, 21 O.O.2d 350.

3. Right of action

County child support enforcement agency was entitled to participate in parentage action following admission of paternity and in absence of evidence of past child support, as agency was necessary party and adjudicated father suffered no prejudice from agency's participation. State ex rel. Donovan v. Zajac (Ohio App. 11 Dist. 1998) 125 Ohio App.3d 245, 708 N.E.2d 254, dismissed, appeal not allowed 81 Ohio St.3d 1521, 692 N.E.2d 1023.

Child and Department of Human Services were not in privity with mother, and, therefore, judgment rendered in mother's paternity action did not present res judicata bar to later action by child and Department. Payne v. Cartee (Ross 1996) 111 Ohio App.3d 580, 676 N.E.2d 946, appeal not allowed 77 Ohio St.3d 1482, 673 N.E.2d 143.

Mother's claim against alleged father was distinct from Department of Human Services' claim for reimbursement of birthing expenses, for purposes of determining whether judgment rendered in mother's paternity action barred Department's later claim. Payne v. Cartee (Ross 1996) 111 Ohio App.3d 580, 676 N.E.2d 946, appeal not allowed 77 Ohio St.3d 1482, 673 N.E.2d 143.

Department of Human Services (DHS), as only entity which provided support for minor children, was only public authority that could bring suit against putative fathers for reimbursement; county Support Enforcement Agency could not bring suit for reimbursement on behalf of DHS. State ex rel. Gillion v. Reese (Cuyahoga 1994) 97 Ohio App.3d 315, 646 N.E.2d 852, appeal not allowed 71 Ohio St.3d 1466, 644 N.E.2d 1388.

Mother who received aid to dependent children from county department of human services had no right to bring action against father to recover child support, as any such right was assigned to county department of human services by operation of law. Vance v. Banks (Cuyahoga 1994) 94 Ohio App.3d 475, 640 N.E.2d 1214, appeal not allowed 70 Ohio St.3d 1447, 639 N.E.2d 115, certiorari denied 115 S.Ct. 1144, 513 U.S. 1170, 130 L.Ed.2d 1103.

Mother's right to initiate action against child's natural father to establish parent and child relationship did not also give her right to enforce parental obligation to support child, where mother received aid to dependent children from county department of human services; right to enforce parental obligation to support depended entirely on who was support provider of child. Vance v. Banks (Cuyahoga 1994) 94 Ohio App.3d 475, 640 N.E.2d 1214, appeal not allowed 70 Ohio St.3d 1447, 639 N.E.2d 115, certiorari denied 115 S.Ct. 1144, 513 U.S. 1170, 130 L.Ed.2d 1103.

In action to establish parent and child relationship, neither county department of human services nor any state agency can be proper party for purpose of initiating action, but can only intervene for limited purpose of collecting or recovering support if it is support provider. Vance v. Banks (Cuyahoga 1994) 94 Ohio App.3d 475, 640 N.E.2d 1214, appeal not allowed 70 Ohio St.3d 1447, 639 N.E.2d 115, certiorari denied 115 S.Ct. 1144, 513 U.S. 1170, 130 L.Ed.2d 1103.

Determination that mother who received aid to dependent children from county department of human services had no right to bring action to enforce father's child support obligation did not deprive mother of her right to be heard and to access to courts; courts remained open to mother when she had legitimate gripe against system. Vance v. Banks (Cuyahoga 1994) 94 Ohio App.3d 475, 640 N.E.2d 1214, appeal not allowed 70 Ohio St.3d 1447, 639 N.E.2d 115, certiorari denied 115 S.Ct. 1144, 513 U.S. 1170, 130 L.Ed.2d 1103.

Plaintiff's action against the biological father seeking reimbursement for necessaries furnished to plaintiff's wife's children born during his marriage is properly dismissed when it is clear from the record that such action was not brought for the benefit of, nor out of concern for, the children involved. Weinman v Larsh, No. C-810383 (1st Dist Ct App, Hamilton, 3-31-82), affirmed by 5 OS(3d) 85, 5 OBR 138, 448 NE(2d) 1384 (1983).

4. Bankruptcy

Although bankruptcy matters are inherently proceedings in equity and must foster equitable results, bankruptcy court would not second-guess judgment rendered by state court in establishing Chapter 7 debtor-biological father's debt for paternity action expenses where debtor was not placed in any worse position than that which existed before bankruptcy and debtor had opportunity to argue merits of debt allocation before the state court. In re Lamb (Bkrtcy.N.D.Ohio 1996) 198 B.R. 511.

Medical expenses arising from paternity action typically are not dischargeable. In re Lamb (Bkrtcy.N.D.Ohio 1996) 198 B.R. 511.

Chapter 7 debtor opposing nondischargeability of debt arising from paternity judgment failed to establish that government engaged in affirmative misconduct, and thus failed to meet burden upon summary judgment to show genuine issue of fact regarding equitable estoppel argument, where debtor alleged that county department of human services delayed in sending medical invoices to debtor's third-party insurance carrier, but debtor offered no proof in support of his claims and did not allege that he either changed his position or detrimentally relied upon any representation by department that it would expeditiously remit bills. In re Lamb (Bkrtcy.N.D.Ohio 1996) 198 B.R. 511.

An $11,000 obligation resulting from the compromise of a paternity action is a support payment to the child that cannot be discharged in the father's bankruptcy action where the amount was based on analysis of what would have been required for support had a declaration of paternity applied from the date of birth to the time of the agreement and from certain medical expenses relating to the birth. In re Wilson (Bkrtcy.S.D.Ohio 1989) 109 B.R. 283.

5. Indigent defendants

In parentage proceedings where the complainant-mothers and their children are recipients of public assistance, the state public defender must, in accordance with RC 120.18, RC 120.28, and RC 120.33, partially reimburse the counties for the cost of representing indigent paternity defendants who face the state as an adversary. OAG 85-090.

3111.16 Continuing jurisdiction

The court has continuing jurisdiction to modify or revoke a judgment or order issued under sections 3111.01 to 3111.19 of the Revised Code to provide for future education and support and a judgment or order issued with respect to matters listed in divisions (C) and (D) of section 3111.13 and division (B) of section 3111.15 of the Revised Code, except that a court entering a judgment or order for the payment of a lump sum or the purchase of an annuity under division (D) of section 3111.13 of the Revised Code may specify that the judgment or order may not be modified or revoked.

(1986 H 476, eff. 9-24-86; 1982 H 245)

Uncodified Law

1992 S 10, § 5: See Uncodified Law under 3111.01.

1982 H 245, § 3: See Uncodified Law under 3111.04.

Historical and Statutory Notes

Ed. Note: Former 3111.16 repealed by 1982 H 245, eff. 6-29-82; 1975 S 145; 1953 H 1; GC 8006-16; Source—GC 12122-1; see now 3111.09 for provisions analogous to former 3111.16.

Pre-1953 H 1 Amendments: 124 v S 65

Library References

Children Out-Of-Wedlock ⚷64.
WESTLAW Topic No. 76H.
C.J.S. Children Out-Of-Wedlock §§ 120, 121.

OJur 3d: 47, Family Law § 1005, 1051
Am Jur 2d: 10, Bastards § 131

Carlin, Baldwin's Ohio Practice, *Merrick-Rippner Probate Law* § 18.2, 18.3, 19.1, 19.2, 19.3, 19.4, 19.5, 19.6, 19.7, 19.8, 19.10, 19.12, 38.4, 98.29, 98.30, 98.31, 105.2, 108.19, 108.20, 108.22, 108.23, 108.24, 108.27, 108.28, 108.31 (1997)

Klein & Darling, Baldwin's Ohio Practice, *Civil Practice* § 1 (1997)

Sowald & Morganstern, Baldwin's Ohio Practice, *Domestic Relations Law* § 3.37, 20.6 (1997)

Notes of Decisions and Opinions

Support modification 1
Vacation of decree 2

---

1. Support modification

Court retains continuing jurisdiction over its orders concerning custody, care and support of children, even when court's initial order was based on agreement by parents of the child; child affected by such an order is considered a ward of the court, which may always reconsider and modify its rulings when changed circumstances require it during child's minority. Singer v. Dickinson (Ohio 1992) 63 Ohio St.3d 408, 588 N.E.2d 806.

Courts have continuing jurisdiction to modify orders for the support of illegitimate children even though the power is not reserved in the original order. (Annotation from former RC 3111.17.) State ex rel. Niven v. Tomblin (Summit 1948) 82 Ohio App. 376, 81 N.E.2d 637, 38 O.O. 51.

A simple assertion of non-paternity is insufficient to invoke the trial court's continuing jurisdiction to modify its child support and health insurance orders. Clippinger v Clippinger, No. CA97-05-010, 1998 WL 8682 (12th Dist Ct App, Preble, 1-12-98).

In a bastardy action a court has continuing jurisdiction until the child involved reaches eighteen, and is not barred from reducing delinquent installments to a lump-sum judgment by any statute of limitations. (Annotation from former RC 3111.17.) State ex rel. Marshall v. Steinbaugh (Ohio Juv. 1939) 138 N.E.2d 252, 73 Ohio Law Abs. 509.

The jurisdiction of the court is continuing as it relates to illegitimate children and an order for support is subject to modification. (Annotation from former RC 3111.17.) State ex rel. Raydel v. Raible (Ohio Com.Pl. 1953) 112 N.E.2d 568, 64 Ohio Law Abs. 438, affirmed 117 N.E.2d 480, 69 Ohio Law Abs. 356, appeal dismissed 162 Ohio St. 74, 120 N.E.2d 590, 54 O.O. 18.

2. Vacation of decree

Juvenile court's continuing jurisdiction over paternity matter authorized court to vacate initial finding of paternity and interim order of child support in light of postjudgment genetic testing which conclusively established putative father's nonpaternity. Cuyahoga Support Enforcement Agency v. Guthrie (Ohio 1999) 84 Ohio St.3d 437, 705 N.E.2d 318.

Although initial judgment of parentage and order requiring putative father to pay future child support were properly vacated in light of postjudgment genetic tests which conclusively established putative father's nonpaternity, he was not entitled to avoid all arrearages that existed due to his own inexcusable neglect; putative father voluntarily and deliberately disregarded initial parentage proceedings, thereby causing delay of finding of nonpaternity. Cuyahoga Support Enforcement Agency v. Guthrie (Ohio 1999) 84 Ohio St.3d 437, 705 N.E.2d 318.

Where HLA test results exclude as the probable father of the child the man adjudged the father of a child in a prior paternity proceeding, the court has continuing jurisdiction to vacate the order of paternity. Haney v Feltner, No. C-830715 (1st Dist Ct App, Hamilton, 7-3-84).

3111.17 Action to determine mother and child relationship

Any interested party may bring an action to determine the existence or nonexistence of a mother and child relationship. Insofar as practicable, the provisions of sections 3111.01 to 3111.19 of the Revised Code that are applicable to the father and child relationship shall apply to an action brought under this section.

(1986 H 476, eff. 9-24-86; 1982 H 245)

Uncodified Law

1992 S 10, § 5: See Uncodified Law under 3111.01.

1982 H 245, § 3: See Uncodified Law under 3111.04.

Historical and Statutory Notes

Ed. Note: Former 3111.17 repealed by 1982 H 245, eff. 6-29-82; 1975 S 145; 1970 S 460; 125 v 184; 1953 H 1; GC 8006-17; Source—GC 12123; see now 3111.13 to 3111.15 for provisions analogous to former 3111.17, and 3111.03, 3111.04, and 3111.15 for annotations from former 3111.17.

Pre-1953 H 1 Amendments: 124 v S 65

Library References

Children Out-Of-Wedlock ⚷34.
Parent and Child ⚷1.
WESTLAW Topic Nos. 76H, 285.
C.J.S. Children Out-Of-Wedlock §§ 49, 85 to 92.
C.J.S. Parent and Child §§ 2 to 4, 10.

OJur 3d: 47, Family Law § 959, 962
Am Jur 2d: 10, Bastards § 75; 59, Parent and Child § 2, 3, 5

Carlin, Baldwin's Ohio Practice, *Merrick-Rippner Probate Law* § 18.2, 18.3, 19.1, 19.2, 19.3, 19.4, 19.5, 19.6, 19.7, 19.8, 19.10, 19.12, 38.4, 98.29, 98.30, 98.31, 105.2, 108.19, 108.20, 108.22, 108.23, 108.24, 108.27, 108.28, 108.31 (1997)
Klein & Darling, Baldwin's Ohio Practice, *Civil Practice* § 1 (1997)
Sowald & Morganstern, Baldwin's Ohio Practice, *Domestic Relations Law* § 3.10, 3.31, 20.64 (1997)

Law Review and Journal Commentaries

Modern Reproductive Technology and Motherhood: The Search for Common Ground and the Recognition of Difference, Comment. 62 U Cin L Rev 1623 (Spring 1994).

Notes of Decisions and Opinions

Child support obligation 2
Evidence 1

---

1. Evidence

In paternity proceedings, the juvenile court may consider insurance payments and disability benefits received by the mother of an illegitimate child in determining her need for medical expenses and support during pregnancy, delivery, and post-natal convalescence. Edwards v. Sadusky (Summit 1982) 4 Ohio App.3d 297, 448 N.E.2d 506, 4 O.B.R. 548.

2. Child support obligation

Lesbian mother's agreement, to accept full financial responsibility for children in exchange for father impregnating mother, was circumstance "which ought reasonably to relieve father" of child support obligation between date of birth and date amicable and cooperative parenting arrangement broke down and, thus, trial court's refusal to order child support to commence at birth was not an abuse of discretion. Myers v. Moschella (Hamilton 1996) 112 Ohio App.3d 75, 677 N.E.2d 1243.

3111.18 New birth record

As used in this section, "birth record" has the meaning given in section 3705.01 of the Revised Code.

Upon the order of a court of this state or upon the request of a court of another state, the department of health shall prepare a new birth record consistent with the findings of the court and shall substitute the new record for the original birth record.

(1988 H 790, eff. 3-16-89; 1982 H 245)

Uncodified Law

1992 S 10, § 5: See Uncodified Law under 3111.01.

1982 H 245, § 3: See Uncodified Law under 3111.04.

Historical and Statutory Notes

Ed. Note: Former 3111.18 repealed by 1982 H 245, eff. 6-29-82; 1953 H 1; GC 8006-18; Source—GC 12124.

Pre-1953 H 1 Amendments: 124 v S 65

Cross References

Vital statistics, birth record of legitimatized child, 3705.09

Library References

Health and Environment ⚿34.
WESTLAW Topic No. 199.
C.J.S. Health and Environment § 41.

OJur 3d: 47, Family Law § 1003

Carlin, Baldwin's Ohio Practice, *Merrick-Rippner Probate Law* § 18.2, 18.3, 19.1, 19.2, 19.3, 19.4, 19.5, 19.6, 19.7, 19.8, 19.10, 19.12, 38.4, 98.29, 98.30, 98.31, 105.2, 108.19, 108.20, 108.22, 108.23, 108.24, 108.27, 108.28, 108.29, 108.31 (1997)

Klein & Darling, Baldwin's Ohio Practice, *Civil Practice* § 1 (1997)

Sowald & Morganstern, Baldwin's Ohio Practice, *Domestic Relations Law* § 3.48 (1997)

3111.19 Compromise agreement; approval by court

After an action has been brought and before judgment, the alleged father and the mother, subject to the approval of the court, may compromise the action by an agreement in which the parent and child relationship is not determined but in which a specific economic obligation is undertaken by the alleged parent in favor of the child. In reviewing the obligation undertaken by the alleged parent, the court shall consider the interest of the child, the factors set forth in division (B)(3) of section 3113.215 of the Revised Code, and the probability of establishing the existence of a parent and child relationship in a trial.

(1993 S 115, eff. 10-12-93; 1982 H 245)

Uncodified Law

1992 S 10, § 5: See Uncodified Law under 3111.01.

1982 H 245, § 3: See Uncodified Law under 3111.04.

Historical and Statutory Notes

Ed. Note: Former 3111.19 repealed by 1982 H 245, eff. 6-29-82; 127 v 1039; 1953 H 1; GC 8006-19; Source—GC 12128. 3111.19 contains provisions analogous to former 3111.07, repealed by 1982 H 245, eff. 6-29-82.

Pre-1953 H 1 Amendments: 124 v S 65

Amendment Note: 1993 S 115 changed a reference to section 3111.13(E) to a reference to section 3113.215(B)(3).

Cross References

Calculation of amount of child support obligation, 3113.215

Library References

Children Out-Of-Wedlock ⚿22.
WESTLAW Topic No. 76H.
C.J.S. Children Out-Of-Wedlock §§ 44 to 46, 51.

OJur 3d: 47, Family Law § 1004

Carlin, Baldwin's Ohio Practice, *Merrick-Rippner Probate Law* § 18.2, 18.3, 19.1, 19.2, 19.3, 19.4, 19.5, 19.6, 19.7, 19.8, 19.10, 19.12, 38.4, 98.29, 98.30, 98.31, 105.2, 108.19, 108.20, 108.22, 108.23, 108.24, 108.27, 108.28, 108.29, 108.31, 108.32 (1997)

Klein & Darling, Baldwin's Ohio Practice, *Civil Practice* § 1 (1997)

Sowald & Morganstern, Baldwin's Ohio Practice, *Domestic Relations Law* § 3.29, 3.40 (1997)

Law Review and Journal Commentaries

Bankruptcy Reform Act of 1994—What the Bankruptcy Code Giveth, Domestic Relations Courts (and Congress) Taketh Away, C.R. "Chip" Bowles. 8 Domestic Rel J Ohio 17 (March/April 1996).

Compromise Settlement in Paternity Action is Res Judicata as to Parentage, Pamela J. MacAdams. 4 Domestic Rel J Ohio 105 (November/December 1992).

Practice Pointer—Parentage Cases—Litigation, Pamela J. MacAdams. 8 Domestic Rel J Ohio 17 (March/April 1996).

Notes of Decisions and Opinions

Action to set aside agreement 2
Bankruptcy 3
Res judicata 1

1. Res judicata

Trial court was required to consider support being paid by father of minor child to child's mother pursuant to agreed settlement entry of previous parentage action in calculating support payable under judgment entered in child's subsequent action to establish parent-child relationship; while prior action was not res judicata with respect to issue of support, both actions served same purpose in that they required payment of money for benefit of child, and child was only entitled to single "support." Cornell v. Brumfield (Ohio App. 4 Dist. 1996) 115 Ohio App.3d 259, 685 N.E.2d 270.

Issues of paternity and support determined in compromise agreement reached by child's parents in parentage action initiated by child's mother were not res judicata with respect to subsequent action against father by child to establish parent-child relationship, despite fact that second action was also initiated by child's mother, in her capacity as child's next friend; mother's status as plaintiff was mere pleading formality, mother and child were not in privity, and child was never party to previous parentage action. Cornell v. Brumfield (Ohio App. 4 Dist. 1996) 115 Ohio App.3d 259, 685 N.E.2d 270.

Agreed entry in parentage action bars any subsequent relitigation of same issues in second parentage case between same parties. Cornell v. Brumfield (Ohio App. 4 Dist. 1996) 115 Ohio App.3d 259, 685 N.E.2d 270.

Legitimation order filed in probate court with consent of mother did not bar subsequent parentage action wherein mother sought child support arrearages; application of doctrine of res judicata would violate state's strong public policy favoring protection of children and their support, health, maintenance and welfare, and would also violate equal protection. Lewis v. Chapin (Cuyahoga 1994) 93 Ohio App.3d 695, 639 N.E.2d 848.

A parentage action brought by a natural mother against a putative father is barred by res judicata where the parties have previously entered into an agreement signed and journalized by the court, providing for the father to pay the mother $20 a week until the minor child's eighteenth birthday and for the mother to release the father from all claims against him; the fact that the agreement failed to determine the parent/child relationship did not render it void since RC 3111.19 expressly provides that the agreement need not make such a determination. Nelson v. Pleasant (Lawrence 1991) 73 Ohio App.3d 479, 597 N.E.2d 1137.

An illegitimate child may not bring a declaratory judgment action asking that the defendant be found to be his putative father and thereby obtain financial support for himself, and also the right to have his surname changed to that of the defendant, where the mother of the child entered into a compromise agreement under RC 3111.07. (Annotation from former RC 3111.07.) In re Paternity (Ohio Com.Pl. 1965) 4 Ohio Misc. 193, 211 N.E.2d 894, 33 O.O.2d 299.

2. Action to set aside agreement

Statute allowing parties in paternity action to enter compromise agreement subject to court approval supersedes rule allowing dismissal by stipulation without court approval. State ex rel. Fowler v. Smith (Ohio 1994) 68 Ohio St.3d 357, 626 N.E.2d 950.

Where a mother enters into agreement not to establish paternity with an alleged father, the child is not bound by the agreement and may subsequently bring a paternity action against the alleged father. Fitzpatrick v. Fitzpatrick (Ohio App. 12 Dist. 1998) 126 Ohio App.3d 476, 710 N.E.2d 778, dismissed, appeal not allowed 82 Ohio St.3d 1441, 695 N.E.2d 264.

Mother's compromise agreement with alleged father did not bar later paternity action brought on behalf of child to recover prospective support and by Department of Human Services to recover birthing expenses, where child was not party to compromise agreement. Payne v. Cartee (Ross 1996) 111 Ohio App.3d 580, 676 N.E.2d 946, appeal not allowed 77 Ohio St.3d 1482, 673 N.E.2d 143.

Overruling stipulation for dismissal of paternity action for past child support, as not in best interests of child, was not an abuse of discretion in light of absence of evidence on alleged father's ability to pay and emancipated child's need for past support. Phelps v. Fowler (Cuyahoga 1995) 107 Ohio App.3d 263, 668 N.E.2d 558, appeal not allowed 75 Ohio St.3d 1452, 663 N.E.2d 332.

Trial court obtained jurisdiction to proceed with adjudication of paternity, notwithstanding prior stipulation for dismissal. Phelps v. Fowler (Cuyahoga 1995) 107 Ohio App.3d 263, 668 N.E.2d 558, appeal not allowed 75 Ohio St.3d 1452, 663 N.E.2d 332.

Parties to a paternity action may enter into settlement agreement concerning the action. Ransome v. Lampman (Miami 1995) 103 Ohio App.3d 8, 658 N.E.2d 313, dismissed, appeal not allowed 73 Ohio St.3d 1449, 654 N.E.2d 985.

As binding contracts, settlement agreements, including those in paternity action, may be enforced through breach of contract action. Ransome v. Lampman (Miami 1995) 103 Ohio App.3d 8, 658 N.E.2d 313, dismissed, appeal not allowed 73 Ohio St.3d 1449, 654 N.E.2d 985.

Mother had remedy by way of breach of contract complaint for putative father's failure to make support payments in accordance with settlement of paternity action, and thus was not entitled to relief from judgment approving the settlement. Ransome v. Lampman (Miami 1995) 103 Ohio App.3d 8, 658 N.E.2d 313, dismissed, appeal not allowed 73 Ohio St.3d 1449, 654 N.E.2d 985.

Where court properly approved compromise agreement entered into by parties to paternity action and there was no indication that mother was forced or coerced into the agreement or that she did not understand the ramifications of entering the agreement, mother was not entitled to relief from judgment under catchall provision, even though she was not experienced in legal matters. Ransome v. Lampman (Miami 1995) 103 Ohio App.3d 8, 658 N.E.2d 313, dismissed, appeal not allowed 73 Ohio St.3d 1449, 654 N.E.2d 985.

Fact that child was not represented by guardian ad litem in paternity proceedings was not sufficient reason to relieve mother from settlement agreement. Ransome v. Lampman (Miami 1995) 103 Ohio App.3d 8, 658 N.E.2d 313, dismissed, appeal not allowed 73 Ohio St.3d 1449, 654 N.E.2d 985.

Mother's motion for relief from judgment approving settlement of paternity action was not timely under catchall provision where it was brought eight years after the judgment and most of the reasons cited in support of motion were in existence immediately after judgment was entered. Ransome v. Lampman (Miami 1995) 103 Ohio App.3d 8, 658 N.E.2d 313, dismissed, appeal not allowed 73 Ohio St.3d 1449, 654 N.E.2d 985.

Child's interests in paternity action conflicted with those of her mother, so that child was entitled to relief from settlement even though mother was not, where it was likely in prosecutor's interest to have a compromise agreement entered into by the parties and mother's motivation in compromising the action may have been merely to cooperate with public authorities so that she might continue to receive public support, whereas child's interests included right to know the identity of her father so that she might enjoy the physical, mental, and emotional support of both of her parents during her lifetime, as well as the bundle of rights which accompany the determination of parentage. Ransome v. Lampman (Miami 1995) 103 Ohio App.3d 8, 658 N.E.2d 313, dismissed, appeal not allowed 73 Ohio St.3d 1449, 654 N.E.2d 985.

Child was entitled to relief from judgment approving settlement of paternity action without determination of paternity even though judgment was entered nearly eight years earlier, as child was quite young and could not have been expected to have sought relief in the interim period. Ransome v. Lampman (Miami 1995) 103 Ohio App.3d 8, 658 N.E.2d 313, dismissed, appeal not allowed 73 Ohio St.3d 1449, 654 N.E.2d 985.

Order of juvenile court, by agreement of parties, awarding custody of child to natural mother and giving support duties and visitation privileges to natural mother's brother-in-law as putative father should not have been made without consideration of best interest of child and vacation of such order on basis that it was unjust was not an abuse of the trial court's discretion. In re Smith (Miami 1984) 16 Ohio App.3d 75, 474 N.E.2d 632, 16 O.B.R. 79.

A minor child is not barred from instituting a later action to determine paternity when a prior action brought in her name has reached judgment through a stipulated agreement. Ransome v Lampman, Nos. 94-CA-20+, 1995 WL 136983, 2d Dist Ct App, Miami, 3-31-95).

Where a plaintiff brought an action to set aside a settlement agreement entered into in a bastardy proceeding and the defendant filed motions and obtained subpoenas duces tecum ordering the plaintiff to appear for a taking of his deposition, and plaintiff failed to do so, a trial court acted properly in ordering him to appear. (Annotation from former RC 3111.07.) Raible v. Raydel (Cuyahoga 1952) 110 N.E.2d 431, 63 Ohio Law Abs. 591, appeal dismissed 158 Ohio St. 328, 109 N.E.2d 319, 49 O.O. 180.

3. Bankruptcy

An obligation for child support arrearages will be discharged in bankruptcy, as between the debtor and the mother, where the obligation arose by agreement in settlement of a paternity proceeding in which the debtor denied paternity, and where no evidence of paternity is before the bankruptcy court. Matter of Gray (Bkrtcy.S.D.Ohio 1984) 41 B.R. 759.

ADMINISTRATIVE SUPPORT ORDERS

Ohio Administrative Code References

CSEA's administrative authority regarding paternity determination and child support orders, OAC Ch 5101:1-32

Library References

Sowald & Morganstern, Baldwin's Ohio Practice, *Domestic Relations Law* § 3.10, 19.2, 20.3, 22.2 (1997)

3111.20 Parental duty of support

(A) As used in sections 3111.20 to 3111.29 of the Revised Code:

(1) "Obligor" means the person required to pay support under an administrative support order.

(2) "Obligee" means the person entitled to receive the support payments under an administrative support order.

(3) "Administrative support order" means an administrative order for the payment of support that is issued by a child support enforcement agency.

(4) "Support" means child support.

(5) "Personal earnings" means compensation paid or payable for personal services, however denominated, and includes, but is not limited to, wages, salary, commissions, bonuses, draws against commissions, profit sharing, and vacation pay.

(6) "Financial institution" means a bank, savings and loan association, or credit union, or a regulated investment company or mutual fund in which a person who is required to pay support has funds on deposit that are not exempt under the law of this state or the United States from execution, attachment, or other legal process.

(7) "Title IV-D case" means any case in which the child support enforcement agency is enforcing the support order pursuant to Title IV-D of the "Social Security Act," 88 Stat. 2351 (1975), 42 U.S.C. 651, as amended.

(8) "Payor" means any person or entity that distributes income to an obligor including the obligor, if the obligor is self-employed; an employer; an employer that is paying the obligor's workers' compensation benefits; the public employees retirement board; the governing entity of any municipal retirement system; the board of trustees of the Ohio police and fire pension fund; the state teachers retirement board; the school employees retirement board; the state highway patrol retirement board; a person paying or otherwise distributing an obligor's income; the bureau of workers' compensation; or any other person or entity, except the director of job and family services with respect to unemployment compensation benefits paid pursuant to Chapter 4141. of the Revised Code.

(9) "Income" means any form of monetary payment including personal earnings; unemployment compensation benefits to the extent permitted by, and in accordance with, sections 2301.371 and 4141.282 of the Revised Code, and federal law governing the department of job and family services; workers' compensation payments; pensions; annuities; allowances; retirement benefits; disability or sick pay; insurance proceeds; lottery prize awards; federal, state, or local government benefits to the extent that the benefits can be withheld or deducted under the law governing the benefits; any form of trust fund or endowment; lump-sum payments; and any other monetary payments.

(B) A man who is presumed to be the natural father of a child pursuant to section 3111.03 of the Revised Code assumes the parental duty of support with respect to the child.

(C) Notwithstanding section 3109.01 of the Revised Code, a parent's duty of support for a child shall continue beyond the age of majority as long as the child continuously attends on a full-time basis any recognized and accredited high school or a court-issued child support order provides that the duty of support continues beyond the age of majority. Except in cases in which a child support order requires the duty of support to continue for any period after the child reaches nineteen years of age, the duty does not continue after the child reaches nineteen years of age. The parental duty of support shall continue during seasonal vacations.

A parent, guardian, or legal custodian of a child, the person with whom the child resides, or the child support enforcement agency of the county in which the child, parent, guardian, or legal custodian of the child resides may file a complaint pursuant to section 2151.231 of the Revised Code in the juvenile court of that county requesting the court to order a parent who neglects or does not assume the parental duty of support to pay an amount for the support of the child and to provide for the health care needs of the child, may contact a child support enforcement agency for assistance in obtaining the order, or may request an administrative officer of a child support enforcement agency to issue an administrative order for the payment of child support and providing for the health care needs of the child pursuant to division (D) of this section. Upon the filing of the complaint or the making of the request, the court shall issue an order requiring the payment of support for the child and providing for the health care needs of the child, pursuant to section 2151.231 of the Revised Code, or the administrative officer, pursuant to division (D) of this section, shall issue an order requiring the payment of support for the child and providing for the health care needs of the child.

A party to a request made under this division may raise the issue of the existence or nonexistence of a parent-child relationship between the presumed natural father and the child unless the presumption is based on acknowledgment of paternity that has become final pursuant to section 2151.232, 3111.211, or 5101.314 of the Revised Code. If a request is made for an administrative order providing for support and health care needs pursuant to division (D) of this section and the issue of the existence or nonexistence of a parent-child relationship is raised, the administrative officer shall treat the request as a request made pursuant to section 3111.22 of the Revised Code and determine the issue pursuant to that section. An administrative order issued pursuant to division (D) of this section does not preclude a party from requesting a determination of the issue of the existence or nonexistence of a parent-child relationship pursuant to this chapter if the issue was not determined with respect to the party in the proceedings conducted pursuant to division (D) of this section or pursuant to an acknowledgment of paternity that has become final under section 2151.232, 3111.211, or

5101.314 of the Revised Code. An order issued pursuant to division (D) of this section shall remain effective until a final and enforceable determination is made pursuant to this chapter that a parent-child relationship does not exist between the presumed natural father and the child or until the occurrence of an event described in division (E)(4)(a) of section 3111.23 of the Revised Code that requires the order to be terminated.

(D) If a request is made pursuant to division (C) of this section or division (A) of section 3111.211 of the Revised Code for an administrative order requiring the payment of child support and providing for the health care needs of the child, the administrative officer shall schedule an administrative hearing to determine, in accordance with sections 3111.23 to 3111.29 and 3113.215 of the Revised Code, the amount of child support either parent is required to pay, the method of paying that child support, and the method of providing for the child's health care. The hearing shall be held not later than sixty days after the request is made pursuant to division (A) of this section or division (A) of section 3111.211 of the Revised Code nor earlier than thirty days after the officer gives the mother and father of the child notice of the action. When an administrative officer issues an administrative order for the payment of support and provision for the child's health care, all of the following apply:

(1) The administrative support order shall require periodic payments of support that may vary in amount, except that, if it is in the best interest of the child, the administrative officer may order a lump sum payment or the purchase of an annuity in lieu of periodic payments of support.

(2) The administrative support order shall require the parents to provide for the health care needs of the child in accordance with section 3111.241 of the Revised Code.

The administrative support order shall include a notice stating that the mother or the father may object to the administrative order by bringing an action for the payment of support and provision for the child's health care under section 2151.321 of the Revised Code in the juvenile court of the county in which the child or the guardian or legal custodian of the child resides, that the action may be brought no later than thirty days after the date of the issuance of the administrative support order, and that, if neither the mother nor the father brings an action for the payment of support and provision for the child's health care within that thirty-day period, the administrative support order is final and enforceable by a court and may be modified and enforced only as provided in sections 3111.20 to 3111.28 and 3113.21 to 3113.219 of the Revised Code.

(2000 H 509, eff. 9-21-00; 1999 H 471, eff. 7-1-00; 1999 H 222, eff. 11-2-99; 1997 H 352, eff. 1-1-98; 1997 H 408, eff. 10-1-97; 1996 H 710, § 7, eff. 6-11-96; 1995 H 167, eff. 6-11-96; 1992 S 10, eff. 7-15-92)

Uncodified Law

1996 H 710, § 15, eff. 6-11-96, reads, in part:

(A) The amendments to sections 2151.231, 2301.34, 2301.35, 2301.351, 2301.358, 2705.02, 3111.20, 3111.21, 3111.22, 3111.23, 3111.241, 3111.242, 3111.27, 3111.28, 3111.99, 3113.21, 3113.214, 3113.215, 3113.99, 4723.07, and 4723.09 of the Revised Code by Sub. H.B. 167 of the 121st General Assembly take effect, and their existing interim versions are correspondingly repealed, on the date this act takes effect and not on November 15, 1996[.]

Historical and Statutory Notes

Ed. Note: Former 3111.20 repealed by 1982 H 245, eff. 6-29-82; 1975 S 145; 127 v 1039; 1953 H 1; GC 8006-20; Source—GC 12129.

Ed. Note: The effective date of the amendment of this section by 1995 H 167 was changed from 11-15-96 to 6-11-96 by 1996 H 710, § 7, eff. 6-11-96.

Pre-1953 H 1 Amendments: 124 v S 65

Amendment Note: 2000 H 509 substituted "and 4141.282" for "of the Revised Code, division (D)(4) of section 4141.28" in division (A)(9); and made other nonsubstantive changes.

Amendment Note: 1999 H 471 substituted "director of job and family services" for "bureau of employment services" in division (A)(8); and substituted "department of job and family services" for "bureau of employment services" in division (A)(9).

Amendment Note: 1999 H 222 substituted "Ohio police and fire pension fund" for "police and firemen's disability and pension fund" in division (A)(8); and made other corrective and nonsubstantive changes.

Amendment Note: 1997 H 352 rewrote this section, which prior thereto read:

"(A) As used in sections 3111.20 to 3111.29 of the Revised Code:

"(1) "Child support enforcement agency" has the same meaning as in section 3111.21 of the Revised Code.

"(2) "Obligor" means the person required to pay support under an administrative support order.

"(3) "Obligee" means the person entitled to receive the support payments under an administrative support order.

"(4) "Administrative support order" means an administrative order for the payment of support that is issued by a child support enforcement agency.

"(5) "Support" means child support.

"(6) "Personal earnings" means compensation paid or payable for personal services, however denominated, and includes, but is not limited to, wages, salary, commissions, bonuses, draws against commissions, profit sharing, and vacation pay.

"(7) "Financial institution" means a bank, savings and loan association, or credit union, or a regulated investment company or mutual fund in which a person who is required to pay support has funds on deposit that are not exempt under the law of this state or the United States from execution, attachment, or other legal process.

"(8) "Title IV-D case" means any case in which the child support enforcement agency is enforcing the support order pursuant to Title IV-D of the "Social Security Act," 88 Stat. 2351 (1975), 42 U.S.C. 651, as amended.

"(B) A man who is presumed to be the natural father of a child pursuant to section 3111.03 of the Revised Code assumes the parental duty of support with respect to the child.

"(C) Notwithstanding section 3109.01 of the Revised Code, a parent's duty of support for a child shall continue beyond the age of majority as long as the child continuously attends on a full-time basis any recognized and accredited high school. The parental duty of support shall continue during seasonal vacations.

"A parent, guardian, or legal custodian of a child, the person with whom the child resides, or the child support enforcement agency of the county in which the child, parent, guardian, or legal custodian of the child resides may file a complaint pursuant to section 2151.231 of the Revised Code in the juvenile court of that county requesting the court to order a parent who neglects or does not assume the parental duty of support to pay an amount for the support of the child, may contact a child support enforcement agency for assistance in obtaining the order, or may request an administrative officer of a child support enforcement agency to issue an administrative order for the payment of child support pursuant to division (D) of this section. Upon the filing of the complaint or the making of the request, the court shall issue an order requiring the payment of support for the child, pursuant to section 2151.231 of the Revised Code, or the administrative officer, pursuant to division (D) of this section, shall issue an order requiring the payment of support for the child.

"A party to a request made under this division may raise the issue of the existence or nonexistence of a parent-child relationship between the presumed natural father and the child. If a request is made for an administrative order of support pursuant to division (D) of this section and the issue of the existence or nonexistence of a parent-child relationship is raised, the administrative officer shall treat the request as a request made pursuant to section 3111.22 of the Revised Code and determine the issue pursuant to that section. The administrative officer may issue an order pursuant to division (D) of this section if the administrative proceeding terminates before a determination of the existence or nonexistence of a parent-child relationship is made and the termination is due to the presumed natural father's failure to sign an acknowledgment of paternity, sign an agreement to be bound by the results of genetic testing, or appear at the administrative hearing without showing good cause for the failure to appear, or the proceedings terminate because of the presumed natural father's failure to submit to genetic testing or submit the child to genetic testing. An administrative order issued pursuant to division (D) of this section does not preclude a party from requesting a determination of the issue of the existence or nonexistence of a parent-child relationship pursuant to this chapter if the issue is not determined with respect to the party in the proceedings conducted pursuant to division (D) of this section. An order issued pursuant to division (D) of this section shall remain effective until a final and enforceable determination is made pursuant to this chapter that a parent-child relationship does not exist between the presumed natural father and the child or until the occurrence of an event described in division (E)(4)(a) of section 3111.23 of the Revised Code that requires the order to be terminated.

"(D) If a request is made pursuant to division (C) of this section for an administrative order requiring the payment of child support, the administrative officer shall schedule an administrative hearing to determine, in accordance with sections 3111.23 to 3111.29 and 3113.215 of the Revised Code, the amount of child support either parent is required to pay and the method of paying that child support. The hearing shall be held not later than sixty days after the issuance of the administrative order nor earlier than thirty days after the officer gives the mother and father of the child notice of the action. When an administrative officer issues an administrative order for the payment of support, all of the following apply:

"(1) An administrative order for the payment of support ordinarily shall be for periodic payments that may vary in amount. In the best interest of the child, the administrative officer may order a lump sum payment or the purchase of an annuity in lieu of periodic payments of support.

"(2) The administrative order for the payment of support shall include a notice stating that the mother or the father may object to the administrative order by bringing an action for the payment of support under section 2151.321 of the Revised Code in the juvenile court of the county in which the child or the guardian or legal custodian of the child resides, that the action may be brought no later than thirty days after the date of the issuance of the administrative order requiring the payment of child support, and that, if neither the mother nor the father brings an action for the payment of support within that thirty-day period, the administrative order requiring the payment of support is final and enforceable by a court and may be modified and enforced only in accordance with sections 3111.20 to 3111.28 and 3113.21 to 3113.219 of the Revised Code."

Amendment Note: 1997 H 408 deleted former division (A)(1); and redesignated former divisions (A)(2) through (A)(8) as new divisions (A)(1) through (A)(7), respectively. Prior to deletion, former division (A)(1) read:

"(1)"Child support enforcement agency" has the same meaning as in section 3111.21 of the Revised Code."

Amendment Note: 1995 H 167 rewrote division (B); divided former division (C) into two paragraphs; deleted "After the probate court enters the acknowledgment upon its journal or the father voluntarily signs the birth certificate as an informant as provided in section 3705.09 of the Revised Code, the" from the end of the first paragraph in division (C); deleted "with custody of the child" after the first occurrence of "parent" and inserted "of a child, the person with whom the child resides" and the second occurrence of "parent" in the first sentence in the second paragraph in division (C); added the third paragraph in division (C); inserted "and enforceable by a court" and "and enforced" in, added a reference to sections 3111.20 to 3111.28 in, and deleted a reference to section 3111.27 from, division (D)(2); and made other nonsubstantive changes.

Cross References

Acknowledgment of paternity, 2105.18
Child support enforcement agencies, administrative officers, 2301.358
Child support enforcement agencies, as social security Title IV-D agency, 2301.35
Child support guidelines, 3113.215
Child support withholding or deduction requirements and notices, 3113.21
Contempt of court, 2705.02
Duty of parents to support children of unemancipated minor children, 3109.19
Notice of default on child support order sent to professional licensing boards, 2301.373
Reports by employers to child support division, entry of information into directory, comparison against case registry, 5101.312
Subrogation of right to workers' compensation benefits to child support obligation, 5101.36
Support order defined, 2301.34
Unemployment compensation benefits, withholding or deduction for child support obligations, 2301.371
Uniform Interstate Family Support Act, receipt of income-withholding order of another state, obligor's payor defined, 3115.32

Ohio Administrative Code References

Income withholding and other "division (D)" orders, OAC 5101:1-30-411

Library References

Children Out-Of-Wedlock ⚿3, 21, 67, 69.
Divorce ⚿306 to 311.5.
Parent and Child ⚿3 to 3.3.
Social Security and Public Welfare ⚿11, 194.19.
WESTLAW Topic Nos. 76H, 134, 285, 356A.
C.J.S. Children Out-of-Wedlock §§ 13 to 17, 40 to 43, 122 to 126, 128, 129.
C.J.S. Divorce §§ 665 to 671, 673, 736.
C.J.S. Parent and Child §§ 14, 49 to 71, 73.
C.J.S. Social Security and Public Welfare §§ 17, 122.

OJur 3d: 47, Family Law § 891, 1036, 1038, 1039 to 1042

Carlin, Baldwin's Ohio Practice, *Merrick-Rippner Probate Law* § 18.2, 18.3, 19.1, 19.2, 19.3, 19.4, 19.6, 19.7, 19.8, 19.10, 98.29, 98.31, 108.13, 108.19, 108.22, 108.29, 108.33, 108.34, 108.39 (1997)
Klein & Darling, Baldwin's Ohio Practice, *Civil Practice* § 52 (1997)
Sowald & Morganstern, Baldwin's Ohio Practice, *Domestic Relations Law* § 3.12, 20.3, 22.5, 22.13, 23.40 (1997)

Law Review and Journal Commentaries

Bankruptcy Reform Act of 1994—What the Bankruptcy Code Giveth, Domestic Relations Courts (and Congress) Taketh Away, C.R. "Chip" Bowles. 8 Domestic Rel J Ohio 17 (March/April 1996).

Finality in Parentage Findings: Perfection or Finality?, Pamela J. MacAdams. 10 Domestic Rel J Ohio 19 (March/April 1998).

Should Children be Penalized Because Their Parents Did Not Marry? A Constitutional Analysis of Section 516 of the New York Family Court Act, Allan E. Mayefsky and Gary von Stange. 26 U Tol L Rev 957 (Summer 1995).

Notes of Decisions and Opinions

Child support enforcement agency assistance 2
Personal earnings, defined 3
Retroactive support 1

---

1. Retroactive support

General precept of making modifications of child support retroactive to the date of filing of request for increase is not mandatory, but is merely a starting point from which a court may use its sound discretion in varying. Pacurar v. Pacurar (Ohio App. 7 Dist. 1999) 132 Ohio App.3d 787, 726 N.E.2d 552.

Reviewing court could not determine that trial court abused its discretion by making increase in former husband's child support obligation retroactive only to date five and one-half months prior to entry of modification order, rather than to date of filing of motion for increase 11 months prior to entry of order, where wife did not supply reviewing court with a transcript of support hearing. Pacurar v. Pacurar (Ohio App. 7 Dist. 1999) 132 Ohio App.3d 787, 726 N.E.2d 552.

Biological father could not be ordered to pay back child support for expenses incurred by child's mother during first 18 years of child's life, where no action for support, or other action which would trigger duty to support, had been commenced during period of child's minority. Snider v. Lillie (Ohio App. 1 Dist. 1997) 131 Ohio App.3d 444, 722 N.E.2d 1036.

An obligor who deliberately redirects part of his income to his new wife to avoid child support obligations perpetrates a fraud upon the court which consequently awards retroactive support payments to remedy the results of the scheme to defraud the court. Leffel v Leffel, No. 97-CA-20, 1997 WL 666102 (2d Dist Ct App, Clark, 10-24-97).

In order to present a cognizable claim for past child support the appropriate action to establish that claim must have been commenced during the child's minority when the legal duty to support exists. Snider v Lillie, No. C-961014, 1997 WL 663521 (1st Dist Ct App, Hamilton, 10-17-97).

The statutory language from RC 3111.20(C) is broad enough to authorize a juvenile court to award child support retroactive to the date of the birth of the child. State ex rel Summit County Human Services Dept v Paynter, No. 16657, 1994 WL 665512 (9th Dist Ct App, Summit, 11-30-94).

2. Child support enforcement agency assistance

County support enforcement agency lacked statutory authority to bring action in its own name against relator's husband for child support when relator and husband were married, did not dispute parentage, and did not receive public assistance; two statutory exceptions permitting agency to bring action in its own name, when probate court enters acknowledgement of paternity upon its journal and when father voluntarily signs birth certificate as informant pursuant to statute, did not apply. In re Owens (Cuyahoga 1994) 104 Ohio App.3d 201, 661 N.E.2d 765, appeal allowed 71 Ohio St.3d 1422, 642 N.E.2d 387, appeal dismissed as improvidently allowed 74 Ohio St.3d 1280, 658 N.E.2d 304.

Trial court's dismissal of child support enforcement agency as party in five child support actions where parentage was established through administrative proceedings violated equal protection clauses of State and Federal Constitutions; statutory scheme, which permits agency to be party in support actions where parentage is established through probate court and where parents are on public assistance, but which does not specifically permit agency to be party when parentage is established through administrative proceedings, did not have rational basis, since enforcement agency can only effectuate its duty to protect best interests of child and public fisc by being joined as party in all child support enforcement actions. Cuyahoga Cty. Support Enforcement Agency v. Lozada (Cuyahoga 1995) 102 Ohio App.3d 442, 657 N.E.2d 372.

It is a violation of the equal protection clauses of the United States and Ohio constitutions to allow the aid and support of the child support enforcement agency in an action for child support brought by parents who have established their parentage through the probate court and residential parents who are on public assistance while denying the aid and support of the child support enforcement agency to parents who have established their parentage through the administrative process. Cuyahoga County Support Enforcement Agency v Lozada, Nos. 67463+, 1995 WL 386965 (8th Dist Ct App, Cuyahoga, 6-29-95).

Dismissal of the child support enforcement agency (CSEA) as a party in an action for child support under RC 3111.21 via RC 2151.231 violates the Ohio and federal Equal Protection Clauses when a similarly situated residential parent who legitimizes a child through probate court is entitled to have the CSEA advocate for a proper child support order in the juvenile court under RC 3111.20, by way of RC 2151.231. Cuyahoga County Support Enforcement Agency v Lozada, No. 67463+, 1995 WL 386965 (8th Dist Ct App, Cuyahoga, 6-29-95).

3. Personal earnings, defined

A company truck given to an employee for use in company business and also used from time to time for personal reasons does not significantly reduce the father's living expenses where he already owns two automobiles for his private use; as a result, the mother's attempt to include the value of the truck in the father's income is rejected. Bahring v Mercer, No. CA96-02-023, 1996 WL 468760 (12th Dist Ct App, Clermont, 8-19-96).

3111.21 Signing, notarizing, and sending of acknowledgment

If the natural mother and alleged father of a child sign an acknowledgment of paternity affidavit prepared pursuant to section 5101.324 of the Revised Code with respect to that child at a child support enforcement agency, the agency shall provide a notary public to notarize the acknowledgment. The agency shall send a signed and notarized acknowledgment of paternity to the division of child support in the department of job and family services pursuant to section 5101.314 of the Revised Code. The agency shall send the acknowledgment no later than ten days after it has been signed and notarized. If the agency knows a man is presumed under section 3111.03 of the Revised Code to be the father of the child, the agency shall not notarize or send an acknowledgment with respect to the child pursuant to this section.

(1999 H 471, eff. 7-1-00; 1997 H 352, eff. 1-1-98)

Uncodified Law

1996 H 710, § 15: See Uncodified Law under 3111.20.

Historical and Statutory Notes

Ed. Note: Former 3111.21 repealed by 1997 H 352, eff. 1-1-98; 1996 H 710, § 7, eff. 6-11-96; 1995 H 167, eff. 6-11-96; 1992 S 10, eff. 7-15-92.

Ed. Note: Prior 3111.21 repealed by 1982 H 245, eff. 6-29-82; 1953 H 1; GC 8006-21; Source—GC 12130.

Ed. Note: The effective date of the amendment of this section by 1995 H 167 was changed from 11-15-96 to 6-11-96 by 1996 H 710, § 7, eff. 6-11-96.

Pre-1953 H 1 Amendments: 124 v S 65

Amendment Note: 1999 H 471 substituted "job and family" for "human".

Cross References

Action for child support order, existence of parent-child relationship, 2151.231
Calculation of child support obligation, potential income defined, 3113.215
Child support enforcement agencies, as social security Title IV-D agency, 2301.35
Child support enforcement agencies, paternity compliance plans, staff to meet with unmarried mothers, 2301.357
Child support withholding or deduction requirements and notices, 3113.21
Contempt of court, 2705.02
Duty of parents to support children of unemancipated minor children, 3109.19
Hospitals, staff to meet with unmarried mothers, 3727.17
Notice of default on child support order sent to professional licensing boards, 2301.373
Support order defined, 2301.34

Ohio Administrative Code References

Parent's responsibility for support of unmarried minors' child(ren), OAC 5101:1-32-04

Library References

Children Out-Of-Wedlock ⟹22, 45, 58, 67.
WESTLAW Topic No. 76H.
C.J.S. Children Out-of-Wedlock §§ 44 to 46, 51, 75, 76, 122 to 126.

OJur 3d: 47, Family Law § 892, 965, 966, 973, 983, 1036, 1041, 1043, 1207
Statute of limitations in illegitimacy or bastardy proceedings. 59 ALR3d 685
Carlin, Baldwin's Ohio Practice, *Merrick-Rippner Probate Law* § 18.2, 18.3, 19.1, 19.2, 19.3, 19.4, 19.6, 19.7, 19.8, 19.10, 19.10.1, 98.29, 98.31, 108.19, 108.22, 108.23, 108.24, 108.29, 108.30, 108.33, 108.34, 108.38, 108.39 (1997)
Klein & Darling, Baldwin's Ohio Practice, *Civil Practice* § 52 (1997)
Sowald & Morganstern, Baldwin's Ohio Practice, *Domestic Relations Law* § 22.4, 22.19 (1997)

Notes of Decisions and Opinions

Administrative order 3
Bankruptcy 1
Child support enforcement agency assistance 2

---

1. Bankruptcy

Paternity suit judgments are nondischargeable under provision of Bankruptcy Code rendering nondischargeable a debt to spouse, former spouse, or child of debtor for alimony to, maintenance for, or support of such spouse or child, in connection with separation agreement, divorce decree or "other order of a court of record." (Annotation from former RC 3111.21.) In re Oberley (Bkrtcy.N.D.Ohio 1993) 153 B.R. 179.

2. Child support enforcement agency assistance

It is a violation of the equal protection clauses of the United States and Ohio constitutions to allow the aid and support of the child support enforcement agency in an action for child support brought by parents who have established their parentage through the probate court and residential parents who are on public assistance while denying the aid and support of the child support enforcement agency to parents who have established their parentage through the administrative process. (Annotation from former RC 3111.21.) Cuyahoga County Support Enforcement Agency v Lozada, Nos. 67463+, 1995 WL 386965 (8th Dist Ct App, Cuyahoga, 6-29-95).

Dismissal of the child support enforcement agency (CSEA) as a party in an action for child support under RC 3111.21 via RC 2151.231 violates the Ohio and federal Equal Protection Clauses when a similarly situated residential parent who legitimizes a child through probate court is entitled to have the CSEA advocate for a proper child support order in the juvenile court under RC 3111.20, by way of RC 2151.231. (Annotation from former RC 3111.21.) Cuyahoga County Support Enforcement Agency v Lozada, No. 67463+, 1995 WL 386965 (8th Dist Ct App, Cuyahoga, 6-29-95).

3. Administrative order

A person is not entitled to relief under Civ R 60(B)(2) or (5) from a judgment of paternity and child support where he signed the child's birth certificate and an administrative order indicating he was the child's biological father even though he knew he was not the biological father because the mother was two months pregnant when he began dating her, and therefore a recent DNA test result showing a 0.00 chance he was the father is not "new evidence" under Civ R 60(B)(2), the specific provision of the rule that prevails over the more general section, (B)(5); although it may appear unfair to require an individual to pay child support for a child not biologically his own, there must be some finality to a judgment and one cannot choose to be a parent and then change his or her mind when the relationship is dissolved. Shaffer v Rusnak, No. 97 CA 26, 1998 WL 429624 (5th Dist Ct App, Guernsey, 7-1-98).

3111.211 Administrative support order before acknowledgment becomes final

(A) If an acknowledgment has been filed and entered into the birth registry pursuant to section 5101.314 of the Revised Code but has not yet become final, either of the persons who signed the acknowledgment may request that an administrative officer of a child support enforcement agency issue an administrative order pursuant to division (B) of this section for payment of child support and providing for the health care needs of the child.

A party to a request made under this section may raise the issue of the existence or nonexistence of a parent and child relationship. If a request is made pursuant to this section and the issue of the existence or nonexistence of a parent and child relationship is raised, the administrative officer shall treat the request as a request made pursuant to section 3111.22 of the Revised Code and determine the issue in accordance with that section. The administrative officer shall promptly notify the division of child support in the department of job and family services that proceedings are being conducted in compliance with section 3111.22 of the Revised Code. On receipt of the notice by the division, the acknowledgment of paternity signed by the parties and filed pursuant to section 5101.314 of the Revised Code shall be considered rescinded.

If the parties do not raise the issue of the existence or nonexistence of a parent and child relationship pursuant to the request made under this section and an administrative order is issued pursuant to division (B) of this section prior to the date the acknowledgment filed and entered on the birth registry under section 5101.314 of the Revised Code becomes final, the acknowledgment shall be considered final as of the date of the issuance of the order. An administrative order issued pursuant to division (B) of this section shall not affect an acknowledgment that becomes final pursuant to section 5101.314 of the Revised Code prior to the issuance of the order.

(B) If a request is made pursuant to division (A) of this section for an administrative order requiring the payment of child support and providing for the health care needs of the child, the administrative officer shall comply with the requirements of division (D) of section 3111.20 of the Revised Code and shall issue a support order in accordance with that division.

(1999 H 471, eff. 7-1-00; 1997 H 352, eff. 1-1-98)

Historical and Statutory Notes

Amendment Note: 1999 H 471 substituted "job and family" for "human" in the second paragraph in division (A).

Cross References

Adoption, consents required, 3107.06
Adoption, exception to requirement of search of putative father registry, 3107.064
Child support enforcement agency, designation, 2301.35
Child support guidelines, 3113.215
Contempt, 2705.02
Duty of parents to support children of unemancipated minor children, complaints regarding, 3109.19
Filing of birth certificate upon acknowledgment of paternity, 3705.09
Juvenile courts, action for child support order, raising issue of existence of parent-child relationship, 2151.231
Notice of child support default sent to licensing boards, child support order defined, 2301.373
Parental duty of support, when arising, 3103.031
Relief from final judgment, court order, or administrative determination, 3113.2111
Support order defined, 2301.34
Support orders, withholding or deduction requirements and notices, 3113.21
Visitation rights of grandparents and other relatives, complaints for, 3109.12

Ohio Administrative Code References

Administrative support order process, OAC 5101:1-32-03
Parent's responsibility for support of unmarried minors' child(ren), OAC 5101:1-32-04

Library References

OJur 3d: 47, Family Law § 892, 908.1, 965, 1008, 1027, 1038, 1039, 1255, 1300

Carlin, Baldwin's Ohio Practice, *Merrick-Rippner Probate Law* § 18.3, 19.1, 19.2, 19.3, 19.4, 19.6, 19.7, 19.8, 19.10, 98.29, 98.30, 98.31, 98.33, 98.37, 105.1, 108.13, 108.19, 108.20, 108.31, 108.33, 108.34, 108.39 (1997)

Sowald & Morganstern, Baldwin's Ohio Practice, *Domestic Relations Law* § 3.12, 3.39, 18.8, 19.2, 23.15 (1997)

3111.22 Administrative support orders based on determinations of existence or nonexistence of parent and child relationships

(A)(1) Except as otherwise provided in division (A)(2) of this section, no person may bring an action under sections 3111.01 to 3111.19 of the Revised Code before requesting an administrative determination of the existence or nonexistence of a parent and child relationship from the child support enforcement agency of the county in which the child or the guardian or legal custodian of the child resides.

(2) If the alleged father of a child is deceased and proceedings for the probate of the estate of the alleged father have been or can be commenced, the court with jurisdiction over the probate proceedings shall retain jurisdiction to determine the existence or nonexistence of a parent and child relationship between the alleged father and any child without an administrative determination being requested from a child support enforcement agency. If an action for divorce, dissolution of marriage, or legal separation, or an action under section 2151.231 of the Revised Code requesting an order requiring the payment of child support and provision for the health care of a child, has been filed in a court of common pleas and a question as to the existence or nonexistence of a parent and child relationship arises, the court in which the original action was filed shall retain jurisdiction to determine the existence or nonexistence of the parent and child relationship without an administrative determination being requested from a child support enforcement agency. If a juvenile court issues a support order under section 2151.231 of the Revised Code relying on a presumption under section 3111.03 of the Revised Code, the juvenile court that issued the support order shall retain jurisdiction if a question as to the existence of a parent and child relationship arises.

(B) Except as provided in division (A)(2) of this section, before a person brings an action pursuant to sections 3111.01 to 3111.19 of the Revised Code to determine the existence or nonexistence of a parent and child relationship, the person shall request the child support enforcement agency of the county in which the child or the guardian or legal custodian of the child resides to determine the existence or nonexistence of a parent and child relationship between the alleged father and the child. If more than one agency receives a request pursuant to this section, the agency that receives the request first shall proceed with the request. The request shall contain all of the following information:

(1) The name, birthdate, and current address of the alleged father of the child;

(2) The name, social security number, and current address of the mother of the child;

(3) The name and last known address of the alleged father of the child;

(4) The name and birthdate of the child.

(C)(1) Upon receiving a request for a determination of the existence or nonexistence of a parent and child relationship in accordance with division (B) of this section, the agency shall assign an administrative officer to consider the request. The administrative officer may schedule a conference with the mother and the alleged father to provide information and the opportunity to sign an acknowledgment of paternity affidavit prepared pursuant to section 5101.324 of the Revised Code. If the mother and alleged father do not sign the affidavit at a conference held by the administrative officer, the administrative officer shall issue an order requiring the child, the mother, and the alleged father to submit to genetic testing. In the order, the agency shall schedule the genetic tests for the mother, alleged father, and child on a date that is no later than forty-five days after the date of assignment of the administrative officer and shall require the tests to be conducted in accordance with the rules adopted by the director of job and family services pursuant to section 2301.35 of the Revised Code.

The agency shall attach a notice to the order and send both in accordance with the Rules of Civil Procedure to the mother and the alleged father. The notice shall state all of the following:

(a) That the agency has been requested to determine the existence of a parent and child relationship between a child and the alleged named father;

(b) The name and birthdate of the child of which the man is alleged to be the natural father;

(c) The name of the mother and the alleged natural father;

(d) The rights and responsibilities of a parent;

(e) That the child, the mother, and the alleged father must submit to genetic testing at the date, time, and place determined by the agency in the order issued pursuant to division (C)(1) of this section;

(f) The administrative procedure for determining the existence of a parent and child relationship;

(g) That if the alleged father or natural mother willfully fails to submit to genetic testing, or the alleged father, natural mother, or the custodian of the child willfully fails to submit the child to genetic testing, the agency shall issue an order that it is inconclusive whether the alleged father is the child's natural father;

(h) That if the alleged father or natural mother willfully fails to submit to genetic testing, or the alleged father, natural mother, or custodian of the child willfully fails to submit the child to genetic testing, they may be found in contempt of court.

(2) The genetic testing shall be conducted by a qualified examiner authorized by the department of job and family services. On completion of the genetic tests, the examiner shall send a complete report of the test results to the agency. The administrative officer shall do one of the following:

(a) If the results of the genetic testing show a ninety-nine per cent or greater probability that the alleged father is the natural father of the child, the administrative officer of the agency shall issue an administrative order that the alleged father is the father of the child who is the subject of the proceeding.

(b) If the results of genetic testing show less than a ninety-nine per cent probability that the alleged father is the natural father of the child but do not exclude the alleged father from being the natural father of the child, the administrative officer shall issue an administrative order stating that it is inconclusive whether the alleged father is the natural father of the child.

(c) If the results of the genetic testing exclude the alleged father from being the natural father of the child, the administrative officer shall issue an administrative order that the alleged father is not the father of the child who is the subject of the proceeding.

An administrative officer shall include with any order the officer issues pursuant to division (C)(2)(a) or (c) of this section a notice that contains the information described in division (D) of this section informing the mother, father, and the guardian or legal custodian of the child of the right to object to the order.

(D) When an administrative officer issues an administrative order determining the existence or nonexistence of a parent and child relationship pursuant to division (C)(2)(a) or (c) of this section, the mother, alleged father, and the guardian or legal custodian of the child may object to the determination by bringing, within thirty days after the date the administrative officer issued the order, an action under sections 3111.01 to 3111.19 of the Revised Code in the juvenile court in the county in which the agency that employs the administrative officer is located. If the mother, alleged father, or guardian or legal custodian does not bring an action within that thirty-day period, the administrative order is final and enforceable by a court and may not be challenged in an action or proceeding under Chapter 3111. of the Revised Code.

(E)(1) If an administrative officer issues an administrative order determining the existence of a parent and child relationship between the alleged father and the child pursuant to division (C)(2)(a) of this section, the administrative officer shall schedule an administrative hearing to determine, in accordance with sections 3111.23 to 3111.29 and 3113.215 of the Revised Code, the amount of child support any parent is required to pay, the method of payment of child support, and the method of providing for the child's health care. The hearing shall be held no later than sixty days after the date of the issuance of the order and no earlier than thirty days after the date the administrative officer gives the mother and the father notice of the administrative hearing. When an administrative officer issues an administrative order for the payment of support and provision for the child's health care, all of the following apply:

(a) The administrative support order shall require periodic payments of support that may vary in amount, except that, if it is in the best interest of the child, the administrative officer may order a lump-sum payment or the purchase of an annuity in lieu of periodic payments of support.

(b) The administrative support order shall require the parents to provide for the health care needs of the child in accordance with section 3111.241 of the Revised Code.

(c) The administrative support order shall include a notice informing the mother, father, and the legal guardian or custodian of the child of the right to object to the order and containing the information described in division (E)(2) of this section.

(2) The mother, father, or the legal guardian or custodian of the child may object to the administrative order by bringing an action for the payment of support and provision for the child's health care under section 2151.231 of the Revised Code in the juvenile court of the county in which the agency that employs the administrative officer is located. The action shall be brought no later than thirty days after the date of the issuance of the administrative support order. If neither the mother nor the father brings an action for the payment of support and provision for the child's health care within that thirty-day period, the administrative support order is final and enforceable by a court and may be modified and enforced only as provided in sections 3111.20 to 3111.28 and 3113.21 to 3113.219 of the Revised Code.

(F) If the alleged natural father or the natural mother willfully fails to submit to genetic testing or if either parent or any other person who is the custodian of the child willfully fails to submit the child to genetic testing, the agency shall enter an administrative order stating that it is inconclusive as to whether the alleged natural father is the natural father of the child and shall provide a notice to the parties informing them that an action may be brought under sections 3111.01 to 3111.19 of the Revised Code to establish a parent and child relationship.

(G) Unless the agency has reason to believe that a person named in the order is a potential victim of domestic violence, any order issued pursuant to this section finding the existence of a parent and child relationship shall contain the full names, addresses, and social security numbers of the mother and father of the child and the full name and address of the child. The agency, as part of an order determining the existence of a parent and child relationship issued pursuant to this section, may order the surname of the child subject to the determination to be changed and order the change to be made on the child's birth record consistent with the order if the parties agree to the change.

(H) An administrative support order issued pursuant to section 3111.21 of the Revised Code prior to January 1, 1998, that is in effect on January 1, 1998, shall remain in effect on and after January 1, 1998, and shall be considered an administrative support order issued pursuant to this section for all purposes.

(I) As used in this section, "birth record" has the same meaning as in section 3705.01 of the Revised Code.

(1999 H 471, eff. 7-1-00; 1997 H 352, eff. 1-1-98; 1996 H 710, § 7, eff. 6-11-96; 1995 H 167, eff. 6-11-96; 1992 S 10, eff. 7-15-92)

Uncodified Law

1996 H 710, § 15: See Uncodified Law under 3111.20.

Historical and Statutory Notes

Ed. Note: Former 3111.22 repealed by 1982 H 245, eff. 6-29-82; 1953 H 1; GC 8006-22; Source—GC 12131.

Ed. Note: The effective date of the amendment of this section by 1995 H 167 was changed from 11-15-96 to 6-11-96 by 1996 H 710, § 7, eff. 6-11-96.

Pre-1953 H 1 Amendments: 124 v S 65

Amendment Note: 1999 H 471 substituted "director of job and family services" for "department of human services" in the introductory paragraph in division (C)(1); substituted "job and family" for "human" in the introductory paragraph in division (C)(2); and substituted "January 1, 1998" for "the effective date of this amendment" three times in division (H).

Amendment Note: 1997 H 352 rewrote this section; see *Baldwin's Ohio Legislative Service Annotated*, 1997, p 9/L-2562, or the OH-LEGIS or OH-LEGIS-OLD database on WESTLAW, for text of previous version.

Amendment Note: 1995 H 167 substituted "a presumption under section 3111.03" for "an acknowledgment of paternity entered upon its journal by the probate court pursuant to section 2105.18" in division (A)(2); inserted "and enforceable by a court" and "and enforced" in, added references to sections 3111.20 to 3111.28 in, and deleted references to section 3111.27 from, divisions (C)(4)(b), (C)(5)(d), and (D)(2); inserted "and enforceable by a court" in division (C)(5)(b)(iv); substituted "3111.23" for "3111.21" in division (C)(5)(c); and made other changes to reflect gender neutral language.

Cross References

Acknowledgment of paternity, rescission, 5101.314
Administrative child support orders, birth record defined, 3705.01
Calculation of child support obligation, potential income defined, 3113.215
Child support enforcement agencies, administrative officers, 2301.358
Child support enforcement agencies, as social security Title IV-D agency, 2301.35
Child support withholding or deduction requirements and notices, 3113.21
Contempt, 2705.02
Duty of parents to support children of unemancipated minor children, 3109.19
Filing of birth certificate upon acknowledgment of paternity, 3705.09
Genetic testing, collection of samples, 2301.356
Notice of default on child support order sent to professional licensing boards, 2301.373
Support order defined, 2301.34

Ohio Administrative Code References

Administrative paternity process, support order process, OAC 5101:1-32-02 et seq.
Parent's responsibility for support of unmarried minors' child(ren), OAC 5101:1-32-04
Title IV-D responsibility in establishing paternity, OAC 5101:1-30-23

Library References

Children Out-Of-Wedlock ⚿30 to 68.
WESTLAW Topic No. 76H.
C.J.S. Children Out-of-Wedlock §§ 41, 46, 47, 49 to 51, 67, 70 to 127.
OJur 3d: 47, Family Law § 968, 1039, 1040 to 1043, 1207, 1255
Carlin, Baldwin's Ohio Practice, *Merrick-Rippner Probate Law* § 18.2, 18.3, 19.1, 19.2, 19.3, 19.4, 19.6, 19.7, 19.8, 19.10, 19.10.1, 19.12, 98.29, 98.31, 108.13, 108.19, 108.22, 108.24, 108.29, 108.30, 108.31, 108.33, 108.34, 108.39 (1997)
Klein & Darling, Baldwin's Ohio Practice, *Civil Practice* § 52 (1997)
Sowald & Morganstern, Baldwin's Ohio Practice, *Domestic Relations Law* § 3.2, 3.3, 3.4, 3.5, 3.6, 3.7, 3.8, 3.9, 3.10, 3.17, 3.19, 3.38, 3.39, 3.42, 3.50, 3.51, 3.58, 15.6, 22.4, 22.5, 22.13, 22.19, 23.14, 23.15 (1997)

Law Review and Journal Commentaries

Bankruptcy Reform Act of 1994—What the Bankruptcy Code Giveth, Domestic Relations Courts (and Congress) Taketh Away, C.R. "Chip" Bowles. 8 Domestic Rel J Ohio 17 (March/April 1996).

Establishing Parentage After Senate Bill 10, Pamela J. MacAdams. 4 Domestic Rel J Ohio 81 (September/October 1992).

Notes of Decisions and Opinions

Bankruptcy 1
Child support enforcement agency assistance 2
Constitutional issues 3
Procedural issues 4

---

1. Bankruptcy

Paternity suit judgments are nondischargeable under provision of Bankruptcy Code rendering nondischargeable a debt to spouse, former spouse, or child of debtor for alimony to, maintenance for, or support of such spouse or child, in connection with separation agreement, divorce decree or "other order of a court of record." In re Oberley (Bkrtcy.N.D.Ohio 1993) 153 B.R. 179.

2. Child support enforcement agency assistance

It is a violation of the equal protection clauses of the United States and Ohio constitutions to allow the aid and support of the child support enforcement agency in an action for child support brought by parents who have established their parentage through the probate court and residential parents who are on public assistance while denying the aid and support of the child support enforcement agency to parents who have established their parentage through the administrative process. Cuyahoga County Support Enforcement Agency v Lozada, Nos. 67463+, 1995 WL 386965 (8th Dist Ct App, Cuyahoga, 6-29-95).

3. Constitutional issues

Trial court's dismissal of child support enforcement agency as party in five child support actions where parentage was established through administrative proceedings violated equal protection clauses of State and Federal Constitutions; statutory scheme, which permits agency to be party in support actions where parentage is established through probate court and where parents are on public assistance, but which does not specifically permit agency to be party when parentage is established through administrative proceedings, did not have rational basis, since enforcement agency can only effectuate its duty to protect best interests of child and public fisc by being joined as party in all child support enforcement actions. Cuyahoga Cty. Support Enforcement Agency v. Lozada (Cuyahoga 1995) 102 Ohio App.3d 442, 657 N.E.2d 372.

4. Procedural issues

Fact that adjudicated father's motion for modification of child support was pending before Juvenile Court did not give Juvenile Court jurisdiction to entertain paternal grandmother's petition for grandparental visitation, where child support obligation was established by virtue of administrative order, over modification of which Juvenile Court lacked jurisdiction. Borkosky v. Mihailoff (Ohio App. 3 Dist. 1999) 132 Ohio App.3d 508, 725 N.E.2d 694.

Domestic relations courts have original jurisdiction to consider parentage issues during pendency of divorce, dissolution, or legal separation actions. Leguillon v. Leguillon (Ohio App. 12 Dist. 1998) 124 Ohio App.3d 757, 707 N.E.2d 571.

Father's duty to support child did not begin until date administrative parentage determination became final, nearly a month after mother and stepfather petitioned to adopt child, and, therefore, father's earlier failure to support child did not obviate need to obtain father's consent to adoption. In re Adoption of Hudnell (Ross 1996) 113 Ohio App.3d 296, 680 N.E.2d 1055.

Despite mother's contention that father's failure to participate in administrative determination of parentage precluded court of common pleas from exercising jurisdiction over parentage action, given apparent conflict in jurisdictional statutes, court of common pleas was not so patently and unambiguously devoid of subject matter jurisdiction that Court of Appeals would issue writ of prohibition prohibiting court of common pleas from exercising jurisdiction while final judgment was pending. State ex rel. Dixon v. Clark Cty. Court of Common Pleas, Juv. Div. (Clark 1995) 103 Ohio App.3d 523, 660 N.E.2d 486.

A motion for summary judgment may lie in paternity proceedings in juvenile court. State ex rel Drews v Ambrosi, No. 73761, 1998 WL 563993 (8th Dist Ct App, Cuyahoga, 9-3-98).

3111.221 Preparation of new birth record pursuant to determination of parent and child relationship

As used in this section, "birth record" has the same meaning as in section 3705.01 of the Revised Code.

If an administrative order determining the existence or nonexistence of a parent and child relationship includes a finding that the child's father is a man other than the man named in the child's birth record as the father or is otherwise at variance with the child's birth record, the agency that made the determination shall notify the department of health of the determination as soon as any period for objection to the determination provided for in former section 3111.21 or section 3111.22 of the Revised Code has elapsed.

On receipt of notice under this section or notice from an agency of another state with authority to make paternity determinations that has made a determination of the existence or nonexistence of a parent and child relationship, the department of health shall prepare a new birth record consistent with the agency's determination and substitute the new record for the original birth record.

(1997 H 352, eff. 1-1-98)

Cross References

Administrative child support orders, birth record defined, 3705.01

Library References

OJur 3d: 47, Family Law § 892

Carlin, Baldwin's Ohio Practice, *Merrick-Rippner Probate Law* § 18.3, 19.1, 19.2, 19.3, 19.4, 19.6, 19.7, 19.10, 98.29, 98.31, 108.19, 108.34, 108.39 (1997)

Sowald & Morganstern, Baldwin's Ohio Practice, *Domestic Relations Law* § 3.4, 22.19 (1997)

3111.23 Withholding or deduction requirements and notices

(A)(1) If an administrative officer of a child support enforcement agency issues an administrative support order under section 3111.20, 3111.211, or 3111.22 of the Revised Code, the agency shall require the withholding or deduction of an amount of the income or assets of the obligor in accordance with division (B) of this section or require the issuance of an order in accordance with section 3111.231 of the Revised Code to ensure that withholding or deduction from the income or assets of the obligor is available from the commencement of the administrative support order for the collection of the support and any arrearages that occur. The agency shall determine the specific withholding or deduction requirements or other requirement applicable to the obligor under the administrative support order in accordance with division (B) of this section and section 3111.231 of the Revised Code and shall include the specific requirements in the notices described in divisions (A)(2) and (B) of this section or in an order described under section 3111.231 of the Revised Code. Any person required to comply with the withholding or deduction requirements shall determine the manner of withholding or deducting an amount of the income or assets of the obligor in accordance with the specific requirements included in the notices described in those divisions without the need for any amendment to the administrative support order. Any person required to comply with an order described in section 3111.231 of the Revised Code shall comply without the need for any amendment to the administrative order. The agency shall include in an administrative support order under section 3111.20, 3111.211, or 3111.22 of the Revised Code a general provision that states the following:

"All child support ordered by this administrative support order shall be withheld or deducted from the income or assets of the obligor pursuant to a withholding or deduction notice issued in accordance with section 3111.23 of the Revised Code or a withdrawal directive issued pursuant to section 3113.214 of the Revised Code and shall be forwarded to the obligee in accordance with sections 3111.23 to 3111.28 of the Revised Code."

(2) In any action in which support is ordered or modified under an administrative support order as described in division (A)(1) of this section, the child support enforcement agency shall determine in accordance with division (B) of this section or section 3111.231 of the Revised Code the types of withholding or deduction requirements or other requirements that should be imposed relative to the obligor under the administrative support order to collect the support due under the order. Within fifteen days after the obligor under the administrative support order is located subsequent to the issuance of the administrative support order or within fifteen days after the default under the administrative support order, whichever is applicable, the agency shall send a notice by regular mail to each person required to comply with a withholding or deduction requirement. The notice shall specify the withholding or deduction requirement and shall contain all of the information set forth in division (B)(1) or (2)(b) of this section that is applicable to the requirement. The notices, plus the notices provided by the child support enforcement agency that require the obligor to notify the agency of any change in the obligor's employment status or of any other change in the status of the obligor's assets, are final and are enforceable by the court. The agency shall provide the notice to the obligor in accordance with division (B)(1)(c) or (2)(c) of this section, whichever is applicable, and shall include with that notice the additional notices described in the particular division that is applicable.

(3)(a) If support is ordered or modified on or after December 31, 1993, under an administrative support order issued under former section 3111.21 or section 3111.20, 3111.211, or 3111.22 of the Revised Code, if the child support enforcement agency has determined in accordance with division (A)(2) of this section the types of withholding or deduction requirements or other requirements that should be imposed relative to the obligor under the support order to collect the support due under the order, if the agency has sent the appropriate withholding or deduction notices or issued and sent an order under section 3111.231 of the Revised Code to the persons required to comply with the withholding or deduction requirements or order that the agency determined should be imposed, and if the agency is notified or otherwise determines that the employment status or other circumstances of the obligor have changed, the agency shall conduct an investigation to determine whether it is more appropriate to impose another type of or an additional withholding or deduction requirement or order regarding the administrative support order and shall issue and send by regular mail one or more notices described in division (B) of this section or an order pursuant to section 3111.231 of the Revised Code that it determines are appropriate. The agency shall immediately cancel any previously issued notice or order that no longer is appropriate and send written notice of the cancellation by regular mail to the person required to comply with the previously issued notice or order. The notices shall be sent within fifteen days after the obligor under the administrative support order is located or within fifteen days after the default under the administrative support order, whichever is applicable. The notices shall specify the withholding or deduction requirement and shall contain all of the information set forth in division (B)(1)(b) or (2)(b) of this section that is applicable. The agency shall provide the notices to the obligor in accordance with division (B)(1)(c) or (2)(c) of this section, whichever is applicable, and shall include with that notice the additional notices described in the particular division that are applicable. The notices are final and are enforceable by the court.

(b) All support orders issued prior to December 31, 1993, under former section 3111.21 or section 3111.20 or 3111.22 of the Revised Code that have not been modified or found in default on or after that date shall be considered to contain the general provision described in division (A)(1) of this section and shall be enforced and modified in the same manner as an order for support issued on or after December 31, 1993.

(4) If, pursuant to division (A)(2) or (A)(3)(a) of this section, a person is sent a withholding or deduction notice described in division (B) of this section or an order issued under section 3111.231 of the Revised Code and the person fails to comply with the notice or order, the child support enforcement agency, in accordance with section 3111.28 of the Revised Code, shall request the court to find the person in contempt pursuant to section 2705.02 of the Revised Code.

(5) The department of job and family services shall adopt standard forms for the support withholding and deduction notices prescribed by divisions (A)(1) to (3) and (B) of this section. All child support enforcement agencies shall use the forms in complying with this section.

(B) If a child support enforcement agency is required by division (A) of this section to issue one or more withholding or deduction notices described in this division, the agency shall issue one or more of the following types of notices to pay the support required under the administrative support order in question and to pay any arrearages:

(1)(a) If the child support enforcement agency determines that the obligor is receiving income from a payor, the agency shall require the payor to withhold from the obligor's income a specified amount for support in satisfaction of the administrative support order, to begin the withholding no later than fourteen working days following the date the notice was mailed to the payor under divisions (A)(2) or (3) and (B)(1)(b) of this section or, if the payor is an employer, no later than the first pay period that occurs after fourteen working days following the date the notice was mailed, to send the amount withheld to the division of child support in the department of job and family services pursuant to section 5101.325 of the Revised Code, to send that amount to the division immediately but not later than seven working days after the date the obligor is paid, and to continue the withholding at intervals specified in the notice until further notice from the child support enforcement agency. To the extent possible, the amount specified in the notice to be withheld shall satisfy the amount ordered for support in the administrative support order plus any arrearages that may be owed by the obligor under any prior court or administrative support order that pertained to the same child or spouse, notwithstanding any applicable limitations of sections 2329.66, 2329.70, 2716.02, 2716.041, and 2716.05 of the Revised Code. However, in no case shall the sum of the amount specified in the notice to be withheld and any fee withheld by the payor as a charge for its services exceed the maximum amount permitted under section 303(b) of the "Consumer Credit Protection Act," 15 U.S.C. 1673(b).

(b) If the agency imposes a withholding requirement under division (B)(1)(a) of this section, the agency, within the applicable period of time specified in division (A) of this section, shall send to the payor by regular mail a notice that contains all of the information set forth in divisions (B)(1)(b)(i) to (xi) of this section. The notice is final and is enforceable by the court. The notice shall contain all of the following:

(i) The amount to be withheld from the obligor's income and a statement that the amount actually withheld for support and other purposes, including the fee described in division (B)(1)(b)(xi) of this section, shall not be in excess of the maximum amounts permitted under section 303(b) of the "Consumer Credit Protection Act," 15 U.S.C. 1673(b);

(ii) A statement that the payor is required to send the amount withheld to the division of child support immediately, but not later than seven working days, after the obligor is paid and is required to report to the agency the date on which the amount was withheld from the obligor's income;

(iii) A statement that the withholding is binding upon the payor until further notice from the agency;

(iv) A statement that if the payor is an employer, the payor is subject to a fine to be determined under the law of this state for discharging the obligor from employment, refusing to employ the obligor, or taking any disciplinary action against the obligor because of the withholding requirement;

(v) A statement that, if the payor fails to withhold income in accordance with the provisions of the notice, the payor is liable for the accumulated amount the payor should have withheld from the obligor's income;

(vi) A statement that the withholding in accordance with the notice and under the provisions of this section has priority over any other legal process under the law of this state against the same income;

(vii) The date on which the notice was mailed and a statement that the payor is required to implement the withholding no later than fourteen working days following the date the notice was mailed or, if the payor is an employer, no later than the first pay period that occurs after fourteen working days following the date the notice was mailed and is required to continue the withholding at the intervals specified in the notice;

(viii) A requirement that the payor promptly notify the child support enforcement agency, in writing, within ten working days after the date of any situation that occurs, including, termination of employment, layoff of the obligor, any leave of absence of the obligor without pay, termination of workers' compensation benefits, or termination of any pension, annuity, allowance, or retirement benefit in which the payor ceases to pay income in an amount sufficient to comply with the administrative order to the obligor and provide the agency with the obligor's last known address;

(ix) A requirement that, if the payor is an employer, the payor identify in the notification given under division (B)(1)(b)(viii) of this section any types of benefits other than personal earnings that the obligor is receiving or is eligible to receive as a benefit of employment or as a result of the obligor's termination of employment, including, but not limited to, unemployment compensation, workers' compensation benefits, severance pay, sick leave, lump sum payments of retirement benefits or contributions, and bonuses or profit-sharing payments or distributions, and the amount of such benefits, and include in the notification the obligor's last known address and telephone number, date of birth, social security number, and case number and, if known, the name and business address of any new employer of the obligor;

(x) A requirement that, no later than the earlier of forty-five days before the lump-sum payment is to be made or, if the obligor's right to the lump-sum payment is determined less than forty-five days before it is to be made, the date on which that determination is made, the payor notify the child support enforcement agency of any lump-sum payments of any kind of one hundred fifty dollars or more that are to be paid to the obligor, hold the lump-sum payments of one hundred fifty dollars or more for thirty days after the date on which the lump-sum payments otherwise would have been paid to the obligor, and, upon order of the agency, pay any specified amount of the lump-sum payment to the division of child support;

(xi) A statement that, in addition to the amount withheld for support, the payor may withhold a fee from the obligor's income as a charge for its services in complying with the notice a specification of the amount that may be withheld.

(c) The agency shall send the notice described in division (B)(1)(b) of this section to the obligor, and shall attach to the notice an additional notice requiring the obligor immediately to notify the child support enforcement agency, in writing, of any change in employment, including self-employment, and of the availability of any other sources of income that can be the subject of any withholding or deduction requirement described in division (B) of this section. The agency shall serve the notices upon the obligor at the same time as service of the administrative support order or, if the administrative support order previously has been issued, shall send the notices to the obligor by regular mail at the obligor's last known address at the same time that it sends the notice described in division (B)(1)(b) of this section to the payor. The notification required of the obligor shall include a description of the nature of any new employment or income source, the name, business address, and telephone number of any new employer or income source, and any other information reasonably required by the agency. No obligor shall fail to give the notification as required by division (B)(1)(c) of this section.

(2)(a) If the child support enforcement agency determines that the obligor has funds on deposit in any account in a financial institution under the jurisdiction of the court, the agency may require any financial institution in which the obligor's funds are on deposit to deduct from the obligor's account a specified amount for support in satisfaction of the administrative support order, to begin the deduction no later than fourteen working days following the date the notice was mailed to the financial institution under divisions (A)(2) or (3) and (B)(2)(b) of this section, to send the amount deducted to the division of child support in the department of job and family services pursuant to section 5101.325 of the Revised Code, to send that amount to the division immediately but not later than seven working days after the date the latest deduction was made, to provide the date on which the amount was deducted, and to continue the deduction at intervals specified in the notice until further notice from the agency. To the extent possible, the amount specified in the notice to be deducted shall satisfy the amount ordered for support in the administrative support order plus any arrearages that may be owed by the obligor under any prior court or administrative support order that pertained to the same child or spouse, notwithstanding the limitations of sections 2329.66, 2329.70, and 2716.13 of the Revised Code.

(b) If the agency imposes a deduction requirement under division (B)(2)(a) of this section, it, within the applicable period of time specified in division (A) of this section, shall send to the financial institution by regular mail a notice that contains all of the information set forth in divisions (B)(2)(b)(i) to (viii) of this section. The notice is final and is enforceable by the court. The notice shall contain all of the following:

(i) The amount to be deducted from the obligor's account;

(ii) A statement that the financial institution is required to send the amount deducted to the division of child support immediately, but not later than seven working days, after the date the last deduction was made and is required to report to the agency the date on which the amount was deducted from the obligor's account;

(iii) A statement that the deduction is binding upon the financial institution until further notice from the court or agency;

(iv) A statement that the withholding in accordance with the notice and under the provisions of this section has priority over any other legal process under the law of this state against the same account;

(v) The date on which the notice was mailed and a statement that the financial institution is required to implement the deduction no later than fourteen working days following the date the notice was mailed and is required to continue the deduction at the intervals specified in the notice;

(vi) A requirement that the financial institution promptly notify the child support enforcement agency, in writing, within ten days after the date of any termination of the account from which the deduction is being made and notify the agency, in writing, of the opening of a new account at that financial institution, the account number of the new account, the name of any other known financial institutions in which the obligor has any accounts, and the numbers of those accounts;

(vii) A requirement that the financial institution include in all notices the obligor's last known mailing address, last known residence address, and social security number;

(viii) A statement that, in addition to the amount deducted for support, the financial institution may deduct a fee from the obligor's account as a charge for its services in complying with the administrative order and a specification of the amount that may be deducted.

(c) The agency shall send the notice described in division (B)(2)(b) of this section to the obligor and shall attach to the notice an additional notice requiring the obligor immediately to notify the child support enforcement agency, in writing, of any change in the status of the account from which the amount of support is being deducted or the opening of a new account with any financial institution, of the commencement of employment, including self-employment, or of the availability of any other sources of income that can be the subject of any withholding or deduction requirement described in division (B) of this section. The agency shall serve the notices upon the obligor at the same time as service of the administrative support order or, if the support order previously has been issued, shall send the notices to the obligor by regular mail at the obligor's last known address at the same time that it sends the notice described in division (B)(2)(b) of this section to the obligor. The additional notice also shall notify the obligor that upon commencement of employment, the obligor may request the agency to cancel its financial institution account deduction notice and instead issue a notice requiring the withholding of an amount from the obligor's personal earnings for support in accordance with division (B)(1) of this section and that upon commencement of employment the agency may cancel its financial institution account deduction notice and instead will issue a notice requiring the withholding of an amount from the obligor's personal earnings for support in accordance with division (B)(1) of this section. The notification required of the obligor shall include a description of the nature of any new accounts opened at a financial institution located in the county in which the agency is located, the name and business address of that financial institution, a description of the nature of any new employment or income source, the name, business address, and telephone number of any new employer or income source, and any other information reasonably required by the agency.

(C) If an agency issues or modifies an administrative support order under section 3111.20, 3111.211, or 3111.22 of the Revised Code and issues one or more notices described in division (B) of this section, the agency to the extent possible shall issue a sufficient number of notices under division (B) of this section to provide that the aggregate amount withheld or deducted under those notices satisfies the amount ordered for support in the administrative support order plus any arrearages that may be owed by the obligor under any prior court or administrative support order that pertained to the same child or spouse, notwithstanding any applicable limitations of sections 2329.66, 2329.70, 2716.02, 2716.041, 2716.05, 2716.13, and 4123.67 of the Revised Code. However, in no case shall the aggregate amount withheld pursuant to a withholding notice issued under division (B)(1) of this section and any fees withheld pursuant to the notice as a charge for services exceed the maximum amount permitted under section 303(b) of the "Consumer Credit Protection Act," 15 U.S.C. 1673(b).

(D) When two or more withholding notices that are described in division (B)(1) of this section are received by a payor, the payor shall comply with all of the requirements contained in the notices to the extent that the total amount withheld from the obligor's income does not exceed the maximum amount permitted under section 303(b) of the "Consumer Credit Protection Act," 15 U.S.C. 1673(b), withhold amounts in accordance with the allocation set forth in divisions (D)(1) and (2) of this section, notify each agency that issued one of the notices of the allocation, and give priority to amounts designated in each notice as current support in the following manner:

(1) If the total of the amounts designated in the notices as current support exceeds the amount available for withholding under section 303(b) of the "Consumer Credit Protection Act," 15 U.S.C. 1673(b), the payor shall allocate to each notice an amount for current support

equal to the amount designated in that notice as current support multiplied by a fraction in which the numerator is the amount of income available for withholding and the denominator is the total amount designated in all of the notices as current support.

(2) If the total of the amounts designated in the notices as current support does not exceed the amount available for withholding under section 303(b) of the "Consumer Credit Protection Act," the payor shall pay all of the amounts designated as current support in the notices and shall allocate to each notice an amount for past-due support equal to the amount designated in that notice as past-due support multiplied by a fraction in which the numerator is the amount of income remaining available for withholding after the payment of current support and the denominator is the total amount designated in all of the notices orders [*sic*] as past-due support.

(E)(1) Except when a provision specifically authorizes or requires service other than as described in this division, service of any notice on any party, a financial institution, or a payor, for purposes of division (A) or (B) of this section, shall be made by ordinary first class mail directed to the addressee at the addressee's last known address, or, in the case of a corporation, at its usual place of doing business. A notice shall be considered to have been served when it is mailed.

(2) Each party to an administrative support order shall notify the child support enforcement agency of the party's current mailing address, current residence address, current residence telephone number, and current driver's license number, at the time of the issuance or modification of the order and, until further notice of the agency that issues the order, shall notify the agency of any change in that information immediately after the change occurs. No person shall fail to give the notice as required by division (E)(2) of this section.

(3) Each administrative support order issued pursuant to this section shall contain a notice that states the following in boldfaced type and in all capital letters:

"EACH PARTY TO THIS SUPPORT ORDER MUST NOTIFY THE CHILD SUPPORT ENFORCEMENT AGENCY IN WRITING OF HIS OR HER CURRENT MAILING ADDRESS, CURRENT RESIDENCE ADDRESS, CURRENT RESIDENCE TELEPHONE NUMBER, CURRENT DRIVER'S LICENSE NUMBER, AND OF ANY CHANGES IN THAT INFORMATION. EACH PARTY MUST NOTIFY THE AGENCY OF ALL CHANGES UNTIL FURTHER NOTICE FROM THE AGENCY. IF YOU ARE THE OBLIGOR UNDER THE SUPPORT ORDER AND YOU FAIL TO MAKE THE REQUIRED NOTIFICATIONS, YOU MAY BE FINED UP TO $50 FOR A FIRST OFFENSE, $100 FOR A SECOND OFFENSE, AND $500 FOR EACH SUBSEQUENT OFFENSE.

IF YOU ARE AN OBLIGOR AND YOU FAIL TO MAKE THE REQUIRED NOTIFICATIONS, YOU MAY NOT RECEIVE NOTICE OF THE FOLLOWING ENFORCEMENT ACTIONS AGAINST YOU: IMPOSITION OF LIENS AGAINST YOUR PROPERTY; LOSS OF YOUR PROFESSIONAL OR OCCUPATIONAL LICENSE, DRIVER'S LICENSE, AND RECREATIONAL LICENSE; WITHHOLDING FROM YOUR INCOME; ACCESS RESTRICTION AND DEDUCTION FROM YOUR ACCOUNTS IN FINANCIAL INSTITUTIONS; AND ANY OTHER ACTION PERMITTED BY LAW TO OBTAIN MONEY FROM YOU TO SATISFY YOUR SUPPORT OBLIGATION."

(4)(a) The parent who is the residential parent and legal custodian of a child for whom an administrative support order is issued or the person who otherwise has custody of a child for whom an administrative support order is issued immediately shall notify, and the obligor under an administrative support order may notify, the child support enforcement agency of any reason for which an administrative support order should terminate, including, but not limited to, the child's attainment of the age of majority if the child no longer attends an accredited high school on a full-time basis; the child ceasing to attend such a high school on a full-time basis after attaining the age of majority; or the death, marriage, emancipation, enlistment in the armed services, deportation, or change of legal or physical custody of the child. Upon receipt of a notice pursuant to this division, the agency immediately shall conduct an investigation to determine if any reason exists for which the administrative support order should terminate. The agency may conduct such an investigation regardless of whether a parent or person with custody sends a notice that the order should terminate. If the agency determines the order should terminate, it immediately shall terminate the administrative support order.

(b) Upon receipt of a notice given pursuant to division (E)(4)(a) of this section, the agency shall direct the division of child support to impound any funds received for the child pursuant to the administrative support order and the agency shall set the case for an administrative hearing for a determination of whether the administrative support order should be terminated or modified or whether the agency should take any other appropriate action.

(c) If the child support enforcement agency terminates an administrative support order pursuant to divisions (E)(4)(a) and (b) of this section, the termination of the support order also terminates any withholding or deduction order as described in division (B) of this section issued prior to December 31, 1993, and any withholding or deduction notice as described in division (B) of this section issued on or after December 31, 1993. Upon the termination of any withholding or deduction order or notice, the agency immediately shall notify each payor or financial institution required to withhold or deduct a sum of money for the payment of support under the terminated withholding or deduction order or notice that the order or notice has been terminated and that it is required to cease all withholding or deduction under the order or notice.

(d) The director of job and family services shall adopt rules that provide for both of the following:

(i) The payment to the appropriate person of any funds that the division of child support has impounded under division (E)(4)(b) of this section, consistent with the agency's determination pursuant to divisions (E)(4)(a) and (b) of this section;

(ii) The return to the appropriate person of any other payments made pursuant to an administrative support order, if the payments were made at any time after the administrative support order has been terminated pursuant to divisions (E)(4)(a) and (b) of this section.

(5) If any party to an administrative support order requests a modification of the administrative support order, the agency shall proceed as provided in section 3111.27 of the Revised Code. If the obligor is in default under the administrative support order, the agency shall proceed as provided in division (B) of section 3113.21 of the Revised Code. If any person otherwise files an action to enforce an administrative support order, the agency shall proceed as provided in sections 3111.20 to 3111.28 of the Revised Code.

(F)(1)(a) Upon receipt of a notice that a lump-sum payment of one hundred fifty dollars or more is to be paid to the obligor, the agency shall do either of the following:

(i) If the obligor is in default under the administrative support order or has any unpaid arrearages under the administrative support order, issue an administrative order requiring the transmittal of the lump-sum payment to the division of child support;

(ii) If the obligor is not in default under the administrative support order and does not have any unpaid arrearages under the support order, issue an administrative order directing the person who gave the notice to the agency to immediately pay the full amount of the lump-sum payment to the obligor.

(b) Upon receipt of notice that a lump-sum payment of less than one hundred fifty dollars is to be paid to the obligor, the agency may take the action described in division (F)(1)(a) of this section.

(2) Upon receipt of any moneys pursuant to division (F)(1)(a) of this section, the division of child support shall pay the amount of the lump-sum payment that is necessary to discharge all of the obligor's arrearages to the obligee and, within two business days after its receipt of the money, any amount that is remaining after the payment of the arrearages to the obligor.

(G)(1) Any administrative support order, or modification of an administrative support order, that is subject to this section shall contain the date of birth and social security number of the obligor.

(2) No withholding or deduction notice described in division (B) of this section shall contain any information other than the information specifically required by division (B) or (G)(3) of this section or by any other section of the Revised Code and any additional information that the issuing agency determines may be necessary to comply with the notice.

(3) Each withholding or deduction notice described in division (B) of this section shall include notice of all of the following:

(a) That the child support enforcement agency may bring an action under section 3111.28 of the Revised Code requesting the court to find the payor or financial institution in contempt pursuant to section 2705.02 of the Revised Code if the payor or financial institution fails to comply with the withholding or deduction notice;

(b) That, if the payor or financial institution fails to comply with the withholding or deduction notice, that failure to comply is contempt pursuant to section 2705.02 of the Revised Code.

(H) No withholding or deduction notice described in division (B) of this section and issued under this section or any other section of the Revised Code shall be terminated solely because the obligor pays any part or all of the arrearages under the administrative support order.

(I)(1) Except as provided in division (I)(2) of this section, if child support arrearages are owed by an obligor to the obligee and to the department of job and family services, any payments received on the arrearages by the division of child support first shall be paid to the obligee until the arrearages owed to the obligee are paid in full.

(2) Division (I)(1) of this section does not apply to the collection of past-due child support from refunds of paid federal taxes pursuant to section 5101.32 of the Revised Code or of overdue child support from refunds of paid state income taxes pursuant to sections 5101.321 and 5747.121 of the Revised Code.

(1999 H 471, eff. 7-1-00; 1998 S 170, eff. 3-30-99; 1997 H 352, eff. 1-1-98; 1997 H 408, eff. 10-1-97; 1996 S 292, eff. 11-6-96; 1996 H 710, § 7, eff. 6-11-96; 1995 H 167, eff. 6-11-96; 1993 H 173, eff. 12-31-93; 1992 S 10)

Uncodified Law

1996 H 710, § 15: See Uncodified Law under 3111.20.

Historical and Statutory Notes

Ed. Note: Former 3111.23 repealed by 1982 H 245, eff. 6-29-82; 1953 H 1; GC 8006-23; Source—GC 12132.

Ed. Note: The effective date of the amendment of this section by 1995 H 167 was changed from 11-15-96 to 6-11-96 by 1996 H 710, § 7, eff. 6-11-96.

Pre-1953 H 1 Amendments: 124 v S 65

Amendment Note: 1999 H 471 substituted "job and family" for "human" in divisions (A)(5), (B)(1)(a), (B)(2)(a), and (I)(1); and substituted "director of job and family services" for "department of human services" in division (E)(4)(d).

Amendment Note: 1998 S 170 substituted "any applicable" for "the" and inserted "2716.041," in division (B)(1)(a); and substituted "any applicable" for "the" and inserted "2716.02, 2716.041, 2716.05," in division (C).

Amendment Note: 1997 H 352 rewrote this section; see *Baldwin's Ohio Legislative Service Annotated*, 1997, p 9/L-2566, or the OH-LEGIS or OH-LEGIS-OLD database on WESTLAW, for text of previous version.

Amendment Note: 1997 H 408 deleted "designated" before and "pursuant to section 2301.35 of the Revised Code" after "for that county" in divisions (B)(1)(a), (B)(2)(a), (B)(3)(a), (B)(4)(a), and (B)(5)(a); and made other nonsubstantive changes.

Amendment Note: 1996 S 292 inserted "and section 2301.42 of the Revised Code and the rules adopted pursuant to division (C) of that section, if child support arrearages are owed by an obligor to the obligee and to the department of human services, any payments received on the arrearages by the child support enforcement agency first shall be paid to the obligee until the arrearages owed to the obligee are paid in full" in division (I)(1); and made changes to reflect gender neutral language and other nonsubstantive changes.

Amendment Note: 1995 H 167 substantially rewrote this section; see *Baldwin's Ohio Legislative Service*, 1995, page 8/L-3038.

Amendment Note: 1993 H 173 rewrote this section; see *Baldwin's Ohio Legislative Service*, 1993 Laws of Ohio, H 173, p 5-1012.

Cross References

Penalty: 3111.99(C), (D)

Alternative retirement plans for employees of public institutions of higher education, exemption from legal process, applicability, 3305.08

Child support enforcement agency, powers and duties, 2301.35

Duty of parents to support children of unemancipated minor children, 3109.19

Income and benefits subject to withholding, 145.56, 742.47, 3307.71, 3309.66, 3770.07, 5505.22

Payments to child support division, 2301.36

Prisoner earnings, distribution for child support, 3113.16

Property exempt from legal purposes, 2329.66

Public employees retirement board, required information, 145.27

Reports by employers to child support division, entry of information into directory, comparison against case registry, 5101.312

School employees retirement board, required information, 3309.22

Teachers retirement board, required information, 3307.21

Ohio Administrative Code References

Collection of child support through the withholding of unemployment compensation, OAC 5101:1-30-79

Enforcement of orders, lump sum payments, OAC 5101:1-30-428, 5101:1-30-49

Income withholding and other "division (D)" orders, OAC 5101:1-30-411 et seq.

Library References

Children Out-Of-Wedlock ⚷64 to 69.
WESTLAW Topic No. 76H.
C.J.S. Children Out-of-Wedlock §§ 120 to 129.

OJur 3d: 45, Exemptions § 48, 49; 47, Family Law § 1041, 1047, 1048, 1244, 1253 to 1261, 1263 to 1267, 1327

Carlin, Baldwin's Ohio Practice, *Merrick-Rippner Probate Law* § 18.2, 18.3, 19.1, 19.2, 19.3, 19.4, 19.6, 19.7, 19.8, 19.10, 92.1, 98.29, 98.31, 108.19, 108.22, 108.24, 108.33, 108.34, 108.38, 108.39 (1997)

Sowald & Morganstern, Baldwin's Ohio Practice, *Domestic Relations Law* § 3.38, 22.6, 22.20, 22.21 (1997)

Wasil, Waite, & Mastrangelo, Ohio Workers' Compensation Law § 15:22

Law Review and Journal Commentaries

Bankruptcy Reform Act of 1994—What the Bankruptcy Code Giveth, Domestic Relations Courts (and Congress) Taketh Away, C.R. "Chip" Bowles. 8 Domestic Rel J Ohio 17 (March/April 1996).

BWC and Self-Insured Employer Liability for Spousal and Child Support, C. Jeffrey Waite. 11 Domestic Rel J Ohio 17 (March/April 1999).

Looking to Unwed Dads to Fill the Public Purse: A Disturbing Wave in Welfare Reform, Roger J.R. Levesque. 32 J Fam L 1 (1993-94).

Notes of Decisions and Opinions

Bankruptcy 2
Consumer Credit Protection Act 1

---

1. Consumer Credit Protection Act

Entire amount ordered for child support may not be withheld from wages if it exceeds guidelines of Consumer Credit Protection Act and when such is case, obligor must supplement payments from withheld wages from other sources, such as additional job, income-producing investments or assets. In re Yeauger (Union 1992) 83 Ohio App.3d 493, 615 N.E.2d 289.

2. Bankruptcy

Automatic stay precluded governmental child support enforcement agency from attempting collection of arrearage from Chapter 13 debtor's postpetition earnings, in that such earnings were property of debtor's bankruptcy estate. In re Walter (Bkrtcy.N.D.Ohio 1993) 153 B.R. 38.

Because child support obligations are typically nondischargeable, in instances where Chapter 13 plan calls for less than full payment of arrearages, relief from automatic stay may be available to allow payee or appropriate governmental agency to pursue only those amounts not provided for in plan. In re Walter (Bkrtcy.N.D.Ohio 1993) 153 B.R. 38.

3111.231 Administrative order requiring obligor to seek employment or participate in work activity

If a child support enforcement agency otherwise required by division (A) of section 3111.23 of the Revised Code to issue a withholding or deduction notice under division (B) of that section is unable to issue the notice because none of the conditions specified in division (B) of that section for issuing the notice apply to the obligor, the agency shall issue an administrative order requiring the obligor, if able to engage in employment, to seek employment or participate in a work activity to which a recipient of assistance under Title IV-A of the "Social Security Act," 49 Stat. 620 (1935), 42 U.S.C.A. 301, as amended, may be assigned as specified in section 407(d) of the "Social Security Act," 42 U.S.C.A. 607(d), as amended. The agency shall include in the order a requirement that the obligor notify the agency on obtaining employment or income, or ownership of any asset with a value of five hundred dollars or more. The agency may issue the order regardless of whether the obligee to whom the obligor owes support is a recipient of assistance under Title IV-A of the "Social Security Act."

If an obligor is ordered to participate in a work activity, the child support enforcement agency shall oversee the obligor's participation in accordance with rules the director of job and family services shall adopt in accordance with Chapter 119. of the Revised Code. The agency may contract with one or more persons or government entities to carry out some or all of its oversight duties.

If an obligor fails to comply with an administrative order, the agency shall submit a request to a court for the court to take action under division (D)(4) of section 3113.21 of the Revised Code.

(1999 H 471, eff. 7-1-00; 1997 H 352, eff. 1-1-98)

Historical and Statutory Notes

Amendment Note: 1999 H 471 substituted "director of job and family services" for "department of human services" in the second paragraph.

Cross References

Payments to child support division, 2301.36

Ohio Administrative Code References

Income withholding and other "division (D)" orders, OAC 5101:1-30-411

Library References

OJur 3d: 47, Family Law § 1253, 1266

Carlin, Baldwin's Ohio Practice, *Merrick-Rippner Probate Law* § 18.3, 19.1, 19.2, 19.3, 19.4, 19.6, 19.7, 19.10, 98.29, 98.31, 108.19, 108.34, 108.39 (1997)

Sowald & Morganstern, Baldwin's Ohio Practice, *Domestic Relations Law* § 22.20 (1997)

3111.24 Withholding fees; combined payments; distributions

(A)(1) For purposes of this section, a withholding or deduction order that was issued prior to December 31, 1993, under division (A)(1), (2), (3), (4), or (5) of section 3111.23 of the Revised Code as the division existed prior to that date and that has not been terminated on or after December 31, 1993, shall be considered to be a withholding or deduction notice issued under divisions (A) and (B)(1) or (2) of section 3111.23 of the Revised Code.

(2) A payor required to withhold a specified amount from the income of an employee pursuant to a withholding notice issued under section 3111.23 of the Revised Code for purposes of support also may deduct from the income of the person, in addition to the amount withheld for purposes of support, a fee of two dollars or an amount not to exceed one per cent of the amount withheld for purposes of support, whichever is greater, as a charge for its services in complying with the withholding requirement included in the withholding notice. A financial institution required to deduct funds from an account pursuant to a deduction notice issued under divisions (A) and (B)(2) of section 3111.23 of the Revised Code for purposes of support may deduct from the account of the person, in addition to the amount deducted for purposes of support, a fee of five dollars or an amount not to exceed the lowest rate that it charges, if any, for a debit transaction in a similar account, whichever is less, as a charge for its service in complying with the deduction requirement included in the deduction notice.

The entire amount withheld or deducted pursuant to a withholding or deduction notice issued under divisions (A) and (B) of section 3111.23 of the Revised Code for purposes of support shall be forwarded to the division of child support in the department of job and family services immediately, but no later than seven working days, after the withholding or deduction, as directed in the withholding or deduction notice.

(B) If a payor or financial institution is required to withhold or deduct a specified amount from the income or savings of more than one obligor pursuant to a withholding or deduction notice issued under divisions (A) and (B) of section 3111.23 of the Revised Code and is required to forward the amounts withheld or deducted to the division of child support, the payor or financial institution may combine all of the amounts to be forwarded in one payment, provided the payment is accompanied by a list that clearly identifies each obligor who is covered by the payment and the portion of the payment that is attributable to that obligor.

(C) Upon receipt of any amount forwarded from a payor or financial institution the division of child support shall distribute the amount to the obligee within two business days of its receipt of the amount forwarded. The director of job and family services may adopt, amend, and rescind rules in accordance with Chapter 119. of the Revised Code to assist in the implementation of this division.

(D) A payor or financial institution shall not be subject to criminal or civil liability for compliance, in accordance with this section, with a withholding or deduction notice issued pursuant to division (B) of section 3111.23 of the Revised Code.

(1999 H 471, eff. 7-1-00; 1997 H 352, eff. 1-1-98; 1993 H 173, eff. 12-31-93; 1992 S 10)

Historical and Statutory Notes

Ed. Note: Former 3111.24 repealed by 1982 H 245, eff. 6-29-82; 1953 H 1; GC 8006-24; Source—GC 12133.

Pre-1953 H 1 Amendments: 124 v S 65

Amendment Note: 1999 H 471 substituted "job and family" for "human" in the second paragraph in division (A)(2); and substituted "director of job and family services" for "department of human services" in division (C).

Amendment Note: 1997 H 352 rewrote this section, which prior thereto read:

"(A)(1) For purposes of this section, a withholding or deduction order that was issued prior to December 31, 1993, under division (A)(1), (2), (3), (4), or (5) of section 3111.23 of the Revised Code as the division existed prior to that date and that has not been terminated on or after December 31, 1993, shall be considered to be a withholding or deduction notice issued under divisions (A) and (B)(1), (2), (3), (4), or (5) of section 3111.23 of the Revised Code.

"(2) An employer required to withhold a specified amount from the personal earnings of an employee pursuant to a withholding notice issued under section 3111.23 of the Revised Code for purposes of support also may deduct from the personal earnings of the person, in addition to the amount withheld for purposes of support, a fee of two dollars or an amount not to exceed one per cent of the amount withheld for purposes of support, whichever is greater, as a charge for its services in complying with the withholding requirement included in the withholding notice. An employer that is paying a person's workers' compensation benefits and that is required to withhold a specified amount from a person's workers' compensation benefits pursuant to a withholding notice issued under divisions (A) and (B)(2) of section 3111.23 of the Revised Code for purposes of support also may deduct from the workers' compensation benefits, in addition to the amount withheld for purposes of support, a fee of two dollars or an amount not to exceed one per cent of the amount withheld for purposes of support, whichever is greater, as a charge for its services in complying with the withholding requirement included in the withholding notice. A financial institution required to deduct funds from an account pursuant to a deduction notice issued under divisions (A) and (B)(5) of section 3111.23 of the Revised Code for purposes of support may deduct from the account of the person, in addition to the amount deducted for purposes of support, a fee of five dollars or an amount not to exceed the lowest rate that it charges, if any, for a debit transaction in a similar account, whichever is less, as a charge for its service in complying with the deduction requirement included in the deduction notice. The public employees retirement board, the board, board of trustees, or other governing entity of any municipal retirement system, the board of trustees of the police and firemen's disability and pension fund, the state teachers retirement board, the school employees retirement board, the state highway patrol retirement board, and a person paying or otherwise distributing an obligor's income required to withhold or deduct a specified amount from an obligor's pension, annuity, allowance, other benefit, or other source of income pursuant to a withholding or deduction notice issued under divisions (A) and (B)(3) or (4) of section 3111.23 of the Revised Code for purposes of support also may deduct from the obligor's pension, annuity, allowance, other benefit, or other source of income, a fee of two dollars or an amount not to exceed one per cent of the amount withheld or deducted, whichever is less, as a charge for its services in complying with the withholding or deduction requirement included in the withholding or deduction notice.

"The entire amount withheld or deducted pursuant to a withholding or deduction notice issued under divisions (A) and (B) of section 3111.23 of the Revised Code for purposes of support shall be forwarded to the child support enforcement agency immediately, but no later than ten working days, after the withholding or deduction, as directed in the withholding or deduction notice.

"(B) If an employer, a financial institution, an employer that is paying an obligor's workers' compensation benefits, the public employees retirement board, the board, board of trustees, or other governing entity of any municipal retirement system, the board of trustees of the police and firemen's disability and pension fund, the state teachers retirement board, the school employees retirement board, the state highway patrol retirement board, the person paying or otherwise distributing an obligor's income, or the bureau of workers' compensation is required to withhold or deduct a specified amount from the personal earnings, payments, pensions, annuities, allowances, benefits, other sources of income, or savings of more than one obligor pursuant to a withholding or deduction notice issued under divisions (A) and (B) of section 3111.23 of the Revised Code and is required to forward the amounts withheld or deducted to the child support enforcement agency, the employer, the public employees retirement board, the board, board of trustees, or other governing entity of any municipal retirement system, the board of trustees of the police and firemen's disability and pension fund, the state teachers retirement board, the school employees retirement board, the state highway patrol retirement board, the person paying or otherwise distributing an obligor's income, the financial institution, the employer that is paying an obligor's workers' compensation benefits, or the bureau of workers' compensation may combine all of the amounts to be forwarded in one payment, provided the payment is accompanied by a list that clearly identifies each obligor who is covered by the payment and the portion of the payment that is attributable to that obligor.

"(C) Upon receipt of any amount forwarded from an employer, a financial institution, an employer that is paying a person's workers' compensation benefits, the public employees retirement board, the board, board of trustees, or other governing entity of any municipal retirement system, the board of trustees of the police and firemen's disability and pension fund, the state teachers retirement board, the school employees retirement board, the state highway patrol retirement board, the person paying or otherwise distributing an obligor's income, or the bureau of workers' compensation under this section, a child support enforcement agency shall distribute the amount to the obligee within two business days of its receipt of the amount forwarded. The department of human services may adopt, amend, and rescind rules in accordance with Chapter 119. of the Revised Code to assist child support enforcement agencies in the implementation of this division."

Amendment Note: 1993 H 173 added division (A)(1); designated division (A)(2); and changed references to administrative withholding orders to references to withholding or deduction requirements and orders throughout divisions (A) and (B).

Library References

Children Out-Of-Wedlock ⚷64 to 69.
WESTLAW Topic No. 76H.
C.J.S. Children Out-of-Wedlock §§ 120 to 129.

OJur 3d: 47, Family Law § 1262, 1263

Carlin, Baldwin's Ohio Practice, *Merrick-Rippner Probate Law* § 18.2, 18.3, 19.1, 19.2, 19.3, 19.4, 19.6, 19.7, 19.8, 19.10, 98.29, 98.31, 108.19, 108.22, 108.24, 108.33, 108.34, 108.38, 108.39 (1997)

Sowald & Morganstern, Baldwin's Ohio Practice, *Domestic Relations Law* § 22.20, 22.21 (1997)

3111.241 Health insurance coverage for children

(A) As used in this section, "insurer" means any person that is authorized to engage in the business of insurance in this state under Title XXXIX of the Revised Code, any health insuring corporation, and any legal entity that is self-insured and provides benefits to its employees or members.

(B) In any proceeding in which an administrative support order is issued under section 3111.20, 3111.211, or 3111.22 of the Revised Code, the child support enforcement agency shall determine the parent responsible for the health care of the children subject to the order and shall include in the order one of the following:

(1) A requirement that the obligor under the child support order obtain health insurance coverage for the children if coverage is available at a reasonable cost through a group health insurance or health care policy, contract, or plan offered by the obligor's employer or through any other group health insurance or health care policy, contract, or plan available to the obligor and if it is not available for a more reasonable cost to the obligee under the administrative child support order;

(2) A requirement that the obligee obtain health insurance coverage for the children if coverage is available through a group health insurance or health care policy, contract, or plan offered by the obligee's employer or through any other group health insurance or health care policy, contract, or plan available to the obligee and if it is available at a more reasonable cost than such coverage is available to the obligor;

(3) If health insurance coverage for the children is not available at a reasonable cost through a group health insurance or health care policy, contract, or plan offered by the obligor's employer or through any other group health insurance or health care policy, contract,

or plan available to the obligor or the obligee, a requirement that the obligor and the obligee share liability for the cost of the medical and health care needs of the children, under an equitable formula established by the agency, and a requirement that if, after the issuance of the order, health insurance coverage for the children becomes available at a reasonable cost through a group health insurance or health care policy, contract, or plan offered by the obligor's or obligee's employer or through any other group health insurance or health care policy, contract, or plan available to the obligor or obligee, the obligor or obligee to whom the coverage becomes available immediately inform the agency of that fact;

(4) A requirement that both the obligor and the obligee obtain health insurance coverage for the children if health insurance coverage is available for the children at a reasonable cost to both the obligor and the obligee and dual coverage by both parents would provide for coordination of medical benefits without unnecessary duplication of coverage.

(C) An administrative support order issued pursuant to section 3111.20 or 3111.22 of the Revised Code shall contain all of the following:

(1) If the obligor is required under division (B)(1) of this section, the obligee is required under division (B)(2) of this section, or both the obligor and obligee are required under division (B)(4) of this section, to provide health insurance coverage for the children, a requirement that the obligor or obligee, whoever is required to obtain health insurance coverage, provide the other parent with information regarding the benefits, limitations, and exclusions of the health insurance coverage, copies of any insurance forms necessary to receive reimbursement, payment, or other benefits under the health insurance coverage, and a copy of any necessary insurance cards, a requirement that the obligor or obligee, whoever is required to obtain health insurance coverage, submit a copy of the administrative order issued pursuant to division (B)(1), (2), or (4) of this section to the insurer at the time that the obligor or obligee, whoever is required to obtain health insurance coverage, makes application to enroll the children in the health insurance or health care policy, contract, or plan, and a requirement that the obligor or obligee, whoever is required to obtain health insurance coverage, furnish written proof to the child support enforcement agency that division (C)(1) of this section has been complied with;

(2) A list of the group health insurance and health care policies, contracts, and plans that the child support enforcement agency determines are available at a reasonable cost to the obligor or to the obligee and the name of the insurer that issues each policy, contract, or plan;

(3) A statement setting forth the name, address, and telephone number of the individual who is to be reimbursed for out-of-pocket medical, optical, hospital, dental, or prescription expenses paid for each child who is the subject of the administrative child support order and a statement that the insurer that provides the health insurance coverage for the children may continue making payment for medical, optical, hospital, dental, or prescription services directly to any health care provider in accordance with the applicable health insurance or health care policy, contract, or plan;

(4) A requirement that the obligor and the obligee designate the children as covered dependents under any health insurance or health care policy, contract, or plan for which they contract;

(5) A requirement that the obligor, the obligee, or both of them under a formula established by the child support enforcement agency pay copayment or deductible costs required under the health insurance or health care policy, contract, or plan that covers the children;

(6) A notice that the employer of the obligor or obligee required to obtain health insurance coverage is required to release to the other parent or the child support enforcement agency upon written request any necessary information on the health insurance coverage, including, but not limited to, the name and address of the insurer and any policy, contract, or plan number, and to otherwise comply with this section and any court order issued under this section;

(7) A statement setting forth the full name and date of birth of each child who is the subject of the administrative child support order;

(8) A requirement that the obligor and the obligee comply with any requirement described in division (B)(1), (2), and (4), and (C)(1) and (4) of this section that is contained in the order issued under section 3111.20, 3111.211, or 3111.22 of the Revised Code no later than thirty days after the issuance of the order.

(9) A notice that, if the obligor or obligee is required to obtain health insurance coverage pursuant to an administrative support order for the children and if the obligor or obligee fails to obtain the health insurance coverage, the child support enforcement agency will comply with division (D) of this section to obtain a court order requiring the obligor or obligee to obtain the health insurance coverage;

(10) A notice that states the following: "If the person required to obtain health care insurance coverage for the children subject to this administrative support order obtains new employment and the health insurance coverage for the children is provided through the previous employer, the agency shall comply with the requirements of division (E) of section 3111.241 of the Revised Code which may result in the issuance of a notice requiring the new employer to take whatever action is necessary to enroll the children in health care insurance coverage provided by the new employer."

(D) If an obligor or obligee required to obtain health insurance coverage pursuant to an administrative support order issued in accordance with this section does not obtain the required health insurance coverage within thirty days after the administrative support order is issued, the child support enforcement agency shall notify the court of common pleas of the county in which the agency is located in writing of the failure to comply with the administrative support order. On receipt of the notice from the agency, the court shall issue an order to the employer of the obligor or obligee required to obtain health insurance coverage requiring the employer to take whatever action is necessary to make application to enroll the obligor or obligee required to obtain health insurance coverage in any available group health insurance or health care policy, contract, or plan with coverage for the children, to submit a copy of the administrative support order to the insurer at the time that the employer makes application to enroll the children in the health insurance or health care policy, contract, or plan, and, if the application is accepted, to deduct from the wages or other income of the obligor or obligee required to obtain health insurance coverage the cost of the coverage for the children. On receipt of any court order under this division, the employer shall take whatever action is necessary to comply with the court order.

(E)(1) If an obligor or obligee is required to obtain health insurance coverage pursuant to an administrative support order in accordance with this section and the obligor or obligee obtains health insurance coverage for the children through an employer and subsequently obtains new employment, the child support enforcement agency shall investigate whether the new employer offers health insurance coverage that would cover the children. If the agency determines that the new employer provides health insurance coverage that would cover the children, the agency shall send a notice described in division (E)(2) of this section and a copy of the administrative support order to the new employer and shall send a copy of the notice to the obligor or obligee, whoever is required to obtain health insurance coverage under the administrative support order. On receipt of the notice, the new employer shall comply with its provisions.

(2) The notice required by division (E)(1) shall contain the following:

(a) A requirement that the new employer take whatever action is necessary to make application to enroll the obligor or obligee, whoever is required to obtain health insurance coverage, in any available group health insurance or health care policy, contract, or plan with coverage for the children;

(b) A requirement that the new employer submit a copy of the administrative support order requiring the obligor or obligee to obtain health care insurance for the children to the insurer at the time that the employer makes application to enroll the children in the health insurance or health care policy, contract, or plan;

(c) A requirement that, if the application is accepted, the new employer deduct from the wages or other income of the obligor or obligee, whoever is required to obtain the health insurance coverage, the cost of the coverage for the children;

(d) A statement that the provisions of the notice are final and enforceable by a court and are incorporated into the administrative support order unless the obligor or obligee required to obtain health insurance coverage, within ten days after the date on which the notice is sent, files a written request with the agency requesting modification of the administrative support order pursuant to section 3111.27 of the Revised Code.

(F) Any administrative support order issued in accordance with, or any court order issued under division (D) of, this section shall be binding upon the obligor and the obligee, their employers, and any insurer that provides health insurance coverage for either of them or their children. The agency shall send a copy of the administrative support order or court order by ordinary mail to the obligor, the obligee, and any employer that is subject to the administrative order or court order.

(G)(1) During the time that any administrative support order issued in accordance with, or court order issued under division (D) of, this section is in effect and after the employer has received a copy of the administrative support order or court order, the employer of the obligor or obligee required to comply with the administrative support order or court order shall comply with the administrative support order or court order and, upon request from the other parent or the agency, shall release to that other parent and the child support enforcement agency all information about the health insurance coverage that is necessary to ensure compliance with this section or any administrative support order issued in accordance with, or court order issued under division (D) of, this section, including, but not limited to, the name and address of the insurer and any policy, contract, or plan number. Any information provided by an employer pursuant to this division shall be used only for the purpose of the enforcement of the administrative support order or court order.

(2) Any employer who receives a copy of the administrative support order or court order shall notify the agency of any change in or the termination of the health insurance coverage that is maintained pursuant to the order.

(3) Any insurer that receives a copy of an administrative support order or court order issued in accordance with this section shall comply with this section, regardless of the residence of the children. If an insurer provides health insurance coverage for the children who are the subject of an administrative child support order in accordance with the administrative support order or court order issued under division (D) of this section, the insurer shall reimburse the parent, who is designated to receive reimbursement in the administrative support order, for covered out-of-pocket medical, optical, hospital, dental, or prescription expenses incurred on behalf of the children.

(H) If an obligee under an administrative child support order issued in accordance with this section is eligible for medical assistance under Chapter 5111. or 5115. of the Revised Code and the obligor has obtained health insurance coverage, the obligee shall notify any physician, hospital, or other provider of medical services for which medical assistance is available of the name and address of the obligor's insurer and of the number of the obligor's health insurance or health care policy, contract, or plan. Any physician, hospital, or other provider of medical services for which medical assistance is available under Chapter 5111. or 5115. of the Revised Code who is notified under this division of the existence of a health insurance or health care policy, contract, or plan with coverage for children who are eligible for medical assistance first shall bill the insurer for any services provided for those children. If the insurer fails to pay all or any part of a claim filed under this division by the physician, hospital, or other medical services provider and the services for which the claim is filed are covered by Chapter 5111. or 5115. of the Revised Code, the physician, hospital, or other medical services provider shall bill the remaining unpaid costs of the services in accordance with Chapter 5111. or 5115. of the Revised Code.

(I) Any obligor who fails to comply with an administrative support order issued in accordance with, or a court order issued under division (D) of, this section is liable to the obligee for any medical expenses incurred as a result of the failure to comply with the order. An obligee who fails to comply with an administrative support order issued in accordance with, or a court order issued under division (D) of, this section is liable to the obligor for any medical expenses incurred as a result of the failure to comply with the order.

(J) Nothing in this section shall be construed to require an insurer to accept for enrollment any child who does not meet the underwriting standards of the health insurance or health care policy, contract, or plan for which application is made.

(K) Whoever violates a court order issued under division (D) of this section may be punished as for contempt pursuant to section 2705.02 of the Revised Code.

(L) An administrative order issued pursuant to this section prior to the effective date of this amendment to provide for the health care needs of children subject to an administrative support order issued pursuant to former section 3111.21 or section 3111.20 or 3111.22 of the Revised Code shall remain in full force and effect and shall be considered a requirement included as part of the administrative support order. The administrative support order shall be subject to the provisions of this section on and after the effective date of this amendment.

(1997 H 352, eff. 1-1-98; 1997 S 67, eff. 6-4-97; 1996 H 710, § 7, eff. 6-11-96; 1995 H 167, eff. 6-11-96; 1995 H 249, eff. 7-17-95; 1992 S 10, eff. 7-15-92)

Uncodified Law

1996 H 710, § 15: See Uncodified Law under 3111.20.

Historical and Statutory Notes

Ed. Note: The effective date of the amendment of this section by 1995 H 167 was changed from 11-15-96 to 6-11-96 by 1996 H 710, § 7, eff. 6-11-96.

Amendment Note: 1997 H 352 rewrote this section; see *Baldwin's Ohio Legislative Service Annotated*, 1997, p 9/L-2581, or the OH-LEGIS or OH-LEGIS-OLD database on WESTLAW, for text of previous version.

Amendment Note: 1997 S 67 replaced references to prepaid dental plans, medical care corporations, health care corporations, dental care corporations and health maintenance organizations with language pertaining to health insuring corporations in division (A); and made other nonsubstantive changes.

Amendment Note: 1995 H 167 added references to section 3111.20 in the first paragraph in division (B) and in division (C); added a reference to Chapter 5111 in the second sentence in division (G); and rewrote division (J), which previously read:

"(J) If any person fails to comply with an administrative order issued under this section, the agency may bring an action under section 3111.242 of the Revised Code in the juvenile court of the county in which the agency is located requesting the court to issue an order requiring the obligor or any other person to comply with the agency's administrative order. If the person fails to comply with any court order issued under this division, he is in contempt of court."

Amendment Note: 1995 H 249 substituted "5115." for "5113." in the first sentence in division (G); substituted "Chapter 5115." for "section 5111.02" in the second sentence in division (G); and inserted "and the services for which the claim is filed are covered by Chapter 5111. or 5115. of the Revised Code" and substituted "5115." for "5113." in the third sentence in division (G).

Cross References

Health insurance coverage, enrollment of child under family coverage, 3924.48, 3924.49

Ohio Administrative Code References

Health insurance, establishment and enforcement, OAC 5101:1-29-353, 5101:1-29-354

Library References

Children Out-Of-Wedlock ⟹67.
Divorce ⟹308.
Parent and Child ⟹3.3(7).
WESTLAW Topic Nos. 76H, 134, 285.
C.J.S. Children Out-of-Wedlock §§ 122 to 126.
C.J.S. Divorce §§ 669 to 671, 673 to 683, 700 to 705, 708.
C.J.S. Parent and Child §§ 81, 89.
OJur 3d: 47, Family Law § 1043, 1268

Carlin, Baldwin's Ohio Practice, *Merrick-Rippner Probate Law* § 18.2, 18.3, 19.1, 19.2, 19.3, 19.4, 19.6, 19.7, 19.8, 19.10, 98.29, 98.31, 108.19, 108.22, 108.24, 108.29, 108.33, 108.34, 108.39 (1997)

Sowald & Morganstern, Baldwin's Ohio Practice, *Domestic Relations Law* § 3.38, 22.15 (1997)

3111.242 Contempt

(A) If an obligor or any other person fails to comply with an administrative order issued under former section 3111.21 or section 3111.20, 3111.211, or 3111.22 of the Revised Code, the child support enforcement agency that issued the administrative order may request the juvenile court of the county in which the agency is located to find the obligor or other person in contempt pursuant to section 2705.02 of the Revised Code.

(B) If an alleged father or natural mother willfully fails to submit to genetic testing, or the alleged father, natural mother, or any other person who is the custodian of the child willfully fails to submit the child to genetic testing, as required by an order for genetic testing issued under section 3111.22 of the Revised Code, the child support enforcement agency that issued the order may request that the juvenile court of the county in which the agency is located find the alleged father, natural mother, or other person in contempt pursuant to section 2705.02 of the Revised Code.

(1997 H 352, eff. 1-1-98; 1996 H 710, § 7, eff. 6-11-96; 1995 H 167, eff. 6-11-96; 1992 S 10, eff. 7-15-92)

Uncodified Law

1996 H 710, § 15: See Uncodified Law under 3111.20.

Historical and Statutory Notes

Ed. Note: The effective date of the amendment of this section by 1995 H 167 was changed from 11-15-96 to 6-11-96 by 1996 H 710, § 7, eff. 6-11-96.

Amendment Note: 1997 H 352 designated division (A) and inserted "former section 3111.21 or", substituted "3111.211" for "3111.21", and deleted ", or 3111.241" after "3111.22", therein; added division (B); and made other nonsubstantive changes.

Amendment Note: 1995 H 167 rewrote this section, which previously read:

"If an obligor or any other person fails to comply with an administrative order issued under section 3111.241 of the Revised Code, the child support enforcement agency that issued the administrative order may request the juvenile court of the county in which the agency is located to issue a court order requiring the obligor or other person to comply with the administrative order or be held in contempt. If the court issues the requested order and if the obligor or other person ordered by the court to comply with the administrative order knowingly fails to immediately comply with the administrative order, he is in contempt of court."

Library References

Children Out-Of-Wedlock ⟹69.
Divorce ⟹311(2).
Parent and Child ⟹3.3(9).
WESTLAW Topic Nos. 76H, 134, 285.
C.J.S. Children Out-of-Wedlock §§ 128, 129.
C.J.S. Divorce §§ 709 to 715.
C.J.S. Parent and Child §§ 80, 85 to 87, 89.

Carlin, Baldwin's Ohio Practice, *Merrick-Rippner Probate Law* § 18.2, 18.3, 19.1, 19.2, 19.3, 19.4, 19.6, 19.7, 19.8, 19.10, 98.29, 98.31, 108.19, 108.22, 108.24, 108.25, 108.33, 108.34, 108.39 (1997)

Sowald & Morganstern, Baldwin's Ohio Practice, *Domestic Relations Law* § 3.3, 22.19 (1997)

OJur 3d: 47, Family Law § 1268

3111.25 Liability for noncompliance with withholding or deduction requirements

(A)(1) For purposes of this section, a withholding or deduction order that was issued prior to December 31, 1993, under division (A)(1), (2), (4), or (5) of section 3111.23 of the Revised Code as the division existed prior to that date and that has not been terminated on or after December 31, 1993, shall be considered to be a withholding or deduction notice issued under divisions (A) and (B)(1) or (2) of section 3111.23 of the Revised Code.

(2) A payor that fails to withhold an amount from an obligor's income for support in accordance with a withholding requirement contained in a withholding notice issued under divisions (A) and (B)(1) of section 3111.23 of the Revised Code or a financial institution that fails to deduct funds from an obligor's account for support in accordance with a deduction

requirement contained in a deduction notice issued under divisions (A) and (B)(2) of section 3111.23 of the Revised Code is liable for the amount that was not withheld or deducted, provided that no payor that is an employer whose normal pay and disbursement cycles make it impossible to comply with a withholding requirement contained in a withholding notice issued under divisions (A) and (B)(1) of section 3111.23 of the Revised Code shall be liable for the amount not withheld if the employer, as soon as possible after the employer's receipt of the withholding notice, provides the agency that issued the withholding notice with written notice of the impossibility and the reasons for the impossibility. An employer who is liable under this provision for an amount that was not withheld shall be ordered by the agency to pay that amount to the division of child support in the department of job and family services, to be disbursed in accordance with the administrative support order for the benefit of the child or spouse.

(B) No payor that is an employer may use a requirement to withhold personal earnings contained in a withholding notice issued under divisions (A) and (B)(1) of section 3111.23 of the Revised Code as a basis for a discharge of, or for any disciplinary action against, an employee, or as a basis for a refusal to employ a person.

(1999 H 471, eff. 7-1-00; 1997 H 352, eff. 1-1-98; 1993 H 173, eff. 12-31-93; 1992 S 10)

Historical and Statutory Notes

Amendment Note: 1999 H 471 substituted "director of job and family services" for "department of human services" in division (A)(2).

Amendment Note: 1997 H 352 rewrote division (A), which prior thereto read:

"(A)(1) For purposes of this section, a withholding or deduction order that was issued prior to December 31, 1993, under division (A)(1), (2), (4), or (5) of section 3111.23 of the Revised Code as the division existed prior to that date and that has not been terminated on or after December 31, 1993, shall be considered to be a withholding or deduction notice issued under divisions (A) and (B)(1), (2), (4), or (5) of section 3111.23 of the Revised Code.

"(2) An employer that fails to withhold an amount from an obligor's personal earnings for support in accordance with a withholding requirement contained in a withholding notice issued under divisions (A) and (B)(1) of section 3111.23 of the Revised Code, an employer that is paying an obligor's workers' compensation benefits and that fails to withhold the obligor's workers' compensation benefits for support in accordance with a withholding requirement contained in a withholding notice issued under divisions (A) and (B)(2) of section 3111.23 of the Revised Code, a financial institution that fails to deduct funds from an obligor's account for support in accordance with a deduction requirement contained in a deduction notice issued under divisions (A) and (B)(5) of section 3111.23 of the Revised Code, or any other person that fails to withhold or deduct an amount from the income of an obligor in accordance with a withholding or deduction requirement contained in a withholding or deduction notice issued under divisions (A) and (B)(4) of section 3111.23 of the Revised Code is liable for the amount that was not withheld or deducted, provided that no employer whose normal pay and disbursement cycles make it impossible to comply with a withholding requirement contained in a withholding notice issued under divisions (A) and (B)(1) of section 3111.23 of the Revised Code shall be liable for the amount not withheld if the employer, as soon as possible after the employer's receipt of the withholding notice, provides the agency that issued the withholding notice with written notice of the impossibility and the reasons for the impossibility. An employer who is liable under this provision for an amount that was not withheld shall be ordered by the agency to pay that amount to the child support enforcement agency, to be disbursed in accordance with the administrative support order for the benefit of the child or spouse."

Amendment Note: 1993 H 173 added division (A)(1); designated division (A)(2); and changed references to administrative withholding orders to references to withholding or deduction requirements and orders throughout.

Library References

Children Out-Of-Wedlock ⚷69.
Divorce ⚷311(2).
Parent and Child ⚷3.3(9).
WESTLAW Topic Nos. 76H, 134, 285.
C.J.S. Children Out-of-Wedlock §§ 128, 129.
C.J.S. Divorce §§ 709 to 715.
C.J.S. Parent and Child §§ 80, 85 to 87, 89.

OJur 3d: 47, Family Law § 1222, 1257, 1267

Carlin, Baldwin's Ohio Practice, *Merrick-Rippner Probate Law* § 18.2, 18.3, 19.1, 19.2, 19.3, 19.4, 19.6, 19.7, 19.8, 19.10, 98.29, 98.31, 108.19, 108.22, 108.24, 108.33, 108.34, 108.38, 108.39 (1997)

Sowald & Morganstern, Baldwin's Ohio Practice, *Domestic Relations Law* § 3.38, 22.21 (1997)

Law Review and Journal Commentaries

Bankruptcy Reform Act of 1994—What the Bankruptcy Code Giveth, Domestic Relations Courts (and Congress) Taketh Away, C.R. "Chip" Bowles. 8 Domestic Rel J Ohio 17 (March/April 1996).

3111.26 Notice of request for determination of existence or nonexistence of parent and child relationship

If a child support enforcement agency is requested to determine the existence or nonexistence of a parent and child relationship pursuant to sections 3111.22 to 3111.29 of the Revised Code, the administrative officer shall provide notice of the determination request pursuant to the Rules of Civil Procedure to the natural mother of the child who is the subject of the request, each man presumed to be the father of the child under section 3111.03 of the Revised Code, and each man alleged to be the natural father of the child. If the agency is unable to obtain service of process on the presumed father, alleged father, or natural mother within the time period described in division (C)(1) of section 3111.22 of the Revised Code, the agency shall proceed with the genetic testing as provided in that section.

(1997 H 352, eff. 1-1-98; 1992 S 10, eff. 7-15-92)

Historical and Statutory Notes

Amendment Note: 1997 H 352 substituted "3111.22" for "3111.21"; and added the second sentence.

Library References

Children Out-Of-Wedlock ⟹39.
WESTLAW Topic No. 76H.
C.J.S. Children Out-of-Wedlock §§ 50, 72 to 74, 92, 94.

OJur 3d: 47, Family Law § 969

Carlin, Baldwin's Ohio Practice, *Merrick-Rippner Probate Law* § 18.2, 18.3, 19.1, 19.2, 19.3, 19.4, 19.6, 19.7, 19.8, 19.10, 98.29, 98.31, 108.19, 108.22, 108.24, 108.33, 108.34, 108.39 (1997)

Sowald & Morganstern, Baldwin's Ohio Practice, *Domestic Relations Law* § 3.3, 22.19 (1997)

3111.27 Review of support orders

(A) No later than May 1, 1992, the director of job and family services shall adopt rules in accordance with Chapter 119. of the Revised Code establishing a procedure substantially similar to the procedure adopted pursuant to section 3113.216 of the Revised Code for determining when existing administrative support orders should be reviewed to determine whether it is necessary or in the best interest of the child who is the subject of the administrative support order to modify:

(1) The support amount ordered under the administrative support order and to calculate any modification to the support amount in accordance with section 3113.215 of the Revised Code;

(2) The provisions for the child's health care needs in the administrative support order and to make the modification in accordance with section 3111.241 of the Revised Code.

(B)(1) If a child support enforcement agency, periodically or upon the request of the obligee or obligor, plans to review an administrative support order in accordance with the rules adopted pursuant to division (A) of this section or otherwise is requested to review an administrative support order, it shall do all the following prior to formally beginning the review:

(a) Establish a date certain upon which the review shall begin;

(b) At least sixty days before formally beginning the review, send the obligor and obligee notice of the planned review and of the date when the review will formally begin;

(c) Request the obligor to provide the agency, no later than the scheduled date for formally beginning the review, with a copy of the obligor's federal income tax return from the previous year, a copy of all pay stubs obtained by the obligor within the preceding six months, a copy of all records evidencing the receipt of salary, wages, or compensation by the obligor within the preceding six months, a list of the group health insurance and health care policies, contracts, and plans available to the obligor and their costs, the current group health insurance or health care policy, contract, or plan under which the obligor is enrolled and its cost, and any other information necessary to properly review the administrative support order, and request the obligee to provide the agency, no later than the scheduled date for review to formally begin, with a copy of the obligee's federal income tax returns from the previous year, a copy of all pay stubs obtained by the obligee within the preceding six months, a copy of all records evidencing the receipt of salary, wages, or compensation by the obligee within the preceding six months, a list of the group health insurance and health care policies, contracts, and plans available to the obligee and their costs, the current group health insurance or health care policy, contract, or plan under which the obligor is enrolled and its cost, and any other information necessary to properly review the administrative support order;

(d) Include in the notice sent pursuant to division (B)(1)(b) of this section, a notice that if either the obligor or obligee fails to comply with the request for information, the agency may bring an action under section 3111.28 of the Revised Code requesting the court to find the obligor and the obligee in contempt pursuant to section 2705.02 of the Revised Code.

(2) If either the obligor or obligee fails to comply with the request made pursuant to division (B)(1)(c) of this section, the agency may bring an action under section 3111.28 of the Revised Code in the court of common pleas of the county in which the agency is located requesting the court to issue an order requiring an obligor and obligee to comply with the agency's request for information pursuant to division (B)(1)(c) of this section. If the obligor or obligee fails to comply with the court order issued pursuant to section 3111.28 of the Revised Code requiring compliance with the administrative request for information, the obligor or obligee is in contempt of court. In the action brought under section 3111.28 of the Revised Code, the agency may request the court to issue an order to require the obligor or obligee to provide the necessary information or to permit the agency to take whatever action is necessary to obtain information and make any reasonable assumptions necessary with respect to the information the person in contempt did not provide to ensure a fair and equitable review of the administrative child support order. If the agency decides to conduct the review based on the reasonable assumptions with respect to the information the person in contempt did not provide, it shall proceed in accordance with the rules adopted by the director of job and family services pursuant to division (A) of this section.

(C)(1) If the agency determines that a modification is necessary and in the best interest of the child who is the subject of the administrative support order, the agency shall calculate the amount the obligor shall pay in accordance with section 3113.215 of the Revised Code. The agency may not deviate from the guidelines set forth in section 3113.215 of the Revised Code.

(2) If the agency cannot set the amount of support the obligor shall pay without deviating from the guidelines set forth in section 3113.215 of the Revised Code, the agency shall bring an action under section 2151.231 of the Revised Code on behalf of the person who requested the agency to review the existing administrative order or if no one requested the review, on behalf of the obligee, in the court of common pleas of the county in which the agency is located requesting the court to issue a support order in accordance with sections 3113.21 to 3113.219 of the Revised Code.

(3) When it reviews an administrative support order pursuant to this section, the agency shall consider whether the provision for the child's health care needs in the administrative support order is adequate. If the agency determines that the administrative support order does not provide adequately for the child's health care needs, the agency shall modify the order in accordance with section 3111.241 of the Revised Code.

(D)(1) If the agency modifies an existing administrative support order, the agency shall provide the obligee and obligor with notice of the change and shall include in the notice a statement that the obligor or obligee may object to the modified administrative support order by initiating an action under section 2151.231 of the Revised Code in the juvenile court of the county in which the mother, the father, the child, or the guardian or custodian of the child resides.

(2) If the agency modifies an existing administrative support order, the modification shall relate back to the first day of the month following the date certain on which the review began under division (B)(1)(a) of this section.

(1999 H 471, eff. 7-1-00; 1997 H 352, eff. 1-1-98; 1996 H 710, § 7, eff. 6-11-96; 1995 H 167, eff. 6-11-96; 1992 S 10, eff. 7-15-92)

Uncodified Law

1996 H 710, § 15: See Uncodified Law under 3111.20.

Historical and Statutory Notes

Ed. Note: The effective date of the amendment of this section by 1995 H 167 was changed from 11-15-96 to 6-11-96 by 1996 H 710, § 7, eff. 6-11-96.

Amendment Note: 1999 H 471 substituted "director of job and family services" for "department of human services" in the introductory paragraph in division (A) and in division (B)(2).

Amendment Note: 1997 H 352 designated division (A)(1) and inserted "the support amount ordered under" and "to the support amount" therein; added division (A)(2); inserted "a list of the group health insurance and health care policies, contracts, and plans available to the obligor and their costs, the current group health insurance or health care policy, contract, or plan under which the obligor is enrolled and its cost," and "a list of the group health insurance and health care policies, contracts, and plans available to the obligee and their costs, the current group health insurance or health care policy, contract, or plan under which the obligor is enrolled and its cost," in division (B)(1)(c); substituted "information" for "income of" twice and inserted "did not provide" twice in division (B)(2); added division (C)(3); redesignated former division (C)(3) ad new division (D)(1); and added division (D)(2).

Amendment Note: 1995 H 167 rewrote division (B)(1)(d); and made other changes to reflect gender neutral language. Prior to amendment, division (B)(1)(d) read:

"(d) Include in the notice sent pursuant to division (B)(1)(b) of this section, a notice that if either the obligor or obligee fails to comply with the request for information, the agency may bring an action under section 3111.28 of the Revised Code requesting the court to issue an order requiring the obligor and the obligee to comply with the administrative request for information and that failure to comply with the court order is contempt of court."

Ohio Administrative Code References

Review and adjustment of IV-D court and administrative child support orders, OAC 5101:1-30-403

Library References

Children Out-Of-Wedlock ⚷67.
Divorce ⚷309.1 to 309.6.
Parent and Child ⚷3.3(8).
WESTLAW Topic Nos. 76H, 134, 285.
C.J.S. Children Out-of-Wedlock §§ 122 to 126.
C.J.S. Divorce §§ 719 to 736.
C.J.S. Parent and Child §§ 80, 82 to 84, 89.

OJur 3d: 47, Family Law § 1000, 1042, 1044, 1045, 1046

Carlin, Baldwin's Ohio Practice, *Merrick-Rippner Probate Law* § 18.2, 18.3, 19.1, 19.2, 19.3, 19.4, 19.6, 19.7, 19.8, 19.10, 98.29, 98.31, 108.19, 108.22, 108.24, 108.33, 108.34, 108.39 (1997)
Sowald & Morganstern, Baldwin's Ohio Practice, *Domestic Relations Law* § 3.4, 3.5, 3.38, 22.11, 22.13 (1997)

Notes of Decisions and Opinions

Procedural issues 1

---

1. Procedural issues

Pursuant to RC 3111.27, the department of human services adopts OAC 5101:1-32-15 and reviewing RC 3111.27 and OAC 5101:1-32-15 and construing them in pari materia, the appeals court concludes (1) after the thirty-two-day period for filing objections to the administrative support order has passed, a party can only seek modification of their order by first filing a request for an administrative review of the order with the CSEA; (2) if the CSEA determines that a modification is necessary and in the best interest of the child, the CSEA shall recalculate the support order by utilizing the child support guidelines set forth in RC 3113.215 and shall modify the order whenever the recalculated support amount has changed by more than ten per cent; (3) moreover, the CSEA shall not deviate from the guidelines in recalculating support; (4) if the CSEA modifies the administrative support order, the obligor or obligee may object to the modified order by initiating an action pursuant to RC 2151.231 in the juvenile court; and (5) objections to the modified administrative support order, however, are not limited by a thirty-day requirement. Kruse v Pinniger, No. L-95-029, 1995 WL 703917 (6th Dist Ct App, Lucas, 12-1-95).

3111.28 Orders requiring compliance with withholding or deduction requirements; contempt

(A) If a payor or a financial institution fails to comply with a withholding or deduction requirement contained in a withholding or deduction notice issued under section 3111.23 of the Revised Code, the child support enforcement agency that issued the withholding or deduction notice shall request the court to find the payor or financial institution in contempt pursuant to section 2705.02 of the Revised Code.

(B) If an obligor or obligee fails to comply with a child support enforcement agency's request for information pursuant to section 3111.27 of the Revised Code, the agency may request the court of common pleas of the county in which the agency is located to issue an order requiring the obligor or obligee to provide the necessary information or to permit the agency to take whatever action is necessary to obtain information and make any reasonable assumptions necessary with respect to the income of the person who failed to comply with the request to ensure a fair and equitable review of the administrative child support order. If the obligor or obligee fails to comply with a court order requiring compliance with the agency's request for information, the obligor or obligee is in contempt of court. If an obligor or obligee is in contempt of court, the agency may request the court to hold the person who failed to comply in contempt or to permit the agency to take whatever action is necessary to obtain information and make any reasonable assumptions necessary with respect to the income of the person who failed to comply with the request to ensure a fair and equitable review of the administrative child support order.

(1997 H 352, eff. 1-1-98; 1996 H 710, § 7, eff. 6-11-96; 1995 H 167, eff. 6-11-96; 1993 H 173, eff. 12-31-93; 1992 S 10)

Uncodified Law

1996 H 710, § 15: See Uncodified Law under 3111.20.

Historical and Statutory Notes

Ed. Note: The effective date of the amendment of this section by 1995 H 167 was changed from 11-15-96 to 6-11-96 by 1996 H 710, § 7, eff. 6-11-96.

Amendment Note: 1997 H 352 rewrote division (A), which prior thereto read:

"(A) If an employer, a financial institution, an employer that is paying the obligor's workers' compensation benefits, the public employees retirement board, the board, board of trustees, or other governing entity of any municipal retirement system, the board of trustees of the police and firemen's disability and pension fund, the state teachers retirement board, the school employees retirement board, the state highway patrol retirement board, the person paying or otherwise distributing an obligor's income, or the bureau of workers' compensation fails to comply with a withholding or deduction requirement contained in a withholding or deduction notice issued under section 3111.23 of the Revised Code, the child support enforcement agency that issued the withholding or deduction notice shall request the court to find the employer, financial institution, employer that is paying the obligor's workers' compensation benefits, public employees retirement board, board, board of trustees, or other governing entity of the municipal retirement system, board of trustees of the police and firemen's disability and pension fund, state teachers retirement board, school employees retirement board, state highway patrol retirement board, person paying or otherwise distributing an obligor's income, or bureau of workers' compensation person in contempt pursuant to section 2705.02 of the Revised Code."

Amendment Note: 1995 H 167 rewrote division (A), which previously read:

"(A) If an employer, a financial institution, an employer that is paying the obligor's workers' compensation benefits, the public employees retirement board, the board, board of trustees, or other governing entity of any municipal retirement system, the board of trustees of the police and firemen's disability and pension fund, the state teacher's retirement board, the school employees retirement board, the state highway patrol retirement board, the person paying or otherwise distributing an obligor's income, or the bureau of workers' compensation fails to comply with a withholding or deduction requirement contained in a withholding or deduction notice issued under section 3111.23 of the Revised Code, the child support enforcement agency that issued the withholding or deduction notice shall request the court to issue a court order requiring the employer, financial institution, employer that is paying the obligor's workers' compensation benefits, public employees retirement board, board, board of trustees, or other governing entity of the municipal retirement system, board of trustees of the police and firemen's disability and pension fund, state teacher's retirement board, school employees retirement board, state highway patrol retirement board, person paying or otherwise distributing an obligor's income, or bureau of workers' compensation person to comply with the withholding or deduction notice sent by the agency immediately or be held in contempt of court. If the court issues the requested order and if the employer, financial institution, employer that is paying the obligor's workers' compensation benefits, public employees retirement board,

board, board of trustees, or other governing entity of the municipal retirement system, board of trustees of the police and firemen's disability and pension fund, state teacher's retirement board, school employees retirement board, state highway patrol retirement board, person paying or otherwise distributing an obligor's income, or bureau of workers' compensation does not comply with the withholding or deduction notice of the agency that is the subject of the court order immediately, it is in contempt of court."

Amendment Note: 1993 H 173 changed references to administrative withholding orders to references to withholding or deduction requirements and notices throughout division (A).

Library References

Children Out-Of-Wedlock ⚷69.
Divorce ⚷311(2).
Parent and Child ⚷3.3(9).
WESTLAW Topic Nos. 76H, 134, 285.
C.J.S. Children Out-of-Wedlock §§ 128, 129.
C.J.S. Divorce §§ 709 to 715.
C.J.S. Parent and Child §§ 80, 85 to 87, 89.

OJur 3d: 47, Family Law § 1045, 1266

Carlin, Baldwin's Ohio Practice, *Merrick-Rippner Probate Law* § 18.2, 18.3, 19.1, 19.2, 19.3, 19.4, 19.6, 19.7, 19.8, 19.10, 98.29, 98.31, 108.19, 108.22, 108.24, 108.33, 108.34. 108.39 (1997)

Law Review and Journal Commentaries

Bankruptcy Reform Act of 1994—What the Bankruptcy Code Giveth, Domestic Relations Courts (and Congress) Taketh Away, C.R. "Chip" Bowles. 8 Domestic Rel J Ohio 17 (March/April 1996).

3111.29 Interference with parentage action

No person, by using physical harassment or threats of violence against another person, shall interfere with the other person in his initiation or continuance of, or attempt to prevent the other person from initiating or continuing, an action under sections 3111.01 to 3111.19 of the Revised Code.

(1992 S 10, eff. 7-15-92)

Cross References

Penalty: 3111.99(B)

Interfering with action to issue or modify support order, 2919.231

Library References

Extortion and Threats ⚷25.1.
WESTLAW Topic No. 165.
C.J.S. Threats and Unlawful Communications §§ 2 to 20.

OJur 3d: 47, Family Law § 963

Carlin, Baldwin's Ohio Practice, *Merrick-Rippner Probate Law* § 18.2, 18.3, 19.1, 19.2, 19.3, 19.4, 19.6, 19.7, 19.8, 19.10, 98.29, 98.31, 108.19, 108.22, 108.24, 108.33, 108.34, 108.39 (1997)

3 Katz & Giannelli, Baldwin's Ohio Practice, *Criminal Law* § 109.12 (1996)

Sowald & Morganstern, Baldwin's Ohio Practice, *Domestic Relations Law* § 3.22 (1997)

NON-SPOUSAL ARTIFICIAL INSEMINATION

Library References

Am Jur 2d: 61, Physicians, Surgeons, and Other Healers § 169, 170, 182, 192

Legal consequences of human artificial insemination. 25 ALR3d 1103

3111.30 Definitions

As used in sections 3111.30 to 3111.38 of the Revised Code:

(A) "Artificial insemination" means the introduction of semen into the vagina, cervical canal, or uterus through instruments or other artificial means.

(B) "Donor" means a man who supplies semen for a non-spousal artificial insemination.

(C) "Non-spousal artificial insemination" means an artificial insemination of a woman with the semen of a man who is not her husband.

(D) "Physician" means a person who is licensed pursuant to Chapter 4731. of the Revised Code to practice medicine or surgery or osteopathic medicine or surgery in this state.

(E) "Recipient" means a woman who has been artificially inseminated with the semen of a donor.

(1986 H 476, eff. 9-24-86)

Cross References

Relief from final judgment, court order, or administrative determination, 3113.2111

Library References

Children Out-Of-Wedlock ⚷1, 20.
WESTLAW Topic No. 76H.
C.J.S. Children Out-of-Wedlock §§ 2 to 12, 34 to 39.

OJur 3d: 47, Family Law § 1014

Carlin, Baldwin's Ohio Practice, *Merrick-Rippner Probate Law* § 18.2, 19.12 (1997)
Dill Calloway, Ohio Nursing Law, Text 10.05(D)

Law Review and Journal Commentaries

Artificial insemination: In the child's best interest? 5 Alb L J Sci & Tech 321 (1996).

Surrogate Parenting: What We Can Learn From Our British Counterparts, Note. 39 Case W Res L Rev 217 (1988-89).

Notes of Decisions and Opinions

Constitutional issues 2
Paternity action by donor 1

1. Paternity action by donor

Failure to comply with medical requirements of artificial insemination statutes would prevent mother from invoking nonspousal artificial insemination statute to obtain dismissal of sperm donor's complaint to determine paternity, custody, support, and visitation. C.O. v. W.S. (Ohio Com.Pl. 1994) 64 Ohio Misc.2d 9, 639 N.E.2d 523.

Artificial insemination statute establishing legal relationship between donor and mother would not apply to prevent paternity adjudication where unmarried woman solicited participation of donor, who was known to her, and where donor and woman agreed that there would be relationship between donor and child. C.O. v. W.S. (Ohio Com.Pl. 1994) 64 Ohio Misc.2d 9, 639 N.E.2d 523.

2. Constitutional issues

Even if artificial insemination statute establishing legal relationship between donor and mother applied, statute was unconstitutional as applied to donor and child insofar as it could be read to absolutely extinguish donor's efforts to assert rights and responsibilities of being father in case in which mother had solicited participation of donor, who was known to her, and donor and mother agreed that there would be relationship between donor and child. C.O. v. W.S. (Ohio Com.Pl. 1994) 64 Ohio Misc.2d 9, 639 N.E.2d 523.

3111.31 Sections applicable to non-spousal artificial insemination

Sections 3111.30 to 3111.38 of the Revised Code deal with non-spousal artificial insemination for the purpose of impregnating a woman so that she can bear a child that she intends to raise as her child. These sections do not deal with the artificial insemination of a wife with the semen of her husband or with surrogate motherhood.

(1986 H 476, eff. 9-24-86)

Library References

Children Out-Of-Wedlock ⚷1, 20.
WESTLAW Topic No. 76H.
C.J.S. Children Out-of-Wedlock §§ 2 to 12, 34 to 39.

Carlin, Baldwin's Ohio Practice, *Merrick-Rippner Probate Law* § 18.2, 19.12, 108.1 (1997)
Sowald & Morganstern, Baldwin's Ohio Practice, *Domestic Relations Law* § 3.47 (1997)

Law Review and Journal Commentaries

Belsito v Clark: Ohio's Battle with "Motherhood," Dawn Wenk. 28 U Tol L Rev 247 (Fall 1996).

3111.32 Supervision by physician

A non-spousal artificial insemination shall be performed by a physician or a person who is under the supervision and control of a physician. Supervision requires the availability of a physician for consultation and direction, but does not necessarily require the personal presence of the physician who is providing the supervision.

(1986 H 476, eff. 9-24-86)

Library References

Physicians and Surgeons ⚷6(1).
WESTLAW Topic No. 299.
C.J.S. Physicians, Surgeons, and Other Health-Care Providers §§ 2, 3, 5, 11, 14, 15, 28.

OJur 3d: 47, Family Law § 1014
Am Jur 2d: 61, Physicians, Surgeons and Other Healers § 169, 170, 182, 192

Rights and obligations resulting from human artificial insemination. 83 ALR4th 295

Carlin, Baldwin's Ohio Practice, *Merrick-Rippner Probate Law* § 18.2, 19.12 (1997)
Dill Calloway, Ohio Nursing Law, Text 10.05(D)

3111.33 Fresh semen; frozen semen; medical history of donor; laboratory studies

(A) In a non-spousal artificial insemination, fresh or frozen semen may be used, provided that the requirements of division (B) of this section are satisfied.

(B)(1) A physician or person under the supervision and control of a physician may use fresh semen for purposes of a non-spousal artificial insemination, only if within one year prior to the supplying of the semen, a complete medical history of the donor, including, but not limited to, any available genetic history of the donor, was obtained by a physician, the donor had a physical examination by a physician, and the donor was tested for blood type and RH [*sic*] factor.

(2) A physician or person under the supervision and control of a physician may use frozen semen for purposes of a non-spousal artificial insemination only if all the following apply:

(a) The requirements set forth in division (B)(1) of this section are satisfied;

(b) In conjunction with the supplying of the semen, the semen or blood of the donor was the subject of laboratory studies that the physician involved in the non-spousal artificial insemination considers appropriate. The laboratory studies may include, but are not limited to, venereal disease research laboratories, karotyping, GC culture, cytomegalo, hepatitis, kemzyme, Tay-Sachs, sickle-cell, ureaplasma, HLTV-III, and chlamydia.

(c) The physician involved in the non-spousal artificial insemination determines that the results of the laboratory studies are acceptable results.

(1986 H 476, eff. 9-24-86)

Library References

Physicians and Surgeons ⚷1, 15(5.1).
Products Liability ⚷46.
WESTLAW Topic Nos. 299, 313A.
C.J.S. Physicians, Surgeons, and Other Health-Care Providers §§ 6, 7, 11, 70, 71, 77, 90, 92, 97 to 100.
C.J.S. Products Liability § 54.

OJur 3d: 47, Family Law § 1014

Am Jur 2d: 61, Physicians, Surgeons and Other Healers § 169, 170, 182, 192
Rights and obligations resulting from human artificial insemination. 83 ALR4th 295

Carlin, Baldwin's Ohio Practice, *Merrick-Rippner Probate Law* § 18.2, 19.12 (1997)
Dill Calloway, Ohio Nursing Law, Text 10.05(D)

Law Review and Journal Commentaries

Artificial insemination: In the child's best interest? 5 Alb L J Sci & Tech 321 (1996).

Federal Regulation of Artificial Insemination Donor Screening Practices: An Opportunity for Law to Co-Evolve with Medicine, Comment. 96 Dick L Rev 37 (Fall 1991).

3111.34 Consents to non-spousal insemination of married woman

The non-spousal artificial insemination of a married woman may occur only if both she and her husband sign a written consent to the artificial insemination as described in section 3111.35 of the Revised Code.

(1986 H 476, eff. 9-24-86)

Library References

Physicians and Surgeons ⚷15(15).
WESTLAW Topic No. 299.
C.J.S. Physicians, Surgeons, and Other Health-Care Providers §§ 70, 97 to 100.

OJur 3d: 47, Family Law § 1015
Am Jur 2d: 61, Physicians, Surgeons and Other Healers § 169, 170, 182, 192

Rights and obligations resulting from human artificial insemination. 83 ALR4th 295

Carlin, Baldwin's Ohio Practice, *Merrick-Rippner Probate Law* § 18.2, 19.12 (1997)
Dill Calloway, Ohio Nursing Law, Text 10.05(D)

Notes of Decisions and Opinions

Consent 1

1. Consent

Although statute requiring a physician to obtain husband's consent prior to performing artificial insemination by nonspousal donor provided no remedy for its breach, husband could maintain claim against physician for fraud. Kerns v. Schmidt (Franklin 1994) 94 Ohio App.3d 601, 641 N.E.2d 280.

Husband stated claim of fraud, independent of any claim of malpractice, against physician by asserting that physician performed artificial insemination by nonspousal donor on his wife without first obtaining his consent; husband alleged that physician assured him there would be no artificial insemination without his consent, that physician breached statutory duty to refrain from performing nonspousal artificial insemination without husband's consent, that physician knew he needed to obtain such consent yet disregarded that requirement with intent to mislead husband, that husband justifiably relied upon physician's assurances, and that husband was damaged by physician's conduct. Kerns v. Schmidt (Franklin 1994) 94 Ohio App.3d 601, 641 N.E.2d 280.

Claim that physician was negligent per se for performing artificial insemination by nonspousal donor on his wife without first obtaining statutorily required consent of husband was subject to statute of limitations for medical claim. Kerns v. Schmidt (Franklin 1994) 94 Ohio App.3d 601, 641 N.E.2d 280.

3111.35 Recipient information and statements; date of insemination to be recorded

(A) Prior to a non-spousal artificial insemination, the physician associated with it shall do the following:

(1) Obtain the written consent of the recipient on a form that the physician shall provide. The written consent shall contain all of the following:

(a) The name and address of the recipient and, if married, her husband;

(b) The name of the physician;

(c) The proposed location of the performance of the artificial insemination;

(d) A statement that the recipient and, if married, her husband consent to the artificial insemination;

(e) If desired, a statement that the recipient and, if married, her husband consent to more than one artificial insemination if necessary;

(f) A statement that the donor shall not be advised by the physician or another person performing the artificial insemination as to the identity of the recipient or, if married, her husband and that the recipient and, if married, her husband shall not be advised by the physician or another person performing the artificial insemination as to the identity of the donor;

(g) A statement that the physician is to obtain necessary semen from a donor and, subject to any agreed upon provision as described in division (A)(1)(n) of this section, that the recipient and, if married, her husband shall rely upon the judgment and discretion of the physician in this regard;

(h) A statement that the recipient and, if married, her husband understand that the physician cannot be responsible for the physical or mental characteristics of any child resulting from the artificial insemination;

(i) A statement that there is no guarantee that the recipient will become pregnant as a result of the artificial insemination;

(j) A statement that the artificial insemination shall occur in compliance with sections 3111.30 to 3111.38 of the Revised Code;

(k) A brief summary of the paternity consequences of the artificial insemination as set forth in section 3111.37 of the Revised Code;

(l) The signature of the recipient and, if married, her husband;

(m) If agreed to, a statement that the artificial insemination will be performed by a person who is under the supervision and control of the physician;

(n) Any other provision that the physician, the recipient, and, if married, her husband agree to include.

(2) Upon request, provide the recipient and, if married, her husband with the following information to the extent the physician has knowledge of it:

(a) The medical history of the donor, including, but not limited to, any available genetic history of the donor and persons related to him by consanguinity, the blood type of the donor, and whether he has an RH [*sic*] factor;

(b) The race, eye and hair color, age, height, and weight of the donor;

(c) The educational attainment and talents of the donor;

(d) The religious background of the donor;

(e) Any other information that the donor has indicated may be disclosed.

(B) After each non-spousal artificial insemination of a woman, the physician associated with it shall note the date of the artificial insemination in his records pertaining to the woman and the artificial insemination, and retain this information as provided in section 3111.36 of the Revised Code.

(1986 H 476, eff. 9-24-86)

Library References

Physicians and Surgeons ⟹15(5.1, 15).
WESTLAW Topic No. 299.
C.J.S. Physicians, Surgeons, and Other Health-Care Providers §§ 70, 71, 77, 90, 92, 97 to 100.

OJur 3d: 47, Family Law § 1015
Am Jur 2d: 61, Physicians, Surgeons and Other Healers § 169, 170, 182, 192

Rights and obligations resulting from human artificial insemination. 83 ALR4th 295

Carlin, Baldwin's Ohio Practice, *Merrick-Rippner Probate Law* § 18.2, 19.12 (1997)
Dill Calloway, Ohio Nursing Law, Text 10.05(D)

3111.36 Physician's files; confidential information; donor information; action for file inspection

(A) The physician who is associated with a non-spousal artificial insemination shall place the written consent obtained pursuant to division (A)(1) of section 3111.35 of the Revised Code, information provided to the recipient and, if married, her husband pursuant to division (A)(2) of that section, other information concerning the donor that he possesses, and other matters concerning the artificial insemination in a file that shall bear the name of the recipient. This file shall be retained by the physician in his office separate from any regular medical chart of the recipient, and shall be confidential, except as provided in divisions (B) and (C) of this section. This file is not a public record under section 149.43 of the Revised Code.

(B) The written consent form and information provided to the recipient and, if married, her husband pursuant to division (A)(2) of section 3111.35 of the Revised Code shall be open to inspection only until the child born as the result of the non-spousal artificial insemination is twenty-one years of age, and only to the recipient or, if married, her husband upon request to the physician.

(C) Information pertaining to the donor that was not provided to the recipient and, if married, her husband pursuant to division (A)(2) of section 3111.35 of the Revised Code and that the physician possesses shall be kept in the file pertaining to the non-spousal artificial insemination for at least five years from the date of the artificial insemination. At the expiration of this period, the physician may destroy such information or retain it in the file.

The physician shall not make this information available for inspection by any person during the five-year period or, if the physician retains the information after the expiration of that period, at any other time, unless the following apply:

(1) A child is born as a result of the artificial insemination, an action is filed by the recipient, her husband if she is married, or a guardian of the child in the domestic relations division or, if there is no domestic relations division, the general division of the court of

common pleas of the county in which the office of the physician is located, the child is not twenty-one years of age or older, and the court pursuant to division (C)(2) of this section issues an order authorizing the inspection of specified types of information by the recipient, husband, or guardian;

(2) Prior to issuing an order authorizing an inspection of information, the court shall determine, by clear and convincing evidence, that the information that the recipient, husband, or guardian wishes to inspect is necessary for or helpful in the medical treatment of the child born as a result of the artificial insemination, and shall determine which types of information in the file are germane to the medical treatment and are to be made available for inspection by the recipient, husband, or guardian in that regard. An order only shall authorize the inspection of information germane to the medical treatment of the child.

(1986 H 476, eff. 9-24-86)

Library References

Physicians and Surgeons ⚷10.
WESTLAW Topic No. 299.
C.J.S. Physicians, Surgeons, and Other Health-Care Providers §§ 53, 57.

OJur 3d: 47, Family Law § 1016
Am Jur 2d: 61, Physicians, Surgeons and Other Healers § 169, 170, 182, 192

Rights and obligations resulting from human artificial insemination. 83 ALR4th 295

Carlin, Baldwin's Ohio Practice, *Merrick-Rippner Probate Law* § 18.2, 19.12 (1997)

3111.37 Husband rather than donor regarded as natural father of child

Note: See also following version of this section, eff. 10-27-00.

(A) If a married woman is the subject of a non-spousal artificial insemination and if her husband consented to the artificial insemination, the husband shall be treated in law and regarded as the natural father of a child conceived as a result of the artificial insemination, and a child so conceived shall be treated in law and regarded as the natural child of the husband. A presumption that arises under division (A)(1) or (2) of section 3111.03 of the Revised Code is conclusive with respect to this father and child relationship, and no action or proceeding under sections 3111.01 to 3111.19 or section 3111.22 of the Revised Code shall affect the relationship.

(B) If a woman is the subject of a non-spousal artificial insemination, the donor shall not be treated in law or regarded as the natural father of a child conceived as a result of the artificial insemination, and a child so conceived shall not be treated in law or regarded as the natural child of the donor. No action or proceeding under sections 3111.01 to 3111.19 or section 3111.22 of the Revised Code shall affect these consequences.

(1997 H 352, eff. 1-1-98; 1986 H 476, eff. 9-24-86)

Note: See also following version of this section, eff. 10-27-00.

3111.37 Husband rather than donor regarded as natural father of child

Note: See also preceding version of this section, in effect until 10-27-00.

(A) If a married woman is the subject of a non-spousal artificial insemination and if her husband consented to the artificial insemination, the husband shall be treated in law and regarded as the natural father of a child conceived as a result of the artificial insemination, and a child so conceived shall be treated in law and regarded as the natural child of the husband. A presumption that arises under division (A)(1) or (2) of section 3111.03 of the Revised Code is conclusive with respect to this father and child relationship, and no action or proceeding under sections 3111.01 to 3111.19 or section 3111.22 or 3113.2111 of the Revised Code shall affect the relationship.

(B) If a woman is the subject of a non-spousal artificial insemination, the donor shall not be treated in law or regarded as the natural father of a child conceived as a result of the artificial insemination, and a child so conceived shall not be treated in law or regarded as the natural child of the donor. No action or proceeding under sections 3111.01 to 3111.19 or section 3111.22 of the Revised Code shall affect these consequences.

(2000 H 242, eff. 10-27-00; 1997 H 352, eff. 1-1-98; 1986 H 476, eff. 9-24-86)
Note: See also preceding version of this section, in effect until 10-27-00.

Historical and Statutory Notes

Amendment Note: 2000 H 242 inserted "or 3113.2111".

Amendment Note: 1997 H 352 inserted "or proceeding" and "or section 3111.22" in divisions (A) and (B).

Library References

Children Out-Of-Wedlock ⚿1.
WESTLAW Topic No. 76H.
C.J.S. Children Out-of-Wedlock §§ 2 to 11.

OJur 3d: 47, Family Law § 1017
Am Jur 2d: 59, Parent and Child § 2, 6, 7, 36, 51
Legal consequences of human artificial insemination. 25 ALR3d 1103

Rights and obligations resulting from human artificial insemination. 83 ALR4th 295

Carlin, Baldwin's Ohio Practice, *Merrick-Rippner Probate Law* § 18.2, 19.7, 19.12, 98.30, 108.19, 108.22 (1997)
Sowald & Morganstern, Baldwin's Ohio Practice, *Domestic Relations Law* § 3.12, 3.14, 3.47 (1997)

Law Review and Journal Commentaries

In re T.R.: Not In Front of the Children, Bill Dickhaut. I Ky Children's Rts J 10 (July 1991).

Notes of Decisions and Opinions

Custody after divorce 1

1. Custody after divorce

Legal parentage, not to be confused with biological parentage, must be established before the issue of custody can properly be decided where the child is the product of artificial insemination of a married woman by a man not her husband. In re Adoption of Reams (Franklin 1989) 52 Ohio App.3d 52, 557 N.E.2d 159, dismissed 50 Ohio St.3d 707, 553 N.E.2d 684.

Where a husband and wife agree to conceive a child by means of artificial insemination, and a child so conceived is born to the parties, it is against public policy for a court to enter a judgment establishing the husband's non-paternity in connection with a divorce of the parties and the remarriage of the mother. Brooks v. Fair (Van Wert 1988) 40 Ohio App.3d 202, 532 N.E.2d 208.

3111.38 Effect of physician's failure to comply with statutes

The failure of a physician or person under the supervision and control of a physician to comply with the applicable requirements of sections 3111.30 to 3111.37 of the Revised Code shall not affect the legal status, rights, or obligations of a child conceived as a result of a non-spousal artificial insemination, a recipient, a husband who consented to the non-spousal artificial insemination of his wife, or the donor. If a recipient who is married and her husband make a good faith effort to execute a written consent that is in compliance with section 3111.35 of the Revised Code relative to a non-spousal artificial insemination, the failure of the written consent to so comply shall not affect the paternity consequences set forth in division (A) of section 3111.37 of the Revised Code.

(1986 H 476, eff. 9-24-86)

Library References

Children Out-Of-Wedlock ⚿1.
WESTLAW Topic No. 76H.
C.J.S. Children Out-of-Wedlock §§ 2 to 11.

Carlin, Baldwin's Ohio Practice, *Merrick-Rippner Probate Law* § 18.2, 19.12 (1997)

PENALTIES

3111.99 Penalties

(A) For purposes of this section, "administrative support order" and "obligor" have the same meaning as in section 3111.20 of the Revised Code.

(B) Whoever violates section 3111.29 of the Revised Code is guilty of interfering with the establishment of paternity, a misdemeanor of the first degree.

(C) An obligor who violates division (B)(1)(c) of section 3111.23 of the Revised Code shall be fined not more than fifty dollars for a first offense, not more than one hundred dollars for a second offense, and not more than five hundred dollars for each subsequent offense.

(D) An obligor who violates division (E)(2) of section 3111.23 of the Revised Code shall be fined not more than fifty dollars for a first offense, not more than one hundred dollars for a second offense, and not more than five hundred dollars for each subsequent offense.

(E) A fine imposed pursuant to division (C) or (D) of this section shall be paid to the division of child support in the department of job and family services or, pursuant to division (H)(4) of section 2301.35 of the Revised Code, the child support enforcement agency. The amount of the fine that does not exceed the amount of arrearage the obligor owes under the administrative support order shall be disbursed in accordance with the support order. The amount of the fine that exceeds the amount of the arrearage under the support order shall be called program income and shall be collected in accordance with section 5101.325 of the Revised Code.

(1999 H 471, eff. 7-1-00; 1997 H 352, eff. 1-1-98; 1996 H 710, § 7, eff. 6-11-96; 1995 H 167, eff. 6-11-96; 1995 S 2, eff. 7-1-96; 1992 S 10, eff. 7-15-92)

Uncodified Law

1996 H 710, § 15: See Uncodified Law under 3111.20.

Historical and Statutory Notes

Ed. Note: The effective date of the amendment of this section by 1995 H 167 was changed from 11-15-96 to 6-11-96 by 1996 H 710, § 7, eff. 6-11-96.

Amendment Note: 1999 H 471 substituted "job and family" for "human" in division (E).

Amendment Note: 1997 H 352 substituted "division of child support in the department of human services or, pursuant to division (H) of section 2301.35 of the Revised Code, the child support enforcement agency" for "child support enforcement agency administering the obligor's child support order" and "called program income and shall be collected in accordance with section 5101.325 of the Revised Code" for "used by the agency for the administration of its program for child support enforcement" in division (E).

Amendment Note: 1995 S 2 deleted the former second sentence, which read:

"If the offender previously has been convicted of or pleaded guilty to a violation of section 3111.29 or 2919.231 of the Revised Code, interfering with the establishment of paternity is a felony of the fourth degree."

Amendment Note: 1995 H 167 added division (A); designated division (B); and added divisions (C), (D), and (E).

Cross References

Child support enforcement agency, powers and duties, 2301.35

Program income fund, child support division depositing funds in, 5101.325

Ohio Administrative Code References

Allocation hierarchy for collections, OAC 5101:1-31-14
Child support administrative fund, OAC 5101:1-31-04
Nonsupport collections, OAC 5101:1-31-11
Program income, OAC 5101:1-31-20

Library References

Children Out-Of-Wedlock ⚷1.
WESTLAW Topic No. 76H.
C.J.S. Children Out-of-Wedlock §§ 2 to 11.

OJur 3d: 47, Family Law § 963

Carlin, Baldwin's Ohio Practice, *Merrick-Rippner Probate Law* § 19.8, 108.19, 108.22, 108.33, 108.34, 108.39 (1997)

Sowald & Morganstern, Baldwin's Ohio Practice, *Domestic Relations Law* § 3.22 (1997)

CHAPTER 3113

Neglect, Abandonment, or Domestic Violence

Cross References

"Abused child" defined, 2151.031
Child support division, requests for assistance from other states in enforcement of support orders, 5101.318
"Dependent child" defined, 2151.04
Domestic violence, criminal sanctions, 2919.25 to 2919.271
"Neglected child" defined, 2151.03
Nonsupport, child endangering, related offenses, 2919.21 to 2919.24
Prevention of child abuse and child neglect, 3109.13 to 3109.18
Reciprocal enforcement of support, Ch 3115
Uniform Interstate Family Support Act, duties and powers of responding tribunal, 3115.16

Ohio Administrative Code References

Child abuse and neglect, OAC Ch 5101:2-35
Child abuse and neglect, supportive services, OAC Ch 5101:2-39
Child support program, OAC Ch 5101:1-29
Children's protective services, OAC Ch 5101:2-34
Collection of past due support by federal tax refund offset, OAC Ch 5101:1-30

Library References

Am Jur 2d: 10, Bastards § 68; 23, Desertion and Nonsupport § 56 et seq.; 24, Divorce and Separation § 772 et seq.; 59, Parent and Child § 72 et seq.
Father's criminal liability for desertion of or failure to support child where divorce decree awards custody to another. 73 ALR2d 960
Carlin, Baldwin's Ohio Practice, *Merrick-Rippner Probate Law* § 19.8, 19.9, 108.19, 108.33, 108.34, 108.39 (1997)
Sowald & Morganstern, Baldwin's Ohio Practice, *Domestic Relations Law* § 23.36 (1997)
Wasil, Waite, & Mastrangelo, Ohio Workers' Compensation Law § 14:4

WESTLAW Electronic Research

See WESTLAW Electronic Research Guide following the Preface.

Law Review and Journal Commentaries

Abandonment of Children as a Civil Wrong: Burnette v Wahl, Comment. 41 Ohio St L J 533 (1980).

Domestic Relations: Legal Responses to Wife Beating: Theory and Practice in Ohio, Note. 16 Akron L Rev 705 (Spring 1983).

Father's Day: Ohio's Child Support Guidelines And The Responsible Father, Comment. 21 Cap U L Rev 1145 (Fall 1992).

Interminable Child Neglect/Custody Cases: Are There Better Alternatives?, Sheila Reynolds and Roy B. Lacoursiere. 21 J Fam L 239 (1982-83).

Judges' Column, Hon. Francine Bruening. (Ed. note: Judge Bruening discusses the Child Support Reorganization Act of House Bill 352, effective 1-1-98.) 21 Lake Legal Views 1 (June 1998).

R.C. 3109.19: Grandparent's Duty to Support Grandchild—Support for Children of Unemancipated Minor Children, Pamela J. MacAdams. 8 Domestic Rel J Ohio 42 (May/June 1996).

FAILURE TO PAY SUPPORT; BOND

3113.01 to 3113.03 Neglect, inability to provide for, and abandonment of child or pregnant woman—Repealed

(1972 H 511, eff. 1-1-74; 1953 H 1; GC 13008 to 13009)

Historical and Statutory Notes

Ed. Note: See now 2919.21 for annotations from former 3113.01.

Pre-1953 H 1 Amendments: 121 v 557; 110 v 7; 99 v 228

3113.04 Suspension of sentence on posting bond; support orders; contempt

(A) Sentence may be suspended if a person, after conviction under section 2919.21 of the Revised Code and before sentence under that section, appears before the court of common pleas in which the conviction took place and enters into bond to the state in a sum fixed by the court at not less than five hundred nor more than one thousand dollars, with sureties approved by the court, conditioned that the person will furnish the child or other dependent with necessary or proper home, care, food, and clothing, or will pay promptly each week for such purpose to the division of child support in the department of job and family services, a sum to be fixed by the agency. The child support enforcement agency shall comply with sections 3113.21 to 3113.219 of the Revised Code when it fixes the sum to be paid to the division.

(B) Each order for child support made or modified under this section shall include as part of the order a general provision, as described in division (A)(1) of section 3113.21 of the Revised Code, requiring the withholding or deduction of income or assets of the obligor under the order as described in division (D) of section 3113.21 of the Revised Code or another type of appropriate requirement as described in division (D)(3), (D)(4) or (H) of that section, to ensure that withholding or deduction from the income or assets of the obligor is available from the commencement of the support order for collection of the support and of any arrearages that occur; a statement requiring all parties to the order to notify the child support enforcement agency in writing of their current mailing address, current residence address, current resident telephone number, current driver's license number, and any changes to that information, and a notice that the requirement to notify the agency of all changes to that information continues until further notice from the court. If any person required to pay child support under an order made under this section on or after April 15, 1985, or modified on or after December 1, 1986, is found in contempt of court for failure to make support payments under the order, the court that makes the finding, in addition to any other penalty or remedy imposed, shall assess all court costs arising out of the contempt proceeding against the person and require the person to pay any reasonable attorney's fees of any adverse party, as determined by the court, that arose in relation to the act of contempt.

(C) Notwithstanding section 3109.01 of the Revised Code, if a court issues a child support order under this section, the order shall remain in effect beyond the child's eighteenth birthday as long as the child continuously attends on a full-time basis any recognized and accredited high school or the order provides that the duty of support of the child continues beyond the child's eighteenth birthday. Except in cases in which the order provides that the duty of support continues for any period after the child reaches nineteen years of age, the order shall not remain in effect after the child reaches age nineteen. Any parent ordered to pay support under a child support order issued under this section shall continue to pay support under the order, including during seasonal vacation periods, until the order terminates.

(1999 H 471, eff. 7-1-00; 1997 H 352, eff. 1-1-98; 1993 H 173, eff. 12-31-93; 1992 S 10; 1990 H 591; 1988 H 708; 1987 H 231; 1986 H 509; 1984 H 614; 1978 S 87; 1972 H 511; 1953 H 1; GC 13010)

Historical and Statutory Notes

Ed. Note: 3113.04 contains provisions analogous to former 2901.41 and 2903.09, repealed by 1972 H 511, eff. 1-1-74.

Pre-1953 H 1 Amendments: 99 v 228, § 1

Amendment Note: 1999 H 471 substituted "job and family" for "human" in division (A).

Amendment Note: 1997 H 352 substituted "division of child support in the department of human services" for "child support enforcement agency" and inserted "to the division" in division (A); deleted "on or after December 31, 1993," before "shall include", substituted "income" for "wages" twice and "(D)(3), (D)(4)" for "(D)(6), (D)(7)", and inserted "current residence telephone number, current driver's license number,", in division (B); inserted "or the order provides that the duty of support of the child continues beyond the child's eighteenth birthday" and added the second sentence in division (C); and made other nonsubstantive changes.

Amendment Note: 1993 H 173 rewrote division (B) before the first semi-colon, which previously read:

"(B) Each order for child support made or modified under this section on or after December 1, 1986, shall be accompanied by one or more orders described in division (D) or (H) of section 3113.21 of the Revised Code, whichever is appropriate under the requirements of that section".

Cross References

Automated system to support enforcement of child support, 5101.322

Child support enforcement agency, adoption of rules, 2301.35

Contempt action for failure to pay support, 2705.031, 2705.05
Criminal nonsupport of dependents, 2919.21
Interfering with action to issue or modify support order, 2919.231
Lottery winner to state under oath whether or not he is in default of support order, 3770.071
Notice of default on child support order sent to professional licensing boards, 2301.373
Payment of child support to bureau of support, procedures on default, 2301.37
Payment of support through withholding of earnings, workers' compensation benefits, unemployment compensation benefits, retirement benefits, or bank account; procedures, 3113.21 et seq.
Support order, defined, 2301.34

Ohio Administrative Code References

Age of majority defined, OAC 5101:1-32-06
Child support program, OAC Ch 5101:1-29
Collection of past due support by federal tax refund offset, OAC Ch 5101:1-30

Library References

Parent and Child ⚷3.3(9)
Social Security and Public Welfare ⚷194.19.
WESTLAW Topic Nos. 285, 356A.
C.J.S. Parent and Child §§ 80, 85 to 87, 89.
C.J.S. Social Security and Public Welfare § 122.

OJur 3d: 29, Criminal Law § 3346; 47, Family Law § 1198, 1201, 1222, 1300, 1301, 1306, 1308
Am Jur 2d: 10, Bastards § 128, 129

Baldwin's Ohio Legislative Service, 1990 Laws of Ohio, H 591—LSC Analysis, p 5-576
Carlin, Baldwin's Ohio Practice, *Merrick-Rippner Probate Law* § 108.1 (1997)
3 Katz & Giannelli, Baldwin's Ohio Practice, *Criminal Law* § 109.9, 109.12 (1996)
Sowald & Morganstern, Baldwin's Ohio Practice, *Domestic Relations Law* § 22.5, 22.21, 23.46 (1997)

Law Review and Journal Commentaries

Bankruptcy Reform Act of 1994—What the Bankruptcy Code Giveth, Domestic Relations Courts (and Congress) Taketh Away, C.R. "Chip" Bowles. 8 Domestic Rel J Ohio 17 (March/April 1996).

Notes of Decisions and Opinions

Action on bond 2
Procedure to suspend sentence 1

---

1. Procedure to suspend sentence

Sentence of conviction under GC 13008 (former RC 3113.01) may be suspended under GC 13010 (RC 3113.04) or GC 13706 (Repealed), the former not being exclusive. Norman v. State (Ohio 1924) 109 Ohio St. 213, 142 N.E. 234, 2 Ohio Law Abs. 68, 21 Ohio Law Rep. 412, 21 Ohio Law Rep. 413, certiorari denied 44 S.Ct. 453, 264 U.S. 595, 68 L.Ed. 867.

When a person convicted under GC 13008 (former RC 3113.01) appears for sentence, and the court thereupon under authority of this section proceeds to make an order covering support and bond, and appoints a trustee, and the convicted forthwith complies with such order and executes and delivers bond, conditioned as provided by this section, such procedure effects a suspension of the sentence provided for in GC 13008 (former RC 3113.01), and the same stands suspended, conditioned upon the continued compliance by the convicted with such order or any modification thereof made under authority of GC 13015 (RC 3113.08). Seaman v. State (Ohio 1922) 106 Ohio St. 177, 140 N.E. 108, 1 Ohio Law Abs. 71, 20 Ohio Law Rep. 462.

Defendant was required to comply with statutory requirement and post bond before sentence for nonsupport could be suspended. State v. Lizanich (Franklin 1994) 93 Ohio App.3d 706, 639 N.E.2d 855.

2. Action on bond

Under this section, suspending sentence of person convicted for nonsupport of minor children on execution of bond for support of children in accordance with order of court, state has no interest in amount that may be recovered in action on bond, but money recovered goes to person who has furnished such support. State ex rel. McCloskey v. McCloskey (Erie 1929) 34 Ohio App. 30, 169 N.E. 823, 7 Ohio Law Abs. 710.

A bond given by a parent to secure compliance with an order of the juvenile court, fixing the amount to be contributed for support of his minor children, and accepted as a condition of the parent's dismissal from a criminal proceeding in such court for nonsupport of the children, is not contrary to public policy, and in case of default of the principal may be enforced against the surety. Anderson v. Anderson (Ohio App. 2 Dist. 1921) 15 Ohio App. 382.

Although a trial court may suspend a sentence of a defendant found guilty of criminal nonsupport if the defendant appears before the court in which the conviction took place, enters into a bond, and furnishes the child with enumerated necessities or pays a weekly sum to the child support enforcement agency which sum is to be fixed by the agency pursuant to RC 3113.04, where there is no evidence a defendant entered into a bond, and where the trial court sets a weekly support amount sua sponte without referring the matter to the child support enforcement agency, the matter must be remanded for further proceedings. State v Locklear, No. 93AP-657, 1993 WL 473260 (10th Dist Ct App, Franklin, 11-9-93).

Where a bond is given in the penal sum of $500, conditioned that the convicted person shall make payments of $4 weekly, a recovery in the full amount of $500 may be had against the sureties where the amount owing is $500 or more, despite the fact that during such period some weekly payments were made by the convicted person. 1935 OAG 4786.

When a bond is given to secure the furnishing of necessaries to an abandoned child, and the amount of the bond is recovered in an action on such bond, the state has no interest in the amount so recovered but the proceeds collected are to be used for the maintenance of the child for whose benefit such bond is given. 1930 OAG 1886.

3113.05 Venue—Repealed

(1972 H 511, eff. 1-1-74; 1953 H 1; GC 13011)

Historical and Statutory Notes

Ed. Note: See now 2901.11 for annotations from former 3113.05.

Pre-1953 H 1 Amendments: 99 v 229, § 2

3113.06 Failure to pay maintenance cost of child

No father, or mother when she is charged with the maintenance, of a child under eighteen years of age, or a mentally or physically handicapped child under age twenty-one, who is legally a ward of a public children services agency or is the recipient of aid pursuant to Chapter 5107. or 5115. of the Revised Code, shall neglect or refuse to pay such agency the reasonable cost of maintaining such child when such father or mother is able to do so by reason of property, labor, or earnings.

An offense under this section shall be held committed in the county in which the agency is located. The agency shall file charges against any parent who violates this section, unless the agency files charges under section 2919.21 of the Revised Code, or unless charges of nonsupport are filed by a relative or guardian of the child, or unless an action to enforce support is brought under Chapter 3115. of the Revised Code.

(1997 H 408, eff. 10-1-97; 1996 H 274, eff. 8-8-96; 1995 H 249, eff. 7-17-95; 1991 H 298, eff. 7-26-91; 1986 H 428; 1972 H 511; 1969 H 361, S 49; 132 v H 390; 1953 H 1; GC 13012, 13014)

Historical and Statutory Notes

Pre-1953 H 1 Amendments: 121 v 538; 99 v 228, 229

Amendment Note: 1997 H 408 changed references to county human services departments and county children services boards to references to public children services agencies in division (D).

Amendment Note: 1996 H 274 deleted "legitimate or illegitimate" before "child under eighteen years of age" in the first paragraph.

Amendment Note: 1995 H 249 removed a reference to Chapter 5113.

Cross References

Penalty: 3113.99

Aid to dependent children, Ch 5107

Automated system to support enforcement of child support, 5101.322

Charge against adult, defendant bound over to grand jury, 2151.43

Criminal nonsupport of dependents, 2919.21

Duty of married person to support self, spouse, and children, duration of duty to support, 3103.03

General assistance, Ch 5113

Lottery winner must state under oath whether or not he is in default of support order, 3770.071

Powers and duties of county children services board, 5153.16

Ohio Administrative Code References

Child support program, OAC Ch 5101:1-29

Collection of past due support by federal tax refund offset, OAC Ch 5101:1-30

Library References

Bail ⟹42.
Infants ⟹228.
Parent and Child ⟹17(2).
Social Security and Public Welfare ⟹194.19.
WESTLAW Topic Nos. 49, 211, 285, 356A.
C.J.S. Bail; Release and Detention Pending Proceedings §§ 6, 9 to 11, 13 to 15, 17, 19, 24 to 29, 31, 32.
C.J.S. Infants §§ 42, 53, 54, 57, 69 to 85.
C.J.S. Parent and Child §§ 166, 168, 169.
C.J.S. Social Security and Public Welfare § 122.

OJur 3d: 27, Criminal Law § 1673, 1739; 28, Criminal Law § 2859; 29, Criminal Law § 3337, 3340, 3346, 3348; 78, Public Welfare § 120

Am Jur 2d: 10, Bastards § 89, 128, 129; 23, Desertion and Nonsupport § 59; 59, Parent and Child § 65, 66, 72 to 74, 82

Parent's obligation to support unmarried minor child who refuses to live with parent. 98 ALR3d 334

Removal by custodial parent of child from jurisdiction in violation of court order as justifying termination, suspension, or reduction of child support payments. 8 ALR4th 1231

Postmajority disability as reviving parental duty to support child. 48 ALR4th 919

Carlin, Baldwin's Ohio Practice, *Merrick-Rippner Probate Law* § 108.3 (1997)

Sowald & Morganstern, Baldwin's Ohio Practice, *Domestic Relations Law* § 20.16, 23.46 (1997)

Law Review and Journal Commentaries

Abandonment of Children as a Civil Wrong: Burnette v Wahl, Comment. 41 Ohio St L J 533 (1980).

Bankruptcy Reform Act of 1994—What the Bankruptcy Code Giveth, Domestic Relations Courts (and Congress) Taketh Away, C.R. "Chip" Bowles. 8 Domestic Rel J Ohio 17 (March/April 1996).

Notes of Decisions and Opinions

1. Ability to pay

The inability of an accused to pay maintenance costs is an excuse or justification peculiarly within the knowledge of the accused and on which he can reasonably be required to adduce supporting evidence; thus, it is an affirmative defense to a violation of RC 3113.06. State v. Wright (Columbiana 1982) 4 Ohio App.3d 291, 448 N.E.2d 499, 4 O.B.R. 541.

In parentage proceedings where the complainant-mothers and their children are recipients of public assistance, the state public defender must, in accordance with RC 120.18, 120.28, and 120.33, partially reimburse the counties for the cost of representing indigent paternity defendants who face the state as an adversary. OAG 85-090.

2. Imprisonment

Imprisonment for violation of RC 3113.06 is not imprisonment for a debt in a "civil action," within the meaning of O Const Art I §15. State v. Wright (Columbiana 1982) 4 Ohio App.3d 291, 448 N.E.2d 499, 4 O.B.R. 541.

Imprisonment imposed for violation of RC 2151.42 is not imprisonment for debt. State v. Ducey (Franklin 1970) 25 Ohio App.2d 50, 266 N.E.2d 233, 54 O.O.2d 80.

3. Penalties

Criminal liability may be imposed on parent for failure to provide child support if children become wards of county department of human services or recipients of Aid to Dependent Children. Columbus v. Bickel (Franklin 1991) 77 Ohio App.3d 26, 601 N.E.2d 61.

By virtue of RC 1.23 the penalty provisions of RC 3113.99(B) apply to the new offense added to RC 3113.06, as amended effective November 7, 1963, which was not an offense under RC 3113.06 prior to such amendment. State v. Knecht (Ohio Com.Pl. 1969) 21 Ohio Misc. 91, 253 N.E.2d 324, 50 O.O.2d 153, 50 O.O.2d 180.

Where an agreement has been entered into pursuant to GC 3070-17 (RC 335.16), such fact does not divert courts of jurisdiction over offenses described in GC 1639-46 (RC 2151.42), GC 13308 (former RC 3113.01), and this section, and parent may be held criminally liable for failure to support a minor child as provided in said sections; juvenile courts have no jurisdiction of felonies, nor over offenses described in GC 13008 (former RC 3113.01) and this section. 1946 OAG 1100.

4. Constitutional issues

RC 3113.06 does not violate the Equal Protection Clause of the US Constitution or O Const Art I §2. State v. Meyer (Greene 1983) 14 Ohio App.3d 69, 470 N.E.2d 156, 14 O.B.R. 81.

Even though RC 3113.06 fails to specifically provide the affirmative defense of inability to pay that is provided under RC 2919.21(B), RC 3113.06 does not unconstitutionally discriminate against parents whose children receive ADC benefits, since the same affirmative defense is available to them pursuant to RC 2901.05(C)(2). State v. Jackson (Greene 1983) 13 Ohio App.3d 416, 469 N.E.2d 872, 13 O.B.R. 503.

The phrases "reasonable cost" and "neglect or refuse" in RC 3113.06 are not so vague or technical as to be unconstitutional. State v. Wright (Columbiana 1982) 4 Ohio App.3d 291, 448 N.E.2d 499, 4 O.B.R. 541.

3113.07 Suspension of sentence on entering into bond; payment of reasonable maintenance cost; requirement to provide for health care needs of child

As used in this section, "executive director" has the same meaning as in section 5153.01 of the Revised Code.

Sentence may be suspended, if a person, after conviction under section 3113.06 of the Revised Code and before sentence thereunder, appears before the court of common pleas in which such conviction took place and enters into bond to the state in a sum fixed by the court at not less than five hundred dollars, with sureties approved by such court, conditioned that such person will pay, so long as the child remains a ward of the public children services agency or a recipient of aid pursuant to Chapter 5107. or 5115. of the Revised Code, to the executive director thereof or to a trustee to be named by the court, for the benefit of such agency or if the child is a recipient of aid pursuant to Chapter 5107. or 5115. of the Revised Code, to the county department of job and family services, the reasonable cost of keeping such child. The amount of such costs and the time of payment shall be fixed by the court.

The court, in accordance with section 3113.217 of the Revised Code, shall include in each support order made under this section the requirement that one or both of the parents provide for the health care needs of the child to the satisfaction of the court.

(1999 H 471, eff. 7-1-00; 1997 H 352, eff. 1-1-98; 1997 H 408, eff. 10-1-97; 1995 H 249, eff. 7-17-95; 1991 H 298, eff. 7-26-91; 1991 H 82; 1986 H 428; 1969 S 49; 132 v H 390; 1953 H 1; GC 13013)

Historical and Statutory Notes

Pre-1953 H 1 Amendments: 121 v 538; 99 v 228

Amendment Note: 1999 H 471 substituted "job and family" for "human" in the second paragraph.

Amendment Note: 1997 H 352 added the third paragraph.

Amendment Note: 1997 H 408 changed references to county human services departments and county children services boards to references to public children services agencies in division (D).

Amendment Note: 1995 H 249 removed references to Chapter 5113.

Cross References

Aid to dependent children, Ch 5107
Disposition of abused, neglected, or dependent child, temporary or permanent custody by public agency, 2151.353, 2151.412 to 2151.414
General assistance, Ch 5113
Interfering with action to issue or modify support order, 2919.231
Notice of default on child support order sent to professional licensing boards, 2301.373
Placing of child in public or private institution, 5103.15
Powers and duties of county children services board, 5153.16
Support payments to bureau of support, 2301.36

Library References

Bail ⚿42.
Infants ⚿228.
Parent and Child ⚿17(7.5).
Social Security and Public Welfare ⚿194.19.
WESTLAW Topic Nos. 49, 211, 285, 356A.
C.J.S. Bail; Release and Detention Pending Proceedings §§ 6, 9 to 11, 13 to 15, 17, 19, 24 to 29, 31, 32.
C.J.S. Infants §§ 42, 53, 54, 57, 69 to 85.
C.J.S. Parent and Child §§ 175, 176.
C.J.S. Social Security and Public Welfare § 122.

OJur 3d: 26, Family Law § 1198, 1201, 1222, 1241, 1300, 1301, 1308; 29, Criminal Law § 3346

Am Jur 2d: 10, Bastards § 128, 129; 23, Desertion and Nonsupport § 109 to 112, 118; 59, Parent and Child § 82

Carlin, Baldwin's Ohio Practice, *Merrick-Rippner Probate Law* § 108.1, 108.38 (1997)
3 Katz & Giannelli, Baldwin's Ohio Practice, *Criminal Law* § 109.12 (1996)
Sowald & Morganstern, Baldwin's Ohio Practice, *Domestic Relations Law* § 22.10 (1997)

Notes of Decisions and Opinions

Funds held by county 1

---

1. Funds held by county

Mandamus will not lie to recover money collected from noncustodial parents and retained by the county, since an action on an account is an adequate remedy. Creasy v. Waller (Ohio 1982) 1 Ohio St.3d 93, 438 N.E.2d 414, 1 O.B.R. 129.

3113.08 Failure to give bond; arrest; sentence or modification of order

Upon failure of the father or mother of a child under eighteen years of age, or of a physically or mentally handicapped child under twenty-one years of age, or the husband of a pregnant woman to comply with any order and undertaking provided for in sections 3113.01[2] to 3113.14, inclusive, of the Revised Code, such person may be arrested by the sheriff or other officer, on a warrant issued on the praecipe of the prosecuting attorney, and brought before the court of common pleas for sentence. Thereupon the court may pass sentence, or for good cause shown, may modify the order as to the time and amount of payments, or take a new

---

[2]Sections 3113.01 to 3113.03 were repealed by 1972 H 511, eff. 1-1-74; see now 2919.21 et seq. for provisions analogous to former 3113.01 to 3113.03.

undertaking and further suspend sentence, whichever is for the best interests of such child or pregnant woman and of the public.

(1996 H 274, eff. 8-8-96; 1953 H 1, eff. 10-1-53; GC 13015)

Historical and Statutory Notes

Pre-1953 H 1 Amendments: 99 v 229, § 5

Amendment Note: 1996 H 274 deleted "legitimate or illegitimate" before "child under eighteen years of age".

Cross References

Issuance of warrant, 2935.08

Library References

Infants ⚷228.
Parent and Child ⚷17(1), 17(7.5).
Social Security and Public Welfare ⚷194.19.
WESTLAW Topic Nos. 211, 285, 356A.
C.J.S. Infants §§ 42, 53, 54, 57, 69 to 85.
C.J.S. Parent and Child §§ 165 to 169, 175, 176.
C.J.S. Social Security and Public Welfare § 122.

OJur 3d: 29, Criminal Law § 3346
Am Jur 2d: 10, Bastards § 128, 129; 23, Desertion and Nonsupport § 109 to 112, 120 to 123; 59, Parent and Child § 82

Law Review and Journal Commentaries

Bankruptcy Reform Act of 1994—What the Bankruptcy Code Giveth, Domestic Relations Courts (and Congress) Taketh Away, C.R. "Chip" Bowles. 8 Domestic Rel J Ohio 17 (March/April 1996).

TRUSTEE

3113.09 Duties of trustee

The trustee appointed by the court of common pleas under sections 3113.04 and 3113.07 of the Revised Code, shall make quarterly reports of the receipts and expenditures of all moneys coming into his hands as provided in sections 3113.01[3] to 3113.14 of the Revised Code, such reports to be made to the board of county commissioners of the county from which the person described in section 3113.01 of the Revised Code was sentenced, or to the department of job and family services. The court may require such trustee to enter into a good and sufficient bond for the faithful performance of the duties imposed on him.

(1999 H 471, eff. 7-1-00; 1986 H 428, eff. 12-23-86; 1953 H 1; GC 13016)

Historical and Statutory Notes

Pre-1953 H 1 Amendments: 99 v 229, § 7

Amendment Note: 1999 H 471 substituted "job and family" for "human".

Library References

Infants ⚷228.
WESTLAW Topic No. 211.
C.J.S. Infants §§ 42, 53, 54, 57, 69 to 85.

OJur 3d: 29, Criminal Law § 3346
Am Jur 2d: 24, Divorce and Separation § 838; 59, Parent and Child § 81

3113.10 Humane society may act as trustee

A humane society, incorporated and existing under the laws of this state, and willing to render its services without compensation, may be appointed by the court of common pleas as trustee under sections 3113.04 and 3113.07 of the Revised Code.

(1953 H 1, eff. 10-1-53; GC 13017)

Historical and Statutory Notes

Pre-1953 H 1 Amendments: 99 v 229, § 6

---

[3]Sections 3113.01 to 3113.03 were repealed by 1972 H 511, eff. 1-1-74; see now 2919.21 et seq. for provisions analogous to former 3113.01 to 3113.03.

Cross References

Humane societies, Ch 1717

Library References

Infants ⚷228.
WESTLAW Topic No. 211.
C.J.S. Infants §§ 42, 53, 54, 57, 69 to 85.
OJur 3d: 29, Criminal Law § 3346
Am Jur 2d: 24, Divorce and Separation § 838; 59, Parent and Child § 81

3113.11 Amount credited convict paid to trustee

When a person is convicted, sentenced, and confined in a workhouse, under sections 3113.01[4] to 3113.14, inclusive, of the Revised Code, the county from which he is so convicted, sentenced, and confined upon the warrant of the county auditor of such county, and out of the general revenue fund thereof, shall pay monthly fifty cents for each day he is so confined, to the trustee appointed by the court under such sections, to be expended by such trustee for the maintenance of the child under sixteen years of age.

(1953 H 1, eff. 10-1-53; GC 13018)

Historical and Statutory Notes

Pre-1953 H 1 Amendments: 103 v 913; 99 v 229, § 7

Library References

Infants ⚷228.
WESTLAW Topic No. 211.
C.J.S. Infants §§ 42, 53, 54, 57, 69 to 85.
OJur 3d: 26, Family Law § 1027
Am Jur 2d: 59, Parent and Child § 81

3113.12 Credit for persons in penitentiary or reformatory—Repealed

(1972 H 494, eff. 7-1-72; 125 v 823; 1953 H 1; GC 13019)

Historical and Statutory Notes

Ed. Note: 1972 H 494, § 3, states that the repeal of RC 3113.12 takes effect 7-1-72. The Ohio Constitution provides that "no law passed by the general assembly shall go into effect until ninety days after it shall have been filed by the governor in the office of the secretary of state" (Art II, § 1c)—*except* for emergency laws and laws providing for tax levies or appropriations for current expenses, which take effect immediately (Art II, § 1d). Since H 494 is apparently not an exception, and 7-1-72 is within the ninety-day period, the effective date of the repeal of RC 3113.12 is probably 7-12-72.

Pre-1953 H 1 Amendments: 102 v 115; 99 v 229, § 7

3113.13 Trustee to be named in mittimus

When a person is imprisoned in a workhouse or state correctional institution under sections 3113.01[5] to 3113.14 of the Revised Code, the name and post-office address of the trustee appointed by the court of common pleas under sections 3113.04 and 3113.07 of the Revised Code shall appear in the mittimus.

(1994 H 571, eff. 10-6-94; 1953 H 1, eff. 10-1-53; GC 13020)

Historical and Statutory Notes

Pre-1953 H 1 Amendments: 99 v 229, § 7

Amendment Note: 1994 H 571 substituted "or state correctional institution" for ", penitentiary, or reformatory".

Library References

Infants ⚷228.
WESTLAW Topic No. 211.
C.J.S. Infants §§ 42, 53, 54, 57, 69 to 85.
OJur 3d: 26, Family Law § 1027

---

[4]Sections 3113.01 to 3113.03 were repealed by 1972 H 511, eff. 1-1-74; see now 2919.21 et seq. for provisions analogous to former 3113.01 to 3113.03.

[5]Sections 3113.01 to 3113.03 were repealed by 1972 H 511, eff. 1-1-74; see now 2919.21 et seq. for provisions analogous to former 3113.01 to 3113.03.

Sowald & Morganstern, Baldwin's Ohio Practice, *Domestic Relations Law* § 3.33 (1997)

MISCELLANEOUS PROVISIONS

3113.14 Continuance of citizenship

Citizenship once acquired in this state by a father or mother of a child living in this state, for the purpose of sections 3113.01[6] to 3113.14 of the Revised Code, shall continue until the child has arrived at the age of sixteen years, provided the child continues to live in this state.

(1996 H 274, eff. 8-8-96; 1953 H 1, eff. 10-1-53; GC 13021)

Historical and Statutory Notes

Pre-1953 H 1 Amendments: 99 v 229, § 4

Amendment Note: 1996 H 274 deleted "legitimate or illegitimate" before "child living in this state", and made other nonsubstantive changes.

Library References

Infants ⚷228.
WESTLAW Topic No. 211.
C.J.S. Infants §§ 42, 53, 54, 57, 69 to 85.

OJur 3d: 29, Criminal Law § 3345

Notes of Decisions and Opinions

Nonresident parent 1

1. Nonresident parent

Nonresident parent may be guilty of violating these sections. (See also State v Sanner, 81 OS 393, 90 NE 1007 (1910).) Burns v. Tarbox (Ohio 1907) 76 Ohio St. 520, 81 N.E. 761, 5 Ohio Law Rep. 167.

PAYMENT OF SUPPORT; ENFORCEMENT PROCEDURES

3113.16 Distribution of prisoner's earnings for child support

(A) As used in this section:

(1) "Child support order" has the same meaning as in section 2301.373 of the Revised Code.

(2) "Default," "obligor," and "obligee" have the same meanings as in section 2301.34 of the Revised Code.

(3) "Prison," "prison term," and "jail" have the same meanings as in section 2929.01 of the Revised Code.

(B) Notwithstanding any other section of the Revised Code, including sections 5145.16 and 5147.30 of the Revised Code, twenty-five per cent of any money earned pursuant to section 5145.16 or 5147.30 of the Revised Code by a prisoner in a prison or jail who has a dependent child receiving assistance under Chapter 5107. of the Revised Code, shall be paid to the state department of job and family services.

(C) Notwithstanding any other section of the Revised Code, including sections 5145.16 and 5147.30 of the Revised Code, and except as provided in division (B) of this section, twenty-five per cent of any money earned pursuant to section 5145.16 or 5147.30 of the Revised Code by a prisoner in a prison or jail who is an obligor in default under a child support order according to the records of the child support enforcement agency administering the order, shall be paid to the agency for distribution to the obligee under the order pursuant to sections 3111.23 to 3111.28 or sections 3113.21 to 3113.219 of the Revised Code.

(1999 H 471, eff. 7-1-00; 1997 S 52, eff. 9-3-97)

---

[6]Sections 3113.01 to 3113.03 were repealed by 1972 H 511, eff. 1-1-74; see now 2919.21 et seq. for provisions analogous to former 3113.01 to 3113.03.

Historical and Statutory Notes

Amendment Note: 1999 H 471 substituted "job and family" for "human" in division (B).

Library References

OJur 3d: 78, Public Welfare § 63, 120

3113.21 Withholding or deduction requirements and notices

(A)(1) In any action in which support is ordered under Chapter 3115. or under section 2151.23, 2151.231, 2151.232, 2151.33, 2151.36, 2151.49, 3105.18, 3105.21, 3109.05, 3109.19, 3111.13, 3113.04, 3113.07, 3113.216, or 3113.31 of the Revised Code, the court shall require the withholding or deduction of income or assets of the obligor in accordance with division (D) of this section or require the issuance of another type of appropriate court order in accordance with division (D)(3) or (4) or (H) of this section to ensure that withholding or deduction from the income or assets of the obligor is available from the commencement of the support order for the collection of the support and any arrearages that occur. The court shall determine the specific withholding or deduction requirements or other appropriate requirements applicable to the obligor under the support order in accordance with divisions (D) and (H) of this section and section 2301.371 of the Revised Code and shall include the specific requirements in the notices described in divisions (A)(2) and (D) of this section or in the court orders described in divisions (A)(2), (D)(3) or (4), and (H) of this section. Any person required to comply with any withholding or deduction requirement shall determine the manner of withholding or deducting from the specific requirement included in the notices described in those divisions without the need for any amendment to the support order, and any person required to comply with a court order described in division (D)(3), (D)(4), or (H) of this section shall comply with the court order without the need for any amendment to the support order. The court shall include in any action in which support is ordered as described in division (A)(1) of this section a general provision that states the following:

"All child support and spousal support under this order shall be withheld or deducted from the income or assets of the obligor pursuant to a withholding or deduction notice or appropriate court order issued in accordance with section 3113.21 of the Revised Code or a withdrawal directive issued pursuant to section 3113.214 of the Revised Code and shall be forwarded to the obligee in accordance with sections 3113.21 to 3113.213 of the Revised Code."

(2) In any action in which support is ordered or modified as described in division (A)(1) of this section, the court shall determine in accordance with divisions (D) and (H) of this section the types of withholding or deduction requirements or other appropriate requirements that should be imposed relative to the obligor under the support order to collect the support due under the order. Within fifteen days after the obligor under the support order is located subsequent to the issuance of the support order or within fifteen days after the default under the support order, whichever is applicable, the court or the child support enforcement agency, as determined by agreement of the court and the agency, shall send a notice by regular mail to each person required to comply with a withholding or deduction requirement. The notice shall specify the withholding or deduction requirement and shall contain all of the information set forth in division (D)(1)(b) or (2)(b) of this section that is applicable to the requirement. If the appropriate requirement is an order of the type described in division (D)(3), (D)(4), or (H) of this section, the court shall issue and send a court order in accordance with that division. The notices and court orders, and the notices provided by the court or child support enforcement agency that require the obligor to notify the agency of any change in the obligor's employment status or of any other change in the status of the obligor's assets, are final and are enforceable by the court. When the court or agency issues a notice, it shall provide the notice to the obligor in accordance with division (D)(1)(c) or (D)(2)(c) of this section, whichever is applicable, and shall include with the notice the additional notices described in the particular division that is applicable.

(3)(a) If support is ordered or modified on or after December 31, 1993, under Chapter 3115. or under section 2151.23, 2151.231, 2151.232, 2151.33, 2151.36, 2151.49, 3105.18, 3105.21, 3109.05, 3109.19, 3111.13, 3113.04, 3113.07, 3113.216, or 3113.31 of the Revised Code, if the court has determined in accordance with division (A)(2) of this section the types of withholding or deduction requirements or other appropriate requirements that should be imposed relative to the obligor under the support order to collect the support due under the order, if the court or a child support enforcement agency has mailed the appropriate notice to the person required to comply with the withholding or deduction requirements that the court has determined should be imposed or the court has issued and sent a court order described in division (D)(3), (D)(4), or (H) of this section containing the other appropriate requirements that the court determined should be imposed, and if the child support enforcement agency is notified or otherwise determines that the employment status or other circumstances of the obligor have changed and that it is more appropriate to impose another type of or an additional withholding or deduction requirement or another type of or additional court order containing another appropriate requirement, the agency immediately shall comply with section 3113.212 of the Revised Code. The notices and court orders issued under this division and section 3113.212 of the Revised Code, and the notices provided by the court or child support enforcement agency that require the obligor to notify the agency of any change in the obligor's employment status or of any other change in the status of the obligor's assets, are final and are enforceable by the court.

(b) All orders for support issued prior to December 31, 1993, under Chapter 3115. or under section 2151.23, 2151.231, 2151.33, 2151.36, 2151.49, 3105.18, 3105.21, 3109.05, 3109.19, 3111.13, 3113.04, 3113.07, 3113.216, or 3113.31 of the Revised Code that have not been modified or subject to division (B) of this section regarding a default under the order on or after that date shall be considered to contain the general provision described in division (A)(1) of this section and shall be enforced and modified in the same manner as an order for support issued on or after December 31, 1993.

(4) The department of job and family services shall adopt standard forms for the support withholding and deduction notices that are prescribed by divisions (A)(1) to (3) and (B) of this section. All courts and child support enforcement agencies shall use the forms in issuing withholding and deduction notices in compliance with this section.

(B)(1)(a) In any action in which support is ordered under Chapter 3115. or under section 2151.23, 2151.231, 2151.232, 2151.33, 2151.36, 2151.49, 3105.18, 3105.21, 3109.05, 3109.19, 3111.13, 3111.20, 3111.211, 3111.22, 3113.04, 3113.07, 3113.216, or 3113.31 of the Revised Code and in which there has been a default under the order, the court shall comply with divisions (B)(1) to (6) of this section.

If the support was ordered prior to December 31, 1993, or pursuant to section 3111.20, 3111.211, or 3111.22 of the Revised Code, the court that issued the order, or in the case of an order pursuant to section 3111.20, 3111.211, or 3111.22 of the Revised Code, the common pleas court of the county in which the child support enforcement agency that issued the order is located, shall reissue the support order under which there has been a default and shall include in the reissued order a general provision as described in this division requiring the withholding or deduction of income or assets of the obligor in accordance with division (D) of this section or requiring the issuance of a court order containing another type of appropriate requirement in accordance with division (D)(3), (D)(4), or (H) of this section to ensure that withholding or deduction from the income or assets is available for the collection of current support and any arrearages that occur. If the support was ordered pursuant to section 3111.20, 3111.211, or 3111.22 of the Revised Code and the support order includes a general provision similar to the one described in this division, the court shall replace the similar general provision with the general provision described in this division. Except for the inclusion or replacement of the general provision, the provisions of the reissued order required under this division shall be identical to those of the support order under which there has been a default.

When support has been ordered under any chapter or section described in this division, the child support enforcement agency shall initiate support withholding when the order is in default. Immediately after the identification of a default under the support order, the child support enforcement agency shall conduct the investigation described in division (B)(1)(b) of this section. Additionally, within fifteen calendar days after the identification of a default under the support order, the child support enforcement agency shall investigate the default and, if it is before July 1, 1999, send advance notice to the obligor. On and after that date, the division of child support in the department of human services shall send the advance notice to the obligor. The advance notice shall include a notice describing the actions that may be taken against the obligor pursuant to sections 2301.353, 2301.373, 2301.374, 2301.375, 2301.42 to 2301.45, and 3113.214 of the Revised Code if the court or agency makes a final and enforceable determination that the obligor is in default pursuant to this division. If the location of the obligor is unknown at the time of the identification of a default under the support order, the division shall send the advance notice to the obligor within fifteen days after the agency locates the obligor. The general provision for the withholding or deduction of income or assets to be included in the reissued support order specifically shall include the following statement:

"All child support and spousal support under this order shall be withheld or deducted from the income or assets of the obligor pursuant to a withholding or deduction notice or appropriate court order issued in accordance with section 3113.21 of the Revised Code or a withdrawal directive issued pursuant to section 3113.214 of the Revised Code and shall be forwarded to the obligee in accordance with sections 3113.21 to 3113.213 of the Revised Code."

(b) After the identification of a default under a support order as described in division (B)(1)(a) of this section, the child support enforcement agency immediately shall conduct an investigation to determine the employment status of the obligor, the obligor's social security number, the name and business address of the obligor's employer, whether the obligor is in default under a support order, the amount of any arrearages, and any other information necessary to enable the court or agency to impose any withholding or deduction requirements and issue the related notices described in division (D) of this section or to issue any court orders described in division (D)(3) or (4) of this section. The agency also shall conduct an investigation under this division when required by division (C)(1)(a) or (b) of this section, shall complete the investigation within twenty days after the obligor or obligee files the motion with the court under division (C)(1)(a) of this section or the court orders the investigation under division (C)(1)(b) of this section.

(2) An advance notice to an obligor required by division (B)(1) of this section shall contain all of the following:

(a) A statement of the date on which the advance notice is sent, the amount of arrearages owed by the obligor as determined by the court or the child support enforcement agency, the types of withholding or deduction requirements and related notices described in division (D) of this section or the types of court orders described in division (D)(3), (D)(4), or (H) of this section that will be issued to pay support and any arrearages, and the amount that will be withheld or deducted pursuant to those requirements;

(b) A statement that any notice for the withholding or deduction of an amount from income or assets apply to all current and subsequent payors of the obligor and financial institutions in which the obligor has an account and that any withholding or deduction requirement and related notice described in division (D) of this section or any court order described in division (D)(3), (D)(4), or (H) of this section that is issued will not be discontinued solely because the obligor pays any arrearages;

(c) An explanation of the administrative and court action that will take place if the obligor contests the inclusion of any of the provisions;

(d) A statement that the contents of the advance notice are final and are enforceable by the court unless the obligor files with the child support enforcement agency, within seven days after the date on which the advance notice is sent, a written request for an administrative hearing to determine if a mistake of fact was made in the notice.

(3) If the obligor requests a hearing regarding the advance notice in accordance with division (B)(2)(d) of this section, the child support enforcement agency shall conduct an administrative hearing no later than ten days after the date on which the obligor files the request for the hearing. No later than five days before the date on which the hearing is to be conducted, the agency shall send the obligor and the obligee written notice of the date, time, place, and purpose of the hearing. The notice to the obligor and obligee also shall indicate that the obligor may present testimony and evidence at the hearing only in regard to the issue of whether a mistake of fact was made in the advance notice.

At the hearing, the child support enforcement agency shall determine whether a mistake of fact was made in the advance notice. If it determines that a mistake of fact was made, the agency shall determine the provisions that should be changed and included in a corrected notice and shall correct the advance notice accordingly. The agency shall send its determinations to the obligor. The agency's determinations are final and are enforceable by the court unless, within seven days after the agency makes its determinations, the obligor files a written motion with the court for a court hearing to determine if a mistake of fact still exists in the advance notice or corrected advance notice.

(4) If, within seven days after the agency makes its determinations under division (B)(3) of this section, the obligor files a written motion for a court hearing to determine if a mistake of fact still exists in the advance notice or the corrected advance notice, the court shall hold a hearing on the request as soon as possible, but no later than ten days, after the request is filed. If the obligor requests a court hearing, no later than five days before the date on which the court hearing is to be held, the court shall send the obligor and the obligee written notice by ordinary mail of the date, time, place, and purpose of the court hearing. The hearing shall be limited to a determination of whether there is a mistake of fact in the advance notice or the corrected advance notice.

If, at a hearing conducted under this division, the court detects a mistake of fact in the advance notice or the corrected advance notice, it immediately shall correct the notice.

(5) Upon exhaustion of all rights of the obligor to contest the withholding or deduction on the basis of a mistake of fact and no later than the expiration of forty-five days after the issuance of the advance notice under division (B)(1) of this section, the court or child support enforcement agency shall issue one or more notices requiring withholding or deduction of income or assets of the obligor in accordance with divisions (A)(2) and (D) of this section, or the court shall issue one or more court orders imposing other appropriate requirements in accordance with division (A)(2) and division (D)(3), (D)(4), or (H) of this section. Thereafter, section 3113.212 of the Revised Code applies in relation to the issuance of the notices and court orders. The notices and court orders issued under this division or section 3113.212 of the Revised Code are final and are enforceable by the court. The court or agency shall send to the obligor by ordinary mail a copy of the withholding or deduction notice, in accordance with division (D) of this section. The failure of the court or agency to give the notice required by this division does not affect the ability of any court to issue any notice or order under this section or any other section of the Revised Code for the payment of support, does not provide any defense to any notice or order for the payment of support that is issued under this section or any other section of the Revised Code, and does not affect any obligation to pay support.

(6) The department of job and family services shall adopt standard forms for the advance notice prescribed by divisions (B)(1) to (5) of this section. All courts and child support enforcement agencies shall use those forms, and the support withholding and deduction notice forms adopted under division (A)(4) of this section, in complying with this section.

(C)(1) In any action in which support is ordered under Chapter 3115. or under section 2151.23, 2151.231, 2151.232, 2151.33, 2151.36, 2151.49, 3105.18, 3105.21, 3109.05, 3109.19, 3111.13, 3113.04, 3113.07, 3113.216, or 3113.31 of the Revised Code, all of the following apply:

(a) The obligor or obligee under the order may file a motion with the court that issued the order requesting the issuance of one or more withholding or deduction notices as described in division (D) of this section to pay the support due under the order. The motion may be filed at any time after the support order is issued. Upon the filing of a motion pursuant to this division, the child support enforcement agency immediately shall conduct, and shall complete within twenty days after the motion is filed, an investigation in accordance with division (B)(1)(b) of this section. Upon the completion of the investigation and the filing of the agency's report under division (B)(1)(b) of this section, the court shall issue one or more appropriate orders described in division (D) of this section.

(b) If any proceedings involving the support order are commenced in the court and if the court has not issued any orders under division (D) of this section as it existed prior to December 31, 1993, with respect to the support order, if the court determines that any orders issued under division (D) of this section as it existed prior to December 31, 1993, no longer are appropriate, if the court on or after December 31, 1993, has not modified or reissued the support order under division (A) or (B) of this section and issued any notices under division (D) or court orders under division (D)(3) or (4) of this section, or if the court on or after December 31, 1993, has modified or reissued the support order under division (A) or (B) of this section and issued one or more notices under division (D) or one or more court orders under division (D)(3) or (4) of this section but determines that the notices or court orders no longer are appropriate, the court, prior to or during any hearings held with respect to the proceedings and prior to the conclusion of the proceedings, shall order the child support enforcement agency to conduct an investigation pursuant to division (B)(1)(b) of this section. Upon the filing of the findings of the agency following the investigation, the court, as necessary, shall issue one or more notices described in division (D) or one or more court orders described in division (D)(3) or (4) of this section or modify any notices previously issued under division (D) or any court orders previously issued under division (D)(3) or (4) of this section.

(c)(i) If a child support enforcement agency, in accordance with section 3113.216 of the Revised Code, requests the court to issue a revised child support order in accordance with a revised amount of child support calculated by the agency, the court shall proceed as described in this division. If neither the obligor nor the obligee requests a court hearing on the revised amount of child support, the court shall issue a revised child support order requiring the obligor to pay the revised amount of child support calculated by the agency. However, if the obligor or the obligee requests a court hearing on the revised amount of child support calculated by the agency, the court, in accordance with division (C)(1)(c)(ii) of this section, shall schedule and conduct a hearing to determine if the revised amount of child support is the appropriate amount and if the amount of child support being paid under the child support order otherwise should be revised.

(ii) If the court is required to schedule and conduct a hearing pursuant to division (C)(1)(c)(i) of this section, the court shall give the obligor, obligee, and agency at least thirty days' notice of the date, time, and location of the hearing; order the obligor to provide the court with a copy of the obligor's federal income tax return from the previous year, a copy of all pay stubs obtained by the obligor within the preceding six months, a copy of all other records evidencing the receipt of any other salary, wages, or compensation by the obligor within the preceding six months, a list of the group health insurance and health care policies, contracts, and plans available to the obligor and their costs, and the current health insurance or health care policy, contract, or plan under which the obligor is enrolled and its cost, if the obligor failed to provide any of those documents to the agency, and order the obligee to provide the court with a copy of the obligee's federal income tax return from the previous year, a copy of all pay stubs obtained by the obligee within the preceding six months, a copy of all other records evidencing the receipt of any other salary, wages, or compensation by the obligee within the preceding six months, a list of the group health insurance and health care policies, contracts, and plans available to the obligee and their costs, and the current health insurance or health care policy, contract, or plan under which the obligee is enrolled and its cost, if the obligee failed to provide any of those documents to the agency; give the obligor and the obligee notice that any willful failure to comply with that court order is contempt of court and, upon a finding by the court that the party is in contempt of court, the court and the agency will take any action necessary to obtain the information or make any reasonable assumptions necessary with respect to the information the person in contempt of court did not provide to ensure a fair and equitable review of the child support order; issue a revised child support order requiring the obligor to pay the revised amount of child support calculated by the agency, if the court determines at the hearing that the revised amount of child support calculated by the agency is the appropriate amount; and determine the appropriate amount of child support and, if necessary, issue a revised child support order requiring the obligor to pay the amount of child support determined by the court, if the court determines that the revised amount of child support calculated by the agency is not the appropriate amount.

(iii) In determining, at a hearing conducted under divisions (C)(1)(c)(i) and (ii) of this section, the appropriate amount of child support to be paid by the obligor, the court shall consider, in addition to all other factors required by law to be considered, the appropriate person, whether it is the obligor, obligee, or both, to be required in accordance with section 3113.217 of the Revised Code to provide health insurance coverage for the children specified in the order, and the cost of health insurance which the obligor, the obligee, or both have been ordered in accordance with section 3113.217 of the Revised Code to obtain for the children specified in the order.

(d)(i) An obligee under a child support order may file a motion with the court that issued the order requesting the court to modify the order to require the obligor to obtain health insurance coverage for the children who are the subject of the order, and an obligor under a child support order may file a motion with the court that issued the order requesting the court to modify the order to require the obligee to obtain health insurance coverage for those children. Upon the filing of such a motion, the court shall order the child support enforcement agency to conduct an investigation to determine whether the obligor or obligee has satisfactory health insurance coverage for the children. Upon completion of its investigation, the agency shall inform the court, in writing, of its determination. If the court determines that neither the obligor nor the obligee has satisfactory health insurance coverage for the children, it shall modify the child support order in accordance with section 3113.217 of the Revised Code.

(ii) An obligor or obligee under a child support order may file a motion with the court that issued the order requesting the court to modify the amount of child support required to be paid under the order because that amount does not adequately cover the medical needs of the child. Upon the filing of such a motion, the court shall determine whether the amount of child support required to be paid under the order adequately covers the medical needs of the child and whether to modify the order, in accordance with division (B)(4) of section 3113.215 of the Revised Code.

(e) Whenever a court modifies, reviews, or otherwise reconsiders a child support order, it may reconsider which parent may claim the children who are the subject of the child support order as dependents for federal income tax purposes as set forth in section 151 of the "Internal Revenue Code of 1986," 100 Stat. 2085, 26 U.S.C. 1, as amended, and shall issue its determination on this issue as part of the child support order. The court in its order may permit the parent who is not the residential parent and legal custodian to claim the children as dependents for federal income tax purposes only if the payments for child support are current in full as ordered by the court for the year in which the children will be claimed as dependents. If the court determines that the parent who is not the residential parent and legal custodian may claim the children as dependents for federal income tax purposes, it shall order the residential parent to take whatever action is necessary pursuant to section 152 of the "Internal Revenue Code of 1986," 100 Stat. 2085, 26 U.S.C. 1, as amended, to enable the parent who is not the residential parent and legal custodian to claim the children as dependents for federal income tax purposes in accordance with the order of the court. Any willful failure of the residential parent to comply with the order of the court is contempt of court.

(f) When issuing or modifying a child support order, the court shall include in the order all of the requirements, specifications, and statements described in division (B) of section 3113.218 of the Revised Code. If the obligor or obligee does not request a court hearing on the revised amount of child support determined by the agency and filed with the court pursuant to section 3113.216 of the Revised Code and the court modifies the order to include the revised amount pursuant to division (C)(1)(c)(i) of this section, the modification shall relate back to the first day of the month following the date certain on which the review of the child support order began pursuant to division (C)(1)(a) of section 3113.216 of the Revised Code. If the obligor or obligee requests a court hearing on the revised amount of child support pursuant to this section and section 3113.216 of the Revised Code and the court, after conducting a hearing, modifies the child support amount under the order, the modification shall relate back to the first day of the month following the date certain on which the review of the child support order began pursuant to division (C)(1)(a) of section 3113.216 of the Revised Code.

(2) In any action in which a support order is issued under Chapter 3115. or under section 2151.23, 2151.231, 2151.232, 2151.33, 2151.36, 2151.49, 3105.18, 3105.21, 3109.05, 3109.19, 3111.13, 3113.04, 3113.07, 3113.216, or 3113.31 of the Revised Code, the court issuing the order also shall conduct a hearing, prior to or at the time of the issuance of the support order, to determine the employment status of the obligor, the obligor's social security number, the name and business address of the obligor's employer, and any other information necessary to enable the court or a child support enforcement agency to issue any withholding or deduction notice described in division (D) of this section or for the court to issue a court order described in division (D)(3) or (4) of this section. The court, prior to the hearing, shall give the obligor notice of the hearing that shall include the date on which the notice is given and notice that the obligor is subject to a requirement for the withholding of a specified amount from income if employed and to one or more other types of withholding or deduction requirements described in division (D) of this section or one or more types of court orders described in division (D)(3) or (4) of this section and that the obligor may present evidence and testimony at the hearing to prove that any of the requirements would not be proper because of a mistake of fact.

The court or child support enforcement agency, immediately upon the court's completion of the hearing, shall issue one or more of the types of notices described in division (D) of this section imposing a withholding or deduction requirement, or the court shall issue one or more types of court orders described in division (D)(3) or (4) of this section.

(D) If a court or child support enforcement agency is required under division (A), (B), or (C) of this section or any other section of the Revised Code to issue one or more withholding or deduction notices described in this division or court orders described in division (D)(3) or (4) of this section, the court shall issue one or more of the following types of notices or court orders, or the agency shall issue one or more of the following types of notices to pay the support required under the support order in question and also, if required by any of those divisions, any other section of the Revised Code, or the court, to pay any arrearages:

(1)(a) If the court or the child support enforcement agency determines that the obligor is receiving income from a payor, the court or agency shall require the obligor's payor to withhold from the obligor's income a specified amount for support in satisfaction of the support order, to begin the withholding no later than fourteen working days following the date the notice was mailed to the employer under divisions (A)(2) or (B) and (D)(1)(b) of this section or, if the payor is an employer, no later than the first pay period that occurs after fourteen working days following the date the notice was mailed, to send the amount withheld to the division of child support in the department of job and family services pursuant to section 5101.325 of the Revised Code, to send that amount to the division immediately but not later than seven days after the date the obligor is paid, and to continue the withholding at intervals specified in the notice until further notice from the court or child support enforcement agency. To the extent possible, the amount specified in the notice to be withheld shall satisfy the amount ordered for support in the support order plus any arrearages that may be owed by the obligor under any prior support order that pertained to the same child or spouse, notwithstanding any applicable limitations of sections 2329.66, 2329.70, 2716.02, 2716.041, and 2716.05 of the Revised Code. However, in no case shall the sum of the amount specified in the notice to be withheld and any fee withheld by the payor as a charge for its services exceed the maximum amount permitted under section 303(b) of the "Consumer Credit Protection Act," 15 U.S.C. 1673(b).

(b) If the court or agency imposes a withholding requirement under division (D)(1)(a) of this section, it, within the applicable period of time specified in division (A), (B), or (C) of this section, shall send to the obligor's payor by regular mail a notice that contains all of the information set forth in divisions (D)(1)(b)(i) to (xi) of this section. The notice is final and is enforceable by the court. The notice shall contain all of the following:

(i) The amount to be withheld from the obligor's income and a statement that the amount actually withheld for support and other purposes, including the fee described in division (D)(1)(b)(xi) of this section, shall not be in excess of the maximum amounts permitted under section 303(b) of the "Consumer Credit Protection Act," 15 U.S.C. 1673(b);

(ii) A statement that the payor is required to send the amount withheld to the division of child support immediately, but not later than seven working days, after the obligor is paid and is required to report to the agency the date on which the amount was withheld from the obligor's income;

(iii) A statement that the withholding is binding upon the payor until further notice from the agency;

(iv) A statement that if the payor is an employer, the payor is subject to a fine to be determined under the law of this state for discharging the obligor from employment, refusing to employ the obligor, or taking any disciplinary action against the obligor because of the withholding requirement;

(v) A statement that, if the payor fails to withhold income in accordance with the provisions of the notice, the payor is liable for the accumulated amount the payor should have withheld from the obligor's income;

(vi) A statement that the withholding in accordance with the notice and under the provisions of this section has priority over any other legal process under the law of this state against the same income;

(vii) The date on which the notice was mailed and a statement that the payor is required to implement the withholding no later than fourteen working days following the date the notice was mailed or, if the payor is an employer, no later than the first pay period that occurs after fourteen working days following the date the notice was mailed and is required to continue the withholding at the intervals specified in the notice;

(viii) A requirement that the payor promptly notify the child support enforcement agency, in writing, within ten working days after the date of any situation that occurs including termination of employment, layoff of the obligor from employment, any leave of absence of the obligor from employment without pay, termination of workers' compensation benefits, or termination of any pension, annuity, allowance, or retirement benefit, in which the payor ceases to pay income in an amount sufficient to comply with the order to the obligor, provide the agency with the obligor's last known address, notify the agency of any new employer or income source, if known, and provide the agency with any new employer's or income source's name, address, and telephone number, if known;

(ix) A requirement that, if the payor is an employer, the payor identify in the notification given under division (D)(1)(b)(viii) of this section any types of benefits other than personal earnings that the obligor is receiving or is eligible to receive as a benefit of employment or as a result of the obligor's termination of employment, including, but not limited to, unemployment compensation, workers' compensation benefits, severance pay, sick leave, lump-sum payments of retirement benefits or contributions, and bonuses or profit-sharing payments or distributions, and the amount of such benefits, and include in the notification the obligor's last known address and telephone number, date of birth, social security number, and court case number and, if known, the name and business address of any new employer of the obligor;

(x) A requirement that, no later than the earlier of forty-five days before the lump-sum payment is to be made or, if the obligor's right to the lump-sum payment is determined less than forty-five days before it is to be made, the date on which that determination is made, the payor notify the child support enforcement agency of any lump-sum payments of any kind of one hundred fifty dollars or more that are to be paid to the obligor, hold the lump-sum payments of one hundred fifty dollars or more for thirty days after the date on which the lump-sum payments otherwise would have been paid to the obligor and, upon order of the court, pay any specified amount of the lump-sum payment to the division of child support;

(xi) A statement that, in addition to the amount withheld for support, the payor may withhold a fee from the obligor's income as a charge for its services in complying with the notice and a specification of the amount that may be withheld.

(c) The court or agency shall send the notice described in division (D)(1)(b) of this section to the obligor and shall attach to the notice an additional notice requiring the obligor immediately to notify the child support enforcement agency, in writing, of any change in the obligor's income source and of the availability of any other sources of income that can be the subject of any withholding or deduction requirement described in division (D) of this section. The court or agency shall serve the notices upon the obligor at the same time as service of the support order or, if the support order previously has been issued, shall send the notices to the obligor by regular mail at the last known address at the same time that it sends the notice described in division (D)(1)(b) of this section to the payor. The notification required of the obligor shall include a description of the nature of any new employment or income source, the name, business address, and telephone number of any new employer or income source, and any other information reasonably required by the court. No obligor shall fail to give the notification required by division (D)(1)(c) of this section.

(2)(a) If the court or child support enforcement agency determines that the obligor has funds on deposit in any account in a financial institution under the jurisdiction of the court, the court or agency may require any financial institution in which the obligor's funds are on deposit to deduct from the obligor's account a specified amount for support in satisfaction of the support order, to begin the deduction no later than fourteen working days following the date the notice was mailed to the financial institution under divisions (A)(2) or (B) and (D)(2)(b) of this section, to send the amount deducted to the division of child support in the department of job and family services pursuant to section 5101.325 of the Revised Code, to send that amount to the division immediately but not later than seven working days after the date the latest deduction was made, to provide the date on which the amount was deducted, and to continue the deduction at intervals specified in the notice until further notice from the court or child support enforcement agency. To the extent possible, the amount specified in the notice to be deducted shall satisfy the amount ordered for support in the support order plus any arrearages that may be owed by the obligor under any prior support order that pertained to the same child or spouse, notwithstanding the limitations of sections 2329.66, 2329.70, and 2716.13 of the Revised Code.

(b) If the court or agency imposes a withholding requirement under division (D)(2)(a) of this section, it, within the applicable period of time specified in division (A), (B), or (C) of this section, shall send to the financial institution by regular mail a notice that contains all of the information set forth in divisions (D)(2)(b)(i) to (viii) of this section. The notice is final and is enforceable by the court. The notice shall contain all of the following:

(i) The amount to be deducted from the obligor's account;

(ii) A statement that the financial institution is required to send the amount deducted to the division of child support immediately, but not later than seven working days, after the date the last deduction was made and is required to report to the child support enforcement agency the date on which the amount was deducted from the obligor's account;

(iii) A statement that the deduction is binding upon the financial institution until further notice from the court or agency;

(iv) A statement that the withholding in accordance with the notice and under the provisions of this section has priority over any other legal process under the law of this state against the same account;

(v) The date on which the notice was mailed and a statement that the financial institution is required to implement the deduction no later than fourteen working days following the date the notice was mailed and is required to continue the deduction at the intervals specified in the notice;

(vi) A requirement that the financial institution promptly notify the child support enforcement agency, in writing, within ten days after the date of any termination of the account from which the deduction is being made and notify the agency, in writing, of the opening of a new account at that financial institution, the account number of the new account, the name of any other known financial institutions in which the obligor has any accounts, and the numbers of those accounts;

(vii) A requirement that the financial institution include in all notices the obligor's last known mailing address, last known residence address, and social security number;

(viii) A statement that, in addition to the amount deducted for support, the financial institution may deduct a fee from the obligor's account as a charge for its services in complying with the notice and a specification of the amount that may be deducted.

(c) The court or agency shall send the notice described in division (D)(2)(b) of this section to the obligor and shall attach to the notice an additional notice requiring the obligor immediately to notify the child support enforcement agency, in writing, of any change in the status of the account from which the amount of support is being deducted or the opening of a new account with any financial institution, of commencement of employment, including self-employment, or of the availability of any other sources of income that can be the subject of any withholding or deduction requirement described in division (D) of this section. The court or agency shall serve the notices upon the obligor at the same time as service of the support order or, if the support order previously has been issued, shall send the notices to the obligor by regular mail at the last known address at the same time that it sends the notice described in division (D)(2)(b) of this section to the financial institution. The additional notice also shall specify that upon commencement of employment, the obligor may request the court or child support enforcement agency to cancel its financial institution account deduction notice and instead issue a notice requiring the withholding of an amount from personal earnings for support in accordance with division (D)(1) of this section and that upon commencement of employment the court may cancel its financial institution account deduction notice under division (D)(2)(b) of this section and instead will issue a notice requiring the withholding of an amount from personal earnings for support in accordance with division (D)(1) of this section. The notification required of the obligor shall include a description of the nature of any new accounts opened at a financial institution under the jurisdiction of the court, the name and business address of that financial institution, a description of the nature of any new employment or income source, the name, business address, and telephone number of any new employer or income source, and any other information reasonably required by the court.

(3) The court may issue an order requiring the obligor to enter into a cash bond with the court. The court shall issue the order as part of the support order or, if the support order previously has been issued, as a separate order. Any cash bond so required shall be in a sum fixed by the court at not less than five hundred nor more than ten thousand dollars, conditioned that the obligor will make payment as previously ordered and will pay any arrearages under any prior support order that pertained to the same child or spouse. The order, along with an additional order requiring the obligor to immediately notify the child support enforcement agency, in writing, if the obligor begins to receive income from a payor, shall be attached to, and shall be served upon the obligor at the same time as service of, the support order or, if the support order previously has been issued, as soon as possible after the issuance of the order under this division. The additional order also shall specify that when the obligor begins to receive income from a payor the obligor may request the court to cancel its bond order and

instead issue a notice requiring the withholding of an amount from income for support in accordance with division (D)(1) of this section and that when the obligor begins to receive income from a payor the court will proceed to collect on the bond, if the court determines that payments due under the support order have not been made and that the amount that has not been paid is at least equal to the support owed for one month under the support order, and will issue a notice requiring the withholding of an amount from income for support in accordance with division (D)(1) of this section. The notification required of the obligor shall include a description of the nature of any new employment, the name and business address of any new employer, and any other information reasonably required by the court.

The court shall not order an obligor to post a cash bond under this division unless the court determines that the obligor has the ability to do so. A child support enforcement agency shall not issue an order of the type described in this division. If a child support enforcement agency is required to issue a withholding or deduction notice under division (D) of this section but the agency determines that no notice of the type described in division (D)(1) or (2) of this section would be appropriate, the agency may request the court to issue a court order under this division, and, upon the request, the court may issue an order as described in this division.

(4) If the obligor is unemployed, has no income, and does not have an account at any financial institution, or on request of a child support enforcement agency made under section 3111.231 of the Revised Code, the court shall issue an order requiring the obligor, if able to engage in employment, to seek employment or participate in a work activity to which a recipient of assistance under Title IV-A of the "Social Security Act," 49 Stat. 620 (1935), 42 U.S.C.A. 301, as amended, may be assigned as specified in section 407(d) of the "Social Security Act," 42 U.S.C.A. 607(d), as amended. The court shall include in the order a requirement that the obligor notify the child support enforcement agency upon obtaining employment, upon obtaining any income, or upon obtaining ownership of any asset with a value of five hundred dollars or more. The court may issue the order regardless of whether the obligee to whom the obligor owes support is a recipient of assistance under Title IV-A of the "Social Security Act." The court shall issue the order as part of a support order or, if a support order previously has been issued, as a separate order. If a child support enforcement agency is required to issue a withholding or deduction notice under division (D) of this section but the agency determines that no notice of the type described in division (D)(1) or (2) of this section would be appropriate, the agency may request the court to issue a court order under division (D)(4) of this section, and, upon the request, the court may issue an order as described in division (D)(4) of this section.

If an obligor is ordered to participate in a work activity, the child support enforcement agency of the county in which the obligor resides shall oversee the obligor's participation in accordance with rules the director of job and family services shall adopt in accordance with Chapter 119. of the Revised Code. A child support enforcement agency may contract with one or more governmental agencies or persons to carry out some or all of its oversight duties.

(E) If a court or child support enforcement agency is required under division (A), (B), or (C) of this section or any other section of the Revised Code to issue one or more notices or court orders described in division (D) of this section, the court or agency to the extent possible shall issue a sufficient number of notices or court orders under division (D) of this section to provide that the aggregate amount withheld or deducted under those notices or court orders satisfies the amount ordered for support in the support order plus any arrearages that may be owed by the obligor under any prior support order that pertained to the same child or spouse, notwithstanding any applicable limitations of sections 2329.66, 2329.70, 2716.02, 2716.041, 2716.05, 2716.13, and 4123.67 of the Revised Code. However, in no case shall the aggregate amount withheld pursuant to a withholding notice issued under division (D)(1) of this section and any fees withheld pursuant to the notice as a charge for services exceed the maximum amount permitted under section 303(b) of the "Consumer Credit Protection Act," 15 U.S.C. 1673(b).

(F)(1) Any withholding or deduction requirement that is contained in a notice described in division (D) of this section and that is required to be issued by division (A), (B), or (C) of this section or any other section of the Revised Code has priority over any order of attachment, any order in aid of execution, and any other legal process issued under state law against the same earnings, payments, or account.

(2) When a payor receives two or more withholding notices that are described in division (D)(1) of this section and that are required to be issued by division (A), (B), or (C) of this section or any other section of the Revised Code, the payor shall comply with all of the requirements contained in the notices to the extent that the total amount withheld from the obligor's income does not exceed the maximum amount permitted under section 303(b) of the "Consumer Credit Protection Act," 15 U.S.C. 1673(b), withhold amounts in accordance with the allocation set forth in divisions (F)(2)(a) and (b) of this section, notify each court or child support enforcement agency that issued one of the notices of the allocation, and give priority to amounts designated in each notice as current support in the following manner:

(a) If the total of the amounts designated in the notices as current support exceeds the amount available for withholding under section 303(b) of the "Consumer Credit Protection Act," 15 U.S.C. 1673(b), the payor shall allocate to each notice an amount for current support equal to the amount designated in that notice as current support multiplied by a fraction in which the numerator is the amount of income available for withholding and the denominator is the total amount designated in all of the notices as current support.

(b) If the total of the amounts designated in the notices as current support does not exceed the amount available for withholding under section 303(b) of the "Consumer Credit Protection Act," 15 U.S.C. 1673(b), the payor shall pay all of the amounts designated as current support in the notices and shall allocate to each notice an amount for past-due support equal to the amount designated in that notice as past-due support multiplied by a fraction in which the numerator is the amount of income remaining available for withholding after the payment of current support and the denominator is the total amount designated in all of the notices as past-due support.

(G)(1) Except when a provision specifically authorizes or requires service other than as described in this division, service of any notice on any party, a financial institution, or payor, for purposes of division (A), (B), (C), or (D) of this section, shall be made by ordinary first class mail directed to the addressee at the last known address, or, in the case of a corporation, at its usual place of doing business. A notice shall be considered to have been served when it is mailed.

(2) Each party to a support order shall notify the child support enforcement agency of the party's current mailing address, current residence address, current residence telephone number, and current driver's license number, at the time of the issuance or modification of the order and, until further notice of the court that issues the order, shall notify the agency of any change in that information immediately after the change occurs. Any willful failure to comply with this division is contempt of court. No person shall fail to give the notice required by division (G)(2) of this section.

(3) Each support order, or modification of a support order, that is subject to this section shall contain a notice that states the following in boldfaced type and in all capital letters:

"EACH PARTY TO THIS SUPPORT ORDER MUST NOTIFY THE CHILD SUPPORT ENFORCEMENT AGENCY IN WRITING OF HIS OR HER CURRENT MAILING ADDRESS, CURRENT RESIDENCE ADDRESS, CURRENT RESIDENCE TELEPHONE NUMBER, CURRENT DRIVER'S LICENSE NUMBER, AND OF ANY CHANGES IN THAT INFORMATION. EACH PARTY MUST NOTIFY THE AGENCY OF ALL CHANGES UNTIL FURTHER NOTICE FROM THE COURT. IF YOU ARE THE OBLIGOR UNDER A CHILD SUPPORT ORDER AND YOU FAIL TO MAKE THE REQUIRED NOTIFICATIONS YOU MAY BE FINED UP TO $50 FOR A FIRST OFFENSE, $100 FOR A SECOND OFFENSE, AND $500 FOR EACH SUBSEQUENT

OFFENSE. IF YOU ARE AN OBLIGOR OR OBLIGEE UNDER ANY SUPPORT ORDER AND YOU WILLFULLY FAIL TO MAKE THE REQUIRED NOTIFICATIONS YOU MAY BE FOUND IN CONTEMPT OF COURT AND BE SUBJECTED TO FINES UP TO $1,000 AND IMPRISONMENT FOR NOT MORE THAN 90 DAYS.

IF YOU ARE AN OBLIGOR AND YOU FAIL TO MAKE THE REQUIRED NOTIFICATIONS YOU MAY NOT RECEIVE NOTICE OF THE FOLLOWING ENFORCEMENT ACTIONS AGAINST YOU: IMPOSITION OF LIENS AGAINST YOUR PROPERTY; LOSS OF YOUR PROFESSIONAL OR OCCUPATIONAL LICENSE, DRIVER'S LICENSE, OR RECREATIONAL LICENSE; WITHHOLDING FROM YOUR INCOME; ACCESS RESTRICTION AND DEDUCTION FROM YOUR ACCOUNTS IN FINANCIAL INSTITUTIONS; AND ANY OTHER ACTION PERMITTED BY LAW TO OBTAIN MONEY FROM YOU TO SATISFY YOUR SUPPORT OBLIGATION."

(4)(a) The parent who is the residential parent and legal custodian of a child for whom a support order is issued or the person who otherwise has custody of a child for whom a support order is issued immediately shall notify, and the obligor under a support order may notify, the child support enforcement agency of any reason for which the support order should terminate, including, but not limited to, the child's attainment of the age of majority if the child no longer attends an accredited high school on a full-time basis and the support order does not provide for the duty of support to continue past the age of majority; the child ceasing to attend such a high school on a full-time basis after attaining the age of majority, if the support order does not provide for the duty of support to continue past the age of majority; or the death, marriage, emancipation, enlistment in the armed services, deportation, or change of legal or physical custody of the child. A willful failure to notify the child support enforcement agency as required by this division is contempt of court. Upon receipt of a notice pursuant to this division, the agency immediately shall conduct an investigation to determine if any reason exists for which the support order should terminate. The agency may conduct such an investigation regardless of whether it received notice under this division. If the agency determines the order should terminate, it immediately shall notify the court that issued the support order of the reason for which the support order should terminate.

(b) Upon receipt of a notice given pursuant to division (G)(4)(a) of this section, the court shall order the division of child support to impound any funds received for the child pursuant to the support order and the court shall set the case for a hearing for a determination of whether the support order should be terminated or modified or whether the court should take any other appropriate action.

(c) If the court terminates a support order pursuant to divisions (G)(4)(a) and (b) of this section, the termination of the support order also terminates any withholding or deduction order as described in division (D) or (H) of this section issued prior to December 31, 1993, and any withholding or deduction notice as described in division (D) of this section or court order as described in division (D)(3), (D)(4), or (H) of this section issued on or after December 31, 1993. Upon the termination of any withholding or deduction order or any withholding or deduction notice, the court immediately shall notify the appropriate child support enforcement agency that the order or notice has been terminated, and the agency immediately shall notify each payor or financial institution required to withhold or deduct a sum of money for the payment of support under the terminated withholding or deduction order or notice that the order or notice has been terminated and that it is required to cease all withholding or deduction under the order or notice.

(d) The director of job and family services shall adopt rules that provide for both of the following:

(i) The return to the appropriate person of any funds that a court has ordered impounded under division (G)(4)(b) of this section if the support order under which the funds were paid has been terminated pursuant to divisions (G)(4)(a) and (b) of this section;

(ii) The return to the appropriate person of any other payments made pursuant to a support order if the payments were made at any time after the support order under which the funds were paid has been terminated pursuant to divisions (G)(4)(a) and (b) of this section.

(5) If any party to a support order requests a modification of the order or if any obligee under a support order or any person on behalf of the obligee files any action to enforce a support order, the court shall notify the child support enforcement agency that is administering the support order or that will administer the order after the court's determination of the request or the action, of the request or the filing.

(6) When a child support enforcement agency receives any notice under division (G) of section 2151.23, section 2301.37, division (E) of section 3105.18, division (C) of section 3105.21, division (A) of section 3109.05, division (F) of section 3111.13, division (B) of section 3113.04, section 3113.21, section 3113.211, section 3113.212, division (K) of section 3113.31, or division (C)(3) of section 3115.31 of the Revised Code, it shall issue the most appropriate notices under division (D) of this section. Additionally, it shall do all of the following:

(a) If the obligor is subject to a withholding notice issued under division (D)(1) of this section and the notice relates to the obligor's change of employment, send a withholding notice under that division to the new employer of the obligor as soon as the agency obtains knowledge of that employer;

(b) If the notification received by the agency specifies that a lump-sum payment of one hundred fifty dollars or more is to be paid to the obligor, notify the court of the receipt of the notice and its contents. The agency may notify the court if the notification specifies that a lump-sum payment of less than one hundred fifty dollars is to be paid to the obligor.

(c) Comply with section 3113.212 of the Revised Code, as appropriate.

(H)(1)(a) For purposes of division (D)(1) of this section, when a person who fails to comply with a support order that is subject to that division derives income from self-employment or commission, is employed by an employer not subject to the jurisdiction of the court, or is in any other employment situation that makes the application of that division impracticable, the court may require the person to enter into a cash bond to the court in a sum fixed by the court at not less than five hundred nor more than ten thousand dollars, conditioned that the person will make payment as previously ordered.

(b) When a court determines at a hearing conducted under division (B) of this section, or a child support enforcement agency determines at a hearing or pursuant to an investigation conducted under division (B) of this section, that the obligor under the order in relation to which the hearing or investigation is conducted is unemployed and has no other source of income and no assets so that the application of divisions (B) and (D) of this section would be impracticable, the court shall issue an order as described in division (D)(4) of this section and shall order the obligor to notify the child support enforcement agency in writing immediately of the receipt of any source of income or of the opening of an account in a financial institution, and to include in the notification a description of the nature of the employment or income source, the name, business address, and telephone number of the employer or income source, and any other information reasonably required by the court.

(2) When a court determines, at a hearing conducted under division (C)(2) of this section, that an obligor is unemployed, is not receiving workers' compensation payments, does not have an account in a financial institution, and has no other source of income and no assets so that the application of divisions (C)(2) and (D) of this section would be impracticable, the court shall issue an order as described in division (D)(4) of this section and shall order the obligor to notify the child support enforcement agency, in writing, immediately of the receipt of any source of income or of the opening of an account in a financial institution, and to include in the notification a description of the nature of the employment or income source, the name, business address, and telephone number of the employer or income source or the name, address, and telephone number of the financial institution, and any other information reasonably required by the court.

(3)(a) Upon receipt of a notice from a child support enforcement agency under division (G)(6) of this section that a lump-sum payment is to be paid to the obligor, the court shall do either of the following:

(i) If the obligor is in default under the support order or has any unpaid arrearages under the support order, issue an order requiring the transmittal of the lump-sum payment to the division of child support.

(ii) If the obligor is not in default under the support order and does not have any unpaid arrearages under the support order, issue an order directing the person who gave the notice to the court to immediately pay the full amount of the lump-sum payment to the obligor.

(b) Upon receipt of any moneys pursuant to division (H)(3)(a) of this section, the division of child support shall pay the amount of the lump-sum payment that is necessary to discharge all of the obligor's arrearages to the obligee and, within two business days after its receipt of the money, any amount that is remaining after the payment of the arrearages to the obligor.

(c) Any court that issued an order prior to December 1, 1986, requiring an employer to withhold an amount from an obligor's personal earnings for the payment of support shall issue a supplemental order that does not change the original order or the related support order requiring the employer to do all of the following:

(i) No later than the earlier of forty-five days before a lump-sum payment is to be made or, if the obligor's right to a lump-sum payment is determined less than forty-five days before it is to be made, the date on which that determination is made, notify the child support enforcement agency of any lump-sum payment of any kind of one hundred fifty dollars or more that is to be paid to the obligor;

(ii) Hold the lump-sum payment for thirty days after the date on which it would otherwise be paid to the obligor, if the lump-sum payment is sick pay, a lump-sum payment of retirement benefits or contributions, or profit-sharing payments or distributions;

(iii) Upon order of the court, pay any specified amount of the lump-sum payment to the division of child support.

(d) If an employer knowingly fails to notify the child support enforcement agency in accordance with division (D) of this section of any lump-sum payment to be made to an obligor, the employer is liable for any support payment not made to the obligee as a result of its knowing failure to give the notice as required by that division.

(I)(1) Any support order, or modification of a support order, that is subject to this section shall contain the date of birth and social security number of the obligor.

(2) No withholding or deduction notice described in division (D) of this section or court order described in division (D)(3) or (4) of this section shall contain any information other than the information specifically required by division (A), (B), (C), or (D) of this section or by any other section of the Revised Code and any additional information that the issuing court determines may be necessary to comply with the notice.

(J) No withholding or deduction notice described in division (D) of this section or court order described in division (D)(3) or (4) of this section and issued under division (A), (B), or (C) of this section or any other section of the Revised Code shall be terminated solely because the obligor pays any part or all of the arrearages under the support order.

(K)(1) Except as provided in division (K)(2) of this section and section 2301.42 of the Revised Code and the rules adopted pursuant to division (C) of that section, if child support arrearages are owed by an obligor to the obligee and to the department of job and family services, any payments received on the arrearages by the division of child support first shall be paid to the obligee until the arrearages owed to the obligee are paid in full.

(2) Division (K)(1) of this section does not apply to the collection of past-due child support from refunds of paid federal taxes pursuant to section 5101.32 of the Revised Code or of overdue child support from refunds of paid state income taxes pursuant to sections 5101.321 and 5747.121 of the Revised Code.

(L)(1) Each court with jurisdiction to issue support orders or orders establishing the existence or nonexistence of a parent and child relationship shall establish rules of court to ensure that the following percentage of all actions to establish the existence or nonexistence of a parent and child relationship, to establish a support requirement, or to modify a previously issued support order be completed within the following time limits:

(a) Seventy-five per cent of all of the actions shall be completed within six months after they were initially filed;

(b) Ninety per cent of all of the actions shall be completed within twelve months after they were initially filed.

(2) If a case involves complex legal issues requiring full judicial review, the court shall issue a temporary support order within the time limits set forth in division (L)(1) of this section, which temporary order shall be in effect until a final support order is issued in the case. All cases in which the imposition of a notice or order under division (D) of this section is contested shall be completed within the period of time specified by law for completion of the case. The failure of a court to complete a case within the required period does not affect the ability of any court to issue any order under this section or any other section of the Revised Code for the payment of support, does not provide any defense to any order for the payment of support that is issued under this section or any other section of the Revised Code, and does not affect any obligation to pay support.

(3)(a) In any Title IV-D case, the judge, when necessary to satisfy the federal requirement of expedited process for obtaining and enforcing support orders, shall appoint magistrates to make findings of fact and recommendations for the judge's approval in the case. All magistrates appointed pursuant to this division shall be attorneys admitted to the practice of law in this state. If the court appoints a magistrate pursuant to this division, the court may appoint any additional administrative and support personnel for the magistrate.

(b) Any magistrate appointed pursuant to division (L)(3)(a) of this section may perform any of the following functions:

(i) The taking of testimony and keeping of a record in the case;

(ii) The evaluation of evidence and the issuance of recommendations to establish, modify, and enforce support orders;

(iii) The acceptance of voluntary acknowledgments of support liability and stipulated agreements setting the amount of support to be paid;

(iv) The entering of default orders if the obligor does not respond to notices in the case within a reasonable time after the notices are issued;

(v) Any other functions considered necessary by the court.

(4) The child support enforcement agency may conduct administrative reviews of support orders to obtain voluntary notices or court orders under division (D) of this section and to correct any errors in the amount of any arrearages owed by an obligor. The obligor and the obligee shall be notified of the time, date, and location of the administrative review at least fourteen days before it is held.

(M)(1) The termination of a support obligation or a support order does not abate the power of any court to collect overdue and unpaid support or to punish any person for a failure to comply with an order of the court or to pay any support as ordered in the terminated support order and does not abate the authority of a child support enforcement agency to issue, in accordance with this section, any notice described in division (D) of this section or of a court to issue, in accordance with this section, any court order as described in division (D)(3) or (4) of this section to collect any support due or arrearage under the support order.

(2) Any court that has the authority to issue a support order shall have all powers necessary to enforce that support order, and all other powers, set forth in this section.

(3) Except as provided in division (M)(4) of this section, a court may not retroactively modify an obligor's duty to pay a delinquent support payment.

(4) A court with jurisdiction over a support order may modify an obligor's duty to pay a support payment that becomes due after notice of a petition to modify the support order has been given to each obligee and to the obligor before a final order concerning the petition for modification is entered.

(N) If an obligor is in default under a support order and has a claim against another person of more than one thousand dollars, the obligor shall notify the child support enforcement agency of the claim, the nature of the claim, and the name of the person against whom the claim exists. If an obligor is in default under a support order and has a claim against another person or is a party in an action for any judgment, the child support enforcement agency or the agency's attorney, on behalf of the obligor, immediately shall file with the court in which the action is pending a motion to intervene in the action or a creditor's bill. The motion to intervene shall be prepared and filed pursuant to Civil Rules 5 and 24(A) and (C).

Nothing in this division shall preclude an obligee from filing a motion to intervene in any action or a creditor's bill.

(O) If an obligor is receiving unemployment compensation benefits, an amount may be deducted from those benefits for purposes of child support, in accordance with sections 2301.371 and 4141.282 of the Revised Code. Any deduction from a source in accordance with those provisions is in addition to, and does not preclude, any withholding or deduction for purposes of support under divisions (A) to (N) of this section.

(P) As used in this section, and in sections 3113.211 to 3113.219 of the Revised Code:

(1) "Financial institution" means a bank, savings and loan association, or credit union, or a regulated investment company or mutual fund in which a person who is required to pay child support has funds on deposit that are not exempt under the law of this state or the United States from execution, attachment, or other legal process.

(2) "Title IV-D case" means any case in which the child support enforcement agency is enforcing the child support order pursuant to Title IV-D of the "Social Security Act," 88 Stat. 2351 (1975), 42 U.S.C. 651, as amended.

(3) "Obligor" means the person who is required to pay support under a support order.

(4) "Obligee" means the person who is entitled to receive the support payments under a support order.

(5) "Support order" means an order for the payment of support and, for orders issued or modified on or after December 31, 1993, includes any notices described in division (D) or (H) of this section that are issued in accordance with this section.

(6) "Support" means child support, spousal support, and support for a spouse or former spouse.

(7) "Personal earnings" means compensation paid or payable for personal services, however denominated, and includes, but is not limited to, wages, salary, commissions, bonuses, draws against commissions, profit sharing, and vacation pay.

(8) "Default" has the same meaning as in section 2301.34 of the Revised Code.

(9) "Payor" means any person or entity that pays or distributes income to an obligor, including the obligor, if the obligor is self-employed; an employer; an employer that is paying the obligor's workers' compensation benefits; the public employees retirement board; the board of trustees, or other governing entity of a municipal retirement system; the board of trustees of the Ohio police and fire pension fund; the state teachers retirement board; the school employees retirement board; the state highway patrol retirement board; the bureau of workers' compensation; or any other person or entity, except the department of job and family services with respect to unemployment compensation benefits paid pursuant to Chapter 4141. of the Revised Code.

(Q) As used in this section, "income" means any form of monetary payment, including personal earnings; workers' compensation payments; unemployment compensation benefits to the extent permitted by, and in accordance with, sections 2301.371 and 4141.282 of the Revised Code, and federal law governing the department of job and family services; pensions; annuities; allowances; private or governmental retirement benefits; disability or sick pay; insurance proceeds; lottery prize awards; federal, state, or local government benefits to the extent that the benefits can be withheld or deducted under the law governing the benefits; any form of trust fund or endowment; lump-sum payments; and any other payment in money.

(2000 H 509, eff. 9-21-00; 1999 H 471, eff. 7-1-00; 1999 H 222, eff. 11-2-99; 1998 S 170, eff. 3-30-99; 1997 H 352, eff. 1-1-98; 1997 H 408, eff. 10-1-97; 1996 S 292, eff. 11-6-96; 1996 H 710, § 8, eff. 8-8-96; 1996 H 710, § 7, eff. 6-11-96; 1996 H 274, § 7, eff. 8-8-96; 1996 H 274, § 1, eff. 8-8-96; 1995 H 167, eff. 6-11-96; 1993 H 173, eff. 12-31-93; 1992 S 331; 1990 S 3, H 514, H 591; 1988 H 242, H 708; 1987 H 231, H 164; 1986 H 509; 1984 H 614; 1982 H 254, H 245, H 515; 1980 H 736; 1979 H 674; 1971 H 504)

Uncodified Law

1995 H 167, § 3, eff. 10-25-95, reads: The General Assembly hereby requests the Supreme Court to promptly adopt rules pursuant to its authority under Ohio Constitution, Article IV, Section 2(B)(1)(g) and consistent with section 4705.021 of the Revised Code that would include as attorney misconduct for which an attorney may be disciplined situations in which a person licensed to practice law in the State of Ohio has been determined pursuant to division (B) of section 3113.21 of the Revised Code by a court or child support enforcement agency to be in default under a child support order.

1993 S 115, § 3, eff. 10-12-93, reads: The General Assembly hereby requests the Supreme Court to create a uniform income withholding form for use by all courts that issue support orders and that are required to issue withholding orders pursuant to division (D) of section 3113.21 of the Revised Code to pay the support required under the support orders issued by the courts.

Historical and Statutory Notes

Ed. Note: 3113.21 is former 3115.23 recodified by 1971 H 504, eff. 10-27-71; 1969 H 361; 132 v H 471.

Ed. Note: The effective date of the amendment of this section by 1996 H 274, § 7, was changed from 11-15-96 to 8-8-96 by 1996 H 710, § 8, eff. 6-11-96.

Ed. Note: The effective date of the amendment of this section by 1995 H 167 was changed from 11-15-96 to 6-11-96 by 1996 H 710, § 7, eff. 6-11-96.

Amendment Note: 2000 H 509 substituted "4141.282" for "division (D)(4) of section 4141.28" in division (O); substituted "and 4141.282" for "of the Revised Code, division (D)(4) of section 4141.28" in division (Q); and made other nonsubstantive changes.

Amendment Note: 1999 H 471 substituted "job and family" for "human" in divisions (A)(4), (B)(6), (D)(1)(a), (D)(2)(a), and (K)(1); substituted "director of job and family services" for "department of human services" in the last paragraph in division (D)(4) and in the introductory paragraph in division (G)(4)(d); and substituted "department of job and family services" for "bureau of employment services" in divisions (P)(9) and (Q).

Amendment Note: 1999 H 222 substituted "Ohio police and fire pension fund" for "police and firemen's disability and pension fund" in division (P)(9); and made other corrective and nonsubstantive changes.

Amendment Note: 1998 S 170 substituted "any applicable" for "the" and inserted "2716.041," in division (D)(1)(a); substituted "any applicable" for "the" and inserted "2716.02, 2716.041, 2716.05," in division (E); substituted "3113.219" for "3113.217" in the first paragraph in division (P); and made other nonsubstantive changes.

Amendment Note: 1997 H 352 rewrote this section; see *Baldwin's Ohio Legislative Service Annotated*, 1997, p 9/L-2592, or the OH-LEGIS or OH-LEGIS-OLD database on WESTLAW, for text of previous version.

Amendment Note: 1997 H 408 deleted "designated" before and "pursuant to section 2301.35 of the Revised Code" after "for that county" in divisions (D)(1)(a), (D)(2)(a), (D)(3)(a), (D)(4)(a), and (D)(5)(a); deleted former division (P)(3); redesignated former divisions (P)(4) through (P)(9) as new divisions (P)(3) through (P)(8), respectively; and made other nonsubstantive changes. Prior to deletion, former division (P)(3) read:

"(3)"Child support enforcement agency" means the child support enforcement agency designated pursuant to section 2301.35 of the Revised Code."

Amendment Note: 1996 S 292 inserted "and section 2301.42 of the Revised Code and the rules adopted pursuant to division (C) of that section, if child support arrearages are owed by an obligor to the obligee and to the department of human services, any payments received on the arrearages by the child support enforcement agency first shall be paid to the obligee until the arrearages owed to the obligee are paid in full" in division (K)(1); and made changes to reflect gender neutral language and other nonsubstantive changes.

Amendment Note: 1996 H 274, § 7, eff. 8-8-96, harmonized the versions of this section as amended by 1995 H 167, § 1, eff. 6-11-96, and 1996 H 274, § 1, eff. 8-8-96; and deleted division (Q), which prior thereto read:

"(Q) This is an interim section effective until November 15, 1996."

Amendment Note: 1996 H 274, § 1, eff. 8-8-96, added references to section 2151.33 throughout; added division (Q); and made changes to reflect gender neutral language.

Amendment Note: 1995 H 167 substantially rewrote this section; see *Baldwin's Ohio Legislative Service*, 1995, page 8/L-3055.

Amendment Note: 1993 H 173 rewrote this section; see *Baldwin's Ohio Legislative Service*, 1993 Laws of Ohio, H 173, p 5-1022.

Cross References

Administrative child support orders, 3111.22
Administrative child support orders, withholding or deduction requirements and notices, 3111.23
Alternative retirement plans for employees of public institutions of higher education, exemption from legal process, applicability, 3305.08
Application for appointment of trustee, 2329.70
Automated system to support enforcement of child support, 5101.322
Bureau of support, payments to bureau or third person, 2301.36
Bureau of support, procedures upon default, 2301.37
Bureaus of support, monthly payment orders, employer not to discharge employee due to orders, 2301.39
Child support division, agreements for access to financial institution account information, definitions, 5101.315
Child support division, obligor and obligee defined, 5101.31
Child support, obligor and obligee defined, 2301.34
Child support agency, prosecuting attorney to seek collection, 2301.372
Child support enforcement agencies, notice of default of obligor, fees, 2301.353
Child support enforcement agency, powers and duties, 2301.35
Contempt action for failure to pay support, 2705.031, 2705.05
Court making or modifying child support order, 2151.23, 3105.21
Custody and support of children, support orders, 3105.21
Default on support order, remedy, 2301.38
Duty of married person to support self, spouse, and children, duration of duty to support, 3103.03
Factors determining amount of support, applicability, 3109.05, 3111.13
Hearings, powers of child support enforcement agencies, 5101.37
Highway patrol retirement system, benefits exempt from execution or garnishment, exception, 5505.22
Juvenile courts, child support orders, 2151.36
Lien on property of obligor in default on child support order, 2301.43
Lottery, award of prizes, rights not assignable, exception, 3770.07
Lottery winner to state under oath whether or not he is in default of support order, hearing, deduction order, 3770.071
Neglect and abandonment, suspension of sentence on posting bond, support orders, contempt, 3113.04
Notice of attorneys in default on child support orders, 4705.021
Ohio works first program, participation constitutes assignment of right of support from other person, 5107.20
Parental duty of support, 3111.20
Paternity proceedings, support orders, contempt, 3111.13
Police and firemen's disability and pension fund, benefits exempt from execution, exceptions, 742.47
Property exempt from execution or garnishment, 2329.66
Public employees deferred compensation program, exemption of benefits from legal process, 148.09
Public employees retirement system, benefits exempt from execution or garnishment, exceptions, 145.56
Reports by employers to child support division, entry of information into directory, comparison against case registry, 5101.312
Review of administrative child support orders, 3111.27
School employees retirement system, benefits exempt, from execution or garnishment, exceptions, 3309.66
Small loans, assignment or order of wages for support, 1321.32, 1321.33
Spousal support, modification, enforcement orders, contempt, 3105.18
State retirement systems, furnishing information to court or child support enforcement agency, 145.27, 742.41, 3307.21, 3309.22, 5505.04
Teachers retirement system, benefits exempt from execution or garnishment, exceptions, 3307.71
Temporary support order pending determination of action objecting to parentage determination, 3111.111
Uniform Interstate Family Support Act, applicability, 3115.14
Uniform Interstate Family Support Act, issuance of support order, 3115.31
Uniform Interstate Family Support Act, notice of registration of order, issuance of withholding notice, 3115.42
Uniform Interstate Family Support Act, receipt of income-withholding order of another state, obligor's payor defined, 3115.32
Workers' compensation benefits exempt from attachment or execution, exceptions, 4123.67

Ohio Administrative Code References

Child support program, OAC Ch 5101:1-29
Collection of past due support by federal tax refund offset, OAC Ch 5101:1-30

Library References

Children Out-Of-Wedlock ⚿23, 69.
Divorce ⚿311(1), 311(2), 311.5.
Exemptions ⚿48, 49.
Infants ⚿228.
Parent and Child ⚿3.3(8), 3.3(9).
Social Security and Public Welfare ⚿194.19.
WESTLAW Topic Nos. 76H, 134, 163, 211, 285, 356A.
C.J.S. Children Out-of-Wedlock §§ 53 to 62, 128, 129.

C.J.S. Divorce §§ 706 to 718, 721.
C.J.S. Exemptions §§ 39, 105 to 121.
C.J.S. Infants §§ 42, 53, 54, 57, 69 to 85.
C.J.S. Parent and Child §§ 80, 82 to 87, 89.
C.J.S. Social Security and Public Welfare § 122.

OJur 3d: 40, Enforcement and Execution of Judgments § 503, 533, 549; 61, Intoxicating Liquors § 387; 62, Investment Securities and Securities Regulation § 53
Am Jur 2d: 10, Bastards § 130; 23, Desertion and Nonsupport § 118; 24, Divorce and Separation § 863
Spouse's right to set off debt owed by other spouse against accrued spousal or child support payments. 11 ALR5th 259
Decrease in income of obligor spouse following voluntary termination of employment as basis for modification of child support award. 39 ALR5th 1

Baldwin's Ohio Legislative Service, 1990 Laws of Ohio, H 591—LSC Analysis, p 5-576
Carlin, Baldwin's Ohio Practice, *Merrick-Rippner Probate Law* § 19.6, 19.7, 19.8, 19.10, 19.10.1, 105.11, 107.160, 107.161, 108.3, 108.13, 108.20, 108.29, 108.30, 108.34, 108.35, 108.36, 108.37, 108.38 (1997)
Gotherman & Babbit, Ohio Municipal Law, Text 10.20(A)
Klein & Darling, Baldwin's Ohio Practice, *Civil Practice* § 24 (1997)
Kurtz & Giannelli, Ohio Juvenile Law (1998 Ed.), Text 27.2, 29.2
Sowald & Morganstern, Baldwin's Ohio Practice, *Domestic Relations Law* § 3.4, 3.5, 3.31, 3.35, 3.41, 3.55, 7.19, 9.11, 9.18, 9.20, 9.98, 10.13, 11.43, 11.44, 12.23, 13.44, 14.3, 15.69, 19.1, 19.12, 19.19, 19.25, 19.27, 20.1, 20.2, 20.3, 20.6, 20.7, 20.8, 20.9, 20.10, 20.21, 20.26, 20.37, 20.49, 20.62, 20.64, 22.5, 22.6, 22.7, 22.8, 22.9, 22.12, 22.13.1, 22.14, 22.15, 22.20, 22.21, 23.16, 23.17, 23.21, 23.35, 23.37, 23.39, 23.40, 23.42, 23.48, 28.21, 29.34, 31.15, 32.10 (1997)
Wasil, Waite, & Mastrangelo, Ohio Workers' Compensation Law §§ 1:2, 4:29, 11:11, 11:12, 11:13, 11:14, 11:15, 11:17, 11:18, 11:19, 11:20, 11:21, 11:108, 14:203, 19:14
Williams, Ohio Consumer Law (2000 Ed.), Text 20.12

Law Review and Journal Commentaries

Bankruptcy Reform Act of 1994—What the Bankruptcy Code Giveth, Domestic Relations Courts (and Congress) Taketh Away, C.R. "Chip" Bowles. 8 Domestic Rel J Ohio 17 (March/April 1996).

BWC and Self-Insured Employer Liability for Spousal and Child Support, C. Jeffrey Waite. 11 Domestic Rel J Ohio 17 (March/April 1999).

Contempt After Emancipation Under R.C. 2705.03(E): Unconstitutional?, Richard L. Innis. 5 Domestic Rel J Ohio 95 (November/December 1993).

Garnishment of Employee Wages in Ohio: Whose Money Is It, Anyway?, Cecilia M. Martaus. 18 Ohio N U L Rev 197 (1991).

Legal Fees v. Child Support Arrearages—Update on Workers' Compensation Awards, Paul J. Buser. 8 Domestic Rel J Ohio 25 (March/April 1996).

Removing Nonconforming Child Support Payments from the Shadow of the Rule Against Retroactive Modification: A Proposal for Judicial Discretion, J. Eric Smithburn. 28 J Fam L 43 (1989-90).

Notes of Decisions and Opinions

---

1. In general

26 USC 152(e) does not preempt a state court's authority to allocate the federal tax dependency exemption to the noncustodial parent. Singer v. Dickinson (Ohio 1992) 63 Ohio St.3d 408, 588 N.E.2d 806.

The allocation of the dependency exemption provided by 26 USC 152(e) may be awarded to the noncustodial parent when that allocation would produce a net tax savings for the parents, thereby furthering the best interest of the child. Singer v. Dickinson (Ohio 1992) 63 Ohio St.3d 408, 588 N.E.2d 806.

In determining whether taxes would be saved by allocating the federal tax dependency exemption to the noncustodial parent, a court should review all pertinent factors, including the parents' gross incomes, the exemptions and deductions to which the parents are otherwise entitled, and the relevant federal, state, and local tax rates. Singer v. Dickinson (Ohio 1992) 63 Ohio St.3d 408, 588 N.E.2d 806.

Trial court in divorce action retains jurisdiction to modify allocation of income tax dependency exemption. Hopton v. Preston (Ohio App. 9 Dist. 1998) 128 Ohio App.3d 571, 716 N.E.2d 226.

Divorced father who was not current in his child support payments could not be awarded federal income tax dependency exemption for child. Davis v. Davis (Lucas 1996) 112 Ohio App.3d 518, 679 N.E.2d 319.

For purposes of defining "disposable earnings" to determine maximum allowable garnishment, support orders are not "amounts required by law to be withheld." Lough v. Robinson (Washington 1996) 111 Ohio App.3d 149, 675 N.E.2d 1272.

Support order is debt and therefore falls within meaning of "garnishment," for purposes of Consumer Credit Protection Act (CCPA). Lough v. Robinson (Washington 1996) 111 Ohio App.3d 149, 675 N.E.2d 1272.

Debtor who was subject to child support order that was 38 percent of his disposable earnings, thereby exceeding 25 percent garnishment limitations of Consumer Credit Protection Act (CCPA), was not subject to further garnishment of wages. Lough v. Robinson (Washington 1996) 111 Ohio App.3d 149, 675 N.E.2d 1272.

Child support order has priority over garnishment by creditors. Lough v. Robinson (Washington 1996) 111 Ohio App.3d 149, 675 N.E.2d 1272.

Child support arrearage which accrued in favor of former wife was not taxable to her. Schultz v. Schultz (Franklin 1996) 110 Ohio App.3d 715, 675 N.E.2d 55.

Although trial court purported to apply statute generally prohibiting retroactive modification of delinquent support, which became effective only after parties were divorced, former husband was granted "credit" against child support arrearages on basis of cohabitation and, thus, actual result was that statute was not applied and retroactive modification of support was effected, barring relief on claim that statute was improperly applied retroactively. Parker v. Parker (Marion 1993) 86 Ohio App.3d 727, 621 N.E.2d 1229.

Trial court could impose wage order for purpose of applying payments to support arrearages which had been reduced to judgment. Cattren v. Cattren (Cuyahoga 1992) 83 Ohio App.3d 111, 614 N.E.2d 770.

The doctrine of laches prevents an award of child support arrearage to a mother who deliberately kept the child from the father for eighteen years where she and her new family moved several times out of state and never requested payment during those years; these actions materially prejudiced the father's rights. Ferree v. Sparks (Warren 1991) 77 Ohio App.3d 185, 601 N.E.2d 568.

Restitution may be ordered paid from child support arrearages received by an obligee after the emancipation of the child for whose benefit the support was ordered where the obligee has been convicted of theft in office. Miller v. Miller (Jackson 1991) 73 Ohio App.3d 721, 598 N.E.2d 167.

A trial court has the authority to modify a child support order with respect to which parent may claim the child as a dependent for the purpose of claiming a federal income tax dependency exemption, but may do so only upon a finding of a substantial change in circumstances, and where the reallocation of the dependency exemption is in the best interest of the child. Hoban v. Hoban (Wayne 1990) 64 Ohio App.3d 257, 580 N.E.2d 1175.

Attorney fees incurred in the process of bringing a contempt motion due to the failure of the noncustodial parent to comply with a prior child support order constitute "child support" within the meaning of RC 3113.21(O)(7) and are subject to mandatory wage withholding. Hamilton v. Hamilton (Franklin 1988) 40 Ohio App.3d 190, 532 N.E.2d 213.

Support garnishments take precedence over creditor garnishments pursuant to RC 3113.21(C); the two may co-exist, however, as long as, combined, they do not exceed the twenty-five per cent limit on wages that are subject to garnishment. Marco v. Wilhelm (Wayne 1983) 13 Ohio App.3d 171, 468 N.E.2d 771, 13 O.B.R. 206.

A father's duty to support a minor child includes an obligation to pay reasonable funeral expenses in the event of the child's death prior to reaching the age of majority, and the juvenile court is justified in ordering the continuation of support payments being made by the father until such funeral expenses have been paid. In re Terrell (Cuyahoga 1976) 48 Ohio App.2d 352, 357 N.E.2d 1113, 2 O.O.3d 353.

The word "employer" as used in RC 3113.21 is not defined or restricted to natural persons or corporations, and is broad enough to include the state and all its departments and agencies. Sheahan v. Department of Liquor Control (Lucas 1974) 44 Ohio App.2d 393, 339 N.E.2d 840, 73 O.O.2d 520.

A parent at a child support hearing makes a false statement under oath when she testifies that she had not worked since January 1994 contrary to an employer's testimony that (1) the parent "was employed by me" to care for his infirm wife, (2) she was paid what "he felt he wanted her to have," and (3) she did not consider caring for the infirm spouse as a job; in addition, cancelled checks show that she was paid on a weekly basis. State v Keller, No. CA97-07-020, 1998 WL 54374 (12th Dist Ct App, Fayette, 2-9-98).

In a dispute involving child support where the judgment entries of the trial court are internally inconsistent and the intention of the court remains unclear and an interpretation of the orders would require sheer conjecture, the matter must be reversed and remanded to the trial court for clarification as in a case where the court's initial child support order does indeed appear to be temporary, but the wage order requiring the obligor's employer to withhold $400 does not. Fountain v Vicario, No. 66922, 1995 WL 33058 (8th Dist Ct App, Cuyahoga, 1-26-95).

Where a child support obligor quits his job in order to become a self-employed independent salesman for a product and his income decreases significantly as a result in the two year period immediately following the change, a motion for the reduction of child support is properly granted based on a change in circumstances so long as the job change is made in good faith with the belief of eventually earning a better income and where there is no evidence the job change is made with an intention to frustrate a child support order. Martin v Custer, No. 1317, 1993 WL 386249 (2d Dist Ct App, Darke, 9-29-93).

Trial court had sufficient evidence before it to issue a seek employment order under RC 3113.21(D)(7) where 1) mother testified that she has made no attempt to be employed since 11/88, has not made any attempt to further her education, does not have a bank or savings account, she could perform jobs that do not require lifting, standing or bending over, and she made no attempt to obtain a job which would not require her to perform these actions and 2) her chiropractor testified that she was able to be employed in some capacity. In re England, No. 92AP-1749, 1993 WL 179994 (10th Dist Ct App, Franklin, 5-18-93).

Pursuant to RC 3113.21, a court may use its contempt powers to compel payment of arrearages of a prior support order even after the child who was the subject of the order has reached the age of majority or been emancipated. In re Cramer, No. 5-92-47 (3d Dist Ct App, Hancock, 4-13-93).

Pursuant to RC 3113.21(M)(1), a court may use its contempt powers to compel payment of arrearages of a prior support order even after the child who was the subject of the order has reached the age of majority or has become emancipated. Smith v Abbott, No. 558 (7th Dist Ct App, Carroll, 12-19-88).

Where the settlor of a trust is to receive the income therefrom and also reserves the power to amend the trust, alimony obligations accrued by him may be satisfied by attachment of both the principal and the income of the trust under RC 3113.21. Clark v Clark, No. 87AP060055 (5th Dist Ct App, Tuscarawas, 12-7-87).

Medical expenses are support within the meaning of RC 3113.21, and thus subject to a wage assignment order because of nonpayment. Soinger v Soinger, No. CA976 (9th Dist Ct App, Medina, 10-29-80).

2. Procedure and notice

Trial court lacks jurisdiction to retroactively modify an in-gross child support order. Lytle v. Lytle (Ohio App. 10 Dist. 1998) 130 Ohio App.3d 697, 720 N.E.2d 1007.

Former husband, designated children's nonresidential parent in divorce decree, was required to demonstrate change of circumstances justifying award of income tax dependency exemption to him, as his motion for such award amounted to motion to modify divorce decree;

original decree provided that former wife was to be children's primary residential parent and was silent as to dependency exemption, and former husband's motion requested new order, clarification of divorce judgment, or modification of divorce judgment as alternative forms of relief. Hopton v. Preston (Ohio App. 9 Dist. 1998) 128 Ohio App.3d 571, 716 N.E.2d 226.

Trial court was not required to consider affidavit of former wife's daughter in support of former wife's claims that she did not know former husband's whereabouts during 18 years prior to filing of her motion to consolidate child support arrearages, where former wife made no effort to proffer daughter's testimony for record and did not submit affidavit until six months after final evidentiary hearing on her motion. Gerlach v. Gerlach (Ohio App. 10 Dist. 1997) 124 Ohio App.3d 246, 705 N.E.2d 1287, dismissed, appeal not allowed 81 Ohio St.3d 1495, 691 N.E.2d 1057.

Retroactive modification of child support beyond date when motion to amend such support is filed is strictly prohibited. Gerlach v. Gerlach (Ohio App. 10 Dist. 1997) 124 Ohio App.3d 246, 705 N.E.2d 1287, dismissed, appeal not allowed 81 Ohio St.3d 1495, 691 N.E.2d 1057.

Trial court did not abuse its discretion in ordering father to provide health insurance for child if it was available to him at reasonable cost, even absent investigation to determine whether father had satisfactory health insurance coverage; based upon history of case, trial court already knew that father had health care coverage. Yost v. Unanue (Stark 1996) 109 Ohio App.3d 294, 671 N.E.2d 1374.

Trial court did not abuse its discretion in making modified child support order retroactive to date that ex-wife's petition was filed, where ex-husband failed to point out any special circumstance to negate application of general rule that modifications should be retroactive. Hamilton v. Hamilton (Lucas 1995) 107 Ohio App.3d 132, 667 N.E.2d 1256, appeal not allowed 75 Ohio St.3d 1425, 662 N.E.2d 27.

If trial court determines that child support order should be modified, it may make modification order effective from date motion for modification was filed. Hamilton v. Hamilton (Lucas 1995) 107 Ohio App.3d 132, 667 N.E.2d 1256, appeal not allowed 75 Ohio St.3d 1425, 662 N.E.2d 27.

Determining whether to make modification of child support order retroactive is a matter within discretion of trial court and cannot be reversed unless trial court abuses its discretion. Hamilton v. Hamilton (Lucas 1995) 107 Ohio App.3d 132, 667 N.E.2d 1256, appeal not allowed 75 Ohio St.3d 1425, 662 N.E.2d 27.

Assertion by creditor that reviewing court was barred by doctrine of res judicata from considering issue of whether debts for child support arrearages were discharged in bankruptcy was not considered on appeal where issue of res judicata was not addressed to trial court and creditor did not assign as error trial court's failure to utilize res judicata. Schindler v. Schindler (Summit 1994) 95 Ohio App.3d 277, 642 N.E.2d 404.

Husband was not entitled to hearing before order was entered withholding his alimony obligation from his civil service retirement benefits, where case involved no issue of arrearages or default. Holloman v. Holloman (Montgomery 1993) 91 Ohio App.3d 279, 632 N.E.2d 575.

Statute governing withholding personal earnings to pay child support does not mandate that trial court make explicit finding on record of obligor's ability to pay before ordering obligor to post bond to secure future payment of child support. High v. High (Allen 1993) 89 Ohio App.3d 424, 624 N.E.2d 801.

Bond is ordered to secure future payment of child support if it has become evident to court that other methods of enforcing support obligation would not be effective. High v. High (Allen 1993) 89 Ohio App.3d 424, 624 N.E.2d 801.

Employee of county child support enforcement agency was not entitled to appear as agency's legal representative at child support termination hearing or to make recommendation as to manner in which father should be ordered to liquidate arrearage, even though agency was required to act as investigator in case in which obligor is seeking termination of support obligation, and employee could have been found to have some knowledge of facts at issue and could have offered evidence as to father's financial ability to settle arrearage; employee was not attorney and was not party to action. Hill v. Hill (Franklin 1993) 88 Ohio App.3d 447, 624 N.E.2d 288.

Trial court had authority to order, sua sponte, liquidation of father's child support arrearage through installment payments, even though child was emancipated. Hill v. Hill (Franklin 1993) 88 Ohio App.3d 447, 624 N.E.2d 288.

Motion for temporary spousal support, child support and custody may be heard and decided directly by referee without oral hearing. Lyon v. Lyon (Scioto 1993) 86 Ohio App.3d 580, 621 N.E.2d 718.

In making an initial decision on temporary support, referee or court need not ordinarily make factual finding as to date or duration of marriage. Lyon v. Lyon (Scioto 1993) 86 Ohio App.3d 580, 621 N.E.2d 718.

Trial court has discretion to order modification of child support retroactive to date of filing of modification motion. Parzynski v. Parzynski (Erie 1992) 85 Ohio App.3d 423, 620 N.E.2d 93, dismissed, jurisdictional motion overruled 67 Ohio St.3d 1450, 619 N.E.2d 419, rehearing denied 67 Ohio St.3d 1513, 622 N.E.2d 660.

Just as it is within trial court's discretion to determine whether to consider new spouse's income when determining amount of child support, it is also within trial court's discretion whether to consider new spouse's income when determining question of who should be awarded income tax dependency exemption. Hutchinson v. Hutchinson (Jackson 1993) 85 Ohio App.3d 173, 619 N.E.2d 466.

Trial court did not abuse its discretion by declining to consider mother's new husband's income in determining whether it was in children's best interest to modify dissolution decree to allow mother to claim children as dependents for tax purposes; court considered fact that new husband earned income, but chose not to include parties' spouses' incomes in ruling on motion. Hutchinson v. Hutchinson (Jackson 1993) 85 Ohio App.3d 173, 619 N.E.2d 466.

Court applies best interest of child test in determining which parent may claim children as dependents for purposes of income tax exemptions. Hutchinson v. Hutchinson (Jackson 1993) 85 Ohio App.3d 173, 619 N.E.2d 466.

A mother is without standing to contest on behalf of her employer a trial court's order establishing wage withholding for support. Wayne Cty. Bur. of Support v. Wolfe (Wayne 1991) 71 Ohio App.3d 765, 595 N.E.2d 421.

When referee contemplates that child support obligor be jailed for his failure to pay child support and arrearages if he has not made substantial efforts to seek employment by date certain, better practice is to schedule purge hearing, just before incarceration, to take place before trial judge, rather than before referee. State ex rel. Burns v. Haines (Montgomery 1989) 55 Ohio App.3d 168, 563 N.E.2d 52.

The authority and jurisdiction of the trial court to entertain legal proceedings to order wages of a defendant held by the department of liquor control is not exclusively controlled by RC 4301.10(B), but stems also from RC 3113.21. Sheahan v. Department of Liquor Control (Lucas 1974) 44 Ohio App.2d 393, 339 N.E.2d 840, 73 O.O.2d 520.

RC 3113.21(A) and 115.46, when construed together, compel an employer, including the state and any of its agencies, after notice is given as required in an action for support pursuant to RC 3113.21, to comply with a court order to pay support by withholding personal earnings. Sheahan v. Department of Liquor Control (Lucas 1974) 44 Ohio App.2d 393, 339 N.E.2d 840, 73 O.O.2d 520.

The jurisdiction of the trial court to enforce RC 3113.21 against the state, or any of its agencies, to compel the withholding of wages of a state employee to satisfy a claim against the state employee is provided by RC 115.46. Sheahan v. Department of Liquor Control (Lucas 1974) 44 Ohio App.2d 393, 339 N.E.2d 840, 73 O.O.2d 520.

A proceeding brought pursuant to RC 3113.21, to withhold wages due a defendant from the department of liquor control, and the order to withhold wages are ancillary to the main legal action against the defendant; are not "any action against the board of liquor control ... or the department of liquor control" within the meaning of RC 4301.31; and are not an order "to restrain the exercise of any power or to compel the performance of any duty" as such phraseology is used in that statute. Sheahan v. Department of Liquor Control (Lucas 1974) 44 Ohio App.2d 393, 339 N.E.2d 840, 73 O.O.2d 520.

Modification of child support, absent special circumstances, should be retroactive to the date economic circumstances of the parties justify it and all the parties have been notified of the request. Wayco v Wayco, No. 1998-CA-00279, 1999 WL 174918 (5th Dist Ct App, Stark, 3-8-99).

A modification of a child support order may not be made retroactive to a date prior to the date that the motion for modification was made. Coffman v Coffman, No. 94-CA-104, 1995 WL 386926 (2d Dist Ct App, Greene, 6-28-95).

A judgment entry regarding an obligor's child support obligation that is still in force and determines an additional arrearage of $6000 is error where no precipitating motion is filed and no notice given the obligor, prior to this determination, that he would be called upon to defend any additional arrearage. McCulloch v McCulloch, No. 93-P-0062, 1994 WL 315782 (11th Dist Ct App, Portage, 6-10-94).

Trial courts may enforce a prior child support order even if the child has reached the age of majority and a father who does not pay the support arrearages may be found in contempt. Cottrill v Barcus, No. CA 9409, 1994 WL 75667 (5th Dist Ct App, Stark, 3-7-94).

The trial court erred in awarding a retroactive modification of child support in violation of RC 3113.21 where the husband had been ordered to pay $408 every two weeks but lost his job and later started a new job at a lower salary, the husband failed to notify the court of his change in status, but reached an oral agreement with the residential parent to pay only $300 per month. Kiser v Quartermaine, No. 93WD037, 1993 WL 496677 (6th Dist Ct App, Wood, 12-3-93).

Where it is evident on the record that an obligor has the financial ability to post a bond to ensure payment of his child support obligations, there is no need to hold a hearing on such ability. Straw v Straw, No. L-87-386 (6th Dist Ct App, Lucas, 9-2-88).

Where the trial court improperly ordered the employer to make wage deductions from a parent ordered to pay child support because such an employer was made a party to the action without advance notice pursuant to Civ R 75 and RC 3113.21, the voluntary appearance of the employer in a motion to dismiss where the employer fails to object to the deficiency in notice cures any defect of notice in the re-entered wage order. Pinkus v Pinkus, No. 43776 (8th Dist Ct App, Cuyahoga, 4-15-82).

A non-resident employer of a parent ordered to pay child support consents to personal jurisdiction by filing a motion to dismiss without raising the issue of the court's in personam jurisdiction, and thus was properly subject to an order requiring wage deductions. Pinkus v Pinkus, No. 43776 (8th Dist Ct App, Cuyahoga, 4-15-82).

Where a court has, pursuant to RC 3113.21(B)(4), issued an order to a child support enforcement agency to conduct an investigation under RC 3113.21(B)(3), including investigation of the obligee, the agency must comply with that order, unless and until the order is changed by orderly and proper judicial proceedings. OAG 93-028.

15 USC 1673 does not apply to lump-sum payments paid to a child support enforcement agency on behalf of an obligor pursuant to RC 3113.21(H)(3) and 3113.21(D)(1)(c); therefore, the county child support enforcement agency may, if necessary, apply 100 per cent of the lump-sum payment to the obligor's arrearages. OAG 88-012.

Under RC 3113.21(B)(3)(b) the findings and recommendations of an investigation ordered by a court under RC 3113.21(B)(3)(a) may be sent through an appropriate means that is reasonably calculated to apprise obligors of their right to a hearing. OAG 87-053.

3. Order; reasonableness

Court's inherent authority to enforce lawfully issued child support order did not end when child was emancipated; court's interest in seeing that its orders were not disobeyed with impunity existed independent of child, General Assembly granted courts jurisdiction to hold contempt proceedings after obligation to support child ended, and state had strong interest in ensuring enforcement of child support obligations due to conditions placed by federal government on Aid for Dependent Children (ADC) program and requirement that families receiving ADC assign their interests in child support to state. Cramer v. Petrie (Ohio 1994) 70 Ohio St.3d 131, 637 N.E.2d 882.

Trial court did not abuse its discretion in ordering husband to pay combined spousal and child support in excess of 50 percent of his net income incident to divorce; state and federal statutory limitations applied only to wage withholdings and not to amounts of underlying awards. Arthur v. Arthur (Ohio App. 5 Dist. 1998) 130 Ohio App.3d 398, 720 N.E.2d 176.

Trial court could not order withholding of over 75 percent of husband's monthly income for spousal support and child support payments incident to divorce, as such withholding exceeded state and federal withholding limits. Arthur v. Arthur (Ohio App. 5 Dist. 1998) 130 Ohio App.3d 398, 720 N.E.2d 176.

Divorce decree which failed to award dependency tax exemption to nonresidential parent amounted to award of exemption to residential parent. Hopton v. Preston (Ohio App. 9 Dist. 1998) 128 Ohio App.3d 571, 716 N.E.2d 226.

Trial court lacked statutory authority to impose restraints on adjudicated father's disposition of Individual Retirement Account (IRA) as security for payment of child support obligations; only statutory provision addressing trial court's power against support obligor's funds on deposit with financial institution authorized attachment of funds in IRA for actual payment of support obligation, and only form of security expressly authorized was cash bond. Church v. Gadd (Ohio App. 11 Dist. 1998) 126 Ohio App.3d 284, 710 N.E.2d 320.

Child support obligor remained obligated for any arrearages and current child support that accrued during his incarceration on criminal charges unrelated to stayed contempt order; however, his incarceration was defense to reinstatement of contempt order. Burchett v. Miller (Ohio App. 6 Dist. 1997) 123 Ohio App.3d 550, 704 N.E.2d 636.

Purge conditions placed upon contemnor were either void or unreasonable; requirement that he seek work following resolution of pending criminal charges impermissibly concerned future compliance, requirement that he pay child support arrearages was unreasonable in light of trial court's knowledge that contemnor was under house arrest and awaiting outcome of unrelated criminal charges which affected his ability to pay support and arrearages, and trial court imposed jail sentence for contempt while contemnor was still incarcerated following resolution of those charges. Burchett v. Miller (Ohio App. 6 Dist. 1997) 123 Ohio App.3d 550, 704 N.E.2d 636.

On reconsideration of child support order, former husband, who was the nonresidential parent of parties' two minor children, was not entitled to one federal income tax dependency exemption, where parties' incomes were comparable. Hurchanik v. Hurchanik (Warren 1996) 110 Ohio App.3d 628, 674 N.E.2d 1260.

When reconsidering child support order, trial court may not exercise its authority to award federal income tax dependency exemption to nonresidential parent unless record shows that doing so will further interest of child. Hurchanik v. Hurchanik (Warren 1996) 110 Ohio App.3d 628, 674 N.E.2d 1260.

Allocation of federal income tax dependency exemption may be awarded to nonresidential parent on reconsideration of child support order when that allocation would produce net tax savings for parents; such savings would occur through allocation to nonresidential parent only if nonresidential parent's taxable income falls into higher tax bracket than tax bracket of residential parent. Hurchanik v. Hurchanik (Warren 1996) 110 Ohio App.3d 628, 674 N.E.2d 1260.

Wife could not be allowed to satisfy her child support arrearages in two years, at time of sale of marital home two years after effective date of division of marital assets in divorce proceeding, despite fact that husband was being allowed to reside with minor children in home for that period before sale of home, where trial court's decision to let husband and children reside in home was based on parties' desire to avoid further disruptions in children's lives. McQuinn v. McQuinn (Butler 1996) 110 Ohio App.3d 296, 673 N.E.2d 1384.

No abuse of discretion occurs merely because trial court chooses to satisfy lump-sum child support arrearage judgment out of division of marital property in divorce proceeding. McQuinn v. McQuinn (Butler 1996) 110 Ohio App.3d 296, 673 N.E.2d 1384.

It is appropriate for trial court to make obligor satisfy his child support arrearages out of his share of net proceeds from sale of marital home. McQuinn v. McQuinn (Butler 1996) 110 Ohio App.3d 296, 673 N.E.2d 1384.

Court-ordered child support is for benefit of children, rather than custodial parent. McQuinn v. McQuinn (Butler 1996) 110 Ohio App.3d 296, 673 N.E.2d 1384.

It is within trial court's authority to reduce arrearages on child support to lump-sum judgment which is enforceable against party, the same as any other judgment. McQuinn v. McQuinn (Butler 1996) 110 Ohio App.3d 296, 673 N.E.2d 1384.

Portion of father's child support arrearage payments to child support enforcement agency were properly directed to mother's current husband, though mother had legal custody, where children lived with husband after his separation from mother during period of arrearages; statute allowed court to take appropriate action, and father was not prejudiced since amount of support did not increase. Palmer v. Harrold (Greene 1995) 101 Ohio App.3d 732, 656 N.E.2d 708.

Garnishment order in parentage proceeding that was under 15% of obligor's aggregate disposable earnings, after deduction of relevant taxes and union dues, was not excessive. Seegert v. Zietlow (Cuyahoga 1994) 95 Ohio App.3d 451, 642 N.E.2d 697.

Trial court's order applying father's expenditures, for travel and legal fees spent in pursuit of enforcement of his visitation rights, to reduce father's child support arrearage did not constitute impermissible, retroactive modification of support obligation, even though expenditures were made prior to father's application for modification of support obligation; there was no modification of amount that was due prior to father's motion, and order dealt only with whether certain amounts should be credited to unamended arrearages. Miller v. Miller (Erie 1993) 92 Ohio App.3d 340, 635 N.E.2d 384, motion overruled 69 Ohio St.3d 1424, 631 N.E.2d 164.

Trial court had jurisdiction to issue order withholding husband's alimony payments from his monthly civil service pension check to enforce alimony award, although husband was not in default of his obligation to pay alimony. Holloman v. Holloman (Montgomery 1993) 91 Ohio App.3d 279, 632 N.E.2d 575.

Legislature never intended that withholding order be treated as modification of alimony award, but only as means of enforcing or easing administration of that award. Holloman v. Holloman (Montgomery 1993) 91 Ohio App.3d 279, 632 N.E.2d 575.

Since father's child support payments were past due, trial court was required to grant state's motion to reduce support arrearages to lump-sum judgment, and court improperly relied on equitable principles to deny state's motion, where state's motion encompassed only unpaid child support; even if trial court believed that order finding paternity was inequitable, fairness of that order was not before court. State ex rel. LaMar v. Stabile (Medina 1993) 90 Ohio App.3d 54, 627 N.E.2d 1076.

Trial court did not abuse its discretion in ruling that former husband was entitled to claim only two of his three children for federal income tax exemption purposes, where trial court stated that it considered evidence as it related to factors set out by Ohio Supreme Court for determination of allocation of dependency exemption, referee recommended that husband be awarded income tax exemption for two oldest children since it would provide greater tax savings for husband, and court found this to be reasonable. Goode v. Goode (Franklin 1993) 89 Ohio App.3d 405, 624 N.E.2d 788.

If court determines that child support order should be modified, it can only make modification order effective from date that motion for modification was filed. Tobens v. Brill (Auglaize 1993) 89 Ohio App.3d 298, 624 N.E.2d 265.

Order modifying child support could only be effective from date that former wife's motion for modification was filed, and not from earlier date when former wife began taking care of minor children in her home. Tobens v. Brill (Auglaize 1993) 89 Ohio App.3d 298, 624 N.E.2d 265.

Father was not prejudiced by trial court's refusal to modify ordered child support arrearages downward by approximately $130 so as to reflect emancipation of father's oldest son, as there was no evidence that father was ever ordered to pay additional support for his youngest child until paternity was adjudicated when child was over 12 years old. Parker v. Parker (Marion 1993) 86 Ohio App.3d 727, 621 N.E.2d 1229.

RC 3113.21 does not provide for seek-work orders for obligees and thus, a trial court errs when it orders a mother who is an obligee to seek employment; moreover, even if the statute permitted the trial court's obligee seek-work order, it is not supported by the evidence where the obligee is the sole caregiver of her leukemia-ridden husband and her five-year-old child and doctors have cautioned her against sending the child to preschool and even kindergarten because of the deleterious effect it might have on the father's health if she contracted ordinary childhood diseases. Chinn v. Weaver (Scioto 1991) 76 Ohio App.3d 64, 600 N.E.2d 1134.

A garnishment order in excess of sixty-five per cent for the collection of child support arrearages is improper. Hockenberry v. Hockenberry (Henry 1992) 75 Ohio App.3d 806, 600 N.E.2d 839.

A trial court's sua sponte judgment in a support action ordering a custodial mother to seek employment is not supported by sufficient evidence in either the record transmitted on appeal nor the referee's report where (1) the mother did not have an opportunity to defend against the court's sua sponte imposition of the seek employment order, (2) the evidence indicated that the imposition of the order may interfere with the mother's plans to attend college, and (3) neither the report nor the trial court's judgment entry adopting the referee's report included any reference to applicable statutes, case authority, or rational for the issuance of the seek employment order. Smith v. Smith (Scioto 1991) 75 Ohio App.3d 679, 600 N.E.2d 396.

Child support arrearages may not be ordered to be paid where the obligor's only source of income is from public assistance received for the benefit of his other children as aid for dependent children benefits are not subject to attachment. Crigger v. Crigger (Franklin 1991) 71 Ohio App.3d 410, 594 N.E.2d 67.

A trial court may not use its contempt powers to seek to enforce a prior child support order by ordering monthly installments to retire arrearages after the children have become emancipated. Crigger v. Crigger (Franklin 1991) 71 Ohio App.3d 410, 594 N.E.2d 67.

A spousal support withholding order in excess of the statutory maximum, i.e. seventy per cent of income, is erroneous and will be vacated. Haase v. Haase (Cuyahoga 1990) 64 Ohio App.3d 758, 582 N.E.2d 1107.

In the absence of factors making it inequitable, the right to interest under RC 1343.03(A) on unpaid child support accrues on the date each installment becomes due, and runs until paid; such interest may be included in a lump-sum judgment for child support arrearages. Allen v. Allen (Summit 1990) 62 Ohio App.3d 621, 577 N.E.2d 126.

An order to withhold fifty-five per cent of an obligor's disposable income for current and past-due child support and alimony obligations is well within statutory contemplation. Perdew v. Perdew (Fulton 1989) 61 Ohio App.3d 735, 573 N.E.2d 1137.

There is no requirement that support withholding orders be "inherently reasonable." Perdew v. Perdew (Fulton 1989) 61 Ohio App.3d 735, 573 N.E.2d 1137.

An order requiring the withholding of seventy-three per cent of the pension benefits of an alimony obligor is improper. Roach v. Roach (Cuyahoga 1989) 61 Ohio App.3d 315, 572 N.E.2d 772.

Absent a written agreement by a child support obligor, a court lacked authority to order wage withholding in the amount of a support obligation under former RC 3113.21, as amended by 1984 H 614, eff. 4-10-85. Brueggeman v. Brueggeman (Hamilton 1987) 34 Ohio App.3d 333, 518 N.E.2d 586.

An order to an employer to withhold wages, entered pursuant to RC 3113.21(A), may be kept in force after the children have reached majority for the purpose of reducing an outstanding judgment for arrearages on a child support order. Wheeler v. Wheeler (Clark 1986) 27 Ohio App.3d 329, 500 N.E.2d 917, 27 O.B.R. 386.

Ohio garnishment law provides for more limited garnishments than the federal statute and is thus not preempted where an obligor is subject to a child support order that amounts to thirty-eight per cent of his disposable earnings; no creditor garnishments are allowable because all of the obligor's remaining disposable earnings are exempt from garnishment pursuant to RC 2329.66. Lough v Robinson, No. 95CA18, 1996 WL 271707 (4th Dist Ct App, Washington, 5-23-96).

By not reducing arrearages to a lump sum judgment, or in the alternative, refraining from issuing a final judgment until an arrearage statement is received from the CSEA, the trial court essentially grants an unspecified award and orders payments on an uncertain obligation and thus abuses its discretion in failing to award a sum certain. Little v Little, No. 94WD045, 1994 WL 573772 (6th Dist Ct App, Wood, 10-14-94).

It is in contravention of the Ohio Constitution for a trial court to utilize civil contempt proceedings and threat of imprisonment to coerce an obligor to pay his past due child support obligation after the emancipation of his children as RC 2705.031 and RC 3113.21 authorize only criminal contempt proceedings against parents having no present obligation to pay child support. Young v Young, No. 93 CA 10, 1994 WL 147793 (2d Dist Ct App, Miami, 4-20-94), reversed by 70 Ohio St.3d 679 (1994).

Although a trial court does not have the authority to use its power of contempt after a child is emancipated or has reached the age of majority, a trial court's reduction of the arrearage accrued prior to the emancipation of the child to judgment and an order for wage withholding of $10 per week until the arrearage is paid is not an abuse of discretion. Hill v Hill, No. 93AP-100, 1993 WL 271044 (10th Dist Ct App, Franklin, 6-30-93).

An order requiring the obligor to post a bond will be reversed where the trial court failed to determine that the obligor had the ability to post such a bond. Gilbert v Ucker, No. CA-3337 (5th Dist Ct App, Licking, 4-14-88).

A referee does not have the authority under RC 3113.21(B)(1) to sign a child support deduction order prior to a final judgment of the court. Blankenship v Blankenship, No. 86-CA-0093 (2d Dist Ct App, Greene, 6-26-87).

The provisions set forth in RC 3113.21 are available to enforce payment of arrearages on an order for child support after the attainment of majority by the minor for whose benefit the support order was made. Heiges v Heiges, No. L-83-323 (6th Dist Ct App, Lucas, 6-8-84).

Proper course of action for parent who cannot comply with support order is to seek modification of order. In re Serre (Ohio Com.Pl. 1996) 77 Ohio Misc.2d 29, 665 N.E.2d 1185.

A court order issued under RC 3113.21(D)(1)(c) does not require an employer of a child support obligor who is subject to a wage withholding order to hold for thirty days lump-sum payments made to the obligor-employee in lieu of vacation, but such payments may be required to be withheld pursuant to court orders issued under RC 3113.21(D)(4). OAG 88-052.

The employer of a child support obligor must obey any order imposed upon him by a court as long as that court has issued an order within its jurisdiction and power. OAG 88-052.

4. Unemployment, workers' compensation, pension, other lump sum benefits

Statute which requires trial courts to order that workers' compensation benefits be paid directly to a child-support enforcement agency in order to satisfy claimant's unpaid child-support obligations does not prohibit trial court's deduction of any attorney's contingent fee from lump-sum workers' compensation payment. Rowan v. Rowan (Ohio 1995) 72 Ohio St.3d 486, 650 N.E.2d 1360.

RC 3113.21(D)(4) authorizes a domestic relations court to issue a "qualified domestic relations order" attaching benefits provided under pension plans qualifying under the Employment Retirement Income Security Act, 29 USC 1001 et seq. Taylor v. Taylor (Ohio 1989) 44 Ohio St.3d 61, 541 N.E.2d 55.

While there is presumption to award federal income tax exemption to custodial parent, trial court has authority to award tax exemption to noncustodial parent if it is demonstrated that there will be net tax savings for parents, which advances best interest of child. Burns v. May (Ohio App. 12 Dist. 1999) 133 Ohio App.3d 351, 728 N.E.2d 19.

Allocation of federal income tax exemption is directly related to support of the child, and trial court's decision to allocate the tax exemption will be upheld provided that its decision will further the best interest of the child. Burns v. May (Ohio App. 12 Dist. 1999) 133 Ohio App.3d 351, 728 N.E.2d 19.

For purposes of allocating tax dependency exemption, best interest of child is furthered when allocation of exemption to noncustodial parent produces net tax savings for parents. Will v. Will (Jackson 1996) 113 Ohio App.3d 8, 680 N.E.2d 197.

Trial court did not abuse its discretion in refusing to consider income of mother's current husband when determining whether mother or father of child should receive federal tax dependency exemption. Will v. Will (Jackson 1996) 113 Ohio App.3d 8, 680 N.E.2d 197.

State law provides manner in which state court may allocate tax dependency exemption. Will v. Will (Jackson 1996) 113 Ohio App.3d 8, 680 N.E.2d 197.

In order to allocate tax dependency exemption to noncustodial parent, trial court must find that interest of child has been furthered. Will v. Will (Jackson 1996) 113 Ohio App.3d 8, 680 N.E.2d 197.

When determining net tax savings of parents for purposes of allocating tax dependency exemption, trial court should review all pertinent factors including parents' gross incomes, exemptions and deductions to which parents are otherwise entitled and relevant federal, state and local income tax rates. Will v. Will (Jackson 1996) 113 Ohio App.3d 8, 680 N.E.2d 197.

Trial court does not abuse its discretion when allocating tax dependency exemption if court chooses to only look at net tax savings and does not look at additional factors such as determining which parent spends more on child or which parent visits more with child. Will v. Will (Jackson 1996) 113 Ohio App.3d 8, 680 N.E.2d 197.

Finding that father was in contempt of postdivorce child support order was supported by evidence that, when father was asked at contempt hearing why he never paid child support from his workers' compensation checks, he stated that to do so would have decreased his income to the point where he would have been eligible for welfare, that father was capable of employment of some sort, and that father had refused to enter work program offered to him as an alternative to incarceration for nonpayment of child support. Watson v. Wolsonovich (Ohio App. 7 Dist. 1996) 112 Ohio App.3d 565, 679 N.E.2d 350.

Trial court has no discretion, under statute regarding disposition of any lump-sum payments to obligor of child support arrearage, to choose amounts to be allocated to arrearage and to obligor. Tardona v. Bell (Butler 1995) 105 Ohio App.3d 44, 663 N.E.2d 679.

Entire lump-sum disbursement to obligor from workers' compensation should have been applied to child support arrearage, rather than equally divided between obligor and obligee, where lump-sum disbursement was greater than $500 statutory minimum and obligor had arrearage greater than amount of disbursement. Tardona v. Bell (Butler 1995) 105 Ohio App.3d 44, 663 N.E.2d 679.

Divorce decree stating the "rate" of child and spousal support in terms of a monthly amount and stating that these amounts were to be paid directly to county child support enforcement agency and to mother, respectively, out of father's Voluntary Separation Incentive (VSI) payments offered by the armed forces to encourage a reduction in force, which court recognized were annual payments, was consistent with federal law prohibiting state courts from altering the normal pay and disbursement cycles of federal entities when those entities are subject to court orders to garnish wages for payment of child and spousal support; trial court determined the appropriate amount of support per month and required that amount sufficient to pay father's obligation for the year be deducted from his VSI payment. McClure v. McClure (Greene 1994) 98 Ohio App.3d 27, 647 N.E.2d 832, appeal not allowed 71 Ohio St.3d 1481, 645 N.E.2d 1260.

Naming error in divorce decree stating that father's child and spousal support obligations were to be paid out of his Voluntary Separation Incentive (VSI) payments, offered by the armed forces to encourage a reduction in force, directly from the United States Air Force when in fact father received his VSI payments from the Defense

Finance and Accounting Service (DFAS) was harmless because trial court had properly sent withholding order to DFAS to compel it to withhold father's support obligations. McClure v. McClure (Greene 1994) 98 Ohio App.3d 27, 647 N.E.2d 832, appeal not allowed 71 Ohio St.3d 1481, 645 N.E.2d 1260.

Order permitting agency that distributed husband's civil service pension checks to deduct fee to cover its costs of complying with order withholding portion of those checks to pay husband's alimony obligation did not amount to modification of alimony award. Holloman v. Holloman (Montgomery 1993) 91 Ohio App.3d 279, 632 N.E.2d 575.

Wife's request that husband's alimony obligation be deducted from his monthly civil service pension check was not barred by laches, although seven and one-half years had passed since entry of divorce decree; although wife was permitted by statute to seek withholding order, she was never obligated to do so, and husband failed to demonstrate how he had been prejudiced. Holloman v. Holloman (Montgomery 1993) 91 Ohio App.3d 279, 632 N.E.2d 575.

Husband's federal civil service retirement benefits were subject to withholding order to satisfy his alimony obligation to his former wife. Holloman v. Holloman (Montgomery 1993) 91 Ohio App.3d 279, 632 N.E.2d 575.

Trial court did not abuse its discretion in ordering former husband to post bond of $1,000 as security for payment of future child support; former husband became delinquent in his child support payments, thus violating wage withholding order issued in previous divorce due to his failure to issue himself paycheck from his corporate earnings in his welding corporation, former husband had exclusive control over compliance with original wage withholding order, and trial court implicitly determined that former husband had ability to post bond. High v. High (Allen 1993) 89 Ohio App.3d 424, 624 N.E.2d 801.

Spendthrift trust can be reached for child support. Albertson v. Ryder (Lake 1993) 85 Ohio App.3d 765, 621 N.E.2d 480.

To qualify as "qualified domestic relations order" (QDRO) excepted from ERISA's antialienation provision, order must relate to provision of child support, alimony payments or marital property rights of spouse, former spouse, child or other dependent of participant, and must be made pursuant to state domestic relations law. Albertson v. Ryder (Lake 1993) 85 Ohio App.3d 765, 621 N.E.2d 480.

Order allowing attachment of father's employer-sponsored savings plan met requirements of "qualified domestic relations order" (QDRO), and, therefore, general antialienation provision of ERISA was inapplicable; order related to child support, juvenile court made order pursuant to domestic relations law requiring parent to support minor children, and juvenile court had jurisdiction to order child support. Albertson v. Ryder (Lake 1993) 85 Ohio App.3d 765, 621 N.E.2d 480.

Statute authorizing income withholding orders from otherwise exempt retirement benefits to provide support payments did not permit trial court that found husband in contempt for failing to pay former wife her share of retirement income that was marital property to order husband to agree to withholding order. Johnson v. Johnson (Montgomery 1993) 85 Ohio App.3d 161, 619 N.E.2d 458.

Trial court is not prohibited from ordering recipient of retirement benefit to divide it to conform to ordered marital property division by himself directing payor of benefit to make payments according to method ordered by court. Johnson v. Johnson (Montgomery 1993) 85 Ohio App.3d 161, 619 N.E.2d 458.

Trial court's order finding husband in contempt for failing to provide former wife with her share of retirement income that was marital property was not functional equivalent of impermissible attachment of or execution against exempt retirement fund; order did not direct the prohibited act, but merely allowed husband to avoid incarceration by taking steps to divide fund, and primary purpose of order was to vindicate court's authority. Johnson v. Johnson (Montgomery 1993) 85 Ohio App.3d 161, 619 N.E.2d 458.

Statute authorizing income withholding orders from otherwise exempt pension or retirement benefits to provide support payments for benefit of spouse, former spouse, or minor child does not permit trial court to execute against or attach retirement benefits. Johnson v. Johnson (Montgomery 1993) 85 Ohio App.3d 161, 619 N.E.2d 458.

Any contractual lien that attorney for adjudicated father had on father's workers' compensation award did not take priority over child support enforcement agency's (CSEA) attachment. Minor Child of Zentack v. Strong (Ohio App. 8 Dist. 1992) 83 Ohio App.3d 332, 614 N.E.2d 1106.

A corporation's offense of failing to notify a support enforcement agency of a lump-sum payment made by it to its employees is an omission to which RC 2901.23(A)(3) applies and to which the mental state of no particular officer is relevant, since in the case of an omission to act, no particular corporate officer or officers are involved; thus, the defense by a corporation that the right hand did not know what the left hand was doing is not available to the corporation in the case of failing to notify a support enforcement agency of a lump-sum payment since the general assembly has dispensed with any particular culpability state for an offense consisting of an omission to discharge a specific duty imposed by law on a corporate organization. Burrs v. Burrs (Montgomery 1991) 66 Ohio App.3d 628, 585 N.E.2d 918.

The use of the words "knowingly" and "knowing" in RC 3113.21(H)(1)(d) is presumably intended to avoid the imposition of liability on an employer as a result of its failure to notify a support enforcement agency of lump-sum payments that may be paid by third parties to its employee, as a result of the termination of his employment, of which the employer has no knowledge; however, the employer cannot reasonably claim that it has no knowledge of payments that it will make, itself, to its employee. Burrs v. Burrs (Montgomery 1991) 66 Ohio App.3d 628, 585 N.E.2d 918.

A trial court which imposes a contempt fine on a corporate employer for its failure to notify a support enforcement agency of a lump-sum payment made by it to its employee is only required to find, beyond a reasonable doubt, that (1) the employer received an order to withhold directing it to notify the support enforcement agency of any pending lump-sum distributions in excess of $500, (2) it failed to notify the support enforcement agency of the pending lump-sum distribution, (3) it made a lump-sum distribution in excess of $500, and (4) at the time that it made the lump-sum distribution, there were existing child support and alimony arrearages; thus, proof of intent on the part of the contemnor is not required. Burrs v. Burrs (Montgomery 1991) 66 Ohio App.3d 628, 585 N.E.2d 918.

The administrator of an alimony obligor's pension plan may properly be joined as a party to an action to secure payment of alimony, although the obligee has waived all rights to the obligor's pension plan. Roach v. Roach (Cuyahoga 1989) 61 Ohio App.3d 315, 572 N.E.2d 772.

Supplemental unemployment benefits paid under a collective bargaining agreement are not "personal earnings" as that term is used in RC 3113.21(D)(1). Robbins v. Robbins (Franklin 1988) 53 Ohio App.3d 6, 557 N.E.2d 823.

The provisions of RC Ch 4123 apply to state-insured and self-insured employers without distinction; thus, workers' compensation benefits paid by a self-insured employer do not constitute personal earnings and are not subject to withholding for the payment of child support or alimony. Industrial Com'n of Ohio v. Sherry (Paulding 1984) 20 Ohio App.3d 32, 484 N.E.2d 212, 20 O.B.R. 34.

Notification to the court that the obligor will be receiving a lump-sum payment from his employer as a holiday bonus does not mean that the court must seize it and apply it to the child support obligation where the obligor is not in default and there is no arrearage other than that created by the agreed entry. Haynie v Haynie, No. 96APF11-1610, 1997 WL 360877 (10th Dist Ct App, Franklin, 6-30-97).

In a case of child support arrearage, the Consumer Credit Protection Act garnishment limits do not apply to lump-sum workers' compensation awards and the trial court must subtract the contingent legal fee amount due from a $20,000 lump-sum workers' compensation award before ordering the remainder of the $20,000 to be applied to the child support arrearage. Coy v Jackson County Child Support Enforcement Agency, No. 96-CA-777, 1996 WL 612473 (4th Dist Ct App, Jackson, 10-15-96).

Allowing a spouse to satisfy her arrearages in child support at the time of sale of the marital home and to further authorize her to incur additional arrearages to be paid when the marital real estate is sold is error. McQuinn v McQuinn, No. CA95-06-099, 1996 WL 165516 (12th Dist Ct App, Butler, 4-8-96).

The domestic relations court has subject matter jurisdiction to determine a third party's interest in the deferred compensation fund of a person whose spouse seeks to attach the fund for an award of support. Zashin, Rich, Sutula & Monastra v Offenberg, No. 68951, 1995 WL 723345 (8th Dist Ct App, Cuyahoga, 12-7-95).

To find an employer in contempt for violation of RC 3113.21(H)(3)(d), the court must determine that (1) the employer received an order directing it to notify the child support enforcement agency of any pending lump-sum payments for retirement benefits owed to the employee; (2) the employer failed to notify the agency of a lump-sum payment in excess of $500 made to the employee; and (3) at the time of the lump-sum distribution a child support arrearage existed against the employee. Sells v Sells, No. 2888, 1995 WL 66369 (9th Dist Ct App, Summit, 2-15-95).

Under a contingent fee agreement, an attorney's lien does not attach until a judgment is rendered in the client's favor and an actual award is granted, and where the client has child support arrearages that have vested prior to the awarding of the client's lump sum workers' compensation claim, the child support arrearages have priority over the attorney's lien. Ruttman v Flores, No. 66079, 1994 WL 677539 (8th Dist Ct App, Cuyahoga, 12-1-94).

Allocation of the dependency exemption for federal tax purposes which is not explicitly decided by the trial court is remanded for determination particularly where there is substantial disparity in the parties' incomes. Winters v Winters, No. 2112, 1994 WL 69885 (4th Dist Ct App, Scioto, 2-24-94).

Trial court has discretion to award attorney fees under a contingency fee contract from a lump-sum payment from the bureau of workers' compensation that has been directed by RC 3113.21(H) to be transmitted to a county child support enforcement agency to reduce obligor's arrearages to obligee since RC 3113.21 does not prohibit a trial court from finding that an equitable interest was established in the fund from the moment of its inception by virtue of a valid contingency fee contract and since such an equitable interest would not be included in any lump-sum payment referred to in RC 3113.21. Stewart v Stewart, No. 93-L-051, 1993 WL 548547 (11th Dist Ct App, Lake, 12-17-93).

The federal Consumer Credit Collection Act limitations on amount of disposable income subject to withholding, referenced in RC 3113.21(E), is inapplicable to lump sum distributions from ESOPs or other voluntary payroll deduction programs. Colwell v Jones, No. 14528 (9th Dist Ct App, Summit, 8-1-90).

The provisions of RC 3113.21(D)(1)(b)(x) require an employer who is subject to a withholding order to notify a child support enforcement agency of a pending lump-sum payment of any kind to be paid to a child support obligor whenever the amount of such lump-sum payment, as calculated prior to any employer withholding or deductions, equals or exceeds $500. OAG 95-007.

5. Constitutional issues

It is a violation of the equal protection clauses of the United States and Ohio constitutions to allow the aid and support of the child support enforcement agency in an action for child support brought by parents who have established their parentage through the probate court and residential parents who are on public assistance while denying the aid and support of the child support enforcement agency to parents who have established their parentage through the administrative process. Cuyahoga County Support Enforcement Agency v Lozada, Nos. 67463+, 1995 WL 386965 (8th Dist Ct App, Cuyahoga, 6-29-95).

6. Laches

Trial court lacked statutory authority retroactively to modify former husband's delinquent child support obligation with respect to children who came to reside with him by mutual agreement after entry of divorce decree which included support order, where former husband did not move for modification of payments after children moved into his home and thus remained legally obligated to make support payments according to original order. Gerlach v. Gerlach (Ohio App. 10 Dist. 1997) 124 Ohio App.3d 246, 705 N.E.2d 1287, dismissed, appeal not allowed 81 Ohio St.3d 1495, 691 N.E.2d 1057.

For purposes of determining applicability of laches defense to former wife's motion to reduce child support arrearages to lump-sum judgment, evidence that former wife maintained close relationship with her two sons who resided with former husband, that both former spouses attended their children's weddings, and that former wife had spoken with former husband at least once on telephone, was sufficient to support trial court's findings that former wife was aware of former husband's whereabouts, as element of former husband's equitable defense of laches. Gerlach v. Gerlach (Ohio App. 10 Dist. 1997) 124 Ohio App.3d 246, 705 N.E.2d 1287, dismissed, appeal not allowed 81 Ohio St.3d 1495, 691 N.E.2d 1057.

Testimony in evidentiary hearing on former wife's motion to consolidate child support arrearages, to effect that former husband's bank had destroyed all records relating to payments made by him during former wife's 18-year delay in bringing suit, and that former husband's father, who could have offered testimony concerning such payments, died prior to commencement of action, constituted some evidence in support of trial court's determination that former wife's motion was barred by laches. Gerlach v. Gerlach (Ohio App. 10 Dist. 1997) 124 Ohio App.3d 246, 705 N.E.2d 1287, dismissed, appeal not allowed 81 Ohio St.3d 1495, 691 N.E.2d 1057.

In order for appellate court to overturn trial court's judgment that recipient-spouse's motion for child support arrearages is barred by doctrine of laches, appellate court must determine that such judgment is against manifest weight of evidence. Gerlach v. Gerlach (Ohio App. 10 Dist. 1997) 124 Ohio App.3d 246, 705 N.E.2d 1287, dismissed, appeal not allowed 81 Ohio St.3d 1495, 691 N.E.2d 1057.

The fact that a woman waited thirteen years before informing a man of the existence of his illegitimate son is held to not bar her claim for child support arrearages or to have prejudiced the father by denying him the chance to be a father to the boy; since the boy is still a minor the court states that the father may still petition for visitation and become involved in the boy's life. State ex rel Scioto County Child Support Agency v Gardner, 113 App(3d) 46, 680 NE(2d) 221 (Scioto 1996).

3113.211 Fees assessed for withholding or deduction of child support; time for distribution

(A)(1) For purposes of this section, a withholding or deduction order that was issued prior to December 31, 1993, under division (D)(1), (2), (3), (4), or (5) of section 3113.21 of the Revised Code as the division existed prior to that date and that has not been terminated on or after December 31, 1993, shall be considered to be a withholding or deduction notice issued under division (D)(1) or (2) of section 3113.21 of the Revised Code.

(2) A payor ordered to withhold a specified amount from the income of an employee under a withholding notice issued under division (A), (B), (C), or (D)(1) of section 3113.21 of the Revised Code for purposes of support also may deduct from the income of the person, in addition to the amount withheld for purposes of support, a fee of two dollars or an amount not to exceed one per cent of the amount withheld for purposes of support, whichever is greater, as a charge for its services in complying with the withholding requirement included in the withholding notice. A financial institution required to deduct funds from an account under a deduction notice issued under division (D)(2) of section 3113.21 of the Revised Code for purposes of support may deduct from the account of the person, in addition to the amount deducted for purposes of support, a fee of five dollars or an amount not to exceed the lowest rate that it charges, if any, for a debit transaction in a similar account, whichever is less, as a charge for its service in complying with the deduction requirement included in the deduction notice.

The entire amount withheld or deducted pursuant to a withholding or deduction notice issued under division (D) of section 3113.21 of the Revised Code for purposes of support shall be forwarded to the division of child support in the department of job and family services immediately, but not later than seven working days after, the withholding or deduction, as directed in the withholding or deduction notice.

(B) If a payor or financial institution is required to withhold or deduct a specified amount from the income or savings of more than one obligor under a withholding or deduction notice issued under division (D) of section 3113.21 of the Revised Code and is required to forward the amounts withheld or deducted to the division of child support, the payor or the financial institution may combine all of the amounts to be forwarded in one payment, provided the payment is accompanied by a list that clearly identifies each obligor who is covered by the payment and the portion of the payment that is attributable to that obligor.

(C) Upon receipt of any amount forwarded from a payor or financial institution the division of child support shall distribute the amount to the obligee within two business days of its receipt of the amount forwarded. The director of job and family services may adopt, revise, or amend rules under Chapter 119. of the Revised Code to assist in the implementation of this division.

(D) A payor or financial institution shall not be subject to criminal or civil liability for compliance, in accordance with this section, with a withholding or deduction notice issued pursuant to division (D) of section 3113.21 of the Revised Code.

(1999 H 471, eff. 7-1-00; 1997 H 352, eff. 1-1-98; 1993 H 173, eff. 12-31-93; 1990 S 3; 1988 H 503, H 708; 1986 H 509)

Historical and Statutory Notes

Amendment Note: 1999 H 471 substituted "job and family" for "human" in the second paragraph in division (A)(2); and substituted "director of job and family services" for "department of human services" in division (C).

Amendment Note: 1997 H 352 rewrote this section, which prior thereto read:

"(A)(1) For purposes of this section, a withholding or deduction order that was issued prior to December 31, 1993, under division (D)(1), (2), (3), (4), or (5) of section 3113.21 of the Revised Code as the division existed prior to that date and that has not been terminated on or after December 31, 1993, shall be considered to be a withholding or deduction notice issued under division (D)(1), (2), (3), (4), or (5) of section 3113.21 of the Revised Code.

"(2) An employer ordered to withhold a specified amount from the personal earnings of an employee under a withholding notice issued under division (A), (B), (C), or (D)(1) of section 3113.21 of the Revised Code for purposes of support also may deduct from the personal earnings of the person, in addition to the amount withheld for purposes of support, a fee of two dollars or an amount not to exceed one per cent of the amount withheld for purposes of support, whichever is greater, as a charge for its services in complying with the withholding requirement included in the withholding notice. An employer that is paying a person's workers' compensation benefits and that is required to withhold a specified amount from a person's workers' compensation benefits under a withholding notice issued under division (D)(2) of section 3113.21 of the Revised Code for purposes of support also may deduct from the workers' compensation benefits, in addition to the amount withheld for purposes of support, a fee of two dollars or an amount not to exceed one per cent of the amount withheld for purposes of support, whichever is greater, as a charge for its services in complying with the withholding requirement included in the withholding notice. A financial institution required to deduct funds from an account under a deduction notice issued under division (D)(5) of section 3113.21 of the Revised Code for purposes of support may deduct from the account of the person, in addition to the amount deducted for purposes of support, a fee of five dollars or an amount not to exceed the lowest rate that it charges, if any, for a debit transaction in a similar account, whichever is less, as a charge for its service in complying with the deduction requirement included in the deduction notice. The public employees retirement board, the board, board of trustees, or other governing entity of any municipal retirement system, the board of trustees of the police and firemen's disability and pension fund, the state teachers retirement board, the school employees retirement board, the state highway patrol retirement board, and a person paying or otherwise distributing an obligor's income required to withhold or deduct a specified amount from an obligor's pension, annuity, allowance, other benefit, or other source of income under a withholding or deduction notice issued under division (D)(3) or (4) of section 3113.21 of the Revised Code for purposes of support also may deduct from the obligor's pension, annuity, allowance, other benefit, or other source of income, a fee of two dollars or an amount not to exceed one per cent of the amount withheld or deducted, whichever is less, as a charge for its services in complying with the withholding or deduction requirement included in the withholding or deduction notice.

"The entire amount withheld or deducted pursuant to a withholding or deduction notice issued under division (D) of section 3113.21 of the Revised Code for purposes of support shall be forwarded to the child support enforcement agency of the county in which that court is located immediately, but not later than ten working days after, the withholding or deduction, as directed in the withholding or deduction notice.

"(B) If an employer, a financial institution, an employer that is paying an obligor's workers' compensation benefits, the public employees retirement board, the board, board of trustees, or other governing entity of any municipal retirement system, the board of trustees of the police and firemen's disability and pension fund, the state teachers retirement board, the school employees retirement board, the state highway patrol retirement board, the person paying or otherwise distributing an obligor's income, or the bureau of workers' compensation is required to withhold or deduct a specified amount from the personal earnings, payments, pensions, annuities, allowances, benefits, other sources of income, or savings of more than one obligor under a withholding or deduction notice issued under division (D) of section 3113.21 of the Revised Code and is required to forward the amounts withheld or deducted to the same child support enforcement agency, the employer, the public employees retirement board, the board, board of trustees, or other governing entity of any municipal retirement system, the board of trustees of the police and firemen's disability and pension fund, the state teachers retirement board, the school employees retirement board, the state highway patrol retirement board, the person paying or otherwise distributing an obligor's income, the financial institution, the employer that is paying an obligor's workers' compensation benefits, or the bureau of workers' compensation may combine all of the amounts to be forwarded in one payment, provided the payment is accompanied by a list that clearly identifies each obligor who is covered by the payment and the portion of the payment that is attributable to that obligor.

"(C) Upon receipt of any amount forwarded from an employer, a financial institution, an employer that is paying a person's workers' compensation benefits, the public employees retirement board, the board, board of trustees, or other governing entity of any municipal retirement system, the board of trustees of the police and firemen's disability and pension fund, the state teachers retirement board, the school employees retirement board, the state highway patrol retirement board, the person paying or otherwise distributing an obligor's income, or the bureau of workers' compensation under this section, a clerk of court or child support enforcement agency shall distribute the amount to the obligee within two business days of its receipt of the amount forwarded. The department of human services may adopt, revise, or amend rules under Chapter 119. of the Revised Code to assist the clerk of court or child support enforcement agency in the implementation of this division."

Amendment Note: 1993 H 173 added division (A)(1); rewrote the final paragraph of division (A)(2); changed references to administrative withholding orders to references to withholding or deduction requirements and orders throughout divisions (A) and (B); and substituted "required" for "ordered" prior to "to withhold or deduct" and deleted "clerk of court or" prior to "child support enforcement agency" in division (B). Prior to amendment, division (A)(1) read:

"The entire amount withheld or deducted pursuant to an order described in division (D) of section 3113.21 of the Revised Code for purposes of support and required to be issued by division (B) or (C) of that section or any other section of the Revised Code shall be forwarded immediately to the clerk of the court issuing the order, or to the child support enforcement agency of the county in which that court is located, as directed in the order."

Cross References

Bureaus of support, monthly payment orders, employer not to discharge employee due to orders, 2301.39
Child support division maintaining separate accounts for deposit of support payments, 5101.325
Child support enforcement agencies, support payments to, applicability, 2301.36
Court making or modifying child support order, 2151.23, 3105.21, 3115.22
Court support enforcement agency, adoption of rules, 2301.35
Factors determining amount of support, applicability, 3109.05, 3111.13

Library References

Children Out-Of-Wedlock ⚷23, 69.
Divorce ⚷311(1), 311(2), 311.5.
Exemptions ⚷48, 49.
Infants ⚷228.
Parent and Child ⚷3.3(8), 3.3(9).
Social Security and Public Welfare ⚷194.19.
WESTLAW Topic Nos. 76H, 134, 163, 211, 285, 356A.
C.J.S. Children Out-of-Wedlock §§ 53 to 62, 128, 129.
C.J.S. Divorce §§ 706 to 718, 721.
C.J.S. Exemptions §§ 39, 105 to 121.
C.J.S. Infants §§ 42, 53, 54, 57, 69 to 85.
C.J.S. Parent and Child §§ 80, 82 to 87, 89.
C.J.S. Social Security and Public Welfare § 122.

Carlin, Baldwin's Ohio Practice, *Merrick-Rippner Probate Law* § 19.6, 19.7, 19.8, 19.10, 19.10.1, 108.3, 108.20, 108.29, 108.30, 108.35, 108.36, 108.37 (1997)
Kurtz & Giannelli, Ohio Juvenile Law (1998 Ed.), Text 27.2, 29.2
Sowald & Morganstern, Baldwin's Ohio Practice, *Domestic Relations Law* § 3.4, 3.5, 3.35, 3.55, 7.19, 9.11, 9.98, 10.13, 11.43, 11.44, 13.44, 14.3, 15.69, 19.1, 20.3, 20.64, 22.20, 22.21, 23.21, 23.35, 23.39, 23.42, 29.34 (1997)

Notes of Decisions and Opinions

1. Constitutional issues

"Poundage fees" for collection of child support by state agency or for withholding of child support by employer are not unconstitutional punishment and do not discriminate against wealthier parents; the fees are not punishment, do not depend on or affect any suspect classification, and are rationally based in the need to offset administrative expenses associated with administering and enforcing child support laws. Childrens and Parents Rights Ass'n of Ohio, Inc., (CAPRA) v. Sullivan (N.D.Ohio 1991) 787 F.Supp. 724.

3113.212 Change in obligor's status; cancellation of orders or notices

(A) When a court has issued a support order, when the court or a child support enforcement agency has issued one or more notices containing one or more of the requirements described in division (D) of section 3113.21 of the Revised Code or when a court has issued one or more court orders described in division (D)(3) or (4) of that section, and when either the child support enforcement agency receives a notification as described in division (D), (G), or (H) of section 3113.21 of the Revised Code that pertains to a change in the source of income or status of accounts in a financial institution of the obligor or the child support enforcement agency otherwise determines that the source of income or status of accounts in a financial institution of the obligor has changed, the child support enforcement agency immediately shall conduct an investigation to determine the obligor's present source of income or assets, and the obligor's address and social security number and shall issue one or more notices described in division (D) of section 3113.21 of the Revised Code that it determines are appropriate. If the agency determines that no notice of the type described in division (D)(1) or (2) of that section would be appropriate, the agency may request the court to issue a court order under division (D)(3) or (4) of that section, and, upon the request, the court may issue an order as described in that division. The notices and court orders are final and are enforceable by the court. The notices shall be mailed within fifteen days after the obligor under the support order is located or within fifteen days after the default under the support order, whichever is applicable.

If the court or child support enforcement agency previously has issued one or more notices containing one or more of the requirements described in division (D) of section 3113.21 of the Revised Code or the court previously has issued one or more court orders described in division (D)(3) or (4) of that section and the child support enforcement agency determines that any of the requirements or court orders no longer are appropriate due to the change, the agency immediately shall cancel any previously issued notice, and the court shall cancel any previously issued court order that no longer is appropriate, the agency shall send written notice of the cancellation by regular mail to the person who was required to comply with the withholding, deduction, or other requirement contained in the canceled notice or court order, and the agency shall issue one or more new notices containing one or more requirements described in division (D) of section 3113.21 of the Revised Code that it determines are appropriate. If the agency determines that no notice of the type described in division (D)(1) or (2) of that section would be appropriate, the agency may request the court to issue a court order under division (D)(3) or (4) of that section, and, upon the request, the court may issue an order as described in that division. The notices and court orders are final and are enforceable by the court. The notices shall be mailed within fifteen days after the obligor under the support order is located or within fifteen days after the default under the support order, whichever is applicable.

(B) When a court or child support enforcement agency has issued one or more notices containing one or more of the requirements described in division (D) of section 3113.21 of the Revised Code requiring withholding by a payor that is not an employer or requiring deduction by a financial institution or a court has issued one or more court orders described in division (D)(3) or (4) of that section and the agency is informed that the obligor has commenced employment, the agency shall issue a notice requiring the withholding of an amount from the person's personal earnings for support, in accordance with division (D)(1) of section 3113.21 of the Revised Code. The notice is final and is enforceable by the court. Additionally, if the court or agency determines that payments due under the support order have not been made and that the amount that has not been paid is at least equal to the support owed for one month under the support order, the court shall proceed to collect on any cash bond and shall order it paid to the division of child support in the department of job and family services.

(C) If a child support enforcement agency sends a notice imposing a withholding or deduction requirement or a court sends a court order imposing any other appropriate requirement to a person under division (A) or (B) of this section, the notice or court order, for purposes of sections 3113.21 to 3113.219 of the Revised Code, also shall be considered to have been issued under division (D) of section 3113.21 of the Revised Code. The notice or court order is final and is enforceable by the court.

(D) If a child support enforcement agency sends a notice imposing a withholding or deduction requirement or any other appropriate requirement to a person under division (A) or (B) of this section or under section 3113.21 of the Revised Code and if the payor or financial institution that is sent the withholding, deduction, or other appropriate notice fails to comply with the notice, the child support enforcement agency shall request the court to issue a court order requiring the payor or financial institution to comply with the withholding, deduction, or other appropriate notice sent by the agency immediately or be held in contempt of court. If the court issues the requested order and if the payor or financial institution does not comply with the withholding, deduction, or other appropriate order of the agency that is the subject of the court order immediately, it is in contempt of court.

(1999 H 471, eff. 7-1-00; 1997 H 352, eff. 1-1-98; 1993 H 173, eff. 12-31-93; 1988 H 708; 1987 H 231; 1986 H 509)

Historical and Statutory Notes

Amendment Note: 1999 H 471 substituted "job and family" for "human" in division (B).

Amendment Note: 1997 H 352 rewrote this section, which prior thereto read:

"(A) When a court has issued a support order, when the court or a child support enforcement agency has issued one or more notices containing one or more of the requirements described in division (D) of section 3113.21 of the Revised Code or when a court has issued one or more court orders described in division (D)(6) or (7) of that section, and when either the child support enforcement agency receives a notification as described in division (D), (G), or (H) of section 3113.21 of the Revised Code that pertains to a change in the employment status, status of the workers' compensation payments, status of the pension, annuity, allowance, benefit, or other source of income, or status of accounts in a financial institution of the obligor or the child support enforcement agency otherwise determines that the employment status, status of the workers' compensation payments, status of the pension, annuity, allowance, benefit, or other source of income, or status of accounts in a financial institution of the obligor has changed, the child support enforcement agency immediately shall conduct an investigation to determine the obligor's present employment status, his employer's address, whether he has any other source of income or assets, and the obligor's address and social security number and shall issue one or more notices described in division (D) of section 3113.21 of the Revised Code that it determines are appropriate. If the agency determines that no notice of the type described in division (D)(1) to (5) of that section would be appropriate, the agency may request the court to issue a court order under division (D)(6) or (7) of that section, and, upon the request, the court may issue an order as described in that division. The notices and court orders are final and are enforceable by the court. The notices shall be mailed within fifteen days after the obligor under the support order is located or within fifteen days after the default under the support order, whichever is applicable.

"If the court or child support enforcement agency previously has issued one or more notices containing one or more of the requirements described in division (D) of section 3113.21 of the Revised Code or the court previously has issued one or more court orders described in division (D)(6) or (7) of that section and the child support enforcement agency determines that any of the requirements or court orders no longer are appropriate due to the change, the agency immediately shall cancel any previously issued notice, and the court shall cancel any previously issued court order that no longer is appropriate, the agency shall send written notice of the cancellation by regular mail to the person who was required to comply with the withholding, deduction, or other requirement contained in the canceled notice or court order, and the agency shall issue one or more new notices containing one or more requirements described in division (D) of section 3113.21 of the Revised Code that it determines are appropriate. If the agency determines that no notice of the type described in division (D)(1) to (5) of that section would be appropriate, the agency may request the court to issue a court order under division (D)(6) or (7) of that section, and, upon the request, the court may issue an order as described in that division. The notices and court orders are final and are enforceable by the court. The notices shall be mailed within fifteen days after the obligor under the support order is located or within fifteen days after the default under the support order, whichever is applicable.

"(B) When a court or child support enforcement agency has issued one or more notices containing one or more of the requirements described in division (D)(2), (3), (4), or (5) of section 3113.21 of the Revised Code or a court has issued one or more court orders described in division (D)(6) or (7) of that section and the agency is informed that the obligor has commenced employment, the agency shall issue a notice requiring the withholding of an amount from the person's personal earnings for support, in accordance with division (D)(1) of section 3113.21 of the Revised Code. The notice is final and is enforceable by the court. Additionally, if the court or agency determines that payments due under the support order have not been made and that the amount that has not been paid is at least equal to the support owed for one month under the support order, the court shall proceed to collect on any cash bond.

"(C) If a child support enforcement agency sends a notice imposing a withholding or deduction requirement or a court sends a court order imposing any other appropriate requirement to a person under division (A) or (B) of this section, the notice or court order, for purposes of sections 3113.21 to 3113.219 of the Revised Code, also shall be considered to have been issued under division (D) of section 3113.21 of the Revised Code. The notice or court order is final and is enforceable by the court.

"(D) If a child support enforcement agency sends a notice imposing a withholding or deduction requirement or any other appropriate requirement to a person under division (A) or (B) of this section or under section 3113.21 of the Revised Code and if the employer, the financial institution, the employer that is paying the obligor's workers' compensation benefits, the public employees retirement board, the board, board of trustees, or other governing entity of the municipal retirement system, the board of trustees of the police and firemen's disability and pension fund, the state teachers retirement board, the school employees retirement board, the state highway patrol retirement board, the person paying or otherwise distributing an obligor's income, or the bureau of workers' compensation that is sent the withholding, deduction, or other appropriate notice fails to comply with the notice, the child support enforcement agency shall request the court to issue a court order requiring the employer, the financial institution, the employer that is paying the obligor's workers' compensation benefits, the public employees retirement board, the board, board of trustees, or other governing entity of the municipal retirement system, the board of trustees of the police and firemen's disability and pension fund, the state teachers retirement board, the school employees retirement board, the state highway patrol retirement board, the person paying or otherwise distributing an obligor's income, or the bureau of workers' compensation to comply with the withholding, deduction, or other appropriate notice sent by the agency immediately or be held in contempt of court. If the court issues the requested order and if the employer, the financial institution, the employer that is paying the obligor's workers' compensation benefits, the public employees retirement board, the board, board of trustees, or other governing entity of the municipal retirement system, the board of trustees of the police and firemen's disability and pension fund, the state teachers retirement board, the school employees retirement board, the state highway patrol retirement board, the person paying or otherwise distributing an obligor's income, or the bureau of workers' compensation does not comply with the withholding, deduction, or other appropriate order of the agency that is the subject of the court order immediately, it is in contempt of court."

Amendment Note: 1993 H 173 rewrote this section, which previously read:

"(A) When a court that has issued a support order and an order described in division (D) of section 3113.21 of the Revised Code receives a notification from a child support enforcement agency pursuant to division (G)(5) of section 3113.21 of the Revised Code that the agency received a notification of the type described in division (D) or (H) of that section that pertains to a change in the employment status, status of the workers' compensation payments, status of the pension, annuity, allowance, benefit, or other source of income, or status of accounts in a financial institution of the obligor, or when a court that has made such an order determines at a hearing conducted on its own motion or on the motion of any person with an interest in the welfare of the subject child or spouse that the employment status, status of the workers' compensation payments, status of the pension, annuity, allowance, benefit, or other source of income, or status of accounts in a financial institution of the obligor has changed, the court immediately shall order the child support enforcement agency to conduct an investigation to determine the obligor's present employment status, his employer's address, whether he has any other source of income or assets, and the obligor's address and social security number and to report its findings to the court within ten days after the issuance of the order to conduct the investigation. The child support enforcement agency shall give the obligor notice, as described in division (B) of section 3113.21 of the Revised Code, of the investigation and of his right to present evidence to the agency as to whether the issuance of any order described in division (D) of section 3113.21 of the Revised Code would be improper because of a mistake in fact.

"If the court previously has issued one or more orders described in division (D) of section 3113.21 of the Revised Code and the court determines that any of the orders no longer is appropriate due to the changes, the court shall immediately cancel any previously issued order that is no longer appropriate, and issue one or more new orders described in division (D) of section 3113.21 of the Revised Code or issue an order of the type described in division (H) of that section, whichever is applicable.

"(B) When a court that has issued an order described in division (D)(2), (3), (4), (5), or (6) of section 3113.21 of the Revised Code is informed that the obligor has commenced employment, the court shall issue an order requiring the withholding of an amount from the person's personal earnings for support, in accordance with division (D)(1) of section 3113.21 of the Revised Code, and, if the court determines that payments due under the support order have not been made and that the amount that has not been paid is at least equal to the support owed for one month under the support order, the court shall proceed to collect on any cash bond."

Cross References

Child support enforcement agency, adoption of rules, 2301.35

Court making or modifying child support order, 2151.23, 3105.21, 3115.22

Factors determining amount of support, applicability, 3109.05, 3111.13

Library References

Children Out-Of-Wedlock ⚷23, 69.
Divorce ⚷311(1), 311(2), 311.5.
Exemptions ⚷48, 49.
Infants ⚷228.
Parent and Child ⚷3.3(8), 3.3(9).
Social Security and Public Welfare ⚷194.19.
WESTLAW Topic Nos. 76H, 134, 163, 211, 285, 356A.
C.J.S. Children Out-of-Wedlock §§ 53 to 62, 128, 129.
C.J.S. Divorce §§ 706 to 718, 721.
C.J.S. Exemptions §§ 39, 105 to 121.
C.J.S. Infants §§ 42, 53, 54, 57, 69 to 85.
C.J.S. Parent and Child §§ 80, 82 to 87, 89.
C.J.S. Social Security and Public Welfare § 122.

Carlin, Baldwin's Ohio Practice, *Merrick-Rippner Probate Law* § 19.6, 19.7, 19.8, 19.10, 19.10.1, 108.3, 108.20, 108.29, 108.30, 108.35, 108.36, 108.37 (1997)

Kurtz & Giannelli, Ohio Juvenile Law (1998 Ed.), Text 27.2, 29.2

Sowald & Morganstern, Baldwin's Ohio Practice, *Domestic Relations Law* § 3.4, 3.5, 3.35, 3.55, 7.19, 9.11, 9.98, 10.13, 11.43, 11.44, 13.44, 14.3, 15.69, 19.1, 20.3, 20.64, 22.21, 23.21, 23.35, 23.39, 23.42, 29.34 (1997)

Law Review and Journal Commentaries

Bankruptcy Reform Act of 1994—What the Bankruptcy Code Giveth, Domestic Relations Courts (and Congress) Taketh Away, C.R. "Chip" Bowles. 8 Domestic Rel J Ohio 17 (March/April 1996).

Notes of Decisions and Opinions

Criminal history records 2
Notice of withholding order 1

1. Notice of withholding order

Issuance of a child support income withholding order without proper notice to the party subject to the withholding order is reversible error pursuant to RC 3113.212 and Civ R 75. Kracht v Kracht, No. 65759, 1994 WL 385967 (8th Dist Ct App, Cuyahoga, 7-21-94).

2. Criminal history records

A contempt citation or bench warrant issued by a court of record against a person for the person's failure to pay spousal or child support, to surrender real property to his spouse, to seek work, to accept responsibility for marital debts, or to appear for a hearing in a civil proceeding does not constitute "criminal history record information," as defined in 28 CFR §§ 20.3(b) and 20.32, for purposes of being entered into the LEADS/NCIC wanted persons data base. OAG 99-029.

3113.213 Contempt for failure to notify court; fine for failure to withhold or notify court; withholding requirement not basis for discharge or refusal to hire

(A)(1) For purposes of this section, a withholding or deduction order that was issued prior to December 31, 1993, under division (D)(1), (2), (4), or (5) of section 3113.21 of the Revised Code as the division existed prior to that date and that has not been terminated on or after December 31, 1993, shall be considered to be a withholding or deduction notice issued under division (D)(1) or (2) of section 3113.21 of the Revised Code.

(2) The failure of any person to send any notification required by division (D) or (H) of section 3113.21 of the Revised Code shall be considered as contempt of court.

(B) A payor that fails to withhold an amount from an obligor's income for support in accordance with a withholding requirement included in a withholding notice issued under division (D)(1) of section 3113.21 of the Revised Code or a financial institution that fails to deduct funds from an obligor's account for support in accordance with a deduction requirement included in a deduction notice issued under division (D)(2) of section 3113.21 of the Revised Code is liable for the amount that was not withheld or deducted, provided that no payor that is an employer whose normal pay and disbursement cycles make it impossible to comply with a withholding requirement contained in a withholding notice issued under division (D)(1) of section 3113.21 of the Revised Code shall be liable for the amount not withheld if the employer, as soon as possible after the employer's receipt of the withholding notice, provides the court or child support enforcement agency that issued the notice with written notice of the impossibility and the reasons for the impossibility. An employer who is liable under this provision for an amount that was not withheld shall be ordered by the court to pay that amount to the division of child support in the department of job and family services, to be disbursed in accordance with the support order for the benefit of the child or spouse.

(C) The court may fine a payor not more than two hundred dollars for failure to withhold income or to notify the court or child support enforcement agency that a situation has occurred causing the payor to cease paying income in an amount sufficient to comply with the order to the obligor, or, in cases in which the obligor is an employer, the obligor is receiving or is eligible to receive a benefit of employment other than personal earnings, as required by a withholding notice issued under division (D)(1) of section 3113.21 of the Revised Code. The court may fine a financial institution not more than two hundred dollars for failure to deduct funds from an account or to notify the court or child support enforcement agency of the termination of an account from which funds are being deducted or the opening of a new account, as required by a deduction notice issued under division (D)(2) of section 3113.21 of the Revised Code.

(D) No payor that is an employer may use a requirement to withhold personal earnings contained in a withholding notice issued under division (D)(1) of section 3113.21 of the Revised Code, as a basis for a discharge of, or for any disciplinary action against, an employee, or as a basis for a refusal to employ a person. The court may fine an employer who so discharges or takes disciplinary action against an employee, or refuses to employ a person, not more than five hundred dollars.

(1999 H 471, eff. 7-1-00; 1997 H 352, eff. 1-1-98; 1993 H 173, eff. 12-31-93; 1988 H 708; 1986 H 509)

Historical and Statutory Notes

Amendment Note: 1999 H 471 substituted "job and family" for "human" in division (B).

Amendment Note: 1997 H 352 rewrote this section, which prior thereto read:

"(A)(1) For purposes of this section, a withholding or deduction order that was issued prior to December 31, 1993, under division (D)(1), (2), (4), or (5) of section 3113.21 of the Revised Code as the division existed prior to that date and that has not been terminated on or after December 31, 1993, shall be considered to be a withholding or deduction notice issued under division (D)(1), (2), (4), or (5) of section 3113.21 of the Revised Code.

"(2) The failure of any person to send any notification required by division (D) or (H) of section 3113.21 of the Revised Code shall be considered as contempt of court.

"(B) An employer that fails to withhold an amount from an obligor's personal earnings for support in accordance with a withholding requirement included in a withholding notice issued under division (D)(1) of section 3113.21 of the Revised Code, an employer that is paying an obligor's workers' compensation benefits and that fails to withhold the obligor's workers' compensation benefits for support in accordance with a withholding requirement included in a withholding notice issued under division (D)(2) of section 3113.21 of the Revised Code, a financial institution that fails to deduct funds from an obligor's account for support in accordance with a deduction requirement included in a deduction notice issued under division (D)(5) of section 3113.21 of the Revised Code, or any other person that fails to withhold or deduct an amount from the income of an obligor in accordance with a withholding or deduction requirement included in a withholding or deduction notice issued under division (D)(4) of section 3113.21 of the Revised Code is liable for the amount that was not withheld or deducted, provided that no employer whose normal pay and disbursement cycles make it impossible to comply with a withholding requirement contained in a withholding notice issued under division (D)(1) of section 3113.21 of the Revised Code shall be liable for the amount not withheld if the employer, as soon as possible after the employer's receipt of the withholding notice, provides the court or child support enforcement agency that issued the notice with written notice of the impossibility and the reasons for the impossibility. An employer who is liable under this provision for an amount that was not withheld shall be ordered by the court to pay that amount to the clerk of the court or the child support enforcement agency, to be disbursed in accordance with the support order for the benefit of the child or spouse.

"(C) The court may fine an employer not more than two hundred dollars for failure to withhold personal earnings or to notify the court or child support enforcement agency that an obligor has terminated employment, has been laid off, has taken a leave of absence without pay, has entered into another situation in which the employer has ceased to pay personal earnings in an amount sufficient to comply with the order to the obligor, or is receiving or is eligible to receive a benefit of employment other than personal earnings, as required by a withholding notice issued under division (D)(1) of section 3113.21 of the Revised Code. The court may fine an employer that is paying an obligor's workers' compensation benefits not more than two hundred dollars for failure to withhold an obligor's workers' compensation benefits or to notify the court or child support enforcement agency of any termination in the payment of the obligor's workers' compensation benefits, as required by a withholding notice issued under division (D)(2) of section 3113.21 of the Revised Code. The court may fine a person who is paying or otherwise distributing the income of an obligor not more than two hundred dollars for failure to withhold or deduct an amount from the income of the obligor or to notify the court or child support enforcement agency of the termination of that income, as required by a withholding or deduction notice issued under division (D)(4) of section 3113.21 of the Revised Code. The court may fine a financial institution not more than two hundred dollars for failure to deduct funds from an account or to notify the court or child support enforcement agency of the termination of an account from which funds are being deducted or the opening of a new account, as required by a deduction notice issued under division (D)(5) of section 3113.21 of the Revised Code.

"(D) No employer may use a requirement to withhold personal earnings contained in a withholding notice issued under division (D)(1) of section 3113.21 of the Revised Code, as a basis for a discharge of, or for any disciplinary action against, an employee, or as a basis for a refusal to employ a person. The court may fine an employer who so discharges or takes disciplinary action against an employee, or refuses to employ a person, not more than five hundred dollars."

Amendment Note: 1993 H 173 added division (A)(1); designated division (A)(2); and changed references to administrative withholding orders to references to withholding or deduction requirements and orders throughout divisions (B) through (D).

Cross References

Bureaus of support, monthly payment orders, employer not to discharge employee due to orders, 2301.39

Child support enforcement agency, adoption of rules, 2301.35

Court making or modifying child support order, 2151.23, 3105.21, 3115.22

Factors determining amount of support, applicability, 3109.05, 3111.13

Library References

Children Out-Of-Wedlock ⚷23, 69.
Divorce ⚷311(1), 311(2), 311.5.
Exemptions ⚷48, 49.
Infants ⚷228.
Parent and Child ⚷3.3(8), 3.3(9).
Social Security and Public Welfare ⚷194.19.
WESTLAW Topic Nos. 76H, 134, 163, 211, 285, 356A.
C.J.S. Children Out-of-Wedlock §§ 53 to 62, 128, 129.
C.J.S. Divorce §§ 706 to 718, 721.
C.J.S. Exemptions §§ 39, 105 to 121.
C.J.S. Infants §§ 42, 53, 54, 57, 69 to 85.
C.J.S. Parent and Child §§ 80, 82 to 87, 89.
C.J.S. Social Security and Public Welfare § 122.

OJur 3d: 39, Employment Relations § 48

Spouse's right to set off debt owed by other spouse against accrued spousal or child support payments. 11 ALR5th 259

Carlin, Baldwin's Ohio Practice, *Merrick-Rippner Probate Law* § 19.6, 19.7, 19.8, 19.10, 19.10.1, 108.20, 108.29, 108.30, 108.35, 108.36 (1997)

Kurtz & Giannelli, Ohio Juvenile Law (1998 Ed.), Text 27.2, 29.2

Siegel & Stephen, Ohio Employment Practices Law (1999 Ed.), Text 1.4, 3.1, 4.10, 20.22

Sowald & Morganstern, Baldwin's Ohio Practice, *Domestic Relations Law* § 3.4, 3.5, 3.35, 3.55, 7.19, 9.11, 9.98, 10.13, 11.43, 11.44, 13.44, 14.3, 15.69, 19.1, 20.2, 20.3,

20.6, 20.64, 22.8, 22.21, 23.21, 23.35, 23.39, 23.42, 29.34 (1997)

Williams, Ohio Consumer Law (2000 Ed.), Text 20.12

Law Review and Journal Commentaries

Bankruptcy Reform Act of 1994—What the Bankruptcy Code Giveth, Domestic Relations Courts (and Congress) Taketh Away, C.R. "Chip" Bowles. 8 Domestic Rel J Ohio 17 (March/April 1996).

"Breach of Public Policy" as an Exception to At-Will Employment, Donald F. Woodcock. 6 Gotherman's Ohio Mun Serv 65 (November/December 1994).

Notes of Decisions and Opinions

1. Discharge from employment

Public policy warrants an exception to the employment-at-will doctrine when an employee is discharged or disciplined for a reason which is prohibited by statute. Greeley v. Miami Valley Maintenance Contractors, Inc. (Ohio 1990) 49 Ohio St.3d 228, 551 N.E.2d 981.

Henceforth, the right of employers to terminate employment at will for "any cause" no longer includes the discharge of an employee where the discharge is in violation of a statute and thereby contravenes public policy. Greeley v. Miami Valley Maintenance Contractors, Inc. (Ohio 1990) 49 Ohio St.3d 228, 551 N.E.2d 981.

In Ohio, a cause of action for wrongful discharge in violation of public policy may be brought in tort. Greeley v. Miami Valley Maintenance Contractors, Inc. (Ohio 1990) 49 Ohio St.3d 228, 551 N.E.2d 981.

No civil action exists for an employee terminated, due to being subject to wage withholding, contrary to RC 3113.213. Greeley v Miami Valley Maintenance Contractors, Inc, No. CA87-12-164 (12th Dist Ct App, Butler, 8-29-88), reversed by 49 OS(3d) 228, 551 NE(2d) 981 (1990).

2. Contempt

A trial court has the authority to determine if an employer is in contempt of a court order for failing to forward child support payments to the bureau of support and award attorney fees if proper. McDaniel v. McDaniel (Cuyahoga 1991) 74 Ohio App.3d 577, 599 N.E.2d 758.

3113.214 Access restrictions and withdrawal directives on financial institution accounts of obligors in default

(A) For the purposes of this section, "access restriction" means that funds may not be withdrawn or transferred.

(B) If, as a result of information obtained pursuant to an agreement under section 5101.315 of the Revised Code, the division of child support in the department of job and family services finds or receives notice that identifies an obligor in default who maintains an account with a financial institution, the division shall, within one business day, enter the information into the case registry established pursuant to section 5101.319 of the Revised Code.

(C) A financial institution that learns, pursuant to an agreement under section 5101.315 of the Revised Code, that an obligor in default maintains an account with the financial institution shall promptly place an access restriction on the account. The access restriction shall remain on the account until the financial institution complies with a withdrawal directive under division (F) of this section or a court or child support enforcement agency orders the financial institution to remove the access restriction.

(D) The child support enforcement agency shall, no later than five business days after information is entered into the case registry pursuant to division (B) of this section, investigate and determine the amount of funds in the account that is available to satisfy the obligor's arrearages under a support order. The financial institution shall cooperate with the agency's investigation.

(E)(1) If a child support enforcement agency that completes an investigation described in division (D) of this section does not find that any person other than the obligor has an ownership interest in the account, it shall issue a withdrawal directive pursuant to division (F) of this section. If the agency finds that a person other than an obligor has an ownership interest in the account, the agency shall send written notice by first-class mail to that person at an address for that person contained in records of the financial institution, except that if the address of that person is not contained in records of the financial institution, the agency shall send the notice to that person in care of another person whose address is contained in records of the financial institution concerning the account.

(2) The notice shall contain both of the following:

(a) A statement of the date the notice is sent, that another of the account holders is an obligor under a support order, the name of the obligor, that the support order is in default, the amount of the arrearage owed by the obligor as determined by the court or child support enforcement agency, the amount that will be withdrawn, the type of account from which the amount will be withdrawn, and the name of the financial institution from which the amount will be withdrawn;

(b) A statement that the person may object to the withdrawal by filing with the agency, no later than ten days after the date on which the notice is sent, a written request for an administrative hearing to determine whether any amount contained in the account is the property of the person to whom the notice is sent and should not be subject to the withdrawal directive.

(3) The person to whom the notice is sent shall have ten days from the date the notice is sent to object to the withdrawal by filing with the agency a written request for an administrative hearing to determine whether any amount contained in the account is the property of that person and should not be subject to the withdrawal directive.

(a) If the person requests it, the agency shall conduct an administrative hearing no later than ten days after the date the person files the request for the hearing. No later than five days before the date the hearing is to be conducted, the agency shall send the person written notice of the date, time, place, and purpose of the hearing.

At the hearing, the agency shall determine whether any amount contained in the account is the property of the person who filed the objection. The person may present testimony and evidence at the hearing only in regard to the issue of whether how much, if any, of the amount contained in the account is the property of the person and should not be subject to withdrawal directive. If the agency determines that any amount contained in the account is the property of the person, the agency shall determine that amount. The agency shall send notice of its determination to the person.

If the agency determines that the total amount in the account is the property of the person, it shall order the financial institution to release the access restriction on the account and shall take no further enforcement action on the account. If the agency determines that some of the funds in the account are the property of the person, it shall order the financial institution to release the access restriction on the account in that amount and shall take no further enforcement action on those funds. The agency shall issue a withdrawal directive pursuant to division (F) of this section for the remaining funds unless, no later than ten days after the agency makes its determination, the person files a written motion with the court of common pleas of the county served by the child support enforcement agency for a hearing to determine whether any amount contained in the account is the property of the person. If the person files a timely motion with the court, the court shall hold a hearing on the request no later than ten days after the request is filed. No later than five days before the date on which the hearing is to be held, the court shall send the person written notice by ordinary mail of the date, time, place, and purpose of the hearing. The hearing shall be limited to a determination of how much, if any of the amount contained in the account is the property of the person.

If the court determines that all of the funds in the account are the property of the person, it shall order the financial institution to release the access restriction on the account and to take no further enforcement action on the account. If the court determines that some of the funds in the account are the property of the person, it shall determine that amount, order the financial institution to release the access restriction on the account in that amount, and order the agency to take no further enforcement action on those funds. If the court determines that any of the funds in the account are not the property of the person, it shall issue a withdrawal directive pursuant to division (F) of this section.

(b) If a person to whom a notice is sent under division (E)(1) of this section fails to file a timely request for an administrative hearing, the agency shall send a withdrawal directive to the financial institution pursuant to division (F) of this section.

(F)(1) Subject to divisions (D) and (E) of this section, an agency that determines that an obligor has funds in an account in a financial institution, shall issue a withdrawal directive to the financial institution. The directive shall require the financial institution to transmit funds from the account to the division of child support.

(2) The withdrawal directive shall contain the following information:

(a) The name, address, and social security number or taxpayer identification number of the obligor;

(b) A statement that the obligor has been determined to be in default under a support order;

(c) The amount of the arrearage owed by the obligor as determined by the court or child support enforcement agency;

(d) The amount of funds that are to be withdrawn from the account and the type of account from which the funds are to be withdrawn.

(3) On receipt of a withdrawal directive, a financial institution shall withdraw the amount specified from the account described in the notice and pay it to the division of child support.

(G) A financial institution is not subject to criminal or civil liability for imposing an access restriction on an account or complying with a withdrawal directive pursuant to this section or for any other action taken in good faith pursuant to this section.

(1999 H 471, eff. 7-1-00; 1997 H 352, eff. 1-1-98)

Uncodified Law

1996 H 710, § 15: See Uncodified Law under 3113.21.

Historical and Statutory Notes

Ed. Note: Former 3313.214 repealed by 1997 H 352, eff. 1-1-98; 1996 H 710, § 8, eff. 8-8-96; 1996 H 710, § 7, eff. 6-11-96; 1996 H 274, § 7, eff. 8-8-96; 1996 H 274, § 1, eff. 8-8-96; 1995 H 167, eff. 6-11-96; 1993 H 173, eff. 12-31-93; 1991 H 298.

Ed. Note: Prior 3113.214 repealed by 1991 H 298, eff. 7-26-91; 1990 S 3; 1986 H 509.

Ed. Note: The effective date of the amendment of this section by 1996 H 274, § 7, was changed from 11-15-96 to 8-8-96 by 1996 H 710, § 8, eff. 6-11-96.

Ed. Note: The effective date of the amendment of this section by 1995 H 167 was changed from 11-15-96 to 6-11-96 by 1996 H 710, § 7, eff. 6-11-96.

Amendment Note: 1999 H 471 substituted "job and family" for "human" in division (B); and substituted "divisions (D) and (E)" for "division (E)" in division (F)(1).

Cross References

Administrative support orders, withholding or deduction requirements and notices, 3111.23

Library References

Divorce ⚿403.

Parent and Child ⚿3.3(9).

WESTLAW Nos. 134, 285.

C.J.S. Divorce § 828.

C.J.S. Parent and Child §§ 80, 85 to 87, 89.

OJur 3d: 47, Family Law § 1312, 1324; 78, Public Welfare § 63, 120

Carlin, Baldwin's Ohio Practice, *Merrick-Rippner Probate Law* § 19.6, 19.7, 19.8, 19.10, 19.10.1, 108.20, 108.29, 108.30, 108.35, 108.36, 108.37 (1997)

Kurtz & Giannelli, Ohio Juvenile Law (1998 Ed.), Text 27.2, 29.2

Sowald & Morganstern, Baldwin's Ohio Practice, *Domestic Relations Law* § 3.4, 3.5, 3.35, 3.55, 7.19, 9.11, 9.98, 10.13, 11.43, 11.44, 13.44, 14.3, 15.69, 19.1, 20.3, 20.64, 23.17, 23.21, 23.35, 23.39, 23.42, 29.34 (1997)

Notes of Decisions and Opinions

Death of obligor 2
Full faith and credit 3
Temporary restraining order 1

1. Temporary restraining order

A domestic relations court has jurisdiction to consider the request of a man who was granted an out-of-state divorce for a temporary restraining order preventing his Ohio employer from withholding part of his pay in response to the other state's support order. (Annotation from former RC 3113.214.) Kass v. Cleveland Metro. Gen. Hosp. (Cuyahoga 1989) 65 Ohio App.3d 264, 583 N.E.2d 1012.

2. Death of obligor

Decedent's duty to pay child support under Indiana dissolution decree did not terminate at his death, even though, under Ohio law, child support order does not survive death of payor spouse unless child support order so provides, where Indiana law allows for child support order to survive death of payor spouse. (Annotation from former RC 3113.214.) Barnett v. Barnett (Lorain 1993) 85 Ohio App.3d 1, 619 N.E.2d 38.

3. Full faith and credit

Full Faith and Credit for Child Support Orders Act, which requires enforcement according to its terms of child support order made by a court of another state, does not violate due process or equal protection and is not an impermissible burden on freedom of travel; statute purports to rely upon full faith and credit clause of the Constitution, and distinctions which result from operation of statute are reasonable and directly related to furtherance of solving a critical national problem, the failure of a significant number of parents to fulfill their responsibilities to support their children. (Annotation from former RC 3113.214.) Paton v. Brill (Franklin 1995) 104 Ohio App.3d 826, 663 N.E.2d 421.

Full Faith and Credit for Child Support Orders Act precluded Ohio court from obtaining jurisdiction to modify amount of child support ordered pursuant to original Maryland divorce decree and subsequently ordered enforced in Ohio pursuant to Ohio Uniform Reciprocal Enforcement of Support Act (URESA). (Annotation from former RC 3113.214.) Paton v. Brill (Franklin 1995) 104 Ohio App.3d 826, 663 N.E.2d 421.

In enforcing judgment of sister state pursuant to full faith and credit clause, court must determine if laws of state that rendered decision allow judgment to be enforced. (Annotation from former RC 3113.214.) Barnett v. Barnett (Lorain 1993) 85 Ohio App.3d 1, 619 N.E.2d 38.

Orders for child support, payable in installments and subject to modification under laws of rendering state, made in divorce or dissolution in that state, are not entitled to full faith and credit in courts of sister state, since they are not considered to be sufficiently final. (Annotation from former RC 3113.214.) Barnett v. Barnett (Lorain 1993) 85 Ohio App.3d 1, 619 N.E.2d 38.

Child support order was modifiable under Indiana law, and, thus, decedent's children's claim against decedent's estate for lump-sum payment, including all child support due them, was not entitled to full faith and credit in Ohio. (Annotation from fomer RC 3113.214.) Barnett v. Barnett (Lorain 1993) 85 Ohio App.3d 1, 619 N.E.2d 38.

Tuition includes only the primary cost of attending college and does not include room, board, and books less any financial aid or scholarships received by the student, in a child support dispute where the parties have a California dissolution judgment and an Ohio court accepts jurisdiction and extends full faith and credit to the California judgment. (Annotation from former RC 3113.214.) Weber v Weber, No. 16278, 1994 WL 11039 (9th Dist Ct App, Summit, 1-5-94).

3113.215 Calculation of amount of child support obligation

(A) As used in this section:

(1) "Income" means either of the following:

(a) For a parent who is employed to full capacity, the gross income of the parent;

(b) For a parent who is unemployed or underemployed, the sum of the gross income of the parent, and any potential income of the parent.

(2) "Gross income" means, except as excluded in this division, the total of all earned and unearned income from all sources during a calendar year, whether or not the income is taxable, and includes, but is not limited to, income from salaries, wages, overtime pay and bonuses to the extent described in division (B)(5)(d) of this section, commissions, royalties, tips, rents, dividends, severance pay, pensions, interest, trust income, annuities, social security benefits, workers' compensation benefits, unemployment insurance benefits, disability insurance benefits, benefits received by and in the possession of the veteran who is the beneficiary for any service-connected disability under a program or law administered by the United States department of veterans' affairs or veterans' administration, spousal support actually received from a person not a party to the support proceeding for which actual gross income is being determined, and all other sources of income; income of members of any branch of the United States armed services or national guard, including, but not limited to, amounts representing base pay, basic allowance for quarters, basic allowance for subsistence, supplemental subsistence allowance, cost of living adjustment, specialty pay, variable housing allowance, and pay for training or other types of required drills; self-generated income; and potential cash flow from any source.

"Gross income" does not include any of the following:

(a) Benefits received from means-tested public assistance programs, including, but not limited to, Ohio works first; prevention, retention, and contingency; supplemental security income; food stamps; or disability assistance;

(b) Benefits for any service-connected disability under a program or law administered by the United States department of veterans' affairs or veterans' administration that have not been distributed to the veteran who is the beneficiary of the benefits and that are in the possession of the United States department of veterans' affairs or veterans' administration;

(c) Child support received for children who were not born or adopted during the marriage at issue;

(d) Amounts paid for mandatory deductions from wages other than taxes, social security, or retirement in lieu of social security, including, but not limited to, union dues;

(e) Nonrecurring or unsustainable income or cash flow items.

(3) "Self-generated income" means gross receipts received by a parent from self-employment, proprietorship of a business, joint ownership of a partnership or closely held corporation, and rents minus ordinary and necessary expenses incurred by the parent in generating the gross receipts. "Self-generated income" includes expense reimbursements or in-kind payments received by a parent from self-employment, the operation of a business, or rents, including, but not limited to, company cars, free housing, reimbursed meals, and other benefits, if the reimbursements are significant and reduce personal living expenses.

(4)(a) "Ordinary and necessary expenses incurred in generating gross receipts" means actual cash items expended by the parent or the parent's business and includes depreciation expenses of replacement business equipment as shown on the books of a business entity.

(b) Except as specifically included in "ordinary and necessary expenses incurred in generating gross receipts" by division (A)(4)(a) of this section, "ordinary and necessary expenses incurred in generating gross receipts" does not include depreciation expenses and other noncash items that are allowed as deductions on any federal tax return of the parent or the parent's business.

(5) "Potential income" means both of the following for a parent that the court, or a child support enforcement agency pursuant to sections 3111.20, 3111.211, and 3111.22 of the Revised Code, determines is voluntarily unemployed or voluntarily underemployed:

(a) Imputed income that the court or agency determines the parent would have earned if fully employed as determined from the parent's employment potential and probable earnings based on the parent's recent work history, the parent's occupational qualifications, and the prevailing job opportunities and salary levels in the community in which the parent resides;

(b) Imputed income from any nonincome-producing assets of a parent, as determined from the local passbook savings rate or another appropriate rate as determined by the court or agency, not to exceed the rate of interest specified in division (A) of section 1343.03 of the Revised Code, if the income is significant.

(6) "Child support order" means an order for the payment of child support.

(7) "Combined gross income" means the combined gross income of both parents.

(8) "Split parental rights and responsibilities" means a situation in which there is more than one child who is the subject of an allocation of parental rights and responsibilities and each parent is the residential parent and legal custodian of at least one of those children.

(9) "Schedule" means the basic child support schedule set forth in division (D) of this section.

(10) "Worksheet" means the applicable worksheet that is used to calculate a parent's child support obligation and that is set forth in divisions (E) and (F) of this section.

(11) "Nonrecurring or unsustainable income or cash flow item" means any income or cash flow item that the parent receives in any year or for any number of years not to exceed three years and that the parent does not expect to continue to receive on a regular basis. "Nonrecur-

ring or unsustainable income or cash flow item" does not include a lottery prize award that is not paid in a lump sum or any other item of income or cash flow that the parent receives or expects to receive for each year for a period of more than three years or that the parent receives and invests or otherwise utilizes to produce income or cash flow for a period of more than three years.

(12) "Extraordinary medical expenses" means any uninsured medical expenses that are incurred for a child during a calendar year and that exceed one hundred dollars for that child during that calendar year.

(B)(1) In any action in which a child support order is issued or modified under Chapter 3115. or section 2151.23, 2151.231, 2151.232, 2151.33, 2151.36, 2151.49, 3105.18, 3105.21, 3109.05, 3109.19, 3111.13, 3113.04, 3113.07, 3113.216, or 3113.31 of the Revised Code, in any other proceeding in which the court determines the amount of child support that will be ordered to be paid pursuant to a child support order, or when a child support enforcement agency determines the amount of child support that will be paid pursuant to an administrative child support order issued pursuant to sections 3111.20, 3111.211, and 3111.22 of the Revised Code, the court or agency shall calculate the amount of the obligor's child support obligation in accordance with the basic child support schedule in division (D) of this section, the applicable worksheet in division (E) or (F) of this section, and the other provisions of this section, shall specify the support obligation as a monthly amount due, and shall order the support obligation to be paid in periodic increments as it determines to be in the best interest of the children. In performing its duties under this section, the court or agency is not required to accept any calculations in a worksheet prepared by any party to the action or proceeding. In any action or proceeding in which the court determines the amount of child support that will be ordered to be paid pursuant to a child support order or when a child support enforcement agency determines the amount of child support that will be paid pursuant to an administrative child support order issued pursuant to sections 3111.20, 3111.211, and 3111.22 of the Revised Code, the amount of child support that would be payable under a child support order, as calculated pursuant to the basic child support schedule in division (D) of this section and pursuant to the applicable worksheet in division (E) of this section, through line 24, or in division (F) of this section, through line 23, is rebuttably presumed to be the correct amount of child support due, and the court or agency shall order that amount to be paid as child support unless both of the following apply with respect to an order issued by a court:

(a) The court, after considering the factors and criteria set forth in division (B)(3) of this section, determines that the amount calculated pursuant to the basic child support schedule and pursuant to the applicable worksheet in division (E) of this section, through line 24, or in division (F) of this section, through line 23, would be unjust or inappropriate and would not be in the best interest of the child.

(b) The court enters in the journal the amount of child support calculated pursuant to the basic child support schedule and pursuant to the applicable worksheet in division (E) of this section, through line 24, or in division (F) of this section, through line 23, its determination that that amount would be unjust or inappropriate and would not be in the best interest of the child, and findings of fact supporting that determination.

(2) In determining the amount of child support to be paid under any child support order, the court, upon its own recommendation or upon the recommendation of the child support enforcement agency, shall or the child support enforcement agency, pursuant to sections 3111.20, 3111.211, and 3111.22 of the Revised Code, shall do all of the following:

(a) If the combined gross income of both parents is less than six thousand six hundred dollars per year, the court or agency shall determine the amount of the obligor's child support obligation on a case-by-case basis using the schedule as a guideline. The court or agency shall review the obligor's gross income and living expenses to determine the maximum amount of child support that it reasonably can order without denying the obligor the means for self-support at a minimum subsistence level and shall order a specific amount of child support, unless the obligor proves to the court or agency that the obligor is totally unable to pay child support and the court or agency determines that it would be unjust or inappropriate to order the payment of child support and enters its determination and supporting findings of fact in the journal.

(b) If the combined gross income of both parents is greater than one hundred fifty thousand dollars per year, the court or agency shall determine the amount of the obligor's child support obligation on a case-by-case basis and shall consider the needs and the standard of living of the children who are the subject of the child support order and of the parents. When the court or agency determines the amount of the obligor's child support obligation for parents with a combined gross income greater than one hundred fifty thousand dollars, the court or agency shall compute a basic combined child support obligation that is no less than the same percentage of the parents' combined annual income that would have been computed under the basic child support schedule and under the applicable worksheet in division (E) of this section, through line 24, or in division (F) of this section, through line 23, for a combined gross income of one hundred fifty thousand dollars, unless the court or agency determines that it would be unjust or inappropriate and would not be in the best interest of the child, obligor, or obligee to order that amount and enters in the journal the figure, determination, and findings.

(c) The court shall not order an amount of child support that deviates from the amount of child support that would otherwise result from the use of the basic child support schedule and the applicable worksheet in division (E) of this section, through line 24, or in division (F) of this section, through line 23, unless both of the following apply:

(i) The court, after considering the factors and criteria set forth in division (B)(3) of this section, determines that the amount calculated pursuant to the basic child support schedule and pursuant to the applicable worksheet in division (E) of this section, through line 24, or in division (F) of this section, through line 23, would be unjust or inappropriate and would not be in the best interest of the child;

(ii) The court enters in the journal the amount of child support calculated pursuant to the basic child support schedule and pursuant to the applicable worksheet in division (E) of this section, through line 24, or in division (F) of this section, through line 23, its determination that that amount would be unjust or inappropriate and would not be in the best interest of the child, and findings of fact supporting that determination.

(3) The court, in accordance with divisions (B)(1) and (2)(c) of this section, may deviate from the amount of support that otherwise would result from the use of the schedule and the applicable worksheet in division (E) of this section, through line 24, or in division (F) of this section, through line 23, in cases in which the application of the schedule and the applicable worksheet in division (E) of this section, through line 24, or in division (F) of this section, through line 23, would be unjust or inappropriate and would not be in the best interest of the child. In determining whether that amount would be unjust or inappropriate and would not be in the best interest of the child, the court may consider any of the following factors and criteria:

(a) Special and unusual needs of the children;

(b) Extraordinary obligations for minor children or obligations for handicapped children who are not stepchildren and who are not offspring from the marriage or relationship that is the basis of the immediate child support determination;

(c) Other court-ordered payments;

(d) Extended times of visitation or extraordinary costs associated with visitation, provided that this division does not authorize and shall not be construed as authorizing any deviation from the schedule and the applicable worksheet in division (E) of this section, through line 24, or in division (F) of this section, through line 23, or any escrowing, impoundment, or withholding of child support because of a denial of or interference with a right of companionship or visitation granted by court order;

(e) The obligor obtains additional employment after a child support order is issued in order to support a second family;

(f) The financial resources and the earning ability of the child;

(g) Disparity in income between parties or households;

(h) Benefits that either parent receives from remarriage or sharing living expenses with another person;

(i) The amount of federal, state, and local taxes actually paid or estimated to be paid by a parent or both of the parents;

(j) Significant in-kind contributions from a parent, including, but not limited to, direct payment for lessons, sports equipment, schooling, or clothing;

(k) The relative financial resources, other assets and resources, and needs of each parent;

(l) The standard of living and circumstances of each parent and the standard of living the child would have enjoyed had the marriage continued or had the parents been married;

(m) The physical and emotional condition and needs of the child;

(n) The need and capacity of the child for an education and the educational opportunities that would have been available to the child had the circumstances requiring a court order for support not arisen;

(o) The responsibility of each parent for the support of others;

(p) Any other relevant factor.

The court may accept an agreement of the parents that assigns a monetary value to any of the factors and criteria listed in division (B)(3) of this section that arc applicable to their situation.

(4) If an obligor or obligee under a child support order requests the court to modify the amount of support required to be paid pursuant to the child support order, the court shall recalculate the amount of support that would be required to be paid under the support order in accordance with the schedule and pursuant to the applicable worksheet in division (E) of this section, through line 24, or in division (F) of this section, through line 23, and if that amount as recalculated is more than ten per cent greater than or more than ten per cent less than the amount of child support that is required to be paid pursuant to the existing child support order, the deviation from the recalculated amount that would be required to be paid under the schedule and the applicable worksheet in division (E) of this section, through line 24, or in division (F) of this section, through line 23, shall be considered by the court as a change of circumstance that is substantial enough to require a modification of the amount of the child support order. In determining pursuant to this division the recalculated amount of support that would be required to be paid under the support order for purposes of determining whether that recalculated amount is more than ten per cent greater than or more than ten per cent less than the amount of child support that is required to be paid pursuant to the existing child support order, the court shall consider, in addition to all other factors required by law to be considered, the cost of health insurance which the obligor, the obligee, or both the obligor and the obligee have been ordered to obtain for the children specified in the order. Additionally, if an obligor or obligee under a child support order requests the court to modify the amount of support required to be paid pursuant to the child support order and if the court determines that the amount of support does not adequately meet the medical needs of the child, the inadequate coverage shall be considered by the court as a change of circumstance that is substantial enough to require a modification of the amount of the child support order. If the court determines that the amount of child support required to be paid under the child support order should be changed due to a substantial change of circumstances that was not contemplated at the time of the issuance of the original child support order or the last modification of the child support order, the court shall modify the amount of child support required to be paid under the child support order to comply with the schedule and the applicable worksheet in division (E) of this section, through line 24, or in division (F) of this section, through line 23, unless the court determines that the amount calculated pursuant to the basic child support schedule and pursuant to the applicable worksheet in division (E) of

this section, through line 24, or in division (F) of this section, through line 23, would be unjust or inappropriate and would not be in the best interest of the child and enters in the journal the figure, determination, and findings specified in division (B)(2)(c) of this section.

(5) When a court computes the amount of child support required to be paid under a child support order or a child support enforcement agency computes the amount of child support to be paid pursuant to an administrative child support order issued pursuant to section 3111.20, 3111.211, or 3111.22 of the Revised Code, all of the following apply:

(a) The parents shall verify current and past income and personal earnings with suitable documents, including, but not limited to, paystubs, employer statements, receipts and expense vouchers related to self-generated income, tax returns, and all supporting documentation and schedules for the tax returns.

(b) The amount of any pre-existing child support obligation of a parent under a child support order and the amount of any court-ordered spousal support paid to a former spouse shall be deducted from the gross income of that parent to the extent that payment under the child support order or that payment of the court-ordered spousal support is verified by supporting documentation.

(c) If other minor children who were born to the parent and a person other than the other parent who is involved in the immediate child support determination live with the parent, the court or agency shall deduct an amount from that parent's gross income that equals the number of such minor children times the federal income tax exemption for such children less child support received for them for the year, not exceeding the federal income tax exemption.

(d) When the court or agency calculates the gross income of a parent, it shall include the lesser of the following as income from overtime and bonuses:

(i) The yearly average of all overtime and bonuses received during the three years immediately prior to the time when the person's child support obligation is being computed;

(ii) The total overtime and bonuses received during the year immediately prior to the time when the person's child support obligation is being computed.

(e) When the court or agency calculates the gross income of a parent, it shall not include any income earned by the spouse of that parent.

(f) The court shall not order an amount of child support for reasonable and ordinary uninsured medical or dental expenses in addition to the amount of the child support obligation determined in accordance with the schedule. The court shall issue a separate order for extraordinary medical or dental expenses, including, but not limited to, orthodontia, psychological, appropriate private education, and other expenses, and may consider the expenses in adjusting a child support order.

(g) When a court or agency calculates the amount of child support to be paid pursuant to a child support order or an administrative child support order, if the combined gross income of both parents is an amount that is between two amounts set forth in the first column of the schedule, the court or agency may use the basic child support obligation that corresponds to the higher of the two amounts in the first column of the schedule, use the basic child support obligation that corresponds to the lower of the two amounts in the first column of the schedule, or calculate a basic child support obligation that is between those two amounts and corresponds proportionally to the parents' actual combined gross income.

(h) When the court or agency calculates gross income, the court or agency, when appropriate, may average income over a reasonable period of years.

(6)(a) If the court issues a shared parenting order in accordance with section 3109.04 of the Revised Code, the court shall order an amount of child support to be paid under the child support order that is calculated in accordance with the schedule and with the worksheet set forth in division (E) of this section, through line 24, except that, if the application of the schedule and the worksheet, through line 24, would be unjust or inappropriate to the children or either parent and would not be in the best interest of the child because of the extraordinary circumstances of the parents or because of any other factors or criteria set forth in division (B)(3) of this section, the court may deviate from the amount of child support that would be ordered in accordance with the schedule and worksheet, through line 24, shall consider those extraordinary circumstances and other factors or criteria if it deviates from that amount, and shall enter in the journal the amount of child support calculated pursuant to the basic child support schedule and pursuant to the applicable worksheet, through line 24, its determination that that amount would be unjust or inappropriate and would not be in the best interest of the child, and findings of fact supporting that determination.

(b) For the purposes of this division, "extraordinary circumstances of the parents" includes, but is not limited to, all of the following:

(i) The amount of time that the children spend with each parent;

(ii) The ability of each parent to maintain adequate housing for the children;

(iii) Each parent's expenses, including, but not limited to, child care expenses, school tuition, medical expenses, and dental expenses.

(7)(a) In any action in which a child support order is issued or modified under Chapter 3115. or section 2151.23, 2151.231, 2151.232, 2151.33, 2151.36, 2151.49, 3105.18, 3105.21, 3109.05, 3109.19, 3111.13, 3113.04, or 3113.31 of the Revised Code or in any other proceeding in which the court determines the amount of child support that will be ordered to be paid pursuant to a child support order and except as otherwise provided in this division, the court shall issue a minimum support order requiring the obligor to pay a minimum amount of fifty dollars a month for child support under the child support order. The court, in its discretion and in appropriate circumstances, may issue a minimum support order requiring the obligor to pay an amount of child support that is less than fifty dollars a month or not requiring the obligor to pay an amount for support. The appropriate circumstances for which a court may issue a minimum support order requiring an obligor to pay an amount of child support that is less than fifty dollars a month or not requiring the obligor to pay an amount for support include, but are not limited to, the nonresidential parent's medically verified or documented physical or mental disability or institutionalization in a facility for persons with a mental illness. If the court issues a minimum support order pursuant to this division and the obligor under the support order is the recipient of need-based public assistance, any unpaid amounts of support due under the support order shall accrue as arrearages from month to month, the obligor's current obligation to pay the support due under the support order is suspended during any period of time that the obligor is receiving need-based public assistance and is complying with any seek work orders issued pursuant to division (D)(4) of section 3113.21 of the Revised Code, and the court, obligee, and child support enforcement agency shall not enforce the obligation of the obligor to pay the amount of support due under the support order during any period of time that the obligor is receiving need-based public assistance and is complying with any seek work orders issued pursuant to division (D)(4) of section 3113.21 of the Revised Code.

(b) Notwithstanding division (B)(7)(a) of this section, if the amount of support payments that federal law requires or permits to be disregarded in determining eligibility for aid under Chapter 5107. of the Revised Code exceeds fifty dollars, instead of fifty dollars the amount of a minimum support order described in division (B)(7)(a) of this section shall be the amount federal law requires or permits to be disregarded.

(C) Except when the parents have split parental rights and responsibilities, a parent's child support obligation for a child for whom the parent is the residential parent and legal custodian shall be presumed to be spent on that child and shall not become part of a child support order, and a parent's child support obligation for a child for whom the parent is not the residential parent and legal custodian shall become part of a child support order. If the parents have split parental rights and responsibilities, the child support obligations of the parents shall be offset, and the court shall issue a child support order requiring the parent with the larger child support obligation to pay the net amount pursuant to the child support order. If neither parent of a child who is the subject of a child support order is the residential parent and legal custodian of the child and the child resides with a third party who is the legal custodian of the child, the court shall issue a child support order requiring each parent to pay that parent's child support obligation pursuant to the child support order.

Whenever a court issues a child support order, it shall include in the order specific provisions for regular, holiday, vacation, and special visitation in accordance with section 3109.05, 3109.11, or 3109.12 of the Revised Code or in accordance with any other applicable section of the Revised Code. The court shall not authorize or permit the escrowing, impoundment, or withholding of any child support payment because of a denial of or interference with a right of visitation included as a specific provision of the child support order or as a method of enforcing the specific provisions of the child support order dealing with visitation.

(D) The following basic child support schedule shall be used by all courts and child support enforcement agencies when calculating the amount of child support that will be paid pursuant to a child support order or an administrative child support order, unless the combined gross income of the parents is less than sixty-six hundred dollars or more than one hundred fifty thousand dollars:

Basic Child Support Schedule

Combined Gross Income	Number of Children					
	One	Two	Three	Four	Five	Six
6600	600	600	600	600	600	600
7200	600	600	600	600	600	600
7800	600	600	600	600	600	600
8400	600	600	600	600	600	600
9000	849	859	868	878	887	896
9600	1259	1273	1287	1301	1315	1329
10200	1669	1687	1706	1724	1743	1761
10800	2076	2099	2122	2145	2168	2192
11400	2331	2505	2533	2560	2588	2616
12000	2439	2911	2943	2975	3007	3039
12600	2546	3318	3354	3390	3427	3463
13200	2654	3724	3765	3806	3846	3887
13800	2761	4029	4175	4221	4266	4311
14400	2869	4186	4586	4636	4685	4735
15000	2976	4342	4996	5051	5105	5159
15600	3079	4491	5321	5466	5524	5583
16200	3179	4635	5490	5877	5940	6003
16800	3278	4780	5660	6254	6355	6423
17400	3378	4924	5830	6442	6771	6843
18000	3478	5069	5999	6629	7186	7262
18600	3578	5213	6169	6816	7389	7682
19200	3678	5358	6339	7004	7592	8102
19800	3778	5502	6508	7191	7796	8341
20400	3878	5647	6678	7378	7999	8558
21000	3977	5790	6847	7565	8201	8774
21600	4076	5933	7015	7750	8402	8989
22200	4176	6075	7182	7936	8602	9204
22800	4275	6216	7345	8116	8798	9413
23400	4373	6357	7509	8297	8994	9623
24000	4471	6498	7672	8478	9190	9832

24600	4570	6639	7836	8658	9386	10042
25200	4668	6780	8000	8839	9582	10251
25800	4767	6920	8163	9020	9778	10461
26400	4865	7061	8327	9200	9974	10670
27000	4963	7202	8490	9381	10170	10880
27600	5054	7332	8642	9548	10351	11074
28200	5135	7448	8776	9697	10512	11246
28800	5216	7564	8911	9845	10673	11418
29400	5297	7678	9045	9995	10833	11592
30000	5377	7792	9179	10143	10994	11764
30600	5456	7907	9313	10291	11154	11936
31200	5535	8022	9447	10439	11315	12107
31800	5615	8136	9581	10587	11476	12279
32400	5694	8251	9715	10736	11636	12451
33000	5774	8366	9849	10884	11797	12623
33600	5853	8480	9983	11032	11957	12794
34200	5933	8595	10117	11180	12118	12966
34800	6012	8709	10251	11328	12279	13138
35400	6091	8824	10385	11476	12439	13310
36000	6171	8939	10519	11624	12600	13482
36600	6250	9053	10653	11772	12761	13653
37200	6330	9168	10787	11920	12921	13825
37800	6406	9275	10913	12058	13071	13988
38400	6447	9335	10984	12137	13156	14079
39000	6489	9395	11055	12215	13242	14170
39600	6530	9455	11126	12294	13328	14261
40200	6571	9515	11197	12373	13413	14353
40800	6613	9575	11268	12451	13499	14444
41400	6653	9634	11338	12529	13583	14534
42000	6694	9693	11409	12607	13667	14624
42600	6735	9752	11479	12684	13752	14714
43200	6776	9811	11549	12762	13836	14804
43800	6817	9871	11619	12840	13921	14894
44400	6857	9930	11690	12917	14005	14985
45000	6898	9989	11760	12995	14090	15075
45600	6939	10049	11830	13073	14174	15165
46200	6978	10103	11897	13146	14251	15250
46800	7013	10150	11949	13203	14313	15316
47400	7048	10197	12000	13260	14375	15382
48000	7083	10245	12052	13317	14437	15448
48600	7117	10292	12103	13374	14498	15514
49200	7152	10339	12155	13432	14560	15580
49800	7187	10386	12206	13489	14622	15646
50400	7222	10433	12258	13546	14684	15712
51000	7257	10481	12309	13603	14745	15778
51600	7291	10528	12360	13660	14807	15844
52200	7326	10575	12412	13717	14869	15910
52800	7361	10622	12463	13774	14931	15976
53400	7396	10669	12515	13832	14992	16042
54000	7431	10717	12566	13889	15054	16108
54600	7468	10765	12622	13946	15120	16178
55200	7524	10845	12716	14050	15232	16298

55800	7582	10929	12814	14159	15350	16425
56400	7643	11016	12918	14273	15474	16558
57000	7704	11104	13021	14388	15598	16691
57600	7765	11192	13125	14502	15722	16824
58200	7825	11277	13225	14613	15842	16953
58800	7883	11361	13324	14723	15961	17079
59400	7941	11445	13423	14832	16079	17206
60000	8000	11529	13522	14941	16197	17333
60600	8058	11612	13620	15050	16315	17460
61200	8116	11696	13719	15160	16433	17587
61800	8175	11780	13818	15269	16552	17714
62400	8233	11864	13917	15378	16670	17840
63000	8288	11945	14011	15481	16783	17958
63600	8344	12024	14102	15582	16893	18075
64200	8399	12103	14194	15683	17002	18193
64800	8454	12183	14285	15784	17111	18310
65400	8510	12262	14376	15885	17220	18427
66000	8565	12341	14468	15986	17330	18544
66600	8620	12421	14559	16087	17439	18661
67200	8676	12500	14650	16188	17548	18778
67800	8731	12579	14741	16289	17657	18895
68400	8786	12659	14833	16390	17767	19012
69000	8842	12738	14924	16491	17876	19129
69600	8897	12817	15015	16592	17985	19246
70200	8953	12897	15107	16693	18094	19363
70800	9008	12974	15196	16791	18201	19476
71400	9060	13047	15281	16885	18302	19585
72000	9111	13120	15366	16979	18404	19694
72600	9163	13194	15451	17073	18506	19803
73200	9214	13267	15536	17167	18608	19912
73800	9266	13340	15621	17261	18709	20021
74400	9318	13413	15706	17355	18811	20130
75000	9369	13487	15791	17449	18913	20239
75600	9421	13560	15876	17543	19015	20347
76200	9473	13633	15961	17636	19116	20456
76800	9524	13707	16046	17730	19218	20565
77400	9576	13780	16131	17824	19320	20674
78000	9627	13853	16216	17918	19422	20783
78600	9679	13927	16300	18012	19523	20892
79200	9731	14000	16385	18106	19625	21001
79800	9782	14073	16470	18200	19727	21109
80400	9834	14147	16555	18294	19829	21218
81000	9885	14220	16640	18387	19930	21326
81600	9936	14292	16723	18480	20030	21434
82200	9987	14364	16807	18573	20131	21541
82800	10038	14439	16891	18665	20235	21651
83400	10090	14514	16979	18762	20340	21763
84000	10142	14589	17066	18859	20444	21875
84600	10194	14663	17154	18956	20549	21987
85200	10246	14738	17241	19052	20653	22099
85800	10298	14813	17329	19149	20758	22211
86400	10350	14887	17417	19246	20863	22323

87000	10403	14962	17504	19343	20967	22435
87600	10455	15037	17592	19440	21072	22547
88200	10507	15111	17679	19537	21176	22659
88800	10559	15186	17767	19633	21281	22771
89400	10611	15261	17855	19730	21386	22883
90000	10663	15335	17942	19827	21490	22995
90600	10715	15410	18030	19924	21595	23107
91200	10767	15485	18118	20021	21700	23219
91800	10819	15559	18205	20118	21804	23331
92400	10872	15634	18293	20215	21909	23443
93000	10924	15709	18380	20311	22013	23555
93600	10976	15783	18468	20408	22118	23667
94200	11028	15858	18556	20505	22223	23779
94800	11080	15933	18643	20602	22327	23891
95400	11132	16007	18731	20699	22432	24003
96000	11184	16082	18818	20796	22536	24115
96600	11236	16157	18906	20892	22641	24227
97200	11289	16231	18994	20989	22746	24339
97800	11341	16306	19081	21086	22850	24451
98400	11393	16381	19169	21183	22955	24563
99000	11446	16450	19255	21279	23062	24676
99600	11491	16516	19334	21366	23156	24777
100200	11536	16583	19413	21453	23250	24878
100800	11581	16649	19491	21539	23345	24978
101400	11625	16714	19569	21625	23437	25077
102000	11670	16779	19646	21710	23530	25177
102600	11714	16844	19724	21796	23623	25276
103200	11759	16909	19801	21881	23715	25375
103800	11803	16974	19879	21967	23808	25475
104400	11847	17039	19956	22052	23901	25574
105000	11892	17104	20034	22138	23994	25673
105600	11934	17167	20108	22220	24083	25769
106200	11979	17232	20186	22305	24176	25868
106800	12023	17297	20263	22391	24269	25968
107400	12068	17362	20341	22476	24361	26067
108000	12110	17425	20415	22559	24451	26162
108600	12155	17490	20493	22644	24543	26262
109200	12199	17555	20570	22730	24636	26361
109800	12243	17620	20648	22815	24729	26460
110400	12286	17683	20722	22897	24818	26556
111000	12331	17748	20800	22983	24911	26655
111600	12375	17813	20877	23068	25004	26755
112200	12419	17878	20955	23154	25096	26854
112800	12462	17941	21029	23236	25186	26949
113400	12506	18006	21107	23322	25278	27049
114000	12551	18071	21184	23407	25371	27148
114600	12595	18136	21262	23493	25464	27247
115200	12640	18202	21339	23578	25557	27347
115800	12682	18264	21414	23660	25646	27442
116400	12727	18329	21491	23746	25739	27542
117000	12771	18394	21569	23831	25832	27641
117600	12815	18460	21646	23917	25924	27740

118200	12858	18522	21721	23999	26013	27836
118800	12902	18587	21798	24084	26106	27935
119400	12947	18652	21876	24170	26199	28034
120000	12991	18718	21953	24256	26292	28134
120600	13034	18780	22028	24338	26381	28229
121200	13078	18845	22105	24423	26474	28329
121800	13123	18910	22183	24509	26567	28428
122400	13167	18976	22260	24594	26659	28527
123000	13210	19038	22335	24676	26749	28623
123600	13254	19103	22412	24762	26841	28722
124200	13299	19168	22490	24847	26934	28821
124800	13343	19234	22567	24933	27027	28921
125400	13386	19296	22642	25015	27116	29016
126000	13430	19361	22719	25101	27209	29115
126600	13474	19426	22797	25186	27302	29215
127200	13519	19492	22874	25272	27395	29314
127800	13561	19554	22949	25354	27484	29410
128400	13606	19619	23026	25439	27576	29509
129000	13650	19684	23104	25525	27669	29608
129600	13695	19750	23181	25610	27762	29708
130200	13739	19815	23259	25696	27855	29807
130800	13783	19879	23335	25780	27946	29905
131400	13828	19945	23414	25868	28041	30007
132000	13874	20012	23494	25955	28136	30108
132600	13919	20079	23573	26043	28231	30210
133200	13963	20143	23649	26127	28323	30308
133800	14008	20210	23729	26215	28418	30410
134400	14054	20276	23808	26302	28513	30511
135000	14099	20343	23887	26390	28608	30613
135600	14143	20407	23964	26474	28699	30711
136200	14188	20474	24043	26561	28794	30813
136800	14234	20541	24123	26649	28889	30914
137400	14279	20607	24202	26737	28984	31016
138000	14323	20671	24278	26821	29075	31114
138600	14368	20738	24358	26908	29170	31215
139200	14414	20805	24437	26996	29265	31317
139800	14459	20872	24516	27083	29361	31419
140400	14503	20936	24593	27168	29452	31517
141000	14549	21002	24672	27255	29547	31618
141600	14594	21069	24751	27343	29642	31720
142200	14639	21136	24831	27430	29737	31822
142800	14683	21200	24907	27515	29828	31920
143400	14729	21267	24986	27602	29923	32021
144000	14774	21333	25066	27690	30018	32123
144600	14820	21400	25145	27777	30113	32225
145200	14865	21467	25225	27865	30208	32327
145800	14909	21531	25301	27949	30300	32424
146400	14963	21596	25377	28041	30396	32526
147000	15006	21659	25452	28124	30486	32622
147600	15049	21722	25527	28207	30576	32718
148200	15090	21782	25599	28286	30662	32810
148800	15133	21845	25674	28369	30752	32907

149400	15176	21908	25749	28452	30842	33003
150000	15218	21971	25823	28534	30931	33099

(E) When a court or child support enforcement agency calculates the amount of child support that will be required to be paid pursuant to a child support order or an administrative child support order in a proceeding in which one parent is the residential parent and legal custodian of all of the children who are the subject of the child support order or the court issues a shared parenting order, the court or child support enforcement agency shall use a worksheet that is identical in content and form to the following worksheet:

"Worksheet
____________County Domestic Relations Court (or)
____________County Child Support Enforcement Agency
Child Support Computation
Sole Residential Parent or
Shared Parenting Order

Name of parties ____

Case No. ______

Number of minor children ______. The following parent was designated as the residential parent and legal guardian (disregard if shared parenting order):

____________ mother; ____________ father.

Father has ______ pay periods annually; mother has ______ pay periods annually.

	Column I Father	Column II Mother	Column III Combined
1a. Annual gross income from employment or, when determined appropriate by the court or agency, average annual gross income from employment over a reasonable period of years (exclude overtime and bonuses)	$______	$______	
b. Amount of overtime and bonuses	Father	Mother	
Yr. 3 (Three years ago)	$______	$______	
Yr. 2 (Two years ago)	$______	$______	
Yr. 1 (Last calendar year)	$______	$______	
Average:	$______	$______	

(Include in Column I and/or Column II the average of the three years or the year 1 amount years or the year one amount, whichever is less, if there exists a reasonable expectation that the total earnings from overtime and/or bonuses during the current calendar year will meet or exceed the amount that is the greater of the average of the three years or the year 1 amount. If, however, there exists a reasonable expectation that the total earnings from overtime/bonuses during the current calendar year will be less than the lower of the average of the three years or the year 1 amount, include only the amount reasonably expected to be earned this year.) . . . . $_____ $_____

2. Annual income from interest and dividends (whether or not taxable) . . . . . . $_____ $_____
3. Annual income from unemployment compensation . . . . $_____ $_____
4. Annual income from workers' compensation or disability insurance benefits . . . . $_____ $_____
5. Other annual income (identify) . . . . $_____ $_____
6. Total annual gross income (add lines 1-5) . $_____ $_____
7. Annual court-ordered support paid for other children . . . . $_____ $_____
8. Adjustment for minor children born to either parent and another parent, which children are living with this parent (number of children times federal income tax exemption less child support received for the year, not to exceed the federal tax exemption) . . . . $_____ $_____
9. Annual court-ordered spousal support paid to a former spouse . . . . $_____ $_____
10. Amount of local income taxes actually paid or estimated to be paid . . . . $_____ $_____
11. For self-employed individuals, deduct 5.6% of adjusted gross income or the actual marginal difference between the actual rate paid by the self-employed individual and the F.I.C.A. rate . . . . $_____ $_____
12. For self-employed individuals, deduct ordinary and necessary business expenses . . . $_____ $_____
13. Total gross income adjustments (add lines 7-12 . . . . $_____ $_____
14. Adjusted annual gross income (subtract line 13 from line 6) . . . . $_____ $_____

15. Combined annual income that is basis for child support order (add line 14, Col. I and Col. II) . . . . $____
16. Percentage parent's income to total income
  a. Father (divide line 14, Col. I by line 15, Col. III) . . . . ____%
  b. Mother (divide line 14, Col. II by line 15, Col. III) . . . . ____ + ____% = 100%
17. Basic combined child support obligation (Refer to basic child support schedule in division (D) of section 3113.215 of the Revised Code; in the first column of the schedule, locate the sum that is nearest to the combined annual income listed in line 15, Col. III of this worksheet, then refer to the column of the schedule that corresponds to the number of children in this family. If the income of the parents is more than one sum, and less than another sum, in the first column of the schedule, you may calculate the basic combined child support obligation based upon the obligation for those two sums.) . . . . $____
18. Annual child care expenses for the children who are the subject of this order that are work, employment training, or education related, as approved by the court or agency (deduct the tax credit from annual cost, whether or not claimed) . $____ $____
19. Marginal, out-of-pocket costs, necessary to provide for health insurance for the children who are the subject of this order . $____ $____
20. Total child care and medical expenses (add lines 18 and 19, Column I and Column II) . . . . $____ $____
21. Combined annual child support obligation for this family (add lines 17 and 20, Column I and Column II) . . . . $____
22. Annual support obligation/parent
  a. Father (multiply line 21, Col. III, by line 16a) . . . . $____
  b. Mother (multiply line 21, Col. III, by line 16b) . . . . $____
23. Adjustment for actual expenses paid for annual child care expenses and marginal, out-of-pocket costs, necessary to provide for health insurance (enter number from line 18 or 19 if applicable) . . . . $____ $____
24. Actual annual obligation (subtract line 23 from line 22a or 22b) . . . . $____ $____

25. Gross household income per party after exchange of child support (add lines 14 and 24 Column I or II for residential parent or, in the case of shared parenting order, the parent to whom child support will be paid; subtract line 24 Column I or II from line 14 for parent who is not the residential parent or, in the case of shared parenting order, the parent who will pay child support) . . . . $_____ $_____
26. Comments, rebuttal, or adjustments to correct figures in lines 24, Column I and 24, Column II if they would be unjust or inappropriate and would not be in best interest of the child or children (specific facts to support adjustments must be included) . . . . $_____ $_____

____

____

____

(Addendum Sheet may be attached)

27. Final figure (this amount reflects final annual child support obligation) . . . . $_____ father/mother obligor
28. For decree: child support per child per week or per month (divide obligor's annual share, line 27, by 12 or 52 and by number of children) . . . . $_____
29. For deduction order: child support per pay period (calculate support per pay period from figure on line 28) plus appropriate processing charge . . . . $_____ $_____

Calculations have been reviewed.

Signatures

____
Father
I do/do not consent.

Sworn to before me and subscribed in my presence, this _____ day of __________, ___.

____
Notary Public

____
Mother
I do/do not consent.

Sworn to before me and subscribed in my presence, this _____ day of __________, ___.

____
Notary Public

____
Attorney for Father

____
Attorney for Mother"

(F) When a court or child support enforcement agency calculates the amount of child support that will be required to be paid pursuant to a child support order in a proceeding in which both parents have split parental rights and responsibilities with respect to the children who are the subject of the child support order, the court or child support enforcement agency shall use a worksheet that is identical in content and form to the following worksheet:

"Worksheet
__________County Domestic Relations Court (or)
__________ County Child Support Enforcement Agency
Child Support Computation
Split Parental Rights and Responsibilities

Name of parties __________

Case No. __________

Number of minor children ______. The following parent was designated residential parent and legal custodian:

__________ mother; __________ father.

Father has ______ pay periods annually; mother has ______ pay periods annually.

	Column I Father	Column II Mother	Column III Combined
1a. Annual gross income from employment or, when determined to be appropriate by the court or agency, average annual gross income from employment over a reasonable period of years (exclude overtime and bonuses)	$_____	$_____	
b. Amount of overtime and bonuses	Father	Mother	
Yr. 3 (Three years ago)	$_____	$_____	
Yr. 2 (Two years ago)	$_____	$_____	
Yr. 1 (Last calendar year)	$_____	$_____	
Average:	$_____	$_____	
(Include in Column I and/or Column II the average of the three years or the year 1 amount, whichever is less, if there exists a reasonable expectation that the total earnings from overtime and/or bonuses during the current calendar year will meet or exceed the amount that is the lower of the average of the three years or the year 1 amount. If, however, there exists a reasonable expectation that the total earnings from overtime/bonuses during the current calendar year will be less than the lower of the average of the three years or the year 1 amount, include only the amount reasonably expected to be earned this year.)	$_____	$_____	
2. Annual income from interest and dividends (whether or not taxable)	$_____	$_____	

	Col. I	Col. II	Col. III
3. Annual income from unemployment compensation	$____	$____	
4. Annual income from workers' compensation or disability insurance benefits	$____	$____	
5. Other annual income (identify)	$____	$____	
6. Total annual gross income (add lines 1-5)	$____	$____	
7. Annual court-ordered support paid for other children	$____	$____	
8. Adjustment for minor children born to either parent and another parent, which children are living with this parent (number of children times federal income tax exemption less child support received for the year, not to exceed the federal tax exemption)	$____	$____	
9. Annual court-ordered spousal support paid to a former spouse	$____	$____	
10. Amount of local income taxes actually paid or estimated to be paid	$____	$____	
11. For self-employed individuals, deduct 5.6% of adjusted gross income or the actual marginal difference between the actual rate paid by the self-employed individual and the F.I.C.A. rate	$____	$____	
12. For self-employed individuals, deduct ordinary and necessary business expenses	$____	$____	
13. Total gross income adjustments (add lines 7-12)	$____	$____	
14. Adjusted annual gross income (subtract line 13 from line 6)	$____	$____	
15. Combined annual income that is basis for child support order (add line 14, Col. I and Col. II)			$____
16. Percentage parent's income to total income			
a. Father (divide line 14, Col. I by line 15, Col. III)	____%		
b. Mother (divide line 14, Col. II by line 15, Col. III)		+ ____%	= 100%
17. Basic combined child support obligation/household			

a. For children for whom the father is the residential parent and legal custodian (Refer to basic child support schedule in division (D) of section 3113.215 of the Revised Code; in the first column of the schedule, locate the sum that is nearest to the combined annual income listed in line 15, Col. III of this worksheet, then refer to the column of the schedule that corresponds to the number of children for whom the father is the residential parent and legal custodian. If the income of the parents is more than one sum, and less than another sum, in the first column of the schedule, you may calculate the basic combined child support obligation based upon the obligation for those two sums.) . $_____

b. For children for whom the mother is the residential parent and the legal custodian. (Refer to basic child support schedule in division (D) of section 3113.215 of the Revised Code; in the first column of the schedule, locate the sum that is nearest to the combined annual income listed in line 15, Col. III of this worksheet, then refer to the column of the schedule that corresponds to the number of children for whom the mother is the residential parent and the legal custodian. If the income of the parents is more than one sum, and less than another sum, in the first column of the schedule, you may calculate the basic combined child support obligation based upon the obligation for those two sums.) . $_____

18. Annual child care expenses for the children who are the subject of this order that are work, employment training, or education related, as approved by the court or agency (deduct the tax credit from annual cost, whether or not claimed)

a. Expenses paid by the father . . . . $_____

b. Expenses paid by the mother . . . . $_____

19. Marginal, out-of-pocket costs, necessary to provide for health insurance for the children who are the subject of this order

a. Costs paid by the father . . . . $_____

b. Costs paid by the mother . . . . $_____

20. Total annual child care and medical expenses

a. Of father (add lines 18a and 19a) . . . . $_____

b. Of mother (add lines 18b and 19b) . . . . . . $_____

21. Total annual child support obligation

a. Of father for child(ren) for whom the mother is the residential parent and legal custodian (add lines 20a and 17b and multiply by line 16a) . . . . $_____

b. Of mother for child(ren) for whom the father is the residential parent and legal custodian (add lines 20b and 17a and multiply by line 16b) . . . . $_____

22. Adjustment for actual expenses paid for annual child care expenses, and marginal, out-of-pocket costs, necessary to provide for health insurance

a. For father (enter number from line 20a) . . . $_____

b. For mother (enter number from line 20b) . . . . $_____

23. Actual annual obligation (subtract line 22a from line 21a and insert in Column I; subtract line 22b from line 21b and insert in Column II) . . . . $_____ $_____

24. Net annual support obligation (greater amount on line 23 Column I or line 23 Column II minus lesser amount on line 23 Column I or line 23 Column II) . . . . $_____ $_____

25. Gross household income per party after exchange of child support . . . . $_____ $_____
(add line 14 and line 24 for the parent receiving a child support payment; subtract line 24 from line 14 for the parent making a child support payment)

26. Comments, rebuttal, or adjustments to correct figures in lines 24, Column I and 24, Column II if they would be unjust or inappropriate and would not be in best interest of the children (specific facts to support adjustments must be included). . . . . $_____ $_____

____

____

____

(Addendum sheet may be attached)

27. Final figure (this amount reflects final annual child support obligation) . . . . $_____ father/mother obligor

28. For decree: child support per child per week or per month (divide obligor's annual share, line 27, by 12 or 52 and by the number of children) . . . . $_____

29. For deduction order: child support per day (calculate support per pay period from figure on line 28) and add appropriate processing charge. $_____
    Calculations have been reviewed.

Signatures ____________________
Father
I do/do not consent.

Sworn to before me and subscribed in my presence, this _____ day of _________, ___.

____
Notary Public

____
Mother
I do/do not consent.

Sworn to before me and subscribed in my presence, this _____ day of _________, ___.

____
Notary Public

____________________ ____________________
Attorney for Father Attorney for Mother"

(G) At least once every four years, the department of job and family services shall review the basic child support schedule set forth in division (D) of this section to determine whether support orders issued in accordance with the schedule and the applicable worksheet in division (E) of this section, through line 24, or in division (F) of this section, through line 23, adequately provide for the needs of the children who are subject to the support orders, prepare a report of its review, and submit a copy of the report to both houses of the general assembly. For each review, the department shall establish a child support guideline advisory council to assist the department in the completion of its reviews and reports. Each council shall be composed of obligors, obligees, judges of courts of common pleas who have jurisdiction over domestic relations cases, attorneys whose practice includes a significant number of domestic relations cases, representatives of child support enforcement agencies, other persons interested in the welfare of children, three members of the senate appointed by the president of the senate, no more than two of whom are members of the same party, and three members of the house of representatives appointed by the speaker of the house, no more than two of whom are members of the same party. The department shall consider input from the council prior to the completion of any report under this section. The advisory council shall cease to exist at the time that it submits its report to the general assembly. Any expenses incurred by an advisory council shall be paid by the department.

On or before March 1, 1993, the department shall submit its initial report under this division to both houses of the general assembly. On or before the first day of March of every fourth year after 1993, the department shall submit a report under this division to both houses of the general assembly.

(2000 H 495, § 5, eff. 7-1-00; 2000 H 495, § 1, eff. 5-9-00; 1999 H 471, eff. 7-1-00; 1997 H 352, eff. 1-1-98; 1997 H 408, eff. 10-1-97; 1996 H 670, eff. 12-2-96; 1996 H 710, § 8, eff. 8-8-96; 1996 H 710, § 7, eff. 6-11-96; 1996 H 274, § 7, eff. 8-8-96; 1996 H 274, § 1, eff. 8-8-96; 1995 H 167, eff. 6-11-96; 1995 H 249, eff. 7-17-95; 1994 S 355, eff. 12-9-94; 1994 H 415, eff. 11-9-94; 1993 H 173, eff. 10-12-93; 1993 S 115; 1990 S 3, H 514, H 591)

Uncodified Law

1996 H 670, § 27: See Uncodified Law under 101.84 for provisions regarding expiration of agencies.

1996 H 710, § 15: See Uncodified Law under 3113.21.

Historical and Statutory Notes

Ed. Note: The effective date of the amendment of this section by 1996 H 274, § 7, was changed from 11-15-96 to 8-8-96 by 1996 H 710, § 8, eff. 6-11-96.

Ed. Note: The effective date of the amendment of this section by 1995 H 167 was changed from 11-15-96 to 6-11-96 by 1996 H 710, § 7, eff. 6-11-96.

Amendment Note: 2000 H 495 § 1 and § 5 deleted references to nineteen hundred dates.

Amendment Note: 1997 H 352 substituted "3111.211" for "3111.21" in division (A)(5), twice in the first paragraph in division (B)(1); and in the first paragraphs in divisions (B)(2) and (B)(5); inserted "2151.231, 2151.232," in the first paragraph in division (B)(1) and in division (B)(7)(a); substituted "(D)(4)" for "(D)(7)" twice in division (B)(7)(a); substituted "processing charge" for "poundage" in line 29 in division (E) and in line 29 in division (F); and made other nonsubstantive changes.

Amendment Note: 1999 H 471 substituted "job and family" for "human" in the first paragraph in division (G).

Amendment Note: 1997 H 408 rewrote division (A)(2) after the first paragraph; redesignated former division (D)(1) as new division (D) and deleted "Except as provided in divisions (D)(2) and (3) of this section," from the beginning thereof; deleted former divisions (D)(2) and (D)(3); reinstated Step 25 in division (E); and made corrective changes and other nonsubstantive changes. Prior to deletion, former divisions (D)(2) and (D)(3) read:

"(2) Until July 1, 1994, or a later date specified pursuant to division (D)(3) of this section, the following basic child support schedule shall be used by all courts and child support enforcement agencies to calculate the amount of child support that will be paid pursuant to a child support order or an administrative child support order when combined gross income is at least six thousand dollars but not more than twenty-one thousand six hundred dollars:

Basic Child Support Schedule

Gross	Number of Children					
Income	One	Two	Three	Four	Five	Six
6000	240	372	468	528	576	612
7200	1068	1308	1428	1608	1656	1692
8400	1884	2244	2388	2688	2736	2784
9600	2052	3180	3348	3768	3816	3876
10800	2208	3432	4308	4848	4896	4968
12000	2439	3684	4620	5208	5676	6060
13200	2654	3924	4920	5556	6048	6456
14400	2869	4186	5208	5880	6408	6840
15600	3079	4491	5508	6204	6756	7224
16800	3278	4780	5796	6528	7116	7608
18000	3478	5069	6072	6840	7464	7980
19200	3678	5358	6339	7140	7788	8352
20400	3878	5647	6678	7440	8112	8688
21600	4078	5935	7018	7755	8448	9036

"(3) The office of budget and management and the department of human services shall conduct a study of the impact on the general revenue fund of implementing the basic child support schedule in division (D)(1) of this section for combined gross incomes of at least six thousand dollars but not more than twenty-one thousand six hundred dollars. If, prior to July 1, 1994, the department and the office conclude from the study that implementing the basic child support schedule in division (D)(1) of this section for those incomes will have a negative impact on the general revenue fund, the department shall inform the controlling board of the impact and recommend to the board continued use of the schedule in division (D)(2) until a date which the department shall specify. On receipt of the department's recommendation, the board shall specify a date for discontinuance of the schedule in division (D)(2), which may be the date recommended by the department or any other date considered appropriate by the board. On the date specified by the board, the schedule in division (D)(2) shall cease to be used and child support shall be calculated pursuant to the schedule in division (D)(1) of this section."

Amendment Note: 1996 H 670 substituted "council" for "commission" five times in the first paragraph in division (G).

Amendment Note: 1996 H 274, § 7, eff. 8-8-96, harmonized the versions of this section as amended by 1995 H 167, eff. 6-11-96, and 1996 H 274, § 1, eff. 8-8-96; and deleted division (H), which prior thereto read:

"(H) This is an interim section effective until November 15, 1996."

Amendment Note: 1996 H 274, § 1, eff. 8-8-96, added references to section 2151.33 throughout; added division (H); and made changes to reflect gender neutral language.

Amendment Note: 1995 H 167 added a reference to section 3111.20 in division (A)(5); added references to section 3109.19 and 3111.20 in the first paragraph of division (B)(1), added a reference to section 3111.20 in division (B)(2) and (5); added a reference to section 3109.19 in division (B)(7)(a); and made other changes to reflect gender neutral language.

Amendment Note: 1995 H 249 removed a reference to general assistance from the second paragraph in division (A)(2); and substituted "(add lines 18b and 19b)" for "18b 19a 19b)" in Line 20.b. in the Worksheet reproduced in division (F).

Amendment Note: 1994 S 355 rewrote this section; see *Baldwin's Ohio Legislative Service*, 1994 Laws of Ohio, S 355, p 5-1324.

Amendment Note: 1994 H 415 inserted "benefits received by and in the possession of the veteran who is the beneficiary for any service-connected disability under a program or law administered by the United States department of veterans' affairs or veterans' administration," and "that have not been distributed to the veteran who is the beneficiary of the benefits and that are in the possession of the United States department of veteran's affairs or veterans' administration" in division (A)(2).

Amendment Note: 1993 H 173 rewrote this section; see *Baldwin's Ohio Legislative Service*, 1993 Laws of Ohio, H 173, p 5-1039.

Amendment Note: 1993 S 115 rewrote this section; see *Baldwin's Ohio Legislative Service*, 1993 Laws of Ohio, S 115, p 5-313.

Cross References

Administrative child support orders, 3111.22

Child support enforcement agency, adoption of rules, 2301.35

Court making or modifying child support order, 2151.23, 3105.21, 3115.22

Custody of children, compromise agreement, factors considered, 3111.19

Custody of children, shared parenting, factors considered, 3109.04

Factors determining amount of support, applicability, 3109.05, 3111.13

Parental duty of support, 3111.20

Review of administrative child support orders, 3111.27

Ohio Administrative Code References

Review and adjustment of IV-D child support orders, OAC 5101:1-30-403

State guidelines for child support awards, OAC 5101:1-30-40

Library References

Divorce ⚿308 to 309.6.
Infants ⚿228.
Parent and Child ⚿3.3(7), 3.3(8).
WESTLAW Nos. 134, 211, 285.
C.J.S. Divorce §§ 669 to 671, 673 to 683, 700 to 705, 719 to 736.
C.J.S. Infants §§ 42, 53, 54, 57, 69 to 85.
C.J.S. Parent and Child §§ 80 to 84, 89.

Am Jur 2d: 24, Divorce and Separation § 1035 et seq.

Divorce and separation: attributing undisclosed income to parent or spouse for purposes of making child or spousal support award. 70 ALR4th 173

Spouse's right to set off debt owed by other spouse against accrued spousal or child support payments. 11 ALR5th 259

Consideration of obligated spouse's earnings from overtime or "second job" held in addition to regular full-time employment in fixing alimony or child support awards. 17 ALR5th 143

Loss of income due to incarceration as affecting child support obligation. 27 ALR5th 540

Treatment of depreciation expenses claimed for tax or accounting purposes in determining ability to pay child or spousal support. 28 ALR5th 46.

Baldwin's Ohio Legislative Service, 1990 Laws of Ohio, H 591—LSC Analysis, p 5-576

Carlin, Baldwin's Ohio Practice, *Merrick-Rippner Probate Law* § 18.2, 19.6, 19.7, 19.8, 19.10, 19.10.1, 107.160, 108.20, 108.29, 108.30, 108.35, 108.36 (1997)

Klein & Darling, Baldwin's Ohio Practice, *Civil Practice* § 86 (1997)

Kurtz & Giannelli, Ohio Juvenile Law (1998 Ed.), Text 27.2, 29.2

Sowald & Morganstern, Baldwin's Ohio Practice, *Domestic Relations Law* § 3.4, 3.5, 3.35, 3.55, 5.12, 7.19, 9.9, 9.10, 9.11, 9.13, 9.35, 9.98, 9.132, 9.161 to 9.163, 10.13, 11.43, 11.44, 11.46, 13.44, 14.3, 15.14, 15.36, 15.38, 15.46, 15.49, 15.58, 15.69, 18.22, 19.1, 19.5 to 19.11, 19.14, 19.15, 19.18, 19.20, 19.30, 20.3, 20.64, 21.23, 22.5, 22.11, 23.21, 23.35, 23.39, 23.42, 25.41, 29.8, 29.11, 29.12, 29.34, 31.14 (1997)

Law Review and Journal Commentaries

Awarding Child Support Against the Impoverished Parent: Straying from Statutory Guidelines and Using SSI in Setting the Amount, Note. 83 Ky L J 653 (1994-95).

Bankruptcy Reform Act of 1994—What the Bankruptcy Code Giveth, Domestic Relations Courts (and Congress) Taketh Away, C.R. "Chip" Bowles. 8 Domestic Rel J Ohio 17 (March/April 1996).

Children At Risk In The Politics Of Child Custody Suits: Acknowledging Their Needs For Nurture, Arlene Browand Huber. 32 J Fam L 33 (Winter 1994).

College Tuition as "Court-Ordered Child Support," Patrice R.T. Yarham. 10 Domestic Rel J Ohio 107 (November/December 1998).

Father's Day: Ohio's Child Support Guidelines And The Responsible Father, Comment. 21 Cap U L Rev 1145 (Fall 1992).

General Assembly Assumes Responsibility for Child Support Guidelines, Mary C. LoPresti. 2 Domestic Rel J Ohio 35 (May/June 1990).

Judges' Column, Hon. Francine Bruening. (Ed. note: Judge Bruening discusses the Child Support Reorganization Act of House Bill 352, effective 1-1-98.) 21 Lake Legal Views 1 (June 1998).

Judicial Activism in Domestic Relations Cases, Hon. V. Michael Brigner. (Ed. note: Judge Brigner lists the powers of a judge hearing custody, support, and visitation matters.) 45 Dayton B Briefs 22 (January 1996).

Looking to Unwed Dads to Fill the Public Purse: A Disturbing Wave in Welfare Reform, Roger J.R. Levesque. 32 J Fam L 1 (Winter 1994).

Malishenko—Child Support Calculation in Shared Parenting Differs from Split Custody, James R. Kirkland. 9 Domestic Rel J Ohio 57 (July/August 1997).

The New Child Support Act—1993 S.B. 115, Richard L. Innis. 5 Domestic Rel J Ohio 73 (September/October 1993).

Ohio's Mandatory Child Support Guidelines: Child Support or Spousal Maintenance?, Note. 42 Case W Res L Rev 297 (1992).

Practice Pointer—Spousal Support from Party to the Proceeding Not Included as Gross Income for Child Support, Lynn B. Schwartz. 6 Domestic Rel J Ohio 52 (July/August 1994).

Practice Pointers, Pamela J. MacAdams. 11 Domestic Rel J Ohio 87 (November/December 1999).

Pro-Rating Child Support for Shared Parenting, James R. Kirkland. 6 Domestic Rel J Ohio 82 (November/December 1994).

R.C. 3113.215—Support Section or Alimony Section?, Joel S. Moskowitz. 2 Domestic Rel J Ohio 89 (November/December 1990).

Support Issues in Paternity Cases, Pamela J. MacAdams. 7 Domestic Rel J Ohio 81 (November/December 1995).

Notes of Decisions and Opinions

---

1. —Underemployment, income

Trial court did not abuse discretion in finding that parent was voluntarily underemployed, for purposes of determining child support obligation; trial court determined parent had accounting degree and ability to earn more as accountant than in chosen field as weaver, and that parent obtained accounting degree to support herself in accounting profession but was enabled by remarriage to pursue full-time career as weaver. Rock v. Cabral (Ohio 1993) 67 Ohio St.3d 108, 616 N.E.2d 218.

Parent need not to have been found to have purposely reduced earnings in effort to reduce child support obligation in order to be found to be voluntarily underemployed within meaning of child support statute; parent's subjective motivations for being voluntarily unemployed or underemployed play no part in determination of whether potential income is to be imputed to that parent in calculation of child support. Rock v. Cabral (Ohio 1993) 67 Ohio St.3d 108, 616 N.E.2d 218.

Question of whether parent is voluntarily unemployed or voluntarily underemployed, for purposes of calculation of child support, is question of fact for trial court; absent abuse of discretion, that factual determination will not be disturbed on appeal. Rock v. Cabral (Ohio 1993) 67 Ohio St.3d 108, 616 N.E.2d 218.

In calculating and awarding child support, a trial court must consider the potential income as well as the gross income of a parent the court determines to be voluntarily unemployed or underemployed. Clark v. Smith (Ohio App. 3 Dist. 1998) 130 Ohio App.3d 648, 720 N.E.2d 973.

Evidence supported trial court's determination that former husband was voluntarily underemployed, despite his testimony that his health concerns prompted him to take lower-paying job. Boggs v. Boggs (Ohio App. 5 Dist. 1997) 118 Ohio App.3d 293, 692 N.E.2d 674.

Voluntary termination of employment or voluntary underemployment does not equate to decrease in ability to support one's children, for purpose of determining whether modification of child support obligation is warranted. Sancho v. Sancho (Union 1996) 114 Ohio App.3d 636, 683 N.E.2d 849.

Evidence supported trial court's determination, in computing child support obligation, that father, who had quit his job as engineer in foreign country and had made no effort to obtain new employment but intended to live off his existing financial resources, was underemployed. Marsh v. Marsh (Allen 1995) 105 Ohio App.3d 747, 664 N.E.2d 1353.

Trial court's finding that child support obligor was not voluntarily underemployed would not be disturbed; despite referee's reference to obligor's income being "imputed," there was no evidence of such. Houts v. Houts (Mercer 1995) 99 Ohio App.3d 701, 651 N.E.2d 1031, appeal not allowed 72 Ohio St.3d 1529, 649 N.E.2d 838.

Trial court properly applied child support statute in determining whether to modify child support, even though motion was filed and reinstated prior to statute's effective date, where hearings on motion and filing of trial court's decision and judgment entry took place after its effective date. Parzynski v. Parzynski (Erie 1992) 85 Ohio App.3d 423, 620 N.E.2d 93, dismissed, jurisdictional motion overruled 67 Ohio St.3d 1450, 619 N.E.2d 419, rehearing denied 67 Ohio St.3d 1513, 622 N.E.2d 660.

For purposes of a child support reduction modification hearing, a former husband's status should have been categorized as "underemployed" and not as "unemployed" where he held a job at the time of the hearing. Ferguson v. Ferguson (Franklin 1992) 76 Ohio App.3d 818, 603 N.E.2d 391.

Husband who claims that his income is limited by his disability has a burden to provide evidence and documentation concerning the extent of his disability once the wife establishes a prima facie case of voluntary unemployment; in such case a husband is found to be voluntarily underemployed by his own testimony that he is able to work part-time as an investigator for a consulting firm, drive, play in a bag-pipe band, cut grass and perform other physical activities. Kelly-Doley v Doley, No. 96-L-217, 1999 WL 262165 (11th Dist Ct App, Lake, 3-12-99).

An obligor has not voluntarily quit his job by choosing to attend college when he is compelled to make that choice because of a disability and the opportunity presented by the Veterans Administration to learn new skills; on the other hand the obligor is voluntarily unemployed in the sense that he could be working a part-time job while attending school. Sharp v Brennan, No. E-97-133, 1998 WL 230567 (6th Dist Ct App, Erie, 5-1-98).

Parent who is physically and mentally able to gain employment is not voluntarily unemployed or underemployed when it is extremely difficult and not in the best interest of the children for the parent to work and pay babysitters when receiving a total of only $25 per month in child support. Spiker v Ullman, No. 768, 1997 WL 598088 (7th Dist Ct App, Monroe, 9-19-97).

A trial court could reasonably consider a mother's diminished income from her decision to abandon her twenty-year gymnastics career after her gymnastics business went bankrupt and she pursued a career in medical assistance in determining whether there has been a substantial change of circumstances warranting modification of the father's child support obligation, as the mother's new career will maintain the child's standard of living and provide a stable income and the mother is not thereby "voluntarily underemployed". Holt v Troha, No. 96-CA-19, 1996 WL 430866 (2d Dist Ct App, Greene, 8-2-96).

An order reducing child support to $20 per week is reversed and the order establishing support at $36 per week is reinstated where the obligor decides to quit his $30,000 employment and to start his own company without regard to its impact on his ability to provide for his two minor children; the trial court could reasonably find that he had failed to give adequate weight to his duty to support his children and on that basis find that he had failed to demonstrate a substantial change of circumstances necessary for modification of child support. Contreras v Contreras, No. 95-CA-61, 1996 WL 239825 (2d Dist Ct App, Miami, 5-10-96).

Imputation of a $36,000 annual salary to a husband who is capable of working as an attorney is an abuse of discretion absent evidence that he is voluntarily underemployed and failed to look for work within his profession; whether defendant should be required to obtain work outside his area of expertise is a factual determination depending on whether it appears he will be unable to find work as an attorney, or whether temporary work outside his profession will interfere with looking for a job. English v Rubino, No. 68901, 1996 WL 157342 (8th Dist Ct App, Cuyahoga, 4-4-96).

According to RC 3113.215, when a court or agency calculates a parent's gross income, it may not take into consideration any income earned by the spouse of such parent; a trial court errs in requiring a defendant obligor's present wife to withdraw monies from her investment account, which was originally funded by an inheritance she received prior to marrying defendant, to assist him in paying the extraordinary medical expenses for the minor children of his previous marriage. Seaver v Ameduri, No. 94-CA-179, 1996 WL 133006 (7th Dist Ct App, Mahoning, 3-20-96).

An obligor is guilty of contempt for failure to comply with child support and medical support orders where he voluntarily terminates his employment and ability to pay his child support prior to, and after, the termination; in addition, the court is not required to modify the ongoing child support order absent a modification request. Jones v Mosley, No. 95APF04-442, 1995 WL 739688 (10th Dist Ct App, Franklin, 12-14-95).

A parent's subjective motivations for being voluntarily underemployed play no part in determining whether potential income is to be imputed to that parent in calculating his support obligation, and an obligor who leaves a medical practice in which he was earning $542,205 to complete his internal medicine residency and earn $32,250 is voluntarily underemployed; the court does not err when it does not deviate downward from the guidelines to avoid giving the child a lavish award because his father is wealthy. Brakora v Haudenschield, No. 6-95-9, 1995 WL 695089 (3d Dist Ct App, Hardin, 11-22-95).

A voluntary reduction in earning ability will be disregarded for purposes of computing a child support obligation and where the wife is the obligor, impairment to her earning ability represented by her having borne two children by a subsequent marriage, is voluntarily undertaken and she is not entitled to deduct from her potential income the child care expenses that would be necessitated by her entering the workforce. Addington v Addington, Nos. 1373+, 1995 WL 599886 (2d Dist Ct App, Darke, 10-11-95).

A parent is "voluntarily underemployed" for the purposes of determining child support payments under RC 3113.215(A) when that parent quits a higher paying job citing underpayment, stress, and time away from his family while he takes a huge pay cut, does not seek medical treatment for stress and voluntarily relinquishes custody of the children. Stark v Stark, No. 93-A-1819 (11th Dist Ct App, Ashtabula, 6-30-94).

Trial court did not err in imputing income of father based on job as gas company employee where father voluntarily left that job and obtained employment elsewhere for less money but was later laid off and could not return to the gas company; RC 3113.215 allows work history to be considered and father was voluntarily underemployed. Bohannon v Bohannon, No. 63982, 1993 WL 437600 (8th Dist Ct App, Cuyahoga, 10-28-93).

Under RC 3113.215(A)(5), voluntary underemployment by husband cannot be shown where a potential position located in another community was not offered to him but he did apply for comparable employment in the area. Higgins v Higgins, No. 92-CA-00132, 1993 WL 221265 (5th Dist Ct App, Licking, 6-7-93).

An employee's refusal to accept overtime work because of a concern that doing so will increase his income and result in higher alimony and child support payments is just cause for an employer to fire the employee under RC 4141.29. In re Cobb, UCBR B95-01393-0000 (8-10-95).

2. —Imputed, income

Trial court did not abuse discretion in determining that $14,000 annually of potential income should be attributed to parent with accounting degree who was voluntarily underemployed as weaver, even though parent argued such sum was twice what she had ever earned on annual basis in any profession; salary range for beginning accountants in parent's community was $15,000 to $22,000 per year. Rock v. Cabral (Ohio 1993) 67 Ohio St.3d 108, 616 N.E.2d 218.

Question of amount of potential income to be imputed to child support obligor who is voluntarily unemployed or voluntarily underemployed, for purposes of calculation of child support, is question of fact for trial court; absent abuse of discretion, that factual determination will not be disturbed on appeal. Rock v. Cabral (Ohio 1993) 67 Ohio St.3d 108, 616 N.E.2d 218.

Better course for courts to follow is to include potential income of child support obligor on child support computation worksheet as "other annual income," although it is appropriate for court to include potential income as "annual gross income from employment" where court sets forth reasons in its journal entry for imputing income to child support obligor and specifically identifies amount of potential income imputed. Rock v. Cabral (Ohio 1993) 67 Ohio St.3d 108, 616 N.E.2d 218.

Imputing income to mother, for purposes of calculating her child support obligation, based upon her apparently voluntary decision to not work and to stay at home with an expected baby was not an abuse of discretion. Clark v. Smith (Ohio App. 3 Dist. 1998) 130 Ohio App.3d 648, 720 N.E.2d 973.

Before a trial court may impute income to a parent in calculating and awarding child support, the trial court must make a finding that the parent is voluntarily unemployed or underemployed. Clark v. Smith (Ohio App. 3 Dist. 1998) 130 Ohio App.3d 648, 720 N.E.2d 973.

The imputed income from husband's unexercised executive employee stock options was "potential cash flow from any source" that was includable in his "gross income," within meaning of statutory procedures for awarding and calculating child support, where the options were given every year, husband could expect to receive them so long as he continued to work in his position with employer, they could be exercised only by the husband in his complete discretion, and they were an integral part of husband's compensation. Murray v. Murray (Ohio App. 12 Dist. 1999) 128 Ohio App.3d 662, 716 N.E.2d 288.

Imputed income from husband's unexercised executive employee stock options was not a "nonrecurring or unsustainable source of income or cash flow item," within meaning of child support statute's exclusion from gross income, where the options were an integral part of husband's compensation and he could expect to receive annual stock options so long as he continued to work in his position with employer. Murray v. Murray (Ohio App. 12 Dist. 1999) 128 Ohio App.3d 662, 716 N.E.2d 288.

In cases where the obligor is a majority shareholder in a corporation, the trial court may impute to the obligor the retained earnings of the corporation when determining child support. Murray v. Murray (Ohio App. 12 Dist. 1999) 128 Ohio App.3d 662, 716 N.E.2d 288.

Trial court abused its discretion by imputing to former husband, who was unemployed, $80,000 in annual income, based on his last prior employment, for child support purposes, where husband had actively sought employment but could not find comparable work at his prior income level, and trial court, by stating that it would take a "miracle" for husband to find work at same salary level, indicated that it knew husband could not find work at that level. Badovick v. Badovick (Ohio App. 8 Dist. 1998) 128 Ohio App.3d 18, 713 N.E.2d 1066.

Factors of parent's employment potential and probable earnings based on the parent's recent work history, job qualifications, and prevailing job opportunities and salary levels in the community in which the parent resides, which are considered in determining amount of "potential income" to be imputed to parent for child support purposes, are mandatory, and a court's failure to consider all three factors will constitute an abuse of discretion. Badovick v. Badovick (Ohio App. 8 Dist. 1998) 128 Ohio App.3d 18, 713 N.E.2d 1066.

Trial court did not abuse its discretion in declining to impute income to wife, by reason of her allegedly voluntary underemployment, for purposes of calculating parties' child support obligations in action for divorce, where wife had history of carpal tunnel syndrome and tendinitis. Zeefe v. Zeefe (Ohio App. 8 Dist. 1998) 125 Ohio App.3d 600, 709 N.E.2d 208.

Former wife's voluntary decision to quit her guidance counseling job and take another one that paid $15,000 less but was in a community closer to her home and children did not warrant imputing potential income to her in determining whether to modify her $550 monthly child support obligation, where she was still working as a counselor and was earning the most she could in the closer community. Shank v. Shank (Ohio App. 3 Dist. 1997) 122 Ohio App.3d 189, 701 N.E.2d 439, appeal not allowed 80 Ohio St.3d 1471, 687 N.E.2d 299.

Trial court may not impute income to parent, for purposes of determining child support obligation, unless it finds that parent is voluntarily unemployed or underemployed. Inscoe v. Inscoe (Ohio App. 4 Dist. 1997) 121 Ohio App.3d 396, 700 N.E.2d 70.

Imputing income to both parties in amount of minimum wage in order to complete child support worksheet was abuse of discretion in proceeding to modify father's child support obligation, where there was no finding that either party was voluntarily unemployed or underemployed, and parties' potential income was not calculated in accordance with statutory factors. Leonard v. Erwin (Adams 1996) 111 Ohio App.3d 413, 676 N.E.2d 552.

Trial court has jurisdiction, upon filing of motion to show cause regarding child support issues, over any matters related to such motion to show cause, including modification of support. Bellamy v. Bellamy (Erie 1996) 110 Ohio App.3d 576, 674 N.E.2d 1227.

Trial court did not abuse its discretion in declining to impute income to mother for purposes of computing father's child support obligation under divorce decree in light of fact that mother was residential parent of parties' two children. Carman v. Carman (Butler 1996) 109 Ohio App.3d 698, 672 N.E.2d 1093.

Potential income could be properly imputed to mother who had few work skills and little work history in the amount of $8,800 per year, which was essentially what she could earn in minimum wage position, in computing child support obligations of mother and father. Marsh v. Marsh (Allen 1995) 105 Ohio App.3d 747, 664 N.E.2d 1353.

Absent evidence or consideration of job opportunities or salary levels within father's field in county in which he was residing, trial court erred by imputing income of $95,000 per year to father based upon what he had earned in his prior employment as engineer in foreign country. Marsh v. Marsh (Allen 1995) 105 Ohio App.3d 747, 664 N.E.2d 1353.

Bonuses received by husband should have been included in his gross income in determining child support. Paulus v. Paulus (Geauga 1994) 95 Ohio App.3d 612, 643 N.E.2d 165, stay denied 70 Ohio St.3d 1444, 639 N.E.2d 112, dismissed, appeal not allowed 71 Ohio St.3d 1420, 642 N.E.2d 386.

Trial court did not abuse its discretion in failing to find that former wife was either voluntarily unemployed or underemployed, in determining former spouses' income for child support purposes. Parzynski v. Parzynski (Erie 1992) 85 Ohio App.3d 423, 620 N.E.2d 93, dismissed, jurisdictional motion overruled 67 Ohio St.3d 1450, 619 N.E.2d 419, rehearing denied 67 Ohio St.3d 1513, 622 N.E.2d 660.

Trial court's decision to impute to father his "potential" income for purposes of child support was not per se abuse of discretion. In re Yeauger (Union 1992) 83 Ohio App.3d 493, 615 N.E.2d 289.

Imputing $62,000 in earnings to husband is not an abuse of discretion where the husband, whose occupation as that of builder and project manager, could easily obtain a job making a minimum of $1000 a week for a gross annual salary of $52,000; in addition, his ability to obtain side jobs as evidenced throughout the marriage would produce a minimum of an additional $10,000 a year. Fasano v Fasano, No. 74040, 1999 WL 285382 (8th Dist Ct App, Cuyahoga, 5-6-99).

Trial court's use of an historical figure of parent's income as the permanent earning capacity of parent was abuse of discretion where court did not make express finding that parent was voluntarily underemployed or unemployed or expressly consider the statutory factors for imputation of income. Slone v Slone, No. 98CA610, 1999 WL 156149 (4th Dist Ct App, Pike, 3-22-99).

A court properly imputes potential interest income of $6242 from a brokerage account to a spouse who liquidates the account to pay her current husband's business debt instead of keeping it for the children's beneficial use in addition to imputing $32,000 for potential income based upon the spouse's ability to find employment as a teacher. Butland v Butland, No. 97APF06-792, 1998 WL 195729 (10th Dist Ct App, Franklin, 4-23-98).

An order finding a father voluntarily unemployed and imputing minimum wage income to him and providing for forty-three dollars per month child support is proper where (1) the father had worked only a few weeks and paid only twenty dollars in child support since his release from prison five years earlier and (2) although he is now an able-bodied college graduate, he chooses to be a house-husband because he and his new wife do not wish to place their children in day care unless he is able to find a job paying more than the $33,000 his wife earns. Woods v Woods, No. 17935, 1997 WL 303660 (9th Dist Ct App, Summit, 5-21-97).

Imputing income for child support purposes that is derived from playing in a band is error where (1) there is no documentation relative to the income derived from the band playing activities, (2) playing in the band is for pleasure and does not produce enough income to exceed equipment costs and other related expenses, and (3) the trial court does not find voluntary unemployment or underemployment as required prior to imputing income. Lacarelli v Lacarelli, No. 95-B-3, 1997 WL 35422 (7th Dist Ct App, Belmont, 1-24-97).

An additional $20,000 of imputed income to the husband for the purpose of calculating child support is error where neither the lower court nor the referee makes a determination of involuntary or voluntary unemployment where the husband had engaged in an auto repair business out of the home during the course of the marriage and the repair work stops when the parties begin having marital difficulties and the divorce action is filed. Tomovcik v Tomovcik, No. 95-JE-22, 1997 WL 28548 (7th Dist Ct App, Jefferson, 1-22-97).

A personal injury settlement of $18,000 due to an automobile accident constitutes income for the calculation of child support even though the obligor incurs medical bills in excess of the settlement amount. Pyles v Hornsby, No. CA96-01-006, 1996 WL 307206 (12th Dist Ct App, Clermont, 6-10-96).

An imputed income figure that is derived from outdated information is error where the court bases its computation on a husband's outdated work history and occupational qualifications and glosses over his testimony regarding recent work history and prevailing job opportunities and salary levels in the community where he lives. Dixon v Dixon, No. 66997, 1995 WL 106137 (8th Dist Ct App, Cuyahoga, 3-9-95).

A trial court does not err in imputing income to a voluntarily underemployed parent with two bachelor degrees and experience in the education profession who is currently working part-time in a department store for minimum wage. Sofonia v Norton, No. 5-93-28, 1993 WL 415321 (3d Dist Ct App, Hancock, 10-6-93).

Debtor's obligation to pay $5 per week to county department of human services for child's past medical expenses was not unreasonable burden on debtor, and, accordingly, obligation could be found nondischargeable as "support," even though it would take debtor over 200 years to pay off entire debt based on weekly payments of $5. In re Oberley (Bkrtcy.N.D.Ohio 1993) 153 B.R. 179.

3. —Business, income

Trial court should not have excluded cost of acquisition of tractor as deduction from current year's income, for determining amount of child support to be paid by obligor who was self-employed farmer, without first considering facts and circumstances of case. Kamm v. Kamm (Ohio 1993) 67 Ohio St.3d 174, 616 N.E.2d 900, on remand.

Acquisition of a capital asset by a self-employed child support obligor may be deductible against such obligor's gross receipts for purpose of computing obligor's statutory child support obligation, providing acquisition is otherwise both "ordinary and necessary" and is acquired by actual cash expenditure. Kamm v. Kamm (Ohio 1993) 67 Ohio St.3d 174, 616 N.E.2d 900, on remand.

Award of child support in divorce action based solely upon husband's "reasonable salary" required remand for recomputation in light of all statutory factors; trial court's journal entry specified that $120,000 was husband's "reasonable salary," but court made no findings as to husband's gross income, retained earnings of husband's business, or value of substantial benefits to husband paid for by his business. Zeefe v. Zeefe (Ohio App. 8 Dist. 1998) 125 Ohio App.3d 600, 709 N.E.2d 208.

Evidence that self-employed former husband had multiplied number of miles he had driven by standard federal mileage deduction was sufficient to prove that former husband was entitled to deduct some car and truck expenses, as cash items, from gross income on which modified child support obligation was to be based. Phillips v. Phillips (Geauga 1996) 113 Ohio App.3d 868, 682 N.E.2d 701.

Self-employed parent must show actual number of miles traveled, but need not show actual cost of each travel expense incurred, in order to be entitled to deduct some portion of car expenses from gross income under child support statute. Phillips v. Phillips (Geauga 1996) 113 Ohio App.3d 868, 682 N.E.2d 701.

Fact that employer required father to work out of state and incur expenses for lodging, food, industrial shoes, tools, and truck maintenance did not entitle father to reduction of his gross income by amount of those expenses, under child support statute authorizing deduction of ordinary and necessary expenses incurred in generating gross receipts received from self-employment, proprietorship of a business, joint ownership of partnership or closely held corporation, where father did not claim to fall within any of those categories. State ex rel. Scioto County Child Support Enforcement Agency v.Gardner (Scioto 1996) 113 Ohio App.3d 46, 680 N.E.2d 221.

Wife's share of husband's pension, which was awarded to wife in divorce proceeding, had to be included in her gross income for purposes of calculating wife's child support obligation, where pension account was in pay status, and wife would receive her share of husband's pension in monthly payments. McQuinn v. McQuinn (Butler 1996) 110 Ohio App.3d 296, 673 N.E.2d 1384.

Although trial court's entry awarding child support, upon former husband's motion for modification, characterized cash payment from former husband's former employer as "buyout," trial court effectively considered payment to be "severance pay," as it was cash payment provided to former husband in lump sum upon termination of employment without fault and represented sum beyond wages, and payment was thus correctly included in former husband's gross income for purpose of child support calculation. McCoy v. McCoy (Meigs 1995) 105 Ohio App.3d 651, 664 N.E.2d 1012.

Generic language of child support statute referring to "nonrecurring or unsustainable income or cash flow items" cannot be used to exclude from gross income, for purpose of child support calculation, a specifically defined category of gross income; where legislature has specifically included severance pay in "gross income," courts are not free to construe general language of statute in manner that renders specific enumeration meaningless. McCoy v. McCoy (Meigs 1995) 105 Ohio App.3d 651, 664 N.E.2d 1012.

Decision to increase husband's gross income, by adding back expenses which he failed to document (including repair and maintenance expenses allegedly incurred in connection with office which he admittedly only rented), was not abuse of divorce court's discretion, for purposes of calculating husband's child support obligation. Mallin v. Mallin (Cuyahoga 1995) 102 Ohio App.3d 717, 657 N.E.2d 856.

Trial court could not use incomplete records of former husband's financial assets and income to compute his child support obligation, but rather had to use its authority to compel former husband to comply with discovery requests and orders to produce documents, even to extent of appointing independent expert to advise court as to former husband's true resources available for child support and taxing costs of expert against former husband. Bowen v. Thomas (Marion 1995) 102 Ohio App.3d 196, 656 N.E.2d 1328.

When determining personal income, for child support purposes, of parent who is only stockholder and who has control of all income and disbursements of corporation, court must consider all of parent's corporate and personal records in order to clarify parent's actual personal financial benefit from corporation, particularly in cases in which sole shareholder obscures his or her personal worth through creative corporate accounting. Bowen v. Thomas (Marion 1995) 102 Ohio App.3d 196, 656 N.E.2d 1328.

For purposes of determining child support in cases involving "corporate proprietorship," which is business operated in form of corporation but having only one individual as shareholder, director, and manager, court has duty to carefully examine evidence of corporate expenses and deductions as related to possible personal income. Matrka v. Matrka (Union 1995) 100 Ohio App.3d 161, 652 N.E.2d 250.

When obligor father sold business formerly awarded to him pursuant to divorce decree, father's income from sale, for child support purposes, should have included only profit from sale, not total amount received from sale of assets, even if father used sale proceeds as if it were income to satisfy his debts and expenses; converting tangible or intangible assets into cash was not income except to extent, if any, that there was profit or gain. Geiger v. Geiger (Franklin 1994) 96 Ohio App.3d 630, 645 N.E.2d 818.

For purposes of determining income of child support obligor, income from sale of assets other than in ordinary course of business includes only profit received on item, not initial investment which may be recouped upon sale. Geiger v. Geiger (Franklin 1994) 96 Ohio App.3d 630, 645 N.E.2d 818.

Monthly loan payments toward purchase of rig by father who was self-employed truck driver were ordinary and necessary, and actual cash expenditures, and thus were deductible from his gross income in calculating his child support obligation. Woods v. Woods (Hancock 1994) 95 Ohio App.3d 222, 642 N.E.2d 45.

Depreciation expenses should not be added to the income of a noncustodial parent who owns his own business and seeks to have weekly child support decreased since it has value only for income tax purposes and cannot be used to pay living expenses. Sizemore v. Sizemore (Montgomery 1991) 77 Ohio App.3d 733, 603 N.E.2d 1032.

Trial court should have considered retained earnings of corporation in which husband was 50% shareholder when ruling upon his motion to modify child support order; though husband had ceased drawing salary from corporation, therby decreasing his taxable income, increase in shareholder's equity, which increased value of husband's stock in corporation, constituted "income" for child support purposes. Williams v. Williams (Scioto 1991) 74 Ohio App.3d 838, 600 N.E.2d 739.

In determining a self-employed dentist's gross income for purposes of computing his child support obligations, equipment costs and leasehold improvements for his dental office are properly excluded as ordinary and necessary business expenses, despite the wife's claim that since such costs were included on her husband's federal tax detail depreciation schedule, they must be included in his gross income under RC 3113.215(A)(4), which excludes from ordinary and necessary business expenses "depreciation expenses and other noncash items that are allowed as deductions on any federal tax return," and is designed to ensure that a parent's gross income is not reduced by any sum not actually expended in the year used for computing child support. Baus v. Baus (Wayne 1991) 72 Ohio App.3d 781, 596 N.E.2d 509.

In determining a self-employed dentist's gross income for purposes of computing his child support obligations, contributions made to his dental employee's retirement plan are properly held to be ordinary and necessary business expenses, even though such contributions were termed "discretionary" given the testimony of the husband's accountant that the contributions were really a necessary cost of doing business if the husband wished to attract and keep good employees. Baus v. Baus (Wayne 1991) 72 Ohio App.3d 781, 596 N.E.2d 509.

Inclusion of one-half of a child support obligor's retained earnings in a Subchapter S corporation of which the obligor father is president in the obligor's gross income for purposes of calculation of child support is improper where (1) the funds are not available to the obligor merely upon his request, although they are included in gross income for income tax purposes, and (2) the plan to retain earnings existed during the parties' marriage and there has been no attempt to shelter the retained earnings to reduce the obligor's child support obligation. Riepenhoff v. Riepenhoff (Jackson 1990) 64 Ohio App.3d 135, 580 N.E.2d 846.

Under the child support guidelines, amounts for depreciation and other non-cash deductible items allowable by the internal revenue service are not deducted from the gross revenue of a person who is self-employed, and significant amounts of reimbursements and in-kind payments received by a self-employed parent are to be counted as income; therefore, a court's taking into consideration amounts on a self-employed parent's tax returns which do not affect cash flow and the fact that the self-employed parent receives a residence and use of an automobile from his business as additional compensation is not arbitrary, unreasonable, or unconscionable. Pruden-Wilgus v. Wilgus (Lucas 1988) 46 Ohio App.3d 13, 545 N.E.2d 647.

Order reducing the amount of child support owed by a former spouse is granted where the spouse presents unrefuted evidence that the hog farming operation he engages in is not a hobby but is for legitimate business purposes; a full deduction in excess of $29,000 for depreciation on two hog buildings and an addition to one of the structures is allowed as ordinary and necessary expenses for replacement business equipment. Beougher v Beougher, No. 10-99-18, 2000 WL 429900 (3d Dist Ct App, Mercer, 4-21-00).

Unexercised stock options given by an employer as part of a compensation package are to be included in the income of the obligor for purposes of calculating his child support obligation even though he has not actually received any cash. Murray v Murray, No. CA98-08-097, 1999 WL 55673 (12th Dist Ct App, Warren, 2-8-99).

Operating losses from a landscaping business cannot be used to reduce income generated from the primary occupation as an orthopedic surgeon for purposes of determining self-generated income under RC 3113.215(A)(3) and 3113.215(A)(4). Muehrcke v Muehrcke, No. 73434, 1998 WL 741942 (8th Dist Ct App, Cuyahoga, 10-22-98).

An obligor's additional compensation in the amount of $4995 due to the requirement that he furnish his own truck, tools and ladders in his work is not "self-generated income" subject to deductions for truck maintenance and insurance for purposes of child support calculations where the obligor is not self-employed and does not own the truck or equipment. Pugsley v Pugsley, No. 15-98-12, 1998 WL 769723 (3d Dist Ct App, Van Wert, 11-6-98).

Certain repair expenditures made by a child support obligor constitute "replacement business equipment" where (1) the obligor is in the business of renting residential property, (2) the rental properties themselves are the business "equipment," and (3) the expenditures are for items that replace broken, obsolete, or worn-out items already existing at the rental properties. Helfrich v Helfrich, No. 97APF08-975, 1998 WL 63528 (10th Dist Ct App, Franklin, 2-10-98).

The inclusion of the total depreciation amount from a spouse's corporate interests into that spouse's self-generated income is improper under RC 3113.215(A), and an order of support based on such erroneous calculation must be reversed and remanded. Sofonia v Norton, No. 5-93-28, 1993 WL 415321 (3d Dist Ct App, Hancock, 10-6-93).

4. —Spousal support, income

Trial court did not abuse its discretion in denying ex-husband's motion to modify his spousal support obligation; although ex-husband's income may have decreased and ex-wife's income increased since time of divorce, substantial gap continued to exist between incomes of parties and that difference weighed heavily against reducing ex-husband's spousal support payments. Fallang v. Fallang (Butler 1996) 109 Ohio App.3d 543, 672 N.E.2d 730, dismissed, appeal not allowed 76 Ohio St.3d 1434, 667 N.E.2d 985.

Where Court of Appeals found insufficient evidence to conclude that Chapter 7 debtor-obligor parent's assumption of joint credit card debt was in the nature of spousal support, and, thus, held that the debt was dischargeable, on remand for recalculation of child support trial court was free to consider the dischargeable nature of the debt when computing obligor's child support obligation. Snyder v. Snyder (Ashtabula 1995) 105 Ohio App.3d 69, 663 N.E.2d 695.

Spousal support obligation paid by one party to child support proceeding to another party could not be considered as "gross income" of other party for purpose of calculating child support on child support worksheet, and similarly, could not be excluded from first party's gross income. Matrka v. Matrka (Union 1995) 100 Ohio App.3d 161, 652 N.E.2d 250.

Spousal support paid by party to child support proceedings should not be deducted from payor's gross income calculation, and should not be included in payee's gross income calculation in determining child support; overruling *Kundrat v Kundrat*, Lake App. No. 92-L-097. Paulus v. Paulus (Geauga 1994) 95 Ohio App.3d 612, 643 N.E.2d 165, stay denied 70 Ohio St.3d 1444, 639 N.E.2d 112, dismissed, appeal not allowed 71 Ohio St.3d 1420, 642 N.E.2d 386.

In determining child support obligation, proper treatment of spousal support payments from one party to the other is not to deduct spousal support from payor's gross income calculation and not include amount received for spousal support in payee's gross income calculation. Parzynski v. Parzynski (Erie 1992) 85 Ohio App.3d 423, 620 N.E.2d 93, dismissed, jurisdictional motion overruled 67 Ohio St.3d 1450, 619 N.E.2d 419, rehearing denied 67 Ohio St.3d 1513, 622 N.E.2d 660.

Spousal support is not to be treated as income to the wife when calculating child support. Goffinet v Goffinet, Nos. CA94-11-197+, (12th Dist Ct App, Butler, 1-22-96).

Spousal support paid by a husband to a wife is not to be included in the wife's gross income in computing child support. Bolen v Bolen, No. 5-94-39, 1995 WL 328103 (3d Dist Ct App, Hancock, 6-5-95).

Spousal support received by a residential parent from an obligor is properly excluded from the calculation of child support under RC 3113.215(A)(2) as only spousal support received from a nonparty to the instant action is to be considered as income. Jackson v Jackson, No. 91-L-112 (11th Dist Ct App, Lake, 10-23-92).

5. —Noncash receipts, income

To value unexercised employee stock options for purposes of determining a child support obligation, the court should account for the options' appreciation in value as determined on the grant and exercise dates which fall into the income year at issue, using the stock price on the date the options were granted and the stock price on the date the options could be exercised, without considering appreciation from years earlier than the income year at issue. Murray v. Murray (Ohio App. 12 Dist. 1999) 128 Ohio App.3d 662, 716 N.E.2d 288.

Although trial courts may not consider new spouse's income when calculating parent's gross income for purposes of child support, trial courts may consider benefits parent receives from new spouse, or from sharing living expenses with another person, when deciding whether to deviate from amount of child support that would otherwise be required by statute. Inscoe v. Inscoe (Ohio App. 4 Dist. 1997) 121 Ohio App.3d 396, 700 N.E.2d 70.

Father was not entitled to credit against child support ordered under divorce decree for military "in-kind" benefits such as free medical benefits for children and access to commissary, post exchange (PX), and army recreational facilities. Carman v. Carman (Butler 1996) 109 Ohio App.3d 698, 672 N.E.2d 1093.

Roll-over Individual Retirement Account (IRA) that was established two years prior to motion to decrease child support and not contributed to in the interim was not "income" for purpose of calculating child support obligation. Rapp v. Rapp (Warren 1993) 89 Ohio App.3d 85, 623 N.E.2d 624.

Even if income from former husband's investment was only "paper income," in that it was applied to recourse note executed by former husband previously as part of initial investment, trial court properly included entire amount in determining former husband's gross income for purpose of calculating his child support obligation. Parzynski v. Parzynski (Erie 1992) 85 Ohio App.3d 423, 620 N.E.2d 93, dismissed, jurisdictional motion overruled 67 Ohio St.3d 1450, 619 N.E.2d 419, rehearing denied 67 Ohio St.3d 1513, 622 N.E.2d 660.

Pension contribution made on former husband's behalf by business in which husband was 50% owner had to be included in determining former husband's gross income for child support purposes. Parzynski v. Parzynski (Erie 1992) 85 Ohio App.3d 423, 620 N.E.2d 93, dismissed, jurisdictional motion overruled 67 Ohio St.3d 1450, 619 N.E.2d 419, rehearing denied 67 Ohio St.3d 1513, 622 N.E.2d 660.

In determining under C P Sup R 75 the amount of support a noncustodial parent is obligated to pay, a court must consider the noncustodial parent's receipt of free housing. Merkel v. Merkel (Montgomery 1988) 51 Ohio App.3d 110, 554 N.E.2d 1346.

Converting a tangible or intangible asset into cash is not income except to the extent, if any, that there is profit or gain, and where a spouse sells business assets, it is error for a divorce court to include the total amount of cash received from the sale in its calculations of gross income for the seller spouse for the purpose of determining child support. Geiger v Geiger, No. 93APF09-1333, 1994 WL 479349 (10th Dist Ct App, Franklin, 9-1-94).

6. Best interest of child

Mother was liable to pay child support to custodial father in amount determined pursuant to Child Support Guidelines, despite prior agreement between mother and father that father would waive child support, where referee found that Guidelines were not unjust or inappropriate and were in best interests of the child. DePalmo v. DePalmo (Ohio 1997) 78 Ohio St.3d 535, 679 N.E.2d 266.

Allowance of deduction for acquisition of capital asset by self-employed child support obligor against such obligor's gross receipts may be grounds for deviation from statutory child support guidelines, providing "best interest of child" is considered. Kamm v. Kamm (Ohio 1993) 67 Ohio St.3d 174, 616 N.E.2d 900, on remand.

Overriding concern of legislation governing procedures which court must follow in calculating and awarding child support is to ensure best interest of child for whom support is being awarded. Rock v. Cabral (Ohio 1993) 67 Ohio St.3d 108, 616 N.E.2d 218.

Definition of "income" as set forth in statute governing calculation of child support obligation is intended to be broad and flexible; such expansive definition is necessary to ensure that best interests of children, the intended beneficiaries of child support awards, are protected. McQuinn v. McQuinn (Butler 1996) 110 Ohio App.3d 296, 673 N.E.2d 1384.

Underlying spirit and policy of child support statutes are concern for best interests of child. Cuyahoga Cty. Support Enforcement Agency v. Lozada (Cuyahoga 1995) 102 Ohio App.3d 442, 657 N.E.2d 372.

If party fails to respond to discovery request for information concerning his or her financial situation and income for purposes of determining child support, trial court has duty to use its full power to obtain complete information on that party's income and financial affairs in order to provide support which is in children's best interest and which reflects standard of living for children that they would have enjoyed if their parents were married and cohabiting. Bowen v. Thomas (Marion 1995) 102 Ohio App.3d 196, 656 N.E.2d 1328.

The best interest of the child is the general principle emphasized when court calculates child support. Houts v. Houts (Mercer 1995) 99 Ohio App.3d 701, 651 N.E.2d 1031, appeal not allowed 72 Ohio St.3d 1529, 649 N.E.2d 838.

7. Findings of fact

Whether court is establishing initial child support order or is modifying order based on agreement between parties that does not include any order for payment of child support, Child Support Guidelines must be followed unless court makes factual determination and sets forth criteria as to why following Guidelines would be unjust or inappropriate and not in best interests of child, and makes actual entry in journal of findings of fact to support that determination. DePalmo v. DePalmo (Ohio 1997) 78 Ohio St.3d 535, 679 N.E.2d 266.

Appellate court must be able to ascertain from trial court's journal entry amount of potential income imputed to spouse in computing child support, and trial court's reasons for imputing such income. Rock v. Cabral (Ohio 1993) 67 Ohio St.3d 108, 616 N.E.2d 218.

Any court-ordered deviation from the applicable worksheet and the basic child support schedule must be entered by the court in its journal and must include findings of fact to support such determination. Marker v. Grimm (Ohio 1992) 65 Ohio St.3d 139, 601 N.E.2d 496.

Proper procedure for determining child support under shared parenting plan is to calculate parties' respective child support obligations using the worksheet provided in relevant statute, then to set off those obligations against each other to yield the "net order" that must be paid by obligor parent, except that trial court may deviate from resulting amount provided it sets forth appropriate findings of fact to support its determination. Beard v. Beard (Ohio App. 11 Dist. 1998) 130 Ohio App.3d 102, 719 N.E.2d 625.

Agreed journal entry was "existing child support order of the court" for purposes of determining whether trial court erred by reducing child support obligation solely upon finding of 10% deviation from support schedule, even though trial court failed to make findings of fact with respect to such deviation; parties waived any error in trial court's adoption of agreed entry, as neither party timely appealed that entry. Smith v. Collins (Summit 1995) 107 Ohio App.3d 100, 667 N.E.2d 1236.

Trial court's findings of fact were insufficient to permit Court of Appeals meaningful review of child support obligor's gross income where obligor testified and provided documentation showing that his gross income was more than $4,000 less than trial court's estimated amount, trial court did not adequately support the income figure it assigned to obligor, and there was no statement by trial court indicating that it was imputing income. Snyder v. Snyder (Ashtabula 1995) 105 Ohio App.3d 69, 663 N.E.2d 695.

Trial court failed to set forth specific findings of fact to support continuing deviation from child support guidelines that parties agreed to in their divorce, and deviation could not serve as basis for rebutting presumption of change of circumstances. Paulus v. Paulus (Geauga 1994) 95 Ohio App.3d 612, 643 N.E.2d 165, stay denied 70 Ohio St.3d 1444, 639 N.E.2d 112, dismissed, appeal not allowed 71 Ohio St.3d 1420, 642 N.E.2d 386.

The trial court is not required to make findings of fact and conclusions of law in modifying a child support order to conform to the child support guidelines where not timely requested by one of the parties. Forest v. Forest (Stark 1993) 82 Ohio App.3d 572, 612 N.E.2d 815.

An order reducing child support from $296.67 monthly to $1.00 "in the best interests of the child and his parents" but lacking findings of fact, and allowing direct payment in contravention of RC 2301.36, will be reversed as an abuse of discretion. Minter v Copes, No. 67614, 1995 WL 363866 (8th Dist Ct App, Cuyahoga, 6-15-95).

8. —Joint custody, modification of child support

Former RC 3113.215(B)(4), which required a trial court to modify a joint custody support order that was ten per cent less than the amount set by the child support guidelines, is an exception to former RC 3109.04(B)(2)(b), which prohibited a court from modifying a joint custody support order without the consent of both custodians. Martin v. Martin (Ohio 1993) 66 Ohio St.3d 110, 609 N.E.2d 537.

Court of common pleas had jurisdiction to modify child support award contained within agreed joint custody plan pursuant to wife's motion based upon husband's increased income and Uniform Child Support Guidelines which were adopted after original plan, despite husband's lack of consent. Santantonio v. Santantonio (Lorain 1993) 88 Ohio App.3d 201, 623 N.E.2d 670, motion overruled 67 Ohio St.3d 1506, 622 N.E.2d 653.

9. —Change of circumstances, modification of child support

Former husband's court-ordered child support obligation for daughter who was initially placed in custody of his former wife did not terminate merely because custody of daughter was transferred to husband. Lytle v. Lytle (Ohio App. 10 Dist. 1998) 130 Ohio App.3d 697, 720 N.E.2d 1007.

Former husband's child support obligation was not subject to modification after former wife voluntarily chose to terminate her employment, to stay home, and to raise child that she had with new husband. Sancho v. Sancho (Union 1996) 114 Ohio App.3d 636, 683 N.E.2d 849.

Trial court could order noncustodial parent to make child support payments, even though noncustodial parent claimed that custodial parent was sharing living expenses with another person, obviating need to modify earlier arrangement; court had discretion to order modification even if supporting parent had resources to provide total amount needed to support child. Faulkner v. Faulkner (Clermont 1996) 114 Ohio App.3d 216, 683 N.E.2d 31.

Evidence supported conclusion that noncustodial parent who relinquished claim to property in favor of custodial parent, in lieu of making periodic child support payments, could now be required to make those payments; circumstances of both parents had changed, with noncustodial parent making nothing at time of decree and $21,382.40 per year at time of hearing on motion for support order modification, and custodial parent's income going from $23,400 per year to $14,248 during same period. Faulkner v. Faulkner (Clermont 1996) 114 Ohio App.3d 216, 683 N.E.2d 31.

Father's criminal conduct resulting in incarceration was voluntary act and, thus, did not constitute substantial change in circumstances warranting modification of his child support obligation. Richardson v. Ballard (Butler 1996) 113 Ohio App.3d 552, 681 N.E.2d 507.

When child support obligor reduces his or her income voluntarily, the reduction does not constitute substantial change in circumstances warranting modification of child support obligation. Richardson v. Ballard (Butler 1996) 113 Ohio App.3d 552, 681 N.E.2d 507.

Modification of award of child support normally requires determination of whether there has been substantial change in circumstances and, if so, redetermination of amount of child support in accordance with support guidelines. Leonard v. Erwin (Adams 1996) 111 Ohio App.3d 413, 676 N.E.2d 552.

Substantial change of circumstances occasioned by father's sale of stock option was contemplated at time original order of child support was issued, contrary to requirement of statute addressing modification of child support obligation; stock option was discussed during hearing conducted to determine father's original child support obligation, and mother had not appealed modification of original child support order dismissing requirement that husband pay 3% of all income realized from exercise of his stock options. Yost v. Unanue (Stark 1996) 109 Ohio App.3d 294, 671 N.E.2d 1374.

Discharge in bankruptcy of ex-wife's obligation on joint debt for which she had agreed to hold former husband harmless was not "change in circumstances" such as might warrant modification of husband's child support obligation, where joint debt from which wife was discharged was obligation owing to husband's mother, and no evidence was presented that husband had made any payment thereon or assumed liability to mother. Mallin v. Mallin (Cuyahoga 1995) 102 Ohio App.3d 717, 657 N.E.2d 856.

In action for modification of residential parent agreement, residential parent was not entitled to child support from nonresidential parent, absent finding that residential parent was no longer able to provide total amount reasonable for support of children, or that nonresidential parent's circumstances had changed substantially, making it in best interest of children to receive support from him. Ricker v. Ricker (Putnam 1995) 102 Ohio App.3d 209, 656 N.E.2d 1337.

Former husband's annual income of $307,692.30 after winning lottery permitted increase in annual child support from $3,276 to $31,215.38, even though former husband claimed that this was more than child actually needed; trial court awarded 10.145% of former husband's annual income, and former wife testified that increased support would enable her to insure that child received quality education, was able to participate in more sports activities, and was able to take piano lessons. Pratt v. McCullough (Warren 1995) 100 Ohio App.3d 479, 654 N.E.2d 372, appeal not allowed 72 Ohio St.3d 1540, 650 N.E.2d 481.

Trial court could not reduce father's child support obligations, where trial court expressly found no substantial change in parties' circumstances and no decrease in father's income. Matrka v. Matrka (Union 1995) 100 Ohio App.3d 161, 652 N.E.2d 250.

On father's motion to modify his child support obligation, evidence supported finding that father's earnings did not decrease, though father's reported earnings decreased from $115,990 three years earlier to $91,750 in previous year, where father was sole stockholder, manager and director of corporate business, gross income of corporation increased from $809,000 two years earlier to $853,000 in previous year, father used corporate work crews to work on remodeling projects on father's home and father's girlfriend's home, and corporation purchased late model sport utility vehicle. Matrka v. Matrka (Union 1995) 100 Ohio App.3d 161, 652 N.E.2d 250.

Father's termination of employment to enroll in law school as full-time student did not amount to substantial change of circumstances warranting reduction of his child support obligation, considering that mother had borne most of financial responsibility for child while father finished his undergraduate degree, putting her own educational goals behind needs of child, that father might be able to secure employment while he attended law school, and that father was given option of paying reduced support while he attended law school and paying accrued balance of award after graduation. Baker v. Grathwohl (Butler 1994) 97 Ohio App.3d 116, 646 N.E.2d 253.

Parent's unemployment may be determined in certain instances to constitute change of circumstances warranting modification of child support obligation, but voluntary termination of employment may not constitute inability to support and may not justify such modification. Baker v. Grathwohl (Butler 1994) 97 Ohio App.3d 116, 646 N.E.2d 253.

Trial court was not required, pursuant to statute requiring recalculation of child support payments upon request for modification, to recalculate support upon reinstating support payments after having suspended payments pursuant to former husband's motion to terminate support; statute required recomputation only upon motion to modify amount of support to be paid. In re Owens (Clark 1994) 96 Ohio App.3d 429, 645 N.E.2d 130.

Divorced husband's misappropriation of funds and his consequent surrender of his license to practice law, his resignation from firm, and his incarceration amounted to voluntary change of circumstances that could not warrant modification of his child support obligation. Brockmeier v. Brockmeier (Hamilton 1993) 91 Ohio App.3d 689, 633 N.E.2d 584, dismissed, jurisdictional motion overruled 69 Ohio St.3d 1408, 629 N.E.2d 1370.

Nonpaying split custodial parent was entitled to have child support obligation terminated upon emancipation of child in paying parent's custody by increasing support payments from paying parent to full amount nonpaying parent would have received absent split custody arrangement. Beckley v. Beckley (Greene 1993) 90 Ohio App.3d 202, 628 N.E.2d 135.

Where an agreement places sole responsibility for support of children on the custodial father and a court determines that the custodial parent is no longer in a position to provide the total amount reasonable for support of the child or that the noncustodial parent's circumstances have changed substantially and it would be in the best interest of the child to receive support from the noncustodial parent, then the court should apply RC 3113.215 to calculate the amount of child support and if appropriate, deviate from the amount according to requirements of RC 3113.215(B)(1). Anderkin v. Lansdell (Clermont 1992) 80 Ohio App.3d 687, 610 N.E.2d 570.

The potential remarriage and fathering of more children are irrelevant to the obligor's responsibility to support his children and the court need not provide for an automatic adjustment to the child support award in the event of the obligor's remarriage. Hockenberry v. Hockenberry (Henry 1992) 75 Ohio App.3d 806, 600 N.E.2d 839.

Insufficient evidence exists upon which to enter an order modifying a child support order where the obligor fails to submit required financial data, in which case the obligee must seek a subpoena duces tecum to compel the obligor's production of the information. In re Dissolution of Marriage of Al-Faour (Franklin 1990) 68 Ohio App.3d 279, 588 N.E.2d 228, dismissed, jurisdictional motion overruled 56 Ohio St.3d 702, 564 N.E.2d 704.

An obligor's sale of his business along with the occurrence of transactions which lead to the reduction of personal and business debt without due regard for the duty to provide for the continuing needs of his children do not constitute the change of circumstances required for a modification of child support; in addition, a child support worksheet must be completed and included in the record for the order or modification to be made and failure to do so constitutes reversible error. Barnard v Kuppin, Nos. C-980360 and C-980400, 1999 WL 699595 (1st Dist Ct App, Hamilton, 9-10-99).

In a case where a child support obligor wins the Ohio lottery jackpot (1) the court properly excludes from the calculations of gross income the obligor's $4.9 million dollar lottery prize as nonrecurring or unsustainable income and by considering only the $250,000 generated from the investment of the prize money, the court follows the mandates of RC 3113.215, (2) the court exceeds its authority when it orders $1000 of the child support to be placed into a trust fund and that a court appointed trustee is in a better position to determine how to utilize the funds and provide for the child's best interests than the custodial parent, and (3) awarding the federal tax dependency exemption to the obligor who provides ninety-three per cent of the child support is not an abuse of discretion. Barlow v Ray, No. 9-96-68, 1997 WL 232241 (3d Dist Ct App, Marion, 5-2-97).

Incarceration does not constitute a substantial change of circumstances warranting modification or suspension of child support during the period of imprisonment where the obligor is incarcerated at the time the original order of support is entered. Green v Green, No. S-96-013, 1997 WL 43279 (6th Dist Ct App, Sandusky, 1-31-97).

Suspension of a child support obligation during the time that an obligor's two sons spend in the custody of the Ohio Department of Youth Services is not error. Sigler v Sigler, No. 15624, 1996 WL 629518 (2d Dist Ct App, Montgomery, 11-1-96).

A trial court did not abuse its discretion in an action to modify a child support order by finding a substantial change in circumstances justifying a ninety-two per cent increase in the father's obligation where his gross income has increased twenty-five per cent and his teenage daughter's financial needs have increased since the divorce due to her involvement in extra-curricular high-school activities, and her driving expenses and increased clothing costs over the previous three years. Holt v Troha, No. 96-CA-19, 1996 WL 430866 (2d Dist Ct App, Greene, 8-2-96).

RC 3113.215(B)(5)(f) does not prohibit the parties to a separation agreement from agreeing that one party will pay all of the children's uninsured medical expenses; however, where a court later modifies the amount of child support pursuant to the guidelines, the court may not order an additional amount of child support for uninsured medical expenses. Thompson v Thompson, No. 93CA21, 1994 WL 649273 (4th Dist Ct App, Pickaway, 11-14-94).

Modification of child support is proper where an obligor is self-employed as a truck driver and seeks to have his monthly loan payment on his tractor-trailer rig deducted as an ordinary and necessary expense incurred by the parent in generating gross receipts. Woods v Woods, No. 5-93-38, 1994 WL 247048 (3d Dist Ct App, Hancock, 6-9-94).

An obligor's decision to quit his present job for a career change, in anticipation of a layoff, in good faith, constitutes a change of circumstances which warrants a modification of child support obligations. Pagliaro v Pagliaro, No. CA93-07-049, 1994 WL 43380 (12th Dist Ct App, Clermont, 2-14-94).

The RC 3113.215(B)(4) 10% deviation provision is not the only change of circumstances to be recognized; RC 3113.215(B)(4) created an additional change of circumstances but did not eliminate a modification of support premised on RC 3109.05 and common law changes of circumstances. In re Grosh, No. 93AP-347, 1993 WL 238877 (10th Dist Ct App, Franklin, 6-24-93).

A compromise agreement establishing paternity and child support entered pursuant to former RC 3111.07 is dispositive between the mother and father only and does not bar a support modification action brought on behalf of the child; as the child's action is not barred, use of RC 3113.215 in the modification proceeding is proper. Carpenter v Digman, No. 91-CA-4 (5th Dist Ct App, Knox, 7-22-91).

The adoption of the child support guidelines found in C P Sup R 75 has extinguished the burden of demonstrating a change of circumstances in order to obtain modification of a child support order. Andreas v Andreas, No. CA-7559 (5th Dist Ct App, Stark, 11-7-88).

On a motion to reduce a child support obligation, where the trial court finds a change of circumstances but orders only a minimal reduction in support not in conformity with the support guidelines, the modification order will be remanded for computation in accordance with the guidelines, absent findings of fact warranting the deviation. Kozloski v Kozloski, No. CA87-10-141 (12th Dist Ct App, Butler, 6-30-88).

10. —Ten percent variation, modification of child support

When court is modifying preexisting order for payment of child support, court must apply ten percent test established by Child Support Guidelines and must follow Guidelines unless court makes factual determination and sets forth criteria as to why following Guidelines would be unjust or inappropriate and not in best interests of child, and makes actual entry in journal of findings of fact to support that determination. DePalmo v. DePalmo (Ohio 1997) 78 Ohio St.3d 535, 679 N.E.2d 266.

Trial court did not abuse its discretion by adopting agreed journal entry as child support order, even though that order deviated from statutory support schedule by more than 10%; evidence showed that father, with full knowledge of support schedule, voluntarily undertook child support obligation in amount greater than statutory level, and nothing in record suggested that such obligation was unjust or inappropriate, or contrary to best interest of children. Smith v. Collins (Summit 1995) 107 Ohio App.3d 100, 667 N.E.2d 1236.

Where father voluntarily agreed to child support obligation that exceeded support schedule by more than 10%, trial court could not reduce that obligation solely upon finding of 10% deviation from support schedule, as such deviation was already contemplated and accepted by parties. Smith v. Collins (Summit 1995) 107 Ohio App.3d 100, 667 N.E.2d 1236.

Increased economic need is not requirement for obtaining increase in child support after divorce as long as it is shown that increase in obligor's income would result in at least 10% change in amount of child support. Pratt v. McCullough (Warren 1995) 100 Ohio App.3d 479, 654 N.E.2d 372, appeal not allowed 72 Ohio St.3d 1540, 650 N.E.2d 481.

In determining whether to increase paying parent's child support obligation in split custodial arrangement based on changed circumstances after child in paying parent's custody was emancipated, whether required ten percent difference between previous support order and recalculated support order existed had to be based on actual prior support order, rather than amount prior support order would have been without split custody arrangement. Beckley v. Beckley (Greene 1993) 90 Ohio App.3d 202, 628 N.E.2d 135.

Evidence supported finding, in dissolution of marriage proceeding in which wife sought modification of husband's child support obligation, that husband had concealed income of over $70,000 in prior child support modification proceeding and, thus, trial court could construe concealment as significant misrepresentation justifying setting aside of earlier child support order; in earlier proceeding, husband's testimony omitted reference to over $70,000 in income related to commissions. In re Marriage of Stearns (Franklin 1993) 88 Ohio App.3d 264, 623 N.E.2d 711.

Trial court did not abuse its discretion in finding change of circumstances that required upward modification of former husband's child support obligation, when proper calculation of child support based on current combined annual gross income of former spouse would result in substantially greater than ten-percent deviation from current child support order of $14,040 annually. Parzynski v. Parzynski (Erie 1992) 85 Ohio App.3d 423, 620 N.E.2d 93, dismissed, jurisdictional motion overruled 67 Ohio St.3d 1450, 619 N.E.2d 419, rehearing denied 67 Ohio St.3d 1513, 622 N.E.2d 660.

C P Sup R 75(B) should be interpreted as requiring reconsideration of the amount of child support only when there is a change in the income of either or both parties that would produce a variance in the support award calculated using the guidelines, before and after the change, in excess of ten per cent. Harrison v. Harrison (Montgomery 1989) 62 Ohio App.3d 343, 575 N.E.2d 853.

Although a greater than ten per cent deviation between child support called for by C P Sup R 75 and the amount of support actually ordered in a dissolution decree entered prior to the adoption of C P Sup R 75 is a sufficient ground upon which to base a modification of child support, under such circumstances, the trial court must hold an evidentiary hearing at which the guidelines set forth in C P Sup R 75, along with any other relevant factors presented by either party, could be considered. Wogoman v. Wogoman (Miami 1989) 44 Ohio App.3d 34, 541 N.E.2d 128.

A party moving for a modification of an order for child support under C P Sup R 75 need only demonstrate a variance in excess of ten per cent between the guideline formula and the extant judgment in order to meet his or her initial burden of proof, and once this burden is satisfied, it is incumbent upon the parties to show how all revelant facts surrounding their situations should affect the amount of child support obligation. (But see Klein v Brewer, No. CA-7605 (5th Dist Ct App, Stark, 1-30-89).) Rohrbach v. Rohrbach (Ashland 1988) 40 Ohio App.3d 92, 531 N.E.2d 773.

In an action to modify a support order, if a court recalculates the amount of support due under RC 3113.215(B)(4), and the amount varies from the original order by more than ten per cent, a trial court's finding of a substantial change of circumstance warranting a modification of support will be affirmed. Birath v Birath, No. 92AP-1603, 1993 WL 290926 (10th Dist Ct App, Franklin, 7-20-93).

In determining whether a child support order should be modified, a substantial change in circumstances must be demonstrated through all requisite factors, statutory or otherwise; the mere adoption of statutory guidelines and the ten per cent variance rule, by itself, is insufficient to support a modification, but modification is proper where the custodial parent's voluntary underemployment is factored in. Mathers v Mathers, No. 92-G-1707 (11th Dist Ct App, Geauga, 3-31-93).

11. Child support worksheet

A child support computation worksheet, required to be used by a trial court in calculating the amount of an obligor's child support obligation in accordance with RC 3113.215, must actually be completed and made a part of the trial court's record. Marker v. Grimm (Ohio 1992) 65 Ohio St.3d 139, 601 N.E.2d 496.

Trial court's failure, in divorce action, to perform statutorily required calculation for temporary child support required remand for recalculation of such support and inclusion in record of calculations and amount of temporary child support separate from award of temporary spousal support. Zeefe v. Zeefe (Ohio App. 8 Dist. 1998) 125 Ohio App.3d 600, 709 N.E.2d 208.

Before trial court can issue or modify child support order, it must calculate amount of obligor's child support obligation in accordance with basic child support schedule, and cannot deviate from child support guidelines unless its journal entry includes determination that calculated support would be unjust or inappropriate and would not be in best interest of the child. Leguillon v. Leguillon (Ohio App. 12 Dist. 1998) 124 Ohio App.3d 757, 707 N.E.2d 571.

Whenever trial court considers modification of child support, it must use properly prepared worksheet to determine amount of child support to be paid and must make such work sheet part of the record to assist appellate court in reviewing the proceedings. Bellamy v. Bellamy (Erie 1996) 110 Ohio App.3d 576, 674 N.E.2d 1227.

Guideline amount of child support is rebuttably presumed to be correct amount due. Carman v. Carman (Butler 1996) 109 Ohio App.3d 698, 672 N.E.2d 1093.

Whether parent is underemployed is factual determination which is to be based on circumstances of each particular case and which will not be disturbed absent an abuse of discretion; such "abuse of discretion" connotes more than an error of law or judgment and indicates that trial court's decision is unreasonable, arbitrary, or unconscionable. Carman v. Carman (Butler 1996) 109 Ohio App.3d 698, 672 N.E.2d 1093.

Child support computation worksheet, required to be used by trial court in calculating amount of obligor's child support obligation, must actually be completed and made part of trial court's record. Fallang v. Fallang (Butler 1996) 109 Ohio App.3d 543, 672 N.E.2d 730, dismissed, appeal not allowed 76 Ohio St.3d 1434, 667 N.E.2d 985.

Child support worksheet must actually be completed by trial court and made part of record upon motion to establish support order, and trial court may not merely adopt by reference worksheets prepared by either party, although worksheet prepared by magistrate and adopted by court is considered as having been completed by trial court. In re Krechting (Clermont 1996) 108 Ohio App.3d 435, 670 N.E.2d 1081.

Trial court committed reversible error in child support modification proceeding by failing to include completed child support computation worksheets in record of case. Smith v. Collins (Summit 1995) 107 Ohio App.3d 100, 667 N.E.2d 1236.

Although trial court did not strictly comply with mandatory statutory procedure in determining former husband's motion to modify child support, error was harmless; although worksheet submitted by former wife was not signed, dated, or notarized, and thus could not be adopted by court, and worksheet adopted by court and included in record was prepared by child support enforcement agency months after child support order was entered, effective appellate review was not precluded by utilizing worksheet untimely prepared, as it would make little sense to remand matter for recalculation under new worksheet containing same information as the one in record. McCoy v. McCoy (Meigs 1995) 105 Ohio App.3d 651, 664 N.E.2d 1012.

In considering motion for modification of child support, trial court must follow statutory procedure requiring it to recalculate amount of support that would have to be paid under support order in accordance with schedule and pursuant to applicable worksheet outlining financial status of both parties and allowing for thorough consideration of financial issues affecting determination of child support. McCoy v. McCoy (Meigs 1995) 105 Ohio App.3d 651, 664 N.E.2d 1012.

Father could not have child support obligation reduced by 36%, to reflect percentage of time that he had physical custody of children under agreed upon shared parenting agreement; statute already covered method of computing child support in those situations. LaLiberte v. LaLiberte (Medina 1995) 105 Ohio App.3d 207, 663 N.E.2d 974.

Trial court could decline to depart from amount of support required to be paid by father to mother, as provided through application of statute and worksheet, even though father claimed that his assumption of physical custody over children for 36% of the time, pursuant to an agreed-upon shared parenting arrangement, made child support amounts required to be paid to mother every month excessive; court had determined that mother needed full amount of child support to maintain children in manner which they would have enjoyed had marriage continued. LaLiberte v. LaLiberte (Medina 1995) 105 Ohio App.3d 207, 663 N.E.2d 974.

Amount shown on properly completed support work sheet is rebuttably presumed to be correct amount of child support due. Mallin v. Mallin (Cuyahoga 1995) 102 Ohio App.3d 717, 657 N.E.2d 856.

Court-ordered deviations from child support schedule and work sheet are not permitted, absent full and strict compliance with statutory requirements. Mallin v. Mallin (Cuyahoga 1995) 102 Ohio App.3d 717, 657 N.E.2d 856.

In determining father's child support obligation, trial court could not deviate downward from presumed child support obligation as calculated on worksheet in accordance with statute, where trial court did not offer any findings of fact or other reasons to justify downward deviation or to show why amount calculated on worksheet was not in best interests of child. Cuyahoga Cty. Support Enforcement Agency v. Lozada (Cuyahoga 1995) 102 Ohio App.3d 442, 657 N.E.2d 372.

Trial court did not have to deduct former husband's alleged child support obligation to another woman in calculating child support to be paid to former wife, absent any evidence to support alleged prior support obligation. Bowen v. Thomas (Marion 1995) 102 Ohio App.3d 196, 656 N.E.2d 1328.

Parties' failure to submit child support computation worksheets as required by statute for purposes of former husband's motion to modify child support would require remand; Court of Appeals was unable to determine with certainty whether financial situation merited modification of child support. Zayed v. Zayed (Cuyahoga 1995) 100 Ohio App.3d 410, 654 N.E.2d 163.

In order to determine whether court abused its discretion in denying modification of child support it is necessary to review, along with record, parties' completed child support computation worksheets, which are required to be submitted by statute. Zayed v. Zayed (Cuyahoga 1995) 100 Ohio App.3d 410, 654 N.E.2d 163.

Juvenile court did not abuse its discretion in parentage action by calculating back child support owed for each year of child's life by use of worksheets with reference to applicable law for each given year, due to dramatic changes in parties' financial situations since child's birth. Seegert v. Zietlow (Cuyahoga 1994) 95 Ohio App.3d 451, 642 N.E.2d 697.

Trial court did not abuse its discretion by adopting referee's calculation of child support obligations that were based on referee's use of child support worksheet mandated by statute, absent any evidence warranting deviation from referee's calculation. Harbeitner v. Harbeitner (Cuyahoga 1994) 94 Ohio App.3d 485, 641 N.E.2d 206, dismissed, appeal not allowed 70 Ohio St.3d 1465, 640 N.E.2d 527.

Trial court's failure to comply with statute by using or consulting required worksheet prior to issuing child support order constituted reversible error. Tobens v. Brill (Auglaize 1993) 89 Ohio App.3d 298, 624 N.E.2d 265.

Court of Appeals could not determine whether trial court erred in ordering former husband to pay any amount of children's uninsured health care costs over $50, where trial court did not follow child support worksheet in arriving at figure that former husband owed for child support, and trial court made no mention that incarcerated former husband had means to pay any child support or any health care costs. Tobens v. Brill (Auglaize 1993) 89 Ohio App.3d 298, 624 N.E.2d 265.

Child support worksheet, as required by statute, must actually be completed for child support order to be made. Tobens v. Brill (Auglaize 1993) 89 Ohio App.3d 298, 624 N.E.2d 265.

Lack of child support worksheets in record and lack of findings of fact supporting deviation downward from Child Support Guidelines recommended amount of $1,108 per month prevented Court of Appeals from having way of reviewing lower court's calculation of support, thus requiring reversal and remand for completion of worksheet, which should have been included in record. Ingalls v. Ingalls (Cuyahoga 1993) 88 Ohio App.3d 570, 624 N.E.2d 368.

Failure to include child support worksheet in record on appeal required reversal and remand for completion of worksheet. McClain v. McClain (Summit 1993) 87 Ohio App.3d 856, 623 N.E.2d 242.

RC 3113.215(E) basically provides a sample worksheet and although it contains signature lines for each party and lines for the notarization of each party's signature the statute does not require a party to sign the worksheet. Stewart v Stewart, Nos. 16649 and 16769, 1998 WL 177558 (2d Dist Ct App, Montgomery, 4-17-98).

RC 3113.215(E) requires the trial court to deduct the child care credit from work-related child care expense before calculating the parties' child support obligation. DeWine v Bennett, No. 96 CA 124, 1997 WL 435701 (2d Dist Ct App, Greene, 8-1-97).

A trial court may not automatically deviate from the amount on line twenty-four of the section (E) worksheet to credit a parent's child support obligation for the time the child resides with the parent; the credit may only be given when a trial court finds that the line twenty-four amount is unjust, inappropriate, and not in the best interest of the child and indicates this finding along with findings of fact in its journal entry. Pauly v Pauly, No. L-95-293, 1996 WL 199185 (6th Dist Ct App, Lucas, 4-26-96), affirmed by 80 Ohio St.3d 386 (1997).

Failure to complete the child support worksheet and make it part of the record constitutes reversible error. Wegner v Heischman, No. 17076, 1995 WL 569119 (9th Dist Ct App, Summit, 9-27-95).

A child support computation worksheet required to be used by a trial court in calculating the amount of an obligor's child support obligation in accordance with RC 3113.215 must actually be completed and made part of the trial court's record. Ober v Ausra, No. 94-P-0037, 1994 WL 738479 (11th Dist Ct App, Portage, 12-23-94).

In a parentage action in juvenile court to establish paternity and to recover past child support, an award of "arrearages" of $4000 for ten and one-half years for a total of $42,000 is an abuse of discretion where the child support worksheet imputes to the father an income of $50,000 per year since the birth of the child, tax returns indicate past income levels considerably less than the imputed amount, and the worksheet does not reflect support payments the father has already made. Harris v Knights, No. 64268, 1994 WL 50699 (8th Dist Ct App, Cuyahoga, 2-17-94).

Where trial court did not include in record worksheet required for calculating child support obligation pursuant to RC 3113.215, and trial court's calculation of change in parents' incomes is not provided for under child support computation worksheet, trial court's judgment is reversed and remanded for calculation and award of support in accordance with procedures set forth in RC 3113.215. Straube v Straube, No. S-92-43, 1993 WL 355648 (6th Dist Ct App, Sandusky, 9-17-93).

Under RC 3113.215, a court that changes the referee's computations must complete a new child support computation worksheet for the parties and appellate court to review. Grant v McNeil, No. CA-9038, 1993 WL 221290 (5th Dist Ct App, Stark, 6-14-93).

Failure by the juvenile court to enter the child support computation worksheet completed by the guardian ad litem into evidence as prescribed by the "literal requirements" of RC 3113.215, as well as its failure to enter a separate order with respect to health insurance coverage as required by RC 3113.217(C), constitutes reversible error. In re Cross, No. C-920113 (1st Dist Ct App, Hamilton, 4-28-93).

Where a trial court imputes income to mother and modifies support she should pay to $247.12 per month (which is not the $278 amount to be computed from the child support schedule in RC 3113.215) and where a trial court does not include in the record a worksheet showing its figure, the award is against the manifest weight of evidence and will be reversed and remanded for completion of the worksheet. Pournaras v Pournaras, No. 62285 (8th Dist Ct App, Cuyahoga, 4-8-93).

12. In general

The terms of RC 3113.215 are mandatory in nature and must be followed literally and technically in all material respects. Marker v. Grimm (Ohio 1992) 65 Ohio St.3d 139, 601 N.E.2d 496.

The parties to a separation agreement may not abrogate the right of a minor child of the marriage to be supported by either parent; prior to the effective date of RC 3113.215 to 3113.218, the parties could, however, agree to allocate the support obligation between themselves in a manner analogous to an indemnity agreement. In re Dissolution of Marriage of Lazor (Ohio 1991) 59 Ohio St.3d 201, 572 N.E.2d 66.

"In-gross child support orders" are orders for one amount of child support entered for multiple children, as opposed to a specific, or per-child order, which specifies an amount of support for each child. Lytle v. Lytle (Ohio App. 10 Dist. 1998) 130 Ohio App.3d 697, 720 N.E.2d 1007.

Trial court must calculate a child support arrearage on the basis of the express language of the most recent court entry relating to the issue of child support; this allows court to change a per-child support order to an in-gross order, or vice versa. Lytle v. Lytle (Ohio App. 10 Dist. 1998) 130 Ohio App.3d 697, 720 N.E.2d 1007.

Presumption that a residential parent's child support obligation is spent on the child is inapplicable under a shared parenting order. Beard v. Beard (Ohio App. 11 Dist. 1998) 130 Ohio App.3d 102, 719 N.E.2d 625.

Appellate review of reasonableness of trial court's award of temporary support in divorce action was precluded by form of award, where trial court addressed temporary child support and spousal support together without indicating which portion of $3,200 monthly award was allocated to each. Zeefe v. Zeefe (Ohio App. 8 Dist. 1998) 125 Ohio App.3d 600, 709 N.E.2d 208.

Arrangement under which court orders party to child support proceeding to relinquish claim to property in lieu of making regular payments toward support, is not "child support order" for purposes of statute governing modification of child support orders. Faulkner v. Faulkner (Clermont 1996) 114 Ohio App.3d 216, 683 N.E.2d 31.

The purpose of the child support system is to protect the child and his or her best interest. Richardson v. Ballard (Butler 1996) 113 Ohio App.3d 552, 681 N.E.2d 507.

Failure of child support obligor to request hearing on determination of amount of future child support constituted waiver. State ex rel. Scioto County Child Support Enforcement Agency v.Gardner (Scioto 1996) 113 Ohio App.3d 46, 680 N.E.2d 221.

Children's psychological care was not "medical, optical, hospital, dental, or prescription services" under child support order and, thus, support obligor could not be compelled to pay portion of uninsured medical expenses for children's psychological care. Myers v. Moschella (Hamilton 1996) 112 Ohio App.3d 75, 677 N.E.2d 1243.

Court is not required to include child's financial resources when determining child support. Powell v. Powell (Athens 1996) 111 Ohio App.3d 418, 676 N.E.2d 556.

For purposes of reviewing trial court's decision whether to include child's financial resources when determining child support obligation, all cases should be evaluated in view of their unique facts and circumstances. Powell v. Powell (Athens 1996) 111 Ohio App.3d 418, 676 N.E.2d 556.

Procedure for computing child support obligations set forth in governing statute is mandatory, and its terms must be followed literally and technically in all material aspects. McQuinn v. McQuinn (Butler 1996) 110 Ohio App.3d 296, 673 N.E.2d 1384.

Four years after dissolution of parties' marriage, Court of Common Pleas did not have jurisdiction to decide parentage and ultimately award child support for child conceived after dissolution through artificial insemination. Bailey v. Bailey (Lawrence 1996) 109 Ohio App.3d 569, 672 N.E.2d 747.

In order for trial court to maintain continuing jurisdiction over issue of child support, there must have been minor child either born or conceived prior to entry of final judgment in dissolution. Bailey v. Bailey (Lawrence 1996) 109 Ohio App.3d 569, 672 N.E.2d 747.

Where trial court follows statutory guidelines for calculating child support, designating one parent, particularly one who earns significantly more than the other, as obligor in shared parenting situation is not ipso facto unconstitutional or abuse of discretion. Fallang v. Fallang (Butler 1996) 109 Ohio App.3d 543, 672 N.E.2d 730, dismissed, appeal not allowed 76 Ohio St.3d 1434, 667 N.E.2d 985.

Money received by father following exercise of his stock option qualified as "nonrecurring income" for purposes of determining whether to modify his child support obligation; father had apparently only exercised his stock option on two occasions, and fact that he accumulated options over period of time in excess of three years did not require option to be treated as income, particularly as he earned no income on options until market value of stock exceeded option price, such that he received no value for accumulated shares of stock until he exercised his stock option. Yost v. Unanue (Stark 1996) 109 Ohio App.3d 294, 671 N.E.2d 1374.

Amended statute governing parental duty to support children should be read to incorporate broad definition of "child support order" contained in statute governing calculation of child support obligation. Mazzuckelli v. Mazzuckelli (Hamilton 1995) 106 Ohio App.3d 554, 666 N.E.2d 620.

Trial court's refusal to give father credit toward his child support obligation for value of child-care services he provided was not against manifest weight of evidence, though father claimed that parties had agreed that he provided child care in lieu of child support obligations, where mother did not testify on agreement, father paid no rent and only minimal contribution to household expenses while residing with mother and her children during his unemployment, and duration of his unemployment was disputed; father failed to provide transcript of proceedings for meaningful review of weight of evidence. Helton v. Helton (Hamilton 1994) 102 Ohio App.3d 733, 658 N.E.2d 1.

Mere fact that ex-wife's housing expenses were allegedly subsidized by her parents, who allowed wife and her children to live in home which parents owned for less than its fair market value, did not necessitate reduction in husband's child support obligation, though ex-wife's housing arrangements with her parents resulted in savings to wife, in light of husband's failure to stay current on child support obligation, including obligation to repay support arrearages. Mallin v. Mallin (Cuyahoga 1995) 102 Ohio App.3d 717, 657 N.E.2d 856.

Trial court may not simply find lack of any evidence upon which to determine party's income and then arbitrarily assign court's own figures to determine child support. Bowen v. Thomas (Marion 1995) 102 Ohio App.3d 196, 656 N.E.2d 1328.

Trial court erred in including expenses for 1993 calendar year in support obligor's 1992 gross income; trial court could use only obligor's income and ordinary and necessary expenses for one year in determining the amount of "gross income" for that year. Houts v. Houts (Mercer 1995) 99 Ohio App.3d 701, 651 N.E.2d 1031, appeal not allowed 72 Ohio St.3d 1529, 649 N.E.2d 838.

Obligor's disposable income and disposable earnings are not considered in determining amount of child support owed. Seegert v. Zietlow (Cuyahoga 1994) 95 Ohio App.3d 451, 642 N.E.2d 697.

In split custody arrangement, even though only one parent actually pays child support, both parents have support obligations flowing to children, and court implicitly orders nonpaying parent to "pay" support to paying parent by reducing paying parent's support obligation. Beckley v. Beckley (Greene 1993) 90 Ohio App.3d 202, 628 N.E.2d 135.

Divorce court is within its discretion to arrive at amounts of spousal support and child support based on different calculations, since calculation for child support is based upon actual wages earned, whereas calculation of spousal support is determined by earning capacity. Frost v. Frost (Franklin 1992) 84 Ohio App.3d 699, 618 N.E.2d 198, motion overruled 66 Ohio St.3d 1489, 612 N.E.2d 1245.

"Calendar year," used for purposes of child support calculation, may or may not coincide with tax year. Frost v. Frost (Franklin 1992) 84 Ohio App.3d 699, 618 N.E.2d 198, motion overruled 66 Ohio St.3d 1489, 612 N.E.2d 1245.

Although court-ordered child support is for the benefit of the children and therefore future obligations cannot be waived by the parents, the custodial parent is nevertheless empowered in certain circumstances to forgive past arrearages. Nelson v. Nelson (Lake 1990) 65 Ohio App.3d 800, 585 N.E.2d 502.

The guidelines set forth in C P Sup R 75 are just that—guidelines; they are not intended to supplant the requirement in RC 3109.05 that courts must consider all relevant factors in determining the amount reasonable or necessary for child support, including the factors expressly stated in the statute. Wogoman v. Wogoman (Miami 1989) 44 Ohio App.3d 34, 541 N.E.2d 128.

Set-off of a wife's judgment of $3475 for attorney fees against the husband's obligation for back child support in the amount of $3080 is within the court's discretion where (1) the action involves the same parties, (2) the amount of debt owed to each party is comparable, and (3) the children are now emancipated; furthermore, a spouse's claim that the husband fails to submit $10,000 worth of medical expenses to his medical insurance carrier must fail where the husband acknowledges that he received the statements but could not submit them to the insurance carrier for reimbursement because they were not bills but statements of charges. Lieberman v Lieberman, No. 74181, 1999 WL 342238 (8th Dist Ct App, Cuyahoga, 5-27-99).

The parent in a shared parenting plan with the greater child support obligation, after being given credit for the time that the child lives with him or her, is the obligor parent, and the obligor parent is required to pay as child support only the difference between his or her greater obligation and the other parent's lesser obligation. Leis v Leis, No. 96-CA-20, 1997 WL 335145 (2d Dist Ct App, Miami, 6-20-97).

A residential parent is entitled to a reduction of the child support obligation in proportion to the time the children reside with the parent. Beard v Beard, No. 96-P-0011, 1997 WL 184766 (11th Dist Ct App, Portage, 4-4-97).

Failure to issue a separate order allocating responsibility for a child's extraordinary medical expenses is error where the court orders a parent to pay one-half of "all uncovered medical expenses, both ordinary and extraordinary" in addition to the amount of child support calculated pursuant to the guidelines. Helfrich v Helfrich, No. 95APF12-1599, 1996 WL 532185 (10th Dist Ct App, Franklin, 9-17-96).

RC 3113.215 requires a standing order to be issued at the time child support is decided regarding the amount and the person responsible for extraordinary medical expenses. Sullivan v Walker, No. 17401, 1996 WL 199556 (9th Dist Ct App, Summit, 4-24-96).

RC 3113.215(B)(5)(f) does not prohibit the parties to a separation agreement from agreeing that one party will pay all of the children's uninsured medical expenses, however, where a court later modifies the amount of child support pursuant to the guidelines, it may not order an additional amount of child support for uninsured medical expenses. Thompson v Thompson, No. 93CA21, 1994 WL 649273 (4th Dist Ct App, Pickaway, 11-14-94).

A father's supplemental security income cannot be included in any calculation of gross income for child support purposes pursuant to RC 3113.215. Chauncey v Chauncey, No. 66197, 1994 WL 530900 (8th Dist Ct App, Cuyahoga, 9-29-94).

It is not an abuse of discretion for a trial court to use the schedule and worksheet in RC 3113.215 to calculate child support arrearages for the years before the statute became law; RC 3113.215 nowhere limits the use of its schedule and worksheet to prospective child support. Persinger v Miller, No. 1305 (2d Dist Ct App, Darke, 3-8-93).

Failure to follow the guidelines for child support in C P Sup R 75 is not error where said guidelines were not in effect at the time of the decree. Jones v Jones, No. 87AP080065 (5th Dist Ct App, Tuscarawas, 4-25-88).

13. Deviation from guidelines

In granting mother's motion to increase child support under shared parenting plan entered pursuant to divorce decree, trial court acted within its discretion in refusing to deviate from amount of child support calculated under statutory schedule and worksheet and grant father credit for extra time children had resided with him. Pauly v. Pauly (Ohio 1997) 80 Ohio St.3d 386, 686 N.E.2d 1108.

Subsection of child support statute expressly stating that it is to be used to calculate child support in cases in which "shared parenting order" has been issued, rather than subsection providing right to offset in child support obligations where parties have "split parental rights and responsibilities," governs computation of child support payments under shared parenting order. Pauly v. Pauly (Ohio 1997) 80 Ohio St.3d 386, 686 N.E.2d 1108.

Statute governing calculation of child support payments under shared parenting order does not provide for automatic credit in parent's child support obligation for time child resides with such parent; however, trial court may deviate from amount of child support calculated under such statute if court finds that amount of child support would be unjust or inappropriate to children or either parent and would not be in best interest of child. Pauly v. Pauly (Ohio 1997) 80 Ohio St.3d 386, 686 N.E.2d 1108.

In determining whether allowance of deduction for acquisition of capital asset by self-employed child support obligor against obligor's gross receipts is grounds for deviation from child support guidelines, trial court may consider, among other factors, comparison of cost of capital asset versus obligor's gross income, comparison of such cost versus new worth of obligor's business, existence of past pattern of acquisition of capital assets as deductions, proximity in time of acquisition of capital asset to date of termination of child support obligation, analysis of necessity of capital asset to maintain or increase past or current levels of income production, and whether capital asset is acquired from current year's income or out of past years' retained savings. Kamm v. Kamm (Ohio 1993) 67 Ohio St.3d 174, 616 N.E.2d 900, on remand.

Deviation from the child support guidelines, set forth in C P Sup R 75, by using a father's net income where the father's living expenses are substantially higher than the mother's due to geographic differences does not constitute an abuse of discretion. Booth v. Booth (Ohio 1989) 44 Ohio St.3d 142, 541 N.E.2d 1028.

Upward deviation in former husband's child support obligation, occasioned by requirement that he pay half of child's tutoring expenses, was just, appropriate, and in child's best interest, where child had failed first grade and was in danger of failing again. Burns v. May (Ohio App. 12 Dist. 1999) 133 Ohio App.3d 351, 728 N.E.2d 19.

Calculation of father's child support by using the income amount father provided on his financial disclosure affidavit and his W-2 form, rather than a higher amount determined by the trial court based on the father's testimony, was not an abuse of discretion; father supported his financial affidavit with appropriate documents, his documentation was from his present employer and represented his current position with that employer, his paycheck stubs demonstrated that his weekly pay fluctuated, and his testimony at trial verified that fluctuation. Clark v. Smith (Ohio App. 3 Dist. 1998) 130 Ohio App.3d 648, 720 N.E.2d 973.

Provisions of statute setting forth guidelines for calculation of child support payments are to be strictly construed by courts in order to ensure uniform, consistent, and fair child support orders, and failure to comply with requirements of statute constitutes reversible error. State ex rel. Scioto County Child Support Enforcement Agency v.Gardner (Scioto 1996) 113 Ohio App.3d 46, 680 N.E.2d 221.

Modified amount of child support was reasonable in light of reasonable needs of children and lifestyle the family had lived during the marriage, despite mother's contention that trial court should not have deviated downward from child support guidelines percentage and despite father's contention that trial court should have deviated further. Schultz v. Schultz (Franklin 1996) 110 Ohio App.3d 715, 675 N.E.2d 55.

It was fair for trial court determining children's expenses in order to compute father's modified child support obligation to divide the common expenses by three, to account for mother and each child of the marriage, despite father's contention that children did not consume two thirds of expenses such as mortgage, car insurance, and car lease payment; children derived benefit from those expenses, which were necessary expenses for their lifestyle. Schultz v. Schultz (Franklin 1996) 110 Ohio App.3d 715, 675 N.E.2d 55.

Child support obligation must be determined on case-by-case basis when combined gross income of both parents is greater than $150,000, but award may not be less than child support guidelines percentage of parents' combined annual income, unless court determines that such award would be unjust, inappropriate, or not in the best interest of children, obligor, or obligee. Schultz v. Schultz (Franklin 1996) 110 Ohio App.3d 715, 675 N.E.2d 55.

Decision whether to deviate from child support guidelines is within trial court's discretion. Carpenter v. Reis (Lucas 1996) 109 Ohio App.3d 499, 672 N.E.2d 702.

Any court-ordered deviation from applicable worksheet and basic child support schedule must be entered by court in its journal and must include findings of fact to support determination. In re Krechting (Clermont 1996) 108 Ohio App.3d 435, 670 N.E.2d 1081.

Trial court could not order ex-husband to visit his multihandicapped child as a form of child support; determination of child support obligation was governed by comprehensive statutory scheme that did not provide for visitation as a form of support. Hamilton v. Hamilton

(Lucas 1995) 107 Ohio App.3d 132, 667 N.E.2d 1256, appeal not allowed 75 Ohio St.3d 1425, 662 N.E.2d 27.

Trial court has discretionary authority, upon motion to modify child support, to deviate from child support amount computed under statute governing such computation and allow residential parent any amounts incurred for respite care due to nonresidential parent's failure to exercise overnight visitation rights. Hamilton v. Hamilton (Lucas 1995) 107 Ohio App.3d 132, 667 N.E.2d 1256, appeal not allowed 75 Ohio St.3d 1425, 662 N.E.2d 27.

In computing child support, obligor was not entitled to have amount deducted from his gross income for support paid to minor child born of prior marriage where obligor provided insufficient verifying documentation of that preexisting child support obligation. Snyder v. Snyder (Ashtabula 1995) 105 Ohio App.3d 69, 663 N.E.2d 695.

Finding that child support obligee's estimated gross income was $17,387 was supported by evidence that obligee earned $8.68 per hour and worked 35 to 37 hours per week at one job, that temporary job paid obligee additional $900 per year, and that trial court's estimated calculation fell within actual calculated range of $16,697.60 to $17,600.32. Snyder v. Snyder (Ashtabula 1995) 105 Ohio App.3d 69, 663 N.E.2d 695.

Father's annual payments on student loans were not deductible from father's income for purposes of determining his child support obligation. Cuyahoga Cty. Support Enforcement Agency v. Lozada (Cuyahoga 1995) 102 Ohio App.3d 442, 657 N.E.2d 372.

Although amount of child support father was obligated to pay was more than ten percent less than amount of support he would be obligated to pay under current guidelines, deviation did not justify modifying support order, where deviation was within contemplation of court and parties when original support order was issued. Baire v. Baire (Greene 1995) 102 Ohio App.3d 50, 656 N.E.2d 984.

Deviation, between amount child support obligor would be required to pay in accordance with current statutory schedule and worksheet and amount he or she is actually obligated to pay, is insufficient to justify modification of support order, unless change of circumstance was not contemplated when original support order was made. Baire v. Baire (Greene 1995) 102 Ohio App.3d 50, 656 N.E.2d 984.

When calculating child support, court must strictly comply with statutory mandates for calculating child support. Houts v. Houts (Mercer 1995) 99 Ohio App.3d 701, 651 N.E.2d 1031, appeal not allowed 72 Ohio St.3d 1529, 649 N.E.2d 838.

Statute providing that, if combined gross income of both parents is less than $6,600 per year, court shall determine amount of obligor's child support obligation on case-by-case basis and shall review obligor's gross income and living expenses to determine maximum amount of child support that it reasonably can order without denying obligor the means for self-support did not apply to case where father's Voluntary Separation Incentive (VSI) payments, offered by the armed forces to encourage a reduction in force, alone were about $17,400 annually. McClure v. McClure (Greene 1994) 98 Ohio App.3d 27, 647 N.E.2d 832, appeal not allowed 71 Ohio St.3d 1481, 645 N.E.2d 1260.

In deviating downward in parentage proceeding from presumably correct amount of child support owed pursuant to child support guidelines, juvenile court erred reversibly in failing to explicitly find that deviation was in best interest of child. Seegert v. Zietlow (Cuyahoga 1994) 95 Ohio App.3d 451, 642 N.E.2d 697.

Trial court which adopted shared-parenting plan granting residential status to father during school year and to mother during summer months could properly determine that strict application of child support guidelines would be inappropriate and accordingly deny child support to father under circumstances that parties stipulated that cost of children's parochial education would be shared in proportion to their relative incomes, both parties were required to carry medical insurance for children, and parties were required to share cost of clothing, school supplies and other ordinary expenses. Eickelberger v. Eickelberger (Butler 1994) 93 Ohio App.3d 221, 638 N.E.2d 130.

Common pleas court's local rule governing child support during visitation when parents resided more than 150 miles apart violated purpose and intent of state statute governing child support, insofar as rule suspended child support during visitation; rationale behind the rule was arbitrary and unreasonable when order was applied without individualized consideration of facts of each case. Gatliff v. Gatliff (Hancock 1993) 89 Ohio App.3d 391, 624 N.E.2d 779.

Trial court's failure to provide for any visitation schedule in its child support order was reversible error, since statutory terms requiring that visitation schedule be devised are mandatory in nature. Tobens v. Brill (Auglaize 1993) 89 Ohio App.3d 298, 624 N.E.2d 265.

Husband's child support obligation provided by statutory child support guidelines could be reduced in dissolution of marriage proceeding by amount husband expended pursuant to separation agreement toward payment of mortgage on former marital residence, taxes, insurance, and maintenance of residence, despite fact that husband would ultimately receive financial gain resulting from those payments because he would have his equity redeemed. In re Marriage of Stearns (Franklin 1993) 88 Ohio App.3d 264, 623 N.E.2d 711.

Trial court did not abuse its discretion in failing to deviate from amount of child support as calculated pursuant to statute, but, rather, trial court satisfied requirement of determining obligation on case-by-case basis in case in which combined gross income of both parents exceeded $120,000 annually; evidence was presented as to standard of living of former spouses and their children, their expenses, and monetary contributions made by both spouses for their eldest daughter's show horse. Parzynski v. Parzynski (Erie 1992) 85 Ohio App.3d 423, 620 N.E.2d 93, dismissed, jurisdictional motion overruled 67 Ohio St.3d 1450, 619 N.E.2d 419, rehearing denied 67 Ohio St.3d 1513, 622 N.E.2d 660.

While statute allows trial court to deviate from amount of child support calculated from schedules and worksheet and in so deviating to consider amount of tax that party actually paid, any such deviation is determined after child support obligation is calculated, not in trial court's computation of parties' gross income. Parzynski v. Parzynski (Erie 1992) 85 Ohio App.3d 423, 620 N.E.2d 93, dismissed, jurisdictional motion overruled 67 Ohio St.3d 1450, 619 N.E.2d 419, rehearing denied 67 Ohio St.3d 1513, 622 N.E.2d 660.

Deviation from the child support guidelines to award child care expenses is improper where the court finds the evidence presented as to child care expenses unreliable.

Hockenberry v. Hockenberry (Henry 1992) 75 Ohio App.3d 806, 600 N.E.2d 839.

Although the child support guidelines set forth in C P Sup R 75 are intended to be used by a court to indicate the appropriate level of child support to be ordered, the court still retains broad discretion to deviate from the guidelines if it substantiates its decision by stating its findings of fact; consequently, a child support order which deviates more than forty per cent from the guidelines may not be an abuse of discretion where the child support obligor incurs increased necessary living expenses due to relocation and remarriage. Hurdelbrink v. Hurdelbrink (Lucas 1989) 45 Ohio App.3d 5, 544 N.E.2d 700, motion overruled 44 Ohio St.3d 715, 542 N.E.2d 1112.

Ordering the mother as the obligee to return one-half of the monthly child support obligation to the father as the obligor during the eight week period of time the minor children will reside with the father during the summer amounts to a deviation and violates the purpose and intent of the statute governing child support as the mother's obligation to provide a custodial residence and other necessities for the children during the period of time in question will not be diminished. Gordon v Gordon, No. 97-JE-31, 2000 WL 34133 (7th Dist Ct App, Jefferson, 3-31-00).

An order for monthly child support is inappropriate in light of the fact that child care costs and needs are provided entirely by medical insurance for a child who has been hospitalized since birth with a severe medical condition. Nienaber v Hestand, No. CA98-12-118, 1999 WL 326190 (12th Dist Ct App, Clermont, 5-17-99).

If less than the statutory guideline amount of child support is being received because of a miscalculation, the custodial parent should not be required to show an increased need of child support to begin receiving the increased amount that is correctly calculated in accordance with the guidelines. Smith v Smith, No. 16183, 1997 WL 435697 (2d Dist Ct App, Montgomery, 7-25-97).

Deviation from child support guidelines is proper in ordering a parent to pay private school tuition where (1) it is in the children's best interest to remain enrolled in private schools considering the level of education they have received during the marriage, (2) the parties can afford to continue the tuition and divide the tuition expenses in proportion to their respective incomes, and (3) the court's order does not extend the tuition payments to education beyond high school. Kaminski v Kaminski, No. CA96-09-073, 1997 WL 89156 (12th Dist Ct App, Clermont, 3-3-97).

Unique musical ability does not constitute special or unusual needs of the child and a further downward deviation in child support for private music lessons is inappropriate. Donaldson v Donaldson, No. 96APF06-766, 1997 WL 35539 (10th Dist Ct App, Franklin, 1-30-97).

Legal enforceability of an obligor's debt to his parents is irrelevant in a court's decision as to whether deviation from child support guidelines is in order. Fitzgerald v Fitzgerald, No. 15982, 1997 WL 24807 (2d Dist Ct App, Montgomery, 1-24-97).

"One-time" earnings of a bonus and dividends which occur not long after the final decree but before a motion to modify are to be considered for purposes of deviating from the child support worksheet. Schneeberger v Schneeberger, No. 70525, 1996 WL 732439 (8th Dist Ct App, Cuyahoga, 12-19-96).

A cost of living adjustment in money values given an obligor for service in the military in Germany is not a cost of living adjustment as contemplated by RC 3113.215 and monies derived from the foreign exchange rate should be disregarded in computing the amount of child support. Ford v Ford, No. 15613, 1996 WL 685787 (2d Dist Ct App, Montgomery, 11-22-96).

A father's voluntary contributions to his teenage daughter's various expenses, along with his contributions to his other children's expenses does not alter his legal obligation to provide support for his minor daughter, and the fact that he chose to contribute more than his legal share of child support does not compel a reduction in his share of child support at a later time, and so circumstances did not require the trial court to deviate from the magistrate's calculations based upon principles of equity. Holt v Troha, No. 96-CA-19, 1996 WL 430866 (2d Dist Ct App, Greene, 8-2-96).

A court errs by deviating from the child support guideline amount of $451.52 per month where the obligor's disabled child receives SSI benefits. Smith v Smith, No. 94-J-9, 1996 WL 71068 (7th Dist Ct App, Jefferson, 2-15-96).

A trial court's deviation from the child support worksheet and its determination that the obligor owes no further retroactive support are valid where (1) the guidelines did not exist in Ohio for the first few years the obligee was seeking retroactive child support, (2) payments were made during the years in question, (3) additional payments were made into an investment account for the child, (4) the obligee accepted these payments without question, and (5) the obligee waited nearly nine years to file an action against the defendant. Hancock v Grimm, No. C-940956, 1995 WL 757833 (1st Dist Ct App, Hamilton, 12-20-95).

A father's continued payment of child support while he has extended summer visitation with his son is not inappropriate; in addition, a court is within its discretion in finding that an eight-year-old child lacks sufficient reasoning ability to make an informed choice with respect to who would be his residential parent. Dicke v Dicke, No. 1-95-23, 1995 WL 657112 (3d Dist Ct App, Allen, 11-7-95).

Worksheet calculations pertaining to child care and health insurance are reversed and remanded for recalculation where the trial court does not deduct the child care tax credit as required by line 18 of the worksheet and on line 19, the figure for the children's health insurance coverage is not specified. Clay v Clay, No. 17014, 1995 WL 434404 (9th Dist Ct App, Summit, 7-19-95).

In a shared parenting situation, a trial court may deviate from the child support schedule and reduce the statutory support obligation by twenty-five per cent, where the obligor also pays spousal support, pays for all child care expenses and provides medical and dental insurance for the children. Clay v Clay, No. 17014, 1995 WL 434404 (9th Dist Ct App, Summit, 7-19-95).

Suspension of court-ordered support during a child's seasonal vacation period is a deviation from child support guidelines and is without statutory authority. In re Price, No. 9-94-44, 1995 WL 81973 (3d Dist Ct App, Marion, 2-13-95).

The use of two worksheets, calculated subsequent to an original child support order, indicates that there were at least two motions to modify before a trial court, and such use of two different worksheets, when only one motion to modify was pending before the court, does not constitute a deviation as contemplated by RC 3113.215. Justinger v Schlegel, No. 11-94-2, 1994 WL 521205 (3d Dist Ct App, Paulding, 9-26-94).

In an action to modify child support where there is no prior worksheet calculation available, it is reversible error for the trial court to use two different worksheets to arrive at the support figure when only one motion for modification was filed; the use of two worksheets does not constitute a justifiable deviation as contemplated by RC 3113.215(B)(3). Justinger v Schlegel, No. 11-94-2, 1994 WL 521205 (3d Dist Ct App, Paulding, 9-26-94).

The trial court erred where it included a husband's navy disability benefit in the calculation of the husband's gross income for purposes of child support, in violation of RC 3113.215. Kennedy v Kennedy, No. 93FU000002, 1993 WL 553608 (6th Dist Ct App, Fulton, 12-30-93).

A local rule which provides for the mandatory suspension of support payments during all but the first week of extended visitation under "long-distance parenting" which applies in situations where the parents live more than 150 miles apart violates the purpose and intent of RC 3113.215 because it does not provide for individualized consideration of the facts of each case and favors obligors living a considerable distance from their children who actually spend fewer days per year with their children than those covered by a more typical visitation schedule providing for visitation of 2-3 days per week, assorted holidays, and a few week long visits during summer vacation. Gatliff v Gatliff, No. 5-93-4, 1993 WL 323693 (3d Dist Ct App, 8-23-93).

The child support guidelines are not a mathematical straitjacket, and the refusal of a domestic relations court to consider evidence supporting deviation from the guidelines constitutes an abuse of discretion. Oyer v Oyer, No. CA88-03-007 (12th Dist Ct App, Madison, 9-19-88).

14. Child's social security benefits

Ex-husband, as disabled parent, was entitled to a full credit in his child support obligation for Social Security payments received by minor child due to his disability. Williams v. Williams (Ohio 2000) 88 Ohio St.3d 441, 727 N.E.2d 895.

Social Security payments made on a minor child's behalf, due to a parent's disability, are not mere gratuities from the federal government, nor do they constitute earnings by the child, for child support purposes; instead, the payments arise simply because the obligor has paid into the Social Security system and was found to be disabled. Williams v. Williams (Ohio 2000) 88 Ohio St.3d 441, 727 N.E.2d 895.

Social Security payments made on a minor child's behalf, due to a parent's disability, are tantamount to earnings by the disabled parent, for purposes of determining parent's child support obligation. Williams v. Williams (Ohio 2000) 88 Ohio St.3d 441, 727 N.E.2d 895.

Granting a disabled parent a credit for Social Security benefits does not retroactively modify the disabled parent's monthly child support obligation; it merely changes the source of the payments. Williams v. Williams (Ohio 2000) 88 Ohio St.3d 441, 727 N.E.2d 895.

Mere fact that husband had financial resources to pay child support was not adequate factual finding to support determination that amount of child support provided by Social Security benefits paid as result of husband's disability was unjust and not in child's best interest, and thus trial court abused its discretion in modifying husband's support obligation to require him to pay $175 per month, where child's Social Security benefits exceeded guideline-determined necessary support, child received substantial increase in support as result of Social Security benefits, and husband's income and financial resources had not increased since support order had last been modified. Fruchtnicht v. Fruchtnicht (Ohio App. 12 Dist. 1997) 122 Ohio App.3d 492, 702 N.E.2d 145.

Husband was entitled to reimbursement of child support overpayment that resulted from child's receipt of lump sum payment of back Social Security benefits, paid as result of husband's disability, where husband paid his child support obligation during period while his social security application was pending. Fruchtnicht v. Fruchtnicht (Ohio App. 12 Dist. 1997) 122 Ohio App.3d 492, 702 N.E.2d 145.

Financial resources and earning ability of a child include Social Security benefits received by a child due to the disability of a parent, for purposes of determining whether to deviate from amount of support calculated under child support guidelines. Fruchtnicht v. Fruchtnicht (Ohio App. 12 Dist. 1997) 122 Ohio App.3d 492, 702 N.E.2d 145.

Trial court did not abuse its discretion by failing to give former husband credit for son's Supplemental Security Income (SSI) benefits when calculating husband's child support arrearage and obligation as to son, who was born with spina bifida; trial court's judgment was not unreasonable, arbitrary, or unconscionable, Court of Appeals would not substitute its judgment for that of trial court, and facts did not support conclusion that child support award was inequitable or resulted in windfall. Powell v. Powell (Athens 1996) 111 Ohio App.3d 418, 676 N.E.2d 556.

Trial court could consider Social Security disability benefits received by child due to stepfather's disability in determining whether to depart downward from guideline amount of support in modifying divorce decree to require child support from mother upon transfer of custody to father. Carpenter v. Reis (Lucas 1996) 109 Ohio App.3d 499, 672 N.E.2d 702.

Governmental benefits received by child due to disability or retirement of child support obligor or child support obligee are "financial resource" of the child that must be considered by trial court when deciding whether to deviate from statutorily determined child support amount. Carpenter v. Reis (Lucas 1996) 109 Ohio App.3d 499, 672 N.E.2d 702.

Trial court had to consider whether social security payments received by children as result of former husband's disability should be credited against former husband's child support arrearage as of date payments were received by children. Young v. Young (Stark 1995) 105 Ohio App.3d 701, 664 N.E.2d 1323.

Trial court's decision, on former husband's motion to modify his child support obligation after his ex-wife began receiving social security benefits as result of her disability, to offset former husband's support obligation with social security disability benefits that child was receiving on account of wife's disability was not abuse of discretion, notwithstanding wife's contention that setoff resulted in windfall for husband and that benefits should be saved to pay for child's future educational needs, where record was devoid of evidence as to child's educational needs or as to parties' agreement thereto. Previte v. Previte (Lake 1994) 99 Ohio App.3d 347, 650 N.E.2d 919, appeal not allowed 71 Ohio St.3d 1503, 646 N.E.2d 1127, reconsideration denied 72 Ohio St.3d 1422, 648 N.E.2d 515.

Social security payments for a child's benefit must be considered in connection with child support payments ordered to be made by the parent whose retirement triggers the payments, but this does not justify crediting the entire monthly benefit amount to child support, nor is the determination of necessary child support unaffected by the receipt of the benefits; the proper method is to deduct all or part of the benefit amount from the guideline-determined necessary support based on the child's best interest and equity to both parents. McNeal v. Cofield (Franklin 1992) 78 Ohio App.3d 35, 603 N.E.2d 436.

In a case pertaining to the interrelationship between child support and social security disability benefits, entitlement to benefits is determined by the father's disabled status and so the children and not the father are entitled to the funds; therefore, (1) where the obligor receives long-term disability through his former employer due to a diabetic and heart condition, (2) the disability insurance policy contains subrogation language providing that, upon allowance of a claim for social security disability benefits for himself and his children, the insurer could demand reimbursement for benefits previously paid, and (3) the retroactive collateral social security benefits received by the obligor's children are not payable to him to satisfy the private insurance subrogation claim. Rigel v Rigel, No. CT98-0021, 1999 WL 436824 (5th Dist Ct App, Muskingum, 6-23-99).

Social security benefits a child receives on behalf of a parent's disability claim is a financial resource of the child that must be considered by the trial court when calculating the parties' child support obligations or in determining whether to deviate from the child support guideline amount. Barnett v Barnett, No. E-97-050, 1997 WL 679630 (6th Dist Ct App, Erie, 10-31-97).

The father as obligor cannot be credited with social security payments occasioned by the death of the mother and received by the custodial grandparents on behalf of the minor child; such payments should be added to the obligor's annual salary to arrive at an annual child support figure. In re Mudrak, No. 94-B-32, 1997 WL 28557 (7th Dist Ct App, Belmont, 1-22-97).

A court errs in failing to credit a father's arrearage in child support payments with the amount of social security disability benefits received by the mother on behalf of the children as a result of the father's disability. Ledford v Ledford, No. CA95-12-215, 1996 WL 688755 (12th Dist Ct App, Butler, 12-2-96).

Social security disability income received by a child as a result of her father's disability is not support for child support enforcement agency purposes; rather, it is credited towards the total support obligation in the worksheet computation of the father's child support obligation rather than in the monthly payment of that obligation to the child support enforcement agency. McClure v McClure, No. 95-CA-86, 1996 WL 562793 (2d Dist Ct App, Greene, 9-27-96).

Social security payments received by a child from the father's retirement benefits should be subtracted from the total guideline-determined necessary child support in accordance with the McNeal formula, and the remaining child support need should be allocated between the parents by percentages in the manner set forth in the guidelines. Dunn v Taylor, No. CA95-04-062, 1996 WL 12876 (12th Dist Ct App, Butler, 1-16-96).

Retroactive lump sum social security payments to a minor child whose father is receiving social security disability payments should be credited to the father's corresponding past child support and medical expense obligations. Slowbe v Slowbe, No. 68739, 1995 WL 723333 (8th Dist Ct App, Cuyahoga, 12-7-95).

A trial court errs when it fails to consider credit toward child support arrearages for social security payments to the disabled obligor's minor children where the arrearages accrue after the children receive the payments. Young v Young, No. 1995CA00023, 1995 WL 498949 (5th Dist Ct App, Stark, 8-14-95).

An obligor may receive credit for any arrearage incurred during the period encompassed by the lump-sum Social Security payment but not for any arrearage that accrued prior to the obligor's disability. Cook v Cook, No. CA-94-10, 1995 WL 495400 (5th Dist Ct App, Morgan, 5-8-95).

15. Discretion

Award of retroactive child support in total amount of $13,750 for 15-month period was not so unreasonable, arbitrary, or unconscionable as to connote abuse of discretion; pursuant to applicable statutory guidelines and 10 percent rule, obligor parent should have paid between $18,000 and $22,000 per month, and would still have had income of over $2 million per year during period at issue had he done so. Frazier v. Daniels (Ohio App. 1 Dist. 1997) 118 Ohio App.3d 425, 693 N.E.2d 289.

Guidelines for amount of child support are mandatory; however, where annual combined gross income of both parents exceeds $150,000 per year, court has some discretion in setting amount of child support. Frazier v. Daniels (Ohio App. 1 Dist. 1997) 118 Ohio App.3d 425, 693 N.E.2d 289.

Appellate court uses abuse of discretion standard when reviewing matters concerning child support. State ex rel. Scioto County Child Support Enforcement Agency v.Gardner (Scioto 1996) 113 Ohio App.3d 46, 680 N.E.2d 221.

Trial court had discretion to exclude testimony of expert economist who allegedly would have testified that, for income levels that are in excess of $150,000 per year, percentage of income spent on children decreases as opposed to remaining at constant percentage level, where expert had not interviewed the parties, had not studied parties' income and expenses, and would not have given testimony directly related to case at hand. Schultz v. Schultz (Franklin 1996) 110 Ohio App.3d 715, 675 N.E.2d 55.

Court of Appeals reviews factual determinations underlying trial court's child support decisions to determine whether trial court abused its discretion. Mallin v. Mallin (Cuyahoga 1995) 102 Ohio App.3d 717, 657 N.E.2d 856.

On motion to modify child support, determinations and recommendations by referee concerning alleged change in circumstances and imputation of income to child support obligor may not be disturbed on appeal absent abuse of discretion. Zayed v. Zayed (Cuyahoga 1995) 100 Ohio App.3d 410, 654 N.E.2d 163.

Upon calculation of child support by trial court pursuant to child support statute, that court's calculation will not be disturbed on appeal absent abuse of discretion. Houts v. Houts (Mercer 1995) 99 Ohio App.3d 701, 651 N.E.2d 1031, appeal not allowed 72 Ohio St.3d 1529, 649 N.E.2d 838.

Father failed to demonstrate abuse of discretion by juvenile court in parentage proceeding in awarding $3,900 in current child support for year of 1993; pursuant to statutory guidelines, "rebuttably presumed" correct amount was $4,542 for 1993 and, despite father's claims to contrary, his disposable income exceeded amount of child support for that year. Seegert v. Zietlow (Cuyahoga 1994) 95 Ohio App.3d 451, 642 N.E.2d 697.

Shared-parenting order in divorce action was not improper on theory it encouraged excessive entanglement between parties in requiring parties to cooperate and communicate by sharing expenses. Eickelberger v. Eickelberger (Butler 1994) 93 Ohio App.3d 221, 638 N.E.2d 130.

Trial court, in determining former spouses' gross income for child support purposes, did not abuse its discretion in failing to permit evidence as to value of individual retirement accounts (IRAs) that former wife received in property settlement. Parzynski v. Parzynski (Erie 1992) 85 Ohio App.3d 423, 620 N.E.2d 93, dismissed, jurisdictional motion overruled 67 Ohio St.3d 1450, 619 N.E.2d 419, rehearing denied 67 Ohio St.3d 1513, 622 N.E.2d 660.

A child support order requiring a noncustodial father to make payments of $100 each month does not constitute an abuse of discretion despite the custodial mother's claim that since the father previously voluntarily made four $200 payments and one $240 payment that he is able to make $200 child support payments each month; the trial court made specific findings concerning the absence of the father's W-2 forms and tax returns and ordered the father to submit the forms and tax returns to the child support enforcement agency and if the information reveals that the father's income is not what it was alleged to be, the agency may request a modification of the amount of child support. Smith v. Smith (Scioto 1991) 75 Ohio App.3d 679, 600 N.E.2d 396.

A trial court errs in considering a roll over IRA created two years earlier as gross income when calculating child support, and the award must be reversed and remanded for a recalculation of income. Rapp v Rapp, No. CA92-10-092, 1993 WL 304370 (12th Dist Ct App, Warren, 8-9-93).

16. Referee's reports

Trial court did not abuse its discretion in adopting recommendations of referee that husband pay off his child support arrearage in installments added to reduced child support obligation, where recommendation was based on child support computation worksheets and affidavits of income, expenses, and financial disclosure. Helton v. Helton (Hamilton 1994) 102 Ohio App.3d 733, 658 N.E.2d 1.

Allowing former wife to testify that former husband forged certain signatures on financial documents involving former husband and others did not impermissibly shift burden of proof on former husband's motion to modify child support, where referee did not rely on testimony in making his report. Zayed v. Zayed (Cuyahoga 1995) 100 Ohio App.3d 410, 654 N.E.2d 163.

Evidence sustained referee's finding that former husband sold his business for $100,000, not $35,000 as claimed by former husband and as stated in purchase agreement, on former husband's motion to modify child support; lawyer who drafted purchase agreement made contemporaneous note that real purchase price was $100,000, and that there was bag full of cash in his office on date business was transferred. Zayed v. Zayed (Cuyahoga 1995) 100 Ohio App.3d 410, 654 N.E.2d 163.

A referee's report need not recite all the evidence, or absence of evidence, regarding each and every factor mentioned in RC 3109.05 and 3113.215. Smith v. Smith (Scioto 1991) 75 Ohio App.3d 679, 600 N.E.2d 396.

An obligor who has remarried becomes voluntarily unemployed when she terminates her employment due to the fact that she is going to have a child and a trial court abuses discretion in releasing her from her obligation to pay child support for a four-year period; the referee's recommendation of child support suspension for a period of six months is more reasonable. Lalama v Lalama, No. 94-CA-62, 1996 WL 79374 (7th Dist Ct App, Mahoning, 2-23-96).

The trial court erred in adopting the referee's report where the referee had deviated from the amount computed on the child support work sheet to impute a forty-hour work week to appellant for income paid by his parents, as well as refused to set off appellant's real property losses against other sources of self-generated income; RC 3113.215 provides a statutorily defined mechanism to adjust for the appellant's perceived greater resources. Bailey v Bailey, No. 93APF12-1694, 1994 WL 530305 (10th Dist Ct App, Franklin, 9-29-94).

17. Enforcement of agreement

Trial court has obligation to test any proposal of parents to see if it meets Child Support Guidelines even if parties agree between themselves to different amount or agree that only one party shall assume all support. DePalmo v. DePalmo (Ohio 1997) 78 Ohio St.3d 535, 679 N.E.2d 266.

Trial court was required to consider support being paid by father of minor child to child's mother pursuant to agreed settlement entry of previous parentage action in calculating support payable under judgment entered in child's subsequent action to establish parent-child relationship; while prior action was not res judicata with respect to issue of support, both actions served same purpose in that they required payment of money for benefit of child, and child was only entitled to single "support." Cornell v. Brumfield (Ohio App. 4 Dist. 1996) 115 Ohio App.3d 259, 685 N.E.2d 270.

Divorce court had no authority to offset former husband's current child support obligation based on ex-wife's bankruptcy discharge from obligation on which she was to hold former husband harmless pursuant to property settlement provisions of divorce decree. Mallin v. Mallin (Cuyahoga 1995) 102 Ohio App.3d 717, 657 N.E.2d 856.

In determination of husband's past-due child support obligation in dissolution of marriage proceeding, husband was not entitled to credit for payments he made under separation agreement for child's vacation; agreement did not call for vacation expenditures to be considered child support and vacation-related costs were sufficiently different from items which parties considered "miscellaneous expenses" for benefit of children. In re Marriage of Stearns (Franklin 1993) 88 Ohio App.3d 264, 623 N.E.2d 711.

In determination of husband's past-due child support obligation in dissolution of marriage proceeding, husband was entitled to credit as "ordinary medical costs" for one half of payments he made under separation agreement for eyeglasses, driving school, and contact lenses for children. In re Marriage of Stearns (Franklin 1993) 88 Ohio App.3d 264, 623 N.E.2d 711.

A domestic relations court may enforce the provisions of an agreement incorporated to a divorce decree that a parent provide financial support for an incompetent adult child, notwithstanding the fact that the child is an adult at the time the decree is issued and may utilize the child support guidelines to determine the appropriate amount of support. O'Connor v. O'Connor (Franklin

1991) 71 Ohio App.3d 541, 594 N.E.2d 1081, motion overruled 62 Ohio St.3d 1409, 577 N.E.2d 362.

Pursuant to the terms of a joint custody agreement between the parties, husband is obligated to pay not only the costs of the children's private school education but also, in years where there is a tuition waiver due to husband's position at work, he must pay child support in the agreed upon amount of $350 per month, per child, despite additional financial obligations husband incurs. Neiheiser v Neiheiser, No. 75184, 2000 WL 23116 (8th Dist Ct App, Cuyahoga, 1-13-00).

The spouse in a divorce proceeding is not entitled to relief from judgment relating to her distribution from the husband's monthly retirement benefit in absence of irregularity or fraud in procurement of the judgment and where the divorce decree and resulting qualified domestic relations order (QDRO) are consent judgments based upon the parties' settlement agreement. Shanks v Shanks, No. 96CA2252, 1997 WL 114397 (4th Dist Ct App, Ross, 3-10-97).

Medical and dental expenses are part of child support pursuant to a formula within a separation agreement providing that the more paid in child support, the less is to be paid in alimony; therefore, the husband's alimony payments are reduced by the $6310 paid in medical and dental expenses. Caldwell v Caldwell, No. 67920, 1996 WL 38874 (8th Dist Ct App, Cuyahoga, 2-1-96).

A court has power to modify a separation agreement incorporated into a decree of divorce where (1) the parties are among the winners of the Ohio Super Lotto, (2) they agree to divide the winnings, (3) the wife seeks to modify the method by which the lottery winnings are distributed, and (4) the husband refuses to pay his former spouse her share of the proceeds stating, "It's mine, I won it, she doesn't deserve it." Leis v Leis, No. 94CA54, 1995 WL 559974 (2d Dist Ct App, Miami, 9-20-95).

A separation agreement that is made part of a divorce decree and provides for spousal and child support cannot interfere with a trial court's statutory requirement to determine whether the defendant's retirement indeed effected a substantial change in circumstances, even though the agreement states that the forced or voluntary retirement of the husband from the military "shall be considered a substantial change for review of the spousal support provisions at such time." Conway v Conway, No. S-93-37, 1994 WL 159776 (6th Dist Ct App, Sandusky, 4-29-94).

18. Juvenile court

A juvenile court must use the child support guidelines when determining the amount of child support to be awarded. In re Stewart, No. 88 CA 15 (2d Dist Ct App, Greene, 11-23-88).

19. Tax exemptions

Statutory subsection providing that amount of any preexisting child support obligation under child support or spousal support order shall be deducted from gross income of parent to extent that payment under order is verified by supporting documentation was not applicable to authorize reduction of amount of father's gross income in child support calculation for minor child by amount of federal income tax exemption for two other children over the age of 18, where father submitted no supporting documentation to verify existence of preexisting court-ordered child support or court-ordered spousal support obligation. State ex rel. Scioto County Child Support Enforcement Agency v.Gardner (Scioto 1996) 113 Ohio App.3d 46, 680 N.E.2d 221.

Child support provision providing that if parent has other minor children living with him, court shall deduct amount from that parent's gross income that equals number of such minor children times federal income tax exemption for such children, less child support received for them for the year, not exceeding federal income tax exemption, was not applicable to provide deduction for other children who were not minors but who might otherwise qualify parent for tax exemption under federal tax code. State ex rel. Scioto County Child Support Enforcement Agency v.Gardner (Scioto 1996) 113 Ohio App.3d 46, 680 N.E.2d 221.

For purposes of allocating tax dependency exemption, best interest of child is furthered when allocation of exemption to noncustodial parent produces net tax savings for parents. Will v. Will (Jackson 1996) 113 Ohio App.3d 8, 680 N.E.2d 197.

Trial court did not abuse its discretion in refusing to consider income of mother's current husband when determining whether mother or father of child should receive federal tax dependency exemption. Will v. Will (Jackson 1996) 113 Ohio App.3d 8, 680 N.E.2d 197.

State law provides manner in which state court may allocate tax dependency exemption. Will v. Will (Jackson 1996) 113 Ohio App.3d 8, 680 N.E.2d 197.

In order to allocate tax dependency exemption to noncustodial parent, trial court must find that interest of child has been furthered. Will v. Will (Jackson 1996) 113 Ohio App.3d 8, 680 N.E.2d 197.

When determining net tax savings of parents for purposes of allocating tax dependency exemption, trial court should review all pertinent factors including parents' gross incomes, exemptions and deductions to which parents are otherwise entitled and relevant federal, state and local income tax rates. Will v. Will (Jackson 1996) 113 Ohio App.3d 8, 680 N.E.2d 197.

Trial court does not abuse its discretion when allocating tax dependency exemption if court chooses to only look at net tax savings and does not look at additional factors such as determining which parent spends more on child or which parent visits more with child. Will v. Will (Jackson 1996) 113 Ohio App.3d 8, 680 N.E.2d 197.

In computing child support, obligor was entitled to have his gross income reduced by amount equaling the federal income tax exemption for two children where obligor presented undisputed but unverified testimony that two minor children born as issue of his current marriage were living with him. Snyder v. Snyder (Ashtabula 1995) 105 Ohio App.3d 69, 663 N.E.2d 695.

Trial court did not err in splitting children's tax exemptions between father and mother even though father, pursuant to shared-parenting plan, was residential parent of children for nine months of year. Eickelberger v. Eickelberger (Butler 1994) 93 Ohio App.3d 221, 638 N.E.2d 130.

Trial court abused its discretion by ordering that tax dependency exemption alternate between the custodial parent and non-residential parent as the record and transcript did not reveal any evidence regarding any tax savings that would result from awarding the tax dependency exemption to one parent or the other. Pentzer v Pentzer, No. CA99-09-026, 2000 WL 190019 (12th Dist Ct App, Fayette, 2-14-00).

A trial court, at the very least, should consider the gross income of the parents, the exemptions and deductions to which they are otherwise entitled, and the relevant federal, state, and local tax rates when allocating a child dependency exemption to a nonresidential parent; where none of this evidence is introduced during the trial court proceedings, a court errs in its decision to reallocate the income tax dependency exemption. Mills v Mills, No. 16-94-10, 1995 WL 232794 (3d Dist Ct App, Wyandot, 4-18-95).

A trial court's award of dependency tax exemptions to the mother is error where the only evidence offered is the gross income of the parties and the court fails to inquire as to the current expenses of the parties, any other family income, the liabilities and tax obligations of the parties, and the economic impact of the income tax exemption on either party. Saunders v Saunders, No. 94CA005855, 1995 WL 98956 (9th Dist Ct App, Lorain, 3-8-95).

A trial court order alternating the federal income tax dependency exemption between the custodial and noncustodial parent annually must be reversed and remanded where the court considered only the parents' gross incomes, but failed to consider the parties' respective exemptions and deductions, the best interest of the child, and the relevant federal, state, and local income tax rates. Maitlen v Maitlen, No. CA-9347, 1993 WL 564220 (5th Dist Ct App, Stark, 12-30-93).

The child support guidelines, C P Sup R 75, do not address the issue of tax exemptions; accordingly, there is no provision for taking into account the tax exemptions and the tax ramifications of child support in considering at what level to place child support. (Annotation from former C P Sup R 75.) In re Lee (Ohio Com.Pl. 1989) 58 Ohio Misc.2d 4, 567 N.E.2d 1350.

20. Income tax returns

On father's motion to modify his child support obligation, evidence supported finding that mother's earnings did not increase, though father alleged that mother was earning more by babysitting, in light of parties' testimony, federal tax returns, corporate tax returns of father's business, and supporting documents. Matrka v. Matrka (Union 1995) 100 Ohio App.3d 161, 652 N.E.2d 250.

Divorced father seeking to modify child support obligation did not adequately verify current income; trial court relied solely upon father's 1992 tax return and past income and personal earnings; father failed to provide adequate supporting documentation for tax return, and testified that only documentation accountant used in preparing return was computer printout from father's bank reflecting deposits and withdrawals but did not consider cancelled checks or receipts. Houts v. Houts (Mercer 1995) 99 Ohio App.3d 701, 651 N.E.2d 1031, appeal not allowed 72 Ohio St.3d 1529, 649 N.E.2d 838.

Although tax return is proper reference to aid in calculating parent's gross income, it is not sole determining factor of what constitutes parent's gross income or ordinary and necessary expenses. Houts v. Houts (Mercer 1995) 99 Ohio App.3d 701, 651 N.E.2d 1031, appeal not allowed 72 Ohio St.3d 1529, 649 N.E.2d 838.

In calculating an obligor's annual income for the computation of child and spousal support, the trial court is not required to rely exclusively on the obligor's gross income as reported on his previous tax return. Showalter v Showalter, No. CA95-11-082, 1996 WL 679681 (12th Dist Ct App, Clermont, 11-25-96).

For purposes of RC 149.43, federal tax return information filed by an individual pursuant to RC 3113.215(B)(5) and a local rule of court is a public record. OAG 91-053.

26 USC 6103, imposing confidentiality on federal income tax returns, is not applicable to a federal income tax return submitted to a court of common pleas by a litigant in connection with a child support determination or modification proceeding in that court. OAG 91-053.

21. —In general, income

Cost of health care insurance paid by husband to cover parties' minor children had to be included in calculation of wife's child support obligation in divorce proceeding. McQuinn v. McQuinn (Butler 1996) 110 Ohio App.3d 296, 673 N.E.2d 1384.

Trial court's determination of party's annual income in domestic relations case will not be disturbed on appeal without showing of abuse of discretion. Fallang v. Fallang (Butler 1996) 109 Ohio App.3d 543, 672 N.E.2d 730, dismissed, appeal not allowed 76 Ohio St.3d 1434, 667 N.E.2d 985.

Trial court's determination in child support modification case that mother's income was approximately $14,500 was supported by competent, credible evidence; mother testified that her annual income from substitute teaching and part-time summer work was $14,502, mother offered into evidence a pay stub dated December 17, 1994, showing her year-to-date income from teaching to be $13,968.15, and mother also testified that she had earned about $500 doing part-time work for her church. Fallang v. Fallang (Butler 1996) 109 Ohio App.3d 543, 672 N.E.2d 730, dismissed, appeal not allowed 76 Ohio St.3d 1434, 667 N.E.2d 985.

Since both parties agreed at child support modification hearing to address only income and not expenses, Court of Appeals would not consider father's argument concerning mother's allegedly inflated expenses. Fallang v. Fallang (Butler 1996) 109 Ohio App.3d 543, 672 N.E.2d 730, dismissed, appeal not allowed 76 Ohio St.3d 1434, 667 N.E.2d 985.

The supplemental security income of an obligor who is disabled may be included in his gross income where he is in contempt for having failed to comply with a preexisting support order established by the court in 1996 and defendant fails to show that the amount of support established in the preexisting order was based on the supplemental security income. State ex rel Miller v Comer, No. 75763, 2000 WL 217796 (8th Dist Ct App, Cuyahoga, 2-24-00).

A temporary part-time job taken only for a sufficient time to pay attorney fees to defend the action brought by the non-custodial parent is included in calculating a child support obligation even though the obligor intends to quit when the fees are paid. Sheard v Sheard, No. CA99-06-115, 1999 WL 1237838 (12th Dist Ct App, Butler, 12-20-99).

A parent who makes significant financial contributions towards the care of his son for nine years prior to the date the complaint for support is filed is relieved of his support obligation for the nine year period where (1) the child has had severe mental and physical disabilities since birth and is confined to a wheelchair, (2) a good faith relationship exists between the mother and father before the support complaint is filed such that the child's financial needs were apparently met, and (3) there is reason to expect that the father's support obligation may last well beyond the time that the child reaches the age of majority. Shocky v Blackburn, No. CA98-07-085, 1999 WL 326174 (12th Dist Ct App, Warren, 5-17-99).

Being the primary caretaker of the children does not lead to a presumption that the particular parent should be the residential parent but should be considered with other statutory factors; in addition, where there is documentation that an obligor is under a duty to support two other children, the trial court must consider such obligation when calculating the current child support obligation. Kunkle v Lupardus, No. 96-P-0014, 1997 WL 158104 (11th Dist Ct App, Portage, 3-28-97).

22. Due process

Grant of child support to custodial parent subsequent to divorce, in absence of any motion therefor or notice to noncustodial parent that custodial parent was seeking support, violated noncustodial parent's due process rights, as noncustodial parent lacked opportunity to prepare her case and provide court with records as to her income, or lack thereof, in anticipation of hearing. Hannas v. Hannas (Ohio App. 11 Dist. 1997) 123 Ohio App.3d 378, 704 N.E.2d 294.

The Americans with Disabilities Act (ADA) does not require that the disabled be provided access to the courts by reasonable accommodation in the form of telephone hearings in a child support case where the wife lives in Tennessee and is unable to travel to Ohio because of her multiple sclerosis condition and the accommodation she requests is a telephone conference to prosecute her objection that the husband is underemployed; a telephonic hearing in such a case would fundamentally alter the nature of a hearing before a trial court rendering it difficult to administer oaths, admit evidence or permit cross-examination. McLaughlin v Pyles, No. 99CA0013, 1999 WL 1062236 (2d Dist Ct App, Clark, 11-24-99).

Reduction in child support obligation to reflect reduced monthly income is error when no hearing on the motion is held to give the obligee an opportunity to present evidence that the obligor, who has started taking college courses to become a physical therapist and reduces his work time in half, is voluntarily underemployed. Trisel v Overholt, No. 15-96-12, 1997 WL 123629 (3d Dist Ct App, Van Wert, 3-20-97).

23. Retroactive support

Statutory guidelines for calculation of child-support obligation where annual combined income of parents exceeds $150,000 apply in calculating award of retroactive support. Frazier v. Daniels (Ohio App. 1 Dist. 1997) 118 Ohio App.3d 425, 693 N.E.2d 289.

24. —Exceeding $150,000, income

Trial court did not abuse its discretion in setting child support according to the same percentage that would be applicable under the statutory schedule and worksheets for parents with combined income greater than $150,000, where the trial court found that husband had ample resources to pay the obligation and the husband did not request a deviation from the schedule and worksheets, though the obligation was a heavy one. Murray v. Murray (Ohio App. 12 Dist. 1999) 128 Ohio App.3d 662, 716 N.E.2d 288.

When the combined income of both parents is greater than $150,000, the appropriate standard for the amount of child support is that amount necessary to maintain for the children the standard of living they would have enjoyed had the marriage continued. Murray v. Murray (Ohio App. 12 Dist. 1999) 128 Ohio App.3d 662, 716 N.E.2d 288.

In setting amount of child support where annual combined income of parents exceeds $150,000, court determines amount of obligor's child-support obligation on case-by-case basis, considers needs and standard of living of child and parents, computes basic combined child-support obligation that is no less than same percentage of parents' combined annual income as applies to combined income of $150,000, and orders that amount as child support, unless it determines that such order would be unjust or inappropriate and would not be in best interest of child, obligor, or obligee. Frazier v. Daniels (Ohio App. 1 Dist. 1997) 118 Ohio App.3d 425, 693 N.E.2d 289.

3113.216 Review of child support orders

(A) As used in this section, "obligor" and "obligee" have the same meanings as in section 3113.21 of the Revised Code.

(B) No later than October 13, 1990, the director of job and family services shall adopt rules pursuant to Chapter 119. of the Revised Code establishing a procedure for determining when existing child support orders should be reviewed to determine whether it is necessary and in the best interest of the children who are the subject of the child support order to change the child support order. The rules shall include, but are not limited to, all of the following:

(1) Any procedures necessary to comply with section 666(a)(10) of Title 42 of the U.S. Code, "Family Support Act of 1988," 102 Stat. 2346, 42 U.S.C. 666(a)(10), as amended, and any regulations adopted pursuant to, or to enforce, that section;

(2) Procedures for determining what child support orders are to be subject to review upon the request of either the obligor or the obligee or periodically by the child support enforcement agency administering the child support order;

(3) Procedures for the child support enforcement agency to periodically review and to review, upon the request of the obligor or the obligee, any child support order that is subject to review to determine whether the amount of child support paid under the child support order should be adjusted in accordance with the basic child support schedule set forth in division (D) of section 3113.215 of the Revised Code or whether the provisions for the child's health care needs under the child support order should be modified in accordance with section 3113.217 of the Revised Code;

(4) Procedures for giving obligors and obligees notice of their right to request a review of a child support order that is determined to be subject to review, notice of any proposed revision of the amount of child support to be paid under the child support order, notice of the procedures for requesting a hearing on any proposed revision of the amount of child support to be paid under a child support order, notice of any administrative hearing to be held on a proposed revision of the amount of child support to be paid under a child support order, at least sixty days' prior notice of any review of their child support order, and notice that a failure to comply with any request for documents or information to be used in the review of a child support order is contempt of court;

(5) Procedures for obtaining the necessary documents and information necessary to review child support orders and for holding administrative hearings on a proposed revision of the amount of child support to be paid under a child support order;

(6) Procedures for adjusting child support orders in accordance with the basic child support schedule set forth in division (D) of section 3113.215 of the Revised Code and the applicable worksheet in division (E) of that section, through line 24, or in division (F) of that section, through line 23;

(7) Procedures for adjusting the provisions of the child support order governing the health care needs of the child pursuant to section 3113.217 of the Revised Code.

(C)(1) If a child support enforcement agency, periodically or upon request of an obligor or obligee, plans to review a child support order in accordance with the rules adopted pursuant to division (B) of this section or otherwise plans to review a child support order, it shall do all of the following prior to formally beginning the review:

(a) Establish a date certain upon which the review will formally begin;

(b) At least sixty days before formally beginning the review, send the obligor and the obligee notice of the planned review and of the date when the review will formally begin;

(c) Request the obligor to provide the agency, no later than the scheduled date for formally beginning the review, with a copy of the obligor's federal income tax return from the previous year, a copy of all pay stubs obtained by the obligor within the preceding six months, a copy of all other records evidencing the receipt of any other salary, wages, or compensation by the obligor within the preceding six months, a list of the group health insurance and health care policies, contracts, and plans available to the obligor and their costs, the current health insurance or health care policy, contract, or plan under which the obligor is enrolled and its cost, and any other information necessary to properly review the child support order, and request the obligee to provide the agency, no later than the scheduled date for formally beginning the review, with a copy of the obligee's federal income tax return from the previous year, a copy of all pay stubs obtained by the obligee within the preceding six months, a copy of all other records evidencing the receipt of any other salary, wages, or compensation by the obligee within the preceding six months, a list of the group health insurance and health care policies, contracts, and plans available to the obligee and their costs, the current health insurance or health care policy, contract, or plan under which the obligee is enrolled and its cost, and any other information necessary to properly review the child support order;

(d) Include in the notice sent pursuant to division (C)(1)(b) of this section, a notice that a willful failure to provide the documents and other information requested pursuant to division (C)(1)(c) of this section is contempt of court.

(2) If either the obligor or the obligee fails to comply with a request for information made pursuant to division (C)(1)(c) of this section, it is contempt of court, and the agency shall notify the court of the failure to comply with the request for information. The agency may request the court to issue an order requiring the obligor or the obligee to provide the information as requested or take whatever action is necessary to obtain the information and make any reasonable assumptions necessary with respect to the information the person in contempt of court did not provide to ensure a fair and equitable review of the child support order. If the agency decides to conduct the review based on reasonable assumptions with

respect to the information the person in contempt of court did not provide, it shall proceed under division (C)(3) of this section in the same manner as if all requested information has been received.

(3) Upon the date established pursuant to division (C)(1)(a) of this section for formally beginning the review of a child support order, the agency shall review the child support order and shall do all of the following:

(a) Calculate a revised amount of child support to be paid under the child support order;

(b) Give the obligor and obligee notice of the revised amount of child support to be paid under the child support order, of their right to request an administrative hearing on the revised amount of child support, of the procedures and time deadlines for requesting the hearing, and that the revised amount of child support will be submitted to the court for inclusion in a revised child support order unless the obligor or obligee requests an administrative hearing on the proposed change within thirty days after receipt of the notice under this division;

(c) If neither the obligor nor the obligee timely requests an administrative hearing on the revised amount of child support to be paid under the child support order, submit the revised amount of child support to the court for inclusion in a revised child support order;

(d) If the obligor or the obligee timely requests an administrative hearing on the revised amount of child support to be paid under the child support order, the agency shall schedule a hearing on the issue, give the obligor and obligee notice of the date, time, and location of the hearing, conduct the hearing in accordance with the rules adopted under division (B) of this section, redetermine at the hearing a revised amount of child support to be paid under the child support order, and give notice of all of the following to the obligor and obligee:

(i) The revised amount of child support to be paid under the child support order;

(ii) That they may request a court hearing on the revised amount of child support;

(iii) That the agency will submit the revised amount of child support to the court for inclusion in a revised child support order, if neither the obligor nor the obligee requests a court hearing on the revised amount of child support.

(e) If neither the obligor nor the obligee requests a court hearing on the revised amount of child support to be paid under the child support order, submit the revised amount of child support to the court for inclusion in a revised child support order.

(4) In calculating a revised amount of child support to be paid under a child support order under division (C)(3)(a) of this section, and in redetermining, at an administrative hearing conducted under division (C)(3)(d) of this section, a revised amount of child support to be paid under a child support order, the child support enforcement agency shall consider, in addition to all other factors required by law to be considered, the following:

(a) The appropriate person, whether it is the obligor, obligee, or both, to be required in accordance with section 3113.217 of the Revised Code to provide health insurance coverage for the children specified in the order;

(b) The cost of health insurance coverage which the obligor, the obligee, or both have been ordered to obtain in accordance with section 3113.217 of the Revised Code for the children specified in the order.

(D) If an obligor or obligee files a request for a court hearing on a revised amount of child support to be paid under a child support order in accordance with division (C) of this section and the rules adopted under division (B) of this section, the court shall conduct a hearing in accordance with division (C)(1)(c) of section 3113.21 of the Revised Code.

(E) A child support enforcement agency is not required to review a child support order pursuant to this section if the review is not otherwise required by section 666(a)(10) of Title 42 of the U.S. Code, "Family Support Act of 1988," 102 Stat. 2346, 42 U.S.C. 666(a)(10), as amended, and any regulations adopted pursuant to, or to enforce, that section and if either of the following apply:

(1) The obligee has made an assignment under section 5107.20 of the Revised Code of the right to receive child support payments, the agency determines that the review would not be in the best interest of the children who are the subject of the child support order, and neither the obligor nor the obligee has requested that the review be conducted;

(2) The obligee has not made an assignment under section 5107.20 of the Revised Code of the right to receive child support payments, and neither the obligor nor the obligee has requested that the review be conducted.

(1999 H 471, eff. 7-1-00; 1997 H 352, eff. 1-1-98; 1997 H 408, eff. 10-1-97; 1993 H 173, eff. 12-31-93; 1993 S 115; 1990 H 591)

Historical and Statutory Notes

Amendment Note: 1999 H 471 substituted "director of job and family services" for "department of human services" in the introductory paragraph in division (B).

Amendment Note: 1997 H 352 inserted "or whether the provisions for the child's health care needs under the child support order should be modified in accordance with section 3113.217 of the Revised Code" in division (B)(3); added division (B)(7); inserted "a list of the group health insurance and health care policies, contracts, and plans available to the obligor and their costs, the current health insurance or health care policy, contract, or plan under which the obligor is enrolled and its cost," and "a list of the group health insurance and health care policies, contracts, and plans available to the obligee and their costs, the current health insurance or health care policy, contract, or plan under which the obligor is enrolled and its cost," in division (C)(1)(c); substituted "information" for "income of" twice and inserted "did not provide" twice in division (C)(2); and rewrote division (C)(4), which prior thereto read:

"(4) In calculating a revised amount of child support to be paid under a child support order under division (C)(3)(a) of this section, and in redetermining, at an administrative hearing conducted under division (C)(3)(d) of this section, a revised amount of child support to be paid under a child support order, the child support enforcement agency shall consider, in addition to all other factors required by law to be considered, the cost of health insurance which the obligor, the obligee, or both the obligor and the obligee have been ordered to obtain for the children specified in the order."

Amendment Note: 1997 H 408 removed a references to "child support enforcement agency" in division (A); substituted "5107.20" for "5107.07" in divisions (E)(1) and (E)(2); and made changes to reflect gender neutral language and other nonsubstantive changes.

Amendment Note: 1993 H 173 substituted "23" for "22" at the end of division (B)(6); and substituted "(C)(1)(c)" for "(B)(7)" in division (D).

Amendment Note: 1993 S 115 substituted "in division (E) of that section, through line 24 or in division (F) of that section, through line 22" for "set forth in division (E) or (F) of that section, through line 18" in division (B)(6).

Cross References

Administrative child support withholding orders, 3111.23
Child support enforcement agency, adoption of rules, 2301.35
Court making or modifying child support order, 2151.23, 3105.21, 3115.22
Factors determining amount of support, applicability, 3109.05, 3111.13
Notice of default on child support order sent to professional licensing boards, 2301.373
Review of administrative child support orders, 3111.27

Ohio Administrative Code References

CSEA administrative review and adjustment hearing procedure, OAC 5101:1-30-404

Library References

Divorce ⟹309.1 to 309.6.
Parent and Child ⟹3.3(8).
Social Security and Public Welfare ⟹194.19.
WESTLAW Nos. 134, 285, 356A.
C.J.S. Divorce §§ 719 to 736.
C.J.S. Parent and Child §§ 80, 82 to 84, 89.
C.J.S. Social Security and Public Welfare § 122.

Am Jur 2d: 24, Divorce and Separation § 1035 et seq.
Divorce and separation: attributing undisclosed income to parent or spouse for purposes of making child or spousal support award. 70 ALR4th 173

Baldwin's Ohio Legislative Service, 1990 Laws of Ohio, H 591—LSC Analysis, p 5-576
Carlin, Baldwin's Ohio Practice, *Merrick-Rippner Probate Law* § 19.6, 19.7, 19.8, 19.10, 19.10.1, 108.20, 108.29, 108.30, 108.35, 108.36, 108.38 (1997)
Kurtz & Giannelli, Ohio Juvenile Law (1998 Ed.), Text 27.2, 29.2
Sowald & Morganstern, Baldwin's Ohio Practice, *Domestic Relations Law* § 3.4, 3.5, 3.35, 3.38, 3.55, 7.19, 9.11, 9.98, 10.13, 11.43, 11.44, 13.44, 14.3, 15.69, 19.1, 19.14, 19.20, 20.3, 20.49, 20.64, 22.2, 22.11, 22.12, 22.13.1, 23.21, 23.35, 23.39, 23.42, 29.34, 31.15 (1997)

Law Review and Journal Commentaries

Establishing And Enforcing The Child Support Obligation: An Evaluation Of Practical Impediments To An Effective System, Comment. 19 Cap U L Rev 1169 (Fall 1990).

Notes of Decisions and Opinions

1. Increase in agreed support amount

A trial court may grant a petition to increase a child support obligation to conform to the child support guidelines despite the lower child support obligation provided for by a separation agreement between the parties. Forest v. Forest (Stark 1993) 82 Ohio App.3d 572, 612 N.E.2d 815.

2. Arrearages

Trial court must calculate a child support arrearage on the basis of the express language of the most recent court entry relating to the issue of child support; this allows court to change a per-child support order to an in-gross order, or vice versa. Lytle v. Lytle (Ohio App. 10 Dist. 1998) 130 Ohio App.3d 697, 720 N.E.2d 1007.

Husband failed to file timely appeal from judgment finding him in arrears on spousal support, but rather improperly used motion for relief from judgment as substitute for direct appeal of judgment, so that Court of Appeals lacked jurisdiction to consider merits of husband's appeal from denial of motion for relief from judgment. Rundle v. Rundle (Ohio App. 8 Dist. 1997) 123 Ohio App.3d 304, 704 N.E.2d 56.

Although court-ordered future child-support obligations cannot be waived by the parents, the custodial parent is empowered in certain circumstances to forgive past arrearages. Nelson v. Nelson (Lake 1990) 65 Ohio App.3d 800, 585 N.E.2d 502.

A child support obligor is not required to pay the original child support arrearages after the parties remarry and then divorce for a second time. Watchowski v Watchowski, No. WD-99-028, 1999 WL 769545 (6th Dist Ct App, Wood, 9-30-99).

"Child support order," as used in RC 3113.216, includes an order that periodic payments be made through the Child Support Enforcement Agency solely for the purpose of satisfying past due child support obligations. Treadway v Ballew, No. 18984, 1998 WL 696888 (9th Dist Ct App, Summit, 10-7-98).

3. Income of obligor

An obligor who deliberately redirects part of his income to his new wife to avoid child support obligations perpetrates a fraud upon the court which consequently awards retroactive support payments to remedy the results of the scheme to defraud the court. Leffel v Leffel, No. 97-CA-20, 1997 WL 666102 (2d Dist Ct App, Clark, 10-24-97).

3113.217 Health insurance coverage for children

(A) As used in this section:

(1) "Obligor" and "obligee" have the same meanings as in section 3113.21 of the Revised Code.

(2) "Insurer" means any person that is authorized to engage in the business of insurance in this state under Title XXXIX of the Revised Code, any health insuring corporation, and any legal entity that is self-insured and provides benefits to its employees or members.

(B) In any action or proceeding in which a child support order is issued or modified under Chapter 3115. or section 2151.23, 2151.231, 2151.232, 2151.33, 2151.36, 2151.49, 3105.21, 3109.05, 3109.19, 3111.13, 3113.04, 3113.07, 3113.216, or 3113.31 of the Revised Code, the court shall determine the parent responsible for the health care of the children subject to the child support order and shall include in the order one of the following:

(1) A requirement that the obligor under the child support order obtain health insurance coverage for the children if coverage is available at a reasonable cost through a group health insurance or health care policy, contract, or plan offered by the obligor's employer or through any other group health insurance or health care policy, contract, or plan available to the obligor and if it is not available for a more reasonable cost through a group health insurance or health care policy, contract, or plan available to the obligee under the child support order;

(2) A requirement that the obligee under the child support order obtain health insurance coverage for the children if coverage is available through a group health insurance or health care policy, contract, or plan offered by the obligee's employer or through any other group health insurance or health care policy, contract, or plan available to the obligee and if it is available at a more reasonable cost than such coverage is available to the obligor;

(3) If health insurance coverage for the children is not available at a reasonable cost through a group health insurance or health care policy, contract, or plan offered by the obligor's employer or through any other group health insurance or health care policy, contract, or plan available to the obligor or the obligee, a requirement that the obligor and the obligee share liability for the cost of the medical and health care needs of the children, under an

equitable formula established by the court, and a requirement that if, after the issuance of the order, health insurance coverage for the children becomes available at a reasonable cost through a group health insurance or health care policy, contract, or plan offered by the obligor's or obligee's employer or through any other group health insurance or health care policy, contract, or plan available to the obligor or obligee, the obligor or obligee to whom the coverage becomes available immediately inform the court of that fact;

(4) A requirement that both the obligor and the obligee obtain health insurance coverage for the children if health insurance coverage is available for the children at a reasonable cost to both the obligor and the obligee and dual coverage by both parents would provide for coordination of medical benefits without unnecessary duplication of coverage.

(C) A child support order issued or modified pursuant to section 2151.23, 2151.231, 2151.232, 2151.33, 2151.36, 2151.49, 3105.21, 3109.05, 3109.19, 3111.13, 3113.04, 3113.07, 3113.216, 3113.31, or 3115.30 of the Revised Code shall contain all of the following:

(1) If the obligor is required under division (B)(1) of this section, the obligee is required under division (B)(2) of this section, or both the obligor and obligee are required under division (B)(4) of this section, to provide health insurance coverage for the children, a requirement that the obligor or obligee, whoever is required to obtain health insurance coverage, provide the other parent with information regarding the benefits, limitations, and exclusions of the health insurance coverage, copies of any insurance forms necessary to receive reimbursement, payment, or other benefits under the health insurance coverage, and a copy of any necessary insurance cards, a requirement that the obligor or obligee, whoever is required to obtain health insurance coverage submit a copy of the court order issued pursuant to division (B)(1), (2), or (4) of this section to the insurer at the time that the obligor or obligee, whoever is required to obtain health insurance coverage makes application to enroll the children in the health insurance or health care policy, contract, or plan, and a requirement that the obligor or obligee, whoever is required to obtain health insurance coverage, furnish written proof to the child support enforcement agency that division (C)(1) of this section has been complied with;

(2) A list of the group health insurance and health care policies, contracts, and plans that the court determines are available at a reasonable cost to the obligor or to the obligee and the name of the insurer that issues each policy, contract, or plan;

(3) A statement setting forth the name, address, and telephone number of the individual who is to be reimbursed for out-of-pocket medical, optical, hospital, dental, or prescription expenses paid for each child who is the subject of the support order and a statement that the insurer that provides the health insurance coverage for the children may continue making payment for medical, optical, hospital, dental, or prescription services directly to any health care provider in accordance with the applicable health insurance or health care policy, contract, or plan;

(4) A requirement that the obligor and the obligee designate the children as covered dependents under any health insurance or health care policy, contract, or plan for which they contract;

(5) A requirement that the obligor, the obligee, or both of them under a formula established by the court pay co-payment or deductible costs required under the health insurance or health care policy, contract, or plan that covers the children;

(6) A notice that the employer of the obligor or obligee required to obtain health insurance coverage is required to release to the other parent or the child support enforcement agency upon written request any necessary information on the health insurance coverage, including, but not limited to, the name and address of the insurer and any policy, contract, or plan number, and to otherwise comply with this section and any court order issued under this section;

(7) A statement setting forth the full name and date of birth of each child who is the subject of the child support order;

(8) A requirement that the obligor and the obligee comply with any requirement described in division (B)(1), (2), and (4), and (C)(1) and (4) of this section that is contained in the order issued under this section no later than thirty days after the issuance of the order.

(9) A notice that, if the obligor or obligee is required to obtain health insurance coverage pursuant to the child support order for the children and if the obligor or obligee fails to obtain the health insurance coverage, the child support enforcement agency shall comply with division (D) of this section to obtain a court order requiring the obligor or obligee to obtain the health insurance coverage;

(10) A notice that states the following: "If the person required to obtain health care insurance coverage for the children subject to this child support order obtains new employment and the health insurance coverage for the children is provided through the previous employer, the agency shall comply with the requirements of division (E) of section 3113.217 of the Revised Code which may result in the issuance of a notice requiring the new employer to take whatever action is necessary to enroll the children in health care insurance coverage provided by the new employer."

(D) If an obligor or obligee required to obtain health insurance coverage pursuant to a child support order issued in accordance with this section does not obtain the required health insurance coverage within thirty days after the child support order is issued, the child support enforcement agency shall notify the court in writing of the failure of the obligor to comply with the child support order. On receipt of the notice from the agency, the court shall issue an order to the employer of the obligor or obligee required to obtain health insurance coverage requiring the employer to take whatever action is necessary to make application to enroll the obligor or obligee required to obtain health insurance coverage in any available group health insurance or health care policy, contract, or plan with coverage for the children, to submit a copy of the child support order to the insurer at the time that the employer makes application to enroll the children in the health insurance or health care policy, contract, or plan, and, if the application is accepted, to deduct from the wages or other income of the obligor or obligee required to obtain health insurance coverage the cost of the coverage for the children. Upon receipt of any order under this division, the employer shall take whatever action is necessary to comply with the order.

(E)(1) If an obligor or obligee is required to obtain health insurance coverage pursuant to a child support order issued in accordance with this section and the obligor or obligee obtains health insurance coverage for the children through an employer and subsequently obtains new employment, the child support enforcement agency shall investigate whether the new employer offers health insurance coverage that would cover the children. If the agency determines that the new employer provides health insurance coverage that would cover the children, the agency shall send a notice described in division (E)(2) of this section and a copy of the child support order to the new employer and shall send a copy of the notice to the obligor or obligee required to obtain health insurance coverage under the child support order. On receipt of the notice, the new employer shall comply with its provisions.

(2) The notice required by division (E)(1) shall contain the following:

(a) A requirement that the new employer take whatever action is necessary to make application to enroll the obligor or obligee required to obtain health insurance coverage in any available group health insurance or health care policy, contract, or plan with coverage for the children;

(b) A requirement that the new employer submit a copy of the child support order requiring the obligor or obligee to obtain health care insurance for the children to the insurer at the time that the employer makes application to enroll the children in the health insurance or health care policy, contract, or plan;

(c) A requirement that, if the application is accepted, the new employer deduct from the wages or other income of the obligor or obligee required to obtain the health insurance coverage the cost of the coverage for the children.

(d) A statement that the provisions of the notice are final and enforceable by a court and are incorporated into the child support order unless the obligor or obligee required to obtain health insurance coverage, within ten days after the date on which the notice is sent, files a written request with the agency requesting modification of the child support order pursuant to section 3113.216 of the Revised Code.

(F) A child support order issued in accordance with, or any order issued under division (D) of, this section shall be binding upon the obligor and the obligee, their employers, and any insurer that provides health insurance coverage for either of them or their children. The court shall send a copy of the child support or other order by ordinary mail to the obligor, the obligee, and any employer that is subject to the order.

(G)(1) During the time that any child support order issued in accordance with, or order issued under division (D) of, this section is in effect and after the employer has received a copy of the order, the employer of the obligor or obligee required to comply with the order shall comply with the order and, upon request from the other parent or the agency, shall release to that parent and the child support enforcement agency all information about the obligor's health insurance coverage that is necessary to ensure compliance with this section or the order, including, but not limited to, the name and address of the insurer and any policy, contract, or plan number. Any information provided by an employer pursuant to this division shall be used only for the purpose of the enforcement of the order.

(2) Any employer who receives a copy of an order described in division (G)(1) of this section shall notify the agency of any change in or the termination of the health insurance coverage that is maintained pursuant to the order.

(3) Any insurer that receives a copy of an order described in division (G)(1) of this section shall comply with this section, regardless of the residence of the children. If an insurer provides health insurance coverage for the children who are the subject of a child support order in accordance with the child support order or an order issued under division (D) of this section, the insurer shall reimburse the parent, who is designated to receive reimbursement in the child support order, for covered out-of-pocket medical, optical, hospital, dental, or prescription expenses incurred on behalf of the children.

(H) If an obligee under a child support order issued in accordance with section 2151.23, 2151.231, 2151.232, 2151.33, 2151.36, 2151.49, 3105.21, 3109.05, 3109.19, 3111.13, 3113.04, 3113.07, 3113.216, 3113.31, or 3115.30 is eligible for medical assistance under Chapter 5111. or 5115. of the Revised Code and the obligor has obtained health insurance coverage, the obligee shall notify any physician, hospital, or other provider of medical services for which medical assistance is available of the name and address of the obligor's insurer and of the number of the obligor's health insurance or health care policy, contract, or plan. Any physician, hospital, or other provider of medical services for which medical assistance is available under Chapter 5111. or 5115. of the Revised Code who is notified under this division of the existence of a health insurance or health care policy, contract, or plan with coverage for children who are eligible for medical assistance first shall bill the insurer for any services provided for those children. If the insurer fails to pay all or any part of a claim filed under this division by the physician, hospital, or other medical services provider and the services for which the claim is filed are covered by Chapter 5111. or 5115. of the Revised Code, the physician, hospital, or other medical services provider shall bill the remaining unpaid costs of the services in accordance with Chapter 5111. or 5115. of the Revised Code.

(I) Any obligor who fails to comply with a child support order issued in accordance with, or an order issued under division (D) of, this section is liable to the obligee for any medical expenses incurred as a result of the failure to comply with the order. An obligee who fails to comply with a child support order issued in accordance with, or an order issued under division (D) of, this section is liable to the obligor for any medical expenses incurred as a result of the failure to comply with the order.

(J) Whoever violates a child support order issued in accordance with, or an order issued under division (D) of, this section may be punished as for contempt under Chapter 2705. of the Revised Code. If an obligor is found in contempt under that chapter for failing to comply with a child support order issued in accordance with, or an order issued under division (D) of, this section and if the obligor previously has been found in contempt under that chapter, the court shall consider the obligor's failure to comply with the order as a change in circumstances for the purpose of modification of the amount of support due under the child support order that is the basis of the order issued under this section.

(K) Nothing in this section shall be construed to require an insurer to accept for enrollment any child who does not meet the underwriting standards of the health insurance or health care policy, contract, or plan for which application is made.

(L) An order issued pursuant to this section prior to the effective date of this amendment to provide for the health care needs of children subject to a child support order issued pursuant to section 2151.23, 2151.231, 2151.232, 2151.33, 2151.36, 2151.49, 3105.21, 3109.05, 3109.19, 3111.13, 3113.04, 3113.07, 3113.216, 3113.31, or 3115.30 of the Revised Code, shall remain in full force and effect and shall be considered a requirement included as part of the child support order. The child support order shall be subject to the provisions of this section on and after the effective date of this amendment.

(1997 H 352, eff. 1-1-98; 1997 H 408, eff. 10-1-97; 1997 S 67, eff. 6-4-97; 1996 H 274, eff. 8-8-96; 1995 H 167, eff. 11-15-95; 1995 H 249, eff. 7-17-95; 1993 H 173, eff. 12-31-93; 1992 S 10; 1990 S 3, H 737, H 591)

Historical and Statutory Notes

Amendment Note: 1997 H 352 rewrote this section; see *Baldwin's Ohio Legislative Service Annotated*, 1997, p 9/L-2639, or the OH-LEGIS or OH-LEGIS-OLD database on WESTLAW, for text of previous version.

Amendment Note: 1997 H 408 removed a references to "child support enforcement agency" in division (A)(1); and made other nonsubstantive changes.

Amendment Note: 1997 S 67 replaced references to prepaid dental plans, medical care corporations, health care corporations, dental care corporations and health maintenance organizations with language pertaining to health insuring corporations in division (A)(2); and made other nonsubstantive changes.

Amendment Note: 1996 H 274 added references to section 2151.33 throughout.

Amendment Note: 1995 H 167 added references to section 3109.19 in division (B), the first paragraph in division (C), and division (D).

Amendment Note: 1995 H 249 substituted "5115." for "5113." in the first sentence in division (H); substituted "Chapter 5111. or 5115." for "section 5111.02" in the second sentence in division (H); and inserted "and the services for which the claim is filed are covered by Chapter 5111. or 5115. of the Revised Code" and substituted "5115." for "5113." in the third sentence in division (H).

Amendment Note: 1993 H 173 added the references to sections 2151.36, 2151.49, 3113.07, and 3113.216 in divisions (B) through (D).

Cross References

Child support enforcement agency, adoption of rules, 2301.35

Court making or modifying child support order, 2151.23, 3105.21, 3115.22

Factors determining amount of support, applicability, 3109.05, 3111.13

Health insurance coverage, enrollment of child under family coverage, 3924.48, 3924.49

Health insurance coverage required, collection of costs by providers from nonobligors prohibited, 1349.01

Juvenile courts, suspension of sentence on condition of child support, provision of health care, 2151.49

Ohio Administrative Code References

Establishment, enforcement of health insurance, OAC 5101:1-29-353, 5101:1-29-354

Library References

Divorce ⚷308.
Parent and Child ⚷3.3(7).
WESTLAW Nos. 134, 285.
C.J.S. Divorce §§ 669 to 671, 673 to 683, 700 to 705, 708.
C.J.S. Parent and Child §§ 81, 89.

Am Jur 2d: 24, Divorce and Separation § 1025, 1044

Baldwin's Ohio Legislative Service, 1990 Laws of Ohio, H 591—LSC Analysis, p 5-576

Carlin, Baldwin's Ohio Practice, *Merrick-Rippner Probate Law* § 19.6, 19.7, 19.8, 19.10, 19.10.1, 108.20, 108.29, 108.30, 108.35, 108.36 (1997)

Kurtz & Giannelli, Ohio Juvenile Law (1998 Ed.), Text 27.2, 29.2

Sowald & Morganstern, Baldwin's Ohio Practice, *Domestic Relations Law* § 3.4, 3.5, 3.35, 3.55, 7.19, 9.11, 9.98, 10.13, 11.43, 11.44, 13.44, 14.3, 15.69, 19.1, 19.10, 19.20, 20.3, 20.64, 22.15, 23.21, 23.35, 23.39, 23.42, 29.34 (1997)

Notes of Decisions and Opinions

Insurance order required 1
Modification 3
Physical handicaps 2

1. Insurance order required

In determining child support obligations, trial court was statutorily required to issue separate orders regarding health insurance for children. Cuyahoga Cty. Support Enforcement Agency v. Lozada (Cuyahoga 1995) 102 Ohio App.3d 442, 657 N.E.2d 372.

Juvenile court had authority to issue nunc pro tunc order under statute requiring court issuing support order to also issue separate order relating to health insurance coverage for child. In re Kessler (Huron 1993) 90 Ohio App.3d 231, 628 N.E.2d 153, motion overruled 68 Ohio St.3d 1437, 625 N.E.2d 625.

Court of Appeals could not determine whether trial court erred in ordering former husband to pay any amount of children's uninsured health care costs over $50, where trial court did not follow child support worksheet in arriving at figure that former husband owed for child support, and trial court made no mention that incarcerated former husband had means to pay any child support or any health care costs. Tobens v. Brill (Auglaize 1993) 89 Ohio App.3d 298, 624 N.E.2d 265.

Failure of a court to issue a separate order regarding health insurance pursuant to RC 3113.217 is plain error. Cuyahoga Support Enforcement Agency v Perrin, No. 68835, 1996 WL 65835 (8th Dist Ct App, Cuyahoga, 2-15-96).

An obligor is guilty of contempt for failure to comply with child support and medical support orders where he voluntarily terminates his employment and ability to pay his child support prior to, and after, the termination; in addition, the court is not required to modify the ongoing child support order absent a modification request. Jones v Mosley, No. 95APF04-442, 1995 WL 739688 (10th Dist Ct App, Franklin, 12-14-95).

A support order requiring both parents to obtain health insurance coverage for their minor children without specifying statutorily designated facts to justify dual coverage under RC 3113.217, will be reversed and remanded as unreasonable. Cogley v Cogley, No. 5-92-41 (3d Dist Ct App, Hancock, 6-16-93).

Failure by the juvenile court to enter the child support computation worksheet completed by the guardian ad litem into evidence as prescribed by the "literal requirements" of RC 3113.215, as well as its failure to enter a separate order with respect to health insurance coverage as required by RC 3113.217(C), constitutes reversible error. In re Cross, No. C-920113 (1st Dist Ct App, Hamilton, 4-28-93).

2. Physical handicaps

It is not an abuse of discretion for a court to order a nonworking custodial parent of a child with cystic fibrosis to pay thirty per cent of all uninsured hospital and medical expenses for the child where the child's pre-existing condition is uninsurable. Azbill v Azbill, No. CA93-12-242, 1995 WL 22689 (12th Dist Ct App, Butler, 1-23-95).

Trial court properly ordered father to continue carrying eighteen-year-old daughter on health insurance policy, where daughter is diabetic, daughter was ruled unruly, RC 2151.353(E)(1) allows court to retain jurisdiction over "physically handicapped" unruly child until age of 21 years, and Code of Federal Regulations for implementation of Americans With Disabilities Act of 1990 considers diabetes a physical impairment qualifying as a disability. In re Kessler, No. H-92-27, 1993 WL 356941 (6th Dist Ct App, Huron, 9-17-93).

3. Modification

Trial court had authority in proceeding to modify child support obligations of divorce decree to modify parties' health insurance obligations, regardless of whether health insurance obligations were addressed in parties' pleadings. Wade v. Wade (Lake 1996) 113 Ohio App.3d 414, 680 N.E.2d 1305.

3113.218 Administration of child support orders by child support enforcement agencies

(A) As used in this section, "child support order" has the same meaning as in section 3113.215 of the Revised Code.

(B) In any action or proceeding in which a child support order is issued or modified on or after July 1, 1990, under Chapter 3115. or section 2151.23, 2151.231, 2151.232, 2151.33, 2151.36, 2151.49, 3105.18, 3105.21, 3109.05, 3109.19, 3111.13, 3113.04, 3113.07, 3113.216, or 3113.31 of the Revised Code, the court that issues or modifies the order shall include in the order, in addition to any provision required by any of those sections or by any other section of the Revised Code, all of the following:

(1) A requirement that, regardless of the frequency or amount of child support payments to be made under the order, the child support enforcement agency that is required to administer the order shall administer it on a monthly basis, in accordance with this section;

(2) A specification of the monthly amount due under the child support order for purposes of its monthly administration, as determined under division (D) of this section;

(3) A statement that payments under the order are to be made in the manner ordered by the court, and that if the payments are to be made other than on a monthly basis, the required monthly administration by the agency does not affect the frequency or the amount of the child support payments to be made under the order.

(C) If a child support enforcement agency is required by statute or court order to administer a child support order that was issued or modified on or after July 1, 1990, the agency shall administer the order on a monthly basis, in accordance with the provisions of the order that contain the information described in division (B) of this section.

(D) If a court issues or modifies a child support order on or after July 1, 1990, and if the child support payments due under the order are to be made other than on a monthly basis, the court shall calculate a monthly amount due under the child support order, for purposes of its monthly administration, in the following manner:

(1) If the child support order is to be paid weekly, multiply the weekly amount of child support due under the order by fifty-two and divide the resulting product by twelve;

(2) If the child support order is to be paid biweekly, multiply the biweekly amount of child support due under the order by twenty-six and divide the resulting product by twelve;

(3) If the child support order is to be paid periodically but is not to be paid weekly, biweekly, or monthly, multiply the periodic amount of child support due by an appropriate number to obtain the annual amount of child support due under the order and divide the annual amount of child support due by twelve.

(E) If the payments under a child support order are to be made other than on a monthly basis, the required monthly administration of the order by a child support enforcement agency pursuant to this section shall not affect the frequency or the amount of the child support payments to be made under the order.

(F) The provisions of this section do not apply in relation to a child support order unless the order was issued or modified on or after July 1, 1990.

(1997 H 352, eff. 1-1-98; 1997 H 408, eff. 10-1-97; 1996 H 274, eff. 8-8-96; 1995 H 167, eff. 11-15-95; 1993 H 173, eff. 12-31-93; 1990 H 591)

Historical and Statutory Notes

Amendment Note: 1997 H 352 inserted "2151.231, 2151.232," in the first paragraph in division (B).

Amendment Note: 1997 H 408 deleted former division (A)(1); redesignated former division (A)(2) as new division (A); and made other nonsubstantive changes. Prior to deletion, former division (A)(1) read:

"(1)"Child support enforcement agency" has the same meaning as in section 3113.21 of the Revised Code."

Amendment Note: 1996 H 274 inserted "2151.33," in the first paragraph in division (B).

Amendment Note: 1995 H 167 added a reference to section 3109.19 in the first paragraph in division (B).

Amendment Note: 1993 H 173 added the references to sections 2151.36, 2151.49, 3113.07, and 3113.216 in the first paragraph of division (B).

Cross References

Child support enforcement agency, adoption of rules, 2301.35

Court making or modifying child support order, 2151.23, 3105.21, 3115.22

Factors determining amount of support, applicability, 3109.05, 3111.13

Ohio Administrative Code References

Billing upon conversion to sets[*sic*], OAC 5101:1-29-714

Monthly administration upon SETS conversion, OAC 5101:1-29-713

Library References

Divorce ⟜311(1), 311.5.

Parent and Child ⟜3.3(9).

WESTLAW Nos. 134, 285.

C.J.S. Divorce §§ 706 to 708, 716 to 718, 721.

C.J.S. Parent and Child §§ 80, 85 to 87, 89.

Baldwin's Ohio Legislative Service, 1990 Laws of Ohio, H 591—LSC Analysis, p 5-576

Carlin, Baldwin's Ohio Practice, *Merrick-Rippner Probate Law* § 19.6, 19.7, 19.8, 19.10, 19.10.1, 108.20, 108.29, 108.30, 108.35, 108.36 (1997)

Kurtz & Giannelli, Ohio Juvenile Law (1998 Ed.), Text 27.2, 29.2
Sowald & Morganstern, Baldwin's Ohio Practice, *Domestic Relations Law* § 3.4, 3.5, 3.35, 3.55, 7.19, 9.11, 9.98, 10.13, 11.43, 11.44, 13.44, 14.3, 15.69, 19.1, 19.20, 20.3, 20.64, 23.21, 23.35, 23.39, 23.42, 29.34 (1997)

Law Review and Journal Commentaries

Bankruptcy Reform Act of 1994—What the Bankruptcy Code Giveth, Domestic Relations Courts (and Congress) Taketh Away, C.R. "Chip" Bowles. 8 Domestic Rel J Ohio 17 (March/April 1996).

Notes of Decisions and Opinions

1. Constitutional issues

It is a violation of the equal protection clauses of the United States and Ohio constitutions to allow the aid and support of the child support enforcement agency in an action for child support brought by parents who have established their parentage through the probate court and residential parents who are on public assistance while denying the aid and support of the child support enforcement agency to parents who have established their parentage through the administrative process. Cuyahoga County Support Enforcement Agency v Lozada, Nos. 67463+, 1995 WL 386965 (8th Dist Ct App, Cuyahoga, 6-29-95).

2. Exceptions

Judgment for payment of a child's college expenses provided for in a separation agreement should not be considered child support and collection thereof should not be made through the Child Support Enforcement Agency.

3113.219 Issuance of new order; interest and costs (pre 1996 H 350 amendment)

Ed. Note: See also following versions, note under Notes of Decisions, and casenote for Ohio Academy of Trial Lawyers v Sheward.

(A) On or after July 1, 1992, when a court issues or modifies a support order under Chapter 3115. or section 2151.23, 2151.231, 2151.33, 2151.36, 2151.49, 3105.18, 3105.21, 3109.05, 3109.19, 3111.13, 3113.04, 3113.07, 3113.216, or 3113.31 of the Revised Code or in any proceeding in which a court determines the amount of support to be paid pursuant to a support order, the court shall determine the date the obligor failed to pay the support required under the support order and the amount of support the obligor failed to pay. If the court determines the obligor has failed at any time to comply with a support order, the court shall issue a new order requiring the obligor to pay support. If the court determines that the failure to pay was willful, the court shall assess interest on the amount of support the obligor failed to pay from the date the court specifies as the original date the obligor failed to comply with the order requiring the payment of support to the date the court issues the new order requiring the payment of support and shall compute the interest at the rate specified in section 1343.03 of the Revised Code. The court shall specify in the support order the amount of interest the court assessed against the obligor and incorporate the amount of interest into the new monthly payment plan.

(B) On or after July 1, 1992, when a court issues or modifies a support order under Chapter 3115. or section 2151.23, 2151.231, 2151.33, 2151.36, 2151.49, 3105.18, 3105.21, 3109.05, 3109.19, 3111.13, 3113.04, 3113.07, 3113.216, or 3113.31 of the Revised Code or in any proceeding in which a court determines the amount of support to be paid pursuant to a support order, the court may include in the support order a statement ordering either party to pay the costs of the action, including, but not limited to, attorney's fees, fees for genetic tests in contested actions under sections 3111.01 to 3111.19 of the Revised Code, and court fees.

(1996 H 274, eff. 8-8-96; 1995 H 167, eff. 11-15-95; 1993 H 173, eff. 12-31-93; 1992 S 10)

Ed. Note: See also following versions, note under Notes of Decisions, and casenote for Ohio Academy of Trial Lawyers v Sheward.

3113.219 Issuance of new order; interest and costs (1996 H 350 amendment)

Ed. Note: See also preceding and following versions, note under Notes of Decisions, and casenote for Ohio Academy of Trial Lawyers v Sheward.

(A) On or after July 1, 1992, when a court issues or modifies a support order under Chapter 3115. or section 2151.23, 2151.231, 2151.33, 2151.36, 2151.49, 3105.18, 3105.21, 3109.05,

3109.19, 3111.13, 3113.04, 3113.07, 3113.216, or 3113.31 of the Revised Code or in any proceeding in which a court determines the amount of support to be paid pursuant to a support order, the court shall determine the date the obligor failed to pay the support required under the support order and the amount of support the obligor failed to pay. If the court determines the obligor has failed at any time to comply with a support order, the court shall issue a new order requiring the obligor to pay support. If the court determines that the failure to pay was willful, the court shall assess interest on the amount of support the obligor failed to pay from the date the court specifies as the original date the obligor failed to comply with the order requiring the payment of support to the date the court issues the new order requiring the payment of support and shall compute the interest at the rate specified in division (A) of section 1343.03 of the Revised Code. The court shall specify in the support order the amount of interest the court assessed against the obligor and incorporate the amount of interest into the new monthly payment plan.

(B) On or after July 1, 1992, when a court issues or modifies a support order under Chapter 3115. or section 2151.23, 2151.231, 2151.33, 2151.36, 2151.49, 3105.18, 3105.21, 3109.05, 3109.19, 3111.13, 3113.04, 3113.07, 3113.216, or 3113.31 of the Revised Code or in any proceeding in which a court determines the amount of support to be paid pursuant to a support order, the court may include in the support order a statement ordering either party to pay the costs of the action, including, but not limited to, attorney's fees, fees for genetic tests in contested actions under sections 3111.01 to 3111.19 of the Revised Code, and court costs.

(1996 H 350, eff. 1-27-97)

Ed. Note: See also preceding and following versions, note under Notes of Decisions, and casenote for Ohio Academy of Trial Lawyers v Sheward.

3113.219 Issuance of new order; interest and costs (1996 H 350 and subsequent amendments)

Ed. Note: See also preceding versions, note under Notes of Decisions, and casenote for Ohio Academy of Trial Lawyers v Sheward.

(A) On or after July 1, 1992, when a court issues or modifies a support order under Chapter 3115. or section 2151.23, 2151.231, 2151.232, 2151.33, 2151.36, 2151.49, 3105.18, 3105.21, 3109.05, 3109.19, 3111.13, 3113.04, 3113.07, 3113.216, or 3113.31 of the Revised Code or in any proceeding in which a court determines the amount of support to be paid pursuant to a support order, the court shall determine the date the obligor failed to pay the support required under the support order and the amount of support the obligor failed to pay. If the court determines the obligor has failed at any time to comply with a support order, the court shall issue a new order requiring the obligor to pay support. If the court determines that the failure to pay was willful, the court shall assess interest on the amount of support the obligor failed to pay from the date the court specifies as the original date the obligor failed to comply with the order requiring the payment of support to the date the court issues the new order requiring the payment of support and shall compute the interest at the rate specified in division (A) of section 1343.03 of the Revised Code. The court shall specify in the support order the amount of interest the court assessed against the obligor and incorporate the amount of interest into the new monthly payment plan.

(B) On or after July 1, 1992, when a court issues or modifies a support order under Chapter 3115. or section 2151.23, 2151.231, 2151.33, 2151.36, 2151.49, 3105.18, 3105.21, 3109.05, 3109.19, 3111.13, 3113.04, 3113.07, 3113.216, or 3113.31 of the Revised Code or in any proceeding in which a court determines the amount of support to be paid pursuant to a support order, the court may include in the support order a statement ordering either party to pay the costs of the action, including, but not limited to, attorney's fees, fees for genetic tests in contested actions under sections 3111.01 to 3111.19 of the Revised Code, and court costs.

(1997 H 352, eff. 1-1-98; 1996 H 350, eff. 1-27-97; 1996 H 274, eff. 8-8-96; 1995 H 167, eff. 11-15-95; 1993 H 173, eff. 12-31-93; 1992 S 10)

Ed. Note: See also preceding versions, note under Notes of Decisions, and casenote for Ohio Academy of Trial Lawyers v Sheward.

Uncodified Law

1996 H 350, § 6, eff. 1-27-97, reads, in part:

(A) The amendments to sections 163.17, 1343.03, 1701.95, 2743.18, 2743.19, 2744.06, 3313.219[7], 3722.08, 4113.52, and 4909.42 of the Revised Code that are made in this act and that pertain to judgment interest shall apply only to civil actions based on tortious conduct and not settled by agreement of the parties that are commenced on or after the effective date of this act.

Historical and Statutory Notes

Amendment Note: 1997 H 352 inserted "2151.232," in division (A).

Amendment Note: 1996 H 350 inserted "division (A) of" in division (A); and substituted "court costs" for "court fees" in division (B).

Amendment Note: 1996 H 274 added references to section 2151.33 throughout.

Amendment Note: 1995 H 167 added references to section 3109.19 throughout.

Amendment Note: 1993 H 173 added the references to sections 3113.07 and 3113.216 in divisions (A) and (B).

Ohio Administrative Code References

Allocation hierarchy for collections, OAC 5101:1-31-14
Child support administrative fund, nonsupport collections, OAC 5101:1-31-04, 5101:1-31-11
Enforcement of the support order, OAC 5101:1-30-428
Program income, OAC 5101:1-31-20

Library References

Divorce ⟹309.1 to 309.6.
Interest ⟹22(1).
Parent and Child ⟹3.3(8), 3.3(9).
WESTLAW Nos. 134, 219, 285.
C.J.S. Divorce §§ 719 to 736, 756 to 760.
C.J.S. Interest and Usury; Consumer Credit § 23.
C.J.S. Parent and Child §§ 80, 82 to 87, 89.
Carlin, Baldwin's Ohio Practice, *Merrick-Rippner Probate Law* § 19.6, 19.7, 19.8, 19.10, 19.10.1, 108.20, 108.29, 108.30, 108.35, 108.36, 108.38 (1997)
Kurtz & Giannelli, Ohio Juvenile Law (1998 Ed.), Text 27.2, 29.2
Sowald & Morganstern, Baldwin's Ohio Practice, *Domestic Relations Law* § 3.4, 3.5, 3.31, 3.35, 3.53, 3.55, 3.56, 3.58, 7.19, 9.11, 9.98, 10.13, 11.43, 11.44, 13.44, 14.2, 14.3, 15.69, 19.1, 19.13, 19.20, 19.23, 20.3, 20.6, 20.64, 23.20, 23.21, 23.35, 23.39, 23.42, 29.34 (1997)

Notes of Decisions and Opinions

Ed. Note: *1996 H 350 was ruled unconstitutional in toto by the Ohio Supreme Court in State ex rel. Ohio Academy of Trial Lawyers v. Sheward (Ohio 1999), 86 Ohio St.3d 451, 715 N.E.2d 1062.*

---

1. Interest

Unless child and spousal support arrearages are reduced to lump-sum judgment, interest cannot be awarded as of time support payments become due unless support orders were issued or modified on or after effective date of statute permitting assessment of interest on delinquent support payments when obligor willfully fails to pay. Mattoni v. Mattoni (Ohio App. 6 Dist. 1997) 118 Ohio App.3d 782, 694 N.E.2d 104, appeal not allowed 79 Ohio St.3d 1422, 680 N.E.2d 158.

A trial court has authority under RC 1343.03(A) to award interest on child support arrearages from the date each installment becomes due. In re Hammond (Hamilton 1992) 78 Ohio App.3d 170, 604 N.E.2d 197.

Interest on child support arrearages accrues from the date the individual child support payments become due and payable, and is calculated pursuant to RC 1343.03(A) at the rate of 6% from July 1, 1962 until July 29, 1980, 8% from July 30, 1980 until July 4, 1982, and 10% thereafter. Sheets v Sheets, No. 94CA17, 1994 WL 728050 (4th Dist Ct App, Gallia, 12-30-94).

A court should not award interest on a lump-sum child support award for back support from the date that each payment was due but unpaid where the original support order was issued in 1965 and RC 3113.219, which allows a court to order a wilfully delinquent obligor to pay interest on a lump-sum award, was not effective until 1992; interest should only be charged from the post-1992 date the lump-sum judgment was ordered. Bloom v McCoil, No. 94OT018, 1994 WL 530843 (6th Dist Ct App, Ottawa, 9-30-94).

Interest under RC 3113.219(A) may not be assessed for time periods prior to July 15, 1992. OAG 93-037.

2. Attorneys fees

Trial court did not abuse its discretion in awarding wife partial attorney fees in dissolution of marriage proceeding in which wife sought modification of husband's child support obligation; child support provisions of separation agreement accounted for far less in child support payments than current statutory child support guidelines.

---

[7] So in original.

In re Marriage of Stearns (Franklin 1993) 88 Ohio App.3d 264, 623 N.E.2d 711.

Trial court was within its discretion in awarding only partial attorney fees to wife in dissolution of marriage proceeding in which wife sought modification of husband's child support obligation, as some litigation involved issues other than increase in child support. In re Marriage of Stearns (Franklin 1993) 88 Ohio App.3d 264, 623 N.E.2d 711.

Trial court did not abuse its discretion in awarding former wife $12,000 of requested $24,000 in attorney fees incurred with respect to motion for modification of former husband's child support obligation. Parzynski v. Parzynski (Erie 1992) 85 Ohio App.3d 423, 620 N.E.2d 93, dismissed, jurisdictional motion overruled 67 Ohio St.3d 1450, 619 N.E.2d 419, rehearing denied 67 Ohio St.3d 1513, 622 N.E.2d 660.

3. Constitutional issues

1996 H 350, which amended more than 100 statutes and a variety of rules relating to tort and other civil actions, and which was an attempt to reenact provisions of law previously held unconstitutional by the Supreme Court of Ohio, is an act of usurpation of judicial power in violation of the doctrine of separation of powers; for that reason, and because of violation of the one-subject rule of the Ohio Constitution, 1996 H 350 is unconstitutional. Ohio Academy of Trial Lawyers v. Sheward (Ohio 1999) 86 Ohio St.3d 451, 715 N.E.2d 1062.

3113.2110 Action for unpaid support

Whenever an obligor fails to make any payment required by a child support order, the obligee or a child support enforcement agency acting on behalf of the obligee may bring an action in the court of common pleas that issued the support order to obtain a judgment on the unpaid amount. Any judgment obtained under this section may be enforced in the same manner as any other judgment of a court of this state.

(1992 S 331, eff. 11-13-92)

Library References

Divorce ⚷311(1), 311.5.
Parent and Child ⚷3.3(9).
WESTLAW Nos. 134, 285.
C.J.S. Divorce §§ 706 to 708, 716 to 718, 721.
C.J.S. Parent and Child §§ 80, 85 to 87, 89.

Am Jur 2d: 24, Divorce & Separation § 1056, 1060

Carlin, Baldwin's Ohio Practice, *Merrick-Rippner Probate Law* § 108.37 (1997)
Kurtz & Giannelli, Ohio Juvenile Law (1998 Ed.), Text 27.2, 29.2

Notes of Decisions and Opinions

1. Lapse of time

Ten years of inactivity before pursuing child support arrearages from obligor did not equitably prevent county child support enforcement agency from pursuing arrearages claims against obligor, even though custodial parent released claims after assigning rights to county. Campbell v. Campbell (Wayne 1993) 87 Ohio App.3d 48, 621 N.E.2d 853.

A claim for child support arrearages is barred by laches where the mother delays asserting her purported right to child support until the child has reached majority, accruing a seven-year arrearage against the father and leading him to conclude that he owed no further support. Smith v Leone, No. 68381, 1995 WL 705256 (8th Dist Ct App, Cuyahoga, 11-30-95).

Claim for overdue child support against decedent's estate by alleged former common-law wife of decedent could be adequately reviewed, and rights to any estate assets to satisfy purported claim could be fairly decided, by someone other than common-law wife herself in role as creditor-fiduciary, where claim for overdue child support arose three decades prior to filing of application to administer estate, which was subject to attack on procedural and jurisdictional grounds. In re Estate of Dalton (Ohio Com.Pl. 1995) 68 Ohio Misc.2d 78, 647 N.E.2d 581.

2. Dismissal of action

Conduct of mother in connection with her motion to collect child support arrears was so irresponsible, contumacious, and dilatory as to provide substantial grounds for dismissal of action, where she disobeyed court order prohibiting use of slanderous statements in pleadings, filed hundreds of documents, most of which required father to respond, and subjected court, judges and staff to unnecessary abuse. In re Reiner (Ohio Com.Pl. 1993) 63 Ohio Misc.2d 487, 635 N.E.2d 68.

3. Death of custodial parent, effect

Emancipated child had right to recover child support arrearages collected by child support agency after death of custodial parent; arrearages were not assets of deceased parent's estate. In re Estate of Antkowiak (Lucas 1994) 95 Ohio App.3d 546, 642 N.E.2d 1154.

Right to collect child support arrearages passes directly to emancipated child upon death of custodial parent absent judgment for arrearages obtained during custodial parent's lifetime. In re Estate of Antkowiak (Lucas 1994) 95 Ohio App.3d 546, 642 N.E.2d 1154.

Existence of child support arrearage upon beneficiary's emancipation and death of custodial parent establishes prima facie case that emancipated child has been denied standard of living to which he or she is entitled and that child has superior claim to arrearages. In re Estate of Antkowiak (Lucas 1994) 95 Ohio App.3d 546, 642 N.E.2d 1154.

In an action by a county child support enforcement agency to collect prebankruptcy child support arrearages, the law in effect at the time the bankruptcy petition is filed rather than the law in effect at the time a court renders its decision determines the dischargeability of the arrearage as a debt. Schindler v Schindler, No. 16413, 1994 WL 189783 (9th Dist Ct App, Summit, 5-18-94).

4. Interest

Interest on child support arrearages accrues from the date the individual child support payments become due and payable, and is calculated pursuant to RC 1343.03(A) at the rate of 6% from July 1, 1962 until July 29, 1980, 8% from July 30, 1980 until July 4, 1982, and 10% thereafter. Sheets v Sheets, No. 94CA17, 1994 WL 728050 (4th Dist Ct App, Gallia, 12-30-94).

5. Constitutional issues

It is a violation of the equal protection clauses of the United States and Ohio constitutions to allow the aid and support of the child support enforcement agency in an action for child support brought by parents who have established their parentage through the probate court and residential parents who are on public assistance while denying the aid and support of the child support enforcement agency to parents who have established their parentage through the administrative process. Cuyahoga County Support Enforcement Agency v Lozada, Nos. 67463+, 1995 WL 386965 (8th Dist Ct App, Cuyahoga, 6-29-95).

3113.2111 Motion for relief from final judgment, court order, or administrative determination

(A)(1) Notwithstanding the provisions to the contrary in Civil Rule 60(B) and in accordance with this section, a person may file a motion for relief from a final judgment, court order, or administrative determination or order that determines that the person or a male minor referred to in division (B) of section 3109.19 of the Revised Code is the father of a child or that requires the person or male minor to pay child support. The person shall file the motion in the court of common pleas of the county in which the original judgment, court order, or administrative determination or order was made.

(2) Upon the motion of any adverse party or upon its own motion, the court in which an action is brought under this section may transfer the action to the county in which an adverse party resides when it appears to the court that the location of the original venue presents a hardship for that adverse party.

(B)(1) Upon the filing of a motion for relief under division (A)(1) of this section, a court shall grant relief from a final judgment, court order, or administrative determination or order that determines that a person or male minor is the father of a child or that requires a person or male minor to pay child support for a child if all of the following apply:

(a) The court receives genetic test results from a genetic test administered no more than six months prior to the filing of the motion for relief that finds that there is a zero per cent probability that the person or male minor is the father of the child.

(b) The person or male minor has not adopted the child.

(c) The child was not conceived as a result of artificial insemination in compliance with sections 3111.30 to 3111.38 of the Revised Code.

(2) A court shall not deny relief from a final judgment, court order, or administrative determination or order that determines that a person or male minor is the father of a child or that requires a person or male minor to pay child support for a child solely because of the occurrence of any of the following acts if the person or male minor at the time of or prior to the occurrence of that act did not know that he was not the natural father of the child:

(a) The person or male minor married the mother of the child.

(b) The person or male minor acknowledged his paternity of the child in a writing sworn to before a notary public.

(c) The person or male minor was named as the child's natural father on the child's birth certificate with the valid consent of the person or male minor.

(d) The person or male minor was required to support the child because of a written voluntary promise or by a court order or an administrative support order.

(e) The person or male minor validly signed the child's birth certificate as an informant as provided in section 3705.09 of the Revised Code as that section existed prior to January 1, 1998.

(f) The person or male minor was named in an acknowledgment of paternity of the child that a court entered upon its journal pursuant to former section 2105.18 of the Revised Code.

(g) The person or male minor was named in an acknowledgment of paternity of the child that has become final under section 2151.232, 3111.211, or 5101.314 of the Revised Code.

(h) The person or male minor was presumed to be the natural father of the child under any of the circumstances listed in section 3111.03 of the Revised Code.

(i) The person or male minor was determined to be the father of the child in a parentage action under Chapter 3111. of the Revised Code.

(j) The person or male minor otherwise admitted or acknowledged himself to be the child's natural father.

(C) A court shall not grant relief from a final judgment, court order, or administrative determination or order that determines that a person or male minor is the father of a child or that requires a person or male minor to pay child support for a child if the court determines, by a preponderance of the evidence, that the person or male minor knew that he was not the natural father of the child before any of the following:

(1) Any act listed in divisions (B)(2)(a) to (g) of this section occurred.

(2) The person or male minor was presumed to be the natural father of the child under any of the circumstances listed in divisions (A)(1) to (4) of section 3111.03 of the Revised Code.

(3) The person or male minor otherwise admitted or acknowledged himself to be the child's father.

(D)(1) In any action for relief instituted under this section, if the genetic test results submitted in connection with the motion for relief are solely provided by the moving party, the court, upon its own motion, may order and, upon the motion of any party to the action, shall order the child's mother, the child, and the alleged father to submit to genetic tests. The clerk of the court shall schedule the genetic testing no later than thirty days after the court issues its order.

(2) If the mother is the custodian of the child and willfully fails to submit the child to genetic testing, if the alleged father of the child willfully fails to submit himself to genetic testing, or if the alleged father is the custodian of the child and willfully fails to submit the child to genetic testing, the court shall issue an order determining the motion for relief against the party failing to submit the party or the child to the genetic testing. If a party shows good cause for failing to submit to genetic testing or for failing to submit the child to genetic testing, the court shall not consider the failure to be willful.

(3) The party requesting the genetic tests shall pay any fees charged for the tests, unless the custodian of the child is represented by the child support enforcement agency in its role as the agency providing enforcement of child support orders, in which case the child support enforcement agency shall pay the costs of genetic testing if it requests the tests. The child support enforcement agency or the person who paid the fees charged for the genetic testing may seek reimbursement for the fees from the person against whom the court assesses the costs of the action.

(4) The genetic tests shall be made by qualified examiners who are authorized by the court or the department of job and family services or by a genetic testing laboratory accredited by the American association of blood banks. An examiner conducting a genetic test, upon the completion of the test, shall send a complete report of the test results to the clerk of the court that ordered the test.

(E) If a court grants a motion that relieves a person or male minor from a final judgment, court order, or administrative determination or order under this section, the granting of the motion does not preclude any person from filing, subsequent to the granting of the motion, an action under Chapter 3111. of the Revised Code to establish a parent-child relationship between the person or male minor who was granted relief and the child who is the subject of the judgment, court order, or administrative determination or order from which relief was granted. A person shall not file more than one action of that type under Chapter 3111. of the Revised Code in any two-year period regarding the person or male minor who was granted relief and the child. A court, pursuant to a motion filed under this division and in accordance with Chapter 3111. of the Revised Code, may enter a judgment in the action that determines the existence of a parent-child relationship between the person or male minor granted relief and the child only if genetic tests taken subsequent to the granting of the motion for relief indicate that there is a statistical probability that the party or the male minor is the natural father of the child. If a person files an action under Chapter 3111. of the Revised Code as described in this division and the court determines that no parent-child relationship exists between the person or the male minor and the child, the court shall require the person who filed the action to pay all court costs of the action and the reasonable attorney's fees of the opposing party.

(F) If a court grants relief from a judgment, court order, or administrative determination or order pursuant to this section and the person who is relieved from the judgment, order, or determination, the male minor, or any relative of the person or male minor has been granted companionship or visitation rights with the child pursuant to an order issued under section 3109.051 or 3109.12 of the Revised Code, the court shall determine whether the order granting those rights should be terminated, modified, or continued.

(G) If a court grants relief from a judgment, court order, or administrative order for the payment of child support pursuant to this section and child support arrearages are owed, the court may issue an order canceling that arrearage. Nothing in this section limits any actions that may be taken by the person or male minor granted relief under this section to recover child support paid under the judgment or order from which relief was granted.

(H) If relief from a judgment, court order, or administrative order for the payment of child support is not granted pursuant to this section, the court shall require the person who filed the motion for relief to pay all court costs of the action and the reasonable attorney's fees of the opposing party.

(I) Except as otherwise provided in this section, a party is entitled to obtain relief under this section regardless of whether the final judgment, court order, or administrative determination or order from which relief is sought was issued prior to, on, or after the effective date of this section.

(J) As used in this section:

(1) "Child support" means support for a child that is included in a support order issued or modified prior to, on, or after the effective date of this section, under former section 3111.21 or section 2151.23, 2151.33, 2151.36, 2151.49, 3105.21, 3109.05, 3109.19, 3111.13, 3111.20, 3111.22, 3111.27, 3113.04, 3113.07, 3113.216, or 3113.31 of the Revised Code.

(2) "Genetic tests" and "genetic testing" have the same meanings as in section 3111.09 of the Revised Code.

(2000 H 242, eff. 10-27-00)

Cross References

Husband rather than donor regarded as natural father, 3111.37

3113.25 Notice to state retirement systems of death of member subject to child support order

A child support enforcement agency that learns that an obligor under a support order administered by the agency who was a member of the public employees retirement system, school employees retirement system, or state teachers retirement system has died shall immediately notify the retirement system that the member was survived by one or more children who are the subject of a child support order.

(1998 H 648, eff. 9-16-98)

Library References

OJur 3d: 48, Family Law § 1236 to 1250, 1253 et seq.

DOMESTIC VIOLENCE

Library References

Sowald & Morganstern, Baldwin's Ohio Practice, *Domestic Relations Law* § 7.16 (1997)

3113.31 Petitions; protection orders concerning domestic violence; support orders; sanctions for violations; notification of law enforcement agencies and courts

(A) As used in this section:

(1) "Domestic violence" means the occurrence of one or more of the following acts against a family or household member:

(a) Attempting to cause or recklessly causing bodily injury;

(b) Placing another person by the threat of force in fear of imminent serious physical harm or committing a violation of section 2903.211 or 2911.211 of the Revised Code;

(c) Committing any act with respect to a child that would result in the child being an abused child, as defined in section 2151.031 of the Revised Code.

(2) "Court" means the domestic relations division of the court of common pleas in counties that have a domestic relations division, and the court of common pleas in counties that do not have a domestic relations division.

(3) "Family or household member" means any of the following:

(a) Any of the following who is residing with or has resided with the respondent:

(i) A spouse, a person living as a spouse, or a former spouse of the respondent;

(ii) A parent or a child of the respondent, or another person related by consanguinity or affinity to the respondent;

(iii) A parent or a child of a spouse, person living as a spouse, or former spouse of the respondent, or another person related by consanguinity or affinity to a spouse, person living as a spouse, or former spouse of the respondent.

(b) The natural parent of any child of whom the respondent is the other natural parent or is the putative other natural parent.

(4) "Person living as a spouse" means a person who is living or has lived with the respondent in a common law marital relationship, who otherwise is cohabiting with the respondent, or who otherwise has cohabited with the respondent within five years prior to the date of the alleged occurrence of the act in question.

(5) "Victim advocate" means a person who provides support and assistance for a person who files a petition under this section.

(B) The court has jurisdiction over all proceedings under this section. The petitioner's right to relief under this section is not affected by the petitioner's leaving the residence or household to avoid further domestic violence.

(C) A person may seek relief under this section on the person's own behalf, or any parent or adult household member may seek relief under this section on behalf of any other family or household member, by filing a petition with the court. The petition shall contain or state:

(1) An allegation that the respondent engaged in domestic violence against a family or household member of the respondent, including a description of the nature and extent of the domestic violence;

(2) The relationship of the respondent to the petitioner, and to the victim if other than the petitioner;

(3) A request for relief under this section.

(D)(1) If a person who files a petition pursuant to this section requests an ex parte order, the court shall hold an ex parte hearing on the same day that the petition is filed. The court, for good cause shown at the ex parte hearing, may enter any temporary orders, with or without bond, including, but not limited to, an order described in division (E)(1)(a), (b), or (c) of this section, that the court finds necessary to protect the family or household member from domestic violence. Immediate and present danger of domestic violence to the family or household member constitutes good cause for purposes of this section. Immediate and present danger includes, but is not limited to, situations in which the respondent has threatened the family or household member with bodily harm or in which the respondent previously has been convicted of or pleaded guilty to an offense that constitutes domestic violence against the family or household member.

(2)(a) If the court, after an ex parte hearing, issues an order described in division (E)(1)(b) or (c) of this section, the court shall schedule a full hearing for a date that is within seven court days after the ex parte hearing. If any other type of protection order that is authorized under division (E) of this section is issued by the court after an ex parte hearing, the court shall schedule a full hearing for a date that is within ten court days after the ex parte hearing. The court shall give the respondent notice of, and an opportunity to be heard at, the full hearing. The court shall hold the full hearing on the date scheduled under this division unless the court grants a continuance of the hearing in accordance with this division. Under any of the following circumstances or for any of the following reasons, the court may grant a continuance of the full hearing to a reasonable time determined by the court:

(i) Prior to the date scheduled for the full hearing under this division, the respondent has not been served with the petition filed pursuant to this section and notice of the full hearing.

(ii) The parties consent to the continuance.

(iii) The continuance is needed to allow a party to obtain counsel.

(iv) The continuance is needed for other good cause.

(b) An ex parte order issued under this section does not expire because of a failure to serve notice of the full hearing upon the respondent before the date set for the full hearing under division (D)(2)(a) of this section or because the court grants a continuance under that division.

(3) If a person who files a petition pursuant to this section does not request an ex parte order, or if a person requests an ex parte order but the court does not issue an ex parte order after an ex parte hearing, the court shall proceed as in a normal civil action and grant a full hearing on the matter.

(E)(1) After an ex parte or full hearing, the court may grant any protection order, with or without bond, or approve any consent agreement to bring about a cessation of domestic violence against the family or household members. The order or agreement may:

(a) Direct the respondent to refrain from abusing the family or household members;

(b) Grant possession of the residence or household to the petitioner or other family or household member, to the exclusion of the respondent, by evicting the respondent, when the residence or household is owned or leased solely by the petitioner or other family or household member, or by ordering the respondent to vacate the premises, when the residence or household is jointly owned or leased by the respondent, and the petitioner or other family or household member;

(c) When the respondent has a duty to support the petitioner or other family or household member living in the residence or household and the respondent is the sole owner or lessee of the residence or household, grant possession of the residence or household to the petitioner or other family or household member, to the exclusion of the respondent, by ordering the respondent to vacate the premises, or, in the case of a consent agreement, allow the respondent to provide suitable, alternative housing;

(d) Temporarily allocate parental rights and responsibilities for the care of, or establish temporary visitation rights with regard to, minor children, if no other court has determined, or is determining, the allocation of parental rights and responsibilities for the minor children or visitation rights;

(e) Require the respondent to maintain support, if the respondent customarily provides for or contributes to the support of the family or household member, or if the respondent has a duty to support the petitioner or family or household member;

(f) Require the respondent, petitioner, victim of domestic violence, or any combination of those persons, to seek counseling;

(g) Require the respondent to refrain from entering the residence, school, business, or place of employment of the petitioner or family or household member;

(h) Grant other relief that the court considers equitable and fair, including, but not limited to, ordering the respondent to permit the use of a motor vehicle by the petitioner or other family or household member and the apportionment of household and family personal property.

(2) If a protection order has been issued pursuant to this section in a prior action involving the respondent and the petitioner or one or more of the family or household members, the court may include in a protection order that it issues a prohibition against the respondent returning to the residence or household. If it includes a prohibition against the respondent returning to the residence or household in the order, it also shall include in the order provisions of the type described in division (E)(7) of this section. This division does not preclude the court from including in a protection order or consent agreement, in circumstances other than those described in this division, a requirement that the respondent be evicted from or vacate the residence or household or refrain from entering the residence, school, business, or place of employment of the petitioner or a family or household member, and, if the court includes any requirement of that type in an order or agreement, the court also shall include in the order provisions of the type described in division (E)(7) of this section.

(3)(a) Any protection order issued or consent agreement approved under this section shall be valid until a date certain, but not later than five years from the date of its issuance or approval.

(b) Subject to the limitation on the duration of an order or agreement set forth in division (E)(3)(a) of this section, any order under division (E)(1)(d) of this section shall terminate on the date that a court in an action for divorce, dissolution of marriage, or legal separation brought by the petitioner or respondent issues an order allocating parental rights and responsibilities for the care of children or on the date that a juvenile court in an action brought by the petitioner or respondent issues an order awarding legal custody of minor children. Subject to the limitation on the duration of an order or agreement set forth in division (E)(3)(a) of this section, any order under division (E)(1)(e) of this section shall terminate on the date that a court in an action for divorce, dissolution of marriage, or legal separation brought by the petitioner or respondent issues a support order or on the date that a juvenile court in an action brought by the petitioner or respondent issues a support order.

(c) Any protection order issued or consent agreement approved pursuant to this section may be renewed in the same manner as the original order or agreement was issued or approved.

(4) A court may not issue a protection order that requires a petitioner to do or to refrain from doing an act that the court may require a respondent to do or to refrain from doing under division (E)(1)(a), (b), (c), (d), (e), (g), or (h) of this section unless all of the following apply:

(a) The respondent files a separate petition for a protection order in accordance with this section.

(b) The petitioner is served notice of the respondent's petition at least forty-eight hours before the court holds a hearing with respect to the respondent's petition, or the petitioner waives the right to receive this notice.

(c) If the petitioner has requested an ex parte order pursuant to division (D) of this section, the court does not delay any hearing required by that division beyond the time specified in that division in order to consolidate the hearing with a hearing on the petition filed by the respondent.

(d) After a full hearing at which the respondent presents evidence in support of the request for a protection order and the petitioner is afforded an opportunity to defend against that evidence, the court determines that the petitioner has committed an act of domestic violence or has violated a temporary protection order issued pursuant to section 2919.26 of the Revised Code, that both the petitioner and the respondent acted primarily as aggressors, and that neither the petitioner nor the respondent acted primarily in self-defense.

(5) No protection order issued or consent agreement approved under this section shall in any manner affect title to any real property.

(6)(a) If a petitioner, or the child of a petitioner, who obtains a protection order or consent agreement pursuant to division (E)(1) of this section or a temporary protection order pursuant to section 2919.26 of the Revised Code and is the subject of a visitation or companionship order issued pursuant to section 3109.051, 3109.11, or 3109.12 of the Revised Code or division (E)(1)(d) of this section granting visitation or companionship rights to the respondent, the court may require the public children services agency of the county in which the court is located to provide supervision of the respondent's exercise of visitation or companionship rights with respect to the child for a period not to exceed nine months, if the court makes the following findings of fact:

(i) The child is in danger from the respondent;

(ii) No other person or agency is available to provide the supervision.

(b) A court that requires an agency to provide supervision pursuant to division (E)(6)(a) of this section shall order the respondent to reimburse the agency for the cost of providing the supervision, if it determines that the respondent has sufficient income or resources to pay that cost.

(7)(a) If a protection order issued or consent agreement approved under this section includes a requirement that the respondent be evicted from or vacate the residence or household or refrain from entering the residence, school, business, or place of employment of the petitioner or a family or household member, the order or agreement shall state clearly that the order or agreement cannot be waived or nullified by an invitation to the respondent from the petitioner or other family or household member to enter the residence, school, business, or place of employment or by the respondent's entry into one of those places otherwise upon the consent of the petitioner or other family or household member.

(b) Division (E)(7)(a) of this section does not limit any discretion of a court to determine that a respondent charged with a violation of section 2919.27 of the Revised Code, with a violation of a municipal ordinance substantially equivalent to that section, or with contempt of court, which charge is based on an alleged violation of a protection order issued or consent agreement approved under this section, did not commit the violation or was not in contempt of court.

(F)(1) A copy of any protection order, or consent agreement, that is issued or approved under this section shall be issued by the court to the petitioner, to the respondent, and to all law enforcement agencies that have jurisdiction to enforce the order or agreement. The court shall direct that a copy of an order be delivered to the respondent on the same day that the order is entered.

(2) All law enforcement agencies shall establish and maintain an index for the protection orders and the approved consent agreements delivered to the agencies pursuant to division (F)(1) of this section. With respect to each order and consent agreement delivered, each agency shall note on the index the date and time that it received the order or consent agreement.

(3) Regardless of whether the petitioner has registered the order or agreement in the county in which the officer's agency has jurisdiction pursuant to division (N) of this section, any officer of a law enforcement agency shall enforce a protection order issued or consent agreement approved by any court in this state in accordance with the provisions of the order or agreement, including removing the respondent from the premises, if appropriate.

(G) Any proceeding under this section shall be conducted in accordance with the Rules of Civil Procedure, except that an order under this section may be obtained with or without bond. An order issued under this section, other than an ex parte order, that grants a protection order or approves a consent agreement, or that refuses to grant a protection order or approve a consent agreement, is a final, appealable order. The remedies and procedures provided in this section are in addition to, and not in lieu of, any other available civil or criminal remedies.

(H) The filing of proceedings under this section does not excuse a person from filing any report or giving any notice required by section 2151.421 of the Revised Code or by any other law. When a petition under this section alleges domestic violence against minor children, the court shall report the fact, or cause reports to be made, to a county, township, or municipal peace officer under section 2151.421 of the Revised Code.

(I) Any law enforcement agency that investigates a domestic dispute shall provide information to the family or household members involved regarding the relief available under this section and section 2919.26 of the Revised Code.

(J) Notwithstanding any provision of law to the contrary, no court shall charge a fee for the filing of a petition pursuant to this section.

(K)(1) Each order for support made or modified under this section shall include as part of the order a general provision, as described in division (A)(1) of section 3113.21 of the Revised Code, requiring the withholding or deduction of income or assets of the obligor under the order as described in division (D) of section 3113.21 of the Revised Code or another type of appropriate requirement as described in division (D)(3), (D)(4), or (H) of that section, to ensure that withholding or deduction from the income or assets of the obligor is available from the commencement of the support order for collection of the support and of any arrearages that occur; a statement requiring all parties to the order to notify the child support enforcement agency in writing of their current mailing address, current residence address, current residence telephone number, current driver's license number, and any changes to that information; and a notice that the requirement to notify the agency of all changes to that information continues until further notice from the court. The court shall comply with sections 3113.21 to 3113.219 of the Revised Code when it makes or modifies an order for child support under this section.

If any person required to pay child support under an order made under this section on or after April 15, 1985, or modified under this section on or after December 31, 1986, is found in contempt of court for failure to make support payments under the order, the court that makes the finding, in addition to any other penalty or remedy imposed, shall assess all court costs arising out of the contempt proceeding against the person and require the person to pay any reasonable attorney's fees of any adverse party, as determined by the court, that arose in relation to the act of contempt.

(2) Notwithstanding section 3109.01 of the Revised Code, if a court issues a child support order under this section, the order shall remain in effect beyond the child's eighteenth birthday as long as the child continuously attends on a full-time basis any recognized and accredited high school or the order provides that the duty of support of the child continues beyond the child's eighteenth birthday. Except in cases in which the order provides that the duty of support continues for any period after the child reaches nineteen years of age, the order shall not remain in effect after the child reaches nineteen years of age. Any parent ordered to pay support under a child support order issued under this section shall continue to pay support under the order, including during seasonal vacation periods, until the order terminates.

(L)(1) A person who violates a protection order issued or a consent agreement approved under this section is subject to the following sanctions:

(a) Criminal prosecution for a violation of section 2919.27 of the Revised Code, if the violation of the protection order or consent agreement constitutes a violation of that section;

(b) Punishment for contempt of court.

(2) The punishment of a person for contempt of court for violation of a protection order issued or a consent agreement approved under this section does not bar criminal prosecution of the person for a violation of section 2919.27 of the Revised Code. However, a person punished for contempt of court is entitled to credit for the punishment imposed upon conviction of a violation of that section, and a person convicted of a violation of that section shall not subsequently be punished for contempt of court arising out of the same activity.

(M) In all stages of a proceeding under this section, a petitioner may be accompanied by a victim advocate.

(N)(1) A petitioner who obtains a protection order or consent agreement under this section or a temporary protection order under section 2919.26 of the Revised Code may provide notice of the issuance or approval of the order or agreement to the judicial and law enforcement officials in any county other than the county in which the order is issued or the agreement is approved by registering that order or agreement in the other county pursuant to division (N)(2) of this section and filing a copy of the registered order or registered agreement with a law enforcement agency in the other county in accordance with that division. A person who obtains a protection order issued by a court of another state may provide notice of the issuance of the order to the judicial and law enforcement officials in any county of this state by registering the order in that county pursuant to section 2919.272 of the Revised Code and filing a copy of the registered order with a law enforcement agency in that county.

(2) A petitioner may register a temporary protection order, protection order, or consent agreement in a county other than the county in which the court that issued the order or approved the agreement is located in the following manner:

(a) The petitioner shall obtain a certified copy of the order or agreement from the clerk of the court that issued the order or approved the agreement and present that certified copy to the clerk of the court of common pleas or the clerk of a municipal court or county court in the county in which the order or agreement is to be registered.

(b) Upon accepting the certified copy of the order or agreement for registration, the clerk of the court of common pleas, municipal court, or county court shall place an endorsement of registration on the order or agreement and give the petitioner a copy of the order or agreement that bears that proof of registration.

(3) The clerk of each court of common pleas, the clerk of each municipal court, and the clerk of each county court shall maintain a registry of certified copies of temporary protection orders, protection orders, or consent agreements that have been issued or approved by courts in other counties and that have been registered with the clerk.

(4) If a petitioner who obtains a protection order or consent agreement under this section or a temporary protection order under section 2919.26 of the Revised Code wishes to register the order or agreement in any county other than the county in which the order was issued or the agreement was approved, pursuant to divisions (N)(1) to (3) of this section, and if the petitioner is indigent, both of the following apply:

(a) If the petitioner submits to the clerk of the court that issued the order or approved the agreement satisfactory proof that the petitioner is indigent, the clerk may waive any fee that otherwise would be required for providing the petitioner with a certified copy of the order or agreement to be used for purposes of divisions (N)(1) to (3) of this section;

(b) If the petitioner submits to the clerk of the court of common pleas or the clerk of a municipal court or county court in the county in which the order or agreement is to be registered satisfactory proof that the petitioner is indigent, the clerk may waive any fee that otherwise would be required for accepting for registration a certified copy of the order or agreement, for placing an endorsement of registration on the order or agreement, or for giving the petitioner a copy of the order or agreement that bears the proof of registration.

(1997 H 352, eff. 1-1-98; 1997 S 1, eff. 10-21-97; 1996 H 438, eff. 7-1-97; 1996 H 274, eff. 8-8-96; 1994 H 335, eff. 12-9-94; 1993 H 173, eff. 12-31-93; 1992 H 536, S 10; 1990 S 3, H 591; 1988 H 172, H 708; 1987 H 231; 1986 H 428, H 509; 1984 H 113, H 614, H 587; 1980 H 920; 1978 H 835)

Uncodified Law

1994 H 335, § 4, eff. 12-9-94, reads: The General Assembly hereby requests the Supreme Court, in consultation with the Department of Human Services, to prescribe a form that is to be filed by a petitioner seeking a civil protection order under section 3113.31 of the Revised Code and that makes reference to all the forms of relief that a court is authorized to grant under division (E) of section 3113.31 of the Revised Code, as amended by this act, contains space for the petitioner to request any of those forms of relief, and includes instructions for completing the form so that a petitioner may file the form without the assistance of an attorney.

Historical and Statutory Notes

Amendment Note: 1997 H 352 deleted "or other services" after "supervision" in division (E)(6)(a)(11) and twice in division (E)(6)(b); deleted "on or after December 31, 1993," before "shall include", substituted "income" for "wages" twice and "(D)(3), (D)(4)" for "(D)(6), (D)(7)", inserted "current residence telephone number, current driver's license number,", and deleted "on or after April 12, 1990," before "shall comply", in the first paragraph in division (K)(1); inserted "or the order provides that the duty of support of the child continues beyond the child's eighteenth birthday" and added the second sentence in division (K)(2); and made other nonsubstantive changes.

Amendment Note: 1997 S 1 rewrote this section; see *Baldwin's Ohio Legislative Service Annotated*, 1997, p 7/L-727, or the OH-LEGIS or OH-LEGIS-OLD database on WESTLAW, for text of previous version.

Amendment Note: 1996 H 438 inserted "or county court" in divisions (N)(2)(a) and (N)(4)(b); inserted "and the clerk of each county court" in division (N)(3); and made changes to reflect gender neutral language.

Amendment Note: 1996 H 274 added division (E)(6); and made changes to reflect gender neutral language.

Amendment Note: 1994 H 335 rewrote this section; see *Baldwin's Ohio Legislative Service*, 1994 Laws of Ohio, H 335, page 5-1350 for text of previous version.

Amendment Note: 1993 H 173 rewrote division (K)(1) before the first semi-colon, which previously read:

"(K)(1) Each order for support made or modified under this section on or after December 1, 1986, shall be accompanied by one or more orders described in division (D) or (H) of section 3113.21 of the Revised Code, whichever is appropriate under the requirements of that section."

Cross References

Anti-stalking protection order, family or household member defined, 2903.214
Bail, temporary protection order violations, 2937.23
Bureau of support, support order defined, 2301.34
Child support enforcement agency, adoption of rules, 2301.35
Child support orders, procedures on default, 2301.37
Commitment of alcoholics and intoxicated persons, 2935.33
Common-law marriage prohibited, 3105.12
Competency of spouse to testify against spouse, 2945.42
Conciliation of marital controversies, Ch 3117
Contempt action for failure to pay support, 2705.031, 2705.05
County children services boards, powers and duties, 5153.16
Crime victims' rights pamphlet, 109.42
Domestic violence arrest policies, protection orders, 2935.032
Domestic violence, 2919.25
Endangering children, 2919.22
Hospitals, domestic violence interview protocols, 3727.08
Interfering with action to issue or modify support order, 2919.231
Medical personnel to report suspected domestic violence, 2921.22
Nonsupport of dependents, 2919.21
Notice of default on child support order sent to professional licensing boards, 2301.373
Peace officer training commission, certificate of training for peace officers, 109.77
Peace officer training commission, powers and duties, 109.73
Peace officer training programs, rulemaking powers, 109.744
Sexual assaults, 2907.02 to 2907.11
Temporary protection orders, 2919.26
Violating protection order or consent agreement, mental evaluation, 2919.271
Violation of protection order or consent agreement, bail schedule, 2919.251

Ohio Administrative Code References

Age of majority defined, OAC 5101:1-32-06
Alleged child abuse and neglect, OAC Ch 5101:2-34
Child abuse and neglect, supportive services, OAC Ch 5101:2-39

Library References

Breach of the Peace ⚷15 to 21.
WESTLAW Topic No. 62.
C.J.S. Breach of the Peace §§ 14 to 22, 25.
C.J.S. Domestic Abuse and Violence §§ 2 to 23.

Am Jur 2d: 6, Assault and Battery § 44, 47
Who has custody or control of child within terms of penal statute punishing cruelty or neglect by one having custody or control. 75 ALR3d 933
Civil liability of physician for failure to diagnose or report battered child syndrome. 97 ALR3d 338
Validity and construction of penal statute prohibiting child abuse. 1 ALR4th 38
Admissibility of expert or opinion testimony on battered wife or battered woman syndrome. 18 ALR4th 1153

Baldwin's Ohio Legislative Service, 1990 Laws of Ohio, H 591—LSC Analysis, p 5-576
Katz & Giannelli, Baldwin's Ohio Practice, *Criminal Law* § 109.9, 109.12, 109.15, 143.51 (1996)
Sowald & Morganstern, Baldwin's Ohio Practice, *Domestic Relations Law* § 2.66, 2.69, 4.12, 4.13, 4.14, 5.1, 5.3, 5.5, 5.6, 5.7, 5.8, 5.9, 5.10, 5.11, 5.12, 5.13, 5.14, 5.15, 5.16, 5.17, 5.18, 5.20, 7.16, 19.1, 20.21, 21.3, 22.5, 25.26 (1997)

Law Review and Journal Commentaries

Caseworker Liability for the Negligent Handling of Child Abuse Reports, Comment. 60 U Cin L Rev 191 (Summer 1991).

Civil Protection Orders in Ohio Domestic Violence Cases, Hon. Mike Brigner. 9 Domestic Rel J Ohio 37 (May/June 1997).

Domestic Relations: Legal Responses to Wife Beating: Theory and Practice in Ohio, Note. 16 Akron L Rev 705 (Spring 1983).

Empowering the Battered Woman: The Use of Criminal Contempt Sanctions to Enforce Civil Protection Orders, David M. Zlotnick. 56 Ohio St L J 1153 (1995).

Felton v. Felton: A Case Study, James Wilsman. 45 Clev St L Rev 579 (1997).

Honor thy father and mother?—The unintended consequences of Ohio's domestic violence preferred arrest policy on Ohio's parents, Richard M. Garner. 11 Ohio Law 12 (January/February 1997).

Major Evidentiary Issues in Prosecutions of Family Abuse Cases, Susan P. Mele. 11 Ohio N U L Rev 245 (1984).

Ohio Revised Code Section 3113.31 And The Constitution: Ohio's Statutory Response To Domestic Violence And Its Double Jeopardy Infirmity, Note. 19 U Dayton L Rev 317 (Fall 1993).

Ohio's Domestic Violence Law, Sarah H. Ramsey. 8 Ohio N U L Rev 895 (1981).

Ohio's New Civil Remedies for Victims of Domestic Violence, Judge June R. Galvin. 8 Ohio N U L Rev 248 (1981).

School Personnel & Mandated Reporting of Child Maltreatment, Kevin S. Mahoney. 24 J L & Educ 227 (Spring 1995).

Selection of Remedies/Temporary Restraining Order or Protective Order—Which is More Effective?, Judith A. Nicely. 2 Domestic Rel J Ohio 37 (May/June 1990).

Spouse Battering and Ohio's Domestic Violence Legislation, Comment. 13 U Tol L Rev 347 (Winter 1982).

Therapists' Liability to the Falsely Accused for Inducing Illusory Memories of Childhood Sexual Abuse—Current Remedies and a Proposed Statute, Joel Jay Finer. 11 J L & Health 45 (1996-97).

Understanding Ohio's new domestic violence law, Francis G. Forchione. 11 Ohio Law 8 (January/February 1997).

Notes of Decisions and Opinions

---

1. Domestic violence defined

Finding that respondent had placed petitioner, who was his former live-in girlfriend, in reasonable fear of serious physical harm by threat of force, and thus had engaged in acts of domestic violence against petitioner which would warrant issuance of civil protection order, was supported by evidence that respondent had left message on petitioner's telephone answering machine saying that he would "surprise" petitioner in court during hearing on pending stalking charges, and had left book with threatening inscription in courtroom where he believed petitioner would see it. Conkle v. Wolfe (Ohio App. 4 Dist. 1998) 131 Ohio App.3d 375, 722 N.E.2d 586.

Domestic violence has occurred and a civil protection order is appropriate where a husband (1) uses offensive language and threatening verbal abuse with cursing against his wife in the presence of their minor children, (2) attempts to cause his wife serious bodily injury, (3) places her in fear of imminent serious physical harm by threatening to kill her, and (4) has engaged in similar conduct on previous occasions. Eichenberger v. Eichenberger (Franklin 1992) 82 Ohio App.3d 809, 613 N.E.2d 678.

A parent commits domestic violence by striking the shoulder of his eleven-year-old son three or four times with the bottom of a closed hand. State v Moser, No. L-98-1111, 1999 WL 550272 (6th Dist Ct App, Wood, 7-30-99).

A petition for domestic violence is granted for acts which result in child abuse and a temporary order is enforced against the mother to protect the child from further domestic violence where (1) the child's fractured forearm injury is at variance with the account provided by the mother, (2) there is improper care and hygiene including constant exposure to filth and grime, and (3) there is an inordinate amount of minor physical injuries while in the care of the mother and a babysitter who was hired by the mother. Tischler v Vahcic, No. 68053, 1995 WL 680928 (8th Dist Ct App, Cuyahoga, 11-16-95).

2. Hearing

Trial court did not abuse its discretion by denying respondent's request for a continuance of full hearing held in connection with request for civil protection order, where request was not made until three weeks after hearing, petitioner did not agree to request, and respondent failed to raise with trial court his claim that he needed continuance to consult with counsel. Conkle v. Wolfe (Ohio App. 4 Dist. 1998) 131 Ohio App.3d 375, 722 N.E.2d 586.

Where the issuance of a domestic protection order is contested, the court must, at the very least, allow for presentation of evidence, both direct and rebuttal, as well as arguments. Deacon v. Landers (Ross 1990) 68 Ohio App.3d 26, 587 N.E.2d 395.

3. Eviction order

RC 3113.31(E)(1)(b) grants a trial court the authority to enter an eviction order without the necessity of a prior protection order. Mallin v. Mallin (Cuyahoga 1988) 44 Ohio App.3d 53, 541 N.E.2d 116.

4. Civil Rule 75

While a court may consider whether there is a pending action for divorce or dissolution and whether a request has been made or an order granted pursuant to Civ R 75, the mere filing of an action for divorce is not a basis on which to deny a civil protection order. Thomas v. Thomas (Franklin 1988) 44 Ohio App.3d 6, 540 N.E.2d 745.

A comparison of RC 3113.31 and Civ R 75 shows that while the relief available under both provisions is somewhat similar, it is directed to a different purpose in that the purpose of a civil protection order issued pursuant to RC 3113.31 is to provide protection from domestic violence and, incidental to that relief, to provide for support and shelter; further, (1) the relief is available to a broader range of petitioners, (2) the scope of relief is broader, (3) there is no residency requirement, and (4) a violation of a civil protection order can form the basis of a criminal offense under RC 2919.27. Civ R 75, though providing for financial support and custody, does so only incidental to a divorce or dissolution and is available only to parties to the action. Thomas v. Thomas (Franklin 1988) 44 Ohio App.3d 6, 540 N.E.2d 745.

5. Petitioners

Trial court did not abuse its discretion in adopting referee's report based upon former wife's testimony and in denying husband's motion for neutral pickup and delivery site for parties' children, which was based on alleged violence that occurred between parties; wife admitted to knocking husband's glasses off his face but denied any other confrontations, arguments, or unpleasantries during visitation, wife testified that it was inconvenient for her to use neutral site because many times she was at work and there was no one to deliver or pick up children, and she preferred that children be able to take their belongings from house to automobile. Goode v. Goode (Franklin 1993) 89 Ohio App.3d 405, 624 N.E.2d 788.

A parent need not live in the same household as his or her adult child and grandchildren in order to petition the court for protective orders on behalf of such adult child and grandchildren pursuant to RC 3113.31. Carney v Pankey, No. 87 CA 85 (7th Dist Ct App, Mahoning, 3-4-88).

6. Double jeopardy

A defendant, having been found guilty of contempt of court for violating a temporary protection order under RC 3113.31, may not subsequently be prosecuted under RC 2919.27 for the exact same act, as such prosecution violates the Double Jeopardy Clause of US Const Am 5 and O Const Art I §10. State v. Vanselow (Ohio Mun. 1991) 61 Ohio Misc.2d 1, 572 N.E.2d 269.

7. Constitutional issues

Telephone company's advanced custom calling service of caller identification, approved by Public Utilities Commission of Ohio (PUCO), did not violate constitutional right against disclosure of personal information as alleged by domestic violence network and consumer representative; interests served by service would outweigh threatened privacy intrusions, and free per-call and per-line blocking features would safeguard against disclosure in comparatively limited instances in which caller had to make particularly sensitive or potentially embarrassing call. Ohio Domestic Violence Network v. Public Utilities Comm. (Ohio 1994) 70 Ohio St.3d 311, 638 N.E.2d 1012.

Approval by Public Utilities Commission of Ohio (PUCO) of telephone company's applications to offer new advanced custom calling services did not constitute "state action" under Fourteenth Amendment as required for finding that approval infringed First and Fourth Amendment rights of domestic violence network and consumer representative, where PUCO did not order company to implement services, but that decision was initiated by and remained with company throughout proceedings. Ohio Domestic Violence Network v. Public Utilities Comm. (Ohio 1994) 70 Ohio St.3d 311, 638 N.E.2d 1012.

Amended version of stalking statute, which extended to five years period prior to acts of harassment during which petitioner must have cohabited with respondent in order for petitioner to be considered a "family member," threats to whom could support issuance of civil protection order, contained no indication that statute was intended to apply retroactively, and thus would be applied only to acts committed after its effective date. Conkle v. Wolfe (Ohio App. 4 Dist. 1998) 131 Ohio App.3d 375, 722 N.E.2d 586.

Proceedings held in connection with wife's petition for civil protection order against her husband, who had allegedly committed act of domestic violence, did not result in husband being placed in jeopardy, as would bar subsequent domestic violence prosecution under Double Jeopardy Clauses of Federal and State Constitutions; civil protection order sought by wife was remedial, and not punitive, in nature. Cleveland v. Hogan (Ohio Mun. 1998) 92 Ohio Misc.2d 34, 699 N.E.2d 1020.

City which brought criminal charge of domestic violence against defendant was not in privity with defendant's wife, who earlier had unsuccessfully petitioned for civil protection order against defendant following incident giving rise to charge, and thus, determination in domestic relations proceeding did not operate to bar prosecution under collateral estoppel aspect of Double Jeopardy Clause; interest of city in enforcing law was different from interest of wife in protecting herself from abuse, and city could not have participated in prior action. Cleveland v. Hogan (Ohio Mun. 1998) 92 Ohio Misc.2d 31, 699 N.E.2d 1020.

RC 3113.31(L)(1), insofar as it purports to allow criminal prosecutions for the same acts that have already been adjudicated in a contempt proceeding, is unconstitutional. State v. Vanselow (Ohio Mun. 1991) 61 Ohio Misc.2d 1, 572 N.E.2d 269.

Plaintiff's wife did not qualify as "state actor," and, thus, viable claim could not be established against wife under federal civil rights statute with regard to violation of plaintiff's due process rights upon service and execution of civil protection order (CPO), even though wife utilized Ohio statute in seeking CPO. Kelm v. Hyatt (C.A.6 (Ohio) 1995) 44 F.3d 415.

Police officers had qualified immunity in civil rights action alleging that service and execution of civil protection order (CPO) constituted breach of peace and wrongful arrest that deprived plaintiff of liberty and property without due process of law, where CPO was executed pursuant to presumably constitutional Ohio statute. Kelm v. Hyatt (C.A.6 (Ohio) 1995) 44 F.3d 415.

Younger abstention was appropriate with regard to husband's claims for injunctive relief in civil rights action alleging that due process was violated by Ohio statute enabling domestic violence victims to receive ex parte civil protection order (CPO), and by Ohio civil rule allowing parties in divorce proceeding to obtain restraining orders without hearing, where underlying divorce case was pending at time that husband filed action, challenged provisions affected underlying divorce and involved important state interests, and there was no reason to question ability or willingness of Ohio courts to address husband's constitutional questions. Kelm v. Hyatt (C.A.6 (Ohio) 1995) 44 F.3d 415.

A protective order issued to prevent relative or household member from abusing other family members creates property right that incurs duty on part of government irrespective of whether the right is created by judicial function at statutory behest of the state legislature, and government has duty to protect beneficiary of such order, and failure to perform the duty may constitute denial of right to procedural due process. Siddle v. City of Cambridge, Ohio (S.D.Ohio 1991) 761 F.Supp. 503.

8. —Effect in divorce action, consent degree

Genuine issue of material fact existed, regarding whether consent agreement was enforceable as final property settlement of parties to divorce action, which precluded summary judgment for wife in divorce proceedings, on issue of property settlement. Cooley v. Cooley (Montgomery 1993) 90 Ohio App.3d 706, 630 N.E.2d 417.

9. Length of time of order

A court is without authority under Ohio Rule of Civil Procedure 60(A) to extend the effective term of a prior protection order by way of filing, more than one year after the initial protective order is issued, without a hearing, a "Corrective Entry and Order" where the terminal limits of the initial protective order are within the scope of RC 3113.31, as amended on December 9, 1994; the trial court's admitted unawareness of the amendment when the order of January 27, 1995 was issued amounts to something other than a clerical mistake since the modification was a substantive change and the action taken by the trial court in the corrective entry was beyond the scope of Civ R 60(A). Harlett v Harlett, No. 15799, 1996 WL 629510 (2d Dist Ct App, Montgomery, 11-1-96).

The language of RC 3113.31(J) declaring that "[n]otwithstanding any provision of law to the contrary, no court shall charge a fee for the filing of a petition" pursuant to that section for a civil protection order does not limit or restrict the discretion and power of a court, following its final disposition of the petition, to enter an order requiring a petitioner to pay whatever charges, costs, fees, deposits, or expenses are imposed by statutory enactment or rule of court as a condition of filing the petition. OAG 96-058.

10. Filing fees

The language of RC 3113.31(J) declaring that "[n]otwithstanding any provision of law to the contrary, no court shall charge a fee for the filing of a petition" pursuant to that section for a civil protection order is to be construed as prohibiting the collection of any charge, cost, fee, deposit, or expense, which is imposed by statutory enactment or rule of court as a condition of filing, at the time that the petition is first submitted to the clerk of court for filing. OAG 96-058.

11. Procedural issues

Court is not precluded by statute or public policy reasons from issuing protection order pursuant to civil domestic violence statute by fact that parties' dissolution or divorce decree already prohibits them from harassing each other. Felton v. Felton (Ohio 1997) 79 Ohio St.3d 34, 679 N.E.2d 672.

When granting protection order pursuant to civil domestic violence statute, trial court must find that petitioner has shown by preponderance of evidence that petitioner or petitioner's family or household members are in danger of domestic violence; abrogating *O'Hara v Dials* (Feb. 2, 1996), Erie App. No. E-95-044, 1996 WL 38810; *Moman v. Smith* (Oct. 14, 1996), Clermont App. No. CA96-05-047, 1996 WL 586771; *Tischler v. Vahcic* (Nov. 16, 1995), Cuyahoga App. No. 68053, 1995 WL 680928; *Coughlin v. Lancione* (Feb. 25, 1992), Franklin App. No. 91AP-950, 1992 WL 40557. Felton v. Felton (Ohio 1997) 79 Ohio St.3d 34, 679 N.E.2d 672.

Original civil protection order under domestic violence statute implicitly included petitioner's three children, although it did not explicitly name them, permitting renewal order to name children as protected persons, where petitioner had been granted custody of children, individual subject to order had been granted visitation, and protection order was drafted to accommodate such visitation. Woolum v. Woolum (Ohio App. 12 Dist. 1999) 131 Ohio App.3d 818, 723 N.E.2d 1135.

Civil protection order under domestic violence statute could be renewed based on evidence that the individual subject to the order had threatened the petitioner and her family since the prior order had expired, even though the threats, in and of themselves, did not rise to level of domestic violence under the statute. Woolum v. Woolum (Ohio App. 12 Dist. 1999) 131 Ohio App.3d 818, 723 N.E.2d 1135.

12. Evidence

Uncontroverted testimony of divorced woman and one other witness concerning violent proclivities of woman's former husband provided sufficient credible evidence to support finding that woman was in danger of domestic violence, warranting issuance of protection order under civil domestic violence statute; woman testified that her former husband's assaults had increased during their marriage, had continued after their divorce, and had culminated in attempted strangling, that he harassed her on telephone, and that she feared he would try to kill her if she angered him. Felton v. Felton (Ohio 1997) 79 Ohio St.3d 34, 679 N.E.2d 672.

Testimony of former husband of petitioner for domestic violence order that he grabbed petitioner by the neck and forced her to the floor, and petitioner's testimony that her former husband choked her, pushed her to the floor, and injured her head and arm, was sufficient to prove that former husband attempted to injure petitioner within scope of statute governing issuance of domestic violence orders. Sroka v. Sroka (Ohio App. 8 Dist. 1997) 121 Ohio App.3d 728, 700 N.E.2d 916.

Husband's appearance to pick up the parties' young son pursuant to a visitation order is insufficient to compel wife to call 911 upon seeing her husband's van outside her apartment and before he starts "banging on the door really hard" which does not reasonably place wife in fear of domestic violence and does not authorize issuance of a temporary protection order. Rush v Rush, No. 74832, 1999 WL 1044482 (8th Dist Ct App, Cuyahoga, 11-18-99).

13. Federal preemption

Stalking statute, which allowed issuance of civil protection orders, did not interfere with execution of, and was not preempted by, federal Gun Control Act, and thus, before entering order barring individual against whom protection order was entered from possessing guns, trial court was required only to determine that individual had committed domestic violence and that enjoining him from possessing firearms was fair and equitable, and was not required to make determination that subject was a "credible threat" to the safety of an intimate partner or child, as would make his possession of a gun unlawful under Act. Conkle v. Wolfe (Ohio App. 4 Dist. 1998) 131 Ohio App.3d 375, 722 N.E.2d 586.

14. —Order to surrender, firearms

When renewing civil protection order pursuant to domestic violence statute, trial court was within its discretion to incorporate the remedy provided in federal Gun Control Act of 1968 by requiring subject individual to surrender all firearms in his possession, although such requirement was not imposed in original protection order. Woolum v. Woolum (Ohio App. 12 Dist. 1999) 131 Ohio App.3d 818, 723 N.E.2d 1135.

3113.32 Records of domestic disputes and violence; procedures

(A) The sheriff of a county, constable or chief of police of a township, and chief of police of a city or village shall keep a separate record of domestic dispute and domestic violence problems on a form prepared and distributed by the superintendent of the bureau of criminal identification and investigation. The forms shall contain spaces for the reporting of all information that the superintendent determines to be relevant to domestic dispute and domestic violence problems, including, but not limited to, the number of domestic dispute and domestic violence problems reported to the law enforcement agency for which the record is kept, the relationship of the complainant and the person allegedly the victim of the domestic violence, if different, to the alleged offender, and the relationship of all other persons involved in the domestic dispute or domestic violence problem, and the action taken by the law enforcement officers who handled the domestic dispute or domestic violence problem. A copy of the record shall be submitted to the bureau each month.

(B) The superintendent of the bureeau [*sic*] of criminal identification and investigation shall receive copies of monthly records of domestic dispute and domestic violence problems kept by local law enforcement agencies and submitted to him under division (A) of this section. The superintendent shall compile the data and annually produce a statistical public report on the incidence of domestic disputes and violence in this state and its political subdivisions. The report shall be prepared in such a manner that there is no identifying data, including the names and addresses of the persons involved in the domestic dispute and domestic violence problems, that would enable any person to determine the identity of any of the persons involved.

(C) The attorney general shall oversee the statistical reporting required pursuant to this section to ensure that it is complete and accurate.

(1984 H 587, eff. 9-25-84)

Historical and Statutory Notes

Ed. Note: Former 3113.32 repealed by 1978 H 835, § 3, eff. 3-27-83; 1978 H 835, § 1.

Library References

Breach of the Peace ⚿15 to 21.
Criminal Law ⚿1226(1).
WESTLAW Topic Nos. 62, 110.

C.J.S. Breach of the Peace §§ 14 to 22, 25.
C.J.S. Criminal Law § 1734.
C.J.S. Domestic Abuse and Violence §§ 2 to 23.

Sowald & Morganstern, Baldwin's Ohio Practice, *Domestic Relations Law* § 4.14, 5.5 (1997)

Notes of Decisions and Opinions

Dismissal of charges 1

1. Dismissal of charges

Trial court lacked authority to dismiss charges of assault and domestic violence against defendant upon request of prosecuting witness, where city attorney had objected to dismissal and indicated that state was prepared to proceed to trial. State v. Wise (Franklin 1994) 99 Ohio App.3d 239, 650 N.E.2d 191.

SHELTERS FOR VICTIMS

Ohio Administrative Code References

Supportive services, OAC 5101:2-39-07

Library References

Sowald & Morganstern, Baldwin's Ohio Practice, *Domestic Relations Law* § 4.14, 7.16 (1997)

3113.33 Definitions

As used in sections 3113.33 to 3113.40 of the Revised Code:

(A) "Domestic violence" means attempting to cause or causing bodily injury to a family or household member, or placing a family or household member by threat of force in fear of imminent physical harm.

(B) "Family or household member" means any of the following:

(1) Any of the following who is residing or has resided with the person committing the domestic violence:

(a) A spouse, a person living as a spouse, or a former spouse of the person committing the domestic violence;

(b) A parent or child of the person committing the domestic violence, or another person related by consanguinity or affinity to the person committing the domestic violence;

(c) A parent or a child of a spouse, person living as a spouse, or former spouse of the person committing the domestic violence, or another person related by consanguinity or affinity to a spouse, person living as a spouse, or former spouse of the person committing the domestic violence;

(d) The dependents of any person listed in division (B)(1)(a), (b), or (c) of this section.

(2) The natural parent of any child of whom the person committing the domestic violence is the other natural parent or is the putative other natural parent.

(C) "Shelter for victims of domestic violence" or "shelter" means a facility that provides temporary residential service or facilities to family or household members who are victims of domestic violence.

(D) "Person living as a spouse" means a person who is living or has lived with the person committing the domestic violence in a common law marital relationship, who otherwise is cohabiting with the person committing the domestic violence, or who otherwise has cohabited with the person committing the domestic violence within five years prior to the date of the alleged occurrence of the act in question.

(1997 S 1, eff. 10-21-97; 1997 H 215, eff. 6-30-97; 1994 H 335, eff. 12-9-94; 1988 H 172, eff. 3-17-89; 1984 H 587; 1980 H 920; 1979 S 46)

Historical and Statutory Notes

Ed. Note: A special endorsement by the Legislative Service Commission states, "Comparison of these amendments [1997 S 1, eff. 10-21-97 and 1997 H 215, eff. 6-30-97] in pursuance of section 1.52 of the Revised Code discloses that they are not irreconcilable so that they are required by that section to be harmonized to give effect to each amendment." In recognition of this rule of construction, changes made by 1997 S 1, eff. 10-21-97, and 1997 H 215, eff. 6-30-97, have been incorporated in the above amendment. See *Baldwin's Ohio Legislative Service Annotated*, 1997, pages 7/L-733 and 8/L-1505, or the OH-LEGIS or OH-LEGIS-OLD database on WESTLAW, for original versions of these Acts.

Amendment Note: 1997 S 1 inserted "or is the putative other natural parent" in division (A)(2); and substituted "five years" for "one year" in division (D).

Amendment Note: 1997 H 215 substituted "3113.40" for "3113.39" in the first paragraph.

Amendment Note: 1994 H 335 designated division (B)(1); redesignated former divisions (B)(1) through (B)(4) as divisions (B)(1)(a) through (B)(1)(d); substituted "(B)(1)(a), (b), or (c)" for "(B)(1), (2), or (3)" in division (B)(1)(d); and added division (B)(2).

Cross References

Common-law marriage prohibited, 3105.12

Pupils under care of shelter for victims of domestic violence, attendance in schools in districts of location of shelters, 3313.64

Pupils under care of shelter for victims of domestic violence, limits on public access to records concerning, 3319.321

Pupils under care of shelter for victims of domestic violence, provision of information to schools, 3313.672

Library References

Asylums ⚷2, 3.
WESTLAW Topic No. 43.
C.J.S. Asylums and Institutional Care Facilities §§ 2 to 8.

Am Jur 2d: 6, Assault and Battery § 44, 47

Who has custody or control of child within terms of penal statute punishing cruelty or neglect by one having custody or control. 75 ALR3d 933

Civil liability of physician for failure to diagnose or report battered child syndrome. 97 ALR3d 338

Validity and construction of penal statute prohibiting child abuse. 1 ALR4th 38

Admissibility of expert or opinion testimony on battered wife or battered woman syndrome. 18 ALR4th 1153

Baldwin's Ohio School Law, Text 23.2

Sowald & Morganstern, Baldwin's Ohio Practice, *Domestic Relations Law* § 2.66, 5.5 (1997)

Law Review and Journal Commentaries

Ohio's New Civil Domestic Violence Law, Pamela J. MacAdams. 7 Domestic Rel J Ohio 19 (March/April 1995).

The Violent Family and the Ambivalent State: Developing a Coherent Policy for State Aid to Victims of Family Violence, Lowell F. Schechter. 20 J Fam L 1 (1981-82).

Notes of Decisions and Opinions

Shelters 1

---

1. Shelters

In RC 3113.33(C), which states that a "'[s]helter for victims of domestic violence' or 'shelter' means a facility that provides temporary residential service or facilities to family or household member who are victims of domestic violence," the word "facility" may be construed to mean the organization that provides the residential service or facilities, and is not limited in meaning to a building or structure. OAG 95-022.

A provision of hotel rooms on a temporary basis to victims of domestic violence and to children of victims, instead of using a particular building or structure dedicated to the shelter of such persons, qualifies as "residential service or facilities" within the meaning of RC 3113.33(C) and RC 3113.36(A)(4). OAG 95-022.

3113.34 Fee for shelters for victims of domestic violence

In addition to any fee established under section 2101.16 of the Revised Code for the issuance of a marriage license, the probate court shall collect and deposit in the county treasury a fee of seventeen dollars for each marriage license issued. This fee, plus the thirty-two-dollar fee collected under division (D) of section 2303.201 of the Revised Code as additional costs in each new action or proceeding for annulment, divorce, or dissolution of marriage, shall be retained in a special fund and shall be expended only to provide financial assistance to shelters for victims of domestic violence and only as provided in sections 3113.35 to 3113.39 of the Revised Code.

(1994 H 335, eff. 12-9-94; 1984 H 319, eff. 12-26-84; 1979 S 46)

Historical and Statutory Notes

Amendment Note: 1994 H 335 inserted ", plus the thirty-two-dollar fee collected under division (D) of section 2303.201 of the Revised Code as additional costs in each new action or proceeding for annulment, divorce, or dissolution of marriage[.]"

Library References

Asylums ⚿2, 3.
WESTLAW Topic No. 43.

C.J.S. Asylums and Institutional Care Facilities §§ 2 to 8.

Notes of Decisions and Opinions

Funds, allocation 1

1. Funds, allocation

Pursuant to RC 3113.35, a board of county commissioners may allocate funds collected under RC 3113.34 to a qualified shelter for victims of domestic violence if the shelter is located within the county or if the shelter is located within a nearby county and serves or will serve the population of the county allocating the funds. OAG 94-063.

3113.35 Application by shelter for funds; notice; payment

(A) A shelter for victims of domestic violence may apply to the board of county commissioners of the county in which it is located or of an adjoining county, the population of which is or will be served by the shelter, for the release of funds to be collected as fees for the issuance of marriage licenses pursuant to section 3113.34 or fees as additional costs in annulment, divorce, or dissolution of marriage actions and proceedings pursuant to division (D) of section 2303.201 of the Revised Code and that are to be used for the funding of the shelter. All applications for funds shall be submitted by the first day of October of the year preceding the calendar year for which the funding is desired, and shall include all of the following:

(1) Evidence that the shelter is incorporated in this state as a nonprofit corporation;

(2) A list of the trustees of the corporation, and a list of the trustees of the shelter, if different;

(3) The proposed budget of the shelter for the following calendar year;

(4) A summary of the services proposed to be offered in the following calendar year;

(5) An estimate of the number of persons to be served during the following calendar year.

(B) Upon receipt of an application for funds from a shelter that meets the criteria set forth in section 3113.36 of the Revised Code, the board of county commissioners shall, on or before the fifteenth day of November of the year in which the application is filed, notify the shelter, in writing, whether it is eligible for funds, and if the shelter is eligible, estimate the amount available for that shelter from the fees to be collected under section 3113.34 or division (D) of section 2303.201 of the Revised Code.

(C) Funds collected as fees for the issuance of marriage licenses pursuant to section 3113.34 or fees as additional costs in annulment, divorce, or dissolution of marriage actions and proceedings pursuant to division (D) of section 2303.201 of the Revised Code that are allocated to shelters under this section shall be paid to the shelters twice annually. Funds collected from the first day of January through the thirtieth day of June of the calendar year following the year in which the application is filed shall be allocated to the shelters by the fifteenth day of July of the year following the year in which the application is filed. Funds collected from the first day of July through the thirty-first day of December of the calendar year following the year in which the application is filed shall be allocated to the shelters by the fifteenth day of January of the year following the end of the collection period.

(1994 H 335, eff. 12-9-94; 1986 H 569, eff. 4-15-86; 1980 H 736; 1979 S 46)

Historical and Statutory Notes

Amendment Note: 1994 H 335 inserted "or fees as additional costs in annulment, divorce, or dissolution of marriage actions and proceedings pursuant to division (D) of section 2303.201" in divisions (A) and (C); and inserted "or division (D) of section 2303.201" in division (B).

Cross References

Nonprofit corporations, Ch 1702

Library References

Asylums ⚿2, 3.

WESTLAW Topic No. 43.

C.J.S. Asylums and Institutional Care Facilities §§ 2 to 8.

Notes of Decisions and Opinions

Adjoining counties 1
Funds, allocation 2

1. Adjoining counties

As used in RC 3113.35, the word "adjoining" is not restricted to counties that share common borders, but extends also to counties that are near one another even though their boundaries do not touch. OAG 94-063.

2. Funds, allocation

Pursuant to RC 3113.35, a board of county commissioners may allocate funds collected under RC 3113.34 to a qualified shelter for victims of domestic violence if the shelter is located within the county or if the shelter is located within a nearby county and serves or will serve the population of the county allocating the funds. OAG 94-063.

3113.36 Qualifications for funding

(A) To qualify for funds under section 3113.35 of the Revised Code, a shelter for victims of domestic violence shall meet all of the following requirements:

(1) Be incorporated in this state as a nonprofit corporation;

(2) Have trustees who represent the racial, ethnic, and socioeconomic diversity of the community to be served, including at least one person who is or has been a victim of domestic violence;

(3) Receive at least twenty-five per cent of its funds from sources other than funds distributed pursuant to section 3113.35 of the Revised Code. These other sources may be public or private, and may include funds distributed pursuant to section 3113.37 of the Revised Code, and contributions of goods or services, including materials, commodities, transportation, office space, or other types of facilities or personal services.

(4) Provide residential service or facilities for children when accompanied by a parent, guardian, or custodian who is a victim of domestic violence and who is receiving temporary residential service at the shelter;

(5) Require persons employed by or volunteering services to the shelter to maintain the confidentiality of any information that would identify individuals served by the shelter.

(B) A shelter for victims of domestic violence does not qualify for funds if it discriminates in its admissions or provision of services on the basis of race, religion, color, age, marital status, national origin, or ancestry. A shelter does not qualify for funds in the second half of any year if its application projects the provision of residential service and such service has not been provided in the first half of that year; such a shelter does not qualify for funds in the following year.

(1979 S 46, eff. 1-18-80)

Cross References

Nonprofit corporations, Ch 1702

Library References

Asylums ⚿2, 3.
WESTLAW Topic No. 43.
C.J.S. Asylums and Institutional Care Facilities §§ 2 to 8.

Notes of Decisions and Opinions

Residential service or facilities, defined 1

1. Residential service or facilities, defined

A provision of hotel rooms on a temporary basis to victims of domestic violence and to children of victims, instead of using a particular building or structure dedicated to the shelter of such persons, qualifies as "residential service or facilities" within the meaning of RC 3113.33(C) and RC 3113.36(A)(4). OAG 95-022.

3113.37 Unused county funds; transfer to domestic violence shelters fund; administration

(A) If in any calendar year a board of county commissioners does not allocate all of the funds collected that year under section 3113.34 or division (D) of section 2303.201 of the

Revised Code to a shelter for victims of domestic violence that applied for them, or if a board receives no application in that year from a shelter that is qualified to receive funds as determined under section 3113.36 of the Revised Code, the funds shall be deposited, on or before the thirty-first day of December of that year, in the state treasury to the credit of the domestic violence shelters fund, which is hereby created. The fund shall be administered by the attorney general for the purpose of providing financial assistance to shelters.

(B) A shelter located in this state may apply to the attorney general for funds. All applications for funds shall be submitted by the first day of February of the year for which the funds are requested and shall contain all of the information set forth in division (A) of section 3113.35 of the Revised Code.

(C) Upon receipt of an application for funds from a shelter that meets the criteria set forth in section 3113.36 of the Revised Code, the attorney general, on or before the fifteenth day of March of the year in which the application is received, shall notify the shelter, in writing, whether it is eligible for funds and, if the shelter is eligible, specify the amount available for that shelter.

(D) Funds allocated under this section shall be paid once annually, on or before the thirtieth day of April of the year in which the application is received.

(1994 H 335, eff. 12-9-94; 1985 H 201, eff. 7-1-85; 1979 S 46)

Historical and Statutory Notes

Amendment Note: 1994 H 335 inserted "or division (D) of section 2303.201" in division (A).

Library References

Asylums ⚿2, 3.
WESTLAW Topic No. 43.
C.J.S. Asylums and Institutional Care Facilities §§ 2 to 8.

3113.38 Criteria for allocation of funds among shelters

If a board of county commissioners or the attorney general receives applications from more than one qualified shelter for victims of domestic violence, and the requests for funds exceed the amount of funds available, funds shall be allocated on the basis of the following priorities:

(A) To shelters in existence on the effective date of this section;

(B) To shelters offering or proposing to offer the broadest range of services and referrals to the community served, including medical, psychological, financial, educational, vocational, child care services, and legal services;

(C) To other qualified shelters.

(1979 S 46, eff. 1-18-80)

Library References

Asylums ⚿2, 3.
WESTLAW Topic No. 43.
C.J.S. Asylums and Institutional Care Facilities §§ 2 to 8.

3113.39 Annual reports of shelters

(A) A shelter for victims of domestic violence that receives funds pursuant to section 3113.35 or 3113.37 of the Revised Code shall file an annual report with the board of county commissioners of the county in which it is located and of the county from which it is receiving funds, if different, and with the attorney general on or before the thirty-first day of March of the year following the year in which funds were received. The annual report shall include statistics on the number of persons served by the shelter, the relationship of the victim of domestic violence to the abuser, the number of referrals made for medical, psychological, financial, educational, vocational, child care services, or legal services, and shall include a compilation report of an independent accountant. No information contained in the report shall identify any person served by the shelter, or enable any person to determine the identity of any such person.

(B) The attorney general shall compile the reports filed pursuant to division (A) of this section annually.

(1984 H 587, eff. 9-25-84; 1979 S 46)

Library References

Asylums ⚷2, 3.
WESTLAW Topic No. 43.
C.J.S. Asylums and Institutional Care Facilities §§ 2 to 8.

3113.40 Domestic violence shelter to determine resident's last known residential address; use of information

When a shelter for victims of domestic violence provides accommodations to a person, the shelter, on admitting the person, shall determine, if possible, the person's last known residential address and county of residence. The information concerning the address and county of residence is confidential and may be released only to a public children services agency pursuant to section 2151.422 of the Revised Code.

(1997 H 215, eff. 6-30-97)

Library References

OJur 3d: 46, Family Law § 319

PENALTIES

3113.99 Penalties

(A) For purposes of this section:

(1) "Child support order" means an order for support issued or modified under Chapter 3115. or section 2151.23, 2151.231, 2151.232, 2151.36, 2151.49, 3105.18, 3105.21, 3109.05, 3111.13, 3113.04, 3113.07, 3113.216, or 3113.31 of the Revised Code.

(2) "Obligor" means a person who is required to pay support under a child support order.

(B) Whoever violates section 3113.06 of the Revised Code is guilty of a misdemeanor of the first degree. If the offender previously has been convicted of or pleaded guilty to a violation of section 3113.06 of the Revised Code or if the court finds that the offender has failed to pay the cost of child maintenance under section 3113.06 of the Revised Code for a total accumulated period of twenty-six weeks out of one hundred four consecutive weeks, whether or not the twenty-six weeks were consecutive, a violation of section 3113.06 of the Revised Code is a felony of the fifth degree.

(C) An obligor who violates division (D)(1)(c) of section 3113.21 of the Revised Code shall be fined not more than fifty dollars for a first offense, not more than one hundred dollars for a second offense, and not more than five hundred dollars for each subsequent offense.

(D) An obligor who violates division (G)(2) of section 3113.21 of the Revised Code shall be fined not more than fifty dollars for a first offense, not more than one hundred dollars for a second offense, and not more than five hundred dollars for each subsequent offense.

(E) A fine amount imposed pursuant to division (C) or (D) of this section shall be paid to the division of child support in the department of job and family services or, pursuant to division (H)(4) of section 2301.35 of the Revised Code, the child support enforcement agency. The amount of the fine that does not exceed the amount of arrearage under the child support order shall be disbursed in accordance with the child support order. The amount of the fine that exceeds the amount of the arrearage order shall be called program income and collected in accordance with section 5101.325 of the Revised Code.

(1999 H 471, eff. 7-1-00; 1997 H 352, eff. 1-1-98; 1996 H 710, § 7, eff. 6-11-96; 1995 H 167, eff. 6-11-96; 1995 S 2, eff. 7-1-96; 1972 H 511, eff. 1-1-74; 1953 H 1)

Uncodified Law

1996 H 710, § 15: See Uncodified Law under 3113.21.

Historical and Statutory Notes

Ed. Note: The effective date of the amendment of this section by 1995 H 167 was changed from 11-15-96 to 6-11-96 by 1996 H 710, § 7, eff. 6-11-96.

Amendment Note: 1999 H 471 substituted "job and family" for "human" in division (E).

Amendment Note: 1997 H 352 inserted "2151.231, 2151.232," in division (A)(1); and substituted "division of child support in the department of human services or, pursuant to division (H) of section 2301.35 of the Revised Code, the child support enforcement agency" for "child support enforcement agency administering the obligor's child support order" and "called program income and shall be collected in accordance with section 5101.325 of the Revised Code" for "used by the agency for the administration of its program for child support enforcement" in division (E).

Amendment Note: 1995 H 167 added division (A); designated division (B); and added divisions (C), (D), and (E).

Amendment Note: 1995 S 2 rewrote this section, which previously read:

"Whoever violates section 3113.06 of the Revised Code is guilty of a felony of the fourth degree."

Cross References

Child support enforcement agency, powers and duties, 2301.35
Penalties and fines for felonies, 2929.11 to 2929.15
Program income fund, child support division depositing funds in, 5101.325

Ohio Administrative Code References

Allocation hierarchy for collections, OAC 5101:1-31-14
Child support administrative fund, OAC 5101:1-31-04
Income withholding procedures, OAC 5101:1-30-413
Nonsupport collections, OAC 5101:1-31-11
Program income, OAC 5101:1-31-20

Library References

Parent and Child ⚿17.
WESTLAW Topic No. 285.
C.J.S. Parent and Child § 165.
Am Jur 2d: 23, Desertion and Nonsupport § 122; 59, Parent and Child § 82

Notes of Decisions and Opinions

In general 2
Constitutional issues 1

---

1. Constitutional issues

RC 3113.01, in its application to the neglect of a mentally handicapped child, is neither unconstitutional and invalid by reason of indefiniteness or uncertainty, nor unconstitutional and invalid by reason of the fact that the trial court could exercise a discretion in determining the extent of the punishment. State v. Turner (Lucas 1965) 3 Ohio App.2d 5, 209 N.E.2d 475, 32 O.O.2d 72.

2. In general

Willful failure to provide for a minor child is a continuing offense. Petition of Perdiak (S.D.Cal. 1958) 162 F.Supp. 76, 6 O.O.2d 478.

CHAPTER 3115

Interstate Family Support

Section

GENERAL PROVISIONS

JURISDICTION

Uniform Interstate Family Support Act (1996)

Table of Jurisdictions Wherein Act Has Been Adopted

For text of Uniform Act, and variation notes and annotation materials for adopting jurisdictions, see Uniform Laws Annotated, Master Edition, Volume 9, Pt. I.

Jurisdiction	Statutory Citation
Alabama	Code 1975, § 30-3A-101 to 30-3A-906.
Alaska	AS 25.25.101 to 25.25.903.
Arizona	A.R.S. § 25-621 to 25-661.
Arkansas	A.C.A. § 9-17-101 to 9-17-902.
California	West's Ann.Cal.Fam.Code § 4900 to 4976.
Colorado	West's C.R.S.A. § 14-5-101 to 14-5-1007.
Connecticut	C.G.S.A. § 46b-212 to 46b-213v.
Delaware	13 Del.C. § 601 to 691.
District of Columbia	D.C.Code 1981 § 30-341.1 to 30-349.1.
Florida	West's F.S.A. § 88.0011 to 88.9051.
Georgia	O.C.G.A. § 19-11-100 to 19-11-191.
Hawaii	HRS § 576B-101 to 576B-902.
Idaho	I.C. § 7-1001 to 7-1059.
Illinois	S.H.A. 750 ILCS 22/100 to 22/990.
Iowa	I.C.A. § 252K.101 to 252K.904.
Kansas	K.S.A. 23-9101 to 23-9903.
Kentucky	Baldwin's KRS 407.5101 to 407.5902.
Louisiana	LSA-Children's Code Arts. 1301.1 to 1308.2.
Maryland	Code, Family Law § 10-301 to 10-359.
Massachusetts	M.G.L.A. c. 209D, § 1-101 to 9-902.
Michigan	M.C.L.A. § 552.101 to 552.1901.
Minnesota	M.S.A. § 518C.101 to 518C.902.
Mississippi	Code 1972, 93-25-1 to 93-25-117.
Missouri	V.A.M.S. § 454.850 to 454.997.
Montana	MCA § 40-5-101 to 40-5-197.
Nebraska	R.R.S. 1943, § 42-701 to 42-751.
Nevada	N.R.S. 130.0902 to 130.802.
New Hampshire	RSA 546-B:1 to 546-B:60.
New Jersey	N.J.S.A. 2A:4-30.65 to 2A:4-30.122.
New Mexico	NMSA 1978, § 40-6A-101 to 40-6A-903.
New York	McKinney's Family Ct. Act, § 580-101 to 580-905.
North Carolina	G.S. 52C-1-100 to 52C-9-902.
North Dakota	NDCC 14-12.2-01 to 14-12.2-49.
Oklahoma	43 Okl.St.Ann. § 601-100 to 601-901.
Oregon	ORS 110.303 to 110.452.
Pennsylvania	Pa. C.S.A. § 7101 to 7901.
Tennessee	T.C.A. § 36-5-2001 to 36-5-2902.
Texas	V.T.C.A. Family Code, § 159.001 to 159.902.
Utah	U.C.A. 1953, 78-45f-100 to 78-45f-901.
Vermont	15B V.S.A. § 101 to 904.
Virginia	Code 1950, § 20-88.32 to 20-88.82.
Virgin Islands	16 V.I.C. § 391 to 451.
Washington	RCWA 26.21.005 to 26.21.916.
West Virginia	Code, 48B-1-101 to 48B-9-903.
Wisconsin	W.S.A. 769.101 to 769.903.

Uncodified Law

1997 H 352, § 3, eff. 1-1-98, reads:

The General Assembly recognizes that in certain instances, the wording of this act differs from that of the Uniform Interstate Family Support Act approved by the National Conference of Commissioners on Uniform State Laws. Any such dissimilarity denotes a technical change or is made to reflect the intent of the Commissioners as expressed in the Comments to the Uniform Interstate Family Support Act.

Cross References

Administration of child support orders by child support enforcement agencies, 3113.218
Calculation of amount of child support obligation, 3113.215
Child support division, requests for assistance from other states in enforcement of support orders, 5101.318
Child support, withholding or deduction requirements and notices, 3113.21
Court of common pleas, bureau of support, 2301.34 et seq.
Duty of married person to support self, spouse and children, duration of duty to support, 3103.03
Factors determining amount of child support, support orders, medical needs, 3109.05
Failure to pay maintenance cost of child, 3113.06
Health insurance coverage for children, 3113.217
Interfering with action to issue or modify support order, 2919.231
Issuance of new child support orders, interest and costs, 3113.219
Judges of the court of domestic relations, juvenile court responsibility, 2301.03
Jurisdiction of juvenile courts, 2151.23
Juvenile court, charges against adult, 2151.43
Uniform child custody jurisdiction law, 3109.21 to 3109.37
Visitation rights, 3109.051

Ohio Administrative Code References

Child support program, OAC Ch 5101:1-29
Collection of past due support by federal tax refund offset, OAC Ch 5101:1-30

Library References

Allowance in state of decedent's domicil for widow's support as enforceable against decedent's real estate, or proceeds thereof, in another state. 13 ALR2d 973

Carlin, Baldwin's Ohio Practice, *Merrick-Rippner Probate Law* § 19.6, 19.8, 105.1, 105.2, 105.5, 107.117, 108.1, 108.3, 108.20, 108.36 (1997)
3 Katz & Giannelli, Baldwin's Ohio Practice, *Criminal Law* § 109.12 (1996)
Klein & Darling, Baldwin's Ohio Practice, *Civil Practice* § 1 (1997)
Sowald & Morganstern, Baldwin's Ohio Practice, *Domestic Relations Law* § 22.9, 23.19, 23.20, 23.31, 23.46 (1997)

WESTLAW Electronic Research

See WESTLAW Electronic Research Guide following the Preface.

Law Review and Journal Commentaries

Abusing the Power to Regulate: The Child Support Recovery Act of 1992, Comment. (Ed. note: Federal encroachment into traditional fields of State criminal law is discussed.) 46 Case W Res L Rev 935 (Spring 1996).

Civil Liberties Versus Governmental Interest: A Constitutional Context for the Impact of Title IV-D of the Social Security Act on Families in the Aid to Families with Dependent Children Program, Note. 5 Cap U L Rev 245 (1976).

Establishing And Enforcing The Child Support Obligation: An Evaluation Of Practical Impediments To An Effective System, Comment. 19 Cap U L Rev 1169 (Fall 1990).

Family Law/Personal Jurisdiction/The Transient Physical Presence Rule And The Death Of Pennoyer v Neff, 95 U.S. 714 (1878), William D. Meily. 38 Columbus B Briefs 6 (April 1989).

Interstate Enforcement of Support Obligations Through Long Arm Statutes and URESA, Note. 18 J Fam L 537 (1979-80).

Interstate Family Support: Ohio's Version of the Uniform Interstate Family Support Act, Cooley R. Howarth, Jr. 10 Domestic Rel J Ohio 49 (July/August 1998).

Origins and Development of the Law of Parental Child Support, Donna Schuele. 27 J Fam L 807 (1988-89).

A Review of the Child Support Enforcement Program, Note. 20 J Fam L 489 (1981-82).

Title I Of The Family Support Act Of 1988—The Quest For Effective National Child Support Enforcement Continues, Note. 29 J Fam L 149 (1990-91).

The Uniform Interstate Family Support Act: The New URESA, Note. 20 U Dayton L Rev 425 (Fall 1994).

Notes of Decisions and Opinions

---

1. Child support modification

Where a URESA action is consolidated with the prior local divorce action, the trial court has no authority pursuant to Civ R 75(I) to modify a party's obligation for child support where the other party to the divorce was not served notice of the modification motion and was not given an opportunity to protect her interests in the modification proceeding; without such jurisdiction, the trial court has no authority to issue a valid, binding judgment, and any order rendered in such action is void ab initio and subject to collateral attack at any time. Rondy v. Rondy (Summit 1983) 13 Ohio App.3d 19, 468 N.E.2d 81, 13 O.B.R. 20.

2. Defense

The parent with legal custody of a child may not avoid an action for payment of support under RC Ch 3115 by pleading the violation of a custody order. State of Iowa ex rel. Cantrell v. Cantrell (Summit 1983) 9 Ohio App.3d 194, 459 N.E.2d 242, 9 O.B.R. 305.

3. Due process

The spouses in a family residing in and domiciliaries of New York separate, one spouse moving to California. The separation agreement provides that custody of the two children will remain with the New York spouse, school vacations were to be visitations to the California spouse. The California spouse obtained a divorce decree from Haiti, and pursuant to one child's request, the New York spouse consented to that child staying in California. Later, the California spouse brought the other child to California without the consent of the New York spouse. The California spouse then sought to establish the Haiti decree as a California judgment, to modify the judgment so as to grant full custody to herself, and to increase the support payments. Although the adequacy of notice given defendant was never challenged in this action for child support, the court held that the exercise of in personam jurisdiction under these circumstances failed to meet the standards of "minimal contacts" (under established doctrine of International Shoe Co v Washington, 326 US 310, 66 SCt 154, 90 LEd 95 (1945)) imposed by the Due Process Clause of the Fourteenth Amendment. Kulko v. Superior Court of California In and For City and County of San Francisco (U.S.Cal. 1978) 98 S.Ct. 1690, 436 U.S. 84, 56 L.Ed.2d 132, rehearing denied 98 S.Ct. 3127, 438 U.S. 908, 57 L.Ed.2d 1150.

4. Federal jurisdiction

In a federal suit based on diversity of citizenship the principle that federal courts will not hear domestic relations disputes does not apply where the claim is that an employer who withheld wages to satisfy an Ohio court's support order converted the funds instead of turning them over to the Cuyahoga support enforcement agency; the federal court will not be delving into the plaintiff's domestic affairs here, the level or appropriateness of the support payments is not at issue, the state court's orders are not questioned, and it is merely alleged that the employer converted withheld wages. Ungrady v. Burns Intern. Sec. Services, Inc. (N.D.Ohio 1991) 767 F.Supp. 849.

The field of domestic relations is a state matter peculiarly unsuited to control by federal courts and under the principles set forth in Barber v Barber, 62 US 582, 16 LEd 226 (1858), federal courts will refuse to exercise jurisdiction over domestic matters regardless of diversity of state citizenship or the presence of the requisite amount in controversy; federal diversity jurisdiction does exist for suits that are actually tort or contract claims and have only overtones of domestic matters, however, and a constitutional claim that is not frivolous may also invoke federal jurisdiction. Taylor v. Wettstein (S.D.Ohio 1989) 746 F.Supp. 713.

GENERAL PROVISIONS

Library References

Sowald & Morganstern, Baldwin's Ohio Practice, *Domestic Relations Law* § 23.43 (1997)

3115.01 Definitions

As used in sections 3115.01 to 3115.59 of the Revised Code:

(A) "Child" means an individual under the age of majority, who is or is alleged to be owed a duty of support by the individual's parent or who is or is alleged to be the beneficiary of a support order directed to the parent.

(B) "Child support order" means an order for the support of a child that provides for monetary support, whether current or in arrears, health care, or reimbursements, and may include related costs and fees, interest, income withholding requirements, attorney fees, and other relief. "Child support order" includes orders under which the child has attained the age of majority under the law of the issuing state and arrearages are owed under the order.

(C) "Duty of support" means an obligation imposed or that may be imposed under law to provide support for a child, spouse, or former spouse, including an unsatisfied obligation to provide support.

(D) "Home state" means the state in which a child lived with a parent or a person acting as a parent for at least six consecutive months immediately preceding the time of filing of a complaint or comparable pleading for support and, if a child is less than six months old, the state in which the child lived from birth with any of them. A period of temporary absence of any of them is counted as part of the six-month or other period.

(E) "Income" includes earnings or other periodic entitlements to money from any source and any other property subject to withholding for support under the law of this state.

(F) "Income withholding order" means an order or other legal process directed to an obligor's payor, as defined in sections 3111.20 and 3113.21 of the Revised Code, to withhold support from the income of the obligor.

(G) "Initiating state" means a state from which a proceeding is forwarded or in which a proceeding is filed for forwarding to a responding state under sections 3115.01 to 3115.59 of the Revised Code or a law or procedure substantially similar to those sections, the uniform reciprocal enforcement of support act, or the revised uniform reciprocal enforcement of support act.

(H) "Initiating tribunal" means the authorized tribunal in an initiating state.

(I) "Issuing state" means the state in which a tribunal issues a support order or renders a judgment determining parentage.

(J) "Issuing tribunal" means the tribunal that issues a support order or renders a judgment determining the existence or nonexistence of a parent and child relationship.

(K) "Law" includes decisional and statutory law and rules and regulations having the force of law.

(L) "Obligee" means any of the following:

(1) An individual to whom a duty of support is or is alleged to be owed or in whose favor a support order has been issued or a judgment determining parentage has been rendered;

(2) A state or political subdivision to which the rights under a duty of support or support order have been assigned or which has independent claims based on financial assistance provided to an individual obligee;

(3) An individual seeking a judgment determining parentage of the individual's child.

(M) "Obligor" means an individual, or the estate of a decedent to which any of the following applies:

(1) The individual or estate owes or is alleged to owe a duty of support;

(2) The individual is alleged but has not been adjudicated to be a parent of a child;

(3) The individual or estate is liable under a support order.

(N) "Register" means to file a support order or judgment determining the existence or nonexistence of a parent and child relationship in a registering tribunal.

(O) "Registering tribunal" means a tribunal in which a support order is registered.

(P) "Responding state" means a state in which a proceeding is filed or to which a proceeding is forwarded for filing from an initiating state under sections 3115.01 to 3115.59 of the Revised Code or a law or procedure substantially similar to those sections, the uniform reciprocal enforcement of support act, or the revised uniform reciprocal enforcement of support act.

(Q) "Responding tribunal" means the authorized tribunal in a responding state.

(R) "Revised uniform reciprocal enforcement of support act" means the act addressing interstate enforcement of support orders adopted in 1968 by the national conference of commissioners on uniform state laws or any law substantially similar to the act adopted by another state.

(S) "Spousal support order" means an order for the support of a spouse or former spouse that provides for monetary support, whether current or in arrears, health care, or reimbursements, and may include related costs and fees, interest, income withholding requirements, attorney fees, and other relief.

(T) "State" has the same meaning as in section 1.59 of the Revised Code, except that it also includes both of the following:

(1) An Indian tribe;

(2) A foreign jurisdiction that has enacted a law or established procedures for issuance and enforcement of support orders that are substantially similar to the procedures under sections 3115.01 to 3115.59 of the Revised Code, the uniform reciprocal enforcement of support act, or the revised uniform reciprocal enforcement of support act.

(U) "Support enforcement agency" means a public official or agency authorized to do any of the following:

(1) Seek enforcement of support orders or laws relating to the duty of support;

(2) Seek establishment or modification of child support;

(3) Seek determination of the existence or nonexistence of a parent and child relationship;

(4) Locate obligors or their assets.

(V) "Support order" means a spousal support order or child support order.

(W) "Tribunal" means any trial court of record of this state and when the context requires, a court, administrative agency, or quasi-judicial entity of any other state authorized to establish, enforce, or modify support orders or to determine parentage.

(X) "Uniform reciprocal enforcement of support act" means the act addressing interstate enforcement of support orders adopted in 1950 and amended in 1952 and 1958 by the national conference of commissioners on uniform state laws or any law substantially similar to the act adopted by another state.

(1997 H 352, eff. 1-1-98)

Historical and Statutory Notes

Ed. Note: Former 3115.01 repealed by 1997 H 352, eff. 1-1-98; 1987 H 231, eff. 10-5-87; 1971 H 504; 126 v 560; 1953 H 1; GC 8007-2.

Pre-1953 H 1 Amendments: 124 v H 1

Ohio Administrative Code References

Services in interstate, Uniform Interstate Family Act, OAC 5101:1-30-50

Library References

Parent and Child ⚷3.4.
WESTLAW Topic No. 285.
C.J.S. Parent and Child § 90.

OJur 3d: 26, Criminal Law § 600, 803; 45, Family Law § 1; 46, Family Law § 400; 47, Family Law § 639, 641, 642, 647 to 649, 1357 to 1368, 1372, 1373, 1375, 1376, 1378, 1379, 1381, 1383, 1385 to 1388, 1390, 1392, 1394, 1396 to 1398, 1400 to 1402, 1406.2; 78, Public Welfare § 120

Am Jur 2d: 23, Desertion and Nonsupport § 118, 130

Reciprocal enforcement of duty to support dependents, construction and application of state statutes providing for. 42 ALR2d 768

State or political subdivision's right to maintain action in another state for support and maintenance of defendant's child, parent, or dependent in plaintiff's institution. 67 ALR2d 771

Determination of paternity of child as within scope of proceeding under Uniform Reciprocal Enforcement of Support Act. 81 ALR3d 1175

Spouse's right to set off debt owed by other spouse against accrued spousal or child support payments. 11 ALR5th 259

Baldwin's Ohio Legislative Service Annotated, 1997 H 352—LSC Analysis, p 9/L-2719

Carlin, Baldwin's Ohio Practice, *Merrick-Rippner Probate Law* § 19.6, 19.8, 108.36 (1997)

Klein & Darling, Baldwin's Ohio Practice, *Civil Practice* § 1 (1997)

Sowald & Morganstern, Baldwin's Ohio Practice, *Domestic Relations Law* § 23.19, 23.31, 23.36, 23.48 (1997)

Notes of Decisions and Opinions

In general 3
Civil action 5
Domicile 2
Duty to support 1
Jurisdiction 4
Modification of support 6
Specific limits on enforcement 7

1. Duty to support

RC 3115.01 et seq. (the Uniform Reciprocal Enforcement of Support Act) imposes upon father, whose wife removes their children of tender ages from this to another state, duty to support children as delineated by law of Ohio. (Annotation from former RC 3115.01.) Porter v. Porter (Ohio 1971) 25 Ohio St.2d 123, 267 N.E.2d 299, 54 O.O.2d 260.

Absent express language to the contrary in the foreign state's order, former spouse has an obligation to provide support for the issue of the marriage, which can be suspended only upon clear and unambiguous language in a decree. Swayne v. Newman (Ohio App. 4 Dist. 1998) 131 Ohio App.3d 793, 723 N.E.2d 1117.

Full Faith and Credit for Child Support Orders Act, which requires enforcement according to its terms of child support order made by a court of another state, does not violate due process or equal protection and is not an impermissible burden on freedom of travel; statute purports to rely upon full faith and credit clause of the Constitution, and distinctions which result from operation of statute are reasonable and directly related to furtherance of solving a critical national problem, the failure of a significant number of parents to fulfill their responsibilities to support their children. (Annotation from former RC 3115.01.) Paton v. Brill (Franklin 1995) 104 Ohio App.3d 826, 663 N.E.2d 421.

Parent's legally imposed duty to support her minor children is not dependent on her awareness of that obligation. (Annotation from former RC 3115.01.) In re Adoption of Kuhlmann (Hamilton 1994) 99 Ohio App.3d 44, 649 N.E.2d 1279.

Past child support is "asset" owned by custodial parent; thus, fact that child may not have been supported by custodial parent to extent that child would have been supported had noncustodial parent been contributing to child's support all along does not relieve noncustodial parent of his duty to support that child from date of birth to majority. (Annotation from former RC 3115.01.) Seegert v. Zietlow (Cuyahoga 1994) 95 Ohio App.3d 451, 642 N.E.2d 697.

A temporary suspension of an existing support order does not affect the nature of an underlying order as a "support order" within the statutory definition which, by its language, encompasses temporary judgments of support. (Annotation from former RC 3115.01.) Snelling v. Gardner (Franklin 1990) 69 Ohio App.3d 196, 590 N.E.2d 330.

2. Domicile

Domicile is a legal relationship between a person and a particular place where the person resides in a particular place at least for some period of time and has the intent to reside in that place permanently or at least indefinitely; residence is encompassed within the definition of domicile; however, a person may have more than one residence but only one domicile. (Annotation from former RC 3115.01.) Snelling v. Gardner (Franklin 1990) 69 Ohio App.3d 196, 590 N.E.2d 330.

3. In general

Child support enforcement agency (CSEA) is a proper party to all actions for the collection of child support. Collins v. Collins (Ohio App. 12 Dist. 1998) 127 Ohio App.3d 281, 712 N.E.2d 800.

Purpose of Uniform Reciprocal Enforcement of Support Act (URESA) action is to facilitate payment of preexisting child support obligations. Bobbs v. Cline (Ohio App. 7 Dist. 1997) 116 Ohio App.3d 46, 686 N.E.2d 556.

Uniform Reciprocal Enforcement of Support Act (URESA) is a measure devised to afford a practical method to enforce legal obligations obligor/noncustodial parent owes to support his or her child or children where obligor has left state in which child or other children reside. (Annotation from former RC 3115.01.) Paton v. Brill (Franklin 1995) 104 Ohio App.3d 826, 663 N.E.2d 421.

The central purpose of URESA is to ensure that the duties of support are enforced, even across state boundaries; convenience to the obligor is not a consideration, but it is the interest of the child that is paramount. (Annotation from former RC 3115.01.) Snelling v. Gardner (Franklin 1990) 69 Ohio App.3d 196, 590 N.E.2d 330.

Uniform Support of Dependents Act is liberally construed. (Annotation from former RC 3115.01.) Skinner v. Fasciano (Cuyahoga 1956) 137 N.E.2d 613, 75 Ohio Law Abs. 409.

4. Jurisdiction

Trial court had subject matter jurisdiction under Ohio version of Uniform Reciprocal Enforcement of Support Act (URESA) to establish child support order against former wife, who was residing in Ohio after obtaining divorce in Kentucky, even though former husband and child who was in his custody still lived in Kentucky, where prior Kentucky court order terminating husband's initial support obligation, and granting him custody, was silent as to any support obligation on wife's part. Swayne v. Newman (Ohio App. 4 Dist. 1998) 131 Ohio App.3d 793, 723 N.E.2d 1117.

In former wife's action to recover child support and alimony arrearages from former husband, trial court had jurisdiction to grant judgment on terms of parties' original separation agreement, although trial court in another county had previously entered judgment on same issues in former wife's action under Uniform Reciprocal Enforcement of Support Act (URESA). In Matter of Shanyfelt (Ohio App. 3 Dist. 1997) 118 Ohio App.3d 243, 692 N.E.2d 642.

Full Faith and Credit for Child Support Orders Act precluded Ohio court from obtaining jurisdiction to modify amount of child support ordered pursuant to original Maryland divorce decree and subsequently ordered enforced in Ohio pursuant to Ohio Uniform Reciprocal Enforcement of Support Act (URESA). (Annotation from former RC 3115.01.) Paton v. Brill (Franklin 1995) 104 Ohio App.3d 826, 663 N.E.2d 421.

A father resides in Ohio for purposes of the Uniform Reciprocal Enforcement of Support Act (URESA) where evidence establishes that he (1) visited Ohio on at least twelve separate occasions, (2) had been employed in Ohio for six weeks, (3) used his sister's Columbus address as a forwarding address, (4) applied for employment in Ohio, and (5) received unemployment benefits in Ohio; thus, a trial court could rightfully assert jurisdiction over the father for purposes of enforcing an out-of-state child support order. (Annotation from former RC 3115.01.) Snelling v. Gardner (Franklin 1990) 69 Ohio App.3d 196, 590 N.E.2d 330.

Trial court's orders modifying, and later suspending, former husband's child support obligations were void ab initio where the motions were granted after the trial court, without notice to former wife, who was residing in Florida, granted former husband's motion to consolidate former wife's Uniform Reciprocal Enforcement of Support Act action, which had been filed by the state of Florida on her behalf, with the prior divorce action, and thus, the trial court's orders were subject to collateral attack at any time. (Annotation from former RC 3115.01.) Rondy v. Rondy (Summit 1983) 13 Ohio App.3d 19, 468 N.E.2d 81, 13 O.B.R. 20.

The division of domestic relations of the common pleas court is a court of record, with jurisdiction, under the provisions of the support of dependents act, to entertain an action to enforce duties of support. (Annotation from former RC 3115.01.) Robinson v. Robinson (Franklin 1964) 8 Ohio App.2d 235, 221 N.E.2d 598, 37 O.O.2d 218.

5. Civil action

An action instituted under RC Ch 3115 to enforce duties of support is a civil action. (Annotation from former RC 3115.01.) Robinson v. Robinson (Franklin 1964) 8 Ohio App.2d 235, 221 N.E.2d 598, 37 O.O.2d 218.

Uniform Support Act is civil in its nature and is not governed by any criminal law. (Annotation from former RC 3115.01.) Burney v. Vance (Ohio Com.Pl. 1969) 17 Ohio Misc. 307, 246 N.E.2d 371, 46 O.O.2d 427.

Prosecuting attorney may bring civil action for separate maintenance and support in accordance with procedure outlined in RC 3115.05. (Annotation from former RC 3115.01.) OAG 70-050.

6. Modification of support

Under Ohio version of Uniform Reciprocal Enforcement of Support Act (URESA), courts do not have subject matter jurisdiction to modify child support obligations set forth in initiating state's orders. Swayne v. Newman (Ohio App. 4 Dist. 1998) 131 Ohio App.3d 793, 723 N.E.2d 1117.

Any determination of support by trial court in former wife's prior action under Uniform Reciprocal Enforcement of Support Act (URESA) was unaffected by subsequent court proceedings which modified support order, unless subsequent order specifically provided for alteration in the URESA payment. In Matter of Shanyfelt (Ohio App. 3 Dist. 1997) 118 Ohio App.3d 243, 692 N.E.2d 642.

Once initial Uniform Reciprocal Enforcement of Support Act (URESA) order is established, a subsequent modification proceeding in divorce action neither automatically nor necessarily modifies initial URESA order; initial URESA order is modified only if divorce court specifically orders modification. (Annotation from former RC 3115.01.) Paton v. Brill (Franklin 1995) 104 Ohio App.3d 826, 663 N.E.2d 421.

Under the Uniform Interstate Family Support Act (UIFSA) an Ohio court is without authority to modify a parent's child support obligation under a New York decree to cease that obligation when the parties' children reach eighteen by applying Ohio law. Vancott-Young v Cummings, No. CA98-09-122, 1999 WL 326149 (12th Dist Ct App, Warren, 5-24-99).

As the primary purpose of RC Ch 3115 is to enforce child support orders effected in foreign jurisdictions rather than to provide for their modification, a petition under RC Ch 3115 to increase a child support order from a different state is properly dismissed. (Annotation from former RC 3115.01.) Briggs v Briggs, No. CA86-09-064 (12th Dist Ct App, Clermont, 3-2-87).

7. Specific limits on enforcement

Child support payments being made by a father may be impounded by the court where the mother denies visitation to the father by removing the children from the state without the consent of the court and without notice or provision of a forwarding address to the father. (Annotation from former RC 3115.01.) Rodriguez v. Rodriguez (Ohio Com.Pl. 1988) 61 Ohio Misc.2d 112, 575 N.E.2d 519.

Determination of the age at which a person becomes an adult, for the purpose of enforcing the provisions of the reciprocal support act, depends upon the state in which the child is living and the state in which the father is living, and not upon the state in which the original divorce was granted. (Annotation from former RC 3115.01.) Burney v. Vance (Ohio Com.Pl. 1969) 17 Ohio Misc. 307, 246 N.E.2d 371, 46 O.O.2d 427.

The Uniform Support of Dependents Act may not be used by a nonresident mother to compel an Ohio resident to support an alleged illegitimate child of his where there has been no judicial determination of the paternity of such child. (Annotation from former RC 3115.01.) Smith v. Smith (Ohio Com.Pl. 1965) 11 Ohio Misc. 25, 224 N.E.2d 925, 40 O.O.2d 136.

3115.02 Remedies cumulative

Remedies provided by sections 3115.01 to 3115.59 of the Revised Code are in addition to, not in substitution for, any other remedies.

(1997 H 352, eff. 1-1-98)

Historical and Statutory Notes

Ed. Note: Former 3115.02 repealed by 1997 H 352, eff. 1-1-98; 1971 H 504, eff. 10-27-71.

Ed. Note: Former 3115.02 was former 3115.22 recodified by 1971 H 504, eff. 10-27-71; 126 v 560.

Ed. Note: Prior 3115.02 recodified as 3115.07 by 1971 H 504, eff. 10-27-71; 126 v 560; 1953 H 1; GC 8007-8.

Pre-1953 H 1 Amendments: 124 v H 1

Cross References

Contempt action for failure to pay support, 2705.031, 2705.05

Court of common pleas, bureau of support, 2301.34 et seq.

Criminal nonsupport of dependents, 2919.21

Payment of support through withholding of earnings, workers' compensation benefits, unemployment compensation benefits, retirement benefits, or bank account; procedures, 3113.21 et seq.

INTERSTATE FAMILY SUPPORT

Ohio Administrative Code References

Child support program, OAC Ch 5101:1-29
Collection of past due support by federal tax refund offset, OAC Ch 5101:1-30

Library References

Parent and Child ⟾3.4(1).
WESTLAW Topic No. 285.
C.J.S. Parent and Child §§ 90 to 92.

OJur 3d: 47, Family Law § 1362, 1406.1, 1406.2; 78, Public Welfare § 120
Am Jur 2d: 23, Desertion and Nonsupport § 134, 135
Determination of paternity of child as within scope of proceeding under Uniform Reciprocal Enforcement of Support Act. 81 ALR3d 1175

Baldwin's Ohio Legislative Service Annotated, 1997 H 352—LSC Analysis, p 9/L-2719
Carlin, Baldwin's Ohio Practice, *Merrick-Rippner Probate Law* § 19.6, 19.8, 108.36 (1997)
Sowald & Morganstern, Baldwin's Ohio Practice, *Domestic Relations Law* § 23.13, 23.19 (1997)

Law Review and Journal Commentaries

Abusing the Power to Regulate: The Child Support Recovery Act of 1992, Comment. (Ed. note: Federal encroachment into traditional fields of State criminal law is discussed.) 46 Case W Res L Rev 935 (Spring 1996).

Reaching Out-Of-State Obligors: Collecting Judgments Through UIFSA and Beyond, Patrice R.T. Yarham. 11 Domestic Rel J Ohio 85 (November/December 1999).

Notes of Decisions and Opinions

In general 2
Enforcement of foreign judgments 1
Paternity 3

---

1. Enforcement of foreign judgments

Neither the Uniform Enforcement of Foreign Judgments Act (UEFJA), 1983 S 23, eff. 7-29-83, RC 2329.021 to 2329.027, nor the Uniform Reciprocal Enforcement of Support Act (URESA), 1971 H 504, eff. 10-27-71, RC Ch 3115, deprives a court of common pleas jurisdiction to decide an action to enforce a foreign judgment. (Annotation from former RC 3115.02.) State ex rel. Ruessman v. Flanagan (Ohio 1992) 65 Ohio St.3d 464, 605 N.E.2d 31.

In former wife's action to recover child support and alimony arrearages from former husband, trial court had jurisdiction to grant judgment on terms of parties' original separation agreement, although trial court in another county had previously entered judgment on same issues in former wife's action under Uniform Reciprocal Enforcement of Support Act (URESA). In Matter of Shanyfelt (Ohio App. 3 Dist. 1997) 118 Ohio App.3d 243, 692 N.E.2d 642.

A petition in an action to enforce a duty of support filed in this state by a court of a sister state, which state has adopted the Uniform Support Act, and which petition complies with the requirements of that act in requesting that a common pleas court of this state make an order for support of a wife alleged to have been abandoned in Pennsylvania by her husband, who is not a resident of Ohio, states a good cause of action; and such petition may be tried under the terms of the Ohio Support of Dependents Act. (Annotation from former RC 3115.22.) Pennsylvania ex rel. Stobie v. Stobie (Summit 1964) 3 Ohio App.2d 18, 209 N.E.2d 457, 32 O.O.2d 79.

2. In general

Any determination of support by trial court in former wife's prior action under Uniform Reciprocal Enforcement of Support Act (URESA) was unaffected by subsequent court proceedings which modified support order, unless subsequent order specifically provided for alteration in the URESA payment. In Matter of Shanyfelt (Ohio App. 3 Dist. 1997) 118 Ohio App.3d 243, 692 N.E.2d 642.

The Uniform Support Act covers children who are minors, and under RC 3115.22 is in addition to and not in substitution of any other remedies authorized by law. (Annotation from former RC 3115.22.) Burney v. Vance (Ohio Com.Pl. 1969) 17 Ohio Misc. 307, 246 N.E.2d 371, 46 O.O.2d 427.

Under the Support of Dependent's Act, mother was entitled to reimbursement of funds expended for the support of herself and her child between the time the father allegedly abandoned his family, and the date of trial of her action for support. (Annotation from former RC 3115.02.) Skinner v. Fasciano (Cuyahoga 1956) 137 N.E.2d 613, 75 Ohio Law Abs. 409.

3. Paternity

The Uniform Support of Dependents Act may not be used by a nonresident mother to compel an Ohio resident to support an alleged illegitimate child of his where there has been no judicial determination of the paternity of such child. (Annotation from former RC 3115.22.) Smith v. Smith (Ohio Com.Pl. 1965) 11 Ohio Misc. 25, 224 N.E.2d 925, 40 O.O.2d 136.

JURISDICTION

Library References

Sowald & Morganstern, Baldwin's Ohio Practice, *Domestic Relations Law* § 23.43 (1997)

3115.03 Bases for jurisdiction over nonresident

In a proceeding to establish, enforce, or modify a support order or to determine the existence or nonexistence of a parent and child relationship, a tribunal of this state may exercise personal jurisdiction over a nonresident individual if any of the following is the case:

(A) The individual is personally served with summons within this state;

(B) The individual submits to the jurisdiction of this state by consent, by entering a general appearance, or by filing a responsive pleading or other document having the effect of waiving any contest to personal jurisdiction;

(C) The individual resided with the child in this state;

(D) The individual resided in this state and provided prenatal expenses or support for the child;

(E) The child resides in this state as a result of the acts or directives of the individual;

(F) The individual engaged in sexual intercourse in this state and the child may have been conceived by that act of intercourse;

(G) The individual registered in the putative father registry maintained pursuant to section 3107.062 of the Revised Code;

(H) There is any other basis for the state to exercise personal jurisdiction over the individual.

(1997 H 352, eff. 1-1-98)

Historical and Statutory Notes

Ed. Note: Former 3115.03 repealed by 1997 H 352, eff. 1-1-98; 1971 H 504, eff. 10-27-71; 126 v 560; 1953 H 1; GC 8007-7, 8007-4.

Pre-1953 H 1 Amendments: 124 v H 1

Ohio Administrative Code References

Personal jurisdiction (long arm jurisdiction), OAC 5101:1-30-51

Library References

Parent and Child ⚷3.4(2).
WESTLAW Topic No. 285.
C.J.S. Parent and Child §§ 93 to 96.

OJur 3d: 47, Family Law § 1364, 1406.1 to 1406.3
Am Jur 2d: 23, Desertion and Nonsupport § 122, 131; 41, Husband and Wife § 329 et seq.
Construction and application of state statutes providing for reciprocal enforcement of duty to support dependents. 42 ALR2d 768
Determination of paternity of child as within scope of proceeding under Uniform Reciprocal Enforcement of Support Act. 81 ALR3d 1175

Baldwin's Ohio Legislative Service Annotated, 1997 H 352—LSC Analysis, p 9/L-2719
Carlin, Baldwin's Ohio Practice, *Merrick-Rippner Probate Law* § 19.6, 19.8, 108.36 (1997)
Sowald & Morganstern, Baldwin's Ohio Practice, *Domestic Relations Law* § 23.32, 23.39, 23.48 (1997)

Law Review and Journal Commentaries

Abusing the Power to Regulate: The Child Support Recovery Act of 1992, Comment. (Ed. note: Federal encroachment into traditional fields of State criminal law is discussed.) 46 Case W Res L Rev 935 (Spring 1996).

Interstate Family Support: Ohio's Version of the Uniform Interstate Family Support Act, Cooley R. Howarth, Jr. 10 Domestic Rel J Ohio 49 (July/August 1998).

Notes of Decisions and Opinions

1. Removal to another state

Where father and his children have been deprived of their rights of visitation with each other by mother's removal of children from this state without father's consent, trial court may condition father's duty to support children upon mother's compliance with reasonable visitation privileges, unless mother is unable fully to support the children. (Annotation from former RC 3115.03.) Porter v. Porter (Ohio 1971) 25 Ohio St.2d 123, 267 N.E.2d 299, 54 O.O.2d 260.

RC 3115.01 et seq. (the Uniform Reciprocal Enforcement of Support Act) imposes upon father, whose wife removes their children of tender ages from this to another state, duty to support children as delineated by law of Ohio. (Annotation from former RC 3115.03.) Porter v. Porter (Ohio 1971) 25 Ohio St.2d 123, 267 N.E.2d 299, 54 O.O.2d 260.

There is no duty on the father of minor children to make support payments to the mother as decreed by another court pursuant to the Uniform Reciprocal Enforcement of Support Act, where the father has obtained a prior order of custody and the mother has removed the children from the jurisdiction of the court contrary to such order. (Annotation from former RC 3115.03.) State of N. J. v. Morales (Franklin 1973) 35 Ohio App.2d 56, 299 N.E.2d 920, 64 O.O.2d 175.

Where a wife abandons her husband without any aggression on his part and takes her children to another state, the husband cannot be compelled to support such children under the uniform enforcement of support laws where he retains a domicile in Ohio, earns his living in Ohio, and apparently is ready, willing and able to support his children in Ohio. (Annotation from former RC 3115.03.) Buliox v. Buliox (Ohio Com.Pl. 1962) 185 N.E.2d 802, 90 Ohio Law Abs. 251, 21 O.O.2d 30.

2. Support of parent

In a proceeding, initiated in Pennsylvania and certified to Ohio under the provisions of the Uniform Dependent's Act to require a son, who is a citizen and resident of Ohio, to contribute to the support of his father, who is a resident of Pennsylvania, the courts of Ohio will determine the liability of such son for such support in accordance with the law of Ohio and, in so doing, will accord to such son any benefit of GC 12431 (former RC 2901.42) to which he may be entitled. (Annotation from former RC 3115.03.) Com. of Pa. ex rel. Department of Public Assistance, Mercer County Bd. of Assistance v. Mong (Ohio 1954) 160 Ohio St. 455, 117 N.E.2d 32, 52 O.O. 340.

3. Modification of support

Minor children are third party beneficiaries of provisions in a divorce decree granting support payments for their benefit, and such benefits may not be modified by the parties to the detriment of the minors. (Annotation from former RC 3115.03.) Rhoades v. Rhoades (Hamilton 1974) 40 Ohio App.2d 559, 321 N.E.2d 242, 69 O.O.2d 488.

4. Support of adult children

The common pleas court is without power to order, in a divorce decree, a father to support a child of the divorced parties after such child reaches the age of twenty-one years. (Annotation from former RC 3115.03.) Sylvester v. Sylvester (Hamilton 1969) 21 Ohio App.2d 58, 254 N.E.2d 699, 50 O.O.2d 104.

Trial court erred in granting a father's motion to terminate support of his child on the grounds that the child had reached eighteen years of age where such child was mentally retarded. (Annotation from former RC 3115.03.) Castle v Castle, No. CA 8092 (2d Dist Ct App, Montgomery, 10-12-83).

5. Bigamous marriage

In a proceeding under the Uniform Support of Dependents Act, defendant was properly held liable for the support of a child born of a bigamous marriage and residing in Pennsylvania following proceedings in a Pennsylvania court. (Annotation from former RC 3115.03.) In re Duncan (Cuyahoga 1961) 172 N.E.2d 478, 85 Ohio Law Abs. 522, 17 O.O.2d 21.

3115.031 Child wrongly held by another

(A) A duty of support of an obligor owed to a minor child is not enforceable pursuant to this chapter during any period of time during which both of the following conditions are met:

(1) The obligor has legal custody of the child;

(2) The obligor does not have physical custody of the child because of the wrongful taking or wrongful continuation of physical custody by another person.

(B) If the state or a political subdivision of the state provides support to a minor child, a duty of support is owed to the child by an obligor, and the duty of support is not enforceable pursuant to division (A) of this section, the state or political subdivision may take all actions necessary to return the child to the obligor.

(1986 H 149, eff. 6-26-86)

Cross References

Child stealing, 2905.04
Interference with custody, 2919.23
Uniform child custody jurisdiction law, 3109.21 to 3109.37

Library References

Parent and Child ⟹3.4(2), 18.
WESTLAW Topic No. 285.
C.J.S. Parent and Child §§ 93 to 96, 130 to 136, 178.

OJur 3d: 47, Family Law § 1387

Am Jur 2d: 24, Divorce and Separation § 1075; 59, Parent and Child § 60

Carlin, Baldwin's Ohio Practice, *Merrick-Rippner Probate Law* § 19.6, 19.8, 108.36 (1997)

3115.04 Procedure when exercising jurisdiction over nonresident

A tribunal of this state exercising personal jurisdiction over a nonresident under section 3115.03 of the Revised Code may apply section 3115.27 of the Revised Code to obtain evidence from another state and section 3115.29 of the Revised Code to obtain discovery through a tribunal of another state. In all other respects, sections 3115.12 to 3115.52 of the Revised Code are not applicable and the tribunal shall apply the procedural and substantive law of this state, including the rules on choice of law other than those established by sections 3115.01 to 3115.59 of the Revised Code.

(1997 H 352, eff. 1-1-98)

Historical and Statutory Notes

Ed. Note: Former 3115.04 repealed by 1997 H 352, eff. 1-1-98; 1971 H 504, eff. 10-27-71; 1953 H 1; GC 8007-5, 8007-6.

Pre-1953 H 1 Amendments: 124 v H 1

Cross References

Extradition, Ch 2963

Governor may issue warrant in certain cases, 107.04

Ohio Administrative Code References

Locating the absent parent, OAC 5101:1-30-01

Personal jurisdiction (long arm jurisdiction), OAC 5101:1-30-51

Library References

Parent and Child ⟹3.4(2).
WESTLAW Topic No. 285.
C.J.S. Parent and Child §§ 93 to 96.

OJur 3d: 26, Criminal Law § 803; 47, Family Law § 1373, 1406.1 to 1406.3

Am Jur 2d: 23, Desertion and Nonsupport § 117, 143 to 147, 151

Construction and application of state statutes providing for reciprocal enforcement of duty to support dependents. 42 ALR2d 768

Determination of paternity of child as within scope of proceeding under Uniform Reciprocal Enforcement of Support Act. 81 ALR3d 1175

Baldwin's Ohio Legislative Service Annotated, 1997 H 352—LSC Analysis, p 9/L-2719

Carlin, Baldwin's Ohio Practice, *Merrick-Rippner Probate Law* § 19.6, 19.8, 108.36 (1997)

Sowald & Morganstern, Baldwin's Ohio Practice, *Domestic Relations Law* § 23.37 (1997)

Notes of Decisions and Opinions

1. Extradition from Ohio

A person in Ohio who intentionally does nothing to support his child in another state, when under the laws of such other state he is required to do so, thereby "commits an act" in Ohio which intentionally results in a crime in such other state, and he may be extradited therefor. (Annotation from former RC 3115.04.) In re Harris (Ohio 1959) 170 Ohio St. 151, 163 N.E.2d 762, 10 O.O.2d 99.

2. Defenses

Where a wife has obtained a warrant for a husband for child desertion from the court of another state, the husband cannot obtain a support order from an Ohio court under the Uniform Support of Dependents Act and thereby be protected from extradition. (Annotation from former RC 3115.04.) Sands v. Sands (Ohio Com.Pl. 1956) 136 N.E.2d 747, 73 Ohio Law Abs. 331, 60 O.O. 181.

3115.05 Initiating and responding tribunal of state

Under sections 3115.01 to 3115.59 of the Revised Code, a tribunal of this state may serve as an initiating tribunal to forward proceedings to another state and as a responding tribunal for proceedings initiated in another state.

(1997 H 352, eff. 1-1-98)

Historical and Statutory Notes

Ed. Note: Former 3115.05 repealed by 1997 H 352, eff. 1-1-98; 1971 H 504, eff. 10-27-71.

Ed. Note: Prior 3115.05 recodified as 3115.08 by 1971 H 504, eff. 10-27-71; 1969 H 361; 126 v 560; 1953 H 1; GC 8007-9.

Pre-1953 H 1 Amendments: 124 v H 1

Ohio Administrative Code References

Proceeding involving two or more states, OAC 5101:1-30-53

Library References

Parent and Child ⟹3.4(2).
WESTLAW Topic No. 285.
C.J.S. Parent and Child §§ 93 to 96.

OJur 3d: 26, Criminal Law § 803; 47, Family Law § 1373, 1406.1, 1406.2, 1406.4
Am Jur 2d: 23, Desertion and Nonsupport § 151
Determination of paternity of child as within scope of proceeding under Uniform Reciprocal Enforcement of Support Act. 81 ALR3d 1175

Baldwin's Ohio Legislative Service Annotated, 1997 H 352—LSC Analysis, p 9/L-2719
Carlin, Baldwin's Ohio Practice, *Merrick-Rippner Probate Law* § 19.6, 19.8, 108.36 (1997)
Sowald & Morganstern, Baldwin's Ohio Practice, *Domestic Relations Law* § 23.32, 23.33, 23.46 (1997)

Notes of Decisions and Opinions

1. Compliance with support order

A person for whom an extradition requisition has been received by the governor of Ohio from a state which has enacted the Uniform Dependent's Act asking for the person's return to the demanding state for desertion or nonsupport, must be relieved of extradition where such person submits to a court of record in this state and complies with the court's order of support, but such court cannot obtain jurisdiction to make such order of support otherwise than in the manner designated in GC 8007-10 (RC 3115.06) et seq.; and where there has been no compliance with the provisions of these sections an obligor may not be relieved of extradition by a mere offer to submit to the jurisdiction of the court of the responding state. (Annotation from former RC 3115.05.) 1953 OAG 3009.

3115.06 Simultaneous proceedings in another state

(A) A tribunal of this state may exercise jurisdiction to issue a support order if the complaint or comparable pleading is filed in this state after a complaint or comparable pleading requesting the issuance of a support order is filed in another state only if all of the following apply:

(1) The complaint or comparable pleading is filed in this state before the expiration of the time allowed in the other state for filing a responsive pleading challenging the exercise of jurisdiction by the other state;

(2) The contesting party timely challenges the exercise of jurisdiction in the other state;

(3) With respect to actions to issue child support orders, this state is the home state of the child.

(B) A tribunal of this state may not exercise jurisdiction to issue a support order if the complaint or comparable pleading is filed in this state before a complaint or comparable pleading requesting the issuance of a support order is filed in another state if any of the following is the case:

(1) The complaint or comparable pleading is filed in the other state before the expiration of the time allowed in this state for filing a responsive pleading challenging the exercise of jurisdiction by this state.

(2) The contesting party timely challenges the exercise of jurisdiction in this state.

(3) With respect to actions to issue child support orders, the other state is the home state of the child.

(1997 H 352, eff. 1-1-98)

Historical and Statutory Notes

Ed. Note: Former 3115.06 repealed by 1997 H 352, eff. 1-1-98; 1971 H 504, eff. 10-27-71.

Ed. Note: Prior 3115.06 recodified as 3115.09 by 1971 H 504, eff. 10-27-71; 126 v 560; 1953 H 1; GC 8007-10.

Pre-1953 H 1 Amendments: 124 v H 1

Ohio Administrative Code References

Proceeding involving two or more states, OAC 5101:1-30-53

Library References

Parent and Child ⚿3.4(2).
WESTLAW Topic No. 285.
C.J.S. Parent and Child §§ 93 to 96.

OJur 3d: 47, Family Law § 1365
Am Jur 2d: 23, Desertion and Nonsupport § 122, 137
Determination of paternity of child as within scope of proceeding under Uniform Reciprocal Enforcement of Support Act. 81 ALR3d 1175

Baldwin's Ohio Legislative Service Annotated, 1997 H 352—LSC Analysis, p 9/L-2719
Carlin, Baldwin's Ohio Practice, *Merrick-Rippner Probate Law* § 19.6, 19.8, 108.36 (1997)
Sowald & Morganstern, Baldwin's Ohio Practice, *Domestic Relations Law* § 23.19, 23.23, 23.33, 23.34 (1997)

Notes of Decisions and Opinions

1. Removal from jurisdiction

There is no duty on the father of minor children to make support payments to the mother as decreed by another court pursuant to the uniform reciprocal enforcement of support act, where the father has obtained a prior order of custody and the mother has removed the children from the jurisdiction of the court contrary to such order. (Annotation from former RC 3115.06.) State of N. J. v. Morales (Franklin 1973) 35 Ohio App.2d 56, 299 N.E.2d 920, 64 O.O.2d 175.

It is error to award pre-judgment interest on unpaid child support where the trial court makes no findings concerning the obligor's presence in any state while he worked outside of Ohio during the time he owed support and his whereabouts and periods of time cannot be determined from the record; on the other hand a claim for recovery of unpaid child support that is filed after the child turns eighteen is not barred by laches where, contrary to the obligor's contention that attempts to locate the mother and child were thwarted and that he was denied the opportunity to establish and maintain a parent-child relationship, he could have enforced his right to visitation through a court order since the mother and child resided at the same address for nineteen years. Chamberlin v Chamberlin, No. 97CA22, 1998 WL 274823 (4th Dist Ct App, Washington, 5-18-98).

2. Prior support order

If an action is not one to enforce a general obligation of support but one to enforce a specific duty of support as embodied within a prior child support order, then the duty of support as provided by the law of the state which had entered the support order is controlling; hence, a prior support order in Ohio is controlling rather than the law of Michigan relating to the duty of support. (Annotation from former RC 3115.06.) Morrison v Morrison, No. 73AP-195 (10th Dist Ct App, Franklin, 2-5-74).

3115.07 Continuing, exclusive jurisdiction

(A) A tribunal of this state has continuing, exclusive jurisdiction over a child support order it issues as long as the obligor, individual obligee, or child subject to the child support order is a resident of this state, unless all of the parties who are individuals have filed written consents with the tribunal of this state for a tribunal of another state to modify the order and assume continuing, exclusive jurisdiction.

(B) A tribunal of this state may not exercise continuing jurisdiction to modify a child support order it issues if the order is modified by a tribunal of another state pursuant to a law adopted by the other state that is substantially similar to sections 3115.01 to 3115.59 of the Revised Code.

(C) If a child support order issued by a tribunal of this state is modified by a tribunal of another state pursuant to a law adopted by the other state that is substantially similar to sections 3115.01 to 3115.59 of the Revised Code, the tribunal of this state loses its continuing, exclusive jurisdiction with regard to prospective enforcement of the order, and may do only the following:

(1) Order collection of support amounts accruing before the modification of the order;

(2) Enforce nonmodifiable aspects of that order;

(3) Provide other appropriate relief for violations of the order that occurred before the effective date of the modification.

(D) A tribunal of this state shall recognize the continuing, exclusive jurisdiction of a tribunal of another state that has issued a child support order pursuant to a law adopted by the other state that is substantially similar to sections 3115.01 to 3115.59 of the Revised Code.

(E) A temporary support order issued ex parte or pending resolution of a jurisdictional conflict does not create continuing, exclusive jurisdiction in the issuing tribunal.

(F) A tribunal of this state has continuing, exclusive jurisdiction over a spousal support order it issues throughout the existence of the support obligation. A tribunal of this state may not modify a spousal support order issued by a tribunal of another state having continuing, exclusive jurisdiction over that order under the law of that state.

(1997 H 352, eff. 1-1-98)

Historical and Statutory Notes

Ed. Note: Former 3115.07 repealed by 1997 H 352, eff. 1-1-98; 1971 H 504, eff. 10-27-71.

Ed. Note: Former 3115.07 was former 3115.02 recodified by 1971 H 504, eff. 10-27-71; 126 v 560; 1953 H 1; GC 8007-8.

Ed. Note: Prior 3115.07 recodified as 3115.12 by 1971 H 504; eff. 10-27-71; 126 v 560; 1953 H 1; GC 8007-11.

Pre-1953 H 1 Amendments: 124 v H 1

Cross References

Aid to dependent children, Ch 5107
County children services, determination of ability to pay cost of care, 5153.19
General assistance, Ch 5113
Placing of child in public or private institution, 5103.15

Ohio Administrative Code References

Continuing exclusive jurisdiction, OAC 5101:1-30-54

Library References

Parent and Child ⟹3.4(2).
WESTLAW Topic No. 285.
C.J.S. Parent and Child §§ 93 to 96.

OJur 3d: 47, Family Law § 1386; 78, Public Welfare § 120
Am Jur 2d: 23, Desertion and Nonsupport § 127, 146; 79, Welfare Laws § 79 to 83
Right of state or its political subdivision to maintain action in another state for support and maintenance of defendant's child, parent, or dependent in plaintiff's institution. 67 ALR2d 771
Determination of paternity of child as within scope of proceeding under Uniform Reciprocal Enforcement of Support Act. 81 ALR3d 1175

Baldwin's Ohio Legislative Service Annotated, 1997 H 352—LSC Analysis, p 9/L-2719
Carlin, Baldwin's Ohio Practice, *Merrick-Rippner Probate Law* § 19.6, 19.8, 108.36 (1997)
Klein & Darling, Baldwin's Ohio Practice, *Civil Practice* § 1 (1997)
Sowald & Morganstern, Baldwin's Ohio Practice, *Domestic Relations Law* § 23.19, 23.20, 23.33, 23.42, 23.43 (1997)

Notes of Decisions and Opinions

1. Modification

Where a state or political subdivision thereof is the petitioner in a URESA action, a court in a local divorce case cannot modify the existing URESA order, even if it so specifically provides, unless the URESA petitioner has had prior notice of the local proceeding, in which modification is to be considered, and an opportunity to protect its interests therein. (Annotation from former RC 3115.07.) San Diego County v. Elavsky (Ohio 1979) 58 Ohio St.2d 81, 388 N.E.2d 1229, 12 O.O.3d 88.

2. Defenses

A violation of a custody order is not a defense to a state's action under the Uniform Reciprocal Enforcement of Support Act for reimbursement of support provided and for current support of a minor child. (Annotation from former RC 3115.07.) State of Iowa ex rel. Cantrell v. Cantrell (Summit 1983) 9 Ohio App.3d 194, 459 N.E.2d 242, 9 O.B.R. 305.

A laches defense is unavailable to a child support obligor who is in arrears in excess of $11,000 where the child support enforcement agency as an agency of the state seeks collection of back child support in order to reimburse the mother for costs incurred in the rearing of the parties' three children and to reimburse the state for sums distributed to her in the form of Aid to Dependent Children (ADC) while the obligor was failing to make support payments. Yeater v Yeater, No. 96-BA-23, 1998 WL 574429 (7th Dist Ct App, Belmont, 8-28-98).

3. Duty to reimburse

Under RC 3115.21, a father's duty to reimburse another state for child support payments pursuant to the Uniform Reciprocal Enforcement of Support Act is conditioned on the mother's inability to pay, and the mother's removal of the child from the jurisdiction in contravention of the court's order is of no consequence. (Annotation from former RC 3115.07.) McCoy v. McCoy (Summit 1977) 53 Ohio App.2d 331, 374 N.E.2d 164, 7 O.O.3d 427.

An order of the domestic relations court suspending a father's obligation to make child support payments precludes a state from seeking reimbursement for assistance provided to the mother and child under URESA. (Annotation from former RC 3115.07.) Minnesota v Monroe, No. 17042, 1995 WL 411393 (9th Dist Ct App, Summit, 7-5-95).

3115.08 Enforcement and modification of support order by tribunal having continuing jurisdiction

(A) A tribunal of this state may serve as an initiating tribunal to request a tribunal of another state to enforce or modify a support order issued in that state.

(B) A tribunal of this state having continuing, exclusive jurisdiction over a support order may act as a responding tribunal to enforce or modify the order. If a party subject to the continuing, exclusive jurisdiction of the tribunal no longer resides in the issuing state, in subsequent proceedings the tribunal may apply section 3115.27 of the Revised Code to obtain evidence from another state and section 3115.29 of the Revised Code to obtain discovery through a tribunal of another state.

(C) A tribunal of this state that lacks continuing, exclusive jurisdiction over a spousal support order may not serve as a responding tribunal to modify a spousal support order of another state.

(1997 H 352, eff. 1-1-98)

Historical and Statutory Notes

Ed. Note: Former 3115.08 repealed by 1997 H 352, eff. 1-1-98; 1971 H 504, eff. 10-27-71.

Ed. Note: Former 3115.08 was former 3115.05 recodified by 1971 H 504, eff. 10-27-71; 1969 H 361; 126 v 560; 1953 H 1; GC 8007-9.

Ed. Note: Prior 3115.08 recodified as 3115.16 by 1971 H 504, eff. 10-27-71; 126 v 560; 1953 H 1; GC 8007-12.

Pre-1953 H 1 Amendments: 124 v H 1

Cross References

Charges against adults; defendant bound over to grand jury, 2151.43

Contempt action for failure to pay support, 2705.031, 2705.05

Jurisdiction of juvenile court, 2151.23

Ohio Administrative Code References

Continuing exclusive jurisdiction, OAC 5101:1-30-54

Library References

Parent and Child ⟹3.4(2).
WESTLAW Topic No. 285.
C.J.S. Parent and Child §§ 93 to 96.

OJur 3d: 47, Family Law § 1364, 1367, 1380; 48, Family Law § 1554
Am Jur 2d: 23, Desertion and Nonsupport § 141

Baldwin's Ohio Legislative Service Annotated, 1997 H 352—LSC Analysis, p 9/L-2719

Carlin, Baldwin's Ohio Practice, *Merrick-Rippner Probate Law* § 19.6, 19.8, 108.36 (1997)

Sowald & Morganstern, Baldwin's Ohio Practice, *Domestic Relations Law* § 23.19, 23.20, 23.33 (1997)

Law Review and Journal Commentaries

Foreign Support Decrees—Overcoming Procedural Barriers, Hon. Judith A. Nicely. 3 Domestic Rel J Ohio 147 (November/December 1991).

Notes of Decisions and Opinions

County of residence 1
Defenses 2

---

1. County of residence

An ex-wife's petition to register a foreign support order in the common pleas court located in the county where she moves after the dissolution of her marriage is not improperly filed on the grounds that her ex-husband resides in the same county since the statute provides that the support order may be filed in the county where the obligee resides and the court of that county cannot refuse jurisdiction. (Annotation from former RC 3115.08.) Nardone v. Nardone (Medina 1989) 63 Ohio App.3d 798, 580 N.E.2d 448.

Responding court in action brought under the Uniform Reciprocal Enforcement of Support Act (URESA) has jurisdiction to enforce duty to pay arrearages under prior support order. (Annotation from former RC 3115.08.) Jacobs v. Jacobs (Lucas 1988) 62 Ohio App.3d 271, 575 N.E.2d 480.

Under the broad wording of RC 3115.08, a trial court has jurisdiction to hear child support actions involving parties residing in different counties within Ohio, as well as parties residing in different states. (Annotation from former RC 3115.08.) Cochenour v Bradley, No. 8-87-13 (3d Dist Ct App, Logan, 11-8-88).

2. Defenses

Mother's claim for child support was not barred by doctrine of laches, although father claimed mother informed him he need not make any more payments;

father demonstrated only that mother had delayed asserting her claim for support, and he failed to show that delay resulted in prejudice to him. (Annotation from former RC 3115.08.) Wise v. Wise (Butler 1993) 86 Ohio App.3d 702, 621 N.E.2d 1213.

A father's claim that the mother's delay in seeking child support results in his losing the opportunity to visit his child during her formative years and incurring additional financial obligations do not constitute material prejudice since he had ample opportunity on his own initiative to request visitation or set aside money for the child's support. Goff v Walters, No. 18981, 1998 WL 791815 (9th Dist Ct App, Summit, 10-28-98).

It is error to award pre-judgment interest on unpaid child support where the trial court makes no findings concerning the obligor's presence in any state while he worked outside of Ohio during the time he owed support and his whereabouts and periods of time cannot be determined from the record; on the other hand a claim for recovery of unpaid child support that is filed after the child turns eighteen is not barred by laches where, contrary to the obligor's contention that attempts to locate the mother and child were thwarted and that he was denied the opportunity to establish and maintain a parent-child relationship, he could have enforced his right to visitation through a court order since the mother and child resided at the same address for nineteen years. Chamberlin v Chamberlin, No. 97CA22, 1998 WL 274823 (4th Dist Ct App, Washington, 5-18-98).

The doctrine of laches is inappropriate in a claim for child support where (1) the mother encourages visitation and a relationship between the father and child, (2) she accepts the father's financial help, and (3) she relies upon his agreement to help her and delays filing formal action. Powers v Eurez, No. 97APF08-1103, 1998 WL 96439 (10th Dist Ct App, Franklin, 3-5-98).

A defense of laches does not apply to a mother's claim for retroactive child support where her seventeen-year delay in bringing the claim does not result in material prejudice to the obligor who at all times during a twelve-year period when he was denied visitation with his son had remedies available to him including an action to establish paternity and visitation rights; in addition, a court errs in failing to address the son's claim for retroactive support which is separate and distinct from the claim brought by his mother, thereby resulting in two claims for recovery of retroactive child support. (Annotation from former RC 3115.08.) Davis v Hamilton County Child Support Enforcement Agency, No. C-950650, 1996 WL 149076 (1st Dist Ct App, Hamilton, 4-3-96).

In a suit for nonpayment of child support brought subsequent to decedent's death where decedent was ordered to make child support payments through the clerk of courts, the defense of laches is not available to the executor of decedent's estate merely on the grounds that decedent's death and the lapse of time since such do not constitute material prejudice. (Annotation from former RC 3115.08.) Heavenridge v Heavenridge, No. CA-479 (12th Dist Ct App, Clinton, 9-21-83).

3115.09 Recognition of controlling child support order

(A) If a proceeding is brought under sections 3115.01 to 3115.59 of the Revised Code, and only one tribunal has issued a child support order, the order of that tribunal shall be recognized as controlling.

(B) If a proceeding is brought under sections 3115.01 to 3115.59 of the Revised Code, and two or more child support orders have been issued by tribunals of this state or another state with regard to the same obligor and child, a tribunal of this state shall do the following:

(1) If only one of the tribunals would have continuing, exclusive jurisdiction, recognize the child support order of that tribunal as controlling.

(2) If more than one of the tribunals would have continuing, exclusive jurisdiction, recognize the child support order issued by the tribunal in the current home state of the child as controlling, but if a child support order has not been issued in the current home state of the child, recognize the child support order most recently issued as controlling.

(3) If none of the tribunals would have continuing, exclusive jurisdiction, the tribunal of this state having jurisdiction over the parties shall issue its own child support order which shall be controlling.

(C) If two or more child support orders have been issued for the same obligor and child and the obligor or the individual obligee resides in this state, a party may request a tribunal of this state to determine which order to recognize as controlling pursuant to division (B) of this section. The request must be accompanied by a certified copy of every support order in effect. The requesting party shall give notice of the request to each party whose rights may be affected by the determination.

(D) The tribunal that issued the controlling child support order under division (A), (B), or (C) of this section is the tribunal that has continuing, exclusive jurisdiction under section 3115.07 of the Revised Code.

(E) A tribunal of this state that determines by order the identity of the controlling child support order under division (B)(1) or (2) of this section or that issues a new controlling child support order under division (B)(3) of this section shall state in the order or child support order the basis upon which the tribunal made its determination.

(F) Within thirty days after issuance of an order recognizing the controlling child support order or a new controlling child support order, the party obtaining the order shall file a certified copy of it with each tribunal that issued or registered an earlier child support order. A party who obtains the order and fails to file a certified copy is subject to appropriate sanctions by a tribunal in which the issue of failure to file arises. The failure to file does not affect the validity or enforceability of the controlling order.

(1997 H 352, eff. 1-1-98)

Historical and Statutory Notes

Ed. Note: Former 3115.09 repealed by 1997 H 352, eff. 1-1-98; 1971 H 504, eff. 10-27-71.

Ed. Note: Former 3115.09 was former 3115.06 recodified by 1971 H 504, eff. 10-27-71; 126 v 560; 1953 H 1; GC 8007-10.

Ed. Note: Prior 3115.09 recodified as 3115.23 by 1971 H 504, eff. 10-27-71; 1953 H 1; GC 8007-15.

Pre-1953 H 1 Amendments: 124 v H 1

Cross References

Adoption, Ch 3107
Commencement of action, venue, Civ R 3
Divorce, alimony, annulment, dissolution of marriage, Ch 3105
Habeas corpus, Ch 2725
Support of children, 3109.05
Uniform child custody jurisdiction law, 3109.21 to 3109.37
Visitation rights, 3109.051

Ohio Administrative Code References

Determining the controlling order, OAC 5101:1-30-541

Library References

Parent and Child ⟹3.4(2).
WESTLAW Topic No. 285.
C.J.S. Parent and Child §§ 93 to 96.

OJur 3d: 47, Family Law § 1370, 1371
Am Jur 2d: 23, Desertion and Nonsupport § 129, 139 to 142
Determination of paternity of child as within scope of proceeding under Uniform Reciprocal Enforcement of Support Act. 81 ALR3d 1175
Baldwin's Ohio Legislative Service Annotated, 1997 H 352—LSC Analysis, p 9/L-2719
Carlin, Baldwin's Ohio Practice, *Merrick-Rippner Probate Law* § 19.6, 19.8, 108.36 (1997)
Klein & Darling, Baldwin's Ohio Practice, *Civil Practice* § 1 (1997)
Sowald & Morganstern, Baldwin's Ohio Practice, *Domestic Relations Law* § 23.20, 23.33, 23.34, 23.43 (1997)

Notes of Decisions and Opinions

---

1. County of residence

An ex-wife's petition to register a foreign support order in the common pleas court located in the county where she moves after the dissolution of her marriage is not improperly filed on the grounds that her ex-husband resides in the same county since the statute provides that the support order may be filed in the county where the obligee resides and the court of that county cannot refuse jurisdiction. (Annotation from former RC 3115.09.) Nardone v. Nardone (Medina 1989) 63 Ohio App.3d 798, 580 N.E.2d 448.

2. Elements

Trial court correctly denied request for enforcement of foreign child support order, where obligor's former wife and children did not mention Uniform Reciprocal Enforcement of Support Act (URESA) in their complaint, nor did they attempt to meet requirements of URESA complaint. (Annotation from former RC 3115.09.) Barnett v. Barnett (Lorain 1993) 85 Ohio App.3d 1, 619 N.E.2d 38.

A complaint for child support under the Uniform Reciprocal Enforcement of Support Act need not explicitly allege that the defendant is the natural father of the child for whom support is sought in order to state a valid cause of action. (Annotation from former RC 3115.09.) McMullen v. Muir (Cuyahoga 1986) 34 Ohio App.3d 241, 517 N.E.2d 1381.

3. Defenses

A defendant need not be permitted to file an answer to a complaint filed under the Uniform Reciprocal Enforcement of Support Act so long as an opportunity to raise any defenses which would normally be asserted in an answer is provided. (Annotation from former RC 3115.09.) McMullen v. Muir (Cuyahoga 1986) 34 Ohio App.3d 241, 517 N.E.2d 1381.

3115.10 Multiple child support orders for two or more obligees

In responding to multiple registrations or complaints for enforcement of two or more child support orders in effect at the same time with regard to the same obligor and different individual obligees, at least one of which was issued by a tribunal of another state, a tribunal of this state shall enforce those orders in the same manner as if the multiple orders had been issued by a tribunal of this state.

(1997 H 352, eff. 1-1-98)

Historical and Statutory Notes

Ed. Note: Former 3115.10 repealed by 1997 H 352, eff. 1-1-98; 1986 H 428, eff. 12-23-86; 1971 H 504, eff. 10-27-71.

Ed. Note: Prior 3115.10 recodified as 3115.22 by 1971 H 504, eff. 10-27-71; 1953 H 1; GC 8007-13, 8007-14.

Pre-1953 H 1 Amendments: 124 v H 1

Cross References

County department of job and family services, Ch 329

Powers and duties of prosecuting attorney, 309.08

Ohio Administrative Code References

Proceeding involving two or more states, OAC 5101:1-30-53

Library References

Parent and Child ⟹3.4(2).
WESTLAW Topic No. 285.
C.J.S. Parent and Child §§ 93 to 96.

OJur 3d: 47, Family Law § 1376
Am Jur 2d: 23, Desertion and Nonsupport § 141
Determination of paternity of child as within scope of proceeding under Uniform Reciprocal Enforcement of Support Act. 81 ALR3d 1175

Baldwin's Ohio Legislative Service Annotated, 1997 H 352—LSC Analysis, p 9/L-2719
Carlin, Baldwin's Ohio Practice, *Merrick-Rippner Probate Law* § 19.6, 19.8, 108.36 (1997)
Sowald & Morganstern, Baldwin's Ohio Practice, *Domestic Relations Law* § 23.34 (1997)

Notes of Decisions and Opinions

Civil action 1
Prosecutors 2

1. Civil action

An action, instituted under RC Ch 3115 to enforce duties of support, is a civil action. (Annotation from former RC 3115.05.) Robinson v. Robinson (Franklin 1964) 8 Ohio App.2d 235, 221 N.E.2d 598, 37 O.O.2d 218.

Prosecuting attorney may bring civil action for separate maintenance and support in accordance with procedure outlined in RC 3115.05. (Annotation from former RC 3115.05.) OAG 70-050.

2. Prosecutors

Persons employed to prosecute child support enforcement actions under RC 2919.21(A)(2) and 3115.10 act in the capacity of assistant county prosecutors. (Annotation from former RC 3115.10.) OAG 89-099.

3115.11 Credit for payments

Amounts collected and credited for a particular period pursuant to a support order issued by a tribunal of another state must be credited against the amounts accruing or accrued for the same period under a support order covering the same parties for the same duty of support issued by the tribunal of this state.

(1997 H 352, eff. 1-1-98)

Historical and Statutory Notes

Ed. Note: Former 3115.11 repealed by 1997 H 352, eff. 1-1-98; 1971 H 504, eff. 10-27-71.

Ed. Note: Prior 3115.11 recodified as 3115.25 by 1971 H 504, eff. 10-27-71; 1953 H 1; GC 8007-16.

Pre-1953 H 1 Amendments: 124 v H 1

Cross References

Awarding parental rights and responsibilities, award to person other than parent, 3109.04

Ohio Administrative Code References

Proceeding involving two or more states, OAC 5101:1-30-53

Library References

Parent and Child ⟹3.4(2).
WESTLAW Topic No. 285.
C.J.S. Parent and Child §§ 93 to 96.

OJur 3d: 47, Family Law § 1371, 1406.1
Am Jur 2d: 23, Desertion and Nonsupport § 141
Determination of paternity of child as within scope of proceeding under Uniform Reciprocal Enforcement of Support Act. 81 ALR3d 1175

Baldwin's Ohio Legislative Service Annotated, 1997 H 352—LSC Analysis, p 9/L-2719
Carlin, Baldwin's Ohio Practice, *Merrick-Rippner Probate Law* § 19.6, 19.8, 108.36 (1997)
Sowald & Morganstern, Baldwin's Ohio Practice, *Domestic Relations Law* § 23.34 (1997)

Notes of Decisions and Opinions

De facto guidelines 1

1. De facto guidelines

An individual who has accepted the burdens of support and care of a minor child with the consent of its parents is a "de facto" guardian and as such has standing to bring an action for child support under the Uniform Reciprocal Enforcement of Support Act despite the lack of a legal decree of custody or of an appointment as guardian ad litem. (Annotation from former RC 3115.11.) McMullen v. Muir (Cuyahoga 1986) 34 Ohio App.3d 241, 517 N.E.2d 1381.

CIVIL PROVISIONS OF GENERAL APPLICATION

3115.12 Proceedings under Act

An individual or a support enforcement agency may commence a proceeding authorized under sections 3115.01 to 3115.59 of the Revised Code by filing a complaint in an initiating tribunal for forwarding to a responding tribunal or by filing a complaint or a comparable pleading directly in a tribunal of another state that has or can obtain personal jurisdiction over the defendant.

(1997 H 352, eff. 1-1-98)

Historical and Statutory Notes

Ed. Note: Former 3115.12 repealed by 1997 H 352, eff. 1-1-98; 1977 H 1, eff. 8-26-77; 1971 H 504, eff. 10-27-71.

Ed. Note: Former 3115.12 was former 3115.07 recodified by 1971 H 504, eff. 10-27-71; 126 v 560; 1953 H 1; GC 8007-11.

Ed. Note: Prior 3115.12 recodified as 3115.26 by 1971 H 504, eff. 10-27-71; 1953 H 1; GC 8007-17.

Pre-1953 H 1 Amendments: 124 v H 1

Ohio Administrative Code References

CSEA responsibilities as initiating or responding agency, OAC 5101:1-30-58, 5101:1-30-581

Library References

Parent and Child ⟹3.4(2).
WESTLAW Topic No. 285.
C.J.S. Parent and Child §§ 93 to 96.

OJur 3d: 47, Family Law § 1372, 1406.1, 1406.2, 1406.4, 1406.6
Am Jur 2d: 23, Desertion and Nonsupport § 131, 161
Determination of paternity of child as within scope of proceeding under Uniform Reciprocal Enforcement of Support Act. 81 ALR3d 1175

Baldwin's Ohio Legislative Service Annotated, 1997 H 352—LSC Analysis, p 9/L-2719
Carlin, Baldwin's Ohio Practice, *Merrick-Rippner Probate Law* § 19.6, 19.8, 108.36 (1997)
Klein & Darling, Baldwin's Ohio Practice, *Civil Practice* § 1 (1997)
Sowald & Morganstern, Baldwin's Ohio Practice, *Domestic Relations Law* § 23.20, 23.35 (1997)

3115.13 Action by minor parent

A minor parent, or a guardian or other legal representative of a minor parent, may maintain a proceeding on behalf of or for the benefit of the minor's child.

(1997 H 352, eff. 1-1-98)

Historical and Statutory Notes

Ed. Note: Former 3115.13 repealed by 1997 H 352, eff. 1-1-98; 1971 H 504, eff. 10-27-71.

Ed. Note: Prior 3115.13 recodified as 3115.20 by 1971 H 504, eff. 10-27-71; 126 v 560; 1953 H 1; GC 8007-18.

Pre-1953 H 1 Amendments: 124 v H 1

Ohio Administrative Code References

CSEA responsibilities as initiating or responding agency, OAC 5101:1-30-58, 5101:1-30-581

Library References

Infants ⟹70, 72(1).
Parent and Child ⟹3.4(2).
WESTLAW Topic Nos. 211, 285.
C.J.S. Infants §§ 215 to 217, 226.
C.J.S. Parent and Child §§ 93 to 96.

OJur 3d: 47, Family Law § 1369, 1406.1
Am Jur 2d: 23, Desertion and Nonsupport § 149
Determination of paternity of child as within scope of proceeding under Uniform Reciprocal Enforcement of Support Act. 81 ALR3d 1175

Baldwin's Ohio Legislative Service Annotated, 1997 H 352—LSC Analysis, p 9/L-2719
Carlin, Baldwin's Ohio Practice, *Merrick-Rippner Probate Law* § 19.6, 19.8, 108.36 (1997)
Sowald & Morganstern, Baldwin's Ohio Practice, *Domestic Relations Law* § 23.20, 23.35 (1997)

3115.14 Application of law of state

Except as otherwise provided by sections 3115.01 to 3115.59 of the Revised Code, a responding tribunal of this state shall apply the procedural and substantive law, including the rules on choice of law, generally applicable to similar proceedings originating in this state and may exercise all powers and provide all remedies available in those proceedings and shall determine the duty of support and the amount of support payable in accordance with sections 3113.21 to 3113.219 and sections 3115.01 to 3115.59 of the Revised Code.

(1997 H 352, eff. 1-1-98)

Historical and Statutory Notes

Ed. Note: Former 3115.14 repealed by 1997 H 352, eff. 1-1-98; 1971 H 504, eff. 10-27-71.

Ed. Note: Former 3115.14 was former 3115.17 recodified by 1971 H 504, eff. 10-27-71; 126 v 560.

Ed. Note: Prior 3115.14 recodified as 3115.21 by 1971 H 504, eff. 10-27-71; 126 v 560; 1953 H 1; GC 8007-19.

Pre-1953 H 1 Amendments: 124 v H 1

Library References

Parent and Child ⟹3.4(1).
WESTLAW Topic No. 285.
C.J.S. Parent and Child §§ 90 to 92.

OJur 3d: 47, Family Law § 1374
Am Jur 2d: 23, Desertion and Nonsupport § 153
Determination of paternity of child as within scope of proceeding under Uniform Reciprocal Enforcement of Support Act. 81 ALR3d 1175

Baldwin's Ohio Legislative Service Annotated, 1997 H 352—LSC Analysis, p 9/L-2719
Carlin, Baldwin's Ohio Practice, *Merrick-Rippner Probate Law* § 19.6, 19.8, 108.36 (1997)
Sowald & Morganstern, Baldwin's Ohio Practice, *Domestic Relations Law* § 23.35, 23.41 (1997)

3115.15 Duties of initiating tribunal

(A) On the filing of a complaint pursuant to section 3115.12 of the Revised Code, an initiating tribunal of this state shall forward three copies of the complaint and its accompanying documents to either of the following:

(1) The responding tribunal or appropriate support enforcement agency in the responding state;

(2) The state information agency of the responding state with a request that they be forwarded to the appropriate tribunal, if the identity of the responding tribunal is unknown, and that receipt be acknowledged.

(B) If a responding state has not enacted a law or procedure substantially similar to sections 3115.01 to 3115.59 of the Revised Code, a tribunal of this state may issue a certificate or other document and make findings required by the law of the responding state. If the responding state is a foreign jurisdiction, the tribunal may specify the amount of support sought and provide other documents necessary to satisfy the requirements of the responding state.

(1997 H 352, eff. 1-1-98)

Historical and Statutory Notes

Ed. Note: Former 3115.15 repealed by 1997 H 352, eff. 1-1-98; 1987 H 231, eff. 10-5-87; 1986 H 428; 1971 H 504, eff. 10-27-71.

Ed. Note: Former 3115.15 was former 3115.21 recodified by 1971 H 504, eff. 10-27-71; 126 v 560.

Ed. Note: Prior 3115.15 repealed by 1971 H 504, eff. 10-27-71; 126 v 560; 1953 H 1; GC 8007-3.

Pre-1953 H 1 Amendments: 124 v H 1

Ohio Administrative Code References

CSEA responsibilities as initiating or responding agency, OAC 5101:1-30-58, 5101:1-30-581

Library References

Parent and Child ⚷3.4(2).
WESTLAW Topic No. 285.
C.J.S. Parent and Child §§ 93 to 96.

OJur 3d: 47, Family Law § 1366, 1375, 1377
Am Jur 2d: 23, Desertion and Nonsupport § 140
Determination of paternity of child as within scope of proceeding under Uniform Reciprocal Enforcement of Support Act. 81 ALR3d 1175

Baldwin's Ohio Legislative Service Annotated, 1997 H 352—LSC Analysis, p 9/L-2719
Carlin, Baldwin's Ohio Practice, *Merrick-Rippner Probate Law* § 19.6, 19.8, 108.36 (1997)
Sowald & Morganstern, Baldwin's Ohio Practice, *Domestic Relations Law* § 23.20, 23.35, 23.36 (1997)

3115.16 Duties and powers of responding tribunal

(A) When a responding tribunal of this state receives a complaint or comparable pleading from an initiating tribunal or directly pursuant to section 3115.12 of the Revised Code, it shall cause the complaint or pleading to be filed and notify the plaintiff where and when it was filed.

(B) A responding tribunal of this state, to the extent otherwise authorized by law, may do one or more of the following consistent with applicable sections of Chapters 3105., 3109., 3111., and 3113. of the Revised Code:

(1) Issue or enforce a support order, modify a child support order, or determine the existence or nonexistence of a parent and child relationship;

(2) Order an obligor to comply with a support order, specifying the amount and the manner of compliance;

(3) Order income withholding;

(4) Determine the amount of any arrearages, and specify a method of payment;

(5) Enforce orders by civil or criminal contempt, or both;

(6) Set aside property for satisfaction of the support order;

(7) Place liens and order execution on the obligor's property;

(8) Order an obligor to keep the tribunal informed of the obligor's current residential address, telephone number, employer, address of employment, and telephone number at the place of employment;

(9) Issue a bench warrant for an obligor who has failed after proper notice to appear at a hearing ordered by the tribunal and enter the bench warrant in any local and state computer systems for criminal warrants;

(10) Order the obligor to seek appropriate employment by specified methods;

(11) Award reasonable attorney's fees and other fees and costs;

(12) Grant any other available remedy.

(C) A responding tribunal of this state shall include in a support order issued under sections 3115.01 to 3115.59 of the Revised Code, or in the documents accompanying the order, the calculations on which the support order is based.

(D) A responding tribunal of this state may not condition the payment of a support order issued under sections 3115.01 to 3115.59 of the revised code [*sic*] upon compliance by a party with provisions for visitation.

(E) If a responding tribunal of this state issues an order under sections 3115.01 to 3115.59 of the Revised Code, the tribunal shall send a copy of the order to the plaintiff and the defendant and to the initiating tribunal, if any.

(1997 H 352, eff. 1-1-98)

Historical and Statutory Notes

Ed. Note: Former 3115.16 repealed by 1997 H 352, eff. 1-1-98; 1986 H 428, eff. 12-23-86; 1971 H 504, eff. 10-27-71.

Ed. Note: Former 3115.16 was former 3115.08 recodified by 1971 H 504, eff. 10-27-71; 126 v 560; 1953 H 1; GC 8007-12.

Ed. Note: Prior 3115.16 repealed by 1971 H 504, eff. 10-27-71; 126 v 560.

Library References

Parent and Child ⟹3.4(2).
WESTLAW Topic No. 285.
C.J.S. Parent and Child §§ 93 to 96.

OJur 3d: 47, Family Law § 1375, 1376
Am Jur 2d: 23, Desertion and Nonsupport § 142
Determination of paternity of child as within scope of proceeding under Uniform Reciprocal Enforcement of Support Act. 81 ALR3d 1175

Baldwin's Ohio Legislative Service Annotated, 1997 H 352—LSC Analysis, p 9/L-2719
Carlin, Baldwin's Ohio Practice, *Merrick-Rippner Probate Law* § 19.6, 19.8, 108.36 (1997)
Sowald & Morganstern, Baldwin's Ohio Practice, *Domestic Relations Law* § 21.23, 23.21, 23.35, 23.36, 23.39 (1997)

Notes of Decisions and Opinions

Notice 2
Representation 1

1. Representation

The failure to provide legal representation to an obligee as required by this section is plain error. (Annotation from former RC 3115.16.) Brown v. Brown (Warren 1984) 16 Ohio App.3d 26, 474 N.E.2d 613, 16 O.B.R. 28.

2. Notice

The requirement of RC 3115.08 that the court cause "notice" of the time and place of hearing to be served on the defendant is satisfied by the issuance of a citation for the defendant to appear. (Annotation from former RC 3115.08.) Robinson v. Robinson (Franklin 1964) 8 Ohio App.2d 235, 221 N.E.2d 598, 37 O.O.2d 218.

A trial court lacks jurisdiction to dismiss a uniform reciprocal enforcement of support action and dissolution of marriage where no notice is served on the former wife, who discovers the dismissal when she attempts to collect child support; in the absence of service, the continuing jurisdiction of the court cannot be invoked and any judgment rendered by the court is void ab initio. (Annotation from former RC 3115.16.) Charnock v Murphy, No. CA94-07-017, 1995 WL 128399 (12th Dist Ct App, Preble, 3-27-95).

3115.17 Inappropriate tribunal

If a complaint or comparable pleading is received by an inappropriate tribunal of this state, the tribunal shall forward the pleading and accompanying documents to an appropriate tribunal in this state or another state and notify the plaintiff where and when the pleading was sent.

(1997 H 352, eff. 1-1-98)

Historical and Statutory Notes

Ed. Note: Former 3115.17 repealed by 1997 H 352, eff. 1-1-98; 1971 H 504, eff. 10-27-71.

Ed. Note: Prior 3115.17 recodified as 3115.14 by 1971 H 504, eff. 10-27-71; 126 v 560.

Ohio Administrative Code References

Direct enforcement of support orders, OAC 5101:1-30-582

Locating the absent parent, OAC 5101:1-30-01

Library References

Parent and Child ⟹3.4(2).
WESTLAW Topic No. 285.
C.J.S. Parent and Child §§ 93 to 96.

OJur 3d: 47, Family Law § 1377, 1378
Am Jur 2d: 23, Desertion and Nonsupport § 130, 132, 146
Determination of paternity of child as within scope of proceeding under Uniform Reciprocal Enforcement of Support Act. 81 ALR3d 1175

Baldwin's Ohio Legislative Service Annotated, 1997 H 352—LSC Analysis, p 9/L-2719
Carlin, Baldwin's Ohio Practice, *Merrick-Rippner Probate Law* § 19.6, 19.8, 108.36 (1997)
Sowald & Morganstern, Baldwin's Ohio Practice, *Domestic Relations Law* § 23.21, 23.35, 23.36 (1997)

3115.18 Duties of support enforcement agency

(A) A support enforcement agency of this state, upon request, shall provide services to a plaintiff in a proceeding under sections 3115.01 to 3115.59 of the Revised Code.

(B) A support enforcement agency that is providing services to the plaintiff, as appropriate, shall do all of the following:

(1) Take all steps necessary to enable an appropriate tribunal in this state or another state to obtain jurisdiction over the defendant;

(2) Request an appropriate tribunal to set a date, time, and place for a hearing;

(3) Make a reasonable effort to obtain all relevant information, including information as to income and property of the parties;

(4) Within two days, not including saturdays [*sic*], sundays [*sic*], and legal holidays, after receipt of a written notice from a tribunal pursuant to sections 3115.01 to 3115.59 of the Revised Code, send a copy of the notice to the plaintiff;

(5) Within two days, not including saturdays [*sic*], sundays [*sic*], and legal holidays, after receipt of a written communication from the defendant or the defendant's attorney, send a copy of the communication to the plaintiff;

(6) Notify the plaintiff if jurisdiction over the defendant cannot be obtained.

(C) Sections 3115.01 to 3115.59 of the Revised Code do not create or negate a relationship of attorney and client or other fiduciary relationship between a support enforcement agency or the attorney for the agency and the individual being assisted by the agency.

(1997 H 352, eff. 1-1-98)

Historical and Statutory Notes

Ed. Note: Former 3115.18 repealed by 1997 H 352, eff. 1-1-98; 1971 H 504, eff. 10-27-71.

Ed. Note: Prior 3115.18 repealed by 1971 H 504, eff. 10-27-71; 126 v 560.

Cross References

Depositions, Civ R 27 to 32

Ohio Administrative Code References

CSEA responsibilities as initiating or responding agency, OAC 5101:1-30-58, 5101:1-30-581

Library References

Parent and Child ⟹3.4.
WESTLAW Topic No. 285.
C.J.S. Parent and Child § 90.

OJur 3d: 47, Family Law § 1382, 1406.1, 1406.2, 1406.5
Am Jur 2d: 23, Desertion and Nonsupport § 134, 143
Determination of paternity of child as within scope of proceeding under Uniform Reciprocal Enforcement of Support Act. 81 ALR3d 1175

Baldwin's Ohio Legislative Service Annotated, 1997 H 352—LSC Analysis, p 9/L-2719
Carlin, Baldwin's Ohio Practice, *Merrick-Rippner Probate Law* § 19.6, 19.8, 108.36 (1997)
Sowald & Morganstern, Baldwin's Ohio Practice, *Domestic Relations Law* § 23.21, 23.35, 23.36 (1997)

3115.19 Duty of attorney general

If the attorney general determines that the support enforcement agency is neglecting or refusing to provide services to an individual, the attorney general may order the agency to perform its duties pursuant to sections 3115.01 to 3115.59 of the Revised Code or may provide those services directly to the individual.

(1997 H 352, eff. 1-1-98)

Historical and Statutory Notes

Ed. Note: Former 3115.19 repealed by 1997 H 352, eff. 1-1-98; 1971 H 504, eff. 10-27-71.

Ed. Note: Prior 3115.19 recodified as 3115.28 by 1971 H 504, eff. 10-27-71; 126 v 560.

Cross References

Common pleas court to grant transactional immunity, procedure, exceptions, 2945.44
Paternity proceedings, self-incrimination, immunity, 3111.12
Perjury, 2921.11
Right against compulsory self-incrimination, O Const I §10
Testimony regarding witness credibility, not waiver of privilege against self-incrimination, Evid R 608

Ohio Administrative Code References

CSEA responsibilities as initiating or responding agency, OAC 5101:1-30-58, 5101:1-30-581

Library References

Parent and Child ⟜3.4.
WESTLAW Topic No. 285.
C.J.S. Parent and Child § 90.

OJur 3d: 47, Family Law § 1384, 1406.1, 1406.2, 1406.5
Am Jur 2d: 23, Desertion and Nonsupport § 143; 43A, Poor Relief and Public Welfare § 60
Determination of paternity of child as within scope of proceeding under Uniform Reciprocal Enforcement of Support Act. 81 ALR3d 1175
Baldwin's Ohio Legislative Service Annotated, 1997 H 352—LSC Analysis, p 9/L-2719
Carlin, Baldwin's Ohio Practice, *Merrick-Rippner Probate Law* § 19.6, 19.8, 108.36 (1997)
Sowald & Morganstern, Baldwin's Ohio Practice, *Domestic Relations Law* § 23.21, 23.35, 23.36 (1997)

3115.20 Private counsel

An individual may employ private counsel to represent the individual in proceedings authorized by sections 3115.01 to 3115.59 of the Revised Code.

(1997 H 352, eff. 1-1-98)

Historical and Statutory Notes

Ed. Note: Former 3115.20 repealed by 1997 H 352, eff. 1-1-98; 1971 H 504, eff. 10-27-71.

Ed. Note: Former 3115.20 was former 3115.13 recodified by 1971 H 504, eff. 10-27-71; 126 v 560; 1953 H 1; GC 8007-18.

Ed. Note: Prior 3115.20 recodified as 3115.29 by 1971 H 504, eff. 10-27-71; 126 v 560.

Cross References

Competency of witnesses, husband and wife, 2945.42
Privileged communications and acts, husband and wife, 2317.02

Ohio Administrative Code References

CSEA responsibilities as initiating or responding agency, OAC 5101:1-30-58, 5101:1-30-581

Library References

Parent and Child ⟜3.4(2).
WESTLAW Topic No. 285.
C.J.S. Parent and Child §§ 93 to 96.

OJur 3d: 47, Family Law § 1383, 1406.1, 1406.2
Am Jur 2d: 23, Desertion and Nonsupport § 134, 144
Determination of paternity of child as within scope of proceeding under Uniform Reciprocal Enforcement of Support Act. 81 ALR3d 1175

Effect, on competency to testify against spouse or on marital communication privilege, of separation or

other marital instability short of absolute divorce. 98 ALR3d 1285
Communication between unmarried couple living together as privileged. 4 ALR4th 422
Existence of spousal privilege where marriage was entered into for purpose of barring testimony. 13 ALR4th 1305

Baldwin's Ohio Legislative Service Annotated, 1997 H 352—LSC Analysis, p 9/L-2719

Carlin, Baldwin's Ohio Practice, *Merrick-Rippner Probate Law* § 19.6, 19.8, 108.36 (1997)
Giannelli & Snyder, Baldwin's Ohio Practice, Evidence § 501.25 (1996)
Sowald & Morganstern, Baldwin's Ohio Practice, *Domestic Relations Law* § 23.21, 23.35, 23.36 (1997)

3115.21 Duties of state information agency

(A) The department of job and family services is the state information agency under sections 3115.01 to 3115.59 of the Revised Code.

(B) The state information agency shall do all of the following:

(1) Compile a list, including addresses, of the tribunals in this state and each support enforcement agency in this state and transmit a copy to the state information agency of every other state that has adopted an act substantially similar to sections 3115.01 to 3115.59 of the Revised Code;

(2) Maintain a register of tribunals and support enforcement agencies received from other states;

(3) Forward to the appropriate tribunal in this state that has jurisdiction over the individual obligee or the obligor or the obligor's property, all documents concerning a proceeding under sections 3115.01 to 3115.59 of the Revised Code received from an initiating tribunal or the state information agency of the initiating state;

(4) Obtain information concerning the location of the obligor and the obligor's property within this state not exempt from execution, by such means as postal verification and federal or state parent locator services, examination of telephone directories, requests for the obligor's address from employers, and examination of governmental records, including, to the extent not prohibited by other law, those relating to real property, vital statistics, law enforcement, taxation, motor vehicles, drivers' licenses, and social security benefits.

(1999 H 471, eff. 7-1-00; 1997 H 352, eff. 1-1-98)

Historical and Statutory Notes

Ed. Note: Former 3115.21 repealed by 1997 H 352, eff. 1-1-98; 1987 H 231, eff. 10-5-87; 1980 H 685; 1971 H 504, eff. 10-27-71.

Ed. Note: Former 3115.21 was former 3115.14 recodified by 1971 H 504, eff. 10-27-71; 126 v 560; 1953 H 1; GC 8007-19.

Ed. Note: Prior 3115.21 recodified as 3115.15 by 1971 H 504, eff. 10-27-71; 126 v 560.

Amendment Note: 1999 H 471 substituted "department of job and family services" for "state department of human services" in division (A).

Cross References

Dispositional hearing, juvenile court may admit any evidence that is material and relevant, Juv R 34
Support of children, 3109.05
Visitation rights, 3109.051

Ohio Administrative Code References

Interstate central registry, OAC 5101:1-30-56

Library References

Infants ⚷133.
Parent and Child ⚷3.4.
WESTLAW Topic Nos. 211, 285.
C.J.S. Criminal Law § 2008.
C.J.S. Infants §§ 57, 69 to 85.
C.J.S. Parent and Child § 90.

OJur 3d: 47, Family Law § 1381, 1393, 1406.1, 1406.2, 1406.5; 48, Family Law § 1764

Am Jur 2d: 23, Desertion and Nonsupport § 134, 138, 142 to 147
Determination of paternity of child as within scope of proceeding under Uniform Reciprocal Enforcement of Support Act. 81 ALR3d 1175
Withholding visitation rights for failure to make alimony or support payments. 65 ALR4th 1155

Baldwin's Ohio Legislative Service Annotated, 1997 H 352—LSC Analysis, p 9/L-2719

Carlin, Baldwin's Ohio Practice, *Merrick-Rippner Probate Law* § 19.6, 19.8, 108.36 (1997)
Sowald & Morganstern, Baldwin's Ohio Practice, *Domestic Relations Law* § 21.23, 23.21, 23.24, 23.35, 23.36 (1997)

Law Review and Journal Commentaries

Retroactive Modification of Accrued and Unpaid Child Support Orders in Ohio, Lon R. Vinion. 56 Ohio St B Ass'n Rep 328 (March 7, 1983).

Notes of Decisions and Opinions

Custody 2
Duty to support 3
Federal jurisdiction 4
Visitation 1

---

1. Visitation

Ohio version of Uniform Reciprocal Enforcement of Support Act (URESA) creates single exception to rule that support issues and visitation and custody issues must be determined separately from each other by allowing court to suspend already established visitation rights if parent owing support has willfully failed to provide such support. (Annotation from former RC 3115.21.) In re Byard (Ohio 1996) 74 Ohio St.3d 294, 658 N.E.2d 735.

Uniform Reciprocal Enforcement of Support Act (URESA) confers subject matter jurisdiction over sole issues of paternity and support; related matters such as visitation and custody are not within court's purview. In Matter of Shanyfelt (Ohio App. 3 Dist. 1997) 118 Ohio App.3d 243, 692 N.E.2d 642.

Provision of Uniform Reciprocal Enforcement of Support Act (URESA) permitting support funds to be impounded because of obligee parent's interference with obligor's right to visitation did not permit suspension of support order, or forgiveness of past-due unpaid support, due to denial or interference with visitation rights. In Matter of Shanyfelt (Ohio App. 3 Dist. 1997) 118 Ohio App.3d 243, 692 N.E.2d 642.

In former wife's action under Uniform Reciprocal Enforcement of Support Act (URESA), trial court did not have statutory authority to refund funds placed in escrow and suspend former husband's support payments contingent upon visitation with his child. In Matter of Shanyfelt (Ohio App. 3 Dist. 1997) 118 Ohio App.3d 243, 692 N.E.2d 642.

Father who was required to pay child support under Uniform Reciprocal Enforcement of Support Act (URESA) but whose claim for visitation was not also considered in URESA proceeding was not deprived of his right to equal protection, since URESA did not create discriminatory classification; simply because statute was written so that it limited scope of matters within jurisdiction of court did not create discriminatory classifications so as to make it violative of equal protection. (Annotation from former RC 3115.21.) Hammitt v. Howard (Franklin 1994) 99 Ohio App.3d 463, 651 N.E.2d 20.

Uniform Reciprocal Enforcement of Support Act (URESA) does not violate due process by addressing issues of child support but not issues of visitation, since it is rationally related to purpose of ensuring that obligations of child support are enforced, even across state lines. (Annotation from former RC 3115.21.) Hammitt v. Howard (Franklin 1994) 99 Ohio App.3d 463, 651 N.E.2d 20.

Trial court's determination that father owed child support under Uniform Reciprocal Enforcement of Support Act (URESA) without addressing issue of visitation did not violate his rights to due process, since he could pursue his right to visitation in another action in another forum. (Annotation from former RC 3115.21.) Hammitt v. Howard (Franklin 1994) 99 Ohio App.3d 463, 651 N.E.2d 20.

Child support rights and visitation rights are separate and distinct and are entitled to separate enforcement. (Annotation from former RC 3115.21.) Hammitt v. Howard (Franklin 1994) 99 Ohio App.3d 463, 651 N.E.2d 20.

Uniform Reciprocal Enforcement of Support Act (URESA), which grants court right to suspend visitation if it finds that obligor has willfully failed to provide child support after having been found financially able to do so, does not address issue of granting visitation, and so does not confer jurisdiction on trial court to allow visitation in first instance in URESA proceeding. (Annotation from former RC 3115.21.) Hammitt v. Howard (Franklin 1994) 99 Ohio App.3d 463, 651 N.E.2d 20.

Suspension of a child support obligation pending three undisturbed visitation periods is not a permissible sanction for interference with a visitation order. (Annotation from former RC 3115.21.) Fry v. Fry (Paulding 1989) 64 Ohio App.3d 519, 582 N.E.2d 11.

RC 3115.21 confers authority on the common pleas court to hear evidence of denial of visitation and to withhold support payments until visitation rights are respected; thus a court errs in finding that it lacks jurisdiction over an obligor's visitation claim. (Annotation from former RC 3115.21.) Sperry v. Hlutke (Cuyahoga 1984) 19 Ohio App.3d 156, 483 N.E.2d 870, 19 O.B.R. 246.

Neither RC 3115.21(B) nor 3109.05(B) authorizes the suspension of a support order or the forgiveness of past due unpaid support because of denial or interference with the obligor's visitation rights. (Annotation from former RC 3115.21.) Brown v. Brown (Warren 1984) 16 Ohio App.3d 26, 474 N.E.2d 613, 16 O.B.R. 28.

2. Custody

The parent with legal custody of a child may not avoid an action for payment of support under RC Ch 3115 by pleading the violation of a custody order. (Annotation from former RC 3115.21.) State of Iowa ex rel. Cantrell v. Cantrell (Summit 1983) 9 Ohio App.3d 194, 459 N.E.2d 242, 9 O.B.R. 305.

3. Duty to support

Under RC 3115.21, a father's duty to reimburse another state for child support payments pursuant to the uniform reciprocal enforcement of support act is conditioned on the mother's inability to pay, and the mother's removal of the child from the jurisdiction in contravention of the court's order is of no consequence. (Annotation from former RC 3115.21.) McCoy v. McCoy (Summit 1977) 53 Ohio App.2d 331, 374 N.E.2d 164, 7 O.O.3d 427.

The duty to pay child support is unaffected by any interference with rights of visitation, and no estoppel to claim child support arrears from a father may be inferred from the mother's withholding of visitation with the child. (Annotation from former RC 3115.21.) French v French, No. 9-95-7, 1995 WL 328110 (3d Dist Ct App, Marion, 5-30-95).

RC 3115.21(A) provides that the duty of support owed to one obligee is unaffected by any interference with the rights of custody or visitation granted by a court; therefore, a trial court errs in reducing a child support arrearage to zero because the obligor has not seen his children since 1972 and because it finds an eleven-year delay in bringing the action unreasonable, especially in light of the fact there is no evidence the obligor ever made any attempt to obtain or exercise visitation with his children. (Annotation from former RC 3115.21.) Greenfield v Cobb, No. 1-93-27, 1993 WL 387114 (3d Dist Ct App, Allen, 9-30-93).

The duty of support is not affected by an order which temporarily suspended an obligor's child support duty, even though the whereabouts of the custodial parent and children are unknown; a foreign state which advances welfare assistance to the custodial parent and children can seek reimbursement from the obligor. (Annotation from former RC 3115.21.) New Mexico v Michelson, No. 1044 (11th Dist Ct App, Portage, 11-17-80).

4. Federal jurisdiction

Trial court committed prejudicial error, in mother's action for arrearages arising from California child support order filed pursuant to Uniform Reciprocal Enforcement of Child Support Act (URESA), in reducing father's total arrearages of $43,255.80 to $0 based on its apparent finding that father's failure to pay child support was excused after he had allegedly been denied visitation with his children and based on its finding that 11-year delay in bringing action was unreasonable; the only two defenses available to respondent in URESA action for enforcement of child support order are that paternity has not been established or that order is void and defense of laches was not applicable. (Annotation from former RC 3115.21.) Greenfield v. Cobb (Allen 1993) 90 Ohio App.3d 618, 630 N.E.2d 66, dismissed, jurisdictional motion overruled 68 Ohio St.3d 1445, 626 N.E.2d 687.

Although matters concerning divorce and alimony have been excepted from federal court jurisdiction based on diversity of the parties' state citizenship since Barber v Barber, 62 US 582, 16 LEd(2d) 226(1859), this rule does not bar a husband's claim in federal court that the former wife intentionally inflicted emotional distress on him by taking their child to another state and denying him visitation rights, or that she interfered with his employment by writing letters to his employer; the court may also hear his counterclaim for enforcement of a state judgment concerning arrearages in alimony and child support. (Annotation from former RC 3115.21.) Drewes v. Ilnicki (C.A.6 (Ohio) 1988) 863 F.2d 469.

3115.22 Pleadings and accompanying documents

(A) A plaintiff seeking issuance or modification of a support order or a determination of the existence or nonexistence of a parent and child relationship under sections 3115.01 to 3115.59 of the Revised Code must verify the complaint. Unless otherwise ordered under section 3115.23 of the Revised Code, the complaint or accompanying documents must provide, so far as known, the name, residential address, and social security numbers of the obligor and the obligee, and the name, sex, residential address, social security number, and date of birth of each child for whom support is sought. The complaint must be accompanied by a certified copy of any support order in effect. The complaint may include any other information that may assist in locating or identifying the defendant.

(B) The complaint must specify the relief sought. The complaint and accompanying documents must conform substantially with the requirements imposed by the forms mandated by federal law for use in cases filed by a support enforcement agency.

(1997 H 352, eff. 1-1-98)

Historical and Statutory Notes

Ed. Note: Former 3115.22 repealed by 1997 H 352, eff. 1-1-98; 1993 H 173, eff. 12-31-93; 1992 S 10; 1990 H 591; 1988 H 708; 1987 H 231; 1986 H 509; 1984 H 614; 1978 S 87; 1971 H 504, eff. 10-27-71.

Ed. Note: Former 3115.22 was former 3115.10 recodified by 1971 H 504, eff. 10-27-71; 1953 H 1; GC 8007-13, 8007-14.

Ed. Note: Prior 3115.22 recodified as 3115.02 by 1971 H 504, eff. 10-27-71; 126 v 560.

Cross References

Automated system to support enforcement of child support, 5101.322

Bureau of support, support enforcement, 2301.34 et seq.

Contempt action for failure to pay support, 2705.031, 2705.05

Execution against property, Ch 2329

Lottery winner must state under oath whether or not he is in default of support order, 3770.071

Nonsupport of dependents, 2919.21

Payment of child support through withholding of personal earnings, workers' compensation benefits, unemployment compensation benefits, retirement benefits, or bank account, 3113.21

Small loans; assignment or order of wages for support, 1321.32, 1321.33

Ohio Administrative Code References

Pleadings and other documents, OAC 5101:1-30-586

Library References

Parent and Child ⚷3.4(2).
WESTLAW Topic No. 285.
C.J.S. Parent and Child §§ 93 to 96.

OJur 3d: 47, Family Law § 1306, 1385, 1390, 1392, 1394, 1406.1, 1406.2, 1406.6
Am Jur 2d: 23, Desertion and Nonsupport § 136 to 138, 150 to 154
Determination of paternity of child as within scope of proceeding under Uniform Reciprocal Entorcement of Support Act. 81 ALR3d 1175
Construction & effect of provision of Uniform Reciprocal Enforcement of Support Act that no support order shall supersede or nullify any other order. 31 ALR4th 347

Baldwin's Ohio Legislative Service Annotated, 1997 H 352—LSC Analysis, p 9/L-2719

Baldwin's Ohio Legislative Service, 1990 Laws of Ohio, H 591—LSC Analysis, p 5-576

Carlin, Baldwin's Ohio Practice, *Merrick-Rippner Probate Law* § 19.6, 19.8, 108.36 (1997)

3 Katz & Giannelli, Baldwin's Ohio Practice, *Criminal Law* § 109.9 (1996)

Klein & Darling, Baldwin's Ohio Practice, *Civil Practice* § 1 (1997)

Sowald & Morganstern, Baldwin's Ohio Practice, *Domestic Relations Law* § 23.21, 23.35, 23.37 (1997)

Law Review and Journal Commentaries

Qualified Domestic Relations Orders, Philip Zukowski and Mary Eaves. 35 Dayton B Briefs 12 (June/July 1986).

Notes of Decisions and Opinions

Constitutional issues 5
Duty to reimburse 2
Federal jurisdiction 4
Modification 3
Orders 1

---

1. Orders

An Alaska trial court's finding that an Ohio exwife gave the Alaska revenue department child support enforcement division actual authority to settle her claims for delinquent child support payments against her exhusband, who was residing in Alaska, is binding on the parties and thus, the exwife's revivor action is barred by the Full Faith and Credit Clause and by res judicata. (Annotation from former RC 3115.22.) Wyatt v. Wyatt (Ohio 1992) 65 Ohio St.3d 268, 602 N.E.2d 1166, rehearing denied 65 Ohio St.3d 1482, 604 N.E.2d 758.

County child support enforcement agency (CSEA) had power to bring action to hold husband in contempt for failure to pay child support arrearage in accordance with prior judgment entry, despite the CSEA's failure to file a motion to intervene in the action, where husband testified that he had not made child support arrearage payment and there was evidence that wife had received Aid to Dependent Children (ADC) benefits. Collins v. Collins (Ohio App. 12 Dist. 1998) 127 Ohio App.3d 281, 712 N.E.2d 800.

While the state has direct financial interest in the enforcement of child support orders, it has no right to participate in the creation of such orders. (Annotation from former RC 3115.22.) Starr v. Starr (Cuyahoga 1996) 109 Ohio App.3d 116, 671 N.E.2d 1097.

An order impounding a child support arrearage pending resolution of a visitation dispute but not determining the amount of a child support arrearage or future child support obligations is not a final, appealable order. (Annotation from former RC 3115.22.) Logan v. Vice (Adams 1992) 79 Ohio App.3d 838, 608 N.E.2d 786.

Statute providing that any person required to pay child support who was found in contempt for failure to make the support payments may be assessed costs and penalties does not limit finding of contempt only to those obligors who fail to make child support payments rather than other payments. (Annotation from former RC 3115.22.) Ankrom v. Ankrom (Cuyahoga 1985) 30 Ohio App.3d 47, 506 N.E.2d 259, 30 O.B.R. 102.

Under Uniform Reciprocal Enforcement of Support Act, state has duty to enforce any support order which might have been issued in it as well as to obtain initial issuance of that support order. (Annotation from former RC 3115.22.) Brown v. Brown (Warren 1984) 16 Ohio App.3d 26, 474 N.E.2d 613, 16 O.B.R. 28.

A magistrate errs in finding that an obligor owes arrearages for all payments not made through the child support enforcement agency where the court fails to afford the obligor an opportunity to rebut the presumption that payments made outside the agency are gifts. Drake v Gozdan, No. 96-CA-0050, 1997 WL 416471 (9th Dist Ct App, Wayne, 7-9-97).

Where there is a lapse of eight and one-half years between a child support agreement of the parties in open court and the filing of a judgment entry which purports to journalize that agreement, a trial court errs in preparing, signing, and filing the judgment entry without notice to the obligor that the matters addressed in the entry are being considered by the court and without granting the opportunity to be heard on the issues affected by the entry. (Annotation from former RC 3115.22.) Rose v Rose, No. 95APF12-1626, 1996 WL 274101 (10th Dist Ct App, Franklin, 5-23-96).

2. Duty to reimburse

Under RC 3115.21, a father's duty to reimburse another state for child support payments pursuant to the uniform reciprocal enforcement of support act is conditioned on the mother's inability to pay, and the mother's removal of the child from the jurisdiction in contravention of the court's order is of no consequence. (Annotation from former RC 3115.22.) McCoy v. McCoy (Summit 1977) 53 Ohio App.2d 331, 374 N.E.2d 164, 7 O.O.3d 427.

Under the uniform support of dependents act, petitioner may obtain reimbursement for funds expended for the support of the petitioner and child of the parties between the time it is alleged that respondent abandoned his family and the date of trial. (Annotation from former RC 3115.10.) Skinner v. Fasciano (Cuyahoga 1956) 137 N.E.2d 613, 75 Ohio Law Abs. 409.

3. Modification

In an action pursuant to RC Ch 3115, the trial court may modify a child support order made in a divorce action in another state. (Annotation from former RC 3115.22.) Ventura County, California, for Dean v Poynter, No. 508 (4th Dist Ct App, Highland, 3-6-84).

4. Federal jurisdiction

A federal court can exercise jurisdiction over the enforcement of support arrearages so long as the arrearages award is not modifiable or does not require interpretation of an ongoing divorce dispute; thus, a district court may decide which of two states' support orders is enforceable. (Annotation from former RC 3115.22.) Taylor v. Wettstein (S.D.Ohio 1989) 746 F.Supp. 713.

5. Constitutional issues

It is a violation of the equal protection clauses of the United States and Ohio constitutions to allow the aid and support of the child support enforcement agency in an action for child support brought by parents who have established their parentage through the probate court and residential parents who are on public assistance while denying the aid and support of the child support enforcement agency to parents who have established their parentage through the administrative process. (Annotation from former RC 3115.22.) Cuyahoga County Support Enforcement Agency v Lozada, Nos. 67463+, 1995 WL 386965 (8th Dist Ct App, Cuyahoga, 6-29-95).

3115.23 Nondisclosure of information in exceptional circumstances

A tribunal shall order that the address of a child or party or other identifying information not be disclosed in a pleading or other document filed in a proceeding under sections 3115.01 to 3115.59 of the Revised Code if a tribunal has made a finding, that may be made ex parte, that the health, safety, or liberty of a party or child would be unreasonably put at risk by the disclosure of identifying information.

(1997 H 352, eff. 1-1-98)

Historical and Statutory Notes

Ed. Note: Former 3115.23 repealed by 1997 H 352, eff. 1-1-98; 1971 H 504, eff. 10-27-71.

Ed. Note: Former 3115.23 was former 3115.09 recodified by 1971 H 504, eff. 10-27-71; 1953 H 1; GC 8007-15.

Ed. Note: Prior 3115.23 recodified as 3113.21 by 1971 H 504, eff. 10-27-71; 1969 H 361; 132 v H 471.

Cross References

Bureau of support, support enforcement, 2301.34 et seq.
Contempt action for failure to pay support, 2705.031, 2705.05

Ohio Administrative Code References

Pleadings and other documents, OAC 5101:1-30-586

Library References

Infants ⚷133.
Parent and Child ⚷3.4.
WESTLAW Topic Nos. 211, 285.
C.J.S. Criminal Law § 2008.
C.J.S. Infants §§ 57, 69 to 85.
C.J.S. Parent and Child § 90.

OJur 3d: 47, Family Law § 1395, 1406.1, 1406.2, 1406.6
Am Jur 2d: 23, Desertion and Nonsupport § 136 to 178
Determination of paternity of child as within scope of proceeding under Uniform Reciprocal Enforcement of Support Act. 81 ALR3d 1175

Baldwin's Ohio Legislative Service Annotated, 1997 H 352—LSC Analysis, p 9/L-2719
Carlin, Baldwin's Ohio Practice, *Merrick-Rippner Probate Law* § 19.6, 19.8, 108.36 (1997)
Klein & Darling, Baldwin's Ohio Practice, *Civil Practice* § 75 (1997)
Sowald & Morganstern, Baldwin's Ohio Practice, *Domestic Relations Law* § 23.21, 23.35, 23.37 (1997)

Notes of Decisions and Opinions

1. Spousal support

A trial court has no power under RC 3115.23 to order the garnishment of wages to pay alimony. (Annotation from former RC 3115.23.) Whitmore v. Whitmore (Wayne 1976) 49 Ohio App.2d 159, 359 N.E.2d 714, 3 O.O.3d 204.

2. Extradition

A person for whom an extradition requisition has been received by the governor of Ohio from a state which has enacted the Uniform Dependent's Act asking for the person's return to the demanding state for desertion or nonsupport, must be relieved of extradition where such person submits to a court of record in this state and complies with the court's order of support, but such court cannot obtain jurisdiction to make such order of support otherwise than in the manner designated in GC 8007-10 (RC 3115.06) et seq.; and where there has been no compliance with the provisions of these sections an obligor may not be relieved of extradition by a mere offer to submit to the jurisdiction of the court of the responding state. (Annotation from former RC 3115.06.) 1953 OAG 3009.

3115.24 Costs and fees

(A) The plaintiff under an action filed pursuant to sections 3115.01 to 3115.59 of the Revised Code may not be required to pay a filing fee or other costs.

(B) If an obligee prevails, a responding tribunal may assess against an obligor filing fees, reasonable attorney's fees, other costs, and necessary travel and other reasonable expenses incurred by the obligee and the obligee's witnesses. The tribunal may not assess fees, costs, or expenses against the obligee or the support enforcement agency of either the initiating or the responding state, except as provided by other law. Attorney's fees may be taxed as costs, and may be ordered paid directly to the attorney, who may enforce the order in the attorney's own name. Payment of support owed to the obligee has priority over fees, costs and expenses.

(C) The tribunal shall order the payment of costs and reasonable attorney's fees if it determines that a hearing was requested primarily for delay.

(1997 H 352, eff. 1-1-98)

Historical and Statutory Notes

Ed. Note: Former 3115.24 repealed by 1997 H 352, eff. 1-1-98; 1997 H 408, eff. 10-1-97; 1994 S 355, eff. 12-9-94; 1992 S 10, eff. 7-15-92; 1990 H 591; 1988 H 242, H 708; 1987 H 231; 1971 H 504, eff. 10-27-71.

Ed. Note: Prior 3115.24 repealed by 1971 H 504, eff. 10-27-71; 132 v H 471.

Cross References

Bureau of support, 2301.34 et seq.
Paternity proceedings, genetic tests, 3111.09
Presumption of paternity, 3111.03

Ohio Administrative Code References

Payment and recovery of costs for interstate cases, OAC 5101:1-30-587

Library References

Parent and Child ⟹3.4(2).
WESTLAW Topic No. 285.
C.J.S. Parent and Child §§ 93 to 96.

OJur 3d: 47, Family Law § 1379, 1406.1, 1406.2
Am Jur 2d: 10, Bastards § 19; 23, Desertion and Nonsupport § 135
Determination of paternity of child as within scope of proceeding under Uniform Reciprocal Enforcement of Support Act. 81 ALR3d 1175
Who may dispute presumption of legitimacy of child conceived or born during wedlock. 90 ALR3d 1032
Baldwin's Ohio Legislative Service Annotated, 1997 H 352—LSC Analysis, p 9/L-2719
Baldwin's Ohio Legislative Service, 1990 Laws of Ohio, H 591—LSC Analysis, p 5-576
Carlin, Baldwin's Ohio Practice, *Merrick-Rippner Probate Law* § 19.6, 19.7, 19.8, 108.22, 108.36 (1997)
Sowald & Morganstern, Baldwin's Ohio Practice, *Domestic Relations Law* § 3.15, 3.35, 23.14, 23.19, 23.24, 23.35, 23.37 (1997)

Law Review and Journal Commentaries

Reaching Out-Of-State Obligors: Collecting Judgments Through UIFSA and Beyond, Patrice R.T. Yarham. 11 Domestic Rel J Ohio 85 (November/December 1999).

Retroactive Modification of Accrued and Unpaid Child Support Orders in Ohio, Lon R. Vinion. 56 Ohio St B Ass'n Rep 328 (March 7, 1983).

Notes of Decisions and Opinions

Paternity determination 1

1. Paternity determination

Under single exception to rule that subject matter jurisdiction under Ohio version of Uniform Reciprocal Enforcement of Support Act (URESA) is limited to matters of child support, court may consider and adjudicate paternity defense. (Annotation from former RC 3115.24.) In re Byard (Ohio 1996) 74 Ohio St.3d 294, 658 N.E.2d 735.

Issues involving "parenting" do not come within exception to rule that subject matter jurisdiction under Ohio version of Uniform Reciprocal Enforcement of Support Act (URESA) is limited to matters of child support, under which court may consider and adjudicate paternity defense. (Annotation from former RC 3115.24.) In re Byard (Ohio 1996) 74 Ohio St.3d 294, 658 N.E.2d 735.

A convicted rapist who alleges in his complaint for writ of mandamus due process and equal protection rights to postconviction DNA testing without legal argument or citation to authority does not sufficiently establish a clear right for purposes of withstanding a motion for summary judgment. (Annotation from former RC 3115.24.) State ex rel. Smith v. Columbus (Ohio 1993) 66 Ohio St.3d 271, 611 N.E.2d 827.

Paternity may be determined by a court in the absence of a defendant at a hearing pursuant to RC 3115.24 where the issue of nonpaternity is raised by the defendant's counsel and the defendant has waived any statutory right to be present by willfully disregarding a subpoena commanding him to appear at the hearing. (Annotation from former RC 3115.24.) McMullen v. Muir (Cuyahoga 1986) 34 Ohio App.3d 241, 517 N.E.2d 1381.

A referee has the power to interview a minor child outside the presence of counsel during a hearing to determine paternity. (Annotation from former RC 3115.24.) McMullen v. Muir (Cuyahoga 1986) 34 Ohio App.3d 241, 517 N.E.2d 1381.

The Uniform Support of Dependents Act may not be used by a nonresident mother to compel an Ohio resident to support an alleged illegitimate child of his where there has been no judicial determination of the paternity of such child. (Annotation from former RC 3111.01.) Smith v. Smith (Ohio Com.Pl. 1965) 11 Ohio Misc. 25, 224 N.E.2d 925, 40 O.O.2d 136.

3115.25 Limited immunity of plaintiff

(A) Participation by a plaintiff in a proceeding before a responding tribunal pursuant to sections 3115.01 to 3115.59 of the Revised Code, whether in person, by private attorney, or through services provided by the support enforcement agency, does not confer personal jurisdiction over the plaintiff in another proceeding.

(B) A plaintiff is not amenable to service of civil process while physically present in this state to participate in a proceeding under sections 3115.01 to 3115.59 of the Revised Code.

(C) The immunity granted by this section does not extend to civil litigation based on acts unrelated to a proceeding under sections 3115.01 to 3115.59 of the Revised Code committed by a party while present in this state to participate in the proceeding.

(1997 H 352, eff. 1-1-98)

Historical and Statutory Notes

Ed. Note: Former 3115.25 repealed by 1997 H 352, eff. 1-1-98; 1971 H 504, eff. 10-27-71.

Ed. Note: Former 3115.25 was former 3115.11 recodified by 1971 H 504, eff. 10-27-71; 1953 H 1; GC 8007-16.

Ed. Note: Prior 3115.25 repealed by 1971 H 504, eff. 10-27-71; 132 v H 471.

Ohio Administrative Code References

Personal jurisdiction (long arm jurisdiction), OAC 5101:1-30-51

Library References

Parent and Child ⚷3.4(2).
WESTLAW Topic No. 285.
C.J.S. Parent and Child §§ 93 to 96.

OJur 3d: 47, Family Law § 1391, 1406.1 to 1406.3
Am Jur 2d: 23, Desertion and Nonsupport § 142, 146

Baldwin's Ohio Legislative Service Annotated, 1997 H 352—LSC Analysis, p 9/L-2719
Carlin, Baldwin's Ohio Practice, *Merrick-Rippner Probate Law* § 19.6, 19.8, 108.36 (1997)
Sowald & Morganstern, Baldwin's Ohio Practice, *Domestic Relations Law* § 23.21, 23.35, 23.37 (1997)

3115.26 Nonparentage as defense

A party who has been previously determined pursuant to law to be the parent of a child may not plead that the party is not the parent of the child as a defense to a proceeding under sections 3115.01 to 3115.59 of the Revised Code.

(1997 H 352, eff. 1-1-98)

Historical and Statutory Notes

Ed. Note: Former 3115.26 repealed by 1997 H 352, eff. 1-1-98; 1971 H 504, eff. 10-27-71.

Ed. Note: Former 3115.26 was former 3115.12 recodified by 1971 H 504, eff. 10-27-71; 1953 H 1; GC 8007-17.

Ohio Administrative Code References

Interstate paternity, OAC 5101:1-30-52

Library References

Children Out-of-Wedlock ⟹21.
Parent and Child ⟹3.4(1).
WESTLAW Topic Nos. 76H, 285.
C.J.S. Children Out-of-Wedlock §§ 40 to 43, 124.
C.J.S. Parent and Child §§ 90 to 92.

OJur 3d: 47, Family Law § 1391, 1406.1 1406.2, 1406.6
Am Jur 2d: 23, Desertion and Nonsupport § 141, 146

Baldwin's Ohio Legislative Service Annotated, 1997 H 352—LSC Analysis, p 9/L-2719

Carlin, Baldwin's Ohio Practice, *Merrick-Rippner Probate Law* § 19.6, 19.8, 108.36 (1997)

Sowald & Morganstern, Baldwin's Ohio Practice, *Domestic Relations Law* § 23.21, 23.35, 23.37, 23.39, 23.44 (1997)

3115.27 Special rules of evidence and procedure

Except as provided in sections 3115.04 and 3115.50 of the Revised Code, in a proceeding under sections 3115.01 to 3115.59 of the Revised Code all the following apply:

(A) The physical presence of the plaintiff in a responding tribunal of this state is not required for the issuance, enforcement, or modification of a support order or the determination of the existence or nonexistence of a parent and child relationship.

(B) A verified complaint, affidavit, document substantially complying with federally mandated forms, and a document incorporated by reference in any of them, not excluded under the hearsay rule if given in person, is admissible in evidence if given under oath by a party or witness residing in another state.

(C) A copy of the record of child support payments certified as a true copy of the original by the custodian of the record may be forwarded to a responding tribunal. The copy is evidence of facts asserted in it, and is admissible to show whether payments were made.

(D) Copies of bills for testing for parentage, and for prenatal and postnatal health care of the mother and child, furnished to the adverse party at least ten days before trial, are admissible in evidence to prove the amount of the charges billed and that the charges were reasonable, necessary, and customary.

(E) Documentary evidence transmitted from another state to a tribunal of this state by telephone, telecopier, or other means that do not provide an original writing may not be excluded from evidence on an objection based on the means of transmission.

(F) A tribunal of this state may permit a party or witness residing in another state to be deposed or to testify by telephone, audiovisual means, or other electronic means at a designated tribunal or other location in that state. A tribunal of this state shall cooperate with tribunals of other states in designating an appropriate location for the deposition or testimony.

(G) If a party called to testify at a civil hearing refuses to answer a question, the trier of fact may draw an adverse inference from the person's silence.

(H) A privilege against disclosure of communications between spouses does not apply.

(I) The defense of immunity based on the relationship of husband and wife or parent and child does not apply.

(1997 H 352, eff. 1-1-98)

Historical and Statutory Notes

Ed. Note: Former 3115.27 repealed by 1997 H 352, eff. 1-1-98; 1971 H 504, eff. 10-27-71.

Cross References

Divorce, annulment, and legal separation actions; allowance of spousal support, child support, and custody pendente lite, Civ R 75

Ohio Administrative Code References

New evidentiary and procedural rules, OAC 5101:1-30-588

Library References

Parent and Child ⚿3.4(2).
WESTLAW Topic No. 285.
C.J.S. Parent and Child §§ 93 to 96.

OJur 3d: 47, Family Law § 1396, 1406.1 to 1406.3, 1406.6
Am Jur 2d: 23, Desertion and Nonsupport § 126, 135
Wife's possession of independent means as affecting her right to alimony pendente lite. 60 ALR3d 728
Wife's possession of independent means as affecting her right to child support pendente lite. 60 ALR3d 832
Baldwin's Ohio Legislative Service Annotated, 1997 H 352—LSC Analysis, p 9/L-2719
Carlin, Baldwin's Ohio Practice, *Merrick-Rippner Probate Law* § 19.6, 19.8, 108.36 (1997)
Sowald & Morganstern, Baldwin's Ohio Practice, *Domestic Relations Law* § 22.10, 23.24, 23.32, 23.33, 23.35, 23.37, 23.39, 23.43 (1997)

Notes of Decisions and Opinions

1. Amount of support

The amount of support ordered in an initial proceeding under the Uniform Reciprocal Enforcement of Support Act must conform to the amount determined in a previous divorce case, but once the URESA order is established it is not modified by a subsequent proceeding in the divorce action, unless the divorce court specifically so provides (RC 3115.27 and 3115.28 harmonized). (Annotation from former RC 3115.27.) San Diego County v. Elavsky (Ohio 1979) 58 Ohio St.2d 81, 388 N.E.2d 1229, 12 O.O.3d 88.

Under traditional method of enforcement of foreign support orders, state courts are deprived by statute of subject-matter jurisdiction to increase amount of support obligation set forth in foreign court's order. McClure v. McClure (Ohio App. 4 Dist. 1997) 119 Ohio App.3d 76, 694 N.E.2d 515.

Trial court did not abuse its discretion in directing husband to pay as temporary support during divorce proceeding child support, spousal support, amount to bring mortgage on marital home current, and mortgage payments thereafter as they became due. (Annotation from former RC 3115.27.) DiLacqua v. DiLacqua (Summit 1993) 88 Ohio App.3d 48, 623 N.E.2d 118.

Trial court did not abuse its discretion by including in calculation of husband's temporary child support obligation $20,000 bonus husband received from his employer, even though most of bonus was used to make mortgage payments on marital home and balance was divided equally between husband and wife; funds at issue were part of husband's obligation to pay temporary spousal support, and distribution of bonus did not constitute distribution of marital property. (Annotation from former RC 3115.27.) DiLacqua v. DiLacqua (Summit 1993) 88 Ohio App.3d 48, 623 N.E.2d 118.

Under the Uniform Reciprocal Enforcement of Support Act, a responding court does not have the jurisdiction to increase the amount in an existing child support order where there is no comparable modification emanating from the court rendered the original support order. (Annotation from former RC 3115.27.) Jacobs v. Jacobs (Lucas 1988) 62 Ohio App.3d 271, 575 N.E.2d 480.

Under Ohio and Illinois law, the amount of child support ordered in an initial proceeding under the Uniform Reciprocal Enforcement of Support Act (URESA) must conform to the amount determined in the previous divorce case. (Annotation from former RC 3115.27.) Taylor v. Wettstein (S.D.Ohio 1989) 746 F.Supp. 713.

2. Jurisdiction

In former wife's action under Uniform Reciprocal Enforcement of Support Act (URESA), trial court had ability to either enforce or deny enforcement of separation agreement's support obligation, but not to modify terms of the support payments. In Matter of Shanyfelt (Ohio App. 3 Dist. 1997) 118 Ohio App.3d 243, 692 N.E.2d 642.

Doctrine of res judicata did not preclude Ohio court from making determination of former husband's child support arrearages based upon original Ohio court order of support, even though Florida court had issued order of support in amount different from that originally ordered by Ohio court; Florida court merely established another support obligation of former husband. Bobbs v. Cline (Ohio App. 7 Dist. 1997) 116 Ohio App.3d 46, 686 N.E.2d 556.

Under Uniform Reciprocal Enforcement of Support Act (URESA), court in Florida, where former husband resided, had no authority to change amount of child support order as issued by court in Ohio, where former wife and children resided and where original decree of dissolution was issued; jurisdiction over children remained in Ohio, and there was no evidence to indicate that Ohio court ordered modification or that parties agreed in writing that Florida court could modify Ohio order. Bobbs v. Cline (Ohio App. 7 Dist. 1997) 116 Ohio App.3d 46, 686 N.E.2d 556.

An Ohio court does not lack jurisdiction in a URESA action where a foreign court has issued an order staying all other proceedings; the foreign order does not purport to relieve the obligor of his support obligations, and, therefore, an Ohio court has jurisdiction to enforce the foreign order. (Annotation from former RC 3115.27.)

Casale v. Casale (Cuyahoga 1989) 61 Ohio App.3d 118, 572 N.E.2d 192.

An Ohio court lacks jurisdiction to modify child support ordered pursuant to a Maryland divorce decree and subsequently ordered pursuant to an Ohio URESA enforcement order where the Maryland court has continuing, exclusive jurisdiction of its child support order because (1) Maryland remains the residence of the mother and children, and (2) the mother has not filed written consent to the Ohio court's modifying and assuming jurisdiction over the order. (Annotation from former RC 3115.27.) Paton v Brill, No. 95APF08-976, 1995 WL 739883 (10th Dist Ct App, Franklin, 12-14-95).

Under RC 3115.27, an Ohio court does not have authority to increase a support order which was originally rendered by a court of another state. (Annotation from former RC 3115.27.) State ex rel Marsh v Jarocki, No. 93-T-4832, 1993 WL 407303 (11th Dist Ct App, Trumbull, 9-30-93).

3115.28 Communications between tribunals

A tribunal of this state may communicate with a tribunal of another state in writing, or by telephone or other means, to obtain information concerning the laws of that state, the legal effect of a judgment, decree, or order of that tribunal, and the status of a proceeding in the other state. A tribunal of this state may furnish similar information by similar means to a tribunal of another state.

(1997 H 352, eff. 1-1-98)

Historical and Statutory Notes

Ed. Note: Former 3115.28 repealed by 1997 H 352, eff. 1-1-98; 1971 H 504, eff. 10-27-71.

Ed. Note: Former 3115.28 was former 3115.19, recodified by 1971 H 504, eff. 10-27-71; 126 v 560.

Ohio Administrative Code References

New evidentiary and procedural rules, OAC 5101:1-30-588

Library References

Parent and Child ⚷3.4(2).
WESTLAW Topic No. 285.
C.J.S. Parent and Child §§ 93 to 96.

OJur 3d: 47, Family Law § 1397, 1406.1, 1406.2, 1406.4
Am Jur 2d: 23, Desertion and Nonsupport § 135, 138

Baldwin's Ohio Legislative Service Annotated, 1997 H 352—LSC Analysis, p 9/L-2719

Carlin, Baldwin's Ohio Practice, *Merrick-Rippner Probate Law* § 19.6, 19.8, 108.36 (1997)
Sowald & Morganstern, Baldwin's Ohio Practice, *Domestic Relations Law* § 23.19, 23.34, 23.35, 23.38, 23.43 (1997)

Notes of Decisions and Opinions

---

1. Amount of support

Where a state or political subdivision thereof is the petitioner in a URESA action, a court in a local divorce case cannot modify the existing URESA order, even if it so specifically provides, unless the URESA petitioner has had prior notice of the local proceeding, in which modification is to be considered, and an opportunity to protect its interests therein. (Annotation from former RC 3115.28.) San Diego County v. Elavsky (Ohio 1979) 58 Ohio St.2d 81, 388 N.E.2d 1229, 12 O.O.3d 88.

The amount of support ordered in an initial proceeding under the Uniform Reciprocal Enforcement of Support Act must conform to the amount determined in a previous divorce case, but once the URESA order is established it is not modified by a subsequent proceeding in the divorce action, unless the divorce court specifically so provides (RC 3115.27 and 3115.28 harmonized). (Annotation from former RC 3115.28.) San Diego County v. Elavsky (Ohio 1979) 58 Ohio St.2d 81, 388 N.E.2d 1229, 12 O.O.3d 88.

Amount of child support ordered by responding court in initial Uniform Reciprocal Enforcement of Support Act (URESA) proceeding must conform to amount set forth in order of initiating court in original divorce action. (Annotation from former RC 3115.28.) Paton v. Brill (Franklin 1995) 104 Ohio App.3d 826, 663 N.E.2d 421.

Evidence supported finding that parties cohabited following their divorce for only two and one-half years for purposes of awarding husband credit for child support, even though witnesses' testimony was confused and conflicting. (Annotation from former RC 3115.28.) Parker v. Parker (Marion 1993) 86 Ohio App.3d 727, 621 N.E.2d 1229.

A common pleas court does not have jurisdiction by way of a petition brought under RC Ch 3115 to modify a child support order effected in a foreign state where the foreign divorce court has not invoked its continuing jurisdiction to modify such order. (Annotation from former RC 3115.28.) Briggs v Briggs, No. CA86-09-064 (12th Dist Ct App, Clermont, 3-2-87).

In an initial proceeding under the Uniform Reciprocal Enforcement of Support Act, codified in Ohio at RC Ch 3115, the amount of child support ordered must conform to the amount determined in the earlier divorce case. (Annotation from former RC 3115.28.) Taylor v. Wettstein (S.D.Ohio 1989) 746 F.Supp. 713.

2. Res judicata

An Alaska trial court's finding that an Ohio exwife gave the Alaska revenue department child support enforcement division actual authority to settle her claims for delinquent child support payments against her exhusband, who was residing in Alaska, is binding on the parties and thus, the exwife's revivor action is barred by the Full Faith and Credit Clause and by res judicata. (Annotation from former RC 3115.28.) Wyatt v. Wyatt (Ohio 1992) 65 Ohio St.3d 268, 602 N.E.2d 1166, rehearing denied 65 Ohio St.3d 1482, 604 N.E.2d 758.

Doctrine of res judicata did not preclude Ohio court from making determination of former husband's child support arrearages based upon original Ohio court order of support, even though Florida court had issued order of support in amount different from that originally ordered by Ohio court; Florida court merely established another support obligation of former husband. Bobbs v. Cline (Ohio App. 7 Dist. 1997) 116 Ohio App.3d 46, 686 N.E.2d 556.

3. Specific duty of support

Trial court did not abuse its discretion in adopting referee's denial of husband's motion to consolidate divorce and action brought under the Uniform Reciprocal Enforcement of Support Act (URESA) for reimbursement of Aid to Families with Dependent Children (AFDC) benefits received by wife for support of minor child. (Annotation from former RC 3115.28.) McDonnold v. McDonnold (Lake 1994) 98 Ohio App.3d 822, 649 N.E.2d 1236.

If an action is not one to enforce a general obligation of support but one to enforce a specific duty of support as embodied within a prior child support order, then the duty of support as provided by the law of the state which had entered the support order is controlling; hence, a prior support order in Ohio is controlling rather than the law of Michigan relating to the duty of support. (Annotation from former RC 3115.28.) Morrison v Morrison, No. 73AP-195 (10th Dist Ct App, Franklin, 2-5-74).

4. Jurisdiction

Under Uniform Reciprocal Enforcement of Support Act (URESA), court in Florida, where former husband resided, had no authority to change amount of child support order as issued by court in Ohio, where former wife and children resided and where original decree of dissolution was issued; jurisdiction over children remained in Ohio, and there was no evidence to indicate that Ohio court ordered modification or that parties agreed in writing that Florida court could modify Ohio order. Bobbs v. Cline (Ohio App. 7 Dist. 1997) 116 Ohio App.3d 46, 686 N.E.2d 556.

Domestic relations court did not lack jurisdiction to hear Uniform Reciprocal Enforcement of Support Act (URESA) action merely because modification proceedings were pending simultaneously in New Jersey divorce court; although divorce court order purported to stay all other proceedings, order did not in any way relieve former husband of his duty to continue paying support, and former husband was merely required to make further support payments in Ohio rather than in New Jersey. (Annotation from former RC 3115.28.) Casale v. Casale (Cuyahoga 1989) 61 Ohio App.3d 118, 572 N.E.2d 192.

Trial court's orders modifying, and later suspending, former husband's child support obligations were void ab initio where the motions were granted after the trial court, without notice to former wife, who was residing in Florida, granted former husband's motion to consolidate former wife's Uniform Reciprocal Enforcement of Support Act action, which had been filed by the state of Florida on her behalf, with the prior divorce action, and thus, the trial court's orders were subject to collateral attack at any time. (Annotation from former RC 3115.28.) Rondy v. Rondy (Summit 1983) 13 Ohio App.3d 19, 468 N.E.2d 81, 13 O.B.R. 20.

An Ohio court has subject matter jurisdiction under the Uniform Reciprocal Enforcement of Support Act (URESA) to establish a support order when a Kentucky court's order changing custody of the child is silent on the issue of support to be paid to the parent receiving custody. Swayne v Newman, No. 98CA2572, 1999 WL 2438 (4th Dist Ct App, Scioto, 12-30-98).

5. Reimbursement

An order of the domestic relations court suspending a father's obligation to make child support payments precludes a state from seeking reimbursement for assistance provided to the mother and child under URESA. (Annotation from former RC 3115.28.) Minnesota v Monroe, No. 17042, 1995 WL 411393 (9th Dist Ct App, Summit, 7-5-95).

3115.29 Assistance with discovery

A tribunal of this state may request a tribunal of another state to assist in obtaining discovery and may, on the request of a tribunal of another state, compel a person over whom it has jurisdiction to respond to a discovery order issued by the requesting tribunal.

(1997 H 352, eff. 1-1-98)

Historical and Statutory Notes

Ed. Note: Former 3115.29 repealed by 1997 H 352, eff. 1-1-98; 1971 H 504, eff. 10-27-71.

Ed. Note: Former 3115.29 was former 3115.20 recodified by 1971 H 504, eff. 10-27-71; 126 v 560.

Ohio Administrative Code References

New evidentiary and procedural rules, OAC 5101:1-30-588

Library References

Parent and Child ⚿3.4(2).

WESTLAW Topic No. 285.

C.J.S. Parent and Child §§ 93 to 96.

OJur 3d: 47, Family Law § 1367, 1406.1 to 1406.4
Am Jur 2d: 23, Desertion and Nonsupport § 128, 136

Baldwin's Ohio Legislative Service Annotated, 1997 H 352—LSC Analysis, p 9/L-2719

Carlin, Baldwin's Ohio Practice, *Merrick-Rippner Probate Law* § 19.6, 19.8, 108.36 (1997)
Sowald & Morganstern, Baldwin's Ohio Practice, *Domestic Relations Law* § 23.21, 23.32, 23.33, 23.35, 23.38, 23.39, 23.43 (1997)

Notes of Decisions and Opinions

In general 1

1. In general

No provision in Ohio version of Uniform Reciprocal Enforcement of Support Act (URESA) grants court subject matter jurisdiction over disputed matter other than paternity and child support. (Annotation from former RC 3115.29.) In re Byard (Ohio 1996) 74 Ohio St.3d 294, 658 N.E.2d 735.

Ohio version of Uniform Reciprocal Enforcement of Support Act (URESA) does not confer subject matter jurisdiction over issues concerning child custody and visitation in action for child support enforcement. (Annotation from former RC 3115.29.) In re Byard (Ohio 1996) 74 Ohio St.3d 294, 658 N.E.2d 735.

3115.30 Receipt and disbursement of payments

A support enforcement agency or tribunal of this state shall disburse promptly any amounts received pursuant to a support order, as directed in the order. The agency or tribunal shall furnish to a requesting party or tribunal of another state a certified statement by the custodian of the record of the amounts and dates of all payments received.

(1997 H 352, eff. 1-1-98)

Historical and Statutory Notes

Ed. Note: Former 3115.30 was repealed by 1997 H 352, eff. 1-1-98, and 1988 H 242, eff. 6-24-88; 1971 H 504, eff. 10-27-71.

Cross References

Child support orders, health insurance coverage, 3113.217

Library References

Parent and Child ⚷3.4(2).
WESTLAW Topic No. 285.
C.J.S. Parent and Child §§ 93 to 96.

OJur 3d: 47, Family Law § 1406.1, 1406.2

Baldwin's Ohio Legislative Service Annotated, 1997 H 352—LSC Analysis, p 9/L-2719

Carlin, Baldwin's Ohio Practice, *Merrick-Rippner Probate Law* § 19.6, 19.8, 108.36 (1997)
Sowald & Morganstern, Baldwin's Ohio Practice, *Domestic Relations Law* § 23.35, 23.38 (1997)

ESTABLISHMENT OF SUPPORT ORDER

3115.31 Issuance of support order

(A) If a support order entitled to recognition under sections 3115.01 to 3115.59 of the Revised Code has not been issued, a responding tribunal of this state may issue a support order if either of the following apply:

(1) The individual seeking the order resides in another state;

(2) The support enforcement agency seeking the order is located in another state.

(B) The tribunal may issue a temporary child support order if any of the following apply:

(1) The defendant has signed a verified statement acknowledging that the defendant is the parent of the child;

(2) The defendant has been determined by or pursuant to law to be the parent;

(3) There is other clear and convincing evidence that the defendant is the child's parent.

(C)(1) If the responding tribunal finds, after giving notice and an opportunity to be heard to the obligor, that the obligor owes a duty of support, it shall issue a support order directed to the obligor and may issue any other order under section 3115.16 of the Revised Code. Support orders made pursuant to sections 3115.01 to 3115.59 of the Revised Code shall require that payments be made to the division of child support in the department of job and family services.

(2) The responding tribunal shall transmit to the initiating tribunal a copy of all orders of support or for reimbursement of support.

(3) Each order for support made or modified under section 3115.16 of the Revised Code, this section, and former section 3115.22 of the Revised Code on or after December 31, 1993, shall include as part of the order a general provision, as described in division (A)(1) of section 3113.21 of the Revised Code, requiring the withholding or deduction of income or assets of the obligor under the order as described in division (D) of section 3113.21 of the Revised Code or another type of appropriate requirement as described in division (D)(3), (D)(4), or (H) of that section, to ensure that withholding or deduction from the income or assets of the obligor is available from the commencement of the support order for collection of the support and of any arrearages that occur; a statement requiring all parties to the order to notify the support enforcement agency in writing of their current mailing address, current residence address, current residence telephone number, current driver's license number, and any changes to that information; and a notice that the requirement to notify the agency of all changes to that information continues until further notice from the tribunal. Any tribunal that makes or modifies an order for support under this section or former section 3115.22 of the Revised Code on or after April 12, 1990, shall comply with sections 3113.21 to 3113.219 of the Revised Code. If any person required to pay child support under an order made under this section or former section 3115.22 of the Revised Code on or after April 15, 1985, or any person required to pay support under an order made or modified under this section or former section 3115.22 of the Revised Code on or after December 31, 1986, is found in contempt of court for failure to make support payments under the order, the tribunal that makes the finding, in addition to any other penalty or remedy imposed, shall assess all court costs arising out of the contempt proceeding against the person and require the person to pay any reasonable attorney's fees of any adverse party, as determined by the tribunal, that arose in relation to the act of contempt.

(1999 H 471, eff. 7-1-00; 1997 H 352, eff. 1-1-98)

Historical and Statutory Notes

Ed. Note: Former 3115.31 repealed by 1997 H 352, eff. 1-1-98; 1986 H 428, eff. 12-23-86; 1971 H 504.

Amendment Note: 1999 H 471 substituted "job and family" for "human" in division (C)(1); and made other nonsubstantive changes.

Cross References

Child support enforcement agency, designation, 2301.35

Nonsupport of dependents, court costs and attorney fees, 2919.21

Support order defined, 2301.34

Support orders, withholding or deduction requirements and notices, 3113.21

Library References

Parent and Child ⚷3.4(2).

WESTLAW Topic No. 285.

C.J.S. Parent and Child §§ 93 to 96.

OJur 3d: 47, Family Law § 1306, 1399, 1406.1, 1406.2, 1406.6

Am Jur 2d: 23, Desertion and Nonsupport § 134

Baldwin's Ohio Legislative Service Annotated, 1997 H 352—LSC Analysis, p 9/L-2719

Carlin, Baldwin's Ohio Practice, *Merrick-Rippner Probate Law* § 19.6, 19.8, 108.36 (1997)

Sowald & Morganstern, Baldwin's Ohio Practice, *Domestic Relations Law* § 19.1, 22.5, 23.31, 23.39, 23.44 (1997)

Law Review and Journal Commentaries

Interviewing Child Victims/Witnesses, Mary A. Lentz. 9 Baldwin's Ohio Sch L J 25 (July/August 1997).

ENFORCEMENT OF ORDER OF ANOTHER STATE WITHOUT REGISTRATION

3115.32 Payor's receipt of income-withholding order of another state

An income withholding order issued in another state may be sent to the individual or entity defined as the obligor's payor under sections 3111.20 and 3113.21 of the Revised Code without first filing a complaint or comparable pleading or registering the order with a tribunal of this state.

(1997 H 352, eff. 1-1-98)

Historical and Statutory Notes

Ed. Note: Former 3115.32 repealed by 1997 H 352, eff. 1-1-98; 1986 H 428, eff. 12-23-86; 1971 H 504.

Cross References

Automated system to support enforcement of child support, 5101.322
Bureau of support, support enforcement, 2301.34 et seq.
Contempt action for failure to pay support, 2705.031, 2705.05
Execution against property, Ch 2329
Lottery winner to state under oath whether or not he is in default of support order, 3770.071
Nonsupport of dependents, 2919.21
Payment of child support through withholding of personal earnings, workers' compensation benefits, unemployment compensation benefits, retirement benefits, or bank account, 3113.21

Ohio Administrative Code References

Direct enforcement of support orders, OAC 5101:1-30-582

Library References

Divorce ⚷403(9).
Parent and Child ⚷3.4(2).
WESTLAW Topic Nos. 134, 285.
C.J.S. Divorce §§ 846 to 849.
C.J.S. Parent and Child §§ 93 to 96.

OJur 3d: 47, Family Law § 1400 to 1406, 1406.1, 1406.2, 1406.7
Am Jur 2d: 23, Desertion and Nonsupport § 148, 149, 155

Baldwin's Ohio Legislative Service Annotated, 1997 H 352—LSC Analysis, p 9/L-2719

Carlin, Baldwin's Ohio Practice, *Merrick-Rippner Probate Law* § 19.6, 19.8, 108.36 (1997)
Klein & Darling, Baldwin's Ohio Practice, *Civil Practice* § 1 (1997)
Sowald & Morganstern, Baldwin's Ohio Practice, *Domestic Relations Law* § 23.25, 23.33, 23.40, 23.41, 23.48 (1997)

Law Review and Journal Commentaries

Retroactive Modification of Accrued and Unpaid Child Support Orders in Ohio, Lon R. Vinion. 56 Ohio St B Ass'n Rep 328 (March 7, 1983).

Notes of Decisions and Opinions

Constitutional issues 4
Enforcement 2
Modification 3
Personal jurisdiction 1

---

1. Personal jurisdiction

Nonresident father who was current on all support payments had committed no tortious injury within state and, thus, no basis existed for exercise of personal jurisdiction over father for purposes of mother's motion for registration of foreign child support order within state. (Annotation from former RC 3115.32.) Bigley v. Bigley (Wayne 1993) 90 Ohio App.3d 310, 629 N.E.2d 45.

As a defense in subsequent actions concerning enforcement or modification of child support, a registering court's lack of personal jurisdiction over the obligor is not waived by the obligor's failure to respond to notice of registration of a foreign support order. (Annotation from former RC 3115.32.) Hudgins v. Hudgins (Henry 1992) 80 Ohio App.3d 707, 610 N.E.2d 582, dismissed, jurisdictional motion overruled 65 Ohio St.3d 1463, 602 N.E.2d 1172.

Infrequent visits of short duration within Ohio and a one time three-month stay in an apartment as required by an employer while the obligor's family stayed in another state do not establish residency for jurisdictional purposes in an action to modify a foreign order for child support. (Annotation from former RC 3115.32.) Hudgins v. Hudgins (Henry 1992) 80 Ohio App.3d 707, 610 N.E.2d 582, dismissed, jurisdictional motion overruled 65 Ohio St.3d 1463, 602 N.E.2d 1172.

In an action for modification and enforcement of a foreign child support order, an obligor who enters Ohio several times a year as required by his employer is not transacting business within this state as contemplated by Civ R 4.3(A)(1) and RC 2307.382. (Annotation from former RC 3115.32.) Hudgins v. Hudgins (Henry 1992) 80 Ohio App.3d 707, 610 N.E.2d 582, dismissed, jurisdictional motion overruled 65 Ohio St.3d 1463, 602 N.E.2d 1172.

2. Enforcement

In determining whether to enforce Indiana child support order after obligor's death, Ohio trial court was required to determine whether Indiana, not Ohio, law allowed collection of child support after death. (Annotation from former RC 3115.32.) Barnett v. Barnett (Lorain 1993) 85 Ohio App.3d 1, 619 N.E.2d 38.

When decedent's duty to pay child support survived his death under Indiana law, decedent's former wife and children could maintain action against decedent's estate in Ohio for any support payments which had accrued and which Indiana courts could not modify retroactively. (Annotation from former RC 3115.32.) Barnett v. Barnett (Lorain 1993) 85 Ohio App.3d 1, 619 N.E.2d 38.

A mother's attempt to use the Uniform Reciprocal Enforcement of Support Act, RC Ch 3115, in a motion to modify an order for child support which had been entered in another county within the state is improper where RC 3115.30 was explicitly repealed for the purpose of eliminating the intrastate use of the Act. (Annotation from former RC 3115.32.) Pastorius v. Pastorius (Union 1992) 81 Ohio App.3d 403, 611 N.E.2d 364.

In action initiated under Uniform Reciprocal Enforcement of Support Act, trial court lacked jurisdiction to compel former husband to pay marital debts in accordance with final decree of foreign court or to find him in contempt for failing to do so. (Annotation from former RC 3115.32.) Thorley v. Thorley (Huron 1991) 77 Ohio App.3d 275, 602 N.E.2d 268.

Ohio court should have registered Tennessee child support order, even though support obligation had been subsequently revoked "temporarily" and not reinstated; temporary suspension of existing support order did not affect nature of underlying order as enforceable support order. (Annotation from former RC 3115.32.) Snelling v. Gardner (Franklin 1990) 69 Ohio App.3d 196, 590 N.E.2d 330.

3. Modification

Trial court lacked authority to modify previous order with respect to child support entered by foreign court, where registration of foreign order under Uniform Reciprocal Enforcement of Support Act (URESA) was not requested and both child support enforcement transmittal form and Uniform Support Petition filed with trial court merely requested establishment of URESA order. McClure v. McClure (Ohio App. 4 Dist. 1997) 119 Ohio App.3d 76, 694 N.E.2d 515.

An Ohio court has subject matter jurisdiction to modify a Pennsylvania child support order once it is registered in Ohio. (Annotation from former RC 3115.32.) Lewis v Lewis, No. 96APF07-868, 1997 WL 128566 (10th Dist Ct App, Franklin, 3-18-97).

Pursuant to RC 3115.32, an Ohio court has subject matter jurisdiction to modify registered foreign child support orders and where an initial motion to modify a registered foreign decree is erroneously dismissed by an Ohio court for lack of subject matter jurisdiction, a second motion to modify a registered foreign decree is not barred under the doctrine of res judicata. (Annotation from former RC 3115.32.) Berry v Berry, No. 13746, 1993 WL 295096 (2d Dist Ct App, Montgomery, 7-28-93).

4. Constitutional issues

Fundamental nature of divorce decree entered in Nebraska and subsequently registered in Ohio, including determination of whether spousal support provisions of such decree were subject to modification, was controlled by Nebraska law, despite former wife's residence in Ohio and parties' prior resort to Ohio law for interpretation of decree in other respects; parties could not, by their conduct, waive Nebraska's entitlement to have its laws given full faith and credit. Peterson v. Peterson (Ohio Com.Pl. 1999) 101 Ohio Misc.2d 34, 721 N.E.2d 515.

3115.33 Employer's compliance with income-withholding order of another state

(A) Upon receipt of an income withholding order, the obligor's employer shall immediately provide a copy of the order to the obligor.

(B) The employer shall treat an income withholding order issued in another state which appears regular on its face as if it had been issued by a tribunal of this state.

(C) Except as otherwise provided in division (D) of this section and section 3115.34 of the Revised Code, the employer shall withhold and distribute the funds as directed in the withholding order by complying with terms of the order that specify:

(1) The duration and amount of periodic payments of support, stated as a sum certain;

(2) The person or agency designated to receive payments and the address to which the payments are to be forwarded;

(3) Medical support, whether in the form of periodic cash payment, stated as a sum certain, or ordering the obligor to provide health insurance coverage under a policy available through the obligor's employment;

(4) The amount of periodic payments of fees and costs for a support enforcement agency, the issuing tribunal, and the obligee's attorney, stated as a sum certain;

(5) The amount of periodic payments of arrearages and interest on arrearages, stated as a sum certain.

(D) An employer shall comply with the law of the state of the obligor's principal place of employment for withholding from income with respect to all of the following:

(1) The employer's fee for processing an income withholding order;

(2) The maximum amount permitted to be withheld from the obligors [*sic*] income;

(3) The times within which the employer must implement the withholding order and forward the support payment.

(1997 H 352, eff. 1-1-98)

Historical and Statutory Notes

Ed. Note: Former 3115.33 repealed by 1997 H 352, eff. 1-1-98; 1971 H 504, eff. 10-27-71.

Ohio Administrative Code References

Direct enforcement of support orders, OAC 5101:1-30-582

Surrender of obligor charged with criminal nonsupport, OAC 5101:1-30-589

Library References

Divorce ⚷403(9).

Parent and Child ⚷3.4(2).

WESTLAW Topic Nos. 134, 285.

C.J.S. Divorce §§ 846 to 849.

C.J.S. Parent and Child §§ 93 to 96.

OJur 3d: 47, Family Law § 1360, 1406.1, 1406.2, 1406.7

Am Jur 2d: 23, Desertion and Nonsupport § 130

Determination of paternity of child as within scope of proceeding under Uniform Reciprocal Enforcement of Support Act. 81 ALR3d 1175

Baldwin's Ohio Legislative Service Annotated, 1997 H 352—LSC Analysis, p 9/L-2719

Carlin, Baldwin's Ohio Practice, *Merrick-Rippner Probate Law* § 19.6, 19.8, 108.36 (1997)

Sowald & Morganstern, Baldwin's Ohio Practice, *Domestic Relations Law* § 23.40 (1997)

3115.34 Compliance with multiple income-withholding orders

If an obligor's employer receives multiple income withholding orders with respect to the earnings of the same obligor, the employer satisfies the terms of the multiple orders if the employer complies with the law of the state of the obligor's principal place of employment to establish the priorities for withholding and allocating income withheld for multiple support obligees.

(1997 H 352, eff. 1-1-98)

Historical and Statutory Notes

Ed. Note: Former 3115.34 repealed by 1997 H 352, eff. 1-1-98; 1971 H 504, eff. 10-27-71.

Ohio Administrative Code References

Direct enforcement of support orders, OAC 5101:1-30-582

Library References

Divorce ⚷403(9).

Parent and Child ⚷3.4(2).

WESTLAW Topic Nos. 134, 285.

C.J.S. Divorce §§ 846 to 849

C.J.S. Parent and Child §§ 93 to 96.

OJur 3d: 47, Family Law § 1361, 1406.1, 1406.2

Am Jur 2d: 23, Desertion and Nonsupport § 129

Determination of paternity of child as within scope of proceeding under Uniform Reciprocal Enforcement of Support Act. 81 ALR3d 1175

Baldwin's Ohio Legislative Service Annotated, 1997 H 352—LSC Analysis, p 9/L-2719

Carlin, Baldwin's Ohio Practice, *Merrick-Rippner Probate Law* § 19.6, 19.8, 108.36 (1997)

Sowald & Morganstern, Baldwin's Ohio Practice, *Domestic Relations Law* § 23.40 (1997)

3115.35 Immunity from civil liability

An employer who complies with an income withholding order issued in another state in accordance with sections 3115.32 to 3115.37 of the Revised Code is not subject to civil liability to an individual or agency with regard to the employer's withholding of support from the obligor's income pursuant to the support order.

(1997 H 352, eff. 1-1-98)

Ohio Administrative Code References

Direct enforcement of support orders, OAC 5101:1-30-582

Library References

Divorce ⚿403(9).
Parent and Child ⚿3.4(2).
WESTLAW Topic Nos. 134, 285.
C.J.S. Divorce §§ 846 to 849.
C.J.S. Parent and Child §§ 93 to 96.

OJur 3d: 47, Family Law § 1406.1, 1406.2, 1406.7

Baldwin's Ohio Legislative Service Annotated, 1997 H 352—LSC Analysis, p 9/L-2719

Carlin, Baldwin's Ohio Practice, *Merrick-Rippner Probate Law* § 19.6, 19.8, 108.36 (1997)

Sowald & Morganstern, Baldwin's Ohio Practice, *Domestic Relations Law* § 23.40 (1997)

3115.36 Penalties for noncompliance

An employer who willfully fails to comply with an income withholding order issued by another state and received for enforcement is subject to the same penalties that may be imposed for noncompliance with an order issued by a tribunal of this state.

(1997 H 352, eff. 1-1-98)

Ohio Administrative Code References

Direct enforcement of support orders, OAC 5101:1-30-582

Library References

Divorce ⚿403(9).
Parent and Child ⚿3.4(2).
WESTLAW Topic Nos. 134, 285.
C.J.S. Divorce §§ 846 to 849.
C.J.S. Parent and Child §§ 93 to 96.

OJur 3d: 47, Family Law § 1406.1, 1406.2, 1406.7

Baldwin's Ohio Legislative Service Annotated, 1997 H 352—LSC Analysis, p 9/L-2719

Carlin, Baldwin's Ohio Practice, *Merrick-Rippner Probate Law* § 19.6, 19.8, 108.36 (1997)

Sowald & Morganstern, Baldwin's Ohio Practice, *Domestic Relations Law* § 23.40 (1997)

3115.37 Contest by obligor

(A) If a person designated as an obligor under an income withholding order issued in another state and received directly by an employer in this state believes that the person is not subject to a support order or does not have a duty of support under any order issued by any tribunal pursuant to which the income withholding order was issued, the person may contest the validity or enforcement of the income withholding order by filing an action for declaratory judgment pursuant to Chapter 2721. of the Revised Code in the court of common pleas in the county in which is located the employer's principal place of business requesting that the court determine whether the person is the obligor subject to a support order or has a duty of support under a support order pursuant to which the income withholding order was issued.

(B) The obligor shall give notice of the action initiated pursuant to Chapter 2721. of the Revised Code to all of the following:

(1) A support enforcement agency providing services to the obligee;

(2) Each employer that has directly received an income withholding order;

(3) The person or agency designated to receive payments in the income withholding order or, if no person or agency is designated, the obligee.

(C) Notwithstanding sections 3115.32 to 3115.36 of the Revised Code, if the court issues an order determining that the person is not an obligor subject to a support order or does not have a duty of support under a support order pursuant to which the income withholding order was issued, the employer shall not enforce the income withholding order against the person.

(1997 H 352, eff. 1-1-98)

Library References

Divorce ⟹403(9)
Parent and Child ⟹3.4(2).
WESTLAW Topic Nos. 134, 285.
C.J.S. Divorce §§ 846 to 849
C.J.S. Parent and Child §§ 93 to 96.

OJur 3d: 47, Family Law § 1406.1, 1406.2, 1406.7

Baldwin's Ohio Legislative Service Annotated, 1997 H 352—LSC Analysis, p 9/L-2719

Carlin, Baldwin's Ohio Practice, *Merrick-Rippner Probate Law* § 19.6, 19.8, 108.36 (1997)

Sowald & Morganstern, Baldwin's Ohio Practice, *Domestic Relations Law* § 23.31, 23.40 (1997)

3115.38 Administrative enforcement of orders

A party seeking to enforce a support order or an income withholding order, or both, issued by a tribunal of another state may send the documents required for registering the order pursuant to sections 3115.39 to 3115.51 of the Revised Code to a support enforcement agency of this state. On receipt of the documents, the support enforcement agency, without initially seeking to register the order, shall consider and, if appropriate, use any administrative procedure authorized by the law of this state to enforce a support order or an income withholding order, or both. If the obligor does not contest administrative enforcement, the order need not be registered. If the obligor contests the validity or administrative enforcement of the order, the support enforcement agency shall register the order pursuant to sections 3115.39 to 3115.51 of the Revised Code.

(1997 H 352, eff. 1-1-98)

Ohio Administrative Code References

Registration of orders, OAC 5101:1-30-55

Library References

Divorce ⟹403(9).
Parent and Child ⟹3.4(2).
WESTLAW Topic Nos. 134, 285.
C.J.S. Divorce §§ 846 to 849.
C.J.S. Parent and Child §§ 93 to 96.

OJur 3d: 47, Family Law § 1406.1, 1406.2, 1406.7

Baldwin's Ohio Legislative Service Annotated, 1997 H 352—LSC Analysis, p 9/L-2719

Carlin, Baldwin's Ohio Practice, *Merrick-Rippner Probate Law* § 19.6, 19.8, 108.36 (1997)

Sowald & Morganstern, Baldwin's Ohio Practice, *Domestic Relations Law* § 23.40 (1997)

ENFORCEMENT AND MODIFICATION OF SUPPORT ORDER AFTER REGISTRATION

3115.39 Procedure to register order for enforcement

(A) A support order or income withholding order of another state may be registered in this state by sending all of the following documents and information to the appropriate tribunal in this state:

(1) A letter of transmittal to the tribunal requesting registration and enforcement;

(2) Two copies, including one certified copy, of all orders to be registered, including any modification of an order;

(3) A sworn statement by the party seeking registration or a certified statement by the custodian of the records showing the amount of any arrearage;

(4) The name of the obligor and all of the following, if known:

(a) The obligor's address and social security number;

(b) The name and address of the obligor's employer and any other source of income of the obligor;

(c) A description and the location of property of the obligor in this state not exempt from execution.

(5) Thc namc and address of the obligee and, if applicable, the agency or person to whom support payments are to be remitted.

(B) On receipt of a request for registration, the registering tribunal shall cause the order to be filed, together with one copy of the documents and information, regardless of their form.

(C) A complaint or comparable pleading seeking a remedy that must be affirmatively sought under other law of this state may be filed at the same time as the request for registration or at a later time. The pleading must specify the grounds for the remedy sought.

(1997 H 352, eff. 1-1-98)

Ohio Administrative Code References

Registration of orders, OAC 5101:1-30-55

Library References

Divorce ⚷403(9).
Parent and Child ⚷3.4(2).
WESTLAW Topic Nos. 134, 285.
C.J.S. Divorce §§ 846 to 849.
C.J.S. Parent and Child §§ 93 to 96.

OJur 3d: 47, Family Law § 1406.1, 1406.2, 1406.7

Baldwin's Ohio Legislative Service Annotated, 1997 H 352—LSC Analysis, p 9/L-2719

Carlin, Baldwin's Ohio Practice, *Merrick-Rippner Probate Law* § 19.6, 19.8, 108.36 (1997)

Sowald & Morganstern, Baldwin's Ohio Practice, *Domestic Relations Law* § 23.37, 23.40, 23.41, 23.43 (1997)

Notes of Decisions and Opinions

Jurisdiction
Subject matter 1

1. —Subject matter, jurisdiction

The minimum contacts requirement of Civ R 4.3 applies to personal jurisdiction, not to subject matter jurisdiction and in regard to a foreign child support order, RC 3115.39 imposes no minimum contact requirement regarding the party outside Ohio who is bound by the order; therefore, the trial court errs when it vacates its prior order registering a Texas decree pursuant to RC 3115.39(B) on a finding that the obligor lacked the minimum contacts with Ohio necessary to register the order here and notwithstanding the Ohio court's having obtained personal jurisdiction over the obligor by service effected pursuant to Civ R 4.3(A) it lacks the subject matter jurisdiction to modify the Texas order. Compton v Compton, No. 99-CA-17, 1999 WL 375578 (2d Dist Ct App, Greene, 6-11-99).

3115.40 Effect of registration for enforcement

A support order or income withholding order issued in another state is registered when the order is filed in the registering tribunal of this state pursuant to section 3115.39 of the Revised Code. A registered order issued in another state that is confirmed pursuant to section 3115.43 or 3115.44 of the Revised Code is enforceable in the same manner and is subject to the same procedures as an order issued by a tribunal of this state. Except as provided in sections 3115.39 to 3115.51 of the Revised Code, a tribunal of this state shall recognize and enforce, but may not modify, a registered order that has been confirmed if the issuing tribunal had jurisdiction.

(1997 H 352, eff. 1-1-98)

Ohio Administrative Code References

Registration of orders, OAC 5101:1-30-55

Library References

Divorce ⚷403(9).
Parent and Child ⚷3.4(2).
WESTLAW Topic Nos. 134, 285.
C.J.S. Divorce §§ 846 to 849.
C.J.S. Parent and Child §§ 93 to 96.

OJur 3d: 47, Family Law § 1406.1, 1406.2, 1406.7

Baldwin's Ohio Legislative Service Annotated, 1997 H 352—LSC Analysis, p 9/L-2719

Carlin, Baldwin's Ohio Practice, *Merrick-Rippner Probate Law* § 19.6, 19.8, 108.36 (1997)

Sowald & Morganstern, Baldwin's Ohio Practice, *Domestic Relations Law* § 23.41, 23.42, 23.43 (1997)

3115.41 Choice of law

The law of the issuing state governs the nature, extent, amount, and duration of current payments and other obligations of support and the payment of arrearages under the order. In a proceeding for arrearages, the statute of limitation under the laws of this state or of the issuing state, whichever is longer, applies.

(1997 H 352, eff. 1-1-98)

Ohio Administrative Code References

Registration of orders, OAC 5101:1-30-55

Library References

Parent and Child ⚷3.4(1).
WESTLAW Topic No. 285.
C.J.S. Parent and Child §§ 90 to 92.

OJur 3d: 47, Family Law § 1406.1, 1406.2, 1406.7

Baldwin's Ohio Legislative Service Annotated, 1997 H 352—LSC Analysis, p 9/L-2719

Carlin, Baldwin's Ohio Practice, *Merrick-Rippner Probate Law* § 19.6, 19.8, 108.36 (1997)

Sowald & Morganstern, Baldwin's Ohio Practice, *Domestic Relations Law* § 23.35, 23.40, 23.41, 23.42, 23.43 (1997)

3115.42 Notice of registration of order

(A) When a support order or income withholding order issued in another state is registered, immediately on registration the registering tribunal shall send notice to the nonregistering party of the registration. The notice must be accompanied by a copy of the registered order and the documents and relevant information described in division (A) of section 3115.39 of the Revised Code.

(B) The notice must inform the nonregistering party of all of the following:

(1) That a registered order that is confirmed pursuant to section 3115.43 or 3115.44 of the Revised Code is enforceable as of the date of registration in the same manner as an order issued by a tribunal of this state;

(2) That a hearing to contest the validity or enforcement of the registered order must be requested pursuant to section 3115.43 of the Revised Code no later than twenty days after the date of mailing or personal service of the notice;

(3) That failure to contest the validity or enforcement of the registered order in a timely manner will result in confirmation of the order and enforcement of the order and the alleged arrearages and precludes further contest of that order with respect to any matter that could have been asserted;

(4) The amount of any alleged arrearages under the support order.

(C) On registration of an income withholding order for enforcement, the registering tribunal shall issue a withholding notice to the obligor's employer pursuant to sections 3113.21 to 3113.219 of the Revised Code.

(1997 H 352, eff. 1-1-98)

Library References

Divorce ⚷403(9).
Parent and Child ⚷3.4(2).
WESTLAW Topic Nos. 134, 285.
C.J.S. Divorce §§ 846 to 849.
C.J.S. Parent and Child §§ 93 to 96.

OJur 3d: 47, Family Law § 1406.1, 1406.2, 1406.7

Baldwin's Ohio Legislative Service Annotated, 1997 H 352—LSC Analysis, p 9/L-2719

Carlin, Baldwin's Ohio Practice, *Merrick-Rippner Probate Law* § 19.6, 19.8, 108.36 (1997)

Sowald & Morganstern, Baldwin's Ohio Practice, *Domestic Relations Law* § 23.42, 23.43 (1997)

3115.43 Procedure to contest validity or enforcement of registered order

(A) A nonregistering party seeking to contest the validity or enforcement of a registered order in this state shall request a hearing no later than twenty days after the date of mailing or personal service of the notice of the registration by filing a motion with the registering tribunal. The nonregistering party may seek to vacate the registration, to assert any defense to an allegation of noncompliance with the registered order, or to contest the remedies being sought or the amount of any alleged arrearages pursuant to section 3115.44 of the Revised Code.

(B) If the nonregistering party fails to make the request pursuant to division (A) of this section in a timely manner, the order is confirmed by operation of law.

(C) If a nonregistering party makes a request pursuant to division (A) of this section in a timely manner, the registering tribunal shall schedule the matter for hearing and give notice to the parties of the date, time, and place of the hearing. At the hearing, the registering tribunal shall determine whether the registered order is to be confirmed.

(1997 H 352, eff. 1-1-98)

Library References

Divorce ⚷403(9).
Parent and Child ⚷3.4(2).
WESTLAW Topic Nos. 134, 285.
C.J.S. Divorce §§ 846 to 849.
C.J.S. Parent and Child §§ 93 to 96.

OJur 3d: 47, Family Law § 1406.1, 1406.2, 1406.7

Baldwin's Ohio Legislative Service Annotated, 1997 H 352—LSC Analysis, p 9/L-2719

Carlin, Baldwin's Ohio Practice, *Merrick-Rippner Probate Law* § 19.6, 19.8, 108.36 (1997)

Sowald & Morganstern, Baldwin's Ohio Practice, *Domestic Relations Law* § 23.31, 23.42, 23.43 (1997)

3115.44 Contest of registration or enforcement

(A) A party contesting the validity or enforcement of a registered order or seeking to vacate the registration has the burden of proving one or more of the following defenses:

(1) The issuing tribunal lacked personal jurisdiction over the contesting party;

(2) The order was obtained by fraud;

(3) The order has been vacated, suspended, or modified by a later order;

(4) The issuing tribunal has stayed the order pending appeal;

(5) There is a defense under the law of this state to the remedy sought;

(6) Full or partial payment has been made;

(7) The applicable statute of limitation under section 3115.41 of the Revised Code precludes enforcement of some or all of the arrearages.

(B) If a party presents evidence establishing a full or partial defense under division (A) of this section, a tribunal may stay enforcement of the registered order, continue the proceeding to permit production of additional relevant evidence, and issue other appropriate orders. An uncontested portion of the registered order may be enforced by all remedies available under the law of this state.

(C) If the contesting party does not establish a defense under division (A) of this section to the validity or enforcement of the order, the registering tribunal shall issue an order confirming the order.

(1997 H 352, eff. 1-1-98)

Library References

Divorce ⚷403(9).
Parent and Child ⚷3.4(2).
WESTLAW Topic Nos. 134, 285.
C.J.S. Divorce §§ 846 to 849.
C.J.S. Parent and Child §§ 93 to 96.

OJur 3d: 47, Family Law § 1406.1, 1406.2, 1406.7

Baldwin's Ohio Legislative Service Annotated, 1997 H 352—LSC Analysis, p 9/L-2719

Carlin, Baldwin's Ohio Practice, *Merrick-Rippner Probate Law* § 19.6, 19.8, 108.36 (1997)

Sowald & Morganstern, Baldwin's Ohio Practice, *Domestic Relations Law* § 23.31, 23.42, 23.43 (1997)

3115.45 Confirmed order

Confirmation of a registered order, whether by operation of law under section 3115.43 of the Revised Code or after notice and hearing pursuant to section 3115.44 of the Revised Code, precludes further contest of the order with respect to any matter that could have been asserted at the time of registration.

(1997 H 352, eff. 1-1-98)

Library References

Divorce ⚷403(9).
Parent and Child ⚷3.4(2).
WESTLAW Topic Nos. 134, 285.
C.J.S. Divorce §§ 846 to 849.

C.J.S. Parent and Child §§ 93 to 96.

OJur 3d: 47, Family Law § 1406.1, 1406.2

Baldwin's Ohio Legislative Service Annotated, 1997 H 352—LSC Analysis, p 9/L-2719
Carlin, Baldwin's Ohio Practice, *Merrick-Rippner Probate Law* § 19.6, 19.8, 108.36 (1997)
Sowald & Morganstern, Baldwin's Ohio Practice, *Domestic Relations Law* § 23.42, 23.43 (1997)

3115.46 Procedure to register child support order of another state for modification

A party or support enforcement agency seeking to modify, or to modify and enforce, a child support order issued in another state shall register that order in this state pursuant to section 3115.39 of the Revised Code. A motion for modification may be filed at the same time as a request for registration, or at a later time. The motion must specify the grounds for modification.

(1997 H 352, eff. 1-1-98)

Library References

Divorce ⚿403(7).
Parent and Child ⚿3.4(2).
WESTLAW Topic Nos. 134, 285.
C.J.S. Divorce § 831.
C.J.S. Parent and Child §§ 93 to 96.

OJur 3d: 47, Family Law § 1406.1, 1406.2, 1406.8
Spouse's right to set off debt owed by other spouse against accrued spousal or child support payments. 11 ALR5th 259

Baldwin's Ohio Legislative Service Annotated, 1997 H 352—LSC Analysis, p 9/L-2719
Carlin, Baldwin's Ohio Practice, *Merrick-Rippner Probate Law* § 19.6, 19.8, 108.36 (1997)
Sowald & Morganstern, Baldwin's Ohio Practice, *Domestic Relations Law* § 23.31, 23.41, 23.43 (1997)

3115.47 Effect of registration for modification

A tribunal of this state may enforce a child support order of another state registered for purposes of modification, in the same manner as if the order had been issued by a tribunal of this state, but the registered order may be modified only if the requirements of section 3115.48 of the Revised Code have been met.

(1997 H 352, eff. 1-1-98)

Library References

Divorce ⚿403(7).
Parent and Child ⚿3.4(2).
WESTLAW Topic Nos. 134, 285.
C.J.S. Divorce § 831.
C.J.S. Parent and Child §§ 93 to 96.

OJur 3d: 47, Family Law § 1406.1, 1406.2, 1406.8
Spouse's right to set off debt owed by other spouse against accrued spousal or child support payments. 11 ALR5th 259

Baldwin's Ohio Legislative Service Annotated, 1997 H 352—LSC Analysis, p 9/L-2719
Carlin, Baldwin's Ohio Practice, *Merrick-Rippner Probate Law* § 19.6, 19.8, 108.36 (1997)
Sowald & Morganstern, Baldwin's Ohio Practice, *Domestic Relations Law* § 23.41, 23.43(1997)

3115.48 Modification of child support order of another state

(A) After a child support order issued in another state has been registered in this state, the responding tribunal of this state may modify that order only if section 3115.50 of the Revised Code does not apply and after notice and hearing it finds either of the following applicable:

(1) The child, the individual obligee, and the obligor subject to the support order do not reside in the issuing state, a petitioner who is a nonresident of this state seeks modification, and the respondent is subject to the personal jurisdiction of the tribunal of this state.

(2) The child, or a party who is an individual, is subject to the personal jurisdiction of the tribunal of this state and all of the parties who are individuals have filed written consents in the issuing tribunal for a tribunal of this state to modify the support order and assume continuing, exclusive jurisdiction over the order. However, if the issuing state is a foreign jurisdiction that has not enacted a law or established procedures substantially similar to the procedures under sections 3115.01 to 3115.59 of the Revised Code, the consent otherwise required of an individual residing in this state is not required for the tribunal to assume jurisdiction to modify the child support order.

(B) Modification of a registered child support order is subject to the same requirements, procedures, and defenses that apply to the modification of an order issued by a tribunal of this state and the order may be enforced and satisfied in the same manner.

(C) A tribunal of this state may not modify any aspect of a child support order that may not be modified under the law of the issuing state. If two or more tribunals have issued child support orders for the same obligor and child, the order that must be recognized as controlling under section 3115.09 of the Revised Code establishes the aspects of the child support order that are nonmodifiable.

(D) On issuance of an order modifying a child support order issued in another state, a tribunal of this state becomes the tribunal having continuing, exclusive jurisdiction.

(1997 H 352, eff. 1-1-98)

Library References

Divorce ⟸403(7).
Parent and Child ⟸3.4(2).
WESTLAW Topic Nos. 134, 285.
C.J.S. Divorce § 831.
C.J.S. Parent and Child §§ 93 to 96.

OJur 3d: 47, Family Law § 1406.1, 1406.2, 1406.8
Spouse's right to set off debt owed by other spouse against accrued spousal or child support payments. 11 ALR5th 259

Baldwin's Ohio Legislative Service Annotated, 1997 H 352—LSC Analysis, p 9/L-2719
Carlin, Baldwin's Ohio Practice, *Merrick-Rippner Probate Law* § 19.6, 19.8, 108.36 (1997)
Sowald & Morganstern, Baldwin's Ohio Practice, *Domestic Relations Law* § 23.41, 23.43 (1997)

Notes of Decisions and Opinions

Emancipation effect 1

1. Emancipation effect

Under the Uniform Interstate Family Support Act (UIFSA) an Ohio court is without authority to modify a parent's child support obligation under a New York decree to cease that obligation when the parties' children reach eighteen by applying Ohio law. Vancott-Young v Cummings, No. CA98-09-122, 1999 WL 326149 (12th Dist Ct App, Warren, 5-24-99).

3115.49 Recognition of order modified in another state

A tribunal of this state shall recognize a modification of its earlier child support order by a tribunal of another state that assumed jurisdiction pursuant to a law adopted by the other state that is substantially similar to sections 3115.01 to 3115.59 of the Revised Code and, upon request, except as otherwise provided in sections 3115.01 to 3115.59 of the Revised Code, shall do all of the following:

(A) Enforce collection of support amounts accruing before the modification of the order;

(B) Enforce only nonmodifiable aspects of that order;

(C) Provide other appropriate relief only for violations of that order that occurred before the effective date of the modification;

(D) Recognize the modifying order of the other state, upon registration, for the purpose of enforcement.

(1997 H 352, eff. 1-1-98)

Library References

Divorce ⟸403(9).
Parent and Child ⟸3.4(2).
WESTLAW Topic Nos. 134, 285.
C.J.S. Divorce §§ 846 to 849.
C.J.S. Parent and Child §§ 93 to 96.

OJur 3d: 47, Family Law § 1406.1, 1406.2, 1406.8
Spouse's right to set off debt owed by other spouse against accrued spousal or child support payments. 11 ALR5th 259

Baldwin's Ohio Legislative Service Annotated, 1997 H 352—LSC Analysis, p 9/L-2719
Carlin, Baldwin's Ohio Practice, *Merrick-Rippner Probate Law* § 19.6, 19.8, 108.36 (1997)
Sowald & Morganstern, Baldwin's Ohio Practice, *Domestic Relations Law* § 23.41, 23.43 (1997)

3115.50 Jurisdiction to modify child support order of another state when individual parties reside in this state

If all of the parties who are individuals reside in this state and the child does not reside in the issuing state, a tribunal of this state has jurisdiction to enforce and to modify the issuing state's child support order in a proceeding to register that order. Sections 3115.01 to 3115.11 and 3115.39 to 3115.51 of the Revised Code and the procedural and substantive laws of this state are applicable, and sections 3115.12 to 3115.38, 3115.52 to 3115.54, 3115.58, and 3115.59 of the Revised Code are not applicable, to a proceeding conducted by a tribunal of this state exercising jurisdiction under this section.

(1997 H 352, eff. 1-1-98)

Library References

Divorce ⟹403(7).
Parent and Child ⟹3.4(2).
WESTLAW Topic Nos. 134, 285.
C.J.S. Divorce § 831.
C.J.S. Parent and Child §§ 93 to 96.

OJur 3d: 47, Family Law § 1406.1, 1406.2, 1406.8
Spouse's right to set off debt owed by other spouse against accrued spousal or child support payments. 11 ALR5th 259

Baldwin's Ohio Legislative Service Annotated, 1997 H 352—LSC Analysis, p 9/L-2719
Carlin, Baldwin's Ohio Practice, *Merrick-Rippner Probate Law* § 19.6, 19.8, 108.36 (1997)
Sowald & Morganstern, Baldwin's Ohio Practice, *Domestic Relations Law* § 23.41, 23.43 (1997)

3115.51 Notice to issuing tribunal of modification

No later than thirty days after issuance of a modified child support order, the party obtaining the modification shall file a certified copy of the order with the issuing tribunal that had continuing, exclusive jurisdiction over the earlier order, and in each tribunal in which the party knows the earlier order has been registered. A party who obtains the order and fails to file a certified copy is subject to appropriate sanctions by a tribunal in which the issue of failure to file arises. The failure to file does not affect the validity or enforceability of the modified order of the new tribunal having continuing, exclusive jurisdiction.

(1997 H 352, eff. 1-1-98)

Library References

Divorce ⟹403(7).
Parent and Child ⟹3.4(2).
WESTLAW Topic Nos. 134, 285.
C.J.S. Divorce § 831.
C.J.S. Parent and Child §§ 93 to 96.

OJur 3d: 47, Family Law § 1406.1, 1406.2, 1406.8
Spouse's right to set off debt owed by other spouse against accrued spousal or child support payments. 11 ALR5th 259

Baldwin's Ohio Legislative Service Annotated, 1997 H 352—LSC Analysis, p 9/L-2719
Carlin, Baldwin's Ohio Practice, *Merrick-Rippner Probate Law* § 19.6, 19.8, 108.36 (1997)
Sowald & Morganstern, Baldwin's Ohio Practice, *Domestic Relations Law* § 23.41, 23.43 (1997)

DETERMINATION OF PARENTAGE

3115.52 Proceeding to determine parentage

(A) A tribunal of this state may serve as an initiating or responding tribunal in a proceeding brought under sections 3115.01 to 3115.59 of the Revised Code or a law or procedure substantially similar to those sections, the uniform reciprocal enforcement of support act, or the revised uniform reciprocal enforcement of support act to determine the existence or nonexistence of a parent and child relationship with respect to the parties.

(B) In a proceeding pursuant to division (A) of this section, a responding tribunal of this state shall comply with sections 3111.01 to 3111.19 of the Revised Code and the rules of this state on choice of law.

(1997 H 352, eff. 1-1-98)

Cross References

Presumptions regarding father-child relationship, 3111.03

Ohio Administrative Code References

Interstate paternity, OAC 5101:1-30-52

Library References

Children Out-of-Wedlock ⚷V.
Parent and Child ⚷3.4.
WESTLAW Topic Nos. 76H, 285.
C.J.S. Parent and Child § 90.

OJur 3d: 47, Family Law § 1406.1, 1406.2
Paternity proceedings: right to jury trial. 51 ALR4th 565

Baldwin's Ohio Legislative Service Annotated, 1997 H 352—LSC Analysis, p 9/L-2719

Carlin, Baldwin's Ohio Practice, *Merrick-Rippner Probate Law* § 19.6, 19.8, 108.36 (1997)

Sowald & Morganstern, Baldwin's Ohio Practice, *Domestic Relations Law* § 3.35, 23.31, 23.44 (1997)

INTERSTATE RENDITION

3115.53 Grounds for rendition

(A) For purposes of this article, "governor" includes an individual performing the functions of the executive authority of a state.

(B) The governor of this state may do either of the following:

(1) Demand that the governor of another state surrender an individual found in the other state who is charged criminally in this state with having failed to pay support under a support order;

(2) On the demand by the governor of another state, surrender an individual found in this state who is charged criminally in the other state with having failed to pay support under a support order.

(C) Notwithstanding section 2963.03 of the Revised Code, sections 2963.01 to 2963.29 and 107.04 of the Revised Code apply to the demand even if the individual whose surrender is demanded was not in the demanding state when the crime was allegedly committed and has not fled therefrom.

(1997 H 352, eff. 1-1-98)

Library References

Parent and Child ⚷3.4.
WESTLAW Topic No. 285.
C.J.S. Parent and Child § 90.

OJur 3d: 26, Criminal Law § 803; 47, Family Law 1406.1, 1406.2, 1406.9

Baldwin's Ohio Legislative Service Annotated, 1997 H 352—LSC Analysis, p 9/L-2719

Carlin, Baldwin's Ohio Practice, *Merrick-Rippner Probate Law* § 19.6, 19.8, 108.36 (1997)

Sowald & Morganstern, Baldwin's Ohio Practice, *Domestic Relations Law* § 23.46 (1997)

3115.54 Conditions of rendition

(A) Before making a demand that the governor of another state surrender an individual pursuant to division (B)(1) of section 3115.53 of the Revised Code, the governor of this state may require a prosecutor of this state to demonstrate that at least sixty days previously the obligee had initiated proceedings for support pursuant to sections 3115.01 to 3115.59 of the Revised Code or that such proceedings would not be effective in enforcing the support order.

(B) If, under a law adopted by another state that is substantially similar to sections 3115.01 to 3115.59 of the Revised Code, the uniform reciprocal enforcement of support act, or the revised uniform reciprocal enforcement of support act, the governor of the other state makes a demand pursuant to division (B)(2) of section 3115.53 of the Revised Code, the governor of this state may require a prosecutor of this state to investigate the demand and report whether a proceeding for support has been initiated or would be effective in enforcing the support order. If it appears that a proceeding would be effective but has not been initiated, the governor of this state may delay honoring the demand for a reasonable time to permit the initiation of a proceeding.

(C) If a proceeding for support has been initiated and the individual whose surrender is demanded prevails, the governor of this state may decline to honor the demand. If the petitioner prevails and the individual whose surrender is demanded is subject to a support order, the governor of this state may decline to honor the demand if the individual is complying with the support order.

(1997 H 352, eff. 1-1-98)

Ohio Administrative Code References

Surrender of obligor charged with criminal nonsupport, OAC 5101:1-30-589

Library References

Parent and Child ⚷3.4.
WESTLAW Topic No. 285.
C.J.S. Parent and Child § 90.

OJur 3d: 26, Criminal Law § 803; 47, Family Law § 1406.1, 1406.2, 1406.9

Baldwin's Ohio Legislative Service Annotated, 1997 H 352—LSC Analysis, p 9/L-2719
Carlin, Baldwin's Ohio Practice, *Merrick-Rippner Probate Law* § 19.6, 19.8, 108.36 (1997)
Sowald & Morganstern, Baldwin's Ohio Practice, *Domestic Relations Law* § 23.46 (1997)

MISCELLANEOUS PROVISIONS

3115.55 Civil Procedure Rules applicable

(A) Any action or proceeding brought pursuant to sections 3115.01 to 3115.59 of the Revised Code is a civil action and shall be governed by the Rules of Civil Procedure unless a different procedure is specifically provided by those sections.

(B) An action under section 3115.31 of the Revised Code to establish a support order, section 3115.37 of the Revised Code to contest direct withholding of support, sections 3115.43 and 3115.44 of the Revised Code to register a support order, section 3115.46 of the Revised Code to register an order for modification, or section 3115.52 of the Revised Code to determine parentage is an original action and shall be governed by the Rules of Civil Procedure. On filing the complaint with the responding tribunal, the clerk of court shall comply with the service of process requirements of the Rules of Civil Procedure.

(C) In any proceeding in which the plaintiff seeks to invoke the continuing jurisdiction of a responding tribunal of this state in order to modify or enforce a support order, notice of the complaint shall be served in the manner provided for service of process under the Rules of Civil Procedure.

(D) If the manner of notice is not specified in this section, or otherwise in this chapter or the Rules of Civil Procedure, notice shall be by first class mail.

(1997 H 352, eff. 1-1-98)

Ohio Administrative Code References

Child support, other procedural matters, OAC 5101:1-30-501

Library References

Parent and Child ⚷3.4(2).
WESTLAW Topic No. 285.
C.J.S. Parent and Child §§ 93 to 96.

OJur 3d: 47, Family Law § 1406.1, 1406.2, 1406.6

Baldwin's Ohio Legislative Service Annotated, 1997 H 352—LSC Analysis, p 9/L-2719

Carlin, Baldwin's Ohio Practice, *Merrick-Rippner Probate Law* § 19.6, 19.8, 108.36 (1997)
Sowald & Morganstern, Baldwin's Ohio Practice, *Domestic Relations Law* § 23.31 (1997)

3115.56 Venue

(A) If this state is the responding state, a complaint seeking enforcement, collection, or modification of an existing support order originally issued in this state shall be filed with the tribunal or child support enforcement agency that issued the original order.

(B) An original action under this chapter shall be filed with the appropriate tribunal of the county pursuant to sections 2151.23 and 2301.03 of the Revised Code in which the respondent resides or is found.

(C) If an obligor contesting the direct withholding of income under section 3115.37 of the Revised Code is not a resident of this state, the complaint shall be filed with the appropriate tribunal located in either of the following:

(1) The county in which the obligor's employer is located, if the order attaches to the income of the obligor paid by the employer;

(2) The county in which an account is located in a financial institution, if the income withholding order attaches the funds in that account.

If venue cannot be determined under division (C)(1) or (2) of this section, the nonresident obligor shall file the complaint with a tribunal located in a county of this state that borders the obligor's county of residence or in Franklin county.

(1997 H 352, eff. 1-1-98)

Ohio Administrative Code References

Child support, other procedural matters, OAC 5101:1-30-501

Library References

Parent and Child ⇐3.4(2).
WESTLAW Topic No. 285.
C.J.S. Parent and Child §§ 93 to 96.

OJur 3d: 47, Family Law § 1406.1, 1406.2

Baldwin's Ohio Legislative Service Annotated, 1997 H 352—LSC Analysis, p 9/L-2719

Carlin, Baldwin's Ohio Practice, *Merrick-Rippner Probate Law* § 19.6, 19.8, 108.36 (1997)
Sowald & Morganstern, Baldwin's Ohio Practice, *Domestic Relations Law* § 23.31, 23.40 (1997)

3115.57 Effect of orders issued prior to effective date of Act

An order issued prior to the effective date of this section pursuant to former Chapter 3115. of the Revised Code shall remain in full force and effect as issued, but may be modified or terminated pursuant to Chapter 3115. of the Revised Code as that chapter exists on and after the effective date of this section. The provisions of section 3115.41 of the Revised Code shall not revive any action that could not be filed prior to the effective date of this section under provisions of former section 3115.06 of the Revised Code.

(1997 H 352, eff. 1-1-98)

Ohio Administrative Code References

Child support, other procedural matters, OAC 5101:1-30-501

Library References

Children Out-of-Wedlock ⇐68 to 69.
Divorce ⇐403(9).
Parent and Child ⇐3.3(8), 3.4(1).
WESTLAW Topic Nos. 76H, 134, 285.
C.J.S. Children Out-of-Wedlock §§ 126 to 129.
C.J.S. Divorce §§ 846 to 849.
C.J.S. Parent and Child §§ 80, 82 to 84, 89 to 92.

OJur 3d: 47, Family Law § 1406.1, 1406.2

Baldwin's Ohio Legislative Service Annotated, 1997 H 352—LSC Analysis, p 9/L-2719
Carlin, Baldwin's Ohio Practice, *Merrick-Rippner Probate Law* § 19.6, 19.8, 108.36 (1997)
Sowald & Morganstern, Baldwin's Ohio Practice, *Domestic Relations Law* § 23.19 (1997)

3115.58 Uniformity of application and construction

Sections 3115.01 to 3115.59 of the Revised Code shall be applied and construed to effectuate its general purpose to make uniform the law of those states that enact a uniform interstate family support act.

(1997 H 352, eff. 1-1-98)

Ohio Administrative Code References

Child support, other procedural matters, OAC 5101:1-30-501

Library References

Parent and Child ⚿3.4(1).
WESTLAW Topic No. 285.
C.J.S. Parent and Child §§ 90 to 92.

OJur 3d: 47, Family Law § 1406.1, 1406.2

Baldwin's Ohio Legislative Service Annotated, 1997 H 352—LSC Analysis, p 9/L-2719
Carlin, Baldwin's Ohio Practice, *Merrick-Rippner Probate Law* § 19.6, 19.8, 108.36 (1997)

3115.59 Severability clause

If any provision of sections 3115.01 to 3115.59 of the Revised Code or its application to any person or circumstance is held invalid, the invalidity does not affect other provisions or applications of those sections which can be given effect without the invalid provision or application, and to this end the provisions of those sections are severable.

(1997 H 352, eff. 1-1-98)

Ohio Administrative Code References

Child support, other procedural matters, OAC 5101:1-30-501

Library References

Parent and Child ⚿3.4(1).
WESTLAW Topic No. 285.
C.J.S. Parent and Child §§ 90 to 92.

OJur 3d: 47, Family Law § 1406.1, 1406.2

Baldwin's Ohio Legislative Service Annotated, 1997 H 352—LSC Analysis, p 9/L-2719
Carlin, Baldwin's Ohio Practice, *Merrick-Rippner Probate Law* § 19.6, 19.8, 108.36 (1997)

CHAPTER 3117

Conciliation of Marital Controversies

Cross References

Conciliation order, procedure, 3105.091
Courts of conciliation, O Const Art IV §19
Domestic violence, content of protection orders, 3113.31
General assembly to grant no divorce or exercise judicial power, O Const Art II §32

Library References

Sowald & Morganstern, Baldwin's Ohio Practice, *Domestic Relations Law* § 6.9, 25.34 (1997)

WESTLAW Electronic Research

See WESTLAW Electronic Research Guide following the Preface.

Law Review and Journal Commentaries

Family Conciliation: Draft Rules for the Settlement of Family Disputes, Morris Wolff. 21 J Fam L 213 (1982-83).

3117.01 Determination of necessity of conciliation procedures

Chapter 3117. of the Revised Code is applicable only in counties in which the court of common pleas determines that social conditions and the number of domestic relations cases in the county render the conciliation procedures provided necessary to proper consideration of such cases or to effectuate conciliation of marital controversies. Such determination shall be made by the judge of the court of common pleas in counties having only one such judge, or by a majority of the judges of the court of common pleas in counties having more than one such judge. A determination to terminate such procedures may be made in the same manner.

(1969 S 74, eff. 11-19-69)

Library References

Divorce ⚷87.5.
WESTLAW Topic No. 134.
C.J.S. Divorce § 131.

OJur 3d: 5A, Alternative Dispute Resolution § 175; 46, Family Law § 328

Am Jur 2d: 24, Divorce and Separation § 331 et seq., 339
"Cooling off period" or lapse of time prior to entry of decree in divorce suit. 62 ALR2d 1262

Sowald & Morganstern, Baldwin's Ohio Practice, *Domestic Relations Law* § 6.1, 6.9 (1997)

3117.02 Conciliation judges

(A) Judges elected under section 2301.03 of the Revised Code as judges of the court of common pleas, division of domestic relations, shall hear all conciliation cases.

(B) In counties having more than one judge of the court of common pleas, but no division of domestic relations, the presiding judge or the judges of that court shall designate, in January of each year, one or more of their number to hear all conciliation cases. A conciliation judge may request that any case before him be assigned by the presiding judge for hearing or other proceedings by any other common pleas judge, whenever in the opinion of the conciliation judge the assignment is necessary to expedite any case. When any case is so assigned, the judge to whom it is assigned acts as a conciliation judge.

(C) The presiding judge of the court of common pleas may appoint a judge of the court of common pleas to act as conciliation judge during any period when a conciliation judge is on vacation, is absent, or is for any reason unable to perform his duties.

(1995 H 151, eff. 12-4-95; 1969 S 74, eff. 11-19-69)

Historical and Statutory Notes

Amendment Note: 1995 H 151 deleted "chief justice," before "presiding judge" in division (B); and made other nonsubstantive changes.

Library References

Divorce ⚷87.5.
WESTLAW Topic No. 134.
C.J.S. Divorce § 131.

OJur 3d: 46, Family Law § 331

Am Jur 2d: 24, Divorce and Separation § 333, 339

Sowald & Morganstern, Baldwin's Ohio Practice, *Domestic Relations Law* § 6.1, 6.9 (1997)

3117.03 Appointment of counselors; duties

In each county having a population over one hundred thousand according to the latest federal decennial census, the court of common pleas may appoint one or more conciliation counselors to assist the court in carrying out its functions under this chapter. Conciliation counselors shall do any of the following, as the court may direct:

(A) Confer with the parties to conciliation proceedings, and make recommendations concerning such proceedings to the conciliation judge;

(B) Hold hearings in conciliation cases;

(C) Cause such statistics to be compiled, reports to be made, and records to be kept, as may be relevant to the work of the court in conciliation cases;

(D) Provide such other assistance as may be relevant to the work of the court in conciliation cases.

(1969 S 74, eff. 11-19-69)

Cross References

Referees, Civ R 53, 75

Library References

Divorce ⟹87.5.
WESTLAW Topic No. 134.
C.J.S. Divorce § 131.

OJur 3d: 46, Family Law § 331

Am Jur 2d: 24, Divorce and Separation § 333, 339

Sowald & Morganstern, Baldwin's Ohio Practice, *Domestic Relations Law* § 6.1, 6.9 (1997)

3117.04 Assistance of probation officer

The probation officer in every county shall, upon request of the conciliation judge, in order to carry out the purposes of this chapter, make investigations and reports and render other assistance in conciliation cases, within the limits of the powers and duties granted and imposed by the laws of this state relating to probation officers.

(1969 S 74, eff. 11-19-69)

Cross References

Court of common pleas, department of probation, 2301.27 et seq.

Library References

Divorce ⟹87.5.
WESTLAW Topic No. 134.
C.J.S. Divorce § 131.

OJur 3d: 46, Family Law § 331

Am Jur 2d: 24, Divorce and Separation § 333, 339

Sowald & Morganstern, Baldwin's Ohio Practice, *Domestic Relations Law* § 6.9 (1997)

3117.05 Petition for conciliation; form; absence of fees

(A) Prior to or during pendency of any action for divorce, annulment, or legal separation, one or both spouses may file in the court of common pleas a petition for conciliation, to preserve the marriage by effecting a reconciliation, or to amicably settle the controversy between the spouses, so as to avoid further litigation over the issues involved.

(B) The petition shall be captioned substantially as follows:

IN THE COURT OF COMMON PLEAS
OF ________ COUNTY, OHIO

In Re:	: No. ________________
______________________	:
and	: PETITION FOR CONCILIATION
______________________	:

(C) The petition shall:

(1) Allege facts showing a controversy between the spouses which may, unless a reconciliation or settlement is achieved, result in dissolution of the marriage or disruption of the household;

(2) State the name and age of each minor child whose welfare may be affected by the controversy;

(3) State the names and addresses of the parties;

(4) Name as respondent any other person who has any relation to the controversy, stating his address if known to the petitioner;

(5) State any other information that the court by rule requires;

(6) Request the aid of the court to effect a reconciliation or an amicable settlement of the controversy between the parties.

(D) The clerk of the court of common pleas shall provide, at the expense of the county, blank forms for petitions for filing pursuant to this chapter. Any employee of the county engaged in conciliation duties shall assist any person at his request in the preparation and presentation of any such petition. All public officers in each county shall refer to the conciliation judge all petitions and complaints made to them in respect to controversies within the purview of this chapter.

(E) No fee shall be charged for filing the petition, nor shall any fee be charged by any officer for the performance of any duty pursuant to this chapter.

(F) Conciliation case files shall be closed, but may be opened for inspection by any party, his counsel, or other proper person, upon written authority of the conciliation judge.

(1990 H 514, eff. 1-1-91; 1969 S 74)

Cross References

Conciliation order, procedure, 3105.091

Library References

Divorce ⚷87.5.
WESTLAW Topic No. 134.
C.J.S. Divorce § 131.

OJur 3d: 5A, Alternative Dispute Resolution § 175; 46, Family Law § 330, 333, 336

Am Jur 2d: 24, Divorce and Separation § 333, 339

Sowald & Morganstern, Baldwin's Ohio Practice, *Domestic Relations Law* § 6.9 (1997)

3117.06 Hearing and notice; conferences; court order

(A) The conciliation judge shall fix a reasonable time and place for hearing on the petition within thirty days after the date it is filed, and shall cause such manner of notice of the filing of the petition and the time and place for hearing as he finds necessary to be given to the parties and respondents. The court may issue a citation to any party or respondent requiring him to appear at the time and place stated in the citation, and may require the attendance of witnesses as in other civil cases.

(B) The court may be convened and hearings held pursuant to this chapter at any time and place within the county, and the hearing may be had in chambers or otherwise, except that if any party, prior to hearing, objects to a different time or place, the time and place for hearing shall be that provided by law for the trial of civil actions.

(C) Hearings and conferences in conciliation proceedings shall be held in private. The court shall exclude all persons except officers and employees of the court, the parties and respondents and their counsel, witnesses, and persons called to the aid of the court in the controversy. Conferences may be held with each party separately, and counsel for one party may be excluded from a hearing or conference when the other party is present without counsel.

(D) Hearings and conferences shall be conducted as informally as possible, and a series of hearings or conferences may be held if it appears necessary to effect a reconciliation or amicable settlement of the controversy between the spouses. The court may, with the consent of the parties, recommend or invoke the aid of physicians, psychologists, clergymen, or other specialists, or persons with expertise in the matter in controversy. Such aid shall be at the expense of the parties, unless the board of county commissioners authorizes and provides for payment for such aid.

(E) Upon hearing, the conciliation judge may make such orders in respect to the conduct of the spouses and the subject matter of the controversy as the court finds necessary to preserve the marriage or implement the reconciliation of the spouses. Such orders shall not be effective for more than thirty days, unless the parties consent to a longer time or to a continuation. Any reconciliation agreement between the parties may be reduced to writing and, with the consent of the parties, a court order may be made pursuant to this section requiring the parties to comply therewith.

(1969 S 74, eff. 11-19-69)

Cross References

Commencement of action, venue, Civ R 3

Library References

Divorce ⟹87.5.
WESTLAW Topic No. 134.
C.J.S. Divorce § 131.

OJur 3d: 5A, Alternative Dispute Resolution § 175; 10, Buildings, Zoning, and Land Controls § 326; 46, Family Law § 333 to 335

Am Jur 2d: 24, Divorce and Separation § 333, 339

Sowald & Morganstern, Baldwin's Ohio Practice, *Domestic Relations Law* § 6.9 (1997)

3117.07 Other actions stayed pending conciliation

During the period beginning with the filing of the petition for conciliation and continuing until expiration of any court order made pursuant to division (E) of section 3117.06 of the Revised Code, neither spouse may file or proceed with any action for divorce, annulment, or legal separation. The pendency of an action for divorce, annulment, or legal separation does not bar proceedings for conciliation under this chapter.

(1990 H 514, eff. 1-1-91; 1969 S 74)

Library References

Divorce ⟹87.5.
WESTLAW Topic No. 134.
C.J.S. Divorce § 131.

OJur 3d: 5A, Alternative Dispute Resolution § 175; 46, Family Law § 329, 330

Am Jur 2d: 24, Divorce and Separation § 331, 332, 339

Sowald & Morganstern, Baldwin's Ohio Practice, *Domestic Relations Law* § 6.9 (1997)

3117.08 Transfer and disposition of conciliation matters; jurisdiction

(A) Whenever it appears at any time during pendency of an action for divorce, annulment, or legal separation that conciliation proceedings may prevent dissolution of the marriage or disruption of the household, the court may transfer the matter to the conciliation judge for proceedings pursuant to this chapter, and the original action shall be stayed pending completion of conciliation proceedings.

(B) Whenever there is a minor child of one or both spouses whose welfare may be affected by the controversy, the conciliation judge shall entertain all conciliation cases properly brought before him. Whenever there is no such minor child, but it appears that reconciliation of the spouses or amicable settlement of the controversy may be achieved, and that conciliation cases involving children will not be seriously impeded by acceptance of the case, the conciliation judge may accept and dispose of conciliation cases in the same manner as in cases involving the welfare of children.

(C) The conciliation judge has jurisdiction over the controversy, the parties, such of the minor children of the parties whose welfare may be affected by the controversy, and all persons having any relation to the controversy, in all conciliation cases properly before him pursuant to this chapter.

(1990 H 514, eff. 1-1-91; 1969 S 74)

Library References

Divorce ⚷87.5.
WESTLAW Topic No. 134.
C.J.S. Divorce § 131.

OJur 3d: 5A, Alternative Dispute Resolution § 175; 46, Family Law § 329, 332

Am Jur 2d: 24, Divorce and Separation § 333, 339

Sowald & Morganstern, Baldwin's Ohio Practice, *Domestic Relations Law* § 6.9 (1997)

INDEX TO TITLE 31
DOMESTIC RELATIONS—CHILDREN

Cross references to another main heading are in CAPITAL LETTERS.

†